Department of Economic and
Social Affairs

Statistics Division

Département des affaires économiques
et sociales

Division de statistique

Statistical Yearbook
Forty-sixth issue

1999
Data available as of
30 November 2001

Annuaire statistique
Quarante-sixième édition

Données disponibles
au 30 novembre 2001

United Nations/Nations Unies • New York, 2002

Note

The designations employed and the presentation of material in this publication do not imply the expression of any opinion whatsoever on the part of the Secretariat of the United Nations concerning the legal status of any country, territory, city or area or of its authorities, or concerning the delimitation of its frontiers or boundaries.

In general, statistics contained in the present publication are those available to the United Nations Secretariat up to November 2001 and refer to 1999/2000 or earlier. They therefore reflect country nomenclature in use in 2001.

The term "country" as used in this publication also refers, as appropriate, to territories or areas.

The designations "developed" and "developing" are intended for statistical convenience and do not necessarily express a judgement about the stage reached by a particular country or area in the development process.

Symbols of United Nations documents are composed of capital letters combined with figures.

Note

Les appellations employées dans la présente publication et la présentation des données qui y figurent n'impliquent de la part du Secrétariat de l'Organisation des Nations Unies aucune prise de position quant au statut juridique des pays, territoires, villes ou zones, ou de leurs autorités, ni quant au tracé de leurs frontières ou limites.

En règle générale, les statistiques contenues dans la présente publication sont celles dont disposait le Secrétariat de l'Organisation des Nations Unies jusqu'à novembre 2001 et portent sur la période finissant à 2000. Elles reflètent donc la nomenclature des pays en vigueur à l'époque.

Le terme « pays », tel qu'il est utilisé ci-après, peut également désigner des territoires ou des zones.

Les appellations « développés » et « en développement » sont employées à des fins exclusivement statistiques et n'expriment pas nécessairement un jugement quant au niveau de développement atteint par tel pays ou telle région.

Les cotes des documents de l'Organisation des Nations Unies se composent de lettres majuscules et de chiffres.

ST/ESA/STAT/SER.S/22

UNITED NATIONS PUBLICATION
Sales No. E/F.01.XVII.1

PUBLICATION DES NATIONS UNIES
Numéro de vente : E/F.01.XVII.1

ISBN 92-1-061191-8
ISSN 0082-8459

Inquiries should be directed to:

SALES SECTION
PUBLISHING DIVISION
UNITED NATIONS
NEW YORK 10017
USA

Adresser toutes demandes de renseignements à la :

SECTION DES VENTES
DIVISION DES PUBLICATIONS
NATIONS UNIES
NEW YORK 10017
ÉTATS-UNIS D'AMÉRIQUE

E-mail: publications@un.org
Internet: http://www.un.org/Pubs

Preface

This is the forty-sixth issue of the United Nations *Statistical Yearbook,* prepared by the Statistics Division, Department of Economic and Social Affairs of the United Nations Secretariat, since 1948. The present issue contains series covering, in general, 1990-1999 or 1991-2000, using for the most part statistics available to the Statistics Division up to 30 November 2001.

The *Yearbook* is based on data compiled by the Statistics Division from over 35 international and national sources. These include the United Nations Statistics Division in the fields of national accounts, industry, energy, transport and international trade, the United Nations Statistics Division and Population Division in the field of demographic statistics, and over 20 offices of the United Nations system and international organizations in other specialized fields.

United Nations agencies and other international, national and specialized organizations which furnished data are listed under "Statistical sources and references" at the end of the *Yearbook.* Acknowledgement is gratefully made for their generous cooperation in providing data.

The Statistics Division also publishes the *Monthly Bulletin of Statistics* [26]*, which provides a valuable complement to the *Yearbook* by covering current international economic statistics for most countries and areas of the world and quarterly world and regional aggregates. Subscribers to the *Monthly Bulletin of Statistics* may also access the *Bulletin* on-line via the World Wide Web on Internet. The *MBS On-line* allows time-sensitive statistics to reach users much faster than the traditional print publication. For further information see <http://www.un.org/Depts/unsd/>.

Recognizing the tremendous worldwide growth in recent years in the use of microcomputers and the corresponding interest in obtaining statistics in machine-readable form for further study and analysis by users, the *Yearbook* has also been published on CD-ROM for IBM-compatible microcomputers, since the thirty-eighth issue. The latest issue on CD-ROM is the forty-fifth[1]. The present issue will also be published on CD-ROM in 2002. Ad hoc or standing orders for the *Yearbook* in hard copy and on CD-ROM may be placed with United Nations Publications sales offices in New York and Geneva. A full list of machine-readable products in statistics available from the United Nations Statistics Division may be obtained, upon request, from the Statistics Division of the United Nations Secretariat, New York or from the Division's Internet home page <http://www.un.org/Depts/unsd/>. The

Préface

La présente édition est la quarante-sixième de l'*Annuaire statistique* des Nations Unies, établi depuis 1948 par la Division de statistique du Département des affaires économiques et sociales du Secrétariat de l'Organisation des Nations Unies. Elle contient des séries qui portent d'une manière générale sur la période 1990 à 1999 ou 1991 à 2000 et pour lesquelles ont été utilisées les informations dont disposait la Division de statistique au 30 novembre 2001.

L'*Annuaire* est établi à partir des données que la Division de statistique a recueillies auprès de plus de 35 sources, internationales et nationales. Ces sources sont: la Division de statistique du Secrétariat de l'Organisation des Nations Unies pour ce qui concerne les comptabilités nationales, l'industrie, l'énergie, les transports et le commerce international, la Division de statistique et la Division de la population du Secrétariat de l'Organisation des Nations Unies pour les statistiques démographiques; et plus de 20 bureaux du système des Nations Unies et d'organisations internationales pour les autres domaines spécialisés.

Les institutions spécialisées des Nations Unies et les autres organisations internationales, nationales et spécialisées qui ont fourni des données sont énumérées dans la section "Sources statistiques et références" figurant à la fin de l'ouvrage. Les auteurs de l'*Annuaire statistique* les remercient de leur généreuse coopération.

La Division de Statistique publie également le *Bulletin Mensuel de Statistiques* [26]*, qui est un complément intéressant à l'*Annuaire Statistique* qui couvre les statistiques économiques courantes sur la plupart des pays et zones du monde et des aggrégats trimestriels, au niveau du monde et des grandes régions. Les abonnés au *Bulletin Mensuel de Statistiques* ont aussi à leur disposition le *Bulletin* en ligne, accessible sur Internet par le "World Wide Web". Grâce à "BMS en ligne" les utilisateurs disposent plus rapidement des données conjoncturelles que par la voie traditionnelle de la publication imprimée. Pour des informations supplémentaires, voir <http://www.un.org/Depts/unsd/>.

En raison de l'expansion extraordinaire que la micro-informatique a connue ces dernières années et de l'intérêt croissant que suscite la présentation de statistiques sur des supports lisibles en machine et exploitables directement par l'utilisateur, l'*Annuaire* a été publiée sur disque compact (CD/ROM) pour micro-ordinateurs IBM et compatibles depuis la publication de la trente-huitième édition. La plus récente édition sur disque compact (CD/ROM) est la quarante-cinquième[1]. La présente édition sera également publiée sur CD/ROM en 2002.

---

*   Numbers in brackets refer to numbered entries in the section "Statistical sources and references" at the end of this book.

*   Les chiffres entre crochets se réfèrent aux entrées numérotées dans la section «Sources statistiques et références» à la fin de l'ouvrage.

Division has also prepared an inventory of over 100 international statistical databases with some form of public access, *StatBase Locator on Disk - UNSTAT's Guide to International Computerized Statistical Databases*.[2]

The organization of the *Yearbook*, described in the Introduction below in more detail, consists of four parts. Part One: World and Region Summary, consists of key world and regional aggregates and totals. In the remaining three parts, the subject matter is generally presented by countries or areas, with world and regional aggregates also shown in some cases. Parts two, three and four cover, respectively, population and social topics, national economic activity and international economic relations. The organization of the population and social topics generally follows the arrangement of subject matter in the United Nations *Handbook on Social Indicators* [47]; economic activity is taken up according to the classes of the United Nations International Standard Industrial Classification of All Economic Activities (ISIC) [49]; and tables on international economic relations cover merchandise trade, international tourism (a major factor in international trade in services and balance of payments) and financial transactions including development assistance. Each chapter ends with brief technical notes on statistical sources and methods for the tables it includes. References to sources and related methodological publications are provided at the end of the *Yearbook* in the section "Statistical sources and references".

Annex I provides complete information on country and area nomenclature, and regional and other groupings used in the *Yearbook*, and annex II lists conversion coefficients and factors used in various tables. Symbols and conventions used in the *Yearbook* are shown in the section "Explanatory notes", preceding the Introduction.

The complete list of tables added to or omitted from the last issue of the *Yearbook* is given in annex III. Tables for which a sufficient amount of new data is not available are not being published in this *Yearbook*. Their titles nevertheless are still listed in the table of contents since it is planned that they will be published in a later issue as new data are compiled by the collecting agency. However, the complete set of tables is retained in the CD-ROM version of the *Yearbook*.

As described more fully in the Introduction below, every attempt has been made to ensure that the series contained in the *Yearbook* are sufficiently comparable to provide a reliable general description of economic and social topics throughout the world. Nevertheless, the reader should carefully consult the footnotes and technical notes for any given table for explanations of general limitations of series presented and specific limitations affecting particular data items; the section "comparability of statistics" should also be consulted. Readers interested in more detailed figures than those shown in the present publication, and in further information on the full range of internationally assembled statistics in

Les commandes individuelles et les abonnements à l'*Annuaire statistique* (édition imprimée ou sur CD/ROM) peuvent être adressées aux bureaux de vente des publications des Nations Unies à New York et à Genève ou sur Internet page d'accueil de la Division <http://www.un.org/Depts/unsd/>. La Division de statistique du Secrétariat de l'Organisation des Nations Unies à New York fournit sur demande la liste complète de produits statistiques disponibles sur supports lisibles en machine. La Division publie également *StatBase Locator on Disk - UNSTAT's Guide to International Computerized Databases*,[2] inventaire de plus de 100 bases de données statistiques internationales accessibles au public.

Le plan de l'*Annuaire*, qui est décrit ci-après de manière plus détaillée dans l'introduction, comprend quatre parties. La première partie, "Aperçu mondial et régional", se compose des principaux agrégats et totaux aux niveaux mondial et régional. Les trois autres sont consacrées à la population et aux questions sociales (deuxième partie), à l'activité économique nationale (troisième partie) et aux relations économiques internationales (quatrième partie). L'organisation de la deuxième partie, "Population et questions sociales", suit généralement le plan adopté par l'ONU "*Manuel des indicateurs sociaux*" [47]; dans la troisième partie, l'activité économique est présentée conformément aux catégories adoptées par l'ONU dans la *Classification internationale type, par industrie, de toutes les branches d'activité économique* [49]; les tableaux de la quatrième partie, consacrée aux relations économiques internationales, portent sur le commerce des marchandises, le tourisme international (élément essentiel du secteur international des services et balance des paiements) et les opérations financières, y compris l'aide au développement. Chaque chapitre termine avec une brève note technique sur les sources et méthodes statistiques utilisées pour les tableaux du chapitre. On trouvera à la fin de l'*Annuaire*, dans la section "Sources statistiques et références", des références aux sources et publications méthodologiques connexes.

L'annexe I donne des renseignements complets sur la nomenclature des pays et des zones et sur la façon dont ceux-ci ont été regroupés pour former les régions et autres entités géographiques utilisées dans l'*Annuaire*; l'annexe II fournit des renseignements sur les coefficients et facteurs de conversion employés dans les différents tableaux. Les divers symboles et conventions utilisés dans l'*Annuaire* sont présentés dans la section "Notes explicatives" qui précède l'introduction.

La liste complète des tableaux ajoutés et supprimés depuis la dernière édition de l'*Annuaire* figure à l'annexe III. Les tableaux pour lesquels on ne dispose pas d'une quantité suffisante des données nouvelles, n'ont pas été publiés dans cet *Annuaire*. Comme ils seront repris dans une prochaine édition à mesure que des données nouvelles seront dépouillées par l'office statistique d'origine, ses titres figurent toujours dans la table des matières. Tous les tableaux sont cependant repris dans l'édition publiée sur CD/ROM.

specialized fields, should also consult the specialized publications listed in the "Statistical sources and references" at the end of the *Yearbook.*

Needless to say, much more can be done to improve the *Yearbook*'s scope, coverage, timeliness, design, and technical notes. The process is inevitably an evolutionary one. Comments on the present *Yearbook* and its future evolution are welcome and should be addressed to the Director, United Nations Statistics Division, New York 10017 USA, or via e-mail to statistics@un.org .

Comme il est précisé ci-après dans l'introduction, aucun effort n'a été épargné afin que les séries figurant dans l'*Annuaire* soient suffisamment comparables pour fournir une description générale fiable de la situation économique et sociale dans le monde entier. Néanmoins, le lecteur devra consulter avec soins les renvois individuels et les notes techniques de chaque tableau pour y trouver l'explication des limites générales imposées aux séries présentées et des limites particulières propres à certains types de données; aussi le lecteur devra consulter la section "comparabilité des statistiques". Les lecteurs qui souhaitent avoir des chiffres plus détaillés que ceux figurant dans le présent volume ou qui désirent se procurer des renseignements sur la gamme complète des statistiques qui ont été compilées à l'échelon international dans tel ou tel domaine particulier devraient consulter les publications énumérées dans la section "Sources statistiques et références".

Inutile de dire qu'il reste beaucoup à faire pour mettre l'*Annuaire* pleinement à jour en ce qui concerne son champ, sa couverture, sa mise à jour, sa conception générale, et ses notes techniques. Il s'agit là inévitablement d'un processus évolutif. Les observations sur la présente édition de l'*Annuaire* et les modifications suggérées pour l'avenir seront reçues avec intérêt et doivent être adressées au Directeur de la Division de statistique de l'ONU, New York, N.Y. 10017 (États-Unis d'Amérique), ou e-mail à statistics@un.org .

---

[1]   *Statistical Yearbook, forty-fifth issue, CD-ROM,* (United Nations publication, Sales No. E.01.XVII.4).

[2]   United Nations publication, Sales No. E.94.XVII.8 (issued on one 3 1/2" diskette for IBM-compatible microcomputers).

[1]   *L'Annuaire statistique, quarante-cinquième édition sur CD-ROM* (Publication des Nations Unies, numéro de vente E.01.XVII.4).

[2]   Publication des Nations Unies, numéro de vente E.94.XVII.8 (sur une disquette de 3,5 inches pour micro-ordinateurs IBM et compatibles).

Contents

Preface... iii
Explanatory notes...................................... xiv
Introduction 1

Part One
World and Region Summary

I.   *World and region summary*
    Tables 1-7 9
    Technical notes 28

Part Two
Population and Social Statistics

II.   *Population and human settlements*
    Tables 8 and 9 33
    Technical notes 53
III.   *Literacy*
    Table 10 55
    Technical notes 63
IV.   *Health, childbearing and nutrition*
    Tables 11-13 65
    Technical notes 87
V.   *Culture and communication*
    Tables 14-21 91
    Technical notes 155

Part Three
Economic Activity

VI.   *National accounts and industrial production*
    Tables 22-26 159
    Technical notes 236
VII.   *Financial statistics*
    Tables 27 and 28 239
    Technical notes 254
VIII.   *Labour force*
    Tables 29 and 30 256
    Technical notes 293
IX.   *Wages and prices*
    Tables 31-33 295
    Technical notes 331
X.   *Agriculture, forestry and fishing*
    Tables 34-40 333
    Technical notes 414
XI.   *Manufacturing*
    A. Food, beverages and tobacco
       Tables 41-44 417
    B. Textiles and leather products
       Tables 45 and 46 466

Table des matières

Préface...iii
Notes explicatives xiv
Introduction 1

Première partie
Aperçu mondial et régional

I.   *Aperçu mondial et régional*
    Tableaux 1 à 7.................................. 9
    Notes techniques 28

Deuxième partie
Population et statistiques sociales

II.   *Population et établissements humains*
    Tableaux 8 et 9 33
    Notes techniques 53
III.   *Alphabétisation*
    Tableau 10 55
    Notes techniques 63
IV.   *Santé, maternité et nutrition*
    Tableaux 11 à 13.......................... 65
    Notes techniques 87
V.   *Culture et communication*
    Tableaux 14 à 21 91
    Notes techniques 155

Troisième partie
Activité économique

VI.   *Comptabilités nationales et production industrielle*
    Tableaux 22 à 26.......................... 159
    Notes techniques 236
VII.   *Statistiques financières*
    Tableaux 27 et 28......................... 239
    Notes techniques 254
VIII.   *Main-d'oeuvre*
    Tableaux 29 et 30......................... 256
    Notes techniques 293
IX.   *Salaires et prix*
    Tableaux 31 à 33.......................... 295
    Notes techniques 331
X.   *Agriculture, forêts et pêche*
    Tableaux 34 à 40 333
    Notes techniques 414
XI.   *Industries manufacturières*
    A. Alimentation, boissons et tabac
       Tableaux 41 à 44 417
    B. Textiles et articles en cuir
       Tableaux 45 et 46 466

C. Wood and wood products; paper
    and paper products
    Tables 47 and 48 478
D. Chemicals and related products
    Tables 49 and 50 490
E. Basic metal industries
    Tables 51 and 52 500
F. Fabricated metal products, machinery
    and equipment
    Tables 53-58 511
    Technical notes 533

XII.   *Transport*
        Tables 59-63 537
        Technical notes 608
XIII.   *Energy*
        Tables 64 and 65 610
        Technical notes 653
XIV.   *Environment*
        Tables 66 and 67 657
        Technical notes 673
XV.   *Science and technology, intellectual
        property*
        Tables 68 and 69 677
        Technical notes 688

Part Four
International Economic Relations

XVI.   *International merchandise trade*
        Tables 70-72 691
        Technical notes 721
XVII.   *International tourism*
        Tables 73-75 725
        Technical notes 773
XVIII. *Balance of payments*
        Table 76 775
        Technical notes 806
XIX.   *International finance*
        Tables 77 and 78 809
        Technical notes 834
XX.   *Development assistance*
        Tables 79-81 837
        Technical notes 855

        Annexes
I.   Country and area nomenclature,
        regional and other groupings 856
II.   Conversion coefficients and factors 868
III.   Tables added and omitted 870

Statistical sources and references 871
Index (English only) 875

C. Bois et produits dérivés; papier
    et produits dérivés
    Tableaux 47 et 48 478
D. Produits chimiques et apparentés
    Tableaux 49 et 50 490
E. Industries métallurgiques de base
    Tableaux 51 et 52 500
F. Fabrications métallurgiques, machines
    et équipements
    Tableaux 53 à 58 511
    Notes techniques 533

XII.   *Transports*
        Tableaux 59 à 63 537
        Notes techniques 608
XIII.   *Energie*
        Tableaux 62 et 63 610
        Notes techniques 653
XIV.   *Environnement*
        Tableaux 66 et 67 657
        Notes techniques 673
XV.   *Science et technologie, propriété
        intellectuelle*
        Tableaux 68 et 69 677
        Notes techniques 688

Quatrième partie
Relations économiques internationales

XVI.   *Commerce international des marchandises*
        Tableaux 70 à 72 691
        Notes techniques 721
XVII.   *Tourisme international*
        Tableaux 73 à 75 725
        Notes techniques 773
XVIII. *Balance des paiements*
        Tableau 76 775
        Notes techniques 806
XIX.   *Finances internationales*
        Tableaux 77 et 78 809
        Notes techniques 834
XX.   *Aide au développement*
        Tableaux 79 à 81 837
        Notes techniques 855

        Annexes
I.   Nomenclature des pays et des zones,
        groupements régionaux et autres
        groupements 856
II.   Coefficients et facteurs de conversion 868
III.   Tableaux ajoutés et supprimés 870
Sources statistiques et références 871

List of tables

Part One
World and Region Summary

Chapter I. *World and region summary*
1.   Selected series of world statistics......................9
2.   Population, rate of increase, birth
      and death rates, surface area and density.........12
3.   Index numbers of total agricultural and
      food production...14
4.   Index numbers of per capita total
      agricultural and food production.....................15
5.   Index numbers of industrial production:
      world and regions...16
6.   Production, trade and consumption
      of commercial energy.....................................24
7.   Total exports and imports:
      index numbers..26

Part Two
Population and Social Statistics

Chapter II. *Population and human settlements*
8.   Population by sex, rate of population
      increase, surface area and density...................33
9.   Population in urban and rural areas,
      rates of growth and largest urban
      agglomeration population...............................45

Chapter III. *Education and literacy*
10.   Illiterate population by sex............................55
*   Education at the primary, secondary and
       tertiary levels
*   Public expenditure on education: total and
       current

Chapter IV. *Health, childbearing and nutrition*
11.   Selected indicators of life expectancy,
       childbearing and mortality.............................65
12.   Estimates of cumulative HIV/AIDS
       infections, AIDS deaths and reported
       AIDS cases...73
       A. Estimated cumulative HIV/AIDS
           infections, AIDS deaths and people
           newly infected with HIV in 2001.............73
       B. Reported AIDS cases to the World
           Health Organization: world and
           regions...73
       C. Reported AIDS cases.............................74
13.   Food supply...81

Liste des tableaux

Première partie
Aperçu mondial et régional

Chapitre I. *Aperçu mondial et régional*
1.   Séries principales de statistiques mondiales......9
2.   Population, taux d'accroissement, taux de
      natalité et taux de mortalité, superficie
      et densité..12
3.   Indices de la production agricole totale
      et de la production alimentaire.......................14
4.   Indices de la production agricole totale et de
      la production alimentaire par habitant............15
5.   Indices de la production industrielle:
      monde et régions..16
6.   Production, commerce et consommation
      d'énergie commerciale...................................24
7.   Exportations et importations totales: indices...26

Deuxième partie
Population et statistiques sociales

Chapitre II. *Population et établissements humains*
8.   Population selon le sexe, taux d'accroissement
      de la population, superficie et densité............33
9.   Population urbaine, population rurale,
      taux d'accroissement et population de
      l'agglomération urbaine la plus peuplée..........45

Chapitre III. *Instruction et alphabétisation*
10.   Population analphabète, selon le sexe............55
*   Enseignement primaire, secondaire et
       supérieur
*   Dépenses publiques afférentes à l'éducation:
       totales et ordinaires

Chapitre IV. *Santé, maternité et nutrition*
11.   Choix d'indicateurs de l'espérance
       de vie, de maternité et de la mortalité...........65
12.   Chiffres estimatifs du nombre cumulé de
       personnes infectées par le VIH ou le SIDA,
       décès dus au SIDA, et cas déclarés
       de SIDA..73
       A. Chiffres estimatifs cumulés du nombre
           de personnes infectées par le VIH ou le
           SIDA, décès dus au SIDA et nouveaux
           cas d'infection à VIH en 2001................73
       B. Cas de SIDA déclarés à l'Organisation
           mondiale de la santé: monde et régions....73
       C. Cas de SIDA déclarés.............................74
13.   Disponibilités alimentaires...........................81

Chapter V. *Culture and communication*
14.   Book production: number of titles
       by UDC classes 91
15.   Daily newspapers 98
16.   Non-daily newspapers and periodicals 105
17.   Television and radio receivers 113
18.   Cinemas: number, seating capacity,
       annual attendance and box office
       receipts 121
19.   Mobile cellular telephone subscribers 127
20.   Telephones.............................. 136
21.   Internet users.............................146

Part Three
Economic Activity

Chapter VI. *National accounts and industrial
              production*
22.   Gross domestic product: total and
       per capita 159
23.   Expenditure on gross domestic product
       at current prices.............................177
24.   Value added by kind of economic activity
       at current prices.............................188
25.   Relationships between the principal national
       accounting aggregates 199
26.   Index numbers of industrial production.........209
*   Government final consumption expenditure
       by function at current prices
*   Private final consumption expenditure by
       type and purpose at current prices

Chapter VII. *Financial statistics*
27.   Rates of discount of central banks.................239
28.   Short-term interest rates 245

Chapter VIII. *Labour force*
29.   Employment by industry.............................256
       A.   ISIC Rev. 2.............................256
       B.   ISIC Rev. 3.............................260
30.   Unemployment.............................275

Chapter IX. *Wages and prices*
31.   Wages in manufacturing 295
32.   Producers prices and wholesale prices 308
33.   Consumer price index numbers.................316

Chapter X. *Agriculture, forestry and fishing*
34.   Agricultural production (index numbers) 333
35.   Cereals.............................342
36.   Oil crops, in oil equivalent.............................350

Chapitre V. *Culture et communication*
14.   Production de livres: nombre de titres
       classés d'après la CDU.............................91
15.   Journaux quotidiens 98
16.   Journaux non quotidiens et périodiques 105
17.   Récepteurs de télévision et de radiodiffusion
       sonore.............................. 113
18.   Cinémas: nombre d'établissements, nombre
       de sièges, fréquentation annuelle et
       recettes guichet.............................121
19.   Abonnés au téléphone mobile.....................127
20.   Téléphones.............................. 136
21.   Usagers d'Internet.............................146

Troixième partie
Activité économique

Chapitre VI. *Comptabilités nationales et
              production industrielle*
22.   Produit intérieur brut: total et par habitant 159
23.   Dépenses imputées au produit intérieur
       brut aux prix courants.............................177
24.   Valeur ajoutée par genre d'activité
       économique aux prix courants 188
25.   Relations entre les principaux agrégats de
       comptabilité nationale 199
26.   Indices de la production industrielle 209
*   Consommation finale des administrations
       publiques par fonction aux prix courants
*   Consommation finale privée par catégorie
       de dépenses et par fonction aux prix
       courants

Chapitre VII. *Statistiques financières*
27.   Taux d'escompte des banques centrales 239
28.   Taux d'intérêt à court terme.............................245

Chapitre VIII. *Main-d'oeuvre*
29.   Emploi par industrie.............................256
       A.   CITI Rév. 2.............................256
       B.   CITI Rév. 3.............................260
30.   Chômage.............................275

Chapitre IX. *Salaires et prix*
31.   Salaires dans les industries manufacturières..295
32.   Prix à la production et des prix de gros.........308
33.   Indices des prix à la consommation 316

Chapitre X. *Agriculture, forêts et pêche*
34.   Production agricole (indices).............................333
35.   Céréales.............................342
36.   Cultures d'huile, en équivalent d'huile 350

37.	Livestock	358		37.	Cheptel	358
38.	Roundwood	377		38.	Bois rond	377
39.	Fish production	384		39.	Production halieutique	384
40.	Fertilizers (production and consumption)	394		40.	Engrais (production et consommation)	394

Chapter XI. *Manufacturing*
    A. Food, beverages and tobacco

41.	Sugar (production and consumption)	417
42.	Meat	428
43.	Beer	453
44.	Cigarettes	459

    B. Textiles and leather products

45.	Fabrics (cotton, wool, cellulosic and non-cellulosic fibres)	466
46.	Leather footwear	473

    C. Wood and wood products; paper and paper products

47.	Sawnwood	478
48.	Paper and paperboard	485

    D. Chemicals and related products

49.	Cement	490
50.	Sulphuric acid	497

    E. Basic metal industries

51.	Pig-iron and crude steel	500
52.	Aluminium	506

    F. Fabricated metal products, machinery and equipment

53.	Radio and television receivers	511
54.	Passenger cars	514
55.	Refrigerators for household use	516
56.	Washing machines for household use	520
57.	Machine tools (drilling/boring machines, lathes, milling machines and metal-working presses)	523
58.	Lorries (trucks)	529

Chapter XII. *Transport*

59.	Railways: traffic	537
60.	Motor vehicles in use	548
61.	Merchant shipping: fleets	566
62.	International maritime transport	584
63.	Civil aviation	593

Chapter XIII. *Energy*

64.	Production, trade and consumption of commercial energy	610
65.	Production of selected energy commodities	638

Chapitre XI. *Industries manufacturières*
    A. Alimentation, boissons et tabac

41.	Sucre (production et consommation)	417
42.	Viande	428
43.	Bière	453
44.	Cigarettes	459

    B. Textiles et articles en cuir

45.	Tissus (coton, laines, fibres cellulosiques et non cellulosiques)	466
46.	Chaussures de cuir	473

    C. Bois et produits dérivés; papier et produits dérivés

47.	Sciages	478
48.	Papiers et cartons	485

    D. Produits chimiques et apparentés

49.	Ciment	490
50.	Acide sulfurique	497

    E. Industries métallurgiques de base

51.	Fonte et acier brut	500
52.	Aluminium	506

    F. Fabrications métallurgiques, machines et équipements

53.	Récepteurs radio et télévision	511
54.	Voitures de tourisme	514
55.	Réfrigérateurs à usage domestique	516
56.	Machines à laver à usage domestique	520
57.	Machines-outils (perceuses, tours, fraiseuses et presses pour le travail des métaux)	523
58.	Camions	529

Chapitre XII. *Transports*

59.	Chemins de fer: trafic	537
60.	Véhicules automobiles en circulation	548
61.	Transports maritimes: flotte marchande	566
62.	Transports maritimes internationaux	584
63.	Aviation civile	593

Chapitre XIII. *Energie*

64.	Production, commerce et consommation d'énergie commerciale	610
65.	Production des principaux biens de l'énergie	638

Chapter XIV. *Environment*
66.   Land.. 657
67.   CO$_2$ emissions estimates............................. 665
*   Water supply and sanitation coverage
*   Threatened species

Chapter XV. *Science and technology, intellectual property*
68.   Researchers, technicians and other supporting staff engaged in research and development 677
69.   Patents 682
*   Gross domestic expenditure on R&D by source of funds

Part Four
International Economic Relations

Chapter XVI. *International merchandise trade*
70.   Total imports and exports 691
71.   Total imports and exports: index numbers............................... 708
72.   Manufactured goods exports........................ 714

Chapter XVII. *International tourism*
73.   Tourist/visitor arrivals by region of origin 725
74.   Tourist/visitor arrivals and tourism expenditure 754
75.   Tourism expenditure in other countries 764

Chapter XVIII. *Balance of payments*
76.   Summary of balance of payments 775

Chapter XIX. *International finance*
77.   Exchange rates 809
78.   Total external and public/publicly guaranteed long-term debt of developing countries 827
       A.   Total external debt 827
       B.   Public and publicly guaranteed long-term debt 829

Chapter XX. *Development assistance*
79.   Disbursements of bilateral and multilateral official development assistance and official aid to individual recipients 837
80.   Net official development assistance from DAC countries to developing countries and multilateral organizations.. 847

Chapitre XIV. *Environnement*
66.   Terres.. 657
67.   Estimations des émissions de CO$_2$ 665
*   Accès à l'eau et à l'assainissement
*   Espèces menacées

Chapitre XV. *Science et technologie, propriété intellectuelle*
68.   Chercheurs, techniciens et autre personnel de soutien employés à des travaux de recherche et de développement 677
69.   Brevets 682
*   Dépenses intérieures brutes de recherche et développement par source de fonds

Quatrième partie
Relations économiques internationales

Chapitre XVI. *Commerce international des marchandises*
70.   Importations et exportations totales 691
71.   Importations et exportations totales: indices 708
72.   Exportations des produits manufacturés........ 714

Chapitre XVII. *Tourisme international*
73.   Arrivées de touristes/visiteurs par régions de provenance................................... 725
74.   Arrivées de touristes/visiteurs et dépenses touristiques................................. 754
75.   Dépenses touristiques dans d'autres pays...... 764

Chapitre XVIII. *Balance des paiements*
76.   Résumé des balances des paiements 775

Chapitre XIX. *Finances internationales*
77.   Cours des changes.................................... 809
78.   Total de la dette extérieure et dette publique extérieure à long terme garantie par l'Etat des pays en développement 827
       A.   Total de la dette extérieure.................... 827
       B.   Dette publique extérieure à long terme garantie par l'Etat 829

Chapitre XX. *Aide au développement*
79.   Versements d'aide publique au développement et d'aide publique bilatérales et multilatérales aux bénéficiaires 837
80.   Aide publique au développement nette de pays du CAD aux pays en développement et aux organisations multilatérales 847

81.   Socio-economic development assistance
       through the United Nations system
              Development grant expenditures 848

81.   Assistance en matière de développement
       socioéconomique fournie par le système
       des Nations Unies
              Aide au développement......................... 848

---

*   This symbol identifies tables presented in previous issues
     of the *Statistical Yearbook* but not contained in the present
     issue because of insufficient new data. These tables will
     be updated in future issues of the *Yearbook* when new data
     become available.

*   Ce symbole indique les tableaux publiés dans les éditions
     précédentes de l'*Annuaire statistique* mais qui n'ont pas été
     repris dans la présente édition fautes de données nouvelles
     suffisantes. Ces tableaux seront actualisés dans les futures
     livraisons de l'*Annuaire* à mesure que des données nouvel-
     les deviendront disponibles.

Explanatory notes

The metric system of weights and measures has been employed throughout the *Statistical Yearbook*. For conversion coefficients and factors, see annex II.

In some cases, the comparability of the statistics is affected by geographical changes. As a general rule, the data relate to a given country or area within its present de facto boundaries. Where statistically important, attention is called to changes in territory by means of a footnote. The reader is referred to annex I, concerning country and area nomenclature, where changes in designation are listed.

Numbers in brackets refer to numbered entries in the section "Statistical sources and references" at the end of this book.

In general, the statistics presented in the present publication are based on information available to the Statistics Division of the United Nations Secretariat up to 30 November 2001.

Symbols and conventions used in the tables:

A point (.) is used to indicate decimals.

A hyphen (-) between years, e.g., 1994-1995, indicates the full period involved, including the beginning and end years; a slash (/) indicates a financial year, school year or crop year, e.g., 1994/95.

Not applicable or not separately reported ..
Data not available ...
Magnitude zero -
Less than half of unit employed   0 or 0.0
Provisional or estimated figure *
United Nations estimate x
Marked break in series #

Details and percentages in the tables do not necessarily add to totals because of rounding.

Notes explicatives

Le système métrique de poids et mesures a été utilisé dans tout l'*Annuaire statistique*. On trouvera à l'annexe II les coefficients et facteurs de conversion.

Dans certains cas, les changements géographiques intervenus influent sur la comparabilité des statistiques. En règle générale, les données renvoient au pays ou zone en question dans ses frontières actuelles effectives. Une note appelle l'attention sur les changements territoriaux, si cela importe du point de vue statistique. Le lecteur est renvoyé à l'annexe I (nomenclature des pays et zones et groupements régionaux) où il trouvera une liste des changements de désignation.

Les chiffres figurant entre crochets se réfèrent aux entrées numérotées dans la liste des sources et références statistiques à la fin de l'ouvrage.

En général, les statistiques qui figurent dans la présente publication sont fondées sur les informations dont disposait la Division de statistique du Secrétariat de l'ONU au 30 novembre 2001.

Signes et conventions employés dans les tableaux:

Les décimales sont précédées d'un point (.).

Un tiret (-) entre des années, par exemple "1994-1995", indique que la période est embrassée dans sa totalité, y compris la première et la dernière année; une barre oblique (/) renvoie à un exercice financier, à une année scolaire ou à une campagne agricole, par exemple "1994/95".

Non applicable ou non communiqué séparément ..
Données non disponibles ...
Néant -
Valeur inférieure à la moitié de la dernière unité retenue   0 ou 0.0
Chiffre provisoire ou estimatif *
Estimation des Nations Unies x
Discontinuité notable dans la série #

Les chiffres étant arrondis, les totaux ne correspondent pas toujours à la somme exacte des éléments ou pourcentages figurant dans les tableaux.

Introduction

This is the forty-sixth issue of the United Nations *Statistical Yearbook*, prepared by the Statistics Division, Department of Economic and Social Affairs of the United Nations Secretariat. It contains series covering, in general, 1990-1999 or 1991-2000, based on statistics available to the Statistics Division up to 30 November 2001.

The major purpose of the *Statistical Yearbook* is to provide in a single volume a comprehensive compilation of internationally available statistics on social and economic conditions and activities, at world, regional and national levels, covering roughly a ten-year period.

Most of the statistics presented in the *Yearbook* are extracted from more detailed, specialized publications prepared by the Statistics Division and by many other international statistical services. Thus, while the specialized publications concentrate on monitoring topics and trends in particular social and economic fields, the *Statistical Yearbook* tables provide data for a more comprehensive, overall description of social and economic structures, conditions, changes and activities. The objective has been to collect, systematize and coordinate the most essential components of comparable statistical information which can give a broad and, to the extent feasible, a consistent picture of social and economic processes at world, regional and national levels.

More specifically, the *Statistical Yearbook* provides systematic information on a wide range of social and economic issues which are of concern in the United Nations system and among the governments and peoples of the world. A particular value of the *Yearbook*, but also its greatest challenge, is that these issues are extensively interrelated. Meaningful analysis of these issues requires systematization and coordination of the data across many fields. These issues include:

— General economic growth and related economic conditions;

— Economic situation in developing countries and progress towards the objectives adopted for the United Nations development decades;

— Population and urbanization, and their growth and impact;

— Employment, inflation and wages;

— Energy production and consumption and the development of new energy sources;

— Expansion of trade;

— Supply of food and alleviation of hunger;

— Financial situation and external payments and receipts;

— Education, training and eradication of illiteracy;

— Improvement in general living conditions;

— Pollution and protection of the environment;

— Assistance provided to developing countries for social and economic development purposes.

Introduction

La présente édition est la quarante-sixième de l'*Annuaire statistique* des Nations Unies, établi par la Division de statistique du Département des affaires économiques et sociales du Secrétariat de l'Organisation des Nations Unies. Elle contient des séries de données qui portent d'une manière générale sur les années 1990 à 1999 ou 1991 à 2000, et pour lesquelles ont été utilisées les informations dont disposait la Division de statistique au 30 novembre 2001.

L'*Annuaire statistique* a principalement pour objet de présenter en un seul volume un inventaire complet de statistiques disponibles sur le plan international et concernant la situation et les activités sociales et économiques aux échelons mondial, régional et national, pour une période d'environ dix ans.

Une bonne partie des données qui figurent dans l'*Annuaire* existent sous une forme plus détaillée dans les publications spécialisées établies par la Division de statistique et par bien d'autres services statistiques internationaux. Alors que les publications spécialisées suivent essentiellement l'évolution dans certains domaines socio-économiques précis, l'*Annuaire statistique* présente les données de manière à fournir une description plus globale et exhaustive des structures, conditions, transformations et activités socio-économiques. On a cherché à recueillir, systématiser et coordonner les principaux éléments de renseignements statistiques comparables, de manière à dresser un tableau général et autant que possible cohérent des processus socio-économiques en cours aux échelons mondial, régional et national.

Plus précisément, l'*Annuaire statistique* a pour objet de présenter des renseignements systématiques sur toutes sortes de questions socio-économiques qui sont liées aux préoccupations actuelles du système des Nations Unies ainsi que des gouvernements et des peuples du monde. Le principal avantage de l'*Annuaire* ▯ et aussi la principale difficulté à surmonter ▯ tient à ce que ces questions sont étroitement interdépendantes. Pour en faire une analyse utile, il est essentiel de systématiser et de coordonner les données se rapportant à de nombreux domaines différents. Ces questions sont notamment les suivantes:

— La croissance économique générale et les aspects connexes de l'économie;

— La situation économique dans les pays en développement et les progrès accomplis vers la réalisation des objectifs des décennies des Nations Unies pour le développement;

— La population et l'urbanisation, leur croissance et leur impact;

— L'emploi, l'inflation et les salaires;

— La production et la consommation d'énergie et la mise en valeur des énergies nouvelles;

— L'expansion des échanges;

— La pollution et la protection de

Organization of the *Yearbook*

The contents of the *Statistical Yearbook* are planned to serve a general readership. The *Yearbook* endeavours to provide information for various bodies of the United Nations system as well as for other international organizations, for governments and non-governmental organizations, for national statistical, economic and social policy bodies, for scientific and educational institutions, for libraries and for the public. Data published in the *Statistical Yearbook* are also of interest to companies and enterprises and to agencies engaged in marketing research.

The 81 tables of the *Yearbook* are grouped into four broad parts:

— Part One: World and Region Summary (chapter I, tables 1-7);

— Part Two: Population and Social Statistics (chapters II-V: tables 8-21);

— Part Three: Economic Activity (chapters VI-XV: tables 22-69);

— Part Four: International Economic Relations (chapters XVI-XX: tables 70-81).

These four parts together present data at two levels of aggregation. The more aggregated information shown in Part One provides an overall picture of development at the world and region levels. More specific and detailed information for analysis concerning individual countries or areas is presented in the three following parts. Each of these is divided into more specific chapters, by topic, and each chapter includes a section after the tables, "Technical notes". These notes provide brief descriptions of major statistical concepts, definitions and classifications required for interpretation and analysis of the data. Systematic information on the methodology used for the computation of the figures can be found in the publications on methodology of the United Nations and its agencies, listed in the section "Statistical sources and references" at the end of the *Yearbook*. Additional general information on statistical methodology is provided in the section below on "Comparability of statistics" and in the explanatory notes following the Introduction.

Part One, World and Region Summary, comprises seven tables highlighting the principal trends in the world as a whole as well as in regions and in the major economic and social sectors. It contains global totals of important aggregate statistics needed for the analysis of economic growth, the structure of the world economy, major changes in world population and expansion of external merchandise trade. The global totals are, as a rule, subdivided into major geographical areas.

Part Two, Population and Social Statistics, comprises 14 tables which contain more detailed statistical series on population, social conditions and levels of living, for example, illiteracy, health, culture and communication.

l'environnement;

— Les approvisionnements alimentaires et la lutte contre la faim;

— La situation financière, les paiements extérieurs et les recettes extérieures;

— L'éducation, la formation et l'élimination de l'analphabétisme;

— L'assistance fournie aux pays en développement à des fins socio-économiques.

Présentation de l'*Annuaire*

Le contenu de l'*Annuaire statistique* a été préparé à l'intention de tous les lecteurs intéressés. Les renseignements fournis devraient pouvoir être utilisés par les divers organismes du système des Nations Unies ainsi que par d'autres organisations internationales, par les gouvernements et les organisations non gouvernementales, par les organismes nationaux de statistique et de politique économique et sociale, par les institutions scientifiques et les établissements d'enseignement, les bibliothèques et les particuliers. Les données publiées dans l'*Annuaire statistique* peuvent également intéresser les sociétés et entreprises, et les organismes spécialisés dans les études de marché.

Les 81 tableaux de l'*Annuaire* sont groupés en quatre parties:

— La première partie: Aperçu mondial et régional (chapitre I, tableaux 1 à 7);

— La deuxième partie: Statistiques démographiques et sociales (chapitres II à V, tableaux 8 à 21);

— La troisième partie: Activité économique (chapitres VI à XV, tableaux 22 à 69);

— La cuatrième partie: Relations économiques internationales (chapitres XVI à XX, tableaux 70 à 81).

Ces quatre parties présentent les données à deux niveaux d'agrégation: les valeurs les plus agrégées qui figurent dans la première partie donnent un tableau global du développement à l'échelon mondial et régional, tandis que les trois autres parties contiennent des renseignements plus précis et détaillés qui se prêtent mieux à une analyse par pays ou par zones. Chacune de ces trois parties est divisée en chapitres portant sur des sujets donnés, et chaque chapitre comprend une section intitulée "Notes techniques" où l'on trouve une brève description des principales notions, définitions et classifications statistiques nécessaires pour interpréter et analyser les données. Les méthodes de calcul utilisées sont décrites de façon systématique dans les publications se référant à la méthodologie des Nations Unies et de leurs organismes, énumérées à la fin de l'*Annuaire* dans la section "Sources et références statistiques". Le lecteur trouvera un complément d'informations générales ci-après dans la section intitulée "Comparabilité des statistiques", ainsi que dans les notes explicatives qui suivent l'introduction.

La première partie, intitulée "Aperçu mondial et régional", comprend sept tableaux présentant les princi-

Of the 48 tables in Part Three, Economic Activity, 23 provide data on national accounts, index numbers of industrial production, interest rates, labour force, wages and prices, transport, energy, environment, science and technology and intellectual property; 25 tables provide data on production in the major branches of the economy (using, in general, the International Standard Industrial Classification, ISIC), namely agriculture, hunting, forestry and fishing, and manufacturing. In an innovation in the general approach of the *Yearbook*, consumption data are combined with the production data in tables on specific commodities, where feasible.

Part Four, International Economic Relations, comprises 12 tables on international merchandise trade, balance of payments, international tourism, international finance and development assistance.

An index (in English only) is provided at the end of the *Yearbook*.

Annexes and regional groupings of countries or areas

The annexes to the *Statistical Yearbook* and the section "Explanatory notes" preceding the Introduction, provide additional essential information on the *Yearbook*'s contents and presentation of data.

Annex I provides information on countries or areas covered in the *Yearbook* tables and on their grouping into geographical regions. The geographical groupings shown in the *Yearbook* are generally based on continental regions unless otherwise indicated. However, strict consistency in this regard is impossible. A wide range of classifications is used for different purposes in the various international agencies and other sources of statistics for the *Yearbook*. These classifications vary in response to administrative and analytical requirements.

Similarly, there is no common agreement in the United Nations system concerning the terms "developed" and "developing" when referring to the stage of development reached by any given country or area, and its corresponding classification in one or the other grouping. The *Yearbook* thus refers more generally to "developed" or "developing" regions on the basis of conventional practice. Following this practice, "developed regions" comprises Northern America, Europe and the former USSR, Australia, Japan and New Zealand, while all of Africa and the remainder of the Americas, Asia and Oceania comprise the "developing regions". These designations are intended for statistical convenience and do not necessarily express a judgement about the stage reached by a particular country or area in the development process.

Annex II provides detailed information on conversion coefficients and factors used in various tables, and annex III provides listings of tables added and omitted in the present edition of the *Yearbook*.

pales tendances dans le monde et dans les régions ainsi que dans les principaux secteurs économiques et sociaux. Elle fournit des chiffres mondiaux pour les principaux agrégats statistiques nécessaires pour analyser la croissance économique, la structure de l'économie mondiale, les principaux changements dans la population mondiale et l'expansion du commerce extérieur de marchandises. En règle générale, les chiffres mondiaux sont ventilés par grandes régions géographiques.

La deuxième partie, intitulée "Statistiques démographiques et sociales", comporte 14 tableaux où figurent des séries plus détaillées concernant la population, les conditions sociales et les niveaux de vie, notamment des données sur l'alphabétisation, la santé, la culture et la communication.

La troisième partie, intitulée "Activité économique", comporte 48 tableaux, 23 qui présentent des statistiques concernant les comptes nationaux, les nombres indices relatifs à la production industrielle, les taux d'intérêt, la population active, les prix et les salaires, le transport, l'énergie, l'environnement, la science et technologie, et la propriété intellectuelle; et 25 qui présentent des données sur la production des principales branches d'activité économique (en utilisant en général la *Classification internationale type, par industrie, de toutes les branches d'activité économique*): agriculture, chasse, sylviculture et pêche, et industries manufacturières. Une innovation a été introduite dans la présentation générale de l'*Annuaire* en ce sens que les tableaux traitant de certains produits de base associent autant que possible les données relatives à la consommation aux valeurs concernant la production.

La quatrième partie, intitulée "Relations économiques internationales", comprend 12 tableaux relatifs au commerce international de marchandises, aux balances des paiements, au tourisme international, aux finances internationales, et à l'aide au développement.

Un index (en anglais seulement) figure à la fin de l'*Annuaire*.

Annexes et groupements régionaux des pays et zones

Les annexes à l'*Annuaire statistique* et la section intitulée "Notes explicatives" qui précède l'introduction, offrent d'importantes informations complémentaires quant à la teneur et à la présentation des données figurant dans le présent ouvrage.

L'annexe I donne des renseignements sur les pays ou zones couverts par les tableaux de l'*Annuaire* et sur leur regroupement en régions géographiques. Sauf indication contraire, les groupements géographiques figurant dans l'*Annuaire* sont généralement fondés sur les régions continentales, mais une présentation absolument systématique est impossible à cet égard car les diverses institutions internationales et autres sources de statisti-

Comparability of statistics

One major aim of the *Statistical Yearbook* is to present series which are as nearly comparable across countries as the available statistics permit. Considerable efforts are also made among the international suppliers of data and by the staff of the *Yearbook* to ensure the compatibility of various series by coordinating time periods, base years, prices chosen for valuation and so on. This is indispensable in relating various bodies of data to each other and to facilitate analysis across different sectors. Thus, for example, relating data on economic output to those on employment makes it possible to derive some trends in the field of productivity; relating data on exports and imports to those on national product allows an evaluation of the relative importance of external trade in different countries and reveals changes in the role of trade over time.

In general, the data presented reflect the methodological recommendations of the United Nations Statistical Commission, issued in various United Nations publications, and of other international bodies concerned with statistics. Publications containing these recommendations and guidelines are listed in the section "Statistical sources and references" at the end of the *Yearbook*. Use of international recommendations not only promotes international comparability of the data but also ensures a degree of compatibility regarding the underlying concepts, definitions and classifications relating to different series. However, much work remains to be done in this area and, for this reason, some tables can serve only as a first source of data, which require further adjustment before being used for more in-depth analytical studies. While on the whole, a significant degree of comparability has been achieved in international statistics, there are many limitations, for a variety of reasons.

One common cause of non-comparability of economic data is different valuations of statistical aggregates such as national income, wages and salaries, output of industries and so forth. Conversion of these and similar series originally expressed in national prices into a common currency, for example into United States dollars, through the use of exchange rates, is not always satisfactory owing to frequent wide fluctuations in market rates and differences between official rates and rates which would be indicated by unofficial markets or purchasing power parities. For this reason, data on national income in United States dollars which are published in the *Yearbook* are subject to certain distortions and can be used as only a rough approximation of the relative magnitudes involved.

The use of different kinds of sources for obtaining data is another cause of incomparability. This is true, for example, in the case of employment and unemployment, where data are collected from such non-comparable sources as sample surveys, social insurance statistics and establishment surveys.

ques employées pour la confection de l'*Annuaire* emploient, selon l'objet de l'exercice, des classifications fort différentes en réponse à diverses exigences d'ordre administratif ou analytique.

Il n'existe pas non plus dans le système des Nations Unies de définition commune des termes "développé" et "en développement" pour décrire le niveau atteint en la matière par un pays ou une zone donnés ni pour les classifier dans l'un ou l'autre de ces groupes. Ainsi, dans l'*Annuaire*, on s'en remet à l'usage pour qualifier les régions de "développées" ou "en développement". Selon cet usage, les régions développées sont l'Amérique septentrionale, l'Europe et l'ancienne URSS, l'Australie, le Japon et la Nouvelle-Zélande, alors que toute l'Afrique et le reste des Amériques, l'Asie et l'Océanie constituent les régions en développement. Ces appellations sont utilisées pour plus de commodité dans la présentation des statistiques et n'impliquent pas nécessairement un jugement quant au stade de développement auquel est parvenu tel pays ou telle zone.

L'annexe II fournit des renseignements sur les coefficients et facteurs de conversion employés dans les différents tableaux, et l'annexe III contient les listes de tableaux qui ont été ajoutés ou omis dans la présente édition de l'*Annuaire*.

Comparabilité des statistiques

L'*Annuaire statistique* a principalement pour objet de présenter des statistiques aussi comparables d'un pays à l'autre que les données le permettent. Les sources internationales de données et les auteurs de l'*Annuaire* ont réalisés des efforts considérables pour faire en sorte que les diverses séries soient compatibles en harmonisant les périodes de référence, les années de base, les prix utilisés pour les évaluations, etc. Cette démarche est indispensable si l'on veut rapprocher divers ensembles de données pour faciliter l'analyse intersectorielle de l'économie. Ainsi, en liant les données concernant la production à celles de l'emploi, on parvient à dégager certaines tendances dans le domaine de la productivité; de même, en associant les données concernant les exportations et importations aux valeurs du produit national, on obtient une évaluation de l'importance relative des échanges extérieurs dans différents pays et de l'évolution du rôle joué par le commerce.

De façon générale, les données sont présentées selon les recommandations méthodologiques formulées par la Commission de statistique de l'ONU et par les autres organisations internationales qui s'intéressent aux statistiques. Les titres des publications contenant ces recommandations et lignes directrices figurent à la fin de l'ouvrage dans la section intitulée "Sources et références statistiques". Le respect des recommandations internationales tend non seulement à promouvoir la comparabilité des données à l'échelon international, mais elle assure également une certaine comparabilité entre les concepts, les définitions et classifications utilisés. Mais comme il

Non-comparability of data may also result from differences in the institutional patterns of countries. Certain variations in social and economic organization and institutions may have an impact on the comparability of the data even if the underlying concepts and definitions are identical.

These and other causes of non-comparability of the data are briefly explained in the technical notes to each chapter.

Statistical sources and reliability and timeliness of data

Statistics and indicators have been compiled mainly from official national and international sources, as these are more authoritative and comprehensive, more generally available as time series and more comparable among countries than other sources. In a few cases, official sources are supplemented by other sources and estimates, where these have been subjected to professional scrutiny and debate and are consistent with other independent sources. The comprehensive international data sources used for most of the tables are presented in the list of "Statistical sources and references" at the end of the *Yearbook*.

Users of international statistics are often concerned about the apparent lack of timeliness in the available data. Unfortunately, most international data are only available with a delay of at least one to three years after the latest year to which they refer. The reasons for the delay are that the data must first be processed by the national statistical services at the country level, then forwarded to the international statistical services and processed again to ensure as much consistency across countries and over time as possible.

reste encore beaucoup à faire dans ce domaine, les données présentées dans certains tableaux n'ont qu'une valeur indicative et nécessiteront des ajustements plus poussés avant de pouvoir servir à des analyses approfondies. Bien que l'on soit parvenu, dans l'ensemble, à un degré de comparabilité appréciable en matière de statistiques internationales, diverses raisons expliquent que subsistent encore de nombreuses limitations.

Une cause commune de non-comparabilité des données réside dans la diversité des méthodes d'évaluation employées pour comptabiliser des agrégats tels que le revenu national, les salaires et traitements, la production des différentes branches d'activité industrielle, etc. Il n'est pas toujours satisfaisant de ramener la valeur des séries de ce type □ exprimée à l'origine en prix nationaux □ à une monnaie commune (par exemple le dollar des États-Unis) car les taux de change du marché connaissent fréquemment de fortes fluctuations tandis que les taux officiels ne coïncident pas avec ceux des marchés officieux ni avec les parités réelles de pouvoir d'achat. C'est pourquoi les données relatives au revenu national, qui sont publiées dans l'*Annuaire* en dollars des États-Unis, souffrent de certaines distorsions et ne peuvent servir qu'à donner une idée approximative des ordres de grandeur relatifs.

Le recours à des sources diverses pour la collecte des données est une autre facteur qui limite la comparabilité, en particulier dans les secteurs de l'emploi et du chômage où les statistiques sont obtenues par des moyens aussi peu comparables que les sondages, le dépouillement des registres d'assurances sociales et les enquêtes auprès des entreprises.

Dans certains cas, les données ne sont pas comparables en raison de différences entre les structures institutionnelles des pays. Certaines variations dans l'organisation et les institutions économiques et sociales peuvent affecter la comparabilité des données même si les concepts et définitions sont fondamentalement identiques.

Ces causes de non-comparabilité des données sont parmi celles qui sont brièvement expliquées dans les notes techniques de chaque chapitre.

Origine, fiabilité et actualité des données

Les statistiques et les indicateurs sont fondés essentiellement sur des données provenant de sources officielles nationales et internationales; c'est en effet la meilleure source si l'on veut des données fiables, complètes et comparables et si l'on a besoin de séries chronologiques. Dans quelques cas, les données officielles sont complétées par des informations et des estimations provenant d'autres sources qui ont été examinées par des spécialistes et confirmées par des sources indépendantes. On trouvera à la fin de l'*Annuaire* la liste des "Sources statistiques et références", qui récapitule les sources des données internationales utilisées pour la plupart des tableaux.

Les utilisateurs des statistiques internationales se plaignent souvent du fait que les données disponibles ne sont pas actualisées. Malheureusement, la plupart des données internationales ne sont disponibles qu'avec un délai de deux ou trois ans après la dernière année à laquelle elles se rapportent. S'l en est ainsi, c'est parce que les données sont d'abord traitées par les services statistiques nationaux avant d'être transmises aux services statistiques internationaux, qui les traitent à nouveau pour assurer la plus grande comparabilité possible entre les pays et entre les périodes.

Part One
World and Region Summary

I
World and region summary (tables 1-7)

This part of the *Statistical Yearbook* presents selected aggregate series on principal economic and social topics for the world as a whole and for the major regions. The topics include population and surface area, agricultural and industrial production, motor vehicles in use, external trade, government financial reserves, and energy production and consumption. More detailed data on individual countries and areas are provided in the subsequent parts of the present *Yearbook*. These comprise Part Two: Population and Social Statistics; Part Three: Economic Activity; and Part Four: International Economic Relations.

Regional totals may contain incomparabilities between series owing to differences in definitions of regions and lack of data for particular regional components. General information on regional groupings is provided in annex I of the *Yearbook*. Supplementary information on regional groupings used in specific series is provided, as necessary, in table footnotes and in the technical notes at the end of chapter I.

Première partie
Aperçu mondial et régional

I
Aperçu mondial et régional (tableaux 1 à 7)

Cette partie de l'*Annuaire statistique* présente, pour le monde entier et ses principales subdivisions, un choix d'agrégats ayant trait à des questions économiques et sociales essentielles: population et superficie, production agricole et industrielle, véhicules automobiles en circulation, commerce extérieur, réserves financières publiques, et la production et la consommation d'énergie. Des statistiques plus détaillées pour divers pays ou zones figurent dans les parties ultérieures de l'*Annuaire*, c'est-à-dire dans les deuxième, troisième et quatrième parties intitulées respectivement: population et statistiques sociales, activités économiques et relations économiques internationales.

Les totaux régionaux peuvent présenter des incomparabilités entre les séries en raison de différences dans la définition des régions et de l'absence de données sur tel ou tel élément régional. A l'annexe I de l'*Annuaire*, on trouvera des renseignements généraux sur les groupements régionaux. Des informations complémentaires sur les groupements régionaux pour certaines séries bien précises sont fournies, lorsqu'il y a lieu, dans les notes figurant au bas des tableaux et dans les notes techniques à la fin du chapitre I.

1
Selected series of world statistics
Séries principales de statistiques mondiales
Population, production, transport, external trade and finance
Population, production, transports, commerce extérieur et finances

Series Séries	Unit or base Unité ou base	1991	1992	1993	1994	1995	1996	1997	1998	1999	2000
World population [1] **Population mondiale** [1]	million	**5385**	**5480**	**5572**	**5630**	**5666**	**5768**	**5849**	**5901**	**5978**	**6055**

Agriculture, forestry and fishing production • Production agricole, forestière et de la pêche
Index numbers • Indices

All commodities Tous produits	1989−91=100	101	104	104	107	109	114	117	118	121	123
Food Produits alimentaires	1989−91=100	101	104	105	108	110	115	118	120	123	125
Crops Cultures	1989−91=100	101	104	104	107	108	115	117	118	120	121
Cereals Céréales	1989−91=100	99	100	100	103	100	109	111	110	111	110
Livestock products Produits de l'élevage	1989−91=100	102	102	103	106	109	111	113	116	119	121

Quantities • Quantités

Oil crops Cultures d'huile	million t.	77	79	80	88	92	93	98	103	109	110
Meat Viande	million t.	137	138	140	144	146	146	151	157	160	162
Roundwood Bois rond	million m³	3273	3199	3187	3193	3243	3231	3286	3182	3291	3353
Fish production Production halieutique	million t.	98.2	100.8	86.6	91.6	91.9	93.5	93.8	86.9	92.9	...

Industrial production • Production industrielle
Index numbers [2] • Indices [2]

All commodities Tous produits	1990=100	100	101	102	107	111	115	121	124	129	137
Mining Mines	1990=100	101	103	104	108	110	113	115	116	114	118
Manufacturing Manufactures	1990=100	100	101	101	106	111	115	122	125	130	140

Quantities • Quantités

Coal Houille	million t.	3460	3526	3462	3592	3745	3804	3834	3711	...	...
Lignite and brown coal Lignite et charbon brun	million t.	1056	1040	995	1002	941	949	929	917	...	...
Crude petroleum Pétrole brut	million t.	2987	3019	3003	3055	3080	3142	3233	3289	...	...
Natural gas Gaz naturel	petajoules pétajoules	76750	76117	78521	80785	85450	89912	90107	90841	...	...
Pig−iron and ferro−alloys Fonte et ferro−alliages	million t.	491	491	494	502	518	511	534	528	532	...
Fabrics • Tissus Cellulosic and non−cellulosic fibres Cellulosiques et non cellulosiques	million m²	18473	18386	17131	12712	13367	13132	13334	13073	12914	...
Cotton and wool Coton et laines	million m²	67972	66483	66921	63405	68640	61770	66968	65084	65375	...
Leather footwear Chaussures de cuir	million pairs	4212	4287	3998	3751	3673	3574	3570	3522	3518	...
Sulphuric acid Acide sulfurique	million t.	98	89	81	81	87	87	90	91	94	...
Refrigerators Réfrigérateurs	million	53	53	56	62	64	63	68	66	71	...
Washing machines Machines à laver	million	46	44	48	49	46	48	53	53	55	...

1
Selected series of world statistics
Population, production, transport, external trade and finance [*cont.*]
Séries principales de statistiques mondiales
Population, production, transports, commerce extérieur et finances [*suite*]

Series Séries	Unit or base Unité ou base	1991	1992	1993	1994	1995	1996	1997	1998	1999	2000
Machine tools · Machines outils											
Drilling and boring machines	thousands										
Perceuses	milliers	117	94	87	73	76	66	67	54	45	...
Lathes	thousands										
Tours	milliers	89	63	49	52	66	65	62	58	52	...
Lorries · Camions											
Assembled	thousands										
Assemblés	milliers	635	598	679	687	761	830	891	846	854	...
Produced	thousands										
Fabriqués	milliers	11070	11628	10473	10437	10049	10082	10336	10329	10066	...
Aluminium	thousands t.										
Aluminium	milliers t.	24078	24516	24978	25085	25485	26884	27971	28677	29047	...
Cement											
Ciment	million t.	1161	1215	1279	1353	1421	1466	1512	1515	1570	
Electricity[3]	billion kWh										
Electricité[3]	milliard kWh	12041	12141	12403	12697	13386	13789	14086	14446	...	...
Fertilizers[4]											
Engrais[4]	million t.	144.5	137.8	132.3	135.8	142.5	146.9	146.6	146.5	148.9	
Sugar, raw											
Sucre, brut	million t.	112.3	117.4	111.9	110.5	117.9	125.1	125.1	126.0	134.9	130.6
Woodpulp											
Pâte de bois	million t.	155.2	152.0	151.3	161.9	161.6	156.6	162.7	160.4	163.8	171.3
Sawnwood											
Sciages	million m³	458	438	431	434	425	421	420	411	423	421
Motor vehicles · Véhicules automobiles											
Passenger cars											
Voitures de tourisme	million	33.63	33.81	31.98	33.60	33.14	33.94	34.20	32.93	...	...
Commercial vehicles											
Véhicules utilitaires	million	11.51	12.13	11.04	11.07	10.72	10.74	10.07	10.74	...	...

Transport · Transports

Motor vehicles in use · Véhicules automobiles en service

Series Séries	Unit or base Unité ou base	1991	1992	1993	1994	1995	1996	1997	1998	1999	2000
Passenger cars	thousands										
Voitures de tourisme	milliers	451928	445742	449990	469303	457763	470587	452101	477096	...	...
Commercial vehicles	thousands										
Véhicules utilitaires	milliers	141930	139575	141023	149548	165368	186867	176943	185943	...	...

External trade · Commerce extérieur

Value · Valeur

Series	Unit	1991	1992	1993	1994	1995	1996	1997	1998	1999	2000
Imports, c.i.f.	billion US$										
Importations c.a.f.	milliard $E.–U.	3554.6	3797.9	3741.5	4255.4	5083.7	5327.6	5505.8	5426.0	5658.0	6373.1
Exports, f.o.b.	billion US$										
Exportations f.o.b.	milliard $E.–U.	3444.2	3688.2	3707.8	4218.5	5045.1	5257.1	5446.0	5370.7	5543.2	6165.1

Quantum: index of exports · Quantum : indice des exportations

Series	Unit	1991	1992	1993	1994	1995	1996	1997	1998	1999	2000
All commodities											
Tous produits	1990=100	105	110	113	123	137	137	166	175	181	199
Manufactures											
Produits manufacturés	1990=100	105	111	115	130	141	152	172	172	180	195

Unit value: index of exports[5] · Valeur unitaire : indice des exportations[5]

Series	Unit	1991	1992	1993	1994	1995	1996	1997	1998	1999	2000
All commodities											
Tous produits	1990=100	98	100	97	101	109	108	97	91	90	92
Manufactures											
Produits manufacturés	1990=100	100	103	99	101	110	106	98	95	91	88

Primary commodities: price indexes[56] · Produits de base : indices des prix[56]

Series	Unit	1991	1992	1993	1994	1995	1996	1997	1998	1999	2000
All commodities											
Tous produits	1980=100	69	71	65	66	72	76	71	56	63	81
Food											
Produits alimentaires	1980=100	85	87	82	87	92	90	87	80	74	69
Non−food: of agricultural origin											
Non alimentaires: d'origine agricole	1980=100	93	91	84	95	106	98	90	81	73	72
Minerals											
Minéraux	1980=100	59	62	55	53	58	67	62	43	57	87

1

Selected series of world statistics
Population, production, transport, external trade and finance [*cont.*]
Séries principales de statistiques mondiales
Population, production, transports, commerce extérieur et finances [*suite*]

Series Séries	Unit or base Unité ou base	1991	1992	1993	1994	1995	1996	1997	1998	1999	2000
Finance • Finances											
International reserves minus gold, billion SDR [7] · Réserves internationales moins l'or, milliard de DTS [7]											
All countries	billion SDR										
Tous les pays	milliard DTS	692.3	720.1	797.8	858.3	988.4	1142.2	1261.3	1244.0	1368.4	1545.5
Position in IMF	billion SDR										
Disponibilité au FMI	milliard DTS	25.9	33.9	32.8	31.7	36.7	38.0	47.1	60.6	54.8	47.4
Foreign exchange	billion SDR										
Devises	milliard DTS	646.2	673.5	750.4	811.8	932.0	1085.7	1193.7	1163.1	1295.2	1479.7
SDR (special drawing rights)	billion SDR										
DTS (droits de tirage spéciaux)	milliard DTS	20.6	12.9	14.6	15.8	19.8	18.5	20.5	20.4	18.5	18.5

Sources:
Databases of the Food and Agriculture Organization of the United Nations (FAO), Rome; the International Monetary Fund (IMF), Washington, D.C.; and the United Nations Statistics Division, New York.

1   Annual data: mid–year estimates.
2   Excluding China and the countries of the former USSR (except Russian Federation and Ukraine).
3   Electricity generated by establishments for public or private use.
4   Year beginning 1 July.
5   Indexes computed in US dollars.
6   Export price indexes.
7   End of period.

Sources:
Les bases de données de l'Organisation des Nations Unies pour l'alimentation et l'agriculture (FAO), Rome; du Fonds Monétaire International (FMI), Washington, D.C.; et de la Division de statistique de l'Organisation des Nations Unies, New York.

1   Données annuelles : estimations au milieu de l'année.
2   Non compris la Chine et les pays de l'ancienne URSS (sauf la Fédération de Russie et Ukraine).
3   L'électricité produite par des entreprises d'utilisation publique ou privée.
4   L'année commençant le 1er juillet.
5   Indice calculé en dollars des Etats–Unis.
6   Indice des prix à l'exportation.
7   Fin de la période.

2
Population, rate of increase, birth and death rates, surface area and density
Population, taux d'accroissement, taux de natalité et taux de mortalité, superficie et densité

Major areas and regions Grandes régions et régions	Mid–year population estimates (millions) Estimations de population au milieu de l'année (millions)								Annual rate of increase Taux d'accroissement annuel % 1995–2000	Birth rate Taux de natalité (0/000)	Death rate Taux de mortalité (0/000)	Surface area (km²) Superficie (km²) (000's) 1999	Density[1] Densité[1] 2000
	1950	1960	1970	1980	1990	1995	1999	2000					
World *Monde*	2 521	3 022	3 696	4 440	5 266	5 666	5 978	6 055	1.3	22	9	135 641	45
Africa **Afrique**	221	277	357	467	615	700	767	784	2.4	38	14	30 306	26
Eastern Africa Afrique orientale	65	82	108	144	192	217	240	247	2.6	42	18	6 356	39
Middle Africa Afrique centrale	26	32	40	52	70	84	93	96	2.7	45	15	6 613	14
Northern Africa Afrique septentrionale	53	67	85	110	142	157	170	173	2.0	28	7	8 525	20
Southern Africa Afrique méridionale	16	20	25	31	39	43	46	47	1.6	28	12	2 675	18
Western Africa Afrique occidentale	61	76	98	128	172	196	216	222	2.5	40	15	6 138	36
Northern America[2] **Amérique septentrionale**[2]	172	204	232	255	282	297	307	310	0.9	14	8	21 517	14
Latin America **Amérique latine**	167	218	285	361	440	480	511	519	1.6	23	6	20 533	25
Caribbean Caraïbes	17	20	25	29	34	36	38	38	1.1	21	8	235	162
Central America Amérique centrale	37	49	67	90	111	123	133	135	1.9	27	5	2 480	55
South America Amérique du Sud	113	145	192	242	295	321	341	346	1.5	22	7	17 819	19
Asia[3] **Asie**[3]	1 402	1 702	2 147	2 641	3 181	3 436	3 634	3 683	1.4	22	8	31 764	116
Eastern Asia Asie orientale	671	791	987	1 178	1 350	1 422	1 473	1 485	0.9	16	7	11 762	126
South–central Asia Asie central et du Sud	499	621	788	990	1 239	1 365	1 466	1 491	1.8	27	9	10 776	138
South–eastern Asia Asie du Sud–Est	182	225	287	360	441	480	511	519	1.5	23	7	4 495	115
Western Asia[3] Asie occidentale[3]	50	66	86	113	150	168	184	188	2.2	30	7	4 731	40
Europe[3] **Europe**[3]	547	605	656	693	722	728	729	729	0.0	10	11	22 986	32
Eastern Europe Europe orientale	219	253	276	295	311	310	308	307	−0.2	10	13	18 813	16
Northern Europe Europe septentrionale	78	82	87	90	92	94	94	94	0.1	12	11	1 749	54
Southern Europe Europe mériodionale	109	118	128	138	143	143	144	144	0.1	10	10	1 316	110
Western Europe Europe occidentale	141	152	165	170	176	181	183	183	0.3	11	10	1 107	166
Oceania[2] **Océanie**[2]	12.6	15.7	19.3	22.7	26.4	28.5	30	30.4	1.3	18	8	8 537	4
Australia and New Zealand Australie et Nouvelle–Zélande	10.1	12.6	15.4	17.7	20.2	21.6	22.5	22.7	1.0	14	8	7 984	3
Melanesia Mélanésie	2.1	2.6	3.3	4.2	5.2	5.8	6.3	6.5	2.2	31	9	541	12
Micronesia Micronésie	0.2	0.2	0.3	0.3	0.4	0.5	0.5	0.5	2.6	36	5	3	181
Polynesia Polynésie	0.2	0.3	0.4	0.5	0.5	0.6	0.6	0.6	1.6	25	5	9	70

2
Population, rate of increase, birth and death rates, surface area and density [*cont.*]
Population, taux d'accroissement, taux de natalité et taux de
mortalité, superficie et densité [*suite*]

Source:
United Nations Division, New York, "Demographic
Yearbook 1999" and the demographic statistics database.

Source:
Organisation des Nations Unies, Division de statistique, New York,
"Annuaire démographique 1999" et la base de données pour les
statistiques démographiques.

1   Population per square kilometre of surface area. Figures
are merely the quotients of population divided by surface
area and are not to be considered as either reflecting
density in the urban sense or as indicating the supporting
power of a territory's land and resources.
2   Hawaii, a state of the United States of America, is included
in Northern America rather than Oceania.
3   The European portion of Turkey is included in Western
Asia rather than Europe.

1   Habitants per kilomètre carré. Il s'agit simplement du quotient calculé
en divisant la population par la superficie et n'est pas considéré
comme indiquant la densité au sens urbain du mot ni l'effectif de
population que les terres et les ressources du territoire sont capables
de nourrir.
2   Hawaii, un Etat des Etats−Unis d'Amérique, est compris en Amérique
septentrionale plutôt qu'en Océanie.
3   La partie européenne de la Turquie est comprise en Asie Occidentale
plutôt qu'en Europe.

3
Index numbers of total agricultural and food production
Indices de la production agricole totale et de la production alimentaire

1989–1991 = 100

Region or area Région ou zone	1991	1992	1993	1994	1995	1996	1997	1998	1999	2000

A. Total agricultural production · Production agricole totale

Region or area Région ou zone	1991	1992	1993	1994	1995	1996	1997	1998	1999	2000
World *Monde*	**101**	**104**	**104**	**107**	**109**	**114**	**117**	**118**	**121**	**123**
Africa Afrique	105	102	106	109	110	122	120	124	127	127
America, North Amérique du Nord	101	108	101	114	109	114	118	119	122	124
America, South Amérique du Sud	103	106	106	112	119	121	125	128	135	138
Asia Asie	103	112	117	122	127	132	137	141	145	147
Europe Europe	100	94	91	86	86	88	88	86	87	87
Oceania Océanie	101	105	107	102	109	116	118	122	126	126
former USSR † l'ex–URSS †	91	...	...	...	...	...	...	...	...	...

B. Food production · Production alimentaire

Region or area Région ou zone	1991	1992	1993	1994	1995	1996	1997	1998	1999	2000
World *Monde*	**101**	**104**	**105**	**108**	**110**	**115**	**118**	**120**	**123**	**124**
Africa Afrique	105	103	107	110	111	122	121	125	128	127
America, North Amérique du Nord	101	108	101	113	110	114	118	120	122	125
America, South Amérique du Sud	103	106	107	115	122	124	129	131	139	142
Asia Asie	103	112	118	123	128	134	138	143	147	150
Europe Europe	100	94	91	86	86	88	89	87	88	87
Oceania Océanie	101	108	112	107	117	126	128	133	138	138
former USSR † l'ex–URSS †	91	...	...	...	...	...	...	...	...	...

Source:
Food and Agriculture Organization of the United Nations (FAO), Rome, "FAO Production Yearbook 2000" and the FAOSTAT database.

† For information on recent changes in country or area nomenclature pertaining to former Czechoslovakia, Germany, Hong Kong Special Administrative Region (SAR) of China, Macao Special Administrative Region (SAR) of China, SFR of Yugoslavia and the former USSR, see Annex I – Country or area nomenclature, regional and other groupings.

Source:
Organisation des Nations Unies pour l'alimentation et l'agriculture (FAO), Rome, "Annuaire FAO de la production 2000 "et la base de données FAOSTAT.

† Pour les modifications récentes de nomenclature de pays ou de zone concernant l'Allemagne, Hong Kong région administrative spéciale (RAS) de Chine, Macao région administrative spéciale (RAS) de Chine, l'ex–Tchécoslovaquie, l'ex–URSS et l'ex–Rfs de Yougoslavie, voir annexe I – Nomenclature des pays ou des zones, groupements régionaux et autres groupements.

4
Index numbers of per capita total agricultural and food production
Indices de la production agricole totale et de la production alimentaire par habitant

1989-1991 = 100

Region or area Région ou zone	1991	1992	1993	1994	1995	1996	1997	1998	1999	2000
A. Per capita total agricultural production · Production agricole totale par habitant										
World ***Monde***	100	100	100	101	102	104	105	106	107	107
Africa Afrique	102	97	98	98	97	105	101	102	102	99
America, North Amérique du Nord	100	105	97	108	103	106	108	108	109	110
America, South Amérique du Sud	101	102	101	105	109	110	112	112	117	118
Asia Asie	101	107	110	112	115	118	121	122	124	125
Europe Europe	100	93	91	85	85	87	88	86	87	86
Oceania Océanie	100	102	102	96	101	106	107	109	111	110
former USSR † l'ex−URSS †	91	...	...	...	...	...	...	...	...	...
B. Per capita food production · Production alimentaire par habitant										
World ***Monde***	99	101	100	102	102	105	106	107	108	108
Africa Afrique	102	98	99	99	98	105	101	103	102	100
America, North Amérique du Nord	99	105	97	108	103	106	108	109	110	111
America, South Amérique du Sud	101	103	102	107	112	112	115	116	121	121
Asia Asie	101	106	110	113	116	119	122	124	126	126
Europe Europe	100	93	91	85	85	87	88	86	87	86
Oceania Océanie	99	105	107	100	109	116	115	118	122	120
former USSR † l'ex−URSS †	90	...	...	...	...	...	...	...	...	...

Source:
Food and Agriculture Organization of the United Nations (FAO), Rome, "FAO Production Yearbook 2000" and the FAOSTAT database.

Source:
Organisation des Nations Unies pour l'alimentation et l'agriculture (FAO), Rome, "Annuaire FAO de la production 2000 "et la base de données FAOSTAT.

† For information on recent changes in country or area nomenclature pertaining to former Czechoslovakia, Germany, Hong Kong Special Administrative Region (SAR) of China, Macao Special Administrative Region (SAR) of China, SFR of Yugoslavia and the former USSR, see Annex I − Country or area nomenclature, regional and other groupings.

† Pour les modifications récentes de nomenclature de pays ou de zone concernant l'Allemagne, Hong Kong région administrative spéciale (RAS) de Chine, Macao région administrative spéciale (RAS) de Chine, l'ex−Tchécoslovaquie, l'ex−URSS et l'ex−Rfs de Yougoslavie, voir annexe I − Nomenclature des pays ou des zones, groupements régionaux et autres groupements.

5

Index numbers of industrial production: world and regions
Indices de la production industrielle: monde et régions
1990=100

Region and industry [ISIC Rev.3] Région et industrie [CITI Rév.3]	Weight(%) Pond.(%)	1992	1993	1994	1995	1996	1997	1998	1999	2000
World · Monde										
Total industry [CDE] **Total, industrie [CDE]**	**100.0**	**100.3**	**101.3**	**102.1**	**106.7**	**111.2**	**114.9**	**121.0**	**123.6**	**128.6**
Total mining [C] **Total, industries extractives[C]**	**9.8**	**101.3**	**102.7**	**103.8**	**107.1**	**109.3**	**112.3**	**114.5**	**115.0**	**114.8**
Coal Houille	1.2	98.7	96.2	91.6	92.7	94.7	95.1	96.2	95.6	95.8
Crude petroleum and natural gas Pétrole brut et gaz naturel	6.6	102.2	104.7	107.2	110.7	112.6	115.7	118.0	118.0	117.4
Metal ores Minerais métalliques	1.0	98.7	97.4	91.6	91.5	95.7	101.3	104.0	108.1	107.2
Total manufacturing [D] **Total, industries manufacturières[D]**	**81.6**	**99.9**	**100.7**	**101.3**	**106.3**	**111.1**	**114.9**	**121.8**	**124.6**	**130.4**
Food, beverages, tobacco Industries alimentaires, boissons, tabac	10.0	102.1	103.7	104.5	108.3	111.1	113.2	116.4	118.5	125.1
Textiles Textiles	3.9	100.8	102.2	101.0	104.6	105.4	106.1	109.5	106.1	106.1
Wearing apparel, leather and footwear Articles d'habillement, cuir et chaussures	2.9	98.2	96.3	94.8	95.5	94.7	92.5	91.1	86.9	82.5
Wood and wood products Bois et articles en bois	1.8	95.7	97.5	97.9	102.4	103.5	103.5	106.6	107.1	108.5
Paper, printing, publishing and recorded media Papier, imprimerie, édition et supports enregistrés	6.3	99.5	101.1	103.1	105.8	107.3	107.4	111.2	111.8	113.0
Chemicals and related products Produits chimiques et alliés	12.7	100.5	103.9	105.6	110.9	114.8	118.4	124.6	126.1	130.8
Non−metallic mineral products Produits minéraux non métalliques	3.5	98.4	99.2	99.3	103.9	108.1	111.0	114.7	112.8	115.3
Basic metals Métallurgie de base	4.9	98.1	96.4	98.0	104.2	108.2	110.2	116.5	113.3	113.3
Fabricated metal products Fabrications d'ouvrages en métaux	12.2	97.4	96.2	97.0	104.3	112.2	116.1	121.7	122.3	120.7
Office and related electrical products Machines de bureau et autres appareils élect.	12.3	102.7	102.0	103.1	111.3	125.1	138.7	156.3	175.5	205.1
Transport equipment Equipement de transports	7.8	99.5	100.9	98.2	102.0	104.9	107.2	117.8	121.4	125.2
Electricity, gas, water [E] **Electricité, gaz et eau [E]**	**8.6**	**103.9**	**104.8**	**107.6**	**110.4**	**114.2**	**118.6**	**120.6**	**123.1**	**126.5**
Developed regions [1] · Régions développées [1]										
Total industry [CDE] **Total, industrie [CDE]**	**100.0**	**99.2**	**99.4**	**99.3**	**103.7**	**107.8**	**110.7**	**116.1**	**119.4**	**123.3**
Total mining [C] **Total, industries extractives [C]**	**5.6**	**100.4**	**99.5**	**100.5**	**104.4**	**105.6**	**108.4**	**109.5**	**107.9**	**104.7**
Coal Houille	0.9	98.1	94.5	88.8	89.3	89.6	89.3	89.7	88.0	87.3
Crude petroleum and natural gas Pétrole brut et gaz naturel	3.3	101.5	101.0	104.4	109.6	111.2	115.5	116.5	113.3	108.8
Metal ores Minerais métalliques	0.6	101.2	102.8	101.7	100.1	99.0	100.9	102.5	102.3	94.5
Total manufacturing [D] **Total, industries manufacturières [D]**	**85.9**	**98.7**	**98.9**	**98.5**	**103.2**	**107.6**	**110.4**	**116.6**	**120.3**	**124.9**
Food, beverages, tobacco Industries alimentaires, boissons, tabac	9.9	101.3	102.2	102.4	105.4	107.0	107.4	109.3	109.7	110.3
Textiles Textiles	2.3	97.4	98.3	95.4	98.3	97.1	94.2	97.5	95.1	92.6
Wearing apparel, leather and footwear Articles d'habillement, cuir et chaussures	2.6	97.8	95.8	93.6	94.7	93.7	90.6	88.6	83.9	78.3
Wood and wood products Bois et articles en bois	2.0	95.1	97.2	97.0	101.9	103.0	102.8	106.3	108.2	110.7

5

Index numbers of industrial production: world and regions [*cont.*]
Indices de la production industrielle: monde et régions [*suite*]
1990=100

Region and industry [ISIC Rev.3] Région et industrie [CITI Rév.3]	Weight(%) Pond.(%)	1992	1993	1994	1995	1996	1997	1998	1999	2000
Paper, printing, publishing and recorded media										
Papier, imprimerie, édition et supports enregistrés	8.9	100.0	101.4	103.6	104.6	104.8	109.4	110.4	111.5	113.3
Chemicals and related products										
Produits chimiques et alliés	13.3	102.9	103.4	108.4	112.1	114.5	121.1	124.4	128.8	132.5
Non−metallic mineral products										
Produits minéraux non métalliques	3.2	94.6	93.1	97.8	100.2	101.1	103.4	104.3	106.9	110.1
Basic metals										
Métallurgie de base	4.6	95.2	94.8	100.2	103.1	103.3	108.6	106.6	106.4	112.3
Fabricated metal products										
Fabrications d'ouvrages en métaux	15.8	95.6	97.7	106.3	116.7	122.6	129.7	134.9	139.5	151.2
Office and related electrical products										
Machines de bureau et autres appareils élect.	11.8	100.3	100.2	107.0	118.6	130.0	145.2	160.1	182.4	222.7
Transport equipment										
Equipement de transports	9.3	96.9	93.1	97.1	98.2	100.0	108.1	114.4	117.6	121.1
Electricity, gas, water [E]										
Electricité, gaz et eau [E]	**8.0**	**104.2**	**106.2**	**107.9**	**111.1**	**114.9**	**115.7**	**117.3**	**120.4**	**124.6**

Developing countries [2] · Pays en développement [2]

Total industry [CDE]										
Total, industrie [CDE]	**100.0**	**108.8**	**112.7**	**118.0**	**124.1**	**130.7**	**138.9**	**138.5**	**143.3**	**153.8**
Total mining [C]										
Total, industries extractives [C]	**24.7**	**105.5**	**106.5**	**109.5**	**112.2**	**115.2**	**118.7**	**121.2**	**119.5**	**125.0**
Coal										
Houille	1.1	101.6	100.8	103.8	111.3	113.7	117.4	119.1	122.3	126.8
Crude petroleum and natural gas										
Pétrole brut et gaz naturel	20.0	107.1	109.0	111.4	113.6	115.8	119.3	12¹.4	119.2	124.5
Metal ores										
Minerais métalliques	2.2	92.0	82.8	85.1	94.6	104.8	108.6	118.2	120.2	130.9
Total manufacturing [D]										
Total, industries manufacturières [D]	**69.4**	**109.9**	**114.6**	**120.5**	**127.6**	**135.4**	**145.2**	**143.2**	**150.0**	**162.5**
Food, beverages, tobacco										
Industries alimentaires, boissons, tabac	12.9	108.4	110.7	115.9	122.0	127.5	131.5	132.6	135.5	139.0
Textiles										
Textiles	6.9	107.2	107.7	112.1	114.6	119.6	123.3	118.6	119.5	122.9
Wearing apparel, leather and footwear										
Articles d'habillement, cuir et chaussures	3.7	97.1	96.3	95.3	95.8	96.0	95.2	94.6	93.8	96.5
Wood and wood products										
Bois et articles bois	1.2	99.1	103.8	106.4	107.6	110.2	110.7	101.2	99.0	99.9
Paper, printing, publishing and recorded media										
Papier, imprimerie, édition et supports enregistrés	3.0	113.2	119.3	126.5	131.3	134.6	139.5	139.0	140.9	145.4
Chemicals and related products										
Produits chimiques et alliés	13.7	107.8	113.9	119.8	125.3	134.1	144.5	144.7	150.4	155.4
Non−metallic mineral products										
Produits minéraux non métalliques	4.0	114.0	119.1	124.0	133.6	142.7	151.1	141.6	148.8	154.0
Basic metals										
Métallurgie de base	4.7	101.3	111.1	120.7	129.3	138.6	147.5	142.8	145.9	152.7
Fabricated metal products										
Fabrications d'ouvrages en métaux	7.0	108.1	112.4	120.4	123.3	131.5	141.6	134.5	140.2	156.4
Office and related electrical products										
Machines de bureau et autres appareils élect.	6.2	109.7	115.3	126.4	142.8	156.9	175.7	182.0	215.8	270.9
Transport equipment										
Equipement de transports	3.9	139.1	149.8	150.7	172.6	181.2	216.8	213.1	229.8	267.6
Electricity, gas, water [E]										
Electricité, gaz et eau [E]	**5.9**	**108.8**	**116.2**	**124.7**	**132.0**	**140.2**	**148.9**	**155.4**	**164.7**	**172.9**

Northern America [3] · Amérique septentrionale [3]

Total industry [CDE]										
Total, industrie [CDE]	**100.0**	**100.3**	**103.9**	**109.7**	**114.9**	**119.9**	**127.9**	**134.8**	**142.1**	**153.2**
Total mining [C]										
Total, industries extractives [C]	**6.5**	**96.5**	**96.9**	**99.5**	**99.8**	**101.2**	**103.2**	**101.3**	**96.8**	**99.3**
Coal										
Houille	0.8	95.6	90.7	99.1	99.0	101.3	104.5	105.6	103.7	104.5

5

Index numbers of industrial production: world and regions [*cont.*]
Indices de la production industrielle: monde et régions [*suite*]
1990=100

Region and industry [ISIC Rev.3] Région et industrie [CITI Rév.3]	Weight(%) Pond.(%)	1992	1993	1994	1995	1996	1997	1998	1999	2000
Crude petroleum and natural gas										
Pétrole brut et gaz naturel	4.4	95.8	97.5	98.9	98.3	99.5	101.0	97.4	91.6	94.9
Metal ores										
Minerais métalliques	0.5	104.3	100.3	97.8	98.9	101.8	102.5	101.7	93.5	92.8
Total manufacturing [D]										
Total, industries manufacturières [D]	**86.7**	**100.4**	**104.3**	**110.6**	**116.3**	**121.7**	**130.8**	**138.9**	**147.4**	**159.7**
Food, beverages, tobacco										
Industries alimentaires, boissons, tabac	11.3	101.9	101.5	105.7	108.4	108.3	109.4	112.3	112.3	114.0
Textiles										
Textiles	1.6	107.1	112.7	118.8	118.9	117.2	118.1	116.9	113.4	109.4
Wearing apparel, leather and footwear										
Articles d'habillement, cuir et chaussures	2.3	100.4	102.6	105.2	105.2	102.9	103.6	98.9	93.3	90.3
Wood and wood products										
Bois et articles bois	2.2	97.9	99.0	103.8	105.5	108.1	112.0	116.4	120.5	117.2
Paper, printing, publishing and recorded media										
Papier, imprimerie, édition et supports enregistrés	11.3	98.6	100.0	101.3	101.8	102.2	107.7	108.1	108.5	110.3
Chemicals and related products										
Produits chimiques et alliés	14.1	103.2	106.1	110.5	113.0	115.8	123.9	128.5	132.8	135.2
Non−metallic mineral products										
Produits minéraux non métalliques	2.4	94.2	96.0	101.5	104.2	110.8	114.9	120.7	124.7	127.5
Basic metals										
Métallurgie de base	3.5	97.0	102.0	109.8	112.1	115.4	121.0	123.2	125.7	128.8
Fabricated metal products										
Fabrications d'ouvrages en métaux	17.4	98.4	106.5	119.1	132.4	142.9	154.2	164.5	174.4	192.4
Office and related electrical products										
Machines de bureau et autres appareils élect.	8.2	107.0	112.6	122.8	142.2	165.9	197.4	232.7	286.5	368.4
Transport equipment										
Equipement de transports	9.5	96.9	101.4	105.9	106.2	107.6	116.9	126.5	130.3	130.2
Electricity, gas, water [E]										
Electricité, gaz et eau [E]	**6.8**	**101.7**	**105.6**	**107.2**	**111.0**	**114.5**	**114.4**	**115.2**	**118.3**	**122.0**

Latin America and the Caribbean
Amérique latine et Caraïbes

Total industry [CDE]										
Total, industrie [CDE]	**100.0**	**103.7**	**107.9**	**115.4**	**116.5**	**122.6**	**130.0**	**131.3**	**128.8**	**134.3**
Total mining [C]										
Total, industries extractives [C]	**11.7**	**104.7**	**105.7**	**111.6**	**119.3**	**128.2**	**135.6**	**140.4**	**136.7**	**136.3**
Coal										
Houille	0.5	95.1	95.2	103.7	110.3	116.6	125.7	126.0	134.8	145.3
Crude petroleum and natural gas										
Pétrole brut et gaz naturel	7.2	109.3	111.7	116.6	125.7	134.6	142.1	148.8	139.2	134.0
Metal ores										
Minerais métalliques	2.7	105.1	104.6	107.6	117.1	128.1	133.1	136.0	146.7	156.5
Total manufacturing [D]										
Total, industries manufacturières [D]	**80.8**	**103.9**	**108.4**	**116.1**	**115.8**	**121.4**	**128.9**	**129.3**	**126.0**	**132.1**
Food, beverages, tobacco										
Industries alimentaires, boissons, tabac	18.3	108.5	109.2	114.0	117.7	121.3	125.2	127.7	130.4	130.9
Textiles										
Textiles	4.1	101.7	97.3	101.1	97.0	99.7	99.1	94.6	93.3	98.2
Wearing apparel, leather and footwear										
Articles d'habillement, cuir et chaussures	4.1	95.5	97.8	100.0	94.8	97.6	97.6	96.0	90.1	94.7
Wood and wood products										
Bois et articles bois	1.2	104.0	110.6	120.3	116.6	128.2	137.4	140.9	136.5	139.6
Paper, printing, publishing and recorded media										
Papier, imprimerie, édition et supports enregistrés	4.9	112.7	119.1	126.1	127.0	129.3	134.4	136.1	134.3	141.1
Chemicals and related products										
Produits chimiques et alliés	16.3	102.2	106.1	112.2	111.1	118.2	125.9	129.6	128.9	132.2
Non−metallic mineral products										
Produits minéraux non métalliques	3.9	105.8	111.9	117.6	114.9	121.3	130.5	132.5	128.4	130.9
Basic metals										
Métallurgie de base	5.0	94.9	99.7	108.8	111.3	120.1	130.5	131.5	127.3	133.5

5

Index numbers of industrial production: world and regions [*cont.*]

Indices de la production industrielle: monde et régions [*suite*]

1990=100

Region and industry [ISIC Rev.3] Région et industrie [CITI Rév.3]	Weight(%) Pond.(%)	1992	1993	1994	1995	1996	1997	1998	1999	2000
Fabricated metal products										
Fabrications d'ouvrages en métaux	7.2	98.3	105.8	117.3	111.6	112.4	121.9	122.4	117.2	129.2
Office and related electrical products										
Machines de bureau et autres appareils élect.	7.5	90.6	98.5	112.6	122.5	132.3	135.4	128.1	118.0	131.8
Transport equipment										
Equipement de transports	5.0	114.8	129.3	144.5	135.6	144.0	168.7	164.5	152.2	173.9
Electricity, gas, water [E]										
Electricité, gaz et eau [E]	**7.5**	**100.7**	**106.1**	**114.3**	**119.6**	**126.8**	**133.6**	**138.7**	**147.0**	**154.2**

Asia · Asie

	Weight(%) Pond.(%)	1992	1993	1994	1995	1996	1997	1998	1999	2000
Total industry [CDE]										
Total, industrie [CDE]	**100.0**	**103.3**	**103.1**	**105.4**	**110.6**	**114.8**	**120.3**	**116.1**	**119.9**	**127.8**
Total mining [C]										
Total, industries extractives [C]	**12.7**	**107.7**	**109.9**	**113.2**	**114.8**	**116.3**	**119.1**	**121.8**	**120.7**	**127.0**
Coal										
Houille	0.7	102.4	100.7	101.3	107.5	108.7	107.1	108.1	109.8	110.8
Crude petroleum and natural gas										
Pétrole brut et gaz naturel	10.5	107.9	110.4	113.3	114.4	115.2	118.2	120.4	119.0	125.5
Metal ores										
Minerais métalliques	0.5	123.3	123.9	138.2	165.8	188.0	194.8	232.8	235.9	266.3
Total manufacturing [D]										
Total, industries manufacturières [D]	**80.3**	**102.0**	**101.0**	**102.7**	**108.4**	**112.9**	**118.8**	**112.8**	**117.3**	**125.6**
Food, beverages, tobacco										
Industries alimentaires, boissons, tabac	8.9	104.5	105.8	109.7	113.3	117.1	118.5	115.7	117.6	121.2
Textiles										
Textiles	4.9	104.8	102.6	105.0	107.2	111.5	115.2	109.0	109.2	110.6
Wearing apparel, leather and footwear										
Articles d'habillement, cuir et chaussures	2.8	97.0	91.2	87.4	86.3	84.0	80.2	75.5	74.6	72.0
Wood and wood products										
Bois et articles bois	1.1	96.7	95.7	94.0	93.3	92.2	89.4	76.0	73.5	72.5
Paper, printing, publishing and recorded media										
Papier, imprimerie, édition et supports enregistrés	5.0	105.6	108.9	111.3	115.2	117.5	119.4	116.3	115.9	115.4
Chemicals and related products										
Produits chimiques et alliés	11.9	106.3	108.7	113.4	120.7	125.8	132.9	129.4	135.2	138.4
Non-metallic mineral products										
Produits minéraux non métalliques	3.8	104.6	104.7	107.2	114.3	118.8	122.5	108.8	114.5	119.8
Basic metals										
Métallurgie de base	6.3	95.7	96.6	98.0	103.3	104.1	109.0	97.7	99.3	107.6
Fabricated metal products										
Fabrications d'ouvrages en métaux	9.9	96.4	92.2	94.9	99.9	104.9	107.9	97.5	97.7	104.9
Office and related electrical products										
Machines de bureau et autres appareils élect.	15.1	100.2	97.7	102.5	113.3	122.6	133.4	132.0	146.4	173.4
Transport equipment										
Equipement de transports	6.8	111.2	107.1	102.2	110.4	114.3	129.1	121.8	130.5	142.7
Electricity, gas, water [E]										
Electricité, gaz et eau [E]	**7.0**	**110.3**	**114.7**	**122.6**	**127.8**	**133.9**	**139.9**	**143.5**	**148.5**	**154.8**

Asia excluding Israel and Japan

Asie à l'exception de l'Israël et du Japon

	Weight(%) Pond.(%)	1992	1993	1994	1995	1996	1997	1998	1999	2000
Total industry [CDE]										
Total, industrie [CDE]	**100.0**	**114.0**	**118.9**	**123.7**	**134.1**	**142.0**	**151.9**	**149.6**	**160.3**	**175.2**
Total mining [C]										
Total, industries extractives [C]	**26.7**	**107.9**	**110.3**	**113.8**	**115.5**	**117.0**	**120.1**	**122.9**	**121.7**	**128.4**
Coal										
Houille	1.5	103.8	102.6	103.7	111.8	112.9	114.8	117.0	118.4	120.9
Crude petroleum and natural gas										
Pétrole brut et gaz naturel	23.0	107.9	110.4	113.3	114.4	115.2	118.2	120.4	119.1	125.5
Metal ores										
Minerais métalliques	1.0	124.1	125.0	140.7	170.6	195.1	202.8	243.8	247.6	280.4
Total manufacturing [D]										
Total, industries manufacturières [D]	**68.2**	**116.2**	**121.6**	**126.6**	**140.4**	**150.6**	**163.1**	**158.2**	**173.5**	**191.9**

5
Index numbers of industrial production: world and regions [*cont.*]
Indices de la production industrielle: monde et régions [*suite*]
1990=100

Region and industry [ISIC Rev.3] Région et industrie [CITI Rév.3]	Weight(%) Pond.(%)	1992	1993	1994	1995	1996	1997	1998	1999	2000
Food, beverages, tobacco Industries alimentaires, boissons, tabac	10.4	110.5	115.5	123.0	133.9	142.7	147.2	144.1	146.9	154.7
Textiles Textiles	8.6	110.2	112.8	118.2	123.8	131.1	136.4	131.0	133.1	136.3
Wearing apparel, leather and footwear Articles d'habillement, cuir et chaussures	3.5	99.7	96.0	91.6	96.5	95.3	92.5	91.3	95.1	96.2
Wood and wood products Bois et articles bois	1.1	103.0	106.8	107.1	111.9	111.1	112.3	95.3	94.1	95.2
Paper, printing, publishing and recorded media Papier, imprimerie, édition et supports enregistrés	2.4	115.9	123.1	131.1	143.7	148.9	153.6	149.1	157.7	158.5
Chemicals and related products Produits chimiques et alliés	13.5	112.1	120.1	126.1	136.5	146.7	159.3	157.1	166.8	173.1
Non−metallic mineral products Produits minéraux non métalliques	4.3	119.9	125.0	129.8	146.5	157.2	166.6	148.0	162.6	169.5
Basic metals Métallurgie de base	5.1	109.2	126.7	137.1	153.8	163.7	171.8	159.4	171.3	180.3
Fabricated metal products Fabrications d'ouvrages en métaux	7.6	115.4	118.0	123.9	132.5	145.7	156.1	142.4	154.4	172.1
Office and related electrical products Machines de bureau et autres appareils élect.	6.3	124.6	128.7	137.9	159.5	177.0	207.8	224.0	291.5	378.9
Transport equipment Equipement de transports	3.8	161.8	170.0	159.2	207.6	216.8	263.3	259.9	301.5	354.8
Electricity, gas, water [E] **Electricité, gaz et eau [E]**	**5.1**	**117.1**	**127.7**	**137.1**	**147.1**	**157.0**	**168.3**	**175.5**	**185.9**	**196.3**

Europe · Europe

Total industry [CDE] **Total, industrie [CDE]**	**100.0**	**95.6**	**92.1**	**93.3**	**95.8**	**96.0**	**99.0**	**102.1**	**104.1**	**109.5**
Total mining [C] **Total, industries extractives [C]**	**6.0**	**100.0**	**100.1**	**104.7**	**107.1**	**111.1**	**109.3**	**105.9**	**105.8**	**105.1**
Coal Houille	1.9	86.9	78.7	69.4	66.9	63.2	58.6	51.0	47.4	44.8
Crude petroleum and natural gas Pétrole brut et gaz naturel	2.8	113.4	121.0	136.0	142.2	154.2	153.4	150.5	151.4	151.3
Metal ores Minerais métalliques	0.5	82.2	69.4	60.5	59.3	52.9	47.4	42.7	38.1	34.7
Total manufacturing [D] **Total, industries manufacturières [D]**	**85.8**	**94.6**	**90.6**	**91.7**	**94.3**	**94.0**	**97.6**	**101.3**	**103.5**	**109.5**
Food, beverages, tobacco Industries alimentaires, boissons, tabac	10.2	98.1	97.7	97.6	97.3	97.2	98.6	99.5	100.4	102.2
Textiles Textiles	4.2	83.6	75.1	68.6	65.3	61.4	62.9	60.7	57.5	57.7
Wearing apparel, leather and footwear Articles d'habillement, cuir et chaussures	3.3	88.8	82.7	76.7	73.4	70.2	68.7	64.6	59.7	57.5
Wood and wood products Bois et articles bois	2.1	93.0	88.8	88.5	90.2	86.4	87.9	91.2	92.6	96.7
Paper, printing, publishing and recorded media Papier, imprimerie, édition et supports enregistrés	5.6	99.9	100.3	103.3	104.6	103.6	108.0	112.1	115.4	118.2
Chemicals and related products Produits chimiques et alliés	12.8	98.0	94.8	98.2	102.3	103.5	108.8	112.5	116.3	121.7
Non−metallic mineral products Produits minéraux non métalliques	4.2	93.9	90.6	93.9	96.1	93.6	95.0	96.9	98.9	102.2
Basic metals Métallurgie de base	4.8	89.3	83.1	85.7	88.8	86.5	90.7	90.9	87.9	92.7
Fabricated metal products Fabrications d'ouvrages en métaux	15.7	90.6	86.3	84.9	90.3	88.3	90.1	92.5	91.7	95.7
Office and related electrical products Machines de bureau et autres appareils élect.	11.7	97.4	95.5	98.9	104.6	108.5	116.1	128.0	139.3	162.7
Transport equipment Equipement de transports	8.2	95.0	84.2	89.1	91.6	93.2	99.8	109.2	112.4	119.4
Electricity, gas, water [E] **Electricité, gaz et eau [E]**	**8.3**	**102.7**	**102.5**	**101.4**	**103.2**	**105.9**	**105.9**	**107.2**	**109.8**	**113.6**

5
Index numbers of industrial production: world and regions [cont.]
Indices de la production industrielle: monde et régions [suite]
1990=100

Region and industry [ISIC Rev.3] Région et industrie [CITI Rév.3]	Weight(%) Pond.(%)	1992	1993	1994	1995	1996	1997	1998	1999	2000
European Union [4] · Union européenne [4]										
Total industry [CDE]										
Total, industrie [CDE]	**100.0**	**98.8**	**96.0**	**100.8**	**104.7**	**105.6**	**109.7**	**114.3**	**117.1**	**123.6**
Total mining [C]										
Total, industries extractives [C]	**3.7**	**100.2**	**101.7**	**108.6**	**111.0**	**113.8**	**111.9**	**111.4**	**112.7**	**109.9**
Coal										
Houille	1.0	89.0	80.4	71.6	70.9	66.6	64.4	57.8	55.7	51.7
Crude petroleum and natural gas										
Pétrole brut et gaz naturel	1.8	110.7	119.6	135.7	139.8	148.9	145.7	146.2	147.5	143.0
Metal ores										
Minerais métalliques	0.1	92.8	74.6	77.9	80.6	74.2	71.4	67.5	61.8	59.0
Total manufacturing [D]										
Total, industries manufacturières [D]	**87.7**	**98.1**	**94.7**	**99.9**	**103.9**	**104.4**	**109.2**	**114.1**	**116.9**	**124.0**
Food, beverages, tobacco										
Industries alimentaires, boissons, tabac	9.8	103.0	104.0	106.3	107.3	108.2	111.1	112.1	114.0	116.7
Textiles										
Textiles	3.3	95.1	90.0	93.0	91.7	88.2	91.9	90.5	87.2	88.3
Wearing apparel, leather and footwear										
Articles d'habillement, cuir et chaussures	3.1	92.4	88.0	89.2	88.8	85.4	83.7	80.6	74.4	71.3
Wood and wood products										
Bois et articles bois	1.8	98.7	98.0	104.9	106.9	103.4	107.1	111.9	115.5	121.5
Paper, printing, publishing and recorded media										
Papier, imprimerie, édition et supports enregistrés	6.9	101.1	101.8	105.6	106.3	105.3	110.1	114.4	118.0	120.5
Chemicals and related products										
Produits chimiques et alliés	14.0	102.9	101.2	107.2	111.6	113.6	119.7	124.4	129.2	135.4
Non-metallic mineral products										
Produits minéraux non métalliques	4.1	95.6	92.4	97.9	100.9	98.3	100.5	103.1	105.4	108.7
Basic metals										
Métallurgie de base	4.4	95.4	91.3	99.2	102.4	100.1	106.3	107.3	104.2	110.9
Fabricated metal products										
Fabrications d'ouvrages en métaux	16.8	93.6	89.7	95.4	104.7	104.8	108.2	112.5	112.6	118.0
Office and related electrical products										
Machines de bureau et autres appareils élect.	11.0	97.9	95.7	102.3	109.5	113.9	121.5	134.3	144.2	169.1
Transport equipment										
Equipement de transports	9.4	95.3	82.7	89.8	93.0	94.7	102.1	112.1	115.8	123.4
Electricity, gas, water [E]										
Electricité, gaz et eau [E]	**8.6**	**105.7**	**106.5**	**107.0**	**109.8**	**114.1**	**114.6**	**116.9**	**120.4**	**124.8**
Oceania · Océanie										
Total industry [CDE]										
Total, industrie [CDE]	**100.0**	**99.4**	**100.9**	**104.7**	**108.0**	**110.8**	**112.7**	**116.6**	**118.2**	**123.0**
Total mining [C]										
Total, industries extractives [C]	**18.8**	**109.9**	**110.4**	**110.6**	**116.3**	**120.1**	**121.8**	**129.6**	**127.5**	**140.8**
Coal										
Houille	5.0	112.3	112.0	112.8	119.3	123.0	123.4	129.4	139.2	150.9
Crude petroleum and natural gas										
Pétrole brut et gaz naturel	5.6	101.6	102.0	100.4	109.7	108.6	109.8	118.3	104.6	127.4
Metal ores										
Minerais métalliques	7.5	116.2	117.6	120.4	120.0	130.9	137.6	145.4	146.0	154.2
Total manufacturing [D]										
Total, industries manufacturières [D]	**66.6**	**95.0**	**97.3**	**102.2**	**104.9**	**107.4**	**109.4**	**112.7**	**116.1**	**119.4**
Food, beverages, tobacco										
Industries alimentaires, boissons, tabac	13.0	102.9	104.3	108.2	110.0	114.2	115.4	124.1	129.1	136.0
Textiles										
Textiles	1.9	91.5	88.5	90.1	88.9	84.6	84.1	84.3	85.2	81.7
Wearing apparel, leather and footwear										
Articles d'habillement, cuir et chaussures	2.0	91.4	88.5	90.2	89.2	84.9	84.3	84.1	84.9	81.7
Wood and wood products										
Bois et articles bois	2.3	95.0	101.6	105.6	110.6	112.3	109.4	111.4	109.4	124.9
Paper, printing, publishing and recorded media										
Papier, imprimerie, édition et supports enregistrés	6.9	92.9	97.2	100.3	104.9	106.3	108.0	107.1	107.1	114.5

5

Index numbers of industrial production: world and regions [cont.]
Indices de la production industrielle: monde et régions [suite]
1990=100

Region and industry [ISIC Rev.3] Région et industrie [CITI Rév.3]	Weight(%) Pond.(%)	1992	1993	1994	1995	1996	1997	1998	1999	2000
Chemicals and related products										
Produits chimiques et alliés	9.2	98.4	100.4	106.0	110.3	116.0	117.6	119.9	127.0	126.8
Non–metallic mineral products										
Produits minéraux non métalliques	3.4	88.1	95.6	98.2	99.7	93.9	95.7	99.6	110.4	93.1
Basic metals										
Métallurgie de base	7.1	96.3	98.8	103.6	102.2	104.9	107.5	108.2	110.5	105.9
Fabricated metal products										
Fabrications d'ouvrages en métaux	8.5	93.4	96.4	102.9	104.8	107.9	111.2	113.2	115.0	118.2
Office and related electrical products										
Machines de bureau et autres appareils élect.	3.2	89.5	90.8	98.3	104.9	108.6	112.3	117.0	118.8	131.5
Transport equipment										
Equipement de transports	6.9	90.0	91.1	98.8	105.2	109.1	112.7	117.3	119.8	132.8
Electricity, gas, water [E]										
Electricité, gaz et eau [E]	**14.6**	**105.9**	**104.9**	**108.6**	**111.2**	**114.4**	**115.7**	**117.6**	**116.2**	**116.8**

Source:
United Nations Statistics Division, New York, "Industrial Commodity Statistics Yearbook 1999" and the industrial statistics database.

1 Northern America (Canada and the United States), Europe, Australia, Israel, Japan, New Zealand and South Africa.
2 Latin America and the Caribbean, Africa (excluding South Africa), Asia (excluding Israel and Japan), Oceania (excluding Australia and New Zealand).
3 Canada and the United States only.
4 Austria, Belgium, Denmark, Finland, France, Germany, Greece, Ireland, Italy, Luxembourg, Netherlands, Portugal, Spain, Sweden and the United Kingdom.

Source :
Organisation des Nations Unies, Division de statistique, New York, "Annuaire de statistiques industrielles par produit 1999" et la base de données pour les statistiques industrielles.

1 Amérique septentrionale (le Canada et les Etats–Unis), Europe, l'Australie, l'Israël, la Nouvelle–Zélande et l'Afrique du Sud.
2 Amérique latine et Caraïbes, Afrique (non compris l'Afrique du Sud), Asie (non compris l'Israël et le Japon), Océanie (non compris l'Australie et la Nouvelle–Zélande).
3 Le Canada et les Etats–Unis seulement.
4 L'Autriche, la Belgique, le Danemark, la Finlande, la France, l'Allemagne, la Grèce, l'Irlande, l'Italie, le Luxembourg, les Pays–Bas, le Portugal, l'Espagne, la Suède et le Royaume–Uni.

Table 6 follows overleaf

Le tableau 6 est présenté au verso

6
Production, trade and consumption of commercial energy
Production, commerce et consommation d'énergie commerciale
Thousand metric tons of oil equivalent and kilograms per capita
Milliers de tonnes d'équivalent pétrole et kilogrammes par habitant

Regions	Year	Primary energy production – Production d'énergie primaire					Changes in stocks	Imports	Exports
		Total Totale	Solids Solides	Liquids Liquides	Gas Gaz	Electricity Electricité	Variations des stocks	Imports Importations	Exports Exportations
World	1992	8 152 847	2 196 956	3 234 825	1 929 084	791 983	36 202	2 916 808	2 826 443
	1993	8 186 693	2 145 566	3 264 364	1 961 804	814 959	− 24 528	2 985 724	2 897 725
	1994	8 361 410	2 224 840	3 302 446	2 003 815	830 310	30 872	2 994 484	2 928 193
	1995	8 558 491	2 292 787	3 345 655	2 055 068	864 980	13 616	3 061 510	3 035 812
	1996	8 788 503	2 329 992	3 409 588	2 156 896	892 027	949	3 237 067	3 164 775
	1997	8 909 172	2 345 804	3 513 854	2 161 009	888 504	47 518	3 359 349	3 304 541
	1998	8 932 349	2 274 060	3 577 185	2 176 603	904 501	51 478	3 405 212	3 412 026
Africa	1992	529 600	97 933	353 965	70 233	7 469	− 4 641	48 226	343 830
	1993	522 886	101 884	340 932	73 091	6 978	− 4 775	49 934	341 394
	1994	526 512	109 338	338 530	70 843	7 801	7 288	54 405	334 384
	1995	555 652	114 928	348 268	84 269	8 187	7 473	56 208	351 411
	1996	569 305	114 464	355 267	90 888	8 686	7 809	54 443	362 703
	1997	594 925	121 643	363 505	100 499	9 278	6 448	53 626	383 240
	1998	606 353	124 042	369 565	102 673	10 073	7 953	56 568	391 254
America, North	1992	2 139 964	558 991	681 444	631 097	268 431	− 9 425	567 740	335 087
	1993	2 126 072	525 854	689 103	637 882	273 234	− 21 058	633 607	329 406
	1994	2 223 199	575 970	686 361	676 425	284 442	28 136	665 946	332 296
	1995	2 226 789	573 336	682 520	675 141	295 793	− 11 056	652 072	354 691
	1996	2 261 860	590 071	675 909	695 631	300 249	− 6 874	688 103	368 383
	1997	2 287 219	605 486	694 972	704 578	282 182	19 847	738 037	384 003
	1998	2 271 834	612 686	679 463	692 328	287 357	39 432	778 860	394 426
America, South	1992	355 061	19 844	239 883	60 229	35 105	2 985	60 999	153 931
	1993	380 795	19 693	253 789	69 524	37 789	1 884	67 322	169 134
	1994	407 780	21 433	270 083	76 577	39 686	− 2 003	71 449	187 356
	1995	430 737	22 992	286 385	79 636	41 725	− 600	74 481	205 530
	1996	463 339	24 862	317 271	77 948	43 258	6 326	81 064	225 930
	1997	494 310	28 205	335 517	85 054	45 534	− 478	85 333	254 728
	1998	503 482	30 413	340 698	86 046	46 325	1 412	88 812	254 784
Asia	1992	2 604 995	866 750	1 276 204	329 514	132 526	13 401	906 567	1 084 902
	1993	2 721 118	889 373	1 331 653	354 908	145 184	5 063	941 687	1 143 093
	1994	2 813 938	938 891	1 353 908	367 055	154 084	− 2 362	944 939	1 110 926
	1995	2 937 369	1 003 486	1 371 788	395 024	167 070	8 301	991 928	1 139 911
	1996	3 031 870	1 036 388	1 393 427	427 964	174 090	− 492	1 066 157	1 166 885
	1997	3 096 621	1 029 143	1 448 369	437 958	181 151	19 790	1 132 575	1 218 563
	1998	3 127 485	970 243	1 519 277	447 099	190 866	731	1 100 538	1 282 769
Europe	1992	2 344 315	541 747	647 876	811 441	343 251	34 288	1 310 999	816 307
	1993	2 254 063	496 081	613 327	798 330	346 324	− 3 705	1 266 022	816 841
	1994	2 199 359	457 869	619 492	783 377	338 621	2 136	1 229 551	858 298
	1995	2 201 597	444 526	621 597	788 902	346 572	7 279	1 258 192	870 575
	1996	2 253 196	428 408	633 610	831 033	360 146	− 5 036	1 315 486	925 128
	1997	2 217 410	416 225	637 164	799 276	364 745	− 77	1 317 037	941 545
	1998	2 191 875	382 325	631 183	814 261	364 107	3 687	1 347 825	954 653
Oceania	1992	178 913	111 691	35 454	26 569	5 199	− 406	22 277	92 385
	1993	181 759	112 680	35 559	28 070	5 450	− 1 938	27 151	97 857
	1994	190 623	121 338	34 072	29 537	5 676	− 2 324	28 194	104 934
	1995	206 347	133 519	35 097	32 096	5 635	2 219	28 629	113 693
	1996	208 933	135 798	34 105	33 432	5 597	− 783	31 814	115 747
	1997	218 687	145 102	34 328	33 644	5 613	1 988	32 741	122 462
	1998	231 319	154 352	36 999	34 195	5 773	− 1 737	32 609	134 140

Source:
United Nations Statistics Division, New York, "Energy Statistics Yearbook 1998" and the energy statistics database.

Source:
Organisation des Nations Unies, Division de statistique, New York, "Annuaire des statistiques de l'énergie 1998" et la base de données pour les statistiques énergétiques.

| Bunkers – Soutes | | | Consumption – Consommation | | | | | | | |
Air Avion	Sea Maritime	Unallocated Nondistribué	Per capita Par habitant	Total Totale	Solids Solides	Liquids Liquides	Gas Gaz	Electricity Electricité	Année	Régions
45 383	113 256	297 341	1 472	7 751 030	2 202 998	2 825 950	1 930 200	791 882	1992	*Monde*
48 466	116 030	306 700	1 465	7 828 022	2 221 974	2 847 474	1 943 960	814 615	1993	
50 576	116 638	324 827	1 459	7 904 788	2 255 468	2 849 273	1 969 758	830 289	1994	
52 535	120 953	313 237	1 427	8 083 847	2 307 316	2 865 021	2 046 775	864 735	1995	
55 431	124 486	332 622	1 454	8 347 307	2 376 767	2 927 290	2 151 256	891 993	1996	
57 584	128 120	374 227	1 436	8 356 531	2 337 909	2 960 275	2 170 348	887 998	1997	
58 795	132 548	367 515	1 405	8 315 199	2 284 537	2 974 556	2 151 978	904 127	1998	
2 114	3 516	33 921	326	199 087	70 735	84 740	36 314	7 298	1992	Afrique
2 348	5 834	27 049	321	200 970	68 052	86 096	39 961	6 862	1993	
2 644	6 876	23 350	323	206 375	73 967	83 281	41 405	7 721	1994	
2 529	6 958	22 226	317	221 263	76 244	87 536	49 417	8 065	1995	
2 742	7 474	15 569	319	227 451	76 099	89 784	53 136	8 433	1996	
2 633	7 241	15 963	319	233 026	79 901	89 595	54 558	8 972	1997	
2 342	6 633	17 032	317	237 708	80 897	93 519	53 685	9 606	1998	
1 483	35 709	17 577	5 303	2 327 272	494 036	925 904	638 696	268 636	1992	Amérique du Nord
1 388	31 704	58 121	5 307	2 360 119	506 643	942 065	638 176	273 235	1993	
1 440	31 375	70 056	5 385	2 425 842	508 198	965 066	668 137	284 441	1994	
1 504	33 058	56 966	5 357	2 443 699	510 638	949 620	687 576	295 865	1995	
1 769	31 362	61 189	5 402	2 494 134	534 259	964 128	695 450	300 297	1996	
1 828	27 687	78 207	5 381	2 513 683	539 512	987 612	704 358	282 201	1997	
1 754	27 873	69 689	5 329	2 517 520	554 019	1 002 323	673 741	287 437	1998	
568	2 064	21 392	770	235 120	17 358	122 579	60 196	34 987	1992	Amérique du Sud
593	2 239	18 173	825	256 094	17 746	131 458	69 189	37 701	1993	
703	2 302	19 452	860	271 418	18 724	136 505	76 591	39 598	1994	
783	2 527	16 761	874	280 216	19 608	139 294	79 591	41 723	1995	
893	2 821	22 077	879	286 357	20 749	144 864	77 502	43 241	1996	
978	3 186	22 459	904	298 769	21 922	147 013	84 284	45 550	1997	
1 115	3 092	24 187	917	307 704	21 923	154 074	85 604	46 104	1998	
14 291	33 816	149 263	675	2 215 889	958 851	804 240	319 561	133 237	1992	Asie
14 194	37 343	150 795	693	2 312 316	1 001 494	835 327	330 227	145 268	1993	
14 777	38 182	162 851	719	2 434 503	1 052 600	860 372	366 435	155 096	1994	
15 812	39 021	163 614	746	2 562 637	1 112 775	889 681	392 727	167 454	1995	
17 014	40 665	179 060	773	2 694 895	1 158 942	931 041	430 316	174 596	1996	
17 449	44 071	203 211	771	2 726 111	1 140 501	949 148	455 034	181 428	1997	
16 698	47 049	202 313	743	2 678 463	1 090 022	936 182	460 592	191 667	1998	
24 411	36 973	78 036	4 444	2 665 299	619 836	848 448	854 490	342 525	1992	Europe
27 290	37 660	54 846	4 309	2 587 152	586 995	809 109	844 948	346 100	1993	
28 314	36 446	50 224	4 084	2 453 493	558 595	761 821	795 318	337 759	1994	
28 997	37 908	54 679	3 380	2 460 350	543 353	756 459	814 546	345 992	1995	
29 929	40 686	54 873	3 464	2 523 102	538 372	753 641	871 260	359 830	1996	
31 512	44 508	52 537	3 382	2 464 421	505 846	746 261	848 080	364 234	1997	
33 488	46 584	52 129	3 363	2 449 159	484 081	747 530	854 007	363 541	1998	
2 517	1 178	− 2 847	4 010	108 362	42 182	40 039	20 942	5 199	1992	Océanie
2 652	1 251	− 2 283	4 059	111 371	41 044	43 418	21 459	5 450	1993	
2 698	1 456	− 1 106	4 064	113 159	43 384	42 227	21 872	5 676	1994	
2 910	1 481	− 1 009	4 121	115 682	44 699	42 432	22 917	5 635	1995	
3 084	1 477	− 146	4 265	121 368	48 347	43 831	23 593	5 597	1996	
3 183	1 426	1 849	4 181	120 520	50 227	40 647	24 033	5 613	1997	
3 398	1 317	2 165	4 271	124 645	53 596	40 928	24 350	5 773	1998	

7
Total exports and imports: index numbers
Exportations et importations totales: indices
Quantum, unit value and terms of trade (1990 = 100)

Quantum, valeur unitaire et termes de l'échange (1990 = 100)

Regions [1]	1993	1994	1995	1996	1997	1998	1999	2000	Régions [1]
Total									**Total**
Exports: Quantum indices [2]	113	123	137	137	166	175	181	199	**Exp.: Indices du quantum [2]**
Exports: Unit value indices US $ [5]	97	101	109	108	97	91	90	92	**Exp.: Indices de la val. unit. en $ E.−U [5]**
Imports: Quantum indices [2]	114	126	138	145	158	166	176	199	**Imp.: Indices du quantum [2]**
Imports: Unit value indices US $ [5]	94	97	106	105	99	93	92	93	**Imp.: Indices de la val. unit. en $ E.−U [5]**
Developed economies [3]									**Economies développées [3]**
Exports: Quantum indices [2]	107	117	127	133	152	159	162	183	**Exp.: Indices du quantum [2]**
Exports: Unit value indices US $ [5]	98	101	109	107	96	93	92	90	**Exp.: Indices de la val. unit. en $ E.−U[5]**
Imports: Quantum indices [2]	107	118	128	134	148	159	170	192	**Imp.: Indices du quantum [2]**
Imports: Unit value indices US $ [5]	92	95	103	101	95	90	88	88	**Imp.: Indices de la val. unit. en $ E.−U[5]**
Terms of trade [7]	106	106	107	105	102	103	105	102	**Termes de l'échange [7]**
North America									**Amérique du Nord**
Exports: Quantum indices [2]	117	127	137	145	161	166	178	188	Exp.: Indices du quantum [2]
Exports: Unit value indices US $ [5]	99	101	107	108	106	102	100	106	Exp.: Indices de la val. unit. en $ E.−U [5]
Imports: Quantum indices [2]	116	129	137	144	162	179	197	228	Imp.: Indices du quantum [2]
Imports: Unit value indices US $ [5]	100	101	106	106	104	98	100	102	Imp.: Indices de la val. unit. en $ E.−U [5]
Terms of trade [7]	100	100	101	101	102	103	99	105	Termes de l'échange [7]
Europe									**Europe**
Exports: Quantum indices [2]	104	115	128	133	156	165	165	190	Exp.: Indices du quantum [2]
Exports: Unit value indices US $ [5]	93	96	106	103	90	88	87	80	Exp.: Indices de la val. unit. en $ E.−U [5]
Imports: Quantum indices [2]	103	112	124	127	142	154	163	182	Imp.: Indices du quantum [2]
Imports: Unit value indices US $ [5]	89	92	101	99	90	87	83	80	Imp.: Indices de la val. unit. en $ E.−U [5]
Terms of trade [7]	105	105	105	104	100	101	105	100	Termes de l'échange [7]
EU +									**UE +**
Exports: Quantum indices [2]	105	116	130	134	158	167	168	195	Exp.: Indices du quantum [2]
Exports: Unit value indices US $ [5]	94	97	106	104	90	88	87	80	Exp.: Indices de la val. unit. en $ E.−U [5]
Imports: Quantum indices [2]	104	114	125	129	144	156	165	186	Imp.: Indices du quantum [2]
Imports: Unit value indices US $ [5]	89	92	100	99	90	87	83	80	Imp.: Indices de la val. unit. en $ E.−U [5]
Terms of trade [7]	106	105	105	105	100	101	105	100	Termes de l'échange [7]
EFTA +									**AELE +**
Exports: Quantum indices [2]	108	117	121	127	143	145	154	147	Exp.: Indices du quantum [2]
Exports: Unit value indices US $ [5]	85	88	101	100	86	81	80	92	Exp.: Indices de la val. unit. en $ E.−U [5]
Imports: Quantum indices [2]	93	102	107	104	124	135	140	124	Imp.: Indices du quantum [2]
Imports: Unit value indices US $ [5]	90	92	106	109	89	85	81	91	Imp.: Indices de la val. unit. en $ E.−U [5]
Terms of trade [7]	95	95	96	92	97	96	99	101	Termes de l'échange [7]
Africa [4]									**Afrique [4]**
Exports: Quantum indices [2]	106	112	103	187	...	...	...	...	Exp.: Indices du quantum [2]
Exports: Unit value indices US $ [5]	97	96	114	66	...	...	...	...	Exp.: Indices de la val. unit. en $ E.−U [5]
Imports: Quantum indices [2]	107	124	150	165	...	...	...	...	Imp.: Indices du quantum [2]
Imports: Unit value indices US $ [5]	101	103	112	100	...	...	...	...	Imp.: Indices de la val. unit. en $ E.−U [5]
Terms of trade [7]	96	93	102	104	...	...	...	...	Termes de l'échange [7]
Asia									**Asie**
Exports: Quantum indices [2]	102	104	108	109	119	117	120	133	Exp.: Indices du quantum [2]
Exports: Unit value indices US $ [5]	123	132	143	132	123	115	121	127	Exp.: Indices de la val. unit. en $ E.−U [5]
Imports: Quantum indices [2]	108	123	138	143	145	137	150	168	Imp.: Indices du quantum [2]
Imports: Unit value indices US $ [5]	96	97	105	105	99	87	88	96	Imp.: Indices de la val. unit. en $ E.−U [5]
Terms of trade [7]	128	137	136	126	124	132	138	132	Termes de l'échange [7]
Oceania									**Océanie**
Exports: Quantum indices [2]	127	136	139	155	167	165	173	190	Exp.: Indices du quantum [2]
Exports: Unit value indices US $ [5]	85	89	97	98	93	82	79	82	Exp.: Indices de la val. unit. en $ E.−U [5]
Imports: Quantum indices [2]	107	121	130	140	148	157	169	175	Imp.: Indices du quantum [2]
Imports: Unit value indices US $ [5]	99	104	110	110	104	95	95	94	Imp.: Indices de la val. unit. en $ E.−U [5]
Terms of trade [7]	86	85	88	88	89	87	83	87	Termes de l'échange [7]
Developing economies [3]									**Economies en développement [3]**
Exports: Quantum indices [2]	131	143	165	172	206	223	239	251	**Exp.: Indices du quantum [2]**
Exports: Unit value indices US $ [5]	95	101	108	110	99	86	86	97	**Exp.: Indices de la val. unit. en $ E.−U [5]**
Imports: Quantum indices [2]	139	152	168	179	190	188	194	221	**Imp.: Indices du quantum [2]**
Imports: Unit value indices US $ [5 6]	97	100	113	113	112	102	104	108	**Imp.: Indices de la val. unit. en $ E.−U [5 6]**
Terms of trade [7]	98	101	96	98	88	84	83	90	**Termes de l'échange [7]**

7
Total exports and imports: index numbers
Quantum, unit value and terms of trade (1990 = 100) [*cont.*]
Exportations et importations totales: indices
Quantum, valeur unitaire et termes de l'échange (1990 = 100) [*suite*]

Regions [1]	1993	1994	1995	1996	1997	1998	1999	2000	Régions [1]
America									**Amérique**
Exports: Quantum indices [2]	117	124	166	160	172	186	194	204	Exp.: Indices du quantum [2]
Exports: Unit value indices US $ [5]	89	97	103	119	122	112	115	130	Exp.: Indices de la val. unit. en $ E.–U [5]
Africa									**Afrique**
Exports: Quantum indices [2]	102	99	124	121	251	315	300	253	Exp.: Indices du quantum [2]
Exports: Unit value indices US $ [5]	81	87	83	93	45	33	34	41	Exp.: Indices de la val. unit. en $ E.–U [5]
Asia									**Asie**
Exports: Quantum indices [2]	138	154	171	184	211	222	245	265	Exp.: Indices du quantum [2]
Exports: Unit value indices US $ [5]	98	104	112	110	103	91	89	98	Exp.: Indices de la val. unit. en $ E.–U [5]
Middle East									**Moyen–Orient**
Exports: Quantum indices [2]	138	135	137	143	154	183	176	137	Exp.: Indices du quantum [2]
Exports: Unit value indices US $ [5]	83	84	93	101	100	73	88	132	Exp.: Indices de la val. unit. en $ E.–U [5]
Other Asia									**Autres pays d'Asie**
Exports: Quantum indices [2]	137	157	177	192	222	229	260	296	Exp.: Indices du quantum [2]
Exports: Unit value indices US $ [5]	102	108	116	112	103	95	89	94	Exp.: Indices de la val. unit. en $ E.–U [5]

Source:
United Nations Statistics Division, New York, trade statistics
database.

Source:
Organisation des Nations Unies, Division de statistique, New York, la base
de donées pour les statistiques du commerce extérieur.

+   For Member States of this grouping, see
Annex I – Other groupings.

+   Pour les Etats membres de ce groupements, voir annexe I – Autres
groupements.

1   The regional analysis in this table is in accordance with
the groupings of countries or areas specified in table 70.

2   Quantum indices are derived from value data and unit value
indices. They are base period weighted.

3   This classification is intended for statistical convenience
and does not necessarily express a judgement about the
stage reached by a particular country in the development
process.

4   South African Customs Union.

5   Regional aggregates are current period weighted.

6   Indices, except those for Europe, are based on estimates
prepared by the International Monetary Fund.

7   Unit value index of exports divided by unit value index of
imports.

1   L'analyse régionale dans ce tableau est conforme aux groupes des pays
ou zones paraissant dans le tableau 70.

2   Les indices du quantum sont calculés à partir des chiffres de la valeur
et des indices de valeur unitaire. Ils sont àcoéfficients de pondération
correspondant à la périod en base.

3   Cette classification est utilisée pour plus de commodité
dans la présentation des statistiques et n'implique pas
nécessairement un jugement quant au stage de développement
auquel est parvenu un pays donné.

4   L'Union douanière d'Afrique australe.

5   Les totaux régionaux sont à coéfficients de pondération
correspondant à la périod en cours.

6   Le calcul des indices, sauf ceux pour l'Europe, sont basés
sur les estimations preparées par le Fonds monétaire
international.

7   Indices de la valeur unitaire des exportations divisé par
l'indice de la valeur unitaire des importations.

Technical notes, tables 1-7

Table 1: The series of world aggregates on population, production, transport, external trade and finance have been compiled from statistical publications and databases of the United Nations and the specialized agencies and other institutions [1, 6, 8, 9, 14, 22, 23, 24, 25]. These sources should be consulted for details on compilation and coverage.

Table 2 presents estimates of population size, rates of population increase, crude birth and death rates, surface area and population density for the world and regions. Unless otherwise specified, all figures are estimates of the order of magnitude and are subject to a substantial margin of error.

The population estimates and rates presented in this table were prepared by the Population Division of the United Nations Secretariat and published in *World Population Prospects: 2000 Revision* [29].

The average annual percentage rates of population growth were calculated by the Population Division of the United Nations Secretariat, using an exponential rate of increase formula.

Crude birth and crude death rates are expressed in terms of the average annual number of births and deaths respectively, per 1,000 mid-year population. These rates are estimated.

Surface area totals were obtained by summing the figures for the individual countries or areas.

Density is the number of persons in the 2000 total population per square kilometre of total surface area.

The scheme of regionalization used for the purpose of making these estimates is presented in annex I. Although some continental totals are given, and all can be derived, the basic scheme presents eight macro regions that are so drawn as to obtain greater homogeneity in sizes of population, types of demographic circumstances and accuracy of demographic statistics.

Tables 3-4: The index numbers in table 3 refer to agricultural production, which is defined to include both crop and livestock products. Seeds and feed are excluded. The index numbers of food refer to commodities which are considered edible and contain nutrients. Coffee, tea and other inedible commodities are excluded.

The index numbers of total agricultural and food production in table 3 are calculated by the Laspeyres formula with the base year period 1989-1991. The latter is provided in order to diminish the impact of annual fluctuations in agricultural output during base years on the indices for the period. Production quantities of each commodity are weighted by 1989-1991 average national producer prices and summed for each year. The index numbers are based on production data for a calendar year.

Notes techniques, tableaux 1 à 7

Tableau 1: Les séries d'agrégats mondiaux sur la population, la production, les transports, le commerce extérieur et les finances ont été établies à partir de publications statistiques et bases de données des Nations Unies et les institutions spécialisées et autres organismes [1, 6, 8, 9, 14, 22, 23, 24, 25]. On doit se référer à ces sources pour tous renseignements détaillés sur les méthodes de calcul et la portée des statistiques.

Le *Tableau 2* présente les estimations mondiales et régionales de la population, des taux d'accroissement de la population, des taux bruts de natalité et de mortalité, de la superficie et de la densité de population. Sauf indication contraire, tous les chiffres sont des estimations de l'ordre de grandeur et comportent une assez grande marge d'erreur.

Les estimations de la population et tous les taux présentés dans ce tableau ont été établis par la Division de la population du Secrétariat des Nations Unies et publiés dans "*World Population Prospects: 2000 Revision*" [29].

Les pourcentages annuels moyens de l'accroissement de la population ont été calculés par la Division de la population du Secrétariat des Nations Unies, sur la base d'une formule de taux d'accroissement exponentiel.

Les taux bruts de natalité et de mortalité sont exprimés, respectivement, sur la base du nombre annuel moyen de naissances et de décès par tranche de 1.000 habitants au milieu de l'année. Ces taux sont estimatifs.

On a déterminé les superficies totales en additionnant les chiffres correspondant aux différents pays ou régions.

La densité est le nombre de personnes de la population totale de 2000 par kilomètre carré de la superficie totale.

Le schéma de régionalisation utilisé aux fins de l'établissement de ces estimations est présenté dans l'annexe I. Bien que les totaux de certains continents soient donnés et que tous puissent être déterminés, le schéma de base présente huit grandes régions qui sont établies de manière à obtenir une plus grande homogénéité en ce qui concerne l'ampleur des populations, les types de conditions démographiques et la précision des statistiques démographiques.

Tableaux 3-4: Les indices du tableau 3 se rapportent à la production agricole, qui est définie comme comprenant à la fois les produits de l'agriculture et de l'élevage. Les semences et les aliments pour les animaux sont exclus de cette définition. Les indices de la production alimentaire se rapportent aux produits considérés comme

As in the past, the series include a large number of estimates made by FAO in cases where figures are not available from official country sources.

Index numbers for the world and regions are computed in a similar way to the country index numbers except that instead of using different commodity prices for each country group, "international commodity prices" derived from the Gheary-Khamis formula are used for all country groupings. This method assigns a single "price" to each commodity.

The indexes in table 4 are calculated as a ratio between the index numbers of total agricultural and food production in table 3 described above and the corresponding index numbers of population.

For further information on the series presented in these tables, see the FAO *Production Yearbook* [6].

Table 5: The index numbers of industrial production are classified according to tabulation categories, divisions and combinations of divisions of the International Standard Industrial Classification of All Economic Activities, Revision 3, (ISIC Rev. 3) [49] for mining (category C), manufacturing (category D), and electricity, gas and water (category E).

The indices indicate trends in value added in constant US dollars. The measure of value added used is the national accounts concept, which is defined as gross output less the cost of materials, supplies, fuel and electricity consumed and services received.

Each series is compiled using the Laspeyres formula, that is, the indices are base-weighted arithmetic means. The weight base year is 1990 and value added, generally at factor values, is used in weighting.

For most countries the estimates of value added used as weights are derived from the results of national industrial censuses or similar inquiries relating to 1990. These data, in national currency, are adjusted to the ISIC where necessary and are subsequently converted into US dollars.

Within each of the ISIC categories (tabulation categories, divisions and combinations of divisions) shown in the tables, the indices for the country aggregations (regions or economic groupings) are calculated directly from the country data. The indices for the World, however, are calculated from the aggregated indices for the groupings of developed and developing countries.

China and the countries of the former USSR (except Russian Federation and Ukraine) are excluded from their respective regions.

Table 6: For a description of the series in table 6, see the technical notes to chapter XIII.

comestibles et contenant des éléments nutritifs. Le café, le thé et les produits non comestibles sont exclus.

Les indices de la production agricole et de la production alimentaire présentés au tableau 3 sont calculés selon la formule de Laspeyres avec les années 1989-1991 comme période de référence, cela afin de limiter l'incidence, sur les indices correspondant à la période considérée, des fluctuations annuelles de la production agricole enregistrée pendant les années de référence. Les chiffres de production de chaque produit sont pondérés par les prix nationaux moyens à la production pour la période 1989-1991 et additionnés pour chaque année. Les indices sont fondés sur les données de production de l'année civile. Comme dans le passé, les séries comprennent un grand nombre d'estimations établies par la FAO lorsqu'elle n'avait pu obtenir de chiffres de sources officielles dans les pays eux-mêmes.

Les indices pour le monde et les régions sont calculés de la même façon que les indices par pays, mais au lieu d'appliquer des prix différents aux produits de base pour chaque groupe de pays, on a utilisé des "prix internationaux" établis d'après la formule de Gheary-Khamis pour tous les groupes de pays. Cette méthode attribue un seul "prix" à chaque produit de base.

Les indices du tableau 4 sont calculés comme ratio entre les indices de la production alimentaire et de la production agricole totale du tableau 3 décrits ci-dessus et les indices de population correspondants.

Pour tout renseignement complémentaire sur les séries présentées dans ces tableaux, voir l'*Annuaire FAO de la production* [6].

Tableau 5: Les indices de la production industrielle sont classés selon les catégories de classement, les divisions ou des combinaisons des divisions de la Classification Internationale type, par industrie, de toutes les branches d'activité économique, Révision 3 (CITI Rev. 3) [49] qui concernent les industries extractives (la catégorie C) et les industries manufacturières (la catégorie D), ainsi que l'électricité, le gaz et l'eau (la catégorie E).

Ces indices représentent les tendances de la valeur ajoutée en dollars constants des Etats-Unis. La mesure utilisée pour la valeur ajoutée correspond à celle qui est appliquée aux fins de la comptabilité nationale, c'est-à-dire égale à la valeur de la production brute diminuée des coûts des matériaux, des fournitures, de la consommation de carburant et d'électricité ainsi que des services reçus.

Chaque série a été établie au moyen de la formule de Laspeyres, ce qui signifie que les indices sont des moyennes arithmétiques affectées de coefficients de pondération. L'année de base de pondération est l'année 1990 et on utilise généralement pour la pondération la valeur ajoutée aux coûts des facteurs.

Table 7: For a description of the series in table 7, see the technical notes to chapter XVI. The composition of the regions is presented in table 70.

Pour la plupart des pays, les estimations de la valeur ajoutée qui sont utilisées comme coefficients de pondération sont tirées des résultats des recensements industriels nationaux ou enquêtes analogues concernant l'année 1990. Ces données, en monnaie nationale, sont ajustées s'il y a lieu aux normes de la CITI et ultérieurement converties en dollars des Etats-Unis.

A l'intérieur de chacune des subdivisions de la CITI (catégories de classement, divisions et combinaisons des divisions) indiquées dans les tableaux, les indices relatifs aux assemblages de pays (régions géographiques ou groupements économiques) sont calculés directement à partir des données des pays. Toutefois, les indices concernant le *Monde* sont calculés à partir des indices agrégés applicables aux groupements de pays développés et de pays en développement.

La Chine et les pays de l'ancienne URSS (sauf la Fédération de Russie et Ukraine) sont exclus de leurs régions respectives.

Tableau 6: On trouvera une description de la série de statistiques du tableau 6 dans les notes techniques du chapitre XIII.

Tableau 7: On trouvera une description de la série de statistiques du tableau 7 dans les notes techniques du chapitre XVI. La composition des régions est présentée au tableau 70.

Part Two
Population and Social Statistics

II
Population (tables 8 and 9)
III
Literacy (table 10)
IV
Health, childbearing and nutrition (tables 11-13)
V
Culture and communication (tables 14-21)

Part Two of the *Yearbook* presents statistical series on a wide range of population and social topics for all countries or areas of the world for which data are available. These include population and population growth, surface area and density; the illiterate population; life expectancy, childbearing and mortality; AIDS cases; food supply; book production; newspapers and periodicals; television and radio receivers; cinemas; telephones; and Internet users.

Deuxième partie
Population et statistiques sociales

II
Population (tableaux 8 et 9)
III
Alphabétisation (tableau 10)
IV
Santé, maternité et nutrition (tableaux 11-13)
V
Culture et communication (tableaux 14 à 21)

La deuxième partie de l'*Annuaire* présente, pour tous les pays ou zones du monde pour lesquels des données sont disponibles, des séries statistiques intéressant une large gamme de questions démographiques et sociales: population et croissance démographique, superficie et densité; la population analphabète; l'espérance de vie, maternité et mortalité; cas de SIDA; disponibilités alimentaires; production de livres; journaux et périodiques; récepteurs de télévision et de radiodiffusion sonore; cinémas; téléphones; et usagers d'Internet.

8
Population by sex, rate of population increase, surface area and density
Population selon le sexe, taux d'accroissement de la population, superficie et densité

Country or area Pays ou zone	Latest census Dernier recensement Date	Both sexes Les deux sexes	Male Masculin	Female Féminin	Mid-year estimates (thousands) Estimations au milieu de l'année (milliers) 1995	1999	Annual rate of increase Taux d'accrois-sement annuel % 1995-99	Surface area (km²) Superficie (km²) 1999	Density Densité 1999[1]
Africa · Afrique									
Algeria[2] Algérie[2]	25 VI 1998	*29 272 343	*14 801 025	*14 471 318	28 060	x30 774	2.3	2 381 741	13
Angola[3] Angola[3]	15 XII 1970	5 646 166	2 943 974	2 702 192	x10 972	x12 479	3.2	1 246 700	10
Benin Bénin	15 II 1992	4 915 555	2 390 336	2 525 219	5 412	*6 059	2.8	112 622	54
Botswana Botswana	21 VIII 1991	1 326 796	634 400	692 396	1 459	*1 611	2.5	581 730	3
Burkina Faso[4] Burkina Faso[4]	10 XII 1996	10 312 609	4 970 882	5 341 727	10 200	x11 616	...	274 000	42
Burundi Burundi	16 VIII 1990	5 139 073	2 473 599	2 665 474	5 982	*6 483	2.0	27 834	233
Cameroon Cameroun	11 IV 1987	10 493 655	...	...	13 277	x14 693	2.5	475 442	31
Cape Verde Cap-Vert	23 VI 1990	341 491	161 494	179 997	386	x418	2.0	4 033	104
Central African Republic République centrafricaine	8 XII 1988	2 463 616	1 210 734	1 252 882	x3 288	x3 550	1.9	622 984	6
Chad[5] Tchad[5]	8 IV 1993	6 279 931	...	...	x6 707	x7 458	2.7	1 284 000	6
Comoros[6] Comores[6]	15 IX 1991	446 817	221 152	225 665	x606	x676	2.7	2 235	302
Congo Congo	22 XII 1984	1 843 421	...	...	x2 561	x2 864	2.8	342 000	8
Côte d'Ivoire[4] Côte d'Ivoire[4]	1 III 1988	10 815 694	5 527 343	5 288 351	14 230	x14 526	...	322 463	45
Dem. Rep. of the Congo Rép. dém du Congo	1 VII 1984	29 916 800	14 543 800	15 373 000	x45 421	x50 335	2.6	2 344 858	21
Djibouti Djibouti	11 XII 1960	81 200	...	...	x601	x629	1.2	23 200	27
Egypt[4] Egypte[4]	19 XI 1996	59 312 914	30 351 390	28 961 524	57 510	x67 226	...	1 001 449	67
Equatorial Guinea[7] Guinée équatoriale[7]	4 VII 1983	300 000	144 760	155 240	x399	x442	2.5	28 051	16
Eritrea Erythrée	9 V 1984	2 748 304	1 374 452	1 373 852	x3 187	x3 719	3.9	117 600	32
Ethiopia Ethiopie	11 X 1994	53 477 265	26 910 698	26 566 567	54 649	*61 672	3.0	1 104 300	56
Gabon Gabon	31 VII 1993	1 014 976	501 784	513 192	x1 077	*1 385	6.3	267 668	5
Gambia Gambie	13 IV 1993	1 025 867	514 530	511 337	x1 111	x1 268	3.3	11 295	112
Ghana Ghana	11 III 1984	12 296 081	6 063 848	6 232 233	x17 649	x19 678	2.7	238 533	82
Guinea[8] Guinée[8]	4 II 1983	4 533 240	...	...	x7 153	x7 360	0.7	245 857	30
Guinea-Bissau Guinée-Bissau	1 XII 1991	983 367	476 210	507 157	x1 086	x1 187	2.2	36 125	33
Kenya[4] Kenya[4]	24 VIII 1999	*28 679 000	*14 165 000	*14 514 000	30 522	x29 549	...	580 367	51
Lesotho Lesotho	14 IV 1996	*1 862 275	...	...	x1 926	x2 108	2.3	30 355	69
Liberia Libéria	1 II 1984	2 101 628	1 063 127	1 038 501	2 760	x2 930	1.5	111 369	26

8
Population by sex, rate of population increase, surface area and density [*cont.*]
Population selon le sexe, taux d'accroissement de la population,
superficie et densité [*suite*]

Country or area Pays ou zone	Latest census Dernier recensement Date	Both sexes Les deux sexes	Male Masculin	Female Féminin	Mid-year estimates (thousands) Estimations au milieu de l'année (milliers) 1995	1999	Annual rate of increase Taux d'accrois- sement annuel % 1995–99	Surface area (km²) Superficie (km²) 1999	Density Densité 1999[1]
Libyan Arab Jamahiriya Jamahiriya arabe libyenne	11 VIII 1995	4 404 986	2 236 943	2 168 043	x4 967	x5 471	2.4	1 759 540	3
Madagascar Madagascar	1 VIII 1993	12 092 157	5 991 171	6 100 986	x13 744	x15 497	3.0	587 041	26
Malawi [4] Malawi [4]	1 IX 1987	7 988 507	3 867 136	4 121 371	9 788	x10 640	...	118 484	90
Mali [9] Mali [9]	17 IV 1998	9 790 492	4 847 436	4 943 056	x9 944	x10 960	2.4	1 240 192	9
Mauritania [10] Mauritanie [10]	5 IV 1988	1 864 236	923 175	941 061	2 284	x2 598	3.2	1 025 520	3
Mauritius Maurice	1 VII 1990	1 056 660	527 760	528 900	1 122	*1 174	1.1	2 040	576
Morocco Maroc	2 IX 1994	26 073 717	...	...	26 386	*28 238	1.7	446 550	63
Mozambique [4] [8] Mozambique [4] [8]	1 VIII 1997	16 099 246	7 714 306	8 384 940	15 820	*17 299	...	801 590	22
Namibia Namibie	21 X 1991	1 409 920	686 327	723 593	x1 543	x1 695	2.3	824 292	2
Niger Niger	20 V 1988	7 248 100	3 590 070	3 658 030	x9 150	x10 400	3.2	1 267 000	8
Nigeria Nigéria	26 XI 1991	88 992 220	44 529 608	44 462 612	x98 952	x108 945	2.4	923 768	118
Reunion [2] Réunion [2]	15 III 1990	597 828	294 256	303 572	x655	x691	1.3	2 510	275
Rwanda Rwanda	15 VIII 1991	7 142 755	...	...	x5 259	x7 235	8.0	26 338	275
St. Helena ex. dep. Sainte–Hélène sans dép.	8 III 1998	5 157	2 612	2 545	...	...	...	122	...
Ascension Ascension	31 XII 1978	849	608	241	...	...	...	88	...
Tristan da Cunha Tristan da Cunha	31 XII 1988	296	139	157	...	...	...	...	...
Sao Tome and Principe Sao Tomé–et–Principe	4 VIII 1991	116 998	57 837	59 161	127	x144	3.1	964	149
Senegal Sénégal	27 V 1988	6 896 808	3 353 599	3 543 209	8 347	*9 279	2.6	196 722	47
Seychelles Seychelles	29 VIII 1997	75 876	37 589	38 287	75	*80	1.6	455	177
Sierra Leone [8] Sierra Leone [8]	15 XII 1985	3 515 812	1 746 055	1 769 757	x4 188	x4 717	3.0	71 740	66
Somalia Somalie	15 II 1987	7 114 431	3 741 664	3 372 767	x8 201	x9 672	4.1	637 657	15
South Africa [8] Afrique du Sud [8]	10 X 1996	40 583 573	19 520 887	21 062 686	39 477	*43 054	2.2	1 221 037	35
Sudan [4] Soudan [4]	15 IV 1993	24 940 683	12 518 638	12 422 045	x26 617	x28 883	...	2 505 813	12
Swaziland Swaziland	11 V 1997	*965 859	...	...	908	x980	1.9	17 364	56
Togo Togo	22 XI 1981	2 703 250	...	...	x4 060	x4 512	2.6	56 785	79
Tunisia Tunisie	20 IV 1994	8 785 711	4 439 289	4 346 422	8 958	*9 457	1.4	163 610	58
Uganda Ouganda	12 I 1991	16 671 705	8 185 747	8 485 958	19 263	*21 620	2.9	241 038	90
United Rep. of Tanzania Rép.–Unie de Tanzanie	28 VIII 1988	23 126 310	11 217 723	11 908 587	28 279	x32 793	3.7	883 749	37
Western Sahara [11] Sahara occidental [11]	31 XII 1970	76 425	43 981	32 444	x248	x284	3.4	266 000	1

8
Population by sex, rate of population increase, surface area and density [cont.]
Population selon le sexe, taux d'accroissement de la population,
superficie et densité [suite]

Country or area Pays ou zone	Latest census Dernier recensement				Mid-year estimates (thousands) Estimations au milieu de l'année (milliers)		Annual rate of increase Taux d'accrois- sement annuel %	Surface area (km²) Superficie (km²)	Density Densité
	Date	Both sexes Les deux sexes	Male Masculin	Female Féminin	1995	1999	1995-99	1999	1999[1]
Zambia Zambie	20 VIII 1990	7 383 097	3 617 577	3 765 520	9 112	*10 407	3.3	752 618	14
Zimbabwe Zimbabwe	18 VIII 1992	10 412 548	5 083 537	5 329 011	11 526	*13 079	3.2	390 757	33
America, North · Amérique du Nord									
Anguilla Anguilla	13 IV 1992	8 960	4 473	4 487	10	13	6.7	96	134
Antigua and Barbuda Antigua-et-Barbuda	28 V 1991	62 922	...	...	68	x67	-0.2	442	152
Aruba [2] Aruba [2]	6 X 1991	66 687	32 821	33 866	82	*94	3.7	193	489
Bahamas Bahamas	1 V 1990	255 095	124 992	130 103	279	x301	1.9	13 878	22
Barbados Barbade	2 V 1990	257 082	...	...	264	*267	0.3	430	621
Belize Belize	12 V 1991	189 774	96 289	93 485	216	x235	2.0	22 696	10
Bermuda [12] Bermudes [12]	20 V 1991	74 837	...	...	60	x64	1.7	53	1 208
British Virgin Islands Iles Vierges britanniques	12 V 1991	17 809	...	...	x19	x21	2.9	151	139
Canada [2][8] Canada [2][8]	14 V 1996	28 846 760	14 170 030	14 676 735	29 354	*30 493	1.0	9 970 610	3
Cayman Islands [2] Iles Caïmanes [2]	15 X 1989	25 355	12 372	12 983	x32	x37	3.6	264	140
Costa Rica [2] Costa Rica [2]	10 VI 1984	2 416 809	1 208 216	1 208 593	3 333	*3 589	1.8	51 100	70
Cuba Cuba	11 IX 1981	9 723 605	4 914 873	4 808 732	10 978	*11 160	0.4	110 861	101
Dominica Dominique	12 V 1991	71 794	35 927	35 867	75	x71	-1.4	751	95
Dominican Republic Rép. dominicaine	24 IX 1993	7 293 390	3 550 797	3 742 593	7 705	*8 325	1.9	48 511	172
El Salvador El Salvador	27 IX 1992	5 118 599	2 485 613	2 632 986	5 669	*6 154	2.1	21 041	292
Greenland [2] Groenland [2]	26 X 1976	49 630	26 856	22 774	56	*56	0.1	2 175 600	-
Grenada [13] Grenade [13]	12 V 1991	85 123	41 893	43 230	x92	x93	0.2	344	270
Guadeloupe [2][14] Guadeloupe [2][14]	15 III 1990	387 034	189 187	197 847	x424	x450	1.5	1 705	264
Guatemala [4] Guatemala [4]	17 IV 1994	8 322 051	...	...	9 976	*11 088	...	108 889	102
Haiti [2] Haïti [2]	30 VIII 1982	5 053 792	2 448 370	2 605 422	7 180	*7 803	2.1	27 750	281
Honduras Honduras	29 V 1988	4 248 561	2 110 106	2 138 455	5 602	*6 385	3.3	112 088	57
Jamaica Jamaïque	7 IV 1991	2 314 479	1 134 386	1 180 093	2 503	x2 590	0.9	10 990	236
Martinique [2] Martinique [2]	15 III 1990	359 579	173 878	185 701	x379	*381	0.2	1 102	346
Mexico [2] Mexique [2]	7 II 2000	*97 361 711	*47 354 386	*50 007 325	90 487	x97 365	1.8	1 958 201	50
Montserrat Montserrat	12 V 1991	10 639	5 290	5 349	x11	x11	0.5	102	108
Netherlands Antilles[2][15] Antilles néerlandaises[2][15]	27 I 1992	189 474	90 707	98 767	205	x215	1.3	800	269

8

Population by sex, rate of population increase, surface area and density [*cont.*]
Population selon le sexe, taux d'accroissement de la population,
superficie et densité [*suite*]

Country or area Pays ou zone	Latest census Dernier recensement				Mid-year estimates (thousands) Estimations au milieu de l'année (milliers)		Annual rate of increase Taux d'accrois- sement annuel % 1995–99	Surface area (km²) Superficie (km²) 1999	Density Densité 1999[1]
	Date	Both sexes Les deux sexes	Male Masculin	Female Féminin	1995	1999			
Nicaragua[2] Nicaragua[2]	25 IV 1995	4 357 099	2 147 105	2 209 994	4 427	*4 936	2.7	130 000	38
Panama Panama	13 V 1990	2 329 329	1 178 790	1 150 539	2 631	*2 809	1.6	75 517	37
Puerto Rico[2][16] Porto Rico[2][16]	1 IV 1990	, 3 522 037	1 705 642	1 816 395	3 719	*3 890	1.1	8 875	438
Saint Kitts and Nevis Saint–Kitts–et–Nevis	12 V 1991	40 618	19 933	20 685	44	x39	−2.7	261	149
Saint Lucia Sainte–Lucie	12 V 1991	133 308	64 645	68 663	145	x152	1.1	539	282
St. Pierre and Miquelon Saint–Pierre et Miquelon	5 III 1990	6 392	...	...	7	x7	–	242	29
St. Vincent and Grenadines [17] St.-Vincent-et- Grenadines [17]	12 V 1991	106 499	53 165	53 334	111	*112	0.3	388	289
Trinidad and Tobago Trinité–et–Tobago	2 V 1990	1 169 572	584 445	585 127	1 260	x1 289	0.6	5 130	251
Turks and Caicos Islands Iles Turques et Caïques	31 V 1990	12 350	6 289	6 061	x14	x16	3.3	430	37
United States [18] Etats–Unis [18]	01 IV 2000	*281 421 906	...	...	263 044	*273 131	0.9	9 363 520	29
United States Virgin Islands [2][16] Iles Vierges américaines [2][16]	1 IV 1990	101 809	49 210	52 599	x97	x94	−0.8	347	271
America, South · Amérique du Sud									
Argentina Argentine	15 V 1991	32 615 528	15 937 980	16 677 548	34 768	*36 578	1.3	2 780 400	13
Bolivia[8] Bolivie[8]	3 VI 1992	6 420 792	3 171 265	3 249 527	7 414	*8 137	2.3	1 098 581	7
Brazil [9][19] Brésil [9][19]	1 VIII 1996	157 070 163	77 442 865	79 627 298	155 822	*165 371	1.5	8 547 403	19
Chile Chili	22 IV 1992	13 348 401	6 553 254	6 795 147	14 210	*15 018	1.4	756 626	20
Colombia Colombie	24 X 1993	33 109 840	16 296 539	16 813 301	38 542	*41 589	1.9	1 138 914	37
Ecuador[20] Equateur[20]	25 XI 1990	9 648 189	4 796 412	4 851 777	11 460	*12 411	2.0	283 561	44
Falkland Is. (Malvinas)[21][22] Iles Falkland (Malvinas) [21]	24 IV 1996	2 564	1 447	1 117	x2	x2	–	12 173	–
French Guyana[2] Guyane française[2]	15 III 1990	114 808	59 798	55 010	x147	x174	4.3	90 000	2
Guyana Guyana	12 V 1991	701 704	344 928	356 776	x830	x855	0.7	214 969	4
Paraguay[8] Paraguay[8]	26 VIII 1992	4 152 588	2 085 905	2 066 683	4 828	*5 356	2.6	406 752	13
Peru[8][19] Pérou[8][19]	11 VII 1993	22 048 356	10 956 375	11 091 981	23 532	*25 232	1.7	1 285 216	20
Suriname Suriname	1 VII 1980	355 240	...	...	409	x415	0.4	163 265	3
Uruguay Uruguay	22 V 1996	3 163 763	1 532 288	1 631 475	3 218	*3 313	0.7	175 016	19
Venezuela[19] Venezuela[19]	20 X 1990	18 105 265	9 019 757	9 085 508	21 844	x23 706	2.0	912 050	26
Asia · Asie									
Afghanistan [23] Afghanistan [23]	23 VI 1979	13 051 358	6 712 377	6 338 981	x19 663	x21 923	2.7	652 090	34

8
Population by sex, rate of population increase, surface area and density [*cont.*]
Population selon le sexe, taux d'accroissement de la population,
superficie et densité [*suite*]

Country or area Pays ou zone	Latest census Dernier recensement				Mid-year estimates (thousands) Estimations au milieu de l'année (milliers)		Annual rate of increase Taux d'accrois- sement annuel %	Surface area (km²) Superficie (km²)	Density Densité
	Date	Both sexes Les deux sexes	Male Masculin	Female Féminin	1995	1999	1995–99	1999	1999[1]
Armenia [9] Arménie [9]	12 I 1989	3 304 776	1 619 308	1 685 468	3 760	*3 795	0.2	29 800	127
Azerbaijan [9] Azerbaïdjan [9]	27 I 1999	*7 953 000	*4 119 000	*3 834 000	7 685	*7 983	1.0	86 600	92
Bahrain Bahreïn	16 XI 1991	508 037	294 346	213 691	578	666	3.6	694	960
Bangladesh Bangladesh	11 III 1991	111 455 185	57 313 929	54 141 256	119 900	x126 947	1.4	143 998	882
Bhutan Bhoutan	11 XI 1969	1 034 774	...	...	x1 847	x2 064	2.8	47 000	44
Brunei Darussalam[8] Brunéi Darussalam[8]	7 VIII 1991	260 482	137 616	122 866	296	*331	2.8	5 765	57
Cambodia [24] Cambodge[24]	3 III 1998	*11 437 656	*5 511 408	*5 926 248	9 836	x10 945	2.7	181 035	60
China [25] [26] Chine [25] [26]	1 VII 1990	1 160 044 618	...	...	x1 220 516	x1 266 838	0.9	9 596 961	132
China, Hong Kong SAR † Chine, Hong Kong RAS †	15 III 1996	6 217 556	3 108 107	3 109 449	6 156	6 843	2.6	1 075	6 366
China, Macao SAR Chine, Macao RAS	30 VIII 1991	385 089	...	...	409	*434	1.5	18	24 111
Cyprus [27] Chypre [27]	1 X 1992	602 025	299 614	302 411	733	*753	0.7	9 251	81
East Timor Timor oriental	31 X 1990	747 750	386 939	360 811	x814	x871	1.7	14 874	59
Georgia [4] [9] Géorgie [4] [9]	12 I 1989	5 400 841	2 562 040	2 838 801	5 417	*5 399	...	69 700	77
India[28] Inde[28]	01 III 2001	*1027015 247	*531277 078	*495738 169	921 989	*986 611	1.7	3 287 263	300
Indonesia[29] Indonésie[29]	31 X 1990	179 378 946	89 463 545	89 915 401	194 755	*207 437	1.6	1 904 569	109
Iran (Islamic Republic of) Iran (Rép. islamique d')	1 X 1996	60 055 488	30 515 159	29 540 329	59 187	*62 746	1.5	1 648 195	38
Iraq Iraq	17 X 1987	16 335 199	8 395 889	7 939 310	x20 095	x22 450	2.8	438 317	51
Israel[2] [30] Israël[2] [30]	4 XI 1995	5 548 523	2 738 175	2 810 348	5 545	*6 125	2.5	21 056	291
Japan[31] Japon[31]	1 X 1995	125 570 246	61 574 398	63 995 848	125 197	x126 505	0.3	377 829	335
Jordan[32] [33] Jordanie[32] [33]	10 XII 1994	4 095 579	2 135 883	1 959 696	x5 734	x6 482	3.1	97 740	66
Kazakhstan [4] Kazakhstan [4]	02 II 1999	*15 049 100	...	...	16 066	*14 942	...	2 724 900	5
Korea, Dem. People's Rep. Corée, Rép. pop. dém. de	31 XII 1993	21 213 378	10 329 699	10 883 679	x22 239	x23 702	1.6	120 538	197
Korea, Republic of [8] [34] Corée, Rép. de [8] [34]	1 XI 1995	44 608 726	22 389 324	22 219 402	45 093	*46 858	1.0	99 268	472
Kuwait Koweït	20 IV 1995	1 575 983	914 324	661 659	1 802	*2 107	3.9	17 818	118
Kyrgyzstan [9] Kirghizistan [9]	24 III 1999	*4 822 938	*2 380 438	*2 442 500	4 590	*4 865	1.5	199 900	24
Lao People's Dem. Rep. Rép. dém. populaire lao	1 III 1985	3 584 803	1 757 115	1 827 688	x4 773	x5 297	2.6	236 800	22
Lebanon[35] [36] Liban[35] [36]	15 XI 1970	2 126 325	1 080 015	1 046 310	x3 009	x3 236	1.8	10 400	311
Malaysia Malaisie	14 VIII 1991	17 563 420	8 876 829	8 686 591	20 689	*22 712	2.3	329 758	69
Maldives Maldives	25 III 1995	244 814	124 622	120 192	x249	*278	2.7	298	931

8
Population by sex, rate of population increase, surface area and density [cont.]
Population selon le sexe, taux d'accroissement de la population,
superficie et densité [suite]

Country or area Pays ou zone	Latest census Dernier recensement				Mid-year estimates (thousands) Estimations au milieu de l'année (milliers)		Annual rate of increase Taux d'accrois- sement annuel %	Surface area (km²) Superficie (km²)	Density Densité
	Date	Both sexes Les deux sexes	Male Masculin	Female Féminin	1995	1999	1995–99	1999	1999[1]
Mongolia Mongolie	5 I 2000	*2 382 525	*1 181 682	*1 200 843	2 299	x2 621	3.3	1 566 500	2
Myanmar[9] Myanmar[9]	31 III 1983	35 307 913	17 518 255	17 789 658	x42 877	x45 059	1.2	676 578	67
Nepal Népal	22 VI 1991	18 491 097	9 220 974	9 270 123	20 341	*22 367	2.4	147 181	152
Occupied Palestinian Territory[37] [38] Territoire palestinien occupé[37] [38]	9 XII 1997	2 601 669	1 322 264	1 279 405	...	...	...	...	...
Oman Oman	1 XII 1993	2 018 074	...	...	2 131	x2 460	3.6	309 500	8
Pakistan[4] [39] Pakistan[4] [39]	2 III 1998	130 579 571	67 840 137	62 739 434	122 360	*134 510	...	796 095	169
Philippines[2] Philippines[2]	1 IX 1995	68 616 536	34 584 170	34 032 366	70 267	*74 746	1.5	300 000	249
Qatar Qatar	1 III 1997	522 023	342 459	179 564	x548	x589	1.8	11 000	54
Saudi Arabia Arabie saoudite	27 IX 1992	16 948 388	9 479 973	7 468 415	x18 253	*19 895	2.2	2 149 690	9
Singapore[40] Singapour[40]	30 VI 1990	2 705 115	1 370 059	1 335 056	3 468	*3 894	2.9	618	6 300
Sri Lanka Sri Lanka	17 III 1981	14 846 750	7 568 253	7 278 497	18 136	*19 043	1.2	65 610	290
Syrian Arab Republic[41] Rép. arabe syrienne[41]	3 IX 1994	13 782 315	7 048 906	6 733 409	14 153	*16 110	3.2	185 180	87
Tajikistan Tadjikistan	20 I 2000	*6 127 000	*3 082 000	*3 045 000	5 836	*6 237	1.7	143 100	44
Thailand Thaïlande	01 IV 2000	*60 606 947	*29 844 870	*30 762 077	59 401	*61 806	1.0	513 115	120
Turkey Turquie	21 X 1990	56 473 035	28 607 047	27 865 988	60 613	*64 385	1.5	774 815	83
Turkmenistan Turkménistan	10 I 1995	4 483 251	2 225 331	2 257 920	4 509	x4 384	−0.7	488 100	9
United Arab Emirates [4] [42] Emirats arabes unis [4] [42]	11 XII 1995	2 377 453	1 579 743	797 710	2 314	x2 398	...	83 600	29
Uzbekistan[9] Ouzbékistan[9]	12 I 1989	19 810 077	9 784 156	10 025 921	22 690	*23 954	1.4	447 400	54
Viet Nam Viet Nam	01 IV 1999	*76 324 753	*37 519 754	*38 804 999	73 962	x78 705	1.6	331 689	237
Yemen [4] Yémen [4]	16 XII 1994	14 587 807	7 473 540	7 114 267	15 369	*17 676	...	527 968	33
Europe · Europe									
Albania Albanie	12 IV 1989	3 182 400	1 638 900	1 543 500	3 609	x3 113	−3.7	28 748	108
Andorra Andorre	11 XI 1954	5 664	...	...	x64	x75	3.9	468	160
Austria[2] Autriche[2]	15 V 1991	7 795 786	3 753 989	4 041 797	8 047	x8 177	0.4	83 859	98
Belarus Bélarus	16 II 1999	*10 045 237	*4 717 621	*5 327 616	10 281	*10 159	−0.3	207 600	49
Belgium[2] Belgique[2]	1 III 1991	9 978 681	4 875 982	5 102 699	10 137	x10 152	−	30 528	333
Bosnia and Herzegovina [2] Bosnie–Herzégovine [2]	31 III 1991	4 377 033	2 183 795	2 193 238	4 180	x3 839	−2.1	51 197	75
Bulgaria Bulgarie	4 XII 1992	8 472 724	...	...	8 406	*8 208	−0.6	110 912	74

8
Population by sex, rate of population increase, surface area and density [*cont.*]
Population selon le sexe, taux d'accroissement de la population,
superficie et densité [*suite*]

Country or area Pays ou zone	Latest census Dernier recensement Date	Both sexes Les deux sexes	Male Masculin	Female Féminin	Mid-year estimates (thousands) Estimations au milieu de l'année (milliers) 1995	1999	Annual rate of increase Taux d'accrois- sement annuel % 1995-99	Surface area (km²) Superficie (km²) 1999	Density Densité 1999[1]
Channel Islands Iles Anglo-Normandes	10 III 1996	143 831	69 638	74 193	143	x152	1.5	195	779
Croatia [2] Croatie [2]	31 III 1991	4 784 265	2 318 623	2 465 642	4 669	*4 554	-0.6	56 538	81
Czech Republic [2] Rép. tchéque [2]	3 III 1991	10 302 215	4 999 935	5 302 280	10 331	*10 283	-0.1	78 866	130
Denmark [2 43] Danemark [2 43]	1 I 1998	5 294 860	2 615 669	2 679 191	5 228	*5 327	0.5	43 094	124
Estonia [9] Estonie [9]	31 III 2000	*1 370 500	*631 900	*738 600	1 484	x1 412	-1.2	45 100	31
Faeroe Islands [2] Iles Féroe [2]	22 IX 1977	41 969	21 997	19 972	x45	x43	-0.9	1 399	31
Finland [2] Finlande [2]	31 XII 1990	4 998 478	2 426 204	2 572 274	5 108	*5 165	0.3	338 145	15
France [44 45 46] France [44 45 46]	5 III 1990	56 634 299	27 553 788	29 080 511	58 139	*59 099	0.4	551 500	107
Germany † [2 47] Allemagne † [2 47]		...	...	...	81 661	*82 087	0.1	357 022	230
Fed. Rep. of Germany [2] Rép. féd. d'Allemagne [2]	25 V 1987	61 077 042	29 322 923	31 754 119	...	...	...	248 647	...
German Dem Rep. (former) [2] l'ex-R. d. allemande [2]	31 XII 1981	16 705 635	7 849 112	8 856 523	...	...	...	108 333	...
Gibraltar [48] Gibraltar [48]	14 X 1991	26 703	13 628	13 075	27	x25	-2.1	6	4 167
Greece [49 50] Grèce [49 50]	17 III 1991	10 259 900	5 055 408	5 204 492	10 454	x10 626	0.4	131 957	81
Holy See [51] Saint-Siège [51]	30 IV 1948	890	548	342	x1	x1	-	-	...
Hungary Hongrie	1 I 1990	10 374 823	4 984 904	5 389 919	10 229	*10 068	-0.4	93 032	108
Iceland [9] Islande [9]	1 XII 1970	204 930	103 621	101 309	267	x279	1.1	103 000	3
Ireland Irlande	28 IV 1996	3 626 087	1 800 232	1 825 855	3 601	*3 745	1.0	70 273	53
Isle of Man Ile de Man	14 IV 1996	71 714	34 797	36 917	72	x78	2.1	572	136
Italy Italie	20 X 1991	59 103 833	...	...	57 301	x57 343	-	301 318	190
Latvia [9] Lettonie [9]	12 I 1989	2 666 567	1 238 806	1 427 761	2 516	*2 432	-0.8	64 600	38
Liechtenstein Liechtenstein	2 XII 1980	25 215	...	...	31	x32	1.0	160	200
Lithuania [9] Lithuanie [9]	12 I 1989	3 674 802	1 738 953	1 935 849	3 715	*3 699	-0.1	65 200	57
Luxembourg[2] Luxembourg[2]	31 III 1991	384 634	188 570	196 064	410	*429	1.2	2 586	166
Malta [52] Malte [52]	16 XI 1985	345 418	169 832	175 586	371	x386	1.0	316	1 222
Monaco [2] Monaco [2]	23 VII 1990	29 972	14 237	15 735	x32	x33	1.1	1	33 268
Netherlands [2 53] Pays-Bas [2 53]	1 I 1991	15 010 445	7 419 501	7 590 944	15 459	*15 810	0.6	41 526	381
Norway [2] Norvège [2]	3 XI 1990	4 247 546	2 099 881	2 147 665	4 359	*4 462	0.6	323 877	14
Poland [54] Pologne [54]	6 XII 1988	37 878 641	18 464 373	19 414 268	38 588	*38 654	-	323 250	120

8

Population by sex, rate of population increase, surface area and density [*cont.*]
Population selon le sexe, taux d'accroissement de la population,
superficie et densité [*suite*]

Country or area Pays ou zone	Latest census Dernier recensement Date	Both sexes Les deux sexes	Male Masculin	Female Féminin	Mid-year estimates (thousands) Estimations au milieu de l'année (milliers) 1995	1999	Annual rate of increase Taux d'accrois- sement annuel % 1995–99	Surface area (km²) Superficie (km²) 1999	Density Densité 1999[1]
Portugal [55] Portugal [55]	15 IV 1991	9 862 540	4 754 632	5 107 908	9 916	*9 989	0.2	91 982	109
Republic of Moldova [4] République de Moldova[4]	12 I 1989	4 337 592	2 058 160	2 279 432	4 348	x4 380	...	33 851	129
Romania Roumanie	7 I 1992	22 810 035	11 213 763	11 596 272	22 681	*22 458	−0.2	238 391	94
Russian Federation [9] Fédération de Russie [9]	12 I 1989	147 021 869	68 713 869	78 308 000	147 774	*145 559	−0.4	17 075 400	9
San Marino Saint−Marin	30 XI 1976	19 149	9 654	9 495	25	x26	1.0	61	426
Slovakia [2] Slovaquie [2]	3 III 1991	5 274 335	2 574 061	2 700 274	5 364	*5 395	0.1	49 012	110
Slovenia [2] Slovénie [2]	31 III 1991	1 965 986	952 611	1 013 375	1 988	*1 989	−	20 256	98
Spain [56] Espagne [56]	1 III 1991	39 433 942	19 338 083	20 095 859	39 210	*39 418	0.1	505 992	78
Svalbard and Jan Mayen Islands [57] Svalbard et Ile Jan−Mayen [57]	1 XI 1960	3 431	2 545	886	...	...	...	62 422	...
Sweden [2] Suède [2]	1 IX 1990	8 587 353	4 242 351	4 345 002	8 837	*8 857	−	449 964	20
Switzerland [2] Suisse [2]	4 XII 1990	6 873 687	3 390 212	3 483 475	7 041	*7 140	0.4	41 284	173
TFYR of Macedonia [2] L'ex−R.y. Macédoine [2]	20 VI 1994	1 945 932	974 255	971 677	1 963	x2 011	0.6	25 713	78
Ukraine [9] Ukraine [9]	12 I 1989	51 452 034	23 745 108	27 706 926	51 728	*50 106	−0.8	603 700	83
United Kingdom [4] [58] Royaume−Uni [4] [58]	21 IV 1991	56 352 200	...	...	58 606	x58 744	...	242 900	242
Yugoslavia [2] Yougoslavie [2]	31 III 1991	10 394 026	5 157 120	5 236 906	10 547	x10 637	0.2	102 173	104
Oceania · Océanie									
American Samoa [2] [16] Samoa américaines [2] [16]	1 IV 1990	46 773	24 023	22 750	56	x66	4.0	199	332
Australia Australie	30 VI 1996	17 892 423	8 849 224	9 043 199	18 072	*18 967	1.2	7 741 220	2
Cook Islands [59] Iles Cook [59]	1 XII 1996	19 103	9 842	9 261	19	x19	−0.5	236	81
Fiji Fidji	25 VIII 1996	775 077	393 931	381 146	796	*806	0.3	18 274	44
French Polynesia [60] Polynésie française [60]	3 IX 1996	219 521	113 830	105 691	216	*228	1.3	4 000	57
Guam [2] [4] [16] Guam [2] [4] [16]	1 IV 1990	133 152	70 945	62 207	149	x164	...	549	299
Kiribati [61] Kiribati [61]	7 XI 1995	*77 658	*38 478	*39 180	*78	x82	1.4	726	113
Marshall Islands Iles Marshall	13 XI 1988	43 380	22 181	21 199	56	x62	2.7	181	343
Micronesia (Fed. States of) Micronésie (Etats féd. de)	18 IX 1994	105 506	53 923	51 583	105	x116	...	702	165
Nauru Nauru	17 IV 1992	9 919	...	...	11	x11	0.5	21	524
New Caledonia [62] Nouvelle−Calédonie [62]	4 IV 1989	164 173	83 862	80 311	194	*206	1.5	18 575	11
New Zealand [63] Nouvelle−Zélande [63]	5 III 1996	3 618 303	1 777 464	1 840 839	3 656	*3 811	1.0	270 534	14
Niue Nioué	17 VIII 1997	*2 088	*1 053	*1 035	x2	x2	−0.8	260	8

8

Population by sex, rate of population increase, surface area and density [*cont.*]
Population selon le sexe, taux d'accroissement de la population,
superficie et densité [*suite*]

Country or area Pays ou zone	Latest census Dernier recensement		Male Masculin	Female Féminin	Mid–year estimates (thousands) Estimations au milieu de l'année (milliers)		Annual rate of increase Taux d'accrois- sement annuel %	Surface area (km²) Superficie (km²)	Density Densité
	Date	Both sexes Les deux sexes			1995	1999	1995–99	1999	1999[1]
Norfolk Island Ile Norfolk	30 VI 1986	2 367	1 170	1 197	...	...	...	36	...
Northern Mariana Islands Iles Mariannes du Nord	1 IV 1990	43 345	...	...	x59	x74	5.7	464	159
Palau Palaos	9 IX 1995	17 225	9 213	8 012	...	...	...	459	...
Papua New Guinea [64] Papouasie–Nouveau– Guinée[64]	11 VII 1990	3 761 954	...	...	4 074	x4 702	3.6	462 840	10
Pitcairn Pitcairn	31 XII 1991	66	...	...	...	...	...	5	...
Samoa Samoa	11 V 1991	161 298	...	...	x168	*169	0.3	2 831	60
Solomon Islands [65] Iles Salomon [65]	23 XI 1986	285 176	147 972	137 204	x379	x430	3.1	28 896	15
Tokelau Tokélaou	11 XII 1991	1 577	...	...	x2	x1	−10.1	12	83
Tonga Tonga	30 XI 1996	97 784	49 615	48 169	98	x98	0.1	650	151
Tuvalu Tuvalu	17 IX 1991	9 043	4 376	4 667	x10	x11	1.8	26	423
Vanuatu Vanuatu	16 V 1989	142 944	73 674	69 270	x169	x186	2.4	12 189	15
Wallis and Futuna Islands Iles Wallis et Futuna	11 XII 1990	13 705	...	...	x14	x14	−0.2	200	70

Source:
United Nations Statistics Division, New York, "Demographic
Yearbook 1999" and the demographic statistics database.

Source:
Organisation des Nations Unies, Division de statistique, New York,
"Annuaire démographique 1999" et la base de données pour les
statistiques démographiques.

† For information on recent changes in country or area
 nomenclature pertaining to former Czechoslovakia, Germany,
 Hong Kong Special Administrative Region (SAR) of China,
 Macao Special Administrative Region (SAR) of China,
 SFR of Yugolasvia and the former USSR, see Annex I –
 Country or area nomenclature, regional and other groupings.

† Pour les modifications récentes de nomenclature de pays ou de
 zone concernant l'Allemagne, Hong Kong région administrative
 spéciale (RAS) de Chine, Macao région administrative spéciale
 (RAS) de Chine, l'ex–Tchécoslovaquie, l'ex–URSS, et Rfs
 de Yougoslavie, voir annexe I – Nomenclature des pays ou des
 zones, groupements régionaux et autres groupements.

* Provisional.
x Estimate for 1995–2000 prepared by the Population Division
 of the United Nations.
1 Population per square kilometre of surface area in 1999. Figures are
 merely the quotients of population divided by surface area and are not
 to be considered either as reflecting density in the urban sense or as
 indicating the supporting power of a territory's land and resources.

2 De jure population.
3 Including the enclave of Cabinda.
4 Rate not computed because of apparent lack of comparability
 between estimates shown for 1995 and 1999.
5 Census results have been adjusted for under–enumeration
 estimated at 1.4 per cent.
6 Census results, excluding Mayotte.
7 Comprising Bioko (which includes Pagalu) and Rio Muni
 (which includes Corisco and Elobeys).

* Données provisoires.
x Estimations pour 1995–2000 établie par la Division de la
 population de l'Organisation des Nations Unies.
1 Nombre d'habitants au kilomètre carré en 1999. Il s'agit
 simplement du quotient du chiffre de la population divisé par
 celui de la superficie: il ne faut pas y voir d'indication de la
 densité au sens urbain du terme ni de l'effectif de population que
 les terres et les ressources du territoire sont capables de nourrir.

2 Population de droit.
3 Y compris l'enclave de Cabinda.
4 On n'a pas calculé le taux parce que les estimations pour 1995 et
 1999 ne paraissent pas comparables.
5 Les résultats du recensement ont été ajustés pour compenser les
 lacunes du dénombrement estimées à 1,4 p. 100.
6 Les résultats du recensement, non compris Mayotte.
7 Comprend Bioko (qui comprend Pagalu) et Rio Muni (qui
 comprend Corisco et Elobeys).

8

Population by sex, rate of population increase, surface area and density [*cont.*]
Population selon le sexe, taux d'accroissement de la population,
superficie et densité [*suite*]

8	Mid−year estimates have been adjusted for under−enumeration. Census data have not been adjusted for under−enumeration, estimated as follows: Bolivia (6.92), Brunei Darussalam (1.06), Canada (...), Guinea (...), Korea, Republic of (1.9), Mozambique (5.1), Paraguay (7.40), Peru (2.35), South Africa (6.8), Sierra Leone (9.0).	8	Les estimations au milieu de l'année tiennent compte d'un ajustement destiné à compenser les lacunes du dénombrement. Les données de recensement ne tiennent pas compte de cet ajustement. En voici le détail: Bolive (6,92), Brunéi Darussalam (1,06), Canada (...), Guinée (...), Corée Rép. de (1,9), Mozambique (5,1), Paraguay (7,40), Pérou (2,35), Afrique de Sud (6,8), Sierra Leone (9,0).
9	Census results for de jure population.	9	Les résultats du recensement. Population de droit.
10	Census results, including an estimate of 224 095 for nomad population	10	Les résultats du recensement, y compris une estimation de 224 095 personnes pour la population nomade.
11	Comprising the Northern Region (former Saguia el Hamra) and Southern Region (former Rio de Oro).	11	Comprend la région septentrionale (ancien Saguia−el−Hamra) et la région méridionale (ancien Rio de Oro).
12	Mid−year estimates for de jure population, but excluding persons residing in institutions.	12	Estimations au milieu de l'année pour la Population de droit, mais non compris les personnes dans les institutions.
13	Including Carriacou and other dependencies in the Grenadines.	13	Y compris Carriacou et les autres dépendances du groupe des îles Grenadines.
14	Including dependencies: Marie−Galante, la Désirade, les Saintes, Petite−Terre, St. Barthélemy and French part of St. Martin.	14	Y compris les dépendances: Marie−Galante, la Désirade, les Saintes, Petite−Terre, Saint−Barthélemy et la partie française de Saint−Martin.
15	Comprising Bonaire, Curaçao, Saba, St. Eustatius and Dutch part of St. Martin.	15	Comprend Bonaire, Curaçao, Saba, Saint−Eustache et la partie néederlandaise de Saint−Martin.
16	Including armed forces stationed in the area.	16	Y compris les militaires en garnison sur le territoire.
17	Including Bequia and other islands in the Grenadines.	17	Y compris Bequia et des autres îles dans les Grenadines.
18	De jure population, but excluding civilian citizens absent from country for extended period of time. Census figures also exclude armed forces overseas.	18	Population de droit, mais non compris les civils hors du pays pendant une période prolongée. Les chiffres de recensement ne comprennent pas également les militaires à l'étranger.
19	Excluding Indian jungle population.	19	Non compris les Indiens de la jungle.
20	Excluding nomadic Indian tribes.	20	Non compris les tribus d'Indiens nomades.
21	Excluding dependencies, of which South Georgia (area 3 755 km²) had an estimated population of 499 in 1964 (494 males, 5 females). The other dependencies namely, the South Sandwich group (surface area 337 km²) and a number of smaller islands, are presumed to be uninhabited.	21	Non compris les dépendances, parmi lesquelles figure la Georgie du Sud (3 755 km²) avec une population estimée à 499 personnes en 1964 (494 du sexe masculin et 5 du sexe féminin). Les autres dépendances, c'est−à−dire le groupe des Sandwich de Sud (superficie: 337 km²) et certaines petites−îles, sont présumées inhabitées.
22	A dispute exists between the governments of Argentina and the United Kingdom of Great Britain and Northern Ireland concerning sovereignty over the Falkland Islands (Malvinas).	22	La souveraineté sur les îles Falkland (Malvinas) fait l'objet d'un différend entre le Gouvernement argentin et le Gouvernement du Royaume−Uni de Grande−Bretagne et d'Irlande du Nord.
23	Census results, excluding nomad population.	23	Les résultats du recensement, non compris la population nomade.
24	Excluding foreign diplomatic personnel and their dependants.	24	Non compris le personnel diplomatique étranger et les membres de leur famille les accompagnant.
25	For statistical purposes, the data for China do not include those for the Hong Kong Special Administrative Region (Hong Kong SAR) and Macao special Administrative Region (Macao SAR).	25	Pour la présentation des statistiques, les données pour Chine ne comprend pas la Région Administrative Spéciale de Hong Kong (Hong Kong RAS) et la Région Administrative Spéciale de Macao (Macao RAS).
26	Census figures for China, as given in the communiqué of the State Statistical Bureau releasing the major figures of the census, includes a population of 6 130 000 for Hong Kong and Macao.	26	Les chiffres du recensement de la Chine, qui figurent dans le communiqué du Bureau du statistique de l'Etat publiant les principaux chiffres du recensement, comprennent la population de Hong Kong et Macao qui s'élève à 6 130 000 personnes.
27	Census results, for government controlled areas.	27	Les résultats du recensement, pour les zones contrôlées par le Gouvernement.
28	Including data for the Indian−held part of Jammu and Kashmir, the final status of which has not yet been determined.	28	Y compris les données pour la partie du Jammu et du Cachemire occupée par l'Inde dont le statut définitif n'a pas encore été déterminé.
29	Figures provided by Indonesia including East Timor, shown separately	29	Les chiffres fournis par l'Indonesie comprennent le Timor oriental, qui fait l'objet d'une rubrique distincte.
30	Including data for East Jerusalem and Israeli residents in certain other territories under occupation by Israeli military forces since June 1967.	30	Y compris les données pour Jérusalem−Est et les résidents israéliens dans certains autres territoires occupés depuis juin 1967 pour les forces armées israéliennes.

8

Population by sex, rate of population increase, surface area and density [*cont.*]
Population selon le sexe, taux d'accroissement de la population,
superficie et densité [*suite*]

31 Comprising Hokkaido, Honshu, Shikoku, Kyushu. Excluding diplomatic personnel outside the country and foreign military and civilian personnel and their dependants stationed in the area.

32 Including military and diplomatic personnel and their families abroad numbering 933 at 1961 census, but excluding foreign military and diplomatic personnel and their families in the country, numbering 389 at 1961 census. Also including registered Palestinian refugees numbering 654 092 and 722 687 at 30 June 1963 and 31 May 1967, respectively.

33 Census results, excluding data for Jordanian territory under occupation since June 1967 by Israeli military forces.

34 Excluding alien armed forces, civilian aliens employed by armed forces, foreign diplomatic personnel and their dependants and Korean diplomatic personnel and their dependants outside the country.

35 Excluding Palestinian refugees in camps.
36 Based on results of sample survey.
37 The figures were received from the Palestinian Authority and refer to the Palestinian population.
38 Census results exclude an estimate for under−enumeration estimated at 2.4 per cent.
39 Excluding data for Jammu and Kashmir, the final status of which has not yet been determined, Junagardh, Manavadar, Gilgit and Baltistan.

40 Census results, excluding transients afloat and non−locally domiciled military and civilian services personnel and their dependants and visitors.

41 Including Palestinian refugees.
42 Comprising 7 sheikdoms of Abu Dhabi, Dubai, Sharjah, Ajaman, Umm al Qaiwain, Ras al Khaimah and Fujairah, and the area lying within the modified Riyadh line as announced in October 1955.

43 Excluding Faeroe Islands and Greenland.
44 Excluding Overseas Departments, namely French Guiana, Guadeloupe, Martinique and Réunion, shown separately.

45 De jure population, but excluding diplomatic personnel outside the country and including foreign diplomatic personnel not living in embassies or consulates.

46 Excluding military personnel stationed outside the country who do not have a personal residence in France.

47 All data shown pertaining to Germany prior to 3 October 1990 are indicated separately for the Federal Republic of Germany and the former German Democratic Republic based on their respective territories at the time indicated.

48 Excluding armed forces.
49 Census results, include armed forces stationed outside the country, but excluding alien armed forces stationed in the area.

50 Estimates include armed forces stationed outside the country, but including alien armed forces stationed in the area.

31 Comprend Hokkaido, Honshu, Shikoku, Kyushu. Non compris le personnel diplomatique hors du pays, les militaires et agents civils étrangers en poste sur le territoire et les membres de leur famille les accompagnant.

32 Y compris les militaires et le personnel diplomatique à l'ètranger et les members de leur famille les accompagnant, au nombre de 933 personnes au recensement de 1961, mais non compris les militaires et le personnel diplomatique étrangers sur le territoire et les membres de leur famille les accompagnant, au nombre de 389 personnes au recensement de 1961. Y compris également les réfugiés de Palestine immatriculés: 654 092 au 30 juin 1963 et 722 687 au 31 mai 1967.

33 Les résultats du recensement, non compris les données pour le territoire jordanien occupé depuis juin 1967 par les forces armées israéliennes.

34 Non compris les militaires étrangers, les civils étrangers employés par les forces armées, le personnel diplomatique étranger et les membres de leur famille les accompagnant et le personnel diplomatique coréen hors du pays et les membres de leur familles les accompagnant.

35 Non compris les réfugiés de Palestine dans les camps.
36 D'après les résultats d'une enquête par sondage.
37 Les chiffres sont fournis par l'autorité palestinienne et comprennent la population palestinienne.
38 Les résultats du recensement n'ont pas été ajustées pour compenser les lacunes de denombrement, estimées à 2,4 p. 100.
39 Non compris les données pour le Jammu et le Cachemire, dont le statut définitif n'a pas encore été déterminé, le Junagardh, la Manavadar, le Gilgit et le Batistan.

40 Les résultats du recensement, non compris les personnes de passage à bord de navires, les militaires et agents civils non résidents et les membres de leur famille les accompagnant, et les visiteurs.

41 Y compris les réfugiés de Palestine.
42 Comprend les sept cheikhats de Abou Dhabi, Dabai, Ghârdja, Adjmân, Oumm−al−Quiwaïn, Ras al Khaîma et Foudjaïra, ainsi que la zone délimitée par la ligne de Riad modifiée comme il a été annoncé en octobre 1955.

43 Non compris les îles Féroé et le Groenland.
44 Non compris les départements d'outre−mer, c'est−à−dire la Guyane française, la Guadeloupe, la Martinique et la Réunion, qui font l'objet de rubriques distinctes.

45 Population de droit, non compris le personnel diplomatique hors du pays et y compris le personnel diplomatique étranger qui ne vivent pas dans les ambassades ou les consulats.

46 Non compris les militaires en garnison hors du pays et sans résidence personnelle en France.

47 Toutes les données se rapportant à l'Allemagne avant le 3 octobre 1990 figurent dans deux rubriques séparées basées sur les territoires respectifs de la République fédérale d'Allemagne et l'ancienne République démocratique allemande selon la période indiquée.

48 Non compris les militaires.
49 Les résultats du recensement, y compris les militaires en garnison hors du pays, mais non compris les militaires étrangers en garnison sur le territoire.

50 Les estimations de la population, y compris les militaires en garnison hors du pays, mais y compris les militaires étrangers en garnison sur le territoire.

8
Population by sex, rate of population increase, surface area and density [*cont.*]
Population selon le sexe, taux d'accroissement de la population,
superficie et densité [*suite*]

51 Data refer to the Vatican City State.

52 Including Gozo and Comino Islands and civilian nationals temporarily outside the country.

53 Census results, based on compilation of continuous accounting and sample surveys.

54 Excluding civilian aliens within the country, but including civilian nationals temporarily outside the country.

55 Including the Azores and Madeira Islands.

56 Including the Balearic and Canary Islands, and Alhucemas, Ceuta, Chafarinas, Melilla and Penon de Vélez de la Gomera.

57 Inhabited only during the winter season. Census data are for total population while estimates refer to Norwegian population only. Included also in the de jure population of Norway.

58 Excluding Channel Islands and Isle of Man, shown separately.

59 Excluding Niue, shown separately, which is part of Cook Islands, but because of remoteness is administered separately.

60 Comprising Austral, Gambier, Marquesas, Rapa, Society and Tuamotu Islands.

61 Including Christmas, Fanning, Ocean and Washington Islands.

62 Including the islands of Huon, Chesterfield, Loyalty, Walpole and Belep Archipelago.

63 Including Campbell and Kermadec Islands (population 20 in 1961, surface area 148 km²) as well as Antipodes, Auckland, Bounty, Snares, Solander and Three Kings island, all of which are uninhabited. Excluding diplomatic personnel and armed forces outside the country, the latter numbering 1 936 at 1966 census; also excluding alien armed forces within the country.

64 Comprising eastern part of New Guinea, the Bismarck Archipelago, Bougainville and Buka of Solomon Islands group and about 600 smaller islands.

65 Comprising the Solomon Islands group (except Bougainville and Buka which are included with Papua New Guinea shown separately), Ontong, Java, Rennel and Santa Cruz Islands.

51 Les données se rapportent à l'Etat de la Cité du Vatican.

52 Y compris les îles de Gozo et de Comino et les civils nationaux temporairement hors du pays.

53 Les résultats du recensement, d'aprés les résultats des dénombrements et enquêtes par sondage continue.

54 Non compris les civils étrangers dans le pays, mais y compris les civils nationaux temporairement hors du pays.

55 Y compris les Açores et Madère.

56 Y compris les Baléares et les Canaries, Al Hoceima, Ceuta, les îles Zaffarines, Melilla et Penon de Vélez de la Gomera.

57 N'est habitée que pendant la saison d'hiver. Les données de recensement se rapportent à la population totale, mais les estimations ne concernent que la population norvégienne, comprise également dans la population de droit de la Norvège.

58 Non compris les îles Anglo-Normandes et l'île de Man, qui font l'objet de rubriques distinctes.

59 Non compris Nioué, qui fait l'objet d'une rubrique distincte et qui fait partie des îles Cook, mais qui, en raison de son éloignement, est administrée séparément.

60 Comprend les îles Australes, Gambier, Marquises, Rapa, de la Societé et Tuamotou.

61 Y compris les îles Christmas, Fanning, Océan et Washington.

62 Y compris les îles Huon, Chesterfield, Loyauté et Walpole, et l'archipel Belep.

63 Y compris les îles Campbell et Kermadec (20 habitants en 1961, superficie: 148 km²) ainsi que les îles Antipodes, Auckland, Bounty, Snares, Solander et Three Kings, qui sont toutes inhabitées. Non compris les personnel diplomatique et les militaires hors du pays, ces derniers au nombre de 1 936 au recensement de 1966; non compris également les militaires étrangers dans le pays.

64 Comprend l'est de la Nouvelle-Guinée, l'archipel Bismarck, Bougainville et Buka (ces deux dernières du group des Salomon) et environ 600 îlots.

65 Comprend les îles Salomon (à l'exception de Bougainville et de Buka dont la population est comprise dans celle de Papouasie-Nouvelle Guinée qui font l'objet d'une rubrique distincte), ainsi que les îles Ontong, Java, Rennel et Santa Cruz.

9
Population in urban and rural areas, rates of growth and largest urban agglomeration population
Population urbaine, population rurale, taux d'accroissement et population de l'agglomération urbaine la plus peuplée

Country or area Pays ou zone	Year Année	Rural % Rurale %	Urban % Urbaine %	Population estimates Estimations de la population Growth rate p.a. (%)[1] Taux d'accroissement p.a. (%)[1]		Population of largest urban agglomeration with 750,000 inhabitants or more in 2000 Population de l'agglomération urbaine la plus peuplée avec 750 000 habitants ou plus en 2000		
				Rural pop. Pop. rurale	Urban pop. Pop. urbaine	Number (000s) Nombre (000s)	% of urban % de urbaine	% of total % de totale
Africa · Afrique								
Algeria	1995	45.7	54.3	0.5	2.8	2295	15.3	8.3
Algérie	2000	42.9	57.1	0.4	2.7	2761	15.9	9.1
Angola	1995	69.0	31.0	2.0	4.9	2149	61.2	19.0
Angola	2000	65.8	34.2	2.0	4.8	2697	60.0	20.5
Benin	1995	61.6	38.4	1.3	4.6	...	...	...
Bénin	2000	57.7	42.3	1.4	4.5	...	...	...
Botswana	1995	52.8	47.2	0.9	2.4	...	...	...
Botswana	2000	51.0	49.0	−0.3	1.4	...	...	...
Burkina Faso	1995	85.0	15.0	2.0	4.3	700	45.4	6.8
Burkina Faso	2000	83.5	16.5	2.6	5.1	831	43.6	7.2
Burundi	1995	92.5	7.5	0.6	4.4	...	...	...
Burundi	2000	91.0	9.0	2.6	6.4	...	...	...
Cameroon	1995	55.3	44.7	0.7	4.1	1317	22.2	9.9
Cameroun	2000	51.1	48.9	0.6	3.6	1642	22.6	11.0
Cape Verde	1995	45.8	54.2	−1.5	5.1	...	...	...
Cap−Vert	2000	37.8	62.2	−1.2	3.9	...	...	...
Central African Rep.	1995	60.9	39.1	1.4	3.1	...	...	...
Rép. centrafricaine	2000	58.8	41.2	0.8	2.8	...	...	...
Chad	1995	77.8	22.2	2.7	4.5	...	...	...
Tchad	2000	76.2	23.8	2.6	4.6	...	...	...
Comoros	1995	69.6	30.4	2.1	4.7	...	...	...
Comores	2000	66.8	33.2	2.0	4.6	...	...	...
Congo	1995	38.9	61.1	0.6	4.3	1055	66.3	40.5
Congo	2000	34.6	65.4	1.1	4.0	1306	66.2	43.3
Côte d'Ivoire	1995	58.3	41.7	1.5	3.0	2880	48.0	20.0
Côte d'Ivoire	2000	56.4	43.6	1.3	3.0	3790	54.3	23.7
Dem. Rep. of the Congo	1995	71.3	28.7	2.1	3.6	4236	32.9	9.4
Rép. dém. du Congo	2000	69.7	30.3	2.6	4.9	5054	32.8	9.9
Djibouti	1995	17.1	82.9	1.6	3.2	...	...	...
Djibouti	2000	16.0	84.0	−0.3	1.3	...	...	...
Egypt	1995	56.9	43.1	2.0	1.6	8860	33.1	14.3
Egypte	2000	57.3	42.7	1.6	1.8	9462	32.7	13.9
Equatorial Guinea	1995	57.8	42.2	0.5	5.3	...	...	...
Guinée équatoriale	2000	51.8	48.2	0.7	4.9	...	...	...
Eritrea	1995	82.9	17.1	2.3	4.6	...	...	...
Erythrée	2000	81.3	18.7	3.7	6.3	...	...	...
Ethiopia	1995	86.0	14.0	2.2	4.6	2173	28.0	3.9
Ethiopie	2000	84.5	15.5	2.0	4.6	2645	27.1	4.2
Gabon	1995	24.1	75.9	−2.5	4.0	...	...	...
Gabon	2000	18.6	81.4	−2.0	3.4	...	...	...
Gambia	1995	72.3	27.7	2.3	5.2	...	...	...
Gambie	2000	69.3	30.7	1.4	4.4	...	...	...
Ghana	1995	65.2	34.8	1.8	2.9	1603	26.6	9.3
Ghana	2000	63.9	36.1	1.7	3.1	1868	26.8	9.7
Guinea	1995	74.6	25.4	1.6	3.7	1039	55.8	14.2
Guinée	2000	72.5	27.5	0.8	3.1	1232	55.0	15.1
Guinea−Bissau	1995	72.4	27.6	1.0	4.8	...	...	...
Guinée−Bissau	2000	68.5	31.5	1.2	4.8	...	...	...
Kenya	1995	71.5	28.5	0.9	5.5	1756	22.6	6.4
Kenya	2000	66.6	33.4	0.4	4.6	2233	21.8	7.3
Lesotho	1995	76.0	24.0	0.6	4.8	...	...	...
Lesotho	2000	72.0	28.0	−0.4	3.4	...	...	...
Liberia	1995	58.0	42.0	6.0	8.4	...	...	...
Libéria	2000	55.1	44.9	4.4	6.8	...	...	...
Libyan Arab Jamahiriya	1995	14.7	85.3	−1.3	2.7	1518	37.4	31.9
Jamah. arabe libyenne	2000	12.4	87.6	−0.2	2.5	1733	37.4	32.8
Madagascar	1995	73.6	26.4	2.1	5.1	1226	33.7	8.9
Madagascar	2000	70.5	29.5	1.9	4.9	1603	34.0	10.0

9
Population in urban and rural areas, rates of growth and largest urban agglomeration population [*cont.*]
Population urbaine, population rurale, taux d'accroissement et population de l'agglomération
urbaine la plus peuplée [*suite*]

Country or area Pays ou zone	Year Année	Population estimates Estimations de la population		Growth rate p.a. (%) [1] Taux d'accroissement p.a. (%) [1]		Population of largest urban agglomeration with 750,000 inhabitants or more in 2000 Population de l'agglomération urbaine la plus peuplée avec 750 000 habitants ou plus en 2000		
		Rural % Rurale %	Urban % Urbaine %	Rural pop. Pop. rurale	Urban pop. Pop. urbaine	Number (000s) Nombre (000s)	% of urban % de urbaine	% of total % de totale
Malawi	1995	86.9	13.1	2.0	4.8	...	...	...
Malawi	2000	85.3	14.7	1.7	4.6			
Mali	1995	73.1	26.9	1.8	5.0	906	33.9	9.1
Mali	2000	69.8	30.2	1.9	5.1	1114	32.5	9.8
Mauritania	1995	49.1	50.9	0.2	5.7	...	...	...
Mauritanie	2000	42.3	57.7	−0.4	5.1			
Mauritius [2]	1995	59.5	40.5	0.6	1.2	...	...	...
Maurice [2]	2000	58.7	41.3	0.2	1.6			
Morocco	1995	48.0	52.0	0.4	3.2	2994	21.2	11.0
Maroc	2000	44.5	55.5	0.3	2.9	3357	20.3	11.2
Mozambique	1995	73.8	26.2	0.7	6.4	921	21.5	5.7
Mozambique	2000	67.9	32.1	0.0	5.1	1094	18.6	6.0
Namibia	1995	71.4	28.6	1.4	3.6	...	...	...
Namibie	2000	69.1	30.9	0.9	3.3			
Niger	1995	81.8	18.2	2.9	5.9	587	35.4	6.4
Niger	2000	79.4	20.6	3.0	6.0	775	34.8	7.2
Nigeria	1995	60.4	39.6	1.2	4.9	6485	16.5	6.5
Nigéria	2000	55.9	44.1	1.0	4.4	8665	17.3	7.6
Reunion	1995	32.2	67.8	−0.8	2.7	...	...	...
Réunion	2000	28.6	71.4	−1.0	2.2			
Rwanda	1995	94.3	5.7	8.4	10.1	...	...	...
Rwanda	2000	93.8	6.2	2.0	4.2			
Saint Helena [3]	1995	37.4	62.6	−4.0	3.2	...	...	...
Sainte−Hélène [3]	2000	29.4	70.6	−3.1	2.3			
Sao Tome and Principe	1995	56.9	43.1	0.4	3.5	...	...	...
Sao Tomé−et−Principe	2000	53.1	47.0	0.4	3.2			
Senegal	1995	56.2	43.8	1.2	4.2	1708	47.0	20.6
Sénégal	2000	52.6	47.4	1.1	4.0	2078	46.5	22.1
Seychelles	1995	40.9	59.1	−1.1	2.8	...	...	...
Seychelles	2000	36.2	63.8	−0.9	2.4			
Sierra Leone	1995	66.7	33.3	0.5	3.5	681	50.2	16.7
Sierra Leone	2000	63.4	36.6	3.4	6.3	800	49.6	18.2
Somalia	1995	74.4	25.6	3.1	5.0	941	49.9	12.8
Somalie	2000	72.5	27.5	3.6	5.8	1157	47.9	13.2
South Africa	1995	47.4	52.6	−0.3	3.1	2463	11.7	6.1
Afrique du Sud	2000	43.1	56.9	−1.1	2.1	2950	12.0	6.8
Sudan	1995	68.7	31.4	0.7	5.0	2249	25.7	8.0
Soudan	2000	63.9	36.1	0.8	4.7	2742	24.4	8.8
Swaziland	1995	75.0	25.0	1.7	3.1	...	...	...
Swaziland	2000	73.6	26.4	0.4	2.2			
Togo	1995	69.2	30.8	2.5	4.9	...	...	...
Togo	2000	66.6	33.4	1.7	4.2			
Tunisia	1995	38.1	61.9	−0.9	2.2	1722	31.1	19.3
Tunisie	2000	34.5	65.5	−0.8	2.1	1892	30.5	20.0
Uganda	1995	87.5	12.5	2.6	5.4	955	37.9	4.8
Ouganda	2000	85.8	14.2	2.7	5.7	1213	36.8	5.2
United Rep. of Tanzania	1995	73.1	26.9	1.1	6.2	1657	19.9	5.4
Rép. Unie de Tanzanie	2000	67.7	32.3	0.7	5.3	2115	18.7	6.0
Western Sahara	1995	7.2	92.8	−5.7	3.9	...	...	...
Sahara occidental	2000	4.6	95.4	−4.2	3.2			
Zambia	1995	60.8	39.2	2.3	2.7	1317	36.5	14.3
Zambie	2000	60.4	39.6	1.7	2.7	1653	40.0	15.9
Zimbabwe	1995	68.2	31.8	0.8	4.0	1410	38.7	12.3
Zimbabwe	2000	64.7	35.3	0.6	3.7	1791	40.2	14.2
America, North · Amerique du Nord								
Anguilla	1995	0.0	100.0	0.0	2.8	...	...	...
Anguilla	2000	0.0	100.0	0.0	2.6			
Antigua and Barbuda	1995	64.2	35.8	0.0	0.9	...	...	...
Antigua−et−Barbuda	2000	63.2	36.8	−0.2	1.1			
Aruba	1995	49.8	50.2	3.5	3.9	...	...	...
Aruba	2000	49.2	50.8	2.9	3.8			

9
Population in urban and rural areas, rates of growth and largest urban agglomeration population [*cont.*]
Population urbaine, population rurale, taux d'accroissement et population de l'agglomération
urbaine la plus peuplée [*suite*]

Country or area Pays ou zone	Year Année	Population estimates Estimations de la population		Growth rate p.a. (%) [1] Taux d'accroissement p.a. (%) [1]		Population of largest urban agglomeration with 750,000 inhabitants or more in 2000 Population de l'agglomération urbaine la plus peuplée avec 750 000 habitants ou plus en 2000		
		Rural % Rurale %	Urban % Urbaine %	Rural pop. Pop. rurale	Urban pop. Pop. urbaine	Number (000s) Nombre (000s)	% of urban % de urbaine	% of total % de totale
Bahamas	1995	13.5	86.5	−1.8	1.9	...	...	...
Bahamas	2000	11.5	88.5	−1.4	1.6	...	...	...
Barbados	1995	52.7	47.3	−0.7	1.5	...	...	...
Barbade	2000	50.0	50.0	−0.8	1.4	...	...	...
Belize	1995	52.0	48.0	2.2	2.2			
Belize	2000	52.0	48.0	1.6	2.1	...	...	...
Bermuda	1995	0.0	100.0	0.0	0.6			
Bermudes	2000	0.0	100.0	0.0	0.6	...	...	...
British Virgin Islands	1995	44.0	56.0	0.5	4.7			
Iles Vierges britanniques	2000	38.9	61.1	0.2	3.8	...	...	...
Canada	1995	22.3	77.7	0.0	1.2	4197	18.4	14.3
Canada	2000	21.3	78.7	−0.2	1.1	4752	19.6	15.4
Cayman Islands	1995	0.0	100.0	0.0	3.6			
Iles Caïmanes	2000	0.0	100.0	0.0	3.2	...	...	...
Costa Rica	1995	43.6	56.4	1.2	3.4	858	42.9	24.2
Costa Rica	2000	41.0	59.0	0.7	2.9	961	40.5	23.9
Cuba	1995	25.4	74.6	−0.2	0.6	2183	26.7	19.9
Cuba	2000	24.7	75.3	−0.4	0.5	2256	26.7	20.1
Dominica	1995	30.7	69.3	−1.2	0.4	...	...	...
Dominique	2000	29.0	71.0	−1.3	0.4	...	...	...
Dominican Republic	1995	37.9	62.1	−0.1	2.7	2242	46.9	29.1
Rép. dominicaine	2000	34.6	65.4	−0.3	2.4	2563	46.8	30.6
El Salvador	1995	46.0	54.0	−0.9	4.3	1140	37.3	20.1
El Salvador	2000	39.7	60.3	−1.1	3.5	1341	35.4	21.4
Greenland	1995	19.1	80.9	−1.1	0.4	...	...	...
Groënland	2000	18.0	82.0	−1.1	0.4	...	...	...
Grenada	1995	64.2	35.8	−0.4	1.5			
Grenade	2000	62.1	37.9	−0.6	1.7	...	...	...
Guadeloupe	1995	0.8	99.2	−12.1	1.0			
Guadeloupe	2000	0.4	99.6	−9.9	0.8	...	...	...
Guatemala	1995	61.4	38.6	2.3	3.2	2577	66.9	25.8
Guatemala	2000	60.3	39.7	2.0	3.4	3242	71.8	28.5
Haiti	1995	67.4	32.6	0.6	3.4	1427	58.2	19.0
Haïti	2000	64.3	35.7	0.5	3.3	1769	60.9	21.7
Honduras	1995	52.5	47.5	0.5	4.7	814	30.5	14.5
Honduras	2000	47.3	52.7	0.3	4.0	949	28.0	14.8
Jamaica	1995	46.3	53.7	−0.2	1.7	...	...	...
Jamaïque	2000	43.9	56.1	−0.3	1.7	...	...	...
Martinique	1995	7.0	93.0	−5.8	1.0	...	...	...
Martinique	2000	5.1	94.9	−4.9	0.8	...	...	...
Mexico	1995	26.6	73.4	0.9	1.9	16791	25.1	18.4
Mexique	2000	25.6	74.4	0.6	1.7	18066	24.6	18.3
Montserrat	1995	87.5	12.5	−20.2	−19.4	...	...	...
Montserrat	2000	87.0	13.0	3.3	4.7	...	...	...
Netherlands Antilles	1995	31.4	68.6	0.6	1.2	...	...	...
Antilles néerlandaises	2000	30.8	69.2	0.2	1.1	...	...	...
Nicaragua	1995	45.5	54.5	2.0	3.3	870	36.1	19.6
Nicaragua	2000	43.9	56.1	1.7	3.3	1009	35.4	19.9
Panama	1995	45.0	55.0	1.1	2.1	998	68.9	37.9
Panama	2000	43.7	56.3	0.7	2.0	1173	73.0	41.1
Puerto Rico	1995	26.7	73.3	−0.4	1.5	1305	47.9	35.1
Porto Rico	2000	24.8	75.2	−0.6	1.3	1388	47.1	35.4
St. Kitts and Nevis	1995	66.0	34.0	−0.8	−0.7	...	...	...
Saint−Kitts−et−Nevis	2000	65.9	34.1	−1.0	−0.2	...	...	...
Saint Lucia	1995	62.8	37.2	0.9	1.5	...	...	...
Sainte−Lucie	2000	62.2	37.8	0.7	1.7	...	...	...
St. Pierre and Miquelon	1995	8.4	91.6	−0.6	0.9	...	...	...
Saint−Pierre−et−Miquelon	2000	7.9	92.1	−0.6	0.8	...	...	...
St. Vincent and the Grenadines	1995	51.9	48.1	−2.1	3.3	...	...	...
St. Vincent−Grenadines	2000	45.2	54.8	−2.0	2.6	...	...	...
Trinidad and Tobago	1995	28.3	71.7	−1.2	1.1	...	...	...
Trinité−et−Tobago	2000	25.9	74.1	−1.2	1.0	...	...	...

9

Population in urban and rural areas, rates of growth and largest urban agglomeration population [*cont.*]
Population urbaine, population rurale, taux d'accroissement et population de l'agglomération
urbaine la plus peuplée [*suite*]

Country or area Pays ou zone	Year Année	Population estimates Estimations de la population		Growth rate p.a. (%)[1] Taux d'accroissement p.a. (%)[1]		Population of largest urban agglomeration with 750,000 inhabitants or more in 2000 Population de l'agglomération urbaine la plus peuplée avec 750 000 habitants ou plus en 2000		
		Rural % Rurale %	Urban % Urbaine %	Rural pop. Pop. rurale	Urban pop. Pop. urbaine	Number (000s) Nombre (000s)	% of urban % de urbaine	% of total % de totale
Turks and Caicos Islands	1995	56.4	43.6	2.9	4.2	...	...	...
Iles Turques et Caiques	2000	54.8	45.2	2.4	4.1	...	...	...
United States	1995	23.9	76.1	0.1	1.3	16343	8.0	6.1
Etats – Unis	2000	22.8	77.2	−0.2	1.2	16732	7.7	5.9
US Virgin Islands	1995	54.5	45.5	0.8	1.6	...	...	...
Iles Vierges américaines	2000	53.6	46.4	0.6	1.7	...	...	...
America, South · Amerique du Sud								
Argentina	1995	12.6	87.5	0.0	1.4	11620	38.2	33.4
Argentine	2000	11.8	88.2	−0.1	1.4	12024	36.8	32.5
Bolivia	1995	40.6	59.4	0.8	3.3	1267	28.8	17.1
Bolivie	2000	37.6	62.4	0.6	3.0	1460	28.1	17.5
Brazil	1995	21.9	78.1	−1.7	2.1	16469	13.2	10.3
Brésil	2000	18.8	81.2	−1.9	1.9	17962	13.0	10.5
Chile	1995	15.6	84.4	−0.5	1.7	5029	41.9	35.4
Chili	2000	14.2	85.8	−0.7	1.5	5467	41.9	35.9
Colombia	1995	28.0	72.0	−0.4	2.6	5716	20.6	14.8
Colombie	2000	25.0	75.0	−0.5	2.2	6771	21.5	16.1
Ecuador	1995	39.7	60.3	0.5	2.9	1843	26.7	16.1
Equateur	2000	37.0	63.0	0.5	2.4	2118	26.6	16.7
Falkland Islands (Malvinas)	1995	21.9	78.1	−1.3	2.0	...	...	...
Iles Falkland (Malvinas)	2000	19.2	80.8	−1.3	1.7	...	...	...
French Guiana	1995	25.2	74.8	3.3	3.6	...	...	...
Guyane française	2000	24.9	75.1	2.7	3.3	...	...	...
Guyana	1995	65.5	34.5	−0.1	1.5	...	...	...
Guyana	2000	63.7	36.3	−0.5	1.4	...	...	...
Paraguay	1995	47.6	52.4	1.0	3.9	1081	42.7	22.4
Paraguay	2000	44.0	56.0	0.9	3.6	1262	41.0	23.0
Peru	1995	29.1	70.9	0.4	2.3	6667	40.0	28.3
Pérou	2000	27.2	72.8	0.2	2.1	7443	39.9	29.0
Suriname	1995	29.8	70.2	−2.4	1.5	...	...	...
Suriname	2000	25.9	74.1	−2.1	1.3	...	...	...
Uruguay	1995	9.5	90.5	−2.4	1.0	1299	44.6	40.4
Uruguay	2000	8.1	91.9	−2.1	0.9	1324	43.2	39.7
Venezuela	1995	14.5	85.5	0.0	2.3	3007	16.1	13.8
Venezuela	2000	13.1	86.9	−0.1	2.1	3153	15.0	13.0
Asia · Asie								
Afghanistan	1995	80.1	19.9	2.1	4.5	2048	54.0	10.7
Afghanistan	2000	78.1	21.9	3.1	5.7	2602	54.6	12.0
Armenia	1995	32.8	67.2	0.1	0.1	1305	51.6	34.7
Arménie	2000	32.8	67.2	−0.2	0.2	1407	55.3	37.1
Azerbaijan	1995	47.1	52.9	1.3	0.5	1847	45.4	24.0
Azerbaïdjan	2000	48.1	51.9	0.6	0.6	1948	46.7	24.2
Bahrain	1995	9.7	90.3	−2.2	2.6	...	...	...
Bahreïn	2000	7.8	92.2	−2.0	2.0	...	...	...
Bangladesh	1995	77.7	22.3	1.4	4.4	9407	34.2	7.6
Bangladesh	2000	75.0	25.0	1.3	4.3	12519	36.4	9.1
Bhutan	1995	94.0	6.0	2.4	6.0	...	...	...
Bhoutan	2000	92.9	7.1	2.3	5.9	...	...	...
Brunei Darussalam	1995	30.8	69.2	0.1	3.0	...	...	...
Brunéi Darussalam	2000	27.8	72.2	−0.1	2.5	...	...	...
Cambodia	1995	85.8	14.2	2.1	6.3	810	50.2	7.1
Cambodge	2000	83.1	16.9	1.7	5.5	1070	48.3	8.2
China [4]	1995	68.6	31.4	−0.4	3.5	13112	3.4	1.1
Chine [4]	2000	64.2	35.8	−0.8	3.2	12887	2.8	1.0
China, Hong Kong SAR †	1995	0.0	100.0	0.0	2.0	6210	100.0	100.0
Chine, Hong Kong RAS †	2000	0.0	100.0	0.0	1.2	6860	100.0	100.0
China, Macao SAR †	1995	1.2	98.8	0.1	1.3	...	...	...
Chine, Macao RAS †	2000	1.2	98.8	−0.3	0.9	...	...	...
Cyprus	1995	31.5	68.5	0.1	1.5	...	...	...
Chypre	2000	30.1	69.9	−0.3	1.2	...	...	...
East Timor	1995	92.5	7.5	−2.6	−2.6	...	...	...
Timor oriental	2000	92.5	7.5	3.9	4.7	...	...	...

9
Population in urban and rural areas, rates of growth and largest urban agglomeration population [*cont.*]
Population urbaine, population rurale, taux d'accroissement et population de l'agglomération
urbaine la plus peuplée [*suite*]

Country or area Pays ou zone	Year Année	Population estimates Estimations de la population		Growth rate p.a. (%) [1] Taux d'accroissement p.a. (%) [1]		Population of largest urban agglomeration with 750,000 inhabitants or more in 2000 Population de l'agglomération urbaine la plus peuplée avec 750 000 habitants ou plus en 2000		
		Rural % Rurale %	Urban % Urbaine %	Rural pop. Pop. rurale	Urban pop. Pop. urbaine	Number (000s) Nombre (000s)	% of urban % de urbaine	% of total % de totale
Georgia	1995	44.4	55.6	−0.7	−0.1	1382	46.5	25.8
Géorgie	2000	43.7	56.3	−1.1	−0.1	1406	47.5	26.7
India	1995	73.4	26.6	1.4	2.5	14111	5.7	1.5
Inde	2000	72.3	27.7	1.2	2.3	16086	5.8	1.6
Indonesia	1995	64.4	35.6	−0.3	4.2	9161	13.0	4.6
Indonésie	2000	59.0	41.0	−0.6	3.6	11018	12.7	5.2
Iran, Islamic Rep. of	1995	39.8	60.2	−0.3	2.9	6687	17.2	10.3
Iran, Rép. islamique d'	2000	36.0	64.0	−0.7	2.4	6979	15.5	9.9
Iraq	1995	31.4	68.6	3.4	2.4	4433	32.2	22.1
Iraq	2000	32.5	67.5	2.7	2.7	4865	31.4	21.2
Israel	1995	9.2	90.8	0.6	2.6	1897	39.0	35.5
Israël	2000	8.4	91.6	0.2	2.2	2001	36.1	33.1
Japan	1995	21.9	78.1	−0.4	0.4	25785	26.3	20.6
Japon	2000	21.3	78.8	−0.6	0.3	26444	26.4	20.8
Jordan	1995	21.7	78.3	2.5	3.0	986	29.7	23.2
Jordanie	2000	21.3	78.7	2.2	3.0	1148	29.7	23.4
Kazakhstan	1995	43.6	56.4	−0.3	−0.7	1127	12.0	6.8
Kazakhstan	2000	44.2	55.8	−0.4	−0.3	1130	12.5	7.0
Korea, Dem.People's Rep.	1995	40.9	59.1	0.3	1.2	2865	22.7	13.4
Corée, R. p. dém. de	2000	39.8	60.2	−0.1	1.2	3124	23.3	14.0
Korea, Republic of	1995	21.8	78.2	−2.9	1.7	10256	29.2	22.8
Corée, République de	2000	18.1	81.9	−2.7	1.3	9888	25.8	21.2
Kuwait	1995	4.5	95.5	0.2	2.6	859	53.2	50.8
Koweït	2000	4.0	96.0	0.5	2.6	879	47.8	45.9
Kyrgyzstan	1995	64.0	36.0	2.0	0.6	...	...	...
Kirghizistan	2000	65.6	34.4	1.2	1.2	...	...	...
Lao People's Dem. Rep.	1995	82.8	17.2	1.9	4.6	...	...	...
Rép. dém. pop. lao	2000	80.7	19.3	1.7	4.6	...	...	...
Lebanon	1995	12.5	87.5	−2.0	2.5	1823	65.7	57.5
Liban	2000	10.3	89.7	−1.5	1.9	2070	66.0	59.2
Malaysia	1995	46.3	53.7	0.4	3.4	1236	11.5	6.2
Malaisie	2000	42.6	57.4	0.1	2.9	1379	10.8	6.2
Maldives	1995	74.3	25.7	2.5	4.4	...	...	...
Maldives	2000	72.4	27.6	2.4	4.6	...	...	...
Mongolia	1995	43.2	56.8	1.1	0.9	661	48.2	27.4
Mongolie	2000	43.4	56.6	1.0	1.3	764	53.3	30.2
Myanmar	1995	74.2	25.8	1.0	2.8	3853	33.6	8.7
Myanmar	2000	72.3	27.7	0.5	2.9	4393	33.2	9.2
Nepal	1995	89.7	10.3	2.1	5.2	...	...	...
Népal	2000	88.2	11.8	1.9	5.1	...	...	...
Occupied Palestinian Terr. [5]	1995	34.6	65.4	3.0	4.3	...	...	...
Terr. palestinien occupé [5]	2000	33.2	66.8	2.6	4.0	...	...	...
Oman	1995	27.2	72.8	0.8	4.1	...	...	...
Oman	2000	24.0	76.0	0.9	4.0	...	...	...
Pakistan	1995	68.2	31.8	2.3	3.5	8468	21.5	6.8
Pakistan	2000	66.9	33.1	2.0	3.5	10032	21.5	7.1
Philippines	1995	46.0	54.0	0.0	3.6	9402	25.5	13.8
Philippines	2000	41.5	58.6	−0.2	3.2	9950	22.5	13.2
Qatar	1995	8.7	91.3	−1.4	2.3	...	...	...
Qatar	2000	7.3	92.7	−1.5	1.7	...	...	...
Saudi Arabia	1995	17.1	82.9	−0.8	4.3	3453	24.4	20.2
Arabie saoudite	2000	13.8	86.2	−0.5	3.6	4549	25.9	22.4
Singapore	1995	0.0	100.0	0.0	2.9	3476	100.0	100.0
Singapour	2000	0.0	100.0	0.0	1.7	4018	100.0	100.0
Sri Lanka	1995	78.2	21.8	0.7	1.9	...	...	...
Sri Lanka	2000	77.2	22.8	0.5	2.4	...	...	...
Syrian Arab Republic	1995	50.0	50.0	2.0	3.2	1870	26.3	13.1
Rép. arabe syrienne	2000	48.6	51.4	1.8	3.2	2229	26.8	13.8
Tajikistan	1995	72.4	27.6	1.2	1.2	...	...	...
Tadjikistan	2000	72.4	27.6	0.7	0.7	...	...	...
Thailand	1995	80.7	19.3	1.2	1.9	6596	58.3	11.2
Thaïlande	2000	80.2	19.8	0.9	2.1	7372	59.2	11.7

9
Population in urban and rural areas, rates of growth and largest urban agglomeration population [*cont.*]
Population urbaine, population rurale, taux d'accroissement et population de l'agglomération
urbaine la plus peuplée [*suite*]

Country or area Pays ou zone	Year Année	Population estimates Estimations de la population		Growth rate p.a. (%) [1] Taux d'accroissement p.a. (%) [1]		Population of largest urban agglomeration with 750,000 inhabitants or more in 2000 Population de l'agglomération urbaine la plus peuplée avec 750 000 habitants ou plus en 2000		
		Rural % Rurale %	Urban % Urbaine %	Rural pop. Pop. rurale	Urban pop. Pop. urbaine	Number (000s) Nombre (000s)	% of urban % de urbaine	% of total % de totale
Turkey	1995	36.3	63.7	0.4	2.3	7662	19.6	12.5
Turquie	2000	34.2	65.8	0.1	1.9	8953	20.4	13.4
Turkmenistan	1995	55.5	44.5	2.3	2.5	...	...	...
Turkménistan	2000	55.2	44.8	1.5	2.3	...	...	...
United Arab Emirates	1995	16.3	83.7	−2.0	2.8	651	33.1	27.7
Emirats arabes unis	2000	13.3	86.7	−1.9	2.2	886	39.2	34.0
Uzbekistan	1995	61.6	38.4	2.3	0.9	2111	24.1	9.3
Ouzbékistan	2000	63.3	36.7	1.4	1.4	2148	23.5	8.6
Viet Nam	1995	77.8	22.2	0.9	3.1	4296	26.6	5.9
Viet Nam	2000	75.9	24.1	0.7	3.1	4619	24.5	5.9
Yemen	1995	76.4	23.6	3.9	5.1	965	27.5	6.5
Yémen	2000	75.3	24.7	3.6	5.3	1327	29.3	7.2
Europe · Europe								
Albania	1995	60.9	39.1	−1.4	1.2	...	...	...
Albanie	2000	57.7	42.3	−0.5	2.1	...	...	...
Andorra	1995	6.6	93.4	7.5	4.4	...	...	...
Andorre	2000	7.6	92.4	6.8	3.8	...	...	...
Austria	1995	33.1	66.9	−0.1	0.2	2060	38.3	25.6
Autriche	2000	32.7	67.3	−0.6	0.1	2065	38.0	25.6
Belarus	1995	31.2	68.8	−0.7	−0.1	1692	23.8	16.4
Bélarus	2000	30.6	69.4	−0.9	−0.2	1667	23.6	16.4
Belgium	1995	3.0	97.0	−2.4	0.3	1140	11.6	11.2
Belgique	2000	2.7	97.3	−2.2	0.2	1135	11.4	11.1
Bosnia and Herzegovina	1995	59.1	40.9	2.3	4.0	...	...	...
Bosnie−Herzégovine	2000	57.0	43.0	0.3	2.2	...	...	...
Bulgaria	1995	32.1	67.9	−0.9	−1.2	1191	20.9	14.2
Bulgarie	2000	32.5	67.5	−1.1	−0.9	1187	22.1	14.9
Channel Islands	1995	70.5	29.5	0.3	−0.3	...	...	...
Iles Anglo−Normandes	2000	71.1	28.9	0.0	0.2	...	...	...
Croatia	1995	44.2	55.8	−0.8	0.8	981	38.0	21.2
Croatie	2000	42.3	57.7	−1.0	0.7	1067	39.7	22.9
Czech Republic	1995	25.4	74.6	−0.1	−0.1	1214	15.8	11.7
République tchèque	2000	25.5	74.5	−0.3	0.0	1203	15.7	11.7
Denmark	1995	14.9	85.1	0.3	0.4	1335	30.0	25.5
Danemark	2000	14.9	85.1	0.2	0.2	1332	29.4	25.0
Estonia	1995	30.1	69.9	−0.9	−1.4	...	...	...
Estonie	2000	30.6	69.4	−1.3	−1.1	...	...	...
Faeroe Islands	1995	64.5	35.6	0.3	2.4	...	...	...
Iles Féroé	2000	62.1	37.9	0.1	2.3	...	...	...
Finland	1995	35.9	64.1	2.9	−1.4	943	28.8	18.5
Finlande	2000	41.0	59.0	0.1	0.1	937	30.7	18.1
France	1995	25.3	74.7	−0.2	0.6	9478	21.8	16.3
France	2000	24.6	75.4	−0.3	0.6	9630	21.6	16.3
Germany	1995	13.5	86.5	−1.5	0.3	6482[8]	9.2[8]	7.9[8]
Allemagne	2000	12.5	87.5	−1.6	0.2	6531[8]	9.1[8]	8.0[8]
Gibraltar	1995	0.0	100.0	0.0	−0.1	...	...	...
Gibraltar	2000	0.0	100.0	0.0	−0.1	...	...	...
Greece	1995	40.8	59.2	−0.1	0.6	3093	49.9	29.6
Grèce	2000	39.9	60.1	−0.6	0.5	3116	48.9	29.4
Holy See [6]	1995	0.0	100.0	0.0	−0.5	...	...	...
Saint−Siège [6]	2000	0.0	100.0	0.0	0.0	...	...	...
Hungary	1995	36.7	63.3	−1.2	−0.1	1911	29.6	18.7
Hongrie	2000	35.5	64.5	−1.3	−0.1	1819	28.3	18.2
Iceland	1995	8.4	91.6	−1.4	1.1	...	...	...
Islande	2000	7.5	92.5	−1.4	0.8	...	...	...
Ireland	1995	42.1	57.9	0.5	1.4	947	45.3	26.2
Irlande	2000	41.0	59.0	0.3	1.4	985	43.9	25.9
Isle of Man	1995	24.8	75.2	0.0	1.5	...	...	...
Ile de Man	2000	23.4	76.6	−0.3	1.2	...	...	...
Italy	1995	33.4	66.6	−0.1	0.2	4251	11.1	7.4
Italie	2000	33.1	66.9	−0.6	0.1	4251	11.0	7.4

9
Population in urban and rural areas, rates of growth and largest urban agglomeration population [*cont.*]
Population urbaine, population rurale, taux d'accroissement et population de l'agglomération
urbaine la plus peuplée [*suite*]

Country or area Pays ou zone	Year Année	Population estimates Estimations de la population		Growth rate p.a. (%) [1] Taux d'accroissement p.a. (%) [1]		Population of largest urban agglomeration with 750,000 inhabitants or more in 2000 Population de l'agglomération urbaine la plus peuplée avec 750 000 habitants ou plus en 2000		
		Rural % Rurale %	Urban % Urbaine %	Rural pop. Pop. rurale	Urban pop. Pop. urbaine	Number (000s) Nombre (000s)	% of urban % de urbaine	% of total % de totale
Latvia	1995	31.0	69.0	4.1	−3.4	833	48.0	33.1
Lettonie	2000	39.6	60.4	−0.6	−0.6	761	52.0	31.4
Liechtenstein	1995	79.0	21.0	1.1	1.6	...	...	...
Liechtenstein	2000	78.6	21.4	0.8	1.9	...	...	...
Lithuania	1995	31.8	68.2	−0.3	0.0	...	...	...
Lituanie	2000	31.5	68.5	−0.7	0.0	...	...	...
Luxembourg	1995	10.9	89.1	−3.6	1.8	...	...	...
Luxembourg	2000	8.5	91.5	−3.1	1.6	...	...	...
Malta	1995	10.6	89.4	−2.5	1.0	...	...	...
Malte	2000	9.1	90.9	−2.4	0.7	...	...	...
Monaco	1995	0.0	100.0	0.0	1.0	...	...	...
Monaco	2000	0.0	100.0	0.0	0.9	...	...	...
Netherlands	1995	11.0	89.0	−0.4	0.6	1102	8.0	7.1
Pays−Bas	2000	10.5	89.5	−0.6	0.5	1105	7.8	7.0
Norway	1995	26.7	73.3	−0.6	0.9	729	22.8	16.7
Norvège	2000	25.3	74.7	−0.8	0.7	779	23.3	17.4
Poland	1995	38.4	61.6	−0.4	0.2	3425	14.4	8.9
Pologne	2000	37.7	62.3	−0.7	0.3	3494	14.5	9.1
Portugal	1995	43.6	56.4	−3.9	2.9	3363	60.1	33.9
Portugal	2000	35.6	64.4	−3.6	1.9	3861	59.8	38.5
Republic of Moldova	1995	55.5	44.5	0.8	−1.6	...	...	...
République de Moldova	2000	58.4	41.6	−0.4	0.0	...	...	...
Romania	1995	45.4	54.6	−0.4	0.0	2040	16.5	9.0
Roumanie	2000	44.9	55.1	−0.7	0.1	2001	16.2	8.9
Russian Federation	1995	27.1	72.9	−0.4	−0.4	8599	8.0	5.8
Fédération de Russie	2000	27.1	72.9	−0.6	−0.6	8367	7.9	5.8
San Marino	1995	10.6	89.4	−0.4	1.5	...	...	...
Saint−Marin	2000	9.8	90.2	−0.5	1.3	...	...	...
Slovakia	1995	43.0	57.0	−0.1	0.3	...	...	...
Slovaquie	2000	42.6	57.4	−0.4	0.4	...	...	...
Slovenia	1995	50.1	49.9	0.3	−0.3	...	...	...
Slovénie	2000	50.8	49.2	−0.1	−0.1	...	...	...
Spain	1995	23.5	76.5	−0.9	0.4	4072	13.4	10.2
Espagne	2000	22.4	77.6	−1.1	0.3	3976	12.8	10.0
Sweden	1995	16.8	83.2	−0.1	0.1	1548	21.1	17.5
Suède	2000	16.7	83.3	−0.3	−0.1	1612	21.9	18.2
Switzerland	1995	32.3	67.7	0.3	0.1	926	19.2	13.0
Suisse	2000	32.6	67.4	−0.2	0.0	939	19.4	13.1
TFYR of Macedonia	1995	40.3	59.7	0.9	0.6	...	...	...
L'ex−R.y. Macédoine	2000	40.6	59.4	0.2	0.4	...	...	...
Ukraine	1995	32.6	67.4	−1.1	−0.6	2626	7.6	5.1
Ukraine	2000	32.1	67.9	−1.2	−0.8	2499	7.4	5.0
United Kingdom	1995	10.8	89.2	−0.2	0.3	7640	14.6	13.0
Royaume−Uni	2000	10.5	89.5	−0.5	0.3	7640	14.4	12.9
Yugoslavia	1995	48.6	51.4	−0.1	0.1	1483	27.4	14.1
Yougoslavie	2000	48.4	51.6	−0.5	0.1	1673	30.7	15.9
Oceania · Océanie								
American Samoa	1995	49.7	50.3	2.5	4.4	...	...	...
Samoa américaines	2000	47.3	52.7	2.1	4.1	...	...	...
Australia [7]	1995	12.2	87.8	−4.3	1.8	3696	23.3	20.5
Australie [7]	2000	9.3	90.7	−3.8	1.4	3907	22.5	20.4
Cook Islands	1995	41.3	58.7	0.5	0.8	...	...	...
Iles Cook	2000	41.0	59.0	0.3	0.9	...	...	...
Fiji	1995	54.5	45.5	−0.3	2.8	...	...	...
Fidji	2000	50.6	49.4	−0.5	2.5	...	...	...
French Polynesia	1995	45.6	54.4	2.4	1.0	...	...	...
Polynésie française	2000	47.3	52.7	1.6	1.6	...	...	...
Guam	1995	61.7	38.3	1.1	1.9	...	...	...
Guam	2000	60.8	39.2	1.6	3.0	...	...	...
Kiribati	1995	63.6	36.4	0.8	2.4	...	...	...
Kiribati	2000	61.8	38.2	0.6	2.4	...	...	...

9
Population in urban and rural areas, rates of growth and largest urban agglomeration population [*cont.*]
Population urbaine, population rurale, taux d'accroissement et population de l'agglomération
urbaine la plus peuplée [*suite*]

Country or area Pays ou zone	Year Année	Rural % Rurale %	Urban % Urbaine %	Growth rate p.a. (%) [1] Taux d'accroissement p.a. (%) [1]		Population of largest urban agglomeration with 750,000 inhabitants or more in 2000 Population de l'agglomération urbaine la plus peuplée avec 750 000 habitants ou plus en 2000		
				Rural pop. Pop. rurale	Urban pop. Pop. urbaine	Number (000s) Nombre (000s)	% of urban % de urbaine	% of total % de totale
Marshall Islands	1995	34.7	65.3	1.0	1.5	...	...	...
Iles Marshall	2000	34.2	65.8	0.8	1.6	...	...	...
Micronesia, Federated States of	1995	72.9	27.1	2.3	3.5	...	...	...
Etats fédèrés de Micron	2000	71.7	28.3	1.9	3.6	...	...	...
Nauru	1995	0.0	100.0	0.0	2.5	...	...	...
Nauru	2000	0.0	100.0	0.0	2.3	...	...	...
New Caledonia	1995	30.2	69.8	−3.2	4.1	...	...	...
Nouvelle−Calédonie	2000	23.1	76.9	−3.0	3.2	...	...	...
New Zealand	1995	14.7	85.3	0.2	1.1	976	31.7	27.1
Nouvelle−Zélande	2000	14.2	85.8	0.0	0.8	1102	34.0	29.2
Niue	1995	68.5	31.5	−1.7	−0.5	...	...	...
Nioué	2000	67.2	32.8	−1.7	−0.2	...	...	...
Northern Mariana Islands	1995	47.3	52.7	4.5	4.5	...	...	...
Iles Mariannes du Nord	2000	47.3	52.7	3.8	4.2	...	...	...
Palau	1995	28.6	71.4	3.6	1.7	...	...	...
Palaos	2000	30.5	69.5	2.1	2.1	...	...	...
Papua New Guinea	1995	83.8	16.2	2.0	3.8	...	...	...
Papouasie−Nvl−Guinée	2000	82.6	17.4	1.9	3.7	...	...	...
Pitcairn	1995	100.0	0.0	3.5	0.0	...	...	...
Pitcairn	2000	100.0	0.0	0.0	0.0	...	...	...
Samoa	1995	78.7	21.3	−0.2	0.7	...	...	...
Samoa	2000	77.9	22.1	0.0	1.4	...	...	...
Solomon Islands	1995	83.0	17.0	2.8	6.3	...	...	...
Iles Salomon	2000	80.3	19.7	2.6	6.0	...	...	...
Tokelau	1995	100.0	0.0	−1.0	0.0	...	...	...
Tokélaou	2000	100.0	0.0	0.0	0.0	...	...	...
Tonga	1995	68.0	32.0	0.1	0.8	...	...	...
Tonga	2000	67.3	32.7	0.0	1.1	...	...	...
Tuvalu	1995	53.2	46.8	−0.7	3.6	...	...	...
Tuvalu	2000	47.8	52.2	−0.8	3.1	...	...	...
Vanuatu	1995	79.9	20.1	2.3	4.2	...	...	...
Vanuatu	2000	78.3	21.7	2.0	4.2	...	...	...
Wallis and Futuna Islands	1995	100.0	0.0	0.6	0.0	...	...	...
Iles Wallis et Futuna	2000	100.0	0.0	0.6	0.0	...	...	...

Source:
United Nations Population Division, New York, "World Urbanization Prospects: The 2001 Revision".

Source:
Organisation des Nations Unies, Division de la population, New York, "World Urbanization Prospects: The 2001 Revision".

† For information on recent changes in the country or area nomenclature pertaining to Hong Kong Special Administrative Region and Macao Special Administrative Region, see Annex I − Country and area nomenclature, regional and other groupings.

† Pour les modifications rxécentes de nomenclature de pays ou de zone concernant Hong Kong (Région administrative spéciale) et Macao région administrative spéciale (RAS) de Chine, voir annexe I − Nomenclature des pays ou des zones, groupements régionaux et autres groupements.

1 Annual rates of growth calculated for the periods 1995 − 2000 and 2000 − 2005.
2 Includes Agalega, Rodrigues and St. Brandon.
3 Including Ascension and Tristan da Cunha.
4 For statistical purposes, the data for China do not include Hong Kong Special Administrative Region and Macao Special Administrative Region of China.
5 Data refer to the Gaza Strip.
6 Data refer to the Vatican City State.
7 Including Christmas Island, Cocos (Keeling) Islands and Norfolk Island.
8 Data refer to the Rhein−Ruhr North agglomeration (Duisburg, Essen, Krefeld, Mühlheim, an der Ruhr, Oberhausen, Bottrop, Gelsenkirchen, Bochum, Dortmund, Hagen, Hamm and Herne).

1 Ces taux d'accroissement annuel ont été calculés pour les périodes 1995 à 2000 et 2000 à 2005.
2 Y comprisAgalega, Rodriguez et St. Brandon.
3 Y compris Ascension et Tristan da Cunha.
4 Le données statistiques relatives à la Chine ne comprennent pas celles qui concernent le région administrative spéciale de Hong Kong et la région administrative spéciale de Macao.
5 Les données se rapportent à la Zone de Gaza.
6 Les données se rapportent à la Cité du Vatican.
7 Y compris les îles Christmas, Cocos (Keeling) et Norfolk.
8 Les données se rapportent à l'agglomération "Rhein−Ruhr North" (Duisburg, Essen, Krefeld, Mühlheim, an der Ruhr, Oberhausen, Bottrop, Gelsenkirchen, Bochum, Dortmund, Hagen, Hamm, et Herne).

Technical notes, tables 8 and 9

Table 8 is based on detailed data on population and its growth and distribution published in the United Nations *Demographic Yearbook* [22], which also provides a comprehensive description of methods of evaluation and limitations of the data.

Unless otherwise indicated, figures refer to de facto (present-in-area) population for the present territory; surface area estimates include inland waters.

Table 9: The statistics on urban and rural population and population in the largest urban agglomeration of each country or area are estimates provided by the Population Division of the United Nations Secretariat [28, 29]. Because of national differences in the specific characteristics that distinguish urban from rural areas, there are no internationally agreed definitions of urban and rural. In most countries, the distinction is mainly based on size of locality. For the latest available census definition of urban areas in a particular country or area, reference should be made to the *Demographic Yearbook 1999* [22].

An urban agglomeration comprises the city or town proper and also the suburban fringe or thickly settled territory lying outside, but adjacent to, its boundaries. The largest urban agglomerations refer to those inhabited by 750,000 people or more.

Annual rates of change in urban and rural population are computed as average annual percentage changes using mid-year population estimates.

Notes techniques, tableaux 8 et 9

Le *tableau 8* est fondé sur des données détaillées sur la population, sa croissance et sa distribution, publiées dans l'*Annuaire démographique* des Nations Unies [22], qui offre également une description complète des méthodes d'évaluation et une indication des limites des données.

Sauf indication contraire, les chiffres se rapportent à la population effectivement présente sur le territoire tel qu'il est actuellement défini; les estimations de superficie comprennent les étendues d'eau intérieures.

Tableau 9 : Les statistiques de la population urbaine, de la population rurale et de la population de l'agglomération urbaine la plus peuplée de chaque pays ou zone sont tirées d'estimations de la Division de la population du Secrétariat des Nations Unies [28, 29]. Il n'existe pas de définition reconnue à l'échelle internationale des zones urbaines et rurales parce que les caractéristiques retenues pour distinguer ces deux types de zone diffèrent d'un pays à un autre. Dans la plupart des pays, cette distinction est essentiellement une fonction de la taille des agglomérations. Pour la définition la plus récente des zones urbaines utilisée dans une région ou un pays donné, se reporter à l'*Annuaire démographique 1999* [22].

L'agglomération urbaine comprend la ville proprement dite et ses faubourgs ou banlieues, et tout territoire à forte densité de population situé à sa périphérie. Les agglomérations urbaines les plus peuplées se rapportent à celles habitées par 750 000 personnes ou plus.

Les taux annuels de variation des populations urbaines et rurales se calculent sur la base de la variation annuelle moyenne en pourcentage déterminée à partir des estimations de la population au milieu de l'année.

10
Illiterate population by sex, aged 15 years and over, estimates and projections
Population analphabète selon le sexe, âgée de 15 ans et plus, estimations et projections

Country or area Pays ou zone	Year [1] Année [1]	Illiterate population (thousands) Population analphabète (milliers)			Percentage of illiterates Pourcentage d'analphabètes		
		Total	M	F	Total	M	F
Africa · Afrique							
Algeria	1990	6 863	2 625	4 238	47.4	36.1	58.9
Algérie	2000	6 640	2 393	4 247	33.3	23.8	42.9
	2002	6 561	2 346	4 216	31.1	22.1	40.3
Benin	1990	1 771	723	1 047	73.6	61.9	84.5
Bénin	2000	2 067	767	1 300	62.6	47.9	76.4
	2002	2 131	776	1 355	60.2	45.2	74.5
Botswana	1990	221	112	109	31.9	34.2	29.7
Botswana	2000	213	115	98	22.8	25.5	20.2
	2002	205	113	92	21.1	23.9	18.4
Burkina Faso	1990	3 978	1 755	2 224	83.6	75.0	92.0
Burkina Faso	2000	4 786	2 056	2 730	76.1	66.1	85.9
	2002	4 948	2 116	2 832	74.3	64.1	84.2
Burundi	1990	1 869	727	1 142	63.0	51.5	73.4
Burundi	2000	1 869	755	1 114	52.0	43.8	59.6
	2002	1 900	778	1 122	49.6	42.2	56.4
Cameroon	1990	2 378	864	1 514	37.5	27.8	46.8
Cameroun	2000	2 062	739	1 322	24.2	17.6	30.5
	2002	1 989	715	1 274	22.1	16.1	27.9
Cape Verde	1990	70	20	50	36.2	23.7	45.7
Cap–Vert	2000	67	17	50	26.2	15.5	34.3
	2002	66	17	48	24.2	14.5	31.9
Central African Republic	1990	1 114	418	696	66.7	52.8	79.3
Rép. centrafricaine	2000	1 107	398	709	53.3	40.3	65.1
	2002	1 094	394	701	50.4	38.0	61.8
Chad [2]	1990	2 266	964	1 303	72.3	63.0	81.2
Tchad [2]	2000	2 391	987	1 405	57.4	48.4	66.0
	2002	2 388	981	1 406	54.2	45.5	62.5
Comoros	1990	129	53	76	46.2	38.6	53.6
Comores	2000	177	73	104	44.1	36.8	51.3
	2002	188	78	110	43.7	36.5	50.9
Congo	1990	397	133	264	32.9	22.9	42.1
Congo	2000	305	95	209	19.3	12.5	25.6
	2002	287	89	198	17.2	11.1	22.9
Côte d'Ivoire	1990	4 073	1 805	2 268	66.7	57.4	76.6
Côte d'Ivoire	2000	4 452	1 955	2 497	53.2	45.5	61.4
	2002	4 456	1 957	2 499	50.4	43.2	58.0
Democratic Republic of the Congo [2]	1990	10 345	3 684	6 661	52.5	38.6	65.6
Rép. dém. du Congo [2]	2000	10 301	3 506	6 795	38.6	26.9	49.8
	2002	10 159	3 433	6 726	35.9	24.8	46.5
Djibouti [2]	1990	138	48	90	47.0	33.2	60.3
Djibouti [2]	2000	131	43	88	35.4	24.4	45.6
	2002	132	43	88	33.5	23.0	43.2
Egypt	1990	17 913	6 773	11 140	52.9	39.6	66.4
Egypte	2000	19 784	7 458	12 326	44.7	33.4	56.2
	2002	20 160	7 615	12 545	43.1	32.2	54.1
Equatorial Guinea	1990	54	14	40	26.7	14.2	38.9
Guinée équatoriale	2000	43	9	33	16.8	7.5	25.6
	2002	41	9	32	15.2	6.9	23.1
Eritrea [2]	1990	863	329	534	53.6	41.5	65.2
Erythrée [2]	2000	952	345	607	44.3	32.7	55.5
	2002	970	350	620	42.4	31.0	53.4
Ethiopia	1990	18 700	8 217	10 483	71.3	62.5	80.2
Ethiopie	2000	20 514	8 938	11 576	60.9	52.8	69.1
	2002	20 700	9 013	11 687	58.5	50.7	66.3
Gambia	1990	397	179	219	74.4	68.2	80.4
Gambie	2000	494	213	280	63.4	56.0	70.6
	2002	504	216	289	61.1	53.5	68.4
Ghana	1990	3 442	1 216	2 226	41.6	29.9	53.0
Ghana	2000	3 271	1 114	2 157	28.5	19.7	37.1
	2002	3 228	1 095	2 133	26.3	18.1	34.3

10

Illiterate population by sex, aged 15 and over,
estimates and projections [cont.]
Population analphabète selon le sexe, âgée de 15 ans et plus,
estimations et projections [suite]

Country or area Pays ou zone	Year [1] Année [1]	Illiterate population (thousands) Population analphabète (milliers)			Percentage of illiterates Pourcentage d'analphabètes		
		Total	M	F	Total	M	F
Guinea–Bissau	1990	413	158	254	72.8	57.5	87.1
Guinée–Bissau	2000	429	155	274	61.5	45.6	76.7
	2002	428	153	275	59.0	43.2	73.9
Kenya	1990	3 499	1 131	2 369	29.2	19.0	39.2
Kenya	2000	3 012	948	2 064	17.6	11.1	24.0
	2002	2 858	902	1 956	15.7	10.0	21.5
Lesotho	1990	223	168	55	22.1	34.6	10.5
Lesotho	2000	216	173	43	16.6	27.5	6.4
	2002	212	171	40	15.7	26.2	5.8
Liberia	1990	834	309	525	60.6	44.7	76.9
Libéria	2000	838	274	565	46.0	29.9	62.3
	2002	883	282	601	43.6	27.7	59.6
Libyan Arab Jamahiriya	1990	774	222	553	31.9	17.1	48.8
Jamahiriya arabe libyenne	2000	699	167	532	20.0	9.2	31.8
	1990	684	158	526	18.3	8.1	29.2
Madagascar [2]	1990	2 838	1 108	1 730	42.0	33.6	50.2
Madagascar [2]	2000	2 966	1 151	1 815	33.5	26.4	40.3
	2002	2 985	1 160	1 825	31.9	25.2	38.4
Malawi	1990	2 370	735	1 635	48.2	31.2	63.8
Malawi	2000	2 301	720	1 582	39.9	25.5	53.5
	2002	2 322	729	1 593	38.2	24.5	51.3
Mali	1990	3 474	1 513	1 961	74.4	67.1	81.3
Mali	2000	3 533	1 501	2 032	58.5	51.1	65.6
	2002	3 527	1 494	2 033	55.2	48.0	62.1
Mauritania	1990	729	293	436	65.2	53.7	76.1
Mauritanie	2000	904	366	538	59.8	49.3	69.9
	2002	941	381	560	58.8	48.5	68.7
Mauritius	1990	149	56	93	20.1	15.2	25.0
Maurice	2000	134	52	82	15.5	12.2	18.7
	2002	130	51	79	14.7	11.7	17.6
Morocco	1990	8 971	3 418	5 553	61.3	47.2	75.1
Maroc	2000	9 778	3 621	6 157	51.1	38.2	63.9
	2002	9 864	3 644	6 220	49.2	36.6	61.7
Mozambique	1990	5 260	1 953	3 308	66.5	50.7	81.6
Mozambique	2000	6 069	2 115	3 954	56.0	39.9	71.3
	2002	6 017	2 074	3 943	53.5	37.7	68.7
Namibia	1990	194	85	109	25.1	22.6	27.6
Namibie	2000	181	86	96	18.0	17.2	18.8
	1990	174	84	90	16.7	16.2	17.2
Niger	1990	3 584	1 616	1 968	88.6	82.0	94.9
Niger	2000	4 674	2 073	2 601	84.1	76.2	91.6
	2002	4 924	2 175	2 750	83.0	74.9	90.7
Nigeria	1990	24 396	9 395	15 001	51.4	40.4	61.9
Nigéria	2000	22 896	8 592	14 304	36.1	27.6	44.3
	2002	22 372	8 373	13 999	33.3	25.4	41.0
Réunion	1990	74	40	33	17.6	20.0	15.4
Réunion	2000	62	35	27	12.2	14.2	10.4
	2002	61	34	26	11.5	13.5	9.7
Rwanda	1990	1 713	665	1 048	46.7	37.0	56.1
Rwanda	2000	1 402	544	858	33.2	26.3	39.8
	2002	1 404	549	855	30.8	24.6	36.8
Senegal	1990	2 864	1 228	1 636	71.7	61.8	81.4
Sénégal	2000	3 284	1 364	1 921	62.7	52.7	72.4
	2002	3 381	1 398	1 982	60.8	50.9	70.3
South Africa	1990	3 995	1 854	2 142	18.8	17.8	19.7
Afrique du Sud	2000	3 869	1 789	2 080	14.7	14.0	15.4
	2002	3 766	1 741	2 025	14.0	13.3	14.6

10
Illiterate population by sex, aged 15 and over,
estimates and projections [*cont.*]
Population analphabète selon le sexe, âgée de 15 ans et plus,
estimations et projections [*suite*]

Country or area Pays ou zone	Year [1] Année [1]	Illiterate population (thousands) Population analphabète (milliers)			Percentage of illiterates Pourcentage d'analphabètes		
		Total	M	F	Total	M	F
Sudan	1990	7 368	2 711	4 657	54.0	39.7	68.4
Soudan	2000	7 537	2 715	4 822	42.2	30.5	53.7
	2002	7 552	2 720	4 832	40.0	28.9	50.9
Swaziland	1990	115	49	66	28.4	26.3	30.1
Swaziland	2000	117	52	66	20.4	19.2	21.4
	1990	117	52	65	19.1	18.0	20.0
Togo	1990	1 066	369	697	55.7	39.5	71.3
Togo	2000	1 072	339	733	42.9	27.6	57.5
	2002	1 069	334	736	40.4	25.6	54.6
Tunisia	1990	2 081	726	1 355	40.9	28.4	53.5
Tunisie	2000	1 935	623	1 312	29.0	18.6	39.4
	2002	1 873	590	1 283	26.8	16.8	36.8
Uganda	1990	3 723	1 280	2 443	43.9	30.7	56.6
Ouganda	2000	3 582	1 207	2 375	32.9	22.5	43.2
	2002	3 590	1 208	2 381	31.1	21.1	40.8
United Rep. of Tanzania	1990	5 042	1 618	3 424	37.0	24.4	49.0
Rép.– Unie de Tanzanie	2000	4 559	1 439	3 119	24.9	16.1	33.5
	2002	4 411	1 395	3 015	22.9	14.7	30.7
Zambia	1990	1 173	375	798	31.9	21.4	41.3
Zambie	2000	1 057	347	710	21.9	14.8	28.5
	2002	1 025	340	685	20.2	13.7	26.3
Zimbabwe	1990	1 060	362	698	19.3	13.4	25.0
Zimbabwe	2000	775	243	532	11.3	7.2	15.3
	2002	710	219	491	10.0	·6.2	13.7
America, North · Amérique du Nord							
Bahamas	1990	10	5	4	5.6	6.4	4.8
Bahamas	2000	10	6	4	4.6	5.5	3.7
	2002	10	6	4	4.5	5.3	3.6
Belize [2]	1990	11	5	6	10.9	10.0	11.8
Belize [2]	2000	10	5	5	6.8	6.7	6.8
	2002	10	5	5	6.3	6.2	6.4
Costa Rica	1990	118	59	59	6.1	6.0	6.2
Costa Rica	2000	120	61	58	4.4	4.5	4.3
	2002	120	62	58	4.2	4.2	4.1
Cuba	1990	396	194	202	4.8	4.8	4.9
Cuba	2000	292	140	152	3.3	3.2	3.4
	2002	276	132	144	3.1	3.0	3.2
Dominican Republic	1990	922	460	463	20.6	20.2	21.0
Rép. dominicaine	2000	931	473	457	16.4	16.4	16.4
	2002	931	475	456	15.7	15.7	15.6
El Salvador	1990	833	345	489	27.5	23.9	30.9
El Salvador	2000	859	358	501	21.3	18.4	23.9
	2002	860	359	501	20.3	17.6	22.8
Guatemala	1990	1 839	737	1 102	38.9	31.1	46.8
Guatemala	2000	2 013	765	1 248	31.4	23.9	38.8
	2002	2 054	773	1 282	30.0	22.6	37.4
Haiti	1990	2 322	1 061	1 261	60.3	57.3	63.1
Haïti	2000	2 445	1 123	1 321	50.2	48.0	52.2
	2002	2 479	1 142	1 337	48.1	46.2	49.9
Honduras	1990	842	410	432	31.5	30.7	32.3
Honduras	2000	961	479	482	25.4	25.3	25.5
	2002	987	494	492	24.3	24.4	24.3
Jamaica	1990	276	164	111	17.9	22.2	14.0
Jamaïque	2000	234	149	85	13.1	17.1	9.3
	2002	227	146	81	12.4	16.3	8.7
Martinique	1990	12	7	5	4.5	5.1	3.9
Martinique	2000	8	4	3	2.6	3.0	2.2
	2002	7	4	3	2.4	2.8	2.0
Mexico	1990	6 206	2 290	3 917	12.1	9.2	15.0
Mexique	2000	5 675	2 120	3 555	8.6	6.6	10.5
	2002	5 565	2 083	3 482	8.1	6.2	9.8

10
Illiterate population by sex, aged 15 and over,
estimates and projections [*cont.*]
Population analphabète selon le sexe, âgée de 15 ans et plus,
estimations et projections [*suite*]

Country or area Pays ou zone	Year[1] Année[1]	Illiterate population (thousands) Population analphabète (milliers)			Percentage of illiterates Pourcentage d'analphabètes		
		Total	M	F	Total	M	F
Netherlands Antilles	1990	6	3	3	4.4	4.4	4.3
Antilles néerlandaises	2000	6	3	3	3.5	3.5	3.5
	2002	6	3	3	3.3	3.4	3.3
Nicaragua	1990	766	374	391	37.2	37.3	37.2
Nicaragua	2000	972	479	493	33.5	33.7	33.2
	2002	1 018	503	515	32.8	33.1	32.5
Panama	1990	170	81	89	11.0	10.3	11.6
Panama	2000	159	73	85	8.1	7.5	8.7
	2002	157	72	85	7.7	7.0	8.3
Puerto Rico	1990	218	103	115	8.5	8.4	8.5
Porto Rico	2000	183	89	93	6.2	6.5	6.0
	2002	176	87	89	5.9	6.2	5.7
Trinidad and Tobago[3]	1990	70	24	46	8.6	5.9	11.4
Trinité−et−Tobago[3]	2000	61	21	39	6.2	4.5	7.9
	2002	58	21	37	5.8	4.2	7.4
America, South · Amérique du Sud							
Argentina	1990	964	447	516	4.3	4.1	4.4
Argentine	2000	848	408	439	3.2	3.2	3.2
	2002	829	402	427	3.0	3.0	3.0
Bolivia	1990	841	246	595	21.8	13.1	30.1
Bolivie	2000	729	197	532	14.5	8.0	20.7
	2002	707	189	518	13.3	7.3	19.2
Brazil	1990	18 427	8 703	9 724	19.1	18.4	19.8
Brésil	2000	17 862	8 781	9 080	14.8	14.9	14.6
	2002	17 626	8 731	8 895	14.0	14.2	13.8
Chile	1990	542	242	300	5.9	5.4	6.4
Chili	2000	456	213	243	4.2	4.0	4.4
	2002	441	208	233	3.9	3.8	4.1
Colombia	1990	2 567	1 218	1 349	11.5	11.1	11.8
Colombie	2000	2 363	1 152	1 210	8.3	8.3	8.3
	2002	2 318	1 138	1 180	7.8	7.8	7.7
Ecuador	1990	772	305	467	12.3	9.7	14.9
Equateur	2000	702	281	421	8.4	6.7	10.0
	2002	687	275	412	7.8	6.3	9.3
Guyana	1990	15	5	10	2.8	2.0	3.6
Guyana	2000	9	3	6	1.5	1.1	1.9
	2002	8	3	5	1.3	1.0	1.7
Paraguay	1990	237	94	143	9.7	7.6	11.7
Paraguay	2000	223	94	130	6.7	5.6	7.8
	2002	223	94	128	6.3	5.3	7.3
Peru	1990	1 930	524	1 405	14.5	8.0	20.9
Pérou	2000	1 728	447	1 280	10.1	5.3	14.7
	2002	1 690	435	1 255	9.4	4.9	13.7
Uruguay	1990	78	42	36	3.4	3.9	3.0
Uruguay	2000	57	32	25	2.3	2.7	1.9
	2002	53	30	23	2.1	2.5	1.7
Venezuela	1990	1 332	596	736	11.0	9.9	12.2
Venezuela	2000	1 183	552	630	7.4	6.9	7.9
	2002	1 150	542	608	6.8	6.5	7.2
Asia · Asie							
Armenia[2]	1990	63	13	50	2.5	1.1	3.9
Arménie[2]	2000	42	9	33	1.6	0.7	2.4
	2002	39	9	30	1.4	0.7	2.1
Bahrain	1990	60	27	33	17.8	13.1	25.3
Bahreïn	2000	54	23	31	12.4	9.1	17.4
	2002	52	23	30	11.5	8.4	15.8
Bangladesh	1990	39 633	16 761	22 871	65.0	53.7	76.9
Bangladesh	2000	49 148	20 453	28 694	58.7	47.7	70.1
	2002	50 997	21 156	29 841	57.4	46.6	68.8
Brunei Darussalam	1990	25	8	16	14.5	9.0	20.6
Brunéi Darussalam	2000	19	6	12	8.5	5.4	11.9
	2002	20	6	14	8.5	5.2	12.1

10
Illiterate population by sex, aged 15 and over,
estimates and projections [*cont.*]
Population analphabète selon le sexe, âgée de 15 ans et plus,
estimations et projections [*suite*]

Country or area Pays ou zone	Year [1] Année [1]	Illiterate population (thousands) Population analphabète (milliers)			Percentage of illiterates Pourcentage d'analphabètes		
		Total	M	F	Total	M	F
Cambodia	1990	2 009	531	1 477	38.3	22.2	52.0
Cambodge	2000	2 129	628	1 501	32.2	20.2	42.9
	2002	2 155	652	1 502	30.8	19.8	40.7
China ††	1990	192 607	58 175	134 431	23.1	13.6	33.1
Chine ††	2000	152 444	40 900	111 543	15.9	8.3	23.7
	2002	145 043	38 103	106 940	14.6	7.5	22.0
China, Hong Kong SAR † [3]	1990	450	107	343	10.0	4.7	15.6
Chine, Hong Kong RAS † [3]	2000	370	105	265	6.5	3.5	9.8
	2002	352	104	249	5.9	3.3	8.9
China, Macao SAR †	1990	26	7	19	9.5	5.4	13.2
Chine, Macao RAS †	2000	22	6	17	6.2	3.1	9.0
	2002	21	5	16	5.7	2.9	8.3
Cyprus	1990	29	6	23	5.7	2.3	9.0
Chypre	2000	18	4	14	2.9	1.3	4.6
	2002	16	3	12	2.5	1.1	3.9
India [3]	1990	274 097	106 541	167 556	50.7	38.1	64.1
Inde [3]	2000	289 106	110 334	178 772	42.8	31.6	54.6
	2002	291 122	110 807	180 314	41.2	30.4	52.7
Indonesia	1990	24 001	7 685	16 316	20.4	13.2	27.4
Indonésie	2000	19 339	5 953	13 385	13.1	8.2	18.0
	2002	18 480	5 660	12 820	12.1	7.5	16.6
Iran (Islamic Rep. of)	1990	11 212	4 262	6 950	36.5	27.5	45.6
Iran (Rép. islamique d')	2000	10 228	3 661	6 568	23.7	16.8	30.7
	2002	9 918	3 508	6 410	21.6	15.2	28.2
Iraq [3]	1990	5 519	2 196	3 323	54.7	43.0	66.8
Iraq [3]	2000	5 982	2 365	3 617	44.1	34.4	54.1
	2002	6 108	2 418	3 690	42.0	32.8	51.5
Israel	1990	294	86	208	9.2	5.5	12.7
Israël	2000	244	70	174	5.4	3.2	7.6
	2002	229	66	164	4.9	2.9	6.8
Jordan	1990	466	129	337	19.0	10.0	28.9
Jordanie	2000	400	99	301	10.3	4.9	16.1
	2002	383	93	290	9.2	4.3	14.5
Korea, Republic of	1990	1 304	254	1 050	4.1	1.6	6.6
Corée, République de	2000	824	158	666	2.2	0.9	3.6
	2002	755	146	609	2.0	0.8	3.2
Kuwait	1990	316	169	148	23.3	20.6	27.4
Koweït	2000	236	112	124	18.0	16.0	20.3
	2002	242	117	125	17.0	15.3	19.0
Lao People's Dem. Rep. [2]	1990	1 492	554	938	63.8	47.4	80.2
Rép. dém. pop. lao [2]	2000	1 563	547	1 016	51.3	35.9	66.8
	2002	1 574	544	1 030	48.6	33.6	63.6
Lebanon	1990	327	92	235	19.7	11.6	26.9
Liban	2000	309	83	226	14.0	7.9	19.7
	2002	301	80	221	13.1	7.3	18.4
Malaysia	1990	2 180	746	1 434	19.2	13.1	25.5
Malaisie	2000	1 842	634	1 208	12.5	8.6	16.6
	2002	1 778	614	1 165	11.6	7.9	15.3
Maldives	1990	6	3	3	5.5	5.4	5.6
Maldives	2000	5	3	3	3.3	3.4	3.2
	2002	5	3	2	3.0	3.1	2.8
Mongolia	1990	23	7	16	1.8	1.1	2.5
Mongolie	2000	18	8	11	1.1	0.9	1.2
	2002	18	8	10	1.0	0.9	1.1
Myanmar	1990	5 023	1 622	3 401	19.3	12.6	25.7
Myanmar	2000	5 035	1 797	3 238	15.3	11.0	19.5
	2002	5 022	1 824	3 198	14.7	10.8	18.5
Nepal	1990	7 426	2 759	4 667	69.5	52.5	86.0
Népal	2000	8 226	2 854	5 373	58.2	40.4	76.0
	2002	8 389	2 881	5 509	55.9	38.3	73.6
Oman	1990	434	176	257	45.3	32.6	61.7
Oman	2000	401	155	247	28.3	19.9	38.4
	2002	393	151	242	25.6	18.0	34.6

10
Illiterate population by sex, aged 15 and over,
estimates and projections [*cont.*]
Population analphabète selon le sexe, âgée de 15 ans et plus,
estimations et projections [*suite*]

Country or area Pays ou zone	Year [1] Année [1]	Illiterate population (thousands) Population analphabète (milliers)			Percentage of illiterates Pourcentage d'analphabètes		
		Total	M	F	Total	M	F
Pakistan Pakistan	1990	43 917	18 035	25 882	64.6	50.7	79.9
	2000	51 685	20 120	31 565	56.8	42.5	72.1
	2002	53 488	20 610	32 878	55.1	41.0	70.3
Philippines Philippines	1990	2 748	1 278	1 471	7.6	7.1	8.1
	2000	2 265	1 092	1 173	4.7	4.5	4.9
	2002	2 187	1 062	1 125	4.3	4.2	4.4
Qatar Qatar	1990	81	59	22	23.0	22.6	24.0
	2000	83	61	22	18.8	19.6	16.9
	2002	82	60	22	17.9	18.9	15.6
Saudi Arabia Arabie saoudite	1990	3 150	1 360	1 790	33.7	23.6	49.8
	2000	3 045	1 265	1 780	23.7	16.9	33.1
	2002	3 032	1 255	1 777	22.0	15.8	30.5
Singapore Singapour	1990	264	65	198	11.1	5.5	16.7
	2000	213	52	162	7.7	3.7	11.6
	2002	203	49	154	7.1	3.5	10.8
Sri Lanka Sri Lanka	1990	1 294	406	888	11.3	7.1	15.3
	2000	1 162	379	783	8.4	5.6	11.0
	2002	1 137	374	763	7.9	5.3	10.4
Syrian Arab Republic Rép. arabe syrienne	1990	2 273	592	1 681	35.2	18.1	52.5
	2000	2 440	563	1 877	25.6	11.7	39.5
	2002	2 470	558	1 912	23.9	10.7	37.2
Tajikistan Tadjikistan	1990	55	12	43	1.8	0.8	2.8
	2000	30	8	22	0.8	0.4	1.2
	2002	27	7	20	0.7	0.4	1.0
Thailand Thaïlande	1990	2 876	873	2 003	7.6	4.6	10.5
	2000	2 067	649	1 418	4.5	2.9	6.1
	2002	1 968	616	1 352	4.2	2.6	5.6
Turkey Turquie	1990	8 049	1 972	6 077	22.1	10.8	33.5
	2000	7 129	1 567	5 562	14.9	6.5	23.5
	2002	6 912	1 488	5 424	13.9	6.0	22.0
United Arab Emirates Emirats arabes unis	1990	383	270	113	28.8	28.6	29.2
	2000	415	299	117	23.7	25.0	20.7
	2002	419	302	117	22.6	24.3	19.2
Uzbekistan [2] Ouzbékistan [2]	1990	163	32	132	1.3	0.5	2.1
	2000	120	30	90	0.8	0.4	1.2
	2002	117	31	86	0.7	0.4	1.1
Viet Nam Viet Nam	1990	3 873	1 071	2 802	9.5	5.5	13.1
	2000	3 525	1 153	2 372	6.6	4.5	8.6
	2002	3 466	1 166	2 301	6.2	4.3	8.0
Yemen Yémen	1990	3 993	1 243	2 750	67.3	44.8	87.1
	2000	5 027	1 519	3 508	53.7	32.5	74.8
	2002	5 134	1 533	3 601	51.1	30.5	71.6
Europe · Europe							
Albania [2] Albanie [2]	1990	510	149	361	23.0	13.2	33.3
	2000	336	88	248	15.3	7.9	23.0
	2002	317	81	236	14.1	7.1	21.3
Belarus Bélarus	1990	56	12	45	0.7	0.3	1.0
	2000	35	10	25	0.4	0.3	0.6
	2002	33	10	23	0.4	0.3	0.5
Bulgaria Bulgarie	1990	194	58	136	2.8	1.7	3.8
	2000	109	34	75	1.6	1.0	2.1
	2002	99	31	68	1.4	0.9	1.9
Croatia Croatie	1990	113	17	96	3.1	1.0	5.1
	2000	64	12	52	1.7	0.7	2.7
	2002	58	11	47	1.5	0.6	2.4
Greece Grèce	1990	417	94	323	5.1	2.3	7.6
	2000	253	66	188	2.8	1.5	4.0
	2002	236	62	174	2.6	1.4	3.7
Hungary Hongrie	1990	78	29	49	0.9	0.7	1.1
	2000	57	21	36	0.7	0.5	0.8
	2002	53	20	34	0.6	0.5	0.8
Italy Italie	1990	1 104	385	719	2.3	1.7	2.9
	2000	770	267	503	1.6	1.1	2.0
	2002	709	246	463	1.4	1.0	1.8

10
Illiterate population by sex, aged 15 and over,
estimates and projections [cont.]
Population analphabète selon le sexe, âgée de 15 ans et plus,
estimations et projections [suite]

Country or area	Year [1]	Illiterate population (thousands) Population analphabète (milliers)			Percentage of illiterates Pourcentage d'analphabètes		
Pays ou zone	Année [1]	Total	M	F	Total	M	F
Latvia	1990	4	2	2	0.2	0.2	0.2
Lettonie	2000	4	2	2	0.2	0.2	0.2
	2002	4	2	2	0.2	0.2	0.2
Lithuania	1990	20	6	13	0.7	0.5	0.9
Lituanie	2000	13	5	8	0.4	0.3	0.5
	2002	12	5	8	0.4	0.3	0.5
Malta	1990	31	16	15	11.5	12.1	11.1
Malte	2000	25	13	12	8.0	8.7	7.3
	2002	23	13	10	7.3	8.1	6.6
Poland	1990	119	48	71	0.4	0.4	0.5
Pologne	2000	84	38	46	0.3	0.3	0.3
	2002	81	37	44	0.3	0.2	0.3
Portugal	1990	1 005	338	667	12.7	9.0	16.1
Portugal	2000	642	206	436	7.8	5.3	10.1
	2002	583	186	398	7.0	4.7	9.1
Republic of Moldova	1990	80	14	67	2.5	0.9	3.9
République de Moldova	2000	38	7	31	1.1	0.5	1.7
	2002	33	7	26	1.0	0.4	1.4
Romania	1990	523	121	403	2.9	1.4	4.4
Roumanie	2000	345	87	258	1.9	1.0	2.7
	2002	317	82	235	1.7	0.9	2.5
Russian Federation	1990	858	202	656	0.8	0.4	1.1
Fédération de Russie	2000	539	159	379	0.4	0.3	0.6
	2002	502	155	347	0.4	0.3	0.5
Slovenia	1990	7	3	4	0.4	0.4	0.5
Slovénie	2000	6	3	3	0.4	0.3	0.4
	2002	6	3	3	0.3	0.3	0.4
Spain	1990	1 181	337	844	3.7	2.2	5.2
Espagne	2000	798	237	561	2.4	1.4	3.2
	2002	739	220	518	2.2	1.3	3.0
Ukraine [2]	1990	237	55	182	0.6	0.3	0.8
Ukraine [2]	2000	163	47	115	0.4	0.3	0.5
	2002	150	46	104	0.4	0.2	0.5
Oceania · Océanie							
Fiji	1990	51	19	32	11.4	8.4	14.5
Fidji	2000	40	14	25	7.1	5.1	9.2
	2002	38	14	24	6.5	4.7	8.3
Papua New Guinea [2]	1990	993	424	568	43.4	35.6	51.8
Papouasie−Nvl−Guinée [2]	2000	1 065	448	618	36.1	29.4	43.2
	2002	1 075	452	623	34.7	28.3	41.5
Samoa [2]	1990	24	12	12	24.8	23.1	26.7
Samoa [2]	2000	22	11	11	19.8	18.8	21.0
	2002	23	11	11	19.3	18.4	20.3

Source:
United Nations Educational, Scientific and Cultural Organization
(UNESCO) Institute for Statistics, Montreal, the UNESCO statistics
database, January 2002.

Source:
L'Institut de statistique de l'Organisation des Nations Unies pour
l'education, la science et la culture (UNESCO), Montréal, la base de
données de l'UNESCO, janvier 2002.

† For information on the recent changes in country or area
   nomenclature pertaining to former Czechoslovakia,
   Germany, Hong Kong Special Administrative Region (SAR)
   of China, Macao Special Administrative Region (SAR) of
   China, SFR of Yugoslavia and the former USSR, see
   Annex I − Country or area nomenclature, regional and
   other groupings.

† Pour les modifications récentes de nomenclature de pays ou de
   zone concernant l'Allemagne, Hong Kong, région administrative
   spéciale (RAS) de Chine, Macao, région administrative spéciale
   (RAS) de Chine, l'ex−Tchécoslovaquie, l'ex−URSS et l'ex−Rfs de
   Yougoslavie, voir annexe I − Nomenclature des pays ou des zones,
   groupements régionaux et autres groupements.

†† For statistical purposes the data for China do not include
    those for Hong Kong Special Administrative Region
    (Hong Kong SAR), Macao Special Administrative
    Region (Macao SAR) and Taiwan province of China.

†† Les données statistiques relatives à la Chine ne comprennent pas
    celles qui concernent la région administrative spéciale de Hong
    Kong (la RAS de Hong Kong), la région administrative spéciale de
    Macao (la RAS de Macao) et la province chinoise de Taiwan.

10
Illiterate population by sex, aged 15 and over,
estimates and projections [*cont.*]
Population analphabète selon le sexe, âgée de 15 ans et plus,
estimations et projections [*suite*]

1   Estimates and projections of UNESCO, as assessed in January 2002 based on statistics collected during national population censuses.
2   Special estimates and projections of UNESCO for countries with no census data, as assessed in February 2000.

3   Estimates and projections of UNESCO, as assessed in 2000.

1   Estimations et projections de l'UNESCO, révisées en janvier 2002 et basées sur les données collectées au cours des recensements nationaux de la population.
2   Estimations et projections spéciales de l'UNESCO, révisées en février 2000 pour les pays pour lesquels on n'a pas de chiffres de recensement.
3   Estimations et projections de l'UNESCO, révisées en 2000.

Technical notes, table 10

Table 10: Data on the illiterate population by sex refer to the population 15 years of age and over. The ability to both read and write, with understanding, a simple sentence on everyday life is used as the criterion of literacy; hence semi-literates (persons who can read but not write) are included with illiterates. Persons for whom literacy is not known are excluded from calculations; consequently the percentage of illiteracy for a given country is based on the number of reported illiterates, divided by the total number of reported literates and illiterates.

Most of the data are the latest illiteracy estimates and projections of UNESCO, as assessed in January 2002 based on statistics collected during national population censuses. Other data include special estimates and projections of UNESCO for countries with no census data, as assessed in February 2000, and estimates and projections of UNESCO, as assessed in 2000.

Notes techniques, tableau 10

Tableau 10: Les données sur la population analphabète selon le sexe se réfèrent à la population âgée de 15 ans et plus. On utilise l'aptitude à lire et à écrire, en le comprenant, une phrase simple sur la vie quotidienne comme critère d'alphabétisme; par conséquent, les semi-alphabètes (c'est-à-dire les personnes qui savent lire, mais non écrire) sont assimilés aux analphabètes. Les personnes dont on ne sait pas si elles savent lire ou écrire sont exclues de ces calculs; par conséquent, le pourcentage d'analphabétisme d'un pays donné est fondé sur le nombre d'analphabètes connus divisé par le total des alphabètes et analphabètes connus.

La plupart des données sont les dernières estimations et projections de l'UNESCO sur l'analphabétisme, révisées en janvier 2002 et basées sur les données collectées au cours des recensements nationaux de la population. Autres données comprennent les estimations et projections spéciales de l'UNESCO, révisées en février 2000 pour les pays pour lesquels on n'a pas de chiffres de recensement, et les estimations et projections de l'UNESCO, révisées en 2000.

11
Selected indicators of life expectancy, childbearing and mortality
Choix d'indicateurs de l'espérance de vie, de la maternité et de la mortalité

Country or area Pays or zone	Year Année	Life expectancy at birth (years) Espérance de vie à la naissance (en années)		Infant mortality rate Taux de mortalité infantile	Total fertility rate Taux de fécondité	Child mortality rate Taux de mortalité juvénile			Maternal mortality rate Taux de mortalité maternale
		M	F	M + F		Year Année	M	F	1990
Africa · Afrique									
Algeria	1990−1995	66.0	68.3	60.0	4.1				
Algérie	1995−2000	67.5	70.3	50.0	3.3	1982[12]	12.5	12.8	160
Angola	1990−1995	43.9	46.9	125.5	7.2				
Angola	1995−2000	43.3	46.0	126.2	7.2		...	...	1500
Benin	1990−1995	50.6	54.3	95.6	6.5				
Bénin	1995−2000	51.8	55.3	87.7	6.1		...	...	990
Botswana	1990−1995	58.6	61.7	61.2	4.9				
Botswana	1995−2000	43.8	44.7	73.9	4.4		...	...	250
Burkina Faso	1990−1995	45.2	47.3	107.2	7.1				
Burkina Faso	1995−2000	44.2	46.2	99.1	6.9		...	...	930
Burundi	1990−1995	40.0	42.5	136.0	6.8				
Burundi	1995−2000	39.6	41.5	120.0	6.8		...	...	1300
Cameroon	1990−1995	51.3	53.7	86.7	5.7				
Cameroun	1995−2000	49.1	50.8	87.3	5.1		...	...	550
Cape Verde	1990−1995	63.5	69.0	64.5	3.9	1985[3]	21.1	19.3	
Cap−Vert	1995−2000	65.5	71.3	55.6	3.6	1990	3.4	3.4	...
Central African Rep.	1990−1995	45.3	48.3	104.2	5.6				
Rép. centrafricaine	1995−2000	42.7	46.0	101.2	5.3	1988[4]	14.9	12.8	700
Chad	1990−1995	43.3	46.1	128.9	6.7				
Tchad	1995−2000	43.9	46.4	122.5	6.7		...	...	1500
Comoros	1990−1995	55.4	59.2	83.7	5.8				
Comores	1995−2000	57.4	60.2	76.3	5.4		...	...	950
Congo	1990−1995	48.7	53.6	78.0	6.3				
Congo	1995−2000	48.8	53.1	72.1	6.3		...	...	890
Côte d'Ivoire	1990−1995	48.6	50.8	94.1	5.7				
Côte d'Ivoire	1995−2000	47.4	48.1	89.0	5.1		...	...	810
Dem. Republic of the Congo	1990−1995	49.9	53.1	94.5	6.7				
Rép. dém du Congo	1995−2000	49.2	51.9	90.6	6.7		...	...	870
Djibouti	1990−1995	45.8	49.0	121.4	6.3				
Djibouti	1995−2000	43.9	46.9	116.6	6.1		...	...	570
Egypt	1990−1995	62.4	65.6	62.8	3.8	1992[3]	10.0	10.7	
Egypte	1995−2000	64.7	67.9	50.8	3.4	1995	2.8	3.0	170
Equatorial Guinea	1990−1995	46.4	49.6	117.1	5.9				
Guinée équatoriale	1995−2000	48.4	51.6	107.7	5.9		...	...	820
Eritrea	1990−1995	48.4	51.6	101.6	6.1				
Erythrée	1995−2000	50.1	53.0	89.3	5.7				1400
Ethiopia	1990−1995	44.8	47.4	121.2	6.8				
Ethiopie	1995−2000	43.6	45.4	114.8	6.8		...	...	1400
Gabon	1990−1995	50.7	53.6	94.2	5.2				
Gabon	1995−2000	51.2	53.7	87.7	5.4		...	...	500
Gambia	1990−1995	42.6	45.5	134.3	5.6				
Gambie	1995−2000	44.0	46.8	125.3	5.2		...	...	1100
Ghana	1990−1995	54.5	57.5	76.6	5.3				
Ghana	1995−2000	55.0	57.6	68.6	4.6				740
Guinea	1990−1995	44.0	45.0	134.6	6.4				
Guinée	1995−2000	46.0	47.0	124.2	6.3		...	...	1600
Guinea−Bissau	1990−1995	41.4	44.5	141.0	6.0				
Guinée−Bissau	1995−2000	42.7	45.5	130.8	6.0		...	...	910
Kenya	1990−1995	54.9	58.1	67.0	5.4				
Kenya	1995−2000	51.2	53.2	64.7	4.6		...	...	650
Lesotho	1990−1995	56.3	58.8	101.5	5.0				
Lesotho	1995−2000	50.7	51.6	108.1	4.8		...	...	610
Liberia	1990−1995	37.5	39.6	165.6	6.8				
Libéria	1995−2000	47.1	49.0	111.4	6.8		...	...	560
Libyan Arab Jamahiriya	1990−1995	67.7	71.3	29.8	4.1				
Jamah. arabe libyenne	1995−2000	68.3	72.2	27.8	3.8		...	...	220
Madagascar	1990−1995	48.5	51.2	108.4	6.2				
Madagascar	1995−2000	50.5	52.8	100.2	6.1		...	...	490

11
Selected indicators of life expectancy, childbearing and mortality [*cont.*]
Choix d'indicateurs de l'espérance de vie, de la maternité et de la mortalité [*suite*]

Country or area Pays or zone	Year Année	Life expectancy at birth (years) Espérance de vie à la naissance (en années)		Infant mortality rate Taux de mortalité infantile	Total fertility rate Taux de fécondité	Child mortality rate Taux de mortalité juvénile			Maternal mortality rate Taux de mortalité maternelle
		M	F	M + F		Year Année	M	F	1990
Malawi	1990−1995	43.4	44.2	150.8	7.2				
Malawi	1995−2000	40.7	40.7	139.8	6.8		...	...	560
Mali	1990−1995	48.5	50.8	137.3	7.0				
Mali	1995−2000	49.8	51.8	130.3	7.0	1987[3 4]	41.5	35.7	1200
Mauritania	1990−1995	47.9	51.1	110.1	6.1				
Mauritanie	1995−2000	48.9	52.1	105.6	6.0		...	...	930
Mauritius [30]	1990−1995	66.4	73.9	20.7	2.3	1995[5]	0.8	0.6	
Maurice [30]	1995−2000	66.9	74.8	18.5	2.0	1997[5 6]	0.5	0.5	120
Morocco	1990−1995	62.8	66.2	63.0	3.9	1993[3]	6.0	5.5	
Maroc	1995−2000	64.8	68.5	52.2	3.4	1996[3]	4.6	4.2	610
Mozambique	1990−1995	42.3	45.3	134.4	6.4				
Mozambique	1995−2000	39.4	41.8	136.7	6.3		...	...	1500
Namibia	1990−1995	52.6	54.8	82.9	5.8				
Namibie	1995−2000	44.9	45.3	78.5	5.3		...	...	370
Niger	1990−1995	42.4	43.0	144.4	8.0				
Niger	1995−2000	43.9	44.5	136.1	8.0		...	...	1200
Nigeria	1990−1995	50.2	51.2	97.5	6.4				
Nigéria	1995−2000	51.0	51.5	88.1	5.9		...	...	1000
Reunion	1990−1995	69.4	78.3	9.0	2.4	1982[17]	0.9	0.8	
Réunion	1995−2000	69.4	78.3	9.0	2.3	1987[17]	0.6	0.6	...
Rwanda	1990−1995	21.7	22.4	135.7	6.7				
Rwanda	1995−2000	38.7	40.2	121.9	6.2		...	...	1300
Senegal	1990−1995	48.3	52.6	67.9	6.1				
Sénégal	1995−2000	50.5	54.2	62.4	5.6		...	...	1200
Sierra Leone	1990−1995	32.9	35.6	194.8	6.5				
Sierra Leone	1995−2000	36.0	38.6	165.4	6.5		...	...	1800
Somalia	1990−1995	38.5	40.1	164.5	7.3				
Somalie	1995−2000	45.4	48.5	122.3	7.3		...	...	1600
South Africa	1990−1995	56.6	64.4	53.9	3.3				
Afrique du Sud	1995−2000	53.9	59.5	58.2	3.1				230
Sudan	1990−1995	51.6	54.4	94.5	5.3				
Soudan	1995−2000	53.6	56.4	85.9	4.9		...	...	660
Swaziland	1990−1995	54.7	59.1	79.2	5.3				
Swaziland	1995−2000	49.3	52.2	86.9	4.8		...	...	560
Togo	1990−1995	50.2	53.3	90.5	6.2				
Togo	1995−2000	50.1	52.6	83.1	5.8		...	...	640
Tunisia	1990−1995	66.5	68.7	35.0	3.1	1994[3]	6.4	5.3	
Tunisie	1995−2000	68.4	70.7	30.3	2.3	1995[3]	5.9	4.8	170
Uganda	1990−1995	40.8	42.3	118.5	7.1				
Ouganda	1995−2000	41.4	42.5	106.5	7.1		...	...	1200
United Republic of Tanzania	1990−1995	51.1	54.1	86.9	5.9				
Rép.−Unie de Tanzanie	1995−2000	50.0	52.3	81.3	5.5		...	...	770
Western Sahara	1990−1995	57.3	60.6	75.9	4.8				
Sahara occidental	1995−2000	59.8	63.1	64.5	4.4		...	...	...
Zambia	1990−1995	45.1	45.4	100.4	6.3				
Zambie	1995−2000	40.9	40.1	93.6	6.1		...	...	940
Zimbabwe	1990−1995	48.6	49.6	70.7	5.5				
Zimbabwe	1995−2000	43.2	42.7	65.0	5.0		...	...	570
America, North · Amérique du Nord									
Bahamas	1990−1995	65.1	73.1	20.8	2.6				
Bahamas	1995−2000	64.8	73.5	18.7	2.4	1994[6]	1.4	0.9	100
Barbados	1990−1995	72.9	77.9	14.0	1.6	1987[5]	0.8	0.2	
Barbade	1995−2000	73.7	78.7	12.4	1.5	1988[5]	0.5	0.5	43
Belize	1990−1995	71.9	74.3	34.3	4.2				
Belize	1995−2000	72.4	75.0	32.5	3.4	1997[3]	6.7	6.0	...
Canada	1990−1995	74.9	81.0	6.3	1.7	1993[8]	0.4	0.3	
Canada	1995−2000	75.7	81.3	5.5	1.6	1995[8]	0.3	0.2	6
Costa Rica	1990−1995	73.5	78.1	13.7	3.0	1994[3]	4.2	3.4	
Costa Rica	1995−2000	74.3	78.9	12.1	2.8	1996[3]	3.5	3.0	55

11
Selected indicators of life expectancy, childbearing and mortality [*cont.*]
Choix d'indicateurs de l'espérance de vie, de la maternité et de la mortalité [*suite*]

Country or area Pays or zone	Year Année	Life expectancy at birth (years) Espérance de vie à la naissance (en années)		Infant mortality rate Taux de mortalité infantile	Total fertility rate Taux de fécondité	Child mortality rate Taux de mortalité juvénile			Maternal mortality rate Taux de mortalité maternelle
		M	F	M + F		Year Année	M	F	1990
Cuba	1990−1995	73.5	77.3	10.0	1.6	1993	0.6	0.6	
Cuba	1995−2000	74.2	78.0	7.5	1.6	1995	0.8	0.6	95
Dominican Republic	1990−1995	64.6	68.8	46.5	3.2				
Rép. dominicaine	1995−2000	65.3	69.9	40.6	2.9		...	...	110
El Salvador	1990−1995	63.3	71.1	40.2	3.5	1986[3]	7.1	6.2	
El Salvador	1995−2000	66.5	72.5	32.0	3.2	1992	1.4	1.3	300
Guadeloupe	1990−1995	72.4	80.1	9.2	2.1				
Guadeloupe	1995−2000	73.6	80.9	8.3	2.1	1985[13]	4.8	4.2	...
Guatemala	1990−1995	59.8	65.5	51.1	5.4	1981	16.0	16.5	
Guatemala	1995−2000	61.4	67.2	46.0	4.9	1985[3]	22.2	20.1	200
Haiti	1990−1995	49.7	54.5	73.8	4.8				
Haïti	1995−2000	49.1	55.0	68.3	4.4		...	...	1000
Honduras	1990−1995	62.8	67.8	45.4	4.9				
Honduras	1995−2000	63.2	68.7	37.1	4.3	1981[5]	4.6	4.3	220
Jamaica	1990−1995	71.9	75.8	24.3	2.8	1989[5]	1.4	1.1	
Jamaïque	1995−2000	72.9	76.8	21.9	2.5	1991[5]	1.3	1.0	120
Martinique	1990−1995	74.7	81.5	7.6	1.9	1990[13]	2.1	2.5	
Martinique	1995−2000	75.5	82.0	7.0	1.8	1992[136]	1.8	1.4	...
Mexico	1990−1995	68.5	74.5	34.0	3.1	1990[3]	8.5	7.1	
Mexique	1995−2000	69.5	75.5	31.0	2.8	1995[3]	5.8	4.7	110
Netherlands Antilles	1990−1995	71.5	77.6	16.3	2.3				
Antilles néerlandaises	1995−2000	72.5	78.4	14.2	2.1	1992[6]	0.9	0.6	...
Nicaragua	1990−1995	63.5	68.7	48.0	4.8				
Nicaragua	1995−2000	65.7	70.4	39.5	4.3		...	...	160
Panama	1990−1995	70.9	75.0	25.1	2.9	1994[3]	4.9	4.1	
Panama	1995−2000	71.8	76.4	21.4	2.6	1996[3]	4.7	4.1	55
Puerto Rico	1990−1995	69.6	79.1	11.6	2.2	1994[3]	2.8	2.4	
Porto Rico	1995−2000	70.4	79.6	11.0	2.0	1997	0.4	0.3	...
St. Lucia	1990−1995	69.3	74.6	16.1	3.1				
Saint−Lucie	1995−2000	70.3	75.6	14.3	2.7		...	...	...
Trinidad and Tobago	1990−1995	70.5	75.2	16.1	2.1	1993	1.1	0.9	
Trinité−et−Tobago	1995−2000	71.5	76.2	14.3	1.7	1995[6]	0.7	0.6	90
United States	1990−1995	72.2	78.9	8.5	2.1	1993	0.5	0.4	
Etats−Unis	1995−2000	73.6	79.4	7.6	2.0	1995	0.4	0.4	12
United States Virgin Islands Iles vierges américaines		...	...	...	...	1990[6]	1.1	...	...
America, South · Amérique du Sud									
Argentina	1990−1995	68.6	75.7	24.3	2.8	1993[3]	5.6	4.5	
Argentine	1995−2000	69.7	76.8	21.8	2.6	1995[3]	5.5	4.5	100
Bolivia	1990−1995	57.7	61.0	75.1	4.8				
Bolivie	1995−2000	59.8	63.2	65.6	4.4		...	...	650
Brazil	1990−1995	62.4	70.1	46.8	2.5	1992[9]	1.3	1.1	
Brésil	1995−2000	63.5	71.4	42.1	2.3	1995[9]	1.2	1.0	220
Chile	1990−1995	71.5	77.4	14.0	2.5	1995[3]	2.9	2.4	
Chili	1995−2000	72.3	78.3	12.8	2.4	1997[3]	2.4	2.0	65
Colombia	1990−1995	64.3	73.0	35.2	3.0	1992[310]	4.8	3.8	
Colombie	1995−2000	67.3	74.3	30.0	2.8	1994[310]	4.2	3.3	100
Ecuador	1990−1995	66.4	71.4	49.7	3.5	1995[11]	2.4	2.3	
Equateur	1995−2000	67.3	72.5	45.6	3.1	1997[11]	2.3	2.1	150
French Guiana	1990−1995	70.4	78.5	35.1	4.1				
Guyane française	1995−2000	71.4	79.3	31.9	4.1		...	...	...
Guyana	1990−1995	61.1	68.1	56.1	2.6				
Guyana	1995−2000	59.8	67.8	56.2	2.5		...	...	...
Paraguay	1990−1995	66.3	70.8	43.3	4.6	1985[3]	5.4	4.8	
Paraguay	1995−2000	67.5	72.0	39.2	4.2	1992	0.7	0.6	160
Peru	1990−1995	64.4	69.2	55.5	3.4	1983[39]	13.1	12.3	
Pérou	1995−2000	65.9	70.9	45.0	3.0	1985[39]	10.8	9.9	280
Suriname	1990−1995	66.5	71.5	33.4	2.5	1980	1.6	1.6	
Suriname	1995−2000	67.5	72.7	29.1	2.2	1995[3]	6.2	4.7	...
Uruguay	1990−1995	69.2	76.9	20.1	2.5	1985[3]	7.5	5.9	
Uruguay	1995−2000	70.5	78.0	17.5	2.4	1990[3]	5.6	4.5	85

11
Selected indicators of life expectancy, childbearing and mortality [cont.]
Choix d'indicateurs de l'espérance de vie, de la maternité et de la mortalité [suite]

Country or area Pays or zone	Year Année	Life expectancy at birth (years) Espérance de vie à la naissance (en années)		Infant mortality rate Taux de mortalité infantile	Total fertility rate Taux de fécondité	Child mortality rate Taux de mortalité juvénile			Maternal mortality rate Taux de mortalité maternelle
		M	F	M + F		Year Année	M	F	1990
Venezuela	1990−1995	69.0	74.7	23.2	3.3	1986[39]	6.5	5.3	
Venezuela	1995−2000	70.0	75.7	20.9	3.0	1990[39]	7.0	5.7	120
Asia - Asie									
Afghanistan	1990−1995	41.8	42.2	167.0	7.0				
Afghanistan	1995−2000	42.3	42.8	164.7	6.9		...	...	1700
Armenia	1990−1995	68.0	74.6	17.2	2.1	1992[12]	1.3	1.2	
Arménie	1995−2000	69.3	75.4	16.9	1.4	1996[12]	0.8	0.7	50
Azerbaijan	1990−1995	65.6	74.0	34.6	2.6				
Azerbaïdjan	1995−2000	67.2	74.5	32.5	1.9	1996[12]	3.7	3.3	22
Bahrain	1990−1995	69.8	74.1	19.6	3.4				
Bahreïn	1995−2000	71.1	75.3	16.4	2.6	1995[3]	4.4	4.1	60
Bangladesh	1990−1995	55.6	55.6	91.2	4.3	1981	14.1	15.8	
Bangladesh	1995−2000	58.1	58.2	78.8	3.8	1986[3]	43.1	41.1	850
Bhutan	1990−1995	56.5	59.0	74.6	5.8				
Bhoutan	1995−2000	59.5	62.0	62.9	5.5		...	...	1600
Brunei Darussalam	1990−1995	72.4	77.1	10.8	3.1				
Brunéi Darussalam	1995−2000	73.4	78.1	9.6	2.8		...	...	60
Cambodia	1990−1995	53.9	57.4	91.3	5.4				
Cambodge	1995−2000	54.3	58.5	83.4	5.3		...	...	900
China ††	1990−1995	66.7	70.5	46.7	1.9				
Chine ††	1995−2000	67.9	72.0	41.4	1.8		...	...	95
China, Hong Kong SAR †	1990−1995	75.5	81.0	5.0	1.2	1995[3]	1.1	1.0	
Chine, Hong Kong RAS †	1995−2000	76.5	82.0	4.2	1.2	1997	0.3	0.2	7
China, Macao SAR †	1990−1995	75.3	80.0	9.7	1.6				
Chine, Macao RAS †	1995−2000	76.1	80.8	8.9	1.2	1997[36]	1.2	1.2	
Cyprus	1990−1995	74.7	79.2	9.1	2.3	1995[3 13]	1.8	1.7	
Chypre	1995−2000	75.5	80.0	8.1	2.0	1997[3 6 13]	0.3	0.1	5
East Timor	1990−1995	44.2	45.9	149.9	4.8				
Timor oriental	1995−2000	46.7	48.4	135.0	4.4		...	...	...
Georgia	1990−1995	68.5	76.8	19.4	1.9				
Géorgie	1995−2000	68.5	76.8	19.4	1.6		...	...	33
India	1990−1995	60.0	60.3	78.7	3.7				
Inde	1995−2000	61.9	62.6	72.5	3.3		...	...	570
Indonesia	1990−1995	61.0	64.5	58.6	3.0				
Indonésie	1995−2000	63.3	67.0	48.4	2.6		...	...	650
Iran (Islamic Republic of)	1990−1995	65.0	66.5	55.2	4.4	1986	3.9	1.4	
Iran (République islamique d')	1995−2000	67.3	68.8	44.0	3.2	1991	5.1	3.9	120
Iraq	1990−1995	57.6	60.1	127.1	5.7	1987[3]	5.7	4.4	
Iraq	1995−2000	57.2	60.3	91.7	5.3	1988[3]	5.7	4.4	310
Israel	1990−1995	75.1	78.8	8.8	2.9	1994[14]	0.3	0.3	
Israël	1995−2000	76.3	80.2	6.3	2.9	1996[14]	0.4	0.4	7
Japan	1990−1995	76.2	82.4	4.4	1.5	1995[15]	0.5	0.4	
Japon	1995−2000	77.0	83.8	3.5	1.4	1997[15]	0.4	0.3	18
Jordan	1990−1995	67.6	69.5	33.0	5.6				
Jordanie	1995−2000	68.5	71.0	26.6	4.7		...	...	150
Kazakhstan	1990−1995	60.5	70.3	40.9	2.5	1991[12]	2.1	1.7	
Kazakhstan	1995−2000	58.6	70.0	44.8	2.1	1997[12]	2.1	1.7	80
Korea, Democratic People's Rep.	1990−1995	66.6	72.1	27.9	2.3				
Corée, R. p. dém. de	1995−2000	60.5	66.0	45.1	2.1	1993[3]	5.6	5.1	70
Korea, Republic of	1990−1995	68.3	76.4	11.8	1.7	1993[16 17]	0.8	0.7	
Corée, République de	1995−2000	70.6	78.1	7.9	1.5	1995[16 17]	0.7	0.7	130
Kuwait	1990−1995	73.3	77.2	14.0	3.2	1994[3]	3.4	3.3	
Koweït	1995−2000	74.1	78.2	12.3	2.9	1996[3]	3.4	3.1	29
Kyrgyzstan	1990−1995	63.2	71.8	40.8	3.4	1992[12]	2.9	2.6	
Kirghizistan	1995−2000	62.8	71.1	43.2	2.9	1996[12]	2.8	2.5	110
Lao People's Democratic Rep.	1990−1995	49.5	52.0	104.4	5.8				
Rép. dém. pop. lao	1995−2000	51.3	53.8	96.6	5.3		...	...	650
Lebanon	1990−1995	67.5	71.0	31.5	2.9				
Liban	1995−2000	71.1	74.1	20.0	2.3		...	...	300
Malaysia	1990−1995	68.7	73.1	15.1	3.6	1995	0.8	0.7	
Malaisie	1995−2000	69.6	74.5	11.6	3.3	1997	0.8	0.7	80

11
Selected indicators of life expectancy, childbearing and mortality [*cont.*]
Choix d'indicateurs de l'espérance de vie, de la maternité et de la mortalité [*suite*]

Country or area Pays or zone	Year Année	Life expectancy at birth (years) Espérance de vie à la naissance (en années) M	F	Infant mortality rate Taux de mortalité infantile M + F	Total fertility rate Taux de fécondité	Child mortality rate Taux de mortalité juvénile Year Année	M	F	Maternal mortality rate Taux de mortalité maternelle 1990
Maldives	1990–1995	64.0	62.0	56.6	6.1	1990	3.8	4.3	
Maldives	1995–2000	66.3	64.5	46.4	5.8	1996[3]	6.6	6.1	...
Mongolia	1990–1995	59.4	63.2	68.1	3.4				
Mongolie	1995–2000	59.9	63.9	65.8	2.7	1998	4.1	3.7	65
Myanmar	1990–1995	53.3	57.6	98.4	3.8				
Myanmar	1995–2000	53.6	58.3	92.2	3.3		...	...	580
Nepal	1990–1995	55.1	54.1	96.1	5.1				
Népal	1995–2000	57.6	57.1	82.6	4.8		...	...	1500
Occupied Palestinian Territory	1990–1995	68.1	71.4	27.3	6.5				
Terr. palestinien occupé	1995–2000	69.8	73.0	24.0	6.0		...	...	
Oman	1990–1995	67.7	71.0	31.2	6.7				
Oman	1995–2000	69.2	72.0	26.6	5.9		...	...	190
Pakistan	1990–1995	57.2	56.9	104.4	5.8				
Pakistan	1995–2000	59.2	58.9	95.3	5.5		...	...	340
Philippines	1990–1995	64.5	68.7	42.5	4.1	1989	4.7	4.3	
Philippines	1995–2000	66.5	70.7	34.4	3.6	1991[5]	2.8	2.5	280
Qatar	1990–1995	67.2	70.3	20.0	4.1				
Qatar	1995–2000	68.1	70.6	13.6	3.7		...	...	...
Saudi Arabia	1990–1995	68.0	70.6	31.2	6.7				
Arabie saoudite	1995–2000	69.9	72.2	25.0	6.2		...	...	130
Singapore	1990–1995	73.9	78.3	6.0	1.8	1996[3 18]	1.1	1.0	
Singapour	1995–2000	74.9	79.3	4.9	1.6	1998[3 5 18]	1.1	1.0	10
Sri Lanka	1990–1995	68.1	73.5	26.6	2.4	1988[3]	4.7	4.1	
Sri Lanka	1995–2000	69.0	74.7	22.9	2.1	1995[3 5]	3.2	2.8	140
Syrian Arab Republic	1990–1995	66.6	69.3	36.4	4.7				
République arabe syrienne	1995–2000	69.4	71.6	26.9	4.0	1984[19]	2.8	2.9	180
Tajikistan	1990–1995	64.2	70.2	56.6	4.4	1991[12]	5.1	4.8	
Tadjikistan	1995–2000	64.2	70.2	56.6	3.7	1993[12]	9.0	8.5	130
Thailand	1990–1995	66.7	71.9	29.4	2.1	1993[3]	2.2	1.7	
Thaïlande	1995–2000	66.7	72.6	25.4	2.1	1997[3 5]	2.0	1.7	200
Turkey	1990–1995	65.0	69.7	54.5	3.1				
Turquie	1995–2000	66.5	71.7	45.7	2.7		...	...	180
Turkmenistan	1990–1995	61.9	68.9	54.8	4.0				
Turkménistan	1995–2000	61.9	68.9	54.8	3.6		...	...	55
United Arab Emirates	1990–1995	71.2	75.7	15.8	3.8				
Emirats arabes unis	1995–2000	73.3	77.6	12.0	3.2				26
Uzbekistan	1990–1995	64.3	70.7	44.5	3.6				
Ouzbékistan	1995–2000	65.3	71.3	41.0	2.9	1997[12]	3.6	3.3	55
Viet Nam	1990–1995	62.9	67.3	47.4	3.3				
Viet Nam	1995–2000	64.9	69.6	40.1	2.5		...	...	160
Yemen	1990–1995	54.9	55.9	92.4	7.6				
Yémen	1995–2000	58.2	60.4	73.8	7.6		...	...	1400
Europe · Europe									
Albania	1990–1995	68.9	74.9	32.4	2.9				
Albanie	1995–2000	69.9	75.9	28.3	2.6		...	...	65
Austria	1990–1995	73.0	79.5	6.9	1.5	1995	0.4	0.3	
Autriche	1995–2000	74.4	80.7	5.4	1.4	1997	0.3	0.2	10
Belarus	1990–1995	64.5	74.9	15.8	1.7	1993[12]	0.9	0.6	
Bélarus	1995–2000	62.8	74.4	12.5	1.3	1997[12]	0.8	0.6	37
Belgium	1990–1995	73.3	80.0	6.9	1.6	1984[20]	0.6	0.6	
Belgique	1995–2000	74.7	81.1	4.4	1.5	1987[20]	0.4	0.4	10
Bosnia and Herzegovina	1990–1995	69.5	75.1	16.9	1.5				
Bosnie–Herzégovine	1995–2000	70.5	75.9	15.0	1.4		...	...	...
Bulgaria	1990–1995	67.7	74.7	15.9	1.5	1994	1.1	0.9	
Bulgarie	1995–2000	67.1	74.8	15.2	1.1	1997	1.2	1.2	27
Channel Islands	1990–1995	74.4	79.1	5.8	1.5				
Iles Anglo–Normandes	1995–2000	75.2	79.9	5.8	1.5		...	...	...
Croatia	1990–1995	68.3	76.5	10.5	1.5	1995	0.3	0.3	
Croatie	1995–2000	69.3	77.3	10.1	1.7	1997	0.4	0.3[6]	...
Czech Republic	1990–1995	68.8	76.2	9.2	1.6	1995	0.4	0.3	
République tchèque	1995–2000	70.9	77.7	5.8	1.2	1997	0.4	0.4	15

11
Selected indicators of life expectancy, childbearing and mortality [*cont.*]
Choix d'indicateurs de l'espérance de vie, de la maternité et de la mortalité [*suite*]

Country or area Pays or zone	Year Année	Life expectancy at birth (years) Espérance de vie à la naissance (en années)		Infant mortality rate Taux de mortalité infantile	Total fertility rate Taux de fécondité	Child mortality rate Taux de mortalité juvénile Year Année			Maternal mortality rate Taux de mortalité maternale
		M	F	M + F			M	F	1990
Denmark	1990–1995	72.5	77.8	6.5	1.7	1994[21]	0.4	0.3	
Danemark	1995–2000	73.4	78.3	5.9	1.7	1997[21]	0.3	0.2[6]	9
Estonia	1990–1995	62.9	74.2	14.6	1.6	1993[12]	0.8	0.8	
Estonie	1995–2000	64.3	75.6	11.1	1.2	1995[12]	1.3	0.8	41
Finland	1990–1995	72.0	79.6	5.0	1.8	1995[22]	0.2	0.3	
Finlande	1995–2000	73.4	80.7	4.4	1.7	1997[22]	0.3	0.2[6]	11
France	1990–1995	73.3	81.4	6.5	1.7	1991[23]	0.4	0.4	
France	1995–2000	74.2	82.0	5.5	1.7	1993[23]	0.4	0.3	15
Germany	1990–1995	72.8	79.3	6.1	1.4	1994	0.4	0.3	
Allemagne	1995–2000	74.0	80.3	5.0	1.3	1996	0.3	0.3	22
Greece	1990–1995	74.9	79.9	8.5	1.4	1994	0.3	0.3	
Grèce	1995–2000	75.4	80.7	6.6	1.3	1997	0.3	0.3	10
Hungary	1990–1995	64.8	73.9	13.3	1.7	1995	0.5	0.4	
Hongrie	1995–2000	66.3	75.1	9.6	1.4	1997	0.5	0.4	30
Iceland	1990–1995	76.3	80.8	4.9	2.2				
Islande	1995–2000	76.6	81.3	4.7	2.0	1996[6]	0.1	0.3	0
Ireland	1990–1995	72.6	78.1	6.7	2.0	1994[5 25]	0.4	0.2	
Irlande	1995–2000	73.5	78.8	6.6	1.9	1996[5 25]	0.3	0.3	10
Italy	1990–1995	74.0	80.5	7.4	1.3	1991	0.3	0.3	
Italie	1995–2000	75.0	81.4	5.6	1.2	1994	0.3	0.3	12
Latvia	1990–1995	62.4	74.0	16.2	1.6	1995[12]	0.9	0.8	
Lettonie	1995–2000	63.7	75.4	15.6	1.1	1997[12]	0.8	0.4[6]	40
Lithuania	1990–1995	64.3	75.6	14.4	1.8	1995[12]	0.8	0.8	
Lituanie	1995–2000	66.1	76.7	10.7	1.4	1997[12]	0.7	0.5	36
Luxembourg	1990–1995	72.4	79.2	7.1	1.7	1994	0.5	0.2	
Luxembourg	1995–2000	73.6	80.1	6.6	1.7	1996[6]	0.4	0.6	0
Malta	1990–1995	74.0	78.4	9.2	2.0	1994[3]	2.2	1.8	
Malte	1995–2000	74.9	80.2	7.7	1.9	1996[3 29]	2.1[6]	2.7	0
Netherlands	1990–1995	74.3	80.2	6.2	1.6	1994[26 27]	0.4	0.3	
Pays–Bas	1995–2000	75.1	80.5	4.6	1.5	1996[26 27]	0.3	0.3	12
Norway	1990–1995	74.3	80.3	5.5	1.9	1995[3 28]	1.2	0.8	
Norvège	1995–2000	75.2	81.1	4.8	1.8	1997[28]	0.3	0.3	6
Poland	1990–1995	67.0	75.9	14.6	1.9	1995	0.5	0.4	
Pologne	1995–2000	68.6	77.0	10.0	1.5	1997	0.4	0.3	19
Portugal	1990–1995	70.9	78.1	9.1	1.5	1995	0.6	0.5	
Portugal	1995–2000	71.6	78.8	6.6	1.5	1997	0.6	0.5	15
Republic of Moldova	1990–1995	63.6	70.9	25.6	2.1	1989[12]	1.7	1.3	
République de Moldova	1995–2000	62.8	70.3	20.5	1.6	1992[12]	1.6	0.9	60
Romania	1990–1995	65.8	73.2	23.5	1.5	1995	1.3	1.0	
Roumanie	1995–2000	66.5	73.3	22.1	1.3	1997	1.2	1.0	130
Russian Federation	1990–1995	60.8	73.1	20.5	1.5	1993[12]	1.2	1.0	
Fédération de Russie	1995–2000	60.2	72.5	16.7	1.2	1995[12]	1.2	0.9	75
Slovakia	1990–1995	67.8	76.2	11.8	1.9				
Slovaquie	1995–2000	68.8	76.8	8.6	1.4	1991	0.6	0.5	...
Slovenia	1990–1995	69.6	77.4	7.5	1.4	1994	0.5	0.3	
Slovénie	1995–2000	71.1	78.6	6.1	1.2	1996[6]	0.3	0.3	13
Spain	1990–1995	73.8	81.0	6.7	1.3	1994	0.4	0.3	
Espagne	1995–2000	74.6	81.8	5.7	1.2	1996	0.4	0.3	7
Sweden	1990–1995	75.5	80.9	5.2	2.0	1994	0.3	0.2	
Suède	1995–2000	76.8	81.8	3.5	1.5	1996	0.2	0.2	7
Switzerland	1990–1995	74.6	81.3	6.0	1.5	1994	0.4	0.3	
Suisse	1995–2000	75.4	81.8	5.1	1.5	1996	0.3	0.3	6
TFYR of Macedonia	1990–1995	69.4	74.0	26.5	1.8	1992	0.9	0.9	
l'ex–R.y. Macédoine	1995–2000	70.6	74.8	18.2	1.9	1997	0.7	0.7	...
Ukraine	1990–1995	62.2	72.0	18.0	1.6	1993[12]	1.1	0.9	
Ukraine	1995–2000	62.7	73.5	15.3	1.3	1995[12]	1.1	0.9	50
United Kingdom	1990–1995	73.7	79.0	6.7	1.8	1995	0.3	0.2	
Royaume–Uni	1995–2000	74.7	79.7	5.9	1.7	1997	0.3	0.2	9
Yugoslavia	1990–1995	69.2	74.5	16.8	2.0	1995	0.7	0.6	
Yougoslavie	1995–2000	69.9	74.6	14.8	1.8	1997	0.6	0.4	...

11
Selected indicators of life expectancy, childbearing and mortality [*cont.*]
Choix d'indicateurs de l'espérance de vie, de la maternité et de la mortalité [*suite*]

Country or area Pays or zone	Year Année	Life expectancy at birth (years) Espérance de vie à la naissance (en années)		Infant mortality rate Taux de mortalité infantile	Total fertility rate Taux de fécondité	Child mortality rate Taux de mortalité juvénile			Maternal mortality rate Taux de mortalité maternelle
		M	F	M + F		Year Année	M	F	1990
Oceania · Océanie									
Australia [31]	1990−1995	74.7	80.6	6.6	1.9	1993[5]	0.5	0.3	
Australie [31]	1995−2000	75.9	81.5	5.4	1.8	1995[5]	0.4	0.3	9
Fiji	1990−1995	64.6	68.8	34.8	3.4	1985[5]	1.8	1.2	
Fidji	1995−2000	66.6	70.3	19.6	3.2	1987[5]	1.1	0.8	90
French Polynesia	1990−1995	67.9	72.8	11.3	3.1				
Polynésie française	1995−2000	69.4	74.4	9.7	2.6	...	...	...	...
Guam	1990−1995	70.4	75.0	12.3	3.7				
Guam	1995−2000	71.4	76.0	11.0	4.0	...	...	...	...
Micronesia [24]	1990−1995	68.2	72.9	25.4	4.1				
Micronésie [24]	1995−2000	69.7	74.2	21.5	4.3	...	...	...	...
New Caledonia	1990−1995	69.2	74.5	11.0	2.9				
Nouvelle−Calédonie	1995−2000	71.5	76.7	7.2	2.6	1994[6]	1.3	1.4	...
New Zealand	1990−1995	73.3	78.9	7.5	2.1	1991[5]	0.5	0.4	
Nouvelle−Zélande	1995−2000	74.5	79.9	6.6	2.0	1996[5]	0.5	0.4	25
Papua New Guinea	1990−1995	52.8	54.7	76.2	5.1				
Papouasie−Nouvelle−Guinée	1995−2000	54.8	56.7	69.0	4.6	...	...	930
Samoa	1990−1995	63.1	69.7	36.1	4.7				
Samoa	1995−2000	65.4	72.0	29.8	4.5	...	...	35
Solomon Islands	1990−1995	64.4	66.4	28.2	5.8				
Iles Salomon	1995−2000	66.4	68.7	24.0	5.6	...	...	...
Vanuatu	1990−1995	64.0	66.9	38.2	4.8				
Vanuatu	1995−2000	66.0	69.0	32.5	4.6	...	...	280

Sources:
United Nations, "World Population Prospects: The 2000 Revision" and "Demographic Yearbook, 1999"; World Health Organization and United Nations Children's Fund, "Revised 1990 Estimates of Maternal Mortality, A New Approach by WHO and UNICEF".

Sources:
Organisation des Nations Unies, "World Population Prospects: The 2000 Revision" et "Annuair démographique 1999"; Organisation mondiale de la la santé et Fonds des Nations Unies pour l'enfance, "Revised 1990 Estimates of Maternal Mortality, A New Approach by WHO and UNICEF".

† For information on recent changes in country or area nomenclature pertaining to former Czechoslovakia, Germany, Hong Kong Special Administrative Region (SAR) of China, Macao Special Administrative Region (SAR) of China, SFR of Yugoslavia and the former USSR, see Annex I− Country or area nomenclature, regional and other groupings.

†† For statistical purposes, the data for China do not include those for Hong Kong Special Administrative Region (Hong Kong SAR), Macao Special Administrative Region (Macao SAR) and Taiwan province of China.

1 Excluding live−born infants dying before registration of birth.

2 For Algerian population only.

3 0−4 years old.

4 Based on the results of the population census.

5 Data tabulated by date of registration rather than occurrence.

6 Rates based on 30 or fewer deaths.

7 For 1983, 1986 and 1987, domicile population only.

8 Including Canadian residents temporarily in the United States, but excludes United States residents temporarily in Canada.

9 Excluding Indian jungle population.
10 Deaths based on burial permits.
11 Excluding nomadic Indian tribes.

† Pour les modifications récentes de nomenclature de pays ou de zone concernant l'Allemagne, Hong Kong région administrative spéciale (RAS) de Chine, Macao région administrative spéciale (RAS) de Chine, l'ex−Tchécoslovaquie, l'ex−URSS et l'ex−Rfs de Yougoslavie, voir annexe I − Nomenclature des pays ou des zones, groupements régionaux et autres groupements.

†† Les données statistiques relatives à la Chine ne comprennent pas celles qui concernent la région administrative spéciale de Hong Kong (la RAS de Hong Kong), la région administrative spéciale de Macao (la RAS de Macao) et la province chinoise de Taiwan.

1 Non compris les enfants nés vivants, décédés avant l'enregistrement de leur naissance.

2 Pour la population algérienne seulement.

3 De 0 à 4 ans.

4 D'après les résultats de recensement de la population.

5 Données exploitées selon la date de l'enregistrement et non la date de l'événement.

6 Taux basés sur 30 décès ou moins.

7 Pour 1983, 1986 et 1987, pour la population dans les domiciles seulement.

8 Y compris les résidents canadiens se trouvant temporairement aux Etats−Unis, mais non compris les résidents des Etats−Unis se trouvant temporairement au Canada.

9 Non compris les Indiens de la jungle.
10 D'après les permis d'inhumer.
11 Non compris les tribus d'Indiens nomades.

11
Selected indicators of life expectancy, childbearing and mortality [*cont.*]
Choix d'indicateurs de l'espérance de vie, de la maternité et de la mortalité [*suite*]

12 Excluding infants born alive after less than 28 weeks' gestation, of less than 1 000 grammes in weight and 35 centimeters in length, who die within seven days of birth.	12 Non compris les enfants nés vivants apès moins de 28 semaines de gestation, pesant moins de 1000 grammes, mesurant moins de 35 centimètres et décédés dans les sept jours qui ont suivi leur naissance.
13 For government controlled areas.	13 Pour les zones contrôlées pour le Gouvernement.
14 Including data for East Jerusalem and Israeli residents in certain other territories under occupation by Israeli military forces since June 1967.	14 Y compris les données pour Jérusalem—Est et les résidents israéliens dans certains autres territoires occupés depuis juin 1967 par les forces armées israéliennes.
15 For Japanese nationals in Japan only; however, rates computed on population, including foreigners except foreign military civilian personnel and their dependants stationed in the area.	15 Pour les nationaux japonais au Japon seulement; toutefois, les taux sont calculés sur la base d'une population comprenant les étrangers, mais ne comprenant les militaires et agents civils étrangers en poste sur le territoire ni les membres de leur famille les accompagnant.
16 Excluding armed forces, civilian aliens employed by armed forces, foreign diplomatic personnel and their dependants and Korean diplomatic personnel and their dependants outside the country.	16 Non compris les militaires étrangers par les forces armées, le personnel diplomatique étranger et les membres de leur famille les accompagnant et le personnel diplomatique coréen hors du pays et les membres de leurs familles les accompagnant.
17 Estimates based on the results of the Continuous Demographic Sample Survey.	17 Les estimations sont basés sur les résultats d'une enquète démographique pour sondage continue.
18 Excluding transients afloat and non–locally domiciled military and civilian services personnel and their dependants.	18 Non compris les personnes de passage à bord de navires, les militaires et agents civils domiciliés hors du territoire et les membres de leur famille les accompagnant.
19 Excluding deaths for which cause is unknown.	19 Non compris les décès dont on ignore la cause.
20 Including armed forces stationed outside the country, but excluding alien armed forces stationed in the area.	20 Y compris les militaires nationaux hors du pays, mais non compris les militaires étranges en garnison sur le territoire.
21 Excluding the Faeroe Islands and Greenland.	21 Non compris les Iles Féroé et le Groenland.
22 Including nationals temporarily outside the country.	22 Y compris les nationaux se trouvant temporairement hors du pays.
23 Including armed forces stationed outside the country.	23 Y compris les militaires en garnison hors du pays.
24 Including Federated States of Micronesia, Kiribati, Marshall Islands, Nauru, Northern Mariana Islands and Palau.	24 Y compris les Etats fédérés de Micronésie, Kiribati, Iles Marshall, Nauru, Iles Mariannes septentrionales et Palaos.
25 Deaths registered within one year of occurrence.	25 Décès enregistrés dans l'année qui suit l'événement.
26 Total including residents outside the country if listed in a Netherlands population register.	26 Y compris les résidents hors du pays, s'ils sont incrits sur un registre de population néerlandais.
27 Urban and rural residence, excluding persons on the Central Register of Population (containing persons belonging in the Netherlands population but having no fixed municipality of residence.	27 La résidence urbaine/rurale, non compris les personnes inscrites sur le Registre centrale de la population (personnes appartenant à la population néerlandasie mais sans résidence fixe dans l'une des municipalités).
28 Including deaths of residents temporarily outside the country.	28 Y compris les résidents se trouvant temporairement hors du pays.
29 Rates computed on population including civilian nationals temporarily outside the country.	29 Taux calculés sur la base d'un chiffre de population qui comprend les civils nationaux temporairement hors du pays.
30 Including Agalega, Rodrigues and Saint Brandon.	30 Y compris Agalega, Rodrigues et Saint Brandon.
31 Including Christmas Island, Cocos (Keeling) Islands and Norfolk Island.	31 Y compris les îles Christmas, Cocos (Keeling) et Norfolk.

12
Estimates of cumulative HIV/AIDS infections, AIDS deaths and reported AIDS cases
Chiffres estimatifs du nombre cumulé de personnes infectées par le VIH ou le SIDA, décès dus au SIDA, et cas déclarés de SIDA

A. Estimated cumulative HIV/AIDS infections, AIDS deaths and people newly infected with HIV in 2001
Chiffres estimatifs cumulés du nombre de personnes infectées par le VIH ou le SIDA, décès dus au SIDA et nouveaux cas d'infection à VIH en 2001

	Number of cases (millions) – Nombre de cas (millions)		
	Total	M	F
Cumulative HIV/AIDS infections **Cumulé de personnes infectées par le VIH**	40.0	...	...
Adults Adultes	37.2	19.6	17.6
Children under 15 years Enfants < 15 ans	2.7	...	...
Aids deaths in 2001 **Décès causés par le SIDA en 2001**	3.0	...	...
Adults Adultes	2.4	1.3	1.1
Children under 15 years Enfants < 15 ans	0.6	...	...
People newly infected with HIV in 2001 **Personnes nouvellement infectées par le VIH en 2001**	5.0	...	...
Adults Adultes	4.3	2.5	1.8
Children under 15 years Enfants < 15 ans	0.8	...	...

B. Reported AIDS cases to the World Health Organization
Cas de SIDA déclarés à l'Organisation mondiale de la santé

Regions Régions	Total reported cases to 1991 Nombre total de cas déclarés jusqu' au 1991	New cases reported in: / Nombre de cas nouveaux déclarés en:								Cumulative total Nombre total cumulé
		1992	1993	1994	1995	1996	1997	1998	1999	
World **Monde**	648742	216005	226427	231186	257553	248689	237620	237632	223505	2561680[1]
Africa Afrique	235854	81626	84402	81477	100162	93722	92789	107796	98834	1007345[1]
North America Amérique du Nord	296474	88875	89220	82699	80505	71547	63940	53924	56449	883633[1]
South America Amérique du Sud	47535	19436	21432	24629	26414	29441	28769	28159	23945	249760[1]
Asia Asie	3058	2396	8007	15616	23639	28319	32319	32918	31672	180612[1]
Europe Europe	61903	22808	22417	25714	25923	24837	19251	14263	12158	230233[1]
Oceania Océanie	3918	864	949	1051	910	823	552	572	447	10097[1]

12 C. Reported AIDS cases • Cas de SIDA déclarés

Country or area Pays ou zone	Total reported cases to 1991 Nombre total de cas déclarés jusqu' au 1991	New cases reported in:/ Nombre de cas nouveaux déclarés en:								
		1992	1993	1994	1995	1996	1997	1998	1999	2000
Africa • Afrique										
Algeria Algérie	100	34	31	53	32	48	39	49	40	58
Angola Angola	724	290	339	361	427	465	1121	1186	453	1271
Benin Bénin	247	218	277	324	214	503	1030	725	650	769
Botswana Botswana	437	534	876	575	1172	1368	2224	2992	...	...
Burkina Faso Burkina Faso	1813	1073	836	1892	1684	1838	2216	2166	2031	1532
Burundi Burundi	5180	1583	799	443	1358	2239	3510	4092	4395	1762
Cameroon Cameroun	921	1308	1385	1761	2766	1485	3950	5410	...	...
Cape Verde Cap–Vert	78	15	18	16	24	36	39	43	64	75
Central African Rep. Rép. centrafricaine	3314	636	290	50	649	2077	0	...	...	...
Chad Tchad	224	363	1010	1268	1132	1242	2748	2030	1664	1704
Comoros Comores	3	3	4	3	2	2	3	2	1	4
Congo Congo	10907	5267	6473	7773	10223	...	...	...	...	...
Côte d'Ivoire Côte d'Ivoire	10790	3863	4015	6566	6727	5935	5949	5685	6427	...
Dem. Rep. of the Congo Rép. dém. du Congo	21001	2070	4215	2637	8329	11572	9642	5809	9953	9848
Djibouti Djibouti	165	144	144	196	231	358	434	111	...	...
Egypt Egypte	29	23	29	22	16	14	25	23	34	44
Equatorial Guinea Guinée équatoriale	7	12	24	16	98	74	111	189	122	222
Eritrea Erythrée	150	219	300	625	727	896	1260	1610	1086	...
Ethiopia Ethiopie	1639	3256	5132	6927	3793	832	7631	9416	11964	13347
Gabon Gabon	215	178	128	204	334	601	932	1212	1111	508
Gambia Gambie	180	56	38	53	32	78	74	126	...	...
Ghana Ghana	7586	2699	2371	2330	2578	3295	3833	4854	7752	6289
Guinea Guinée	441	236	328	543	610	922	1005	1648	1069	1646
Guinea–Bissau Guinée–Bissau	172	118	165	254	77	37	217	...	120	...
Kenya Kenya	25704	11569	12204	8588	9133	6844	4885	2565	...	...
Lesotho Lesotho	52	139	166	238	341	936	2203	3242	3563	3760
Liberia Libéria	10	9	4	13	11	8	59	114	79	81
Libyan Arab Jamah. Jamah. arabe libyenne	12	3	2	3	2	3	7	33	4	5
Madagascar Madagascar	3	1	6	9	6	1	6	2	0	2
Malawi Malawi	22300	4655	4916	4732	5209	5406	3705	1878	1711	...
Mali Mali	853	460	672	609	454	594	711	620	290	...
Mauritania Mauritanie	45	18	94	56	103	98	...	...	...	...

12 C. Reported AIDS cases [*cont.*] • Cas de SIDA déclarés [*suite*]

Country or area Pays ou zone	Total reported cases to 1991 Nombre total de cas déclarés jusqu' au 1991	New cases reported in:/ Nombre de cas nouveaux déclarés en:								
		1992	1993	1994	1995	1996	1997	1998	1999	2000
Mauritius Maurice	13	6	5	6	6	4	6	2	7	8
Morocco Maroc	98	30	44	77	57	66	92	93	165	112
Mozambique Mozambique	340	322	164	534	1380	2086	1661	4376	6361	7800
Namibia Namibie	...	430	355	452	1836	2687	3797	5158	6878	4503
Niger Niger	505	304	453	467	621	652	217	425	940	1014
Nigeria Nigéria	599	484	719	1114	2829	2980	3815	18490	16188	9715
Réunion Réunion	72	16	25	23	30	0	0	...	...	...
Rwanda Rwanda	6578	2908	1220	0	2072	3847	1350	3948	671	...
Sao Tome and Principe Sao Tomé–et–Principe	9	2	2	1	4	6	11	25	10	19
Senegal Sénégal	552	96	263	534	396	327	225	311	208	...
Seychelles Seychelles	...	1	3	3	6	6	5	5	8	4
Sierra Leone Sierra Leone	51	37	23	22	29	62	67	26	...	...
Somalia Somalie	13	...	...	...	...	...	...	...	...	...
South Africa Afrique du Sud	1283	887	1882	3816	4219	738	...	...	...	...
Sudan Soudan	508	184	191	201	257	221	270	511	517	652
Swaziland Swaziland	61	216	165	120	154	613	1466	733	1259	...
Togo Togo	1278	824	1330	1284	1710	1527	1211	1623	998	262
Tunisia Tunisie	134	38	52	50	65	54	62	44	42	...
Uganda Ouganda	30190	6362	4641	4927	2192	3032	1962	1406	1149	...
United Rep. of Tanzania Rép. Unie de Tanzanie	43186	15871	13506	6096	4499	8426	8595	8675	8850	11673
Zambia Zambie	24531	3376	2894	1963	5950	4552	1676	...	...	...
Zimbabwe Zimbabwe	10551	8180	9174	10647	13356	12029	6732	4113	...	...
America, North • Amérique du Nord										
Anguilla Anguilla	5	0	0	0	0	0	0	...	...	...
Antigua and Barbuda Antigua–et–Barbuda	17	14	23	16	7	13	7	2	14	...
Aruba Aruba	11	3	1	0	22	0	0	0	...	...
Bahamas Bahamas	834	264	296	317	388	375	387	323	314	...
Barbados Barbade	252	78	88	119	95	130	113	168	133	23
Belize Belize	30	20	29	45	28	38	30	37	90	46
Bermuda Bermudes	197	21	33	44	48	40	14	17	10	...
British Virgin Islands Iles Vierges britanniques	6	2	2	1	3	0	3	1	2	...
Canada Canada	7962	1810	1859	1855	1727	1184	793	734	584	644
Cayman Islands Iles Caïmanes	11	4	0	4	0	3	1	2	1	...

12 C. Reported AIDS cases [*cont.*] • Cas de SIDA déclarés [*suite*]

Country or area Pays ou zone	Total reported cases to 1991 Nombre total de cas déclarés jusqu' au 1991	New cases reported in:/ Nombre de cas nouveaux déclarés en:								
		1992	1993	1994	1995	1996	1997	1998	1999	2000
Costa Rica										
Costa Rica	327	125	126	173	214	214	250	281	215	177
Cuba										
Cuba	108	71	82	102	116	99	129	150	173	105
Dominica										
Dominique	42	6	15	6	5	14	19	12	15	...
Dominican Republic										
Rép. dominicaine	1838	390	407	429	500	444	419	393	434	186
El Salvador										
El Salvador	316	116	177	384	383	418	414	352	425	...
Grenada										
Grenade	33	4	21	7	18	18	10	7	...	...
Guadeloupe										
Guadeloupe	310	81	135	104	106	73	0	0	...	...
Guatemala										
Guatemala	277	94	178	110	141	835	649	397	730	519
Haiti										
Haïti	4164	806	0	0	0	0	3932	0	...	...
Honduras										
Honduras	2039	861	1201	1123	1221	1086	1261	1492	1136	369
Jamaica										
Jamaïque	361	135	219	335	511	491	609	643	892	903
Martinique										
Martinique	193	44	44	49	41	42	23	...	...	...
Mexico										
Mexique	14637	3988	3950	4129	4252	4142	4054	4014	4094	610
Montserrat										
Montserrat	6	0	1	0	0	0	0	1	...	...
Netherlands Antilles										
Antilles néerlandaises	92	31	36	0	76	0	0	0	...	...
Nicaragua										
Nicaragua	29	10	24	38	21	28	20	30	36	36
Panama										
Panama	368	118	204	289	344	380	463	563	534	263
Saint Kitts and Nevis										
Saint–Kitts–et–Nevis	33	4	3	7	6	6	3	1	5	...
Saint Lucia										
Sainte–Lucie	33	8	12	13	10	14	15	10	21	...
St. Vincent and the Grenadines										
St. Vincent–et–Grenadines	37	7	8	16	6	28	31	45	51	...
Trinidad and Tobago										
Trinité–et–Tobago	888	279	280	247	324	323	291	355	397	...
Turks and Caicos Islands										
Iles Turques et Caïques	21	4	14	0	0	0	0	0	...	...
United States										
Etats–Unis	260997	79477	79752	72737	69892	61109	50000	43894	46143	42156
America, South • Amérique du Sud										
Argentina										
Argentine	1905	1132	1466	2181	2184	2622	2297	1899	1401	528
Bolivia										
Bolivie	49	24	22	19	14	11	17	40	21	...
Brazil										
Brésil	36660	15060	16829	18341	20357	22943	23546	24017	20009	15013
Chile										
Chili	537	200	247	315	350	421	529	445	518	178
Colombia										
Colombie	2804	934	740	1361	910	1095	589	...	...	...
Ecuador										
Equateur	198	69	89	116	70	65	128	186	325	313
French Guiana										
Guyane française	271	73	52	70	78	62	35	0	...	...
Guyana										
Guyana	230	162	107	105	192	144	115	222	338	...
Paraguay										
Paraguay	49	30	55	35	50	78	96	27	49	...

12 C. Reported AIDS cases [*cont.*] • Cas de SIDA déclarés [*suite*]

Country or area Pays ou zone	Total reported cases to 1991 Nombre total de cas déclarés jusqu' au 1991	New cases reported in:/ Nombre de cas nouveaux déclarés en:								
		1992	1993	1994	1995	1996	1997	1998	1999	2000
Peru Pérou	1585	748	709	840	1090	1177	1078	1031	1009	615
Suriname Suriname	106	28	35	26	20	...	120	112	103	...
Uruguay Uruguay	245	90	103	119	127	156	173	180	172	...
Venezuela Venezuela	2896	886	978	1101	972	667	46	0	...	...
Asia • Asie										
Armenia Arménie	3	0	0	0	0	7	2	2	8	3
Azerbaijan Azerbaïdjan	0	0	0	1	1	2	5	3	8	19
Bahrain Bahreïn	4	6	3	5	10	9	14	11	8	8
Bangladesh Bangladesh	1	0	0	0	6	0	3	0	...	...
Bhutan Bhoutan	...	...	...	...	...	...	1	1	1	...
Brunei Darussalam Brunéi Darussalam	2	0	1	2	4	2	2	0	2	3
Cambodia Cambodge	906	...	1	14	91	300	572	1494	2256	3684
China †† Chine ††	8	5	23	29	52	38	126	136	230	233
China, Hong Kong SAR † Chine, Hong Kong RAS †	60	14	19	37	45	70	64	63	61	67
China, 'Macao SAR † Chine, Macao RAS †	2	2	2	2	0	1	2	4	2	4
Cyprus Chypre	32	2	7	11	5	18	10	6	13	24
Georgia Géorgie	5	4	0	2	3	2	6	2	7	14
India Inde	102	140	252	523	1091	888	2108	1148	...	...
Indonesia Indonésie	25	10	17	15	20	31	34	75	57	166
Iran, Islamic Rep. of Iran, Rép. islamique d'	44	16	32	19	16	27	40	21	...	...
Iraq Iraq	7	6	21	37	16	15	2	4	0	...
Israel Israël	163	46	47	32	45	67	45	36	137	50
Japan Japon	129	51	86	136	169	234	250	231	300	327
Jordan Jordanie	21	7	8	6	2	4	12	11	3	14
Kazakhstan Kazakhstan	...	...	2	1	2	2	8	9	5	8
Korea, Dem.People's Rep. Corée, Rép. pop. dém. de	0	0	0	0	0	0	0	...	...	...
Korea, Republic of Corée, République de	8	2	6	11	14	22	33	35	34	21
Kuwait Koweït	6	2	2	5	4	5	2	19	4	12
Kyrgyzstan Kirghizistan	15	0	0	0	2	2	2	6	...	...
Lao People's Dem. Rep. Rép. dém. populaire lao	1	0	5	4	4	16	48	27	18	27
Lebanon Liban	40	7	22	12	18	5	8	35	...	...
Malaysia Malaisie	82	73	71	105	233	347	568	875	1200	1168

12 C. Reported AIDS cases [*cont.*] • Cas de SIDA déclarés [*suite*]

Country or area Pays ou zone	Total reported cases to 1991 Nombre total de cas déclarés jusqu' au 1991	New cases reported in:/ Nombre de cas nouveaux déclarés en:								
		1992	1993	1994	1995	1996	1997	1998	1999	2000
Maldives Maldives	1	0	1	1	4	1	2	0	0	1
Mongolia Mongolie	0	0	0	0	0	0	0	0	1	0
Myanmar Myanmar	6	41	142	286	618	690	554	231	...	...
Occupied Palestinian Terr. Terr. palestinien occupé	6	6	1	3	3	1	9	3	1	...
Oman Oman	121	35	38	60	41	27	43	28	36	32
Pakistan Pakistan	46	18	16	9	19	20	19	23	17	15
Philippines Philippines	85	19	36	56	52	52	23	42	77	42
Qatar Qatar	75	5	8	8	6	2	4	3	9	3
Saudi Arabia Arabie saoudite	44	6	12	38	37	100	112	39	26	...
Singapore Singapour	35	18	22	48	56	92	88	125	140	143
Sri Lanka Sri Lanka	12	10	11	14	11	11	9	15	...	...
Syrian Arab Republic Rép. arabe syrienne	20	3	3	4	6	9	8	8	7	3
Tajikistan Tadjikistan	0	0	0	0	0	0	0	0	0	0
Thailand Thaïlande	870	1806	6949	13923	20686	24709	26713	27128	26003	23352
Turkey Turquie	61	28	29	34	34	37	38	29	28	46
Turkmenistan Turkménistan	0	1	0	0	0	0	0	...	...	...
United Arab Emirates Emirats arabes unis	9	3	1	2	1	2	1	1	2	...
Uzbekistan Ouzbékistan	0	1	1	0	0	2	1	2	1	3
Viet Nam Viet Nam	...	...	106	118	201	390	688	953	970	1164
Yemen Yémen	1	3	4	3	11	60	40	34	...	...
Europe • Europe										
Albania Albanie	0	0	0	2	5	1	2	1	0	4
Austria Autriche	674	199	204	188	214	142	130	111	89	84
Belarus Bélarus	3	5	2	2	3	0	2	4	5	0
Belgium Belgique	1049	250	224	237	237	219	136	165	98	105
Bosnia & Herzegovina Bosnie–Herzégovine	11	1	1	2	5	3	5	3	2	2
Bulgaria Bulgarie	12	6	6	10	1	10	8	3	11	16
Croatia Croatie	42	8	10	17	15	17	17	12	15	18
Czech Republic République tchèque	23	9	15	12	13	18	21	8	16	13
Denmark Danemark	925	194	236	249	229	161	108	71	73	60
Estonia Estonie	0	1	1	1	4	7	3	4	2	3
Finland Finlande	96	23	24	46	37	25	17	20	10	16

12 C. Reported AIDS cases [*cont.*] • Cas de SIDA déclarés [*suite*]

Country or area Pays ou zone	Total reported cases to 1991 Nombre total de cas déclarés jusqu' au 1991	New cases reported in:/ Nombre de cas nouveaux déclarés en:								
		1992	1993	1994	1995	1996	1997	1998	1999	2000
France France	17709	5141	5582	5797	5483	4837	2835	2098	1785	1772
Germany Allemagne	6809	1635	1846	1862	1783	1630	1416	943	578	1474
Greece Grèce	544	149	160	123	310	212	239	146	137	143
Hungary Hongrie	81	33	32	23	31	46	31	36	37	27
Iceland Islande	21	4	6	4	3	3	2	2	5	1
Ireland Irlande	238	69	74	62	53	78	30	41	41	21
Italy Italie	10670	4147	4532	5440	6062	5376	3782	2483	2201	1903
Latvia Lettonie	3	1	3	2	0	8	3	11	17	24
Lithuania Lituanie	3	1	0	2	1	3	3	8	7	8
Luxembourg Luxembourg	45	12	20	13	15	12	10	10	5	10
Malta Malte	22	4	3	5	3	4	2	4	1	3
Monaco Monaco	7	10	7	9	4	2	1	0	0	0
Netherlands Pays–Bas	1943	533	435	461	468	448	342	291	234	192
Norway Norvège	262	50	64	74	67	56	34	36	23	38
Poland Pologne	85	40	42	94	120	96	117	132	113	109
Portugal Portugal	831	383	465	609	692	896	893	873	1011	1125
Republic of Moldova République de Moldova	2	0	2	0	2	1	10	4	5	4
Romania Roumanie	...	...	400	484	608	719	701	583	359	631
Russian Federation Fédération de Russie	54	54	21	27	39	57	13	94	39	50
San Marino Saint–Marin	0	0	0	0	0	4	4	4	2	1
Slovakia Slovaquie	3	1	3	4	2	0	5	3	2	4
Slovenia Slovénie	19	4	7	6	14	10	1	14	9	7
Spain Espagne	11254	5272	5472	7066	6754	6930	6058	4192	3458	2958
Sweden Suède	645	126	176	181	198	156	77	63	74	54
Switzerland Suisse	2220	643	672	711	736	543	565	423	262	257
TFYR of Macedonia L'ex–R.y. Macédonie	3	4	5	8	5	2	1	3	5	4
Ukraine Ukraine	8	4	10	10	37	159	193	287	580	648
United Kingdom Royaume–Uni	5413	1470	1601	1770	1571	1854	1378	963	790	737
Yugoslavia Yougoslavie	174	87	54	101	99	92	56	114	57	66
Oceania • Océanie										
American Samoa Samoa américaines	0	0	0	0	0	0	0	0	0	1
Australia Australie	3429	788	844	954	805	658	371	301	181	212
Cook Islands Iles Cook	0	0	0	0	0	0	0	0	0	0

12 C. Reported AIDS cases [*cont.*] · Cas de SIDA déclarés [*suite*]

Country or area / Pays ou zone	Total reported cases to 1991 Nombre total de cas déclarés jusqu' au 1991	New cases reported in:/ Nombre de cas nouveaux déclarés en:								
		1992	1993	1994	1995	1996	1997	1998	1999	2000
Fiji Fidji	4	1	1	2	0	0	0	0	4	3
French Polynesia Polynésie française	52	3	5	1	4	2	2	2	1	0
Guam Guam	12	2	5	11	2	10	5	7	8	2
Kiribati Kiribati	2	0	0	0	0	2	2	4	5	2
Marshall Islands Iles Marshall	2	...	0		...	0	...	0	0	0
Micronesia, Federated States of Micronésie, Etats fédérés de	2	0	0	0	0	0	0	0	1	0
New Caledonia Nouvelle – Calédonie	32	1	10	9	5	2	9	3	4	5
New Zealand Nouvelle – Zélande	325	50	70	44	49	76	43	29	33	27
Niue Nioué	0	0	0	0	0	0	0	0	0	0
Northern Mariana Islands Iles Mariannes du Nord	...	0	0	0	0	0	0	5	2	3
Palau Palaos	...	...	...	...	0	0	0	0	0	0
Papua New Guinea Papouasie – Nvl – Guinée	55	19	12	26	44	69	120	220	207	0
Samoa Samoa	1	0	0	2	1	2	0	0	0	0
Solomon Islands Iles Salomon	...	...	...	...	...	...	...	...	0	0
Tokelau Tokélaou	...	...	...	...	...	...	...	...	0	0
Tonga Tonga	2	0	1	2	0	2	0	1	1	0
Wallis and Futuna Islands Iles Wallis – et – Futuna	...	...	1	...	...	...	0	0	0	0

Source:
Joint United Nations Programme on HIV/AIDS (UNAIDS) and
World Health Organization (WHO), Geneva, "Aids epidemic
update: December 2001" and the UNAIDS/WHO HIV/AIDS
database.

Source:
Programme commun des Nations Unies sur le VIH/SIDA (ONUSIDA)
et l'Organisation mondiale de la santé (OMS), Genève, "Le point sur
l'épidémie de SIDA: décembre 2001" et la base de données sur le VIH
et le SIDA de l'ONUSIDA/OMS.

† For information on recent changes in country or area
  nomenclature pertaining to former Czechoslovakia, Germany,
  Hong Kong Special Administrative Region (SAR) of China,
  Macao Special Administrative Region (SAR) of China,
  SFR of Yugoslavia and the former USSR, see Annex I –
  Country or area nomenclature, regional and other groupings.

†† For statistical purposes, the data for China do not
  include those for the Hong Kong Special Administrative
  Region (Hong Kong SAR), Macao Special Administrative
  Region (Macao SAR) and Taiwan province of China.

1 Total includes AIDS cases with unreported year of diagnosis.

† Pour les modifications récentes de nomenclature de pays ou de zone
  concernant l'Allemagne, Hong Kong région administrative spéciale (RAS)
  de Chine), Macao région administrative spéciale (RAS) de Chine,
  l'ex – Tchécoslovaquie, l'ex – URSS et l'ex – Rfs de Yougoslavie, voir
  annex I – Nomenclature des pays ou des zones, groupements régionaux et
  autres groupements.

†† Les données statistiques relatives à la Chine ne comprennent pas
  celles qui concernent la région administrative spéciale de
  Hong Kong (la RAS de Hong Kong), la région administrative spéciale
  de Macao (la RAS de Macao) et la province chinoise de Taiwan.

1 Y compris les cas de SIDA pour lesquels l'année de diagnostic n'a pas
  été précisée.

13
Food Supply
Disponibilités alimentaires
Calories, protein and fat: per capita per day
Calories, protéine et lipides : par habitant, par jour

Country or area	Calories (number) Calories (nombre)			Protein (grams) Protéine (grammes)			Fat (grams) Lipides (grammes)		
Pays ou zone	1985−87	1987−89	1997−99	1985−87	1987−89	1997−99	1985−87	1987−89	1997−99
World **Monde**	**2274.0**	**2286.9**	**2616.6**	**62.2**	**62.5**	**71.9**	**63.5**	**64.4**	**75.0**
Africa · Afrique									
Algeria Algérie	2742.0	2833.4	2933.5	74.1	76.6	80.4	59.8	65.3	70.8
Angola Angola	1794.1	1744.6	1878.6	46.0	43.0	39.6	41.9	44.2	37.5
Benin Bénin	2060.1	2110.9	2498.4	51.4	52.2	59.6	44.4	40.6	41.1
Botswana Botswana	2361.2	2383.8	2278.0	72.6	72.4	70.5	48.8	56.5	59.5
Burkino Faso Burkina Faso	2066.0	2202.8	2292.6	61.3	65.6	66.9	45.8	45.6	49.7
Burundi Burundi	1968.5	1888.5	1660.1	62.3	57.5	49.2	14.8	14.1	11.0
Cameroon Cameroun	2201.3	2145.3	2259.4	51.7	51.4	53.7	45.7	45.3	45.5
Cape Verde Cap−Vert	2951.2	2983.2	3155.5	73.5	76.1	72.3	63.7	70.9	93.6
Central African Rep. Rép. centrafricaine	1889.4	1897.5	1968.4	36.8	38.1	42.1	59.0	63.1	60.8
Chad Tchad	1683.5	1676.9	2139.3	49.2	49.4	66.2	39.3	40.4	68.1
Comoros Comores	1788.7	1848.3	1811.3	39.1	41.0	42.6	35.8	36.6	41.6
Congo Congo	2323.4	2295.8	2173.0	47.6	46.4	44.2	54.5	55.4	48.7
Côte d'Ivoire Côte d'Ivoire	2607.1	2541.4	2566.0	53.4	53.1	49.0	50.0	49.0	51.3
Dem. Rep. of the Congo Rép. dém. du Congo	2137.9	2135.2	1713.1	35.0	34.2	27.3	32.5	33.4	24.9
Djibouti Djibouti	1908.7	1917.9	2102.6	46.5	50.3	45.0	46.6	43.5	60.4
Egypt Egypte	3082.6	3113.5	3316.8	80.1	81.8	91.7	63.8	62.0	56.0
Eritrea Erythrée	...	...	1709.0	...	...	54.7	...	...	22.5
Ethiopia Ethiopie	...	...	1808.9	...	...	52.7	...	...	22.2
Ethiopia including Eritrea Ethiopie y compris Erythrée	1704.0	1713.6	...	49.9	49.4	...	25.0	24.2	...
Gabon Gabon	2517.3	2490.7	2517.0	76.8	73.2	71.1	43.9	48.2	55.0
Gambia Gambie	2431.1	2439.6	2573.9	54.4	52.7	52.2	49.2	52.0	70.1
Ghana Ghana	1955.5	2011.0	2545.7	43.6	44.7	50.5	38.0	38.9	36.6
Guinea Guinée	1982.1	1920.0	2198.0	44.9	44.3	47.1	41.9	38.9	52.5
Guinea−Bissau Guinée−Bissau	2473.3	2428.2	2301.6	49.5	49.6	46.2	70.4	60.1	59.5
Kenya Kenya	2110.7	1992.9	1933.8	56.4	54.0	50.6	41.3	42.4	45.9
Lesotho Lesotho	2284.4	2259.6	2308.5	65.5	64.1	64.4	35.6	36.1	32.9
Liberia Libéria	2473.1	2524.7	2083.7	47.9	48.2	38.0	53.1	43.9	58.2
Libyan Arab Jamahirya Jamah. arabe libyenne	3302.8	3304.9	3290.7	82.3	82.6	83.4	100.9	106.3	99.7
Madagascar Madagascar	2282.8	2163.5	2004.4	54.4	51.7	47.2	31.6	31.2	30.5
Malawi Malawi	2046.6	1985.4	2115.2	58.7	56.3	53.7	31.7	28.6	27.6

13
Food Supply
Calories, protein and fat: per capita per day [cont.]
Disponibilités alimentaires
Calories, protéine et lipides : par habitant, par jour [suite]

Country or area Pays ou zone	Calories (number) Calories (nombre)			Protein (grams) Protéine (grammes)			Fat (grams) Lipides (grammes)		
	1985–87	1987–89	1997–99	1985–87	1987–89	1997–99	1985–87	1987–89	1997–99
Mali Mali	2217.3	2303.6	2237.7	62.7	64.5	65.6	43.9	48.8	45.6
Mauritania Mauritanie	2502.2	2551.5	2689.7	79.2	79.1	75.3	63.3	64.1	65.0
Mauritius Maurice	2729.0	2751.9	2951.0	62.3	65.4	74.9	68.9	68.3	86.1
Morocco Maroc	2954.0	3016.9	3030.5	79.8	82.9	80.9	57.3	59.4	58.8
Mozambique Mozambique	1792.4	1798.8	1923.2	33.3	32.9	37.7	35.1	38.9	35.2
Namibia Namibie	2263.9	2223.3	2091.4	64.8	63.2	56.6	37.3	37.4	35.3
Niger Niger	2048.5	2062.9	2007.9	55.4	57.2	56.2	31.2	30.3	33.9
Nigeria Nigéria	2129.6	2224.1	2813.1	50.1	52.8	62.6	53.6	53.5	67.9
Rwanda Rwanda	2204.5	2026.7	2020.5	54.1	48.5	47.0	17.1	15.9	22.2
Sao Tome and Principe Sao Tomé–et–Principe	2116.8	2178.5	2198.7	44.6	46.8	44.2	87.2	91.8	72.8
Senegal Sénégal	2324.8	2157.1	2283.6	70.8	68.5	64.1	58.9	48.6	72.0
Seychelles Seychelles	2282.4	2325.0	2415.5	65.2	66.0	77.4	47.9	49.8	71.4
Sierra Leone Sierra Leone	2029.1	1973.7	2079.9	42.7	41.5	46.4	59.8	58.6	52.5
Somalia Somalie	1942.1	1902.6	1553.9	62.2	62.2	49.8	69.4	67.3	55.7
South Africa Afrique du Sud	2871.6	2871.6	2837.5	74.1	74.5	71.4	72.1	71.5	71.2
Sudan Soudan	2166.6	2173.0	2365.8	64.0	64.9	74.9	65.2	62.1	73.5
Swaziland Swaziland	2548.3	2584.7	2549.7	63.6	65.3	64.4	43.5	49.6	56.7
Togo Togo	2115.5	2153.5	2511.4	50.4	52.2	60.3	33.9	41.3	42.9
Tunisia Tunisie	3060.3	3117.1	3341.3	84.7	84.9	90.6	80.8	83.3	94.7
Uganda Ouganda	2091.0	2202.7	2183.9	47.3	50.3	48.3	23.4	25.9	29.7
United Rep. of Tanzania Rép. Unie de Tanzanie	2245.4	2223.9	1926.1	55.7	55.7	46.7	31.2	32.0	30.7
Zambia Zambie	2037.0	2040.5	1936.4	52.9	52.4	48.7	29.7	29.8	28.9
Zimbabwe Zimbabwe	2114.2	2134.7	2084.5	52.4	53.7	49.1	47.2	49.8	49.4
America, North · Amérique du Nord									
Antigua and Barbuda Antigua et Barbuda	2303.6	2381.4	2415.7	82.1	84.3	81.1	90.4	96.5	85.3
Bahamas Bahamas	2737.9	2792.8	2518.5	81.8	82.7	78.0	92.7	95.2	77.1
Barbados Barbade	3122.7	3197.3	3139.6	95.2	97.8	88.9	101.2	106.8	104.7
Belize Belize	2542.1	2568.5	2897.9	68.0	68.1	65.5	73.6	73.6	72.7
Bermuda Bermudes	3133.5	3031.3	2941.9	107.7	106.5	92.0	132.0	127.0	123.8
Canada Canada	3066.1	3036.0	3145.1	95.2	95.6	100.2	130.2	129.4	124.5
Costa Rica Costa Rica	2695.1	2729.0	2767.1	65.0	66.2	71.8	65.9	66.9	72.9
Cuba Cuba	3089.2	3062.8	2452.5	73.5	72.3	55.6	82.5	81.9	47.1
Dominica Dominique	2764.2	2938.2	2998.5	69.3	74.0	81.2	74.6	81.7	79.3

13

Food Supply
Calories, protein and fat: per capita per day [*cont.*]
Disponibilités alimentaires
Calories, protéine et lipides : par habitant, par jour [*suite*]

Country or area	Calories (number) Calories (nombre)			Protein (grams) Protéine (grammes)			Fat (grams) Lipides (grammes)		
Pays ou zone	1985−87	1987−89	1997−99	1985−87	1987−89	1997−99	1985−87	1987−89	1997−99
Dominican Republic Rép. dominicaine	2374.1	2304.9	2322.1	50.5	50.9	50.8	56.0	59.9	78.9
El Salvador El Salvador	2337.8	2360.6	2493.1	55.3	56.2	61.1	51.7	53.6	55.3
Grenada Grenade	2438.4	2610.0	2686.9	69.4	70.3	66.6	83.5	90.9	93.8
Guatemala Guatemala	2336.7	2396.3	2229.0	60.0	62.3	57.4	41.4	42.2	46.5
Haiti Haïti	1918.8	1788.6	1925.8	48.9	46.8	43.3	35.4	28.8	35.9
Honduras Honduras	2186.9	2259.2	2366.9	51.7	53.4	57.5	53.9	57.9	64.8
Jamaica Jamaïque	2592.9	2620.9	2739.6	63.3	64.6	67.6	66.2	67.0	76.5
Mexico Mexique	3139.7	3085.0	3148.2	83.1	80.6	86.1	84.9	82.7	89.8
Netherlands Antilles Antilles néerlandaises	2649.5	2608.4	2620.7	83.0	83.8	81.6	95.3	89.9	100.1
Nicaragua Nicaragua	2356.7	2290.9	2233.6	57.9	55.8	55.8	43.3	43.4	48.0
Panama Panama	2484.1	2282.3	2463.7	64.0	59.5	64.8	71.0	62.9	73.0
Saint Kitts and Nevis Saint−Kitts−et−Nevis	2518.1	2620.3	2674.3	65.9	69.2	74.2	84.4	89.0	82.0
Saint Lucia Sainte−Lucie	2555.5	2606.7	2829.2	73.5	78.4	83.9	65.7	60.2	72.7
St. Vincent and the Grenadines St. Vincent−et−Grenadines	2473.2	2432.5	2527.8	59.5	60.6	64.6	65.1	66.2	77.3
Trinidad and Tobago Trinité−et−Tobago	2960.6	2828.7	2696.3	77.5	68.3	63.0	84.5	76.0	72.3
United States Etats−Unis	3379.2	3435.1	3711.0	105.2	106.6	113.3	139.7	139.3	145.0
America, South · Amérique du Sud									
Argentina Argentine	3113.2	3027.3	3165.5	101.0	98.0	101.8	110.6	107.2	113.8
Bolivia Bolivie	2132.5	2153.9	2222.6	56.1	55.8	56.3	46.9	49.4	63.9
Brazil Brésil	2705.7	2769.0	2971.3	65.7	67.1	78.0	70.2	76.9	88.2
Chile Chili	2499.9	2491.5	2855.6	66.0	67.2	78.4	55.9	56.9	85.4
Colombia Colombie	2279.5	2351.5	2577.8	49.5	51.5	60.7	50.8	53.6	66.5
Ecuador Equateur	2365.5	2499.3	2702.1	48.1	50.8	57.1	73.1	77.9	92.1
Guyana Guyana	2495.2	2455.5	2558.1	56.2	56.6	75.1	35.7	30.4	50.7
Paraguay Paraguay	2592.5	2546.3	2574.3	68.8	69.6	75.1	71.0	67.7	82.7
Peru Pérou	2215.9	2252.9	2550.5	55.2	55.6	64.7	48.6	48.3	48.2
Suriname Suriname	2488.3	2421.3	2611.1	61.8	60.7	64.7	47.8	46.1	66.7
Uruguay Uruguay	2622.2	2572.1	2843.6	80.2	80.3	92.9	89.9	90.8	98.5
Venezuela Venezuela	2563.6	2579.9	2280.6	63.4	63.7	60.1	78.0	76.9	60.1
Asia · Asie									
Afghanistan Afghanistan	2062.6	2118.7	1800.7	57.1	59.0	54.9	38.0	38.3	37.2
Armenia Arménie	...	...	2158.4	...	...	61.6	...	...	43.6
Azerbaijan Azerbaïdjan	...	...	2132.7	...	...	63.9	...	...	35.1

13
Food Supply
Calories, protein and fat: per capita per day [*cont.*]
Disponibilités alimentaires
Calories, protéine et lipides : par habitant, par jour [*suite*]

Country or area	Calories (number) Calories (nombre)			Protein (grams) Protéine (grammes)			Fat (grams) Lipides (grammes)		
Pays ou zone	1985−87	1987−89	1997−99	1985−87	1987−89	1997−99	1985−87	1987−89	1997−99
Bangladesh Bangladesh	2036.6	2060.2	2121.7	44.0	44.2	45.7	18.2	19.7	19.8
Brunei Darussalam Brunéi Darussalam	2811.6	2817.3	2755.2	82.5	83.3	75.8	67.4	75.0	65.8
Cambodia Cambodge	1697.6	1803.4	1974.3	41.0	43.1	44.3	18.8	20.0	28.8
China †† Chine ††	2617.9	2625.5	3037.2	62.2	63.3	82.4	43.4	46.5	77.5
China, Hong Kong SAR † Chine, Hong Kong RAS †	3132.6	3260.9	3187.6	92.1	93.3	102.9	115.9	131.3	131.7
China, Macao SAR † Chine, Macao RAS †	2606.4	2591.6	2569.6	74.9	71.5	68.3	97.7	100.4	116.0
Cyprus Chypre	3164.9	3092.5	3457.7	94.2	98.6	110.0	131.9	131.1	143.3
Georgia Géorgie	...	...	2402.5	...	...	68.4	...	...	42.4
India Inde	2224.0	2301.9	2434.0	54.6	56.5	58.6	37.1	39.4	46.6
Indonesia Indonésie	2446.4	2561.6	2902.7	52.9	55.5	64.2	44.2	48.4	57.4
Iran (Islamic Republic of) Iran (Rép. islamique d')	2770.8	2797.0	2928.2	72.0	73.6	77.6	60.9	58.8	61.1
Iraq Iraq	3472.3	3504.0	2416.3	88.9	89.0	52.3	79.5	81.1	68.6
Israel Israël	3374.5	3418.4	3560.9	108.4	111.1	114.7	119.7	121.9	131.2
Japan Japon	2787.6	2828.9	2778.5	91.7	94.3	92.3	76.3	78.5	81.9
Jordan Jordanie	2732.7	2754.9	2811.7	76.1	74.4	73.9	71.1	70.3	83.0
Kazakhstan Kazakhstan	...	...	2608.4	...	...	83.9	...	...	61.3
Korea, Dem. People's Rep. Corée, Rép. pop. dém. de	2560.2	2557.8	2082.5	80.9	82.1	60.8	43.4	45.5	33.3
Korea, Republic of Corée, République de	2955.0	3033.1	3051.1	79.5	81.8	86.2	44.3	48.7	70.8
Kuwait Koweït	3014.7	3030.4	3138.8	91.1	90.4	98.0	96.3	98.1	95.0
Kyrgyzstan Kirghizistan	...	...	2732.4	...	...	89.5	...	...	53.1
Lao People's Democratic Rep. Rép. dém. populaire lao	2076.0	2057.0	2148.9	50.4	49.6	53.7	21.5	21.8	26.5
Lebanon Liban	3008.9	3085.1	3230.9	78.7	77.8	83.1	90.9	93.8	102.9
Malaysia Malaisie	2589.5	2634.1	2924.7	58.3	59.6	75.3	86.6	90.4	87.5
Maldives Maldives	2250.2	2290.8	2365.9	83.9	84.1	90.6	39.4	44.5	49.0
Mongolia Mongolie	2269.5	2249.9	2004.0	74.5	73.6	75.2	76.0	75.1	73.4
Myanmar Myanmar	2718.1	2681.6	2787.5	69.4	68.2	70.6	46.6	44.5	46.0
Nepal Népal	2109.1	2330.7	2292.9	55.2	60.4	59.8	28.0	30.7	30.9
Pakistan Pakistan	2197.1	2247.2	2477.8	54.0	55.0	63.5	49.5	54.4	65.3
Philippines Philippines	2183.1	2251.5	2331.6	50.2	52.6	55.4	32.3	37.2	45.2
Saudi Arabia Arabie saoudite	2657.1	2687.5	2957.2	75.6	75.4	82.1	79.6	80.8	80.9
Sri Lanka Sri Lanka	2328.5	2265.4	2350.9	48.1	48.1	52.6	43.6	43.2	46.2
Syrian Arab Republic Rép. arabe syrienne	3228.1	3184.7	3328.0	87.4	85.6	84.9	85.4	84.8	95.9
Tajikistan Tadjikistan	...	...	1975.2	...	...	49.9	...	...	42.0

13

Food Supply
Calories, protein and fat: per capita per day [*cont.*]
Disponibilités alimentaires
Calories, protéine et lipides : par habitant, par jour [*suite*]

Country or area Pays ou zone	Calories (number) Calories (nombre)			Protein (grams) Protéine (grammes)			Fat (grams) Lipides (grammes)		
	1985−87	1987−89	1997−99	1985−87	1987−89	1997−99	1985−87	1987−89	1997−99
Thailand Thaïlande	2186.7	2222.6	2413.5	49.2	49.0	54.6	39.3	41.5	49.0
Turkey Turquie	3466.3	3529.9	3486.9	102.1	101.0	97.0	86.9	94.3	98.0
Turkmenistan Turkménistan	...	...	2658.6	...	...	75.5	...	...	73.0
United Arab Emirates Emirats arabes unis	3045.8	3029.4	3165.6	98.2	96.1	100.0	97.0	93.3	100.9
Uzbekistan Ouzbékistan	...	...	2912.2	...	...	82.8	...	...	73.2
Viet Nam Viet Nam	2272.4	2208.6	2502.4	50.7	50.0	58.5	25.8	26.6	38.2
Yemen Yémen	2075.7	2165.8	2040.1	58.0	60.2	55.2	37.3	37.4	38.7
Europe • Europe									
Albania Albanie	2638.9	2616.9	2682.7	78.2	77.9	89.8	59.4	61.8	80.4
Austria Autriche	3398.5	3426.2	3640.6	97.2	98.8	106.8	154.0	152.8	158.0
Belarus Bélarus	...	...	3206.3	...	...	91.7	...	...	98.7
Belgium−Luxembourg Belgique−Luxembourg	3441.4	3502.7	3625.1	102.5	102.5	102.8	151.7	156.4	159.2
Bosnia and Herzegovina Bosnie−Herzégovine	...	...	2932.7	...	...	83.4	...	...	51.3
Bulgaria Bulgarie	3650.9	3696.5	2795.9	108.5	111.3	86.4	119.9	122.8	96.6
Croatia Croatie	...	...	2539.1	...	...	63.1	...	...	72.5
Czech Republic République tchèque	...	...	3242.0	...	...	95.3	...	...	114.4
Czechoslovakia (former) † Tchécoslovaquie (anc.) †	3470.1	3564.9	...	102.6	106.1	...	132.0	135.9	...
Denmark Danemark	3171.5	3214.5	3374.4	98.9	102.6	103.5	128.4	133.1	131.7
Estonia Estonie	...	...	3075.6	...	...	98.9	...	...	95.8
Finland Finlande	2955.6	3082.9	3138.1	93.3	98.0	101.5	124.6	125.8	128.2
France France	3499.1	3551.9	3556.1	115.8	115.9	115.4	156.5	162.4	164.7
Germany Allemagne	3467.2	3481.3	3374.4	100.9	101.4	94.8	140.4	141.7	147.5
Greece Grèce	3448.5	3559.5	3655.7	108.1	110.5	117.8	136.2	140.1	152.1
Hungary Hongrie	3654.6	3733.5	3414.6	105.2	106.2	88.5	146.7	153.0	138.5
Iceland Islande	3220.9	3156.8	3259.3	127.8	118.1	114.2	133.8	126.0	133.1
Ireland Irlande	3634.1	3619.4	3618.2	115.8	116.9	112.0	142.8	141.9	135.1
Italy Italie	3486.2	3544.0	3591.7	107.0	108.4	111.6	142.9	148.2	150.9
Latvia Lettonie	...	...	2930.0	...	...	79.0	...	...	92.4
Lithuania Lituanie	...	...	3012.6	...	...	92.4	...	...	78.3
Malta Malte	3113.0	3232.2	3475.3	95.5	99.1	111.9	111.9	114.3	112.6
Netherlands Pays−Bas	3079.7	3162.0	3233.7	94.4	94.6	105.4	130.8	135.2	140.1
Norway Norvège	3244.9	3203.7	3386.2	101.3	99.5	103.5	137.4	132.9	138.8
Poland Pologne	3427.4	3484.3	3342.9	103.8	105.2	98.9	115.3	117.7	111.9

13
Food Supply
Calories, protein and fat: per capita per day [*cont.*]
Disponibilités alimentaires
Calories, protéine et lipides : par habitant, par jour [*suite*]

Country or area	Calories (number) Calories (nombre)			Protein (grams) Protéine (grammes)			Fat (grams) Lipides (grammes)		
Pays ou zone	1985−87	1987−89	1997−99	1985−87	1987−89	1997−99	1985−87	1987−89	1997−99
Portugal									
Portugal	3194.4	3365.5	3681.0	93.0	98.7	117.0	100.5	110.4	132.2
Republic of Moldova									
République de Moldova	...	...	2718.8	...	...	63.2	...	...	55.0
Romania									
Roumanie	2988.8	2943.1	3258.1	92.8	91.1	101.8	90.2	86.7	86.5
Russian Federation									
Fédération de Russie	...	...	2861.6	...	...	87.7	...	...	75.7
Slovakia									
Slovaquie	...	...	3078.4	...	...	81.2	...	...	115.7
Slovenia									
Slovénie	...	...	3018.6	...	...	100.2	...	...	112.3
Spain									
Espagne	3110.6	3192.2	3330.8	99.2	102.2	109.5	125.2	132.9	148.9
Sweden									
Suède	2947.6	2944.3	3084.9	95.4	95.3	99.1	122.9	123.0	127.4
Switzerland									
Suisse	3353.6	3345.6	3279.0	95.6	94.7	90.1	153.6	152.6	146.5
TFYR of Macedonia									
L'ex−R.y. Macédoine	...	...	2857.8	...	...	72.7	...	...	78.3
Ukraine									
Ukraine	...	...	2828.7	...	...	79.9	...	...	73.4
United Kingdom									
Royaume−Uni	3200.0	3212.8	3272.8	92.0	91.1	95.9	137.3	136.3	142.8
Yugoslavia									
Yougoslavie	...	...	2910.2	...	...	84.9	...	...	119.3
Yugoslavia, SFR †									
Yougoslavie, Rfs †	3660.0	3644.0		103.2	102.3	...	114.3	117.2	...
USSR (former) †									
URSS (anc.) †	3376.8	3378.5		106.0	106.4	...	101.8	104.9	...
Oceania · Océanie									
Australia									
Australie	3153.6	3183.5	3140.7	108.4	109.3	105.4	124.1	128.1	128.8
Fiji									
Fidji	2599.2	2608.3	2919.6	64.0	66.1	72.9	85.1	92.6	103.6
French Polynesia									
Polynésie française	2798.9	2821.6	2937.5	80.0	82.3	97.7	102.0	102.0	111.2
Kiribati									
Kiribati	2490.4	2502.4	2942.8	61.3	63.0	70.7	92.0	90.5	102.3
New Caledonia									
Nouvelle−Calédonie	2872.0	2833.5	2784.9	79.3	77.1	82.3	105.2	101.9	112.7
New Zealand									
Nouvelle−Zélande	3146.7	3143.8	3130.3	98.6	96.4	97.8	126.8	126.1	114.2
Papua New Guinea									
Papouasie−Nvl−Guinée	2223.6	2200.0	2179.3	48.2	47.6	45.5	42.1	42.4	42.4
Solomon Islands									
Iles Salomon	2239.9	2159.6	2218.6	56.9	56.3	50.9	46.5	44.5	40.7
Vanuatu									
Vanuatu	2748.6	2727.9	2750.3	64.5	61.2	59.3	102.1	101.0	88.4

Source:
Food and Agriculture Organization of the United Nations (FAO), Rome,
FAOSTAT Nutrition database.

Source:
Organisation des Nations Unies pour l'alimentation et l'agriculture
(FAO), Rome, les données alimentaires de FAOSTAT.

† For information on the recent changes in country or area nomenclature
pertaining to former Czechoslovakia, Germany, Hong Kong Special
Administrative Region (SAR) of China, Macao Special Administrative
Region (SAR) of China, SFR of Yugoslavia and the former USSR, see
see Annex I − Country or area nomenclature, regional and other groupings.

† Pour les modifications récentes de nomenclature de pays ou de
zone concernant l'Allemagne, Hong Kong, région administrative
spéciale (RAS) de Chine, Macao, région administrative spéciale
(RAS) de Chine, l'ex−Tchécoslovaquie, l'ex−URSS et l'ex−Rfs de
Yougoslavie, voir annexe I − Nomenclature des pays ou des zones,
groupements régionaux et autres groupements.

†† For statistical purposes, the data for China do not include
those for Hong Kong Special Administrative Region
(Hong Kong SAR) and Macao Special Administrative Region
(Macao SAR).

†† Les données statistiques relatives à la Chine ne comprennent
pas celles qui concernent la région administrative spéciale de
Hong Kong (la RAS de Hong Kong) et la région administrative
spéciale de Macao (la RAS de Macao).

Technical notes, tables 11-13

Table 11: "Life expectancy at birth", "Infant mortality rate" and "Total fertility rate" are taken from the estimates and projections prepared by the Population Division of the United Nations Secretariat, published in *World Population Prospects: The 2000 Revision* [29].

"Life expectancy at birth" is an overall estimate of the expected average number of years to be lived by a female or male newborn. Many developing countries lack complete and reliable statistics of births and deaths based on civil registration, so various estimation techniques are used to calculate life expectancy using other sources of data, mainly population censuses and demographic surveys. Life expectancy at birth by sex gives a statistical summary of current differences in male and female mortality across all ages. However, trends and differentials in infant and child mortality rates are the predominant influence on trends and differentials in life expectancy at birth in most developing countries. Thus, life expectancy at birth is of limited usefulness in these countries in assessing levels and differentials in male and female mortality at other ages.

"Infant mortality rate" is the total number of deaths in a given year of children less than one year old divided by the total number of live births in the same year, multiplied by 1,000. It is an approximation of the number of deaths per 1,000 children born alive who die within one year of birth. In most developing countries where civil registration data are deficient, the most reliable sources are demographic surveys of households. Where these are not available, other sources and general estimates are made which are necessarily of limited reliability. Where countries lack comprehensive and accurate systems of civil registration, infant mortality statistics by sex are difficult to collect or to estimate with any degree of reliability because of reporting biases, and thus are not shown here.

"Total fertility rate" is the average number of children that would be born alive to a hypothetical cohort of women if, throughout their reproductive years, the age-specific fertility rates for the specified year remained unchanged.

"Child mortality rate" is defined as the annual number of deaths among children aged 1-4 years per 1,000 population of the same age. These series have been compiled by the Statistics Division of the United Nations Secretariat for the *Demographic Yearbook* [22] and are subject to the limitations of national reporting in this field.

Data on maternal mortality are estimated by the World Health Organization and the United Nations Educational, Scientific and Cultural Organization and published in *Revised 1990 Estimates of Maternal Mortality*

Notes techniques, tableaux 11 à 13

Tableau 11: L'"espérance de vie à la naissance", le "taux de mortalité infantile" et le "taux de fécondité" sont proviennent des estimations et projections de la Division de la population du Secrétariat de l'ONU, qui ont publiées dans *World Population Prospects: The 2000 Revision* [29].

L'"espérance de vie à la naissance" est une estimation globale du nombre d'années qu'un nouveau-né de sexe masculin ou féminin vivant, peut s'attendre à vivre. Comme dans beaucoup de pays en développement, les registres d'état civil ne permettent pas d'établir des statistiques fiables et complètes des naissances et des décès, diverses techniques d'estimation ont été utilisées pour calculer l'espérance de vie à partir d'autres sources et notamment des recensements et enquêtes démographiques. Sur la base des statistiques de l'espérance de vie par sexe, on peut calculer la différence entre la longévité des hommes et celle des femmes à tous les âges. Cependant, ce sont les tendances et les écarts des taux de mortalité infantile et juvénile qui influent de façon prépondérante sur les tendances et les écarts de l'espérance de vie à la naissance dans la plupart des pays en développement. Ainsi, l'espérance de vie à la naissance ne revêt qu'une utilité limitée dans ce pays pour évaluer les niveaux et les écarts de la mortalité des femmes et des hommes à des âges plus avancés.

Le "taux de mortalité infantile" correspond au nombre total de décès au cours d'une année donnée des enfants de moins de 5 ans divisé par le nombre total de naissances vivantes au cours de la même année, multiplié par 1 000. Il s'agit d'une approximation du nombre de décès pour 1 000 enfants nés vivants qui meurent la première année. Dans la plupart des pays en développement, où les données d'état civil sont déficientes, les sources les plus fiables sont les enquêtes démographiques auprès des ménages. Lorsque de telles enquêtes ne sont pas réalisées, d'autres sources sont utilisées et des estimations générales sont réalisées qui sont nécessairement d'une fiabilité limitée. Lorsqu'il n☐' a pas dans les pays de systèmes complets et exacts d'enregistrement des faits d'état civil, les statistiques de la mortalité infantile par sexe sont difficiles à rassembler ou à estimer avec quelque fiabilité que ce soit en raison des distorsions de la notification; elles ne sont donc pas indiquées ici.

Le "taux de fécondité" est le nombre moyen d'enfants que mettrait au monde une cohorte hypothétique de femmes si, pendant toutes leurs années d'âge reproductif, les taux de fécondité par âge de l'année en question restaient inchangés.

Le "taux de mortalité juvénile" est par définition le nombre de décès d'enfants âgés de 1 à 4 ans pour 1 000

[35]. The revised 1990 estimates were developed using a dual strategy: existing national maternal mortality estimates were adjusted to account for under-reporting and misclassification; and a simple model was developed to predict values for countries with no data. The model uses two widely available independent variables - general fertility rates and proportion of births that are assisted by a trained person - to predict maternal mortality. A detailed description of the methodology used is found in *Modelling maternal mortality in the developing world* [41].

Table 12: Data on acquired immunodeficiency syndrome (AIDS) have been compiled and estimated by the Joint United Nations Programme on HIV/AIDS (UNAIDS) and the World Health Organization (WHO). UNAIDS is composed of the United Nations Children's Fund, the United Nations Development Programme, the United Nations Population Fund, the United Nations International Drug Control Programme, the United Nations Educational, Scientific and Cultural Organization, the World Health Organization and the World Bank. Data are published in the *AIDS epidemic update* [33].

Table 13: Estimates on food supply are published by the Food and Agriculture Organization of the United Nations in *Food Balance Sheets* [5], in which the data give estimates of total and per caput food supplies per day available for human consumption during the reference period in terms of quantity and, by applying appropriate food composition factors for all primary and processed products, also in terms of caloric value and protein and fat content. Calorie supplies are reported in kilocalories. The traditional unit of calories is being retained for the time being until the proposed kilojoule gains wider acceptance and understanding (1 calorie = 4.19 kilojoules). Per caput supplies in terms of product weight are derived from the total supplies available for human consumption (i.e. Food) by dividing the quantities of Food by the total population actually partaking of the food supplies during the reference period, i.e. the present in-area (de facto) population within the present geographical boundaries of the country. In other words, nationals living abroad during the reference period are excluded, but foreigners living in the country are included. Adjustments are made wherever possible for part-time presence or absence, such as temporary migrants, tourists and refugees supported by special schemes (if it has not been possible to allow for the amounts provided by such schemes under imports). In almost all cases, the population figures used are the mid-year estimates published by the United Nations Population Division.

Per caput supply figures shown in the commodity balances therefore represent only the average supply available for the population as a whole and do not nec-

enfants de cet âge. Cette série a été compilée par la Division de statistique du Secrétariat de l'ONU pour l'*Annuaire démographique* [22] et les données qui sont incluses sont présentées sous réserve de mises en garde formulées à leur sujet.

Les données concernant la mortalité maternelle sont tirées des chiffres estimatifs de l'OMS et de l'UNICEF, publiés dans "*Revised 1990 Estimates of Maternal Mortality*" [35]. Les chiffres révisés de 1990 ont été calculés en combinant deux méthodes: d'une part on a ajusté les chiffres nationaux existants de mortalité maternelle pour tenir compte des déclarations lacunaires et des erreurs de classement; de l'autre, on a mis au point un modèle simple permettant de prédire les taux pour les pays où les données font défaut, à partir de deux variables indépendantes qui sont largement disponibles: les taux globaux de fécondité, et la proportion d'accouchements bénéficiant de l'aide d'une personne qualifiée. On trouvera cette méthode exposée en détail dans "*Modelling Maternal Mortality in the Developing World*" [41].

Tableau 12: Les données sur le syndrome d'immunodéficience acquise (SIDA) ont été compilées et estimées par le Programme commun des Nations Unies sur le VIH/SIDA (ONUSIDA) et l'Organisation mondiale de la santé (OMS). L'ONUSIDA se compose du Fonds des Nations Unies pour l'enfance, du Programme des Nations Unies pour le développement, du Fonds des Nations Unies pour la population, du Programme des Nations Unies pour le contrôle international des drogues, de l'Organisation des Nations pour l'éducation, la science et la culture, de l'Organisation mondiale de la santé et de la Banque mondiale. Les données sont publiées dans "*AIDS epidemic update*" [33].

Tableau 13: Les estimations sur les disponibilités alimentaires sont publiées par l'Organisation des Nations Unies pour l'alimentation et l'agriculture dans les *Bilans alimentaires* [5] où les données donnent des estimations des disponibilités alimentaires totales et par habitant par jour pour la consommation humaine durant la période de référence, en quantité, en calories, en protéines et en lipides. Les calories sont exprimées en kilocalories. L'unité traditionnelle pour les calories n'est pas utilisée pour l'instant jusqu'à ce que le kilojoule soit plus largement accepté (1 calorie = 4,19 kilojoules). Les disponibilités par habitant exprimées en poids du produit sont calculées à partir des disponibilités totales pour la consommation humaine (c'est-à-dire "Alimentation humaine") en divisant ce chiffre par la population totale qui a effectivement eu accès aux approvisionnements alimentaires durant la période de référence, c'est-à-dire par la population présente (de facto) dans les limites géographiques actuelles du pays. En d'autres termes, les ressortissants du pays vivant à l'étranger durant la

essarily indicate what is actually consumed by individuals. Even if they are taken as an approximation of per caput consumption, it is important to bear in mind that there could be considerable variation in consumption between individuals.

période de référence sont exclus, mais les étrangers vivant dans le pays sont inclus. Des ajustements ont été opérés chaque fois que possible pour tenir compte des présences ou des absences de durée limitée, comme dans le cas des imigrants/émigrants temporaires, des touristes et des réfugiés bénéficiant de programmes alimentaires spéciaux (s'il n'a pas été possible de tenir compte des vivres fournis à ce titre à travers les importations). Dans la plupart des cas, les données démographiques utilisés sont les estimations au milieu de l'année publiées par la Division de la population des Nations Unies.

Les disponibilités alimentaires par habitant figurant dans les bilans ne représentent donc que les disponibilités moyennes pour l'ensemble de la population et n'indiquent pas nécessairement la consommation effective des individus. Même si elles sont considérées comme une estimation approximative de la consommation par habitant, il importe de ne pas oublier que la consommation peut varier beaucoup selon les individus.

14
Book production: number of titles by UDC classes
Production de livres : nombre de titres classés d'après la CDU

Country or area Pays ou zone	Year Année	Total	Gener- alities Géné- ralités	Philo- sophy Philo- sophie	Reli- gion	Social sciences Sciences sociales	Philo- logy Philo- logie	Pure sciences Sciences pures	Applied sciences Sciences appli- quées	Arts Beaux arts	Litera- ture Litté- rature	Geogr/ History Géogr., histoire
Africa · Afrique												
Algeria	1994	323	22	21	9	97	4	42	14	10	72	32
Algérie	1996[1]	670	39	21	112	96	34	71	157	30	77	33
	1999	133	...	4	2	57	1	11	46	2	10	0
Angola	1985	47	...	...	...	1	...	...	...	...	46	...
Angola	1995	22	...	...	...	...	...	...	...	...	22	...
Benin[2]	1992[1]	647	10	4	...	534	7	12	77	...	...	3
Bénin[2]	1994	84	5	...	1	22	6	6	37	1	5	1
Botswana[2]	1980	97	...	...	...	67	...	6	19	2	...	3
Botswana[2]	1991	158	8	...	...	125	1	10	11	...	...	3
Burkina Faso[2]	1985	4	...	...	...	1	...	...	...	...	3	...
Burkina Faso[2]	1995	17	1	...	...	3	...	...	...	1	11	1
	1996[1]	12	1	...	...	1	...	...	1	...	9	...
Cameroon												
Cameroun	1999	13	...	...	4	...	...	...	2	...	7	...
Dem. Rep. of the Congo[2]												
Rép. dém. du Congo[2]	1992	64	...	1	30	27	...	...	5	...	...	1
Egypt	1993	3108	289	58	329	220	238	190	280	118	378	176
Egypte	1995	2215	92	66	307	180	226	206	331	140	515	152
	1999	1410	96	18	200	126	215	219	150	44	256	86
Eritrea												
Erythrée	1993	106	...	...	...	37	33	29	7	...	...	...
Ethiopia	1990	385	32	1	15	179	11	24	71	9	32	11
Ethiopie	1991	240	36	...	23	66	11	8	44	3	31	18
	1999	444	40	...	63	203	8	6	77	8	18	21
Gambia	1991[2]	21	...	...	...	15	...	...	5	...	...	1
Gambie	1994	21	...	...	4	5	4	6	1	...	...	1
	1996[3]	14	...	...	...	10	...	...	2	...	...	2
Ghana	1980	209	10	4	52	65	3	5	27	2	35	6
Ghana	1992	28	...	1	6	7	3	...	5	2	4	...
Kenya	1990	348	2	...	115	47	56	26	41	12	23	26
Kenya	1991[1]	239	7	...	84	48	26	13	34	1	19	7
	1994[1][2]	300	3	3	76	73	41	19	41	13	12	14
Libyan Arab Jamahiriya												
Jamahiriya arabe libyenne	1994	26	...	2	2	2	1	2	5	...	11	1
Madagascar	1994	114	...	6	37	29	6	6	11	...	11	8
Madagascar	1995	131	3	3	32	44	2	2	13	4	19	9
	1996	119	1	3	25	22	2	4	36	6	18	2
Malawi	1994	243	10	...	41	92	11	11	40	10	24	4
Malawi	1995	182	10	...	44	81	5	5	18	5	14	...
	1996[2][4]	117	...	...	1	76	14	10	5	3	...	8
Mali	1984[5]	160	...	...	...	98	19	17	23	...	...	3
Mali	1995[1][2]	14	1	...	...	1	...	...	1	...	11	...
Mauritius	1994	84	9	1	1	35	3	1	6	1	15	12
Maurice	1995	64	4	1	3	20	6	1	4	2	18	5
	1996	80	1	4	4	14	4	1	6	6	32	8
Morocco	1995	940	275	8	58	273	12	9	37	24	134	110
Maroc	1996	918	33	13	45	359	12	13	135	107	136	65
	2000	386	25	3	34	151	5	1	33	12	75	47
Namibia												
Namibie	1990	106	7	...	2	57	...	2	18	2	14	4
Niger[2]												
Niger[2]	1991	5	...	...	...	...	...	...	...	...	5	...
Nigeria	1992	1562	55	14	142	733	104	71	196	30	148	69
Nigéria	1994	1008	11	7	121	458	53	72	114	37	60	75
	1995	1314	18	36	203	530	91	80	116	52	133	55
Reunion	1980	99	...	...	5	23	...	12	16	10	24	9
Réunion	1985	73	1	...	6	15	2	2	12	4	18	13
	1992	69	1	...	...	20	...	4	5	12	14	13
South Africa	1994	4574	116	40	491	1034	315	363	911	189	907	208
Afrique du Sud	1995	5418	136	33	516	1262	566	330	1002	156	1227	190
	1999	325	...	...	...	325	...	...	...	...	...	...

14
Book production: number of titles by UDC classes [cont.]
Production de livres : nombre de titres classés d'après la CDU [suite]

Country or area Pays ou zone	Year Année	Total	Generalities Généralités	Philosophy Philosophie	Religion	Social sciences Sciences sociales	Philology Philologie	Pure sciences Sciences pures	Applied sciences Sciences appliquées	Arts Beaux arts	Literature Littérature	GeogrHistory Géogr., historie
Tunisia	1994[1]	569	18	26	11	130	4	9	39	11	286	27
Tunisie	1995[1]	563	8	25	7	132	23	9	19	24	166	150
	1996	720	24	18	14	138	6	4	38	23	338	111
Uganda	1992	162	4	2	...	77	...	...	78	...	...	1
Ouganda	1993[17]	314	...	...	4	10	43	35	14	...	4	11
	1996[1]	288	...	...	7	...	45	41	7	...	4	9
United Republic of Tanzania	1980	512	31	4	94	151	17	50	86	57	22	...
Rép.–Unie de Tanzanie	1984[2]	363	17	1	41	195	6	7	77	4	9	6
	1990[2]	172	...	1	18	45	2	7	40	3	47	9
Zimbabwe	1985	544	5	2	15	132	141	58	89	16	66	20
Zimbabwe	1990	349	6	...	14	153	22	16	70	7	56	5
	1992	232	6	...	15	107	15	3	48	7	24	7
America, North • Amérique du Nord												
Canada	1995	17931	467	336	406	6261	411	888	2625	745	3213	1211
Canada	1996	19900	480	403	534	7902	503	911	3530	1171	2854	1612
	1999	22941	594	516	740	8182	620	1101	3634	1402	4248	1904
Cuba												
Cuba	1999	953	75	11	6	253	15	43	74	34	380	62
Honduras												
Honduras	1999	26	...	...	...	13	1	...	...	...	12	...
United States [9]	1994	51863	2208	1741	2730	11072	700	3021	8384	3146	8836	4704
Etats–Unis [9]	1995	62039	2751	2068	3324	12840	732	3323	9891	4238	11537	5657
	1996	68175	3027	2333	3803	14225	898	3725	10762	4245	13221	6583
America, South • Amérique du Sud												
Argentina [1]	1994	9065	279	996	607	2594	86	28	920	404	2778	373
Argentine [1]	1995	9113	157	437	492	2823	91	89	866	580	2664	476
	1996	9850	339	818	541	2529	111	111	900	490	2520	525
Bolivia												
Bolivie	1999	350			...	...		...	...		...	...
Brazil [1 11]	1992	27557	1749	1388	3175	5022	376	352	683	391	3037	721
Brésil [1 11]	1993	20141	1480	1225	3005	4430	919	1451	2355	491	3713	1072
	1994	21574	2013	2281	2823	5629	941	773	2341	1051	2358	1364
Chile	1992	1820	13	59	127	587	34	58	183	43	548	168
Chili	1995	2469	18	59	158	707	33	71	261	80	860	222
	1999	1443	3	44	112	394	31	30	125	43	538	123
Colombia	1980	5492	700	70	155	1408	107	430	671	441	1170	340
Colombie	1984	15041	1078	239	352	2784	290	1098	6067	997	1501	635
	1991[1]	1481	141	28	88	570	43	40	243	52	216	60
Ecuador	1994[2]	11	...	...	...	...	1	...	...	1	9	...
Equateur	1995[2]	12	...	...	...	...	1	...	...	...	11	...
	1999	1870	36	62	28	1077	125	74	101	60	237	70
Guyana [2]	1989	46	1	...	...	29	...	...	4	3	4	5
Guyana [2]	1994[12]	33	...	...	...	5	9	10	9	...	...	...
	1996	42	3	...	2	23	...	1	1	3	4	5
Paraguay												
Paraguay	1993	152	11	2	4	71	6	4	14	2	28	10
Peru	1994	1993	65	81	59	697	39	88	321	111	328	204
Pérou	1995	1294	49	29	56	453	74	79	134	106	167	147
	1996	612	44	24	25	266	13	27	66	11	97	39
Suriname [2]												
Suriname [2]	1996	47	18	1	16	6	2	...	2	...	1	1
Uruguay	1991	1143	6	68	35	340	17	81	205	33	276	82
Uruguay	1996	934	22	33	33	264	9	29	201	77	193	73
	1999	644	16	19	7	194	6	5	123	28	181	65
Venezuela [2]	1994	3660	147	141	138	1003	86	160	794	301	625	265
Venezuela [2]	1995	4225	229	217	186	1106	85	187	1032	243	636	304
	1996	3468	87	210	188	955	81	136	608	274	682	247
Asia • Asie												
Afghanistan	1980	273	40	3	5	126	13	26	35	3	4	18
Afghanistan	1990	2795	165	25	170	1045	30	125	680	95	200	260
Armenia	1994[2]	224	...	4	3	19	17	15	14	10	84	28
Arménie	1996[2]	396	2	4	13	52	13	10	32	15	123	47
	1999	516	20	23	25	131	12	21	32	27	188	37

14
Book production: number of titles by UDC classes [*cont.*]
Production de livres : nombre de titres classés d'après la CDU [*suite*]

Country or area Pays ou zone	Year Année	Total	Gener- alities Géné- ralités	Philo- sophy Philo- sophie	Reli- gion	Social sciences Sciences sociales	Philo- logy Philo- logie	Pure sciences Sciences pures	Applied sciences Sciences appli- quées	Arts Beaux arts	Litera- ture Litté- rature	Geogr- History Géogr., historie
Azerbaijan	1994	375	12	11	20	157	17	1	20	4	128	5
Azerbaïdjan	1995	498	10	11	22	144	13	12	44	17	176	49
	1996	542	12	10	25	167	21	17	44	9	209	28
Bahrain [2]												
Bahreïn [2]	1996	40	6	...	...	7	...	...	1	...	14	12
Brunei Darussalam	1985[2]	25	9	...	...	1	...	11	2	...	...	2
Brunéi Darussalam	1990[1 13]	25	2	...	...	13	2	...	...	...	8	...
	1992[1 2]	45	4	3	7	24	2	2	1	1	...	1
China †† [6]	1990[1]	73923	2588	1206	./.	36231	2403	3087	12196	5727	7756	2729
Chine †† [6]	1993	92972	3098	1222	./.	48796	2724	3248	15311	5560	9488	3525
	1994	100951	3013	1156	./.	55380	3175	3673	15783	5350	9735	3686
China, Macao SAR †	1996	67	2	...	...	44	3	...	2	13	2	1
Chine, Macao RAS †	1999	389	5	1	11	103	...	10	31	80	91	57
Cyprus	1995	1128	48	3	47	365	36	28	214	124	153	110
Chypre	1996	930	22	6	30	341	84	27	181	121	61	57
	1999	931	21	10	32	381	87	20	154	94	80	52
Georgia	1995	1104	574	17	17	81	23	36	67	10	216	63
Géorgie	1996[2]	581	4	17	18	124	38	49	74	16	190	51
	1999	697	476	14	17	84	14	16	7	4	65	0
India	1994	11460	307	412	848	2188	233	584	1183	297	4350	1058
Inde	1995	11643	382	377	948	2501	150	486	1278	274	4078	1169
	1996	11903	505	354	764	2504	256	593	1314	298	4423	892
Indonesia	1992[2]	6303	191	148	892	1192	294	186	788	64	231	246
Indonésie	1996[3]	4018	245	82	438	805	263	497	749	115	480	144
	1999	121	17	...	...	88	...	...	16	...	...	...
Iran, Islamic Rep. of	1995[1]	13031	384	383	2834	972	907	1021	1227	226	535	1189
Iran, Rép. islamique d'	1996[1]	15073	438	537	3293	1025	947	1244	1787	443	157	576
	1999	14783	612	706	4504	1319	1486	1844	2426	733	247	906
Israel	1985	2214	25	40	173	230	50	79	71	44	718	234
Israël	1992[7]	2310	22	53	182	263	92	101	85	31	638	173
	1998	2317	55	77	148	534	66	251	229	39	732	186
Japan [1]	1985[7]	45430	1529	1608	679	10708	2493	2709	7349	5698	10506	2151
Japon [1]	1992[2]	35496	539	1539	638	8529	917	1142	6276	5532	8525	1859
	1996[2]	56221	1149	1791	1078	12770	1402	1363	12155	10046	11924	2543
Jordan	1993[1 2]	500	15	11	77	115	14	13	37	10	136	72
Jordanie	1995	465	15	9	74	106	10	19	26	22	128	56
	1996	511	25	8	60	122	16	39	45	21	116	59
Kazakhstan	1995	1115	65	12	17	339	50	44	197	31	291	69
Kazakhstan	1996	1226	53	22	23	464	44	58	202	39	253	68
	1999	1223	52	13	21	579	40	89	173	18	166	72
Korea, Republic of	1994	34204	579	640	1844	6584	2371	2025	3856	6315	8885	1105
Corée, République de	1995	35864	1854	947	2146	4300	4421	2692	4422	6614	6958	1510
	1996[1 2]	30487	303	678	1605	3201	1384	359	3513	6543	4164	716
Kuwait	1985[14]	250	3	6	5	103	18	56	14	21	12	12
Koweït	1992[15]	196	17	5	17	18	...	102	6	15	13	3
	1999	219	36	13	31	71	1	8	9	5	19	26
Kyrgyzstan	1994	328	31	2	3	193	16	3	29	5	46	...
Kirghizistan	1995	407	16	3	6	177	17	15	58	4	97	14
	1996	351	11	5	3	176	16	19	25	8	73	15
Lao People's Dem. Rep.	1991[1]	58	...	...	1	31	2	...	2	1	20	1
Rép. dém. pop. lao	1992[1 2]	64	...	...	1	7	11	...	6	...	36	3
	1995[2]	88	...	...	2	41	6	6	9	2	15	7
Malaysia	1995	6465	101	41	659	1259	748	530	598	190	2053	286
Malaisie	1996	5843	73	36	606	1088	1043	685	538	221	1259	294
	1999	5084	157	59	547	1058	662	526	614	222	998	241
Mongolia	1986	889	...	...	...	467	6	16	181	41	178	...
Mongolie	1990	717	49	...	...	300	2	45	103	...	218	...
	1992[2]	285	26	12	5	36	6	17	20	9	135	19
Myanmar	1992	3785	11	78	720	18[10]	./.	66	26	1274	1584	8
Myanmar	1993	3660	...	73	713	26[10]	./.	82	22	1171	1551	22
	1999	227	106	...	1	76	20	16	1	1	4	2
Occupied Palestinian Terr. [2]												
Terr. palestinien occupé [2]	1996	114	3	2	8	47	3	12	21	...	10	8
Oman	1992[1]	24	1	...	3	...	9	...	1	...	...	10
Oman	1996[2]	7	...	...	4	...	...	...	1	...	1	1
	1999	12	...	1	5	...	...	...	1	5	...	...

14
Book production: number of titles by UDC classes [cont.]
Production de livres : nombre de titres classés d'après la CDU [suite]

Country or area Pays ou zone	Year Année	Total	Gener- alities Géné- ralités	Philo- sophy Philo- sophie	Reli- gion	Social sciences Sciences sociales	Philo- logy Philo- logie	Pure sciences Sciences pures	Applied sciences Sciences appli- quées	Arts Beaux arts	Litera- ture Litté- rature	Geogr- History Géogr., historie
Philippines [1]	1995	1229	65	23	47	290	51	31	157	18	199	14
Philippines [1]	1996	1507	22	18	34	378	65	43	68	17	249	33
	1999	1380	63	15	41	631	79	53	117	79	227	75
Qatar [1]	1994	371	23	6	26	149	15	60	41	4	11	36
Qatar [1]	1995	419	21	5	70	84	36	120	40	5	16	22
	1996[3]	209	9	3	26	88	7	19	27	6	12	12
Saudi Arabia	1980	218	3	...	67	27	2	1	11	4	61	31
Arabie saoudite	1996[2]	3900	209	154	1042	620	250	404	363	128	421	309
Sri Lanka	1995	3933	350	29	306	2082	137	63	268	69	489	140
Sri Lanka	1996	4115	338	29	28	2505	139	55	390	33	483	115
	1999	4655	426	368	533	1384	169	68	347	103	1110	147
Syrian Arab Republic	1980[2]	95	...	4	...	22	...	4	1	3	34	4
Rép. arabe syrienne	1992[1]	598	144	24	62	79	13	1	89	25	112	49
Tajikistan	1994	231	...	3	1	24	7	16	47	8	60	22
Tadjikistan	1995	226	...	6	2	58	17	22	42	3	33	10
	1996[2]	132	...	5		18	11	14	19	9	27	12
Thailand	1991	7676	429	198	273	2415	260	539	2271	411	477	403
Thaïlande	1992	7626	413	189	302	2341	234	591	2235	443	457	421
	1996	8142	464	202	275	2456	259	617	2371	407	644	447
Turkey	1995	6275	185	162	397	2053	175	211	1106	257	1224	505
Turquie	1996	6546	128	231	636	1551	181	222	764	229	2035	569
	1999	2920	45	139	255	649	82	68	285	91	1096	210
Turkmenistan	1992	565	47	5	6	147	21	72	74	18	136	39
Turkménistan	1994[2]	450	1	5	7	150	23	46	60	20	121	17
United Arab Emirates	1990[4]	281	6	3	37	16	86	104	17	...	...	12
Emirats arabes unis	1992	302	10	3	46	20	85	99	9	3	...	27
	1993[4]	293	...	3	68	2	83	99	9	2	...	27
Uzbekistan	1993[6]	1340	./.	118	./.	54	71	./.	136	./.	605	./.
Ouzbékistan	1995	1200	18	20	20	414	60	60	213	11	316	68
	1996	1003	8	7	22	367	44	42	158	10	277	68
Viet Nam [6]	1991	3429	./.	./.	./.	444	./.	./.	395	./.	979	./.
Viet Nam [6]	1992	4707	./.	./.	./.	683	./.	./.	603	./.	1024	./.
	1993	5581	./.	./.	./.	647	./.	./.	646	./.	1502	./.
Europe · Europe												
Albania	1980	948	21	2	...	211	63	103	223	46	237	42
Albanie	1985	939	9	6	...	189	75	159	281	42	139	39
	1991	381	12	...	4	28	35	74	127	20	63	18
Andorra	1992	56	3	...	1	15	1	3	4	7	10	12
Andorre	1994[1]	57	...	...	...	24	...	3	4	5	15	6
	1999	172	5	...	1	45	4		17	46	27	27
Austria [8]	1994	7987	229	246	284	2758	229	847	703	922	1181	588
Autriche [8]	1995	8222	406	255	239	2948	239	657	738	929	1208	603
	1996	8056	243	289	289	2851	209	651	682	963	1188	691
Belarus	1994	3346	161	68	184	790	169	187	792	77	813	105
Bélarus	1995	3205	132	74	181	756	125	147	665	61	952	112
	1996	3809	214	84	153	930	146	182	776	100	1127	97
Belgium [16]	1985	8327	169	240	480	1235	291	343	1153	890	2807	719
Belgique [16]	1990	12157	303	285	458	2530	335	461	1886	1074	3673	1152
	1991	13913	300	311	686	2847	478	817	2228	1325	3696	1225
Bulgaria	1995	5400	204	238	156	1045	162	276	765	154	2104	296
Bulgarie	1996	4840	155	256	156	1060	130	195	576	129	1935	248
	1999	4971	170	235	205	1029	159	211	715	178	1803	266
Croatia	1996	1718	7	41	68	329	30	55	170	31	317	21
Croatie	1998	3626[20]	75	126	262	858	73	116	639	170	818	128
	1999	2309[20]	78	83	209	655	5	106	398	110	554	111
Czech Republic	1995	8994	314	283	321	1447	243	732	1178	524	3374	578
République tchèque	1996	10244	187	363	289	1928	369	972	1471	662	3261	742
	1999	12551	358	387	363	2440	396	1277	1771[21]	781	3708	1070
Denmark	1995	12478	368	554	339	2509	328	913	3006	797	2432	1232
Danemark	1996	12352	233	536	294	2460	347	863	3036	923	2561	1099
	1999	14455	306	642	381	2914	338	1090	3228	864	3369	1323
Estonia	1995	2635	191	86	74	634[10]	./.	195	307	176	851	121
Estonie	1996	2628	181	92	93	571[10]	./.	193	341	176	885	96
	1999	3265	122	86	99	718	0	274	519	186	1082	179

14
Book production: number of titles by UDC classes [cont.]
Production de livres : nombre de titres classés d'après la CDU [suite]

Country or area Pays ou zone	Year Année	Total	Gener-alities Géné-ralités	Philo-sophy Philo-sophie	Reli-gion	Social sciences Sciences sociales	Philo-logy Philo-logie	Pure sciences Sciences pures	Applied sciences Sciences appli-quées	Arts Beaux arts	Litera-ture Litté-rature	Geogr-History Géogr., historie
Finland	1995	13494	315	266	390	3385	438	1212	3537	870	1947	1134
Finlande	1996	13104	325	240	355	3189	411	1215	3477	807	1898	1187
	1999	13173	294	238	318	3068	364	1169	3252	760	2144	1566
France	1993	41234	731	1890	1322	7893	1010	1971	5578	3308	12401	5130
France	1994	45311	1029	2053	1407	8306	1029	2140	6226	3538	13524	6059
	1995	34766	706	1392	1252	7315	877	1576	4120	2620	10545	4363
Germany	1994	70643	6255	3594	3815	16259[10]	./.	2532	10062	5797	13015	9314
Allemagne	1995	74174	6991	3861	3637	16816[10]	./.	2637	10410	6810	13571	9441
	1996	71515	6287	3580	3718	16210	3176	2756	10550	5921	9622	9695
Greece	1990	3255	95	79	183	511	80	134	154	224	1474	321
Grèce	1991	4066	143	158	289	638	159	157	260	246	1633	383
	1995[1]	4134	152	98	204	613	190	254	287	284	1598	454
Holy See [19]	1992[1]	205	5	37	117	31	7	...	...	...	...	8
Saint–Siège [19]	1995	298	...	48	198	42	1	...	...	2	...	7
	1996	228	...	38	105	78	2	...	...	...	5	...
Hungary	1995	9314	207	306	468	1376	438	649	1483	598	3064	725
Hongrie	1996	9193	399	336	394	1313	478	602	1446	534	2717	974
	1999	10352	290	378	593	1121	602	854	1609	565	3338	1002
Iceland	1994	1429	36	22	37	276	123	110	166	124	382	153
Islande	1995	1522	29	25	65	331	105	94	169	122	438	144
	1996	1527	29	30	43	354	124	114	168	107	414	144
Italy	1995	34470	783	2045	2041	6572	860	1265	3663	3609	9225	4407
Italie	1996	35236	723	2146	2232	6698	763	1173	3898	4264	8539	4800
	1999	32365[22]	603	2075	2338	6446	608	1110	3537	3353	7826	4469
Latvia	1995	1968	75	78	78	378	56	54	148	67	426	88
Lettonie	1996	1965	91	63	87	414	67	54	166	87	364	65
	1999	2178	104	131	104	627	158	102	343	87	385	137
Lithuania	1995	3164	152	92	160	630	203	223	653	155	773	123
Lituanie	1996	3645	206	81	163	712	222	270	669	183	961	178
	1999	4097	301	126	153	794	309	320	509	215	1151	219
Luxembourg	1992	586	44	9	10	240	2	9	61	108	48	55
Luxembourg	1993	640	19	...	11	292	5	7	85	118	46	57
	1994	681	64	13	15	246	2	19	49	118	67	88
Malta	1992	395	9	7	76	155	17	6	17	22	34	52
Malte	1993	417	8	11	80	163	18	4	16	29	41	47
	1995	404	4	6	78	159	8	4	13	28	47	57
Monaco	1985	121	35	15	8	2	...	2	6	26	15	12
Monaco	1990	41	3	...	1	1	...	1	8	22	2	3
	1999	178[20]	14	1	10	14	...	11	1	18	1	2
Netherlands [1]	1991	16017	84	612	823	1615	307	351	2581	880	3082	1278
Pays–Bas [1]	1992	15997	71	628	833	1701	233	358	2502	874	3251	1393
	1993	34067	70	710	788	1883	334	215	2310	2826	2950	1364
Norway	1995[78]	7265	184	148	307	1010	111	218	644	413	3110	1120
Norvège	1996[78]	6900	160	162	281	1215	138	288	707	384	2831	734
	1999	4985	162	141	242	814	69	143	556	315	2130	413
Poland	1995	11925	238	382	900	1885	670	1083	2210	575	2895	1087
Pologne	1996	14104	265	456	1078	2958	616	1291	2654	678	2828	1280
	1999	19192	676	589	1274	3829	823	1545	3304	1045	4176	1931
Portugal [11]	1993[6]	6089	286	./.	./.	830	./.	./.	410	159	2021	./.
Portugal [11]	1994[6]	6667	./.	./.	./.	789	./.	401	./.	192	1934	./.
	1996	7868	312	178	233	1207	17	190	506	260	4554	411
Republic of Moldova	1995	1016	41	19	48	385	37	47	272	19	109	39
République de Moldova	1996	921	52	9	22	456	21	27	165	15	124	30
	1999	1166	181	23	22	320	44	76	215	25	177	83
Romania	1995	5517	98	237	231	650	323	643	1161	120	1804	250
Roumanie	1996	7199	213	275	301	913	431	989	1485	105	2182	305
	1999	7874	925	207	357	943	24	761	1629	134	2466[23]	428
Russian Federation	1994	30390	2860	896	957	5965	995	2644	6849	704	7176	1344
Fédération de Russie	1995	33623	2968	1038	854	7719	988	2790	6783	685	7704	2094
	1996	36237	3362	1275	984	8801	1171	2869	7003	664	8493	1615
Slovakia	1994	3481	63	143	164	656	139	271	774	146	938	187
Slovaquie	1996	3800	72	129	248	753	135	337	844	192	879	211
	1999	3153	69	123	264	681	97	254	684	117	711	153
Slovenia	1994	2906	57	117	106	536	125	263	481	393	631	197
Slovénie	1995	3194	72	119	123	623	117	295	461	400	763	221
	1996	3441	82	123	135	659	123	319	620	438	680	262

14
Book production: number of titles by UDC classes [*cont.*]
Production de livres : nombre de titres classés d'après la CDU [*suite*]

Country or area Pays ou zone	Year Année	Total	Gener-alities Géné-ralités	Philo-sophy Philo-sophie	Reli-gion	Social sciences Sciences sociales	Philo-logy Philo-logie	Pure sciences Sciences pures	Applied sciences Sciences appli-quées	Arts Beaux arts	Litera-ture Litté-rature	Geogr-History Géogr., historie
Spain	1995	48467	1723	1761	1890	9423	1772	2790	6711	3574	14492	4331
Espagne	1996	46330	1504	1744	1941	9324	2102	3000	6907	3763	11695	4350
	1999	59174	1446	2455	1962	10899	2064	3245	8800	5032	18145	5126
Sweden	1994	13822	317	401	577	2722	428	919	3038	923	3226	1271
Suède	1995	12700	332	313	464	2429	434	936	2823	817	3104	1048
	1996	13496	396	328	502	2685	464	900	3285	850	2876	1210
Switzerland	1995	15771	272	702	736	3770	223	1581	3427	1610	1759	817
Suisse	1996	15371	296	639	737	3852	230	1396	3300	1731	1669	693
	1999	18273	336	825	1101	4885	306	1761	3862	1881	2379	937
TFYR of Macedonia	1995	885	7	12	7	365	14	23	72	58	248	79
L'ex−R.y. Macédoine	1996	892	24	13	31	400	14	40	49	39	245	37
	1999	733	29	7	8	345	25	27	46	47	174	25
Ukraine	1994	4882	141	86	169	1097	183	249	1388	273	1055	241
Ukraine	1995	6225	260	155	253	1471	234	393	1592	272	1227	368
	1999	6282	198	121	186	2960	137	213	1086	100	1011	270
United Kingdom	1994	95015	2445	3063	4278	19791	3858	10764	10969	9927	19139	10781
Royaume−Uni	1995	101764	2096	3168	5575	21632	3264	9364	16205	8938	20029	11493
	1996	107263	2082	3548	5003	23889	3563	9417	16616	9431	21686	12028
Yugoslavia	1994	2799	117	62	48	908	4	76	409	165	846	164
Yougoslavie	1995	3531	121	54	75	1023	3	151	624	225	975	280
	1996	5367	206	102	136	1515	6	234	791	302	1613	462
Oceania · Océanie												
Australia	1985	10251	427	82	363	3623	447	609	2016	946	842	896
Australie	1989[16]	10723	353	135	333	3997	277	627	1753	966	1205	1077
	1994[16]	10835	218	151	246	4453	157	511	1730	700	1812	857
Fiji	1980	110	3	...	...	4	31	19	26	11	...	16
Fidji	1994[18]	401	...	...	...	22	21	40	39	2	...	21
New Zealand Nouvelle−Zélande	1999	5405	182	50	119	2173	401	400	798	357	535	390
Papua New Guinea Papouasie−Nvl−Guinée	1991	122	8	...	19	64	1	6	16	4	...	4

Source:
United Nations Educational, Scientific and Cultural Organization (UNESCO) Institute for Statistics, Montreal, the UNESCO statistics database, January 2002.

Source:
L'Institut de statistique de l'Organisation des Nations Unies pour l'éducation, la science et la culture (UNESCO), Montréal, la base de données de l'UNESCO, janvier 2002.

† For information on the recent changes in country or area nomenclature pertaining to former Czechoslovakia, Germany, Hong Kong Special Administrative Region (SAR) of China, Macao Special Administrative Region (SAR) of China, SFR of Yugoslavia and the former USSR, see Annex I − Country or area nomenclature, regional and other groupings.

†† For statistical purposes, the data for China do not include those for the Hong Kong Special Administrative Region (Hong Kong SAR), Macao Special Administrative Region (Macao SAR) and Taiwan province of China.

1 Not including pamphlets.
2 First editions only.
3 Data refer to school textbooks and government publications only.
4 Data refer to school textbooks only.
5 Data refer to school textbooks, government publications and university theses only.
6 Works indicated by the symbol ./. are distributed without specification among other classes for which a figure is shown.
7 Not including government publications.
8 Not including school textbooks.

† Pour les modifications récentes de nomenclature de pays ou de zone concernant l'Allemagne, Hong Kong, (Région administrative spéciale de Chine), Macao (Région administrative spéciale de Chine), l'ex−Tchécoslovaquie, l'ex−URSS et l'ex−Rfs de Yougoslavie, voir annexe I − Nomenclature des pays ou des zones, groupements régionaux et autres groupements.

†† Les données statistiques relatives à la Chine ne comprennent pas celles qui concernent la région administrative spéciale de Hong Kong (la RAS de Hong Kong) la région spéciale de Macao (la RAS de Macao) et la province chinoise de Taiwan.

1 Non compris les brochures.
2 Premières éditions seulement.
3 Les données se réfèrent aux manuels scolaires et aux publications officielles seulement.
4 Les données se réfèrent aux manuels scolaires seulement.
5 Les données se réfèrent aux manuels scolaires, aux publications officielles et aux thèses universitaires seulement.
6 Les ouvrages représentés par le symbole ./. sont distribués sans spécification entre les autres catégories pour lesquelles un chiffre est donné.
7 Non compris les publications officielles.
8 Non compris les manuels scolaires.

14
Book production: number of titles by UDC classes [*cont.*]
Production de livres : nombre de titres classés d'après la CDU [*suite*]

9 Not including pamphlets, school textbooks, government publications and university theses but including juvenile titles for which a class breakdown is not available.

10 Data on philology are included with those on literature.

11 Including reprints.
12 Data refer to school textbooks and chidren's books only.

13 Data refer to school textbooks, chidren's books and government publications only.
14 Data refer to school textbooks, chidren's books, government publications and university theses only.

15 Government publications only.
16 The figures do not represent the total book production, but only those actually received in the National Library.

17 Popularization of science books for children are included in the total but not distributed.
18 Data refer only to books published by the Ministry of Education and the government printing department.

19 Refers to the Vatican City State.
20 The total includes unclassified titles.
21 Includes books on trade, communication, transport and tourism.

22 Estimate.
23 Including children's books.

9 Non compris les brochures, les manuels scolaires, les publications officielles et les thèses universitaires ma: compris les livres pour jeunes pour lesquels repartitic catégories n'est pas disponible.

10 Les données relatives à la philologie sont comprises ε celles de la littérature.

11 Y compris les réimpressions.
12 Les données se réfèrent aux manuels scolaires et aux pour enfants saulement.

13 Les données se réfèrent aux manuels scolaires, aux li· pour enfants et aux publications officielles seulement
14 Les données se réfèrent aux manuels scolaires, aux li· pour enfants, aux publications officielles et aux thése universitaires seulement.

15 Publications officielles seulement.
16 Les chiffres ne représentent pas la totalité de l'éditio livres mais seulement le nombre de titres enregistrés Bibliothèque Nationale.

17 Les livres pour enfants destinés à la vulgarisation des sciences sont inclus dans le total mais ne sont pas rép
18 Les données se réfèrent seulement aux livres publiés Ministére de l'Education et le départment des public du gouvernement.

19 Concerne la Cité du Vatican.
20 Le total comprend des titres non classifiés.
21 Y compris les ouvrages relatifs au commerce, à la communication, au transport, et au tourisme.

22 Estimation.
23 Y compris des livres pour enfants.

15
Daily newspapers
Journaux quotidiens

Country or area Pays ou zone	Number of titles Nombre de titres				Circulation Diffusion Total (000)				Per 1000 inhabitants Pour 1000 habitants			
	1995	1996	1997	1998	1995	1996	1997	1998	1995	1996	1997	1998
Africa • Afrique												
Algeria Algérie	8	5	18	24	1 440	1 080	761	796	51.0	38.0	25.9	26.5
Angola Angola	5	5	...	...	122	* 128	...	...	11.0	* 11.0	...	...
Benin Bénin	1	1	...	...	3	12	...	...	0.5	2.2	...	...
Botswana Botswana	1	1	...	...	45	40	...	...	31.0	27.0	...	...
Burkina Faso Burkina Faso	3	4	...	...	* 15	* 14	...	...	* 1.4	1.3	...	...
Burundi Burundi	1	1	1	1	20	20	1	1	3.2	3.2	0.2	0.2
Cameroon Cameroun	2	2	...	...	85	91	...	...	6.4	6.7	...	...
Central African Rep. Rép. centrafricaine	1	3	...	...	* 2	6	...	...	* 0.6	1.8	...	...
Chad Tchad	1	1	2	2	2	2	...	...	0.2	0.2	...	...
Congo Congo	6	6	...	...	* 20	...	...	...	* 7.8	8.0	...	...
Côte d'Ivoire Côte d'Ivoire	9	12	...	...	198	231	...	...	15.0	17.0	...	...
Dem. Rep. of the Congo Rép. dém. du Congo	9	9	...	...	* 120	* 124	...	...	* 2.6	* 2.7	...	...
Egypt Egypte	15	17	14	...	2 373	* 2 400	2 100	...	38.0	* 40.0	32.4	...
Equatorial Guinea Guinée équatoriale	1	1	...	...	* 2	* 2	...	...	* 5.0	* 4.9	...	...
Ethiopia Ethiopie	4	4	2	2	* 92	86	23	23	* 1.7	1.5	0.4	0.4
Gabon Gabon	2	2	...	...	* 30	33	...	...	* 28.0	29.0	...	...
Gambia Gambie	1	1	...	...	1	2	...	...	0.9	1.7	...	...
Ghana Ghana	4	4	...	...	* 310	250	...	...	* 18.0	14.0	...	...
Guinea-Bissau Guinée-Bissau	1	1	...	...	6	6	...	...	5.5	5.4	...	...
Kenya Kenya	4	4	...	...	264	263	...	...	9.7	9.4	...	...
Lesotho Lesotho	* 2	* 2	...	...	* 14	* 15	...	...	* 7.3	* 7.6	...	...
Liberia Libéria	* 8	6	...	...	* 35	* 35	...	...	* 17.0	...	...	...
Libyan Arab Jamahiriya Jamah. arabe libyenne	4	4	...	...	* 71	* 71	...	...	* 14.0	* 14.0	...	...
Madagascar Madagascar	6	5	...	...	59	66	...	...	4.3	4.6	...	...
Malawi Malawi	* 1	5	...	...	* 25	...	...	...	* 2.6	3.0	...	...
Mali Mali	* 2	3	...	...	* 11	* 12	...	...	* 1.1	* 1.2	...	...
Mauritania Mauritanie	1	2	...	...	* 1	* 1	...	...	* 0.4	* 0.5	...	...
Mauritius Maurice	5	6	8	6	80	85	88	82	72.0	75.0	77.7	71.7
Morocco Maroc	20	22	21	22	630	704	662	715	24.0	26.0	24.6	26.1
Mozambique Mozambique	3	2	12	12	* 80	49	43	43	* 4.6	2.7	2.3	2.3

15
Daily newspapers [cont.]
Journaux quotidiens [suite]

Country or area	Number of titles Nombre de titres				Circulation Diffusion							
					Total (000)				Per 1000 inhabitants Pour 1000 habitants			
Pays ou zone	1995	1996	1997	1998	1995	1996	1997	1998	1995	1996	1997	1998
Namibia												
Namibie	4	4	...	...	* 30	30	...	...	* 19.0	19.0	...	...
Niger												
Niger	2	1	...	...	4	2	...	...	0.4	0.2	...	...
Nigeria												
Nigéria	27	25	...	...	* 1 950	* 2 740	...	...	* 20.0	* 24.0	...	...
Réunion												
Réunion	3	3	...	...	* 57	55	...	...	* 87.0	83.0	...	...
Rwanda												
Rwanda	1	1	...	...	* 1	...	...	...	* 0.1	...	...	...
Senegal												
Sénégal	3	1	4	5	48	45	...	...	5.8	5.3	...	...
Seychelles												
Seychelles	1	1	...	...	3	3	...	...	45.0	...	...	...
Sierra Leone												
Sierra Leone	1	1	...	...	20	20	...	...	4.8	4.7	...	...
Somalia												
Somalie	1	2	...	...	* 10	* 10	...	...	* 1.2	...	...	...
South Africa												
Afrique du Sud	* 17	17	...	...	* 1 300	1 288	...	...	* 35.0	32.0	...	...
Sudan												
Soudan	5	5	20	20	* 650	* 737	...	...	* 24.0	* 27.0	...	...
Swaziland												
Swaziland	3	3	...	...	* 15	* 24	...	...	* 17.0	...	...	...
Togo												
Togo	* 1	1	...	...	* 10	* 15	...	...	* 2.5	* 3.6	...	...
Tunisia												
Tunisie	8	8	...	...	270	280	...	...	30.0	31.0	...	...
Uganda												
Ouganda	2	2	...	...	40	40	...	...	2.1	2.1	...	...
United Rep. of Tanzania												
Rép.−Unie de Tanzanie	4	3	...	...	121	* 120	...	...	4.0	* 3.9	...	...
Zambia												
Zambie	3	3	...	...	107	114	...	...	13.0	12.0	...	...
Zimbabwe												
Zimbabwe	2	2	...	...	192	209	...	...	18.0	19.0	...	...
America, North • Amérique du Nord												
Antigua and Barbuda												
Antigua−et−Barbuda	* 1	1	...	...	* 6	6	...	...	* 91.0	...	...	...
Aruba												
Aruba	13	13	...	...	73	73	...	...	896.0	852.0	...	...
Bahamas												
Bahamas	* 3	3	...	...	* 35	28	...	...	* 125.0	...	...	...
Barbados												
Barbade	* 2	2	...	...	* 41	53	...	...	* 155.0	...	...	...
Belize												
Belize	−	−	...	...	−	−	...	...	−	−	...	...
Bermuda												
Bermudes	1	1	...	...	17	17	...	...	274.0	272.0	...	...
Canada												
Canada	107	107	...	...	4 881	4 718	...	...	165.0	159.0	...	...
Cayman Islands												
Iles Caïmanes	* 1	1	...	...	* 8	9	...	...	* 250.0	...	...	...
Costa Rica												
Costa Rica	* 5	6	9	10	* 300	320	...	...	* 84.0	94.0	...	...
Cuba												
Cuba	17	17	...	...	* 1 300	* 1 300	...	...	* 119.0	* 118.0	...	...
Dominican Republic												
République dominicaine	* 11	12	10	10	* 264	* 416	1 263	1 263	* 34.0	* 52.0	156.0	153.4
El Salvador												
El Salvador	* 6	5	4	4	* 280	278	219	171	* 49.0	48.0	37.0	28.3
Greenland												
Groenland	−	2	...	...	−	* 1	...	...	−	...	...	...

15
Daily newspapers [cont.]
Journaux quotidiens [suite]

Country or area	Number of titles Nombre de titres				Circulation Diffusion Total (000)				Per 1000 inhabitants Pour 1000 habitants			
Pays ou zone	1995	1996	1997	1998	1995	1996	1997	1998	1995	1996	1997	1998
Guadeloupe												
Guadeloupe	* 1	1	...	...	* 35	35	...	...	* 82.0	81.0	...	...
Guatemala												
Guatemala	* 5	7	...	...	* 240	* 338	...	...	* 24.0	* 33.0	...	...
Haiti												
Haïti	* 4	4	...	...	* 25	20	...	...	* 3.3	2.5	...	...
Honduras												
Honduras	* 5	7	...	...	* 240	* 320	...	...	* 42.0	* 55.0	...	...
Jamaica												
Jamaïque	* 3	3	...	...	* 160	* 158	...	...	* 65.0	* 62.0	...	...
Martinique												
Martinique	* 1	1	...	...	* 32	30	...	...	* 84.0	78.0	...	...
Mexico												
Mexique	301	295	...	...	9 338	9 030	...	...	102.0	97.0	...	...
Netherlands Antilles												
Antilles néerlandaises	* 6	6	...	...	* 53	70	...	...	* 258.0	334.0	...	...
Nicaragua												
Nicaragua	* 4	4	...	...	* 130	* 135	...	...	* 29.0	* 30.0	...	...
Panama												
Panama	* 7	7	...	...	* 160	166	...	...	* 61.0	62.0	...	...
Puerto Rico												
Porto Rico	* 3	3	...	...	* 475	475	...	...	* 128.0	127.0	...	...
Saint Vincent and Grenadines												
Saint–Vincent–et–Grenadines	1	1	...	...	1	1	...	...	9.1	9.0	...	...
Trinidad and Tobago												
Trinité–et–Tobago	* 4	4	...	...	* 150	156	...	...	* 119.0	123.0	...	...
United States												
Etats–Unis	1 533	1 520	...	...	58 193	56 990	...	...	218.0	212.0	...	...
US Virgin Islands												
Iles Vierges américaines	2	3	...	...	24	42	...	...	247.0	437.0	...	...
America, South • Amérique du Sud												
Argentina												
Argentine	* 190	181	34	34	* 4 300	* 4 320	1 427	1 346	* 124.0	123.0	40.0	37.3
Bolivia												
Bolivie	* 17	18	27	29	* 410	* 420	8 626[1]	7 884[2]	* 55.0	* 55.0	...	...
Brazil												
Brésil	352	380	400	372	6 551	* 6 472	6 892	7 163	41.0	40.0	42.1	43.2
Chile												
Chili	56	52	...	...	* 1 400	* 1 410	...	...	* 99.0	* 98.0	...	...
Colombia												
Colombie	* 34	37	...	...	* 1 500	* 1 800	...	...	* 39.0	* 46.0	...	...
Ecuador												
Equateur	* 24	29	11	11	* 800	* 820	569	529	* 70.0	* 70.0	47.7	43.4
French Guiana												
Guyane française	1	1	...	...	2	2	...	...	11.0	10.0	...	...
Guyana												
Guyana	2	2	...	...	39	42	...	...	47.0	...	...	...
Paraguay												
Paraguay	* 5	5	...	...	* 200	213	...	...	* 41.0	43.0	...	...
Peru												
Pérou	* 48	* 74	...	64	* 2 000	* 2 000	...	...	* 85.0	...	...	...
Suriname												
Suriname	2	2	2	2	50	50	29	28	122.0	...	69.2	67.6
Uruguay												
Uruguay	36	36	...	...	* 950	* 950	...	...	* 295.0	* 293.0	...	...
Venezuela												
Venezuela	* 89	86	...	...	* 4 500	* 4 600	...	...	* 206.0	* 206.0	...	...
Asia • Asie												
Afghanistan												
Afghanistan	* 15	12	...	...	* 200	113	...	...	* 10.0	5.6	...	...
Armenia												
Arménie	7	11	8	7	* 85	...	22	25	* 24.0	23.0	6.3	6.9
Azerbaijan												
Azerbaïdjan	3	6	...	...	* 210	...	...	...	* 28.0	27.0	...	...

15
Daily newspapers [*cont.*]
Journaux quotidiens [*suite*]

Country or area	Number of titles Nombre de titres				Circulation Diffusion Total (000)				Per 1000 inhabitants Pour 1000 habitants			
Pays ou zone	1995	1996	1997	1998	1995	1996	1997	1998	1995	1996	1997	1998
Bahrain Bahreïn	* 3	4	...	...	* 65	67	...	...	* 117.0	...	...	...
Bangladesh Bangladesh	* 51	37	221	233	* 950	1 117	* 6 325	* 6 658	* 8.0	9.3	* 51.6	* 53.4
Brunei Darussalam Brunéi Darussalam	* 1	1	...	...	* 20	21	...	...	* 68.0	69.0	...	...
Cambodia Cambodge	...	2	...	...	...	17	...	...	...	1.7	...	...
China †† Chine ††	...	...	...	...	...	...	...	...	...	...	...	...
China, Hong Kong SAR † Chine, Hong Kong RAS †	46	52	...	...	* 4 500	* 5 000	...	...	* 723.0	* 786.0	...	...
China, Macao SAR † Chine, Macao RAS †	* 9	10	...	...	* 250	* 200	...	...	* 582.0	* 455.0	...	...
Cyprus Chypre	10	9	8	7	84	84	76	79	113.0	...	99.6	102.5
India Inde	...	...	5 044[3]	...	...	...	46 452[3]	...	...	...	48.1[3]	...
Indonesia Indonésie	74	69	81	172	4 701	4 665	4 975	4 713	24.0	24.0	24.5	22.8
Iran, Islamic Rep. of Iran, Rép. islamique d'	27	32	...	...	1 446	1 651	...	...	23.0	28.0	...	...
Iraq Iraq	* 4	4	...	...	* 530	407	...	...	* 26.0	19.0	...	...
Israel Israël	* 34	34	...	...	* 1 500	* 1 650	...	...	* 269.0	* 290.0	...	...
Japan Japon	121	122	...	...	72 047	72 705	...	...	574.0	578.0	...	...
Jordan Jordanie	4	4	8	8	250	250	350	352	44.0	58.0	57.1	55.8
Korea, Dem.People's Rep. Corée, Rép. pop. dém. de	* 11	3	...	...	* 5 000	* 4 500	...	...	* 225.0	* 199.0	...	...
Korea, Republic of Corée, République de	* 62	60	...	...	* 17 700	...	...	...	* 394.0	393.0	...	...
Kuwait Koweït	9	8	...	...	655	635	...	...	388.0	374.0	...	...
Kyrgyzstan Kirghizistan	2	3	...	...	52	67	...	...	11.0	...	...	...
Lao People's Dem. Rep. République dém. pop. lao	* 3	3	...	...	* 14	18	...	...	* 2.9	3.7	...	...
Lebanon Liban	14	15	...	...	* 330	* 435	...	...	* 110.0	* 107.0	...	...
Malaysia Malaisie	44	42	...	...	2 800	3 345	...	...	139.0	158.0	...	...
Maldives Maldives	* 2	2	...	...	* 3	5	...	...	* 12.0	...	...	...
Mongolia Mongolie	3	4	...	3	70	68	...	...	29.0	27.0	...	...
Myanmar Myanmar	5	5	...	...	446	449	420	400	10.0	10.0	9.6	9.1
Nepal Népal	* 28	29	168	175	* 160	* 250	...	...	* 7.5	* 11.0	...	...
Oman Oman	4	4	5	5	63	63	...	...	29.0	29.0	...	...
Pakistan Pakistan	* 223	264	359[4]	...	* 2 800	...	3 915[4]	...	* 21.0	23.0	27.2[4]	...
Philippines Philippines	* 42	47	...	...	* 4 200	5 700	...	...	* 61.0	79.0	...	...
Qatar Qatar	4	5	...	...	80	90	...	...	146.0	...	...	...
Saudi Arabia Arabie saoudite	12	13	1	1	1 060	1 105	5 911	6 419	58.0	57.0	303.5	318.1
Singapore Singapour	* 8	8	...	...	* 1 000	1 095	...	...	* 301.0	324.0	...	...

15
Daily newspapers [cont.]
Journaux quotidiens [suite]

| Country or area | Number of titles Nombre de titres | | | | Circulation Diffusion | | | | | | | |
| Pays ou zone | | | | | Total (000) | | | | Per 1000 inhabitants Pour 1000 habitants | | | |
	1995	1996	1997	1998	1995	1996	1997	1998	1995	1996	1997	1998
Sri Lanka												
Sri Lanka	9	9	...	...	515	530	...	...	29.0	29.0	...	...
Syrian Arab Republic												
Rép. arabe syrienne	8	8	...	...	274	287	...	...	19.0	20.0	...	...
Tajikistan												
Tadjikistan	* 2	2	...	...	* 80	* 120	...	...	* 14.0	* 20.0	...	...
Thailand												
Thaïlande	35	30	...	...	2 700	3 800	...	...	46.0	63.0	...	...
Turkey [5]												
Turquie [5]	57	57	700	720	5 600	6 845	...	...	91.0	111.0	...	...
United Arab Emirates												
Emirats arabes unis	* 8	7	...	...	* 310	384	...	...	* 140.0	156.0	...	...
Uzbekistan												
Ouzbékistan	3	3	...	...	84	75	...	...	3.7	3.3	...	...
Viet Nam												
Viet Nam	10	10	...	...	294	300	...	...	4.0	4.0	...	...
Yemen												
Yémen	* 3	* 3	...	...	* 230	* 230	...	...	* 15.0	* 15.0	...	...
Europe • Europe												
Albania												
Albanie	* 3	5	...	...	* 130	116	...	...	* 41.0	36.0	...	...
Andorra												
Andorre	* 3	3	...	...	* 4	* 4	...	...	* 62.0	* 60.0	...	...
Austria												
Autriche	17	17	17	17	2 088	* 2 382	...	...	261.0	296.0	...	...
Belarus												
Bélarus	* 10	8	19	20	* 1 800	...	1 437	1 559	* 173.0	...	138.8	151.1
Belgium												
Belgique	31	30	...	...	1 628	1 625	...	...	161.0	160.0	...	...
Bosnia and Herzegovina												
Bosnie – Herzégovine	* 2	3	...	...	* 520	...	...	...	* 152.0	...	...	...
Bulgaria												
Bulgarie	* 17	17	...	...	* 2 200	2 145	...	...	* 259.0	257.0	...	...
Croatia												
Croatie	9	10	...	...	480	515	...	...	107.0	115.0	...	...
Czech Republic												
République tchèque	23	21	99	103	2 950	2 620	...	...	286.0	254.0	...	...
Denmark												
Danemark	37	37	37	36	1 610	1 628	1 615	1 613	308.0	309.0	307.3	306.1
Estonia												
Estonie	15	15	15	16	243	255	...	...	164.0	174.0	...	...
Faeroe Islands												
Iles Féroé	1	1	...	...	6	6	...	...	134.0	145.0	...	...
Finland												
Finlande	56	56	56	56	2 368	2 332	2 336	2 343	464.0	455.0	454.4	454.6
France [6]												
France [6]	* 80	117	...	...	* 12 200	* 12 700	...	...	* 210.0	* 218.0	...	...
Germany												
Allemagne	389	375	402	398	25 600	25 500	25 200	25 000	313.0	311.0	307.1	305.2
Gibraltar												
Gibraltar	* 2	2	1	1	* 6	* 6	6	6	* 231.0	...	230.8	240.0
Greece												
Grèce	* 160	156	198	207	* 1 600	...	251[7]	237[7]	* 153.0	153.0	23.8[7]	22.4[7]
Holy See [8]												
Saint – Siège [8]	1	1	...	...	140 000	147 059	...	...	70.0	70.0	...	...
Hungary												
Hongrie	41	40	33	33	2 022	1 895	466	469	198.0	186.0	45.9	46.3
Iceland												
Islande	5	5	4	3	140	* 145	100	...	522.0	...	365.0	...
Ireland												
Irlande	7	6	...	...	546	543	...	...	151.0	150.0	...	...
Italy												
Italie	76	78	...	...	5 722	5 960	...	...	100.0	104.0	...	...

15
Daily newspapers [cont.]
Journaux quotidiens [suite]

Country or area	Number of titles Nombre de titres				Circulation Diffusion Total (000)				Per 1000 inhabitants Pour 1000 habitants			
Pays ou zone	1995	1996	1997	1998	1995	1996	1997	1998	1995	1996	1997	1998
Latvia Lettonie	21	24	...	...	437	616	...	...	172.0	247.0	...	...
Liechtenstein Liechtenstein	2	2	...	...	19	19	...	...	617.0	602.0	...	...
Lithuania Lituanie	19	19	20	20	417	344	100	108	112.0	93.0	26.9	29.3
Luxembourg Luxembourg	5	5	...	...	135	135	...	...	332.0	...	...	...
Malta Malte	* 3	2	3	3	* 50	48	...	...	* 133.0	...	...	...
Monaco Monaco	1	1	...	...	8	...	...	...	251.0	...	...	...
Netherlands Pays–Bas	39	38	...	...	4 752	4 753	...	...	307.0	306.0	...	...
Norway Norvège	83	83	82	81	2 582	2 578	2 598	2 592	594.0	588.0	591.0	586.6
Poland Pologne	63	55	55	52	4 846	4 351	4 194	4 168	126.0	113.0	108.4	107.7
Portugal Portugal	28	27	31	...	728	740	316	...	74.0	75.0	32.0	...
Republic of Moldova République de Moldova	2	4	5	6	200	261	480	660	46.0	60.0	109.7	150.8
Romania Roumanie	93	106	74	95	...	...	...	...	...	300.0	...	...
Russian Federation Fédération de Russie	292	285	...	...	17 919	15 517	...	...	121.0	105.0	...	...
San Marino Saint–Marin	3	3	3	3	2	2	2	2	72.0	...	69.2	69.2
Slovakia Slovaquie	20	19	21	19	1 051	989	1 324	939	196.0	185.0	246.5	174.6
Slovenia Slovénie	7	7	5	5	390	397	343	340	196.0	199.0	171.9	170.6
Spain Espagne	86	87	...	...	4 046	3 931	...	...	102.0	100.0	...	...
Sweden Suède	95	94	94	94	4 096	3 933	3 881	3 820	465.0	445.0	438.2	430.4
Switzerland Suisse	98	88	78	74	2 754	2 383	2 680	2 620	386.0	337.0	369.6	...
TFYR of Macedonia L'ex–R.y.Macédoine	3	3	4	4	54	41	2 817	3 206	28.0	21.0	...	...
Ukraine Ukraine	36	44	53	41	2 322	2 780	3 495	5 059	45.0	54.0	68.4	99.5
United Kingdom Royaume–Uni	100	99	...	...	20 101	19 332	...	...	345.0	329.0	...	...
Yugoslavia Yougoslavie	17	18	...	...	850	1 128	...	...	80.0	107.0	...	...
Oceania • Océanie												
American Samoa Samoa américaines	* 1	2	...	...	* 2	5	...	...	* 35.0	...	...	...
Australia Australie	* 69	65	...	...	* 5 340	* 5 370	...	...	* 298.0	* 293.0	...	...
Cook Islands Iles Cook	1	1	...	...	2	2	...	...	106.0	...	...	...
Fiji Fidji	* 1	1	...	...	* 35	40	...	...	* 46.0	...	...	...
French Polynesia Polynésie française	* 4	4	...	...	* 24	* 24	...	...	* 112.0	...	...	...
Guam Guam	1	1	...	...	25	28	...	...	165.0	178.0	...	...
New Caledonia Nouvelle–Calédonie	* 3	3	...	...	* 23	* 24	...	...	* 119.0	* 121.0	...	...
New Zealand Nouvelle–Zélande	25	23	28	28	828	804	821	786	226.0	216.0	218.4	207.0

15
Daily newspapers [*cont.*]
Journaux quotidiens [*suite*]

| Country or area | Number of titles Nombre de titres | | | | Circulation Diffusion Total (000) | | | | Per 1000 inhabitants Pour 1000 habitants | | | |
Pays ou zone	1995	1996	1997	1998	1995	1996	1997	1998	1995	1996	1997	1998
Papua New Guinea Papouasie – Nouv. – Guinée	* 2	2	...	...	* 65	65	...	...	* 15.0	15.0	...	...
Tonga Tonga	* 1	1	...	...	* 7	7	...	...	* 72.0	...	...	...

Source:
United Nations Educational, Scientific and Cultural Organization (UNESCO) Institute for Statistics, Montreal, the UNESCO statistics database, January 2002.

Data prior to 1997 may not be comparable to data for later years due to UNESCO's use of different sources.

† For information on recent changes in country or area nomenclature pertaining to former Czechoslovakia, Germany, Hong Kong Special Administrative Region (SAR) of China, Macao Special Administrative Region (SAR) of China, SFR Yugoslavia and former USSR, see Annex I – Country or area nomenclature, regional and other groupings.

†† For statistical purposes, the data for China do not include those for the Hong Kong Special Administrative Region (Hong Kong SAR) and Macao Special Administrative Region (Macao SAR) and Taiwan province of China.

1 Estimate for 10 out of 27 titles.
2 Estimate for 10 out of 29 titles.
3 Includes tri–weeklies and bi–weeklies.
4 Newspapers and periodicals.
5 Data do not include local newspapers.
6 Including DOM–TOM.
7 Includes Athens circulation only.
8 Refer to Vatican City State.

Source:
L'Institut de statistique de l'Organisation des Nations Unies pour l'éducation, la science et la culture (UNESCO), Montréal, la base de données de l'UNESCO, janvier 2002.

Les données antérieures à 1997 peuvent n'être pas comparables à celles des années suivantes, l'UNESCO ayant utilisé des sources différentes.

† Pour les modifications récentes de nomenclature de pays ou de zone concernant l'Allemagne, Hong Kong (Région administrative spéciale de Chine), Macao (Région administrative spéciale de Chine), l'ex–Tchécoslovaquie, l'ex–URSS, Rfs de Yougoslavie, voir annexe I – Nomenclature des pays ou des zones, groupements zones, groupements régionaux et autres groupments.

†† Les données statistiques relatives à la Chine ne comprennent pas celles qui concernent la région administrative spéciale de Hong Kong (la RAS de Hong Kong) et la province chinoise Macao (la RAS de Macao) et la province chinoise de Taiwan.

1 L'estimation ne comprend que 10 titres sur 27.
2 L'estimation ne comprend que 10 titres sur 29.
3 Y compris les journaux paraissant deux ou tois fois par semaine.
4 Journaux quotidiens et périodiques.
5 Les données n'incluent pas les journaux locaux.
6 Y compris les DOM TOM.
7 Les données de diffusion ne comprennent que celles d'Athènes.
8 Concerne la Cité du Vatican.

16
Non-daily newspapers and periodicals
Journaux non quotidiens et périodiques

| | Non-daily newspapers Journaux non quotidiens | | | | Periodicals Périodiques | | | |
| | | | Circulation Diffusion | | | | Circulation Diffusion | |
Country or area Pays ou zone	Year§ Année§	Number Nombre	Total (000)	Per 1000 inhabitants Pour 1000 habitants	Year§ Année§	Number Nombre	Total (000)	Per 1000 inhabitants Pour 1000 habitants
Africa · Afrique								
Algeria	1997	64	1 196	41	...	...	...	...
Algérie	1998	82	909	30	1990	48	803	32
Angola								
Angola	1988	* 2	* 7	* 1	...	...	...	...
Benin	1996	4	* 66	* 12	...	...	...	...
Bénin	1999	2	...	...	1999	106	110	19
Botswana	1995	5	79	53	...	...	...	...
Botswana	1996	3	51	33	1992	14	177	130
Burkina Faso	1991	58	...	...	...	...	...	...
Burkina Faso	1995	9	42	4	1990	37	24	3
Burundi	1997	5	...	...	...	...	...	...
Burundi	1998	5	...	...	...	...	...	...
Cameroon	1988	25	315	29	1988	58	127	* 11
Cameroun	1996	7	152	11	...	...	...	...
Cape Verde	1995	6	21	55	...	...	...	...
Cap-Vert	1996	4	* 20	* 51	...	...	...	...
Central African Republic	1995	1	2	1	...	...	...	...
Rép. centrafricaine	1996	7	13	4	...	...	...	...
Chad	1997	14	...	...	1997	51	...	...
Tchad	1998	10	...	...	1998	53	...	...
Comoros								
Comores	1995	1	0.3	1	...	...	...	...
Congo	1990	3	139	63	1990	* 3	* 34	15
Congo	1995	15	38	15	...	...	...	...
Côte d'Ivoire	1995	13	235	17	...	...	...	...
Côte d'Ivoire	1996	15	251	18	...	...	...	...
Democratic Rep. of the Congo	1985	7	...	...	...	...	...	...
Rép. dém. du Congo	1990	77	...	...	...	...	...	...
Djibouti	1988	2	* 7	* 15	1989	* 7	* 7	* 14[1]
Djibouti	1995	1	1	1	...	...	...	...
Egypt	1995	40	1 442	23	1995	258	2 373	38
Egypte	1997	46	1 470	23	1997	259	2 332	36
Ethiopia	1997	85	338	5	1997	7	598	10
Ethiopie	1998	78	402	6	1998	10	688	11
Gabon								
Gabon	1988	1	20	18	...	...	...	...
Gambia	1990	6	* 7	* 8	1990	10	885	961
Gambie	1996	4	* 6	* 5	...	...	...	...
Ghana								
Ghana	1990	87	1 111	73	1990	121	774	52
Guinea	1990	* 1	* 10	* 2	1990	* 3	* 5	* 1
Guinée	1996	1	20	3	...	...	...	...
Guinea-Bissau								
Guinée-Bissau	1988	* 1	* 2	* 2	...	...	...	...
Kenya	1995	7	484	18	...	...	...	...
Kenya	1996	7	524	19	...	...	...	...
Lesotho	1988	* 3	* 45	* 26	...	...	...	...
Lesotho	1996	7	74	37	...	...	...	...
Liberia								
Libéria	1988	* 8	* 25	* 10	...	...	...	...
Libyan Arab Jamahiriya								
Jamah. arabe libyenne	1988	* 1	* 15	* 4	...	...	...	...
Madagascar	1994	31	90	7	1994	55	* 108	* 7
Madagascar	1995	31	* 90	* 7	...	...	...	...
Malawi	1992	4	133	14	...	...	...	...
Malawi	1996	4	* 120	* 12	...	...	...	...

16
Non–daily newspapers and periodicals [*cont.*]
Journaux non quotidiens et périodiques [*suite*]

	Non–daily newspapers Journaux non quotidiens				Periodicals Périodiques			
			Circulation Diffusion				Circulation Diffusion	
Country or area Pays ou zone	Year[§] Année[§]	Number Nombre	Total (000)	Per 1000 inhabitants Pour 1000 habitants	Year[§] Année[§]	Number Nombre	Total (000)	Per 1000 inhabitants Pour 1000 habitants
Mauritius	1997	36	18	16	1997	39	39	34
Maurice	1998	36	...	...	1998	42	42	37
Morocco	1997	807	...	...	1997	828	4 684	174
Maroc	1998	693	...	...	1998	715	4 422	162
Mozambique	1997	44	187	10	1997	32	83	5
Mozambique	1998	44	187	10	1998	32	83	4
Namibia	1990	18	71	53	...	...	...	...
Namibie	1996	2	16	10	...	...	...	...
Niger	1995	5	15	2	...	...	...	...
Niger	1996	5	14	2	...	...	...	...
Nigeria								
Nigéria	1988	11	45	0	1988	92	495	5
Réunion								
Réunion	1988	* 4	* 20	* 34	...	...	...	...
Rwanda	1992	15	...	...	...	...	...	...
Rwanda	1996	2	123	22	1992	15	101	14
Saint Helena	1997	...	...	...	1997	4	...	...
Sainte Hélène	1998	...	...	...	1998	4	...	...
Sao Tome & Principe								
Sao Tomé–et–Principe	1988	* 2	* 2	* 18	...	...	...	...
Senegal	1997	74	...	...	1997	32	...	...
Sénégal	1998	79	...	...	1998	38	...	...
Seychelles	1995	3	7	93	...	...	...	...
Seychelles	1996	3	7	92	...	...	...	...
Sierra Leone								
Sierra Leone	1988	* 6	* 65	* 17	...	...	...	...
Somalia	1988	* 4	* 13	* 2	...	...	...	...
Somalie	1996	2	...	...	...	...	...	...
South Africa	1995	46	1 265	34	...	...	...	...
Afrique du Sud	1996	48	1 110	29	1991	11	2 149	57
Sudan	1997	6	...	...	1997	54	...	...
Soudan	1998	6	...	...	1998	54	...	...
Swaziland								
Swaziland	1988	* 1	* 7	* 10	...	...	...	...
Togo								
Togo	1988	* 1	* 5	* 2	...	...	...	...
Tunisia	1995	25	775	87	...	...	...	...
Tunisie	1996	25	900	99	1996	170	1 748	190
Uganda	1995	4	74	4	...	...	...	...
Ouganda	1996	4	67	3	1990	26	158	10
United Rep. of Tanzania								
Rép.–Unie de Tanzanie	1988	* 9	* 450	* 19	...	...	...	...
Zambia	1985	11	285	44	...	...	...	...
Zambie	1988	* 1	* 72	* 9	...	...	...	...
Zimbabwe	1985	4	233	28	...	...	...	...
Zimbabwe	1990	16	428	44	1990	28	680	69
America, North · Amérique du Nord								
Antigua and Barbuda	1992	4	...	...	...	...	...	...
Antigua–et–Barbuda	1996	4	...	...	...	...	...	...
Bahamas								
Bahamas	1988	* 2	* 13	* 52	...	...	...	...
Barbados	1985	4	* 80	* 317	...	...	...	...
Barbade	1990	4	* 95	* 369	...	...	...	...
Belize	1990	7	37	197	...	...	...	...
Belize	1996	6	80	363	...	...	...	...
Bermuda	1995	2	13	215	...	...	...	...
Bermudes	1996	2	13	213	...	...	...	...
British Virgin Islands	1990	2	4	248	...	...	...	...
Iles Vierges brit.	1996	2	4	182	...	...	...	...

16
Non–daily newspapers and periodicals [cont.]
Journaux non quotidiens et périodiques [suite]

Country or area Pays ou zone	Non–daily newspapers Journaux non quotidiens				Periodicals Périodiques			
			Circulation Diffusion				Circulation Diffusion	
	Year[§] Année[§]	Number Nombre	Total (000)	Per 1000 inhabitants Pour 1000 habitants	Year[§] Année[§]	Number Nombre	Total (000)	Per 1000 inhabitants Pour 1000 habitants
Canada	1985	1 265	15 567	600	...	...	...	...
Canada	1996	* 1 071	* 21 235	* 709	1992	1 400	37 108	1 303
Cayman Islands Iles Caïmanes	1988	* 1	* 4	* 167	...	...	...	...
Costa Rica	1997	22	...	...	1997	235	206	...
Costa Rico	1998	25	...	...	...	...	...	...
Cuba	1995	24	422	38	...	...	...	...
Cuba	1996	24	456	41	1996	14	285	26
Dominica	1992	1	5	63	...	...	...	...
Dominique	1996	1	5	64	...	...	...	...
Dominican Republic	1997	6	183	23	1997	132	1 263	156
République dominicaine	1998	6	183	22	1998	132	1 263	153
El Salvador	1995	6	48	9	...	...	...	...
El Salvador	1996	6	52	9	1996	45	774	133
Greenland	1985	3	15	273	...	...	...	...
Groenland	1988	* 3	* 15	* 264	...	...	...	...
Grenada	1995	1	13	136	...	...	...	...
Grenade	1996	4	14	151	1996	4	89	967
Guadeloupe Guadeloupe	1988	* 9	* 28	* 74	...	...	...	...
Guatemala Guatemala	1988	* 1	* 7	* 1	...	...	...	...
Haiti Haïti	1988	* 4	* 16	* 3	...	...	...	...
Honduras Honduras	1988	* 1	* 5	* 1	...	...	...	...
Martinique Martinique	1988	* 7	* 28	* 80	...	...	...	...
Mexico	1995	21	648	7	...	...	...	...
Mexique	1996	23	620	7	1994	158	13 097	146
Montserrat	1997	1	1	90	...	...	...	...
Montserrat	1998	1	1	90	...	...	...	...
Netherlands Antilles Antilles néerlandaises	1988	* 1	* 3	* 16	...	...	...	...
Nicaragua Nicaragua	1988	* 8	* 140	* 40	...	...	...	...
Panama Panama	1988	3	* 50	* 22	...	...	...	...
Puerto Rico Porto Rico	1988	* 4	* 106	* 31	...	...	...	...
Saint Kitts and Nevis	1993	2	6	147	1993	10	44	1 048
Saint Kitts–et–Nevis	1996	2	10	239	...	...	...	...
Saint Lucia	1995	5	34	236	...	...	...	...
Sainte Lucie	1996	5	34	233	...	...	...	...
Saint Pierre and Miquelon	1992	1	2	294	...	...	...	...
Saint–Pierre et Miquelon	1996	1	2	293	...	...	...	...
Saint Vincent and the Grenadines	1995	6	34	305	...	...	...	...
Saint–Vincent–et–les Grenadines	1996	6	34	302	...	...	...	...
Trinidad and Tobago	1990	5	125	103	...	...	...	...
Trinité–et–Tobago	1996	5	* 150	* 118	...	...	...	...
Turks and Caicos Islands	1992	1	10	799	...	...	...	...
Iles Turques et Caïques	1996	1	5	344	...	...	...	...
United States	1994	9 728	70 000	265	...	...	...	...
Etats–Unis	1995	* 9 728	* 70 000	* 262	...	...	...	...
United States Virgin Is. Iles Vierges américaines	1988	* 2	* 4	* 33	...	...	...	...
America, South · Amérique du Sud								
Argentina	1992	* 7	* 350	* 10	1997	60	3 412	96
Argentine	1998	...	...	...	1998	71	3 639	101

16
Non-daily newspapers and periodicals [*cont.*]
Journaux non quotidiens et périodiques [*suite*]

Country or area Pays ou zone	Non-daily newspapers Journaux non quotidiens				Periodicals Périodiques			
			Circulation Diffusion				Circulation Diffusion	
	Year[§] Année[§]	Number Nombre	Total (000)	Per 1000 inhabitants Pour 1000 habitants	Year[§] Année[§]	Number Nombre	Total (000)	Per 1000 inhabitants Pour 1000 habitants
Bolivia								
Bolivie	1988	* 8	* 16	* 2	...	...	...	...
Brazil	1997	892	...	...	...	...	...	...
Brésil	1998	1 251	...	...	...	...	...	...
Chile	1995	68	...	...	...	...	...	...
Chili	1996	63	...	...	1992	417	* 3 450	* 255
Colombia	1995	4[3]	58[3]	2	...	...	...	...
Colombie	1996	5[3]	65[3]	2	...	...	...	...
Ecuador	1997	34	150	13	1997	133	820	69
Equateur	1998	45	175	14	1998	146	1 615	133
Falkland Islands (Malvinas)	1995	2	1	410	...	...	...	...
Iles Falkland (Malvinas)	1996	3	1	453	...	...	...	...
French Guiana								
Guyane française	1988	* 2	* 7	* 66	...	...	...	...
Guyana								
Guyana	1988	* 6	* 84	* 106	...	...	...	...
Paraguay								
Paraguay	1988	* 2	* 16	* 4	...	...	...	...
Peru	1988	* 12	* 374	* 18	1988	45	90	4
Pérou	1998	7	...	...	...	...	...	...
Suriname	1997	9	65[10]	147[10]	1997	4	4	8
Suriname	1998	9	63[10]	153[10]	1998	8	8	20
Uruguay	1995	76	...	...	...	...	...	...
Uruguay	1996	62	...	...	...	...	...	...
Venezuela								
Venezuela	1988	* 45	* 450	* 24	...	...	...	...
Asia · Asie								
Afghanistan	1991	31	...	...	...	...	...	...
Afghanistan	1992	13	...	...	1988	105	...	...
Armenia	1997	100	116	33	1997	40	26	7
Arménie	1998	119	215	61	1998	75	49	14
Azerbaijan	1995	238	...	...	1997	34	57	7
Azerbaïdjan	1996	251	...	...	1998	38	50	7
Bahrain								
Bahreïn	1993	5	17	31	1993	26	73	138
Bangladesh	1997	275	* 4 249	35	1997	275	4 543	37
Bangladesh	1998	290	* 4 473	36	1998	219	4 783	38
Bhutan	1992	1	11	6	...	...	...	...
Bhoutan	1996	1	11	6	...	...	...	...
Brunei Darussalam	1992	2	57	210	1992	15	132	483
Brunéi Darussalam	1996	1	45	149	...	...	...	...
China ††	1993	943[4]	136 268[4]	...	...	...	...	...
Chine ††	1994	1 015[4]	131 481[4]	...	1992	6 486	205 060	173
China, Hong Kong SAR †	1995	8	...	...	...	...	...	...
Chine, Hong-Kong RAS †	1996	11	...	...	1992	598[6]	...	...
China, Macao SAR †								
Chine, Macao RAS †	1992	* 3	...	...	1992	16	...	...
Cyprus	1997	31	185	242	1997	30	310	403
Chypre	1998	31	185	240	1998	29	290	376
India	1995	32 702[2]	43 192[2]	...	...	...	...	...
Inde	1997	36 661	5 926	6	...	...	...	...
Indonesia	1997	94	5 130	25	1997	114	4 390	22
Indonésie	1998	433	7 838	38	1998	266	4 156	20
Iran, Islamic Rep. of								
Iran, Rép. islamique d'	1990	50	* 470	* 8	1990	318	6 166	104
Iraq	1985	22	...	...	...	...	...	...
Iraq	1988	* 12	* 465	* 27	...	...	...	...
Israel	1985	83	...	...	...	...	...	...
Israël	1988	* 80	...	...	...	...	...	...

16
Non-daily newspapers and periodicals [cont.]
Journaux non quotidiens et périodiques [suite]

| Country or area Pays ou zone | Non-daily newspapers Journaux non quotidiens | | | | Periodicals Périodiques | | | |
| | | | Circulation Diffusion | | | | Circulation Diffusion | |
	Year[§] Année[§]	Number Nombre	Total (000)	Per 1000 inhabitants Pour 1000 habitants	Year[§] Année[§]	Number Nombre	Total (000)	Per 1000 inhabitants Pour 1000 habitants
Japan	1995	6	...	...	...	...	...	...
Japon	1996	6	...	...	1992	2 926	...	...
Jordan	1997	13	...	...	1997	256	144	23
Jordanie	1998	13	...	...	1998	270	148	23
Korea, Dem. People's Rep. of								
Corée, Rép. pop. dém.	1988	* 2	...	...	...	...	...	...
Kuwait	1995	57	...	...	...	...	...	...
Koweït	1996	78	...	...	...	...	...	...
Kyrgyzstan	1995	140	1 092	239	...	...	...	...
Kirghizistan	1996	146	896	195	...	...	...	...
Lao People's Dem. Rep.								
Rép. dém. pop. lao	1988	* 4	* 20	* 5				
Lebanon								
Liban	1988	* 15	* 240	* 94	...	...	...	...
Malaysia	1995	39	2 500	124	...	...	...	...
Malaisie	1996	44	1 424	69	1992	25	996	53
Maldives	1985	15	5	25	...	...	...	...
Maldives	1988	* 4	* 5	* 25	...	...	...	...
Mongolia	1996	30	137	55	...	...	...	...
Mongolie	1998	26	3 835	1 487	1990	45	...	...
Myanmar	1988	* 4	* 246	* 6	1997	7	8 931	203
Myanmar	1998	...	...	...	1998	7	15 449	352
Nepal	1997	2 144	...	...	1997	2 312	...	...
Népal	1998	2 288	...	...	1998	2 463	...	...
Oman	1997	24[9]	...	...	1997	24	...	...
Oman	1998	24[9]	...	...	1998	24	...	...
Pakistan	1991	719[2]	1 957[2]	...	...	...	...	...
Pakistan	1997	782[2]	1 830[2]	13[2]	...	...	...	...
Philippines	1993	218	472	7	...	...	...	...
Philippines	1995	243	153	2	1990	1 570	* 9 468	* 156
Qatar	1995	* 1	* 7	* 13	...	...	...	...
Qatar	1996	* 1	* 7	* 13	1994	11	47	87
Saudi Arabia	1995	168	* 2 150	* 118	...	...	...	...
Arabie saoudite	1996	185	...	...	1994	471	...	...
Singapore	1995	2	...	...	...	...	...	...
Singapour	1996	2	...	...	...	...	...	...
Sri Lanka	1995	38	2 520	141	...	...	...	...
Sri Lanka	1996	40	2 665	147	...	...	...	...
Syrian Arab Republic	1995	5	55	4	...	...	...	...
Rép. arabe syrienne	1996	5	57	4	1996	30	192	13
Tajikistan	1995	92	399	69	...	...	...	...
Tadjikistan	1996	73	153	26	1996	11	130	22
Thailand	1995	280	1 850	32	...	...	...	...
Thaïlande	1996	320	2 550	43	1992	1 522	...	...
Turkey	1997	400	...	...	1997	1 590	...	...
Turquie	1998	425	...	...	1998	1 670	...	...
United Arab Emirates	1980	1	20	20	...	...	...	...
Emirats arabes unis	1985	1	25	16	1990	80	922	614
Uzbekistan	1995	338	1 507	67	...	...	...	...
Ouzbékistan	1996	350	1 404	61	1996	81	684	30
Viet Nam	1995	184	2 910	39	...	...	...	...
Viet Nam	1996	214	4 023	54	1996	338	2 710	36
Europe • Europe								
Albania	1980	29	59	22	...	...	...	...
Albanie	1989	42	65	20	1989	143	3 477	1 074
Andorra								
Andorre	1992	4	* 8	* 143	...	...	...	...
Austria	1997	151	...	...	1997	2 637	...	...
Autriche	1998	155	...	...	1998	2 685	...	...

16
Non-daily newspapers and periodicals [*cont.*]
Journaux non quotidiens et périodiques [*suite*]

Country or area Pays ou zone	Non-daily newspapers Journaux non quotidiens				Periodicals Périodiques			
			Circulation Diffusion				Circulation Diffusion	
	Year[§] Année[§]	Number Nombre	Total (000)	Per 1000 inhabitants Pour 1000 habitants	Year[§] Année[§]	Number Nombre	Total (000)	Per 1000 inhabitants Pour 1000 habitants
Belarus	1997	539	7 823	756	1997	302	1 647	159
Bélarus	1998	560	8 973	870	1998	318	1 687	164
Belgium	1991	3	...	...	1992	13 706		
Belgique	1992	3	* 40	* 4	1996	772	1 740	205
Bosnia and Herzegovina	1991	23	3 488	837	...	...	...	...
Bosnie-Herzégovine	1992	22	2 508	635	...	...	...	...
Bulgaria	1995	1 000[5]	8 810[5]	1 037	...	...	...	...
Bulgarie	1996	869[5]	5 791[5]	685	...	...	...	...
Croatia	1995	766	437	97	...	...	...	...
Croatie	1996	767	584	130	1990	352	6 357	1 407
Czech Republic	1997	1 126	...	...	1997	4 038	...	...
République tchèque	1998	1 169	...	...	1998	4 168	...	...
Denmark	1997	11	1 501	286	1997	140	6 263	1 192
Danemark	1998	11	1 509	286	1998	133	5 782	1 097
Estonia	1997	87	...	...	1997	572	2 044	1 412
Estonie	1998	93	...	...	1998	578	1 830	1 280
Faeroe Islands	1991	8	6	129	...	...	...	...
Iles Féroé	1992	7	6	130	...	...	...	...
Finland	1997	158	1 003	195	1997	5 612	...	...
Finlande	1998	155	965	187	1998	5 712	...	...
France	1994	295	2 856	49	...	...	...	...
France	1995	278	1 714	30	1991	2 672	120 018	2 105
Germany	1997	33	6 500	79	1997	9 010	395	5
Allemagne	1998	33	6 500	79	1998	9 203	397	5
Gibraltar	1997	3	4	154	...	...	...	...
Gibraltar	1998	3	4	160	...	...	...	...
Greece	1997	...	66	6	1997	1 558	...	...
Grèce	1998	1 286	69	7	1998	1 570	...	...
Holy See								
Saint-Siège	1992	...	...	...	1992	48	...	102
Hungary	1997	55	53	5	1997	473	478	47
Hongrie	1998	29	33	3	1998	433	457	45
Iceland	1995	113	...	...	1997	1 021	...	...
Islande	1996	84	...	...	1998	880	...	...
Ireland	1995	55	1 538	426	...	...	...	...
Irlande	1996	77	1 561	430	...	...	...	...
Italy	1994	231	1 428	25	...	...	...	...
Italie	1995	274	2 132	37	1994	9 951	80 469	1 408
Latvia	1995	265	2 478	977	...	...	...	...
Lettonie	1996	228	1 433	573	1994	213	1 660	645
Liechtenstein	1991	3	3	96	...	...	...	...
Liechtenstein	1996	1	14	449	...	...	...	...
Lithuania	1997	419	114	31	1997	797	...	...
Lituanie	1998	395	106	29	1998	807	...	...
Luxembourg	1995	5	32	79	...	...	...	...
Luxembourg	1996	5	70	170	1990	508	...	...
Malta	1997	9	...	...	1997	447	...	...
Malte	1998	9	...	...	1998	471	...	...
Monaco	1995	5	50	1 572	...	...	...	...
Monaco	1996	5	50	1 554	1992	3	38	1 226
Netherlands	1995	63[3]	585[3]	38	...	...	...	...
Pays-Bas	1996	63[3]	590[3]	38	1990	367	19 283	1 290
Norway	1997	72	370	84	...	...	...	...
Norvège	1998	74	383	87	1994	8 017	...	...
Poland	1997	28	933	24	1997	4 718	67 739	1 751
Pologne	1998	28	870	22	1998	5 297	72 336	1 868
Portugal	1996	182	* 3 800	* 385	1994	984	10 208	1 039
Portugal	1997	559	113	11	1997	702	180	18
Republic of Moldova	1997	208	598	137	1997	81	182	42
République de Moldova	1998	239	801	183	1998	86	210	48

16
Non-daily newspapers and periodicals [cont.]
Journaux non quotidiens et périodiques [suite]

Country or area Pays ou zone	Non-daily newspapers Journaux non quotidiens				Periodicals Périodiques			
			Circulation Diffusion				Circulation Diffusion	
	Year[8] Année[8]	Number Nombre	Total (000)	Per 1000 inhabitants Pour 1000 habitants	Year[8] Année[8]	Number Nombre	Total (000)	Per 1000 inhabitants Pour 1000 habitants
Romania	1980	24	746	34	1997	1 781	...	...
Roumanie	1985	24	742	33	1998	1 455	...	...
Russian Federation	1995	4 809	103 542	699	...	...	...	...
Fédération de Russie	1996	4 596	98 558	666	1996	2 751	387 832	2 618
San Marino	1997	8	12	462	1997	15	9	346
Saint-Marin	1998	8	12	462	1998	17	10	385
Slovakia	1997	402	2 787	519	1997	734	10 107	1 881
Slovaquie	1998	374	3 751	698	1998	8 376	11 210	2 085
Slovenia	1997	196	...	...	1997	1 126	...	...
Slovénie	1998	242	...	...	1998	1 177	...	...
Spain	1995	14[6]	4 980[6]	126	...	...	...	...
Espange	1996	12[6]	4 850[6]	122	...	...	...	...
Sweden	1997	66	356	40	1997	393	22 063	2 491
Suède	1998	70	376	42	1998	381	21 832	2 460
Switzerland	1997	124	1 194	165	...	...	...	...
Suisse	1998	119	1 144	...	1994	* 60	* 4 561	* 640
TFYR of Macedonia	1997	33	2 967	1 493	1997	104	5 619	2 828
L'ex-R.y. Macédoine	1998	26	2 818	1 410	1998	93	3 913	1 957
Ukraine	1997	2 275	25 361	497	1997	817	3 096	61
Ukraine	1998	2 351	33 894	666	1998	1 009	5 215	103
United Kingdom	1995	473[3]	6 600[3]	113	...	...	...	...
Royaume-Uni	1996	478[3]	6 220[3]	106	...	...	...	...
Yugoslavia	1995	573	3 781	358	...	...	...	...
Yugoslavie	1996	602	3 935	371	1994	395	...	...
Oceania · Océanie								
American Samoa	1992	2	4	85	...	...	...	...
Samoa américaines	1996	1	3	48	...	...	...	...
Australia	1995	96	379	21	...	...	...	...
Australie	1996	98	383	21	...	...	...	...
Cook Islands	1995	1	1	53	...	...	...	...
Iles Cook	1996	1	1	53	...	...	...	...
Fiji								
Fidji	1988	* 7	* 99	* 138	...	...	...	...
French Polynesia								
Polynésie française	1988	* 1	* 4	* 19				
Guam								
Guam	1988	* 4	* 26	* 203	...	...	...	...
Kiribati								
Kiribati	1988	* 2	* 4	* 57				
Marshall Islands								
Iles Marshall	1996	1	10	177	...	...	...	...
New Caledonia								
Nouvelle-Calédonie	1988	* 1	* 5	* 31	...	...	...	...
New Zealand	1997	8	...	...	1997	164	4 524	1 203
Nouvelle-Zélande	1998	8	...	...	1998	188	5 500	1 449
Niue	1992	1	2	860	...	...	...	...
Nioué	1996	1	* 2	* 941	1992	8	54	3
Norfolk Island								
Ile Norfolk	1992	1	1	21	...	...	...	...
Papua New Guina								
Papouasie-Nvl-Guinée	1988	* 4	* 78	* 21	...	...	...	...
Samoa								
Samoa	1988	* 5	* 23	* 143	...	...	...	...
Solomon Islands	1988	4	12	40	...	...	...	...
Iles Salomon	1996	3	9	23	...	...	...	...
Tokelau								
Tokélaou	1988	* 1	* 2	* 750	...	...	...	...
Tonga								
Tonga	1988	* 2	* 9	* 96	...	...	...	...

16
Non–daily newspapers and periodicals [*cont.*]
Journaux non quotidiens et périodiques [*suite*]

Country or area Pays ou zone	Non–daily newspapers Journaux non quotidiens				Periodicals Périodiques			
			Circulation Diffusion				Circulation Diffusion	
	Year[§] Année[§]	Number Nombre	Total (000)	Per 1000 inhabitants Pour 1000 habitants	Year[§] Année[§]	Number Nombre	Total (000)	Per 1000 inhabitants Pour 1000 habitants
Tuvalu	1992	1	0.3	32	...	...	...	...
Tuvalu	1996	1	0.3	28	...	...	...	...
Vanuatu	1992	1	2	11	...	...	...	...
Vanuatu	1996	2	4	23	...	...	...	...

Source:

United Nations Educational, Scientific and Cultural Organization (UNESCO) Institute for Statistics, Montreal, the UNESCO statistics database, January 2002.

[§] Data prior to 1997 may not be comparable to data for later years due to UNESCO's use of different sources.

† For information on recent changes in country or area nomenclature pertaining to Hong Kong Special Administrative Region (SAR) of China, Macao Special Administrative Region (SAR) of China, see Annex I – Country or area nomenclature, regional and other groupings.

†† For statistical purposes, the data for China do not include those for the Hong Kong Special Administrative Region (Hong Kong SAR), Macao Special Administrative Region (Macao SAR) and Taiwan province of China.

1 Data on periodicals refer only to periodicals for the general public.
2 Data on non–dailies include periodicals.
3 Data refer to regional/local non–dailies only.
4 Data on non–dailies include daily newspapers.
5 Data include regional editions.
6 Data refer to weekly newspapers only.
7 Data include the district newspapers and the home bulletins.
8 Data refer only to newspapers purchased and do not include satellite publications.
9 Data include titles issued once a week and titles issued less frequently.
10 Circulation includes only 3 out of 9 titles.

Source:

L'Institut de statistique de l'Organisation des Nations Unies pour l'éducation, la science et la culture (UNESCO), Montréal, la base de données de l'UNESCO, janvier 2002.

[§] Les données antérieures à 1997 peuvent n'être pas comparables à celles des années suivantes, l'UNESCO ayant utilisé des sources différentes.

† Pour les modifications récentes de nomenclature de pays ou de zone concernant Hong Kong (Région administrative spéciale de Chine), Macao (Région administrative spéciale de Chine), voir annexe I – Nomenclature des pays ou des zones, groupements régionaux et autres groupements.

†† Les données statistiques relatives à la Chine ne comprennent pas celles qui concernent la région administrative spéciale de Hong Kong (la RAS de Hong Kong) et la région administrative administrative spéciale de Macao (la RAS de Macao) et la province chinoise de Taiwan

1 Les données relatives aux périodiques se réfèrent seulement aux périodiques destinés au grand public.
2 Les données relatives aux journaux non quotidiens comprennent les périodiques.
3 Les données se réfèrent aux journaux non quotidiens régionaux/locaux seulement.
4 Les données relatives aux journaux non quotidiens comprennent les journaux quotidiens.
5 Les données comprennent les éditions régionales.
6 Les données ne concernent que les journaux hebdomadaires.
7 Les données comprennent les journaux de quartier et les bulletins locaux.
8 Les données se réfèrent seulement aux journaux payants et n'incluent pas les éditions satellites.
9 Les données comprennent les titres paraissant une fois par semaine ou moins fréquemment.
10 Les chiffres de diffusion ne comprennent que 3 titres sur 9.

17
Television and radio receivers
Récepteurs de télévision et de radiodiffusion sonore

Country or area Pays ou zone	Code [1]	Number (Thousands) Nombre (Milliers)				Per 1000 inhabitants Pour 1000 habitants			
		1996	1997	1998	1999	1996	1997	1998	1999
Africa • Afrique									
Algeria	T	3 000	3 100	3 200	3 300	104	105	106	107
Algérie	R	6 870	7 100	...	...	239	242	...	...
Angola	T	100	150	170	190	9	13	14	15
Angola	R	600	630	750	840	53	54	62	67
Benin	T	50	60	254	263	9	11	44	44
Bénin	R	600	620	2 574	2 661	109	110	445	448
Botswana [2]	T	29	31	32	33	19	20	20	21
Botswana [2]	R	230	237	...	...	152	154	...	...
Burkina Faso	T	90	100	120	130	8	9	11	11
Burkina Faso	R	344	370	...	...	32	34	...	...
Burundi	T	20	25	80	100	3	4	12	15
Burundi	R	425	440	1 000	1 000	68	69	155	152
Cameroon	T	400	450	480	500	30	32	34	34
Cameroun	R	2 200	2 270	...	...	162	163	...	...
Cape Verde	T	1	2	2	2	3	5	5	5
Cap–Vert	R	71	73	...	...	183	183	...	...
Central African Rep.	T	17	18	19	20	5	5	5	6
Rép. centrafricaine	R	270	283	...	...	81	83	...	...
Chad	T	9	10	10	11	1	1	1	1
Tchad	R	1 620	1 670	...	...	235	236	...	...
Comoros	T	3	3	3	...	4	4	4	...
Comores	R	87	90	...	...	140	141	...	...
Congo	T	30	33	35	...	11	12	13	...
Congo	R	330	341	...	...	125	126	...	...
Côte d'Ivoire	T	870	937	1 000	944	63	67	70	65
Côte d'Ivoire	R	2 200	2 260	...	...	159	161	.	...
Democratic Republic of the Congo	T	90	95	100	...	2	2	2	...
Rép. démocratique du Congo	R	15 970	18 030	...	...	341	376	...	...
Djibouti	T	27	28	29	30	44	45	47	48
Djibouti	R	50	52	53	54	82	84	85	86
Egypt	T	7 500	7 700	7 900	11 400	118	119	120	170
Egypte	R	20 000	20 500	...	...	315	317	...	...
Equatorial Guinea	T	40	45	50	...	98	107	116	...
Guinée équatoriale	R	175	180	...	...	427	429	...	...
Eritrea	T	25	40	50	60	8	12	14	16
Erythreé	R	330	1 200	1 500	1 800	100	350	419	484
Ethiopia [3]	T	300	320	340	350	5	5	5	5
Ethiopie [3]	R	11 300	11 750	12 000	12 000	188	191	190	185
Gabon	T	60	63	200	300	54	55	171	251
Gabon	R	201	208	500	600	182	183	428	501
Gambia [2]	T	4	4	4	4	3	3	3	3
Gambie [2]	R	189	196	300	500	164	165	244	394
Ghana	T	1 650	1 730	1 900	2 266	91	93	99	115
Ghana	R	4 250	4 400	13 200	13 390	234	236	689	680
Guinea	T	250	312	330	343	34	43	45	47
Guinée	R	350	357	373	380	48	49	51	52
Guinea–Bissau Guinée–Bissau	R	47	49	...	...	42	43	...	...
Kenya [3]	T	580	620	640	660	21	22	22	22
Kenya [3]	R	3 000	3 070	...	6 383	108	108	...	216
Lesotho	T	27	29	31	33	14	14	15	16
Lesotho	R	100	104	...	...	51	52	...	...
Liberia	T	60	70	75	76	27	29	28	26
Libéria	R	715	790	...	...	325	329	...	...
Libyan Arab Jamahiriya	T	680	730	750	760	134	140	140	139
Jamah. arabe libyenne	R	1 300	1 350	...	...	256	259	...	...
Madagascar	T	305	325	340	360	22	22	23	23
Madagascar	R	2 950	3 050	...	...	208	209	...	...
Malawi	T	23	25	26	27	2	2	3	3
Malawi	R	2 525	2 600	4 929	...	257	258	476	...
Mali	T	120	125	130	140	12	12	12	13
Mali	R	550	570	...	...	54	55	...	...

17
Television and radio receivers [*cont.*]
Récepteurs de télévision et de radiodiffusion sonore [*suite*]

Country or area Pays ou zone	Code[1]	Number (Thousands) Nombre (Milliers)				Per 1000 inhabitants Pour 1000 habitants			
		1996	1997	1998	1999	1996	1997	1998	1999
Mauritania	T	193	221	231	247	80	90	91	95
Mauritanie	R	350	360	...	...	146	146	...	...
Mauritius	T	252	258	260	285	224	228	227	248
Maurice	R	415	420	...	...	369	371	...	...
Morocco	T	4 300	4 400	4 500	4 600	163	164	164	165
Maroc	R	6 500	6 640	...	...	246	247	...	...
Mozambique	T	70	90	95	100	4	5	5	5
Mozambique	R	700	730	...	...	39	40	...	...
Namibia[4]	T	50	60	63	65	32	37	38	38
Namibie[4]	R	225	232	...	...	142	143	...	...
Niger	T	250	260	270	285	26	27	27	15
Niger	R	650	680	685	690	69	70	68	36
Nigeria	T	6 500	6 900	7 200	7 500	64	66	68	69
Nigéria	R	22 700	23 500	...	...	224	226	...	...
Réunion	T	123	127	130	...	185	189	191	...
Réunion	R	170	173	...	...	256	257	...	...
Rwanda	T	1	1	1	...	0.09	0.1	0.09	...
Rwanda	R	550	601	...	...	100	101	...	...
Saint Helena	T	1	1	2	2	242	247	250	267
Sainte−Hélène	R	3	3	3	3	500	500	500	500
Sao Tome and Principe	T	25	30	32	33	185	217	227	229
Sao Tomé−et−Principe	R	37	38	45	...	274	275	319	...
Senegal	T	350	361	370	375	41	41	41	41
Sénégal	R	1 200	1 240	...	...	140	141	...	...
Seychelles	T	11	16	16	16	149	219	217	214
Seychelles	R	40	42	...	...	541	560	...	...
Sierra Leone	T	51	53	60	62	12	12	13	13
Sierra Leone	R	1 080	1 120	1 250	...	252	253	274	...
Somalia	T	129	135	138	140	15	15	15	14
Somalie	R	450	470	...	...	53	53	...	...
South Africa[2]	T	5 232	5 399	5 450	5 500	137	139	138	138
Afrique du Sud[2]	R	13 400	13 750	...	...	351	355	...	...
Sudan	T	2 300	2 380	2 450	5 000	85	86	87	173
Soudan	R	7 360	7 550	12 961	13 868	271	272	458	480
Swaziland[2]	T	100	105	108	110	111	114	113	112
Swaziland[2]	R	150	155	...	...	167	168	...	...
Togo	T	70	73	80	100	17	17	18	22
Togo	R	910	940	1 000	1 100	218	219	227	244
Tunisia	T	900	1 500	1 700	1 800	99	163	182	190
Tunisie	R	2 000	1 320	1 340	1 490	220	143	144	158
Uganda	T	525	550	580	600	27	28	28	28
Ouganda	R	2 500	2 600	...	...	128	130	...	...
United Rep. of Tanzania	T	600	650	670	690	20	21	21	21
Rép.−Unie de Tanzanie	R	8 550	8 800	...	...	279	280	...	...
Zambia[2]	T	660	850	1 200	1 300	79	99	137	145
Zambie[2]	R	1 000	1 030	1 200	1 436	119	120	137	160
Zimbabwe[3]	T	350	370	390	400	32	33	34	35
Zimbabwe[3]	R	1 100	1 140	...	4 488	100	102	...	389
America, North • Amérique du Nord									
Anguilla	T	1	1	1	1	125	125	125	125
Anguilla	R	3	3	...	...	375	375	...	...
Antigua and Barbuda	T	31	31	32	33	470	470	478	493
Antigua−et−Barbuda	R	35	36	...	...	530	545	...	...
Aruba	T	20	20	21	22	233	222	223	224
Aruba	R	45	50	...	...	523	556	...	...
Bahamas	T	66	70	72	73	231	241	243	243
Bahamas	R	210	215	...	...	734	739	...	...
Barbados	T	75	76	77	78	282	285	287	290
Barbade	R	236	237	168	175	887	888	627	651
Belize[2]	T	40	41	42	43	183	183	183	183
Belize[2]	R	129	133	...	...	589	594	...	...
Bermuda[2]	T	66	66	70	70	1 048	1 048	1 094	1 094
Bermudes[2]	R	82	82	...	...	1 302	1 302	...	...

17
Television and radio receivers [cont.]
Récepteurs de télévision et de radiodiffusion sonore [suite]

Country or area Pays ou zone	Code [1]	Number (Thousands) Nombre (Milliers)				Per 1000 inhabitants Pour 1000 habitants			
		1996	1997	1998	1999	1996	1997	1998	1999
British Virgin Islands	T	4	4	4	4	211	200	200	190
Iles Vierges brit.	R	9	9	...	...	474	450	...	...
Canada	T	21 053	21 450	...	...	703	709	...	...
Canada	R	30 678	31 398	...	...	1 024	1 038	...	...
Cayman Islands	T	6	7	7	8	182	206	194	216
Iles Caïmanes	R	35	36	...	...	1 061	1 059	...	...
Costa Rica	T	800	850	870	900	219	227	227	229
Costa Rica	R	950	980	...	3 045	260	261	...	774
Cuba	T	2 600	2 660	2 700	2 750	236	240	245	248
Cuba	R	3 870	3 900	...	...	351	352	...	...
Dominica	T	13	15	16	17	183	211	225	232
Dominica	R	46	46	...	...	648	648	...	...
Dominican Republic	T	730	770	790	...	92	95	96	...
République dominicaine	R	1 410	1 440	...	...	177	178	...	...
El Salvador	T	850	1 000	1 097	1 177	147	169	182	191
El Salvador	R	2 680	2 750	2 850	2 940	463	465	472	478
Greenland	T	21	22	23	...	375	393	411	...
Groënland	R	26	27	...	...	464	482	...	...
Grenada	T	32	33	34	35	348	355	366	376
Grenade	R	56	57	...	...	609	613	...	...
Guadeloupe	T	116	118	120	122	269	270	271	271
Guadeloupe	R	110	113	...	...	255	259	...	...
Guatemala	T	620	640	660	680	61	61	61	61
Guatemala	R	800	835	...	...	78	79	...	...
Haiti	T	36	38	40	42	5	5	5	5
Haïti	R	400	415	...	...	52	53	...	...
Honduras	T	550	570	590	600	95	95	96	95
Honduras	R	2 380	2 450	...	...	409	410	...	...
Jamaica	T	450	460	480	490	180	183	189	191
Jamaïque	R	1 200	1 215	2 019	...	481	483	796	...
Martinique	T	55	58	60	62	144	150	154	158
Martinique	R	80	82	...	...	209	212	...	...
Mexico	T	22 000	24 200	25 000	26 500	237	257	261	272
Mexique	R	30 000	31 000	...	...	324	329	...	...
Montserrat	T	2	3	3	3	182	273	273	273
Montserrat	R	7	7	...	...	636	636	...	...
Netherlands Antilles	T	67	69	70	71	322	327	329	330
Antilles néerlandaises	R	214	217	...	...	1 029	1 028	...	...
Nicaragua	T	310	320	330	340	68	68	69	69
Nicaragua	R	1 200	1 240	1 300	...	264	265	270	...
Panama	T	500	510	530	540	187	187	192	192
Panama	R	800	815	...	...	299	299	...	...
Puerto Rico [5]	T	1 200	1 220	1 250	1 270	320	323	328	331
Porto Rico [5]	R	2 820	2 840	...	...	752	751	...	...
Saint Kitts and Nevis	T	10	10	10	10	250	256	256	256
Saint−Kitts−et−Nevis	R	28	28	...	...	700	718	...	...
Saint Lucia	T	52	54	55	56	356	365	367	368
Sainte−Lucie	R	109	111	...	...	747	750	...	...
Saint Pierre and Miquelon	T	4	4	4	4	667	571	571	571
Saint−Pierre−et−Miquelon	R	4	4	...	...	667	571	...	...
Saint Vincent and Grenadines	T	24	25	26	26	216	223	228	230
Saint−Vincent−et−Grenadines	R	76	77	...	...	685	688	...	...
Trinidad and Tobago	T	419	425	430	435	330	333	335	337
Trinité−et−Tobago	R	670	680	...	...	528	532	...	...
Turks and Caicos Is.									
Iles Turques et Caïques	R	7	8	...	...	467	533	...	...
United States	T	223 000	229 000	231 000	233 000	828	843	843	844
Etats−Unis	R	570 000	575 000	...	...	2 116	2 116	...	...
US Virgin Islands	T	68	69	70	71	708	726	745	755
Iles Vierges américaines	R	106	107	...	...	1 104	1 126	...	...
America, South • Amérique du Sud									
Argentina [4]	T	10 000	10 300	10 600	...	284	289	293	...
Argentine [4]	R	23 850	24 300	...	...	677	681	...	...
Bolivia	T	875	900	930	960	115	116	117	118
Bolivie	R	5 110	5 250	...	...	673	675	...	...

17
Television and radio receivers [cont.]
Récepteurs de télévision et de radiodiffusion sonore [suite]

Country or area Pays ou zone	Code [1]	Number (Thousands) Nombre (Milliers)				Per 1000 inhabitants Pour 1000 habitants			
		1996	1997	1998	1999	1996	1997	1998	1999
Brazil	T	45 643	50 573	53 768	56 000	283	309	324	333
Brésil	R	70 000	71 000	...	...	433	434	...	...
Chile	T	3 300	3 400	3 500	3 600	229	232	236	240
Chili	R	5 100	5 180	...	...	354	354	...	...
Colombia	T	7 614	7 766	11 288	11 613	194	194	277	279
Colombie	R	20 600	21 000	21 781	22 418	524	524	534	539
Ecuador	T	2 000	2 300	2 500	2 640	171	193	205	213
Equateur	R	4 000	4 500	4 800	5 040	342	377	394	406
Falkland Islands (Malvinas)	T	1	1	2	2	650	700	750	750
Iles Falkland (Malvinas)	R	1	1	...	...	500	500	...	...
French Guiana	T	30	35	37	...	196	219	222	...
Guyane française	R	100	104	...	...	654	650	...	...
Guyana	T	45	50	55	60	54	59	65	70
Guyana	R	415	420	375	400	496	498	441	468
Paraguay	T	850	900	1 000	1 100	171	177	191	205
Paraguay	R	900	925	...	...	182	182	...	...
Peru	T	3 400	3 500	3 600	3 700	142	144	145	147
Pérou	R	6 500	6 650	...	...	271	273	...	...
Suriname	T	90	95	98	100	220	231	237	241
Suriname	R	295	300	...	...	720	728	...	...
Uruguay	T	1 720	1 735	1 750	1 760	531	531	532	531
Uruguay	R	1 955	1 970	...	...	603	603	...	...
Venezuela	T	3 800	4 000	4 300	4 386	170	176	185	185
Venezuela	R	10 500	10 750	6 919	7 011	471	472	298	296
Asia • Asie									
Afghanistan	T	250	270	290	300	12	13	14	14
Afghanistan	R	2 550	2 750	...	...	125	132	...	...
Armenia	T	820	825	840	850	230	232	238	241
Arménie	R	840	850	...	...	236	239	...	...
Azerbaijan	T	1 600	1 800	1 950	1 980	210	236	254	257
Azerbaïdjan	R	170	175	...	...	22	23	...	...
Bahrain	T	257	260	265	270	451	446	445	446
Bahreïn	R	330	338	24	39	579	580	40	64
Bangladesh	T	870	900	920	940	7	7	7	7
Bangladesh	R	6 000	6 150	...	...	50	50	...	...
Bhutan	T	12	12	13	13	6	6	6	6
Bhoutan	R	35	37	...	...	18	19	...	...
Brunei Darussalam	T	190	196	200	205	632	636	635	637
Brunéi Darussalam	R	90	93	...	...	299	302	...	...
Cambodia	T	90	94	96	98	9	9	9	9
Cambodge	R	1 300	1 340	...	...	127	128	...	...
China ††	T	321 000	340 000	360 000	370 000	265	279	286	291
Chine	R	412 797	417 000	...	...	341	342	...	...
China, Hong Kong SAR † [2]	T	2 450	2 680	2 884	3 105	385	412	433	457
Chine, Hong Kong RAS † [2]	R	4 300	4 450	...	...	676	683	...	...
China, Macao SAR †	T	119	121	123	125	270	268	268	268
Chine, Macao RAS †	R	155	160	215	219	352	356	469	468
Cyprus	T	112	115	117	120	149	151	152	154
Chypre	R	300	310	...	...	398	406	...	...
Georgia	T	2 560	2 570	2 580	2 585	494	502	510	516
Georgie	R	3 010	3 020	...	...	580	590	...	...
India [2]	T	60 000	66 000	70 000	75 000	63	68	71	75
Inde [2]	R	113 500	116 000	...	...	119	120	...	...
Indonesia	T	25 000	27 000	28 000	30 000	125	133	136	143
Indonésie	R	31 000	31 500	...	...	155	155	...	...
Iran, Islamic Rep. of [7]	T	9 000	9 000	10 300	10 300	142	139	157	154
Iran, Rép. islamique d' [7]	R	16 600	17 000	17 400	...	262	263	265	...
Iraq	T	1 700	1 750	1 800	1 850	82	83	83	82
Iraq	R	4 700	4 850	...	...	228	229	...	...
Israel [8]	T	1 900	1 900	1 900	2 000	332	324	318	328
Israël [8]	R	3 000	3 070	...	...	524	524	...	...
Japan	T	88 000	89 200	90 000	91 000	700	708	713	719
Japon	R	120 000	120 500	...	...	954	956	...	...

17
Television and radio receivers [*cont.*]
Récepteurs de télévision et de radiodiffusion sonore [*suite*]

Country or area Pays ou zone	Code [1]	Number (Thousands) Nombre (Milliers)				Per 1000 inhabitants Pour 1000 habitants			
		1996	1997	1998	1999	1996	1997	1998	1999
Jordan	T	480	500	520	540	81	82	82	83
Jordanie	R	1 600	1 660	...	...	269	271	...	...
Kazakhstan	T	3 870	3 880	3 890	3 900	235	237	238	240
Kazakhstan	R	6 460	6 470	...	...	393	395	...	...
Korea, Dem.People's Rep.	T	1 080	1 200	1 300	1 300	48	52	56	55
Corée, Rép. pop. dém. de	R	3 300	3 360	...	...	146	146	...	...
Korea, Republic of	T	15 258	15 746	16 421	16 896	336	344	356	364
Corée, République de	R	47 000	47 500	...	...	1 036	1 039	...	...
Kuwait	T	860	875	890	910	510	505	491	480
Koweït	R	1 160	1 175	1 190	1 200	688	678	657	633
Kyrgyzstan	T	200	210	220	230	44	45	47	49
Kirghizistan	R	515	520	...	...	112	113	...	...
Lao People's Dem. Rep.	T	49	49	50	51	10	10	10	10
République dém. pop. lao	R	700	730	...	...	143	145	...	...
Lebanon	T	1 096	1 107	1 120	1 150	355	352	351	355
Liban	R	2 750	2 850	...	...	892	907	...	...
Malaysia	T	3 500	3 600	3 700	3 800	170	172	173	174
Malaisie	R	8 900	9 100	...	...	433	434	...	...
Maldives	T	10	10	11	11	40	39	39	38
Maldives	R	33	34	...	...	129	129	...	...
Mongolia	T	149	150	152	153	60	59	59	58
Mongolie	R	350	360	...	...	140	142	...	...
Myanmar	T	311	317	320	323	7	7	7	7
Myanmar	R	4 150	4 200	3 155	3 157	96	96	72	72
Nepal	T	79	82	85	150	4	4	4	6
Népal	R	810	840	...	...	37	38	...	...
Oman	T	1 361	1 395	1 400	1 415	610	605	588	575
Oman	R	1 340	1 400	...	...	601	607	...	...
Pakistan	T	7 600	9 000	12 500	16 000	54	62	84	105
Pakistan	R	12 900	13 500	...	...	92	94	...	...
Philippines	T	7 500	7 800	8 000	8 200	107	109	110	110
Philippines	R	11 000	11 500	...	...	157	161	...	...
Qatar	T	300	460	490	510	538	808	846	866
Qatar	R	250	256	...	...	448	450	...	...
Saudi Arabia	T	4 900	5 100	5 300	5 500	260	262	263	263
Arabie saoudite	R	6 000	6 250	...	...	319	321	...	...
Singapore [2]	T	1 100	1 110	1 120	1 200	326	324	322	341
Singapour [2]	R	2 500	2 550	...	...	741	744	...	...
Sri Lanka	T	1 500	1 700	1 800	1 900	83	93	98	102
Sri Lanka	R	3 800	3 850	...	...	210	211	...	...
Syrian Arab Republic	T	1 040	1 050	1 060	1 070	71	70	69	68
Rép. arabe syrienne	R	4 000	4 150	...	...	275	278	...	...
Tajikistan	T	1 653	1 700	1 900	2 000	283	287	316	328
Tadjikistan	R	800	850	...	...	137	143	...	...
Thailand [4]	T	12 500	14 200	15 115	16 700	211	238	251	274
Thaïlande [4]	R	12 000	13 959	...	...	203	234	...	...
Turkey	T	19 719	20 000	21 000	21 500	316	315	326	328
Turquie	R	11 000	11 300	...	33 406	176	178	...	510
Turkmenistan	T	850	855	865	870	205	202	201	198
Turqmenistan	R	1 200	1 225	...	...	289	289	...	...
United Arab Emirates	T	675	700	720	740	299	303	306	309
Emirats arabes unis	R	800	820	...	...	354	355	...	...
Uzbekistan	T	6 250	6 400	6 600	6 700	274	276	280	280
Ouzbekistan	R	10 500	10 800	...	...	460	465	...	...
Viet Nam	T	13 500	14 000	14 250	14 500	180	183	184	184
Viet Nam	R	8 050	8 200	...	...	107	107	...	...
Yemen	T	4 300	4 500	4 800	5 000	274	276	284	286
Yémen	R	1 000	1 050	...	...	64	64	...	...
Europe • Europe									
Albania	T	380	405	430	455	121	129	137	146
Albanie	R	800	810	...	...	254	259	...	...
Andorra	T	26	27	30	33	388	386	417	440
Andorre	R	15	16	...	...	224	229	...	...

17
Television and radio receivers [*cont.*]
Récepteurs de télévision et de radiodiffusion sonore [*suite*]

Country or area Pays ou zone	Code[1]	Number (Thousands) Nombre (Milliers)				Per 1000 inhabitants Pour 1000 habitants			
		1996	1997	1998	1999	1996	1997	1998	1999
Austria	T	4 000	4 100	4 200	4 300	497	506	516	526
Autriche	R	6 000	6 080	...	...	745	751	...	...
Belarus	T	3 100	3 200	3 300	3 400	299	309	320	331
Bélarus	R	3 000	3 020	...	...	289	292	...	...
Belgium	T	5 100	5 200	5 300	5 400	505	513	523	532
Belgique	R	8 050	8 075	...	...	796	797	...	...
Bosnia and Herzegovina	T	410	420	430	430	120	119	117	112
Bosnie−et−Herzégovine	R	900	940	...	940	263	267	...	245
Bulgaria	T	3 056	3 310	3 400	3 550	362	394	408	429
Bulgarie	R	4 500	4 510	...	...	533	537	...	...
Croatia	T	1 200	1 220	1 250	1 280	267	272	279	286
Croatie	R	1 500	1 510	...	...	334	337	...	...
Czech Republic	T	4 400	4 600	4 800	5 000	427	447	467	487
Républic Tchèque	R	8 261	8 270	...	...	801	803	...	...
Denmark	T	2 900	3 000	3 100	4 100	553	571	588	776
Danemark	R	6 000	6 020	...	7 000	1 145	1 145	...	1 325
Estonia	T	660	700	720	800	450	484	504	567
Estonie	R	1 000	1 010	1 300	1 400	682	698	910	992
Faeroe Islands	T	16	17	44	45	364	375	1 023	1 047
Iles Féroé	R	25	26	70	80	568	591	1 628	1 860
Finland	T	2 700	3 200	3 350	3 320	527	622	650	643
Finlande	R	7 100	7 670	7 540	8 080	1 385	1 492	1 463	1 564
France	T	35 000	35 500	36 000	36 500	601	607	613	620
France	R	55 000	55 300	...	...	944	946	...	...
Germany	T	40 400	46 850	47 590	47 660	493	571	581	581
Allemagne	R	77 500	77 800	...	...	946	948	...	...
Gibraltar	T	10	10	10	10	385	385	400	400
Gibraltar	R	37	37	...	...	1 423	1 423	...	...
Greece	T	4 800	4 900	5 000	5 100	456	464	472	480
Grèce	R	5 000	5 020	...	...	475	475	...	...
Holy See	T	2	2	2	...	...	...	...	...
Saint−Siège									
Hungary	T	4 400	4 450	4 500	4 500	432	438	445	447
Hongrie	R	7 000	7 010	...	...	687	690	...	...
Iceland	T	130	135	139	141	480	493	504	505
Islande	R	250	260	280	300	923	949	1 014	1 075
Ireland[2]	T	1 390	1 470	1 500	1 505	382	402	407	406
Irlande[2]	R	2 500	2 550	...	...	688	697	...	...
Italy	T	27 800	27 800	28 000	28 200	485	485	488	492
Italie	R	50 000	50 500	...	...	872	880	...	...
Latvia	T	1 483	1 500	1 550	1 808	593	610	639	757
Lettonie	R	1 750	1 760	...	1 674	700	715	...	701
Liechtenstein	T	14	15	15	...	452	453	469	...
Liechtenstein	R	21	21	...	...	677	656	...	...
Lithuania	T	1 395	1 450	1 550	1 555	376	391	420	422
Lituanie	R	1 850	1 900	...	1 850	498	513	...	502
Luxembourg	T	240	245	248	255	583	588	588	599
Luxembourg	R	280	285	...	...	680	683	...	...
Malta[4]	T	186	196	206	212	492	515	536	549
Malte[4]	R	250	255	...	...	661	669	...	...
Monaco	T	24	25	25	25	750	758	758	758
Monaco	R	34	34	...	...	1 063	1 030	...	...
Netherlands	T	8 300	8 400	8 450	8 500	534	538	539	540
Pays−Bas	R	15 000	15 300	...	...	965	980	...	...
Norway	T	2 500	2 550	2 600	2 900	572	580	588	653
Norvège	R	4 000	4 030	...	...	915	917	...	...
Poland	T	12 839	14 000	14 500	15 000	332	362	375	387
Pologne	R	20 000	20 200	...	...	517	522	...	...
Portugal	T	5 000	5 200	5 400	5 600	507	527	547	567
Portugal	R	3 000	3 020	...	...	304	306	...	...
Republic of Moldova	T	1 300	1 300	1 300	1 300	297	297	297	297
Rép. de Moldova	R	3 200	3 220	3 240	3 250	731	736	740	742
Romania	T	5 100	5 250	5 400	7 000	225	233	240	312
Roumanie	R	7 190	7 200	...	7 500	318	319	...	335

17
Television and radio receivers [*cont.*]
Récepteurs de télévision et de radiodiffusion sonore [*suite*]

Country or area Pays ou zone	Code [1]	Number (Thousands) Nombre (Milliers)				Per 1000 inhabitants Pour 1000 habitants			
		1996	1997	1998	1999	1996	1997	1998	1999
Russian Federation	T	57 000	57 300	62 000	...	385	388	421	...
Fédération de Russie	R	61 000	61 500	...	...	413	417	...	...
San Marino	T	22	23	23	23	896	865	873	875
Saint−Marin	R	35	35	35	...	1 404	1 346	1 346	...
Slovakia	T	2 065	2 160	2 220	2 250	385	402	413	418
Slovaquie	R	3 100	5 200	5 200	...	578	968	967	...
Slovenia	T	680	700	710	720	341	351	356	362
Slovénie	R	800	805	...	...	401	404	...	...
Spain	T	20 000	19 900	20 000	22 000	505	502	505	555
Espagne	R	13 000	13 100	...	...	328	331	...	...
Sweden	T	4 400	4 500	4 700	4 900	498	508	530	551
Suède	R	8 000	8 250	...	...	906	932	...	...
Switzerland	T	3 200	3 310	3 500	3 700	445	457	...	...
Suisse	R	7 000	7 100	...	...	972	979	...	...
TFYR of Macedonia	T	203	206	...	...	253	252	250	273
L'ex−R.y. de Macédoine	R	400	410	...	...	500	500	500	550
Ukraine	T	19 700	20 000	21 000	22 000	384	392	413	433
Ukraine	R	45 000	45 050	...	...	878	882	...	...
United Kingdom [2]	T	37 300	37 800	38 000	38 800	635	643	648	661
Royaume−Uni [2]	R	84 000	84 500	...	...	1 431	1 437	...	...
Yugoslavia	T	2 700	2 750	2 900	2 950	255	259	273	277
Yougoslavie	R	3 100	3 150	...	...	292	296	...	...
Oceania • Océanie									
American Samoa	T	13	14	15	15	220	230	230	227
Samoa américaines	R	55	57	...	...	932	934	...	...
Australia [3]	T	12 800	13 000	13 200	13 400	706	709	713	716
Australie [3]	R	25 000	25 500	...	...	1 378	1 391	...	...
Cook Islands	T	3	3	3	3	158	146	147	147
Iles Cook	R	14 [9]	14	4	4	737 [9]	737	194	195
Fiji	T	75	78	80	89	97	99	101	110
Fidji	R	490	500	527	545	631	636	662	677
French Polynesia	T	40	41	42	43	183	184	192	193
Polynésie française	R	125	128	...	...	571	574	...	...
Guam	T	105	106	108	110	677	671	671	671
Guam	R	216	221	...	...	1 394	1 399	...	...
Kiribati	T	2	2	2	2	22	22	22	23
Kiribati	R	17	17	20	28	215	213	247	341
Micronesia (Fed. States of)	T	2	2	2	2	20	21	20	20
Micron (États fédérés de)	R	8	...	...	...	70	...	...	...
Nauru	T	636	636	...	...	0.4	1	1	...
Nauru	R	7	7	...	...	36	45	45	...
New Caledonia	T	81	90	95	101	408	446	461	481
Nouvelle−Calédonie	R	104	107	112	117	525	530	544	557
New Zealand [2]	T	1 845	1 926	1 950	1 975	496	512	514	516
Nouvelle−zélande [2]	R	3 700	3 750	...	...	995	997	...	...
Niue	T	0.3	0.3	0.4	0.4	175	175	180	185
Nioué	R	1	1	...	...	500	500	...	...
Papua New Guinea	T	17	18	20	60	4	4	4	13
Papouasie−Nouv.−Guinée	R	400	410	...	...	91	91	...	...
Samoa	T	8	8	9	10	44	47	52	56
Samoa	R	...	178	...	...	...	1 035	...	...
Solomon Islands	T	3	4	6	7	8	10	14	16
Iles Salomon	R	55	57	...	...	140	141	...	...
Tokelau	T	0.1	0.1	0.1	0.1	110	115	120	125
Tokélaou	R	1	1	...	...	1 000	1 000	...	...
Tonga	T	5	5	6	6	52	51	56	61
Tonga	R	60	61	...	65	619	622	...	663
Tuvalu	T	0.1	0.1	0.1	0.1	9	9	9	9
Tuvalu	R	4	4	...	...	364	364	...	...
Vanuatu	T	2	2	2	2	11	11	12	12
Vanuatu	R	60	62	...	...	347	350	...	...
Wallis and Futuna Islands	T	1	1	1	1	93	93	96	100
Iles Wallis−et−Futuna									

17
Television and radio receivers [*cont.*]
Récepteurs de télévision et de radiodiffusion sonore [*suite*]

Source:
United Nations Educational, Scientific and Cultural Organization
(UNESCO) Institute for Statistics, Montreal, the UNESCO
statistics database, January 2002.

†   For information on recent changes in country or area
nomenclature pertaining to former Czechoslovakia, Germany,
Hong Kong Special Administrative Region (SAR) of China,
Macao Special Administrative Region (SAR) of China,
SFR of Yugoslavia and the former USSR, see Annex I –
Country or area nomenclature, regional and other groupings.

†† For statistical purposes, the data for China do not
include those for the Hong Kong Special Administrative
Region (Hong Kong SAR), Macao Special Administrative
Region (Macao SAR) and Taiwan province of China.

1   T: Estimated number of television receivers in use.
    R: Estimated number of radio receivers in use.
2   Data refer to fiscal years beginning 1 April.
3   Data refer to fiscal years ending 30 June.
4   Data refer to fiscal years ending 30 Sept.
5   Data refer to Puerto Rico Telephone Authority.
6   For 1990, data refer to fiscal year ending Nov.
7   Data refer to fiscal years beginning 22 March.
8   Data prior to 1986 refer to fiscal years beginning 1 April.
9   1996: Data refer to year ending Nov. 1997.

Source:
L'Institut de statistiques de l'Organisation des Nations Unies pour
l'éducation, la science et la culture (UNESCO), Montréal, la base de
données de l'UNESCO, janvier 2002.

†   Pour les modifications récentes de nomenclature de pays
ou de zone concernant l'Allemagne, Hong Kong, région
administrative spéciale (RAS) de Chine, Macao, région
administrative spéciale (RAS) de Chine, l'ex–Tchécoslovaquie,
l'ex–URSS et l'ex–Rfs de Yougoslavie, voir annexe I –
Nomenclature des pays ou des zones, groupements
régionaux et autres groupements.

†† Les données statistiques relatives à la Chine ne comprennent
pas celles qui concernent la région administrative spéciale de
Hong Kong (la RAS de Hong Kong), la région administrative
spéciale de Macao (la RAS de Macao) et la province chinoise
de Taiwan.

1   T: Estimation du nombre de récepteurs de télévision en service.
    R: Estimation du nombre de récepteurs de radiodiffusion
     sonore en service.
2   Les données se réfèrent aux années fiscales commençant le 1er avril.
3   Les données se réfèrent aux années fiscales finissant le 30e juin.
4   Les données se réfèrent aux années fiscales finissant le 30e sept.
5   Les données se réfèrent au "Puerto Rico Telephone Authority".
6   Pour 1990, les données se réfèrent aux années fiscales finissant en nov.
7   Les données se réfèrent aux années fiscales commençant le 22e mars.
8   Antérieur à 1986, les données se réfèrent aux années fiscales
commençant le 1er avril.
9   1996: les données se réfèrent à l'année finissant en nov. 1997.

18
Cinemas: number, seating capacity, annual attendance and box office receipts
Cinémas: nombre d'établissements, nombre de sièges, fréquentation annuelle et recettes guichet

Country or area Pays ou zone	Year Année	Cinemas – Cinémas Number Nombre	Seating capacity Sièges No. (000)	P. 1000	Annual attendance Fréquentation annuelle No. (000000)	P. capita P. habitant	Gross receipts Recettes brutes Total (000000)	Currency Monnaie
Africa • Afrique								
Algeria	1985	216	110.0	5.0	20.5	0.9	109.0	dinar
Algérie	1996	136	...	...	0.6	0.0	...	dinar
	1997	136	...	...	0.6	0.0	...	
Benin	1993	23[1]	9.4	1.9	0.7	0.1	116.0	CFA franc
Bénin	1996	3	2.5	0.5	0.3	0.1	56.0	franc CFA
	1997	3	2.5	0.4	0.3	0.0	58.0	
Burkina Faso	1986	23	24.0	3.0	6.2	0.8	890.0	CFA franc
Burkina Faso	1996	35	55.0	5.1	4.7	0.4	838.0	franc CFA
	1997	35	55.0	5.0	4.9	0.4	870.0	
Cameroon	1985	197[1]	39.8	4.0	...	...	...	CFA franc
Cameroun	1990	230[1]	38.9	3.4	...	...	...	franc CFA
	1991	232[1]	39.9	3.4	...	...	...	
Congo	1994	28[1]	11.2	4.5	...	...	...	CFA franc
Congo	1995	30[1]	4.4	1.7	...	...	...	franc CFA
Côte d'Ivoire	1992	60	70.0	5.6	7.9	0.6	...	CFA franc
Côte d'Ivoire	1993	60	70.0	5.5	7.3	0.6	...	franc CFA
Egypt	1991	149	126.0	2.2	16.5	0.3	23.0	pound
Egypte	1994	138	106.0	1.7	12.9	0.2	37.0	livre
	1996	122	96.1	1.5	10.6	0.2	46.0	
Guinea	1985	29	61.2	12.3	2.6	0.5	...	syli
Guinée	1990	88	46.4	8.1	4.4	0.8	897.0	syli
	1991	80	41.0	6.8	3.9	0.6	793.0	
Kenya	1993	42[1]	7.0	0.3	5.8	0.2	...	shilling
Kenya	1998	20	6.6	0.2	0.6	0.0	0.0	shilling
	1999	20	6.6	0.2	0.9	0.0	0.1	
Libyan Arab Jamahiriya	1998	27	14.4	2.7	2.9	0.5	1.4	dinar
Jamah. arabe libyenne	1999	27	14.4	2.6	2.9	0.5	1.4	dinar
Madagascar	1990	20	...	...	0.7	0.1	356.0	franc
Madagascar	1991	11	...	...	0.4	0.0	209.0	franc
Mauritius	1993	16	14.0	12.8	0.7	0.7	*22.0	rupee
Maurice	1998	25	13.0	11.4	1.3	1.1	...	roupie
	1999	32	16.0	13.9	1.3	1.2	...	
Morocco	1995	185	131.0	5.0	17.3	0.7	103.0	dirham
Maroc	1996	183	130.0	4.9	16.3	0.6	114.0	dirham
	1997	175	124.0	4.6	14.3	0.5	111.0	
Rwanda	1980	10	3.1	0.6	0.3	0.1	52.0	franc
Rwanda	1985	34	9.3	1.5	...	...	...	franc
	1990	4	1.9	0.3	...	...	...	
United Rep. of Tanzania	1986	31	16.4	0.7	4.2	0.2	167.0	shilling
Rép.–Unie de Tanzanie	1990	28	12.4	0.5	1.9	*0.1	183.0	shilling
	1991	28	12.4	0.5	1.9	*0.1	148.0	
Zimbabwe	1991	24	12.2	1.2	1.8	0.2	7.6	dollar
Zimbabwe	1998	22	4.1	0.4	1.5	0.1	3.9	dollar
	1999	22	4.1	0.4	1.2	0.1	2.3	
America, North • Amérique du Nord								
Barbados	1990	3	...	...	0.0	0.0	...	dollar
Barbade	1991	4	...	...	0.0	0.0	...	dollar
Bermuda	1998	4	1.0	15.4	0.3	5.0	...	dollar
Bermudes	1999	4	1.0	15.4	0.3	5.0	...	dollar
Canada	1990	742	722.0	26.0	79.0	2.8	439.0[2]	dollar
Canada	1998	685	588.9	19.3	99.1	3.2	714.7	dollar
	1999	692	646.7	21.0	112.8	3.7	857.0	
Costa Rica	1985	105	...	...	0.2	*0.1	...	colon
Costa Rica	1994	38	...	...	1.5	0.4	760.0	colón
	1995	39	...	...	1.7	0.5	1 058.0	
Cuba	1993	903[1]	187.9	17.3	23.8	2.2	6.4	peso
Cuba	1996	944	193.3	17.5	10.8	1.0	5.8	peso
	1997	782	172.5	15.6	9.2	0.8	6.4	

18
Cinemas: number, seating capacity, annual attendance and box office receipts [*cont.*]
Cinémas: nombre d'établissements, nombre de sièges, fréquentation annuelle et recettes guichet [*suite*]

Country or area Pays ou zone	Year Année	Cinemas – Cinémas Number Nombre	Seating capacity Sièges No. (000)	P. 1000	Annual attendance Fréquentation annuelle No. (000000)	P. capita P. habitant	Gross receipts Recettes brutes Total (000000)	Currency Monnaie
Mexico	1997	1842	...	...	95.0	1.0		peso
Mexique	1998	2105	627.3	6.5	104.0	1.1	81.0	peso
	1999	2320	624.1	6.4	120.0	1.2	134.5	
Nicaragua	1998	6	1.8	0.4	0.7	0.2	22.0[3]	dollar [3]
Nicaragua	1999	10	2.7	0.5	1.2	0.2	34.0[3]	dollar [3]
United States	1992	25105	...	...	971.2	3.7	4 650.0	dollar
Etats – Unis	1993	25737	...	...	1 180.0	4.5	4 980.0	dollar
	1994	26586	...	...	1 210.0	4.6	5 250.0	
America, South · Amérique du Sud								
Argentina	1992	280	...	...	7.8	0.2	...	peso
Argentine	1996	523	...	...	21.5	0.6	...	peso
	1997	635	...	...	26.6	0.7	...	
Bolivia	1997	72	...	...	1.2	0.2	11.0	boliviano
Bolivie	1998	27	...	...	...	...	...	boliviano
	1999	27	...	...	...	...	...	
Chile	1993	*133	*75.9	*5.5	8.0	*0.6	...	peso
Chili	1998	208	74.6	5.0	3.7	0.2	...	peso
	1999	255	81.9	5.5	4.6	0.3	...	
Colombia	1985	586	277.3	8.8	56.1	1.8	4 642.0	peso
Colombie	1998	258	...	...	18.4	0.5	43.5[3]	peso
	1999	277	43.0	1.0	...	...	...	
Ecuador	1986	118	110.0	11.8	11.1	1.2	884.0	sucre
Equateur	1990	161	77.6	7.6	7.8	0.8	3 162.0	sucre
	1991	134	75.3	7.2	6.8	0.6	4 949.0	
Peru	1996	124	...	...	3.0	0.1	19.0	inti
Pérou	1997	116	...	...	4.1	0.2	25.0	inti
Suriname	1996	1	0.8	1.9	0.2	0.4	...	guilder
Suriname	1997	1	0.8	1.9	0.1	0.3	...	florin
Venezuela	1993	218	132.0	6.3	18.3	0.9	1 896.0	bolivar
Venezuela	1996	220	138.7	62.2	6.2	0.3	6 142.0	bolivar
	1997	241	139.5	61.2	6.4	0.3	10 353.0	
Asia · Asie								
Armenia	1993	577[1]	118.5	33.1	...	...	44.0	dram
Arménie	1994	599[1]	124.9	34.9	...	...	...	dram
	1995	599[1]	124.9	34.9	...	...	...	
Azerbaijan	1997	234	376.0	49.2	0.2	0.0	1 785.0	manat
Azerbaïdjan	1998	187	317.0	41.3	0.2	0.0	1 358.0	manat
	1999	184	296.0	38.5	0.2	0.0	1 307.0	
Bahrain	1980	6	4.0	11.5	...	...	...	dinar
Bahreïn	1985	6	4.0	9.7	1.1	2.6	...	dinar
	1989	6	3.2	6.7	0.6	1.3	...	
China ††	1985	182948[1]	...	...	21 756.4	20.3	...	yuan
Chine ††	1990	146184[1]	...	...	16 107.3	13.9	2 225.0	yuan
	1991	139639[1]	...	...	14 428.4	12.3	2 365.0	
China, Hong Kong SAR †	1991	166	...	...	...	...	1 557.0	dollar
Chine, Hong Kong RAS †	1994	186	99.9	16.4	35.0	5.7	1 449.0	dollar
	1995	184	94.8	15.2	28.0	4.5	1 368.0	
China, Macao SAR †	1998	7	5.0	10.9	0.2	0.4	...	pataca
Chine, Macao RAS †	1999	5	5.0	10.7	0.2	0.4	...	pataca
Cyprus	1997	29	8.0	10.5	0.9	1.2	...	pound
Chypre	1998	26	9.3	12.1	1.0	1.3	3.0	livre
	1999	28	9.6	12.3	0.8	1.1	2.6	
Georgia	1993	290[1]	106.8	19.9	30.4	5.7	91 093.0	rouble
Géorgie	1996	97	22.8	4.4	20.5	4.0	...	rouble
	1997	97	22.8	4.5	18.7	3.7	...	
India	1985	12696[1]	6 034.3	7.9	4 921.0	6.4	4 500.0	rupee
Inde	1990	*13550[1]	*6611.4	*7.8	4 300.0	5.1	...	roupie
	1991	*13448[1]	*6751.4	*7.8	4 300.0	5.0	...	
Indonesia	1985	1902	962.1	5.7	...	...	...	rupiah
Indonésie	1996	1009	674.4	3.4	...	...	...	rupiah
	1997	1009	674.4	3.3	...	...	...	
Iran (Islamic Rep. of)	1993	277	171.4	2.9	29.0	0.5	12 616.0	rial
Iran (Rép. islamique de)	1994	294	197.0	3.2	56.0	0.9	...	rial
	1995	287	173.0	2.8	26.0	0.4	...	

18

Cinemas: number, seating capacity, annual attendance and box office receipts [*cont.*]

Cinémas: nombre d'établissements, nombre de sièges, fréquentation annuelle et recettes guichet [*suite*]

Country or area Pays ou zone	Year Année	Number Nombre	Seating capacity Sièges No. (000)	P. 1000	Annual attendance Fréquentation annuelle No. (000000)	P. capita P. habitant	Gross receipts Recettes brutes Total (000000)	Currency Monnaie
Israel	1992	241	71.1	14.2	...	...	...	shekel
Israël	1993	256	63.9	12.3	...	...	...	shekel
	1994	266	62.5	11.6	10.0	1.9	...	
Japan	1993	1734	...	...	130.7	1.0	163 700.0	yen
Japon	1994	1747	...	...	123.0	1.0	153 590.0	yen
	1995	1776	...	...	127.0	1.0	...	
Jordan	1989	61	94.0	20.9	1.0	0.2	...	dinar
Jordanie	1992	35	...	...	0.2	0.0	...	dinar
	1993	35	...	...	0.2	0.0	...	
Kazakhstan	1993	5947[1]	...	...	39.4	2.4	2.3	tenge
Kazakhstan	1994	1896	389.8	23.5	13.2	0.8	24.0	tenge
	1995	1580	346.7	21.0	6.2	0.4	39.0	
Korea, Republic of	1997	241	...	...	47.5	1.0	238 446.0	won
Corée, République de	1998	507	182.0	3.9	50.2	1.1	258 354.2	won
	1999	588	195.0	4.2	54.7	1.2	286 213.9	
Kuwait	1992	14	...	...	0.4	0.2	...	dinar
Kowëit	1993	7	...	...	0.7	0.4	...	dinar
	1994	6	...	...	0.8	0.5	...	
Kyrgyzstan	1997	571[1]	80.8	17.5	0.4	0.1	2.1	som
Kirghizistan	1998	296	...	...	0.4	0.1	1.7	som
	1999	293	...	...	0.3	0.1	1.6	
Lao People's Dem. Rep.	1990	31[1]	6.6	1.6	1.4	0.3	340.0	kip
Rép. dém. pop. lao	1991	31[1]	6.6	1.5	1.0	0.2	245.0	kip
Lebanon	1997	36	35.6	11.3	35.6	11.3	249 163.0	pound
Liban	1998	105	38.7	12.1	108.7	34.1	760 970.0	livre
	1999	105	38.7	12.0	108.7	33.6	760 970.0	
Malaysia	1997	106	37.6	1.8	16.1	0.8	...	ringgit
Malaisie	1998	...	...	...	0.3	0.0	6.0	ringgit
	1999	...	...	...	0.3	0.0	8.6	
Mongolia	1980	520	...	...	15.3	9.2	...	tughrik
Mongolie	1985	562	...	...	19.1	10.0	...	tughrik
	1989	581	...	...	20.1	9.3	...	
Myanmar	1991	163	127.2	3.1	...	...	...	kyat
Myanmar	1992	162	125.3	3.0	...	...	...	kyat
	1993	163	126.0	3.0	...	...	...	
Oman								rial
Oman	1998	17	4.7	2.0	0.4	0.2	...	rial
Pakistan	1997	652	...	...	9.7	0.1	243.0	rupee
Pakistan	1998	574	...	...	...	...	...	roupie
	1999	574	...	...	...	...	...	
Qatar	1980	4	4.0	17.4	1.2	5.2	7.7	riyal
Qatar	1989	4	4.0	8.6	0.3	0.6	...	riyal
Singapore	1993	80	...	...	20.0	6.2	...	dollar
Singapour	1994	80	...	...	17.9	5.5	...	dollar
	1995	80	...	...	18.1	5.5	...	
Sri Lanka	1985	318	201.0	12.5	36.5	2.3	39.0	rupee
Sri Lanka	1992	255	142.0	8.2	29.2	1.7	222.0	roupie
	1993	259	143.0	8.1	27.2	1.5	223.0	
Syrian Arab Republic	1989	77	40.0	3.3	7.0	0.6	...	pound
Rép. arabe syrienne	1992	56	24.8	1.9	4.0	0.3	9.5	livre
	1993	55	23.8	1.8	3.9	0.3	12.0	
Tajikistan	1993	916[1]	200.2	35.8	12.7	2.3	235.0	rouble
Tadjikistan	1994	514[1]	108.0	19.1	2.5	0.4	3.3	rouble
	1995	172[1]	39.0	6.8	0.4	0.1	6.0	
Turkey	1993	320	...	...	15.0	0.3	392 135.0	lira
Turquie	1996	300	115.0	1.8	9.5	0.2	...	livre
	1997	344	118.0	1.9	11.3	0.2	...	
Uzbekistan	1992	3357	669.2	31.4	64.2	3.0	...	rouble
Ouzbékistan	1993	2777	609.3	28.0	29.0	1.3	...	rouble
Viet Nam	1980	1107[1]	...	...	288.9	5.4	...	dong
Viet Nam	1985	1394[1]	...	...	345.8	5.8	...	dong
	1988	1451[1]	...	...	240.0	3.8	...	

18
Cinemas: number, seating capacity, annual attendance and box office receipts [*cont.*]
Cinémas: nombre d'établissements, nombre de sièges, fréquentation annuelle et recettes guichet [*suite*]

Country or area Pays ou zone	Year Année	Cinemas – Cinémas Number Nombre	Seating capacity Sièges No. (000)	P. 1000	Annual attendance Fréquentation annuelle No. (000000)	P. capita P. habitant	Gross receipts Recettes brutes Total (000000)	Currency Monnaie
Europe • Europe								
Austria	1995	412[1]	72.7	9.1	11.9	1.5	847.0	schilling
Autriche	1996	423[1]	64.2	8.0	12.3	1.5	904.0	schilling
	1997	441[1]	73.3	9.0	13.7	1.7	1 025.0	
Belarus	1993	4168	744.3	71.8	29.5	2.8	2 581.0	rouble
Bélarus	1994	3900	712.9	68.6	18.7	1.8	3 515.0	rouble
	1995	3780	700.1	67.4	12.5	1.2	19 290.0	
Belgium	1997	438	...	...	22.1	2.2	4 157.0	franc
Belgique	1998	463	...	...	25.4	2.5	5 062.7	franc
	1999	463	...	...	21.9	2.2	4 333.1	
Bulgaria	1997	216	98.0	11.7	3.2	0.4	4 389.0	lev
Bulgarie	1998	205	94.0	11.3	3.2	0.4	10 730.0	lev
	1999	191	83.0	10.0	1.9	0.2	8 009.0	
Croatia	1997	146[1]	53.0	11.8	3.2	0.7	53.0	kuna
Croatie	1998	147	52.0	11.6	2.7	0.6	52.1	kuna
	1999	141	52.0	11.6	2.3	0.5	42.2	
Czech Republic	1997	851	300.0	29.1	9.8	1.0	437.0	koruna
République tchèque	1998	722	290.0	28.2	9.3	0.9	509.0	couronne
	1999	713	292.0	28.5	8.4	0.8	496.0	
Denmark	1997	321[1]	51.0	9.7	10.8	2.1	390.0	krone
Danemark	1998	167	51.0	9.7	11.0	2.1	429.7	couronne
	1999	169	52.0	9.8	10.9	2.1	428.0	
Estonia	1997	200	...	...	1.0	0.7	29.0	kroon
Estonie	1998	2[4]	...	...	1.0	0.7	46.5	couronne
	1999	2[4]	...	...	0.9	0.6	40.5	
Finland	1995	330	58.4	11.4	5.3	1.0	194.0	markka
Finlande	1996	325	57.2	11.2	5.5	1.1	197.0	markka
	1997	321	55.5	10.8	5.9	1.1	217.0	
France	1995	4365	919.2	15.8	130.1	2.2	4 523.0	franc
France	1996	3214	954.0	16.4	137.0	2.3	4 762.0	franc
	1997	4655	942.0	16.1	148.0	2.5	5 143.0	
Germany	1997	4182[1]	772.0	9.4	143.0	1.7	1 469.0	deutsche mark
Allemagne	1998	4491	801.0	9.8	148.9	1.8	1 600.2	deutsche mark
	1999	4712	835.0	10.2	149.0	1.8	1 580.5	
Gibraltar								pound stg.
Gibraltar	1980	4	2.3	80.7	0.2	6.7	...	livre stg.
Greece	1990	584	392.0	38.4	...	...	...	drachma
Grèce	1991	584	392.0	38.1	...	...	...	drachme
	1994	320	...	...	6.5	0.6	8 800.0	
Hungary	1996	558	117.0	11.5	13.3	1.3	2 884.0	forint
Hongrie	1997	652	121.0	11.9	16.6	1.6	4 727.0	forint
	1998	606	121.0	12.0	14.6	1.4	5 302.3	
Iceland	1997	32	10.0	36.6	1.5	5.4	800.0	krona
Islande	1998	45	9.0	32.6	1.5	5.5	808.4	couronne
	1999	46	9.0	32.3	1.5	5.5	930.1	
Ireland	1992	189	43.0	12.2	8.3	2.3	21.0	pound
Irlande	1993	184	...	...	9.3	2.6	24.0	livre
	1994	191	...	...	10.4	2.9	27.0	
Italy	1995	3816	...	...	90.7	1.6	797 396.0	lira
Italie	1996	4004	472.0	8.2	96.5	1.7	875 154.0	lire
	1998	4603	...	...	...	...	...	
Latvia	1997	118	23.0	9.3	1.3	0.5	1.2	lats
Lettonie	1998	116	24.0	9.9	1.4	0.6	1.6	lats
	1999	114	26.0	10.9	1.4	0.6	1.8	
Lithuania	1997	124	28.2	7.6	0.5	0.1	2.2	litas
Lituanie	1998	113	26.8	7.3	1.6	0.4	10.6	litai
	1999	105	26.1	7.1	1.8	0.5	11.9	
Luxembourg	1992	17	3.1	7.9	0.6	1.5	114.0	franc
Luxembourg	1993	17	3.1	7.8	0.7	1.8	134.0	franc
	1994	17	3.1	7.7	0.7	1.8	133.0	
Malta	1990	10	7.0	19.8	0.3	0.7	...	lira
Malte	1991	10	7.0	19.6	0.3	0.7	...	lire
	1992	10	7.0	19.3	0.3	0.8	...	

18
Cinemas: number, seating capacity, annual attendance and box office receipts [*cont.*]
Cinémas: nombre d'établissements, nombre de sièges, fréquentation annuelle et recettes guichet [*suite*]

Country or area Pays ou zone	Year Année	Cinemas – Cinémas Number Nombre	Seating capacity Sièges No. (000)	Seating capacity Sièges P. 1000	Annual attendance Fréquentation annuelle No. (000000)	Annual attendance Fréquentation annuelle P. capita P. habitant	Gross receipts Recettes brutes Total (000000)	Currency Monnaie
Monaco	1980	3	1.4	52.7	0.1	3.8	...	franc
Monaco	1990	4	1.6	53.4	0.1	3.7	3.9	franc
Netherlands	1994	423	90.6	5.9	16.0	1.0	188.0	guilder
Pays – Bas	1996	440	90.8	5.8	16.8	1.1	202.0	florin
	1997	444	88.8	5.7	18.9	1.2	233.0	
Norway	1997	631	90.1	20.5	10.9	2.5	487.0	krone
Norvège	1998	604	88.0	19.9	11.5	2.6	574.2	couronne
	1999	605	89.0	20.0	11.4	2.6	579.6	
Poland	1997	686	200.0	5.2	24.3	0.6	168.0	zloty
Pologne	1998	686	201.0	5.2	20.3	0.5	203.3	zloty
	1999	695	211.0	5.4	27.5	0.7	337.5	
Portugal	1997	595	97.1	9.8	...	...	...	escudo
Portugal	1998	621	180.0	18.2	14.8	1.5	9 383.3	escudo
	1999	584	183.0	18.5	15.2	1.5	10 500.8	
Republic of Moldova	1997	50	23.0	5.3	0.2	0.0	0.3	leu
République de Moldova	1998	48	28.8	6.6	0.2	0.0	...	leu
	1999	48	28.8	6.6	0.1	0.0	...	
Romania	1997	469	149.0	6.6	9.5	0.4	36 333.0	leu
Roumanie	1998	296	250.0	11.1	6.8	0.3	60 936.0	leu
	1999	311	200.0	8.9	4.2	0.2	46 380.0	
Russian Federation	1997	1746	778.9	5.3	16.2	0.1	49.0	rouble
Fédération de Russie	1998	1568	691.0	4.7	20.2	0.1	131.6	rouble
	1999	1416	613.0	4.2	19.1	0.1	311.9	
San Marino	1995	2	1.8	72.3	0.1	2.0	253.0	lira
Saint – Marin	1996	3	1.8	70.6	0.1	2.7	354.0	lire
	1997	3	1.9	74.4	0.1	3.0	468.0	
Slovakia	1997	296	83.6	15.6	4.0	0.8	159.0	koruna
Slovaquie	1998	296	83.5	15.5	4.1	0.8	194.0	couronne
	1999	335	95.3	17.7	3.0	0.6	160.3	
Slovenia	1997	91	27.0	13.5	2.5	1.3	1 376.0	tolar
Slovénie	1998	90	24.0	12.0	2.6	1.3	1 295.9	tolar
	1999	83	22.0	11.1	2.0	1.0	856.7	
Spain	1997	2530	...	...	101.0	2.6	56 841.0	peseta
Espagne	1998	3025	...	...	112.1	2.8	66 763.4	peseta
	1999	3354	...	...	131.3	3.3	82 504.1	
Sweden	1997	1164	435.0	49.1	15.2	1.7	...	krona
Suède	1998	...	...	...	...	...	1 050.1	couronne
	1999	...	...	...	...	...	1 110.6	
Switzerland	1997	502	110.9	15.3	15.6	2.1	205.0	franc
Suisse	1998	499	191.0	...	15.9	...	211.6	franc
	1999	384	230.8	...	15.4	...	204.2	
TFYR of Macedonia	1995	38	14.0	7.1	0.2	0.1	22.0	dinar
L'ex – R.Y. Macédoine	1996	39	14.0	7.1	0.3	0.1	26.0	dinar
	1997	37	10.0	5.0	0.5	0.2	45.0	
Ukraine	1997	10768[1]	2 477.0	48.5	7.3	0.1	3.3	hryvnia
Ukraine	1998	9040	2 088.1	41.1	53.1	1.0	33.2	hryvina
	1999	7795	1 837.4	36.1	51.4	1.0	48.0	
United Kingdom	1993	1890	...	...	113.4	2.0	343.0	pound stg.
Royaume – Uni	1994	1969	553.0	9.5	124.4	2.1	364.0	live stg.
	1995	2019	...	...	114.6	2.0	384.0	
Yugoslavia	1997	195[1]	80.0	7.5	5.3	0.5	55.0	dinar
Yougoslavie	1998	164	67.0	6.3	5.2	0.5	61.2	dinar
	1999	165	70.0	6.6	3.9	0.4	64.7	
Oceania · Océanie								
Australia	1995	1137	332.0	18.5	69.0	3.8	502.0	dollar
Australie	1996	1251	356.0	19.6	74.0	4.1	537.0	dollar
	1997	1422	387.0	21.1	76.0	4.1	584.0	
New Zealand	1997	285	...	...	16.5	4.4	112.0	dollar
Nouvellé – Zélande	1998	290	...	...	16.3	4.3	...	dollar
	1999	315	...	...	16.8	4.4	...	

18
Cinemas: number, seating capacity, annual attendance and box office receipts [*cont.*]
Cinémas: nombre d'établissements, nombre de sièges, fréquentation annuelle et recettes guichet [*suite*]

Source:
United Nations Educational, Scientific and Cultural Organization
(UNESCO) Institute for Statistics, Montreal, the UNESCO statistics
database, January 2002.

†   For information on recent changes in country or area
     nomenclature pertaining to former Czechoslovakia,
     Germany, Hong Kong Special Administrative Region (SAR) of
     China, Macao Special Administrative Region (SAR) of China, SFR
     of Yugoslavia and former USSR, see Annex I – Country or area
     nomenclature, regional and other groupings.

††   For statistical purposes, the data for China do not include those
     for the Hong Kong Special Administrative Region (Hong Kong SAR),
     Macao Special Administrative Region (Macao SAR) and Taiwan
     province of China.

1   Data on number of cinemas include mobile units used for
     non−commercial exhibitions.
2   Receipts do not include taxes.
3   U.S. dollars.
4   Fixed cinemas only.

Source:
L'Institut de statistiques de l'Organisation des Nations Unies pour
l'éducation, la science et la culture (UNESCO), Montréal, la base de
données de l'UNESCO, janvier 2002

†   Pour les modifications récentes de nomenclature de pays
     ou de zone concernant l'Allemagne, Hong Kong, région
     administrative spéciale (RAS) de Chine, Macao région
     administrative spéciale (RAS) de Chine, l'ex−Tchécoslovaquie
     l'ex−URSS, et l'ex−Rfs de Yougoslavie voir annex I – ou
     des pays ou des zones, groupements régionaux et autres
     groupements.

††   Les données statistiques relatives à la Chine ne comprennent
     pas celles qui concernent la région administrative spéciale de
     Hong Kong (la RAS de Hong Kong), la région administrative
     spécial de Macao (la RAS de Macao) et la province chinoise de
     Taiwan.

1   Les données sur le nombre de cinémas comprennent les cinémas
     itinérants non commerciaux.
2   Les recettes ne tiennent pas compte des taxes.
3   Dollars des Etats−Unis.
4   Etablissements fixes seulement.

19
Mobile cellular telephone subscribers
Abonnés au téléphone mobile
Number
Nombre

Country or area Pays ou zone	1991	1992	1993	1994	1995	1996	1997	1998	1999	2000
Africa · Afrique										
Algeria Algérie	4 781	4 781	4 781	1 348	4 691	11 700	17 400	18 000	72 000	86 000
Angola Angola	0	0	1 100	1 824	1 994	3 298	7 052	9 820	24 000	25 806
Benin Bénin	0	0	0	0	1 050	2 707	4 295	6 286	...	...
Botswana[1] Botswana[1]	0	0	0	0	0	0	0	22 980	120 000	...
Burkina Faso Burkina Faso	0	0	0	0	0	525	1 503	2 730	5 036	25 000
Burundi Burundi	0	0	353	378	564	561	619	620	800	...
Cameroon Cameroun	0	0	0	1 600	2 800	3 500	4 200	...	...	...
Cape Verde Cap-Vert	0	0	0	0	0	0	20	1 020	8 068	19 729
Central African Rep. Rép. centrafricaine	0	0	0	0	44	1 071	1 370	1 633	4 162	4 967
Congo Congo	0	0	0	0	0	1 000	...	3 390	...	...
Côte d'Ivoire Côte d'Ivoire	0	0	0	0	0	13 549	36 000	91 212	257 134	...
Dem. Rep. of the Congo Rép. dém. du Congo	0	...	...	...	8 500	7 200[2]	8 900[2]	10 000[2]	...	...
Djibouti Djibouti	0	0	0	0	0	110	203	220	280	...
Egypt[3] Egypte[3]	4 500	4 913	6 877	7 371	7 368	7 369	65 378	90 786	480 974	1 359 900
Equatorial Guinea Guinée équatoriale	0	0	0	0	0	61	300	297	...	...
Ethiopia[3] Ethiopie[3]	0	0	0	0	0	0	0	0	6 740	17 757
Gabon Gabon	0	280	1 200	2 581	4 000	6 800	9 500	9 694	8 891	120 000
Gambia[1] Gambie[1]	0	204	457	812	1 442	3 096	4 734	5 048	5 307	...
Ghana Ghana	0	400	1 742	3 336	6 200	12 766	21 866	41 753	70 026	130 045
Guinea Guinée	0	0	42	812	950	950	2 868	21 567	25 182	42 112
Kenya[3] Kenya[3]	0	1 100	1 162	1 990	2 279	2 826	6 767	10 756	23 757	35 000
Lesotho[1] Lesotho[1]	0	0	0	0	0	1 262	3 500	9 831	...	...
Libyan Arab Jamah. Jamah. arabe libyenne	0	0	0	0	0	0	10 000[2]	20 000	...	...
Madagascar Madagascar	0	0	0	300	1 300	2 300	4 100	12 784	35 752	...

19
Mobile cellular telephone subscribers
Number [*cont.*]

Abonnés au téléphone mobile
Nombre [*suite*]

Country or area Pays ou zone	1991	1992	1993	1994	1995	1996	1997	1998	1999	2000
Malawi Malawi	0	0	0	0	382	3 700	7 000	10 500	22 500	...
Mali Mali	0	0	0	0	0	1 187	2 842	4 473	...	...
Mauritania Mauritanie	0	0	0	0	0	0	0	0	0	7 133
Mauritius Maurice	* 2 500	2 912	4 037	5 706	11 735	20 843	42 515	60 448	102 119	120 330
Morocco Maroc	1 500	3 217	6 725	13 794	29 511	42 942	74 472	116 645	374 353	2 342 000
Mozambique Mozambique	0	0	0	0	0	0	2 500	6 725	12 243	21 969
Namibia [4] Namibie [4]	0	0	0	0	3 500	6 644	12 500	19 500	30 000	82 000
Niger Niger	0	0	0	0	0	0	98	1 349	...	...
Nigeria Nigéria	0	0	9 049	12 800	13 000	14 000	15 000	20 000	25 000	30 000
Réunion Réunion	0	0	0	0	5 500	14 000	26 700	50 300	111 000	257 190
Rwanda Rwanda	0	0	0	0	0	0	0	5 000	11 000	20 000
Senegal Sénégal	0	0	0	98	122	1 412	6 942	27 487	87 879	195 508
Seychelles [1] Seychelles [1]	0	0	0	0	50	1 043	2 247	5 190	16 316	24 482
Sierra Leone Sierra Leone	0	0	0	0	0	0	0	0	0	5 700
South Africa [1] Afrique du Sud [1]	7 100	12 510	40 000	340 000	535 000	953 000	1 574 000	2 600 000	5 269 000	...
Sudan Soudan	0	0	0	0	0	2 200	3 800	8 600	13 000	23 000
Swaziland [1] Swaziland [1]	0	0	0	0	0	0	0	4 700	14 000	...
Togo Togo	0	0	0	0	0	2 995	7 500	17 000	25 000	
Tunisia Tunisie	1 239	1 974	2 269	2 709	3 185	5 439	7 656	38 973	55 258	...
Uganda [3] Ouganda [3]	0	0	0	0	1 747	4 000	5 000	30 000	56 358	...
United Rep. of Tanzania Rép.-Unie de Tanzanie	0	0	0	371	3 500	9 038	20 200	37 940	50 950	180 200
Zambia [15] Zambie [15]	0	0	0	0	1 547	2 721	4 550	8 260	28 190	...
Zimbabwe [3] Zimbabwe [3]	0	0	0	0	0	0	5 734	19 000	174 000	...
Anguilla Anguilla	**America, North · Amérique du Nord**									
	...	...	...	...	160	359	707	787	...	...

19
Mobile cellular telephone subscribers
Number [*cont.*]

Abonnés au téléphone mobile
Nombre [*suite*]

Country or area Pays ou zone	1991	1992	1993	1994	1995	1996	1997	1998	1999	2000
Antigua and Barbuda[1] Antigua-et-Barbuda[1]	...	...	...	...	...	1 300	...	1 500	8 500	22 000
Aruba Aruba	0	20	...	...	1 718	3 000	3 402	5 380	12 000	...
Bahamas Bahamas	2 020	2 600	2 401	...	4 100	4 948	6 152	8 072	15 911	31 524
Barbados[1] Barbade[1]	486	796	1 560	2 967	4 614	6 283	8 013	12 000	30 000	...
Belize[1] Belize[1]	0	0	400	832	1 547	2 184	3 023	3 584	6 469	7 154
Bermuda[1] Bermudes[1]	1 440	1 936	3 400	5 127	6 324	7 980	...	12 572	...	...
British Virgin Islands[1] Iles Vierges britanniques[1]	...	...	...	...	...	1 200	...	...	...	...
Canada Canada	775 831	1 026 611	1 332 982	1 865 779	2 589 780	3 420 318	4 265 778	5 354 133	6 876 000	8 751 338
Cayman Islands[1] Iles Caïmanes[1]	559	988	1 260	1 813	2 534	...	4 109	5 170	8 410	10 700
Costa Rica Costa Rica	0	3 008	4 533	6 985	18 750	46 531	64 387	108 770	138 727	209 064
Cuba Cuba	0	234	500	1 152	1 939	2 427	2 994	4 056	5 136	6 536
Dominica[1] Dominique[1]	0	0	0	0	0	461	...	650	...	...
Dominican Republic Rép. dominicaine	5 605	7 190	10 364	20 990	55 979	73 402	133 463	255 912	420 080	...
El Salvador El Salvador	0	0	1 632	4 868	13 475	23 270	40 163	106 114	382 610	...
Greenland Groenland	0	171	438	964	2 052	4 122	6 481	8 899	13 521	15 977
Grenada Grenade	147	181	282	350	400	570	976	1 410	2 012	4 300
Guadeloupe Guadeloupe	0	0	0	0	0	...	...	14 227	88 080	169 840
Guatemala Guatemala	1 221	2 141	2 990	10 462	29 999	43 421	64 194	111 445	337 800	...
Haiti Haïti	0	0	0	0	0	0	0	10 000	25 000	...
Honduras Honduras	0	0	0	0	0	2 311	14 427	34 896	78 588	155 271
Jamaica[1] Jamaïque[1]	2 447	7 628	15 221	26 106	45 138	54 640	65 995	78 624	144 388	366 952
Martinique Martinique	0	0	0	0	0	...	15 000	55 000	102 000	162 080
Mexico Mexique	160 898	312 647	386 132	569 251	688 513	1 021 900	1 740 814	3 349 475	7 731 635[6]	14 073 741[6]
Montserrat Montserrat	...	59	59	71	84	250	325	250	300	...
Netherlands Antilles Antilles néerlandaises	...	...	5 710	8 486	11 698	13 977	* 14 500	16 000	...	...

19
Mobile cellular telephone subscribers
Number [cont.]

Abonnés au téléphone mobile
Nombre [suite]

Country or area Pays ou zone	1991	1992	1993	1994	1995	1996	1997	1998	1999	2000
Nicaragua Nicaragua	0	0	324	2 183	4 400	5 100	7 560	18 310	44 229	...
Panama Panama	0	0	0	0	0	7 000	18 542	85 883	232 888	...
Puerto Rico[7] Porto Rico[7]	33 410	60 000	95 000	175 000	287 000	329 000	367 000	580 000	813 800	...
Saint Kitts and Nevis[1] Saint-Kitts-et-Nevis[1]	...	...	...	...	...	300	205	440	700	...
Saint Lucia[1] Sainte-Lucie[1]	...	...	...	524	1 000	1 400	1 600	1 900	...	...
St. Vincent-Grenadines[1] St. Vincent-Grenadines[1]	...	* 70	* 83	* 150	* 215	* 280	346	750	1 420	2 361
Trinidad and Tobago[1] Trinité-et-Tobago[1]	426	1 277	1 679	2 599	6 353	14 000	17 547	26 307	38 659	133 198
United States Etats-Unis	7 557 148	11 032 753	16 009 461	24 134 420	33 785 660	44 042 992	55 312 292	69 209 320	86 047 000	110 040 544
United States Virgin Is. Iles Vierges américaines	...	...	...	...	...	...	16 000	25 000	...	...
	America, South · Amérique du Sud									
Argentina[4] Argentine[4]	25 000	46 590	112 000	241 163	340 743	568 000	1 588 000	2 530 000	4 434 000	6 049 963
Bolivia Bolivie	500	1 556	2 651	4 056	10 000	20 300	118 433	239 272	420 344	...
Brazil Brésil	6 700	32 000	182 000	574 009	1 285 533	2 498 154	4 550 000	7 760 563	15 032 698	23 200 000
Chile Chili	36 136	64 438	85 186	115 691	197 314	319 474	409 740	964 248	2 260 687	3 401 525
Colombia Colombie	0	0	0	86 805	274 590	522 857	1 264 763	1 800 229	1 966 535	2 256 801
Ecuador Equateur	0	0	0	18 920	54 380	59 779	126 505	242 812	383 185	...
French Guiana Guyane française	0	0	0	0	0	0	0	4 000	18 000	39 830
Guyana Guyana	0	841	1 029	1 251	1 243	1 200	1 400	1 454	2 815	...
Paraguay Paraguay	0	1 500	3 390	7 660	15 807	32 860	84 240	231 520	1 047 568	...
Peru Pérou	5 700	21 550	36 300	52 200	73 543	200 972	421 814	742 642	1 013 314	...
Suriname Suriname	0	0	1 078	1 382	1 687	2 416	2 258	6 007	17 500	41 048
Uruguay Uruguay	0	1 712	4 969	6 825	39 904	79 701	99 318	154 505	316 131	440 196
Venezuela * Venezuela *	16 600	78 560	182 600	319 000	403 800	581 700	1 071 900	2 009 757	3 784 735	5 255 983
	Asia · Asie									
Armenia Arménie	0	0	0	0	0	300	5 000	7 000	8 148	...

19
Mobile cellular telephone subscribers
Number [*cont.*]

Abonnés au téléphone mobile
Nombre [*suite*]

Country or area Pays ou zone	1991	1992	1993	1994	1995	1996	1997	1998	1999	2000
Azerbaijan Azerbaïdjan	0	0	0	500	6 000	17 000	40 000	65 000	180 000	430 000
Bahrain Bahreïn	7 354	9 683	11 360	17 616	27 600	40 080	58 543	92 063	133 468	205 727
Bangladesh[3] Bangladesh[3]	0	250	500	1 104	2 500	4 000[2]	26 000[2]	75 000	149 000	...
Brunei Darussalam Brunéi Darussalam	3 025	4 103	8 304	15 623	35 881	43 524	45 000	49 129	66 000	...
Cambodia Cambodge	0	0	4 810	10 239	14 100	23 098	33 556	61 345	89 117	130 547
China †† Chine ††	47 544	176 943	638 000	1 568 000	3 629 000	6 853 000	13 233 000	23 863 000	43 296 000	85 260 000
China, Hong Kong SAR†[1] Chine, Hong Kong RAS†[1]	189 664	233 324	290 843	484 823	798 373	1 361 861	2 229 862	3 174 369	4 275 048	5 447 346
China, Macao SAR † Chine, Macao RAS †	4 847	10 513	15 135	21 445	35 881	44 788	50 624	65 320	88 561	117 961
Cyprus Chypre	5 131	9 739	15 288	22 938	44 453	70 781	91 968	116 429	151 649	218 324
Georgia Géorgie	0	0	0	0	150	2 300	30 000	60 000	102 500	...
India[1] Inde[1]	0	0	0	0	76 680	327 967	881 839	1 195 400	1 884 311	3 577 095
Indonesia Indonésie	24 528	35 546	53 438	78 024	210 643	562 517	916 173	1 065 820	2 220 969	3 669 327
Iran (Islamic Rep. of)[8] Iran (Rép. islamique d')[8]	0	0	0	9 200	15 902	59 967	238 942	389 974	490 478	962 595
Israel Israël	23 000	36 104	64 484	133 425	445 456	1 047 582	1 672 442	2 147 000	2 880 000	4 400 000
Japan[19] Japon[19]	1 378 108	1 712 545	2 131 367	4 331 369	11 712 137	26 906 512	38 253 892	47 307 592	56 845 592	66 784 376
Jordan Jordanie	1 462	1 462	1 456	1 446	12 400	16 100[2]	45 037	82 429	118 417	388 949
Kazakhstan Kazakhstan	0	0	0	400	4 600	9 798	11 202	29 700	49 500	...
Korea, Republic of Corée, République de	166 108	271 927	471 784	960 258	1 641 293	3 180 989	6 878 786	14 018 612	23 442 724	26 816 398
Kuwait Koweït	43 000	51 000	64 311	85 195	117 609	151 063	210 000	250 000	300 000	476 000
Kyrgyzstan Kirghizistan	0	0	0	0	0	0	0	1 350	2 574	9 000
Lao People's Dem. Rep. Rép. dém. pop. lao	0	290	340	625	1 539	3 790	4 915	6 453	12 078	...
Lebanon * Liban *	0	0	0	0	120 000	198 000	373 900	505 300	627 000	...
Malaysia Malaisie	130 000	200 573	340 022	571 720	1 005 066	1 520 320	2 000 000	2 200 000	2 990 000	3 600 000
Maldives Maldives	0	0	0	0	0	20	1 290	1 600	2 926	7 660
Mongolia Mongolie	0	0	0	0	0	900	2 000	9 032	34 562	107 500

19
Mobile cellular telephone subscribers
Number [*cont.*]

Abonnés au téléphone mobile
Nombre [*suite*]

Country or area Pays ou zone	1991	1992	1993	1994	1995	1996	1997	1998	1999	2000
Myanmar Myanmar	0	0	643	1 920	2 766	7 260	8 492	8 516	11 389	29 333
Nepal[10] Népal[10]	0	0	0	0	0	0	0	0	5 500	10 226
Occupied Palestinian Terr.[11] Terr. palestinien occupé[11]	...	...	...	...	20 000	25 000	40 000	...	...	...
Oman Oman	3 672	4 721	5 616	6 751	8 052	12 934	59 822	103 032	124 119	164 348
Pakistan[3] Pakistan[3]	8 500	13 500	16 000	24 662	43 000	65 000	110 000	206 908	278 830	...
Philippines Philippines	34 600	56 044	102 400	171 903	493 862	959 024	1 343 620	1 733 652	2 849 980	6 300 000
Qatar Qatar	4 057	4 233	4 289	9 790	18 469	28 772	43 476	65 786	84 365	119 460
Saudi Arabia Arabie saoudite	15 331	15 828	15 910	15 959	16 008	190 736	332 068	627 321	836 628	1 375 881
Singapore[1] Singapour[1]	81 906	120 000	179 000	235 630	306 000	431 010	848 600	1 094 700	1 630 800	2 747 400
Sri Lanka Sri Lanka	1 973	4 000	13 000	29 182	53 124	71 029	114 888	174 202	256 655	451 262
Syrian Arab Republic Rép. arabe syrienne	0	0	0	0	0	0	0	0	4 000	27 000
Tajikistan Tadjikistan	0	0	0	0	0	102	320	420	625	570
Thailand[4] Thaïlande[4]	123 551	250 584	413 557	737 283	1 297 826	1 844 627	2 203 905	1 976 957	2 339 401	2 660 000
Turkey Turquie	47 828	61 395	84 187	174 779	437 130	806 339	1 609 809	3 506 127	8 121 517	16 133 405
Turkmenistan Turkménistan	0	0	0	0	0	0	2 500	3 000	4 000	...
United Arab Emirates Emirats arabes unis	43 008	48 919	70 586	91 488	128 968	193 834	309 373	493 278	832 267	1 428 115
Uzbekistan Ouzbékistan	0	0	500	902	3 731	9 510	17 232	26 826	40 389	53 128
Viet Nam Viet Nam	0	800	4 060	12 500	23 500	68 910	160 457	222 700	328 671	...
Yemen Yémen	0	1 550	5 170	8 191	8 250	8 810	12 245	16 146	27 677	32 000
Europe · Europe										
Albania Albanie	0	0	0	0	0	2 300	3 300	5 600	11 008	29 791
Andorra Andorre	0	770	780	784	2 825	5 488	8 618	14 117	20 600	...
Austria Autriche	115 402	172 453	220 859	278 199	383 535	598 708	1 159 700	2 292 900	4 206 000	6 450 000
Belarus Bélarus	0	0	324	1 724	5 897	6 548	8 167	12 155	23 457	49 353
Belgium Belgique	51 420	61 460	67 771	128 071	235 258	478 172	974 494	1 756 287	3 186 602	5 577 000

19
Mobile cellular telephone subscribers
Number [*cont.*]

Abonnés au téléphone mobile
Nombre [*suite*]

Country or area Pays ou zone	1991	1992	1993	1994	1995	1996	1997	1998	1999	2000
Bosnia and Herzegovina Bosnie-Herzégovine	0	0	0	0	0	1 500	9 000	25 181	52 607	219 714
Bulgaria Bulgarie	0	0	1 000	6 500	20 920	26 588	70 000	127 000	350 000	738 000
Croatia Croatie	2 019	6 320	11 382	21 664	33 688	64 943	120 420	182 500	295 000	1 033 000
Czech Republic République tchèque	1 242	4 651	14 043	30 429	48 900	200 315	526 339	965 476	1 944 553	4 346 009
Denmark Danemark	175 943	211 063	357 589	503 500	822 264	1 316 592	1 444 016	1 931 101	2 628 585	3 543 128
Estonia Estonie	570	2 498	7 224	13 774	30 452	69 500	144 200	247 000	387 000	557 000
Faeroe Islands Iles Féroé	1 429	1 718	1 605	1 960	2 558	3 265	4 701	6 516	10 761	...
Finland Finlande	319 137	386 021	489 174	675 565	1 039 126	1 502 003	2 162 574	2 946 948	3 363 589	3 760 000
France France	375 000	436 700	572 000	883 000	1 302 496	2 462 700	5 817 300	11 210 100	21 433 500	29 052 360
Germany † Allemagne †	532 251	971 890	1 774 378	2 490 500	3 725 000	5 512 000	8 276 000	13 913 000	23 470 000	48 145 000
Gibraltar Gibraltar	0	0	0	0	660	1 002	1 620	2 445	3 648	5 558
Greece Grèce	0	0	48 000	153 000	273 000	532 000	937 700	2 047 000	3 904 000	5 951 000
Hungary Hongrie	8 477	23 292	45 712	143 000	265 000	473 100	705 786	1 070 154	1 628 153	3 000 413
Iceland Islande	12 889	15 251	17 409	21 845	30 883	46 805	65 368	104 280	172 614	188 200
Ireland[1] Irlande[1]	32 000	44 000	61 100	88 000	158 000	288 600	533 000	946 000	1 655 000	2 490 000
Italy Italie	568 000	783 000	1 207 175	2 240 000	3 923 000	6 422 000	11 737 904	20 489 000	30 296 000	42 243 000
Latvia Lettonie	0	1 027	3 800	8 364	15 003	28 500	77 100	167 460	274 344	401 272
Liechtenstein Liechtenstein	...	...	...	...	...	...	...	7 500	9 500	14 743
Lithuania[12] Lituanie[12]	0	267	1 242	4 512	14 795	50 973	165 337	267 615	332 000	524 000
Luxembourg Luxembourg	1 139	1 120	5 082	12 895	26 838	45 000	67 208	130 500	209 000	380 000
Malta Malte	2 280	3 500	5 300	7 500	10 791	12 500	17 691	22 531	37 541	114 444
Monaco Monaco	0	0	1 150	2 559	3 005	5 400	7 200	12 000	...	...
Netherlands Pays-Bas	115 000	166 000	216 000	321 000	539 000	1 016 000	1 717 000	3 351 000	6 745 460	10 710 000
Norway Norvège	234 423	282 918	371 403	588 478	981 305	1 261 445	1 676 763	2 106 414	2 744 793	3 151 000
Poland Pologne	0	2 195	15 699	38 942	75 000	216 900	812 200	1 928 042	3 956 500	6 747 000

19
Mobile cellular telephone subscribers
Number [*cont.*]

Abonnés au téléphone mobile
Nombre [*suite*]

Country or area Pays ou zone	1991	1992	1993	1994	1995	1996	1997	1998	1999	2000
Portugal Portugal	12 600	37 262	101 300	173 508	340 845	663 651	1 506 958	3 074 633	4 671 458	6 664 951
Republic of Moldova République de Moldova	0	0	0	0	14	920	2 200	7 000	18 000	132 343
Romania Roumanie	0	0	800	2 775	9 068	17 000	201 000	643 000	1 355 500	2 499 000
Russian Federation Fédération de Russie	300	6 000	10 000	27 744	88 526	223 002	484 883	747 160	1 370 630	2 861 650
San Marino Saint-Marin	...	900	1 300	1 900	2 340	2 279	2 350	4 980	9 580	...
Slovakia Slovaquie	119	1 537	3 125	5 946	12 315	28 658	200 140	465 364	918 039	1 293 736
Slovenia Slovénie	523	3 500	6 500	16 332	27 301	41 205	93 611	161 606	613 780	1 085 590
Spain Espagne	108 451	180 296	257 261	411 930	944 955	2 997 645	4 337 696	7 051 264	12 300 000	24 736 000
Sweden Suède	568 200	656 000	774 500	1 381 000	2 008 000	2 492 000	3 169 000	4 109 000	5 165 000	6 338 000
Switzerland Suisse	174 557	215 061	257 703	332 165	447 167	662 713	1 044 379	1 698 565	3 057 509	4 618 000
TFYR of Macedonia L'ex-R.y. Macédoine	0	0	0	0	0	1 058	12 362	30 087	47 737	115 748
Ukraine Ukraine	0	0	65	5 000	14 000	30 000	57 200	115 500	216 567	818 524
United Kingdom[1] Royaume-Uni[1]	1 260 000	1 507 000	2 268 000	3 940 000	5 735 785	7 248 355	8 841 000	14 878 000	27 185 000[13]	40 017 000
Yugoslavia * Yougoslavie *	0	0	0	0	0	14 800	87 000	240 000	605 697	1 303 609
Oceania · Océanie										
American Samoa Samoa américaines	...	700	900	1 200	2 000	2 500	2 550	2 650	2 377	...
Australia[3] Australie[3]	291 459	497 000	690 000	1 220 000	2 242 000	3 990 000	4 578 000	5 342 000	6 501 000	8 550 000
Cook Islands[1] Iles Cook[1]	...	...	...	...	...	182[14]	196	285	506	...
Fiji Fidji	0	0	0	1 100	2 200	3 700	5 200	8 000	23 380	...
French Polynesia Polynésie française	0	0	0	0	1 150	2 719	5 427	11 060	21 929	...
Guam Guam	867	1 301	1 907	4 098	4 965	5 803	5 673	...	20 000	...
Kiribati Kiribati	0	0	0	0	0	0	0	22	200	...
Marshall Islands Iles Marshall	0	0	0	280	264	365	466	345	443	447
Nauru Nauru	0	0	150	450	* 500	600	750	850	...	...
New Caledonia Nouvelle-Calédonie	0	0	0	0	825	2 060	5 198	13 040	25 450	49 948

19
Mobile cellular telephone subscribers
Number [*cont.*]
Abonnés au téléphone mobile
Nombre [*suite*]

Country or area Pays ou zone	1991	1992	1993	1994	1995	1996	1997	1998	1999	2000
New Zealand[1] Nouvelle-Zélande[1]	72 300	100 200	143 800	239 200	365 000	492 800	566 200	790 000	1 395 000	1 542 000
Northern Mariana Islands Iles Mariannes du Nord	...	...	732	765	1 200	...	...	...	2 905[15]	...
Papua New Guinea Papouasie-Nvl-Guinée	0	0	0	0	0	2 285	3 857	5 558	7 059	...
Samoa Samoa	0	0	0	0	0	0	1 545	3 000[16]	3 000	...
Solomon Islands[1] Iles Salomon[1]	0	0	0	144	230	337	658	702	1 093	1 151
Tonga Tonga	0	0	0	0	300	302	120	130	140	...
Vanuatu Vanuatu	0	0	0	64	121	154	207	220	300	365

Source:
International Telecommunication Union (ITU), Geneva,
"Yearbook of Statistics, Telecommunication Services,
Chronological Time Series 1990-1999" and the ITU database.

† For information on recent changes in country or
area nomenclature pertaining to former Czechoslovakia,
Germany, Hong Kong Special Administrative Region (SAR) of
China, Macao Special Administrative Region (SAR) of China,
SFR of Yugoslavia and the former USSR, see Annex I - Country
or area nomenclature, regional and other groupings.

†† For statistical purposes, the data for
China do not include those for Hong Kong Special
Administrative Region (Hong Kong SAR), Macao Special
Administrative Region (Macao SAR) and Taiwan province of
China.

1 Data refer to fiscal years beginning 1 April.

2 ITU estimate.
3 Data refer to fiscal years ending 30 June.

4 Data refer to fiscal years ending 30 September.

5 Zamtel (Zambian Telecommunications Company Limited) only.

6 Includes Personal Communication Systems.
7 Data refer to Puerto Rico Telephone Authority.
8 Data refer to fiscal years beginning 22 March.

9 Including PHS.
10 Data refer to fiscal years ending 15 July.

11 Users use Israel cellular network.

12 Not including radiotelephone connections of "Altaj" System.

13 Data refer to fiscal years ending December.

14 As of May 1997.
15 As of 31 March 2000.
16 As of 10 February 1998.

Source:
Union internationale des télécommunications (UIT), Genève,
"Yearbook of Statistics, Telecommunication Services,
Chronological Time Series 1990-1999" et la base de données
de l'UIT.

† Pour les modifications récentes de nomenclature
de pays ou de zone concernant l'Allemagne, Hong Kong, région
administrative spéciale (RAS) de Chine, Macao, région
administrative spéciale (RAS) de Chine,
l'ex-Tchécoslovaquie, l'ex-URSS et l'ex-Rfs de Yougoslavie,
voir annexe I - Nomenclature des pays ou des zones,
groupements régionaux et autres groupements.

†† Les données statistiques relatives à
la Chine ne comprennent pas celles qui concernent la région
administrative spéciale de Hong Kong (la RAS de Hong Kong),
la région administrative spéciale de Macao (la RAS de Macao)
et la province chinoise de Taiwan.

1 Les données se réfèrent aux années fiscales commençant le
1er avril.
2 Estimations de l'UIT.
3 Les données se réfèrent aux années fiscales finissant le 30e
juin.
4 Les données se réfèrent aux années fiscales finissant le 30e
septembre.
5 "Zamtel (Zambian Telecommunications Company Limited)"
seulement.
6 Y compris "Sistema de Comunicación Personal".
7 Les données se réfèrent à "Puerto Rico Telephone Authority".
8 Les données se réfèrent aux années fiscales commençant le
22e mars.
9 Y compris "PHS"
10 Les données se réfèrent aux années fiscales finissant le 15e
juillet.
11 Les abonnés utilisent le réseau israélien de téléphonie
mobile.
12 Non compris les connections radio-téléphonique du systéme
d'Altaj.
13 Les données se réfèrent aux années fiscales finissant
décembre.
14 Dès mai 1997.
15 Dès le 31e mars 2000.
16 Dès le 10 février 1998.

20
Telephones
Téléphones
Main telephone lines in operation and per 100 inhabitants
Nombre de lignes téléphoniques en service et pour 100 habitants

Country or area Pays ou zone	Number (000) Nombre (000)					Per 100 inhabitants Pour 100 habitants				
	1995	1996	1997	1998	1999	1995	1996	1997	1998	1999
Africa · Afrique										
Algeria Algérie	1 176	1 278	1 400	1 477	1 600	4.1	4.4	4.8	4.9	5.2
Angola Angola	53[1]	53[1]	62[1]	65[1]	67[1]	0.5	0.5	0.5	0.5	0.5
Benin Bénin	28	33	36	38	...	0.5	0.6	0.6	0.7	...
Botswana[2] Botswana[2]	60	72	86	102	124	4.1	4.8	5.6	6.5	7.7
Burkina Faso Burkina Faso	30	34	36	41	47	0.3	0.3	0.3	0.4	0.4
Burundi Burundi	17	15	16	18	19	0.3	0.2	0.3	0.3	0.3
Cameroon Cameroun	66	71	75	94	95	0.5	0.5	0.5	0.7	0.6
Cape Verde Cap-Vert	22	25	33	40	47	5.5	6.4	8.2	9.8	11.2
Central African Rep. Rép. centrafricaine	8	10	10	10	10	0.3	0.3	0.3	0.3	0.3
Chad Tchad	5	6	7	9	10	0.1	0.1	0.1	0.1	0.1
Comoros Comores	4	5	6	6	7	0.7	0.8	0.8	0.9	1.0
Congo Congo	21	* 22	* 22	* 22	* 22	0.8	0.8	0.8	0.8	0.8
Côte d'Ivoire Côte d'Ivoire	116	130	142	170	219	0.9	1.0	1.0	1.2	1.5
Dem. Rep. of the Congo Rép. dém. du Congo	* 36	* 36	* 21	* 20	* 20	0.1	0.1	0.0	0.0	0.0
Djibouti Djibouti	8	8	8	8	9	1.3	1.3	1.3	1.3	1.4
Egypt[3] Egypte[3]	2 716	3 025	3 453	3 972	4 686	4.7	5.1	5.7	6.5	7.5
Equatorial Guinea Guinée équatoriale	* 3[4]	* 4	* 4	* 6	...	0.6	0.9	0.9	1.3	...
Eritrea Erythrée	18	19	22	24	27	0.5	0.5	0.6	0.7	0.7
Ethiopia[3] Ethiopie[3]	142	149	157	164	194	0.2	0.3	0.3	0.3	0.3
Gabon Gabon	32	35	37	39	38	3.0	3.2	3.3	3.3	3.2
Gambia[2 5] Gambie[2 5]	19	21	25	26	29	1.8	1.9	2.1	2.1	2.3
Ghana Ghana	63	78	106	144	159	0.4	0.4	0.6	0.8	0.8
Guinea Guinée	11	16	20	37	46	0.1	0.2	0.3	0.5	0.6
Guinea-Bissau Guinée-Bissau	7	8	8	8	...	0.7	0.7	0.7	0.7	...

20
Telephones
Main telephone lines in operation and per 100 inhabitants [cont.]
Téléphones
Nombre de lignes téléphoniques en service et pour 100 habitants [suite]

Country or area Pays ou zone	Number (000) Nombre (000)					Per 100 inhabitants Pour 100 habitants				
	1995	1996	1997	1998	1999	1995	1996	1997	1998	1999
Kenya[3] Kenya[3]	256	267	272	288	305	0.8	0.9	0.9	1.0	1.0
Lesotho[2] Lesotho[2]	18	16	20	21	...	0.9	0.8	1.0	1.0	...
Liberia Libéria	* 5	* 5	6	* 7	* 7	0.2	0.2	0.2	0.2	0.2
Libyan Arab Jamah. Jamah. arabe libyenne	318	380	400	500	* 550	5.9	6.8	7.2	9.1	10.1
Madagascar Madagascar	37	39	43	47	50	0.2	0.3	0.3	0.3	0.3
Malawi Malawi	34	35	37	37	41	0.4	0.3	0.4	0.4	0.4
Mali Mali	17	21	23	27	...	0.2	0.2	0.2	0.3	...
Mauritania Mauritanie	9	10	13	15	17	0.4	0.4	0.5	0.6	0.6
Mauritius Maurice	148	184	223	245	257	13.2	16.2	19.5	21.2	21.9
Mayotte Mayotte	5	7	9	12	10	4.7	5.6	7.5	9.5	7.3
Morocco Maroc	1 128	1 208	1 301	1 393	1 471	4.2	4.4	4.7	5.0	5.3
Mozambique Mozambique	60	61	66	75	78	0.3	0.3	0.4	0.4	0.4
Namibia[6] Namibie[6]	78	86	100	106	108	5.1	5.4	6.2	6.4	6.4
Niger Niger	14	15	16	18	...	0.2	0.2	0.2	0.2	...
Nigeria Nigéria	405	413	400	407	* 410	0.4	0.4	0.4	0.4	0.4
Réunion Réunion	219	226	236	243	268	33.1	33.9	35.1	35.6	38.9
Rwanda Rwanda	* 7	10	12	11	13	0.1	0.2	0.2	0.2	0.2
Saint Helena[2] Sainte-Hélène[2]	2	2	2	2	2	28.8	29.8	31.1	31.9	32.4
Sao Tome and Principe Sao Tomé-et-Principe	2	3	4	4	5	2.0	1.9	3.1	3.0	3.1
Senegal Sénégal	82	95	116	140	166	1.0	1.1	1.3	1.6	1.8
Seychelles[2] Seychelles[2]	13	16	18	19	20	17.4	20.6	23.1	23.8	24.4
Sierra Leone Sierra Leone	17	17	17	17	18	0.4	0.4	0.4	0.4	0.4
Somalia Somalie	* 15	* 15	* 15	* 15	* 15	0.2	0.2	0.2	0.2	0.2
South Africa[2] Afrique du Sud[2]	4 002	4 259	4 645	5 075	5 493	10.1	10.5	11.3	12.0	12.5

20
Telephones
Main telephone lines in operation and per 100 inhabitants [cont.]
Téléphones
Nombre de lignes téléphoniques en service et pour 100 habitants [suite]

Country or area Pays ou zone	Number (000) Nombre (000)					Per 100 inhabitants Pour 100 habitants				
	1995	1996	1997	1998	1999	1995	1996	1997	1998	1999
Sudan Soudan	75	99	113	162	251	0.3	0.4	0.4	0.6	0.9
Swaziland[2] Swaziland[2]	21	23	25	29	31	2.3	2.4	2.7	3.0	3.1
Togo Togo	22	24	25	31	38	0.5	0.6	0.6	0.7	0.8
Tunisia Tunisie	522	585	654	752	850	5.8	6.4	7.1	8.1	9.0
Uganda[3] Ouganda[3]	39	48	54	57	57[7]	0.2	0.2	0.3	0.3	0.3
United Rep. of Tanzania Rép.-Unie de Tanzanie	90	93	105	122	150	0.3	0.3	0.3	0.4	0.5
Zambia[2] Zambie[2]	77	78	77	78	83	0.9	0.9	0.9	0.9	0.9
Zimbabwe[3] Zimbabwe[3]	152	175	212	237	239	1.4	1.6	1.9	2.1	2.1
America, North · Amérique du Nord										
Anguilla Anguilla	4	4	5	6	...	51.3	55.2	67.8	68.9	...
Antigua and Barbuda[2] Antigua-et-Barbuda[2]	26	28	31	34	37	38.8	40.8	43.9	46.8	48.9
Aruba Aruba	* 27	34	33	35	37	33.5	39.1	36.7	37.3	37.2
Bahamas Bahamas	84	89	98	106	111	30.0	31.5	34.0	35.8	36.9
Barbados[2] Barbade[2]	90	97	108	113	115	34.5	36.5	40.8	42.2	42.7
Belize[2] Belize[2]	29	30	31	32	36	13.4	13.3	13.7	14.1	15.4
Bermuda[2] Bermudes[2]	46	49	52	54	55	73.7	75.8	81.0	84.0	85.7
British Virgin Islands[2] Iles Vierges britanniques[2]	9	10	...	...	...	51.3	51.3	...	...	...
Canada Canada	17 763	17 974	18 660	19 294	19 957	60.5	60.6	62.2	63.8	65.4
Cayman Islands[2] Iles Caïmanes[2]	19	...	19	28	32	62.7	...	52.0	72.1	78.8
Costa Rica Costa Rica	479	526	685	742	803	14.4	15.5	18.9	19.3	20.4
Cuba Cuba	353	356	371	388	434	3.2	3.2	3.4	3.5	3.9
Dominica[2] Dominique[2]	18	19	* 19	20	21	24.1	25.2	25.6	26.5	27.9
Dominican Republic Rép. dominicaine	583	618	706	764	821	7.4	7.7	8.7	9.3	9.8
El Salvador El Salvador	285	325	360	483	468	5.0	5.6	6.1	8.0	7.6
Greenland Groenland	20	21	23	25	26	35.1	37.7	41.7	44.6	45.7

20
Telephones
Main telephone lines in operation and per 100 inhabitants [*cont.*]
Téléphones
Nombre de lignes téléphoniques en service et pour 100 habitants [*suite*]

Country or area Pays ou zone	Number (000) Nombre (000)					Per 100 inhabitants Pour 100 habitants				
	1995	1996	1997	1998	1999	1995	1996	1997	1998	1999
Grenada Grenade	23	24	27	27	29	26.0	26.7	29.0	29.8	31.5
Guadeloupe Guadeloupe	165	171	* 180	197	201	39.0	39.6	41.2	44.5	44.7
Guatemala Guatemala	286	338	430	* 517	611	2.9	3.3	4.1	4.8	5.5
Haiti Haïti	60	60	60	65	70	0.8	0.8	0.8	0.8	0.9
Honduras Honduras	161	190	234	250	279	2.7	3.1	3.8	4.0	4.4
Jamaica[2] Jamaïque[2]	290	357	416	463	487	11.6	14.2	16.4	18.2	19.0
Martinique Martinique	161	163	170	172	172	41.7	42.2	43.8	44.3	43.8
Mexico[8] Mexique[8]	8 801	8 826	9 254	9 927	10 927	9.4	9.3	9.7	10.4	11.2
Montserrat Montserrat	5	5	4	...	...	44.7	57.9	62.2	...	...
Netherlands Antilles Antilles néerlandaises	* 76	76	* 77	* 78	* 79	36.6	36.3	36.5	36.6	36.8
Nicaragua Nicaragua	97	111	123	141	150	2.2	2.6	2.8	3.0	3.0
Panama Panama	304	325	366	419	462	11.6	12.2	13.4	15.1	16.4
Puerto Rico[9][10] Porto Rico[9][10]	1 196	1 254	1 322	1 262	1 295	32.1	33.2	34.5	32.7	33.3
Saint Kitts and Nevis[2] Saint-Kitts-et-Nevis[2]	14	16	17	18	20	36.3	39.7	43.8	47.1	51.8
Saint Lucia[2] Sainte-Lucie[2]	31	34	37	40	44	21.0	23.0	24.7	26.6	28.9
Saint Pierre and Miquelon Saint-Pierre-et-Miquelon	* 4	4	4	4	5	57.9	61.0	66.0	65.8	69.1
St. Vincent-Grenadines[2] St. Vincent-Grenadines[2]	18	19	20	21	24	16.5	17.4	18.4	18.8	20.9
Trinidad and Tobago[2] Trinité-et-Tobago[2]	209	220	243	264	279	16.8	17.4	19.1	20.6	21.6
United States[11] Etats-Unis[11]	159 735	165 047	172 452	179 822	183 521	60.7	62.2	64.4	66.5	67.3
United States Virgin Is. Iles Vierges américaines	58	59	62	65	67	51.2	51.5	53.2	54.8	56.2
America, South · Amérique du Sud										
Argentina[6] Argentine[6]	5 622	6 227	6 852	7 323	7 357	16.2	17.7	19.2	20.3	20.1
Bolivia Bolivie	247	* 349	384	452	502	3.3	4.6	4.9	5.7	6.2
Brazil[12] Brésil[12]	13 263	15 106	17 039	19 987	* 24 985	8.5	9.6	10.7	12.1	14.9
Chile Chili	1 818	2 151	2 693	3 047	3 109	12.7	14.9	18.4	20.6	20.7

20
Telephones
Main telephone lines in operation and per 100 inhabitants [*cont.*]
Téléphones
Nombre de lignes téléphoniques en service et pour 100 habitants [*suite*]

Country or area Pays ou zone	Number (000) Nombre (000)					Per 100 inhabitants Pour 100 habitants				
	1995	1996	1997	1998	1999	1995	1996	1997	1998	1999
Colombia Colombie	3 873	4 645	5 395	6 367	6 665	10.0	11.8	13.5	15.6	16.0
Ecuador Equateur	698	750	819	991	1 130	6.1	6.4	6.9	8.1	9.1
Falkland Is. (Malvinas)[2] Iles Falkland (Malvinas)[2]	2	2	2	2	2	72.9	74.7	84.2	91.3	96.6
French Guiana Guyane française	42	44	47	46	49	27.9	28.9	29.2	27.7	28.3
Guyana Guyana	45	50	55	60	64	5.4	6.0	6.5	7.0	7.5
Paraguay Paraguay	167	176	218	261	268	3.5	3.6	4.3	5.0	5.0
Peru Pérou	1 109	1 435	1 646	1 555	1 628	4.7	6.0	6.8	6.3	6.5
Suriname Suriname	54	57	64	67	71	13.2	13.8	15.5	16.3	17.1
Uruguay Uruguay	622	669	761	824	897	19.5	20.9	23.4	25.0	27.1
Venezuela Venezuela	2 463	2 667	2 804	2 592	2 551	11.4	11.7	12.2	11.2	10.8
Asia · Asie										
Afghanistan Afghanistan	* 29	* 29	* 29	* 29	* 29	0.1	0.1	0.1	0.1	0.1
Armenia Arménie	583	580	568	557	547	15.5	15.3	15.0	15.7	15.5
Azerbaijan Azerbaïdjan	640	645	658	680	730	8.5	8.5	8.6	8.9	9.5
Bahrain Bahreïn	141	144	152	158	165	24.2	24.1	24.6	24.5	24.9
Bangladesh[3] Bangladesh[3]	287	316	368	413	433	0.2	0.3	0.3	0.3	0.3
Bhutan Bhoutan	5	6	6	10	12	0.9	1.0	1.0	1.6	1.8
Brunei Darussalam Brunéi Darussalam	68	79	77	78	79	24.0	25.8	25.0	24.7	24.6
Cambodia[13] Cambodge[13]	9	15	20	24	28	0.1	0.2	0.2	0.2	0.2
China †† Chine ††	40 706	54 947	70 310	87 421	108 716	3.3	4.4	5.6	7.0	8.6
China, Hong Kong SAR†[2] Chine, Hong Kong RAS†[2]	3 278	3 451	3 647	3 729	3 869	53.2	54.7	55.6	56.1	57.6
China, Macao SAR † Chine, Macao RAS †	153	161	170	174	178	37.4	38.8	40.2	40.4	40.8
Cyprus[14] Chypre[14]	347	366	386	405	424	53.9	56.3	58.6	60.8	63.0
Georgia Géorgie	554	567	617	629	672	10.2	10.5	11.3	11.5	12.3
India[2] Inde[2]	11 978	14 543	17 802	21 594	26 511	1.3	1.5	1.9	2.2	2.7

20
Telephones
Main telephone lines in operation and per 100 inhabitants [cont.]
Téléphones
Nombre de lignes téléphoniques en service et pour 100 habitants [suite]

Country or area Pays ou zone	Number (000) Nombre (000)					Per 100 inhabitants Pour 100 habitants				
	1995	1996	1997	1998	1999	1995	1996	1997	1998	1999
Indonesia Indonésie	3 291	4 186	4 982	5 572	6 080	1.7	2.1	2.5	2.7	2.9
Iran (Islamic Rep. of)[15] Iran (Rép. islamique d')[15]	5 090	5 825	6 503	7 355	8 371	8.6	9.7	10.7	11.9	13.3
Iraq[3] Iraq[3]	* 675	675	675	675	675	3.4	3.3	3.2	3.1	3.0
Israel Israël	2 343	2 539	2 656	2 819	2 877	41.7	44.1	45.0	47.1	47.1
Japan[2] Japon[2]	62 292[16]	64 037[16]	65 735[16]	67 488[16]	70 530[16]	49.6	50.9	52.1	53.4	55.7
Jordan Jordanie	317	346	416	511	565	5.8	6.2	7.2	8.3	8.7
Kazakhstan Kazakhstan	1 963	1 917	1 805	1 775	1 760	11.9	11.6	11.0	10.9	10.8
Korea, Dem. P. R. Corée, R. p. dém. de	* 1 100	* 1 100	* 1 100	* 1 100	* 1 100	5.0	4.9	4.8	4.7	4.6
Korea, Republic of[17] Corée, République de[17]	18 600	19 601	20 422	20 089	20 518	41.2	43.0	44.4	43.3	43.8
Kuwait Koweït	382	392	412	427	456	22.6	22.4	23.1	23.6	24.0
Kyrgyzstan Kirghizistan	357	342	351	368	371	7.9	7.5	7.6	7.9	7.9
Lao People's Dem. Rep. Rép. dém. pop. lao	17	19	25	28	35	0.4	0.4	0.5	0.6	0.7
Lebanon Liban	* 330	461	562	620	* 650	11.0	14.9	17.9	19.4	20.1
Malaysia Malaisie	3 332	3 771	4 223	4 384	4 431	16.6	17.8	19.5	20.2	20.3
Maldives Maldives	14	15	18	20	22	5.7	5.8	6.6	7.2	8.0
Mongolia Mongolie	78	84	87	103	103	3.4	3.6	3.7	4.1	3.9
Myanmar Myanmar	158	179	214	229	249	0.4	0.4	0.5	0.5	0.6
Nepal[18] Népal[18]	84	113	140	208	253	0.4	0.5	0.7	1.0	1.1
Occupied Palestinian Terr. Terr. palestinien occupé	80	84	111	167	222	3.5	3.3	4.0	5.8	7.2
Oman Oman	170	198	201	220	220	7.9	8.6	8.6	9.2	8.9
Pakistan[3] Pakistan[3]	2 127	2 377	2 558	2 756	2 986	1.7	1.8	2.0	2.1	2.2
Philippines Philippines	1 410	1 787[19]	2 078[19]	2 492[17]	2 892[17]	2.1	2.6	2.9	3.4	3.9
Qatar Qatar	123	134	142	151	155	22.3	23.9	24.9	26.0	26.3
Saudi Arabia Arabie saoudite	1 719	1 796	1 877	2 167	2 706	9.4	9.5	9.6	10.7	12.9

20
Telephones
Main telephone lines in operation and per 100 inhabitants [*cont.*]
Téléphones
Nombre de lignes téléphoniques en service et pour 100 habitants [*suite*]

Country or area Pays ou zone	Number (000) Nombre (000)					Per 100 inhabitants Pour 100 habitants				
	1995	1996	1997	1998	1999	1995	1996	1997	1998	1999
Singapore[2] Singapour[2]	1 429	1 563	1 685	1 778	1 877	41.2	43.3	45.1	46.0	48.2
Sri Lanka Sri Lanka	206	255	342	524	672	1.1	1.4	1.9	2.8	3.6
Syrian Arab Republic Rép. arabe syrienne	958	1 199	1 313	1 463	1 600	6.8	8.2	8.7	9.4	9.9
Tajikistan Tadjikistan	263	247	226	221	213	4.5	4.2	3.8	3.7	3.5
Thailand[6] Thaïlande[6]	3 482	4 200	4 827	5 038	5 216	5.9	7.0	8.0	8.4	8.6
Turkey Turquie	13 216	14 286	15 744	16 960	18 054	21.1	22.4	25.0	26.5	27.8
Turkmenistan Turkménistan	320	338	354	354	359	7.1	7.4	8.0	8.2	8.2
United Arab Emirates Emirats arabes unis	672	738	835	915	975	28.8	32.7	35.1	38.9	40.7
Uzbekistan Ouzbékistan	1 544	1 531	1 541	1 537	1 599	6.8	6.6	6.5	6.4	6.6
Viet Nam Viet Nam	775	1 186	1 333	1 744	2 106	1.1	1.6	1.7	2.2	2.7
Yemen Yémen	187	205	220	250	372	1.2	1.3	1.3	1.5	2.1
Europe · Europe										
Albania Albanie	42	64	87	116	140	1.2	1.7	2.3	3.1	3.6
Andorra Andorre	30	31	32	33	34	43.8	43.6	43.1	43.9	44.7
Austria[20] Autriche[20]	3 797	3 902	3 969	3 997	3 862	47.2	48.4	49.2	49.1	47.2
Belarus Bélarus	1 968	2 128	2 313	2 490	2 638	19.2	20.8	22.6	24.3	25.7
Belgium[20] Belgique[20]	4 682	4 814	4 964	5 073	5 100	46.2	47.4	48.7	50.0	50.2
Bosnia and Herzegovina Bosnie-Herzégovine	238	272	303	333	368	6.0	7.0	8.0	9.1	9.6
Bulgaria Bulgarie	2 563	2 647	2 681	2 758	2 833	30.5	31.7	32.3	33.1	34.2
Croatia Croatie	1 287	1 389	1 488	1 558	1 634	28.3	30.9	33.2	34.8	36.5
Czech Republic République tchèque	2 444	2 817	3 280	3 741	3 806	23.6	27.3	31.8	36.4	37.1
Denmark Danemark	3 193	3 251	3 341	3 496	3 638	61.2	61.9	63.3	66.0	68.5
Estonia Estonie	412	439	469	499	515	27.7	29.9	32.1	34.4	35.7
Faeroe Islands Iles Féroé	22	23	24	24	25	50.5	52.7	53.8	54.4	55.7
Finland[17] Finlande[17]	2 810	2 842	2 861	2 855	2 850	54.3	55.4	55.6	55.3	55.2

20
Telephones
Main telephone lines in operation and per 100 inhabitants [*cont.*]
Téléphones
Nombre de lignes téléphoniques en service et pour 100 habitants [*suite*]

Country or area Pays ou zone	Number (000) Nombre (000)					Per 100 inhabitants Pour 100 habitants				
	1995	1996	1997	1998	1999	1995	1996	1997	1998	1999
France[20] France[20]	32 400	32 900	33 700	34 099	34 100	56.0	56.7	57.9	58.4	58.2
Germany † Allemagne †	42 000[21]	44 100[21]	45 200[21]	46 530	48 500	51.3	53.8	55.1	56.7	59.0
Gibraltar Gibraltar	17	18	19	20	22	61.2	64.6	68.5	74.8	80.2
Greece Grèce	5 163	5 329	5 431	5 536	5 611	49.4	50.9	51.6	52.2	52.8
Hungary Hongrie	2 157	2 651	3 095	3 423	3 726	21.1	26.0	30.4	33.6	37.1
Iceland[22] Islande[22]	149	155	168	178	189	55.5	57.6	61.4	64.8	67.7
Ireland[2] Irlande[2]	1 310	1 390	1 500	1 600	1 770	36.3	38.3	41.1	43.5	47.8
Italy Italie	24 845	25 259	25 698	25 986	26 506	43.3	44.0	44.8	45.3	46.2
Latvia Lettonie	705	739	740	742	732	27.9	29.5	29.8	30.2	30.0
Liechtenstein Liechtenstein	20	20	20	20	20	63.3	64.2	63.0	61.8	60.9
Lithuania[5] Lituanie[5]	941	993	1 054	1 113	1 153	25.4	26.8	28.5	30.1	31.2
Luxembourg[23] Luxembourg[23]	234	258	280	293	311	57.3	62.6	66.9	69.2	72.4
Malta Malte	171	181	187	192	198	45.9	48.3	49.3	49.9	51.2
Monaco Monaco	31	32	32	33	...	97.0	99.0	96.4	99.1	...
Netherlands[20] Pays-Bas[20]	8 124	8 431	8 860	9 337	9 610	52.4	54.0	56.6	59.3	60.7
Norway[20] Norvège[20]	2 476	2 589	2 735	2 935	3 176	56.7	58.9	61.9	66.0	70.9
Poland Pologne	5 728	6 532	7 510	8 812	10 175	14.8	16.9	19.4	22.8	26.3
Portugal[20] Portugal[20]	3 643	3 822	4 002	4 117	4 230	36.7	38.5	40.2	41.3	42.3
Republic of Moldova République de Moldova	566	593	627	657	555	13.0	13.7	14.4	15.0	12.7
Romania Roumanie	2 968	3 176	3 398	3 599	3 740	13.1	14.0	15.1	16.0	16.7
Russian Federation Fédération de Russie	25 019	25 915	28 250	29 246	30 949	16.9	17.6	19.2	19.9	21.0
San Marino Saint-Marin	16	17	18	19	20	64.3	68.3	70.5	77.3	76.0
Slovakia Slovaquie	1 118	1 246	1 392	1 539	1 655	20.8	23.2	25.8	28.5	30.7
Slovenia Slovénie	615	663	710	726	752	30.9	33.4	35.8	36.4	37.8

20

Telephones

Main telephone lines in operation and per 100 inhabitants [cont.]

Téléphones

Nombre de lignes téléphoniques en service et pour 100 habitants [suite]

Country or area Pays ou zone	Number (000) Nombre (000)					Per 100 inhabitants Pour 100 habitants				
	1995	1996	1997	1998	1999	1995	1996	1997	1998	1999
Spain Espagne	15 095	15 413	15 854	16 289	16 480	38.5	39.2	40.3	41.4	41.0
Sweden Suède	6 013	6 032	6 010	5 965	5 889	68.0	68.2	67.9	67.4	66.5
Switzerland[20] Suisse[20]	4 480	4 571	4 688	4 884	5 061	63.4	64.5	66.1	68.6	70.8
TFYR of Macedonia L'ex-R.y. Macédoine	351	367	408	439	471	17.9	18.5	20.5	21.9	23.4
Ukraine Ukraine	8 311	9 241	9 410	9 698	10 074	16.1	18.1	18.5	19.1	19.9
United Kingdom[2] Royaume-Uni[2]	29 411	30 678	31 879	32 829[24]	33 750	50.2	52.2	54.0	55.4	56.7
Yugoslavia Yougoslavie	2 017	2 082	2 182	2 319	2 281	19.1	19.7	20.6	21.8	21.4
Oceania · Océanie										
American Samoa Samoa américaines	10	13	13	14	14	18.5	21.6	22.1	21.4	21.2
Australia[3] Australie[3]	8 900	9 170	9 498	9 844	9 857	49.2	50.1	51.3	52.6	52.1
Cook Islands[2] Iles Cook[2]	5	5	5	5	5	27.1	26.9	26.9	27.5	28.0
Fiji Fidji	65	70	72	77	82	8.4	9.0	9.2	9.7	10.1
French Polynesia Polynésie française	49	51	52	53	52	22.1	23.0	23.0	23.2	22.6
Guam Guam	69	70	71	75	78	46.1	45.8	45.3	46.6	47.2
Kiribati Kiribati	2	2	2	3	4	2.6	2.6	3.1	3.4	4.3
Marshall Islands Iles Marshall	3	3	3	4	4	5.7	5.9	5.8	6.2	6.2
Micronesia (Fed. States of) Micron (Etats fédérés de)	8	8	8	9	...	7.3	7.5	7.5	8.0	...
Nauru Nauru	* 2	2	2	2	...	14.1	14.3	14.5	15.0	...
New Caledonia Nouvelle-Calédonie	44	46	47	49	51	23.6	24.1	24.1	23.9	24.1
New Zealand[2] Nouvelle-Zélande[2]	1 719	1 782	1 840	1 868	1 889	47.3	48.4	48.6	49.3	49.6
Northern Mariana Islands Iles Mariannes du Nord	15	21	20	21	25	32.2	42.8	40.0	40.4	48.0
Papua New Guinea Papouasie-Nvl-Guinée	44	47	54	57	60	1.1	1.1	1.3	1.3	1.3
Samoa Samoa	8	8	8	8	9	4.7	5.0	5.0	4.9	4.8
Solomon Islands[2 25] Iles Salomon[2 25]	7	7	8	8	8	1.7	1.8	1.9	1.9	1.9

20
Telephones
Main telephone lines in operation and per 100 inhabitants [cont.]
Téléphones
Nombre de lignes téléphoniques en service et pour 100 habitants [suite]

Country or area Pays ou zone	Number (000) Nombre (000)					Per 100 inhabitants Pour 100 habitants				
	1995	1996	1997	1998	1999	1995	1996	1997	1998	1999
Tonga Tonga	7	8	7	9	9	6.7	7.9	7.4	8.6	9.3
Tuvalu Tuvalu	1	1	1	1	1	5.1	5.0	4.9	5.5	5.5
Vanuatu Vanuatu	4	4	5	5	* 6	2.5	2.6	2.7	2.8	3.0
Wallis and Futuna Islands Iles Wallis et Futuna	1	1	1	1	2	9.6	10.3	9.9	9.8	10.6

Source:
International Telecommunication Union (ITU), Geneva,
"Yearbook of Statistics, Telecommunication Services,
Chronological Time Series 1990-1999" and the ITU database.

† For information on recent changes in country or
area nomenclature pertaining to former Czechoslovakia,
Germany, Hong Kong Special Administrative Region (SAR) of
China, Macao Special Administrative Region (SAR) of China,
SFR of Yugoslavia and the former USSR, see Annex I - Country
or area nomenclature, regional and other groupings.

†† For statistical purposes, the data for
China do not include those for Hong Kong Special
Administrative Region (Hong Kong SAR), Macao Special
Administrative Region (Macao SAR) and Taiwan province of
China.

1 Data refer to Angola Telecom.
2 Data refer to fiscal years beginning 1 April.

3 Data refer to fiscal years ending 30 June.

4 Malabo and Bata.
5 Excluding public call offices.
6 Data refer to fiscal years ending 30 September.

7 Including data from MTN.
8 Lines in service.
9 Switched access lines.
10 Data refer to Puerto Rico Telephone Authority.
11 Data up to 1980 refer to main stations reported by FCC.
    From 1981, data refer to "Local Loops".
12 Conventional telephony terminals in service.
13 Since 1994 WLL lines included.
14 Excluding 8,960 main lines in the occupied areas.

15 Data refer to fiscal years beginning 22 March.

16 Main lines with ISDN channels.
17 Telephone subscribers (Finland: from 1996 the basis for the
    compilation of the statistics changed).
18 Data refer to fiscal years ending 15 July.

19 ITU estimate.
20 Including ISDN channels.
21 Only Deutsche Telekom.
22 Including PABX.
23 Including digital lines.
24 OFTEL estimate.
25 Billable lines.

Source:
Union internationale des télécommunications (UIT), Genève,
"Yearbook of Statistics, Telecommunication Services,
Chronological Time Series 1990-1999" et la base de données
de l'UIT.

† Pour les modifications récentes de nomenclature
de pays ou de zone concernant l'Allemagne, Hong Kong, région
administrative spéciale (RAS) de Chine, Macao, région
administrative spéciale (RAS) de Chine,
l'ex-Tchécoslovaquie, l'ex-URSS et l'ex-Rfs de Yougoslavie,
voir annexe I - Nomenclature des pays ou des zones,
groupements régionaux et autres groupements.

†† Les données statistiques relatives à
la Chine ne comprennent pas celles qui concernent la région
administrative spéciale de Hong Kong (la RAS de Hong Kong),
la région administrative spéciale de Macao (la RAS de Macao)
et la province chinoise de Taiwan.

1 Les données se réfèrent à "Angola Telecom".
2 Les données se réfèrent aux années fiscales commençant le
  1er avril.
3 Les données se réfèrent aux années fiscales finissant le 30e
  juin.
4 Malabo et Bata.
5 Cabines publiques exclues.
6 Les données se réfèrent aux années fiscales finissant le 30e
  septembre.
7 Y compris les données du MTN.
8 Lignes en service.
9 Lignes d'accès par communication.
10 Les données se réfèrent à "Puerto Rico Telephone Authority".
11 Les données pour 1980 se réfèrent aux stations principales.
   Dès 1981, les données se réfèrent aux "Local Loops".
12 Terminaux classiques en service.
13 Dès 1994, y compris les lignes "WLL".
14 Non compris 8960 lignes principales dans les territoires
   occupés.
15 Les données se réfèrent aux années fiscales commençant le
   22e mars.
16 Lignes principales inclu RNIS.
17 Abonnés au téléphone. (Finland : à compter de 1996, la base
   de calcul des statistiques à changé).
18 Les données se réfèrent aux années fiscales finissant le 15e
   juillet.
19 Estimation de l'UIT.
20 RNIS inclu.
21 Deutsche Telekom seulement.
22 PABX inclu.
23 Y compris lignes digitales.
24 Estimation de l'OFTEL.
25 Lignes payables.

21
Internet users
Usagers d'Internet
Estimated number
Nombre estimatif

Country or area Pays ou zone	1991	1992	1993	1994	1995	1996	1997	1998	1999	2000
	Africa · Afrique									
Algeria Algérie	...	...	...	100	500	500	1 000	2 000	20 000	50 000
Angola Angola	...	...	...	...	...	100	750	2 500	10 000	30 000
Benin Bénin	...	...	...	...	...	100	500	2 000	10 000	...
Botswana[1] Botswana[1]	0	0	0	...	1 000	2 500	5 000	10 000	12 000	...
Burkina Faso Burkina Faso	...	...	...	...	...	100	800	1 000	4 000	10 000
Burundi Burundi	0	0	0	0	0	50	75	150	2 000	...
Cameroon Cameroun	...	...	...	...	...	...	1 000	2 000	20 000	...
Cape Verde Cap-Vert	...	...	...	...	...	...	1 000	2 000	5 000	8 000
Central African Rep. Rép. centrafricaine	...	...	...	...	...	59	200	200	1 000	1 500
Chad Tchad	...	...	...	...	...	...	50	335	1 000	...
Comoros Comores	...	...	...	...	...	...	0	200	800	1 500
Congo Congo	...	...	...	...	...	100	100	100	500	...
Côte d'Ivoire Côte d'Ivoire	...	...	...	...	30	1 300	3 000	10 000	20 000	...
Dem. Rep. of the Congo Rép. dém. du Congo	...	...	...	...	...	50	100	200	500	...
Djibouti Djibouti	...	...	...	...	100	200	550	650	750	...
Egypt[2] Egypte[2]	...	...	600	4 000	20 000	40 000	60 000	100 000	200 000	450 000
Equatorial Guinea Guinée équatoriale	...	...	...	...	...	...	200	470	500	...
Eritrea Erythrée	...	...	0	0	0	0	300	300	900	5 000
Ethiopia[2] Ethiopie[2]	...	...	...	...	10	1 000	3 000	6 000	8 000	10 000
Gabon[3] Gabon[3]	...	...	...	...	...	0	550	2 000	3 000	15 000
Gambia[1] Gambie[1]	...	...	...	...	100	400	600	2 500	3 000	...
Ghana Ghana	...	...	...	...	60	1 000	5 000	6 000	20 000	30 000
Guinea Guinée	...	...	...	10	50	150	300	500	5 000	8 000
Guinea-Bissau Guinée-Bissau	...	...	...	...	...	...	200	300	1 500	...

21
Internet users
Estimated number [*cont.*]
Usagers d'Internet
Nombre estimatif [*suite*]

Country or area Pays ou zone	1991	1992	1993	1994	1995	1996	1997	1998	1999	2000
Kenya[2] Kenya[2]	...	...	...	...	200	2 500	10 000	15 000	35 000	200 000
Lesotho[1] Lesotho[1]	...	...	...	...	...	50	100	200	1 000	...
Liberia Libéria	...	...	...	...	...	...	100	100	300	...
Madagascar Madagascar	...	...	...	...	...	500	2 000	9 000	25 000	30 000
Malawi Malawi	...	...	...	...	...	...	500	2 000	10 000	...
Mali Mali	...	...	...	...	...	200	1 000	1 000	10 000	...
Mauritania Mauritanie	...	...	...	...	...	...	100	1 000	12 500	...
Mauritius Maurice	...	...	...	...	...	2 100	5 500	30 000	55 000	87 000
Morocco Maroc	...	...	...	...	1 000	1 552	6 000	40 000	50 000	100 000
Mozambique Mozambique	...	...	...	...	...	500	2 000	3 500	15 000	...
Namibia[4] Namibie[4]	...	...	...	...	110	116	1 000	5 000	6 000	30 000
Niger Niger	...	...	...	...	...	100	200	300	3 000	
Nigeria Nigéria	...	...	...	...	...	10 000	20 000	30 000	100 000	...
Réunion Réunion	...	...	...	...	...	...	...	9 000	10 000	...
Rwanda Rwanda	...	...	...	...	...	50	100	800	5 000	5 000
Sao Tome and Principe Sao Tomé-et-Principe	...	...	...	...	...	...	...	400	500	6 500
Senegal Sénégal	...	...	...	...	60	1 000	2 500	7 500	30 000	40 000
Seychelles[1] Seychelles[1]	...	...	...	...	...	500	1 000	2 000	5 000	6 000
Sierra Leone Sierra Leone	...	...	0	0	0	100	200	600	2 000	20 000
Somalia Somalie	...	...	...	...	0	0	0	100	200	...
South Africa[1] Afrique du Sud[1]	10 000	60 000	140 000	330 000	460 000	618 000	800 000	1 266 000	1 820 000	2 400 000
Sudan Soudan	...	...	...	0	0	0	700	2 000	5 000	10 000
Swaziland[1] Swaziland[1]	...	...	...	...	10	500	900	1 000	5 000	...
Togo Togo	0	0	0	0	0	500	5 000	7 500	15 000	20 000
Tunisia Tunisie	...	...	...	650	1 000	2 500	4 000	10 000	30 000	100 000

21
Internet users
Estimated number [*cont.*]
Usagers d'Internet
Nombre estimatif [*suite*]

Country or area Pays ou zone	1991	1992	1993	1994	1995	1996	1997	1998	1999	2000
Uganda[2] Ouganda[2]	...	...	...	...	600	1 000	2 300	15 000	25 000	...
United Rep. of Tanzania Rép.-Unie de Tanzanie	...	...	...	...	...	500	2 500	3 000	25 000	115 000
Zambia[1] Zambie[1]	...	...	...	600	800	850	900	3 000	15 000	...
Zimbabwe[2] Zimbabwe[2]	...	...	...	200	900	2 000	4 000	10 000	20 000	...
America, North · Amérique du Nord										
Antigua and Barbuda[1] Antigua-et-Barbuda[1]	...	...	...	...	1 500	2 000	2 500	3 000	4 000	5 000
Aruba Aruba	...	...	...	...	...	2 300	...	...	4 000	...
Bahamas Bahamas	...	...	...	...	2 700	5 000	3 967	6 908	11 307	13 130
Barbados[1] Barbade[1]	...	...	...	...	20	1 000	2 000	5 000	6 000	...
Belize[1] Belize[1]	...	...	...	...	100	2 000	3 000	5 000	10 000	15 000
Bermuda[1] Bermudes[1]	...	...	...	...	4 200	10 000	15 000	20 000	25 000	...
Canada Canada	160 000	260 000	340 000	690 000	1 220 000	2 000 000	4 500 000	7 500 000	11 000 000	12 700 000
Cayman Islands[1] Iles Caïmanes[1]	...	...	0	0	1 300	...	...	...	...	...
Costa Rica Costa Rica	...	36	2 700	9 500	14 500	30 000	60 000	100 000	150 000	250 000
Cuba Cuba	...	...	...	...	10	3 500	7 500	25 000	34 800	60 000
Dominica[1] Dominique[1]	...	...	...	...	377	800	...	2 000	2 000	...
Dominican Republic Rép. dominicaine	...	...	...	...	1 400	6 200	10 000	20 000	25 000	...
El Salvador El Salvador	...	...	...	...	...	2 628	10 000	30 000	40 000	...
Greenland Groenland	...	...	...	36	30	1 000	4 434	8 187	12 102	17 841
Grenada Grenade	0	0	0	0	0	300	1 000	1 500	2 500	4 113
Guadeloupe Guadeloupe	...	...	...	...	...	100	1 000	2 000	4 000	...
Guatemala Guatemala	...	...	...	...	300	2 000	10 000	50 000	65 000	...
Haiti Haïti	...	...	...	...	...	600	...	2 000	6 000	...
Honduras Honduras	...	...	...	...	2 055	2 500	10 000	18 000	20 000	40 000
Jamaica[1] Jamaïque[1]	...	...	...	900	2 700	14 700	20 000	50 000	60 000	...

21
Internet users
Estimated number [*cont.*]
Usagers d'Internet
Nombre estimatif [*suite*]

Country or area Pays ou zone	1991	1992	1993	1994	1995	1996	1997	1998	1999	2000
Martinique Martinique	...	...	...	...	...	...	...	2 000	5 000	...
Mexico Mexique	5 000	15 000	25 000	39 000	94 000	187 000	595 700	1 222 379	1 822 198	2 712 375
Netherlands Antilles Antilles néerlandaises	...	...	...	...	...	500	...	...	2 000	...
Nicaragua Nicaragua	...	...	...	600	1 400	4 000	10 000	15 000	20 000	
Panama Panama	...	...	...	200	1 500	6 000	15 000	30 000	45 000	
Puerto Rico Porto Rico				1 000	5 000	10 000	50 000	100 000	200 000	...
Saint Kitts and Nevis[1] Saint-Kitts-et-Nevis [1]	...	...	...	...	...	850	1 000	1 500	2 000	...
Saint Lucia[1] Sainte-Lucie [1]	...	...	...	...	450	1 000	1 500	2 000	3 000	...
St. Vincent-Grenadines[1] St. Vincent-Grenadines [1]	...	...	...	...	139	522	1 000	2 000	3 000	3 500
Trinidad and Tobago[1] Trinité-et-Tobago [1]	...	...	...	...	1 960	5 000	10 000	20 000	30 000	42 750
United States Etats-Unis	3 000 000	4 500 000	5 500 000	8 500 000	20 000 000	30 000 000	40 000 000	60 000 000	74 100 000	95 354 000
United States Virgin Is. Iles Vierges américaines	...	...	...	1 000	3 000	5 000	7 500	10 000	12 000	...
America, South · Amérique du Sud										
Argentina[4] Argentine[4]	...	1 000	10 000	15 000	30 000	50 000	100 000	200 000	500 000	2 500 000
Bolivia Bolivie	...	...	...	...	5 000	14 000	35 000	52 000	78 000	...
Brazil Brésil	5 000	20 000	40 000	60 000	170 000	740 000	1 310 000	2 500 000	3 500 000	5 000 000
Chile Chili	...	5 000	10 000	20 000	50 000	100 000	156 875	250 000	625 000	1 757 379
Colombia Colombie	...	...	...	38 371	68 560	122 500	208 000	433 000	664 000	878 000
Ecuador Equateur	...	550	1 800	3 900	5 000	10 000	13 000	15 000	35 000	...
French Guiana Guyane française	...	...	...	...	...	500	1 000	1 500	2 000	...
Guyana Guyana	...	...	...	...	...	500	1 000	2 000	3 000	...
Paraguay Paraguay	...	...	...	...	...	1 000	5 000	10 000	20 000	...
Peru Pérou	...	...	...	2 000	8 000	* 60 000	100 000	200 000	400 000	...
Suriname Suriname	...	...	...	...	500	1 000	4 494	7 587	8 715	11 709
Uruguay Uruguay	...	...	...	2 000	10 000	60 000	110 000	230 000	330 000	370 000

21
Internet users
Estimated number [*cont.*]
Usagers d'Internet
Nombre estimatif [*suite*]

Country or area Pays ou zone	1991	1992	1993	1994	1995	1996	1997	1998	1999	2000
Venezuela Venezuela	...	2 500	8 800	12 000	27 000	56 000	90 000	185 000	525 000	950 000
Asia · Asie										
Armenia Arménie	...	...	...	300	1 700	3 000	3 500	4 000	30 000	...
Azerbaijan Azerbaïdjan	...	...	...	110	160	500	2 000	3 000	8 000	12 000
Bahrain Bahreïn	...	...	...	...	2 000	5 000	10 000	20 000	30 000	40 000
Bangladesh[2] Bangladesh[2]	...	...	...	...	...	...	1 000	5 000	50 000	...
Bhutan Bhoutan	...	...	...	...	...	...	...	...	500	...
Brunei Darussalam Brunéi Darussalam	...	...	...	...	3 000	10 000	15 000	20 000	25 000	...
Cambodia Cambodge	...	...	...	...	...	...	700	2 000	4 000	6 000
China †† Chine ††	...	...	2 000	14 000	60 000	160 000	400 000	2 100 000	8 900 000	22 500 000
China, Hong Kong SAR†[1] Chine, Hong Kong RAS†[1]	7 000	50 000	80 000	170 000	200 000	300 000	675 000	947 000	1 734 000	2 283 000
China, Macao SAR † Chine, Macao RAS †	...	...	...	150	1 153	3 037	10 000	30 000	40 000	60 000
Cyprus Chypre	...	350	400	800	3 000	5 000	33 000	68 000	88 000	120 000
Georgia Géorgie	...	...	...	...	600	2 000	3 000	5 000	20 000	...
India[1] Inde[1]	...	1 000	2 000	10 000	250 000	450 000	700 000	1 400 000	2 800 000	5 000 000
Indonesia Indonésie	...	...	...	2 000	50 000	100 000	250 000	500 000	900 000	1 450 000
Iran (Islamic Rep. of)[5] Iran (Rép. islamique d')[5]	...	...	...	250	2 600	10 000	30 000	65 000	100 000	250 000
Israel Israël	10 000	15 000	20 000	30 000	50 000	120 000	250 000	600 000	800 000	1 100 000
Japan[1] Japon[1]	50 000	120 000	500 000	1 000 000	2 000 000	5 500 000	11 550 000	16 940 000	27 060 000	47 080 000
Jordan Jordanie	...	...	...	...	1 000	2 000	27 354	60 816	120 000	127 317
Kazakhstan Kazakhstan	...	...	...	84	1 800	5 000	10 000	20 000	70 000	...
Korea, Republic of Corée, République de	20 000	43 000	110 000	138 000	366 000	731 000	1 634 000	3 103 000	10 860 000	19 040 000
Kuwait Koweït	...	...	1 700	2 600	3 500	15 000	40 000	60 000	100 000	150 000
Kyrgyzstan Kirghizistan	...	...	...	...	...	...	...	3 500	10 000	51 600
Lao People's Dem. Rep. Rép. dém. pop. lao	...	...	...	...	...	...	...	500	2 000	...

21
Internet users
Estimated number [*cont.*]
Usagers d'Internet
Nombre estimatif [*suite*]

Country or area Pays ou zone	1991	1992	1993	1994	1995	1996	1997	1998	1999	2000
Lebanon Liban	...	...	...	...	2 500	5 000	45 000	100 000	200 000	300 000
Malaysia Malaisie	...	200	5 000	20 000	40 000	200 000	600 000	1 500 000	2 500 000	3 500 000
Maldives Maldives	0	0	0	0	0	575	800	1 500	3 000	6 000
Mongolia Mongolie	...	...	...	...	200	415	2 600	3 400	12 000	30 000
Myanmar Myanmar	...	...	...	...	...	...	...	...	500	...
Nepal[6] Népal[6]	0	0	0	0	200	1 000	5 000	15 000	35 000	50 000
Oman Oman	...	...	...	...	...	...	10 000	20 000	50 000	90 000
Pakistan[2] Pakistan[2]	...	...	...	...	160	4 000	37 800	61 900	80 000	...
Philippines Philippines	...	...	...	4 000	20 000	40 000	100 000	150 000	1 320 000	2 000 000
Qatar Qatar	...	...	...	...	1 000	5 000	17 000	20 000	24 000	30 000
Saudi Arabia Arabie saoudite	...	...	...	...	2 000	5 000	10 000	20 000	100 000	200 000
Singapore[1] Singapour[1]	5 000	15 000	25 000	40 000	100 000	300 000	500 000	750 000	950 000	1 200 000
Sri Lanka Sri Lanka	...	...	...	500	1 000	10 000	30 000	55 000	65 000	121 500
Syrian Arab Republic Rép. arabe syrienne	0	0	0	0	0	0	5 000	10 000	20 000	30 000
Tajikistan Tadjikistan	...	...	...	...	...	...	...	...	2 000	2 000
Thailand[4] Thaïlande[4]	0	60	5 000	20 000	40 000	80 000	150 000	200 000	800 000	1 200 000
Turkey Turquie	...	...	5 000	30 000	50 000	120 000	300 000	450 000	1 500 000	2 000 000
United Arab Emirates Emirats arabes unis	...	...	...	...	2 503[7]	9 669	90 000	200 000	400 000	735 000
Uzbekistan Ouzbékistan	...	...	...	...	350	1 000	2 500	5 000	7 500	...
Viet Nam Viet Nam	...	...	...	...	...	100	3 000	10 000	100 000	...
Yemen Yémen	...	...	...	...	...	100	2 500	4 000	10 000	19 000
Europe · Europe										
Albania Albanie	...	...	...	...	350	1 000	1 500	2 000	2 500	...
Andorra Andorre	...	...	...	...	...	1 000	2 000	4 500	5 000	...
Austria Autriche	20 000	50 000	60 000	110 000	150 000	250 000	360 000	710 000	1 250 000	2 100 000

21
Internet users
Estimated number [*cont.*]
    Usagers d'Internet
    Nombre estimatif [*suite*]

Country or area Pays ou zone	1991	1992	1993	1994	1995	1996	1997	1998	1999	2000
Belarus Bélarus	...	...	...	50	300	3 000	5 000	7 500	50 000	180 000
Belgium Belgique	2 000	10 000	20 000	70 000	100 000	300 000	500 000	800 000	1 200 000	2 000 000
Bosnia and Herzegovina Bosnie-Herzégovine	...	...	...	...	...	500	2 000	5 000	7 000	...
Bulgaria Bulgarie	...	...	200	1 650	10 000	60 000	100 000	150 000	234 600	...
Croatia Croatie	...	...	4 500	12 500	24 000	40 000	80 000	150 000	200 000	...
Czech Republic République tchèque	...	...	60 000	130 000	150 000	200 000	300 000	400 000	700 000	1 000 000
Denmark Danemark	10 000	20 000	30 000	70 000	200 000	300 000	600 000	1 000 000	1 500 000	1 950 000
Estonia Estonie	...	1 000	4 500	17 000	40 000	50 000	80 000	150 000	200 000	366 600
Faeroe Islands Iles Féroé	...	...	...	...	...	500	1 000	2 000	3 000	...
Finland Finlande	70 000	95 000	130 000	250 000	710 000	860 000	1 000 000	1 311 000	1 667 000	1 927 000
France France	60 000	115 000	225 000	275 000	950 000	1 500 000	2 500 000	3 700 000	5 370 000	8 500 000
Germany † Allemagne †	200 000	350 000	375 000	750 000	1 500 000	2 500 000	5 500 000	8 100 000	14 400 000	24 000 000
Gibraltar Gibraltar	...	...	...	...	...	...	765	1 201	1 707	5 530
Greece Grèce	5 000	5 000	20 000	40 000	80 000	150 000	200 000	350 000	750 000	1 000 000
Hungary Hongrie	350	5 000	20 000	50 000	70 000	100 000	200 000	400 000	600 000	715 000
Iceland Islande	1 300	4 000	7 000	18 000	30 000	40 000	75 000	100 000	150 000	168 000
Ireland[1] Irlande[1]	2 000	6 000	10 000	20 000	40 000	80 000	150 000	300 000	679 000	784 000
Italy Italie	20 000	40 000	70 000	110 000	300 000	585 000	1 300 000	2 600 000	5 000 000	6 000 000
Latvia Lettonie	...	...	...	...	...	20 000	50 000	80 000	105 000	150 000
Lithuania Lituanie	...	...	...	...	...	10 000	35 000	70 000	103 000	...
Luxembourg Luxembourg	...	600	1 200	2 000	6 500	23 000	30 000	* 50 000	75 000	100 000
Malta Malte	...	...	...	...	850	4 000	15 000	25 000	30 000	40 000
Netherlands Pays-Bas	80 000	130 000	160 000	330 000	600 000	900 000	1 000 000	1 600 000	3 000 000	3 800 000
Norway Norvège	60 000	95 000	120 000	180 000	280 000	800 000	1 300 000	1 600 000	2 000 000	2 200 000
Poland Pologne	2 000	20 000	50 000	150 000	250 000	500 000	800 000	1 581 000	2 100 000	2 800 000

21
Internet users
Estimated number [*cont.*]
Usagers d'Internet
Nombre estimatif [*suite*]

Country or area Pays ou zone	1991	1992	1993	1994	1995	1996	1997	1998	1999	2000
Portugal Portugal	10 000	25 000	45 000	72 000	90 000	230 000	270 000	500 000	700 000	5 962 000
Republic of Moldova République de Moldova	...	...	...	36	150	200	1 200	11 000	25 000	...
Romania Roumanie	...	...	850	6 000	17 000	50 000	100 000	500 000	600 000	800 000
Russian Federation Fédération de Russie	...	1 000	20 000	80 000	220 000	400 000	700 000	1 200 000	1 500 000	2 000 000
Slovakia Slovaquie	...		6 800	17 000	28 000	100 000	190 000	500 000	600 000	650 000
Slovenia Slovénie	...	...	8 000	21 000	57 000	100 000	150 000	200 000	250 000	...
Spain Espagne	10 000	30 000	50 000	110 000	150 000	526 000	1 100 000	1 733 000	2 830 000	5 387 800
Sweden Suède	100 000	130 000	150 000	300 000	450 000	800 000	2 100 000	2 961 000	3 666 000	4 048 000
Switzerland Suisse	80 000	120 000	150 000	190 000	250 000	322 000	548 000	1 200 000	1 761 000	2 134 000
TFYR of Macedonia L'ex-R.y. Macédoine	...	...	...	...	800	1 500	10 000	20 000	30 000	
Ukraine Ukraine	...	...	400	7 000	22 000	50 000	100 000	150 000	200 000	...
United Kingdom[1] Royaume-Uni[1]	100 000	150 000	300 000	600 000	1 100 000	2 400 000	4 310 000	8 000 000	12 500 000	15 400 000
Yugoslavia Yougoslavie	...	...	...	...	...	20 000	50 000	65 000	80 000	400 000
Oceania · Océanie										
Australia[2] Australie[2]	190 000	310 000	350 000	400 000	500 000	600 000	1 600 000	3 000 000	6 000 000	6 700 000
Micronesia (Fed. States of) Micron (Etats fédérés de)	...	...	...	...	...	300	616	976	2 000	...
Fiji Fidji	...	...	50	60	70	500	1 750	5 000	7 500	...
French Polynesia Polynésie française	...	...	...	...	...	200	480	3 000	5 000	...
Guam Guam	...	...	...	...	500	2 000	3 000	4 000	5 000	...
Kiribati Kiribati	...	...	...	...	...	...	...	500	1 000	...
Marshall Islands Iles Marshall	0	0	0	0	0	19		...	...	500
New Caledonia Nouvelle-Calédonie	...	...	...	...	10	500	2 000	4 000	12 000	24 000
New Zealand[1] Nouvelle-Zélande[1]	...	10 000	22 500	115 000	180 000	300 000	550 000	600 000	700 000	830 000
Papua New Guinea Papouasie-Nvl-Guinée	...	...	...	...	...	50	...	...	2 000	135 000
Samoa Samoa	...	...	...	...	...	...	300	400	500	...

21
Internet users
Estimated number [*cont.*]
Usagers d'Internet
Nombre estimatif [*suite*]

Country or area Pays ou zone	1991	1992	1993	1994	1995	1996	1997	1998	1999	2000
Solomon Islands[1] Iles Salomon[1]	...	...	...	...	90	1 000	1 500	2 000	2 000	2 000
Tonga Tonga	...	...	...	...	120	160	500	750	1 000	...
Vanuatu Vanuatu	...	...	...	...	...	100	1 000	2 000	3 000	...

Source:
International Telecommunication Union (ITU), Geneva,
"Yearbook of Statistics, 1990-1999" and the ITU database.

†   For information on recent changes in country or
area nomenclature pertaining to former Czechoslovakia,
Germany, Hong Kong Special Administrative Region (SAR) of
China, Macao Special Administrative Region (SAR) of China,
SFR of Yugoslavia and the former USSR, see Annex I - Country
or area nomenclature, regional and other groupings.

††   For statistical purposes, the data for
China do not include those for Hong Kong Special
Administrative Region (Hong Kong SAR), Macao Special
Administrative Region (Macao SAR) and Taiwan province of
China.

1   Data refer to fiscal years beginning 1 April.

2   Data refer to fiscal years ending 30 June.

3   Number of subscribers.
4   Data refer to fiscal years ending 30 September.

5   Data refer to fiscal years beginning 22 March.

6   Data refer to fiscal years ending 15 July.

7   Internet Dial-up customers.

Source:
Union internationale des télécommunications (UIT), Genève,
"Annuaire statistique, 1990-1999" et la base de données de
l'UIT.

†   Pour les modifications récentes de nomenclature
de pays ou de zone concernant l'Allemagne, Hong Kong, région
administrative spéciale (RAS) de Chine, Macao, région
administrative spéciale (RAS) de Chine,
l'ex-Tchécoslovaquie, l'ex-URSS et l'ex-Rfs de Yougoslavie,
voir annexe I - Nomenclature des pays ou des zones,
groupements régionaux et autres groupements.

††   Les données statistiques relatives à
la Chine ne comprennent pas celles qui concernent la région
administrative spéciale de Hong Kong (la RAS de Hong Kong),
la région administrative spéciale de Macao (la RAS de Macao)
et la province chinoise de Taiwan.

1   Les données se réfèrent aux années fiscales commençant le
    1er avril.
2   Les données se réfèrent aux années fiscales finissant le 30e
    juin.
3   Nombre d'abonnés.
4   Les données se réfèrent aux années fiscales finissant le 30e
    septembre.
5   Les données se réfèrent aux années fiscales commençant le
    22e mars.
6   Les données se réfèrent aux années fiscales finissant le 15e
    juillet.
7   Clients accédant à l'Internet par numérotation.

Technical notes, tables 14-21

Tables 14-18: The data on books, newspapers, periodicals, television and radio receivers and cinemas have been compiled from the UNESCO Institute for Statistics database and from earlier editions of the UNESCO *Statistical Yearbook* [31].

Table 14: Data on books by subject groups cover printed books and pamphlets and, unless otherwise stated, refer to first editions and re-editions as well as to reprints that do not require a new ISBN. The grouping by subject follows the Universal Decimal Classification (UDC).

Table 15: For the purposes of this table, a daily general interest newspaper is defined as a publication devoted primarily to recording general news. It is considered to be "daily" if it appears at least four times a week. It should be noted that data prior to 1997 may not be comparable to data for later years due to UNESCO's use of different sources.

Table 16: For the purposes of this table, a non-daily general interest newspaper is defined as a publication which is devoted primarily to recording general news and which is published three times a week or less. Under the category of periodicals are included publications of periodical issue, other than newspapers, containing information of a general or of a specialized nature. It should be noted that data prior to 1997 may not be comparable to data for later years due to UNESCO's use of different sources.

Table 17: The data show the estimated number of television receivers in use (indicated by T) and the estimated number of radio receivers in use (indicated by R) as well as receivers per 1,000 inhabitants. The figures refer to 31 December of the year stated. In these tables the term "receivers" relates to all types of receivers for broadcasts to the general public, including those connected to a cable distribution system. Private sets installed in public places are also included as well as communal receivers.

Table 18: The data refer to fixed cinemas and mobile units regularly used for commercial exhibition of long films of 1,600 metres and over. The term fixed cinema used in this table refers to establishments possessing their own equipment and includes indoor cinemas (those with a permanent fixed roof over most of the seating accommodation), outdoor cinemas and drive-ins (establishments designed to enable the audience to watch a film while seated in their automobile). Mobile units are defined as projection units equipped and used to serve more than one site.

The capacity of fixed cinemas refers to the number of seats in indoor and outdoor cinemas plus the number

Notes techniques, tableaux 14 à 21

Tableaux 14 à 18 : Les données concernant les livres, les journaux, les périodiques, les récepteurs de télévision et de radiodiffusion sonore, et les cinémas proviennent de la base de données de l'Institut de statistique de l'UNESCO et des éditions précédentes de l'*Annuaire statistique* de l'UNESCO [31].

Tableau 14: Les données concernant la production de livres par groupes de sujets se rapportent aux livres et brochures imprimés, sauf indication contraire, aux premières éditions et aux rééditions, ainsi qu'aux réimpressions qui ne nécessitent pas un nouveau numéro de ISBN. Les sujets sont groupés selon la Classification décimale universelle (CDU).

Tableau 15: Dans ce tableau, par "journal quotidien d'information générale", on entend une publication qui a essentiellement pour objet de rendre compte des événements courants. Il est considéré comme "quotidien" s'il paraît au moins quatre fois par semaine. Les données antérieures à 1997 peuvent n'être pas comparables à celles des années suivantes, l'UNESCO ayant utilisé des sources différentes.

Tableau 16: Aux fins de ce tableau, par "journal non quotidien d'information générale", on entend une publication qui a essentiellement pour objet de rendre compte des événements courants et qui est publié trois fois par semaine ou moins. La catégorie périodique comprend les publications périodiques autres que les journaux, contenant des informations de caractère général ou spécialisé. Les données antérieures à 1997 peuvent n'être pas comparables à celles des années suivantes, l'UNESCO ayant utilisé des sources différentes.

Tableau 17: Les données de ces tableaux indiquent le nombre estimatif de récepteurs de télévision en usage (indiqués par un T), et le nombre estimatif de récepteurs de radiodiffusion sonore en usage (indiqués par R) ainsi que les récepteurs pour 1000 habitants. Les chiffres se rapportent au 31 décembre de l'année indiquée. Dans ces tableaux, le terme "récepteurs" désigne tous les types de récepteurs permettant de capter les émissions destinées au grand public, y compris ceux qui sont reliés à un système de distribution par cable. Les récepteurs privés installés dans des endroits publics sont également inclus, de même que les récepteurs communautaires.

Tableau 18: Les données concernent les établissements fixes et les cinémas itinérants d'exploitation commerciale de films d'une longueur de 1600 mètres et plus. Le terme établissement fixe désigne tout établissement doté de son propre équipement; il englobe les salles fermées (c'est-à-dire celles où un toit fixe recouvre la plupart des places assises), les cinémas de plein air et les cinémas pour automobilistes ou drive-ins

of places for automobiles, multiplied by a factor of 4 in the case of drive-ins.

Cinema attendance is calculated from the number of tickets sold during a given year.

As a rule, figures refer only to commercial establishments but in the case of mobile units, it is possible that the figures for some countries may also include non-commercial units. Gross receipts are given in the national currency of each country.

The statistics included in *Tables 19-21* were obtained from the statistics database and the *Yearbook of Statistics, Telecommunication Services* [18] of the International Telecommunication Union.

Table 19: The number of mobile cellular telephone subscribers refers to users of portable telephones subscribing to an automatic public mobile telephone service using cellular technology which provides access to the Public Switched Telephone Network (PSTN).

Table 20: This table shows the number of main lines in operation and the main lines in operation per 100 inhabitants for the years indicated. Main telephone lines refer to the telephone lines connecting a customer's equipment to the Public Switched Telephone Network (PSTN) and which have a dedicated port on a telephone exchange. Note that in most countries, main lines also include public telephones. Main telephone lines per 100 inhabitants is calculated by dividing the number of main lines by the population and multiplying by 100.

Table 21: Internet user data is based on reported estimates, derivations based on reported Internet Access Provider subscriber counts, or calculated by multiplying the number of hosts by an estimated multiplier. However, comparisons of user data are misleading because there is no standard definition of frequency (e.g., daily, weekly, monthly) or services used (e.g., e-mail, World Wide Web).

(conçus pour permettre aux spectateurs d'assister à la projection sans quitter leur voiture). Les cinémas itinérants sont définis comme groupes mobiles de projection équipés de manière à pouvoir être utilisés dans des lieux différents.

La capacité des cinémas fixes se réfère au nombre de sièges dans les salles fermées et les cinémas de plein air, plus le nombre de places d'automobiles multiplié par le facteur 4 dans le cas des drive-ins.

La fréquentation des cinémas est calculée sur la base du nombre de billets vendus au cours d'une année donnée.

En général, les statistiques présentées ne concernent que les établissements commerciaux: toutefois, dans le cas des cinémas itinérants, il se peut que les données relatives à certains pays tiennent compte aussi des établissements non-commerciaux. Les recettes brutes sont indiquées en monnaie nationale de chaque pays.

Les données présentées dans les *Tableaux 19 à 21* proviennent de la base de données et *l'Annuaire statistique, Services de télécommunications* [18] de l'Union internationale des télécommunications.

Tableau 19: Les abonnés mobiles désignent les utilisateurs de téléphones portatifs abonnés à un service automatique public de téléphones mobiles ayant accès au Réseau de téléphone public connecté (RTPC).

Tableau 20: Ce tableau indique le nombre de lignes principales en service et les lignes principales en service pour 100 habitants pour les années indiquées. Les lignes principales sont des lignes téléphoniques qui relient l'équipement terminal de l'abonné au Réseau de téléphone public connecté (RTPC) et qui possèdent un accès individualisé aux équipements d'un central téléphonique. Pour la plupart des pays, le nombre de lignes principales en service indiqué comprend également les lignes publiques. Le nombre de lignes principales pour 100 habitants se calcule en divisant le nombre de lignes principales par la population et en multipliant par 100.

Tableau 21: Les chiffres relatifs aux usagers d'Internet sont basés sur les estimations communiquées, calculés à partir des chiffres issus de dénombrements d'abonnés aux services de fournisseurs d'accès, ou obtenus en multipliant le nombre d'hôtes par un facteur estimatif. Mais les comparaisons de chiffres relatifs aux usagers prêtent à confusion, car il n'existe pas de définition normalisée de la fréquence (quotidienne, hebdomadaire, mensuelle) ni des services utilisés (courrier électronique, Web).

Part Three
Economic Activity

VI
National accounts and industrial production (tables 22-26)
VII
Financial statistics (tables 27 and 28)
VIII
Labour force (tables 29 and 30)
IX
Wages and prices (tables 31-33)
X
Agriculture, forestry and fishing (tables 34-40)
XI
Manufacturing (tables 41-58)
XII
Transport (tables 59-63)
XIII
Energy (tables 64 and 65)
XIV
Environment (tables 66 and 67)
XV
Science and technology, intellectual property (tables 68 and 69)

Part Three of the *Yearbook* presents statistical series on production and consumption for a wide range of economic activities, and other basic series on major economic topics, for all countries or areas of the world for which data are available. Included are basic tables on national accounts, finance, labour force, wages and prices, a wide range of agricultural, mined and manufactured commodities, transport, energy, environment, research and development personnel and intellectual property.

International economic topics such as external trade are covered in Part Four.

Troisième partie
Activité économique

VI
Comptabilités nationales et production industrielle (tableaux 22 à 26)
VII
Statistiques financières (tableaux 27 et 29)
VIII
Main-d'oeuvre (tableaux 29 et 30)
IX
Salaires et prix (tableaux 31 à 33)
X
Agriculture, forêts et pêche (tableaux 34 à 40)
XI
Industries manufacturières (tableaux 41 à 58)
XII
Transports (tableaux 59 à 63)
XIII
Energie (tableaux 64 et 65)
XIV
Environnement (tableaux 66 et 67)
XV
Science et technologie, propriété intellectuelle (tableaux 68 et 69)

La troisième partie de l'*Annuaire* présente, pour une large gamme d'activités économiques, des séries statistiques sur la production et la consommation, et, pour tous les pays ou zones du monde pour lesquels des données sont disponibles, d'autres séries fondamentales ayant trait à des questions économiques importantes. Y figurent des tableaux de base consacrés à la comptabilité nationale, aux finances, à la main-d'oeuvre, aux salaires et aux prix, à un large éventail de produits agricoles, miniers et manufacturés, aux transports, à l'énergie, à l'environnement, au personnel employé à des travaux de recherche et développement, et à la propriété intellectuelle.

Les questions économiques internationales comme le commerce extérieur sont traitées dans la quatrième partie.

22
Gross domestic product: total and per capita
Produit intérieur brut : total et par habitant

In US dollars (millions) [1] at current and constant 1990 prices; per capita US dollars;
real rates of growth

En dollars E.−U. (millions) [1] aux prix courants et constants de 1990; par habitant en dollars E.−U.;
taux de l'accroissement réels

Country or area Pays ou zone	1991	1992	1993	1994	1995	1996	1997	1998	1999
World Monde									
At current prices	23 377 273	23 894 371	24 478 158	26 315 179	29 145 966	29 875 621	29 730 388	29 566 880	30 703 679
Per capita	4 383	4 412	4 453	4 718	5 152	5 208	5 112	5 016	5 140
At constant prices	22 943 374	23 222 617	23 484 240	24 115 261	24 755 638	25 575 295	26 470 994	27 044 553	27 835 339
Growth rates	1.2	1.2	1.1	2.7	2.7	3.3	3.5	2.2	2.9
Albania Albanie									
At current prices	1 010	676	1 228	1 949	2 479	2 689	2 294	3 058	3 676
Per capita	306	206	378	606	778	850	730	975	1 174
At constant prices	1 563	1 450	1 589	1 721	1 950	2 128	1 978	2 136	2 291
Growth rates	−28.0	−7.2	9.6	8.3	13.3	9.1	−7.0	8.0	7.3
Algeria Algérie									
At current prices	46 670	49 216	50 962	42 426	42 017	46 845	48 046	50 816	51 350
Per capita	1 835	1 893	1 919	1 565	1 519	1 662	1 673	1 738	1 726
At constant prices	61 148	62 127	60 760	60 050	62 332	64 701	65 412	68 748	71 086
Growth rates	−1.2	1.6	−2.2	−1.2	3.8	3.8	1.1	5.1	3.4
Andorra Andorre									
At current prices	774	888	776	825	1 003	1 096	1 053	1 148	1 229
Per capita	14 001	15 253	12 628	12 729	14 701	15 301	14 023	14 602	14 939
At constant prices	704	709	701	716	736	752	778	808	838
Growth rates	2.3	0.7	−1.2	2.2	2.7	2.3	3.4	3.9	3.7
Angola Angola									
At current prices	12 186	13 995	10 142	10 437	4 994	6 584	6 962	7 407	7 502
Per capita	1 233	1 368	957	951	440	563	578	597	588
At constant prices	10 330	9 727	7 394	7 493	8 359	9 326	9 861	10 491	10 625
Growth rates	0.3	−5.8	−24.0	1.3	11.6	11.6	5.7	6.4	1.3
Anguilla Anguilla									
At current prices	56	61	66	74	75	79	88	94	101
Per capita	6 383	6 734	7 120	7 719	7 575	7 767	8 381	8 670	9 079
At constant prices	52	56	60	65	62	65	71	75	80
Growth rates	−3.7	7.3	7.3	7.4	−4.3	4.3	9.2	6.5	6.0
Antigua and Barbuda Antigua−et−Barbuda									
At current prices	409	424	457	500	494	540	581	622	645
Per capita	6 503	6 710	7 204	7 865	7 737	8 442	9 047	9 659	9 979
At constant prices	402	406	426	453	430	453	479	497	513
Growth rates	2.7	0.8	5.1	6.2	−5.0	5.4	5.6	3.9	3.1
Argentina Argentine									
At current prices	189 709	228 779	236 755	257 696	258 097	272 242	293 006	298 280	282 910
Per capita	5 753	6 845	6 990	7 509	7 423	7 730	8 214	8 257	7 735
At constant prices	156 190	172 284	183 055	193 738	188 226	198 629	214 739	223 063	216 342
Growth rates	10.5	10.3	6.3	5.8	−2.8	5.5	8.1	3.9	−3.0
Armenia Arménie									
At current prices	9 117	321	464	648	1 287	1 597	1 639	1 885	1 859
Per capita	2 539	88	126	174	342	423	433	498	491
At constant prices	13 789	8 025	7 319	7 714	8 247	8 733	9 021	9 671	10 058
Growth rates	−8.8	−41.8	−8.8	5.4	6.9	5.9	3.3	7.2	4.0
Australia Australie									
At current prices	316 591	313 887	305 860	346 954	376 651	417 598	419 986	372 723	403 633
Per capita	18 478	18 065	17 367	19 444	20 842	22 826	22 687	19 905	21 319
At constant prices	311 221	322 696	335 965	351 162	367 063	380 959	398 937	417 031	436 767
Growth rates	0.4	3.7	4.1	4.5	4.5	3.8	4.7	4.5	4.7
Austria Autriche									
At current prices	169 567	190 480	185 906	199 511	235 597	231 731	206 668	210 913	208 179
Per capita	21 768	24 233	23 434	24 946	29 279	28 692	25 548	26 070	25 748
At constant prices	167 845	170 097	170 970	175 316	178 922	182 467	184 636	189 946	193 886
Growth rates	3.4	1.3	0.5	2.5	2.1	2.0	1.2	2.9	2.1
Azerbaijan Azerbaïdjan									
At current prices	15 269	445	1 571	1 193	2 417	3 177	3 962	4 117	4 098
Per capita	2 097	60	210	157	315	409	505	520	513
At constant prices	21 858	16 931	13 020	10 461	9 224	9 340	9 882	10 969	11 781
Growth rates	−0.7	−22.5	−23.1	−19.7	−11.8	1.3	5.8	11.0	7.4

22

Gross domestic product: total and per capita
In US dollars (millions) [1] at current and constant 1990 prices; per capita US dollars;
real rates of growth [cont.]
Produit intérieur brut : total et par habitant
En dollars E.–U. (millions) [1] aux prix courants et constants de 1990; par habitant en dollars E.–U.;
taux de l'accroissement réels [suite]

Country or area Pays ou zone	1991	1992	1993	1994	1995	1996	1997	1998	1999
Bahamas Bahamas									
At current prices	2 888	2 857	2 854	3 053	3 069	3 278	3 451	3 670	3 994
Per capita	11 087	10 732	10 487	10 989	10 841	11 384	11 807	12 385	13 302
At constant prices	2 950	2 780	2 722	2 775	2 805	2 923	3 020	3 110	3 297
Growth rates	−3.2	−5.8	−2.1	2.0	1.1	4.2	3.3	3.0	6.0
Bahrain Bahreïn									
At current prices	4 241	4 433	4 648	4 861	5 054	5 361	5 578	5 433	5 878
Per capita	8 373	8 468	8 600	8 728	8 824	9 125	9 274	8 839	9 369
At constant prices	4 189	4 515	4 888	5 004	5 112	5 270	5 433	5 693	5 605
Growth rates	4.6	7.8	8.3	2.4	2.2	3.1	3.1	4.8	−1.6
Bangladesh Bangladesh									
At current prices	24 770	24 340	26 041	29 103	32 315	33 570	35 107	36 253	39 139
Per capita	220	211	220	241	261	266	272	275	291
At constant prices	25 157	26 285	27 393	28 611	30 143	31 915	33 694	35 599	37 435
Growth rates	4.2	4.5	4.2	4.4	5.4	5.9	5.6	5.7	5.2
Barbados Barbados									
At current prices	1 697	1 589	1 651	1 737	1 883	2 008	2 219	2 405	2 500
Per capita	6 571	6 126	6 338	6 642	7 169	7 616	8 386	9 055	9 380
At constant prices	1 649	1 546	1 570	1 629	1 673	1 741	1 787	1 872	1 927
Growth rates	−4.2	−6.2	1.5	3.8	2.7	4.1	2.6	4.8	2.9
Belarus Bélarus									
At current prices	49 486	4 746	6 723	5 922	10 409	14 240	13 714	13 473	8 970
Per capita	4 809	460	651	573	1 008	1 381	1 333	1 313	877
At constant prices	63 665	57 529	53 133	46 444	41 628	42 797	47 676	51 633	53 389
Growth rates	−1.2	−9.6	−7.6	−12.6	−10.4	2.8	11.4	8.3	3.4
Belgium Belgique									
At current prices	202 332	226 230	214 792	232 925	275 744	268 208	243 540	250 391	248 411
Per capita	20 234	22 545	21 330	23 051	27 202	26 384	23 898	24 517	24 277
At constant prices	201 165	204 335	201 259	207 228	212 407	214 494	222 066	228 047	233 850
Growth rates	2.0	1.6	−1.5	3.0	2.5	1.0	3.5	2.7	2.5
Belize Belize									
At current prices	433	485	530	552	587	604	615	630	675
Per capita	2 284	2 513	2 705	2 769	2 888	2 912	2 905	2 907	3 045
At constant prices	422	453	472	484	503	510	527	535	569
Growth rates	4.2	7.2	4.2	2.6	3.9	1.3	3.4	1.5	6.4
Benin Bénin									
At current prices	1 878	2 152	2 106	1 497	2 009	2 208	2 141	2 306	2 360
Per capita	390	432	409	281	366	391	369	387	386
At constant prices	1 932	2 009	2 080	2 171	2 271	2 397	2 534	2 648	2 780
Growth rates	4.7	4.0	3.5	4.4	4.6	5.5	5.7	4.5	5.0
Bermuda Bermudes									
At current prices	1 705	1 720	1 864	1 914	2 083	2 194	2 330	2 457	2 544
Per capita	28 729	28 785	30 988	31 611	34 177	35 763	37 732	39 531	40 664
At constant prices	1 661	1 593	1 668	1 677	1 795	1 847	1 915	1 944	1 974
Growth rates	1.6	−4.1	4.7	0.6	7.0	2.9	3.7	1.5	1.5
Bhutan Bhoutan									
At current prices	242	245	236	271	307	331	399	398	435
Per capita	140	140	133	151	168	177	208	202	214
At constant prices	295	308	327	362	387	408	440	471	502
Growth rates	3.5	4.5	6.1	11.0	6.8	5.5	7.8	7.1	6.5
Bolivia Bolivie									
At current prices	5 343	5 644	5 735	5 981	6 715	7 397	7 967	8 571	8 402
Per capita	794	819	812	826	906	974	1 025	1 077	1 032
At constant prices	5 124	5 208	5 431	5 684	5 950	6 210	6 486	6 794	6 835
Growth rates	5.3	1.6	4.3	4.7	4.7	4.4	4.4	4.7	0.6
Bosnia & Herzegovina Bosnie−Herzégovine									
At current prices	14 377	1 377	1 222	1 088	2 029	2 778	3 300	4 045	4 207
Per capita	3 451	348	329	309	593	810	936	1 098	1 094
At constant prices	11 438	8 452	6 170	6 571	8 740	11 187	12 865	15 438	19 455
Growth rates	−12.1	−26.1	−27.0	6.5	33.0	28.0	15.0	20.0	26.0
Botswana Botswana									
At current prices	4 105	4 287	4 528	4 564	5 123	5 260	5 578	5 504	5 526

22
Gross domestic product: total and per capita
In US dollars (millions) [1] at current and constant 1990 prices; per capita US dollars;
real rates of growth [*cont.*]
Produit intérieur brut : total et par habitant
En dollars E.–U. (millions) [1] aux prix courants et constants de 1990; par habitant en dollars E.–U.;
taux de l'accroissement réels [*suite*]

Country or area Pays ou zone	1991	1992	1993	1994	1995	1996	1997	1998	1999
Per capita	3 214	3 259	3 346	3 285	3 601	3 621	3 769	3 660	3 625
At constant prices	4 282	4 279	4 457	4 577	4 878	5 224	5 641	5 878	6 223
Growth rates	6.3	−0.1	4.2	2.7	6.6	7.1	8.0	4.2	5.9
Brazil Brésil									
At current prices	407 759	390 594	438 391	546 222	704 177	774 948	801 584	775 342	592 989
Per capita	2 712	2 558	2 829	3 474	4 415	4 793	4 891	4 669	3 525
At constant prices	470 012	467 277	490 483	519 046	540 966	555 142	575 401	574 764	577 810
Growth rates	1.1	−0.6	5.0	5.8	4.2	2.6	3.6	−0.1	0.5
British Virgin Islands Iles Vierges britanniques									
At current prices	315	345	364	431	479	511	574	612	654
Per capita	17 661	18 638	19 045	21 811	23 477	24 278	26 459	27 394	28 452
At constant prices	305	313	324	342	360	368	390	395	406
Growth rates	2.0	2.5	3.5	5.7	5.0	2.3	5.9	1.3	3.0
Brunei Darussalam Brunéi Darussalam									
At current prices	3 832	4 030	4 075	4 377	5 217	5 450	5 422	4 846	4 844
Per capita	14 496	14 821	14 580	15 249	17 719	18 074	17 579	15 376	15 055
At constant prices	3 736	3 695	3 713	3 781	3 895	4 034	4 199	4 240	4 346
Growth rates	4.0	−1.1	0.5	1.8	3.0	3.6	4.1	1.0	2.5
Bulgaria Bulgarie									
At current prices	7 629	8 604	10 833	9 708	13 106	9 830	10 141	12 257	12 403
Per capita	881	1 000	1 268	1 145	1 559	1 181	1 232	1 507	1 543
At constant prices	19 294	17 894	17 630	17 950	18 323	16 472	15 313	15 854	16 245
Growth rates	−6.9	−7.3	−1.5	1.8	2.1	−10.1	−7.0	3.5	2.5
Burkina Faso Burkina Faso									
At current prices	2 877	3 070	2 939	1 887	2 390	2 583	2 424	2 626	2 628
Per capita	311	323	301	188	233	246	226	239	234
At constant prices	3 143	3 221	3 196	3 234	3 363	3 564	3 733	3 963	4 111
Growth rates	9.9	2.5	−0.8	1.2	4.0	6.0	4.8	6.2	3.7
Burundi Burundi									
At current prices	1 167	1 087	977	1 071	1 000	902	960	887	803
Per capita	203	186	164	178	165	147	156	143	128
At constant prices	1 210	1 231	1 145	1 110	1 032	943	946	989	1 036
Growth rates	5.3	1.8	−7.0	−3.1	−7.0	−8.6	0.4	4.5	4.7
Cambodia Cambodge									
At current prices	1 900	1 980	2 263	2 436	3 078	3 172	3 063	2 736	3 036
Per capita	191	192	212	221	270	270	253	220	238
At constant prices	1 540	1 648	1 715	1 783	1 901	2 006	2 059	2 085	2 169
Growth rates	7.6	7.0	4.1	3.9	6.7	5.5	2.6	1.3	4.0
Cameroon Cameroun									
At current prices	13 211	13 904	12 269	6 762	8 945	9 370	9 201	9 736	9 984
Per capita	1 106	1 132	973	522	674	689	661	684	686
At constant prices	13 772	13 352	13 153	12 726	13 122	13 774	14 476	15 200	15 869
Growth rates	−3.8	−3.1	−1.5	−3.2	3.1	5.0	5.1	5.0	4.4
Canada Canada									
At current prices	586 979	568 680	552 968	553 374	579 233	601 588	624 142	598 250	634 899
Per capita	20 920	20 024	19 248	19 052	19 733	20 288	20 845	19 796	20 822
At constant prices	561 739	566 859	579 905	607 325	623 965	633 508	661 313	683 148	714 526
Growth rates	−1.9	0.9	2.3	4.7	2.7	1.5	4.4	3.3	4.6
Cape Verde Cap−Vert									
At current prices	321	358	362	409	491	496	509	543	584
Per capita	921	1 007	994	1 099	1 289	1 275	1 278	1 331	1 400
At constant prices	312	322	345	369	397	407	434	469	507
Growth rates	1.4	3.0	7.3	6.9	7.5	2.6	6.6	8.0	8.0
Cayman Islands Iles Caïmanes									
At current prices	513	573	621	674	708	747	814	859	889
Per capita	18 718	20 086	20 930	21 872	22 120	22 491	23 650	24 069	24 064
At constant prices	498	495	500	502	500	501	503	511	518
Growth rates	1.3	−0.6	0.9	0.5	−0.5	0.2	0.5	1.5	1.5
Central African Rep. Rép. centrafricaine									
At current prices	1 284	1 382	1 251	822	1 099	1 031	958	1 010	1 010
Per capita	425	446	393	252	328	301	274	282	277
At constant prices	1 289	1 207	1 211	1 270	1 346	1 303	1 377	1 444	1 488
Growth rates	−0.6	−6.4	0.3	4.9	6.0	−3.2	5.7	4.9	3.1

22

Gross domestic product: total and per capita
In US dollars (millions) [1] at current and constant 1990 prices; per capita US dollars;
real rates of growth [*cont.*]

Produit intérieur brut : total et par habitant
En dollars E.−U. (millions) [1] aux prix courants et constants de 1990; par habitant en dollars E.−U.;
taux de l'accroissement réels [*suite*]

Country or area Pays ou zone	1991	1992	1993	1994	1995	1996	1997	1998	1999
Chad Tchad									
At current prices	1 321	1 325	1 030	830	1 006	1 060	994	1 091	974
Per capita	220	215	162	127	149	153	139	147	128
At constant prices	1 328	1 434	1 206	1 292	1 325	1 352	1 393	1 477	1 460
Growth rates	8.5	8.0	−15.9	7.1	2.6	2.0	3.1	6.0	−1.1
Chile Chili									
At current prices	34 650	41 882	44 474	50 919	65 215	68 568	75 287	73 064	67 658
Per capita	2 601	3 092	3 229	3 639	4 589	4 755	5 148	4 929	4 505
At constant prices	32 739	36 759	39 327	41 572	45 990	49 400	53 051	55 133	54 503
Growth rates	8.0	12.3	7.0	5.7	10.6	7.4	7.4	3.9	−1.1
China †† Chine ††									
At current prices	406 090	483 047	601 078	542 534	700 219	816 490	898 244	946 311	991 203
Per capita	353	416	512	457	584	675	736	768	798
At constant prices	423 447	483 576	548 859	618 015	682 907	748 466	814 331	877 849	940 176
Growth rates	9.2	14.2	13.5	12.6	10.5	9.6	8.8	7.8	7.1
China, Hong Kong SAR † Chine, Hong Kong RAS †									
At current prices	86 025	100 682	116 018	130 801	139 241	154 120	171 143	163 712	158 990
Per capita	14 879	17 145	19 415	21 482	22 423	24 314	26 430	24 757	23 579
At constant prices	78 567	83 488	88 607	93 393	97 029	101 467	106 422	100 902	103 953
Growth rates	5.1	6.3	6.1	5.4	3.9	4.6	4.9	−5.2	3.0
Colombia Colombie									
At current prices	48 033	51 411	59 241	79 936	92 503	97 147	106 671	99 082	86 643
Per capita	1 347	1 413	1 597	2 114	2 400	2 474	2 668	2 435	2 093
At constant prices	47 847	49 782	52 463	55 514	58 402	59 602	61 647	61 941	59 285
Growth rates	2.0	4.0	5.4	5.8	5.2	2.1	3.4	0.5	−4.3
Comoros Comores									
At current prices	247	266	264	186	215	213	194	197	193
Per capita	455	477	459	314	352	340	299	296	281
At constant prices	237	257	264	250	241	240	240	240	242
Growth rates	−5.4	8.5	3.0	−5.3	−3.9	−0.4	0.0	0.0	1.0
Congo Congo									
At current prices	2 725	2 933	2 684	1 769	2 116	2 526	2 285	1 944	2 244
Per capita	1 185	1 236	1 096	701	813	942	827	683	766
At constant prices	2 866	2 941	2 912	2 752	2 862	3 043	2 959	3 067	3 017
Growth rates	2.4	2.6	−1	−5.5	4.0	6.3	−2.7	3.6	−1.6
Cook Islands Iles Cook									
At current prices	70	72	81	96	102	102	95	76	78
Per capita	3 773	3 872	4 302	5 074	5 365	5 367	4 962	3 927	4 026
At constant prices	68	73	75	78	75	75	73	71	73
Growth rates	7.1	6.0	3.9	3.9	−4.4	−0.2	−2.8	−2.3	2.7
Costa Rica Costa Rica									
At current prices	5 637	6 738	7 521	8 317	9 233	9 391	9 952	10 867	11 572
Per capita	1 793	2 076	2 246	2 409	2 598	2 571	2 655	2 829	2 942
At constant prices	5 838	6 290	6 688	6 991	7 169	7 129	7 394	7 892	8 548
Growth rates	2.3	7.7	6.3	4.5	2.5	−0.6	3.7	6.7	8.3
Côte d'Ivoire Côte d'Ivoire									
At current prices	11 531	12 033	11 153	8 314	11 105	12 075	11 571	12 336	12 666
Per capita	890	902	814	592	772	820	769	803	808
At constant prices	11 900	11 825	11 778	12 031	12 879	13 748	14 567	15 222	15 883
Growth rates	0.1	−0.6	−0.4	2.1	7.1	6.7	6.0	4.5	4.3
Croatia Croatie									
At current prices	22 464	10 241	10 903	14 583	18 811	19 872	20 146	21 320	19 739
Per capita	4 951	2 244	2 375	3 160	4 060	4 278	4 331	4 582	4 242
At constant prices	19 556	17 265	15 879	16 812	17 961	19 038	20 276	20 823	20 715
Growth rates	−21.1	−11.7	−8.0	5.9	6.8	6.0	6.5	2.7	−0.5
Cuba Cuba									
At current prices	16 248	14 905	15 095	19 198	21 737	22 815	22 952	23 901	24 639
Per capita	1 517	1 382	1 391	1 760	1 983	2 071	2 074	2 150	2 208
At constant prices	17 544	15 513	13 205	13 299	13 626	14 694	15 060	15 248	16 199
Growth rates	−10.7	−11.6	−14.9	0.7	2.5	7.8	2.5	1.2	6.2
Cyprus Chypre									
At current prices	5 760	6 902	6 584	7 414	8 850	8 916	8 495	9 037	9 103
Per capita	8 327	9 796	9 164	10 131	11 899	11 825	11 139	11 734	11 715

22

Gross domestic product: total and per capita
In US dollars (millions) [1] at current and constant 1990 prices; per capita US dollars;
real rates of growth [cont.]

Produit intérieur brut : total et par habitant
En dollars E.–U. (millions) [1] aux prix courants et constants de 1990; par habitant en dollars E.–U.;
taux de l'accroissement réels [suite]

Country or area Pays ou zone	1991	1992	1993	1994	1995	1996	1997	1998	1999
At constant prices	5 619	6 145	6 188	6 547	6 914	7 045	7 215	7 573	7 914
Growth rates	0.7	9.4	0.7	5.8	5.6	1.9	2.4	5.0	4.5
Czech Republic République tchèque									
At current prices	25 570	29 816	34 998	41 091	52 035	57 921	53 000	56 402	53 782
Per capita	2 480	2 890	3 389	3 977	5 037	5 610	5 139	5 476	5 229
At constant prices	30 835	30 676	30 695	31 377	33 241	34 513	34 623	33 817	32 917
Growth rates	−11.6	−0.5	0.1	2.2	5.9	3.8	0.3	−2.3	−2.7
Dem. Rep. of the Congo Rép. dém. du Congo									
At current prices	9 088	8 204	10 708	5 721	5 542	5 492	5 686	5 542	5 749
Per capita	236	205	256	132	124	119	120	115	116
At constant prices	8 562	7 666	6 629	6 372	6 417	6 475	6 060	5 848	4 971
Growth rates	−8.4	−10.5	−13.5	−3.9	0.7	0.9	−6.4	−3.5	−15.0
Denmark Danemark									
At current prices	134 082	147 092	138 828	151 829	180 237	182 954	168 365	173 683	174 280
Per capita	26 018	28 452	26 758	29 154	34 476	34 862	31 960	32 850	32 853
At constant prices	134 848	135 671	135 669	143 085	147 024	150 727	155 456	159 406	162 085
Growth rates	1.1	0.6	0.0	5.5	2.8	2.5	3.1	2.5	1.7
Djibouti Djibouti									
At current prices	466	482	482	511	510	496	491	498	515
Per capita	898	913	907	953	935	887	850	833	835
At constant prices	443	445	453	451	447	421	426	435	450
Growth rates	−3.1	0.5	2.0	−0.6	−0.9	−5.7	1.2	2.1	3.5
Dominica Dominica									
At current prices	177	189	198	213	220	234	242	254	267
Per capita	2 489	2 663	2 787	2 998	3 102	3 297	3 412	3 589	3 778
At constant prices	170	174	176	179	182	187	190	195	202
Growth rates	1.8	2.0	1.0	2.1	1.7	2.8	1.4	2.6	3.5
Dominican Republic Rép. dominicaine									
At current prices	7 884	8 797	9 512	10 347	11 814	13 189	14 923	15 685	17 221
Per capita	1 097	1 203	1 279	1 368	1 535	1 684	1 874	1 936	2 091
At constant prices	7 667	8 262	8 510	8 879	9 298	9 972	10 791	11 581	12 543
Growth rates	0.8	7.8	3.0	4.3	4.7	7.3	8.2	7.3	8.3
Ecuador Equateur									
At current prices	11 752	12 656	14 304	16 606	17 939	19 040	19 769	19 723	13 760
Per capita	1 119	1 178	1 303	1 480	1 565	1 627	1 656	1 620	1 109
At constant prices	11 222	11 622	11 858	12 371	12 661	12 911	13 348	13 403	12 421
Growth rates	5.0	3.6	2.0	4.3	2.3	2.0	3.4	0.4	−7.3
Egypt Egypte									
At current prices	35 100	40 999	45 938	50 615	59 168	65 907	74 036	80 979	87 173
Per capita	611	700	769	832	954	1 044	1 151	1 236	1 307
At constant prices	56 794	57 078	59 978	62 346	65 188	68 524	72 155	76 327	80 900
Growth rates	0.3	0.5	5.1	3.9	4.6	5.1	5.3	5.8	6.0
El Salvador El Salvador									
At current prices	5 313	5 961	6 955	8 090	9 477	10 290	11 105	11 945	12 358
Per capita	1 020	1 121	1 281	1 458	1 671	1 777	1 878	1 980	2 007
At constant prices	5 518	5 935	6 373	6 754	7 186	7 308	7 618	7 884	8 089
Growth rates	3.6	7.5	7.4	6.0	6.4	1.7	4.2	3.5	2.6
Equatorial Guinea Guinée équatoriale									
At current prices	165	179	181	118	178	302	606	555	847
Per capita	457	485	477	303	445	735	1 440	1 283	1 907
At constant prices	161	178	189	199	228	294	503	614	706
Growth rates	−1.1	10.7	6.3	5.1	14.3	29.1	71.2	22.0	15.1
Eritrea Erythrée									
At current prices	...	715	504	619	629	670	702	751	779
Per capita	...	227	160	196	197	207	212	220	221
At constant prices	...	780	756	830	855	913	985	1 014	1 044
Growth rates	...	...	−3.0	9.8	2.9	6.8	7.9	3.0	3.0
Estonia Estonie									
At current prices	10 466	1 100	1 634	2 278	3 550	4 358	4 634	5 210	5 066
Per capita	6 694	710	1 070	1 514	2 393	2 977	3 206	3 649	3 591
At constant prices	10 357	8 881	8 127	7 964	8 306	8 631	9 547	9 997	9 767
Growth rates	−13.5	−14.2	−8.5	−2.0	4.3	3.9	10.6	4.7	−2.3

22
Gross domestic product: total and per capita
In US dollars (millions) [1] at current and constant 1990 prices; per capita US dollars;
real rates of growth [cont.]

Produit intérieur brut : total et par habitant
En dollars E.−U. (millions) [1] aux prix courants et constants de 1990; par habitant en dollars E.−U.;
taux de l'accroissement réels [suite]

Country or area Pays ou zone	1991	1992	1993	1994	1995	1996	1997	1998	1999
Ethiopia including Eritrea	**Ethiopie y compris Erythrée**								
At current prices	9 573	...	...	...	...	...	...	...	...
Per capita	186	...	...	...	...	...	...	...	...
At constant prices	8 113	...	...	...	...	...	...	...	...
Growth rates	−6.0	...	...	...	...	...	...	...	...
Ethiopia Ethiopie									
At current prices	...	7 419	5 354	5 184	5 502	5 973	6 180	6 329	6 200
Per capita	...	147	103	96	99	105	106	106	101
At constant prices	...	7 500	8 397	8 530	9 056	10 017	10 535	10 478	11 139
Growth rates	...	...	12.0	1.6	6.2	10.6	5.2	−0.5	6.3
Fiji Fidji									
At current prices	1 384	1 532	1 636	1 826	1 990	2 121	2 130	1 660	1 830
Per capita	1 897	2 075	2 188	2 409	2 592	2 728	2 707	2 087	2 275
At constant prices	1 301	1 352	1 375	1 445	1 481	1 527	1 514	1 536	1 638
Growth rates	−2.7	3.9	1.7	5.1	2.5	3.1	−0.9	1.5	6.6
Finland Finlande									
At current prices	123 482	108 702	86 237	99 992	129 290	127 541	122 419	129 335	129 665
Per capita	24 652	21 592	17 040	19 661	25 312	24 881	23 811	25 096	25 112
At constant prices	128 236	123 976	122 553	127 399	132 253	137 555	146 210	154 218	160 409
Growth rates	−6.3	−3.3	−1.1	4.0	3.8	4.0	6.3	5.5	4.0
France France									
At current prices	1 220 133	1 346 103	1 276 044	1 350 801	1 553 131	1 554 361	1 406 121	1 446 950	1 432 364
Per capita	21 396	23 484	22 151	23 338	26 714	26 625	23 994	24 601	24 267
At constant prices	1 227 606	1 245 740	1 234 688	1 260 197	1 281 244	1 295 375	1 320 875	1 365 613	1 405 541
Growth rates	1.0	1.5	−0.9	2.1	1.7	1.1	2.0	3.4	2.9
French Guiana Guyane française									
At current prices	1 312	1 507	1 411	1 482	1 675	1 672	1 500	1 518	1 488
Per capita	10 829	12 001	10 881	11 077	12 110	11 678	10 106	9 870	9 342
At constant prices	1 341	1 448	1 406	1 492	1 516	1 540	1 565	1 590	1 616
Growth rates	11.9	8.0	−2.9	6.1	1.6	1.6	1.6	1.6	1.6
French Polynesia Polynesie française									
At current prices	2 975	3 265	3 479	3 741	4 112	4 123	3 742	3 735	3 717
Per capita	14 922	16 059	16 794	17 735	19 150	18 877	16 844	16 535	16 188
At constant prices	3 045	3 160	3 263	3 682	3 597	3 656	3 698	3 737	3 836
Growth rates	3.9	3.8	3.3	12.8	−2.3	1.6	1.1	1.1	2.7
Gabon Gabon									
At current prices	5 403	5 593	5 406	4 191	4 959	5 630	5 341	4 666	4 504
Per capita	5 611	5 642	5 300	3 995	4 599	5 081	4 693	3 994	3 756
At constant prices	5 759	5 572	5 792	6 005	6 304	6 556	6 851	6 995	6 596
Growth rates	6.1	−3.2	4.0	3.7	5.0	4.0	4.5	2.1	−5.7
Gambia Gambie									
At current prices	298	329	337	339	405	428	432	436	434
Per capita	309	328	324	314	363	371	363	354	342
At constant prices	292	305	308	312	301	317	334	348	362
Growth rates	1.7	4.5	0.9	1.3	−3.4	5.3	5.4	4.0	4.2
Georgia Géorgie									
At current prices	10 941	716	1 335	1 246	2 842	4 229	4 957	4 928	4 043
Per capita	2 005	132	247	232	531	793	933	930	765
At constant prices	17 729	9 769	6 906	6 188	6 349	7 060	7 858	8 086	8 110
Growth rates	−21.1	−44.9	−29.3	−10.4	2.6	11.2	11.3	2.9	0.3
Germany † Allemagne †									
At current prices	1 770 370	2 020 427	1 956 911	2 091 706	2 458 256	2 383 421	2 114 402	2 150 631	2 112 061
Per capita	22 152	25 122	24 186	25 718	30 103	29 109	25 788	26 218	25 749
At constant prices	1 807 206	1 847 714	1 827 622	1 870 507	1 902 805	1 917 388	1 944 178	1 984 092	2 014 986
Growth rates	...	2.2	−1.1	2.3	1.7	0.8	1.4	2.1	1.6
Ghana Ghana									
At current prices	7 000	6 884	5 966	5 441	6 458	6 926	6 884	7 474	7 556
Per capita	450	430	363	322	373	391	380	404	400
At constant prices	6 557	6 812	7 148	7 382	7 679	8 032	8 441	8 825	9 311
Growth rates	5.3	3.9	4.9	3.3	4.0	4.6	5.1	4.6	5.5
Greece Grèce									
At current prices	91 176	100 325	94 266	100 260	117 564	124 361	120 933	121 513	125 088
Per capita	8 924	9 761	9 115	9 639	11 246	11 845	11 478	11 500	11 811

22
Gross domestic product: total and per capita
In US dollars (millions) [1] at current and constant 1990 prices; per capita US dollars;
real rates of growth [*cont.*]
Produit intérieur brut : total et par habitant
En dollars E.−U. (millions) [1]   aux prix courants et constants de 1990; par habitant en dollars E.−U.;
taux de l'accroissement réels [*suite*]

Country or area Pays ou zone	1991	1992	1993	1994	1995	1996	1997	1998	1999
At constant prices	88 777	89 168	88 359	89 648	91 327	93 481	96 679	100 216	103 673
Growth rates	3.4	0.4	−0.9	1.5	1.9	2.4	3.4	3.7	3.5
Grenada Grenade									
At current prices	210	214	213	224	236	251	269	286	307
Per capita	2 309	2 346	2 330	2 439	2 558	2 720	2 898	3 079	3 295
At constant prices	206	206	200	206	211	220	230	242	257
Growth rates	3.0	−0.3	−2.6	2.8	2.5	4.1	4.6	5.3	6.2
Guadeloupe Guadeloupe									
At current prices	2 909	3 395	3 461	3 946	4 439	4 575	4 453	4 697	4 645
Per capita	7 354	8 498	8 595	9 726	10 854	11 089	10 697	11 177	10 953
At constant prices	2 293	2 460	2 639	2 835	2 711	2 828	3 089	3 217	3 237
Growth rates	−17.9	7.3	7.3	7.4	−4.3	4.3	9.2	4.1	0.6
Guatemala Guatemala									
At current prices	9 406	10 441	11 400	12 983	14 656	15 783	17 797	19 008	18 149
Per capita	1 048	1 133	1 205	1 336	1 469	1 541	1 692	1 760	1 637
At constant prices	7 930	8 314	8 640	8 989	9 434	9 712	10 129	10 612	10 986
Growth rates	3.7	4.8	3.9	4.0	5.0	2.9	4.3	4.8	3.5
Guinea Guinée									
At current prices	3 016	2 974	3 177	3 395	3 682	3 932	3 916	3 779	3 631
Per capita	474	450	463	478	502	522	508	480	453
At constant prices	2 895	2 982	3 122	3 247	3 390	3 542	3 654	3 837	3 981
Growth rates	4.8	3.0	4.7	4.0	4.4	4.5	3.2	5.0	3.7
Guinea−Bissau Guinée−Bissau									
At current prices	234	221	170	255	179	138	109	116	124
Per capita	241	221	166	242	166	125	97	101	106
At constant prices	240	249	253	270	284	296	311	327	355
Growth rates	3.0	3.6	1.6	6.9	4.9	4.4	5.1	5.1	8.7
Guyana Guyana									
At current prices	348	374	467	545	622	706	749	725	647
Per capita	477	510	634	738	837	945	999	961	854
At constant prices	420	453	490	534	558	602	640	631	643
Growth rates	6.0	7.8	8.2	9.0	4.6	7.9	6.3	−1.3	1.8
Haiti Haïti									
At current prices	2 352	1 532	1 551	2 057	2 330	2 754	3 110	3 522	3 973
Per capita	334	214	213	278	310	360	400	446	496
At constant prices	2 620	2 275	2 219	2 035	2 126	2 183	2 208	2 276	2 331
Growth rates	0.2	−13.2	−2.4	−8.3	4.4	2.7	1.1	3.1	2.4
Holy See [2] Saint−Siège [2]									
At current prices	15	15	11	10	10	10	10	10	10
Per capita	19 125	18 458	13 241	12 193	11 960	12 835	12 084	12 645	12 806
At constant prices	16	16	16	16	17	17	17	18	18
Growth rates	1.4	0.8	−0.9	2.2	2.9	1.1	1.8	1.5	1.4
Honduras Honduras									
At current prices	3 068	3 419	3 506	3 432	3 960	4 081	4 698	5 217	5 356
Per capita	612	662	659	628	704	706	791	855	856
At constant prices	3 148	3 325	3 532	3 486	3 628	3 762	3 929	4 045	3 969
Growth rates	3.3	5.6	6.2	−1.3	4.1	3.7	4.5	2.9	−1.9
Hungary Hongrie									
At current prices	34 160	38 069	39 441	42 415	44 669	45 163	45 724	47 049	48 225
Per capita	3 306	3 695	3 838	4 138	4 373	4 440	4 516	4 671	4 813
At constant prices	32 210	31 223	31 044	31 958	32 432	32 866	34 370	36 039	37 661
Growth rates	−11.9	−3.1	−0.6	2.9	1.5	1.3	4.6	4.9	4.5
Iceland Islande									
At current prices	6 729	6 910	6 086	6 220	6 980	7 315	7 474	8 268	8 815
Per capita	26 145	26 585	23 192	23 479	26 105	27 107	27 446	30 093	31 814
At constant prices	6 321	6 109	6 167	6 390	6 429	6 796	7 159	7 523	7 857
Growth rates	1.2	−3.3	0.9	3.6	0.6	5.7	5.3	5.1	4.4
India Inde									
At current prices	287 426	288 648	281 773	321 896	364 498	384 372	417 380	427 202	449 955
Per capita	334	329	315	353	393	407	435	438	453
At constant prices	325 623	343 273	360 282	386 727	416 326	445 269	465 598	497 053	528 999
Growth rates	0.4	5.4	5.0	7.3	7.7	7.0	4.6	6.8	6.4

22

Gross domestic product: total and per capita
In US dollars (millions) [1] at current and constant 1990 prices; per capita US dollars;
real rates of growth [cont.]

Produit intérieur brut : total et par habitant
En dollars E.–U. (millions) [1] aux prix courants et constants de 1990; par habitant en dollars E.–U.;
taux de l'accroissement réels [suite]

Country or area Pays ou zone	1991	1992	1993	1994	1995	1996	1997	1998	1999
Indonesia Indonésie									
At current prices	128 169	139 116	158 007	176 893	202 131	227 369	215 749	100 097	140 964
Per capita	691	738	824	909	1 023	1 134	1 060	485	674
At constant prices	124 642	133 642	143 336	154 143	166 814	179 856	188 308	163 450	163 820
Growth rates	8.9	7.2	7.3	7.5	8.2	7.8	4.7	−13.2	0.2
Iran (Islamic Rep. of) [3] Iran (Rép. islamique d') [3]									
At current prices	97 923	101 453	73 838	73 414	102 335	134 361	158 496	187 422	238 554
Per capita	1 634	1 657	1 183	1 156	1 583	2 043	2 368	2 752	3 445
At constant prices	103 606	109 534	111 277	112 111	116 848	124 698	129 299	131 646	135 069
Growth rates	11.5	5.7	1.6	0.7	4.2	6.7	3.7	1.8	2.6
Iraq [4] Iraq [4]									
At current prices	18 771	35 999	45 745	46 146	44 298	45 227	56 534	65 014	70 215
Per capita	1 056	1 965	2 422	2 370	2 210	2 194	2 669	2 989	3 144
At constant prices	18 614	21 365	14 950	15 081	14 477	14 781	18 476	21 248	22 947
Growth rates	−66.1	14.8	−30.0	0.9	−4.0	2.1	25.0	15.0	8.0
Ireland Irlande									
At current prices	47 762	53 646	50 283	54 775	66 389	73 011	79 983	86 265	93 413
Per capita	13 566	15 179	14 147	15 302	18 396	20 044	21 731	23 181	24 825
At constant prices	48 214	49 826	51 167	54 112	59 380	63 946	70 814	76 875	84 427
Growth rates	1.9	3.3	2.7	5.8	9.7	7.7	10.7	8.6	9.8
Israel Israël									
At current prices	63 559	70 781	70 956	80 024	92 791	101 806	105 008	103 688	103 797
Per capita	13 651	14 679	14 187	15 446	17 346	18 498	18 599	17 941	17 564
At constant prices	59 926	64 396	66 815	71 694	76 628	80 400	82 533	84 346	86 210
Growth rates	7.3	7.5	3.8	7.3	6.9	4.9	2.7	2.2	2.2
Italy Italie									
At current prices	1 161 241	1 231 407	993 392	1 025 404	1 097 210	1 232 882	1 164 846	1 190 929	1 171 005
Per capita	20 440	21 630	17 409	17 930	19 148	21 482	20 272	20 709	20 355
At constant prices	1 117 764	1 126 266	1 116 312	1 140 955	1 174 315	1 187 150	1 208 708	1 227 218	1 244 703
Growth rates	1.4	0.8	−0.9	2.2	2.9	1.1	1.8	1.5	1.4
Jamaica Jamaïque									
At current prices	3 732	3 353	4 214	4 221	5 113	3 950	3 868	3 841	3 800
Per capita	1 564	1 394	1 736	1 723	2 069	1 585	1 539	1 516	1 487
At constant prices	4 270	4 329	4 381	4 423	4 456	4 393	4 302	4 271	4 226
Growth rates	0.5	1.4	1.2	1.0	0.7	−1.4	−2.1	−0.7	−1.1
Japan Japon									
At current prices	3 402 192	3 719 044	4 275 087	4 689 066	5 137 383	4 599 322	4 212 258	3 808 100	4 346 919
Per capita	27 444	29 903	34 270	37 478	40 944	36 553	33 384	30 101	34 276
At constant prices	3 082 846	3 114 353	3 124 058	3 144 198	3 190 451	3 351 568	3 404 998	3 319 572	3 326 307
Growth rates	3.8	1.0	0.3	0.6	1.5	5.1	1.6	−2.5	0.2
Jordan Jordanie									
At current prices	4 193	5 203	5 569	6 078	6 512	6 645	6 976	7 306	7 541
Per capita	1 222	1 431	1 445	1 496	1 533	1 507	1 535	1 566	1 576
At constant prices	4 094	4 752	5 017	5 444	5 767	5 800	5 877	5 817	5 893
Growth rates	1.8	16.1	5.6	8.5	5.9	0.6	1.3	−1.0	1.3
Kazakhstan Kazakhstan									
At current prices	46 286	6 237	11 722	11 916	16 640	21 035	22 165	22 311	15 961
Per capita	2 756	371	700	714	1 002	1 273	1 348	1 365	982
At constant prices	62 816	55 673	49 883	43 597	40 022	40 183	40 866	40 089	40 771
Growth rates	−9.7	−11.4	−10.4	−12.6	−8.2	0.4	1.7	−1.9	1.7
Kenya Kenya									
At current prices	8 043	7 951	5 520	7 024	9 047	9 257	10 614	11 465	10 649
Per capita	330	317	213	264	331	330	370	390	355
At constant prices	8 655	8 587	8 617	8 844	9 234	9 616	9 817	9 975	10 105
Growth rates	1.4	−0.8	0.4	2.6	4.4	4.1	2.1	1.6	1.3
Kiribati Kiribati									
At current prices	34	34	33	40	46	50	48	45	51
Per capita	465	459	441	520	596	633	606	564	627
At constant prices	30	30	30	32	34	35	36	39	41
Growth rates	6.9	−1.6	0.8	7.2	6.5	2.6	2.3	8.3	6.1
Korea, Dem. P. R. Corée, R.p. dém.									
At current prices	15 598	13 881	11 711	9 360	5 229	10 588	10 323	10 273	10 369
Per capita	770	675	562	443	245	490	474	468	469

22
Gross domestic product: total and per capita
In US dollars (millions) [1] at current and constant 1990 prices; per capita US dollars;
real rates of growth [*cont.*]

Produit intérieur brut : total et par habitant
En dollars E.–U. (millions) [1] aux prix courants et constants de 1990; par habitant en dollars E.–U.;
taux de l'accroissement réels [*suite*]

Country or area Pays ou zone	1991	1992	1993	1994	1995	1996	1997	1998	1999
At constant prices	15 898	14 674	14 057	13 804	13 169	12 682	11 820	11 690	12 415
Growth rates	−5.1	−7.7	−4.2	−1.8	−4.6	−3.7	−6.8	−1.1	6.2
Korea, Republic of Corée, République de									
At current prices	295 234	314 737	345 716	402 525	489 256	520 203	476 487	320 748	411 648
Per capita	6 821	7 201	7 833	9 035	10 884	11 475	10 426	6 964	8 871
At constant prices	275 932	290 936	306 913	332 234	361 867	386 294	405 651	381 970	417 195
Growth rates	9.2	5.4	5.5	8.3	8.9	6.8	5.0	−5.8	9.2
Kuwait Kowëit									
At current prices	11 014	19 869	23 956	24 859	26 554	31 085	30 368	25 617	30 015
Per capita	5 254	9 957	12 816	14 141	15 705	18 525	17 754	14 437	16 244
At constant prices	11 289	21 141	28 326	30 716	31 049	34 138	33 107	28 803	33 165
Growth rates	−38.9	87.3	34.0	8.4	1.1	10.0	−3.0	−13.0	15.1
Kyrgyzstan Kirghizistan									
At current prices	10 571	767	993	1 109	1 492	4 365	4 795	4 902	5 079
Per capita	2 382	172	221	245	327	945	1 022	1 028	1 048
At constant prices	11 832	10 300	8 663	6 921	6 548	7 013	7 703	7 875	8 159
Growth rates	−7.7	−12.9	−15.9	−20.1	−5.4	7.1	9.8	2.2	3.6
Lao People's Dem. Rep. Rép. dém. pop. lao									
At current prices	1 028	1 180	1 328	1 544	1 764	1 874	1 747	1 292	1 467
Per capita	243	271	298	338	376	390	355	256	285
At constant prices	900	964	1 020	1 103	1 181	1 262	1 349	1 403	1 476
Growth rates	4.0	7.0	5.8	8.1	7.0	6.9	6.9	4.0	5.2
Latvia Lettonie									
At current prices	16 380	1 364	2 172	3 649	4 453	5 137	5 527	5 966	6 135
Per capita	6 168	519	839	1 431	1 770	2 064	2 240	2 434	2 519
At constant prices	16 799	10 943	9 316	9 375	9 300	9 613	10 242	10 644	10 653
Growth rates	−10.4	−34.9	−14.9	0.6	−0.8	3.4	6.5	3.9	0.1
Lebanon [4] Liban [4]									
At current prices	4 151	5 465	7 537	8 923	10 965	5 162	5 343	5 503	5 448
Per capita	1 493	1 904	2 536	2 902	3 461	1 589	1 610	1 628	1 585
At constant prices	3 888	4 063	4 348	4 696	5 001	5 201	5 383	5 544	5 489
Growth rates	38.3	4.5	7.0	8.0	6.5	4.0	3.5	3.0	−1.0
Lesotho Lesotho									
At current prices	690	822	815	835	933	943	1 024	890	923
Per capita	402	468	455	456	499	495	527	450	460
At constant prices	646	680	704	728	760	835	903	861	886
Growth rates	3.8	5.3	3.5	3.4	4.4	10.0	8.1	−4.6	2.8
Liberia [4] Libéria [4]									
At current prices	1 491	1 671	1 878	2 112	2 385	573	651	668	698
Per capita	710	816	937	1 056	1 166	266	282	267	258
At constant prices	1 185	1 013	1 013	667	667	681	773	794	830
Growth rates	−10.0	−14.6	0.0	−34.1	0.0	2.0	13.5	2.7	4.6
Libyan Arab Jamah. Jamah. arabe libyenne									
At current prices	31 363	32 047	22 600	22 049	22 540	23 203	22 511	26 574	27 139
Per capita	7 127	7 141	4 941	4 729	4 740	4 781	4 543	5 248	5 244
At constant prices	29 624	28 379	27 074	26 478	26 055	26 367	26 710	25 909	26 427
Growth rates	4.7	−4.2	−4.6	−2.2	−1.6	1.2	1.3	−3.0	2.0
Liechtenstein Liechtenstein									
At current prices	981	1 032	1 009	1 120	1 324	1 283	1 117	1 150	1 141
Per capita	33 570	34 870	33 677	36 937	43 138	41 281	35 478	36 094	35 376
At constant prices	951	950	945	950	955	958	974	994	1 010
Growth rates	−0.8	−0.1	−0.5	0.5	0.5	0.3	1.7	2.1	1.5
Lithuania Lituanie									
At current prices	23 697	1 921	2 668	4 250	6 026	7 892	9 550	10 708	10 611
Per capita	6 346	514	715	1 142	1 622	2 127	2 576	2 891	2 867
At constant prices	18 993	14 956	12 529	11 305	11 677	12 231	12 928	13 596	13 032
Growth rates	−5.7	−21.3	−16.2	−9.8	3.3	4.7	5.7	5.2	−4.1
Luxembourg Luxembourg									
At current prices	11 520	13 329	13 565	15 397	18 265	18 200	17 459	18 341	19 328
Per capita	29 791	33 991	34 087	38 123	44 581	43 822	41 491	43 039	44 797
At constant prices	11 600	12 118	13 174	13 727	14 247	14 659	15 723	16 512	17 750
Growth rates	6.1	4.5	8.7	4.2	3.8	2.9	7.3	5.0	7.5

22

Gross domestic product: total and per capita
In US dollars (millions) [1] at current and constant 1990 prices; per capita US dollars;
real rates of growth [*cont.*]

Produit intérieur brut : total et par habitant
En dollars E.−U. (millions) [1] aux prix courants et constants de 1990; par habitant en dollars E.−U.;
taux de l'accroissement réels [*suite*]

Country or area Pays ou zone	1991	1992	1993	1994	1995	1996	1997	1998	1999
Madagascar Madagascar									
At current prices	2 673	2 996	3 366	2 972	3 155	3 987	3 546	3 741	3 715
Per capita	217	237	259	222	229	281	242	248	239
At constant prices	2 886	2 920	2 981	2 979	3 030	3 095	3 209	3 336	3 491
Growth rates	−6.3	1.2	2.1	−0.1	1.7	2.1	3.7	3.9	4.7
Malawi Malawi									
At current prices	2 178	1 858	2 031	1 210	1 474	2 418	2 575	1 773	1 921
Per capita	226	190	207	122	147	237	246	165	174
At constant prices	2 020	1 872	2 053	1 843	2 128	2 319	2 431	2 506	2 676
Growth rates	8.7	−7.3	9.7	−10.2	15.5	9.0	4.8	3.1	6.8
Malaysia Malaisie									
At current prices	49 135	59 152	66 895	74 482	88 833	100 850	100 169	72 489	78 735
Per capita	2 688	3 161	3 494	3 804	4 438	4 929	4 791	3 395	3 613
At constant prices	48 227	52 512	57 708	63 025	69 219	76 143	81 718	75 698	79 970
Growth rates	9.5	8.9	9.9	9.2	9.8	10.0	7.3	−7.4	5.6
Maldives Maldives									
At current prices	163	191	216	239	269	301	340	366	390
Per capita	735	832	914	984	1 075	1 168	1 278	1 335	1 382
At constant prices	156	166	176	188	201	217	237	258	280
Growth rates	7.7	6.3	6.2	6.6	7.2	7.9	9.1	9.1	8.5
Mali Mali									
At current prices	2 451	2 786	2 590	1 813	2 310	2 669	2 535	2 716	2 801
Per capita	272	302	274	187	233	262	242	253	254
At constant prices	2 505	2 747	2 633	2 738	2 903	3 196	3 403	3 597	3 786
Growth rates	−0.2	9.7	−4.2	4.0	6.1	10.1	6.5	5.7	5.2
Malta Malte									
At current prices	2 496	2 743	2 459	2 722	3 245	3 333	3 338	3 507	3 627
Per capita	6 865	7 468	6 629	7 267	8 588	8 754	8 706	9 091	9 349
At constant prices	2 457	2 572	2 687	2 839	3 019	3 140	3 292	3 403	3 542
Growth rates	6.3	4.7	4.5	5.7	6.3	4.0	4.9	3.4	4.1
Marshall Islands Iles Marshall									
At current prices	72	80	87	95	105	97	92	95	97
Per capita	1 595	1 733	1 869	2 006	2 205	2 006	1 880	1 914	1 920
At constant prices	69	69	72	70	76	64	58	60	60
Growth rates	1.1	0.0	4.1	−3.8	9.8	−15.9	−9.4	2.5	0.8
Martinique Martinique									
At current prices	3 684	4 173	4 055	4 273	4 838	4 863	4 377	4 617	4 566
Per capita	10 140	11 408	11 016	11 545	12 996	12 986	11 621	12 183	11 979
At constant prices	3 408	3 463	3 520	3 577	3 635	3 695	3 755	3 910	3 936
Growth rates	−4.0	1.6	1.6	1.6	1.6	1.6	1.6	4.1	0.6
Mauritania Mauritanie									
At current prices	1 136	1 146	894	903	971	985	959	830	808
Per capita	556	547	416	408	427	420	396	332	313
At constant prices	1 085	1 127	1 162	1 193	1 248	1 295	1 342	1 382	1 439
Growth rates	3.4	3.8	3.1	2.7	4.6	3.7	3.6	3.0	4.1
Mauritius Maurice									
At current prices	2 738	3 189	3 205	3 510	3 973	4 307	4 104	4 042	4 192
Per capita	2 565	2 956	2 938	3 182	3 566	3 830	3 619	3 536	3 638
At constant prices	2 661	2 827	2 985	3 102	3 247	3 436	3 636	3 827	3 958
Growth rates	4.1	6.2	5.6	3.9	4.7	5.8	5.8	5.3	3.4
Mexico Mexique									
At current prices	314 451	363 609	403 193	420 773	286 166	332 337	400 870	420 852	490 247
Per capita	3 708	4 209	4 583	4 698	3 140	3 585	4 252	4 392	5 036
At constant prices	273 802	283 737	289 272	302 044	283 417	298 022	318 204	333 941	346 163
Growth rates	4.2	3.6	2.0	4.4	−6.2	5.2	6.8	4.9	3.7
Micronesia (Fed. States of) Micron (Etats fédérés de)									
At current prices	173	187	208	211	224	26	222	224	230
Per capita	1 779	1 877	2 031	2 013	2 083	233	1 952	1 918	1 922
At constant prices	167	176	190	188	194	190	182	181	182
Growth rates	8.9	5.2	8.1	−1.2	3.5	−2.3	−3.9	−0.6	0.2
Monaco Monaco									
At current prices	649	720	688	733	848	855	778	806	803
Per capita	21 396	23 484	22 151	23 338	26 714	26 625	23 994	24 601	24 267

22

Gross domestic product: total and per capita
In US dollars (millions) [1] at current and constant 1990 prices; per capita US dollars;
real rates of growth [*cont.*]

Produit intérieur brut : total et par habitant
En dollars E.−U. (millions) [1] aux prix courants et constants de 1990; par habitant en dollars E.−U.;
taux de l'accroissement réels [*suite*]

Country or area Pays ou zone	1991	1992	1993	1994	1995	1996	1997	1998	1999
At constant prices	648	676	690	704	716	724	738	763	785
Growth rates	1.0	4.2	2.1	2.1	1.7	1.1	2.0	3.4	2.9
Mongolia Mongolie									
At current prices	2 566	1 435	793	886	1 235	1 203	1 071	992	872
Per capita	1 133	621	338	372	512	493	435	399	348
At constant prices	2 846	2 575	2 498	2 555	2 717	2 783	2 893	2 994	3 084
Growth rates	−9.2	−9.5	−3.0	2.3	6.3	2.4	4.0	3.5	3.0
Montserrat Montserrat									
At current prices	60	63	66	68	64	52	40	38	39
Per capita	5 519	5 738	6 008	6 281	6 286	5 677	5 221	6 248	8 238
At constant prices	57	58	60	60	56	44	32	31	31
Growth rates	−20.9	2.7	2.5	0.9	−7.6	−21.4	−26.5	−3.2	−0.7
Morocco Maroc									
At current prices	27 837	28 451	26 802	30 352	32 985	36 672	33 514	37 193	37 040
Per capita	1 107	1 109	1 024	1 137	1 212	1 322	1 186	1 292	1 263
At constant prices	27 619	26 505	26 237	28 954	27 050	30 328	29 709	31 588	31 638
Growth rates	6.9	−4.0	−1.0	10.4	−6.6	12.1	2.0	6.3	0.2
Mozambique Mozambique									
At current prices	1 371	1 098	1 174	1 291	1 369	1 651	1 998	2 257	2 407
Per capita	98	75	78	82	84	98	116	128	134
At constant prices	1 554	1 428	1 552	1 668	1 740	1 864	2 075	2 323	2 549
Growth rates	4.9	−8.1	8.7	7.5	4.3	7.1	11.3	12.0	9.7
Myanmar [4] Myanmar [4]									
At current prices	20 625	22 617	23 983	25 777	27 568	29 344	31 002	32 538	34 402
Per capita	500	538	560	591	622	651	677	700	730
At constant prices	20 625	22 617	23 983	25 777	27 568	29 344	31 002	32 538	34 402
Growth rates	−0.7	9.7	6.0	7.5	6.9	6.4	5.7	5.0	5.7
Namibia Namibie									
At current prices	2 483	2 823	2 628	2 978	3 224	3 122	3 234	3 044	2 990
Per capita	1 745	1 924	1 742	1 925	2 035	1 925	1 952	1 800	1 734
At constant prices	2 532	2 712	2 666	2 835	2 940	3 003	3 082	3 156	3 232
Growth rates	8.2	7.1	−1.7	6.4	3.7	2.1	2.6	2.4	2.4
Nauru Nauru									
At current prices	51	46	41	42	41	41	37	32	34
Per capita	5 242	4 604	3 973	3 984	3 767	3 710	3 284	2 767	2 830
At constant prices	49	46	42	39	36	34	31	31	30
Growth rates	−3.7	−7.3	−7.3	−7.3	−7.3	−7.3	−7.3	−1.9	−1.9
Nepal Népal									
At current prices	3 231	3 499	3 528	4 034	4 224	4 391	4 836	4 495	4 903
Per capita	174	184	181	202	207	210	225	205	218
At constant prices	3 745	3 899	4 049	4 382	4 534	4 776	5 017	5 134	5 336
Growth rates	6.4	4.1	3.8	8.2	3.5	5.3	5.0	2.3	3.9
Netherlands Pays−Bas									
At current prices	302 166	335 207	325 979	351 433	414 799	411 826	376 602	391 263	393 703
Per capita	20 073	22 115	21 360	22 877	26 832	26 483	24 085	24 894	24 929
At constant prices	302 081	308 199	310 549	320 556	327 801	337 760	350 554	363 396	376 391
Growth rates	2.3	2.0	0.8	3.2	2.3	3.0	3.8	3.7	3.6
Netherlands Antilles Antilles néerlandaises									
At current prices	1 910	1 998	2 129	2 288	2 360	2 471	2 504	2 530	2 515
Per capita	10 022	10 297	10 759	11 347	11 518	11 902	11 933	11 950	11 783
At constant prices	1 923	1 992	1 992	2 026	2 052	2 023	1 987	1 971	1 914
Growth rates	5.8	3.6	0.0	1.7	1.3	−1.4	−1.8	−0.8	−2.9
New Caledonia Nouvelle−Calédonie									
At current prices	2 654	2 924	3 070	3 039	3 628	3 607	3 326	3 143	3 068
Per capita	15 159	16 299	16 695	16 120	18 792	18 254	16 463	15 224	14 550
At constant prices	2 629	2 655	2 673	2 743	2 905	2 919	2 978	2 882	2 908
Growth rates	3.9	1.0	0.7	2.6	5.9	0.5	2.0	−3.2	0.9
New Zealand Nouvelle−Zélande									
At current prices	41 694	40 057	43 677	51 322	60 019	65 258	64 813	52 944	55 290
Per capita	12 257	11 608	12 464	14 431	16 652	17 898	17 597	14 247	14 754
At constant prices	42 574	43 082	45 805	48 271	50 103	51 388	52 404	52 420	54 730
Growth rates	−1.2	1.2	6.3	5.4	3.8	2.6	2.0	0.0	4.4

22
Gross domestic product: total and per capita
In US dollars (millions) [1] at current and constant 1990 prices; per capita US dollars;
real rates of growth [*cont.*]
Produit intérieur brut : total et par habitant
En dollars E.–U. (millions) [1] aux prix courants et constants de 1990; par habitant en dollars E.–U.;
taux de l'accroissement réels [*suite*]

Country or area Pays ou zone	1991	1992	1993	1994	1995	1996	1997	1998	1999
Nicaragua Nicaragua									
At current prices	1 738	1 843	1 967	1 831	1 888	1 974	2 023	2 125	2 266
Per capita	442	455	471	426	427	433	432	442	459
At constant prices	2 210	2 218	2 210	2 283	2 382	2 494	2 622	2 728	2 864
Growth rates	−0.2	0.4	−0.4	3.3	4.3	4.7	5.1	4.0	5.0
Niger Niger									
At current prices	2 352	2 370	2 244	1 580	1 901	2 009	1 875	2 069	2 089
Per capita	295	288	264	179	209	213	192	205	200
At constant prices	2 568	2 401	2 436	2 533	2 599	2 688	2 777	3 007	3 076
Growth rates	2.5	−6.5	1.4	4.0	2.6	3.4	3.3	8.3	2.3
Nigeria [4] Nigéria [4]									
At current prices	32 695	31 784	31 791	41 568	66 759	56 366	58 358	51 807	52 384
Per capita	369	349	339	431	672	552	556	480	473
At constant prices	33 966	34 952	35 871	36 230	37 169	39 547	40 758	41 535	41 998
Growth rates	4.8	2.9	2.6	1.0	2.6	6.4	3.1	1.9	1.1
Norway Norvège									
At current prices	117 757	126 307	116 111	122 926	146 602	157 615	154 971	147 029	152 943
Per capita	27 620	29 465	26 934	28 356	33 631	35 963	35 176	33 206	34 377
At constant prices	119 051	122 940	126 302	133 239	138 365	145 140	151 953	154 993	156 347
Growth rates	3.1	3.3	2.7	5.5	3.8	4.9	4.7	2.0	0.9
Oman Oman									
At current prices	11 341	12 452	12 493	12 919	13 803	15 278	15 837	14 162	15 691
Per capita	6 103	6 445	6 229	6 213	6 409	6 857	6 877	5 953	6 386
At constant prices	12 391	13 443	14 269	14 818	15 534	15 983	16 971	17 470	17 301
Growth rates	6.0	8.5	6.1	3.8	4.8	2.9	6.2	2.9	−1.0
Pakistan Pakistan									
At current prices	51 138	53 741	56 233	61 864	68 009	68 434	66 888	67 323	67 024
Per capita	454	466	477	513	550	539	513	503	487
At constant prices	50 940	51 915	53 938	56 699	59 540	60 270	62 259	64 692	66 436
Growth rates	7.8	1.9	3.9	5.1	5.0	1.2	3.3	3.9	2.7
Palau Palaos									
At current prices	94	100	100	109	116	144	143	119	126
Per capita	6 051	6 278	6 100	6 529	6 779	8 190	7 964	6 507	6 722
At constant prices	88	89	91	89	90	91	92	88	88
Growth rates	3.9	1.5	2.0	−1.9	0.8	0.8	0.8	−4.0	0.2
Panama Panama									
At current prices	5 842	6 641	7 253	7 734	7 906	8 110	8 613	9 097	9 551
Per capita	2 390	2 666	2 858	2 992	3 005	3 029	3 164	3 287	3 397
At constant prices	5 814	6 290	6 634	6 823	6 942	7 110	7 425	7 732	8 050
Growth rates	9.4	8.2	5.5	2.9	1.8	2.4	4.4	4.1	4.1
Papua New Guinea Papouasie−Nvl−Guinée									
At current prices	3 788	4 292	4 878	5 216	4 510	5 114	4 816	3 718	3 568
Per capita	982	1 083	1 200	1 250	1 054	1 167	1 073	809	759
At constant prices	3 528	4 017	4 748	5 030	4 863	5 239	5 035	4 845	5 024
Growth rates	9.5	13.8	18.2	5.9	−3.3	7.7	−3.9	−3.8	3.7
Paraguay Paraguay									
At current prices	6 249	6 446	6 875	7 854	9 016	9 629	9 612	8 596	7 741
Per capita	1 440	1 445	1 501	1 670	1 867	1 943	1 889	1 646	1 445
At constant prices	5 395	5 492	5 719	5 896	6 173	6 252	6 413	6 387	6 419
Growth rates	2.5	1.8	4.1	3.1	4.7	1.3	2.6	−0.4	0.5
Peru Pérou									
At current prices	34 545	36 083	34 834	44 910	53 574	55 751	58 964	57 005	51 977
Per capita	1 573	1 614	1 532	1 942	2 277	2 328	2 420	2 299	2 060
At constant prices	30 100	29 971	31 399	35 425	38 461	39 416	42 075	41 900	42 480
Growth rates	2.8	−0.4	4.8	12.8	8.6	2.5	6.7	−0.4	1.4
Philippines Philippines									
At current prices	45 418	52 976	54 368	64 084	74 120	82 847	82 239	65 410	76 559
Per capita	727	829	831	958	1 085	1 187	1 154	899	1 032
At constant prices	44 055	44 204	45 140	47 120	49 325	52 208	54 907	54 581	56 395
Growth rates	−0.6	0.3	2.1	4.4	4.7	5.8	5.2	−0.6	3.3
Poland Pologne									
At current prices	76 477	84 354	85 995	98 534	126 318	142 965	143 132	158 102	154 162
Per capita	2 000	2 199	2 236	2 557	3 273	3 701	3 704	4 091	3 991

22

Gross domestic product: total and per capita
In US dollars (millions) [1] at current and constant 1990 prices; per capita US dollars;
real rates of growth [*cont.*]

Produit intérieur brut : total et par habitant
En dollars E.–U. (millions) [1] aux prix courants et constants de 1990; par habitant en dollars E.–U.;
taux de l'accroissement réels [*suite*]

Country or area Pays ou zone	1991	1992	1993	1994	1995	1996	1997	1998	1999
At constant prices	54 838	56 264	58 389	61 401	65 675	69 647	74 383	81 149	84 529
Growth rates	−7.0	2.6	3.8	5.2	7.0	6.0	6.8	9.1	4.2
Portugal Portugal									
At current prices	80 360	96 980	85 912	90 430	107 412	112 535	105 808	110 872	112 242
Per capita	8 128	9 811	8 686	9 132	10 832	11 329	10 631	11 116	11 229
At constant prices	72 597	74 424	73 598	75 247	77 392	79 852	82 786	86 039	88 646
Growth rates	2.3	2.5	−1.1	2.2	2.9	3.2	3.7	3.9	3.0
Puerto Rico Porto Rico									
At current prices	34 630	36 923	39 691	42 647	45 341	48 187	53 875	59 946	65 389
Per capita	9 721	10 258	10 910	11 596	12 196	12 824	14 187	15 622	16 868
At constant prices	33 761	35 330	36 808	38 482	39 374	41 296	43 986	47 253	49 237
Growth rates	4.6	4.6	4.2	4.5	2.3	4.9	6.5	7.4	4.2
Qatar Qatar									
At current prices	6 884	7 646	7 157	7 374	8 138	9 059	11 298	10 460	11 786
Per capita	14 734	15 946	14 586	14 711	15 896	17 328	21 164	19 200	21 220
At constant prices	7 302	8 011	7 964	8 151	8 391	8 795	10 909	12 054	13 477
Growth rates	−0.8	9.7	−0.6	2.3	2.9	4.8	24.0	10.5	11.8
Republic of Moldova République de Moldova									
At current prices	14 800	463	500	1 109	1 441	1 663	1 929	1 698	1 161
Per capita	3 386	106	115	255	332	384	446	394	270
At constant prices	15 708	11 153	11 019	7 592	7 486	6 902	6 992	6 390	6 109
Growth rates	−17.5	−29.0	−1.2	−31.1	−1.4	−7.8	1.3	−8.6	−4.4
Réunion Réunion									
At current prices	5 554	6 382	5 953	6 352	7 420	7 564	6 929	7 172	7 184
Per capita	9 029	10 180	9 314	9 752	11 183	11 198	10 082	10 263	10 116
At constant prices	5 292	5 475	5 711	5 839	5 998	6 169	6 360	6 553	6 750
Growth rates	1.6	3.5	4.3	2.3	2.7	2.9	3.1	3.0	3.0
Romania Roumanie									
At current prices	28 852	19 578	26 361	30 073	35 477	35 315	34 945	38 158	31 293
Per capita	1 246	849	1 150	1 319	1 564	1 562	1 550	1 695	1 392
At constant prices	37 834	34 517	35 045	36 423	39 023	40 563	37 700	35 657	34 510
Growth rates	−1.1	−8.8	1.5	3.9	7.1	3.9	−7.1	−5.4	−3.2
Russian Federation Fédération de Russie									
At current prices	799 143	85 572	172 941	278 809	337 892	419 014	435 968	276 608	183 815
Per capita	5 375	575	1 163	1 878	2 281	2 836	2 959	1 884	1 257
At constant prices	918 905	785 662	717 309	626 930	601 083	580 046	584 854	556 196	574 106
Growth rates	−5.0	−14.5	−8.7	−12.6	−4.1	−3.5	0.8	−4.9	3.2
Rwanda Rwanda									
At current prices	1 701	1 630	1 579	969	1 038	1 135	1 505	1 635	1 538
Per capita	263	272	289	191	209	217	262	255	217
At constant prices	2 277	2 410	2 211	1 101	1 480	1 714	1 933	2 117	2 240
Growth rates	−2.5	5.9	−8.3	−50.2	34.4	15.8	12.8	9.5	5.8
Saint Kitts and Nevis Saint–Kitts–et–Nevis									
At current prices	165	182	198	222	231	247	275	294	309
Per capita	3 970	4 429	4 874	5 497	5 780	6 227	6 986	7 534	7 974
At constant prices	166	172	180	190	197	209	223	227	231
Growth rates	3.9	3.5	5.0	5.5	3.7	5.8	6.8	1.9	2.0
Saint Lucia Sainte–Lucie									
At current prices	448	497	498	519	554	571	578	628	658
Per capita	3 360	3 686	3 646	3 756	3 968	4 046	4 048	4 344	4 505
At constant prices	419	449	450	456	461	475	471	493	508
Growth rates	0.6	7.3	0.3	1.4	1.1	2.9	−0.8	4.6	3.1
St. Vincent–Grenadines St. Vincent–Grenadines									
At current prices	212	232	238	242	263	277	294	316	340
Per capita	1 991	2 161	2 204	2 223	2 397	2 512	2 645	2 830	3 018
At constant prices	201	215	232	225	243	246	254	268	280
Growth rates	1.4	6.9	7.9	−2.9	8.3	1.2	3.1	5.7	4.2
Samoa Samoa									
At current prices	112	118	119	189	193	217	236	221	238
Per capita	698	737	744	1 189	1 220	1 372	1 492	1 395	1 505
At constant prices	109	107	109	105	112	120	121	126	132
Growth rates	−2.4	−2.3	2.4	−3.7	6.4	7.3	1.0	3.4	5.3

22
Gross domestic product: total and per capita
In US dollars (millions) [1] at current and constant 1990 prices; per capita US dollars;
real rates of growth [*cont.*]
    Produit intérieur brut : total et par habitant
    En dollars E.–U. (millions) [1] aux prix courants et constants de 1990; par habitant en dollars E.–U.;
    taux de l'accroissement réels [*suite*]

Country or area Pays ou zone	1991	1992	1993	1994	1995	1996	1997	1998	1999
San Marino Saint–Marin									
At current prices	477	512	419	439	476	542	519	537	535
Per capita	20 341	21 543	17 358	17 898	19 136	21 491	20 302	20 759	20 421
At constant prices	454	458	454	464	477	482	491	499	506
Growth rates	1.4	0.8	−0.9	2.2	2.9	1.1	1.8	1.5	1.4
Sao Tome and Principe Sao Tomé–et–Principe									
At current prices	57	46	48	50	45	45	44	30	35
Per capita	487	386	393	401	360	350	335	228	257
At constant prices	51	52	52	53	54	55	56	58	59
Growth rates	1.6	1.5	1.5	1.4	2.6	1.9	1.7	2.6	2.5
Saudi Arabia Arabie saoudite									
At current prices	118 034	123 204	118 516	120 167	127 811	141 322	146 494	128 377	139 383
Per capita	7 468	7 646	7 235	7 201	7 478	8 023	8 033	6 782	7 095
At constant prices	114 906	118 112	117 360	117 963	118 515	120 167	123 378	125 318	125 819
Growth rates	9.8	2.8	−0.6	0.5	0.5	1.4	2.7	1.6	0.4
Senegal Sénégal									
At current prices	5 500	6 027	5 431	3 642	4 476	4 653	4 377	4 666	4 798
Per capita	732	782	688	450	539	547	502	521	522
At constant prices	5 676	5 802	5 673	5 836	6 136	6 454	6 780	7 163	7 526
Growth rates	−0.4	2.2	−2.2	2.9	5.2	5.2	5.0	5.6	5.1
Seychelles Seychelles									
At current prices	374	434	469	483	508	499	579	594	620
Per capita	5 302	6 042	6 431	6 509	6 748	6 538	7 479	7 578	7 804
At constant prices	379	406	431	428	425	433	532	571	583
Growth rates	2.7	7.2	6.2	.8	−0.6	1.9	22.8	7.4	2.0
Sierra Leone Sierra Leone									
At current prices	652	655	823	927	941	950	832	662	680
Per capita	159	160	201	227	231	232	202	158	159
At constant prices	617	533	500	501	487	475	443	444	392
Growth rates	−2.8	−13.6	−6.2	0.2	−2.8	−2.5	−6.6	0.1	−11.6
Singapore Singapour									
At current prices	43 719	49 685	58 372	70 849	85 161	92 746	96 318	84 275	86 488
Per capita	14 124	15 618	17 829	21 008	24 500	25 873	26 051	22 118	22 072
At constant prices	40 167	42 668	47 109	52 064	56 568	60 453	65 145	65 407	68 907
Growth rates	7.3	6.2	10.4	10.5	8.7	6.9	7.8	0.4	5.4
Slovakia Slovaquie									
At current prices	10 844	11 757	11 996	13 747	17 392	18 781	19 452	20 363	18 837
Per capita	2 054	2 217	2 252	2 571	3 242	3 493	3 613	3 778	3 492
At constant prices	13 236	12 364	11 881	12 464	13 324	14 202	15 130	15 750	16 049
Growth rates	−14.5	−6.6	−3.9	4.9	6.9	6.6	6.5	4.1	1.9
Slovenia Slovénie									
At current prices	12 673	12 523	12 673	14 386	18 744	18 858	18 202	19 585	20 011
Per capita	6 561	6 429	6 449	7 267	9 419	9 451	9 119	9 822	10 052
At constant prices	15 835	14 970	15 395	16 215	16 881	17 435	18 102	18 788	19 733
Growth rates	−8.9	−5.5	2.8	5.3	4.1	3.3	3.8	3.8	5.0
Solomon Islands Iles Salomon									
At current prices	186	209	245	282	322	355	376	319	346
Per capita	566	614	696	774	854	911	932	763	801
At constant prices	172	190	195	205	219	226	224	219	221
Growth rates	2.2	10.7	2.4	5.1	6.7	3.5	−1.0	−2.2	1.0
Somalia Somalie									
At current prices	614	551	1 006	1 126	1 122	1 260	1 482	1 926	2 021
Per capita	85	77	140	156	153	167	191	238	240
At constant prices	1 051	925	925	731	731	759	739	757	773
Growth rates	−1.0	−12.0	0.0	−21.0	0.0	3.9	−2.7	2.5	2.1
South Africa Afrique du Sud									
At current prices	120 226	130 514	130 406	135 778	151 113	143 840	148 366	133 962	131 127
Per capita	3 240	3 449	3 381	3 454	3 775	3 530	3 579	3 180	3 067
At constant prices	110 873	108 504	109 842	113 395	116 928	121 782	124 856	125 639	127 185
Growth rates	−1.0	−2.1	1.2	3.2	3.1	4.2	2.5	0.6	1.2
Spain Espagne									
At current prices	551 939	602 811	500 114	505 013	584 187	608 812	558 567	582 138	595 943
Per capita	14 001	15 253	12 628	12 729	14 701	15 301	14 023	14 602	14 939

22
Gross domestic product: total and per capita
In US dollars (millions) [1] at current and constant 1990 prices; per capita US dollars;
real rates of growth [cont.]
Produit intérieur brut : total et par habitant
En dollars E.–U. (millions) [1] aux prix courants et constants de 1990; par habitant en dollars E.–U.;
taux de l'accroissement réels [suite]

Country or area Pays ou zone	1991	1992	1993	1994	1995	1996	1997	1998	1999
At constant prices	525 315	528 925	522 770	534 383	548 964	561 424	580 524	602 978	625 432
Growth rates	2.3	0.7	−1.2	2.2	2.7	2.3	3.4	3.9	3.7
Sri Lanka Sri Lanka									
At current prices	8 937	9 623	10 341	11 720	12 924	13 957	15 104	15 657	15 673
Per capita	518	551	585	656	716	766	821	843	836
At constant prices	8 318	8 682	9 282	9 807	10 349	10 738	11 430	11 972	12 491
Growth rates	4.8	4.4	6.9	5.6	5.5	3.8	6.4	4.7	4.3
Sudan Soudan									
At current prices	44 531	7 058	8 881	12 783	12 514	8 259	10 642	10 092	9 569
Per capita	1 754	271	333	468	448	289	365	339	315
At constant prices	35 674	37 255	38 282	40 338	42 477	43 739	46 670	49 003	51 946
Growth rates	6.0	4.4	2.8	5.4	5.3	3.0	6.7	5.0	6.0
Suriname [4] Suriname [4]									
At current prices	1 034	1 006	836	479	519	758	848	1 015	688
Per capita	2 560	2 483	2 057	1 174	1 269	1 846	2 059	2 454	1 657
At constant prices	1 034	1 006	836	857	911	1 115	1 224	1 217	1 278
Growth rates	3.4	−2.6	−16.9	2.4	6.3	22.4	9.8	−0.6	5.0
Swaziland Swaziland									
At current prices	879	970	987	1 062	1 267	1 219	1 312	1 210	1 185
Per capita	1 118	1 213	1 218	1 293	1 517	1 431	1 507	1 359	1 304
At constant prices	881	892	921	953	982	1 017	1 055	1 076	1 097
Growth rates	2.5	1.3	3.3	3.5	3.0	3.6	3.7	2.0	2.0
Sweden Suède									
At current prices	247 839	256 360	192 415	206 890	240 187	261 910	237 479	237 765	238 681
Per capita	28 763	29 542	22 022	23 540	27 211	29 595	26 807	26 844	26 968
At constant prices	235 271	231 926	226 776	236 112	244 826	247 466	252 368	259 817	269 645
Growth rates	−1.1	−1.4	−2.2	4.1	3.7	1.1	2.0	3.0	3.8
Switzerland Suisse									
At current prices	232 680	243 464	236 731	261 363	307 263	295 979	256 038	262 111	258 358
Per capita	33 728	34 964	33 701	36 930	43 165	41 417	35 748	36 563	36 031
At constant prices	226 586	226 299	225 209	226 409	227 550	228 275	232 104	236 881	240 541
Growth rates	−0.8	−0.1	−0.5	0.5	0.5	0.3	1.7	2.1	1.5
Syrian Arab Republic [4] Rép. arabe syrienne [4]									
At current prices	27 756	33 107	36 860	45 087	50 866	38 714	39 215	39 607	39 845
Per capita	2 175	2 521	2 732	3 255	3 577	2 652	2 617	2 576	2 525
At constant prices	25 793	29 268	30 783	33 139	35 045	36 620	37 094	37 464	37 689
Growth rates	7.9	13.5	5.2	7.7	5.8	4.5	1.3	1.0	0.6
Tajikistan Tadjikistan									
At current prices	7 661	2 614	683	730	568	1 044	922	1 320	959
Per capita	1 415	475	122	129	99	179	156	221	159
At constant prices	10 072	7 050	5 901	4 644	4 068	3 389	3 447	3 629	3 753
Growth rates	−8.7	−30.0	−16.3	−21.3	−12.4	−16.7	1.7	5.3	3.4
Thailand Thaïlande									
At current prices	98 249	111 456	125 199	144 493	168 010	181 867	150 617	112 089	123 986
Per capita	1 769	1 978	2 192	2 494	2 861	3 054	2 495	1 832	2 000
At constant prices	92 690	100 195	108 577	118 276	128 809	136 446	134 076	120 520	125 531
Growth rates	8.6	8.1	8.4	8.9	8.9	5.9	−1.7	−10.1	4.2
TFYR of Macedonia L'ex–R.y. Macédoine									
At current prices	4 685	2 317	2 544	3 384	4 475	4 413	3 699	3 504	3 432
Per capita	2 437	1 199	1 310	1 734	2 279	2 232	1 857	1 745	1 697
At constant prices	4 195	3 919	3 627	3 563	3 523	3 565	3 616	3 723	3 822
Growth rates	−6.2	−6.6	−7.5	−1.8	−1.1	1.2	1.4	2.9	2.7
Togo Togo									
At current prices	1 469	1 676	1 244	982	1 307	1 450	1 400	1 511	1 500
Per capita	416	466	339	262	340	366	342	356	342
At constant prices	1 585	1 526	1 317	1 532	1 666	1 733	1 816	1 925	1 966
Growth rates	0.9	−3.7	−13.7	16.3	8.8	4.0	4.8	6.0	2.1
Tonga Tonga									
At current prices	149	147	145	163	175	187	185	163	155
Per capita	1 551	1 526	1 502	1 676	1 795	1 916	1 883	1 659	1 574
At constant prices	132	132	137	144	162	156	154	154	157
Growth rates	6.4	0.3	3.7	5.0	12.5	−3.7	−1.4	0.1	2.2

22
Gross domestic product: total and per capita
In US dollars (millions) [1] at current and constant 1990 prices; per capita US dollars;
real rates of growth [*cont.*]
Produit intérieur brut : total et par habitant
En dollars E.−U. (millions) [1] aux prix courants et constants de 1990; par habitant en dollars E.−U.;
taux de l'accroissement réels [*suite*]

Country or area Pays ou zone	1991	1992	1993	1994	1995	1996	1997	1998	1999
Trinidad and Tobago Trinité−et−Tobago									
At current prices	5 308	5 440	4 577	4 947	5 324	5 770	5 914	6 115	6 596
Per capita	4 338	4 410	3 680	3 946	4 217	4 543	4 631	4 767	5 119
At constant prices	5 204	5 118	5 044	5 224	5 423	5 631	5 812	6 069	6 488
Growth rates	2.7	−1.6	−1.5	3.6	3.8	3.8	3.2	4.4	6.9
Tunisia Tunisie									
At current prices	13 009	15 497	14 608	15 633	18 030	19 587	18 899	19 936	21 032
Per capita	1 563	1 825	1 688	1 775	2 016	2 161	2 061	2 151	2 247
At constant prices	12 795	13 793	14 096	14 543	15 251	16 334	17 216	18 069	19 198
Growth rates	3.9	7.8	2.2	3.2	4.9	7.1	5.4	5.0	6.2
Turkey Turquie									
At current prices	151 041	159 095	180 422	130 652	169 319	181 465	189 878	200 307	184 761
Per capita	2 640	2 729	3 039	2 162	2 753	2 901	2 985	3 098	2 813
At constant prices	152 073	161 174	174 136	164 635	176 476	188 838	203 054	208 709	198 234
Growth rates	0.9	6.0	8.0	−5.5	7.2	7.0	7.5	2.8	−5.0
Turkmenistan Turkménistan									
At current prices	8 492	4 145	5 725	2 844	2 639	2 380	2 681	2 759	3 269
Per capita	2 252	1 069	1 435	694	627	551	606	609	705
At constant prices	10 505	14 245	14 458	12 044	11 117	11 128	9 859	10 362	12 020
Growth rates	−4.7	35.6	1.5	−16.7	−7.7	0.1	−11.4	5.1	16.0
Tuvalu Tuvalu									
At current prices	10	11	10	11	12	13	14	14	16
Per capita	1 135	1 180	1 040	1 223	1 240	1 383	1 420	1 399	1 556
At constant prices	10	10	11	12	11	12	13	15	15
Growth rates	3.6	2.8	4.1	10.3	−5.0	10.3	3.5	14.9	6.1
Uganda Ouganda									
At current prices	3 028	3 252	3 367	5 280	6 170	6 344	6 865	7 126	6 800
Per capita	170	177	178	271	307	306	322	325	301
At constant prices	3 941	4 124	4 415	4 882	5 352	5 665	5 920	6 240	6 614
Growth rates	5.5	4.6	7.1	10.6	9.6	5.9	4.5	5.4	6.0
Ukraine Ukraine									
At current prices	171 086	20 970	32 713	36 755	37 009	44 559	50 151	41 883	30 328
Per capita	3 293	404	631	710	718	870	986	830	606
At constant prices	224 305	186 173	159 737	123 157	108 132	97 272	94 365	92 530	92 068
Growth rates	−10.6	−17.0	−14.2	−22.9	−12.2	−10.0	−3.0	−1.9	−0.5
United Arab Emirates Emirats arabes unis									
At current prices	33 920	35 413	35 745	38 268	42 807	47 993	49 353	46 471	50 396
Per capita	16 217	16 368	16 026	16 688	18 198	19 933	20 062	18 516	19 700
At constant prices	33 706	34 658	34 368	35 124	37 617	41 531	42 340	39 364	40 348
Growth rates	0.2	2.8	−0.8	2.2	7.1	10.4	1.9	−7.0	2.5
United Kingdom Royaume−Uni									
At current prices	1 030 900	1 067 379	958 904	1 036 983	1 126 740	1 179 577	1 318 524	1 410 433	1 441 786
Per capita	17 845	18 408	16 477	17 755	19 226	20 063	22 361	23 854	24 323
At constant prices	973 158	973 867	996 539	1 040 252	1 069 251	1 096 542	1 135 057	1 165 033	1 189 637
Growth rates	−1.5	0.1	2.3	4.4	2.8	2.6	3.5	2.6	2.1
United Rep. of Tanzania Rép.−Unie de Tanzanie									
At current prices	4 957	4 601	4 258	4 511	5 255	6 496	7 692	8 382	8 389
Per capita	184	165	147	151	170	204	236	251	245
At constant prices	4 377	4 457	4 509	4 537	4 698	4 896	5 058	5 311	5 594
Growth rates	2.8	1.8	1.2	0.6	3.6	4.2	3.3	5.0	5.3
United States Etats−Unis									
At current prices	5 930 700	6 261 800	6 582 900	6 993 300	7 338 400	7 751 100	8 239 000	8 699 200	9 191 962
Per capita	23 038	24 067	25 031	26 305	27 306	28 532	30 002	31 343	32 778
At constant prices	5 723 816	5 898 430	6 054 933	6 299 333	6 467 453	6 698 329	6 995 331	7 300 706	7 603 624
Growth rates	−0.5	3.1	2.7	4.0	2.7	3.6	4.4	4.4	4.1
Uruguay Uruguay									
At current prices	10 047	11 858	13 832	16 279	18 046	19 124	19 967	20 831	19 519
Per capita	3 213	3 766	4 361	5 095	5 607	5 899	6 115	6 333	5 891
At constant prices	8 632	9 312	9 591	10 199	10 020	10 549	11 083	11 581	11 208
Growth rates	3.2	7.9	3.0	6.3	−1.8	5.3	5.1	4.5	−3.2
Uzbekistan Ouzbékistan									
At current prices	35 171	2 298	5 479	6 514	10 049	7 680	15 373	14 599	16 693
Per capita	1 676	107	250	292	441	331	650	606	682

22
Gross domestic product: total and per capita
In US dollars (millions) [1] at current and constant 1990 prices; per capita US dollars;
real rates of growth [*cont.*]
Produit intérieur brut : total et par habitant
En dollars E.–U. (millions) [1]   aux prix courants et constants de 1990; par habitant en dollars E.–U.;
taux de l'accroissement réels [*suite*]

Country or area Pays ou zone	1991	1992	1993	1994	1995	1996	1997	1998	1999
At constant prices	48 448	43 049	42 067	39 858	39 515	40 202	42 263	44 123	46 064
Growth rates	−0.5	−11.1	−2.3	−5.3	−0.9	1.7	5.1	4.4	4.4
Vanuatu Vanuatu									
At current prices	182	190	196	214	243	253	254	232	229
Per capita	1 185	1 202	1 202	1 281	1 412	1 427	1 399	1 240	1 193
At constant prices	171	170	178	182	191	196	200	205	201
Growth rates	12.1	−0.7	4.5	2.5	4.7	2.6	2.4	2.1	−2.0
Venezuela Venezuela									
At current prices	53 462	60 423	60 048	58 417	77 389	70 538	88 704	95 450	102 222
Per capita	2 676	2 955	2 871	2 733	3 543	3 162	3 894	4 107	4 312
At constant prices	53 326	56 558	56 714	55 381	57 570	57 456	61 116	61 050	56 671
Growth rates	9.7	6.1	0.3	−2.3	4.0	−0.2	6.4	−0.1	−7.2
Viet Nam Viet Nam									
At current prices	7 642	9 867	13 181	16 286	20 743	24 657	27 609	27 458	28 800
Per capita	113	143	188	227	285	333	368	361	373
At constant prices	6 858	7 450	8 052	8 763	9 599	10 496	11 351	12 006	12 579
Growth rates	6.0	8.6	8.1	8.8	9.5	9.3	8.2	5.8	4.8
Yemen Yémen									
At current prices	12 177	15 227	18 392	22 556	11 001	6 958	5 729	5 161	5 739
Per capita	1 002	1 190	1 363	1 589	739	447	353	305	326
At constant prices	12 668	13 288	13 677	13 615	14 737	15 387	16 187	16 591	17 139
Growth rates	0.3	4.9	2.9	−0.5	8.2	4.4	5.2	2.5	3.3
Yugoslavia Yougoslavie									
At current prices	25 754	18 696	13 169	13 862	14 681	15 548	17 000	17 774	14 382
Per capita	2 516	1 810	1 264	1 321	1 392	1 470	1 606	1 680	1 361
At constant prices	25 091	18 090	12 525	12 843	13 628	14 428	14 632	13 965	10 995
Growth rates	−11.6	−27.9	−30.8	2.5	6.1	5.9	1.4	−4.6	−21.3
Zambia Zambie									
At current prices	3 377	3 307	3 274	3 347	3 470	3 286	3 932	3 352	3 293
Per capita	408	388	374	373	376	347	405	337	323
At constant prices	3 741	3 675	3 926	3 791	3 705	3 946	4 081	3 999	4 041
Growth rates	0.0	−1.7	6.8	−3.4	−2.3	6.5	3.4	−2	1.0
Zimbabwe Zimbabwe									
At current prices	8 180	6 746	6 553	6 889	7 128	7 475	8 235	5 600	5 408
Per capita	778	626	595	613	621	638	690	460	436
At constant prices	9 251	8 416	8 528	9 111	9 052	9 713	10 026	10 274	10 325
Growth rates	5.5	−9.0	1.3	6.8	−0.6	7.3	3.2	2.5	0.5

Source:
United Nations Statistics Division, New York, the
national accounts database.

† For information on recent changes in country or area
nomenclature pertaining to former Czechoslovakia, Germany,
Hong Kong Special Administrative Region (SAR) of China,
Macao Special Administrative Region (SAR) of China,
SFR of Yugoslavia and the former USSR, see Annex I –
Country or area nomenclature, regional and other groupings.

†† For statistical purposes, the data for China do not
include those for the Hong Kong Special Administrative
Region (Hong Kong SAR), Macao Special Administrative
Region (Macao SAR) and Taiwan province of China.

1 The conversion rates used to translate national currency
data into United States dollars are the period averages of
market exchange rates (MERs) for members of the
International Monetary Fund (IMF). These rates, which are

Source:
Organisation des Nations Unies, Division de statistique, New York,
la base de données sur les comptes nationaux.

† Pour les modifications récentes de nomenclature de pays
ou de zone concernant l'Allemagne, Hong Kong, région
administrative spéciale (RAS) de Chine, Macao, région
administrative spéciale (RAS) de Chine, l'ex–Tchécoslovaquie,
l'ex–URSS et l'ex–Rfs de Yougoslavie, voir annexe I –
Nomenclature des pays ou des zones, groupements
régionaux et autres groupements.

†† Les données statistiques relatives à la Chine ne comprennent
pas celles qui concernent la région administrative spéciale de
Hong Kong (la RAS de Hong Kong), la région administrative
spéciale de Macao (la RAS de Macao) et la province chinoise
de Taiwan.

1 Les taux de conversion utilisés pour exprimer les données
nationales en dollars des États–Unis sont, pour les membres du
Fonds monétaire international (FMI), les moyennes pour la
période considérée des taux de change du marché. Ces derniers,

22

Gross domestic product: total and per capita
In US dollars (millions) [1] at current and constant 1990 prices; per capita US dollars;
real rates of growth [*cont.*]

Produit intérieur brut : total et par habitant
En dollars E.–U. (millions) [1] aux prix courants et constants de 1990; par habitant en dollars E.–U.;
taux de l'accroissement réels [*suite*]

published in the *International Financial Statistics*, are communicated to the IMF by national central banks and consist of three types of rates:

a) Market rates, determined largely by market forces;
b) Official rates, determined by government authorities;
c) Principal rates, for countries maintaining multiple exchange rate arrangements.

Market rates always take priority and official rates are used only when a free market rate is not available.

For non–members of the IMF, averages of the United Nations operational rates, used for accounting purposes in UN transactions with member countries, are applied. These are based on official, commercial and/or tourist rates of exchange.

It should be noted that there are practical constraints in the use of MERs for conversion purposes, particularly in the case of countries with multiple exchange rates, those coping with inordinate levels of inflation or experiencing misalignments caused by market fluctuations, the use of which may result in excessive fluctuations or distortions in the dollar income levels of a number of countries. Caution is therefore urged when making inter–country comparisons of incomes as expressed in US dollars.

2   Data refer to the Vatican City State.
3   Weighted rates of exchange were used for the period 1987 – 1992.
4   For Iraq, Lebanon, Liberia, Myanmar, Nigeria, Suriname and Syrian Arab Republic price–adjusted rates of exchange (PARE) were used due to large distortions in the levels of per capita GDP with the use of IMF market exchange rates.

qui sont publiés dans "Statistiques financières internationales," sont communiqués au FMI par les banques centrales nationales et reposent sur trois types de taux :

a) Taux du marché, déterminés surtout par les facteurs du marché;
b) Taux officiels, déterminés par les pouvoirs publics;
c) Taux principaux, pour les pays pratiquant différents arrangements en matière de taux de change.

On donne toujours la priorité aux taux du marché, n'utilisant les taux officiels que lorsqu'il n'y a pas de taux du marché libre.

Pour les pays qui ne sont pas membres du FMI, on utilise des moyennes des taux de change opérationnels de l'ONU (qui servent à des fins comptables, pour les opérations de l'ONU avec les les pays qui en sont membres). Ces taux reposent sur les taux de change officiels, les taux du commerce et/ou les taux touristiques.

Il est à noter qu'on se heurte à des difficultés pratiques en utilisant les taux de change du marché pour convertir les données en monnaie nationale, surtout dans le cas des pays qui pratiquent plusieurs taux de change et de ceux qui connaissent des taux d'inflation exceptionnels ou des décalages provenant des fluctuations du marché; on risque en les utilisant d'aboutir à des fluctuations excessives ou à des distorsions du revenu en dollars de certains pays. Les comparaisons de revenu entre pays sont donc sujettes à caution lorsqu'on se fonde sur le revenu en dollars des États–Unis.

2   Les données se rapportent à l'Etat de la Cité du Vatican.
3   Pour la période 1987 à 1992, on a utilisé des taux de change pondérés.
4   Pour l'Iraq, le Liban, le Libéria, le Myanmar, le Nigéria, le Suriname et le République arabe syrienne on a utilisé des taux de change corrigés des prix, car les taux de change du marché publiés par le FMI induisent des distorsions importantes dans les montants du produit intérieur brut par habitant.

23
Expenditure on gross domestic product at current prices
Dépenses imputées au produit intérieur brut aux prix courants

Percentage distribution
Répartition en pourcentage

Country or area Pays ou zone	Year Année	GDP at current prices (Million nat. cur.) PIB aux prix courants (Mil. monnaie nat.)	% of GDP − en % du PIB					
			Govt. final consumption expenditure Consom. finale des admin. publiques	Household final consumption expenditure Consom. finale des ménages	Changes in inventories Variation des stocks	Gross fixed capital formation Formation brute de capital fixe	Exports of goods and services Exportations de biens et services	Imports of goods and services Importations de biens et services
Albania Albanie	1988 1989 1990	17 001 18 674 16 812	9.5 8.8 10.2	63.3 61.0 72.7	−2.6 0.4 −10.1	31.9 31.3 34.6	−2.0[1] −1.5[1] −7.4[1]	... ...
Algeria Algérie	1994 1995 1996	1 487 404 2 002 638 2 564 739	17.7 17.0 15.8	56.3 55.5 52.0	4.1 4.6 0.2	27.4 27.1 24.9	23.0 26.6 30.9	28.5 30.8 23.9
Angola Angola	1988 1989 1990	239 640 278 866 308 062	32.9 28.9 28.5	45.5 48.2 44.7	−0.0 0.9 0.6	14.6 11.2 11.1	32.8 33.8 38.9	25.8 23.1 23.8
Anguilla Anguilla	1997 1998 1999	240 255 284	18.6 14.1 19.7	73.8 74.1 86.3	... ...	25.0 31.4 37.7	76.2 87.2 67.3	93.6 107.1 113.3
Antigua and Barbuda Antigua−et−Barbuda	1984 1985 1986	468 541 642	18.5 18.3 18.9	69.8 71.5 69.7	... ...	23.6 28.0 36.1	73.7 75.7 75.2	85.6 93.5 99.9
Argentina Argentine	1997 1998 1999	292 859 298 131 282 769	12.1 11.9 12.9	70.7 70.7 69.7	... ...	19.4[2] 19.9[2] 19.1[2]	10.6 10.4 9.8	12.7 12.9 11.5
Armenia[3] Arménie[3]	1997 1998 1999	804 300[4] 955 400[4] 987 100[4]	11.2 11.1 10.7	103.5[5] 100.1[5] 95.7[5]	2.9 2.9 3.0	16.2 16.2 16.5	20.3 19.0 21.0	58.3 52.8 49.7
Aruba[3] Aruba[3]	1994	2 381	16.8	48.6	0.5	29.3	80.4	75.6
Australia[3][6] Australie[3][6]	1997 1998 1999	565 881 593 311[4] 630 050[4]	18.2 18.2 18.8	58.9 59.4 59.1	0.2 0.8 0.3	23.5 23.8 23.8	20.1 18.8 19.9	21.0 21.3 22.4
Austria[3] Autriche[3]	1997 1998 1999	2 513 476[4] 2 614 661[4] 2 712 034[4]	19.7 19.6 19.8	57.3[5] 57.0[5] 56.6[5]	0.7[7] 0.6[7] 0.3[7]	23.5 23.5 23.7	42.7 43.5 45.1	44.3 44.1 45.6
Azerbaijan[3] Azerbaïdjan[3]	1998 1999 2000	17 203 100[4] 18 576 200[4] 21 939 800[4]	15.2 19.0 14.2	80.0[5] 76.1[5] 62.7[5]	−2.1 −2.0 −1.7	35.5 25.0 20.5	22.7 28.4 46.0	54.5 42.5 38.5
Bahamas[3] Bahamas[3]	1993 1994 1995	2 854[4] 3 053[4] 3 069[4]	14.3 16.7 15.8	69.6 67.3 67.7	1.2 1.0 0.5	18.4 20.1 22.7	53.2 51.4 54.7	51.6 53.5 59.3
Bahrain Bahreïn	1994 1995 1996	1 828 1 900 2 016	24.4 24.0 21.2	29.4 26.4 24.5	1.8[4] −7.5[4] −2.8[4]	32.3 28.3 22.2	98.4 112.1 120.9	86.3 83.2 86.1
Bangladesh[6] Bangladesh[6]	1995 1996 1997	1 301 600[4] 1 403 045[4] 1 540 923[4]	13.6 14.1 14.8	78.8 78.4 77.3	... ...	17.0 17.3 16.3	14.2 15.4 16.8	23.9 23.2 23.4
Barbados Barbade	1997 1998 1999	4 413 4 747 4 970	21.0 20.7 20.7	63.1 63.0 65.9	0.1 0.2 0.6	17.8 18.2 18.8	55.3 53.1 50.8	57.3 55.2 56.8
Belarus[3] Bélarus[3]	1997 1998 1999	366 830 100[4] 702 161 100[4] 3 026 063 700[4]	20.3 19.9 19.5	57.1[5] 57.8[5] 58.6[5]	1.6 0.8 −2.6	25.2 25.9 26.3	59.9 59.1 59.2	65.7 63.9 61.6
Belgium[3] Belgique[3]	1997 1998 1999	8 727 011 9 081 545 9 423 280	21.3 21.2 21.4	53.8[5] 54.0[5] 53.6[5]	−0.2 −0.0 −0.1	20.6 20.9 21.3	75.7 75.7 76.5	71.2 71.7 72.8
Belize[3] Belize[3]	1997 1998 1999	1 231 1 258 1 377	17.0 17.4 17.1	66.5 67.3 65.1	1.6 3.1 10.3	22.0 21.3 19.3	53.8 52.9 51.3	60.9 62.1 63.2
Benin Bénin	1989 1990 1991	479 200 502 300 535 500	13.0 13.2 12.0	81.4 80.4 82.6	−0.6 0.8 0.9	12.5 13.4 13.6	18.3 20.4 22.0	24.5 28.2 31.1
Bermuda[13] Bermudes[13]	1997 1998 1999[3]	2 330 2 457 2 624	11.7 12.9 12.4	63.7[5] 64.4[5] 64.3[5]	... ...	13.7 15.1 15.7	60.0 58.4 59.0	49.2 50.8 50.2

23
Expenditure on gross domestic product at current prices
Percentage distribution [cont.]
Dépenses imputées au produit intérieur brut aux prix courants
Répartition en pourcentage [suite]

Country or area Pays ou zone	Year Année	GDP at current prices (Million nat. cur.) PIB aux prix courants (Mil. monnaie nat.)	% of GDP – en % du PIB					
			Govt. final consumption expenditure Consom. finale des admin. publiques	Household final consumption expenditure Consom. finale des ménages	Changes in inventories Variation des stocks	Gross fixed capital formation Formation brute de capital fixe	Exports of goods and services Exportations de biens et services	Imports of goods and services Importations de biens et services
Bhutan Bhoutan	1996	11 714	21.4	40.3	1.1	46.9	34.0	43.7
	1997	14 477	25.5	35.8	2.1	46.0	33.0	42.3
	1998	16 420	25.8	36.3	2.5	44.8	33.2	42.6
Bolivia Bolivie	1997	41 644	13.9	74.7	0.7	19.0	21.1	29.4
	1998	47 001	14.1	75.1	0.3	22.8	20.0	32.4
	1999	48 605	14.6	76.2	−0.6	19.4	17.4	27.1
Botswana [3] [8] Botswana [3] [8]	1997	17 740	26.6	30.0[5]	1.8	24.1	55.7	38.2
	1998	20 163	27.0	30.4[5]	4.4	25.6	56.5	44.0
	1999	21 524	30.6	32.2[5]	7.7	29.1	46.7	46.3
Brazil [3] Brésil [3]	1997	870 743	18.2	62.7	1.6	19.9	7.5	9.9
	1998	913 735	18.8	62.1	1.5	19.6	7.6	9.6
	1999	960 858	18.9	61.8	1.5	18.9	10.6	11.7
British Virgin Islands Iles Vierges brit.	1987	117	17.3	73.7	2.3	36.9	95.5	125.7
	1988	131	20.1	68.9	2.7	34.3	107.6	133.5
	1989	156	20.7	64.9	2.6	31.6	104.8	124.6
Brunei Darussalam Brunéi Darussalam	1982	9 126	10.0	5.5	−0.0	12.4	89.3	17.2
	1983	8 124	11.4	9.5	−0.0	9.9	88.3	19.0
	1984	8 069	31.1	−5.6	0.0	6.5	84.5	16.5
Bulgaria [3] Bulgarie [3]	1998	21 577 020[4]	15.1	72.9[5][9]	3.6	13.2	48.0	50.9
	1999	22 776 444[4]	15.9	74.8[5][9]	3.1	15.9	44.1	51.9
	2000	25 453 649[4]	17.7	72.2[5][9]	0.4	16.2	58.5	64.1
Burkina Faso Burkina Faso	1991	811 676	14.7	76.2	1.4	21.8	11.4	25.4
	1992	812 590	14.4	76.2	−0.2	21.3	9.7	21.4
	1993	832 349	14.4	77.2	0.8	20.4	9.7	22.5
Burundi Burundi	1990	196 656	19.5	83.0	−0.6	16.4	8.0	26.2
	1991	211 898	17.0	83.9	−0.5	18.1	10.0	28.5
	1992	226 384	15.6	82.9	0.4	21.1	9.0	29.0
Cambodia Cambodge	1997	9 149 243[4]	6.0	87.9	1.3	13.0	33.3	44.5
	1998	10 531 368[4]	5.6	89.0	−0.9	12.9	35.9	46.2
	1999	11 470 479[4]	6.3	86.4	2.5	15.8	37.2	49.1
Cameroon [3] [6] Cameroun [3] [6]	1996	4 793 080	79.8[10]	...	−0.2	13.1	24.7	17.4
	1997	5 370 580	82.0[10]	...	0.1	12.8	24.0	19.0
	1998	5 744 000	82.9[10]	...	−0.1	13.5	24.0	20.4
Canada [3] Canada [3]	1997	864 200[4]	19.8	57.8[5]	1.2	19.4	39.9	38.3
	1998	887 480[4]	19.7	58.6[5]	0.6	19.6	41.8	40.5
	1999	943 288[4]	19.0	57.8[5]	0.4	19.8	43.7	40.8
Cape Verde Cap–Vert	1993	29 078	23.3	83.5	−1.0	40.0	18.0	63.8
	1994	33 497	21.6	83.0	0.7	43.7	18.4	67.3
	1995	37 705	22.8	86.3	2.0	38.8	16.6	66.5
Cayman Islands Iles Caïmanes	1989	474[4]	14.1	65.0	...	23.2	60.1	68.8
	1990	590[4]	14.2	62.5	...	21.4	64.1	58.5
	1991	616[4]	15.1	62.5	...	21.8	58.9	52.8
Central African Rep. Rép. centrafricaine	1990	388 647	15.6	82.1	−0.1	12.9	18.2	28.6
	1991	360 942	17.5	80.6	−0.2	12.9	17.8	28.6
	1992	376 748	16.1	80.7	−0.7	9.8	17.7	25.1
Chad Tchad	1992	350 632	17.6	75.6	...	8.7	17.6	19.5
	1993	291 691	24.1	83.1	...	7.7	19.9	34.8
	1994	460 851	12.8	56.0	...	9.8	22.7	1.3
Chile Chili	1997	31 567 287	10.5	65.0	1.7	25.5	28.1	30.9
	1998	33 630 367	11.2	65.5	1.4	26.0	26.7	30.9
	1999	34 422 796	12.0	64.1	0.2	21.9	29.0	27.2
China †† [3] Chine †† [3]	1997	7 489 430	11.6	46.5	4.4	33.6	22.9	19.1
	1998	7 985 330	11.9	46.2	2.8	35.3	21.5	17.7
	1999	8 242 970	12.5	47.8	1.2	35.8	21.9	19.2
China, Hong Kong SAR † Chine, Hong Kong RAS †	1997	1 323 862	8.6	60.3[5]	0.9	33.6	132.5	135.9
	1998	1 261 437	9.3	60.4[5]	−1.2	30.4	129.1	128.0
	1999	1 233 133	9.9	59.6[5]	−0.5	25.7	133.2	127.9
Colombia [3] Colombie [3]	1995	84 439 109	14.9	65.7[5]	3.4[7]	22.4	14.5	21.0
	1996	100 711 389	18.0	65.5[5]	0.6[7]	21.6	15.2	20.8
	1997	121 707 501	19.9	65.1[5]	0.7[7]	20.2	14.8	20.8

23
Expenditure on gross domestic product at current prices
Percentage distribution [cont.]
Dépenses imputées au produit intérieur brut aux prix courants
Répartition en pourcentage [suite]

			% of GDP − en % du PIB					
Country or area Pays ou zone	Year Année	GDP at current prices (Million nat. cur.) PIB aux prix courants (Mil. monnaie nat.)	Govt. final consumption expenditure Consom. finale des admin. publiques	Household final consumption expenditure Consom. finale des ménages	Changes in inventories Variation des stocks	Gross fixed capital formation Formation brute de capital fixe	Exports of goods and services Exportations de biens et services	Imports of goods and services Importations de biens et services
Comoros	1989	63 397	27.6	77.8	4.6	14.4	14.9	39.3
Comores	1990	66 370	25.7	79.7	8.0	12.2	11.7	37.3
	1991	69 248	25.3	80.9	4.0	12.3	15.5	38.0
Congo	1987	690 523	20.6	56.6[5]	−1.1	20.9	41.7	38.6
Congo	1988	658 964	21.1	60.1[5]	−1.0	19.6	40.6	40.4
	1989	773 524	18.7	52.8[5]	−0.5	16.4	47.6	35.0
Costa Rica[3]	1997	2 956 558	13.4	71.2	0.9	18.5	41.0	45.0
Costa Rica[3]	1998	3 571 523	13.2	69.3	−0.5	21.0	48.0	50.9
	1999	4 343 922	12.8	63.5	−2.5	19.8	53.7	47.2
Côte d'Ivoire	1994	4 616 000	18.1	60.4[5]	2.2	10.2	39.6	30.5
Côte d'Ivoire	1995	5 543 000	16.9	64.1[5]	1.9	12.2	37.0	32.1
	1996	6 177 000	16.0	65.1[5]	−4.1	13.7	41.0	31.7
Croatia[3]	1998	137 604	26.6	58.9	0.7	23.3	39.6	49.2
Croatie[3]	1999	142 698	27.8	57.1	0.3	23.1	40.6	48.9
	2000	157 510	26.5	57.2	1.0	21.0	45.0	50.6
Cuba	1996	22 815[4]	24.2	70.6	−2.8	9.9	15.6	18.3
Cuba	1997	22 952[4]	24.0	71.7	−2.2	9.9	16.5	19.4
	1998	23 901[4]	23.6	71.0	−2.3	10.2	16.2	19.3
Cyprus	1997	4 371[4]	18.8	66.0	0.8	19.0	47.1	52.0
Chypre	1998	4 695[4]	19.3	67.5	1.5	19.2	43.5	51.1
	1999	5 009[4]	17.5	66.1	1.2	18.2	44.6	88.3
Czech Republic[3]	1997	1 668 800	19.9	53.3[5]	3.0[7]	30.8	56.9	62.9
République tchèque[3]	1998	1 798 300	19.0	52.8[5]	2.4[7]	28.3	60.7	62.2
	1999	1 836 300	19.7	53.4[5]	...	26.4	63.6	65.2
Dem. Rep. of the Congo	1987	326 946	22.4	77.1	5.3	20.3	63.2	88.2
Rép. dém. du Congo	1988	622 822	37.2	...	3.7	19.0	81.0	...
	1989	2 146 811	14.4	...	3.2	13.4	46.5	...
Denmark[3]	1997	1 116 324	25.5	50.2[5]	1.2[7]	19.6	36.4	32.9
Danemark[3]	1998	1 168 996	25.7	50.6[5]	1.2[7]	20.5	35.4	33.4
	1999	1 229 585	25.5	49.6[5]	−0.0[7]	20.2	37.4	32.7
Djibouti	1996	88 233	33.6	63.7	−0.9	19.3	40.3	56.8
Djibouti	1997	87 289	34.7	59.5	0.2	21.4	42.2	57.8
	1998	88 461	29.0	67.4	0.2	23.2	43.4	63.0
Dominica	1989	423	20.5	71.5	1.5	38.8	41.0	73.4
Dominique	1990	452	20.3	64.1	1.1	39.7	50.1	75.3
	1991	479	20.0	71.4	1.1	40.2	46.4	79.1
Dominican Republic[3]	1994	179 130	4.6	76.8	3.4	17.9	37.4	40.2
Rép. dominicaine[3]	1995	209 646	4.3	78.6	3.3	16.1	34.5	36.7
	1996	232 993	4.7	81.4	3.6	17.3	18.1	25.1
Ecuador	1998	107 421 048	11.7	70.4	3.7	21.0	25.3	32.0
Equateur	1999	161 350 379	10.4	65.5	−1.9	14.8	37.1	25.8
	2000	343 820 986	9.3	63.2	1.1	15.8	40.7	30.0
Egypt[6]	1989	87 741	11.0	71.7	5.5	25.6	22.0	35.8
Egypte[6]	1990	110 143	10.0	76.3	−0.6	22.4	28.1	36.2
	1991	136 190	8.9	80.8	0.1	17.9	29.5	37.2
El Salvador	1997	97 428	9.1	86.7	−1.0	16.1	24.1	35.0
El Salvador	1998	104 907	9.7	84.7	0.9	16.6	25.2	37.0
	1999	109 086	10.1	85.8	0.1	16.2	25.1	37.3
Equatorial Guinea	1989	42 256	22.2	54.3	−0.0	19.6	40.4	36.6
Guinée équatoriale	1990	44 349	15.3	53.2	−3.1	34.6	59.7	59.7
	1991	46 429	14.4	75.9	−2.3	18.4	28.4	34.7
Estonia[3]	1998	73 325[4]	21.8	59.5[5]	−0.3	29.7	79.9	90.4
Estonie[3]	1999	75 297[4]	23.7	58.4[5]	−0.4	25.1	77.0	83.0
	2000	84 382[4]	22.2	58.6[5]	0.6	23.5	96.5	100.8
Ethiopia[11]	1997	41 465	10.9	79.2	...	19.1	16.2	23.3
Ethiopie[11]	1998	44 896	14.2	78.4	...	19.0	16.2	26.4
	1999	48 949	16.0	81.4	...	20.8	14.5	30.2
Fiji	1994	2 674[4]	16.5	71.1	1.5	12.3	56.4	59.4
Fidji	1995	2 799[4]	16.1	71.0	1.1	12.0	54.7	58.2
	1996	2 976[4]	16.2	69.2	1.4	9.6	59.4	59.0

23
Expenditure on gross domestic product at current prices
Percentage distribution *[cont.]*
Dépenses imputées au produit intérieur brut aux prix courants
Répartition en pourcentage *[suite]*

Country or area Pays ou zone	Year Année	GDP at current prices (Million nat. cur.) PIB aux prix courants (Mil. monnaie nat.)	% of GDP − en % du PIB					
			Govt. final consumption expenditure Consom. finale des admin. publiques	Household final consumption expenditure Consom. finale des ménages	Changes in inventories Variation des stocks	Gross fixed capital formation Formation brute de capital fixe	Exports of goods and services Exportations de biens et services	Imports of goods and services Importations de biens et services
Finland [3] Finlande [3]	1997	635 532[4]	22.4	50.9[5]	0.4	18.0	39.1	30.9
	1998	689 523[4]	21.7	50.2[5]	1.0	18.7	38.8	30.0
	1999	721 958[4]	21.5	50.4[5]	0.5	18.8	37.5	29.3
France [3] France [3]	1997	8 207 091	24.2	55.0[5]	−0.1[7]	18.0	25.5	22.5
	1998	8 536 312	23.5	55.0[5]	0.4[7]	18.3	26.1	23.5
	1999	8 818 797	23.7	54.8[5]	0.0[7]	19.0	26.1	23.6
French Guyana Guyane française	1990	6 526	35.0	64.4	−0.2	47.8	67.3	114.3
	1991	7 404	34.4	60.1	1.5	40.5	81.1	117.6
	1992	7 976	34.2	58.9	1.5	30.8	65.4	90.8
French Polynesia Polynésie française	1991	305 211	39.3	63.9	−0.2	18.4	9.3	30.7
	1992	314 265	47.8	63.9	0.0	16.7	8.3	27.4
	1993	329 266	38.3	61.5	−0.2	16.2	10.5	26.4
Gabon Gabon	1987	1 020 600	23.7	48.6	...	26.7[2]	41.3	40.3
	1988	1 013 600	21.8	48.1	...	36.2[2]	37.3	43.4
	1989	1 168 066	18.4	48.4	...	23.3[2]	50.3	40.3
Gambia [6] Gambie [6]	1991	2 920	13.0	83.7	...	18.2	45.3	60.1
	1992	3 078	13.2	81.2	...	22.4	45.2	61.9
	1993	3 243	15.1	78.1	...	27.1	36.6	56.9
Georgia [3] Georgie [3]	1998	5 041[4]	9.4	86.3[5]	2.0	21.1	16.4	37.0
	1999	5 665[4]	10.7	84.0[5]	2.2	13.7	19.1	38.1
	2000	5 956[4]	9.1	96.3[5]	1.9	15.6	23.3	40.2
Germany [3] Allemagne [3]	1998	3 784 400	19.1	57.5[5]	0.5[7]	21.3	28.9	27.3
	1999	3 877 200	19.0	57.8[5]	0.9[7]	21.3	29.4	28.5
	2000	3 982 000	18.8	58.2[5]	1.2[7]	21.4	33.3	32.8
Ghana Ghana	1994	5 205 200	13.7	73.7	1.4	22.6	22.5	33.9
	1995	7 752 600	12.1	76.2	−1.1	21.1	24.5	32.8
	1996	11 339 200	12.0	76.1	0.9	20.6	24.9	34.5
Greece [3] Grèce [3]	1997	33 103 840	15.2	72.2[5]	0.2	20.0	19.4	27.0
	1998	35 872 501	15.3	71.8[5]	0.3	21.6	19.9	28.9
	1999	38 147 219	15.0	71.1[5]	−0.2	22.5	20.2	28.6
Grenada Grenade	1990	541	20.5	64.9	3.1	38.9	44.4	71.8
	1991	567	18.8	69.2	3.7	40.0	45.4	77.1
	1992	578	19.9	66.5	2.1	32.4	38.6	59.4
Guadeloupe Guadeloupe	1990	15 201	30.8	92.8	1.1	33.9	4.9	63.5
	1991	16 415	31.0	87.3	1.0	33.0	6.1	58.4
	1992	17 972	29.3	84.1	1.3	27.8	4.5	47.0
Guatemala Guatemala	1996	95 479	5.1	87.0	−0.6	13.3	17.8	22.6
	1997	107 943	4.9	86.9	−1.0	14.8	17.9	23.6
	1998	121 548	6.2	86.6	−0.2	15.7	17.9	26.2
Guinea−Bissau Guinée−Bissau	1990	510 094	11.4	100.9	0.9	13.8	12.0	39.0
	1991	854 985	12.6	100.6	0.9	10.4	13.4	38.0
	1992	1 530 010	10.7	111.1	...	26.5[2]	8.2	56.5
Guyana Guyana	1997	106 678	20.4	44.2	...	44.2[2]	−9.5[1]	...
	1998	108 002	21.4	48.6	...	41.5[2]	−11.7[1]	...
	1999	120 668	24.8	44.2	...	37.7[2]	−10.3[1]	...
Haiti [12] Haïti [12]	1997	51 578	103.1[10]	...	...	12.5	11.5	27.1
	1998	59 055	102.5[10]	...	...	12.9	13.2	28.6
	1999	66 425	101.8[10]	...	...	13.1	13.3	28.2
Honduras Honduras	1995	37 507	9.3	63.5	7.6	24.0	43.7	48.1
	1996	47 774	9.5	65.1	7.1	23.3	47.0	52.0
	1997	61 084	8.8	64.9	6.4	23.6	46.5	50.2
Hungary [3] Hongrie [3]	1997	8 540 669	21.9	50.3[5]	5.5	22.2	45.5	45.5
	1998	10 087 434	21.7	50.8[5]	6.0	23.6	50.6	52.7
	1999	11 436 482	21.4	52.3[5]	5.0	23.8	52.8	55.3
Iceland [3] Islande [3]	1997	524 679	21.5	57.1[5]	−0.0	20.9	36.4	35.8
	1998	577 406	22.1	57.6[5]	0.2	24.6	35.3	39.8
	1999	624 606	22.9	58.8[5]	0.0	22.8	34.3	38.8
India [13] Inde [13]	1996	13 619 520[4]	10.7	65.5	−1.2	23.0	10.6	11.8
	1997	15 156 460[4]	11.3	64.1	0.7	22.7	10.9	12.2
	1998	17 626 090[4]	12.3	63.3	0.4	21.4	11.2	12.6

23

Expenditure on gross domestic product at current prices
Percentage distribution *[cont.]*

Dépenses imputées au produit intérieur brut aux prix courants
Répartition en pourcentage *[suite]*

Country or area Pays ou zone	Year Année	GDP at current prices (Million nat. cur.) PIB aux prix courants (Mil. monnaie nat.)	% of GDP − en % du PIB					
			Govt. final consumption expenditure Consom. finale des admin. publiques	Household final consumption expenditure Consom. finale des ménages	Changes in inventories Variation des stocks	Gross fixed capital formation Formation brute de capital fixe	Exports of goods and services Exportations de biens et services	Imports of goods and services Importations de biens et services
Indonesia	1996	532 567 000	7.6	62.4[5]	1.1	29.6	25.8	26.4
Indonésie	1997	627 695 000	6.8	61.7[5]	3.4	28.3	27.9	28.1
	1998	1 002 334 000	5.4	66.2[5]	−3.0	22.1	50.5	41.2
Iran (Islamic Republic of) [3][14]	1997	281 018 300	14.4	49.8[5]	3.6[4]	29.9	18.2	15.9
Iran (Rép. islamique d') [3][14]	1998	317 638 900	15.9	56.8[5]	−2.3[4]	31.4	14.1	15.9
	1999	429 142 600	15.2	52.5[5]	−2.2[4]	28.7	20.8	15.0
Iraq	1989	21 026	28.5	53.4	−11.0	30.0	21.3	22.2
Iraq	1990	23 297	26.4	50.5	−4.2	26.7	18.5	17.8
	1991	19 940	35.3	48.2	2.6	16.5	2.7	5.3
Ireland [3]	1997	52 760[4]	15.2	51.5[5]	1.2[7]	20.3	79.8	67.2
Irlande [3]	1998	60 582[4]	14.5	50.2[5]	1.5[7]	21.9	86.8	75.4
	1999	69 052[4]	14.0	49.0[5]	−0.0[7]	23.4	87.6	73.8
Israel [3]	1997	367 300	27.8	56.9[5]	0.2	20.9	29.1	34.9
Israël [3]	1998	400 605	27.8	56.7[5]	−0.0	19.2	30.4	34.1
	1999	437 377	27.7	56.8[5]	1.3	18.8	34.0	38.6
Italy [3]	1997	1 983 850 000	18.2	58.9[5]	0.8[7]	18.1	26.4	22.4
Italie [3]	1998	2 067 703 000	18.0	59.0[5]	1.2[7]	18.4	26.5	23.1
	1999	2 128 165 000	18.1	59.5[5]	1.4[7]	18.9	25.5	23.5
Jamaica [3]	1996	221 763	14.4	66.5	0.2	31.6	47.8	60.4
Jamaïque [3]	1997	242 762	16.4	65.7	0.2	31.5	42.6	56.5
	1998	257 392	17.8	64.8	0.2	28.2	44.3	55.3
Japan	1997	509 645 300	9.7	60.0[5]	0.5	28.6	11.1	9.9
Japon	1998	498 499 300	10.2	61.1[5]	−0.1	26.8	11.1	9.1
	1999	495 144 500	10.3	62.0[5]	0.0	26.1	10.4	8.7
Jordan	1996	4 711	25.6	69.0	1.1	30.7	55.1	81.5
Jordanie	1997	4 946	26.6	69.8	−0.1	26.8	51.2	74.3
	1998	5 180	26.4	71.2	0.7	22.8	48.6	69.7
Kazakhstan [3]	1997	1 672 143[4]	12.4	70.5[5]	−0.7	16.3	34.9	37.4
Kazakhstan [3]	1998	1 733 264[4]	10.8	73.3[5]	0.1	14.2	30.3	34.9
	1999	2 016 456[4]	10.6	72.4[5]	1.6	13.0	42.5	40.1
Kenya	1997	31 168	16.2	72.7	0.9	17.6	28.0	35.4
Kenya	1998	34 606	16.4	73.9	0.9	16.5	25.0	32.6
	1999	37 446	17.0	71.6	1.0	15.1	25.0	29.6
Korea, Republic of [3]	1997	453 276 389	10.1	56.3[5]	−0.9[7]	35.1	34.7	35.7
Corée, Rép. de [3]	1998	444 366 540	11.0	54.8[5]	−8.6[7]	29.8	49.4	36.1
	1999	483 777 785	10.1	55.7[5]	−1.1[7]	28.0	42.1	35.3
Kuwait	1995	7 925	33.0	41.3	1.2	13.9	53.6	43.0
Koweït	1996	9 307	27.6	45.9	...	13.3[2]	52.9	39.7
	1997	9 212	27.6	47.2	...	13.5[2]	52.6	40.8
Kyrgyzstan [3]	1997	30 686	17.3	68.9[5]	9.3[7]	12.4	38.3	46.2
Kirghizistan [3]	1998	34 181	17.9	88.2[5]	2.6[7]	12.9	36.5	58.0
	1999	48 744	19.1	77.6[5]	2.3[7]	15.7	42.2	57.0
Latvia [3]	1997	3 276	19.1	66.6[5]	4.1[7]	18.7	51.0	59.5
Lettonie [3]	1998	3 590	21.4	64.5[5]	0.3[7]	27.3	51.3	64.8
	1999	3 897	17.9	65.7[5]	2.2	24.5	43.8	54.1
Lebanon	1994	14 992 000	121.4[10]	...	...	36.4	8.4	66.3
Liban	1995	17 779 000	117.7[10]	...	...	36.3	11.0	64.9
Lesotho [3]	1997	4 720	16.9	113.5[5]	−1.0	55.0	27.6	112.0
Lesotho [3]	1998	4 921	20.8	112.6[5]	−1.9	49.0	26.8	107.4
	1999	5 637	21.1	105.4[5]	−1.0	47.0	24.1	96.6
Liberia	1987	1 090[4]	13.2	65.5	0.6	11.1	40.2	32.7
Libéria	1988	1 158[4]	11.8	63.3[5]	0.3	10.0	39.0	27.8
	1989	1 194[4]	11.9	55.0[5]	0.3	8.1	43.7	23.1
Libyan Arab Jamah.	1983	8 805	32.7	39.2[5]	−1.1	25.1	42.1	38.0
Jamah. arabe libyenne	1984	8 013	33.6	38.6[5]	0.5	25.3	41.4	39.4
	1985	8 277	31.7	37.6[5]	0.4	19.7	37.4	26.7
Lithuania [3]	1997	38 340	19.0	65.0[5]	2.2[7]	24.4	54.5	65.1
Lithuanie [3]	1998	42 990	24.4	63.1[5]	0.1[7]	24.3	47.2	59.1
	1999	42 655	22.2	65.5[5]	0.6[7]	22.1	39.7	50.1

23
Expenditure on gross domestic product at current prices
Percentage distribution *[cont.]*
Dépenses imputées au produit intérieur brut aux prix courants
Répartition en pourcentage *[suite]*

| Country or area Pays ou zone | Year Année | GDP at current prices (Million nat. cur.) PIB aux prix courants (Mil. monnaie nat.) | % of GDP – en % du PIB | | | | | |
			Govt. final consumption expenditure Consom. finale des admin. publiques	Household final consumption expenditure Consom. finale des ménages	Changes in inventories Variation des stocks	Gross fixed capital formation Formation brute de capital fixe	Exports of goods and services Exportations de biens et services	Imports of goods and services Importations de biens et services
Luxembourg[3]	1997	624 581	17.3	46.3[5]	0.3[7]	20.1	109.8	93.8
Luxembourg[3]	1998	665 735	16.8	45.2[5]	0.3[7]	19.2	113.7	95.1
	1999	731 822	17.7	43.4[5]	0.4[7]	22.4	113.4	97.3
Madagascar	1990	4 601 600	8.0	86.0	...	17.0	15.9	26.9
Madagascar	1991	4 906 400	8.6	92.2	...	8.2	17.3	26.2
	1992	5 584 500	8.2	90.0	...	11.6	15.6	25.3
Malawi	1994	10 319	28.3	74.4[15]	...	12.0	31.8	40.7
Malawi	1995	20 923	21.9	30.4[15]	...	11.9	32.2	38.2
	1996	33 918	17.5	56.1[15]	...	11.2	15.5	27.1
Malaysia	1997	281 795	10.8	45.3[5]	−0.2	43.1	93.2	92.3
Malaisie	1998	284 472	10.0	41.5[5]	−0.1	26.8	114.4	92.6
	1999	299 194	11.2	41.7[5]	0.1	22.3	121.7	97.0
Maldives	1982	454	14.3	80.8	0.4	22.7	−18.3[1]	...
Maldives	1983	466	16.3	82.6	2.6	35.6	−37.1[1]	...
	1984	537	17.7	77.5	1.5	39.5	−36.1[1]	...
Mali	1990	683 300	15.2	79.0	2.2	20.0	17.3	33.7
Mali	1991	691 400	15.3	85.1	−2.4	20.0	17.5	35.5
	1992	737 400	14.2	82.2	2.7	17.6	17.8	34.6
Malta	1997	1 288	20.5	62.4	0.2[4]	25.3	85.1	93.5
Malte	1998	1 362	19.7	62.1	−0.8[4]	24.5	87.7	93.2
	1999	1 447	18.7	63.1	0.8[4]	22.8	91.3	96.7
Martinique	1990	19 320	29.7	83.6	1.9	26.7	8.4	50.3
Martinique	1991	20 787	28.8	84.0	1.4	25.6	7.4	47.1
	1992	22 093	28.7	84.3	−0.9	23.6	6.8	42.5
Mauritania	1986	59 715	14.3	85.4	1.5	22.7	55.4	79.4
Mauritanie	1987	67 216	13.6	82.6	1.7	20.8	48.3	67.0
	1988	72 635	14.2	79.6	1.4	17.0	49.1	61.3
Mauritius	1997	86 428	12.1	63.5	2.2	27.1	62.9	67.7
Maurice	1998	97 842	11.7	63.5	2.1	23.6	67.2	68.0
	1999	106 495	11.9	65.3	−1.5	27.9	64.9	68.4
Mexico[3]	1997	3 174 275	9.9	64.3[5]	6.3[16]	19.5	30.4	30.4
Méxique[3]	1998	3 844 917	10.4	67.3[5]	3.3[16]	20.9	30.8	32.8
	1999	4 620 600	10.0	68.1[5]	2.2[16]	21.0	30.8	32.1
Mongolia	1996	659 698	71.2[10]	...	...	22.4[2]	...	...
Mongolie	1997	846 344	70.0[10]	...	...	25.3[2]	...	...
	1998	833 727	81.0[10]	...	...	27.3[2]	...	...
Montserrat	1984	94	20.6	96.4	2.7	23.7	13.6	56.9
Montserrat	1985	100	20.3	96.3	1.5	24.7	11.7	54.4
	1986	114	18.7	89.5	2.8	33.0	10.1	53.9
Morocco	1997	318 342	17.8	65.3	0.0	20.7	26.9	23.1
Maroc	1998	342 558	18.1	64.0	0.1	22.4	27.3	22.7
	1999	343 131	19.3	61.1	−0.2	24.3	29.0	24.4
Mozambique	1992	2 764 000	21.6	93.5	...	43.5[2]	26.7	85.3
Mozambique	1997[3]	40 126 200	8.4	89.2	...	18.9[2]	12.8	29.2
	1998[3]	43 557 100	9.4	88.2	...	23.3[2]	11.6	32.5
Myanmar[13]	1996	791 980	88.5[10]	...	−2.7	14.9	0.7	1.5
Myanmar[13]	1997	1 109 554	88.1[10]	...	−0.9	13.5	0.6	1.3
	1998	1 559 996	89.4[10]	...	−0.7	11.8	0.5	1.0
Namibia[3]	1998	18 858[4]	29.3	58.8	2.7	23.6	45.9	57.8
Namibie[3]	1999	21 230[4]	28.8	57.4	0.2	23.6	46.7	56.2
	2000	24 145[4]	26.1	56.3	0.4	23.2	41.8	46.9
Nepal[17]	1996	248 913	9.2	76.9	4.8	22.5	22.3	35.8
Népal[17]	1997	280 513	8.9	77.1	3.7	21.7	26.3	37.7
	1998	296 547	9.3	81.2	−0.5	21.2	23.1	34.3
Netherlands[3]	1997	734 853	22.9	49.4[5]	0.1[7]	21.4	61.2	55.1
Pays−Bas[3]	1998	776 161	23.0	49.5[5]	0.2[7]	21.7	60.9	55.3
	1999	814 336	23.2	50.1[5]	−0.3[7]	22.3	60.6	55.8
Netherlands Antilles	1992	3 548	25.3	58.3[5]	2.3	22.1	81.5	89.6
Antilles néerlandaises	1993	3 766	27.7	57.6[5]	0.4	20.9	76.1	82.7
	1994	4 218	26.2	64.2[5]	0.7	18.5	72.8	82.4

23

Expenditure on gross domestic product at current prices
Percentage distribution [cont.]
Dépenses imputées au produit intérieur brut aux prix courants
Répartition en pourcentage [suite]

Country or area Pays ou zone	Year Année	GDP at current prices (Million nat. cur.) PIB aux prix courants (Mil. monnaie nat.)	% of GDP − en % du PIB					
			Govt. final consumption expenditure Consom. finale des admin. publiques	Household final consumption expenditure Consom. finale des ménages	Changes in inventories Variation des stocks	Gross fixed capital formation Formation brute de capital fixe	Exports of goods and services Exportations de biens et services	Imports of goods and services Importations de biens et services
New Caledonia	1990	250 427[4]	32.6	57.3	−1.1	24.4	22.0	35.4
Nouvelle−Calédonie	1991	272 235[4]	32.8	53.8	1.3	23.9	20.1	32.2
	1992	281 427[4]	33.7	56.7	0.1	23.7	16.8	31.4
New Zealand [13]	1997	98 024[4]	15.1	63.4[5]	0.9	20.2	29.0	28.4
Nouvelle−Zélande [13]	1998	98 913[4]	15.3	65.0[5]	−0.1	19.2	30.7	30.0
	1999	103 528[4]	15.8	64.4[5]	1.1	19.5	31.9	32.8
Nicaragua	1997	18 601	17.1	95.8	0.4	31.1	37.4	81.8
Nicaragua	1998	22 881	16.0	88.8	0.4	31.9	35.2	76.7
	1999	26 107	18.9	94.8	0.3	43.1	34.6	91.7
Niger	1988	678 200	15.5	65.9	7.9	11.9	20.7	21.9
Niger	1989	692 600	18.0	73.0	−0.1	12.3	18.6	21.8
	1990	682 300	17.2	74.1	1.1	11.7	16.8	20.9
Nigeria	1992	549 809	3.7	73.5	0.1	10.7	35.8	23.8
Nigéria	1993	701 473	3.9	76.6	0.1	11.5	32.6	24.8
	1994	914 334	3.5	82.1	0.0	9.3	23.8	18.6
Norway [3]	1997	1 096 170	19.9	47.5[5]	1.7	23.0	40.9	33.4
Norvège [3]	1998	1 109 348	21.4	49.8[5]	2.7	25.0	37.2	36.7
	1999	1 192 826	21.2	48.5[5]	...	22.2	39.0	33.0
Oman [3]	1997	6 090	23.2	47.5	0.1	17.7	48.3	36.7
Oman [3]	1998	5 416	25.9	57.2	0.0	24.0	39.3	46.4
	1999	6 000	23.9	49.2	0.1	14.8	46.5	34.4
Pakistan [6]	1997	2 677 656	11.3	72.1	2.7	15.0	16.5	17.5
Pakistan [6]	1998	2 913 514	10.4	76.1	1.6	13.2	15.6	17.0
	1999	3 173 685	11.4	75.7	1.6	13.3	16.2	18.3
Panama	1997	8 658	16.2	54.3	4.6	26.5	98.1	99.7
Panama	1998	9 345	16.1	56.5	4.0	28.1	89.9	94.6
	1999	9 557	15.6	57.0	2.9	29.6	76.5	81.6
Papua New Guinea	1990	3 076	24.8	59.0	−0.7	25.1	40.6	48.9
Papouasie−Nouvelle−	1991	3 606	22.4	60.1	−0.6	28.0	42.3	52.2
Guinée	1992	4 140	22.5	57.9	...	23.8	45.2	49.3
Paraguay	1993	11 991 719	6.7	81.3	0.9	22.0	36.9	47.9
Paraguay	1994	14 960 131	6.8	88.4	0.9	22.5	34.2	52.8
	1995	17 699 000	7.2	85.3	0.9	23.1	35.0	51.2
Peru	1996	148 278	9.5	71.2	2.1	21.9	12.2	16.8
Pérou	1997	172 389	9.3	69.4	1.6	23.4	13.0	16.7
	1998	183 179	9.5	71.4	1.3	22.9	11.7	16.8
Philippines	1997	2 426 743[4]	13.2	72.6	0.4	24.4	49.0	59.3
Philippines	1998	2 678 187[4]	13.2	73.9	−0.8	21.0	51.9	58.5
	1999	2 996 371[4]	12.9	72.1	−0.3	19.0	51.1	50.1
Poland [3]	1997	472 350	16.0	63.7[5]	1.1	23.5	25.5	29.8
Pologne [3]	1998	553 560	15.4	63.6[5]	1.0	25.1	28.2	33.4
	1999	615 560	15.4	64.6[5]	0.9	25.5	26.1	32.5
Portugal [3]	1997	18 581 524[4]	19.2	63.8[5]	0.6[7]	23.9	30.6	38.1
Portugal [3]	1998	19 992 891[4]	19.2	64.5[5]	0.6[7]	24.7	30.9	39.9
	1999	21 312 929[4]	20.0	64.8[5]	0.7[7]	24.9	29.9	40.2
Puerto Rico [6]	1997	54 133	13.1	59.5[5]	0.1	17.1	68.2	58.0
Porto Rico [6]	1998	60 039	12.5	57.7[5]	0.8	19.3	69.5	59.7
	1999	63 150	11.4	57.9[5]	0.5	19.3	72.9	62.1
Qatar	1997	41 124	29.8	22.7	0.8	34.6	48.3	36.2
Qatar	1998	37 330	31.6	25.3	1.1	30.9	51.1	40.0
	1999	44 397	26.6	21.4	0.9	20.5	59.8	29.3
Republic of Moldova [3]	1998	9 122	24.7	76.2[5]	3.8	22.1	45.0	71.8
Rép. de Moldova [3]	1999	12 322	15.3	74.7[5]	4.4	18.4	52.3	65.2
	2000	15 980	15.2	82.8[5]	4.1	18.2	52.3	72.5
Réunion	1992	33 787	28.4	76.1	2.1	28.6	3.4	38.6
Réunion	1993	33 711	28.6	76.4	−0.4	25.7	3.1	36.2
	1994	35 266	28.9	78.0	0.1	28.1	2.9	38.0
Romania [3]	1998	368 260 700	14.0	72.7[5]	2.1[7]	19.4	23.7	31.8
Roumanie [3]	1999	521 735 500	12.3	72.0[5]	1.5[7]	18.5	30.1	34.3
	2000	796 533 700	12.5	73.9[5]	1.0[7]	18.5	34.1	39.9

23
Expenditure on gross domestic product at current prices
Percentage distribution [cont.]
Dépenses imputées au produit intérieur brut aux prix courants
Répartition en pourcentage [suite]

Country or area Pays ou zone	Year Année	GDP at current prices (Million nat. cur.) PIB aux prix courants (Mil. monnaie nat.)	% of GDP − en % du PIB					
			Govt. final consumption expenditure Consom. finale des admin. publiques	Household final consumption expenditure Consom. finale des ménages	Changes in inventories Variation des stocks	Gross fixed capital formation Formation brute de capital fixe	Exports of goods and services Exportations de biens et services	Imports of goods and services Importations de biens et services
Russian Federation [3] Fédération de Russie [3]	1998 1999 2000	2 741 100 4 757 200[4] 7 063 400[4]	18.7 14.7 14.6	57.9[5] 54.8[5] 49.1[5]	−1.5 −0.8 −0.7	17.7 16.1 18.3	30.7 43.9 45.8	23.5 26.9 24.9
Rwanda Rwanda	1990 1991 1992	192 900 212 900 217 300	17.2 21.6 25.1	82.9 82.2 76.8	−0.9 −1.5 −0.0	12.4 11.9 14.9	7.7 9.8 7.4	19.2 23.9 24.2
Saint Kitts−Nevis Saint−Kitts−et−Nevis	1997 1998 1999	742 775 812	19.3 19.1 21.6	52.0 54.3 64.7	... ...	44.1[2] 43.0[2] 37.3[2]	53.6 53.5 46.2	68.8 69.9 69.8
Saint Lucia Sainte−Lucie	1996 1997 1998	1 543 1 562 1 695	16.9 18.2 18.5	64.4 65.5 65.5	... ...	24.7 26.8 24.7	61.8 62.0 60.7	67.9 72.4 69.4
Saint Vincent−Grenadines St.−Vincent−et− Grenadines	1997 1998 1999	793 858 888	18.9 18.3 18.4	79.7 78.8 69.4	... ...	29.6 31.7 32.5	49.8 49.5 53.7	78.1 78.3 74.0
Sao Tome and Principe Sao Tomé−et−Principe	1986 1987 1988	2 478[4] 3 003[4] 4 221[4]	30.3 24.8 21.2	76.1 63.1 71.8	0.9 1.1 ...	13.6 15.4 15.7[2]	... ...	50.8 43.1 66.8
Saudi Arabia [6] Arabie saoudite [6]	1997 1998 1999	548 620 480 773 521 988	27.6 32.6 29.9	37.6 41.3 38.8	1.0 1.1 1.0	18.7 20.2 18.3	45.8 35.5 39.8	30.7 30.7 27.9
Senegal Sénégal	1996 1997 1998	2 380 000[4] 2 555 000 2 753 000	12.0 11.3 11.2	78.9 76.4 74.5	2.2	16.3 18.0[2] 20.2[2]	30.6 34.0 32.8	40.0 39.7 38.6
Seychelles Seychelles	1996 1997 1998	2 500 2 845 3 060	29.4 25.8 27.7	47.6 51.5 52.4	−0.8 3.8 ...	32.9 30.3 37.8[2]	−9.9[1] −9.2[1] −15.7[1]	... ...
Sierra Leone [6] Sierra Leone [6]	1988 1989 1990	43 947 82 837 150 175	7.5 6.6 10.4	86.7 84.7 77.9	0.8 0.5 1.8	12.7 13.5 10.1	14.5 19.7 25.4	22.3 25.1 25.7
Singapore [3] Singapour [3]	1997 1998 1999	140 466[4] 138 529[4] 143 981[4]	9.4 10.0 9.7	40.2 39.4 40.4	0.5 −4.3 0.3	38.8 37.1 32.5	12.9[1] 19.6[1] 19.0[1]	... ...
Slovakia [3] Slovaquie [3]	1997 1998 1999	686 087 750 761 815 330	21.2 21.5 19.5	52.0[5] 53.3[5] 54.0[5]	0.7 −1.9 1.1	35.9 38.0 30.8	58.0 61.2 61.5	67.8 72.2 66.9
Slovenia [3] Slovénie [3]	1998 1999 2000	3 253 751 3 648 401 4 035 518	20.3 20.2 20.8	55.7[5] 55.8[5] 54.9[5]	1.0 1.0 1.1	24.6 27.4 26.7	56.6 52.5 59.1	58.2 56.9 62.7
Solomon Islands Iles Salomon	1986 1987 1988	253 293 367	33.3 36.3 31.4	63.1 63.1 68.6	1.0 2.7 2.7	25.2 20.4 30.0	52.6 55.9 52.4	75.2 78.4 85.0
Somalia Somalie	1985 1986 1987	87 290 118 781 169 082	10.6 9.7 11.1	90.5 89.1 88.8	2.9 1.0 4.8	8.9 16.8 16.8	4.2 5.8 5.9	17.0 22.4 27.2
South Africa [3] Afrique du Sud [3]	1997 1998 1999	683 744[4] 735 086[4] 795 575[4]	19.8 20.0 19.4	63.0 63.4 63.3	−0.3 −0.7 −0.2	16.3 16.8 15.2	24.6 25.9 25.9	23.5 24.7 23.1
Spain [3] Espagne [3]	1997 1998 1999	82 059 500 87 545 400 93 693 400	17.6 17.5 17.3	59.3[5] 59.2[5] 59.3[5]	0.2 0.3 0.5	21.9 22.9 24.2	26.8 27.3 27.3	25.8 27.3 28.7
Sri Lanka Sri Lanka	1996 1997 1998	771 414[4] 891 067 1 011 326	14.5 14.2 14.1	68.7 67.0 66.7	0.3 0.1 0.1	25.7 25.7 25.6	35.0 36.6 36.1	43.7 43.5 42.5
Sudan [6] Soudan [6]	1994 1996 1997	5 522 838 10 330 678 16 769 372	4.6 7.5 5.4	84.1 81.9 85.6	6.8 9.6 5.7	9.4 12.3 12.2	4.6 8.0 10.2	9.5 19.2 19.2
Suriname Suriname	1996 1997 1998	303 970 340 220 407 130	14.7 17.7 18.7	58.9 60.2 71.5	6.2 5.9 ...	29.1 24.0 23.2[2]	65.5 57.4 42.3	74.4 65.1 55.7

23

Expenditure on gross domestic product at current prices
Percentage distribution *[cont.]*

Dépenses imputées au produit intérieur brut aux prix courants
Répartition en pourcentage *[suite]*

Country or area Pays ou zone	Year Année	GDP at current prices (Million nat. cur.) PIB aux prix courants (Mil. monnaie nat.)	% of GDP – en % du PIB					
			Govt. final consumption expenditure Consom. finale des admin. publiques	Household final consumption expenditure Consom. finale des ménages	Changes in inventories Variation des stocks	Gross fixed capital formation Formation brute de capital fixe	Exports of goods and services Exportations de biens et services	Imports of goods and services Importations de biens et services
Swaziland [3] [8]	1996	5 307	22.3	59.1	0.9	28.9	80.4	91.5
Swaziland [3] [8]	1997	6 268	26.1	54.6	0.9	32.3	78.9	92.9
	1998	7 041	25.6	53.0	...	34.4	84.4	97.4
Sweden [3]	1997	1 823 799	26.5	50.6[5]	0.4	15.2	42.7	35.4
Suède [3]	1998	1 905 349	26.7	50.2[5]	0.8	16.0	43.7	37.4
	1999	1 994 854	26.9	50.2[5]	0.2	16.8	43.7	37.8
Switzerland	1997	371 372	14.1	61.3[5]	0.6	19.6	39.6	35.3
Suisse	1998	380 940	14.0	60.9[5]	1.2	20.0	40.2	36.2
	1999	388 976	13.6	61.2[5]	0.1	19.9	42.1	37.0
Syrian Arab Rep.	1997	745 569	11.4	69.1	...	20.9	32.4	33.8
Rép. arabe syrienne	1998	790 444	11.2	68.6	...	20.6	30.5	30.9
	1999	821 327	11.4	69.5	...	18.8	32.2	31.9
Tajikistan [3]	1997	518 400[4]	10.6	60.0[5]	2.0	17.7	81.8	85.4
Tadjikistan [3]	1998	1 025 200[4]	7.8	68.9[5]	2.0	13.4	49.7	57.5
	1999	1 344 900[4]	8.6	70.0[5]	1.9	17.2	67.9	66.4
Thailand	1996	4 609 000[4]	10.2	54.5	0.6	41.1	39.2	45.5
Thaïlande	1997	4 727 000[4]	10.0	55.5	−0.5	33.3	47.9	46.5
	1998	4 635 000[4]	10.8	54.6	−1.9	22.2	58.6	42.7
TFYR of Macedonia [3]	1997	184 982	17.2	73.7[5]	5.0	17.4	36.9	50.2
L'ex–République yougo–	1998	190 827	17.6	73.8[5]	5.2	17.8	43.5	57.8
slave de Macédoine [3]	1999	195 285	17.0	72.4[5]	3.1	17.9	44.0	54.4
Togo	1984	304 800	14.0	66.0	−1.5	21.2	51.9	51.6
Togo	1985	332 500	14.2	66.0	5.2	22.9	48.3	56.7
	1986	363 600	14.4	69.0	5.3	23.8	35.6	48.2
Tonga [8]	1981	54	14.2	122.8	2.2	23.9	26.3	67.3
Tonga [8]	1982	64	16.8	121.0	1.4	23.1	25.7	63.9
	1983	73	14.2	125.9	1.0	28.1	19.7	70.0
Trinidad and Tobago	1992	23 118	17.8	57.5	0.2	13.6	39.4	28.5
Trinité–et–Tobago	1993	24 491	16.4	61.9	0.4	12.9	40.5	30.6
	1994	29 312	14.8	55.4	0.4	12.3	42.6	27.8
Tunisia [3]	1997	20 898	15.8	60.2	1.8	24.7	43.8	46.2
Tunisie [3]	1998	22 581	15.7	60.7	2.0	24.9	43.0	46.4
	1999	24 672	15.6	60.4	0.8	25.4	42.6	44.8
Turkey	1997	28 835 883 000[4]	12.3	68.0	−1.3	26.4	24.6	30.4
Turquie	1998	52 224 945 000[4]	12.7	69.2	−0.4	24.6	24.3	27.9
	1999	77 374 802 000[4]	15.2	72.7	1.5	21.8	23.2	26.9
Turkmenistan [3]	1995	652 044	8.4	60.6[5]	10.4[7]	23.1	142.5	145.0
Turkménistan [3]	1996	7 751 754[4]	7.1	49.2[5]	8.7[7]	41.3	105.8	107.0
	1997	11 108 783[4]	13.3	68.4[5]	7.7[7]	40.9	51.3	82.4
Uganda	1997	7 230 521[4]	9.6	92.3	−0.1	16.9	11.5	25.5
Ouganda	1998	8 298 977[4]	9.2	90.6	...	17.3	10.4	28.2
	1999	9 132 410[4]	9.2	91.0	...	20.1	10.3	28.5
Ukraine [3]	1997	93 365	23.9	57.7[5]	1.6[7]	19.8	40.6	43.7
Ukraine [3]	1998	102 593	21.6	59.9[5]	1.2[7]	19.6	41.9	44.2
	1999	130 038	22.0	57.4[5]	−1.8[7]	19.3	52.0	49.0
United Arab Emirates	1990	124 008	16.3	38.6	1.0	19.4	65.4	40.8
Emirats arabes unis	1991	124 500	16.9	41.4	1.1	20.7	67.6	47.7
	1992	128 400	17.8	45.5	1.2	23.2	69.1	56.8
United Kingdom [3]	1997	805 402	18.4	64.3[5]	0.5[7]	16.7	28.5	28.4
Royaume–Uni [3]	1998	851 653	18.2	64.8[5]	0.6[7]	17.4	26.5	27.4
	1999	891 583	18.4	65.8[5]	−0.2[7]	17.8	25.8	27.5
United Rep. of Tanzania	1992	1 130 596	7.1	90.7	2.8	29.9	15.1	45.7
Rép.–Unie de Tanzanie	1993	1 404 369	9.1	86.8	3.2	29.0	20.5	48.6
	1994	1 822 570	7.7	89.6	3.2	27.5	26.4	54.4
United States [3]	1997	8 256 500	14.6	67.0[5]	...	18.6	11.7	12.8
Etats–Unis [3]	1998	8 728 800	14.3	67.0[5]	...	19.2	11.1	12.8
	1999	9 237 000	14.2	67.9[5]	...	19.9	10.7	13.5
Uruguay	1997	204 938	12.4	72.5	0.8	14.3	20.5	20.5
Uruguay	1998	235 393	12.6	72.6	0.7	14.9	19.8	20.5
	1999	238 820	13.8	72.6	0.7	14.6	18.0	19.6

23
Expenditure on gross domestic product at current prices
Percentage distribution *[cont.]*
Dépenses imputées au produit intérieur brut aux prix courants
Répartition en pourcentage *[suite]*

Country or area Pays ou zone	Year Année	GDP at current prices (Million nat. cur.) PIB aux prix courants (Mil. monnaie nat.)	% of GDP − en % du PIB					
			Govt. final consumption expenditure Consom. finale des admin. publiques	Household final consumption expenditure Consom. finale des ménages	Changes in inventories Variation des stocks	Gross fixed capital formation Formation brute de capital fixe	Exports of goods and services Exportations de biens et services	Imports of goods and services Importations de biens et services
Uzbekistan [3] Ouzbékistan [3]	1998	1 419 400	20.7	62.8[5]	−15.6	30.3	23.7	22.0
	1999	2 128 700	20.6	62.1[5]	−10.0	27.1	0.1	...
	2000	3 194 500	19.7	63.7[5]	−9.1	25.0	0.7	...
Vanuatu Vanuatu	1993	23 779[4]	28.4	49.2	2.3	25.5	45.3	53.8
	1994	24 961[4]	27.7	49.2	2.3	26.5	47.3	57.2
	1995	27 255[4]	25.4	46.9	2.1	29.8	44.2	53.6
Venezuela Venezuela	1998	52 482 472	7.5	71.8[5]	2.8	19.0	19.9	21.1
	1999	62 577 039	7.5	69.1[5]	2.4	15.7	21.6	16.4
	2000	81 924 193	7.0	63.1[5]	3.0	14.5	29.4	17.0
Viet Nam [3] Viet Nam [3]	1997	313 623 000[4]	8.1	71.8	1.6	26.7	−8.1[1]	...
	1998	361 017 000[4]	7.6	70.9	2.0	27.0	−7.3[1]	...
	1999	399 942 000[4]	7.3	68.2	1.8	25.4	−2.2[1]	...
Yemen [3] Yémen [3]	1997	888 808	13.1	64.3	3.3	21.6	35.8	38.2
	1998	849 321	14.7	67.8	1.0	31.5	27.6	42.6
	1999	1 128 825	13.8	69.0	2.1	21.4	36.4	42.8
Yugoslavia [3] Yougoslavie [3]	1996	79 396	22.1	72.6	4.9	11.9	15.8	27.4
	1997	112 355	25.0	65.5[5]	6.4[7]	11.7	17.8	26.3
	1998	154 584	27.0	69.0[5]	1.8[7]	11.2	22.5	31.5
Yugoslavia, SFR † Yougoslavie, SFR †	1988	15 833[4]	14.2	50.1	19.9	17.2	29.5	30.4
	1989	235 395[4]	14.4	47.4	28.0	14.5	25.3	29.2
	1990	1 147 787[4]	17.6	66.1	7.3	14.7	23.7	29.4
Zambia Zambie	1989	58 706	73.3	13.5	...	19.9	25.2	31.8
	1990	123 487	54.7	14.1	...	30.7	34.3	33.8
	1991	234 504	60.4	14.3	...	24.6	26.4	25.7
Zimbabwe Zimbabwe	1996	84 759	17.1	64.0[5]	0.5	18.2	36.5	36.3
	1997	102 074	16.7	72.2[5]	0.1	18.0	37.6	44.6
	1998	135 722	15.6	69.0[5]	−0.4	17.6	45.9	47.8

Source:
United Nations Statistics Division, New York,
national accounts database.

† For information on recent changes in country or area
nomenclature pertaining to former Czechoslovakia, Germany,
Hong Kong Special Administrative Region (SAR) of China,
Macao Special Administrative Region (SAR) of China,
SFR of Yugoslavia and the former USSR, see Annex I − Country
or area nomenclature, regional and other groupings.

†† For statistical purposes, the data for China do not
include those for the Hong Kong Special Administrative
Region (Hong Kong SAR), Macao Special Administrative
Region (Hong Kong SAR) and Taiwan province of China.

1 Net exports.
2 Gross capital formation.
3 Data classified according to SNA 93.
4 Including statistical discrepancy.
5 Including "Non−profit institutions serving households" (NPISHs)
final consumption expenditure.
6 Data refer to fiscal years beginning 1 July.
7 Including acquisitions less disposals of valuables.
8 Data refer to fiscal years ending 30 June.
9 Including government consumption expenditure on collective goods.

Source:
Organisation des Nations Unies, Division de statistique,
New York, la base de données sur les comptes nationaux.

† Pour les modifications récentes de nomenclature de pays
ou de zone concernant l'Allemagne, Hong Kong région
administrative spéciale (RAS) de Chine, Macao région administrative
spéciale (RAS) de Chine, l'ex−Tchécoslovaquie, l'ex−URSS et l'ex−
Rfs de Yougoslavie, voir annexe I − Nomenclature des pays ou des
zones, groupements régionaux et autres groupements.

†† Les données statistiques relatives à la Chine ne comprennent
pas celles qui concernent la région administrative spéciale de
Hong Kong (la RAS de Hong Kong), la région administrative
spéciale de Macao (la RAS de Macao) et la province chinoise
de Taiwan.

1 Exportations nettes.
2 Formation brute de capital.
3 Les données sont classifiées selon le SCN 1993.
4 Y compris divergence statistique.
5 Y compris la consommation finale des institutions sans but lucratif
au service des ménages.
6 Les données se réfèrent aux années fiscales commençant le 1er juillet.
7 Y compris les acquisitions moins cessions d'objets de valeur.
8 Les données se réfèrent aux années fiscales finissant le 30e juin.
9 Y compris la consommation des administrations publiques sur des
biens collectifs.

23
Expenditure on gross domestic product at current prices
Percentage distribution *[cont.]*
Dépenses imputées au produit intérieur brut aux prix courants
Répartition en pourcentage *[suite]*

10 Including household final consumption expenditure.	10 Y compris la consommation finale des ménages.
11 Data refer to fiscal years ending 7 July.	11 Les données se réfèrent aux années fiscales commençant le 7e juillet.
12 Data refer to fiscal years ending 30 September.	12 Les données se réfèrent aux années fiscales finissant le 30e septembre.
13 Data refer to fiscal years beginning 1 April.	13 Les données se réfèrent aux années fiscales commençant le 1er avril.
14 Data refer to fiscal years beginning 21 March.	14 Les données se réfèrent aux années fiscales commençant le 21e mars.
15 Including changes in inventories.	15 Y compris les variations des stocks.
16 Excluding acquisitions less disposals of valuables.	16 Non compris les acquisitions moins cessions d'objets de valeur.
17 Data refer to fiscal years ending 15 July.	17 Les données se réfèrent aux années fiscales finissant le 15e juillet.

24
Value added by kind of economic activity at current prices
Valeur ajoutée par genre d'activité économique aux prix courants
Percentage distribution
Répartition en pourcentage

% of Value added − % de la valeur ajoutée

Country or area Pays ou zone	Year Année	Value added (Mil. nat.cur.) Valeur ajoutée (Mil. mon.nat.)	Agriculture, hunting, forestry & fishing Agriculture, chasse, sylviculture et pêche	Mining & quarrying Industries extractives	Manufac- turing Industries manufac- turières	Electricity, gas and water Electricité, gaz et eau	Con- struc- tion Con- struc- tion	Wholesale/ retail trade, restaurants and hotels Commerce, restaurants, hôtels	Transport, storage & commu- nication Transports, entrepôts, communi- cations	Other activities Autres activités
Albania [1] Albanie [1]	1997	341 716	56.0	12.4 [6] [7]	...	...	11.2	17.6 [2]	2.7	...
	1998	460 631	54.4	11.9 [6] [7]	...	...	12.6	18.0 [2]	3.0	...
	1999	506 205	52.6	11.9 [6] [7]	...	...	13.5	18.8 [2]	3.3	...
Algeria Algérie	1994	1 155 644	12.6	30.1	12.5	1.2	13.1	21.0	6.5	2.9
	1995	1 566 580	12.5	33.8	10.9	1.2	12.2	19.8	6.4	3.2
	1996	2 039 189	13.6	37.6	9.4	1.2	10.7	17.3	7.3	2.9
Angola Angola	1988	237 046	16.0	27.1	8.3	0.2	4.1	11.7 [3]	3.5	29.1
	1989	276 402	19.2	29.6	6.2	0.2	3.3	11.3 [3]	3.0	27.1
	1990	305 353	18.0	33.0	5.0	0.1	2.9	10.8 [3]	3.2	27.1
Anguilla Anguilla	1997	194 [4]	3.8	1.0	0.8	3.7	14.7	40.2	15.9	30.2
	1998	209 [4]	3.8	1.0	1.0	3.8	14.8	39.7	15.3	29.2
	1999	233 [4]	3.0	0.9	1.3	4.3	16.7	38.2	14.6	30.5
Antigua and Barbuda Antigua−et−Barbuda	1986	567 [4]	4.3	1.7	3.8	3.5	8.9	23.6	15.6	38.5
	1987	649 [4]	4.5	2.2	3.5	3.5	11.3	24.1	15.6	35.3
	1988	776 [4]	4.1	2.2	3.1	4.0	12.7	23.7	14.3	35.9
Argentina Argentine	1997	273 093 [5]	5.6	2.1	19.5	2.0	5.5	18.0	8.4	38.9
	1998	278 632 [5]	5.7	1.5	19.1	2.1	6.0	18.1	8.5	39.0
	1999	266 125 [5]	4.6	1.8	18.2	2.3	6.0	17.2	8.5	41.4
Armenia [1] Arménie [1]	1997	760 200	31.2	...	24.6 [6] [7]	...	8.6	9.6	8.0	18.2
	1998	884 500	33.4	...	22.3 [6] [7]	...	8.7	9.4	7.4	18.8
	1999	917 300	28.3	...	23.4 [6] [7]	...	9.5	9.7	7.8	21.3
Aruba Aruba	1994	2 225	0.5 [7]	...	5.8	3.5	7.0	28.6	9.2	45.4
Australia [1] [8] Australie [1] [8]	1996	494 838	3.5	4.8	13.5	2.7	5.9	13.8	9.2	46.7
	1997	525 523	3.4	4.7	13.7	2.5	6.2	13.6	9.1	46.8
	1998	554 711	3.3	4.1	13.4	2.4	6.5	14.0	9.1	47.3
Austria [1] Autriche [1]	1997	2 367 296	2.4	0.4	20.0	2.6	8.0	16.6	7.3	42.7
	1998	2 461 187	2.3	0.3	20.2	2.6	8.2	16.6	7.3	42.5
	1999	2 530 308	2.1	0.4	20.1	2.5	8.4	16.8	7.1	42.6
Azerbaijan [1] Azerbaïdjan [1]	1997	14 675 500	21.5	...	28.4 [6] [7]	...	12.6	6.2	11.3	20.0
	1998	16 591 100	18.6	...	23.5 [6] [7]	...	13.4	6.1	12.4	25.9
	1999	15 328 900	23.3	...	25.2 [6] [7]	...	10.1	5.5	15.5	20.5
Bahamas [1] Bahamas [1]	1993	2 404	3.3	0.7	3.7	4.0	3.6	27.0	10.9	46.8
	1994	2 608	3.8	0.7	3.4	4.6	3.1	26.0	11.9	46.4
	1995	2 656	3.8	1.0	3.0	4.4	2.7	26.5	11.1	46.6
Bahrain Bahreïn	1994	2 009	0.9	14.3	16.0	1.5	5.5	10.4	10.8	40.7
	1995	2 071	1.0	15.4	20.2	1.7	5.1	9.8	7.9	38.9
	1996	2 188	1.0	18.1	18.0	1.6	4.5	9.5	8.4	38.9
Bangladesh [8] Bangladesh [8]	1995	1 301 600	30.0	0.0	9.6	2.2	5.9	9.0	11.4	32.0
	1996	1 403 045	29.3	0.0	9.3	2.2	5.9	8.9	11.5	32.9
	1997	1 540 923	28.9	0.0	9.4	2.1	5.9	8.9	11.2	33.5
Barbados Barbade	1997	3 629 [4]	5.3	0.6	6.2	3.2	5.6	29.7	10.0	39.5
	1998	3 913 [4]	3.9	0.6	6.2	3.3	5.7	30.3	10.2	39.8
	1999	4 145 [4]	4.9	0.7	6.3	3.2	5.8	29.1	10.4	39.7
Belarus [1] Bélarus [1]	1998	620 839 100	13.6	...	35.1 [6] [7]	...	6.6	10.7	11.2	22.8
	1999	2 687 694 200	14.3	...	33.6 [6] [7]	...	6.5	10.8	12.9	21.9
	2000	7 996 200	15.0	...	32.0 [6] [7]	...	6.5	10.6	13.5	22.5
Belgium [1] Belgique [1]	1997	8 142 842	1.7	0.2	19.9	3.0	4.9	13.3	6.9	50.3
	1998	8 483 500	1.5	0.2	19.5	2.9	4.7	13.2	6.9	51.1
	1999	8 773 377	1.4	0.2	18.7	2.7	5.0	13.5	6.8	51.8
Belize [1] Belize [1]	1997	1 040	19.8	0.6	13.8	3.0	5.6	18.4	10.5	37.5
	1998	1 051	19.1	0.6	13.2	3.4	5.7	18.9	10.4	37.9
	1999	1 154	18.8	0.6	12.8	2.7	6.3	...	10.6	35.6
Benin Bénin	1987	430 800	36.3	1.2	7.8	0.9	3.5	17.0	8.5	24.7
	1988	451 080	37.2	0.9	8.9	1.0	3.3	18.7	8.1	21.9
	1989	465 735	38.0	0.9	9.2	0.9	3.3	17.6	7.8	22.2

24
Value added by kind of economic activity at current prices
Percentage distribution *[cont.]*
Valeur ajoutée par genre d'activité économique aux prix courants
Répartition en pourcentage *[suite]*

			% of Value added − % de la valeur ajoutée							
Country or area Pays ou zone	Year Année	Value added (Mil. nat.cur.) Valeur ajoutée (Mil. mon.nat.)	Agriculture, hunting, forestry & fishing Agriculture, chasse, sylviculture et pêche	Mining & quarrying Industries extractives	Manufac− turing Industries manufac− turières	Electricity, gas and water Electricité, gaz et eau	Con− struc− tion Con− struc− tion	Wholesale/ retail trade, restaurants and hotels Commerce, restaurants, hôtels	Transport, storage & commu− nication Transports, entrepôts, communi− cations	Other activities Autres activités
Bhutan	1996	11 558[4]	39.3	2.3	12.1	9.5	9.0	7.8	7.4	12.6
Bhoutan	1997	14 498[4]	36.4	2.1	11.0	11.9	10.1	7.0	7.1	14.4
	1998	16 288[4]	36.7	2.4	11.1	11.0	10.6	7.0	7.5	13.7
Bolivia	1997	37 720	16.5	7.0	16.0	3.0	3.2	12.1	12.0	30.3
Bolivie	1998	42 498	13.7	7.2	16.3	2.7	4.3	11.2	13.1	31.5
	1999	44 476	13.6	6.4	15.9	3.0	3.8	10.8	12.9	33.5
Botswana [1][9]	1997	17 024	3.5	40.6	5.2	1.9	6.0	10.5	3.4	29.0
Botswana [1][9]	1998	19 320	3.6	39.7	5.2	1.9	6.0	10.4	3.5	29.7
	1999	20 477	3.2	32.7	5.5	2.2	6.6	11.4	4.0	34.3
Brazil [1]	1992	701	6.2	1.3	21.3	2.4	6.2	7.5[3][31]	4.3	50.8
Brésil [1]	1993	16 552	5.8	0.9	22.2	2.4	6.3	7.1[3][31]	4.1	51.3
	1994	352 827	8.6	0.9	23.5	2.7	8.0	8.3[3][31]	4.3	43.7
British Virgin Islands	1987	108	4.0	0.2	3.2	3.8	6.0	29.8	11.4	41.6
Iles Vierges brit.	1988	121	3.6	0.2	3.1	4.0	6.1	28.3	11.9	42.8
	1989	141	3.4	0.2	3.0	3.7	6.7	27.9	15.0	40.1
Brunei Darussalam	1996	7 886	2.5	34.7[10]	...	1.0	5.8	11.9	4.8	39.3
Brunéi Darussalam	1997	8 268	2.6	33.6[10]	...	1.0	6.2	12.1	4.9	39.6
	1998	8 331	2.8	31.6[10]	...	1.1	6.5	12.6	5.1	40.4
Bulgaria [1]	1998	19 203 204	21.1	1.5	19.1	4.3	3.7	9.7	8.2	32.3
Bulgarie [1]	1999	19 890 889	17.3	1.7	16.6	4.8	3.7	9.7	8.7	37.5
	2000	22 532 628	14.5	1.7	17.4	5.0	3.6	11.7	10.5	35.5
Burkina Faso	1991	780 492	33.8	0.9	14.2	0.9	5.7	1.7	4.1	...
Burkina Faso	1992	782 551	32.7	0.9	19.5	1.1	5.7	1.6	4.2	...
	1993	808 487	33.9	0.8	14.7	1.3	5.6	1.7	4.4	...
Burundi	1988	149 067	48.9	1.0[6]	16.5	...	2.9	12.9	2.6	15.2
Burundi	1989	175 627	47.0	1.2[6]	18.5	...	3.3	10.8	3.3	16.0
	1990	192 050	52.4	0.8[6]	16.8	...	3.4	4.9	3.1	18.5
Cambodia	1997	8 735 386	44.2	0.2	11.3	0.5	4.8	17.4	6.1	15.6
Cambodge	1998	10 076 543	43.8	0.2	13.4	0.5	4.1	16.5	5.8	15.8
	1999	10 974 385	41.4	0.2	13.7	0.4	5.4	16.9	6.5	15.6
Cameroon [1][8]	1996	4 467 110	22.0	5.5	21.3	0.9	3.2	21.0	5.2	20.9
Cameroun [1][8]	1997	5 013 530	23.6	5.6	21.3	0.8	2.1	19.9	5.8	20.8
	1998	5 362 130	23.6	5.6	21.3	0.8	2.1	19.9	5.8	20.8
Canada [1]	1995	699 685[4]	2.8	4.0	19.2	3.6	5.1	13.4	7.5	44.5
Canada [1]	1996	722 775[4]	2.9	4.7	18.8	3.6	5.1	13.2	7.4	44.3
	1997	761 852[4]	2.5	4.5	18.9	3.4	5.4	13.7	7.5	44.1
Cape Verde	1993	27 264	14.7	1.0	7.5	1.4	11.6	17.8	18.9	27.0
Cap−Vert	1994	31 175	13.8	0.9	7.5	1.4	11.1	18.9	20.2	26.2
	1995	35 256	14.6	1.1	7.3	1.9	10.1	18.6	18.0	28.5
Cayman Islands	1989	473	0.4	0.6	1.9	3.2	11.0	24.5	11.0	47.6
Iles Caïmanes	1990	580	0.3	0.3	1.6	3.1	9.7	24.5	10.9	49.8
	1991	605	0.3	0.3	1.5	3.1	9.1	22.8	10.7	52.1
Central African Rep.	1983	243 350	40.8	2.5	7.8	0.5	2.1	21.2[3]	4.2	20.8
Rép. centrafricaine	1984	268 725	40.7	2.8	8.1	0.9	2.7	21.7[3]	4.3	18.8
	1985	308 549	42.4	2.5	7.5	0.8	2.6	22.0[3]	4.2	17.9
Chad	1992	297 361[4]	34.7	0.3	18.1	0.7	1.2	34.3[11]	...	10.7[12]
Tchad	1993	250 850[4]	32.1	0.2	18.7	0.9	1.1	33.8[11]	...	13.1[12]
	1994	347 578[4]	29.4	0.3	17.9	0.7	1.6	40.1[11]	...	10.0[12]
Chile	1996	26 361 928[5]	7.2	7.5	20.4	3.2	7.6	13.6	7.6	33.0
Chili	1997	29 476 765[5]	7.1	6.9	20.3	3.1	8.2	13.7	7.9	32.7
	1998	31 767 117[5]	7.2	4.5	19.2	2.9	8.5	14.8	8.3	34.6
China ††	1995	5 847 810	20.5	...	42.3[6][7]	...	6.5	8.4	5.2	17.0
Chine ††	1996	6 788 460	20.4	...	42.8[6][7]	...	6.7	8.2	5.1	16.8
	1997	7 477 240	18.7	...	42.5[6][7]	...	6.7	8.4	6.1	17.7
China, Hong Kong SAR †	1997	1 323 198[4]	0.1	0.0	6.0	2.2	5.4	23.7	8.5	54.0
Chine, Hong Kong RAS †	1998	1 260 422[4]	0.1	0.0	5.6	2.7	5.5	22.9	8.7	54.5
	1999	1 247 790[4]	0.1	0.0	5.3	2.8	5.2	22.8	8.8	55.1

24
Value added by kind of economic activity at current prices
Percentage distribution *[cont.]*
Valeur ajoutée par genre d'activité économique aux prix courants
Répartition en pourcentage *[suite]*

% of Value added − % de la valeur ajoutée

Country or area Pays ou zone	Year Année	Value added (Mil. nat.cur.) Valeur ajoutée (Mil. mon.nat.)	Agriculture, hunting, forestry & fishing Agriculture, chasse, sylviculture et pêche	Mining & quarrying Industries extractives	Manufac− turing Industries manufac− turières	Electricity, gas and water Electricité, gaz et eau	Con− struc− tion Con− struc− tion	Wholesale/ retail trade, restaurants and hotels Commerce, restaurants, hôtels	Transport, storage & commu− nication Transports, entrepôts, communi− cations	Other activities Autres activités
Colombia [1]	1995	82 058 289	14.4	4.0	15.2	3.2	7.7	12.4	7.4	35.7
Colombie [1]	1996	99 204 630	13.0	4.2	14.6	3.4	6.7	12.0	7.0	39.1
	1997	119 370 200	12.9	3.6	14.1	3.5	6.5	11.6	7.2	40.8
Comoros	1989	64 731	40.0	...	3.9	0.8	3.4	25.1	3.9	22.8
Comores	1990	67 992	40.4	...	4.1	0.9	3.1	25.1	4.1	22.3
	1991	71 113	40.8	...	4.2	0.9	2.7	25.1	4.2	22.1
Congo	1987	678 106	12.2	22.9	8.8	1.6	3.2	15.1	10.5	25.8
Congo	1988	643 830	14.2	17.1	8.8	2.0	2.7	16.7	11.3	27.2
	1989	757 088	13.3	28.6	7.2	1.9	1.8	14.7	9.3	23.3
Cook Islands	1984	44	14.9	0.2	4.8	1.0	2.1	25.4	10.3	41.3
Iles Cook	1985	53	14.1	0.1	4.5	0.1	2.6	25.6	10.6	42.3
	1986	64	12.5	0.1	5.0	1.1	3.7	22.6	12.0	43.1
Costa Rica [1]	1997	2 774 612	12.8	0.1	21.9	3.0	3.7	18.7	8.8	31.1
Costa Rica [1]	1998	3 358 182	· 12.4	0.1	22.8	2.7	4.1	18.9	8.5	30.5
	1999	4 105 111	10.3	0.2	28.8	2.5	4.1	17.3	8.2	28.7
Côte d'Ivoire	1994	4 551 000	25.6	0.2	17.6	1.7	1.8	...	6.0	18.7
Côte d'Ivoire	1995	5 110 000	26.6	0.3	18.1	1.7	2.2	...	5.4	18.0
	1996	5 684 000	27.2	0.4	19.0	1.7	2.6	...	5.0	17.1
Croatia [1]	1998	116 293	9.4	0.6	21.2	3.2[32]	6.6	14.9	8.4	35.6
Croatie [1]	1999	122 948	9.2	0.5	21.5	3.1[32]	6.5	14.5	8.5	36.2
	2000	136 480	· 9.1	25.8[6 10]	...	...	5.6	15.1	9.2	35.2
Cuba	1996	22 392[4]	6.9	1.5	37.4	2.2	5.3	21.3	4.5	21.0
Cuba	1997	22 601[4]	6.8	1.5	37.2	2.2	5.4	21.4	4.5	21.1
	1998	23 515[4]	6.3	1.5	37.9	2.0	5.5	21.4	4.5	20.9
Cyprus	1997	4 162	4.3	0.3	11.8	2.1	8.4	22.1	8.6	42.5
Chypre	1998	4 497	4.4	0.3	11.3	2.1	8.0	22.4	8.9	42.6
	1999	4 820	4.2	0.3	10.8	2.0	7.7	22.3	8.7	49.6
Czech Republic [1]	1997	1 548 900	4.7	2.0	28.6	3.8	8.6	14.0	7.8	30.5
République tchèque [1]	1998	1 672 100	...	...	...	...	8.0	...	9.3	15.7
	1999	1 677 600	...	...	...	...	7.5	...	9.7	15.8
Denmark [1]	1997	985 673	3.3	1.4	16.8	2.5	4.5	14.7	7.9	48.9
Danemark [1]	1998	1 026 370	2.9	0.9	16.5	2.2	5.0	14.7	8.2	49.0
	1999	1 083 721	2.7	1.2	15.8	2.1	4.7	14.7	8.0	49.6
Djibouti	1996	75 617[4]	3.5	0.2	2.9	6.8[13]	5.7	16.0	22.0	43.9
Djibouti	1997	75 111[4]	3.6	0.2	2.9	6.6[13]	6.1	16.3	23.4	42.1
	1998	77 401[4]	3.6	0.2	2.8	5.3[13]	6.5	16.6	26.3	39.9
Dominica	1989	367[4]	24.4	0.8	6.7	2.7	6.8	11.9	14.7	32.1
Dominique	1990	402[4]	24.1	0.8	6.6	2.8	7.0	12.1	14.9	31.8
	1991	427[4]	23.8	0.9	6.4	3.0	6.8	12.3	15.2	31.6
Dominican Republic [1]	1994	165 808	10.8	1.1	20.2[14 15]	1.4	7.7	16.4[3]	9.8	32.6
Rép. dominicaine [1]	1995	193 436	10.1	1.3	19.6[14 15]	1.7	7.7	17.3[3]	9.0	33.3
	1996	228 022	8.9	1.0	19.3[14 15]	1.8	7.3	20.4[3]	8.8	32.5
Ecuador	1998	103 676 217[5]	12.5	5.8[16]	22.7	0.3	5.1	20.9	9.9	22.8
Equateur	1999	156 065 932[5]	12.6	11.8[16]	22.0	0.3	4.7	19.0	9.7	20.0
	2000	329 698 057[5]	11.6	16.7[16]	20.3	0.3	4.5	18.2	9.4	19.0
Egypt [8]	1989	81 341	19.5	4.8[29]	18.0	1.3[17]	5.5	21.9	9.2	19.8
Egypte [8]	1990	103 344	17.2	10.6[29]	16.9	1.4[17]	5.1	21.0	10.5	17.3
	1991	125 485	16.5	10.6[29]	17.1	1.6[17]	4.8	21.2	11.3	16.8
El Salvador	1997	94 567[5]	13.8	0.5	21.6	1.6	4.4	20.2[3]	8.1	29.7
El Salvador	1998	102 001[5]	12.4	0.4	22.0	2.1	4.5	19.8[3]	8.3	30.4
	1999	106 500[5]	11.0	0.4	23.0	1.9	4.5	19.5[3]	8.6	31.0
Equatorial Guinea	1989	40 948	56.1	...	1.3	3.1	3.7	8.8	2.0	25.0
Guinée équatoriale	1990	42 765	53.6	...	1.3	3.4	3.8	7.6	2.2	28.0
	1991	43 932	53.1	...	1.4	3.1	3.0	7.6	1.9	30.0
Estonia [1]	1998	65 918	6.3	1.2	16.4	3.7	6.4	17.7	13.8	34.5
Estonie [1]	1999	68 283	5.7	1.2	15.2	3.5	5.4	17.3	14.5	37.2
	2000	75 578	5.3	1.2	16.6	3.4	5.6	17.4	14.9	35.6

24
Value added by kind of economic activity at current prices
Percentage distribution [cont.]
      Valeur ajoutée par genre d'activité économique aux prix courants
      Répartition en pourcentage [suite]

% of Value added − % de la valeur ajoutée

Country or area Pays ou zone	Year Année	Value added (Mil. nat.cur.) Valeur ajoutée (Mil. mon.nat.)	Agriculture, hunting, forestry & fishing Agriculture, chasse, sylviculture et pêche	Mining & quarrying Industries extractives	Manufac− turing Industries manufac− turières	Electricity, gas and water Electricité, gaz et eau	Con− struc− tion Con− struc− tion	Wholesale/ retail trade, restaurants and hotels Commerce, restaurants, hôtels	Transport, storage & commu− nication Transports, entrepôts, communi− cations	Other activities Autres activités
Ethiopia incl. Eritrea [18]	1990	11 436[4]	41.1	0.2	11.1	1.5	3.6	9.6	7.2	25.7
Ethiopie y comp. Eryth. [18]	1991	12 295[4]	41.0	0.3	10.3	1.5	3.2	9.4	7.1	27.3
	1992	12 544[4]	50.3	0.3	9.1	1.3	2.8	10.2	5.4	20.6
Fiji	1987	1 399[4]	21.9	2.2	11.2	3.1	3.6	14.9	9.5	33.5
Fidji	1988	1 518[4]	18.4	4.1	9.0	3.4	4.0	18.6	10.7	31.8
	1989	1 759[4]	18.5	3.2	9.9	3.1	3.8	21.5	9.6	30.3
Finland [1]	1997	562 722	4.2	0.3	24.3	2.4	4.6	12.1	9.8	42.3
Finlande [1]	1998	609 714	3.8	0.3	25.1	2.3	5.0	12.0	10.0	41.6
	1999	638 749	3.6	0.3	24.3	2.1	5.5	12.1	10.1	42.1
France	1995	7 349 082	2.5	0.4	20.1	2.4	4.7	15.8	5.9	48.1
France	1996	7 505 238	2.4	0.4	20.0	2.5	4.5	15.6	5.9	48.6
	1997	7 747 705	2.4	0.4	20.3	2.4	4.5	15.4	5.9	48.8
French Guiana	1990	6 454	10.1	7.6	...	0.7	12.8	13.5	7.7	47.5
Guyane française	1991	7 385	7.4	7.6	...	0.5	12.1	13.1	12.3	47.0
	1992	8 052	7.2	9.0	...	0.6	10.8	11.9	11.4	49.1
French Polynesia	1991	305 211	4.1	...	7.5	1.8	5.7	...	...	29.3
Polynésie française	1992	314 265	3.8	...	7.5	2.1	5.9	...	...	29.5
	1993	329 266	3.9	...	6.7	2.1	5.7	...	...	29.0
Gabon	1987	986 000	10.9	28.4	7.1[15]	2.7	7.2	9.2	8.1	26.5
Gabon	1988	965 700	11.2	22.6	7.3[15]	3.0	5.2	14.4	9.1	27.3
	1989	1 128 400	10.4	32.3	5.7[15]	2.5	5.5	12.4	8.2	23.1
Gambia [8]	1991	2 962	22.3	0.0	5.5	0.9	4.4	39.1	10.9	17.0
Gambie [8]	1992	3 100	18.4	0.0	5.7	1.0	4.7	41.7	11.2	17.4
	1993	3 296	20.2	0.0	5.1	1.0	4.5	38.3	12.5	18.4
Georgia [1]	1998	4 843	27.8	...	17.7[6 7]	...	4.8	13.3	10.9	25.5
Géorgie [1]	1999	5 391	26.0	...	18.4[6 7]	...	3.9	15.0	12.1	24.5
	2000	5 656	21.1	...	18.6[6 7]	...	4.0	17.6	13.3	25.4
Germany [1]	1997	3 441 010	1.3	0.3	22.3	2.3	6.0	11.7	5.7	50.4
Allemagne [1]	1998	3 547 540	1.2	0.3	22.5	2.3	5.6	11.9	5.7	50.6
	1999	3 612 620	1.2	0.3	22.3	2.0	5.3	11.6	5.6	51.7
Ghana	1994	4 686 000	42.0	6.3	10.1	3.0	8.3	6.4	4.8	19.2
Ghana	1995	7 040 200	42.7	5.3	10.3	2.9	8.3	6.5	4.3	19.8
	1996	10 067 000	43.9	5.3	9.7	3.0	8.5	6.5	4.2	18.9
Greece [1]	1997	30 169 626	8.5	0.6	12.2	2.0	7.3	21.5	6.3	41.6
Grèce [1]	1998	32 635 985	8.1	0.6	11.6	2.2	7.5	21.8	6.5	41.6
	1999	34 485 641	7.7	0.5	11.7	2.3	8.3	21.5	6.4	41.6
Grenada	1989	393[4]	18.7	0.4	5.3	2.9	10.3	18.8	13.9	34.4
Grenade	1990	440[4]	16.2	0.4	5.1	3.0	10.1	18.7	13.7	32.8
	1991	463[4]	14.9	0.4	5.3	3.1	10.4	19.5	14.3	32.1
Guadeloupe	1990	15 036	6.7	5.4[10]	...	1.0	7.4	18.3	5.9	55.2
Guadeloupe	1991	16 278	7.3	6.1[10]	...	1.4	7.0	16.5	6.0	55.5
	1992	17 968	6.7	6.9[10]	...	1.7	6.5	16.2	7.9	54.1
Guinea−Bissau	1989	358 875	44.6	7.9[6 10]	...	...	9.7	25.7	3.6	8.5
Guinée−Bissau	1990	510 094	44.6	8.2[6 10]	...	...	10.0	25.7	3.7	7.8
	1991	854 985	44.7	8.5[6 10]	...	...	8.4	25.8	3.9	8.7
Guyana	1997	89 744[4]	43.2	17.3	3.7[6]	...	5.0	4.3[3]	5.8	20.7
Guyana	1998	90 471[4]	40.5	16.0	3.5[6]	...	5.4	4.6[3]	6.9	23.1
	1999	102 098[4]	41.7	13.6	3.6[6]	...	4.7	4.2[3]	7.0	25.3
Honduras	1995	32 626[4]	21.5	1.9	17.8	5.4	5.5	12.0	4.7	31.0
Honduras	1996	41 171[4]	22.3	1.9	18.1	6.2	4.6	11.9	4.4	30.6
	1997	52 872[4]	22.6	1.7	18.0	6.2	4.3	11.8	4.8	30.4
Hungary [1]	1997	7 555 986	5.9	0.4	23.9	3.8	4.6	13.5	9.7	38.2
Hongrie [1]	1998	8 873 463	5.5	0.3	24.1	3.9	4.6	13.5	9.9	38.3
	1999	9 994 623	4.9	0.3	23.8	3.9	4.6	13.4	10.2	39.0
Iceland [1]	1995	382 754	11.7	0.1	16.4	3.9	7.1	14.1	8.8	31.9
Islande [1]	1996	412 033	11.4	0.1	16.4	3.7	6.6	14.3	8.5	32.5
	1997	448 828	9.6	0.1	16.9	3.8	7.1	13.3	7.8	34.3

24

Value added by kind of economic activity at current prices
Percentage distribution *[cont.]*
Valeur ajoutée par genre d'activité économique aux prix courants
Répartition en pourcentage *[suite]*

			% of Value added – % de la valeur ajoutée							
Country or area Pays ou zone	Year Année	Value added (Mil. nat.cur.) Valeur ajoutée (Mil. mon.nat.)	Agriculture, hunting, forestry & fishing Agriculture, chasse, sylviculture et pêche	Mining & quarrying Industries extractives	Manufac– turing Industries manufac– turières	Electricity, gas and water Electricité, gaz et eau	Con– struc– tion Con– struc– tion	Wholesale/ retail trade, restaurants and hotels Commerce, restaurants, hôtels	Transport, storage & commu– nication Transports, entrepôts, communi– cations	Other activities Autres activités
India [19] Inde [19]	1996	12 691 470[4]	28.8	2.2	18.3	2.5	5.1	13.8	6.7	22.6
	1997	14 209 410[4]	27.5	2.3	17.7	2.4	5.6	13.8	7.0	23.7
	1998	16 509 650[4]	28.6	2.0	16.5	2.4	5.7	13.3	6.9	24.5
Indonesia Indonésie	1996	532 567 000[20]	16.7	8.7	25.6	1.3	7.9	16.4[3]	6.6	17.0
	1997	627 695 000[20]	16.1	8.9	26.8	1.2	7.5	15.9[3]	6.1	17.6
	1998	1 002 334 000[20]	18.1	13.7	24.5	1.1	5.6	16.7[3]	5.2	15.2
Iran (Islamic Rep. of) [1] [21] Iran (Rép. islamique d') [1] [21]	1997	284 205 500	14.2	14.9	13.7	1.0	4.4	16.1	8.3	27.3
	1998	321 306 100	16.5	9.5	13.7	1.1	4.0	17.1	7.8	30.4
	1999	431 360 300	14.2	15.4	13.4	1.0	3.9	15.6	7.8	28.7
Iraq Iraq	1993	146 912[4]	30.9	0.1	5.5	0.3	5.3	24.4[22]	13.0	20.5
	1994	721 603[4]	42.1	0.0	3.2	0.1	1.3	27.2[22]	14.8	11.3
	1995	2 320 671[4]	54.1	–0.1	3.8	0.0	1.2	8.8[22]	22.2	10.0
Ireland [1] Irlande [1]	1996	40 802	6.8	0.8	28.7	1.8	5.4	13.6	5.7	37.2
	1997	46 926	5.6	0.9	30.1	1.7	5.7	13.6	5.6	36.8
	1998	54 461	4.7	0.6	30.7	1.5	6.1	13.2	5.7	37.6
Israel Israël	1995	204 335	2.3	17.8[10]	...	1.1	8.0	11.4	7.2	52.2
	1996	236 833	2.0	17.5[10]	...	1.0	8.1	11.2	6.4	53.7
	1997	242 650	2.0	19.5[10]	...	1.1	0.8	11.9	6.5	58.2
Italy [1] Italie [1]	1997	1 856 824 000	3.1	0.5	21.2	2.1	4.9	16.8	7.2	44.2
	1998	1 920 288 000	3.0	0.4	21.3	2.2	4.8	16.8	7.4	44.0
	1999	1 966 976 000	3.0	0.5	20.8	2.3	4.8	16.9	7.5	44.3
Jamaica [1] Jamaïque [1]	1997	240 462[5]	7.3	5.1	14.9	3.0	10.6	21.0	9.5	28.4
	1998	254 053[5]	7.3	4.4	14.0	3.2	10.3	21.0	10.2	29.5
	1999	276 974[5]	6.6	4.1	13.9	3.6	10.4	20.2	10.4	30.7
Japan Japon	1996	520 832 400	1.8	0.2	23.5	2.7	9.9	11.6[3]	6.4	44.0
	1997	530 188 000	1.6	0.2	23.5	2.8	9.4	11.6[3]	6.3	44.6
	1998	519 201 600	1.7	0.2	22.6	2.9	8.9	11.3[3]	6.3	46.2
Jordan Jordanie	1993	3 271[4]	5.9	3.3	13.1	2.4	8.7	9.7	14.9	41.9
	1994	3 626[4]	5.3	2.8	15.5	2.3	8.3	10.4	14.3	40.9
	1995	3 955[4]	4.3	4.0	14.7	2.5	7.5	10.5	14.5	41.9
Kazakhstan [1] Kazakhstan [1]	1995	976 600	12.8	0.6	33.1[6]	...	6.7	17.9	11.1	17.8
	1996	1 356 000	12.7	0.4	31.9[6]	...	4.6	18.0	11.8	20.6
	1997	1603 300	11.9	0.5	32.3[6]	...	4.4	16.3	12.2	22.4
Kenya Kenya	1997	28 784[4]	25.5	0.1	9.5	1.1	3.7	19.1	7.3	30.3
	1998	32 057[4]	24.5	0.1	9.7	0.8	3.7	20.0	6.7	30.5
	1999	34 246[4]	21.8	0.1	10.1	0.8	4.0	22.6	6.5	29.8
Korea, Republic of [1] Corée, Rép. de [1]	1997	455 590 846[5]	5.3	0.4	28.7	2.1	11.6	11.4	6.5	33.9
	1998	448 988 063[5]	4.9	0.4	30.5	2.4	10.0	10.2	7.0	34.6
	1999	487 906 668[5]	5.0	0.4	31.5	2.6	8.7	10.8	7.0	34.1
Kuwait Koweït	1995	8 022	0.4	39.1	11.1	–0.4	3.0	7.7	4.5	34.5
	1996	9 421	0.4	43.8	11.7	–0.1	2.6	6.7	4.2	30.7
	1997	9 402	0.4	39.2	13.1	0.1	2.6	6.9	4.5	33.2
Kyrgyzstan [1] Kirghizistan [1]	1998	31 444	39.2	0.2	18.0[6]	...	4.9	13.7	4.9	19.1
	1999	45 201	37.6	0.2	23.7[6]	...	3.3	13.9	5.2	16.2
	2000	57 909	39.4	0.2	23.4[6]	...	3.3	13.8	2.7	17.3
Latvia [1] Lettonie [1]	1998	3 096	4.3	0.2	17.9	5.3	6.9	18.1	16.7	30.7
	1999	3 411	4.5	0.1	15.3	4.4	7.1	18.9	15.3	34.3
	2000	3 820	4.5	0.1	14.5	3.9	6.8	19.3	16.2	34.8
Lebanon Liban	1982	12 600	8.5	...	13.0	5.4	3.4	28.3	3.7	37.5
	1994	15 038 000	12.0	...	...	...	9.4	28.7	2.8	8.3
	1995	17 982 000	12.4	...	...	...	9.2	30.1	2.8	7.4
Lesotho [1] Lesotho [1]	1997	4 293[4]	16.0	0.1	15.9	7.3	18.2	10.6	3.8	28.1
	1998	4 521[4]	17.4	0.1	17.2	5.0	15.8	10.3	3.6	30.7
	1999	5 182[4]	16.9	0.1	16.4	5.9	17.9	9.4	3.3	30.5
Liberia Libéria	1987	1 009[4]	37.8	10.4	7.2	1.9	3.2	6.0	7.5	26.0
	1988	1 080[4]	38.2	10.7	7.4	1.7	2.7	5.9	7.3	26.1
	1989	1 119[4]	36.7	10.9	7.3	1.7	2.4	5.7	7.1	28.3

24
Value added by kind of economic activity at current prices
Percentage distribution *[cont.]*
Valeur ajoutée par genre d'activité économique aux prix courants
Répartition en pourcentage *[suite]*

% of Value added − % de la valeur ajoutée

Country or area Pays ou zone	Year Année	Value added (Mil. nat.cur.) Valeur ajoutée (Mil. mon.nat.)	Agriculture, hunting, forestry & fishing Agriculture, chasse, sylviculture et pêche	Mining & quarrying Industries extractives	Manufacturing Industries manufacturières	Electricity, gas and water Electricité, gaz et eau	Construction Construction	Wholesale/retail trade, restaurants and hotels Commerce, restaurants, hôtels	Transport, storage & communication Transports, entrepôts, communications	Other activities Autres activités
Libyan Arab Jamah.	1983	8 482[4]	3.0	48.8[23]	3.2	0.9	10.4	6.1	4.6	23.0
Jamah. arabe libyenne	1984	7 681[4]	3.4	40.9[23]	3.9	1.2	11.1	7.9	5.3	26.4
	1985	8 050[4]	3.5	41.6[23]	4.5	1.3	11.4	7.0	5.0	25.8
Lithuania [1]	1998	38 035	10.3	0.5	18.8	4.6	8.6	17.8	9.6	30.0
Lithuanie [1]	1999	38 054	8.4	0.7	17.6	4.5	7.9	16.9	11.4	32.4
	2000	40 674	7.6	1.1	21.0	4.2	6.2	16.5	12.2	31.2
Luxembourg [1]	1997	629 667	0.9	0.1	13.0	1.3	5.6	12.5	9.6	57.0
Luxembourg [1]	1998	666 118	0.7	0.1	13.4	1.3	5.7	12.4	9.8	56.4
	1999	734 129	0.7	0.1	11.5	1.2	5.5	11.9	10.9	58.2
Madagascar	1983	1 187 400	44.2	15.6[6 10]	...	...	...	30.4	...	9.7
Madagascar	1984	1 323 100	43.9	16.2[6 10]	...	...	...	30.3	...	9.7
	1985	1 500 600	43.5	16.9[6 10]	...	...	...	30.1	...	9.5
Malawi	1984	1 322	37.4	...	18.6	1.8	2.0	6.8	4.9	28.6
Malawi	1985	1 540	34.7	...	17.5	1.5	2.2	12.8	4.8	26.4
	1986	1 694	34.5	...	20.3	1.2	2.0	11.5	3.5	27.1
Malaysia	1997	292 838	10.7	6.6	27.3	2.6	6.3	14.2	6.4	25.8
Malaisie	1998	301 554	12.5	6.4	27.0	2.8	4.9	14.4	6.6	25.5
	1999	313 518	10.2	6.5	30.2	2.8	4.5	13.9	6.7	25.2
Mali	1990	655 600	47.8	1.6	8.1[14]	3.8[24]	...	18.8	4.9	15.1
Mali	1991	662 500	46.1	1.7	6.9[14]	4.3[24]	...	20.2	5.0	15.9
	1992	707 000	47.2	1.5	7.0[14]	4.4[24]	...	19.3	5.0	15.6
Malta	1995	989[4]	2.8	3.5[24]	24.4	6.2	...	13.3[3]	6.7	43.1
Malte	1996	1 058[4]	2.9	3.4[24]	23.4	5.6	...	12.6[3]	6.4	45.2
	1997	1 111[4]	3.0	3.4[24]	22.7	6.7	...	12.2[3]	6.2	46.1
Marshall Islands	1995	105	14.9	0.3	2.6	2.0	10.2	17.0	6.2	46.8
Iles Marshall	1996	95	14.3	0.3	1.6	2.7	7.0	18.7	7.3	48.2
	1997	90	14.3	0.4	1.7	3.1	7.0	17.9	7.9	47.7
Martinique	1990	18 835	5.7	7.9[10]	...	2.5	4.9	18.9	6.2	53.9
Martinique	1991	20 377	5.7	7.8[10]	...	2.4	5.3	18.9	6.3	53.6
	1992	21 869	5.1	8.1[10]	...	2.2	5.2	18.4	6.5	54.5
Mauritania	1987	60 302[4]	32.3	8.3	12.1	...	6.3	13.0	5.1	22.8
Mauritanie	1988	65 069[4]	32.4	7.7	13.0	...	6.3	13.2	5.1	22.3
	1989	75 486[4]	34.2	10.4	10.3	...	6.4	...	4.9	14.5
Mauritius	1997	78 023[4]	8.5	0.2	23.4	2.0	5.8	16.9	11.4	31.8
Maurice	1998	87 991[4]	8.3	0.1	23.9	1.5	5.7	16.8	11.8	31.9
	1999	94 895[4]	5.2	0.1	24.0	1.2	6.0	17.5	12.2	33.8
Mexico [1]	1996	2 353 489	5.9	1.5	21.0	1.1	4.1	21.0	9.9	35.4
Mexique [1]	1997	2 915 601	5.5	1.5	21.1	1.2	4.4	21.0	10.4	34.9
	1998	3 554 791	5.2	1.3	21.1	1.2	4.6	19.8	10.7	36.1
Mongolia	1996	625 005	45.2	10.8	5.2	2.4	2.8	11.8	7.7	14.1
Mongolie	1997	792 989	37.6	15.0	5.7	3.2	2.3	16.4	8.1	12.1
	1998	775 578	39.5	8.8	5.0	4.3	2.6	15.3	10.4	14.2
Montserrat	1985	90[4]	4.8	1.3	5.7	3.7	7.9	18.0	11.5	47.2
Montserrat	1986	103[4]	4.3	1.4	5.6	3.7	11.3	18.7	11.6	43.4
	1987	118[4]	4.1	1.3	5.7	3.2	11.5	22.1	11.1	41.0
Morocco	1995	271 520	15.2	1.9	19.0	8.7[13 16]	4.6	13.9	6.4	30.2
Maroc	1996	310 240	19.9	1.8	17.6	8.2[13 16]	4.3	13.8	6.0	28.8
	1997	309 810	15.9	2.3	18.1	8.7[13 16]	4.8	13.9	6.4	30.3
Myanmar [19]	1996	791 980	60.1	0.6	7.1	0.3[17]	2.4	22.6[3]	3.5	3.4
Myanmar [19]	1997	1 109 554	59.4	0.6	7.1	0.1[17]	2.4	23.2[3]	3.9	3.1
	1998	1 559 996	59.1	0.5	7.2	0.1[17]	2.4	23.9[3]	4.0	2.7
Namibia [1]	1998	17 037	10.8	10.8	12.0	2.6	3.1	12.2	6.5	41.9
Namibie [1]	1999	18 843	10.5	11.2	11.1	2.7	2.6	12.3	6.6	42.8
	2000	21 691	12.7	12.7	11.0	2.4	3.0	12.2	6.5	39.5
Nepal [25]	1997	269 570[4]	40.4	0.6	9.2[26]	1.7	10.9	11.3	7.2	18.9
Népal [25]	1998	285 702[4]	39.4	0.5	9.3[26]	1.6	10.2	11.8	7.8	19.5
	1999	323 009[4]	40.1	0.5	9.1[26]	1.5	9.9	12.0	7.5	19.4

24

Value added by kind of economic activity at current prices
Percentage distribution [cont.]
Valeur ajoutée par genre d'activité économique aux prix courants
Répartition en pourcentage [suite]

Country or area Pays ou zone	Year Année	Value added (Mil. nat.cur.) Valeur ajoutée (Mil. mon.nat.)	Agriculture, hunting, forestry & fishing Agriculture, chasse, sylviculture et pêche	Mining & quarrying Industries extractives	Manufacturing Industries manufacturières	Electricity, gas and water Electricité, gaz et eau	Construction Construction	Wholesale/ retail trade, restaurants and hotels Commerce, restaurants, hôtels	Transport, storage & communication Transports, entrepôts, communications	Other activities Autres activités
Netherlands [1]	1997	676 874	3.1	2.9	17.1	1.7	5.4	14.8	7.4	47.7
Pays–Bas [1]	1998	714 347	3.0	2.4	17.1	1.7	5.4	14.9	7.6	48.3
	1999	748 807	2.7	1.9	16.8	1.7	5.8	15.1	7.4	49.6
Netherlands Antilles	1992	3 755	0.7[7]	...	6.9	4.2	6.1	25.3	11.6	45.3
Antilles néerlandaises	1993	3 994	0.8[7]	...	6.1	3.4	6.0	24.4	12.3	46.9
	1994	4 476	0.8[7]	...	6.3	2.8	5.7	24.1	13.8	46.4
New Caledonia	1994	306 748	1.9	7.4	6.6	1.5	6.0	23.0[3]	6.3	47.4
Nouvelle–Calédonie	1995	329 296	1.8	8.7	6.0	1.5	5.7	22.2[3]	6.3	47.7
	1996	335 482	1.7	8.5	5.7	1.6	5.0	22.8[3]	6.7	47.8
New Zealand [19]	1993	77 599	8.7	1.5	18.7	3.0	3.4	16.2	8.4	40.3
Nouvelle–Zélande [19]	1994	83 096	7.8	1.3	19.3	2.9	3.7	16.6	8.5	40.0
	1995	87 808	7.5	1.2	18.9	2.7	3.8	16.6	8.7	40.6
Nicaragua	1996	16 204	32.6	0.8	16.2	1.2	3.9	23.5	3.5	18.3
Nicaragua	1997	18 601	32.6	0.8	15.9	1.2	4.1	23.4	3.5	18.5
	1998	22 881	35.3	0.9	14.9	1.2	4.2	22.5	3.4	17.7
Niger	1985	627 027	37.9	8.3	7.4	2.3	3.6	16.3	4.4	19.9
Niger	1986	622 426	37.3	7.6	7.9	2.6	4.6	14.6	4.2	21.1
	1987	632 248	34.6	7.8	9.0	2.8	5.3	14.1	4.3	22.2
Nigeria	1992	549 809[4]	26.5	46.6	5.7	0.3	1.1	11.5[27]	1.7	6.7
Nigéria	1993	701 473[4]	33.1	35.9	6.2	0.2	1.1	14.6[27]	2.2	6.8
	1994	914 334[4]	38.2	25.0	7.1	0.2	1.1	17.5[27]	3.5	7.3
Norway	1995	831 067	2.8	13.4	13.4	2.8	3.8	11.9	10.5	41.4
Norvège	1996	911 370	2.4	17.2	12.5	2.3	3.9	11.3	10.2	40.2
	1997	970 655	2.2	16.8	12.4	2.4	4.2	11.5	10.3	40.1
Oman [1]	1997	6 202[5]	2.6	39.7	3.9	1.1	3.1	13.3	6.7	29.6
Oman [1]	1998	5 532[5]	2.8	30.5	4.5	1.2	3.7	16.1	8.1	33.0
	1999	6 117[5]	2.6	38.9	4.2	1.2	2.3	13.3	7.1	30.4
Pakistan [8]	1997	2 480 884[4]	27.3	0.5	15.8	3.8	3.6	15.2[3]	10.2	23.5
Pakistan [8]	1998	2 711 078[4]	27.2	0.5	15.6	4.0	3.3	15.2[3]	10.2	24.0
	1999	2 922 924[4]	26.1	0.6	15.3	4.1	3.3	15.1[3]	10.5	25.0
Panama	1997	8 693[5]	6.9	0.3	8.7	3.6	4.3	20.8	13.9	41.4
Panama	1998	9 391[5]	7.0	0.4	8.0	3.4	4.6	19.4	14.8	42.4
	1999	9 634[5]	6.7	0.5	7.6	3.7	5.0	17.9	15.8	42.7
Papua New Guinea	1989	2 964	28.9	11.9	11.4	1.7	5.4	11.1[3]	5.5	24.2
Papouasie–Nouv.– Guinée	1990	2 996	29.7	15.1	9.2	1.7	5.2	9.9[3]	6.4	22.8
	1991	3 515	26.6	17.4	9.8	1.7	6.4	10.2[3]	6.9	20.9
Paraguay	1993	11 991 719	24.5	0.4	16.5	3.4	5.9	30.4[3]	3.9	15.0
Paraguay	1994	14 960 131	23.7	0.4	15.7	3.9	6.0	30.5[3]	3.9	15.9
	1995	17 699 000	24.8	0.3	15.7	4.3	6.0	29.5[3]	3.7	15.8
Peru	1996	149 092	7.0	1.9	22.1	1.6	10.8	16.9	5.0	34.7
Pérou	1997	174 201	6.5	1.9	21.8	1.7	11.5	16.8	5.2	34.6
	1998	185 055	6.6	1.7	21.4	1.8	11.3	16.7	5.3	35.3
Philippines	1997	2 426 743	18.9	0.7	22.3	2.7	6.4	14.9[3]	4.9	29.2
Philippines	1998	2 678 187	17.4	0.8	21.8	2.9	5.9	15.4[3]	5.2	30.8
	1999	2 996 371	17.6	0.6	21.5	2.9	5.4	15.9[3]	5.3	30.7
Poland [1]	1997	412 870	5.5	3.5	22.4	3.4	7.9	22.1	6.5	28.7
Pologne [1]	1998	485 177	4.8	2.9	21.5	3.2	8.7	21.8	6.4	30.8
	1999	536 565	3.9	2.6	21.0	3.5	8.8	22.1	6.6	31.5
Portugal	1993	13 270 959	3.8	23.8	26.1	4.1	6.0	16.8	5.8	...
Portugal	1994	14 190 807	4.1	...	26.4	4.0	6.0	16.6	5.9	36.8
	1995	15 294 193	4.1	...	26.2	3.9	6.4	16.5	6.1	36.9
Puerto Rico [8]	1997	54 848	0.8	0.1	41.9	2.5	2.6[28]	14.4	4.8	33.0
Porto Rico [8]	1998	60 427	0.6	0.1	44.1	2.1	2.6[28]	14.1	4.5	32.0
	1999	63 326	0.7	0.1	43.3	2.3	2.9[28]	14.4	4.1	32.3
Qatar	1997	41 958	0.7	41.4	8.1	1.1	6.8	6.6	3.5	31.7
Qatar	1998	38 361	0.7	33.9	7.7	1.6	7.1	8.2	4.9	36.0
	1999	45 432	0.6	43.9	7.2	1.4	4.8	7.1	4.3	30.8

24
Value added by kind of economic activity at current prices
Percentage distribution *[cont.]*
       Valeur ajoutée par genre d'activité économique aux prix courants
       Répartition en pourcentage *[suite]*

% of Value added − % de la valeur ajoutée

Country or area Pays ou zone	Year Année	Value added (Mil. nat.cur.) Valeur ajoutée (Mil. mon.nat.)	Agriculture, hunting, forestry & fishing Agriculture, chasse, sylviculture et pêche	Mining & quarrying Industries extractives	Manufac- turing Industries manufac- turières	Electricity, gas and water Electricité, gaz et eau	Con- struc- tion Con- struc- tion	Wholesale/ retail trade, restaurants and hotels Commerce, restaurants, hôtels	Transport, storage & commu- nication Transports, entrepôts, communi- cations	Other activities Autres activités
Republic of Moldova [1]	1998	8 154	28.8	0.2	15.6	2.8	3.5	12.4	8.2	28.4
Rép. de Moldova [1]	1999	11 692	26.2	0.2	13.8	3.9	3.5	17.0	8.7	26.7
	2000	14 963	26.2	0.2	16.2	2.4	2.8	15.3	9.6	27.3
Réunion	1990	27 417	4.0	9.1[10]	...	4.7	5.9	20.5	4.0	51.7
Réunion	1991	30 371	3.7	9.1[10]	...	4.1	7.1	19.9	4.6	51.5
	1992	32 832	3.5	9.0[10]	...	4.1	6.8	20.0	4.5	52.2
Romania [1]	1998	332 699 900	16.1	30.4[6][10]	...	...	5.9	15.2	9.7	22.7
Roumanie [1]	1999	469 591 100	15.5	30.9[6][10]	...	...	5.4	...	...	48.3
	2000	719 834 100	12.6	30.5[6][10]	...	...	5.3	...	...	51.5
Russian Federation [1]	1998	2 494 800	5.7	...	30.0[6][7]	...	7.1	18.9	11.2	27.0
Fédération de Russie [1]	1999	4 147 400	6.9	...	32.7[6][7]	...	5.9	22.0	10.2	22.3
	2000	5 427 400	8.3	...	37.6[6][7]	...	7.8	24.4	9.7	12.3
Rwanda	1987	166 760	39.2	0.2	15.0	0.6	7.2	14.2	7.1	16.5
Rwanda	1988	171 700	39.3	0.2	14.5	0.7	7.1	13.2	7.4	17.6
	1989	184 380	41.1	0.4	13.5	0.5	7.0	13.2	7.0	17.3
Saint Kitts−Nevis	1997	671[4]	5.2	0.3	9.7	1.8	10.4	22.5	7.0	43.2
Saint−Kitts−et−Nevis	1998	697[4]	3.9	0.3	9.2	1.8	11.5	23.0	6.8	43.6
	1999	731[4]	3.4	0.3	9.7	1.8	12.2	22.3	7.0	43.4
Saint Lucia	1996	1 409[4]	8.2	0.4	6.2	3.6	7.1	24.7	17.4	32.4
Sainte−Lucie	1997	1 454[4]	7.0	0.4	5.8	3.7	7.0	25.4	17.7	32.9
	1998	1 544[4]	7.5	0.4	5.3	4.1	7.2	25.6	17.3	32.6
Saint Vincent−Grenadines	1997	706[4]	9.5	0.3	7.4	5.4	11.9	17.1	20.3	28.2
St.−Vincent−et−Gren.	1998	764[4]	10.2	0.3	6.5	5.4	13.4	17.4	19.6	27.2
.	1999	790[4]	10.0	0.3	5.9	5.6	12.3	18.4	19.7	27.8
Sao Tome and Principe	1986	2 259	29.2	...	2.3	0.3	3.4	19.4	5.3	40.1
Sao Tomé−et−Principe	1987	2 797	31.5	...	1.3	1.4	3.8	17.1	5.6	39.2
	1988	3 800	32.1	...	1.7	1.0	4.2	18.8	4.1	38.1
Saudi Arabia [8]	1997	545 481	6.1	37.3	9.3	0.2	8.5	6.8	6.0	25.8
Arabie saoudite [8]	1998	477 210	7.1	27.6	10.0	0.2	9.9	7.8	7.0	30.4
	1999	519 419	6.6	31.8	9.6	0.2	9.3	7.2	6.6	28.7
Senegal	1996	2 380 000	20.6	0.8	12.8	2.2	3.6	26.3	10.0	23.6
Sénégal	1997	2 555 000	20.0	1.1	12.5	2.2	3.8	26.7	10.9	22.7
	1998	2 753 000	18.2	1.0	12.8	2.2	4.0	27.7	11.1	23.0
Seychelles	1997	2 845	3.3	...	14.3[7][14]	3.0	7.5	9.5	40.0	22.4
Seychelles	1998	3 060	3.0	...	14.4[7][14]	3.0	9.0	8.8	40.3	21.5
	1999	3 157	3.2	...	15.5[7][14]	3.1	10.9	8.2	37.6	21.6
Sierra Leone [8]	1988	42 364	39.3	6.3	7.7	0.3	2.6	20.9	10.5	12.3
Sierra Leone [8]	1989	81 921	37.3	7.0	7.1	0.2	1.9	25.0	10.8	10.6
	1990	148 652	35.3	9.5	8.7	0.1	1.3	20.3	8.9	15.9
Singapore [1]	1997	148 436	0.2[7]	...	21.8	2.0	9.0	17.2	10.6	39.2
Singapour [1]	1998	146 630	0.2[7]	...	21.8	2.1	9.5	16.1	10.6	39.7
	1999	153 796	0.2[7]	...	24.2	1.8	7.5	16.6	10.7	39.0
Slovakia [1]	1997	632 861	5.0	1.0	24.4	3.7	7.5	22.5	10.4	34.8
Slovaquie [1]	1998	680 357	4.6	0.9	24.5	2.7	7.1	...	10.9	17.8
	1999	736 202	4.5	1.0	24.2	4.1	5.8	...	11.1	18.4
Slovenia [1]	1998	2 857 241[4]	4.1	1.3	27.4	3.4	5.6	14.4	8.2	35.8
Slovénie [1]	1999	3 179 760[4]	3.6	1.2	27.0	3.1	6.2	14.5	8.1	36.3
	2000	3 562 382[4]	3.2	1.0	27.2	3.2	6.0	14.5	7.9	36.9
Solomon Islands	1984	199	53.5	−0.2	3.6	0.9	3.8	10.6	5.2	22.6
Iles Salomon	1985	213	50.4	−0.7	3.8	1.0	4.2	10.4	5.1	25.8
	1986	224	48.3	−1.2	4.5	1.2	5.1	8.4	5.8	27.9
Somalia	1985	84 050[4]	66.1	0.3	4.9	0.1	2.2	10.1	6.7	9.5
Somalie	1986	112 584[4]	62.5	0.4	5.5	0.2	2.7	10.3	7.3	11.1
	1987	163 175[4]	64.9	0.3	5.1	−0.5	2.9	10.7	6.8	9.8
South Africa [1]	1997	625 418	4.0	6.5	19.9	3.3	3.1	13.7	9.2	40.2
Afrique du Sud [1]	1998	670 383	3.6	6.5	19.3	3.1	3.1	13.3	9.5	41.6
	1999	723 247	3.4	6.1	18.8	3.0	2.9	13.2	9.9	42.8

24

Value added by kind of economic activity at current prices
Percentage distribution [cont.]
Valeur ajoutée par genre d'activité économique aux prix courants
Répartition en pourcentage [suite]

% of Value added − % de la valeur ajoutée

Country or area Pays ou zone	Year Année	Value added (Mil. nat.cur.) Valeur ajoutée (Mil. mon.nat.)	Agriculture, hunting, forestry & fishing Agriculture, chasse, sylviculture et pêche	Mining & quarrying Industries extractives	Manufacturing Industries manufacturières	Electricity, gas and water Electricité, gaz et eau	Construction Construction	Wholesale/ retail trade, restaurants and hotels Commerce, restaurants, hôtels	Transport, storage & communication Transports, entrepôts, communications	Other activities Autres activités
Spain	1994	64 878 000	3.3	0.5	20.5	2.7	7.9	22.5	5.7	36.8
Espagne	1995	69 906 400	3.0	...	18.4	...	8.1	...	...	13.7
	1996	73 229 800	3.5	...	17.9	...	7.8	...	...	13.8
Sri Lanka	1996	744 865	19.0	1.2	18.3	2.2	7.3	23.0	10.4	18.6
Sri Lanka	1997	863 283	18.4	1.1	19.1	1.9	7.0	23.3	10.7	18.5
	1998	985 586	17.8	0.9	18.8	1.9	6.9	23.7	10.9	19.0
Sudan [8]	1994	4 440 648	40.5	6.5[10]	...	0.7	3.8	46.6[11 12]	...	1.9
Soudan [8]	1996	9 015 824	37.1	9.6[10]	...	0.9	5.0	44.4[11 12]	...	3.0
	1997	15 865 432	40.5	9.1[10]	...	0.8	6.9	39.8[11 12]	...	2.8
Suriname	1996	272 100[4]	14.3	8.9	10.9	7.5	2.5	24.8	11.2	24.0
Suriname	1997	293 870[4]	11.4	7.2	11.4	8.0	3.0	27.1	11.4	25.9
	1998	361 210[4]	9.1	6.9	10.8	7.0	3.1	24.8	11.5	34.1
Swaziland [1 9]	1996	4 285	17.9	1.1	31.5	2.4	4.8	8.7	5.2	28.5
Swaziland [1 9]	1997	4 956	16.2	0.9	35.5	2.1	4.7	8.9	4.8	26.9
	1998	5 360	15.9	0.9	36.0	2.0	5.0	8.9	4.8	26.5
Sweden [1]	1996	1 615 329	2.1	0.3	21.3	2.9	4.3	11.7	8.1	49.2
Suède [1]	1997	1 676 770	...	...	...	...	...	...	...	...
	1998	1 738 935	...	...	...	...	...	...	...	...
Switzerland	1985	234 650	3.5	...	25.1	2.1	7.4	17.8	6.2	37.9
Suisse	1990	324 289	3.0	...	23.7	1.9	8.1	18.7	5.7	39.0
	1991	343 983	2.9	...	22.6	1.9	7.8	16.6	5.8	42.4
Syrian Arab Rep.	1997	745 569	25.8	16.7	7.1	1.0	3.8	20.0	11.6	14.1
Rép. arabe syrienne	1998	790 444	29.4	13.5	7.7	1.5	3.7	19.2	11.2	13.7
	1999	821 327	24.0	19.8	5.6	1.6	3.3	18.6	12.7	14.5
Tajikistan [1]	1997	472 200	35.1	...	25.9[6 7]	...	3.0	22.7	3.2	10.1
Tadjikistan [1]	1998	950 700	27.1	...	23.2[6 7]	...	4.2	24.2	4.5	16.9
	1999	1 209 300	18.7	...	21.6[6 7]	...	3.4	16.0	2.1	38.2
Thailand	1996	4 049 000	12.6	1.3	26.6	2.5	8.0	18.9	8.4	21.6
Thaïlande	1997	4 185 000	12.9	1.7	26.6	2.6	5.9	20.0	8.7	21.5
	1998	4 160 000	14.9	1.7	27.4	2.7	3.8	19.5	8.6	21.4
TFYR of Macedonia [1]	1997	163 086	12.7	...	26.1[7]	3.0	6.2	14.2	6.9	30.8
L'ex−R.y. Macédoine [1]	1998	169 094	11.8	...	27.0[7]	2.9	6.4	14.3	7.2	30.4
	1999	171 948	11.0	...	25.8[7]	2.8	7.2	15.0	8.2	30.0
Trinidad and Tobago	1997	36 302[5]	2.4	25.0	7.8	1.6	8.9	15.6	9.3	29.4
Trinité−et−Tobago	1998	37 682[5]	2.2	20.0	8.4	2.2	9.9	16.9	9.6	30.7
	1999	41 140[5]	2.2	21.5	8.1	2.1	10.3	16.9	9.3	29.7
Tunisia [1]	1997	18 850	14.6	4.1	20.5	2.2[13]	4.9	16.1[3]	8.6	29.0
Tunisie [1]	1998	20 232	14.0	3.7	20.6	2.3[13]	5.1	16.7[3]	8.6	29.1
	1999	22 093	14.5	4.2	20.1	2.1[13]	5.1	16.8[3]	8.6	28.6
Turkey	1995	7 748 669 630	15.7	1.3	22.6	2.5	5.5	20.5	12.7	19.3
Turquie	1996	15 022 756 540	16.6	1.2	20.8	2.7	5.7	20.1	12.9	19.9
	1997	29 235 581 840	15.0	1.2	21.3	2.5	5.9	20.7	13.8	20.9
Turkmenistan [1]	1998	13 629 143	25.9	...	31.2[6 7]	...	13.4	3.7	8.0	17.8
Turkménistan [1]	1999	17 000 000	26.0	...	32.0[6 7]	...	11.0	...	...	31.0
	2000	23 000 000	26.2	...	37.1[6 7]	...	9.5	...	...	27.1
Uganda	1997	6 565 455[4]	42.4	0.6	8.7	1.4	7.5	13.9	4.5	20.9
Ouganda	1998	7 568 986[4]	43.5	0.6	8.8	1.3	7.6	13.7	4.5	20.0
	1999	8 356 013[4]	42.5	0.6	9.2	1.3	8.2	13.7	5.0	19.6
Ukraine [1]	1997	82 100	14.3	...	30.3[6 7]	...	5.8	9.0	14.4	26.2
Ukraine [1]	1998	88 000	14.1	...	31.4[6 7]	...	5.6	8.6	14.3	25.9
	1999	109 200	14.2	...	34.4[6 7]	...	4.9	8.5	14.1	23.9
United Arab Emirates	1988	90 137[4]	1.8	33.2	9.1	2.3	9.8	11.3	5.6	26.8
Emirats arabes unis	1989	104 730[4]	1.8	37.3	8.3	2.1	9.1	10.2	5.4	25.7
	1990	127 737[4]	1.6	45.4	7.2	1.8	7.8	8.8	4.6	22.7
United Kingdom	1993	571 363[4]	1.8	2.1	20.3	2.6	5.1	13.8[15]	8.1	46.2
Royaume−Uni	1994	607 800[4]	1.7	2.2	20.4	2.4	5.1	13.7[15]	8.1	46.6
	1995	634 789[4]	1.8	2.4	20.7	2.2	5.1	13.8[15]	8.0	45.9

24
Value added by kind of economic activity at current prices
Percentage distribution *[cont.]*
Valeur ajoutée par genre d'activité économique aux prix courants
Répartition en pourcentage *[suite]*

% of Value added — % de la valeur ajoutée

Country or area Pays ou zone	Year Année	Value added (Mil. nat.cur.) Valeur ajoutée (Mil. mon.nat.)	Agriculture, hunting, forestry & fishing Agriculture, chasse, sylviculture et pêche	Mining & quarrying Industries extractives	Manufac- turing Industries manufac- turières	Electricity, gas and water Electricité, gaz et eau	Con- struc- tion Con- struc- tion	Wholesale/ retail trade, restaurants and hotels Commerce, restaurants, hôtels	Transport, storage & commu- nication Transports, entrepôts, communi- cations	Other activities Autres activités
United Rep. of Tanzania	1992	1 060 631[4]	54.4	1.8	7.8[14]	1.9	4.5	15.4	5.1	9.1
Rép.—Unie de Tanzanie	1993	1 343 237[4]	54.4	1.4	7.8[14]	2.1	4.9	14.6	6.3	8.5
	1994	1 740 521[4]	54.5	1.5	7.3[14]	2.2	5.0	14.6	6.2	8.8
United States	1994	6 919 100	1.8	1.4	17.7	2.8	3.9	16.3	5.9	50.2
Etats—Unis	1995	7 296 500	1.6	1.4	17.8	2.8	4.0	16.1	5.8	50.6
	1996	7 695 300	1.7	1.5	17.5	2.7	4.0	16.1	5.7	50.7
Uruguay	1997	209 920	7.4	0.2	18.6	3.7	5.2	14.4	7.7	42.9
Uruguay	1998	242 339	6.9	0.2	18.3	3.8	5.5	13.6	7.8	43.8
	1999	249 425	5.4	0.2	16.0	3.8	6.0	13.5	8.4	46.6
Uzbekistan [1]	1998	1 212 700	31.3	...	17.4[6 7]	...	8.8	9.9	7.9	24.7
Ouzbékistan [1]	1999	1 842 900	33.5	...	16.5[6 7]	...	7.8	10.4	8.0	23.7
	2000	2 788 100	34.9	...	15.8[6 7]	...	7.0	10.9	9.3	22.2
Vanuatu	1996	28 227	24.9	...	5.0	1.7	5.6	32.0	7.3	23.5
Vanuatu	1997	29 477	25.2	...	4.9	1.7	5.5	32.4	7.3	23.1
	1998	29 545	23.1	...	4.9	1.8	4.6	34.3	7.4	23.9
Venezuela	1998	50 571 669	4.9	10.7[30]	14.8[16]	1.7[13]	6.8	17.4	9.7	34.1
Venezuela	1999	60 336 461	4.8	13.8[30]	13.6[16]	1.5[13]	5.6	16.2	9.5	34.9
	2000	79 133 481	4.1	20.3[30]	13.7[16]	1.4[13]	4.8	14.5	9.0	32.2
Viet Nam [1]	1997	313 623 000	25.8	6.3	16.5	2.7	6.5	19.2	4.0	19.0
Viet Nam [1]	1998	361 017 000	25.8	6.7	17.1	2.9	5.8	18.9	3.9	18.9
	1999	399 942 000	25.4	8.4	17.7	2.9	5.4	18.2	3.9	18.0
Yemen [1]	1997	875 477	15.8	28.3	10.5	0.8	4.7	10.1	12.1	17.8
Yémen [1]	1998	847 533	19.4	16.4	10.2	0.9	5.3	11.2	14.4	22.2
	1999	1 128 359	16.4	29.3	8.2	0.7	4.7	8.9	11.6	20.1
Yugoslavia [1]	1997	103 160	19.3	5.5	22.8	4.7	5.3	8.4	8.6	25.4
Yougoslavie [1]	1998	141 182	18.1	5.1	24.3	4.3	5.3	9.7	9.7	23.6
Yugoslavia, SFR †	1988	14 645	11.2	2.7	40.3	2.2	6.2	7.6	11.1	18.6
Yougoslavie, SFR †	1989	224 684	11.3	2.4	41.4	1.7	6.4	6.6	10.5	19.7
	1990	966 420	12.9	2.5	31.2	1.7	7.9	8.5	12.3	23.1
Zambia	1989	55 850[4]	11.4	18.0	23.3	0.6	5.4	16.0	5.6	19.7
Zambie	1990	114 675[4]	12.4	22.0	22.2	0.6	5.5	11.5	6.0	19.9
	1991	220 351[4]	12.8	15.3	28.0	0.9	5.0	10.9	7.2	20.0
Zimbabwe	1996	76 274[4]	21.9	1.7	17.4	3.2[13]	2.2	19.8	5.5	28.3
Zimbabwe	1997	90 246[4]	18.9	1.5	17.0	3.2[13]	2.8	19.0	5.7	31.8
	1998	118 145[4]	19.3	2.1	16.4	2.6[13]	3.1	19.2	5.7	31.7

Source:
United Nations Statistics Division, New York,
national accounts database.

† For information on recent changes in country or area
nomenclature pertaining to former Czechoslovakia, Germany,
Hong Kong Special Administrative Region (SAR) of China,
Macao Special Administrative Region (SAR) of China,
SFR of Yugoslavia and the former USSR, see Annex I —
Country or area nomenclature, regional and other groupings.

†† For statistical purposes, the data for China do not
include those for the Hong Kong Special Administrative
Region (Hong Kong SAR), Macao Special Administrative
Region (Macao SAR) and Taiwan province of China.

Source:
Organisation des Nations Unies, Division de statistique,
New York, la base de données sur les comptes nationaux.

† Pour les modifications récentes de nomenclature de pays
ou de zone concernant l'Allemagne, Hong Kong, région
administrative spéciale (RAS) de Chine, Macao, région
administrative spéciale (RAS) de Chine, l'ex—Tchécoslovaquie,
l'ex—URSS et l'ex—Rfs de Yougoslavie, voir annexe I —
Nomenclature des pays ou des zones, groupements
régionaux et autres groupements.

††Les données statistiques relatives à la Chine ne comprennent
pas celles qui concernent la région administrative spéciale de
Hong Kong (la RAS de Hong Kong), la région administrative
spéciale de Macao (la RAS de Macao) et la province chinoise
de Taiwan.

24
Value added by kind of economic activity at current prices
Percentage distribution *[cont.]*
Valeur ajoutée par genre d'activité économique aux prix courants
Répartition en pourcentage *[suite]*

1 Data classified according to 1993 SNA.	1 Les données sont classifiées selon le SCN 1993.
2 Including "other activities".	2 Y compris "autres activitiés".
3 Restaurants and hotels are included in "other activities".	3 Restaurants et hôtels sont incluses dans "autres activités".
4 Value added at factor cost.	4 Valeur ajoutée au coût des facteurs.
5 Value added at producers' prices.	5 Valeur ajoutée aux prix à la production.
6 Including electricity, gas and water.	6 Y compris l'électricité, le gaz et l'eau.
7 Including mining and quarrying.	7 Y compris industries extractives.
8 Data refer to fiscal year beginning 1 July.	8 Les données se réfèrent à l'année fiscale commençant le 1er juillet.
9 Data refer to fiscal year ending 30 June.	9 Les données se réfèrent à l'année fiscale finissant le 30e juin.
10 Including manufacturing.	10 Y compris les industries manufacturières.
11 Including "transport, storage and communication".	11 Y compris transports, entrepôts et communications.
12 "Other activities," refer only to public administration and defence; compulsory social security; all other services and activities are included in "wholesale and retail trade".	12 Les "autres activités" ne comprennent que l'administration publique et la défense, et la sécurité sociale obligatoire. Tous les autres services et activités sont compris dans le commerce de gros et de détail.
13 Excluding gas.	13 Non compris le gaz.
14 Including handicrafts.	14 Y compris l'artisanat.
15 Including repair services.	15 Y compris les services de réparation.
16 Including petroleum refining.	16 Y compris le raffinage du pétrole.
17 Electricity only. Gas and water are included in "other activities".	17 Seulement électricité. Le gaz et l'eau sont incluses dans
18 Data refer to fiscal year ending 7 July.	18 Les données se réfèrent à l'année fiscale finissant le 7e juillet.
19 Data refer to fiscal year beginning 1 April.	19 Les données se réfèrent à l'année fiscale commençant le 1er avril.
20 Including taxes less subsidies on products.	20 Impôts compris, moins les subventions aux produits.
21 Data refer to fiscal year beginning 21 March.	21 Les données se réfèrent à l'année fiscale commençant le 21e mars.
22 Distribution of petroleum products and gas is included in wholesale and retail trade".	22 La distribution des produits pétroliers et du gaz est comprise dans le commerce de gros et de détail.
23 Including gas and oil production.	23 Y compris la production de gaz et de pétrole.
24 Including construction.	24 Y compris construction.
25 Data refer to fiscal year ending 15 July.	25 Les données se réfèrent à l'année fiscale finissant le 15e juillet.
26 Including cottage industries.	26 Y compris artisanat.
27 Including import duties.	27 Droits d'importation compris.
28 Contract construction only.	28 Construction sous contrat seulement.
29 Refers to oil and its products.	29 Concerne le pétrole et les produits pétroliers.
30 Including crude petroleum and natural gas production.	30 Y compris la production de pétrole brut et de gas naturel.
31 Excluding repair of motor vehicles, motorcyles and personal and household goods.	31 Non compris les réparations de véhicules à moteur, de motorcycles et d'articles personnels et ménagers.
32 Excluding electricity and gas.	32 Non compris l'électricité et le gaz.

25
Relationships between the principal national accounting aggregates
Relations entre les principaux agrégats de comptabilité nationale
As a percentage of GDP
En pourcentage du PIB

As a percentage of GDP – En pourcentage du PIB

Country or area Pays ou zone	Year Année	GDP at current prices (Mil. nat.cur.) PIB aux prix courants (Mil. mon.nat.)	Plus: Net factor income from the rest of world Plus : Rev. net des facteurs reçu du reste du monde	Equals: Gross national income Égal : Revenue national brut	Plus: Net curr. transfers from the rest of the world Plus : Transferts courants nets reçus du reste du monde	Equals: Gross national disposable income Égal : Revenu national brut disponible	Less: Final consumption Moins : Consommation finale	Equals: Gross savings Égal : Épargne brute	Consumption of fixed capital Consommation de capital fixe
Algeria	1994	1 487 404	−3.9	96.1	6.7	102.8	74.0	28.8	8.2
Algérie	1995	2 002 638	−5.1	94.9	5.8	100.7	72.5	28.2	7.1
	1996	2 564 739	−4.6	95.4	3.5	98.9	67.8	31.1	10.7
Angola	1988	239 640	−11.1	88.9	−1.9	87.0	78.4	8.6	...
Angola	1989	278 866	−10.5	89.5	−1.6	87.9	77.1	10.8	...
	1990	308 062	−12.4	87.6	−4.2	83.4	73.2	10.2	...
Argentina	1996	272 150	−1.9	98.1	0.2	...	82.5	...	...
Argentine	1997	292 859	−2.1	97.9	0.2	...	82.8	...	...
	1998	298 131	−2.6	97.4	0.2	...	82.6	...	...
Australia [1][2]	1996	533 632	−3.6	96.4	0.0	96.4	77.0	19.3	15.3
Australie [1][2]	1997	565 881	−3.2	96.8	0.0	96.8	77.1	19.7	15.5
	1998	593 311	−3.0	97.7	0.0	97.7	77.6	20.1	15.7
Austria [1]	1997	2 513 476	−0.6	99.4	−0.4	99.0	77.0	22.0	14.3
Autriche [1]	1998	2 614 661	−0.8	99.2	−0.6	98.6	76.6	22.0	14.3
	1999	2 712 034	−1.6	98.4	−0.5	97.9	76.5	21.4	14.3
Azerbaijan [1]	1995	10 669 000	−0.2	99.8	4.6	104.4	97.1	...	14.1
Azerbaïdjan [1]	1996	13 663 200	0.1	100.1	2.1	102.2	99.7	...	11.1
	1997	15 791 400	0.1	100.1	1.2	101.3	87.1	...	14.1
Bahamas [1]	1993	2 854	...	97.4	...	...	83.9	...	...
Bahamas [1]	1994	3 053	...	97.1	...	...	84.0	...	...
	1995	3 069	...	96.8	...	...	83.4	...	...
Bahrain	1994	1 828	...	82.4	...	...	53.8	...	...
Bahreïn	1995	1 900	...	85.3	...	...	50.3	...	...
	1996	2 016	...	83.9	...	...	45.7	...	...
Bangladesh [2]	1995	1 301 600	...	104.6	...	106.7	92.5	14.3	7.2
Bangladesh [2]	1996	1 403 045	...	105.1	...	107.3	92.5	14.8	7.2
	1997	1 540 923	...	104.9	...	106.9	92.1	14.8	7.1
Belgium [1]	1997	8 727 011	0.8	100.8	−0.8	100.0	75.1	24.9	14.4
Belgique [1]	1998	9 081 545	0.7	100.7	−0.9	99.8	75.1	24.7	14.5
	1999	9 423 280	0.8	100.8	−1.2	99.6	75.0	24.5	14.7
Belize [1]	1997	1 231	...	96.1	...	100.1	83.5	...	4.9
Belize [1]	1998	1 258	...	94.9	...	100.2	84.8	...	4.7
	1999	1 377	...	95.1	...	...	82.3	...	5.9
Benin	1987	469 554	...	98.2	8.7	106.9	96.5	10.4	...
Bénin	1988	482 434	...	97.9	9.3	107.2	95.3	11.9	...
	1989	479 200	...	99.2	11.1	110.2	94.4	12.6	...
Bermuda [1][3]	1994	1 914	...	202.3	...	...	82.1	...	...
Bermudes [1][3]	1995	2 083	...	206.1	...	...	77.9	...	...
	1996	2 194	...	206.0	...	...	77.0	...	...
Bhutan	1996	11 714	−10.6	89.4	3.2	92.6	61.7	30.9	8.1
Bhoutan	1997	14 477	−7.9	92.1	4.9	97.0	61.2	35.8	8.2
	1998	16 420	...	93.6	4.9	98.5	62.1	36.5	8.2
Bolivia	1990	15 443	−4.6	95.4	2.9	98.3	88.6	9.7	...
Bolivie	1991	19 132	−4.0	96.0	2.6	98.6	89.9	8.7	...
	1992	22 014	−3.5	96.5	2.8	99.3	92.3	7.0	...
Botswana [1][4]	1997	17 740	−3.9	96.1	−0.3	95.8	56.5	39.3	12.5
Botswana [1][4]	1998	20 163	−0.1	99.9	−0.4	99.5	57.5	42.0	12.0
	1999	21 524	−1.6	98.4	−0.1	98.2	62.8	35.4	12.3
Brazil [1]	1997	870 743	...	100.0	−1.8	98.2	80.9	17.4	...
Brésil [1]	1998	913 735	...	100.0	−2.3	97.7	80.8	16.9	...
	1999	960 858	...	100.0	−3.4	96.6	80.7	15.9	...

25
Relationships between the principal national accounting aggregates
As a percentage of GDP *[cont.]*
Relations entre les printicpaux agrégats de comptabilité nationale
En pourcentage du PIB *[suite]*

As a percentage of GDP – En pourcentage du PIB

Country or area Pays ou zone	Year Année	GDP at current prices (Mil. nat.cur.) PIB aux prix courants (Mil. mon.nat.)	Plus: Net factor income from the rest of world Plus : Rev. net des facteurs reçu du reste du monde	Equals: Gross national income Égal : Revenue national brut	Plus: Net curr. transfers from the rest of the world Plus : Transferts courants nets reçus du reste du monde	Equals: Gross national disposable income Égal : Revenu national brut disponible	Less: Final consump– tion Moins : Consom– mation finale	Equals: Gross savings Égal : Épargne brute	Consump– tion of fixed capital Consom– mation de capital fixe
British Virgin Islands	1987	117	9.3	109.3	1.7	110.9	91.0	19.9	11.6
Iles Vierges britanniques	1988	131	8.8	108.8	1.6	110.4	88.9	21.5	10.8
	1989	156	8.5	108.5	1.5	109.9	85.6	24.3	14.9
Bulgaria [1]	1995	880 322	−3.3	96.7	0.1	96.8	85.9	...	8.7
Bulgarie [1]	1996	1 748 701	−4.0	96.0	1.0	97.0	88.5	...	8.2
	1997	17 055 205	−3.5	96.5	2.3	98.9	83.1	...	6.8
Burkina Faso	1991	811 676	0.3	100.3	1.5	...	90.9	...	...
Burkina Faso	1992	812 590	0.2	100.2	1.9	...	90.6	...	...
	1993	832 349	−0.1	99.9	1.9	...	91.6	...	...
Burundi	1990	196 656	...	98.0	...	...	102.5	...	4.2
Burundi	1991	211 898	...	99.0	...	...	100.9	...	...
	1992	226 384	...	98.7	...	...	98.5	...	...
Cambodia	1994	6 201 001	...	92.1	...	...	104.7	...	...
Cambodge	1995	7 542 711	...	95.1	...	...	95.6	...	...
	1996	8 324 792	...	93.6	...	...	95.5	...	...
Cameroon [1 2]	1994	3 754 530	...	94.6	0.0	94.7	84.4	10.2	...
Cameroun [1 2]	1995	4 465 080	...	95.2	0.5	95.8	80.3	15.5	...
	1996	4 793 080	...	95.7	0.3	95.9	79.8	16.1	...
Canada [1]	1997	864 200	−3.2	96.8	0.1	96.9	77.6	19.3	12.8
Canada [1]	1998	887 480	−3.3	96.7	0.1	96.8	78.3	18.5	13.0
	1999	943 288	−3.1	96.9	0.1	97.0	76.8	20.2	12.7
Cape Verde	1993	29 078	...	166.4	...	...	106.8	...	...
Cap–Vert	1994	33 497	...	161.3	...	...	104.5	...	...
	1995	37 705	...	163.5	...	...	109.1	...	...
Cayman Islands	1989	474	−10.8	89.2	...	92.0	79.3	12.7	8.0
Iles Caïmanes	1990	590	−10.3	89.7	...	92.2	76.8	15.4	7.1
	1991	616	−9.4	90.6	...	93.0	77.6	15.4	7.6
Chile	1997	31 567 287	...	96.4	0.7	97.1	75.5	21.6	9.2
Chili	1998	33 630 367	...	97.3	0.6	97.9	76.7	21.2	9.6
	1999	34 422 796	...	97.3	0.7	97.9	76.1	21.8	...
China †† [1]	1997	7 446 260	...	98.2	...	...	...	...	...
Chine †† [1]	1998	7 834 520	...	98.2	...	...	...	...	...
	1999	8 191 090	−1.8	98.2	...	...	...	...	...
China, Hong Kong SAR †	1997	1 323 862	0.8	100.8	−0.9	99.8	68.9	30.9	...
Chine, Hong Kong RAS †	1998	1 261 437	2.3	102.3	−1.0	101.3	69.8	31.5	...
	1999	1 233 133	2.2	102.2	−0.9	101.3	69.4	31.8	...
Colombia [1]	1995	84 439 109	−1.7	98.3	5.4	103.7	80.6	23.0	...
Colombie [1]	1996	100 711 389	−2.1	97.9	3.9	101.8	83.5	18.3	...
	1997	121 707 501	−2.2	97.8	3.0	101.2	85.0	16.2	...
Comoros	1989	63 397	...	100.7	...	...	...	...	...
Comores	1990	66 370	...	99.8	12.3	112.1	105.5	6.7	...
	1991	69 248	...	99.6	...	...	...	...	...
Congo	1986	640 407	−6.5	93.5	−1.3	92.2	84.4	7.8	24.4
Congo	1987	690 523	−11.1	88.9	−1.6	87.3	77.2	10.2	23.8
	1988	658 964	−13.7	86.3	−1.8	84.5	81.2	3.3	22.0
Costa Rica [1]	1997	2 956 558	−1.9	98.1	1.0	99.1	84.6	14.4	5.9
Costa Rica [1]	1998	3 571 523	−3.2	96.8	0.8	97.6	82.4	15.2	5.9
	1999	4 343 922	−11.1	88.9	0.7	89.7	76.2	13.4	5.9
Côte d'Ivoire	1994	4 616 000	−8.0	91.9	2.4	...	78.5	...	...
Côte d'Ivoire	1995	5 543 000	−7.8	92.4	−1.2	...	81.0	...	...
	1996	6 177 000	−8.6	91.4	−2.7	...	81.1	...	...
Cuba	1996	22 815	...	97.8	1.7	101.1	94.8	6.3	...
Cuba	1997	22 952	...	97.9	1.9	101.3	95.7	5.6	...
	1998	23 901	...	97.5	1.3	100.9	94.6	6.4	...

25
Relationships between the principal national accounting aggregates
As a percentage of GDP [cont.]
Relations entre les printicpaux agrégats de comptabilité nationale
En pourcentage du PIB [suite]

Country or area Pays ou zone	Year Année	GDP at current prices (Mil. nat.cur.) PIB aux prix courants (Mil. mon.nat.)	Plus: Net factor income from the rest of world Plus : Rev. net des facteurs reçu du reste du monde	Equals: Gross national income Égal : Revenue national brut	Plus: Net curr. transfers from the rest of the world Plus : Transferts courants nets reçus du reste du monde	Equals: Gross national disposable income Égal : Revenu national brut disponible	Less: Final consump- tion Moins : Consom- mation finale	Equals: Gross savings Égal : Épargne brute	Consump- tion of fixed capital Consom- mation de capital fixe
Cyprus	1997	4 371	0.9	100.9	...	101.7	84.8	...	10.6
Chypre	1998	4 695	0.6	100.6	...	101.2	86.8	...	10.6
	1999	5 009	0.4	100.4	...	100.7	83.6	...	10.5
Czech Republic [1]	1995	1 381 049	−0.5	99.5	1.1	100.6	70.7	29.9	18.2
République tchèque [1]	1996	1 572 257	−1.1	98.9	0.7	99.6	71.4	28.1	17.0
	1997	1 668 860	−1.2	98.8	0.7	99.5	73.2	26.3	19.8
Dem. Rep. of the Congo	1983	59 134	...	95.7	...	...	...	...	2.9
Rép. dém. du Congo	1984	99 723	...	88.5	...	...	...	...	2.5
	1985	147 263	...	97.2	...	...	...	...	2.9
Denmark [1]	1997	1 116 324	−1.4	98.6	−1.7	96.9	75.7	21.2	14.9
Danemark [1]	1998	1 168 996	−1.1	98.9	−1.7	97.2	76.3	20.9	14.9
	1999	1 229 585	−0.4	99.6	−2.1	97.4	75.1	22.4	15.0
Djibouti	1996	88 233	...	100.0	9.4	...	97.3	...	...
Djibouti	1997	87 289	...	99.9	8.3	...	94.2	...	...
	1998	88 461	...	99.9	8.3	...	96.4	...	...
Dominica	1989	423	...	101.0	...	...	92.0	...	...
Dominique	1990	452	...	101.1	...	...	84.4	...	...
	1991	479	...	101.0	...	...	91.4	...	...
Dominican Republic [1]	1994	179 130	−2.2	97.8	6.7	104.5	81.4	23.1	3.6
Rép. dominicaine [1]	1995	209 646	−2.3	97.7	6.2	103.9	82.9	21.0	4.0
	1996	232 993	−5.5	99.0	6.4	105.4	86.1	19.4	4.0
Ecuador	1998	107 421 048	−8.2	91.8	3.9	95.7	82.0	13.7	...
Equateur	1999	161 350 379	−12.7	87.3	8.1	95.3	75.8	19.5	...
	2000	343 820 986	−14.7	85.3	8.1	93.4	72.4	21.0	...
Egypt [2]	1980	17 149	4.3	104.3	1.5	...	81.6	...	...
Egypte [2]	1981	20 222	1.3	101.3	1.3	...	81.7	...	...
El Salvador	1997	97 428	...	99.2	12.1	111.3	95.8	15.5	...
El Salvador	1998	104 907	...	98.7	12.5	111.2	94.4	16.8	...
	1999	109 086	...	97.7	12.5	110.2	95.9	14.3	...
Estonia [1]	1996	52 446	0.0	100.0	2.3	102.4	84.8	17.6	10.8
Estonie [1]	1997	64 324	−3.1	96.9	2.5	99.4	81.2	18.2	11.5
	1998	73 325	−1.6	98.4	2.8	101.3	81.3	19.9	13.7
Ethiopia [5]	1997	41 465	...	99.5	7.0	106.5	...	...	...
Ethiopie [5]	1998	44 896	...	99.6	8.3	107.9	...	...	...
	1999	48 949	...	99.6	7.6	107.2	...	...	...
Fiji	1991	2 042	−1.4	105.1	−1.6	103.6	92.1	11.5	8.2
Fidji	1992	2 302	−1.7	101.5	−0.9	100.7	88.1	12.5	7.9
	1993	2 522	−0.6	100.2	−0.5	99.7	87.4	12.3	7.3
Finland [1]	1997	635 532	−2.0	98.0	−0.6	97.4	73.4	24.1	16.7
Finlande [1]	1998	689 523	−2.4	97.6	−0.8	96.8	71.9	24.9	16.2
	1999	721 958	−1.9	98.1	−0.8	97.3	71.9	25.4	16.1
France [1]	1997	8 207 091	0.2	100.2	−0.8	99.6	79.2	20.5	12.7
France [1]	1998	8 536 312	0.4	100.4	−0.8	99.8	78.6	21.0	12.7
	1999	8 818 797	0.5	100.5	...	...	78.5	...	12.7
French Guiana	1990	6 526	−1.9	98.1	36.3	134.4	99.4	35.0	...
Guyane française	1991	7 404	−5.8	94.2	35.9	130.1	94.5	35.6	...
	1992	7 976	−6.9	93.1	36.4	129.6	93.1	36.4	...
Gabon	1987	1 020 600	−6.2	93.8	−4.2	89.7	72.4	17.3	19.2
Gabon	1988	1 013 600	−7.4	92.6	−7.6	85.0	69.9	15.1	12.0
	1989	1 168 066	−8.6	91.4	−6.1	85.3	66.8	18.5	14.5
Gambia [2]	1991	2 920	...	98.3	...	115.7	96.7	19.0	11.7
Gambie [2]	1992	3 078	...	98.7	...	114.1	94.4	19.7	12.3
	1993	3 243	...	98.5	...	114.4	93.3	21.1	12.9

25
Relationships between the principal national accounting aggregates
As a percentage of GDP *[cont.]*
Relations entre les printicpaux agrégats de comptabilité nationale
En pourcentage du PIB *[suite]*

As a percentage of GDP − En pourcentage du PIB

Country or area Pays ou zone	Year Année	GDP at current prices (Mil. nat.cur.) PIB aux prix courants (Mil. mon.nat.)	Plus: Net factor income from the rest of world Plus : Rev. net des facteurs reçu du reste du monde	Equals: Gross national income Égal : Revenue national brut	Plus: Net curr. transfers from the rest of the world Plus : Transferts courants nets reçus du reste du monde	Equals: Gross national disposable income Égal : Revenu national brut disponible	Less: Final consump- tion Moins : Consom- mation finale	Equals: Gross savings Égal : Épargne brute	Consump- tion of fixed capital Consom- mation de capital fixe
Georgia [1]	1995	3 694[9]	...	97.9	4.0	101.9	91.2	10.7	11.2
Georgie [1]	1996	5 300[9]	...	101.7	2.0	103.7	93.2	10.5	11.6
	1997	6 431[9]	...	102.6	3.9	106.5	100.0	6.5	11.7
Germany [1]	1998	3 784 400	−0.7	99.3	−1.0	98.3	76.6	21.6	14.7
Allemagne [1]	1999	3 877 200	−0.8	99.2	−1.0	98.2	76.8	21.4	14.7
	2000	3 982 000	−0.8	99.2	−1.0	98.2	77.0	21.2	14.8
Ghana	1994	5 205 200	...	98.0	...	...	...	...	7.9
Ghana	1995	7 752 600	...	98.0	...	...	...	...	6.6
	1996	11 339 200	...	98.1	...	...	...	...	7.1
Greece [1]	1997	33 103 840	2.3	102.3	2.9	105.2	87.4	17.8	8.9
Grèce [1]	1998	35 872 501	2.3	102.3	2.8	105.1	87.1	18.0	8.9
	1999	38 147 219	2.6	102.6	2.6	105.2	86.1	19.1	8.7
Grenada	1984	275	...	98.9	...	...	...	...	...
Grenade	1985	311	...	98.9	...	...	...	...	...
	1986	350	...	99.2	...	...	...	...	...
Guadeloupe	1990	15 201	−2.5	97.5	37.3	134.8	123.6	11.2	...
Guadeloupe	1991	16 415	−3.4	96.6	35.4	132.0	118.3	13.7	...
	1992	17 972	−3.0	97.0	36.6	133.6	113.4	20.2	...
Guatemala	1996	95 479	−1.5	98.5	3.4	101.9	91.7	10.2	...
Guatemala	1997	107 943	−1.3	98.7	3.4	102.1	91.4	10.8	...
	1998	121 548	−0.8	99.2	3.8	103.0	92.4	10.6	...
Guinea−Bissau	1986	46 973	−1.7	98.3	2.9	...	102.8	...	...
Guinée−Bissau	1987	92 375	−0.5	99.5	4.1	103.6	100.8	2.8	...
Guyana	1997	106 678	...	90.2	...	...	64.6	...	...
Guyana	1998	108 002	...	92.2	...	...	70.1	...	...
	1999	120 668	...	89.9	...	...	69.0	...	...
Haiti [6]	1995	35 207	...	98.7	22.8	121.5	108.1	13.4	2.2
Haïti [6]	1996	43 234	...	99.6	17.1	116.7	104.9	11.8	2.3
	1997	51 789	...	99.6	14.1	113.7	103.7	10.0	2.0
Honduras	1995	37 507	...	93.2	6.7	99.9	72.8	27.0	6.0
Honduras	1996	47 774	...	93.6	6.8	100.3	74.6	25.7	5.9
	1997	61 084	...	94.9	6.6	101.5	73.7	27.4	5.5
Hungary [1]	1996	6 893 934	−7.3	92.7	...	...	73.9	...	...
Hongrie [1]	1997	8 540 669	−8.4	91.6	...	...	72.3	...	...
	1998	10 087 434	−8.7	91.3	...	...	72.4	...	...
Iceland [1]	1997	524 679	−2.3	97.7	0.0	97.7	78.6	19.1	13.5
Islande [1]	1998	577 406	−2.2	97.8	−0.2	97.6	79.7	17.9	13.1
	1999	624 606	−2.3	97.7	−0.1	97.6	81.7	15.9	13.1
India [3]	1996	13 619 520	−1.0	99.0	3.2	102.3	76.2	23.3	9.9
Inde [3]	1997	15 156 460	−0.9	99.1	2.9	102.0	75.5	24.7	9.9
	1998	17 626 090	−0.8	99.2	2.5	101.6	75.6	22.3	9.4
Indonesia	1996	532 567 000	...	97.3	...	...	69.9	...	5.0
Indonésie	1997	627 695 000	...	97.1	...	...	68.5	...	5.0
	1998	1002 334 000	...	94.6	...	...	71.6	...	4.9
Iran (Islamic Rep. of) [1][7]	1997	281 018 300	−0.4	99.6	...	99.6	64.2	35.4	26.2
Iran (Rép. islamique d') [1][7]	1998	317 638 900	0.5	100.5	...	100.5	72.7	27.9	25.4
	1999	429 142 600	0.2	100.2	...	100.2	67.7	32.5	22.1
Iraq	1989	21 026	...	96.7	...	95.9	81.9	14.0	8.7
Iraq	1990	23 297	...	96.7	...	96.5	76.8	19.6	8.8
	1991	19 940	...	96.7	...	97.4	83.5	13.9	9.6
Ireland [1]	1997	52 760	−10.2	89.8	0.6	90.4	66.7	23.8	9.8
Irlande [1]	1998	60 582	−10.8	89.2	0.3	89.5	64.7	24.8	10.1
	1999	69 052	−13.3	86.7	0.3	86.9	63.0	23.9	10.3

25
Relationships between the principal national accounting aggregates
As a percentage of GDP *[cont.]*
Relations entre les printicpaux agrégats de comptabilité nationale
En pourcentage du PIB *[suite]*

Country or area Pays ou zone	Year Année	GDP at current prices (Mil. nat.cur.) PIB aux prix courants (Mil. mon.nat.)	Plus: Net factor income from the rest of world Plus : Rev. net des facteurs reçu du reste du monde	Equals: Gross national income Égal : Revenue national brut	Plus: Net curr. transfers from the rest of the world Plus : Transferts courants nets reçus du reste du monde	Equals: Gross national disposable income Égal : Revenu national brut disponible	Less: Final consump- tion Moins : Consom- mation finale	Equals: Gross savings Égal : Épargne brute	Consump- tion of fixed capital Consom- mation de capital fixe
Israel [1] Israël [1]	1996 1997 1998	327 371 367 300 400 605	−3.2 −3.3 −2.7	96.1 95.3 95.7	6.1 5.8 5.9	102.2 101.1 101.6	84.4 84.0 83.8	17.8 17.2 17.8	13.0 13.3 13.7
Italy [1] Italie [1]	1997 1998 1999	1 983 850 000 2 067 703 000 2 128 165 000	−0.9 −1.1 −0.8	99.1 98.9 99.2	−0.4 −0.5 −0.3	98.7 98.4 98.9	77.0 77.0 77.7	21.7 21.4 21.2	13.5 13.5 13.7
Jamaica Jamaïque	1987 1988 1989	16 640 19 458 23 400	−11.4 −10.1 −10.5	84.8 86.2 84.5	3.7 12.2 7.5	88.4 98.4 92.0	73.5 74.4 72.6	14.9 24.0 19.3	7.9 7.0 7.5
Japan Japon	1997 1998 1999	509 645 300 498 499 300 495 144 500	1.3 1.4 1.1	101.3 101.4 101.1	−0.2 −0.2 ...	101.1 101.2 ...	69.7 71.3 ...	31.0 29.6 ...	16.1 16.7 ...
Jordan Jordanie	1996 1997 1998	4 711 4 946 5 180	−2.4 −1.0 −0.1	97.6 99.0 99.9	25.4 24.5 21.5	123.0 123.5 121.4	94.6 96.4 97.6	... ...	11.0 11.4 11.5
Kazakhstan [1] Kazakhstan [1]	1994 1995 1996	423 469 1 014 190 1 415 750	0.5 0.9 0.0	99.5 99.1 99.1	1.7 0.8 0.7	101.2 99.9 99.8	88.3 82.4 79.8	12.9 17.5 20.1	19.9 18.1 14.3
Kenya Kenya	1997 1998 1999	31 168 34 606 37 446	... ...	97.8 98.5 98.5	6.0 5.0 6.3	... ...	88.9 263.7 88.6	... ...	... ...
Korea, Republic of [1] Corée, Rép. de [1]	1997 1998 1999	453 276 389 444 366 540 483 777 785	−0.5 −1.5 −1.1	99.5 98.5 98.9	0.2 1.0 0.5	99.6 99.6 99.3	66.3 65.8 65.8	33.3 33.8 33.5	11.3 13.1 13.6
Kuwait Koweït	1995 1996 1997	7 925 9 307 9 212	... ...	118.4 116.7 120.7	−5.5 −4.8 −4.7	112.9 111.9 116.0	74.3 73.5 74.8	38.6 38.4 41.2	9.0 7.4 7.6
Krygyzstan [1] Kirghizistan [1]	1994 1995 1996	12 019 16 145 23 399	... ...	98.4 98.8 97.9	5.5 5.1 6.1	104.0 103.8 104.1	97.3 94.5 100.6	6.7 9.3 3.4	10.2 10.2 12.7
Latvia [1] Lettonie [1]	1994 1995 1996	2 043 2 349 2 829	−0.2 0.5 0.8	99.8 100.5 100.8	3.6 1.5 1.8	103.4 102.0 102.6	78.8 84.8 89.3	24.6 17.2 13.4	12.5 12.2 10.7
Lesotho [1] Lesotho [1]	1997 1998 1999	4 720 4 921 5 637	38.4 32.3 27.1	138.4 132.3 127.1	24.0 19.5 20.0	162.4 151.8 147.2	130.5 133.4 126.5	31.9 18.4 20.7	... ...
Liberia Libéria	1987 1988 1989	1 090 1 158 1 194	... ...	83.2 84.2 84.9	... ...	... ...	... ...	... ...	8.6 8.3 8.5
Libyan Arab Jamah. Jamah. arabe libyenne	1983 1984 1985	8 805 8 013 8 277	... ...	91.0 92.7 96.7	−0.2 −0.3 −0.2	90.9 92.4 96.5	72.0 72.2 69.2	18.9 20.2 27.3	5.0 5.7 5.8
Lithuania [1] Lituanie [1]	1995 1996 1997	24 103 31 569 38 340	... −1.2 −2.1	99.8 98.8 97.6	1.8 1.8 2.4	101.6 100.7 100.0	87.1 85.3 84.0	14.5 15.3 13.5	8.7 9.7 10.0
Luxembourg [1] Luxembourg [1]	1997 1998 1999	624 581 665 735 731 822	2.2 −1.7 −9.2	102.2 98.3 90.8	... ...	... ...	63.6 61.9 61.1	... ...	13.4 13.1 12.1
Madagascar Madagascar	1980	689 800	...	99.9	...	...	...	...	...
Malawi Malawi	1994 1995 1996	10 319 20 923 33 918	... ...	104.7 93.7 69.5	... ...	... ...	... ...	... ...	... ...

25

Relationships between the principal national accounting aggregates
As a percentage of GDP [cont.]
Relations entre les printicpaux agrégats de comptabilité nationale
En pourcentage du PIB [suite]

As a percentage of GDP – En pourcentage du PIB

Country or area / Pays ou zone	Year / Année	GDP at current prices (Mil. nat.cur.) PIB aux prix courants (Mil. mon.nat.)	Plus: Net factor income from the rest of world Plus: Rev. net des facteurs reçu du monde	Equals: Gross national income Égal: Revenue national brut	Plus: Net curr. transfers from the rest of the world Plus: Transferts courants nets reçus du reste du monde	Equals: Gross national disposable income Égal: Revenu national brut disponible	Less: Final consumption Moins: Consommation finale	Equals: Gross savings Égal: Épargne brute	Consumption of fixed capital Consommation de capital fixe
Malaysia	1997	281 795	−5.4	94.6	−1.2	93.5	56.1	37.3	...
Malaisie	1998	284 472	−5.4	94.6	−3.5	91.1	51.5	39.6	...
	1999	299 194	−6.5	93.5	−2.7	90.9	52.9	38.0	...
Mali	1990	683 300	−1.2	98.8	11.5	110.3	94.3	16.1	3.9
Mali	1991	691 400	−1.3	98.7	13.0	111.9	100.4	11.5	4.0
	1992	737 400	−1.2	98.8	11.4	110.2	96.4	13.8	3.5
Malta	1997	1 288	...	100.3	...	...	...	...	...
Malte	1998	1 362	...	98.0	...	...	...	...	...
	1999	1 447	...	100.0	...	...	...	...	...
Martinique	1990	19 320	−4.2	95.8	33.7	...	113.3	...	...
Martinique	1991	20 787	−4.4	95.6	30.7	...	112.8	...	...
	1992	22 093	−3.9	96.1	33.4	...	113.1	...	...
Mauritania	1987	67 216	−5.1	94.9	8.1	...	96.2	...	...
Mauritanie	1988	72 635	−5.6	94.4	7.9	...	93.7	...	...
	1989	83 520	−3.6	96.4	9.0	...	...	...	...
Mauritius	1997	86 428	−0.4	99.6	2.8	102.3	75.5	26.8	...
Maurice	1998	97 842	−0.7	99.3	2.3	101.7	75.2	26.5	...
	1999	106 495	−0.4	99.6	3.4	103.0	77.2	25.8	...
Mexico [1]	1996	2 525 575	−4.1	95.9	1.4	97.2	74.8	22.5	10.8
Mexique [1]	1997	3 174 275	−3.1	96.9	1.3	98.2	74.2	24.0	10.2
	1998	3 844 917	−3.2	96.8	1.4	98.2	77.8	20.5	10.3
Mongolia	1996	659 698	...	98.8	...	...	...	...	6.0
Mongolie	1997	846 344	...	95.0	...	...	...	...	8.4
	1998	833 727	...	99.3	...	...	...	...	10.5
Morocco	1997	318 342	...	...	6.6	103.5	83.1	20.4	...
Maroc	1998	342 558	...	...	...	104.2	82.1	22.1	...
	1999	343 131	...	...	...	103.8	80.4	...	...
Mozambique	1984	109 000	...	100.0	...	...	...	...	3.7
Mozambique	1985	147 000	...	100.0	...	...	...	...	2.7
	1986	167 000	...	100.6	...	...	...	...	...
Myanmar [3]	1996	791 980	0.0	100.0	...	100.0	88.5	11.4	2.3
Myanmar [3]	1997	1 109 554	0.0	100.0	...	100.0	88.1	11.9	1.9
	1998	1 559 996	0.0	100.0	...	100.0	89.4	10.6	1.7
Namibia [1]	1998	18 858	...	102.6	11.9	114.5	88.0	...	13.2
Namibie [1]	1999	21 230	...	100.8	12.2	113.1	86.3	...	13.5
	2000	24 145	...	100.9	13.1	114.0	82.3	...	13.2
Nepal [8]	1996	248 913	1.4	101.4	0.4	101.8	86.2	15.6	1.8
Népal [8]	1997	280 513	1.7	101.7	0.4	102.0	86.0	16.0	2.0
	1998	296 547	2.0	102.0	0.4	102.4	90.5	11.9	2.4
Netherlands [1]	1997	734 853	1.8	101.8	−0.9	100.9	72.3	28.6	14.9
Pays−Bas [1]	1998	776 161	1.1	101.1	−0.8	100.3	72.5	27.9	14.8
	1999	814 336	0.8	100.8	−0.5	100.3	73.3	27.1	14.8
Netherlands Antilles	1992	3 548	3.4	103.4	...	107.9	83.6	24.3	11.4
Antilles néerlandaises	1993	3 766	1.6	101.6	...	105.8	85.4	20.4	12.6
	1994	4 218	3.8	103.8	...	106.6	90.4	16.2	13.1
New Zealand [3]	1996	94 940	−8.4	91.6	0.8	92.4	77.3	15.1	9.7
Nouvelle−Zélande [3]	1997	98 025	−6.9	93.1	0.5	93.5	78.4	15.1	9.9
	1998	98 913	−7.7	92.3	0.3	92.6	80.3	12.4	10.2
Nicaragua	1981	24 483	...	95.9	...	...	...	...	4.2
Nicaragua	1982	28 350	...	95.1	...	...	...	...	4.2
	1983	32 920	...	98.0	...	...	...	...	4.5
Niger	1982	663 022	−3.1	96.9	1.5	98.4	85.1	13.3	8.7
Niger	1983	687 142	−3.1	96.9	1.1	98.0	88.8	9.5	9.3
	1984	638 406	...	96.2	1.6	97.8	88.2	11.3	10.4

25
Relationships between the principal national accounting aggregates
As a percentage of GDP *[cont.]*
Relations entre les printicpaux agrégats de comptabilité nationale
En pourcentage du PIB *[suite]*

As a percentage of GDP – En pourcentage du PIB

Country or area Pays ou zone	Year Année	GDP at current prices (Mil. nat.cur.) PIB aux prix courants (Mil. mon.nat.)	Plus: Net factor income from the rest of world Plus : Rev. net des facteurs reçu du reste du monde	Equals: Gross national income Égal : Revenue national brut	Plus: Net curr. transfers from the rest of the world Plus : Transferts courants nets reçus du reste du monde	Equals: Gross national disposable income Égal : Revenu national brut disponible	Less: Final consump– tion Moins : Consom– mation finale	Equals: Gross savings Égal : Épargne brute	Consump– tion of fixed capital Consom– mation de capital fixe
Nigeria Nigéria	1992 1993 1994	549 809 701 473 914 334	−11.7 −10.5 −7.2	88.3 89.5 92.8	2.3 2.5 1.2	90.6 92.0 94.0	77.2 80.6 85.5	13.4 11.5 8.5	3.0 2.5 2.0
Norway [1] Norvège [1]	1997 1998 1999	1 096 170 1 109 348 1 192 826	−1.0 −0.7 −1.0	99.0 99.3 99.0	−0.9 −1.0 −1.1	98.1 98.3 97.9	67.4 71.2 69.7	30.7 27.1 28.3	15.2 16.3 16.1
Oman [1] Oman [1]	1997 1998 1999	6 090 5 416 6 000	... ...	97.3 96.3 95.8	... ...	... ...	70.8 83.1 73.1	... ...	10.3 12.0 ...
Pakistan [2] Pakistan [2]	1997 1998 1999	2 677 656 2 913 514 3 173 685	... ...	99.1 99.1 98.3	... ...	... ...	83.3 86.5 87.1	... ...	6.8 7.0 ...
Panama Panama	1997 1998 1999	8 658 9 345 9 557	... ...	94.8 93.5 91.7	1.7 1.7 1.7	96.5 95.2 93.5	70.5 72.7 72.6	26.0 22.5 20.9	6.9 7.1 7.5
Papua New Guinea Papouasie−Nouv.−Guinée	1990 1991 1992	3 076 3 606 4 140	−3.8 −3.3 ...	96.2 96.7 97.3	3.2 3.4 ...	99.4 100.2 ...	83.9 82.5 ...	15.5 17.7 ...	11.0 11.6 ...
Paraguay Paraguay	1993 1994 1995	11 991 719 14 960 131 17 699 000	... ...	100.4 100.5 100.9	... ...	100.4 100.5 100.9	88.0 95.2 92.5	12.4 5.3 8.4	7.8 7.8 7.8
Peru Pérou	1996 1997 1998	148 278 172 389 183 179	... ...	97.3 97.5 97.7	... ...	... ...	80.6 78.7 80.9	... ...	... ...
Philippines Philippines	1997 1998 1999	2 426 743 2 678 187 2 996 371	4.2 5.1 5.3	104.2 105.1 105.3	2.8 1.3 2.0	107.0 106.4 107.3	85.8 87.2 85.1	21.2 19.2 22.3	8.6 ... ...
Poland [1] Pologne [1]	1996 1997 1998	387 827 472 350 553 560	−0.8 −0.8 −0.7	99.2 99.2 99.3	1.2 1.4 1.8	... ...	79.7 79.8 79.0	20.7 20.9 22.0	... ...
Portugal [1] Portugal [1]	1997 1998 1999	18 581 524 19 992 891 21 312 929	−1.4 −1.3 −1.3	98.6 98.7 98.7	3.2 3.3 3.1	101.7 102.0 101.9	82.9 83.7 84.8	18.8 18.3 17.1	15.0 14.9 15.0
Puerto Rico [2] Porto Rico [2]	1997 1998 1999	54 133 60 039 63 150	−35.5 −36.7 −34.9	64.5 63.3 61.9	13.2 14.4 12.5	77.7 77.7 74.4	72.6 70.1 69.4	... ...	6.7 6.9 7.1
Réunion Réunion	1990 1991 1992	28 374 31 339 33 787	−2.5	97.5 100.7 98.4	44.3 42.7 43.6	... ...	108.1 103.5 104.5	... ...	... ...
Romania [1] Roumanie [1]	1994 1995 1996	49 773 200 72 135 500 108 919 600	... ...	... ...	2.2 1.2 ...	... ...	77.3 81.3 82.6	... ...	... ...
Russian Federation [1] Fédération de Russie [1]	1992 1993 1994	19 005 500 171 509 500 610 745 200	... ...	98.0 98.5 99.4	3.1 0.7 0.0	101.1 99.2 99.4	48.3 60.2 68.6	52.7 39.0 30.8	12.8 16.9 20.2
Rwanda Rwanda	1987 1988 1989	171 430 177 920 190 220	−1.6 −2.0 −1.2	98.4 98.0 98.8	2.5 2.9 2.4	100.9 100.9 101.3	93.5 93.6 95.4	7.4 7.3 9.4	6.5 6.9 7.6
Saint Kitts−Nevis Saint−Kitts−et−Nevis	1996 1997 1998	663 742 775	−7.4 −8.1 −9.7	108.8 107.6 106.2	6.8 5.8 10.6	115.6 113.3 116.8	81.2 71.3 73.4	34.4 42.0 43.4	... ...
Saint Lucia Sainte−Lucie	1996 1997 1998	1 543 1 562 1 695	... ...	92.6 92.3 92.8	3.6 3.6 3.4	96.2 95.9 96.2	81.4 83.7 84.0	14.8 12.3 12.2	... ...

25
Relationships between the principal national accounting aggregates
As a percentage of GDP *[cont.]*
Relations entre les princtpaux agrégats de comptabilité nationale
En pourcentage du PIB *[suite]*

As a percentage of GDP – En pourcentage du PIB

Country or area Pays ou zone	Year Année	GDP at current prices (Mil. nat.cur.) PIB aux prix courants (Mil. mon.nat.)	Plus: Net factor income from the rest of world Plus : Rev. net des facteurs reçu du reste du monde	Equals: Gross national income Égal : Revenue national brut	Plus: Net curr. transfers from the rest of the world Plus : Transferts courants nets reçus du reste du monde	Equals: Gross national disposable income Égal : Revenu national brut disponible	Less: Final consumption Moins : Consommation finale	Equals: Gross savings Égal : Épargne brute	Consumption of fixed capital Consommation de capital fixe
Saint Vincent – Grenadines St. – Vincent – et – Gren.	1997	793	−4.4	95.7	4.4	100.1	98.6	0.0	...
	1998	858	−4.5	95.3	3.3	99.8	97.1	0.0	...
	1999	888	−6.6	95.8	4.4	100.2	87.7	14.2	...
Saudi Arabia [2] Arabie saoudite [2]	1996	529 250	−2.8	97.2	−13.2	84.0	65.5	18.5	10.0
	1997	548 620	−2.6	97.4	−12.3	85.1	65.2	19.9	10.0
	1998	480 773	−1.6	98.4	−13.4	84.9	73.9	11.1	10.0
Senegal Sénégal	1996	2 380 000	...	108.1	...	...	91.0	...	...
	1997	2 555 000	...	104.1	...	...	87.7	...	...
	1998	2 753 000	...	104.2	...	...	85.7	...	...
Seychelles Seychelles	1996	2 500	−3.0	98.0	3.1	99.4	77.1	21.0	9.6
	1997	2 845	...	99.3	...	...	77.3	...	...
	1998	3 060	...	97.6	...	...	80.1	...	...
Sierra Leone [2] Sierra Leone [2]	1988	43 947	−0.9	100.9	0.6	101.5	94.3	7.3	5.8
	1989	82 837	−0.8	100.8	0.5	101.3	91.3	10.0	5.9
	1990	150 175	−5.0	95.0	0.7	95.7	88.4	7.3	5.6
Singapore [1] Singapour [1]	1997	140 466	6.2	106.2	−1.3	105.0	49.6	57.2	12.3
	1998	138 529	7.2	107.2	−1.4	105.8	49.4	58.2	13.9
	1999	143 981	7.4	107.4	−1.4	106.0	50.1	57.8	14.0
Slovakia [1] Slovaquie [1]	1993	390 600	−0.3	94.2	0.8	95.0	78.7	21.1	16.0
	1994	466 200	−0.8	93.7	0.5	94.1	72.8	26.4	13.8
	1995	546 032	−0.1	94.6	0.4	94.9	70.9	28.8	12.8
Slovenia [1] Slovénie [1]	1993	1 435 095	−0.4	...	...	...	...	...	...
Solomon Islands Iles Salomon	1984	222	...	94.2	...	100.8	78.2	22.6	5.9
	1985	237	...	95.0	...	101.0	91.6	9.4	6.7
	1986	253	...	92.6	...	115.7	94.8	20.9	7.6
Somalia Somalie	1985	87 290	...	97.8	...	...	101.1	...	...
	1986	118 781	...	96.3	...	...	98.8	...	...
	1987	169 608	...	96.8	...	...	99.9	...	...
South Africa [1] Afrique du Sud [1]	1997	683 744	...	97.8	−0.5	97.3	82.9	14.5	12.7
	1998	735 086	...	97.6	−0.6	97.1	83.3	14.3	12.9
	1999	795 575	...	97.5	−0.7	96.8	82.7	14.6	13.0
Spain [1] Espagne [1]	1997	82 059 500	−0.8	99.2	0.3	99.5	76.8	22.6	13.0
	1998	87 545 400	−0.9	99.1	0.2	99.3	76.7	22.6	13.2
	1999	93 693 400	−1.3	98.7	0.2	99.0	76.7	22.3	12.7
Sri Lanka Sri Lanka	1996	771 414	−1.4	98.6	5.1	103.7	83.2	20.9	5.2
	1997	891 067	−1.1	98.9	5.2	104.1	81.2	22.9	5.2
	1998	1 011 326	−1.1	98.9	5.4	104.3	80.8	23.5	5.1
Sudan [2] Soudan [2]	1991	421 819	...	85.5	...	104.0	86.0	18.0	7.0
	1992	948 448	...	99.7	...	102.2	88.2	14.0	6.4
	1993	1 881 289	...	99.8	...	100.6	88.3	12.3	7.1
Suriname Suriname	1996	303 970	...	100.3	0.2	100.5	73.6	26.9	9.6
	1997	340 220	...	99.7	−0.3	99.8	77.9	21.9	9.3
	1998	407 130	...	100.1	−0.2	...	90.2	...	9.5
Swaziland [1][4] Swaziland [1][4]	1992	2 771	...	103.9	...	113.7	81.5	...	...
	1993	3 231	...	97.6	...	107.8	73.7	...	...
	1994	3 788	...	96.0	...	102.7	74.1	...	...
Sweden [1] Suède [1]	1997	1 823 799	−2.8	97.2	−0.7	96.6	77.1	19.5	13.6
	1998	1 905 349	−2.1	97.9	−0.9	97.1	77.0	20.1	13.7
	1999	1 994 854	−1.2	98.8	−0.9	97.9	77.1	20.8	13.9
Switzerland Suisse	1996	365 833	4.7	104.7	−1.2	103.5	75.6	27.9	16.3
	1997	371 372	6.9	106.9	−1.2	104.7	75.4	30.3	15.8
	1998	380 940	7.3	107.3	...	...	74.9	31.0	15.7

25

Relationships between the principal national accounting aggregates
As a percentage of GDP *[cont.]*

Relations entre les printicpaux agrégats de comptabilité nationale
En pourcentage du PIB *[suite]*

As a percentage of GDP − En pourcentage du PIB

Country or area Pays ou zone	Year Année	GDP at current prices (Mil. nat.cur.) PIB aux prix courants (Mil. mon.nat.)	Plus: Net factor income from the rest of world Plus : Rev. net des facteurs reçu du reste du monde	Equals: Gross national income Égal : Revenue national brut	Plus: Net curr. transfers from the rest of the world Plus : Transferts courants nets reçus du reste du monde	Equals: Gross national disposable income Égal : Revenu national brut disponible	Less: Final consump- tion Moins : Consom- mation finale	Equals: Gross savings Égal : Épargne brute	Consump- tion of fixed capital Consom- mation de capital fixe
Thailand	1996	4 609 000	−2.2	97.8	0.4	98.2	64.6	33.6	12.0
Thaïlande	1997	4 727 000	−2.6	97.4	0.4	97.8	65.5	32.3	13.3
	1998	4 635 000	−3.6	96.6	0.4	96.9	65.4	31.5	14.7
TYFR of Macedonia [1]	1991	935	...	99.4	−0.4	99.0	85.5	13.5	12.0
L'ex−R.y. Macédoine [1]	1992	12 005	...	96.9	−0.4	96.6	83.8	12.8	27.1
	1993	58 145	...	97.7	0.7	98.4	88.9	9.5	22.2
Togo									
Togo	1980	238 872	−1.8	98.2	6.3	104.4	80.3	24.1	7.5
Tonga [4]	1981	54	6.3	106.3	23.7	130.0	136.9	...	4.6
Tonga [4]	1982	64	6.9	106.9	35.8	142.7	137.9	...	4.5
	1983	73	4.4	104.4	27.1	130.5	140.0	...	4.0
Trinidad and Tobago	1995	31 697	−9.2	90.7	...	...	...	...	...
Trinité−et−Tobago	1996	34 448	−9.1	91.5	...	...	...	...	...
	1997	36 552	−6.3	94.8	...	...	...	...	...
Tunisia [1]	1997	20 898	−4.8	95.2	4.1	99.3	76.0	23.3	9.5
Tunisie [1]	1998	22 581	−4.2	95.8	4.1	100.0	76.5	23.5	9.6
	1999	24 672	−4.1	95.9	4.2	100.1	76.0	24.1	9.6
Turkey	1997	28 835 883 000	1.9	101.9	0.0	101.9	80.3	21.6	6.1
Turquie	1998	52 224 945 000	2.5	102.5	0.0	102.5	81.9	20.6	6.3
	1999	77 374 802 000	1.1	101.1	0.0	101.1	87.9	13.2	6.9
Ukraine [1]	1996	81 519	...	98.7	1.1	99.9	79.9	20.0	18.0
Ukraine [1]	1997	93 365	...	98.7	1.7	100.4	81.6	18.8	18.6
	1998	102 593	...	98.0	2.6	100.6	81.5	19.1	18.8
United Arab Emirates	1988	87 106	...	100.3	−1.2	99.1	65.8	33.3	16.5
Emirats arabes unis	1989	100 976	...	100.4	−0.7	99.7	61.7	38.0	15.0
	1990	124 008	...	99.0	−8.9	90.1	54.9	35.1	13.0
United Kingdom [1]	1997	805 402	1.1	101.1	−0.3	100.8	82.7	18.0	11.7
Royaume−Uni [1]	1998	851 653	1.3	101.3	−0.3	100.9	83.0	18.0	11.6
	1999	891 583	0.6	100.6	−0.1	100.5	84.2	16.3	11.6
United Rep. of Tanzania	1992	1 130 596	...	93.8	25.0	118.8	97.8	20.9	3.2
Rép.−Unie de Tanzanie	1993	1 404 369	...	95.7	20.8	116.5	95.9	20.6	2.6
	1994	1 822 570	...	96.2	20.9	117.1	97.3	19.8	2.7
United States [1]	1997	8 256 500	0.1	99.7	−0.6	99.2	81.6	17.9	11.5
Etats−Unis [1]	1998	8 728 800	0.0	100.2	−0.6	99.7	81.3	18.4	11.6
	1999	9 237 000	−0.1	100.7	−0.6	100.1	82.1	18.1	11.9
Uruguay	1997	204 938	−1.4	98.6	0.3	98.9	84.9	14.0	...
Uruguay	1998	235 393	−1.3	98.7	0.3	98.9	85.1	13.8	...
	1999	238 820	−1.4	98.6	0.3	98.9	86.4	12.5	...
Vanuatu	1996	28 227	...	91.1	...	...	...	...	...
Vanuatu	1997	29 477	...	91.7	...	...	...	...	...
	1998	29 545	...	93.5	...	...	...	...	...
Venezuela	1998	52 482 472	−1.6	98.0	−0.1	97.9	79.3	18.5	7.8
Venezuela	1999	62 577 039	−1.2	98.5	−0.1	98.6	76.6	22.0	7.6
	2000	81 924 193	...	99.0	−0.1	98.9	70.1	28.8	7.2
Yemen [1]	1997	888 808	−8.6	91.4	17.5	109.0	77.5	31.5	6.5
Yémen [1]	1998	849 321	−5.6	94.4	19.1	113.5	82.5	31.0	9.3
	1999	1 128 825	−9.4	90.6	17.3	107.9	82.8	25.1	8.4
Yugoslavia, SFR †	1988	15 833	...	105.0	...	...	64.3	...	12.2
Yougoslavie, SFR †	1989	235 395	...	106.9	...	...	61.9	...	12.1
	1990	1 147 787	...	108.7	...	...	83.7	...	11.2
Zimbabwe	1996	84 759	...	96.5	2.8	99.3	81.1	18.2	...
Zimbabwe	1997	102 074	...	95.1	2.9	98.0	88.9	9.1	...
	1998	135 722	...	93.3	4.0	97.2	84.6	12.6	...

25
Relationships between the principal national accounting aggregates
As a percentage of GDP *[cont.]*
Relations entre les printicpaux agrégats de comptabilité nationale
En pourcentage du PIB *[suite]*

Source:
United Nations Statistics Division, New York, the
national accounts database.

† For information on recent changes in country or area
nomenclature pertaining to former Czechoslovakia, Germany,
Hong Kong Special Administrative Region (SAR) of China,
Macao Special Administrative Region (SAR) of China,
SFR of Yugoslavia and the former USSR, see Annex I – Country
or area nomenclature, regional and other groupings.

†† For statistical purposes, the data for China do not
include those for the Hong Kong Special Administrative
Region (Hong Kong SAR), Macao Special Administrative
Region (Hong Kong SAR) and Taiwan province of China.

1 Data classified according to 1993 SNA.
2 Data refer to fiscal years beginning 1 July.

3 Data refer to fiscal years beginning 1 April.

4 Data refer to fiscal years ending 30 June.

5 Data refer to fiscal years ending 7 July.

6 Data refer to fiscal years ending 30 September.

7 Data refer to fiscal years beginning 21 March.

8 Data refer to fiscal years ending 15 July.

9 Data in Russian rubles.

Source:
Organisation des Nations Unies, Division de statistique,
New York, la base de données sur les comptes nationaux.

† Pour les modifications récentes de nomenclature de pays ou de
zone concernant l'Allemagne, Hong Kong région administrative
spéciale (RAS) de Chine, Macao région administrative
spéciale (RAS) de Chine, l'ex–Tchécoslovaquie, l'ex–URSS
et l'ex–Rfs de Yougoslavie, voir annex I – Nomenclature des
pays ou des zones, groupements régionaux et autres groupments.

†† Les données statistiques relatives à la Chine ne comprennent
pas celles qui concernent la région administrative spéciale de
Hong Kong (la RAS de Hong Kong), la région administrative
spéciale de Macao (la RAS de Macao) et la province chinoise
de Taiwan.

1 Les données sont classifiées selon le SCN 1993.
2 Les données se réfèrent aux années fiscales commençant le
1er juillet.

3 Les données se réfèrent aux années fiscales commençant le
1er avril.

4 Les données se réfèrent aux années fiscales finissant le
30e juin.

5 Les données se réfèrent aux années fiscales finissant le
7e juillet.

6 Les données se réfèrent aux années fiscales finissant le
30e septembre.

7 Les données se réfèrent aux années fiscales commençant le
21e mars.

8 Les données se réfèrent aux années fiscales finissant le
15e juillet.

9 Les données sont exprimées en roubles.

26
# Index numbers of industrial production
# Indices de la production industrielle
1990=100

Country or area and industry [ISIC Rev.3] Pays ou zone et industrie [CITI Rév.3]	1993	1994	1995	1996	1997	1998	1999	2000
Africa · Afrique								
Algeria Algérie								
Total industry [CDE]								
Total, industrie [CDE]	92.9	86.8	86.0	79.6	77.0	82.2	82.5	83.2
Total mining [C]								
Total, industries extractives [C]	83.0	80.9	79.7	76.2	67.0	69.5	74.1	73.3
Total manufacturing [D]								
Total, industries manufacturières [D]	87.5	79.7	76.4	67.8	62.9	68.6	67.5	66.1
Food, beverages, tobacco								
Aliments, boissons, tabac	99.0	95.0	87.7	83.7	81.9	93.9	92.5	84.6
Textiles,wearing apparel, leather, footwear								
Textiles, habillement, cuir et chaussures	79.2	72.3	64.6	46.1	41.5	45.7	33.6	30.5
Chemicals, petroleum, rubber and plastic prod.								
Prod. chimiques, pétroliers, caoutch. et plast.	94.7	92.6	94.1	88.6	95.1	93.7	97.6	98.3
Basic metals								
Métaux de base	93.1	85.5	96.9	64.4	52.2	61.0	72.8	70.3
Metal products								
Produits métalliques	80.0	64.3	75.0	56.7	44.8	48.3	53.4	54.7
Electricity [E]								
Electricité [E]	122.7	125.8	125.1	130.7	135.8	147.6	158.1	161.9
Cameroon [1] Cameroun [1]								
Total industry [DE]								
Total, industrie [DE]	98.5	99.4	106.7	126.9	124.9	129.2	...	...
Total manufacturing [D]								
Total, industries manufacturières [D]	94.8	96.7	106.1	127.5	124.7	128.5	...	...
Electricity, gas and water [E]								
Electricité, gaz et eau [E]	110.0	108.8	109.2	118.5	124.2	132.1	...	...
Central African Republic République centrafricaine								
Total industry [CDE]								
Total, industrie [CDE]	85.4	93.3	83.9	84.7	...	...	...	...
Total mining [C]								
Total, industries extractives [C]	114.5	120.6	110.3	103.4	...	...	...	...
Total manufacturing [D]								
Total, industries manufacturières [D]	69.4	65.7	93.2	76.2	...	...	...	...
Electricity, gas and water [E]								
Electricité, gaz et eau [E]	100.3	90.2	106.8	103.1	...	...	...	...
Côte d'Ivoire Côte d'Ivoire								
Total industry [CDE]								
Total, industrie [CDE]	97.9	101.0	111.5	125.0	139.6	155.2	159.6	147.1
Total mining [C]								
Total, industries extractives [C]	27.3	27.3	290.9	709.1	654.5	490.9	500.9	432.7
Total manufacturing [D]								
Total, industries manufacturières [D]	97.3	99.1	101.8	108.2	120.9	141.8	142.0	129.1
Food, beverages, tobacco								
Aliments, boissons, tabac	107.2	99.3	97.1	105.1	113.3	123.4	135.6	129.3
Textiles and wearing apparel								
Textiles et habillement	95.9	97.9	128.9	129.9	151.5	211.3	203.1	137.1
Chemicals, petroleum, rubber and plastic prod.								
Prod. chimiques, pétroliers, caoutch. et plast.	90.0	101.6	98.1	104.9	117.7	129.0	123.5	113.5
Metal products								
Produits métalliques	80.6	84.2	98.9	102.8	101.1	111.2	98.7	93.3
Electricity and water [E]								
Electricité et eau [E]	109.9	116.2	139.6	154.1	185.6	188.3	219.1	218.5
Egypt [2] Egypte [2]								
Total industry [CDE]								
Total, industrie [CDE]	103.3	104.8	105.8	117.5	131.7	...	...	...
Total mining [C]								
Total, industries extractives [C]	107.7	108.0	106.1	104.2	120.7	...	...	...
Total manufacturing [D]								
Total, industries manufacturières [D]	99.5	101.3	101.2	121.8	135.6	...	...	...
Food, beverages, tobacco								
Aliments, boissons, tabac	113.1	118.7	124.4	140.3	146.8	...	...	...

26
Index numbers of industrial production [*cont.*]
Indices de la production industrielle [*suite*]
1990=100

Country or area and industry [ISIC Rev.3] Pays ou zone et industrie [CITI Rév.3]	1993	1994	1995	1996	1997	1998	1999	2000
Textiles and wearing apparel								
Textiles et habillement	88.7	89.2	93.4	81.1	87.8	...	...	...
Chemicals, petroleum, rubber and plastic prod.								
Prod. chimiques, pétroliers, caoutch. et plast.	105.3	104.3	96.8	121.0	119.3	...	...	...
Basic metals								
Métaux de base	89.5	97.0	102.8	124.2	113.1	...	...	...
Metal products								
Produits métalliques	92.0	95.3	96.3	131.7	175.6	...	...	...
Electricity, gas and water [E]								
Electricité, gaz et eau [E]	**125.4**	**126.8**	**129.4**	**136.6**	**143.2**	...	...	...
Ethiopia [2] Ethiopie [2]								
Total industry [CDE]								
Total, industrie [CDE]	**96.1**	**102.1**	**110.6**	**115.9**	**123.1**	**131.9**	**143.1**	...
Total mining [C]								
Total, industries extractives [C]	**297.4**	**234.4**	**255.2**	**288.5**	**326.0**	**366.7**	**410.9**	...
Total manufacturing [D]								
Total, industries manufacturières [D]	**87.5**	**95.2**	**103.7**	**111.6**	**118.1**	**127.1**	**134.4**	...
Electricity and water [E]								
Electricité et eau [E]	**113.3**	**119.1**	**125.6**	**116.4**	**123.2**	**127.8**	**152.6**	...
Gabon Gabon								
Total industry [CDE]								
Total, industrie [CDE]	**71.0**	**71.0**	**86.0**	**87.2**	**84.4**	...	...	...
Total mining [C]								
Total, industries extractives [C]	**60.0**	**64.0**	**81.6**	**81.3**	**77.3**	...	...	...
Total manufacturing [D]								
Total, industries manufacturières [D]	**109.7**	**97.3**	**102.9**	**108.2**	**107.8**	...	...	...
Food, beverages, tobacco								
Aliments, boissons, tabac	107.2	96.0	99.4	103.4	103.8	...	...	...
Textiles								
Textiles	78.7	55.8	61.4	48.7	44.5	...	...	...
Chemicals and chemical products								
Produits chimiques	100.7	96.1	101.1	101.1	89.5	...	...	...
Electricity and water [E]								
Electricité et eau [E]	**104.3**	**104.3**	**105.8**	**120.8**	**127.9**	...	...	...
Ghana Ghana								
Total industry [CDE] [3]								
Total, industrie [CDE] [3]	**143.1**	**161.4**	**176.6**	**183.6**	**170.9**	**185.6**	**197.7**	**200.1**
Total mining [C]								
Total, industries extractives [C]	**200.2**	**216.8**	**250.9**	**251.7**	**274.2**	**353.2**	**398.4**	**385.8**
Total manufacturing [D]								
Total, industries manufacturières [D]	**137.5**	**159.4**	**173.1**	**181.1**	**159.1**	**163.1**	**170.2**	**176.1**
Food, beverages, tobacco								
Aliments, boissons, tabac	116.3	118.6	121.7	126.7	133.0	133.7	129.9	130.7
Textiles,wearing apparel, leather, footwear								
Textiles, habillement, cuir et chaussures	159.7	127.3	145.4	148.8	147.2	148.3	148.5	149.1
Chemicals, petroleum, rubber and plastic prod.								
Prod. chimiques, pétroliers, caoutch. et plast.	81.2	175.4	188.9	197.0	209.1	169.8	183.7	199.9
Basic metals								
Métaux de base	307.0	364.2	414.3	421.2	447.1	344.1	366.3	366.6
Metal products								
Produits métalliques	185.9	203.6	182.1	210.7	221.6	217.4	213.3	213.4
Electricity [E]								
Electricité [E]	**107.9**	**104.8**	**105.7**	**114.3**	**118.7**	**122.6**	**126.4**	**124.5**
Kenya Kenya								
Total industry [CD] [3]								
Total, industrie [CD] [3]	**106.0**	**107.8**	**111.7**	**117.2**	**124.9**	**135.9**	...	...
Total mining [C]								
Total, industries extractives [C]	**103.5**	**95.7**	**100.4**	**121.0**	**142.7**	**144.6**	...	...
Total manufacturing [D]								
Total, industries manufacturières [D]	**106.1**	**108.1**	**112.0**	**117.1**	**124.5**	**135.7**	...	...
Food, beverages, tobacco								
Aliments, boissons, tabac	103.1	100.8	113.4	110.1	109.9	111.9	...	...
Textiles,wearing apparel, leather, footwear								
Textiles, habillement, cuir et chaussures	109.9	86.6	63.1	60.3	56.5	55.7	...	...

26
Index numbers of industrial production [*cont.*]
Indices de la production industrielle [*suite*]
1990=100

Country or area and industry [ISIC Rev.3] Pays ou zone et industrie [CITI Rév.3]	1993	1994	1995	1996	1997	1998	1999	2000
Chemicals, petroleum, rubber and plastic prod. Prod. chimiques, pétroliers, caoutch. et plast.	144.9	140.8	147.5	153.7	170.4	177.9	...	...
Metal products Produits métalliques	105.8	113.6	117.0	138.2	138.8	121.1	...	...
Malawi Malawi								
Total industry [DE] **Total, industrie [DE]**	**98.0**	**93.2**	**94.5**	**97.8**	**97.0**	**93.9**	**85.4**	**86.1**
Total manufacturing [D] **Total, industries manufacturières [D]**	**95.1**	**88.2**	**89.7**	**92.8**	**89.8**	**84.6**	**72.8**	**71.9**
Food, beverages, tobacco Aliments, boissons, tabac	99.7	101.2	96.2	97.9	99.1	99.1	48.1	46.6
Textiles,wearing apparel, leather, footwear Textiles, habillement, cuir et chaussures	103.1	93.4	73.7	67.2	107.6	107.6	163.7	100.9
Electricity and water [E] **Electricité et eau [E]**	**114.4**	**121.2**	**121.0**	**125.2**	**136.4**	**145.6**	**143.6**	**155.0**
Mali Mali								
Total industry [DE] **Total, industrie [DE]**	**93.3**	**102.8**	**124.7**	**132.4**	**151.5**	**174.7**	**166.3**	...
Food, beverages, tobacco Aliments, boissons, tabac	90.9	93.5	93.2	97.2	102.6	97.2	92.0	...
Wearing apparel Habillement	128.9	108.6	121.4	131.5	168.0	171.6	147.8	...
Chemicals and chemical products Produits chimiques	78.4	80.2	87.6	98.6	93.3	88.6	79.9	...
Morocco Maroc								
Total industry [CD] [3] **Total, industrie [CD]** [3]	**102.6**	**108.2**	**112.3**	**116.0**	**121.6**	**124.1**	**125.5**	...
Total mining [C] [4] **Total, industries extractives [C]** [4]	**90.1**	**98.1**	**96.9**	**99.3**	**108.1**	**106.4**	**104.1**	**100.6**
Total manufacturing [D] [5] **Total, industries manufacturières [D]** [5]	**103.6**	**108.0**	**111.6**	**115.1**	**119.9**	**122.9**	**125.7**	**130.1**
Food, beverages, tobacco Aliments, boissons, tabac	98.3	107.1	108.9	113.4	113.1	117.6	116.5	...
Textiles,wearing apparel, leather, footwear Textiles, habillement, cuir et chaussures	105.3	107.4	111.6	115.2	121.7	124.4	122.6	...
Chemicals, petroleum, rubber and plastic prod. Prod. chimiques, pétroliers, caoutch. et plast.	105.2	110.3	108.2	107.8	115.5	115.1	126.9	...
Basic metals Métaux de base	99.6	101.3	114.6	112.5	126.7	125.3	139.8	...
Metal products Produits métalliques	102.8	104.2	106.3	108.9	114.1	112.7	119.2	...
Electricity [E] **Electricité [E]**	**107.5**	**118.6**	**130.3**	**136.0**	**144.8**	**146.7**	**142.9**	...
Namibia Namibie								
Total industry [CDE] **Total, industrie [CDE]**	**104.4**	**115.4**	...	...	...	...	...	...
Total mining [C] **Total, industries extractives [C]**	**104.0**	**115.0**	...	...	...	...	...	...
Total manufacturing [D] **Total, industries manufacturières [D]**	**118.3**	**128.8**	...	...	...	...	...	...
Electricity and water [E] **Electricité et eau [E]**	**59.3**	**72.8**	...	...	...	...	...	...
Nigeria Nigéria								
Total industry [CDE] **Total, industrie [CDE]**	**100.8**	**98.9**	**98.5**	**101.3**	**107.6**	**102.5**	...	...
Total mining [C] **Total, industries extractives [C]**	**108.3**	**105.2**	**108.1**	**112.1**	**122.9**	**116.5**	...	...
Total manufacturing [D] **Total, industries manufacturières [D]**	**89.3**	**88.5**	**83.7**	**84.7**	**85.0**	**81.7**	...	...
Electricity [E] **Electricité [E]**	**113.9**	**122.4**	**120.4**	**117.5**	**115.1**	**111.0**	...	...
Senegal Sénégal								
Total industry [CDE] **Total, industrie [CDE]**	**87.9**	**89.0**	**103.4**	**99.7**	**101.5**	**105.5**	**107.6**	**107.2**

26
Index numbers of industrial production [*cont.*]
Indices de la production industrielle [*suite*]
1990=100

Country or area and industry [ISIC Rev.3] Pays ou zone et industrie [CITI Rév.3]	1993	1994	1995	1996	1997	1998	1999	2000
Total mining [C]								
Total, industries extractives [C]	**78.8**	**74.4**	**75.4**	**74.9**	**84.0**	**80.7**	**93.4**	**95.0**
Total manufacturing [D] [3]								
Total, industries manufacturières [D] [3]	**88.7**	**91.1**	**109.0**	**104.1**	**103.7**	**109.4**	**108.8**	**107.5**
Food, beverages, tobacco								
Aliments, boissons, tabac	88.3	90.9	98.9	85.0	79.7	88.2	89.9	86.7
Textiles								
Textiles	73.6	75.2	66.0	71.4	70.9	69.0	55.5	57.0
Chemicals, petroleum, rubber and plastic prod.								
Prod. chimiques, pétroliers, caoutch. et plast.	106.4	98.2	128.2	119.4	137.2	136.6	124.8	117.4
Metal products								
Produits métalliques	90.6	92.1	125.7	118.6	118.3	121.5	123.7	117.8
Electricity and water [E]								
Electricité et eau [E]	**108.7**	**110.8**	**120.5**	**124.2**	**132.2**	**136.9**	**140.8**	**146.6**
South Africa Afrique du Sud								
Total industry [CDE] [3]								
Total, industrie [CDE] [3]	**97.1**	**98.9**	**102.9**	**104.4**	**107.4**	**104.7**	**104.3**	**107.5**
Total mining [C]								
Total, industries extractives [C]	**102.4**	**100.9**	**100.1**	**98.4**	**100.5**	**99.4**	**97.5**	**96.5**
Total manufacturing [D]								
Total, industries manufacturières [D]	**93.9**	**96.3**	**102.4**	**104.0**	**106.9**	**103.6**	**103.9**	**108.6**
Food and beverages								
Aliments et boissons	98.9	99.5	103.5	105.1	105.6	104.3	103.1	101.0
Textiles,wearing apparel, leather, footwear								
Textiles, habillement, cuir et chaussures	96.6	102.5	110.6	104.4	108.3	100.0	99.1	98.0
Chemicals, petroleum, rubber and plastic prod.								
Prod. chimiques, pétroliers, caoutch. et plast.	102.9	105.8	111.6	112.1	115.0	114.2	117.3	118.6
Basic metals								
Métaux de base	87.8	95.0	109.8	119.2	124.2	120.8	123.3	141.8
Metal products								
Produits métalliques	89.5	94.0	105.3	108.3	112.0	107.6	106.2	115.2
Electricity [E]								
Electricité [E]	**105.6**	**109.9**	**112.9**	**121.0**	**127.2**	**124.2**	**122.8**	**127.3**
Swaziland Swaziland								
Total industry [CDE] [3]								
Total, industrie [CDE] [3]	**102.5**	**112.7**	**122.4**	**122.7**	**137.3**	**139.8**	**134.4**	**135.0**
Total mining [C]								
Total, industries extractives [C]	**99.3**	**106.3**	**103.0**	**99.4**	**80.7**	**102.6**	**88.1**	**67.9**
Total manufacturing [D]								
Total, industries manufacturières [D]	**101.4**	**112.1**	**122.8**	**122.0**	**138.3**	**140.0**	**133.9**	**135.8**
Electricity, gas and water [E]								
Electricité, gaz et eau [E]	**119.3**	**122.5**	**124.0**	**139.7**	**142.7**	**149.2**	**156.7**	**146.2**
Tunisia Tunisie								
Total industry [CDE]								
Total, industrie [CDE]	**112.1**	**117.7**	**121.4**	**124.7**	**130.1**	**139.1**	**146.5**	**154.5**
Total mining [C]								
Total, industries extractives [C]	**100.4**	**96.5**	**97.6**	**102.9**	**100.1**	**107.2**	**110.2**	**107.0**
Total manufacturing [D]								
Total, industries manufacturières [D]	**116.4**	**125.5**	**130.0**	**132.5**	**140.7**	**150.7**	**159.2**	**171.3**
Food, beverages, tobacco								
Aliments, boissons, tabac	112.5	118.4	116.7	121.7	136.2	137.6	151.1	159.8
Textiles,wearing apparel, leather, footwear								
Textiles, habillement, cuir et chaussures	130.7	145.4	157.4	158.3	166.2	179.7	184.8	204.1
Chemicals, petroleum, rubber and plastic prod.								
Prod. chimiques, pétroliers, caoutch. et plast.	109.3	121.2	128.6	134.5	138.6	149.3	151.7	159.1
Basic metals								
Métaux de base	99.3	96.5	96.3	97.1	101.1	96.6	115.2	119.9
Metal products								
Produits métalliques	111.9	121.6	120.6	127.8	135.4	156.4	172.6	186.8
Electricity and water [E]								
Electricité et eau [E]	**113.0**	**119.6**	**126.0**	**128.7**	**136.5**	**144.3**	**157.1**	**166.0**
Uganda Ouganda								
Total manufacturing [D]								
Total, industries manufacturières [D]	**138.6**	**167.4**	**212.9**	**253.5**	**293.6**	**326.7**	**351.5**	**349.8**

26

Index numbers of industrial production [*cont.*]

Indices de la production industrielle [*suite*]

1990=100

Country or area and industry [ISIC Rev.3] Pays ou zone et industrie [CITI Rév.3]	1993	1994	1995	1996	1997	1998	1999	2000
Food, beverages, tobacco Aliments, boissons, tabac	126.7	163.2	203.2	248.5	255.9	282.5	302.0	302.7
Textiles,wearing apparel, leather, footwear Textiles, habillement, cuir et chaussures	80.8	69.2	86.2	92.1	125.8	130.4	141.2	110.7
Chemicals, rubber and plastic prod. Prod. chimiques, caoutchouc et plastiques	212.0	259.3	376.2	388.9	526.3	621.0	669.5	675.4
Basic metals Métaux de base	240.5	362.0	455.4	446.3	1164.0	1278.0	1454.0	1306.0
Metal products Produits métalliques	307.6	361.9	381.2	486.3	402.7	298.9	264.5	235.8
United Rep. of Tanzania Rép.–Unie de Tanzanie								
Total manufacturing [D] **Total, industries manufacturières [D]**	**96.5**	**87.8**	**91.2**	**92.1**	**97.4**	**105.3**	**108.8**	**...**
Food, beverages, tobacco Aliments, boissons, tabac	99.8	90.5	93.8	107.1	121.2	125.1	124.0	...
Textiles, leather and footwear Textiles, cuir et chaussures	81.2	68.2	65.6	63.2	58.9	69.1	67.9	...
Chemicals, rubber and plastic prod. Prod. chimiques, caoutchouc et plastiques	83.8	92.1	82.0	70.7	68.9	73.4	86.6	...
Basic metals Métaux de base	128.6	105.7	45.7	14.3	13.3	37.1	7.6	...
Metal products Produits métalliques	42.8	45.5	33.9	38.8	35.7	33.4	32.9	...
Zambia Zambie								
Total industry [CDE] [3] **Total, industrie [CDE]** [3]	**92.3**	**80.6**	**75.5**	**77.3**	**79.4**	**80.5**	**70.5**	**72.3**
Total mining [C] **Total, industries extractives [C]**	**93.2**	**77.2**	**69.1**	**79.0**	**79.1**	**89.5**	**64.1**	**66.4**
Total manufacturing [D] **Total, industries manufacturières [D]**	**89.2**	**80.6**	**78.5**	**71.9**	**74.5**	**64.4**	**68.7**	**75.0**
Food, beverages, tobacco Aliments, boissons, tabac	138.0	123.6	123.2	88.6	67.3	64.3	70.3	70.9
Textiles and wearing apparel Textiles et habillement	57.1	54.1	48.0	61.5	104.6	79.1	86.0	89.8
Chemicals, petroleum, rubber and plastic prod. Prod. chimiques, pétroliers, caoutch. et plast.	86.5	66.7	60.0	83.4	69.3	67.7	57.8	101.7
Basic metals Métaux de base	116.2	108.9	103.7	81.8	68.9	77.1	79.5	81.8
Metal products Produits métalliques	74.8	63.8	67.0	45.5	43.8	46.9	39.0	43.5
Electricity and water [E] **Electricité et eau [E]**	**101.2**	**104.7**	**106.4**	**91.9**	**106.5**	**97.9**	**98.9**	**100.6**
Zimbabwe Zimbabwe								
Total industry [CDE] [3] **Total, industrie [CDE]** [3]	**87.8**	**97.2**	**89.4**	**90.2**	**91.8**	**90.7**	**...**	**...**
Total mining [C] **Total, industries extractives [C]**	**96.2**	**109.3**	**116.0**	**111.4**	**110.8**	**119.8**	**113.9**	**...**
Total manufacturing [D] **Total, industries manufacturières [D]**	**85.8**	**94.0**	**81.2**	**84.0**	**86.7**	**82.6**	**78.2**	**...**
Food, beverages, tobacco Aliments, boissons, tabac	92.7	94.7	94.2	96.0	99.3	100.7	96.0	...
Textiles,wearing apparel, leather, footwear Textiles, habillement, cuir et chaussures	88.5	91.6	50.3	50.5	50.5	51.6	50.3	...
Chemicals, petroleum, rubber and plastic prod. Prod. chimiques, pétroliers, caoutch. et plast.	81.5	93.6	84.1	86.2	118.0	88.2	84.5	...
Basic metals and metal products Métaux de base et produtis métalliques	71.2	83.8	81.4	88.4	92.6	78.9	66.4	...
Electricity [E] **Electricité [E]**	**78.5**	**86.8**	**83.3**	**80.1**	**78.3**	**72.7**	**...**	**...**
America, North · Amérique du Nord								
Barbados Barbade								
Total industry [CDE] **Total, industrie [CDE]**	**88.5**	**93.4**	**100.3**	**100.5**	**104.6**	**112.5**	**113.3**	**111.5**

26

Index numbers of industrial production [*cont.*]
Indices de la production industrielle [*suite*]
1990=100

Country or area and industry [ISIC Rev.3] Pays ou zone et industrie [CITI Rév.3]	1993	1994	1995	1996	1997	1998	1999	2000
Total mining [C]								
Total, industries extractives [C]	**87.6**	**90.3**	**90.8**	**81.3**	**84.3**	**128.4**	**149.6**	**127.4**
Total manufacturing [D]								
Total, industries manufacturières [D]	**85.9**	**91.0**	**98.4**	**98.5**	**102.6**	**107.3**	**105.5**	**104.9**
Food, beverages, tobacco								
Aliments, boissons, tabac	104.5	109.2	114.3	116.4	123.4	132.2	128.7	126.0
Wearing apparel								
Habillement	44.1	26.9	24.6	22.4	23.2	17.0	16.0	17.2
Chemicals, petroleum products								
Produits chimiques et pétroliers	81.4	80.5	94.9	96.4	110.5	54.4	48.1	38.5
Metal products								
Produits métalliques	102.3	94.1	102.2	108.8	105.6	89.4	82.6	80.6
Electricity and gas [E]								
Electricité et gaz [E]	**104.3**	**108.4**	**115.8**	**120.2**	**124.8**	**135.8**	**143.1**	**143.0**
Belize Belize								
Total industry [DE]								
Total, industrie [DE]	**111.5**	**118.4**	**122.7**	**123.1**	**129.9**	**124.5**	...	...
Total manufacturing [D]								
Total, industries manufacturières [D]	**109.3**	**115.9**	**120.2**	**120.4**	**126.4**	**118.2**	...	...
Food, beverages, tobacco								
Aliments, boissons, tabac	108.5	115.9	123.5	124.2	131.5	122.2	...	...
Wearing apparel								
Habillement	118.9	91.8	54.9	55.3	55.4	59.6	...	...
Chemicals and chemical products								
Produits chimiques	162.5	249.3	241.8	224.8	195.6	193.8	...	...
Metal products								
Produits métalliques	43.0	33.3	27.4	22.1	18.4	15.5	...	...
Electricity and water [E]								
Electricité et eau [E]	**132.7**	**142.2**	**147.1**	**149.5**	**164.1**	**185.7**	...	...
Canada Canada								
Total industry [CDE]								
Total, industrie [CDE]	**101.3**	**107.9**	**112.8**	**114.3**	**119.3**	**122.2**	**127.6**	**134.8**
Total mining [C]								
Total, industries extractives [C]	**111.5**	**116.7**	**120.7**	**122.2**	**126.0**	**123.8**	**119.6**	**127.6**
Total manufacturing [D]								
Total, industries manufacturières [D]	**98.6**	**106.1**	**111.4**	**112.8**	**119.3**	**124.2**	**132.0**	**139.5**
Food, beverages, tobacco								
Aliments, boissons, tabac	102.7	106.1	107.2	106.5	105.8	109.5	111.2	113.4
Textiles,wearing apparel, leather, footwear								
Textiles, habillement, cuir et chaussures	96.0	102.4	108.5	106.0	113.7	113.3	112.6	111.5
Chemicals, petroleum, rubber and plastic prod.								
Prod. chimiques, pétroliers, caoutch. et plast.	101.2	108.6	112.2	115.9	120.7	126.6	132.6	136.0
Basic metals								
Métaux de base	113.0	114.1	116.9	119.2	125.8	126.9	129.1	131.7
Metal products								
Produits métalliques	98.8	112.8	125.3	125.4	137.8	146.5	163.5	186.0
Electricity, gas and water [E]								
Electricité, gaz et eau [E]	**104.4**	**107.4**	**111.6**	**114.0**	**113.0**	**111.4**	**114.8**	**119.9**
Costa Rica Costa Rica								
Total industry [DE] [3]								
Total, industrie [DE] [3]	**120.2**	**125.4**	**130.4**	**131.4**	**141.1**	**156.5**	**190.8**	**187.3**
Total manufacturing [D]								
Total, industries manufacturières [D]	**121.4**	**125.9**	**131.1**	**131.7**	**141.9**	**158.0**	**196.7**	**190.9**
Food, beverages, tobacco								
Aliments, boissons, tabac	128.8	130.4	139.4	143.2	153.2	163.1	169.2	169.0
Textiles,wearing apparel, leather, footwear								
Textiles, habillement, cuir et chaussures	109.3	108.1	105.2	97.2	93.2	97.0	87.1	83.3
Chemicals, petroleum, rubber and plastic prod.								
Prod. chimiques, pétroliers, caoutch. et plast.	132.0	137.8	139.2	132.4	137.1	120.2	120.4	124.3
Metal products								
Produits métalliques	122.1	141.0	141.1	145.0	159.7	149.7	145.8	141.0
Electricity and water [E]								
Electricité et eau [E]	**114.0**	**122.5**	**126.3**	**129.6**	**136.7**	**148.7**	**158.6**	**168.1**

26
Index numbers of industrial production [*cont.*]
Indices de la production industrielle [*suite*]
1990=100

Country or area and industry [ISIC Rev.3] Pays ou zone et industrie [CITI Rév.3]	1993	1994	1995	1996	1997	1998	1999	2000
Dominican Republic Rép. dominicaine								
Total industry [CDE]								
Total, industrie [CDE]	**110.8**	**120.7**	**123.8**	**127.3**	**136.5**	**141.9**	**150.2**	**164.0**
Total mining [C]								
Total, industries extractives [C]	**49.7**	**93.5**	**102.3**	**104.7**	**108.0**	**90.8**	**89.4**	**97.6**
Total manufacturing [D]								
Total, industries manufacturières [D]	**118.2**	**122.3**	**125.1**	**127.8**	**137.4**	**145.2**	**154.4**	**168.3**
Electricity [E]								
Electricité [E]	**155.8**	**161.6**	**155.1**	**171.0**	**188.3**	**214.4**	**231.8**	**257.4**
El Salvador El Salvador								
Total industry [CDE]								
Total, industrie [CDE]	**111.8**	**120.1**	**128.3**	**131.0**	**141.4**	**150.8**	**156.3**	**163.1**
Total mining [C]								
Total, industries extractives [C]	**127.5**	**141.4**	**150.9**	**152.5**	**162.3**	**170.9**	**171.6**	**176.8**
Total manufacturing [D]								
Total, industries manufacturières [D]	**114.6**	**123.0**	**131.5**	**133.8**	**144.5**	**154.0**	**159.8**	**166.9**
Food, beverages, tobacco								
Aliments, boissons, tabac	110.7	116.4	121.1	123.0	128.3	134.6	138.1	143.8
Textiles,wearing apparel, leather, footwear								
Textiles, habillement, cuir et chaussures	99.3	102.7	112.1	110.3	117.0	121.3	119.2	125.5
Chemicals, petroleum, rubber and plastic prod.								
Prod. chimiques, pétroliers, caoutch. et plast.	116.7	127.8	132.4	130.7	137.1	151.1	164.0	155.9
Basic metals and metal products								
Métaux de base et produtis métalliques	104.5	113.7	126.9	137.4	144.8	159.1	160.7	160.2
Electricity [E]								
Electricité [E]	**31.6**	**34.2**	**36.3**	**50.5**	**51.5**	**56.9**	**58.1**	**57.1**
Guatemala Guatemala								
Total industry [CDE]								
Total, industrie [CDE]	**112.4**	**116.2**	**121.2**	**125.0**	...	...	...	...
Total mining [C]								
Total, industries extractives [C]	**156.2**	**162.9**	**185.6**	**229.9**	...	...	...	...
Total manufacturing [D]								
Total, industries manufacturières [D]	**108.8**	**112.0**	**115.6**	**117.8**	...	...	...	...
Food, beverages, tobacco								
Aliments, boissons, tabac	109.3	112.7	116.8	119.4	...	...	...	...
Textiles,wearing apparel, leather, footwear								
Textiles, habillement, cuir et chaussures	108.6	111.9	114.5	116.1	...	...	...	...
Chemicals, rubber and plastic products								
Prod. chimiques, caoutchouc et plastiques	108.8	112.4	116.4	118.6	...	...	...	...
Basic metals and metal products								
Métaux de base et produtis métalliques	108.3	111.6	115.1	117.2	...	...	...	...
Electricity and water [E]								
Electricité et eau [E]	**129.5**	**136.8**	**148.6**	**157.5**	...	...	...	...
Haiti [6] Haïti [6]								
Total manufacturing [D]								
Total, industries manufacturières [D]	**45.6**	**32.6**	**39.2**	**42.6**	**43.8**	**46.1**	**47.6**	**50.8**
Food, beverages, tobacco								
Aliments, boissons, tabac	39.1	38.4	36.7	43.3	46.4	46.1	61.7	71.4
Chemicals and chemical products								
Produits chimiques	109.7	100.1	126.6	224.6	220.1	237.6	237.9	244.7
Honduras Honduras								
Total industry [CDE]								
Total, industrie [CDE]	**114.3**	**111.8**	**119.6**	**127.2**	**135.1**	**140.0**	**143.9**	**151.3**
Total mining [C]								
Total, industries extractives [C]	**119.4**	**115.3**	**133.3**	**143.1**	**150.0**	**155.6**	**163.9**	**168.0**
Total manufacturing [D]								
Total, industries manufacturières [D]	**114.4**	**112.6**	**118.8**	**124.2**	**131.9**	**136.4**	**139.9**	**146.8**
Food, beverages, tobacco								
Aliments, boissons, tabac	160.9	207.1	261.0	317.4	388.0	425.6	473.4	518.8
Textiles,wearing apparel, leather, footwear								
Textiles, habillement, cuir et chaussures	182.4	218.8	301.5	397.9	495.4	553.1	638.8	693.2
Chemicals, petroleum, rubber and plastic prod.								
Prod. chimiques, pétroliers, caoutch. et plast.	157.6	190.3	287.8	305.9	358.4	409.9	459.2	506.2

26
Index numbers of industrial production [*cont.*]
Indices de la production industrielle [*suite*]
1990=100

Country or area and industry [ISIC Rev.3] Pays ou zone et industrie [CITI Rév.3]	1993	1994	1995	1996	1997	1998	1999	2000
Basic metals Métaux de base	122.2	147.8	200.6	231.6	274.0	288.2	319.2	358.0
Metal products Produits métalliques	126.2	159.8	193.2	226.0	251.7	288.0	323.4	357.9
Electricity, gas and water [E] Électricité, gaz et eau [E]	109.4	101.6	116.4	134.4	144.5	151.6	154.7	166.4
Mexico Mexique								
Total industry [CDE] [7] Total, industrie [CDE] [7]	108.2	113.4	104.5	115.2	125.8	133.7	139.4	148.5
Total mining [C] Total, industries extractives [C]	104.2	107.3	104.0	112.4	117.4	120.6	118.1	122.8
Total manufacturing [D] Total, industries manufacturières [D]	107.1	111.5	105.9	117.3	129.0	138.5	144.3	154.6
Food, beverages, tobacco Aliments, boissons, tabac	110.9	114.5	114.5	118.4	122.2	130.3	135.5	140.4
Textiles and wearing apparel Textiles et habillement	99.7	100.8	94.4	109.2	120.6	125.0	129.1	135.9
Chemicals, petroleum, rubber and plastic prod. Prod. chimiques, pétroliers, caoutch. et plast.	101.0	104.4	103.5	110.3	117.8	124.9	127.9	131.9
Basic metals Métaux de base	99.8	106.0	110.3	130.9	145.5	151.3	151.9	157.4
Metal products Produits métalliques	110.1	117.5	105.4	129.0	153.5	171.0	182.9	208.3
Electricity, gas and water [E] Électricité, gaz et eau [E]	106.2	111.3	113.6	118.8	125.1	127.3	137.4	145.9
Panama Panama								
Total industry [CDE] [3] Total, industrie [CDE] [3]	124.5	130.0	132.2	135.4	146.2	153.8	149.1	146.8
Total mining [C] Total, industries extractives [C]	318.0	351.9	341.9	277.0	534.0	674.3	691.9	728.2
Total manufacturing [D] Total, industries manufacturières [D]	125.7	129.9	130.1	130.5	137.9	143.6	137.6	130.4
Food, beverages, tobacco Aliments, boissons, tabac	116.1	122.4	121.5	125.3	133.7	143.5	135.2	131.8
Textiles, wearing apparel, leather, footwear Textiles, habillement, cuir et chaussures	119.7	113.2	112.0	101.4	96.2	90.9	78.3	70.8
Chemicals, petroleum, rubber and plastic prod. Prod. chimiques, pétroliers, caoutch. et plast.	131.1	119.9	128.3	153.8	158.6	165.6	165.7	153.7
Basic metals Métaux de base	196.0	170.0	202.4	226.9	301.3	251.5	358.4	274.4
Metal products Produits métalliques	120.4	129.3	140.5	146.9	157.7	168.1	157.5	167.5
Electricity and water [E] Électricité et eau [E]	118.3	126.4	132.3	144.6	159.1	168.9	167.0	175.5
Trinidad and Tobago Trinité–et–Tobago								
Total industry [DE] Total, industrie [DE]	114.5	130.7	140.6	148.6	158.0	175.8	195.4	205.8
Total manufacturing [D] [3] Total, industries manufacturières [D] [3]	114.6	131.2	141.2	149.3	158.9	176.7	196.7	207.6
Food, beverages, tobacco Aliments, boissons, tabac	93.6	103.6	104.0	104.8	107.4	159.5	163.2	221.4
Textiles, leather and footwear Textiles, cuir et chaussures	56.9	48.6	46.8	47.6	67.8	96.5	208.3	266.6
Chemicals and petroleum products Produits chimiques et pétroliers	91.0	90.9	82.9	91.4	120.1	173.4	203.8	236.3
Metal products Produits métalliques	124.3	133.4	145.5	174.0	158.0	214.7	220.0	227.3
Electricity [E] Électricité [E]	110.3	116.6	122.3	125.5	130.0	146.9	155.4	148.6
United States Etats–Unis								
Total industry [CDE] Total, industrie [CDE]	104.6	110.3	115.6	120.8	129.1	135.5	141.2	149.0
Total mining [C] Total, industries extractives [C]	95.4	97.6	97.3	98.8	100.5	98.3	93.5	95.4

26
Index numbers of industrial production [*cont.*]
Indices de la production industrielle [*suite*]
1990=100

Country or area and industry [ISIC Rev.3] Pays ou zone et industrie [CITI Rév.3]	1993	1994	1995	1996	1997	1998	1999	2000
Total manufacturing [D] **Total, industries manufacturières [D]**	**105.3**	**111.6**	**117.5**	**123.2**	**132.8**	**140.3**	**147.0**	**155.9**
Food, beverages, tobacco Aliments, boissons, tabac	101.4	105.6	108.5	108.4	109.6	112.5	112.4	114.1
Textiles,wearing apparel, leather, footwear Textiles, habillement, cuir et chaussures	107.4	111.3	110.9	108.9	109.2	105.7	100.7	97.1
Chemicals, petroleum, rubber and plastic prod. Prod. chimiques, pétroliers, caoutch. et plast.	106.4	110.6	113.0	115.8	124.1	128.6	132.9	135.2
Basic metals Métaux de base	101.0	109.4	111.7	115.0	120.6	122.9	125.4	128.5
Metal products Produits métalliques	106.9	116.5	127.7	139.3	154.9	171.1	189.7	217.9
Electricity and gas [E] **Électricité et gaz [E]**	**105.8**	**107.2**	**111.0**	**114.6**	**114.8**	**116.1**	**119.1**	**122.5**
America, South · Amérique du Sud								
Argentina Argentine **Total manufacturing [D]** **Total, industries manufacturières [D]**	**128.7**	**134.6**	**125.2**	**133.2**	**145.7**	**148.6**	**136.3**	**134.6**
Food, beverages, tobacco Aliments, boissons, tabac	124.1	133.0	135.1	135.6	142.5	149.9	151.1	145.8
Textiles,wearing apparel, leather, footwear Textiles, habillement, cuir et chaussures	102.7	107.4	99.1	109.0	106.3	96.1	81.4	77.5
Chemicals, petroleum, rubber and plastic prod. Prod. chimiques, pétroliers, caoutch. et plast.	132.4	140.5	128.9	141.4	154.2	157.0	148.3	148.7
Basic metals Métaux de base	90.2	98.9	104.5	116.7	129.8	132.1	113.4	127.2
Metal products Produits métalliques	161.5	167.5	138.0	152.1	179.0	185.4	142.8	142.8
Bolivia Bolivie **Total industry [CDE] [3]** **Total, industrie [CDE] [3]**	**120.2**	**121.9**	**136.1**	**135.5**	**139.5**	**142.4**	**138.3**	**139.6**
Total mining [C] **Total, industries extractives [C]**	**123.7**	**120.2**	**142.0**	**135.3**	**137.2**	**136.6**	**127.2**	**127.4**
Total manufacturing [D] **Total, industries manufacturières [D]**	**115.9**	**122.4**	**127.9**	**133.2**	**138.8**	**144.9**	**146.1**	**148.1**
Food, beverages, tobacco Aliments, boissons, tabac	116.5	120.6	127.6	134.7	135.4	141.8	146.6	154.3
Textiles,wearing apparel, leather, footwear Textiles, habillement, cuir et chaussures	142.2	155.8	172.6	176.1	194.7	198.6	180.6	181.4
Chemicals, petroleum, rubber and plastic prod. Prod. chimiques, pétroliers, caoutch. et plast.	101.0	110.7	116.5	132.3	147.6	149.9	156.8	142.9
Basic metals Métaux de base	130.4	134.0	102.5	95.7	111.1	86.8	89.3	92.8
Metal products Produits métalliques	116.3	135.9	131.9	121.3	122.6	125.2	116.4	116.2
Electricity, gas and water [E] **Électricité, gaz et eau [E]**	**123.7**	**142.0**	**155.5**	**170.0**	**184.2**	**196.2**	**204.6**	**211.0**
Brazil Brésil **Total industry [CD]** **Total, industrie [CD]**	**100.8**	**108.5**	**110.4**	**112.4**	**116.7**	**114.3**	**113.6**	**121.0**
Total mining [C] **Total, industries extractives [C]**	**102.3**	**107.2**	**110.7**	**121.5**	**130.3**	**146.4**	**159.8**	**178.9**
Total manufacturing [D] **Total, industries manufacturières [D]**	**101.3**	**109.2**	**111.0**	**112.3**	**116.3**	**112.6**	**110.7**	**117.3**
Food, beverages, tobacco Aliments, boissons, tabac	106.2	108.2	117.0	122.3	124.8	123.7	126.3	123.8
Textiles,wearing apparel, leather, footwear Textiles, habillement, cuir et chaussures	93.3	94.3	88.3	84.5	78.9	74.4	74.1	78.4
Chemicals, petroleum, rubber and plastic prod. Prod. chimiques, pétroliers, caoutch. et plast.	96.7	102.6	103.5	109.1	114.3	116.8	116.9	119.1
Basic metals and metal products Métaux de base et produtis métalliques	100.5	116.2	121.9	122.4	127.3	116.3	108.5	122.7

26
Index numbers of industrial production [*cont.*]
Indices de la production industrielle [*suite*]
1990=100

Country or area and industry [ISIC Rev.3] Pays ou zone et industrie [CITI Rév.3]	1993	1994	1995	1996	1997	1998	1999	2000
Chile Chili								
Total industry [CDE] [3]								
Total, industrie [CDE] [3]	122.4	127.0	136.5	148.3	158.5	163.1	171.9	179.3
Total mining [C]								
Total, industries extractives [C]	123.2	131.4	146.2	178.8	197.1	208.3	240.6	253.9
Total manufacturing [D]								
Total, industries manufacturières [D]	121.5	124.1	131.8	135.4	142.3	143.6	143.2	148.1
Food, beverages, tobacco								
Aliments, boissons, tabac	121.2	131.1	137.9	138.9	138.8	133.9	135.7	139.2
Textiles,wearing apparel, leather, footwear								
Textiles, habillement, cuir et chaussures	103.7	94.4	93.0	91.7	85.7	74.7	65.8	65.1
Chemicals, petroleum, rubber and plastic prod.								
Prod. chimiques, pétroliers, caoutch. et plast.	123.4	132.2	144.3	155.0	170.9	179.7	186.3	206.0
Basic metals								
Métaux de base	103.6	99.6	106.8	109.7	118.8	126.8	130.6	99.4
Metal products								
Produits métalliques	142.7	145.5	153.7	155.5	174.4	164.5	151.9	161.9
Electricity [E]								
Electricité [E]	127.0	137.5	146.2	164.7	177.2	189.9	204.1	215.5
Colombia Colombie								
Total industry [CDE] [3]								
Total, industrie [CDE] [3]	106.2	108.9	118.0	125.6	130.2	135.2	...	...
Total mining [C]								
Total, industries extractives [C]	99.6	98.5	120.6	149.2	157.6	176.0	...	...
Total manufacturing [D]								
Total, industries manufacturières [D]	109.5	113.5	115.9	112.8	115.5	113.8	98.5	108.1
Food, beverages, tobacco								
Aliments, boissons, tabac	103.6	104.4	108.9	109.1	109.7	110.3	100.0	98.8
Textiles,wearing apparel, leather, footwear								
Textiles, habillement, cuir et chaussures	102.0	93.9	92.4	91.0	95.5	112.8	98.1	115.0
Chemicals, petroleum, rubber and plastic prod.								
Prod. chimiques, pétroliers, caoutch. et plast.	107.2	112.3	114.7	112.0	112.8	109.0	98.2	106.9
Basic metals								
Métaux de base	112.0	126.8	129.4	122.7	139.0	127.0	121.5	161.8
Metal products								
Produits métalliques	118.1	128.2	134.5	128.4	137.2	127.3	95.0	107.8
Electricity [E]								
Electricité [E]	108.5	116.4	122.9	125.4	128.3	129.6	124.6	...
Ecuador Equateur								
Total manufacturing [D]								
Total, industries manufacturières [D]	120.6	135.1	141.8	145.2	148.1	149.3	141.8	163.0
Food, beverages, tobacco								
Aliments, boissons, tabac	108.1	110.6	113.4	115.6	117.2	120.4	118.2	119.8
Textiles, leather and footwear								
Textiles, cuir et chaussures	77.8	81.6	82.9	84.6	86.3	84.1	79.3	95.3
Chemicals, petroleum, rubber and plastic prod.								
Prod. chimiques, pétroliers, caoutch. et plast.	140.2	157.1	161.4	165.1	168.9	172.3	156.1	174.0
Basic metals								
Métaux de base	139.0	154.3	152.8	154.9	156.5	156.9	145.9	194.1
Metal products								
Produits métalliques	144.8	184.2	194.7	192.9	195.0	196.5	129.7	177.4
Paraguay Paraguay								
Total manufacturing [D]								
Total, industries manufacturières [D]	103.5	105.1	108.2	105.8	105.6	106.7	106.7	...
Food, beverages, tobacco								
Aliments, boissons, tabac	108.6	117.0	121.6	122.7	127.3	128.6	132.7	...
Textiles, wearing apparel, leather and footwear								
Textiles, habillement, cuir et chaussures	100.8	89.7	98.3	96.4	80.8	85.7	84.0	...
Chemicals, petroleum, rubber and plastic prod.								
Prod. chimiques, pétroliers, caoutch. et plast.	92.3	89.9	76.3	67.8	62.8	59.8	57.9	...
Basic metals								
Métaux de base	106.0	85.2	88.6	85.2	80.5	76.7	73.5	...
Metal products								
Produits métalliques	86.2	54.6	54.8	54.6	54.3	54.3	54.3	...

26
Index numbers of industrial production [cont.]
Indices de la production industrielle [suite]
1990=100

Country or area and industry [ISIC Rev.3] Pays ou zone et industrie [CITI Rév.3]	1993	1994	1995	1996	1997	1998	1999	2000
Peru Pérou								
Total industry [CDE] [7] **Total, industrie [CDE]** [7]	**107.2**	**120.9**	**131.3**	**134.6**	**143.7**	**143.1**	**145.0**	**150.3**
Total mining [C] **Total, industries extractives [C]**	**107.8**	**120.7**	**125.9**	**132.4**	**144.3**	**152.3**	**170.3**	**174.4**
Total manufacturing [D] **Total, industries manufacturières [D]**	**106.9**	**124.7**	**131.5**	**133.5**	**140.6**	**135.6**	**142.1**	**152.0**
Food, beverages, tobacco Aliments, boissons, tabac	100.5	120.3	120.0	120.9	124.4	119.0	135.3	143.8
Textiles,wearing apparel, leather, footwear Textiles, habillement, cuir et chaussures	99.7	134.8	147.8	150.7	158.1	146.8	141.8	159.1
Chemicals, petroleum, rubber and plastic prod. Prod. chimiques, pétroliers, caoutch. et plast.	130.0	156.5	164.4	177.9	200.4	190.7	195.0	210.2
Basic metals Métaux de base	125.5	170.6	179.8	195.3	207.8	218.3	219.2	230.3
Metal products Produits métalliques	77.9	106.2	128.7	104.5	108.7	110.1	83.6	91.9
Electricity [E] **Electricité [E]**	**112.3**	**124.6**	**125.0**	**132.4**	**149.2**	**160.8**	**163.9**	**171.4**
Suriname Suriname								
Total industry [CDE] **Total, industrie [CDE]**	**100.0**	**96.0**	**105.0**	**109.0**	**113.0**	**112.0**	**104.0**	**...**
Total mining [C] **Total, industries extractives [C]**	**98.0**	**101.0**	**103.0**	**107.0**	**174.0**	**200.0**	**...**	**...**
Total manufacturing [D] **Total, industries manufacturières [D]**	**107.0**	**84.0**	**111.0**	**113.0**	**116.0**	**96.0**	**88.0**	**...**
Food, beverages, tobacco Aliments, boissons, tabac	87.6	92.9	89.9	108.8	110.6	120.8	140.2	...
Leather, leather products and footwear Cuir, produits en cuir et chaussures	76.0	85.0	...	...	...	...	...	...
Rubber and plastics products Prod. caoutchouc et plastiques	124.0	151.0	...	...	...	...	...	...
Electricity, gas and water [E] **Electricité, gaz et eau [E]**	**96.0**	**67.0**	**94.0**	**114.0**	**132.0**	**150.0**	**81.0**	**59.0**
Uruguay Uruguay								
Total manufacturing [D] **Total, industries manufacturières [D]**	**81.1**	**83.4**	**86.1**	**89.6**	**94.7**	**99.9**	**91.4**	**92.1**
Food, beverages, tobacco Aliments, boissons, tabac	101.5	108.0	109.4	117.1	127.3	129.9	129.5	123.9
Textiles,wearing apparel, leather, footwear Textiles, habillement, cuir et chaussures	97.2	101.0	84.4	89.7	92.9	78.3	61.0	64.9
Chemicals, petroleum, rubber and plastic prod. Prod. chimiques, pétroliers, caoutch. et plast.	87.4	89.9	97.7	96.8	96.9	99.9	93.2	96.4
Basic metals Métaux de base	85.5	78.4	74.3	72.9	79.5	82.8	78.2	75.0
Metal products Produits métalliques	87.0	107.3	67.1	51.4	64.0	87.8	69.9	81.0
Asia · Asie								
Armenia [8] **Arménie** [8]								
Total industry [CDE] **Total, industrie [CDE]**	**...**	**...**	**100.0**	**101.4**	**102.4**	**100.2**	**105.5**	**112.3**
Total mining [C] **Total, industries extractives [C]**	**...**	**...**	**100.0**	**116.1**	**110.2**	**143.1**	**166.3**	**207.4**
Total manufacturing [D] **Total, industries manufacturières [D]**	**...**	**...**	**100.0**	**99.0**	**101.9**	**97.1**	**107.3**	**114.7**
Electricity [E] **Electricité [E]**	**...**	**...**	**100.0**	**108.3**	**105.2**	**105.7**	**100.0**	**102.6**
Azerbaijan Azerbaïdjan								
Total industry [CDE] **Total, industrie [CDE]**	**50.9**	**38.3**	**30.1**	**28.1**	**28.2**	**28.8**	**29.9**	**31.9**
Total mining [C] **Total, industries extractives [C]**	**78.0**	**72.0**	**53.0**	**51.9**	**51.6**	**64.2**	**77.0**	**77.9**
Total manufacturing [D] **Total, industries manufacturières [D]**	**48.8**	**35.4**	**27.5**	**24.8**	**25.0**	**22.0**	**20.0**	**23.1**

26
Index numbers of industrial production [cont.]
Indices de la production industrielle [suite]
1990=100

Country or area and industry [ISIC Rev.3] Pays ou zone et industrie [CITI Rév.3]	1993	1994	1995	1996	1997	1998	1999	2000
Electricity [E]								
Electricité [E]	76.5	67.7	63.5	67.2	62.6	65.8	66.5	69.0
Bangladesh ² Bangladesh ²								
Total industry [CDE]								
Total, industrie [CDE]	129.9	140.5	150.0	159.3	165.4	168.8	182.1	197.3
Total mining [C]								
Total, industries extractives [C]	125.2	132.9	146.9	157.6	156.4	166.8	168.5	197.6
Total manufacturing [D]								
Total, industries manufacturières [D]	131.1	142.2	150.9	160.4	165.7	181.1	186.8	200.4
Food, beverages, tobacco								
Aliments, boissons, tabac	133.6	147.5	160.8	156.0	154.9	164.3	165.0	176.0
Textiles,wearing apparel, leather, footwear								
Textiles, habillement, cuir et chaussures	133.7	135.0	148.3	167.7	181.8	212.3	228.7	242.0
Chemicals, petroleum, rubber and plastic prod.								
Prod. chimiques, pétroliers, caoutch. et plast.	139.5	154.5	157.2	168.9	162.5	169.0	161.2	168.4
Basic metals								
Métaux de base	66.4	117.6	195.8	170.4	184.7	205.8	174.8	182.1
Metal products								
Produits métalliques	85.5	79.4	85.5	79.5	89.9	129.8	99.0	102.5
Electricity [E]								
Electricité [E]	119.2	126.6	140.4	148.5	153.5	166.9	178.8	190.7
China, Hong Kong SAR † Chine, Hong Kong RAS †								
Total industry [DE] ³								
Total, industrie [DE] ³	104.7	101.3	102.8	99.7	99.3	92.7	87.1	87.4
Total manufacturing [D]								
Total, industries manufacturières [D]	102.0	101.8	102.8	98.9	98.2	89.7	84.0	83.5
Food, beverages, tobacco								
Aliments, boissons, tabac	111.8	113.5	113.0	112.0	111.5	101.3	99.7	96.6
Textiles and wearing apparel								
Textiles and habillement	100.6	100.3	99.4	94.3	93.2	85.8	83.8	86.6
Chemicals and other non−metallic mineral prod.								
Prod. chimiques et minéraux non−métalliques	81.1	74.1	70.2	70.3	71.2	61.8	52.6	45.0
Basic metals and metal products								
Métaux de base et produtis métalliques	102.8	105.4	113.0	106.5	103.4	95.4	91.3	90.6
Electricity and gas [E]								
Electricité et gaz [E]	124.5	98.1	102.7	105.1	107.4	114.9	109.7	116.4
Cyprus Chypre								
Total industry [CDE]								
Total, industrie [CDE]	98.0	101.4	102.9	99.6	99.5	102.3	104.0	108.6
Total mining [C]								
Total, industries extractives [C]	122.0	132.1	121.7	118.8	123.4	147.4	157.4	163.4
Total manufacturing [D]								
Total, industries manufacturières [D]	93.0	96.3	96.8	91.9	91.3	92.3	92.6	96.3
Food, beverages, tobacco								
Aliments, boissons, tabac	98.8	108.2	108.4	102.7	100.2	100.0	103.4	107.5
Textiles,wearing apparel, leather, footwear								
Textiles, habillement, cuir et chaussures	75.1	74.6	71.7	60.2	57.6	58.7	54.5	50.2
Chemicals, petroleum, rubber and plastic prod.								
Prod. chimiques, pétroliers, caoutch. et plast.	94.3	100.4	103.6	101.8	106.5	105.3	105.3	106.2
Metal products								
Produits métalliques	115.4	117.0	122.2	121.0	122.0	124.2	128.0	138.7
Electricity, gas and water [E]								
Electricité, gaz et eau [E]	125.0	133.4	143.5	151.5	154.7	166.4	177.2	189.0
India ⁹ Inde ⁹								
Total industry [CDE]								
Total, industrie [CDE]	109.1	119.1	134.6	142.7	152.2	158.6	169.0	177.5
Total mining [C]								
Total, industries extractives [C]	105.6	116.0	127.2	124.7	133.4	132.4	133.7	138.7
Total manufacturing [D]								
Total, industries manufacturières [D]	107.6	117.3	133.9	143.7	153.3	160.0	171.4	180.6
Food, beverages, tobacco								
Aliments, boissons, tabac	98.7	113.0	120.4	127.0	133.2	136.3	143.1	152.1
Textiles,wearing apparel, leather, footwear								
Textiles, habillement, cuir et chaussures	116.8	116.5	136.8	150.3	159.0	153.6	164.0	172.1

26
Index numbers of industrial production [*cont.*]
Indices de la production industrielle [*suite*]
1990=100

Country or area and industry [ISIC Rev.3] Pays ou zone et industrie [CITI Rév.3]	1993	1994	1995	1996	1997	1998	1999	2000
Chemicals, petroleum, rubber and plastic prod. Prod. chimiques, pétroliers, caoutch. et plast.	106.2	112.5	124.1	129.2	144.3	155.3	166.7	181.0
Basic metals Métaux de base	131.1	148.4	171.8	183.3	188.2	183.5	192.6	196.2
Metal products Produits métalliques	95.1	108.2	123.7	133.9	139.9	152.3	168.4	176.6
Electricity [E] **Electricité [E]**	**122.5**	**132.9**	**143.7**	**149.4**	**159.2**	**169.5**	**181.9**	**189.1**
Indonesia Indonésie								
Total industry [CDE] [3] **Total, industrie [CDE]** [3]	**120.6**	**127.0**	**134.5**	**136.7**	**142.2**	**129.6**	**127.7**	**135.1**
Total mining [C] **Total, industries extractives [C]**	**106.4**	**107.2**	**108.7**	**110.6**	**112.3**	**112.9**	**105.3**	**110.6**
Total manufacturing [D] **Total, industries manufacturières [D]**	**137.3**	**149.7**	**163.8**	**164.8**	**173.7**	**142.0**	**144.7**	**150.0**
Food, beverages, tobacco Aliments, boissons, tabac	136.1	142.1	163.4	169.8	164.8	152.8	142.6	139.6
Textiles,wearing apparel, leather, footwear Textiles, habillement, cuir et chaussures	151.1	161.9	170.4	167.3	172.9	177.9	193.4	178.0
Chemicals, petroleum, rubber and plastic prod. Prod. chimiques, pétroliers, caoutch. et plast.	145.4	157.9	170.1	182.0	193.5	177.4	186.4	181.4
Basic metals Métaux de base	213.3	232.9	282.0	279.6	293.5	228.6	251.7	308.2
Metal products Produits métalliques	92.1	111.9	124.8	119.1	144.4	63.8	70.3	106.0
Electricity [E] **Electricité [E]**	**137.6**	**155.8**	**180.3**	**206.2**	**234.5**	**266.1**	**302.0**	**333.9**
Iran (Islamic Rep. of) Iran (Rép. islamique d')								
Total manufacturing [D] **Total, industries manufacturières [D]**	**121.3**	**129.4**	**138.1**	**146.1**	**150.0**	**180.0**	**185.0**	...
Food and beverages Aliments et boissons	129.5	134.4	150.1	163.8	178.3	185.6	197.8	...
Textiles, wearing apparel, leather, footwear Textiles, habillement, cuir et chaussures	120.8	129.1	127.8	138.5	140.9	137.1	133.2	...
Chemical, rubber and plastic products Prod. chimiques, caoutchouc et plastiques	109.3	116.9	128.6	146.0	154.6	148.2	158.5	...
Metal products Produits métalliques	191.1	157.0	181.7	194.8	264.9	284.7	318.5	...
Israel Israël								
Total industry [CD] **Total, industrie [CD]**	**124.1**	**132.5**	**143.7**	**151.4**	**154.0**	**158.4**	**160.6**	**176.8**
Total mining [C] **Total, industries extractives [C]**	**124.3**	**134.8**	**148.7**	**160.3**	**156.0**	**162.4**	**160.9**	**157.1**
Total manufacturing [D] **Total, industries manufacturières [D]**	**124.1**	**132.5**	**143.4**	**151.1**	**153.9**	**158.3**	**160.7**	**177.4**
Food, beverages, tobacco Aliments, boissons, tabac	112.6	119.7	130.3	130.5	134.4	135.4	137.3	137.5
Textiles Textiles	110.5	119.8	128.4	121.4	121.4	125.4	131.4	124.0
Chemicals, petroleum, rubber and plastic prod. Prod. chimiques, pétroliers, caoutch. et plast.	131.3	145.7	157.7	170.4	171.3	187.0	185.8	192.1
Basic metals Métaux de base	121.4	138.7	165.9	175.6	178.1	167.7	166.9	170.0
Metal products Produits métalliques	123.3	133.9	146.4	150.8	153.9	157.6	156.7	168.7
Japan Japon								
Total industry [CDE] **Total, industrie [CDE]**	**91.2**	**92.4**	**95.4**	**97.7**	**101.1**	**94.4**	**95.3**	**100.6**
Total mining [C] **Total, industries extractives [C]**	**100.0**	**99.8**	**96.2**	**97.6**	**89.2**	**83.2**	**82.8**	**82.5**
Total manufacturing [D] **Total, industries manufacturières [D]**	**91.2**	**92.1**	**95.1**	**97.3**	**100.8**	**93.7**	**94.4**	**100.0**
Food, beverages, tobacco Aliments, boissons, tabac	100.0	101.6	100.9	101.8	101.3	98.6	99.9	101.1

26
Index numbers of industrial production [*cont.*]
Indices de la production industrielle [*suite*]
1990=100

Country or area and industry [ISIC Rev.3] Pays ou zone et industrie [CITI Rév.3]	1993	1994	1995	1996	1997	1998	1999	2000
Textiles,wearing apparel, leather, footwear Textiles, habillement, cuir et chaussures	84.2	80.4	74.8	72.2	69.9	62.0	57.8	53.7
Chemicals, petroleum, rubber and plastic prod. Prod. chimiques, pétroliers, caoutch. et plast.	100.3	104.0	109.0	110.3	113.7	108.9	112.0	113.1
Basic metals Métaux de base	91.2	90.9	94.1	93.3	97.6	86.5	86.1	94.5
Metal products Produits métalliques	89.2	90.4	95.1	99.9	104.9	97.6	98.4	106.7
Electricity and gas [E] **Electricité et gaz [E]**	**107.0**	**114.0**	**116.6**	**120.3**	**123.1**	**124.5**	**126.1**	**130.0**
Jordan Jordanie								
Total industry [CDE] **Total, industrie [CDE]**	**116.7**	**123.4**	**138.8**	**131.5**	**138.2**	**141.8**	**142.3**	**147.8**
Total mining [C] **Total, industries extractives [C]**	**86.9**	**93.4**	**108.5**	**110.0**	**112.9**	**107.9**	**115.7**	**117.2**
Total manufacturing [D] **Total, industries manufacturières [D]**	**120.6**	**127.0**	**136.8**	**130.2**	**138.1**	**142.4**	**139.6**	**146.9**
Food, beverages, tobacco Aliments, boissons, tabac	124.1	132.8	150.5	138.7	125.6	162.2	163.3	211.7
Textiles,wearing apparel, leather, footwear Textiles, habillement, cuir et chaussures	87.7	84.4	82.2	94.4	89.8	88.6	71.0	63.9
Chemicals, petroleum, rubber and plastic prod. Prod. chimiques, pétroliers, caoutch. et plast.	91.8	91.4	120.9	96.1	124.6	117.8	103.8	105.9
Basic metals Métaux de base	105.1	89.0	84.6	91.9	66.0	54.5	63.6	59.8
Electricity and gas [E] **Electricité et gaz [E]**	**135.0**	**143.9**	**163.1**	**174.9**	**182.8**	**202.1**	**212.2**	**214.0**
Korea, Republic of Corée, Rép. de								
Total industry [CDE] **Total, industrie [CDE]**	**121.2**	**134.5**	**150.6**	**163.3**	**171.1**	**159.9**	**198.6**	**231.9**
Total mining [C] **Total, industries extractives [C]**	**79.9**	**78.7**	**73.6**	**72.1**	**69.1**	**53.6**	**57.8**	**57.0**
Total manufacturing [D] **Total, industries manufacturières [D]**	**121.1**	**134.5**	**150.6**	**163.1**	**170.5**	**159.2**	**199.1**	**233.0**
Food, beverages, tobacco Aliments, boissons, tabac	112.1	119.9	119.9	126.0	124.9	114.9	123.8	127.8
Textiles,wearing apparel, leather, footwear Textiles, habillement, cuir et chaussures	77.3	75.2	72.2	67.9	59.2	48.4	51.6	53.3
Chemicals, petroleum, rubber and plastic prod. Prod. chimiques, pétroliers, caoutch. et plast.	149.7	159.7	172.6	193.6	218.6	199.6	221.6	231.4
Basic metals Métaux de base	128.9	139.9	153.6	163.0	172.4	151.5	173.0	187.9
Metal products Produits métalliques	129.2	153.4	185.3	210.0	225.3	218.5	310.8	398.3
Electricity and gas [E] **Electricité et gaz [E]**	**139.2**	**160.5**	**182.1**	**204.6**	**224.6**	**216.9**	**243.7**	**273.0**
Malaysia Malaisie								
Total industry [CDE] **Total, industrie [CDE]**	**132.4**	**148.9**	**168.3**	**186.9**	**206.7**	**191.9**	**209.2**	**249.1**
Total mining [C] **Total, industries extractives [C]**	**109.3**	**113.2**	**123.3**	**130.5**	**133.7**	**135.1**	**130.8**	**130.5**
Total manufacturing [D] **Total, industries manufacturières [D]**	**142.0**	**163.2**	**186.3**	**209.2**	**235.2**	**211.0**	**238.0**	**297.4**
Food, beverages, tobacco Aliments, boissons, tabac	106.5	114.6	121.5	132.2	142.7	137.3	155.7	182.4
Textiles,wearing apparel, leather, footwear Textiles, habillement, cuir et chaussures	133.2	147.4	155.8	156.4	164.6	154.5	160.8	173.4
Chemicals, petroleum, rubber and plastic prod. Prod. chimiques, pétroliers, caoutch. et plast.	137.1	155.1	173.8	201.8	239.3	237.5	270.2	307.6
Basic metals Métaux de base	148.1	170.0	191.6	224.5	253.8	179.6	257.9	271.5
Metal products Produits métalliques	174.7	213.8	256.0	283.7	319.8	277.0	317.5	437.4

26

Index numbers of industrial production [*cont.*]

Indices de la production industrielle [*suite*]

1990=100

Country or area and industry [ISIC Rev.3] Pays ou zone et industrie [CITI Rév.3]	1993	1994	1995	1996	1997	1998	1999	2000
Electricity [E] **Electricité [E]**	144.9	164.8	188.2	212.2	242.3	250.6	260.2	276.2
Mongolia Mongolie								
Total industry [CDE] **Total, industrie [CDE]**	59.1	61.3	68.6	66.9	69.9	127.7	73.2	74.7
Total mining [C] **Total, industries extractives [C]**	121.2	154.8	187.4	201.1	235.1	218.4	226.7	240.1
Total manufacturing [D] **Total, industries manufacturières [D]**	42.4	36.5	40.8	36.5	33.5	29.9	29.0	26.9
Food and beverages Aliments et boissons	40.8	35.6	42.5	32.1	30.1	29.6	25.8	25.3
Textiles,wearing apparel, leather, footwear Textiles, habillement, cuir et chaussures	31.4	25.8	30.6	23.7	22.3	20.9	23.7	24.1
Chemicals and chemical products Produits chimiques	74.3	68.1	69.9	68.1	67.2	72.0	75.5	75.8
Basic metals Métaux de base	34.4	49.6	102.1	94.8	170.8	146.1	148.1	136.1
Electricity and gas [E] **Electricité et gaz [E]**	101.7	123.6	130.2	125.3	122.0	127.7	131.6	134.9
Myanmar [1] Myanmar [1]								
Total industry [CDE] [3] **Total, industrie [CDE] [3]**	118.3	128.5	139.0	145.3	...	...	...	...
Total mining [C] **Total, industries extractives [C]**	130.4	152.3	173.5	186.0	...	...	...	...
Total manufacturing [D] **Total, industries manufacturières [D]**	116.9	126.1	135.5	141.3	...	...	...	...
Food and beverages Aliments et boissons	118.0	122.8	128.5	132.5	...	...	...	...
Textiles,wearing apparel, leather, footwear Textiles, habillement, cuir et chaussures	116.0	160.9	175.7	174.7	...	...	...	...
Chemicals and petroleum products Prod. chimiques, pétroliers, caoutch. et plast.	96.6	127.7	182.0	173.0	...	...	...	...
Basic metals and other non−metallic mineral prod. Métaux de base et minéraux non−métalliques	113.9	103.6	107.2	112.8	...	...	...	...
Metal products Produits métalliques	116.6	132.8	175.3	236.3	...	...	...	...
Electricity [E] **Electricité [E]**	128.1	137.4	153.5	161.1	...	...	...	...
Pakistan [1] Pakistan [1]								
Total industry [CDE] [3] **Total, industrie [CDE] [3]**	116.7	114.2	123.6	122.4	130.6	135.0	134.8	141.4
Total mining [C] **Total, industries extractives [C]**	100.0	98.4	107.8	111.0	109.9	108.5	106.4	115.6
Total manufacturing [D] **Total, industries manufacturières [D]**	117.1	118.9	122.7	120.0	129.2	133.8	133.6	144.8
Electricity and gas [E] **Electricité et gaz [E]**	122.8	130.1	137.8	142.9	150.1	156.0	156.9	133.8
Singapore Singapour								
Total manufacturing [D] **Total, industries manufacturières [D]**	118.8	134.2	148.0	153.0	160.0	159.4	181.5	209.2
Food, beverages, tobacco Aliments, boissons, tabac	114.4	120.8	121.4	122.3	115.6	102.5	104.9	104.6
Textiles,wearing apparel, leather, footwear Textiles, habillement, cuir et chaussures	75.3	66.8	54.3	44.0	43.0	46.0	47.9	54.8
Chemicals, petroleum, rubber and plastic prod. Prod. chimiques, pétroliers, caoutch. et plast.	115.1	124.8	126.1	131.4	149.1	166.9	192.1	200.8
Basic metals Métaux de base	109.3	111.2	101.4	101.6	106.7	88.6	94.1	99.8
Metal products Produits métalliques	111.0	123.7	131.6	130.1	134.7	131.7	148.7	178.7
Sri Lanka Sri Lanka								
Total manufacturing [D] **Total, industries manufacturières [D]**	118.6	125.0	131.6	123.1	119.8	116.5	...	...

26
Index numbers of industrial production [*cont.*]
Indices de la production industrielle [*suite*]
1990=100

Country or area and industry [ISIC Rev.3] Pays ou zone et industrie [CITI Rév.3]	1993	1994	1995	1996	1997	1998	1999	2000
Food, beverages, tobacco								
Aliments, boissons, tabac	107.4	128.9	135.2	120.7	120.9	116.2	...	...
Textiles,wearing apparel, leather, footwear								
Textiles, habillement, cuir et chaussures	169.5	162.2	150.3	147.5	159.9	170.4	...	...
Chemicals, petroleum, rubber and plastic prod.								
Prod. chimiques, pétroliers, caoutch. et plast.	100.1	105.2	120.1	144.1	114.2	111.2	...	...
Basic metals								
Métaux de base	90.2	92.9	91.9	100.2	99.3	100.9	...	...
Metal products								
Produits métalliques	101.3	118.2	128.1	122.5	153.8	156.5	...	...
Syrian Arab Republic Rép. arabe syrienne								
Total industry [CDE]								
Total, industrie [CDE]	**116.6**	**125.7**	**129.5**	**130.8**	**138.6**	**141.2**	**141.2**	...
Total mining [C]								
Total, industries extractives [C]	**136.9**	**142.9**	**148.8**	**148.8**	**150.3**	**151.8**	**150.3**	...
Total manufacturing [D]								
Total, industries manufacturières [D]	**107.0**	**114.1**	**117.6**	**118.8**	**128.2**	**129.3**	**129.3**	...
Food, beverages, tobacco								
Aliments, boissons, tabac	103.8	108.2	120.4	120.6	133.7	123.5	131.2	...
Textiles,wearing apparel, leather, footwear								
Textiles, habillement, cuir et chaussures	95.4	97.1	96.5	95.7	104.5	105.6	110.5	...
Chemicals, petroleum, rubber and plastic prod.								
Prod. chimiques, pétroliers, caoutch. et plast.	114.9	130.4	121.1	128.0	142.8	154.1	137.8	...
Basic metals								
Métaux de base	108.3	74.6	73.2	106.8	119.2	116.3	107.5	...
Metal products								
Produits métalliques	180.5	246.1	292.9	276.4	254.8	230.7	261.8	...
Electricity and water [E]								
Electricité et eau [E]	**101.3**	**118.2**	**129.9**	**140.3**	**149.4**	**167.5**	**184.4**	...
Tajikistan Tadjikistan								
Total industry [CDE]								
Total, industrie [CDE]	**67.0**	**50.0**	**43.0**	**33.0**	**32.0**	**35.0**	**37.0**	...
Total mining [C]								
Total, industries extractives [C]	**75.0**	**65.0**	**64.0**	**62.0**	**76.0**	**84.0**	**84.0**	...
Total manufacturing [D]								
Total, industries manufacturières [D]	**66.0**	**49.0**	**41.0**	**30.0**	**27.0**	**28.0**	**32.0**	...
Electricity, gas and water [E]								
Electricité, gaz et eau [E]	**99.0**	**96.0**	**95.0**	**93.0**	**104.0**	**107.0**	**120.0**	...
Thailand Thaïlande								
Total manufacturing [D]								
Total, industries manufacturières [D]	**130.2**	**138.8**	**150.8**	**163.3**	**162.6**	**145.6**	**163.8**	**168.8**
Turkey Turquie								
Total industry [CDE]								
Total, industrie [CDE]	**115.0**	**107.8**	**117.0**	**123.9**	**137.2**	**138.4**	**131.1**	**138.5**
Total mining [C]								
Total, industries extractives [C]	**95.2**	**104.1**	**104.7**	**108.1**	**114.5**	**125.9**	**115.0**	**110.1**
Total manufacturing [D]								
Total, industries manufacturières [D]	**112.3**	**101.8**	**110.5**	**117.7**	**131.2**	**130.8**	**123.4**	**130.4**
Food, beverages, tobacco								
Aliments, boissons, tabac	114.1	118.7	125.0	136.5	147.2	152.6	149.6	157.3
Textiles,wearing apparel, leather, footwear								
Textiles, habillement, cuir et chaussures	92.5	89.3	102.5	111.6	119.7	114.5	107.3	117.2
Chemicals, petroleum, rubber and plastic prod.								
Prod. chimiques, pétroliers, caoutch. et plast.	110.6	106.2	122.6	125.4	138.2	140.7	137.2	136.5
Basic metals								
Métaux de base	110.1	104.1	110.7	119.2	130.7	131.4	129.0	133.9
Metal products								
Produits métalliques	134.8	96.9	120.7	138.5	172.3	172.6	157.6	188.6
Electricity, gas and water [E]								
Electricité, gaz et eau [E]	**128.1**	**136.0**	**149.8**	**165.6**	**179.2**	**192.8**	**202.3**	**217.0**
Europe · Europe								
Albania [10] Albanie [10]								
Total industry [CDE]								
Total, industrie [CDE]	**100.0**	**88.0**	**76.1**	**63.0**	**40.8**	**62.8**	**45.4**	**92.3**

26
Index numbers of industrial production [*cont.*]
Indices de la production industrielle [*suite*]
1990=100

Country or area and industry [ISIC Rev.3] Pays ou zone et industrie [CITI Rév.3]	1993	1994	1995	1996	1997	1998	1999	2000
Total mining [C] **Total, industries extractives [C]**	100.0	93.2	86.5	75.9	47.1	48.6	35.8	31.5
Total manufacturing [D] **Total, industries manufacturières [D]**	100.0	85.9	71.8	58.2	53.7	49.2	55.8	83.5
Electricity, gas and water [E] **Electricité, gaz et eau [E]**	100.0	115.0	130.0	170.4	150.8	149.0	157.9	135.9
Austria Autriche								
Total industry [CDE] **Total, industrie [CDE]**	92.5	93.6	112.3	113.4	120.6	130.5	138.4	151.0
Total mining [C] **Total, industries extractives [C]**	78.6	75.4	89.7	89.9	86.7	93.2	96.3	100.3
Total manufacturing [D] **Total, industries manufacturières [D]**	90.5	91.9	112.8	113.6	121.8	132.9	140.9	155.6
Food, beverages, tobacco Aliments, boissons, tabac	99.7	94.5	97.9	98.0	106.2	110.9	114.8	118.7
Textiles,wearing apparel, leather, footwear Textiles, habillement, cuir et chaussures	87.2	79.5	75.9	72.1	73.9	75.8	70.9	69.7
Chemicals, petroleum, rubber and plastic prod. Prod. chimiques, pétroliers, caoutch. et plast.	102.8	98.8	109.7	111.4	114.1	122.6	126.7	138.6
Basic metals Métaux de base	83.4	89.8	105.0	101.1	116.8	120.3	119.6	134.8
Metal products Produits métalliques	82.2	90.1	121.4	124.8	135.2	159.5	185.1	215.8
Electricity, gas and water [E] **Electricité, gaz et eau [E]**	121.4	119.2	114.1	117.4	119.6	121.6	128.8	129.3
Belarus [8] Belarus [8]								
Total industry [CDE] **Total, industrie [CDE]**	...	...	100.0	103.5	123.0	138.3	152.5	164.7
Total mining [C] **Total, industries extractives [C]**	...	...	100.0	99.0	111.7	118.6	123.9	117.2
Total manufacturing [D] **Total, industries manufacturières [D]**	...	...	100.0	104.3	125.6	143.9	159.8	174.8
Electricity, gas and water [E] **Electricité, gaz et eau [E]**	...	...	100.0	98.4	103.9	96.2	101.4	98.6
Belgium Belgique								
Total industry [CDE] **Total, industrie [CDE]**	93.0	94.7	100.6	101.4	106.0	109.6	110.8	116.4
Total mining [C] **Total, industries extractives [C]**	101.4	103.3	145.1	154.8	164.5	169.2	181.7	195.2
Total manufacturing [D] **Total, industries manufacturières [D]**	98.3	100.1	106.5	107.0	112.2	115.4	116.8	123.9
Food, beverages, tobacco Aliments, boissons, tabac	101.8	99.8	107.5	108.4	113.4	115.9	111.2	115.6
Textiles,wearing apparel, leather, footwear Textiles, habillement, cuir et chaussures	93.5	93.1	86.9	79.0	81.1	78.4	73.3	75.7
Chemicals, petroleum, rubber and plastic prod. Prod. chimiques, pétroliers, caoutch. et plast.	105.2	104.9	112.9	117.2	129.6	130.4	139.3	152.2
Basic metals Métaux de base	95.0	103.3	106.8	104.5	104.9	108.1	108.4	112.2
Metal products Produits métalliques	87.6	89.8	99.3	100.5	105.4	110.8	114.5	118.2
Electricity, gas and water [E] **Electricité, gaz et eau [E]**	101.1	102.7	106.0	109.9	112.0	119.5	119.6	116.8
Bulgaria [8] Bulgarie [8]								
Total industry [CDE] **Total, industrie [CDE]**	...	...	100.0	105.1	94.6	87.1	79.0	83.2
Total mining [C] **Total, industries extractives [C]**	...	...	100.0	115.5	105.2	105.8	93.0	89.2
Total manufacturing [D] **Total, industries manufacturières [D]**	...	...	100.0	104.8	92.2	82.1	74.7	78.2
Electricity, gas and water [E] **Electricité, gaz et eau [E]**	...	...	100.0	101.6	108.3	119.3	102.4	115.0

26
Index numbers of industrial production [*cont.*]
Indices de la production industrielle [*suite*]
1990=100

Country or area and industry [ISIC Rev.3] Pays ou zone et industrie [CITI Rév.3]	1993	1994	1995	1996	1997	1998	1999	2000
Croatia Croatie								
Total industry [CDE]								
Total, industrie [CDE]	57.4	55.9	56.1	57.8	61.7	64.0	63.2	64.2
Total mining [C]								
Total, industries extractives [C]	77.6	73.9	75.7	73.4	73.1	71.4	72.7	74.1
Total manufacturing [D]								
Total, industries manufacturières [D]	54.7	53.4	53.2	53.9	56.0	57.8	56.1	57.7
Food, beverages, tobacco								
Aliments, boissons, tabac	63.8	66.5	68.2	70.1	65.3	67.5	64.0	64.1
Textiles,wearing apparel, leather, footwear								
Textiles, habillement, cuir et chaussures	58.9	55.3	49.6	43.0	44.6	44.6	40.0	39.7
Chemicals, petroleum, rubber and plastic prod.								
Prod. chimiques, pétroliers, caoutch. et plast.	58.7	60.3	62.3	60.3	60.0	58.0	58.7	61.9
Basic metals								
Métaux de base	42.2	42.1	34.7	31.5	39.6	46.3	40.1	41.8
Metal products								
Produits métalliques	43.9	40.1	41.0	42.6	47.7	50.6	51.0	50.8
Electricity, gas and water [E]								
Electricité, gaz et eau [E]	108.1	99.8	104.7	131.3	163.0	177.2	189.5	180.5
Czech Republic Rép. tchèque								
Total industry [CDE]								
Total, industrie [CDE]	68.3	69.8	75.9	77.4	80.8	82.1	79.5	83.8
Total mining [C]								
Total, industries extractives [C]	69.7	70.1	69.1	70.1	68.1	64.1	56.4	60.7
Total manufacturing [D]								
Total, industries manufacturières [D]	56.7	56.7	61.4	62.4	66.4	68.1	66.3	69.6
Electricity, gas and water [E]								
Electricité, gaz et eau [E]	94.5	94.5	98.5	102.1	99.4	97.9	94.5	100.3
Denmark Danemark								
Total industry [CD]								
Total, industrie [CD]	101.0	111.0	116.0	118.0	124.1	126.8	129.2	137.2
Total mining [C]								
Total, industries extractives [C]	91.0	97.0	97.0	100.3	85.7	91.5	91.2	91.7
Total manufacturing [D]								
Total, industries manufacturières [D]	101.0	111.0	116.0	118.0	124.4	126.9	129.3	137.5
Food, beverages, tobacco								
Aliments, boissons, tabac	106.6	113.4	109.6	107.5	113.5	112.3	112.0	115.1
Textiles,wearing apparel, leather, footwear								
Textiles, habillement, cuir et chaussures	93.5	98.5	97.1	100.2	98.4	102.9	97.6	101.4
Chemicals, petroleum, rubber and plastic prod.								
Prod. chimiques, pétroliers, caoutch. et plast.	106.5	118.3	126.3	131.0	141.0	147.1	165.8	185.4
Basic metals								
Métaux de base	121.8	129.9	132.7	125.2	138.4	135.9	133.8	158.6
Metal products								
Produits métalliques	95.5	108.8	117.6	121.9	127.1	130.9	130.6	141.8
Estonia Estonie								
Total industry [CDE]								
Total, industrie [CDE]	48.9	47.4	48.3	49.7	57.0	59.3	57.3	64.9
Total mining [C]								
Total, industries extractives [C]	54.1	53.5	51.1	54.1	53.8	51.6	43.5	47.0
Total manufacturing [D]								
Total, industries manufacturières [D]	46.6	45.2	46.5	47.5	56.3	59.4	58.0	66.9
Electricity [E]								
Electricité [E]	57.9	56.5	55.4	58.8	57.0	55.0	52.0	52.0
Finland Finlande								
Total industry [CDE]								
Total, industrie [CDE]	97.1	107.9	114.5	118.6	129.7	140.2	148.8	164.9
Total mining [C]								
Total, industries extractives [C]	94.4	106.8	105.4	106.1	130.5	99.7	131.7	105.1
Total manufacturing [D]								
Total, industries manufacturières [D]	96.2	107.4	114.9	118.4	130.3	142.5	151.6	169.9
Food, beverages, tobacco								
Aliments, boissons, tabac	103.9	103.3	106.6	110.5	114.4	114.9	119.7	121.3

26
Index numbers of industrial production [*cont.*]
Indices de la production industrielle [*suite*]
1990=100

Country or area and industry [ISIC Rev.3] Pays ou zone et industrie [CITI Rév.3]	1993	1994	1995	1996	1997	1998	1999	2000
Textiles,wearing apparel, leather, footwear								
Textiles, habillement, cuir et chaussures	73.3	80.1	73.8	75.3	75.8	76.1	76.6	75.6
Chemicals, petroleum, rubber and plastic prod.								
Prod. chimiques, pétroliers, caoutch. et plast.	103.5	116.2	118.1	121.9	127.1	135.7	138.6	147.7
Basic metals								
Métaux de base	117.0	126.2	133.9	141.5	150.5	158.1	164.4	174.0
Metal products								
Produits métalliques	97.9	118.9	143.9	155.7	178.5	221.7	256.0	330.6
Electricity, gas and water [E]								
Electricité, gaz et eau [E]	**107.5**	**113.8**	**112.0**	**122.2**	**121.9**	**123.5**	**123.1**	**124.2**
France France								
Total industry [CDE]								
Total, industrie [CDE]	**95.0**	**99.1**	**101.5**	**102.4**	**106.3**	**111.8**	**114.1**	**118.0**
Total mining [C]								
Total, industries extractives [C]	**84.0**	**82.6**	**82.2**	**75.4**	**73.6**	**73.0**	**73.8**	**74.9**
Total manufacturing [D]								
Total, industries manufacturières [D]	**93.1**	**97.6**	**99.8**	**100.4**	**105.2**	**111.3**	**113.6**	**117.5**
Food, beverages, tobacco								
Aliments, boissons, tabac	101.2	103.2	104.8	106.9	110.0	111.2	113.4	113.4
Textiles,wearing apparel, leather, footwear								
Textiles, habillement, cuir et chaussures	82.8	84.3	80.1	70.9	69.3	67.3	61.0	56.5
Chemicals, petroleum, rubber and plastic prod.								
Prod. chimiques, pétroliers, caoutch. et plast.	104.8	110.5	113.2	115.7	121.0	127.1	129.4	135.9
Basic metals								
Métaux de base	87.4	96.6	97.1	94.6	102.0	105.0	102.9	109.3
Metal products								
Produits métalliques	88.6	93.0	96.2	98.5	104.9	114.4	118.3	123.5
Electricity and gas [E]								
Electricité et gaz [E]	**113.1**	**113.4**	**118.2**	**122.6**	**120.3**	**121.5**	**124.3**	**128.3**
Germany [11] **Allemagne** [11]								
Total industry [CDE]								
Total, industrie [CDE]	**90.5**	**93.9**	**95.9**	**96.5**	**99.8**	**104.1**	**105.7**	**112.8**
Total mining [C]								
Total, industries extractives [C]	**85.7**	**82.8**	**79.6**	**75.1**	**72.5**	**67.5**	**66.6**	**63.0**
Total manufacturing [D]								
Total, industries manufacturières [D]	**90.1**	**93.9**	**96.0**	**96.4**	**100.2**	**105.1**	**106.8**	**114.8**
Food, beverages, tobacco								
Aliments, boissons, tabac	99.9	102.0	102.4	103.7	104.9	104.3	107.2	114.3
Textiles,wearing apparel, leather, footwear								
Textiles, habillement, cuir et chaussures	79.6	72.7	69.6	64.8	63.2	62.2	57.5	57.0
Chemicals, petroleum, rubber and plastic prod.								
Prod. chimiques, pétroliers, caoutch. et plast.	93.2	99.2	102.1	105.2	110.7	112.7	116.3	120.4
Basic metals								
Métaux de base	85.5	92.3	93.6	88.6	97.2	98.0	94.7	101.7
Metal products								
Produits métalliques	86.7	90.9	92.3	93.3	98.1	106.2	108.8	122.8
Electricity and gas [E]								
Electricité et gaz [E]	**98.2**	**99.1**	**101.1**	**106.7**	**105.9**	**106.1**	**106.7**	**107.4**
Greece Grèce								
Total industry [CDE]								
Total, industrie [CDE]	**95.1**	**95.7**	**97.9**	**99.1**	**99.9**	**106.8**	**109.7**	**118.1**
Total mining [C]								
Total, industries extractives [C]	**86.6**	**89.5**	**91.7**	**95.3**	**94.4**	**92.9**	**87.2**	**99.3**
Total manufacturing [D]								
Total, industries manufacturières [D]	**94.6**	**93.8**	**95.7**	**95.9**	**96.5**	**101.9**	**102.6**	**108.8**
Food, beverages, tobacco								
Aliments, boissons, tabac	112.0	115.3	120.3	117.7	124.0	126.8	127.9	132.0
Textiles,wearing apparel, leather, footwear								
Textiles, habillement, cuir et chaussures	86.2	80.3	75.7	73.3	66.8	64.1	63.2	66.1
Chemicals, petroleum, rubber and plastic prod.								
Prod. chimiques, pétroliers, caoutch. et plast.	93.0	97.5	100.8	105.5	107.7	120.5	122.6	127.2
Basic metals								
Métaux de base	92.4	93.6	102.0	99.4	112.1	106.6	113.5	128.7

26
Index numbers of industrial production [*cont.*]
Indices de la production industrielle [*suite*]
1990=100

Country or area and industry [ISIC Rev.3] Pays ou zone et industrie [CITI Rév.3]	1993	1994	1995	1996	1997	1998	1999	2000
Metal products								
Produits métalliques	98.6	89.9	89.7	87.2	86.1	98.2	101.1	110.7
Electricity and gas [E]								
Electricité et gaz [E]	**108.1**	**114.1**	**118.3**	**123.5**	**124.9**	**142.1**	**158.4**	**176.5**
Hungary Hongrie								
Total industry [CDE]								
Total, industrie [CDE]	**76.7**	**84.0**	**87.9**	**90.9**	**100.9**	**113.4**	**125.2**	**148.2**
Total mining [C]								
Total, industries extractives [C]	**72.6**	**60.1**	**52.1**	**53.4**	**48.9**	**38.9**	**39.2**	**36.0**
Total manufacturing [D]								
Total, industries manufacturières [D]	**74.7**	**81.7**	**85.9**	**88.8**	**101.8**	**118.2**	**132.8**	**160.6**
Food, beverages, tobacco								
Aliments, boissons, tabac	81.4	85.8	87.4	87.0	80.7	81.3	83.5	88.7
Textiles,wearing apparel, leather, footwear								
Textiles, habillement, cuir et chaussures	63.1	66.2	63.2	61.8	62.4	72.0	78.6	85.6
Chemicals, petroleum, rubber and plastic prod.								
Prod. chimiques, pétroliers, caoutch. et plast.	74.0	78.1	78.1	76.5	78.3	84.8	76.8	80.6
Basic metals								
Métaux de base	55.9	65.2	74.0	80.9	90.6	87.9	83.9	97.9
Metal products								
Produits métalliques	71.1	83.0	91.7	139.6	305.6	518.7	938.5	1186.0
Electricity and gas [E]								
Electricité et gaz [E]	**81.7**	**83.1**	**84.7**	**89.0**	**89.8**	**89.7**	**88.5**	**87.1**
Ireland Irlande								
Total industry [CDE]								
Total, industrie [CDE]	**119.3**	**133.4**	**160.8**	**173.0**	**204.2**	**244.5**	**280.7**	**324.0**
Total mining [C]								
Total, industries extractives [C]	**101.7**	**104.5**	**154.1**	**151.6**	**129.7**	**119.6**	**142.2**	**175.0**
Total manufacturing [D]								
Total, industries manufacturières [D]	**119.8**	**135.0**	**163.7**	**176.8**	**211.9**	**257.0**	**295.6**	**342.2**
Food, beverages, tobacco								
Aliments, boissons, tabac	116.4	125.0	138.7	140.9	144.0	151.6	158.8	167.1
Textiles,wearing apparel, leather, footwear								
Textiles, habillement, cuir et chaussures	92.2	91.7	76.2	76.4	76.6	78.0	68.6	57.2
Chemicals, rubber and plastic prod.								
Prod. chimiques, caoutch. et plast.	150.4	178.0	226.0	262.6	357.4	498.6	622.7	707.8
Basic metals								
Métaux de base	94.6	99.3	119.5	117.7	113.5	111.8	109.9	112.5
Metal products								
Produits métalliques	110.4	124.8	165.4	179.5	208.1	238.5	267.4	352.6
Electricity, gas and water [E]								
Electricité, gaz et eau [E]	**117.5**	**123.3**	**125.3**	**132.5**	**138.1**	**142.0**	**154.0**	**162.2**
Italy Italie								
Total industry [CDE]								
Total, industrie [CDE]	**96.5**	**101.5**	**107.0**	**106.0**	**109.6**	**111.6**	**111.7**	**115.2**
Total mining [C]								
Total, industries extractives [C]	**99.2**	**106.1**	**114.1**	**116.8**	**123.8**	**123.1**	**123.0**	**112.3**
Total manufacturing [D]								
Total, industries manufacturières [D]	**95.9**	**100.9**	**106.5**	**105.3**	**108.8**	**110.7**	**110.3**	**113.6**
Food, beverages, tobacco								
Aliments, boissons, tabac	104.1	104.3	105.1	104.8	107.5	109.9	113.8	116.4
Textiles,wearing apparel, leather, footwear								
Textiles, habillement, cuir et chaussures	97.9	104.5	107.6	106.0	110.0	107.3	102.5	103.2
Chemicals, petroleum, rubber and plastic prod.								
Prod. chimiques, pétroliers, caoutch. et plast.	98.4	102.6	105.3	104.9	110.8	112.1	112.1	114.8
Basic metals								
Métaux de base	100.9	111.4	115.7	115.6	118.0	117.8	108.9	116.6
Metal products								
Produits métalliques	89.0	94.5	105.5	105.5	108.1	109.8	107.8	112.3
Electricity and gas [E]								
Electricité et gaz [E]	**103.2**	**107.2**	**111.5**	**112.2**	**115.3**	**119.6**	**124.2**	**131.9**
Latvia Lettonie								
Total industry [CDE]								
Total, industrie [CDE]	**44.2**	**39.8**	**38.4**	**40.5**	**46.1**	**47.5**	**39.0**	**40.2**

26
Index numbers of industrial production [*cont.*]
Indices de la production industrielle [*suite*]
1990=100

Country or area and industry [ISIC Rev.3] Pays ou zone et industrie [CITI Rév.3]	1993	1994	1995	1996	1997	1998	1999	2000
Total mining [C]								
Total, industries extractives [C]	**38.0**	**46.6**	**38.7**	**39.7**	**42.8**	**45.4**	**48.0**	**52.3**
Total manufacturing [D]								
Total, industries manufacturières [D]	**41.8**	**36.8**	**35.2**	**37.7**	**44.2**	**45.8**	**36.4**	**38.1**
Food, beverages, tobacco								
Aliments, boissons, tabac	44.9	39.0	38.8	47.1	56.2	59.3	52.5	64.4
Textiles,wearing apparel, leather, footwear								
Textiles, habillement, cuir et chaussures	36.8	29.0	24.5	32.8	35.0	34.5	25.9	28.0
Chemicals, rubber and plastic prod.								
Prod. chimiques, caoutch. et plast.	54.9	35.8	36.9	36.4	43.1	40.8	21.9	19.5
Basic metals								
Métaux de base	61.0	68.0	56.0	55.8	78.2	133.1	182.5	182.4
Metal products								
Produits métalliques	32.9	29.7	26.5	27.8	34.4	31.7	22.3	27.1
Electricity, gas and water [E]								
Electricité, gaz et eau [E]	**59.7**	**58.6**	**58.4**	**57.3**	**56.9**	**57.6**	**54.1**	**52.5**
Lithuania [8] **Lituanie** [8]								
Total industry [CDE]								
Total, industrie [CDE]	...	...	100.0	104.1	108.8	117.8	106.1	109.4
Total mining [C]								
Total, industries extractives [C]	...	...	100.0	122.0	136.3	185.7	173.2	194.7
Total manufacturing [D]								
Total, industries manufacturières [D]	...	...	100.0	100.9	106.6	115.4	104.7	110.8
Electricity, gas and water [E]								
Electricité, gaz et eau [E]	...	...	100.0	106.7	96.8	99.9	80.0	69.5
Luxembourg **Luxembourg**								
Total industry [CDE]								
Total, industrie [CDE]	**95.2**	**100.9**	**102.0**	**102.1**	**107.4**	**116.8**	**118.6**	**124.5**
Total mining [C]								
Total, industries extractives [C]	**114.8**	**105.6**	**96.7**	**86.9**	**86.4**	**96.9**	**104.2**	**105.2**
Total manufacturing [D]								
Total, industries manufacturières [D]	**94.3**	**100.1**	**101.0**	**101.3**	**107.2**	**116.9**	**118.9**	**124.8**
Food and beverages								
Aliments et boissons	101.8	105.2	103.7	103.2	103.3	104.9	109.5	110.5
Textiles,wearing apparel, leather, footwear								
Textiles, habillement, cuir et chaussures	108.9	119.4	116.0	94.4	108.1	114.6	106.3	114.1
Chemicals, rubber and plastic products								
Prod. chimiques, caoutchouc et plastiques	94.7	107.5	111.2	116.8	123.2	148.1	135.7	145.5
Basic metals								
Métaux de base	92.2	91.0	83.7	78.4	86.1	75.4	95.6	100.9
Metal products								
Produits métalliques	90.8	96.4	105.7	112.7	113.1	128.6	128.9	129.6
Electricity and gas [E]								
Electricité et gaz [E]	**106.0**	**111.0**	**117.5**	**116.6**	**115.4**	**119.8**	**117.3**	**125.6**
Malta **Malte**								
Total industry [CDE]								
Total, industrie [CDE]	**132.8**	**149.6**	**166.0**	**158.2**	...	...	...	...
Total mining [C]								
Total, industries extractives [C]	**159.0**	**195.4**	**247.3**	**274.7**	...	...	...	...
Total manufacturing [D]								
Total, industries manufacturières [D]	**134.2**	**152.6**	**165.0**	**154.8**	...	...	...	...
Food, beverages, tobacco								
Aliments, boissons, tabac	116.1	122.3	126.7	132.5	...	...	...	...
Textiles,wearing apparel, leather, footwear								
Textiles, habillement, cuir et chaussures	102.4	116.7	102.5	110.6	...	...	...	...
Chemicals, petroleum, rubber and plastic prod.								
Prod. chimiques, pétroliers, caoutch. et plast.	141.6	154.8	170.3	176.9	...	...	...	...
Metal products								
Produits métalliques	132.0	151.4	175.8	161.6	...	...	...	...
Electricity and water [E]								
Electricité et eau [E]	**124.6**	**131.7**	**137.5**	**142.7**	...	...	...	...
Netherlands **Pays−Bas**								
Total industry [CDE]								
Total, industrie [CDE]	**100.4**	**105.3**	**108.5**	**111.1**	**111.3**	**114.0**	**116.5**	**119.9**

26
Index numbers of industrial production [*cont.*]
Indices de la production industrielle [*suite*]
1990=100

Country or area and industry [ISIC Rev.3] Pays ou zone et industrie [CITI Rév.3]	1993	1994	1995	1996	1997	1998	1999	2000
Total mining [C]								
Total, industries extractives [C]	**112.5**	**111.3**	**112.2**	**127.2**	**116.8**	**114.0**	**106.7**	**104.2**
Total manufacturing [D]								
Total, industries manufacturières [D]	**98.0**	**104.0**	**107.6**	**108.1**	**110.9**	**114.6**	**118.1**	**122.4**
Food, beverages, tobacco								
Aliments, boissons, tabac	107.6	114.2	118.1	120.2	120.6	120.0	124.0	127.3
Textiles,wearing apparel, leather, footwear								
Textiles, habillement, cuir et chaussures	85.9	84.1	79.7	78.9	79.1	81.3	80.0	82.3
Chemicals, petroleum, rubber and plastic prod.								
Prod. chimiques, pétroliers, caoutch. et plast.	98.3	108.4	114.2	111.8	111.3	112.1	119.9	126.0
Basic metals								
Métaux de base	97.3	108.9	110.1	107.3	116.2	118.6	119.5	122.0
Metal products								
Produits métalliques	95.7	100.4	104.5	106.5	110.0	117.5	120.1	126.5
Electricity, gas and water [E]								
Electricité, gaz et eau [E]	**104.9**	**106.8**	**109.3**	**114.5**	**106.5**	**107.7**	**113.1**	**115.5**
Norway Norvège								
Total industry [CDE]								
Total, industrie [CDE]	**112.2**	**120.1**	**127.2**	**134.1**	**138.7**	**137.8**	**137.5**	**141.5**
Total mining [C] [12]								
Total, industries extractives [C] [12]	**97.0**	**103.2**	**106.3**	**105.7**	**109.8**	**105.6**	**104.5**	**108.1**
Total manufacturing [D]								
Total, industries manufacturières [D]	**102.1**	**108.1**	**111.5**	**114.6**	**118.4**	**122.0**	**119.3**	**116.0**
Food, beverages, tobacco								
Aliments, boissons, tabac	104.0	108.6	110.4	112.5	113.6	112.7	109.1	107.2
Textiles,wearing apparel, leather, footwear								
Textiles, habillement, cuir et chaussures	93.7	102.8	99.2	100.5	99.1	94.3	82.4	75.8
Chemicals, petroleum, rubber and plastic prod.								
Prod. chimiques, pétroliers, caoutch. et plast.	98.5	102.7	103.6	105.4	107.6	109.7	109.7	108.2
Basic metals								
Métaux de base	101.6	109.9	108.6	111.6	115.7	121.6	125.4	126.7
Metal products								
Produits métalliques	116.2	120.1	123.9	128.7	133.8	145.4	142.7	135.6
Electricity and gas [E]								
Electricité et gaz [E]	**98.6**	**93.4**	**101.5**	**86.4**	**92.2**	**96.5**	**101.3**	**117.8**
Poland Pologne								
Total industry [CDE]								
Total, industrie [CDE]	**100.7**	**112.9**	**123.8**	**135.5**	**150.7**	**157.7**	**165.3**	**177.7**
Total mining [C]								
Total, industries extractives [C]	**88.4**	**92.4**	**91.9**	**93.1**	**91.6**	**79.6**	**76.4**	**75.4**
Total manufacturing [D]								
Total, industries manufacturières [D]	**104.2**	**118.4**	**132.1**	**147.3**	**167.3**	**178.2**	**188.2**	**203.1**
Food, beverages, tobacco								
Aliments, boissons, tabac	118.1	132.8	143.8	155.7	167.9	180.3	182.4	182.4
Textiles,wearing apparel, leather, footwear								
Textiles, habillement, cuir et chaussures	89.3	100.9	102.4	107.5	125.4	125.4	120.7	'120.2
Chemicals, petroleum, rubber and plastic prod.								
Prod. chimiques, pétroliers, caoutch. et plast.	116.3	131.6	146.4	156.7	173.3	173.6	183.2	206.3
Basic metals								
Métaux de base	74.9	87.4	100.7	100.7	113.8	108.0	97.9	107.3
Metal products								
Produits métalliques	86.2	100.5	116.2	135.4	167.7	191.7	208.9	232.6
Electricity, gas and water [E]								
Electricité, gaz et eau [E]	**87.7**	**91.9**	**92.7**	**93.1**	**95.3**	**97.1**	**99.3**	**108.4**
Portugal Portugal								
Total industry [CDE]								
Total, industrie [CDE]	**95.2**	**94.9**	**99.4**	**100.8**	**103.3**	**107.4**	**110.8**	**111.4**
Total mining [C]								
Total, industries extractives [C]	**94.4**	**89.3**	**87.5**	**86.4**	**86.4**	**88.0**	**85.5**	**86.8**
Total manufacturing [D]								
Total, industries manufacturières [D]	**92.2**	**92.5**	**95.9**	**97.4**	**101.7**	**104.3**	**105.8**	**106.1**
Food, beverages, tobacco								
Aliments, boissons, tabac	98.0	94.8	97.1	99.3	102.1	106.6	110.9	114.9

26

Index numbers of industrial production [*cont.*]

Indices de la production industrielle [*suite*]

1990=100

Country or area and industry [ISIC Rev.3] Pays ou zone et industrie [CITI Rév.3]	1993	1994	1995	1996	1997	1998	1999	2000
Textiles,wearing apparel, leather, footwear								
Textiles, habillement, cuir et chaussures	88.5	86.5	88.6	85.3	83.9	80.8	76.3	71.4
Chemicals, petroleum, rubber and plastic prod.								
Prod. chimiques, pétroliers, caoutch. et plast.	78.9	82.9	84.3	87.0	92.0	94.2	99.4	100.0
Basic metals								
Métaux de base	96.2	97.9	103.8	100.3	114.0	116.7	131.1	128.8
Metal products								
Produits métalliques	91.1	92.3	100.7	109.4	117.1	127.0	141.6	156.4
Electricity and gas [E]								
Electricité et gaz [E]	**108.0**	**106.7**	**117.1**	**118.2**	**113.4**	**124.6**	**144.6**	**146.0**
Romania Roumanie								
Total industry [CDE]								
Total, industrie [CDE]	**58.0**	**59.9**	**65.5**	**69.2**	**64.6**	**53.6**	**50.9**	**54.4**
Total mining [C]								
Total, industries extractives [C]	**82.1**	**83.4**	**83.0**	**83.6**	**78.8**	**67.7**	**63.1**	**66.2**
Total manufacturing [D]								
Total, industries manufacturières [D]	**53.9**	**55.9**	**62.6**	**67.1**	**63.1**	**51.6**	**49.2**	**53.2**
Food, beverages, tobacco								
Aliments, boissons, tabac	61.2	68.4	70.7	71.8	62.1	61.9	62.5	69.9
Textiles,wearing apparel, leather, footwear								
Textiles, habillement, cuir et chaussures	60.2	67.5	73.5	78.5	78.1	52.3	52.0	56.8
Chemicals, petroleum, rubber and plastic prod.								
Prod. chimiques, pétroliers, caoutch. et plast.	57.6	54.5	58.1	53.2	44.6	38.8	35.0	39.1
Basic metals								
Métaux de base	55.2	57.1	67.4	61.8	62.7	62.2	43.1	53.8
Metal products								
Produits métalliques	60.3	60.4	73.8	87.3	88.3	68.2	62.7	57.8
Electricity, gas and water [E]								
Electricité, gaz et eau [E]	**76.8**	**76.7**	**79.2**	**79.7**	**70.3**	**61.6**	**57.8**	**57.6**
Russian Federation Fédération de Russie								
Total industry [CDE]								
Total, industrie [CDE]	**64.9**	**51.3**	**49.4**	**47.4**	**48.7**	**46.1**	**50.6**	**57.1**
Total mining [C]								
Total, industries extractives [C]	**76.9**	**71.5**	**70.8**	**60.0**	**61.5**	...	...	...
Total manufacturing [D]								
Total, industries manufacturières [D]	**62.9**	**45.3**	**43.4**	**37.1**	**34.0**	...	...	...
Food, beverages, tobacco								
Aliments, boissons, tabac	82.0	67.4	58.6	52.1	50.0	50.3	...	...
Textiles,wearing apparel, leather, footwear								
Textiles, habillement, cuir et chaussures	51.1	25.9	18.4	14.0	12.7	9.8	...	...
Chemicals, petroleum, rubber and plastic prod.								
Prod. chimiques, pétroliers, caoutch. et plast.	57.5	43.2	45.3	41.1	40.3	39.7	...	...
Basic metals								
Métaux de base	64.9	55.8	59.7	59.1	59.7	57.1	...	...
Metal products								
Produits métalliques	62.9	37.1	29.6	16.4	12.6	10.7	...	...
Electricity and gas [E]								
Electricité et gaz [E]	**90.9**	**82.7**	**80.0**	**78.2**	**76.4**	**74.5**	**73.6**	**75.4**
Slovakia Slovaquie								
Total industry [CDE]								
Total, industrie [CDE]	**70.2**	**73.7**	**79.8**	**81.8**	**82.8**	**86.7**	**84.3**	**91.9**
Total mining [C]								
Total, industries extractives [C]	**44.5**	**43.0**	**42.8**	**45.2**	**50.5**	**44.9**	**47.8**	**46.4**
Total manufacturing [D]								
Total, industries manufacturières [D]	**67.8**	**70.9**	**78.2**	**80.0**	**81.3**	**86.3**	**82.4**	**90.8**
Electricity, gas and water [E]								
Electricité, gaz et eau [E]	**102.0**	**118.8**	**116.8**	**122.3**	**118.6**	**111.7**	**115.8**	**124.3**
Slovenia Slovénie								
Total industry [CDE]								
Total, industrie [CDE]	**73.9**	**78.7**	**80.2**	**81.0**	**81.8**	**84.8**	**84.4**	...
Total mining [C]								
Total, industries extractives [C]	**79.0**	**75.0**	**75.6**	**75.9**	**77.3**	**77.1**	**73.9**	...
Total manufacturing [D]								
Total, industries manufacturières [D]	**72.4**	**77.2**	**79.3**	**80.2**	**80.4**	**83.6**	**83.6**	...

26
Index numbers of industrial production [*cont.*]
Indices de la production industrielle [*suite*]
1990=100

Country or area and industry [ISIC Rev.3] Pays ou zone et industrie [CITI Rév.3]	1993	1994	1995	1996	1997	1998	1999	2000
Food, beverages, tobacco								
Aliments, boissons, tabac	77.5	79.4	79.7	83.4	80.0	79.1	79.0	...
Textiles,wearing apparel, leather, footwear								
Textiles, habillement, cuir et chaussures	74.6	72.1	73.5	71.4	70.4	71.0	70.3	...
Chemicals, petroleum, rubber and plastic prod.								
Prod. chimiques, pétroliers, caoutch. et plast.	71.7	80.2	82.5	85.2	70.9	72.9	72.6	...
Basic metals								
Métaux de base	69.4	75.7	79.3	72.1	62.8	63.9	59.5	...
Metal products								
Produits métalliques	66.5	74.9	79.5	81.7	70.3	76.2	75.4	...
Electricity [E]								
Electricité [E]	**93.5**	**100.8**	**100.5**	**101.3**	**109.6**	**113.3**	**107.2**	**...**
Spain Espagne								
Total industry [CDE]								
Total, industrie [CDE]	**91.6**	**98.3**	**102.9**	**102.2**	**109.2**	**115.1**	**118.1**	**122.8**
Total mining [C]								
Total, industries extractives [C]	**87.0**	**93.3**	**98.0**	**92.5**	**90.2**	**90.3**	**88.4**	**89.4**
Total manufacturing [D]								
Total, industries manufacturières [D]	**90.5**	**98.2**	**103.3**	**102.6**	**110.1**	**116.9**	**119.6**	**123.7**
Food, beverages, tobacco								
Aliments, boissons, tabac	100.2	104.1	102.3	99.3	106.7	111.5	111.5	110.5
Textiles,wearing apparel, leather, footwear								
Textiles, habillement, cuir et chaussures	78.5	86.5	84.7	80.8	84.4	86.0	83.5	82.0
Chemicals, petroleum, rubber and plastic prod.								
Prod. chimiques, pétroliers, caoutch. et plast.	95.1	105.7	109.2	109.4	116.8	122.7	129.3	130.3
Basic metals								
Métaux de base	93.8	103.3	109.7	106.6	113.9	119.1	120.2	136.8
Metal products								
Produits métalliques	84.5	94.3	107.0	109.4	119.1	129.1	130.3	138.5
Electricity and gas [E]								
Electricité et gaz [E]	**99.6**	**100.1**	**101.5**	**102.1**	**108.6**	**110.0**	**116.8**	**126.8**
Sweden Suède								
Total industry [CD]								
Total, industrie [CD]	**91.9**	**101.9**	**112.1**	**114.7**	**122.6**	**127.4**	**129.8**	**141.0**
Total mining [C]								
Total, industries extractives [C]	**94.6**	**98.7**	**105.3**	**104.3**	**100.4**	**100.1**	**96.8**	**98.5**
Total manufacturing [D]								
Total, industries manufacturières [D]	**91.9**	**101.9**	**112.2**	**114.8**	**123.0**	**127.7**	**130.4**	**141.8**
Food, beverages, tobacco								
Aliments, boissons, tabac	99.0	103.0	106.5	111.3	110.0	110.8	110.9	109.8
Textiles,wearing apparel, leather, footwear								
Textiles, habillement, cuir et chaussures	70.5	76.8	78.8	76.7	77.1	74.6	68.0	68.5
Chemicals, petroleum, rubber and plastic prod.								
Prod. chimiques, pétroliers, caoutch. et plast.	116.2	114.2	113.0	117.3	123.1	125.0	128.4	138.4
Basic metals								
Métaux de base	103.5	122.7	130.2	132.2	137.5	137.2	134.6	140.9
Metal products								
Produits métalliques	88.0	107.5	134.7	141.1	157.7	170.1	182.9	210.1
Switzerland Suisse								
Total industry [CDE]								
Total, industrie [CDE]	**96.9**	**101.0**	**103.1**	**103.0**	**107.8**	**111.8**	**115.5**	**125.2**
Total manufacturing [D]								
Total, industries manufacturières [D]	**96.9**	**100.0**	**103.1**	**103.4**	**108.1**	**112.5**	**116.1**	**126.9**
Food, beverages, tobacco								
Aliments, boissons, tabac	101.0	100.0	102.0	102.6	95.8	95.3	96.7	95.8
Textiles and wearing apparel								
Textiles et habillement	89.6	90.4	93.5	89.9	88.8	85.8	81.0	78.9
Chemicals and chemical products								
Produits chimiques	112.9	130.0	142.9	157.4	179.6	194.0	217.1	232.9
Basic metals and metal products								
Métaux de base et produtis métalliques	97.1	98.9	101.0	99.4	106.1	110.0	110.6	124.7
Electricity, gas and water [E]								
Electricité, gaz et eau [E]	**110.2**	**118.2**	**113.6**	**110.8**	**115.5**	**116.4**	**122.7**	**122.3**

26
Index numbers of industrial production [*cont.*]
Indices de la production industrielle [*suite*]
1990=100

Country or area and industry [ISIC Rev.3] Pays ou zone et industrie [CITI Rév.3]	1993	1994	1995	1996	1997	1998	1999	2000
TFYR of Macedonia L'ex−R.y. Macédonie								
Total industry [CDE]								
Total, industrie [CDE]	**60.4**	**53.7**	**48.0**	**49.5**	**50.3**	**52.6**	**51.2**	**53.5**
Ukraine Ukraine								
Total industry [CDE]								
Total, industrie [CDE]	**82.0**	**59.6**	**52.4**	**49.7**	**48.8**	**48.0**	**50.2**	**56.7**
Total mining [C]								
Total, industries extractives [C]	**67.6**	**56.1**	**49.7**	**47.1**	**48.6**	**47.4**	**48.8**	**51.7**
Total manufacturing [D]								
Total, industries manufacturières [D]	**82.0**	**57.6**	**49.7**	**47.2**	**47.0**	**46.6**	**48.3**	**56.0**
Food, beverages, tobacco								
Aliments, boissons, tabac	71.4	60.7	54.4	...	...	...	...	...
Textiles,wearing apparel, leather, footwear								
Textiles, habillement, cuir et chaussures	96.6	59.3	38.0	...	...	...	...	...
Chemicals, petroleum, rubber and plastic prod.								
Prod. chimiques, pétroliers, caoutch. et plast.	64.0	46.7	41.6	...	...	...	...	...
Basic metals								
Métaux de base	64.5	41.8	38.9	...	...	...	...	...
Metal products								
Produits métalliques	108.9	70.2	57.1	...	...	...	...	...
Electricity, gas and water [E]								
Electricité, gaz et eau [E]	**84.6**	**74.0**	**69.6**	**64.9**	**63.2**	**63.1**	**61.5**	**60.3**
United Kingdom Royaume−Uni								
Total industry [CDE]								
Total, industrie [CDE]	**99.3**	**104.5**	**106.3**	**107.4**	**108.5**	**109.4**	**109.9**	**111.6**
Total mining [C]								
Total, industries extractives [C]	**114.9**	**132.1**	**136.4**	**140.9**	**139.3**	**142.4**	**147.5**	**145.8**
Total manufacturing [D]								
Total, industries manufacturières [D]	**96.4**	**100.8**	**102.4**	**102.8**	**104.1**	**104.6**	**104.5**	**106.2**
Food, beverages, tobacco								
Aliments, boissons, tabac	101.8	105.0	103.0	104.8	107.0	105.3	105.1	103.7
Textiles,wearing apparel, leather, footwear								
Textiles, habillement, cuir et chaussures	90.2	92.0	89.2	87.4	86.6	79.5	73.9	70.0
Chemicals, petroleum, rubber and plastic prod.								
Prod. chimiques, pétroliers, caoutch. et plast.	107.1	113.4	119.2	118.2	119.5	120.6	121.7	125.7
Basic metals								
Métaux de base	88.2	89.9	93.0	94.0	95.3	92.2	87.6	83.3
Metal products								
Produits métalliques	91.5	97.3	100.6	102.6	105.5	109.9	112.3	117.2
Electricity, gas and water [E]								
Electricité, gaz et eau [E]	**111.9**	**113.1**	**115.6**	**121.7**	**122.2**	**124.4**	**126.5**	**130.8**
Yugoslavia Yougoslavie								
Total industry [CDE]								
Total, industrie [CDE]	**40.1**	**40.5**	**42.4**	**45.5**	**49.7**	**51.4**	**38.9**	**43.3**
Total mining [C]								
Total, industries extractives [C]	**73.6**	**73.4**	**77.1**	**76.5**	**81.8**	**81.3**	**66.3**	**72.4**
Total manufacturing [D]								
Total, industries manufacturières [D]	**34.2**	**34.5**	**35.5**	**39.4**	**45.3**	**47.3**	**33.6**	**38.4**
Food, beverages, tobacco								
Aliments, boissons, tabac	58.0	59.1	62.8	64.2	61.9	71.2	68.7	69.2
Textiles,wearing apparel, leather, footwear								
Textiles, habillement, cuir et chaussures	33.9	33.5	28.3	30.0	31.8	36.0	25.6	30.1
Chemicals, petroleum, rubber and plastic prod.								
Prod. chimiques, pétroliers, caoutch. et plast.	26.7	30.6	33.6	45.8	65.3	75.3	41.3	46.7
Basic metals								
Métaux de base	22.3	23.2	27.7	39.7	49.1	53.3	29.1	39.4
Metal products								
Produits métalliques	26.9	25.0	24.9	28.1	31.2	37.0	25.1	28.8
Electricity, gas and water [E]								
Electricité, gaz et eau [E]	**83.5**	**86.4**	**90.8**	**93.1**	**98.5**	**99.2**	**93.6**	**95.0**
Oceania · Océanie								
Australia [2] Australie [2]								
Total industry [CDE]								
Total, industrie [CDE]	**101.7**	**105.5**	**108.7**	**112.2**	**114.0**	**117.7**	**121.4**	**127.2**

26
Index numbers of industrial production [*cont.*]
Indices de la production industrielle [*suite*]
1990=100

Country or area and industry [ISIC Rev.3] Pays ou zone et industrie [CITI Rév.3]	1993	1994	1995	1996	1997	1998	1999	2000
Total mining [C] [13] **Total, industries extractives [C]** [13]	**112.8**	**114.8**	**122.5**	**132.0**	**133.6**	**137.8**	**139.5**	**156.3**
Total manufacturing [D] **Total, industries manufacturières [D]**	**96.9**	**101.2**	**103.3**	**105.7**	**107.9**	**111.3**	**115.7**	**119.2**
Food, beverages, tobacco Aliments, boissons, tabac	103.9	107.7	108.8	112.7	114.4	123.6	131.4	139.7
Textiles,wearing apparel, leather, footwear Textiles, habillement, cuir et chaussures	88.4	89.6	87.5	83.0	82.3	83.8	84.9	79.6
Chemicals, petroleum, rubber and plastic prod. Prod. chimiques, pétroliers, caoutch. et plast.	100.6	105.6	108.8	115.1	117.2	120.5	128.1	127.6
Basic metals and metal products Métaux de base et produtis métalliques	94.9	100.9	103.3	106.8	109.7	112.5	115.6	120.0
Electricity, gas and water [E] **Electricité, gaz et eau [E]**	**105.1**	**108.9**	**111.8**	**113.4**	**113.1**	**117.1**	**118.8**	**122.1**
Fiji Fidji								
Total industry [CDE] **Total, industrie [CDE]**	**110.7**	**116.2**	**119.4**	**103.7**	**108.6**	**110.5**	**117.9**	...
Total mining [C] **Total, industries extractives [C]**	**92.0**	**94.0**	**92.9**	**118.3**	**124.1**	**99.0**	**117.7**	...
Total manufacturing [D] **Total, industries manufacturières [D]**	**110.7**	**116.2**	**118.8**	**87.7**	**93.2**	**96.3**	**100.1**	...
Food, beverages, tobacco Aliments, boissons, tabac	106.0	116.0	111.7	110.6	96.1	99.5	108.0	...
Textiles and wearing apparel Textiles et habillement	124.8	106.3	144.2	190.2	244.0	318.4	346.9	...
Chemicals and chemical products Produits chimiques	114.4	113.7	107.3	100.0	121.8	133.8	117.2	...
Electricity and water [E] **Electricité et eau [E]**	**115.2**	**123.9**	**129.3**	**139.0**	**142.4**	**147.3**	**161.4**	...
New Zealand [14] **Nouvelle−Zélande** [14]								
Total industry [CDE] **Total, industrie [CDE]**	**100.3**	**106.3**	**111.9**	**114.4**	**116.4**	**118.0**	**113.6**	**117.4**
Total mining [C] [15] **Total, industries extractives [C]** [15]	**119.7**	**123.4**	**121.4**	**123.9**	**136.8**	**139.3**	**134.2**	**135.8**
Total manufacturing [D] **Total, industries manufacturières [D]**	**97.4**	**103.8**	**110.7**	**112.8**	**114.9**	**116.9**	**111.8**	**116.9**
Food, beverages, tobacco Aliments, boissons, tabac	105.7	109.7	114.4	119.8	119.8	126.7	121.2	123.4
Textiles,wearing apparel, leather, footwear Textiles, habillement, cuir et chaussures	87.9	92.5	95.1	90.1	88.8	78.6	77.6	81.4
Chemicals, petroleum, rubber and plastic prod. Prod. chimiques, pétroliers, caoutch. et plast.	98.9	108.8	120.0	122.1	118.6	115.2	120.0	121.8
Basic metals and metal products Métaux de base et produtis métalliques	95.9	106.5	112.9	114.0	120.6	121.7	114.9	123.9
Electricity, gas and water [E] **Electricité, gaz et eau [E]**	**101.0**	**106.2**	**110.0**	**115.8**	**105.8**	**103.7**	**105.3**	**101.6**

Source:
United Nations Statistics Division, New York, "Industrial Commodity
Statistics Yearbook 1999" and the industrial statistics database.

Source:
Organisation des Nations Unies, New York, "Annuaire de
statistiques industrielles par produit 1999" et la base de données
pour les statistiques industrielles.

†   For information on recent changes in country or area
     nomenclature pertaining to former Czechoslovakia, Germany,
     Hong Kong Special Administrative Region (SAR) of China,
     Macao Special Administrative Region (SAR) of China,
     SFR of Yugolasvia and the former USSR, see Annex I −
     Country or area nomenclature, regional and other groupings.

†   Pour les modifications récentes de nomenclature de pays ou
     de zone concernant l'Allemagne, Hong Kong (Région
     administrative spéciale de Chine), Macao (Région
     administrative spéciale de Chine), l'ex−Tchécoslovaquie,
     l'ex−URSS, Rfs de Yougoslavie, voir annexe I −
     Nomenclature des pays ou des zones, groupements
     régionaux et autres groupments.

26

Index numbers of industrial production [*cont.*]

Indices de la production industrielle [*suite*]

1990=100

Figures relate to 12 months beginning 1 July of the year stated.
Figures relate to 12 months ending 30 June of the year stated.
Calculated by the Statistics Division of the United Nations
from component national indices.
Excluding coal mining and crude petroleum.
Excluding petroleum refineries.
Figures relate to 12 months ending 30 September of
the year stated.
Including construction.
Base: 1995 = 100.
Figures relate to 12 months beginning 1 April of the year stated.
0 Base: 1993 = 100.
1 Base: 1991 = 100.
2 Excluding gas and oil extraction.
3 Excluding services to mining.
4 Figures relate to 12 months ending 31 March of the year stated.
5 Including forestry and fishing.

1 Les chiffres se rapportent à 12 mois commençant le 1 juillet
de l'année indiquée.
2 Les chiffres se rapportent à 12 mois finissant le 30 juin
de l'année indiquée.
3 Calculé par la Division de Statistiques de l'Organisation
des Nations Unies à partir d'indices nationaux plus détaillés.
4 Non compris l'extraction du charbon et de pétrole brut.
5 Non compris les raffineries de pétrole.
6 Les chiffres se rapportent à 12 mois finissant le 30 septembre
de l'année indiquée.
7 Y compris la construction.
8 Base de référence: 1995=100.
9 Les chiffres se rapportent à 12 mois commençant le 1 avril
de l'année indiquée.
10 Base de référence: 1993=100.
11 Base de référence: 1991=100.
12 Non compris l'extraction de gaz et de pétrole brut.
13 Non compris les services relatifs aux mines.
14 Les chiffres se rapportent à 12 mois finissant le 31 mars
de l'année indiquée.
15 Y compris l'exploitation forestière et la pêche.

Technical notes, tables 22-26

Detailed internationally comparable data on national accounts are compiled and published annually by the Statistics Division, Department of Economic and Social Affairs of the United Nations Secretariat. Data for national accounts aggregates for countries or areas are based on the concepts and definitions contained in *A System of National Accounts* (1968 SNA) [57] and in *System of National Accounts 1993* (1993 SNA) [58]. A summary of the conceptual framework, classifications and definitions of transactions is found in the annual United Nations publication, *National Accounts Statistics: Main Aggregates and Detailed Tables* [27].

The national accounts data shown in this publication offer, in the form of analytical tables, a summary of selected principal national accounts aggregates based on official detailed national accounts data of some 180 countries and areas. Every effort has been made to present the estimates of the various countries or areas in a form designed to facilitate international comparability. The data for the majority of countries or areas has been compiled according to the 1968 SNA. Data for those countries or areas which have started to follow the concepts and definitions of the 1993 SNA is indicated with a footnote. To the extent possible, any other differences in concept, scope, coverage and classification are footnoted as well. Detailed footnotes identifying these differences are also available in the annual national accounts publication mentioned above. Such differences should be taken into account in order to avoid misleading comparisons among countries or areas.

Table 22 shows gross domestic product (GDP) and GDP per capita in US dollars at current prices, and GDP at constant 1990 prices and the corresponding rates of growth. The table is designed to facilitate international comparisons of levels of income generated in production. In order to present comparable coverage for as many countries as possible, the official GDP national currency data are supplemented by estimates prepared by the Statistics Division, based on a variety of data derived from national and international sources. The conversion rates used to translate national currency data into US dollars are the period averages of market exchange rates (MERs) for members of the International Monetary Fund (IMF). These rates, which are published in the *International Financial Statistics* [15], are communicated to the IMF by national central banks and consist of three types: (a) market rates, determined largely by market forces; (b) official rates, determined by government authorities; and (c) principal rates for countries maintaining multiple exchange rate arrangements. Market rates always take priority and official rates are used only when a free market rate is not available.

Notes techniques, tableaux 22 à 26

La Division de statistique du Département des affaires économiques et sociales du Secrétariat de l'Organisation des Nations Unies établit et publie chaque année des données détaillées, comparables au plan international, sur les comptes nationaux. Les données relatives aux agrégats des différents pays et territoires sont établies en fonction des concepts et des définitions du *Système de comptabilité nationale* (SCN de 1968) [57] et du *Système de comptabilité nationale* (SCN de 1993) [58]. On trouvera un résumé de l'appareil conceptuel, des classifications et des définitions des opérations dans *National Accounts Statistics: Main Aggregates and Detailed Tables* [27], publication annuelle des Nations Unies.

Les chiffres de comptabilité nationale présentés ici récapitulent sous forme de tableaux analytiques un choix d'agrégats essentiels de comptabilité nationale, issus des comptes nationaux détaillés de quelque 180 pays et territoires. On n'a rien négligé pour présenter les chiffres des différents pays et territoires sous une forme facilitant les comparaisons internationales. Pour la plupart des pays, les chiffres ont été établis selon le SCN de 1968. Les données des pays et territoires qui ont commencé à appliquer les concepts et les définitions du SCN de 1993 sont signalées par une note. Dans toute la mesure possible, on signale également au moyen de notes les cas où les concepts, la portée, la couverture et la classification ne seraient pas les mêmes. Il y a en outre des notes détaillées explicitant ces différences dans la publication annuelle mentionnée plus haut. Il y a lieu de tenir compte de ces différences pour éviter de tenter des comparaisons qui donneraient matière à confusion.

Le *tableau 22* fait apparaître le produit intérieur brut (PIB) total et par habitant, exprimé en dollars des États-Unis aux prix courants et à prix constants (base 1990), ainsi que les taux de croissance correspondants. Le tableau est conçu pour faciliter les comparaisons internationales du revenu issu de la production. Afin que la couverture soit comparable pour le plus grand nombre possible de pays, la Division de statistique s'appuie non seulement sur les chiffres officiels du PIB exprimé dans la monnaie nationale, mais aussi sur diverses données provenant de sources nationales et internationales. Les taux de conversion utilisés pour exprimer les données nationales en dollars des États-Unis sont, pour les membres du Fonds monétaire international (FMI), les moyennes pour la période considérée des taux de change du marché. Ces derniers, publiés dans *Statistiques financières internationales* [15], sont communiqués au FMI par les banques centrales des pays et reposent sur trois types de taux : a) taux du marché, déterminés dans une large mesure par les facteurs du marché; b) taux officiels, déterminés par les pouvoirs publics; c) taux principaux, pour les pays pratiquant diffé-

For non-members of the IMF, averages of the United Nations operational rates, used for accounting purposes in United Nations transactions with member countries, are applied. These are based on official, commercial and/or tourist rates of exchange.

It should be noted that there are practical constraints in the use of MERs for conversion purposes. Their use may result in excessive fluctuations or distortions in the dollar income levels of a number of countries particularly in those with multiple exchange rates, those coping with inordinate levels of inflation or countries experiencing misalignments caused by market fluctuations. Caution is therefore urged when making inter-country comparisons of incomes as expressed in US dollars.

The GDP constant price series, based primarily on data officially provided by countries or areas and partly on estimates made by the Statistics Division, are transformed into index numbers and rebased to 1990=100. The resulting data are then converted into US dollars at the rate prevailing in the base year 1990. The growth rates are based on the estimates of GDP at constant 1990 prices. The growth rate of the year in question is obtained by dividing the GDP of that year by the GDP of the preceding year.

Table 23 features the percentage distribution of GDP at current prices by expenditure breakdown. It shows the portions of GDP spent on consumption by the government and the household (including the non-profit institutions serving households) sector, the portions spent on gross fixed capital formation, on changes in inventories, and on exports of goods and services, deducting imports of goods and services. The percentages are derived from official data reported to the United Nations by the countries and published in the annual national accounts publication.

Table 24 shows the percentage distribution of value added originating from the various industry components of the *International Standard Industrial Classification of All Economic Activities, Revision 3* (ISIC Rev. 3) [49]. This table reflects the economic structure of production in the different countries or areas. The percentages are based on official value added estimates at current prices broken down by the kind of economic activity: agriculture, hunting, forestry and fishing (categories A+B); mining and quarrying (C); manufacturing (D); electricity, gas and water supply (E); construction (F); wholesale and retail trade, repair of motor vehicles, motorcycles and personal and household goods, restaurants and hotels (G+H); transport, storage and communications (I) and other activities comprised of financial intermediation (J), real estate, renting and business activities (K), public administration and defence, compulsory social security (L), education (M), health and social

rents arrangements en matière de taux de change. On donne toujours la priorité aux taux du marché, n'utilisant les taux officiels que lorsqu'on n'a pas de taux du marché libre.

Pour les pays qui ne sont pas membres du FMI, on utilise les moyennes des taux de change opérationnels de l'ONU (qui servent à des fins comptables pour les opérations de l'ONU avec les pays qui en sont membres). Ces taux reposent sur les taux de change officiels, les taux du commerce et/ou les taux touristiques.

Il est à noter que l'utilisation des taux de change du marché pour la conversion des données se heurte à des obstacles pratiques. On risque, ce faisant, d'aboutir à des fluctuations excessives ou à des distorsions du revenu en dollars de certains pays, surtout dans le cas des pays qui pratiquent plusieurs taux de change et de ceux qui connaissent des taux d'inflation exceptionnels ou des décalages provenant des fluctuations du marché. Les comparaisons de revenu entre pays sont donc sujettes à caution lorsqu'on se fonde sur le revenu exprimé en dollars des États-Unis.

La série de statistiques du PIB à prix constants est fondée principalement sur des données officiellement communiquées par les pays, et en partie sur des estimations de la Division de statistique; les données permettent de calculer des indices, la base 100 correspondant à 1990. Les chiffres ainsi obtenus sont alors convertis en dollars des États-Unis au taux de change de l'année de base (1990). Les taux de croissance sont calculés à partir des estimations du PIB aux prix constants de 1990. Le taux de croissance de l'année considérée est obtenu en divisant le PIB de l'année par celui de l'année précédente.

Le *tableau 23* montre la répartition (en pourcentage) du PIB aux prix courants par catégorie de dépense. Il indique la part du PIB consacrée aux dépenses de consommation des administrations publiques et du secteur des ménages (y compris les institutions sans but lucratif au service des ménages), celle qui est consacrée à la formation brute de capital fixe, celle qui correspond aux variations de stocks et celle qui correspond aux exportations de biens et services, déduction faite des importations de biens et services. Ces pourcentages sont calculés à partir des chiffres officiels communiqués à l'ONU par les pays, publiés dans l'ouvrage annuel.

Le *tableau 24* montre la répartition (en pourcentage) de la valeur ajoutée par branche d'activité, selon le classement retenu dans la *Classification internationale type, par industrie, de toutes les branches d'activité économique, Révision 3* (CITI Rev. 3) [49]. Il rend donc compte de la structure économique de la production dans chaque pays. Les pourcentages sont établis à partir des chiffres officiels de valeur ajoutée, aux prix courants, ventilés selon les différentes catégories d'activité économique : agriculture, chasse, sylviculture et pêche (catégories

work (N), other community, social and personal service activities (O) and private households with employed persons (P).

Table 25 presents the relationships between the principal national accounting aggregates, namely: gross domestic product (GDP), gross national income (GNI), gross national disposable income (GNDI) and gross saving. GNI is the term used in the 1993 SNA instead of the term Gross National Product (GNP) which was used in the 1968 SNA. The ratio of each aggregate to GDP is derived cumulatively by adding net primary income (or net factor income) from the rest of the world, (GNI); adding net current transfers from the rest of the world, (GNDI) and deducting final consumption to arrive at gross saving. Net national income, net national disposable income and net saving can be derived by deducting consumption of fixed capital from the corresponding gross values mentioned above.

Table 26: The national indices in this table are shown for the categories "Mining", "Manufacturing" and "Electricity, gas and water". These categories are classified according to Tabulation Categories C, D and E of the ISIC Revision 3 [49]. Major deviations from ISIC in the scope of the indices for the above categories are indicated by footnotes to the table.

The category "Total industry" covers Mining, Manufacturing and Electricity, gas and water. The indices for "Total industry", however, are the combination of the components shown and share all deviations from ISIC as footnoted for the component series.

For the purpose of presentation, the national indices have been rebased to 1990=100, where necessary.

A + B); activités extractives (C); activités de fabrication (D); production et distribution d'électricité, de gaz et d'eau (E); construction (F); commerce de gros et de détail, réparation de véhicules automobiles, de motocycles et de biens personnels et domestiques, hôtels et restaurants (G + H); transports, entreposage et communications (I) et intermédiation financière (J); immobilier, locations et activités de services aux entreprises (K); administration publique et défense, sécurité sociale obligatoire (L); éducation (M); santé et action sociale (N); autres activités de services collectifs, sociaux et personnels (O); et ménages privés employant du personnel domestique (P).

Le *tableau 25* montre les rapports entre les principaux agrégats de la comptabilité nationale, à savoir le produit intérieur brut (PIB), le revenu national brut (RNB), le revenu national brut disponible et l'épargne brute. Le revenu national brut est l'agrégat qui remplace dans le SCN de 1993 le produit national brut, utilisé dans le SCN de 1968. Chacun d'entre eux est obtenu par rapport au PIB, en ajoutant les revenus primaires nets (ou revenus nets de facteurs) engendrés dans le reste du monde, pour obtenir le revenu national brut; en ajoutant les transferts courants nets reçus de non-résidents, pour obtenir le revenu national disponible; en soustrayant la consommation finale pour obtenir l'épargne brute. Le revenu national net, le revenu national disponible net et l'épargne nette s'obtiennent en déduisant de la valeur brute correspondante la consommation de capital fixe.

Tableau 26: Les définitions des catégories "Mines", "Industries manufacturières" et "Electricité, gaz et eau", pour lesquelles des indices nationaux sont donnés dans ce tableau correspondent aux catégories C, D et E des tableaux de la CITI Révision 3 [49]. Toutes différences importantes par rapport à la CITI dans la portée des indices de ces catégories sont indiquées dans les notes du tableau.

La catégorie "Total, industrie" couvre Mines, Industries manufacturières et Electricité, gaz et eau. Toutefois, les indices de cette catégorie "Total, industrie" ne portent que sur la combinaison des indices partiels indiqués, et partagent toutes les différences par rapport à la CITI notées dans le cas des indices partiels.

Pour les besoins de la présentation, les indices nationaux ont été dans certains cas recalculés en prenant 1990=100 comme base de référence.

27
Rates of discount of central banks
Taux d'escompte des banques centrales
Per cent per annum, end of period
Pour cent par année, fin de la période

Country or area Pays ou zone	1991	1992	1993	1994	1995	1996	1997	1998	1999	2000
Albania Albanie	...	40.00	34.00	25.00	20.50	24.00	32.00	23.44	18.00	10.82
Algeria Algérie	11.50	11.50	11.50	21.00	14.00	13.00	11.00	9.50	8.50	6.00
Angola Angola	...	...	...	...	160.00	2.00	48.00	58.00	120.00	150.00
Armenia Arménie	...	30.00	210.00	210.00	77.80	26.00	65.10	...	...	...
Aruba Aruba	9.50	9.50	9.50	9.50	9.50	9.50	9.50	9.50	6.50	6.50
Australia Australie	10.99	6.96	5.83	5.75	5.75	...	...	...	...	...
Austria Autriche	8.00	8.00	5.25	4.50	3.00	2.50	2.50	2.50	...	...
Azerbaijan Azerbaïdjan	...	12.00	100.00	200.00	80.00	20.00	12.00	14.00	10.00	10.00
Bahamas Bahamas	9.00	7.50	7.00	6.50	6.50	6.50	6.50	6.50	5.75	5.75
Bangladesh Bangladesh	9.25	8.50	6.00	5.50	6.00	7.00	8.00	8.00	7.00	7.00
Barbados Barbade	18.00	12.00	8.00	9.50	12.50	12.50	9.00	9.00	10.00	10.00
Belarus Bélarus	...	30.00	210.00	480.00	66.00	8.30	8.90	9.60	23.40	# 80.00
Belgium Belgique	8.50	7.75	5.25	4.50	3.00	2.50	2.75	2.75	...	...
Belize Belize	12.00	12.00	12.00	12.00	12.00	12.00	12.00	12.00	12.00	12.00
Benin Bénin	11.00	12.50	10.50	10.00	7.50	6.50	6.00	6.25	5.75	6.50
Bolivia Bolivie	...	...	...	...	...	16.50	13.25	14.10	12.50	10.00
Botswana Botswana	12.00	14.25	14.25	13.50	13.00	13.00	12.50	12.50	13.25	14.25
Brazil Brésil	...	...	...	...	...	25.34	45.09	39.41	21.37	# 18.52
Bulgaria Bulgarie	54.00	41.00	52.00	72.00	34.00	180.00	6.65	5.08	4.46	4.63
Burkina Faso Burkina Faso	11.00	12.50	10.50	10.00	7.50	6.50	6.00	6.25	5.75	6.50
Burundi Burundi	10.00	11.00	10.00	10.00	10.00	10.00	12.00	12.00	12.00	14.00
Cameroon Cameroun	10.75	12.00	11.50	# 7.75	8.60	7.75	7.50	7.00	7.30	7.00
Canada Canada	7.67	7.36	4.11	7.43	5.79	3.25	4.50	5.25	5.00	6.00
Central African Rep. Rép. centrafricaine	10.75	12.00	11.50	# 7.75	8.60	7.75	7.50	7.00	7.60	7.00

27
Rates of discount of central banks
Per cent per annum, end of period [cont.]
Taux d'escompte des banques centrales
Pour cent par année, fin de la période [suite]

Country or area Pays ou zone	1991	1992	1993	1994	1995	1996	1997	1998	1999	2000
Chad Tchad	10.75	12.00	11.50	# 7.75	8.60	7.75	7.50	7.00	7.60	7.00
Chile Chili	...	...	7.96	13.89	7.96	11.75	7.96	9.12	7.44	8.73
China †† Chine ††	7.20	7.20	10.08	10.08	10.44	9.00	8.55	4.59	3.24	3.24
China, Hong Kong SAR† Chine, Hong Kong RAS†	...	4.00	4.00	5.75	6.25	6.00	7.00	6.25	7.00	8.00
Colombia Colombie	44.98	34.42	33.49	44.90	40.42	35.05	31.32	42.28	23.05	18.28
Congo Congo	10.75	12.00	11.50	# 7.75	8.60	7.75	7.50	7.00	7.60	7.00
Costa Rica Costa Rica	42.50	29.00	35.00	37.75	38.50	35.00	31.00	37.00	34.00	31.50
Côte d'Ivoire Côte d'Ivoire	11.00	12.50	10.50	10.00	7.50	6.50	6.00	6.25	5.75	6.50
Croatia Croatie	...	1 889.39	34.49	8.50	8.50	6.50	5.90	5.90	7.90	5.90
Cyprus Chypre	6.50	6.50	6.50	6.50	6.50	# 7.50	7.00	7.00	7.00	7.00
Czech Republic République tchèque	...	...	8.00	8.50	9.50	10.50	13.00	7.50	5.00	5.00
Dem. Rep. of the Congo Rép. dém. du Congo	55.00	55.00	95.00	145.00	125.00	238.00	13.00	22.00	120.00	120.00
Denmark Danemark	9.50	9.50	6.25	5.00	4.25	3.25	3.50	3.50	3.00	4.75
Ecuador Equateur	49.00	49.00	33.57	44.88	59.41	46.38	37.46	61.84	64.40	# 13.16
Egypt Egypte	20.00	18.40	16.50	14.00	13.50	13.00	12.25	12.00	12.00	12.00
Equatorial Guinea Guinée équatoriale	10.75	12.00	11.50	# 7.75	8.60	7.75	7.50	7.00	7.60	7.00
Ethiopia Ethiopie	3.00	5.25	12.00	12.00	12.00	...	...	...	...	...
Fiji Fidji	8.00	6.00	6.00	6.00	6.00	6.00	1.88	2.50	2.50	8.00
Finland Finlande	8.50	9.50	5.50	5.25	4.88	4.00	4.00	3.50	...	...
Gabon Gabon	10.75	12.00	11.50	# 7.75	8.60	7.75	7.50	7.00	7.60	7.00
Gambia Gambie	15.50	17.50	13.50	13.50	14.00	14.00	14.00	12.00	10.50	10.00
Germany Allemagne	8.00	8.25	5.75	4.50	3.00	2.50	2.50	2.50	...	...
Ghana Ghana	20.00	30.00	35.00	33.00	45.00	45.00	45.00	37.00	27.00	27.00
Greece Grèce	19.00	19.00	21.50	20.50	18.00	16.50	14.50	...	# 11.81	8.10
Guinea Guinée	19.00	19.00	17.00	17.00	18.00	18.00	15.00	...	...	11.50

27
Rates of discount of central banks
Per cent per annum, end of period [cont.]
Taux d'escompte des banques centrales
Pour cent par année, fin de la période [suite]

Country or area Pays ou zone	1991	1992	1993	1994	1995	1996	1997	1998	1999	2000
Guinea-Bissau Guinée-Bissau	42.00	45.50	41.00	26.00	39.00	54.00	6.00	6.25	5.75	6.50
Guyana Guyana	32.50	24.30	17.00	20.25	17.25	12.00	11.00	11.25	13.25	11.75
Hungary Hongrie	22.00	21.00	22.00	25.00	28.00	23.00	20.50	17.00	14.50	11.00
Iceland Islande	21.00	# 16.63	...	4.70	5.93	5.70	6.55	# 8.50	10.00	12.40
India Inde	12.00	12.00	12.00	12.00	12.00	12.00	9.00	9.00	8.00	8.00
Indonesia Indonésie	18.47	13.50	8.82	12.44	13.99	12.80	20.00	38.44	12.51	14.53
Ireland Irlande	10.75	...	7.00	6.25	6.50	6.25	6.75	4.06	...	...
Israel Israël	14.23	10.39	9.78	17.01	14.19	...	...	...	...	...
Italy Italie	12.00	12.00	8.00	7.50	9.00	7.50	5.50	3.00	...	...
Japan Japon	4.50	3.25	1.75	1.75	0.50	0.50	0.50	0.50	0.50	0.50
Jordan Jordanie	8.50	8.50	8.50	8.50	8.50	8.50	7.75	9.00	8.00	6.50
Kazakhstan Kazakhstan	...	...	170.00	230.00	# 52.50	35.00	18.50	25.00	18.00	14.00
Kenya Kenya	20.27	20.46	45.50	21.50	24.50	26.88	32.27	17.07	26.46	19.47
Korea, Republic of Corée, République de	7.00	7.00	5.00	5.00	5.00	5.00	5.00	3.00	3.00	3.00
Kuwait Koweït	7.50	7.50	5.75	7.00	7.25	7.25	7.50	7.00	6.75	7.25
Lao People's Dem. Rep. Rép. dém. pop. lao	...	23.67	25.00	30.00	32.08	35.00	...	35.00	34.89	35.17
Latvia Lettonie	...	...	27.00	25.00	24.00	9.50	4.00	4.00	4.00	3.50
Lebanon Liban	18.04	16.00	20.22	16.49	19.01	25.00	30.00	30.00	25.00	20.00
Lesotho Lesotho	18.00	15.00	13.50	13.50	15.50	17.00	15.60	19.50	19.00	15.00
Libyan Arab Jamah. Jamah. arabe libyenne	5.00	5.00	5.00	...	...	...	...	3.00	5.00	5.00
Malawi Malawi	13.00	20.00	25.00	40.00	50.00	27.00	23.00	43.00	47.00	50.23
Malaysia Malaisie	7.70	7.10	5.24	4.51	6.47	7.28	...	...	...	...
Mali Mali	11.00	12.50	10.50	10.00	7.50	6.50	6.00	6.25	5.75	6.50
Malta Malte	5.50	5.50	5.50	5.50	5.50	5.50	5.50	5.50	4.75	4.75
Mauritania Mauritanie	7.00	7.00	...	...	...	...	...	...	...	...

27
Rates of discount of central banks
Per cent per annum, end of period [cont.]
Taux d'escompte des banques centrales
Pour cent par année, fin de la période [suite]

Country or area Pays ou zone	1991	1992	1993	1994	1995	1996	1997	1998	1999	2000
Mauritius Maurice	11.30	8.30	8.30	13.80	11.40	11.82	10.46	17.19	...	...
Mongolia Mongolie	...	...	628.80	180.00	150.00	109.00	45.50	23.30	11.40	8.65
Morocco Maroc	...	...	...	7.17	...	...	...	6.04	5.42	5.00
Mozambique Mozambique	...	...	...	69.70	57.75	32.00	12.95	9.95	9.95	9.95
Myanmar Myanmar	11.00	11.00	11.00	11.00	12.50	15.00	15.00	15.00	12.00	10.00
Namibia Namibie	20.50	16.50	14.50	15.50	17.50	17.75	16.00	18.75	11.50	11.25
Nepal Népal	13.00	13.00	11.00	11.00	11.00	11.00	9.00	9.00	9.00	7.50
Netherlands Pays-Bas	8.50	7.75	5.00	...	...	...	...	...	...	...
Netherlands Antilles Antilles néerlandaises	6.00	6.00	5.00	5.00	6.00	6.00	6.00	6.00	6.00	6.00
New Zealand Nouvelle-Zélande	8.30	9.15	5.70	9.75	9.80	8.80	9.70	5.60	5.00	6.50
Nicaragua Nicaragua	15.00	15.00	11.75	10.50	...	...	...	...	...	...
Niger Niger	11.00	12.50	10.50	10.00	7.50	6.50	6.00	6.25	5.75	6.50
Nigeria Nigéria	15.50	17.50	26.00	13.50	13.50	13.50	13.50	13.50	18.00	14.00
Norway Norvège	10.00	11.00	7.00	6.75	6.75	6.00	5.50	10.00	7.50	9.00
Pakistan Pakistan	10.00	10.00	10.00	# 15.00	17.00	20.00	18.00	16.50	13.00	13.00
Papua New Guinea Papouasie-Nvl-Guinée	9.30	7.12	6.39	...	...	...	...	...	...	...
Paraguay Paraguay	19.75	24.00	27.17	19.15	20.50	15.00	20.00	20.00	20.00	20.00
Peru Pérou	67.65	48.50	28.63	16.08	18.44	18.16	15.94	18.72	17.80	14.00
Philippines Philippines	14.00	14.30	9.40	8.30	10.83	11.70	14.64	12.40	7.89	13.81
Poland Pologne	36.00	32.00	29.00	28.00	25.00	22.00	24.50	18.25	19.00	21.50
Portugal Portugal	20.00	21.96	11.00	8.88	8.50	6.70	5.31	3.00	...	...
Russian Federation Fédération de Russie	...	...	...	...	160.00	48.00	28.00	60.00	55.00	25.00
Rwanda Rwanda	14.00	11.00	11.00	11.00	16.00	16.00	10.75	11.38	11.19	11.69
Sao Tome and Principe Sao Tomé-et-Principe	45.00	45.00	30.00	32.00	50.00	35.00	55.00	29.50	17.00	17.00
Senegal Sénégal	11.00	12.50	10.50	10.00	7.50	6.50	6.00	6.25	5.75	6.50

27
Rates of discount of central banks
Per cent per annum, end of period [*cont.*]

Taux d'escompte des banques centrales
Pour cent par année, fin de la période [*suite*]

Country or area Pays ou zone	1991	1992	1993	1994	1995	1996	1997	1998	1999	2000
Seychelles Seychelles	1.00	1.00	1.00	1.00	1.00	1.00	1.00	1.00	1.00	1.00
Slovakia Slovaquie	...	...	12.00	12.00	9.75	8.80	8.80	8.80	8.80	8.80
Slovenia Slovénie	...	...	...	...	14.62	11.42	13.78	8.55	8.35	11.85
South Africa Afrique du Sud	17.00	14.00	12.00	13.00	15.00	17.00	16.00	# 19.32	12.00	12.00
Spain Espagne	12.50	13.25	9.00	7.38	9.00	6.25	4.75	3.00	...	...
Sri Lanka Sri Lanka	17.00	17.00	17.00	17.00	17.00	17.00	17.00	17.00	16.00	25.00
Swaziland Swaziland	13.00	12.00	11.00	12.00	15.00	16.75	15.75	18.00	12.00	11.00
Sweden Suède	8.00	# 10.00	5.00	7.00	7.00	3.50	2.50	2.00	1.50	2.00
Switzerland Suisse	7.00	6.00	4.00	3.50	1.50	1.00	1.00	1.00	0.50	# 3.20
Syrian Arab Republic Rép. arabe syrienne	5.00	5.00	5.00	5.00	5.00	5.00	5.00	5.00	5.00	5.00
Thailand Thaïlande	11.00	11.00	9.00	9.50	10.50	10.50	12.50	12.50	4.00	4.00
TFYR of Macedonia L'ex-R.y. Macédoine	...	...	295.00	33.00	15.00	9.20	8.90	8.90	8.90	7.90
Togo Togo	11.00	12.50	10.50	10.00	7.50	6.50	6.00	6.25	5.75	6.50
Trinidad and Tobago Trinité-et-Tobago	11.50	13.00	13.00	13.00	13.00	13.00	13.00	13.00	13.00	13.00
Tunisia Tunisie	11.88	11.38	8.88	8.88	8.88	7.88	...	...	...	...
Turkey Turquie	48.00	48.00	48.00	55.00	50.00	50.00	67.00	67.00	60.00	60.00
Uganda Ouganda	46.00	41.00	24.00	15.00	13.30	15.85	14.08	9.10	15.75	18.86
Ukraine Ukraine	...	80.00	240.00	252.00	110.00	40.00	35.00	60.00	45.00	27.00
United Rep. of Tanzania Rép.-Unie de Tanzanie	...	14.50	14.50	67.50	47.90	19.00	16.20	17.60	20.20	10.70
United States Etats-Unis	3.50	3.00	3.00	4.75	5.25	5.00	5.00	4.50	5.00	6.00
Uruguay Uruguay	219.00	162.40	164.30	182.30	178.70	160.30	95.50	73.70	66.39	57.26
Venezuela Venezuela	43.00	52.20	71.25	48.00	49.00	45.00	45.00	60.00	38.00	38.00
Viet Nam Viet Nam	...	...	...	...	...	18.90	10.80	12.00	6.00	6.00
Yemen Yémen	...	...	...	...	...	29.13	19.31	...	22.81	...
Zambia Zambie	...	47.00	72.50	20.50	40.20	47.00	17.70	...	...	...

27
Rates of discount of central banks
Per cent per annum, end of period [*cont.*]
Taux d'escompte des banques centrales
Pour cent par année, fin de la période [*suite*]

Country or area Pays ou zone	1991	1992	1993	1994	1995	1996	1997	1998	1999	2000
Zimbabwe Zimbabwe	20.00	29.50	28.50	29.50	29.50	27.00	31.50	# 39.50	74.41	57.84

Source:
International Monetary Fund (IMF), Washington, D.C.,
"International Financial Statistics," November 2001 and the
IMF database.

† For information on recent changes in country or
area nomenclature pertaining to former Czechoslovakia,
Germany, Hong Kong Special Administrative Region (SAR) of
China, Macao Special Administrative Region (SAR) of China,
SFR of Yugoslavia and the former USSR, see Annex I - Country
or area nomenclature, regional and other groupings.

†† For statistical purposes, the data for
China do not include those for Hong Kong Special
Administrative Region (Hong Kong SAR), Macao Special
Administrative Region (Macao SAR) and Taiwan province of
China.

Source:
Fonds monétaire international (FMI), Washington,
D.C.,"Statistiques Financières Internationales," novembre
2001 et la base de données du FMI.

† Pour les modifications récentes de nomenclature
de pays ou de zone concernant l'Allemagne, Hong Kong, région
administrative spéciale (RAS) de Chine, Macao, région
administrative spéciale (RAS) de Chine,
l'ex-Tchécoslovaquie, l'ex-URSS et l'ex-Rfs de Yougoslavie,
voir annexe I - Nomenclature des pays ou des zones,
groupements régionaux et autres groupements.

†† Les données statistiques relatives à
la Chine ne comprennent pas celles qui concernent la région
administrative spéciale de Hong Kong (la RAS de Hong Kong),
la région administrative spéciale de Macao (la RAS de Macao)
et la province chinoise de Taiwan.

28
Short-term interest rates
Taux d'intérêt à court terme
Treasury bill and money market rates: per cent per annum
Taux des bons du Trésor et du marché monétaire : pour cent par année

Country or area Pays ou zone	1991	1992	1993	1994	1995	1996	1997	1998	1999	2000
Albania Albanie										
Treasury bill										
Bons du Trésor	...	...	...	...	13.84	17.81	32.59	27.49	17.54	10.80
Algeria Algérie										
Treasury bill										
Bons du Trésor	9.50	9.50	9.50	16.50	...	...	...	# 9.96	10.05	7.95
Money market										
Marché monétaire	...	...	...	19.80	# 21.05	18.47	11.80	10.40	10.43	6.77
Antigua and Barbuda Antigua-et-Barbuda										
Treasury bill										
Bons du Trésor	7.00	7.00	7.00	7.00	7.00	7.00	7.00	7.00	7.00	7.00
Argentina Argentine										
Money market										
Marché monétaire	71.33	15.11	6.31	7.66	9.46	6.23	6.63	6.81	6.99	8.15
Armenia Arménie										
Treasury bill										
Bons du Trésor	...	...	...	...	37.81	# 43.95	57.54	46.99	55.10	24.40
Money market										
Marché monétaire	...	...	...	...	...	48.56	36.41	27.84	23.65	18.63
Australia Australie										
Treasury bill										
Bons du Trésor	9.96	6.27	5.00	5.69	# 7.64	7.02	5.29	4.84	4.76	5.98
Money market										
Marché monétaire	10.47	6.44	5.11	5.18	# 7.50	7.20	5.50	4.99	# 4.78	5.90
Austria Autriche										
Money market										
Marché monétaire	9.10	9.35	7.22	5.03	4.36	3.19	3.27	3.36	...	...
Azerbaijan Azerbaïdjan										
Treasury bill										
Bons du Trésor	...	...	...	...	...	...	12.23	14.10	18.31	16.73
Bahamas Bahamas										
Treasury bill										
Bons du Trésor	6.49	5.32	3.96	1.88	3.01	4.45	4.35	3.84	1.97	1.03
Bahrain Bahreïn										
Treasury bill										
Bons du Trésor	5.90	3.78	3.33	4.81	6.07	5.49	5.68	5.53	5.46	6.56
Money market										
Marché monétaire	6.31	3.99	3.53	5.18	6.24	5.69	...	5.69	5.58	6.89
Barbados Barbade										
Treasury bill										
Bons du Trésor	9.34	10.88	5.44	7.26	8.01	6.85	3.61	5.61	5.83	5.29
Belgium Belgique										
Treasury bill										
Bons du Trésor	9.24	9.36	8.52	5.57	4.67	3.19	3.38	3.51	2.72	4.02
Money market										
Marché monétaire	# 9.38	9.38	8.21	5.72	4.80	3.24	3.46	3.58	...	...
Belize Belize										
Treasury bill										
Bons du Trésor	6.71	5.38	4.59	4.27	4.10	3.78	3.51	3.83	5.91	5.91
Benin Bénin										
Money market										
Marché monétaire	10.94	11.44	...	...	...	...	...	4.81	4.95	4.95
Bolivia Bolivie										
Treasury bill										
Bons du Trésor	...	...	...	17.89	24.51	19.93	13.65	12.33	14.07	10.99

28
Short-term interest rates
Treasury bill and money market rates: per cent per annum [*cont.*]
Taux d'intérêt à court terme
Taux des bons du Trésor et du marché monétaire : pour cent par année [*suite*]

Country or area Pays ou zone	1991	1992	1993	1994	1995	1996	1997	1998	1999	2000
Money market Marché monétaire	...	...	...	...	22.42	20.27	13.97	12.57	13.49	7.40
Brazil Brésil										
Treasury bill Bons du Trésor	...	...	...	...	49.93	25.73	24.79	28.57	26.39	18.51
Money market Marché monétaire	847.54	1 574.28	3 284.44	4 820.64	53.37	27.45	25.00	29.50	26.26	17.59
Bulgaria Bulgarie										
Treasury bill Bons du Trésor	...	48.11	45.45	57.72	48.27	114.31	78.35	6.02	5.43	4.21
Money market Marché monétaire	48.67	52.39	48.07	66.43	53.09	119.88	66.43	2.48	2.93	3.02
Burkina Faso Burkina Faso										
Money market Marché monétaire	10.94	11.44	...	...	...	...	...	4.81	4.95	4.95
Canada Canada										
Treasury bill Bons du Trésor	8.73	6.59	4.84	5.54	6.89	4.21	3.26	4.73	4.72	5.49
Money market Marché monétaire	7.40	6.79	3.79	5.54	5.71	3.01	4.34	5.11	4.76	5.80
Chile Chili										
Money market Marché monétaire	...	...	...	...	...	...	...	...	...	10.09
China, Hong Kong SAR† Chine, Hong Kong RAS†										
Treasury bill Bons du Trésor	...	3.83	3.17	5.66	5.55	4.45	7.50	5.04	4.94	5.69
Money market Marché monétaire	4.63	3.81	4.00	5.44	6.00	5.13	4.50	5.50	5.75	7.13
Colombia Colombie										
Money market Marché monétaire	...	...	...	...	22.40	28.37	23.83	35.00	18.81	10.87
Côte d'Ivoire Côte d'Ivoire										
Money market Marché monétaire	10.94	11.44	...	...	...	...	...	4.81	4.95	4.95
Croatia Croatie										
Money market Marché monétaire	...	951.20	1 370.50	26.93	21.13	19.26	10.18	14.48	13.72	8.85
Denmark Danemark										
Money market Marché monétaire	9.78	11.35	# 11.49	6.30	6.19	3.98	3.71	4.27	3.37	4.98
Dominica Dominique										
Treasury bill Bons du Trésor	6.50	6.48	6.40	6.40	6.40	6.40	6.40	6.40	6.40	6.40
Dominican Republic Rép. dominicaine										
Money market Marché monétaire	...	...	...	...	...	14.70	13.01	16.68	15.30	18.28
Egypt Egypte										
Treasury bill Bons du Trésor	...	...	...	...	...	...	8.80	8.80	9.00	9.10
El Salvador El Salvador										
Money market Marché monétaire	...	...	...	...	...	...	10.43	9.43	10.68	6.93

28
Short-term interest rates
Treasury bill and money market rates: per cent per annum [*cont.*]
Taux d'intérêt à court terme
Taux des bons du Trésor et du marché monétaire : pour cent par année [*suite*]

Country or area Pays ou zone	1991	1992	1993	1994	1995	1996	1997	1998	1999	2000
Estonia Estonie										
Money market										
Marché monétaire	...	...	...	5.67	4.94	3.53	6.45	11.66	5.39	4.57
Ethiopia Ethiopie										
Treasury bill										
Bons du Trésor	3.00	5.25	12.00	12.00	12.00	7.22	3.97	3.48	3.65	2.74
Fiji Fidji										
Treasury bill										
Bons du Trésor	5.61	3.65	2.91	2.69	3.15	2.98	2.60	2.00	2.00	3.63
Money market										
Marché monétaire	4.28	3.06	2.91	4.10	3.95	2.43	1.91	1.27	1.27	2.58
Finland Finlande										
Money market										
Marché monétaire	13.08	13.25	7.77	5.35	5.75	3.63	3.23	3.57	2.96	4.39
France France										
Treasury bill										
Bons du Trésor	9.69	10.49	8.41	5.79	6.58	3.84	3.35	3.45	2.72	4.23
Money market										
Marché monétaire	9.49	10.35	8.75	5.69	6.35	3.73	3.24	3.39	...	...
Georgia Géorgie										
Money market										
Marché monétaire	...	...	...	...	...	43.39	26.58	43.26	34.61	18.17
Germany † Allemagne †										
Treasury bill										
Bons du Trésor	8.27	8.32	6.22	5.05	4.40	3.30	3.32	3.42	2.88	4.32
Money market										
Marché monétaire	8.84	9.42	7.49	5.35	4.50	3.27	3.18	3.41	2.73	4.11
Ghana Ghana										
Treasury bill										
Bons du Trésor	29.23	19.38	30.95	27.72	35.38	41.64	42.77	34.33	26.37	36.28
Greece Grèce										
Treasury bill										
Bons du Trésor	22.50	22.50	20.25	17.50	14.20	11.20	11.38	10.30	8.30	# 6.22
Money market										
Marché monétaire	...	...	...	24.60	16.40	13.80	12.80	13.99	...	...
Grenada Grenade										
Treasury bill										
Bons du Trésor	6.50	6.50	6.50	6.50	6.50	6.50	6.50	6.50	6.50	6.50
Guatemala Guatemala										
Money market										
Marché monétaire	...	...	...	...	...	...	7.77	6.62	9.23	9.33
Guinea-Bissau Guinée-Bissau										
Money market										
Marché monétaire	10.94	11.45	...	...	...	...	...	4.81	4.95	4.95
Guyana Guyana										
Treasury bill										
Bons du Trésor	30.94	25.75	16.83	17.66	17.51	11.35	8.91	8.33	11.31	9.88
Haiti Haïti										
Treasury bill										
Bons du Trésor	...	...	...	...	...	...	14.13	16.21	7.71	12.33
Hungary Hongrie										
Treasury bill										
Bons du Trésor	34.48	22.65	17.22	26.93	32.04	23.96	20.13	17.83	14.68	11.03

28
Short-term interest rates
Treasury bill and money market rates: per cent per annum [*cont.*]
Taux d'intérêt à court terme
Taux des bons du Trésor et du marché monétaire : pour cent par année [*suite*]

Country or area Pays ou zone	1991	1992	1993	1994	1995	1996	1997	1998	1999	2000
Iceland Islande										
Treasury bill										
Bons du Trésor	14.25	# 11.30	8.35	4.95	7.22	6.97	7.04	7.40	8.61	11.12
Money market										
Marché monétaire	14.85	12.38	8.61	4.96	6.58	6.96	7.38	8.12	9.24	11.61
India Inde										
Money market										
Marché monétaire	19.35	15.23	8.64	7.14	15.57	11.04	5.29	...	...	...
Indonesia Indonésie										
Money market										
Marché monétaire	14.91	11.99	8.66	9.74	13.64	13.96	27.82	62.79	23.58	10.32
Ireland Irlande										
Treasury bill										
Bons du Trésor	10.12	...	# 9.06	5.87	6.19	5.36	6.03	5.37	...	...
Money market										
Marché monétaire	10.45	15.12	10.49	# 5.75	5.45	5.74	6.43	3.23	3.14	4.84
Israel Israël										
Treasury bill										
Bons du Trésor	14.50	11.79	10.54	11.77	14.37	15.54	13.88	12.17	...	...
Italy Italie										
Treasury bill										
Bons du Trésor	12.54	14.32	10.58	9.17	10.85	8.46	6.33	4.59	3.01	4.53
Money market										
Marché monétaire	# 12.21	14.02	10.20	8.51	10.46	8.82	6.88	4.99	2.95	4.39
Jamaica Jamaïque										
Treasury bill										
Bons du Trésor	25.56	34.36	28.85	42.98	27.65	37.95	21.14	25.65	20.75	18.24
Japan Japon										
Money market										
Marché monétaire	7.46	4.58	# 3.06	2.20	1.21	0.47	0.48	0.37	0.06	0.11
Kazakhstan Kazakhstan										
Treasury bill										
Bons du Trésor	...	...	...	214.34	48.98	28.91	15.15	23.59	15.63	6.59
Kenya Kenya										
Treasury bill										
Bons du Trésor	16.59	16.53	49.80	23.32	18.29	22.25	22.87	22.83	13.87	12.05
Korea, Republic of Corée, République de										
Money market										
Marché monétaire	17.03	14.32	12.12	12.45	12.57	12.44	13.24	14.98	5.01	5.16
Kuwait Koweït										
Treasury bill										
Bons du Trésor	...	...	...	6.32	7.35	6.93	6.98	...	...	...
Money market										
Marché monétaire	...	...	7.43	6.31	7.43	6.98	7.05	7.24	6.32	6.82
Kyrgyzstan Kirghizistan										
Treasury bill										
Bons du Trésor	...	...	...	143.13	34.90	40.10	35.83	43.67	47.19	32.26
Money market										
Marché monétaire	...	...	...	...	...	...	...	43.98	43.71	24.26
Lao People's Dem. Rep. Rép. dém. pop. lao										
Treasury bill										
Bons du Trésor	...	...	...	...	20.46	...	...	23.66	30.00	29.94
Latvia Lettonie										
Treasury bill										
Bons du Trésor	...	...	...	...	28.24	16.27	4.73	5.27	6.23	3.83

28
Short-term interest rates
Treasury bill and money market rates: per cent per annum [cont.]
Taux d'intérêt à court terme
Taux des bons du Trésor et du marché monétaire : pour cent par année [suite]

Country or area Pays ou zone	1991	1992	1993	1994	1995	1996	1997	1998	1999	2000
Money market Marché monétaire	...	...	...	37.18	22.39	13.08	3.76	4.42	4.72	2.97
Lebanon Liban										
Treasury bill Bons du Trésor	17.47	22.40	18.27	15.09	19.40	15.19	13.42	12.70	11.57	11.18
Lesotho Lesotho										
Treasury bill Bons du Trésor	15.75	14.20	13.10	9.44	12.40	13.89	14.83	15.47	12.45	9.06
Libyan Arab Jamah. Jamah. arabe libyenne										
Money market Marché monétaire	4.00	4.00	4.00	...	...	...	...	4.00	4.00	4.00
Lithuania Lituanie										
Treasury bill Bons du Trésor	...	...	...	...	26.82	20.95	8.64	10.69	11.14	...
Money market Marché monétaire	...	...	...	69.48	26.73	20.26	9.55	6.12	6.26	3.60
Luxembourg Luxembourg										
Money market Marché monétaire	9.10	8.93	8.09	5.16	4.26	3.29	3.36	3.48	...	...
Madagascar Madagascar										
Money market Marché monétaire	15.00	15.00	...	0.00	29.00	10.00	...	11.24	...	16.00
Malawi Malawi										
Treasury bill Bons du Trésor	11.50	15.62	23.54	27.68	46.30	30.83	18.31	32.98	42.85	39.52
Malaysia Malaisie										
Treasury bill Bons du Trésor	7.27	7.66	6.48	3.68	5.50	6.41	6.41	6.86	3.53	2.86
Money market Marché monétaire	7.83	8.01	6.53	4.65	5.78	# 6.98	7.61	8.46	3.38	2.66
Maldives Maldives										
Money market Marché monétaire	7.00	7.00	5.00	5.00	6.80	6.80	6.80	6.80	6.80	6.80
Mali Mali										
Money market Marché monétaire	10.94	11.44	...	...	...	...	...	4.81	4.95	4.95
Malta Malte										
Treasury bill Bons du Trésor	4.46	4.58	4.60	4.29	4.65	4.99	5.08	5.41	5.15	4.89
Mauritius Maurice										
Money market Marché monétaire	12.24	9.05	7.73	10.23	10.35	9.96	9.43	8.99	10.01	7.66
Mexico Mexique										
Treasury bill Bons du Trésor	19.28	15.62	14.99	14.10	48.44	31.39	19.80	24.76	21.41	15.24
Money market Marché monétaire	23.58	18.87	17.39	16.47	# 60.92	33.61	21.91	26.89	24.10	16.96
Morocco Maroc										
Money market Marché monétaire	...	...	...	12.29	10.06	8.42	7.89	6.30	5.64	5.41
Mozambique Mozambique										
Treasury bill Bons du Trésor	...	...	...	...	...	...	...	...	...	16.97

28
Short-term interest rates
Treasury bill and money market rates: per cent per annum [*cont.*]
Taux d'intérêt à court terme
Taux des bons du Trésor et du marché monétaire : pour cent par année [*suite*]

Country or area Pays ou zone	1991	1992	1993	1994	1995	1996	1997	1998	1999	2000
Money market Marché monétaire	...	...	...	...	...	...	...	...	9.92	16.12
Namibia Namibie Treasury bill Bons du Trésor	...	13.88	12.16	11.35	13.91	15.25	15.69	17.24	13.28	10.26
Nepal Népal Treasury bill Bons du Trésor	8.80	9.00	4.50	6.50	9.90	11.51	2.52	3.70	4.30	5.30
Netherlands Pays-Bas Money market Marché monétaire	9.01	9.27	7.10	5.14	4.22	2.89	3.07	3.21	...	...
Netherlands Antilles Antilles néerlandaises Treasury bill Bons du Trésor	...	...	4.83	4.48	5.46	5.66	5.77	5.82	6.15	6.15
New Zealand Nouvelle-Zélande Treasury bill Bons du Trésor	9.74	6.72	6.21	6.69	8.82	9.09	7.53	7.10	4.58	6.39
Niger Niger Money market Marché monétaire	10.94	11.44	...	...	...	...	...	4.81	4.95	4.95
Nigeria Nigéria Treasury bill Bons du Trésor	...	17.89	24.50	12.87	12.50	12.25	12.00	12.26	17.82	15.50
Norway Norvège Money market Marché monétaire	10.58	13.71	7.64	5.70	5.54	4.97	3.77	6.03	6.87	6.72
Pakistan Pakistan Treasury bill Bons du Trésor	...	12.47	13.03	11.26	12.49	13.61	# 15.74	...	...	8.38
Money market Marché monétaire	7.64	7.51	11.00	8.36	11.52	11.40	12.10	10.76	9.04	8.57
Papua New Guinea Papouasie-Nvl-Guinée Treasury bill Bons du Trésor	10.33	8.88	6.25	6.85	17.40	14.44	9.94	21.18	22.70	17.00
Paraguay Paraguay Money market Marché monétaire	12.39	21.59	22.55	18.64	20.18	16.35	12.48	20.74	17.26	10.70
Philippines Philippines Treasury bill Bons du Trésor	21.48	16.02	12.45	12.71	11.76	12.34	12.89	15.00	10.00	9.91
Poland Pologne Treasury bill Bons du Trésor	...	44.03	33.16	28.81	25.62	20.32	21.58	19.09	13.14	16.62
Money market Marché monétaire	49.93	# 29.49	24.51	23.32	25.82	20.63	22.43	20.59	13.58	18.16
Portugal Portugal Treasury bill Bons du Trésor	14.20	12.88	...	...	7.75	5.75	4.43	...	...	...
Money market Marché monétaire	15.50	# 17.48	13.25	10.62	8.91	7.38	5.78	4.34	2.71	...
Republic of Moldova République de Moldova Treasury bill Bons du Trésor	...	...	...	...	52.90	39.01	23.63	30.54	28.49	22.20

28
Short-term interest rates
Treasury bill and money market rates: per cent per annum [*cont.*]
Taux d'intérêt à court terme
Taux des bons du Trésor et du marché monétaire : pour cent par année [*suite*]

Country or area Pays ou zone	1991	1992	1993	1994	1995	1996	1997	1998	1999	2000
Money market Marché monétaire	...	...	...	...	...	...	28.10	30.91	32.60	20.77
Romania Roumanie										
Treasury bill Bons du Trésor	...	...	...	...	...	51.09	85.72	63.99	74.21	51.86
Russian Federation Fédération de Russie										
Treasury bill Bons du Trésor	...	...	...	...	168.04	86.07	23.43	...	...	12.12
Money market Marché monétaire	...	...	...	...	190.43	47.65	20.97	50.56	14.79	7.14
Saint Kitts and Nevis Saint-Kitts-et-Nevis										
Treasury bill[1] Bons du Trésor[1]	6.50	6.50	6.50	6.50	6.50	6.50	6.50	6.50	6.50	6.50
Saint Lucia Sainte-Lucie										
Treasury bill Bons du Trésor	7.00	7.00	7.00	7.00	7.00	7.00	7.00	7.00	7.00	7.00
St. Vincent-Grenadines St. Vincent-Grenadines										
Treasury bill Bons du Trésor	6.50	6.50	6.50	6.50	6.50	6.50	6.50	6.50	6.50	6.50
Senegal Sénégal										
Money market Marché monétaire	10.94	11.44	...	...	...	...	...	4.81	4.95	4.95
Seychelles Seychelles										
Treasury bill Bons du Trésor	13.00	13.00	12.91	12.36	12.15	11.47	10.50	7.96	4.50	4.50
Sierra Leone Sierra Leone										
Treasury bill Bons du Trésor	50.67	78.63	28.64	12.19	14.73	29.25	12.71	22.10	32.42	26.22
Singapore Singapour										
Treasury bill Bons du Trésor	1.20	0.90	1.35	0.65	0.71	1.15	1.90	1.15	0.40	2.48
Money market Marché monétaire	4.76	2.74	2.50	3.68	2.56	2.93	4.35	5.00	2.04	2.57
Slovakia Slovaquie										
Money market Marché monétaire	...	...	...	...	...	...	...	...	...	8.08
Slovenia Slovénie										
Treasury bill Bons du Trésor	...	...	...	...	...	...	...	...	8.63	10.94
Money market Marché monétaire	...	67.58	39.15	29.08	12.18	13.98	9.71	7.45	6.87	6.95
Solomon Islands Iles Salomon										
Treasury bill Bons du Trésor	13.71	13.50	12.15	11.25	12.50	12.75	12.88	6.00	6.00	...
South Africa Afrique du Sud										
Treasury bill Bons du Trésor	16.68	13.77	11.31	10.93	13.53	15.04	15.26	16.53	12.85	10.11
Money market Marché monétaire	17.02	14.11	10.83	10.24	13.07	15.54	15.59	17.11	13.06	9.54
Spain Espagne										
Treasury bill Bons du Trésor	12.45	12.44	10.53	8.11	9.79	7.23	5.02	3.79	3.01	4.61
Money market Marché monétaire	13.20	13.01	12.33	7.81	8.98	7.65	5.49	4.34	2.72	4.11

28
Short-term interest rates
Treasury bill and money market rates: per cent per annum [*cont.*]
Taux d'intérêt à court terme
Taux des bons du Trésor et du marché monétaire : pour cent par année [*suite*]

Country or area Pays ou zone	1991	1992	1993	1994	1995	1996	1997	1998	1999	2000
Sri Lanka Sri Lanka										
Treasury bill										
Bons du Trésor	13.75	16.19	16.52	12.68	16.81	# 17.40	...	12.59	12.51	14.02
Money market										
Marché monétaire	25.42	21.63	25.65	18.54	41.87	24.33	18.42	15.74	16.69	17.30
Swaziland Swaziland										
Treasury bill										
Bons du Trésor	12.67	12.34	8.25	8.35	10.87	13.68	14.37	13.09	11.19	8.30
Money market										
Marché monétaire	10.61	10.25	9.73	7.01	8.52	9.77	10.35	10.63	8.86	5.54
Sweden Suède										
Treasury bill										
Bons du Trésor	11.59	12.85	8.35	7.40	8.75	5.79	4.11	4.19	3.12	3.95
Money market										
Marché monétaire	11.81	18.42	9.08	7.36	8.54	6.28	4.21	4.24	3.14	3.81
Switzerland Suisse										
Treasury bill										
Bons du Trésor	7.74	7.76	4.75	3.97	2.78	1.72	1.45	1.32	1.17	2.93
Money market										
Marché monétaire	7.73	7.47	4.94	3.85	2.89	1.78	1.35	1.22	0.93	# 3.50
Thailand Thaïlande										
Money market										
Marché monétaire	11.15	6.93	6.54	7.25	10.96	9.23	14.59	13.02	1.77	1.95
Togo Togo										
Money market										
Marché monétaire	10.94	11.44	...	...	...	...	...	4.81	4.95	4.95
Trinidad and Tobago Trinité-et-Tobago										
Treasury bill										
Bons du Trésor	7.67	9.26	9.45	9.99	8.41	10.44	9.83	11.93	10.40	10.56
Tunisia Tunisie										
Money market										
Marché monétaire	11.79	11.73	10.48	8.81	8.81	8.64	6.88	6.89	5.99	5.88
Turkey Turquie										
Treasury bill										
Bons du Trésor	67.01	72.17	...	...	...	...	...	...	...	33.32
Money market										
Marché monétaire	72.75	65.35	62.83	136.47	72.30	76.24	70.32	74.60	73.53	56.72
Uganda Ouganda										
Treasury bill										
Bons du Trésor	34.17	...	# 21.30	12.52	8.75	11.71	10.59	7.77	7.43	13.19
Ukraine Ukraine										
Money market										
Marché monétaire	...	...	...	...	...	...	22.05	40.41	44.98	18.34
United Kingdom Royaume-Uni										
Treasury bill										
Bons du Trésor	10.85	8.94	5.25	5.15	6.33	5.77	6.48	6.82	5.04	5.80
Money market										
Marché monétaire	11.77	9.39	5.46	4.76	5.98	5.89	6.56	7.09	5.11	5.71
United Rep. of Tanzania Rép.-Unie de Tanzanie										
Treasury bill										
Bons du Trésor	...	...	34.00	35.09	40.33	15.30	9.59	11.83	10.05	9.78
United States Etats-Unis										
Treasury bill										
Bons du Trésor	5.41	3.46	3.02	4.27	5.51	5.02	5.07	4.82	4.66	5.84
Money market [2]										
Marché monétaire[2]	5.69	3.52	3.02	4.20	5.84	5.30	5.46	5.35	4.97	6.24

28
Short-term interest rates
Treasury bill and money market rates: per cent per annum [cont.]
Taux d'intérêt à court terme
Taux des bons du Trésor et du marché monétaire : pour cent par année [suite]

Country or area Pays ou zone	1991	1992	1993	1994	1995	1996	1997	1998	1999	2000
Uruguay Uruguay										
Treasury bill										
Bons du Trésor	...	...	...	44.60	39.40	29.20	23.18	...	...	...
Money market										
Marché monétaire	...	...	...	39.82	36.81	28.47	23.43	20.48	13.96	14.82
Vanuatu Vanuatu										
Money market										
Marché monétaire	7.00	5.92	6.00	6.00	6.00	6.00	6.00	8.65	6.99	5.58
Venezuela Venezuela										
Money market										
Marché monétaire	...	...	...	...	...	16.70	12.47	18.58	7.48	8.14
Viet Nam Viet Nam										
Treasury bill										
Bons du Trésor	...	...	26.40	...	...	...	...	...	...	5.42
Yemen Yémen										
Treasury bill										
Bons du Trésor	...	...	...	...	...	25.20	15.97	12.53	20.57	14.07
Zambia Zambie										
Treasury bill										
Bons du Trésor	...	...	124.03	74.21	39.81	52.78	29.48	24.94	36.19	31.37
Zimbabwe Zimbabwe										
Treasury bill										
Bons du Trésor	14.44	26.16	33.04	29.22	27.98	24.53	22.07	32.78	50.48	64.78
Money market										
Marché monétaire	17.49	34.77	34.18	30.90	29.64	26.18	25.15	37.22	53.13	64.98

Source:
International Monetary Fund (IMF), Washington, D.C.,
"International Financial Statistics," November 2001 and the
IMF database.

† For information on recent changes in country or
area nomenclature pertaining to former Czechoslovakia,
Germany, Hong Kong Special Administrative Region (SAR) of
China, Macao Special Administrative Region (SAR) of China,
SFR of Yugoslavia and the former USSR, see Annex I - Country
or area nomenclature, regional and other groupings.

1 Including Anguilla.
2 Federal funds rate.

Source:
Fonds monétaire international (FMI), Washington,
D.C.,"Statistiques Financières Internationales," novembre
2001 et la base de données du FMI.

† Pour les modifications récentes de nomenclature
de pays ou de zone concernant l'Allemagne, Hong Kong, région
administrative spéciale (RAS) de Chine, Macao, région
administrative spéciale (RAS) de Chine,
l'ex-Tchécoslovaquie, l'ex-URSS et l'ex-Rfs de Yougoslavie,
voir annexe I - Nomenclature des pays ou des zones,
groupements régionaux et autres groupements.

1 Y compris Anguilla.
2 Taux des fonds du système fédérale.

Technical notes, tables 27 and 28

Detailed information and current figures relating to tables 27 and 28 are contained in *International Financial Statistics*, published by the International Monetary Fund [15] and in the United Nations *Monthly Bulletin of Statistics* [26].

Table 27: The discount rates shown represent the rates at which the central bank lends or discounts eligible paper for deposit money banks, typically shown on an end-of-period basis.

Table 28: The rates shown represent short-term treasury bill rates and money market rates. The treasury bill rate is the rate at which short-term securities are issued or traded in the market. The money market rate is the rate on short-term lending between financial institutions.

Notes techniques, tableaux 27 et 28

Les informations détaillées et les chiffres courants concernant les tableaux 27 et 28 figurent dans les *Statistiques financières internationales* publiées par le Fonds monétaire international [15] et dans le *Bulletin mensuel de statistique* des Nations Unies [26].

Tableau 27: Les taux d'escomptes indiqués représentent les taux que la banque centrale applique à ses prêts ou auquel elle réescompte les effets escomptables des banques créatrices de monnaie (généralement, taux de fin de période).

Tableau 28: Les taux indiqués représentent le taux des bons du Trésor et le taux du marché monétaire à court terme. Le taux des bons du Trésor est le taux auquel les effets à court terme sont émis ou négociés sur le marché. Le taux du marché monétaire est le taux prêteur à court terme entre institutions financières.

Table 29 follows overleaf

   Le tableau 29 est présenté au verso

29
Employment by industry
Emploi par industrie

A. ISIC Rev. 2 [+] · CITI Rév. 2 [+]

Persons employed, by branch of economic activity (thousands)
Personnes employées, par branches d'activité économique (milliers)

Country or area Pays ou zone	Year Année	Total employment (000s) Emploi total (000s) M	F	Agriculture, hunting, forestry and fishing Agriculture, chasse, sylviculture, pêche M	F	Mining and quarrying Industries extractives M	F	Manufacturing Industries manufacturières M	F	Electricity, gas, Electricité, gaz, M
Bangladesh [11]	1989	29386.0	20761.0	17735.0	14836.0	82.0	6.0	2491.0	4484.0	14.0
Bangladesh [11]	1990	30443.0	19716.0	16560.0	16743.0	15.0	...	4240.0	1685.0	39.0
	1996[12]	33765.0	20832.0	18382.0	16148.0	22.0	1.0	2586.0	1499.0	90.0
Barbados [12]	1994	54.1	46.6	3.5	2.4	...	...	5.2	4.8	0.9
Barbade [12]	1995	57.7	52.1	3.2	1.9	...	...	5.4	6.3	0.8
	1999	65.5	56.9	3.4	1.8	...	...	5.4	4.9	1.4
Belarus [7]	1992	4891.4	...	1089.7	...	24.5	...	1329.1	...	34.7
Belarus [7]	1993	4827.7	...	1048.8	...	29.6	...	1311.8	...	38.1
	1994	4700.9	...	995.7	...	27.2	...	1245.6	...	38.7
Belize [19]	1993	43.4	18.7	14.7	0.9	0.3	...	5.0	2.2	1.0
Belize [19]	1994	43.0	19.0	13.3	0.8	0.3	...	5.0	1.7	1.0
Brazil [11 17 21]	1996	41244.0	26677.0	11285.0	5256.0	645.0	124.0	6080.0	2330.0	...
Brésil [11 17 21]	1997	41978.0	27354.0	11254.0	5516.0	658.0	116.0	6101.0	2406.0	...
	1998	42312.0	27650.0	10996.0	5342.0	712.0	150.0	5910.0	2320.0	...
Chile [1 2 14]	1996[37]	3609.0	1689.7	727.3	89.1	87.2	3.4	631.1	228.6	36.6
Chili [1 2 14]	1997	3631.7	1748.5	697.8	78.1	84.0	3.8	632.5	228.3	27.3
	1998	3624.8	1807.6	702.1	82.3	76.6	5.3	591.3	227.3	34.0
China †† [7 17 38 39]	1996	688500.0	...	329100.0	...	9020.0	...	97630.0	...	2730.0
Chine †† [7 17 38 39]	1997	696000.0	...	330049.0	...	8676.0	...	96108.0	...	2834.0
	1998	699570.0	...	332320.0	...	7210.0	...	83190.0	...	2830.0
China, Hong Kong SAR † [1 2 41]	1997	1928.1	1263.4	7.7	2.8	0.4	...	285.7	165.0	17.0
Chine, Hong Kong RAS † [1 2 41]	1998	1869.1	1281.0	6.5	2.9	0.2	...	243.3	142.3	15.6
	1999	1821.5	1311.5	6.5	2.7	0.3	...	223.8	135.6	15.2
Colombia [17 43 44 45]	1997	3247.4	2410.0	45.0	11.0	18.8	2.0	673.0	480.7	29.2
Colombie [17 43 44 45]	1998	3194.6	2460.3	43.3	14.8	11.0	3.4	624.7	474.4	23.4
	1999	3121.8	2518.8	50.6	13.2	12.8	2.5	573.1	466.6	26.4
Cyprus [1]	1993	165.7	103.0	18.7	12.8	0.7	...	25.5	19.3	1.4
Chypre [1]	1994	166.9	107.4	18.5	11.6	0.7	...	25.6	18.3	1.3
	1995	173.0	112.1	18.8	11.7	0.8	...	25.9	18.1	1.3
Ecuador [11 17 20]	1996	1794.5	1094.4	170.2	20.9	15.2	1.6	283.0	141.1	8.1
Equateur [11 17 20]	1997	1909.6	1152.6	187.2	22.2	10.7	0.5	307.5	167.8	8.4
	1998	1920.8	1230.4	202.4	28.2	10.4	0.2	303.7	159.3	12.9
El Salvador [11]	1996	1285.1	771.4	517.9	60.6	1.5	0.2	188.8	181.9	7.3
El Salvador [11]	1997	1292.1	783.9	492.4	54.7	1.6	0.1	175.8	158.3	14.1
	1998	1345.8	881.7	502.2	55.9	1.7	0.2	199.7	215.9	7.7
Honduras [1 11 17]	1997	1374.5	714.0	722.0	50.7	2.9	0.1	170.6	191.1	5.6
Honduras [1 11 17]	1998	1400.8	734.2	680.9	57.6	4.4	0.1	177.1	191.3	5.8
	1999	1472.1	826.9	732.5	73.6	2.3	1.5	180.2	196.6	6.6
Indonesia [17]	1995[11]	51686.0	31729.0	22773.0	15012.0	540.0	118.0	5804.0	4920.0	189.0
Indonésie [17]	1996[11]	52990.0	32711.8	23001.5	14718.7	612.5	161.7	5877.6	4895.5	147.5
	1997[2]	53971.0	33079.0	21960.0	13889.0	710.0	186.0	6189.0	5026.0	214.0
Jamaica [1 42 59]	1996	553.3	406.5	171.6	45.8	5.5	0.8	57.4	43.0	5.4
Jamaïque [1 42 59]	1997	556.9	399.4	162.5	40.2	4.6	0.8	52.4	35.0	4.0
	1998	553.7	400.6	160.5	39.6	4.5	0.7	55.7	29.1	4.0
Japan [2 61]	1997	38920.0	26650.0	1900.0	1590.0	60.0	10.0	9170.0	5250.0	310.0
Japon [2 61]	1998	38580.0	26560.0	1860.0	1580.0	50.0	10.0	8920.0	4900.0	330.0
	1999	38310.0	26320.0	1850.0	1510.0	50.0	10.0	8730.0	4710.0	320.0
Malaysia [1 49]	1997	5657.7	2911.5	1067.4	413.8	34.0	4.5	1195.7	806.8	44.1
Malaisie	1998	5718.9	2880.7	1185.0	431.5	25.3	3.1	1146.9	761.0	44.2
	1999	5851.2	2986.6	1222.3	401.4	33.9	3.9	1187.9	802.9	43.5
Morocco [2 20]	1997	3222.0	1001.8	172.6	44.1	35.3	1.1	589.2	453.9	35.1
Maroc [2 20]	1998	3238.3	930.0	160.7	44.9	42.3	1.4	599.5	389.8	36.5
	1999	3226.3	948.2	181.1	57.3	39.1	1.7	584.5	366.2	33.0

Construction Construction		Trade, restaurants and hotels Commerce, restaurants, hôtels		Transport, storage, communications Transports, entrepôts, communications		Financing, insurance, real est.,bus. services Services financières, immob., et apparentées		Community, social and personal services Services fournis à la collectivité, services soc. et pers.	
M	F	M	F	M	F	M	F	M	F
610.0	51.0	3909.0	220.0	1268.0	9.0	229.0	8.0	1606.0	188.0
485.0	41.0	4262.0	123.0	1600.0	11.0	284.0	12.0	1647.0	262.0
936.0	80.0	5573.0	488.0	2263.0	45.0	197.0	16.0	3343.0	1748.0
7.4^{15}	0.3^{15}	6.9^{16}	8.4^{16}	3.1	1.1	2.2	4.1	10.8	19.8
8.5^{15}	0.3^{15}	8.1^{16}	8.5^{16}	3.7	1.3	2.3	5.3	20.3	21.8
13.2	0.8	12.5	17.0	3.3	1.2	13.6	16.7	12.7	13.7
418.8	...	340.8	...	350.9	...	31.0	...	1069.6	...
369.1	...	405.3	...	328.9	...	33.6	...	1075.6	...
328.9	...	422.3	...	318.0	...	40.9	...	1099.7	...
3.8	0.1	1.1	2.0	2.9	0.5	0.3	0.6	1.6	1.1
3.5	0.1	1.3	1.9	3.2	0.5	0.5	0.7	1.4	1.4
4234.0	104.0	5573.0	3498.0	2304.0	249.0	825.0	483.0	10298.0	14633.0
4486.0	98.0	5614.0	3609.0	2507.0	252.0	818.0	460.0	10538.0	14898.0
4787.0	193.0	5639.0	3778.0	2501.0	285.0	842.0	467.0	10925.0	15115.0
402.6	14.4	522.5	409.4	349.9	44.0	231.3	138.1	620.4	757.5
474.1	14.7	523.0	452.8	353.1	47.9	233.4	143.1	606.4	776.0
434.6	13.9	545.1	460.4	373.6	59.1	252.4	153.3	615.2	802.5
34080.0	...	45110.0	...	20130.0	...	3760.0	...	18390.0	...
34479.0	...	47943.0	...	20599.0	...	3952.0	...	18031.0	...
33270.0	...	46450.0	...	20090.0	...	4080.0	...	19650.0	...
291.0	17.4	534.5	433.5	281.3	68.4	239.0	165.9	271.3	408.1
290.6	18.9	514.4	447.3	285.7	67.3	242.7	168.9	270.2	431.1
270.0	19.2	493.5	447.8	275.1	67.6	261.5	176.1	270.0	460.6
326.2	24.2	764.1	676.6	366.8	49.3	316.9	211.4	695.4	939.3
326.2	26.2	763.7	668.1	355.4	56.3	312.3	206.8	730.5	997.6
244.1	25.4	784.4	698.7	386.3	55.7	305.2	194.6	728.9	1050.2
23.5	1.5	37.3	30.2	12.2	4.6	10.3	9.1	33.5	24.7
23.4	1.4	38.3	32.5	12.9	4.9	11.0	10.0	32.7	27.8
24.1	1.6	40.3	34.3	13.4	5.1	11.8	10.8	34.2	29.6
164.1	7.3	447.4	426.5	156.3	11.1	90.8	42.3	458.7	440.3
178.7	6.4	458.9	412.0	164.2	11.4	96.5	42.0	495.9	487.3
181.0	4.9	489.9	462.6	181.3	17.7	113.0	50.8	425.3	502.6
127.9	4.0	175.9	223.0	85.2	6.1	13.0	14.1	167.6	280.7
134.7	4.0	187.4	257.7	90.1	6.6	16.9	13.3	179.1	288.0
117.9	3.3	228.4	327.5	84.8	5.2	49.7	32.9	153.7	239.9
86.7	1.6	157.3	236.5	43.0	3.8	26.8	14.6	159.6	214.5
108.8	1.8	183.5	256.4	48.9	5.7	36.5	15.9	154.8	204.3
114.3	3.5	182.3	306.8	51.8	4.2	31.2	18.7	170.8	220.3
3667.0	109.0	7059.0	7273.0	3383.0	103.0	475.0	162.0	7796.0	3958.0
3675.8	120.4	7871.8	8230.8	3850.2	92.6	501.7	188.1	7442.0	4286.4
4050.0	150.0	8404.0	8817.0	4023.0	115.0	447.0	209.0	7972.0	4666.0
78.8	2.4	72.3	126.8	39.8	8.6	27.4	27.1	94.9	150.2
77.6	1.9	80.4	125.8	43.6	10.7	35.8	30.7	95.2	151.3
75.8	2.6	77.2	127.2	46.6	11.3	27.5	30.4	101.0	157.6
5730.0	1120.0	7300.0	7450.0	3380.0	740.0	3180.0	2570.0	7710.0	7720.0
5550.0	1070.0	7290.0	7540.0	3290.0	760.0	3310.0	2630.0	7770.0	7890.0
5550.0	1020.0	7250.0	7590.0	3310.0	750.0	3350.0	2630.0	7650.0	7890.0
740.7	50.3	945.0	632.9	368.1	55.3	257.6	189.6	1003.0	751.5
700.4	45.5	982.6	633.3	364.7	57.0	247.4	178.4	1022.6	764.9
677.6	45.2	1006.2	654.5	361.8	58.5	274.2	192.0	1043.8	821.6
371.6	5.4	810.4	75.7	186.8	10.3	65.9	29.9	932.8	371.3
338.7	4.9	860.2	88.2	191.9	7.9	60.6	25.4	923.2	357.6
362.4	4.5	825.7	89.2	204.8	12.0	69.3	30.8	918.7	380.2

29
Employment by industry [*cont.*]
Emploi par industrie [*suite*]

A. ISIC Rev. 2 [+] – CITI Rév. 2 [+]

Persons employed, by branch of economic activity (thousands)
Personnes employées, par branches d'activité économique (milliers)

Country or area Pays ou zone	Year Année	Total employment (000s) Emploi total (000s)		Agriculture, hunting, forestry and fishing Agriculture, chasse, sylviculture, pêche		Mining and quarrying Industries extractives		Manufacturing Industries manufacturières		Electricity, gas, wa[...] Electricité, gaz, ea[...]	
		M	F	M	F	M	F	M	F	M	
Myanmar [1 7]	1994	16817.0	...	11551.0	...	87.0	...	1250.0	...	17.0	
Myanmar [1 7]	1997	17964.0	...	11381.0	...	132.0	...	1573.0	...	21.0	
	1998	18359.0	...	11507.0	...	121.0	...	1666.0	...	48.0	
Nicaragua [7]	1997	1369.9		574.5		6.7	...	117.2	...	5.9	
Nicaragua [7]	1998	1441.8		609.2		9.7	...	122.0	...	5.8	
	1999	1544.2	...	655.3	...	11.7	...	125.3	...	5.8	
Pakistan [1 11 71]	1995	27591.0	3816.0	12125.0	2571.0	38.0	...	2897.0	362.0	256.0	[...]
Pakistan [1 11 71]	1996	28275.0	3913.0	12426.0	2635.0	39.0	...	2969.0	371.0	263.0	[...]
	1997	29581.0	4599.0	12040.0	3051.0	35.0	...	3336.0	457.0	332.0	2[...]
Paraguay [1 11 20]	1993[73]	326.5	243.2	8.0	1.2	0.2	...	68.2	32.5	3.5	[...]
Paraguay [1 11 20]	1994	616.0	433.6	36.9	3.5	1.8	...	126.7	53.1	10.1	[...]
	1996	684.8	505.6	48.1	14.1	0.1	...	121.3	49.2	6.3	2[...]
Philippines [2 17 74]	1997	17437.0	10451.0	8295.0	2965.0	113.0	11.0	1489.0	1265.0	119.0	20[...]
Philippines [2 17 74]	1998	17654.0	10608.0	8375.0	2898.0	98.0	6.0	1480.0	1207.0	119.0	2[...]
	1999	17924.0	11709.0	8367.0	2976.0	82.0	7.0	1451.0	1327.0	118.0	26[...]
Puerto Rico [1 77]	1997	668.0	464.0	30.0	2.0	1.0	...	98.0	65.0	13.0	2[...]
Porto Rico [1 77]	1998	667.0	470.0	27.0	1.0	1.0	...	98.0	62.0	12.0	2[...]
	1999	669.0	480.0	23.0	1.0	1.0	...	94.0	62.0	11.0	2[...]
Sri Lanka [11 14 82]	1995	3661.0	1655.0	1298.5	686.9	49.3	7.2	415.7	448.4	23.9	0[...]
Sri Lanka [11 14 82]	1996	3797.4	1789.5	1244.2	718.5	58.4	10.3	429.9	408.2	20.8	3[...]
	1998	3855.3	2090.8	1451.6	1020.7	68.3	9.8	479.5	435.1	30.2	5[...]
Suriname [42]	1994	51.3	26.6	4.1	0.6	2.8	0.4	5.1	1.2	1.0	0[...]
Suriname [42]	1995	54.4	28.1	4.8	0.9	3.2	...	5.3	1.1	1.0	
	1996	57.8	29.4	4.6	0.5	4.1	0.1	6.0	1.3	1.2	0[...]
Thailand [1 13 85]	1997	18121.0	15041.3	8949.5	7741.7	41.4	5.4	2223.6	2068.3	143.3	35[...]
Thaïlande [1 13 85]	1998	17666.8	14471.1	9231.2	7240.5	33.1	8.1	2135.4	2054.0	149.8	27[...]
	1999	17721.2	14365.9	8826.0	6737.3	40.6	11.2	2224.8	2169.6	124.6	33[...]
Trinidad and Tobago [2]	1996	282.5	161.7	35.3	7.3	15.1	2.1	31.9	12.8	5.8	1[...]
Trinité–et–Tobago [2]	1997	294.5	165.3	37.2	6.5	15.5	2.1	33.2	13.6	4.8	1[...]
	1998	305.5	173.8	33.1	5.9	16.0	2.5	37.2	14.3	5.1	1[...]
Turkey [1 17 43]	1997	15364.0	5450.0	4657.0	3562.0	174.0	3.0	2919.0	684.0	101.0	11[...]
Turquie [1 17 43]	1998	15587.0	6371.0	5074.0	4460.0	167.0	4.0	2667.0	632.0	96.0	10[...]
	1999	15167.0	6882.0	5127.0	4970.0	131.0	2.0	2479.0	638.0	71.0	7[...]
Ukraine [7]	1997	19835.0	...	4988.0	...	730.0	...	3628.0	...	...	
Ukraine [7]	1998	19415.0	...	5060.0	...	687.0	...	3540.0	...	...	
	1999	18790.0	...	4961.0	...	639.0	...	3319.0	...	...	
United States [1 77 93]	1997	69685.0	59873.0	2662.0	875.0	543.0	92.0	14152.0	6683.0	1188.0	305[...]
Etats–Unis [1 77 93]	1998	70693.0	60771.0	2657.0	852.0	535.0	85.0	14138.0	6595.0	1162.0	334[...]
	1999	71446.0	62042.0	2539.0	877.0	495.0	69.0	13647.0	6423.0	1145.0	324[...]
Uruguay [18 20 42]	1995	707.2	498.8	49.9	7.8	1.6	0.2	138.5	78.2	13.3	2[...]
Uruguay [18 20 42]	1998	635.3	468.4	36.4	6.9	1.4	0.2	116.1	61.8	8.5	2[...]
	1999	623.7	458.4	36.2	5.7	1.4	...	112.2	58.5	7.2	3.[...]
Uzbekistan	1993	...	...	...	...	...	...	560.2	519.2	...	
Ouzbékistan	1994	...	...	...	...	...	...	537.8	506.3	...	
	1995	...	...	...	...	...	...	498.3	469.3	...	
Venezuela [1 2]	1995	5186.0	2481.0	990.9	44.3	63.4	9.0	743.4	298.0	54.5	11.4[...]
Venezuela [1 2]	1996	5249.6	2569.6	1013.1	43.3	69.1	8.6	715.0	290.4	50.2	13.4[...]
	1997	5451.8	2835.0	852.8	41.3	80.1	10.4	789.9	332.6	55.3	10.9[...]
Viet Nam [7]	1995	...	...	...	...	...	...	3227.2	...	...	
Viet Nam [7]	1996	...	...	...	...	...	...	3288.8	...	...	
	1997	...	...	...	...	...	...	3292.5	...	...	

Construction Construction		Trade, restaurants and hotels Commerce, restaurants, hôtels		Transport, storage, communications Transports, entrepôts, communications		Financing, insurance, real est.,bus. services Services financières, immob., et apparentées		Community, social and personal services Services fournis à la collectivité, services soc. et pers.	
M	F	M	F	M	F	M	F	M	F
292.0	...	1450.0	...	420.0	...	486.0	...	1264.0	...
378.0	...	1746.0	...	470.0	...	577.0	...	1686.0	...
400.0	...	1781.0	...	495.0	...	597.0	...	1744.0	...
58.7	...	233.8	...	45.0	...	15.6	...	241.0	...
63.2	...	245.5	...	46.8	...	17.4	...	251.0	...
88.1	...	259.2	...	49.7	...	20.1	...	261.5	...
2218.0	45.0	4446.0	109.0	1558.0	34.0	234.0	8.0	3797.0	686.0
2273.0	46.0	4557.0	111.0	1597.0	35.0	240.0	8.0	3891.0	704.0
2284.0	23.0	4868.0	128.0	1934.0	16.0	333.0	3.0	4407.0	917.0
41.8	...	79.4	73.4	24.0	3.6	29.1	15.3	72.2	116.5
89.2	...	151.1	159.0	48.7	6.2	30.5	16.8	121.0	193.4
82.5	...	198.9	199.7	56.5	5.2	41.0	15.9	130.0	219.5
1606.0	35.0	1493.0	2726.0	1676.0	94.0	404.0	277.0	2239.0	3057.0
1480.0	31.0	1511.0	2817.0	1780.0	105.0	408.0	287.0	2398.0	3234.0
1485.0	21.0	1657.0	2962.0	1893.0	116.0	407.0	309.0	2454.0	3335.0
63.0	3.0	141.0	92.0	32.0	11.0	17.0	20.0	274.0	268.0
70.0	3.0	134.0	96.0	33.0	13.0	18.0	23.0	272.0	271.0
80.0	4.0	138.0	93.0	34.0	10.0	17.0	25.0	271.0	281.0
281.7	18.7	469.4	87.7	230.0	14.7	57.2	34.3	573.0	320.5
309.2	11.7	552.6	152.5	234.2	25.3	78.8	39.2	691.1	392.0
295.2	14.0	469.5	124.2	251.5	16.5	85.5	31.6	607.7	398.9
4.1	0.1	7.5	3.9	4.4	0.7	2.2	1.3	18.0	17.7
7.0	0.1	8.1	4.8	3.0	0.9	3.4	1.5	16.1	17.5
7.6	0.2	8.9	6.0	5.6	1.2	2.2	1.7	13.9	18.1
1596.8	423.8	2194.0	2407.0	871.7	108.5	...	...	2094.3	2247.7
1082.4	197.1	2076.5	2387.0	798.7	124.0	...	...	2156.8	2427.4
1064.4	220.9	2229.0	2506.9	873.3	115.8	...	...	2331.0	2561.4
40.1	3.9	39.1	42.5	25.0	5.7	19.2	17.2	71.2	68.3
47.0	3.8	37.5	43.5	25.6	6.2	20.7	18.1	72.9	70.2
53.9	4.9	38.4	44.9	29.3	6.2	19.0	20.0	73.2	73.9
1296.0	27.0	2617.0	298.0	882.0	44.0	373.0	143.0	2345.0	679.0
1306.0	30.0	2601.0	300.0	917.0	36.0	358.0	157.0	2400.0	742.0
1170.0	22.0	2636.0	308.0	830.0	32.0	374.0	146.0	2350.0	757.0
1194.0	...	1589.0	...	1438.0	...	213.0	...	...	...
1097.0	...	1514.0	...	1400.0	...	213.0	...	...	...
974.0	...	1604.0	...	1329.0	...	197.0	...	...	...
7518.0	784.0	14118.0	12659.0	5351.0	2338.0	7014.0	7754.0	17138.0	28384.0
7721.0	798.0	14367.0	12836.0	5436.0	2375.0	7431.0	8021.0	17246.0	28875.0
8101.0	886.0	14448.0	13124.0	5670.0	2416.0	7871.0	8182.0	17530.0	29740.0
84.8	1.9	135.3	101.2	58.8	10.4	43.8	30.9	181.2	265.2
81.0	1.7	127.7	95.9	57.0	9.9	39.5	30.9	167.6	258.7
88.7	2.2	120.6	93.7	54.1	12.3	40.1	31.7	163.2	251.3
...	...	...	...	...	...	...	...	...	...
...	...	...	...	...	...	...	...	...	...
...	...	...	...	...	...	...	...	...	...
600.2	24.5	104.3	690.6	437.7	40.6	256.1	170.1	992.3	1187.1
580.9	19.2	1027.7	765.5	485.0	36.8	299.1	182.9	1001.8	1204.1
668.0	26.4	1130.7	854.9	487.8	46.6	281.0	185.3	1092.3	1319.4
995.6	...	...	...	781.0	...	...	...	...	...
975.1	...	...	...	855.6	...	...	...	...	...
976.5	...	...	...	856.0	...	...	...	...	...

29
Employment by industry [cont.]
Emploi par industrie [suite]

B. ISIC Rev. 3 [+] · CITI Rév. 3 [+]

Persons employed, by branch of economic activity (thousands)
Personnes employées, par branches d'activité économique (milliers)

Country or area Pays ou zone	Sex	Year Année	Total employment (000s) Emploi total (000s)	Agriculture, hunting and forestry Agriculture, chasse et sylviculture	Fishing Pêche	Mining and quarrying Activités extractives	Manufacturing Activités de fabrication	Electricity, gas and water supply Production et distribution d'électricité, de gaz et d'eau	Construc Construc
Argentina [11 13 97] Argentine [11 13 97]	M	1996	4604.4	41.3	9.1	19.5	898.9	55.1	5
	F	1996	2765.5	5.1	0.8	0.9	312.0	9.2	
	M	1997	4897.0	47.8	6.8	21.3	981.5	52.1	6
	F	1997	2961.5	6.8	0.4	0.9	310.3	9.9	
	M	1998	5057.0	50.1	5.9	18.0	966.8	47.6	6
	F	1998	3221.6	7.0	0.0	1.0	312.8	8.6	
Australia [1 2 99] Australie [1 2 99]	M	1997	...	...	11.6	67.8	831.1	56.6	5
	F	1997	...	...	2.7	6.8	304.3	8.9	
	M	1998	...	...	10.6	69.4	812.5	54.0	5
	F	1998	...	...	2.7	7.3	285.8	11.1	
	M	1999	...	...	12.0	63.7	787.6	53.1	5
	F	1999	...	...	2.3	6.1	287.5	11.3	
Austria [2] Autriche [2]	M	1997	2129.2	129.9	0.3	7.4	558.2	33.0	29
	F	1997	1590.3	120.0	...	1.6	199.9	5.3	2
	M	1998	2125.7	124.5	0.2	9.8	560.3	31.8	29
	F	1998	1597.5	117.2	0.1	1.8	196.7	4.1	2
	M	1999	2139.7	119.8	0.2	9.9	564.4	27.4	31
	F	1999	1622.7	110.5	0.1	1.3	198.9	3.8	2
Azerbaijan [7] Azerbaïdjan [7]	T	1989[8 9]	2880.0	...	...	...	...	...	
	T	1998	3701.5	1565.8	...	58.4	143.0	55.0	17
	T	1999	3701.9	1566.3	0.5	58.8	143.2	55.1	17
Bahamas [8 17] Bahamas [8 17]	M	1996	70.4	5.7	...	1.3	2.8	...	1
	F	1996	59.4	0.7	...	0.4	2.6	...	
	M	1997	71.3	4.3	...	1.4	2.7	...	1
	F	1997	63.9	0.9	0.5	...	2.7	...	
	M	1998	74.6	4.4	...	1.2	2.9	...	1
	F	1998	69.8	0.6	0.3	...	2.5	...	
Belgium [2 17 18] Belgique [2 17 18]	M	1997	22770.1	69.4	...	9.9	570.9	29.1	24
	F	1997	1562.1	32.5	...	1.3	187.4	4.5	1
	M	1998	2270.4	61.4	...	8.8	570.4	33.1	23
	F	1998	1587.1	24.9	...	1.4	178.6	4.4	1
	M	1999	2321.5	...	...	...	...	...	1
	F	1999	1585.6	...	...	...	...	...	
Bolivia [1 11 20] Bolivie [1 11 20]	M	1994	676.7	16.0	...	13.6	139.4	4.8	11
	F	1994	519.6	3.5	...	1.4	77.0	0.6	1
	M	1995	708.0	21.4	...	16.9	147.7	3.8	10
	F	1995	548.5	6.2	...	1.6	83.5	1.2	2
	M	1996[17]	736.0	15.7	0.3	17.6	156.9	8.7	10
	F	1996[17]	618.6	12.5	...	2.1	92.1	1.5	2
Bulgaria [7 8] Bulgarie [7 8]	T	1997	3157.4	800.4	...	60.5	752.4	58.5	13
	T	1998	3152.5	825.2	...	55.5	723.2	57.8	12
	T	1999	3072.0	818.2	...	47.9	663.0	57.9	12
Canada [2 32] Canada [2 32]	M	1997	7648.8	352.0	30.7	160.0	1496.3	86.0	65
	F	1997	6291.7	133.2	4.7	27.7	570.6	30.2	7
	M	1998	7802.6	359.0	29.2	151.6	1556.7	90.8	67
	F	1998	6523.8	141.1	4.8	30.0	589.9	26.6	8
	M	1999[22]	7865.8	349.0	28.9	132.8	1589.2	87.8	69
	F	1999[22]	6665.3	139.2	4.4	23.5	628.1	28.0	7

Wholesale and retail trade; repair of motor vehicles motorcycles and personal and household goods / Commerce de gros de détail; réparation de véhicules automobiles, de motorcycles et de biens personnels et domestiques	Hotels and restaurants / Hôtels et restaurants	Transport, storage and communications / Transports, entreposage et communications	Financial intermediation / Inter médiation financière	Real estate, renting and business activities / Immobilier, locations et activités de services aux entreprises	Public admin. and defence; compulsory social sec. Admin. publique et défense; séc. sociale obligatoire	Education / Education	Health and social work / Santé et action sociale	Other community, social and personal service act. / Autres act. de services collectifs, sociaux et personnels	Private households with employed persons / Ménages privés employant du personnel domestique	Extra-territorial org. and bodies / Org. et organismes extra-territoriaux
1043.6	134.9	517.7	102.9	312.3	368.9	102.7	148.9	246.5	54.1	0.5
479.2	74.2	54.9	73.1	201.4	193.2	384.7	285.4	143.5	522.9	1.0
1040.5	128.8	532.5	121.3	339.5	376.1	118.7	161.6	270.6	55.7	1.1
524.1	81.3	71.0	74.0	194.3	209.0	414.1	320.9	147.9	570.2	...
1070.2	133.4	562.4	115.0	358.7	412.5	131.0	161.3	281.0	37.4	...
597.3	96.3	72.4	86.9	213.1	241.8	472.6	335.4	166.7	584.7	1.7
942.2	178.8	410.7	...	...	...	...	...	...	1.9	0.7
777.8	224.8	140.0	...	...	...	...	...	...	9.6	0.7
975.2	183.4	401.2	...	...	...	...	...	...	1.7	0.6
799.5	224.4	143.6	...	...	...	...	...	...	9.0	0.7
1001.3	188.5	415.1	...	...	...	...	...	...	1.4	0.5
839.6	230.0	155.0	...	...	...	...	...	...	8.1	0.3
269.2	81.5	183.6	71.5	119.5	169.4	67.1	71.2	72.7	0.7	2.4
311.2	134.0	48.8	70.8	119.5	93.7	143.8	222.3	82.2	13.3	2.8
265.7	82.5	190.9	71.8	113.2	161.7	69.8	72.4	73.2	0.4	4.0
315.9	133.5	51.0	67.1	119.7	90.8	148.0	226.3	85.2	13.6	1.8
269.5	76.4	197.1	71.8	114.2	157.4	71.1	74.6	72.6	0.4	2.7
323.3	135.8	57.2	70.0	126.3	90.3	149.2	226.7	89.0	11.9	2.1
...	...	...	...	...	...	...	...	...	...	...
724.3	10.1	169.0	17.2	49.3	162.6	295.2	170.5	106.8	0.3	...
724.7	10.3	169.9	18.4	48.7	163.7	292.2	171.5	107.1	0.3	...
8.0	8.7	7.7	4.9	...	...	...	...	...	19.2	...
10.4	11.7	3.7	6.2	...	...	...	...	...	23.0	...
8.0	9.2	7.9	5.0	...	...	...	...	...	20.7	...
9.6	12.2	4.0	7.4	...	...	...	...	...	25.9	...
8.7	9.3	7.5	5.9	...	...	...	...	...	20.3	...
11.4	12.8	4.3	8.1	...	...	...	...	...	28.4	...
299.7	65.8	229.2	233.9	...	519.0	...	...	...	9.5	...
249.2	63.8	56.3	171.3	...	766.8	...	...	...	15.5	...
299.3	69.2	215.1	260.6	...	507.3	...	...	...	9.0	...
264.6	64.4	53.6	187.6	...	772.8	...	...	...	16.7	...
...	...	...	...	...	...	...	...	...	...	...
...	...	...	...	...	...	...	...	...	...	...
131.9	18.1	83.5	8.8	23.5	45.6	48.5[104]	...	26.6[105]	...	1.8
193.6	53.0	6.0	4.1	11.5	12.0	70.4[104]	...	82.6[105]	...	0.9
146.4	18.9	89.1	7.7	23.9	43.2	47.6[104]	...	33.3[105]	...	2.0
201.5	53.6	5.9	5.7	11.7	13.7	69.0[104]	...	91.3[105]	...	1.3
149.7	18.9	93.7	8.2	27.3	51.9	30.9	17.3	22.6	6.2	0.7
209.4	61.9	5.4	6.3	13.8	22.8	46.7	26.7	22.4	92.5	0.3
310.4	72.1	228.2	40.0	98.7	78.9	242.6	177.6	98.1	...	...
337.2	70.5	236.7	37.6	102.9	80.7	233.1	167.1	95.9	...	...
337.7	68.2	232.9	35.8	95.2	91.7	232.0	165.1	102.7	...	...
1354.0	370.1	736.1	209.5	835.1	444.5	357.0	270.8	277.4	14.7	...
1046.3	529.4	324.3	399.3	661.8	345.3	581.4	1127.6	362.1	70.8	...
1359.7	383.6	737.6	207.7	903.4	435.5	349.3	281.2	267.5	14.7	...
1092.8	532.9	343.5	387.9	730.1	352.7	593.4	1184.0	353.3	77.0	1.5
1391.5	374.0	775.3	213.4	912.7	415.0	354.6	271.1	272.7	5.7	...
1122.1	550.7	328.6	405.5	739.9	357.3	628.0	1173.3	365.5	92.7	1.5

29
Employment by industry [*cont.*]
Emploi par industrie [*suite*]

B. ISIC Rev. 3 [+] — CITI Rév. 3 [+]

Persons employed, by branch of economic activity (thousands)
Personnes employées, par branches d'activité économique (milliers)

Country or area Pays ou zone	Sex Sex	Year Année	Total employment (000s) Emploi total (000s)	Agriculture, hunting and forestry Agriculture, chasse et sylviculture	Fishing Pêche	Mining and quarrying Activités extractives	Manufacturing Activités de fabrication	Electricity, gas and water supply Production et distribution d'électricité, de gaz et d'eau	Construct Construct
China, Macao SAR † [1 42] Chine, Macao RAS † [1 42]	M	1997	...	...	...	...	...	...	
	F	1997	...	...	...	...	...	...	
	M	1998	109.8	0.2	...	...	13.4	1.1	1
	F	1998	91.2	0.1	...	...	28.0	0.3	
	M	1999	106.4	0.1	...	...	13.6	1.0	1
	F	1999	96.1	...	...	...	30.9	0.2	
Costa Rica [1 17 43] Costa Rica [1 17 43]	M	1997	849.2	224.9	5.9	1.5	129.3	11.1	8
	F	1997	378.1	22.2	0.2	...	61.7	2.5	
	M	1998	887.5	233.1	5.6	1.6	132.4	11.1	8
	F	1998	412.5	22.7	0.1	...	71.1	2.0	
	M	1999	879.6	230.5	6.2	1.9	133.4	11.8	8
	F	1999	420.5	19.7	0.1	0.2	70.6	1.4	
Croatia [2] Croatie [2]	M	1997[17]	863.6	141.5	2.8	6.3	204.6	25.2	7
	F	1997[17]	729.4	138.5	...	...	138.5	4.6	1
	M	1998[14]	832.2	264.0	2.4	7.3	184.3	22.8	8
	F	1998[14]	711.6	123.1	...	...	139.1	5.8	1
	M	1999[14]	802.2	125.2	3.6	7.6	188.5	20.8	8
	F	1999[14]	689.5	118.3	0.3	1.2	136.5	5.4	9
Czech Republic [2 14] Rép. tchèque [2 14]	M	1997	2786.0	188.0	...	73.0	814.0	70.0	44
	F	1997	2141.0	92.0	...	15.0	539.0	22.0	4
	M	1998	2751.0	171.0	...	73.0	806.0	74.0	41
	F	1998	2101.0	85.0	...	10.0	538.0	20.0	3
	M	1999	2691.0	165.0	...	66.0	787.0	64.0	41
	F	1999	2074.0	78.0	...	9.0	515.0	17.0	3
Denmark [107] Danemark [107]	M	1996	1440.7	74.4	5.4	2.8	351.0	13.4	155
	F	1996	1186.5	23.7		0.7	159.6	3.3	14
	M	1997	1464.7	73.3	5.3	2.4	353.6	13.3	159
	F	1997	1217.3	20.3	...	0.6	159.1	3.3	16
	M	1998	1460.1	72.0	4.7	2.4	356.1	16.9	159
	F	1998	1232.3	19.9		0.8	160.0	3.6	18
Dominican Republic Rép. dominicaine	M	1997	1891.4	502.5	...	7.5	332.7	13.7	150
	F	1997	760.6	16.5	...	0.9	150.7	6.6	3
Egypt [1 49]	M	1997[13]	12813.0	3642.3	87.0	41.2	1925.4	177.1	1134
	F	1997[13]	3017.0	1218.0	3.9	0.8	208.1	15.6	18
	M	1998[17]	13187.0	3665.1	98.8	57.6	1814.5	187.1	1269
	F	1998[17]	2996.0	1058.0	0.8	11.4	227.7	16.3	17
Estonia [46] Estonie [46]	M	1997	338.8	34.3	6.3	6.3	80.3	12.8	42
	F	1997	309.5	19.3	...	...	63.8	4.8	5
	M	1998	330.7	33.1	4.5	7.0	76.2	13.2	42
	F	1998	309.5	19.8	...	...	63.3	5.0	5
	M	1999[19]	315.2	31.4	2.8	7.6	70.4	12.8	36
	F	1999[19]	299.8	19.8	...	...	58.1	5.5	3
Finland [46] Finlande [46]	M	1997	1167.0	101.0	2.0	5.0	307.0	18.0	121
	F	1997	1027.0	49.0	1.0	1.0	129.0	4.0	8
	M	1998	1199.0	95.0	2.0	5.0	314.0	18.0	129
	F	1998	1048.0	47.0	...	1.0	133.0	4.0	10
	M	1999	1227.0	97.0	2.0	4.0	321.0	18.0	138
	F	1999	1090.0	46.0	...	1.0	140.0	4.0	11

Wholesale and retail trade; repair of motor vehicles motorcycles and personal and household goods / Commerce de gros et détail; répa-...on de véhicules automobiles, de motorcycles et de biens personnels et domestiques	Hotels and restaurants / Hôtels et restaurants	Transport, storage and communications / Transports, entreposage et communications	Financial intermediation / Inter médiation financière	Real estate, renting and business activities / Immobilier, locations et activités de services aux entreprises	Public admin. and defence; compulsory social sec. / Admin. publique et défense; séc. sociale obligatoire	Education / Education	Health and social work / Santé et action sociale	Other community, social and personal service act. / Autres act. de services collectifs, sociaux et personnels	Private households with employed persons / Ménages privés employant du personnel domestique	Extra-territorial org. and bodies / Org. et organismes extra-territoriaux
...	...	...	...	...	...	...	...	...	...	...
...	...	...	...	...	...	...	...	...	...	...
19.2	12.0	10.3	2.2	6.2	11.0	2.1	1.3	11.0	0.4	...
14.3	11.1	3.4	3.4	2.1	5.4	4.6	2.8	9.0	4.5	...
17.1	11.0	11.2	2.7	6.6	12.0	2.9	1.6	11.3	0.2	...
14.2	10.7	3.8	3.4	3.1	4.8	6.3	3.6	8.4	5.4	...
121.0	23.7	59.6	16.2	2.6	...	21.0	23.5	113.5	6.8	0.7
58.5	31.0	6.1	9.6	0.7	...	47.2	29.5	37.3	67.2	0.6
129.4	26.3	65.4	19.0	3.5	...	21.5	27.4	114.8	6.9	1.9
63.9	32.2	7.9	10.5	1.1	...	50.3	32.0	42.9	71.1	1.0
126.1	30.4	66.9	12.9	3.8	...	21.2	24.7	115.1	6.9	1.4
77.7	34.4	7.7	7.5	1.6	...	44.2	31.1	43.7	76.6	0.8
92.7	36.3	83.4	8.8	29.8	77.8	23.6	20.1	27.3	...	3.4
117.8	45.0	24.7	23.7	25.4	45.4	55.0	69.2	22.5	3.6	...
89.0	38.7	86.9	7.9	34.0	67.4	21.1	20.0	28.9	...	...
117.1	43.7	23.6	24.9	26.4	41.0	54.2	72.6	23.0	3.8	...
90.2	34.3	79.1	9.6	29.9	62.3	18.7	19.3	25.9	0.3	...
107.0	39.7	22.0	25.0	26.7	43.1	62.1	69.6	19.0	3.1	...
292.0	78.0	259.0	32.0	134.0	200.0	70.0	52.0	77.0	...	1.0
362.0	97.0	117.0	67.0	117.0	122.0	233.0	224.0	90.0	1.0	1.0
300.0	69.0	266.0	37.0	139.0	191.0	65.0	51.0	91.0	...	1.0
355.0	96.0	113.0	65.0	110.0	138.0	216.0	214.0	102.0	1.0	1.0
299.0	67.0	252.0	322.0	145.0	202.0	67.0	53.0	79.0	...	1.0
338.0	92.0	118.0	67.0	118.0	134.0	229.0	235.0	90.0	2.0	2.0
212.6	26.7	132.0	39.2	115.4	86.7	88.9	75.7	56.9	0.6	0.6
146.6	42.5	52.5	44.1	73.7	80.8	104.3	368.3	62.6	6.6	0.5
214.7	29.6	134.5	36.1	128.6	88.3	86.0	74.1	61.7	0.6	0.4
151.0	44.4	50.9	43.7	80.5	80.0	113.4	383.2	63.3	4.1	0.3
211.6	28.1	131.9	37.9	138.1	89.5	80.1	70.5	56.7	0.8	0.4
156.1	43.2	50.0	41.3	89.5	78.8	113.7	388.3	61.8	4.6	0.5
356.1	59.5	190.0	17.3	...	99.5	...	...	152.2	...	...
176.1	55.8	12.9	16.8	...	25.9	...	...	295.3	...	...
1550.6	203.9	881.4	138.1	182.4	1221.8	1040.2	228.9	280.1	30.2	...
195.2	13.2	41.8	41.9	24.6	343.5	674.9	181.5	24.3	9.3	...
1676.1	244.7	909.9	139.7	240.9	1279.8	1028.0	250.4	292.0	31.5	...
273.8	32.3	44.2	34.6	25.3	348.8	637.2	235.4	24.3	8.8	...
41.4	2.5	42.7	2.0	20.5	18.2	13.1	4.9	11.0	...	...
49.2	12.0	16.7	5.5	14.6	16.0	45.9	32.0	21.9	...	...
40.1	2.4	41.8	2.7	21.6	19.0	11.9	4.8	10.3	...	...
50.5	11.9	16.5	5.9	17.3	17.6	44.6	30.3	19.9	...	...
37.6	1.9	40.8	3.4	22.6	20.7	11.5	5.0	10.6	...	...
51.4	11.1	14.2	5.4	18.2	18.8	43.1	30.1	18.9	...	...
137.0	19.0	119.0	15.0	111.0	76.0	48.0	37.0	47.0	...	...
126.0	47.0	45.0	33.0	81.0	57.0	98.0	273.0	69.0	4.0	...
141.0	22.0	122.0	15.0	117.0	81.0	50.0	37.0	47.0	...	...
128.0	49.0	47.0	31.0	87.0	56.0	104.0	277.0	68.0	3.0	...
143.0	24.0	121.0	14.0	125.0	79.0	53.0	38.0	47.0	...	...
135.0	52.0	48.0	32.0	97.0	59.0	102.0	283.0	74.0	4.0	...

29
Employment by industry [*cont.*]
Emploi par industrie [*suite*]

B. ISIC Rev. 3 [+] − CITI Rév. 3 [+]

Persons employed, by branch of economic activity (thousands)
Personnes employées, par branches d'activité économique (milliers)

Country or area Pays ou zone	Sex Sexe	Year Année	Total employment (000s) Emploi total (000s)	Agriculture, hunting and forestry Agriculture, chasse et sylviculture	Fishing Pêche	Mining and quarrying Activités extractives	Manufacturing Activités de fabrication	Electricity, gas and water supply Production et distribution d'électricité, de gaz et d'eau	Construc Construc
Germany [2 17] Allemagne [2 17]	M	1997	20549.0	652.0	5.0	179.0	6102.0	274.0	28
	F	1997	15256.0	391.0	...	23.0	2373.0	65.0	3
	M	1998	20509.0	639.0	6.0	167.0	6068.0	241.0	27
	F	1998	15351.0	377.0	...	15.0	2393.0	64.0	4
	M	1999	20659.0	653.0	5.0	148.0	6115.0	249.0	27
	F	1999	15743.0	367.0	...	13.0	2417.0	62.0	4
Greece [14 18 42] Grèce [14 18 42]	M	1996	2470.3	437.2	13.5	16.3	395.4	33.6	2
	F	1996	1401.6	334.3	1.1	0.9	180.7	7.2	
	M	1997	2439.0	424.5	13.2	16.6	380.5	33.4	2
	F	1997	1415.1	326.1	1.2	0.7	178.2	7.4	
	M	1998[2]	2504.2	396.8	10.1	17.4	406.7	29.4	2
	F	1998[2]	1463.0	296.7	0.6	0.9	171.2	5.9	
Hungary [46] Hongrie [46]	M	1997	2043.5	216.5	...	23.9	511.3	72.2	2
	F	1997	1602.8	71.3	...	3.3	352.8	25.2	
	M	1998	2041.7	211.6	...	21.4	535.5	72.6	2
	F	1998	1656.0	67.2	...	4.3	376.6	23.9	
	M	1999	2103.1	204.5	...	19.4	551.7	65.4	2
	F	1999	1708.4	65.9	...	5.0	377.2	24.4	
Iceland [1 13 69] Islande [1 13 69]	M	1996	76.1	4.0	6.5	0.1	15.4	0.9	
	F	1996	65.9	2.5	0.6	...	8.7	0.2	
	M	1997	76.4	3.5	5.9	0.1	15.8	0.9	
	F	1997	65.6	2.4	0.4	...	8.9	0.3	
	M	1998	79.1	3.9	5.6	0.1	15.3	1.2	
	F	1998	68.9	2.7	0.6	...	9.4	0.3	
Ireland [2 13] Irlande [2 13]	M	1997	840.3	123.2	2.2	6.0	183.9	10.5	10
	F	1997	539.7	16.0	...	0.4	86.0	1.7	
	M	1998	899.9	116.1	3.4	4.7	193.8	9.9	12
	F	1998	594.6	16.1	0.4	0.4	90.4	2.0	
	M	1999	947.3	117.7	2.7	5.3	200.4	10.0	13
	F	1999	643.9	15.1	0.4	0.4	91.0	1.8	
Israel [1 2 56] Israël [1 2 56]	M	1997	1155.4	39.8	...	284.8	...	15.5	13
	F	1997	884.8	9.1	...	113.4	...	3.3	
	M	1998[22]	1155.2	37.7	...	279.5	...	16.4	12
	F	1998[22]	917.2	9.8	...	106.7	...	3.6	
	M	1999	1176.2	38.8	...	281.1	...	15.9	1
	F	1999	960.5	10.8	...	108.7	...	3.3	
Italy [2 57 58] Italie [2 57 58]	M	1997	13221.0	793.0	41.0	59.0	3363.0	168.0	147
	F	1997	7192.0	409.0	2.0	8.0	1476.0	23.0	9
	M	1998	13273.0	767.0	43.0	65.0	3421.0	169.0	145
	F	1998	7345.0	389.0	2.0	9.0	1500.0	22.0	9
	M	1999	13330.0	737.0	42.0	61.0	3442.0	156.0	148
	F	1999	7533.0	352.0	3.0	10.0	1487.0	20.0	9
Kazakhstan [7] Kazakhstan [7]	T	1996	6361.0	...	...	...	...	...	
	T	1997	6308.0	...	...	...	...	...	
	T	1998	6127.0	1353.9	5.9	123.7	627.0	125.5	22
Korea, Republic of [1 2] Corée, République de [1 2]	M	1997	12420.0	1152.0	83.0	24.0	2885.0	66.0	178
	F	1997	8686.0	1124.0	26.0	2.0	1597.0	11.0	21
	M	1998	11910.0	1241.0	58.0	21.0	2553.0	52.0	143
	F	1998	8084.0	1158.0	24.0	...	1345.0	9.0	14
	M	1999	11978.0	1189.0	59.0	19.0	2563.0	52.0	135
	F	1999	8303.0	1075.0	26.0	1.0	1443.0	9.0	12

Wholesale and retail trade; repair of motor vehicles motorcycles and personal and household goods Commerce de gros et de détail; répa- ...on de véhicules automobiles, de motorcycles et de biens personnels et domestiques	Hotels and restaurants Hôtels et restaurants	Transport, storage and communications Transports, entreposage et communi- cations	Financial inter- mediation Inter médiation financière	Real estate, renting and business activities Immobilier, locations et activités de services aux entreprises	Public admin. and defence; compulsory social sec. Admin. publique et défense; séc. sociale obligatoire	Education Education	Health and social work Santé et action sociale	Other community, social and personal service act. Autres act. de services collectifs, sociaux et personnels	Private households with employed persons Ménages privés employant du personnel domestique	Extra- territorial org. and bodies Org. et organismes extra- territoriaux
2384.0	481.0	1390.0	622.0	1290.0	1917.0	673.0	881.0	803.0	7.0	17.0
2727.0	652.0	552.0	635.0	1185.0	1377.0	1215.0	2556.0	969.0	127.0	12.0
2435.0	482.0	1382.0	638.0	1348.0	1872.0	697.0	914.0	820.0	9.0	22.0
2719.0	648.0	538.0	635.0	1233.0	1302.0	1230.0	2620.0	1006.0	141.0	14.0
2442.0	492.0	1396.0	639.0	1422.0	1859.0	697.0	927.0	839.0	8.0	22.0
2766.0	696.0	557.0	652.0	1316.0	1319.0	1251.0	2738.0	1040.0	133.0	15.0
400.0	137.1	220.7	50.6	93.2	187.2	87.9	64.6	80.3	3.5	0.3
228.7	92.2	33.3	41.6	65.1	87.6	136.3	106.0	49.7	35.8	0.2
407.4	131.6	214.5	53.2	96.7	188.3	87.3	64.9	76.9	3.9	0.5
235.2	98.3	32.2	43.6	63.5	91.0	142.6	105.2	48.6	37.8	0.3
413.1	145.9	212.2	50.9	109.3	185.5	92.8	65.4	84.6	2.5	1.3
254.7	103.4	32.5	45.4	85.0	93.1	148.2	119.8	50.9	52.2	0.7
241.4	59.6	228.4	28.1	77.9	168.3	70.9	57.4	85.5	0.3	1.5
255.4	61.3	81.6	55.2	68.4	125.5	226.0	174.7	82.0	0.5	0.7
220.2	57.2	216.0	26.6	91.4	160.7	73.5	57.0	84.4	0.7	1.8
252.0	64.4	85.9	55.2	71.6	133.6	232.0	180.8	87.4	0.8	1.2
241.6	63.9	222.8	26.6	102.2	160.8	71.9	56.5	81.9	0.6	0.7
275.9	69.3	85.5	54.3	81.7	141.1	235.0	182.7	87.9	1.4	0.7
11.2	1.9	6.7	1.9	5.1	2.8	3.2	3.0	4.2	...	0.3
8.2	2.4	3.4	2.7	3.6	3.2	6.3	17.9	5.4	...	0.3
11.1	2.0	6.2	1.7	5.1	3.3	3.0	3.3	4.1	...	0.7
9.0	2.2	3.6	2.6	3.8	2.7	6.0	17.6	5.3	...	0.2
11.2	2.0	6.6	1.8	5.7	4.1	3.1	3.0	4.4	...	0.7
9.4	2.5	4.1	2.8	3.8	2.9	6.5	17.7	5.4	...	0.1
108.8	32.7	51.4	22.7	48.7	45.0	33.4	27.1	36.3	1.4	0.6
84.5	43.7	13.6	27.6	35.6	27.2	59.8	92.6	37.2	5.2	0.6
115.3	39.4	59.9	22.8	58.8	45.0	33.9	25.8	33.9	0.6	0.1
92.3	53.7	20.2	32.5	51.5	27.4	66.2	86.9	34.4	8.3	0.1
118.2	41.8	72.0	26.3	72.9	45.1	32.6	24.9	35.9	0.9	0.3
105.1	60.8	23.9	34.8	61.8	29.3	67.9	95.1	38.1	7.6	0.3
160.5	42.2	93.6	31.1	116.0	65.1	60.1	47.2	50.0	2.6	0.5
102.6	33.3	30.8	42.5	88.4	48.6	186.1	137.0	46.4	29.8	0.8
164.7	45.6	92.7	31.6	119.7	67.0	62.8	52.4	51.6	2.5	1.2
107.7	35.0	29.7	41.2	97.0	45.4	199.4	150.4	47.1	29.9	1.0
169.3	51.1	100.3	31.9	127.4	65.6	64.2	52.2	50.2	5.0	1.1
112.3	39.0	35.3	41.8	97.3	50.6	203.6	159.7	49.0	35.1	0.7
2086.0	379.0	896.0	425.0	690.0	1347.0	427.0	557.0	468.0	40.0	11.0
1148.0	311.0	203.0	222.0	463.0	578.0	1003.0	704.0	380.0	163.0	7.0
2077.0	378.0	884.0	439.0	729.0	1345.0	422.0	557.0	471.0	43.0	12.0
1189.0	298.0	213.0	235.0	488.0	594.0	1004.0	724.0	407.0	172.0	6.0
2066.0	400.0	910.0	434.0	774.0	1343.0	416.0	547.0	469.0	43.0	11.0
1242.0	339.0	223.0	236.0	562.0	600.0	1029.0	742.0	428.0	158.0	6.0
...	...	...	...	...	...	...	...	...	...	...
...	...	...	...	...	...	...	...	...	...	...
1404.6	67.9	560.2	37.9	183.5	178.7	521.7	325.9	186.8	0.1	...
2161.0	587.0	1033.0	323.0	756.0	502.0	465.0	104.0	473.0	8.0	12.0
1755.0	1303.0	129.0	438.0	383.0	145.0	638.0	225.0	472.0	221.0	1.0
2151.0	563.0	1045.0	357.0	771.0	571.0	488.0	113.0	467.0	5.0	18.0
1667.0	1190.0	124.0	404.0	323.0	174.0	656.0	247.0	421.0	197.0	1.0
2172.0	586.0	1080.0	351.0	855.0	610.0	463.0	120.0	483.0	4.0	17.0
1732.0	1234.0	122.0	372.0	347.0	260.0	659.0	261.0	442.0	197.0	...

29
Employment by industry [*cont.*]
Emploi par industrie [*suite*]

B. ISIC Rev. 3 ⁺ — CITI Rév. 3 ⁺

Persons employed, by branch of economic activity (thousands)
Personnes employées, par branches d'activité économique (milliers)

Country or area Pays ou zone	Sex Sex	Year Année	Total employment (000s) Emploi total (000s)	Agriculture, hunting and forestry Agriculture, chasse et sylviculture	Fishing Pêche	Mining and quarrying Activités extractives	Manufacturing Activités de fabrication	Electricity, gas and water supply Production et distribution d'électricité, de gaz et d'eau	Construct Construct
Kyrgyzstan	M	1997	907.9	435.1	...	6.9	82.4	14.3	4
Kirghizistan	F	1997	781.4	380.5	...	2.0	61.3	4.7	1
	M	1998	918.7	450.4	...	6.3	78.7	15.3	4
	F	1998	786.2	385.0	...	1.9	64.6	5.0	
	M	1999	971.6	501.9	0.5	7.7	74.1	16.6	3
	F	1999	792.7	421.9	0.1	1.8	52.9	5.5	
Latvia ² ¹⁷ ⁸⁰	M	1997	527.1	117.9	3.5	0.3	108.1	19.0	4
Lettonie ² ¹⁷ ⁸⁰	F	1997	487.8	86.5	1.4	0.2	83.8	5.5	
	M	1998	533.5	108.5	3.7	1.1	105.3	17.8	4
	F	1998	473.7	75.6	1.2	0.2	77.1	6.6	
	M	1999	515.0	83.5	3.2	1.1	102.6	16.6	5
	F	1999	474.5	63.5	0.8	0.1	72.9	6.4	
Lithuania ¹ ⁴²	M	1997	828.7	191.9	...	158.7		32.3	9
Lituanie ¹ ⁴²	F	1997	742.0	132.6	...	135.7		12.2	1
	M	1998	823.3	199.5	...	155.1		28.1	9
	F	1998	774.3	136.6	...	146.2		9.9	
	M	1999	812.0	194.7	...	145.1		29.3	9
	F	1999	786.3	128.1	...	145.3		10.6	
Luxembourg ⁷ ⁵⁰	T	1997	227.1	5.1	...	0.3	32.4	1.5	2
Luxembourg ⁷ ⁵⁰	T	1998	237.0	5.0	...	0.3	32.5	1.5	2
	T	1999	248.3	...	...	...			
Mauritius ¹ ⁴³	M	1995	299.3	45.9	...	1.9	68.1	4.1	4
Maurice ¹ ⁴³	F	1995	137.0	17.3	...	0.1	57.4	0.3	
Mexico ¹⁴ ⁴³	M	1997	24795.5	7246.7	190.9	99.1	4013.9	161.2	170
Mexique ¹⁴ ⁴³	F	1997	12564.3	1574.2	8.4	9.3	2251.0	26.3	5
	M	1998	25663.1	6508.6	171.4	140.8	4473.5	155.1	205
	F	1998	12954.4	1133.3	4.0	11.9	2510.5	27.6	6
	M	1999	26049.7	6855.8	153.3	122.5	4675.5	168.7	211
	F	1999	13019.4	1192.8	6.7	10.8	2669.3	24.5	4
Netherlands ⁴⁹	M	1996	4109.0	188.0	...	9.0	849.0	34.0	39
Pays–Bas ⁴⁹	F	1996	2862.0	71.0	...	...	229.0	7.0	3
	M	1997	4194.0	180.0	5.0	12.0	858.0	36.0	41
	F	1997	3000.0	74.0	...	...	245.0	6.0	3
	M	1998	4289.0	167.0	...	10.0	856.0	40.0	41
	F	1998	3109.0	70.0	...	...	247.0	7.0	38
Netherlands Antilles ² ¹⁷ ⁶⁸	M	1996	31.7	0.4	...	0.0	4.8	0.8	4
Antilles néerlandaises ² ¹⁷ ⁶⁸	F	1996	25.2	0.1	...	0.0	1.1	0.2	0
	M	1997	30.5	0.5	...	0.0	4.3	0.8	4
	F	1997	25.8	0.1	...	0.0	1.0	0.1	0
	M	1998	29.5	0.5	...	0.0	3.9	0.8	4
	F	1998	24.7	0.1	...	0.1	0.9	0.1	0
New Zealand ¹ ²	M	1997	958.0	104.1	2.5	4.3	197.1	8.8	102
Nouvelle–Zealande ¹ ²	F	1997	777.9	42.9	0.9	0.6	85.9	1.9	13
	M	1998	947.5	98.8	3.5	3.6	202.1	8.1	97
	F	1998	777.5	44.1	0.5	0.6	87.6	2.0	13
	M	1999	956.6	108.5	3.8	3.1	195.3	7.1	98
	F	1999	793.7	52.6	0.6	0.4	83.1	1.8	11
Norway ⁶⁹	M	1997	1183.0	62.0	16.0	23.0	242.0	17.0	127
Norvègge ⁶⁹	F	1997	1009.0	23.0	2.0	6.0	86.0	4.0	9
	M	1998	1207.0	60.0	17.0	28.0	239.0	16.0	134
	F	1998	1036.0	26.0	2.0	6.0	82.0	3.0	11
	M	1999	1208.0	60.0	16.0	26.0	222.0	15.0	134
	F	1999	1050.0	25.0	2.0	6.0	77.0	3.0	12

Wholesale and retail trade; repair of motor vehicles motorcycles and personal and household goods mmerce de gros de détail; répa– on de véhicules automobiles, de otorcycles et de biens personnels et domestiques	Hotels and restaurants Hôtels et restaurants	Transport, storage and communications Transports, entreposage et communi- cations	Financial inter- mediation Inter médiation financière	Real estate, renting and business activities Immobilier, locations et activités de services aux entreprises	Public admin. and defence; compulsory social sec. Admin. publique et défense; séc. sociale obligatoire	Education Education	Health and social work Santé et action sociale	Other community, social and personal service act. Autres act. de services collectifs, sociaux et personnels	Private households with employed persons Ménages privés employant du personnel domestique	Extra- territorial org. and bodies Org. et organismes extra- territoriaux
86.2	6.0	65.4	3.1	21.7	44.6	46.6	23.0	26.5	...	...
88.5	6.1	13.9	4.1	19.6	15.8	92.8	65.6	15.6	...	...
82.9	6.9	61.9	4.4	23.5	47.2	47.7	23.2	28.9	...	...
97.3	7.0	13.4	3.7	15.4	15.8	91.6	61.3	15.0	...	...
102.5	5.7	52.6	3.3	17.4	50.0	46.4	22.3	28.4	3.5	...
81.2	5.8	13.2	3.8	11.3	15.7	94.3	62.9	14.6	1.3	...
61.8	4.4	61.4	3.4	17.2	34.6	17.9	8.5	19.8	0.7	...
79.2	11.1	24.5	6.5	12.3	25.2	72.7	43.3	28.2	1.2	...
65.2	3.8	57.4	4.6	20.0	41.3	20.5	11.8	21.4	1.0	0.1
86.6	13.0	24.6	8.0	16.7	29.5	62.1	41.6	24.1	0.9	...
72.2	5.4	56.8	3.5	23.5	43.6	19.9	8.4	20.3	1.0	...
78.8	16.2	28.0	7.3	21.5	34.8	70.2	43.5	23.1	2.3	...
112.8	8.5	66.0	6.7	24.5	42.6	33.2	21.0	32.8	0.5	...
121.6	17.5	32.5	7.8	23.7	31.1	101.2	79.2	33.9	1.3	...
110.9	6.2	69.1	7.2	23.2	48.3	35.8	19.1	27.5	0.7	...
114.5	19.6	34.9	12.4	21.8	28.9	114.8	87.0	36.8	1.5	...
113.7	6.8	69.6	5.9	24.3	51.5	36.0	17.4	26.5	0.6	...
109.8	23.5	30.8	10.6	21.7	34.0	126.8	95.3	37.4	3.4	0.6
35.5	10.9	17.2	22.9	25.8	11.5	10.9	14.1	9.2	5.3	...
37.2	11.0	19.0	24.0	29.3	11.4	11.1	14.4	9.4	5.6	...
...	...	...	...	...	...	...	...	...	...	...
41.9	11.2	24.9	...	8.6	21.2	18.0	...	12.1	...	...
15.4	3.3	2.7	...	4.6	5.4	16.1	...	13.9	...	...
3344.9	743.5	1402.0	213.0	741.9	1097.7	752.9	388.6	2428.6	159.3	101.2
3099.6	839.5	117.5	153.5	404.5	488.9	1077.2	572.5	460.7	1394.0	25.9
3643.5	815.2	1539.5	175.8	766.1	1134.1	785.2	341.6	2628.1	187.6	120.0
3160.7	1009.6	153.6	140.0	390.1	472.9	1108.0	668.8	482.1	1583.8	24.4
3502.0	827.2	1548.2	178.7	732.8	1186.7	731.4	365.1	2573.0	179.0	124.5
3080.4	980.2	190.3	124.0	423.9	541.6	991.5	659.6	521.5	1528.4	26.5
648.0	113.0	321.0	132.0	423.0	343.0	214.0	210.0	136.0	...	...
512.0	131.0	102.0	104.0	297.0	157.0	228.0	736.0	145.0	25.0	...
668.0	118.0	314.0	139.0	448.0	361.0	203.0	215.0	139.0	...	...
542.0	134.0	109.0	113.0	313.0	168.0	223.0	772.0	164.0	21.0	...
686.0	120.0	333.0	148.0	498.0	348.0	219.0	221.0	147.0	...	...
534.0	147.0	109.0	116.0	334.0	117.0	246.0	807.0	171.0	20.0	...
5.5	1.5	2.9	1.5	2.2	3.8	0.8	1.0	1.4	0.1	0.2
5.3	2.5	1.2	2.2	1.3	2.1	2.0	3.4	1.9	1.8	0.1
5.3	1.6	2.9	1.4	2.4	3.6	0.9	0.9	1.3	0.1	0.1
5.4	2.4	1.3	2.3	1.4	2.2	1.9	3.4	2.0	2.0	0.1
5.1	1.6	2.8	1.4	2.5	3.6	0.9	0.9	1.2	0.1	...
5.3	2.1	1.3	2.3	1.4	2.1	1.8	3.3	1.8	1.9	0.1
151.0	33.6	71.8	25.5	88.0	49.6	40.6	22.0	46.4	7.6	0.2
136.0	55.0	31.4	34.3	75.9	48.5	91.3	104.2	38.9	14.9	0.3
146.8	34.9	72.2	22.4	92.9	46.2	37.8	24.6	51.9	1.0	0.3
134.7	53.6	31.0	31.1	75.4	50.8	89.2	108.9	44.6	7.4	0.4
155.6	33.2	75.1	23.1	93.5	48.2	34.3	25.8	48.9	0.8	0.4
129.2	53.4	35.4	30.7	81.3	50.3	91.1	115.2	47.6	7.2	0.2
178.0	22.0	115.0	25.0	102.0	89.0	65.0	63.0	36.0	...	...
157.0	44.0	49.0	27.0	62.0	62.0	105.0	321.0	48.0	6.0	...
181.0	25.0	119.0	25.0	109.0	89.0	64.0	65.0	37.0	...	...
160.0	45.0	51.0	26.0	70.0	63.0	109.0	324.0	51.0	6.0	...
187.0	23.0	120.0	26.0	121.0	89.0	61.0	66.0	39.0	...	...
151.0	49.0	50.0	28.0	79.0	63.0	118.0	330.0	51.0	5.0	...

29
Employment by industry [*cont.*]
Emploi par industrie [*suite*]

B. ISIC Rev. 3 [+] — CITI Rév. 3 [+]

Persons employed, by branch of economic activity (thousands)
Personnes employées, par branches d'activité économique (milliers)

Country or area Pays ou zone	Sex	Year Année	Total employment (000s) Emploi total (000s)	Agriculture, hunting and forestry Agriculture, chasse et sylviculture	Fishing Pêche	Mining and quarrying Activités extractives	Manufacturing Activités de fabrication	Electricity, gas and water supply Production et distribution d'électricité, de gaz et d'eau	Construc Construc
Panama [7] Panama [7]	M	1997	603.1	153.2	9.3	1.8	65.9	6.9	5
	F	1997	306.0	6.7	0.3	0.2	30.3	2.2	
	M	1998	624.3	151.7	8.8	0.7	63.1	6.6	6
	F	1998	312.2	5.4	0.4	0.1	29.1	2.5	
	M	1999	638.0	151.4	10.0	0.9	64.2	5.8	7
	F	1999	323.4	5.7	0.4		29.8	1.1	
Peru [14 20 42] Pérou [14 20 42]	M	1997	3825.9	344.5	32.2	46.8	627.0	24.7	35
	F	1997	2918.9	136.3	2.1	2.2	333.7	1.0	1
	M	1998	3918.5	247.6	25.5	59.2	608.2	21.6	38
	F	1998	3010.8	94.4	0.4	3.4	317.4	3.1	
	M	1999	3980.4	250.9	63.1	28.3	555.7	35.1	37
	F	1999	3230.8	104.1	2.2	3.0	341.9	6.3	
Poland [2 112] Pologne [2 112]	M	1996	8213.0	1814.0	10.0	372.0	1941.0	215.0	83
	F	1996	6756.0	1484.0	2.0	46.0	1189.0	56.0	8
	M	1997	8397.0	1726.0	12.0	347.0	1969.0	225.0	91
	F	1997	6780.0	1378.0	...	41.0	1213.0	56.0	8
	M	1998	8470.0	1631.0	11.0	339.0	1970.0	210.0	97
	F	1998	6884.0	1304.0	1.0	41.0	1235.0	55.0	9
Portugal Portugal	M	1997[42]	2511.4	285.4	14.6	14.3	558.8	31.8	39
	F	1997[42]	2034.6	315.4	1.5	1.5	395.7	5.5	1
	M	1998[2]	2641.4	299.9	20.5	14.0	635.5	27.9	49
	F	1998[2]	2110.5	317.4	1.6	1.9	494.6	4.0	1
	M	1999[2]	2663.1	281.2	19.0	12.3	610.5	30.8	52
	F	1999[2]	2173.8	312.7	0.4	0.8	496.0	3.2	1
Republic of Moldova [1 7] République de Moldova [1 7]	T	1997	1646.0	683.0	1.0	4.0	167.0	20.0	5
	T	1998	1642.0	749.0	1.0	4.0	155.0	23.0	5
	T	1999	1495.0	730.0	1.0	3.0	135.0	22.0	4
Romania [2] Roumanie [2]	M	1997	6004.2	2113.7	7.5	190.3	1384.7	178.5	40
	F	1997	5045.8	2188.5	1.3	35.0	1058.9	55.9	6
	M	1998	5885.1	2166.3	6.6	171.1	1284.9	183.2	37
	F	1998	4959.8	2168.3	0.9	30.8	1028.8	51.8	5
	M	1999	5799.1	2249.8	6.5	158.8	1198.5	178.5	348
	F	1999	4976.6	2241.8	1.1	27.6	966.3	45.1	4
Russian Federation [17 113] Fédération de Russie [17 113]	M	1997	31554.0	4874.0	180.0	878.0	6511.0	1082.0	2928
	F	1997	28467.0	2214.0	28.0	250.0	5065.0	425.0	873
	M	1998	30486.0	4540.0	135.0	802.0	6146.0	1173.0	2634
	F	1998	27374.0	1962.0	19.0	247.0	4743.0	459.0	785
	M	1999	31524.0	4659.0	133.0	925.0	6513.0	1126.0	2627
	F	1999	28884.0	2328.0	25.0	285.0	5002.0	451.0	818
San Marino [42 78] Saint–Marin [42 78]	M	1996	10.3	0.2	...	...	3.7	...	1
	F	1996	6.4	0.1	...	...	1.6	...	0
	M	1997	10.6	0.1	...	...	3.9	...	1
	F	1997	6.7	0.1	...	...	1.6	...	0
	M	1998	11.0	0.1	...	...	4.1	...	1
	F	1998	6.9	0.1	...	...	1.7	...	0

Wholesale and retail trade; repair of motor vehicles and personal and household goods / Commerce de gros et détail; répa- ration de véhicules automobiles, de motorcycles et de biens personnels et domestiques	Hotels and restaurants / Hôtels et restaurants	Transport, storage and communications / Transports, entreposage et communications	Financial inter- mediation / Inter médiation financière	Real estate, renting and business activities / Immobilier, locations et activités de services aux entreprises	Public admin. and defence; compulsory social sec. / Admin. publique et défense; séc. sociale obligatoire	Education / Education	Health and social work / Santé et action sociale	Other community, social and personal service act. / Autres act. de services collectifs, sociaux et personnels	Private households with employed persons / Ménages privés employant du personnel domestique	Extra- territorial org. and bodies / Org. et organismes extra- territoriaux
105.2	16.6	51.9	8.9	19.8	40.8	16.0	10.5	28.5	5.8	4.3
62.9	17.5	10.2	13.9	8.8	28.4	32.1	18.3	24.3	46.4	1.5
113.3	16.5	55.2	10.0	24.4	40.8	17.0	11.7	31.8	5.9	1.2
64.6	17.4	8.1	14.1	9.7	27.1	35.0	19.7	29.2	47.1	1.2
113.7	18.1	62.2	10.0	25.8	41.1	17.4	11.7	27.8	5.7	1.6
69.0	21.4	10.8	13.9	13.6	27.0	32.8	19.1	29.8	45.4	0.8
867.1	107.4	475.8	42.7	275.0	204.8	202.6	64.9	148.8	11.2	...
1103.2	331.0	41.4	23.3	95.1	57.2	245.7	108.4	171.5	249.6	...
925.3	139.2	522.1	39.6	262.9	233.4	231.9	72.9	128.9	19.2	...
1116.0	373.5	58.0	35.9	97.3	74.1	289.1	100.2	156.0	286.1	...
956.6	111.0	568.9	42.6	270.4	258.2	225.3	63.4	169.8	11.3	...
1120.4	359.6	49.3	33.7	137.1	90.7	326.2	101.7	203.2	342.4	...
889.0	60.0	645.0	87.0	234.0	423.0	243.0	179.0	264.0	1.0	...
1005.0	142.0	245.0	199.0	178.0	323.0	725.0	843.0	225.0	12.0	...
950.0	71.0	685.0	100.0	257.0	452.0	223.0	186.0	288.0	...	...
1042.0	139.0	250.0	211.0	182.0	329.0	718.0	871.0	252.0	8.0	...
1003.0	72.0	710.0	110.0	275.0	440.0	239.0	188.0	294.0	...	1.0
1114.0	147.0	247.0	244.0	189.0	340.0	732.0	868.0	263.0	8.0	...
382.2	104.1	137.3	79.2	121.4	196.9	69.8	47.3	72.3	0.5	1.4
253.9	116.1	42.0	42.3	95.7	120.5	228.3	161.5	119.0	118.5	0.7
388.4	103.3	140.2	55.8	91.0	196.1	67.1	38.8	62.2	1.7	1.6
266.2	141.7	37.4	31.4	84.7	104.4	208.3	161.7	91.5	143.2	1.0
407.1	102.5	130.2	53.8	100.5	202.1	69.4	45.8	71.6	1.7	2.5
286.3	146.3	37.6	30.6	102.7	105.0	208.4	186.1	94.1	142.9	1.1
258.0	18.0	72.0	10.0	36.0	48.0	151.0	91.0	35.0	...	...
190.0	18.0	77.0	10.0	37.0	52.0	148.0	88.0	32.0	...	...
135.0	15.0	70.0	10.0	35.0	49.0	137.0	80.0	29.0	...	...
401.6	57.0	432.5	31.3	95.0	395.5	122.7	81.9	110.1	...	...
481.0	104.4	126.5	58.9	72.6	104.8	312.9	276.6	102.7	...	...
421.4	49.8	399.6	26.8	85.6	392.5	125.8	80.4	112.0	...	...
504.5	92.3	129.7	54.9	68.4	112.1	302.3	255.0	105.6	...	...
412.8	42.2	369.3	25.0	74.7	411.5	129.1	72.2	122.1	...	...
513.4	81.7	130.4	62.0	66.4	121.1	294.1	268.3	108.2	...	...
2961.0	124.0	3805.0	260.0	939.0	2714.0	1104.0	760.0	2434.0	...	...
4178.0	561.0	1711.0	626.0	921.0	1515.0	4583.0	3416.0	2100.0	...	...
2914.0	130.0	3743.0	243.0	988.0	2723.0	1145.0	767.0	2404.0	...	...
4113.0	559.0	1590.0	569.0	889.0	1534.0	4476.0	3368.0	2064.0	...	...
2933.0	177.0	3772.0	264.0	938.0	3082.0	1186.0	778.0	2411.0	...	...
4275.0	661.0	1715.0	540.0	852.0	1507.0	4697.0	3555.0	2173.0	...	...
1.1	0.3	0.3	0.3	0.5	1.4	0.2	0.3	0.3	...	...
1.1	0.3	0.1	0.2	0.3	0.7	0.7	0.6	0.4	0.1	0.0
1.1	0.3	0.3	0.3	0.5	1.5	0.2	0.3	0.3	0.0	...
1.1	0.3	0.1	0.2	0.4	0.7	0.7	0.7	0.4	0.1	0.0
1.1	0.3	0.3	0.3	0.5	1.5	0.2	0.3	0.3	0.0	0.0
1.1	0.3	0.1	0.2	0.4	0.8	0.8	0.7	0.4	0.1	0.0

29
Employment by industry [cont.]
Emploi par industrie [suite]

B. ISIC Rev. 3 [+] — CITI Rév. 3 [+]

Persons employed, by branch of economic activity (thousands)
Personnes employées, par branches d'activité économique (milliers)

Country or area Pays ou zone	Sex	Year Année	Total employment (000s) Emploi total (000s)	Agriculture, hunting and forestry Agriculture, chasse et sylviculture	Fishing Pêche	Mining and quarrying Activités extractives	Manufacturing Activités de fabrication	Electricity, gas and water supply Production et distribution d'électricité, de gaz et d'eau	Construction Construc…
Singapore [2][17] Singapour [2][17]	M	1997	1081.0	3.9	...	0.5	247.9	10.5	1
	F	1997	749.4	1.2	...	0.1	166.2	1.6	
	M	1998	1089.6	3.5	...	1.3	245.2	6.7	1
	F	1998	780.1	0.9	...	0.2	159.2	1.6	
	M	1999	1087.2	4.5	...	1.0	236.2	7.3	1
	F	1999	798.6	1.0	...	0.4	159.4	1.5	2
Slovakia [1][2][115] Slovaquie [1][2][115]	M	1997	1217.0	138.9	...	35.8	330.2	45.9	18
	F	1997	988.9	63.4	...	6.9	236.6	10.5	
	M	1998	1210.4	125.8	...	30.6	337.1	45.5	18
	F	1998	988.2	55.6	...	5.0	236.6	7.7	
	M	1999	1163.7	111.8	...	25.9	325.8	43.6	1
	F	1999	968.4	45.4	...	3.9	221.7	9.3	
Slovenia [2][14] Slovénie [2][14]	M	1997	482.0	57.0	...	6.0	171.0	12.0	4
	F	1997	416.0	52.0	...	...	119.0	2.0	
	M	1998	487.0	57.0	...	8.0	171.0	7.0	4
	F	1998	420.0	51.0	...	...	118.0	1.0	
	M	1999	482.0	51.0	...	6.0	169.0	6.0	4
	F	1999	410.0	45.0	...	...	109.0	1.0	
Spain [77][80] Espagne [77][80]	M	1997	8266.9	737.4	50.3	63.0	1878.1	73.6	119
	F	1997	4497.7	273.6	6.0	3.7	553.4	8.6	4
	M	1998	8517.4	741.7	49.6	54.4	1984.3	77.0	125
	F	1998	4687.4	263.7	5.6	5.3	578.9	8.0	4
	M	1999	8790.9	701.9	49.5	56.3	2018.2	74.9	140
	F	1999	5026.6	256.5	6.8	6.8	616.3	11.4	6
Sweden [83] Suède [83]	M	1997	2042.0	80.0	2.0	7.0	557.0	25.0	20
	F	1997	1880.0	27.0	...	...	202.0	8.0	1
	M	1998	2079.0	74.0	2.0	8.0	560.0	25.0	20
	F	1998	1901.0	26.0	...	1.0	202.0	7.0	1
	M	1999	2121.0	76.0	2.0	8.0	558.0	23.0	1
	F	1999	1946.0	26.0	...	1.0	198.0	8.0	20
Switzerland [1][2][14][116] Suisse [1][2][14][116]	M	1997	2116.7	118.0	...	498.0	...	...	22
	F	1997	1648.9	61.0	...	192.0	...	...	3
	M	1998	2146.3	119.0	...	507.0	...	...	22
	F	1998	1686.7	63.0	...	186.0	...	...	3
	M	1999	2157.3	126.0	...	501.0	...	...	3
	F	1999	1704.7	65.0	...	177.0	...	...	3
Tajikistan [7] Tadjikistan [7]	M	1994	1057.0	1002.0	...	...	208.0	28.0	10
	F	1994	797.0	...	...	...	...	...	
	M	1995	1038.0	1095.0	...	...	183.0	24.0	8
	F	1995	815.0	...	...	...	...	...	
	M	1996	927.0	1026.0	...	...	181.0	21.0	68
	F	1996	804.0	...	...	...	...	...	
United Kingdom [13][77] Rouyame–Uni [13][77]	M	1997	14792.3	355.3	13.6	92.1	3646.5	139.5	1708
	F	1997	12022.0	124.0	1.6	12.7	1360.3	40.2	16
	M	1998	14998.6	337.5	16.4	86.4	3673.1	138.7	1730
	F	1998	12117.0	108.5	2.6	13.8	1337.5	41.9	17
	M	1999	15138.5	317.2	14.4	87.6	3586.9	134.9	1754
	F	1999	12303.9	91.4	1.6	13.6	1299.3	52.7	174

Wholesale and retail trade; repair of motor vehicles motorcycles and personal and household goods / Commerce de gros de détail; répaon de véhicules automobiles, de otorcycles et de iens personnels et domestiques	Hotels and restaurants / Hôtels et restaurants	Transport, storage and communications / Transports, entreposage et communications	Financial intermediation / Inter médiation financière	Real estate, renting and business activities / Immobilier, locations et activités de services aux entreprises	Public admin. and defence; compulsory social sec. / Admin. publique et défense; séc. sociale obligatoire	Education / Education	Health and social work / Santé et action sociale	Other community, social and personal service act. / Autres act. de services collectifs, sociaux et personnels	Private households with employed persons / Ménages privés employant du personnel domestique	Extra–territorial org. and bodies / Org. et organismes extra–territoriaux
173.6	53.2	163.2	44.1	92.2	91.7	47.3	...	43.2	...	1.1
120.9	50.6	46.7	62.3	75.0	23.4	91.1	...	91.9	...	1.0
166.1	61.0	157.2	45.4	104.3	93.4	41.7	...	50.5	...	1.6
115.1	57.9	49.2	63.1	80.0	25.1	95.9	...	111.4	...	1.1
165.8	61.6	152.8	43.9	110.6	94.8	44.5	...	52.5	...	1.2
113.1	59.7	50.9	60.7	86.2	27.0	97.5	...	119.9	...	1.0
106.8	21.8	112.2	8.3	42.6	84.7	33.4	29.6	41.5	...	1.1
147.3	38.3	48.2	21.9	31.9	75.6	133.2	117.3	39.1	1.7	0.8
110.8	21.2	118.7	9.6	45.1	80.2	32.0	29.9	37.2	0.1	0.1
151.5	41.4	50.9	27.5	32.2	73.7	133.3	116.4	35.7	2.7	0.2
103.1	23.9	116.5	10.6	48.6	80.5	35.0	28.7	38.0	0.1	0.1
157.3	41.0	49.5	26.1	31.5	69.9	131.8	126.3	34.9	1.9	0.1
51.0	14.0	41.0	6.0	20.0	17.0	11.0	8.0	17.0	...	...
56.0	25.0	10.0	14.0	20.0	19.0	41.0	34.0	16.0	1.0	...
55.0	15.0	39.0	5.0	26.0	19.0	14.0	9.0	15.0	...	...
56.0	23.0	12.0	13.0	21.0	22.0	46.0	33.0	15.0	1.0	...
53.0	14.0	42.0	5.0	25.0	25.0	14.0	9.0	17.0	...	...
56.0	19.0	11.0	15.0	24.0	24.0	46.0	36.0	19.0	...	...
1225.6	443.9	637.9	231.6	418.3	537.5	283.6	201.1	247.8	39.6	0.1
898.2	336.6	115.8	103.9	374.1	284.7	462.8	513.3	220.1	296.1	1.8
1252.5	437.1	640.2	228.6	454.7	532.7	293.3	205.8	256.5	48.8	0.5
927.0	360.6	131.4	104.6	403.8	293.4	493.5	508.4	240.0	313.4	2.4
1261.8	453.4	654.3	241.8	495.4	553.9	297.4	226.7	255.6	45.6	0.7
1004.0	395.4	151.6	121.2	435.6	333.7	504.5	516.7	260.5	344.4	0.8
282.0	42.0	184.0	34.0	238.0	107.0	90.0	96.0	95.0	...	...
216.0	62.0	83.0	47.0	154.0	104.0	189.0	666.0	106.0	...	...
288.0	44.0	192.0	36.0	250.0	105.0	94.0	103.0	93.0	...	...
215.0	67.0	79.0	48.0	161.0	103.0	199.0	667.0	106.0	...	...
289.0	49.0	197.0	37.0	271.0	104.0	104.0	103.0	92.0	...	...
223.0	65.0	78.0	48.0	175.0	104.0	212.0	673.0	114.0	...	...
319.0	45.0	155.0	117.0	230.0	110.0	98.0	108.0	93.0	...	...
305.0	74.0	67.0	76.0	140.0	80.0	152.0	291.0	170.0	...	...
307.0	38.0	158.0	119.0	245.0	120.0	91.0	117.0	96.0	...	...
312.0	79.0	65.0	84.0	148.0	94.0	148.0	294.0	176.0	...	...
315.0	39.0	156.0	116.0	247.0	120.0	99.0	115.0	92.0	...	...
295.0	73.0	82.0	80.0	151.0	94.0	152.0	313.0	183.0	...	...
90.0	...	63.0	...	...	...	175.0	101.0	...	...	...
...	...	...	...	...	...	...	...	...	...	...
87.0	...	58.0	...	...	...	168.0	88.0	...	...	...
...	...	...	...	...	...	...	...	...	...	...
69.0	...	58.0	...	...	...	161.0	84.0	...	...	...
...	...	...	...	...	...			...	...	...
2122.7	502.2	1305.8	563.4	1535.5	876.9	606.8	545.6	655.8	42.7	16.8
2043.5	736.6	413.4	623.8	1110.0	717.5	1390.3	2397.3	730.0	116.4	8.9
2127.7	491.3	1331.6	590.7	1611.2	878.8	596.4	582.7	702.9	32.4	16.9
2003.0	752.6	437.8	607.5	1180.1	696.3	1455.9	2399.2	757.9	112.5	4.4
2152.2	459.4	1359.5	558.1	1751.1	902.1	664.2	601.6	694.4	35.9	12.1
2110.3	705.6	453.2	613.7	1242.2	734.5	1518.0	2413.1	745.7	102.5	6.2

29
Employment by industry [*cont.*]
Emploi par industrie [*suite*]

Source:
International Labour Office (ILO), Geneva, "Yearbook of Labour
Statistics 2000" and the ILO labour statistics database.

+ Countries using the latest version of the International Standard
Industrial Classification of all Economic Activities, Revision 3
(ISIC Revision 3), are presented in Part B. Countries using the
former classification, ISIC Revision 2, are presented in Part A.

† For information on the recent changes in country or area
nomenclature pertaining to former Czechoslovakia, Germany,
Hong Kong Special Administrative Region (SAR) of China,
Macao Special Administrative Region (SAR) of China, SFR of
Yugoslavia and the former USSR, see Annex I – Country or area
nomenclature, regional and other groupings.

†† For statistical purposes the data for China do not include
those for Hong Kong Special Administrative Region
(Hong Kong SAR), Macao Special Administrative
Region (Macao SAR) and Taiwan province of China.

1   Civilian labour force employed.
2   Persons aged 15 years and over.
3   Data classified according to ANZSIC; previously classified by ASIC.
4   Estimates based on 1986 census benchmarks.
5   Estimates based on the 1991 Census of Population and Housing.

6   Including armed forces, except conscripts not employed before their
military service.
7   Both sexes.
8   Excluding armed forces.
9   Private agriculture and street vendors.
10 Including mining and quarrying.
11 Persons aged 10 years and over.
12 Year ending in June of the year indicated.
13 Average of less than 12 months.
14 One quarter of each year.
15 Including quarrying.
16 Wholesale and retail trade.
17 One month of each year.
18 Including professional army; excluding compulsory military service.
19 Persons aged 15 to 69 years.
20 Urban areas.
21 Excluding rural population of Rondônia, Acre, Amazonas, Roraima,
Pará and Amapa.
22 Beginning this year, methodology revised; data not strictly
comparable.
23 Including electricity, gas, water and sanitary services.
24 Excluding restaurants and hotels.
25 Excluding storage.
26 Including international and other extra–territorial bodies and
activities not adequately defined.
27 Including restaurants, hotels and storage; excluding sanitary services
and international bodies.
28 State and cooperative sector.
29 Including veterinary services.
30 Including major divisions 2 and 4.
31 Excluding veterinary services, radio and TV broadcasting, repair and
instillation services.
32 Excluding full–time members of the armed forces.
33 Beginning this year, revised series.
34 Including repair and installation services.
35 Including sanitary services.
36 Excluding repair and installation services and sanitary services.

37 Beginning this year, sample design revised.
38 Excluding armed forces and reemployed retired persons.
39 Whole national economy.
40 Excluding business services.

Source:
Bureau international du travail (BIT), Genève, "Annuaire des statistiques
du travail 2000" et la base de données du BIT.

+ On trouvera dans la partie B les chiffres relatifs aux pays qui appliquent
la version la plus récente de la Classification internationale type, par
industrie, de toutes les branches d'activité économique, Révision 3
(CITI Rév. 3). Les pays qui utilisent encore la classification dans sa
version précédente (Révision 2) figurent à la partie A.

† Pour les modifications récentes de nomenclature de pays ou de
zone concernant l'Allemagne, Hong Kong, région administrative
spéciale (RAS) de Chine, Macao, région administrative spéciale
(RAS) de Chine, l'ex–Tchécoslovaquie, l'ex–URSS et l'ex–Rfs de
Yougoslavie, voir annexe I – Nomenclature des pays ou des zones,
groupements régionaux et autres groupements.

†† Les données statistiques relatives à la Chine ne comprennent pas celles
qui concernent la région administrative spéciale de Hong Kong (la RAS
de Hong Kong), la région administrative spéciale de Macao (la RAS de
Macao) et la province chinoise de Taiwan.

1   Main–d'œuvre civile occupée.
2   Personnes âgées de 15 ans et plus.
3   Données classifiées selon l'ANZSIC; précédemment classifiées par l'ASIC.
4   Estimations basées sur les données de calage du recensement de 1986.
5   Estimations basées sur le recensement de la population et de l'habitat de
1991.
6   Y compris les forces armées, sauf les conscrits n'ayant pas travaillé avant
leur service militaire.
7   Les deux sexes.
8   Non compris les forces armées.
9   L'agriculture privée et les marchands ambulants.
10 Y compris les industries extractives.
11 Personnes âgées de 10 ans et plus.
12 Année se terminant en juin de l'année indiquée.
13 Moyenne de moins de douze mois.
14 Un trimestre de chaque année.
15 Y compris les carrières.
16 Commerce de gros et de détail.
17 Un mois de chaque année.
18 Y compris les militaires de carrière; non compris les militaires du contingent
19 Personnes âgées de 15 à 69 ans.
20 Régions urbaines.
21 Non compris la population rurale de Rondônia, Acre, Amazonas,
Roraima, Pará et Amapá.
22 A partir de cette année, méthodologie révisée; les données ne sont pas
strictement comparables.
23 Y compris l'électricité, le gaz, l'eau et les services sanitaires.
24 Non compris les restaurants et hôtels.
25 Non compris les entrepôts.
26 Y compris les organisations internationales et autres organismes extra–
territoriaux et les activités mal designées.
27 Y compris les restaurants, hôtels et entrepôts; non compris les services
sanitaires et les organismes internationaux.
28 Secteur d'Etat et coopératif.
29 Y compris les services vétérinaires.
30 Y compris les branches 2 et 4.
31 Non compris les services vétérinaires, de réparation et d'installation, et la
radiodiffusion et télévision.
32 Non compris les membres à temps complet des forces armées.
33 A partir de cette année, série révisée.
34 Y compris les services de réparation et d'installation.
35 Y compris les services sanitaires.
36 Non compris les services de réparation et d'installation, et les services
sanitaires.
37 A partir de cette année, plan d'échantillonnage révisé.
38 Non compris les forces armées et les retraités réemployés.
39 Ensemble de l'économie nationale.
40 Non compris les services aux entreprises.

29
Employment by industry [*cont.*]
Emploi par industrie [*suite*]

41 Including unpaid family workers who worked for one hour or more.	41 Y compris les travailleurs familiaux non rémunérés ayant travaillé une heure ou plus.
42 Persons aged 14 years and over.	42 Personnes âgées de 14 ans et plus.
43 Persons aged 12 years and over.	43 Personnes âgées de 12 ans et plus.
44 7 main cities of the country.	44 7 villes principales du pays.
45 Estimates based on the 1993 Census results.	45 Estimations basées sur les résultats du Recensement de 1993.
46 Persons aged 15 to 74 years.	46 Personnes âgées de 15 à 74 ans.
47 Data classified according to ISIC, Rev. 3.	47 Données classifiées selon la CITI, Rév. 3.
48 Including electricity, gas and water.	48 Y compris l'électricité, le gaz et l'eau.
49 Persons aged 15 to 64 years.	49 Personnes âgées de 15 à 64 ans.
50 Including armed forces.	50 Y compris les forces armées.
51 Revised industrial classification: data for major divisions 6, 8 and 9 not strictly comparable.	51 Classification industrielle révisée: les données relatives aux branches 6, 8 et 9 ne sont pas strictement comparables.
52 Including repairs.	52 Y compris les réparations.
53 5 major cities.	53 5 villes principales.
54 Including mining and quarrying, electricity, gas and water.	54 Y compris les industries extractives, l'électricité, le gaz et l'eau.
55 Non—material activities; incl. major division 8.	55 Activités non matérielles; y compris la branche 8.
56 Including the residents of East Jerusalem.	56 Y compris les résidents de Jérusalem—Est.
57 Including permanent members of institutional households.	57 Y compris les membres permanents des ménages collectifs.
58 Including conscripts.	58 Y compris les conscrits.
59 Data classified according to ISIC, Rev. 1.	59 Données classifiées selon la CITI, Rév. 1.
60 Including major division 6.	60 Y compris la branche 6.
61 Including self—defence forces.	61 Y compris les forces d'autodéfense.
62 Excluding hotels.	62 Non compris les hôtels.
63 Including hotels.	63 Y compris les hôtels.
64 Excluding real estate and business services.	64 Non compris les affaires immobilières et les services aux entreprises.
65 Including real estate, business services and activities not adequately defined.	65 Y compris les affaires immobilières, les services aux entreprises et les activitiés mal désignées.
66 Including activities not adequately defined.	66 Y compris les activités mal désignées.
67 Beginning 1992: questionnaire revised.	67 A partir de 1992: questionnaire révisé.
68 Curaçao.	68 Curaçao.
69 Persons aged 16 to 74 years.	69 Personnes âgées de 16 à 74 ans.
70 Beginning 2nd quarter 1988: methodology revised.	70 A partir du 2e trimestre de 1988: méthodologie révisée.
71 July of preceding year to June of current year.	71 Juillet de l'année précédente à juin de l'année en cours.
72 Computed from 1987—88 survey results.	72 Calculé sur la base des résultats de l'enquête de 1987—88.
73 Asunción metropolitan area.	73 Région métropolitaine d'Asunción.
74 Including members of the armed forces living in private households.	74 Y compris les membres des forces armées vivant en ménages privés.
75 Including restaurants and hotels.	75 Y compris les restaurants et hôtels.
76 Including the Azores and Madeira.	76 Y compris les Açores et Madère.
77 Persons aged 16 years and over.	77 Personnes âgées de 16 ans et plus.
78 31st Dec. of each year.	78 31 déc. de chaque année.
79 Beginning this year, new industrial classification.	79 A partir de cette année, nouvelle classification industrielle.
80 Excluding compulsory military service.	80 Non compris les militaires du contingent.
81 Whole country.	81 Ensemble du pays.
82 Excluding Northern and Eastern provinces.	82 Non compris les provinces du Nord et de l'Est.
83 Persons aged 16 to 64 years.	83 Personnes âgées de 16 à 64 ans.
84 Persons aged 11 years and over.	84 Personnes âgées de 11 ans et plus.
85 Persons aged 13 years and over.	85 Personnes âgées de 13 ans et plus.
86 Including financing, insurance and real estate; excl. restaurants and hotels.	86 Y compris les banques, les assurances et affaires immobilières; non compris les restaurants et hôtels.
87 Including financing, insurance, real estate and business services.	87 Y compris les banques, les assurances, les affaires immobilières et les services aux enterprises.
88 Beginning this year, figures revised on the basis of the 1990 census results.	88 A partir de cette année, données révisées sur la base des résultats du Recensement de 1990.
89 Excluding unpaid family workers and employees in private domestic services.	89 Non compris les travailleurs familiaux non rémunérés et les personnes occupées àdes services domestiques privés.
90 Including major divisions 2, 4 and 5.	90 Y compris les branches 2, 4 et 5.
91 Including major divisions 7, 8 and 9.	91 Y compris les branches 7, 8 et 9.
92 Employed persons including armed forces; excluding private domestic service and unpaid family workers.	92 Personnes occupées y compris les forces armées; n.c. les service domestiques privés et les travailleurs familiaux non rémunérés.
93 Estimates based on 1990 census benchmarks.	93 Estimations basées sur les données de calage du recensement de 1990.
94 Including hotels, excluding sanitary services.	94 Y compris les hôtels; non compris les services sanitaires.
95 Including major divisions 1 and 4.	95 Y compris les branches 1 et 4.
96 Including agriculture, hunting, forestry and fishing.	96 Y compris l'agriculture, la chasse, la sylviculture et la pêche.
97 28 urban agglomerations.	97 28 agglomérations urbaines.

29
Employment by industry [*cont.*]
Emploi par industrie [*suite*]

98 Gran Buenos Aires.
99 Estimates based on 1996 census of population benchmarks.

100 Including Fishing.
101 Including real estate, renting and business activities.

102 Including tabulation categories M, N and O.
103 Including extra-territorial organizations and bodies.
104 Including health and social work.
105 Including private households with employed persons.
106 Including persons on child-care leave.
107 Persons aged 15 to 66 years.
108 Including manufacturing.
109 Hong Kong Standard Industrial Classification. Prior to March 1991: ISIC.
110 Including public administration and defense; compulsory social security.
111 Including tabulation categories P and Q.
112 Excluding regular military living in barracks and conscripts.

113 Persons aged 15 to 72 years.
114 Population census.
115 Excluding persons on child-care leave.
116 Excluding seasonal/border workers.
117 Including tabulation categories C, D and E.

98 Gran Buenos Aires.
99 Estimations basées sur les données de calage du recensement de population de 1996.

100 Y Compris la pêche.
101 Y compris les activités immobilières locations et activités de services aux entreprises.
102 Y compris les catégories de classement M, N et O.
103 Y compris les organisations et organismes extra-territoriaux.
104 Y compris la santé et action sociale.
105 Y compris les ménages privés employant du personnel domestique.
106 Y compris les personnes en congé parental.
107 Personnes âgées de 15 à 66 ans.
108 Y compris les activités de fabrication.
109 Classification industrielle type de Hong Kong. Avant mars 1991: CITI.
110 Y compris l'administration publique et la défense; la sécurité sociale obligatoire.
111 Y compris les catégories de classement P et Q.
112 Non compris les militaires de carrière vivant des casernes et les conscrits.
113 Personnes âgées de 15 à 72 ans.
114 Recensement de population.
115 Non compris les personnes en congé parental.
116 Non compris les travailleurs saisonniers et frontaliers.
117 Y compris les catégories de classement C, D et E.

30
Unemployment
Chômage
Number (thousands) and percentage unemployed
Nombre (milliers) et pourcentage des chômeurs

Country or area § Pays ou zone §	1990	1991	1992	1993	1994	1995	1996	1997	1998	1999
Albania Albanie										
MF [IV]	150.7	139.8	...	...	...	...	...	...	...	...
% MF [IV]	9.5	9.1	...	...	...	...	...	...	...	...
Algeria Algérie										
MF [IV] [1]	1 156.0	1 261.0	1 482.0	1 519.0	1 660.0	2 105.0	...	2 311.0	...	...
M [IV] [1]	1 069.0	1 155.0	1 348.0	...	...	1 626.0	...	2 031.0	...	...
F [IV] [1]	87.0	106.0	134.0	...	...	478.0	...	280.0	...	...
% MF [IV] [1]	19.8	20.6	23.0	23.2	24.4	27.9	...	28.7	...	...
% M [IV] [1]	...	21.7	24.2	...	...	26.0	...	26.9	...	...
% F [IV] [1]	...	17.0	20.3	...	...	38.4	...	24.0	...	...
Angola Angola										
MF [III] [2]	...	...	...	...	...	...	19.0	...	...	...
M [III] [2]	...	...	...	...	...	...	15.5	...	...	...
F [III] [2]	...	...	...	...	...	...	3.5	...	...	...
Argentina Argentine										
MF [I] [5]	332.1[34]	257.3[34]	305.2[36]	493.9[36]	595.1[36]	963.6[36]	1 531.4[67]	1 375.1[67]	1 218.7[67]	...
M [I] [5]	212.6[34]	158.4[34]	186.2[36]	253.9[36]	325.0[36]	508.1[36]	866.1[67]	731.4[67]	680.0[67]	...
F [I] [5]	119.4[34]	98.8[34]	119.0[36]	240.1[36]	270.1[36]	455.6[36]	665.3[67]	643.7[67]	538.7[67]	...
% MF [I] [5]	7.3[34]	5.8[34]	6.7[36]	10.1[36]	12.1[36]	18.8[36]	17.2[67]	14.9[67]	12.8[67]	...
% M [I] [5]	7.3[34]	5.6[34]	6.4[36]	8.5[36]	10.7[36]	16.5[36]	15.8[67]	13.0[67]	11.9[67]	...
% F [I] [5]	7.3[34]	6.1[34]	7.0[36]	12.7[36]	14.4[36]	22.3[36]	19.4[67]	17.9[67]	14.3[67]	...
Armenia Arménie										
MF [I] [1,15]	...	...	...	...	...	...	...	423.7	...	...
M [I] [1,15]	...	...	...	...	...	...	...	247.0	...	...
F [I] [1,15]	...	...	...	...	...	...	...	176.7	...	...
% MF [I] [1,15]	...	...	...	...	...	...	...	36.4	...	...
% M [I] [1,15]	...	...	...	...	...	...	...	38.0	...	...
% F [I] [1,15]	...	...	...	...	...	...	...	34.4	...	...
Australia Australie										
MF [I] [1]	584.8[8]	814.5[8]	925.1[8]	939.2[8]	855.5[8]	764.5[9]	779.4[9]	786.5[9]	746.5[9]	685.4[9]
M [I] [1]	332.3[8]	489.5[8]	566.2[8]	574.0[8]	505.6[8]	453.4[9]	456.0[9]	457.9[9]	434.5[9]	393.4[9]
F [I] [1]	252.5[8]	325.0[8]	358.9[8]	365.1[8]	349.9[8]	311.1[9]	323.4[9]	328.7[9]	312.0[9]	292.0[9]
% MF [I] [1]	6.9[8]	9.6[8]	10.8[8]	10.9[8]	9.7[8]	8.5[9]	8.5[9]	8.6[9]	8.0[9]	7.2[9]
% M [I] [1]	6.7[8]	9.9[8]	11.4[8]	11.5[8]	10.0[8]	8.8[9]	8.8[9]	8.7[9]	8.2[9]	7.3[9]
% F [I] [1]	7.2[8]	9.2[8]	10.0[8]	10.1[8]	9.4[8]	8.1[9]	8.3[9]	8.3[9]	7.7[9]	7.1[9]
Austria Autriche										
MF [I] [1]	114.8	125.4	132.4	158.8	138.4	143.7	160.4	164.8	165.0	146.7
M [I] [1]	63.0	70.9	74.4	88.1	72.6	71.4	86.5	87.3	88.4	81.7
F [I] [1]	51.8	54.5	58.0	70.7	65.7	72.2	73.9	77.5	76.6	65.0
MF [III] [1]	165.8	185.0	193.1	222.3	214.9	215.7	230.5	233.3	237.8	221.7
M [III] [1]	89.0	99.0	107.2	126.7	120.6	120.0	128.0	128.6	129.4	121.5
F [III] [1]	76.8	86.0	85.9	95.6	94.4	95.7	102.5	104.8	108.4	100.2
% MF [I] [1]	3.2	3.5	3.7	4.3	3.6	3.7	4.1	4.2	4.2	3.8
% M [I] [1]	3.0	3.3	3.5	4.1	3.3	3.2	3.9	3.9	4.0	3.7
% F [I] [1]	3.6	3.7	3.8	4.5	4.0	4.3	4.5	4.6	4.6	3.9
% MF [III] [1]	5.4	5.8	5.9	6.8	6.5	6.6	7.0	7.1	7.2	6.7
% M [III] [1]	4.9	5.3	5.7	6.7	6.4	6.4	6.9	6.9	6.9	6.5
% F [III] [1]	6.0	6.5	6.2	6.9	6.7	6.8	7.3	7.4	7.5	6.9
Azerbaijan Azerbaïdjan										
MF [III] [10]	...	4.0	6.4	19.5	23.6	28.3	31.9	38.3	42.3	45.2
M [III] [10]	...	1.5	2.8	7.7	9.2	11.4	13.1	16.2	18.2	19.6
F [III] [10]	...	2.5	3.6	11.8	14.4	16.9	18.8	22.1	24.1	25.6
% MF [III] [10]	...	0.1	0.2	0.5	0.7	0.8	0.9	1.0	1.1	1.2
% M [III] [10]	...	0.1	0.1	0.4	0.5	0.6	0.7	0.8	0.9	1.0
% F [III] [10]	...	0.2	0.2	0.7	0.9	1.0	1.1	1.2	1.4	1.4
Bahamas Bahamas										
MF [I] [1,4]	...	16.0	20.0	18.0	18.4	15.6	16.9	14.7	12.1	...
M [I] [1,4]	...	8.4	9.8	9.2	9.2	7.5	6.6	6.5	4.7	...
F [I] [1,4]	...	7.7	10.2	8.7	9.3	8.1	10.3	8.2	7.4	...
% MF [I] [1,4]	...	12.3	14.8	13.1	13.3	10.9	11.5	9.8	7.7	...
% M [I] [1,4]	...	12.2	13.8	12.8	12.6	10.1	8.6	8.3	5.9	...
% F [I] [1,4]	...	12.4	16.0	13.4	14.0	11.8	14.7	11.3	9.6	...

30
Unemployment
Number (thousands) and percentage unemployed [*cont.*]
Chômage
Nombre (milliers) et pourcentage des chômeurs [*suite*]

Country or area [§] Pays ou zone [§]	1990	1991	1992	1993	1994	1995	1996	1997	1998	1999
Bahrain Bahreïn										
MF [III] [11]	3.0	3.3	3.0	3.6	4.2	5.1	...	6.1	4.1	3.8
M [III] [11]	2.1	2.4	2.2	2.9	2.7	3.4	...	4.1	2.7	2.6
F [III] [11]	0.8	0.9	0.9	0.7	1.4	1.7	...	2.0	1.4	1.1
Bangladesh Bangladesh										
MF [I] [5]	997.0	...	...	...	...	...	1 417.0[12]	...	...	...
M [I] [5]	616.0	...	...	...	...	...	933.0[12]	...	...	...
F [I] [5]	379.0	...	...	...	...	...	484.0[12]	...	...	...
% MF [I] [5]	1.9	...	...	...	...	...	2.5[12]	...	...	...
% M [I] [5]	2.0	...	...	...	...	...	2.7[12]	...	...	...
% F [I] [5]	1.9	...	...	...	...	...	2.3[12]	...	...	...
Barbados Barbade										
MF [I] [1]	18.6[6]	20.9	28.7	30.9	28.2	26.9	...	...	...	...
M [I] [1]	6.6[6]	8.6	13.2	14.0	12.1	11.4	...	...	...	...
F [I] [1]	12.0[6]	12.3	15.5	16.9	16.1	15.5	...	...	...	...
% MF [I] [1]	15.0[6]	17.1	23.0	24.5	21.9	19.7	...	...	...	...
% M [I] [1]	10.3[6]	13.3	20.4	21.5	18.3	16.5	...	...	...	...
% F [I] [1]	20.2[6]	21.4	25.7	27.7	25.6	22.9	...	...	...	...
Belarus Bélarus										
MF [III] [4]	...	2.3	24.0	66.3	101.2	131.0	182.5	126.2	105.9	95.4
M [III] [4]	...	0.5	4.4	22.3	36.7	46.7	66.1	42.1	35.3	34.1
F [III] [4]	...	1.8	19.6	44.0	64.5	84.3	116.4	84.1	70.6	61.3
% MF [III] [4]	...	0.1	0.5	1.4	2.1	2.7	3.9	2.8	2.3	2.0
% M [III] [4]	...	...	0.2	0.9	1.6	2.2	...	...	...	...
% F [III] [4]	...	0.1	0.7	1.6	2.4	3.3	...	...	...	...
Belgium Belgique										
MF [I] [2 4]	285.1	282.4	316.1	335.2	405.4	390.1	404.0	375.1	384.0	375.0
M [I] [2 4]	109.1	110.9	137.1	149.1	188.5	178.9	181.7	173.2	179.3	179.4
F [I] [2 4]	176.1	171.5	179.0	186.1	216.9	211.2	222.3	201.9	204.7	196.6
MF [III] [13]	402.8	429.5	472.9	549.7	588.7	596.9	588.2	570.0	541.0	507.5
M [III] [13]	161.3	178.0	199.1	237.5	257.0	259.6	255.6	249.6	237.4	224.7
F [III] [13]	241.5	251.5	273.8	312.2	331.6	337.3	332.7	320.5	303.6	282.9
% MF [I] [2 4]	7.2	7.0	7.7	8.2	9.8	9.3	9.6	8.9	9.1	8.6
% M [I] [2 4]	4.5	4.6	5.7	6.2	7.7	7.3	7.4	7.1	7.3	7.2
% F [I] [2 4]	11.4	10.7	10.7	11.1	12.7	12.2	12.8	11.4	11.4	10.4
% MF [III] [13]	9.6	10.2	11.2	12.9	13.8	13.9	13.7	13.1	12.4	11.6
% M [III] [13]	6.6	7.3	8.1	9.7	10.6	10.7	10.5	10.2	9.7	9.2
% F [III] [13]	13.9	14.3	15.3	17.1	18.0	18.1	17.7	16.8	15.9	14.7
Belize Belize										
MF [I] [14]	...	...	...	6.7	7.7	...	...	...	...	...
M [I] [14]	...	...	...	3.5	4.3	...	...	...	...	...
F [I] [14]	...	...	...	3.2	3.5	...	...	...	...	...
% MF [I] [14]	...	...	...	9.8	11.1	...	...	...	...	...
% M [I] [14]	...	...	...	7.5	9.0	...	...	...	...	...
% F [I] [14]	...	...	...	14.5	15.1	...	...	...	...	...
Bermuda Bermudes										
MF [III]	0.1	0.2	...	...	...	...	...	...	...	...
Bolivia Bolivie										
MF [I] [5 15]	71.8	62.1	59.3	69.6	38.8	47.5	58.7[4]	...	...	...
M [I] [5 15]	39.7	34.6	34.5	43.2	23.5	24.3	29.5[4]	...	...	...
F [I] [5 15]	32.1	27.4	24.8	26.3	15.3	23.1	29.2[4]	...	...	...
% MF [I] [5 15]	7.3	5.9	5.5	6.0	3.1	3.6	4.2[4]	...	...	...
% M [I] [5 15]	6.9	5.7	5.5	6.5	3.4	3.3	3.7[4]	...	...	...
% F [I] [5 15]	7.8	6.2	5.6	5.3	2.9	4.0	4.5[4]	...	...	...
Brazil Brésil										
MF [I] [4 5 16]	2 367.5	...	4 573.3[17]	4 395.6	...	4 509.8	5 076.2	5 881.8	6 922.6	...
M [I] [4 5 16]	1 582.4	...	2 355.1[17]	2 305.9	...	2 327.9	2 498.3	2 854.9	3 301.1	...
F [I] [4 5 16]	785.1	...	2 218.2[17]	2 089.7	...	2 181.9	2 577.9	3 026.9	3 621.5	...
% MF [I] [4 5 16]	3.7	...	6.5[17]	6.2	...	6.1	7.0	7.8	9.0	...
% M [I] [4 5 16]	3.8	...	5.6[17]	5.4	...	5.3	5.7	6.4	7.2	...
% F [I] [4 5 16]	3.4	...	8.0[17]	7.4	...	7.3	8.8	10.0	11.6	...

30
Unemployment
Number (thousands) and percentage unemployed [*cont.*]
Chômage
Nombre (milliers) et pourcentage des chômeurs [*suite*]

Country or area [§] Pays ou zone [§]	1990	1991	1992	1993	1994	1995	1996	1997	1998	1999
Bulgaria Bulgarie										
MF [I] [1]	...	...	...	814.7	731.1	589.7	505.2	512.8	497.4	534.0
M [I] [1]	...	...	...	421.3	392.0	305.9	268.6	271.9	269.2	288.0
F [I] [1]	...	...	...	393.4	339.1	283.8	236.6	240.9	228.2	245.9
MF [III] [4]	65.1	419.1	576.9	626.1	488.4	423.8	478.8	523.5	465.2	610.6
M [III] [4 18]	22.7	190.7	274.5	298.4	223.0	188.0	215.4	236.5	211.1	284.5
F [III] [4 19]	42.4	228.4	302.4	327.7	265.4	235.8	263.4	287.1	254.1	326.1
% MF [I] [1]	...	...	...	21.4	20.2	16.5	14.2	14.4	...	...
% M [I] [1]	...	...	...	20.9	20.2	16.2	14.2	14.3	...	...
% F [I] [1]	...	...	...	22.0	20.3	16.8	14.1	14.4	...	...
% MF [III] [4]	1.7	11.1	15.3	16.4	12.4	11.1	12.5	13.7		
Burkina Faso Burkina Faso										
MF [III] [20]	42.0	34.8	29.8	29.6	26.6	13.9	13.5	9.2	9.4	7.5
M [III] [20]	37.4	30.4	25.9	24.9	24.0	11.8	11.0	7.6	7.8	6.2
F [III] [20]	4.6	4.4	3.9	4.6	2.7	2.1	2.5	1.6	1.6	1.4
Burundi Burundi										
MF [III] [21]	14.5	13.8	7.3	...	...	...	...	...	...	...
M [III] [21]	...	9.6	...	...	...	...	...	...	...	...
F [III] [21]	...	4.2	...	...	...	...	...	...	...	...
Canada Canada										
MF [I] [1 22 23]	1 163.9	1 491.7	1 640.2	1 648.8	1 540.7	1 422.1	1 469.2	1 413.5	1 305.1	1 190.1[17]
M [I] [1 22 23]	649.2	866.1	966.2	952.0	884.5	801.1	822.5	779.1	727.4	668.2[17]
F [I] [1 22 23]	514.7	625.6	674.0	696.8	656.2	621.0	646.7	634.3	577.7	521.9[17]
% MF [I] [1 22 23]	8.1	10.4	11.3	11.2	10.4	9.5	9.7	9.2	8.3	7.6[17]
% M [I] [1 22 23]	8.1	10.9	12.1	11.8	10.8	9.8	9.9	9.2	8.5	7.8[17]
% F [I] [1 22 23]	8.1	9.7	10.4	10.6	9.9	9.2	9.4	9.2	8.1	7.3[17]
Cape Verde Cap–Vert										
MF [III]	0.3	0.3	0.2	0.6	0.6	0.6	...	...	...	...
Central African Republic République centrafricaine										
MF [III] [24]	7.8	7.7	5.8	5.6	9.9	7.6	...	...	...	...
M [III] [24]	7.1	7.2	5.2	5.2	9.2	6.7	...	...	...	...
F [III] [24]	0.7	0.5	0.5	0.4	0.6	0.9	...	...	...	...
Chad Tchad										
MF [III]	2.4	4.4	...	16.3	...	...	...	...	...	...
M [III]	2.3	2.8	...	13.3	...	...	...	...	...	...
F [III]	0.1	0.1	...	2.9	...	...	...	...	...	...
Chile Chili										
MF [I] [1 25]	268.9	253.6	217.1	233.6	311.3	248.1	302.0[26]	303.6	419.2	...
M [I] [1 25]	184.8	168.6	132.1	147.6	193.9	158.4	180.9[26]	180.8	271.1	...
F [I] [1 25]	84.0	85.0	85.1	86.0	117.4	89.8	121.1[26]	122.8	148.1	...
% MF [I] [1 25]	5.7	5.3	4.4	4.5	5.9	4.7	5.4[26]	5.3	7.2	...
% M [I] [1 25]	5.7	5.1	4.1	4.2	5.4	4.4	4.8[26]	4.7	7.0	...
% F [I] [1 25]	5.7	5.8	5.6	5.1	6.8	5.3	6.7[26]	6.6	7.6	...
China †† Chine ††										
MF [IV] [4 27]	3 832.0	3 522.0	3 603.0	4 201.0	4 764.0	5 196.0	5 528.0	5 768.0	5 710.0	5 750.0
M [IV] [4 27 28]	1 313.0	1 207.0	1 298.0	1 394.0	1 258.0	...	2 637.0	2 737.0	2 705.0	...
F [IV] [4 27 28]	1 814.0	1 677.0	1 700.0	1 925.0	1 752.0	...	2 891.0	3 031.0	3 005.0	...
% MF [IV] [4 27]	2.5	2.3	2.3	2.6	2.8	2.9	3.0	3.0	3.1	3.1
% M [IV] [4 27 28]	0.9	0.8	...	0.9	0.8	...	...	...	...	...
% F [IV] [4 27 28]	1.2	1.1	...	1.2	1.1	...	...	...	...	...
China, Hong Kong SAR † Chine, Hong Kong RAS †										
MF [I] [1 29]	36.6	50.4	54.7	56.3	56.2	95.6	88.8	72.6	155.4	209.4
M [I] [1 29]	23.3	33.8	35.3	35.8	37.7	62.3	59.8	46.3	102.3	142.1
F [I] [1 29]	13.3	16.6	19.4	20.6	18.6	33.3	29.0	26.4	53.1	67.3
% MF [I] [1 29]	1.3	1.8	2.0	2.0	1.9	3.2	2.8	2.2	4.7	6.3
% M [I] [1 29]	1.3	1.9	2.0	2.0	2.1	3.4	3.1	2.3	5.2	7.2
% F [I] [1 29]	1.3	1.6	1.9	1.9	1.7	2.9	2.3	2.0	4.0	4.9
China, Macao SAR † Chine, Macao RAS †										
MF [I] [2]	5.3[4]	5.3[4]	3.8	3.7	4.4	6.7	8.7	6.5	9.6	13.8
M [I] [2]	2.5[4]	2.6[4]	2.1	2.2	2.4	4.3	5.4	4.2	6.6	9.4
F [I] [2]	2.8[4]	2.7[4]	1.8	1.5	2.0	2.4	3.3	2.3	3.1	4.4
% MF [I] [2]	3.2[4]	3.0[4]	2.2	2.1	2.5	3.6	4.3	3.2	4.6	6.4
% M [I] [2]	2.5[4]	2.5[4]	2.1	2.2	2.4	4.1	4.7	2.7	5.7	8.1
% F [I] [2]	4.1[4]	3.7[4]	2.4	2.0	2.6	3.0	3.7	2.5	3.3	4.4

30
Unemployment
Number (thousands) and percentage unemployed [*cont.*]
Chômage
Nombre (milliers) et pourcentage des chômeurs [*suite*]

Country or area [§] Pays ou zone [§]	1990	1991	1992	1993	1994	1995	1996	1997	1998	1999
Colombia Colombie										
MF [I] [4 30 31]	491.6	522.0[32]	505.3[32]	447.0[32]	442.3[32]	521.9[32]	735.2[32]	782.1[32]	998.3[32]	1 415.4[32]
M [I] [4 30 31]	232.8	225.9[32]	204.0[32]	174.0[32]	163.3[32]	230.2[32]	336.3[32]	353.5[32]	457.2[32]	649.8[32]
F [I] [4 30 31]	258.8	296.1[32]	301.3[32]	273.1[32]	279.0[32]	291.7[32]	398.9[32]	428.6[32]	541.1[32]	765.6[32]
% MF [I] [4 30 31]	10.2	9.8[32]	9.2[32]	7.8[32]	7.6[32]	8.7[32]	12.0[32]	12.1[32]	15.0[32]	20.1[32]
% M [I] [4 30 31]	8.1	7.4[32]	6.5[32]	5.3[32]	4.9[32]	6.8[32]	9.6[32]	9.8[32]	12.5[32]	17.2[32]
% F [I] [4 30 31]	13.2	13.1[32]	12.6[32]	11.0[32]	11.2[32]	11.3[32]	15.1[32]	15.1[32]	18.0[32]	23.3[32]
Costa Rica Costa Rica										
MF [I] [4 30]	49.5	59.1	44.0	46.9	49.4	63.5	75.9	74.3	76.5	83.3
M [I] [4 30]	31.7	35.5	26.4	28.9	28.7	39.1	45.3	43.5	40.6	45.6
F [I] [4 30]	17.8	23.5	17.6	18.0	20.7	24.4	30.6	30.8	36.0	37.7
% MF [I] [4 30]	4.6	5.5	4.1	4.1	4.2	5.2	6.2	5.7	5.6	6.0
% M [I] [4 30]	4.2	4.8	3.5	3.6	3.5	4.6	5.3	4.9	4.4	4.9
% F [I] [4 30]	5.9	7.4	5.4	5.3	5.8	6.5	8.3	7.5	8.0	8.2
Côte d'Ivoire Côte d'Ivoire										
MF [III] [10 33]	140.2	136.9	114.9	...	...	...	...	...	...	...
M [III] [10 33]	99.0	...	88.2	...	...	...	...	...	...	...
F [III] [10 33]	41.3	...	26.7	...	...	...	...	...	...	...
Croatia Croatie										
MF [I] [1]	...	...	...	...	...	...	170.2[4]	175.2[4]	198.5	234.0
M [I] [1]	...	...	...	...	...	...	88.3[4]	90.7[4]	100.9	117.4
F [I] [1]	...	...	...	...	...	...	82.0[4]	84.5[4]	97.5	116.6
MF [III]	161.0	254.0	267.0	251.0	243.0	241.0	261.0	278.0	288.0	322.0
M [III]	70.0	121.0	126.0	113.0	113.0	117.0	131.0	141.0	139.0	153.0
F [III]	91.0	133.0	141.0	138.0	130.0	124.0	130.0	137.0	149.0	169.0
% MF [I] [1]	...	...	...	...	...	...	10.0[4]	9.9[4]	11.4	13.5
% M [I] [1]	...	...	...	...	...	...	9.5[4]	9.5[4]	11.9	12.8
% F [I] [1]	...	...	...	...	...	...	10.5[4]	10.4[4]	12.1	14.5
% MF [III]	8.2	14.9	17.2	16.8	...	...	...	...	...	...
% M [III]	6.2	12.8	14.8	14.0	...	...	...	...	...	...
% F [III]	10.9	17.6	20.1	20.1	...	...	...	...	...	...
Cyprus Chypre										
MF [III] [2 34]	5.1	8.3	5.2	7.6	8.0	7.9	9.4	10.4	10.4	11.4
M [III] [2 34]	2.5	3.8	2.4	3.2	3.7	3.6	4.3	5.0	5.4	5.6
F [III] [2 34]	2.6	4.5	2.8	4.4	4.3	4.3	5.1	5.4	5.0	5.8
% MF [III] [2 34]	1.8	3.0	1.8	2.7	2.7	2.6	3.1	3.4	3.3	3.6
% M [III] [2 34]	1.4	2.2	1.8	1.8	2.0	1.9	2.3	2.7	2.8	2.9
% F [III] [2 34]	2.5	4.4	2.6	4.1	3.9	3.7	4.3	4.5	4.2	4.8
Czech Republic République tchèque										
MF [I] [1 25]	...	...	...	214.6[35]	222.4[35]	192.8[35]	210.3[35]	280.7[35]	379.6	470.4
M [I] [1 25]	...	...	...	93.5[35]	106.1[35]	90.2[35]	97.5[35]	122.7[35]	165.4	222.3
F [I] [1 25]	...	...	...	121.1[35]	116.3[35]	102.7[35]	112.8[35]	158.0[35]	214.3	248.1
MF [III] [4]	39.0	222.0	135.0	185.0	166.0	153.0	186.0	269.0	387.0	488.0
M [III] [4]	19.0	95.0	57.0	81.0	70.0	65.0	81.0	117.0	182.0	240.0
F [III] [4]	20.0	127.0	78.0	104.0	96.0	88.0	105.0	152.0	205.0	248.0
% MF [I] [1 25]	...	...	...	4.2[35]	4.3[35]	3.7[35]	4.1[35]	5.4[35]	7.3	9.0
% M [I] [1 25]	...	...	...	3.3[35]	3.7[35]	3.1[35]	3.4[35]	4.2[35]	5.7	7.6
% F [I] [1 25]	...	...	...	5.3[35]	5.1[35]	4.5[35]	4.9[35]	6.9[35]	9.3	10.7
% MF [III] [4]	0.7	4.1	2.6	3.5	3.2	2.9	3.5	5.2	7.5	9.4
% M [III] [4]	0.7	3.5	2.2	3.0	2.5	2.3	2.8	4.1	6.3	8.2
% F [III] [4]	0.8	4.8	3.0	4.1	4.0	3.6	4.3	6.7	9.0	10.8
Denmark Danemark										
MF [I] [25]	242.4[36]	264.8[36]	261.8[36]	308.8[36]	222.0[37]	195.5[37]	194.5[37]	174.2[37]	155.3[37]	...
M [I] [25]	122.8[36]	129.3[36]	127.9[36]	159.2[36]	107.0[37]	85.6[37]	87.6[37]	74.8[37]	68.5[37]	...
F [I] [25]	119.6[36]	135.5[36]	134.0[36]	149.6[36]	115.0[37]	109.9[37]	107.0[37]	99.5[37]	86.9[37]	...
MF [III] [38]	271.7	296.1	318.3	348.8	343.4	288.4	245.6	220.2	182.7	158.2
M [III] [38]	124.0	137.2	148.8	168.6	163.9	134.1	115.8	99.4	81.0	72.8
F [III] [38]	147.7	158.9	169.5	180.2	179.6	154.3	129.8	120.8	101.8	85.4
% MF [I] [25 37]	...	...	...	...	8.0	7.0	6.9	6.1	5.5	...
% M [I] [25 37]	...	...	...	...	7.1	5.6	5.7	4.9	4.5	...
% F [I] [25 37]	...	...	...	...	9.0	8.6	8.3	7.6	6.6	...
% MF [III] [38]	9.7	10.6	11.3	12.4	12.2	10.3	8.8	7.9	6.6	5.7
% M [III] [38]	8.4	9.2	10.0	11.3	11.0	9.0	7.8	6.7	5.5	4.9
% F [III] [38]	11.3	12.1	12.9	13.7	13.6	12.0	10.1	9.4	7.8	6.5

30
Unemployment
Number (thousands) and percentage unemployed [*cont.*]
Chômage
Nombre (milliers) et pourcentage des chômeurs [*suite*]

Country or area [§] Pays ou zone [§]	1990	1991	1992	1993	1994	1995	1996	1997	1998	1999
Dominican Republic République dominicaine										
MF [IV]	...	547.5[2]	611.8[2]	599.3[2]	456.6[2]	452.1[2]	505.7[5]	503.7[2]	...	...
M [IV]	...	229.7[2]	223.5[2]	217.9[2]	185.1[2]	187.3[2]	218.6[5]	199.0[2]	...	...
F [IV]	...	317.8[2]	388.3[2]	381.4[2]	271.6[2]	264.8[2]	287.2[5]	304.7[2]	...	...
% MF [IV]	...	19.7[2]	20.3[2]	19.9[2]	16.0[2]	15.8[2]	16.6[5]	15.9[2]	...	...
% M [IV]	...	12.5[2]	11.7[2]	11.4[2]	10.0[2]	10.2[2]	10.6[5]	9.5[2]	...	...
% F [IV]	...	33.1[2]	34.9[2]	34.8[2]	26.0[2]	26.2[2]	28.4[5]	28.6[2]	...	...
Ecuador Equateur										
MF [I] [4 5 15]	150.2	158.0	263.2	240.8	207.2	212.7	334.6	311.6	409.3	...
M [I] [4 5 15]	67.0	69.0	105.3	108.6	101.8	104.2	156.1	143.4	174.5	...
F [I] [4 5 15]	83.2	89.1	157.9	132.3	105.4	108.4	178.5	168.3	233.8	...
% MF [I] [4 5 15]	6.1	5.8	8.9	8.3	7.1	6.9	10.4	9.2	11.5	...
% M [I] [4 5 15]	4.3	4.1	6.0	6.2	5.8	5.5	8.0	7.0	8.4	...
% F [I] [4 5 15]	9.1	8.5	13.2	11.5	9.3	8.8	14.0	12.7	16.0	...
Egypt Egypte										
MF [I] [39]	1 346.4[4]	1 463.4[4]	1 415.7[6]	1 800.6[6]	1 877.4[6]	1 916.9[6]	...	1 446.4[6]	1 447.5[4]	...
M [I] [39]	602.3[4]	692.1[4]	768.1[6]	955.8[6]	963.3[6]	997.2[6]	...	701.5[6]	703.3[4]	...
F [I] [39]	744.1[4]	771.3[4]	647.6[6]	844.8[6]	914.1[6]	919.7[6]	...	744.9[6]	744.5[4]	...
% MF [I] [39]	8.6[4]	9.6[4]	9.0[6]	10.9[6]	11.0[6]	11.3[6]	...	8.4[6]	8.2[4]	...
% M [I] [39]	5.2[4]	5.9[4]	6.4[6]	7.5[6]	7.4[6]	7.6[6]	...	5.2[6]	5.1[4]	...
% F [I] [39]	17.9[4]	21.3[4]	17.0[6]	22.3[6]	22.8[6]	24.1[6]	...	19.8[6]	19.9[4]	...
El Salvador El Salvador										
MF [I] [5]	97.9[15]	72.5[15]	81.0[15]	109.0	162.3	163.4	171.0	180.0	175.7	...
M [I] [5]	54.8[15]	43.9[15]	47.5[15]	148.0	110.7	116.8	117.5	136.0	119.9	...
F [I] [5]	43.1[15]	28.6[15]	33.5[15]	51.0	51.6	46.6	53.4	44.0	55.8	...
% MF [I] [5]	10.0[15]	7.5[15]	7.9[15]	9.9	7.7	7.7	7.7	8.0	7.3	...
% M [I] [5]	10.1[15]	8.3[15]	8.4[15]	11.8	8.4	8.7	8.4	9.5	8.2	...
% F [I] [5]	9.8[15]	6.6[15]	7.2[15]	6.8	6.4	5.9	6.5	5.3	6.0	...
Estonia Estonie										
MF [I]	5.3[14]	12.0[14]	29.1[14]	49.6[14]	56.7[14]	70.9[14]	71.9[14]	69.4[36]	70.2[36]	81.1[25 36]
M [I]	2.5[14]	6.1[14]	16.3[14]	26.0[14]	28.9[14]	40.6[14]	40.4[14]	37.9[36]	40.0[36]	47.0[25 36]
F [I]	2.8[14]	6.0[14]	12.8[14]	23.7[14]	27.8[14]	30.3[14]	31.6[14]	31.5[36]	30.2[36]	34.1[25 36]
MF [III] [40]	...	0.9	14.9	16.3	15.3	15.6	17.3	...	18.8	28.2
M [III] [40]	...	0.3	7.5	7.5	6.4	5.1	5.2	...	...	...
F [III] [40]	...	0.6	7.4	8.8	8.9	10.5	12.1	...	...	...
% MF [I]	0.6[14]	1.5[14]	3.7[14]	6.5[14]	7.6[14]	9.7[14]	10.0[14]	9.7[36]	9.9[36]	11.7[25 36]
% M [I]	0.6[14]	1.4[14]	3.9[14]	6.5[14]	7.3[14]	10.6[14]	10.7[14]	10.1[36]	10.8[36]	13.0[25 36]
% F [I]	0.7[14]	1.5[14]	3.4[14]	6.6[14]	7.9[14]	8.8[14]	9.2[14]	9.2[36]	8.9[36]	10.2[25 36]
% MF [III] [40]	...	0.1	1.7	1.9	2.2	...	...	...	2.2	3.2
% M [III] [40]	...	0.1	1.6	1.7	...	...	...	...	...	...
% F [III] [40]	...	0.2	1.8	2.1	...	...	...	...	...	...
Ethiopia Ethiopie										
MF [III] [12]	...	44.3	70.9	62.9	64.7	37.5	44.9	34.6	29.5	25.7
M [III] [12]	...	24.9	52.0	40.4	37.5	14.0	16.6	19.1	16.6	14.3
F [III] [12]	...	19.4	18.8	22.6	27.2	23.5	28.3	15.4	12.9	11.4
Ethiopia incl. Eritrea Ethiopie y compris Erythrée										
MF [III] [12]	44.2	...	...	...	...	...	...	...	...	...
M [III] [12]	25.8	...	...	...	...	...	...	...	...	...
F [III] [12]	18.4	...	...	...	...	...	...	...	...	...
Fiji Fidji										
MF [IV] [1]	16.0	15.0	14.2	15.8	16.1	15.4	...	...	...	...
% MF [IV] [1]	6.4	5.9	5.4	5.9	5.7	5.4	...	...	...	...
Finland Finlande										
MF [I] [36 41]	82.0	169.0	292.0	405.0	408.0	382.0	363.0	314.0	285.0	261.0
M [I] [36 41]	49.0	106.0	178.0	235.0	235.0	204.0	186.0	160.0	143.0	130.0
F [I] [36 41]	33.0	62.0	114.0	170.0	174.0	178.0	176.0	154.0	142.0	131.0
MF [III] [1 41 42]	94.0	181.0	319.0	436.0	467.0	451.0	434.0	398.0	362.0	337.0
M [III] [1 41 42]	52.0	108.0	186.0	245.0	257.0	244.0	231.0	207.0	183.0	169.0
F [III] [1 41 42]	42.0	73.0	133.0	191.0	210.0	207.0	203.0	191.0	179.0	168.0
% MF [I] [36 41]	3.1	6.6	11.6	16.2	16.4	15.2	14.4	12.5	11.3	10.1
% M [I] [36 41]	3.5	7.8	13.3	17.7	17.8	15.3	14.0	12.1	10.7	9.6
% F [I] [36 41]	2.7	5.1	9.6	14.4	14.9	15.1	14.8	13.0	11.9	10.7

30
Unemployment
Number (thousands) and percentage unemployed [*cont.*]
Chômage
Nombre (milliers) et pourcentage des chômeurs [*suite*]

Country or area [§] Pays ou zone [§]	1990	1991	1992	1993	1994	1995	1996	1997	1998	1999
France France										
MF [I] [1 4]	...	...	...	2 781.0	3 115.0	2 935.0	3 098.7	3 152.0	3 050.2	3 059.7
M [I] [1 4]	...	...	...	1 302.0	1 503.0	1 360.0	1 460.9	1 523.0	1 436.7	1 452.1
F [I] [1 4]	...	...	...	1 479.0	1 612.0	1 575.0	1 637.8	1 629.0	1 613.4	1 607.7
MF [III] [40 43]	2 504.7	2 709.1	2 911.2	3 172.0	3 329.2	2 976.2[44]	3 063.0	3 102.4	2 976.8	2 772.1
M [III] [40 43]	1 148.7	1 266.4	1 404.6	1 603.9	1 664.5	1 457.7[44]	1 519.8	1 545.7	1 464.1	1 357.5
F [III] [40 43]	1 355.9	1 442.7	1 506.6	1 568.1	1 664.7	1 518.5[44]	1 543.2	1 556.7	1 512.6	1 333.3
MF [IV] [1]	2 204.9	2 348.9	2 590.7	2 929.0	3 104.0	2 931.0	3 137.0	3 192.0	...	...
M [IV] [1]	947.8	1 031.8	1 168.3	1 401.0	1 488.0	1 371.0	1 502.0	1 554.0	...	...
F [IV] [1]	1 257.0	1 317.1	1 422.5	1 528.0	1 616.0	1 559.0	1 635.0	1 638.0	...	...
% MF [I] [1 4]	...	...	10.1	11.1	12.4	11.6	12.1	12.3	11.8	11.9
% M [I] [1 4]	...	...	7.9	9.4	10.8	9.8	10.4	10.8	10.2	10.2
% F [I] [1 4]	...	...	12.8	13.3	14.3	13.9	14.2	14.2	13.8	13.6
% MF [IV] [1]	8.9	9.4	10.3	11.6	12.3	11.6	12.3	12.4	...	...
% M [IV] [1]	6.7	7.3	8.3	10.0	10.6	9.8	10.6	11.0	...	...
% F [IV] [1]	11.7	12.0	12.9	13.7	14.3	13.8	14.3	14.3	...	...
French Guiana Guyane française										
MF [III] [40 45]	4.4	4.7	6.9	8.1	...	...	...	...	...	...
M [III] [40 45]	2.3	2.5	4.0	4.7	...	...	...	...	...	...
F [III] [40 45]	2.1	2.2	3.0	3.4	...	...	...	...	...	...
% MF [III] [40 45]	13.9	9.7	...	...	...	...	...	...	...	...
% M [III] [40 45]	11.7	8.2	...	...	...	...	...	...	...	...
% F [III] [40 45]	17.6	11.6	...	...	...	...	...	...	...	...
French Polynesia Polynésie française										
MF [III] [2]	0.6	0.6	...	...	...	...	...	...	3.8	...
Georgia Géorgie										
MF [I] [1]	...	...	...	...	...	...	...	...	291.0	277.5
M [I] [1]	...	...	...	...	...	...	...	...	159.7	160.1
F [I] [1]	...	...	...	...	...	...	...	...	131.3	117.4
% MF [I] [1]	...	...	...	...	...	...	...	...	14.5	13.8
% M [I] [1]	...	...	...	...	...	...	...	...	15.4	15.3
% F [I] [1]	...	...	...	...	...	...	...	...	13.9	12.2
Germany Allemagne										
MF [I] [1 4]	...	2 642.0	3 186.0	3 799.0	4 160.0	4 035.0	3 473.0	3 890.0	3 849.0	3 503.0
M [I] [1 4]	...	1 251.0	1 422.0	1 792.0	2 051.0	1 991.0	1 858.0	2 083.0	2 074.0	1 905.0
F [I] [1 4]	...	1 392.0	1 764.0	2 007.0	2 110.0	2 044.0	1 614.0	1 806.0	1 775.0	1 598.0
MF [III] [4 39]	...	...	2 894.2	3 447.1	3 493.3	3 521.0	3 848.4	4 308.1	3 965.4	3 943.0
M [III] [4 39]	...	...	1 344.6	1 672.3	1 721.2	1 764.9	1 996.1	2 220.5	2 046.8	2 013.0
F [III] [4 39]	...	...	1 549.6	1 774.8	1 772.1	1 756.1	1 852.3	2 087.6	1 918.6	1 930.0
% MF [I] [1 4]	...	6.6	7.9	9.5	10.3	10.1	8.8	9.8	9.7	8.8
% M [I] [1 4]	...	5.4	6.2	7.8	8.9	8.7	8.2	9.2	9.2	8.4
% F [I] [1 4]	...	8.2	10.3	11.7	12.3	11.9	9.6	10.6	10.4	9.2
% MF [III] [4 39]	...	...	8.2	9.9	10.0	10.2	11.2	12.5	11.4	11.2
% M [III] [4 39]	...	...	...	...	...	9.2	10.4	11.6	10.7	10.5
% F [III] [4 39]	...	...	...	...	...	11.4	12.1	13.5	12.2	12.0
Ghana Ghana										
MF [III] [46]	30.2	30.7	30.6	39.4	37.0	40.5	...	...	...	...
M [III] [46]	26.6	27.5	27.5	36.2	34.5	...	...	...	...	...
F [III] [46]	3.2	3.3	3.1	3.2	2.4	...	...	...	...	...
Gibraltar Gibraltar										
MF [III] [47]	0.4	0.9	1.8	2.1	2.4	2.1	1.9	1.7	0.5	...
M [III] [47]	0.3	0.7	1.3	1.4	1.5	1.3	1.2	1.1	0.3	...
F [III] [47]	0.1	0.2	0.5	0.8	0.9	0.8	0.7	0.6	0.2	...
Greece Grèce										
MF [I] [25]	280.8[2]	301.1[2]	349.8[2]	398.2[2]	403.8[2]	424.7[2]	446.4[2]	440.4[2]	478.5[1]	...
M [I] [25]	107.1[2]	120.8[2]	137.9[2]	164.5[2]	170.4[2]	176.1[2]	167.1[2]	173.0[2]	188.8[1]	...
F [I] [25]	173.7[2]	180.3[2]	211.9[2]	233.7[2]	233.4[2]	248.6[2]	279.3[2]	267.3[2]	289.8[1]	...
MF [III] [1]	140.2	173.2	184.7	175.9	179.8	...	...	...	...	...
M [III] [1]	68.1	83.9	89.7	87.9	87.3	...	...	...	...	...
F [III] [1]	72.1	89.3	95.0	87.9	92.4	...	...	...	...	...
% MF [I] [25]	7.0[2]	7.7[2]	8.7[2]	9.7[2]	9.6[2]	10.0[2]	10.3[2]	10.3[2]	10.8[1]	...
% M [I] [25]	4.3[2]	4.8[2]	5.4[2]	6.4[2]	6.5[2]	6.7[2]	6.3[2]	6.6[2]	7.0[1]	...
% F [I] [25]	11.7[2]	12.9[2]	14.2[2]	15.2[2]	14.9[2]	15.4[2]	16.6[2]	15.9[2]	16.5[1]	...
% MF [III] [1]	6.4	7.3	7.6	7.1	7.2	...	...	...	...	...
Greenland Groenland										
MF [III]	1.3	1.7	1.9	1.8	1.8	2.0	2.0	1.9	...	...

30
Unemployment
Number (thousands) and percentage unemployed [*cont.*]
Chômage
Nombre (milliers) et pourcentage des chômeurs [*suite*]

Country or area [§] Pays ou zone [§]	1990	1991	1992	1993	1994	1995	1996	1997	1998	1999
Guadeloupe Guadeloupe										
MF [III] [40]	29.4[4]	34.3[4]	...	38.8	42.9	...	...	...	...	...
Guam Guam										
MF [I] [40]	1.3	1.7	1.8	2.6	...	...	...	...	...	...
% MF [I] [40]	2.8	3.5	3.9	5.5	...	...	...	...	...	...
Guatemala Guatemala										
MF [III] [5 48]	1.8	1.7	1.6	1.0	1.3	1.4	...	...	...	...
M [III] [5 48]	1.3	1.0	1.1	0.7	0.9	0.9	...	...	...	...
F [III] [5 48]	0.5	0.7	0.5	0.3	0.4	0.5	...	...	...	...
Honduras Honduras										
MF [I] [45]	61.7	72.1	53.9	...	...	59.1	89.4	69.4	87.7	89.3
M [I] [45]	41.4	46.0	37.8	...	...	40.3	58.9	45.4	55.5	56.7
F [I] [45]	20.3	26.1	16.1	...	...	18.8	30.4	23.9	32.2	32.6
% MF [I] [45]	4.8	4.6	3.1	...	...	3.2	4.3	3.2	3.9	3.7
% M [I] [45]	4.4	4.2	3.2	...	...	3.1	4.2	3.2	3.8	3.7
% F [I] [45]	6.2	5.6	3.0	...	...	3.4	4.4	3.2	4.2	3.8
Hungary Hongrie										
MF [I] [36]	...	...	444.2	518.9	451.2	416.5	400.1	348.8	313.0	284.7
M [I] [36]	...	...	265.9	316.0	274.8	261.5	243.7	214.1	189.2	170.7
F [I] [36]	...	...	178.3	202.9	176.4	155.0	156.4	134.7	123.8	114.0
MF [III] [4]	79.5[49]	406.1[49]	663.0[49]	632.1[49]	519.6[49]	495.9	477.5	464.0	404.1	404.5
M [III] [4]	49.1[49]	239.0[49]	390.0[49]	376.1[49]	302.6[49]	285.3	275.4	...	...	...
F [III] [4]	30.4[49]	167.1[49]	273.0[49]	256.0[49]	217.0[49]	210.6	202.1	...	...	...
% MF [I] [36]	...	...	9.8	11.9	10.7	10.2	9.9	8.7	7.8	7.0
% M [I] [36]	...	...	10.7	13.2	11.8	10.7	10.7	9.5	8.5	7.5
% F [I] [36]	...	...	8.7	10.4	9.4	8.7	8.8	7.8	7.0	6.3
% MF [III] [4]	1.7[49]	8.5[49]	12.3[49]	12.1[49]	10.4[49]	12.0	10.7	10.4	9.6	9.6
% M [III] [4 49]	1.8	9.2	14.0	14.2	11.7	...	...	...	...	...
% F [III] [4 49]	1.4	7.6	10.5	10.1	8.9	...	...	...	...	...
Iceland Islande										
MF [I] [6 50]	...	3.6	6.2	7.6	7.7	7.2	5.5	5.7	4.2	...
M [I] [6 50]	...	1.7	2.9	3.8	4.0	3.8	2.7	2.6	1.8	...
F [I] [6 50]	...	1.9	3.2	3.8	3.8	3.4	2.8	3.1	2.3	...
MF [III] [40]	2.3	1.9	3.9	5.6	6.2	6.5	5.8	5.2	3.8	...
M [III] [40]	1.1	1.0	1.9	2.7	2.9	3.1	2.5	2.0	1.4	...
F [III] [40]	1.2	0.9	1.9	2.9	3.4	3.5	3.3	3.2	2.4	...
% MF [I] [6 50]	...	2.5	4.3	5.3	5.3	4.9	3.7	3.9	2.7	...
% M [I] [6 50]	...	2.3	3.8	5.0	5.1	4.8	3.4	3.3	2.3	...
% F [I] [6 50]	...	2.9	4.9	5.6	5.5	4.9	4.1	4.5	3.3	...
% MF [III] [40]	1.8	1.5	3.0	4.3	4.8	5.0	4.3	3.9	2.8	...
% M [III] [40]	1.4	1.3	2.6	3.6	3.9	4.1	3.2	2.6	1.8	...
% F [III] [40]	2.2	1.7	3.6	5.4	6.1	6.2	5.8	5.6	5.5	...
India Inde										
MF [III] [24]	34 631.8	36 300.0	36 758.4	36 275.5	36 691.5	36 742.3	37 430.0	39 140.0	40 090.0	40 371.0
M [III] [24]	27 932.0	28 992.0	29 105.0	28 410.0	28 647.0	28 722.0	29 050.0	30 107.0	30 563.0	30 439.0
F [III] [24]	6 700.0	7 308.0	7 653.0	7 865.0	8 045.0	8 020.0	8 380.0	9 033.0	9 526.0	9 933.0
Indonesia Indonésie										
MF [I] [4]	1 951.6[5]	2 032.4[5]	2 198.8[5]	...	...	...	3 624.8[5]	4 197.3[1]	5 062.5[1]	...
M [I] [4 5]	1 155.2	1 147.3	1 292.1	...	...	...	1 851.8	...	...	...
F [I] [4 5]	796.4	885.1	906.7	...	...	...	1 773.0	...	...	...
MF [III] [1]	862.0	782.9	814.9	754.1	1 198.3	953.2	1 041.8	1 542.2	1 191.7	...
% MF [I] [4]	...	...	...	...	...	...	4.0[5]	4.7[1]	5.5[1]	...
Ireland Irlande										
MF [I] [16]	172.4	198.5	206.6	220.1	211.0	177.4	179.0	159.0	126.6	96.9
M [I] [16]	108.4	124.9	132.3	138.6	131.9	110.4	109.8	97.1	78.8	59.4
F [I] [16]	63.9	73.6	74.4	81.4	79.1	67.1	69.1	62.0	47.8	37.5
MF [III] [40]	224.7	254.0	283.1	294.3	282.4	276.9	279.2	254.4	227.1	192.2
M [III] [40]	152.1	170.5	187.2	193.8	184.4	178.5	175.6	155.8	135.7	112.7
F [III] [40]	72.6	83.5	96.0	100.5	98.0	99.3	103.6	98.5	91.4	79.5
% MF [I] [16]	12.9	14.7	15.1	15.7	14.7	12.2	11.9	10.3	7.8	5.7
% M [I] [16]	12.5	14.2	15.0	15.6	14.7	12.1	11.9	10.4	8.1	5.9
% F [I] [16]	13.8	15.5	15.2	15.8	14.8	12.2	11.9	10.3	7.4	5.5
% MF [III] [40]	17.2	19.0	...	16.7	15.1	14.1	11.8	10.1	7.6	5.8

30
Unemployment
Number (thousands) and percentage unemployed [*cont.*]
      Chômage
      Nombre (milliers) et pourcentage des chômeurs [*suite*]

Country or area § Pays ou zone §	1990	1991	1992	1993	1994	1995	1996	1997	1998	1999
Isle of Man Ile de Man										
MF [III]	0.6	1.0	1.4	1.7	1.6	1.5	1.2	0.7	0.4	0.3
M [III]	0.4	0.7	1.0	1.2	1.2	1.1	0.9	0.5	0.3	0.2
F [III]	0.1	0.3	0.4	0.4	0.4	0.4	0.3	0.2	0.1	0.1
% MF [III]	2.1	3.0[51]	4.3	4.9	4.7	4.4	3.4	...	...	0.8
% M [III]	2.6	3.9[51]	5.4	...	...	...	4.4	...	...	1.0
% F [III]	1.3	1.9[51]	2.7	...	...	...	2.1	...	...	0.5
Israel Israël										
MF [I] [1 53]	158.0[52]	187.4[52]	207.5[52]	194.9[52]	158.3[52]	145.0	144.1	169.8	193.4[17]	208.5
M [I] [1 53]	82.2[52]	89.9[52]	99.7[52]	96.2[52]	71.7[52]	66.6	70.8	84.6	100.4[17]	108.8
F [I] [1 53]	75.8[52]	97.5[52]	107.8[52]	98.7[52]	86.6[52]	78.4	73.3	85.2	93.0[17]	99.7
% MF [I] [1 53]	9.6[52]	10.6[52]	11.2[52]	10.0[52]	7.8[52]	6.9	6.7	7.7	8.5[17]	8.9
% M [I] [1 53]	8.4[52]	8.6[52]	9.2[52]	8.5[52]	6.2[52]	5.6	5.8	6.8	8.0[17]	8.5
% F [I] [1 53]	11.3[52]	13.4[52]	13.9[52]	12.1[52]	10.0[52]	8.6	7.8	8.8	9.2[17]	9.4
Italy Italie										
MF [I]	2 621.0[2]	2 653.0[2]	2 799.0[2]	2 299.0[1 17]	2 508.0[1]	2 638.0[1]	2 653.0[1]	2 688.0[1]	2 745.0[1]	2 669.0[1]
M [I]	1 102.0[2]	1 142.0[2]	1 226.0[2]	1 094.0[1 17]	1 234.0[1]	1 280.0[1]	1 286.0[1]	1 294.0[1]	1 313.0[1]	1 266.0[1]
F [I]	1 519.0[2]	1 511.0[2]	1 572.0[2]	1 205.0[1 17]	1 274.0[1]	1 358.0[1]	1 367.0[1]	1 394.0[1]	1 431.0[1]	1 404.0[1]
% MF [I]	11.0[2]	10.9[2]	11.4[2]	9.8[1 17]	10.7[1]	11.3[1]	11.4[1]	11.5[1]	11.7[1]	11.4[1]
% M [I]	7.3[2]	7.5[2]	7.9[2]	7.6[1 17]	8.6[1]	8.9[1]	8.9[1]	9.0[1]	9.1[1]	8.8[1]
% F [I]	17.1[2]	16.8[2]	17.2[2]	13.5[1 17]	14.3[1]	15.2[1]	15.3[1]	15.6[1]	16.0[1]	15.7[1]
Jamaica Jamaïque										
MF [I] [2]	166.6	168.7	169.2	176.7	167.4	186.7	183.0	186.9	175.0	...
M [I] [2]	52.8	54.2	54.1	62.1	54.9	66.9	61.3	64.8	61.4	...
F [I] [2]	113.8	114.5	115.2	114.6	112.5	119.8	121.7	122.1	113.5	...
% MF [I] [2]	15.7	15.7	15.4	16.3	15.4	16.2	16.0	...	...	...
% M [I] [2]	9.3	9.4	9.4	10.9	9.6	10.8	9.9	...	...	...
% F [I] [2]	23.1	22.8	22.2	22.4	21.8	22.5	23.0	...	...	...
Japan Japon										
MF [I] [1]	1 340.0	1 360.0	1 420.0	1 660.0	1 920.0	2 100.0	2 250.0	2 300.0	2 790.0	3 170.0
M [I] [1]	770.0	780.0	820.0	950.0	1 120.0	1 230.0	1 340.0	1 350.0	1 680.0	1 940.0
F [I] [1]	570.0	590.0	600.0	710.0	800.0	870.0	910.0	950.0	1 110.0	1 230.0
% MF [I] [1]	2.1	2.1	2.2	2.5	2.9	3.2	3.4	3.4	4.1	4.7
% M [I] [1]	2.0	2.0	2.1	2.4	2.8	3.1	3.4	3.4	4.2	4.8
% F [I] [1]	2.2	2.2	2.2	2.6	3.0	3.2	3.3	3.4	4.0	4.5
Kazakhstan Kazakhstan										
MF [III] [10]	...	6.0	34.0	40.5	70.1	139.6	282.4	257.5	251.9	251.4
M [III] [10]	...	2.0	9.0	12.1	24.7	55.7	104.0	86.0	95.5	102.0
F [III] [10]	...	4.0	25.0	28.4	45.4	83.9	178.4	171.5	156.4	149.4
MF [IV]	...	6.0	70.5	78.1	170.0	203.2	391.7	382.8	382.0	264.0
M [IV]	...	1.0	21.0	...	103.8	88.5	156.6	139.5	161.9	117.0
F [IV]	...	5.0	19.0	...	66.2	114.7	235.1	243.3	220.1	147.0
% MF [III] [10]	...	0.1	0.4	0.6	1.1	2.1	4.2	3.8	3.7	3.9
% M [III] [10]	...	...	...	...	0.7	1.6	2.9	2.4	2.6	...
% F [III] [10]	...	...	...	...	1.4	2.7	5.6	5.5	5.0	...
% MF [IV]	...	...	...	...	7.5	11.0	13.0	13.0	13.7	...
Korea, Republic of Corée, République de										
MF [I] [1 54]	454.0	438.0	466.0	551.0	490.0	420.0	426.0	556.0	1 461.0	1 353.0
M [I] [1 54]	321.0	289.0	306.0	376.0	335.0	280.0	291.0	352.0	983.0	911.0
F [I] [1 54]	133.0	149.0	161.0	175.0	155.0	140.0	135.0	204.0	478.0	442.0
% MF [I] [1 54]	2.4	2.3	2.4	2.8	2.4	2.0	2.0	2.6	6.8	6.3
% M [I] [1 54]	2.9	2.5	2.6	3.2	2.7	2.3	2.3	2.8	7.6	7.1
% F [I] [1 54]	1.8	1.9	2.1	2.2	1.9	1.7	1.6	2.3	5.6	5.1
Kuwait Koweït										
MF [III] [10]	...	...	...	...	...	...	...	8.6	8.9	...
M [III] [10]	...	...	...	...	...	...	...	7.2	7.3	...
F [III] [10]	...	...	...	...	...	...	...	1.4	1.6	...
Kyrgyzstan Kirghizistan										
MF [III]	...	...	1.8	2.9	12.6	50.4	77.2	54.6	55.9	54.7
M [III]	...	...	0.5	0.9	4.9	20.5	32.5	22.7	22.6	24.2
F [III]	...	...	1.3	2.0	7.7	29.9	44.7	31.9	33.3	30.6

30
Unemployment
Number (thousands) and percentage unemployed [*cont.*]
Chômage
Nombre (milliers) et pourcentage des chômeurs [*suite*]

Country or area [§] Pays ou zone [§]	1990	1991	1992	1993	1994	1995	1996	1997	1998	1999
Latvia Lettonie										
MF [I] [4]	...	...	...	...	...	227.0[14]	216.7[1]	171.2[1]	160.6[1]	167.3[1]
M [I] [4]	...	...	...	...	...	126.5[14]	117.9[1]	88.0[1]	82.9[1]	94.4[1]
F [I] [4]	...	...	...	...	...	100.5[14]	98.8[1]	83.2[1]	77.7[1]	72.9[1]
MF [III] [10]	...	...	31.3	76.7	83.9	83.2	90.8	84.9	111.4	109.5
M [III] [10]	...	...	12.9	35.9	40.4	39.7	41.1	34.5	46.2	46.7
F [III] [10]	...	...	18.4	40.8	43.6	43.5	49.7	50.4	65.2	62.8
% MF [I] [4]	...	...	...	...	...	18.9[14]	18.3[1]	14.4[1]	13.8[1]	14.5[1]
% M [I] [4]	...	...	...	...	...	19.7[14]	18.9[1]	14.3[1]	13.5[1]	15.5[1]
% F [I] [4]	...	...	...	...	...	18.0[14]	17.7[1]	14.6[1]	14.1[1]	13.3[1]
% MF [III] [10]	...	...	2.3	5.8	6.5	6.6	7.2	7.0	9.2	9.1
% M [III] [20]	...	...	1.8	5.2	6.1	6.1	6.4	5.6	7.5	7.6
% F [III] [10]	...	...	2.8	6.4	6.9	7.0	8.1	8.5	11.0	10.7
Lebanon Liban										
MF [IV]	...	...	...	...	...	...	...	116.1	...	...
Lithuania Lituanie										
MF [I] [2]	...	...	...	...	347.2	347.1	317.4	257.2	244.9	263.3
M [I] [2]	...	...	...	...	...	...	155.4	137.1	137.2	150.3
F [I] [2]	...	...	...	...	...	...	162.0	120.1	107.7	113.0
MF [III] [10]	...	4.8	66.5	65.5	78.0	127.7	109.4	120.2	122.8	177.4
M [III] [10]	...	...	38.1	33.5	36.7	57.4	49.8	58.3	61.7	94.6
F [III] [10]	...	...	28.4	32.0	41.3	70.3	59.6	61.9	61.1	82.8
% MF [I] [2]	...	...	...	...	17.4	17.1	16.4	14.1	13.3	14.1
% M [I] [2]	...	...	...	...	...	...	...	14.2	14.3	15.6
% F [I] [2]	...	...	...	...	...	...	...	13.9	12.2	12.6
% MF [III] [10]	...	0.3	3.5	3.5	4.5	7.3	6.2	6.7	6.5	10.0
% M [III] [10]	...	...	4.3	3.7	4.4	6.6	5.7	6.6	6.5	10.6
% F [III] [10]	...	...	2.8	3.3	4.5	8.1	6.7	6.9	7.0	9.3
Luxembourg Luxembourg										
MF [III] [55]	2.1	2.3	2.7	3.5	4.6	5.1	5.7	6.4[56]	5.5	5.4
M [III] [55]	1.2	1.4	1.6	2.0	2.8	2.9	3.2	3.6[56]	2.9	2.8
F [III] [55]	0.8	0.9	1.2	1.5	1.9	2.2	2.5	2.8[56]	2.6	2.5
% MF [III] [55]	1.3	1.4	1.6	2.1	2.7	3.0	3.3	3.3[56]	3.1	2.9
Madagascar Madagascar										
MF [III] [4 57]	16.8	9.3	6.2	5.3	3.6	3.3	...	...	...	...
Malaysia Malaisie										
MF [I] [39]	315.2	...	271.2	316.8	...	248.1	216.8	214.9	284.0	313.7
MF [III] [1]	61.2	48.6	45.2	35.6	26.8	24.0	23.3	23.1	33.4	31.8
% MF [I] [39]	5.1	...	3.7	3.0	...	2.8	2.5	2.5	3.2	3.4
Malta Malte										
MF [III] [4 58]	5.1	4.9	5.5	6.2	5.6	5.2	6.2	7.1	7.4	7.7
M [III] [4 58]	4.3	4.0	4.5	5.3	4.8	4.4	5.2	6.0	6.4	6.6
F [III] [4 58]	0.8	0.9	1.1	0.9	0.8	0.8	1.1	1.1	1.0	1.1
% MF [III] [4 58]	3.9	3.6	4.0	4.5	4.1	3.7	4.4	5.0	5.1	5.3
% M [III] [4 58]	4.4	4.0	4.4	5.2	4.8	4.3	5.0	5.8	6.1	6.3
% F [III] [4 58]	2.3	2.6	3.0	2.5	2.2	2.3	2.9	2.8	2.5	2.6
Mauritius Maurice										
MF [III] [1 59]	12.8	10.6	7.9	6.7	6.6	8.5	10.4	10.7	10.7	12.1
M [III] [1 59]	7.3	5.2	3.4	2.6	2.5	3.4	4.5	4.6	4.6	5.3
F [III] [1 59]	5.5	5.4	4.6	4.1	4.2	5.0	5.9	6.0	6.1	6.8
Mexico Mexique										
MF [I] [25 30]	...	694.9	...	819.1	...	1 677.4	1 354.7	984.9	889.6	682.3
M [I] [25 30]	...	373.1	...	495.4	...	1 100.2	860.7	544.7	513.0	387.2
F [I] [25 30]	...	321.8	...	323.7	...	577.2	494.0	440.2	376.6	295.1
% MF [I] [25 30]	...	2.2	...	2.4	...	4.7	3.7	2.6	2.3	1.7
% M [I] [25 30]	...	1.7	...	2.1	...	4.6	3.5	2.1	2.0	1.5
% F [I] [25 30]	...	3.4	...	3.1	...	5.0	4.1	3.4	2.8	2.2
Mongolia Mongolie										
MF [III] [10]	...	...	...	...	...	...	...	...	48.3	...
M [III] [10]	...	...	...	...	...	...	...	...	22.7	...
F [III] [10]	...	...	...	...	...	...	...	...	25.6	...
% MF [III] [10]	...	...	...	...	...	...	...	...	5.7	...
% M [III] [10]	...	...	...	...	...	...	...	...	5.2	...
% F [III] [10]	...	...	...	...	...	...	...	...	6.3	...

30
Unemployment
Number (thousands) and percentage unemployed [*cont.*]
Chômage
Nombre (milliers) et pourcentage des chômeurs [*suite*]

Country or area [§] Pays ou zone [§]	1990	1991	1992	1993	1994	1995	1996	1997	1998	1999
Morocco Maroc										
MF [I] [1 15]	601.2	695.5	649.9	680.8	...	1 111.7	871.2	844.7	969.2	1 161.8
M [I] [1 15]	401.4	459.3	400.7	469.1	...	631.5	568.1	574.8	676.1	808.2
F [I] [1 15]	199.8	236.2	249.2	211.7	...	480.2	303.1	269.9	293.0	353.6
% MF [I] [1 15]	15.8	17.3	16.0	15.9	...	22.9	18.1	16.9	19.1	22.0
% M [I] [1 15]	14.2	15.3	13.0	14.2	...	18.7	16.1	15.3	17.5	20.3
% F [I] [1 15]	20.4	23.3	25.3	21.7	...	32.2	23.6	21.8	24.4	27.6
Myanmar Myanmar										
MF [III] [60]	555.3	559.0	502.6	518.2	541.5	...	...	535.3	451.5	425.3
Netherlands Pays–Bas										
MF [I] [39 61]	516.0	490.0	386.0	437.0	492.0	523.0	489.0	422.0	337.0	...
M [I] [39 61]	227.0	226.0	181.0	217.0	254.0	255.0	228.0	196.0	155.0	...
F [I] [39 61]	288.0	264.0	205.0	220.0	239.0	268.0	262.0	227.0	181.0	...
MF [III] [39 62]	346.0	319.0	336.0	415.0	486.0	464.0	440.0	375.0	286.0	221.5
M [III] [39 62]	209.0	187.0	195.0	241.0	283.0	260.0	240.0	199.0	156.0	...
F [III] [39 62]	137.0	132.0	141.0	174.0	203.0	204.0	201.0	176.0	132.0	...
% MF [I] [39 61]	7.5	7.0	5.5	6.2	6.8	7.1	6.6	5.5	4.4	...
% M [I] [39 61]	5.4	5.3	4.3	5.2	6.0	5.9	5.3	4.5	3.5	...
% F [I] [39 61]	10.7	9.5	7.3	7.6	8.1	8.8	8.4	7.0	5.5	...
% MF [III] [39]	5.9	5.4	5.3	6.5	7.5	7.0	6.6	5.5	4.1	3.2
% M [III] [39]	5.4	4.9	4.9	6.0	7.0	6.4	5.9	4.8	...	...
% F [III] [39]	6.8	6.3	6.1	7.3	8.3	8.1	7.8	6.5	...	...
Netherlands Antilles Antilles néerlandaises										
MF [I] [1 63]	9.8	8.6	8.2	8.2	8.0	8.2	9.3	10.1	10.8	...
M [I] [1 63]	...	3.8	3.5	3.8	3.7	3.3	3.7	4.3	4.8	...
F [I] [1 63]	...	4.7	4.8	4.4	4.3	4.9	5.6	5.8	6.0	...
% MF [I] [1 63]	17.0	14.6	13.9	13.6	12.8	13.1	14.0	15.3	16.7	...
% M [I] [1 63]	...	11.7	10.5	11.4	11.0	9.9	10.5	12.4	14.1	...
% F [I] [1 63]	...	18.1	17.9	16.2	15.0	17.0	10.1	10.4	19.4	...
New Caledonia Nouvelle–Calédonie										
MF [III] [40]	5.7	6.3	6.6	6.8	7.4	7.4	7.7	7.9	8.3	...
New Zealand Nouvelle–Zélande										
MF [I] [1]	124.5	167.6	169.8	158.8	140.4	111.5	112.3	123.3	139.1	127.8
M [I] [1]	74.0	99.8	101.1	94.0	81.7	61.8	61.9	67.9	77.4	72.4
F [I] [1]	50.5	67.7	68.7	64.8	58.6	49.7	50.4	55.5	61.8	55.4
MF [III] [46 64]	163.8	196.0	216.9	212.7	186.5	157.7	154.0	168.9	193.9	213.8[4]
M [III] [46 64]	112.1	135.9	149.8	143.2	124.1	103.1	100.0	107.3	121.8[4]	126.3[4]
F [III] [46 64]	51.7	60.1	67.1	69.4	62.4	54.6	54.0	61.6	68.0[4]	87.5[4]
% MF [I] [1]	7.8	10.3	10.3	9.5	8.1	6.3	6.1	6.6	7.5	6.8
% M [I] [1]	8.2	10.9	10.9	10.0	8.5	6.2	6.1	6.6	7.6	7.0
% F [I] [1]	7.2	9.5	9.6	8.9	7.7	6.3	6.1	6.7	7.4	6.5
Nicaragua Nicaragua										
MF [IV] [5]	145.6	194.2	...	...	...	244.7	225.1	208.4	215.5	...
M [IV] [5]	78.5	104.8	...	...	...	162.3	149.2	138.2	142.9	...
F [IV] [5]	67.1	89.4	...	...	...	82.4	75.9	70.2	72.6	...
% MF [IV] [5]	11.1	14.0	...	...	...	16.9	14.9	13.3	13.3	...
% M [IV] [5]	9.0	11.3	...	...	...	15.9	14.0	12.6	8.8	...
% F [IV] [5]	15.4	19.4	...	...	...	19.3	17.1	14.8	14.5	...
Nigeria Nigéria										
MF [III] [1]	57.1	60.2	64.0	68.6	...	...	...	...	...	...
Norway Norvège										
MF [I] [50]	112.0	116.0	126.0	127.0	116.0	107.0	108.0	93.0	75.0	75.0
M [I] [50]	66.0	68.0	76.0	77.0	70.0	61.0	58.0	49.0	40.0	42.0
F [I] [50]	46.0	48.0	50.0	50.0	46.0	46.0	50.0	44.0	35.0	33.0
MF [III] [40]	92.7[65]	100.7	114.4	118.1	110.3	102.2	90.9	73.5	56.0	59.6[17]
M [III] [40]	57.1[65]	62.8	71.0	73.3	65.7	57.7	50.4	39.9	29.8	33.5[17]
F [III] [40]	35.6[65]	37.9	43.3	44.8	44.5	44.5	40.6	33.6	26.2	26.0[17]
% MF [I] [50]	5.2	5.5	5.9	6.0	5.4	4.9	4.9	4.1	3.2	3.2
% M [I] [50]	5.6	5.9	6.5	6.6	6.0	5.2	4.8	4.0	3.2	3.2
% F [I] [50]	4.8	5.0	5.1	5.2	4.7	4.6	4.9	4.2	3.3	3.3
% MF [III] [40]	4.3[65]	4.7	5.4	5.5	5.2	4.7	4.2	3.3	2.4	2.6[17]
% M [III] [40]	4.8[65]	5.3	6.1	6.3	5.6	4.9	4.1	...	...	...
% F [III] [40]	3.7[65]	3.9	4.5	4.7	4.5	4.5	3.9	...	...	...

30
Unemployment
Number (thousands) and percentage unemployed [cont.]
Chômage
Nombre (milliers) et pourcentage des chômeurs [suite]

Country or area § Pays ou zone §	1990	1991	1992	1993	1994	1995	1996	1997	1998	1999
Pakistan Pakistan										
MF [I] [5 67]	963.0[66]	1 922.0	1 845.0	1 516.0	1 591.0	1 783.0	1 827.0	2 227.0	...	...
M [I] [5 67]	932.0[66]	1 190.0	1 134.0	1 024.0	1 083.0	1 179.0	1 208.0	1 302.0	...	...
F [I] [5 67]	31.0[66]	732.0	711.0	492.0	508.0	604.0	619.0	925.0	...	...
MF [III] [68]	238.8	221.7	204.3	...	...	...	...	...	...	...
% MF [I] [5 67]	3.1[66]	6.3	5.9	4.7	4.8	5.4	5.4	6.1	...	...
% M [I] [5 67]	3.4[66]	4.5	4.3	3.8	3.9	4.1	4.1	4.2	...	...
% F [I] [5 67]	0.9[66]	16.8	14.2	10.3	10.0	13.7	13.7	16.8	...	...
Panama Panama										
MF [I] [1 4]	...	138.4	134.4	124.7	135.5	141.2	144.9	140.3	147.1	128.0
M [I] [1 4]	...	72.8	65.6	60.2	67.7	70.7	74.8	72.5	69.5	62.1
F [I] [1 4]	...	65.6	68.7	64.5	67.7	70.5	70.1	67.8	77.6	65.9
% MF [I] [1 4]	...	16.2	14.7	13.3	14.0	14.0	14.3	13.4	13.6	11.8
% M [I] [1 4]	...	12.6	10.8	9.7	10.7	10.8	11.3	10.7	10.0	8.9
% F [I] [1 4]	...	22.6	22.3	20.2	20.4	20.1	20.0	18.1	19.9	16.9
Paraguay Paraguay										
MF [I]	34.1[30 69]	26.6[30 69]	29.1[30 69]	30.5[5 69]	48.1[5 15]	...	105.7[5 15]	...	...	...
M [I]	20.3[30 69]	16.6[30 69]	20.1[30 69]	19.1[5 69]	31.7[5 15]	...	58.1[5 15]	...	...	...
F [I]	13.8[30 69]	10.0[30 69]	8.9[30 69]	11.4[5 69]	16.5[5 15]	...	47.5[5 15]	...	...	...
% MF [I]	6.6[30 69]	5.1[30 69]	5.3[30 69]	5.1[5 69]	4.4[5 15]	...	8.2[5 15]	...	...	...
% M [I]	6.6[30 69]	5.4[30 69]	6.4[30 69]	5.5[5 69]	4.9[5 15]	...	7.8[5 15]	...	...	...
% F [I]	6.5[30 69]	4.7[30 69]	3.8[30 69]	4.5[5 69]	3.7[5 15]	...	8.6[5 15]	...	...	...
Peru Pérou										
MF [I] [2 15 25]	...	...	...	...	...	...	461.6	565.0	582.5	624.9
M [I] [2 15 25]	...	...	...	...	...	...	247.4	279.9	274.4	322.8
F [I] [2 15 25]	...	...	...	...	...	...	214.2	285.1	308.1	392.2
% MF [I] [2 15 25]	...	...	...	...	...	...	7.0	7.7	7.8	8.0
% M [I] [2 15 25]	...	...	...	...	...	...	6.4	6.8	6.5	7.5
% F [I] [2 15 25]	...	...	...	...	...	...	7.9	8.9	9.3	8.6
Philippines Philippines										
MF [I] [1 4]	1 993.0	2 267.0	2 263.0	2 379.0	2 317.0	2 342.0	2 195.0	2 377.0	3 016.0	2 997.0
M [I] [1 4]	1 099.0	1 290.0	1 303.0	1 384.0	1 362.0	1 354.0	1 293.0	1 411.0	1 857.0	1 876.0
F [I] [1 4]	893.0	977.0	959.0	995.0	955.0	988.0	902.0	966.0	1 159.0	1 121.0
% MF [I] [1 4]	8.1	9.0	8.6	8.9	8.4	8.4	7.4	7.9	9.6	9.4
% M [I] [1 4]	7.1	8.1	7.9	8.2	7.9	7.7	7.0	7.5	9.5	9.5
% F [I] [1 4]	9.8	10.5	9.8	10.0	9.4	9.4	8.2	8.5	9.8	9.2
Poland Pologne										
MF [I] [1]	...	...	...	2 427.0	2 474.0	2 277.0	2 108.0	1 923.0	1 808.0	...
M [I] [1]	...	...	...	1 183.0	1 207.0	1 119.0	1 015.0	889.0	843.0	...
F [I] [1]	...	...	...	1 244.0	1 266.0	1 157.0	1 093.0	1 035.0	965.0	...
MF [III] [1 10]	1 126.1	2 155.6	2 509.3	2 889.6	2 838.0	2 628.8	2 359.5	1 826.4	1 831.4	2 349.8
M [III] [1 10]	552.4	1 021.5	1 170.5	1 382.3	1 343.0	1 180.2	983.9	723.2	760.1	1 042.5
F [III] [1 10]	573.7	1 134.1	1 338.8	1 507.3	1 495.0	1 448.6	1 375.6	1 103.2	1 071.3	1 307.3
% MF [I] [1]	...	...	...	14.0	14.4	13.3	12.3	11.2	10.5	...
% M [I] [1]	...	...	...	12.6	13.1	12.1	11.0	9.6	9.1	...
% F [I] [1]	...	...	...	15.6	16.0	14.7	13.9	13.2	12.3	...
% MF [III] [1 10]	6.5	11.8	13.6	16.4	16.0	15.2	13.2	10.5	10.4	13.0
% M [III] [1 10]	5.8	10.6	11.9	15.0	14.7	...	...	...	...	...
% F [III] [1 10]	7.1	13.5	15.5	17.9	17.3	...	...	...	...	...
Portugal Portugal										
MF [I]	231.1[5]	207.5[5]	194.1[2]	257.5[2]	323.8[2]	338.4[2]	343.9[2]	324.1[2]	247.9[1]	...
M [I]	90.0[5]	77.6[5]	90.7[2]	120.0[2]	155.8[2]	165.8[2]	167.0[2]	158.5[2]	107.6[1]	...
F [I]	141.1[5]	129.9[5]	103.4[2]	137.5[2]	168.1[2]	172.1[2]	177.0[2]	165.6[2]	140.4[1]	...
% MF [I]	4.7[5]	4.1[5]	4.1[2]	5.4[2]	6.7[2]	7.1[2]	7.2[2]	6.7[2]	5.0[1]	...
% M [I]	3.2[5]	2.8[5]	3.4[2]	4.5[2]	5.9[2]	6.3[2]	6.4[2]	6.0[2]	3.9[1]	...
% F [I]	6.6[5]	5.8[5]	4.9[2]	6.5[2]	7.8[2]	8.1[2]	8.2[2]	7.5[2]	6.2[1]	...
Puerto Rico Porto Rico										
MF [I] [40 42]	160.0	186.0	197.0	206.0	175.0	170.0	172.0	176.0	175.0	153.0
M [I] [40 42]	115.0	131.0	139.0	144.0	121.0	117.0	114.0	112.0	112.0	102.0
F [I] [40 42]	45.0	55.0	58.0	62.0	54.0	53.0	58.0	64.0	63.0	51.0
% MF [I] [40 42]	14.1	16.0	16.6	17.0	14.6	13.7	13.4	13.5	13.3	11.8
% M [I] [40 42]	16.2	17.9	19.0	19.5	16.5	15.6	14.9	14.4	14.4	13.2
% F [I] [40 42]	10.7	12.6	12.8	13.2	11.5	10.8	11.2	12.1	11.8	9.6

30
Unemployment
Number (thousands) and percentage unemployed [*cont.*]
      Chômage
      Nombre (milliers) et pourcentage des chômeurs [*suite*]

Country or area § Pays ou zone §	1990	1991	1992	1993	1994	1995	1996	1997	1998	1999
Republic of Moldova Réublique de Moldova										
MF [III] [4]	...	0.1	15.0	14.1	20.6	24.5	23.4	28.0	32.0	...
M [III] [4]	...	...	5.9	5.5	7.7	8.4	7.5	10.3	13.0	...
F [III] [4]	...	0.1	9.1	8.9	12.9	16.1	15.9	17.7	19.0	...
% MF [III] [4]	...	...	0.7	0.7	1.1	1.0	...	...	...	...
Réunion Réunion										
MF [III] [40]	53.8	59.3	80.1	80.2	...	...	...	...	...	...
M [III] [4 40]	28.4	30.4	41.9	43.1	...	...	...	...	...	...
F [III] [4 40]	25.4	28.8	38.2	37.1	...	...	...	...	...	...
% MF [III] [40]	23.0	25.4	34.3	34.4	...	...	...	...	...	...
Romania Roumanie										
MF [I]	...	...	...	...	971.0[24]	967.9[24]	790.9[1]	706.5[1]	732.4[1]	789.9[1]
M [I]	...	...	...	...	488.2[24]	487.6[24]	399.1[1]	364.2[1]	410.3[1]	462.5[1]
F [I]	...	...	...	...	482.8[24]	480.3[24]	391.7[1]	342.2[1]	322.1[1]	327.4[1]
MF [III] [4]	...	337.4	929.0	1 164.7	1 223.9	998.4	657.6	881.4	1 025.1	1 130.3
M [III] [4]	...	129.0	366.0	479.2	530.6	446.9	302.2	452.8	539.9	600.2
F [III] [4]	...	208.4	563.0	685.5	693.3	551.5	355.4	428.6	485.2	530.1
% MF [I]	...	...	...	...	8.2[24]	8.0[24]	6.7[1]	6.0[1]	6.3[1]	6.8[1]
% M [I]	...	...	...	...	7.7[24]	7.5[24]	6.3[1]	5.7[1]	6.5[1]	7.4[1]
% F [I]	...	...	...	...	8.7[24]	8.6[24]	7.3[1]	6.4[1]	6.1[1]	6.2[1]
% MF [III] [4]	...	3.0	8.2	10.4	10.9	9.5	6.6	8.8	10.3	11.5
% M [III] [4]	...	2.2	6.2	8.1	9.0	7.9	5.7	8.5	10.2	11.6
% F [III] [4]	...	4.0	10.3	12.9	12.9	11.4	7.5	9.1	10.5	11.4
Russian Federation Fédération de Russie										
MF [I] [4 70]	...	...	3 877.0	4 305.0	5 702.0	6 712.0	6 732.0	8 058.0	8 876.0	9 323.0
M [I] [4 70]	...	...	2 026.0	2 280.0	3 074.0	3 616.0	3 662.0	4 371.0	4 787.0	4 966.0
F [I] [4 70]	...	...	1 851.0	2 025.0	2 628.0	3 096.0	3 070.0	3 687.0	4 090.0	4 357.0
MF [III] [4]	...	61.9	577.7	836.0	1 637.0	2 327.0	2 506.0	1 990.0	1 929.0	1 263.0
M [III] [4]	...	18.8	160.7	268.0	586.0	872.0	930.0	721.0	682.0	383.0
F [III] [4]	...	43.1	417.0	567.0	1 051.0	1 455.0	1 576.0	1 278.0	1 247.0	880.0
% MF [I] [4 70]	...	...	5.2	5.9	8.1	9.5	9.7	11.8	13.3	13.4
% M [I] [4 70]	...	...	5.2	5.9	8.3	9.7	10.0	12.2	13.6	13.6
% F [I] [4 70]	...	...	5.2	5.8	7.9	9.2	9.3	11.5	13.0	13.1
% MF [III] [4]	...	0.1	0.8	5.7	7.5	8.9	9.9	11.3	13.3	...
Saint Helena Sainte—Hélène										
MF [III]	0.2	0.2	0.2	0.2	0.3	0.3	0.4	0.4	0.5	...
M [III]	0.1	0.1	0.1	0.1	0.2	0.2	0.2	0.3	0.3	...
F [III]	0.1	0.1	0.1	0.1	0.1	0.1	0.1	0.1	0.1	...
Saint Pierre and Miquelon Sainte—Pierre—et—Miquelon										
MF [III] [18]	...	...	...	0.4	...	...	...	...	...	...
San Marino Saint—Marin										
MF [IV] [10]	0.6[2]	0.5[2]	0.5[2]	0.6[2]	0.6[2]	0.5[2]	0.6[1]	0.5[1]	0.6[1]	...
M [IV] [10]	0.2[2]	0.1[2]	0.1[2]	0.2[2]	0.1[2]	0.1[2]	0.1[1]	0.1[1]	0.1[1]	...
F [IV] [10]	0.5[2]	0.3[2]	0.4[2]	0.4[2]	0.4[2]	0.4[2]	0.5[1]	0.4[1]	0.4[1]	...
% MF [IV] [10]	5.5[2]	4.3[2]	4.2[2]	5.1[2]	3.9[2]	3.9[2]	5.1[1]	4.4[1]	4.1[1]	...
% M [IV] [10]	2.4[2]	2.3[2]	2.0[2]	2.6[2]	1.6[2]	1.5[2]	2.0[1]	1.9[1]	1.8[1]	...
% F [IV] [10]	9.7[2]	6.9[2]	7.1[2]	8.1[2]	7.4[2]	7.0[2]	8.8[1]	7.3[1]	6.9[1]	...
Senegal Sénégal										
MF [III] [33 71]	10.4	14.4	12.0	10.2	...	...	...	...	...	...
M [III] [33 71]	8.3	13.1	10.0	9.0	...	...	...	...	...	...
F [III] [33 71]	2.1	1.3	2.0	1.2	...	...	...	...	...	...
Singapore Singapour										
MF [I] [14]	25.8[72]	30.0	43.4	43.7	43.8	47.2	53.8	45.5	62.1	90.1
M [I] [14]	17.6[72]	18.7	26.4	25.2	24.9	28.4	31.0	26.8	35.5	51.4
F [I] [14]	8.2[72]	11.3	17.0	18.5	18.9	18.8	22.8	18.7	26.6	38.7
MF [III] [2]	1.7	1.2	1.0	1.0	1.0	1.1	1.5	2.6	4.4	5.9
M [III] [2]	1.2	0.8	0.7	0.7	0.7	0.7	0.8	1.2	2.3	3.2
F [III] [2]	0.5	0.4	0.3	0.3	0.4	0.4	0.7	1.4	2.1	2.7
% MF [I] [14]	1.7[72]	1.9	2.7	2.7	2.6	2.7	3.0	2.4	3.2	4.6
% M [I] [14]	1.9[72]	2.0	2.7	2.6	2.5	2.7	2.9	2.4	3.2	4.5
% F [I] [14]	1.3[72]	1.8	2.6	2.8	2.8	2.8	3.1	2.4	3.3	4.6

30
Unemployment
Number (thousands) and percentage unemployed [*cont.*]
Chômage
Nombre (milliers) et pourcentage des chômeurs [*suite*]

Country or area [§] Pays ou zone [§]	1990	1991	1992	1993	1994	1995	1996	1997	1998	1999
Slovakia Slovaquie										
MF [I] [1 73]	...	...	...	...	333.5	323.7	284.2	297.5	317.1	416.8
M [I] [1 73]	...	...	...	...	179.9	171.4	140.7	151.8	167.5	226.6
F [I] [1 73]	...	...	...	...	153.5	152.4	143.5	145.6	149.6	190.3
MF [III]	...	169.0	285.5	323.2	366.2	349.8	324.3	336.7	379.5	485.2
M [III]	...	83.4	141.1	167.2	189.5	174.8	155.1	162.9	193.0	265.8
F [III]	...	85.6	144.4	156.0	176.6	175.0	169.2	173.8	186.5	219.4
% MF [I] [1 73]	...	...	...	...	13.7	13.1	11.3	11.8	12.5	16.2
% M [I] [1 73]	...	...	...	...	13.3	12.6	10.2	10.9	11.9	15.9
% F [I] [1 73]	...	...	...	...	14.1	13.8	12.7	12.8	13.2	16.4
% MF [III]	...	6.6	11.4	12.9	14.4	13.8	12.6	12.9	13.7	17.3
% M [III]	...	6.4	11.1	12.7	13.9	12.8	11.3	11.7	13.3	17.9
% F [III]	...	6.9	11.7	13.0	15.0	14.8	14.1	14.3	14.1	16.6
Slovenia Slovénie										
MF [I] [1 4]	...	...	...	85.0	85.0	70.0	69.0	69.0	75.0	71.0
M [I] [1 4]	...	...	...	49.0	48.0	39.0	38.0	36.0	40.0	37.0
F [I] [1 4]	...	...	...	36.0	37.0	31.0	31.0	32.0	35.0	34.0
MF [III] [1]	44.6	75.1	102.6	129.1	127.1	...	...	125.2	126.1	119.0
M [III] [1]	23.2	41.5	57.5	72.5	70.0	...	...	64.1	63.2	58.8
F [III] [1]	21.4	33.6	45.1	56.6	57.0	...	...	61.1	62.9	60.2
% MF [I] [1 4]	...	...	...	9.1	9.0	7.4	7.3	7.1	7.7	7.4
% M [I] [1 4]	...	...	...	9.9	9.5	7.7	7.5	7.0	7.6	7.2
% F [I] [1 4]	...	...	...	8.3	8.4	7.0	7.0	7.3	7.7	7.6
% MF [III] [1]	4.7	8.2	11.5	14.4	14.4	...	...	...	...	...
% M [III] [1]	4.5	8.5	12.1	15.3	15.1	...	...	...	...	...
% F [III] [1]	4.8	7.9	10.8	13.5	13.7	...	...	...	...	...
South Africa Afrique du Sud										
MF [III] [1 74 75]	110.7	247.8	287.8	313.3	271.3	273.0	295.7	309.6	...	...
M [III] [1 74 75]	77.3	176.6	201.1	221.3	184.8	186.7	197.4	207.8	...	...
F [III] [1 74 75]	33.3	71.2	86.7	92.6	86.6	86.2	98.3	101.8	...	...
% MF [III]	...	...	...	...	4.4	4.5	5.1	5.4	...	...
Spain Espagne										
MF [I] [40]	2 441.2	2 463.7	2 788.5	3 481.3	3 738.1	3 583.5	3 540.0	3 356.5	3 060.3	2 605.5
M [I] [40]	1 166.1	1 191.9	1 384.5	1 836.7	1 911.9	1 753.9	1 724.0	1 581.6	1 364.3	1 102.0
F [I] [40]	1 275.1	1 271.8	1 404.1	1 644.6	1 826.2	1 829.7	1 816.1	1 774.9	1 696.1	1 503.5
MF [III] [55]	2 350.0	2 289.0	2 259.9	2 537.9	2 647.0	2 449.0	2 275.4	2 118.7	1 889.5	1 651.6
M [III] [55]	942.5	910.7	954.2	1 193.0	1 283.5	1 156.0	1 064.9	968.4	818.2	682.2
F [III] [55]	1 407.5	1 378.3	1 305.7	1 344.9	1 363.5	1 292.9	1 210.4	1 150.3	1 071.3	964.4
% MF [I] [40]	16.3	16.4	18.4	22.7	24.2	22.9	22.2	20.8	18.8	15.9
% M [I] [40]	12.0	12.3	14.3	19.0	18.8	18.2	17.6	16.1	13.8	11.1
% F [I] [40]	24.2	23.8	25.6	29.2	31.4	30.6	29.6	28.3	26.6	23.0
% MF [III] [55]	15.7	15.2	14.9	16.6	17.1	20.3	...	...	...	...
% M [III] [55]	9.7	9.4	9.9	12.3	13.3	12.0	...	...	...	...
% F [III] [55]	26.7	25.8	23.8	23.9	23.4	21.6	...	...	...	...
Sri Lanka Sri Lanka										
MF [I] [5 25]	1 005.1[76]	843.3[77]	817.6[77]	874.1[77]	813.3[77]	759.1[77]	710.3[77]	...	701.0[77]	612.7[77]
M [I] [5 25]	395.8[76]	380.0[77]	408.7[77]	349.3[77]	390.5[77]	352.9[77]	328.2[77]	...	296.2[77]	330.7[77]
F [I] [5 25]	609.2[76]	463.3[77]	409.0[77]	524.8[77]	422.8[77]	406.2[77]	382.0[77]	...	404.8[77]	282.0[77]
% MF [I] [5 25]	14.4[76]	14.1[77]	14.1[77]	14.7[77]	13.6[77]	12.5[77]	11.3[77]	10.7[77]	10.6[77]	...
% M [I] [5 25]	9.1[76]	10.0[77]	10.6[77]	9.1[77]	9.9[77]	8.8[77]	8.0[77]	8.0[77]	7.1[77]	...
% F [I] [5 25]	23.5[76]	21.2[77]	21.0[77]	25.2[77]	20.8[77]	19.7[77]	17.6[77]	16.2[77]	16.2[77]	...
Sudan Soudan										
MF [III]	70.1	19.9[78]	5.3[78]	...	...	...	...	...	...	...
M [III]	44.4	10.2[78]	3.7[78]	...	...	...	...	...	...	...
F [III]	25.7	9.7[78]	1.6[78]	...	...	...	...	...	...	...
Suriname Suriname										
MF [I] [2]	15.4[6]	...	18.5	14.4	11.3	7.6	10.7	...	...	...
M [I] [2]	7.2[6]	...	9.1	7.3	6.6	4.1	4.9	...	...	...
F [I] [2]	8.2[6]	...	9.4	7.1	4.7	3.4	5.8	...	...	...
MF [III] [79]	3.9	3.7	1.4	1.0	0.6	0.9	0.9	...	...	...
M [III] [79]	1.2	1.1	0.5	0.4	0.1	0.3	0.3	...	...	...
F [III] [79]	2.8	2.6	0.9	0.6	0.4	0.6	0.6	...	...	...
% MF [I] [2]	15.8[6]	...	17.2	14.7	12.7	8.4	11.0	...	...	...
% M [I] [2]	12.5[6]	...	13.7	12.0	11.4	7.0	7.9	...	...	...
% F [I] [2]	20.6[6]	...	23.1	19.2	15.0	10.9	16.4	...	...	...

30
Unemployment
Number (thousands) and percentage unemployed [*cont.*]
Chômage
Nombre (milliers) et pourcentage des chômeurs [*suite*]

Country or area [§] Pays ou zone [§]	1990	1991	1992	1993	1994	1995	1996	1997	1998	1999
Sweden Suède										
MF [I] [55]	75.0	134.0	233.0	356.0[17]	340.0	333.0	347.0	342.0	276.0	241.0
M [I] [55]	40.0	78.0	144.0	218.0[17]	202.0	190.0	192.0	188.0	154.0	133.0
F [I] [55]	36.0	56.0	89.0	137.0[17]	138.0	142.0	155.0	154.0	122.0	107.0
MF [III] [55]	66.4	114.6	309.8	447.4	438.4	436.2	407.6	367.0	285.6	276.7
M [III] [55]	35.6	66.4	186.1	262.6	250.7	238.2	220.2	199.5	156.3	151.7
F [III] [55]	30.9	48.1	123.7	184.8	187.7	198.0	187.3	167.4	129.3	125.0
% MF [I] [55]	1.6	3.0	5.2	8.2[17]	8.0	7.7	8.0	8.0	6.5	5.6
% M [I] [55]	1.7	3.3	6.3	9.7[17]	9.1	8.5	8.5	8.4	6.9	5.9
% F [I] [55]	1.6	2.6	4.2	6.6[17]	6.7	6.9	7.5	7.5	6.0	5.2
Switzerland Suisse										
MF [I] [1 25]	...	68.2	108.7	144.6	150.1	129.0	144.6	162.1	141.8	121.6
M [I] [1 25]	...	26.7	49.7	68.0	76.3	63.6	74.7	94.7	70.0	59.2
F [I] [1 25]	...	41.4	59.0	76.7	73.8	65.4	69.9	67.4	71.8	62.4
MF [III] [1]	18.1	39.2	92.3	163.1	171.0	153.3	168.6	188.3	139.7	98.6
M [III] [1]	9.8	22.7	54.7	96.6	98.0	85.5	96.8	108.7	77.1	52.6
F [III] [1]	8.3	16.5	37.6	66.6	73.1	67.8	71.8	79.6	62.6	46.0
% MF [I] [1 25]	...	1.8	2.8	3.7	3.9	3.3	3.7	4.1	3.6	3.1
% M [I] [1 25]	...	1.2	2.3	3.1	3.5	2.9	3.4	4.3	3.2	2.7
% F [I] [1 25]	...	2.5	3.5	4.6	4.4	3.9	4.1	3.9	4.1	3.5
% MF [III] [1]	0.5	1.1	2.5	4.5	4.7	4.2	4.7	5.2	3.9	2.7
% M [III] [1]	0.4	1.1	2.5	4.4	4.4	3.9	4.4	4.9	3.5	2.4
% F [III] [1]	0.6	1.2	2.7	4.7	5.2	4.8	5.1	5.7	4.4	3.3
Tajikistan Tadjikistan										
MF [III]	...	...	6.8	21.6	32.1	37.5	45.7	51.1	...	...
M [III]	...	...	4.2	12.4	17.1	20.2	22.8	24.1	...	...
F [III]	...	...	2.6	9.2	15.0	17.3	22.9	27.0	...	...
% MF [III]	...	...	0.4	1.2	1.7	2.0	2.6	2.7	...	...
% M [III]	...	...	0.4	1.2	1.6	1.9	2.4	2.4	...	...
% F [III]	...	...	0.4	1.1	1.8	2.1	2.8	2.9	...	...
Thailand Thaïlande										
MF [I] [6 80]	710.0	869.3	456.3	494.4	422.8	375.0	353.9	292.5	1 137.9	985.7
M [I] [6 80]	347.4	350.1	224.1	217.3	196.2	167.1	186.5	154.4	625.2	546.4
F [I] [6 80]	362.5	519.1	232.2	277.0	226.5	207.9	167.4	138.1	512.7	439.3
% MF [I] [6 80]	2.2	2.7	1.4	1.5	1.3	1.1	1.1	0.9	3.4	3.0
% M [I] [6 80]	2.1	2.0	1.3	1.2	1.1	0.9	1.0	0.8	3.4	3.0
% F [I] [6 80]	2.4	3.5	1.5	1.8	1.5	1.4	1.1	0.9	3.4	3.0
TFYR of Macedonia L'ex–R.y. Macédoine										
MF [III]	156.3	164.8	172.1	174.8	185.9	216.2	238.0	253.0	...	...
M [III]	76.0	82.0	87.0	89.0	96.0	101.0	110.0	138.0	...	...
F [III]	80.0	83.0	85.0	86.0	90.0	115.0	128.0	115.0	...	...
% MF [III]	23.6[81]	24.5	26.3	27.7	30.0	35.6	38.8	...	...	...
% M [III]	19.4[81]	20.1	22.1	23.6	25.8	31.9	35.0	...	...	...
% F [III]	29.7[81]	31.3	32.5	33.7	36.4	41.7	44.5	...	...	...
Trinidad and Tobago Trinité–et–Tobago										
MF [I] [1 82 83]	93.6	91.2	99.2	99.9	93.9	89.4	86.1	81.2	79.4	...
M [I] [1 82 83]	55.1	49.6	54.3	56.3	51.5	49.5	43.1	41.3	39.0	...
F [I] [1 82 83]	38.5	41.5	44.9	43.7	42.4	39.9	43.0	39.9	40.4	...
% MF [I] [1 82 83]	20.0	18.5	19.6	19.8	18.4	17.2	16.2	15.0	14.2	...
% M [I] [1 82 83]	17.8	15.7	17.0	17.6	16.1	15.1	13.2	12.3	11.3	...
% F [I] [1 82 83]	24.2	23.4	23.9	23.4	22.3	20.6	21.0	19.4	18.9	...
Tunisia Tunisie										
MF [III] [60]	152.2	133.1	136.9	142.2	160.2	189.7	180.9	...	...	...
M [III] [60]	103.6	89.4	89.0	94.8	132.7	160.4	115.9	...	...	...
F [III] [60]	48.6	43.7	47.9	47.4	27.5	29.3	64.9	...	...	...
Turkey Turquie										
MF [I] [4 30 84]	1 615.0	1 787.0	1 745.0	1 722.0	1 740.0	1 522.0	1 332.0	1 545.0	1 547.0	1 730.0
M [I] [4 30 84]	1 103.0	1 300.0	1 237.0	1 225.0	1 218.0	1 052.0	956.0	994.0	1 041.0	1 259.0
F [I] [4 30 84]	512.0	486.0	508.0	497.0	522.0	470.0	376.0	550.0	416.0	471.0
MF [III] [2]	979.5[85]	859.0[85]	840.1[85]	682.6[85]	469.3[4]	401.3[4]	416.8[4]	463.0[4]	465.2[4]	...
M [III] [2]	808.8[85]	706.8[85]	695.5[85]	571.7[85]	382.2[4]	324.7[4]	341.8[4]	382.1[4]	386.0[4]	...
F [III] [2]	170.7[85]	152.2[85]	144.6[85]	111.0[85]	87.1[4]	76.6[4]	75.0[4]	81.2[4]	79.2[4]	...
% MF [I] [4 30 84]	7.5	8.4	8.0	8.0	7.9	6.6	5.8	6.9	6.2	7.3
% M [I] [4 30 84]	7.5	8.9	8.2	8.2	7.7	6.6	5.9	6.1	6.3	7.7
% F [I] [4 30 84]	7.5	7.3	7.6	7.5	8.2	6.8	5.5	9.2	6.1	6.4

30
Unemployment
Number (thousands) and percentage unemployed [*cont.*]
Chômage
Nombre (milliers) et pourcentage des chômeurs [*suite*]

Country or area [§] Pays ou zone [§]	1990	1991	1992	1993	1994	1995	1996	1997	1998	1999
Ukraine Ukraine										
MF [I] [4 86]	...	...	...	...	...	1 437.0	1 997.5	2 330.1	2 937.1	2 698.8
M [I] [4 86]	...	...	...	...	...	805.7	1 057.2	1 216.9	1 515.1	1 435.5
F [I] [4 86]	...	...	...	...	...	631.3	940.3	1 113.2	1 422.0	1 263.3
MF [III] [10 87]	...	...	...	83.9	82.2	126.9	351.1	637.1	1 003.2	1 174.5
M [III] [10 87]	...	...	...	21.2	22.5	34.7	115.3	220.6	382.8	444.9
F [III] [10 87]	...	...	...	62.7	59.7	92.2	235.8	416.5	620.4	729.6
% MF [I] [4 86]	...	...	...	...	...	5.6	7.6	8.9	11.3	11.9
% M [I] [4 86]	...	...	...	...	...	6.3	8.0	9.5	11.9	12.2
% F [I] [4 86]	...	...	...	...	...	4.9	7.3	8.4	10.8	11.5
%MF [III] [10 87]	...	...	...	0.4	0.4	0.6	1.6	3.1	4.8	5.8
%M [III] [10 87]	...	...	...	0.2	0.2	0.3	1.1	2.2	3.7	7.1
%F [III] [10 87]	...	...	...	0.6	0.6	0.9	2.3	4.0	5.9	4.4
United Kingdom Royaume−Uni										
MF [I] [6 40]	1 973.8	2 413.6	2 769.2	2 935.5	2 737.6	2 460.4	2 340.1	2 037.3	1 776.4	1 751.7
M [I] [6 40]	1 164.6	1 513.9	1 865.2	1 986.4	1 826.1	1 611.8	1 549.0	1 305.8	1 097.8	1 095.2
F [I] [6 40]	809.1	899.7	903.9	949.2	911.6	848.6	791.0	731.5	678.6	656.5
MF [II] [42 88 89]	1 664.5	2 291.9	2 778.6	2 919.2	2 636.5	2 325.7	2 122.2	1 602.4	1 362.4	1 263.1
M [II] [42 88 89]	1 232.3	1 737.1	2 126.0	2 236.0	2 014.4	1 770.0	1 610.3	...	...	...
F [II] [42 88 89]	432.2	554.9	652.6	683.1	622.6	555.6	511.9	...	...	...
% MF [I] [6 40]	6.8	8.4	9.7	10.3	9.6	8.6	8.2	7.1	6.1	6.0
% M [I] [6 40]	7.1	9.2	11.5	12.4	11.4	10.1	9.6	8.1	6.8	6.7
% F [I] [6 40]	6.5	7.2	7.3	7.6	7.3	6.8	6.3	5.7	5.3	5.1
% MF [II] [42 88 89]	5.9	8.1	9.9	10.4	9.4	8.3	7.6	5.7	4.7	4.3
% M [II] [42 88 89]	7.6	10.7	13.3	14.0	12.6	11.3	10.3	...	...	...
% F [II] [42 88 89]	3.5	4.6	5.4	5.6	5.1	4.5	4.2	...	...	...
United States Etats−Unis										
MF [I] [40 90]	7 047.0	8 628.0	9 613.0	8 940.0	7 996.0[17]	7 404.0	7 236.0	6 739.0	6 210.0	5 880.0
M [I] [40 90]	3 906.0	4 946.0	5 523.0	5 055.0	4 367.0[17]	3 983.0	3 880.0	3 577.0	3 266.0	3 066.0
F [I] [40 90]	3 140.0	3 683.0	4 090.0	3 885.0	3 629.0[17]	3 421.0	3 356.0	3 162.0	2 944.0	2 814.0
% MF [I] [40 90]	5.6	6.8	7.5	6.9	6.1[17]	5.6	5.4	4.9	4.5	4.2
% M [I] [40 90]	5.7	7.2	7.9	7.2	6.2[17]	5.6	5.4	4.9	4.4	4.1
% F [I] [40 90]	5.5	6.4	7.0	6.6	6.0[17]	5.6	5.4	5.0	4.6	4.3
United States Virgin Is. Iles Vierges américaines										
MF [III] [91]	1.3	1.4	1.7	1.9	2.8	2.7	2.4	2.7	...	...
% MF [III] [91]	2.8	2.8	3.5	3.5	5.6	5.7	5.2	5.9	...	...
Uruguay Uruguay										
MF [I] [2 15]	105.7	111.0	112.8	105.0	120.1	137.5	...	...	123.8	137.7
M [I] [2 15]	50.6	52.6	49.6	46.9	53.2	61.5	...	...	53.7	59.4
F [I] [2 15]	55.1	58.4	63.2	58.1	66.9	76.0	...	...	70.1	78.3
% MF [I] [2 15]	8.5	9.0	9.0	8.3	9.2	10.2	...	...	10.1	11.3
% M [I] [2 15]	6.9	7.2	6.9	6.5	7.1	8.0	...	...	7.8	8.7
% F [I] [2 15]	10.9	11.6	11.9	10.9	12.1	13.2	...	...	13.0	14.6
Uzbekistan Ouzbékistan										
MF [III]	...	...	20.2	29.0	29.4	31.0	...	...	...	...
M [III]	...	...	7.9	11.3	12.1	12.1	...	...	...	...
F [III]	...	...	12.3	17.7	17.3	18.9	...	...	...	...
% MF [III]	...	...	0.2	0.4	0.4	0.4	...	...	...	...
% M [III]	...	...	0.2	0.2	0.3	0.3	...	...	...	...
% F [III]	...	...	0.3	0.5	0.5	0.5	...	...	...	...
Venezuela Venezuela										
MF [I] [1]	743.4	701.7	582.4	503.5	687.4	874.7	1 042.9	1 060.7	1 092.6	1 525.5
M [I] [1]	514.1	481.7	418.7	371.2	442.4	1 016.8	1 210.0	592.4	616.4	...
F [I] [1]	229.2	220.0	163.7	132.3	245.0	366.3	437.9	468.3	476.2	...
% MF [I] [1]	10.4	9.5	7.7	6.7	8.7	10.3	11.8	11.4	11.2	14.9
% M [I] [1]	10.4	9.6	8.1	7.1	8.2	9.1	10.4	9.8	9.9	...
% F [I] [1]	10.3	9.4	6.8	5.6	9.7	12.9	14.5	14.2	13.4	...

30
Unemployment
Number (thousands) and percentage unemployed [*cont.*]
Chômage
Nombre (milliers) et pourcentage des chômeurs [*suite*]

Source:
International Labour Office (ILO), Geneva, "Yearbook of Labour Statistics 2000" and the ILO labour statistics database.

§   I   = Labour force sample surveys.
   II = Social insurance statistics.
   III = Employment office statistics.
   IV = Official estimates.

†   For information on recent changes in country or area nomenclature pertaining to former Czechoslovakia, Germany, Hong Kong Special Administrative Region of China, Macao Special Administrative Region of China, SFR Yugoslavia and former USSR, see Annex I – Country or area nomenclature, regional and other groupings.

†† For statistical purposes, the data for China do not include those for the Hong Kong Special Administrative Region, Macao Special Administrative Region of China and Taiwan province of China.

1   Persons aged 15 years and over.
2   Persons aged 14 years and over.
3   Gran Buenos Aires.
4   One month of each year.
5   Persons aged 10 years and over.
6   Average of less than 12 months.
7   28 urban agglomerations.
8   Estimates based on the 1991 Census of Population and Housing.
9   Estimates based on 1996 census of population benchmarks.
10 31st December of each year.
11 Private sector.
12 Year ending in June of the year indicated.
13 Beginning April 1985, excluding some elderly unemployed no longer applicants for work.
14 Persons aged 15 to 69 years.
15 Urban areas.
16 Excluding rural population of Rondônia, Acre, Amazonas, Roraima, Pará and Amapá.
17 Beginning this year, methodology revised; data not strictly comparable.
18 Persons aged 16 to 60 years.
19 Persons aged 16 to 55 years.
20 Four employment offices.
21 Bujumbura.
22 Excluding full–time members of the armed forces.
23 Excluding residents of the Territories and indigenous persons living on reserves.
24 Bangui.
25 One quarter of each year.
26 Beginning this year, sample design revised.
27 Unemployed in urban areas.
28 Young people aged 16 to 25 years.
29 Excluding unpaid family workers who worked for one hour or more.
30 Persons aged 12 years and over.
31 7 main cities of the country.
32 Estimates based on the 1993 Census results.
33 Persons aged 14 to 55 years.

Source:
Bureau international du Travail (BIT), Genève, "Annuaire des statistiques du travail 2000" et la base de données du BIT.

§   I   = Enquêtes par sondage sur la main–d'oeuvre.
   II = Statistiques d'assurances sociales.
   III = Statistiques des bureaux de placement.
   IV = Evaluations officielles.

†   Pour les modifications récentes de nomenclature de pays ou de zone concernant l'Allemagne, Hong Kong (Région administrative spéciale de Chine), Macao (Région administrative spéciale de Chine), l'ex–Tchécoslovaquie, l'ex–URSS et l'ex–Rfs de Yougoslavie, voir annexe I – Nomenclature de pays ou des zones, groupements régionaux et autres groupements.

†† Les données statistiques relatives à la Chine ne comprennent pas celles qui concernent la région administrative spéciale de Hong Kong, la région administrative spéciale de Macao et la province chinoise de Taiwan.

1   Personnes âgées de 15 ans et plus.
2   Personnes âgées de 14 ans et plus.
3   Gran Buenos Aires.
4   Un mois de chaque année.
5   Personnes âgées de 10 ans et plus.
6   Moyenne de moins de douze mois.
7   28 agglomérations urbaines.
8   Estimations basées sur le recensement de la population et de l'habitat de 1991.
9   Estimations basées sur les données de calage du recensement de population de 1996.
10 31 décembre de chaque année.
11 Secteur privé.
12 Année se terminant en juin de l'année indiquée.
13 A partir d'avril 1985, non compris certains chômeurs âgés devenus non demandeurs d'emploi.
14 Personnes âgées de 15 à 69 ans.
15 Régions urbaines.
16 Non compris la population rurale de Rondônia, Acre, Amazonas, Roraima, Pará et Amapá.
17 A partir de cette année, méthodologie révisée; les données ne sont pas strictement comparables.
18 Personnes âgées de 16 à 60 ans.
19 Personnes âgées de 16 à 55 ans.
20 Quatre bureaux de placement.
21 Bujumbura.
22 Non compris les membres à temps complet des forces armées.
23 Non compris les habitants des Territoires " et les populations indigènes vivant dans les réserves."
24 Bangui.
25 Un trimestre de chaque année.
26 A partir de cette année, plan d'échantillonnage révisé.
27 Chômeurs dans les régions urbaines.
28 Jeunes gens de 16 à 25 ans.
29 Non compris les travailleurs familiaux non rémunérés ayant travaillé une heure ou plus.
30 Personnes âgées de 12 ans et plus.
31 7 villes principales du pays.
32 Estimations basées sur les résultats du Recensement de 1993.
33 Personnes âgées de 14 à 55 ans.

30
Unemployment
Number (thousands) and percentage unemployed [*cont.*]
Chômage
Nombre (milliers) et pourcentage des chômeurs [*suite*]

34 The data relate to the government−controlled areas.

35 Excluding persons on child care leave actively seeking a job.
36 Persons aged 15 to 74 years.
37 Persons aged 15 to 66 years.
38 Persons aged 16 to 66 years.
39 Persons aged 15 to 64 years.
40 Persons aged 16 years and over.
41 Excluding elderly unemployment pensioners no longer seeking work.
42 Excluding persons temporarily laid off.
43 Beginning October 1982: series revised on the basis of new administrative procedures adopted in 1986.
44 Excluding registered applicants for work who worked more than 78 hours during the month.
45 Cayenne and Kourou.
46 Persons aged 15 to 60 years.
47 Persons aged 15 to 65 years.
48 Guatemala city.
49 Including unemployed temporarily unable to undertake work (child−care allowance, military service, etc.).
50 Persons aged 16 to 74 years.
51 Rates calculated on basis of 1991 Census.
52 Including workers from the Judea, Samaria and Gaza areas.

53 Including the residents of East Jerusalem.
54 Beginning 1992, series revised on basis of 1995 Population Census.
55 Persons aged 16 to 64 years.
56 Beginning this year, series revised.
57 6 provincial capitals.
58 Persons aged 16 to 61 years.
59 Excluding Rodrigues.
60 Persons aged 18 years and over.
61 Beginning 1993, persons working or seeking work for less than 12 hours per week are no longer included.

62 Persons seeking work for 20 hours or more a week.

63 Curaçao.
64 Including students seeking vacation work.

65 Annual average calculated using December data as at 12 December.
66 Computed from 1987−88 survey results.
67 July of preceding year to June of current year.
68 Persons aged 18 to 60 years.
69 Asunción metropolitan area.
70 Persons aged 15 to 72 years.
71 Dakar.
72 Population census.
73 Excluding persons on child−care leave.
74 Excluding Transkei, Bophuthatswana, Venda, Ciskei, Kwazulu, KaNgwane, Qwa Qwa, Gazankulu, Lebowa and KwaNdebele.
75 Whites, Coloureds and Asians; eligibility rules for registration not specified.
76 Whole country.
77 Excluding Northern and Eastern provinces.
78 Khartoum province.
79 Beginning 1987, change in registration system; unemployed must re−register every 3 months.
80 Persons aged 13 years and over.
81 Labour force denominator excluded self−employed.

82 New series according to 1980 population census.
83 Excluding unemployed not previously employed.

34 Les données se réfèrent aux régions sous contrôle gouvernemental.
35 Non compris les personnes en congé parental cherchant activement un travail.
36 Personnes âgées de 15 à 74 ans.
37 Personnes âgées de 15 à 66 ans.
38 Personnes âgées de 16 à 66 ans.
39 Personnes âgées de 15 à 64 ans.
40 Personnes âgées de 16 ans et plus.
41 Non compris les chômeurs indemnisés âgés ne recherchant plus de travail.
42 Non compris les personnes temporairement mises à pied.
43 A partir d'octobre 1982: série révisée sur la base de nouvelles procédures administratives adoptées en 1986.
44 Non compris les demandeurs d'emploi inscrits ayant travaillé plus de 78 heures dans le mois.
45 Cayenne et Kourou.
46 Personnes âgées de 15 à 60 ans.
47 Personnes âgées de 15 à 65 ans.
48 Ville de Guatemala.
49 Y compris chômeurs qui temporairement ne peuvent travailler (allocation congé parental, service militaire, etc.).
50 Personnes âgées de 16 à 74 ans.
51 Taux calculés sur la base du Recensement de 1991.
52 Y compris les travailleurs des régions de Judée, Samarie et Gaza.
53 Y compris les résidents de Jérusalem−Est.
54 A partir de 1992, série révisée sur la base du Recensement de la population de 1995.
55 Personnes âgées de 16 à 64 ans.
56 A partir de cette année, série révisée.
57 6 chefs−lieux de province.
58 Personnes âgées de 16 à 61 ans.
59 Non compris Rodriguez.
60 Personnes âgées de 18 ans et plus.
61 A partir de 1993, ne sont plus comprises les personnes qui travaillent, ou qui cherchent moins de 12 heures de travail par semaine.
62 Personnes à la recherche d'un travail de 20 heures ou plus par semaine.
63 Curaçao.
64 Y compris les étudiants qui cherchent un emploi pendant les vacances.
65 Moyenne annuelle calculée en utilisant pour le mois de décembre les données du 12 décembre.
66 Calculé sur la base des résultats de l'enquête de 1987−88.
67 Juillet de l'année précédente à juin de l'année en cours.
68 Personnes âgées de 18 à 60 ans.
69 Région métropolitaine d'Asunción.
70 Personnes âgées de 15 à 72 ans.
71 Dakar.
72 Recensement de population.
73 Non compris les personnes en congé parental.
74 Non compris Transkei, Bophuthatswana, Venda, Ciskei, Kwazulu, KaNgwane, Qwa Qwa, Gazankulu, Lebowa et KwaNdebele.
75 Blancs, personnes de couleur et asiatiques; conditions d'éligibilité pour l'enregistrement non spécifiées.
76 Ensemble du pays.
77 Non compris les provinces du Nord et de l'Est.
78 Province de Khartoum.
79 A partir de 1987, modification du système d'enregistrement; les chômeurs doivent se réinscrire tous les 3 mois.
80 Personnes âgées de 13 ans et plus.
81 La main−d'oeuvre du dénominateur excluait les travailleurs indépendants.
82 Nouvelle série selon le recensement de population de 1980.
83 Non compris les chômeurs n'ayant jamais travaillé.

30
Unemployment
Number (thousands) and percentage unemployed [*cont.*]
Chômage
Nombre (milliers) et pourcentage des chômeurs [*suite*]

84 Beginning 1988, figures revised on the basis of the 1990 census results.
85 Annual averages.
86 Persons aged 15–70 years.
87 Men aged 16 to 59 years; women aged 16 to 54 years.
88 Beginning April 1983: excluding some categories of men aged 60 and over; February 1986: data not strictly comparable as a result of changes in compilation date; September 1988: excluding most under 18–year–olds; September 1989: excluding some men formerly employed in the coal mining industry.

89 Claimants at unemployment benefits offices.
90 Estimates based on 1990 census benchmarks.

91 Persons aged 16 to 65 years.

84 A partir de 1988, données révisées sur la base des résultats du Recensement de 1990.
85 Moyennes annuelles.
86 Personnes âgées de 15 à 70 ans.
87 Hommes âgés de 16 à 59 ans; femmes âgées de 16 à 54 ans.
88 A partir d'avril 1983: non compris certaines catégories d'hommes âgés de 60 ans et plus; de février 1986: données non strictement comparables en raison d'un changement de date de traitement; de septembre 1988: non compris la plupart des moins de 18 ans; septembre 1989: non compris certains hommes ayant précédemment travaillé dans l'industrie charbonnière.
89 Demandeurs auprès des bureaux de prestations de chômage.
90 Estimations basées sur les données de calage du recensement de 1990.
91 Personnes âgées de 16 à 65 ans.

Technical notes, tables 29 and 30

Detailed data on labour force and related topics are published in the ILO *Yearbook of Labour Statistics* [13]. The series shown in the *Statistical Yearbook* give an overall picture of the availability and disposition of labour resources and, in conjunction with other macro-economic indicators, can be useful for an overall assessment of economic performance. The ILO *Yearbook of Labour Statistics* provides a comprehensive description of the methodology underlying the labour series. Brief definitions of the major categories of labour statistics are given below.

"Employment" is defined to include persons above a specified age who, during a specified period of time, were in one of the following categories:

(a)　"Paid employment", comprising persons who perform some work for pay or profit during the reference period or persons with a job but not at work due to temporary absence, such as vacation, strike, education leave;

(b)　"Self-employment", comprising employers, own-account workers, members of producers cooperatives, persons engaged in production of goods and services for own consumption and unpaid family workers;

(c)　Members of the armed forces, students, homemakers and others mainly engaged in non-economic activities during the reference period who, at the same time, were in paid employment or self-employment are considered as employed on the same basis as other categories.

"Unemployment" is defined to include persons above a certain age and who, during a specified period of time were:

(a)　"Without work", i.e. were not in paid employment or self-employment;

(b)　"Currently available for work", i.e. were available for paid employment or self-employment during the reference period; and

(c)　"Seeking work", i.e. had taken specific steps in a specified period to find paid employment or self-employment.

Persons not considered to be unemployed include:

(a)　Persons intending to establish their own business or farm, but who had not yet arranged to do so and who were not seeking work for pay or profit;

(b)　Former unpaid family workers not at work and not seeking work for pay or profit.

For various reasons, national definitions of employment and unemployment often differ from the recommended international standard definitions and thereby limit international comparability. Intercountry comparisons are also complicated by a variety of types

Notes techniques, tableaux 29 et 30

Des données détaillées sur la main-d'oeuvre et des sujets connexes sont publiées dans l'*Annuaire des Statistiques du Travail* du BIT [13]. Les séries indiquées dans l'*Annuaire des Statistiques* donnent un tableau d'ensemble des disponibilités de main-d'œuvre et de l'emploi de ces ressources et, combinées à d'autres indicateurs économiques, elles peuvent être utiles pour une évaluation générale de la performance économique. L'*Annuaire des statistiques du Travail* du BIT donne une description complète de la méthodologie employée pour établir les séries sur la main-d'œuvre. On trouvera ci-dessous quelques brèves définitions des grandes catégories de statistiques du travail.

Le terme "Emploi" désigne les personnes dépassant un âge déterminé qui, au cours d'une période donnée, se trouvaient dans l'une des catégories suivantes:

(a)　La catégorie "emploi rémunéré", composée des personnes faisant un certain travail en échange d'une rémunération ou d'un profit pendant la période de référence, ou les personnes ayant un emploi, mais qui ne travaillaient pas en raison d'une absence temporaire (vacances, grève, congé d'études);

(b)　La catégorie "emploi indépendant" regroupe les employeurs, les travailleurs indépendants, les membres de coopératives de producteurs et les personnes s'adonnant à la production de biens et de services pour leur propre consommation et la main-d'œuvre familiale non rémunérée;

(c)　Les membres des forces armées, les étudiants, les aides familiales et autres personnes qui s'adonnaient essentiellement à des activités non économiques pendant la période de référence et qui, en même temps, avaient un emploi rémunéré ou indépendant, sont considérés comme employés au même titre que les personnes des autres catégories.

Par "chômeurs", on entend les personnes dépassant un âge déterminé et qui, pendant une période donnée, étaient:

(a)　"sans emploi", c'est-à-dire sans emploi rémunéré ou indépendant;

(b)　"disponibles", c'est-à-dire qui pouvaient être engagées pour un emploi rémunéré ou pouvaient s'adonner à un emploi indépendant au cours de la période de référence; et

(c)　"à la recherche d'un emploi", c'est-à-dire qui avaient pris des mesures précises à un certain moment pour trouver un emploi rémunéré ou un emploi indépendant.

Ne sont pas considérés comme chômeurs:

(a)　Les personnes qui, pendant la période de référence, avaient l'intention de créer leur propre entre-

of data collection systems used to obtain information on employed and unemployed persons.

Table 29 presents absolute figures on the distribution of employed persons by economic activity. In part A the figures are according to Revision 2 (ISIC 2) of the *International Standard Industrial Classification* [49], and in part B according to ISIC 3. In part A, the column for total employment includes economic activities not adequately defined and that are not accounted for in the other categories. Data are arranged as far as possible according to the major divisions of economic activity of the *International Standard Industrial Classification of All Economic Activities* [49].

Table 30: Figures are presented in absolute numbers and in percentages. Data are normally annual averages of monthly, quarterly or semi-annual data.

The series generally represent the total number of persons wholly unemployed or temporarily laid off. Percentage figures, where given, are calculated by comparing the number of unemployed to the total members of that group of the labour force on which the unemployment data are based.

prise ou exploitation agricole, mais n'avaient pas encore pris les dispositions nécessaires à cet effet et qui n'étaient pas à la recherche d'un emploi en vue d'une rémunération ou d'un profit;

(b)   Les anciens travailleurs familiaux non rémunérés qui n'avaient pas d'emploi et n'étaient pas à la recherche d'un emploi en vue d'une rémunération ou d'un profit.

Pour diverses raisons, les définitions nationales de l'emploi et du chômage diffèrent souvent des définitions internationales types recommandées, limitant ainsi les possibilités de comparaison entre pays. Ces comparaisons se trouvent en outre compliquées par la diversité des systèmes de collecte de données utilisés pour recueillir des informations sur les personnes employées et les chômeurs.

Le *tableau 29* présente les effectifs de personnes employées par activité économique. Dans la partie A, les chiffres sont classés en fonction de la Révision 2 de la *Classification internationale type, par Industrie, de toutes les branches d'activité économique* [49] et dans la partie B en fonction de la Révision 3. Dans la partie A, l'emploi total inclut les personnes employées à des activités économiques mal définies et qui ne sont pas classées ailleurs. Les données sont ventilées autant que possible selon les branches d'activité économique de la *Classification internationale type, par industrie, de toutes les activités économiques* [49].

Tableau 30: Les chiffres sont présentés en valeur absolue et en pourcentage. Les données sont normalement des moyennes annuelles des données mensuelles, trimestrielles ou semestrielles.

Les séries représentent généralement le nombre total des chômeurs complets ou des personnes temporairement mises à pied. Les données en pourcentage, lorsqu'elles figurent au tableau, sont calculées par comparaison du nombre de chômeurs au nombre total des personnes du groupe de main-d'œuvre sur lequel sont basées les données relatives au chômage.

31
Wages in manufacturing
Salaires dans les industries manufacturières
By hour, day, week or month
Par heure, jour, semaine ou mois

Country or area and unit Pays ou zone et unité	1990	1991	1992	1993	1994	1995	1996	1997	1998	1999
Albania: lek Albanie : lek										
MF - month mois[12]	554.0	665.0	...	...	...	...	...	...	...	...
Algeria: Algerian dinar Algérie : dinar algérien										
MF - month mois[3]	...	...	6 430.0	8 012.0	8 937.0	10 462.0	12 323.0	...	...	...
Argentina: Argentine peso Argentine : peso argentin										
MF - hour heure[3 4 6]	10 030.8[5]	24 941.2[5]	3.2	3.6	3.8	3.9	4.0	4.1	4.1	4.2
Armenia: dram Arménie : dram										
MF - month mois[3]	263.0[7]	348.0[7]	1 574.0[7]	13 208.0[7]	2 470.0	7 680.0	12 464.0	17 656.0	21 278.0	...
Australia: Australian dollar Australie : dollar australien										
MF - hour heure[8 9]	12.9	13.3	13.7	14.0	14.7[10]	15.6	16.4[3]	...	17.4[3]	...
M - hour heure[8 9]	13.5	13.8	14.2	14.6	15.2[10]	16.1	16.9[3]	...	18.0[3]	...
F - hour heure[8 9]	11.1	11.7	12.0	12.4	13.0[10]	13.7	14.3[3]	...	15.2[3]	...
Austria: Austrian schilling, euro Autriche : schilling autrichien, euro										
MF - month mois[3]	...	...	...	...	...	26 020.0	27 239.0	27 776.0	28 455.0	...
M - month mois[3]	...	...	...	...	...	28 815.0	30 084.0	30 667.0	31 471.0	...
F - month mois[3]	...	...	...	...	...	19 903.0	20 667.0	21 051.0	21 480.0	...
MF - month mois[1]	25 151.0	26 583.0	28 183.0	29 572.0	30 790.0	32 173.0	...	...	...	...
Azerbaijan: manat Azerbaïdjan : manat										
MF - month mois	218.7[11]	400.2[11]	3 282.6[11]	3 109.2	21 009.0	95 556.7	146 174.7	200 030.1[3]	202 082.6[3]	244 087.1[3]
Bahrain: Bahrain dinar Bahreïn : dinar de Bahreïn										
MF - month mois[12 13]	224.5	220.2	203.9	190.0	188.0	...	...	...	257.0	227.0
M - month mois[12 13]	277.0	286.0	288.0	277.0	275.0	...	...	...	276.0	250.0
F - month mois[12 13]	172.0	155.0	120.0	103.0	100.0	...	...	...	125.0	109.0
Bangladesh: taka Bangladesh : taka										
MF - day jour[14 15 16]	...	56.1	59.9	...	...	...	...	...	...	...
M - day jour[14 15 16]	...	60.9	62.1	...	...	...	...	...	...	...
F - day jour[14 15 16]	...	30.1	31.3	...	...	...	...	...	...	...
MF - day jour[14 17 18]	55.9	21.8	23.0	...	...	...	...	...	...	...
M - day jour[14 17 18]	61.1	22.8	24.0	...	...	...	...	...	...	...
F - day jour[14 17 18]	30.1	15.9	17.2	...	...	...	...	...	...	...
Barbados: Barbados dollar Barbade : dollar de la Barbade										
MF - week semaine[6]	251.5[8]	255.7	...							
Belarus: Belarussian rouble Bélarus : rouble bélarussien										
MF - month mois	283.0[19]	596.0	5 852.0	68 866.0	115 536.0	...	...	...	...	...
Belgium: Belgian franc, euro Belgique : franc belge, euro										
MF - hour heure[6 8]	342.4	363.1	379.6	395.9	411.8	388.2[3]	398.2[3]	406.8[3]	...	...
M - hour heure[6 8]	364.0	385.7	403.8	420.7	438.0	405.5[3]	416.2[3]	425.2[3]	...	...
F - hour heure[6 8]	271.2	287.7	300.2	313.4	325.3	320.9[3]	331.0[3]	335.8[3]	...	...
MF - month mois[8 20]	86 673.0	91 950.0	95 615.0	98 702.0	101 426.0	104 773.0[3]	106 983.0[3]	109 980.0[3]	...	...
M - month mois[8 20]	95 285.0	101 007.0	104 757.0	107 877.0	110 656.0	113 618.0[3]	116 279.0[3]	119 233.0[3]	...	...
F - month mois[8 20]	60 211.0	64 116.0	67 524.0	70 506.0	73 061.0	80 118.0[3]	82 096.0[3]	85 194.0[3]	...	...

31
Wages in manufacturing
By hour, day, week or month [*cont.*]
Salaires dans les industries manufacturières
Par heure, jour, semaine ou mois [*suite*]

Country or area and unit Pays ou zone et unité	1990	1991	1992	1993	1994	1995	1996	1997	1998	1999
Bolivia: boliviano Bolivie : boliviano										
MF - month mois[8 21 22 23]	493.1	620.9	689.6	761.3	891.5	959.0	1 094.0	...	...	...
Botswana: pula Botswana : pula										
MF - month mois[8 24]	383.0	403.0	511.0	606.0	537.0	582.0	617.0	633.0	632.0[3]	...
M - month mois[3 8 24]	...	...	...	...	...	...	...	...	821.0	...
F - month mois[3 8 24]	...	...	...	...	...	...	...	...	447.0	...
Brazil: real Brésil : real										
MF - month mois[8]	26 076.0[25]	136 699.0[25]	1 562.0[26]	33 978.0[26]	793 056.6[26]	504.9	597.2	637.1	...	...
M - month mois[8]	29 850.0[25]	156 457.0[25]	2 779.0[26]	38 861.0[26]	905 566.4[26]	569.7	669.6	711.0	...	...
F - month mois[8]	15 990.0[25]	84 818.0[25]	963.0[26]	20 895.0[26]	491 201.2[26]	333.0	403.9	438.8	...	...
British Virgin Islands: US dollar Iles Vierges britanniques : dollar des Etats-Unis										
MF - hour heure[3]	7.3	6.1	6.0	6.3	6.1	...	...	...	...	...
M - hour heure[3]	...	...	...	...	7.2	...	...	...	...	...
F - hour heure[3]	...	...	...	...	4.4	...	...	...	...	...
Bulgaria: lev Bulgarie : lev										
MF - month mois[27]	335.8	916.9	2 244.2[28]	3 481.2[28]	5 356.0[28]	8 448.0[28]	15 276.0[3 29]	148 460.0[3 29]	194 612.0[3 29]	205.9[3 29]
M - month mois[3 29]	...	...	...	...	...	...	17 794.0	172 043.0	224 492.0	...
F - month mois[3 29]	...	...	...	...	...	...	12 658.0	123 423.0	163 045.0	...
Canada: Canadian dollar Canada : dollar canadien										
MF - hour heure[3 6 31 32]	14.2	14.9	15.4	15.7	16.0	16.2	16.7	16.9	17.2	17.2
MF - week semaine[3 31]	599.4	624.7	652.9	669.4	685.8	694.6	716.6	736.7	755.9	755.9
Chile: Chilean peso Chili : peso chilien										
MF - month mois[8 33]	130 650.0	173 012.0	211 780.0	116 457.0[34]	141 844.0	159 085.0	176 480.0	189 753.0	200 773.0	203 540.0
China ††: yuan Chine †† : yuan										
MF - month mois[3 35]	172.3	190.8	219.6	279.0	356.9	430.8	470.2	494.4	588.7	649.5
China, Hong Kong SAR†: Hong Kong dollar Chine, Hong Kong RAS† : dollar de Hong Kong										
MF - month mois[20 21]	5 685.8	6 382.8	7 163.5	7 897.5	8 780.4	9 508.3	10 323.8	11 331.2	11 711.6	11 853.0
M - month mois[20 21]	6 262.3	7 020.7	7 878.2	8 677.8	9 499.6	10 421.4	11 260.0	12 165.2	12 555.7	12 893.2
F - month mois[20 21]	5 022.6	5 718.4	6 445.4	7 180.2	8 098.4	8 684.2	9 390.4	10 467.0	10 915.9	10 846.7
MF - day jour[6 14]	179.5	200.7	218.6	241.7	266.6	278.0	296.9	322.6	335.3	334.7
M - day jour[6 14]	224.5	249.9	274.8	313.8	333.5	357.7	386.3	423.8	430.6	422.6
F - day jour[6 14]	155.8	173.6	189.6	206.8	226.3	233.5	245.3	258.8	262.9	268.9
China, Macao SAR †: Macao pataca Chine, Macao RAS † : pataca de Macao										
MF - month mois[36 37]	2 058.0[8]	2 232.0[8]	2 509.0	2 926.0	3 111.0	3 210.0	3 124.0	3 323.0	3 138.0[3]	2 911.0[3]
M - month mois[36 37]	...	...	3 321.0	3 865.0	4 015.0	4 388.0	4 541.0	5 016.0	4 789.0[3]	4 701.0[3]
F - month mois[36 37]	...	...	2 222.0	2 447.0	2 624.0	2 682.0	2 677.0	2 842.0	2 694.0[3]	2 501.0[3]
Colombia: Colombian peso Colombie : peso colombien										
MF - month mois[8 38 39]	...	94 946.0	177 028.0	145 767.0	209 630.0	225 995.0	275 905.0	322 695.0	441 965.0	455 252.0
MF - month mois[8 36 38 39]	...	95 496.0	117 853.0	163 389.0	225 272.0	248 615.0	274 231.0	329 437.0	446 445.0	427 313.0

31
Wages in manufacturing
By hour, day, week or month [cont.]
Salaires dans les industries manufacturières
Par heure, jour, semaine ou mois [suite]

Country or area and unit Pays ou zone et unité	1990	1991	1992	1993	1994	1995	1996	1997	1998	1999
Cook Islands: Cook Islands dollar Iles Cook : dollar des Iles Cook										
MF - week semaine[8]	137.0	...	...	187.0	...	...	...	...	...	...
M - week semaine[8]	160.0	...	...	194.0	...	...	...	...	...	...
F - week semaine[8]	111.0	...	...	177.0	...	...	...	...	...	...
Costa Rica: Costa Rican colón Costa Rica : colón costa-ricien										
MF - month mois[8]	20 037.0	27 229.0	32 949.0	38 631.0	44 720.0	54 365.0	63 894.0	75 672.0	85 899.0[3]	97 774.5[3]
M - month mois[8]	21 887.0	30 152.0	36 427.0	42 225.0	49 059.0	60 273.0	69 627.0	78 917.0	91 493.0[3]	106 594.0[3]
F - month mois[8]	16 262.0	21 733.0	26 282.0	30 556.0	35 335.0	42 739.0	50 028.0	67 531.0	73 122.0[3]	77 969.3[3]
Croatia: kuna Croatie : kuna										
MF - month mois	4 218.0[40]	7 447.0[40]	34 024.0[40]	518.0	1 186.0	1 672.0	3 034.0[3]	3 358.0[3]	3 681.0[3]	3 869.0[3]
Cuba: Cuban peso Cuba : peso cubain										
MF - month mois[2]	...	180.0	179.0	180.0	192.0	211.0	210.0	212.0	214.0	...
Cyprus: Cyprus pound Chypre : livre chypriote										
MF - month mois[8 20 33 41]	504.0	542.0	558.0	640.0	672.0	710.0	758.0	762.0	769.2[3]	806.0[3]
M - month mois[8 20 33 41]	586.0	626.0	678.0	738.0	770.0	822.0	864.0	871.0	897.1[3]	932.4[3]
F - month mois[8 20 33 41]	314.0	349.0	384.0	419.0	455.0	476.0	504.0	530.0	520.5[3]	560.7[3]
MF - week semaine[6 8 33 41]	74.2	80.3	89.0	101.0	104.1	113.4	130.1	117.5	...	...
M - week semaine[6 8 33 41]	98.8	105.6	116.4	134.2	132.3	143.4	170.8	145.0	166.5[3]	...
F - week semaine[6 8 33 41]	56.8	63.0	69.9	75.8	81.2	86.1	90.1	92.4	96.4[3]	...
Czech Republic: Czech koruna République tchèque : couronne tchèque										
MF - month mois[3]	...	...	...	5 652.0[42]	6 631.0[42]	7 854.0[43]	9 259.0[43]	10 411.0[44]	11 500.0[44]	12 268.0[44]
Denmark: Danish krone Danemark : couronne danoise										
MF - hour heure[3]	...	...	...	...	...	152.8	163.5	167.3	174.6	...
M - hour heure[3]	...	...	...	...	...	160.2	172.9	176.5	183.3	...
F - hour heure[3]	...	...	...	...	...	135.5	143.1	147.4	154.8	...
MF - hour heure[6 41 45]	99.9	104.6	108.3	...	...	...	...	...	...	...
M - hour heure[6 41 45]	103.8	108.5	112.2	...	...	...	...	...	...	...
F - hour heure[6 41 45]	87.8	92.1	95.4	...	...	...	...	...	...	...
Dominican Republic: Dominican peso Rép. dominicaine : peso dominicain										
MF - hour heure[36 46]	...	10.4	12.2	11.3	17.4	16.6	18.0	21.6	...	...
MF - month mois[21]	1 120.0	1 456.0	1 456.0	1 456.0	1 675.0	2 010.0	...	...	...	...
Ecuador: sucre Equateur : sucre										
MF - hour heure[6]	467.9	669.4	1 088.6	1 676.1	2 113.1	2 469.3[3]	3 226.7[3]	4 380.4[3]	...	...
MF - month mois[3 47]	...	...	...	...	...	1 302.7	1 726.4	2 179.7	...	...
Egypt: Egyptian pound Egypte : livre égyptienne										
MF - week semaine[6 8 13]	54.0	55.0	62.0	70.0	77.0	84.0	93.0[3]	103.0[3]	...	...
M - week semaine[6 8 13]	56.0	57.0	64.0	72.0	80.0	87.0	97.0[3]	107.0[3]	...	...
F - week semaine[6 8 13]	38.0	41.0	48.0	54.0	57.0	64.0	87.0[3]	80.0[3]	...	...
El Salvador: El Salvadoran colón El Salvador : cólon salvadorien										
MF - hour heure[6]	3.3	4.1	4.6	5.4	6.2	6.9	7.5	...	10.3	10.7

31
Wages in manufacturing
By hour, day, week or month [cont.]
Salaires dans les industries manufacturières
Par heure, jour, semaine ou mois [suite]

Country or area and unit Pays ou zone et unité	1990	1991	1992	1993	1994	1995	1996	1997	1998	1999
M - hour heure[6]	3.4	4.5	4.8	5.6	6.4	7.0	7.7	...	12.0	12.1
F - hour heure[6]	3.2	3.7	4.5	5.2	6.0	6.8	7.3	...	9.0	9.2
MF - month mois[3 21]	...	...	...	...	...	...	...	...	1 993.4	...
M - month mois[3 21]	...	...	...	...	...	...	...	...	2 348.5	
F - month mois[3 21]	...	...	...	...	...	...	...	...	1 646.0	
Eritrea: Nakfa Erythrée : Nakfa										
MF - month mois[3 21]	...	...	...	...	...	...	478.5	...	...	...
M - month mois[3 21]	...	...	...	...	...	...	522.0	...	...	...
F - month mois[3 21]	...	...	...	...	...	...	346.5	...	...	...
Estonia: Estonian kroon Estonie : couronne estonienne										
MF - month mois	359.8[48]	850.7[48]	536.0[3]	1 036.0[3]	1 784.0[3]	2 421.0[3]	2 991.0[3]	3 578.0[3]	4 081.0[3]	4 117.0[3]
Fiji: Fiji dollar Fidji : dollar des Fidji										
MF - day jour[6 8 14]	11.4	...		13.9	...	...	16.3	15.1	...	...
Finland: Finnish markka, euro Finlande : markka finlandais, euro										
MF - hour heure[6 49]	47.7	50.7	52.3	53.5	55.8	60.1	...	...	...	...
M - hour heure[6 49]	51.1	53.9	55.4	56.8	59.2	63.4	...	...	...	...
F - hour heure[6 49]	39.5	42.1	43.4	44.4	46.6	50.3	...	...	...	...
MF - month mois[3 50]	...	...	...	...	...	11 004.0	11 434.0	11 677.0	12 054.0	...
M - month mois[3 50]	...	...	...	...	...	11 810.0	12 240.0	12 523.0	12 880.0	...
F - month mois[3 50]	...	...	...	...	...	9 232.0	9 674.0	9 842.0	10 237.0	...
France: French franc, euro France : franc français, euro										
MF - hour heure[6 8]	45.5	47.5	49.4	50.6	51.8	52.8	54.2	55.4	...	...
M - hour heure[6 8]	48.4	50.5	52.4	53.7	54.9	55.8	57.2	58.5	...	...
F - hour heure[6 8]	38.2	39.7	41.2	42.5	43.3	44.3	45.4	46.3	...	...
MF - month mois[3]	...	...	...	...	...	...	...	13 600.0	13 860.0	...
M - month mois[3]	...	...	...	...	...	...	...	14 520.0	14 770.0	...
F - month mois[3]	...	...	...	...	...	...	...	11 210.0	11 490.0	...
Gambia: dalasi Gambie : dalasi										
MF - month mois[3 51 52]	...	...	...	1 008.6	1 045.5	...	...	...	969.7	...
Georgia: lari Géorgie : lari										
MF - month mois[3]	...	...	...	...	...	...	...	51.2	68.9	87.4
M - month mois[3]	...	...	...	...	...	...	...	...	...	101.1
F - month mois[3]	...	...	...	...	...	...	...	...	...	63.3
Germany † Allemagne †										
MF - hour heure[3 6]	...	...	...	...	...	...	25.7	26.2	26.8	27.5
M - hour heure[3 6]	...	...	...	...	...	...	27.0	27.4	28.0	28.8
F - hour heure[3 6]	...	...	...	...	...	...	20.0	20.3	20.8	21.4
F. R. Germany: deutsche mark R. f. Allemagne : deutsche mark										
MF - hour heure[6]	20.1[53]	21.3[53]	22.5[53]	23.8[53]	24.6[53]	25.5[3]	26.4[3]	26.8[3]	27.4[3]	...

31
Wages in manufacturing
By hour, day, week or month [*cont.*]
Salaires dans les industries manufacturières
Par heure, jour, semaine ou mois [*suite*]

Country or area and unit Pays ou zone et unité	1990	1991	1992	1993	1994	1995	1996	1997	1998	1999
M - hour heure[6]	21.3[53]	22.6[53]	23.8[53]	25.0[53]	25.8[53]	26.8[3]	27.7[3]	28.0[3]	28.6[3]	...
F - hour heure[6]	15.5[53]	16.5[53]	17.5[53]	18.5[53]	19.0[53]	19.7[3]	20.5[3]	20.8[3]	21.3[3]	...
German D. R.(former): deutsche mark R. d. allemande (anc.) : deutsche mark										
MF - hour heure[6]	...	9.4	11.9	13.9	15.5	17.0[3]	18.0[3]	18.6[3]	19.2[3]	...
M - hour heure[6]	...	9.7	12.3	14.4	16.2	17.8[3]	18.8[3]	19.5[3]	20.1[3]	...
F - hour heure[6]	...	8.4	10.5	11.9	13.0	14.1[3]	15.0[3]	15.4[3]	15.9[3]	...
Ghana: cedi Ghana : cedi										
MF - month mois[8]	45 045.0	34 226.0	...	...	...	...	...	...	...	...
Gibraltar: Gibraltar pound Gibraltar : livre de Gibraltar										
MF - week semaine[6 8 54]	238.5	214.1	239.4	252.2	233.3	279.3	307.3	...	...	...
M - week semaine[6 8 54]	247.7	254.4	254.5	272.7	246.0	295.3	345.0			
F - week semaine[6 8 54]	151.7	148.8	161.7	166.0	171.5	193.8	192.5			
Greece: drachma Grèce : drachme										
MF - hour heure[6 13]	661.3	772.1	878.2	970.8	1 097.9	1 243.3	1 349.9	1 470.5	1 539.8	...
M - hour heure[6 13]	733.8	854.7	967.5	1 063.6	1 200.1	1 353.3	1 459.8	1 585.9	1 653.0	
F - hour heure[6 13]	575.3	673.2	765.3	851.4	963.4	1 088.6	1 183.4	1 287.8	1 355.8	
MF - month mois[13 20]	169 842.0	200 303.0	229 596.0	259 853.0	293 627.0	332 568.0	363 857.0	399 599.0	423 142.0	...
M - month mois[13 20]	183 440.0	216 176.0	247 723.0	280 219.0	319 082.0	358 318.0	391 700.0	430 889.0	456 488.0	
F - month mois[13 20]	125 467.0	148 938.0	171 921.0	195 542.0	218 400.0	244 904.0	278 996.0	303 900.0	323 153.0	
Guam: US dollar Guam : dollar des Etats-Unis										
MF - hour heure[6 8 12]	8.1	9.1	9.3	10.1	10.4	10.6	...	...	...	...
Guatemala: quetzal Guatemala : quetzal										
MF - month mois	473.6	577.9	686.2	775.2	868.1	1 138.0	1 368.9	1 430.0	1 541.0	1 602.3
Guinea: Guinean franc Guinée : franc guinéen										
MF - month mois[21]	80 000.0	85 000.0	110 000.0	110 000.0	130 000.0	130 000.0	153 000.0	...	...	...
Hungary: forint Hongrie : forint										
MF - month mois[3 44 50]	...	...	21 107.0	26 317.0	32 500.0	39 554.0	48 195.0	58 915.0	68 872.0	76 335.0[55]
M - month mois[3 44 50]	...	...	24 319.0	30 422.0	37 429.0	45 466.0	55 437.0	68 396.0	79 892.0	
F - month mois[3 44 50]	...	...	17 014.0	21 109.0	26 175.0	31 853.0	38 897.0	46 897.0	54 985.0	
MF - month mois[6 44]	11 167.0[56]	13 992.0[56]	17 636.0	21 751.0	...	...	...			
Iceland: Icelandic króna Islande : couronne islandaise										
MF - month mois[3 57]	...	...	...	...	...	...	...	...	...	119 800.0
India: Indian rupee Inde : roupie indienne										
MF - month mois[6]	988.4	1 019.3	932.6	977.4	960.5	1 211.0	1 188.8	1 137.3	...	...
Ireland: Irish pound, euro Irlande : livre irlandaise, euro										
MF - hour heure[6 8 58]	5.4	5.6	5.9	6.2	6.3	6.5	6.6	6.9	7.2	...
M - hour heure[6 8 41]	6.0	6.3	6.6	7.0	7.0	7.1	7.3	7.5	7.9	
F - hour heure[6 8 41]	4.2	4.4	4.7	5.0	5.1	5.3	5.4	5.6	5.9	
Isle of Man: pound sterling Ile de Man : livre sterling										
MF - hour heure[3 8]	...	...	...	...	...	6.9	6.6	7.1	7.8	9.1

31
Wages in manufacturing
By hour, day, week or month [cont.]
Salaires dans les industries manufacturières
Par heure, jour, semaine ou mois [suite]

Country or area and unit Pays ou zone et unité	1990	1991	1992	1993	1994	1995	1996	1997	1998	1999
M - hour heure[38]	...	...	...	...	...	6.9	7.0	7.6	8.9	9.4
F - hour heure[38]	...	...	...	...	...	6.7	5.0	5.7	5.7	7.5
MF - week semaine[8]	...	...	207.0	225.0	238.1	285.2[3]	272.4[3]	292.7[3]	313.3[3]	377.1[3]
M - week semaine[8]	...	...	...	276.0	251.8	288.6[3]	294.6[3]	320.5[3]	366.0[3]	408.9[3]
F - week semaine[8]	...	...	...	148.0	199.4	266.2[3]	196.1[3]	215.8[3]	209.6[3]	241.1[3]
Israel: new sheqel Israël : nouveau sheqel										
MF - month mois[59]	2 668.8	3 080.0	3 514.0	3 917.0	4 427.0[3]	5 061.0[3]	5 757.0[3]	6 676.0[3]	7 418.0[3]	8 227.0[3]
Italy: Italian lira, euro Italie : lire italienne, euro										
MF - month mois[36]	100.0[60]	109.5[60]	115.7[60]	120.5[60]	124.3[60]	128.7[60]	101.8[61]	105.7[61]	108.6[61]	110.9[61]
MF - month mois[3 20]	100.0[60]	110.2[60]	116.8[60]	121.9[60]	126.1[60]	131.3[60]	102.2[61]	106.4[61]	109.6[61]	112.1[61]
Jamaica: Jamaican dollar Jamaïque : dollar jamaïcain										
MF - week semaine	450.6[62]	701.0	895.0	...	...	...				
Japan: yen Japon : yen										
MF - month mois[8 63 64]	...	...	...	...	276 700.0	278 800.0	283 700.0	287 200.0	289 600.0	291 100.0
M - month mois[8 63 64]	...	...	...	...	317 000.0	318 200.0	322 500.0	325 600.0	327 900.0	327 700.0
F - month mois[8 63 64]	...	...	...	...	175 500.0	177 900.0	181 800.0	184 500.0	187 300.0	189 000.0
MF - month mois[65]	352 020.0	368 011.0	372 594.0	371 356.0	...	...	...	...	...	...
M - month mois[65]	436 135.0	450 336.0	454 482.0	...	...	...	...	...	...	...
F - month mois[65]	180 253.0	193 112.0	198 058.0	...	...	...	...	...	...	...
Jordan: Jordan dinar Jordanie : dinar jordanien										
MF - day jour[8 52]	4.6	4.6	4.8	4.9	5.2	5.3	5.6	5.7	5.9	...
M - day jour[8 52]	4.8	4.9	5.0	5.1	5.4	5.5	5.8	6.0	6.2	...
F - day jour[8 52]	2.7	3.0	2.9	3.1	3.3	3.4	3.6	3.6	3.7	...
Kazakhstan: tenge Kazakhstan : tenge										
MF - month mois	277.0[66]	489.0[66]	5 675.0[66]	144.0	2 263.0	6 520.0	9 288.0	11 092.0	11 357.0[3]	13 434.0[3]
M - month mois[3]	...	...	...	...	...	...	...	...	12 246.0	...
F - month mois[3]	...	...	...	...	...	...	...	...	9 641.0	...
Kenya: Kenya shilling Kenya : shilling du Kenya										
MF - month mois[8 67]	3 064.6	3 324.2	...	...	4 920.5	6 228.7	4 998.6	5 510.8	...	...
M - month mois[8 67]	3 159.8	3 430.1	...	...	4 878.6	6 867.7	...	5 294.3	...	...
F - month mois[8 67]	2 317.7	2 515.8	...	...	5 168.5	3 314.4	...	6 509.5	...	...
Korea, Republic of: Korean won Corée, République de : won coréen										
MF - month mois[33 47]	590.8	690.3	798.5	885.4[3]	1 022.5[3]	1 123.9[3]	1 261.2[3]	1 326.2[3]	1 284.5[3]	1 475.5[3]
M - month mois[33 47]	724.5	842.8	963.8	1 055.5[3]	1 206.7[3]	1 314.7[3]	1 463.4[3]	1 527.2[3]	1 467.3[3]	1 686.3[3]
F - month mois[33 47]	364.3	428.1	497.3	551.4[3]	638.9[3]	711.1[3]	795.6[3]	852.0[3]	820.1[3]	933.1[3]
Kyrgyzstan: Kyrgyz som Kirghizistan : som kirghize										
MF - month mois[3]	1.3	2.1	15.1	118.1	280.4	377.1	652.1	844.7	988.8	1 280.8
Latvia: lats Lettonie : lats										
MF - month mois[3]	1.6[2]	3.2[2]	22.5	46.2	60.5[45]	86.5[45]	95.2[45]	114.7[45]	128.3[45]	129.0[45]

31
Wages in manufacturing
By hour, day, week or month [cont.]
Salaires dans les industries manufacturières
Par heure, jour, semaine ou mois [suite]

Country or area and unit Pays ou zone et unité	1990	1991	1992	1993	1994	1995	1996	1997	1998	1999
M - month mois[3]	...	...	24.0	...	66.2[45]	94.6[45]	101.4[45]	121.5[45]	136.1[45]	137.5[45]
F - month mois[3]	...	...	20.1	...	54.8[45]	77.8[45]	88.3[45]	107.9[45]	119.2[45]	118.5[45]
Lithuania: litas Lituanie : litas										
MF - month mois[3 8 50]	...	...	...	...	...	...	...	824.0	973.0	1 010.0
M - month mois[3 8 50]	...	...	...	...	...	...	...	909.0	1 089.0	1 135.0
F - month mois[3 8 50]	...	...	...	...	...	...	...	733.0	847.0	875.0
Luxembourg: Luxembourg franc, euro Luxembourg : franc luxembourgeois, euro										
MF - hour heure[6 8]	379.0	400.0	425.0	446.0	468.0	478.0	484.0	465.0[3]	471.0[3]	...
M - hour heure[6 8]	399.0	420.0	446.0	466.0	486.0	495.0	504.0	485.0[3]	491.0[3]	...
F - hour heure[6 8]	248.0	265.0	278.0	300.0	314.0	316.0	320.0	336.0[3]	337.0[3]	...
MF - month mois[8 20]	118 555.0	124 885.0	133 958.0	136 802.0	138 170.0	139 190.0	140 155.0	145 916.0[3]	144 489.0[3]	...
M - month mois[8 20]	129 207.0	135 258.0	144 648.0	146 876.0	148 197.0	147 878.0	148 131.0	156 645.0[3]	154 403.0[3]	...
F - month mois[8 20]	72 152.0	77 096.0	83 632.0	88 607.0	89 493.0	93 576.0	95 441.0	97 881.0[3]	98 940.0[3]	...
Malawi: Malawi kwacha Malawi : kwacha malawien										
MF - month mois	176.8	154.8	167.8	173.8	184.7	195.8	...	...	...	...
Malaysia: ringgit Malaisie : ringgit										
MF - month mois	660.0	719.0	794.0	848.0	928.0	1 002.0	1 115.0	1 210.0	...	...
M - month mois	885.0	952.0	1 037.0	1 082.0	1 161.0	1 242.0	1 343.0	1 449.0	...	...
F - month mois	443.0	495.0	558.0	612.0	677.0	719.0	842.0	912.0	...	...
Mauritius: Mauritian rupee Maurice : roupie mauricienne										
MF - month mois[8 20]	3 105.0[68]	3 684.0	4 016.0	4 411.0	5 162.0	5 659.0	5 972.0	6 282.0	6 912.0	7 034.0
MF - day jour[8 69]	60.5[68]	84.0	93.0	109.0	122.0	132.0	138.0	148.7	161.4	166.0
Mexico: Mexican peso Mexique : peso mexicain										
MF - hour heure[3 6]	4.2	5.2	6.4	6.5	7.2	8.3	10.2	12.4	14.8	17.8
MF - month mois[3]	...	947.8	...	1 014.9	...	1 220.6	1 404.2	1 651.8	2 077.2	2 377.7
M - month mois[3]	...	1 124.1	...	1 122.3	...	1 338.3	1 526.3	1 816.7	2 286.0	2 632.9
F - month mois[3]	...	558.9	...	750.1	...	919.9	1 104.1	1 281.7	1 622.4	1 835.9
Myanmar: kyat Myanmar : kyat										
M - month mois[62 70]	...	631.9	880.5	985.3	...	...	...	1 043.3	1 054.3	1 066.0
F - month mois[62 70]	...	670.9	866.8	940.2	...	...	...	998.9	1 010.6	1 190.9
Namibia: Namibia dollar Namibie : Dollar namibia										
MF - month mois	...	...	1 201.0	...	...	...	...	...	...	...
Netherlands: Netherlands guilder, euro Pays-Bas : florin néerlandais, euro										
MF - hour heure	21.5[8 58]	22.3[8 58]	22.7[8 58]	23.4[8 58]	27.9[71]	28.9[71]	30.2[3 72]	31.1[3 72]	32.0[71]	...
M - hour heure	22.8[8 41]	23.5[8 41]	23.9[8 41]	24.5[8 41]	29.1[71]	30.1[71]	31.4[3 72]	32.3[3 72]	33.4[71]	...
F - hour heure	17.1[8 41]	17.8[8 41]	18.3[8 41]	19.0[8 41]	22.2[71]	22.6[71]	24.0[3 72]	24.8[3 72]	25.7[71]	...
MF - month mois[3 50 72]	...	...	...	...	4 052.0[8]	4 184.0[8]	4 369.0	4 472.0	4 614.0[8]	...
M - month mois[3 50 72]	...	...	...	...	4 186.0[8]	4 318.0[8]	4 497.0	4 601.0	4 750.0[8]	...

31
Wages in manufacturing
By hour, day, week or month [*cont.*]
Salaires dans les industries manufacturières
Par heure, jour, semaine ou mois [*suite*]

Country or area and unit Pays ou zone et unité	1990	1991	1992	1993	1994	1995	1996	1997	1998	1999
F - month mois[3 50 72]	...	...	...	...	3 194.0[8]	3 270.0[8]	3 474.0	3 567.0	3 684.0[8]	...
Netherlands Antilles: Netherlands Antillean guilder Antilles néerlandaises : florin des Antilles néerlandaises										
MF - month mois[3 73]	...	2 319.0	2 416.0	2 441.0	2 445.0	2 364.0	2 475.0	2 546.0	2 507.0	...
New Zealand: New Zealand dollar Nouvelle-Zélande : dollar néo-zélandais										
MF - hour heure[8 74]	13.3	13.8	14.2	14.3	14.4[3]	14.8[3]	15.4[3]	15.9[3]	16.3[3]	16.9[3]
M - hour heure[8 74]	14.3	14.8	15.1	15.2	15.3[3]	15.7[3]	16.3[3]	16.8[3]	17.2[3]	17.7[3]
F - hour heure[8 74]	10.6	11.0	11.5	11.6	11.9[3]	12.2[3]	12.7[3]	13.2[3]	13.7[3]	14.3[3]
Nicaragua: córdoba Nicaragua : córdoba										
MF - hour heure	590.1[47 75]	4.7	8.0	8.8	9.4	10.0	11.0	11.2	12.0	12.0
MF - month mois	143 589.0[47 75]	1 140.6	1 951.2	2 150.0	2 282.4	2 443.6	2 672.0	2 724.0	2 846.0	3 014.3
Norway: Norwegian krone Norvège : couronne norvégienne										
MF - hour heure[6 41 67]	92.5	97.3	100.4	103.2	106.1	109.8	114.4	118.9	125.5	...
M - hour heure[6 41 67]	94.6	99.5	102.7	105.4	108.5	112.3	117.0	121.6	128.3	...
F - hour heure[6 41 67]	81.8	86.7	89.2	91.8	94.6	97.8	102.2	106.1	112.4	...
MF - month mois[3 8 50 72]	...	...	...	...	...	...	...	20 005.0	21 417.0	22 441.0
M - month mois[3 8 50 72]	...	...	...	...	...	...	...	...	...	23 039.0
F - month mois[3 8 50 72]	...	...	...	...	...	...	...	...	...	20 017.0
Pakistan: Pakistan rupee Pakistan : roupie pakistanaise										
MF - month mois	1 735.0	...	...	1 502.0	1 956.0	2 970.0	2 878.0	3 211.5		
Panama: balboa Panama : balboa										
MF - month mois[3 8 37]	...	...	...	...	...	...	...	...	247.0	250.9
M - month mois[3 8 37]	...	...	...	...	...	...	...	...	249.8	259.0
F - month mois[3 8 37]	...	...	...	...	...	...	...	...	238.5	241.3
MF - month mois	515.0[52]	537.0[52]	524.0[52]	590.0[52]	587.0[52]	...	597.0[3 76]	...	...	...
Paraguay: guaraní Paraguay : guaraní										
MF - month mois	220 548.0	273 537.0	298 682.0	380 096.0	480 081.0	610 414.0	686 436.0	761 675.0	898 598.0	741 416.0
M - month mois	234 234.0	292 787.0	342 552.0	407 117.0	507 072.0	645 759.0	721 289.0	800 340.0	947 853.0	923 124.0
F - month mois	155 744.0	196 738.0	177 754.0	298 952.0	389 558.0	485 113.0	563 271.0	628 963.0	729 160.0	404 458.0
Peru: new sol Pérou : nouveau sol										
MF - month mois[20 21]	14.9[8]	322.7[8]	565.0[8]	860.6[8]	1 451.1[8]	...	1 624.6[3 77]	1 875.2[3 77]	2 067.0[3 77]	2 155.6[3 77]
MF - day jour[6 14]	0.3[8]	6.0[8]	10.1[8]	14.8[8]	21.9[8]	24.0[3 8 78]	22.6[3 77]	24.5[3 77]	24.9[3 77]	25.6[3 77]
Philippines: Philippine peso Philippines : peso philippin										
MF - month mois[13 79]	4 108.0	4 831.0	5 386.0	5 584.0	6 272.0	6 654.0	...	...	...	...
M - month mois[13 79]	...	...	...	6 223.0	7 063.0	7 529.0	...	...	...	...
F - month mois[13 79]	...	...	...	4 741.0	5 277.0	5 592.0	...	...	...	...
Poland: new zloty Pologne : nouveau zloty										
MF - month mois[67]	995.5[19 47 80]	1 620.1[47 80]	2 679.4[47 80]	361.9[3]	494.9[3]	656.7[3]	832.8[3]	1 014.9[3]	1 164.4[3]	1 598.9[3]
Portugal: Portuguese escudo, euro Portugal : escudo portugais, euro										
MF - hour heure[6]	324.0	370.0	419.0	436.4	...	470.0	498.0	539.0	703.0[3]	...
M - hour heure[6]	368.0	419.0	480.0	485.7	...	551.0	586.0	626.0	832.0[3]	...

31
Wages in manufacturing
By hour, day, week or month [cont.]
Salaires dans les industries manufacturières
Par heure, jour, semaine ou mois [suite]

Country or area and unit Pays ou zone et unité	1990	1991	1992	1993	1994	1995	1996	1997	1998	1999
F - hour heure[6]	254.0	295.0	326.0	390.1	...	378.0	402.0	434.0	545.0[3]	...
MF - month mois	...	...	...	...	...	100 700.0	107 800.0	116 100.0	120 803.0[3]	122 327.0[3]
M - month mois	...	...	...	...	...	118 900.0	127 200.0	136 900.0	140 720.0[3]	146 138.0[3]
F - month mois	...	...	...	...	...	78 100.0	83 900.0	88 900.0	94 837.0[3]	94 057.0[3]
Puerto Rico: US dollar Porto Rico : dollar des Etats-Unis										
MF - hour heure[6]	6.0	6.3	6.6	7.0	7.2	7.4	7.7	8.0	8.4	8.9
Republic of Moldova: Moldovan leu République de Moldova : leu moldove										
MF - month mois	287.6[81]	475.2[81]	3 676.2[81]	37.8	143.2	209.5	282.2[3 44]	352.0[3 44]	399.0[3 44]	492.6[3 44]
Romania: Romanian leu Roumanie : leu roumain										
MF - month mois[3]	...	...	23 582.0	71 779.0	169 435.0	268 436.0	424 587.0	826 902.0	1 198 560.0	...
MF - month mois[6]	3 146.0[27]	6 842.0[27]	17 959.0	54 245.0	126 260.0	...	...	...	...	...
Russian Federation: ruble Fédération de Russie : ruble										
MF - month mois	302.0	584.0	6 466.0	57 633.0	198 593.0	464 792.0[3]	748 189.0[3]	919.0[3 82]	1 026.0[3 82]	...
San Marino: Italian lira Saint-Marin : lire italienne										
MF - day jour	84 835.0	102 579.0	111 611.0	113 772.0	120 131.0	127 347.0	135 278.0	142 712.0	149 357.0	...
Seychelles: Seychelles rupee Seychelles : roupie seychelloises										
MF - month mois[83]	2 187.0[84]	2 259.0[84]	2 349.0	2 454.0	2 422.0	2 513.0	2 646.0	2 727.0	...	...
Singapore: Singapore dollar Singapour : dollar singapourien										
MF - month mois	1 395.0	1 551.8	1 686.2	1 817.8	1 995.3	2 157.3	2 319.5	2 486.7	2 716.0[3 85]	2 803.0[3]
M - month mois	1 797.5	1 970.1	2 127.4	2 266.2	2 473.8	2 644.0	2 815.2	2 999.7	3 311.0[3 85]	3 384.0[3]
F - month mois	983.3	1 096.8	1 190.7	1 294.5	1 415.4	1 541.2	1 674.4	1 811.0	1 916.0[3 85]	2 007.0[3]
Slovakia: Slovak koruna Slovaquie : couronne slovaque										
MF - month mois	3 262.0	3 757.0[3 86]	4 370.0[3 86]	5 234.0[3 86]	6 193.0[3 86]	7 194.0[3 86]	8 230.0[3 86]	9 197.0[3 87]	10 001.0[3 87]	10 758.0[3]
Slovenia: tolar Slovénie : tolar										
MF - month mois[3]	8 698.0	14 737.0	43 305.0	62 491.0	79 347.0	92 877.0	106 144.0	118 960.0	131 958.0	144 110.0
Solomon Islands: Solomon Islands dollar Iles Salomon : dollar des Iles Salomon										
MF - month mois[18]	433.0	403.0	...	572.0	579.0	632.0	987.0	...	...	...
South Africa: rand Afrique du Sud : rand										
MF - month mois[88]	1 660.0	1 890.0	2 195.0	2 446.0	...	...	...	...	...	...
Spain: peseta, euro Espagne : peseta, euro										
MF - hour heure	902.0	994.0	1 080.0	1 159.0	1 221.0	1 263.0	1 311.0[3]	1 372.0[3]	1 429.0[3]	1 463.0[3]
Sri Lanka: Sri Lanka rupee Sri Lanka : roupie sri-lankaise										
MF - hour heure[6 62]	9.5	11.2	11.8	13.7	15.1	16.5	17.9	18.2	20.3	22.0
M - hour heure[6 62]	9.8	11.7	12.3	14.1	15.6	17.1	17.9	18.4	20.8	22.3
F - hour heure[6 62]	8.9	9.4	10.4	12.7	13.8	16.2	17.6	16.3	16.4	18.1
MF - day jour[6 62]	82.1	100.5	104.8	116.8	134.6	145.4	151.2	166.3	174.2	199.2
M - day jour[6 62]	85.1	106.1	107.7	120.3	139.0	151.7	151.6	167.8	175.6	203.9
F - day jour[6 62]	74.8	79.2	96.7	105.7	120.0	136.2	138.7	142.5	145.7	165.8

31
Wages in manufacturing
By hour, day, week or month [cont.]
Salaires dans les industries manufacturières
Par heure, jour, semaine ou mois [suite]

Country or area and unit Pays ou zone et unité	1990	1991	1992	1993	1994	1995	1996	1997	1998	1999
Sudan: Sudanese pound Soudan : livre soudanaise										
MF - month mois[6]	375.4	...	1 210.3	...	...	...	...	...	...	...
Swaziland: lilangeni Swaziland : lilangeni										
M - month mois[8 12 16]	1 380.0	1 415.0	1 486.0	1 146.0	1 861.0	2 134.0	2 388.0	2 948.0	...	...
F - month mois[8 12 16]	1 001.0	845.0	835.0	1 869.0	1 252.0	1 507.0	1 530.0	1 850.0	...	...
M - month mois[8 12 18]	324.0	318.0	372.0	409.0	424.0	558.0	681.0	863.0	...	...
F - month mois[8 12 18]	284.0	286.0	305.0	382.0	346.0	483.0	572.0	542.0	...	...
Sweden: Swedish krona Suède : couronne suédoise										
MF - hour heure[6 41]	87.3[89]	91.7[89]	98.3[89]	98.5[89 90]	102.4[89 90]	107.0[89 90]	115.0[89 90]	101.2[90 91]	105.1[90 92]	...
M - hour heure[6 41]	89.5[89]	93.8[89]	100.7[89]	100.7[89 90]	104.5[89 90]	109.1[89 90]	117.4[89 90]	103.3[90 91]	107.0[90 92]	...
F - hour heure[6 41]	79.5[89]	83.7[89]	90.1[89]	90.1[89 90]	94.2[89 90]	98.2[89 90]	105.7[89 90]	93.3[90 91]	97.6[90 92]	...
Switzerland: Swiss franc Suisse : franc suisse										
M - hour heure[6 8 41]	23.4	25.0	26.2	26.8	...	...	...	...	...	...
F - hour heure[6 8 41]	15.9	17.0	17.8	18.4	...	...	...	...	...	...
MF - month mois[3 93]	...	...	...	...	5 462.0	...	5 565.0	...	5 717.0	...
M - month mois[3 93]	...	...	...	...	5 881.0	...	5 970.0	...	6 128.0	...
F - month mois[3 93]	...	...	...	...	4 151.0	...	4 280.0	...	4 413.0	...
Tajikistan: Tajik ruble Tadjikistan : ruble tadjik										
MF - month mois[28]	...	405.4[94]	2 522.9[94]	26 905.1[94]	65 162.0[94]	1 559.0	8 080.0	14 977.0	...	...
Thailand: baht Thaïlande : baht										
MF - month mois[8 21 95]	3 357.0	3 688.0	3 986.0	4 138.0	4 229.0[96]	4 994.0[96]	5 502.0[96]	5 935.0[96]	6 389.0[96]	5 921.0[96]
M - month mois[8 21 95]	...	4 728.0	5 159.0	5 145.0	5 205.0[96]	6 234.0[96]	...	...	...	...
F - month mois[8 21 95]	...	3 016.0	3 329.0	3 558.0	3 715.0[96]	4 250.0[96]	...	...	...	...
Tonga: pa'anga Tonga : pa'anga										
MF - week semaine[8]	42.6	51.4	51.3	58.3	62.6	...	...	...	...	...
Trinidad and Tobago: Trinidad and Tobago dollar Trinité-et-Tobago : dollar de la Trinité-et-Tobago										
MF - week semaine[3]	724.5	731.3	732.3	755.0	739.9	790.6	810.1	865.4	908.7	...
Turkey: Turkish lira Turquie : livre turque										
MF - hour heure[3 13 47 62 97]	...	...	...	...	...	...	173.6	333.3	...	...
MF - month mois[3 13 47 62 98]	...	...	...	...	...	...	38 992.0	77 250.0	...	...
MF - day jour[8]	30 582.2	61 620.4	88 144.3	135 236.0	191 118.5	...	757 277.0	1 640 856.4	...	...
M - day jour[8]	31 231.1	62 140.3	91 204.1	138 746.1	191 858.8	...	758 475.1	1 661 886.1	...	...
F - day jour[8]	25 299.5	56 660.2	84 558.2	122 720.8	189 297.3	...	747 788.8	1 611 526.4	...	...
Ukraine: hryvnia Ukraine : hryvnia										
MF - month mois	263.0[99]	532.2[99]	7 494.8[99]	173.3[100]	1 499.9[100]	7 716.7[100]	131.7	148.9	157.4	188.0
United Kingdom: pound sterling Royaume-Uni : livre sterling										
MF - hour heure[101 102]	6.1	6.7	7.1	7.5	7.6	7.9	8.2	8.5	9.1	9.5
M - hour heure[101 102]	6.5	7.2	7.7	8.0	8.1	8.4	8.8	9.1	9.7	10.1
F - hour heure[101 102]	4.5	4.9	5.3	5.6	5.7	6.0	6.2	6.6	7.0	7.5

31
Wages in manufacturing
By hour, day, week or month [*cont.*]
Salaires dans les industries manufacturières
Par heure, jour, semaine ou mois [*suite*]

Country or area and unit Pays ou zone et unité	1990	1991	1992	1993	1994	1995	1996	1997	1998	1999
United States: US dollar Etats-Unis : dollar des Etats-Unis										
MF - hour heure[6][103]	10.8	11.2	11.5	11.7	12.1	12.4	12.8	13.2	13.5	13.9
United States Virgin Is.: US dollar Iles Vierges américaines : dollar des Etats-Unis										
MF - hour heure[6]	11.9	12.5	13.7	15.0	15.2	15.8	17.0	18.1	...	...
Uruguay: Uruguayan peso Uruguay : peso uruguayen										
MF - month mois[12]	3 453.2[104]	7 371.5[104]	12 564.4[104]	20 197.5[104]	28 849.4[104]	38 710.5[104]	113.3[105]	135.2[105]	151.2[105]	159.7[105]
Zimbabwe: Zimbabwe dollar Zimbabwe : dollar zimbabwéen										
MF - month mois[106]	796.1	928.1	1 123.3	1 242.1	1 559.1	1 913.8	2 301.1	2 951.5	3 699.6	5 261.5

Source:
International Labour Office (ILO), Geneva, "Yearbook of Labour Statistics, 2000" and ILO database.

† For information on recent changes in country or area nomenclature pertaining to former Czechoslovakia, Germany, Hong Kong Special Administrative Region (SAR) of China, Macao Special Administrative Region (SAR) of China, SFR of Yugoslavia and the former USSR, see Annex I - Country or area nomenclature, regional and other groupings.

†† For statistical purposes, the data for China do not include those for Hong Kong Special Administrative Region (Hong Kong SAR), Macao Special Administrative Region (Macao SAR) and Taiwan province of China.

1 Including mining and quarrying.
2 State sector.
3 Data classified according to ISIC, Rev.3.
4 Hourly wage rates.
5 Australes; 1 peso = 10,000 australes.
6 Wages earners.
7 Roubles; 1 dram = 200 roubles.
8 One month of each year.
9 Full-time adult non-managerial employees.

10 New industrial classification.
11 Roubles; 1 manat is equivalent to 10 roubles.
12 Private sector.
13 Establishments with 10 or more persons employed.
14 Daily wage rates.
15 Managerial, administrative, technical, and production workers.
16 Skilled wage earners.
17 Clerical, sales and service workers.

18 Unskilled wage earners.
19 Socialised sector.
20 Salaried employees.
21 Monthly wage rates.
22 Private sector establishments with 5 or more employees.
23 La Paz and El Alto.
24 Citizens only.
25 Cruzeiros; 1 real = approximately 2750 x 1000 cruzeiros.
26 Figures in thousands. Cruzeiros; 1 real = approximately 2750 x 1000 cruzeiros.

Source:
Bureau international du Travail (BIT), Genève, "Annuaire des statistiques du travail, 2000" et la base de données du BIT.

† Pour les modifications récentes de nomenclature de pays ou de zone concernant l'Allemagne, Hong Kong, région administrative spéciale (RAS) de Chine, Macao, région administrative spéciale (RAS) de Chine, l'ex-Tchécoslovaquie, l'ex-URSS et l'ex-Rfs de Yougoslavie, voir annexe I - Nomenclature des pays ou des zones, groupements régionaux et autres groupements.

†† Les données statistiques relatives à la Chine ne comprennent pas celles qui concernent la région administrative spéciale de Hong Kong (la RAS de Hong Kong), la région administrative spéciale de Macao (la RAS de Macao) et la province chinoise de Taiwan.

1 Y compris les industries extractives.
2 Secteur d'Etat.
3 Données classifiées selon la CITI, Rev.3.
4 Taux de salaire horaires.
5 Australes; 1 peso = 10,000 australes.
6 Ouvriers.
7 Roubles; 1 dram = 200 roubles.
8 Un mois de chaque année.
9 Salariés adultes à plein temps, non compris les cadres dirigeants.
10 Nouvelle classification industrielle.
11 Roubles; 1 manat équivaut à 10 roubles.
12 Secteur privé.
13 Etablissements occupant 10 personnes et plus.
14 Taux de salaire journaliers.
15 Directeurs, cadres administratifs supérieurs, personnel technique et travailleurs à la production.
16 Ouvriers qualifiés.
17 Personnel administratif, personnel commercial et spécialisé dans les services.
18 Ouvriers non qualifiés.
19 Secteur socialisé.
20 Employés.
21 Taux de salaire mensuels.
22 Etablissements du secteur privé occupant 5 salariés ou plus.
23 La Paz et El Alto
24 Nationaux seulement.
25 Cruzeiros; 1 real = environ 2750 x 1000 cruzeiros.
26 Données en milliers. Cruzeiros; 1 real = environ 2750 x 1000 cruzeiros.

31
Wages in manufacturing
By hour, day, week or month [cont.]
Salaires dans les industries manufacturières
Par heure, jour, semaine ou mois [suite]

27 State and cooperative sector.
28 Including major divisions 2 and 4.
29 Employees under labour contract.
30 New denomination: 1 new lev = 1000 old leva.
31 Including overtime payments.
32 Employees paid by the hour.
33 Including family allowances and the value of payments in kind.
34 Beginning April: sample design and methodology revised.

35 State-owned units, urban collective-owned units and other ownership units.
36 Total employment.
37 Median.
38 Estimates based on the results of the 1993 Census.
39 7 main cities.
40 Dinars; 1 kuna = 1,000 dinars.
41 Adults.
42 Enterprises with 25 or more employees.
43 Enterprises with 100 or more employees.
44 Enterprises with 20 or more employees.
45 One quarter of each year.
46 Estimations based on National Accounts.
47 Figures in thousands.
48 Roubles; 1 kroon = 10 roubles.
49 Including mining, quarrying and electricity.
50 Full-time employees.
51 Survey results influenced by a low response rate.

52 Establishments with 5 or more persons employed.
53 Including family allowances paid directly by the employers.

54 Excluding part-time workers and juveniles.
55 Enterprises with 5 or more employees.
56 All legal economic units.

57 Adult employees; excluding overtime payments and payments in kind.
58 Including juveniles.
59 Including payments subject to income tax.
60 Index of hourly wage rates (1990=100).
61 Index of hourly wage rates (Dec.1995=100).
62 Average of less than 12 months.
63 Regular scheduled cash earnings.
64 Private sector; establishments with 10 or more regular employees.
65 Including family allowances and mid- and end-of-year bonuses.
66 Roubles; 1 tenge = 500 roubles.
67 Including the value of payments in kind.
68 Excluding sugar and tea factories.
69 Wage-earners on daily rates of pay.

70 Regular employees.
71 One month of each year. Data classified according to ISIC, Rev.3. Excluding overtime payments.

72 Excluding overtime payments.
73 Curaçao.
74 Establishments with the equivalent of more than 2 full-time paid employees.
75 Old córdobas; 1 new córdoba = 1,000 old córdobas.

76 Incorporated entreprises.

27 Secteur d'Etat et coopératif.
28 Y compris les branches 2 et 4.
29 Salariés sous contrat de travail.
30 Nouvelle dénomination: 1 nouveau lev = 1000 anciens leva.
31 Y compris la rémunération des heures supplémentaires.
32 Salariés rémunérés à l'heure.
33 Y compris les allocations familiales et la valeur des paiements en nature.
34 A partir d'avril: plan d'échantillonnage et méthodologie révisés.
35 Unités d'Etat, unités collectives urbaines et autres.

36 Emploi total.
37 Médiane.
38 Estimations basées sur les résultats du Recensement de 1993.
39 7 villes principales.
40 Dinars; 1 kuna = 1?000 dinars.
41 Adultes.
42 Entreprises occupant 25 salariés et plus.
43 Entreprises occupant 100 salariés et plus.
44 Entreprises occupant 20 salariés et plus.
45 Un trimestre de chaque année.
46 Estimations basées sur la Comptabilité nationale.
47 Données en milliers.
48 Roubles; 1 couronne = 10 roubles.
49 Y compris les industries extractives et l'électricité.
50 Salariés à plein temps.
51 Résultats de l'enquête influencés par un taux de réponse faible.
52 Etablissements occupant 5 personnes et plus.
53 Y compris les allocations familiales payées directement par l'employeur.
54 Non compris les travailleurs à temps partiel et les jeunes.
55 Entreprises occupant 5 salariés et plus.
56 Ensemble des unités économiques dotées d'un statut juridique.
57 Salariés adultes; n.c. la rémunération des heures supplémentaires et la valeur des paiements en nature.
58 Y compris les jeunes gens.
59 Y compris les versements soumis à l'impôt sur le revenu.
60 Indice des taux de salaires horaires (1990=100).
61 Indice des taux de salaires horaires (déc.1995=100).
62 Moyenne de moins de douze mois.
63 Gains en espèce tarifés réguliers.
64 Secteur privé; établissements occupant 10 salariés stables ou plus.
65 Y compris les allocations familiales et les primes de milieu et de fin d'année.
66 Roubles; 1 tenge = 500 roubles.
67 Y compris la valeur des paiements en nature.
68 Non compris les fabriques de sucre et de thé.
69 Ouvriers rémunérés sur la base de taux de salaire journaliers.
70 Salariés stables.
71 Un mois de chaque année. Données classifiées selon la CITI, Rev.3. Non compris la rémunération des heures supplémentaires.
72 Non compris la rémunération des heures supplémentaires.
73 Curaçao.
74 Etablissements occupant plus de l'équivalent de 2 salariés à plein temps.
75 Anciens córdobas; 1 nouveau córdoba = 1?000 anciens córdobas.
76 Entreprises constituées en sociétés.

31
Wages in manufacturing
By hour, day, week or month [cont.]
Salaires dans les industries manufacturières
Par heure, jour, semaine ou mois [suite]

77 Annual averages. Urban areas.
78 Lima.
79 Computed on the basis of annual wages.
80 Zlotyche; 1 new zloty = 10,000 zlotyche.
81 Roubles; 1 leu = approximately 417 roubles.
82 New denomination: 1 new rouble = 1000 old roubles.

83 Earnings are exempted from income tax.
84 Including electricity and water.
85 Beginning this year, methodology revised.
86 Excluding enterprises with less than 25 employees.
87 Excluding enterprises with less than 20 employees.
88 Including employers' non-statutory contributions to certain funds.
89 One quarter of each year. Including holidays and sick-leave payments and the value of payments in kind.

90 Private sector. Data classified according to ISIC, Rev.3.
91 One quarter of each year. Excluding holidays, sick-leave and overtime payments.

92 Average of less than 12 months. Excluding holidays, sick-leave and overtime payments.

93 Standardised monthly earnings (40 hours x 4 1/3 weeks).
94 Roubles; 1 Tajik rouble = 100 roubles.
95 Average wage rates for normal/usual hours of work.

96 Excluding public enterprises.
97 Excluding overtime payments and irregular bonuses and allowances.
98 Including overtime payments and irregular bonuses and allowances.
99 Roubles; 1 rouble = 25 karbovanets.
100 Figures in thousands. Karbovanets: 1 hrivna = 100,000 karbovanets.
101 One month of each year. Data classified according to ISIC, Rev.3.
102 Excluding Northern Ireland. Full-time employees on adult rates of pay. Excluding overtime payments.
103 Private sector; production workers.
104 Index of average monthly earnings (October - December 1984 = 100).
105 Index of average monthly earnings (December 1995 = 100).
106 Including employers' contributions to pension, provident and other funds.

77 Moyennes annuelles. Régions urbaines.
78 Lima.
79 Calculés sur la base de salaires annuels.
80 Zlotyche; 1 nouveau zloty = 10?000 zlotyche.
81 Roubles; 1 leu = environ 417 roubles.
82 Nouvelle dénomination: 1 nouveau rouble = 1000 anciens roubles.
83 Les gains sont exempts de l'impôt sur le revenu.
84 Y compris l'électricité et l'eau.
85 A partir de cette année, méthodologie révisée.
86 Non compris les entreprises occupant moins de 25 salariés.
87 Non compris les entreprises occupant moins de 20 salariés.
88 Y compris les cotisations des employeurs à certains fonds privés.
89 Un trimestre de chaque année. Y compris les versements pour les vacances et congés de maladie et la valeur des paiements en nature.
90 Secteur privé. Données classifiées selon la CITI, Rev.3.
91 Un trimestre de chaque année. Non compris les

versements pour les vacances, congés maladie ainsi que la rémunération des heures supplémentaires.
92 Moyenne de moins de douze mois. Non compris les versements pour les vacances, congés maladie ainsi que la rémunération des heures supplémentaires.
93 Gains mensuels standardisés (40 heures x 4 1/3 semaines).
94 Roubles; 1 rouble Tajik = 100 roubles.
95 Taux de salaire moyens pour la durée normale/usuelle du travail.
96 Non compris les entreprises publiques.
97 Non compris la rémunération des heures supplémentaires et les prestations versées irrégulièrement.
98 Y compris la rémunération des heures suppl émentaires et les prestations versées irrégulièrement.
99 Roubles; 1 rouble = 25 karbovanets.
100 Données en milliers. Karbovanets; 1 hrivna = 100,000 karbovanets.
101 Un mois de chaque année. Données classifiées selon la CITI, Rev.3.
102 Non compris l'Irlande du Nord. Salariés à plein temps rémunérés sur la base de taux de salaire pour adultes. Non compris la rémunération des heures supplémentaires.
103 Secteur privé; travailleurs à la production.
104 Indices des gains mensuels moyens (octobre - decembre 1984 = 100).
105 Indices des gains mensuels moyens (decembre 1995 = 100).
106 Y compris les cotisations des employeurs aux fonds de pension, de prévoyance et autres fonds.

32
Producers prices and wholesale prices
Prix à la production et des prix de gros
Index numbers: 1990 = 100
Indices : 1990 = 100

Country or area and groups	1994	1995	1996	1997	1998	1999	2000	Pays ou zone et groupes
Argentina								**Argentine**
Domestic supply[12]	226	241	248	249	241	232	241	Offre intérieure[12]
Domestic production	229	243	252	253	245	236	247	Production intérieure
Agricultural products[2]	223	245	283	254	237	189	184	Produits agricoles[2]
Industrial products[23]	232	247	248	252	249	241	244	Produits industriels[23]
Import products[3]	190	211	204	196	187	177	177	Produits importés[3]
Australia								**Australie**
Industrial products[2345]	106	110	111	112	109	114	...	Produits industriels[2345]
Raw materials[4]	103	106	102	105	102	111	...	Matières premières[4]
Austria								**Autriche**
Domestic supply[26]	101	102	102	102	102	101	105	Offre intérieure[26]
Agricultural products	91	86	76	74	77	75	77	Produits agricoles
Consumers' goods[2]	105	107	106	106	107	106	110	Biens de consommation[2]
Capital goods[2]	100	100	101	101	100	98	96	Biens d'équipement[2]
Bangladesh								**Bangladesh**
Domestic supply[246]	115	121	127	128	135	144	141	Offre intérieure[246]
Agricultural products[247]	113	119	126	126	133	146	142	Produits agricoles[247]
Industrial products[2347]	122	125	131	132	137	128	138	Produits industriels[2347]
Raw materials[4]	107	117	120	123	...	134	131	Matières premières[4]
Belgium								**Belgique**
Domestic supply	99	102	102	104	103	...	...	Offre intérieure
Agricultural products[2]	104	106	107	111	109	107	111	Produits agricoles[2]
Industrial products	99	101	102	104	103	102	111	Produits industriels
Intermediate products	94	97	98	99	97	97	111	Produits intermédiaires
Consumers' goods	101	107	108	111	110	109	112	Biens de consommation
Capital goods	107	108	109	109	109	108	108	Biens d'équipement
Bolivia								**Bolivie**
Agricultural products	151	167	185	...	...	...	...	Produits agricoles
Industrial products	...	...	174	179	187	190	200	Produits industriels
Import products	167	179	194	...	...	...	...	Produits importés
Brazil								**Brésil**
Domestic supply[89]	100	159	169	181	189	220	261	Offre intérieure[89]
Agricultural products[89]	100	163	172	200	215	252	306	Produits agricoles[89]
Industrial products[89]	100	155	165	172	175	203	237	Produits industriels[89]
Raw materials[89]	100	150	162	179	179	212	251	Matières premières[89]
Consumers' goods[89]	100	169	177	192	212	243	288	Biens de consommation[89]
Capital goods[8]	100	155	172	176	178	198	220	Biens d'équipement[8]
Canada								**Canada**
Raw materials[10]	108	118	122	120	103	111	136	Matières premières[10]
Chile								**Chili**
Domestic supply	159	171	181	184	188	198	220	Offre intérieure
Domestic production	163	178	190	195	197	205	229	Production intérieure
Agricultural products	163	180	193	197	204	200	216	Produits agricoles
Industrial products[6]	168	179	190	193	198	210	235	Produits industriels[6]
Import products	136	140	147	145	152	165	182	Produits importés

32
Producers prices and wholesale prices
Index numbers: 1990 = 100 [cont.]
Prix à la production et des prix de gros
Indices : 1990 = 100 [suite]

Country or area and groups	1994	1995	1996	1997	1998	1999	2000	Pays ou zone et groupes
China, Hong Kong SAR†								**Chine, Hong Kong RAS†**
Industrial products	108	111	111	111	109	107	107	Produits industriels
Colombia								**Colombie**
Domestic supply[2][11]	55	64	73	86	97	100	...	Offre intérieure[2][11]
Domestic production[11]	54	62	72	85	97	100	...	Production intérieure[11]
Agricultural products[11]	56	63	73	90	99	100	...	Produits agricoles[11]
Industrial products[11]	55	64	73	84	97	100	...	Produits industriels[11]
Import products[11]	60	72	76	88	99	100	...	Produits importés[11]
Raw materials[11]	56	62	71	84	94	100	...	Matières premières[11]
Intermediate products[11]	57	66	75	87	98	100	...	Produits intermédiaires[11]
Croatia								**Croatie**
Industrial products[12]	97	98	99	100	98	101	111	Produits industriels[12]
Consumers' goods[12]	92	94	98	100	99	99	100	Biens de consommation[12]
Capital goods[12]	103	100	102	100	101	105	110	Biens d'équipement[12]
Cyprus								**Chypre**
Industrial products	112	117	122	122	124	126	135	Produits industriels
Czech Republic								**République tchèque**
Agricultural products	120	129	140	146	147	131	...	Produits agricoles
Denmark								**Danemark**
Domestic supply[2][9]	100	103	104	106	105	106	...	Offre intérieure[2][9]
Domestic production[2][9]	100	103	105	107	106	107	...	Production intérieure[2][9]
Import products[9]	100	103	103	105	104	104	...	Produits importés[9]
Consumers' goods	101	103	104	106	106	106	...	Biens de consommation
Ecuador								**Equateur**
Agricultural products	...	12	...	...	...	...	110	Produits agricoles
Egypt								**Egypte**
Domestic supply[4][6]	153	163	176	183	186	188	185	Offre intérieure[4][6]
Raw materials[4]	104	113	133	140	133	132	129	Matières premières[4]
Intermediate products[4]	138	151	162	165	169	163	162	Produits intermédiaires[4]
Capital goods[4]	145	153	158	163	165	159	158	Biens d'équipement[4]
El Salvador								**El Salvador**
Domestic supply[13]	125	138	145	147	138	136	...	Offre intérieure[13]
Domestic production	131	133	147	148	142	147	...	Production intérieure
Import products	117	125	130	126	119	119	...	Produits importés
Finland								**Finlande**
Domestic supply	106	107	106	108	106	106	115	Offre intérieure
Domestic production	103	104	102	104	105	104	111	Production intérieure
Import products	119	119	120	121	115	115	130	Produits importés
Raw materials	105	108	105	107	100	98	109	Matières premières
Consumers' goods	110	107	108	109	112	113	114	Biens de consommation
Capital goods	105	105	105	108	109	109	113	Biens d'équipement
France								**France**
Agricultural products	88	89	89	90	90	86	88	Produits agricoles
Germany †								**Allemagne †**
Domestic supply[14]	102	104	104	105	103	102	106	Offre intérieure[14]
Domestic production[14]	100	103	100	101	100	...	...	Production intérieure[14]

32
Producers prices and wholesale prices
Index numbers: 1990 = 100 [*cont.*]
Prix à la production et des prix de gros
Indices : 1990 = 100 [*suite*]

Country or area and groups	1994	1995	1996	1997	1998	1999	2000	Pays ou zone et groupes
Agricultural products[14]	92	92	91	93	88	84	89	Produits agricoles[14]
Import products[14]	97	97	96	97	97	97	108	Produits importés[14]
Raw materials[14]	95	97	92	99	88	...	...	Matières premières[14]
Intermediate products[14]	...	...	100	101	100	...	...	Produits intermédiaires[14]
Consumers' goods[14]	105	106	107	108	108	...	...	Biens de consommation[14]
Capital goods[14]	105	106	107	108	109	...	...	Biens d'équipement[14]
Greece								**Grèce**
Domestic supply[15 16]	153	166	176	182	189	193	208	Offre intérieure[15 16]
Domestic production[15 16]	154	166	179	186	192	199	215	Production intérieure[15 16]
Agricultural products[15 17]	152	164	171	178	192	198	204	Produits agricoles[15 17]
Industrial products[15 16]	154	166	180	187	193	200	216	Produits industriels[15 16]
Import products[15 16]	157	166	170	174	183	184	196	Produits importés[15 16]
Guatemala								**Guatemala**
Domestic supply	155	166	202	222	228	236	260	Offre intérieure
India								**Inde**
Domestic supply[18]	151	165	174	184	197	203	210	Offre intérieure[18]
Agricultural products[18]	158	173	189	201	225	237	249	Produits agricoles[18]
Industrial products[3 18]	146	162	169	176	184	188	188	Produits industriels[3 18]
Raw materials[18 19]	154	170	181	189	210	219	223	Matières premières[18 19]
Indonesia								**Indonésie**
Domestic supply[16]	121	135	145	158	319	355	404	Offre intérieure[16]
Domestic production	139	157	168	179	296	326	406	Production intérieure
Agricultural products	156	186	209	233	393	533	604	Produits agricoles
Industrial products[3]	131	146	151	156	258	325	344	Produits industriels[3]
Import products[16]	113	120	127	136	313	325	349	Produits importés[16]
Raw materials	108	125	141	161	357	352	452	Matières premières
Intermediate products	123	135	141	148	317	342	376	Produits intermédiaires
Consumers' goods	127	141	151	164	299	395	440	Biens de consommation
Capital goods	121	128	132	139	248	291	296	Biens d'équipement
Iran (Islamic Rep. of)								**Iran (Rép. islamique d')**
Domestic supply[27]	301	483	582	644	740	860	1 013	Offre intérieure[27]
Domestic production[27]	302	423	573	619	749	868	1 015	Production intérieure[27]
Agricultural products[27]	268	409	505	541	690	822	943	Produits agricoles[27]
Industrial products[27]	291	415	493	486	536	663	882	Produits industriels[27]
Import products[27]	314	477	668	731	798	910	1 067	Produits importés[27]
Raw materials[27]	287	410	572	598	608	691	832	Matières premières[27]
Ireland								**Irlande**
Domestic supply[2 20]	108	110	111	110	112	112	119	Offre intérieure[2 20]
Agricultural products[2 20]	106	108	103	96	96	91	...	Produits agricoles[2 20]
Industrial products[2 3 20]	108	111	112	111	112	113	120	Produits industriels[2 3 20]
Capital goods[7]	110	113	115	117	120	123	128	Biens d'équipement[7]
Israel								**Israël**
Industrial products[16]	150	166	180	192	201	214	218	Produits industriels[16]
Italy								**Italie**
Domestic supply[2 16]	117	130	132	134	135	...	...	Offre intérieure[2 16]
Agricultural products[27]	109	122	127	124	...	...	...	Produits agricoles[27]

32
Producers prices and wholesale prices
Index numbers: 1990 = 100 [cont.]
Prix à la production et des prix de gros
Indices : 1990 = 100 [suite]

Country or area and groups	1994	1995	1996	1997	1998	1999	2000	Pays ou zone et groupes
Industrial products[2][16]	119	130	133	136	...	...	...	Produits industriels[2][16]
Consumers' goods	120	129	133	134	136	...	...	Biens de consommation
Capital goods	116	130	133	137	139	...	...	Biens d'équipement
Japan								**Japon**
Domestic supply[2]	95	94	93	95	93	91	91	Offre intérieure[2]
Domestic production	97	96	95	94	94	92	93	Production intérieure
Agricultural products[7]	98	90	90	90	85	88	86	Produits agricoles[7]
Industrial products[7]	97	96	95	95	94	92	93	Produits industriels[7]
Import products	98	104	103	102	92	93	102	Produits importés
Raw materials	80	80	88	93	83	78	89	Matières premières
Intermediate products	93	93	92	94	92	90	91	Produits intermédiaires
Consumers' goods	99	97	96	97	96	95	94	Biens de consommation
Capital goods	97	95	93	93	93	90	88	Biens d'équipement
Jordan								**Jordanie**
Domestic supply[2]	119	117	119	121	122	116	...	Offre intérieure[2]
Korea, Republic of								**Corée, République de**
Domestic supply	112	117	121	125	141	107	140	Offre intérieure
Agricultural products[7][21]	128	134	134	136	142	157	151	Produits agricoles[7][21]
Industrial products	109	115	117	121	139	134	137	Produits industriels
Raw materials	110	118	126	140	169	157	192	Matières premières
Intermediate products	108	116	117	123	153	139	145	Produits intermédiaires
Consumers' goods	118	121	126	131	144	147	147	Biens de consommation
Capital goods	110	112	112	114	139	132	128	Biens d'équipement
Kuwait								**Koweït**
Domestic supply	108	110	115	114	112	111	111	Offre intérieure
Agricultural products	105	113	111	112	115	109	...	Produits agricoles
Raw materials	103	103	110	115	114	115	...	Matières premières
Intermediate products	110	111	119	123	121	114	...	Produits intermédiaires
Consumers' goods	115	117	126	128	128	126	...	Biens de consommation
Capital goods	92	95	98	89	84	86	...	Biens d'équipement
Latvia								**Lettonie**
Domestic supply[22]	254	284	323	336	343	329	331	Offre intérieure[22]
Lithuania								**Lituanie**
Domestic supply	28 445	36 504	42 796	44 611	41 636	42 912	51 238	Offre intérieure
Luxembourg								**Luxembourg**
Industrial products	94	98	94	95	97	93	98	Produits industriels
Import products	107	111	106	109	112	110	116	Produits importés
Intermediate products	88	92	86	88	90	84	90	Produits intermédiaires
Consumers' goods[23]	101	103	104	104	104	104	105	Biens de consommation[23]
Capital goods	106	108	111	112	114	113	117	Biens d'équipement
Malaysia								**Malaisie**
Domestic supply	109	113	115	118	131	127	131	Offre intérieure
Domestic production	110	115	118	121	135	130	134	Production intérieure
Import products	103	104	104	107	117	116	118	Produits importés
Mexico								**Mexique**
Domestic supply[6][24]	151	214	278	327	379	438	474	Offre intérieure[6][24]

32
Producers prices and wholesale prices
Index numbers: 1990 = 100 [*cont.*]
Prix à la production et des prix de gros
Indices : 1990 = 100 [*suite*]

Country or area and groups	1994	1995	1996	1997	1998	1999	2000	Pays ou zone et groupes
Agricultural products	167	206	287	333	349	434	514	Produits agricoles
Raw materials	138	211	287	325	358	400	447	Matières premières
Consumers' goods[7 24]	158	222	288	349	404	455	503	Biens de consommation[7 24]
Capital goods[6 7 24]	150	207	266	312	363	418	457	Biens d'équipement[6 7 24]
Morocco								**Maroc**
Domestic supply	117	125	130	128	132	134	...	Offre intérieure
Agricultural products	119	132	140	134	138	136	141	Produits agricoles
Industrial products	116	120	124	126	129	130	...	Produits industriels
Netherlands								**Pays-Bas**
Industrial products	102	100	101	104	102	102	110	Produits industriels
Import products	92	100	104	109	102	106	132	Produits importés
Raw materials	95	100	101	104	99	99	111	Matières premières
Intermediate products	100	100	101	104	100	100	111	Produits intermédiaires
Consumers' goods	105	100	102	104	103	104	111	Biens de consommation
Capital goods	104	100	101	103	105	106	107	Biens d'équipement
New Zealand								**Nouvelle-Zélande**
Agricultural products[2 12]	...	101	99	100	99	99	110	Produits agricoles[2 12]
Industrial products[2 12 25]	...	102	101	100	101	102	109	Produits industriels[2 12 25]
Intermediate products[12 26]	...	99	100	100	101	102	108	Produits intermédiaires[12 26]
Norway								**Norvège**
Domestic supply	105	107	108	110	110	112	117	Offre intérieure
Import products	98	99	98	97	98	96	101	Produits importés
Raw materials	96	98	97	101	100	101	109	Matières premières
Intermediate products	104	109	110	111	113	113	116	Produits intermédiaires
Consumers' goods	108	109	111	113	114	116	119	Biens de consommation
Capital goods	108	111	112	113	114	115	116	Biens d'équipement
Pakistan								**Pakistan**
Domestic supply[2 4 6]	144	168	199	237	227	229	238	Offre intérieure[2 4 6]
Agricultural products[4]	165	184	206	221	236	237	241	Produits agricoles[4]
Industrial products[4]	151	165	185	189	195	201	204	Produits industriels[4]
Raw materials[4]	155	179	216	233	256	245	236	Matières premières[4]
Panama								**Panama**
Domestic supply	108	111	113	111	106	109	119	Offre intérieure
Peru								**Pérou**
Domestic supply	1 111	1 228	1 344	1 443	1 548	1 624	1 694	Offre intérieure
Domestic production	1 103	1 226	1 341	...	1 545	1 606	1 673	Production intérieure
Agricultural products[27]	1 330	1 468	1 592	1 763	2 061	1 891	1 793	Produits agricoles[27]
Industrial products[3 7]	1 035	1 155	1 264	1 355	1 437	1 525	1 616	Produits industriels[3 7]
Import products	1 035	1 116	1 230	1 295	1 376	1 513	1 608	Produits importés
Philippines								**Philippines**
Domestic supply[28]	127	131	143	...	162	172	175	Offre intérieure[28]
Romania								**Roumanie**
Industrial products	3 999	7 391	11 236	28 390	37 810	53 757	81 488	Produits industriels
Singapore								**Singapour**
Domestic supply[6]	87	87	85	81	79	80	88	Offre intérieure[6]

32
Producers prices and wholesale prices
Index numbers: 1990 = 100 [cont.]
Prix à la production et des prix de gros
Indices : 1990 = 100 [suite]

Country or area and groups	1994	1995	1996	1997	1998	1999	2000	Pays ou zone et groupes
Domestic production[2 3 29]	80	81	77	70	67	67	72	Production intérieure[2 3 29]
Import products[29]	91	91	87	84	83	85	92	Produits importés[29]
Slovenia								**Slovénie**
Agricultural products	858	972	1 077	1 149	1 198	1 206	...	Produits agricoles
Industrial products	1 015	1 145	1 222	1 297	1 374	1 404	...	Produits industriels
Consumers' goods	1 082	1 212	1 305	1 408	1 533	1 535	...	Biens de consommation
Capital goods	973	1 028	1 104	1 115	1 136	1 217	...	Biens d'équipement
South Africa								**Afrique du Sud**
Domestic supply[30]	139	152	164	175	181	190	209	Offre intérieure[30]
Domestic production[30]	143	157	168	181	188	197	212	Production intérieure[30]
Agricultural products	155	166	174	188	191	194	202	Produits agricoles
Industrial products[3]	139	153	166	180	188	195	210	Produits industriels[3]
Import products	125	134	141	148	153	164	189	Produits importés
Spain								**Espagne**
Domestic supply[16]	111	118	120	121	120	121	...	Offre intérieure[16]
Consumers' goods	115	121	126	127	127	129	...	Biens de consommation
Capital goods	109	113	116	117	118	119	...	Biens d'équipement
Sri Lanka								**Sri Lanka**
Domestic supply	134	146	172	188	199	198	...	Offre intérieure
Domestic production	141	151	168	179	188	194	...	Production intérieure
Import products	121	134	151	161	161	161	...	Produits importés
Consumers' goods	130	138	173	189	203	203	...	Biens de consommation
Capital goods	156	172	182	192	210	227	...	Biens d'équipement
Sweden								**Suède**
Domestic supply[2 16 31]	111	120	118	119	119	120	127	Offre intérieure[2 16 31]
Domestic production[2 16 31]	107	116	116	117	117	117	121	Production intérieure[2 16 31]
Import products[16 31]	117	124	120	122	121	124	134	Produits importés[16 31]
Switzerland								**Suisse**
Domestic supply[2 6]	100	100	98	98	97	95	98	Offre intérieure[2 6]
Domestic production[2 6]	102	102	99	99	98	98	98	Production intérieure[2 6]
Agricultural products[2]	97	91	85	84	81	79	83	Produits agricoles[2]
Industrial products	102	103	101	100	99	98	98	Produits industriels
Import products[6]	96	96	92	94	92	90	96	Produits importés[6]
Raw materials	103	93	88	89	84	81	88	Matières premières
Consumers' goods	104	104	103	103	103	104	104	Biens de consommation
Thailand								**Thaïlande**
Domestic supply[2 9]	109	119	125	130	147	138	157	Offre intérieure[2 9]
Agricultural products	113	133	145	148	171	147	145	Produits agricoles
Industrial products[3]	108	117	120	125	139	136	141	Produits industriels[3]
Raw materials	110	134	138	144	173	138	139	Matières premières
Intermediate products	109	118	123	128	150	144	142	Produits intermédiaires
Consumers' goods	119	123	130	137	160	148	151	Biens de consommation
TFYR of Macedonia								**L'ex-R.y. Macédoine**
Domestic supply[32]	88	93	92	96	100	100	109	Offre intérieure[32]
Consumers' goods[32]	89	90	92	97	100	101	103	Biens de consommation[32]

32
Producers prices and wholesale prices
Index numbers: 1990 = 100 [cont.]
Prix à la production et des prix de gros
Indices : 1990 = 100 [suite]

Country or area and groups	1994	1995	1996	1997	1998	1999	2000	Pays ou zone et groupes
Capital goods[32]	89	90	92	96	100	102	103	Biens d'équipement[32]
Trinidad and Tobago								**Trinité-et-Tobago**
Industrial products	112	116	119	122	124	126	...	Produits industriels
Tunisia								**Tunisie**
Agricultural products	122	135	...	147	153	...	...	Produits agricoles
Industrial products	108	192	199	...	...	...	...	Produits industriels
Turkey								**Turquie**
Domestic supply[2 16 33]	880	1 638	2 881	5 238	9 000	13 776	20 861	Offre intérieure[2 16 33]
Agricultural products	788	1 638	3 054	5 707	10 659	15 117	...	Produits agricoles
Industrial products	890	1 611	2 746	4 959	8 265	12 991	...	Produits industriels
United Kingdom								**Royaume-Uni**
Agricultural products	106	116	114	99	90	86	84	Produits agricoles
Industrial products[3]	116	120	123	123	123	123	124	Produits industriels[3]
Raw materials	95	103	102	94	85	87	97	Matières premières
United States								**Etats-Unis**
Domestic supply[2]	104	107	110	110	107	108	114	Offre intérieure[2]
Agricultural products[2]	95	96	109	101	93	88	89	Produits agricoles[2]
Industrial products[2 34]	104	109	110	111	108	109	116	Produits industriels[2 34]
Raw materials	93	94	104	102	89	90	110	Matières premières
Intermediate products	103	109	110	110	107	108	113	Produits intermédiaires
Consumers' goods	104	106	110	110	109	111	202	Biens de consommation
Capital goods	109	111	113	113	112	112	113	Biens d'équipement
Uruguay								**Uruguay**
Domestic supply[2 6 35]	515	703	887	1 032	1 128	1 118	1 194	Offre intérieure[2 6 35]
Domestic production[35]	534	735	919	1 069	1 168	1 158	1 237	Production intérieure[35]
Agricultural products[35]	523	748	918	1 067	1 170	1 062	1 146	Produits agricoles[35]
Industrial products[6 35]	546	742	934	1 086	1 184	1 208	1 285	Produits industriels[6 35]
Venezuela								**Venezuela**
Domestic supply[6]	363	573	1 164	1 511	1 846	2 145	2 427	Offre intérieure[6]
Domestic production[6]	372	597	1 191	1 580	1 966	2 313	2 703	Production intérieure[6]
Agricultural products[6]	316	500	793	1 089	1 635	2 265	3 682	Produits agricoles[6]
Industrial products[6]	367	579	1 194	1 545	1 863	2 136	2 438	Produits industriels[6]
Import products[6]	341	514	1 098	1 339	1 548	1 727	1 894	Produits importés[6]
Yugoslavia								**Yougoslavie**
Domestic supply[32]	15	28	64	75	100	135	...	Offre intérieure[32]
Agricultural products[32]	15	28	64	75	100	144	336	Produits agricoles[32]
Industrial products[32]	22	35	67	80	100	144	298	Produits industriels[32]
Consumers' goods[32]	20	35	66	80	100	142	264	Biens de consommation[32]
Capital goods[32]	22	36	68	75	100	160	360	Biens d'équipement[32]
Zambia								**Zambie**
Domestic supply	1 743	2 603	...	...	...	...	...	Offre intérieure
Domestic production	1 475	2 081	...	...	...	...	...	Production intérieure
Agricultural products	2 431	2 900	...	...	...	...	...	Produits agricoles
Industrial products	1 426	2 751	...	...	...	...	...	Produits industriels
Consumers' goods	1 847	5 475	...	...	...	...	...	Biens de consommation
Capital goods	1 390	1 718	...	...	...	...	...	Biens d'équipement

32
Producers prices and wholesale prices
Index numbers: 1990 = 100 [cont.]
Prix à la production et des prix de gros
Indices : 1990 = 100 [suite]

Country or area and groups	1994	1995	1996	1997	1998	1999	2000	Pays ou zone et groupes
Zimbabwe								**Zimbabwe**
Domestic supply	315	380	445	503	662	1 048	...	Offre intérieure
Domestic production	315	381	446	503	661	1 048	...	Production intérieure

Source:
United Nations Statistics Division, New York, price
statistics database.

† For information on recent changes in country or
area nomenclature pertaining to former Czechoslovakia,
Germany, Hong Kong Special Administrative Region (SAR) of
China, Macao Special Administrative Region (SAR) of China,
SFR of Yugoslavia and the former USSR, see Annex I - Country
or area nomenclature, regional and other groupings.

1 Domestic agricultural products only.
2 Including exported products.
3 Manufacturing industry only.
4 Annual average refers to average of 12 months beginning
   July.
5 Prices relate only to products for sale or transfer to other
   sectors or for use as capital equipment.

6 Excluding mining and quarrying.
7 Including imported products.
8 Base: 1994=100.
9 Agricultural products and products of manufacturing
   industry.
10 Valued at purchasers' values.
11 Base: 1999=100.
12 Base: 1997=100.
13 San Salvador.
14 Base: 1991=100.
15 Finished products only.
16 Excluding electricity, gas and water.
17 Including mining and quarrying.
18 Annual average refers to average of 12 months beginning
   April.
19 Primary articles include food, non-food articles and
   minerals.
20 Excluding Value Added Tax.
21 Including marine foods.
22 Base: 1992=100.
23 Beginning 1994, durable goods only.
24 Mexico City.
25 Including all outputs of manufacturing.
26 Including all industrial inputs.
27 Excluding fishing.
28 Metro Manila.
29 Not a sub-division of the domestic supply index.
30 Excluding gold mining.
31 Excluding agriculture.
32 Base: 1998=100.
33 Excluding industrial finished goods.
34 Excluding foods and feeds production.
35 Montevideo.

Source:
Organisation des Nations Unies, Division de statistique, New
York, la base de données pour les statistiques des prix.

† Pour les modifications récentes de nomenclature
de pays ou de zone concernant l'Allemagne, Hong Kong, région
administrative spéciale (RAS) de Chine, Macao, région
administrative spéciale (RAS) de Chine,
l'ex-Tchécoslovaquie, l'ex-URSS et l'ex-Rfs de Yougoslavie,
voir annexe I - Nomenclature des pays ou des zones,
groupements régionaux et autres groupements.

1 Produits agricoles interiéurs seulement.
2 Y compris les produits exportés.
3 Industries manufacturières seulement.
4 La moyenne annuelle est la moyenne de douze mois de compter
   à partir de juillet.
5 Uniquement les prix des produits destinés à être vendus ou
   transférés à d'autres secteurs ou à être utilisés comme
   biens d'équipement.
6 Non compris les industries extractives.
7 Y compris les produits importés.
8 Base: 1994=100.
9 Produits agricoles at produits des industries
   manufacturières.
10 A la valeur d'acquisition.
11 Base : 1999=100.
12 Base: 1997=100.
13 San Salvador.
14 Base : 1991=100.
15 Produits finis uniquement.
16 Non compris l'électricité, le gaz et l'eau.
17 Y compris les industries extractives.
18 La moyenne annuelle est la moyenne de 12 mois de compter à
   partir d'avril.
19 Les articles primaires comprennent des articles des produits
   alimentaires, non-alimentaires et des minéraux.
20 Non compris taxe sur la valeur ajoutée.
21 Y compris l'alimentation marine.
22 Base : 1992=100.
23 De compter à partir de 1994, biens durables seulement.
24 Mexico.
25 Y compris toute la production du secteur manufacturière.
26 Tous les intrants industriels.
27 Non compris la pêche.
28 L'agglomération de Manille.
29 N'est pas un élément de l'indice de l'offre intérieure.
30 Non compris l'extraction de l'or.
31 Non compris l'agriculture.
32 Base : 1998=100.
33 Non compris les produits finis industriels.
34 Non compris les produits alimentaires et d'affouragement.
35 Montevideo.

33
Consumer price index numbers
Indices des prix à la consommation
All items and food; 1990 = 100

Ensemble des prix et alimentation; 1990 = 100

Country or area Pays ou zone	1990	1991	1992	1993	1994	1995	1996	1997	1998	1999
Afghanistan[1,2] **Afghanistan**[1,2]	100	144	...	...	...	...	...	...	...	...
Food Aliments[1]	100	...	...	...	...	...	...	...	...	...
Albania[4] **Albanie**[4]	23[3]	31	100	185	227	244	276	367	443	444
Food[4,5] Aliments[4,5]	21[3]	45[3]	100	187	214	229	263	358	433	432
Algeria **Algérie**	100	125	164	200	263	338	407	431	458	468
Food Aliments	100	121	152	189	266	343	417	437	467	472
American Samoa[2] **Samoa américaines**[2]	100	104	109	109	111	113	118	...	...	...
Food Aliments	100	104	108	107	108	109	112	...	...	...
Angola[1] **Angola**[1]	...	100[6]	399[6]	5 904[6]	61 982[6]	2 771[7]	117 653[7]	375 531[7]	...	...
Food Aliments[1]	...	100[6]	409[6]	6 856[6]	70 425[6]	2 533[7]	100 167[7]	201 844[7]	...	...
Anguilla **Anguilla**	100	105	108	111	116	117	121	122	125	126
Food Aliments	100	104	107	111	113	116	119	120	119	122
Antigua and Barbuda **Antigua-et-Barbuda**	100	106	...	100[8]	106[8]	108[8,9]	112[8]	112[8]	116[8]	117[8]
Food Aliments	100	106	...	100[8]	112[8]	115[8,9]	119[8]	118[8]	119[8]	123[8]
Argentina[1,10] **Argentine**[1,10]	100	272	339	375	391	404	405	407	411	406
Food Aliments[1,10]	100	261	340	375	380	391	389	387	393	379
Armenia[7] **Arménie**[7]	...	...	...	0	100	276	328	373	406	408
Food Aliments[7]	...	...	...	0	100	291	334	362	384	362
Aruba **Aruba**	100	106	110	115	123	127[11]	131	135	137	...
Food Aliments	100	105	109	113	120	125[11]	130	134	136	...
Australia **Australie**	100	103	104	106	108	113	116	116	117	119
Food Aliments	100	103	105	107	109	113	116	119	122	126
Austria **Autriche**	100	103	107	111	115	117	119[11]	121	122	123
Food Aliments	100	104	108	111	113	113	114[11]	116	118	118
Azerbaijan[8] **Azerbaïdjan**[8]	...	1	8	100	1 764	9 025	10 817	11 218	11 131	10 182
Food[5,8] Aliments[5,8]	...	1	7	100	1 793	9 369	11 016	10 964	10 817	9 630
Bahamas **Bahamas**	100	107	113	116	118	121[11]	122	123	125	126

33
Consumer price index numbers
All items and food; 1990 = 100 [*cont.*]
Indices des prix à la consommation
Ensemble des prix et alimentation; 1990 = 100 [*suite*]

Country or area Pays ou zone	1990	1991	1992	1993	1994	1995	1996	1997	1998	1999
Food Aliments	100	109	111	112	111	113[11]	116	118	121	121
Bahrain **Bahreïn**	**100**	**101**	**101**	**103**	**104**	**107**	**107**	**100**[12]	**100**[12]	**98**[12]
Food Aliments	100	102	102	102	101	107	108	100[12]	101[12]	100[12]
Bangladesh[7 13] **Bangladesh**[7 13]	...	...	...	...	100	110	113	119	129	...
Food[7 13] Aliments[7 13]	...	...	...	...	100	111	113	118	130	...
Barbados **Barbade**	**100**	**106**	**113**	**114**	**114**	**117**[11]	**120**	**129**	**127**	**129**
Food Aliments	100	105	105	105	105	110[11]	115	130	124	128
Belarus **Bélarus**	**100**	**9**[4]	**100**[4]	**1 290**[4]	**29 946**[4]	**242 349**[4]	**370 043**[4]	**606 280**[4]	**1 049 047**[4]	**4 130 518**[4]
Food Aliments	100	9[4]	100[4]	1 515[4]	37 477[4]	285 492[4]	427 011[4]	725 423[4]	1 275 657[4]	5 264 124[4]
Belgium **Belgique**	**100**	**103**[11]	**106**	**109**	**111**	**113**	**115**[11]	**117**	**118**	**119**
Food Aliments	100	102[11]	102	101	103	104	105[11]	107	109	109
Belize **Belize**	**100**	**106**	**102**[6]	**104**[6]	**107**[6]	**110**[6]	**117**[6]	**118**[6]	**117**[6]	**115**[6]
Food Aliments	100	106	103[56]	105[56]	106[56]	109[56]	116[56]	118[56]	116[56]	115[56]
Benin[14] **Bénin**[14]	...	...	**100**	**101**[9]	**140**	**160**	**166**	**172**[11]	**182**	**182**
Food[1] Aliments[1]	100	100	100[4]	100[49]	135[4]	161[4]	183[4 11]	189[4]	203[4]	202[4]
Bermuda **Bermudes**	**100**	**104**	**107**	**110**	**112**	**115**	**118**	**121**	**123**	**126**
Food Aliments	100	103	103	105	106	110	113	116	119	121
Bhutan **Bhoutan**	**100**	**112**	**130**	**145**	**155**	**170**	**185**	**197**	**217**	...
Food[5] Aliments[5]	100	113	134	145	150	165	180	187	208	...
Bolivia[14] **Bolivie**[14]	**100**	**120**	**136**	**148**	**159**	**176**	**197**	**207**	**223**	**227**
Food[14] Aliments[14]	100	120	138	147	160	180	205	212	224	...
Botswana **Botswana**	**100**	**112**	**130**[11]	**148**	**164**	**181**	**200**[11]	**217**	**231**	**248**
Food Aliments	100	112	133[11]	151	165	183	207[11]	228	242	259
Brazil **Brésil**	**100**	**533**	**5 605**	**113 626**	**100**[7]	**166**[7]	**192**[7]	**205**[7]	**212**[7]	**222**[7]
Food Aliments	100	489	5 367	109 994	100[7]	158[7]	168[7]	169[7]	174[7]	180[7]
British Virgin Islands **Iles Vierges britanniques**	**100**	**106**	**110**	**113**	**117**	**123**	**129**	...	...	...

33
Consumer price index numbers
All items and food; 1990 = 100 [cont.]
Indices des prix à la consommation
Ensemble des prix et alimentation; 1990 = 100 [suite]

Country or area Pays ou zone	1990	1991	1992	1993	1994	1995	1996	1997	1998	1999
Food Aliments	100	107	109	109	115	120	124	...	...	...
Brunei Darussalam **Brunéi Darussalam**	**100**	**102**	**103**	**107**	**110**	**117**	**119**	**121**	**120**	**...**
Food Aliments	100	103	103	106	107	110	113	118	118	...
Bulgaria **Bulgarie**	**100**	**439**	**787**	**1 228**	**2 296**	**3 722**	**8 300**	**98 132**	**120 008**	**122 155**
Food Aliments	100	475	830	1 296	2 484	3 968	8 664	106 100	128 552	118 044
Burkina Faso[1] **Burkina Faso**[1]	**100**	**103**	**100**	**101**	**126**	**136**	**144**	**...**	**...**	**...**
Food[1] Aliments[1]	100	110	101	96	113	126	145	...	...	...
Burundi[1] **Burundi**[1]	**100**	**109**	**111**[11]	**122**	**140**	**166**	**...**	**...**	**...**	**...**
Food[1] Aliments[1]	100	107	105[11]	121	143	171	...	...	...	...
Cambodia[1 15] **Cambodge**[1 15]	**...**	**...**	**...**	**...**	**...**	**100**	**107**	**116**	**133**	**138**
Food[1 15] Aliments[1 15]	...	...	...	...	...	100	108	115[5]	131[5]	141[5]
Cameroon[7] **Cameroun**[7]	**...**	**...**	**...**	**...**	**100**	**109**	**113**	**119**	**123**	**125**
Food[7] Aliments[7]	...	...	...	...	100	108	112	120	123	125
Canada **Canada**	**100**	**106**	**107**[11]	**109**	**109**	**112**	**114**	**115**	**116**	**118**
Food Aliments	100	105	104[11]	106	107	109	111	112	114	116
Cape Verde **Cap-Vert**	**100**	**106**	**112**	**119**	**122**	**133**	**141**	**153**	**160**	**166**
Food Aliments	100	109	119	123	126	140	148	162	170	176
Cayman Islands **Iles Caïmanes**	**100**	**108**	**111**	**114**	**118**	**120**	**123**	**126**	**130**	**...**
Food Aliments	100	102	103	106	108	110	114	119	121	...
Central African Rep.[1 2] **Rép. centrafricaine**[1 2]	**100**	**97**	**96**	**94**	**117**	**139**	**144**	**146**	**145**	**...**
Food[1] Aliments[1]	100	96	95	91	113	139	147	148	...	...
Chad[1] **Tchad**[1]	**100**	**104**	**101**	**92**	**131**	**143**	**161**	**170**	**193**	**...**
Food[1] Aliments[1]	100	109	104	90	136	143	164	178	184	...
Chile[1] **Chili**[1]	**100**	**122**	**141**	**158**	**177**	**191**	**205**	**218**	**229**[11]	**236**
Food[1] Aliments[1]	100	126	148	165	181	196	207	222	231[11]	231
China †† **Chine** ††	**100**	**105**	**113**	**132**	**166**	**193**	**210**	**215**	**214**	**211**
Food Aliments	100	102	113	132	174	214	230	230	223	213

33
Consumer price index numbers
All items and food; 1990 = 100 [cont.]
Indices des prix à la consommation
Ensemble des prix et alimentation; 1990 = 100 [suite]

Country or area Pays ou zone	1990	1991	1992	1993	1994	1995	1996	1997	1998	1999
China, Hong Kong SAR† **Chine, Hong Kong RAS†**	**100**	**111**	**122**	**133**	**144**	**157**	**167**	**177**	**182**	**175**
Food Aliments	100	111	122	131	140	149	155	161	164	161
China, Macao SAR † **Chine, Macao RAS †**	**100**[2]	**110**[2]	**118**[2]	**126**[2]	**134**[2,11]	**145**[2]	**152**[2]	**158**[2,11]	**158**[2]	**97**[16,17]
Food Aliments	100	109	118	126	135[11]	146	152	158[11]	159	152
Colombia[18] **Colombie**[18]	**100**	**130**	**167**	**203**	**250**	**302**	**364**	**432**	**520**[11]	**578**
Food[18] Aliments[18]	100	130	168	194	234	280	326	379	465[11]	491
Congo[1] **Congo**[1]	**100**	**98**	**94**	**99**	**141**	**154**	**170**	**202**	**194**	**...**
Food[1] Aliments[1]	100	96	88	94	139	149	159	...	...	...
Cook Islands[1] **Iles Cook**[1]	**100**	**106**	**110**	**118**	**121**	**122**	**121**	**120**	**121**	**...**
Food[1,19] Aliments[1,19]	100	102	106	113	115	115	114	114	116	...
Costa Rica[20] **Costa Rica**[20]	**100**	**129**	**157**	**172**	**195**	**241**	**283**	**320**	**358**	**394**
Food[20] Aliments[20]	100	126	156	173	197	100[15,21]	119[15,21]	136[15,21]	156[15,21]	171[15,21]
Côte d'Ivoire[1,6,18] **Côte d'Ivoire**[1,6,18]	**98**[9]	**100**	**104**	**107**	**135**[11]	**...**	**...**	**...**	**...**	**...**
Food[1,6,18] Aliments[1,6,18]	98[9]	100	103	107	131[11]	...	...	...	...	...
Croatia **Croatie**	**100**	**224**	**1 646**	**26 104**	**54 088**	**56 251**	**58 670**	**61 074**	**65 032**	**67 259**
Food Aliments	100	223	1 832	26 707	53 696	54 112	55 844	58 305	62 270	62 294
Cyprus **Chypre**	**100**	**105**	**112**	**117**	**123**[11]	**126**	**130**	**134**	**137**	**140**
Food Aliments	100	107	115	117	126[11]	128	132	139	145	148
Czech Republic **République tchèque**	**100**	**157**	**174**	**210**	**231**[11]	**252**	**275**	**298**	**330**	**337**
Food[22] Aliments[22]	100	144	158	184	201[11]	222	240	252	267	261
Denmark **Danemark**	**100**	**102**	**105**	**106**	**108**	**110**	**113**	**115**	**117**	**120**
Food Aliments	100	101	102	102	105	108	110	114	116	117
Dominica **Dominique**	**100**	**106**	**111**	**113**	**113**	**115**	**116**	**119**	**...**	**...**
Food Aliments	100	105	114	117	112	114	116	120	...	...
Dominican Republic[23] **Rép. dominicaine**[23]	**100**	**147**	**153**	**161**	**175**	**197**	**207**	**224**	**...**	**...**
Food Aliments	100	149	149	154	164	188	197	212	...	...
Ecuador **Equateur**	**100**	**149**	**230**	**333**	**424**	**522**[24]	**649**	**847**	**1 153**	**1 749**

33
Consumer price index numbers
All items and food; 1990 = 100 [cont.]
Indices des prix à la consommation
Ensemble des prix et alimentation; 1990 = 100 [suite]

Country or area Pays ou zone	1990	1991	1992	1993	1994	1995	1996	1997	1998	1999
Food[5] Aliments[5]	100	149	229	325	405	489[24]	598	814	1 146	1 574
Egypt **Egypte**	**100**	**120**	**136**	**153**	**165**	**179**	**192**	**200**	**207**	**218**[11]
Food[5] Aliments[5]	100	117	127	136	149	164	176	184	191	203[11]
El Salvador[14] **El Salvador**[14]	**100**	**114**	**127**	**151**	**167**	**183**	**201**	**210**	**216**	**217**
Food[5 14] Aliments[5 14]	100	118	133	167	193	206	232	244	248	246
Estonia **Estonie**	...	**100**[6]	**1 176**[6]	**2 232**[6]	**3 296**[6]	**4 252**[6]	**5 232**[6]	**5 817**[6]	**108**[12]	**112**[12]
Food Aliments	...	100[6]	1 037[6]	1 804[6]	2 451[6]	2 838[6]	3 355[6]	3 540[6]	105[12]	101[12]
Ethiopia[1] **Ethiopie**[1]	**100**[2]	**136**[2]	**150**[2]	**155**[2]	**167**[2]	**184**[2]	**178**[29]	**100**[12 25]	**101**[12 25]	**105**[12 2]
Food[1] Aliments[1]	100	141	158	160	177	199	189[9]	100[12 26]	102[12 26]	111[12 2]
Faeroe Islands **Iles Féroé**	**100**	**104**	**106**	**111**	**114**	**118**	**121**	...	...	...
Food Aliments	100	105	110	116	123	133	138	...	...	...
Falkland Is. (Malvinas)[1] **Iles Falkland (Malvinas)**[1]	**100**	**105**	**112**	**113**	**113**	**117**	**123**	**125**	**128**	...
Food[1] Aliments[1]	100	104	110	116	119	124	128	124	...	...
Fiji **Fidji**	**100**	**107**	**112**	**118**	**118**[11]	**121**	**125**	**129**	**136**	**139**
Food[27] Aliments[27]	100	102	101	108	109[11]	109	112	117	126	128
Finland **Finlande**	**100**	**104**	**107**	**110**	**111**	**112**[11]	**113**	**114**	**116**	**117**
Food[28] Aliments[28]	100	103	103	102	102	95[11]	93	94	96	96
France **France**	**100**	**103**	**106**	**108**	**110**	**112**	**114**	**115**	**116**	**117**[11]
Food Aliments	100	103	104	104	105	106	107	109	111	111[11]
French Guiana **Guyane française**	**100**	...	**105**	**107**	**109**	**111**	**112**	**113**	**114**	**114**[11]
Food Aliments	100	...	102	104	105	107	108	109	111	110[11]
French Polynesia **Polynésie française**	**100**	**101**	**102**	**104**	**106**	**107**	**108**	**109**	**111**	**112**
Food Aliments	100	99	100	102	105	107	108	111	112	112
Gabon[16] **Gabon**[16]	**100**[9]	**100**	**90**	**91**	**121**	**133**	**138**	**144**	**147**	**146**
Food[16] Aliments[16]	101[9]	100	83	85	111	120	121	129	133	132
Gambia[1] **Gambie**[1]	**100**	**119**	**119**	**127**	**129**	**138**	**139**	**143**	**144**	**142**
Food[1] Aliments[1]	100	108	118	128	126	137	139	141	146	151

33
Consumer price index numbers
All items and food; 1990 = 100 [*cont.*]
Indices des prix à la consommation
Ensemble des prix et alimentation; 1990 = 100 [*suite*]

Country or area Pays ou zone	1990	1991	1992	1993	1994	1995	1996	1997	1998	1999
Georgia[15] Géorgie[5][15]	...	...	...	...	38	100	139	149	155	184
Food[5][15] Aliments[5][15]	...	...	...	...	42	100	133	139	145	171
Germany[6] Allemagne[6]	...	100	105	110	113	115[24]	116	118	120	120
Food[6][29] Aliments[6][29]	...	100	103	105	107	102[24]	102	104	105	103
Ghana Ghana	100	118	130	163	203	323	474	606	720[11]	...
Food Aliments	100	109	120	150	189	307	417	504	610[11]	...
Gibraltar Gibraltar	100	108	115	121	121	124	126	128	130	131[11]
Food Aliments	100	107	112	114	113	114	117	120	122	124[11]
Greece Grèce	100	120	138	158	176[11]	191	207	218	229	235
Food Aliments	100	119	136	153	164[24]	178	190	198	207	212
Greenland Groenland	100	104	106	107	108	109	111	112	113	114[11]
Food[5] Aliments[5]	100	105	106	107	107	113	118	120	122	101[16]
Grenada Grenade	100	103	107	109	112	115	118	120	...	...
Food[5] Aliments[5]	100	102	102	107	112	118	123	123	...	...
Guadeloupe Guadeloupe	100	103	106	108[11][30]	110	112	114	115	117[11]	118
Food Aliments	100	102	103	106[11][30]	108	111	113	114	117[11]	117
Guam Guam	100	110	121	132	154	162	...	100[12]	100[12]	...
Food Aliments	100	118	136	160	208	226	...	100[12]	101[12]	...
Guatemala[1] Guatemala[1]	100	135	149	169	190	206	229	250	266	280
Food[1] Aliments[1]	100	132	142	162	189	205	229	244	256	261
Guinea[1] Guinée[1]	100	119	140	149	156	164	169	...	...	...
Food[1] Aliments[1]	100	116	131	148	154	167	169	...	...	...
Guyana[16] Guyana[16][14]	62[9]	100	126	138	155[11]	174	186	193	202	...
Food[16][14] Aliments[16][14]	65[9]	100	125	133	149[11]	174	187	189	196	...
Haiti[10] Haïti[10]	100	115	131	166	243	228	...	...	...	...
Food[10] Aliments[10]	100	115	126	160	226	216	...	...	...	...
Honduras Honduras	100	134	146	161	196	254	315	378	430	480
Food Aliments	100	144	153	172	219	281	350	420	469	506

33
Consumer price index numbers
All items and food; 1990 = 100 [cont.]
Indices des prix à la consommation
Ensemble des prix et alimentation; 1990 = 100 [suite]

Country or area Pays ou zone	1990	1991	1992	1993	1994	1995	1996	1997	1998	1999
Hungary **Hongrie**	**100**	**135**	**166**[11]	**203**	**242**	**310**	**383**	**453**	**518**	**570**
Food Aliments	100	122	146[11]	188	232	304	357	419	480	494
Iceland **Islande**	**100**	**107**	**111**	**115**	**117**	**119**	**122**	**124**	**126**	**130**
Food[19] Aliments[19]	100	103	104	106	104	107	110	114	117	121
India[1 31] **Inde**[1 31]	**100**	**112**	**127**	**139**	**153**	**168**	**177**	**195**	**229**	**246**
Food[1 31] Aliments[1 31]	100	116	129	144	160	179	187	201	236	230
Indonesia **Indonésie**	**100**	**109**	**118**	**129**	**140**	**153**	**165**	**176**	**278**[11]	**335**
Food Aliments	100	108	116	124	138	156	171	186	358[11]	448
Iran (Islamic Rep. of) **Iran (Rép. islamique d')**	**100**	**118**	**148**	**180**	**236**	**353**	**455**	**534**	**637**	**771**
Food[5] Aliments[5]	100	119	159	193	255	405	506	557	688	856
Ireland **Irlande**	**100**	**103**	**106**	**108**	**111**	**113**	**115**	**117**[11]	**120**	**122**
Food Aliments	100	101	103	103	107	110	112	114[11]	119	123
Isle of Man **Ile de Man**	**100**	**107**	**112**	**115**	**118**	**121**	**124**	**127**	**131**	**133**
Food Aliments	100	108	113	118	121	126	133	135	143	...
Israel **Israël**	**100**	**119**	**133**	**148**[11]	**166**	**183**	**203**	**222**	**234**	**246**
Food Aliments	100	114	128	135[11]	150	161	177	193	204	218
Italy **Italie**	**100**	**106**[11]	**112**	**117**	**121**	**128**	**133**[11]	**135**	**138**	**140**
Food Aliments	100[32]	107[11 32]	112[32 33]	114[32 34]	118[32 34]	126[32 34]	131[11 32 34]	131[32 34]	132[32 34]	133[29]
Jamaica **Jamaïque**	**100**	**151**	**268**	**327**	**442**	**530**	**669**	**734**	**797**	**...**
Food Aliments	100	155	275	333	461	554	688	742	794	...
Japan **Japon**	**100**	**103**	**105**	**106**	**107**	**107**[11]	**107**	**109**	**110**	**109**
Food Aliments	100	105	105	107	107	106[11]	106	108	109	109
Jordan **Jordanie**	**100**	**108**	**112**[11]	**116**	**120**	**123**	**131**	**135**[11]	**139**	**140**
Food Aliments	100	111	114[11]	117	123	126	135	144[11]	150	149
Kazakhstan[4] **Kazakhstan**[4]	**...**	**3**[3]	**100**	**703**	**13 899**	**38 389**	**53 476**	**62 776**	**67 246**	**72 834**
Food[4] Aliments[4]	...	5[3]	100	691	13 465	35 521	47 882	50 946	53 208	57 162
Kenya[1 18] **Kenya**[1 18]	**100**[11]	**119**	**154**	**225**	**291**	**297**	**319**	**357**	**378**	**...**

33
Consumer price index numbers
All items and food; 1990 = 100 [*cont.*]
Indices des prix à la consommation
Ensemble des prix et alimentation; 1990 = 100 [*suite*]

Country or area Pays ou zone	1990	1991	1992	1993	1994	1995	1996	1997	1998	1999
Food[1][18] Aliments[1][18]	100[11]	124	167	242	317	310	335	388	402	...
Kiribati[1] **Kiribati[1]**	**100**	**106**	**110**	**117**	**123**	**127**	**127**	**127**[9]	...	...
Food[1] Aliments[1]	100	104	107	113	117	123	121	120[9]	...	...
Korea, Republic of **Corée, République de**	**100**	**109**	**116**	**122**	**129**	**135**[11]	**142**	**148**	**159**	**160**
Food Aliments	100	112	119	124	135	140[11]	145	151	164	169
Kuwait[35] **Koweit[35]**	**110**[9]	**120**[9]	**119**	**120**	**123**	**126**	**130**	**131**	**131**	...
Food[35] Aliments[35]	112[9]	124[9]	121	115	117	120	127	127	128	...
Kyrgyzstan[4] **Kirghizistan[4]**	...	...	**100**	**1 186**	**3 329**	**4 776**	**6 303**	**7 780**	**8 593**	**11 678**
Food[4] Aliments[4]	...	...	100	1 066	2 785	3 898	5 504	6 874	7 593	10 705
Latvia[6] **Lettonie[6]**	...	**100**	**1 051**	**2 199**	**2 989**	**3 735**[11]	**4 393**	**4 766**	**4 986**	**5 102**
Food[6][28] Aliments[6][28]	...	100	848	1 104	1 470	1 708[11]	1 919	1 969	1 995	1 974
Lebanon[1] **Liban[1]**	**100**	**148**	**268**	**310**	**331**	**413**	**438**	**447**	...	...
Food[1] Aliments[1]	100	143	258	301	324	350	379	377	...	...
Lesotho **Lesotho**	**100**	**118**	**138**	**157**	**168**	**185**	**202**	...	...	...
Food[5] Aliments[5]	100	118	146	161	171	193	214	...	...	...
Liberia[1][9][35] **Libéria[1][9][35]**	**108**	...	...	...	...	...	...	...	...	...
Food[1][9][36] Aliments[1][9][36]	125	...	...	...	...	...	...	...	...	...
Lithuania[6] **Lituanie[6]**	...	**100**	**1 121**	**5 718**	**9 845**	**13 749**	**17 135**	**18 656**	**19 602**	**19 751**
Food[6] Aliments[6]	...	100	1 038	5 204	8 380	11 679	14 812	15 815	16 036	15 534
Luxembourg[17] **Luxembourg[17]**	**100**	**103**	**106**	**110**	**113**	**115**	**116**	**118**	**119**	**120**
Food[28] Aliments[28]	100	103	104	104	105	108	109	110[11]	113	114
Madagascar[1][2][37] **Madagascar[1][2][37]**	**100**	**109**	**124**	**137**	**190**	**283**	**339**	**355**	**377**	**414**
Food[1][37] Aliments[1][37]	100	109	127	138	193	291	346	360	382	428
Malawi **Malawi**	**100**	**108**	**133**	**164**	**221**	**404**	**556**	**607**	**788**	**1 141**
Food Aliments	100	108	139	176	243	469	681	737	941	1 346
Malaysia **Malaisie**	**100**	**104**	**109**	**113**	**117**	**121**	**126**	**129**	**136**	**222**
Food Aliments	100	105	112	114	120	126	133	139	151	158

33
Consumer price index numbers
All items and food; 1990 = 100 [*cont.*]
Indices des prix à la consommation
Ensemble des prix et alimentation; 1990 = 100 [*suite*]

Country or area Pays ou zone	1990	1991	1992	1993	1994	1995	1996	1997	1998	1999
Maldives[1] **Maldives**[1]	**100**	**115**	**134**	**161**	**166**	**176**	**187**	**201**	**196**	...
Food[15] Aliments[15]	100	113	129	152	158	177	193	231	219	...
Mali **Mali**	**100**	**101**	**95**	**95**	**117**	...	**142**	...	...	...
Food Aliments	100	103	93	93	116	...	147	...	...	...
Malta **Malte**	**100**	**103**	**104**[11]	**109**	**113**	**118**[11]	**120**	**124**	**127**	**129**
Food[27] Aliments[27]	100	102	102[11]	107	111	115[11]	119	120	123	...
Marshall Islands[14] **Iles Marshall**[14]	...	...	**100**	**105**	**111**	**119**	...	...	...	...
Martinique **Martinique**	**100**	**103**	**107**	**111**[11]	**113**	**116**	**117**	**119**	**120**	...
Food[5] Aliments[5]	100	103	106	109[11]	111	113	114	116	119	...
Mauritania **Mauritanie**	**100**	**106**	**116**	**127**	**132**	**141**	**148**	**154**	**167**	...
Food Aliments	100	103	110	121	125	135	145	151	165	...
Mauritius **Maurice**	**100**	**107**	**112**[11]	**124**	**133**	**141**	**150**	**160**[11]	**171**	**183**
Food Aliments	100	104	100[4]	114[4]	124[4]	132[4]	139[4]	146[4][11]	158[4]	168[4]
Mexico **Mexique**	**100**	**123**	**142**	**156**	**166**[11]	**225**	**302**	**364**	**422**	**492**
Food[5] Aliments[5]	100	120	134	142	150[11]	209	296	352	409	474
Morocco **Maroc**	**100**	**108**	**114**	**120**	**126**	**134**	**138**	**139**	**143**	**144**
Food[5] Aliments[5]	100	109	116	123	132	143	144	142	146	145
Myanmar[1] **Myanmar**[1]	**100**	**132**	**161**	**213**	**264**	**330**	**384**	**498**	**755**	**893**
Food[1] Aliments[1]	100	137	168	234	281	354	421	548	835	997
Namibia[1] **Namibie**[1]	**100**	**113**	**132**	**144**	**159**	**175**	**189**	**206**	**219**	...
Food[1] Aliments[1]	100	106	126	135	152	170	181	195	201	...
Nepal **Népal**	**100**	**116**	**135**	**145**	**158**	**170**	**186**	**193**	**212**	...
Food Aliments	100	118	139	147	159	171	189	194	...	...
Netherlands **Pays-Bas**	**100**	**103**	**106**	**109**	**112**	**114**	**117**[11]	**119**	**122**	**124**
Food[5] Aliments[5]	100	103	106	107	109	109	110[11]	112	114	116
Netherlands Antilles[1] **Antilles néerlandaises**[1]	**100**	**104**	**105**	**108**	**110**	**113**	**117**[11]	**120**	**122**	**122**
Food[1] Aliments[1]	100	107	110	114	116	122	129[11]	132	133	136

33
Consumer price index numbers
All items and food; 1990 = 100 [cont.]
Indices des prix à la consommation
Ensemble des prix et alimentation; 1990 = 100 [suite]

Country or area Pays ou zone	1990	1991	1992	1993	1994	1995	1996	1997	1998	1999
New Caledonia **Nouvelle-Calédonie**[1]	**100**	**104**	**107**	**109**[11]	**113**	**114**	**116**	**118**	**119**	**120**
Food[1] Aliments[1]	100	103	106	110[11]	114	115	118	123	124	125
New Zealand **Nouvelle-Zélande**	**100**	**103**	**104**	**105**	**107**	**111**	**113**	**115**	**116**	**116**
Food Aliments	100	101	101	102	102	103	104	107	110	111
Nicaragua **Nicaragua**	**100**	**2 842**	**3 767**	**4 534**	**4 886**[11]	**5 421**	**6 050**	**6 608**	**7 470**	**8 308**
Food Aliments	100	2 851	3 503	3 904	4 208[11]	4 711	5 248	5 724	6 541	6 898
Niger[12] **Niger**[12]	**100**	**92**	...	...	...	...	...	...	...	...
Food[1] Aliments[1]	100	88	...	...	...	...	...	...	...	...
Nigeria[38] **Nigéria**[38]	**100**	**113**	**163**	**257**	**403**	**688**	**901**	**975**	**1 076**	...
Food[38] Aliments[38]	100	112	164	259	380	654	851	924	985	...
Niue **Nioué**	**100**	**105**	**110**	**112**	**114**	**115**	...	...	...	...
Food Aliments	100	104	107	110	111	113	...	...	...	...
Norfolk Island[6] **Ile Norfolk**[6]	...	**100**	**102**	**106**	**110**	**113**	**117**	...	...	...
Food[6] Aliments[6]	...	100	101	103	106	112	117	...	...	...
Northern Mariana Islands[1] **Iles Mariannes du Nord**[1]	**100**	**107**	**117**	**122**	**125**	**128**	**131**	**133**	**133**	...
Food[1] Aliments[1]	100	108	112	116	118	119	121	121	120	...
Norway **Norvège**	**100**	**103**	**106**	**108**	**110**	**112**	**114**	**117**	**119**	**122**
Food Aliments	100	102	103	102	103	105	107	110	116	119
Oman[1] **Oman**[1]	**100**	**105**	**106**	**107**	**106**	**105**	**105**	**105**	**104**	**105**
Food[15] Aliments[15]	100	103	102	101	100	102	104	105	104	104
Pakistan **Pakistan**	**100**	**112**	**122**[11]	**135**	**151**	**170**	**188**	**209**	**222**	**231**
Food Aliments	100	111	123[11]	135	155	177	193	217	229	238
Panama[1] **Panama**[1]	**100**	**101**	**103**	**104**	**105**	**106**	**107**	**109**	**109**	**111**
Food[1] Aliments[1]	100	102	106	106	108	108	109	110	110	111
Papua New Guinea **Papouasie-Nvl-Guinée**	**100**	**107**	**112**	**117**	**120**	**141**	**158**	...	...	...
Food Aliments	100	108	111	114	116	137	156	...	...	...
Paraguay[1] **Paraguay**[1]	**100**	**124**	**143**	**169**	**204**	**231**	**254**	**272**	**303**	...

33
Consumer price index numbers
All items and food; 1990 = 100 [*cont.*]
Indices des prix à la consommation
Ensemble des prix et alimentation; 1990 = 100 [*suite*]

Country or area Pays ou zone	1990	1991	1992	1993	1994	1995	1996	1997	1998	1999
Food[1] Aliments[1]	100	120	138	161	195	224	237	247	275	...
Peru[1 10] **Pérou**[1 10]	**100**	**510**	**884**	**1 314**	**1 626**[11]	**1 806**	**2 015**	**2 187**	**2 346**	**2 427**
Food[1 10] Aliments[1 10]	100	448	770	1 150	1 352[24]	1 479	1 659	1 776	1 923	1 918
Philippines Philippines	**100**	**119**	**129**	**139**	**149**	**161**	**176**	**186**	**204**	**218**
Food[5] Aliments[5]	100	115	123	131	141	154	170	175	191	201
Poland Pologne	**100**	**170**	**244**	**330**	**436**	**557**	**668**	**767**	**100**[16]	**107**[16]
Food[32] Aliments[32]	100	151	207	274	363	462	550	620	100[16]	102[16]
Portugal[2] **Portugal**[2]	**100**	**111**	**121**[11]	**129**	**136**	**142**	**146**	**149**[11]	**153**	**157**
Food[29] Aliments[29]	100	110	118[11]	121	127	132	135	136[11]	140	143
Puerto Rico Porto Rico	**100**	**103**	**106**	**109**	**113**	**118**	**124**	**131**	**138**	**146**
Food Aliments	100	105	111	118	127	140	153	169	188	206
Qatar Qatar	**100**	**104**	**108**	**107**	**108**	**111**	**119**	**122**	**126**	**129**
Food[5] Aliments[5]	100	106	106	98	93	104	108	108	112	112
Republic of Moldova[4] **République de Moldova**[4]	...	**7**	**100**	**1 714**	**10 059**	**13 064**	**16 135**	**18 034**	**19 422**	**27 046**
Food[4] Aliments[4]	...	7	100	1 418	7 844	10 168	12 148	13 004	13 525	17 954
Réunion Réunion	**100**[11 30]	**104**	**107**	**111**	**114**	**116**	**118**	**119**	**121**[11]	**122**
Food Aliments	100[11 30]	105	107	111	112	113	115	117	120[11]	119
Romania Roumanie	**100**	**275**	**310**[6]	**1 105**[6]	**2 617**[6]	**3 461**[6]	**4 805**[6]	**12 241**[6]	**19 474**[6]	**28 394**[6]
Food Aliments	100	299	337[6]	1 174[6]	2 774[6]	3 657[6]	4 987[6]	12 536[6]	18 607[6]	23 789[6]
Russian Federation[6] **Fédération de Russie**[6]	...	**100**	**1 630**	**15 869**	**64 688**	**192 521**	**284 429**[11]	**326 484**	**416 814**	**773 814**
Food[6] Aliments[6]	...	100	1 690	16 760	67 339	210 975	287 151[11]	323 749	412 044	810 254
Rwanda[1] **Rwanda**[1]	**100**	**120**	**131**	**147**	...	...	...	...	...	...
Food[1] Aliments[1]	100	114	122	...	...	...	...	...	...	...
Saint Helena Sainte-Hélène	**100**	**104**	**109**[11]	**118**	**123**	**128**	**134**	**137**	**139**	**142**
Food Aliments	100	102	106[11]	112	116	121	126	126	124	126
Saint Kitts and Nevis[1] **Saint-Kitts-et-Nevis**[1]	**100**	**104**	**107**	**109**	**111**	**114**	**116**	...	...	...
Food[1] Aliments[1]	100	106	111	113	117	119	123	...	...	...

33
Consumer price index numbers
All items and food; 1990 = 100 [cont.]
Indices des prix à la consommation
Ensemble des prix et alimentation; 1990 = 100 [suite]

Country or area Pays ou zone	1990	1991	1992	1993	1994	1995	1996	1997	1998	1999
Saint Lucia **Sainte-Lucie**	**100**	**106**	**113**	**113**	**116**	**123**	**124**	**124**	**128**	**132**
Food Aliments	100	109	114	114	119	128	128	124	130	133
Saint Pierre and Miquelon **Saint-Pierre-et-Miquelon**	**100**	**105**	**...**	**...**	**...**	**...**	**...**	**100**[12]	**101**[12]	**102**[12]
Food Aliments	100	104	...	...	...	...	...	100[12]	102[12]	104[12]
St. Vincent-Grenadines[1] **St. Vincent-Grenadines**[1]	**100**	**106**	**110**	**115**	**115**	**118**	**123**	**124**	**126**	**128**
Food[1] Aliments[1]	100	109	113	116	116	120	128	127	124	125
Samoa[2] **Samoa**[2]	**100**	**99**	**107**	**109**	**129**	**130**	**139**	**155**	**137**	**...**
Food Aliments	100	92	102	102	127	128	144	160	123	...
San Marino **Saint-Marin**	**100**	**107**	**115**	**121**	**125**[11]	**132**	**137**[11]	**140**	**143**	**...**
Food Aliments	100	105	111	118	123[11]	128	132[11]	136	139	...
Saudi Arabia[39] **Arabie saoudite**[39]	**100**	**105**	**104**	**105**	**106**	**111**	**112**	**112**	**111**	**110**
Food[5 39] Aliments[5 39]	100	108	112	113	111	112	114	116	117	114
Senegal[1] **Sénégal**[1]	**100**	**98**	**98**	**98**	**129**	**139**	**143**	**...**	**...**	**...**
Food[1] Aliments[1]	100	97	96	94	131	143	145	...	...	...
Seychelles **Seychelles**	**100**	**102**	**105**	**107**	**109**	**108**	**107**	**108**	**111**	**...**
Food Aliments	100	102	104	107	100	99	96	98	...	...
Sierra Leone[1] **Sierra Leone**[1]	**100**	**183**	**258**	**...**	**...**	**...**	**...**	**...**	**...**	**...**
Food[1] Aliments[1]	100	186	264	...	...	...	...	...	...	...
Singapore **Singapour**	**100**	**103**	**106**	**108**	**112**	**113**	**115**	**117**	**117**	**117**
Food Aliments	100	101	103	104	107	110	112	114	115	116
Slovakia **Slovaquie**	**100**	**161**	**177**	**218**	**248**	**272**	**288**	**305**	**326**	**360**
Food[28] Aliments[28]	100	152	163	197	231	260	270	286	303	311
Slovenia[14] **Slovénie**[14]	**100**	**215**	**662**	**880**	**1 065**	**1 208**	**1 327**	**1 438**	**1 552**	**1 647**
Food[14 19] Aliments[14 19]	100	212	649	816	1 005	1 162	1 271	1 378	1 495	1 555
Solomon Islands[1] **Iles Salomon**[1]	**100**	**114**	**126**	**134**[11]	**152**	**167**	**186**	**202**	**226**	**245**
Food[1 32] Aliments[1 32]	100	117	130	136[11]	152	163	185	205	232	258
South Africa **Afrique du Sud**	**100**	**115**	**131**	**144**	**157**	**171**	**183**	**199**	**213**	**224**

33
Consumer price index numbers
All items and food; 1990 = 100 [cont.]
Indices des prix à la consommation
Ensemble des prix et alimentation; 1990 = 100 [suite]

Country or area Pays ou zone	1990	1991	1992	1993	1994	1995	1996	1997	1998	1999
Food Aliments	100	120	150	160	182	198	210	230	244	256
Spain Espagne	100	106	112[24]	117	123	129	133	136	138	142
Food[5] Aliments[5]	100	104	107[24]	108	115	121	125	126	128	130
Sri Lanka[1] Sri Lanka[1]	100	112	125	140	151	163	189	207	227	237
Food[1] Aliments[1]	100	112	125	139	152	162	193	214	238	247
Sudan[18] Soudan[18]	100	222	473	953	2 068	3 482	8 192	...	...	...
Food[5 18] Aliments[5 18]	100	236	457	...	...	...	...	...	...	...
Suriname[1] Suriname[1]	100	126	181	441	2 065	6 934	6 879	7 371	8 773	...
Food[1] Aliments[1]	100	119	184	485	2 364	7 842	7 267	7 209	8 244	...
Swaziland[18] Swaziland[18]	100	102	122	137	157	180	204	212[11]	228	...
Food[18] Aliments[18]	100	114	128	144	172	206	233	265[11]	281	...
Sweden Suède	100	109	112	117	120	123	123	124	124	125
Food Aliments	100	105	99	100	102	103	96	96	97	99
Switzerland Suisse	100	106	110	114[11]	115	117	118	118	118	119
Food Aliments	100	105	105	106[11]	106	107	106	107	108	108
Syrian Arab Republic Rép. arabe syrienne	100	109	121	137	154	170	185	189	188	184
Food Aliments	100	106	113	126	145	155	169	173	169	162
Tajikistan Tadjikistan	100	184	1 951	43 622	148 095	804 305	2 977 539	5 112 434	...	...
Food Aliments	100	189	2 477	75 096	189 918	1 066 009	4 065 760	7 172 001	...	...
Thailand Thaïlande	100	106	110	114	120[11]	126	134	141	153	153
Food Aliments	100	107	112	114	122[11]	132	144	154	168	167
TFYR of Macedonia L'ex-R.y. Macédoine	100	211	3 397	15 692	35 826	41 444	42 401	43 499	43 468	43 154
Food Aliments	100	205	3 462	15 434	34 419	37 382	37 336	38 910	38 833	38 216
Togo[1] Togo[1]	100	100	102	102	143[11]	165	173	187	184	...
Food[1 27] Aliments[1 27]	100	96	99	98	129	100[15]	106[15]	121[15]	117[15]	...
Tonga[2] Tonga[2]	100	109	118	119	120[11]	122	126	129	133	138
Food Aliments	100	106	119	115	114	117	126	130	138	145

33
Consumer price index numbers
All items and food; 1990 = 100 [cont.]
Indices des prix à la consommation
Ensemble des prix et alimentation; 1990 = 100 [suite]

Country or area Pays ou zone	1990	1991	1992	1993	1994	1995	1996	1997	1998	1999
Trinidad and Tobago **Trinité-et-Tobago**	**100**	**104**	**111**	**122**	**133**[11]	**140**	**145**	**150**	**159**	**164**
Food Aliments	100	106	115	137	161[11]	188	208	228	262	285
Tunisia **Tunisie**	**100**[24]	**108**	**115**	**119**	**125**	**132**	**137**	**142**	**147**	**151**
Food Aliments	100[24]	109	114	117	122	132	137	143	147	150
Turkey **Turquie**	**100**	**166**	**282**	**469**	**967**	**1 872**	**339**[7]	**630**[7]	**1 163**[7]	**1 917**[7]
Food[5] Aliments[5]	100	167	286	468	983	1 938	331[7]	637[7]	1 162[7]	1 727[7]
Tuvalu[1 14] **Tuvalu**[1 14]	**100**	**106**	**100**	**102**	**104**	**109**	**110**	**112**	**112**	...
Food[1] Aliments[1]	100	106	97	99	103	109	110	110	110	...
Uganda[14] **Ouganda**[14]	**100**	**128**	**197**	**207**	**228**	**243**	**260**	...	...	...
Food[14] Aliments[14]	100	124	205	197	228	238	254	...	...	...
Ukraine[4] **Ukraine**[4]	...	...	**100**	**4 835**	**47 923**	**228 471**	**411 775**	**477 190**	**527 663**	**647 356**
Food[4 5] Aliments[4 5]	...	...	100	5 514	49 582	226 059	357 921	399 575	446 690	570 891
United Kingdom **Royaume-Uni**	**100**	**106**	**110**	**112**	**114**	**118**	**121**	**125**	**129**	**131**
Food Aliments	100	105	107	109	110	115	118	119	120	120
United Rep. of Tanzania[40] **Rép.-Unie de Tanzanie**[40]	**100**	**129**	**157**	**197**	**254**	**336**	**406**	**471**	**532**	...
Food[40] Aliments[40]	100	132	160	196	260	347	417	490	562	...
United States **Etats-Unis**	**100**	**104**	**107**	**111**	**113**	**117**	**120**	**123**	**125**	**127**
Food Aliments	100	104	105	107	110	113	116	119	122	125
Uruguay[1] **Uruguay**[1]	**100**	**202**	**340**	**524**	**759**	**1 079**	**1 385**	**1 661**[11]	**1 839**	**1 943**
Food[1] Aliments[1]	100	185	297	449	632	894	1 105	1 308[11]	1 444	1 498
Vanuatu[14] **Vanuatu**[14]	**100**	**106**	**111**	**115**	**117**	**120**	**121**	**124**	**129**	...
Food[14] Aliments[14]	100	103	104	108	109	113	112	113	117	...
Venezuela **Venezuela**	**100**	**133**	**175**	**239**	**381**	**609**	**1 224**	**1 819**	**2 448**	**2 986**
Food[5] Aliments[5]	100	134	175	231	366	585	1 096	1 585	2 182	2 516
Yugoslavia **Yougoslavie**	**100**	**222**	**20 021**	...	**24**[12]	**43**[12]	**82**[12]	**100**[12]	**130**[12]	**145**[12]
Food Aliments	100	200	19 217	...	27[12]	46[12]	84[12]	100[12]	133[12]	144[12]
Zambia[18] **Zambie**[18]	**100**	**193**	**573**	**1 655**	**2 521**	**3 381**	**4 590**[24]	**5 662**	**7 045**	...

33
Consumer price index numbers
All items and food; 1990 = 100 [cont.]
Indices des prix à la consommation
Ensemble des prix et alimentation; 1990 = 100 [suite]

Country or area Pays ou zone	1990	1991	1992	1993	1994	1995	1996	1997	1998	1999
Food[5][18] Aliments[5][18]	100	191	608	1 781	2 665	3 568	5 203[24]	6 279	7 803	...
Zimbabwe Zimbabwe	**100**	**123**	**175**	**224**	**273**	**335**	**407**	**484**	**637**	**1 010**
Food[27] Aliments[27]	100	113	193	267	337	429	545	641	893	1 500

Source:
International Labour Office (ILO), Geneva, "Yearbook of Labour Statistics 2000" and the ILO labour statistics database.

† For information on recent changes in country or area nomenclature pertaining to former Czechoslovakia, Germany, Hong Kong Special Administrative Region (SAR) of China, Macao Special Administrative Region (SAR) of China, SFR of Yugoslavia and the former USSR, see Annex I - Country or area nomenclature, regional and other groupings.

†† For statistical purposes, the data for China do not include those for Hong Kong Special Administrative Region (Hong Kong SAR), Macao Special Administrative Region (Macao SAR) and Taiwan province of China.

1 Data refer to the index of the capital city.
2 Excluding Rent.
3 One month of each year.
4 Index base: 1992 = 100.
5 Including tobacco.
6 Index base: 1991 = 100.
7 Index base: 1994 = 100.
8 Index base 1993 = 100.
9 Average of less than twelve months.
10 Metropolitan area.
11 Series linked to former series.
12 Index base 1997 = 100.
13 Government officials.
14 Urban areas.
15 Index base: 1995 = 100.
16 Index base 1998 = 100.
17 Including rent.
18 Low income group.
19 Excluding beverages.
20 Central area.
21 Including alcoholic beverages and tobacco.
22 Including tobacco, beverages and public catering.
23 Including direct taxes.
24 Series replacing former series.
25 Beginning September 1996: including "rent".
26 Beginning September 1996: excluding beverages.
27 Excluding beverages and tobacco.
28 Excluding alcoholic beverages and tobacco.
29 Excluding alcoholic beverages.
30 All households.
31 Industrial workers.
32 Including alcoholic beverages.
33 Beginning February 1992: excluding tobacco.
34 Excluding tobacco.
35 Index base: 1989 = 100.
36 Index base: 1988 = 100.
37 Madagascans.
38 Rural and urban areas.
39 All cities.
40 Tanganyika.

Source:
Bureau international du Travail (BIT), Genève, "Annuaire des statistiques du travail 2000" et la base de données du BIT.

† Pour les modifications récentes de nomenclature de pays ou de zone concernant l'Allemagne, Hong Kong, région administrative spéciale (RAS) de Chine, Macao, région administrative spéciale (RAS) de Chine, l'ex-Tchécoslovaquie, l'ex-URSS et l'ex-Rfs de Yougoslavie, voir annexe I - Nomenclature des pays ou des zones, groupements régionaux et autres groupements.

†† Les données statistiques relatives à la Chine ne comprennent pas celles qui concernent la région administrative spéciale de Hong Kong (la RAS de Hong Kong), la région administrative spéciale de Macao (la RAS de Macao) et la province chinoise de Taiwan.

1 Les données se réfèrent à l'indice de la capitale.
2 Non compris le groupe loyer.
3 Un mois de chaque année.
4 Indices base: 1992 = 100.
5 Y compris le tabac.
6 Indices base: 1991 = 100.
7 Indices base: 1994 = 100.
8 Indices base 1993 = 100.
9 Moyenne de moins de douze mois.
10 Région métropolitaine.
11 Série enchaînée à la précédente.
12 Indices base 1997 = 100.
13 Fonctionnaires.
14 Régions urbaines.
15 Indices base: 1995 = 100.
16 Indices base 1998 = 100.
17 Y compris le groupe loyer.
18 Familles à revenu modique.
19 Non compris les boissons.
20 Région centrale.
21 Y compris les boissons alcoolisées et le tabac.
22 Y compris le tabac, les boissons et la restauration.
23 Y compris les impôts directs.
24 Série remplaçant la précédente.
25 A partir de septembre 1996: y compris le groupe loyer.
26 A partir de septembre 1996: non compris les boissons.
27 Non compris les boissons et le tabac.
28 Non compris les boissons alcoolisées et le tabac.
29 Non compris les boissons alcooliques.
30 Ensemble des ménages.
31 Travailleurs de l'industrie.
32 Y compris les boissons alcoolisées.
33 A partir de février 1992: non compris le tabac.
34 Non compris le tabac.
35 Indices base: 1989 = 100.
36 Indices base: 1988 = 100.
37 Malgaches.
38 Régions rurales et urbaines.
39 Ensemble des villes.
40 Tanganyika.

Technical notes, tables 31-33

Table 31: The series generally relate to the average earnings per worker in manufacturing industries, according to the *International Standard Industrial Classification of All Economic Activities* (ISIC) Revision 2 or Revision 3 [49]. The data cover all employees (i.e. wage earners and salaried employees) of both sexes, irrespective of age. Data which refer exclusively to wage earners (i.e. manual or production workers), or to salaried employees (i.e. non-manual workers) are footnoted. Earnings generally include bonuses, cost of living allowances, taxes, social insurance contributions payable by the employed person and, in some cases, payments in kind, and normally exclude social insurance contributions payable by the employers, family allowances and other social security benefits. The time of year to which the figures refer is not the same for all countries. In some cases, the series may show wage rates instead of earnings; this is indicated in footnotes.

Table 32: Producer prices are prices at which producers sell their output on the domestic market or for export. Wholesale prices, in the strict sense, are prices at which wholesalers sell their goods on the domestic market or for export. In practice, many national wholesale price indexes are a mixture of producer and wholesale prices for domestic goods representing prices for purchases in large quantities from either source. In addition, these indexes may cover the prices of goods imported in quantity for the domestic market either by producers or by retail or wholesale distributors.

Producer or wholesale price indexes normally cover the prices of the characteristic products of agriculture, forestry and fishing, mining and quarrying, manufacturing, and electricity, gas and water supply. Prices are normally measured in terms of transaction prices, including non-deductible indirect taxes less subsidies, in the case of domestically-produced goods and import duties and other non-deductible indirect taxes less subsidies in the case of imported goods.

The Laspeyres index number formula is generally used and, for the purpose of the presentation, the national index numbers have been recalculated, where necessary, on the reference base 1990=100.

The price index numbers for each country are arranged according to the following scheme:
(a)   Components of supply
    Domestic supply
    Domestic production for domestic market
    Agricultural products
    Industrial products
    Imported products

Notes techniques, tableaux 31 à 33

Tableau 31: Les séries se rapportent généralement aux gains moyens des salariés des industries manufacturières (activités de fabrication), suivant la *Classification internationale type, par industrie, de toutes les branches d'activité économique* (CITI, Rev. 2 ou Rev.3) [49]. Les données portent sur l'ensemble des salariés (qu'ils perçoivent un salaire ou un traitement au mois) des deux sexes, indépendamment de leur âge. Lorsque les données portent exclusivement sur les salariés horaires (ouvriers, travailleurs manuels) ou sur les employés percevant un traitement (travailleurs autres que manuels, cadres), le fait est signalé par une note. Les gains comprennent en général les primes, les indemnités pour coût de la vie, les impôts, les cotisations de sécurité sociale à la charge de l'employé, et dans certains cas des paiements en nature, mais ne comprennent pas en règle générale la part patronale des cotisations d'assurance sociale, les allocations familiales et les autres prestations de sécurité sociale. La période de l'année visée par les données n'est pas la même pour tous les pays. Dans certains cas, les séries visent les taux horaires et non pas les gains, ce qui est alors signalé en note.

Tableau 32: Les prix à la production sont les prix auxquels les producteurs vendent leur production sur le marché intérieur ou à l'exportation. Les prix de gros, au sens strict du terme, sont les prix auxquels les grossistes vendent sur le marché intérieur ou à l'exportation. En pratique, les indices nationaux des prix de gros combinent souvent les prix à la production et les prix de gros de biens nationaux représentant les prix d'achat par grandes quantités au producteur ou au grossiste. En outre, ces indices peuvent s'appliquer aux prix de biens importés en quantités pour être vendus sur le marché intérieur par les producteurs, les détaillants ou les grossistes.

Les indices de prix de gros ou de prix à la production comprennent aussi en général les prix des produits provenant de l'agriculture, de la sylviculture et de la pêche, des industries extractives (mines et carrières), de l'industrie manufacturière ainsi que les prix de l'électricité, de gaz et de l'eau. Les prix sont normalement ceux auxquels s'effectue la transaction, y compris les impôts indirects non déductibles, mais non compris les subventions dans le cas des biens produits dans le pays et y compris les taxes à l'importation et autres impôts indirects non déductibles, mais non compris les subventions dans le cas des biens importés.

On utilise généralement la formule de Laspeyres et, pour la présentation, on a recalculé les indices nationaux, le cas échéant, en prenant comme base de référence 1990=100.

(b)   Stage of processing
          Raw materials
          Intermediate products
(c)   End-use
          Consumers' goods
          Capital goods

A description of the general methods used in compiling the related national indexes is given in the United Nations *1977 Supplement to the Statistical Yearbook and the Monthly Bulletin of Statistics* [56].

Table 33: Unless otherwise stated, the consumer price index covers all the main classes of expenditure on all items and on food. Monthly data for many of these series and descriptions of them may be found in the United Nations *Monthly Bulletin of Statistics* [26] and the United Nations *1977 Supplement to the Statistical Yearbook and the Monthly Bulletin of Statistics* [56].

Les indices des prix pour chaque pays sont présentés suivant la classification ci-après:
(a)   Eléments de l'offre
          Offre intérieure
          Production nationale pour le marché intérieur
          Produits agricoles
          Produits industriels
          Produits importés
(b)   Stade de la transformation
          Matières premières
          Produits intermédiaires
(c)   Utilisation finale
          Biens de consommation
          Biens d'équipement

Les méthodes générales utilisées pour calculer les indices nationaux correspondants sont exposées dans: *1977 Supplément à l'Annuaire statistique et au Bulletin mensuel de statistique* des Nations Unies [56].

Tableau 33: Sauf indication contraire, les indices des prix à la consommation donnés englobent tous les groupes principaux de dépenses pour l'ensemble des prix et alimentation. Les données mensuelles pour plusieurs de ces séries et définitions figurent dans le *Bulletin mensuel de statistique* [26] et dans le *1977 Supplément à l'Annuaire statistique et au Bulletin mensuel de statistique* des Nations Unies [56].

34
Agricultural production
Production agricole
Index numbers: 1989-91 = 100
Indices : 1989-91 = 100

Country or area Pays ou zone	Agriculture Agriculture					Food Produits alimentaires				
	1996	1997	1998	1999	2000	1996	1997	1998	1999	2000
Africa · Afrique										
Algeria Algérie	141.1	113.3	129.1	131.7	125.5	143.1	114.2	130.5	133.0	126.7
Angola Angola	126.8	127.4	146.1	138.9	140.3	128.4	128.9	148.2	141.4	142.7
Benin Bénin	154.7	166.6	163.4	164.6	163.6	134.9	151.8	149.2	150.6	149.4
Botswana Botswana	106.3	94.5	90.3	93.7	96.0	106.4	94.6	90.4	93.8	96.1
Burkina Faso Burkina Faso	126.5	132.6	144.0	138.7	138.7	126.7	122.8	137.2	133.4	133.4
Burundi Burundi	95.9	94.2	89.3	91.2	84.8	97.6	97.1	91.5	91.6	86.1
Cameroon Cameroun	126.8	120.0	126.4	132.8	131.9	126.8	122.9	126.1	135.3	136.2
Cape Verde Cap-Vert	122.7	108.1	128.7	139.0	135.7	123.0	108.4	129.0	139.4	136.1
Central African Rep. Rép. centrafricaine	129.5	126.8	128.3	126.7	132.7	129.5	125.8	130.1	132.3	138.0
Chad Tchad	123.2	133.4	161.6	141.9	143.6	121.1	132.8	160.9	141.4	143.4
Comoros Comores	111.3	113.2	122.3	129.0	124.9	112.5	114.8	122.9	130.7	126.1
Congo Congo	114.9	112.2	114.8	115.9	115.9	115.7	113.0	115.6	116.7	116.7
Côte d'Ivoire Côte d'Ivoire	118.6	126.8	128.2	130.8	135.2	128.1	130.1	127.5	128.8	134.4
Dem. Rep. of the Congo Rép. dém. du Congo	94.4	93.7	93.4	90.3	87.8	95.1	94.5	94.6	91.8	89.6
Djibouti Djibouti	85.8	86.5	87.2	88.3	88.7	85.8	86.5	87.2	88.3	88.7
Egypt Egypte	136.2	143.1	141.5	150.5	152.0	137.5	145.0	145.3	154.8	156.5
Equatorial Guinea Guinée équatoriale	88.2	79.5	81.7	86.9	82.3	99.1	90.5	94.2	100.4	93.8
Eritrea Erythrée	104.2	103.7	150.3	139.2	112.0	104.3	103.7	151.3	140.0	112.3
Ethiopia Ethiopie	123.5	124.8	115.7	122.5	118.6	124.7	126.1	116.2	123.4	119.4
Gabon Gabon	109.3	113.0	115.4	117.9	117.8	107.7	110.2	112.3	114.8	114.8
Gambia Gambie	69.5	90.6	88.5	126.6	126.6	69.4	91.2	89.5	128.1	128.1
Ghana Ghana	149.5	144.8	158.8	165.7	165.7	148.7	143.9	157.5	164.6	164.6
Guinea Guinée	129.4	135.1	142.7	145.2	145.4	132.1	137.5	143.9	145.1	145.3
Guinea-Bissau Guinée-Bissau	115.2	119.5	122.2	127.2	127.2	115.3	119.7	122.6	127.3	127.3

34
Agricultural production
Index numbers: 1989-91 = 100 [cont.]
Production agricole
Indices : 1989-91 = 100 [suite]

Country or area Pays ou zone	Agriculture Agriculture					Food Produits alimentaires				
	1996	1997	1998	1999	2000	1996	1997	1998	1999	2000
Kenya Kenya	108.0	107.5	109.6	106.9	101.0	105.7	107.5	107.2	104.9	100.4
Lesotho Lesotho	111.8	116.6	96.9	95.4	95.6	111.3	115.9	98.1	96.4	95.9
Libyan Arab Jamah. Jamah. arabe libyenne	126.5	132.3	153.3	136.7	142.2	127.4	133.5	156.1	137.9	143.8
Madagascar Madagascar	107.8	109.4	108.9	112.4	105.5	109.5	111.7	110.8	114.4	107.5
Malawi Malawi	123.1	121.9	134.9	145.2	145.7	119.7	114.7	142.1	158.5	155.8
Mali Mali	119.8	123.9	130.4	133.6	133.6	111.9	112.9	121.4	126.5	126.5
Mauritania Mauritanie	107.2	105.0	104.1	103.9	107.4	107.2	105.0	104.1	103.9	107.4
Mauritius Maurice	104.2	110.6	105.9	83.3	103.9	108.2	116.0	111.3	87.0	109.1
Morocco Maroc	114.0	96.9	111.2	98.6	89.7	114.7	96.8	111.4	98.7	89.4
Mozambique Mozambique	122.6	131.0	140.3	142.4	114.8	122.5	130.1	138.5	140.7	113.4
Namibia Namibie	118.3	85.9	95.3	96.6	101.3	118.4	85.3	94.9	95.9	100.8
Niger Niger	120.7	97.4	147.1	141.3	140.3	120.3	97.1	147.1	141.0	140.0
Nigeria Nigéria	139.4	142.8	148.9	153.3	153.3	139.9	143.2	149.4	153.9	153.9
Réunion Réunion	110.4	119.8	114.1	118.8	118.8	111.0	120.5	114.7	119.6	119.5
Rwanda Rwanda	75.0	77.9	84.1	90.1	97.5	75.9	78.3	84.7	91.0	99.1
Sao Tome and Principe Sao Tomé-et-Principe	137.2	141.2	151.9	163.0	166.4	137.1	141.0	151.7	162.7	166.5
Senegal Sénégal	107.4	101.8	100.5	119.5	119.3	108.1	101.7	100.8	121.0	120.8
Seychelles Seychelles	136.9	142.1	128.0	133.8	136.2	138.6	142.7	128.3	134.9	137.4
Sierra Leone Sierra Leone	97.1	103.0	95.0	82.8	76.4	97.2	101.9	94.7	85.3	78.1
South Africa Afrique du Sud	100.6	100.8	95.5	101.2	106.1	103.0	103.6	97.9	103.6	109.4
Sudan Soudan	152.7	153.7	156.1	154.5	157.9	154.5	156.6	159.7	158.2	160.2
Swaziland Swaziland	92.3	86.1	86.4	90.2	91.1	97.3	88.0	90.1	93.1	94.1
Togo Togo	128.7	136.1	133.2	140.7	141.1	128.6	133.1	126.5	136.5	137.0
Tunisia Tunisie	142.1	97.5	123.1	129.0	127.1	144.2	98.2	124.6	130.8	128.6

34
Agricultural production
Index numbers: 1989-91 = 100 [cont.]
Production agricole
Indices : 1989-91 = 100 [suite]

Country or area Pays ou zone	Agriculture Agriculture					Food Produits alimentaires				
	1996	1997	1998	1999	2000	1996	1997	1998	1999	2000
Uganda Ouganda	109.8	109.5	117.2	121.2	131.0	102.6	105.4	113.5	116.2	127.9
United Rep. of Tanzania Rép.-Unie de Tanzanie	105.1	99.8	104.4	106.3	100.3	102.9	97.4	104.8	106.9	100.7
Zambia Zambie	112.3	100.1	95.0	107.3	117.2	113.7	98.7	93.4	105.9	116.8
Zimbabwe Zimbabwe	110.2	114.3	110.0	110.3	126.1	102.9	105.8	93.5	103.0	115.7
America, North · Amérique du Nord										
Antigua and Barbuda Antigua-et-Barbuda	98.6	98.6	98.6	98.6	98.6	98.9	98.9	98.9	98.9	98.9
Bahamas Bahamas	128.6	137.9	148.0	146.7	138.2	128.6	137.9	148.0	146.7	138.2
Barbados Barbade	105.6	96.7	97.2	99.1	100.1	105.6	96.7	97.2	99.1	100.1
Belize Belize	147.2	161.5	153.1	161.5	161.5	147.2	161.5	153.1	161.5	161.5
Bermuda Bermudes	78.1	78.4	78.4	78.4	78.4	78.1	78.4	78.4	78.4	78.4
British Virgin Islands Iles Vierges britanniques	104.0	104.0	104.0	104.0	104.0	104.0	104.0	104.0	104.0	104.0
Canada Canada	117.7	116.2	124.0	131.7	132.9	117.7	116.1	123.7	131.7	133.5
Cayman Islands Iles Caïmanes	84.9	84.9	84.9	84.9	84.9	84.9	84.9	84.9	84.9	84.9
Costa Rica Costa Rica	128.0	125.3	136.6	142.2	137.8	133.2	130.8	141.5	148.9	143.0
Cuba Cuba	64.4	63.0	59.3	62.3	63.4	63.8	62.2	58.3	61.4	62.8
Dominica Dominique	91.3	92.1	84.3	85.8	85.9	90.5	91.3	83.5	84.9	85.1
Dominican Republic Rép. dominicaine	104.4	104.8	106.4	103.6	107.8	106.0	105.4	104.8	107.5	110.9
El Salvador El Salvador	101.5	109.8	108.2	116.7	114.8	102.0	117.6	116.5	119.2	121.1
Greenland Groenland	105.7	105.9	105.8	105.8	105.8	106.1	106.3	106.1	106.1	106.1
Grenada Grenade	93.1	99.0	85.6	93.4	95.0	93.1	99.0	85.6	93.4	95.0
Guadeloupe Guadeloupe	90.6	113.8	108.2	108.2	108.2	90.6	113.8	108.2	108.2	108.2
Guatemala Guatemala	114.2	118.1	120.7	120.6	120.7	120.1	122.3	126.2	121.7	121.4
Haiti Haïti	91.2	94.1	93.3	95.0	101.1	92.6	95.7	94.9	96.5	102.8
Honduras Honduras	115.2	115.5	117.8	115.5	114.9	112.3	110.6	112.0	107.6	105.4
Jamaica Jamaïque	124.2	117.4	117.7	121.3	122.4	124.6	117.7	118.3	121.8	122.8

34
Agricultural production
Index numbers: 1989-91 = 100 [*cont.*]
Production agricole
Indices : 1989-91 = 100 [*suite*]

Country or area Pays ou zone	Agriculture Agriculture					Food Produits alimentaires				
	1996	1997	1998	1999	2000	1996	1997	1998	1999	2000
Martinique Martinique	112.8	120.2	120.0	120.0	120.0	112.8	120.2	120.0	120.0	120.0
Mexico Mexique	117.0	121.8	123.1	127.3	131.0	117.1	122.7	124.0	129.2	133.8
Montserrat Montserrat	110.2	110.2	110.2	110.2	110.2	110.2	110.2	110.2	110.2	110.2
Netherlands Antilles Antilles néerlandaises	130.0	163.4	170.7	161.4	160.3	130.0	163.4	170.7	161.4	160.3
Nicaragua Nicaragua	114.2	118.7	124.3	151.6	157.0	121.4	122.9	130.3	156.8	165.1
Panama Panama	105.0	100.6	103.0	102.1	114.7	105.3	100.8	103.2	102.3	115.5
Puerto Rico Porto Rico	83.0	81.8	81.8	81.8	81.8	82.7	81.7	81.7	81.7	81.7
Saint Kitts and Nevis Saint-Kitts-et-Nevis	102.4	134.3	112.5	96.5	93.9	102.6	134.6	112.8	96.7	94.2
Saint Lucia Sainte-Lucie	91.6	81.0	67.3	75.6	74.1	91.6	81.0	67.3	75.6	74.1
St. Vincent-Grenadines St. Vincent-Grenadines	82.7	71.3	76.1	73.5	77.3	82.2	70.7	75.6	72.9	76.7
Trinidad and Tobago Trinité-et-Tobago	112.8	110.6	99.2	112.0	117.1	114.3	111.2	100.4	113.5	118.5
United States Etats-Unis	114.5	118.7	119.5	121.2	123.8	114.3	118.6	120.7	121.9	124.7
United States Virgin Is. Iles Vierges américaines	103.4	103.4	103.4	103.4	103.4	103.4	103.4	103.4	103.4	103.4
America, South · Amérique du Sud										
Argentina Argentine	120.3	122.6	131.5	134.7	135.5	122.0	125.3	134.8	139.0	140.4
Bolivia Bolivie	129.8	139.6	136.6	133.7	148.1	128.8	139.2	136.4	133.2	149.5
Brazil Brésil	122.0	126.9	129.2	139.6	144.5	125.2	130.5	131.9	142.5	146.9
Chile Chili	127.9	131.6	133.5	131.2	131.1	128.7	132.7	134.6	132.1	132.0
Colombia Colombie	107.1	108.5	111.2	111.1	112.8	112.1	115.1	116.2	117.9	119.8
Ecuador Equateur	141.5	147.5	121.4	145.8	150.9	142.2	154.1	127.8	150.1	155.4
Falkland Is. (Malvinas) Iles Falkland (Malvinas)	84.4	91.9	90.3	90.3	90.3	71.6	87.0	86.4	86.4	86.4
French Guiana Guyane française	136.5	129.5	118.4	110.1	110.1	136.5	129.5	118.4	110.1	110.1
Guyana Guyana	189.1	192.4	176.3	195.5	195.5	189.6	192.9	176.9	196.2	196.2
Paraguay Paraguay	105.4	108.8	113.0	120.3	116.1	116.1	124.8	127.9	137.6	132.4
Peru Pérou	133.1	140.6	142.2	161.5	165.8	134.8	144.9	147.2	166.8	170.1

34
Agricultural production
Index numbers: 1989-91 = 100 [cont.]
Production agricole
Indices : 1989-91 = 100 [suite]

Country or area Pays ou zone	Agriculture Agriculture					Food Produits alimentaires				
	1996	1997	1998	1999	2000	1996	1997	1998	1999	2000
Suriname Suriname	89.1	90.3	77.4	81.4	82.3	89.1	90.3	77.4	81.5	82.3
Uruguay Uruguay	121.4	129.8	129.6	129.8	122.0	128.0	136.7	137.8	141.0	132.8
Venezuela Venezuela	110.7	117.7	113.2	115.7	112.1	111.9	119.3	114.9	117.8	114.5
Asia · Asie										
Armenia Arménie	79.8	72.2	75.7	76.6	74.1	80.6	72.9	76.3	77.2	74.7
Azerbaijan Azerbaïdjan	59.4	52.9	57.4	61.2	66.4	63.0	58.3	64.2	69.7	74.0
Bahrain Bahreïn	116.1	105.4	108.6	127.0	127.2	116.1	105.4	108.6	127.0	127.2
Bangladesh Bangladesh	109.4	111.6	115.2	130.3	133.6	109.8	111.3	115.2	128.2	131.6
Bhutan Bhoutan	115.2	116.6	116.6	114.4	114.4	115.2	116.7	116.7	114.4	114.4
Brunei Darussalam Brunéi Darussalam	127.1	157.6	182.9	180.6	180.7	127.6	158.3	183.8	181.5	181.5
Cambodia Cambodge	128.5	132.1	134.4	147.2	142.9	128.4	132.2	134.5	147.7	143.3
China †† Chine ††	144.5	153.9	159.7	164.8	170.7	148.2	157.2	165.4	171.4	177.3
Cyprus Chypre	112.6	103.8	110.5	118.0	110.2	112.1	103.5	110.5	118.0	110.1
Georgia Géorgie	75.6	80.1	72.2	75.1	69.8	86.1	92.3	80.1	82.0	75.4
India Inde	119.4	121.9	122.4	127.8	126.9	119.1	122.4	122.6	128.3	127.4
Indonesia Indonésie	122.4	119.4	117.2	119.8	120.2	122.7	119.8	117.2	120.4	120.8
Iran (Islamic Rep. of) Iran (Rép. islamique d')	138.1	134.6	154.4	144.3	145.8	138.1	134.6	155.1	143.8	145.4
Iraq Iraq	100.6	90.3	93.8	80.6	67.6	102.4	91.4	94.8	81.1	67.6
Israel Israël	111.8	111.4	115.5	109.2	111.4	111.2	110.5	115.1	111.3	113.6
Japan Japon	95.3	95.6	91.4	92.4	93.1	95.9	96.1	91.9	92.9	93.6
Jordan Jordanie	116.2	141.0	151.1	124.3	134.2	115.3	141.9	152.9	125.8	136.4
Kazakhstan Kazakhstan	61.2	60.5	49.5	67.4	59.9	62.0	62.0	50.7	69.7	61.5
Korea, Republic of Corée, République de	119.3	124.7	124.0	125.1	123.1	120.4	126.1	125.2	126.1	124.1
Kuwait Koweït	158.1	139.4	154.2	165.3	168.1	160.1	140.5	155.7	166.6	169.1
Kyrgyzstan Kirghizistan	89.8	97.9	100.8	106.3	107.7	99.8	109.0	111.5	117.2	117.4

34
Agricultural production
Index numbers: 1989-91 = 100 [cont.]
Production agricole
Indices : 1989-91 = 100 [suite]

Country or area Pays ou zone	Agriculture Agriculture					Food Produits alimentaires				
	1996	1997	1998	1999	2000	1996	1997	1998	1999	2000
Lao People's Dem. Rep. Rép. dém. pop. lao	111.7	125.0	129.2	150.6	156.7	112.8	126.7	131.1	157.2	152.4
Lebanon Liban	137.5	137.3	144.9	140.7	148.0	135.3	135.1	142.4	138.2	145.3
Malaysia Malaisie	120.6	121.2	119.3	124.7	126.7	128.7	131.2	130.1	138.7	141.2
Maldives Maldives	113.5	115.9	120.9	131.2	132.4	113.5	115.9	120.9	131.2	132.4
Mongolia Mongolie	91.2	88.2	90.9	94.3	85.4	90.9	88.2	90.7	94.1	84.4
Myanmar Myanmar	135.7	136.4	138.7	154.4	160.0	135.5	136.0	138.1	154.9	160.4
Nepal Népal	114.9	118.3	118.7	120.8	124.9	115.2	118.7	119.0	121.2	125.3
Occupied Palestinian Terr.[1] Terr. palestinien occupé[1]	101.3	102.0	102.0	102.0	102.0	101.3	102.0	102.0	102.0	102.0
Oman Oman	109.2	114.7	114.7	112.8	113.3	108.4	113.9	113.9	112.0	112.5
Pakistan Pakistan	127.6	129.2	134.7	138.5	140.2	135.0	137.1	144.3	144.4	146.6
Philippines Philippines	119.6	122.3	112.5	114.9	119.2	121.2	123.9	113.7	116.6	121.1
Qatar Qatar	173.5	173.2	137.8	170.1	175.2	173.5	173.2	137.8	170.1	175.2
Saudi Arabia Arabie saoudite	69.0	89.7	89.2	84.5	84.5	67.9	89.0	88.4	83.6	83.6
Singapore Singapour	42.3	37.5	41.4	39.5	39.5	42.3	37.5	41.4	39.5	39.5
Sri Lanka Sri Lanka	106.7	110.6	114.6	117.3	116.4	104.6	108.1	113.7	117.2	115.7
Syrian Arab Republic Rép. arabe syrienne	147.7	137.8	165.8	139.0	152.1	150.4	132.5	166.8	136.0	151.3
Tajikistan Tadjikistan	51.8	50.2	48.4	47.3	54.3	54.0	53.1	49.0	50.2	61.6
Thailand Thaïlande	116.5	118.4	114.3	115.9	116.8	114.7	116.6	112.3	114.2	114.7
Turkey Turquie	109.1	108.5	116.4	110.5	108.9	109.4	107.7	116.0	110.1	108.5
Turkmenistan Turkménistan	68.1	78.2	85.1	99.4	94.2	97.6	105.7	126.1	136.5	136.4
United Arab Emirates Emirats arabes unis	198.8	252.3	263.2	262.5	275.1	199.9	253.8	264.9	264.0	276.9
Uzbekistan Ouzbékistan	91.7	95.2	98.7	97.8	96.3	104.7	110.5	113.4	117.3	117.6
Viet Nam Viet Nam	136.9	143.6	150.7	162.0	169.5	134.1	138.9	146.2	155.5	159.7
Yemen Yémen	115.1	122.2	133.2	130.6	133.3	113.8	120.5	131.3	128.5	130.9

34
Agricultural production
Index numbers: 1989-91 = 100 [cont.]
Production agricole
Indices : 1989-91 = 100 [suite]

Country or area Pays ou zone	Agriculture Agriculture					Food Produits alimentaires				
	1996	1997	1998	1999	2000	1996	1997	1998	1999	2000
Europe · Europe										
Austria Autriche	102.0	104.8	106.9	105.3	100.9	102.0	104.8	106.9	105.3	100.9
Belarus Bélarus	64.9	62.3	65.6	59.4	59.4	64.8	62.7	65.8	59.9	59.5
Belgium-Luxembourg Belgique-Luxembourg	115.0	113.8	113.6	114.3	111.9	115.0	113.8	113.5	114.2	111.8
Bulgaria Bulgarie	62.6	68.7	67.3	66.1	64.9	63.6	69.4	68.8	67.8	64.9
Croatia Croatie	60.2	59.4	71.3	67.3	66.9	59.7	58.9	70.8	67.0	66.8
Czech Republic République tchèque	79.3	78.1	80.2	81.6	69.9	79.3	78.4	80.3	81.6	69.9
Denmark Danemark	101.9	104.0	106.4	104.2	105.8	101.9	104.0	106.4	104.2	105.8
Estonia Estonie	46.8	44.2	40.8	40.9	46.4	46.8	44.2	40.8	40.9	46.4
Faeroe Islands Iles Féroé	104.6	105.8	105.7	96.7	96.7	104.6	105.8	105.7	96.7	96.7
Finland Finlande	92.0	95.1	84.8	88.3	96.3	92.0	95.0	84.8	88.3	96.3
France France	106.0	106.5	107.5	107.9	106.8	106.1	106.6	107.6	107.9	106.8
Germany Allemagne	91.5	92.9	94.0	96.6	95.9	91.5	92.9	93.9	96.4	95.6
Greece Grèce	106.0	102.6	101.6	103.7	103.1	104.3	99.3	97.8	100.0	98.7
Hungary Hongrie	76.0	78.3	78.1	74.4	67.5	76.2	78.5	78.2	74.5	67.5
Iceland Islande	92.8	92.7	94.9	100.5	102.2	93.9	93.7	95.9	101.5	103.4
Ireland Irlande	105.7	103.0	107.0	115.1	112.5	106.2	103.5	107.5	115.8	113.1
Italy Italie	101.9	100.7	101.2	106.5	104.8	102.4	101.2	101.8	107.2	105.4
Latvia Lettonie	45.8	52.2	46.0	41.5	46.7	45.9	52.4	46.1	41.4	46.7
Liechtenstein Liechtenstein	91.1	91.1	91.1	91.1	91.1	91.1	91.1	91.1	91.1	91.1
Lithuania Lituanie	70.4	71.2	65.9	61.7	62.8	70.5	71.4	66.1	61.9	63.0
Malta Malte	139.9	137.4	136.9	130.7	134.2	140.1	137.5	137.1	130.9	134.4
Netherlands Pays-Bas	102.8	95.9	98.1	104.2	102.3	102.9	96.0	98.3	104.5	102.6
Norway Norvège	97.6	96.9	96.1	96.0	95.0	97.4	96.8	95.9	95.9	94.9
Poland Pologne	87.8	84.9	90.8	86.4	85.3	88.2	85.4	91.2	86.8	85.9

34
Agricultural production
Index numbers: 1989-91 = 100 [cont.]
Production agricole
Indices : 1989-91 = 100 [suite]

Country or area Pays ou zone	Agriculture Agriculture					Food Produits alimentaires				
	1996	1997	1998	1999	2000	1996	1997	1998	1999	2000
Portugal Portugal	102.5	96.8	94.2	106.5	102.2	102.5	96.7	94.0	106.6	102.2
Republic of Moldova République de Moldova	55.7	63.3	45.5	41.5	45.9	56.7	64.3	45.6	41.6	46.2
Romania Roumanie	94.0	102.4	87.9	97.9	88.2	95.0	103.6	88.8	99.0	89.0
Russian Federation Fédération de Russie	67.3	67.8	58.8	61.0	60.9	67.9	68.6	59.4	61.8	61.7
Slovakia Slovaquie	76.5	81.9	78.0	77.7	70.2	77.0	82.4	78.6	78.2	70.6
Slovenia Slovénie	102.6	99.6	101.2	95.0	92.2	102.6	99.5	101.2	95.0	92.2
Spain Espagne	108.0	114.3	110.6	111.0	114.4	107.9	114.0	110.1	110.4	114.0
Sweden Suède	99.6	101.6	100.9	96.8	104.3	99.5	101.5	100.8	96.7	104.3
Switzerland Suisse	97.8	93.2	99.5	94.1	97.1	97.7	93.2	99.5	94.1	97.2
TFYR of Macedonia L'ex-R.y. Macédoine	92.2	94.3	97.5	99.2	97.1	94.0	93.7	95.2	96.9	94.7
Ukraine Ukraine	53.4	55.3	46.7	46.5	49.1	53.7	55.7	47.1	46.9	49.4
United Kingdom Royaume-Uni	101.0	99.7	99.9	99.0	97.8	101.1	99.7	99.7	98.6	97.8
Yugoslavia Yougoslavie	103.5	99.6	94.4	83.2	80.7	103.7	99.7	94.5	83.1	80.7
Oceania · Océanie										
American Samoa Samoa américaines	96.2	96.2	96.2	96.2	96.2	96.2	96.2	96.2	96.2	96.2
Australia Australie	117.2	118.3	123.4	131.1	129.5	130.2	129.6	136.8	146.9	144.1
Cocos (Keeling) Islands Iles des Cocos (Keeling)	101.7	101.7	101.7	101.7	101.7	101.7	101.7	101.7	101.7	101.7
Cook Islands Iles Cook	80.5	89.4	103.0	96.9	96.9	80.0	89.0	102.7	96.8	96.8
Fiji Fidji	108.3	97.2	81.5	86.1	86.1	108.5	97.4	81.7	86.3	86.3
French Polynesia Polynésie française	95.6	94.1	79.0	92.6	92.6	95.6	94.1	78.9	92.5	92.5
Guam Guam	110.8	110.8	110.8	110.8	110.8	110.8	110.8	110.8	110.8	110.8
Kiribati Kiribati	127.2	127.2	133.1	115.6	116.1	127.2	127.2	133.1	115.6	116.1
Nauru Nauru	105.4	105.6	105.6	105.6	105.6	105.4	105.6	105.6	105.6	105.6
New Caledonia Nouvelle-Calédonie	121.7	125.9	129.4	128.8	128.8	123.3	127.6	131.1	130.6	130.6
New Zealand Nouvelle-Zélande	114.0	120.2	120.6	114.4	119.6	120.1	127.2	128.2	121.7	127.7

34
Agricultural production
Index numbers: 1989-91 = 100 [cont.]
Production agricole
Indices: 1989-91 = 100 [suite]

Country or area Pays ou zone	Agriculture Agriculture					Food Produits alimentaires				
	1996	1997	1998	1999	2000	1996	1997	1998	1999	2000
Niue Nioué	100.7	100.7	100.7	100.7	100.7	100.7	100.7	100.7	100.7	100.7
Papua New Guinea Papouasie-Nvl-Guinée	111.2	110.5	113.4	119.7	120.1	111.8	111.3	111.0	117.2	117.7
Samoa Samoa	94.2	94.2	94.2	94.2	94.2	93.8	93.8	93.8	93.8	93.8
Solomon Islands Iles Salomon	125.5	131.0	134.6	138.1	140.5	125.6	131.1	134.7	138.2	140.6
Tokelau Tokélaou	108.5	108.5	108.5	108.5	108.5	108.5	108.5	108.5	108.5	108.5
Tonga Tonga	76.6	76.5	76.1	76.3	76.3	76.6	76.6	76.2	76.3	76.3
Tuvalu Tuvalu	99.2	99.2	99.2	99.2	99.2	99.2	99.2	99.2	99.2	99.2
Vanuatu Vanuatu	105.3	122.7	126.9	107.6	125.5	105.2	122.7	126.9	107.5	125.4
Wallis and Futuna Islands Iles Wallis et Futuna	101.5	101.5	101.5	101.5	101.5	101.5	101.5	101.5	101.5	101.5

Source:
Food and Agriculture Organization of the United
Nations (FAO), Rome, "FAO Production Yearbook 2000" and the
FAOSTAT database.

1 Data refer to the Gaza Strip.

Source:
Organisation des Nations Unies pour l'alimentation et
l'agriculture (FAO), Rome, "Annuaire FAO de la production
2000" et la base de données FAOSTAT.

1 Les données se rapportent à la Zone de Gaza.

35
Cereals
Céréales
Production: thousand metric tons
Production : milliers de tonnes

Region, country or area / Région, pays ou zone	1991	1992	1993	1994	1995	1996	1997	1998	1999	2000
World *Monde*	1 889 270	1 972 820	1 903 090	1 956 770	1 896 509	2 070 194	2 098 136	2 081 766	2 076 843	2 049 415
Africa **Afrique**	104 534	88 922	99 817	110 811	97 671	124 667	110 640	115 753	111 922	112 405
Algeria Algérie	3 810	3 330	1 454	965	2 140	4 902	870	3 026	1 540	1 226
Angola Angola	372	402	322	285	296	525	457	621	550	550[1]
Benin Bénin	587	609	627	646	725	714	906	867	890	872
Botswana Botswana	50	20	43	52	42	111	31	12	20	22[1]
Burkina Faso Burkina Faso	2 455	2 477	2 552	2 492	2 308	2 465	2 309	2 657	2 453[1]	2 453[1]
Burundi Burundi	300	306	300	* 225	* 269	* 273	* 305	261	265	245
Cameroon Cameroun	1 048	917	959	910	1 238	1 314	1 296	1 499	1 055	1 489
Cape Verde Cap-Vert	8	10	12	8[1]	8	10	9[1]	10[1]	11[1]	11[1]
Central African Rep. Rép. centrafricaine	92	94	94	101	113	126	138	148	173	176
Chad Tchad	812	977	680	1 073	907	878	986	1 353	1 153	1 248
Comoros Comores	20	20	21	21	21	21	21	21	21	21[1]
Congo Congo	6	6	7	7	6	* 5	* 4	2	2[1]	2[1]
Côte d'Ivoire Côte d'Ivoire	1 286	1 319	1 511	1 599	1 690	1 494	1 963	1 864	1 827	1 827[1]
Dem. Rep. of the Congo Rép. dém. du Congo	1 507	1 553	1 655	1 708	1 550	1 557	1 633	1 692	1 649	1 621
Egypt Egypte	13 864	14 611	14 961	15 012	16 097	16 542	18 071	17 964	19 384	20 046[1]
Eritrea Erythrée	...	...	87	259	* 123	* 83	* 95	* 449	319	182[1]
Ethiopia incl. Eritrea Ethiopie comp. Erythrée	5 811	5 035	...	...	...	...	...	...	...	...
Ethiopia Ethiopie	...	...	5 295	5 245	6 740	9 379	9 473	7 197	8 406	7 845
Gabon Gabon	25	26	27	29	30[1]	31[1]	32[1]	32[1]	32[1]	32[1]
Gambia Gambie	111	96	97	95	98	103	104	114	144	144
Ghana Ghana	1 436	1 254	1 645	1 594	1 797	1 770	1 669	1 788	1 686	1 686[1]
Guinea Guinée	686	683	711	718	825	879	927	985	973	973[1]
Guinea-Bissau Guinée-Bissau	179	169	181	190	201	174	190	200[1]	212	212[1]

35

Cereals
Production: thousand metric tons [*cont.*]
Céréales
Production : milliers de tonnes [*suite*]

Region, country or area Région, pays ou zone	1991	1992	1993	1994	1995	1996	1997	1998	1999	2000
Kenya Kenya	2 773	2 849	2 530	3 663	3 275	2 773	2 767	3 062	2 644	2 197
Lesotho Lesotho	67	94	153	223	81	256	206	171	174	149[1]
Liberia Libéria	100[1]	110[1]	* 65	* 50	* 56	* 94	* 168	* 210	200[1]	200[1]
Libyan Arab Jamah. Jamah. arabe libyenne	258[1]	218[1]	180[1]	165[1]	146	160	206	238[1]	251[1]	238[1]
Madagascar Madagascar	2 497	2 591	2 724	2 517	2 642	2 685	2 742	2 610	2 829	2 460
Malawi Malawi	1 680	689	2 137	1 109	1 778	1 943	1 349	1 904	2 655	2 463
Mali Mali	2 414	1 809	2 228	2 457	2 173	2 219	2 149	2 552	2 952	2 952[1]
Mauritania Mauritanie	105	107	169	207	222	234	154	189	193	263
Mauritius Maurice	2	2	2	1	0	0	0	0	0	0[1]
Morocco Maroc	8 665	2 950	2 818	9 639	1 783	10 104	4 098	6 632	3 859	2 006
Mozambique Mozambique	546	242	765	791	1 127	1 379	1 531	1 688	1 821	1 476
Namibia Namibie	115	31	75	116	62	89	173	55	72	140
Niger Niger	2 384	2 253	2 023	2 428	2 094	2 230	1 695	2 958	2 823	2 738
Nigeria Nigéria	18 615	19 597	20 091	20 373	22 513	21 665	21 853	22 040	22 405	22 405[1]
Réunion Réunion	13	16	14	17	17	16	17[1]	17[1]	17[1]	17[1]
Rwanda Rwanda	341	240	234	133	142	183	223	194	179	240
Sao Tome and Principe Sao Tomé-et-Principe	4	4	4	4	* 3	2[1]	1	2[1]	1	2
Senegal Sénégal	946	856	1 086	943	1 059	976	783	720	963	963[1]
Sierra Leone Sierra Leone	560	534	542	466	408	444	467	373	280	222
Somalia Somalie	256	209	165	405	285	290	284[1]	232	208	313
South Africa Afrique du Sud	11 289	5 044	12 792	15 967	7 491	13 648	13 230	10 098	10 025	13 245
Sudan Soudan	4 637	5 438	3 102	5 146	3 305	5 202	4 261	5 595	3 066	3 292
Swaziland Swaziland	142	58	75	101	79	152	110	126	114	73
Togo Togo	465	495	634	559	550	687	748	624	759	759[1]
Tunisia Tunisie	2 556	2 199	1 917	660	622	2 869	1 056	1 667	1 819	1 095

35
Cereals
Production: thousand metric tons [*cont.*]
Céréales
Production : milliers de tonnes [*suite*]

Region, country or area Région, pays ou zone	1991	1992	1993	1994	1995	1996	1997	1998	1999	2000
Uganda Ouganda	1 576	1 743	1 880	1 936	2 030	1 588	1 625	1 911	1 825	2 111
United Rep. of Tanzania Rép.-Unie de Tanzanie	3 777	3 533	3 917	3 550	4 629	4 719	3 390	4 495	3 977	3 556
Zambia Zambie	1 225	612	1 758	1 170	882	1 573	1 137	798	1 057	1 435
Zimbabwe Zimbabwe	2 060	481	2 498	2 780	987	3 127	2 723	1 829	1 987	2 513
America, North **Amérique du Nord**	**362 802**	**435 429**	**341 317**	**434 410**	**359 099**	**429 116**	**419 389**	**434 712**	**423 376**	**430 378**
Bahamas Bahamas	1 [1]	1 [1]	0 [1]	0	0	0	0	0	0	0
Barbados [1] Barbade [1]	2	2	2	2	2	2	2	2	2	2
Belize Belize	37	32	37	30	38	50	54	46	49 [1]	49 [1]
Canada Canada	53 855	49 701	51 676	46 724	49 315	58 465	49 526	50 897	53 911	51 315
Costa Rica Costa Rica	260	272	208	229	223	329	271	314	312	287
Cuba Cuba	484	418	227	301	305	474	546	392	555	555 [1]
Dominican Republic Rép. dominicaine	526	629	498	417	548	535	564	530	611	556
El Salvador El Salvador	729	992	909	727	889	857	764	841	846	793
Guatemala Guatemala	1 382	1 514	1 446	1 296	1 164	1 140	954	1 155	1 199	1 199 [1]
Haiti Haïti	400	452	420 [1]	425 [1]	410 [1]	412	490 [1]	403	450 [1]	431
Honduras Honduras	692	687	691	674	770	784	757	590	563	607
Jamaica Jamaïque	3	4	4	4	4	4	3	2	2	2 [1]
Mexico Mexique	23 673	26 889	25 200	26 810	26 883	29 311	28 062	29 123	28 424	29 550
Nicaragua Nicaragua	388	498	588	521	622	674	608	618	559	751
Panama Panama	337	337	329	348	310	323	239	338	322	401
St. Vincent-Grenadines St. Vincent-Grenadines	2 [1]	2	2	2	2	1	1	2	2	2
Trinidad and Tobago Trinité-et-Tobago	19	26	21	23	15	23	12	12	12 [1]	12 [1]
United States Etats-Unis	280 013	352 973	259 057	355 877	277 600	335 731	336 536	349 446	335 556	343 866
America, South **Amérique du Sud**	**73 990**	**85 131**	**84 464**	**87 996**	**91 718**	**93 219**	**99 348**	**95 858**	**100 373**	**103 416**
Argentina Argentine	21 591	25 444	25 097	25 270	24 209	30 507	35 824	37 632	34 634	38 110

35
Cereals
Production: thousand metric tons [cont.]
Céréales
Production : milliers de tonnes [suite]

Region, country or area Région, pays ou zone	1991	1992	1993	1994	1995	1996	1997	1998	1999	2000
Bolivia Bolivie	1 011	819	1 078	1 008	1 096	1 254	1 252	1 077	1 169	1 257
Brazil Brésil	36 682	44 058	43 073	45 849	49 642	44 962	44 876	40 743	47 493	46 597
Chile Chili	2 864	2 901	2 643	2 619	2 766	2 578	3 077	3 098	2 168	2 598
Colombia Colombie	3 948	3 674	3 522	3 631	3 435	3 177	3 207	2 893	3 286	3 362
Ecuador Equateur	1 444	1 631	1 902	2 061	1 900	1 947	1 815	1 485	1 915	2 341
French Guiana Guyane française	29	24	28	25	25	31	31	25	20	20[1]
Guyana Guyana	254	288	349	396	506	547	571	535	603	603[1]
Paraguay Paraguay	830	985	950	815	1 522	1 210	1 450	1 156	1 163	1 266[1]
Peru Pérou	1 729	1 522	2 013	2 408	2 135	2 338	2 583	2 830	3 389	3 313
Suriname Suriname	229	261	217	218	242	220	213	189	180	175
Uruguay Uruguay	1 074	1 558	1 491	1 515	1 811	2 222	2 057	2 046	2 185	1 817
Venezuela Venezuela	2 305	1 966	2 100	2 181	2 428	2 225	2 391	2 149	2 167	1 958
Asia Asie	868 834	930 596	936 949	923 429	943 859	996 603	995 834	1 015 693	1 028 735	987 498
Afghanistan Afghanistan	2 724	2 420	2 900	3 102	3 052	3 252	3 683	3 876	3 397	1 913
Armenia Arménie	...	307	312	233	257	323	254	323	297	216
Azerbaijan Azerbaïdjan	...	1 325	1 137	1 024	909	1 010	1 119	940	1 006	1 530
Bangladesh Bangladesh	28 462	28 654	28 297	26 513	27 702	29 622	29 673	31 575	36 479	37 785
Bhutan Bhoutan	106	106	118[1]	133[1]	151[1]	165[1]	174	174	159	159[1]
Brunei Darussalam Brunéi Darussalam	1	1	1	* 1	* 1	* 0	* 0	* 0	0[1]	0[1]
Cambodia Cambodge	2 460	2 281	2 429	2 268	3 373	3 455	3 457	3 564	4 094	3 857
China †† Chine ††	398 464	404 269	407 931	396 460	418 665	453 665	445 931	458 396	455 192	408 431
Cyprus Chypre	65	182	205	162	145	141	48	66	127	47
Georgia Géorgie	...	496	403	471	501	630	892	589	771	327
India Inde	193 101	201 468	208 627	211 941	210 013	218 750	226 646	226 946	232 488	239 814
Indonesia Indonésie	50 944	56 235	54 641	53 510	57 990	60 409	58 148	59 369	60 070	60 169

35
Cereals
Production: thousand metric tons [*cont.*]
Céréales
Production : milliers de tonnes [*suite*]

Region, country or area Région, pays ou zone	1991	1992	1993	1994	1995	1996	1997	1998	1999	2000
Iran (Islamic Rep. of) Iran (Rép. islamique d')	14 447	15 811	16 287	16 691	17 032	16 083	15 823	18 985	14 186	12 513
Iraq Iraq	2 673	2 959	3 239	2 829	2 538	2 999	2 211	2 511	1 595[1]	795[1]
Israel Israël	277	343	297	184	309	264	187	213	99	134
Japan Japon	13 070	14 286	10 737	15 787	14 122	13 668	13 320	11 934	12 263	12 769
Jordan Jordanie	107	157	114	111	125	97	96	93	27	52
Kazakhstan Kazakhstan	...	29 649	21 533	16 375	9 476	11 210	12 359	6 380	14 249	11 583
Korea, Dem. P. R. Corée, R. p. dém. de	8 836	8 681	9 137	7 215	3 787	2 596	2 866	4 422	3 987	3 118
Korea, Republic of Corée, République de	7 853	7 846	7 042	7 305	6 877	7 617	7 676	7 132	7 701	7 498
Kuwait Koweït	0[1]	2[1]	2[1]	2	2	3	2	3	3	3[1]
Kyrgyzstan Kirghizistan	...	1 603	1 597	1 065	1 045	1 407	1 615	1 608	1 617	1 550
Lao People's Dem. Rep. Rép. dém. pop. lao	1 292	1 561	1 298	1 633	1 466	1 490	1 738	1 784	2 199	2 232
Lebanon Liban	83	88	81	79	100	94	90	94	93[1]	96[1]
Malaysia Malaisie	1 961	2 049	2 142	2 179	2 170	2 273	2 168	1 994	2 094	2 094[1]
Mongolia Mongolie	597	496	474	328	261	219	240	194	172	190
Myanmar Myanmar	13 651	15 342	17 263	18 727	18 483	18 238	17 195	17 640	20 772	20 643
Nepal Népal	5 520	4 902	5 773	5 375	6 078	6 367	6 416	6 360	6 465	6 986
Occupied Palestinian Terr.[2] Terr. palestinien occupé[2]	1	1	1	1	1	1	1	1	1	1
Oman[1] Oman[1]	5	5	5	6	6	6	6	6	6	6
Pakistan Pakistan	21 138	22 123	23 870	22 338	24 816	25 163	24 994	27 621	27 456	29 923
Philippines Philippines	14 329	14 132	14 232	14 669	14 702	15 629	15 600	12 377	16 371	16 901
Qatar Qatar	4	4	5	4	4	5	6	6	6	6[1]
Saudi Arabia Arabie saoudite	4 574	4 703	5 043	4 860	2 669	1 932	2 339	2 202	2 452	2 452[1]
Sri Lanka Sri Lanka	2 430	2 374	2 609	2 722	2 850	2 099	2 269	2 731	2 894	2 804
Syrian Arab Republic Rép. arabe syrienne	3 294	4 368	5 393	5 397	6 098	5 995	4 325	5 275	3 276	3 503
Tajikistan Tadjikistan	...	261	258	250	244	525	539	482	455	455

35

Cereals
Production: thousand metric tons [*cont.*]
Céréales
Production : milliers de tonnes [*suite*]

Region, country or area Région, pays ou zone	1991	1992	1993	1994	1995	1996	1997	1998	1999	2000
Thailand Thaïlande	24 462	23 864	22 013	25 339	26 399	27 124	27 605	27 613	27 906	28 262
Turkey Turquie	31 148	29 157	31 749	27 014	28 134	29 344	29 747	33 182	26 557	26 657
Turkmenistan Turkménistan	...	732	1 009	1 120	1 102	545	759	1 278	1 567	1 768
United Arab Emirates Emirats arabes unis	2	3	1	1	1	1	1[1]	0	0	0[1]
Uzbekistan Ouzbékistan	...	2 178	2 165	2 502	3 223	3 558	3 768	4 132	4 312	3 048
Viet Nam Viet Nam	20 294	22 338	23 719	24 672	26 141	27 933	29 175	30 758	33 146	34 484
Yemen Yémen	448	811	834	802	810	664	646	833	700	695
Europe **Europe**	**303 558**	**406 878**	**413 000**	**383 815**	**376 049**	**390 784**	**440 808**	**386 327**	**376 485**	**384 222**
Albania Albanie	446	430	686	666	662	519	616	621	512	580
Austria Autriche	5 045	4 323	4 206	4 436	4 455	4 493	5 009	4 776	4 806	4 457
Belarus Bélarus	...	7 061	7 315	5 938	5 314	5 478	5 920	4 495	3 412	* 4 820
Belgium-Luxembourg Belgique-Luxembourg	2 215	2 165	2 311	2 174	2 144	2 571	2 393	2 541	2 493	2 511
Bosnia and Herzegovina Bosnie-Herzégovine	...	1 080[1]	962[1]	847[1]	* 671	* 841	* 1 242	* 1 327	* 1 274	1 311
Bulgaria Bulgarie	8 974	6 560	5 666	6 409	6 514	3 380	6 152	5 345	5 132	4 545
Croatia Croatie	...	2 356	2 733	2 596	2 760	2 762	3 179	3 210	2 883	2 070
Czechoslovakia-former† Tchécoslovaquie(anc.) †	11 939	10 198	...	...	...	...	...	...	...	...
Czech Republic République tchèque	...	...	6 486	6 790	6 611	6 654	6 995	6 676	6 935	6 455
Denmark Danemark	9 231	6 954	8 203	7 800	9 043	9 218	9 529	9 344	8 781	9 598
Estonia Estonie	...	592	811	510	513	629	651	576	402	647
Finland Finlande	3 429	2 603	3 340	3 400	3 333	3 697	3 807	2 773	2 879	4 006
France France	60 335	60 639	55 626	53 407	53 545	62 599	63 432	68 661	64 817	66 542
Germany † Allemagne †	39 268	34 758	35 549	36 336	39 863	42 136	45 486	44 575	44 461	45 304
Greece Grèce	6 183	5 035	4 856	5 272	4 903	4 683	4 705	4 359	4 601	4 171
Hungary Hongrie	15 832	10 007	8 543	11 749	11 297	11 344	14 139	13 038	11 405	9 956
Ireland Irlande	1 964	2 017	1 627	1 610	1 796	2 142	1 944	1 865	2 011	1 963

35

Cereals
Production: thousand metric tons [*cont.*]
Céréales
Production : milliers de tonnes [*suite*]

Region, country or area Région, pays ou zone	1991	1992	1993	1994	1995	1996	1997	1998	1999	2000
Italy Italie	19 219	19 891	19 772	19 187	19 693	20 900	19 898	20 699	21 002	20 744
Latvia Lettonie	...	1 146	1 234	899	692	961	1 036	964	784	928
Lithuania Lituanie	...	2 198	2 673	2 098	1 907	2 615	2 945	2 717	2 049	2 658
Malta Malte	7	7	7	7	7	7	11	11	11	12
Netherlands Pays-Bas	1 252	1 350	1 466	1 355	1 505	1 659	1 373	1 465	1 367	1 649
Norway Norvège	1 482	1 010	1 402	1 271	1 227	1 345	1 288	1 412	1 299	1 322
Poland Pologne	27 812	19 962	23 417	21 763	25 905	25 298	25 399	27 159	25 750	22 341
Portugal Portugal	1 789	1 338	1 449	1 645	1 446	1 673	1 559	1 622	1 690	1 686
Republic of Moldova République de Moldova	...	1 978	3 219	1 628	2 611	1 976	3 487	2 385	2 138	2 021
Romania Roumanie	19 307	12 288	15 493	18 184	19 883	14 200	22 107	15 454	17 034	9 594
Russian Federation Fédération de Russie	...	103 794	96 225	78 650	61 902	67 589	86 801	46 969	53 845	64 088
Slovakia Slovaquie	...	...	3 157	3 700	3 489	3 322	3 740	3 485	2 829	2 201
Slovenia Slovénie	...	429	457	571	453	487	544	557	469	502
Spain Espagne	19 457	14 479	17 479	15 231	11 574	22 366	19 324	22 557	17 996	24 602
Sweden Suède	5 160	3 760	5 242	4 472	4 860	5 995	5 986	5 618	4 931	6 200
Switzerland Suisse	1 313	1 213	1 292	1 249	1 281	1 348	1 223	1 264	1 056	1 138
TFYR of Macedonia L'ex-R.y. Macédoine	...	624	479	648	725	546	610	660	740	621
Ukraine Ukraine	...	35 550	42 725	32 960	32 360	23 486	34 396	25 689	23 953	23 760
United Kingdom Royaume-Uni	22 635	22 063	19 482	19 948	21 859	24 571	23 527	22 795	22 126	23 983
Yugoslavia Yougoslavie	...	7 019	7 411	8 409	9 245	7 294	10 355	8 667	8 615	5 238
Yugoslavia, SFR† Yougoslavie, Rfs†	19 263	...	...	...	...	...	...	...	...	...
Oceania **Océanie**	**19 592**	**25 863**	**27 542**	**16 308**	**28 113**	**35 804**	**32 118**	**33 422**	**35 951**	**31 496**
Australia Australie	18 748	25 097	26 709	15 437	27 331	34 870	31 107	32 533	35 038	30 589
Fiji Fidji	30	23	23	20	20	19	19	6	19[1]	19[1]
New Caledonia Nouvelle-Calédonie	1	1	1	1	1	2	2	2	2	2[1]

35
Cereals
Production: thousand metric tons [*cont.*]
Céréales
Production : milliers de tonnes [*suite*]

Region, country or area Région, pays ou zone	1991	1992	1993	1994	1995	1996	1997	1998	1999	2000
New Zealand Nouvelle-Zélande	808	736	803	843	752	904	980	869	876	870
Papua New Guinea Papouasie-Nvl-Guinée	5[1]	5[1]	6[1]	7[1]	8[1]	9[1]	10	10[1]	11[1]	11[1]
Solomon Islands Iles Salomon	0[1]	0[1]	0[1]	0[1]	0[1]	0[1]	0[1]	* 1	* 5	5[1]
Vanuatu Vanuatu	1[1]	1[1]	1[1]	1[1]	1[1]	1[1]	1	1	1[1]	1[1]
USSR - former † URSS (anc.) †	155 960	...	...	...	...	...	...	...	...	...

Source:
Food and Agriculture Organization of the United
Nations (FAO), Rome, "FAO Production Yearbook 2000" and the
FAOSTAT database.

† For information on recent changes in country or
area nomenclature pertaining to former Czechoslovakia,
Germany, Hong Kong Special Administrative Region (SAR) of
China, Macao Special Administrative Region (SAR) of China,
SFR of Yugoslavia and the former USSR, see Annex I - Country
or area nomenclature, regional and other groupings.

1 FAO estimate.
2 Data refer to the Gaza Strip.

Source:
Organisation des Nations Unies pour l'alimentation et
l'agriculture (FAO), Rome, "Annuaire FAO de la production
2000" et la base de données FAOSTAT.

† Pour les modifications récentes de nomenclature
de pays ou de zone concernant l'Allemagne, Hong Kong, région
administrative spéciale (RAS) de Chine, Macao, région
administrative spéciale (RAS) de Chine,
l'ex-Tchécoslovaquie, l'ex-URSS et l'ex-Rfs de Yougoslavie,
voir annexe I - Nomenclature des pays ou des zones,
groupements régionaux et autres groupements.

1 Estimation de la FAO.
2 Les données se rapportent à la Zone de Gaza.

36
Oil crops, in oil equivalent
Cultures d'huile, en équivalent d'huile
Production: thousand metric tons
Production : milliers de tonnes

Region, country or area Région, pays ou zone	1991	1992	1993	1994	1995	1996	1997	1998	1999	2000
World *Monde*	77 427	78 749	80 061	88 439	91 938	93 409	98 341	103 005	108 943	109 669
Africa Afrique	5 691	5 453	5 824	5 917	6 198	7 072	6 659	6 802	7 339	7 068
Algeria Algérie	55	97	84	76	67	108	109	67	119	116[1]
Angola Angola	64	68	70	73	72	74	73	75	67	67[1]
Benin Bénin	65	63	73	70	89	93	94	89	91	91
Botswana Botswana	1	1[1]	1	1[1]	1	2	2[1]	3[1]	3[1]	3[1]
Burkina Faso Burkina Faso	71	85	96	97	103	109	98	118	114[1]	114[1]
Burundi Burundi	8	8	8	6	7	6	6	6	6	5
Cameroon Cameroun	217	206	212	218	222	277	225	228	252	253
Cape Verde Cap-Vert	1	1	1	1	1	1	1	1	1	1
Central African Rep. Rép. centrafricaine	49	52	53	57	61	64	67	68	66	66
Chad Tchad	97	91	78	87	113	123	142	183	147	147[1]
Comoros Comores	7	7	7	7	9	9	10	10	10	10[1]
Congo Congo	26	26	26	27	27	27[1]	25	25[1]	26[1]	26[1]
Côte d'Ivoire Côte d'Ivoire	390	407	409	404	359	375	366	356	356	356[1]
Dem. Rep. of the Congo Rép. dém. du Congo	395	401	417	420	422	358	335	327	322	318
Egypt Egypte	157	171	215	183	206	224	207	186	197	214[1]
Equatorial Guinea Guinée équatoriale	7[1]	7[1]	7[1]	7[1]	7[1]	7[1]	6[1]	6[1]	6	6[1]
Eritrea Erythrée	...	...	7	8	11	7	6	8	7[1]	7[1]
Ethiopia incl. Eritrea Ethiopie comp. Erythrée	143	144	...	...	...	...	...	...	...	...
Ethiopia Ethiopie	...	...	144	144	144	147	150	157	158	147[1]
Gabon Gabon	13	12	13	13	13	12	13	12[1]	12[1]	12[1]
Gambia Gambie	29	20	27	28	26	17	27	25	41	41
Ghana Ghana	169	189	198	219	216	204	210	251	237[1]	237[1]

36
Oil crops, in oil equivalent
Production: thousand metric tons [*cont.*]
Cultures d'huile, en équivalent d'huile
Production : milliers de tonnes [*suite*]

Region, country or area Région, pays ou zone	1991	1992	1993	1994	1995	1996	1997	1998	1999	2000
Guinea Guinée	98	105	114	114	118	126	130	131	134[1]	134[1]
Guinea-Bissau Guinée-Bissau	19	18	18	19	19	19	20	20	21	21
Kenya Kenya	32	27	30	33	32	32	35	35	32	31
Liberia Libéria	30	30	36[1]	39[1]	43[1]	41[1]	42[1]	48[1]	49[1]	49[1]
Libyan Arab Jamah. Jamah. arabe libyenne	22	26	31	35	41	45	46	47	47	47
Madagascar Madagascar	28	26	30	27	28	30	31	30	30	30
Malawi Malawi	24	11	25	15	21	29	28	39	40	40
Mali Mali	108	96	95	120	107	105	108	105	104	104
Mauritania Mauritanie	1	1	1	1	2	2	2	2[1]	2[1]	2[1]
Mauritius Maurice	1	1	1	1	1	0	1	0	0	0
Morocco Maroc	169	157	122	141	104	229	158	183	119	110
Mozambique Mozambique	113	104	106	102	112	118	124	132	132	92
Namibia Namibie	0	0	1	0	0	0	0	0	1	1
Niger Niger	14	18	8	21	32	60	27	30	33	34
Nigeria Nigéria	1 579	1 613	1 695	1 767	1 889	2 036	2 162	2 213	2 350	2 350
Rwanda Rwanda	5	8	5	4	5	4	3	3	3	4
Sao Tome and Principe Sao Tomé-et-Principe	5	5	5	5	5[1]	5[1]	5[1]	5[1]	6	8
Senegal Sénégal	228	184	199	215	251	207	179	186	260	260
Seychelles [1] Seychelles [1]	1	0	0	0	0	0	0	0	0	0
Sierra Leone Sierra Leone	72	70	69	79	71	74	78	64	55	51
Somalia Somalie	17	8	12	12	13	13	13	11[1]	12[1]	13[1]
South Africa Afrique du Sud	335	137	209	227	278	417	273	323	552	307
Sudan Soudan	143	280	251	352	420	476	488	394	486	467
Swaziland Swaziland	5	2	3	2	2	4	5	6	5	5[1]

36
Oil crops, in oil equivalent
Production: thousand metric tons [*cont.*]
Cultures d'huile, en équivalent d'huile
Production : milliers de tonnes [*suite*]

Region, country or area Région, pays ou zone	1991	1992	1993	1994	1995	1996	1997	1998	1999	2000
Togo Togo	30	37	36	39	41	47	41	40	43	43[1]
Tunisia Tunisie	296	153	236	83	72	347	116	215	222	227
Uganda Ouganda	92	95	103	99	101	99	100	106	116	120
United Rep. of Tanzania Rép.-Unie de Tanzanie	135	137	129	122	139	141	136	126	130	131
Zambia Zambie	23	11	32	22	28	32	29	28	30	31
Zimbabwe Zimbabwe	100	38	77	77	49	89	106	76	86	122
America, North **Amérique du Nord**	**15 176**	**15 463**	**14 672**	**19 481**	**17 152**	**17 546**	**19 781**	**20 900**	**20 851**	**20 562**
Canada Canada	2 189	1 926	2 779	3 656	3 360	2 718	3 349	3 907	4 362	3 556
Costa Rica Costa Rica	87	86	96	101	106	110	115	122	122	148
Cuba Cuba	7	7	8	8	8	8	8	8	8	8
Dominica Dominique	2[1]	2	2	2[1]	2[1]	2[1]	2[1]	1[1]	1[1]	1[1]
Dominican Republic Rép. dominicaine	44	42	44	50	49	50	48	50	52	50
El Salvador El Salvador	18	17	17	13	15	14	15	15	16	16
Grenada[1] Grenade[1]	1	1	1	1	1	1	1	1	1	1
Guatemala Guatemala	43	49	46	53	59	73	91	89	94	94
Haiti Haïti	16[1]	13	13[1]	13[1]	13[1]	13	14[1]	12	13[1]	12
Honduras Honduras	88	95	92	92	91	94	92	104	95	164
Jamaica Jamaïque	13	16	16	16	16	16	16	16	16	16[1]
Mexico Mexique	405	323	313	335	331	347	365	383	366	320
Nicaragua Nicaragua	22	18	20	35	28	32	31	27	35	37
Panama Panama	3	3	3[1]	2	2	2	2[1]	2[1]	2[1]	2
Puerto Rico Porto Rico	1	1	1	1	1	1	1	1[1]	1[1]	1[1]
Saint Lucia[1] Sainte-Lucie[1]	3	3	3	2	2	2	3	2	2	2

36
Oil crops, in oil equivalent
Production: thousand metric tons [*cont.*]
Cultures d'huile, en équivalent d'huile
Production : milliers de tonnes [*suite*]

Region, country or area Région, pays ou zone	1991	1992	1993	1994	1995	1996	1997	1998	1999	2000
St. Vincent-Grenadines St. Vincent-Grenadines	3	3	3	3	3	3	3	3	3	3
Trinidad and Tobago[1] Trinité-et-Tobago[1]	5	7	7	4	3	3	3	3	3	3
United States Etats-Unis	12 226	12 851	11 207	15 093	13 062	14 057	15 622	16 153	15 658	16 126
America, South **Amérique du Sud**	**8 546**	**8 968**	**9 194**	**10 365**	**11 510**	**11 151**	**11 561**	**14 130**	**14 895**	**14 902**
Argentina Argentine	4 020	3 753	3 440	4 009	4 855	4 921	4 482	6 083	6 768	6 267
Bolivia Bolivie	84	79	104	146	183	180	231	249	186	271
Brazil Brésil	3 260	3 995	4 463	4 928	5 068	4 573	5 270	6 198	6 212	6 645
Chile Chili	38	36	16	14	15	16	16	23	32	24
Colombia Colombie	410	375	394	435	469	492	522	497	571	595
Ecuador Equateur	217	215	221	255	221	226	275	299	208	326
Guyana Guyana	6	6	7	8	10	10	10	8	8	8
Paraguay Paraguay	351	369	404	413	490	520	542	599	674	580
Peru Pérou	51	41	48	54	64	69	61	52	66	66
Suriname Suriname	3	4	4	3	3	2	1	1	1	1
Uruguay Uruguay	30	31	27	30	54	51	51	37	71	19
Venezuela Venezuela	75	63	66	71	78	91	99	84	97	99
Asia **Asie**	**34 754**	**37 504**	**39 651**	**41 851**	**44 184**	**45 707**	**47 151**	**47 314**	**49 770**	**52 633**
Afghanistan Afghanistan	29	29	29	29	29	29	29	29[1]	29[1]	29[1]
Azerbaijan Azerbaïdjan	...	31	26	27	24	23	12	11	10	11
Bangladesh Bangladesh	150	159	163	157	161	159	162	163	162	164
Bhutan[1] Bhoutan[1]	1	1	1	1	1	1	1	1	1	1
Cambodia Cambodge	19	19	19	16	16	18	23	19	20	20[1]
China †† Chine ††	10 104	9 885	10 893	11 880	12 485	12 145	12 455	12 869	13 555	15 334
Cyprus Chypre	2	5	3	3	3	3	2	3	4	4

36
Oil crops, in oil equivalent
Production: thousand metric tons [*cont.*]
Cultures d'huile, en équivalent d'huile
Production : milliers de tonnes [*suite*]

Region, country or area Région, pays ou zone	1991	1992	1993	1994	1995	1996	1997	1998	1999	2000
Georgia Géorgie	...	3	1	3	3	2	13	10	17	19[1]
India Inde	7 374	8 396	8 094	8 528	8 707	9 314	9 022	9 230	8 516	8 606
Indonesia Indonésie	5 272	6 035	6 268	6 902	7 472	8 033	8 689	9 040	9 626	10 337
Iran (Islamic Rep. of) Iran (Rép. islamique d')	73	80	80	117	92	106	102	106	106	106[1]
Iraq Iraq	18	36	44	37	39	41	40	41	39	27[1]
Israel Israël	28	39	31	27	36	39	34	33	24	24[1]
Japan Japon	51	50	30	36	38	45	36	36	42	51
Jordan Jordanie	9	18	7	21	14	20	13	30	14	36
Kazakhstan Kazakhstan	...	109	81	86	82	57	56	66	86	91
Korea, Dem. P. R. Corée, R. p. dém. de	82	75	72	76	73	76	68	65	65	67[1]
Korea, Republic of Corée, République de	62	62	52	53	57	53	54	50	43	46
Kyrgyzstan Kirghizistan	...	5	5	5	7	8	7	8	10	10
Lao People's Dem. Rep. Rép. dém. pop. lao	5	7	7	7	9	9	9	10	8	11
Lebanon Liban	12	26	14[1]	20	15[1]	24	23	25	23[1]	26[1]
Malaysia Malaisie	7 118	7 397	8 615	8 398	9 080	9 692	10 431	9 567	12 072	12 387
Maldives Maldives	* 2	2	* 2	2	2	2[1]	2[1]	2[1]	2[1]	2
Myanmar Myanmar	312	264	311	299	376	433	416	392	408	506
Nepal Népal	46	45	47	49	53	53	55	52	56	57
Occupied Palestinian Terr.[2] Terr. palestinien occupé[2]	1	1	1	1	1	1	1	1	1	1
Pakistan Pakistan	849	657	593	628	763	717	725	700	851	842
Philippines Philippines	1 199	1 298	1 551	1 535	1 660	1 552	1 785	1 574	820	820
Saudi Arabia Arabie saoudite	2	2	2	2	2	2	2	2	2	2[1]
Sri Lanka Sri Lanka	220	230	221	264	277	255	264	254	258	258[1]
Syrian Arab Republic Rép. arabe syrienne	127	211	169	192	176	243	213	296	208	287[1]

36
Oil crops, in oil equivalent
Production: thousand metric tons [cont.]
Cultures d'huile, en équivalent d'huile
Production : milliers de tonnes [suite]

Region, country or area Région, pays ou zone	1991	1992	1993	1994	1995	1996	1997	1998	1999	2000
Tajikistan Tadjikistan	...	46	50	51	39	29	33	36	30	34
Thailand Thaïlande	666	706	718	761	804	837	876	895	1 139	952
Turkey Turquie	680	755	646	815	749	959	721	969	740	741
Turkmenistan Turkménistan	...	132	115	133	125	42	61	68	99	100
Uzbekistan Ouzbékistan	...	400	413	390	391	336	366	320	368	320
Viet Nam Viet Nam	236	244	265	266	290	315	314	304	280	265
Yemen Yémen	4	6	6	6	7	8	9	10	10	11
Europe **Europe**	**9 144**	**10 585**	**9 903**	**10 041**	**12 009**	**10 941**	**12 059**	**12 327**	**14 284**	**12 931**
Albania Albanie	10	6	6	7	9	7	8	12	11	12
Austria Autriche	88	98	113	142	134	71	76	90	112	88
Belarus Bélarus	...	23	17	16	22	20	20	30	34	43 [1]
Belgium-Luxembourg Belgique-Luxembourg	14	9	10	12	14	13	* 12	* 13	15	18
Bosnia and Herzegovina Bosnie-Herzégovine	...	3 [1]	3 [1]	2 [1]	2	2	* 2	* 2	* 2	2 [1]
Bulgaria Bulgarie	192	254	183	252	323	222	186	221	256	186
Croatia Croatie	...	38	39	33	38	26	28	52	71	55
Czechoslovakia-former† Tchécoslovaquie (anc.) †	246	216	...	...	...	...	...	...	...	...
Czech Republic République tchèque	...	...	161	195	280	221	237	298	412	368
Denmark Danemark	276	155	159	141	119	96	112	137	157	157 [1]
Estonia Estonie	...	1 [1]	1 [1]	1	3	4	4	7	11	14
Finland Finlande	36	50	48	41	49	34	35	27	34	33
France France	2 003	1 598	1 317	1 590	1 946	1 986	2 221	2 195	2 536	2 168
Germany Allemagne	1 190	1 090	1 185	1 241	1 245	821	1 169	1 394	1 783	1 514
Greece Grèce	524	497	457	547	616	571	525	581	556	562
Hungary Hongrie	397	346	300	304	368	420	289	342	474	290

36
Oil crops, in oil equivalent
Production: thousand metric tons [*cont.*]
Cultures d'huile, en équivalent d'huile
Production : milliers de tonnes [*suite*]

Region, country or area Région, pays ou zone	1991	1992	1993	1994	1995	1996	1997	1998	1999	2000
Ireland Irlande	9	7	3	6	5	4	5	6	2	2[1]
Italy Italie	1 289	860	911	976	1 139	888	1 240	1 018	1 213	1 001
Latvia Lettonie	...	1	2	1	1	1	1	1	5	5
Lithuania Lituanie	...	4	2	6	10	10	15	28	45	35
Netherlands Pays-Bas	11	7	6	6	5	3	4	3	5	4
Norway Norvège	2	3	6	5	* 5	* 5	* 5	5	4	4
Poland Pologne	402	292	230	295	532	177	231	425	438	372
Portugal Portugal	115	61	85	73	87	84	86	89	133	130
Republic of Moldova République de Moldova	...	82	81	62	96	130	83	83	120	115
Romania Roumanie	297	350	315	335	407	473	382	492	613	459
Russian Federation Fédération de Russie	...	1 476	1 313	1 209	1 865	1 273	1 283	1 370	1 840	1 708
Slovakia Slovaquie	...	...	52	62	94	100	105	91	146	102
Slovenia Slovénie	...	2	2	2	1	1	0	0	0	0[1]
Spain Espagne	1 108	1 278	1 170	1 050	645	1 544	1 890	1 486	1 042	1 317
Sweden Suède	110	108	137	81	76	54	50	49	64	48
Switzerland Suisse	20	18	20	14	18	18	21	21	18	20
TFYR of Macedonia L'ex-R.y. Macédoine	...	17	8	8	10	10	7	6	6	4
Ukraine Ukraine	...	953	891	666	1 203	888	971	966	1 195	1 524
United Kingdom Royaume-Uni	553	517	496	520	498	566	617	645	766	444
Yugoslavia Yougoslavie	...	165	174	138	146	196	138	146	167	124
Yugoslavia, SFR† Yougoslavie, Rfs†	251	...	...	...	...	...	...	...	...	...
Oceania Océanie	**732**	**776**	**818**	**785**	**885**	**991**	**1 130**	**1 532**	**1 804**	**1 573**
American Samoa[1] Samoa américaines[1]	1	1	1	1	1	1	1	1	1	1
Australia Australie	269	249	260	248	361	396	554	928	1 176	935

36
Oil crops, in oil equivalent
Production: thousand metric tons [*cont.*]
Cultures d'huile, en équivalent d'huile
Production : milliers de tonnes [*suite*]

Region, country or area Région, pays ou zone	1991	1992	1993	1994	1995	1996	1997	1998	1999	2000
Cocos (Keeling) Islands[1] Iles des Cocos (Keeling)[1]	1	1	1	1	1	1	1	1	1	1
Cook Islands Iles Cook	1[1]	0	1	0	1[1]	1[1]	1	1	1[1]	1[1]
Fiji Fidji	26	32	26	25	25[1]	28[1]	28	27	28[1]	28[1]
French Polynesia[1] Polynésie française[1]	11	11	11	11	12	12	11	8	10	10
Guam[1] Guam[1]	5	5	5	5	5	5	5	5	5	5
Kiribati Kiribati	* 10	* 11	* 11	* 11	* 11	* 13	* 13	* 14	11	10
New Caledonia[1] Nouvelle-Calédonie[1]	2	2	2	2	2	2	2	2	2	2
New Zealand Nouvelle-Zélande	1	1	1	2	2	2	2	2	2	2
Papua New Guinea Papouasie-Nvl-Guinée	284	332	363	344	337	402	372	398	438	438[1]
Samoa[1] Samoa[1]	12	13	17	17	17	17	17	17	17	17
Solomon Islands Iles Salomon	51	61	62	61	69	69	71	72	72	72[1]
Tonga Tonga	4	4[1]	4[1]	4[1]	3	3[1]	3[1]	3[1]	3[1]	3[1]
Vanuatu Vanuatu	35	34	34	34	36	38	48	51	36	48
USSR - former † URSS (anc.) †	3 383	...	...	...	...	...	...	...	...	...

Source:
Food and Agriculture Organization of the United
Nations (FAO), Rome, "FAO Production Yearbook 2000" and the
FAOSTAT database.

† For information on recent changes in country or
area nomenclature pertaining to former Czechoslovakia,
Germany, Hong Kong Special Administrative Region (SAR) of
China, Macao Special Administrative Region (SAR) of China,
SFR of Yugoslavia and the former USSR, see Annex I - Country
or area nomenclature, regional and other groupings.

1 FAO estimate.
2 Data refer to the Gaza Strip.

Source:
Organisation des Nations Unies pour l'alimentation et
l'agriculture (FAO), Rome, "Annuaire FAO de la production
2000" et la base de données FAOSTAT.

† Pour les modifications récentes de nomenclature
de pays ou de zone concernant l'Allemagne, Hong Kong, région
administrative spéciale (RAS) de Chine, Macao, région
administrative spéciale (RAS) de Chine,
l'ex-Tchécoslovaquie, l'ex-URSS et l'ex-Rfs de Yougoslavie,
voir annexe I - Nomenclature des pays ou des zones,
groupements régionaux et autres groupements.

1 Estimation de la FAO.
2 Les données se rapportent à la Zone de Gaza.

37
Livestock
Cheptel

Thousand head

Milliers de têtes

Region, country or area	1993	1994	1995	1996	1997	1998	1999	2000	Région, pays ou zone
World									**Monde**
Cattle and buffaloes	1459973	1475595	1491696	1499536	1493521	1499484	1503097	1515098	Bovine et buffles
Sheep and goats	1748948	1763451	1756949	1766671	1735864	1753143	1767193	1777916	Ovine et caprins
Pigs	877 038	883 191	900 213	860 954	836 676	880 425	903 889	908 104	Porcine
Horses	60 301	60 265	60 844	60 403	58 881	58 532	58 930	58 808	Chevaline
Asses	43 480	43 749	44 177	43 951	43 051	43 238	43 472	43 398	Asine
Mules	15 024	14 900	14 948	14 123	13 515	13 520	13 614	13 571	Mulassière
Africa									**Afrique**
Cattle and buffaloes	197 343	200 134	204 927	214 267	220 391	226 257	228 627	230 616	Bovine et buffles
Sheep and goats	398 776	416 488	420 278	427 538	441 307	448 589	451 057	450 420	Ovine et caprins
Pigs	17 831	18 392	18 711	18 787	19 239	19 482	19 423	18 777	Porcine
Horses	4 766	4 800	4 818	4 830	4 814	4 829	4 853	4 850	Chevaline
Asses	14 652	14 813	14 996	14 915	15 094	15 174	15 181	15 254	Asine
Mules	1 371	1 367	1 379	1 358	1 345	1 351	1 353	1 355	Mulassière
Algeria									**Algérie**
Cattle and buffaloes	1 314	1 269	1 267	1 228	1 255	1 317	1 650	1 650[1]	Bovine et buffles
Sheep and goats	21 348	20 386	20 081	20 460	19 876	20 900	21 600	21 600[1]	Ovine et caprins
Pigs [1]	6	6	6	6	6	6	6	6	Porcine [1]
Horses	73	67	62	60	52	55[1]	55[1]	55[1]	Chevaline
Asses	259	226	224	210	199	200[1]	200[1]	202[1]	Asine
Mules	88	81	80	76	69	70[1]	71[1]	72[1]	Mulassière
Angola									**Angola**
Cattle and buffaloes	3 100[1]	3 000[1]	3 000	3 309	* 3 556	* 3 898	* 3 900	* 4 042	Bovine et buffles
Sheep and goats	1 745[1]	1 690[1]	* 1 700	18 501	* 2 000	* 2 166	* 2 336	* 2 500	Ovine et caprins
Pigs	800[1]	790[1]	800	8101	820[1]	810[1]	800[1]	800[1]	Porcine
Horses [1]	1	1	1	1	1	1	1	1	Chevaline [1]
Asses [1]	5	5	5	5	5	5	5	5	Asine [1]
Benin									**Bénin**
Cattle and buffaloes	* 1 140	1 223	1 294	1 350	1 399	1 345	1 438	1 438[1]	Bovine et buffles
Sheep and goats	2 120[1]	2 150[1]	1 575[1]	1 614	1 688[1]	1 721	1 828	1 828[1]	Ovine et caprins
Pigs	* 536	555	566	584	580[1]	470	470[1]	470[1]	Porcine
Horses [1]	6	6	6	6	6	6	6	6	Chevaline [1]
Asses [1]	1	1	1	1	1	1	1	1	Asine [1]
Botswana									**Botswana**
Cattle and buffaloes	1 821	2 200[1]	2 530	2 249	2 270[1]	2 250[1]	2 300[1]	2 350[1]	Bovine et buffles
Sheep and goats	2 088	2 088	2 961	2 554	2 580[1]	2 400[1]	2 470[1]	2 550[1]	Ovine et caprins
Pigs	4	4[1]	1	3	5[1]	2[1]	5[1]	6[1]	Porcine
Horses	31	31	35	30[1]	33[1]	32[1]	33[1]	33[1]	Chevaline
Asses	231	231	303	336	330[1]	320[1]	325[1]	330[1]	Asine
Mules [1]	3	3	3	3	3	3	3	3	Mulassière [1]
Burkina Faso									**Burkina Faso**
Cattle and buffaloes	4 178	4 261	4 346	4 433	4 522	4 612	4 704	4 704[1]	Bovine et buffles
Sheep and goats	12 546	12 923	13 310	13 709	14 121	14 544	14 980	14 980[1]	Ovine et caprins
Pigs	541	552	563	575	587	598	610	610[1]	Porcine
Horses	23	* 23	23	23	24	24	24	24[1]	Chevaline
Asses	436	445	454	463	472	482	491	491[1]	Asine
Burundi									**Burundi**
Cattle and buffaloes	465[1]	400[1]	350[1]	330[1]	* 311	346	329	320[1]	Bovine et buffles
Sheep and goats	1 340[1]	1 270[1]	1 150[1]	1 000[1]	850[1]	822	759[1]	670[1]	Ovine et caprins
Pigs	90[1]	85[1]	80[1]	75[1]	70[1]	73	61	50[1]	Porcine
Cameroon									**Cameroun**
Cattle and buffaloes [1]	5 110	5 250	5 400	5 550	5 700	5 900	5 900	5 900	Bovine et buffles [1]
Sheep and goats [1]	7 530	7 550	7 600	7 640	7 670	7 700	7 730	7 730	Ovine et caprins [1]
Pigs [1]	1 390	1 400	1 410	1 415	1 420	1 425	1 430	1 430	Porcine [1]
Horses [1]	15	15	16	16	16	16	17	17	Chevaline [1]
Asses [1]	36	36	36	37	37	37	37	38	Asine [1]
Cape Verde									**Cap−Vert**
Cattle and buffaloes	18	18	19	21	21[1]	22[1]	22	22	Bovine et buffles
Sheep and goats	152	143[1]	122	118	119[1]	125[1]	121	118	Ovine et caprins
Pigs	326	512	450	455[1]	560[1]	636[1]	640[1]	640[1]	Porcine
Asses	13[1]	13[1]	13	14[1]	14[1]	14[1]	14[1]	14[1]	Asine
Mules	2[1]	2[1]	2[1]	2[1]	2[1]	2[1]	2[1]	2[1]	Mulassière

37

Livestock
Thousand head [*cont.*]
Cheptel
Milliers de têtes [*suite*]

Region, country or area	1993	1994	1995	1996	1997	1998	1999	2000	Région, pays ou zone
Central African Rep.									**Rép. centrafricaine**
Cattle and buffaloes	2 674	2 735	2 797	2 861	2 926	* 2 992	2 951	2 950¹	Bovine et buffles
Sheep and goats	1 927	2 037	2 152	2 274	2 404	* 2 540	* 2 684	2 810¹	Ovine et caprins
Pigs	502	524	547	571	596	* 622	* 649	650¹	Porcine
Chad									**Tchad**
Cattle and buffaloes	4 517	4 528	4 539	4 860	5 451	5 582	5 595¹	5 595¹	Bovine et buffles
Sheep and goats	5 175	5 330	5 490	6 235	7 189	7 371	7 550¹	7 550¹	Ovine et caprins
Pigs	16	17	18	* 18	* 19	20¹	21¹	21¹	Porcine
Horses	210	214	218¹	* 224	190	194	198	198¹	Chevaline
Asses	248	253	258¹	* 275	346	347	350	350¹	Asine
Comoros									**Comores**
Cattle and buffaloes	* 44	* 45	* 46	* 47	* 48	* 50	51¹	52¹	Bovine et buffles
Sheep and goats	* 147¹	* 150¹	* 153¹	* 156¹	* 158¹	* 160	160¹	160¹	Ovine et caprins
Asses ¹	5	5	5	5	5	5	5	5	Asine ¹
Congo									**Congo**
Cattle and buffaloes	68¹	69¹	70¹	72¹	75	72	70¹	77¹	Bovine et buffles
Sheep and goats	407¹	409¹	409¹	409¹	401	394¹	395¹	401¹	Ovine et caprins
Pigs	46¹	47¹	46¹	46¹	45	44¹	45¹	46¹	Porcine
Côte d'Ivoire									**Côte d'Ivoire**
Cattle and buffaloes	1 205	1 231	1 258	1 286	1 312	1 330¹	1 350¹	1 350¹	Bovine et buffles
Sheep and goats	2 173	2 229	2 284	2 341	2 399	2 440¹	2 483¹	2 483¹	Ovine et caprins
Pigs	392	403	414	290	271	275¹	280¹	280¹	Porcine
Dem. Rep. of the Congo									**Rép. dém. du Congo**
Cattle and buffaloes	1 225	1 127	1 150¹	1 060	982	881	853	822	Bovine et buffles
Sheep and goats	5 135	5 372	* 5 395	5 286	5 403	5 629	5 136	5 056	Ovine et caprins
Pigs	1 142	1 152	1 170	1 117	1 144	1 154	1 100	1 049	Porcine
Djibouti									**Djibouti**
Cattle and buffaloes	200¹	* 213	* 247	* 266	267¹	268¹	269¹	269¹	Bovine et buffles
Sheep and goats	967¹	* 971	* 965	* 972	973¹	974¹	977¹	978¹	Ovine et caprins
Asses	8¹	8¹	* 8	* 8	8¹	9¹	9¹	9¹	Asine
Egypt									**Egypte**
Cattle and buffaloes	6 227¹	* 5 909	6 014	* 6 014	6 213	6 366	6 330¹	6 380¹	Bovine et buffles
Sheep and goats	6 724	* 7 003	7 352	* 7 352	7 447	7 613	8 661¹	7 750¹	Ovine et caprins
Pigs	27¹	27	27¹	27¹	28¹	29¹	29¹	30¹	Porcine
Horses	35¹	* 39	* 42	* 41	43¹	45¹	46¹	46¹	Chevaline
Asses ¹	2 950	3 100	3 112	2 980	2 990	2 995	3 000	3 050	Asine ¹
Mules ¹	1	1	1	1	1	1	1	1	Mulassière ¹
Equatorial Guinea									**Guinée équatoriale**
Cattle and buffaloes ¹	5	5	5	5	5	5	5	5	Bovine et buffles ¹
Sheep and goats ¹	44	44	44	44	44	44	44	44	Ovine et caprins ¹
Pigs ¹	5	5	5	5	5	5	5	5	Porcine ¹
Eritrea									**Erythrée**
Cattle and buffaloes	* 1 269	* 1 290	* 1 312	* 1 600	* 1 928	* 2 026	2 100¹	1 800¹	Bovine et buffles
Sheep and goats ¹	2 910	2 970	3 030	3 090	3 150	3 210	3 270	3 040	Ovine et caprins ¹
Ethiopia									**Ethiopie**
Cattle and buffaloes	29 450¹	29 450¹	29 825	31 207	32 612	35 372	35 095	35 000¹	Bovine et buffles
Sheep and goats ¹	38 400	38 400	38 500	38 600	38 700	38 800	38 950	37 800	Ovine et caprins ¹
Pigs ¹	20	20	21	22	23	24	25	24	Porcine ¹
Horses ¹	2 750	2 750	2 750	2 750	2 750	2 750	2 750	2 750	Chevaline ¹
Asses ¹	5 200	5 200	5 200	5 200	5 200	5 200	5 200	5 200	Asine ¹
Mules ¹	630	630	630	630	630	630	630	630	Mulassière ¹
Gabon									**Gabon**
Cattle and buffaloes	37	38¹	* 38	36	33	34¹	35¹	36¹	Bovine et buffles
Sheep and goats	256	260¹	265¹	270¹	275¹	280¹	285¹	289¹	Ovine et caprins
Pigs	207	207¹	208¹	209¹	210¹	211¹	212¹	213¹	Porcine
Gambia									**Gambie**
Cattle and buffaloes	305	279	290	322	346	360¹	370¹	370¹	Bovine et buffles
Sheep and goats	329	370	376¹	398	432	455¹	465¹	465¹	Ovine et caprins
Pigs	14	14	14	14	14	14¹	14¹	14¹	Porcine
Horses	17	18	18¹	13	16	17¹	17¹	17¹	Chevaline
Asses	36	33	34¹	25	33	34¹	35¹	35¹	Asine
Ghana									**Ghana**
Cattle and buffaloes	1 169	1 187	1 217	1 248	1 260	1 273	1 285¹	1 285¹	Bovine et buffles
Sheep and goats	4 350	4 473	4 420	4 759	5 101	5 256	5 365¹	5 365¹	Ovine et caprins
Pigs	408	419	351	318	353	352	350¹	350¹	Porcine

37

Livestock
Thousand head [*cont.*]
Cheptel
Milliers de têtes [*suite*]

Region, country or area	1993	1994	1995	1996	1997	1998	1999	2000	Région, pays ou zone
Horses	2	2	2[1]	2[1]	2[1]	2[1]	2[1]	2[1]	Chevaline
Asses	12	12	12[1]	13[1]	13[1]	13[1]	13[1]	13[1]	Asine
Guinea									**Guinée**
Cattle and buffaloes	1 768	1 874	2 202	2 246	2 291	2 337	2 368	2 368[1]	Bovine et buffles
Sheep and goats	1 038	1 074	1 341	1 389	1 438	1 489	1 551	1 551[1]	Ovine et caprins
Pigs	35	41	46	48	51	53	54	54[1]	Porcine
Horses [1]	2	2	3	3	3	3	3	3	Chevaline [1]
Asses	2[1]	2[1]	* 2	2[1]	2[1]	2[1]	2[1]	2[1]	Asine
Guinea–Bissau									**Guinée–Bissau**
Cattle and buffaloes	475[1]	480[1]	490[1]	500[1]	510[1]	520[1]	530[1]	530[1]	Bovine et buffles
Sheep and goats	525[1]	540[1]	550[1]	565[1]	580[1]	595[1]	610[1]	610[1]	Ovine et caprins
Pigs	310[1]	320[1]	325[1]	330[1]	335[1]	340[1]	345[1]	345[1]	Porcine
Horses	2[1]	2[1]	2[1]	2[1]	2[1]	2[1]	2[1]	2[1]	Chevaline
Asses	5[1]	5[1]	5[1]	5[1]	5[1]	5[1]	5[1]	5[1]	Asine
Kenya									**Kenya**
Cattle and buffaloes	13 000[1]	13 250[1]	* 13 567	* 13 838	13 414	* 13 002	* 13 392	* 13 794	Bovine et buffles
Sheep and goats	19 000[1]	18 666	18 317	18 3301	18 400	18 600[1]	17 700[1]	16 600[1]	Ovine et caprins
Pigs	170[1]	196	196	225	226	230[1]	200[1]	170[1]	Porcine
Horses [1]	2	2	2	2	2	2	2	2	Chevaline [1]
Lesotho									**Lesotho**
Cattle and buffaloes	658	578	580	539	601	496	510[1]	520[1]	Bovine et buffles
Sheep and goats	1 988	2 152	1 880	1 683	1 749	1 243	1 280[1]	1 330[1]	Ovine et caprins
Pigs	60	46	66	64	58	60[1]	63[1]	65[1]	Porcine
Horses	107	113	100	98	100[1]	95[1]	98[1]	100[1]	Chevaline
Asses	139	140	146	153	155[1]	150[1]	152[1]	154[1]	Asine
Mules [1]	1	1	1	1	1	1	1	1	Mulassière [1]
Liberia									**Libéria**
Cattle and buffaloes [1]	36	36	36	36	36	36	36	36	Bovine et buffles [1]
Sheep and goats [1]	430	430	430	430	430	430	430	430	Ovine et caprins [1]
Pigs [1]	120	120	120	120	120	120	120	120	Porcine [1]
Libyan Arab Jamah.									**Jamah. arabe libyenne**
Cattle and buffaloes	155[1]	* 140	* 145	* 145	142[1]	180[1]	190[1]	143[1]	Bovine et buffles
Sheep and goats [1]	6 220	* 6 260	* 6 400	* 7 200	8 420	8 800	6 800	7 000	Ovine et caprins [1]
Horses	29[1]	* 30	* 35	* 40	43[1]	44[1]	45[1]	46[1]	Chevaline
Asses	30[1]	* 20	* 21	* 25	27[1]	28[1]	29[1]	30[1]	Asine
Madagascar									**Madagascar**
Cattle and buffaloes	10 287	10 298	10 309	10 320	10 331	10 342	10 353	10 364	Bovine et buffles
Sheep and goats	* 2 127	* 2 173	* 2 220	2 085	2 110[1]	2 130[1]	2 150[1]	2 170[1]	Ovine et caprins
Pigs	1 526	1 558	1 592	1 629	1 662	1 650[1]	1 500[1]	900[1]	Porcine
Malawi									**Malawi**
Cattle and buffaloes	800[1]	680[1]	690[1]	700	750[1]	740[1]	750[1]	760[1]	Bovine et buffles
Sheep and goats	1 000[1]	1 100[1]	1 200[1]	1 358	1 370[1]	1 355[1]	1 370[1]	1 385[1]	Ovine et caprins
Pigs	240[1]	245[1]	247	220	230[1]	220[1]	230[1]	240[1]	Porcine
Asses	2[1]	2[1]	2	2[1]	2[1]	2[1]	2[1]	2[1]	Asine
Mali									**Mali**
Cattle and buffaloes	5 227	5 380	5 541	5 708	5 882	6 058	6 200[1]	6 200[1]	Bovine et buffles
Sheep and goats	11 955	12 553	13 179	13 838	14 500[1]	14 500	14 550[1]	14 550[1]	Ovine et caprins
Pigs	61	62	63	64	65	65	65[1]	65[1]	Porcine
Horses	92	101	112	123	136	136[1]	136[1]	136[1]	Chevaline
Asses	600	612	625	638	652	652[1]	652[1]	652[1]	Asine
Mauritania									**Mauritanie**
Cattle and buffaloes	1 200	1 100	1 111	1 122	1 353	1 394	1 433	1 435[1]	Bovine et buffles
Sheep and goats	* 8 800	* 8 800	* 8 814	10 332	10 332	10 335[1]	10 340[1]	10 340[1]	Ovine et caprins
Horses	18[1]	* 19	* 19	* 19	20[1]	20[1]	20[1]	20[1]	Chevaline
Asses [1]	155	155	155	155	156	156	157	157	Asine [1]
Mauritius									**Maurice**
Cattle and buffaloes [1]	29	29	25	31	* 22	* 25	* 27	* 29	Bovine et buffles [1]
Sheep and goats [1]	102	97	98	97	98	99	100	101	Ovine et caprins [1]
Pigs	15	17[1]	18[1]	19[1]	* 20	* 20	* 20	* 20	Porcine
Morocco									**Maroc**
Cattle and buffaloes	2 348	2 343	2 371	2 408	2 547	2 569	2 560	2 675	Bovine et buffles
Sheep and goats	15 735	17 282	17 403	19 131	20 077	19 743	21 691	22 420	Ovine et caprins
Pigs	10[1]	10[1]	10[1]	10[1]	10	8	8[1]	8[1]	Porcine
Horses	162	165	162	156	145	147	150[1]	150[1]	Chevaline

37
Livestock
Thousand head [*cont.*]
Cheptel
Milliers de têtes [*suite*]

Region, country or area	1993	1994	1995	1996	1997	1998	1999	2000	Région, pays ou zone
Asses	905	916	954	919	949	980	980[1]	980[1]	Asine
Mules	526	527	540	523	516	524	524[1]	524[1]	Mulassière
Mozambique									**Mozambique**
Cattle and buffaloes [1]	1 260	1 240	1 250	1 270	1 290	1 300	1 310	1 320	Bovine et buffles [1]
Sheep and goats [1]	501	497	501	504	508	511	514	517	Ovine et caprins [1]
Pigs [1]	170	168	170	172	174	176	178	180	Porcine [1]
Asses [1]	19	18	19	20	21	22	23	23	Asine [1]
Namibia									**Namibie**
Cattle and buffaloes	2 074	2 036	2 031	1 990	2 055	2 192	2 294	2 063	Bovine et buffles
Sheep and goats	4 232	4 259	4 026	3 985	4 250	3 797	3 907	3 750[1]	Ovine et caprins
Pigs	20	18	20	19	17	15	19	17[1]	Porcine
Horses	57	59	58	57	57	53	66	62[1]	Chevaline
Asses	71[1]	72[1]	71[1]	70[1]	71[1]	69[1]	701	68[1]	Asine
Mules	7[1]	7[1]	7[1]	7[1]	7[1]	7[1]	71	7[1]	Mulassière
Niger									**Niger**
Cattle and buffaloes	1 872	1 968	2 008	2 048	2 089	2 131	2 174	* 2 217	Bovine et buffles
Sheep and goats	8 885	9 244	9 504	9 718	* 10 176	* 10 447	10 826	10 900[1]	Ovine et caprins
Pigs [1]	39	39	39	39	39	39	39	39	Porcine [1]
Horses	* 89	* 90	* 93	* 96	* 99	* 102	100[1]	100[1]	Chevaline
Asses	* 476	* 486	* 505	* 525	* 546	* 568	530[1]	530[1]	Asine
Nigeria									**Nigéria**
Cattle and buffaloes	14 807	14 881	15 405	18 680	19 610	19 700[1]	19 830	19 830[1]	Bovine et buffles
Sheep and goats	38 500	38 500[1]	38 500[1]	38 500[1]	42 660	43 700[1]	44 800[1]	44 800[1]	Ovine et caprins
Pigs	3 836	3 989	4 149	4 315	4 487	4 667[1]	4 855[1]	4 855[1]	Porcine
Horses [1]	204	204	204	204	204	204	204	204	Chevaline [1]
Asses [1]	1 000	1 000	1 000	1 000	1 000	1 000	1 000	1 000	Asine [1]
Réunion									**Réunion**
Cattle and buffaloes	25	26	26	26	* 27	27[1]	27[1]	27[1]	Bovine et buffles
Sheep and goats	33	33	32	32	* 40	40[1]	40[1]	40[1]	Ovine et caprins
Pigs	86	82	86	86	* 89	89[1]	89[1]	89[1]	Porcine
Rwanda									**Rwanda**
Cattle and buffaloes	500[1]	454	465	500[1]	570[1]	650[1]	726	725[1]	Bovine et buffles
Sheep and goats	* 1 615	* 1 655	* 770	* 869	* 921	* 977	* 924	1 020[1]	Ovine et caprins
Pigs	* 146	* 150	* 120	* 134	* 142	* 149	160	160[1]	Porcine
Sao Tome and Principe									**Sao Tomé−et−Principe**
Cattle and buffaloes [1]	4	4	4	4	4	4	4	4	Bovine et buffles [1]
Sheep and goats [1]	7	7	7	7	7	7	7	7	Ovine et caprins [1]
Pigs [1]	2	2	2	2	2	2	2	2	Porcine [1]
Senegal									**Sénégal**
Cattle and buffaloes	* 2 754	* 2 760	* 2 829	2 835[1]	2 913	2 955[1]	2 960[1]	2 960[1]	Bovine et buffles
Sheep and goats	* 7 518	* 7 800	7 900[1]	7 750[1]	7 811	7 895[1]	7 895[1]	7 895[1]	Ovine et caprins
Pigs [1]	320	322	324	326	328	330	330	330	Porcine [1]
Horses	498	500[1]	502[1]	504[1]	506[1]	508[1]	510[1]	510[1]	Chevaline
Asses	364	364[1]	368[1]	372[1]	376[1]	380[1]	384[1]	384[1]	Asine
Seychelles									**Seychelles**
Cattle and buffaloes [1]	2	2	2	1	1	1	1	1	Bovine et buffles [1]
Sheep and goats [1]	5	5	5	5	5	5	5	5	Ovine et caprins [1]
Pigs	18	18	18	18	18	18	18	18	Porcine [1]
Sierra Leone									**Sierra Leone**
Cattle and buffaloes	360	370[1]	380[1]	390[1]	400[1]	410[1]	420[1]	420[1]	Bovine et buffles
Sheep and goats	468	488[1]	510[1]	525[1]	540[1]	553[1]	565[1]	565[1]	Ovine et caprins
Pigs	50[1]	50[1]	50[1]	50[1]	50[1]	50[1]	52	52[1]	Porcine
Somalia									**Somalie**
Cattle and buffaloes	4 200[1]	5 000	5 200[1]	5 400[1]	5 600[1]	5 300[1]	5 000[1]	5 100[1]	Bovine et buffles
Sheep and goats	22 500[1]	25 000	26 000[1]	26 600[1]	27 000[1]	26 000[1]	25 000[1]	25 400[1]	Ovine et caprins
Pigs [1]	4	4	4	4	5	4	4	4	Porcine [1]
Horses [1]	1	1	1	1	1	1	1	1	Chevaline [1]
Asses [1]	18	19	20	20	21	19	19	20	Asine [1]
Mules [1]	18	19	19	20	20	18	18	19	Mulassière [1]
South Africa									**Afrique du Sud**
Cattle and buffaloes	12 503	12 584	13 015	13 389	13 667	13 772	13 565	* 13 700	Bovine et buffles
Sheep and goats	35 017	35 536	35 241	35 608	35 830	35 903	35 137	35 200[1]	Ovine et caprins
Pigs	1 493	1 511	1 628	1 603	1 617	1 641	1 531	1 535[1]	Porcine
Horses [1]	235	240	245	250	255	260	258	255	Chevaline [1]

37
Livestock
Thousand head [*cont.*]
Cheptel
Milliers de têtes [*suite*]

Region, country or area	1993	1994	1995	1996	1997	1998	1999	2000	Région, pays ou zone
Asses [1]	210	210	210	210	210	210	210	210	Asine [1]
Mules [1]	14	14	14	14	14	14	14	14	Mulassière [1]
Sudan									**Soudan**
Cattle and buffaloes	* 27 571	29 000[1]	30 077	31 669	33 103	34 584	35 825	37 093	Bovine et buffles
Sheep and goats	* 58 545	70 464	72 395[1]	72 418	75 872	79 709	80 000[1]	80 600[1]	Ovine et caprins
Horses [1]	23	23	24	24	25	25	26	26	Chevaline [1]
Asses [1]	670	675	678	680	700	720	730	740	Asine [1]
Mules [1]	1	1	1	1	1	1	1	1	Mulassière [1]
Swaziland									**Swaziland**
Cattle and buffaloes	608	626	642	656	658	660	602	610[1]	Bovine et buffles
Sheep and goats	449	455[1]	459	465	465[1]	462[1]	458[1]	470[1]	Ovine et caprins
Pigs	30	30[1]	30	31	32[1]	30[1]	31[1]	33[1]	Porcine
Horses	1	1	1[1]	1[1]	1[1]	1[1]	1[1]	1[1]	Chevaline
Asses	15	15	15[1]	15[1]	15[1]	15[1]	15[1]	15[1]	Asine
Togo									**Togo**
Cattle and buffaloes	248	248[1]	239	217	206	223	215[1]	215[1]	Bovine et buffles
Sheep and goats	3 100	2 850[1]	2 740[1]	1 932	1 598	1 850	1 850[1]	1 850[1]	Ovine et caprins
Pigs	8501	850[1]	850[1]	850[1]	850[1]	850[1]	850[1]	850[1]	Porcine
Horses [1]	2	2	2	2	2	2	2	2	Chevaline [1]
Asses [1]	3	3	3	3	3	3	3	3	Asine [1]
Tunisia									**Tunisie**
Cattle and buffaloes	659	662	654	680[1]	701	770[1]	780[1]	790[1]	Bovine et buffles
Sheep and goats	8 527	7 488	7 426	7 650[1]	7 554	7 900[1]	7 950[1]	8 000[1]	Ovine et caprins
Pigs [1]	6	6	6	6	6	6	6	6	Porcine [1]
Horses [1]	56	56	56	56	56	56	56	56	Chevaline [1]
Asses [1]	230	230	230	230	230	230	230	230	Asine [1]
Mules [1]	81	81	81	81	81	81	81	81	Mulassière [1]
Uganda									**Ouganda**
Cattle and buffaloes	5 370	5 106	5 233	5 301	5 460	5 651	5 820	5 966	Bovine et buffles
Sheep and goats	* 5 160	5 300[1]	5 400[1]	5 470[1]	* 5 544	5 560[1]	5 620[1]	5 680[1]	Ovine et caprins
Pigs	900[1]	910[1]	920[1]	930[1]	940	950[1]	960[1]	970[1]	Porcine
Asses [1]	17	17	17	18	18	18	18	18	Asine [1]
United Rep. of Tanzania									**Rép.–Unie de Tanzanie**
Cattle and buffaloes	* 13 618	* 13 752	* 13 888	* 14 025	* 14 163	* 14 302	14 350[1]	14 380[1]	Bovine et buffles
Sheep and goats	* 13 201	* 13 637	13 670[1]	13 750[1]	13 850[1]	13 950[1]	14 050[1]	14 150[1]	Ovine et caprins
Pigs	* 335	* 335	340[1]	330[1]	335[1]	340[1]	345[1]	350[1]	Porcine
Asses [1]	177	178	178	176	177	178	179	180	Asine [1]
Zambia									**Zambie**
Cattle and buffaloes	* 3 204	3 200[1]	3 000[1]	2 800[1]	* 2 100	* 2 176	* 2 273	* 2 373	Bovine et buffles
Sheep and goats	* 667	700[1]	724[1]	747[1]	* 780	* 989	* 1 189	* 1 389	Ovine et caprins
Pigs	300[1]	310[1]	300[1]	320[1]	* 316	* 320	* 324	* 330	Porcine
Asses [1]	2	2	2	2	2	2	2	2	Asine [1]
Zimbabwe									**Zimbabwe**
Cattle and buffaloes	* 4 180	4 300[1]	4 500	5 436	5 400[1]	5 450	5 500[1]	5 550[1]	Bovine et buffles
Sheep and goats	2 920[1]	3 030[1]	3 102	3 236	3 210[1]	3 270	3 295[1]	3 320[1]	Ovine et caprins
Pigs	* 210	* 246	277	266	260[1]	270	272[1]	275[1]	Porcine
Horses [1]	23	24	25	25	25	25	26	26	Chevaline [1]
Asses [1]	103	104	105	105	104	105	106	107	Asine [1]
Mules [1]	1	1	1	1	1	1	1	1	Mulassière [1]
America, North									**Amérique du Nord**
Cattle and buffaloes	**161 992**	**163 999**	**165 367**	**166 169**	**165 459**	**163 174**	**161 193**	**160 459**	**Bovine et buffles**
Sheep and goats	**33 920**	**32 811**	**31 825**	**30 975**	**29 966**	**29 581**	**28 987**	**29 290**	**Ovine et caprins**
Pigs	**92 554**	**91 373**	**93 783**	**92 208**	**90 557**	**98 506**	**95 804**	**93 157**	**Porcine**
Horses	**14 102**	**14 077**	**14 135**	**14 196**	**14 179**	**14 089**	**14 176**	**14 196**	**Chevaline**
Asses	**3 689**	**3 699**	**3 730**	**3 750**	**3 750**	**3 750**	**3 751**	**3 756**	**Asine**
Mules	**3 696**	**3 706**	**3 736**	**3 755**	**3 753**	**3 749**	**3 753**	**3 755**	**Mulassière**
Antigua and Barbuda									**Antigua–et–Barbuda**
Cattle and buffaloes [1]	16	16	16	16	16	16	16	16	Bovine et buffles [1]
Sheep and goats [1]	25	25	24	24	24	24	24	24	Ovine et caprins [1]
Pigs [1]	2	2	2	2	2	2	2	2	Porcine [1]
Horses [1]	1	1	0	0	0	0	0	0	Chevaline [1]
Asses [1]	2	2	1	1	1	1	1	1	Asine [1]

37
Livestock
Thousand head [*cont.*]
Cheptel
Milliers de têtes [*suite*]

Region, country or area	1993	1994	1995	1996	1997	1998	1999	2000	Région, pays ou zone
Bahamas									**Bahamas**
Cattle and buffaloes	1[1]	1	1	1	1[1]	1[1]	1	1[1]	Bovine et buffles
Sheep and goats	20[1]	20	21	22	22[1]	22[1]	20	20[1]	Ovine et caprins
Pigs	5[1]	5	* 5	5	5[1]	5[1]	6	6[1]	Porcine
Barbados									**Barbade**
Cattle and buffaloes [1]	28	28	28	28	24	23	23	23	Bovine et buffles [1]
Sheep and goats [1]	46	46	46	46	46	46	46	46	Ovine et caprins [1]
Pigs [1]	30	30	30	30	31	33	33	33	Porcine [1]
Horses [1]	1	1	1	1	1	1	1	1	Chevaline [1]
Asses [1]	2	2	2	2	2	2	2	2	Asine [1]
Mules [1]	2	2	2	2	2	2	2	2	Mulassière [1]
Belize									**Belize**
Cattle and buffaloes	* 58	59[1]	60	62[1]	60[1]	58[1]	59[1]	59[1]	Bovine et buffles
Sheep and goats [1]	5	4	4	4	4	4	4	4	Ovine et caprins [1]
Pigs	25[1]	24[1]	22	23[1]	23[1]	23[1]	24[1]	24[1]	Porcine
Horses [1]	5	5	5	5	5	5	5	5	Chevaline [1]
Mules [1]	4	4	4	4	4	4	4	4	Mulassière [1]
Bermuda									**Bermudes**
Cattle and buffaloes [1]	1	1	1	1	1	1	1	1	Bovine et buffles [1]
Sheep and goats	1[1]	1	0[1]	0	0[1]	0[1]	0[1]	0[1]	Ovine et caprins
Pigs	1[1]	1[1]	1[1]	1	1[1]	1[1]	1[1]	1[1]	Porcine
Horses	1[1]	1	1[1]	1[1]	1[1]	1[1]	1[1]	1[1]	Chevaline
British Virgin Islands									**Iles Vierges britanniques**
Cattle and buffaloes [1]	2	2	2	2	2	2	2	2	Bovine et buffles [1]
Sheep and goats [1]	16	16	16	16	16	16	16	16	Ovine et caprins [1]
Pigs [1]	2	2	2	2	2	2	2	2	Porcine [1]
Canada									**Canada**
Cattle and buffaloes	11 860	12 012	12 709	13 402	13 409	13 215	12 902	12 786	Bovine et buffles
Sheep and goats [1]	660	667	645	672	656	642	679	725	Ovine et caprins [1]
Pigs	10 744	10 534	11 291	11 588	11 480	11 985	12 409	12 242	Porcine
Horses [1]	370	350	380	376	400	380	380	385	Chevaline [1]
Mules [1]	4	4	4	4	4	4	4	4	Mulassière [1]
Cayman Islands									**Iles Caïmanes**
Cattle and buffaloes	1[1]	1[1]	1[1]	1[1]	1[1]	1[1]	1[1]	1[1]	Bovine et buffles
Costa Rica									**Costa Rica**
Cattle and buffaloes	* 2 122	* 1 894	* 1 645	* 1 585	* 1 529	* 1 527	* 1 617	1 715	Bovine et buffles
Sheep and goats [1]	4	4	4	4	4	4	4	4	Ovine et caprins [1]
Pigs	340	350	300	300	315[1]	360[1]	390[1]	390[1]	Porcine
Horses [1]	114	114	115	115	115	115	115	115	Chevaline [1]
Asses [1]	7	7	8	8	8	8	8	8	Asine [1]
Mules [1]	5	5	5	5	5	5	5	5	Mulassière [1]
Cuba									**Cuba**
Cattle and buffaloes	4 583	4 617	4 632	4 601	4 606	4 644	4 406	4 700[1]	Bovine et buffles
Sheep and goats [1]	410	410	415	429	449	472	518	450	Ovine et caprins [1]
Pigs [1]	2 300	2 300	2 300	2 400	2 400	2 400	2 500	2 800	Porcine [1]
Horses	608	597	583	568	525	434	450[1]	450[1]	Chevaline
Asses	6	6	6	6	6	6	6[1]	6[1]	Asine
Mules	33	33	32	30	28	24	25[1]	25[1]	Mulassière
Dominica									**Dominique**
Cattle and buffaloes [1]	13	13	13	13	13	13	13	13	Bovine et buffles [1]
Sheep and goats [1]	17	17	17	17	17	17	17	17	Ovine et caprins [1]
Pigs [1]	5	5	5	5	5	5	5	5	Porcine [1]
Dominican Republic									**Rép. dominicaine**
Cattle and buffaloes	* 2 371	* 2 366	2 302	2 435	2 481	2 528	1 904	1 904	Bovine et buffles
Sheep and goats	691[1]	700[1]	705[1]	705[1]	705	435	269	2751	Ovine et caprins
Pigs	850[1]	900[1]	950[1]	950[1]	960	960	540	539	Porcine
Horses [1]	329	329	329	329	329	330	330	330	Chevaline [1]
Asses [1]	145	145	145	145	145	145	145	145	Asine [1]
Mules [1]	135	135	135	135	135	135	138	138	Mulassière [1]
El Salvador									**El Salvador**
Cattle and buffaloes	1 197	1 262	1 125	1 287	1 162	1 038	1 141	1 212	Bovine et buffles
Sheep and goats [1]	20	20	21	21	21	21	21	21	Ovine et caprins [1]
Pigs	336	223	295	306	294	3 120	248	300	Porcine

37
Livestock
Thousand head [*cont.*]
Cheptel
Milliers de têtes [*suite*]

Region, country or area	1993	1994	1995	1996	1997	1998	1999	2000	Région, pays ou zone
Horses [1]	96	96	96	96	96	96	96	96	Chevaline [1]
Asses [1]	3	3	3	3	3	3	3	3	Asine [1]
Mules [1]	24	24	24	24	24	24	24	24	Mulassière [1]
Greenland									**Groenland**
Sheep and goats [1]	22	22	22	22	22	22	22	22	Ovine et caprins [1]
Grenada									**Grenade**
Cattle and buffaloes	4[1]	4[1]	4	4[1]	4[1]	4[1]	4[1]	4[1]	Bovine et buffles
Sheep and goats	21[1]	21[1]	20	20[1]	20[1]	20[1]	20[1]	20[1]	Ovine et caprins
Pigs	5[1]	5[1]	5	5[1]	5[1]	5[1]	5[1]	5[1]	Porcine
Asses [1]	1	1	1	1	1	1	1	1	Asine [1]
Guadeloupe									**Guadeloupe**
Cattle and buffaloes	56	60	63[1]	651	80	80[1]	80[1]	80[1]	Bovine et buffles
Sheep and goats [1]	66	66	66	64	67	67	67	67	Ovine et caprins
Pigs [1]	14	14	17	15	15	15	15	15	Porcine [1]
Horses [1]	1	1	1	1	1	1	1	1	Chevaline [1]
Guatemala									**Guatemala**
Cattle and buffaloes	2 400	2 300	2 293	2 291	* 2 337	* 2 330	2 300[1]	2 300[1]	Bovine et buffles
Sheep and goats	545	604	628	660	660[1]	660[1]	661[1]	661[1]	Ovine et caprins
Pigs	715	796	753	773	802	826	825[1]	825[1]	Porcine
Horses [1]	115	116	117	118	118	118	119	120	Chevaline [1]
Asses [1]	9	9	9	10	10	10	10	10	Asine [1]
Mules [1]	38	38	38	38	38	38	39	39	Mulassière [1]
Haiti									**Haïti**
Cattle and buffaloes	* 1 251	* 1 234	1 250	1 246	1 270	1 300	1 300[1]	1 430	Bovine et buffles
Sheep and goats	1 243[1]	1 245[1]	* 1 242	* 1 380	* 1 605	* 1 756	1 757[1]	2 094	Ovine et caprins
Pigs	* 350	* 360	390	485	600	800	800[1]	1 000	Porcine
Horses [1]	460	470	480	490	490	490	490	500	Chevaline [1]
Asses [1]	210	210	210	210	210	210	210	215	Asine [1]
Mules [1]	80	80	80	80	80	80	80	82	Mulassière [1]
Honduras									**Honduras**
Cattle and buffaloes	2 077	* 2 286	2 111	2 127	2 061	2 200	2 061	1 950[1]	Bovine et buffles
Sheep and goats	40	41[1]	41[1]	41[1]	43[1]	43[1]	44[1]	44[1]	Ovine et caprins
Pigs	596	600[1]	600[1]	640[1]	670[1]	700[1]	798[1]	800[1]	Porcine
Horses [1]	172	173	174	175	176	177	178	179	Chevaline [1]
Asses [1]	22	23	23	23	23	23	23	23	Asine [1]
Mules [1]	69	69	69	69	69	69	70	70	Mulassière [1]
Jamaica									**Jamaïque**
Cattle and buffaloes [1]	460	440	450	420	400	400	400	400	Bovine et buffles [1]
Sheep and goats [1]	441	441	441	441	442	442	441	441	Ovine et caprins [1]
Pigs [1]	200	200	200	180	180	180	180	180	Porcine [1]
Horses [1]	4	4	4	4	4	4	4	4	Chevaline [1]
Asses [1]	23	23	23	23	23	23	23	23	Asine [1]
Mules [1]	10	10	10	10	10	10	10	10	Mulassière [1]
Martinique									**Martinique**
Cattle and buffaloes	30	30	30[1]	30[1]	30[1]	30[1]	30[1]	30[1]	Bovine et buffles
Sheep and goats [1]	72	70	64	64	64	64	64	64	Ovine et caprins [1]
Pigs [1]	36	36	33	33	33	33	33	33	Porcine [1]
Horses [1]	2	2	2	2	2	2	2	2	Chevaline [1]
Mexico									**Mexique**
Cattle and buffaloes	* 30 649	* 30 702	* 30 191	29 301	30 772	30 500	30 293	30 293[1]	Bovine et buffles
Sheep and goats	17 176[1]	* 16 355[1]	16 328	15 750	* 15 195	* 15 371[1]	15 500[1]	15 500[1]	Ovine et caprins
Pigs	16 832	16 200	15 923	15 405	15 735	14 994	13 855	* 13 690	Porcine
Horses [1]	6 185	6 190	6 200	6 250	6 250	6 250	6 250	6 250	Chevaline [1]
Asses [1]	3 190	3 200	3 230	3 250	3 250	3 250	3 250	3 250	Asine [1]
Mules [1]	3 210	3 220	3 250	3 270	3 270	3 270	3 270	3 270	Mulassière [1]
Montserrat									**Montserrat**
Cattle and buffaloes [1]	10	10	10	10	10	10	10	10	Bovine et buffles [1]
Sheep and goats [1]	12	12	12	12	12	12	12	12	Ovine et caprins [1]
Pigs [1]	1	1	1	1	1	1	1	1	Porcine [1]
Netherlands Antilles									**Antilles néerlandaises**
Cattle and buffaloes [1]	1	1	1	1	1	1	1	1	Bovine et buffles [1]
Sheep and goats [1]	19	20	19	20	19	20	20	20	Ovine et caprins [1]
Pigs [1]	2	2	2	2	2	2	2	2	Porcine [1]
Asses [1]	3	3	3	3	3	3	3	3	Asine [1]

37

Livestock
Thousand head [*cont.*]
Cheptel
Milliers de têtes [*suite*]

Region, country or area	1993	1994	1995	1996	1997	1998	1999	2000	Région, pays ou zone
Nicaragua									**Nicaragua**
Cattle and buffaloes	1 688	1 730	1 750	1 807	* 1 712	* 1 668	* 1 693	* 1 660	Bovine et buffles
Sheep and goats	10[1]	10[1]	10[1]	11	10[1]	10[1]	10[1]	11[1]	Ovine et caprins
Pigs [1]	430	330	392	366	385	400	400	400	Porcine [1]
Horses [1]	248	247	246	245	245	245	245	245	Chevaline [1]
Asses [1]	8	8	8	8	9	9	9	9	Asine [1]
Mules [1]	45	46	46	46	46	46	46	46	Mulassière [1]
Panama									**Panama**
Cattle and buffaloes	1 437	1 454	1 456	1 442	1 362	1 382	1 360	1 360	Bovine et buffles
Sheep and goats	5[1]	* 5	5[1]	5[1]	5[1]	5[1]	5[1]	5	Ovine et caprins
Pigs	266	257	261	244	240	252	278	280	Porcine
Horses	156[1]	* 164	165[1]	165[1]	165[1]	165[1]	166[1]	166[1]	Chevaline
Mules	4[1]	* 4	4[1]	4[1]	4[1]	4[1]	4[1]	4[1]	Mulassière
Puerto Rico									**Porto Rico**
Cattle and buffaloes	429	429	368	371	388	388[1]	388[1]	388[1]	Bovine et buffles
Sheep and goats [1]	29	28	26	16	21	21	21	21	Ovine et caprins [1]
Pigs	194	196	205	182	175	175[1]	175[1]	175[1]	Porcine
Horses [1]	23	24	24	24	24	24	24	24	Chevaline [1]
Asses [1]	2	2	2	2	2	2	2	2	Asine [1]
Mules [1]	3	3	3	3	3	3	3	3	Mulassière [1]
Saint Kitts and Nevis									**Saint−Kitts−et−Nevis**
Cattle and buffaloes	4	4[1]	4[1]	4[1]	4	4[1]	4[1]	4[1]	Bovine et buffles
Sheep and goats	24	24[1]	24	26	24[1]	21[1]	22[1]	22[1]	Ovine et caprins
Pigs	2[1]	2	2	3	3[1]	3[1]	3	3[1]	Porcine
Saint Lucia									**Sainte−Lucie**
Cattle and buffaloes [1]	12	12	12	12	12	12	12	12	Bovine et buffles [1]
Sheep and goats	25[1]	24[1]	23[1]	22	22[1]	22[1]	22[1]	22[1]	Ovine et caprins
Pigs	14[1]	14[1]	14[1]	15	15[1]	15[1]	15[1]	15[1]	Porcine
Horses [1]	1	1	1	1	1	1	1	1	Chevaline [1]
Asses [1]	1	1	1	1	1	1	1	1	Asine [1]
Mules [1]	1	1	1	1	1	1	1	1	Mulassière [1]
St. Vincent−Grenadines									**St. Vincent−Grenadines**
Cattle and buffaloes	6[1]	6[1]	6[1]	6[1]	6[1]	6[1]	6[1]	6[1]	Bovine et buffles
Sheep and goats	18[1]	18[1]	19[1]	19[1]	19[1]	19[1]	19[1]	19[1]	Ovine et caprins
Pigs	9[1]	9[1]	9[1]	9[1]	9[1]	9[1]	9[1]	10[1]	Porcine
Asses [1]	1	1	1	1	1	1	1	1	Asine [1]
Trinidad and Tobago									**Trinité−et−Tobago**
Cattle and buffaloes	41	41	41	41[1]	40[1]	39[1]	40[1]	40[1]	Bovine et buffles
Sheep and goats [1]	71	71	71	71	71	71	71	71	Ovine et caprins
Pigs	45[1]	31	32	34	43[1]	40[1]	41[1]	41[1]	Porcine
Horses [1]	1	1	1	1	1	1	1	1	Chevaline [1]
Asses [1]	2	2	2	2	2	2	2	2	Asine [1]
Mules [1]	2	2	2	2	2	2	2	2	Mulassière [1]
United States									**Etats−Unis**
Cattle and buffaloes	99 176	100 976	102 785	103 548	101 656	99 744	99 115	98 048	Bovine et buffles
Sheep and goats	12 161	11 796	10 839	10 365	9 674	9 225	8 585	8 565[1]	Ovine et caprins
Pigs	58 202	57 940	59 738	58 201	56 124	61 158	62 206	59 337	Porcine
Horses	5 210[1]	5 190[1]	5 210[1]	5 230[1]	5 230[1]	5 250	5 317	5 320[1]	Chevaline
Asses [1]	52	52	52	52	52	52	52	52	Asine [1]
Mules [1]	28	28	28	28	28	28	28	28	Mulassière [1]
United States Virgin Is.									**Iles Vierges américaines**
Cattle and buffaloes [1]	8	8	8	8	8	8	8	8	Bovine et buffles [1]
Sheep and goats [1]	7	7	7	7	7	7	7	7	Ovine et caprins [1]
Pigs [1]	3	3	3	3	3	3	3	3	Porcine [1]
America, South									**Amérique du Sud**
Cattle and buffaloes	285 225	290 987	296 584	295 020	298 681	300 940	302 579	307 277	**Bovine et buffles**
Sheep and goats	117 640	116 544	114 945	103 568	102 581	100 117	99 447	98 762	**Ovine et caprins**
Pigs	54 288	56 337	57 603	50 865	52 108	53 279	52 715	53 279	**Porcine**
Horses	15 129	15 308	15 587	15 004	15 093	15 128	15 522	15 537	**Chevaline**
Asses	4 018	4 030	4 062	3 951	3 969	3 954	3 997	4 012	**Asine**
Mules	3 346	3 342	3 311	2 611	2 621	2 620	2 748	2 763	**Mulassière**
Argentina									**Argentine**
Cattle and buffaloes	52 665	53 157	53 500	54 000	54 500	54 600	55 000[1]	55 000[1]	Bovine et buffles
Sheep and goats	* 28 210	* 27 478	* 25 173	* 21 330	* 20 723	* 19 682[1]	* 18 500[1]	19 000[1]	Ovine et caprins
Pigs	2 850[1]	3 300	3 100	3 100	3 200	3 500[1]	4 200[1]	4 200[1]	Porcine

37
Livestock
Thousand head [cont.]
Cheptel
Milliers de têtes [suite]

Region, country or area	1993	1994	1995	1996	1997	1998	1999	2000	Région, pays ou zone
Horses	* 3 300	3 300[1]	3 300[1]	3 300[1]	3 300[1]	3 300[1]	3 600[1]	3 600[1]	Chevaline
Asses [1]	90	90	90	90	90	90	95	95	Asine [1]
Mules [1]	174	175	175	175	175	175	180	180	Mulassière [1]
Bolivia									**Bolivie**
Cattle and buffaloes	5 794	5 912	6 000	6 118	6 238	6 387	6 556	6 725	Bovine et buffles
Sheep and goats	8 982	9 165	9 380	9 539[1]	9 728	9 905	10 075[1]	10 252[1]	Ovine et caprins
Pigs	2 273	2 331	2 405	2 482	2 569	2 637	2 715	2 793	Porcine
Horses [1]	322	322	322	322	322	322	322	322	Chevaline [1]
Asses [1]	631	631	631	631	631	631	631	631	Asine [1]
Mules [1]	81	81	81	81	81	81	81	81	Mulassière [1]
Brazil									**Brésil**
Cattle and buffaloes	156 633	159 815	162 870	159 335	162 394	164 172	164 570	168 621	Bovine et buffles
Sheep and goats	28 627	29 315	29 608	22 162	22 502	22 433	23 500[1]	23 500[1]	Ovine et caprins
Pigs	34 184	35 142	36 062	29 202	29 637	30 007	27 425	27 320	Porcine
Horses	6 314	6 356	6 394	5 705	5 832	5 867	5 900[1]	5 900[1]	Chevaline
Asses	1 302	1 313	1 344	1 232	1 249	1 233	1 250[1]	1 250[1]	Asine
Mules	1 993	1 987	1 990	1 286	1 295	1 292	1 400[1]	1 400[1]	Mulassière
Chile									**Chili**
Cattle and buffaloes	3 557	3 692	3 814	3 858	4 142	4 160	4 134	4 068	Bovine et buffles
Sheep and goats	5 229[1]	5 249[1]	5 225[1]	5 116[1]	4 573	4 494[1]	4 856	4 884	Ovine et caprins
Pigs	1 288	1 407	1 490	1 486	1 655	1 962	2 221	2 465	Porcine
Horses [1]	500	500	550	580	600	600	600	600	Chevaline [1]
Asses [1]	28	28	28	28	28	28	28	28	Asine [1]
Mules [1]	10	10	10	10	10	10	10	10	Mulassière [1]
Colombia									**Colombie**
Cattle and buffaloes	25 324	* 25 634	25 551	* 26 088	25 673	25 764	25 614	26 000[1]	Bovine et buffles
Sheep and goats	3 500	3 500[1]	* 3 505	* 3 503	3 332	3 045	3 311	3 320[1]	Ovine et caprins
Pigs	2 635	2 600[1]	2 500	2 431	2 480	2 452	2 765	2 800[1]	Porcine
Horses	2 200[1]	2 300[1]	2 450	2 450[1]	2 450[1]	2 450[1]	2 500[1]	2 500[1]	Chevaline
Asses [1]	710	710	710	710	710	710	715	715	Asine [1]
Mules	622[1]	622[1]	586	590[1]	590[1]	590[1]	595[1]	595[1]	Mulassière
Ecuador									**Equateur**
Cattle and buffaloes	4 803	4 937	4 995	5 105	5 150	5 076	5 106	5 110	Bovine et buffles
Sheep and goats	1 979	2 059	1 987	2 018	2 112	2 361	2 465	2 415	Ovine et caprins
Pigs	2 461	2 546	2 618	2 621	2 708	2 708	2 786	2 870	Porcine
Horses	510[1]	515[1]	520[1]	520[1]	520[1]	520[1]	521[1]	521[1]	Chevaline
Asses	263[1]	264[1]	265[1]	266[1]	267[1]	268[1]	269[1]	269[1]	Asine
Mules	152[1]	153[1]	154[1]	155[1]	156[1]	157[1]	157[1]	157[1]	Mulassière
Falkland Is. (Malvinas)									**Iles Falkland (Malvinas)**
Cattle and buffaloes	5	5	5	4	5	4	4[1]	4[1]	Bovine et buffles
Sheep and goats	721	727	717	686	707	708	708[1]	708[1]	Ovine et caprins
Horses	1	1	1	1	1	1	1[1]	1[1]	Chevaline
French Guiana									**Guyane française**
Cattle and buffaloes	8	8	8	9	9[1]	9[1]	9[1]	9[1]	Bovine et buffles
Sheep and goats	4	4	4	4[1]	4[1]	4[1]	4[1]	4[1]	Ovine et caprins
Pigs	9	9	9	10	11[1]	11[1]	11[1]	11[1]	Porcine
Guyana									**Guyana**
Cattle and buffaloes [1]	240	260	250	240	230	220	220	220	Bovine et buffles [1]
Sheep and goats [1]	209	209	209	209	209	209	209	209	Ovine et caprins [1]
Pigs [1]	35	25	20	20	20	20	20	20	Porcine [1]
Horses [1]	2	2	2	2	2	2	2	2	Chevaline [1]
Asses [1]	1	1	1	1	1	1	1	1	Asine [1]
Paraguay									**Paraguay**
Cattle and buffaloes	8 600[1]	9 100[1]	9 788	9 765	9 794	* 9 833	* 9 863	* 9 910	Bovine et buffles
Sheep and goats	500[1]	508	509[1]	511[1]	510	* 525	* 527	* 550	Ovine et caprins
Pigs	2 485[1]	2 500[1]	2 525[1]	2 268[1]	2 300[1]	2 300[1]	2 500[1]	2 700[1]	Porcine
Horses	339	370	411[1]	478[1]	400[1]	400[1]	400[1]	400[1]	Chevaline
Asses [1]	32	32	32	32	32	32	32	32	Asine [1]
Mules [1]	14	14	14	14	14	14	14	14	Mulassière [1]
Peru									**Pérou**
Cattle and buffaloes	3 955	4 062	4 513	4 646	4 560	4 657	4 903	4 903[1]	Bovine et buffles
Sheep and goats	13 660	13 950	14 614	14 736	15 156	15 577	16 468[1]	16 468[1]	Ovine et caprins
Pigs	2 317	2 442	2 401	2 533	2 481	2 531	2 788	2 788[1]	Porcine
Horses [1]	665	665	665	665	665	665	675	690	Chevaline [1]

37
Livestock
Thousand head [*cont.*]
Cheptel
Milliers de têtes [*suite*]

Region, country or area	1993	1994	1995	1996	1997	1998	1999	2000	Région, pays ou zone
Asses [1]	520	520	520	520	520	520	535	550	Asine [1]
Mules [1]	224	224	224	224	224	224	235	250	Mulassière [1]
Suriname									**Suriname**
Cattle and buffaloes	98[1]	100[1]	103	99	98	101	103[1]	107[1]	Bovine et buffles
Sheep and goats	17[1]	16[1]	13	16	17	18	21	24	Ovine et caprins
Pigs	36[1]	37	20	20	21	20	25	32	Porcine
Uruguay									**Uruguay**
Cattle and buffaloes	10 217	10 511	10 450	10 651	10 553	10 297	10 504	* 10 800	Bovine et buffles
Sheep and goats [1]	23 316	21 245	20 220	19 762	18 295	16 510	14 424	13 047	Ovine et caprins [1]
Pigs	260[1]	280	270[1]	270	270[1]	330[1]	360[1]	380[1]	Porcine
Horses [1]	480	480	470	480	500	500	500	500	Chevaline [1]
Asses [1]	1	1	1	1	1	1	1	1	Asine [1]
Mules [1]	4	4	4	4	4	4	4	4	Mulassière [1]
Venezuela									**Venezuela**
Cattle and buffaloes	13 325	13 796	14 737	15 103	15 337	15 661	15 992	15 800[1]	Bovine et buffles
Sheep and goats	2 687[1]	3 119[1]	3 781	3 978	4 714[1]	4 647[1]	4 381[1]	4 381[1]	Ovine et caprins
Pigs	3 456	3 716	4 182	4 422	4 756	4 800[1]	4 900[1]	4 900[1]	Porcine
Horses [1]	495	495	500	500	500	500	500	500	Chevaline [1]
Asses [1]	440	440	440	440	440	440	440	440	Asine [1]
Mules [1]	72	72	72	72	72	72	72	72	Mulassière [1]
Asia									**Asie**
Cattle and buffaloes	587 200	597 212	610 562	615 146	607 463	616 631	623 706	633 234	**Bovine et buffles**
Sheep and goats	785 711	801 301	820 169	849 166	812 017	832 568	853 839	868 711	**Ovine et caprins**
Pigs	479 662	489 861	511 342	486 227	464 549	502 914	525 330	535 553	**Porcine**
Horses	17 974	17 912	18 045	18 177	16 695	16 731	16 900	16 880	**Chevaline**
Asses	20 111	20 228	20 445	20 406	19 315	19 516	19 714	19 560	**Asine**
Mules	6 294	6 171	6 221	6 113	5 512	5 528	5 489	5 426	**Mulassière**
Afghanistan									**Afghanistan**
Cattle and buffaloes	1 800[1]	2 100[1]	* 2 410	* 2 641	* 2 895	* 3 173	3 478	3 478[1]	Bovine et buffles
Sheep and goats	16 400[1]	16 600[1]	* 16 594	* 18 574	* 20 641	* 22 803	25 063	25 373[1]	Ovine et caprins
Horses	200[1]	100[1]	100[1]	100[1]	100[1]	100[1]	104	104[1]	Chevaline
Asses	500[1]	600[1]	* 704	* 753	* 805	* 860	920	920[1]	Asine
Mules [1]	23	23	23	24	26	28	30	30	Mulassière [1]
Armenia									**Arménie**
Cattle and buffaloes	499[1]	502[1]	504[1]	508[1]	510[1]	466[1]	* 469	479[1]	Bovine et buffles
Sheep and goats	873	* 736	* 636	604	* 579	* 521	* 546	* 551	Ovine et caprins
Pigs	84	81	82	80	54	57	86	71	Porcine
Horses	9	11	12	12	13	13	12	12	Chevaline
Asses	4[1]	3[1]	3[1]	3[1]	3[1]	3[1]	3[1]	3[1]	Asine
Azerbaijan									**Azerbaïdjan**
Cattle and buffaloes	2 017[1]	1 911[1]	1 928[1]	1 980	2 083	2 137	2 200[1]	2 235[1]	Bovine et buffles
Sheep and goats	* 4 901	* 4 539	* 4 558	4 644	4 922	5 267	5 513	* 5 790	Ovine et caprins
Pigs	67	48	33	30	23	21	26	20	Porcine
Horses	35	35	38	43	49	53	56	61	Chevaline
Asses	24	20	22	25	28	31	33	36	Asine
Bahrain									**Bahreïn**
Cattle and buffaloes	13[1]	12[1]	11	12	12	13	13[1]	11	Bovine et buffles
Sheep and goats	36[1]	35[1]	33	34	35	33	33[1]	34[1]	Ovine et caprins
Bangladesh									**Bangladesh**
Cattle and buffaloes	24 435	* 24 643	* 24 859	24 401	* 24 816	24 220	24 480[1]	24 480[1]	Bovine et buffles
Sheep and goats	26 956	* 29 080[1]	* 31 400[1]	34 436	35 636	34 610	34 921[1]	34 921[1]	Ovine et caprins
Bhutan									**Bhoutan**
Cattle and buffaloes [1]	433	439	439	439	439	439	439	439	Bovine et buffles [1]
Sheep and goats [1]	95	101	101	101	101	101	101	101	Ovine et caprins [1]
Pigs [1]	74	75	75	75	75	75	75	75	Porcine [1]
Horses [1]	29	30	30	30	30	30	30	30	Chevaline [1]
Asses [1]	18	18	18	18	18	18	18	18	Asine [1]
Mules [1]	10	10	10	10	10	10	10	10	Mulassière [1]
Brunei Darussalam									**Brunéi Darussalam**
Cattle and buffaloes	5	6	6	6	8	8	8[1]	8[1]	Bovine et buffles
Sheep and goats	5	4	4	3	3	4	4[1]	4[1]	Ovine et caprins
Pigs	5[1]	5[1]	4[1]	5[1]	5[1]	5[1]	6[1]	6[1]	Porcine
Cambodia									**Cambodge**
Cattle and buffaloes	3 366	3 431	3 543	3 544	3 514	3 555[1]	3 600[1]	3 710[1]	Bovine et buffles

37

Livestock
Thousand head [cont.]
Cheptel
Milliers de têtes [suite]

Region, country or area	1993	1994	1995	1996	1997	1998	1999	2000	Région, pays ou zone
Pigs	2 123	2 024	2 039	2 151	2 438	2 500[1]	2 550[1]	2 600[1]	Porcine
Horses [1]	20	21	21	22	22	23	25	25	Chevaline [1]
China									**Chine**
Cattle and buffaloes *	108 000	113 473	123 484	123 055	112 570	121 964	124 552	127 181	Bovine et buffles *
Sheep and goats *	207 533	217 670	240 840	277 542	237 593	256 073	269 309	279 496	Ovine et caprins *
Pigs *	394 070	402 943	424 787	398 617	373 644	408 425	429 212	437 551	Porcine *
Horses *	10 019	9 961	10 040	10 074	8 717	8 914	8 983	8 916	Chevaline *
Asses *	10 983	10 891	10 923	10 745	9 444	9 528	9 558	9 348	Asine *
Mules *	5 610	5 498	5 552	5 389	4 780	4 806	4 739	4 673	Mulassière *
Cyprus									**Chypre**
Cattle and buffaloes	56	61	64	68	70	62	56	56[1]	Bovine et buffles
Sheep and goats	485	473	465	470	492	535	562	562[1]	Ovine et caprins
Pigs	342	369	356	374	400	415	431	455	Porcine
Horses [1]	1	1	1	1	1	1	1	1	Chevaline [1]
Asses [1]	5	5	5	5	5	5	5	5	Asine [1]
Mules [1]	2	2	2	2	2	2	2	2	Mulassière [1]
Georgia									**Géorgie**
Cattle and buffaloes	1 023[1]	* 949	* 964	* 994	1 026[1]	1 043[1]	1 066[1]	1 138[1]	Bovine et buffles
Sheep and goats	1 192	958	793	725	652	584	587	633	Ovine et caprins
Pigs	476	365	367	353	333	330	366	411	Porcine
Horses	17	20	21	24	26	28	30	30[1]	Chevaline
Asses [1]	2	2	3	3	3	3	3	3	Asine [1]
India									**Inde**
Cattle and buffaloes	* 290 570	293 220	295 868	298 552	301 273	* 303 030	* 306 967	* 312 572	Bovine et buffles
Sheep and goats	* 168 186	170 358	172 550	174 773	177 032	* 178 462	* 180 130	* 180 900	Ovine et caprins
Pigs	* 13 500	13 783	14 306	14 848	15 411	* 16 005	16 500[1]	16 500[1]	Porcine
Horses [1]	980	990	990	990	990	990	990	990	Chevaline [1]
Asses	1 000[1]	1 000[1]	1 000[1]	1 000[1]	1 000[1]	1 000[1]	1 000[1]	1 000[1]	Asine
Mules	200[1]	200[1]	200[1]	200[1]	200[1]	200[1]	200[1]	200[1]	Mulassière
Indonesia									**Indonésie**
Cattle and buffaloes	13 886	14 472	14 670	14 987	15 003	14 463	14 961	14 961[1]	Bovine et buffles
Sheep and goats	17 742	19 511	20 336	21 565	21 860	20 704	21 623	21 623[1]	Ovine et caprins
Pigs	8 704	8 858	7 720	7 597	8 233	7 798	9 353	9 353[1]	Porcine
Horses	582	611	609	579	582	567	579	579[1]	Chevaline
Iran (Islamic Rep. of)									**Iran (Rép. islamique d')**
Cattle and buffaloes	8 426	8 640	8 794	8 948	9 103	9 259	8 521	8 600[1]	Bovine et buffles
Sheep and goats	75 443	76 042	76 646	77 256	78 117	79 002	79 657	81 000[1]	Ovine et caprins
Horses	133	150[1]	150[1]	150[1]	150[1]	130[1]	120[1]	150[1]	Chevaline
Asses	* 1 400	* 1 400	* 1 400	* 1 400	* 1 490	* 1 400	* 1 554	1 600[1]	Asine
Mules	* 137	* 137	* 137	* 137	* 147	* 137	* 173	175[1]	Mulassière
Iraq									**Iraq**
Cattle and buffaloes	1 588[1]	* 1 441[1]	* 1 260[1]	1 100[1]	* 1 363	1 384[1]	1 389[1]	1 415[1]	Bovine et buffles
Sheep and goats	11 050[1]	9 825[1]	8 850[1]	6 405[1]	* 8 050	8 200[1]	8 300[1]	8 380[1]	Ovine et caprins
Horses [1]	51	51	* 47	46	47	48	46	47	Chevaline [1]
Asses	360[1]	380[1]	* 396	368[1]	380[1]	385[1]	375[1]	380[1]	Asine
Mules [1]	12	12	12	12	12	13	11	11	Mulassière [1]
Israel									**Israël**
Cattle and buffaloes	366	387	391	391	380	388	388	388[1]	Bovine et buffles
Sheep and goats	430	435	421	420	435	424	420	420[1]	Ovine et caprins
Pigs [1]	118	120	143	145	165	163	163	163	Porcine [1]
Horses [1]	4	4	4	4	4	4	4	4	Chevaline [1]
Asses [1]	5	5	5	5	5	5	5	5	Asine [1]
Mules [1]	2	2	2	2	2	2	2	2	Mulassière [1]
Japan									**Japon**
Cattle and buffaloes	5 024	4 989	4 916	4 828	4 750	4 708	4 658	* 4 588	Bovine et buffles
Sheep and goats	61	56	50	47	45	42[1]	43[1]	42[1]	Ovine et caprins
Pigs	10 783	10 621	10 250	9 900	9 823	9 904	9 879	* 9 880	Porcine
Horses	27	28	29[1]	26[1]	27	28[1]	22[1]	22[1]	Chevaline
Jordan									**Jordanie**
Cattle and buffaloes	46[1]	62	58	48	52	56[1]	57[1]	57[1]	Bovine et buffles
Sheep and goats	4 029	2 979	3 034	3 182	2 926	2 585	2 213	2 230[1]	Ovine et caprins
Horses [1]	4	4	4	4	4	4	4	4	Chevaline [1]
Asses [1]	19	19	18	18	18	18	18	18	Asine [1]
Mules [1]	3	3	3	3	3	3	3	3	Mulassière [1]

37
Livestock
Thousand head [*cont.*]
Cheptel
Milliers de têtes [*suite*]

Region, country or area	1993	1994	1995	1996	1997	1998	1999	2000	Région, pays ou zone
Kazakhstan									**Kazakhstan**
Cattle and buffaloes [1]	9 587	9 358	8 083	6 870	5 435	4 316	3 967	4 007	Bovine et buffles [1]
Sheep and goats	34 420	34 209	25 132	19 585	13 679	10 384	* 10 069	* 10 481	Ovine et caprins
Pigs	2 591	2 445	1 983	1 623	1 036	879	892	1 034	Porcine
Horses	1 704	1 777	1 636	1 557	1 310	1 083	986	942	Chevaline
Asses [1]	45	40	40	40	35	29	29	29	Asine [1]
Korea, Dem. P. R.									**Corée, R. p. dém. de**
Cattle and buffaloes	900[1]	911	886	629	545	565	580[1]	600[1]	Bovine et buffles [1]
Sheep and goats	1 250[1]	1 401	972[1]	961	1 237	1 673	2 085	2 290[1]	Ovine et caprins
Pigs	4 000[1]	3 572	2 674	2 290	1 859	2 475	2 970	2 970[1]	Porcine
Horses [1]	46	47	45	40	40	44	45	45	Mulassière [1]
Korea, Republic of									**Corée, République de**
Cattle and buffaloes	2 814	2 945	3 147	3 395	3 280	2 922	2 486	2 486[1]	Bovine et buffles
Sheep and goats	560	605	682	676	605	540	506	506[1]	Ovine et caprins
Pigs	5 928	5 955	6 461	6 517	7 096	7 544	7 864	7 864[1]	Porcine
Horses	5	6	6	7	8	8	8	8[1]	Chevaline
Kuwait									**Koweït**
Cattle and buffaloes	11	15	20	19	21	18	20[1]	20[1]	Bovine et buffles
Sheep and goats	192	258	376	491	564	551	580[1]	600[1]	Ovine et caprins
Horses [1]	1	1	1	1	1	1	1	1	Chevaline
Kyrgyzstan									**Kirghizistan**
Cattle and buffaloes	1 122	1 062	920	869	848	885	911	932	Bovine et buffles
Sheep and goats	* 8 742	7 322	5 076	4 275	3 716	* 3 405	* 3 536	* 3 498	Ovine et caprins
Pigs	247	169	118	114	88	93	105	105	Porcine
Horses	313	322	299	308	314	320[1]	325[1]	328[1]	Chevaline
Asses [1]	10	10	10	10	9	8	8	8	Asine [1]
Lao People's Dem. Rep.									**Rép. dém. pop. lao**
Cattle and buffaloes	2 154	2 249	2 337	2 398	2 451	2 219	1 936	* 1 993	Bovine et buffles
Sheep and goats	126	142	153	159	165	122	94	* 100	Ovine et caprins
Pigs	1 625	1 673	1 724	1 772	1 813	1 432	1 036	* 1 101	Porcine
Horses	29[1]	29[1]	29[1]	26[1]	26[1]	27[1]	28[1]	28[1]	Chevaline
Lebanon									**Liban**
Cattle and buffaloes	75[1]	77	* 60	70	69	80	76	77[1]	Bovine et buffles
Sheep and goats	686[1]	662	* 688[1]	795	819	800	814	825[1]	Ovine et caprins
Pigs	48[1]	53	54[1]	58	59[1]	60	62[1]	64[1]	Porcine
Horses	8[1]	* 7	* 5	5	5[1]	6[1]	6[1]	6[1]	Chevaline
Asses	23[1]	23[1]	24[1]	24[1]	25[1]	25[1]	25[1]	25[1]	Asine
Mules	7[1]	7[1]	6[1]	5	6[1]	6[1]	6[1]	6[1]	Mulassière
Malaysia									**Malaisie**
Cattle and buffaloes	901	893	881	850	842	875	879	879[1]	Bovine et buffles
Sheep and goats	581	554	504	442	409	402	406	406[1]	Ovine et caprins
Pigs	2 718	3 203	3 150	3 103	3 171	2 934	1 829	1 829[1]	Porcine
Horses [1]	5	5	4	4	4	5	5	5	Chevaline
Mongolia									**Mongolie**
Cattle and buffaloes	2 819	2 731	3 005	3 317	3 476	3 613	3 726	3 500[1]	Bovine et buffles
Sheep and goats	20 260	19 886	21 028	22 239	22 695	24 431	25 756	24 000[1]	Ovine et caprins
Pigs	49	29	23	24	19	21	21[1]	19[1]	Porcine
Horses	2 200	2 190	2 409	2 648	2 771	2 893	3 059	3 080[1]	Chevaline
Myanmar									**Myanmar**
Cattle and buffaloes	11 722	11 821	12 060	12 386	12 600	12 829	13 131	13 405	Bovine et buffles
Sheep and goats	1 397	1 417	1 492	1 558	1 632	1 688	1 732	1 782	Ovine et caprins
Pigs	2 655	2 728	2 944	3 229	3 358	3 501	3 715	3 914	Porcine
Horses	120	120[1]	120[1]	120[1]	120[1]	120[1]	120[1]	120[1]	Chevaline
Mules [1]	8	8	8	8	8	8	8	8	Mulassière [1]
Nepal									**Népal**
Cattle and buffaloes	9 310	9 722	10 116	10 311	10 387	10 468	10 501	10 531[1]	Bovine et buffles
Sheep and goats	6 363	6 439	6 568	6 642	6 792	6 950	7 060	7 370[1]	Ovine et caprins
Pigs	605	612	636	670	724	766	825	900[1]	Porcine
Occupied Palestinian Terr. [2]									**Terr. palestinien occupé** [2]
Cattle and buffaloes [1]	3	3	3	3	3	3	3	3	Bovine et buffles [1]
Sheep and goats [1]	40	40	40	40	40	40	40	40	Ovine et caprins [1]
Oman									**Oman**
Cattle and buffaloes [1]	142	144	144	145	146	147	148	149	Bovine et buffles [1]
Sheep and goats [1]	883	884	884	870	880	884	888	909	Ovine et caprins [1]
Asses [1]	26	26	26	27	27	28	28	29	Asine [1]

37
Livestock
Thousand head [*cont.*]
Cheptel
Milliers de têtes [*suite*]

Region, country or area	1993	1994	1995	1996	1997	1998	1999	2000	Région, pays ou zone
Pakistan									**Pakistan**
Cattle and buffaloes	36 519	37 033	37 559	40 697	41 640	42 614	43 600	44 700	Bovine et buffles
Sheep and goats	67 893	70 315	72 829	64 713	66 318	67 983	69 700	71 500	Ovine et caprins
Horses	354	350	346	334	331	327	327[1]	327[1]	Chevaline
Asses	3 775	3 901	4 000	4 200	4 300	4 500	4 500[1]	4 500[1]	Asine
Mules	76	77	78	132	142	151	151[1]	151[1]	Mulassière
Philippines									**Philippines**
Cattle and buffaloes	4 490	4 496	4 728	4 970	5 234	5 408	5 443	5 571	Bovine et buffles
Sheep and goats [1]	5 760	6 025	6 213	6 260	6 530	6 810	6 810	6 810	Ovine et caprins [1]
Pigs	7 954	8 227	8 941	9 026	9 752	10 210	10 398	10 398[1]	Porcine
Horses [1]	210	220	220	220	230	230	230	230	Chevaline [1]
Qatar									**Qatar**
Cattle and buffaloes	12	13	14	14	14	14	15	14[1]	Bovine et buffles
Sheep and goats	308	340	360	372	376	381	389	394[1]	Ovine et caprins
Horses	1	1	1	1	4	4[1]	4[1]	4[1]	Chevaline
Saudi Arabia									**Arabie saoudite**
Cattle and buffaloes	229	243	253	259	277	294	297	297[1]	Bovine et buffles
Sheep and goats	11 270	11 840	11 961	12 193	11 886	* 11 771	* 11 881	11 881[1]	Ovine et caprins
Horses	3[1]	3	3	3	3[1]	3[1]	3[1]	3[1]	Chevaline
Asses	100[1]	107	102	101	101[1]	100[1]	100[1]	100[1]	Asine
Singapore									**Singapour**
Sheep and goats [1]	1	1	0	0	0	0	0	0	Ovine et caprins [1]
Pigs [1]	150	180	190	190	190	190	190	190	Porcine [1]
Sri Lanka									**Sri Lanka**
Cattle and buffaloes	2 498	2 494	2 468	2 405	2 305	2 320	2 344	2 344[1]	Bovine et buffles
Sheep and goats	602	608	610	547	531	531	527	527[1]	Ovine et caprins
Pigs	90	94	87	85	80	76	74	74[1]	Porcine
Horses [1]	2	2	2	2	2	2	2	2	Chevaline [1]
Syrian Arab Republic									**Rép. arabe syrienne**
Cattle and buffaloes	708	722	776	812	858	934	980	923[1]	Bovine et buffles
Sheep and goats	11 133	12 292	13 138	14 201	14 930	16 526	15 044	15 600[1]	Ovine et caprins
Pigs	1[1]	1	1[1]	1[1]	1[1]	1[1]	1[1]	1[1]	Porcine
Horses	27	27	27	28	27	28[1]	29[1]	30[1]	Chevaline
Asses	185	201	200	191	190	195[1]	196[1]	198[1]	Asine
Mules	21	18	17	18	18	19[1]	19[1]	20[1]	Mulassière
Tajikistan									**Tadjikistan**
Cattle and buffaloes	1 244	1 250	1 199	1 147	1 082	1 050	1 037	1 042	Bovine et buffles
Sheep and goats	2 997	* 2 906	* 2 700	* 2 494	* 2 293	* 2 222	* 2 195	* 2 183	Ovine et caprins
Pigs	46	46	32	6	2	1	1	1	Porcine
Horses	53[1]	50[1]	48[1]	47[1]	45[1]	45[1]	46[1]	46[1]	Chevaline
Asses [1]	36	35	34	33	32	33	32	32	Asine [1]
Thailand									**Thaïlande**
Cattle and buffaloes	12 277	11 862	11 004	10 611	9 762	* 8 847[1]	* 8 594[1]	8 200[1]	Bovine et buffles
Sheep and goats	262	232	208	140	167	* 171[1]	* 172	172[1]	Ovine et caprins
Pigs	4 985	5 435	5 369	6 129	6 894	* 8 772	* 7 682	7 682[1]	Porcine
Horses	18	14	17	12	15	15[1]	16[1]	16[1]	Chevaline
Turkey									**Turquie**
Cattle and buffaloes	12 303	12 226	12 206	12 044	12 121	11 379	11 207	11 207[1]	Bovine et buffles
Sheep and goats	49 870	47 674	45 210	42 902	42 023	38 614	37 492	37 492[1]	Ovine et caprins
Pigs	12	9	8	5	5	5	5	5[1]	Porcine
Horses	483	450	437	415	391	345	330	330[1]	Chevaline
Asses	895	841	809	731	689	640	603	603[1]	Asine
Mules	181	172	169	169	154	142	133	133[1]	Mulassière
Turkmenistan									**Turkménistan**
Cattle and buffaloes	1 004	1 104	1 181	1 199	* 959	950[1]	880[1]	850[1]	Bovine et buffles
Sheep and goats	* 6 265	* 6 314	* 6 503	* 6 574	* 5 775	5 870[1]	6 025[1]	5 968[1]	Ovine et caprins
Pigs	212	159	128	82	65[1]	55[1]	48[1]	46[1]	Porcine
Horses [1]	22	20	18	17	17	16	16	16	Chevaline [1]
Asses [1]	26	25	25	26	26	25	25	25	Asine [1]
United Arab Emirates									**Emirats arabes unis**
Cattle and buffaloes	60	65	69	74	* 79	98	106	110[1]	Bovine et buffles
Sheep and goats	1 116	1 194	1 277	1 367	* 1 398[1]	1 565	1 674	1 667[1]	Ovine et caprins
Uzbekistan									**Ouzbékistan**
Cattle and buffaloes	5 275	5 431	5 484	5 204	5 100	5 200	5 225	5 268	Bovine et buffles
Sheep and goats	9 368	* 10 400	10 049	* 9 322	* 8 200	* 8 600	* 9 422	* 9 556	Ovine et caprins

37
Livestock
Thousand head [*cont.*]
Cheptel
Milliers de têtes [*suite*]

Region, country or area	1993	1994	1995	1996	1997	1998	1999	2000	Région, pays ou zone
Pigs	529	391	350	208	100	70	80	80	Porcine
Horses	123	120[1]	145	146	* 146	150[1]	155[1]	155[1]	Chevaline
Asses	158	162[1]	165[1]	168[1]	169[1]	165[1]	165[1]	165[1]	Asine
Viet Nam									**Viet Nam**
Cattle and buffaloes	6 294	6 444	6 602	6 754	6 848	6 939	7 019	* 7 034	Bovine et buffles
Sheep and goats	353	428	551	513	515	514	471	544	Ovine et caprins
Pigs	14 874	15 588	16 306	16 922	17 636	18 132	18 886	20 194	Porcine
Horses	133	131	127	126	120	123	150	180[1]	Chevaline
Yemen									**Yémen**
Cattle and buffaloes	1 163	1 151	1 174	1 181	1 201	1 263	1 282	1 283	Bovine et buffles
Sheep and goats	7 012	6 941	7 080	7 480	8 148	8 616	8 871	8 975	Ovine et caprins
Horses [1]	3	3	3	3	3	3	3	3	Chevaline [1]
Asses	500	* 500	500[1]	500[1]	500[1]	500[1]	500[1]	500[1]	Asine
Europe									**Europe**
Cattle and buffaloes	**195 097**	**187 860**	**178 493**	**172 777**	**164 841**	**155 998**	**150 688**	**146 570**	**Bovine et buffles**
Sheep and goats	**223 614**	**213 461**	**199 271**	**186 180**	**182 185**	**178 106**	**172 036**	**168 548**	**Ovine et caprins**
Pigs	**227 765**	**222 023**	**213 619**	**207 788**	**205 089**	**200 903**	**205 394**	**202 330**	**Porcine**
Horses	**7 900**	**7 757**	**7 857**	**7 803**	**7 708**	**7 374**	**7 102**	**6 968**	**Chevaline**
Asses	**1 001**	**970**	**935**	**919**	**914**	**835**	**819**	**806**	**Asine**
Mules	**316**	**314**	**303**	**288**	**286**	**272**	**271**	**272**	**Mulassière**
Albania									**Albanie**
Cattle and buffaloes	656	820	840	806	771	705	720	720[1]	Bovine et buffles
Sheep and goats	3 205	4 177	4 130	3 232	3 006	2 923	3 061[1]	3 061[1]	Ovine et caprins
Pigs	93	98	100	98	97	83	81	81[1]	Porcine
Horses	58	62	71	74	70	65	65[1]	65[1]	Chevaline
Asses	114	113[1]	113[1]	113[1]	113[1]	113[1]	113[1]	113[1]	Asine
Mules	26	25[1]	25[1]	25[1]	25[1]	25[1]	25[1]	25[1]	Mulassière
Austria									**Autriche**
Cattle and buffaloes	2 532	2 334	2 329	2 326	2 272	2 198	* 2 172	* 2 150	Bovine et buffles
Sheep and goats	364	381	392	419	435	442	415	415[1]	Ovine et caprins
Pigs	3 629	3 820	3 729	3 706	3 664	3 680	* 3 810	* 3 790	Porcine
Horses	57	65	67	72	73	74	75	75[1]	Chevaline
Belarus									**Bélarus**
Cattle and buffaloes	6 221	5 851	5 403	5 054	4 855	4 801	4 686	4 326	Bovine et buffles
Sheep and goats	381	301	284	262	213	186	162	150	Ovine et caprins
Pigs	4 308	4 181	4 005	3 895	3 715	3 686	3 698	3 566	Porcine
Horses	215	215	220	229	232	233	229	221	Chevaline
Asses [1]	8	8	8	8	8	9	9	9	Asine [1]
Belgium−Luxembourg									**Belgique−Luxembourg**
Cattle and buffaloes	3 303	3 289	3 369	3 363	3 280	3 184	3 186	3 085	Bovine et buffles
Sheep and goats	180	176	170	173	174	* 167	* 170[1]	* 164[1]	Ovine et caprins
Pigs	6 963	6 948	7 053	7 225	7 194	7 436	7 632	7 322	Porcine
Horses	65	66	66	66	67	67[1]	67[1]	67[1]	Chevaline
Bosnia & Herzegovina									**Bosnie−Herzégovine**
Cattle and buffaloes [1]	666	571	520	391	413	* 427	* 443	* 463	Bovine et buffles
Sheep and goats	700[1]	600[1]	520[1]	473[1]	378[1]	* 581	* 633	* 662	Ovine et caprins
Pigs [1]	300	300	290	180	162	154	155	150	Porcine [1]
Horses	16[1]	17[1]	18[1]	18	19	19	20[1]	20[1]	Chevaline
Bulgaria									**Bulgarie**
Cattle and buffaloes	996	768	652	645	593	622	681	691	Bovine et buffles
Sheep and goats	5 426	4 440	4 193	4 216	3 868	3 814	3 822	3 595	Ovine et caprins
Pigs	2 680	2 071	1 986	2 140	1 500	1 480	1 721	1 512	Porcine
Horses	114	113	133	151	170	126	133	141	Chevaline
Asses	303	297	276	281	287	225	221	208	Asine
Mules	21	23	16	17	17	17	16[1]	16[1]	Mulassière
Croatia									**Croatie**
Cattle and buffaloes	590	519	493	462	451	443	439	427	Bovine et buffles
Sheep and goats	629	552	560	532	552	511	566	608[1]	Ovine et caprins
Pigs	1 262	1 347	1 175	1 196	1 175	1 166	1 362	1 233	Porcine
Horses	22	22	21	21	19	16	13	11	Chevaline
Asses	12	7	4[1]	4[1]	4[1]	4[1]	4[1]	4[1]	Mulassière
Czech Republic									**République tchèque**
Cattle and buffaloes	2 512	2 161	2 030	1 989	1 866	1 701	1 657	1 574	Bovine et buffles
Sheep and goats	299	241	210	176	159	128	120	116	Ovine et caprins

37
Livestock
Thousand head [*cont.*]
Cheptel
Milliers de têtes [*suite*]

Region, country or area	1993	1994	1995	1996	1997	1998	1999	2000	Région, pays ou zone
Pigs	4 599	4 071	3 867	4 016	4 080	4 013	4 001	3 688	Porcine
Horses	19	18	19	19	19	20	23	24	Chevaline
Denmark									**Danemark**
Cattle and buffaloes	2 195	2 105	2 091	2 093	2 030	1 977	1 887	1 850	Bovine et buffles
Sheep and goats	157	145	145	170	142	156	143	143[1]	Ovine et caprins
Pigs	10 870	10 923	11 084	10 842	11 383	12 004	11 626	11 551	Porcine
Horses	20	18	18	20	39	38	40	40[1]	Chevaline
Estonia									**Estonie**
Cattle and buffaloes	615	463	420	370	343	326	308	286	Bovine et buffles
Sheep and goats	124	83	62	50	39	36	31	29	Ovine et caprins
Pigs	541	424	460	449	298	306	326	281	Porcine
Horses	7	5	5	5	4	4	4	4	Chevaline
Faeroe Islands									**Iles Féroé**
Cattle and buffaloes [1]	2	2	2	2	2	2	2	2	Bovine et buffles [1]
Sheep and goats [1]	68	68	68	68	68	68	68	68	Ovine et caprins [1]
Finland									**Finlande**
Cattle and buffaloes	1 232	1 230	1 185	1 179	1 150	1 101	1 087	1 087[1]	Bovine et buffles
Sheep and goats	67	84	85	120	157	135	115	115[1]	Ovine et caprins
Pigs	1 309	1 300	1 295	1 395	1 467	1 401	1 351	1 351[1]	Porcine
Horses	49	49	50	52	55	56	56	56[1]	Chevaline
France									**France**
Cattle and buffaloes	20 328	20 099	20 524	20 661	20 664	20 023	20 265	20 527	Bovine et buffles
Sheep and goats	11 451	12 560	11 389	11 744	11 665	11 516	11 439	11 195	Ovine et caprins
Pigs	13 015	14 291	14 593	14 530	14 976	14 501	14 682	14 635	Porcine
Horses	329	332	338	338	340	347	348	349	Chevaline
Asses [1]	20	18	18	18	17	17	16	16	Asine [1]
Mules	12	13	13	14	14	14	14	15	Mulassière
Germany									**Allemagne**
Cattle and buffaloes	16 207	15 897	15 962	15 890	15 760	15 227	14 942	14 658	Bovine et buffles
Sheep and goats	2 476	2 461	2 435	2 495	2 429	2 417	2 385	2 235	Ovine et caprins
Pigs	26 514	26 075	24 698	23 737	24 283	24 795	26 294	* 27 049	Porcine
Horses	531	599	652	652	670	600	524	476	Chevaline
Greece									**Grèce**
Cattle and buffaloes	588	580	579	582	581	597[1]	578[1]	591[1]	Bovine et buffles
Sheep and goats	14 031	14 084	14 181	14 394	14 466	14 830	* 14 276	* 14 334	Ovine et caprins
Pigs	1 001	1 014	1 009	994	987	938	933	906	Porcine
Horses	40	38	36	35	33	32	33[1]	33[1]	Chevaline
Asses	111	103	95	89	83	78	78[1]	78[1]	Asine
Mules	50	47	44	41	39	37	37[1]	37[1]	Mulassière
Hungary									**Hongrie**
Cattle and buffaloes	1 159	999	910	928	909	871	873	857	Bovine et buffles
Sheep and goats	* 1 781	1 288	999	1 065	980	987	1 058	1 094[1]	Ovine et caprins
Pigs	5 364	5 002	4 356	5 032	5 289	4 931	5 479	5 335	Porcine
Horses	73	72	78	71	79	72	70	65[1]	Chevaline
Asses	4[1]	4[1]	4[1]	4[1]	4[1]	4[1]	4[1]	4[1]	Asine
Iceland									**Islande**
Cattle and buffaloes	74	72	73	75	75	76	75	72	Bovine et buffles
Sheep and goats	489	499	459	464	478	490	491	465	Ovine et caprins
Pigs [1]	40	41	42	43	43	43	43	43	Porcine [1]
Horses	77	79	78	81	80	78	77	771	Chevaline
Ireland									**Irlande**
Cattle and buffaloes	6 265	6 308	6 410	6 757	6 757	6 992	7 093	6 708	Bovine et buffles
Sheep and goats	6 125	5 991	5 775	5 583	5 391	5 634	5 624	5 393	Ovine et caprins
Pigs	1 423	1 487	1 498	1 542	1 665	1 717	1 801	1 763	Porcine
Horses	52[1]	48[1]	40[1]	45[1]	52[1]	50[1]	76	70	Chevaline
Asses [1]	11	10	10	10	10	10	10	10	Asine [1]
Mules [1]	1	1	1	1	1	1	1	1	Mulassière [1]
Italy									**Italie**
Cattle and buffaloes	7 704	7 560	7 272	7 414	7 313	7 328	7 320	* 7 357	Bovine et buffles
Sheep and goats	11 667	11 839	12 129	12 041	12 363	12 241	12 135	* 12 334	Ovine et caprins
Pigs	8 244	8 348	8 023	8 061	8 171	8 281	8 225	* 8 403	Porcine
Horses	316	323	324	315	305[1]	290[1]	288[1]	280[1]	Chevaline
Asses	39	33	* 30	26	25[1]	23[1]	23[1]	23[1]	Asine
Mules	18	17	16	12	12[1]	11[1]	10[1]	10[1]	Mulassière

37
Livestock
Thousand head [*cont.*]
Cheptel
Milliers de têtes [*suite*]

Region, country or area	1993	1994	1995	1996	1997	1998	1999	2000	Région, pays ou zone
Latvia									**Lettonie**
Cattle and buffaloes	1 144	678	551	537	509	477	434	378	Bovine et buffles
Sheep and goats	171	120	94	81	49	38	37	35	Ovine et caprins
Pigs	867	482	501	553	460	430	421	405	Porcine
Horses	28	26	27	27	26	23	19	19	Chevaline
Liechtenstein									**Liechtenstein**
Cattle and buffaloes	6[1]	6[1]	6[1]	6[1]	6[1]	6[1]	6[1]	6[1]	Bovine et buffles
Sheep and goats	3[1]	3	3[1]	3[1]	3[1]	3[1]	3[1]	3[1]	Ovine et caprins
Pigs	3[1]	3[1]	3[1]	3[1]	3[1]	3[1]	3[1]	3[1]	Porcine
Lithuania									**Lituanie**
Cattle and buffaloes	1 701	1 384	1 152	1 065	1 054	1 016	923	898	Bovine et buffles
Sheep and goats	61	55	52	47	45	43	40	39	Ovine et caprins
Pigs	1 360	1 196	1 260	1 270	1 128	1 200	1 159	936	Porcine
Horses	80	81	78	78	81	78	75	75[1]	Chevaline
Malta									**Malte**
Cattle and buffaloes	22	20	19	21	21[1]	19[1]	20[1]	19	Bovine et buffles
Sheep and goats	24[1]	25[1]	25	25	25[1]	25[1]	25[1]	25[1]	Ovine et caprins
Pigs	109[1]	111[1]	103	69	70[1]	70[1]	70[1]	80	Porcine
Horses [1]	1	1	1	1	1	1	1	1	Chevaline [1]
Asses [1]	1	1	1	1	1	1	1	1	Asine [1]
Netherlands									**Pays—Bas**
Cattle and buffaloes	4 797	4 716	4 654	4 557	4 411	4 283	4 206	* 4 200	Bovine et buffles
Sheep and goats	1 973	1 830	1 750	1 729	1 584	1 526	1 554	1 554[1]	Ovine et caprins
Pigs	14 964	14 565	14 397	* 13 958	* 14 253	* 11 438	* 13 418	* 13 140	Porcine
Horses	92	97	100	107	112	114	116	116[1]	Chevaline
Norway									**Norvège**
Cattle and buffaloes	975	980	998	1 006	1 018	1 036	1 042	1 042[1]	Bovine et buffles
Sheep and goats	2 375	2 524	2 586	2 620	2 511	2 481	2 483[1]	2 483[1]	Ovine et caprins
Pigs	748	748	768	7681	692	689	690	690[1]	Porcine
Horses	21	22	22	23	24	26	26[1]	26[1]	Chevaline
Poland									**Pologne**
Cattle and buffaloes	7 643	7 696	7 306	7 136	7 307	6 955	6 555	6 083	Bovine et buffles
Sheep and goats	1 268	870	713	552	491	453	392	362	Ovine et caprins
Pigs	18 860	19 467	20 418	17 964	18 135	19 168	18 538	17 122	Porcine
Horses	841	622	636	569	558	561	567[1]	570[1]	Chevaline
Portugal									**Portugal**
Cattle and buffaloes *	1 345	1 323	1 329	1 324	1 311	1 285	1 267	1 245	Bovine et buffles *
Sheep and goats	6 983	6 827	6 719[1]	6 599[1]	7 081[1]	6 585[1]	* 6 643[1]	6 650[1]	Ovine et caprins
Pigs	2 547	2 666	2 416	2 402	2 344	2 365	2 341	* 2 330	Porcine
Horses [1]	25	25	23	25	22	24	20	20	Chevaline [1]
Asses [1]	160	160	160	150	150	140	130	130	Asine [1]
Mules [1]	70	70	70	60	60	50	50	50	Mulassière [1]
Republic of Moldova									**République de Moldova**
Cattle and buffaloes	971	916	832	726	646	551	452	416	Bovine et buffles
Sheep and goats	1 357	1 445	1 507	1 423	1 372	1 128	* 1 105	* 1 069	Ovine et caprins
Pigs	1 487	1 165	1 061	1 015	950	798	807	705	Porcine
Horses	51	55	59	61	63	66	68[1]	68[1]	Chevaline
Asses	2	2	2[1]	2[1]	2[1]	2[1]	2[1]	2[1]	Asine
Romania									**Roumanie**
Cattle and buffaloes	3 683	3 957	3 481	3 496	3 435	3 235	3 143	3 155	Bovine et buffles
Sheep and goats	12 884	12 275	11 642	11 086	10 317	9 547	8 994	8 526	Ovine et caprins
Pigs	9 852	9 262	7 758	7 960	8 235	7 097	7 194	5 951	Porcine
Horses	721	751	784	806	816	822	839	842[1]	Chevaline
Asses [1]	34	33	32	31	30	31	31	31	Asine [1]
Russian Federation									**Fédération de Russie**
Cattle and buffaloes	52 248	48 932	43 320	39 720	35 124	31 536	28 496	27 516[1]	Bovine et buffles
Sheep and goats	51 369	43 713	34 540	28 027	22 772	18 774	15 556	* 15 720	Ovine et caprins
Pigs	31 520	28 557	24 859	22 631	19 115	17 348	17 248	18 300	Porcine
Horses	2 556	2 500	2 431	2 363	2 197	2 013	1 800	1 750[1]	Chevaline
Asses	22	26	26[1]	27[1]	26[1]	25[1]	25[1]	25[1]	Asine
Slovakia									**Slovaquie**
Cattle and buffaloes	1 203	993	916	929	892	803	705	665	Bovine et buffles
Sheep and goats	592	436	422	453	445	444	377	391	Ovine et caprins
Pigs	2 269	2 179	2 037	2 076	1 985	1 810	1 593	1 562	Porcine
Horses	11	11	10	10	10	10	10[1]	10[1]	Chevaline

37
Livestock
Thousand head [*cont.*]
Cheptel
Milliers de têtes [*suite*]

Region, country or area	1993	1994	1995	1996	1997	1998	1999	2000	Région, pays ou zone
Slovenia									**Slovénie**
Cattle and buffaloes	504	478	477	496	486	446	453	471	Bovine et buffles
Sheep and goats	30	39	50	52	74	88	87	87[1]	Ovine et caprins
Pigs	602	592	571	592	552	578	592	558	Porcine
Horses	9	9	8	8	8	10	10[1]	10[1]	Chevaline
Spain									**Espagne**
Cattle and buffaloes	4 976	5 018	5 248	5 512	5 925	5 884	5 965	6 203	Bovine et buffles
Sheep and goats	27 452	26 819	26 215	23 928	26 989	27 454	26 351	* 26 573	Ovine et caprins
Pigs	18 260	18 234	18 345	18 163	19 557	21 562	22 597	23 682	Porcine
Horses	248	248	248	248	248	248	248	248[1]	Chevaline
Asses	140	140	140	140	140	140	140	140[1]	Asine
Mules	117	117	117	117	117	117	117	117	Mulassière
Sweden									**Suède**
Cattle and buffaloes	1 809	1 827	1 777	1 790	1 781	1 739	1 713	1 713[1]	Bovine et buffles
Sheep and goats	471	484	462	469	442	421	437	437[1]	Ovine et caprins
Pigs	2 277	2 328	2 313	2 349	2 351	2 286	2 115	1 918	Porcine
Horses	79[1]	86	83	85[1]	87	87[1]	87[1]	87[1]	Chevaline
Switzerland									**Suisse**
Cattle and buffaloes	1 745	1 755	1 756	1 772	1 673	1 641	1 609	1 600	Bovine et buffles
Sheep and goats	481	496	489	495	478	482	485	515	Ovine et caprins
Pigs	1 692	1 660	1 611	1 580	1 395	1 487	1 452	1 450	Porcine
Horses	54	51[1]	46[1]	43	46	46[1]	46[1]	45[1]	Chevaline
Asses [1]	2	2	2	2	2	2	2	2	Asine [1]
TFYR of Macedonia									**L'ex−R.y. Macédoine**
Cattle and buffaloes	286	281	282	284	296	298	291	291[1]	Bovine et buffles
Sheep and goats	2 351	2 459	2 466	2 320	1 814	1 805	1 550	1 600[1]	Ovine et caprins
Pigs	173	185	172	175	192	184	197	197[1]	Porcine
Horses	62	62	62	66	66	60	60	60[1]	Chevaline
Ukraine									**Ukraine**
Cattle and buffaloes	22 457	21 607	19 624	17 557	15 313	12 759	11 722	10 627	Bovine et buffles
Sheep and goats	7 237	6 863	5 575	4 099	3 047	2 362	2 026	1 885	Ovine et caprins
Pigs	16 175	15 298	13 946	13 144	11 236	9 479	10 083	10 073	Porcine
Horses	707	716	737	756	754	737	721	698	Chevaline
Asses [1]	19	15	15	14	13	13	12	12	Asine [1]
United Kingdom									**Royaume−Uni**
Cattle and buffaloes	11 729	11 834	11 733	11 913	11 633	11 519	11 423	11 133	Bovine et buffles
Sheep and goats	43 901	43 295	42 771	41 530	42 823	44 471	44 656	42 261	Ovine et caprins
Pigs	7 754	7 892	7 627	7 590	8 072	8 146	7 284	6 482	Porcine
Horses [1]	173	173	173	173	173	173	173	173	Chevaline [1]
Yugoslavia									**Yougoslavie**
Cattle and buffaloes	2 010	1 832	1 968	1 944	1 915	1 910	1 852	1 481	Bovine et buffles
Sheep and goats	3 014	2 914	3 004	2 966	2 859	2 714	2 521	2 158	Ovine et caprins
Pigs	4 092	3 693	4 192	4 446	4 216	4 150	4 372	4 087	Porcine
Horses	82	82	96	93	90	86	76	76[1]	Chevaline
Oceania									**Océanie**
Cattle and buffaloes	**33 115**	**35 403**	**35 762**	**36 155**	**36 686**	**36 484**	**36 304**	**36 943**	**Bovine et buffles**
Sheep and goats	**189 286**	**182 847**	**170 461**	**169 244**	**167 807**	**164 182**	**161 827**	**162 184**	**Ovine et caprins**
Pigs	**4 938**	**5 205**	**5 154**	**5 079**	**5 135**	**5 341**	**5 223**	**5 009**	**Porcine**
Horses	**429**	**412**	**402**	**392**	**392**	**382**	**377**	**377**	**Chevaline**
Asses	**9**	**9**	**9**	**9**	**9**	**9**	**9**	**9**	**Asine**
American Samoa									**Samoa américaines**
Pigs [1]	11	11	11	11	11	11	11	11	Porcine [1]
Australia									**Australie**
Cattle and buffaloes	24 062	25 758	25 731	26 377	26 780	26 852	26 578	26 716	Bovine et buffles
Sheep and goats	138 343	132 801	121 092[1]	121 346[1]	120 458[1]	117 711	115 656[1]	115 893[1]	Ovine et caprins
Pigs	2 646	2 775	2 653	2 526	2 555	2 768	2 626	2 433	Porcine
Horses	272	250[1]	240[1]	230[1]	230[1]	220[1]	220[1]	220[1]	Chevaline
Asses	2	2[1]	2[1]	2[1]	2[1]	2[1]	2[1]	2[1]	Asine
Cook Islands									**Iles Cook**
Sheep and goats	7	8	7	3	3[1]	3[1]	3[1]	3[1]	Ovine et caprins
Pigs	25	28	32	40	40[1]	40[1]	40[1]	40[1]	Porcine
Fiji									**Fidji**
Cattle and buffaloes	315	334	354	350[1]	350[1]	345	350[1]	350[1]	Bovine et buffles
Sheep and goats	204	211	218	214	237	242[1]	242[1]	242[1]	Ovine et caprins

37
Livestock
Thousand head [*cont.*]
Cheptel
Milliers de têtes [*suite*]

Region, country or area	1993	1994	1995	1996	1997	1998	1999	2000	Région, pays ou zone
Pigs	110	115	121	120[1]	115[1]	112	115[1]	115[1]	Porcine
Horses [1]	43	44	44	44	44	44	44	44	Chevaline [1]
French Polynesia									**Polynésie française**
Cattle and buffaloes	8[1]	7	8[1]	6[1]	8[1]	9[1]	10[1]	10[1]	Bovine et buffles
Sheep and goats	15[1]	16	16[1]	16[1]	16[1]	16[1]	17[1]	17[1]	Ovine et caprins
Pigs	38	40	39[1]	37[1]	35[1]	35[1]	37[1]	37[1]	Porcine
Horses [1]	2	2	2	2	2	2	2	2	Chevaline [1]
Guam									**Guam**
Sheep and goats [1]	1	1	1	1	1	1	1	1	Ovine et caprins [1]
Pigs [1]	4	4	4	4	4	4	4	4	Porcine [1]
Kiribati									**Kiribati**
Pigs	9[1]	9[1]	9[1]	10[1]	10[1]	10[1]	10	12[1]	Porcine
Micronesia (Federated States of)									**Micron (Etats fédérés de)**
Cattle and buffaloes [1]	...	...	14	14	14	14	14	14	Bovine et buffles [1]
Sheep and goats [1]	...	...	4	4	4	4	4	4	Ovine et caprins [1]
Pigs [1]	...	...	32	32	32	32	32	32	Porcine [1]
Nauru									**Nauru**
Pigs [1]	3	3	3	3	3	3	3	3	Porcine [1]
New Caledonia									**Nouvelle−Calédonie**
Cattle and buffaloes	120[1]	113	110[1]	120[1]	120[1]	122[1]	123[1]	123[1]	Bovine et buffles
Sheep and goats	19[1]	16[1]	16[1]	3[1]	3[1]	2[1]	2[1]	2[1]	Ovine et caprins
Pigs	39[1]	38[1]	37[1]	38[1]	38[1]	40[1]	40[1]	40[1]	Porcine
Horses	12[1]	12[1]	12[1]	12[1]	12[1]	12[1]	12[1]	12[1]	Chevaline
New Zealand									**Nouvelle−Zélande**
Cattle and buffaloes	8 308	8 887	9 272	9 017	9 145	8 873	8 960	* 9 457	Bovine et buffles
Sheep and goats	50 651	49 750	49 072	47 622	47 049	46 166	45 866	* 45 986[1]	Ovine et caprins
Pigs	395	423	431	424	407	351	369	* 344	Porcine
Horses	80	85[1]	85[1]	85[1]	85[1]	85[1]	80[1]	80[1]	Chevaline
Niue									**Nioué**
Pigs [1]	2	2	2	2	2	2	2	2	Porcine [1]
Papua New Guinea									**Papouasie−Nvl−Guinée**
Cattle and buffaloes	94[1]	93[1]	90[1]	88[1]	87	86[1]	87[1]	87[1]	Bovine et buffles
Sheep and goats	6[1]	7[1]	7[1]	6[1]	* 8	8[1]	8[1]	8[1]	Ovine et caprins
Pigs	1 200[1]	1 300[1]	1 400[1]	1 450[1]	1 500	1 550[1]	1 550[1]	1 550[1]	Porcine
Horses [1]	2	2	2	2	2	2	2	2	Chevaline [1]
Samoa									**Samoa**
Cattle and buffaloes [1]	25	26	26	26	26	26	26	26	Bovine et buffles [1]
Pigs [1]	178	179	179	179	179	179	179	179	Porcine [1]
Horses [1]	3	3	3	3	3	3	3	3	Chevaline [1]
Asses [1]	7	7	7	7	7	7	7	7	Asine [1]
Solomon Islands									**Iles Salomon**
Cattle and buffaloes [1]	10	10	10	10	10	10	10	12	Bovine et buffles [1]
Pigs	55[1]	55[1]	55[1]	56[1]	57[1]	57[1]	58[1]	59[1]	Porcine
Tokelau									**Tokélaou**
Pigs [1]	1	1	1	1	1	1	1	1	Porcine [1]
Tonga									**Tonga**
Cattle and buffaloes	10[1]	10[1]	9	9[1]	9[1]	9[1]	9[1]	9[1]	Bovine et buffles
Sheep and goats	16[1]	16[1]	14	14[1]	14[1]	14[1]	14[1]	14[1]	Ovine et caprins
Pigs	94[1]	94[1]	81	81[1]	81[1]	81[1]	81[1]	81[1]	Porcine
Horses	11[1]	11[1]	11[1]	11[1]	11[1]	11[1]	11[1]	11[1]	Chevaline
Tuvalu									**Tuvalu**
Pigs	13[1]	13[1]	13[1]	13[1]	13[1]	13[1]	131	13[1]	Porcine
Vanuatu									**Vanuatu**
Cattle and buffaloes	150	* 151	* 151	151[1]	151[1]	151[1]	151[1]	152[1]	Bovine et buffles
Sheep and goats	12	12	12	12[1]	12[1]	12[1]	12[1]	12[1]	Ovine et caprins
Pigs	60	60	60	61[1]	61[1]	62[1]	62[1]	62[1]	Porcine
Horses [1]	3	3	3	3	3	3	3	3	Chevaline [1]
Wallis and Futuna Islands									**Iles Wallis et Futuna**
Sheep and goats [1]	7	7	7	7	7	7	7	7	Ovine et caprins [1]
Pigs [1]	25	25	25	25	25	25	25	25	Porcine [1]

37
Livestock
Thousand head [*cont.*]
Cheptel
Milliers de têtes [*suite*]

Source:
Food and Agriculture Organization of the United Nations (FAO),
Rome, FAOSTAT Database.

† For information on recent changes in country or area
nomenclature pertaining to former Czechoslovakia, Germany,
Hong Kong Special Administrative Region (SAR) of China,
Macao Special Administrative Region (SAR) of China,
SFR Yugoslavia and former USSR, see Annex I − Country or
area nomenclature, regional and other groupings.

1   FAO estimate.
2   Data refer to the Gaza Strip.

Source:
Organisation des Nations Unies pour l'alimentation et
l'agriculture (FAO), Rome, la base de données FAOSTAT.

† Pour les modifications récentes de nomenclature de pays
ou de zone concernant l'Allemagne, Hong−Kong (Région
administrative spéciale de Chine), l'ex−Tchécoslovaquie, Macao
(Région administrative spéciale de chine), l'ex−URSS,
Rfs de Yougoslavie, voir annexe I − Nomenclature des pays ou des
zones, groupements régionaux et autres groupments.

1   Estimation de la FAO.
2   Les données se rapportent à la Zone de Gaza.

38
Roundwood
Bois rond

Production (solid volume of roundwood without bark): million cubic metres

Production (volume solide de bois rond sans écorce) : millions de mètres cubes

Region, country or area Région, pays ou zone	1991	1992	1993	1994	1995	1996	1997	1998	1999	2000
World *Monde*	**3 272.9**	**3 199.1**	**3 186.6**	**3 193.3**	**3 242.7**	**3 230.6**	**3 286.1**	**3 181.9**	**3 291.2**	**3 352.5**
Africa Afrique	**504.4**	**522.4**	**538.1**	**551.1**	**568.3**	**576.2**	**582.5**	**584.9**	**588.9**	**596.4**
Algeria Algérie	6.1	6.3	6.6	6.7	6.8	7.0	7.2	7.3	7.4	7.5
Angola Angola	3.3	3.4	3.7	3.7	3.8	3.9	4.0	4.1	4.2	4.3
Benin Bénin	5.9[1]	6.0[1]	6.0[1]	6.1[1]	6.1	6.2	6.2	6.2	6.2	6.2[1]
Botswana[1] Botswana[1]	0.7	0.7	0.7	0.7	0.7	0.7	0.7	0.7	0.7	0.7
Burkina Faso Burkina Faso	9.8[1]	10.0[1]	10.3[1]	10.6	10.8	11.0	11.1	11.3	7.8	8.0
Burundi Burundi	6.0	6.1	6.3	6.6	6.8	7.1	7.4[1]	7.7	5.6	5.8
Cameroon Cameroun	11.0	11.0	11.3	11.9	12.3	12.6	12.2	11.9	11.9	12.1
Central African Rep. Rép. centrafricaine	3.4	3.7	3.7	3.6	3.6	3.2	3.4	3.5	2.9	3.0
Chad Tchad	5.3	5.4	5.6	5.8[1]	5.9[1]	6.0[1]	6.2[1]	6.3[1]	6.5[1]	6.6[1]
Congo Congo	2.2	2.3	2.3	2.4	2.5	2.2	2.7	1.8	1.8	1.8
Côte d'Ivoire Côte d'Ivoire	10.8	10.9	11.2	11.9	11.9	11.7	11.6	11.8	11.7	11.9
Dem. Rep. of the Congo Rép. dém. du Congo	49.8	52.9	57.0	60.1	62.1	63.7	64.9	66.0	67.4[1]	68.6[1]
Egypt Egypte	14.4[1]	14.7[1]	15.1[1]	15.4[1]	15.5[1]	15.8	16.0[1]	16.1	16.3	16.4
Equatorial Guinea Guinée équatoriale	0.6	0.6	0.6	0.7	0.8	0.8[1]	0.8[1]	0.8[1]	0.8[1]	0.8[1]
Eritrea Erythrée	...	...	1.7	1.8	1.9	1.9	2.0	2.1	2.2	2.2[1]
Ethiopia incl. Eritrea Ethiopie comp. Erythrée	76.1	79.1	...	...	...	...	...	...	...	...
Ethiopia Ethiopie	...	...	78.5	80.8	82.5	83.7	85.5	86.5	88.2	89.9
Gabon Gabon	1.8	2.0	2.3	2.6	2.8	2.9	3.3	3.3[1]	2.8	3.1
Gambia Gambie	0.5[1]	0.6[1]	0.6	0.6	0.6	0.6	0.6	0.6	0.6	0.7[1]
Ghana Ghana	12.4	16.3	19.9	22.5	22.0	21.9	22.0	21.9	21.9	21.8
Guinea Guinée	10.9	8.2	8.3	8.6	12.6[1]	12.7[1]	8.7	8.7	12.2[1]	12.1[1]
Guinea-Bissau[1] Guinée-Bissau[1]	0.6	0.6	0.6	0.6	0.6	0.6	0.6	0.6	0.6	0.6
Kenya Kenya	19.0	19.6	20.1	20.4	20.8	21.0	21.3	21.3	21.5	21.6

38
Roundwood
Production (solid volume of roundwood without bark): million cubic metres [*cont.*]
Bois rond
Production (volume solide de bois rond sans écorce) : millions de mètres cubes [*suite*]

Region, country or area Région, pays ou zone	1991	1992	1993	1994	1995	1996	1997	1998	1999	2000
Lesotho Lesotho	1.3	1.4	1.4	1.4	1.5	1.5	1.6	1.6	2.0[1]	2.0[1]
Liberia Libéria	4.1	4.2	3.8	3.4[1]	3.0[1]	3.1	3.5	4.1	4.5[1]	5.1[1]
Libyan Arab Jamah.[1] Jamah. arabe libyenne[1]	0.6	0.6	0.6	0.6	0.6	0.6	0.7	0.7	0.7	0.7
Madagascar Madagascar	8.5	8.9	9.1	9.4	9.8	10.1	9.2	9.2	9.5	9.7
Malawi Malawi	5.6	5.7	5.5	5.6[1]	5.4[1]	5.3[1]	5.3[1]	5.4[1]	5.4[1]	5.5[1]
Mali Mali	4.4[1]	4.5[1]	4.6[1]	4.8[1]	4.8	4.9	5.0[1]	5.0[1]	5.1[1]	5.1[1]
Mauritania[1] Mauritanie[1]	1.2	1.2	1.2	1.3	1.3	1.3	1.3	1.4	1.4	1.4
Morocco Maroc	7.7	7.6	7.3	1.6	1.5	1.5	0.8	1.7	1.1	1.1
Mozambique Mozambique	16.0	16.4	16.8[1]	17.3	17.9	17.9[1]	18.0[1]	18.0[1]	18.0[1]	18.0
Niger[1] Niger[1]	6.2	6.5	6.8	7.0	7.2	7.4	7.6	7.8	8.0	8.2
Nigeria Nigéria	60.0	61.1	62.3	63.8	65.0	66.2	67.7	67.8	68.3[1]	68.8
Rwanda Rwanda	3.0	3.1	3.1	2.6	5.4	5.8	7.4	7.5	7.8	7.8
Senegal Sénégal	5.4	5.5	5.6[1]	5.6[1]	5.6[1]	5.7[1]	5.8[1]	5.8[1]	5.9[1]	5.9[1]
Sierra Leone Sierra Leone	4.7	4.7	4.6	4.5[1]	4.7[1]	4.7[1]	5.1[1]	5.2[1]	5.3[1]	5.5[1]
Somalia[1] Somalie[1]	6.6	7.1	7.2	7.4	7.6	8.0	8.3	8.6	9.0	9.3
South Africa Afrique du Sud	24.8	27.9	28.2	30.5	32.0	32.4	33.2	30.6	30.6	30.6
Sudan Soudan	18.3	18.0	18.0	18.1	18.3[1]	18.4[1]	18.4[1]	18.6[1]	18.7[1]	18.9[1]
Swaziland Swaziland	1.5	1.5	1.5	1.5	1.5	1.5	1.5	0.9	0.9	0.9
Togo Togo	4.9	5.1	5.3	5.4	5.5	5.5	5.6	5.7	5.7	5.8
Tunisia Tunisie	2.1	2.1	2.2	2.2	2.2	2.2	2.3	2.3	2.3	2.3
Uganda Ouganda	31.7	32.7	33.4	34.4[1]	34.9	35.4	36.0	36.4	36.9	37.3[1]
United Rep. of Tanzania Rép.-Unie de Tanzanie	20.9	21.7	22.0	22.3	22.6	22.8	22.9	23.0	23.1	23.1
Zambia Zambie	7.3	7.6	7.9	8.3	8.2[1]	8.1[1]	8.0[1]	8.0[1]	8.1[1]	8.1[1]
Zimbabwe Zimbabwe	7.0	7.0	7.0	8.1	8.4	8.6	8.9	9.0	9.3	9.3
America, North **Amérique du Nord**	**725.3**	**749.2**	**751.4**	**769.6**	**777.4**	**770.8**	**769.6**	**764.1**	**776.9**	**782.6**

38
Roundwood
Production (solid volume of roundwood without bark): million cubic metres [*cont.*]

Bois rond
Production (volume solide de bois rond sans écorce) : millions de mètres cubes [*suite*]

Region, country or area Région, pays ou zone	1991	1992	1993	1994	1995	1996	1997	1998	1999	2000
Bahamas Bahamas	0.1	0.1	0.1	0.1	0.1	0.1	0.1	0.0	0.0	0.0
Belize[1] Belize[1]	0.2	0.2	0.2	0.2	0.2	0.2	0.2	0.2	0.2	0.2
Canada Canada	160.2	169.9	176.2	183.2	188.4	189.8	191.2	176.6	186.4	187.4
Costa Rica Costa Rica	4.5	4.6	4.6	5.1	5.2	5.2	5.2	5.2	5.2	5.2
Cuba Cuba	3.3	3.4	3.5	3.6[1]	3.6[1]	3.5[1]	3.5[1]	3.5[1]	1.6	3.3[1]
Dominican Republic Rép. dominicaine	0.6	0.6	0.6	0.6[1]	0.6[1]	0.6[1]	0.6[1]	0.6[1]	0.6[1]	0.6[1]
El Salvador El Salvador	4.7	3.8[1]	3.9[1]	3.9[1]	4.7	4.3	5.2	5.1	5.2	4.8
Guatemala Guatemala	11.7	12.1	13.0	13.4	13.6	13.5	13.8	14.1[1]	14.7	15.0
Haiti[1] Haïti[1]	1.9	2.0	2.0	2.1	2.1	2.2	2.2	2.2	2.2	2.2
Honduras Honduras	9.3	9.1	9.1	9.3	9.1	9.3	9.4	9.5	9.6	9.5
Jamaica Jamaïque	0.9	0.7	0.6	0.7	0.6	0.8	0.8	0.8	0.9	0.9[1]
Mexico Mexique	41.8	42.0	41.3	41.6	42.5	43.3	44.3	45.0	45.4	45.7
Nicaragua Nicaragua	5.9	5.8	5.8	5.8	5.8	5.9	5.8	5.9[1]	5.9[1]	6.0[1]
Panama Panama	1.5	1.5	1.5	1.5	1.5	1.4	1.4	1.3	1.3	1.4
Trinidad and Tobago Trinité-et-Tobago	0.1	0.1	0.1	0.1	0.2	0.1	0.1	0.1	0.1	0.1
United States Etats-Unis	478.6	493.4	488.8	498.4	499.3	490.6	485.9	494.0	497.6	500.4
America, South **Amérique du Sud**	**277.5**	**286.5**	**289.6**	**300.4**	**306.5**	**304.8**	**303.8**	**303.0**	**332.7**	**338.0**
Argentina Argentine	9.9	10.4	9.8	10.1	10.6	11.4	6.9	5.7	10.6	10.6
Bolivia Bolivie	2.4	2.6	2.7	2.9	2.9	2.9	3.0	2.3	2.6	2.6
Brazil Brésil	198.4	202.5	205.7	208.9	211.1	212.3	213.5	213.7	231.6	235.4
Chile Chili	24.5	28.4	29.9	31.1	34.6	29.8	30.0	31.7	34.0	35.7
Colombia Colombie	10.5	9.7	9.6	9.5	9.5	9.5	9.6	8.2	11.9	12.1
Ecuador Equateur	6.3	6.4	4.7	9.4	10.0	10.6	11.5	10.9	10.7	10.8
French Guiana Guyane française	0.2[1]	0.2[1]	0.1	0.1	0.1[1]	0.1[1]	0.1[1]	0.1[1]	0.1[1]	0.1[1]
Guyana Guyana	1.1	1.1	1.2	1.3	1.4	1.4	1.5	1.3	1.3	1.2

38
Roundwood
Production (solid volume of roundwood without bark): million cubic metres [*cont.*]
Bois rond
Production (volume solide de bois rond sans écorce) : millions de mètres cubes [*suite*]

Region, country or area Région, pays ou zone	1991	1992	1993	1994	1995	1996	1997	1998	1999	2000
Paraguay Paraguay	8.6	8.6	8.8	9.0	9.3	9.3	9.4	9.5	9.6	9.6[1]
Peru Pérou	7.7	7.8	8.2	9.0	8.0	7.9	8.4	9.2	9.2	8.7
Suriname Suriname	0.1	0.1	0.1	0.1	0.1	0.3	0.2	0.2	0.1	0.2
Uruguay Uruguay	4.0	4.2	4.4	4.5	4.6	4.7	5.0	5.5	5.6	5.7
Venezuela Venezuela	3.9	4.3	4.4	4.4	4.3	4.6	4.7	4.6	5.3	5.2
Asia Asie	1 049.1	1 057.6	1 059.0	1 053.8	1 052.4	1 061.4	1 055.5	1 014.3	1 008.6	998.6
Afghanistan[1] Afghanistan[1]	2.2	2.3	2.4	2.5	2.6	2.7	2.8	2.9	3.0	3.0
Armenia Arménie	...	0.0	0.0	0.0	0.0	0.0	0.1	0.0	0.0	0.0[1]
Bangladesh Bangladesh	28.6	28.6	28.6	28.6	28.5	28.5	28.5	28.5	28.5	28.5
Bhutan Bhoutan	3.9	4.0	3.9	3.9[1]	3.9[1]	4.0[1]	4.0[1]	4.1[1]	4.2[1]	4.3[1]
Brunei Darussalam Brunéi Darussalam	0.2	0.2	0.2	0.2[1]	0.2[1]	0.2[1]	0.2[1]	0.2[1]	0.2[1]	0.2[1]
Cambodia Cambodge	11.9[1]	11.8	11.8	12.1	12.0	11.9[1]	11.8[1]	11.6[1]	11.2	10.9
China †† Chine ††	282.4	289.0	298.8	303.5	305.7	312.8	311.2	298.5	291.4	287.5
Cyprus Chypre	0.1	0.0	0.1	0.0	0.0	0.0	0.0	0.0	0.0	0.0
India Inde	306.2	308.5	311.3	312.8	313.4	314.5	316.4	317.2	318.3	319.5
Indonesia Indonésie	162.8	158.8	154.8	148.2	143.6	143.1	139.1	123.1	121.8	120.3
Iran (Islamic Rep. of) Iran (Rép. islamique d')	1.5	1.4	1.6	1.6	1.5	1.4	1.5	1.3	1.1	1.1
Iraq Iraq	0.1[1]	0.1[1]	0.1[1]	0.1[1]	0.1[1]	0.1[1]	0.2	0.2	0.1[1]	0.1[1]
Israel Israël	0.1	0.1	0.1	0.1	0.1	0.1	0.1	0.1	0.1	0.1
Japan Japon	28.1	27.3	25.7	24.6	23.1	23.2	22.3	19.6	19.1	18.1
Jordan[1] Jordanie[1]	0.1	0.1	0.2	0.2	0.2	0.2	0.1	0.2	0.2	0.2
Kazakhstan Kazakhstan	...	0.5	0.3	0.3	0.3	0.3	0.3	0.0[1]	0.0[1]	0.0[1]
Korea, Dem. P. R. Corée, R. p. dém. de	5.1	5.2	5.4	5.5	5.6	6.1[1]	6.5[1]	6.9[1]	6.9[1]	7.0[1]
Korea, Republic of Corée, République de	3.9	3.7	3.7	3.7	3.8	3.6	3.5	3.9	4.1	4.0
Lao People's Dem. Rep. Rép. dém. pop. lao	6.3	6.0	6.3	6.4	6.7	6.5	6.5	6.4[1]	6.7[1]	6.7[1]

38
Roundwood
Production (solid volume of roundwood without bark): million cubic metres [*cont.*]
Bois rond
Production (volume solide de bois rond sans écorce) : millions de mètres cubes [*suite*]

Region, country or area Région, pays ou zone	1991	1992	1993	1994	1995	1996	1997	1998	1999	2000
Lebanon Liban	0.1	0.1	0.1	0.1[1]	0.1[1]	0.1[1]	0.1[1]	0.1[1]	0.0	0.0
Malaysia Malaisie	45.3	48.9	41.8	40.1	39.3	39.3	35.0	25.1	25.2	26.4
Mongolia[1] Mongolie[1]	0.9	0.9	0.9	0.8	0.6	0.6	0.6	0.6	0.6	0.6
Myanmar Myanmar	21.5	21.7	21.2	20.7	21.1	21.5	22.1	22.3[1]	22.6	22.8
Nepal Népal	13.0	13.0[1]	13.1[1]	13.0[1]	13.1[1]	13.1[1]	13.2[1]	13.2[1]	13.3[1]	13.4[1]
Pakistan Pakistan	23.8	24.2	24.2	24.3	24.2	25.0	32.1	31.8	33.1	26.8
Philippines Philippines	19.5	18.8	18.3	18.2	17.9	17.6	17.4	17.3	17.4	17.4
Sri Lanka Sri Lanka	9.9	9.7	9.9	10.2	10.4	10.4	6.8	6.6	6.6	6.5
Syrian Arab Republic Rép. arabe syrienne	0.1	0.1	0.1	0.1[1]	0.1[1]	0.1[1]	0.1[1]	0.1[1]	0.1[1]	0.1[1]
Thailand Thaïlande	24.5	24.2	24.0	23.7	23.5	23.4	23.4	23.4	23.4	23.4
Turkey Turquie	15.3	17.0	18.9	16.8	19.3	19.4	18.1	17.7	17.6	17.8
Viet Nam Viet Nam	31.6	31.2	31.2	31.2[1]	31.2[1]	31.2[1]	31.3[1]	31.2[1]	31.3[1]	31.2[1]
Yemen[1] Yémen[1]	0.2	0.2	0.2	0.2	0.2	0.3	0.3	0.3	0.3	0.3
Europe **Europe**	**316.4**	**538.8**	**500.6**	**468.0**	**486.3**	**466.2**	**522.2**	**463.2**	**529.6**	**577.3**
Albania Albanie	2.6	2.6	0.6	0.4	0.4	0.4	0.4	* 0.0	0.2	0.4
Austria Autriche	15.6	12.8	12.9	15.0	14.4	15.6	15.3	14.0	14.1	13.3
Belarus Bélarus	...	11.4	10.0	10.0	10.0	15.7	17.6	5.9	6.6	6.1
Belgium Belgique	...	...	...	...	...	...	...	...	4.4	4.5
Belgium-Luxembourg Belgique-Luxembourg	4.8	4.2	4.2	4.3	4.1	4.0	4.0	4.8	...	...
Bulgaria Bulgarie	3.7	3.5	3.5	2.7	2.8	3.2	3.0	3.2	4.4	4.8
Croatia Croatie	...	2.0	2.5	2.8	2.6	2.5	3.1	3.4	3.5	3.5
Czechoslovakia-former† Tchécoslovaquie(anc.) †	15.3	...	...	...	...	...	...	...	...	...
Czech Republic République tchèque	...	...	10.4	12.0	12.4	12.6	13.5	14.0	14.2	14.4
Denmark Danemark	2.3	2.2	2.3	2.3	2.3	2.3	2.1	1.5	1.5	3.1
Estonia Estonie	...	2.1	2.4	3.6	3.7	3.9	5.4	6.1	6.7	8.9

38
Roundwood
Production (solid volume of roundwood without bark): million cubic metres [*cont.*]
Bois rond
Production (volume solide de bois rond sans écorce) : millions de mètres cubes [*suite*]

Region, country or area Région, pays ou zone	1991	1992	1993	1994	1995	1996	1997	1998	1999	2000
Finland Finlande	34.9	38.5	42.2	48.7	50.2	46.6	51.3	53.7	53.6	54.3
France France	43.6	42.4	39.4	42.2	43.4	40.4	41.1	35.5	43.0	50.2
Germany † Allemagne †	33.6	33.0	33.2	39.8	39.3	37.0	38.2	39.1	37.6	49.1
Greece Grèce	2.5	2.3	2.2	2.1	2.0	2.0	1.7	1.7	2.2	2.2
Hungary Hongrie	5.5	5.0	4.5	4.5	4.3	3.7	4.2	4.2	5.8	5.9
Ireland Irlande	1.7	2.0	1.8	2.0	2.2	2.3	2.2	2.3	2.6	2.7
Italy Italie	8.3	8.4	8.8	9.5	9.7	9.1	9.1	9.5	11.1	9.3
Latvia Lettonie	...	2.5	4.9	5.7	6.9	8.1	8.7	10.0	14.0	14.5
Lithuania Lituanie	...	3.2	4.5	4.0	6.0	5.5	5.1	4.9	4.9	5.3
Luxembourg Luxembourg	...	...	...	...	...	...	...	...	0.3	0.3 [1]
Netherlands Pays-Bas	1.1	1.3	1.1	1.0	1.1	1.0	1.1	1.0	1.0	1.0
Norway Norvège	11.3	10.1	9.7	8.7	9.0	8.4	8.3	8.2	8.4	8.2
Poland Pologne	17.0	18.8	18.6	18.8	20.4	20.3	21.7	23.1	24.3	25.7
Portugal Portugal	10.8	10.3	10.2	9.8	9.4	9.0	9.0	8.5	9.0	9.4
Republic of Moldova République de Moldova	...	0.0	0.0	0.0	0.0	0.4	0.4	0.4	0.0	0.1
Romania Roumanie	13.0	12.4	8.8	11.9	12.2	12.3	13.5	11.6	12.7	13.1
Russian Federation Fédération de Russie	...	227.9	174.6	111.8	116.2	96.8	134.7	95.0	143.6	158.1
Slovakia Slovaquie	...	...	5.2	5.3	5.3	5.5	4.9	5.5	5.3	5.2
Slovenia Slovénie	...	1.7	1.1	1.9	1.9	2.0	2.2	2.1	2.1	2.3
Spain Espagne	15.2	13.9	13.8	15.3	16.1	15.6	15.6	14.9	14.8	14.8
Sweden Suède	51.4	53.5	54.0	56.3	63.6	56.3	60.2	60.6	58.7	61.8
Switzerland Suisse	4.6	4.6	4.4	4.7	4.7	4.1	4.5	4.3	4.7	10.4
TFYR of Macedonia L'ex-R.y. Macédoine	...	0.0	0.9	0.8	0.8	0.8	0.8	0.7	0.8	1.0
Ukraine Ukraine	...	0.0	0.0	0.0	0.0	10.4	10.1	6.1 [1]	5.9 [1]	5.9 [1]
United Kingdom Royaume-Uni	6.4	6.3	7.8	8.6	7.6	7.1	7.5	7.3	7.5	7.5

38
Roundwood
Production (solid volume of roundwood without bark): million cubic metres [cont.]
Bois rond
Production (volume solide de bois rond sans écorce) : millions de mètres cubes [suite]

Region, country or area Région, pays ou zone	1991	1992	1993	1994	1995	1996	1997	1998	1999	2000
Yugoslavia Yougoslavie	...	0.0	0.0	1.3	1.3	1.3	1.3	0.0	0.0	0.0
Yugoslavia, SFR† Yougoslavie, Rfs†	11.4	...	...	...	...	...	...	...	...	...
Oceania Océanie	43.9	44.7	48.0	50.3	51.7	51.2	52.7	52.3	54.5	59.6
Australia Australie	20.4	20.7	21.9	23.3	24.3	24.4	25.2	26.8	26.6	30.5
Fiji Fidji	0.3	0.3	0.5	0.6	0.6	0.6	0.5	0.5	0.5	0.5
New Zealand Nouvelle-Zélande	14.3	15.1	16.0	16.3	16.9	16.4	17.1	15.3	17.7	18.9
Papua New Guinea Papouasie-Nvl-Guinée	8.2	8.0	8.8	9.3	8.8	8.8	8.8	8.6	8.6	8.6
Samoa [1] Samoa [1]	0.1	0.1	0.1	0.1	0.1	0.1	0.1	0.1	0.1	0.1
Solomon Islands Iles Salomon	0.5	0.5	0.5	0.8	0.9	0.9 [1]	0.9 [1]	0.9 [1]	0.9 [1]	0.9 [1]
Vanuatu Vanuatu	0.1 [1]	0.1 [1]	0.1 [1]	0.1 [1]	0.1 [1]	0.1 [1]	0.1 [1]	0.1 [1]	0.1	0.1
USSR - former † URSS (anc.) †	356.4	...	...	...	...	...	...	...	...	...

Source:
Food and Agriculture Organization of the United
Nations (FAO), Rome, "FAO Yearbook of Forest Products 2000"
and the FAOSTAT database (19 December 2001).

† For information on recent changes in country or
area nomenclature pertaining to former Czechoslovakia,
Germany, Hong Kong Special Administrative Region (SAR) of
China, Macao Special Administrative Region (SAR) of China,
SFR of Yugoslavia and the former USSR, see Annex I - Country
or area nomenclature, regional and other groupings.

1 FAO estimate.

Source:
Organisation des Nations Unies pour l'alimentation et
l'agriculture (FAO), Rome, "Annuaire FAO des produits
forestiers 2000" et la base de données FAOSTAT (19 décembre
2001).

† Pour les modifications récentes de nomenclature
de pays ou de zone concernant l'Allemagne, Hong Kong, région
administrative spéciale (RAS) de Chine, Macao, région
administrative spéciale (RAS) de Chine,
l'ex-Tchécoslovaquie, l'ex-URSS et l'ex-Rfs de Yougoslavie,
voir annexe I - Nomenclature des pays ou des zones,
groupements régionaux et autres groupements.

1 Estimation de la FAO.

39
Fish production
Production halieutique
Capture and aquaculture: metric tons
Capture et aquaculture : tonnes

Country or area Pays ou zone	Capture production Captures 1995	1996	1997	1998	1999	Aquaculture production Production de l'aquaculture 1995	1996	1997	1998	1999
World Monde	91 871 300	93 531 000	93 766 300	86 933 100	92 866 600	24 493 000	26 747 400	28 728 200	30 793 500	33 310 300
Afghanistan[1] Afghanistan[1]	1 300	1 300	1 250	1 200	1 200	...	...	...	...	...
Albania Albanie	1 379	2 125	1 013	2 683	2 745	340[1]	323[1]	97	124	310
Algeria Algérie	105 872	81 989	91 580	92 346	105 693	369	322	322	283	250
American Samoa Samoa américaines	151	207	438	585	474	...	...	...	...	...
Angola Angola	122 781	137 815	136 058	145 811	177 497	...	...	...	...	...
Anguilla[1] Anguilla[1]	150	200	250	250	250	...	...	...	...	...
Antigua and Barbuda Antigua-et-Barbuda	1 429	2 798	3 372	2 878	3 185	...	...	...	...	...
Argentina Argentine	1 155 784	1 250 132	1 353 254	1 128 689	1 024 804	1 474	1 322[1]	1 314[1]	1 040[1]	1 218
Armenia Arménie	821	580	580	698	447	1 120	650	670	437	430[1]
Aruba Aruba	130	150	205	182	175	...	...	...	...	...
Australia Australie	205 464	203 963	198 010	205 414	216 346	22 395	25 323	26 637	28 106	33 729
Austria Autriche	404	450	465	451	432	2 921	2 952	3 021	2 912	3 070
Azerbaijan Azerbaïdjan	10 478	6 627	5 119	4 678	4 700[1]	516	419	364	211	235[1]
Bahamas Bahamas	9 557	9 866	10 439	10 124	10 473	24	1	1[1]	1[1]	1[1]
Bahrain Bahreïn	9 389	12 940	10 050	9 849	10 290	3	3	4[1]	4[1]	5
Bangladesh Bangladesh	792 389	814 787	829 426	839 141	924 056	317 073	379 088	432 135	514 842	620 114
Barbados Barbade	3 539	3 444	2 753	3 594	3 206	...	...	...	...	...
Belarus Bélarus	715	821	499	457	450[1]	5 463	6 038	4 322	4 727	5 359
Belgium Belgique	35 599	30 823	30 500	30 835	29 876	846	946	846	846	846
Belize Belize	1 716	977	10 444	17 164	39 940	950	1 004	1 397	1 642	3 163
Benin Bénin	44 379	42 175	43 784	42 139	38 542	...	...	...	...	...
Bermuda Bermudes	449	485	455	468	460	...	...	...	...	...
Bhutan[1] Bhoutan[1]	310	300	300	300	300	30	30	30	30	30

39
Fish production
Capture and aquaculture: metric tons [*cont.*]
Production halieutique
Capture et aquaculture : tonnes [*suite*]

Country or area Pays ou zone	Capture production Captures					Aquaculture production Production de l'aquaculture				
	1995	1996	1997	1998	1999	1995	1996	1997	1998	1999
Bolivia Bolivie	5 692	5 988	6 038	6 055	6 052	616	380	387	385	398
Bosnia and Herzegovina[1] Bosnie-Herzégovine[1]	2 500	2 500	2 500	2 500	2 500	...	...	...	...	...
Botswana[1] Botswana[1]	2 000	2 000	2 000	2 000	2 000	...	...	...	...	...
Brazil Brésil	706 708	715 482	744 585	706 789	655 000[1]	46 202	77 690[1]	87 673	103 915	119 750[1]
British Virgin Islands Iles Vierges britanniques	532	506	105	116	115	...	...	...	...	...
Brunei Darussalam Brunéi Darussalam	4 719	7 405	4 521	5 049	3 186	103	119	156	172	122
Bulgaria Bulgarie	8 191	8 854	11 237	18 946	10 556	4 615[1]	4 727[1]	5 437	4 252	7 780
Burkina Faso Burkina Faso	8 000	8 000	8 000	8 335	7 600	0	30	45	55[1]	60
Burundi Burundi	21 101	3 041	20 296	13 426	9 199	50[1]	50[1]	50[1]	55[1]	55
Cambodia Cambodge	102 999	94 710	102 800	107 900	269 100	9 511	9 600	11 800	14 100	15 000
Cameroon Cameroun	91 131[1]	92 400[1]	93 000[1]	94 800[1]	95 000[1]	57[1]	58[1]	67	67	67[1]
Canada Canada	848 891	904 665	970 955	1 013 747	1 021 916	65 207	71 378	80 917	91 156	113 600
Cape Verde Cap-Vert	8 495	9 155	9 627	9 460	10 371	...	...	...	...	...
Cayman Islands Iles Caïmanes	125	110	125	125	125	...	...	...	...	...
Central African Rep. Rép. centrafricaine	13 750[1]	14 000[1]	14 250[1]	14 500[1]	15 000	210[1]	150[1]	80	80	117
Chad Tchad	90 000	100 000	85 000	84 000	84 000[1]	...	...	...	...	...
Channel Islands Iles Anglo-Normandes	2 949[1]	4 346	4 238	4 117	3 601	114	191	130	196	249
Chile Chili	7 433 902	6 690 942	5 810 764	3 265 383	5 050 528	157 083	217 903	272 346	293 044	274 216
China †† Chine ††	12562706	14182107	15722344	17229927	17240032	15855653	17714570	19315623	20795367	22789887
China, Hong Kong SAR† Chine, Hong Kong RAS†	194 999	183 856	186 000	180 000	127 780	8 571	8 418	8 310	6 439	6 052
China, Macao SAR † Chine, Macao RAS †	1 604	1 418	1 500[1]	1 500[1]	1 500[1]	...	...	...	...	...
Colombia Colombie	120 699	130 829	147 918	132 862	117 949	36 630	29 990	43 710	45 933	52 947
Comoros[1] Comores[1]	13 000	12 700	12 500	12 500	12 200	...	...	...	...	...
Congo Congo	45 776	45 473	38 082	44 455[1]	43 696[1]	139	106	99	140[1]	190

39
Fish production
Capture and aquaculture: metric tons [*cont.*]
Production halieutique
Capture et aquaculture : tonnes [*suite*]

Country or area Pays ou zone	Capture production Captures					Aquaculture production Production de l'aquaculture				
	1995	1996	1997	1998	1999	1995	1996	1997	1998	1999
Cook Islands Iles Cook	1 090	973[1]	1 010[1]	1 000[1]	1 000[1]	0	0	0	0	0
Costa Rica Costa Rica	21 193	23 375	24 213	20 983	25 679	6 756	6 986	7 000	8 716	9 324
Côte d'Ivoire Côte d'Ivoire	70 189	72 197	67 151	72 528	76 000	386	1 128	450	862	1 000
Croatia Croatie	16 265	18 233	17 035	22 329	19 291	4 007	2 889	3 510	5 958	6 228
Cuba Cuba	80 059	85 492	84 956	67 076	67 262	21 859	36 337	44 050	46 712	55 163
Cyprus Chypre	2 570	5 246	16 019	18 865	5 273	452	787	969	1 178	1 422
Czech Republic République tchèque	3 929	3 524	3 321	3 952	4 190	18 679	18 200	17 560	17 231	18 775
Dem. Rep. of the Congo Rép. dém. du Congo	158 627	163 010	162 211	178 041	208 448	600[1]	600[1]	550[1]	500[1]	414
Denmark Danemark	1 999 033	1 681 517	1 826 852	1 557 335	1 405 011	44 730	41 924	39 697	42 368	42 653
Djibouti[1] Djibouti[1]	350	350	350	350	350	...	...	...	...	...
Dominica Dominique	950	1 030	1 079	1 212	1 200[1]	4	4[1]	5[1]	5[1]	5[1]
Dominican Republic Rép. dominicaine	17 977	13 811	14 509	10 171	8 521	2 206	789	677	810	748
East Timor Timor oriental	0	0	0	0	513[1]	...	...	...	...	...
Ecuador Equateur	505 395	702 974	548 988	310 022	497 872	106 397	108 720	135 297	146 590	127 375
Egypt Egypte	310 790	320 230	342 759	362 741	380 504	61 815	75 837	73 454	139 389	226 276
El Salvador El Salvador	14 533	12 822	10 626	14 994	15 232	518	402	351	384	235
Equatorial Guinea Guinée équatoriale	2 306	5 040	6 090	6 005	7 001	...	...	...	...	...
Eritrea Erythrée	3 720	3 267	1 057	1 658	7 042	...	...	...	...	...
Estonia Estonie	132 028	108 446	123 613	118 714	111 793	315	272	260	260	200
Ethiopia Ethiopie	6 325	8 770	10 370	14 000	15 858	55[1]	38[1]	24[1]	14[1]	0
Faeroe Islands Iles Féroé	288 857	303 703	329 736	376 379	358 044	8 611	17 584	22 538	20 558	39 507
Falkland Is. (Malvinas) Iles Falkland (Malvinas)	29 065	32 171	17 941	44 746	39 146	...	...	...	...	...
Fiji Fidji	28 836	25 029	27 755	28 158	36 713	180[1]	235	345	298	1 758
Finland Finlande	167 484	179 077	180 185	171 690	160 569	17 345	17 659	16 426	16 024	15 449

39
Fish production
Capture and aquaculture: metric tons [*cont.*]
Production halieutique
Capture et aquaculture : tonnes [*suite*]

Country or area / Pays ou zone	Capture production / Captures					Aquaculture production / Production de l'aquaculture				
	1995	1996	1997	1998	1999	1995	1996	1997	1998	1999
France / France	614 373	562 289	573 165	548 764	578 071	280 685	285 584	287 472	268 251	267 578
French Guiana / Guyane française	8 089	7 977	7 702	7 709	7 700[1]	...	...	7	18	20[1]
French Polynesia / Polynésie française	9 020	9 910	11 670	12 473	12 336	61	67	56	53	48
Gabon / Gabon	40 437[1]	45 300	43 584	53 494	52 882	39	62	57	158	558
Gambia / Gambie	23 752	31 601	32 254	29 002	30 000[1]	...	4	4[1]	4[1]	4[1]
Georgia / Géorgie	3 560[1]	2 453	2 583	3 001	1 500[1]	157	101	61	96	100[1]
Germany / Allemagne	239 890	236 411	259 769	266 664	238 925	58 096	75 237	59 433	67 020	73 567
Ghana / Ghana	352 976	477 173	446 797	442 759	492 776	550[1]	550[1]	400	420[1]	430
Greece / Grèce	165 767	163 015	170 487	127 531	136 699	32 644	39 852	48 838	59 926	79 265
Greenland / Groenland	128 890	116 018	120 596	128 590	160 253	...	...	...	...	...
Grenada / Grenade	1 487	1 278	1 408	1 712	1 631	0	0	0	0	1
Guadeloupe / Guadeloupe	9 500	9 570	10 450	9 114	9 150[1]	30	30	20	14	14[1]
Guam / Guam	185	121	158	253	223	216[1]	220[1]	220[1]	220[1]	230[1]
Guatemala / Guatemala	8 253	7 653	6 896	10 847	11 028	3 675	3 421	4 407	3 124	4 850
Guinea / Guinée	67 860	63 360	62 441	69 764	87 314	4	4	0	0	0
Guinea-Bissau / Guinée-Bissau	6 329	7 000[1]	7 250[1]	6 000[1]	5 000[1]	...	...	...	...	...
Guyana / Guyana	47 900[1]	48 583	53 998	52 840	53 844	230[1]	250[1]	270[1]	300[1]	606
Haiti[1] / Haïti[1]	5 517	5 245	5 301	5 259	5 000	...	...	...	...	...
Honduras / Honduras	20 961	13 116	15 378	6 230[1]	7 215	7 241[1]	10 065[1]	9 274[1]	8 147[1]	8 180[1]
Hungary / Hongrie	7 314	7 606	7 406	7 265	7 514	9 360	8 080	9 334	10 222	11 947
Iceland / Islande	1 612 548	2 060 168	2 205 944	1 681 951	1 736 267	3 485	3 687	3 663	3 868	3 897
India / Inde	3 219 583	3 474 064	3 517 084	3 214 765	3 316 815	1 686 346	1 783 491	1 862 288	2 029 831	2 035 488
Indonesia / Indonésie	3 503 779	3 557 623	3 790 790	3 964 897	4 149 420	641 092	733 098	662 547	629 797	647 640
Iran (Islamic Rep. of) / Iran (Rép. islamique d')	341 383	351 725	342 287	367 212	387 200	28 636	29 977	30 279	33 237	31 800

39
Fish production
Capture and aquaculture: metric tons [*cont.*]
Production halieutique
Capture et aquaculture : tonnes [*suite*]

Country or area Pays ou zone	Capture production Captures					Aquaculture production Production de l'aquaculture				
	1995	1996	1997	1998	1999	1995	1996	1997	1998	1999
Iraq Iraq	28 208	30 737	31 302	22 574	24 606	2 600	2 500	3 400	7 500	2 183
Ireland Irlande	384 632	333 030	292 673	324 760	285 921	27 366	34 925	36 854	42 375	43 856
Isle of Man Ile de Man	3 734	3 537	4 289	2 214	2 608	...	...	...	...	...
Israel Israël	4 941	5 229	5 204	6 300	5 884	16 180	17 553	18 264	18 556	18 777
Italy Italie	396 791	365 899	343 693	317 789	294 155	230 725	209 373	211 719	246 625	246 368
Jamaica Jamaïque	10 367[1]	12 504[1]	8 198	6 560	8 508	3 550[1]	3 500[1]	3 450	3 410	4 150
Japan Japon	5 966 615	5 933 440	5 926 113	5 263 384	5 176 460	820 123	829 352	806 534	766 812	759 262
Jordan Jordanie	425	440	450	470	510	170	181	200	293	515
Kazakhstan Kazakhstan	48 402	44 273	31 826	23 089	25 758	1 948[1]	1 682	1 921	1 106	1 193
Kenya Kenya	192 706	180 988	161 054	172 592	205 287	1 302	579	199	153	300
Kiribati Kiribati	30 309	31 829	29 351	33 485	48 205	17[1]	9	7	4	13
Korea, Dem. P. R. Corée, R. p. dém. de	327 083	253 125	236 462	220 000[1]	210 000[1]	73 946	80 896	70 174	68 500[1]	68 500[1]
Korea, Republic of Corée, République de	2 319 915	2 413 713	2 204 047	2 026 934	2 119 668	368 155	358 046	392 367	327 462	303 106
Kuwait Koweït	8 616	8 255	7 826	7 799	6 271	90	90	254[1]	250[1]	264
Kyrgyzstan Kirghizistan	185	160[1]	120[1]	80[1]	48	179	161[1]	150[1]	150[1]	150
Lao People's Dem. Rep. Rép. dém. pop. lao	25 850	25 850	26 000	26 808	30 041	14 400	14 400	14 000	14 050	30 362
Latvia Lettonie	149 194	142 644	105 682	102 331	125 389	525	380	345	425	468
Lebanon Liban	4 085	4 135	3 655	3 520	3 560	300	350	300	400	300
Lesotho Lesotho	26[1]	28[1]	30[1]	30[1]	30	14[1]	14[1]	14[1]	8[1]	4
Liberia Libéria	8 829	7 408	8 580	10 830	15 472	0	0	0	0	0
Libyan Arab Jamah.[1] Jamah. arabe libyenne[1]	34 400	32 976	31 877	32 511	32 450	100	100	100	100	100
Lithuania Lituanie	57 368	88 514	44 002	66 578	33 594	1 714	1 537	1 516	1 516	1 650
Madagascar Madagascar	115 653	114 475	116 391	118 499	131 571	4 712	5 602	8 582	8 492	9 486[1]
Malawi Malawi	53 664	63 569	56 340	41 111	45 392	226[1]	240[1]	231[1]	229[1]	590

39
Fish production
Capture and aquaculture: metric tons [*cont.*]
Production halieutique
Capture et aquaculture : tonnes [*suite*]

Country or area Pays ou zone	Capture production Captures					Aquaculture production Production de l'aquaculture				
	1995	1996	1997	1998	1999	1995	1996	1997	1998	1999
Malaysia Malaisie	1 112 375	1 130 372	1 172 922	1 153 719	1 251 768	132 745	109 063	107 984	133 635	155 127
Maldives Maldives	104 784	120 508	116 257	128 968	133 547	...	...	...	...	...
Mali Mali	132 900	111 910	99 550	98 000	98 536	100[1]	60[1]	60[1]	60[1]	230
Malta Malte	4 387	9 027	875	980	1 033	904	1 552	1 800	1 950	2 002
Marshall Islands Iles Marshall	381[1]	2 772	370[1]	400[1]	400[1]	...	...	...	...	...
Martinique Martinique	5 300	3 266	5 000	5 500	5 000[1]	77	58	66	55	40
Mauritania Mauritanie	53 063	55 482	47 267	47 916	47 811	...	...	...	...	...
Mauritius Maurice	16 395	11 869	14 025	12 026	12 004	176	165	118	83	85
Mayotte Mayotte	646	1 217	1 534	1 570	1 500[1]	...	1	2[1]	2[1]	2[1]
Mexico Mexique	1 329 469	1 464 084	1 489 020	1 174 742	1 202 178	25 580	31 339	39 500	40 989	48 414
Micronesia (Fed. States of) Micron (Etats fédérés de)	9 038[1]	9 724[1]	10 332[1]	15 529[1]	11 886[1]	0	0	0	0	0
Monaco[1] Monaco[1]	3	3	3	3	3	...	...	...	...	...
Mongolia Mongolie	158	221	180	311	524	...	...	...	...	...
Montserrat Montserrat	48	38	45	46	50[1]	...	...	...	...	...
Morocco Maroc	848 951	642 886	791 906	710 436	745 431	2 072	2 226[1]	2 290	2 115	2 752
Mozambique Mozambique	26 833	34 915	42 056	38 344	35 560	37	4	0	0	0
Myanmar Myanmar	758 214	804 830	830 346	872 971	851 581	74 255	68 115	87 304	85 250	94 246
Namibia Namibie	292 372	266 912	282 151	337 482	299 151	50[1]	50[1]	45[1]	45[1]	45
Nauru[1] Nauru[1]	450	400	350	300	250	...	...	...	...	...
Nepal Népal	11 230	11 230	11 230	12 000	12 752	9 918	10 649	11 977	12 866	13 028
Netherlands Pays-Bas	438 092	410 798	451 799	536 626	514 611	83 938	99 871	98 210	120 094	108 785
Netherlands Antilles[1] Antilles néerlandaises[1]	1 020	1 000	900	900	900	4	4	5	5	5
New Caledonia Nouvelle-Calédonie	2 644	2 998	2 428	3 105	3 152	940	1 005	1 152	1 596	1 936
New Zealand Nouvelle-Zélande	544 242	421 104	596 017	636 219	594 084	70 391	74 800	76 850	93 807	91 650

39
Fish production
Capture and aquaculture: metric tons [*cont.*]
Production halieutique
Capture et aquaculture : tonnes [*suite*]

Country or area Pays ou zone	Capture production Captures					Aquaculture production Production de l'aquaculture				
	1995	1996	1997	1998	1999	1995	1996	1997	1998	1999
Nicaragua Nicaragua	10 995	15 442	16 176	19 892	20 569	2 310	2 299	3 452	4 788	4 198
Niger Niger	3 616	4 156	6 328	7 013	11 000	35	11	13	12	14
Nigeria Nigéria	349 482	337 993	387 923	463 024	455 628	16 619[1]	17 944[1]	17 682	20 458	21 737
Niue[1] Nioué[1]	120	120	120	120	120	...	...	...	...	...
Northern Mariana Islands Iles Mariannes du Nord	192	225	250	235	193	...	...	...	...	...
Norway Norvège	2 524 111	2 648 457	2 856 597	2 850 565	2 620 073	277 636	321 542	367 298	408 862	466 035
Occupied Palestinian Terr.[2] Terr. palestinien occupé[2]	1 229	2 493	3 791	3 625	3 600[1]	...	...	...	...	...
Oman Oman	139 864	121 852	120 408	106 637	108 809	...	...	...	10	10
Pakistan Pakistan	526 849	537 432	589 731	596 980	654 530	14 868[1]	13 557	15 464	17 369	20 076[1]
Palau Palaos	1 956	1 990	1 751	1 777	1 800[1]	3	2	2	1	1
Panama Panama	203 029	153 937	166 503	202 854	120 498	5 503	5 079	7 217	10 161	3 236
Papua New Guinea[1] Papouasie-Nvl-Guinée[1]	42 730	38 077	46 880	67 265	53 746	21	23	20	17	17
Paraguay Paraguay	21 000[1]	22 000	28 000	25 000[1]	25 000[1]	190[1]	350[1]	350[1]	95	95[1]
Peru Pérou	8 937 342	9 515 048	7 869 871	4 338 437	8 429 290	5 769	6 912	7 381	7 732	8 275
Philippines Philippines	1 860 491	1 783 593	1 805 806	1 833 458	1 870 450	361 540	349 442	330 441	312 077	328 375
Pitcairn[1] Pitcairn[1]	8	8	8	8	8	...	...	...	...	...
Poland Pologne	426 235	341 299	353 661	238 262	235 111	25 111	27 700	28 680	29 791	33 711
Portugal Portugal	260 584	260 422	221 923	223 961	207 707	4 981	5 364	7 185	7 536	7 523
Puerto Rico Porto Rico	2 516	2 311	2 634	2 118	2 107	136	113	91	306	352
Qatar Qatar	4 271	4 739	5 032	5 279	4 207	...	1	2	...	...
Republic of Moldova République de Moldova	709	603	569	491	500[1]	1 401	1 067	1 202	1 129	1 130[1]
Réunion Réunion	4 821	5 173	5 883	6 363	5 812	4	4	134	63	63
Romania Roumanie	49 275	18 259	8 446	9 061	7 843	19 830[1]	13 900[1]	11 168	9 614	8 998
Russian Federation Fédération de Russie	4 311 809	4 676 666	4 661 853	4 454 759	4 141 157	62 018	52 899	53 171	63 195	68 615

39
Fish production
Capture and aquaculture: metric tons [*cont.*]
Production halieutique
Capture et aquaculture : tonnes [*suite*]

Country or area Pays ou zone	Capture production Captures					Aquaculture production Production de l'aquaculture				
	1995	1996	1997	1998	1999	1995	1996	1997	1998	1999
Rwanda Rwanda	3 300 [1]	2 952	4 428	6 641	6 433	79 [1]	100 [1]	118 [1]	128	300
Saint Helena Sainte-Hélène	840	744	862	1 007	572	...	...	...	...	...
Saint Kitts and Nevis Saint-Kitts-et-Nevis	192	352	216	407	352	4 [1]	4 [1]	4 [1]	4 [1]	5
Saint Lucia Sainte-Lucie	1 188	1 274	1 311	1 314	1 718	1	2	3	2	1
Saint Pierre and Miquelon Saint-Pierre-et-Miquelon	317	747	3 571	6 108	5 892	...	...	...	...	...
St. Vincent-Grenadines St. Vincent-Grenadines	1 015	921 [1]	6 092	33 891	15 573	...	...	...	...	...
Samoa Samoa	2 519	2 511	6 543	7 014	9 750	0	0	1	0	0
Sao Tome and Principe Sao Tomé-et-Principe	3 565	3 980	3 338	3 477	3 756	...	...	...	...	...
Saudi Arabia Arabie saoudite	45 609	47 708	49 314	51 329	46 897	2 696	3 835	4 690	5 101	5 052
Senegal Sénégal	358 617	436 259	506 966	425 766	418 125	60	78	74	23 [1]	155
Seychelles Seychelles	4 008	4 707	12 994	21 123	37 765	195	278	584	649	227
Sierra Leone Sierra Leone	64 870	67 304 [1]	72 628	63 065	59 407	25 [1]	30 [1]	30 [1]	30 [1]	30
Singapore Singapour	10 102	9 943	9 250	8 155	5 052	3 625	3 567	4 088	3 706	4 029
Slovakia Slovaquie	1 949	1 413	1 386	1 362	1 391	1 617	954	1 254	648	872
Slovenia Slovénie	2 141	2 343	2 345	2 210	2 009	789	869	917	909	1 206
Solomon Islands [1] Iles Salomon [1]	66 541	57 211	61 510	59 993	82 334	13	13	13	13	13
Somalia [1] Somalie [1]	27 950	26 050	24 150	22 250	20 250	...	...	...	...	...
South Africa Afrique du Sud	575 654	440 327	514 464	558 857	588 001	3 520	2 981	4 186	5 072	4 143
Spain Espagne	1 147 724 [1]	1 131 618	1 150 098	1 215 645	1 167 242	223 950	231 556	239 136	313 518	317 796
Sri Lanka Sri Lanka	229 421	222 448	235 560	259 830	271 595	6 329 [1]	6 102 [1]	6 440	10 020	8 305
Sudan Soudan	44 000	45 000	47 000	49 500	49 500	1 000	1 000 [1]	1 000	1 000	1 000
Suriname Suriname	13 000 [1]	13 150 [1]	13 000 [1]	12 960 [1]	12 960 [1]	1 [1]	1 [1]	1 [1]	106	106 [1]
Swaziland Swaziland	60 [1]	60 [1]	65 [1]	70 [1]	70 [1]	88	93	66	81	61
Sweden Suède	404 572	370 881	357 406	410 886	351 253	7 573	8 267	6 709	5 504	6 064

39
Fish production
Capture and aquaculture: metric tons [*cont.*]
Production halieutique
Capture et aquaculture : tonnes [*suite*]

Country or area Pays ou zone	Capture production Captures					Aquaculture production Production de l'aquaculture				
	1995	1996	1997	1998	1999	1995	1996	1997	1998	1999
Switzerland Suisse	1 588	1 841	1 859	1 809	1 840	1 161	1 161	1 150	1 150	1 135
Syrian Arab Republic Rép. arabe syrienne	5 782	5 773	6 131	7 097	7 945	5 857	6 355	5 596	7 233	6 079
Tajikistan Tadjikistan	100	0	0	0	0	284	93	71	81	80[1]
Thailand Thaïlande	3 013 268	3 004 678	2 877 622	2 900 320	3 004 900	559 504	556 155	539 855	607 673	602 807
TFYR of Macedonia L'ex-R.y. Macédoine	208	78	130	131	135	1 297	911	879	1 257	1 669
Togo Togo	12 201	15 098	14 290	16 655	22 924	20	21	20	25	150
Tokelau[1] Tokélaou[1]	200	200	200	200	200	...	...	...	...	...
Tonga Tonga	2 597	2 915	2 739	3 903	3 663	...	...	...	...	...
Trinidad and Tobago Trinité-et-Tobago	13 000[1]	14 360	15 000	14 500[1]	15 000[1]	24[1]	24[1]	25[1]	27[1]	27[1]
Tunisia Tunisie	83 355	83 734	87 012	88 075	92 075	960	1 351	1 875	1 842	1 095
Turkey Turquie	633 968	527 826	459 153	487 700	575 097	21 607	33 201	45 450	56 700	63 000
Turkmenistan Turkménistan	9 740	9 014	8 169	7 010	8 789	1 669	307	605	559	503
Turks and Caicos Islands Iles Turques et Caïques	1 395[1]	1 297[1]	1 250[1]	1 318	1 300[1]	5	3[1]	4[1]	4[1]	4[1]
Tuvalu Tuvalu	399	400[1]	400[1]	400[1]	400[1]	...	...	...	...	...
Uganda Ouganda	208 789	195 088	218 026	220 628	226 097	194	210	360	360[1]	360
Ukraine Ukraine	378 650	417 119	373 005	462 308	407 856	35 368	32 709	30 000	28 332	33 816
United Arab Emirates Emirats arabes unis	105 884	107 000	114 358	114 739	117 607	0	0	0	0	0
United Kingdom Royaume-Uni	909 928	865 145	886 261	920 355	837 759	93 838	109 901	129 715	137 421	154 800
United Rep. of Tanzania Rép.-Unie de Tanzanie	359 800	323 921	356 960	348 000	310 020	200[1]	200[1]	250[1]	250[1]	250
United States Etats-Unis	5 224 566	5 001 483	4 983 463	4 708 980	4 749 645	413 411	393 331	438 331	445 123	478 679
United States Virgin Is. Iles Vierges américaines	800[1]	800[1]	800[1]	800[1]	800[1]	0	0	0	0	0
Uruguay Uruguay	126 446	123 330	136 943	140 609	103 012	20[1]	21	19	19	31
Uzbekistan Ouzbékistan	3 611	1 494	3 075	2 799	2 871	10 197	5 006	7 490	6 966	5 665
Vanuatu[1] Vanuatu[1]	60 038	49 639	69 848	74 589	94 581	...	...	...	...	...

39
Fish production
Capture and aquaculture: metric tons [*cont.*]
Production halieutique
Capture et aquaculture : tonnes [*suite*]

Country or area Pays ou zone	Capture production Captures					Aquaculture production Production de l'aquaculture				
	1995	1996	1997	1998	1999	1995	1996	1997	1998	1999
Venezuela Venezuela	500 927	496 025	469 686	505 536	411 877	5 653	7 336	8 565	10 670	10 730
Viet Nam Viet Nam	999 860[1]	1 028 500[1]	1 078 668	1 130 660	1 200 000[1]	451 948[1]	432 500[1]	494 000	521 870	594 910[1]
Wallis and Futuna Islands Iles Wallis et Futuna	170	180	176	206	206[1]	...	...	...	...	...
Yemen Yémen	102 964	101 241	112 834	127 627	123 252	...	...	...	...	...
Yugoslavia Yougoslavie	4 167	4 030	3 873	2 910[1]	1 253	2 373	2 896	3 493	7 353[1]	8 687
Zambia Zambie	66 465	61 562	65 923	69 938	67 327	4 081	4 770	4 718	4 159	4 180[1]
Zimbabwe Zimbabwe	16 463	16 387	18 156	16 386	12 406	150[1]	170[1]	170[1]	170[1]	185
Areas not specified **Zones non spécifiées**	**360 484**	**251 357**	**233 556**	**246 807**	**246 924**	...	...	...	...	...

Source:
Food and Agriculture Organization of the United
Nations (FAO), Rome, FAOSTAT Fisheries database.

† For information on recent changes in country or
area nomenclature pertaining to former Czechoslovakia,
Germany, Hong Kong Special Administrative Region (SAR) of
China, Macao Special Administrative Region (SAR) of China,
SFR of Yugoslavia and the former USSR, see Annex I - Country
or area nomenclature, regional and other groupings.

†† For statistical purposes, the data for
China do not include those for Hong Kong Special
Administrative Region (Hong Kong SAR) and Macao Special
Administrative Region (Macao SAR).

1 FAO estimate.
2 Data refer to the Gaza Strip.

Source:
Organisation des Nations Unies pour l'alimentation et
l'agriculture (FAO), Rome, les données des pêches de
FAOSTAT.

† Pour les modifications récentes de nomenclature
de pays ou de zone concernant l'Allemagne, Hong Kong, région
administrative spéciale (RAS) de Chine, Macao, région
administrative spéciale (RAS) de Chine,
l'ex-Tchécoslovaquie, l'ex-URSS et l'ex-Rfs de Yougoslavie,
voir annexe I - Nomenclature des pays ou des zones,
groupements régionaux et autres groupements.

†† Les données statistiques relatives à
la Chine ne comprennent pas celles qui concernent la région
administrative spéciale de Hong Kong (la RAS de Hong Kong)
et la région administrative spéciale de Macao (la RAS de
Macao).

1 Estimation de la FAO.
2 Les données se rapportent à la Zone de Gaza.

40
Fertilizers
Engrais

Nitrogenous, phosphate and potash: thousand metric tons
Azotés, phosphatés et pottasiques : milliers de tonnes

Country or area Pays ou zone	Production Production					Consumption Consommation				
	1995/96	1996/97	1997/98	1998/99	1999/00	1995/96	1996/97	1997/98	1998/99	1999/00
World Monde										
Nitrogenous fertilizers										
Engrais azotés	86 356.8	90 379.0	87 603.0	88 482.0	90 849.9	78 417.4	82 552.6	81 497.5	82 623.0	85 529.6
Phosphate fertilizers										
Engrais phosphatés	33 452.8	33 572.7	32 810.7	33 023.1	32 648.8	30 655.4	31 120.5	33 346.1	33 224.4	33 149.9
Potash fertilizers										
Engrais potassiques	22 703.6	22 963.3	26 156.6	24 976.6	25 424.5	20 625.5	20 882.0	22 620.9	22 384.6	22 680.7
Africa Afrique										
Nitrogenous fertilizers										
Engrais azotés	2 522.1	2 605.5	2 451.2	2 654.8	2 813.9	2 104.4	2 313.8	2 258.3	2 385.2	2 448.0
Phosphate fertilizers										
Engrais phosphatés	2 306.6	2 458.5	2 264.2	2 430.6	2 515.7	926.7	971.7	944.0	942.3	984.0
Potash fertilizers										
Engrais potassiques	...	...	...	...	...	418.4	468.1	473.3	478.2	528.1
Algeria Algérie										
Nitrogenous fertilizers										
Engrais azotés	* 12.0	* 8.3	* 28.4	* 40.7	57.2	* 18.4	* 14.0	* 36.0	* 44.0	* 63.9
Phosphate fertilizers *										
Engrais phosphatés *	12.3	...	...	23.4	8.7	15.2	11.0	35.0	30.8	30.9
Potash fertilizers *										
Engrais potassiques *	...	...	...	...	...	12.8	13.0	26.0	33.2	51.0
Angola Angola										
Nitrogenous fertilizers *										
Engrais azotés *	...	...	...	...	...	2.0	2.0	2.0	2.3	2.3
Phosphate fertilizers *										
Engrais phosphatés *	...	...	...	...	...	3.0	2.0	...	...	...
Potash fertilizers *										
Engrais potassiques *	...	...	...	...	...	3.0	2.0	...	1.1	1.1
Benin Bénin										
Nitrogenous fertilizers										
Engrais azotés	...	...	...	...	...	* 14.0	14.5	18.8	* 15.3	* 34.6
Phosphate fertilizers										
Engrais phosphatés	...	...	...	...	...	* 15.0	10.3	12.6	* 14.6	* 10.4
Potash fertilizers *										
Engrais potassiques *	...	...	...	...	...	7.0	5.9	7.6	7.8	11.7
Botswana Botswana										
Nitrogenous fertilizers										
Engrais azotés	...	...	...	...	...	2.1	3.2	* 3.5	3.7	* 4.1
Phosphate fertilizers										
Engrais phosphatés	...	...	...	...	...	0.1	0.1	* 0.2	* 0.3	* 0.3
Potash fertilizers										
Engrais potassiques	...	...	...	...	...	0.0	0.0	* 0.1	* 0.2	* 0.2
Burkina Faso Burkina Faso										
Nitrogenous fertilizers										
Engrais azotés	...	...	...	...	...	11.4	11.5	24.4	* 16.4	* 16.9
Phosphate fertilizers										
Engrais phosphatés	* 0.3	* 0.3	* 0.3	* 0.3	* 0.3	6.7	6.3	9.9	* 17.8	* 17.9
Potash fertilizers										
Engrais potassiques	...	...	...	...	...	6.3	6.3	8.3	* 16.0	* 16.0
Burundi Burundi										
Nitrogenous fertilizers *										
Engrais azotés *	...	...	...	...	...	1.0	1.0	1.0	1.4	1.8
Phosphate fertilizers										
Engrais phosphatés	...	...	...	...	...	* 2.0	* 1.8	...	1.2	* 1.4
Potash fertilizers										
Engrais potassiques	...	...	...	...	...	...	...	...	1.0	0.8
Cameroon Cameroun										
Nitrogenous fertilizers										
Engrais azotés	...	...	...	...	...	* 15.0	* 18.0	* 18.9	16.5	* 26.3
Phosphate fertilizers										
Engrais phosphatés	...	...	...	...	...	* 5.0	* 5.0	7.0	7.6	* 10.2
Potash fertilizers										
Engrais potassiques	...	...	...	...	...	* 10.0	* 11.0	13.3	15.4	* 13.5

40
Fertilizers
Nitrogenous, phosphate and potash: thousand metric tons [*cont.*]
Engrais
Azotés, phosphatés et potassiques : milliers de tonnes [*suite*]

Country or area	Production Production					Consumption Consommation				
Pays ou zone	1995/96	1996/97	1997/98	1998/99	1999/00	1995/96	1996/97	1997/98	1998/99	1999/00
Cape Verde Cap−Vert										
Nitrogenous fertilizers										
Engrais azotés	...	...	...	...	...	...	...	...	0.1	0.2
Central African Rep. Rép. centrafricaine										
Nitrogenous fertilizers *										
Engrais azotés *	...	...	...	...	...	0.1	0.1	0.1	0.2	0.2
Phosphate fertilizers *										
Engrais phosphatés *	...	...	...	...	...	0.1	0.1	0.1	0.2	0.2
Potash fertilizers *										
Engrais potassiques *	...	...	...	...	...	0.1	0.1	0.1	0.2	0.2
Chad Tchad										
Nitrogenous fertilizers										
Engrais azotés	...	...	...	...	...	3.6	* 7.5	* 3.5	* 10.7	* 11.0
Phosphate fertilizers										
Engrais phosphatés	...	...	...	...	...	* 2.0	* 2.4	* 2.4	1.7	* 2.0
Potash fertilizers										
Engrais potassiques	...	...	...	...	...	* 3.0	* 2.0	* 2.0	4.4	* 4.5
Comoros Comores										
Nitrogenous fertilizers *										
Engrais azotés *	...	...	...	...	...	0.1	0.1	0.1	0.1	0.1
Phosphate fertilizers *										
Engrais phosphatés *	...	...	...	...	...	0.1	0.1	0.1	0.1	0.1
Potash fertilizers *										
Engrais potassiques *	...	...	...	...	...	0.1	0.1	0.1	0.1	0.1
Congo Congo										
Nitrogenous fertilizers *										
Engrais azotés *	...	...	...	...	...	1.0	2.0	2.0	2.0	2.0
Phosphate fertilizers *										
Engrais phosphatés *	...	...	...	...	...	...	1.0	1.0	1.0	1.0
Potash fertilizers *										
Engrais potassiques *	...	...	...	...	...	1.0	1.0	1.0	2.0	2.0
Côte d'Ivoire Côte d'Ivoire										
Nitrogenous fertilizers *										
Engrais azotés *	...	...	...	...	...	36.0	41.5	60.0	50.0	40.7
Phosphate fertilizers *										
Engrais phosphatés *	...	...	...	...	...	16.0	15.0	25.0	25.0	15.0
Potash fertilizers *										
Engrais potassiques *	...	...	...	...	...	14.0	14.0	25.0	15.0	15.0
Dem. Rep. of the Congo Rép. dém. du Congo										
Nitrogenous fertilizers										
Engrais azotés	...	...	...	...	...	* 3.0	* 2.0	...	1.7	0.3
Phosphate fertilizers										
Engrais phosphatés	...	...	...	...	...	* 3.0	* 2.0	...	0.3	0.3
Potash fertilizers										
Engrais potassiques	...	...	...	...	...	* 3.0	* 2.0	...	1.0	0.2
Egypt Egypte										
Nitrogenous fertilizers										
Engrais azotés	931.0	1 019.4	* 943.8	* 1 111.0	1 191.5	956.8	* 1 002.6	* 915.0	* 1 014.0	1 002.7
Phosphate fertilizers										
Engrais phosphatés	162.9	* 201.6	* 195.3	* 174.0	172.5	* 135.0	* 121.9	* 134.5	* 128.6	* 140.0
Potash fertilizers										
Engrais potassiques	...	...	...	...	...	* 21.4	* 33.0	29.2	28.5	45.0
Eritrea Erythrée										
Nitrogenous fertilizers										
Engrais azotés	...	...	...	...	...	1.4	3.8	* 5.0	* 5.0	5.4
Phosphate fertilizers										
Engrais phosphatés	...	...	...	...	...	* 0.2	* 1.2	* 1.0	* 1.5	5.5
Ethiopia Ethiopie										
Nitrogenous fertilizers										
Engrais azotés	...	...	...	...	...	45.5	81.0	54.2	* 75.1	79.8
Phosphate fertilizers										
Engrais phosphatés	...	...	...	...	...	* 88.8	* 96.5	77.6	89.0	88.1

40

Fertilizers

Nitrogenous, phosphate and potash: thousand metric tons [*cont.*]

Engrais

Azotés, phosphatés et potassiques : milliers de tonnes [*suite*]

Country or area Pays ou zone	Production Production					Consumption Consommation				
	1995/96	1996/97	1997/98	1998/99	1999/00	1995/96	1996/97	1997/98	1998/99	1999/0
Gabon Gabon										
Nitrogenous fertilizers *										
Engrais azotés *	...	...	...	...	...	0.1	0.1	0.1	0.0	0.
Phosphate fertilizers *										
Engrais phosphatés *	...	...	...	...	...	0.1	0.1	0.1	0.2	0.
Potash fertilizers *										
Engrais potassiques *	...	...	...	...	...	0.2	...	...	0.0	0.
Gambia Gambie										
Nitrogenous fertilizers										
Engrais azotés	...	...	...	...	...	0.3	0.2	* 0.3	* 2.3	* 1.
Phosphate fertilizers *										
Engrais phosphatés *	...	...	...	...	...	0.4	0.4	0.5	0.1	0.
Potash fertilizers *										
Engrais potassiques *	...	...	...	...	...	0.2	0.2	0.3	0.1	0.
Ghana Ghana										
Nitrogenous fertilizers										
Engrais azotés	...	...	...	...	...	3.21	* 7.2	8.7	7.3	* 5.
Phosphate fertilizers										
Engrais phosphatés	...	...	...	...	...	2.51	* 3.5	6.0	3.7	* 4.
Potash fertilizers										
Engrais potassiques	...	...	...	...	...	4.01	* 6.7	6.7	4.3	* 2.
Guinea Guinée										
Nitrogenous fertilizers										
Engrais azotés	...	...	...	...	...	2.8	2.4	0.7	1.1	* 1.0
Phosphate fertilizers										
Engrais phosphatés	...	...	...	...	...	1.4	1.0	0.6	1.4	* 1.4
Potash fertilizers										
Engrais potassiques	...	...	...	...	...	0.9	0.8	0.5	0.7	* 0.8
Guinea−Bissau Guinée−Bissau										
Nitrogenous fertilizers *										
Engrais azotés *	...	...	...	...	...	0.1	0.1	0.1	0.2	0.2
Phosphate fertilizers										
Engrais phosphatés	...	...	...	...	...	0.11	* 0.1	* 0.1	* 0.2	* 0.2
Potash fertilizers										
Engrais potassiques	...	...	...	...	...	0.11	* 0.1	* 0.1	* 0.2	* 0.2
Kenya Kenya										
Nitrogenous fertilizers										
Engrais azotés	...	...	...	...	...	33.0	* 63.0	* 51.0	* 53.0	* 59.3
Phosphate fertilizers *										
Engrais phosphatés *	...	...	...	...	...	40.0	75.8	69.4	57.1	83.0
Potash fertilizers *										
Engrais potassiques *	...	...	...	...	...	5.4	22.0	14.0	17.0	10.9
Lesotho Lesotho										
Nitrogenous fertilizers										
Engrais azotés	...	...	...	...	...	1.9	2.1	1.6	* 1.8	1.9
Phosphate fertilizers										
Engrais phosphatés	...	...	...	...	...	2.01	* 2.0	* 2.0	* 2.1	1.9
Potash fertilizers										
Engrais potassiques	...	...	...	...	...	2.01	* 2.0	* 2.0	* 2.1	1.3
Libyan Arab Jamah. Jamah. arabe libyenne										
Nitrogenous fertilizers										
Engrais azotés	* 409.5	* 398.8	* 383.4	408.0	386.9	* 30.0	* 16.6	* 17.5	* 16.1	* 21.1
Phosphate fertilizers *										
Engrais phosphatés *	...	...	...	...	...	55.0	40.4	40.9	27.0	34.7
Potash fertilizers *										
Engrais potassiques *	...	...	...	...	...	4.0	5.4	3.3	3.5	6.7
Madagascar Madagascar										
Nitrogenous fertilizers										
Engrais azotés	...	...	...	...	...	7.7	8.9	3.6	3.6	2.1
Phosphate fertilizers										
Engrais phosphatés	...	...	...	...	...	2.7	4.6	3.0	2.7	1.5
Potash fertilizers										
Engrais potassiques	...	...	...	...	...	2.1	3.1	2.9	2.4	0.9

40
Fertilizers
Nitrogenous, phosphate and potash: thousand metric tons [*cont.*]
Engrais
Azotés, phosphatés et potassiques : milliers de tonnes [*suite*]

Country or area Pays ou zone	Production Production					Consumption Consommation				
	1995/96	1996/97	1997/98	1998/99	1999/00	1995/96	1996/97	1997/98	1998/99	1999/00
Malawi Malawi										
Nitrogenous fertilizers * Engrais azotés *	...	...	...	...	...	28.2	37.9	41.2	34.8	30.0
Phosphate fertilizers Engrais phosphatés	...	...	...	...	...	10.3	* 14.3	* 12.6	* 11.9	* 11.8
Potash fertilizers * Engrais potassiques *	...	...	...	...	...	5.0	6.0	3.0	3.5	3.5
Mali Mali										
Nitrogenous fertilizers * Engrais azotés *	...	...	...	...	...	12.0	12.0	25.6	17.4	7.4
Phosphate fertilizers * Engrais phosphatés *	...	...	...	...	...	8.0	8.7	12.0	15.8	7.9
Potash fertilizers * Engrais potassiques *	...	...	...	...	...	7.0	6.6	10.2	12.7	7.4
Mauritania Mauritanie										
Nitrogenous fertilizers Engrais azotés	...	...	...	...	...	* 4.0	* 5.0	1.5	...	...
Phosphate fertilizers * Engrais phosphatés *	...	...	...	...	...	...	...	0.2	...	...
Mauritius Maurice										
Nitrogenous fertilizers Engrais azotés	15.6	16.2	14.3	* 14.4	* 14.5	12.3	13.1	11.8	* 12.4	* 12.2
Phosphate fertilizers * Engrais phosphatés *	...	...	...	...	...	5.1	8.0	7.0	6.0	5.7
Potash fertilizers Engrais potassiques	...	...	...	...	...	14.3	16.7	14.7	* 14.7	* 15.1
Morocco Maroc										
Nitrogenous fertilizers Engrais azotés	* 269.2	* 257.7	* 261.9	* 271.0	* 273.1	* 144.9	* 124.5	174.1	* 174.2	168.9
Phosphate fertilizers Engrais phosphatés	* 935.8	* 990.0	923.9	* 958.6	* 961.9	* 79.5	* 109.0	* 98.0	* 98.0	102.0
Potash fertilizers Engrais potassiques	...	...	...	...	...	* 57.8	* 56.5	* 55.2	* 51.0	56.9
Mozambique Mozambique										
Nitrogenous fertilizers * Engrais azotés *	...	...	...	...	...	5.0	7.0	1.5	3.8	8.0
Phosphate fertilizers * Engrais phosphatés *	...	...	...	...	...	0.3	0.3	2.6	1.6	...
Potash fertilizers * Engrais potassiques *	...	...	...	...	...	2.5	0.8	2.4	2.6	...
Namibia Namibie										
Nitrogenous fertilizers * Engrais azotés *	...	...	...	...	...	...	...	...	0.1	0.1
Phosphate fertilizers * Engrais phosphatés *	...	...	...	...	...	...	...	...	...	0.2
Niger Niger										
Nitrogenous fertilizers Engrais azotés	...	...	...	...	...	5.2	* 5.5	* 0.5	* 0.5	* 1.1
Phosphate fertilizers Engrais phosphatés	...	...	...	...	...	2.6	* 2.0	...	...	* 1.7
Potash fertilizers Engrais potassiques	...	...	...	...	...	2.2	* 1.5	* 0.2	...	...
Nigeria Nigéria										
Nitrogenous fertilizers Engrais azotés	* 138.0	* 114.3	* 41.2	* 71.0	* 80.5	* 100.0	105.0	* 77.3	* 143.4	* 117.2
Phosphate fertilizers * Engrais phosphatés *	0.9	9.5	5.0	10.5	5.0	50.0	32.5	21.4	39.2	29.9
Potash fertilizers * Engrais potassiques *	...	...	...	...	...	33.0	36.0	39.0	24.8	26.0
Réunion Réunion										
Nitrogenous fertilizers * Engrais azotés *	...	...	...	...	...	3.5	3.5	2.0	2.1	2.1
Phosphate fertilizers * Engrais phosphatés *	...	...	...	...	...	2.0	1.6	2.0	1.5	1.5

40
Fertilizers
Nitrogenous, phosphate and potash: thousand metric tons [*cont.*]
Engrais
Azotés, phosphatés et potassiques : milliers de tonnes [*suite*]

Country or area Pays ou zone	Production Production					Consumption Consommation				
	1995/96	1996/97	1997/98	1998/99	1999/00	1995/96	1996/97	1997/98	1998/99	1999/0
Potash fertilizers * Engrais potassiques *	...	...	...	...	...	0.9	4.0	3.0	2.0	2.
Rwanda Rwanda										
Nitrogenous fertilizers * Engrais azotés *	...	...	...	...	...	...	0.1	0.1	0.1	0.
Phosphate fertilizers * Engrais phosphatés *	...	...	...	...	...	...	0.1	0.2	0.1	0.
Potash fertilizers * Engrais potassiques *	...	...	...	...	...	...	0.1	0.1	0.1	0.
Senegal Sénégal										
Nitrogenous fertilizers * Engrais azotés *	28.7	24.8	30.4	25.0	24.2	5.2	8.0	7.1	8.8	9.
Phosphate fertilizers * Engrais phosphatés *	39.5	35.4	55.0	67.5	48.0	8.0	9.6	10.8	11.0	11.
Potash fertilizers * Engrais potassiques *	...	...	...	...	...	3.0	4.0	5.0	7.0	8.
Sierra Leone Sierra Leone										
Nitrogenous fertilizers * Engrais azotés *	...	...	...	...	...	1.0	1.0	1.0	0.1	..
Phosphate fertilizers * Engrais phosphatés *	...	...	...	...	...	1.0	1.0	1.0	0.1	..
Potash fertilizers * Engrais potassiques *	...	...	...	...	...	1.0	1.0	1.0	0.1	
Somalia Somalie										
Nitrogenous fertilizers * Engrais azotés *	...	...	...	...	...	...	0.5	0.5	0.5	0.5
South Africa Afrique du Sud										
Nitrogenous fertilizers Engrais azotés	* 420.0	452.0	465.0	411.4	443.1	* 386.0	405.0	406.2	415.5	417.5
Phosphate fertilizers Engrais phosphatés	* 373.2	* 397.7	* 378.4	378.8	401.2	* 240.0	255.9	225.0	218.3	227.0
Potash fertilizers Engrais potassiques	...	...	...	...	...	* 141.0	143.0	131.0	136.0	159.0
Sudan Soudan										
Nitrogenous fertilizers * Engrais azotés *	...	...	...	...	...	31.7	76.8	69.0	26.2	70.3
Phosphate fertilizers Engrais phosphatés	...	...	...	...	...	* 20.0	* 18.6	* 8.4	* 11.5	21.3
Swaziland Swaziland										
Nitrogenous fertilizers Engrais azotés	...	...	...	...	...	1.6	1.5	* 1.6	* 2.0	* 1.7
Phosphate fertilizers Engrais phosphatés	...	...	...	...	...	2.5	1.7	* 1.8	* 1.9	* 1.9
Potash fertilizers * Engrais potassiques *	...	...	...	...	...	1.0	1.0	1.8	1.9	1.9
Togo Togo										
Nitrogenous fertilizers Engrais azotés	...	...	...	...	...	5.9	8.1	* 6.0	* 6.6	* 8.5
Phosphate fertilizers Engrais phosphatés	...	...	...	...	...	7.8	4.7	* 5.4	* 5.3	* 4.2
Potash fertilizers Engrais potassiques	...	...	...	...	...	2.8	4.8	* 5.4	* 5.3	* 4.2
Tunisia Tunisie										
Nitrogenous fertilizers Engrais azotés	214.2	223.9	* 190.4	* 225.9	259.9	* 40.0	* 52.0	* 51.5	63.3	* 65.0
Phosphate fertilizers Engrais phosphatés	* 741.7	* 788.0	* 673.3	782.0	880.1	* 35.0	* 41.0	40.0	44.5	* 43.0
Potash fertilizers * Engrais potassiques *	...	...	...	...	...	2.0	4.0	5.0	6.0	4.2
Uganda Ouganda										
Nitrogenous fertilizers Engrais azotés	...	...	...	...	...	* 0.8	* 0.2	* 0.2	1.8	2.1
Phosphate fertilizers Engrais phosphatés	...	...	...	...	...	* 0.2	* 0.2	* 0.2	0.9	1.3

40
Fertilizers
Nitrogenous, phosphate and potash: thousand metric tons [*cont.*]
Engrais
Azotés, phosphatés et potassiques : milliers de tonnes [*suite*]

Country or area	Production Production					Consumption Consommation				
Pays ou zone	1995/96	1996/97	1997/98	1998/99	1999/00	1995/96	1996/97	1997/98	1998/99	1999/00
Potash fertilizers										
Engrais potassiques	...	...	...	...	...	* 0.3	* 0.2	* 0.2	0.8	1.1
United Rep. of Tanzania **Rép.−Unie de Tanzanie**										
Nitrogenous fertilizers										
Engrais azotés	...	...	...	...	...	* 15.0	20.2	* 24.9	19.3	12.5
Phosphate fertilizers										
Engrais phosphatés	...	...	...	...	...	* 7.0	7.0	* 8.3	* 4.9	6.2
Potash fertilizers										
Engrais potassiques	...	...	...	...	...	* 5.0	4.0	6.7	5.6	2.2
Zambia Zambie										
Nitrogenous fertilizers *										
Engrais azotés *	4.0	4.1	4.0	2.3	2.0	34.0	27.5	32.6	13.2	29.7
Phosphate fertilizers *										
Engrais phosphatés *	...	...	...	...	...	13.0	13.9	14.1	13.5	13.5
Potash fertilizers *										
Engrais potassiques *	...	...	...	...	...	8.0	10.0	10.0	10.0	10.0
Zimbabwe Zimbabwe										
Nitrogenous fertilizers										
Engrais azotés	79.9	* 86.0	* 88.4	* 74.1	* 81.0	77.6	94.0	* 94.0	* 95.0	* 100.0
Phosphate fertilizers *										
Engrais phosphatés *	40.0	36.0	33.0	35.5	38.0	38.0	37.0	44.0	42.0	43.0
Potash fertilizers										
Engrais potassiques	...	...	...	...	...	* 31.0	* 37.0	* 37.0	* 38.0	42.0
America, North Amérique du Nord										
Nitrogenous fertilizers										
Engrais azotés	19 939.0	20 966.5	19 111.8	18 748.9	17 958.7	14 312.2	14 636.5	14 685.9	14 857.8	14 718.8
Phosphate fertilizers										
Engrais phosphatés	11 304.0	11 717.0	9 840.5	9 838.1	9 258.6	5 125.4	5 391.7	5 399.1	5 133.1	5 156.3
Potash fertilizers										
Engrais potassiques	8 809.2	8 985.4	10 970.4	9 508.6	9 095.5	5 399.7	5 622.1	5 644.3	5 326.7	5 390.6
Bahamas Bahamas										
Nitrogenous fertilizers *										
Engrais azotés *	...	...	...	...	...	0.1	0.2	0.1	0.1	0.1
Phosphate fertilizers *										
Engrais phosphatés *	...	...	...	...	...	...	0.1	0.1	0.1	0.1
Potash fertilizers										
Engrais potassiques	...	...	...	...	...	* 0.1	* 0.1	0.1	* 0.1	* 0.1
Barbados Barbade										
Nitrogenous fertilizers *										
Engrais azotés *	...	...	...	...	...	2.0	2.0	2.0	1.8	1.8
Phosphate fertilizers *										
Engrais phosphatés *	...	...	...	...	...	* 0.2	* 0.2	* 0.2	0.2	* 0.2
Potash fertilizers *										
Engrais potassiques *	...	...	...	...	...	1.0	1.0	1.0	1.0	1.0
Belize Belize										
Nitrogenous fertilizers *										
Engrais azotés *	...	...	...	...	...	1.3	1.0	1.3	2.1	1.2
Phosphate fertilizers										
Engrais phosphatés	...	...	...	...	...	* 2.7	* 1.3	2.5	* 2.7	* 2.8
Potash fertilizers *										
Engrais potassiques *	...	...	...	...	...	1.0	1.0	1.0	1.0	1.0
Bermuda Bermudes										
Nitrogenous fertilizers *										
Engrais azotés *	...	...	...	...	...	0.1	0.1	0.1	0.1	0.1
Canada Canada										
Nitrogenous fertilizers										
Engrais azotés	4 018.9	* 3 864.2	* 3 654.3	* 3 737.1	* 3 981.2	1 576.2	1 670.6	* 1 652.7	* 1 625.8	* 1 610.0
Phosphate fertilizers *										
Engrais phosphatés *	381.0	383.0	372.6	357.8	273.0	658.4	703.5	717.0	666.6	641.0
Potash fertilizers *										
Engrais potassiques *	7 966.2	8 151.4	9 535.1	8 605.9	8 230.0	333.2	322.2	356.3	356.6	332.0
Costa Rica Costa Rica										
Nitrogenous fertilizers *										
Engrais azotés *	44.0	56.0	41.0	32.0	35.0	70.0	89.0	100.0	104.0	80.1

40
Fertilizers
Nitrogenous, phosphate and potash: thousand metric tons [*cont.*]
Engrais
Azotés, phosphatés et potassiques : milliers de tonnes [*suite*]

Country or area Pays ou zone	Production Production					Consumption Consommation				
	1995/96	1996/97	1997/98	1998/99	1999/00	1995/96	1996/97	1997/98	1998/99	1999/00
Phosphate fertilizers * Engrais phosphatés *	...	...	...	...	...	20.0	28.2	31.0	33.0	20.6
Potash fertilizers Engrais potassiques	...	...	...	...	...	32.0	32.0	60.0	61.0	72.1
Cuba Cuba										
Nitrogenous fertilizers * Engrais azotés *	55.0	60.0	62.0	50.0	50.0	100.0	100.0	133.0	107.0	72.3
Phosphate fertilizers * Engrais phosphatés *	...	...	...	...	...	40.0	32.0	35.0	14.8	18.4
Potash fertilizers * Engrais potassiques *	...	...	...	...	...	104.0	103.0	71.4	47.5	56.0
Dominica Dominique										
Nitrogenous fertilizers Engrais azotés	...	...	...	...	...	1.1	0.9	* 1.0	* 1.0	* 1.0
Phosphate fertilizers Engrais phosphatés	...	...	...	...	...	1.1	0.9	* 1.0	* 1.0	* 1.0
Potash fertilizers Engrais potassiques	...	...	...	...	...	1.1	0.9	* 1.0	* 1.0	* 1.0
Dominican Republic Rép. dominicaine										
Nitrogenous fertilizers Engrais azotés	...	...	...	...	...	* 50.0	* 50.0	* 55.4	* 51.3	53.4
Phosphate fertilizers * Engrais phosphatés *	...	...	...	...	...	21.0	17.9	22.0	20.3	18.3
Potash fertilizers * Engrais potassiques *	...	...	...	...	...	23.0	24.0	31.5	26.2	22.5
El Salvador El Salvador										
Nitrogenous fertilizers Engrais azotés	...	...	...	...	...	41.9	* 60.0	* 72.1	* 58.4	* 62.4
Phosphate fertilizers * Engrais phosphatés *	...	...	...	...	...	21.0	22.0	13.1	16.0	13.1
Potash fertilizers * Engrais potassiques *	...	...	...	...	...	7.0	9.8	9.2	9.8	10.5
Guadeloupe Guadeloupe										
Nitrogenous fertilizers * Engrais azotés *	...	...	...	...	...	1.0	1.5	1.5	6.1	6.8
Phosphate fertilizers Engrais phosphatés	...	...	...	...	...	* 1.0	* 1.0	* 1.0	4.8	* 7.0
Potash fertilizers * Engrais potassiques *	...	...	...	...	...	1.0	1.0	1.0	6.7	5.8
Guatemala Guatemala										
Nitrogenous fertilizers Engrais azotés	...	...	...	...	...	* 115.0	* 110.0	118.6	* 115.0	* 108.2
Phosphate fertilizers * Engrais phosphatés *	...	...	...	...	...	39.0	37.0	76.0	81.0	36.0
Potash fertilizers * Engrais potassiques *	...	...	...	...	...	32.0	36.0	42.0	27.0	36.9
Haiti Haïti										
Nitrogenous fertilizers Engrais azotés	...	...	...	...	...	* 5.4	* 4.0	8.5	6.3	5.0
Phosphate fertilizers Engrais phosphatés	...	...	...	...	...	* 1.0	* 2.0	2.0	2.2	1.7
Potash fertilizers Engrais potassiques	...	...	...	...	...	* 1.0	* 1.0	2.0	2.5	2.0
Honduras Honduras										
Nitrogenous fertilizers * Engrais azotés *	...	...	...	...	...	72.3	49.8	82.9	93.9	109.5
Phosphate fertilizers Engrais phosphatés	...	...	...	...	...	8.31	* 19.2	* 24.2	* 23.0	* 25.3
Potash fertilizers * Engrais potassiques *	...	...	...	...	...	8.3	13.6	36.6	23.0	24.0
Jamaica Jamaïque										
Nitrogenous fertilizers Engrais azotés	...	...	...	...	...	8.1	* 8.1	9.0	8.9	9.2

40
Fertilizers
Nitrogenous, phosphate and potash: thousand metric tons [*cont.*]
Engrais
Azotés, phosphatés et potassiques : milliers de tonnes [*suite*]

Country or area	Production Production					Consumption Consommation				
Pays ou zone	1995/96	1996/97	1997/98	1998/99	1999/00	1995/96	1996/97	1997/98	1998/99	1999/00
Phosphate fertilizers										
Engrais phosphatés	...	...	...	...	...	* 5.0	* 5.3	6.0	5.2	5.0
Potash fertilizers										
Engrais potassiques	...	...	...	...	...	13.4	* 10.4	8.4	9.3	8.8
Martinique Martinique										
Nitrogenous fertilizers *										
Engrais azotés *	...	...	...	...	...	3.0	5.3	3.9	6.4	3.0
Phosphate fertilizers *										
Engrais phosphatés *	...	...	...	...	...	1.0	0.6	1.0	4.4	0.6
Potash fertilizers *										
Engrais potassiques *	...	...	...	...	...	5.8	9.8	4.7	10.3	7.6
Mexico Mexique										
Nitrogenous fertilizers										
Engrais azotés	* 1 314.0	* 1 487.4	* 1 290.9	1 189.8	* 948.0	* 1 049.0	1 207.4	* 1 197.0	* 1 336.0	* 1 300.0
Phosphate fertilizers *										
Engrais phosphatés *	423.0	434.0	462.8	479.4	515.3	182.0	309.0	257.0	295.0	349.0
Potash fertilizers *										
Engrais potassiques *	...	...	...	...	...	55.0	120.0	190.1	173.3	165.9
Nicaragua Nicaragua										
Nitrogenous fertilizers										
Engrais azotés	...	...	...	...	...	* 25.0	25.9	37.1	* 21.3	20.2
Phosphate fertilizers										
Engrais phosphatés	...	...	...	...	...	* 3.0	* 10.6	* 8.9	* 9.0	9.4
Potash fertilizers										
Engrais potassiques	...	...	...	...	...	* 3.0	4.2	6.8	* 7.7	* 6.3
Panama Panama										
Nitrogenous fertilizers										
Engrais azotés	...	...	...	...	...	* 16.7	* 27.4	21.4	21.3	* 15.9
Phosphate fertilizers										
Engrais phosphatés	...	...	...	...	...	* 9.0	* 12.5	9.5	9.2	* 10.2
Potash fertilizers										
Engrais potassiques	...	...	...	...	...	* 2.0	* 4.4	5.5	9.4	* 7.3
Saint Kitts and Nevis Saint−Kitts−et−Nevis										
Nitrogenous fertilizers										
Engrais azotés	...	...	...	...	...	0.6	0.6	* 0.8	* 0.8	* 0.8
Phosphate fertilizers										
Engrais phosphatés	...	...	...	...	...	0.4	0.4	* 0.5	* 0.5	* 0.5
Potash fertilizers										
Engrais potassiques	...	...	...	...	...	0.3	0.3	* 0.4	* 0.4	* 0.4
Saint Lucia Sainte−Lucie										
Nitrogenous fertilizers										
Engrais azotés	...	...	...	...	...	7.01	9.0	9.6	* 2.2	* 2.0
Phosphate fertilizers *										
Engrais phosphatés *	...	...	...	...	...	2.0	2.0	2.0	...	2.5
Potash fertilizers *										
Engrais potassiques *	...	...	...	...	...	2.0	2.0	2.0	...	0.8
St. Vincent−Grenadines St. Vincent−Grenadines										
Nitrogenous fertilizers *										
Engrais azotés *	...	...	...	...	...	1.0	1.0	1.0	1.3	1.3
Phosphate fertilizers *										
Engrais phosphatés *	...	...	...	...	...	1.0	1.0	1.0	1.3	1.3
Potash fertilizers *										
Engrais potassiques *	...	...	...	...	...	1.0	1.0	1.0	1.3	1.3
Trinidad and Tobago Trinité−et−Tobago										
Nitrogenous fertilizers *										
Engrais azotés *	263.1	272.9	277.5	240.7	276.0	3.0	6.0	6.0	5.0	5.0
Phosphate fertilizers *										
Engrais phosphatés *	...	...	...	...	...	1.0	1.0	1.0	0.4	0.3
Potash fertilizers										
Engrais potassiques	...	...	...	...	...	* 3.0	3.4	* 3.6	* 1.4	* 0.6
United States Etats−Unis										
Nitrogenous fertilizers										
Engrais azotés	14 244.0	15 226.0	13 786.1	13 499.2	12 668.5	11 161.4	11 205.6	11 169.7	11 281.5	* 11 249.2

40
Fertilizers
Nitrogenous, phosphate and potash: thousand metric tons [*cont.*]
Engrais
Azotés, phosphatés et potassiques : milliers de tonnes [*suite*]

Country or area	Production Production					Consumption Consommation				
Pays ou zone	1995/96	1996/97	1997/98	1998/99	1999/00	1995/96	1996/97	1997/98	1998/99	1999/0
Phosphate fertilizers										
Engrais phosphatés	10 500.0	10 900.0	9 005.2	9 000.9	8 470.3	4 107.1	4 183.7	4 186.8	3 942.1	* 3 991.
Potash fertilizers										
Engrais potassiques	843.0	834.0	1 435.3	902.7	865.5	4 769.5	4 921.0	4 808.7	4 550.3	* 4 626.
United States Virgin Is.	**Iles Vierges américaines**									
Nitrogenous fertilizers *										
Engrais azotés *	...	...	...	...	...	1.0	1.0	1.0	0.3	0.
Phosphate fertilizers *										
Engrais phosphatés *	...	...	...	...	...	0.3	0.3	0.3	0.3	0.
America, South Amérique du Sud										
Nitrogenous fertilizers										
Engrais azotés	1 529.5	1 565.8	1 575.9	1 364.2	1 457.6	2 319.3	2 675.2	2 896.9	2 915.1	3 113.9
Phosphate fertilizers										
Engrais phosphatés	1 358.0	1 400.3	1 418.7	1 463.4	1 446.7	1 858.0	2 503.9	2 839.9	2 871.2	2 782.2
Potash fertilizers										
Engrais potassiques	276.1	419.5	516.4	636.5	709.8	2 113.2	2 430.0	2 805.1	2 715.1	2 716.0
Argentina Argentine										
Nitrogenous fertilizers										
Engrais azotés	58.3	* 80.7	* 97.1	* 68.1	64.0	* 318.8	* 510.3	* 476.4	* 425.7	457.3
Phosphate fertilizers										
Engrais phosphatés	...	...	...	...	...	* 182.5	* 306.9	* 302.6	* 320.7	340.1
Potash fertilizers										
Engrais potassiques	...	...	...	...	...	* 23.4	* 38.0	* 30.6	32.1	* 26.0
Bolivia Bolivie										
Nitrogenous fertilizers										
Engrais azotés	...	...	...	...	...	2.8	4.0	4.9	1.3	0.9
Phosphate fertilizers										
Engrais phosphatés	...	...	...	...	...	3.6	4.3	7.1	2.9	0.7
Potash fertilizers										
Engrais potassiques	...	...	...	...	...	0.3	0.8	0.6	0.8	0.4
Brazil Brésil										
Nitrogenous fertilizers										
Engrais azotés	795.6	779.0	808.4	728.0	847.6	1 140.1	1 250.9	1 438.1	1 545.5	1 671.6
Phosphate fertilizers										
Engrais phosphatés	1 264.7	1 305.1	1 354.1	1 369.0	1 357.8	1 275.2	1 704.8	2 004.4	2 022.4	1 936.0
Potash fertilizers										
Engrais potassiques	224.1	240.7	281.4	326.5	347.8	1 790.6	2 064.3	2 397.4	2 283.2	2 248.5
Chile Chili										
Nitrogenous fertilizers *										
Engrais azotés *	111.0	111.0	115.0	94.3	95.4	215.0	225.0	220.0	215.5	235.3
Phosphate fertilizers *										
Engrais phosphatés *	5.0	4.0	...	...	...	140.0	145.0	160.0	173.0	164.7
Potash fertilizers *										
Engrais potassiques *	52.0	178.8	235.0	310.0	362.0	50.0	53.0	55.0	81.6	74.5
Colombia Colombie										
Nitrogenous fertilizers *										
Engrais azotés *	92.7	109.0	92.3	69.3	67.0	241.4	236.0	265.2	296.8	299.8
Phosphate fertilizers *										
Engrais phosphatés *	9.3	10.0	9.2	9.3	9.3	108.0	113.0	123.1	127.0	111.3
Potash fertilizers *										
Engrais potassiques *	...	...	...	...	...	136.8	136.0	168.4	172.1	187.0
Ecuador Equateur										
Nitrogenous fertilizers										
Engrais azotés	...	...	...	...	...	* 56.0	* 65.0	* 90.6	87.0	* 52.0
Phosphate fertilizers										
Engrais phosphatés	...	...	...	...	...	* 21.0	23.0	* 32.1	* 29.5	42.0
Potash fertilizers *										
Engrais potassiques *	...	...	...	...	...	24.0	30.0	39.9	44.1	66.4
French Guiana Guyane française										
Nitrogenous fertilizers *										
Engrais azotés *	...	...	...	...	...	1.0	1.0	1.0	0.4	0.4
Phosphate fertilizers *										
Engrais phosphatés *	...	...	...	...	...	0.3	0.3	0.3	0.4	0.4

40
Fertilizers
Nitrogenous, phosphate and potash: thousand metric tons [*cont.*]
Engrais
Azotés, phosphatés et potassiques : milliers de tonnes [*suite*]

Country or area	Production Production					Consumption Consommation				
Pays ou zone	1995/96	1996/97	1997/98	1998/99	1999/00	1995/96	1996/97	1997/98	1998/99	1999/00
Potash fertilizers *										
Engrais potassiques *	...	...	...	...	...	0.1	0.1	0.1	0.4	0.4
Guyana Guyana										
Nitrogenous fertilizers										
Engrais azotés	...	...	...	...	...	* 12.0	* 10.9	14.0	* 13.8	* 10.0
Phosphate fertilizers *										
Engrais phosphatés *	...	...	...	...	...	1.0	1.4	0.7	0.9	3.6
Potash fertilizers *										
Engrais potassiques *	...	...	...	...	...	2.0	1.0	1.0	0.2	0.6
Paraguay Paraguay										
Nitrogenous fertilizers *										
Engrais azotés *	...	...	...	...	...	10.0	14.0	15.0	20.5	18.5
Phosphate fertilizers *										
Engrais phosphatés *	...	...	...	...	...	5.0	5.0	22.0	29.4	25.9
Potash fertilizers *										
Engrais potassiques *	...	...	...	...	...	8.0	14.0	22.0	22.0	21.0
Peru Pérou										
Nitrogenous fertilizers										
Engrais azotés	* 15.9	* 12.6	* 11.5	* 3.0	...	* 129.2	* 133.1	* 149.7	121.8	171.1
Phosphate fertilizers										
Engrais phosphatés	* 1.0	* 2.4	* 2.5	* 3.0	3.5	* 14.3	* 33.6	* 45.8	* 47.4	43.7
Potash fertilizers										
Engrais potassiques	...	...	...	...	...	* 9.8	* 18.6	* 26.7	* 24.8	33.2
Suriname Suriname										
Nitrogenous fertilizers										
Engrais azotés	...	...	...	...	...	* 4.0	* 7.0	* 6.8	* 5.7	6.3
Phosphate fertilizers *										
Engrais phosphatés *	...	...	...	...	...	0.1	0.1	0.1	0.8	...
Potash fertilizers *										
Engrais potassiques *	...	...	...	...	...	0.2	0.2	0.2	1.1	0.5
Uruguay Uruguay										
Nitrogenous fertilizers										
Engrais azotés	...	...	...	...	...	* 21.0	* 47.0	* 47.0	52.5	49.8
Phosphate fertilizers										
Engrais phosphatés	* 5.0	* 9.3	* 9.3	* 9.3	* 9.5	* 40.0	* 102.5	* 80.4	* 65.5	69.6
Potash fertilizers										
Engrais potassiques	...	...	...	...	...	* 5.0	* 4.0	* 1.8	* 11.0	15.8
Venezuela Venezuela										
Nitrogenous fertilizers *										
Engrais azotés *	456.0	473.5	451.6	401.5	383.6	168.0	171.0	168.3	128.6	140.9
Phosphate fertilizers *										
Engrais phosphatés *	73.0	69.5	43.6	72.8	66.6	67.0	64.0	61.3	51.4	44.2
Potash fertilizers *										
Engrais potassiques *	...	...	...	...	...	63.0	70.0	61.4	41.7	41.7
Asia Asie										
Nitrogenous fertilizers										
Engrais azotés	40 494.0	42 832.3	43 490.1	45 442.2	47 760.1	45 082.2	47 655.6	46 542.3	47 480.3	49 932.9
Phosphate fertilizers										
Engrais phosphatés	11 984.8	11 853.8	12 691.6	13 032.1	13 045.1	16 492.2	15 761.8	17 809.4	18 159.1	18 406.3
Potash fertilizers										
Engrais potassiques	2 648.2	2 801.6	2 669.3	2 782.9	3 018.1	6 561.8	6 224.6	7 440.0	7 858.6	8 364.1
Afghanistan Afghanistan										
Nitrogenous fertilizers *										
Engrais azotés *	10.0	5.0	5.0	5.0	5.0	...	5.0	5.0	6.0	5.0
Phosphate fertilizers *										
Engrais phosphatés *	...	...	...	...	...	...	...	...	1.0	...
Armenia Arménie										
Nitrogenous fertilizers										
Engrais azotés	...	...	...	...	...	* 7.0	* 8.0	* 8.0	9.6	6.2
Azerbaijan Azerbaïdjan										
Nitrogenous fertilizers *										
Engrais azotés *	...	...	...	...	...	34.0	16.6	20.0	13.0	14.0
Phosphate fertilizers *										
Engrais phosphatés *	...	...	...	...	...	...	...	2.7	2.8	...

40
Fertilizers
Nitrogenous, phosphate and potash: thousand metric tons [*cont.*]
Engrais
Azotés, phosphatés et potassiques : milliers de tonnes [*suite*]

Country or area	Production Production					Consumption Consommation				
Pays ou zone	1995/96	1996/97	1997/98	1998/99	1999/00	1995/96	1996/97	1997/98	1998/99	1999/
Potash fertilizers										
Engrais potassiques	* 8.0	* 3.0	* 5.0	...	...	* 5.0	...	1.0	...	
Bahrain Bahreïn										
Nitrogenous fertilizers										
Engrais azotés	...	...	...	214.3	227.6	* 0.2	* 0.2	* 0.2	0.7	0
Phosphate fertilizers										
Engrais phosphatés	...	...	...	0.3	...	* 0.2	* 0.2	* 0.2	* 0.3	* 0
Potash fertilizers										
Engrais potassiques	...	...	...	...	...	* 0.2	* 0.2	* 0.2	0.2	* 0
Bangladesh Bangladesh										
Nitrogenous fertilizers										
Engrais azotés	981.6	* 965.7	868.2	* 1 010.1	* 1 027.5	943.0	* 996.1	876.6	* 882.5	* 1 006
Phosphate fertilizers										
Engrais phosphatés	* 60.0	49.4	38.9	* 41.1	52.8	* 158.0	117.5	116.8	* 161.4	* 162
Potash fertilizers										
Engrais potassiques	...	...	...	...	...	* 94.0	* 117.0	115.8	* 126.6	* 132
Bhutan Bhoutan										
Nitrogenous fertilizers *										
Engrais azotés *	...	...	...	...	...	0.1	0.1	0.1	...	
Cambodia Cambodge										
Nitrogenous fertilizers										
Engrais azotés	...	...	...	...	...	* 6.0	* 4.3	* 18.9	0.0	* 3.
Phosphate fertilizers *										
Engrais phosphatés *	...	...	...	...	...	3.0	2.7	3.0	0.0	4.
Potash fertilizers										
Engrais potassiques	...	...	...	...	...	* 0.8	* 0.8	...	0.0	
China Chine										
Nitrogenous fertilizers										
Engrais azotés	* 19 035.1	* 21 042.8	* 20 232.1	* 21 530.0	23 448.6	* 23 781.5	* 25 275.0	* 22 949.7	* 22 887.0	* 24 391.
Phosphate fertilizers										
Engrais phosphatés	* 6 091.3	* 5 822.0	* 6 419.0	* 6 713.0	6 430.0	* 8 911.7	* 8 118.0	* 9 277.0	* 9 457.0	* 8 893.
Potash fertilizers										
Engrais potassiques	* 223.0	* 218.0	* 170.0	* 183.0	* 218.0	2 887.0	2 591.0	3 420.0	3 744.0	* 3 391.
Cyprus Chypre										
Nitrogenous fertilizers										
Engrais azotés	...	...	...	...	...	12.9	13.8	10.8	10.8	10.
Phosphate fertilizers										
Engrais phosphatés	...	...	...	...	...	10.2	9.5	7.8	7.5	7.
Potash fertilizers										
Engrais potassiques	...	...	...	...	...	2.4	2.2	1.8	2.0	1.
Georgia Géorgie										
Nitrogenous fertilizers *										
Engrais azotés *	42.5	53.7	76.3	55.3	93.9	26.0	27.2	31.5	30.0	40.
Phosphate fertilizers *										
Engrais phosphatés *	...	...	...	...	...	5.0	5.0	5.0	4.0	..
India Inde										
Nitrogenous fertilizers										
Engrais azotés	8 728.1	8 593.3	10 083.1	10 477.3	* 10 757.1	9 822.9	10 315.9	10 901.9	11 353.8	11 886.
Phosphate fertilizers										
Engrais phosphatés	2 614.7	2 603.6	3 079.5	* 3 186.9	3 173.4	2 897.5	2 978.5	* 3 913.6	* 4 112.2	4 753.
Potash fertilizers										
Engrais potassiques	...	...	...	...	...	1 155.8	1 043.1	1 372.5	* 1 331.5	1 733.
Indonesia Indonésie										
Nitrogenous fertilizers										
Engrais azotés	* 2 822.0	* 2 986.4	* 2 992.6	* 2 899.1	* 2 840.6	* 1 844.0	* 2 084.0	* 1 706.6	* 2 120.9	1 959.3
Phosphate fertilizers *										
Engrais phosphatés *	325.2	355.0	237.6	237.6	307.5	385.2	331.9	280.0	361.8	300.0
Potash fertilizers *										
Engrais potassiques *	...	...	...	...	...	300.0	300.0	241.0	245.0	400.0
Iran (Islamic Rep. of) Iran (Rép. islamique d')										
Nitrogenous fertilizers										
Engrais azotés	* 500.1	* 688.8	* 727.8	579.4	661.1	* 633.0	685.1	829.7	609.0	687.8
Phosphate fertilizers										
Engrais phosphatés	* 82.5	* 136.1	* 93.3	104.7	101.0	* 379.0	* 374.1	340.0	262.1	284.9

40
Fertilizers
Nitrogenous, phosphate and potash: thousand metric tons [*cont.*]
Engrais
Azotés, phosphatés et potassiques : milliers de tonnes [*suite*]

Country or area	Production Production					Consumption Consommation				
Pays ou zone	1995/96	1996/97	1997/98	1998/99	1999/00	1995/96	1996/97	1997/98	1998/99	1999/00
Potash fertilizers										
Engrais potassiques	...	...	...	...	...	* 5.2	* 20.0	37.1	68.3	155.1
Iraq Iraq										
Nitrogenous fertilizers *										
Engrais azotés *	218.0	235.0	235.0	235.0	255.0	225.0	240.5	242.7	251.2	271.7
Phosphate fertilizers *										
Engrais phosphatés *	90.0	90.0	90.0	90.0	90.0	108.4	103.9	111.6	132.1	134.1
Potash fertilizers										
Engrais potassiques	...	...	...	...	...	* 0.5	* 10.0	* 2.5	...	0.7
Israel Israël										
Nitrogenous fertilizers *										
Engrais azotés *	75.0	76.0	88.0	87.0	82.2	50.0	65.0	61.0	61.0	64.8
Phosphate fertilizers										
Engrais phosphatés	* 216.0	* 222.0	* 244.0	* 250.0	* 285.0	* 22.0	* 19.0	* 23.0	23.0	* 23.0
Potash fertilizers										
Engrais potassiques	* 1 326.0	* 1 500.0	* 1 488.0	* 1 668.0	* 1 702.0	* 32.0	* 35.0	* 36.0	37.0	* 37.0
Japan Japon										
Nitrogenous fertilizers										
Engrais azotés	872.5	883.4	829.7	799.4	802.4	527.5	511.7	494.0	476.0	479.5
Phosphate fertilizers										
Engrais phosphatés	307.0	278.0	263.0	248.9	233.4	631.4	610.1	592.5	561.3	568.6
Potash fertilizers										
Engrais potassiques	* 23.2	* 21.4	* 19.6	* 15.7	* 18.0	* 482.2	* 441.2	* 422.0	381.3	388.8
Jordan Jordanie										
Nitrogenous fertilizers										
Engrais azotés	* 131.2	120.8	127.9	* 149.6	* 135.5	* 6.0	5.1	10.9	14.8	13.0
Phosphate fertilizers										
Engrais phosphatés	* 335.5	308.7	279.4	338.7	* 326.9	* 8.0	11.2	9.1	4.6	* 5.0
Potash fertilizers										
Engrais potassiques	* 1 068.0	* 1 059.2	986.7	916.2	1 080.1	* 2.0	* 3.0	* 4.0	* 4.0	* 5.0
Kazakhstan Kazakhstan										
Nitrogenous fertilizers *										
Engrais azotés *	74.0	78.7	17.0	5.0	7.7	64.0	67.1	15.1	14.3	28.2
Phosphate fertilizers *										
Engrais phosphatés *	129.0	125.0	74.0	9.2	27.2	25.0	57.9	35.0	0.2	2.1
Potash fertilizers *										
Engrais potassiques *	...	...	...	...	...	6.0	6.0	6.0	6.0	2.1
Korea, Dem. P. R. Corée, R. p. dém. de										
Nitrogenous fertilizers										
Engrais azotés	* 75.0	* 72.0	* 72.0	* 72.0	* 72.0	* 84.0	* 72.4	* 149.3	* 128.3	130.0
Phosphate fertilizers *										
Engrais phosphatés *	20.0	20.0	20.0	10.0	10.0	20.0	20.0	21.0	26.0	39.0
Potash fertilizers *										
Engrais potassiques *	...	...	...	...	...	0.2	0.6	0.8	2.9	29.0
Korea, Republic of Corée, République de										
Nitrogenous fertilizers										
Engrais azotés	617.0	663.0	* 659.0	* 584.0	* 584.2	* 478.0	455.9	* 507.0	* 451.0	* 451.0
Phosphate fertilizers										
Engrais phosphatés	* 421.0	* 409.0	* 438.0	* 421.0	* 425.0	* 227.0	208.5	* 223.0	* 188.0	* 188.0
Potash fertilizers *										
Engrais potassiques *	...	...	...	...	...	274.0	244.0	262.0	228.0	233.0
Kuwait Koweït										
Nitrogenous fertilizers										
Engrais azotés	* 390.8	* 356.3	* 348.5	361.3	330.7	* 1.0	* 2.0	* 1.2	* 1.0	1.1
Kyrgyzstan Kirghizistan										
Nitrogenous fertilizers *										
Engrais azotés *	...	...	...	...	...	22.0	25.0	25.0	27.2	28.3
Phosphate fertilizers										
Engrais phosphatés	...	...	...	...	...	* 1.0	* 1.0	* 1.0	1.1	1.2
Potash fertilizers										
Engrais potassiques	...	...	...	...	...	* 5.0	* 5.0	* 5.0	0.2	0.0
Lao People's Dem. Rep. Rép. dém. pop. lao										
Nitrogenous fertilizers										
Engrais azotés	...	...	...	...	...	2.1	* 2.0	* 5.0	2.9	4.5

40
Fertilizers
Nitrogenous, phosphate and potash: thousand metric tons [*cont.*]
Engrais
Azotés, phosphatés et potassiques : milliers de tonnes [*suite*]

Country or area	Production Production					Consumption Consommation				
Pays ou zone	1995/96	1996/97	1997/98	1998/99	1999/00	1995/96	1996/97	1997/98	1998/99	1999/
Phosphate fertilizers										
Engrais phosphatés	...	...	...	...	...	3.9	* 1.3	* 2.6	1.5	3
Potash fertilizers										
Engrais potassiques	...	...	...	...	...	0.1	* 0.5	* 0.2	* 0.3	* 0
Lebanon Liban										
Nitrogenous fertilizers										
Engrais azotés	...	...	...	...	...	25.0	* 22.0	21.9	* 23.4	* 21
Phosphate fertilizers *										
Engrais phosphatés *	81.0	95.0	115.0	86.0	75.0	15.0	30.0	32.0	32.0	32
Potash fertilizers										
Engrais potassiques	...	...	...	...	...	4.0	* 4.0	* 5.0	* 5.0	* 9
Malaysia Malaisie										
Nitrogenous fertilizers										
Engrais azotés	* 290.0	* 290.0	* 231.7	* 316.6	* 385.3	* 286.0	* 255.0	344.0	* 460.5	* 463
Phosphate fertilizers *										
Engrais phosphatés *	...	...	...	...	...	206.0	230.0	238.0	233.0	264
Potash fertilizers *										
Engrais potassiques *	...	...	...	...	...	600.0	646.0	670.0	756.0	793
Mongolia Mongolie										
Nitrogenous fertilizers										
Engrais azotés	...	...	...	...	...	* 2.0	* 2.0	5.0	* 4.2	* 2.
Phosphate fertilizers										
Engrais phosphatés	...	...	...	...	...	...	...	1.0	...	
Myanmar Myanmar										
Nitrogenous fertilizers										
Engrais azotés	65.5	73.6	56.1	51.6	63.8	115.2	130.9	135.5	* 123.0	* 125.
Phosphate fertilizers										
Engrais phosphatés	...	...	...	...	...	* 57.2	* 33.0	35.2	34.5	* 29.
Potash fertilizers *										
Engrais potassiques *	...	...	...	...	...	7.6	10.0	7.2	2.3	2.
Nepal Népal										
Nitrogenous fertilizers *										
Engrais azotés *	...	...	...	...	...	70.0	75.0	77.4	64.0	66.8
Phosphate fertilizers										
Engrais phosphatés	...	...	...	...	...	21.3	* 25.0	* 28.5	* 20.0	* 20.
Potash fertilizers										
Engrais potassiques	...	...	...	...	...	2.4	* 3.0	* 1.6	* 1.8	* 1.
Oman Oman										
Nitrogenous fertilizers										
Engrais azotés	...	...	...	...	...	* 6.0	4.9	3.5	6.7	5.
Phosphate fertilizers										
Engrais phosphatés	...	...	...	...	...	* 0.9	* 0.9	1.0	0.7	0.8
Potash fertilizers										
Engrais potassiques	...	...	...	...	...	* 0.9	* 0.9	1.0	0.7	* 0.8
Pakistan Pakistan										
Nitrogenous fertilizers										
Engrais azotés	1 690.0	1 681.5	1 660.5	1 795.2	2 041.4	1 991.0	1 985.1	2 087.6	2 091.9	2 210.8
Phosphate fertilizers										
Engrais phosphatés	96.1	80.6	67.5	90.8	223.5	494.4	419.5	551.3	465.0	595.8
Potash fertilizers										
Engrais potassiques	...	...	...	...	...	29.7	8.4	20.4	21.2	17.7
Philippines Philippines										
Nitrogenous fertilizers										
Engrais azotés	215.3	255.7	213.0	164.6	162.7	397.3	* 482.5	* 548.1	408.9	480.6
Phosphate fertilizers										
Engrais phosphatés	* 264.4	* 273.4	217.1	192.7	180.8	* 129.7	* 145.8	* 148.7	118.5	140.1
Potash fertilizers										
Engrais potassiques	...	...	...	...	...	* 71.4	* 108.5	112.3	98.5	120.9
Qatar Qatar										
Nitrogenous fertilizers										
Engrais azotés	407.6	400.3	* 672.3	* 767.0	757.2	* 6.0	1.2	1.2	* 1.0	* 1.0
Saudi Arabia Arabie saoudite										
Nitrogenous fertilizers *										
Engrais azotés *	1 027.0	1 063.7	981.1	1 079.8	1 063.6	153.0	171.0	181.0	200.0	207.1

40
Fertilizers
Nitrogenous, phosphate and potash: thousand metric tons [*cont.*]
Engrais
Azotés, phosphatés et potassiques : milliers de tonnes [*suite*]

Country or area	Production					Consumption				
Pays ou zone	1995/96	1996/97	1997/98	1998/99	1999/00	1995/96	1996/97	1997/98	1998/99	1999/00
Phosphate fertilizers *										
Engrais phosphatés *	122.8	129.7	119.8	136.9	150.0	121.0	138.0	131.0	121.0	127.0
Potash fertilizers *										
Engrais potassiques *	...	...	...	...	...	10.0	8.0	9.0	9.0	19.9
Singapore Singapour										
Nitrogenous fertilizers										
Engrais azotés	...	...	...	...	...	3.4	2.8	1.9	2.5	2.3
Phosphate fertilizers										
Engrais phosphatés	...	...	...	...	...	0.1	0.2	0.1	* 0.9	* 0.7
Potash fertilizers *										
Engrais potassiques *	...	...	...	...	...	1.0	0.2	0.1	0.7	0.7
Sri Lanka Sri Lanka										
Nitrogenous fertilizers										
Engrais azotés	...	...	...	...	...	115.9	117.6	122.5	142.2	163.8
Phosphate fertilizers										
Engrais phosphatés	9.0	9.5	8.3	10.2	8.5	34.4	35.0	30.1	29.1	33.7
Potash fertilizers										
Engrais potassiques	...	...	...	...	...	55.7	58.6	56.1	61.6	61.6
Syrian Arab Republic Rép. arabe syrienne										
Nitrogenous fertilizers										
Engrais azotés	* 48.7	* 71.3	* 68.7	120.0	105.0	236.3	227.4	236.8	218.4	251.2
Phosphate fertilizers										
Engrais phosphatés	* 28.0	91.7	* 84.2	* 96.6	66.1	* 99.0	124.0	124.6	103.3	111.9
Potash fertilizers										
Engrais potassiques	...	...	...	...	...	6.5	5.8	7.0	7.4	8.3
Tajikistan Tadjikistan										
Nitrogenous fertilizers										
Engrais azotés	* 14.0	* 4.1	* 4.0	* 4.0	* 4.0	* 40.0	* 32.1	41.2	28.3	* 30.0
Phosphate fertilizers *										
Engrais phosphatés *	...	...	...	...	...	25.0	25.0	25.0	7.7	10.0
Potash fertilizers *										
Engrais potassiques *	...	...	...	...	...	5.0	5.0	5.0	0.1	...
Thailand Thaïlande										
Nitrogenous fertilizers										
Engrais azotés	...	...	* 56.0	* 79.0	* 70.4	728.0	* 811.0	* 784.0	* 905.0	* 1 070.9
Phosphate fertilizers										
Engrais phosphatés	...	...	43.0	85.0	110.0	* 453.0	* 436.0	* 423.0	* 455.0	* 454.7
Potash fertilizers										
Engrais potassiques	...	...	...	...	...	326.0	* 273.0	* 274.0	* 277.0	* 276.1
Turkey Turquie										
Nitrogenous fertilizers										
Engrais azotés	938.8	923.5	* 921.6	* 922.1	* 730.8	1 053.7	1 147.7	* 1 167.0	* 1 392.0	* 1 484.0
Phosphate fertilizers										
Engrais phosphatés	392.1	* 424.9	* 501.8	* 392.0	* 438.0	579.6	578.0	* 592.4	* 700.2	* 637.9
Potash fertilizers										
Engrais potassiques	...	...	...	...	...	67.1	* 73.5	* 66.3	* 88.5	* 80.6
Turkmenistan Turkménistan										
Nitrogenous fertilizers *										
Engrais azotés *	105.0	110.0	100.0	58.0	51.0	105.0	110.0	153.0	58.0	63.2
Phosphate fertilizers										
Engrais phosphatés	* 2.0	...	...	5.0	5.0	* 16.0	* 20.0	* 20.0	* 5.0	* 5.0
Potash fertilizers *										
Engrais potassiques *	...	...	...	...	...	10.0	12.0	14.0	...	...
United Arab Emirates Emirats arabes unis										
Nitrogenous fertilizers										
Engrais azotés	* 293.6	* 258.4	* 299.6	* 258.9	271.9	* 25.0	* 24.5	* 24.2	* 23.6	* 25.1
Phosphate fertilizers *										
Engrais phosphatés *	...	...	...	...	...	4.0	3.3	3.7	5.0	5.0
Potash fertilizers *										
Engrais potassiques *	...	...	...	...	...	3.0	3.0	3.0	5.7	6.1
Uzbekistan Ouzbékistan										
Nitrogenous fertilizers *										
Engrais azotés *	775.5	825.3	809.3	731.8	699.8	300.0	220.0	678.0	643.0	622.0

40

Fertilizers
Nitrogenous, phosphate and potash: thousand metric tons [*cont.*]
Engrais
Azotés, phosphatés et potassiques : milliers de tonnes [*suite*]

Country or area Pays ou zone	Production Production					Consumption Consommation				
	1995/96	1996/97	1997/98	1998/99	1999/00	1995/96	1996/97	1997/98	1998/99	1999/00
Phosphate fertilizers *										
Engrais phosphatés *	168.2	194.3	122.1	141.4	147.0	124.0	150.0	122.1	141.4	135.0
Potash fertilizers *										
Engrais potassiques *	...	...	...	...	...	50.0	75.0	75.0	75.0	75.0
Viet Nam Viet Nam										
Nitrogenous fertilizers *										
Engrais azotés *	50.0	54.0	54.0	29.9	22.3	843.0	947.0	1 039.0	1 300.0	1 121.3
Phosphate fertilizers *										
Engrais phosphatés *	129.0	136.0	136.0	144.0	179.0	313.0	398.0	337.0	378.0	433.3
Potash fertilizers										
Engrais potassiques	...	...	...	...	...	* 58.0	* 110.0	* 185.0	* 270.0	380.0
Yemen Yémen										
Nitrogenous fertilizers *										
Engrais azotés *	...	...	...	...	...	10.1	8.1	19.3	32.7	31.6
Phosphate fertilizers *										
Engrais phosphatés *	...	...	...	...	...	2.0	...	...	0.8	0.3
Potash fertilizers *										
Engrais potassiques *	...	...	...	...	...	1.0	...	...	0.9	0.3
Europe Europe										
Nitrogenous fertilizers										
Engrais azotés	21 514.3	22 060.2	20 642.1	19 880.3	20 449.1	13 753.8	14 286.2	14 116.8	13 839.3	14 061.1
Phosphate fertilizers										
Engrais phosphatés	5 845.2	5 569.7	5 942.3	5 642.0	5 795.4	4 892.7	5 112.8	4 876.0	4 697.3	4 447.0
Potash fertilizers										
Engrais potassiques	10 970.1	10 756.8	12 000.5	12 048.7	12 601.1	5 754.7	5 788.7	5 866.3	5 632.6	5 312.8
Albania Albanie										
Nitrogenous fertilizers *										
Engrais azotés *	...	...	...	...	...	10.0	5.5	4.2	18.1	6.0
Phosphate fertilizers *										
Engrais phosphatés *	1.0	3.0	3.0	2.0	2.0	1.0	1.0	1.0	5.0	5.0
Potash fertilizers										
Engrais potassiques	...	...	...	...	...	...	...	...	0.1	0.1
Austria Autriche										
Nitrogenous fertilizers										
Engrais azotés	* 222.0	* 240.0	* 227.0	* 248.0	* 273.0	* 125.0	* 133.0	* 128.0	* 128.0	128.0
Phosphate fertilizers										
Engrais phosphatés	* 44.0	* 72.0	* 64.0	* 70.0	* 65.0	52.0	* 60.0	* 57.0	57.0	55.0
Potash fertilizers										
Engrais potassiques	...	...	...	...	...	* 60.0	72.0	* 69.0	61.6	60.0
Belarus Bélarus										
Nitrogenous fertilizers *										
Engrais azotés *	429.0	449.6	378.9	442.5	483.6	230.0	260.0	282.3	280.0	280.0
Phosphate fertilizers *										
Engrais phosphatés *	46.1	91.5	128.2	127.0	130.0	43.0	95.0	100.0	100.0	100.0
Potash fertilizers *										
Engrais potassiques *	2 789.0	2 716.0	3 247.0	3 451.0	3 613.0	250.0	422.0	475.0	535.0	475.0
Belgium–Luxembourg	**Belgique–Luxembourg**									
Nitrogenous fertilizers *										
Engrais azotés *	699.0	660.0	838.0	838.0	877.0	167.0	172.0	171.0	171.0	166.0
Phosphate fertilizers *										
Engrais phosphatés *	140.0	108.0	130.0	128.0	132.0	51.0	46.0	44.0	47.0	45.0
Potash fertilizers *										
Engrais potassiques *	...	...	...	...	...	91.0	96.0	92.0	91.0	88.0
Bosnia and Herzegovina	**Bosnie–Herzégovine**									
Nitrogenous fertilizers *										
Engrais azotés *	...	...	...	...	...	5.0	3.0	3.0	23.0	28.0
Phosphate fertilizers										
Engrais phosphatés	...	...	...	...	...	5.0	* 3.0	* 3.0	* 12.0	* 7.0
Potash fertilizers *										
Engrais potassiques *	...	...	...	...	...	5.0	3.0	3.0	12.0	7.0
Bulgaria Bulgarie										
Nitrogenous fertilizers										
Engrais azotés	833.0	835.2	* 694.9	* 362.9	269.8	* 112.0	* 152.0	* 157.8	* 135.0	110.6

40
Fertilizers
Nitrogenous, phosphate and potash: thousand metric tons [*cont.*]
Engrais
Azotés, phosphatés et potassiques : milliers de tonnes [*suite*]

Country or area	Production Production					Consumption Consommation				
Pays ou zone	1995/96	1996/97	1997/98	1998/99	1999/00	1995/96	1996/97	1997/98	1998/99	1999/00
Phosphate fertilizers										
Engrais phosphatés	53.1	* 80.0	109.8	* 83.1	44.3	11.1	13.0	11.0	* 9.0	6.0
Potash fertilizers *										
Engrais potassiques *	...	...	...	...	...	...	27.0	31.0	25.0	6.0
Croatia Croatie										
Nitrogenous fertilizers										
Engrais azotés	291.0	* 305.9	324.1	242.0	300.9	* 93.0	* 101.6	* 152.0	95.0	104.9
Phosphate fertilizers										
Engrais phosphatés	89.6	86.8	88.7	75.5	80.7	44.2	48.2	* 56.0	38.3	43.7
Potash fertilizers										
Engrais potassiques	...	...	...	...	...	* 47.0	52.5	67.9	43.4	51.0
Czech Republic République tchèque										
Nitrogenous fertilizers										
Engrais azotés	* 302.9	* 305.0	264.4	284.4	* 269.3	* 232.7	* 262.3	* 225.8	219.1	* 209.6
Phosphate fertilizers										
Engrais phosphatés	* 30.0	* 24.8	24.6	25.7	* 18.3	* 61.0	* 50.4	46.6	51.2	* 35.4
Potash fertilizers										
Engrais potassiques	...	...	...	...	15.8	* 54.0	* 34.0	41.4	29.8	24.0
Denmark Danemark										
Nitrogenous fertilizers *										
Engrais azotés *	165.0	150.0	160.0	142.0	143.0	291.0	288.0	283.0	263.0	252.0
Phosphate fertilizers										
Engrais phosphatés	* 58.0	* 46.0	* 47.0	* 46.0	* 47.0	* 49.0	* 53.0	* 50.0	47.0	* 41.0
Potash fertilizers *										
Engrais potassiques *	...	...	...	...	...	98.0	108.0	103.0	102.0	98.0
Estonia Estonie										
Nitrogenous fertilizers										
Engrais azotés	55.8	* 52.3	* 41.8	* 29.3	* 40.4	* 19.0	* 16.6	20.5	24.9	19.6
Phosphate fertilizers										
Engrais phosphatés	* 1.3	...	...	...	...	3.8	2.6	4.3	4.4	4.0
Potash fertilizers										
Engrais potassiques	...	...	...	...	...	...	...	* 3.0	3.1	3.7
Finland Finlande										
Nitrogenous fertilizers										
Engrais azotés	* 247.0	* 231.0	* 238.0	* 230.0	* 225.0	183.0	174.0	177.0	* 175.0	* 176.0
Phosphate fertilizers										
Engrais phosphatés	* 122.0	105.0	* 95.0	96.0	97.0	72.9	57.0	56.0	* 53.0	53.0
Potash fertilizers										
Engrais potassiques	...	...	...	...	...	84.9	* 82.0	* 81.0	* 81.0	* 82.0
France France										
Nitrogenous fertilizers										
Engrais azotés	* 1 490.0	* 1 616.0	* 1 484.0	* 1 470.0	* 1 450.0	2 392.0	2 525.1	* 2 513.1	* 2 488.1	* 2 571.0
Phosphate fertilizers *										
Engrais phosphatés *	513.0	558.0	527.6	433.7	435.7	1 031.4	1 051.9	1 038.8	1 011.2	966.0
Potash fertilizers										
Engrais potassiques	* 802.0	* 751.0	* 665.3	* 417.1	* 311.3	1 491.1	1 488.2	* 1 436.9	* 1 337.7	* 1 216.0
Germany † Allemagne †										
Nitrogenous fertilizers										
Engrais azotés	* 1 174.0	* 1 269.0	1 125.0	* 1 175.0	* 1 194.6	1 769.2	1 758.0	1 788.4	1 903.0	2 014.4
Phosphate fertilizers										
Engrais phosphatés	* 110.0	* 203.0	194.0	* 184.0	* 185.0	401.9	415.1	409.5	406.8	420.3
Potash fertilizers										
Engrais potassiques	* 3 278.0	* 3 334.0	* 3 423.0	* 3 582.0	* 3 544.9	649.0	645.8	658.9	628.7	599.2
Greece Grèce										
Nitrogenous fertilizers *										
Engrais azotés *	275.0	316.0	240.0	231.0	228.8	315.0	340.0	307.0	298.0	291.0
Phosphate fertilizers *										
Engrais phosphatés *	146.0	162.0	125.0	132.0	134.0	136.0	145.0	132.0	120.0	119.0
Potash fertilizers *										
Engrais potassiques *	...	...	...	...	...	54.0	75.0	65.0	60.0	59.0
Hungary Hongrie										
Nitrogenous fertilizers										
Engrais azotés	219.7	260.9	251.4	* 213.5	* 209.8	246.8	318.5	* 285.8	* 300.0	* 300.0

40

Fertilizers
Nitrogenous, phosphate and potash: thousand metric tons [*cont.*]
Engrais
Azotés, phosphatés et potassiques : milliers de tonnes [*suite*]

Country or area Pays ou zone	Production Production					Consumption Consommation				
	1995/96	1996/97	1997/98	1998/99	1999/00	1995/96	1996/97	1997/98	1998/99	1999/00
Phosphate fertilizers Engrais phosphatés	26.0	28.5	* 26.5	* 16.0	* 15.0	56.0	* 74.7	* 73.5	* 37.6	* 40.0
Potash fertilizers Engrais potassiques	...	...	...	...	...	* 65.4	* 61.7	67.8	* 51.0	* 47.0
Iceland Islande										
Nitrogenous fertilizers Engrais azotés	8.7	12.3	* 12.0	* 11.5	* 12.0	10.0	11.6	* 11.8	* 12.5	* 13.5
Phosphate fertilizers * Engrais phosphatés *	...	...	...	...	...	5.1	3.5	4.1	4.2	4.2
Potash fertilizers * Engrais potassiques *	...	...	...	...	...	3.5	3.8	3.4	2.0	4.2
Ireland Irlande										
Nitrogenous fertilizers * Engrais azotés *	307.0	288.0	326.0	311.0	277.1	425.0	394.0	397.0	417.1	429.0
Phosphate fertilizers * Engrais phosphatés *	...	...	...	...	...	141.0	128.0	113.0	115.7	115.0
Potash fertilizers Engrais potassiques	...	...	...	...	...	* 182.0	* 160.0	149.0	* 150.9	* 156.0
Italy Italie										
Nitrogenous fertilizers Engrais azotés	* 660.0	* 535.0	* 537.0	* 456.0	* 389.5	918.9	* 876.0	* 855.0	* 898.0	* 866.0
Phosphate fertilizers * Engrais phosphatés *	216.0	198.0	170.0	170.0	170.0	542.0	575.0	501.0	569.0	514.0
Potash fertilizers * Engrais potassiques *	...	...	...	...	...	405.0	414.0	413.0	395.0	392.0
Latvia Lettonie										
Nitrogenous fertilizers * Engrais azotés *	...	...	...	...	...	12.0	14.0	19.0	31.5	33.6
Phosphate fertilizers * Engrais phosphatés *	...	...	...	...	...	4.0	6.0	8.1	10.7	10.5
Potash fertilizers Engrais potassiques	...	...	...	...	...	* 6.0	* 5.0	* 8.0	* 7.0	10.3
Lithuania Lituanie										
Nitrogenous fertilizers Engrais azotés	* 294.4	* 300.2	* 322.9	* 447.3	452.6	* 40.0	* 79.0	* 81.1	83.4	* 94.0
Phosphate fertilizers Engrais phosphatés	* 120.0	* 146.1	* 192.8	246.9	324.9	* 30.0	* 10.0	* 18.2	* 18.4	39.0
Potash fertilizers * Engrais potassiques *	...	...	...	...	...	48.0	30.0	38.0	38.0	50.0
Malta Malte										
Nitrogenous fertilizers Engrais azotés	...	...	...	...	...	* 1.0	* 1.0	* 1.0	1.2	0.5
Phosphate fertilizers Engrais phosphatés	...	...	...	...	...	...	...	...	0.2	0.1
Potash fertilizers Engrais potassiques	...	...	...	...	...	...	...	...	0.2	0.1
Netherlands Pays−Bas										
Nitrogenous fertilizers Engrais azotés	* 1 595.0	* 1 513.0	* 1 586.0	* 1 576.0	* 1 425.0	* 390.0	400.6	* 375.0	* 350.0	* 343.0
Phosphate fertilizers Engrais phosphatés	* 338.0	* 271.0	* 402.0	* 405.0	* 355.0	* 70.0	* 65.0	60.0	* 62.0	* 59.0
Potash fertilizers Engrais potassiques	...	...	...	...	...	* 75.0	* 72.0	66.7	* 72.8	* 73.0
Norway Norvège										
Nitrogenous fertilizers * Engrais azotés *	595.0	595.0	570.0	570.0	575.0	112.0	112.0	112.0	106.0	106.0
Phosphate fertilizers * Engrais phosphatés *	236.0	265.0	236.0	236.0	240.0	32.0	32.0	30.0	30.0	30.0
Potash fertilizers * Engrais potassiques *	...	...	...	...	...	66.0	65.0	63.0	64.0	63.0
Poland Pologne										
Nitrogenous fertilizers Engrais azotés	1 575.1	1 548.0	* 1 557.4	* 1 575.6	* 1 359.5	851.9	* 910.0	* 1 009.7	862.0	861.3

40

Fertilizers
Nitrogenous, phosphate and potash: thousand metric tons [*cont.*]
Engrais
Azotés, phosphatés et potassiques : milliers de tonnes [*suite*]

Country or area	Production Production					Consumption Consommation				
Pays ou zone	1995/96	1996/97	1997/98	1998/99	1999/00	1995/96	1996/97	1997/98	1998/99	1999/00
Phosphate fertilizers										
Engrais phosphatés	* 496.0	* 442.0	* 473.6	* 480.2	* 373.2	301.7	310.0	* 289.6	308.4	296.8
Potash fertilizers										
Engrais potassiques	...	...	...	...	...	357.6	376.1	* 400.9	386.7	368.4
Portugal Portugal										
Nitrogenous fertilizers *										
Engrais azotés *	124.0	135.0	143.0	148.0	138.0	125.0	132.0	121.0	130.0	130.0
Phosphate fertilizers *										
Engrais phosphatés *	56.0	57.0	56.0	56.0	56.0	71.0	76.0	67.0	73.0	77.0
Potash fertilizers *										
Engrais potassiques *	...	...	...	...	...	48.0	50.0	48.0	50.0	50.0
Republic of Moldova République de Moldova										
Nitrogenous fertilizers *										
Engrais azotés *	...	...	...	...	...	60.0	60.0	62.0	5.9	5.8
Phosphate fertilizers *										
Engrais phosphatés *	...	...	...	...	...	40.0	40.0	42.0	...	...
Potash fertilizers *										
Engrais potassiques *	...	...	5.0	...	...	15.0	16.0	17.0	17.0	...
Romania Roumanie										
Nitrogenous fertilizers										
Engrais azotés	* 1 227.0	* 1 250.0	663.7	* 314.1	517.9	* 233.0	* 266.0	* 220.0	* 268.0	* 181.5
Phosphate fertilizers										
Engrais phosphatés	197.0	201.8	* 135.8	* 96.2	* 110.2	* 127.0	* 141.0	* 85.0	* 80.0	* 46.2
Potash fertilizers *										
Engrais potassiques *	...	...	...	...	...	3.4	15.0	10.0	12.0	8.6
Russian Federation Fédération de Russie										
Nitrogenous fertilizers *										
Engrais azotés *	4 856.0	4 900.0	4 187.0	4 629.5	5 110.9	1 000.0	984.0	950.0	738.0	1 050.2
Phosphate fertilizers *										
Engrais phosphatés *	1 933.0	1 575.0	1 853.0	1 688.0	2 000.7	350.0	376.0	320.0	211.0	155.7
Potash fertilizers *										
Engrais potassiques *	2 814.0	2 618.0	3 403.0	3 461.0	4 050.0	400.0	220.0	280.0	230.0	224.8
Slovakia Slovaquie										
Nitrogenous fertilizers										
Engrais azotés	* 183.1	* 210.8	* 283.8	* 218.9	* 201.6	72.0	77.6	* 72.5	81.8	65.4
Phosphate fertilizers										
Engrais phosphatés	* 36.6	* 36.7	* 16.0	* 26.0	* 26.0	16.8	20.9	* 17.8	* 20.5	13.1
Potash fertilizers										
Engrais potassiques	...	...	...	...	...	* 18.7	* 20.2	* 17.1	* 17.1	10.6
Slovenia Slovénie										
Nitrogenous fertilizers										
Engrais azotés	...	...	...	...	...	* 35.0	24.2	34.1	34.8	34.4
Phosphate fertilizers										
Engrais phosphatés	...	...	...	...	...	* 17.0	* 17.5	17.5	18.8	19.8
Potash fertilizers										
Engrais potassiques	...	...	...	...	...	* 22.0	* 21.6	22.3	23.0	24.5
Spain Espagne										
Nitrogenous fertilizers										
Engrais azotés	844.7	881.7	918.5	* 791.0	916.7	912.8	1 153.1	1 041.9	* 1 184.2	* 1 180.0
Phosphate fertilizers										
Engrais phosphatés	413.3	* 333.0	* 349.0	* 369.0	* 382.0	509.9	* 581.0	* 589.0	* 653.0	* 643.0
Potash fertilizers										
Engrais potassiques	* 650.0	680.5	640.0	* 496.0	549.8	* 446.0	* 458.0	* 468.0	* 513.0	491.0
Sweden Suède										
Nitrogenous fertilizers										
Engrais azotés	* 123.0	* 107.0	* 103.0	* 103.0	* 111.0	192.3	204.6	205.6	179.2	189.4
Phosphate fertilizers										
Engrais phosphatés	* 18.0	* 16.0	* 15.0	* 15.0	* 18.0	* 49.0	49.9	49.7	* 40.9	* 40.4
Potash fertilizers										
Engrais potassiques	...	...	...	...	...	* 52.0	52.8	53.7	45.0	46.8
Switzerland Suisse										
Nitrogenous fertilizers *										
Engrais azotés *	22.0	13.0	13.0	18.0	18.0	65.0	62.0	60.0	60.0	58.7

40
Fertilizers
Nitrogenous, phosphate and potash: thousand metric tons [*cont.*]
Engrais
Azotés, phosphatés et potassiques : milliers de tonnes [*suite*]

Country or area	Production					Consumption				
Pays ou zone	1995/96	1996/97	1997/98	1998/99	1999/00	1995/96	1996/97	1997/98	1998/99	1999/00
Phosphate fertilizers *										
Engrais phosphatés *	3.0	...	...	...	...	27.0	26.0	25.0	25.0	24.0
Potash fertilizers *										
Engrais potassiques *	...	...	...	...	...	43.0	37.0	36.0	36.0	35.0
TFYR of Macedonia L'ex−R.y. Macédoine										
Nitrogenous fertilizers										
Engrais azotés	7.9	* 6.0	* 6.5	* 6.5	* 7.0	25.2	* 30.4	* 28.1	* 25.2	* 25.0
Phosphate fertilizers										
Engrais phosphatés	6.3	* 8.0	* 7.0	7.0	7.5	6.0	* 7.0	* 9.2	* 9.5	10.5
Potash fertilizers										
Engrais potassiques	...	...	...	...	...	* 6.0	* 6.0	* 9.4	* 4.5	8.0
Ukraine Ukraine										
Nitrogenous fertilizers										
Engrais azotés	* 1 830.0	* 2 083.3	* 2 021.8	* 1 725.0	1 965.2	* 625.0	* 373.0	* 413.0	* 405.8	327.2
Phosphate fertilizers										
Engrais phosphatés	* 294.0	* 326.5	* 266.7	* 213.7	* 134.0	* 130.0	* 97.0	* 104.0	76.6	62.0
Potash fertilizers										
Engrais potassiques	* 55.1	* 39.3	* 52.2	* 33.6	21.3	* 135.0	* 55.0	* 45.0	32.0	28.5
United Kingdom Royaume−Uni										
Nitrogenous fertilizers *										
Engrais azotés *	729.0	896.0	952.0	958.0	965.0	1 328.0	1 451.0	1 363.0	1 290.0	1 303.0
Phosphate fertilizers *										
Engrais phosphatés *	88.0	111.0	190.0	190.0	200.0	390.0	416.0	408.0	347.0	320.0
Potash fertilizers *										
Engrais potassiques *	582.0	618.0	565.0	608.0	495.0	473.0	509.0	499.0	450.0	423.0
Yugoslavia Yougoslavie										
Nitrogenous fertilizers *										
Engrais azotés *	129.0	95.0	171.0	112.3	42.0	129.0	160.5	185.1	153.4	106.6
Phosphate fertilizers *										
Engrais phosphatés *	14.0	14.0	16.0	24.0	12.0	14.0	19.0	35.0	24.0	26.3
Potash fertilizers *										
Engrais potassiques *	...	...	...	...	...	...	35.0	24.0	25.0	29.0
Oceania Océanie										
Nitrogenous fertilizers										
Engrais azotés	357.9	348.7	331.8	391.5	410.5	845.5	985.2	997.3	1 145.3	1 254.9
Phosphate fertilizers										
Engrais phosphatés	654.2	573.4	653.4	617.0	587.2	1 360.4	1 378.7	1 477.6	1 421.4	1 374.0
Potash fertilizers										
Engrais potassiques	...	...	...	...	...	377.7	348.5	391.8	373.3	369.0
Australia Australie										
Nitrogenous fertilizers *										
Engrais azotés *	281.0	278.7	250.8	299.0	302.5	671.3	824.6	839.4	979.0	1 089.0
Phosphate fertilizers										
Engrais phosphatés	* 407.3	* 333.4	* 383.4	* 357.0	327.2	* 965.3	* 985.3	* 1 090.1	* 1 039.0	* 987.6
Potash fertilizers *										
Engrais potassiques *	...	...	...	...	...	230.8	206.0	254.6	232.0	226.5
Fiji Fidji										
Nitrogenous fertilizers *										
Engrais azotés *	...	...	...	...	...	10.0	10.0	10.2	8.9	6.4
Phosphate fertilizers *										
Engrais phosphatés *	...	...	...	...	...	3.0	4.0	4.0	3.2	2.0
Potash fertilizers *										
Engrais potassiques *	...	...	...	...	...	5.0	5.0	5.0	6.3	6.0
French Polynesia Polynésie française										
Nitrogenous fertilizers										
Engrais azotés	...	...	...	...	...	* 0.4	* 0.4	* 0.4	* 0.4	0.5
Phosphate fertilizers										
Engrais phosphatés	...	...	...	...	...	* 0.4	* 0.4	* 0.4	* 0.4	0.3
Potash fertilizers										
Engrais potassiques	...	...	...	...	...	* 0.2	* 0.2	* 0.2	* 0.2	0.4
New Caledonia Nouvelle−Calédonie										
Nitrogenous fertilizers *										
Engrais azotés *	...	...	...	...	...	0.3	0.3	0.3	0.3	0.3

40
Fertilizers
Nitrogenous, phosphate and potash: thousand metric tons [*cont.*]
Engrais
Azotés, phosphatés et potassiques : milliers de tonnes [*suite*]

Country or area	Production Production					Consumption Consommation				
Pays ou zone	1995/96	1996/97	1997/98	1998/99	1999/00	1995/96	1996/97	1997/98	1998/99	1999/00
Phosphate fertilizers *										
Engrais phosphatés *	...	...	...	...	...	1.0	1.0	1.0	0.3	0.3
Potash fertilizers *										
Engrais potassiques *	...	...	...	...	...	0.3	0.3	0.3	0.3	0.3
New Zealand Nouvelle−Zélande										
Nitrogenous fertilizers *										
Engrais azotés *	76.9	70.0	81.0	92.5	108.0	155.5	140.0	138.9	153.5	156.0
Phosphate fertilizers *										
Engrais phosphatés *	246.9	240.0	270.0	260.0	260.0	387.7	385.0	379.1	376.0	380.0
Potash fertilizers *										
Engrais potassiques *	...	...	...	...	...	139.4	135.0	129.7	132.0	133.0
Palau Palaos										
Nitrogenous fertilizers *										
Engrais azotés *	...	...	...	...	...	...	1.9	...	...	...
Papua New Guinea Papouasie−Nvl−Guinée										
Nitrogenous fertilizers *										
Engrais azotés *	...	...	...	...	...	8.0	8.0	8.1	3.2	2.7
Phosphate fertilizers *										
Engrais phosphatés *	...	...	...	...	...	3.0	3.0	3.0	2.5	3.8
Potash fertilizers *										
Engrais potassiques *	...	...	...	...	...	2.0	2.0	2.0	2.5	2.8

Source:
Food and Agriculture Organization of the United
Nations (FAO), Rome, FAOSTAT Agriculture Database
and the Fertilizer Yearbook 2000.

† For information on recent changes in country or area
nomenclature pertaining to former Czechoslovakia,
Germany, Hong Kong Special Administrative Region
(SAR) of China, Macao Special Administrative Region
(SAR) of China, SFR of Yugoslavia and the former
USSR, see Annex 1 − Country or area nomenclature,
regional and other groupings.

1   FAO estimate.

Source:
Organisation des Nations Unies pour l'alimentation et
l'agriculture (FAO), Rome, les données de l'agriculture de
FAOSTAT et l'Annuaire des Engrais 2000.

† Pour les modifications récentes de nomenclature de pays
ou de zone concernant l'Allemagne, Hong Kong, région
administrative spéciale (RAS) de Chine, Macao, région
administrative spéciale (RAS) de Chine, l'ex−Tchécoslovaquie,
l'ex−URSS et l'ex−Rfs de Yougoslavie, voir annexe I −
Nomenclature des pays ou des zones, groupements
régionaux et autres groupements.

1 Estimation de FAO.

Technical notes, tables 34-40

The series shown on agriculture and fishing have been furnished by the Food and Agriculture Organization of the United Nations (FAO). They refer mainly to:

(a)   Long-term trends in the growth of agricultural output and the food supply;

(b)   Output of principal agricultural commodities.

Agricultural production is defined to include all crops and livestock products except those used for seed and fodder and other intermediate uses in agriculture; for example deductions are made for eggs used for hatching. Intermediate input of seeds and fodder and similar items refer to both domestically produced and imported commodities. For further details, reference may be made to FAO Yearbooks [4, 6, 7, 8, 9]. FAO data are also available through the Internet (http://www.fao.org).

Table 34: "Agriculture" relates to the production of all crops and livestock products. The "Food Index" includes those commodities which are considered edible and contain nutrients.

The index numbers of agricultural output and food production are calculated by the Laspeyres formula with the base year period 1989-1991. The latter is provided in order to diminish the impact of annual fluctuations in agricultural output during base years on the indices for the period. Production quantities of each commodity are weighted by 1989-1991 average national producer prices and summed for each year. The index numbers are based on production data for a calendar year. These may differ in some instances from those actually produced and published by the individual countries themselves due to variations in concepts, coverage, weights and methods of calculation. Efforts have been made to estimate these methodological differences to achieve a better international comparability of data. The series include a large amount of estimates made by FAO in cases where no official or semi-official figures are available from the countries.

Detailed data on agricultural production and trade are published by FAO in its *Production Yearbook* [6] and *Trade Yearbook* [7].

Table 35: The data on the production of cereals relate to crops harvested for dry grain only. Cereals harvested for hay, green feed or used for grazing are excluded.

Table 36: Oil crops, or oil-bearing crops, are those crops yielding seeds, nuts or fruits which are used mainly for the extraction of culinary or industrial oils, excluding essential oils. In this table, data for oil crops represent the total production of oil seeds, oil nuts and oil fruits harvested in the year indicated and expressed

Notes techniques, tableaux 34 à 40

Les séries présentées sur l'agriculture et la pêche ont été fournies par l'Organisation des Nations Unies pour l'alimentation et l'agriculture (FAO) et portent principalement sur:

(a)   Les tendances à long terme de la croissance de la production agricole et des approvisionnements alimentaires;

(b)   La production des principales denrées agricoles.

La production agricole se définit comme comprenant l'ensemble des produits agricoles et des produits de l'élevage à l'exception de ceux utilisés comme semences et comme aliments pour les animaux, et pour les autres utilisations intermédiaires en agriculture; par exemple, on déduit les œufs utilisés pour la reproduction. L'apport intermédiaire de semences et d'aliments pour les animaux et d'autres éléments similaires se rapportent à la fois à des produits locaux et importés. Pour tous détails complémentaires, on se reportera aux annuaires de la FAO [4, 6, 7, 8, 9]. Des statistiques peuvent également être consultées sur le site Web de la FAO (http://www.fao.org).

Tableau 34: L'"Agriculture" se rapporte à la production de tous les produits de l'agriculture et de l'élevage. L'"Indice des produits alimentaires" comprend les produits considérés comme comestibles et qui contiennent des éléments nutritifs.

Les indices de la production agricole et de la production alimentaire sont calculés selon la formule de Laspeyres avec les années 1989-1991 pour période de base. Le choix d'une période de plusieurs années permet de diminuer l'incidence des fluctuations annuelles de la production agricole pendant les années de base sur les indices pour cette période. Les quantités produites de chaque denrée sont pondérées par les prix nationaux moyens à la production de 1989-1991, et additionnées pour chaque année. Les indices sont fondés sur les données de production d'une année civile. Ils peuvent différer dans certains cas des indices effectivement établis et publiés par les pays eux-mêmes par suite de différences dans les concepts, la couverture, les pondérations et les méthodes de calcul. On s'est efforcé d'estimer ces différences méthodologiques afin de rendre les données plus facilement comparables à l'échelle internationale. Les séries comprennent une grande quantité d'estimations faites par la FAO dans les cas où les pays n'avaient pas fourni de chiffres officiels ou semi-officiels.

Des chiffres détaillés de production et d'échange sont publiés dans l'*Annuaire FAO de la production* [6] et l'*Annuaire FAO du commerce* [7].

Tableau 35: Les données sur la production de cé-

in terms of oil equivalent and cake/meal equivalent. That is to say, these figures do not relate to the actual production of vegetable oils and cake/meal, but to the potential production if the total amounts produced from all oil crops were processed into oil and cake/meal in producing countries in the same year in which they were harvested. Naturally, the total production of oil crops is never processed into oil in its entirety, since depending on the crop, important quantities are also used for seed, feed and food. However, although oil and cake/meal extraction rates vary from country to country, in this table the same extraction rate for each crop has been applied for all countries. Moreover. it should be borne in mind that the crops harvested during the latter months of the year are generally processed into oil during the following year.

In spite of these deficiencies in coverage, extraction rates and time reference, the data reported here are useful as they provide a valid indication of year-to-year changes in the size of total oil-crop production. The actual production of vegetable oils in the world is about 80 percent of the production reported here. In addition, about two million tonnes of vegetable oils are produced every year from crops which are not included among those defined above. The most important of these oils are maize-germ oil and rice-bran oil. The actual world production of cake/meal derived from oil crops is also about 80 percent of the production reported in the table.

Table 37: The data refer to livestock numbers grouped into twelve-month periods ending 30 September of the year stated and cover all domestic animals irrespective of their age and place or purpose of their breeding.

Table 38: The data on roundwood refer to wood in the rough, wood in its natural state as felled or otherwise harvested, with or without bark, round, split, roughly squared or in other form (i.e. roots, stumps, burls, etc.). It may also be impregnated (e.g. telegraph poles) or roughly shaped or pointed. It comprises all wood obtained from removals, i.e. the quantities removed from forests and from trees outside the forest, including wood recovered from natural, felling and logging losses during the period — calendar year or forest year.

Table 39: The data cover production from sea and inland fisheries and aquaculture and are expressed in terms of live weight. They generally include crustaceans and molluscs but exclude seaweed and aquatic mammals such as whales and dolphins. Sea fisheries data include landings by domestic craft in foreign ports and exclude the landings by foreign craft in domestic ports. The flag of the vessel is considered as the paramount indication of the nationality of the catch.

Table 40: The data generally refer to the fertilizer

réales se rapportent uniquement aux céréales récoltées pour le grain sec; celles cultivées pour le foin, le fourrage vert ou le pâturage en sont exclues.

Tableau 36: On désigne sous le nom de cultures oléagineuses l'ensemble des cultures produisant des graines, des noix ou des fruits, essentiellement destinées à l'extraction d'huiles alimentaires ou industrielles, à l'exclusion des huiles essentielles. Dans ce tableau, les chiffres se rapportent à la production totale de graines, noix et fruits oléagineux récoltés au cours de l'année de référence et sont exprimés en équivalent d'huile et en équivalent de tourteau/farine. En d'autres termes, ces chiffres ne se rapportent pas à la production effective mais à la production potentielle d'huiles végétales et de tourteau/farine dans l'hypothèse où les volumes totaux de produits provenant de toutes les cultures d'oléagineux seraient transformés en huile et en tourteau/farine dans les pays producteurs l'année même où ils ont été récoltés. Bien entendu, la production totale d'oléagineux n'est jamais transformée intégralement en huile, car des quantités importantes qui varient suivant les cultures sont également utilisées pour les semailles, l'alimentation animale et l'alimentation humaine. Toutefois, bien que les taux d'extraction d'huile et de tourteau/farine varient selon les pays, on a appliqué dans ce tableau le même taux à tous les pays pour chaque oléagineux. En outre, il ne faut pas oublier que les produits récoltés au cours des derniers mois de l'année sont généralement transformés en huile dans le courant de l'année suivante.

En dépit de ces imperfections qui concernent le champ d'application, les taux d'extraction et les périodes de référence, les chiffres présentés ici sont utiles, car ils donnent une indication valable des variations de volume que la production totale d'oléagineux enregistre d'une année à l'autre. La production mondiale effective d'huiles végétales atteint 80 pour cent environ de la production indiquée ici. En outre, environ 2 millions de tonnes d'huiles végétales sont produites chaque année à partir de cultures non comprises dans les catégories définies ci-dessus. Les principales sont l'huile de germes de maïs et l'huile de son de riz. La production mondiale effective tourteau/farine d'oléagineux représente environ 80 pour cent de production indiquée dans le tableau.

Tableau 37: Les statistiques sur les effectifs du cheptel sont groupées en périodes de 12 mois se terminant le 30 septembre de l'année indiquée et s'entendent de tous les animaux domestiques, quel que soit leur âge, leur emplacement ou le but de leur élevage.

Tableau 38: Les données sur le bois rond se réfèrent au bois brut, bois à l'état naturel, tel qu'il a été abattu ou récolté autrement, avec ou sans écorce, fendu, grossièrement équarri ou sous une autre forme (par

year 1 July-30 June.

Nitrogenous fertilizers: data refer to the nitrogen content of commercial inorganic fertilizers.

Phosphate fertilizers: data refer to commercial phosphoric acid (P_2O_5) and cover the P_2O_5 of superphosphates, ammonium phosphate and basic slag.

Potash fertilizers: data refer to K_2O content of commercial potash, muriate, nitrate and sulphate of potash, manure salts, kainit and nitrate of soda potash.

Data on fertilizer production, consumption and trade are available in FAO's *Fertilizer Yearbook* [4].

exemple, racines, souches, loupes, etc.). Il peut être également imprégné (par exemple, dans le cas des poteaux télégraphiques) et dégrossi ou taillé en pointe. Cette catégorie comprend tous les bois provenant des quantités enlevées en forêt ou provenant des arbres poussant hors forêt, y compris le volume récupéré sur les déchets naturels et les déchets d'abattage et de transport pendant la période envisagée (année civile ou forestière).

Tableau 39: Les données ont trait à la pêche maritime et intérieure et l'aquaculture, et sont exprimées en poids vif. Elles comprennent, en général, crustacés et mollusques, mais excluent les plantes marines et les mammifères aquatiques (baleines, dauphins, etc.). Les données de pêche maritime comprennent les quantités débarquées par des bateaux nationaux dans des ports étrangers et excluent les quantités débarquées par des bateaux étrangers dans des ports nationaux. Le pavillon du navire est considéré comme la principale indication de la nationalité de la prise.

Tableau 40: Les données sur les engrais se rapportent en général à une période d'un an comptée du 1er juillet au 30 juin.

Engrais azotés: les données se rapportent à la teneur en azote des engrais commerciaux inorganiques.

Engrais phosphatés: les données se rapportent à l'acide phosphorique (P_2O_5) et englobent la teneur en (P_2O_5) des superphosphates, du phosphate d'ammonium et des scories de déphosphoration.

Engrais potassiques: les données se rapportent à la teneur en K_2O des produits potassiques commerciaux, muriate, nitrate et sulfate de potasse, sels d'engrais, kainite et nitrate de soude potassique.

On trouvera des chiffres relatifs à la production, à la consommation et aux échanges d'engrais dans l'*Annuaire FAO des engrais* [4].

41
Sugar
Sucre

Production and consumption: thousand metric tons; consumption per capita: kilograms
Production et consommation : milliers de tonnes ; consommation par habitant : kilogrammes

Country or area Pays ou zone	1991	1992	1993	1994	1995	1996	1997	1998	1999	2000
World Monde										
Production	112 254	117 443	111 942	110 458	117 883	125 048	125 094	125 948	134 892	130 574
Consumption	108 860	112 237	111 347	112 914	116 516	120 052	122 631	122 768	126 526	128 038
Consumption per cap.(kg)	19	21	20	20	20	21	21	20	21	21
	Africa · Afrique									
Algeria Algérie										
Consumption *	850	880	825	800	775	750	650	800	900	935
Consumption per cap.(kg)	33	34	31	29	28	26	22	27	29	29
Angola Angola										
Production *	30	25	20	20	30	25	28	32	32	30
Consumption *	100	110	110	95	100	110	110	85	120	130
Consumption per cap.(kg)	11	10	11	9	9	10	9	7	10	10
Benin Bénin										
Production *	5	4	5	4	5	5	4	4	4	5
Consumption *	20	25	30	35	45	45	40	40	45	46
Consumption per cap.(kg)	4	5	6	7	8	8	7	7	7	7
Botswana Botswana										
Consumption	55	50	45	45	40	40	30	45	45	46
Consumption per cap.(kg)	41	37	31	32	27	27	20	29	28	28
Burkina Faso Burkina Faso										
Production	* 29	31	* 32	* 33	* 32	* 33	* 34	* 30	30	* 30
Consumption	* 30	32	* 35	* 35	* 35	* 35	* 42	* 50	* 45	* 46
Consumption per cap.(kg)	3	3	4	3	3	3	4	5	4	4
Burundi Burundi										
Production	14	10	10	12	10	8	8	24	23	24
Consumption	11	15	17	20	25	20	12	22	23	24
Consumption per cap.(kg)	2	3	3	4	4	3	2	4	4	4
Cameroon Cameroun										
Production	* 76	* 72	* 67	* 57	* 59	* 52	* 44	* 46	* 52	41
Consumption *	80	80	80	83	85	85	80	95	95	95
Consumption per cap.(kg)	7	7	6	6	6	6	6	7	9	8
Cape Verde Cap–Vert										
Consumption *	12	13	15	15	15	17	18	12	12	13
Consumption per cap.(kg)	37	39	41	40	39	40	41	33	31	32
Central African Rep. Rép. centrafricaine										
Consumption *	3	3	4	4	3	5	5	5	4	4
Consumption per cap.(kg)	1	1	1	1	1	2	2	1	1	1
Chad Tchad										
Production	* 30	* 30	32	* 32	* 30	* 30	* 34	* 31	* 32	* 32
Consumption *	40	40	40	43	47	50	46	55	55	57
Consumption per cap.(kg)	7	7	6	7	8	9	9	11	11	12
Comoros Comores										
Consumption	4	4	4	3	3	3	2	5	5	6
Consumption per cap.(kg)	7	7	7	5	5	4	3	8	8	8
Congo Congo										
Production	21	30	26	* 29	38	42	* 45	* 45	* 35	* 40
Consumption	* 17	18	16	* 17	* 28	* 28	* 30	* 30	* 30	* 40
Consumption per cap.(kg)	7	8	7	7	11	11	11	11	11	14
Côte d'Ivoire Côte d'Ivoire										
Production	* 155	* 160	* 155	141	* 160	* 134	* 132	126	152	189
Consumption	* 160	* 165	* 165	126	* 160	* 170	* 170	137	* 170	* 180
Consumption per cap.(kg)	13	13	12	9	11	12	12	10	12	12
Dem. Rep. of the Congo Rép. dém. du Congo										
Production *	88	90	85	85	80	50	86	51	65	75
Consumption *	95	100	105	105	110	110	90	80	75	70
Consumption per cap.(kg)	3	3	3	3	3	2	2	2	2	1
Djibouti Djibouti										
Consumption	9	12	10	11	12	11	10	10	12	13
Consumption per cap.(kg)	17	22	18	19	20	18	16	16	19	20
Egypt Egypte										
Production *	1 060	1 060	1 090	1 190	1 125	1 222	1 228	1 152	1 269	1 450
Consumption	* 1 745	1 750	* 1 675	* 1 700	* 1 775	* 1 850	* 2 000	* 2 075	* 2 150	* 2 250
Consumption per cap.(kg)	32	32	30	30	31	31	33	34	32	33

41
Sugar
Production and consumption: thousand metric tons; consumption per capita: kilograms [*cont.*]
Sucre
Production et consommation : milliers de tonnes ; consommation par habitant : kilogrammes [*suite*]

Country or area Pays ou zone	1991	1992	1993	1994	1995	1996	1997	1998	1999	2000
Eritrea Erythrée										
Consumption	...	...	...	...	...	...	10	10	8	8
Ethiopia Ethiopie										
Production	* 161	165	* 185	95	128	180	126	219	235	251
Consumption	* 160	* 160	142	107	96	206	145	185	199	246
Consumption per cap.(kg)	3	3	3	2	2	4	3	3	3	4
Gabon Gabon										
Production *	22	15	18	17	16	15	16	17	16	17
Consumption *	16	10	15	17	17	16	16	17	18	19
Consumption per cap.(kg)	15	10	15	16	16	14	14	14	13	11
Gambia Gambie										
Consumption *	35	35	40	40	45	30	40	45	50	58
Consumption per cap.(kg)	37	40	39	37	41	26	34	37	40	44
Ghana Ghana										
Consumption *	95	105	120	123	120	120	130	140	145	145
Consumption per cap.(kg)	6	7	7	7	7	7	7	7	7	7
Guinea Guinée										
Production *	18	18	20	19	20	21	22	22	25	25
Consumption *	55	65	70	75	75	75	80	80	85	90
Consumption per cap.(kg)	9	11	11	11	11	10	11	11	12	12
Guinea−Bissau Guinée−Bissau										
Consumption	3	3	2	3	4	4	7	4	5	7
Consumption per cap.(kg)	3	3	2	3	3	4	6	3	4	6
Kenya Kenya										
Production	471	404	414	329	418	423	436	488	512	437
Consumption	537	600	609	620	* 510	* 500	* 525	* 650	662	663
Consumption per cap.(kg)	21	22	22	21	17	16	16	22	22	22
Liberia Libéria										
Production	1	1	1	1	0	0	0	0	0	0
Consumption	6	6	6	8	8	7	6	10	8	10
Consumption per cap.(kg)	2	2	2	3	3	3	2	4	3	3
Libyan Arab Jamah. Jamah. arabe libyenne										
Consumption *	160	160	160	160	150	180	220	220	220	225
Consumption per cap.(kg)	37	36	34	33	28	32	38	41	40	40
Madagascar Madagascar										
Production	96	97	104	83	94	* 95	* 96	95	* 85	70
Consumption	87	88	85	90	78	* 90	* 95	* 95	* 95	* 98
Consumption per cap.(kg)	8	7	6	7	6	6	7	6	6	6
Malawi Malawi										
Production	210	209	137	213	241	234	210	210	187	209
Consumption	130	152	162	149	164	173	178	158	137	127
Consumption per cap.(kg)	15	17	18	16	17	17	17	15	13	12
Mali Mali										
Production	* 30	25	* 25	* 25	* 25	* 26	* 26	* 33	* 31	* 32
Consumption	* 80	80	* 85	* 90	* 90	* 65	* 60	* 80	* 75	* 85
Consumption per cap.(kg)	8	8	8	9	9	6	6	8	7	8
Mauritania Mauritanie										
Consumption *	60	60	55	70	80	85	90	120	130	140
Consumption per cap.(kg)	29	28	26	32	35	36	37	47	50	52
Mauritius Maurice										
Production	648	681	604	530	572	624	658	667	396	604
Consumption	42	41	39	39	39	40	42	43	42	42
Consumption per cap.(kg)	40	38	36	37	36	36	37	37	36	35
Morocco Maroc										
Production	498	453	507	482	455	434	442	499	522	556
Consumption	778	811	829	830	894	967	996	1 002	1 018	1 034
Consumption per cap.(kg)	31	32	32	32	34	36	37	36	36	36
Mozambique Mozambique										
Production	* 25	* 30	* 20	* 20	* 30	* 30	* 42	39	46	* 45
Consumption *	45	50	70	73	60	55	50	60	70	75
Consumption per cap.(kg)	3	3	5	5	4	3	3	4	4	4
Namibia Namibie										
Consumption *	...	...	...	15	16	25	35	40	45	46

41

Sugar
Production and consumption: thousand metric tons; consumption per capita: kilograms [*cont.*]
Sucre
Production et consommation : milliers de tonnes ; consommation par habitant : kilogrammes [*suite*]

Country or area Pays ou zone	1991	1992	1993	1994	1995	1996	1997	1998	1999	2000
Niger Niger										
Production	...	...	0	0	* 10	15	15	* 5	* 10	* 10
Consumption *	25	23	25	25	30	35	40	45	50	55
Consumption per cap.(kg)	3	3	3	3	3	4	4	5	5	5
Nigeria Nigéria										
Production	* 56	* 46	* 46	* 48	* 37	* 27	* 15	* 15	* 17	36
Consumption *	480	600	625	600	500	600	650	700	700	760
Consumption per cap.(kg)	5	6	6	6	5	6	6	7	6	7
Réunion [1] Réunion [1]										
Production	215	227	184	177	195	205	207	* 195	* 234	* 222
Rwanda Rwanda										
Production	4	4	4	3	1	0	0	0	0	0
Consumption	11	12	* 12	* 7	* 4	* 4	* 4	* 3	* 3	* 3
Consumption per cap.(kg)	2	2	2	1	1	1	1	0	0	0
Senegal Sénégal										
Production	* 85	* 90	* 90	* 95	* 81	* 85	* 91	90	* 95	* 90
Consumption	* 115	128	* 135	* 145	* 165	* 175	* 180	* 170	* 170	* 165
Consumption per cap.(kg)	15	16	17	18	19	20	20	18	18	18
Sierra Leone Sierra Leone										
Production *	5	3	4	4	4	5	6	6	7	7
Consumption *	18	19	17	17	18	19	14	15	15	20
Consumption per cap.(kg)	4	5	4	4	4	4	3	3	3	4
Somalia Somalie										
Production *	30	28	20	18	20	20	19	19	20	15
Consumption *	37	43	47	80	110	110	135	150	170	180
Consumption per cap.(kg)	4	5	5	10	13	13	15	16	18	18
South Africa Afrique du Sud										
Production	2 462	1 715	1 282	1 777	1 732	2 471	2 419	2 985	2 547	2 691
Consumption	1 382	1 327	1 303	1 480	1 381	1 330	1 656	1 367	1 223	1 296
Consumption per cap.(kg)	36	34	33	38	35	33	40	32	28	30
Sudan Soudan										
Production	* 490	* 515	* 485	* 510	486	543	538	610	635	680
Consumption	* 475	* 480	* 500	* 515	* 460	* 480	* 480	391	396	430
Consumption per cap.(kg)	19	18	18	18	17	18	17	14	14	15
Swaziland Swaziland										
Production	517	495	458	474	419	458	457	537	571	553
Consumption	52	73	103	141	174	188	187	250	275	246
Consumption per cap.(kg)	65	100	122	160	191	200	200	263	281	246
Togo Togo										
Production *	5	5	5	5	5	5	3	3	3	3
Consumption *	30	30	19	28	32	35	45	50	50	55
Consumption per cap.(kg)	8	8	5	7	8	8	11	11	11	12
Tunisia Tunisie										
Production	22	28	25	25	29	29	28	15	9	2
Consumption	215	246	250	258	257	272	283	287	292	294
Consumption per cap.(kg)	27	30	30	29	29	30	31	31	31	31
Uganda Ouganda										
Production *	45	58	54	48	76	109	145	111	137	130
Consumption *	45	46	55	65	100	100	150	150	150	155
Consumption per cap.(kg)	2	2	3	4	5	5	7	7	7	7
United Rep. of Tanzania Rép.-Unie de Tanzanie										
Production	* 115	* 105	* 120	* 130	* 110	* 100	84	* 110	114	* 130
Consumption *	115	120	120	115	120	160	175	200	200	208
Consumption per cap.(kg)	4	4	4	4	4	6	6	6	6	6
Zambia Zambie										
Production	134	155	147	* 150	151	166	174	173	* 210	* 190
Consumption	105	111	86	* 105	152	154	74	* 85	* 115	* 145
Consumption per cap.(kg)	13	13	10	12	17	16	8	8	11	14
Zimbabwe Zimbabwe										
Production	3462	9	51	524	512	337	574	571	583	571
Consumption	294	234	229	253	292	287	335	305	376	374
Consumption per cap.(kg)	29	22	21	23	25	24	27	24	29	28

41

Sugar
Production and consumption: thousand metric tons; consumption per capita: kilograms [*cont.*]
Sucre
Production et consommation : milliers de tonnes ; consommation par habitant : kilogrammes [*suite*]

Country or area Pays ou zone	1991	1992	1993	1994	1995	1996	1997	1998	1999	2000
America, North · Amerique du Nord										
Bahamas Bahamas										
Consumption	10	10	10	9	11	12	10	10	10	11
Consumption per cap.(kg)	39	39	36	34	41	43	35	33	33	35
Barbados Barbade										
Production	67	* 55	* 48	* 51	* 55	59	62	46	53	58
Consumption	11	* 12	* 11	* 13	* 14	16	16	15	* 15	* 16
Consumption per cap.(kg)	42	46	42	50	54	60	62	55	56	55
Belize Belize										
Production	103	108	108	108	115	113	131	123	124	128
Consumption	9	9	11	13	13	15	16	15	15	15
Consumption per cap.(kg)	47	47	54	63	60	69	68	64	61	61
Bermuda Bermudes										
Consumption	2	2	2	2	2	2	1	2	1	2
Consumption per cap.(kg)	33	27	33	26	25	25	17	25	17	25
Canada Canada										
Production *	150	125	124	169	167	158	115	104	118	123
Consumption *	1 100	1 120	1 150	1 175	1 200	1 225	1 225	1 200	1 200	1 235
Consumption per cap.(kg)	41	41	40	41	41	41	41	40	39	40
Costa Rica Costa Rica										
Production	279	301	* 305	* 325	* 355	* 332	* 319	* 381	* 378	246
Consumption	183	186	* 190	* 193	* 195	* 225	* 220	* 210	* 210	208
Consumption per cap.(kg)	64	63	63	59	59	66	64	60	59	57
Cuba Cuba										
Production	7 233	7 219	4 246	4 017	3 259	4 529	4 318	3 291	3 875	4 057
Consumption [3]	956	942	796	664	581	* 670	733	713	711	705
Consumption per cap.(kg)	89	87	73	61	53	61	66	64	64	63
Dominican Republic Rép. dominicaine										
Production	628	593	621	579	508	* 670	687	409	421	438
Consumption	251	277	290	295	300	* 350	274	337	* 350	298
Consumption per cap.(kg)	34	37	38	38	39	45	34	42	42	35
El Salvador El Salvador										
Production	186	233	* 250	* 275	* 300	* 352	414	487	585	562
Consumption	* 150	116	* 165	* 175	* 190	* 210	232	237	234	236
Consumption per cap.(kg)	28	21	30	32	34	36	39	39	38	38
Guadeloupe [1] Guadeloupe [1]										
Production	53	38	63	58	33	49	57	38	65	65[4]
Guatemala Guatemala										
Production	1 038	1 165	1 226	1 131	1 362	1 318	1 390	1 682	1 687	1 675
Consumption	348	368	391	416	417	372	392	408	460	468
Consumption per cap.(kg)	37	38	39	43	42	36	37	39	42	38
Haiti Haïti										
Production *	25	20	20	15	5	8	9	10	10	5
Consumption *	90	95	85	85	120	115	120	130	165	170
Consumption per cap.(kg)	14	14	12	12	17	16	16	17	21	21
Honduras Honduras										
Production	175	* 185	* 190	* 185	* 215	* 240	* 251	* 277	190	320
Consumption	161	* 170	* 180	* 200	* 225	* 235	* 235	* 230	235	236
Consumption per cap.(kg)	31	31	32	37	40	41	39	37	37	36
Jamaica Jamaïque										
Production	234	228	219	223	214	236	233	183	212	210
Consumption	116	117	123	120	92	115	113	120	98	129
Consumption per cap.(kg)	48	48	50	49	37	46	44	47	38	50
Martinique [1] Martinique [1]										
Production	6	6	7	7	8	8	7	7	6	6[4]
Mexico Mexique										
Production	3 882	3 885	4 353	3 849	4 588	4 784	5 048	5 287	5 030	4 816
Consumption	4 545	4 301	4 449	4 370	4 423	4 229	4 231	4 293	* 4 400	4 619
Consumption per cap.(kg)	56	48	49	49	49	46	45	45	45	47
Netherlands Antilles Antilles néerlandaises										
Consumption *	10	10	6	8	9	8	12	15	20	21
Consumption per cap.(kg)	39	39	23	40	45	38	57	56	95	100

41
Sugar
Production and consumption: thousand metric tons; consumption per capita: kilograms [*cont.*]
Sucre
Production et consommation : milliers de tonnes ; consommation par habitant : kilogrammes [*suite*]

Country or area Pays ou zone	1991	1992	1993	1994	1995	1996	1997	1998	1999	2000
Nicaragua Nicaragua										
Production	* 225	* 190	* 185	* 210	* 220	* 314	* 354	330	351	398
Consumption	* 140	* 135	* 150	* 155	* 160	* 180	* 180	217	179	157
Consumption per cap.(kg)	35	33	35	35	36	40	48	45	36	31
Panama Panama										
Production	* 127	* 157	150	148	127	142	166	181	177	161
Consumption	* 64	63	63	63	66	69	73	* 75	* 85	* 95
Consumption per cap.(kg)	36	25	25	24	25	26	27	27	30	33
Saint Kitts and Nevis Saint−Kitts−et−Nevis										
Production	20	* 20	* 25	* 30	* 25	20	30	24	* 20	* 20
Consumption	2	* 2	* 2	* 2	* 2	* 2	* 2	* 2	* 2	* 3
Consumption per cap.(kg)	41	41	41	43	50	50	50	50	50	63
Trinidad and Tobago Trinité−et−Tobago										
Production	104	114	108	127	117	117	120	79	92	115
Consumption	61	55	59	63	84	73	87	72	70	78
Consumption per cap.(kg)	49	43	47	50	67	58	68	57	55	59
United States Etats−Unis										
Production	6 477	6 805	7 045	6 921	7 238	6 593	6 731	7 159	* 8 243	8 080
Consumption	7 887	8 098	8 192	8 454	8 580	8 701	8 800	9 049	8 993	8 992
Consumption per cap.(kg)	31	32	32	32	33	33	33	33	33	33
America, South • Amerique du Sud										
Argentina Argentine										
Production	* 1 560	1 379	1 093	1 202	1 612	1 393	1 649	1 749	* 1 882	* 1 580
Consumption	* 1 140	1 174	* 1 200	1 296	1 350	1 347	* 1 350	* 1 350	* 1 450	* 1 485
Consumption per cap.(kg)	35	36	36	38	39	38	38	37	40	40
Bolivia Bolivie										
Production	* 230	* 220	* 220	* 235	* 230	* 270	* 277	282	293	311
Consumption	* 185	* 190	* 200	* 210	* 215	* 225	* 235	287	290	* 293
Consumption per cap.(kg)	28	28	28	29	29	30	30	36	36	35
Brazil Brésil										
Production	9 453	9 925	10 097	12 270	13 835	14 718	16 371	19 168	20 646	16 464
Consumption	7 276	* 7 349	* 7 575	* 7 874	* 8 230	* 8 490	* 8 900	* 9 150	* 9 500	* 9 725
Consumption per cap.(kg)	50	49	50	51	53	54	56	57	57	58
Chile Chili										
Production	363	529	492	503	596	459	390	511	487	457
Consumption	518	588	598	615	650	* 700	* 720	728	729	683
Consumption per cap.(kg)	39	43	43	44	46	49	49	49	49	45
Colombia Colombie										
Production	1 633	1 813	1 833	1 964	2 069	2 149	2 136	2 126	2 241	2 391
Consumption [5]	1 318	1 262	1 158	1 140	1 128	1 206	1 192	1 240	1 281	1 343
Consumption per cap.(kg)	40	38	34	30	29	31	30	30	31	32
Ecuador Equateur										
Production	* 335	387	366	312	358	419	190	* 354	* 420	* 500
Consumption	* 375	439	361	* 400	355	* 375	396	* 410	* 420	* 433
Consumption per cap.(kg)	36	41	33	36	31	32	33	34	34	34
Guyana Guyana										
Production	168	255	255	265	258	287	283	263	336	273
Consumption	26	24	22	23	24	24	25	25	25	24
Consumption per cap.(kg)	32	30	27	28	29	29	30	29	29	28
Paraguay Paraguay										
Production *	105	95	105	100	90	116	108	114	112	90
Consumption	90	* 91	* 100	* 103	* 105	* 110	* 110	* 110	* 110	* 115
Consumption per cap.(kg)	21	20	22	22	22	22	22	21	21	21
Peru Pérou										
Production	579	474	434	543	633	612	693	570	* 655	* 725
Consumption	673	665	669	715	730	745	826	* 850	* 900	* 950
Consumption per cap.(kg)	31	30	30	31	31	31	34	34	36	37
Suriname Suriname										
Production *	5	5	5	7	10	7	10	5	7	10
Consumption *	18	18	16	17	20	18	17	18	19	20
Consumption per cap.(kg)	45	43	39	41	50	44	42	44	46	49
Uruguay Uruguay										
Production	79	73	* 35	* 22	* 20	* 15	* 19	* 14	* 9	* 8
Consumption	88	92	* 95	100	* 105	* 125	* 145	* 115	101	* 102
Consumption per cap.(kg)	28	30	30	31	33	39	44	35	31	31

41
Sugar
Production and consumption: thousand metric tons; consumption per capita: kilograms [*cont.*]
Sucre
Production et consommation : milliers de tonnes ; consommation par habitant : kilogrammes [*suite*]

Country or area Pays ou zone	1991	1992	1993	1994	1995	1996	1997	1998	1999	2000
Venezuela Venezuela										
Production	567	483	* 569	* 530	* 523	* 559	* 594	* 590	* 535	* 645
Consumption	731	642	* 725	* 780	* 800	* 820	* 840	* 855	* 870	* 893
Consumption per cap.(kg)	37	34	35	37	37	37	37	37	37	37
Asia · Asie										
Afghanistan Afghanistan										
Consumption *	40	50	50	46	50	45	50	55	60	60
Consumption per cap.(kg)	2	3	3	2	3	2	2	3	3	3
Armenia Arménie										
Consumption *	...	70	60	50	50	60	60	65	70	72
Consumption per cap.(kg)	...	19	17	13	13	16	16	17	19	19
Azerbaijan Azerbaïdjan										
Consumption	...	* 220	* 205	* 180	* 170	* 170	123	157	* 160	* 170
Consumption per cap.(kg)	...	30	28	24	22	22	16	20	20	21
Bangladesh Bangladesh										
Production *	231	231	205	249	278	194	138	159	162	110
Consumption *	275	285	300	315	285	290	300	270	300	350
Consumption per cap.(kg)	3	3	3	3	2	2	2	2	2	3
Brunei Darussalam Brunéi Darussalam										
Consumption	9	8	8	8	8	6	4	7	5	6
Consumption per cap.(kg)	35	28	27	27	26	20	11	21	16	18
Cambodia Cambodge										
Consumption *	5	10	15	20	22	40	55	65	75	85
Consumption per cap.(kg)	1	1	2	2	2	4	5	6	7	7
China †† Chine ††										
Production	6 944	8 864	8 093	6 325	6 148	* 7 091	7 415	8 904	8 527	7 616
Consumption	* 7 350	7 615	* 7 720	* 7 900	* 8 200	* 8 250	* 7 800	* 8 300	* 8 700	* 8 600
Consumption per cap.(kg)	6	6	7	7	7	7	6	7	7	7
China, Hong Kong SAR † Chine, Hong Kong RAS †										
Consumption *	153	155	158	160	160	180	180	180	180	183
Consumption per cap.(kg)	27	27	27	27	26	29	28	27	26	26
China, Macao SAR † Chine, Macao RAS †										
Consumption	3	3	3	4	5	6	7	7	7	7
Consumption per cap.(kg)	9	8	8	10	12	13	16	16	16	17
Cyprus Chypre										
Consumption *	27	28	30	32	35	30	30	30	30	31
Consumption per cap.(kg)	38	39	42	44	48	41	41	40	39	38
Georgia Géorgie										
Production	...	2	1	0	0	0	0	0	0	0
Consumption *	...	153	100	60	70	90	95	100	105	108
Consumption per cap.(kg)	...	28	18	11	13	17	19	20	21	24
India Inde										
Production	13 113	13 873	* 11 750	11 745	15 337	16 892	14 440	14 281	17 406	20 247
Consumption	11 721	12 387	* 12 989	* 13 700	* 13 900	15 254	14 971	15 272	15 750	16 546
Consumption per cap.(kg)	14	14	15	15	15	16	16	16	17	17
Indonesia Indonésie										
Production	2 259	2 313	2 490	2 461	2 103	2 100	2 189	1 493	* 1 490	* 1 685
Consumption	2 526	2 441	2 724	2 941	3 341	3 074	* 3 350	2 736	* 2 750	* 3 375
Consumption per cap.(kg)	14	13	15	15	17	16	17	13	14	16
Iran (Islamic Rep. of) Iran (Rép. islamique d')										
Production	* 813	* 933	930	902	905	692	848	863	* 940	* 920
Consumption *	1 400	1 500	1 550	1 600	1 675	1 750	1 800	1 800	1 900	1 960
Consumption per cap.(kg)	25	26	27	27	28	29	30	29	30	31
Iraq Iraq										
Consumption *	300	325	350	375	285	250	350	350	400	405
Consumption per cap.(kg)	16	17	18	19	14	12	16	16	18	18
Israel Israël										
Production	0	0	0	0	0	0	0	0	0	0
Consumption *	280	295	305	320	330	340	350	360	365	375
Consumption per cap.(kg)	57	58	58	59	60	60	60	60	60	60
Japan Japon										
Production	1 005	1 023	861	826	870	882	783	870	913	842
Consumption	2 846	2 773	2 678	2 657	2 600	2 579	2 471	2 427	2 541	2 413
Consumption per cap.(kg)	23	22	22	21	21	21	20	19	20	19

41

Sugar
Production and consumption: thousand metric tons; consumption per capita: kilograms [*cont.*]
Sucre
Production et consommation : milliers de tonnes ; consommation par habitant : kilogrammes [*suite*]

Country or area Pays ou zone	1991	1992	1993	1994	1995	1996	1997	1998	1999	2000
Jordan Jordanie										
Consumption	* 175	* 185	171	183	174	170	* 170	* 150	* 180	* 185
Consumption per cap.(kg)	39	40	35	33	30	29	28	24	28	28
Kazakhstan Kazakhstan										
Production	...	* 105	* 100	* 87	45	* 84	* 87	* 85	* 80	* 80
Consumption *	...	495	465	400	390	380	370	370	375	383
Consumption per cap.(kg)	...	29	28	25	24	24	24	25	25	26
Korea, Dem. P. R. Corée, R.p. dém. de										
Consumption	120	125	* 125	* 81	* 55	* 55	* 48	30	* 60	* 95
Consumption per cap.(kg)	5	6	5	4	3	2	2	1	3	4
Korea, Republic of Corée, République de										
Consumption [6]	857	860	852	945	1 041	1 107	1 113	986	966	1 012
Consumption per cap.(kg)	20	20	19	21	23	24	24	21	21	21
Kuwait Koweït										
Consumption *	40	48	50	55	60	65	65	70	70	73
Consumption per cap.(kg)	19	34	34	34	33	34	33	35	33	33
Kyrgyzstan Kirghizistan										
Production	...	* 15	* 10	* 23	* 35	* 35	26	36	45	57
Consumption *	...	135	145	130	125	125	110	110	100	110
Consumption per cap.(kg)	...	30	32	29	27	27	23	23	21	22
Lao People's Dem. Rep. Rép. dém. pop. lao										
Consumption *	8	9	12	14	15	15	15	16	20	21
Consumption per cap.(kg)	2	2	3	3	3	3	3	3	4	4
Lebanon Liban										
Production	...	5	19	23	29	30	32	37	40	34
Consumption	* 115	* 115	* 115	* 120	* 120	* 120	* 120	* 125	* 130	122
Consumption per cap.(kg)	44	43	40	41	40	39	38	39	40	37
Malaysia Malaisie										
Production *	105	105	105	110	110	107	108	100	107	108
Consumption *	700	720	800	875	950	1 025	1 050	1 075	1 110	1 125
Consumption per cap.(kg)	39	39	42	44	46	48	49	49	49	48
Maldives Maldives										
Consumption	8	9	9	9	8	8	7	8	5	6
Consumption per cap.(kg)	36	39	38	36	32	31	27	30	18	21
Mongolia Mongolie										
Consumption	55	50	45	43	45	40	40	19	10	25
Consumption per cap.(kg)	25	22	19	19	20	17	17	8	4	9
Myanmar Myanmar										
Production	35	50	47	48	42	46	55	51	43	75
Consumption	* 36	* 42	* 47	* 50	* 50	* 55	* 50	31	69	* 85
Consumption per cap.(kg)	1	1	1	1	1	1	1	1	2	2
Nepal Népal										
Production	25	20	* 25	* 40	* 60	* 80	* 90	* 120	* 150	* 110
Consumption	40	40	* 41	* 50	* 75	* 80	* 95	* 130	* 140	* 153
Consumption per cap.(kg)	2	2	2	3	4	4	5	6	6	7
Pakistan Pakistan										
Production	2 227	2 543	2 750	3 196	3 116	2 662	2 635	3 503	3 712	* 2 614
Consumption	2 555	2 670	2 747	2 945	2 971	3 033	* 3 023	* 3 085	* 3 196	* 3 330
Consumption per cap.(kg)	21	22	22	23	23	23	22	24	24	24
Philippines Philippines										
Production	1 911	1 919	2 091	2 098	1 562	1 895	1 954	1 549	1 913	1 826
Consumption	1 565	1 643	1 739	1 922	1 765	1 956	1 959	1 958	1 854	2 052
Consumption per cap.(kg)	25	26	27	28	25	27	27	26	25	27
Saudi Arabia Arabie saoudite										
Consumption *	475	500	520	535	550	550	550	550	520	560
Consumption per cap.(kg)	29	30	30	30	30	29	28	27	26	29
Singapore Singapour										
Consumption *	200	210	210	250	250	280	290	270	280	285
Consumption per cap.(kg)	73	75	73	74	72	78	78	70	72	73
Sri Lanka Sri Lanka										
Production	67	60	69	70	70	73	63	20	* 19	* 15
Consumption	* 360	* 360	* 405	* 450	* 500	* 525	* 550	550	* 550	* 575
Consumption per cap.(kg)	21	21	23	25	28	29	30	29	29	30

41
Sugar
Production and consumption: thousand metric tons; consumption per capita: kilograms [*cont.*]
Sucre
Production et consommation : milliers de tonnes ; consommation par habitant : kilogrammes [*suite*]

Country or area Pays ou zone	1991	1992	1993	1994	1995	1996	1997	1998	1999	2000
Syrian Arab Republic Rép. arabe syrienne										
Production	195	193	199	198	172	197	191	107	* 102	* 100
Consumption *	430	450	550	600	650	675	695	715	720	730
Consumption per cap.(kg)	34	39	41	43	46	46	46	46	45	44
Tajikistan Tadjikistan										
Consumption *	...	110	115	100	95	80	70	65	60	60
Consumption per cap.(kg)	...	20	20	17	16	14	12	11	10	9
Thailand Thaïlande										
Production	4 248	5 078	3 825	4 168	5 447	6 154	6 243	4 143	5 456	6 157
Consumption	1 189	1 264	1 368	1 480	1 645	1 706	1 829	1 834	1 776	1 816
Consumption per cap.(kg)	21	22	23	25	28	28	30	30	29	29
Turkey Turquie										
Production	1 983	1 961	1 894	1 877	1 405	2 002	2 187	2 784	2 491	2 273
Consumption	1 737	* 1 752	* 1 810	* 1 795	* 1 800	* 1 900	2 107	2 074	1 836	* 2 150
Consumption per cap.(kg)	30	30	30	30	30	31	34	33	29	33
Turkmenistan Turkménistan										
Consumption *	...	100	105	95	80	75	70	70	70	70
Consumption per cap.(kg)	...	26	27	22	18	16	17	14	16	16
Uzbekistan Ouzbékistan										
Production	...	...	...	...	...	...	...	11	* 20	11
Consumption	...	* 475	* 450	* 375	* 360	* 350	* 350	* 350	* 355	359
Consumption per cap.(kg)	...	22	21	17	16	15	15	15	15	15
Viet Nam Viet Nam										
Production	* 475	* 495	* 510	* 475	* 525	* 550	* 559	657	* 878	1 155
Consumption	* 510	* 520	* 570	* 590	* 625	* 625	* 625	* 675	700	* 810
Consumption per cap.(kg)	8	8	8	8	9	8	8	9	9	10
Yemen Yémen										
Consumption *	250	285	300	285	285	350	375	375	390	410
Consumption per cap.(kg)	22	24	24	19	19	22	23	22	22	22
Europe • Europe										
Albania Albanie										
Production	* 15	* 17	* 10	* 10	* 10	9	* 3	* 3	* 3	* 3
Consumption *	68	65	85	80	80	80	65	65	65	70
Consumption per cap.(kg)	21	19	25	23	22	22	17	17	21	22
Austria Autriche										
Production	507	436	497	501	* 481[1]	* 535[1]	* 529[1]	* 533[1]	* 545[1]	* 447[1]
Consumption [7]	425	426	412	406	...	...	...	...	...	...
Consumption per cap.(kg)	54	54	52	50	...	...	...	...	...	...
Belarus Bélarus										
Production	...	106	129	134	139	144	179	180	151	186
Consumption	...	345	337	376	355	358	380	405[8]	* 357	380
Consumption per cap.(kg)	...	34	33	27	35	35	37	40	36	38
Belgium – Luxembourg [1] Belgique – Luxembourg [1]										
Production	1 049	1 039	1 118	1 005	999	1 036	1 106	863	* 1 186	* 1 024
Bosnia – Herzegovina Bosnie – Herzégovine										
Production *	...	...	25	15	10	15	15	10	10	15
Consumption *	...	...	30	30	30	30	45	85	90	105
Consumption per cap.(kg)	...	...	7	7	7	7	11	20	21	25
Bulgaria Bulgarie										
Production *	65	35	15	10	15	7	6	5	2	2
Consumption	160	* 250	* 250	* 250	* 260	* 260	* 260	* 260	* 225	* 255
Consumption per cap.(kg)	18	29	30	30	31	31	31	32	27	31
Croatia Croatie										
Production	...	...	86	125	191	212	154	151	114	57
Consumption *	...	...	150	155	200	220	220	220	180	180
Consumption per cap.(kg)	...	...	31	33	43	49	46	44	40	39
Czechoslovakia (former) † Tchécoslovaquie (anc.) †										
Production	* 790	743	...	...	...	...	...	...	...	...
Consumption *	800	795	...	...	...	...	...	...	...	...
Consumption per cap.(kg)	51	51	...	...	...	...	...	...	...	...
Czech Republic République tchèque										
Production	...	...	563	465	550	654	648	535	420	434
Consumption	...	...	* 485	435	* 435	412	* 425	438	* 450	440
Consumption per cap.(kg)	...	...	47	42	42	40	41	43	44	43

41

Sugar
Production and consumption: thousand metric tons; consumption per capita: kilograms [*cont.*]

Sucre
Production et consommation : milliers de tonnes ; consommation par habitant : kilogrammes [*suite*]

Country or area Pays ou zone	1991	1992	1993	1994	1995	1996	1997	1998	1999	2000
Denmark [1] Danemark [1]										
Production	527	446	542	510	448	536	603	585	589	* 579
Estonia Estonie										
Consumption	...	* 40	* 40	* 40	* 40	37	* 50	* 55	* 65	* 70
Consumption per cap.(kg)	...	26	26	27	27	25	34	38	46	51
Finland Finlande										
Production [9]	163	153	154	113	164[1]	135[1]	175[1]	133[1]	180[1]	* 166[1]
Consumption [10]	213	227	242	219	...	...	...	...	...	...
Consumption per cap.(kg)	42	45	48	43	...	...	...	...	...	...
France [1] France [1]										
Production	4 413	4 723	4 724	4 364	4 564	4 543	5 134	4 637	4 914	* 4 685
Germany [1] Allemagne [1]										
Production	4 251	4 401	4 359	3 672	3 826	4 203	4 045	4 037	4 300	* 4 550
Gibraltar Gibraltar										
Consumption	3	3	3	4	4	4	4	3	3	3
Consumption per cap.(kg)	79	76	74	117	133	133	133	100	83	83
Greece [1] Grèce [1]										
Production	262	320	* 333	* 271	* 312	* 288	* 396	* 220	* 252	* 400
Hungary Hongrie										
Production	* 700	391	248	434	515	554	460	461	446	309
Consumption	575	608	382	398	430	462	448	386	399	367
Consumption per cap.(kg)	56	59	37	39	42	45	44	38	40	37
Iceland Islande										
Consumption	* 14	* 15	* 15	16	* 16	* 15	* 13	* 13	* 12	* 13
Consumption per cap.(kg)	54	58	58	58	59	54	48	46	43	45
Ireland [1] Irlande [1]										
Production *	232	242	191	232	242	247	223	238	235	221
Italy [1] Italie [1]										
Production	1 641	2 032	1 542	1 621	1 621	1 561	1 891	* 1 735	* 1 853	* 1 687
Latvia Lettonie										
Production	...	* 30	* 35	* 25	* 35	* 40	* 49	71	* 70	68
Consumption	...	* 151	* 145	* 110	* 100	* 90	* 90	* 85	82	78
Consumption per cap.(kg)	...	57	56	43	40	36	36	35	34	32
Lithuania Lituanie										
Production	...	85	* 70	59	105	* 75	117	137	121	137
Consumption	...	116	* 110	* 105	104	* 125	98	119	* 110	95
Consumption per cap.(kg)	...	31	30	28	28	34	27	32	30	26
Malta Malte										
Consumption	13	17	17	* 18	* 19	* 20	* 20	* 20	* 22	* 23
Consumption per cap.(kg)	37	46	47	50	51	54	53	53	58	59
Netherlands [1] Pays–Bas [1]										
Production *	1 137	1 295	1 232	1 051	1 074	1 125	1 109	897	1 217	1 153
Norway Norvège										
Consumption	177	178	177	184	177	* 180	* 185	* 185	* 185	* 186
Consumption per cap.(kg)	42	41	41	43	41	41	42	42	42	41
Poland Pologne										
Production	1 778	1 595	2 155	1 503	1 734	2 380	2 112	2 242	1 968	2 104
Consumption	1 660	1 618	1 691	* 1 700	* 1 700	* 1 700	* 1 750	1 708	* 1 720	* 1 730
Consumption per cap.(kg)	43	42	44	44	44	44	45	44	45	45
Portugal [1] Portugal [1]										
Production *	1	2	4	6	6	3	71	66	76	60
Republic of Moldova République de Moldova										
Production	...	* 180	* 220	167	215	231	203	186	108	102
Consumption *	...	175	175	175	175	175	160	150	125	105
Consumption per cap.(kg)	...	40	40	40	40	40	37	35	29	24
Romania Roumanie										
Production	344	280	141	206	202	226	204	189	86	54
Consumption *	565	615	475	480	480	500	510	520	530	550
Consumption per cap.(kg)	24	24	21	21	21	22	23	23	24	25
Russian Federation Fédération de Russie										
Production	...	2 437	* 2 717	* 1 650	2 241	1 851	1 337	1 370	1 651	1 705
Consumption	...	6 145	5 034	4 957	5 108	5 235	5 308	* 5 450	5 565	5 707
Consumption per cap.(kg)	...	41	34	34	35	35	36	37	38	40

41

Sugar
Production and consumption: thousand metric tons; consumption per capita: kilograms [*cont.*]
Sucre
Production et consommation : milliers de tonnes ; consommation par habitant : kilogrammes [*suite*]

Country or area Pays ou zone	1991	1992	1993	1994	1995	1996	1997	1998	1999	2000
Slovakia Slovaquie										
Production	...	...	* 150	* 130	* 145	* 140	237	170	213	140
Consumption *	...	...	150	150	175	200	220	220	225	230
Consumption per cap.(kg)	...	...	28	28	33	37	41	41	42	43
Slovenia Slovénie										
Production	...	...	41	45	65	71	67	51	* 60	44
Consumption *	...	...	76	110	110	110	110	110	105	110
Consumption per cap.(kg)	...	...	50	55	55	55	55	56	53	55
Spain [1] Espagne [1]										
Production	949	1 032	1 237	1 116	1 111	1 228	1 142	1 327	1 071	* 1 208
Sweden Suède										
Production [11]	266	333	413	370	357[1]	398[1]	396[1]	400[1]	448[1]	448[1]
Consumption	380	382	388	457	...	...	...	...	...	...
Consumption per cap.(kg)	44	44	44	52	...	...	...	...	...	...
Switzerland Suisse										
Production	136	137	* 150	* 130	* 140	* 194	* 200	191	177	* 231
Consumption	307	311	* 310	* 310	* 315	* 310	* 315	206	328	* 338
Consumption per cap.(kg)	46	46	45	44	45	44	44	29	46	47
TFYR of Macedonia L'ex–R.y. Macédoine										
Production	...	...	7	6	7	18	* 15	40	43	32
Consumption *	...	...	35	40	45	50	50	60	80	85
Consumption per cap.(kg)	...	...	17	19	23	25	25	30	40	42
Ukraine Ukraine										
Production	...	3 824	* 4 160	3 632	3 801	* 2 935	* 2 170	2 041	1 640	1 689
Consumption	...	2 881	* 2 575	* 2 492	* 2 200	* 2 100	* 1 800	1 739	* 1 800	* 1 875
Consumption per cap.(kg)	...	55	49	48	43	41	35	34	36	38
United Kingdom [1] Royaume–Uni [1]										
Production	1 326	1 476	1 436	1 373	* 1 326	1 605	1 592	1 439	1 540	* 1 440
Yugoslavia Yougoslavie										
Production	* 900	* 500	* 127	* 210	* 156	* 285	239	213	248	* 170
Consumption	* 810	* 725	* 350	* 325	* 300	* 300	299	* 300	* 300	* 275
Consumption per cap.(kg)	...	69	33	31	28	28	28	28	28	26
Yugoslavia, SFR † Yougoslavie, Rfs †										
Production	900	...	...	...	...	...	...	...	...	...
Consumption *	810	...	...	...	...	...	...	...	...	...
Consumption per cap.(kg)	34	...	...	...	...	...	...	...	...	...
Oceania · Océanie										
Australia Australie										
Production	3 195	4 363	4 488	5 222	5 119	5 618	5 883	5 085	5 514	4 417
Consumption	835	829	909	911	926	976	1 003	1 003	* 1 005	1 220
Consumption per cap.(kg)	48	47	52	51	51	53	54	54	53	64
Fiji Fidji										
Production	456	451	451	543	458	474	369	278	377	353
Consumption [12]	44	45	46	43	48	48	51	44	38	41
Consumption per cap.(kg)	59	60	60	56	63	62	66	56	50	54
New Zealand Nouvelle–Zélande										
Consumption	* 175	* 178	* 180	* 183	* 185	* 200	* 220	158	198	212
Consumption per cap.(kg)	52	52	52	51	51	54	59	42	52	56
Papua New Guinea Papouasie–Nvl–Guinée										
Production	* 35	* 30	* 30	* 35	* 35	* 35	39	41	47	41
Consumption	* 27	* 27	* 28	* 27	* 27	* 30	37	36	38	35
Consumption per cap.(kg)	7	7	7	7	7	7	9	8	8	7
Samoa Samoa										
Production	2	2	2	2	2	2	2	2	2	2
Consumption	3	3	3	4	4	3	3	3	2	2
Consumption per cap.(kg)	13	12	12	15	14	10	9	9	7	7
USSR (former) · URSS (ancienne)										
USSR (former) † URSS (anc.) †										
Production	6 898	...	...	...	...	...	...	...	...	...
Consumption *	11 908	...	...	...	...	...	...	...	...	...
Consumption per cap.(kg)	41	...	...	...	...	...	...	...	...	...

41
Sugar
Production and consumption: thousand metric tons; consumption per capita: kilograms [*cont.*]
Sucre
Production et consommation : milliers de tonnes ; consommation par habitant : kilogrammes [*suite*]

Source:
International Sugar Organization (ISO), London, "Sugar
Yearbook 2000" and the ISO database.

† For information on recent changes in country or
area nomenclature pertaining to former Czechoslovakia,
Germany, Hong Kong Special Administrative Region (SAR) of
China, Macao Special Administrative Region (SAR) of China,
SFR of Yugoslavia and the former USSR, see Annex I − Country
or area nomenclature, regional and other groupings.

†† For statistical purposes, the data for
China do not include those for Hong Kong Special
Administrative Region (Hong Kong SAR), Macao Special
Administrative Region (Macao SAR) and Taiwan province of
China.

1   Source: Food and Agriculture Organization of the United
    Nations.
2   3,268 tons lost in fire.
3   Including non−human consumption: 1984− 31,191 tons; 1985−
    77,946 tons; 1986− 8,831 tons; 1987− 64,646 tons; 1988−
    46,834 tons; 1989− 167,173 tons; 1990− 129,608 tons; 1991−
    92,446 tons; 1993− 94,156 tons; 1994− 92,313 tons.

4   FAO estimate.
5   Including non−human consumption: 1983 − 6,710 tons; 1984 −
    19,797 tons; 1985− 79,908 tons; 1986− 98,608 tons; 1987−
    147,262 tons; 1988− 122,058 tons; 1989− 52,230 tons; 1991−
    13,541 tons; 1994− 12,178 tons; 1995− 10,211 tons; 1996−
    14,648 tons; 2000− 31,836 tons.
6   Including consumption of mono−sodium glutamate, lysine and
    other products: 1987− 44,600 tons; 1988− 92,200 tons; 1989−
    94,500 tons; 1990− 89,400 tons; 1991− 77,300 tons; 1992−
    75,800 tons; 1993− 89,800 tons; 1994− 170,384 tons; 1995−
    200,863 tons; 1996− 257,763 tons; 1997− 257,310 tons; 1998−
    258,247 tons; 2000− 159,027 tons.

7   Including non−human consumption: 1981 − 7,255 tons; 1982 −
    11,501 tons; 1983−4,988 tons; 1984− 9,002 tons; 1986− 7,862
    tons; 1987− 9,989 tons; 1988− 12,384 tons; 1989− 8,288 tons;
    1990− 5,387 tons; 1991− 11,799 tons; 1993− 9,348 tons.
8   Including non−human consumption: 1998 − 15,652 tons.
9   Of which 1 041 tons of sugar produced from imported Estonian
    beet in 1993 and 1 145 tons in 1994.
10 Including non−human consumption: 1980− 22,850 tons; 1981−
    18,840 tons; 1982− 17,270 tons; 1983− 15,075 tons;
    1984−16,775 tons; 1985− 12,812 tons; 1986− 26,552 tons;
    1987− 31,312 tons; 1988− 20,912 tons.
11 Including sales from government stocks: 1983−4,238
    tons;1984−3,602 tons; 1985−3,181 tons; 1988−4,324 tons;
    1989−2,771 tons.
12 Including 11,572 tons sold to other Pacific Island nations
    in 1994; 12,520 tons in 1995; 14,154 tons in 1996; 13,109
    tons in 1997; 5,305 tons in 1998.

Source:
Organisation internationale du sucre (OIS), Londres,
"Annuaire du sucre 2000" et la base de données de l'OIS.

† Pour les modifications récentes de nomenclature
de pays ou de zone concernant l'Allemagne, Hong Kong,
région administrative spéciale (RAS) de Chine, Macao,
région administrative spéciale (RAS) de Chine,
l'ex−Tchécoslovaquie, l'ex−URSS et l'ex−Rfs de
Yougoslavie, voir annexe I − Nomenclature des pays ou
des zones, groupements régionaux et autres groupements.

†† Les données statistiques relatives à la Chine ne
comprennent pas celles qui concernent la région
administrative spéciale de Hong Kong (la RAS de
Hong Kong), la région administrative spéciale de Macao
(la RAS de Macao) et la province chinoise de Taiwan.

1   Source: Organisation des Nations Unies pour l'alimentation
    et l'agriculture.
2   Dont 3 268 tonnes détruites par le feu.
3   Dont consommation non humaine : 1984− 31 119 tonnes; 1985-
    77 946 tonnes; 1986− 8 831 tonnes; 1987− 64 646 tonnes;
    1988− 46 834 tonnes; 1989− 167 173 tonnes; 1990− 129 608
    tonnes; 1991− 92 446 tonnes; 1993− 94 156 tonnes; 1994− 92
    313 tonnes.
4   Estimation de FAO.
5   Dont consommation non humaine : 1983 − 6 701 tonnes; 1984
    − 19 797 tonnes; 1985− 79 908 tonnes; 1986− 98 608 tonnes;
    1987− 147 262 tonnes; 1988− 122 058 tonnes; 1989− 52 230
    tonnes; 1991− 13 541 tonnes; 1994− 12 178 tonnes; 1995−
    10 211 tonnes; 1996− 14 648 tons; 2000− 31 836 tonnes.
6   Y compris la consommation des produits du glutamate
    monosodium, lysine et autres: 1987− 44 600 tonnes ; 1988− 92
    200 tonnes; 1989− 94 500 tonnes; 1990− 89 400 tonnes; 1991−
    77 300 tonnes ; 1992− 75 800 tonnes; 1993− 89 800 tonnes;
    1994− 170 384 tonnes; 1995− 200 863 tonnes; 1996− 257 763
    tonnes; 1997− 257 310 tonnes; 1998− 258 247 tonnes; 2000−
    159 027 tonnes.
7   Y compris la consommation non humaine : 1981−7 255 tonnes;
    1982−11 501 tonnes; 1983− 4 988 tonnes; 1986− 7 862 tonnes;
    1987− 9 989 tonnes; 1988− 12 384 tonnes; 1989− 8 288 tonnes;
    1990− 5 387 tonnes; 1991− 11 799 tonnes; 1993− 9 348 tonnes.
8   Dont la consommation non humaine: 1998 − 15 652 tonnes.
9   Dont 1 041 tonnes de sucre à l'aide de betteraves importées
    d'Estonie en 1993 et 1 145 tonnes en 1994.
10 Dont consommation non humaine : 1980− 22 850 tonnes; 1981-
    18 640 tonnes; 1982− 17 270 tonnes; 1983− 15 075 tonnes;
    1984− tonnes; 1985− 12 812 tonnes; 1986− 26 552 tonnes;
    1987− 31 312 tonnes; 1988− 20 912 tonnes.
11 Dont ventes par prélèvement dans les réserves publiques :
    1983− 4 238 tonnes; 1984− 3 602 tonnes; 1985− 3 181 tonnes;
    1988− 4 324 tonnes; 1989− 2 771 tonnes.
12 Y compris 11 572 tonnes vendues à autres îles pacifiques en
    1994; 12 520 tonnes en 1995; 14 154 tonnes en 1996; 13 109
    tonnes en 1997; et 5 305 tonnes en 1998.

42

Meat
Viande

Production: thousand metric tons
Production : milliers de tonnes

Region, country or area Région, pays ou zone	1991	1992	1993	1994	1995	1996	1997	1998	1999	2000
World *Monde*	137 122	138 273	140 268	143 794	145 987	146 121	150 796	156 555	159 939	162 437
Beef,veal & buffalo Boeuf,veau et buffle	56 348	55 526	55 101	55 916	56 902	57 409	58 254	58 026	58 995	60 233
Pork Porc	70 901	72 838	75 038	77 539	78 534	78 426	82 146	87 647	89 867	90 909
Mutton,lamb & goat Mouton,agneau et caprin	9 872	9 909	10 129	10 339	10 550	10 285	10 396	10 882	11 077	11 294
Africa Afrique	5 800	5 884	5 870	5 802	5 960	6 086	6 339	6 526	6 648	6 726
Beef,veal & buffalo Boeuf,veau et buffle	3 641	3 717	3 664	3 549	3 597	3 702	3 887	3 980	4 098	4 195
Pork Porc	578	548	540	542	601	578	589	606	613	582
Mutton,lamb & goat Mouton,agneau et caprin	1 581	1 620	1 667	1 711	1 762	1 806	1 863	1 941	1 937	1 949
Algeria Algérie	247	260	276	279	279	289	281	282	293	299
Beef,veal & buffalo Boeuf,veau et buffle	94	97	98	101	101	99	102	103	117	117
Mutton,lamb & goat Mouton,agneau et caprin	152	164	178	178	178	190	179	179	175	182
Angola Angola	88	95	96	96	97	107	115	123	124	124
Beef,veal & buffalo Boeuf,veau et buffle	60	66	66	65	65	71	77	85	85	85
Pork Porc	23	24	25	25	26	28	29	29	29	29
Mutton,lamb & goat Mouton,agneau et caprin	5	5	6	6	6	8	9	9	10	11
Benin Bénin	27	28	29	30	32	33	34	33	33	33
Beef,veal & buffalo Boeuf,veau et buffle	16	16	16	17	18	19	20	20	21	21
Pork Porc	6	6	6	6	7	8	8	6	6	6
Mutton,lamb & goat Mouton,agneau et caprin	6	6	6	6	7	6	6	7	6	6
Botswana Botswana	54	56	55	45	55	52	47	45	45	46
Beef,veal & buffalo Boeuf,veau et buffle	44	47	49	38	46	44	38	37	37	38
Pork Porc	1	0	0	0	0	1	0	1	1	1
Mutton,lamb & goat Mouton,agneau et caprin	9	8	7	6	9	8	8	7	7	8
Burkina Faso Burkina Faso	75	75	77	77	78	88	91	94	96	96
Beef,veal & buffalo Boeuf,veau et buffle	38	39	40	40	40	47	50	51	52	52
Pork Porc	6	6	6	6	6	7	8	8	8	8
Mutton,lamb & goat Mouton,agneau et caprin	30	31	31	31	32	33	34	35	36	36
Burundi Burundi	22	24	25	23	22	22	18	19	18	15
Beef,veal & buffalo Boeuf,veau et buffle	12	14	14	12	12	13	10	11	9	9

42
Meat
Production: thousand metric tons [*cont.*]
Viande
Production : milliers de tonnes [*suite*]

Region, country or area Région, pays ou zone	1991	1992	1993	1994	1995	1996	1997	1998	1999	2000
Pork Porc	5	5	5	5	5	5	4	4	4	3
Mutton,lamb & goat Mouton,agneau et caprin	5	5	6	6	5	5	4	3	4	4
Cameroon **Cameroun**	**119**	**122**	**126**	**129**	**132**	**134**	**137**	**139**	**139**	**139**
Beef,veal & buffalo Boeuf,veau et buffle	74	77	79	81	83	85	88	90	90	90
Pork Porc	17	17	17	17	18	18	18	18	18	18
Mutton,lamb & goat Mouton,agneau et caprin	28	28	30	30	31	31	31	31	31	31
Cape Verde **Cap-Vert**	**5**	**5**	**8**	**6**	**9**	**4**	**6**	**8**	**8**	**7**
Beef,veal & buffalo Boeuf,veau et buffle	0	0	0	0	0	1	1	1	0	0
Pork Porc	4	4	7	5	8	3	5	6	7	7
Mutton,lamb & goat Mouton,agneau et caprin	0	0	1	1	0	0	0	1	1	0
Central African Rep. **Rép. centrafricaine**	**56**	**58**	**60**	**61**	**65**	**81**	**70**	**72**	**72**	**83**
Beef,veal & buffalo Boeuf,veau et buffle	42	44	45	45	48	61	50	51	51	60
Pork Porc	8	8	9	9	10	11	12	12	12	12
Mutton,lamb & goat Mouton,agneau et caprin	6	6	6	7	8	8	8	9	9	11
Chad **Tchad**	**94**	**99**	**91**	**79**	**90**	**98**	**98**	**109**	**108**	**108**
Beef,veal & buffalo Boeuf,veau et buffle	75	79	70	57	68	74	73	83	81	81
Mutton,lamb & goat Mouton,agneau et caprin	19	20	21	21	22	24	25	26	27	27
Comoros **Comores**	**1**	**1**	**1**	**1**	**1**	**1**	**1**	**1**	**1**	**1**
Beef,veal & buffalo Boeuf,veau et buffle	1	1	1	1	1	1	1	1	1	1
Congo **Congo**	**5**	**5**	**5**	**5**	**5**	**5**	**5**	**5**	**5**	**5**
Beef,veal & buffalo Boeuf,veau et buffle	2	2	2	2	2	2	2	2	2	2
Pork Porc	2	2	2	2	2	2	2	2	2	2
Mutton,lamb & goat Mouton,agneau et caprin	1	1	1	1	1	1	1	1	1	1
Côte d'Ivoire **Côte d'Ivoire**	**56**	**58**	**59**	**60**	**64**	**60**	**60**	**61**	**62**	**62**
Beef,veal & buffalo Boeuf,veau et buffle	33	34	34	34	36	37	38	38	39	39
Pork Porc	15	15	16	16	19	14	12	13	13	13
Mutton,lamb & goat Mouton,agneau et caprin	8	9	9	9	9	10	10	10	10	10
Dem. Rep. of the Congo **Rép. dém. du Congo**	**79**	**82**	**84**	**85**	**84**	**79**	**82**	**82**	**77**	**76**
Beef,veal & buffalo Boeuf,veau et buffle	19	20	20	19	17	15	16	14	14	14

42

Meat
Production: thousand metric tons [*cont.*]
Viande
Production : milliers de tonnes [*suite*]

Region, country or area Région, pays ou zone	1991	1992	1993	1994	1995	1996	1997	1998	1999	2000
Pork										
Porc	39	41	42	43	44	42	43	43	41	41
Mutton,lamb & goat										
Mouton,agneau et caprin	20	21	22	23	23	23	24	24	22	22
Djibouti										
Djibouti	**7**	**7**	**8**	**8**	**8**	**8**	**8**	**8**	**8**	**8**
Beef,veal & buffalo										
Boeuf,veau et buffle	3	3	3	3	3	3	4	4	4	4
Mutton,lamb & goat										
Mouton,lamb & goat	4	4	4	4	4	4	4	4	4	4
Egypt										
Egypte	**412**	**424**	**446**	**472**	**488**	**546**	**644**	**658**	**687**	**714**
Beef,veal & buffalo										
Boeuf,veau et buffle	335	343	361	382	394	453	548	560	571	595
Pork										
Porc	3	3	3	3	3	3	3	3	3	3
Mutton,lamb & goat										
Mouton,agneau et caprin	74	78	83	87	91	91	93	95	113	116
Eritrea										
Erythrée	...	...	**19**	**20**	**20**	**22**	**25**	**27**	**30**	**26**
Beef,veal & buffalo										
Boeuf,veau et buffle	...	...	9	10	10	12	14	16	18	15
Mutton,lamb & goat										
Mouton,agneau et caprin	...	...	9	10	10	10	10	11	12	11
Ethiopia incl. Eritrea										
Ethiopie comp. Erythrée	**395**	**394**	...	...	...	...	...	...	...	...
Beef,veal & buffalo										
Boeuf,veau et buffle	245	244	...	...	...	...	...	...	...	...
Pork										
Porc	1	1	...	...	...	...	...	...	...	...
Mutton,lamb & goat										
Mouton,agneau et caprin	149	149	...	...	...	...	...	...	...	...
Ethiopia										
Ethiopie	...	...	**370**	**374**	**379**	**412**	**415**	**420**	**436**	**427**
Beef,veal & buffalo										
Boeuf,veau et buffle	...	...	230	230	235	267	270	274	290	285
Pork										
Porc	...	...	1	1	1	1	1	1	1	1
Mutton,lamb & goat										
Mouton,agneau et caprin	...	...	139	143	143	144	144	144	145	141
Gabon										
Gabon	**4**	**5**	**5**	**5**	**5**	**5**	**5**	**5**	**5**	**5**
Beef,veal & buffalo										
Boeuf,veau et buffle	1	1	1	1	1	1	1	1	1	1
Pork										
Porc	3	3	3	3	3	3	3	3	3	3
Mutton,lamb & goat										
Mouton,agneau et caprin	1	1	1	1	1	1	1	1	1	1
Gambia										
Gambie	**4**	**4**	**4**	**4**	**5**	**5**	**5**	**5**	**5**	**5**
Beef,veal & buffalo										
Boeuf,veau et buffle	3	3	3	3	3	3	3	3	3	3
Mutton,lamb & goat										
Mouton,agneau et caprin	1	1	1	1	1	1	1	2	2	2
Ghana										
Ghana	**42**	**40**	**40**	**41**	**40**	**40**	**33**	**35**	**35**	**35**
Beef,veal & buffalo										
Boeuf,veau et buffle	21	20	20	20	21	21	12	14	14	14

42

Meat
Production: thousand metric tons [*cont.*]
Viande
Production : milliers de tonnes [*suite*]

Region, country or area Région, pays ou zone	1991	1992	1993	1994	1995	1996	1997	1998	1999	2000
Pork Porc	10	9	9	9	8	7	8	8	8	8
Mutton,lamb & goat Mouton,agneau et caprin	11	11	11	11	11	12	13	13	13	13
Guinea **Guinée**	**14**	**15**	**16**	**17**	**20**	**20**	**21**	**22**	**22**	**22**
Beef,veal & buffalo Boeuf,veau et buffle	10	11	12	12	15	15	15	15	16	16
Pork Porc	1	1	1	1	1	1	1	2	2	2
Mutton,lamb & goat Mouton,agneau et caprin	3	3	3	3	4	4	4	5	5	5
Guinea-Bissau **Guinée-Bissau**	**14**	**14**	**15**	**15**	**15**	**16**	**16**	**16**	**16**	**16**
Beef,veal & buffalo Boeuf,veau et buffle	3	4	4	4	4	4	4	4	4	4
Pork Porc	9	9	10	10	10	10	10	10	11	11
Mutton,lamb & goat Mouton,agneau et caprin	1	1	1	1	1	1	2	2	2	2
Kenya **Kenya**	**313**	**297**	**292**	**298**	**307**	**329**	**339**	**314**	**320**	**318**
Beef,veal & buffalo Boeuf,veau et buffle	247	230	225	230	240	260	270	243	252	255
Pork Porc	7	7	8	9	9	10	10	10	9	8
Mutton,lamb & goat Mouton,agneau et caprin	59	60	59	59	58	58	58	61	59	55
Lesotho **Lesotho**	**22**	**23**	**25**	**22**	**23**	**21**	**24**	**20**	**19**	**19**
Beef,veal & buffalo Boeuf,veau et buffle	13	14	15	13	14	12	15	12	11	11
Pork Porc	2	2	3	2	3	3	3	3	3	3
Mutton,lamb & goat Mouton,agneau et caprin	7	7	7	7	6	6	6	5	5	5
Liberia **Libéria**	**6**	**6**	**6**	**6**	**6**	**6**	**6**	**6**	**6**	**6**
Beef,veal & buffalo Boeuf,veau et buffle	1	1	1	1	1	1	1	1	1	1
Pork Porc	4	4	4	4	4	4	4	4	4	4
Mutton,lamb & goat Mouton,agneau et caprin	1	1	1	1	1	1	1	1	1	1
Libyan Arab Jamah. **Jamah. arabe libyenne**	**60**	**56**	**61**	**53**	**58**	**59**	**82**	**130**	**49**	**49**
Beef,veal & buffalo Boeuf,veau et buffle	31	27	26	22	22	15	39	43	15	15
Mutton,lamb & goat Mouton,agneau et caprin	30	29	35	31	36	45	43	87	34	34
Madagascar **Madagascar**	**209**	**212**	**215**	**217**	**224**	**226**	**229**	**230**	**231**	**202**
Beef,veal & buffalo Boeuf,veau et buffle	143	144	145	145	146	147	147	148	148	148
Pork Porc	57	58	60	62	68	70	72	72	74	44
Mutton,lamb & goat Mouton,agneau et caprin	9	9	10	10	10	9	10	10	10	10

42

Meat
Production: thousand metric tons [cont.]
Viande
Production : milliers de tonnes [suite]

Region, country or area Région, pays ou zone	1991	1992	1993	1994	1995	1996	1997	1998	1999	2000
Malawi										
Malawi	**31**	**32**	**32**	**30**	**31**	**32**	**35**	**33**	**34**	**34**
Beef,veal & buffalo										
Boeuf,veau et buffle	17	17	18	14	14	16	18	17	17	17
Pork										
Porc	11	11	11	12	12	11	12	11	12	12
Mutton,lamb & goat										
Mouton,agneau et caprin	4	4	4	4	4	5	5	5	5	5
Mali										
Mali	**122**	**128**	**126**	**130**	**135**	**138**	**146**	**152**	**152**	**152**
Beef,veal & buffalo										
Boeuf,veau et buffle	74	78	81	83	85	86	88	91	94	94
Pork										
Porc	2	2	2	2	2	2	2	3	3	3
Mutton,lamb & goat										
Mouton,agneau et caprin	46	48	43	45	48	50	55	58	56	56
Mauritania										
Mauritanie	**41**	**38**	**29**	**30**	**31**	**35**	**35**	**34**	**33**	**33**
Beef,veal & buffalo										
Boeuf,veau et buffle	20	18	9	9	10	10	10	10	10	10
Mutton,lamb & goat										
Mouton,agneau et caprin	21	20	20	21	21	25	25	24	23	23
Mauritius										
Maurice	**3**	**4**	**4**	**4**	**4**	**4**	**4**	**4**	**4**	**4**
Beef,veal & buffalo										
Boeuf,veau et buffle	2	2	3	3	2	2	2	3	3	3
Pork										
Porc	1	1	1	1	1	1	1	1	1	1
Morocco										
Maroc	**270**	**274**	**273**	**250**	**255**	**216**	**268**	**256**	**272**	**283**
Beef,veal & buffalo										
Boeuf,veau et buffle	149	145	150	125	122	103	125	120	130	140
Pork										
Porc	1	1	1	1	1	1	1	1	1	1
Mutton,lamb & goat										
Mouton,agneau et caprin	120	128	122	125	132	112	142	135	141	142
Mozambique										
Mozambique	**53**	**51**	**53**	**51**	**52**	**52**	**53**	**53**	**54**	**54**
Beef,veal & buffalo										
Boeuf,veau et buffle	39	36	38	36	37	37	38	38	38	38
Pork										
Porc	12	12	12	12	12	12	13	13	13	13
Mutton,lamb & goat										
Mouton,agneau et caprin	3	3	3	3	3	3	3	3	3	3
Namibia										
Namibie	**66**	**67**	**69**	**70**	**63**	**61**	**47**	**51**	**52**	**53**
Beef,veal & buffalo										
Boeuf,veau et buffle	46	49	49	49	48	46	30	38	39	40
Pork										
Porc	2	2	2	3	3	2	3	2	2	2
Mutton,lamb & goat										
Mouton,agneau et caprin	18	16	18	17	13	13	15	11	12	11
Niger										
Niger	**57**	**66**	**67**	**69**	**71**	**74**	**76**	**78**	**80**	**80**
Beef,veal & buffalo										
Boeuf,veau et buffle	25	32	33	34	35	36	38	39	40	40
Pork										
Porc	1	1	1	1	1	1	1	1	1	1

42

Meat
Production: thousand metric tons [*cont.*]
Viande
Production : milliers de tonnes [*suite*]

Region, country or area Région, pays ou zone	1991	1992	1993	1994	1995	1996	1997	1998	1999	2000
Mutton,lamb & goat Mouton,agneau et caprin	32	33	33	34	35	36	37	38	39	39
Nigeria **Nigéria**	**482**	**431**	**461**	**478**	**514**	**545**	**584**	**602**	**622**	**622**
Beef,veal & buffalo Boeuf,veau et buffle	205	210	244	264	267	280	294	297	298	298
Pork Porc	106	47	39	34	67	47	56	65	78	78
Mutton,lamb & goat Mouton,agneau et caprin	170	174	178	180	180	218	234	240	246	246
Réunion **Réunion**	**10**	**11**	**11**	**12**	**12**	**12**	**14**	**14**	**14**	**14**
Beef,veal & buffalo Boeuf,veau et buffle	1	1	1	1	1	1	1	1	1	1
Pork Porc	9	10	10	10	10	10	12	13	13	13
Rwanda **Rwanda**	**22**	**21**	**20**	**18**	**16**	**17**	**19**	**22**	**24**	**25**
Beef,veal & buffalo Boeuf,veau et buffle	14	13	12	10	10	11	14	16	18	18
Pork Porc	3	3	3	3	2	2	2	2	2	2
Mutton,lamb & goat Mouton,agneau et caprin	5	5	5	5	3	4	4	5	5	6
Senegal **Sénégal**	**75**	**78**	**80**	**82**	**83**	**82**	**84**	**85**	**85**	**85**
Beef,veal & buffalo Boeuf,veau et buffle	44	44	45	46	46	46	48	48	48	48
Pork Porc	7	7	7	7	7	7	7	7	7	7
Mutton,lamb & goat Mouton,agneau et caprin	25	27	28	29	29	29	29	29	29	29
Seychelles **Seychelles**	**1**	**1**	**1**	**1**	**1**	**1**	**1**	**1**	**1**	**1**
Pork Porc	1	1	1	1	1	1	1	1	1	1
Sierra Leone **Sierra Leone**	**9**	**9**	**9**	**9**	**10**	**10**	**10**	**10**	**10**	**10**
Beef,veal & buffalo Boeuf,veau et buffle	5	5	6	6	6	6	6	6	7	7
Pork Porc	2	2	2	2	2	2	2	2	2	2
Mutton,lamb & goat Mouton,agneau et caprin	1	1	1	1	1	1	1	2	2	2
Somalia **Somalie**	**114**	**88**	**95**	**99**	**107**	**114**	**122**	**135**	**131**	**135**
Beef,veal & buffalo Boeuf,veau et buffle	41	36	42	44	50	54	61	62	58	59
Mutton,lamb & goat Mouton,agneau et caprin	73	52	53	55	57	60	61	73	73	75
South Africa **Afrique du Sud**	**981**	**1 042**	**930**	**828**	**794**	**744**	**732**	**770**	**818**	**855**
Beef,veal & buffalo Boeuf,veau et buffle	700	745	651	554	521	481	484	518	553	590
Pork Porc	113	130	120	119	127	128	120	124	117	117
Mutton,lamb & goat Mouton,agneau et caprin	168	167	159	155	146	135	128	128	148	148

42

Meat
Production: thousand metric tons [*cont.*]
Viande
Production : milliers de tonnes [*suite*]

Region, country or area Région, pays ou zone	1991	1992	1993	1994	1995	1996	1997	1998	1999	2000
Sudan **Soudan**	**361**	**379**	**394**	**417**	**462**	**469**	**505**	**529**	**542**	**563**
Beef,veal & buffalo Boeuf,veau et buffle	231	226	215	212	225	226	250	265	276	296
Mutton,lamb & goat Mouton,agneau et caprin	129	153	179	205	237	242	255	264	266	267
Swaziland **Swaziland**	**17**	**18**	**19**	**18**	**18**	**18**	**18**	**19**	**19**	**20**
Beef,veal & buffalo Boeuf,veau et buffle	13	14	15	14	14	13	14	14	14	14
Pork Porc	1	1	1	1	1	1	2	2	2	2
Mutton,lamb & goat Mouton,agneau et caprin	3	3	3	3	3	3	3	3	4	4
Togo **Togo**	**22**	**24**	**24**	**24**	**25**	**24**	**23**	**24**	**24**	**24**
Beef,veal & buffalo Boeuf,veau et buffle	5	5	5	5	7	7	7	7	7	7
Pork Porc	10	11	12	12	12	12	12	12	12	12
Mutton,lamb & goat Mouton,agneau et caprin	7	7	7	7	7	5	4	5	5	5
Tunisia **Tunisie**	**88**	**91**	**99**	**101**	**105**	**108**	**106**	**112**	**116**	**107**
Beef,veal & buffalo Boeuf,veau et buffle	41	44	48	49	50	52	50	53	58	47
Mutton,lamb & goat Mouton,agneau et caprin	46	47	51	52	54	56	55	58	58	60
Uganda **Ouganda**	**151**	**155**	**163**	**158**	**161**	**163**	**165**	**171**	**175**	**176**
Beef,veal & buffalo Boeuf,veau et buffle	84	86	92	84	86	88	89	93	96	97
Pork Porc	46	48	49	50	51	51	52	53	54	54
Mutton,lamb & goat Mouton,agneau et caprin	21	22	23	24	24	24	25	25	25	25
United Rep. of Tanzania **Rép.-Unie de Tanzanie**	**238**	**241**	**247**	**250**	**251**	**254**	**257**	**264**	**269**	**271**
Beef,veal & buffalo Boeuf,veau et buffle	197	199	203	205	206	209	211	218	223	224
Pork Porc	9	9	9	9	10	9	9	10	10	10
Mutton,lamb & goat Mouton,agneau et caprin	32	33	34	35	36	36	36	36	37	37
Zambia **Zambie**	**49**	**50**	**54**	**56**	**50**	**53**	**41**	**42**	**44**	**48**
Beef,veal & buffalo Boeuf,veau et buffle	37	38	42	43	38	40	28	27	29	32
Pork Porc	10	9	10	10	10	10	10	10	11	11
Mutton,lamb & goat Mouton,agneau et caprin	2	2	2	3	3	3	3	4	4	5
Zimbabwe **Zimbabwe**	**106**	**117**	**94**	**88**	**98**	**92**	**98**	**99**	**121**	**127**
Beef,veal & buffalo Boeuf,veau et buffle	84	94	75	67	73	67	74	74	95	101

42

Meat
Production: thousand metric tons [*cont.*]
Viande
Production : milliers de tonnes [*suite*]

Region, country or area Région, pays ou zone	1991	1992	1993	1994	1995	1996	1997	1998	1999	2000
Pork Porc	11	11	8	10	13	13	12	13	13	13
Mutton,lamb & goat Mouton,agneau et caprin	11	11	11	11	11	12	12	12	13	13
America, North **Amérique du Nord**	**22 847**	**23 617**	**23 512**	**24 626**	**25 240**	**25 030**	**25 190**	**26 359**	**27 116**	**27 265**
Beef,veal & buffalo Boeuf,veau et buffle	13 156	13 290	13 239	13 999	14 445	14 632	14 661	14 861	15 276	15 502
Pork Porc	9 434	10 071	10 024	10 392	10 571	10 183	10 319	11 288	11 632	11 560
Mutton,lamb & goat Mouton,agneau et caprin	257	256	250	235	224	214	211	209	208	204
Antigua and Barbuda **Antigua-et-Barbuda**	1	1	1	1	1	1	1	1	1	1
Beef,veal & buffalo Boeuf,veau et buffle	1	1	1	1	1	1	1	1	1	1
Barbados **Barbade**	**5**	**5**	**5**	**5**	**5**	**5**	**5**	**5**	**5**	**5**
Beef,veal & buffalo Boeuf,veau et buffle	1	1	1	1	1	1	1	1	1	1
Pork Porc	4	4	4	4	4	4	4	4	4	4
Belize **Belize**	**3**	**3**	**3**	**3**	**3**	**3**	**3**	**2**	**2**	**2**
Beef,veal & buffalo Boeuf,veau et buffle	1	2	1	1	1	1	2	1	1	1
Pork Porc	1	1	1	1	1	1	1	1	1	1
Canada **Canada**	**1 973**	**2 118**	**2 065**	**2 139**	**2 214**	**2 255**	**2 343**	**2 548**	**2 811**	**2 946**
Beef,veal & buffalo Boeuf,veau et buffle	866	899	860	899	928	1 016	1 076	1 148	1 238	1 260
Pork Porc	1 096	1 208	1 194	1 229	1 276	1 228	1 257	1 390	1 562	1 675
Mutton,lamb & goat Mouton,agneau et caprin	10	11	11	11	10	11	10	10	11	11
Costa Rica **Costa Rica**	**111**	**100**	**102**	**115**	**116**	**117**	**107**	**107**	**102**	**100**
Beef,veal & buffalo Boeuf,veau et buffle	94	81	82	91	92	96	86	82	75	83
Pork Porc	17	19	20	23	24	20	21	25	27	16
Cuba **Cuba**	**184**	**126**	**130**	**130**	**137**	**144**	**147**	**169**	**178**	**187**
Beef,veal & buffalo Boeuf,veau et buffle	90	77	66	60	64	68	68	69	73	75
Pork Porc	91	47	63	69	72	74	78	98	103	110
Mutton,lamb & goat Mouton,agneau et caprin	2	2	1	1	1	2	2	2	2	2
Dominica **Dominique**	**1**	**1**	**1**	**1**	**1**	**1**	**1**	**1**	**1**	**1**
Beef,veal & buffalo Boeuf,veau et buffle	0	0	0	0	0	1	1	1	1	1
Dominican Republic **Rép. dominicaine**	**125**	**129**	**141**	**140**	**144**	**146**	**146**	**146**	**141**	**131**
Beef,veal & buffalo Boeuf,veau et buffle	84	83	86	81	80	80	79	80	83	69

42

Meat
Production: thousand metric tons [*cont.*]
Viande
Production : milliers de tonnes [*suite*]

Region, country or area Région, pays ou zone	1991	1992	1993	1994	1995	1996	1997	1998	1999	2000
Pork										
Porc	38	43	53	57	62	63	64	64	58	61
Mutton,lamb & goat										
Mouton,agneau et caprin	2	3	3	3	3	3	3	2	1	1
El Salvador										
El Salvador	**34**	**33**	**36**	**35**	**38**	**38**	**45**	**45**	**45**	**42**
Beef,veal & buffalo										
Boeuf,veau et buffle	24	22	25	27	27	27	35	34	34	34
Pork										
Porc	11	11	11	8	11	11	10	10	11	8
Guadeloupe										
Guadeloupe	**4**	**4**	**4**	**5**	**5**	**4**	**5**	**5**	**5**	**5**
Beef,veal & buffalo										
Boeuf,veau et buffle	3	3	3	3	3	3	3	3	3	3
Pork										
Porc	1	1	1	1	1	1	1	1	1	1
Guatemala										
Guatemala	**68**	**57**	**67**	**70**	**73**	**74**	**74**	**75**	**68**	**66**
Beef,veal & buffalo										
Boeuf,veau et buffle	52	41	48	52	54	54	54	54	47	45
Pork										
Porc	13	14	17	15	16	16	17	18	18	18
Mutton,lamb & goat										
Mouton,agneau et caprin	2	2	2	3	3	3	3	3	3	3
Haiti										
Haïti	**44**	**49**	**52**	**53**	**51**	**57**	**59**	**64**	**64**	**76**
Beef,veal & buffalo										
Boeuf,veau et buffle	25	27	29	28	24	28	28	31	31	40
Pork										
Porc	15	18	19	21	23	24	25	27	27	28
Mutton,lamb & goat										
Mouton,agneau et caprin	4	4	4	4	4	5	5	6	6	7
Honduras										
Honduras	**58**	**58**	**58**	**59**	**37**	**40**	**41**	**45**	**38**	**38**
Beef,veal & buffalo										
Boeuf,veau et buffle	45	44	45	45	23	25	26	28	21	21
Pork										
Porc	13	13	13	14	14	15	15	16	17	17
Jamaica										
Jamaïque	**23**	**26**	**24**	**25**	**25**	**24**	**23**	**23**	**23**	**23**
Beef,veal & buffalo										
Boeuf,veau et buffle	16	18	16	16	17	16	15	14	15	15
Pork										
Porc	5	6	7	7	7	7	7	7	7	7
Mutton,lamb & goat										
Mouton,agneau et caprin	2	2	2	2	2	2	2	2	2	2
Martinique										
Martinique	**5**	**5**	**5**	**4**	**4**	**4**	**4**	**4**	**4**	**4**
Beef,veal & buffalo										
Boeuf,veau et buffle	3	3	2	2	2	3	3	3	3	3
Pork										
Porc	2	2	2	2	2	2	2	2	2	2
Mexico										
Mexique	**2 066**	**2 138**	**2 148**	**2 307**	**2 401**	**2 306**	**2 345**	**2 409**	**2 462**	**2 521**
Beef,veal & buffalo										
Boeuf,veau et buffle	1 189	1 247	1 256	1 365	1 412	1 330	1 340	1 380	1 401	1 415
Pork										
Porc	812	820	822	873	922	910	939	961	992	1 035

42

Meat
Production: thousand metric tons [*cont.*]
Viande
Production : milliers de tonnes [*suite*]

Region, country or area Région, pays ou zone	1991	1992	1993	1994	1995	1996	1997	1998	1999	2000
Mutton,lamb & goat Mouton,agneau et caprin	66	71	70	69	68	65	65	69	68	72
Montserrat **Montserrat**	**1**	**1**	**1**	**1**	**1**	**1**	**1**	**1**	**1**	**1**
Beef,veal & buffalo Boeuf,veau et buffle	1	1	1	1	1	1	1	1	1	1
Nicaragua **Nicaragua**	**55**	**56**	**61**	**56**	**54**	**55**	**57**	**52**	**54**	**55**
Beef,veal & buffalo Boeuf,veau et buffle	45	48	52	51	49	50	52	46	48	49
Pork Porc	9	9	8	5	5	5	5	6	6	6
Panama **Panama**	**74**	**73**	**76**	**76**	**78**	**84**	**79**	**82**	**81**	**78**
Beef,veal & buffalo Boeuf,veau et buffle	61	59	60	60	61	66	60	64	60	57
Pork Porc	12	15	16	16	17	19	19	19	21	21
Puerto Rico **Porto Rico**	**50**	**39**	**36**	**34**	**32**	**29**	**29**	**29**	**29**	**29**
Beef,veal & buffalo Boeuf,veau et buffle	19	21	19	18	16	14	16	16	16	16
Pork Porc	30	18	17	15	15	15	13	13	13	13
Saint Lucia **Sainte-Lucie**	**1**	**1**	**1**	**1**	**1**	**1**	**1**	**1**	**1**	**1**
Beef,veal & buffalo Boeuf,veau et buffle	1	1	1	1	1	1	1	1	1	0
Pork Porc	1	1	1	1	1	1	1	1	1	1
St. Vincent-Grenadines **St. Vincent-Grenadines**	**1**	**1**	**1**	**1**	**1**	**1**	**1**	**1**	**1**	**1**
Pork Porc	1	1	1	1	1	1	1	1	1	1
Trinidad and Tobago **Trinité-et-Tobago**	**4**	**4**	**3**	**3**	**3**	**3**	**4**	**3**	**3**	**3**
Beef,veal & buffalo Boeuf,veau et buffle	1	1	1	1	1	1	1	1	1	1
Pork Porc	2	2	2	2	2	2	2	2	2	2
United States **Etats-Unis**	**17 956**	**18 587**	**18 488**	**19 361**	**19 812**	**19 635**	**19 667**	**20 540**	**20 994**	**20 946**
Beef,veal & buffalo Boeuf,veau et buffle	10 534	10 612	10 584	11 194	11 585	11 749	11 714	11 803	12 123	12 311
Pork Porc	7 258	7 817	7 751	8 027	8 097	7 764	7 835	8 623	8 758	8 532
Mutton,lamb & goat Mouton,agneau et caprin	165	158	153	140	130	122	118	114	113	103
United States Virgin Is. **Iles Vierges américaines**	**1**	**1**	**1**	**1**	**1**	**1**	**1**	**1**	**1**	**1**
Beef,veal & buffalo Boeuf,veau et buffle	1	1	1	1	1	1	1	1	1	1
America, South **Amérique du Sud**	**11 951**	**12 048**	**12 304**	**12 760**	**13 409**	**14 163**	**14 023**	**13 811**	**14 528**	**15 215**
Beef,veal & buffalo Boeuf,veau et buffle	**9 598**	**9 578**	**9 739**	**10 114**	**10 639**	**11 265**	**11 181**	**10 794**	**11 331**	**11 895**

42
Meat
Production: thousand metric tons [*cont.*]
Viande
Production : milliers de tonnes [*suite*]

Region, country or area Région, pays ou zone	1991	1992	1993	1994	1995	1996	1997	1998	1999	2000
Pork Porc	**1 992**	**2 124**	**2 214**	**2 274**	**2 412**	**2 572**	**2 514**	**2 701**	**2 867**	**2 986**
Mutton,lamb & goat Mouton,agneau et caprin	**362**	**346**	**351**	**372**	**358**	**327**	**328**	**316**	**329**	**335**
Argentina Argentine	**3 151**	**3 014**	**3 062**	**3 057**	**2 955**	**2 914**	**2 914**	**2 664**	**2 888**	**3 149**
Beef,veal & buffalo Boeuf,veau et buffle	2 918	2 784	2 808	2 783	2 688	2 694	2 712	2 452	2 653	2 900
Pork Porc	142	157	182	182	178	148	137	156	181	190
Mutton,lamb & goat Mouton,agneau et caprin	92	73	72	92	88	71	65	57	54	59
Bolivia Bolivie	**215**	**210**	**205**	**214**	**221**	**229**	**236**	**244**	**250**	**258**
Beef,veal & buffalo Boeuf,veau et buffle	132	126	130	136	140	143	147	151	155	160
Pork Porc	65	67	58	60	62	66	69	72	74	76
Mutton,lamb & goat Mouton,agneau et caprin	17	17	17	19	20	20	20	21	21	21
Brazil Brésil	**5 745**	**6 019**	**6 176**	**6 556**	**7 265**	**7 884**	**7 541**	**7 549**	**8 044**	**8 374**
Beef,veal & buffalo Boeuf,veau et buffle	4 511	4 716	4 807	5 136	5 710	6 187	5 922	5 794	6 182	6 460
Pork Porc	1 120	1 188	1 250	1 300	1 430	1 600	1 518	1 652	1 752	1 804
Mutton,lamb & goat Mouton,agneau et caprin	114	115	119	120	125	97	101	102	110	110
Chile Chili	**376**	**355**	**389**	**417**	**445**	**458**	**486**	**508**	**488**	**540**
Beef,veal & buffalo Boeuf,veau et buffle	230	200	224	240	258	259	262	256	226	253
Pork Porc	129	138	147	161	172	185	209	235	244	269
Mutton,lamb & goat Mouton,agneau et caprin	18	17	18	17	15	13	15	17	18	18
Colombia Colombie	**846**	**742**	**750**	**793**	**849**	**881**	**915**	**917**	**891**	**922**
Beef,veal & buffalo Boeuf,veau et buffle	701	595	603	646	702	730	763	766	724	754
Pork Porc	133	135	134	133	133	135	135	135	150	152
Mutton,lamb & goat Mouton,agneau et caprin	12	13	13	13	14	16	17	16	16	16
Ecuador Equateur	**194**	**200**	**213**	**216**	**245**	**264**	**270**	**265**	**284**	**290**
Beef,veal & buffalo Boeuf,veau et buffle	113	113	126	127	149	153	156	158	164	174
Pork Porc	76	82	81	82	89	103	107	100	110	108
Mutton,lamb & goat Mouton,agneau et caprin	5	5	6	6	7	7	8	7	9	8
Falkland Is. (Malvinas) Iles Falkland (Malvinas)	**1**	**1**	**1**	**1**	**1**	**1**	**1**	**1**	**1**	**1**
Mutton,lamb & goat Mouton,agneau et caprin	1	1	1	1	1	1	1	1	1	1
French Guiana Guyane française	**1**	**1**	**1**	**1**	**2**	**2**	**2**	**2**	**2**	**2**

42

Meat
Production: thousand metric tons [*cont.*]
Viande
Production : milliers de tonnes [*suite*]

Region, country or area Région, pays ou zone	1991	1992	1993	1994	1995	1996	1997	1998	1999	2000
Beef,veal & buffalo Boeuf,veau et buffle	1	0	0	0	0	0	0	0	0	0
Pork Porc	1	1	1	1	1	1	1	1	1	1
Guyana **Guyana**	**5**	**6**	**6**	**6**	**5**	**5**	**4**	**4**	**4**	**4**
Beef,veal & buffalo Boeuf,veau et buffle	3	4	4	5	4	4	3	3	3	3
Pork Porc	1	1	1	1	1	1	1	1	1	1
Mutton,lamb & goat Mouton,agneau et caprin	1	1	1	1	1	1	1	1	1	1
Paraguay **Paraguay**	**343**	**363**	**355**	**356**	**359**	**345**	**347**	**353**	**369**	**390**
Beef,veal & buffalo Boeuf,veau et buffle	219	233	225	225	226	226	226	231	246	239
Pork Porc	121	126	127	128	130	116	117	119	120	148
Mutton,lamb & goat Mouton,agneau et caprin	3	3	3	3	3	3	3	3	3	3
Peru **Pérou**	**206**	**212**	**209**	**205**	**213**	**220**	**233**	**243**	**263**	**269**
Beef,veal & buffalo Boeuf,veau et buffle	109	111	107	102	107	110	118	124	134	136
Pork Porc	69	73	76	78	80	83	87	91	93	95
Mutton,lamb & goat Mouton,agneau et caprin	28	28	26	26	26	27	28	29	37	38
Suriname **Suriname**	**5**	**4**	**4**	**3**	**3**	**2**	**3**	**3**	**3**	**4**
Beef,veal & buffalo Boeuf,veau et buffle	3	3	2	2	2	2	2	2	2	2
Pork Porc	2	1	1	2	1	1	1	1	1	2
Uruguay **Uruguay**	**405**	**415**	**396**	**450**	**412**	**491**	**536**	**531**	**536**	**530**
Beef,veal & buffalo Boeuf,veau et buffle	320	329	310	361	338	407	454	450	458	453
Pork Porc	22	22	23	23	22	21	22	26	27	26
Mutton,lamb & goat Mouton,agneau et caprin	63	64	64	66	52	64	60	55	51	51
Venezuela **Venezuela**	**458**	**507**	**536**	**483**	**435**	**469**	**535**	**528**	**505**	**482**
Beef,veal & buffalo Boeuf,veau et buffle	337	365	394	351	316	350	415	406	384	360
Pork Porc	111	133	133	125	112	113	111	113	114	114
Mutton,lamb & goat Mouton,agneau et caprin	9	8	10	8	7	7	9	9	8	8
Asia **Asie**	**43 209**	**47 964**	**51 493**	**55 191**	**56 941**	**56 546**	**62 136**	**65 800**	**67 779**	**70 340**
Beef,veal & buffalo Boeuf,veau et buffle	**7 836**	**9 520**	**10 428**	**11 027**	**11 809**	**11 768**	**12 869**	**13 270**	**13 565**	**13 884**
Pork Porc	**31 416**	**33 887**	**36 245**	**39 145**	**39 843**	**39 643**	**43 969**	**46 865**	**48 258**	**50 348**

42
Meat
Production: thousand metric tons [*cont.*]
Viande
Production : milliers de tonnes [*suite*]

Region, country or area Région, pays ou zone	1991	1992	1993	1994	1995	1996	1997	1998	1999	2000
Mutton,lamb & goat **Mouton,agneau et caprin**	**3 956**	**4 556**	**4 819**	**5 019**	**5 289**	**5 135**	**5 298**	**5 664**	**5 956**	**6 108**
Afghanistan **Afghanistan**	**219**	**216**	**223**	**240**	**257**	**283**	**312**	**343**	**374**	**374**
Beef,veal & buffalo Boeuf,veau et buffle	86	86	97	113	130	143	156	171	187	187
Mutton,lamb & goat Mouton,agneau et caprin	133	129	125	127	127	141	156	172	187	187
Armenia **Arménie**	**...**	**58**	**43**	**42**	**42**	**44**	**45**	**47**	**45**	**48**
Beef,veal & buffalo Boeuf,veau et buffle	...	33	30	29	30	33	35	35	32	32
Pork Porc	...	17	5	6	5	6	5	7	8	11
Mutton,lamb & goat Mouton,agneau et caprin	...	8	8	7	7	6	5	5	5	5
Azerbaijan **Azerbaïdjan**	**...**	**82**	**73**	**68**	**66**	**71**	**76**	**84**	**86**	**90**
Beef,veal & buffalo Boeuf,veau et buffle	...	50	44	44	41	44	48	50	52	53
Pork Porc	...	5	3	2	2	2	2	1	1	2
Mutton,lamb & goat Mouton,agneau et caprin	...	27	26	22	23	26	26	32	33	36
Bahrain **Bahreïn**	**8**	**8**	**8**	**10**	**9**	**9**	**9**	**8**	**8**	**8**
Beef,veal & buffalo Boeuf,veau et buffle	1	1	1	1	1	1	1	1	1	1
Mutton,lamb & goat Mouton,agneau et caprin	7	7	7	9	9	9	9	7	7	7
Bangladesh **Bangladesh**	**223**	**230**	**240**	**250**	**258**	**273**	**294**	**293**	**303**	**303**
Beef,veal & buffalo Boeuf,veau et buffle	143	145	147	150	151	156	169	165	174	174
Mutton,lamb & goat Mouton,agneau et caprin	80	86	93	100	107	118	126	129	130	130
Bhutan **Bhoutan**	**7**	**7**	**7**	**7**	**7**	**7**	**7**	**7**	**7**	**7**
Beef,veal & buffalo Boeuf,veau et buffle	6	6	6	6	6	6	6	6	6	6
Pork Porc	1	1	1	1	1	1	1	1	1	1
Brunei Darussalam **Brunéi Darussalam**	**2**	**2**	**2**	**2**	**1**	**2**	**2**	**2**	**5**	**5**
Beef,veal & buffalo Boeuf,veau et buffle	2	2	1	2	1	2	2	2	5	5
Cambodia **Cambodge**	**103**	**127**	**132**	**129**	**134**	**139**	**151**	**155**	**158**	**162**
Beef,veal & buffalo Boeuf,veau et buffle	41	45	47	48	52	53	54	55	55	57
Pork Porc	62	82	85	81	82	86	97	100	103	105
China †† **Chine ††**	**28 584**	**30 743**	**33 586**	**36 902**	**38 748**	**38 414**	**43 521**	**46 979**	**48 621**	**51 096**
Beef,veal & buffalo Boeuf,veau et buffle	1 579	1 845	2 375	2 806	3 598	3 585	4 431	4 825	5 078	5 384
Pork Porc	25 824	27 647	29 836	32 613	33 401	33 015	37 155	39 899	41 048	43 058

42

Meat
Production: thousand metric tons [*cont.*]
Viande
Production : milliers de tonnes [*suite*]

Region, country or area Région, pays ou zone	1991	1992	1993	1994	1995	1996	1997	1998	1999	2000
Mutton, lamb & goat Mouton, agneau et caprin	1 181	1 251	1 375	1 483	1 749	1 815	1 935	2 255	2 495	2 654
Cyprus **Chypre**	**43**	**45**	**51**	**54**	**56**	**58**	**60**	**61**	**64**	**64**
Beef, veal & buffalo Boeuf, veau et buffle	5	5	5	4	5	5	5	4	4	4
Pork Porc	32	34	39	43	43	46	46	47	49	49
Mutton, lamb & goat Mouton, agneau et caprin	7	7	7	7	8	8	8	10	11	11
Georgia **Géorgie**	...	**103**	**92**	**98**	**105**	**109**	**109**	**93**	**89**	**94**
Beef, veal & buffalo Boeuf, veau et buffle	...	40	40	44	53	54	56	43	41	48
Pork Porc	...	57	45	47	44	46	47	42	41	41
Mutton, lamb & goat Mouton, agneau et caprin	...	6	7	7	8	9	7	8	7	6
India **Inde**	**3 505**	**3 606**	**3 737**	**3 814**	**3 875**	**3 937**	**3 995**	**4 011**	**4 086**	**4 120**
Beef, veal & buffalo Boeuf, veau et buffle	2 452	2 535	2 632	2 682	2 716	2 751	2 782	2 781	2 832	2 863
Pork Porc	434	445	469	477	495	514	533	543	560	560
Mutton, lamb & goat Mouton, agneau et caprin	619	626	635	655	663	672	680	688	694	696
Indonesia **Indonésie**	**976**	**1 024**	**1 130**	**1 144**	**1 026**	**1 094**	**1 141**	**1 092**	**1 231**	**1 231**
Beef, veal & buffalo Boeuf, veau et buffle	310	342	398	385	359	396	401	389	400	400
Pork Porc	572	583	622	660	572	600	633	622	748	748
Mutton, lamb & goat Mouton, agneau et caprin	94	99	111	100	94	99	107	82	84	84
Iran (Islamic Rep. of) **Iran (Rép. islamique d')**	**572**	**595**	**612**	**628**	**642**	**668**	**715**	**744**	**703**	**703**
Beef, veal & buffalo Boeuf, veau et buffle	228	237	246	256	265	287	309	326	306	306
Mutton, lamb & goat Mouton, agneau et caprin	344	358	366	372	377	380	406	418	397	397
Iraq **Iraq**	**54**	**74**	**92**	**84**	**73**	**59**	**73**	**75**	**76**	**76**
Beef, veal & buffalo Boeuf, veau et buffle	33	45	55	51	43	37	46	47	47	48
Mutton, lamb & goat Mouton, agneau et caprin	22	29	38	33	31	22	27	28	28	29
Israel **Israël**	**53**	**52**	**51**	**57**	**58**	**61**	**65**	**62**	**63**	**63**
Beef, veal & buffalo Boeuf, veau et buffle	38	37	36	41	41	44	46	44	44	44
Pork Porc	9	9	9	9	11	11	12	12	12	12
Mutton, lamb & goat Mouton, agneau et caprin	6	6	7	7	7	7	6	6	6	6
Japan **Japon**	**2 058**	**2 026**	**2 034**	**1 993**	**1 923**	**1 821**	**1 814**	**1 816**	**1 818**	**1 804**
Beef, veal & buffalo Boeuf, veau et buffle	575	592	594	602	601	555	530	529	540	534

42
Meat
Production: thousand metric tons [*cont.*]
Viande
Production : milliers de tonnes [*suite*]

Region, country or area Région, pays ou zone	1991	1992	1993	1994	1995	1996	1997	1998	1999	2000
Pork Porc	1 483	1 434	1 440	1 390	1 322	1 266	1 283	1 286	1 277	1 270
Jordan **Jordanie**	**18**	**17**	**19**	**16**	**16**	**16**	**15**	**22**	**21**	**19**
Beef,veal & buffalo Boeuf,veau et buffle	3	2	3	4	4	3	4	3	4	4
Mutton,lamb & goat Mouton,agneau et caprin	15	14	16	12	12	13	12	19	17	16
Kazakhstan **Kazakhstan**	...	**1 056**	**1 131**	**1 052**	**867**	**740**	**623**	**546**	**548**	**546**
Beef,veal & buffalo Boeuf,veau et buffle	...	596	662	642	548	463	398	351	349	342
Pork Porc	...	217	194	158	113	110	82	79	83	101
Mutton,lamb & goat Mouton,agneau et caprin	...	243	275	252	206	167	143	117	116	103
Korea, Dem. P. R. **Corée, R. p. dém. de**	**271**	**211**	**187**	**173**	**150**	**131**	**108**	**139**	**164**	**165**
Beef,veal & buffalo Boeuf,veau et buffle	30	30	31	32	31	22	19	20	20	21
Pork Porc	235	175	150	135	115	105	84	112	134	134
Mutton,lamb & goat Mouton,agneau et caprin	6	6	6	6	4	4	6	8	10	11
Korea, Republic of **Corée, République de**	**664**	**928**	**977**	**1 003**	**1 023**	**1 138**	**1 237**	**1 318**	**1 249**	**1 210**
Beef,veal & buffalo Boeuf,veau et buffle	132	174	204	214	221	248	338	376	305	266
Pork Porc	530	752	770	786	799	887	896	939	941	941
Mutton,lamb & goat Mouton,agneau et caprin	2	2	3	3	3	3	4	3	3	3
Kuwait **Koweït**	**9**	**18**	**26**	**50**	**40**	**41**	**41**	**40**	**40**	**35**
Beef,veal & buffalo Boeuf,veau et buffle	0	1	1	1	2	2	2	2	2	2
Mutton,lamb & goat Mouton,agneau et caprin	9	17	25	49	38	39	39	38	38	33
Kyrgyzstan **Kirghizistan**	...	**193**	**194**	**177**	**167**	**169**	**165**	**168**	**170**	**170**
Beef,veal & buffalo Boeuf,veau et buffle	...	88	88	82	85	86	95	95	95	98
Pork Porc	...	36	25	18	28	29	26	30	29	29
Mutton,lamb & goat Mouton,agneau et caprin	...	70	82	76	54	54	45	43	47	43
Lao People's Dem. Rep. **Rép. dém. pop. lao**	**40**	**42**	**45**	**48**	**58**	**58**	**61**	**63**	**70**	**67**
Beef,veal & buffalo Boeuf,veau et buffle	18	19	21	22	28	28	30	31	38	33
Pork Porc	22	23	25	26	29	30	31	31	32	33
Lebanon **Liban**	**31**	**34**	**38**	**38**	**33**	**32**	**43**	**47**	**50**	**52**
Beef,veal & buffalo Boeuf,veau et buffle	15	16	16	15	12	10	20	22	25	27
Pork Porc	4	4	5	6	7	8	8	8	9	9

42
Meat
Production: thousand metric tons [*cont.*]
Viande
Production : milliers de tonnes [*suite*]

Region, country or area Région, pays ou zone	1991	1992	1993	1994	1995	1996	1997	1998	1999	2000
Mutton,lamb & goat Mouton,agneau et caprin	13	14	16	17	14	14	14	16	16	16
Malaysia **Malaisie**	**251**	**269**	**282**	**305**	**305**	**301**	**305**	**285**	**274**	**274**
Beef,veal & buffalo Boeuf,veau et buffle	18	18	19	19	21	22	23	22	24	24
Pork Porc	233	251	263	285	283	278	282	262	250	250
Mutton,lamb & goat Mouton,agneau et caprin	1	1	1	1	1	1	1	1	1	1
Mongolia **Mongolie**	**224**	**194**	**178**	**177**	**182**	**212**	**191**	**199**	**211**	**186**
Beef,veal & buffalo Boeuf,veau et buffle	84	76	65	64	69	90	87	86	94	80
Pork Porc	4	2	1	1	1	0	0	1	1	1
Mutton,lamb & goat Mouton,agneau et caprin	136	116	113	112	112	121	104	112	117	105
Myanmar **Myanmar**	**172**	**177**	**179**	**182**	**190**	**196**	**216**	**220**	**263**	**238**
Beef,veal & buffalo Boeuf,veau et buffle	108	109	110	111	113	116	119	121	121	122
Pork Porc	58	61	61	63	69	72	89	91	133	104
Mutton,lamb & goat Mouton,agneau et caprin	7	7	7	7	8	8	8	9	9	11
Nepal **Népal**	**179**	**181**	**182**	**188**	**195**	**199**	**211**	**217**	**220**	**224**
Beef,veal & buffalo Boeuf,veau et buffle	137	137	138	144	150	152	161	165	167	170
Pork Porc	10	10	10	11	11	12	12	13	14	15
Mutton,lamb & goat Mouton,agneau et caprin	32	33	33	34	34	35	37	39	39	40
Occupied Palestinian Terr. **Terr. palestinien occupé**	**2**[1]	**2**[1]	**2**[1]	**3**[1]	**3**[1]	**3**[1]	**3**[1]	**3**[1]	**3**[1]	**3**
Beef,veal & buffalo[1] Boeuf,veau et buffle[1]	1	1	1	1	1	1	1	1	1	1
Mutton,lamb & goat[1] Mouton,agneau et caprin[1]	1	1	1	1	1	1	1	1	1	1
Oman **Oman**	**19**	**18**	**19**	**19**	**18**	**18**	**18**	**18**	**19**	**19**
Beef,veal & buffalo Boeuf,veau et buffle	3	3	3	3	3	3	3	3	3	3
Mutton,lamb & goat Mouton,agneau et caprin	16	16	16	16	15	15	15	16	16	16
Pakistan **Pakistan**	**1 215**	**1 287**	**1 363**	**1 444**	**1 530**	**1 275**	**1 307**	**1 342**	**1 375**	**1 410**
Beef,veal & buffalo Boeuf,veau et buffle	696	731	768	807	847	811	830	853	875	897
Mutton,lamb & goat Mouton,agneau et caprin	519	556	595	637	683	464	477	489	500	513
Philippines **Philippines**	**854**	**814**	**897**	**930**	**983**	**1 051**	**1 121**	**1 175**	**1 228**	**1 240**
Beef,veal & buffalo Boeuf,veau et buffle	127	130	137	136	147	161	189	212	223	235
Pork Porc	702	658	731	765	805	860	901	933	973	973

42

Meat
Production: thousand metric tons [cont.]
Viande
Production : milliers de tonnes [suite]

Region, country or area Région, pays ou zone	1991	1992	1993	1994	1995	1996	1997	1998	1999	2000
Mutton,lamb & goat Mouton,agneau et caprin	25	26	28	30	31	30	31	31	32	32
Qatar **Qatar**	**14**	**12**	**12**	**13**	**14**	**8**	**8**	**8**	**8**	**9**
Mutton,lamb & goat Mouton,agneau et caprin	14	12	12	13	14	8	8	8	8	8
Saudi Arabia **Arabie saoudite**	**106**	**112**	**114**	**119**	**114**	**106**	**101**	**104**	**110**	**110**
Beef,veal & buffalo Boeuf,veau et buffle	27	28	29	30	26	18	16	19	19	19
Mutton,lamb & goat Mouton,agneau et caprin	79	84	85	89	88	88	85	85	91	91
Singapore **Singapour**	**82**	**85**	**86**	**88**	**87**	**84**	**84**	**84**	**50**	**50**
Pork Porc	81	84	85	87	86	84	84	84	50	50
Mutton,lamb & goat Mouton,agneau et caprin	1	1	1	1	0	0	0	0	0	0
Sri Lanka **Sri Lanka**	**32**	**35**	**33**	**36**	**37**	**33**	**34**	**33**	**31**	**33**
Beef,veal & buffalo Boeuf,veau et buffle	28	31	29	31	32	29	30	29	28	29
Pork Porc	2	2	2	2	2	2	2	2	2	2
Mutton,lamb & goat Mouton,agneau et caprin	2	2	2	3	3	2	2	2	2	2
Syrian Arab Republic **Rép. arabe syrienne**	**162**	**146**	**127**	**156**	**170**	**190**	**196**	**204**	**229**	**229**
Beef,veal & buffalo Boeuf,veau et buffle	33	29	29	31	34	40	42	44	47	47
Mutton,lamb & goat Mouton,agneau et caprin	129	118	98	126	137	150	154	160	182	182
Tajikistan **Tadjikistan**	**...**	**65**	**55**	**58**	**51**	**45**	**29**	**28**	**28**	**30**
Beef,veal & buffalo Boeuf,veau et buffle	...	41	34	36	31	34	26	15	15	13
Pork Porc	...	4	1	1	1	0	0	0	0	0
Mutton,lamb & goat Mouton,agneau et caprin	...	20	20	21	19	11	3	13	13	17
Thailand **Thaïlande**	**723**	**753**	**798**	**839**	**827**	**841**	**849**	**750**	**671**	**651**
Beef,veal & buffalo Boeuf,veau et buffle	320	318	338	348	337	329	300	275	244	224
Pork Porc	402	433	459	489	489	511	549	475	426	426
Mutton,lamb & goat Mouton,agneau et caprin	1	2	1	1	1	1	1	1	1	1
Turkey **Turquie**	**715**	**674**	**666**	**697**	**671**	**672**	**763**	**738**	**723**	**723**
Beef,veal & buffalo Boeuf,veau et buffle	348	309	303	325	299	305	385	364	354	354
Pork Porc	0	0	0	0	0	1	0	0	0	0
Mutton,lamb & goat Mouton,agneau et caprin	367	365	363	372	372	366	378	374	368	368
Turkmenistan **Turkménistan**	**...**	**88**	**100**	**100**	**104**	**107**	**107**	**123**	**127**	**127**

42

Meat
Production: thousand metric tons [*cont.*]
Viande
Production : milliers de tonnes [*suite*]

Region, country or area Région, pays ou zone	1991	1992	1993	1994	1995	1996	1997	1998	1999	2000
Beef,veal & buffalo Boeuf,veau et buffle	...	46	50	51	51	52	55	61	63	65
Pork Porc	...	7	5	4	3	1	1	1	1	1
Mutton,lamb & goat Mouton,agneau et caprin	...	35	45	45	50	53	51	61	63	62
United Arab Emirates **Emirats arabes unis**	**37**	**36**	**41**	**44**	**46**	**48**	**50**	**45**	**46**	**47**
Beef,veal & buffalo Boeuf,veau et buffle	6	6	6	7	9	10	13	14	15	15
Mutton,lamb & goat Mouton,agneau et caprin	31	30	35	36	38	39	37	30	31	31
Uzbekistan **Ouzbékistan**	...	**427**	**479**	**483**	**491**	**447**	**471**	**497**	**503**	**516**
Beef,veal & buffalo Boeuf,veau et buffle	...	323	378	390	392	362	387	400	403	413
Pork Porc	...	36	27	20	16	9	4	15	16	17
Mutton,lamb & goat Mouton,agneau et caprin	...	68	74	73	83	76	80	82	84	87
Viet Nam **Viet Nam**	**883**	**995**	**1 051**	**1 137**	**1 191**	**1 232**	**1 284**	**1 400**	**1 499**	**1 598**
Beef,veal & buffalo Boeuf,veau et buffle	165	173	171	176	180	175	175	167	176	185
Pork Porc	716	820	878	958	1 007	1 052	1 104	1 228	1 318	1 409
Mutton,lamb & goat Mouton,agneau et caprin	2	2	3	3	4	5	5	5	5	5
Yemen **Yémen**	**77**	**79**	**79**	**78**	**79**	**81**	**86**	**90**	**93**	**93**
Beef,veal & buffalo Boeuf,veau et buffle	37	38	39	40	41	42	43	45	47	47
Mutton,lamb & goat Mouton,agneau et caprin	40	41	40	38	38	39	43	45	46	46
Europe **Europe**	**34 177**	**44 741**	**43 098**	**41 400**	**40 358**	**40 361**	**39 065**	**39 807**	**39 651**	**38 600**
Beef,veal & buffalo **Boeuf,veau et buffle**	**11 535**	**17 073**	**15 613**	**14 843**	**13 959**	**13 644**	**13 179**	**12 512**	**12 131**	**12 125**
Pork **Porc**	**21 083**	**25 778**	**25 586**	**24 740**	**24 649**	**25 010**	**24 310**	**25 717**	**26 015**	**24 960**
Mutton,lamb & goat **Mouton,agneau et caprin**	**1 558**	**1 890**	**1 899**	**1 818**	**1 751**	**1 708**	**1 575**	**1 579**	**1 506**	**1 515**
Albania **Albanie**	**43**	**49**	**52**	**60**	**63**	**56**	**55**	**55**	**58**	**62**
Beef,veal & buffalo Boeuf,veau et buffle	21	23	24	28	31	33	33	32	34	36
Pork Porc	9	11	13	14	14	6	7	7	6	7
Mutton,lamb & goat Mouton,agneau et caprin	13	15	15	19	18	17	16	17	18	20
Austria **Autriche**	**759**	**780**	**767**	**757**	**723**	**766**	**769**	**796**	**709**	**709**
Beef,veal & buffalo Boeuf,veau et buffle	236	247	223	212	196	221	206	197	203	203
Pork Porc	517	527	538	539	521	538	556	592	499	499
Mutton,lamb & goat Mouton,agneau et caprin	6	6	6	6	7	7	7	7	7	7

42

Meat
Production: thousand metric tons [*cont.*]
Viande
Production : milliers de tonnes [*suite*]

Region, country or area Région, pays ou zone	1991	1992	1993	1994	1995	1996	1997	1998	1999	2000
Belarus **Bélarus**	...	**824**	**700**	**641**	**582**	**554**	**556**	**594**	**570**	**465**
Beef,veal & buffalo Boeuf,veau et buffle	...	495	411	384	316	277	256	271	262	239
Pork Porc	...	323	284	252	263	273	298	320	305	223
Mutton,lamb & goat Mouton,agneau et caprin	...	6	6	5	4	4	3	3	3	3
Belgium-Luxembourg **Belgique-Luxembourg**	**1 305**	**1 316**	**1 378**	**1 380**	**1 405**	**1 436**	**1 377**	**1 393**	**1 290**	**1 252**
Beef,veal & buffalo Boeuf,veau et buffle	381	359	373	355	357	362	340	303	281	260
Pork Porc	915	951	1 001	1 019	1 043	1 070	1 033	1 085	1 005	987
Mutton,lamb & goat Mouton,agneau et caprin	8	6	4	5	5	5	4	4	5	5
Bosnia and Herzegovina **Bosnie-Herzégovine**	...	**48**	**48**	**40**	**35**	**27**	**24**	**27**	**27**	**27**
Beef,veal & buffalo Boeuf,veau et buffle	...	30	30	23	16	13	10	12	12	13
Pork Porc	...	14	15	15	17	11	11	12	12	12
Mutton,lamb & goat Mouton,agneau et caprin	...	4	3	2	3	3	3	3	3	3
Bulgaria **Bulgarie**	**543**	**506**	**449**	**343**	**366**	**388**	**334**	**356**	**364**	**340**
Beef,veal & buffalo Boeuf,veau et buffle	108	135	117	89	65	80	57	56	53	56
Pork Porc	362	311	277	207	256	252	227	247	258	230
Mutton,lamb & goat Mouton,agneau et caprin	73	60	56	47	45	56	50	53	53	53
Croatia **Croatie**	...	**104**	**96**	**91**	**83**	**80**	**83**	**88**	**90**	**90**
Beef,veal & buffalo Boeuf,veau et buffle	...	37	34	28	26	22	26	26	23	23
Pork Porc	...	65	60	60	56	56	55	60	64	64
Mutton,lamb & goat Mouton,agneau et caprin	...	3	2	2	2	2	2	2	2	2
Czechoslovakia-former† **Tchécoslovaquie (anc.) †**	**1 190**	**1 162**	...	...	...	...	...	...	...	...
Beef,veal & buffalo Boeuf,veau et buffle	354	319	...	...	...	...	...	...	...	...
Pork Porc	827	834	...	...	...	...	...	...	...	...
Mutton,lamb & goat Mouton,agneau et caprin	9	8	...	...	...	...	...	...	...	...
Czech Republic **République tchèque**	...	...	**836**	**645**	**676**	**669**	**623**	**613**	**591**	**475**
Beef,veal & buffalo Boeuf,veau et buffle	...	...	216	170	170	164	156	134	136	110
Pork Porc	...	...	615	471	502	502	464	476	452	361
Mutton,lamb & goat Mouton,agneau et caprin	...	...	5	4	4	4	4	3	3	3
Denmark **Danemark**	**1 486**	**1 589**	**1 709**	**1 712**	**1 677**	**1 673**	**1 697**	**1 793**	**1 800**	**1 810**

42
Meat
Production: thousand metric tons [*cont.*]
Viande
Production : milliers de tonnes [*suite*]

Region, country or area Région, pays ou zone	1991	1992	1993	1994	1995	1996	1997	1998	1999	2000
Beef,veal & buffalo										
Boeuf,veau et buffle	213	217	203	189	182	178	175	162	157	159
Pork										
Porc	1 272	1 370	1 504	1 521	1 494	1 494	1 521	1 629	1 642	1 650
Mutton,lamb & goat										
Mouton,agneau et caprin	2	2	2	2	2	2	2	2	1	1
Estonia										
Estonie	...	97	79	63	62	54	49	52	53	50
Beef,veal & buffalo										
Boeuf,veau et buffle	...	45	43	31	26	22	19	19	22	18
Pork										
Porc	...	50	35	30	35	32	30	32	31	32
Mutton,lamb & goat										
Mouton,agneau et caprin	...	2	1	1	1	1	0	0	0	0
Faeroe Islands										
Iles Féroé	1	1	1	1	1	1	1	1	1	1
Mutton,lamb & goat										
Mouton,agneau et caprin	1	1	1	1	1	1	1	1	1	1
Finland										
Finlande	300	295	277	280	265	270	281	279	273	267
Beef,veal & buffalo										
Boeuf,veau et buffle	122	117	106	108	96	97	100	94	90	90
Pork										
Porc	177	176	169	171	168	172	180	185	182	176
Mutton,lamb & goat										
Mouton,agneau et caprin	1	1	1	1	2	1	1	1	1	1
France										
France	3 968	3 936	3 893	3 890	3 975	4 053	4 089	4 104	4 124	4 043
Beef,veal & buffalo										
Boeuf,veau et buffle	2 026	1 877	1 704	1 627	1 683	1 737	1 720	1 632	1 609	1 590
Pork										
Porc	1 773	1 903	2 034	2 116	2 144	2 161	2 219	2 328	2 377	2 315
Mutton,lamb & goat										
Mouton,agneau et caprin	170	156	155	147	148	155	150	144	138	138
Germany										
Allemagne	6 043	5 419	5 257	5 064	5 052	5 160	5 056	5 246	5 604	5 258
Beef,veal & buffalo										
Boeuf,veau et buffle	2 181	1 790	1 570	1 420	1 408	1 482	1 448	1 367	1 447	1 363
Pork										
Porc	3 813	3 585	3 646	3 604	3 602	3 635	3 564	3 834	4 113	3 850
Mutton,lamb & goat										
Mouton,agneau et caprin	50	44	41	40	42	43	44	44	44	45
Greece										
Grèce	359	360	350	349	353	352	355	361	331	335
Beef,veal & buffalo										
Boeuf,veau et buffle	79	76	73	71	72	71	70	69	67	66
Pork										
Porc	140	145	136	137	137	136	142	143	138	143
Mutton,lamb & goat										
Mouton,agneau et caprin	140	139	141	142	143	145	143	148	127	126
Hungary										
Hongrie	1 059	894	771	682	638	723	638	619	712	712
Beef,veal & buffalo										
Boeuf,veau et buffle	123	123	97	72	58	50	55	47	45	45
Pork										
Porc	931	764	672	608	578	671	581	570	664	664
Mutton,lamb & goat										
Mouton,agneau et caprin	6	6	2	1	2	2	2	3	3	3

42

Meat
Production: thousand metric tons [*cont.*]
Viande
Production : milliers de tonnes [*suite*]

Region, country or area Région, pays ou zone	1991	1992	1993	1994	1995	1996	1997	1998	1999	2000
Iceland **Islande**	**15**	**15**	**15**	**16**	**15**	**15**	**15**	**16**	**17**	**18**
Beef,veal & buffalo Boeuf,veau et buffle	3	3	3	4	3	3	3	3	4	4
Pork Porc	3	3	3	3	3	4	4	4	5	5
Mutton,lamb & goat Mouton,agneau et caprin	9	9	9	9	9	8	8	8	9	9
Ireland **Irlande**	**825**	**861**	**837**	**753**	**779**	**836**	**866**	**912**	**977**	**903**
Beef,veal & buffalo Boeuf,veau et buffle	554	565	526	445	477	535	568	590	640	570
Pork Porc	179	202	212	215	212	211	220	239	251	250
Mutton,lamb & goat Mouton,agneau et caprin	92	95	99	93	89	90	79	83	86	83
Italy **Italie**	**2 599**	**2 645**	**2 640**	**2 619**	**2 603**	**2 670**	**2 633**	**2 598**	**2 710**	**2 710**
Beef,veal & buffalo Boeuf,veau et buffle	1 182	1 218	1 188	1 171	1 181	1 182	1 161	1 113	1 165	1 161
Pork Porc	1 333	1 342	1 371	1 369	1 346	1 410	1 396	1 412	1 472	1 475
Mutton,lamb & goat Mouton,agneau et caprin	85	86	81	79	76	78	76	73	73	73
Latvia **Lettonie**	...	**224**	**179**	**124**	**112**	**67**	**63**	**63**	**55**	**54**
Beef,veal & buffalo Boeuf,veau et buffle	...	120	107	68	48	27	26	26	21	22
Pork Porc	...	101	68	54	63	40	37	36	35	32
Mutton,lamb & goat Mouton,agneau et caprin	...	4	4	2	1	1	0	0	0	0
Lithuania **Lituanie**	...	**383**	**254**	**199**	**182**	**173**	**178**	**178**	**170**	**149**
Beef,veal & buffalo Boeuf,veau et buffle	...	226	162	116	87	83	90	81	77	73
Pork Porc	...	155	90	82	93	89	87	96	91	75
Mutton,lamb & goat Mouton,agneau et caprin	...	2	2	2	2	1	1	1	1	1
Malta **Malte**	**10**	**10**	**10**	**11**	**10**	**10**	**12**	**12**	**12**	**11**
Beef,veal & buffalo Boeuf,veau et buffle	2	2	2	2	2	2	2	2	2	2
Pork Porc	8	8	9	9	9	9	10	10	10	9
Netherlands **Pays-Bas**	**2 232**	**2 238**	**2 376**	**2 294**	**2 218**	**2 222**	**1 956**	**2 266**	**2 235**	**2 144**
Beef,veal & buffalo Boeuf,veau et buffle	623	635	611	603	580	580	565	535	508	485
Pork Porc	1 591	1 585	1 747	1 673	1 622	1 624	1 376	1 715	1 711	1 643
Mutton,lamb & goat Mouton,agneau et caprin	18	18	18	17	16	18	15	16	16	16
Norway **Norvège**	**190**	**201**	**200**	**206**	**208**	**217**	**221**	**221**	**224**	**223**
Beef,veal & buffalo Boeuf,veau et buffle	80	85	84	88	85	86	89	91	91	93

42
Meat
Production: thousand metric tons [cont.]
Viande
Production : milliers de tonnes [suite]

Region, country or area Région, pays ou zone	1991	1992	1993	1994	1995	1996	1997	1998	1999	2000
Pork Porc	85	91	90	91	96	103	105	106	109	106
Mutton,lamb & goat Mouton,agneau et caprin	24	25	26	27	27	27	26	24	25	24
Poland **Pologne**	**2 643**	**2 602**	**2 401**	**2 111**	**2 354**	**2 483**	**2 323**	**2 457**	**2 429**	**2 243**
Beef,veal & buffalo Boeuf,veau et buffle	663	544	480	421	386	415	429	430	385	341
Pork Porc	1 947	2 036	1 903	1 681	1 962	2 064	1 891	2 026	2 043	1 900
Mutton,lamb & goat Mouton,agneau et caprin	33	23	18	8	6	5	3	1	2	2
Portugal **Portugal**	**420**	**416**	**451**	**438**	**435**	**450**	**442**	**454**	**468**	**466**
Beef,veal & buffalo Boeuf,veau et buffle	127	124	117	95	104	99	109	96	97	98
Pork Porc	263	265	307	316	305	325	306	332	346	343
Mutton,lamb & goat Mouton,agneau et caprin	30	27	27	27	27	26	27	26	25	25
Republic of Moldova **République de Moldova**	...	**191**	**151**	**127**	**110**	**106**	**104**	**86**	**88**	**72**
Beef,veal & buffalo Boeuf,veau et buffle	...	73	68	62	47	39	35	24	24	21
Pork Porc	...	114	79	61	60	64	66	58	61	48
Mutton,lamb & goat Mouton,agneau et caprin	...	4	3	4	3	3	3	4	4	3
Romania **Roumanie**	**1 245**	**1 138**	**1 105**	**1 114**	**950**	**880**	**916**	**862**	**834**	**865**
Beef,veal & buffalo Boeuf,veau et buffle	317	250	252	258	202	177	185	183	170	182
Pork Porc	834	789	761	775	673	631	667	620	610	626
Mutton,lamb & goat Mouton,agneau et caprin	94	100	92	81	75	71	64	60	54	57
Russian Federation **Fédération de Russie**	...	**6 746**	**6 150**	**5 659**	**4 859**	**4 565**	**4 140**	**3 931**	**3 497**	**3 532**
Beef,veal & buffalo Boeuf,veau et buffle	...	3 632	3 359	3 240	2 733	2 630	2 394	2 247	1 868	2 126
Pork Porc	...	2 784	2 432	2 103	1 865	1 705	1 546	1 505	1 485	1 250
Mutton,lamb & goat Mouton,agneau et caprin	...	330	359	316	261	230	200	178	143	156
Slovakia **Slovaquie**	...	...	**337**	**314**	**304**	**314**	**322**	**288**	**227**	**208**
Beef,veal & buffalo Boeuf,veau et buffle	...	...	93	67	59	61	66	59	50	43
Pork Porc	...	...	241	244	243	251	255	227	176	164
Mutton,lamb & goat Mouton,agneau et caprin	...	...	3	2	2	2	2	2	2	2
Slovenia **Slovénie**	...	**79**	**117**	**123**	**112**	**117**	**114**	**106**	**111**	**111**
Beef,veal & buffalo Boeuf,veau et buffle	...	38	52	52	51	54	54	45	43	43
Pork Porc	...	41	65	71	61	63	59	61	67	67

42

Meat
Production: thousand metric tons [cont.]
Viande
Production : milliers de tonnes [suite]

Region, country or area Région, pays ou zone	1991	1992	1993	1994	1995	1996	1997	1998	1999	2000
Mutton,lamb & goat Mouton,agneauet caprin	...	0	0	0	0	0	1	1	1	1
Spain **Espagne**	**2 630**	**2 690**	**2 817**	**2 849**	**2 925**	**3 159**	**3 238**	**3 645**	**3 809**	**3 900**
Beef,veal & buffalo Boeuf,veau et buffle	509	539	488	484	508	565	592	651	678	697
Pork Porc	1 877	1 918	2 089	2 124	2 175	2 356	2 401	2 744	2 893	2 962
Mutton,lamb & goat Mouton,agneauet caprin	244	233	241	241	242	238	245	250	239	240
Sweden **Suède**	**409**	**412**	**437**	**454**	**456**	**460**	**482**	**477**	**472**	**464**
Beef,veal & buffalo Boeuf,veau et buffle	137	130	142	142	143	138	149	143	143	140
Pork Porc	268	278	291	308	309	319	329	330	325	320
Mutton,lamb & goat Mouton,agneau et caprin	4	4	4	4	3	4	4	3	4	4
Switzerland **Suisse**	**445**	**436**	**422**	**394**	**404**	**385**	**373**	**385**	**379**	**362**
Beef,veal & buffalo Boeuf,veau et buffle	174	165	156	142	147	159	152	147	146	131
Pork Porc	265	264	260	246	251	220	214	232	226	225
Mutton,lamb & goat Mouton,agneau et caprin	6	6	6	6	6	6	6	6	7	6
TFYR of Macedonia **L'ex-R.y. Macédoine**	...	**30**	**31**	**30**	**26**	**26**	**23**	**22**	**22**	**22**
Beef,veal & buffalo Boeuf,veau et buffle	...	8	8	8	7	7	8	7	7	7
Pork Porc	...	10	10	10	9	9	9	9	9	9
Mutton,lamb & goat Mouton,agneauet caprin	...	12	13	13	10	10	7	6	6	6
Ukraine **Ukraine**	...	**2 870**	**2 422**	**2 387**	**2 032**	**1 869**	**1 664**	**1 482**	**1 466**	**1 496**
Beef,veal & buffalo Boeuf,veau et buffle	...	1 656	1 379	1 427	1 186	1 048	930	793	791	803
Pork Porc	...	1 180	1 013	916	807	789	710	668	656	675
Mutton,lamb & goat Mouton,agneauet caprin	...	35	30	44	40	32	24	21	19	18
United Kingdom **Royaume-Uni**	**2 384**	**2 361**	**2 292**	**2 387**	**2 409**	**2 094**	**2 111**	**2 190**	**2 086**	**1 990**
Beef,veal & buffalo Boeuf,veau et buffle	1 020	971	881	943	996	708	696	697	678	708
Pork Porc	979	992	1 012	1 053	1 012	1 004	1 094	1 142	1 047	923
Mutton,lamb & goat Mouton,agneauet caprin	385	398	399	391	401	382	321	351	361	359
Yugoslavia **Yougoslavie**	...	**816**	**790**	**794**	**899**	**986**	**883**	**782**	**767**	**767**
Beef,veal & buffalo Boeuf,veau et buffle	...	201	231	197	227	242	209	127	104	104
Pork Porc	...	592	534	571	644	713	644	625	640	640
Mutton,lamb & goat Mouton,agneauet caprin	...	23	25	26	29	31	31	30	23	23

42

Meat
Production: thousand metric tons [*cont.*]
Viande
Production : milliers de tonnes [*suite*]

Region, country or area Région, pays ou zone	1991	1992	1993	1994	1995	1996	1997	1998	1999	2000
Yugoslavia, SFR† **Yougoslavie, Rfs†**	**1 075**	...	...	...	...	...	...	...	...	...
Beef,veal & buffalo Boeuf,veau et buffle	301	...	...	...	...	...	...	...	...	...
Pork Porc	716	...	...	...	...	...	...	...	...	...
Mutton,lamb & goat Mouton,agneau et caprin	57	...	...	...	...	...	...	...	...	...
Oceania **Océanie**	**3 965**	**4 020**	**3 991**	**4 015**	**4 078**	**3 935**	**4 043**	**4 252**	**4 216**	**4 290**
Beef,veal & buffalo Boeuf,veau et buffle	2 321	2 347	2 418	2 383	2 452	2 398	2 477	2 610	2 593	2 632
Pork Porc	401	430	429	448	459	441	445	470	482	473
Mutton,lamb & goat Mouton,agneau et caprin	1 243	1 242	1 144	1 184	1 167	1 096	1 121	1 172	1 141	1 185
Australia **Australie**	**2 755**	**2 807**	**2 809**	**2 827**	**2 786**	**2 662**	**2 721**	**2 938**	**3 002**	**3 007**
Beef,veal & buffalo Boeuf,veau et buffle	1 760	1 791	1 826	1 825	1 803	1 745	1 810	1 955	2 011	1 988
Pork Porc	312	336	328	344	351	334	336	358	370	363
Mutton,lamb & goat Mouton,agneau et caprin	683	681	655	658	631	583	575	624	622	656
Cook Islands **Iles Cook**	**0**	**0**	**0**	**0**	**0**	**1**	**1**	**1**	**1**	**1**
Pork Porc	0	0	0	0	0	1	1	1	1	1
Fiji **Fidji**	**14**	**14**	**13**	**13**	**13**	**13**	**14**	**14**	**14**	**14**
Beef,veal & buffalo Boeuf,veau et buffle	10	10	9	9	9	9	9	9	10	10
Pork Porc	3	3	3	4	3	3	4	3	4	4
Mutton,lamb & goat Mouton,agneau et caprin	1	1	1	1	1	1	1	1	1	1
French Polynesia **Polynésie française**	**1**	**1**	**1**	**2**	**2**	**1**	**1**	**1**	**1**	**1**
Pork Porc	1	1	1	1	1	1	1	1	1	1
Kiribati **Kiribati**	**1**	**1**	**1**	**1**	**1**	**1**	**1**	**1**	**1**	**1**
Pork Porc	1	1	1	1	1	1	1	1	1	1
Micronesia (Fed. States of) **Micron (Etats fédérés de)**	**0**	**0**	**0**	**0**	**1**	**1**	**1**	**1**	**1**	**1**
Pork Porc	0	0	0	0	1	1	1	1	1	1
New Caledonia **Nouvelle-Calédonie**	**4**	**5**	**5**	**5**	**5**	**6**	**5**	**6**	**6**	**6**
Beef,veal & buffalo Boeuf,veau et buffle	3	3	4	4	4	4	4	4	4	4
Pork Porc	1	1	1	1	1	1	1	1	1	1
New Zealand **Nouvelle-Zélande**	**1 143**	**1 143**	**1 109**	**1 111**	**1 215**	**1 194**	**1 240**	**1 231**	**1 130**	**1 198**

42

Meat
Production: thousand metric tons [cont.]
Viande
Production : milliers de tonnes [suite]

Region, country or area / Région, pays ou zone	1991	1992	1993	1994	1995	1996	1997	1998	1999	2000
Beef,veal & buffalo										
Boeuf,veau et buffle	540	536	572	537	629	633	646	634	561	623
Pork										
Porc	44	47	49	49	51	50	49	50	50	48
Mutton,lamb & goat										
Mouton,agneau et caprin	559	560	488	525	535	511	544	547	519	527
Papua New Guinea										
Papouasie-Nvl-Guinée	**29**	**32**	**35**	**38**	**41**	**42**	**44**	**45**	**45**	**45**
Beef,veal & buffalo										
Boeuf,veau et buffle	2	2	2	2	2	2	2	2	2	2
Pork										
Porc	27	30	33	36	39	40	42	44	44	44
Samoa										
Samoa	**5**	**4**	**5**	**5**	**5**	**5**	**5**	**5**	**5**	**5**
Beef,veal & buffalo										
Boeuf,veau et buffle	1	1	1	1	1	1	1	1	1	1
Pork										
Porc	4	4	4	4	4	4	4	4	4	4
Solomon Islands										
Iles Salomon	**2**	**2**	**2**	**2**	**2**	**2**	**2**	**2**	**2**	**3**
Beef,veal & buffalo										
Boeuf,veau et buffle	1	0	0	0	0	0	0	0	0	1
Pork										
Porc	2	2	2	2	2	2	2	2	2	2
Tonga										
Tonga	**2**	**2**	**2**	**2**	**2**	**2**	**2**	**2**	**2**	**2**
Pork										
Porc	2	2	1	1	1	1	1	1	1	1
Vanuatu										
Vanuatu	**6**	**6**	**6**	**7**	**6**	**6**	**7**	**6**	**7**	**7**
Beef,veal & buffalo										
Boeuf,veau et buffle	3	3	4	4	4	4	4	4	4	4
Pork										
Porc	2	3	3	3	3	3	3	3	3	3
USSR - former †										
URSS (anc.) †	**15 174**	...	...	...	...	...	...	...	...	...
Beef,veal & buffalo										
Boeuf,veau et buffle	8 261	...	...	...	...	...	...	...	...	...
Pork										
Porc	5 997	...	...	...	...	...	...	...	...	...
Mutton,lamb & goat										
Mouton,agneau et caprin	916	...	...	...	...	...	...	...	...	...

Source:
Food and Agriculture Organization of the United
Nations (FAO), Rome, "FAO Production Yearbook 2000" and the
FAOSTAT database.

† For information on recent changes in country or
area nomenclature pertaining to former Czechoslovakia,
Germany, Hong Kong Special Administrative Region (SAR) of
China, Macao Special Administrative Region (SAR) of China,
SFR of Yugoslavia and the former USSR, see Annex I - Country
or area nomenclature, regional and other groupings.

1 Data refer to the Gaza Strip.

Source:
Organisation des Nations Unies pour l'alimentation et
l'agriculture (FAO), Rome, "Annuaire FAO de la production
2000" et la base de données FAOSTAT.

† Pour les modifications récentes de nomenclature
de pays ou de zone concernant l'Allemagne, Hong Kong, région
administrative spéciale (RAS) de Chine, Macao, région
administrative spéciale (RAS) de Chine,
l'ex-Tchécoslovaquie, l'ex-URSS et l'ex-Rfs de Yougoslavie,
voir annexe I - Nomenclature des pays ou des zones,
groupements régionaux et autres groupements.

1 Les données se rapportent à la Zone de Gaza.

43
Beer
Bière
Production: thousand hectolitres
Production : milliers d'hectolitres

Country or area Pays ou zone	1990	1991	1992	1993	1994	1995	1996	1997	1998	1999
Albania Albanie	187	76	18	5	72	89	9	151	92	82
Algeria Algérie	325	301	337	421	398	402	377	379	382	383
Angola Angola	410	484	345	...	...	...	...	...	...	...
Argentina Argentine	6 170	7 979	9 518	10 305	11 272	10 913	11 615	12 687	12 395	12 133
Armenia Arménie	513	419	149	70	70	53	29	50	133	84
Australia Australie	19 540	18 970	18 040	17 760	17 840	17 700	17 118	17 615	17 570	17 290
Austria Autriche	9 799	9 971	10 176	11 465	10 070	9 767	9 445	9 303	8 837	8 884
Azerbaijan Azerbaïdjan	5 876	5 159	1 855	148	114	22	13	16	12	69
Barbados Barbade	77	66	58	67	73	74	76	75	87	76
Belarus Bélarus	3 283	3 389	2 736	2 146	1 489	1 518	2 013	2 413	2 604	2 730
Belgium Belgique	14 141	13 799	14 259	...	15 055	15 110	14 648	14 758	14 763	15 166
Belize Belize	34	36	38	68	56	49	41	37	42	...
Bolivia Bolivie	1 031	1 278	1 333	1 121	1 262	* 1 429	...	...	...	...
Botswana Botswana	1 214	1 211	1 289	1 374	1 305	1 366	1 351	1 005	1 019	1 591
Brazil Brésil	43 849	54 545	43 509	45 336	52 556	67 284	63 559	66 582	66 453	62 491
Bulgaria Bulgarie	6 507	4 880	4 695	4 247	4 792	4 331	4 402	3 031	3 796	4 045
Burkina Faso Burkina Faso	350	394	71	258	...	...	...	...	...	...
Burundi Burundi	1 107	981	1 007	1 044	...	...	...	...	...	...
Cameroon Cameroun	...	4 324	3 834	4 373	2 073	2 933	...	...	...	...
Central African Rep. Rép. centrafricaine	...	270	285	124	450	269	...	...	...	...
Chad Tchad	116	144	129	117	110	95	...	...	...	...
Chile Chili	2 658	2 791	3 349	3 623	3 303	3 551	3 459	3 640	3 666	3 343
China ††[12] Chine ††[12]	6 922	8 380	10 206	11 920	14 142	15 688	137 664	154 610	162 693	...
Colombia Colombie	15 098	...	14 574	...	15 739	20 525	...	18 290	16 461	...

43

Beer
Production: thousand hectolitres [*cont.*]
Bière
Production : milliers d'hectolitres [*suite*]

Country or area Pays ou zone	1990	1991	1992	1993	1994	1995	1996	1997	1998	1999
Congo Congo	566	686	708	759	...	...	...	...	...	...
Croatia Croatie	2 800	2 248	2 720	2 481	3 122	3 166	3 292	3 607	3 759	...
Cyprus Chypre	342	331	370	341	359	352	331	333	365	405
Czech Republic République tchèque	18 936	17 902	18 982	17 366	17 876	17 687	18 057	18 558	18 290	17 946
Denmark[2] Danemark[2]	9 362	...	9 775	9 435	9 410	9 903	9 591	9 181	8 044	8 205
Dominica Dominique	...	...	...	...	...	3	14	11	11	8
Dominican Republic Rép. dominicaine	1 376	1 459	1 956	1 992	2 190	2 082	447	2 593	2 993	3 484
Ecuador Equateur	...	...	1 826	1 525	1 131	3 201	2 163	238	633	...
Egypt Egypte	500	440	420	350	360	360	380	...	...	...
Estonia Estonie	77	675	426	419	477	492	459	543	744	957
Ethiopia[3] Ethiopie[3]	500	435	428	522	634	724	876	843	831	921
Fiji Fidji	194	183	173	167	160	150	170	170	170	...
Finland Finlande	4 151	4 418	4 685	4 579	4 524	4 702	4 980	4 840	4 341	4 733
France France	19 109	18 654	18 512	18 291	17 688	18 311	17 140	17 010	16 551	...
French Polynesia Polynésie française	121	124	129	...	...	...	...	...	...	...
Gabon Gabon	819	814	785	905	801	816	...	...	...	...
Georgia Géorgie	...	...	235	120	63	65	48	79	97	126
Germany † Allemagne †	...	112 071	114 089	111 075	113 428	111 875	108 938	108 729	106 993	...
F. R. Germany R. f. Allemagne	99 150	...	...	...	...	...	...	...	...	...
German D. R.(former) R. d. allemande (anc.)	15 885	...	...	...	...	...	...	...	...	...
Greece Grèce	3 961	3 772	4 025	4 088	4 376	4 024	3 766	3 950	3 886	...
Grenada Grenade	25	25	26	18	24	...	...	...	...	...
Guatemala Guatemala	...	974	1 172	1 327	805	1 471	1 655	1 303	1 363	...
Guyana Guyana	109	124	143	145	97	...	...	...	...	...

43

Beer
Production: thousand hectolitres [*cont.*]
Bière
Production : milliers d'hectolitres [*suite*]

Country or area Pays ou zone	1990	1991	1992	1993	1994	1995	1996	1997	1998	1999
Hungary Hongrie	9 918	9 570	9 162	7 877	8 082	7 697	7 270	6 973	7 163	6 996
Iceland Islande	35	30	32	41	54	52	63	64	71	77
India[4] Inde[4]	1 915	2 136	2 233	3 053	2 778	3 700	4 255	4 331	4 332	3 632
Indonesia Indonésie	1 042	1 043	1 145	871	779	1 136	...	531	502	...
Ireland Irlande	5 236[5]	...	...	...	...	8 132	10 765	12 095	12 580	...
Israel Israël	567	532	511	587	508	...	...	...	...	...
Italy Italie	11 248	11 049	10 489	9 873	10 258	10 616	9 559	10 379	11 073	11 123
Jamaica Jamaïque	887	715	828	786	760	662	690	674	670	656
Japan[6] Japon[6]	65 636	69 157	70 106	69 642	71 007	67 971	69 082	66 370	61 759	58 901
Kazakhstan Kazakhstan	2 980	31 330	23 011	1 692	129	812	636	693	850	824
Kenya Kenya	3 311	3 140	3 686	3 589	3 250	3 474	2 759	...	...	...
Korea, Republic of Corée, République de	13 045	15 928	15 673	15 252	17 176	17 554	17 210	16 907	14 080	14 866
Kyrgyzstan Kirghizistan	41	45	31	19	12	12	14	14	13	12
Lao People's Dem. Rep. Rép. dém. pop. lao	...	...	...	...	102	151	...	...	...
Latvia Lettonie	874	1 295	859	546	638	653	645	715	721	953
Lithuania Lituanie	1 502	1 412	1 426	1 164	1 353	1 093	1 139	1 413	1 559	1 847
Luxembourg Luxembourg	600	572	569	558	531	518	484	481	469	450
Madagascar Madagascar	298	236	226	228	219	246	347	234	297	...
Malawi Malawi	752	763	774	763	811	289	277	292	206	684
Malaysia Malaisie	1 401	1 413	...	...	...	...	...	...	...	...
Mali Mali	34	38	41	40	43	52	60	...	...	...
Mauritius Maurice	281	291	295	292	283	309	312	339	376	358
Mexico Mexique	38 734	41 092	42 262	43 630	45 060	44 205	48 111	51 315	54 569	57 905
Mozambique Mozambique	353	227	211	204	118	244	374	631	75	95
Myanmar[7] Myanmar[7]	24	30	19	24	13	...	...	...	...	...

43
Beer
Production: thousand hectolitres [cont.]
Bière
Production : milliers d'hectolitres [suite]

Country or area Pays ou zone	1990	1991	1992	1993	1994	1995	1996	1997	1998	1999
Nepal[1] Népal[1]	...	...	123	144	149	168	183	215	139	188
Netherlands[29] Pays-Bas[29]	20 055	19 863	20 419	19 720	21 200	22 380	22 670	23 780	23 040	23 799
New Zealand[2] Nouvelle-Zélande[2]	3 890	3 627	3 637	3 519	3 568	3 488	3 435	3 214	3 206	3 148
Nigeria Nigéria	7 877	8 108	11 438	16 860	1 561	1 461	...	...	...	...
Norway Norvège	2 281	...	2 273	...	...	2 255	...	2 396	1 833	2 651
Panama Panama	1 066	1 219	1 163	1 204	1 291	1 274	1 206	...	...	...
Paraguay Paraguay	1 070	1 150	1 140	1 710	...	...	...	...	...	...
Peru Pérou	5 685	6 774	6 764	7 060	6 957	7 817	7 435	7 431	6 557	6 168
Poland Pologne	11 294	13 633	14 139	12 585	14 099	15 205	16 667	19 281	21 017	23 360
Portugal Portugal	6 919	6 309	6 923	6 662	6 902	7 220	6 958	6 766	7 072	6 947
Puerto Rico Porto Rico	751	773	654	477	438	397	360	317	263	259
Republic of Moldova République de Moldova	762	660	410	297[10]	233[10]	276[10]	226[10]	238[10]	278[10]	214[10]
Romania Roumanie	10 527	9 803	10 014	9 929	9 047	8 768	8 118	7 651	9 989	11 133
Russian Federation Fédération de Russie	33 600	33 300	27 900	24 700	21 800	21 400	20 800	26 100	33 600	44 500
Saint Kitts and Nevis Saint-Kitts-et-Nevis	17	17	16	17	17	17	20	19	...	...
Seychelles Seychelles	53	59	70	65	58	58	63	71	72	68
Slovakia Slovaquie	4 607	4 082	3 686	3 967	4 974	4 369	4 666	5 577	4 478	4 473
Slovenia Slovénie	2 456	2 203	1 783	1 978	2 075	2 087	2 223	2 138	2 000	2 022
South Africa Afrique du Sud	17 750	17 710	18 290	...	...	...	...	...	...	...
Spain Espagne	27 940	26 482	24 279	21 353	25 587	25 396	24 520	24 786	22 428	26 007
Suriname Suriname	122	122	71	107	69	65	72	...	...	...
Sweden Suède	4 711	4 663	4 969	5 087	5 379	5 471	5 318	5 078	4 763	4 718
Switzerland[2] Suisse[2]	4 143	4 137	4 020	3 804	3 828	3 672	...	...	...	...
Syrian Arab Republic Rép. arabe syrienne	99	99	102	104	102	102	102	97	97	121

43

Beer
Production: thousand hectolitres [*cont.*]
Bière
Production : milliers d'hectolitres [*suite*]

Country or area Pays ou zone	1990	1991	1992	1993	1994	1995	1996	1997	1998	1999
Tajikistan Tadjikistan	317	364	135	82	67	47	6	6	9	7
Thailand Thaïlande	2 635	2 840	3 252	4 153	5 230	6 473	7 591	8 742	9 770	10 422
TFYR of Macedonia L'ex-R.y. Macédoine	958	928	861	952	725	620	622	600	578	652
Trinidad and Tobago Trinité-et-Tobago	412	487	395	424	482	428	419	407	517	522
Tunisia Tunisie	426	407	494	601	689	659	662	780	813	912
Turkey Turquie	3 544	4 188	4 843	5 524	6 019	6 946	7 381	7 656	7 130	7 188
Turkmenistan Turkménistan	442	465	372	287	218	113	17	44	29	...
Uganda Ouganda	194	195	187	239	308	512	642	896	1 105	1 178
Ukraine Ukraine	13 778	13 093	10 997	9 086	9 087	7 102	6 025	6 125	6 842	8 407
USSR - former † URSS (anc.) †	62 507	...	...	...	...	...	...	...	...	...
United Kingdom Royaume-Uni	70 800	...	...	...	66 161	59 337	61 262	64 736	60 806	...
United Rep. of Tanzania Rép.-Unie de Tanzanie	450	498	493	570	568	893	125	148	...	...
United States[5] Etats-Unis[5]	236 670	...	237 029	237 345	237 987	...	233 485	...	...	...
Uruguay Uruguay	...	...	...	817	...	998	815	921	860	...
Uzbekistan Ouzbékistan	1 746	1 759	1 434	1 363	1 291	724	677	619	...	...
Viet Nam Viet Nam	1 000	1 312	1 685	...	...	4 650	5 330	5 810	6 700	* 6 480
Yemen Yémen	50	100	40	...	...	...	...	...	...	...
Yugoslavia Yougoslavie	6 105	5 460	4 413	3 019	5 043	5 611	5 987	6 106	6 630	6 786

Source:
United Nations Statistics Division, New York, "Industrial Commodity Statistics Yearbook 1999" and the industrial statistics database.

† For information on recent changes in country or area nomenclature pertaining to former Czechoslovakia, Germany, Hong Kong Special Administrative Region (SAR) of China, Macao Special Administrative Region (SAR) of China, SFR of Yugoslavia and the former USSR, see Annex I - Country or area nomenclature, regional and other groupings.

Source:
Organisation des Nations Unies, Division de statistique, New York, "Annuaire de statistiques industrielles par produit 1999" et la base de données pour les statistiques industrielles.

† Pour les modifications récentes de nomenclature de pays ou de zone concernant l'Allemagne, Hong Kong, région administrative spéciale (RAS) de Chine, Macao, région administrative spéciale (RAS) de Chine, l'ex-Tchécoslovaquie, l'ex-URSS et l'ex-Rfs de Yougoslavie, voir annexe I - Nomenclature des pays ou des zones, groupements régionaux et autres groupements.

43

Beer
Production: thousand hectolitres [*cont.*]

Bière
Production : milliers d'hectolitres [*suite*]

†† For statistical purposes, the data for
China do not include those for Hong Kong Special
Administrative Region (Hong Kong SAR), Macao Special
Administrative Region (Macao SAR) and Taiwan province of
China.

1 Original data in metric tons.
2 Sales.
3 Twelve months ending 7 July of the year stated.

4 Production by large and medium scale establishments only.
5 Twelve months ending 30 September of year stated.

6 Twelve months beginning 1 April of year stated.

7 Government production only.
8 Twelve months beginning 16 July of year stated.

9 Production by establishments employing 20 or more persons.
10 Excluding Transnistria region.

†† Les données statistiques relatives à
la Chine ne comprennent pas celles qui concernent la région
administrative spéciale de Hong Kong (la RAS de Hong Kong),
la région administrative spéciale de Macao (la RAS de Macao)
et la province chinoise de Taiwan.

1 Données d'origine exprimées en tonnes.
2 Ventes.
3 Période de douze mois finissant le 7 juillet de l'année
indiquée.
4 Production des grandes et moyennes entreprises seulement.
5 Période de douze mois finissant le 30 septembre de l'année
indiquée.
6 Période de douze mois commençant le 1er avril de l'année
indiquée.
7 Production de l'Etat seulement.
8 Période de douze mois commençant le 16 juillet de l'année
indiquée.
9 Production des établissements occupant 20 personnes ou plus.
10 Non compris la région de Transnistria.

44
Cigarettes
Cigarettes
Production: millions
Production : millions

Country or area Pays ou zone	1990	1991	1992	1993	1994	1995	1996	1997	1998	1999
Albania [1] Albanie [1]	4 947	1 703	1 393	1 395	929	685	4 830	414	764	63
Algeria [1] Algérie [1]	18 775	17 848	16 426	16 260	16 345	16 419	15 840	15 543	17 891	18 324
Angola [2] Angola [2]	2 400	2 400	2 400	...	...	...	...	...	...	...
Argentina Argentine	1 657	1 727	1 845	1 929	1 975	1 963	1 971	1 940	1 967	1 996
Armenia Arménie	8 102	6 614	3 927	1 878	2 014	1 043	152	815	2 489	3 132
Australia [3] Australie [3]	36 263	34 977	* 34 000	...	...	...	...	...	...	...
Austria Autriche	14 961	16 406	15 836	16 247	16 429	16 297	...	...	...	...
Azerbaijan Azerbaïdjan	6 453	7 256	4 855	5 277	3 179	1 926	766	827	241	416
Bangladesh [4] Bangladesh [4]	12 289	13 604	12 535	11 516	12 655	17 379	16 222	18 601	...	...
Barbados Barbade	135 [1]	124 [1]	115 [1]	133 [1]	150 [1]	65	...	...	...	...
Belarus Bélarus	16 399	15 009	8 847	8 670	7 378	6 228	6 267	6 787	7 296	9 259
Belgium Belgique	27 758 [5]	27 303 [5]	29 576 [5]	27 173 [5]	21 366	18 826	17 471	18 061	17 519	14 712
Belize Belize	101	104	104	105	101	95	79	88	94	...
Bolivia Bolivie	97	102	116	119	1 490	* 170	...	...	...	...
Brazil [2] Brésil [2]	173 987	175 396	169 000	...	...	...	...	...	...	...
Bulgaria Bulgarie	73 000	79 749	48 558	32 098	53 664	74 603	57 238	43 315	33 181	25 715
Burkina Faso Burkina Faso	822	983	979	943	...	...	...	...	...	...
Burundi Burundi	384	450	453	517	...	...	...	...	...	...
Cambodia [2] Cambodge [2]	4 200	4 200	4 200	...	...	...	...	...	...	...
Cameroon [2] Cameroun [2]	4 900	5 000	5 000	...	...	...	...	...	...	...
Canada Canada	46 111 [2]	46 815 [2]	45 500 [2]	...	...	50 775	49 362	47 263	...	...
Central African Rep. Rép. centrafricaine	25	26	21	12	21	30	...	...	...	...
Chad Tchad	248	476	415	499	508	569	...	...	...	...
Chile Chili	10 198	10 259	11 167	10 793	10 801	10 891	11 569	12 522	12 904	13 271

44

Cigarettes
Production: millions [*cont.*]
Cigarettes
Production : millions [*suite*]

Country or area Pays ou zone	1990	1991	1992	1993	1994	1995	1996	1997	1998	1999
China †† Chine ††	1 648 765	1 613 245	1 642 340	1 655 630	...	...	...	...		...
China, Hong Kong SAR†[56] Chine, Hong Kong RAS†[56]	21 700	32 721	36 513	25 759	24 747	22 767	21 386	20 929	13 470	...
China, Macao SAR †[178] Chine, Macao RAS †[178]	500	500	500	500	450	450	450	...	...	...
Colombia Colombie	14 490[2]	13 585[2]	14 877	...	11 566	10 491	...	11 662	12 472	
Congo[1] Congo[1]	* 645	581	431	622	...	...	...	...	...	
Costa Rica Costa Rica	2 030[2]	2 000[2]	2 000[2]	16[17]	16[17]	16[17]	16[17]	...	...	...
Côte d'Ivoire[2] Côte d'Ivoire[2]	4 500	4 500	4 500	...	...	...	...	...	...	
Croatia Croatie	12 437	11 655	12 833	11 585	12 672	12 110	11 548	11 416	11 987	...
Cyprus Chypre	4 601	5 497	6 177	3 530	2 493	2 528	2 728	3 662	4 362	4 783
Czech Republic République tchèque	18 119	...	...	...	...	...	...	...	...	
Dem. Rep. of the Congo[2] Rép. dém. du Congo[2]	5 200	5 200	5 200	...	...	...	...	...	...	
Denmark[9] Danemark[9]	11 387	11 407	11 439	10 980	11 448	11 902	11 804	12 262	12 392	11 749
Dominican Republic Rép. dominicaine	4 535	4 170	4 432	4 356	4 696	4 092	4 192	3 972	4 098	4 005
Ecuador Equateur	* 4 600	* 4 600	3 000	3 079	2 515	1 734	1 745	1 678	1 997	...
Egypt Egypte	39 837	40 154	42 516	38 844	39 145	42 469	46 000	50 000	52 000	51 000
El Salvador El Salvador	1 655[2]	1 620[2]	1 620[2]	...	...	1 701	1 756	...	...	...
Estonia Estonie	4 165	3 577	1 780	2 630	2 287	1 864	954	...	...	
Ethiopia[10] Ethiopie[10]	2 258	2 416	1 879	1 932	1 468	1 583	1 862	2 024	2 029	1 829
Fiji Fidji	531	514	484	506	483	437	439	450	410	...
Finland Finlande	8 974	8 180	8 106	7 237	7 232	6 542	5 910	...	...	...
France France	55 495	50 311	* 53 312	47 912	48 188	46 361	46 931	44 646	43 304	...
Gabon Gabon	328	358	399	334	288	297	...	...	...	...
Georgia Géorgie	...	...	4 953	3 593	3 256	1 840	1 183	917	601	1 327
Germany † Allemagne †	...	...	...	204 730	222 791	...	...	...	...	...

44

Cigarettes
Production: millions [*cont.*]
Cigarettes
Production : millions [*suite*]

Country or area Pays ou zone	1990	1991	1992	1993	1994	1995	1996	1997	1998	1999
F. R. Germany R. f. Allemagne	177 905	...	...	...	...	...	...	...	...	...
German D. R.(former) R. d. allemande (anc.)	22 469	...	...	...	...	...	...	...	...	...
Ghana Ghana	1 805	* 2 100	* 2 100	...	...	...	...	...		
Greece Grèce	26 175	27 700	* 29 250	30 427	32 843	39 291	38 268	36 909	21 427	...
Grenada Grenade	22	20	20	19	15	...	...	...	...	...
Guatemala Guatemala	1 955 [2]	870	2 001 [2]	2 010	1 390	2 616	1 725	2 198	4 184	...
Guyana Guyana	247	307	318	302	314	...	...	...	...	...
Haiti Haïti	1 027	985	970	1 110	722	...	...	...		
Honduras [2] Honduras [2]	2 862	2 300	2 200	...	...	...	...	...	...	
Hungary Hongrie	28 212	26 124	26 835	28 728	29 518	25 709	27 594	26 057	26 849	22 985
India [11] Inde [11]	61 162	65 130	61 413	71 842	71 038	69 589	73 841	83 162	...	82 504
Indonesia Indonésie	...	...	34 382	34 757	36 421	38 768	...	220 157	271 177	...
Iran (Islamic Rep. of) Iran (Rép. islamique d')	12 319 [12]	* 11 565 [12]	10 171 [12]	7 835 [12]	7 939 [12]	9 787 [13]	11 860 [13]	10 304 [13]	14 335 [13]	...
Iraq [2] Iraq [2]	26 000	13 000	5 794	...	...	...	...	...	...	...
Ireland Irlande	6 218	6 377	* 7 850	7 300 [17]	7 000 [17]	7 500 [17]	7 500 [17]	4 605	6 452	6 176
Israel Israël	5 440	5 590 [1]	5 742 [1]	5 525 [1]	5 638 [1]	4 933 [1]	4 793 [1]	...	...	...
Italy Italie	61 736 [1]	57 634 [1]	53 799 [1]	54 943 [1]	55 175 [1]	50 247 [1]	51 489 [1]	51 894 [1]	50 785	45 159
Jamaica Jamaïque	1 380	1 219	1 299	1 224	1 273	1 216	1 219	1 175	1 160	1 078
Japan [14] Japon [14]	268 100	275 000	279 000	...	...	...	...	...	...	
Jordan Jordanie	3 185	3 719	3 091	3 465	4 191	3 675	4 738	...	...	...
Kazakhstan Kazakhstan	...	9 536	8 997	10 664	9 393	12 080	19 121	24 109	21 747	18 773
Kenya Kenya	6 647	6 473	7 193	7 267	7 319	7 932	8 436	...	...	...
Korea, Republic of Corée, République de	91 923	94 336	96 648	96 887	90 774	87 959	94 709	96 725	101 011	95 995
Kyrgyzstan Kirghizistan	3 974	4 015	3 120	3 428	1 943	1 332	975	716	862	2 103
Lao People's Dem. Rep. Rép. dém. pop. lao	1 200 [2]	1 200 [2]	1 200 [2]	...	936	1 062	...	...		

44

Cigarettes
Production: millions [cont.]
Cigarettes
Production : millions [suite]

Country or area Pays ou zone	1990	1991	1992	1993	1994	1995	1996	1997	1998	1999
Latvia Lettonie	5 209	4 765	3 435	2 589	2 093	2 101	1 876	1 775	2 018	1 916
Lebanon Liban	4 000[2]	4 000[2]	4 000[2]	...	...	# 535[1]	539[1]	...	...	...
Liberia[2] Libéria[2]	22	22	22	...	...	...	...	...	...	...
Libyan Arab Jamah.[2] Jamah. arabe libyenne[2]	3 500	3 500	3 500	...	...	...	...	...	...	...
Lithuania Lituanie	6 654	6 438	5 269	3 435	3 860	4 876	4 538	5 755	7 427	8 217
Madagascar[1] Madagascar[1]	1 476	1 950	2 223	2 304	2 003	2 354	2 957	2 826	3 303	...
Malawi Malawi	1 061	951	1 000	1 020	1 127	1 160	975	731	501	...
Malaysia[1] Malaisie[1]	17 331	17 498	16 574	15 568	15 762	15 918	16 896	20 236	18 410	15 504
Mali Mali	17	23	24	23	20	22	21	...	...	...
Malta[2] Malte[2]	1 475	1 475	1 475	...	...	...	...	...	...	...
Mauritius Maurice	1 000	1 034	1 060	1 269	1 300	1 215	1 193	1 144	1 034	979
Mexico Mexique	55 380	54 680	55 988	53 435	53 402	56 821	59 907	57 618	60 407	59 492
Morocco Maroc	640	602	515	...	...	...	...	...	...	...
Mozambique Mozambique	1 030	217	124	377	343	106	250	250	950	1 084
Myanmar[15] Myanmar[15]	979	682	396	426	440	752	1 727	1 991	2 040	2 270
Nepal[16] Népal[16]	...	...	6 963	7 846	6 894	7 430	8 067	7 944	8 127	7 315
Netherlands[9][17] Pays-Bas[9][17]	71 992	74 767	78 479	71 254	88 069	97 727	...	...	...	...
New Zealand Nouvelle-Zélande	4 489	4 014	3 466	3 381	3 396[9]	3 338[9]	3 660[9]	3 449[9]	3 263[9]	3 010[9]
Nicaragua[2] Nicaragua[2]	2 400	2 400	2 400	...	...	...	...	...	...	...
Nigeria Nigéria	10 380	9 405	8 608	9 384	338	256	...	...	...	...
Norway[2] Norvège[2]	1 480	1 730	1 825	...	...	...	...	...	...	...
Pakistan[4] Pakistan[4]	32 279	29 887	29 673	29 947	35 895	32 747	45 506	46 101	48 215	51 579
Panama Panama	810	771	806	903	1 204	1 136	663	...	...	...
Paraguay Paraguay	992	827	777	...	...	...	...	...	...	...
Peru Pérou	2 585	2 696	2 501	2 511	2 752	3 041	3 358	3 028	3 115	3 580

44
Cigarettes
Production: millions [*cont.*]
Cigarettes
Production : millions [*suite*]

Country or area Pays ou zone	1990	1991	1992	1993	1994	1995	1996	1997	1998	1999
Philippines[17] Philippines[17]	7 175	7 071	6 771	7 135	7 300	7 440	7 440	...	...	...
Poland Pologne	91 497	90 407	86 571	90 713	98 394	100 627	95 293	95 798	96 741	95 056
Portugal Portugal	17 547	17 361	15 619	15 335	13 610	13 215	12 780	13 234	15 781	17 742
Republic of Moldova République de Moldova	9 088	9 164	8 582	8 790[18]	8 001[18]	7 108[18]	9 657[18]	9 539[18]	7 512[18]	8 731[18]
Romania[3] Roumanie[3]	18 090	17 722	17 781	15 222	14 532	14 747	16 536	25 943	...	...
Russian Federation Fédération de Russie	115 321	112 326	107 763	100 162	91 601	99 545	112 319	140 077	195 806	266 031
Senegal[2] Sénégal[2]	3 350	3 350	3 350	...	...	...	...	...	...	...
Seychelles Seychelles	67	69	62	65	49	56	62	70	61	60
Sierra Leone[2] Sierra Leone[2]	1 200	1 200	1 200	...	...	...	...	...	...	...
Singapore[2] Singapour[2]	9 620	10 500	11 760	...	...	...	...	...	...	...
Slovakia Slovaquie	8 589	8 721	...	...	...	...	...	...	...	...
Slovenia Slovénie	5 179	4 798	5 278	4 851	4 722	4 543	4 909	5 767	7 555	8 032
South Africa Afrique du Sud	40 792	40 163	35 563	34 499	...	...	...	...	...	...
Spain Espagne	75 995	81 843	76 696	80 103	81 886	78 676	77 675	77 315	81 940	74 873
Sri Lanka Sri Lanka	5 621	5 789	5 359	5 649	5 656	5 822	6 160	* 5 712	5 797	5 412
Sudan[2] Soudan[2]	750	750	750	...	...	...	...	...	...	...
Suriname Suriname	487	337	419	454	443	472	483	...	...	...
Sweden Suède	9 648	9 594	9 841	7 420	8 032	7 193	7 251	6 237	5 692	6 060
Switzerland Suisse	31 771	32 943	33 740	34 713	39 906	41 976	42 955	37 638	34 453	32 139
Syrian Arab Republic[1] Rép. arabe syrienne[1]	6 855	7 974	8 093	7 185	7 773	9 699	8 528	10 137	10 398	10 991
Tajikistan Tadjikistan	5 022	4 467	2 607	1 901	1 644	964	604	153	191	209
Thailand Thaïlande	38 180	39 697	40 691	42 043	45 359	43 020	48 173	43 387	34 585	31 146
Trinidad and Tobago Trinité-et-Tobago	701[1]	881[1]	656[1]	638	593	920	1 102	1 386	1 680	1 945
Tunisia Tunisie	6 852	7 790	7 797	6 965	7 128	7 421	7 159	7 735	9 813	11 066

44
Cigarettes
Production: millions [*cont.*]
Cigarettes
Production : millions [*suite*]

Country or area Pays ou zone	1990	1991	1992	1993	1994	1995	1996	1997	1998	1999
Turkey[1] Turquie[1]	63 055	71 106	67 549	74 845	85 093	80 700	73 787	74 984	81 616	75 135
Uganda Ouganda	1 290	1 688	1 575	1 412	1 459	1 576	1 702	1 864	1 866	1 688
Ukraine Ukraine	69 397	66 645	60 990	40 571	47 083	48 033	44 900	54 488	59 275	54 105
USSR - former † URSS (anc.) †	313 082	...	...	...	...	...	...	...	...	...
United Kingdom Royaume-Uni	112 000	127 000	* 126 538	146 138	165 479	155 103	166 496	167 670	152 998	...
United Rep. of Tanzania Rép.-Unie de Tanzanie	3 742	3 870	3 789	3 893	3 383	3 699	3 733	4 710		
United States Etats-Unis	709 700	694 500	718 500	661 000	725 500	746 500	754 500	719 600	679 700	611 929
Uruguay Uruguay	3 900[2]	3 900[2]	3 900[2]	3 736	...	3 561	6 044	6 870	9 209	...
Uzbekistan Ouzbékistan	4 370	4 897	4 150	4 151	3 379	2 742	5 172	8 521	...	...
Venezuela[2] Venezuela[2]	23 560	24 236	24 400	...	...	...	...	...	...	...
Viet Nam Viet Nam	24 990	25 960	* 24 600	...	...	...	...	...	...	...
Yemen Yémen	5 968[1 7]	6 790[1 7]	6 294[1 7]	8 844[1 7]	5 423[1 7]	6 540	6 740	6 800	...	...
Yugoslavia Yougoslavie	...	17 605	15 654	16 053	12 972	12 686	13 176	10 988	14 597	13 126
Yugoslavia, SFR† Yougoslavie, Rfs†	58 200	...	...	...	...	...	...	...	...	...
Zambia[2] Zambie[2]	1 500	1 500	1 500	...	...	...	...	...	...	...
Zimbabwe[2] Zimbabwe[2]	2 600	3 240	3 025	...	...	...	...	...	...	...

Source:
United Nations Statistics Division, New York, "Industrial
Commodity Statistics Yearbook 1999" and the industrial
statistics database.

† For information on recent changes in country or
area nomenclature pertaining to former Czechoslovakia,
Germany, Hong Kong Special Administrative Region (SAR) of
China, Macao Special Administrative Region (SAR) of China,
SFR of Yugoslavia and the former USSR, see Annex I - Country
or area nomenclature, regional and other groupings.

†† For statistical purposes, the data for
China do not include those for Hong Kong Special
Administrative Region (Hong Kong SAR), Macao Special
Administrative Region (Macao SAR) and Taiwan province of
China.

Source:
Organisation des Nations Unies, Division de statistique, New
York, "Annuaire de statistiques industrielles par produit
1999" et la base de données pour les statistiques
industrielles.

† Pour les modifications récentes de nomenclature
de pays ou de zone concernant l'Allemagne, Hong Kong, région
administrative spéciale (RAS) de Chine, Macao, région
administrative spéciale (RAS) de Chine,
l'ex-Tchécoslovaquie, l'ex-URSS et l'ex-Rfs de Yougoslavie,
voir annexe I - Nomenclature des pays ou des zones,
groupements régionaux et autres groupements.

†† Les données statistiques relatives à
la Chine ne comprennent pas celles qui concernent la région
administrative spéciale de Hong Kong (la RAS de Hong Kong),
la région administrative spéciale de Macao (la RAS de Macao)
et la province chinoise de Taiwan.

44

Cigarettes
Production: millions [*cont.*]

Cigarettes
Production : millions [*suite*]

1 Original data in units of weight. Computed on the basis of one million cigarettes per ton.	1 Données d'origine exprimées en poids. Calcul sur la base d'un million cigarettes par tonne.
2 Source: U.S. Department of Agriculture, (Washington, D.C.).	2 Source: "U.S. Department of Agriculture," (Washington, D.C.).
3 Including cigars.	3 Y compris les cigares.
4 Twelve months ending 30 June of year stated.	4 Période de douze mois finissant le 30 juin de l'année indiquée.
5 Including cigarillos.	5 Y compris les cigarillos.
6 1999 data are confidential.	6 Pour 1999, les données sont confidentielles.
7 Source: Food and Agriculture Organization of the United Nations (FAO), (Rome).	7 Source: Organisation des Nations Unies pour l'alimentation et l'agriculture (FAO), (Rome).
8 Beginning 1997, data are confidential.	8 Pour 1999, les données sont confidentielles.
9 Sales.	9 Ventes.
10 Twelve months ending 7 July of the year stated.	10 Période de douze mois finissant le 7 juillet de l'année indiquée.
11 Production by large and medium scale establishments only.	11 Production des grandes et moyennes entreprises seulement.
12 Production by establishments employing 50 or more persons.	12 Production des établissements occupant 50 personnes ou plus.
13 Production by establishments employing 10 or more persons.	13 Production des établissements occupant 10 personnes ou plus.
14 Twelve months beginning 1 April of year stated.	14 Période de douze mois commençant le 1er avril de l'année indiquée.
15 Government production only.	15 Production de l'Etat seulement.
16 Twelve months beginning 16 July of year stated.	16 Période de douze mois commençant le 16 juillet de l'année indiquée.
17 Production by establishments employing 20 or more persons.	17 Production des établissements occupant 20 personnes ou plus.
18 Excluding Transnistria region.	18 Non compris la région de Transnistria.

45
Fabrics
Tissus

Woven cotton, wool, cellulosic and non−cellulosic fibres: million square metres
Tissus de coton, laines, fibres cellulosiques et non cellulosiques : millions de mètres carrés

Country or area Pays ou zone	1990	1991	1992	1992	1994	1995	1996	1997	1998	1999
A. Cotton · Coton										
Armenia Arménie	34	10	5	2	0	0	1	0	0	0
Australia [1] Australie [1]	38	36[2]	40	41	50	52	64	61	62	56
Austria Autriche	108	100	86	83	83	101	96	95	101	74
Azerbaijan Azerbaïdjan	102	95	77	98	78	58	24	17	7	1
Bangladesh [1] Bangladesh [1]	63	63	63	63	63	63	63	63	...	...
Belarus Bélarus	144	144	119	92	25	34	45	48	72	50
Belgium Belgique	399	379	337	331	232	232[3]	267[3]	270[3]	283[3]	274[3]
Bolivia [4] Bolivie [4]	2	1	1	0	0	* 0	...	...	...	...
Brazil [4] Brésil [4]	1 901[56]	1 679[56]	1 616[56]	1 568[56]	1 566[5]	1 354	1 318	1 278	1 209	1 270
Bulgaria Bulgarie	254[7]	138[7]	102[7]	83[7]	86[7]	93[7]	85[7]	98[7]	96[4]	62[4]
Cameroon [4] Cameroun [4]	...	18	21	18	35	24	...	...	...	...
Chad Tchad	58	60	81	...	...	...	...	...	...	...
Chile [4] Chili [4]	31	24	23	32	28	29	34	31	27	21
China †† [4] Chine †† [4]	22 557	21 719	22 783	24 263	25 243	31 091	24 987	29 730	28 800	29 875
China, Hong Kong SAR † Chine, Hong Kong RAS †	* 818	753	807	755	692	658	540	506	...	...
China, Macao SAR † Chine, Macao RAS †	...	...	...	15	10	8	9	9	10	11
Congo [4] Congo [4]	11	7	6	2	...	...	...	...	...	...
Croatia Croatie	39	30	29	29	23	22	19	34	39	...
Czech Republic République tchèque	529	381	293	337	340	358	330	346	331	267
Egypt Egypt	603	609	613	329	494	414	321	290	...	...
Estonia Estonie	169	168	111	55	74	90	120	130	127	95
Ethiopia [8] Ethiopie [8]	65	32	30	36	61	50	48	35	38	43
Finland [7] Finlande [7]	41	24	20	20	19	8	9	...	...	...
France [3] France [3]	836	760	753	761	691	...	...	...	...	...
Georgia Géorgie	...	...	13	7	2	1	1	0	0	0
Germany † Allemagne †	...	929	763	687	635	444	466	489	506	...
F. R. Germany † [7] R. f. Allemagne † [7]	896	...	...	...	...	...	...	...	...	...
former German D. R. † l'ex−R. d. allemande †	213	...	...	...	...	...	...	...	...	...

45

Fabrics
Woven cotton, wool, cellulosic and non−cellulosic fibres: million square metres [*cont.*]

Tissus
Tissus de coton, laines, fibres cellulosiques et non cellulosiques : millions de mètres carrés [*suite*]

Country or area Pays ou zone	1990	1991	1992	1992	1994	1995	1996	1997	1998	1999
Greece Grèce	...	...	...	119[5]	94[5]	72[5]	...	...	29	...
Hungary [7] Hongrie [7]	206	133	86	78	76	66	...	79	44	48
India Inde	15 177	16 478	17 582	19 648	...	...	...	...	...	...
Italy [3] Italie [3]	1 618	1 529	1 352	1 293	1 383	1 441	1 413	1 462	1 506	1 427
Japan Japon	1 765	1 603	1 465	1 205	1 180	1 029	916	917	842	774
Kazakhstan Kazakhstan	...	134	135	136	85	21	21	14	10	9
Kenya Kenya	45	27	31	28	27	22	28	...	...	...
Korea, Republic of [7] Corée, République de [7]	620	608	483	480	447	379	...	...	...	...
Kyrgyzstan Kirghizistan	105	119	119	65	49	21	25	20	13	12
Latvia Lettonie	54	45	22	0	0	2	6	9	12	12
Lithuania Lituanie	98	106	89	48	42	35	35	62	64	57
Madagascar [4] Madagascar [4]	59	57	50	42	44	34	27	32	23	...
Mexico [3] Mexique [3]	371	335	284	413	291	276	256	246	273	259
Myanmar [4] [9] Myanmar [4] [9]	47	27	22	16	13	16	118	112	130	214
Netherlands [3] Pays−Bas [3]	83	81	70	...	...	...	...	...	...	...
Nigeria Nigéria	316	395	420	393	124	113	...	...	...	...
Norway [3] Norvège [3]	* 13	11	10	7	8	6	6	...	...	...
Pakistan [11] Pakistan [11]	295[10]	293[10]	308[10]	325[10]	315	322	327	333	340	385
Paraguay [4] Paraguay [4]	18	23	23	24	...	...	...	...	...	...
Poland [7] [12] Pologne [7] [12]	474	332	290	284	321	263	295	303	275	234
Portugal Portugal	544[3]	511[3]	355[3]	388	421	418	401	412	444	405
Republic of Moldova République de Moldova	170	165	150	1[13]	0[13]	0[13]	0[13]	0[13]	0[13]	0[13]
Romania [7] Roumanie [7]	536	437	289	271	294	275	212	173	170	143
Russian Federation Fédération de Russie	6 201	5 949	3 799	2 822	1 631	1 401	1 120	1 374	1 241	1 455
Slovakia Slovaquie	...	...	...	78	76	90	57	...	125[3]	32[3]
Slovenia Slovénie	136[12]	102[12]	78[12]	81	81	71	53	...	...	...
South Africa Afrique du Sud	175	170	138	166	195	228	246	269	223	224
Spain Espagne	766[3][14]	773[3][14]	748[3][14]	523	622	689	...	...	...	...
Switzerland [4] Suisse [4]	103	81	77	74	82	70	...	...	...	...

45

Fabrics
Woven cotton, wool, cellulosic and non−cellulosic fibres: million square metres [*cont.*]
Tissus
Tissus de coton, laines, fibres cellulosiques et non cellulosiques : millions de mètres carrés [*suite*]

Country or area Pays ou zone	1990	1991	1992	1992	1994	1995	1996	1997	1998	1999
Syrian Arab Republic [3] Rép. arabe syrienne [3]	214[15]	221	205	222	213	184	186	198	199	...
Tajikistan Tadjikistan	122	102	58	57	34	28	17	8	13	11
TFYR of Macedonia L'ex−R.y. Macédoine	39	25	21	19	23	15	16	8	12	6
Turkey [4] Turquie [4]	715[16]	626	648	532	432	414	395	580	479	471
Turkmenistan Turkménistan	29	28	29	29	20	17	18	14	15	...
Uganda [7] Ouganda [7]	8[17]	9[17]	10[17]	7[17]	4	...	...	...	...	...
Ukraine Ukraine	614	561	509	262	145	87	54	28	57	27
USSR (former) † [7] URSS (anc.) † [7]	8 647	...	...	...	...	...	...	...	...	...
United Kingdom [4] Royaume−Uni [4]	202	184	170	130	103	96	99	93	88	...
United Rep. of Tanzania Rép.−Unie de Tanzanie	46	38	49	40	24	10	13	27	...	...
United States Etats−Unis	3 732	3 682	3 846	3 682	3 740	3 753	4 010	4 246	3 974	3 721
Uzbekistan Ouzbékistan	469	392	474	482	433	456	445	425	...	...
Viet Nam Viet Nam	380	335[4]	325[4]	...	...	...	...	...	...	...
Yugoslavia [6] [17] Yougoslavie [6] [17]	65	45	39	27	24	19	22	18	23	21
B. Wool · Laines										
Algeria [4] Algérie [4]	13	16	13	...	...	...	...	...	...	...
Armenia Arménie	8	4	3	1	0	0	0	0	0	0
Australia [1] Australie [1]	8	8	8	8	8	8	7	6	7	6
Austria Autriche	9	8	8	5	3	2	12	13	17	13
Azerbaijan Azerbaïdjan	11	9	7	5	2	1	0	0	0	0
Belarus Bélarus	51	49	39	40	20	8	8	9	10	10
Belgium [18] Belgique [18]	5	6	4	4	...	...	...	...	...	...
Bolivia [4] Bolivie [4]	0	0	0	0	0	* 0	...	...	...	...
Bulgaria [7] Bulgarie [7]	47	26	22	23	21	20	18	17	10[4]	8[4]
China †† [4] Chine †† [4]	487	514	558	388	413	1 079	758	640	442	451
China, Hong Kong SAR † Chine, Hong Kong RAS †	0	0	...	...	...	...	...	...	...	...
Croatia Croatie	9	5	6	7	7	7	5	3	2	...
Czech Republic République tchèque	58	49	46	43	34	32	30	28	28	20
Denmark [19] Danemark [19]	1[10]	1[10]	1[10]	1	1	1	1	1	0	0
Ecuador [4] Equateur [4]	...	...	3	2	2	3	2	0	2	2

45

Fabrics
Woven cotton, wool, cellulosic and non−cellulosic fibres: million square metres [cont.]
Tissus
Tissus de coton, laines, fibres cellulosiques et non cellulosiques : millions de mètres carrés [suite]

Country or area Pays ou zone	1990	1991	1992	1992	1994	1995	1996	1997	1998	1999
Egypt Egypt	23	23	23	9	14	14	8	8	...	...
Estonia Estonie	7	7	4	1	0	0	0	0	0	0
Ethiopia Ethiopie	...	...	...	...	0	0	0	0	0	0
Finland *[7] Finlande *[7]	0	0	0	0	...	...	...	...	...	...
France France	16	14	13	9	37	...	...	...	...	...
Georgia Géorgie	...	...	0	2	1	0	0	0	0	
Germany † Allemagne †	...	121	119	97	...	87	87	87	79	...
F. R. Germany †[7] R. f. Allemagne †[7]	108	...	...	...	...	...	...	...	...	
former German D. R. † l'ex−R. d. allemande †	38	...	...	...	...	...	...	...	...	
Greece Grèce	2[37]	3[37]	2[37]	3	2	2	2	3	3	...
Hungary [7] Hongrie [7]	11	7	4	3	1	1	...	0	...	...
Iceland Islande	0	0	0	0	0	...	...	...	...	...
Ireland [7] Irlande [7]	2	...	...	...	...	...	...	...	...	...
Italy [3] Italie [3]	418	428	445	426	443	433	431	445	396	...
Japan [10] Japon [10]	335	345	326	287	286	249	247	247	213	199
Kazakhstan Kazakhstan	...	31	23	20	10	3	2	2	1	0
Kenya Kenya	0	...	...	0	9	1	1	...	...	
Korea, Republic of Corée, République de	20[7]	20[7]	20[7]	19[7]	20	18	17	14	7	6
Kyrgyzstan Kirghizistan	15	13	11	9	4	2	3	3	2	1
Latvia Lettonie	17	11	8	2	0[7]	0[7]	0[7]	0[7]	0[7]	...
Lithuania Lituanie	22	22	17	12	9	10	13	12	14	11
Mexico [3] Mexique [3]	9	8	11	12	9	12	16	20	19	19
Mongolia [4] Mongolie [4]	2	1	1	0	0	0	0	0	0	0
Netherlands [7] Pays−Bas [7]	4	4	4	...	...	...	...	...	...	
Norway [3] Norvège [3]	...	1	2	1	2	2	2	2	2	...
Paraguay [4] Paraguay [4]	0	0	0	0	...	...	...	...	...	
Poland [7][20] Pologne [7][20]	98	67	50	48	51	50	50	49	45	35
Portugal Portugal	34[3]	29[3]	12	10	9	8	6	6	8	9
Republic of Moldova République de Moldova	0	0	0	0[13]	0[13]	0[13]	0[13]	0[13]	0[13]	0[13]
Romania [7] Roumanie [7]	107	100	69	68	65	68	50	34	22	18

45

Fabrics

Woven cotton, wool, cellulosic and non−cellulosic fibres: million square metres [*cont.*]

Tissus

Tissus de coton, laines, fibres cellulosiques et non cellulosiques : millions de mètres carrés [*suite*]

Country or area Pays ou zone	1990	1991	1992	1992	1994	1995	1996	1997	1998	1999
Russian Federation Fédération de Russie	583	492	351	270	114	107	67	63	52	61
Slovakia Slovaquie	19[7]	12[7]	11[7]	10[7]	10[7]	10[4]	11[4]	11[4]	10[3]	7[3]
Slovenia Slovénie	10	15	15	13	10	7	3	...	...	1
South Africa [21] Afrique du Sud [21]	19	15	11	10	11	10	9	9	7	
Spain [3] Espagne [3]	31[14]	31[14]	28[14]	17	14	15	...	...	...	
Sweden Suède	1	...	...	0[3]	...	...	...	...	...	
Switzerland [21] Suisse [21]	9	10	8	7	7	5	...	...	...	
Syrian Arab Republic [3] Rép. arabe syrienne [3]	1	0	1	2	2	4	5	8	14	...
Tajikistan Tadjikistan	2	2	3	3	1	0	0	0	0	0
TFYR of Macedonia L'ex−R.y. Macédoine	11	10	9	7	5	6	4	4	4	3
Turkey [4] Turquie [4]	42	36	35	38	38	50	59	78	77	78
Turkmenistan Turkménistan	3	3	3	3	3	3	3	3	3	...
Ukraine Ukraine	86	79	76	60	26	19	12	14	8	6
USSR (former) † URSS (anc.) †	865	...	...	...	...	...	...	...	...	
United Kingdom Royaume−Uni	20[22]	* 39	* 37	* 33	* 38	...	...	...	...	
United States Etats−Unis	118	142	147	154	149	136	127	138	111	65
Uzbekistan Ouzbékistan	1	1	1	1	1	1	1	0	...	
Yugoslavia [17] [23] Yougoslavie [17] [23]	39	24	21	13	13	11	11	10	9	7

C. Cellulosic and non−cellulosic fibres · Fibres cellulosiques et non cellulosiques

Australia [1] [2] [24] Australie [1] [2] [24]	179	185	186	185	...	...	...	...	...	...
Austria Autriche	101	66	73	47	41	60	...	...	...	...
Belarus Bélarus	210[15]	175	147	135	80	35	40	67	77	72
Belgium Belgique	3 959[25]	3 887[25]	4 263[25]	4 780[25]	644[3]	879[3]	901[3]	973[3]	1 018[3]	1 015[3]
Bolivia [4] Bolivie [4]	0	1	1	2	2	* 2	...	...	...	...
China, Hong Kong SAR † Chine, Hong Kong RAS †	0	1	2	3	3	1	...	21	...	...
Colombia Colombie	...	...	3[3]	24[3]	20[3]	22[3]	...	93[4]	85[4]	...
Croatia Croatie	19	12	12	14	11	9	8	11	11	...
Czech Republic République tchèque	85	32	35	29	...	...	...	...	...	...
Ecuador [4] Equateur [4]	...	...	23	39	36	36	21	0	21	20
Ethiopia [8] Ethiopie [8]	5	3	2	4	4	5	5	4	5	4

45
Fabrics
Woven cotton, wool, cellulosic and non−cellulosic fibres: million square metres [*cont.*]
Tissus
Tissus de coton, laines, fibres cellulosiques et non cellulosiques : millions de mètres carrés [*suite*]

Country or area Pays ou zone	1990	1991	1992	1992	1994	1995	1996	1997	1998	1999
Finland [7] Finlande [7]	27	* 17	* 14	* 14	* 11	* 8	* 8	...	...	...
France France	2 670	2 766	3 520	2 894	2 887	...	...	...	...	...
Germany † Allemagne †	...	1 478	1 360	1 155	1 117	1 330	1 177	1 226	1 270	...
F. R. Germany † [7] R. f. Allemagne † [7]	1 473	...	...	...	...	...	...	...	...	...
Greece [26][27] Grèce [26][27]	...	...	...	19	29	15	...	...	...	...
Hungary [7] Hongrie [7]	45	35	22	20	19	19	...	...	# 98	232
Japan [10] Japon [10]	3 379	3 266	3 178	2 761	2 580	2 461	2 440	2 499	2 135	1 935
Korea, Republic of Corée, République de	3 432	3 482	3 097	2 462	2 543	2 596	...	...	...	...
Lithuania Lituanie	40	35	26	18	...	8	6	43	47	40
Mexico [3] Mexique [3]	514	453	453	559	527	490	624	639	623	627
Nepal [4] Népal [4]	...	...	16	18	23	20	25	25	26	24
Netherlands [3][28] Pays−Bas [3][28]	203	203	189	...	...	...	...	...	...	...
Poland [7] Pologne [7]	113	88	98	85	106	103	95	95	87	58
Portugal Portugal	15[3]	430[3]	486[3]	133	129	127	131	138	151	134
Republic of Moldova [15] République de Moldova [15]	51	44	22	...	...	...	...	...	...	...
Russian Federation [4] Fédération de Russie [4]	744	674	537	391	167	114	65	56	50	78
Slovakia Slovaquie	30	27	184	...	13	...	...	...	79[3]	68[3]
Slovenia Slovénie	8	7	6	5	10	24	42	...	...	35
Spain [3] Espagne [3]	570[14]	534[14]	466[14]	627	786	1 004	...	...	...	...
Sweden [3] Suède [3]	33	30	21	18	23	24	38	28	28	21
FYR of Macedonia L'ex−R.y. Macédoine	6	5	3	2	1	1	1	1	1	0
Turkey [4] Turquie [4]	108	110	151	179	255	225	246	225	240	215
Ukraine [4] Ukraine [4]	229	194	153	132	42	15	6	5	5	3
United Kingdom [3] Royaume−Uni [3]	...	...	...	26	19	...	...	...	...	...
Yugoslavia Yougoslavie	...	4	4	4	2	2	1	1	1	0

Source:
United Nations Statistics Division, New York, "Industrial Commodity Statistics Yearbook 1999" and the industrial statistics database.

Source:
Organisation des Nations Unies, Division de statistique, New York, "Annuaire de statistiques industrielles par produit 1999" et la base de données pour les statistiques industrielles.

45

Fabrics
Woven cotton, wool, cellulosic and non−cellulosic fibres: million square metres [*cont.*]
Tissus
Tissus de coton, laines, fibres cellulosiques et non cellulosiques : millions de mètres carrés [*suite*]

† For information on recent changes in country or area nomenclature pertaining to former Czechoslovakia, Germany, Hong Kong Special Administrative Region (SAR) of China, Macao Special Administrative Region (SAR) of China, SFR of Yugoslavia and the former USSR, see Annex I − Country or area nomenclature, regional and other groupings.

†† For statistical purposes, the data for China do not include those for Hong Kong Special Administrative Region (Hong Kong SAR), Macao Special Administrative Region (Macao SAR) and Taiwan province of China.

1   Twelve months ending 30 June of year stated.

2   Including pile and chenille fabrics of non−cellulosic fibres.
3   Original data in metric tons.
4   Original data in metres.
5   Including cotton fabrics after undergoing finishing processes.
6   Including mixed cotton fabrics.
7   After undergoing finishing processes.
8   Twelve months ending 7 July of the year stated.

9   Production by government−owned enterprises only.
10 Including finished fabrics and blanketing made of synthetic fibers.
11 Factory production only.
12 Including fabrics of cotton substitutes.
13 Excluding Transnistria region.
14 Including household production.
15 Including silk fabrics.
16 Government production only.
17 Including cellulosic fabrics.
18 Including woollen blankets and carpets.
19 Sales.
20 Including fabrics of wool substitutes.
21 Pure woollen fabrics only.
22 Deliveries of woollen and worsted fabrics, except blankets, containing, by weight, more than 15 per cent wool or animal fibres. Including finished fabrics.

23 Including mixed wool fabrics.
24 Excluding pile and chenille fabrics.
25 Including blankets and carpets of cellulosic and non−cellulosic fibres.
26 Including fabrics after undergoing finishing processes.
27 Including mixed fabrics.
28 Including linen and jute fabrics.

† Pour les modifications récentes de nomenclature de pays ou de zone concernant l'Allemagne, Hong Kong, régi administrative spéciale (RAS) de Chine, Macao, région administrative spéciale (RAS) de Chine, l'ex−Tchécoslovaquie, l'ex−URSS et l'ex−Rfs de Yougoslav: voir annexe I − Nomenclature des pays ou des zones, groupements régionaux et autres groupements.

†† Les données statistiques relatives à la Chine ne comprennent pas celles qui concernent la région administrative spéciale de Hong Kong (la RAS de Hong Kong), la région administrative spéciale de Macao (la RAS de Macao) et la province chinoise de Taiwan.

1   Période de douze mois finissant le 30 juin de l'année indiquée.
2   Y compris les tissus bouclés et tissus chenille de fibres non−cellulosiques.
3   Données d'origine exprimées en tonnes.
4   Données d'origine exprimées en mètres.
5   Y compris les tissus de cotton, après opérations de finition.
6   Y compris les tissus de cotton mélangé.
7   Après opérations de finition.
8   Période de douze mois finissant le 7 juillet de l'année indiquée.
9   Production des établissements d'Etat seulement.
10 Y compris les tissus finis et les couvertures en fibres synthétiques.
11 Production des fabriques seulement.
12 Y compris les tissus de succédanés de coton.
13 Non compris la région de Transnistria.
14 Y compris la production ménagère.
15 Y compris les tissus de soie.
16 Production de l'Etat seulement.
17 Y compris les tissus en fibres cellulosiques.
18 Y compris les couvertures et tapis en laine.
19 Ventes.
20 Y compris les tissus de succédanés de laine.
21 Tissus de laine pure seulement.
22 Quantités livrées de tissus de laine cardée et peignée, à l'exception des couvertures, contenant, en poids, plus de 15 p. 100 de laine ou de fibres animales. Y compris les tissus finis.
23 Y compris les tissus de laine mélangée.
24 Non compris les tissus bouclés et tissus chenille.
25 Y compris les couvertures et les tapis en fibres cellulosiques et non cellulosiques.
26 Y compris les tissus, après opérations de finition.
27 Y compris les tissus mélangés.
28 Y compris les tissus de lin et de jute.

46
Leather footwear
Chaussures de cuir
Production: thousand pairs
Production : milliers de paires

Country or area Pays or zone	1990	1991	1992	1993	1994	1995	1996	1997	1998	1999
Albania Albanie	5 990	1 881	1 214	1 818	266	267	...	...	...	...
Algeria Algérie	16 376	11 824	9 040	7 171	6 467	3 986	2 320	2 542	1 249	1 167
Angola Angola	143	95	48	...	...	...	...	...	...	...
Armenia Arménie	18 740	11 340	5 661	3 517	1 612	656	305	87	65	24
Australia [12] Australie [12]	1 875	1 935	383	283	315	278	...	...	...	...
Austria Autriche	16 553[3]	16 760[3]	14 842[3]	13 229[3]	12 767[3]	12 743	10 120	10 615	10 919	...
Azerbaijan Azerbaïdjan	15 207	10 491	5 221	4 329	3 057	799	495	313	315	54
Belarus Bélarus	46 764	45 343	37 207	33 412	26 358	13 004	11 381	15 587	16 223	16 534
Belgium Belgique	3 562	3 454	3 190	2 267	...	...	...	...	...	...
Bolivia Bolivie	833	862	1 152	1 308	1 381	* 1 222	...	...	...	...
Brazil Brésil	141 000	152 925	156 540	190 026	146 540	124 272	163 042	159 861	142 734	145 393
Bulgaria Bulgarie	27 214	17 048	13 421	10 785	10 244	11 980	8 915	6 838	6 401	4 591
Burkina Faso Burkina Faso	500	1 271	1 200[4]	...	...	...	...	...	...	...
Cameroon Cameroun	1 800[5]	1 800[4]	1 900[4]	...	...	...	...	...	...	...
Canada[4] Canada[4]	15 100	16 000	16 000	...	...	...	...	...	...	...
Cape Verde Cap-Vert	...	...	...	...	...	192	...	...	...	...
Central African Rep. Rép. centrafricaine	200	200[4]	200[4]	...	...	...	...	...	...	...
Chile Chili	7 577	9 231	9 311	9 270	8 317	7 410	7 134	7 008	6 777	6 237
China †† Chine ††	1 202 565	1 328 950	1 613 647	...	...	...	...	...	...	...
China, Hong Kong SAR† Chine, Hong Kong RAS†	73 496	140 000[4]	8 433	...	...	...	1 499	752[6]	178[6]	120[6]
Colombia Colombie	28 100[4]	30 000[4]	20 651	19 471	20 933	18 277	...	18 736[7]	16 635[7]	...
Congo Congo	* 300[7]	300[4]	300[4]	...	...	...	...	...	...	...
Côte d'Ivoire Côte d'Ivoire	1 800	1 800[4]	1 800[4]	...	...	...	...	...	...	...
Croatia Croatie	26 107	11 717	11 240	13 449	12 459	9 521	9 271	9 598	8 742	...

46
Leather footwear
Production: thousand pairs [*cont.*]
Chaussures de cuir
Production : milliers de paires [*suite*]

Country or area Pays or zone	1990	1991	1992	1993	1994	1995	1996	1997	1998	1999
Cuba Cuba	13 400	13 000[4]	13 400[4]	...	...	...	...	...	...	...
Cyprus Chypre	10 447	10 591	6 199	3 835	3 820[8]	3 444[8]	2 507[8]	2 309[8]	2 100[8]	1 710[8]
Czech Republic République tchèque	71 047	41 400	36 948	32 293	23 323	22 115	21 572	13 455	10 099	8 373
Dem. Rep. of the Congo[4] Rép. dém. du Congo[4]	900	900	900							
Denmark[4] Danemark[4]	4 400	4 400	4 600	...	...	...	...	...	...	
Dominican Republic[4] Rép. dominicaine[4]	2 100	2 000	2 200	...	...	...	...	...	...	
Ecuador Equateur	1 500	1 600[4]	1 936	1 691	1 672	1 744	1 507	2	1	...
Egypt Egypte	48 325	48 311	48 390	48 385	48 394	48 444	48 300	48 131	...	...
El Salvador El Salvador	3 600	3 700[4]	3 800[4]	...	...	...	...	...	...	
Estonia Estonie	7 209	6 301	3 208	1 035	827	682	711	793	803	840
Ethiopia[9] Ethiopie[9]	5 367	3 374	2 419	3 083	2 871	3 751	3 773	6 925	6 252	7 477[5]
Finland Finlande	4 752	3 683	3 606	3 291	3 421	3 186	3 220	2 928	3 499	2 650
France[5] France[5]	194 700	169 221	160 320	151 124	154 898	151 704	139 442	135 447	125 524	114 540
Georgia Géorgie	...	...	2 614	1 046	224	50	48	101	95	101
Germany † Allemagne †	...	84 435	63 672	55 485	47 193	45 491	40 675	36 948	38 441	...
F. R. Germany R. f. Allemagne	64 358	...	...	...	...	...	...	...	...	...
German D. R.(former) R. d. allemande (anc.)	61 822	...	...	...	...	...	...	...	...	...
Greece Grèce	12 260	10 712	9 264	8 166	6 922	7 032	6 769	6 202	5 716	...
Haiti[4] Haïti[4]	500	500	600	...	...	...	...	...	...	...
Hungary Hongrie	27 426	20 757	14 752	12 783	12 499	12 178	...	...	...	14 386
Iceland Islande	39	46	18	...	...	...	9	8	...	...
India[10] Inde[10]	198 404	201 449	207 181	188 746	158 263	181 462	157 095	137 837	180 490	134 524
Indonesia[11] Indonésie[11]	61 657	87 571	...	# 250 053	272 529	249 509	...	238 335	258 780	...
Iran (Islamic Rep. of) Iran (Rép. islamique d')	23 374[12]	20 944[12]	25 129[12]	21 756[12]	17 598[12]	29 807[13]	28 310[13]	27 267[13]	22 362[13]	...
Iraq Iraq	4 400	5 000[4]	4 087	...	...	...	...	...	...	...

46
Leather footwear
Production: thousand pairs [cont.]
Chaussures de cuir
Production : milliers de paires [suite]

Country or area Pays or zone	1990	1991	1992	1993	1994	1995	1996	1997	1998	1999
Ireland Irlande	1 403	3 000[4]	3 200[4]	...	...	...	...	...	...	...
Italy[4] Italie[4]	320 200	310 200	295 000	...	...	...	...	...	...	...
Jamaica[4] Jamaïque[4]	700	700	800	...	...	...	...	...	...	...
Japan[13][14] Japon[13][14]	54 054	53 351	52 455	47 703	51 503	49 525	48 819	47 573	42 573	37 546
Kenya Kenya	1 605	1 190	1 480	1 571	1 774	2 018	2 089	...	...	...
Korea, Republic of Corée, République de	24 440	28 923	27 617	19 085	16 806	15 309	...	...	...	...
Kyrgyzstan Kirghizistan	11 569	9 646	5 757	3 528	1 512	755	605	332	135	85
Lao People's Dem. Rep. Rép. dém. pop. lao	...	...	...	...	240	150	...	...	...	...
Latvia Lettonie	10 648	7 778	5 764	2 687	1 633	1 032	939	753	753	350
Lithuania Lituanie	11 884	11 154	7 702	3 657	1 565	1 961	2 004	1 663	1 654	1 686
Madagascar Madagascar	807[11]	837[11]	702[11]	306[11]	180	136	158	126	115	...
Mali Mali	...	127	104	86	106	99	98	...	...	...
Mexico Mexique	38 931	36 911	33 141	62 315	56 948	44 006	50 340	52 586	47 072	43 916
Mongolia Mongolie	4 223	3 994	2 245	1 031	407	325	146	41	33	7
Mozambique Mozambique	347	242	148	153	87	29	...	12	10	7
Nepal Népal	600[4]	700[4]	800[15]	823[15]	700[15]	685[15]	649[15]	550[15]	550[15]	* 605[15]
Netherlands[5][16][17] Pays-Bas[5][16][17]	5 598	5 255	5 289	6 315	5 455	5 492	...	...	...	...
New Zealand[1] Nouvelle-Zélande[1]	4 977[18]	4 022[18]	3 765[18]	3 525[18]	3 590[18]	3 119[18]	2 676[18]	2 222[18]	1 484[18]	1 650[19]
Nicaragua Nicaragua	* 1 100	1 200[4]	1 300[4]	...	...	...	...	...	...	...
Nigeria Nigéria	3 779	7 093	4 538	4 554	1 182	1 255	...	...	...	...
Norway Norvège	900[7]	900[4]	1 000[4]	...	...	...	...	...	...	...
Panama Panama	1 508	1 600[4]	1 377	1 483	1 294	1 287	1 058	...	...	...
Paraguay Paraguay	5 300	5 500[4]	5 600[4]	...	...	...	...	...	...	...
Peru[4] Pérou[4]	18 800	19 000	20 000	...	...	...	...	...	...	...
Philippines[4] Philippines[4]	10 000	12 000	15 000	...	...	...	...	...	...	...

46
Leather footwear
Production: thousand pairs [*cont.*]
Chaussures de cuir
Production : milliers de paires [*suite*]

Country or area Pays or zone	1990	1991	1992	1993	1994	1995	1996	1997	1998	1999
Poland Pologne	98 200	66 857	55 181	47 905	53 236	59 783	66 620	68 513	54 491	48 538
Portugal Portugal	75 378	39 658	60 463	75 422	71 648	68 070	69 439	71 949	68 179	75 054
Republic of Moldova République de Moldova	23 196	20 751	14 504	4 897[20]	2 267[20]	1 506[20]	1 429[20]	1 032[20]	739[20]	704[20]
Romania Roumanie	80 670	63 196	41 237	41 893	45 666	48 239	44 838	34 365	30 341	30 491
Russian Federation Fédération de Russie	385 262	356 147	231 005	153 343	80 776	54 254	38 428	34 541	24 998	30 821
Senegal Sénégal	302	153	644	508	...	...	...	...	...	...
Singapore Singapour	2 800[7]	3 000[4]	3 100[4]	...	...	...	...	...	...	...
Slovakia Slovaquie	44 330	26 744	22 875	18 332	13 577	46 438	13 188	10 300	9 772	7 643
Slovenia Slovénie	11 042	9 124	9 492	8 923	8 683	6 951	5 739	5 976	5 641	4 779
South Africa[5] Afrique du Sud[5]	51 633	49 318	42 251	44 492	41 078	39 071[21]	38 858[21]	35 486[21]	29 581[21]	24 926[21]
Spain Espagne	117 199	115 190	106 959	74 883	104 788	140 141	155 218	165 417	177 464	...
Sri Lanka Sri Lanka	339	276	272	274	...	...	...	...	...	...
Sudan[4] Soudan[4]	4 000	3 000	3 000	...	...	...	...	...	...	...
Sweden Suède	1 904	2 500[4]	3 000[4]	1 013	676	372	1 104	1 202	430	501
Switzerland Suisse	4 039	3 385	3 065	3 291	3 232	2 490	...	...	...	...
Tajikistan Tadjikistan	10 903	8 567	5 476	4 044	929	612	394	107	123	72
TFYR of Macedonia L'ex-R.y. Macédoine	6 340	4 238	3 786	2 031	1 760	1 121	1 200	1 507	1 382	1 953
Togo Togo	100	100[4]	100[4]	...	...	...	...	...	...	...
Tunisia Tunisie	10 380	11 590	13 220	12 870	14 100	16 580	18 380	20 300	...	...
Turkmenistan Turkménistan	5 142	4 246	3 231	3 358	1 938	1 910	1 546	1 108	561	...
Ukraine Ukraine	196 466	183 888	147 703	105 814	40 309	20 757	13 175	10 580	11 389	11 875
USSR - former † URSS (anc.) †	843 245	...	...	...	...	...	...	...	...	...
United Kingdom Royaume-Uni	92 673[22]	41 000[4]	43 000[4]	70 837	69 637	61 141	62 157	54 423	45 155	...
United Rep. of Tanzania Rép.-Unie de Tanzanie	459	328	168	55	89	339	121	152	...	...
United States Etats-Unis	184 568	168 992	164 904	171 733	156 712	146 979	127 315	127 876	115 808	87 065

46
Leather footwear
Production: thousand pairs [*cont.*]
Chaussures de cuir
Production : milliers de paires [*suite*]

Country or area Pays or zone	1990	1991	1992	1993	1994	1995	1996	1997	1998	1999
Uzbekistan Ouzbékistan	46 685	45 443	40 491	40 466	28 202	5 654	5 591	5 547	...	...
Viet Nam Viet Nam	5 827	6 188	5 672	...	...	46 440	61 785	79 289	77 037	* 81 780
Yugoslavia Yougoslavie	26 191	18 149	16 169	10 590	8 824	5 982	6 461	6 848	6 976	3 892

Source:
United Nations Statistics Division, New York, "Industrial
Commodity Statistics Yearbook 1999" and the industrial
statistics database.

† For information on recent changes in country or
area nomenclature pertaining to former Czechoslovakia,
Germany, Hong Kong Special Administrative Region (SAR) of
China, Macao Special Administrative Region (SAR) of China,
SFR of Yugoslavia and the former USSR, see Annex I - Country
or area nomenclature, regional and other groupings.

†† For statistical purposes, the data for
China do not include those for Hong Kong Special
Administrative Region (Hong Kong SAR), Macao Special
Administrative Region (Macao SAR) and Taiwan province of
China.

1 Twelve months ending 30 June of year stated.

2 Excluding sporting footwear.
3 Beginning 1995, data are confidential.
4 Source: Food and Agriculture Organization of the United
Nations (FAO), (Rome).
5 Including rubber footwear.
6 Excluding other footwear for confidentiality purposes.

7 Including rubber and plastic footwear.

8 Including other footwear, house footwear, sandals and other
light footwear. Also including rubber footwear.

9 Twelve months ending 7 July of the year stated.

10 Production by large and medium scale establishments only.
11 Including plastic footwear.
12 Production by establishments employing 50 or more persons.
13 Production by establishments employing 10 or more persons.
14 Shipments.
15 Twelve months beginning 16 July of year stated.

16 Production by establishments employing 20 or more persons.
17 Sales.
18 Including non-leather footwear.
19 Sports footwear only.
20 Excluding Transnistria region.
21 Excluding children's footwear.
22 Manufacturers' sales.

Source:
Organisation des Nations Unies, Division de statistique, New
York, "Annuaire de statistiques industrielles par produit
1999" et la base de données pour les statistiques
industrielles.

† Pour les modifications récentes de nomenclature
de pays ou de zone concernant l'Allemagne, Hong Kong, région
administrative spéciale (RAS) de Chine, Macao, région
administrative spéciale (RAS) de Chine,
l'ex-Tchécoslovaquie, l'ex-URSS et l'ex-Rfs de Yougoslavie,
voir annexe I - Nomenclature des pays ou des zones,
groupements régionaux et autres groupements.

†† Les données statistiques relatives à
la Chine ne comprennent pas celles qui concernent la région
administrative spéciale de Hong Kong (la RAS de Hong Kong),
la région administrative spéciale de Macao (la RAS de Macao)
et la province chinoise de Taiwan.

1 Période de douze mois finissant le 30 juin de l'année
indiquée.
2 A l'exclusion des chaussures sportif.
3 Pour 1995, les données sont confidentielles.
4 Source: Organisation des Nations Unies pour l'alimentation
et l'agriculture (FAO), (Rome).
5 Y compris les chaussures en caoutchouc.
6 A l'exclusion d'autres chaussures, pour raisons de
confidentialité.
7 Y compris les chaussures en caoutchouc et en matière
plastique.
8 Y compris les autres chaussures, chaussures de maison,
sandales et autres chaussures légères. Y compris également
les chaussures en caoutchouc.
9 Période de douze mois finissant le 7 juillet de l'année
indiquée.
10 Production des grandes et moyennes entreprises seulement.
11 Y compris les chaussures en matière plastique.
12 Production des établissements occupant 50 personnes ou plus.
13 Production des établissements occupant 10 personnes ou plus.
14 Expéditions.
15 Période de douze mois commençant le 16 juillet de l'année
indiquée.
16 Production des établissements occupant 20 personnes ou plus.
17 Ventes.
18 Y compris les chaussures en matières autres que le cuir.
19 Les chaussures de sport seulement
20 Non compris la région de Transnistria.
21 Non compris les chaussures pour enfants.
22 Ventes des fabricants.

47
Sawnwood
Sciages

Production (sawn): thousand cubic metres
Production (sciés) : milliers de mètres cubes

Region, country or area Région, pays ou zone	1991	1992	1993	1994	1995	1996	1997	1998	1999	2000
World *Monde*	457 613	437 648	431 298	434 041	424 459	421 321	420 069	410 612	423 083	420 954
Africa **Afrique**	7 949	8 102	7 850	8 490	8 243	7 867	7 505	7 507	7 472	7 667
Algeria[1] Algérie[1]	13	13	13	13	13	13	13	13	13	13
Angola Angola[1]	5	5	5	5	5	5	5	5	5	5
Benin Bénin	27	24	24[1]	24[1]	15	11	12	13	13	13[1]
Burkina Faso Burkina Faso	2	2[1]	2[1]	1	1	1	2	1	1	1[1]
Burundi Burundi	3	3	20	21	43	33	33[1]	33[1]	80[1]	83[1]
Cameroon Cameroun	563[1]	577[1]	579[1]	647[1]	676[1]	685[1]	560	588	600	650
Central African Rep. Rép. centrafricaine	60	68	60[1]	73	70	61	72	91	79	102
Chad Tchad	2	2	2	2[1]	2	2	2[1]	2[1]	2[1]	2[1]
Congo Congo	54	52	52[1]	57	62	59	64	73	74	74[1]
Côte d'Ivoire Côte d'Ivoire	608	623	587	708	706	596	613	623	611	603
Dem. Rep. of the Congo Rép. dém. du Congo	105	105[1]	105[1]	75	65	85	90	80	80[1]	80[1]
Egypt Egypte	0	0	0	0	0	0	0	3	4	4
Equatorial Guinea Guinée équatoriale	13	8	7	4	4	4[1]	4[1]	4[1]	4[1]	4[1]
Ethiopia incl. Eritrea Ethiopie comp. Erythrée	12	12[1]	...	...	...	...	...	...	...	...
Ethiopia Ethiopie	...	...	33	45	40	33	60	60[1]	60[1]	60[1]
Gabon Gabon	* 85	* 155	* 153	* 173	100[1]	50[1]	30[1]	60	59	68
Gambia[1] Gambie[1]	1	1	1	1	1	1	1	1	1	1
Ghana Ghana	400	420	504	801	612	604	575	590	454	243
Guinea Guinée	70	63	65	72	85	85[1]	25	26	26[1]	26[1]
Guinea-Bissau[1] Guinée-Bissau[1]	16	16	16	16	16	16	16	16	16	16
Kenya[1] Kenya[1]	185	185	185	185	185	185	185	185	185	185
Liberia Libéria	* 75	* 125	* 90	90[1]	90[1]	90[1]	90[1]	90[1]	90[1]	90[1]
Libyan Arab Jamah.[1] Jamah. arabe libyenne[1]	31	31	31	31	31	31	31	31	31	31

47
Sawnwood
Production (sawn): thousand cubic metres [*cont.*]
Sciages
Production (sciés) : milliers de mètres cubes [*suite*]

Region, country or area Région, pays ou zone	1991	1992	1993	1994	1995	1996	1997	1998	1999	2000
Madagascar Madagascar	233	238[1]	144	74	84[1]	84[1]	84[1]	84[1]	102	485
Malawi Malawi	* 43	43[1]	45	45[1]	45[1]	45[1]	45[1]	45[1]	45[1]	45[1]
Mali[1] Mali[1]	13	13	13	13	13	13	13	13	13	13
Mauritius Maurice	5	4	5	4	2	3	3[1]	5	5	5[1]
Morocco[1] Maroc[1]	83	83	83	83	83	83	83	83	83	83
Mozambique Mozambique	18	16[1]	30[1]	30	42	42[1]	33	28	28[1]	28[1]
Niger Niger	0	1[1]	4[1]	4[1]	4[1]	4[1]	4[1]	4[1]	4[1]	4[1]
Nigeria Nigéria	2 719	2 715	2 711	2 533	2 356	2 178	2 000	2 000[1]	2 000[1]	2 000[1]
Réunion Réunion	2	2[1]	2[1]	2[1]	2[1]	2[1]	2[1]	2[1]	2[1]	2[1]
Rwanda Rwanda	36	36	36	26	54	59	74	76	79	79[1]
Sao Tome and Principe[1] Sao Tomé-et-Principe[1]	5	5	5	5	5	5	5	5	5	5
Senegal Sénégal	23	23[1]	23[1]	23[1]	23[1]	23[1]	23[1]	23[1]	23[1]	23[1]
Sierra Leone Sierra Leone	9	9[1]	5	5[1]	5[1]	5[1]	5[1]	5[1]	5[1]	5[1]
Somalia[1] Somalie[1]	14	14	14	14	14	14	14	14	14	14
South Africa Afrique du Sud	* 1 792	1 818	1 383	1 499	1 574	1 574[1]	1 574[1]	1 498	1 498[1]	1 498[1]
Sudan Soudan	2	3	3	45	45	45[1]	45[1]	51[1]	51[1]	51[1]
Swaziland Swaziland	75	75	75	80[1]	90[1]	100[1]	102	102[1]	102[1]	102[1]
Togo Togo	2	3	3[1]	8	14	15	17	18	21	19
Tunisia Tunisie	17	6	19	20	20[1]	20[1]	20[1]	20[1]	20[1]	20[1]
Uganda Ouganda	30[1]	96	107	140[1]	200	215	229	245	264	264[1]
United Rep. of Tanzania[1] Rép.-Unie de Tanzanie[1]	156	48	39	24	24	24	24	24	24	24
Zambia Zambie	94	112	318	367	320[1]	245[1]	157[1]	157[1]	157[1]	157
Zimbabwe Zimbabwe	250	250[1]	250[1]	401	401	418	465	416	438	386
America, North **Amérique du Nord**	**158 270**	**168 640**	**169 803**	**175 837**	**169 948**	**177 007**	**181 173**	**185 024**	**195 075**	**193 659**
Bahamas[1] Bahamas[1]	1	1	1	1	1	1	1	1	1	1

47
Sawnwood
Production (sawn): thousand cubic metres [*cont.*]
Sciages
Production (sciés) : milliers de mètres cubes [*suite*]

Region, country or area Région, pays ou zone	1991	1992	1993	1994	1995	1996	1997	1998	1999	2000
Belize[1] Belize[1]	14	14	14	20	35	35	35	35	35	35
Canada Canada	52 040	56 318	59 774	61 650	60 436	62 828	64 764	65 109	69 579	69 639
Costa Rica Costa Rica	412	772	798	746[1]	780[1]	780[1]	780[1]	780[1]	780[1]	812
Cuba[1] Cuba[1]	130	130	130	130	130	130	130	130	146	146
El Salvador El Salvador	70[1]	70[1]	70[1]	70[1]	70[1]	70[1]	58	58[1]	58[1]	58[1]
Guadeloupe[1] Guadeloupe[1]	1	1	1	1	1	1	1	1	1	1
Guatemala Guatemala	55[1]	90[1]	398	417	355	355[1]	355[1]	355[1]	355[1]	355[1]
Haiti[1] Haïti[1]	14	14	14	14	14	14	14	14	14	14
Honduras Honduras	303	411	364	361	231	322	379	369	404	437
Jamaica Jamaïque	32	27	24	63	63	64	65	66	66[1]	66[1]
Martinique Martinique	1[1]	1	1[1]	1[1]	1[1]	1[1]	1[1]	1[1]	1[1]	1[1]
Mexico Mexique	* 2 696	2 696[1]	2 560	2 693	2 329	2 543	2 961	3 260	3 110[1]	3 110[1]
Nicaragua Nicaragua	80[1]	61	65	27	74	160	148	148[1]	148[1]	148[1]
Panama Panama	16	37	37	37	37	19	17	8	46	48
Trinidad and Tobago Trinité-et-Tobago	42	59	35	58	64	29	38	27	12	37
United States Etats-Unis	102 363	107 937	105 516	109 547	105 326	109 654	111 425	114 661	120 318	118 750
America, South **Amérique du Sud**	**25 930**	**26 705**	**25 474**	**27 190**	**28 390**	**29 990**	**29 926**	**29 023**	**28 422**	**29 579**
Argentina Argentine	950[1]	1 472	998	1 080	1 329	1 711	1 170	1 377	1 408	1 408[1]
Bolivia Bolivie	125[1]	230	268	185	162	181	180	515	259	254
Brazil Brésil	18 628[1]	18 628[1]	18 628[1]	18 691	19 091	19 091[1]	19 091[1]	18 591	17 280	18 100
Chile Chili	3 218	3 020	3 113	3 364	3 802	4 140	4 661	4 551	5 254	5 698
Colombia Colombie	813[1]	758	694	644	644	1 134	1 085	160	870	915
Ecuador Equateur	865	908	196	1 600	1 696	1 886	2 075	2 079	1 455	1 455[1]
French Guiana Guyane française	19[1]	19[1]	18	15	15[1]	15[1]	15[1]	15[1]	15[1]	15[1]
Guyana Guyana	50[1]	50[1]	50[1]	77	101	97	57	24	25	29

47
Sawnwood
Production (sawn): thousand cubic metres [*cont.*]
Sciages
Production (sciés) : milliers de mètres cubes [*suite*]

Region, country or area Région, pays ou zone	1991	1992	1993	1994	1995	1996	1997	1998	1999	2000
Paraguay Paraguay	313	357	357[1]	357[1]	400[1]	500[1]	550[1]	550[1]	550[1]	550[1]
Peru Pérou	477	500	592	649	630	693	482	590	835	623
Suriname Suriname	40	43	33	29	29[1]	40	41	41[1]	28	78
Uruguay Uruguay	205	269	269[1]	269[1]	269[1]	269[1]	269[1]	269[1]	269[1]	269[1]
Venezuela Venezuela	227	451	258	230	222	233	250	261	174	185
Asia Asie	**100 069**	**97 200**	**101 601**	**98 045**	**95 767**	**89 188**	**79 663**	**64 654**	**64 554**	**54 313**
Afghanistan[1] Afghanistan[1]	400	400	400	400	400	400	400	400	400	400
Bangladesh[1] Bangladesh[1]	79	79	79	79	70	70	70	70	70	70
Bhutan Bhoutan	35	21	18	18[1]	18[1]	18[1]	18[1]	18[1]	18[1]	18[1]
Brunei Darussalam Brunéi Darussalam	90	90	90	90[1]	90[1]	90[1]	90[1]	90[1]	90[1]	90[1]
Cambodia Cambodge	122	132[1]	155[1]	195	140	100	71	40	10	3
China †† Chine ††	20 942[1]	19 756[1]	25 709[1]	25 603[1]	25 603[1]	27 410[1]	20 982	18 733[1]	16 717[1]	7 202[1]
Cyprus Chypre	16	14	17	15	15	16	14	11	12	9
India Inde	17 460	17 460[1]	17 460[1]	17 460[1]	17 460[1]	8 400	8 400	8 400	8 400	7 900
Indonesia Indonésie	8 638	8 438	8 338	6 838	6 638	7 338	7 238	2 523	2 427	2 427[1]
Iran (Islamic Rep. of) Iran (Rép. islamique d')	173	187	170	178	159	144	141	129	96	106
Iraq Iraq	8[1]	8[1]	8[1]	8[1]	8[1]	8[1]	8[1]	12	12[1]	12[1]
Japan Japon	28 264[1]	27 277[1]	26 260[1]	25 906[1]	24 493[1]	23 844[1]	21 709	18 625	17 952	17 094
Kazakhstan Kazakhstan	...	0	0	0	0	0	0	* 182	* 182	* 77
Korea, Dem. P. R.[1] Corée, R. p. dém. de[1]	280	280	280	280	280	280	280	280	280	280
Korea, Republic of Corée, République de	4 041	3 513	3 249	3 862	3 440	4 291	4 759	2 240	4 300	4 300[1]
Kyrgyzstan Kirghizistan	...	0	0	0	0	0	2	* 23	* 23	* 23
Lao People's Dem. Rep. Rép. dém. pop. lao	300	170[1]	262	331	465	320	560	250[1]	350[1]	350[1]
Lebanon Liban	11	9	9	9[1]	9[1]	9[1]	9[1]	9[1]	9[1]	9[1]
Malaysia Malaisie	8 993	9 369	9 395	8 858	8 382[1]	8 382[1]	7 326	5 241	5 387	5 740

47
Sawnwood
Production (sawn): thousand cubic metres [*cont.*]
Sciages
Production (sciés) : milliers de mètres cubes [*suite*]

Region, country or area Région, pays ou zone	1991	1992	1993	1994	1995	1996	1997	1998	1999	2000
Mongolia Mongolie	270	124	84	50	61	170[1]	200[1]	300[1]	300[1]	300[1]
Myanmar Myanmar	282	302	339	347[1]	347[1]	351	372	337	298	343
Nepal Népal	620	620[1]	620[1]	620[1]	620[1]	620[1]	620[1]	620[1]	620[1]	620[1]
Pakistan Pakistan	1 520	1 450	1 503	1 127	1 266	1 280	1 024	1 051	1 075	1 075[1]
Philippines Philippines	729	647	440	407	286	313	351	216	288	128
Singapore[1] Singapour[1]	30	25	25	25	25	25	25	25	25	25
Sri Lanka Sri Lanka	5	5	5[1]	5[1]	6	5	5[1]	5[1]	5[1]	5[1]
Syrian Arab Republic[1] Rép. arabe syrienne[1]	9	9	9	9	9	9	9	9	9	9
Thailand Thaïlande	939	1 076	715	568	426	307	426	103	178	294
Turkey Turquie	4 928	4 891	5 241	4 037	4 331	4 268	3 833	3 990	4 300	4 683
Viet Nam Viet Nam	885	849	721	721[1]	721[1]	721[1]	721[1]	721[1]	721[1]	721[1]
Europe **Europe**	**80 668**	**131 095**	**120 303**	**117 813**	**115 106**	**110 342**	**114 791**	**117 122**	**119 896**	**127 534**
Albania Albanie	382[1]	382[1]	4	5	5[1]	5[1]	5	28	35	90
Austria Autriche	7 239	7 020	6 786	7 572	7 804	8 200	8 450	8 737	9 628	10 390
Belarus Bélarus	...	1 693	1 545	1 545[1]	1 545[1]	1 545[1]	1 545[1]	* 2 131	2 175	2 437
Belgium Belgique	...	...	...	...	...	...	...	...	1 056	1 056[1]
Belgium-Luxembourg Belgique-Luxembourg	1 244	1 184	1 184[1]	1 209	1 150	1 100	1 150	1 267	...	...
Bosnia and Herzegovina[1] Bosnie-Herzégovine[1]	...	20	20	20	20	20	20	20	20	20
Bulgaria Bulgarie	1 114	324	253	253[1]	253[1]	253[1]	253[1]	253[1]	325	308
Croatia Croatie	...	651	699	601	578	598	644	676	685	685[1]
Czechoslovakia-former† Tchécoslovaquie(anc.) †	3 621	...	...	...	...	...	...	...	...	...
Czech Republic République tchèque	...	...	3 025	3 155	3 490	3 405	3 393	3 427	3 584	4 106
Denmark Danemark	861	620	583	583[1]	583[1]	583[1]	583[1]	238	344	364
Estonia Estonie	...	300	300[1]	341	350	400	729[1]	850	1 200	1 200
Finland Finlande	6 460	7 330	8 570	10 290	9 940	9 780	11 430	12 300	12 768	13 380

47
Sawnwood
Production (sawn): thousand cubic metres [*cont.*]
Sciages
Production (sciés) : milliers de mètres cubes [*suite*]

Region, country or area Région, pays ou zone	1991	1992	1993	1994	1995	1996	1997	1998	1999	2000
France France	10 974	10 488	9 132	9 649	9 848	9 600	9 607	10 220	10 236	12 283
Germany † Allemagne †	13 322	13 496	11 522	13 567	14 105	14 267	14 730	14 972	16 096	16 745
Greece Grèce	387	337	337[l]	337[l]	337[l]	337[l]	130	137	140	137
Hungary Hongrie	936	667	480	417	230	285	317	298	308	291
Ireland Irlande	386[l]	575	637	709	678	687	642	675	811	888
Italy Italie	1 850	1 823	1 700	1 808	1 850	1 650	1 751	1 600	1 630	1 590
Latvia Lettonie	...	740	446	950	1 300	1 614	2 700	3 200	3 640	4 030
Lithuania Lituanie	...	105[l]	699	760	940	1 450	1 250	1 150	1 150	1 300
Luxembourg Luxembourg	...	...	...	...	...	...	...	...	133	133[l]
Netherlands Pays-Bas	425	405	389	383	426	359	401	349	362	390
Norway Norvège	2 262	2 362	2 315	2 415	2 210	2 420	2 520	2 525	2 336	2 463
Poland Pologne	3 205	4 082	4 260	5 300	3 842	3 747	4 214	4 320	4 137	4 140
Portugal Portugal	1 970	1 550	1 494	1 670	1 731	1 731[l]	1 731[l]	1 490	1 430	1 427
Republic of Moldova République de Moldova	...	0	0	31	25	29	30	30	6	5
Romania Roumanie	2 233	2 460	2 460[l]	1 727	1 777	1 693	1 861	2 200	2 818	3 396
Russian Federation Fédération de Russie	...	53 370	40 890	30 720	26 500	21 913	20 600	19 580	19 100	20 250
Slovakia Slovaquie	...	...	550	700	646	629	767	1 265	744	744[l]
Slovenia Slovénie	...	403	513	513	511	496	510	664	455	455[l]
Spain Espagne	3 162	2 468	2 717	2 755	3 262	3 080	3 080	3 178	3 178[l]	3 178[l]
Sweden Suède	11 463	12 128	12 738	13 816	14 944	14 370	15 669	15 124	14 858	15 089
Switzerland Suisse	1 727	1 525	1 410	1 320	1 479	1 355	1 280	1 400[l]	1 525	1 625
TFYR of Macedonia L'ex-R.y. Macédoine	...	0	63	57	42	40	34	27	37	36
United Kingdom Royaume-Uni	2 241	2 097	2 112	2 225	2 295	2 291	2 356	2 382	2 537	2 492
Yugoslavia Yougoslavie	...	490[l]	470[l]	410[l]	410	410[l]	410[l]	410[l]	410[l]	410[l]

47

Sawnwood
Production (sawn): thousand cubic metres [*cont.*]
  Sciages
  Production (sciés) : milliers de mètres cubes [*suite*]

Region, country or area Région, pays ou zone	1991	1992	1993	1994	1995	1996	1997	1998	1999	2000
Yugoslavia, SFR† Yougoslavie, Rfs†	3 204	...	...	...	...	...	...	...	...	...
Oceania **Océanie**	**5 427**	**5 907**	**6 268**	**6 667**	**7 006**	**6 927**	**7 013**	**7 283**	**7 664**	**8 202**
Australia Australie	2 858	3 041	3 187	3 431	3 691	3 530	3 481	3 711	3 673	3 977
Fiji Fidji	141[1]	91[1]	111	112	102	102[1]	133	131	64	72
New Caledonia Nouvelle-Calédonie	3	2	2	3	3[1]	3[1]	3[1]	3[1]	3[1]	3[1]
New Zealand Nouvelle-Zélande	2 263	2 544	2 805	2 861	2 950	3 032	3 136	3 178	3 653	3 879
Papua New Guinea Papouasie-Nvl-Guinée	117[1]	183	118	218	218	218[1]	218[1]	218[1]	218[1]	218[1]
Samoa Samoa	21	21	21	21[1]	21[1]	21[1]	21[1]	21[1]	21[1]	21
Solomon Islands Iles Salomon	16[1]	16[1]	16[1]	12	12[1]	12[1]	12[1]	12[1]	12[1]	12[1]
Tonga Tonga	1[1]	1[1]	1[1]	1[1]	1[1]	1[1]	1[1]	2	2[1]	2[1]
Vanuatu Vanuatu	7	7	7	7[1]	7[1]	7[1]	7[1]	7[1]	18	18
USSR - former † URSS (anc.) †	79 300	...	...	...	...	...	...	...	...	...

Source:
Food and Agriculture Organization of the United
Nations (FAO), Rome, "FAO Yearbook of Forest Products 2000"
and the FAOSTAT database (19 December 2001).

† For information on recent changes in country or
area nomenclature pertaining to former Czechoslovakia, Hong
Kong Special Administrative Region (SAR) of China, Macao
Special Administrative Region (SAR) of China, SFR of
Yugoslavia and the former USSR, see Annex I - Country or
area nomenclature, regional and other groupings.

1 FAO estimate.

Source:
Organisation des Nations Unies pour l'alimentation et
l'agriculture (FAO), Rome, "Annuaire FAO des produits
forestiers 2000" et la base de données FAOSTAT (19 décembre
2001).

† Pour les modifications récentes de nomenclature
de pays ou de zone concernant l'Allemagne, Hong Kong, région
administrative spéciale (RAS) de Chine, Macao, région
administrative spéciale (RAS) de Chine,
l'ex-Tchécoslovaquie, l'ex-URSS et l'ex-Rfs de Yougoslavie,
voir annexe I - Nomenclature des pays ou des zones,
groupements régionaux et autres groupements.

1 Estimation de la FAO.

48
Paper and paperboard
Papiers et cartons
Production: thousand metric tons
Production : milliers de tonnes

Region, country or area Région, pays ou zone	1991	1992	1993	1994	1995	1996	1997	1998	1999	2000
World *Monde*	243 336	245 002	252 028	268 277	282 041	284 048	301 308	301 267	315 211	323 139
Africa **Afrique**	2 658	2 605	2 519	2 437	2 624	2 634	2 885	2 980	2 914	2 916
Algeria Algérie	* 91	91[1]	93	87	* 78	* 56	* 65	* 55	* 44	44[1]
Cameroon Cameroun	5[1]	5[1]	5[1]	5[1]	5[1]	5[1]	0	0	0[1]	0[1]
Dem. Rep. of the Congo Rép. dém. du Congo	1[1]	3	3[1]	3[1]	3[1]	3[1]	3[1]	3[1]	3[1]	3[1]
Egypt Egypte	208	201	* 220	* 219	* 221	221[1]	* 282	343	343[1]	343[1]
Ethiopia incl. Eritrea Ethiopie comp. Erythrée	6	3	...	...	...	...	...	...	...	...
Ethiopia Ethiopie	...	...	7	7	6	8	10	6	9	9
Kenya Kenya	* 92	176	176[1]	* 108	* 113	129	129[1]	129[1]	129[1]	129[1]
Libyan Arab Jamah.[1] Jamah. arabe libyenne[1]	6	6	6	6	6	6	6	6	6	6
Madagascar Madagascar	5	5	6	5	4	3	4	5	2	4[1]
Morocco Maroc	* 117	102	99	103	106	106[1]	107	110	109	109[1]
Mozambique Mozambique	2[1]	2[1]	1[1]	1[1]	1[1]	1[1]	0	0	0[1]	0[1]
Nigeria Nigéria	29	21	5	3	6	21	19	19	19	19
South Africa Afrique du Sud	* 1 905	* 1 800	* 1 710	* 1 684	1 871	1 871[1]	2 047	2 105	2 041	2 041[1]
Sudan Soudan	* 3	3[1]	3[1]	3[1]	3[1]	3[1]	3[1]	3[1]	3[1]	3[1]
Tunisia Tunisie	72	71	* 80	* 92	* 90	90[1]	97	88	* 94	94[1]
Uganda Ouganda	* 3	3[1]	3[1]	3[1]	3[1]	3[1]	3[1]	3[1]	3[1]	3[1]
United Rep. of Tanzania[1] Rép.-Unie de Tanzanie[1]	25	25	25	25	25	25	25	25	25	25
Zambia Zambie	2	2	4	2	2[1]	2[1]	4[1]	4[1]	4[1]	4[1]
Zimbabwe Zimbabwe	86	86	73	81	81	81	81	76	80	80[1]
America, North **Amérique du Nord**	92 389	94 724	97 399	101 968	107 536	105 823	111 272	109 388	113 229	111 660
Canada Canada	16 559	16 585	17 557	18 348	18 713	18 414	18 969	18 875	20 280	20 852
Costa Rica Costa Rica	19[1]	19[1]	19[1]	* 20	20[1]	20[1]	20[1]	20[1]	20[1]	20[1]
Cuba Cuba	* 118	* 60	* 57	57[1]	57[1]	57[1]	57[1]	57[1]	57[1]	57[1]

48
Paper and paperboard
Production: thousand metric tons [*cont.*]
Papiers et cartons
Production : milliers de tonnes [*suite*]

Region, country or area Région, pays ou zone	1991	1992	1993	1994	1995	1996	1997	1998	1999	2000
Dominican Republic Rép. dominicaine	10	10	7	7	7	21	21[1]	130	130[1]	130[1]
El Salvador El Salvador	17	17	17	17	17	56	56[1]	56[1]	56[1]	56[1]
Guatemala Guatemala	14	14	14	25	31	31[1]	31[1]	31[1]	31[1]	31[1]
Honduras Honduras	0	0	0	0	90	103	88	95	95[1]	95[1]
Jamaica Jamaïque	4	5	3	3[1]	0	0[1]	0[1]	0[1]	0[1]	0[1]
Mexico Mexique	2 896[1]	* 2 825	2 447	2 518	* 3 047	3 047[1]	3 491	3 673	3 784	3 865
Panama Panama	28	28	28	28[1]	28[1]	28[1]	28[1]	...	...	...
United States Etats-Unis	72 724	75 161	77 250	80 945	85 526	84 046	88 511	86 451	88 776	86 554
America, South Amérique du Sud	**7 986**	**8 082**	**8 208**	**8 812**	**9 204**	**9 247**	**9 970**	**9 456**	**9 635**	**9 940**
Argentina Argentine	* 963	976	850	* 961	1 025	991	1 133	978	1 012	1 012[1]
Bolivia Bolivie	0	0	0	0[1]	2	2	2[1]	2[1]	0[1]	0[1]
Brazil Brésil	4 888	4 913	5 352	5 730	5 856	5 885	6 475	6 524	6 255	6 473
Chile Chili	486	508	526	553	573	680	614	642	795	861
Colombia Colombie	521	629	595	672	690	693	704	712	733	741
Ecuador Equateur	129	160	103	78	83	86	91	91[1]	91[1]	91[1]
Paraguay Paraguay	13	13	13	13[1]	13[1]	13[1]	13[1]	13[1]	13[1]	13[1]
Peru Pérou	279	141	79	94	140	140[1]	140[1]	63	63[1]	63[1]
Uruguay Uruguay	75	83	83[1]	83[1]	86	86[1]	* 90	* 88	* 92	92[1]
Venezuela Venezuela	632	659	607	628	736	671	708	343	581	594
Asia Asie	**60 339**	**63 168**	**65 822**	**71 791**	**77 457**	**81 636**	**85 286**	**85 474**	**91 558**	**94 984**
Bangladesh Bangladesh	104	97[1]	* 150	* 160	120[1]	90[1]	70	46	46[1]	46[1]
China †† Chine ††	18 640	20 049	22 077	25 627	28 517	30 913	31 763	* 32 303	34 237	35 529
India Inde	2 362	2 528	2 626	* 2 859	* 3 025	3 025[1]	* 3 000	* 3 350	3 795	3 850
Indonesia Indonésie	* 1 755	* 2 263	2 600[1]	* 3 054	* 3 425	* 4 121	* 4 822	* 5 487	6 978	6 977
Iran (Islamic Rep. of) Iran (Rép. islamique d')	235	190	260	205	205	205	205	20	25	46

48
Paper and paperboard
Production: thousand metric tons [*cont.*]
Papiers et cartons
Production : milliers de tonnes [*suite*]

Region, country or area Région, pays ou zone	1991	1992	1993	1994	1995	1996	1997	1998	1999	2000
Iraq Iraq	13	13[1]	13[1]	* 18	18[1]	18[1]	18[1]	20	20[1]	20[1]
Israel Israël	200	215	213	229	275	275[1]	275[1]	242	275[1]	275[1]
Japan Japon	29 053	28 324	27 764	28 527	29 664	30 014	31 014	29 886	30 631	31 794
Jordan Jordanie	* 15	15[1]	29	31	31[1]	31[1]	32	32[1]	32[1]	32[1]
Korea, Dem. P. R.[1] Corée, R. p. dém. de[1]	80	80	80	80	80	80	80	80	80	80
Korea, Republic of Corée, République de	4 922	5 504	5 804	6 435	* 6 878	7 681	8 334	7 750	8 875	9 763
Lebanon Liban	42	42[1]	42[1]	42[1]	42[1]	42[1]	42[1]	42[1]	42[1]	42[1]
Malaysia Malaisie	293	636	663	574	665	674	711	761	859	791
Myanmar Myanmar	11[1]	11[1]	15	15[1]	15[1]	15[1]	39	41	37	40[1]
Nepal Népal	13	13[1]	13[1]	13[1]	13[1]	13[1]	13[1]	13[1]	13[1]	13[1]
Pakistan Pakistan	206	229	362	403	420	447	500	594	631	631
Philippines Philippines	473	570	* 518	* 518	* 613	613[1]	613[1]	* 780	* 894	870
Singapore Singapour	* 85	85[1]	* 96	* 97	* 87	87[1]	87[1]	87[1]	87[1]	87[1]
Sri Lanka Sri Lanka	23	26	29	31	28	25	25[1]	25[1]	25[1]	25[1]
Syrian Arab Republic Rép. arabe syrienne	1	1[1]	1[1]	1[1]	1[1]	1[1]	1[1]	1[1]	1[1]	1[1]
Thailand Thaïlande	958	1 150	1 306	1 664	1 970	2 036	2 271	2 367	2 434	2 315
Turkey Turquie	747	1 013	1 032	1 102	1 240	1 105	1 246	1 357	1 349	1 566
Viet Nam Viet Nam	108	115	129	* 106	* 125	125[1]	125[1]	190	192	192[1]
Europe **Europe**	**67 541**	**73 695**	**75 205**	**80 208**	**82 065**	**81 524**	**88 588**	**90 585**	**94 493**	**99 921**
Albania Albanie	44[1]	44[1]	44[1]	44[1]	44[1]	44[1]	44[1]	44[1]	1	3
Austria Autriche	3 090	3 252	3 301	3 603	3 599	3 653	3 816	4 009	4 142	4 386
Belarus Bélarus	...	267	175	131	131	131	131	195	208	216
Belgium Belgique	...	...	...	...	...	...	...	...	1 727	1 727
Belgium-Luxembourg Belgique-Luxembourg	1 233	1 147	1 147[1]	1 088	1 088[1]	1 432	1 432[1]	1 831	...	...
Bulgaria Bulgarie	258	153	139	148	150	150	150	153	126	126

48
Paper and paperboard
Production: thousand metric tons [*cont.*]
Papiers et cartons
Production : milliers de tonnes [*suite*]

Region, country or area Région, pays ou zone	1991	1992	1993	1994	1995	1996	1997	1998	1999	2000
Croatia Croatie	...	100	114	248	325	304	393	403	417	417
Czechoslovakia-former† Tchécoslovaquie (anc.) †	1 087	...	...	...	...	...	...	...	...	...
Czech Republic République tchèque	...	...	643	700	738	714	772	768	770	809
Denmark Danemark	356	317	339	345	345[1]	345[1]	391	393	397	410[1]
Estonia Estonie	...	42	42	42	42	53	35	43	48	53
Finland Finlande	8 777	9 153	9 990	10 909	10 942	10 442	12 149	12 703	12 947	13 509
France France	7 442	7 691	7 975	8 701	8 619	8 556	9 143	9 161	9 603	10 006
Germany † Allemagne †	12 904	13 214	13 034	14 457	14 827	14 733	15 930	16 311	16 742	18 182
Greece Grèce	387	387[1]	750	750[1]	750[1]	750[1]	478	622	545	494
Hungary Hongrie	364	348	292	328	321	363	820	434	456	506
Ireland Irlande	36	0	0	0	0	0[1]	0[1]	42	42	43
Italy Italie	5 795	6 040	6 019	6 705	6 810	6 954	8 032	8 254	8 568	9 002
Latvia Lettonie	...	45	10	4	6	8	16	18	19	16[1]
Lithuania Lituanie	...	50	31	23	29	31	25	37	37	53
Netherlands Pays-Bas	2 862	2 835	2 855	3 011	2 967	2 987	3 159	3 180	3 256	3 332
Norway Norvège	1 784	1 683	1 958	2 148	2 261	2 096	2 129	2 260	2 241	2 301
Poland Pologne	1 066	1 147	1 183	1 326	1 477	1 528	1 660	1 718	1 839	1 926
Portugal Portugal	877	959	878	949	977	1 026	1 080	1 136	1 163	1 290[1]
Romania Roumanie	359	359[1]	359[1]	288	364	332	324	301	289	340
Russian Federation Fédération de Russie	...	5 765	4 459	3 412	4 073	3 224	3 339	3 595	4 535	5 239
Slovakia Slovaquie	...	...	303	299	327	467	526	597	578	662
Slovenia Slovénie	...	413	401	460	449	456	430	491	417	411
Spain Espagne	3 576	3 449	3 348	3 503	3 684	3 768	3 968	3 545	4 435	4 755
Sweden Suède	8 349	8 378	8 781	9 284	9 159	9 018	9 756	9 879	10 071	10 774

48
Paper and paperboard
Production: thousand metric tons [*cont.*]
Papiers et cartons
Production : milliers de tonnes [*suite*]

Region, country or area Région, pays ou zone	1991	1992	1993	1994	1995	1996	1997	1998	1999	2000
Switzerland Suisse	1 259 [1]	1 305	1 332	1 450	1 435	1 461	1 583	1 592	1 748	1 777
TFYR of Macedonia L'ex-R.y. Macédoine	...	0	22	24	34	21	21	15	14	17
Ukraine Ukraine	...	...	...	...	...	288	261	261 [1]	373	373
United Kingdom Royaume-Uni	4 951	5 152	5 282	5 829	6 093	6 189	6 479	6 477	6 576	6 605
Yugoslavia Yougoslavie	...	...	...	...	...	...	117	117 [1]	163	163
Yugoslavia, SFR† Yougoslavie, Rfs†	685	...	...	...	...	...	...	...	...	...
Oceania Océanie	**2 833**	**2 728**	**2 875**	**3 061**	**3 155**	**3 185**	**3 308**	**3 385**	**3 381**	**3 718**
Australia Australie	2 018	1 990	2 039	2 197	2 252	2 320	2 418	2 541	2 564	2 844
New Zealand Nouvelle-Zélande	815	738	836	864	903	865	890	844	817	874
USSR - former † URSS (anc.) †	**9 590**	...	...	...	...	...	...	...	...	...

Source:
Food and Agriculture Organization of the United
Nations (FAO), Rome, "FAO Yearbook of Forest Products 2000"
and the FAOSTAT database (19 December 2001).

† For information on recent changes in country or
area nomenclature pertaining to former Czechoslovakia, Hong
Kong Special Administrative Region (SAR) of China, Macao
Special Administrative Region (SAR) of China, SFR of
Yugoslavia and the former USSR, see Annex I - Country or
area nomenclature, regional and other groupings.

1 FAO estimate.

Source:
Organisation des Nations Unies pour l'alimentation et
l'agriculture (FAO), Rome, "Annuaire FAO des produits
forestiers 2000" et la base de données FAOSTAT (19 décembre
2001).

† Pour les modifications récentes de nomenclature
de pays ou de zone concernant l'Allemagne, Hong Kong, région
administrative spéciale (RAS) de Chine, Macao, région
administrative spéciale (RAS) de Chine,
l'ex-Tchécoslovaquie, l'ex-URSS et l'ex-Rfs de Yougoslavie,
voir annexe I - Nomenclature des pays ou des zones,
groupements régionaux et autres groupements.

1 Estimation de la FAO.

49
Cement
Ciment

Production: thousand metric tons
Production : milliers de tonnes

Country or area Pays ou zone	1990	1991	1992	1993	1994	1995	1996	1997	1998	1999
Afghanistan Afghanistan	100[1]	109[1]	* 115[2]	* 115[2]	* 115[2]	* 115[2]	* 116[2]	* 116[2]	* 116[2]	* 116[2]
Albania Albanie	644	311	197	198	240	240	204	100	84	107
Algeria Algérie	6 337	6 323	7 093	6 951	6 093	6 783	7 470	7 146	7 836	7 587
Angola Angola	305	314	370	* 250[2]	* 240[2]	* 200[2]	* 270[2]	301[2]	* 350[2]	* 350[2]
Argentina Argentine	3 612	4 399	5 051	5 647	6 306	5 477	5 117	6 769	7 092	7 187
Armenia Arménie	1 466	1 507	368	198	122	228	281	293	314	287
Australia Australie	6 535	5 725	5 897	6 628	7 017	6 606	6 524	6 701	6 277	6 620
Austria Autriche	4 903[3]	5 017[3]	5 029[3]	4 941[3]	4 828[3]	3 806	3 900[3]	3 944	...	...
Azerbaijan Azerbaïdjan	990	923	827	643	467	196	223	303	201	171
Bangladesh[4] Bangladesh[4]	337	275	272	207	324	316	426	610	* 588	* 756
Barbados Barbade	213	144	71	64	76	76	108	176	257	257
Belarus Bélarus	2 258	2 402	2 263	1 908	1 488	1 235	1 467	1 876	2 035	1 998
Belgium Belgique	6 924	7 184	8 073	7 569	7 542	7 501	6 996	6 996	6 852	9 252
Benin[2] Bénin[2]	300	320	370	506	465	579	* 360	* 450	* 520	* 520
Bhutan[2] Bhoutan[2]	...	116	116	108	* 120	* 140	* 160	* 160	* 150	* 150
Bolivia Bolivie	524	621	630	629	789	869	859[5]	970[5]	1 095[5]	1 163[5]
Brazil Brésil	25 850	27 491	23 902	24 845	25 229	28 256	34 559	37 995	39 942	40 248
Bulgaria Bulgarie	4 710	2 374	2 132	2 007	1 910	2 070	2 137	1 654	1 742	2 060
Cameroon Cameroun	624[2]	521[2]	620[2]	* 620[2]	* 479[2]	522	305[2]	350[2]	400[2]	* 500[2]
Canada Canada	11 745	9 372	8 592	9 394	10 584	10 440	11 587	* 11 736	12 064	* 12 624
Chile Chili	2 115	2 251	2 660	3 024	3 001	3 304	3 627	3 718	3 890	2 508
China †† Chine ††	209 711	244 656	308 217	367 878	421 180	475 606	491 189	511 738	536 000	573 000
China, Hong Kong SAR† Chine, Hong Kong RAS†	1 808	1 677	1 644	1 712	1 927	1 913	2 027	1 925	1 539	1 387
Colombia Colombie	6 360	6 389	9 163	18 205	9 273	9 908	...	10 878	8 673	* 6 720
Congo Congo	90	102	124	95	87	98	43	20	0	0

49

Cement
Production: thousand metric tons [cont.]
Ciment
Production : milliers de tonnes [suite]

Country or area Pays ou zone	1990	1991	1992	1993	1994	1995	1996	1997	1998	1999
Costa Rica[2] Costa Rica[2]	...	* 700	* 700	860	940	865	830	940	1 085	* 1 100
Côte d'Ivoire * [2] Côte d'Ivoire * [2]	500	500	510	500	1 100	1 000	1 000	1 100	650	650
Croatia Croatie	2 655	1 742	1 771	1 683	2 055	1 708	1 842	2 184	3 873	...
Cuba Cuba	3 696	1 851[5]	1 134[5]	1 049[5]	1 085[5]	1 456[5]	1 438[5]	1 701[5]	1 713[5]	* 1 800[2]
Cyprus Chypre	1 133	1 134	1 132	1 089	1 053	1 024	1 021	910	1 207	1 157
Czech Republic République tchèque	6 434	5 610	6 145	5 393	5 252	4 831	5 016	4 874	4 599	4 241
Dem. Rep. of the Congo[2] Rép. dém. du Congo[2]	461	* 250	174	149	166	235	241	125	* 100	* 100
Denmark[6] Danemark[6]	1 656	2 019	2 072	2 270	2 427	2 584	2 629	2 683	2 667	2 534
Dominican Republic Rép. dominicaine	1 109	1 235	1 365	1 271	1 276	1 450	1 642	1 822	1 872	2 295
Ecuador Equateur	1 792	1 774	2 072	2 155	2 452	2 549	2 601	...	2 539	...
Egypt Egypte	14 111	16 427	15 454	12 576	13 544	14 237	15 569	15 569	15 480	11 933
El Salvador El Salvador	641[5]	694[5]	760[5]	659[5]	915[5]	914[5]	938[5]	1 029[5]	988[5]	* 1 032
Estonia Estonie	938	905	483	354	403	418	388	422	321	358
Ethiopia[7] Ethiopie[7]	324	270	237	377	464	609	672	775	497	470
Fiji Fidji	78	79	85	80	94	91	84	96	89	...
Finland Finlande	1 649	1 343	1 133	835	864	907	975	* 960[2]	* 1 104	* 1 164
France France	26 230	25 089	21 584	19 222	20 020	19 724	18 337	18 309	19 434	20 302
Gabon Gabon	112	126	116[2]	132[2]	126[2]	154[2]	185[2]	* 200[2]	196[2]	* 200[2]
Georgia Géorgie	...	...	426	278	89	59	85	94	199	341
Germany † Allemagne †	...	...	37 331	36 649	40 217	38 858	37 006	37 210	38 464	* 38 100
F. R. Germany R. f. Allemagne	30 456	...	...	...	...	...	...	...	...	...
German D. R.(former) R. d. allemande (anc.)	7 316	...	...	...	...	...	...	...	...	...
Ghana[2] Ghana[2]	675	750	1 020	1 200	1 350	* 1 300	* 1 500	* 1 700	1 630	1 870
Greece Grèce	13 142	13 151	12 761	12 492	12 633	10 914	13 391	13 660	14 207	...
Guadeloupe Guadeloupe	291	339	292	276	283	* 230	* 230[2]	* 230[2]	* 230[2]	* 230[2]

49

Cement
Production: thousand metric tons [*cont.*]
Ciment
Production : milliers de tonnes [*suite*]

Country or area Pays ou zone	1990	1991	1992	1993	1994	1995	1996	1997	1998	1999
Guatemala Guatemala	897[5]	450	658[5]	1 018[5]	1 163[5]	1 257	1 173	1 480	1 496	...
Haiti Haïti	180	211	216[5]	228[5]	228[5]	...	...	...	...	...
Honduras Honduras	326	402	760[5]	933[5]	1 000[5]	995[5]	948[5]	1 068[5]	1 026[5]	1 211[5]
Hungary Hongrie	3 933	2 529	2 236	2 533	2 793	2 875	2 747	2 811	2 999	2 980
Iceland Islande	114	106	100	86	81	82	90	110	118	131
India Inde	46 170	52 013	53 936	57 326	63 461	67 722	73 261	82 873	87 646	100 230
Indonesia Indonésie	14 786	13 480	14 048	19 610	24 564	23 136	* 24 648	20 702	* 22 344	* 24 024
Iran (Islamic Rep. of)[8] Iran (Rép. islamique d')[8]	14 429	13 996	15 094	16 321	16 250	16 904	17 703	18 349	20 049	...
Iraq Iraq	13 000	* 5 000	2 453	* 2 000[2]	* 2 000[2]	2 108[2]	* 1 600[2]	* 1 700[2]	* 2 000[2]	* 2 000[2]
Ireland[2] Irlande[2]	* 1 630	* 1 600	* 1 600	1 450	1 623	1 730	1 933	2 100	* 2 000	* 2 000
Israel Israël	2 868	3 340	3 960	4 536	4 800	6 204	6 723	5 916	...	...
Italy Italie	40 544	40 301	41 034	33 771	32 698	33 716	33 327	33 718	35 512	36 827
Jamaica Jamaïque	421	390	480	441	445	518	559	588	558	503
Japan Japon	84 445	89 564	88 252	88 046	91 624	90 474	94 492	91 938	81 328	80 120
Jordan Jordanie	1 733	1 675	2 651	3 437	3 392	3 415	3 512	3 250	2 650	...
Kazakhstan Kazakhstan	8 301	7 575	6 436	3 963	2 033	1 772	1 115	657	622	838
Kenya Kenya	1 515	1 423	1 507	1 417	1 470	1 670	1 575	1 440	...	...
Korea, Dem. P. R. *[2] Corée, R. p. dém. de *[2]	16 000	16 000	17 000	17 000	17 000	17 000	17 000	17 000	17 000	16 000
Korea, Republic of Corée, République de	33 914	39 167	44 444	47 313	52 088	56 101	58 434	60 317	46 791	48 579
Kuwait Koweït	800	300[2]	534	956	1 232	* 1 363	1 113[9]	...	2 310	...
Kyrgyzstan Kirghizistan	1 387	1 320	1 096	692	426	310	546	658	709	386
Lao People's Dem. Rep. Rép. dém. pop. lao	...	...	...	...	7	59	...	...	...	...
Latvia Lettonie	744	720	340	114	244	204	325	246	366	301
Lebanon Liban	* 900[2]	* 900[2]	2 163	2 591	2 948	3 470	3 430	...	...	...
Liberia Libéria	50	* 2[2]	* 8[2]	* 8[2]	* 3[2]	* 5[2]	* 15[2]	* 7[2]	* 10[2]	* 15[2]

49

Cement
Production: thousand metric tons [cont.]
Ciment
Production : milliers de tonnes [suite]

Country or area Pays ou zone	1990	1991	1992	1993	1994	1995	1996	1997	1998	1999
Libyan Arab Jamah. Jamah. arabe libyenne	4	4	4	4	4	3	3	3	3	3
Lithuania Lituanie	3 359	3 126	1 485	727	736	649	656	714	788	666
Luxembourg Luxembourg	636	688	695	719	711	714	667	683	699	742
Madagascar Madagascar	29	32	30	36	8	38	44	36	44	...
Malawi Malawi	101	112	108	117	122	124	88	70	83	104
Malaysia Malaisie	5 881	7 451	8 366	8 797	9 928	10 713	12 349	12 668	10 397	10 104
Mali Mali	4	11	16	14	14	13	21	...	...	...
Martinique Martinique	277	291	262	234	231	* 225	* 220^2	* 220^2	* 220^2	* 220^2
Mauritania^2 Mauritanie^2	...	105	122	111	374	120	* 100	* 80	* 50	* 50
Mexico Mexique	24 683	25 208	27 114	28 725	31 594	25 295	26 174	29 685	30 915	31 958
Mongolia Mongolie	441	227	133	82	86	109	106	* 112^2	109	104
Morocco Maroc	5 381	5 777	6 223	6 175	6 284	6 399	6 585	7 236	7 155	7 194
Mozambique Mozambique	80	63	73	60	62	146	179	217	264	266
Myanmar^{10} Myanmar^{10}	420	443	472	400	477	525	513	524	371	343
Nepal^{11} Népal^{11}	107	136^2	237	248	315	327	309	227	139	191
Netherlands Pays-Bas	3 682$^{6\ 12}$	3 571$^{6\ 12}$	3 296$^{6\ 12}$	3 142$^{6\ 12}$	3 180^2	3 180^2	3 140^2	* 3 300^2	...	...
New Caledonia Nouvelle-Calédonie	64	* 68	90	100	97	98	89	84	...	...
New Zealand Nouvelle-Zélande	681	581	599	684	* 900^2	* 950^2	974^2	976^2	* 975^2	* 975^2
Nicaragua Nicaragua	* 140^5	239^2	277^2	255^2	309^2	324^2	360^2	377^2	377^2	* 350^2
Niger Niger	19	20	29	31	26	31	29^2	* 30^2	* 30^2	* 30^2
Nigeria Nigéria	2 974	3 418	3 367	3 247	1 275	1 573	...	...	...	...
Norway Norvège	1 260	1 293	1 242	1 368	1 464	1 613	1 690	...	...	...
Oman Oman	1 000^9	1 100^9	1 120^9	1 128^9	1 163^9	1 174^9	1 260^2	1 247^9	...	...
Pakistan^4 Pakistan^4	7 488	7 762	8 321	8 558	8 100	7 913	9 567	9 536	9 364	9 635
Panama Panama	325	300^2	473	620^5	678^5	658^5	651	756^5	750^2	* 760^2

49
Cement
Production: thousand metric tons [cont.]
Ciment
Production : milliers de tonnes [suite]

Country or area Pays ou zone	1990	1991	1992	1993	1994	1995	1996	1997	1998	1999
Paraguay Paraguay	344	343	476	476	529	624	627	603	586	556
Peru Pérou	2 185	2 137	2 080	2 327	3 177	3 645	3 678	4 092	4 069	3 327
Philippines Philippines	6 360	6 804	6 540	7 932	9 576	10 566	12 429[2]	14 681[2]	12 888[2]	12 556[2]
Poland Pologne	12 518	12 012	11 908	12 200	13 834	13 914	13 959	15 003	14 970	15 555
Portugal Portugal	7 188	7 342	7 728	7 662	7 756	8 030	8 444	9 395	9 784	10 079
Puerto Rico Porto Rico	1 305	1 296	1 266	1 303	1 356	1 398	1 508	1 586	1 646	1 757
Qatar Qatar	267	367	354	400	470	475	486	584	857	959
Republic of Moldova République de Moldova	2 288	1 809	705	110[13]	39[13]	49[13]	40[13]	122[13]	74[13]	50[13]
Réunion Réunion	336	350	344	325	321	313	290	268	275	...
Romania Roumanie	9 468	6 692	6 271	6 158	5 998	6 842	6 956	6 553	7 300	6 252
Russian Federation Fédération de Russie	83 034	77 463	61 699	49 903	37 220	36 466	27 791	26 688	26 018	28 529
Rwanda Rwanda	60	60	60	60	10	36	42	61	60	66
Saudi Arabia Arabie saoudite	12 696[9]	12 106[9]	15 301[9]	16 584	17 013	15 772	16 391	15 448	15 776	16 381
Senegal Sénégal	471	503	602	591	697	694	810	854	847	1 030
Singapore Singapour	1 848	2 199	* 1 900[2]	* 2 980[2]	* 3 100[2]	* 3 200[2]	* 3 300[2]	* 3 300[2]	* 3 300[2]	* 3 250[2]
Slovakia Slovaquie	3 781	2 680	3 374	2 656	2 879	2 981	4 234	5 856	3 066	3 084
Slovenia Slovénie	1 142	1 801	1 568	1 291	1 667	1 807	1 064	1 113	1 149	1 222
South Africa Afrique du Sud	6 563	6 147	5 850	6 135	7 068	7 437	7 664	7 891	7 676	8 211
Spain Espagne	28 092	27 576	24 612	21 658	25 884	27 220	26 339	27 860	...	...
Sri Lanka Sri Lanka	579	620	553	466	* 925[2]	956	670	* 966	* 1 100[2]	* 1 150[2]
Sudan [2] Soudan [2]	* 167	* 170	* 250	* 250	* 160	391	* 380	291	* 300	* 350
Suriname Suriname	55	24	11	17	18	* 60[2]	* 60[2]	* 65[2]	* 65[2]	* 65[2]
Sweden Suède	5 000	4 493	2 289	2 152	2 138	2 550	2 503	2 272	2 372	2 307
Switzerland Suisse	5 206	4 716	4 260	* 4 000[2]	* 4 370[2]	4 024[2]	3 638[2]	3 568[2]	* 3 600[2]	* 3 600[2]
Syrian Arab Republic Rép. arabe syrienne	3 049	3 078	3 515	3 906	4 344	4 804	4 817	4 838	5 016	5 134

49
Cement
Production: thousand metric tons [cont.]
Ciment
Production : milliers de tonnes [suite]

Country or area Pays ou zone	1990	1991	1992	1993	1994	1995	1996	1997	1998	1999
Tajikistan Tadjikistan	1 067	1 013	447	262	178	78	49	36	18	33
Thailand Thaïlande	18 054	19 164	21 711	26 300	29 929	34 051	38 749	37 136	22 722	25 354
TFYR of Macedonia L'ex-R.y. Macédoine	639	606	516	499	486	523	490	610	461	563
Togo[2] Togo[2]	399	388	350	* 350	* 286	350	413	421	565	* 560
Trinidad and Tobago Trinité-et-Tobago	438	486	482	527	583	559	617	677	700	740
Tunisia Tunisie	4 311	4 195	4 184	4 508	4 605	4 998	4 566	4 378	4 588	4 864
Turkey Turquie	24 299	26 029	28 455	31 134	29 356	33 153	35 214	36 035	38 175	34 258
Turkmenistan Turkménistan	1 085	904	1 050	1 118	690	437	438	601	750	...
Uganda Ouganda	27	27	38	52	45	84	195	290	321	347
Ukraine Ukraine	22 729	21 745	20 121	15 012	11 435	7 627	5 021	5 101	5 591	5 828
USSR - former † URSS (anc.) †	137 321	...	...	...	...	...	...	...	...	...
United Arab Emirates Emirats arabes unis	3 800[9]	3 710[9]	4 328[9]	4 734[9]	4 968[9]	5 071[9]	* 6 000[2]	* 5 250[2]	* 6 000[2]	* 6 000[2]
United Kingdom Royaume-Uni	14 740	12 297	11 006	11 039	12 307	11 805	12 214	12 638	12 409	12 697
United Rep. of Tanzania Rép.-Unie de Tanzanie	664	1 022	677	749	686	739	726	621	...	...
United States Etats-Unis	70 944	67 193	69 585	73 807	77 948	76 906	79 266	82 582	83 931	85 952
Uruguay Uruguay	469	458	552	610	701	593	656	753[5]	907[5]	866[5]
Uzbekistan Ouzbékistan	6 385	6 191	5 934	5 277	4 780	3 419	3 277	3 286	...	...
Venezuela Venezuela	5 996	6 336	6 585	6 876	4 562	* 6 900	7 568[5]	7 867[5]	7 869[5]	7 875[5]
Viet Nam Viet Nam	2 534	3 127	3 926	* 4 200[2]	* 4 700[2]	5 828	6 585	8 019	9 738	* 10 381
Yemen Yémen	828	718	820	1 000	898	1 100	1 028	1 038	...	...
former Yemen Arab Rep. * l'ex-Yémen rép. arabe *	700	798	...	...	...	...	...	...	...	...
Yugoslavia Yougoslavie	2 723	2 411	2 036	1 088	1 612	1 696	2 212	2 011	2 253	1 575
Yugoslavia, SFR† Yougoslavie, Rfs†	7 956	...	...	...	...	...	...	...	...	...

49
Cement
Production: thousand metric tons [*cont.*]
Ciment
Production : milliers de tonnes [*suite*]

Country or area Pays ou zone	1990	1991	1992	1993	1994	1995	1996	1997	1998	1999
Zambia Zambie	432	376	347[2]	* 350[2]	280[2]	312[2]	348[2]	384[2]	351[2]	* 350[2]
Zimbabwe Zimbabwe	924	949	829	816	624	948	996	954	...	...

Source:
United Nations Statistics Division, New York, "Industrial Commodity Statistics Yearbook 1999" and the industrial statistics database.

† For information on recent changes in country or area nomenclature pertaining to former Czechoslovakia, Germany, Hong Kong Special Administrative Region (SAR) of China, Macao Special Administrative Region (SAR) of China, SFR of Yugoslavia and the former USSR, see Annex I - Country or area nomenclature, regional and other groupings.

†† For statistical purposes, the data for China do not include those for Hong Kong Special Administrative Region (Hong Kong SAR), Macao Special Administrative Region (Macao SAR) and Taiwan province of China.

1 Twelve months beginning 21 March of year stated.

2 Source: U.S. Geological Survey, (Washington, D.C.).
3 Beginning 1997, data are confidential.
4 Twelve months ending 30 June of year stated.

5 Source: United Nations Economic Commission for Latin America and the Caribbean (ECLAC), (Santiago).
6 Sales.
7 Twelve months ending 7 July of the year stated.

8 Production by establishments employing 50 or more persons.
9 Source: Arab Gulf Cooperation Council (GCC).
10 Government production only.
11 Twelve months beginning 16 July of year stated.

12 Production by establishments employing 20 or more persons.
13 Excluding Transnistria region.

Source:
Organisation des Nations Unies, Division de statistique, New York, "Annuaire de statistiques industrielles par produit 1999" et la base de données pour les statistiques industrielles.

† Pour les modifications récentes de nomenclature de pays ou de zone concernant l'Allemagne, Hong Kong, région administrative spéciale (RAS) de Chine, Macao, région administrative spéciale (RAS) de Chine, l'ex-Tchécoslovaquie, l'ex-URSS et l'ex-Rfs de Yougoslavie, voir annexe I - Nomenclature des pays ou des zones, groupements régionaux et autres groupements.

†† Les données statistiques relatives à la Chine ne comprennent pas celles qui concernent la région administrative spéciale de Hong Kong (la RAS de Hong Kong), la région administrative spéciale de Macao (la RAS de Macao) et la province chinoise de Taiwan.

1 Période de douze mois commençant le 21 mars de l'année indiquée.
2 Source: "U.S. Geological Survey", (Washington, D.C.).
3 A partir de 1997, les données sont confidentielles.
4 Période de douze mois finissant le 30 juin de l'année indiquée.
5 Source: Commission économique des Nations Unies pour l'Amérique Latine et des Caraïbes (CEPAL), (Santiago).
6 Ventes.
7 Période de douze mois finissant le 7 juillet de l'année indiquée.
8 Production des établissements occupant 50 personnes ou plus.
9 Source: "Arab Gulf Cooperation Council", (GCC).
10 Production de l'Etat seulement.
11 Période de douze mois commençant le 16 juillet de l'année indiquée.
12 Production des établissements occupant 20 personnes ou plus.
13 Non compris la région de Transnistrie.

50
Sulphuric acid
Acide sulfurique
Production: thousand metric tons
Production : milliers de tonnes

Country or area Pays ou zone	1990	1991	1992	1993	1994	1995	1996	1997	1998	1999
Albania Albanie	68	21	11	6	4	...	0	0	0	0
Algeria Algérie	39	46	52	55	40	45	42	55	45	48
Argentina Argentine	209	243	219	206	204	226	220	...	...	...
Australia[1] Australie[1]	1 464	986	816	868	833	...	...	...	...	...
Azerbaijan Azerbaïdjan	603	552	269	141	56	24	31	53	24	26
Bangladesh[1] Bangladesh[1]	3	10	8	7	6	5	9	4	...	...
Belarus Bélarus	1 177	998	616	399	291	437	549	698	640	614
Belgium Belgique	1 906[2]	1 936[2]	1 906[2]	1 593[2]	717[3]	673[3]	678[3]	668[3]	596[3]	709[3]
Bolivia Bolivie	1	1	0	1	3	* 1	...	...	...	...
Brazil Brésil	3 451	3 634	3 257	3 724	4 112	4 043	4 308	4 638	4 624	4 882
Bulgaria Bulgarie	522	356	404	409	428	454	525	556	499	456
Canada Canada	3 830	3 676	3 776	3 713	4 059	3 844	4 278	* 4 100	4 333	...
Chile Chili	347	804	887	920	1 174	1 427	1 518	1 864	1 983	2 436
China †† Chine ††	11 969	13 329	14 087	13 365	15 365	18 110	18 836	20 369	21 710	23 560
Colombia Colombie	76	...	91	77	103	86	...	95	93	...
Croatia Croatie	242	187	278	178	206	233	223	202	164	...
Cyprus Chypre	0	0	...	...	...	...	...	...	...	...
Czech Republic République tchèque	910	588	522	383	337	340	345	333	327	318
Denmark[5] Danemark[5]	90[4]	37[4]	38[4]	...	5	25	19	2	...	...
Egypt Egypte	92	101	111	122	112	133	299	84	...	...
Estonia Estonie	547	460	46	...	0	...	...	...	...	...
Finland Finlande	1 010	1 015	1 087	1 179	1 084	1 159	1 288	2 182	2 496	2 857
France France	3 771	3 627	2 871	2 357	2 227	2 382[6]	2 263[6]	2 243[6]	2 231[6]	...
Germany † Allemagne †	...	3 064	...	...	2 781[6]	1 387	1 225	1 370	1 601	...
F. R. Germany R. f. Allemagne	3 221	...	...	...	...	...	...	...	...	...

50
Sulphuric acid
Production: thousand metric tons [cont.]
Acide sulfurique
Production : milliers de tonnes [suite]

Country or area Pays ou zone	1990	1991	1992	1993	1994	1995	1996	1997	1998	1999
German D. R.(former) R. d. allemande (anc.)	431	...	...	...	...	...	...	...	...	...
Greece Grèce	950	841	617	550	623	753	1 544	1 655	814	...
Hungary[7] Hongrie[7]	263	141	99	77	80	114	94	89	62	53
India Inde	3 272	3 904	4 183	3 730	3 745	4 402	4 988	4 830	5 366	5 686
Indonesia Indonésie	40	52	52	42	35	35	...	224	314	...
Israel Israël	154	...	...	...	...	...	...	...	...	...
Italy Italie	2 038	1 853	1 733	1 430	1 975	2 161	2 214	2 214	2 013	1 627
Japan Japon	6 887	7 057	7 100	6 937	6 594	6 888	6 851	6 828	6 739	6 943
Kazakhstan Kazakhstan	3 151	2 815	2 349	1 179	681	695	653	635	605	685
Lithuania Lituanie	412	368	141	129	212	344	425	504	619	800
Mexico Mexique	455	362	195	178	375	...	...	...	...	...
Netherlands Pays-Bas	...	...	...	...	...	500[6]	418[6]	356[6]	429[6]	487[5 8]
Norway Norvège	...	...	615	...	...	...	...	...	...	...
Pakistan[1] Pakistan[1]	90	93	98	100	102	80	69	31	28	27
Peru Pérou	172	207	143	229	215	216	429	411	541	592
Poland Pologne	1 721	1 088	1 244	1 145	1 452	1 861	1 761	1 741	1 707	1 505
Portugal Portugal	260	51	...	...	2[6]	3[6]	10[6]	11[6]	15[6]	...
Romania Roumanie	1 111	745	572	527	491	477	422	329	229	234
Russian Federation Fédération de Russie	12 767	11 597	9 704	8 243	6 334	6 946	5 764	6 247	5 840	7 148
Slovakia Slovaquie	178	94	...	...	...	...	62[6]	73	68	16
Slovenia Slovénie	125	86	121	114	123	116	103	109	128	126
Spain Espagne	2 848	1 628	1 724	1 199	1 375	2 847	2 265	2 817	3 134[6]	...
Sweden Suède	855	928	...	...	487	507	572[6]	566	383	415
Syrian Arab Republic Rép. arabe syrienne	8	8	10	10	...	...	...	...	...	...
Thailand[9] Thaïlande[9]	72	82	...	...	...	...	...	...	...	...

50
Sulphuric acid
Production: thousand metric tons [*cont.*]
Acide sulfurique
Production : milliers de tonnes [*suite*]

Country or area Pays ou zone	1990	1991	1992	1993	1994	1995	1996	1997	1998	1999
TFYR of Macedonia L'ex-R.y. Macédoine	97	102	95	89	72	82	99	105	101	88
Tunisia Tunisie	3 425	3 421	3 644	3 547	4 161	4 239	4 423	4 256	4 657	4 858
Turkey Turquie	716	532	642	757	730	765	798[6]	947	913	828
Turkmenistan Turkménistan	843	788	353	206	70	76	120	31	47	...
Ukraine Ukraine	5 011	4 186	3 000	1 843	1 646	1 593	1 577	1 438	1 354	1 393
USSR - former † URSS (anc.) †	27 267	...	...	...	...	...	...	...	...	...
United Kingdom Royaume-Uni	1 997	1 852	1 568	1 268	1 266	1 293	643[6]	613[6]	716	...
United States Etats-Unis	40 222[10]	12 842[11]	12 340[11]	11 900[11]	11 300[11]	11 500[11]	10 900[11]	10 700[11]	10 600[11]	10 400[11]
Uzbekistan Ouzbékistan	2 859	2 393	1 476	1 361	805	1 016	984	870	...	...
Venezuela Venezuela	210	277	253	...	...	...	...	...	...	...
Viet Nam Viet Nam	8	9	7	...	...	10	18	15	23	* 24
Yugoslavia Yougoslavie	886	582	302	80	24	87	231	177	211	30

Source:
United Nations Statistics Division, New York, "Industrial Commodity Statistics Yearbook 1999" and the industrial statistics database.

Source:
Organisation des Nations Unies, Division de statistique, New York, "Annuaire de statistiques industrielles par produit 1999" et la base de données pour les statistiques industrielles.

† For information on recent changes in country or area nomenclature pertaining to former Czechoslovakia, Germany, Hong Kong Special Administrative Region (SAR) of China, Macao Special Administrative Region (SAR) of China, SFR of Yugoslavia and the former USSR, see Annex I - Country or area nomenclature, regional and other groupings.

†† For statistical purposes, the data for China do not include those for Hong Kong Special Administrative Region (Hong Kong SAR), Macao Special Administrative Region (Macao SAR) and Taiwan province of China.

1 Twelve months ending 30 June of year stated.

2 Production by establishments employing 5 or more persons.
3 Incomplete coverage.
4 Excluding quantities consumed by superphosphate industry.

5 Sales.
6 Source: United Nations Economic Commission for Europe (ECE), (Geneva).
7 Including regenerated sulphuric acid.
8 Production by establishments employing 20 or more persons.
9 Strength of acid not known.
10 Including data for government-owned, but privately-operated plants.
11 Sold or used by producers.

† Pour les modifications récentes de nomenclature de pays ou de zone concernant l'Allemagne, Hong Kong, région administrative spéciale (RAS) de Chine, Macao, région administrative spéciale (RAS) de Chine, l'ex-Tchécoslovaquie, l'ex-URSS et l'ex-Rfs de Yougoslavie, voir annexe I - Nomenclature des pays ou des zones, groupements régionaux et autres groupements.

†† Les données statistiques relatives à la Chine ne comprennent pas celles qui concernent la région administrative spéciale de Hong Kong (la RAS de Hong Kong), la région administrative spéciale de Macao (la RAS de Macao) et la province chinoise de Taiwan.

1 Période de douze mois finissant le 30 juin de l'année indiquée.
2 Production des établissements occupant 5 personnes ou plus.
3 Couverture incomplète.
4 Non compris les quantités utilisées par l'industrie des superphosphates.
5 Ventes.
6 Source: Commission économique des Nations Unies pour l'Europe (CEE), (Genève).
7 Y compris l'acide sulfurique régénéré.
8 Production des établissements occupant 20 personnes ou plus.
9 Titre de l'acide inconnu.
10 Y compris les données relatives à des usines appartenant à l'Etat mais exploitées par des entreprises privées.
11 Vendu ou utilisé par les producteurs.

51
Pig iron and crude steel
Fonte et acier brut
Production: thousand metric tons
Production : milliers de tonnes

Country or area Pays ou zone	1990	1991	1992	1993	1994	1995	1996	1997	1998	1999
A. Pig-iron • Fonte										
Algeria Algérie	1 054	893	944	925	919	962	850	526	757	807
Argentina Argentine	1 908	1 366	971	980	1 392	1 524	1 966[1]	2 066[1]	* 2 148[1]	* 2 010[1]
Australia[2] Australie[2]	6 188	5 600	6 394	7 209	7 449	7 449	7 554	7 545	7 928	7 513
Austria Autriche	3 452	3 439	3 074	3 070	3 320	3 878	3 416	3 966	4 021	3 913[3][4]
Belgium[4] Belgique[4]	9 416	9 353	8 524	8 179	8 976	9 204	8 628	8 076	8 616	8 436
Brazil Brésil	21 141	22 695	23 057	23 900	25 092	25 021	23 978	24 962	25 111	24 549
Bulgaria Bulgarie	1 143	961	849	1 014	1 470	1 607	1 504	1 643	1 389[1]	1 130[1]
Canada Canada	7 344	8 268	8 621	8 628	8 112	8 460	8 638	8 670	8 937	8 783[1]
Chile[4] Chili[4]	722	700	873[1]	917[1]	886[1]	855[1]	* 996[1]	* 941[1]	* 993[1]	* 1 033[1]
China †† Chine ††	62 380	67 000	75 890	87 389	97 410	105 293	107 225	115 114	118 629	125 392
Colombia Colombie	347	300	308[1]	238[1]	245[1]	282[1]	274[1]	322[1]	* 256[1]	* 266[1]
Croatia[4] Croatie[4]	209	69	* 40[1]	* 40[1]	* 40[1]	* 0[1]	* 0[1]	* 0[1]	...	...
Czech Republic République tchèque	6 107	5 090[4]	5 010	4 656	5 274	5 545	4 898	5 276	5 165	4 137
Egypt[1] Egypte[1]	1 100	1 250	1 062	1 326	1 148	1 062	1 050	1 000	1 300	1 400
Finland[4] Finlande[4]	2 283	2 332	2 452	2 595	2 597	2 242	2 457	2 784	2 916	2 954[1]
France France	14 100	13 416	13 057	12 396	13 008	12 860	12 108	13 424	13 602	13 852[5]
Georgia Géorgie	...	501[4][5]	242[4]	# 12	1	4	4	4	1	1
Germany †[5] Allemagne †[5]	...	30 608	28 202	26 705	29 632	29 599	27 340	30 462	29 705	27 934
Greece[1] Grèce[1]	160	160	...	...	...	...	...	...	...	...
Hungary Hongrie	1 697	1 314	1 179	1 407	1 595[5]	1 515[5]	1 496[5]	1 140[5]	1 259[5]	1 310[5]
India[1] Inde[1]	12 600	14 176	15 126	17 913	20 593	21 499	23 168	23 325	23 170	23 340
Iran (Islamic Rep. of) Iran (Rép. islamique d')	* 1 000[4]	1 952[1][4]	2 053[1][4]	1 961[1][4]	1 883[1][4]	1 532[1][4]	1 867[1][4]	2 053[1]	* 2 117[1]	* 2 112[1]
Italy Italie	11 852	10 561	10 432	11 188	11 161	11 677	10 321	11 477	10 791	10 829
Japan Japon	80 229	79 985	73 144	73 738	73 776	74 905	74 597	78 520	74 981	74 520

51
Pig iron and crude steel
Production: thousand metric tons [*cont.*]
Fonte et acier brut
Production : milliers de tonnes [*suite*]

Country or area Pays ou zone	1990	1991	1992	1993	1994	1995	1996	1997	1998	1999
Kazakhstan[6] Kazakhstan[6]	5 226	4 953	4 666	3 552	2 435	2 530	2 536	3 089	2 594	3 438
Korea, Dem. P. R. * [1] Corée, R. p. dém. de * [1]	...	...	...	...	...	500	500	500	250	250
Korea, Republic of Corée, République de	15 477	18 883	19 581	22 193	21 169	22 344	23 010	22 712	23 093	23 328
Luxembourg[4] Luxembourg[4]	2 645	2 463	2 255	2 412	1 927	1 028	829	438	...	...
Mexico Mexique	2 378	2 313	2 220	2 515	3 359	3 660	4 404	4 464	4 532	4 822[1]
Morocco[14] Maroc[14]	15	15	15	15	* 15	* 15	* 15	* 15	* 15	* 15
Netherlands[4] Pays-Bas[4]	4 960	4 697	4 849	5 405	5 443[78]	5 530[78]	5 544[78]	5 805[78]	5 562[78]	5 307[5]
Norway[14] Norvège[14]	54	61	70	73	* 70	* 70	* 70	* 70	* 70	* 60
Peru[1] Pérou[1]	93	207	147	147	* 150	* 247	* 273	* 264	* 283	* 237
Poland Pologne	8 352	6 297	6 315	6 105	6 866	7 373	6 540	7 295	6 129	5 233
Portugal Portugal	336	252	408	396	420	408[4]	420[4]	431[14]	365[14]	* 389[14]
Romania Roumanie	6 355	4 525	3 110	3 190	3 496	4 203	4 025	4 557	4 541	2 969
Russian Federation Fédération de Russie	59 078	48 628	45 990	40 744	36 480	39 676	37 079	37 277	34 582	40 695
Slovakia[4] Slovaquie[4]	3 561	3 163	2 952[5]	3 205	3 330	3 207	2 928	3 072[5]	2 756[5]	2 897[5]
South Africa[1] Afrique du Sud[1]	6 257	6 968	7 352	6 940	6 982	7 137	6 876	6 192	* 5 650	* 4 587
Spain[5] Espagne[5]	5 440	5 397	4 764	5 394	5 447	5 106	4 127	3 927	4 236	4 058
Sweden Suède	2 696	2 851	2 883	2 844	3 036	3 020	3 130	3 072	3 156	3 816
Switzerland Suisse	129	105	102	82	88	97	100[1]	* 100[1]	* 100[1]	* 100[1]
TFYR of Macedonia[4] L'ex-R.y. Macédoine[4]	84	...	13	20	20	* 20[1]	* 20[1]	* 0[1]	* 0[1]	* 0[1]
Tunisia[6] Tunisie[6]	148	162	147	154	145	152	145	152	123	180
Turkey Turquie	354	332	286	296	326	246[6]	363[6]	337[6]	171[6]	192[6]
Ukraine Ukraine	44 612	36 435	36 948	28 160	20 837	18 314	18 110	21 060	21 239	23 315
USSR - former †[9] URSS (anc.) †[9]	110 166	...	...	...	...	...	...	...	...	...
United Kingdom Royaume-Uni	12 320	11 884	11 542	11 534	11 943	12 236	12 830	13 056	12 746	12 139
United States Etats-Unis	49 668	44 123	47 377	48 200	49 400	50 900	49 400	49 600	48 200	46 300

51
Pig iron and crude steel
Production: thousand metric tons [cont.]
Fonte et acier brut
Production : milliers de tonnes [suite]

Country or area Pays ou zone	1990	1991	1992	1993	1994	1995	1996	1997	1998	1999
Venezuela Venezuela	314	0[10]	0[10]	0[10]	0[10]	0[10]	...	...	...	...
Yugoslavia[4] Yougoslavie[4]	...	526	512	62	17	109	565	907[5]	792	128
Yugoslavia, SFR† Yougoslavie, Rfs†	2 313	...	...	...	...	...	...	...	...	...
Zimbabwe[4] Zimbabwe[4]	521	* 535[1]	* 507[1]	* 211[1]	* 100[1]	* 209[1]	* 210[1]	* 216[1]	* 217[1]	* 228[1]

B. Crude steel · Acier brut

Country or area Pays ou zone	1990	1991	1992	1993	1994	1995	1996	1997	1998	1999
Albania Albanie	79	16	0	15	19	22	22	22	22	16
Algeria Algérie	769	797	768	798	772	780	590	361	581	675
Angola *[1 11] Angola *[1 11]	10	10	10	9	9	9	9	9	9	9
Argentina Argentine	3 636	2 972	2 680	2 870	3 274	3 575	4 069	4 157	4 210	3 797
Australia Australie	7 576[2]	7 141[2]	5 205	7 628[2]	7 807[2]	8 052[2]	7 944[2]	8 088[2]	8 356[2]	7 678[2]
Austria Autriche	4 395	4 186	3 953	4 149	4 398	* 4 990	* 4 442	* 5 181	* 5 283	1 406[3]
Azerbaijan Azerbaïdjan	1 361	1 127	809	461	77	39	3	25	8	0
Bangladesh[2 11] Bangladesh[2 11]	90	58[1]	36[1]	32[1]	34[1]	36[1]	27	23	35[1]	36[1]
Belarus Bélarus	1 112	1 123	1 105[5]	946[5]	880	744	886	1 220	1 411	1 448
Belgium Belgique	11 546	11 419	10 386	10 237	11 268	11 544	10 752	10 716	11 400	10 908
Bosnia and Herzegovina[5] Bosnie-Herzégovine[5]	...	...	...	...	...	...	52	72[11]	75[11]	60[11]
Brazil Brésil	20 631	22 617	23 934	25 207	25 747	25 093	25 248	26 168	25 776	25 017
Bulgaria Bulgarie	2 184	1 615	1 551	1 941	2 491	2 724	2 457	2 628	2 216[1]	1 846
Canada Canada	12 281	13 079	14 027	14 369[1]	13 897[1]	14 415[1]	14 735[1]	15 554[1]	15 930[1]	16 300[1]
Chile[11] Chili[11]	768	804	1 008	1 020	996	948	1 178[1]	1 167[1]	1 171[1]	1 288[1]
China †† Chine ††	68 858	73 881	84 252	89 556	92 617	95 360	100 056	108 942	115 590	124 260
Colombia Colombie	733	700	657	715	702	714[1]	677[1]	710[1]	622[1]	* 523[1]
Croatia Croatie	424[11]	214[11]	102[11]	74[5 11]	63[11]	46[5]	47[5]	70[5]	101[5]	75[5]
Cuba[11] Cuba[11]	270	270	134[1]	91[1]	131[1]	207[1]	231[1]	342[1]	284[1]	* 300[1]
Czech Republic République tchèque	9 997	7 972	7 349	6 732	7 075	7 003	6 519	6 593	6 059	5 453

51
Pig iron and crude steel
Production: thousand metric tons [*cont.*]
Fonte et acier brut
Production : milliers de tonnes [*suite*]

Country or area Pays ou zone	1990	1991	1992	1993	1994	1995	1996	1997	1998	1999
Denmark[8] Danemark[8]	...	...	...	...	2	6	4	3	3	10
Ecuador[11] Equateur[11]	20	20	20[1]	27[1]	32[1]	35[1]	* 20[1]	44[1]	46[1]	53[1]
Egypt[1] Egypte[1]	2 326	2 541	2 524	2 772	2 622	2 642	2 618	2 717	* 2 500	* 2 619
Finland Finlande	2 860	2 890	3 077	3 257	3 420	3 176	3 301	3 734	3 952[5]	3 956[5]
France France	19 304	18 708	18 190	17 313	18 242	18 100	17 633	19 767	20 126	20 200
Georgia Géorgie	...	...	532	224	122	175	165	205	112	14
Germany † Allemagne †	...	41 997	39 962	37 705	40 963	42 051[5]	39 792[5]	10 591[5]	10 218[5]	42 062[5]
Greece Grèce	999	980	924	980	852	936	852	1 020	1 104	960
Hungary Hongrie	2 808[5]	1 860[5]	1 560[5]	1 752[5]	1 932[5]	1 860[5]	1 878[5]	1 690[5]	1 940	1 920
India Inde	16 479	17 577	18 723	13 351	13 356	13 378	13 439	13 416	23 899[1]	24 704[1]
Indonesia[1] Indonésie[1]	2 890	3 250	3 171	1 948	3 220	3 500	4 100	3 800	* 2 700	* 2 800
Iran (Islamic Rep. of)[1] Iran (Rép. islamique d')[1]	1 430	2 200	2 940	3 672	4 498	4 696	5 415	6 322	5 600	* 6 071
Iraq * [1 11] Iraq * [1 11]	150	20	100	300	300	300	300	200	200	800
Ireland Irlande	325	293	257	326	288	312	336	336[5]	355[5]	337[5]
Israel * [1] Israël * [1]	144	90	109	120	180	200	203	203	203	200
Italy Italie	25 647	25 270	24 924	25 967	26 212	27 907	24 391	25 870	25 782	24 780
Japan Japon	110 339	109 648	98 132	99 632	98 295	101 640	98 801	104 545	93 548	94 192
Kazakhstan Kazakhstan	6 753	6 377	6 063	4 557	2 968	3 026	3 216	3 880	3 116	4 105
Korea, Dem. P. R. * [1] Corée, R. p. dém. de * [1]	8 000	8 000	8 100	8 100	8 100	1 500	1 500	1 000	1 000	1 000
Korea, Republic of Corée, République de	23 247	26 126	28 177	33 141	33 887	37 639	39 643	43 405	40 299	41 502
Latvia Lettonie	550	374	246	300	332	280	293	465	471	484[5]
Lithuania[12] Lituanie[12]	7	4	3	2	1	1	0	1	1	1
Luxembourg[11] Luxembourg[11]	3 560	3 379	3 068	3 293	3 073	2 613	2 501	2 580	2 477	2 600
Mexico Mexique	8 221	7 462	7 848	8 188	8 690	9 948	9 852	10 560	10 812	...
Morocco[1] Maroc[1]	* 7	* 7	* 7	* 7	* 7	* 7	* 5	5	* 5	* 5

51
Pig iron and crude steel
Production: thousand metric tons [cont.]
Fonte et acier brut
Production : milliers de tonnes [suite]

Country or area Pays ou zone	1990	1991	1992	1993	1994	1995	1996	1997	1998	1999
Netherlands Pays-Bas	5 412	5 171	5 439	6 000	6 172	6 409	6 326	6 641	6 377[11]	6 075[11]
New Zealand[1 11] Nouvelle-Zélande[1 11]	719	806	759	853	766	842	680	680	* 756	* 744
Nigeria[11] Nigéria[11]	220	200	* 200[1]	* 150[1]	* 58[1]	* 36[1]	* 0[1]	* 0[1]	* 2[1]	* 0[1]
Norway Norvège	376	438[5]	446[5]	505[5]	456[5]	503[5]	511[5]	564[5]	639[5]	595[5]
Peru Pérou	284	404	343	417	506[1]	* 512[1]	* 678[1]	* 607[1]	* 631[1]	* 568[1]
Philippines[1] Philippines[1]	# 600	605	497	623	473	* 923	* 920	* 950	* 950	* 900
Poland Pologne	11 501	10 440[5]	9 864[5]	9 936[5]	11 112[5]	11 892[5]	10 668[5]	11 592[5]	9 916[5]	8 759[5]
Portugal Portugal	744	576	768	780	744	828	840[5]	879[5]	907[5]	1 013[5]
Republic of Moldova[12] République de Moldova[12]	712	623	653	# 1[13]	1[13]	0[13]	0[13]	0[13]	0[13]	0[13]
Romania Roumanie	10 624	7 509	5 614	5 629	5 943	6 697	6 216	6 790	6 405	4 431
Russian Federation Fédération de Russie	89 623	77 100	67 028	58 346	48 812	51 590	49 253	48 502	43 673	51 517
Saudi Arabia[1 11] Arabie saoudite[1 11]	1 833	1 785	1 825	2 318	2 411	2 451	2 683	2 539	2 356	* 2 610
Slovakia[11] Slovaquie[11]	4 779	4 107	4 498	3 922	3 974	3 958	253	255	36	16
Slovenia Slovénie	505	289	401	357	424	408	94	99	98	79
South Africa Afrique du Sud	8 691	9 358	8 970[1]	8 726[1]	8 525[1]	8 741[1]	7 999[1]	8 311[1]	7 506[1]	* 6 925[1]
Spain Espagne	* 12 818	12 846[5]	12 600[5]	12 960[5]	13 440[5]	13 932[5]	12 166[5]	13 677[5]	14 819[5]	14 875[5]
Sweden Suède	4 455	4 248	4 356	4 596	4 956	4 920	4 908	5 148	5 172	5 066
Switzerland Suisse	1 105[5]	955[5]	1 238[5]	1 254[5]	1 100[5]	850[5]	750[5]	1 000[1]	1 000[1]	* 1 000[1]
Thailand[11] Thaïlande[11]	685[1]	711[1]	779[1]	972[1]	1 391[1]	2 134[1]	2 143[1]	2 101	1 619	1 474
TFYR of Macedonia[11] L'ex-R.y. Macédoine[11]	227	209	162	133	67	31	21	27	45	47
Tunisia[12] Tunisie[12]	176	193	182	182	183	201	186	195	171	231
Turkey Turquie	12 225	12 323	15 387	15 198	15 861	14 438	17 189	17 795	17 002	16 821
Uganda Ouganda	0	* 20[1]	* 20[1]	* 20[1]	* 10[1]	* 12[1]	* 12[1]	* 15[1]	* 15[1]	* 15
Ukraine Ukraine	54 555	46 767	43 285	33 709	24 635	22 761	22 718	25 972	24 789	27 873
USSR - former † URSS (anc.) †	162 326	...	...	...	...	...	...	...	...	...

51
Pig iron and crude steel
Production: thousand metric tons [cont.]
Fonte et acier brut
Production : milliers de tonnes [suite]

Country or area Pays ou zone	1990	1991	1992	1993	1994	1995	1996	1997	1998	1999
United Arab Emirates[11][14] Emirats arabes unis[11][14]	40	30	40	40	...	...	...	...	...	...
United Kingdom Royaume-Uni	17 841	16 475	16 212	16 625	17 286	17 604	17 992	18 499	17 315	16 284
United States Etats-Unis	89 726	79 738	84 322	88 800	91 200	95 200	95 500	98 500	98 600	97 400
Uruguay[11] Uruguay[11]	34	41[1]	55[1]	36[1]	36[1]	40[1]	34[1]	39[1]	* 52[1]	* 47[1]
Venezuela Venezuela	3 140	2 933	2 446	2 568	3 524[1]	3 568[1]	3 941[1]	4 019[1]	3 700[1]	3 261[1]
Viet Nam[11] Viet Nam[11]	101	149	196	* 270[1]	* 301[1]	* 271[1]	* 311[1]	* 330	* 320[1]	* 450[1]
Yugoslavia Yougoslavie	...	164	96	51	44	28	45	46	45	29
Yugoslavia, SFR† Yougoslavie, Rfs†	3 608	...	...	...	...	...	...	...	...	...
Zimbabwe[1][11] Zimbabwe[1][11]	580	581	547	221	187	210	212	214	212	* 228

Source:
United Nations Statistics Division, New York, "Industrial Commodity Statistics Yearbook 1999" and the industrial statistics database.

† For information on recent changes in country or area nomenclature pertaining to former Czechoslovakia, Germany, Hong Kong Special Administrative Region (SAR) of China, Macao Special Administrative Region (SAR) of China, SFR of Yugoslavia and the former USSR, see Annex I - Country or area nomenclature, regional and other groupings.

†† For statistical purposes, the data for China do not include those for Hong Kong Special Administrative Region (Hong Kong SAR), Macao Special Administrative Region (Macao SAR) and Taiwan province of China.

1 Source: U.S. Geological Survey, (Washington, D.C.).
2 Twelve months ending 30 June of year stated.

3 1999 data for foundry pig-iron and crude steel for casting, are confidential.
4 Pig-iron for steel making only.
5 Source: Annual Bulletin of Steel Statistics for Europe, America and Asia, United Nations Economic Commission of Europe (Geneva).
6 Foundry pig-iron only.
7 Production by establishments employing 20 or more persons.
8 Sales.
9 Including other ferro-alloys.
10 Source: United Nations Economic Commission for Latin America and the Caribbean (ECLAC), (Santiago).
11 Ingots only.
12 Crude steel for casting only.
13 Excluding Transnistria region.
14 Source: Statistical Yearbook of the OIC countries.

Source:
Organisation des Nations Unies, Division de statistique, New York, "Annuaire de statistiques industrielles par produit 1999" et la base de données pour les statistiques industrielles.

† Pour les modifications récentes de nomenclature de pays ou de zone concernant l'Allemagne, Hong Kong, région administrative spéciale (RAS) de Chine, Macao, région administrative spéciale (RAS) de Chine, l'ex-Tchécoslovaquie, l'ex-URSS et l'ex-Rfs de Yougoslavie, voir annexe I - Nomenclature des pays ou des zones, groupements régionaux et autres groupements.

†† Les données statistiques relatives à la Chine ne comprennent pas celles qui concernent la région administrative spéciale de Hong Kong (la RAS de Hong Kong), la région administrative spéciale de Macao (la RAS de Macao) et la province chinoise de Taiwan.

1 Source: "U. S. Geological Survey", (Washington, D. C.).
2 Période de douze mois finissant le 30 juin de l'année indiquée.
3 1999, les données pour la fonte de moulage et l'acier brut pour moulages sont confidentielles.
4 La fonte d'affinage seulement.
5 Source: Bulletin annuel de statistiques de l'acier pour l'Europe, l'Amérique et l'Asie, Commission économique des Nations Unies pour l'Europe (Genève).
6 La fonte de moulage seulement.
7 Production des établissements occupant 20 personnes ou plus.
8 Ventes.
9 Y compris les autres ferro-alliages.
10 Source: Commission économique des Nations Unies pour l'Amérique Latine et des Caraïbes (CEPAL), (Santiago).
11 L'acier brut (lingots) seulement.
12 L'acier brut pour moulages seulement.
13 Non compris la région de Transnistria.
14 Source: Annuaire statistique des pays de OCI.

52
Aluminium
Aluminium

Production: thousand metric tons
Production : milliers de tonnes

Country or area Pays ou zone	1990	1991	1992	1993	1994	1995	1996	1997	1998	1999
Argentina **Argentine**	169	184	172	185	188	193	200	* 203	203[1]	206[2]
Primary 1re fusion	163	166	153	171	173	183	185	187	187	206
Secondary[1] 2ème fusion[1]	6	18	19	14	14	10	16	16	16	...
Australia[3] **Australie[3]**	* 1 268	1 265	1 234	1 341	1 439	1 285	1 331	1 395	1 589	1 686
Primary[3] 1re fusion[3]	1 235	1 235	1 194	1 306	1 384	1 285	1 331	1 395	1 589	1 686
Secondary[3] 2ème fusion[3]	33	30	40[1]	35[1]	55[1]	...	...	...	...	...
Austria **Autriche**	246	206	* 78	43[1]	53[1]	94[1]	98[1]	119[1]	126[1]	...
Primary 1re fusion	159	89	33	0[1]	0[1]	0[1]	0[1]	0[1]	0[1]	...
Secondary 2ème fusion	87[4]	117[4]	45[1]	43[1]	53[1]	94[1]	98[1]	119[1]	126[1]	...
Bahrain **Bahreïn**	213	214	293	448	451	449	456	490[2]	501[2]	502
Belgium[1] **Belgique[1]**	3	3	0	0	0	0	0	0	0	...
Brazil **Brésil**	996[1]	1 206[1]	1 260[1]	1 249[1]	1 276[1]	1 305[1]	1 343[1]	1 369[1]	1 371[1]	1 250[2]
Primary 1re fusion	931[1]	1 139[1]	1 193[1]	1 172[1]	1 185[1]	1 188[1]	1 197[1]	1 189[1]	1 208[1]	1 250[1]
Secondary[1] 2ème fusion[1]	65	66	67	77	91	117	146	180	163	...
Cameroon **Cameroun**	88[1]	86[1]	83[1]	87[1]	81[1]	71	82[1]	91[2]	82[2]	92[2]
Canada **Canada**	1 635[1]	1 889[1]	2 058[1]	2 399[1]	2 352[1]	2 269[1]	2 384[1]	2 433[1]	2 485[1]	2 390
Primary 1re fusion	1 567[1]	1 822	1 972[1]	2 309[1]	2 255[1]	2 172[1]	2 283[1]	2 327[1]	2 374[1]	2 390
Secondary[1] 2ème fusion[1]	68	68	86	90	97	97	101	106	111	...
China †† **Chine ††**	854	900	1 096	1 255	1 498	1 870	1 896	2 180	2 362	2 809
Colombia **Colombie**	...	...	0	1	...	0	...	...	...	...
Croatia **Croatie**	75	54	29	26	26	31	33	35[2]	16	35[2]
Czechoslovakia-former† **Tchécoslovaquie (anc.) †**	70	66	...	...	...	...	...	...	...	...
Primary 1re fusion	30	49	...	...	...	...	...	...	...	...
Secondary 2ème fusion	40	17	...	...	...	...	...	...	...	...
Denmark **Danemark**	11[1]	12[1]	16[5]	21[5]	22[5]	28[5]	27[5]	35[5]	34[5]	34[5]
Egypt[6] **Egypte[6]**	141	141	139	139	149	136	150	119	187[1]	187
Finland * **Finlande ***	5	4	5	4	4	5	5	...	...	...

52

Aluminium
Production: thousand metric tons [*cont.*]

Aluminium
Production : milliers de tonnes [*suite*]

Country or area Pays ou zone	1990	1991	1992	1993	1994	1995	1996	1997	1998	1999
France **France**	**533**[7]	**472**[7]	**637**[7]	**627**[7]	**709**[7]	**364**	**380**	**399**	**424**	**455**
Primary 1re fusion	325	255	414	425	481	364	380	399	424	455
Secondary[7] 2ème fusion[7]	208	217	222	203	227	...	...	...	...	...
Germany † **Allemagne †**	...	**740**	**655**	**610**	**559**	**576**	**577**	**572**	**612**	**634**
Primary 1re fusion	...	690	603	552	503	576	577	572	612[2]	634
Secondary 2ème fusion	...	50	52	58	56	...	...	...	...	...
F. R. Germany **R. f. Allemagne**	**760**	...	...	...	...	...	...	...	...	...
Primary[8] 1re fusion[8]	720	...	...	...	...	...	...	...	...	...
German D. R.(former)[7] **R. d. allemande (anc.)[7]**	**83**	...	...	...	...	...	...	...	...	...
Primary[7] 1re fusion[7]	41	...	...	...	...	...	...	...	...	...
Secondary[7] 2ème fusion[7]	42	...	...	...	...	...	...	...	...	...
Ghana **Ghana**	**174**	**175**	**180**[1]	**175**[1]	**141**[1]	**135**[1]	**137**[1]	**152**[1]	**56**[1]	**114**[2]
Greece **Grèce**	**226**	**175**	**174**	**148**	**142**	**132**	**141**	**132**	**161**	**161**
Hungary **Hongrie**	**81**	**63**	**27**	**29**	**31**	**35**	**94**	**98**	**92**	**89**
Primary 1re fusion	75	63	27	29	31	35	94	98	92	89
Secondary 2ème fusion	6	...	...	...	...	...	...	...	...	...
Iceland **Islande**	**87**	**89**	**89**	**95**	**99**	**100**	**102**	**123**	**160**	**161**
India **Inde**	**428**	**504**	**499**	**478**	**479**	**518**	**516**	**539**	**542**[2]	**550**[2]
Indonesia **Indonésie**	**192**	**173**	**214**	**202**	**222**[1]	**228**[1]	**223**[1]	**219**[1]	**133**[1]	*** 100**[2]
Iran (Islamic Rep. of) **Iran (Rép. islamique d')**	**73**	**110**	**119**	**107**[1]	**142**[1]	**145**[1]	**96**[1]	**125**[1]	**135**[1]	**109**[2]
Primary 1re fusion	59[1]	70[1]	79[1]	92[1]	116[1]	119[1]	70[1]	99[1]	109[1]	109[2]
Secondary[1] 2ème fusion[1]	14	39	39	15	26	26	26	26	26	...
Italy **Italie**	**581**	**566**	**514**	**502**	**551**	**590**	**561**	**631**	**690**	**689**
Primary 1re fusion	232	218	161	156	175	178	184	188	187	187
Secondary 2ème fusion	350	348	353	346	376	412	377	443	503	502
Japan[7] **Japon[7]**	**1 141**	**1 148**	**1 112**	**1 044**	**1 215**	**1 227**	**1 238**	**1 330**	**1 207**	**1 158**
Primary 1re fusion	51	52	38	39	41	46	46	53	51	...

52
Aluminium
Production: thousand metric tons [*cont.*]
Aluminium
Production : milliers de tonnes [*suite*]

Country or area Pays ou zone	1990	1991	1992	1993	1994	1995	1996	1997	1998	1999
Secondary[7] 2ème fusion[7]	1 090	1 096	1 074	1 006	1 175	1 181	1 191	1 277	1 155	1 158
Korea, Republic of **Corée, République de**	13	14	...	...	...	...	...	...	...	...
Mexico **Mexique**	122	122	79	100	74	92	167	184	186	196
Primary 1re fusion	57	43	17	25	29	33	69	71	68	70
Secondary[2] 2ème fusion[2]	66	80	62	74	46	59	98	112	118	126
Netherlands **Pays-Bas**	392	368	378	367	405	408	298[1]	312[1]	366[1]	* 265[2]
Primary 1re fusion	258	254	227	228	230	216	227[1]	232[1]	264[1]	265[2]
Secondary 2ème fusion	134	114	150	139	175	192	71[1]	80[1]	102[1]	...
New Zealand **Nouvelle-Zélande**	265[1]	263[1]	250[1]	285[1]	277[1]	281[1]	293[1]	318[1]	326[1]	300[2]
Primary 1re fusion	260[1]	259[1]	243[1]	277[1]	269[1]	273[1]	285[1]	310[1]	318[1]	300[2]
Secondary[1] 2ème fusion[1]	5	5	7	7	8	8	8	8	8	...
Norway **Norvège**	* 887	* 889	878	* 943	* 906	* 919	* 923	977[1]	1 058[1]	1 034[2]
Primary 1re fusion	867	858	838	887	857	847	863	919[1]	995[1]	1 034[2]
Secondary[1] 2ème fusion[1]	20	31	40	56	49	72	60	59	62	...
Poland **Pologne**	46	46	44	47	50	56	52	54	54	51
Portugal **Portugal**	9	8	12	12	12	3[1]	3[1]	3[1]	3[1]	...
Romania[7 9] **Roumanie**[7 9]	178	167	120	116	122	144	145	164	175	174
Primary[7 9] 1re fusion[7 9]	168	158	112	112	120	141	141	162	174	174
Secondary[7] 2ème fusion[7]	10	9	8	4	3	3	4	2	1[9]	0[9]
Russian Federation[2] **Fédération de Russie**[2]	...	...	2 700	2 820	2 670	2 724	2 874	2 906	3 005	3 146
Slovakia **Slovaquie**	70	66	...	19	4	25	311	110[1]	121	109
Primary 1re fusion	30	49	...	18	4	25	311	110[1]	115	...
Secondary 2ème fusion	40	17	...	1	...	...	...	...	6	...
Slovenia **Slovénie**	100	90	85	83	77	58	27	9	10	9
South Africa[2] **Afrique du Sud**[2]	170	169	173	175	172	229	570	673	693	687
Spain **Espagne**	442[1]	451[1]	456[1]	456[1]	442[1]	469[1]	515[1]	533[1]	570[1]	360[2]
Primary 1re fusion	355[1]	355[1]	359[1]	356[1]	338[1]	362[1]	362[1]	360[1]	360[1]	360[2]

52
Aluminium
Production: thousand metric tons [cont.]
Aluminium
Production : milliers de tonnes [suite]

Country or area Pays ou zone	1990	1991	1992	1993	1994	1995	1996	1997	1998	1999
Secondary[1] 2ème fusion[1]	87	96	97	100	104	107	154	173	210	...
Suriname **Suriname**	**31**	**31**	**32**	**30**	**27**	**28**	**29**	**32**[2]	**29**[2]	**10**[2]
Sweden **Suède**	**126**[1]	**116**	**96**[1]	**101**[1]	**105**[1]	**117**[1]	**123**[1]	**123**[1]	**123**[1]	**96**[2]
Primary 1re fusion	96[1]	97[1]	77[1]	82[1]	84[1]	94[1]	98[1]	98[1]	96[1]	96[2]
Secondary[1] 2ème fusion[1]	30	17	19	19	22	23	25	25	27	...
Switzerland **Suisse**	*** 106**	*** 102**	*** 63**	*** 41**	*** 30**	**26**[1]	**33**[1]	**35**[1]	**47**[1]	**30**[2]
Primary 1re fusion	72	66	52	36	24	21	27[1]	27[1]	32[1]	30[2]
Secondary[1] 2ème fusion[1]	35	36	11	4	6	5	6	8	15	...
Tajikistan **Tadjikistan**	**...**	**...**	*** 400**[2]	**252**	**237**	**237**	**198**	**189**	**196**	**229**
Primary 1re fusion	...	...	* 400[2]	252	237	237	198	189	196	229
TFYR of Macedonia **L'ex-R.y. Macédoine**	**5**	**6**	**6**	**6**	**7**	**5**	**5**	**5**	**7**	**6**
Turkey **Turquie**	**61**	**56**	**61**	**59**	**60**	**62**	**62**	**62**	**62**	**62**
Primary 1re fusion	60	56	61	59	60	62	62	62	62	62
Ukraine * [2] **Ukraine *** [2]	**...**	**...**	**100**	**100**	**100**	**98**	**90**	**101**	**107**	**112**
USSR - former †* [2] **URSS (anc.) †*** [2]	**2 800**	**...**	**...**	**...**	**...**	**...**	**...**	**...**	**...**	**...**
Primary * [2] 1re fusion * [2]	2 200	...	...	...	...	...	...	...	...	...
Secondary * [2] 2ème fusion * [2]	600	...	...	...	...	...	...	...	...	...
United Kingdom[7] **Royaume-Uni**[7]	**491**	**489**	**442**	**475**	**456**	**468**	**501**	**490**	**533**	**528**
Primary[7] 1re fusion[7]	290	294	244	239	231	238	240	248	258	270
Secondary 2ème fusion	201	195	197	236	224	230	261	243	275	258
United States[7] **Etats-Unis**[7]	**6 441**	**6 411**	**6 802**	**6 635**	**6 389**	**6 565**	**6 887**	**7 153**	**7 153**	**7 529**
Primary 1re fusion	4 048	4 121	4 042	3 695	3 299	3 375	3 577	3 603	3 713	3 779
Secondary[7] 2ème fusion[7]	2 393	2 290	2 760	2 940	3 090	3 190	3 310	3 550	3 440	3 750
Venezuela **Venezuela**	**609**	**620**	**542**	**602**	**617**[1]	**654**[1]	**656**[1]	**662**[1]	**606**[1]	**570**[2]
Primary 1re fusion	599	610	508	568	585[1]	627[1]	635[1]	641[1]	584[1]	570[2]
Secondary[1] 2ème fusion[1]	10	10	35	35	32	28	21	21	21	...
Yugoslavia **Yougoslavie**	**...**	**76**	**67**	**26**	**4**	**17**	**37**	**67**	**61**	**73**

52
Aluminium
Production: thousand metric tons [*cont.*]
Aluminium
Production : milliers de tonnes [*suite*]

Country or area Pays ou zone	1990	1991	1992	1993	1994	1995	1996	1997	1998	1999
Primary 1re fusion	...	76	67	26	4	17	37	66	61	73
Secondary 2ème fusion	...	0	0	0	0	0	0	1	0	...
Yugoslavia, SFR† **Yougoslavie, Rfs†**	**291**	...	...	...	...	...	...	...	...	...
Primary * 1re fusion *	290	...	...	...	...	...	...	...	...	...
Secondary * 2ème fusion *	1	...	...	...	...	...	...	...	...	...

Source:
United Nations Statistics Division, New York, "Industrial Commodity Statistics Yearbook 1999" and the industrial statistics database.

† For information on recent changes in country or area nomenclature pertaining to former Czechoslovakia, Germany, Hong Kong Special Administrative Region (SAR) of China, Macao Special Administrative Region (SAR) of China, SFR of Yugoslavia and the former USSR, see Annex I - Country or area nomenclature, regional and other groupings.

†† For statistical purposes, the data for China do not include those for Hong Kong Special Administrative Region (Hong Kong SAR), Macao Special Administrative Region (Macao SAR) and Taiwan province of China.

1 Source: World Metal Statistics, (London).
2 Source: U.S. Geological Survey, (Washington, D.C.).
3 Twelve months ending 30 June of year stated.

4 Secondary metal production only.
5 Sales.
6 Including aluminium plates, shapes and bars.
7 Including alloys.
8 Source: Metallgesellschaft Aktiengesellschaft, (Frankfurt).

9 Including pure content of virgin alloys.

Source:
Organisation des Nations Unies, Division de statistique, New York, "Annuaire de statistiques industrielles par produit 1999" et la base de données pour les statistiques industrielles.

† Pour les modifications récentes de nomenclature de pays ou de zone concernant l'Allemagne, Hong Kong, région administrative spéciale (RAS) de Chine, Macao, région administrative spéciale (RAS) de Chine, l'ex-Tchécoslovaquie, l'ex-URSS et l'ex-Rfs de Yougoslavie, voir annexe I - Nomenclature des pays ou des zones, groupements régionaux et autres groupements.

†† Les données statistiques relatives à la Chine ne comprennent pas celles qui concernent la région administrative spéciale de Hong Kong (la RAS de Hong Kong), la région administrative spéciale de Macao (la RAS de Macao) et la province chinoise de Taiwan.

1 Source: "World Metal Statistics," (Londres).
2 Source: U.S. Geological Survey, (Washington, D.C.).
3 Période de douze mois finissant le 30e juin de l'année indiquée.
4 Production du métal de deuxième fusion seulement.
5 Ventes.
6 Y compris les tôles, les profilés et les barres d'aluminium.
7 Y compris les alliages.
8 Source: "Metallgesellschaft Aktiengesellschaft", (Francfort).
9 Y compris la teneur pure des alliages de première fusion.

53
Radio and television receivers
Récepteurs radio et télévision
Production: thousands
Production : milliers

Country or area Pays ou zone	Radio receivers Récepteurs radio					Television receivers Récepteurs télévision				
	1995	1996	1997	1998	1999	1995	1996	1997	1998	1999
Albania Albanie	0	0	0	0	0	0	0	0	0	0
Algeria Algérie	...	...	...	...	...	194	250	172	251	173
Argentina Argentine	...	...	...	...	...	949	1 096	1 630	1 592	1 335
Azerbaijan Azerbaïdjan	0	0	0	0	0	4	1	1	3	0
Bangladesh Bangladesh	4	11	20	10	13	79	64	94	...	...
Belarus Bélarus	277	138	170	114	195	250	314	454	468	516
Brazil Brésil	4 729	2 941	4 211	2 753	2 039	6 424	8 644	7 976	5 711	4 328
Bulgaria Bulgarie	2	0	...	...	...	10	11	6	3	2
China †† Chine ††	...	...	...	...	...	34 962	35 418	36 372	42 809	49 113
China, Hong Kong SAR†[1] Chine, Hong Kong RAS†[1]	1 698	...	...	...	...	...	...	...	...	...
Colombia Colombie	...	...	...	...	...	129	...	58	50	...
Croatia Croatie	0	0	...	...	...	0	0	...	...	...
Czech Republic République tchèque	...	...	...	...	...	66	74	180	567	707
Ecuador Equateur	...	...	...	...	...	5	0	...	...	...
Egypt Egypte	...	...	...	...	...	288	336	114	...	30
Finland Finlande	82	...	...	...	...	308	191	...	...	...
France France	...	...	3 853	4 586	2 961	...	...	...	...	...
Georgia Géorgie	...	...	...	...	...	0	2	2	1	1
Germany † Allemagne †	3 182	3 342	3 632	3 884	...	3 218	1 965	...	1 269	...
Hungary Hongrie	103	310	528	2 328	2 412	274	...	...	...	...
India Inde	116	47	33	2	0	2 190	1 949	2 370	2 461	2 561
Indonesia[2] Indonésie[2]	3 805	...	4 177	# 80	...	...	...	...	...	...
Iran (Islamic Rep. of)[3] Iran (Rép. islamique d')[3]	45	56	76	127	...	253	453	751	769	...
Italy Italie	...	...	...	...	...	2 780	2 677	1 920	1 659	1 627

53
Radio and television receivers
Production: thousands [*cont.*]

Récepteurs radio et télévision
Production : milliers [*suite*]

Country or area Pays ou zone	Radio receivers Récepteurs radio					Television receivers Récepteurs télévision				
	1995	1996	1997	1998	1999	1995	1996	1997	1998	1999
Japan Japon	7 181	2 638	2 434	2 623	2 678	9 022	7 568	7 559	6 567	4 386
Kazakhstan Kazakhstan	12	3	3	3	...	47	74	61	103	112
Korea, Republic of Corée, République de	0	...	...	...	...	18 722	21 469	16 428	12 763	15 556
Kyrgyzstan Kirghizistan	...	...	...	...	...	7	0	0	4	1
Latvia Lettonie	9	10	10	2	2	...	...	...	...	...
Lithuania Lituanie	...	...	...	...	...	55	57	52	84	187
Malaysia Malaisie	38 767	29 431	33 491	30 265	32 957	9 461	8 901	7 774	8 035	7 611
Mexico Mexique	...	...	...	...	...	181	205	...	...	...
Pakistan Pakistan	...	...	...	...	...	101	278	186	107	128
Poland Pologne	225	206	143	154	132	1 138	1 615	3 020	4 436	5 121
Portugal Portugal	...	4 372	4 552	5 076	5 939	...	...	...	...	...
Republic of Moldova[4] République de Moldova[4]	16	67	94	51	7	47	31	19	10	3
Romania Roumanie	29[2]	76[2]	28[2]	10[2]	0[2]	369	275	89	134	56
Russian Federation Fédération de Russie	988	477	342	235	332	1 005	313	327	329	281
Slovakia Slovaquie	...	...	...	...	...	...	...	...	304	311
Slovenia Slovénie	...	0	0	0	0	130	179	0	231	244
Spain Espagne	54	82	313	508	357	5 392	...	...	...	...
Syrian Arab Republic Rép. arabe syrienne	...	...	...	...	...	71	124	128	151	150
Trinidad and Tobago Trinité-et-Tobago	0	0	...	...	...	3	1	...	...	...
Tunisia Tunisie	...	...	...	...	...	93	90	108	90	104
Turkey Turquie	...	...	...	...	...	1 859	2 510	4 657	5 795	6 941
Ukraine Ukraine	125	47	25	10	27	315	118	50	93	81
United Kingdom Royaume-Uni	1 480	1 531	2 095	2 164		...	...	...	...	...
United Rep. of Tanzania Rép.-Unie de Tanzanie	76	54	56	...	...	...	...	...	...	...

53
Radio and television receivers
Production: thousands [*cont.*]

Récepteurs radio et télévision
Production : milliers [*suite*]

Country or area Pays ou zone	Radio receivers Récepteurs radio					Television receivers Récepteurs télévision				
	1995	1996	1997	1998	1999	1995	1996	1997	1998	1999
United States[5] Etats-Unis[5]	...	...	...	...	...	12 132	11 440	11 476	10 715	11 122
Uzbekistan Ouzbékistan	...	...	...	...	...	65	140	269	...	...
Yugoslavia Yougoslavie	0	1	0	0	0	31	24	25	30	13

Source:
United Nations Statistics Division, New York, "Industrial Commodity Statistics Yearbook 1999" and the industrial statistics database.

† For information on recent changes in country or area nomenclature pertaining to former Czechoslovakia, Germany, Hong Kong Special Administrative Region (SAR) of China, Macao Special Administrative Region (SAR) of China, SFR of Yugoslavia and the former USSR, see Annex I - Country or area nomenclature, regional and other groupings.

†† For statistical purposes, the data for China do not include those for Hong Kong Special Administrative Region (Hong Kong SAR), Macao Special Administrative Region (Macao SAR) and Taiwan province of China.

1 Beginning 1996, data are confidential.
2 Including radio with tape recording unit.

3 Production by establishments employing 10 or more persons.
4 Excluding Transnistria region.
5 Shipments.

Source:
Organisation des Nations Unies, Division de statistique, New York, "Annuaire de statistiques industrielles par produit 1999" et la base de données pour les statistiques industrielles.

† Pour les modifications récentes de nomenclature de pays ou de zone concernant l'Allemagne, Hong Kong, région administrative spéciale (RAS) de Chine, Macao, région administrative spéciale (RAS) de Chine, l'ex-Tchécoslovaquie, l'ex-URSS et l'ex-Rfs de Yougoslavie, voir annexe I - Nomenclature des pays ou des zones, groupements régionaux et autres groupements.

†† Les données statistiques relatives à la Chine ne comprennent pas celles qui concernent la région administrative spéciale de Hong Kong (la RAS de Hong Kong), la région administrative spéciale de Macao (la RAS de Macao) et la province chinoise de Taiwan.

1 A partir de 1996, les données sont confidentielles.
2 Y compris les récepteurs de radio avec appareil enregistreur à bande magnétique incorporés.
3 Production des établissements occupant 10 personnes ou plus.
4 Non compris la région de Transnistria.
5 Expéditions.

54
Passenger cars
Voitures de tourisme
Production: thousands
Production : milliers

Country or area Pays ou zone	1990	1991	1992	1993	1994	1995	1996	1997	1998	1999
Argentina[1] Argentine[1]	81	114	221	287	338	227	269	366	353	225
Australia Australie	361	278	270	285	310	294	305	304	313	340
Austria Autriche	15	14	...	...	...	...	...	...	...	...
Brazil[2] Brésil[2]	267	293	338	392	367	271	245	253	242	221
Canada Canada	940	890	901	838	...	...	...	...	...	...
China ††* Chine ††*	...	40	...	...	...	...	...	...	...	...
Czech Republic République tchèque	188	...	...	...	...	...	...	...	...	...
Ecuador Equateur	...	...	...	...	...	...	...	...	27	...
Egypt Egypte	10	9	7	4	7	8	14	13	13	12
Finland[1] Finlande[1]	30	39	13	7	...	...	0	...	...	...
France France	3 293	3 190	3 326	2 837	3 176	...	...	...	...	...
Germany † Allemagne †	...	4 647	4 895	3 875	4 222	...	4 713[1]	...	...	...
F. R. Germany R. f. Allemagne	4 634	...	...	...	...	...	...	...	...	...
German D. R.(former) R. d. allemande (anc.)	145	...	...	...	...	...	...	...	...	...
Hungary Hongrie	...	...	...	...	...	...	...	...	90	125
India[3] Inde[3]	177	164	162	210	262	331	400	384	393	577
Indonesia Indonésie	16	26	28	20	85	19	...	11	56	...
Italy[3] Italie[3]	1 873	1 632	1 475	1 116	1 340	1 422	1 244	1 563	1 379	1 384
Japan Japon	9 948	9 753	9 379	8 494	7 801	7 611	7 864	8 491	8 056	8 100
Korea, Republic of[1] Corée, République de[1]	935	1 119	1 259	1 528	1 755	1 999	2 256	2 313	1 577	2 158
Mexico Mexique	611[1]	730[1]	799[1]	861	887	705	802	858	947	988
Netherlands[1 4 5] Pays-Bas[1 4 5]	122	84	95	80	92	98	...	...	...	...
Poland Pologne	266	167	219	334	338	366	441	520	592	647
Romania Roumanie	100	84	74	93	56	70	97	109	104	89

54
Passenger cars
Production: thousands [*cont.*]
  Voitures de tourisme
  Production : milliers [*suite*]

Country or area Pays ou zone	1990	1991	1992	1993	1994	1995	1996	1997	1998	1999
Russian Federation Fédération de Russie	1 103	1 030	963	956	798	835	868	986	840	954
Slovakia Slovaquie	3	4	...	5	8	22	32	42	125	127
Slovenia Slovénie	68	79	84	58	74	88	89	...	...	119
Spain Espagne	1 696	1 787	1 817	1 774[14]	2 146[14]	2 254[14]	2 334[14]	2 278[14]	2 468[14]	2 473[14]
Sweden Suède	216	178	205	173	193	...	207	219	214	235
Ukraine Ukraine	156	156	135	140	94	59	7	2	26	10
USSR - former † URSS (anc.) †	1 259	...	...	...	...	...	...	...	...	...
United Kingdom Royaume-Uni	1 302	1 340	1 291	1 504	1 654	1 735	1 707	1 818	1 709	...
United States[6] Etats-Unis[6]	6 081	5 441	5 684	5 956	* 6 614	...	...	...	...	...
Yugoslavia Yougoslavie	179	76	22	8	8	8	9	10	12	8
Yugoslavia, SFR† Yougoslavie, Rfs†	289	...	...	...	...	...	...	...	...	...

Source:
United Nations Statistics Division, New York, "Industrial Commodity Statistics Yearbook 1999" and the industrial statistics database.

† For information on recent changes in country or area nomenclature pertaining to former Czechoslovakia, Germany, Hong Kong Special Administrative Region (SAR) of China, Macao Special Administrative Region (SAR) of China, SFR of Yugoslavia and the former USSR, see Annex I - Country or area nomenclature, regional and other groupings.

†† For statistical purposes, the data for China do not include those for Hong Kong Special Administrative Region (Hong Kong SAR), Macao Special Administrative Region (Macao SAR) and Taiwan province of China.

1 Including assembly.
2 Excluding station wagons.
3 Excluding production for armed forces.
4 Sales.
5 Production by establishments employing 20 or more persons.
6 Factory sales.

Source:
Organisation des Nations Unies, Division de statistique, New York, "Annuaire de statistiques industrielles par produit 1999" et la base de données pour les statistiques industrielles.

† Pour les modifications récentes de nomenclature de pays ou de zone concernant l'Allemagne, Hong Kong, région administrative spéciale (RAS) de Chine, Macao, région administrative spéciale (RAS) de Chine, l'ex-Tchécoslovaquie, l'ex-URSS et l'ex-Rfs de Yougoslavie, voir annexe I - Nomenclature des pays ou des zones, groupements régionaux et autres groupements.

†† Les données statistiques relatives à la Chine ne comprennent pas celles qui concernent la région administrative spéciale de Hong Kong (la RAS de Hong Kong), la région administrative spéciale de Macao (la RAS de Macao) et la province chinoise de Taiwan.

1 Y compris le montage.
2 Non compris les stations-wagons.
3 Non compris la production destinée aux forces armées.
4 Ventes.
5 Production des établissements occupant 20 personnes ou plus.
6 Ventes des fabriques.

55
Refrigerators for household use
Réfrigérateurs à usage domestique
Production: thousands
Production : milliers

Country or area Pays ou zone	1990	1991	1992	1993	1994	1995	1996	1997	1998	1999
Algeria Algérie	387	388	317	183	119	131	137	175	215	181
Angola Angola	1	2	2	...	...	...	...	...	...	...
Antigua and Barbuda[1] Antigua-et-Barbuda[1]	...	...	...	3	3	...	...	...	...	...
Argentina Argentine	265	439	554	688	494	49	45	401	424	354
Australia Australie	329	389	363	421	444	423	403	398	441	427
Azerbaijan Azerbaïdjan	330	313	223	228	97	25	7	0	3	1
Belarus Bélarus	728	743	740	738	742	746	754	795	802	802
Brazil Brésil	2 441	2 445	1 704	2 098	2 721	3 242	3 776	3 592	3 034	2 796
Bulgaria Bulgarie	82	65	106	81	69	49	36	21	58	47
Chile Chili	89	86	136	192	221	272	213	268	229	242
China †† Chine ††	4 631	4 699	4 858	5 967	7 681	9 185	9 797	10 444	10 600	12 100
Colombia Colombie	...	...	306	396	465	465	...	...	...	...
Denmark[2] Danemark[2]	278	269	294	261	808	1 502	1 276	1 523	1 589	1 560
Ecuador Equateur	...	...	66	72	111	156	17	133	88	...
Egypt Egypte	246	260	232	204	236	236	250	...	...	...
Finland Finlande	166	150	144	128	134	104	68	102	107	...
France France	596	556	566	487	554	...	...	...	...	...
Germany † Allemagne †	...	4 226	4 298	3 838	3 794	...	2 747	...	...	...
F. R. Germany R. f. Allemagne	4 037	...	...	...	...	...	...	...	...	...
German D. R.(former) R. d. allemande (anc.)	1 005	...	...	...	...	...	...	...	...	...
Greece Grèce	119	85	80	...	...	...	...	...	...	...
Guyana Guyana	6	8	6	5	5	...	...	...	...	...
Hungary Hongrie	438	443	483	520	603	714	736	835	708	849
India Inde	1 220	1 133	997	1 382	1 668	1 913	1 705	1 600	1 902	2 012

55
Refrigerators for household use
Production: thousands [*cont.*]
Réfrigérateurs à usage domestique
Production : milliers [*suite*]

Country or area Pays ou zone	1990	1991	1992	1993	1994	1995	1996	1997	1998	1999
Indonesia Indonésie	196	194	...	172	469	291	...	573	417	...
Iran (Islamic Rep. of) Iran (Rép. islamique d')	649[3]	829[3]	896[3]	789[3]	629[3]	575[4]	756[4]	702[4]	1 104[4]	...
Iraq Iraq	...	...	35	...	...	...	...	...	...	...
Italy Italie	4 199	4 484	4 285	4 753	5 033	5 908	5 402	5 562	6 280	6 582
Japan Japon	5 048	5 212	4 425	4 351	4 952	5 013	5 163	5 369	4 851	4 543
Kazakhstan Kazakhstan	...	...	...	13	...	...	...	...	...	...
Kenya Kenya	21	...	...	...	...	...	...	...	...	...
Korea, Republic of Corée, République de	2 827	3 228	3 296	3 585	3 943	3 975	4 292	4 257	3 790	...
Kyrgyzstan Kirghizistan	...	0	1	0	3	1	0	0	...	...
Lithuania Lituanie	263	254	137	207	183	187	138	172	154	153
Malaysia Malaisie	212	266	288	250	266	295	257	249	206	194
Mexico Mexique	396	487	541	1 065	1 356	1 256	1 447	1 942	1 986	2 083
Mozambique Mozambique	1	...	...	...	...	...	...	...	...	...
Myanmar[5] Myanmar[5]	0	0	...	...	...	...	...	...	...	...
Nigeria Nigéria	...	77	52	53	20	19	...	...	...	...
Peru Pérou	46	70	54	57	86	161	81	101	118	42
Poland Pologne	604	553	500	588	605	585	584	705	714	726
Portugal Portugal	464	529	251	224	244	...	173	211	257	300
Republic of Moldova République de Moldova	133	118	55	58[6]	53[6]	24[6]	1[6]	2[6]	0[6]	...
Romania[7] Roumanie[7]	393	389	402	435	383	435	446	429	366	323
Russian Federation Fédération de Russie	3 615	3 566	2 972	3 049	2 283	1 531	966	1 108	956	1 041
Slovakia Slovaquie	449	515	552	482	371	330	393	258	228	206
Slovenia Slovénie	844	720	661	665	797	863	592	692	756	780
South Africa[8] Afrique du Sud[8]	352	356	318	318	321	365	411	388	399	440
Spain Espagne	1 285	1 410	1 322	1 240	1 461	1 269	1 260	1 960	2 415	2 107

55
Refrigerators for household use
Production: thousands [cont.]

Réfrigérateurs à usage domestique
Production : milliers [suite]

Country or area Pays ou zone	1990	1991	1992	1993	1994	1995	1996	1997	1998	1999
Sweden Suède	584	562	562	549	582	610	478	523	545	604
Syrian Arab Republic Rép. arabe syrienne	40	85	129	150	148	156	155	138	137	...
Tajikistan Tadjikistan	167	145	61	18	3	0	1	2	1	2
Thailand[9] Thaïlande[9]	855	789	...	...	...	...	2 246	2 384	1 631	...
TFYR of Macedonia L'ex-R.y. Macédoine	156	136	139	98	95	51	20	12	7	...
Trinidad and Tobago Trinité-et-Tobago	14	13	10	3	3	1	0	...	...	...
Tunisia Tunisie	64	82	123	141	129	...	...	...	...	...
Turkey Turquie	986	1 019	1 040	1 254	1 258	1 680	1 612	1 945	1 993	2 079
Ukraine Ukraine	903	883	838	757	653	562	431	382	390	409
USSR - former †[7] URSS (anc.) †[7]	6 499	...	...	...	...	...	...	...	...	...
United Kingdom Royaume-Uni	1 312	...	...	1 033	1 094	1 256	1 225	1 249	1 096	...
United States[10][11] Etats-Unis[10][11]	7 015	7 599	9 676	10 306	11 276	11 005	11 132	12 092	11 279	11 716
Uzbekistan Ouzbékistan	201	212	85	82	20	19	13	13	...	...
Yugoslavia Yougoslavie	215	109	85	39	41	50	51	81	48	5

Source:
United Nations Statistics Division, New York, "Industrial
Commodity Statistics Yearbook 1999" and the industrial
statistics database.

† For information on recent changes in country or
area nomenclature pertaining to former Czechoslovakia,
Germany, Hong Kong Special Administrative Region (SAR) of
China, Macao Special Administrative Region (SAR) of China,
SFR of Yugoslavia and the former USSR, see Annex I - Country
or area nomenclature, regional and other groupings.

†† For statistical purposes, the data for
China do not include those for Hong Kong Special
Administrative Region (Hong Kong SAR), Macao Special
Administrative Region (Macao SAR) and Taiwan province of
China.

Source:
Organisation des Nations Unies, Division de statistique, New
York, "Annuaire de statistiques industrielles par produit
1999" et la base de données pour les statistiques
industrielles.

† Pour les modifications récentes de nomenclature
de pays ou de zone concernant l'Allemagne, Hong Kong, région
administrative spéciale (RAS) de Chine, Macao, région
administrative spéciale (RAS) de Chine,
l'ex-Tchécoslovaquie, l'ex-URSS et l'ex-Rfs de Yougoslavie,
voir annexe I - Nomenclature des pays ou des zones,
groupements régionaux et autres groupements.

†† Les données statistiques relatives à
la Chine ne comprennent pas celles qui concernent la région
administrative spéciale de Hong Kong (la RAS de Hong Kong),
la région administrative spéciale de Macao (la RAS de Macao)
et la province chinoise de Taiwan.

55
Refrigerators for household use
Production: thousands [*cont.*]

Réfrigérateurs à usage domestique
Production : milliers [*suite*]

1 Twelve months beginning 21 March of year stated.	1 Période de douze mois commençant le 21 mars de l'année indiquée.
2 Sales.	2 Ventes.
3 Production by establishments employing 50 or more persons.	3 Production des établissements occupant 50 personnes ou plus.
4 Production by establishments employing 10 or more persons.	4 Production des établissements occupant 10 personnes ou plus.
5 Government production only.	5 Production de l'Etat seulement.
6 Excluding Transnistria region.	6 Non compris la région de Transnistria.
7 Including freezers.	7 Y compris les congélateurs.
8 Including deep freezers and deep freeze-refrigerator combinations.	8 Y compris congélateurs-conservateurs et congélateurs combinés avec un réfrigérateur.
9 Beginning 1999, series discontinued.	9 A partir de 1999, les séries ont été discontinuées.
10 Electric domestic refrigerators only.	10 Réfrigérateurs électriques de ménage seulement.
11 Shipments.	11 Expéditions.

56

Washing machines for household use
Machines à laver à usage domestique

Production: thousands
Production : en milliers

Country or area Pays or zone	1990	1991	1992	1993	1994	1995	1996	1997	1998	1999
Argentina Argentine	...	436	756	801	702	458	524	603	...	...
Armenia Arménie	110	74	9	0	0	1	0	...		
Australia Australie	343	295	295	328	314	310	266	268	321	354
Austria Autriche	77	...	...	...	...	...	...	...	...	
Belarus Bélarus	33	57	62	71	77	37	61	88	91	92
Belgium[12] Belgique[12]	60	99	138	49			...		...	...
Brazil Brésil	552	948	849	1 167	1 461	1 681	2 160	2 095	1 851	1 940
Bulgaria Bulgarie	90	74	69	42	41	26	24	5	...	...
Chile Chili	177	203	301	386	447	434	310	...	...	...
China †† Chine ††	6 627	6 872	7 079	8 959	10 941	9 484	10 747	12 545	12 073	13 422
Colombia Colombie	...	...	41	41	50	45	...	...	...	...
Croatia Croatie	3	1	1	0	0	0	0	0		
Czechoslovakia-former† Tchécoslovaquie (anc.) †	451	376	...	...	...	...	...	...	...	
Czech Republic République tchèque	249	...	...	...	...	...	...	...	...	...
Denmark[3] Danemark[3]	...	...	...	...	0	0	0	0	0	0
Ecuador Equateur	...	...	...	...	...	11	12	...	...	...
Egypt Egypte	179	202	198	200	209	198	200	201	...	...
France[2] France[2]	1 637	1 645	1 713	1 943	2 244	2 200	1 868	1 933	1 941	2 229
Germany † Allemagne † German D. R.(former) R. d. allemande (anc.)	... 556	...	...	...	...	2 703	2 816	3 035	3 370	
Greece Grèce	...	...	...	31	20	15	10	...	...	...
Hungary Hongrie	315	220	219	...	...	...	...	...	...	
Indonesia Indonésie	17	19	27	32	44	13	...	86	33	
Iran (Islamic Rep. of) Iran (Rép. islamique d')	19 [4]	43 [4]	63 [4]	59 [4]	79 [4]	98 [5]	159 [5]	194 [5]	190 [5]	...
Israel[6] Israël[6]	13	...	...	...	...	...	...	...	...	...

56
Washing machines for household use
Production: thousands [*cont.*]

Machines à laver à usage domestique
Production : en milliers [*suite*]

Country or area Pays or zone	1990	1991	1992	1993	1994	1995	1996	1997	1998	1999
Italy Italie	4 372	5 044	5 140	5 693	6 251	6 996	7 135	7 967	8 119	7 367
Japan Japon	5 576	5 587	5 225	5 163	5 042	4 876	5 006	4 818	4 468	4 287
Kazakhstan Kazakhstan	...	391	370	255	88	46	23	11	3	2
Korea, Republic of Corée, République de	2 163	2 157	1 896	2 199	2 443	2 827	2 878	2 967	2 643	...
Kyrgyzstan Kirghizistan	234	209	94	77	17	4	3	2	0	...
Latvia Lettonie	570	427	18	18	10	8	3	3	2	2
Mexico Mexique	558	611	646	1 085	1 185	882	1 091	1 448	1 512	1 593
Peru Pérou	9	6	5	3	5	6	3	1	0	0
Poland Pologne	482	336	363	402	449	419	445	412	416	448
Portugal Portugal	34	7	...	...	...	...	...	...	...	...
Republic of Moldova République de Moldova	298	194	102	123[7]	81[7]	49[7]	54[7]	46[7]	43[7]	18[7]
Romania Roumanie	205	188	159	161	109	125	138	82	36	28
Russian Federation Fédération de Russie	5 419	5 541	4 289	3 901	2 122	1 294	762	800	862	999
Slovakia Slovaquie	202	144	122	100	...	...	...	...	...	...
Slovenia Slovénie	315	318	188	189	200	220	291	405	474	447
South Africa Afrique du Sud	109	87	44	52	55	57	55	44	44	45
Spain Espagne	1 425	1 522	1 540	1 334	1 632	1 655	1 945	2 270	2 281	...
Sweden Suède	107	103	91	94	113	106	103	120	119	122
Syrian Arab Republic Rép. arabe syrienne	44	29	41	47	50	78	80	72	68	...
Thailand[8] Thaïlande[8]	...	...	...	...	...	...	541	794	800	...
Turkey Turquie	743	837	802	980	780	873	1 015	1 485	1 408	1 249
Ukraine Ukraine	788	830	805	643	422	213	149	147	138	127
USSR - former † URSS (anc.) †	7 818	...	...	...	...	...	...	...	...	...
United States[2] Etats-Unis[2]	6 428	6 404	6 566	6 739	7 081	6 605	6 873	6 942	7 504	7 991
Uzbekistan Ouzbékistan	...	13	9	10	9	14	4	4	...	...

56
Washing machines for household use
Production: thousands [cont.]
Machines à laver à usage domestique
Production : en milliers [suite]

Country or area Pays ou zone	1990	1991	1992	1993	1994	1995	1996	1997	1998	1999
Yugoslavia Yougoslavie	...	94	68	39	63	36	33	33	30	12

Source:
United Nations Statistics Division, New York, "Industrial
Commodity Statistics Yearbook 1999" and the industrial
statistics database.

† For information on recent changes in country or
area nomenclature pertaining to former Czechoslovakia,
Germany, Hong Kong Special Administrative Region (SAR) of
China, Macao Special Administrative Region (SAR) of China,
SFR of Yugoslavia and the former USSR, see Annex I - Country
or area nomenclature, regional and other groupings.

†† For statistical purposes, the data for
China do not include those for Hong Kong Special
Administrative Region (Hong Kong SAR), Macao Special
Administrative Region (Macao SAR) and Taiwan province of
China.

1 Production by establishments employing 5 or more persons.
2 Shipments.
3 Sales.
4 Production by establishments employing 50 or more persons.
5 Production by establishments employing 10 or more persons.
6 Marketed local production.
7 Excluding Transnistria region.
8 Beginning 1999, series discontinued.

Source:
Organisation des Nations Unies, Division de statistique, New
York, "Annuaire de statistiques industrielles par produit
1999" et la base de données pour les statistiques
industrielles.

† Pour les modifications récentes de nomenclature
de pays ou de zone concernant l'Allemagne, Hong Kong, région
administrative spéciale (RAS) de Chine, Macao, région
administrative spéciale (RAS) de Chine,
l'ex-Tchécoslovaquie, l'ex-URSS et l'ex-Rfs de Yougoslavie,
voir annexe I - Nomenclature des pays ou des zones,
groupements régionaux et autres groupements.

†† Les données statistiques relatives à
la Chine ne comprennent pas celles qui concernent la région
administrative spéciale de Hong Kong (la RAS de Hong Kong),
la région administrative spéciale de Macao (la RAS de Macao)
et la province chinoise de Taiwan.

1 Production des établissements occupant 5 personnes ou plus.
2 Expéditions.
3 Ventes.
4 Production des établissements occupant 50 personnes ou plus.
5 Production des établissements occupant 10 personnes ou plus.
6 Production locale commercialisée.
7 Non compris la région de Transnistria.
8 A partir de 1999, les séries ont été discontinuées.

57
Machine tools
Machines-outils

Production: number
Production : nombre

Country or area Pays ou zone	1990	1991	1992	1993	1994	1995	1996	1997	1998	1999

A. Drilling and boring machines · Perceuses

Country or area Pays ou zone	1990	1991	1992	1993	1994	1995	1996	1997	1998	1999
Algeria Algérie	412	210	122	30	...	...	...	...	...	...
Azerbaijan Azerbaïdjan	594	643	428	86	102	112	49	24	29	1
Bangladesh Bangladesh	131	...	...	...	...	...	...	...		...
Bulgaria Bulgarie	4 729	1 959	996	759	850	864	953	906	955	906
Croatia Croatie	619	458	346	255	...	4 369	3 212	1 134	31	...
Czech Republic République tchèque	897	1 131	...	...	...	...	1 235	1 263	1 352	986
Denmark [1] Danemark [1]	348	394	223	197	...	...	...	...	...	...
Finland Finlande	59	42	54	78	88	106	109	...	67	13
France [2] France [2]	2 500	1 460	1 212	...	...	...	...	...	...	...
Germany † Allemagne †	...	...	15 085	21 222	15 955	13 049	11 730	...	11 396	
F. R. Germany R. f. Allemagne	14 158	...	...	...	...	...	...	...		...
Hungary Hongrie	1 929	1 257	75	78	15	4	...	...	...	...
Indonesia Indonésie	89	437	1 000	52	...	12 155	...	...	5 153	...
Japan Japon	40 171	33 929	22 973	14 496	11 936	14 678	16 414	17 097	12 531	9 377
Korea, Republic of [3] Corée, République de [3]	7 662	8 150	7 336	7 416	11 107	10 861	8 025	8 741	1 491	2 805
Lithuania Lituanie	...	...	...	...	...	749	437	333	192	171
Mexico Mexique	2 138	2 187	855	487	...	...	...	...	...	...
Poland Pologne	2 238	2 995	1 858	1 348	998	771	840	1 253	917	624
Portugal Portugal	...	...	75	52		...	...	...	...	...
Russian Federation Fédération de Russie	16 192	16 020	12 835	10 607	5 291	5 021	3 088	2 522	1 877	1 898
Slovakia Slovaquie	4	10	...	0	...	...	...	...	...	...
Slovenia Slovénie	137	114	60	0	...	...	...	4	0	...
Spain Espagne	3 688	2 567	2 060	886	1 738	2 313	2 185	2 689	3 317	4 732
Sweden Suède	...	...	...	...	...	...	...	3 158	3 661	2 996

57
Machine tools
Production: number [*cont.*]
Machines-outils
Production : nombre [*suite*]

Country or area Pays ou zone	1990	1991	1992	1993	1994	1995	1996	1997	1998	1999
Turkey Turquie	8	57	239	41	185	12	37	50	0	0
Ukraine Ukraine	4 482	7 970	11 113	12 996	3 745	1 337	563	667	418	306
United Kingdom Royaume-Uni	...	...	...	901	1 061	...	...	...	...	...
United States[1] Etats-Unis[1]	8 828	7 603	7 542	7 182	...	10 465	7 927	6 234	5 812	5 096
Yugoslavia Yougoslavie	...	924	607	276	206	328	100	106	133	111

B. Lathes • Tours

Country or area Pays ou zone	1990	1991	1992	1993	1994	1995	1996	1997	1998	1999
Algeria Algérie	270	273	310	194	118	196	189	110	14	171
Armenia Arménie	2 735	2 633	1 079	486	395	190	141	81	71	33
Austria[4] Autriche[4]	1 726	1 647	1 421	915	709	1 482	1 452	801	1 914	...
Bangladesh[5] Bangladesh[5]	4	13	3	1	1	...	...	...	...	...
Belarus Bélarus	...	...	162	332	57	70	93	117	131	96
Bulgaria Bulgarie	5 014	4 744	3 587	2 197	1 979	2 496	2 513	2 315	1 761	1 611
Colombia Colombie	...	...	97	103	155	112	...	...	...	...
Croatia Croatie	605	584	463	358	...	52	68	98	144	...
Czech Republic République tchèque	1 736	1 405	1 017	709	685	735	943	932	994	989
Denmark[1] Danemark[1]	545	384	279	374	...	...	...	...	...	...
Finland Finlande	4	1	1	1	2	3	2	...	...	...
France[6] France[6]	1 400	988	942	11	546	...	...	...	...	...
Georgia Géorgie	...	...	1 001	348	109	57	18	28	21	2
Germany † Allemagne †	...	...	7 689	4 755	5 322	8 232	6 375	5 542	6 070	...
F. R. Germany R. f. Allemagne	7 612	...	...	...	...	...	...	...	...	...
Hungary Hongrie	663	304	63	135	33	7	...	...	...	...
Indonesia Indonésie	2	45	42	46	96	166	...	23	4	...
Japan Japon	32 659	26 216	16 155	12 343	14 961	20 339	21 443	23 357	22 652	16 924
Korea, Republic of Corée, République de	10 597	11 324	6 643	6 931	10 265	12 526	11 094	8 357	4 809	6 542

57
Machine tools
Production: number [*cont*]
   Machines-outils
   Production : nombre [*suite*]

Country or area Pays ou zone	1990	1991	1992	1993	1994	1995	1996	1997	1998	1999
Latvia Lettonie	...	...	...	28	87	36	26	20	29	...
Lithuania Lituanie	81	95	110	93	27	64	4	1	6	6
Poland Pologne	5 178	2 184	1 105	910	900	1 012	1 037	900	963	732
Portugal Portugal	101	87	...	...	...	...	...	...	...	...
Romania Roumanie	3 702	2 883	1 583	489	312	471	587	681	573	330
Russian Federation Fédération de Russie	14 747	9 850	7 079	6 506	3 807	3 269	2 095	2 135	1 798	1 681
Slovakia Slovaquie	4 326	4 417	...	1 637	1 566	1 549	3 121	3 084	1 660	1 786
Spain Espagne	1 353	1 265	925	1 237	1 713	2 475	2 887	3 080	3 509	3 559
Sweden Suède	...	...	...	...	...	...	259	40	22	23
Turkey Turquie	43	23	2	10	59	12	16	0	0	0
Ukraine Ukraine	3 283	3 300	2 420	1 619	867	808	338	352	234	213
United Kingdom Royaume-Uni	5 742	...	...	2 429	2 941	3 568	3 845	3 077	3 377	...
United States[6] Etats-Unis[6]	3 247	2 658	2 409	3 042	3 662	4 643	4 190	5 058	5 089	3 807
Yugoslavia Yougoslavie	...	514	338	67	135	206	110	256	213	231

C. Milling machines • Fraiseuses

Country or area Pays ou zone	1990	1991	1992	1993	1994	1995	1996	1997	1998	1999
Algeria Algérie	267	150	103	81	124	119	124	75	80	72
Armenia Arménie	951	759	410	0	63	73	47	188	82	27
Austria[4] Autriche[4]	458	526	844	223	209	625	362	284	279	...
Bangladesh Bangladesh	144	...	...	...	...	...	...	...	...	...
Belarus Bélarus	143	150	56	13	0	1	3	5	3	2
Bulgaria Bulgarie	1 240	961	432	324	200	227	295	412	104	139
Croatia Croatie	623	212	168	192	...	77	90	165	224	...
Czech Republic République tchèque	1 470	1 706	1 358	...	...	...	1 109	1 039	1 117	821
Denmark[1] Danemark[1]	...	201	200	0	0	0	...	...	...	...
France[6] France[6]	700	496	401	7	394	...	...	...	...	...

57
Machine tools
Production: number [*cont.*]
Machines-outils
Production : nombre [*suite*]

Country or area Pays ou zone	1990	1991	1992	1993	1994	1995	1996	1997	1998	1999
Germany † Allemagne † F. R. Germany	...	...	...	6 680	6 327	...	5 213	5 335	5 348	...
R. f. Allemagne German D. R.(former)	12 150	...	...	...	...	...	...	...	...	...
R. d. allemande (anc.)	3 051	...	...	...	...	...	...	...	...	...
Greece Grèce	1 805	1 452	...	...	...	...	...	...	4	...
Hungary Hongrie	136	297	256	50	3	...	...	...	...	...
Indonesia Indonésie	21	...	...	50	...	...	...	...	...	...
Japan Japon	8 492	7 584	3 913	2 007	1 791	1 832	2 198	2 368	2 019	1 022
Korea, Republic of Corée, République de	3 775	3 994	2 509	2 824	4 667	5 293	3 952	2 900	825	2 242
Latvia Lettonie	...	...	...	12	44	44	9	26	78	...
Lithuania Lituanie	1 538	1 303	1 035	450	341	255	213	161	130	58
Poland Pologne	1 196	834	500	248	260	274	281	354	257	222
Romania Roumanie	1 196	1 355	764	436	162	341	458	403	321	333
Russian Federation Fédération de Russie	4 555	4 233	4 144	3 424	1 560	897	622	591	641	724
Slovenia Slovénie	...	13	12	15	26	27	...	...	...	...
Spain Espagne	7 062	4 169	4 553	788	1 458	1 600	1 852	1 605	2 986	3 075
Sweden Suède	98	...	48	22	27	25	...	...	...	...
Turkey Turquie	169	86	39	85	107	84	169	75	1	0
Ukraine Ukraine	1 341	1 208	1 040	752	195	90	48	161	168	45
United Kingdom Royaume-Uni	...	...	...	824	856	493	268	240	245	...
United States[6] Etats-Unis[6]	4 787	2 772	2 581	3 386	4 087	4 747	4 102	4 240	3 416	2 749
Yugoslavia Yougoslavie	...	15	...	...	...	...	...	...	...	3

D. Metal-working presses • Presses pour le travail des métaux

Armenia Arménie	292	206	45	100	29	43	34	31	18	11
Brazil Brésil	1 182	1 853	1 194	1 763	1 836	1 858	1 657	1 678	1 531	1 102
Colombia Colombie	...	...	16 992	13 366	22 661	26 344	...	...	...	...

57
Machine tools
Production: number [*cont.*]
Machines-outils
Production : nombre [*suite*]

Country or area Pays ou zone	1990	1991	1992	1993	1994	1995	1996	1997	1998	1999
Czech Republic République tchèque	113	82	106	47	60	114	231	239	...	...
Finland Finlande	126	98	17	6	180	1 764	2 159	2 101	2 285	2 315
France[6] France[6]	1 300	1 235	1 385	970	605	...	...	...	...	...
Germany † Allemagne †	...	17 726	55 997	18 939	23 284	16 399	...	21 531	...	...
F. R. Germany R. f. Allemagne	16 643	...	...	...	...	...	...	...	...	...
German D. R.(former) R. d. allemande (anc.)	1 781	...	...	...	...	...	...	...	...	...
Greece Grèce	328	320	355	...	...	...	...	...	...	...
Japan Japon	22 571	19 173	12 458	9 516	9 531	10 512	10 068	11 575	8 546	7 285
Latvia Lettonie	15	3	...	...	...	...	...	...	...	...
Poland Pologne	50	44	13	11	8	2	2	15	...	...
Portugal Portugal	255	102	742	670	649	...	...	...	...	...
Slovakia Slovaquie	1 311	829	261	184	301	282	199	73	276	195
Slovenia Slovénie	1 334	119	92	145	153	215	719	...	...	...
Spain Espagne	1 600	2 152	1 687	2 436	723	5 452	...	...	...	...
Ukraine Ukraine	575	666	268	277	117	146	35	42	38	29
United Kingdom Royaume-Uni	...	...	...	667	615	...	...	827	...	...
United States[6] Etats-Unis[6]	7 285	5 912	5 822	6 236	10 947	5 045	11 023	12 084	12 559	12 301
Yugoslavia Yougoslavie	...	979	1 046	167	54	114	53	47	66	29

Source:
United Nations Statistics Division, New York, "Industrial Commodity Statistics Yearbook 1999" and the industrial statistics database.

† For information on recent changes in country or area nomenclature pertaining to former Czechoslovakia, Germany, Hong Kong Special Administrative Region (SAR) of China, Macao Special Administrative Region (SAR) of China, SFR of Yugoslavia and the former USSR, see Annex I - Country or area nomenclature, regional and other groupings.

Source:
Organisation des Nations Unies, Division de statistique, New York, "Annuaire de statistiques industrielles par produit 1999" et la base de données pour les statistiques industrielles.

† Pour les modifications récentes de nomenclature de pays ou de zone concernant l'Allemagne, Hong Kong, région administrative spéciale (RAS) de Chine, Macao, région administrative spéciale (RAS) de Chine, l'ex-Tchécoslovaquie, l'ex-URSS et l'ex-Rfs de Yougoslavie, voir annexe I - Nomenclature des pays ou des zones, groupements régionaux et autres groupements.

57
Machine tools
Production: number [*cont.*]

Machines-outils
Production : nombre [*suite*]

1 Sales.
2 Limited coverage.
3 Drilling machines only.
4 1999 data are confidential.
5 Twelve months ending 30 June of year stated.

6 Shipments.

1 Ventes.
2 Couverture limitée.
3 Perceuses seulement.
4 1999, les données sont confidentielles.
5 Période de douze mois finissant le 30 juin de l'année indiquée.
6 Expéditions.

58
Lorries (trucks)
Camions

Production: number
Production : nombre

Country or area Pays ou zone	1990	1991	1992	1993	1994	1995	1996	1997	1998	1999
A. Assembled • Assemblés										
Algeria Algérie	3 564	3 164	2 434	2 304	1 230	2 570	2 136	1 293	1 798	1 583
Bangladesh Bangladesh	504	1 090	715	452	642	1 047	922	1 000	...	...
Belgium [1 2] Belgique [1 2]	65 667	88 937	70 532	56 244	...	...	...	...	...	...
Chile [3] Chili [3]	8 028	9 400	14 352	16 584	15 960	...	...	...	...	...
Colombia Colombie	12 660 [3]	8 900 [3]	10 116 [3]	13 992 [3]	15 660 [3]	...	...	736	903	...
Greece Grèce	1 715	1 534	1 920	62		57	128	...	219	...
Iran (Islamic Rep. of) Iran (Rép. islamique d')	22 198 [4]	32 672 [4]	34 842 [4]	21 234 [4]	15 785 [4]	8 836 [5]	19 777 [5]	16 761 [5]	38 141 [5]	...
Israel Israël	1 074	864	852	836	1 260	1 217	1 199	...	...	...
Kenya Kenya	1 701	1 296	315	310	428	1 103	1 430	...	...	...
Malaysia [6] Malaisie [6]	73 733	78 926	34 711	34 711	42 618	55 961	78 571	94 977	19 693	44 951
Morocco [3] Maroc [3]	10 784	12 775	11 976	9 734	...	...	...	...	...	...
Myanmar [7] Myanmar [7]	166	117	85	172	846	500	550	255	31	102
New Zealand * [6] Nouvelle-Zélande * [6]	13 500	13 500	10 210	...	...	...	...	...	...	...
Nigeria Nigéria	...	4 378	2 683	1 097	696	715	...	...	...	...
Pakistan [8] Pakistan [8]	13 324	13 911	13 270	13 700	6 522	5 857	9 864	12 733	11 736	9 210
Peru [3] Pérou [3]	2 921	2 000	600	768	...	...	...	...	...	...
Slovakia Slovaquie	...	...	...	...	...	...	1 421	709	312	72
Slovenia Slovénie	451	611	...	1	...	...	...	...	...	...
South Africa Afrique du Sud	107 922	97 178	93 599	96 772	118 221	147 792	132 383	132 338	117 092	113 483
Thailand [3] Thaïlande [3]	236 221	206 172	223 680	323 508	324 780	...	...	...	...	...
Trinidad and Tobago [3] Trinité-et-Tobago [3]	1 124	1 711	1 698	1 083	621	0	0	...	...	...
Tunisia Tunisie	1 024	1 065	768	922	1 084	616	954	1 003	1 016	770
Turkey Turquie	27 014	29 967	37 195	49 827	21 591	35 930	50 471	73 946	67 985	44 457
United Rep. of Tanzania [9] Rép.-Unie de Tanzanie [9]	637	479	171	40	115	0	0	0	...	...

58
Lorries (trucks)
Production: number [cont.]
Camions
Production : nombre [suite]

Country or area Pays ou zone	1990	1991	1992	1993	1994	1995	1996	1997	1998	1999
Venezuela Venezuela	12 000	24 000	30 000	...	...	...	...	...	...	...
Yugoslavia Yougoslavie	...	0	0	0		0		...	0	0
Yugoslavia, SFR† Yougoslavie, Rfs†	451	...	...	...	...	...	...	...	...	...

B. Produced • Fabriqués

Country or area Pays ou zone	1990	1991	1992	1993	1994	1995	1996	1997	1998	1999
Argentina[10] Argentine[10]	16 869	22 388	36 999	50 805	64 022	...	...	...	...	
Armenia Arménie	9 410	6 823	3 171	1 247	446	232	114	27	51	2
Australia[8 11] Australie[8 11]	25 958	17 666	14 550	15 459	...	...	...	...	...	
Austria Autriche	736[12]	5 168[12]	4 089[12]	3 565[12]	3 098[12]	2 903	...	...	...	
Azerbaijan Azerbaïdjan	3 104	3 246	402	93	8	2	1	0	0	0
Belarus Bélarus	42 034	38 178	32 951	30 771	21 264	12 902	10 671	13 002	12 799	13 370
Brazil[13] Brésil[13]	51 597	49 295	32 025	47 876	64 137	70 495	48 712	63 744	63 773	55 277
Bulgaria Bulgarie	7 285[10]	2 778[10]	945[10]	406[10]	321	259	66	43	...	...
Canada[14] Canada[14]	789 932	789 600	901 000	838 000	...	...	...	...	...	
China †† Chine ††	289 700	382 500	476 700	597 897	662 600	595 997	625 100	573 600	...	...
Croatia Croatie	...	...	4	7	...	5	8	10	96	...
Czech Republic République tchèque	36 322	20 419	14 030	33 873	30 103	22 052	27 036	39 537	39 098	23 113
Egypt Egypte	1 371	1 127	1 529	1 208	1 379	1 241	738	328	...	...
Finland[10] Finlande[10]	910	545	578	435	546	540	492	493	687	721
France France	539 796	461 640	494 124	373 200	453 344	...	...	...	...	...
Georgia Géorgie	...	...	650	384	137	209	95	82	39	38
Germany † Allemagne †	...	356 059	325 901	240 014	259 575	...	240 604[10]	272 916[10]	292 581[10]	
F. R. Germany R. f. Allemagne	315 010	...	...	...	...	...	...	...	...	
German D. R.(former) R. d. allemande (anc.)	31 360	...	...	...	...	...	...	...	...	...
Hungary[3] Hongrie[3]	840	480	360	...	...	...	...	...	...	...
India[3 14] Inde[3 14]	145 200	146 400	141 600	148 800	163 200	...	...	...	...	...

58
Lorries (trucks)
Production: number [*cont.*]
Camions
Production : nombre [*suite*]

Country or area Pays ou zone	1990	1991	1992	1993	1994	1995	1996	1997	1998	1999
Indonesia Indonésie	1 280	26	174	...	2 890	4 755	...	575	465 464	...
Italy Italie	234 393	229 860	194 616	155 476	191 288	234 354	188 852	256 062	278 322	288 038
Japan Japon	3 486 618	3 433 790	3 053 477	2 674 941	2 689 340	2 519 319	2 417 370	2 410 124	1 930 965	1 742 111
Korea, Republic of[10] Corée, République de[10]	237 384	245 232	293 260	310 639	332 263	331 328	340 179	297 565	182 218	264 212
Kyrgyzstan Kirghizistan	24 270	23 621	14 818	5 026	206	8	1	12	...	...
Mexico Mexique	199 123[10]	238 804[10]	269 591[10]	222 807	217 359	210 072	396 377	468 931	445 125	451 880
Netherlands[15 16] Pays-Bas[15 16]	11 305	10 316	10 034	9 538	13 938	15 818	...	...	...	...
Poland[17] Pologne[17]	38 956	20 100	17 657	18 811	21 356	30 662	44 159	57 254	56 080	62 719
Romania Roumanie	8 457	7 592	4 456	4 433	3 044	3 098	3 142	1 956	1 263	900
Russian Federation Fédération de Russie	665 201	615 868	582 963	466 925	185 018	142 483	134 130	145 850	141 484	174 625
Slovakia Slovaquie	...	...	...	744	369	663	1 421	709	312	72
Slovenia Slovénie	1 721	1 513	377	424	397	277	195	...	...	16
Spain Espagne	302 400[14]	244 164	256 070	17 923[10 16]	32 217[10 16]	50 255[10 16]	73 319[10 16]	280 708[10 16]	343 699[10 16]	366 702[10 16]
Sweden Suède	74 400[14]	75 000[14]	...	...	...	...	...	51 378	30 582	30 399
Ukraine Ukraine	27 680	25 096	33 386	23 052	11 741	6 492	4 164	3 386	4 768	7 769
United Kingdom Royaume-Uni	258 026	207 304	239 936	320 456	372 633	247 022	188 215	189 464	185 152	...
United States Etats-Unis	3 720 000	3 372 000	4 118 578	...	...	...	...	...	...	...
Yugoslavia Yougoslavie	8 421	8 601	4 169	287	685	708	824	1 278	1 139	407
Yugoslavia, SFR† Yougoslavie, Rfs†	9 989	...	...	...	...	...	...	...	...	...

Source:
United Nations Statistics Division, New York, "Industrial Commodity Statistics Yearbook 1999" and the industrial statistics database.

Source:
Organisation des Nations Unies, Division de statistique, New York, "Annuaire de statistiques industrielles par produit 1999" et la base de données pour les statistiques industrielles.

58

Lorries (trucks)
Production: number [*cont.*]

Camions
Production : nombre [*suite*]

† For information on recent changes in country or
area nomenclature pertaining to former Czechoslovakia,
Germany, Hong Kong Special Administrative Region (SAR) of
China, Macao Special Administrative Region (SAR) of China,
SFR of Yugoslavia and the former USSR, see Annex I - Country
or area nomenclature, regional and other groupings.

†† For statistical purposes, the data for
China do not include those for Hong Kong Special
Administrative Region (Hong Kong SAR), Macao Special
Administrative Region (Macao SAR) and Taiwan province of
China.

1 Production by establishments employing 5 or more persons.
2 Shipments.
3 Including motor coaches and buses.
4 Production by establishments employing 50 or more persons.
5 Production by establishments employing 10 or more persons.
6 Including vans and buses.
7 Government production only.
8 Twelve months ending 30 June of year stated.

9 Including buses.
10 Including assembly.
11 Finished and partly finished.
12 Beginning 1995, data are confidential.
13 Trucks only.
14 Excluding production for armed forces.
15 Beginning 1986, production by establishments employing 20 or
   more persons.
16 Sales.
17 Including special-purpose vehicles.

† Pour les modifications récentes de nomenclature
de pays ou de zone concernant l'Allemagne, Hong Kong, région
administrative spéciale (RAS) de Chine, Macao, région
administrative spéciale (RAS) de Chine,
l'ex-Tchécoslovaquie, l'ex-URSS et l'ex-Rfs de Yougoslavie,
voir annexe I - Nomenclature des pays ou des zones,
groupements régionaux et autres groupements.

†† Les données statistiques relatives à
la Chine ne comprennent pas celles qui concernent la région
administrative spéciale de Hong Kong (la RAS de Hong Kong),
la région administrative spéciale de Macao (la RAS de Macao)
et la province chinoise de Taiwan.

1 Production des établissements occupant 5 personnes ou plus.
2 Expéditions.
3 Y compris les autocars et autobus.
4 Production des établissements occupant 50 personnes ou plus.
5 Production des établissements occupant 10 personnes ou plus.
6 Y compris les autobus et les camionnettes.
7 Production de l'Etat seulement.
8 Période de douze mois finissant le 30 juin de l'année
   indiquée.
9 Y compris les autobus.
10 Y compris le montage.
11 Finis et semi-finis.
12 A partir de 1985, les données sont confidentielles.
13 Les camions seulement.
14 Non compris la production destinée aux forces armées.
15 A partir de 1986, production des établissements occupant 20
   prsonnes ou plus.
16 Ventes.
17 Y compris véhicules à usages spéciaux.

Technical notes, tables 41-58

Industrial activity includes mining and quarrying, manufacturing and the production of electricity, gas and water. These activities correspond to the major divisions 2, 3 and 4 respectively of the *International Standard Industrial Classification of All Economic Activities* [49].

Many of the tables are based primarily on data compiled for the United Nations *Industrial Commodity Statistics Yearbook* [24]. Data taken from alternate sources are footnoted.

The methods used by countries for the computation of industrial output are, as a rule, consistent with those described in the United Nations *International Recommendations for Industrial Statistics* [48] and provide a satisfactory basis for comparative analysis. In some cases, however, the definitions and procedures underlying computations of output differ from approved guidelines. The differences, where known, are indicated in the footnotes to each table.

A.   *Food, beverages and tobacco*

Table 41: The statistics on sugar were obtained from the database and the *Sugar Yearbook* [16] of the International Sugar Organization. The data shown cover the production and consumption of centrifugal sugar from both beet and cane, and refer to calendar years.

The consumption data relate to the apparent consumption of centrifugal sugar in the country concerned, including sugar used for the manufacture of sugar-containing products whether exported or not and sugar used for purposes other than human consumption as food. Unless otherwise specified, the statistics are expressed in terms of raw value (i.e. sugar polarizing at 96 degrees). However, where exact information is lacking, data are expressed in terms of sugar "tel quel" and are footnoted accordingly. The world and regional totals also include data for countries not shown separately whose sugar consumption was less than 10 thousand metric tons.

Table 42: The data refer to meat from animals slaughtered within the national boundaries irrespective of the origin of the animals. Production figures of beef, veal, buffalo meat, pork (including bacon and ham), mutton, lamb and goat meat are in terms of carcass weight, excluding edible offals, tallow and lard. All data refer to total meat production, i.e from both commercial and farm slaughter.

Table 43: The data refer to beer made from malt, including ale, stout, porter.

Table 44 presents data on cigarettes only.

Notes techniques, tableaux 41 à 58

L'activité industrielle comprend les industries extractives (mines et carrières), les industries manufacturières et la production d'électricité, de gaz et d'eau. Ces activités correspondent aux grandes divisions 2, 3 et 4, respectivement, de la *Classification internationale type par industrie de toutes les branches d'activité économique* [49].

Un grand nombre de ces tableaux sont établis principalement sur la base de données compilées pour l'*Annuaire de statistiques industrielles par produit* des Nations Unies [24]. Les données tirées des autres sources sont signalées par une note.

En règle générale, les méthodes employées par les pays pour le calcul de leur production industrielle sont conformes à celles dans *Recommandations internationales concernant les statistiques industrielles* des Nations Unies [48] et offrent une base satisfaisante pour une analyse comparative. Toutefois, dans certains cas, les définitions des méthodes sur lesquelles reposent les calculs de la production diffèrent des directives approuvées. Lorsqu'elles sont connues, les différences sont indiquées par une note.

A.   *Alimentation, boissons et tabac*

Tableau 41: Les données sur le sucre proviennent de la base de données et de l'*Annuaire du sucre* [16] de l'Organisation internationale du sucre. Les données présentées portent sur la production et la consommation de sucre centrifugé à partir de la betterave et de la canne à sucre, et se rapportent à des années civiles.

Les données de la consommation se rapportent à la consommation apparente de sucre centrifugé dans le pays en question, y compris le sucre utilisé pour la fabrication de produits à base de sucre, exportés ou non, et le sucre utilisé à d'autres fins que pour la consommation alimentaire humaine. Sauf indication contraire, les statistiques sont exprimés en valeur brute (sucre polarisant à 96°). Toutefois, en l'absence d'informations exactes, les données sont exprimées en sucre tel quel, accompagnées d'une note. Les totaux mondiaux et régionaux comprennent également les données relatives aux pays où la consommation de sucre est inférieure à 10.000 tonnes.

Le *tableau 42* indique la production de viande provenant des animaux abattus à l'intérieur des frontières nationales, quelle que soit leur origine. Les chiffres de production de viande de bœuf, de veau, de la viande de buffle, de porc (y compris le bacon et le jambon), de mouton et d'agneau (y compris la viande de chèvre) se rapportent à la production en poids de carcasses et ne comprennent pas le saindoux, le suif et les abats comestibles. Toutes les données se rapportent à la production totale de viande, c'est-à-dire à la fois aux animaux abattus à des

B.   *Textiles and leather products*

Table 45: The data on cotton fabrics refer to woven fabrics of cotton at the loom stage before undergoing finishing processes such as bleaching, dyeing, printing, mercerizing, lazing, etc.; those on wool refer to woollen and worsted fabrics before undergoing finishing processes. Fabrics of fine hair are excluded.

The data on woven fabrics of cellulosic and non-cellulosic fibres include fabrics of continuous and discontinuous rayon and acetate fibres, and non-cellulosic fibres other than textile glass fibres. Pile and chenille fabrics at the loom stage are also included.

Table 46: The data refer to the total production of leather footwear for children, men and women and all other footwear such as footwear with outer soles of wood or cork, sports footwear and orthopedic leather footwear. House slippers and sandals of various types are included, but rubber footwear is excluded.

C.   *Wood and wood products; paper and paper products*

Table 47: The data refer to the aggregate of sawnwood and sleepers, coniferous or non-coniferous. The data cover wood planed, unplaned, grooved, tongued and the like, sawn lengthwise or produced by a profile-chipping process, and planed wood which may also be finger-jointed, tongued or grooved, chamfered, rabbeted, V-jointed, beaded and so on. Wood flooring is excluded. Sleepers may be sawn or hewn.

Table 48 presents statistics on the production of all paper and paper board. The data cover newsprint, printing and writing paper, construction paper and paperboard, household and sanitary paper, special thin paper, wrapping and packaging paper and paperboard.

D.   *Chemicals and related products*

Table 49: Statistics on all hydraulic cements used for construction (portland, metallurgic, aluminous, natural, and so on) are shown.

Table 50: The data refer to H_2SO_4 in terms of pure monohydrate sulphuric acid, including the sulphuric acid equivalent of oleum or fuming sulphuric acid.

E.   *Basic metal industries*

Table 51 includes foundry and steel making pig-iron. Figures on crude steel include both ingots and steel for castings. In selected cases, data are obtained from the United States Bureau of Mines (Washington, D.C.), the Latin American Iron and Steel Institute (Santiago) and the United Nations Economic Commission for Europe. Detailed references to sources of data are given in the United Nations *Industrial Commodity Statistics Yearbook* [24].

Table 52: The data refer to aluminium obtained by electrolytic reduction of alumina (primary) and re-

fins commerciales et des animaux sacrifiés à la ferme.

Tableau 43: Les données se rapportent à la bière produite à partir du malte, y compris ale, stout et porter (bière anglaise, blonde et brune).

Le *Tableau 44* se rapporte seulement aux cigarettes.

B.   *Textiles et articles en cuir*

Tableau 45: Les données sur les tissus de coton et de laine se rapportent aux tissus de coton, avant les opérations de finition, c'est-à-dire avant d'être blanchis teints, imprimés, mercerisés, glacés, etc., et aux tissus de laine cardée ou peignée, avant les opérations de finition. A l'exclusion des tissus de poils fins.

Les données sur les tissus de fibres cellulosiques et non-cellulosiques comprennent les tissus sortant du métier à tisser de fibres de rayonne et d'acétate et tissus composés de fibres non cellulosiques, autres que les fibres de verre, continues ou discontinues. Cette rubrique comprend les velours, peluches, tissus boucles et tissus chenille.

Tableau 46: Les données se rapportent à la production totale de chaussures de cuir pour enfants, hommes et dames et toutes les autres chaussures telles que chaussures à semelles en bois ou en liège, chaussures pour sports et orthopédiques en cuir. Chaussures en caoutchouc ne sont pas compris.

C.   *Bois et produits dérivés; papier et produits dérivés*

Tableau 47: Les données sont un agrégat des sciages de bois de conifères et de non-conifères et des traverses de chemins de fer. Elles comprennent les bois rabotés, non rabotés, rainés, languetés, etc. sciés en long ou obtenus à l'aide d'un procédé de profilage par enlèvement de copeaux et les bois rabotés qui peuvent être également à joints digitiformes languetés ou rainés, chanfreinés, à feuillures, à joints en V, à rebords, etc. Cette rubrique ne comprend pas les éléments de parquet en bois. Les traverses de chemin de fer comprennent les traverses sciées ou équaries à la hache.

Le *tableau 48* présente les statistiques sur la production de tout papier et carton. Les données comprennent le papier journal, les papiers d'impression et d'écriture, les papiers et cartons de construction, les papiers de ménage et les papiers hygiéniques, les papiers minces spéciaux, les papiers d'empaquetage et d'emballage et carton.

D.   *Produits chimiques et apparentés*

Tableau 49: Les données sur tous les ciments hydrauliques utilisés dans la construction (portland métallurgique, alumineux, naturel, etc.) sont présentées.

Tableau 50: Les données se rapportent au H_2SO_4 sur la base de l'acide sulfurique monohydraté, y compris l'équivalent en acide sulfurique de l'oléum ou acide sulfurique fumant.

melting metal waste or scrap (secondary).

F.   Fabricated metal products, machinery and equipment

Table 53 presents data on the total production of all kinds of radio and television receivers.

Table 54: Passenger cars include three-and four-wheeled road motor vehicles other than motorcycle combinations, intended for the transport of passengers and seating not more than nine persons (including the driver), which are manufactured wholly or mainly from domestically-produced parts and passenger cars shipped in "knocked-down" form for assembly abroad.

Table 55: The data refer to refrigerators of the compression type or of the absorption type, of the sizes commonly used in private households. Insulated cabinets to contain an active refrigerating element (block ice) but no machine are excluded.

Table 56: These washing machines usually include electrically-driven paddles or rotating cylinders (for keeping the cleaning solution circulating through the fabrics) or alternative devices. Washing machines with attached wringers or centrifugal spin driers, and centrifugal spin driers designed as independent units, are included.

Table 57: The data on machine tools presented in this table include drilling and boring machines, lathes, milling machines, and metal-working presses. Drilling and boring machines refer to metal-working machines fitted with a baseplate, stand or other device for mounting on the floor, or on a bench, wall or another machine. Lathes refer to metal-working lathes of all kinds, whether or not automatic, including slide lathes, vertical lathes, capstan and turret lathes, production (or copying) lathes. Milling machines refer to metal-working machines designed to work a plane or profile surface by means of rotating tools, known as milling cutters. Metal-working presses are mechanical, hydraulic and pneumatic presses used for forging, stamping, cutting out, etc. Forge hammers are excluded. Detailed product definitions are given in the United Nations *Industrial Commodity Statistics Yearbook* [24].

Table 58 presents data on lorries, distinguishing between lorries assembled from imported parts and those manufactured wholly or mainly from domestically-produced parts. Both include road motor vehicles designed for the conveyance of goods, including vehicles specially equipped for the transport of certain goods, and articulated vehicles (that is, units made up of a road motor vehicle and a semi-trailer). Ambulances, prison vans and special purpose lorries and vans, such as fire-engines are excluded.

E.   Industries métallurgiques de base

Tableau 51: Les données se rapportent à la production de fonte et d'acier. Les données sur l'acier brut comprennent les lingots et l'acier pour moulage. Dans certains cas, les données proviennent du United States Bureau of Mines (Washington, D.C.), de l'Institut latino-américain du fer et de l'acier (Santiago) et de la Commission économique pour l'Europe. Pour plus de détails sur les sources de données, se reporter à *l'Annuaire des statistiques industrielles par produit* des Nations Unies [24].

Tableau 52: Les données se rapportent à la production d'aluminium obtenue par réduction électrolytique de l'alumine (production primaire) et par refusion de déchets métalliques (production secondaire).

F.   Fabrications métallurgiques, machines et équipements

Tableau 53: Les données sur la production totale de postes récepteurs de radiodiffusion et de télévision de toutes sortes sont présentées.

Tableau 54: Les voitures de tourisme comprennent les véhicules automobiles routiers à trois ou quatre roues, autres que les motocycles, destinés au transport de passagers, dont le nombre de places assises (y compris celle du conducteur) n'est pas supérieur à neuf et qui sont construits entièrement ou principalement avec des pièces fabriqués dans le pays, et les voitures destinées au transport de passagers exportées en pièces détachées pour être montées à l'étranger.

Tableau 55: Les données se rapportent aux appareils frigorifiques du type à compression ou à absorption de la taille des appareils communément utilisés dans les ménages. Cette rubrique ne comprend pas les glacières conçues pour contenir un élément frigorifique actif (glace en bloc) mais non un équipement frigorifique.

Tableau 56: Ces machines à laver comprennent généralement des pales ou des cylindres rotatifs (destinés à assurer le brassage continu du liquide et du linge) ou des dispositifs à mouvements alternés, mus électriquement. Cette rubrique comprend les machines à laver avec essoreuses à rouleau ou essoreuses centrifuges et les essoreuses centrifuges conçues comme des appareils indépendants.

Tableau 57: Les données sur les machines-outils présentés dans ce tableau comprennent les perceuses, tours, fraiseuses, et presses pour le travail des métaux. Perceuses se rapportent aux machines-outils pour le travail des métaux, munies d'un socle, d'un pied ou d'un autre dispositif permettant de les fixer au sol, à un établi, à une paroi ou à une autre machine. Tours se rapportent aux tours à métaux, de tous types, automatiques ou non, y compris les tours parallèles, les tours verticaux, les tours à revolver, les tours à reproduire. Fraiseuses se rapportent aux machines-outils pour le travail des métaux conçues

pour usiner une surface plane ou un profil au moyen d'outils tournants appelés fraises. Presses pour le travail des métaux se rapportent aux presses à commande mécanique, hydraulique et pneumatique servant à forger, à estamper, à matricer etc. Cette rubrique ne comprend pas les outils agissant par chocs. Pour plus de détails sur les description des produits se reporter à l'*Annuaire des statistiques industrielles par produit* [24] des Nations Unies.

Tableau 58 présente les données sur les camions et fait la distinction entre les camions assemblés à partir de pièces importées et les camions qui sont montés entièrement ou principalement avec des pièces importées. Les deux comprennent les véhicules automobiles routiers conçus pour le transport des marchandises, y compris les véhicules spécialement équipés pour le transport de certaines marchandises, et les véhicules articulés (c'est-à-dire les ensembles composés d'un véhicule automobile routier et d'une semi-remorque). Cette rubrique ne comprend pas les ambulances, les voitures cellulaires et les camions à usages spéciaux, tels que les voitures-pompes à incendie.

59
Railways: traffic
Chemins de fer : trafic
Passenger and net ton-kilometres: millions
Voyageurs et tonnes-kilomètres nettes : millions

Country or area Pays ou zone	1991	1992	1993	1994	1995	1996	1997	1998	1999	2000
Albania Albanie										
Passenger-kilometres										
Voyageurs-kilomètres	317	191	223	215	197	168	95	116	121	183
Net ton-kilometres										
Tonnes-kilomètres	278	60	54	53	53	42	23	25	26	28
Algeria Algérie										
Passenger-kilometres										
Voyageurs-kilomètres	3 192	2 904	3 009	2 234	1 574	1 826	1 360	1 163	1 069	1 142
Net ton-kilometres										
Tonnes-kilomètres	2 710	2 523	2 296	2 261	1 946	2 194	2 892	2 174	2 033	1 980
Argentina Argentine										
Passenger-kilometres[1]										
Voyageurs-kilomètres[1]	8 882	6 749	4 171	4 905	7 017	8 524	9 324	9 652	9 102	8 939
Net ton-kilometres										
Tonnes-kilomètres	5 460	4 388	4 477	6 613	7 613	8 505	9 835	9 852	9 101	8 696
Armenia Arménie										
Passenger-kilometres										
Voyageurs-kilomètres	320	446	435	353	166	84	84	52	46	47
Net ton-kilometres										
Tonnes-kilomètres	4 177	1 260	451	378	403	351	381	420	323	354
Australia Australie										
Net ton-kilometres[2]										
Tonnes-kilomètres[2]	88 260	89 276	92 123	97 779	99 727	104 311	114 500	125 200	127 400	134 200
Austria Autriche										
Passenger-kilometres										
Voyageurs-kilomètres	9 428	9 799	9 599	9 384	9 755	9 824	8 477	8 313	8 166	...
Net ton-kilometres										
Tonnes-kilomètres	12 981	12 321	11 922	13 164	13 857	14 066	14 993	15 552	15 762	...
Azerbaijan Azerbaïdjan										
Passenger-kilometres										
Voyageurs-kilomètres	1 975	1 629	1 330	1 081	791	558	491	533	422	493
Net ton-kilometres										
Tonnes-kilomètres	30 477	13 781	7 300	3 312	2 384	2 778	3 515	4 702	5 052	5 770
Bangladesh Bangladesh										
Passenger-kilometres[3]										
Voyageurs-kilomètres[3]	4 587	5 348	5 112	4 570	4 037	3 333	3 754	3 855	...	...
Net ton-kilometres[3]										
Tonnes-kilomètres[3]	651	718	641	641	760	689	782	804	...	...
Belarus Bélarus										
Passenger-kilometres[4]										
Voyageurs-kilomètres[4]	15 795	18 017	19 500	16 063	12 505	11 657	12 909	13 268	16 874	17 722
Net ton-kilometres										
Tonnes-kilomètres	65 551	56 441	42 919	27 963	25 510	26 018	30 636	30 370	30 529	31 425
Belgium Belgique										
Passenger-kilometres										
Voyageurs-kilomètres	6 771	6 798	6 694	6 638	6 757	6 788	6 984	7 097	7 354	...
Net ton-kilometres										
Tonnes-kilomètres	8 187	8 346	7 581	8 081	7 287	7 244	7 465	7 600	7 392	...
Benin Bénin										
Passenger-kilometres										
Voyageurs-kilomètres	63	62	75	107	116	117	121	111	108	100
Net ton-kilometres										
Tonnes-kilomètres	277	238	225	253	207	178	218	219	204	89
Bolivia Bolivie										
Passenger-kilometres										
Voyageurs-kilomètres	350	334	279	277	240	197	225	270	271	259

59
Railways: traffic
Passenger and net ton-kilometres: millions [*cont.*]
Chemins de fer : trafic
Voyageurs et tonnes-kilomètres nettes : millions [*suite*]

Country or area Pays ou zone	1991	1992	1993	1994	1995	1996	1997	1998	1999	2000
Net ton-kilometres Tonnes-kilomètres	682	714	695	782	758	780	839	908	832	856
Botswana Botswana										
Passenger-kilometres Voyageurs-kilomètres	103	75	95	119	110	81	82	71	75	...
Net ton-kilometres Tonnes-kilomètres	...	...	585	569	687	668	1 049	1 278	1 037	...
Brazil Brésil										
Passenger-kilometres[5] Voyageurs-kilomètres[5]	18 859	15 668	14 040	15 758	9 936	9 048	7 876	7 224	6 528	...
Net ton-kilometres[6] Tonnes-kilomètres[6]	121 414	116 599	124 677	133 735	136 460	128 796	138 724	142 446	140 817	...
Bulgaria Bulgarie										
Passenger-kilometres Voyageurs-kilomètres	4 866	5 393	5 837	5 059	4 693	5 065	5 886	4 740	3 819	3 472
Net ton-kilometres[7] Tonnes-kilomètres[7]	8 585	7 758	7 702	7 774	8 595	7 549	7 444	6 152	5 297	5 538
Cambodia Cambodge										
Passenger-kilometres Voyageurs-kilomètres	42	69	97	39	38	22	51	44	50	15
Net ton-kilometres Tonnes-kilomètres	12	22	28	16	6	4	37	76	76	91
Cameroon Cameroun										
Passenger-kilometres Voyageurs-kilomètres	530	445	352	317	301	306	283	292	311	...
Net ton-kilometres Tonnes-kilomètres	679	613	653	812	607	869	850	888	916	...
Canada Canada										
Passenger-kilometres Voyageurs-kilomètres	1 426	1 439	1 413	1 440	1 473	1 519	1 515	1 458	1 593	...
Net ton-kilometres Tonnes-kilomètres	262 425[7]	252 454[7]	257 805[7]	288 864[7]	280 474	282 489	306 943	299 508	298 836	...
Chile Chili										
Passenger-kilometres Voyageurs-kilomètres	1 125	1 010	938	816	691	644	552	519	637	736
Net ton-kilometres Tonnes-kilomètres	2 717	2 738	2 496	2 371	2 262	2 366	2 330	2 650	2 896	3 141
China †† Chine ††										
Passenger-kilometres[8] Voyageurs-kilomètres[8]	282 810	315 224	348 330	363 605	354 570	332 537	358 486	377 342	413 593	...
Net ton-kilometres[8] Tonnes-kilomètres[8]	1 097 200	1 157 555	1 195 464	1 245 750	1 287 025	1 297 046	1 325 330	1 251 707	1 283 840	...
China, Hong Kong SAR† Chine, Hong Kong RAS†										
Passenger-kilometres[9] Voyageurs-kilomètres[9]	2 912	3 121	3 269	3 497	3 662	3 914	4 172	4 252	4 321	4 533
Net ton-kilometres[9] Tonnes-kilomètres[9]	65	61	51	47	41	30	24	15	15	15
Colombia Colombie										
Passenger-kilometres Voyageurs-kilomètres	79	16	...	...	...	...	...	...	...	...
Net ton-kilometres[7] Tonnes-kilomètres[7]	298	243	459	666	753	747	736	658	373	...
Congo Congo										
Passenger-kilometres Voyageurs-kilomètres	435	421	312	227	302	360	235	242	9	...
Net ton-kilometres Tonnes-kilomètres	397	350	257	122	267	289	139	135	21	...

59
Railways: traffic
Passenger and net ton-kilometres: millions [cont.]
Chemins de fer : trafic
Voyageurs et tonnes-kilomètres nettes : millions [suite]

Country or area Pays ou zone	1991	1992	1993	1994	1995	1996	1997	1998	1999	2000
Croatia Croatie										
Passenger-kilometres										
Voyageurs-kilomètres	1 503	981	951	962	943	1 029	981	921	943	985
Net ton-kilometres										
Tonnes-kilomètres	3 617	1 770	1 592	1 563	1 974	1 717	1 876	2 001	1 849	1 822
Cuba Cuba										
Passenger-kilometres										
Voyageurs-kilomètres	3 026	2 594	2 512	2 353	2 188	2 156	1 962	1 750	1 499	1 853
Net ton-kilometres										
Tonnes-kilomètres	1 368	1 059	764	653	745	871	859	822	806	804
Czech Republic République tchèque										
Passenger-kilometres										
Voyageurs-kilomètres	13 557	11 753	8 548	8 481	8 023	8 111	7 710	7 001	6 929	7 266
Net ton-kilometres[10]										
Tonnes-kilomètres[10]	32 679	31 116	25 579	24 393	25 395	24 174	22 173	19 529	17 625	18 183
Denmark Danemark										
Passenger-kilometres										
Voyageurs-kilomètres	4 659	4 798	4 737	4 847	4 783	4 718	4 990	5 369	...	...
Net ton-kilometres[11]										
Tonnes-kilomètres [11]	1 858	1 870	1 751	2 008	1 985	1 757	1 983	2 058	...	...
Ecuador Equateur										
Passenger-kilometres										
Voyageurs-kilomètres	53	53	39	27	47	51	47	44	5	...
Net ton-kilometres										
Tonnes-kilomètres	2	3	3	9	3	1	0	14	0	...
Egypt Egypte										
Passenger-kilometres[2]										
Voyageurs-kilomètres[2]	42 992	46 517	49 025	51 098	52 839	55 888	60 617	64 077	68 423	...
Net ton-kilometres [2]										
Tonnes-kilomètres[2]	2 162	3 213	3 142	3 621	4 073	4 117	3 969	4 012	3 464	...
El Salvador El Salvador										
Passenger-kilometres										
Voyageurs-kilomètres	8	6	6	6	5	7	7	6	8	...
Net ton-kilometres										
Tonnes-kilomètres	35	38	35	30	13	17	17	24	19	...
Estonia Estonie										
Passenger-kilometres										
Voyageurs-kilomètres	1 273	950	722	537	421	309	261	236	238	263
Net ton-kilometres										
Tonnes-kilomètres	6 545	3 646	4 152	3 612	3 846	4 198	5 141	6 079	7 295	8 102
Ethiopia Ethiopie										
Passenger-kilometres[12][13]										
Voyageurs-kilomètres[12][13]	150	152	230	280	293	218	206	151	...	...
Net ton-kilometres[12][13]										
Tonnes-kilomètres[12][13]	116	118	112	102	93	104	106	90	...	...
Finland Finlande										
Passenger-kilometres										
Voyageurs-kilomètres	3 230	3 057	3 007	3 037	3 184	3 254	3 376	3 377	3 415	3 405
Net ton-kilometres[14]										
Tonnes-kilomètres[14]	7 634	7 848	9 259	9 949	9 293	8 806	9 856	9 885	9 753	10 107
France France										
Passenger-kilometres										
Voyageurs-kilomètres	62 300	62 230	58 610	58 930	55 560	59 770	61 830	64 460	66 590	...
Net ton-kilometres[15]										
Tonnes-kilomètres[15]	51 480	50 380	45 830	49 720	49 170	50 500	54 820	55 090	54 350	...

59
Railways: traffic
Passenger and net ton-kilometres: millions [*cont.*]
Chemins de fer : trafic
Voyageurs et tonnes-kilomètres nettes : millions [*suite*]

Country or area Pays ou zone	1991	1992	1993	1994	1995	1996	1997	1998	1999	2000
Georgia Géorgie										
Passenger-kilometres										
Voyageurs-kilomètres	2 135	1 210	917	1 165	371	380	294	397	349	450
Net ton-kilometres										
Tonnes-kilomètres	12 117	3 512	1 554	955	1 246	1 141	2 006	2 574	3 139	3 910
Germany † Allemagne †										
Passenger-kilometres										
Voyageurs-kilomètres	57 034	57 240	58 003	61 962	74 970	75 975	73 917	72 389	73 587	75 081
Net ton-kilometres										
Tonnes-kilomètres	82 219	72 848	66 660	71 814	70 863	69 713	73 763	74 051	71 455	76 108
Ghana Ghana										
Passenger-kilometres										
Voyageurs-kilomètres	159	135	118	196	213	209	...	...	...	...
Net ton-kilometres										
Tonnes-kilomètres	226	109	137	149	157	160	...	...	...	...
Greece Grèce										
Passenger-kilometres										
Voyageurs-kilomètres	1 995	2 004	1 726	1 399	1 569	1 752	1 783	1 552	...	...
Net ton-kilometres[16]										
Tonnes-kilomètres[16]	605	563	523	325	306	350	330	322	...	...
Guatemala Guatemala										
Passenger-kilometres										
Voyageurs-kilomètres	12 531	9 151	3 427	991	...	...	...	...	...	...
Net ton-kilometres										
Tonnes-kilomètres	47 233	66 472	29 186	25 295	14 242	836	...	...	...	...
Hungary Hongrie										
Passenger-kilometres										
Voyageurs-kilomètres	9 861	9 184	8 432	8 508	8 441	8 582	8 669	8 884	9 514	9 693
Net ton-kilometres										
Tonnes-kilomètres	11 938	10 015	7 708	7 707	8 422	7 634	8 149	8 150	7 734	8 095
India Inde										
Passenger-kilometres[17]										
Voyageurs-kilomètres[17]	314 564	300 103	296 245	319 365	341 999	357 013	379 897	403 884	430 666	...
Net ton-kilometres[17]										
Tonnes-kilomètres[17]	250 238	252 388	252 411	249 564	270 489	277 567	284 249	281 513	305 201	...
Indonesia Indonésie										
Passenger-kilometres										
Voyageurs-kilomètres	9 767	10 458	12 337	13 728	15 500	15 223	15 518	16 970	17 820	19 228
Net ton-kilometres										
Tonnes-kilomètres	3 470	3 779	3 955	3 854	4 172	4 700	5 030	4 963	5 035	4 997
Iran (Islamic Rep. of) Iran (Rép. islamique d')										
Passenger-kilometres										
Voyageurs-kilomètres	4 585	5 298	6 422	6 479	7 294	7 044	6 103	5 637	6 451	...
Net ton-kilometres										
Tonnes-kilomètres	7 701	8 002	9 124	10 700	11 865	13 638	14 400	12 638	14 082	...
Iraq Iraq										
Passenger-kilometres										
Voyageurs-kilomètres	436	926	1 566	2 334	2 198	...	...	...	...	...
Net ton-kilometres[18]										
Tonnes-kilomètres[18]	326	1 100	1 587	1 901	1 120	...	...	...	...	...
Ireland Irlande										
Passenger-kilometres										
Voyageurs-kilomètres	1 290	1 226	1 274	1 260	1 291	1 295	1 388	1 490	...	...
Net ton-kilometres										
Tonnes-kilomètres	600	633	575	569	602	570	522	469	523	...
Israel Israël										
Passenger-kilometres										
Voyageurs-kilomètres	186	198	214	231	269	294	346	383	529	781

59
Railways: traffic
Passenger and net ton-kilometres: millions [*cont.*]
Chemins de fer : trafic
Voyageurs et tonnes-kilomètres nettes : millions [*suite*]

Country or area Pays ou zone	1991	1992	1993	1994	1995	1996	1997	1998	1999	2000
Net ton-kilometres Tonnes-kilomètres	1 091	1 098	1 072	1 089	1 176	1 152	992	1 049	1 128	1 169
Italy Italie										
Passenger-kilometres Voyageurs-kilomètres	46 427	48 361	47 101	48 900	49 700	50 300	49 500	47 285	49 424	43 752
Net ton-kilometres[18] Tonnes-kilomètres[18]	21 680	21 830	20 226	22 564	24 050	23 314	25 285	24 704	23 781	25 019
Japan Japon										
Passenger-kilometres Voyageurs-kilomètres	396 472	403 245	401 864	402 513	393 907	400 712	301 510	391 073	418 281	...
Net ton-kilometres Tonnes-kilomètres	27 292	26 899	25 619	25 946	23 695	24 991	18 661	23 136	22 676	...
Jordan Jordanie										
Passenger-kilometres Voyageurs-kilomètres	2	2	2	2	1	1	2	2	2	2
Net ton-kilometres Tonnes-kilomètres	791	797	711	676	698	735	625	596	585	671
Kazakhstan Kazakhstan										
Passenger-kilometres Voyageurs-kilomètres	19 365	19 671	20 507	17 362	13 159	14 188	12 802	10 668	8 859	10 215
Net ton-kilometres Tonnes-kilomètres	374 230	286 109	192 258	146 778	124 502	112 688	106 425	103 045	91 700	124 983
Kenya Kenya										
Passenger-kilometres Voyageurs-kilomètres	715	563	395	401	363	371	393	432	306	302
Net ton-kilometres Tonnes-kilomètres	1 943	1 784	1 479	1 172	1 456	1 309	1 068	1 111	1 492	1 557
Korea, Republic of Corée, République de										
Passenger-kilometres Voyageurs-kilomètres	31 454	32 118	31 048	28 859	29 292	29 580	30 073	32 976	28 606	...
Net ton-kilometres Tonnes-kilomètres	14 494	14 256	14 658	14 070	13 838	12 947	12 710	10 372	10 072	...
Kyrgyzstan Kirghizistan										
Passenger-kilometres Voyageurs-kilomètres	200	235	296	172	87	92	93	59	31	44
Net ton-kilometres Tonnes-kilomètres	2 415	1 589	923	629	403	481	472	466	354	348
Latvia Lettonie										
Passenger-kilometres Voyageurs-kilomètres	3 930	3 656	2 359	1 794	1 256	1 149	1 154	1 059	984	715
Net ton-kilometres[11] Tonnes-kilomètres[11]	16 739	10 115	9 852	9 520	9 757	12 412	13 970	12 995	12 210	13 310
Lithuania Lituanie										
Passenger-kilometres Voyageurs-kilomètres	3 225	2 740	2 700	1 574	1 130	954	842	800	745	611
Net ton-kilometres[19] Tonnes-kilomètres[19]	17 748	11 337	11 030	7 996	7 220	8 103	8 622	8 265	7 849	8 918
Luxembourg Luxembourg										
Passenger-kilometres Voyageurs-kilomètres	272	255	262	289	286	284	295	300	310	332
Net ton-kilometres Tonnes-kilomètres	713	672	647	686	566	574	613	624	660	683
Madagascar Madagascar										
Passenger-kilometres Voyageurs-kilomètres	...	...	...	...	...	...	81	35	28	19
Net ton-kilometres[7,20] Tonnes-kilomètres[7,20]	...	...	...	...	...	...	81	71	44	26

59
Railways: traffic
Passenger and net ton-kilometres: millions [*cont.*]
Chemins de fer : trafic
Voyageurs et tonnes-kilomètres nettes : millions [*suite*]

Country or area Pays ou zone	1991	1992	1993	1994	1995	1996	1997	1998	1999	2000
Malawi Malawi										
Passenger-kilometres [17]										
Voyageurs-kilomètres [17]	92	72	46	20	22	26	17	21	19	...
Net ton-kilometres [17]										
Tonnes-kilomètres [17]	56	52	43	58	74	57	46	55	62	...
Malaysia Malaisie										
Passenger-kilometres [21]										
Voyageurs-kilomètres [21]	1 763	1 618	1 543	1 348	1 270	1 370	1 492	1 397	1 313	1 220
Net ton-kilometres [21]										
Tonnes-kilomètres [21]	1 262	1 081	1 157	1 463	1 416	1 397	1 336	992	908	917
Mali Mali										
Net ton-kilometres										
Tonnes-kilomètres	...	208	191	220	254	405	...	...	...	...
Mexico Mexique										
Passenger-kilometres										
Voyageurs-kilomètres	4 686	4 794	3 219	1 855	1 899	1 799	1 508	460	254	91
Net ton-kilometres										
Tonnes-kilomètres	32 698	34 197	35 672	37 315	37 613	41 723	42 442	48 873	47 273	48 916
Mongolia Mongolie										
Passenger-kilometres										
Voyageurs-kilomètres	596	630	583	790	680	733	951	981	1 010	1 067
Net ton-kilometres										
Tonnes-kilomètres	3 013	2 756	2 531	2 132	2 280	2 529	2 254	2 815	3 492	4 283
Morocco Maroc										
Passenger-kilometres										
Voyageurs-kilomètres	2 345	2 233	1 904	1 881	1 564	1 776	1 856	1 875	1 880	1 956
Net ton-kilometres										
Tonnes-kilomètres	4 523	5 001	4 415	4 679	4 621	4 757	4 835	4 827	4 795	4 650
Myanmar Myanmar										
Passenger-kilometres										
Voyageurs-kilomètres	4 481	4 606	4 706	4 390	4 178	4 294	3 784	3 948	4 112	4 451
Net ton-kilometres [7]										
Tonnes-kilomètres [7]	581	601	663	726	659	748	674	988	1 043	1 222
Netherlands Pays-Bas										
Passenger-kilometres										
Voyageurs-kilomètres	15 195	14 980	14 788	14 439	13 977	14 131	14 485	14 879	...	...
Net ton-kilometres										
Tonnes-kilomètres	3 038	2 764	2 681	2 830	3 097	3 123	3 406	3 778	...	...
New Zealand Nouvelle-Zélande										
Net ton-kilometres [2]										
Tonnes-kilomètres [2]	2 364	2 475	2 468	2 835	3 202	3 260	3 505	3 547	3 636	4 040
Nigeria Nigéria										
Passenger-kilometres										
Voyageurs-kilomètres	475	451	55	220	161	170	179	...	...	...
Net ton-kilometres										
Tonnes-kilomètres	282	203	162	141	108	114	120	...	...	...
Norway Norvège										
Passenger-kilometres										
Voyageurs-kilomètres	2 153	2 201	2 341	2 398	2 381	2 120	2 425	2 495	2 689	2 634
Net ton-kilometres										
Tonnes-kilomètres	2 675	2 294	2 873	2 678	2 715	2 641	2 401	2 144	2 454	2 399
Pakistan Pakistan										
Passenger-kilometres [3]										
Voyageurs-kilomètres [3]	18 159	16 759	16 274	18 044	18 905	19 114	18 771	18 979	18 761	...
Net ton-kilometres [3]										
Tonnes-kilomètres [3]	5 964	5 860	5 940	5 660	5 078	4 538	4 444	3 939	3 612	...

59
Railways: traffic
Passenger and net ton-kilometres: millions [*cont.*]
Chemins de fer : trafic
Voyageurs et tonnes-kilomètres nettes : millions [*suite*]

Country or area Pays ou zone	1991	1992	1993	1994	1995	1996	1997	1998	1999	2000
Panama Panama										
Passenger-kilometres[23] Voyageurs-kilomètres[23]	7 379[22]	4 731[22]	2 315[22]	2 619[24 25]	1 069[24]	122[24]	9[24]	...	...	...
Net ton-kilometres[23 26] Tonnes-kilomètres[23 26]	2 268	2 475	1 669	1 199	1 728	710	306	...	...	...
Paraguay Paraguay										
Passenger-kilometres Voyageurs-kilomètres	1	1	1	...	...	...	...	...	...	...
Net ton-kilometres Tonnes-kilomètres	3	3	3	...	...	...	...	...	...	...
Peru Pérou										
Passenger-kilometres[7] Voyageurs-kilomètres[7]	320	226	165	240	231	222	210	180	144	...
Net ton-kilometres[7] Tonnes-kilomètres[7]	860	837	850	864	843	878	833	892	891	...
Philippines Philippines										
Passenger-kilometres Voyageurs-kilomètres	182	121	102	106	163	69	175	181	171	123
Net ton-kilometres[27] Tonnes-kilomètres[27]	2	1	5	3	4	0	0	0	...	...
Poland Pologne										
Passenger-kilometres Voyageurs-kilomètres	40 115	32 571	30 865	27 610	26 635	26 569	25 806	25 664	26 198	24 093
Net ton-kilometres Tonnes-kilomètres	65 146	57 763	64 359	65 788	69 116	68 332	68 651	61 760	55 471	54 448
Portugal Portugal										
Passenger-kilometres Voyageurs-kilomètres	5 692	5 494	5 397	5 149	4 840	4 503[28]	4 563[28]	4 602[28]	4 380	...
Net ton-kilometres Tonnes-kilomètres	1 784	1 767	1 786	1 826	2 342	2 178	2 632	2 340	2 562	...
Republic of Moldova République de Moldova										
Passenger-kilometres Voyageurs-kilomètres	1 280	1 718[4]	1 661[4]	1 204[4]	1 019[4]	882[4]	789[4]	656[4]	343[4]	315[4]
Net ton-kilometres Tonnes-kilomètres	11 883	7 861	4 965	3 533	3 134	2 897	2 937	2 575	1 191	1 513
Romania Roumanie										
Passenger-kilometres[29] Voyageurs-kilomètres[29]	25 429	24 269	19 402	18 313	18 879	18 356	15 795	13 422	12 304	11 632
Net ton-kilometres Tonnes-kilomètres	37 853	28 170	25 170	24 704	27 179	26 877	24 789	19 708	15 927	17 982
Russian Federation Fédération de Russie										
Passenger-kilometres Voyageurs-kilomètres	255 000	253 200	272 200	227 100	192 200	181 200	170 300	152 900	141 000	167 100
Net ton-kilometres Tonnes-kilomètres	2 326 000	1 967 000	1 608 000	1 195 000	1 214 000	1 131 000	1 100 000	1 020 000	1 205 000	1 373 000
Saudi Arabia Arabie saoudite										
Passenger-kilometres Voyageurs-kilomètres	144	135	136	153	159	170	192	222	224	...
Net ton-kilometres Tonnes-kilomètres	726	915	868	927	728	691	726	856	938	...
Senegal Sénégal										
Passenger-kilometres Voyageurs-kilomètres	173	...	...	...	...	...	...	...	...	...
Net ton-kilometres Tonnes-kilomètres	485	...	...	...	...	...	...	...	...	...
Slovakia Slovaquie										
Passenger-kilometres Voyageurs-kilomètres	6 002	5 453	4 569	4 548	4 202	3 769	3 057	3 092	2 968	2 870

59
Railways: traffic
Passenger and net ton-kilometres: millions [*cont.*]
Chemins de fer : trafic
Voyageurs et tonnes-kilomètres nettes : millions [*suite*]

Country or area Pays ou zone	1991	1992	1993	1994	1995	1996	1997	1998	1999	2000
Net ton-kilometres Tonnes-kilomètres	17 255	16 697	14 201	12 236	13 674	12 017	12 373	11 753	9 859	11 234
Slovenia Slovénie										
Passenger-kilometres Voyageurs-kilomètres	614	547	566	590	595	613	616	645	623	705
Net ton-kilometres Tonnes-kilomètres	3 246	2 573	2 262	2 448	3 076	2 550	2 852	2 859	2 784	2 857
South Africa Afrique du Sud										
Passenger-kilometres[30][31] Voyageurs-kilomètres[30][31]	1 205	1 038	895	686	1 007	1 198	1 393	1 775	1 794	3 930
Net ton-kilometres[30][31] Tonnes-kilomètres[30][31]	93 255	88 817	91 472	92 538	98 798	99 818	99 773	103 866	102 777	106 786
Spain Espagne										
Passenger-kilometres Voyageurs-kilomètres	16 361	17 579	16 490	16 142	16 582	16 637	17 883	18 875	19 659	...
Net ton-kilometres[7] Tonnes-kilomètres[7]	10 802	9 550	8 132	9 048	10 419	10 219	11 488	11 801	12 029	...
Sri Lanka Sri Lanka										
Passenger-kilometres[32] Voyageurs-kilomètres[32]	2 690	2 613	2 822	3 202	3 321	3 103	3 146	3 206	3 393	...
Net ton-kilometres[32] Tonnes-kilomètres[32]	169	177	159	154	136	107	98	108	106	...
Sudan Soudan										
Passenger-kilometres Voyageurs-kilomètres	1 020	177	1 183	...	...	...	...	...	...	...
Net ton-kilometres Tonnes-kilomètres	2 030	2 120	2 240	...	...	...	...	...	...	...
Swaziland Swaziland										
Net ton-kilometres Tonnes-kilomètres	...	...	...	675	743	684	670	653	677	875
Sweden Suède										
Passenger-kilometres Voyageurs-kilomètres	5 745	5 587	6 001	6 063	6 364	6 216[33]	6 770[33]	6 997[33]	7 434[33]	...
Net ton-kilometres Tonnes-kilomètres	18 818	19 204	18 581	19 062	19 390	18 835[33]	19 114[33]	19 019[33]	18 905[33]	19 945[33]
Switzerland Suisse										
Passenger-kilometres Voyageurs-kilomètres	13 834	13 209	13 384	13 836	13 408	13 326	14 104	...	...	...
Net ton-kilometres Tonnes-kilomètres	8 659	8 212	7 821	8 586	8 626	7 847	8 629	...	...	...
Syrian Arab Republic Rép. arabe syrienne										
Passenger-kilometres Voyageurs-kilomètres	1 314	1 254	855	769	498	454	294	182	187	...
Net ton-kilometres Tonnes-kilomètres	1 238	1 699	1 097	1 190	1 285	1 864	1 472	1 430	1 577	...
Tajikistan Tadjikistan										
Passenger-kilometres[34] Voyageurs-kilomètres[34]	888	103	117	366	134	95	129	121	61	73
Net ton-kilometres[34] Tonnes-kilomètres[34]	9 881	641	329	2 169	2 115	1 719	1 384	1 458	1 282	1 326
Thailand Thaïlande										
Passenger-kilometres[32] Voyageurs-kilomètres[32]	12 820	13 669	13 702	13 814	12 975	12 205	11 804	10 947	9 894	10 040
Net ton-kilometres[32] Tonnes-kilomètres[32]	3 365	3 075	3 059	3 072	3 242	3 286	3 410	2 874	2 929	3 347
TFYR of Macedonia L'ex-R.y. Macédoine										
Passenger-kilometres Voyageurs-kilomètres	200	109	66	67	65	120	141	150	150	176

59
Railways: traffic
Passenger and net ton-kilometres: millions [*cont.*]
Chemins de fer : trafic
Voyageurs et tonnes-kilomètres nettes : millions [*suite*]

Country or area Pays ou zone	1991	1992	1993	1994	1995	1996	1997	1998	1999	2000
Net ton-kilometres Tonnes-kilomètres	712	577	493	151	169	271	279	408	380	527
Tunisia Tunisie										
Passenger-kilometres [16] Voyageurs-kilomètres [16]	1 020	1 078	1 057	1 038	996	988	1 094	1 133	1 196	1 243
Net ton-kilometres [7 35] Tonnes-kilomètres [7 35]	1 813	2 015	2 012	2 225	2 317	2 329	2 338	2 349	2 365	2 279
Turkey Turquie										
Passenger-kilometres Voyageurs-kilomètres	6 048	6 259	7 147	6 335	5 797	5 229	5 840	6 160	6 147	5 813
Net ton-kilometres Tonnes-kilomètres	8 093	8 383	8 517	8 339	8 632	9 018	9 717	8 377	8 265	9 731
Uganda Ouganda										
Passenger-kilometres [36] Voyageurs-kilomètres [36]	60	63	60	35	30	25	5	0	0	0
Net ton-kilometres Tonnes-kilomètres	139	119	130	208	245	184	148	148	200	210
Ukraine Ukraine										
Passenger-kilometres Voyageurs-kilomètres	70 968	76 196	75 896	70 882	63 759	59 080	54 540	49 938	47 600	51 767
Net ton-kilometres Tonnes-kilomètres	402 290	307 761	246 356	200 422	195 762	160 384	160 433	158 693	156 336	172 840
United Kingdom Royaume-Uni										
Passenger-kilometres [17 37] Voyageurs-kilomètres [17 37]	32 466	31 718	30 363	28 650	30 039	32 135	34 660	36 270	38 349	...
Net ton-kilometres [17 37] Tonnes-kilomètres [17 37]	15 300	15 550	13 765	12 979	13 136	15 144	16 949	17 369	18 409	...
United Rep. of Tanzania Rép.-Unie de Tanzanie										
Passenger-kilometres Voyageurs-kilomètres	990	...	...	...	...	...	...	...	...	...
Net ton-kilometres Tonnes-kilomètres	983	...	...	...	...	...	...	...	...	...
United States Etats-Unis										
Passenger-kilometres [38] Voyageurs-kilomètres [38]	10 095	9 803	9 976	9 529	8 924	8 127	8 314	8 568	8 509	8 970
Net ton-kilometres [39] Tonnes-kilomètres [39]	1 516 754	1 557 492	1 619 588	1 753 020	1 906 300	1 979 719	1 969 428	2 009 696	2 237 707	2 144 131
Uruguay Uruguay										
Passenger-kilometres [40] Voyageurs-kilomètres [40]	0	0	221	467	...	...	17	14	10	...
Net ton-kilometres Tonnes-kilomètres	203	215	178	188	184	182	204	244	272	...
Uzbekistan Ouzbékistan										
Passenger-kilometres Voyageurs-kilomètres	5	6	5	5	3	2	2	2	2	2
Net ton-kilometres Tonnes-kilomètres	71	41	36	19	17	20	17	16	14	15
Venezuela Venezuela										
Passenger-kilometres Voyageurs-kilomètres	55	47	44	31	12	...	...	...	...	...
Net ton-kilometres Tonnes-kilomètres	40	36	26	47	53	...	...	...	...	...
Viet Nam Viet Nam										
Passenger-kilometres Voyageurs-kilomètres	1 767	1 752	1 921	1 796	2 133	2 261	2 476	2 542	2 722	3 086

59

Railways: traffic
Passenger and net ton-kilometres: millions [*cont.*]
Chemins de fer : trafic
Voyageurs et tonnes-kilomètres nettes : millions [*suite*]

Country or area Pays ou zone	1991	1992	1993	1994	1995	1996	1997	1998	1999	2000
Net ton-kilometres Tonnes-kilomètres	1 103	1 077	978	1 370	1 751	1 684	1 533	1 369	1 446	1 921
Yemen Yémen Passenger-kilometres Voyageurs-kilomètres	...	...	...	1 714	2 051	2 260	2 492	...	...	...
Yugoslavia Yougoslavie Passenger-kilometres Voyageurs-kilomètres	...	2 800	3 379	2 525	2 611	1 830	1 744	1 622	860	1 436
Net ton-kilometres [7] Tonnes-kilomètres [7]	...	4 409	1 699	1 387	1 855	2 062	2 432	2 793	1 267	1 969
Yugoslavia, SFR† Yougoslavie, Rfs† Passenger-kilometres Voyageurs-kilomètres	2 935	...	...	...	...	...	...	...	...	...
Net ton-kilometres [7] Tonnes-kilomètres [7]	5 760	...	...	...	...	...	...	...	...	...
Zambia Zambie Passenger-kilometres Voyageurs-kilomètres	584	547	690	702	778	749	755	586	...	...
Net ton-kilometres Tonnes-kilomètres	141	...	123	151	90	666	758	702	...	...
Zimbabwe Zimbabwe Net ton-kilometres [2 41] Tonnes-kilomètres [2 41]	5 413	5 887	4 581	4 489	7 180	4 990	5 115	9 122	4 375	3 326

Source:
United Nations Statistics Division, New York, transport
statistics database.

† For information on recent changes in country or
area nomenclature pertaining to former Czechoslovakia,
Germany, Hong Kong Special Administrative Region (SAR) of
China, Macao Special Administrative Region (SAR) of China,
SFR of Yugoslavia and the former USSR, see Annex I - Country
or area nomenclature, regional and other groupings.

†† For statistical purposes, the data for
China do not include those for Hong Kong Special
Administrative Region (Hong Kong SAR), Macao Special
Administrative Region (Macao SAR) and Taiwan province of
China.

1 Including urban transport only.
2 Data refer to fiscal years ending 30 June.

3 Data refer to fiscal years beginning 1 July.

4 Including passengers carried without revenues.
5 Including urban railways traffic.
6 Including service traffic, animals, baggage and parcels.

7 Including service traffic.
8 May include service traffic.
9 Kowloon - Canton Railway only.
10 Including only state-owned railways.
11 Including passengers' baggage and parcel post (Latvia: also
mail).

Source:
Organisation des Nations Unies, Division de statistique, New
York, la base de données pour les statistiques des
transports.

† Pour les modifications récentes de nomenclature
de pays ou de zone concernant l'Allemagne, Hong Kong, région
administrative spéciale (RAS) de Chine, Macao, région
administrative spéciale (RAS) de Chine,
l'ex-Tchécoslovaquie, l'ex-URSS et l'ex-Rfs de Yougoslavie,
voir annexe I - Nomenclature des pays ou des zones,
groupements régionaux et autres groupements.

†† Les données statistiques relatives à
la Chine ne comprennent pas celles qui concernent la région
administrative spéciale de Hong Kong (la RAS de Hong Kong),
la région administrative spéciale de Macao (la RAS de Macao)
et la province chinoise de Taiwan.

1 Les chemins de fer urbains seulement.
2 Les données se réfèrent aux années fiscales finissant le 30e
juin.
3 Les données se réfèrent aux années fiscales commençant le
1er juillet.
4 Y compris passagers transportés gratuitement.
5 Y compris le trafic de chemins-de-fer urbains.
6 Y compris le trafic de service, les animaux, les baggages et
les colis.
7 Y compris le trafic de service.
8 Le trafic de service peut être compris.
9 Chemin de fer de Kowloon - Canton seulement.
10 Y compris chemins-de-fer de l'état seulement.
11 Y compris les bagages des voyageurs et les colis postaux
(Lettonie : courrier aussi).

59
Railways: traffic
Passenger and net ton-kilometres: millions [*cont.*]

Chemins de fer : trafic
Voyageurs et tonnes-kilomètres nettes : millions [*suite*]

12 Including traffic of Djibouti portion of Djibouti-Addis Ababa line.
13 Data refer to fiscal years beginning 7 July.

14 Beginning 1995, wagon loads traffic only.

15 Including passengers' baggage.
16 Including military traffic (Greece: also government traffic).
17 Data refer to fiscal years beginning 1 April.

18 Excluding livestock.
19 Prior to 1994, data refer to operated ton-kilometres which is the weight in tons of freight carried multiplied by the distance in kilometres actually run; beginning 1994, data refer to net ton-kilometres which is the weight in tons of freight carried multiplied by distance in kilometres.

20 Including baggage and service traffic.

21 Peninsular Malaysia only.
22 National Railway of Chiriqui only.
23 Beginning August 1997, railways operations closed.
24 Panama Railway and National Railway of Chiriqui.

25 Beginning April, Panama Railway resumed operations.

26 Panama Railway only.
27 Freight train operations suspended from November 1995 to August 1996 due to typhoon damages.

28 Excluding river traffic of the railway company.

29 Including military and government personnel.
30 Data refer to fiscal years ending 31 March.

31 Beginning 1998, excluding Namibia.
32 Data refer to fiscal years ending 30 September.

33 Including Swedish State Railways and MTAB.
34 Beginning 1992, decline due to border changes affecting the Dushanbe branch of the Csredniya Niyatskaya (Central Asia) Railway Co.
35 Ordinary goods only.
36 Beginning late 1997, passenger services suspended.
37 Excluding Northern Ireland.
38 Beginning 1986, excluding commuter railroads.

39 Class I railways only.
40 Passenger transport suspended from 1988 to 1992.

41 Including traffic in Botswana.

12 Y compris le trafic de la ligne Djibouti-Addis Abeba en Djibouti.
13 Les données se réfèrent aux années fiscales commençant le 7e juillet.
14 A compter de 1995, y compris trafic de charge de waggon seulement.
15 Y compris les bagages des voyageurs.
16 Y compris le trafic militaire (Grèce: et de l'Etat aussi).

17 Les données se réfèrent aux années fiscales commençant le 1er avril.
18 Non compris le bétail.
19 Avant de 1994, les données se réfèrent aux tonnes-kilomètres transportées, c'est-à-dire le produit du poids et de la distance effectivement parcourue. A partir de l'année 1994, l'unité utilisée est la tonne-kilomètre nette, c'est-à dire le produit du poids et de la distance pour lequel un paiement à été effectué.
20 Y compris bagages et les transports pour les besoins du service.
21 Malasie péninsulaire seulement.
22 Chemin de fer national de Chiriqui seulement.
23 A cessé de fonctionner en août 1997.
24 Chemin de fer de Panama et chemin de fer national de Chiriqui.
25 A compter d'avril, les Chemins de fer de Panama a recommencé des opérations.
26 Chemin de fer de Panama seulement.
27 Les opérations de train de marchandises interrompues pendant la période de novembre 1995 à août 1996 à cause des dommages de typhon.
28 Non compris le trafic fluvial de la compagnie des chemins de fer.
29 Y compris les militaires et les fonctionnaires.
30 Les données se réfèrent aux années fiscales finissant le 31e mars.
31 A partir de 1988, non compris la Namibie.
32 Les données se réfèrent aux années fiscales finissant le 30e septembre.
33 Y compris chemins-de-fer de l'état y MTAB.
34 A compter de 1992, réduction imputable à des changements de frontière affectant la ligne de Douchanbé de la Compagnie Csredniya Niyatskaya (Asie centrale).
35 Petite vitesse seulement.
36 A compter de l'année de 1997, transport passager interrompu.
37 Non compris l'Irlande du Nord.
38 A partir de 1986, non compris les chemins de fer de banlieue.
39 Réseaux de catégorie 1 seulement.
40 Transport passager interrompu pendant la période 1988 à 1992.
41 Y compris le trafic en Botswana.

60
Motor vehicles in use
Véhicules automobiles en circulation
Passenger cars and commercial vehicles: thousand units
Voitures de tourisme et véhicules utilitaires : milliers de véhicules

Country or area Pays or zone	1991	1992	1993	1994	1995	1996	1997	1998	1999	2000
World Monde										
Passenger cars[1]										
Voitures de tourisme[1]	451 927.6	445 741.8	449 989.7	469 302.6	457 762.8	470 586.6	452 101.3	477 095.8	...	...
Commercial vehicles[1]										
Véhicules utilitaires[1]	141 929.8	139 575.4	141 022.8	149 548.2	165 367.5	186 867.0	176 943.2	185 943.1	...	...
Afghanistan Afghanistan										
Passenger cars										
Voitures de tourisme	31.0	31.0	1.6	1.6	1.6	4.1	4.6	4.9	5.4	6.2
Commercial vehicles										
Véhicules utilitaires	25.0	25.0	0.6	0.6	0.6	4.5	5.3	5.4	6.2	7.0
Albania Albanie										
Passenger cars										
Voitures de tourisme	...	...	56.7	67.9	58.6	67.2	76.8	90.7	99.0	114.5
Commercial vehicles										
Véhicules utilitaires	...	...	39.3	51.1	29.1	30.6	33.2	37.1	40.9	43.0
Algeria Algérie										
Passenger cars										
Voitures de tourisme	1 502.6	1 528.3	1 547.8	1 555.8	1 562.1	1 588.0	1 615.1	1 634.4	1 676.8	1 721.8
Commercial vehicles										
Véhicules utilitaires	903.9	917.2	926.0	930.8	933.1	958.1	952.7	963.9	986.7	1 010.5
American Samoa Samoa américaines										
Passenger cars										
Voitures de tourisme	4.2	5.0	4.6	4.6	4.7	5.4	5.3	5.7	6.2	...
Commercial vehicles										
Véhicules utilitaires	0.3	0.3	0.5	0.4	0.4	0.5	0.5	0.7	0.7	...
Angola Angola										
Passenger cars[1]										
Voitures de tourisme[1]	122.0	122.0	19.3	20.4	22.1	24.1	26.2	28.2	...	...
Commercial vehicles[1]										
Véhicules utilitaires[1]	41.0	42.2	16.6	17.5	19.1	21.7	26.2	30.6	...	...
Antigua and Barbuda Antigua-et-Barbuda										
Passenger cars										
Voitures de tourisme	19.2	13.5	14.8	15.0	15.1	21.6[2]	23.7[2]	24.0[2]	...	...
Commercial vehicles										
Véhicules utilitaires	3.8	3.5	4.6	4.8	4.8	...	...	...	...	...
Argentina Argentine										
Passenger cars										
Voitures de tourisme	4 405.0	4 809.0	4 856.0	4 427.0	4 665.0	4 783.9	4 904.3	6 047.8	...	...
Commercial vehicles										
Véhicules utilitaires	1 554.0	1 648.0	1 664.0	1 342.0	1 233.0	4 254.0	1 172.0	1 094.0	1 029.0	1 004.0
Australia Australie										
Passenger cars[3]										
Voitures de tourisme[3]	7 734.1	7 913.2	8 050.0	8 209.0	8 660.6	9 021.5	9 239.5	9 560.6	...	...
Commercial vehicles[3]										
Véhicules utilitaires[3]	1 915.4	2 041.3	2 043.0	2 151.0	1 990.3	2 075.6	2 111.7	2 177.4	...	...
Austria Autriche										
Passenger cars[4]										
Voitures de tourisme[4]	3 100.0	3 244.9	3 367.6	3 479.6	3 599.6	3 691.7	3 782.5	3 887.2	4 009.6	4 097.0
Commercial vehicles[4 5]										
Véhicules utilitaires[4 5]	657.6	674.6	685.7	698.2	710.1	721.1	736.2	752.1	758.0	770.0
Azerbaijan Azerbaïdjan										
Passenger cars										
Voitures de tourisme	260.0	258.3	263.3	276.4	278.3	273.7	271.3	281.3	311.6	332.1
Commercial vehicles										
Véhicules utilitaires	148.5	141.3	132.3	127.5	125.5	122.9	115.6	117.6	122.8	133.4
Bahamas Bahamas										
Passenger cars										
Voitures de tourisme	69.0[1]	44.7[1]	46.1[1]	54.4	67.1	86.6[6]	89.7[6]	67.4[1]	...	...

60
Motor vehicles in use
Passenger cars and commercial vehicles: thousand units [*cont.*]
Véhicules automobiles en circulation
Voitures de tourisme et véhicules utilitaires : milliers de véhicules [*suite*]

Country or area Pays or zone	1991	1992	1993	1994	1995	1996	1997	1998	1999	2000
Commercial vehicles Véhicules utilitaires	14.0[1]	11.5[1]	11.9[1]	9.3	13.7	16.9[6]	17.6[6]	16.8[1]	...	...
Bahrain Bahreïn										
Passenger cars Voitures de tourisme	105.7	113.8	122.9	130.7	135.4	140.0	147.9	160.2	169.6	...
Commercial vehicles Véhicules utilitaires	25.0	26.5	28.2	29.4	30.5	31.5	32.8	34.5	35.7	
Bangladesh Bangladesh										
Passenger cars Voitures de tourisme	44.2	45.6	46.6	48.1	51.1	55.8	61.2	65.0	...	...
Commercial vehicles Véhicules utilitaires	82.2	87.5	92.4	99.4	111.7	126.8	138.1	145.9	...	
Barbados Barbade										
Passenger cars[7] Voitures de tourisme[7]	42.9	41.3	46.4	43.5	47.2	49.8	53.6	57.5	62.1	...
Commercial vehicles[8] Véhicules utilitaires[8]	5.8	5.6	5.8	5.8	7.1	6.9	7.9	8.6	9.4	...
Belarus Bélarus										
Passenger cars Voitures de tourisme	657.2	722.8	773.6	875.6	939.6	1 035.8	1 132.8	1 279.2	1 351.1	1 448.5
Belgium Belgique										
Passenger cars Voitures de tourisme	3 934.0	3 991.6	4 079.5	4 208.1	4 270.3	4 336.1	4 412.1	4 488.5	4 580.0	4 675.1
Commercial vehicles Véhicules utilitaires	414.3	420.0	427.7	444.4	457.1	471.8	491.3	510.1	539.0	563.2
Belize Belize										
Passenger cars[6][9] Voitures de tourisme[6][9]	...	...	...	...	16.1	17.0	19.1	19.3	21.0	21.5
Commercial vehicles[6][9] Véhicules utilitaires[6][9]	...	...	...	...	3.0	3.1	3.6	3.7	3.9	3.9
Benin Bénin										
Passenger cars[1] Voitures de tourisme[1]	22.0	22.0	7.1	7.3	7.3	7.3	7.3	7.3	...	...
Commercial vehicles[1] Véhicules utilitaires[1]	12.0	12.2	5.3	5.5	5.7	5.8	6.0	6.2	...	...
Bermuda Bermudes										
Passenger cars Voitures de tourisme	20.1	19.7	20.1	20.7	21.1	21.2	21.6	22.0	22.6	...
Commercial vehicles Véhicules utilitaires	3.6	3.9	4.0	4.2	4.4	4.1	4.2	5.0	4.2	...
Bolivia Bolivie										
Passenger cars Voitures de tourisme	131.2	146.6	164.7	183.7	201.9	220.3	234.1	274.1	295.1	304.6
Commercial vehicles Véhicules utilitaires	80.2	87.7	95.3	103.4	112.2	119.8	124.8	138.0	147.2	151.7
Botswana Botswana										
Passenger cars Voitures de tourisme	20.8	23.4	26.3	27.1	30.5	26.7	28.2	37.0	44.5	...
Commercial vehicles Véhicules utilitaires	45.3	49.2	55.0	60.9	63.7	48.1	52.3	58.7	67.9	...
Brazil Brésil										
Passenger cars[1] Voitures de tourisme[1]	12 128.0	7 855.5	8 098.4	9 524.0	10 320.5	12 666.0	9 385.8	10 828.8	...	...
Commercial vehicles[1] Véhicules utilitaires[1]	1 075.0	1 170.8	1 839.0	2 378.7	2 520.4	2 896.0	2 087.5	2 429.5	...	...
British Virgin Islands Iles Vierges britanniques										
Passenger cars[2] Voitures de tourisme[2]	6.5	6.9	6.7	7.0	...	...	...	...	...	...

60
Motor vehicles in use
Passenger cars and commercial vehicles: thousand units [*cont.*]
Véhicules automobiles en circulation
Voitures de tourisme et véhicules utilitaires : milliers de véhicules [*suite*]

Country or area Pays ou zone	1991	1992	1993	1994	1995	1996	1997	1998	1999	2000
Brunei Darussalam Brunéi Darussalam										
Passenger cars										
Voitures de tourisme	114.1	122.0	130.0	135.9	141.7	150.1	163.1	170.2	176.0	...
Commercial vehicles										
Véhicules utilitaires	11.9	13.7	14.5	15.4	16.3	17.3	18.3	19.1	19.4	...
Bulgaria Bulgarie										
Passenger cars										
Voitures de tourisme	1 359.0	1 411.3	1 505.5	1 587.9	1 647.6	1 707.0	1 730.5	1 809.4	1 908.4	1 992.8
Commercial vehicles										
Véhicules utilitaires	209.8	224.5	243.2	255.4	264.2	270.7	273.2	283.8	293.5	301.7
Burkina Faso Burkina Faso										
Passenger cars										
Voitures de tourisme	25.0	27.4	29.9	32.0	35.5[1]	35.5[1]	35.5[1]	35.5[1]	...	...
Commercial vehicles										
Véhicules utilitaires	21.0	22.2	23.4	24.0	19.5[1]	19.5[1]	19.5[1]	19.5[1]	...	...
Burundi Burundi										
Passenger cars										
Voitures de tourisme	16.4	17.5	18.5	17.5	8.2[1]	8.2[1]	8.2[1]	8.2[1]	...	...
Commercial vehicles										
Véhicules utilitaires	11.3	11.8	12.3	10.2	11.8[1]	11.8[1]	11.8[1]	11.8[1]	...	...
Cambodia Cambodge										
Passenger cars										
Voitures de tourisme	5.6	10.8	6.8	7.4	8.0	6.3	8.4	8.0	8.5	8.3
Commercial vehicles										
Véhicules utilitaires	2.9	0.9	0.7	1.7	2.1	1.4	1.8	1.6	1.5	3.1
Cameroon Cameroun										
Passenger cars										
Voitures de tourisme	104.6	98.1	92.8	88.3	94.7	100.9	102.2	105.8	110.7	115.9
Commercial vehicles										
Véhicules utilitaires	45.0	42.9	39.0	37.6	39.6	40.6	41.6	43.2	45.3	47.4
Canada Canada										
Passenger cars[4]										
Voitures de tourisme[4]	12 577.6	12 781.1	12 926.8	13 122.5	13 182.9	13 251.1	13 486.9	13 887.3	16 538.0	16 860.5
Commercial vehicles[4]										
Véhicules utilitaires[4]	3 399.4	3 349.5	3 346.1	3 401.8	3 420.3	3 476.2	3 526.9	3 625.8	649.1[10]	668.0[10]
Cape Verde Cap-Vert										
Passenger cars										
Voitures de tourisme	4.4	5.5	6.5	7.7	8.0	9.3	10.3	11.4	13.5	...
Commercial vehicles										
Véhicules utilitaires	1.2	1.2	1.3	2.0	2.0	2.2	2.5	2.8	3.1	...
Cayman Islands Îles Caïmanes										
Passenger cars										
Voitures de tourisme	10.8	11.3	11.6	12.3	13.5	14.9	16.0	15.8	17.9	19.8
Commercial vehicles										
Véhicules utilitaires	2.6	2.6	2.7	2.8	9.1	3.4	3.7	3.6	4.1	4.4
Central African Rep. Rép. centrafricaine										
Passenger cars										
Voitures de tourisme	9.2	8.0	10.4	11.9	8.9	...	...	...	...	...
Commercial vehicles										
Véhicules utilitaires	2.3	1.7	2.4	2.8	3.5	...	...	...	...	...
Chad Tchad										
Passenger cars[11]										
Voitures de tourisme[11]	8.5	9.0	9.5	9.5	8.7	...	...	...	...	...
Commercial vehicles[11]										
Véhicules utilitaires[11]	6.5	7.0	7.2	7.2	12.4	...	...	...	...	...
Chile Chili										
Passenger cars										
Voitures de tourisme	765.5	826.8	896.5	914.3	1 026.0	1 121.2	1 175.8	1 236.9	1 323.8	...

60

Motor vehicles in use
Passenger cars and commercial vehicles: thousand units [*cont.*]
Véhicules automobiles en circulation
Voitures de tourisme et véhicules utilitaires : milliers de véhicules [*suite*]

Country or area Pays or zone	1991	1992	1993	1994	1995	1996	1997	1998	1999	2000
Commercial vehicles[13] Véhicules utilitaires[13]	192.0[12]	198.8[12]	211.0[12]	492.7[14]	540.0[14]	585.7[14]	620.5[14]	656.0[14]	691.1[14]	...
China †† Chine ††										
Passenger cars Voitures de tourisme	1 852.4	2 261.6	2 859.8	3 497.4	4 179.0	4 880.2	5 805.6	6 548.3	...	...
Commercial vehicles Véhicules utilitaires	3 986.2	4 414.5	5 010.0	5 603.3	5 854.3	5 750.3	6 012.3	6 278.9	...	...
China, Hong Kong SAR† Chine, Hong Kong RAS†										
Passenger cars Voitures de tourisme	229.3	254.6	277.5	297.3	303.3	311.2	332.8	336.2	339.6	350.4
Commercial vehicles Véhicules utilitaires	132.4	134.4	135.6	137.0	134.2	133.7	135.9	133.4	132.3	133.2
China, Macao SAR † Chine, Macao RAS †										
Passenger cars[13] Voitures de tourisme[13]	26.2	29.9	32.6	34.0	34.5	38.9	42.9	46.3	47.8	48.9
Commercial vehicles[13] Véhicules utilitaires[13]	6.5	6.5	6.6	6.3	6.2	6.3	6.6	6.6	7.4	7.1
Colombia Colombie										
Passenger cars[1] Voitures de tourisme[1]	715.0	715.0	761.7	688.1	718.9	800.0	584.1	725.4	...	...
Commercial vehicles[1] Véhicules utilitaires[1]	665.0	665.0	672.6	385.1	405.6	530.0	339.1	420.9	...	...
Congo Congo										
Passenger cars[1] Voitures de tourisme[1]	26.0	26.0	29.0	29.0	29.0	29.0	29.0	29.0	...	...
Commercial vehicles[1] Véhicules utilitaires[1]	20.0	20.1	16.6	16.6	16.6	16.6	16.6	16.6	...	...
Costa Rica Costa Rica										
Passenger cars Voitures de tourisme	180.8[4]	204.2[4]	220.1[4]	238.5[4]	254.8[4]	272.9[4]	294.1	316.8	326.5	...
Commercial vehicles Véhicules utilitaires	96.3[4]	110.3[4]	114.9[4]	127.1[4]	141.4[4]	151.1[4]	153.1	164.8	169.8	...
Côte d'Ivoire Côte d'Ivoire										
Passenger cars[1] Voitures de tourisme[1]	155.0	155.3	109.9	109.9	111.9	74.2	76.2	78.1	...	...
Commercial vehicles[1] Véhicules utilitaires[1]	90.0	90.3	46.1	47.1	50.3	35.3	35.3	36.3	...	...
Croatia Croatie										
Passenger cars Voitures de tourisme	735.7	669.8	646.2	698.4	710.9	835.7	932.3	1 000.0	1 063.5	1 124.8
Commercial vehicles Véhicules utilitaires	58.4	53.6	55.0	68.5	77.4	99.5	114.5	120.6	123.4	127.2
Cyprus Chypre										
Passenger cars Voitures de tourisme	190.1	198.2	203.6	210.4	219.7	226.8	235.0	249.2	257.0	267.6
Commercial vehicles Véhicules utilitaires	84.9	89.9	93.5	98.0	104.9	108.0	109.7	113.6	115.8	119.6
Czech Republic République tchèque										
Passenger cars Voitures de tourisme	2 435.6	2 522.4	2 693.9	2 967.3[15]	3 113.5[15]	3 349.0[15]	3 547.7[15]	3 687.5[15]	3 695.8[15]	3 720.3
Commercial vehicles[16] Véhicules utilitaires[16]	511.8	523.3	515.2	469.5[17]	490.0[17]	537.1[17]	562.3[17]	604.0[17]	583.3[17]	595.8
Denmark Danemark										
Passenger cars[4 18] Voitures de tourisme[4 18]	1 593.9	1 604.6	1 618.3	1 611.2	1 679.0	1 738.9	1 783.1	1 817.1	...	...
Commercial vehicles[4 18] Véhicules utilitaires[4 18]	309.4	376.6	326.4	335.6	347.6	353.6	359.8	371.5	...	...

60
Motor vehicles in use
Passenger cars and commercial vehicles: thousand units [*cont.*]
Véhicules automobiles en circulation
Voitures de tourisme et véhicules utilitaires : milliers de véhicules [*suite*]

Country or area Pays or zone	1991	1992	1993	1994	1995	1996	1997	1998	1999	2000
Djibouti Djibouti										
Passenger cars[11]										
Voitures de tourisme [11]	13.0	13.0	13.5	13.5	...	...	...	...	...	...
Commercial vehicles[11]										
Véhicules utilitaires [11]	2.5	3.0	3.0	3.0	...	...	...	...	...	...
Dominica Dominique										
Passenger cars										
Voitures de tourisme	4.5	4.8	5.8	7.0	7.4	7.9	8.3	8.7	...	...
Commercial vehicles[19]										
Véhicules utilitaires [19]	3.4	2.8	2.7	2.8	2.9	3.3	3.3	3.4	...	...
Dominican Republic Rép. dominicaine										
Passenger cars										
Voitures de tourisme	144.7	138.1	174.4	...	183.8	271.0	331.0	392.7	436.9	495.6
Commercial vehicles										
Véhicules utilitaires	98.6[20]	97.5[20]	118.5[20]	...	106.2	145.1	174.9	220.2	247.2	283.0
Ecuador Equateur										
Passenger cars										
Voitures de tourisme	181.2	194.5	202.4	219.8	253.5	268.2	276.5	301.4	322.3	...
Commercial vehicles										
Véhicules utilitaires	206.0	232.7	231.4	243.4	244.0	248.4	256.3	257.6	272.0	...
Egypt Egypte										
Passenger cars										
Voitures de tourisme	1 081.0	1 117.0	1 143.0	1 225.0	1 313.0	1 372.0	1 439.0	1 525.0	1 616.0	1 700.0
Commercial vehicles										
Véhicules utilitaires	389.0	408.0	423.0	445.0	466.0	484.0	508.0	539.0	577.0	600.0
El Salvador El Salvador										
Passenger cars										
Voitures de tourisme	53.0	80.5	88.4	86.9	113.8	121.8	129.8	136.6	142.2	148.0
Commercial vehicles										
Véhicules utilitaires	65.0	140.2	165.9	195.5	209.9	218.6	227.3	235.4	243.0	250.8
Estonia Estonie										
Passenger cars										
Voitures de tourisme	261.1	283.5	317.4	337.8	383.4	406.6	427.7	451.0	458.7	463.9
Commercial vehicles										
Véhicules utilitaires	85.7	83.0	82.8	60.0	72.6	78.0	83.1	86.9	87.2	88.2
Ethiopia Ethiopie										
Passenger cars[21]										
Voitures de tourisme [21]	40.2	40.0	47.0	52.7	60.0	62.4	66.2	68.9	71.0	...
Commercial vehicles[21]										
Véhicules utilitaires[21]	20.2	18.8	16.0	17.0	23.3	29.0	30.3	34.0	34.6	...
Fiji Fidji										
Passenger cars[22]										
Voitures de tourisme[22]	42.0	44.0	45.3	47.7	49.7	51.7	50.4	51.7	...	...
Commercial vehicles[23]										
Véhicules utilitaires[23]	41.9	43.8	44.8	46.4	47.5	48.5	48.0	48.6	...	...
Finland Finlande										
Passenger cars										
Voitures de tourisme	1 922.5	1 936.3	1 872.9	1 872.6	1 900.9	1 942.8	1 948.1	2 021.1	2 082.6	2 134.7
Commercial vehicles[24]										
Véhicules utilitaires[24]	273.4	271.2	261.4	257.5	260.1	266.9	275.4	289.7	303.2	314.2
France France										
Passenger cars										
Voitures de tourisme	23 810.0	24 020.0	24 385.0	24 900.0	25 100.0	25 500.0	26 090.0	26 810.0	27 480.0	...
Commercial vehicles[25]										
Véhicules utilitaires[25]	5 190.0	5 209.0	5 238.0	5 314.0	5 374.0	5 437.0	5 561.0	5 680.0	5 790.0	...

60
Motor vehicles in use
Passenger cars and commercial vehicles: thousand units [*cont.*]
Véhicules automobiles en circulation
Voitures de tourisme et véhicules utilitaires : milliers de véhicules [*suite*]

Country or area Pays or zone	1991	1992	1993	1994	1995	1996	1997	1998	1999	2000
French Guiana Guyane française										
Passenger cars[1]										
Voitures de tourisme[1]	27.0	27.7	29.1	24.4	26.5	28.2	28.2	28.2	...	...
Commercial vehicles[1]										
Véhicules utilitaires[1]	10.0	10.4	10.6	7.6	8.1	8.9	9.4	9.4		
Gabon Gabon										
Passenger cars[11]										
Voitures de tourisme[11]	23.0	23.0	24.0	24.0	23.0	...	...	...	...	...
Commercial vehicles[11]										
Véhicules utilitaires[11]	17.0	17.0	17.5	18.0	10.0	...	...	...	...	...
Gambia Gambie										
Passenger cars										
Voitures de tourisme	6.7	7.4	6.1	6.2	6.4	...	...	...	...	...
Commercial vehicles										
Véhicules utilitaires	2.5	2.8	3.4	3.5	3.5	...	...	...	...	...
Georgia Géorgie										
Passenger cars										
Voitures de tourisme	479.3	479.0	485.9	452.3	360.6	323.6	265.6	260.4	247.9	244.9
Commercial vehicles										
Véhicules utilitaires	96.5	138.6	147.7	101.2	104.3	90.7	79.6	71.0	68.9	66.8
Germany † Allemagne †										
Passenger cars										
Voitures de tourisme	32 087.6	36 042.4	38 772.5	39 765.4	40 404.3	40 987.5	41 372.0	41 673.8	42 323.7	42 839.9
Commercial vehicles										
Véhicules utilitaires	...	...	...	2 619.3	2 754.9	2 851.4	2 931.3	3 023.9	3 166.4	...
Ghana Ghana										
Passenger cars[1]										
Voitures de tourisme[1]	90.0	90.0	30.4	30.7	30.8	31.2	31.9	32.6	...	...
Commercial vehicles[1]										
Véhicules utilitaires[1]	43.0	44.2	31.5	33.1	35.7	38.4	38.4	38.4	...	...
Gibraltar Gibraltar										
Passenger cars										
Voitures de tourisme	18.1	24.0	18.0	18.5	18.4	19.0[1]	20.5[1]	21.9[1]	...	...
Commercial vehicles										
Véhicules utilitaires	2.6	2.9	1.1	1.2	1.0	12.2[1]	12.3[1]	12.4[1]	...	...
Greece Grèce										
Passenger cars										
Voitures de tourisme	1 777.5	1 829.1	1 958.5	2 074.1	2 204.8	2 339.4	2 500.1	2 675.7	2 928.9	...
Commercial vehicles										
Véhicules utilitaires	814.9	820.5	848.9	872.6	908.4	939.9	977.5	1 013.7	1 050.9	...
Greenland Groenland										
Passenger cars[4]										
Voitures de tourisme[4]	1.9	2.0	2.1	1.9	1.9	2.6	1.8	2.0	2.4	...
Commercial vehicles[4]										
Véhicules utilitaires[4]	1.5	1.5	1.4	1.6	1.4	1.2	1.5	1.4	1.5	...
Grenada Grenade										
Passenger cars[26]										
Voitures de tourisme[26]	...	...	...	...	9.7	10.3	11.4	12.7	14.1	15.5
Commercial vehicles										
Véhicules utilitaires	...	...	...	...	2.2	2.4	2.7	3.1	3.6	3.9
Guadeloupe Guadeloupe										
Passenger cars[1]										
Voitures de tourisme[1]	89.0	94.7	101.6	90.5	97.0	106.5	107.6	108.7	...	...
Commercial vehicles[1]										
Véhicules utilitaires[1]	35.0	36.0	37.5	26.6	28.9	32.5	34.1	35.6	...	...
Guam Guam										
Passenger cars										
Voitures de tourisme	72.8	76.7	74.7	65.1	79.8	79.1	67.8	69.0	66.4	64.5

60

Motor vehicles in use
Passenger cars and commercial vehicles: thousand units [*cont.*]
Véhicules automobiles en circulation
Voitures de tourisme et véhicules utilitaires : milliers de véhicules [*suite*]

Country or area Pays or zone	1991	1992	1993	1994	1995	1996	1997	1998	1999	2000
Commercial vehicles Véhicules utilitaires	29.7	30.2	30.6	27.5	34.7	33.8	28.9	28.9	27.4	26.6
Guatemala Guatemala										
Passenger cars Voitures de tourisme	...	...	...	...	...	...	...	646.5	...	...
Commercial vehicles Véhicules utilitaires	...	...	...	...	...	...	...	21.2	...	...
Guinea Guinée										
Passenger cars Voitures de tourisme	65.6	23.1[11]	24.0[11]	24.0[11]	23.2[11]	...	...	...	...	...
Commercial vehicles Véhicules utilitaires	29.0	13.0[11]	13.5[11]	14.0[11]	13.0[11]	...	...	...	...	...
Guinea-Bissau Guinée-Bissau										
Passenger cars[11] Voitures de tourisme[11]	3.3	3.5	...	...	...	...	...	...	...	...
Commercial vehicles[11] Véhicules utilitaires[11]	2.4	2.5	...	...	...	...	...	...	...	...
Guyana Guyana										
Passenger cars[1] Voitures de tourisme[1]	24.0	24.0	9.5	9.5	9.5	9.5	9.5	9.5	...	...
Commercial vehicles[1] Véhicules utilitaires[1]	9.0	9.0	2.6	2.7	2.9	3.0	3.1	3.2	...	...
Haiti Haïti										
Passenger cars Voitures de tourisme	32.0	32.0	32.0	30.0	49.0	59.0	...	...	93.0	...
Commercial vehicles Véhicules utilitaires	21.0	21.0	21.0	30.0	29.0	35.0	...	...	61.6	...
Honduras Honduras										
Passenger cars Voitures de tourisme	43.7	68.5	...	15.1[1]	16.1[1]	16.3[1]	16.5[1]	17.2[1]	...	...
Commercial vehicles Véhicules utilitaires	92.9	102.0	...	45.3[1]	48.0[1]	48.6[1]	49.1[1]	53.9[1]	...	...
Hungary Hongrie										
Passenger cars Voitures de tourisme	2 015.5	2 058.3	2 091.6	2 176.9	2 245.4	2 264.2	2 297.1	2 218.0	2 255.5	2 364.7
Commercial vehicles Véhicules utilitaires	289.6	288.9	296.2	318.5	345.0	351.3	360.9	355.4	363.0	384.3
Iceland Islande										
Passenger cars Voitures de tourisme	120.9	120.1	116.2	116.2	119.2	124.9	132.5	140.4	151.4	158.9
Commercial vehicles[27] Véhicules utilitaires[27]	16.0	16.0	15.6	15.6	16.0	16.6	17.5	18.1	19.4	21.1
India Inde										
Passenger cars Voitures de tourisme	2 954.0	3 205.0	3 361.0	3 569.0	3 841.0	4 204.0	4 662.0	5 056.0	...	...
Commercial vehicles[28] Véhicules utilitaires[28]	4 220.0	4 641.0	4 961.0	5 192.0	5 623.0	6 327.0	6 876.0	7 541.0	...	...
Indonesia Indonésie										
Passenger cars Voitures de tourisme	1 494.6	1 590.8	1 700.5	1 890.3	2 107.3	2 409.1	2 639.5	2 772.5	2 897.8	3 038.9
Commercial vehicles Véhicules utilitaires	1 592.7	1 666.0	1 729.0	1 903.6	2 024.7	2 030.2	2 160.0	2 220.5	2 273.2	2 373.4
Iran (Islamic Rep. of) Iran (Rép. islamique d')										
Passenger cars[1 29] Voitures de tourisme[1 29]	1 557.0	1 557.0	779.8	819.6	819.6	454.2	572.9	684.5	...	...
Commercial vehicles[1 29] Véhicules utilitaires[1 29]	561.0	584.1	589.2	589.2	589.2	346.4	346.4	355.1	...	...

60
Motor vehicles in use
Passenger cars and commercial vehicles: thousand units [cont.]
Véhicules automobiles en circulation
Voitures de tourisme et véhicules utilitaires : milliers de véhicules [suite]

Country or area Pays or zone	1991	1992	1993	1994	1995	1996	1997	1998	1999	2000
Iraq Iraq										
Passenger cars										
Voitures de tourisme	660.1	670.2	672.4	678.5	680.1	...	...	...	...	...
Commercial vehicles										
Véhicules utilitaires	295.0	299.5	309.3	317.2	319.9	...	...	...	...	...
Ireland Irlande										
Passenger cars[30 31 32]										
Voitures de tourisme[30 31 32]	843.2	865.4	898.3	947.2	999.7	1 067.8	1 145.9	1 209.2	1 283.4	...
Commercial vehicles[19 30]										
Véhicules utilitaires[19 30]	155.2	152.0	142.9	143.9	150.5	155.9	168.2	181.0	193.1	...
Israel Israël										
Passenger cars										
Voitures de tourisme	857.4	932.4	992.9	1 064.9	1 131.0	1 195.1	1 252.0	1 298.0	1 341.3	1 396.9
Commercial vehicles										
Véhicules utilitaires	178.0	200.0	217.0	250.0	263.0	279.0	292.0	297.9	308.8	328.0
Italy Italie										
Passenger cars										
Voitures de tourisme	28 434.9	29 429.6	29 652.0	29 665.3	30 149.6	30 467.1	30 741.9	31 370.8	31 953.2	...
Commercial vehicles										
Véhicules utilitaires	2 529.6	2 763.0	2 663.0	2 745.5	2 863.5	3 177.7	3 253.7	3 336.4	3 409.5	...
Jamaica Jamaïque										
Passenger cars										
Voitures de tourisme	77.8	73.0	81.1	86.8	104.0	120.7	156.8	...	...	...
Commercial vehicles										
Véhicules utilitaires	29.8	30.5	36.2	41.3	49.1	52.8	56.1	...	...	...
Japan Japon										
Passenger cars[33 34]										
Voitures de tourisme[33 34]	37 076.0	38 964.0	40 772.0	42 679.0	44 680.0	46 869.0	48 611.0	49 896.0	51 165.0	52 738.0
Commercial vehicles[33]										
Véhicules utilitaires[33]	21 575.0	21 383.0	21 132.0	20 916.0	20 676.0	20 334.0	19 859.0	19 821.0	18 869.0	18 463.6
Jordan Jordanie										
Passenger cars[4]										
Voitures de tourisme[4]	166.8	181.5	175.3	164.0	188.0	212.2	202.1	200.0	213.0	255.8
Commercial vehicles[4]										
Véhicules utilitaires[4]	61.4	51.5	63.8	75.3	76.7	80.6	85.1	106.9	109.0	104.5
Kazakhstan Kazakhstan										
Passenger cars										
Voitures de tourisme	848.9	916.1	955.9	991.7	1 034.1	997.5	973.3	971.2	987.7	...
Commercial vehicles										
Véhicules utilitaires	453.5	456.9	456.4	428.1	390.9	360.4	315.3	277.1	257.4	...
Kenya Kenya										
Passenger cars										
Voitures de tourisme	163.6	165.1	171.5	171.6	172.8	202.7	211.9	225.1	238.9	244.8
Commercial vehicles										
Véhicules utilitaires	120.6	158.1	162.2	162.3	163.3	187.7	196.1	204.3	212.7	217.8
Korea, Republic of Corée, République de										
Passenger cars[35]										
Voitures de tourisme[35]	2 727.9	3 461.1	4 271.3	5 148.7	6 006.3	6 893.6	7 586.5	7 580.9	7 837.2	...
Commercial vehicles[35]										
Véhicules utilitaires[35]	1 505.1	1 745.1	1 976.6	2 226.7	2 429.2	2 625.6	2 791.2	2 854.0	3 291.3	...
Kuwait Koweït										
Passenger cars										
Voitures de tourisme	554.7	579.8	600.0	629.7	662.9	701.2	540.0	585.0	624.0	...
Commercial vehicles										
Véhicules utilitaires	149.8	151.1	147.0	148.7	153.5	160.0	115.0	124.0	130.0	...
Kyrgyzstan Kirghizistan										
Passenger cars										
Voitures de tourisme	212.6	215.0	188.3	140.0	197.5	172.4	176.1	187.7	187.3	189.8

60
Motor vehicles in use
Passenger cars and commercial vehicles: thousand units [*cont.*]
Véhicules automobiles en circulation
Voitures de tourisme et véhicules utilitaires : milliers de véhicules [*suite*]

Country or area Pays or zone	1991	1992	1993	1994	1995	1996	1997	1998	1999	2000
Latvia Lettonie										
Passenger cars										
Voitures de tourisme	328.5	350.0	367.5	251.6	331.8	379.9	431.8	482.7	525.6	556.8
Commercial vehicles										
Véhicules utilitaires	83.3	83.3	72.1	73.5	85.1	90.2	95.4	96.5	101.8	108.6
Lebanon Liban										
Passenger cars										
Voitures de tourisme	...	...	943.1	1 141.7	1 197.5	1 250.5	1 299.4[36]	1 335.7[36]	...	...
Commercial vehicles										
Véhicules utilitaires	...	...	77.3	82.9	84.7	87.4	859.3[36]	95.4[36]	...	...
Liberia Libéria										
Passenger cars[1]										
Voitures de tourisme[1]	...	...	17.4	17.4	17.4	17.4	17.4	17.4	...	...
Commercial vehicles[1]										
Véhicules utilitaires[1]	...	...	10.7	10.7	10.7	10.7	10.7	10.7	...	...
Libyan Arab Jamah. Jamah. arabe libyenne										
Passenger cars										
Voitures de tourisme	450.0[11]	448.0[11]	448.0[11]	448.0[11]	448.0[11]	829.0	859.0	...	...	...
Commercial vehicles										
Véhicules utilitaires	330.0[11]	322.0[11]	322.0[11]	322.0[11]	322.0[11]	357.5	362.4	...	...	...
Lithuania Lituanie										
Passenger cars										
Voitures de tourisme	530.8	565.3	597.7	652.8	718.5	785.1	882.1	980.9	1 089.3	1 172.4
Commercial vehicles										
Véhicules utilitaires	107.7	112.5	115.1	118.2	125.9	104.8	108.6	114.6	112.2	113.7
Luxembourg Luxembourg										
Passenger cars										
Voitures de tourisme	191.6	200.7	208.8	217.8	229.0	231.7	236.8	244.1	253.4	...
Commercial vehicles[5]										
Véhicules utilitaires[5]	38.0	40.2	42.2	45.6	48.1	47.8	49.2	51.1	53.6	...
Madagascar Madagascar										
Passenger cars										
Voitures de tourisme	47.0[1]	10.9[1]	11.1[1]	11.1[1]	11.1[1]	11.1[1]	11.3[1]	64.0	...	...
Commercial vehicles										
Véhicules utilitaires	33.0[1]	12.6[1]	13.3[1]	13.3[1]	13.3[1]	13.9[1]	15.5[1]	9.1	...	...
Malawi Malawi										
Passenger cars[4]										
Voitures de tourisme[4]	# 6.6	5.3	1.8	2.3	1.5	1.6	...	...	...	...
Commercial vehicles[4]										
Véhicules utilitaires[4]	2.7	2.7	1.4	1.8	2.2	1.9	...	...	...	...
Malaysia Malaisie										
Passenger cars										
Voitures de tourisme	170.1	131.0	132.8	186.6	256.4	325.7	379.5	163.8	300.4	350.4
Commercial vehicles[24]										
Véhicules utilitaires[24]	49.3	43.7	33.5	49.9	74.9	102.7	96.5	19.0	28.6	36.8
Maldives Maldives										
Passenger cars										
Voitures de tourisme	0.1	0.1	0.1	0.2	0.1	0.2	0.2	0.2	0.2	0.3
Commercial vehicles										
Véhicules utilitaires	0.1	0.1	0.2	0.2	0.1	0.1	0.2	0.2	0.2	0.4
Mali Mali										
Passenger cars										
Voitures de tourisme	21.0	21.0	6.3	6.3	6.3	6.3[1]	6.3[1]	6.3[1]	...	...
Commercial vehicles										
Véhicules utilitaires	8.0	8.4	6.6	6.8	7.2	7.6[1]	7.6[1]	7.6[1]	...	...

60
Motor vehicles in use
Passenger cars and commercial vehicles: thousand units [*cont.*]
Véhicules automobiles en circulation
Voitures de tourisme et véhicules utilitaires : milliers de véhicules [*suite*]

Country or area Pays or zone	1991	1992	1993	1994	1995	1996	1997	1998	1999	2000
Malta Malte										
Passenger cars Voitures de tourisme	121.6	125.0	152.6	170.6	199.3	166.2	183.8	191.8	201.8	211.3
Commercial vehicles Véhicules utilitaires	21.7	35.4	50.9	55.7	40.8	39.4	47.4	49.5	51.2	52.6
Martinique Martinique										
Passenger cars[1] Voitures de tourisme[1]	96.0	102.6	80.8	86.7	95.0	...	...	...	...	...
Commercial vehicles[1] Véhicules utilitaires[1]	31.0	31.9	19.3	20.0	21.5	...	...	...	...	...
Mauritania Mauritanie										
Passenger cars[1] Voitures de tourisme[1]	8.0	8.0	5.0	5.1	5.1	5.2	5.3	5.4	...	...
Commercial vehicles[1] Véhicules utilitaires[1]	5.0	5.5	5.0	5.3	5.6	6.0	6.3	6.6	...	...
Mauritius Maurice										
Passenger cars Voitures de tourisme	48.6	52.4	55.8	59.6	63.6	68.1	73.4	78.5	83.0	87.5
Commercial vehicles Véhicules utilitaires	18.7	20.6	22.1	23.3	24.4	25.3	26.6	29.1	31.7	34.2
Mexico Mexique										
Passenger cars[4] Voitures de tourisme[4]	7 220.0	7 750.0	8 112.0	7 772.0	8 074.0	8 437.0	9 023.0	9 761.0	10 282.0	10 444.0
Commercial vehicles[4] Véhicules utilitaires[4]	3 404.0	3 601.0	3 695.0	3 759.0	3 751.0	3 773.0	4 034.0	4 282.0	4 569.0	5 043.0
Morocco Maroc										
Passenger cars[13] Voitures de tourisme[13]	707.1	778.9	849.3	944.0	992.0	1 018.1	1 060.3	1 108.7	1 161.9	...
Commercial vehicles[13] Véhicules utilitaires[13]	295.5	307.4	316.7	332.1	343.2	351.6	365.7	382.0	400.3	...
Mozambique Mozambique										
Passenger cars[1] Voitures de tourisme[1]	84.0	84.0	84.0	27.2	27.2	27.2	27.2	27.2	...	...
Commercial vehicles[1] Véhicules utilitaires[1]	26.0	26.2	26.8	14.3	14.4	14.5	14.5	14.5	...	...
Myanmar Myanmar										
Passenger cars[4] Voitures de tourisme[4]	88.6	100.2	115.9	125.4	145.4	171.3	177.9	177.6	171.1	173.9
Commercial vehicles[4] Véhicules utilitaires[4]	56.6	59.7	66.6	58.2	63.1	68.3	74.8	75.9	83.4	90.4
Nepal Népal										
Passenger cars Voitures de tourisme	24.1	26.2	28.4	31.5	34.5	39.8	42.8	46.9	49.4	...
Commercial vehicles Véhicules utilitaires	...	9.3	103.7	99.5	113.8	131.8	147.9	164.2	185.8	...
Netherlands Pays-Bas										
Passenger cars[4 37] Voitures de tourisme[4 37]	5 205.0	5 247.0	5 341.0	5 456.0	5 581.0	5 664.0	5 810.0	5 931.0	6 120.0	...
Commercial vehicles[4 37] Véhicules utilitaires[4 37]	565.0	590.0	631.0	652.0	654.0	666.0	695.0	738.0	806.0	...
New Caledonia Nouvelle-Calédonie										
Passenger cars Voitures de tourisme	55.0[1]	56.7[1]	58.5[1]	50.4[1]	52.8[1]	55.1[1]	57.9[1]	76.4[2]	80.3[2]	83.5[2]
Commercial vehicles[1] Véhicules utilitaires[1]	20.0	21.2	22.6	17.2	18.4	20.8	23.0	...	...	...

60
Motor vehicles in use
Passenger cars and commercial vehicles: thousand units [*cont.*]
Véhicules automobiles en circulation
Voitures de tourisme et véhicules utilitaires : milliers de véhicules [*suite*]

Country or area Pays or zone	1991	1992	1993	1994	1995	1996	1997	1998	1999	2000
New Zealand Nouvelle-Zélande										
Passenger cars[38]										
Voitures de tourisme[38]	1 551.3	1 554.9	1 575.6	1 615.9	1 665.0	1 655.8	1 697.2	1 768.2	1 855.8	1 905.6
Commercial vehicles[38]										
Véhicules utilitaires[38]	323.6	330.9	344.9	396.2	411.9	403.0	407.8	422.6	433.6	438.1
Nicaragua Nicaragua										
Passenger cars										
Voitures de tourisme	61.4	67.2	68.4	72.4	72.7	65.1	58.1	63.1	65.1	...
Commercial vehicles										
Véhicules utilitaires	54.8	69.5	66.3	69.5	81.8	82.9	70.6	78.9	82.9	...
Niger Niger										
Passenger cars										
Voitures de tourisme	18.0[11]	16.0[1]	16.0[11]	16.0[11]	16.0[11]	...	...	...	...	...
Commercial vehicles										
Véhicules utilitaires	18.0[11]	18.0[1]	18.0[11]	18.0[11]	18.0[11]	...	...	...	...	...
Nigeria Nigéria										
Passenger cars[39]										
Voitures de tourisme[39]	27.3	37.4	63.6	45.4	46.1	40.7	52.3	...	...	...
Commercial vehicles[39]										
Véhicules utilitaires[39]	1.1	4.6	1.4	6.8	8.6	10.5	13.5			
Norway Norvège										
Passenger cars[4]										
Voitures de tourisme[4]	1 614.6	1 619.4	1 633.0	1 653.7	1 684.7	1 661.2	1 758.0	1 786.0	1 813.6	1 851.9
Commercial vehicles[4 40]										
Véhicules utilitaires[4 40]	334.3	341.6	352.5	366.3	382.0	392.1	412.2	427.0	440.0	451.0
Oman Oman										
Passenger cars[41]										
Voitures de tourisme[41]	169.2	171.3	184.3	194.5	204.0	220.4	245.1	279.1	310.4	...
Commercial vehicles[42]										
Véhicules utilitaires[42]	88.1	84.4	86.6	88.2	89.3	92.0	101.2	110.7	117.6	...
Pakistan Pakistan										
Passenger cars[4]										
Voitures de tourisme[4]	594.9	659.0	670.0	690.9	772.6	816.1	863.0	930.1	1 004.3	1 066.1
Commercial vehicles[4]										
Véhicules utilitaires[4]	235.8	262.9	269.6	285.8	305.8	333.6	351.7	379.0	406.4	434.5
Panama Panama										
Passenger cars										
Voitures de tourisme	144.2	149.9	161.2	169.8	178.3	188.3	198.7	212.6	...	...
Commercial vehicles										
Véhicules utilitaires	47.3	50.4	55.0	56.5	60.4	60.5	64.2	68.4	...	...
Papua New Guinea Papouasie-Nvl-Guinée										
Passenger cars										
Voitures de tourisme	...	11.5[11]	13.0[11]	11.5[11]	20.0[11]	21.7[1]	21.7[1]	21.7[1]	...	...
Commercial vehicles										
Véhicules utilitaires	...	29.8[11]	32.0[11]	30.8[11]	35.0[11]	81.1[1]	85.5[1]	89.7[1]	...	...
Paraguay Paraguay										
Passenger cars										
Voitures de tourisme	190.9	221.1	250.7	...	...	...	...	...	...	...
Commercial vehicles										
Véhicules utilitaires	30.7	34.9	37.7	...	...	...	...	...	...	...
Peru Pérou										
Passenger cars										
Voitures de tourisme	379.1	402.4	418.6	444.2	505.8	557.0	595.8	645.9	684.6	731.3
Commercial vehicles										
Véhicules utilitaires	244.9	270.6	288.8	316.6	356.8	379.5	389.9	409.8	429.7	459.6

60
Motor vehicles in use
Passenger cars and commercial vehicles: thousand units [*cont.*]
Véhicules automobiles en circulation
Voitures de tourisme et véhicules utilitaires : milliers de véhicules [*suite*]

Country or area Pays or zone	1991	1992	1993	1994	1995	1996	1997	1998	1999	2000
Philippines Philippines										
Passenger cars										
Voitures de tourisme	1 118.6	1 223.9	1 364.0	1 483.9	1 623.5	1 802.5	1 933.1	1 992.4	2 082.8	...
Commercial vehicles										
Véhicules utilitaires	156.1	172.2	189.7	207.3	220.9	249.6	274.7	263.0	276.6	...
Poland Pologne										
Passenger cars										
Voitures de tourisme	6 112.2	6 504.7	6 770.6	7 153.1	7 517.3	8 054.4	8 533.5	8 890.8	9 282.8	...
Commercial vehicles[43]										
Véhicules utilitaires[43]	1 240.2	1 299.5	1 321.9	1 395.1	1 442.3	1 522.2	1 579.0	1 657.1	1 777.9	...
Portugal Portugal										
Passenger cars[44][45]										
Voitures de tourisme[44][45]	2 774.7	3 049.8	3 295.1	3 532.0	3 751.0	4 002.6[46]	4 272.5[46]	4 587.3[46]	4 931.7[46]	...
Commercial vehicles[45]										
Véhicules utilitaires[45]	881.2[13]	964.0	1 050.1	1 158.6	1 218.8	1 292.2[46]	1 383.9[46]	1 492.4[46]	1 600.1[46]	...
Puerto Rico Porto Rico										
Passenger cars[3]										
Voitures de tourisme[3]	1 321.9	1 347.0	1 393.3	1 484.7	1 597.0	1 726.4	1 840.6	1 962.3	2 038.9	2 035.3
Commercial vehicles[3]										
Véhicules utilitaires[3]	192.1	201.5	239.6	257.7	270.6	290.2	288.8	298.9	306.6	...
Qatar Qatar										
Passenger cars										
Voitures de tourisme	114.5	123.6	132.1	137.6	143.4	151.9	164.7	178.0	188.0	199.6
Commercial vehicles										
Véhicules utilitaires	53.9	57.5	61.5	65.8	69.5	73.8	79.1	85.0	88.9	92.9
Republic of Moldova République de Moldova										
Passenger cars										
Voitures de tourisme	218.1	166.3[47]	166.4[47]	169.4[47]	165.9[47]	173.6[47]	206.0[47]	222.8[47]	232.3[47]	...
Commercial vehicles[48]										
Véhicules utilitaires[48]	14.3	10.1[47]	8.9[47]	7.8[47]	12.9[47]	11.5[47]	10.4[47]	9.2[47]	8.1[47]	6.9[47]
Réunion Réunion										
Passenger cars										
Voitures de tourisme	112.0	119.3	127.8	133.1	142.1	150.6	159.3	167.9	180.6	247.8[2]
Commercial vehicles										
Véhicules utilitaires	34.4	36.6	39.2	40.9	43.6	46.2	49.0	51.6	54.0	...
Romania Roumanie										
Passenger cars										
Voitures de tourisme	1 432.0	1 593.0	1 793.0	2 020.0	2 197.0	2 392.0	2 605.0	2 822.0	2 980.0	...
Commercial vehicles										
Véhicules utilitaires	291.0	311.0	336.0	362.0	385.0	409.0	428.0	456.0	489.0	...
Russian Federation Fédération de Russie										
Passenger cars[49]										
Voitures de tourisme[49]	9 712.7	10 531.3	11 518.3	12 863.5	14 195.3	15 815.0	17 613.6	18 819.6	19 717.8	20 353.0
Commercial vehicles										
Véhicules utilitaires	2 779.3	2 847.9	2 924.0	3 006.0	3 078.1	3 041.1	3 103.1	3 108.2	3 196.2	3 232.4
Rwanda Rwanda										
Passenger cars										
Voitures de tourisme	15.0[11]	7.9[11]	...	...	1.2	3.2	5.8	7.7	9.2	10.7
Commercial vehicles										
Véhicules utilitaires	10.0[11]	2.0[11]	...	...	1.7	4.6	9.0	11.3	13.6	16.3
Saint Kitts and Nevis Saint-Kitts-et-Nevis										
Passenger cars										
Voitures de tourisme	3.9	4.1	4.5	4.8	5.2	5.5	6.3	6.3	7.7	...
Commercial vehicles										
Véhicules utilitaires	2.7	2.3	2.4	2.4	2.3	2.5	2.4	2.9	3.9	...

60
Motor vehicles in use
Passenger cars and commercial vehicles: thousand units [*cont.*]
Véhicules automobiles en circulation
Voitures de tourisme et véhicules utilitaires : milliers de véhicules [*suite*]

Country or area Pays or zone	1991	1992	1993	1994	1995	1996	1997	1998	1999	2000
Saint Lucia Sainte-Lucie										
Passenger cars										
Voitures de tourisme	9.1	9.3	10.1	11.4	12.5	13.5	...	...	...	
Commercial vehicles										
Véhicules utilitaires	8.4	9.3	10.5	9.5	...	10.8	...	...	...	
St. Vincent-Grenadines St. Vincent-Grenadines										
Passenger cars										
Voitures de tourisme	5.3	5.0	5.4	5.7	5.3	6.1	7.4	8.0	8.7	9.1
Commercial vehicles										
Véhicules utilitaires	2.8	2.0	3.1	3.2	3.7	3.2	3.8	4.1	3.9	4.0
Saudi Arabia Arabie saoudite										
Passenger cars[2,50]										
Voitures de tourisme[2,50]	5 117.4	5 328.5	5 588.0	5 861.6	6 111.1	6 333.9	6 580.0	7 046.0	...	...
Senegal Sénégal										
Passenger cars[11]										
Voitures de tourisme[11]	97.0	100.0	102.0	105.0	106.0	...	...	...	...	...
Commercial vehicles[11]										
Véhicules utilitaires[11]	40.0	45.0	46.0	45.0	48.0	...	...	...	...	...
Seychelles Seychelles										
Passenger cars										
Voitures de tourisme	4.7	4.9	6.1	5.6	5.5	6.2	6.7	6.5	6.4	...
Commercial vehicles										
Véhicules utilitaires	1.3	1.5	1.8	1.8	1.9	2.0	2.1	2.2	2.2	
Sierra Leone Sierra Leone										
Passenger cars[1]										
Voitures de tourisme[1]	36.0	36.0	32.4	32.4	32.4	32.4	32.4	32.4	...	...
Commercial vehicles[1]										
Véhicules utilitaires[1]	12.0	12.0	11.9	11.9	11.9	11.9	11.9	11.9		
Singapore Singapour										
Passenger cars										
Voitures de tourisme	300.1	302.8	321.9	340.6	363.9	384.5	396.4	395.2	403.2	413.5
Commercial vehicles										
Véhicules utilitaires	130.1	131.5	135.2	136.8	140.0	142.7	144.8	142.6	141.3	137.2
Slovakia Slovaquie										
Passenger cars										
Voitures de tourisme	906.1	953.2	994.9	994.0	1 015.8	1 058.4	1 135.9	1 196.1	1 236.4	1 274.2
Commercial vehicles										
Véhicules utilitaires	127.5	134.7	130.6	131.2	131.5	127.2	135.0	144.4	149.4	153.2
Slovenia Slovénie										
Passenger cars										
Voitures de tourisme	602.9	615.7	641.7	667.2	709.6	740.9	778.3	813.4	848.3	868.3
Commercial vehicles										
Véhicules utilitaires	33.6	34.0	34.7	36.6	40.2	42.6	44.9	52.0	54.3	56.8
Somalia Somalie										
Passenger cars[11]										
Voitures de tourisme[11]	10.5	10.5	10.7	11.8	12.0	...	...	...	...	...
Commercial vehicles[11]										
Véhicules utilitaires[11]	12.0	11.5	12.0	12.2	12.0	...	...	...	...	...
South Africa Afrique du Sud										
Passenger cars										
Voitures de tourisme	3 698.2[32]	3 739.2[32]	3 488.6[1]	3 814.9[1]	3 830.8[1]	3 846.8[1]	3 664.0[1]	3 952.2[1]	3 966.3[51]	...
Commercial vehicles										
Véhicules utilitaires	1 519.9[52]	1 551.4[52]	1 784.9[1]	1 596.8[1]	1 625.5[1]	1 653.5[1]	1 868.0[1]	1 868.0[1]	2 248.1[53]	...
Spain Espagne										
Passenger cars										
Voitures de tourisme	12 537.1	13 102.3	13 440.7	13 733.8	14 212.3	14 753.8	15 297.4	16 050.1	16 847.4	...

60
Motor vehicles in use
Passenger cars and commercial vehicles: thousand units [cont.]
Véhicules automobiles en circulation
Voitures de tourisme et véhicules utilitaires : milliers de véhicules [suite]

Country or area Pays or zone	1991	1992	1993	1994	1995	1996	1997	1998	1999	2000
Commercial vehicles Véhicules utilitaires	2 615.0	2 773.4	2 859.6	2 952.8	3 071.6	3 200.3	3 360.1	3 561.5	3 788.7	...
Sri Lanka Sri Lanka										
Passenger cars[4] Voitures de tourisme[4]	180.1	189.5	197.3	210.1	228.9	246.5	261.6	284.3	309.5	...
Commercial vehicles[4] Véhicules utilitaires[4]	152.7	159.9	166.3	175.3	184.3	191.5	199.2	211.2	227.1	...
Sudan Soudan										
Passenger cars[11] Voitures de tourisme[11]	116.0	116.0	30.8	30.8	30.8	...	...	...	...	...
Commercial vehicles[11] Véhicules utilitaires[11]	57.0	57.0	35.9	35.9	35.9	...	...	...	...	...
Suriname Suriname										
Passenger cars Voitures de tourisme	38.7	42.6	46.6	42.2	49.3	46.4	50.2	55.4	59.9	61.4
Commercial vehicles Véhicules utilitaires	15.5	16.0	18.2	17.9	17.3	19.5	20.5	21.1	22.5	23.5
Swaziland Swaziland										
Passenger cars[6] Voitures de tourisme[6]	...	...	25.4	26.6	28.1	29.8	31.9	...	...	...
Commercial vehicles[6] Véhicules utilitaires[6]	...	...	32.9	32.1	35.4	37.2	39.7	...	...	...
Sweden Suède										
Passenger cars Voitures de tourisme	3 619.4	3 588.4	3 566.0	3 594.2	3 630.8	3 654.9	3 702.8	3 790.7	3 890.2	3 998.6
Commercial vehicles Véhicules utilitaires	324.1	319.2	316.0	317.8	322.3	326.5	336.6	352.9	369.2	388.6
Switzerland Suisse										
Passenger cars[30] Voitures de tourisme[30]	3 057.8	3 091.2	3 109.5	3 165.0	3 229.2	3 268.1	3 323.4	3 383.2	3 467.3	3 545.2
Commercial vehicles[30] Véhicules utilitaires[30]	291.3	291.3	288.8	292.4	299.3	300.7	302.7	306.4	313.6	318.8
Syrian Arab Republic Rép. arabe syrienne										
Passenger cars Voitures de tourisme	126.9	128.0	149.8	159.1	166.5	173.6	175.9	179.0	180.7	...
Commercial vehicles Véhicules utilitaires	121.9	136.7	162.3	188.4	224.0	251.4	269.1	282.6	313.5	...
Tajikistan Tadjikistan										
Passenger cars Voitures de tourisme	...	...	...	175.0	166.4	151.5	154.1	146.6	141.7	117.1
Commercial vehicles Véhicules utilitaires	...	...	...	10.9	9.8	9.6	10.2	13.3	16.4	16.8
Thailand Thaïlande										
Passenger cars[54] Voitures de tourisme[54]	1 279.2	1 396.6	1 598.2	1 798.8	1 913.2	2 098.6	2 350.4	2 529.2	2 650.5	...
Commercial vehicles[55] Véhicules utilitaires[55]	1 541.2	1 763.5	2 091.1	2 384.1	2 735.6	3 149.3	3 534.9	3 746.7	4 065.3	...
TFYR of Macedonia L'ex-R.y. Macédoine										
Passenger cars Voitures de tourisme	250.0	280.0	290.0	263.0	286.0	284.0	289.0	289.0	290.0	300.0
Commercial vehicles Véhicules utilitaires	18.9	22.1	23.0	19.9	22.1	21.8	22.2	22.6	22.5	23.3
Togo Togo										
Passenger cars[1] Voitures de tourisme[1]	25.0	25.0	18.2	74.6	74.7	74.7	74.7	74.7	...	...
Commercial vehicles[1] Véhicules utilitaires[1]	16.0	16.1	11.6	34.6	34.6	34.6	34.6	34.6	...	...

60

Motor vehicles in use
Passenger cars and commercial vehicles: thousand units [*cont.*]
Véhicules automobiles en circulation
Voitures de tourisme et véhicules utilitaires : milliers de véhicules [*suite*]

Country or area Pays or zone	1991	1992	1993	1994	1995	1996	1997	1998	1999	2000
Tonga Tonga										
Passenger cars										
Voitures de tourisme	2.8	3.3	4.7	5.3	7.7	8.6	9.0	9.7	10.8	...
Commercial vehicles										
Véhicules utilitaires	3.1	3.7	5.0	5.9	8.1	9.7	8.9	9.4	10.4	...
Trinidad and Tobago Trinité-et-Tobago										
Passenger cars										
Voitures de tourisme	162.5	166.7	159.0	162.1	166.8	180.2	194.3	213.4	229.4	...
Commercial vehicles										
Véhicules utilitaires	39.4	40.8	39.2	40.2	42.2	44.9	47.7	51.1	53.9	...
Tunisia Tunisie										
Passenger cars										
Voitures de tourisme	262.7	277.6	299.1	327.0	356.3	379.2	415.2	445.6	482.7	...
Commercial vehicles[56]										
Véhicules utilitaires[56]	140.3	151.6	165.3	177.7	189.3	201.5	217.1	233.0	250.3	...
Turkey Turquie										
Passenger cars[57]										
Voitures de tourisme[57]	1 864.3	2 181.4	2 619.9	2 861.6	3 058.5	3 274.1	3 570.1	3 838.3	4 072.3	...
Commercial vehicles[27]										
Véhicules utilitaires[27]	469.0	490.9	518.4	530.4	617.1	642.3	683.5	715.1	730.7	...
Uganda Ouganda										
Passenger cars										
Voitures de tourisme	17.8	19.0	20.5	24.2	28.9	35.6	42.0	46.9	48.3	49.0
Commercial vehicles										
Véhicules utilitaires	25.2	26.9	29.4	35.0	44.1	52.4	59.1	66.7	72.6	74.3
Ukraine Ukraine										
Passenger cars										
Voitures de tourisme	3 657.0	3 884.8	4 206.5	4 384.1	4 603.1	4 872.3	5 024.0	5 127.3	5 210.8	5 250.1
United Arab Emirates Emirats arabes unis										
Passenger cars										
Voitures de tourisme	241.3	257.8	297.1	332.5	321.6	346.3	...	...	...	...
Commercial vehicles										
Véhicules utilitaires	47.1	65.8	78.8	87.2	84.2	89.3	...	...	...	...
United Kingdom Royaume-Uni										
Passenger cars[58]										
Voitures de tourisme[58]	21 515.0	20 973.0	21 291.0	21 740.0	21 949.9	22 819.0	23 450.0	23 881.0	24 594.0	...
Commercial vehicles[58]										
Véhicules utilitaires[58]	2 438.0	3 008.0	2 990.0	2 994.0	2 987.3	3 035.0	3 104.0	3 167.0	3 333.0	...
United Rep. of Tanzania Rép.-Unie de Tanzanie										
Passenger cars[1]										
Voitures de tourisme[1]	44.0	44.0	13.6	13.6	13.8	13.8	13.8	13.8	...	...
Commercial vehicles[1]										
Véhicules utilitaires[1]	55.0	57.2	33.7	35.4	37.5	42.5	42.5	42.5	...	...
United States Etats-Unis										
Passenger cars[59]										
Voitures de tourisme[59]	185 510.4	187 737.4	187 291.5	191 071.6	193 963.4	198 662.1	199 972.7	203 565.8	207 048.2	211 940.8
Commercial vehicles										
Véhicules utilitaires	7 703.0	7 780.8	7 959.6	7 258.3	7 404.9	7 703.0	7 780.8	7 959.6	8 447.8	8 520.2
Uruguay Uruguay										
Passenger cars										
Voitures de tourisme	389.6	418.0	425.6	444.8	464.5	485.1	516.9	578.3	662.3	...
Commercial vehicles										
Véhicules utilitaires	48.6	45.0	44.3	46.2	45.8	48.4	50.3	53.9	57.8	...
Vanuatu Vanuatu										
Passenger cars[1]										
Voitures de tourisme[1]	4.5	4.0	2.7	7.1	7.4	2.7	2.7	2.7	...	...

60
Motor vehicles in use
Passenger cars and commercial vehicles: thousand units *[cont.]*
Véhicules automobiles en circulation
Voitures de tourisme et véhicules utilitaires : milliers de véhicules *[suite]*

Country or area Pays or zone	1991	1992	1993	1994	1995	1996	1997	1998	1999	2000
Commercial vehicles[1] Véhicules utilitaires[1]	2.1	2.2	2.7	1.7	1.8	3.2	3.5	3.8	...	...
Venezuela Venezuela										
Passenger cars Voitures de tourisme	1 688.0	1 753.0	1 805.0	1 813.0	1 823.0	1 393.5[1]	...	...	...	...
Commercial vehicles Véhicules utilitaires	538.0	559.0	576.0	578.0	581.0	664.6[1]	...	...	...	...
Viet Nam Viet Nam										
Commercial vehicles Véhicules utilitaires	28.2	38.7	41.5	33.8	39.1	41.5	41.5	49.4	57.8	...
Yemen Yémen										
Passenger cars Voitures de tourisme	118.3	140.6	176.1	196.5	224.1	259.4	327.1	380.6	...	...
Commercial vehicles Véhicules utilitaires	204.6	223.0	251.8	266.4	291.7	345.3	413.1	422.1	...	...
Zambia Zambie										
Passenger cars Voitures de tourisme	...	3.0	3.0	3.9	5.7	3.7	...	...	...	...
Commercial vehicles Véhicules utilitaires	...	4.0	2.7	4.2	7.3	3.9	...	...	...	...
Zimbabwe Zimbabwe										
Passenger cars Voitures de tourisme	300.0	310.0	328.3	349.1	384.0	422.4	464.7	521.0	534.6	544.5
Commercial vehicles Véhicules utilitaires	28.4	30.4	32.5	34.5	37.9	42.2	46.4	54.3	58.5	67.7

Source:
United Nations Statistics Division, New York, transport
statistics database.

† For information on recent changes in country or
area nomenclature pertaining to former Czechoslovakia,
Germany, Hong Kong Special Administrative Region (SAR) of
China, Macao Special Administrative Region (SAR) of China,
SFR of Yugoslavia and the former USSR, see Annex I - Country
or area nomenclature, regional and other groupings.

†† For statistical purposes, the data for
China do not include those for Hong Kong Special
Administrative Region (Hong Kong SAR), Macao Special
Administrative Region (Macao SAR) and Taiwan province of
China.

1 Source: World Automotive Market Report, Auto and Truck
International (Illinois).
2 Including commercial vehicles.
3 Data refer to fiscal years beginning 1 July.

4 Including vehicles operated by police or other governmental
security organizations.
5 Including farm tractors.
6 Excluding government vehicles.
7 Including buses and coaches.

8 Including pick-ups.
9 Number of licensed vehicles.
10 Including only vehicles (trucks) weighing 4,500 kilograms to
14,999 kilograms and vehicles (tractor-trailers and Class A
trucks) weighing 15,000 kilograms or more.

Source:
Organisation des Nations Unies, Division de statistique, New
York, la base de données pour les statistiques des
transports.

† Pour les modifications récentes de nomenclature
de pays ou de zone concernant l'Allemagne, Hong Kong, région
administrative spéciale (RAS) de Chine, Macao, région
administrative spéciale (RAS) de Chine,
l'ex-Tchécoslovaquie, l'ex-URSS et l'ex-Rfs de Yougoslavie,
voir annexe I - Nomenclature des pays ou des zones,
groupements régionaux et autres groupements.

†† Les données statistiques relatives à
la Chine ne comprennent pas celles qui concernent la région
administrative spéciale de Hong Kong (la RAS de Hong Kong),
la région administrative spéciale de Macao (la RAS de Macao)
et la province chinoise de Taiwan.

1 Source : "World Automotive Market Report, Auto and Truck
International" (Illinois).
2 Y compris véhicules utilitaires.
3 Les données se réfèrent aux années fiscales commençant le
1er juillet.
4 Y compris véhicules de la police ou d'autres services
gouvernementales d'ordre public.
5 Y compris tracteurs agricoles.
6 Non compris les véhicules des administrations publiques.
7 Voitures de tourisme privées seulement, non compris voitures
de louage y taxis.
8 Y compris fourgonnettes.
9 Nombre de véhicules automobiles licensés.
10 Y compris seulement véhicules (camions) pesant de 4,500
kilogrammes à 14,999 kilogrammes et véhicules
(semi-remorques et camions de Classe A) pesant 15,000

60
Motor vehicles in use
Passenger cars and commercial vehicles: thousand units [*cont.*]
Véhicules automobiles en circulation
Voitures de tourisme et véhicules utilitaires : milliers de véhicules [*suite*]

11 Source: AAMA Motor Vehicle Facts and Figures, American Automobile Manufacturers Association (Michigan).
12 Excluding pick-ups.
13 Including special-purpose vehicles.
14 Including minibuses.
15 Including vans.
16 Including special-purpose commercial vehicles and farm tractors.
17 Excluding vans.
18 Excluding Faeroe Islands.
19 Including large public service excavators and trench diggers.
20 Including dump trucks and motor scooters.
21 Data refer to fiscal years ending 7 July.

22 Including private and government cars, rental and hired cars.

23 Including pick-ups, ambulances, light and heavy fire engines and all other vehicles such as trailers, cranes, loaders, forklifts, etc.

24 Excluding tractors.
25 Including only trailers and semi-trailer combinations less than 10 years old.
26 Including "other, not specified", registered motor vehicles.

27 Excluding tractors and semi-trailer combinations.
28 Including goods vehicles, tractors, trailers, three-wheeled passengers and goods vehicles and other miscellaneous vehicles which are not separately classified.

29 Data refer to fiscal years ending 20 March.

30 Data refer to fiscal years ending 30 September.

31 Including school buses.
32 Including mini-buses equipped for transport of nine to fifteen passengers.
33 Excluding small vehicles.
34 Including cars with a seating capacity of up to 10 persons.
35 Numbered of registered motor vehicles.
36 Source: United Nations Economic and Social Commission for Western Asia (ESCWA).
37 Excluding diplomatic corps vehicles.
38 Data refer to fiscal years ending 31 March.

39 Newly registered.
40 Including hearses (Norway: registered before 1981).
41 Excluding taxis.
42 Trucks only.
43 Excluding buses and tractors, but including special lorries.

44 Including light miscellaneous vehicles.
45 Excluding Madeira and Azores.
46 Including vehicles no longer in circulation.
47 Excluding Transnistria region.
48 For the period 1980 - 1994, including motor vehicles for general use owned by Ministry of Transport. For the period 1995 - 2000, including motor vehicles owned by enterprises with main activity as road transport enterprises.
49 Beginning 1996, data provided by State Inspection for security of road traffic of the Russian Federation Ministry

kilogrammes ou plus.
11 Source : AAMA Motor Vehicle Facts and Figures, American Automobile Manufacturers Association (Michigan).
12 Non compris fourgonnettes.
13 Y compris véhicules à usages spéciaux.
14 Y compris minibuses.
15 Y compris fourgons.
16 Y compris véhicules utilitaires à usages spéciaux et tracteurs agricoles.
17 Non compris fourgons.
18 Non compris Iles Féroés.
19 Y compris les grosses excavatrices et machines d'excavation de tranchées de travaux publics.
20 Y compris camions-bennes et scooters.
21 Les données se réfèrent aux années fiscales finissant le 7e juillet.

22 Y compris les voitures particulières et celles des administrations publiques, les voitures de location et de louage.
23 Y compris les fourgonnettes, les ambulances, les voitures de pompiers légères pompiers légèresd et lourdes, et tous autres véhicules tels que remoques, grues, chargeuses, chariots élévateurs à fourches, etc.

24 Non compris tracteurs.
25 Y compris les légères remorques et semi-remorques de moins de 10 ans seulement.
26 Y compris "autres, non-spécifiés", véhicules automobiles enregistrés.
27 Non compris ensembles tracteur-remorque et semi-remorque.
28 Y compris véhicules de transport de marchandises, camions-remorques, remorques, véhicules à trois roues (passagers et marchandises) et autres véhicules divers qui ne font pas l'objet d'une catégorie separée.

29 Les données se réfèrent aux années fiscales finissant le 20e mars.
30 Les données se réfèrent aux années fiscales finissant le 30e septembre
31 Y compris l'autobus de l'école.
32 Y compris mini-buses ayant une capacité de neuf à quinze passagers.
33 Non compris véhicules petites.
34 Y compris véhicules comptant jusqu'à 10 places.
35 Nombre de véhicules automobiles enregistrés.
36 Source : Commission économique et sociale pour l'Asie occidentale (CESAO).
37 Non compris véhicules des diplomates.
38 Les données se réfèrent aux années fiscales finissant le 31e mars.
39 Enregistrés récemment.
40 Y compris corbillards (Norvège : enregistrés avant de 1981).
41 Non compris taxis.
42 Camions seulement.
43 Non compris autobus et tracteurs, mais y compris camions spéciaux.
44 Y compris les véhicules légers divers.
45 Non compris Madère et Azores.
46 Y compris véhicules retirés de la circulation.
47 Non compris région de Transnistria.
48 Pour la période 1980 - 1994, y compris les véhicules à moteur d'usage général appartenant au Ministère des transports. Pour la période 1995 - 2000, y compris les véhicules pour les entreprises de transport.
49 A partir de 1996, données fournies par l'Inspecteurat d'Etat pour la sécurité routière du Ministère de l'Intérieur de la

60
Motor vehicles in use
Passenger cars and commercial vehicles: thousand units [*cont.*]
Véhicules automobiles en circulation
Voitures de tourisme et véhicules utilitaires : milliers de véhicules [*suite*]

of Internal Affairs.
50 Including motorcycles.
51 Including all minibuses and passenger vehicles which transport fewer than 12 persons.
52 Including hearses, ambulances, fire-engines and jeeps specifically registered as commercial vehicles.
53 Including vehicles which transport 12 persons or more and all light and heavy load vehicles, whether self-propelled or semi-trailer.
54 Including micro-buses and passenger pick-ups.
55 Including pick-ups, taxis, cars for hire, small rural buses.
56 Beginning 1987, including trailers.
57 Including vehicles seating not more than eight persons, including the driver.
58 Figures prior to 1992 were derived from vehicle taxation class; beginning 1992, figures derived from vehicle body type.
59 Including motorcycles (prior to 1993 only), mini-vans, sport-utility vehicles and pick-up trucks.

Fédération de Russie.
50 Y compris motocyclettes.
51 Y compris tous les minibus et véhicules qui transportant moins de 12 passagers.
52 Y compris corbillards, ambulances, voitures de pompiers et jeeps spécifiquement immatriculés comme véhicules utilitaires.
53 Y compris véhicules transportant 12 personnes ou plus et tous véhicules poids légèrs ou poids lourds, auto-propulsés ou semi-remorque.
54 Y compris les microbus et les camionnettes de transport de passagers.
55 Y compris les camionnettes, les taxis, les voitures de louage, les petits autobus ruraux.
56 A compter de l'année 1987, y compris remorques.
57 Y compris véhicules dont le nombre de places assises (y compris celle du conducteur) n'est pas supérieur à huit.
58 Les chiffres antérieurs à 1992 ont été calculés selon les catégories fiscales de véhicules; à partir de 1992, ils ont été calculés selon les types de carrosserie.
59 Y compris motocyclettes (antérieur à 1993 seulement), fourgonettes, véhicules de la classe quatre-x-quatre et camionettes légères.

61
Merchant shipping: fleets
Transports maritimes : flotte marchande
Total, Oil tankers and Ore and bulk carrier fleets: thousand gross registered tons
Total, Pétroliers et Minéraliers et transporteurs de vracs : milliers de tonneaux de jauge brute

Flag Pavillon	1991	1992	1993	1994	1995	1996	1997	1998	1999	2000
A. Total · Totale										
World Monde	**436 027**	**445 169**	**457 915**	**475 859**	**490 662**	**507 873**	**522 197**	**531 893**	**543 610**	**558 054**
Africa · Afrique										
Algeria Algérie	921	921	921	936	980	983	983	1 005	1 005	961
Angola Angola	93	94	88	90	90	82	68	74	66	66
Benin Bénin	2	2	1	1	1	1	1	1	1	1
Cameroon Cameroun	34	35	36	36	37	37	11	13	14	14
Cape Verde Cap-Vert	22	22	23	22	16	15	21	20	21	21
Comoros Comores	3	2	2	2	2	2	2	1	1	20
Congo Congo	9	9	10	9	12	6	7	4	4	3
Côte d'Ivoire Côte d'Ivoire	82	75	103	62	40	13	11	10	10	9
Dem. Rep. of the Congo Rép. dém. du Congo	56	29	15	15	15	15	15	13	13	13
Djibouti Djibouti	3	3	4	4	4	4	4	4	4	4
Egypt Egypte	1 257	1 122	1 149	1 262	1 269	1 230	1 288	1 368	1 368	1 346
Equatorial Guinea Guinée équatoriale	6	7	2	3	3	21	35	59	44	46
Eritrea Erythrée	...	...	0	0	12	1	7	7	16	16
Ethiopia incl. Eritrea Ethiopie comp. Erythrée	84	70	..	...	...	...	...	...	...	...
Ethiopia Ethiopie	...	...	69	83	80	86	86	83	96	92
Gabon Gabon	25	25	36	28	32	33	35	27	16	13
Gambia Gambie	3	2	2	3	1	1	2	2	2	2
Ghana Ghana	135	135	118	106	114	135	130	115	118	119
Guinea Guinée	9	5	6	8	7	7	9	11	11	11
Guinea-Bissau Guinée-Bissau	4	4	4	5	5	6	6	6	6	7
Kenya Kenya	13	14	16	16	18	20	21	21	21	21
Liberia Libéria	52 427	55 918	53 919	57 648	59 801	59 989	60 058	60 492	54 107	51 451
Libyan Arab Jamah. Jamah. arabe libyenne	840	720	721	739	733	681	686	567	439	434

61
Merchant shipping: fleets
Total, Oil tankers and Ore and bulk carrier fleets: thousand gross registered tons [*cont.*]
Transports maritimes : flotte marchande
Total, Pétroliers et Minéraliers et transporteurs de vracs : milliers de tonneaux de jauge brute [*suite*]

Flag Pavillon	1991	1992	1993	1994	1995	1996	1997	1998	1999	2000
Madagascar Madagascar	73	45	34	36	38	39	40	42	43	44
Mauritania Mauritanie	42	43	44	42	39	43	43	48	49	49
Mauritius Maurice	82	122	194	206	238	244	275	206	150	91
Morocco Maroc	483	479	393	362	383	403	417	444	448	467
Mozambique Mozambique	37	39	36	36	38	45	39	35	36	37
Namibia Namibie	0	17	36	44	52	59	55	55	55	63
Nigeria Nigéria	493	516	515	473	479	447	452	452	432	438
Réunion Réunion	21	21	...	...	...	...	...	...	...	...
Saint Helena Sainte-Hélène	...	...	...	...	...	0	1	1	1	1
Sao Tome and Principe Sao Tomé-et-Principe	1	3	3	3	3	3	3	10	42	173
Senegal Sénégal	55	58	66	50	48	50	51	51	48	50
Seychelles Seychelles	4	4	4	4	5	4	5	18	24	22
Sierra Leone Sierra Leone	21	26	26	24	23	19	19	19	17	17
Somalia Somalie	17	17	18	17	16	14	11	11	6	7
South Africa Afrique du Sud	340	336	346	331	340	371	383	384	379	380
Sudan Soudan	45	45	64	57	48	42	42	43	43	43
Togo Togo	22	12	12	1	1	1	2	2	43	5
Tunisia Tunisie	276	280	269	141	160	158	180	193	200	208
United Rep. of Tanzania Rép.-Unie de Tanzanie	39	41	43	43	46	45	46	36	36	38
America, North · Amérique du Nord										
Anguilla Anguilla	5	5	4	3	2	2	2	1	1	1
Antigua and Barbuda Antigua-et-Barbuda	811	802	1 063	1 507	1 842	2 176	2 214	2 788	3 622	4 224
Bahamas Bahamas	17 541	20 616	21 224	22 915	23 603	24 409	25 523	27 716	29 483	31 445
Barbados Barbade	8	51	49	76	292	497	888	688	725	733
Belize Belize	...	37	148	280	517	1 016	1 761	2 382	2 368	2 251
Bermuda Bermudes	3 037	3 338	3 140	2 904	3 048	3 462	4 610	4 811	6 187	5 752

61
Merchant shipping: fleets
Total, Oil tankers and Ore and bulk carrier fleets: thousand gross registered tons [*cont.*]
Transports maritimes : flotte marchande
Total, Pétroliers et Minéraliers et transporteurs de vracs : milliers de tonneaux de jauge brute [*suite*]

Flag Pavillon	1991	1992	1993	1994	1995	1996	1997	1998	1999	2000
British Virgin Islands Iles Vierges britanniques	7	7	6	5	5	5	5	4	4	74
Canada Canada	2 685	2 610	2 541	2 490	2 401	2 406	2 527	2 501	2 496	2 658
Cayman Islands Iles Caïmanes	395	363	383	383	368	827	844	1 282	1 165	1 796
Costa Rica Costa Rica	14	8	8	8	7	6	6	6	6	6
Cuba Cuba	770	671	626	444	410	291	203	158	130	120
Dominica Dominique	2	2	4	2	2	2	3	3	2	2
Dominican Republic Rép. dominicaine	12	12	13	12	12	12	11	9	10	10
El Salvador El Salvador	2	2	2	1	1	1	1	1	2	2
Greenland Groenland	57	55	...	...	...	...	...	...	...	...
Grenada Grenade	1	1	1	1	5	1	1	1	1	1
Guadeloupe Guadeloupe	5	6	...	...	...	...	...	...	...	...
Guatemala Guatemala	1	2	1	1	1	1	1	1	5	5
Haiti Haïti	1	1	1	1	0	1	2	1	1	1
Honduras Honduras	816	1 045	1 116	1 206	1 206	1 198	1 053	1 083	1 220	1 111
Jamaica Jamaïque	14	11	11	7	9	9	10	4	4	4
Martinique Martinique	1	1	...	...	...	...	...	...	...	...
Mexico Mexique	1 196	1 114	1 125	1 179	1 129	1 128	1 145	1 085	918	883
Montserrat Montserrat	1	1	...	...	...	...	...	...	...	...
Netherlands Antilles Antilles néerlandaises	568 [t]	841 [t]	1 039	1 047	1 197	1 168	1 067	971	1 110	1 235
Nicaragua Nicaragua	5	4	4	4	4	4	4	4	4	4
Panama Panama	44 949	52 486	57 619	64 710	71 922	82 131	91 128	98 222	105 248	114 382
Puerto Rico Porto Rico	16	9	...	...	...	...	...	...	...	...
Saint Kitts and Nevis Saint-Kitts-et-Nevis	0	0	0	0	0	0	0	0	0	0
Saint Lucia Sainte-Lucie	2	2	2	2	1	1	...	...	...	...
Saint Pierre and Miquelon Saint-Pierre-et-Miquelon	3	6	...	...	...	...	...	...	...	...

61
Merchant shipping: fleets
Total, Oil tankers and Ore and bulk carrier fleets: thousand gross registered tons [*cont.*]
Transports maritimes : flotte marchande
Total, Pétroliers et Minéraliers et transporteurs de vracs : milliers de tonneaux de jauge brute [*suite*]

Flag Pavillon	1991	1992	1993	1994	1995	1996	1997	1998	1999	2000
St. Vincent-Grenadines St. Vincent-Grenadines	4 221	4 698	5 287	5 420	6 165	7 134	8 374	7 875	7 105	7 026
Trinidad and Tobago Trinité-et-Tobago	22	24	23	27	28	19	19	19	22	22
Turks and Caicos Islands Iles Turques et Caïques	5	4	4	3	2	2	2	1	1	1
United States Etats-Unis	18 565	14 435	14 087	13 655	12 761	12 025	11 789	11 852	12 026	11 111
America, South · Amérique du Sud										
Argentina Argentine	1 709	873	773	716	595	586	579	499	477	464
Bolivia Bolivie	...	...	...	...	...	...	2	16	179	178
Brazil Brésil	5 883	5 348	5 216	5 283	5 077	4 530	4 372	4 171	3 933	3 809
Chile Chili	619	580	624	721	761	691	722	753	820	842
Colombia Colombie	313	250	238	142	144	122	118	112	97	81
Ecuador Equateur	384	348	286	270	168	178	145	171	309	301
Falkland Is. (Malvinas) Iles Falkland (Malvinas)	10	14	15	16	20	30	38	39	45	53
French Guiana Guyane française	1	1	...	...	...	...	...	...	...	...
Guyana Guyana	16	17	17	15	15	16	17	16	14	16
Paraguay Paraguay	35	33	31	33	39	44	44	45	43	45
Peru Pérou	605	433	411	321	341	346	337	270	285	257
Suriname Suriname	13	13	13	8	8	8	8	6	6	5
Uruguay Uruguay	105	127	149	125	124	100	121	107	62	67
Venezuela Venezuela	970	871	971	920	787	697	705	665	657	667
Asia · Asie										
Azerbaijan Azerbaïdjan	...	637	667	621	655	636	633	651	654	647
Bahrain Bahreïn	262	138	103	167	166	164	194	284	292	256
Bangladesh Bangladesh	456	392	388	380	379	436	419	414	378	370
Brunei Darussalam Brunéi Darussalam	348	364	365	366	366	369	369	362	362	362
Cambodia Cambodge	...	4	6	6	60	206	439	616	999	1 447
China †† Chine ††	14 299	13 899	14 945	15 827	16 943	16 993	16 339	16 503	16 315	16 499

61
Merchant shipping: fleets
Total, Oil tankers and Ore and bulk carrier fleets: thousand gross registered tons [cont.]
Transports maritimes : flotte marchande
Total, Pétroliers et Minéraliers et transporteurs de vracs : milliers de tonneaux de jauge brute [suite]

Flag Pavillon	1991	1992	1993	1994	1995	1996	1997	1998	1999	2000
China, Hong Kong SAR† Chine, Hong Kong RAS†	5 876	7 267	7 664	7 703	8 795	7 863	5 771	6 171	7 973	10 242
China, Macao SAR † Chine, Macao RAS †	3	3	2	2	2	2	2	2	4	4
Cyprus Chypre	20 298	20 487	22 842	23 293	24 653	23 799	23 653	23 302	23 641	23 206
Georgia Géorgie	...	...	0	439	282	206	128	118	132	119
India Inde	6 517	6 546	6 575	6 485	7 127	7 127	6 934	6 777	6 915	6 662
Indonesia Indonésie	2 337	2 367	2 440	2 678	2 771	2 973	3 195	3 252	3 241	3 384
Iran (Islamic Rep. of) Iran (Rép. islamique d')	4 583	4 571	4 444	3 803	2 902	3 567	3 553	3 347	3 546	4 234
Iraq Iraq	931	902	902	885	858	857	572	511	511	511
Israel Israël	604	664	652	646	599	679	794	752	728	612
Japan Japon	26 407	25 102	24 248	22 102	19 913	19 201	18 516	17 780	17 063	15 257
Jordan Jordanie	135	61	71	61	21	41	43	42	42	42
Kazakhstan Kazakhstan	...	...	...	9	12	9	10	9	9	11
Korea, Dem. P. R. Corée, R. p. dém. de	511	602	671	696	715	693	667	631	658	653
Korea, Republic of Corée, République de	7 821	7 407	7 047	7 004	6 972	7 558	7 430	5 694	5 735	6 200
Kuwait Koweït	1 373	2 258	2 218	2 017	2 057	2 028	1 984	2 459	2 456	2 415
Lao People's Dem. Rep. Rép. dém. pop. lao	0	0	3	3	3	3	3	2	2	2
Lebanon Liban	274	293	249	258	285	275	297	263	322	363
Malaysia Malaisie	1 755	2 048	2 166	2 728	3 283	4 175	4 842	5 209	5 245	5 328
Maldives Maldives	42	52	55	68	85	96	98	101	90	78
Myanmar Myanmar	1 046	947	711	683	523	687	568	492	540	446
Oman Oman	23	15	16	15	16	16	15	15	17	19
Pakistan Pakistan	358	380	360	375	398	444	435	401	308	260
Philippines Philippines	8 626	8 470	8 466	9 413	8 744	9 034	8 849	8 508	7 650	7 002
Qatar Qatar	485	392	431	557	482	562	648	744	749	715
Saudi Arabia Arabie saoudite	1 321	1 016	998	1 064	1 187	1 208	1 164	1 278	1 208	1 260
Singapore Singapour	8 488	9 905	11 035	11 895	13 611	16 448	18 875	20 370	21 780	21 491

61
Merchant shipping: fleets
Total, Oil tankers and Ore and bulk carrier fleets: thousand gross registered tons [*cont.*]
Transports maritimes : flotte marchande
Total, Pétroliers et Minéraliers et transporteurs de vracs : milliers de tonneaux de jauge brute [*suite*]

Flag Pavillon	1991	1992	1993	1994	1995	1996	1997	1998	1999	2000
Sri Lanka Sri Lanka	333	285	294	294	227	242	217	189	195	150
Syrian Arab Republic Rép. arabe syrienne	109	144	209	279	352	420	415	428	440	465
Thailand Thaïlande	725	917	1 116	1 374	1 743	2 042	2 158	1 999	1 956	1 945
Turkey Turquie	4 107	4 136	5 044	5 453	6 268	6 426	6 567	6 251	6 325	5 833
Turkmenistan Turkménistan	...	...	...	23	32	40	39	38	44	42
United Arab Emirates Emirats arabes unis	889	884	804	1 016	961	890	924	933	786	979
Viet Nam Viet Nam	574	616	728	773	700	808	766	784	865	1 002
Yemen Yémen	17	16	24	25	27	25	26	25	25	28
Europe · Europe										
Albania Albanie	59	59	59	59	63	43	30	29	21	24
Austria Autriche	139	140	160	134	92	95	83	68	71	90
Belgium Belgique	314	241	218	233	240	278	169	127	132	144
Bulgaria Bulgarie	1 367	1 348	1 314	1 295	1 166	1 150	1 128	1 091	1 036	990
Channel Islands Iles Anglo-Normandes	4	3	3	3	2	3	3	2	2	2
Croatia Croatie	...	210	193	247	333	580	871	896	869	734
Czechoslovakia-former† Tchécoslovaquie(anc.) †	361	238	...	...	...	...	...	...	...	...
Czech Republic République tchèque	...	...	228	173	140	78	16	...	...	...
Denmark Danemark	5 698	5 269	5 293	5 698	5 747	5 885	5 754	5 687	5 809	6 823
Estonia Estonie	...	680	686	695	598	545	602	522	453	379
Faeroe Islands Iles Féroé	115	111	100	100	104	109	105	103	104	103
Finland Finlande	1 053	1 197	1 354	1 404	1 519	1 511	1 559	1 629	1 658	1 620
France[2] France[2]	3 879	3 869	4 252	4 242	4 086	4 291	4 570	4 738	4 766	4 681
Germany † Allemagne †	5 971	5 360	4 979	5 696	5 626	5 842	6 950	8 084	6 514	6 552
Gibraltar Gibraltar	1 410	492	384	331	307	306	297	314	451	604
Greece Grèce	22 753	25 739	29 134	30 162	29 435	27 507	25 288	25 225	24 833	26 402
Hungary Hongrie	104	92	45	45	45	50	27	15	12	...

61
Merchant shipping: fleets
Total, Oil tankers and Ore and bulk carrier fleets: thousand gross registered tons [*cont.*]
Transports maritimes : flotte marchande
Total, Pétroliers et Minéraliers et transporteurs de vracs : milliers de tonneaux de jauge brute [*suite*]

Flag Pavillon	1991	1992	1993	1994	1995	1996	1997	1998	1999	2000
Iceland Islande	168	177	174	175	209	218	215	198	192	187
Ireland Irlande	195	199	184	190	213	219	235	184	219	248
Isle of Man Ile de Man	1 937	1 628	1 563	2 093	2 300	3 140	4 759	4 203	4 729	5 431
Italy Italie	8 122	7 513	7 030	6 818	6 699	6 594	6 194	6 819	8 048	9 049
Latvia Lettonie	...	1 207	1 155	1 034	798	723	319	118	118	98
Lithuania Lituanie	...	668	639	661	610	572	510	481	424	434
Luxembourg Luxembourg	1 703	1 656	1 327	1 143	881	878	820	932	1 343	1 079
Malta Malte	6 916	11 005	14 163	15 455	17 678	19 479	22 984	24 075	28 205	28 170
Netherlands Pays-Bas	3 305	3 346	3 086	3 349	3 409	3 995	3 880	4 263	4 814	5 168
Norway Norvège	23 586	22 231	21 536	22 388	21 551	21 806	22 839	23 136	23 446	22 604
Poland Pologne	3 348	3 109	2 646	2 610	2 358	2 293	1 878	1 424	1 319	1 119
Portugal Portugal	887	972	1 002	882	897	676	952	1 130	1 165	1 191
Romania Roumanie	3 828	2 981	2 867	2 689	2 536	2 568	2 345	2 088	1 221	767
Russian Federation Fédération de Russie	...	16 302	16 814	16 504	15 202	13 755	12 282	11 090	10 649	10 486
Slovakia Slovaquie	...	...	...	6	19	19	15	15	15	15
Slovenia Slovénie	...	2	2	9	2	2	2	2	2	2
Spain Espagne	3 617 [3]	2 643 [3]	1 752	1 560	1 619	1 675	1 688	1 838	1 903	2 030
Sweden Suède	3 174	2 884	2 439	2 797	2 955	3 002	2 754	2 552	2 947	2 887
Switzerland Suisse	286	346	300	336	381	400	434	383	439	429
Ukraine Ukraine	...	5 222	5 265	5 279	4 613	3 825	2 690	2 033	1 775	1 546
United Kingdom Royaume-Uni	4 670	4 081	4 117	4 430	4 413	3 872	3 486	4 085	4 331	5 532
Yugoslavia Yougoslavie	...	2	2	2	2	2	2	5	4	4
Yugoslavia, SFR† Yougoslavie, Rfs†	3 293	...	...	...	...	...	...	...	...	...
Oceania · Océanie										
Australia Australie	1 709	2 689	2 862	3 012	2 853	2 718	2 607	2 188	2 084	1 912

61
Merchant shipping: fleets
Total, Oil tankers and Ore and bulk carrier fleets: thousand gross registered tons [*cont.*]
Transports maritimes : flotte marchande
Total, Pétroliers et Minéraliers et transporteurs de vracs : milliers de tonneaux de jauge brute [*suite*]

Flag Pavillon	1991	1992	1993	1994	1995	1996	1997	1998	1999	2000
Cook Islands Iles Cook	7	5	5	5	4	5	6	7	7	6
Fiji Fidji	50	64	39	31	32	36	36	29	29	29
French Polynesia Polynésie française	20	23	...	...	...	...	...	...	...	...
Guam Guam	1	1	...	...	...	...	...	...	...	...
Kiribati Kiribati	4	5	5	5	6	6	6	4	4	4
Marshall Islands Iles Marshall	1 698	1 676	2 198	2 149	3 099	4 897	6 314	6 442	6 762	9 745
Micronesia (Fed. States of) Micron (Etats fédérés de)	8	9	9	9	8	9	9	10	10	10
Nauru Nauru	15	5	1	...	...	...	...	...	...	...
New Caledonia Nouvelle-Calédonie	14	14	...	...	...	...	...	...	...	...
New Zealand Nouvelle-Zélande	269	238	218	246	307	386	367	336	265	180
Papua New Guinea Papouasie-Nvl-Guinée	36	46	47	47	49	57	60	61	65	73
Samoa Samoa	6	6	6	6	6	...	1	3	3	2
Solomon Islands Iles Salomon	8	8	7	8	8	10	10	10	10	9
Tonga Tonga	40	11	12	10	12	11	12	22	25	25
Tuvalu Tuvalu	1	12	70	51	64	57	55	49	43	59
Vanuatu Vanuatu	2 173	2 064	1 946	1 998	1 874	1 711	1 578	1 602	1 444	1 379
Wallis and Futuna Islands Iles Wallis et Futuna	42	80	80	105	108	92	111	111	159	135
USSR - former † · URSS (anc.) †										
USSR - former † URSS (anc.) †	26 405	...	...	...	...	...	...	...	...	...

B. Oil tankers · Pétroliers

World *Monde*	138 897	138 149	143 077	144 595	143 521	146 366	147 108	151 036	154 092	155 429
Africa · Afrique										
Algeria Algérie	39	32	32	35	35	34	34	33	33	19
Angola Angola	2	2	2	2	2	2	3	3	3	3
Cape Verde Cap-Vert	1	0	0	0	0	0	1	1	1	1
Côte d'Ivoire Côte d'Ivoire	0	0	0	1	1	1	1	1	1	1

61
Merchant shipping: fleets
Total, Oil tankers and Ore and bulk carrier fleets: thousand gross registered tons [*cont.*]
Transports maritimes : flotte marchande
Total, Pétroliers et Minéraliers et transporteurs de vracs : milliers de tonneaux de jauge brute [*suite*]

Flag Pavillon	1991	1992	1993	1994	1995	1996	1997	1998	1999	2000
Egypt Egypte	262	170	195	245	222	222	223	210	209	208
Equatorial Guinea Guinée équatoriale	...	...	...	...	...	...	...	5	...	...
Eritrea Erythrée	...	...	...	...	...	...	...	2	2	2
Ethiopia incl. Eritrea Ethiopie comp. Erythrée	4	4	...	...	...	...	...	...	...	...
Ethiopia Ethiopie	...	...	4	4	4	4	...	2	2	2
Gabon Gabon	1	1	1	1	1	1	1	1	1	1
Ghana Ghana	1	1	1	1	1	1	2	6	6	6
Kenya Kenya	4	4	4	4	4	5	5	5	5	5
Liberia Libéria	26 700	27 440	26 273	28 275	29 002	28 044	26 699	26 361	21 298	19 759
Libyan Arab Jamah. Jamah. arabe libyenne	581	581	581	579	572	505	511	395	267	267
Madagascar Madagascar	5	9	9	9	11	11	11	11	11	11
Mauritius Maurice	...	...	...	...	53	53	53	...	...	...
Morocco Maroc	10	14	14	14	14	12	12	12	12	12
Mozambique Mozambique	1	1	1	0	0	0	...	...	...	...
Nigeria Nigéria	225	235	236	245	251	252	250	252	265	265
Sao Tome and Principe Sao Tomé-et-Principe	...	...	...	...	...	...	...	...	1	7
Sierra Leone Sierra Leone	1	1	1	1	1	1	1	1	3	...
Somalia Somalie	...	...	...	...	...	...	...	...	1	1
South Africa Afrique du Sud	1	1	1	1	1	4	3	3	3	3
Sudan Soudan	1	1	1	1	1	1	1	1	1	1
Tunisia Tunisie	27	27	6	6	9	7	7	22	20	20
United Rep. of Tanzania Rép.-Unie de Tanzanie	3	4	5	4	5	5	5	4	4	4
America, North · Amérique du Nord										
Antigua and Barbuda Antigua-et-Barbuda	14	5	7	2	4	4	4	7	5	5
Bahamas Bahamas	8 738	9 812	9 680	10 393	10 326	10 863	10 810	11 982	13 158	13 504
Barbados Barbade	...	44	44	44	44	22	350	350	350	350

61
Merchant shipping: fleets
Total, Oil tankers and Ore and bulk carrier fleets: thousand gross registered tons [cont.]
Transports maritimes : flotte marchande
Total, Pétroliers et Minéraliers et transporteurs de vracs : milliers de tonneaux de jauge brute [suite]

Flag Pavillon	1991	1992	1993	1994	1995	1996	1997	1998	1999	2000
Belize Belize	...	4	9	59	22	67	338	360	321	348
Bermuda Bermudes	1 987	2 058	1 838	1 569	1 586	1 586	2 069	2 144	2 652	2 152
Canada Canada	233	162	153	153	118	110	254	255	250	329
Cayman Islands Iles Caïmanes	72	31	31	6	6	87	114	318	123	304
Cuba Cuba	78	71	67	71	64	27	8	8	3	3
Dominican Republic Rép. dominicaine	1	1	1	1	1	1	1	...	...	...
Honduras Honduras	149	144	119	85	97	103	107	108	131	143
Jamaica Jamaïque	2	2	2	2	2	2	2	2	2	2
Mexico Mexique	507	479	478	425	425	425	435	409	464	460
Netherlands Antilles Antilles néerlandaises	...	32[1]	32	32	139	215	158	135	135	135
Panama Panama	13 976	16 454	18 273	18 649	19 513	20 910	21 272	22 680	23 856	27 588
St. Vincent-Grenadines St. Vincent-Grenadines	378	834	1 112	941	1 101	1 228	1 061	913	569	450
Trinidad and Tobago Trinité-et-Tobago	...	...	...	...	...	...	...	...	1	1
Turks and Caicos Islands Iles Turques et Caïques	1	1	1	1	...	...	...	...	...	...
United States Etats-Unis	8 069	5 493	5 013	4 500	3 987	3 630	3 372	3 436	3 491	3 176
America, South · Amérique du Sud										
Argentina Argentine	542	221	107	124	107	114	105	102	100	83
Bolivia Bolivie	...	...	...	...	...	...	...	...	18	25
Brazil Brésil	1 947	1 930	2 068	2 112	2 090	1 803	1 854	1 825	1 770	1 642
Chile Chili	26	4	4	41	71	93	93	100	100	100
Colombia Colombie	11	6	6	6	6	6	6	6	6	6
Ecuador Equateur	116	112	75	77	77	81	80	93	223	219
Paraguay Paraguay	1	2	2	2	2	4	4	4	4	4
Peru Pérou	177	131	131	68	80	76	76	31	31	19
Suriname Suriname	2	2	2	2	2	2	2	2	2	2
Uruguay Uruguay	47	46	46	46	46	48	48	48	6	6

61
Merchant shipping: fleets
Total, Oil tankers and Ore and bulk carrier fleets: thousand gross registered tons [cont.]
Transports maritimes : flotte marchande
Total, Pétroliers et Minéraliers et transporteurs de vracs : milliers de tonneaux de jauge brute [suite]

Flag Pavillon	1991	1992	1993	1994	1995	1996	1997	1998	1999	2000
Venezuela Venezuela	478	455	437	420	361	275	275	222	222	212
Asia · Asie										
Azerbaijan Azerbaïdjan	...	197	222	180	188	181	180	176	176	176
Bahrain Bahreïn	2	2	2	55	54	54	55	54	54	1
Bangladesh Bangladesh	51	51	51	51	51	59	59	59	61	62
Cambodia Cambodge	...	...	...	...	...	...	...	...	7	31
China †† Chine ††	1 840	1 721	2 117	2 278	2 295	2 190	2 014	2 029	2 084	2 250
China, Hong Kong SAR† Chine, Hong Kong RAS†	756	880	818	697	669	396	22	340	515	734
Cyprus Chypre	5 996	4 677	4 960	4 634	4 341	3 733	3 779	3 848	3 987	4 165
Georgia Géorgie	...	...	...	220	136	115	73	73	76	8
India Inde	1 805	2 009	2 112	2 337	2 553	2 622	2 515	2 530	2 698	2 526
Indonesia Indonésie	595	594	608	646	738	849	844	841	830	805
Iran (Islamic Rep. of) Iran (Rép. islamique d')	2 945	2 944	2 765	2 135	1 234	1 860	1 844	1 592	1 754	2 101
Iraq Iraq	725	720	719	719	698	698	422	361	361	361
Israel Israël	0	1	1	1	1	1	1	1	1	1
Japan Japon	7 204	7 167	7 249	6 421	6 033	5 819	5 510	5 434	5 006	3 742
Jordan Jordanie	50	50	50	50	...	...	...	...	...	...
Korea, Dem. P. R. Corée, R. p. dém. de	13	112	115	115	116	4	5	6	6	6
Korea, Republic of Corée, République de	543	612	620	524	399	380	385	328	404	607
Kuwait Koweït	1 044	1 706	1 548	1 343	1 343	1 343	1 313	1 662	1 644	1 628
Lebanon Liban	2	2	2	2	1	2	2	1	1	1
Malaysia Malaisie	249	256	257	382	412	589	689	854	918	868
Maldives Maldives	5	6	6	6	6	6	6	6	4	3
Myanmar Myanmar	9	3	3	3	3	45	3	3	3	3
Oman Oman	0	...	1	0	0	0	0	0	0	0
Pakistan Pakistan	43	50	50	50	49	49	50	50	50	50

61
Merchant shipping: fleets
Total, Oil tankers and Ore and bulk carrier fleets: thousand gross registered tons [*cont.*]
Transports maritimes : flotte marchande
Total, Pétroliers et Minéraliers et transporteurs de vracs : milliers de tonneaux de jauge brute [*suite*]

Flag Pavillon	1991	1992	1993	1994	1995	1996	1997	1998	1999	2000
Philippines Philippines	376	388	414	419	147	158	163	162	159	154
Qatar Qatar	160	125	125	177	105	183	263	263	263	214
Saudi Arabia Arabie saoudite	561	265	277	210	238	258	203	220	218	219
Singapore Singapour	3 543	4 182	4 684	4 959	5 102	6 614	7 787	8 781	9 619	9 118
Sri Lanka Sri Lanka	78	74	74	74	3	5	5	5	5	2
Thailand Thaïlande	100	172	184	190	196	385	411	364	361	364
Turkey Turquie	772	828	903	954	821	709	514	503	584	625
Turkmenistan Turkménistan	...	...	...	1	3	3	3	2	2	2
United Arab Emirates Emirats arabes unis	334	458	326	502	519	410	426	369	248	240
Viet Nam Viet Nam	91	15	91	94	19	20	22	63	105	136
Yemen Yémen	2	2	2	2	2	2	2	2	2	5
Europe · Europe										
Belgium Belgique	12	2	2	3	2	2	2	4	4	4
Bulgaria Bulgarie	293	283	284	256	216	194	163	145	145	143
Croatia Croatie	...	7	7	19	6	8	13	11	11	9
Denmark Danemark	2 061	834	787	788	1 053	1 024	741	379	494	1 171
Estonia Estonie	...	6	6	10	10	6	6	7	8	6
Faeroe Islands Iles Féroé	...	1	1	1	1	3	2	2	2	2
Finland Finlande	209	256	307	303	303	303	303	303	303	304
France France	1 674	1 696[2]	1 869[2]	1 957[2]	1 943[2]	1 797[2]	2 049[2]	2 248[2]	2 198[2]	2 108[2]
Germany † Allemagne †	249	89	89	83	14	11	17	9	8	29
Gibraltar Gibraltar	1 123	319	276	271	272	272	263	233	288	342
Greece Grèce	9 095	10 876	13 273	13 386	12 836	13 066	11 894	12 587	13 158	13 681
Iceland Islande	1	0	2	2	2	2	2	2	2	2
Ireland Irlande	19	8	8	9	9	3	3	0	0	0
Isle of Man Ile de Man	...	801	744	1 059	872	1 023	2 401	1 893	2 409	2 877

61
Merchant shipping: fleets
Total, Oil tankers and Ore and bulk carrier fleets: thousand gross registered tons [cont.]
Transports maritimes : flotte marchande
Total, Pétroliers et Minéraliers et transporteurs de vracs : milliers de tonneaux de jauge brute [suite]

Flag Pavillon	1991	1992	1993	1994	1995	1996	1997	1998	1999	2000
Italy Italie	2 685	2 115	1 949	2 181	1 956	1 781	1 608	1 547	1 660	1 639
Latvia Lettonie	...	533	536	483	323	279	137	9	9	7
Lithuania Lituanie	...	17	12	13	8	5	5	4	4	4
Luxembourg Luxembourg	264	107	55	3	3	165	165	244	543	311
Malta Malte	2 412	3 086	5 176	5 699	6 793	7 370	9 043	9 848	12 151	11 595
Netherlands Pays-Bas	618	364	407	403	405	412	18	16	25	29
Norway Norvège	10 904	9 220	9 265	8 962	8 779	8 895	9 244	8 993	9 195	7 949
Poland Pologne	136	89	89	88	7	6	5	5	5	6
Portugal Portugal	460	657	723	552	490	217	349	416	416	354
Romania Roumanie	679	520	446	438	429	429	249	204	68	67
Russian Federation Fédération de Russie	...	2 436	2 507	2 378	2 294	1 917	1 646	1 608	1 429	1 402
Spain Espagne	1 488	917[3]	452	430	437	515	510	585	583	600
Sweden Suède	862	692	368	370	385	392	307	105	102	103
Ukraine Ukraine	...	80	80	84	81	79	89	62	56	56
United Kingdom Royaume-Uni	2 316	1 179	1 176	1 185	1 115	876	476	625	544	538
Yugoslavia, SFR† Yougoslavie, Rfs†	264	...	...	...	...	...	...	...	...	...
Oceania · Océanie										
Australia Australie	708	780	780	779	579	467	380	226	226	226
Fiji Fidji	4	4	3	3	3	3	3	3	3	3
Kiribati Kiribati	...	...	...	...	2	2	2	...	...	...
Marshall Islands Iles Marshall	...	1 146	1 601	1 560	1 502	2 721	3 388	3 561	4 313	5 462
New Zealand Nouvelle-Zélande	80	73	54	54	76	61	61	73	73	20
Papua New Guinea Papouasie-Nvl-Guinée	2	3	3	3	3	7	4	3	3	2
Vanuatu Vanuatu	233	184	24	15	38	40	14	11	11	11
Wallis and Futuna Islands Iles Wallis et Futuna	...	50	50	75	75	75	75	75	75	50

61
Merchant shipping: fleets
Total, Oil tankers and Ore and bulk carrier fleets: thousand gross registered tons [*cont.*]
Transports maritimes : flotte marchande
Total, Pétroliers et Minéraliers et transporteurs de vracs : milliers de tonneaux de jauge brute [*suite*]

Flag Pavillon	1991	1992	1993	1994	1995	1996	1997	1998	1999	2000
USSR - former † · URSS (anc.) †										
USSR - former † URSS (anc.) †	4 068	...	...	...	...	...	...	...	...	...

C. Ore and bulk carrier fleets · Minéraliers et transporteurs de vracs

	1991	1992	1993	1994	1995	1996	1997	1998	1999	2000
World *Monde*	**135 884**	**139 042**	**140 915**	**144 914**	**151 694**	**157 382**	**162 169**	**158 565**	**158 957**	**161 186**
Africa · Afrique										
Algeria Algérie	172	172	172	172	172	172	172	172	172	173
Egypt Egypte	343	343	343	420	510	487	575	613	601	546
Gabon Gabon	...	...	11	11	24	24	24	12	...	...
Liberia Libéria	15 629	17 035	15 640	15 970	16 373	16 744	17 711	16 739	14 426	10 533
Mauritius Maurice	47	80	116	120	2	2	4	4	4	4
Morocco Maroc	92	92	...	...	...	...	...	...	...	...
Nigeria Nigéria	...	1	1	1	...	...	...	...	...	...
Tunisia Tunisie	37	37	37	37	38	38	38	27	17	17
America, North · Amérique du Nord										
Antigua and Barbuda Antigua-et-Barbuda	3	43	90	93	102	174	174	294	196	194
Bahamas Bahamas	4 872	4 312	4 515	4 269	4 501	4 425	4 728	4 990	4 943	4 833
Barbados Barbade	...	...	...	...	74	226	268	174	174	174
Belize Belize	...	...	5	5	20	160	195	190	210	178
Bermuda Bermudes	199	213	147	165	248	301	1 018	1 089	1 910	1 911
Canada Canada	1 414	1 425	1 377	1 371	1 335	1 347	1 352	1 352	1 338	1 307
Cayman Islands Iles Caïmanes	54	69	100	136	104	282	282	455	526	634
Cuba Cuba	62	31	30	1	1	1	2	2	2	2
Honduras Honduras	57	92	90	118	138	115	114	77	133	101
Mexico Mexique	48	...	...	...	...	...	...	...	...	...
Netherlands Antilles Antilles néerlandaises	...	113[1]	131	146	71	108	108	...	...	2
Panama Panama	13 669	17 327	19 280	22 169	26 726	33 019	38 617	40 319	42 726	45 734

61
Merchant shipping: fleets
Total, Oil tankers and Ore and bulk carrier fleets: thousand gross registered tons [*cont.*]
Transports maritimes : flotte marchande
Total, Pétroliers et Minéraliers et transporteurs de vracs : milliers de tonneaux de jauge brute [*suite*]

Flag Pavillon	1991	1992	1993	1994	1995	1996	1997	1998	1999	2000
St. Vincent-Grenadines St. Vincent-Grenadines	1 004	1 816	1 798	1 939	2 328	2 627	3 202	2 858	2 656	2 672
United States Etats-Unis	2 168	1 550	1 539	1 546	1 513	1 301	1 275	1 268	1 268	1 271
America, South · Amérique du Sud										
Argentina Argentine	365	62	62	62	62	34	34	34	34	34
Bolivia Bolivie	...	...	...	...	...	...	...	7	49	28
Brazil Brésil	2 855	2 378	2 199	2 214	2 077	1 890	1 706	1 501	1 453	1 437
Chile Chili	296	279	297	306	294	191	213	188	203	217
Colombia Colombie	81	63	63	...	...	...	...	...	...	...
Ecuador Equateur	27	22	22	22	...	...	...	...	...	...
Peru Pérou	129	64	49	31	31	15	...	...	15	...
Venezuela Venezuela	147	96	147	147	111	111	111	126	116	126
Asia · Asie										
Bahrain Bahreïn	...	8	8	8	8	8	33	33	33	43
Bangladesh Bangladesh	...	...	...	...	7	7	7	6	6	6
Cambodia Cambodge	...	...	...	...	...	95	146	169	305	405
China †† Chine ††	5 206	5 405	5 714	5 960	6 677	6 781	6 464	6 832	6 648	6 618
China, Hong Kong SAR† Chine, Hong Kong RAS†	3 925	4 864	5 466	5 570	6 405	5 749	4 211	4 208	5 233	6 947
Cyprus Chypre	10 234	10 816	12 277	12 317	13 084	12 653	11 819	11 090	11 511	11 437
Georgia Géorgie	...	...	...	170	104	48	0	0	0	0
India Inde	3 134	2 912	2 939	2 740	3 183	3 081	3 013	2 832	2 748	2 663
Indonesia Indonésie	149	170	170	170	205	222	335	358	380	335
Iran (Islamic Rep. of) Iran (Rép. islamique d')	1 059	1 047	1 049	1 048	1 015	1 015	1 015	990	957	1 148
Israel Israël	22	22	22	23	12	12	12	...	...	...
Japan Japon	8 652	8 509	7 336	6 615	5 445	4 956	4 558	3 869	3 556	3 243
Jordan Jordanie	13	...	10	10	21	40	40	21	21	11
Korea, Dem. P. R. Corée, R. p. dém. de	79	84	130	128	107	107	96	50	53	63

61
Merchant shipping: fleets
Total, Oil tankers and Ore and bulk carrier fleets: thousand gross registered tons [*cont.*]
Transports maritimes : flotte marchande
Total, Pétroliers et Minéraliers et transporteurs de vracs : milliers de tonneaux de jauge brute [*suite*]

Flag Pavillon	1991	1992	1993	1994	1995	1996	1997	1998	1999	2000
Korea, Republic of Corée, République de	4 463	3 931	3 575	3 659	3 706	3 650	3 542	2 809	2 708	2 915
Kuwait Koweït	...	...	...	...	...	...	...	17	17	17
Lebanon Liban	44	55	46	46	81	73	124	108	152	191
Malaysia Malaisie	319	449	556	798	982	1 272	1 305	1 448	1 513	1 568
Maldives Maldives	21	19	11	11	11	11	...	...	...	...
Myanmar Myanmar	569	553	415	358	215	310	298	283	301	231
Pakistan Pakistan	...	17	17	88	115	159	158	125	30	...
Philippines Philippines	6 262	6 040	5 999	6 496	6 138	6 334	5 951	5 597	4 822	4 366
Qatar Qatar	...	...	70	141	142	142	142	142	142	142
Saudi Arabia Arabie saoudite	...	12	12	12	12	12	12	12	...	...
Singapore Singapour	2 132	2 626	2 889	3 209	3 766	4 344	4 358	4 585	4 695	4 753
Sri Lanka Sri Lanka	93	93	93	93	93	93	95	77	77	77
Syrian Arab Republic Rép. arabe syrienne	14	24	32	48	48	45	14	22	30	26
Thailand Thaïlande	32	69	158	224	387	480	567	491	476	443
Turkey Turquie	2 331	2 263	3 036	3 253	4 007	4 168	4 444	4 023	3 939	3 303
Turkmenistan Turkménistan	...	...	...	...	...	...	...	...	5	3
United Arab Emirates Emirats arabes unis	32	60	27	47	35	37	20	20	20	0
Viet Nam Viet Nam	21	' 21	21	21	21	63	94	94	94	122
Europe · Europe										
Austria Autriche	71	63	85	49	...	...	...	...	...	...
Belgium Belgique	...	...	...	...	...	56	...	...	...	...
Bulgaria Bulgarie	601	613	589	578	502	532	542	532	518	518
Croatia Croatie	...	32	3	19	19	186	469	517	504	438
Czechoslovakia-former† Tchécoslovaquie (anc.) †	276	153	...	...	...	...	...	...	...	...
Czech Republic République tchèque	...	...	153	112	98	78	16	...	...	...
Denmark Danemark	525	563	498	569	493	521	522	522	464	356

61
Merchant shipping: fleets
Total, Oil tankers and Ore and bulk carrier fleets: thousand gross registered tons [*cont.*]
Transports maritimes : flotte marchande
Total, Pétroliers et Minéraliers et transporteurs de vracs : milliers de tonneaux de jauge brute [*suite*]

Flag Pavillon	1991	1992	1993	1994	1995	1996	1997	1998	1999	2000
Estonia Estonie	...	160	160	160	160	160	160	96	65	33
Finland Finlande	89	72	71	71	80	80	80	90	90	90
France France	406	343[2]	463[2]	462[2]	291[2]	448[2]	355[2]	354[2]	539[2]	538[2]
Germany † Allemagne †	695	377	308	285	238	48	2	2	2	2
Gibraltar Gibraltar	192	73	58	28	...	...	...	...	16	16
Greece Grèce	10 802	11 638	12 482	12 988	12 795	10 705	9 472	8 771	7 709	8 077
Iceland Islande	...	0	0	0	0	0	0	0	0	0
Ireland Irlande	9	3	3	3	...	...	...	...	8	26
Isle of Man Ile de Man	...	304	171	223	414	756	831	783	732	795
Italy Italie	2 228	2 200	1 829	1 549	1 535	1 553	1 303	1 525	1 851	2 049
Lithuania Lituanie	...	112	116	111	111	110	110	110	110	100
Luxembourg Luxembourg	993	879	669	555	365	86	86	86	93	6
Malta Malte	2 772	5 103	5 854	6 196	6 857	7 478	8 623	8 616	9 984	10 533
Netherlands Pays-Bas	359	244	98	99	99	68	68	77	77	10
Norway Norvège	7 091	5 912	4 924	4 865	4 010	3 858	3 908	4 041	3 913	3 863
Poland Pologne	1 636	1 667	1 524	1 511	1 455	1 455	1 360	1 082	993	851
Portugal Portugal	197	75	27	85	127	128	128	188	160	261
Romania Roumanie	1 698	1 082	1 089	980	850	865	865	788	320	138
Russian Federation Fédération de Russie	...	1 903	1 821	1 757	1 768	1 767	1 568	1 031	889	864
Spain Espagne	732	504	223	59	68	23	39	42	42	42
Sweden Suède	415	209	119	45	52	44	38	32	32	29
Switzerland Suisse	252	312	268	307	351	370	389	349	393	393
Ukraine Ukraine	...	1 199	1 195	1 196	729	452	254	207	161	100
United Kingdom Royaume-Uni	743	122	104	74	74	67	64	48	33	52
Yugoslavia, SFR† Yougoslavie, Rfs†	1 707	...	...	...	...	...	...	...	...	...

61
Merchant shipping: fleets
Total, Oil tankers and Ore and bulk carrier fleets: thousand gross registered tons [*cont.*]
Transports maritimes : flotte marchande
Total, Pétroliers et Minéraliers et transporteurs de vracs : milliers de tonneaux de jauge brute [*suite*]

Flag Pavillon	1991	1992	1993	1994	1995	1996	1997	1998	1999	2000
Oceania · Océanie										
Australia Australie	1 004	987	1 030	1 049	1 011	1 039	1 036	893	801	624
Marshall Islands Iles Marshall	...	440	506	539	701	1 095	1 666	1 602	1 255	2 067
New Zealand Nouvelle-Zélande	13	22	25	25	25	25	12	12	12	12
Vanuatu Vanuatu	1 132	1 052	1 117	1 008	841	706	620	708	518	506
USSR - former † · URSS (anc.) †										
USSR - former † URSS (anc.) †	3 902	...	...	...	...	...	...	...	...	...

Source:
Lloyd's Register of Shipping, London, "World Fleet
Statistics 2000" and previous issues.

† For information on recent changes in country or
area nomenclature pertaining to former Czechoslovakia,
Germany, Hong Kong Special Administrative Region (SAR) of
China, Macao Special Administrative Region (SAR) of China,
SFR of Yugoslavia and the former USSR, see Annex I - Country
or area nomenclature, regional and other groupings.

†† For statistical purposes, the data for
China do not include those for Hong Kong Special
Administrative Region (Hong Kong SAR), Macao Special
Administrative Region (Macao SAR) and Taiwan province of
China.

1 Including Aruba.
2 Including French Antarctic Territory.
3 Including Canary Islands.

Source:
"Lloyd's Register of Shipping", Londres, "World Fleet
Statistics 2000" et éditions précédentes.

† Pour les modifications récentes de nomenclature
de pays ou de zone concernant l'Allemagne, Hong Kong, région
administrative spéciale (RAS) de Chine, Macao, région
administrative spéciale (RAS) de Chine,
l'ex-Tchécoslovaquie, l'ex-URSS et l'ex-Rfs de Yougoslavie,
voir annexe I - Nomenclature des pays ou des zones,
groupements régionaux et autres groupements.

†† Les données statistiques relatives à
la Chine ne comprennent pas celles qui concernent la région
administrative spéciale de Hong Kong (la RAS de Hong Kong),
la région administrative spéciale de Macao (la RAS de Macao)
et la province chinoise de Taiwan.

1 Y compris Aruba.
2 Y compris le territoire antarctique français.
3 Y compris les Iles Canaries.

62
International maritime transport
Transports maritimes internationaux
Vessels entered and cleared: thousand net registered tons
Navires entrés et sortis : milliers de tonneaux de jauge nette

Country or area Pays ou zone	1991	1992	1993	1994	1995	1996	1997	1998	1999	2000
Albania Albanie										
Vessels entered										
Navires entrés	...	...	288	576	1 002	1 218	1 053	1 419	1 115	2 212
Vessels cleared										
Navires sortis	...	...	121	198	309	213	123	61	29	72
Algeria Algérie										
Vessels entered										
Navires entrés	86 254	85 577	84 744	86 500	88 502	93 913	103 201	106 256	113 681	117 918
Vessels cleared										
Navires sortis	86 213	85 730	84 659	86 767	88 865	93 676	103 187	106 036	113 627	117 937
American Samoa Samoa américaines										
Vessels entered[1]										
Navires entrés[1]	848	618	440	581	526	452	725	589	884	...
Vessels cleared[1]										
Navires sortis[1]	848	618	440	581	526	452	725	589	884	...
Antigua and Barbuda Antigua-et-Barbuda										
Vessels entered										
Navires entrés	...	...	...	...	...	57 386	94 907	...	...	...
Vessels cleared										
Navires sortis	...	...	...	...	...	544 328	667 126			
Argentina Argentine										
Vessels entered[3]										
Navires entrés[3]	36 664[2]	11 379[4]	20 092[5]	12 345[4]	...	...	...	...	...	...
Australia Australie										
Vessels entered[16]										
Navires entrés[16]	...	...	...	...	2 299	2 268	2 231	...	1 864	1 730
Azerbaijan Azerbaïdjan										
Vessels entered										
Navires entrés	...	115	142	127	925	1 022	2 007	3 967	4 015	5 118
Vessels cleared										
Navires sortis	...	1 849	1 568	2 289	1 751	1 702	1 737	1 483	624	703
Bahrain Bahreïn										
Vessels entered										
Navires entrés	1	1	1	1	1	2	2	...	...	...
Bangladesh Bangladesh										
Vessels entered[7]										
Navires entrés[7]	4 997	5 375	4 835	4 832	6 013	5 928	5 488	5 794	6 509	...
Vessels cleared[7]										
Navires sortis[7]	2 816	2 943	3 103	2 556	3 094	3 136	2 866	2 556	2 949	...
Barbados Barbade										
Vessels entered										
Navires entrés	11 894	13 342	12 195	13 703	12 780	14 002	15 146	16 893	14 470	15 875
Belgium Belgique										
Vessels entered										
Navires entrés	211 767	236 323	229 915	239 678	253 427	297 664	337 862	367 684	386 211	...
Vessels cleared										
Navires sortis	165 185	189 286	190 795	201 448	210 144	297 610	333 694	360 987	375 519	...
Benin Bénin										
Vessels entered										
Navires entrés	993	937	1 134	1 163	1 192	1 321	1 296	1 289	1 095	1 184
Brazil Brésil										
Vessels entered										
Navires entrés	65 461	65 794	74 314	78 757	79 732	82 593	86 720	92 822	78 775	...
Vessels cleared										
Navires sortis	166 047	164 152	173 624	185 291	197 955	192 889	209 331	216 273	217 811	...

62
International maritime transport
Vessels entered and cleared: thousand net registered tons [*cont.*]
Transports maritimes internationaux
Navires entrés et sortis : milliers de tonneaux de jauge nette [*suite*]

Country or area Pays ou zone	1991	1992	1993	1994	1995	1996	1997	1998	1999	2000
Cambodia Cambodge										
Vessels entered[8]										
Navires entrés[8]	135	468	463	608	647	726	715	781	1 056	1 313
Vessels cleared										
Navires sortis	158	124	193	182	214	145	293	319	191	179
Cameroon Cameroun										
Vessels entered[3][9]										
Navires entrés[3][9]	5 426	5 344	5 279	964	1 543	1 157	1 159	1 154	1 234	1 215
Canada Canada										
Vessels entered[10]										
Navires entrés[10]	58 690	58 724	56 769	60 417	62 415	66 166	74 422	81 539	82 976	...
Vessels cleared[10]										
Navires sortis[10]	116 974	109 263	108 587	116 279	114 040	117 452	124 999	120 349	122 282	...
Cape Verde Cap-Vert										
Vessels entered										
Navires entrés	...	...	...	3 409	3 628	3 601	3 590	4 296	...	...
China, Hong Kong SAR† Chine, Hong Kong RAS†										
Vessels entered										
Navires entrés	138 102	160 193	184 166	201 919	216 437	229 444	250 303	261 694	267 255	300 606
Vessels cleared										
Navires sortis	138 023	160 436	184 023	201 607	217 539	229 474	250 399	261 552	267 419	300 522
China, Macao SAR † Chine, Macao RAS †										
Vessels entered[6]										
Navires entrés[6]	...	...	...	...	...	...	...	...	...	10 736
Colombia Colombie										
Vessels entered[3]										
Navires entrés[3]	23 732	21 967	24 874	28 138	32 191	35 787	40 863	50 712	68 649	52 442
Vessels cleared										
Navires sortis	23 809	22 056	24 967	27 919	31 813	34 585	39 562	48 530	65 790	50 787
Congo Congo										
Vessels entered										
Navires entrés	6 480	6 318	6 176	5 665	6 449	7 645	...	...	...	...
Costa Rica Costa Rica										
Vessels entered										
Navires entrés	2 942	3 326	3 684	4 004	4 202	4 135	3 555	4 024	...	...
Vessels cleared										
Navires sortis	2 045	2 510	2 760	2 983	3 070	2 992	2 941	3 405	...	...
Croatia Croatie										
Vessels entered										
Navires entrés	9 831	4 419	4 686	5 028	6 023	13 587[6]	16 131[6]	16 410[6]	14 685[6]	13 925
Vessels cleared										
Navires sortis	4 937	2 156	3 251	4 161	4 297	10 393[6]	11 502[6]	11 912[6]	11 374[6]	12 686
Cyprus Chypre										
Vessels entered										
Navires entrés	12 860	14 791	14 918	15 350	15 700	19 033	16 478	15 955	18 001	20 571
Dominica Dominique										
Vessels entered										
Navires entrés	...	...	...	2 214	2 252	2 289	2 145	2 218	...	...
Dominican Republic Rép. dominicaine										
Vessels entered										
Navires entrés	6 698	7 489	7 563	8 421	8 751	9 238	10 113	10 719	13 603	14 245
Vessels cleared										
Navires sortis	736	796	788	770	1 162	1 341	1 822	1 673	1 609	2 170
Ecuador Equateur										
Vessels entered										
Navires entrés	2 389	2 563	2 719	3 006	3 665	3 283	3 263	3 158	2 019	...
Vessels cleared										
Navires sortis	13 916	15 208	15 459	16 958	18 010	17 450	18 277	16 937	18 051	...

62
International maritime transport
Vessels entered and cleared: thousand net registered tons [*cont.*]
Transports maritimes internationaux
Navires entrés et sortis : milliers de tonneaux de jauge nette [*suite*]

Country or area Pays ou zone	1991	1992	1993	1994	1995	1996	1997	1998	1999	2000
Egypt Egypte										
Vessels entered Navires entrés	38 555	39 606	41 253	44 726	48 008	47 824	48 866	40 834	36 333	...
Vessels cleared Navires sortis	28 047	33 059	34 307	37 377	41 257	43 386	40 924	33 711	32 186	...
El Salvador El Salvador										
Vessels entered Navires entrés	2 270	3 008	3 012	3 393	3 185	3 345	5 633	7 969	3 374	...
Vessels cleared Navires sortis	589	834	938	861	625	822	550	490	566	...
Estonia Estonie										
Vessels entered Navires entrés	...	...	3 419	2 376[6]	...	...	...	...	...	...
Vessels cleared Navires sortis	...	...	3 087	3 813[6]	...	...	...	...	...	...
Fiji Fidji										
Vessels entered Navires entrés	3 136	3 381	2 876	2 843	4 065	4 070	...	...	...	...
Finland Finlande										
Vessels entered[3] Navires entrés[3]	112 418	119 238	117 003	111 934	127 711	131 338	144 923	148 690	153 149	155 635
Vessels cleared[3] Navires sortis[3]	111 948	119 040	121 946	117 143	132 879	135 650	148 366	150 969	154 700	152 143
France France										
Vessels entered[11 12] Navires entrés[11 12]	1 751 943	1 825 276	1 861 742	1 941 433	1 893 000	1 975 705	2 215 239	21 642 115	2 119 434	...
Gambia Gambie										
Vessels entered[1] Navires entrés[1]	1 075	1 117	1 153	...	...	...	...	...	...	...
Germany † Allemagne †										
Vessels entered Navires entrés	...	225 984	221 741	223 363	221 226	251 500	260 553	263 470	271 978	...
Vessels cleared Navires sortis	...	199 441	196 456	201 316	197 339	229 959	235 110	237 071	249 225	...
F. R. Germany R. f. Allemagne										
Vessels entered Navires entrés	181 086	...	...	...	...	...	...	...	...	...
Vessels cleared Navires sortis	156 178	...	...	...	...	...	...	...	...	...
Gibraltar Gibraltar										
Vessels entered Navires entrés	291	321	307	276	256	...	...	...	...	...
Greece Grèce										
Vessels entered Navires entrés	36 679	37 789	32 429	33 048	38 573	38 549	38 704	...	...	...
Vessels cleared Navires sortis	20 118	20 401	18 467	21 087	21 940	21 356	19 359	...	...	...
Guadeloupe Guadeloupe										
Vessels entered[3] Navires entrés[3]	2 579	...	...	...	...	...	...	...	...	...
Guatemala Guatemala										
Vessels entered Navires entrés	2 349	2 747	3 367	4 008	3 976	3 680	4 505	...	...	...
Vessels cleared Navires sortis	1 740	2 025	2 266	2 280	2 854	3 275	3 815	...	...	...
Haiti Haïti										
Vessels entered[13] Navires entrés[13]	987	583	897	529	1 285	1 680	1 304	...	...	...

62
International maritime transport
Vessels entered and cleared: thousand net registered tons [*cont.*]
Transports maritimes internationaux
Navires entrés et sortis : milliers de tonneaux de jauge nette [*suite*]

Country or area Pays ou zone	1991	1992	1993	1994	1995	1996	1997	1998	1999	2000
India Inde										
Vessels entered[14][15] Navires entrés[14][15]	18 982	30 125	27 825	39 619	47 857	48 358	47 055	48 512	60 850	...
Vessels cleared[14][15] Navires sortis[14][15]	23 423	34 660	36 325	42 885	48 497	44 494	45 819	39 031	41 187	...
Indonesia Indonésie										
Vessels entered Navires entrés	113 380	128 571	140 861	155 869	163 597	259 096	286 314	246 838	252 893	266 246
Vessels cleared Navires sortis	34 903	38 178	41 993	48 857	48 753	75 055	97 885	82 711	73 938	77 842
Iran (Islamic Rep. of) Iran (Rép. islamique d')										
Vessels entered Navires entrés	12 218	12 772	11 218	13 795	14 686	17 155	27 756	46 937	62 828	64 114
Ireland Irlande										
Vessels entered[3] Navires entrés[3]	32 892	33 857	36 408	37 896	45 968	54 602	165 925[6]	176 228[6]	190 818[6]	...
Vessels cleared Navires sortis	12 495	12 109	13 199	15 113	15 890	16 787	16 463	16 669	17 645	
Italy Italie										
Vessels entered Navires entrés	184 693	175 940	168 545	180 175	181 733	190 910	226 977	250 830	277 384	...
Vessels cleared Navires sortis	80 303	79 600	84 044	91 288	96 505	160 757	132 532	152 655	167 550	...
Jamaica Jamaïque										
Vessels entered Navires entrés	...	...	...	9 892	10 531	12 339	12 815	...	...	...
Vessels cleared Navires sortis	...	4 859	5 576	5 599	5 730	6 043	6 457	6 553	...	...
Japan Japon										
Vessels entered[3] Navires entrés[3]	402 190	398 240	397 582	410 164	412 163	422 256	438 111	425 193	446 482	461 903
Jordan Jordanie										
Vessels entered Navires entrés	1 690	2 041	2 143	1 910	2 382	2 735	2 997	2 608	2 551	2 505
Vessels cleared Navires sortis	385	392	347	576	...	...	...	...	...	...
Kenya Kenya										
Vessels entered[39] Navires entrés[39]	5 897	7 112	7 917	8 269	7 973	8 694	8 442	8 559	8 284	8 837
Korea, Republic of Corée, République de										
Vessels entered Navires entrés	317 046	348 767	383 311	430 872	487 851	537 163	578 373	586 629	691 166	...
Vessels cleared Navires sortis	316 670	350 906	381 545	429 538	485 357	542 600	584 164	595 072	695 598	...
Kuwait Koweït										
Vessels entered Navires entrés	...	6 230	6 248	9 775	10 723	9 676	9 171	9 357	...	...
Vessels cleared Navires sortis	...	619	944	1 184	1 222	1 223	1 285	1 178	...	...
Libyan Arab Jamah. Jamah. arabe libyenne										
Vessels entered Navires entrés	6 592	5 850	6 492	5 277	5 142	5 638	5 980	6 245	5 304	...
Vessels cleared Navires sortis	327	456	556	572	751	624	647	739	815	...
Lithuania Lituanie										
Vessels entered[36] Navires entrés[36]	...	...	...	...	25 642	32 187	34 259	35 680	32 438	37 138

62
International maritime transport
Vessels entered and cleared: thousand net registered tons [*cont.*]
Transports maritimes internationaux
Navires entrés et sortis : milliers de tonneaux de jauge nette [*suite*]

Country or area Pays ou zone	1991	1992	1993	1994	1995	1996	1997	1998	1999	2000
Vessels cleared[3][6] Navires sortis[3][6]	...	...	...	...	25 477	31 383	34 161	35 658	32 419	37 044
Madagascar Madagascar										
Vessels entered[3] Navires entrés[3]	...	...	...	...	...	...	4 169	3 920	2 629	4 842
Malaysia Malaisie										
Vessels entered[16] Navires entrés[16]	101 170	108 170	109 300	110 330	...	...	...	...	...	...
Vessels cleared[16] Navires sortis[16]	101 230	109 070	109 000	110 650	...	...	...	...	...	...
Malta Malte										
Vessels entered Navires entrés	5 087	7 049	6 802	7 657	9 404	9 830	11 597	13 738	16 725	17 299
Vessels cleared Navires sortis	2 377	3 160	3 534	2 471	2 887	3 779	4 976	2 493	5 084	7 528
Mauritius Maurice										
Vessels entered[3] Navires entrés[3]	6 157	5 277	5 271	5 500	5 356	4 999	5 485	5 925	6 725	6 387
Vessels cleared Navires sortis	6 188	5 447	5 219	5 550	5 313	5 140	5 263	5 924	6 129	6 087
Mexico Mexique										
Vessels entered Navires entrés	19 069	21 520	20 241	21 919	19 697	27 533	33 317	43 185	44 614	45 276
Vessels cleared Navires sortis	94 440	97 464	101 688	100 757	103 355	117 598	125 571	125 682	119 284	125 864
Morocco Maroc										
Vessels entered[17] Navires entrés[17]	19 769	21 578	22 436	22 633	24 034	26 271	27 088	27 478	29 918	30 170
Myanmar Myanmar										
Vessels entered Navires entrés	698	879	1 278	1 587	2 388	2 286	2 230	2 955	2 729	4 545
Vessels cleared Navires sortis	667	1 205	1 408	1 612	1 624	1 108	794	1 235	1 656	2 252
Netherlands Pays-Bas										
Vessels entered[6] Navires entrés[6]	374 428	383 164	375 906	403 355	431 997	441 281	456 522	472 977	...	...
Vessels cleared[6] Navires sortis[6]	232 349	239 572	237 817	258 152	280 667	291 089	290 813	301 559	...	...
New Zealand Nouvelle-Zélande										
Vessels entered[6] Navires entrés[6]	38 069	27 983	37 603	39 700	48 827	...	...	...	...	...
Vessels cleared[6] Navires sortis[6]	36 158	27 508	35 128	37 421	42 985	...	...	...	...	...
Nigeria Nigéria										
Vessels entered Navires entrés	2 350	2 352	2 776	1 908	1 846[18]	2 043	2 464	...	...	...
Vessels cleared Navires sortis	3 092	2 275	2 830	1 879	1 852[18]	2 104	2 510	...	...	...
Norway Norvège										
Vessels entered[19] Navires entrés[19]	...	...	82 369	112 247	139 252	147 192	148 060	148 764	155 805	...
Oman Oman										
Vessels entered Navires entrés	1 939	1 819	2 190	2 119	2 099	2 110	2 226	2 102	2 087	...
Vessels cleared Navires sortis	5 156	2 745	1 146	1 192	1 309	5 529	6 781	7 147	7 008	...
Pakistan Pakistan										
Vessels entered[7] Navires entrés[7]	16 289	19 401	18 785	20 195	21 268	22 632	26 915	26 502	26 702	...

62
International maritime transport
Vessels entered and cleared: thousand net registered tons [*cont.*]
Transports maritimes internationaux
Navires entrés et sortis : milliers de tonneaux de jauge nette [*suite*]

Country or area Pays ou zone	1991	1992	1993	1994	1995	1996	1997	1998	1999	2000
Vessels cleared[7] Navires sortis[7]	7 692	7 382	7 284	8 287	7 411	7 728	5 748	6 983	7 296	...
Panama Panama										
Vessels entered Navires entrés	1 660	1 959	2 178	2 404	2 766	3 263	4 431	9 879	12 008	13 301
Vessels cleared Navires sortis	1 492	1 513	1 560	1 643	1 972	2 367	2 927	6 453	7 298	7 369
Peru Pérou										
Vessels entered Navires entrés	6 115	7 012	6 066	7 145	7 454	7 516	6 701	7 675	6 948	6 901
Vessels cleared Navires sortis	9 815	8 852	9 186	4 930	4 640	4 731	6 082	4 688	5 696	6 499
Philippines Philippines										
Vessels entered Navires entrés	28 969	29 876	32 388	38 222	40 876	...	...	...	...	...
Vessels cleared Navires sortis	22 442	19 411	22 431	25 582	27 829	...	...	...	...	...
Poland Pologne										
Vessels entered Navires entrés	13 116	15 573	15 544	14 816	18 316	20 997	24 280	25 549	24 161	26 176
Vessels cleared Navires sortis	18 277	20 031	23 222	25 552	25 269	25 566	28 877	30 065	30 062	32 225
Portugal Portugal										
Vessels entered Navires entrés	34 909	36 415	32 654	34 544	36 095	...	...	...	...	...
Réunion Réunion										
Vessels entered[17] Navires entrés[17]	2 103	2 375	2 421	2 349	2 715	2 595	2 755	3 065	3 059	3 266
Russian Federation Fédération de Russie										
Vessels entered[3] Navires entrés[3]	...	...	...	...	...	...	...	67 110	82 544	76 376
Vessels cleared[3] Navires sortis[3]	...	...	...	...	...	...	...	68 830	82 939	76 369
Saint Helena Sainte-Hélène										
Vessels entered Navires entrés	216	244	319	254	55	...	...	...	...	...
Saint Lucia Sainte-Lucie										
Vessels entered Navires entrés	1 761	1 331	...	...	4 755	5 317	6 803	...	...	...
St. Vincent-Grenadines St. Vincent-Grenadines										
Vessels entered Navires entrés	1 143	1 233	1 336	1 037	932	1 204	1 253	1 274	1 478	1 674
Vessels cleared Navires sortis	1 083	1 233	1 336	1 037	932	1 204	1 253	1 274	1 478	1 674
Samoa Samoa										
Vessels entered Navires entrés	527	425	530	563	579	544	662	685	827	...
Senegal Sénégal										
Vessels entered Navires entrés	8 985	9 447	9 625	...	...	...	...	...	...	...
Vessels cleared Navires sortis	8 987	9 477	9 769	...	...	...	...	...	...	...
Seychelles Seychelles										
Vessels entered Navires entrés	769	778	871	764	879	872	1 059	1 099	1 139	...

62
International maritime transport
Vessels entered and cleared: thousand net registered tons [*cont.*]
Transports maritimes internationaux
Navires entrés et sortis : milliers de tonneaux de jauge nette [*suite*]

Country or area Pays ou zone	1991	1992	1993	1994	1995	1996	1997	1998	1999	2000
Singapore Singapour										
Vessels entered[20]										
Navires entrés[20]	70 345	81 334	92 655	101 107	104 014	117 723	130 333	140 922	141 523	145 383
Vessels cleared[20]										
Navires sortis[20]	70 119	81 245	92 477	101 017	104 123	117 662	130 237	140 838	141 745	145 415
Slovakia Slovaquie										
Vessels entered[21]										
Navires entrés[21]	...	...	387	379	374	401	367	381	336	...
Slovenia Slovénie										
Vessels entered										
Navires entrés	3 850	3 774	3 963	4 049	4 280	5 067	5 960	6 686	7 774	...
Vessels cleared										
Navires sortis	2 321	2 128	2 362	2 095	2 388	2 251	3 254	3 652	4 395	
South Africa Afrique du Sud										
Vessels entered[6]										
Navires entrés[6]	13 396	13 309	13 437	13 037	13 285	14 075	14 383	13 559	12 695	12 041
Vessels cleared[6]										
Navires sortis[6]	402 011	439 645	441 053	472 025	515 278	586 492	629 033	631 059	606 231	577 520
Spain Espagne										
Vessels entered										
Navires entrés	132 398	134 847	130 171	137 951	154 134	149 874	152 951	170 817	184 362	...
Vessels cleared										
Navires sortis	43 226	43 255	46 942	47 813	48 176	51 657	54 243	56 449	56 817	...
Sri Lanka Sri Lanka										
Vessels entered										
Navires entrés	20 545	22 087	24 955	25 120	25 368	29 882	33 188	36 011	37 399	...
Suriname Suriname										
Vessels entered										
Navires entrés	1 294	1 335	1 265	1 301	1 167	1 270	1 307	1 411	1 344	...
Vessels cleared										
Navires sortis	1 617	1 723	1 595	1 714	1 926	2 018	2 137	2 206	2 391	...
Sweden Suède										
Vessels entered										
Navires entrés	63 922[6]	64 654[6]	62 159[6]	74 334[6]	82 386[6]	88 828[6]	95 655[6]	101 977[6]	158 718[22]	...
Vessels cleared										
Navires sortis	56 475[6]	58 075[6]	55 058[6]	63 026[6]	73 139[6]	79 888[6]	82 877[6]	84 722[6]	143 200[22]	...
Syrian Arab Republic Rép. arabe syrienne										
Vessels entered[39]										
Navires entrés[39]	2 446	2 836	3 525	3 433	2 884	2 901	2 640	2 622	2 928	...
Vessels cleared[3]										
Navires sortis[3]	2 351	2 992	3 459	3 537	2 701	2 792	2 573	2 562	2 845	...
Thailand Thaïlande										
Vessels entered										
Navires entrés	40 878	47 639	39 647	46 527	58 759	53 033	54 489	35 764	41 106	...
Vessels cleared										
Navires sortis	22 741	23 584	22 205	24 692	28 689	22 231	23 757	24 920	31 125	...
Tonga Tonga										
Vessels entered										
Navires entrés	1 950	...	...	...	...	...	...	...	...	...
Tunisia Tunisie										
Vessels entered[6]										
Navires entrés[6]	23 725	26 842	28 746	32 498	36 205	38 513	42 749	43 546	52 441	56 632
Vessels cleared[6]										
Navires sortis[6]	23 695	26 883	28 753	32 462	36 232	38 541	42 561	43 513	52 464	56 551
Turkey Turquie										
Vessels entered										
Navires entrés	47 818	46 990	56 687	52 925	57 170	59 861	78 174	142 303[6]	136 456[6]	...

62
International maritime transport
Vessels entered and cleared: thousand net registered tons [*cont.*]
Transports maritimes internationaux
Navires entrés et sortis : milliers de tonneaux de jauge nette [*suite*]

Country or area Pays ou zone	1991	1992	1993	1994	1995	1996	1997	1998	1999	2000
Vessels cleared Navires sortis	45 719	45 961	55 329	51 303	56 221	58 766	77 952	89 712[6]	88 661[6]	...
Ukraine Ukraine										
Vessels entered Navires entrés	19 236	16 640	5 072	3 381	4 270	3 287	3 108	4 843	5 085	6 840
Vessels cleared Navires sortis	40 142	45 374	29 120	25 189	21 916	21 550	28 765	36 027	44 030	4 270
United States Etats-Unis										
Vessels entered[10 23] Navires entrés[10 23]	320 439	321 169	340 507	363 896	352 411	371 107	410 157	431 565	440 341	464 358
Vessels cleared[10 23] Navires sortis[10 23]	298 837	293 452	277 520	281 709	303 707	305 250	318 435	327 092	302 344	332 445
Uruguay Uruguay										
Vessels entered Navires entrés	3 764	3 862	4 036	5 297	5 414	5 505	5 844	5 262	4 386	...
Vessels cleared Navires sortis	12 553	13 141	16 059	20 266	24 608	24 975	26 844	24 499	21 596	...
Venezuela Venezuela										
Vessels entered Navires entrés	19 882	19 758	22 087	21 657	21 009	...	...	...	...	...
Vessels cleared Navires sortis	11 500	15 194	17 211	12 045	8 461	...	...	...	...	...
Yemen Yémen										
Vessels entered Navires entrés	10 075	11 439	12 459	9 323	10 353	10 477	10 268	11 210	...	...
Vessels cleared Navires sortis	3 238	11 207	12 243	10 386	10 524	4 562	5 958	9 851	...	..
Yugoslavia Yougoslavie										
Vessels entered Navires entrés	1 180	626	...	...	805	1 960	1 828	1 589	1 810	...
Vessels cleared Navires sortis	1 128	511	...	...	769	1 155	1 360	1 091	1 083	...

Source:
United Nations Statistics Division, New York, transport
statistics database.

† For information on recent changes in country or
area nomenclature pertaining to former Czechoslovakia,
Germany, Hong Kong Special Administrative Region (SAR) of
China, Macao Special Administrative Region (SAR) of China,
SFR of Yugoslavia and the former USSR, see Annex I - Country
or area nomenclature, regional and other groupings.

1 Data refer to fiscal years ending 30 June.

2 Comprises Buenos Aires, Bahía Blanca, La Plata, Quequén, Mar
del Plata, Paraná Inferior, Paraná Medio and Rosario.
3 Including vessels in ballast.
4 Buenos Aires only.
5 Comprising Buenos Aires, Rosario, Lib. Gral. San Martin,
Quequén and La Plata.
6 Gross registered tons.
7 Data refer to fiscal years beginning 1 July.

Source:
Organisation des Nations Unies, Division de statistique, New
York, la base de données pour les statistiques des
transports.

† Pour les modifications récentes de nomenclature
de pays ou de zone concernant l'Allemagne, Hong Kong, région
administrative spéciale (RAS) de Chine, Macao, région
administrative spéciale (RAS) de Chine,
l'ex-Tchécoslovaquie, l'ex-URSS et l'ex-Rfs de Yougoslavie,
voir annexe I - Nomenclature des pays ou des zones,
groupements régionaux et autres groupements.

1 Les données se réfèrent aux années fiscales finissant le 30
juin.
2 Buenos Aires, Bahía Blanca, La Plata, Quequén, Mar del
Plata, Paraná Inferior, Paraná Medio et Rosario.
3 Y compris navires sur lest.
4 Buenos Aires seulement.
5 Buenos Aires, Rosario, Lib. Gral. San Martín, Quequén et La
Plata.
6 Tonneaux de jauge brute.
7 Les données se réfèrent aux années fiscales finissant le 1er

62

International maritime transport
Vessels entered and cleared: thousand net registered tons [*cont.*]

Transports maritimes internationaux
Navires entrés et sortis : milliers de tonneaux de jauge nette [*suite*]

8 Sihanoukville Port and Phnom Penh Port.
9 All entrances counted.
10 Including Great Lakes international traffic (Canada: also St. Lawrence).
11 Taxable volume in thousands of cubic metres.
12 Including national maritime transport.
13 Port-au-Prince.
14 Data refer to fiscal years beginning 1 April.

15 Excluding minor and intermediate ports.
16 Data for Sarawak include vessels in ballast and all entrances counted.
17 Including vessels cleared.
18 Data cover only the first three quarters of the year.

19 Gross tonnage for a sample of Norwegian ports.
20 Vessels exceeding 75 gross registered tons.
21 Inland waterway system.
22 Break in series. Beginning 1999, data are based on a survey of all ports in Sweden.

23 Excluding traffic with United States Virgin Islands.

juillet.
8 Port de Sihanoukville et Port de Phnom Penh.
9 Toutes entrées comprises.
10 Y compris trafic international des Grands Lacs (Canada: et du St. Laurent).
11 Volume taxable en milliers de mètres cubes.
12 Y compris transports maritimes nationaux.
13 Port-au-Prince.
14 Les données se réfèrent aux années fiscales finissant le 1er avril.
15 Non compris les ports petits et moyens.
16 Les données pour Sarawak comprennent navires sur lest et toutes entrées comprises.
17 Y compris navires sortis.
18 Les données se réfèrent aux premieres trois trimestres de l'année.
19 Tonnage brute pour un échantillon de ports norvègiens.
20 Navires dépassant 75 tonneaux de jauge brute.
21 Transport fluvial.
22 Discontinuité dans la série. A compter de 1999, les données sont basées sur une enquête menée auprès de tous les ports de Suède.
23 Non compris le trafic avec les Iles Vierges américaines.

63
Civil Aviation
Aviation civile
Passengers on scheduled services (thousands); Kilometres (millions)
Passagers sur les services réguliers (milliers); Kilomètres (millions)

Country or area and traffic	Total Totale 1996	1997	1998	1999	International Internationaux 1996	1997	1998	1999	Pays ou zone et trafic
World									**Monde**
Kilometres flown	20601	21635	22430	23672	9322	9963	10589	11231	Kilomètres parcourus
Passengers carried	1391085	1456147	1470730	1558628	412084	437688	457151	491126	Passagers transportés
Passenger–km	2431695	2571962	2627056	2793003	1380670	1467863	1511533	1619369	Passagers–km
Total ton–km	317154	344013	348480	369881	206871	227282	231389	247284	Total tonnes–km
Africa [1]									**Afrique [1]**
Kilometres flown	488	522	532	574	355	388	408	445	Kilomètres parcourus
Passengers carried	28399	29696	29076	31195	14320	15517	16062	17617	Passagers transportés
Passenger–km	53070	56258	55736	62223	43580	46988	47448	53226	Passagers–km
Total ton–km	6279	6657	6830	7598	5353	5778	6031	6719	Total tonnes–km
Algeria									**Algérie**
Kilometres flown	31	34	31	32	14	17	16	21	Kilomètres parcourus
Passengers carried	3494	3518	3382	2937	1406	1525	1436	1663	Passagers transportés
Passenger–km	2863	3130	3012	2991	1616	1874	1785	2226	Passagers–km
Total ton–km	274	299	292	286	158	183	177	214	Total tonnes–km
Angola									**Angola**
Kilometres flown	8	8	8	7	5	5	5	4	Kilomètres parcourus
Passengers carried	585	555	553	531	165	125	125	120	Passagers transportés
Passenger–km	880	620	622	597	660	368	369	355	Passagers–km
Total ton–km	141	97	95	92	120	73	71	68	Total tonnes–km
Benin [2]									**Bénin [2]**
Kilometres flown	3	3	3	3	3	3	3	3	Kilomètres parcourus
Passengers carried	75	86	91	84	75	86	91	84	Passagers transportés
Passenger–km	225	242	258	235	225	242	258	235	Passagers–km
Total ton–km	37	38	38	36	37	38	38	36	Total tonnes–km
Botswana									**Botswana**
Kilometres flown	2	2	3	3	1	2	2	2	Kilomètres parcourus
Passengers carried	104	116	124	144	75	88	92	108	Passagers transportés
Passenger–km	51	55	57	67	37	41	42	50	Passagers–km
Total ton–km	5	5	5	6	3	4	4	5	Total tonnes–km
Burkina Faso [2]									**Burkina Faso [2]**
Kilometres flown	4	3	3	4	3	3	3	4	Kilomètres parcourus
Passengers carried	138	97	102	147	112	94	99	132	Passagers transportés
Passenger–km	258	248	264	269	250	247	263	264	Passagers–km
Total ton–km	40	39	39	39	39	39	39	39	Total tonnes–km
Burundi									**Burundi**
Kilometres flown	...	1	1	...	...	1	1	...	Kilomètres parcourus
Passengers carried	9	12	12	...	8	12	12	...	Passagers transportés
Passenger–km	2	8	8	...	2	8	8	...	Passagers–km
Total ton–km	...	1	1	...	...	1	1	...	Total tonnes–km
Cameroon									**Cameroun**
Kilometres flown	7	6	6	6	6	5	5	5	Kilomètres parcourus
Passengers carried	362	279	290	293	202	175	189	204	Passagers transportés
Passenger–km	649	547	568	597	560	490	492	533	Passagers–km
Total ton–km	100	84	108	106	91	78	100	99	Total tonnes–km
Cape Verde									**Cap–Vert**
Kilometres flown	3	5	5	5	1	3	3	4	Kilomètres parcourus
Passengers carried	129	237	236	252	31	87	87	114	Passagers transportés
Passenger–km	188	268	269	334	157	218	219	287	Passagers–km
Total ton–km	18	25	26	32	14	20	21	27	Total tonnes–km
Central African Rep. [2]									**Rép. centrafricaine [2]**
Kilometres flown	3	3	3	3	3	3	3	3	Kilomètres parcourus
Passengers carried	75	86	91	84	75	86	91	84	Passagers transportés
Passenger–km	225	242	258	235	225	242	258	235	Passagers–km
Total ton–km	37	38	38	36	37	38	38	36	Total tonnes–km
Chad [2]									**Tchad [2]**
Kilometres flown	3	3	3	3	3	3	3	3	Kilomètres parcourus
Passengers carried	93	93	98	84	78	86	91	84	Passagers transportés
Passenger–km	233	247	263	235	226	242	258	235	Passagers–km
Total ton–km	37	39	38	36	37	38	38	36	Total tonnes–km

63
Civil Aviation
Passengers on scheduled services (thousands); Kilometres (millions) [*cont.*]
Aviation civile
Passagers sur les services réguliers (milliers); Kilomètres (millions) [*suite*]

Country or area and traffic	Total Totale				International Internationaux				Pays ou zone et trafic
	1996	1997	1998	1999	1996	1997	1998	1999	
Comoros									**Comores**
Kilometres flown	...	...	...	...	...	...	...	...	Kilomètres parcourus
Passengers carried	27	...	...	...	5	...	...	...	Passagers transportés
Passenger−km	3	...	...	...	1	...	...	...	Passagers−km
Total ton−km	...	...	...	...	...	...	...	...	Total tonnes−km
Congo [2]									**Congo** [2]
Kilometres flown	4	5	5	4	3	3	3	3	Kilomètres parcourus
Passengers carried	253	237	241	132	80	88	93	87	Passagers transportés
Passenger−km	279	305	321	263	227	245	261	240	Passagers−km
Total ton−km	42	44	44	39	37	39	38	36	Total tonnes−km
Côte d'Ivoire [2]									**Côte d'Ivoire** [2]
Kilometres flown	5	4	4	6	4	4	4	6	Kilomètres parcourus
Passengers carried	179	158	162	260	154	148	153	233	Passagers transportés
Passenger−km	307	302	318	381	292	297	313	366	Passagers−km
Total ton−km	44	44	44	50	43	43	43	48	Total tonnes−km
Egypt									**Egypte**
Kilometres flown	62	65	63	68	57	59	58	62	Kilomètres parcourus
Passengers carried	4282	4416	4022	4620	2802	2931	2793	3065	Passagers transportés
Passenger−km	8742	9018	8036	9074	8040	8310	7470	8355	Passagers−km
Total ton−km	993	1029	989	1097	929	965	938	1032	Total tonnes−km
Equatorial Guinea									**Guinée équatoriale**
Kilometres flown	...	0	0	...	...	0	0	...	Kilomètres parcourus
Passengers carried	15	21	21	...	15	8	7	...	Passagers transportés
Passenger−km	7	4	4	...	7	1	1	...	Passagers−km
Total ton−km	1	0	0	...	1	...	...	...	Total tonnes−km
Ethiopia									**Ethiopie**
Kilometres flown	26	28	27	29	23	24	22	25	Kilomètres parcourus
Passengers carried	743	772	790	861	477	496	460	617	Passagers transportés
Passenger−km	1889	1966	1881	2458	1781	1834	1743	2358	Passagers−km
Total ton−km	302	317	318	371	292	305	304	362	Total tonnes−km
Gabon									**Gabon**
Kilometres flown	7	8	8	8	5	6	6	6	Kilomètres parcourus
Passengers carried	431	469	467	423	167	195	194	226	Passagers transportés
Passenger−km	728	826	829	782	650	745	748	712	Passagers−km
Total ton−km	100	112	111	124	93	105	103	117	Total tonnes−km
Ghana									**Ghana**
Kilometres flown	6	6	6	9	6	6	6	9	Kilomètres parcourus
Passengers carried	197	211	210	304	197	211	210	304	Passagers transportés
Passenger−km	655	702	705	1097	655	702	705	1097	Passagers−km
Total ton−km	91	99	97	151	91	99	97	151	Total tonnes−km
Guinea									**Guinée**
Kilometres flown	1	1	1	1	1	1	1	1	Kilomètres parcourus
Passengers carried	36	36	36	59	31	31	31	59	Passagers transportés
Passenger−km	55	55	55	94	50	50	50	94	Passagers−km
Total ton−km	6	6	6	10	5	5	5	10	Total tonnes−km
Guinea−Bissau									**Guinée−Bissau**
Kilometres flown	...	0	0	...	...	0	0	...	Kilomètres parcourus
Passengers carried	21	21	20	...	8	8	8	...	Passagers transportés
Passenger−km	10	10	10	...	6	6	6	...	Passagers−km
Total ton−km	1	1	1	...	1	1	1	...	Total tonnes−km
Kenya									**Kenya**
Kilometres flown	17	19	21	24	14	15	17	19	Kilomètres parcourus
Passengers carried	779	836	1138	1358	463	470	658	808	Passagers transportés
Passenger−km	1838	1824	2091	2513	1709	1689	1883	2286	Passagers−km
Total ton−km	214	216	243	292	203	203	223	271	Total tonnes−km
Lesotho									**Lesotho**
Kilometres flown	1	0	1	0	1	0	1	0	Kilomètres parcourus
Passengers carried	17	10	28	1	17	7	23	1	Passagers transportés
Passenger−km	6	3	9	0	6	3	8	0	Passagers−km
Total ton−km	1	0	1	0	1	0	1	0	Total tonnes−km
Libyan Arab Jamahiriya									**Jamah. arabe libyenne**
Kilometres flown	4	4	4	4	...	...	...	...	Kilomètres parcourus
Passengers carried	639	571	571	571	...	...	...	...	Passagers transportés
Passenger−km	412	377	377	377	...	...	...	...	Passagers−km
Total ton−km	33	30	27	27	...	...	...	...	Total tonnes−km

63
Civil Aviation
Passengers on scheduled services (thousands); Kilometres (millions) [*cont.*]
Aviation civile
Passagers sur les services réguliers (milliers); Kilomètres (millions) [*suite*]

ntry or area and traffic	Total Totale				International Internationaux				Pays ou zone et trafic
	1996	1997	1998	1999	1996	1997	1998	1999	
Madagascar									**Madagascar**
metres flown	8	9	9	12	4	4	7	7	Kilomètres parcourus
engers carried	542	575	318	635	119	131	145	168	Passagers transportés
enger–km	659	758	718	1037	484	570	646	841	Passagers–km
l ton–km	85	98	94	126	68	79	86	107	Total tonnes–km
awi									**Malawi**
metres flown	3	3	3	2	2	2	2	1	Kilomètres parcourus
engers carried	153	158	158	112	76	79	79	63	Passagers transportés
enger–km	115	336	337	224	80	299	300	150	Passagers–km
l ton–km	14	33	33	21	10	31	31	14	Total tonnes–km
i ²									**Mali ²**
metres flown	3	3	3	3	3	3	3	3	Kilomètres parcourus
engers carried	75	86	91	84	75	86	91	84	Passagers transportés
enger–km	225	242	258	235	225	242	258	235	Passagers–km
l ton–km	37	38	38	36	37	38	38	36	Total tonnes–km
uritania ²									**Mauritanie ²**
metres flown	4	4	4	4	3	3	3	3	Kilomètres parcourus
engers carried	235	245	250	187	99	110	115	103	Passagers transportés
enger–km	306	324	340	290	250	267	283	255	Passagers–km
l ton–km	44	46	46	41	39	41	40	38	Total tonnes–km
uritius									**Maurice**
metres flown	22	26	24	29	21	25	23	28	Kilomètres parcourus
engers carried	717	804	810	831	674	743	743	756	Passagers transportés
enger–km	3515	3917	3826	4073	3488	3881	3788	4027	Passagers–km
al ton–km	458	538	526	539	456	535	523	535	Total tonnes–km
rocco									**Maroc**
metres flown	45	49	56	63	42	45	51	59	Kilomètres parcourus
sengers carried	2301	2638	3012	3392	1790	2023	2265	2587	Passagers transportés
enger–km	4665	5321	5868	6614	4489	5124	5625	6355	Passagers–km
al ton–km	396	417	573	667	380	401	549	641	Total tonnes–km
zambique									**Mozambique**
metres flown	3	4	4	5	1	1	2	2	Kilomètres parcourus
sengers carried	163	188	201	235	54	65	73	87	Passagers transportés
senger–km	260	291	295	326	151	170	163	171	Passagers–km
al ton–km	27	32	33	36	15	19	19	20	Total tonnes–km
mibia									**Namibie**
metres flown	8	8	9	7	6	7	7	5	Kilomètres parcourus
sengers carried	237	214	229	201	213	183	200	165	Passagers transportés
senger–km	890	906	630	548	870	882	614	528	Passagers–km
al ton–km	109	118	59	49	107	116	57	47	Total tonnes–km
er ²									**Niger ²**
metres flown	3	3	3	3	3	3	3	3	Kilomètres parcourus
sengers carried	75	86	91	84	75	86	91	84	Passagers transportés
senger–km	225	242	258	235	225	242	258	235	Passagers–km
al ton–km	37	38	38	36	37	38	38	36	Total tonnes–km
geria									**Nigéria**
metres flown	4	5	5	7	2	2	2	4	Kilomètres parcourus
sengers carried	221	318	313	668	66	44	49	162	Passagers transportés
senger–km	273	221	245	560	164	100	122	370	Passagers–km
al ton–km	30	27	32	82	21	14	18	61	Total tonnes–km
o Tome and Principe									**Sao Tomé–et–Principe**
metres flown	...	0	0	0	...	0	0	0	Kilomètres parcourus
sengers carried	23	25	24	34	14	15	15	20	Passagers transportés
senger–km	9	9	9	13	4	5	5	6	Passagers–km
al ton–km	1	1	1	1	...	0	0	1	Total tonnes–km
negal ²									**Sénégal ²**
metres flown	4	4	3	3	3	3	3	3	Kilomètres parcourus
sengers carried	155	166	121	103	124	135	91	84	Passagers transportés
senger–km	247	265	267	241	238	256	258	235	Passagers–km
al ton–km	39	40	39	37	38	40	38	36	Total tonnes–km
ychelles									**Seychelles**
metres flown	8	8	9	9	7	7	8	8	Kilomètres parcourus
sengers carried	373	384	369	347	132	133	113	110	Passagers transportés
senger–km	784	847	755	735	773	836	743	725	Passagers–km
al ton–km	94	106	84	85	93	105	83	84	Total tonnes–km

63
Civil Aviation
Passengers on scheduled services (thousands); Kilometres (millions) [*cont.*]
Aviation civile
Passagers sur les services réguliers (milliers); Kilomètres (millions) [*suite*]

Country or area and traffic	Total Totale				International Internationaux				Pays ou zone et trafic
	1996	1997	1998	1999	1996	1997	1998	1999	
Sierra Leone									**Sierra Leone**
Kilometres flown	...	...	...	0	...	...	...	0	Kilomètres parcourus
Passengers carried	15	...	...	19	15	...	...	19	Passagers transportés
Passenger–km	24	...	...	30	24	...	...	30	Passagers–km
Total ton–km	2	...	...	3	2	...	...	3	Total tonnes–km
South Africa									**Afrique du Sud**
Kilometres flown	121	131	128	144	60	69	75	84	Kilomètres parcourus
Passengers carried	7183	7274	6480	7374	1625	1808	1913	2189	Passagers transportés
Passenger–km	15957	16825	16997	19021	10723	11928	12869	14247	Passagers–km
Total ton–km	1747	1918	2046	2381	1239	1449	1636	1904	Total tonnes–km
Sudan									**Soudan**
Kilometres flown	13	7	6	7	6	5	4	4	Kilomètres parcourus
Passengers carried	491	333	499	390	315	211	311	245	Passagers transportés
Passenger–km	650	471	148	693	522	384	126	588	Passagers–km
Total ton–km	107	66	19	94	73	50	16	80	Total tonnes–km
Swaziland									**Swaziland**
Kilometres flown	1	1	1	1	1	1	1	1	Kilomètres parcourus
Passengers carried	54	41	41	12	54	41	41	12	Passagers transportés
Passenger–km	57	43	43	13	57	43	43	13	Passagers–km
Total ton–km	5	4	4	1	5	4	4	1	Total tonnes–km
Togo [2]									**Togo** [2]
Kilometres flown	3	3	3	3	3	3	3	3	Kilomètres parcourus
Passengers carried	75	86	91	84	75	86	91	84	Passagers transportés
Passenger–km	225	242	258	235	225	242	258	235	Passagers–km
Total ton–km	37	38	38	36	37	38	38	36	Total tonnes–km
Tunisia									**Tunisie**
Kilometres flown	18	24	27	27	18	24	27	27	Kilomètres parcourus
Passengers carried	1371	1779	1888	1923	1371	1779	1888	1923	Passagers transportés
Passenger–km	2118	2479	2683	2762	2118	2479	2683	2762	Passagers–km
Total ton–km	212	249	266	282	212	249	266	282	Total tonnes–km
Uganda									**Ouganda**
Kilometres flown	2	2	2	5	2	2	2	2	Kilomètres parcourus
Passengers carried	100	100	100	179	100	100	100	36	Passagers transportés
Passenger–km	110	110	110	356	110	110	110	198	Passagers–km
Total ton–km	11	11	11	54	11	11	11	37	Total tonnes–km
United Rep. of Tanzania									**Rép.–Unie de Tanzanie**
Kilometres flown	4	4	5	3	2	3	3	2	Kilomètres parcourus
Passengers carried	224	218	220	190	85	93	89	75	Passagers transportés
Passenger–km	190	231	236	176	119	165	171	115	Passagers–km
Total ton–km	20	26	25	18	12	18	18	12	Total tonnes–km
Zambia									**Zambie**
Kilometres flown	...	1	1	1	...	1	1	1	Kilomètres parcourus
Passengers carried	...	50	49	42	...	42	42	36	Passagers transportés
Passenger–km	...	45	44	34	...	43	42	32	Passagers–km
Total ton–km	...	5	4	3	...	4	4	3	Total tonnes–km
Zimbabwe									**Zimbabwe**
Kilometres flown	13	16	19	13	11	13	16	10	Kilomètres parcourus
Passengers carried	654	771	706	567	290	302	310	248	Passagers transportés
Passenger–km	881	914	955	918	740	724	791	788	Passagers–km
Total ton–km	234	224	234	114	220	208	221	102	Total tonnes–km
America, North [1]									**Amérique du Nord** [1]
Kilometres flown	**9547**	**9912**	**10224**	**10908**	**2102**	**2240**	**2473**	**2601**	**Kilomètres parcourus**
Passengers carried	**617339**	**639612**	**640789**	**688567**	**80372**	**82704**	**85779**	**91296**	**Passagers transportés**
Passenger–km	**1005200**	**1058636**	**1086197**	**1154217**	**312073**	**328718**	**339436**	**361495**	**Passagers–km**
Total ton–km	**118516**	**127555**	**130124**	**137802**	**43073**	**47720**	**49173**	**52481**	**Total tonnes–km**
Antigua and Barbuda									**Antigua–et–Barbuda**
Kilometres flown	12	12	12	11	12	12	12	11	Kilomètres parcourus
Passengers carried	1098	1250	1245	1371	1098	1250	1245	1371	Passagers transportés
Passenger–km	267	250	251	276	267	250	251	276	Passagers–km
Total ton–km	24	23	23	26	24	23	23	26	Total tonnes–km
Bahamas									**Bahamas**
Kilometres flown	5	2	2	7	2	1	1	3	Kilomètres parcourus
Passengers carried	978	704	701	1719	472	296	294	944	Passagers transportés
Passenger–km	234	140	140	366	170	76	76	244	Passagers–km
Total ton–km	21	13	13	42	16	7	7	28	Total tonnes–km

Transport   Transports

63

Civil Aviation
Passengers on scheduled services (thousands); Kilometres (millions) [*cont.*]
Aviation civile
Passagers sur les services réguliers (milliers); Kilomètres (millions) [*suite*]

Country or area and traffic	Total Totale				International Internationaux				Pays ou zone et trafic
	1996	1997	1998	1999	1996	1997	1998	1999	
Canada									**Canada**
Kilometres flown	497	519	547	570	273	293	317	337	Kilomètres parcourus
Passengers carried	22856	23981	24653	24039	10045	10945	11382	11875	Passagers transportés
Passenger–km	56018	61862	63801	65323	36764	40928	42071	43728	Passagers–km
Total ton–km	6961	7667	7751	7929	4838	5382	5402	5599	Total tonnes–km
Costa Rica									**Costa Rica**
Kilometres flown	23	24	28	27	22	23	25	24	Kilomètres parcourus
Passengers carried	918	992	1070	1055	865	899	933	923	Passagers transportés
Passenger–km	1965	1915	2004	2145	1958	1903	1983	2112	Passagers–km
Total ton–km	245	248	289	245	242	247	287	242	Total tonnes–km
Cuba									**Cuba**
Kilometres flown	20	26	34	26	15	20	28	22	Kilomètres parcourus
Passengers carried	929	1117	1138	1259	416	592	647	684	Passagers transportés
Passenger–km	2649	3543	4791	3712	2340	3228	4470	3463	Passagers–km
Total ton–km	292	388	524	421	267	362	497	392	Total tonnes–km
Dominican Republic									**Rép. dominicaine**
Kilometres flown	1	1`	1	0	1	1	1	0	Kilomètres parcourus
Passengers carried	30	34	34	10	30	34	34	10	Passagers transportés
Passenger–km	14	16	16	5	14	16	16	5	Passagers–km
Total ton–km	1	1	1	0	1	1	1	0	Total tonnes–km
El Salvador									**El Salvador**
Kilometres flown	22	17	22	28	22	17	22	26	Kilomètres parcourus
Passengers carried	1800	1006	1585	1624	1800	1006	1525	1467	Passagers transportés
Passenger–km	2181	1898	2292	5091	2181	1898	2284	5025	Passagers–km
Total ton–km	212	190	253	502	212	190	252	496	Total tonnes–km
Guatemala									**Guatemala**
Kilometres flown	6	5	7	5	6	4	7	5	Kilomètres parcourus
Passengers carried	300	508	794	506	300	432	760	472	Passagers transportés
Passenger–km	530	368	480	342	530	337	469	331	Passagers–km
Total ton–km	71	77	50	33	71	75	49	32	Total tonnes–km
Jamaica									**Jamaïque**
Kilometres flown	18	22	23	35	17	22	23	35	Kilomètres parcourus
Passengers carried	1388	1400	1454	1670	1322	1400	1454	1670	Passagers transportés
Passenger–km	2117	2677	2961	3495	2107	2677	2961	3495	Passagers–km
Total ton–km	217	264	293	377	216	264	293	377	Total tonnes–km
Mexico									**Mexique**
Kilometres flown	245	308	360	368	101	141	176	179	Kilomètres parcourus
Passengers carried	14678	17752	18685	19263	3844	4773	4728	5049	Passagers transportés
Passenger–km	19636	24065	25976	27847	8971	11228	11703	12939	Passagers–km
Total ton–km	1861	2333	2566	2742	883	1142	1241	1377	Total tonnes–km
Nicaragua									**Nicaragua**
Kilometres flown	1	1	1	1	1	1	1	1	Kilomètres parcourus
Passengers carried	51	51	52	59	51	51	52	59	Passagers transportés
Passenger–km	85	85	93	67	85	85	93	67	Passagers–km
Total ton–km	17	17	10	7	17	17	10	7	Total tonnes–km
Panama									**Panama**
Kilometres flown	14	18	21	24	14	18	21	24	Kilomètres parcourus
Passengers carried	689	772	856	933	689	772	856	933	Passagers transportés
Passenger–km	872	1094	1373	1697	872	1094	1373	1697	Passagers–km
Total ton–km	114	152	174	215	114	152	174	215	Total tonnes–km
Trinidad and Tobago									**Trinité–et–Tobago**
Kilometres flown	20	18	21	25	20	18	21	24	Kilomètres parcourus
Passengers carried	897	807	880	1112	897	807	880	1046	Passagers transportés
Passenger–km	2658	2392	2567	2720	2658	2392	2567	2715	Passagers–km
Total ton–km	265	239	315	309	265	239	315	309	Total tonnes–km
United States									**Etats–Unis**
Kilometres flown	8665	8928	9134	9759	1598	1659	1809	1888	Kilomètres parcourus
Passengers carried	571072	587992	586402	632440	58813	58580	60126	63644	Passagers transportés
Passenger–km	919816	957379	978498	1039643	255916	261741	268253	284008	Passagers–km
Total ton–km	108684	115856	117773	124817	36228	39541	40540	43254	Total tonnes–km
America, South									**Amérique du Sud**
Kilometres flown	**927**	**1023**	**1099**	**1088**	**444**	**466**	**445**	**426**	**Kilomètres parcourus**
Passengers carried	**53497**	**58522**	**63745**	**62391**	**12711**	**13332**	**13731**	**13523**	**Passagers transportés**
Passenger–km	**77786**	**86036**	**91204**	**86711**	**48653**	**53012**	**53043**	**49626**	**Passagers–km**
Total ton–km	**10400**	**12035**	**12559**	**11599**	**7280**	**8277**	**8568**	**7735**	**Total tonnes–km**

63
Civil Aviation
Passengers on scheduled services (thousands); Kilometres (millions) [*cont.*]
Aviation civile
Passagers sur les services réguliers (milliers); Kilomètres (millions) [*suite*]

Country or area and traffic	Total Totale				International Internationaux				Pays ou zone et trafic
	1996	1997	1998	1999	1996	1997	1998	1999	
Argentina									**Argentine**
Kilometres flown	133	155	157	170	64	74	54	53	Kilomètres parcourus
Passengers carried	7913	8603	8623	9192	2193	2120	2108	1980	Passagers transportés
Passenger–km	13360	14348	14379	14024	8267	8602	8447	7621	Passagers–km
Total ton–km	1447	1566	1597	1559	994	1055	1055	970	Total tonnes–km
Bolivia									**Bolivie**
Kilometres flown	24	28	28	21	15	17	19	15	Kilomètres parcourus
Passengers carried	1783	2251	2115	1873	542	705	773	659	Passagers transportés
Passenger–km	1634	2143	2179	1851	1166	1548	1629	1398	Passagers–km
Total ton–km	223	274	273	186	177	215	218	147	Total tonnes–km
Brazil									**Brésil**
Kilometres flown	428	468	535	530	166	172	173	156	Kilomètres parcourus
Passengers carried	22011	24196	29137	28273	4174	4582	4648	3980	Passagers transportés
Passenger–km	37671	42242	46978	42224	22296	25492	25479	21504	Passagers–km
Total ton–km	5166	5716	5980	5333	3348	3697	3627	3088	Total tonnes–km
Chile									**Chili**
Kilometres flown	97	109	117	107	55	59	63	65	Kilomètres parcourus
Passengers carried	3622	4693	5095	5188	1224	1613	1768	2056	Passagers transportés
Passenger–km	6787	8769	9679	10650	4481	5691	6300	7438	Passagers–km
Total ton–km	1419	1865	2124	2107	1175	1543	1768	1766	Total tonnes–km
Colombia									**Colombie**
Kilometres flown	97	117	125	120	43	50	57	60	Kilomètres parcourus
Passengers carried	8342	9099	9051	8665	1115	1136	1320	1553	Passagers transportés
Passenger–km	5991	6934	7350	7848	2980	3400	3835	4659	Passagers–km
Total ton–km	836	1392	1436	1348	551	855	1061	985	Total tonnes–km
Ecuador									**Equateur**
Kilometres flown	15	23	23	16	9	18	18	11	Kilomètres parcourus
Passengers carried	1925	1791	2048	1387	385	503	674	351	Passagers transportés
Passenger–km	1663	2035	2282	1388	1123	1455	1788	976	Passagers–km
Total ton–km	181	235	286	157	130	180	239	118	Total tonnes–km
Guyana									**Guyana**
Kilometres flown	3	3	3	2	2	2	2	2	Kilomètres parcourus
Passengers carried	126	126	126	70	59	59	59	70	Passagers transportés
Passenger–km	248	248	249	277	230	230	231	277	Passagers–km
Total ton–km	26	26	26	28	23	23	24	28	Total tonnes–km
Paraguay									**Paraguay**
Kilometres flown	7	4	5	5	6	4	5	4	Kilomètres parcourus
Passengers carried	260	196	222	232	213	196	222	217	Passagers transportés
Passenger–km	474	215	247	244	454	215	247	239	Passagers–km
Total ton–km	42	19	22	22	40	19	22	21	Total tonnes–km
Peru									**Pérou**
Kilometres flown	33	40	41	27	17	17	18	6	Kilomètres parcourus
Passengers carried	2328	2725	2774	1900	555	510	508	150	Passagers transportés
Passenger–km	2634	2964	3014	1590	1613	1521	1526	450	Passagers–km
Total ton–km	251	276	286	149	153	140	144	42	Total tonnes–km
Suriname									**Suriname**
Kilometres flown	5	7	7	6	5	7	7	6	Kilomètres parcourus
Passengers carried	195	279	278	194	190	275	274	190	Passagers transportés
Passenger–km	883	1068	1072	726	883	1067	1071	725	Passagers–km
Total ton–km	106	127	127	91	106	127	127	91	Total tonnes–km
Uruguay									**Uruguay**
Kilometres flown	5	6	7	8	5	6	7	8	Kilomètres parcourus
Passengers carried	504	544	557	728	504	544	557	728	Passagers transportés
Passenger–km	640	627	642	839	640	627	642	839	Passagers–km
Total ton–km	62	57	70	94	62	57	70	94	Total tonnes–km
Venezuela									**Venezuela**
Kilometres flown	80	63	52	75	57	40	22	39	Kilomètres parcourus
Passengers carried	4487	4020	3720	4690	1557	1090	820	1590	Passagers transportés
Passenger–km	5800	4444	3133	5050	4520	3164	1848	3500	Passagers–km
Total ton–km	639	483	332	526	520	364	213	383	Total tonnes–km
Asia [1]									**Asie** [1]
Kilometres flown	3864	4102	4189	4321	2353	2540	2593	2729	**Kilomètres parcourus**
Passengers carried	337237	345483	336963	351455	113764	117496	116720	127479	**Passagers transportés**
Passenger–km	605604	636050	621807	665643	423548	445638	439870	480286	**Passagers–km**
Total ton–km	86943	93944	91631	100049	69987	76098	74427	82323	**Total tonnes–km**

63
Civil Aviation
Passengers on scheduled services (thousands); Kilometres (millions) [*cont.*]
Aviation civile
Passagers sur les services réguliers (milliers); Kilomètres (millions) [*suite*]

ntry or area and traffic	Total Totale				International Internationaux				Pays ou zone et trafic
	1996	1997	1998	1999	1996	1997	1998	1999	
hanistan									**Afghanistan**
metres flown	6	6	3	3	3	6	2	2	Kilomètres parcourus
engers carried	256	90	53	140	112	51	27	36	Passagers transportés
enger–km	286	158	88	129	212	136	72	90	Passagers–km
l ton–km	40	50	24	19	32	48	22	15	Total tonnes–km
cnia									**Arménie**
metres flown	9	8	9	8	9	8	9	8	Kilomètres parcourus
engers carried	358	368	365	343	358	368	365	343	Passagers transportés
enger–km	747	767	765	639	747	767	765	639	Passagers–km
l ton–km	79	80	80	70	79	80	80	70	Total tonnes–km
rbaijan									**Azerbaïdjan**
metres flown	21	17	9	10	5	13	7	8	Kilomètres parcourus
engers carried	1233	982	669	572	175	517	311	188	Passagers transportés
enger–km	1743	1283	843	614	291	1021	632	390	Passagers–km
l ton–km	183	159	169	113	36	119	145	90	Total tonnes–km
rain [5]									**Bahreïn** [5]
metres flown	22	19	19	21	22	19	19	21	Kilomètres parcourus
engers carried	1200	1165	1207	1307	1200	1165	1207	1307	Passagers transportés
senger–km	2759	2501	2653	2836	2759	2501	2653	2836	Passagers–km
l ton–km	367	333	357	387	367	333	357	387	Total tonnes–km
gladesh									**Bangladesh**
metres flown	19	20	20	21	17	19	19	20	Kilomètres parcourus
sengers carried	1252	1315	1162	1215	765	846	855	892	Passagers transportés
senger–km	2995	3233	3422	3515	2897	3141	3358	3448	Passagers–km
l ton–km	406	494	524	545	396	486	519	538	Total tonnes–km
utan									**Bhoutan**
metres flown	1	1	1	1	1	1	1	1	Kilomètres parcourus
sengers carried	35	36	36	31	35	36	36	31	Passagers transportés
senger–km	46	49	49	41	46	49	49	41	Passagers–km
l ton–km	4	4	4	4	4	4	4	4	Total tonnes–km
nei Darussalam									**Brunéi Darussalam**
metres flown	24	28	35	25	24	28	35	25	Kilomètres parcourus
sengers carried	857	1088	877	808	857	1088	877	808	Passagers transportés
senger–km	2712	2906	2972	2563	2712	2906	2972	2563	Passagers–km
l ton–km	353	378	386	380	353	378	386	380	Total tonnes–km
**ina †† **									**Chine ††**
metres flown	590	639	730	784	111	107	127	138	Kilomètres parcourus
sengers carried	51770	52277	53481	55853	6778	4790	5086	6005	Passagers transportés
senger–km	70605	72964	75823	80575	16128	15781	17181	19877	Passagers–km
al ton–km	7649	8259	8893	10115	2498	2709	3047	3845	Total tonnes–km
ina, Hong Kong SAR † [8]									**Chine, Hong Kong RAS †** [8]
metres flown	...	112	228	228	...	112	228	228	Kilomètres parcourus
sengers carried	...	5957	12203	12593	...	5957	12203	12593	Passagers transportés
senger–km	...	20283	42964	43907	...	20283	42964	43907	Passagers–km
al ton–km	...	4278	8274	8759	...	4278	8274	8759	Total tonnes–km
prus									**Chypre**
metres flown	19	20	20	20	19	20	20	20	Kilomètres parcourus
sengers carried	1214	1278	1346	1337	1214	1278	1346	1337	Passagers transportés
senger–km	2561	2657	2711	2687	2561	2657	2711	2687	Passagers–km
al ton–km	272	278	284	285	272	278	284	285	Total tonnes–km
orgia									**Géorgie**
metres flown	5	3	7	5	4	3	5	5	Kilomètres parcourus
sengers carried	152	110	205	159	149	110	175	159	Passagers transportés
senger–km	288	206	409	307	287	206	340	307	Passagers–km
al ton–km	28	20	45	30	28	20	34	30	Total tonnes–km
dia									**Inde**
metres flown	171	194	200	190	68	66	68	66	Kilomètres parcourus
sengers carried	13395	16536	16547	16005	3229	3447	3478	3640	Passagers transportés
senger–km	22317	24620	24722	24215	12198	12700	12947	13100	Passagers–km
al ton–km	2566	2737	2776	2734	1579	1573	1607	1624	Total tonnes–km
donesia									**Indonésie**
metres flown	256	199	155	122	92	88	56	47	Kilomètres parcourus
sengers carried	17139	12937	9603	8047	3633	3120	2017	1927	Passagers transportés
senger–km	25081	23718	15974	14544	14929	15670	9770	9329	Passagers–km
al ton–km	2986	2797	1826	1560	2015	2007	1173	1022	Total tonnes–km

63
Civil Aviation
Passengers on scheduled services (thousands); Kilometres (millions) [*cont.*]
Aviation civile
Passagers sur les services réguliers (milliers); Kilomètres (millions) [*suite*]

Country or area and traffic	Total Totale				International Internationaux				Pays ou zone et trafic
	1996	1997	1998	1999	1996	1997	1998	1999	
Iran (Islamic Rep. of)									**Iran (Rép. islamique d')**
Kilometres flown	50	70	68	63	15	21	22	23	Kilomètres parcourus
Passengers carried	7610	9804	9303	8277	938	1309	1404	1388	Passagers transportés
Passenger–km	6634	8963	8539	7852	1933	2642	2632	2704	Passagers–km
Total ton–km	708	901	856	799	270	324	322	339	Total tonnes–km
Israel									**Israël**
Kilometres flown	74	75	79	86	67	69	72	80	Kilomètres parcourus
Passengers carried	3695	3754	3699	4033	2715	2714	2741	2984	Passagers transportés
Passenger–km	11793	11776	12418	13515	11512	11493	12152	13225	Passagers–km
Total ton–km	2179	2195	2241	2259	2154	2175	2217	2233	Total tonnes–km
Japan									**Japon**
Kilometres flown	727	777	828	841	370	399	426	440	Kilomètres parcourus
Passengers carried	95914	94998	101701	105960	15641	16235	16388	18057	Passagers transportés
Passenger–km	141812	151048	154402	162798	79049	84098	85608	91463	Passagers–km
Total ton–km	19142	20627	20896	22348	13607	14755	14905	16144	Total tonnes–km
Jordan									**Jordanie**
Kilometres flown	42	40	35	36	42	40	35	36	Kilomètres parcourus
Passengers carried	1299	1353	1187	1252	1293	1353	1187	1252	Passagers transportés
Passenger–km	4750	4900	4065	4195	4748	4900	4065	4195	Passagers–km
Total ton–km	731	721	596	579	731	721	596	579	Total tonnes–km
Kazakhstan									**Kazakhstan**
Kilometres flown	20	20	35	33	7	7	25	25	Kilomètres parcourus
Passengers carried	568	568	726	667	158	158	318	318	Passagers transportés
Passenger–km	1330	1330	1533	1477	640	640	1149	1149	Passagers–km
Total ton–km	137	137	162	156	72	72	123	123	Total tonnes–km
Korea, Dem. P. R.									**Corée, R. p. dém. de**
Kilometres flown	3	5	3	2	1	3	3	2	Kilomètres parcourus
Passengers carried	254	280	64	59	38	64	64	59	Passagers transportés
Passenger–km	207	286	192	178	113	192	192	178	Passagers–km
Total ton–km	22	30	19	18	11	19	19	18	Total tonnes–km
Korea, Republic of									**Corée, République de**
Kilometres flown	323	365	319	336	271	306	266	285	Kilomètres parcourus
Passengers carried	33003	35506	27109	31319	9938	10262	8973	10646	Passagers transportés
Passenger–km	55751	59372	47711	56116	47664	50485	40982	48806	Passagers–km
Total ton–km	11549	13210	11605	13424	10770	12346	10929	12692	Total tonnes–km
Kuwait									**Koweït**
Kilometres flown	43	43	45	36	43	43	45	36	Kilomètres parcourus
Passengers carried	2133	2114	2190	2130	2133	2114	2190	2130	Passagers transportés
Passenger–km	6073	5997	6207	6158	6073	5997	6207	6158	Passagers–km
Total ton–km	929	912	932	829	929	912	932	829	Total tonnes–km
Kyrgyzstan									**Kirghizistan**
Kilometres flown	10	8	9	9	2	2	6	6	Kilomètres parcourus
Passengers carried	488	423	427	312	30	52	143	136	Passagers transportés
Passenger–km	625	531	519	532	136	189	407	463	Passagers–km
Total ton–km	59	52	60	56	13	19	50	50	Total tonnes–km
Lao People's Dem. Rep.									**Rép. dém. pop. lao**
Kilometres flown	1	1	1	2	1	1	1	1	Kilomètres parcourus
Passengers carried	125	125	124	197	31	31	31	54	Passagers transportés
Passenger–km	48	48	48	78	20	20	20	34	Passagers–km
Total ton–km	5	5	5	8	2	2	2	4	Total tonnes–km
Lebanon									**Liban**
Kilometres flown	19	21	20	20	19	21	20	20	Kilomètres parcourus
Passengers carried	775	857	716	719	775	857	716	719	Passagers transportés
Passenger–km	1857	2116	1504	1288	1857	2116	1504	1288	Passagers–km
Total ton–km	252	319	247	222	252	319	247	222	Total tonnes–km
Malaysia									**Malaisie**
Kilometres flown	173	183	189	207	121	128	140	158	Kilomètres parcourus
Passengers carried	15118	15592	13654	14985	6086	6274	6105	6770	Passagers transportés
Passenger–km	26862	28698	29372	33708	22377	24004	25392	29253	Passagers–km
Total ton–km	3620	3777	3777	4431	3199	3332	3407	4014	Total tonnes–km
Maldives									**Maldives**
Kilometres flown	2	3	4	5	1	2	3	4	Kilomètres parcourus
Passengers carried	207	189	247	344	167	170	192	273	Passagers transportés
Passenger–km	252	292	355	501	247	283	331	470	Passagers–km
Total ton–km	26	33	42	62	26	32	40	59	Total tonnes–km

63
Civil Aviation
Passengers on scheduled services (thousands); Kilometres (millions) [*cont.*]
Aviation civile
Passagers sur les services réguliers (milliers); Kilomètres (millions) [*suite*]

untry or area and traffic	Total Totale				International Internationaux				Pays ou zone et trafic
	1996	1997	1998	1999	1996	1997	1998	1999	
ongolia									**Mongolie**
ometres flown	13	4	8	6	2	2	4	3	Kilomètres parcourus
ssengers carried	662	240	255	225	45	121	95	98	Passagers transportés
senger – km	525	195	469	436	130	147	331	325	Passagers – km
al ton – km	48	18	50	46	13	14	35	35	Total tonnes – km
anmar									**Myanmar**
ometres flown	8	9	8	9	5	6	5	5	Kilomètres parcourus
ssengers carried	676	575	522	537	205	192	148	145	Passagers transportés
senger – km	392	385	345	355	197	206	156	152	Passagers – km
al ton – km	44	46	40	40	33	33	25	24	Total tonnes – km
pal									**Népal**
ometres flown	11	11	11	9	7	7	7	8	Kilomètres parcourus
ssengers carried	755	755	754	583	385	385	385	452	Passagers transportés
senger – km	908	908	908	1023	855	855	855	1004	Passagers – km
al ton – km	99	99	99	108	94	94	94	106	Total tonnes – km
nan [3]									**Oman [3]**
ometres flown	27	26	27	30	26	24	26	29	Kilomètres parcourus
ssengers carried	1620	1678	1768	1933	1461	1507	1590	1768	Passagers transportés
senger – km	3277	3197	3405	3435	3146	3055	3257	3295	Passagers – km
al ton – km	413	384	415	437	402	374	404	427	Total tonnes – km
kistan									**Pakistan**
ometres flown	74	78	75	73	52	56	53	52	Kilomètres parcourus
ssengers carried	5375	5883	5414	4972	2473	2632	2568	2443	Passagers transportés
ssenger – km	10580	11658	10972	10466	8574	9413	8922	8550	Passagers – km
tal ton – km	1398	1479	1408	1293	1180	1243	1186	1085	Total tonnes – km
ilippines									**Philippines**
ometres flown	81	96	40	53	58	73	28	37	Kilomètres parcourus
ssengers carried	7263	7475	3944	5004	2816	2902	1306	1922	Passagers transportés
ssenger – km	15132	16392	7503	10292	12848	13966	5918	8405	Passagers – km
tal ton – km	1893	2086	925	1303	1663	1847	785	1112	Total tonnes – km
atar [3]									**Qatar [3]**
ometres flown	22	19	19	21	22	19	19	21	Kilomètres parcourus
ssengers carried	1200	1165	1207	1307	1200	1165	1207	1307	Passagers transportés
ssenger – km	2759	2501	2653	2836	2759	2501	2653	2836	Passagers – km
tal ton – km	367	333	357	387	367	333	357	387	Total tonnes – km
udi Arabia									**Arabie saoudite**
ometres flown	118	117	120	128	68	68	71	76	Kilomètres parcourus
ssengers carried	11706	11738	11816	12328	3873	3895	3895	4074	Passagers transportés
ssenger – km	18980	18949	18820	19618	13126	13061	12875	13357	Passagers – km
tal ton – km	2592	2650	2645	2783	1991	2038	2030	2138	Total tonnes – km
ngapore									**Singapour**
ometres flown	245	270	293	326	245	270	293	326	Kilomètres parcourus
ssengers carried	11841	12981	13316	15283	11841	12981	13316	15283	Passagers transportés
ssenger – km	53647	55459	58174	65471	53647	55459	58174	65471	Passagers – km
tal ton – km	9296	10128	10381	11824	9296	10128	10381	11824	Total tonnes – km
i Lanka									**Sri Lanka**
lometres flown	21	22	23	28	21	22	23	28	Kilomètres parcourus
ssengers carried	1171	1232	1213	1422	1171	1232	1213	1422	Passagers transportés
ssenger – km	3816	4249	4136	5156	3816	4249	4136	5156	Passagers – km
tal ton – km	507	569	553	669	507	569	553	669	Total tonnes – km
rian Arab Republic									**Rép. arabe syrienne**
lometres flown	11	12	13	12	11	11	13	12	Kilomètres parcourus
ssengers carried	599	694	665	668	578	615	643	581	Passagers transportés
ssenger – km	1068	1235	1410	1287	1058	1205	1398	1259	Passagers – km
tal ton – km	113	127	140	134	113	124	139	131	Total tonnes – km
ajikistan									**Tadjikistan**
lometres flown	7	7	5	4	2	2	3	3	Kilomètres parcourus
ssengers carried	594	594	217	156	44	44	105	79	Passagers transportés
ssenger – km	1825	1825	322	229	222	222	275	197	Passagers – km
tal ton – km	166	166	32	23	19	19	28	20	Total tonnes – km
hailand									**Thaïlande**
lometres flown	140	153	158	163	118	131	136	142	Kilomètres parcourus
ssengers carried	14078	14236	15015	15950	8175	8445	9147	10100	Passagers transportés
ssenger – km	29801	30827	34340	38345	26498	27633	31049	35057	Passagers – km
tal ton – km	4075	4460	4682	5184	3744	4139	4355	4854	Total tonnes – km

63
Civil Aviation
Passengers on scheduled services (thousands); Kilometres (millions) [*cont.*]
Aviation civile
Passagers sur les services réguliers (milliers); Kilomètres (millions) [*suite*]

Country or area and traffic	Total Totale				International Internationaux				Pays ou zone et trafic
	1996	1997	1998	1999	1996	1997	1998	1999	
Turkey									**Turquie**
Kilometres flown	101	113	123	134	74	84	90	98	Kilomètres parcourus
Passengers carried	8464	9380	10132	10097	3376	3812	3988	4065	Passagers transportés
Passenger–km	10947	12379	13037	13350	8199	9372	9792	10002	Passagers–km
Total ton–km	1192	1363	1371	1514	953	1107	1092	1223	Total tonnes–km
Turkmenistan									**Turkménistan**
Kilometres flown	15	15	11	9	...	...	6	9	Kilomètres parcourus
Passengers carried	523	523	890	220	...	...	250	220	Passagers transportés
Passenger–km	1093	1093	832	640	...	...	511	640	Passagers–km
Total ton–km	101	101	79	74	...	...	49	74	Total tonnes–km
United Arab Emirates [3]									**Emirats arabes unis** [3]
Kilometres flown	82	85	94	106	82	85	94	106	Kilomètres parcourus
Passengers carried	4063	4720	5264	5848	4063	4720	5264	5848	Passagers transportés
Passenger–km	11352	13519	15633	18154	11352	13519	15633	18154	Passagers–km
Total ton–km	1743	2107	2403	2950	1743	2107	2403	2950	Total tonnes–km
Uzbekistan									**Ouzbékistan**
Kilometres flown	23	23	33	37	2	2	23	27	Kilomètres parcourus
Passengers carried	1566	1566	1401	1658	36	36	673	878	Passagers transportés
Passenger–km	3460	3460	2609	3328	145	145	2258	2952	Passagers–km
Total ton–km	321	321	284	370	20	20	252	335	Total tonnes–km
Viet Nam									**Viet Nam**
Kilometres flown	29	35	33	31	17	22	20	18	Kilomètres parcourus
Passengers carried	2108	2527	2373	2600	713	925	899	994	Passagers transportés
Passenger–km	2954	3785	3644	3831	1884	2511	2371	2523	Passagers–km
Total ton–km	352	448	426	445	234	306	285	303	Total tonnes–km
Yemen									**Yémen**
Kilometres flown	11	13	12	15	9	12	11	13	Kilomètres parcourus
Passengers carried	588	707	765	731	366	408	462	480	Passagers transportés
Passenger–km	849	1076	1104	1031	790	987	1017	960	Passagers–km
Total ton–km	86	115	120	114	80	106	111	107	Total tonnes–km
Europe [1]									**Europe** [1]
Kilometres flown	**5050**	**5299**	**5629**	**6045**	**3714**	**3969**	**4310**	**4679**	**Kilomètres parcourus**
Passengers carried	**309630**	**337120**	**356166**	**381397**	**177827**	**195590**	**212517**	**229568**	**Passagers transportés**
Passenger–km	**584821**	**627072**	**669007**	**720219**	**479774**	**518162**	**560344**	**603478**	**Passagers–km**
Total ton–km	**82232**	**90617**	**94522**	**99950**	**71718**	**79625**	**83633**	**88458**	**Total tonnes–km**
Albania									**Albanie**
Kilometres flown	...	1	0	0	...	1	0	0	Kilomètres parcourus
Passengers carried	13	55	21	20	13	55	21	20	Passagers transportés
Passenger–km	4	35	7	7	4	35	7	7	Passagers–km
Total ton–km	...	3	1	1	...	3	1	1	Total tonnes–km
Austria									**Autriche**
Kilometres flown	111	118	126	131	106	113	121	127	Kilomètres parcourus
Passengers carried	4719	5154	5880	6057	4402	4829	5510	5694	Passagers transportés
Passenger–km	8791	10066	11923	13380	8693	9959	11814	13271	Passagers–km
Total ton–km	1035	1201	1411	1694	1026	1191	1400	1683	Total tonnes–km
Belarus									**Bélarus**
Kilometres flown	36	9	9	8	11	9	9	8	Kilomètres parcourus
Passengers carried	843	231	226	212	293	231	226	212	Passagers transportés
Passenger–km	2342	399	397	338	537	399	397	338	Passagers–km
Total ton–km	216	39	40	33	52	39	40	33	Total tonnes–km
Belgium									**Belgique**
Kilometres flown	153	159	197	219	153	159	197	219	Kilomètres parcourus
Passengers carried	5174	6872	8748	9965	5174	6872	8748	9965	Passagers transportés
Passenger–km	9011	11277	15338	17692	9011	11277	15338	17692	Passagers–km
Total ton–km	1419	1706	1853	2128	1419	1706	1853	2128	Total tonnes–km
Bosnia and Herzegovina									**Bosnie–Herzégovine**
Kilometres flown	...	...	1	1	...	...	1	1	Kilomètres parcourus
Passengers carried	...	...	50	60	...	...	50	60	Passagers transportés
Passenger–km	...	...	40	42	...	...	40	42	Passagers–km
Total ton–km	...	...	5	5	...	...	5	5	Total tonnes–km
Bulgaria									**Bulgarie**
Kilometres flown	21	20	22	20	20	19	21	18	Kilomètres parcourus
Passengers carried	718	722	828	735	637	655	750	650	Passagers transportés
Passenger–km	1812	1796	2026	1512	1776	1766	1992	1478	Passagers–km
Total ton–km	188	194	214	149	185	192	211	146	Total tonnes–km

63
Civil Aviation
Passengers on scheduled services (thousands); Kilometres (millions) [*cont.*]
Aviation civile
Passagers sur les services réguliers (milliers); Kilomètres (millions) [*suite*]

Country or area and traffic	Total Totale				International Internationaux				Pays ou zone et trafic
	1996	1997	1998	1999	1996	1997	1998	1999	
Croatia									**Croatie**
Kilometres flown	9	9	10	10	7	8	8	8	Kilomètres parcourus
Passengers carried	727	767	828	833	402	417	465	503	Passagers transportés
Passenger−km	486	469	544	560	369	367	436	460	Passagers−km
Total ton−km	48	45	52	53	37	35	42	44	Total tonnes−km
Czech Republic									**République tchèque**
Kilometres flown	28	30	32	36	28	29	32	36	Kilomètres parcourus
Passengers carried	1394	1448	1606	1853	1380	1437	1606	1853	Passagers transportés
Passenger−km	2368	2442	2637	2870	2364	2439	2637	2870	Passagers−km
Total ton−km	237	244	264	286	236	244	264	286	Total tonnes−km
Denmark [4]									**Danemark** [4]
Kilometres flown	75	80	81	82	61	66	69	72	Kilomètres parcourus
Passengers carried	5892	6236	5947	5971	3498	3832	3976	4249	Passagers transportés
Passenger−km	5466	5669	5669	5883	4661	4891	4990	5300	Passagers−km
Total ton−km	679	729	725	769	599	651	657	708	Total tonnes−km
Estonia									**Estonie**
Kilometres flown	4	5	6	7	4	5	6	7	Kilomètres parcourus
Passengers carried	149	231	297	302	149	231	294	300	Passagers transportés
Passenger−km	114	147	177	228	114	147	177	228	Passagers−km
Total ton−km	11	14	17	22	11	14	17	22	Total tonnes−km
Finland									**Finlande**
Kilometres flown	82	92	95	81	63	72	73	60	Kilomètres parcourus
Passengers carried	5597	6002	6771	6050	3301	3577	3986	3391	Passagers transportés
Passenger−km	8731	9575	10714	7802	7748	8475	9467	6592	Passagers−km
Total ton−km	1031	1170	1250	967	945	1073	1140	861	Total tonnes−km
France [5]									**France** [5]
Kilometres flown	609	669	726	819	418	432	486	564	Kilomètres parcourus
Passengers carried	41253	42344	43826	48693	17795	17329	18494	21437	Passagers transportés
Passenger−km	81594	84037	90225	101449	55978	54823	59584	67462	Passagers−km
Total ton−km	13151	13750	14033	14279	10475	10622	10784	10909	Total tonnes−km
Germany									**Allemagne**
Kilometres flown	653	704	736	788	566	593	625	680	Kilomètres parcourus
Passengers carried	40118	45805	49417	54247	26068	29202	31281	34963	Passagers transportés
Passenger−km	77765	86189	90393	104602	72011	79338	82922	96402	Passagers−km
Total ton−km	13850	14822	15301	16950	13215	14093	14522	16108	Total tonnes−km
Greece									**Grèce**
Kilometres flown	66	68	68	75	50	52	53	54	Kilomètres parcourus
Passengers carried	6396	7061	6403	6267	2599	2872	2621	2630	Passagers transportés
Passenger−km	8533	9261	8561	8306	7427	8026	7455	7234	Passagers−km
Total ton−km	933	1013	936	899	822	891	829	796	Total tonnes−km
Hungary									**Hongrie**
Kilometres flown	30	32	35	39	30	32	35	39	Kilomètres parcourus
Passengers carried	1563	1635	1749	1944	1563	1635	1749	1944	Passagers transportés
Passenger−km	2077	2346	2510	2861	2077	2346	2510	2861	Passagers−km
Total ton−km	219	249	267	301	219	249	267	301	Total tonnes−km
Iceland									**Islande**
Kilometres flown	26	28	33	35	24	25	31	35	Kilomètres parcourus
Passengers carried	1239	1334	1593	1350	958	1056	1298	1350	Passagers transportés
Passenger−km	2872	3216	3774	4096	2800	3147	3712	4096	Passagers−km
Total ton−km	317	351	426	458	310	344	420	458	Total tonnes−km
Ireland									**Irlande**
Kilometres flown	59	70	78	90	58	68	77	88	Kilomètres parcourus
Passengers carried	7677	8964	10401	11949	7253	8522	9917	11398	Passagers transportés
Passenger−km	6732	7260	8510	11026	6664	7201	8442	10953	Passagers−km
Total ton−km	700	767	889	1121	694	762	883	1115	Total tonnes−km
Italy									**Italie**
Kilometres flown	300	338	344	368	218	242	239	254	Kilomètres parcourus
Passengers carried	25838	28184	28037	28049	11195	11507	11113	11092	Passagers transportés
Passenger−km	36157	38240	38122	39519	28432	29289	28889	29951	Passagers−km
Total ton−km	5060	5247	5261	5526	4274	4327	4338	4586	Total tonnes−km
Latvia									**Lettonie**
Kilometres flown	9	6	6	5	9	6	6	5	Kilomètres parcourus
Passengers carried	276	229	222	199	276	229	222	199	Passagers transportés
Passenger−km	260	217	174	132	260	217	174	132	Passagers−km
Total ton−km	23	20	16	12	23	20	16	12	Total tonnes−km

63
Civil Aviation
Passengers on scheduled services (thousands); Kilometres (millions) [*cont.*]
Aviation civile
Passagers sur les services réguliers (milliers); Kilomètres (millions) [*suite*]

Country or area and traffic	Total Totale				International Internationaux				Pays ou zone et trafic
	1996	1997	1998	1999	1996	1997	1998	1999	
Lithuania									**Lituanie**
Kilometres flown	8	9	10	11	8	9	10	11	Kilomètres parcourus
Passengers carried	214	237	259	250	214	236	259	249	Passagers transportés
Passenger−km	304	301	307	272	304	301	307	272	Passagers−km
Total ton−km	29	30	31	27	29	30	31	27	Total tonnes−km
Luxembourg									**Luxembourg**
Kilometres flown	6	36	43	57	6	36	43	57	Kilomètres parcourus
Passengers carried	639	560	701	843	639	560	701	843	Passagers transportés
Passenger−km	421	281	454	738	421	281	454	738	Passagers−km
Total ton−km	39	2286	2287	2573	39	2286	2287	2573	Total tonnes−km
Malta									**Malte**
Kilometres flown	20	20	20	24	20	20	20	24	Kilomètres parcourus
Passengers carried	1038	1054	1143	1421	1038	1054	1143	1421	Passagers transportés
Passenger−km	1663	1681	1888	2320	1663	1681	1888	2320	Passagers−km
Total ton−km	155	157	177	214	155	157	177	214	Total tonnes−km
Monaco									**Monaco**
Kilometres flown	...	0	0	1	...	0	0	1	Kilomètres parcourus
Passengers carried	44	44	44	75	44	44	44	75	Passagers transportés
Passenger−km	1	1	1	2	1	1	1	2	Passagers−km
Total ton−km	...	0	0	0	...	0	0	0	Total tonnes−km
Netherlands [6]									**Pays−Bas** [6]
Kilometres flown	386	364	390	422	377	363	390	421	Kilomètres parcourus
Passengers carried	17114	17161	17950	18540	16724	17084	17879	18409	Passagers transportés
Passenger−km	62397	66132	68597	70117	62160	66124	68590	70099	Passagers−km
Total ton−km	9959	10590	10864	11204	9937	10589	10864	11202	Total tonnes−km
Norway [4]									**Norvège** [4]
Kilometres flown	121	130	134	151	56	60	62	70	Kilomètres parcourus
Passengers carried	12727	13759	14279	15020	3461	3871	4068	4367	Passagers transportés
Passenger−km	8688	9158	9480	9874	4751	5041	5171	5432	Passagers−km
Total ton−km	969	1061	1082	1154	606	663	673	722	Total tonnes−km
Poland									**Pologne**
Kilometres flown	40	45	46	49	37	42	42	45	Kilomètres parcourus
Passengers carried	1806	1998	2061	2141	1521	1690	1724	1791	Passagers transportés
Passenger−km	3917	4204	4255	4632	3830	4111	4155	4528	Passagers−km
Total ton−km	430	478	483	498	422	470	475	489	Total tonnes−km
Portugal									**Portugal**
Kilometres flown	96	95	98	102	78	76	78	83	Kilomètres parcourus
Passengers carried	4806	5296	5832	6054	2813	3170	3462	3604	Passagers transportés
Passenger−km	8423	9342	10107	10070	7041	7889	8475	8595	Passagers−km
Total ton−km	985	1094	1157	1128	836	936	981	976	Total tonnes−km
Republic of Moldova									**République de Moldova**
Kilometres flown	5	2	4	2	5	2	4	2	Kilomètres parcourus
Passengers carried	190	46	118	43	190	46	118	43	Passagers transportés
Passenger−km	240	61	146	97	240	61	146	97	Passagers−km
Total ton−km	23	6	14	9	23	6	14	9	Total tonnes−km
Romania									**Roumanie**
Kilometres flown	24	26	22	24	21	23	20	22	Kilomètres parcourus
Passengers carried	913	995	921	980	739	775	758	844	Passagers transportés
Passenger−km	1823	1702	1712	1757	1753	1617	1647	1704	Passagers−km
Total ton−km	180	167	167	171	173	159	161	166	Total tonnes−km
Russian Federation									**Fédération de Russie**
Kilometres flown	724	609	581	550	214	198	212	196	Kilomètres parcourus
Passengers carried	22117	20419	18685	18600	6001	5915	5960	5190	Passagers transportés
Passenger−km	52710	49278	46158	45863	18715	18135	18811	16862	Passagers−km
Total ton−km	5643	5269	4931	5036	2222	2145	2179	2088	Total tonnes−km
Slovakia									**Slovaquie**
Kilometres flown	2	2	3	3	2	2	3	2	Kilomètres parcourus
Passengers carried	63	81	107	111	41	59	82	75	Passagers transportés
Passenger−km	80	103	128	117	72	95	119	105	Passagers−km
Total ton−km	7	10	11	10	7	9	10	9	Total tonnes−km
Slovenia									**Slovénie**
Kilometres flown	7	7	8	9	7	7	8	9	Kilomètres parcourus
Passengers carried	393	404	460	555	393	404	460	555	Passagers transportés
Passenger−km	380	375	411	515	380	375	411	515	Passagers−km
Total ton−km	38	37	41	50	38	37	41	50	Total tonnes−km

63
Civil Aviation
Passengers on scheduled services (thousands); Kilometres (millions) [*cont.*]
Aviation civile
Passagers sur les services réguliers (milliers); Kilomètres (millions) [*suite*]

Country or area and traffic	Total Totale				International Internationaux				Pays ou zone et trafic
	1996	1997	1998	1999	1996	1997	1998	1999	
Spain									**Espagne**
Kilometres flown	285	305	331	365	156	159	179	200	Kilomètres parcourus
Passengers carried	27759	30316	31594	33559	7674	8227	8971	9581	Passagers transportés
Passenger–km	34102	37240	40042	44172	21715	23595	26027	29035	Passagers–km
Total ton–km	3807	4093	4378	4828	2618	2780	3038	3360	Total tonnes–km
Sweden [4]									**Suède** [4]
Kilometres flown	120	132	143	150	78	83	89	94	Kilomètres parcourus
Passengers carried	9879	11327	11878	12933	4782	5264	5571	5785	Passagers transportés
Passenger–km	8925	9749	10249	10607	6611	6972	7198	7312	Passagers–km
Total ton–km	1073	1191	1234	1309	863	939	959	1001	Total tonnes–km
Switzerland									**Suisse**
Kilometres flown	211	230	263	295	206	225	258	289	Kilomètres parcourus
Passengers carried	10468	12482	14299	16209	9299	11204	12868	14735	Passagers transportés
Passenger–km	22264	26314	29415	33309	22035	26072	29147	33030	Passagers–km
Total ton–km	3743	4462	4897	5195	3717	4438	4870	5167	Total tonnes–km
TFYR of Macedonia									**L'ex–R.y. Macédoine**
Kilometres flown	7	5	5	7	7	5	5	7	Kilomètres parcourus
Passengers carried	287	250	295	488	287	250	295	488	Passagers transportés
Passenger–km	410	285	328	599	410	285	328	599	Passagers–km
Total ton–km	38	27	31	57	38	27	31	57	Total tonnes–km
Ukraine									**Ukraine**
Kilometres flown	36	36	37	31	22	29	30	24	Kilomètres parcourus
Passengers carried	1151	1190	1064	891	630	887	807	661	Passagers transportés
Passenger–km	1792	1853	1720	1312	1330	1658	1556	1165	Passagers–km
Total ton–km	176	186	188	138	133	168	173	125	Total tonnes–km
United Kingdom [79]									**Royaume–Uni** [79]
Kilometres flown	940	809	885	845	834	698	768	977	Kilomètres parcourus
Passengers carried	64209	56227	61625	48941	49181	40360	45017	67928	Passagers transportés
Passenger–km	167577	136371	151880	153697	161366	129725	144933	161541	Passagers–km
Total ton–km	24104	17912	19589	20021	23562	17331	18984	20692	Total tonnes–km
Oceania [1]									**Océanie** [1]
Kilometres flown	**726**	**777**	**757**	**735**	**354**	**360**	**360**	**351**	**Kilomètres parcourus**
Passengers carried	**44982**	**45714**	**43990**	**43622**	**13091**	**13048**	**12343**	**11643**	**Passagers transportés**
Passenger–km	**105214**	**107911**	**103104**	**103991**	**73043**	**75345**	**71392**	**71257**	**Passagers–km**
Total ton–km	**12783**	**13205**	**12813**	**12883**	**9461**	**9783**	**9558**	**9568**	**Total tonnes–km**
Australia									**Australie**
Kilometres flown	466	500	479	474	189	196	193	194	Kilomètres parcourus
Passengers carried	30075	30954	30180	30007	6777	6783	6894	6579	Passagers transportés
Passenger–km	72594	75873	73647	75575	45238	47771	46525	47436	Passagers–km
Total ton–km	8707	9137	8929	9107	5898	6243	6116	6236	Total tonnes–km
Fiji									**Fidji**
Kilometres flown	17	20	20	20	13	13	13	13	Kilomètres parcourus
Passengers carried	480	517	516	525	305	334	334	361	Passagers transportés
Passenger–km	1217	2000	2000	2159	1195	1956	1956	2120	Passagers–km
Total ton–km	195	200	200	218	193	196	196	214	Total tonnes–km
Kiribati									**Kiribati**
Kilometres flown	1	1	1	...	...	0	0	...	Kilomètres parcourus
Passengers carried	28	28	28	...	3	3	3	...	Passagers transportés
Passenger–km	11	11	11	...	7	7	7	...	Passagers–km
Total ton–km	2	2	2	...	1	1	1	...	Total tonnes–km
Marshall Islands									**Iles Marshall**
Kilometres flown	2	2	1	1	1	1	1	0	Kilomètres parcourus
Passengers carried	41	33	32	19	13	11	9	5	Passagers transportés
Passenger–km	45	26	20	12	28	17	12	7	Passagers–km
Total ton–km	7	2	2	1	5	2	1	1	Total tonnes–km
Nauru									**Nauru**
Kilometres flown	2	2	2	3	2	2	2	3	Kilomètres parcourus
Passengers carried	137	137	137	143	137	137	137	143	Passagers transportés
Passenger–km	243	243	243	254	243	243	243	254	Passagers–km
Total ton–km	24	24	24	25	24	24	24	25	Total tonnes–km
New Zealand									**Nouvelle–Zélande**
Kilometres flown	156	173	174	172	92	93	98	100	Kilomètres parcourus
Passengers carried	9597	9435	8655	8892	3122	3324	2773	2829	Passagers transportés
Passenger–km	22052	20983	19014	19322	19148	18273	16352	16679	Passagers–km
Total ton–km	2841	2816	2700	2746	2555	2492	2479	2529	Total tonnes–km

63
Civil Aviation
Passengers on scheduled services (thousands); Kilometres (millions) [*cont.*]
Aviation civile
Passagers sur les services réguliers (milliers); Kilomètres (millions) [*suite*]

Country or area and traffic	Total Totale				International Internationaux				Pays ou zone et trafic
	1996	1997	1998	1999	1996	1997	1998	1999	
Papua New Guinea									**Papouasie – Nvl – Guinée**
Kilometres flown	14	15	15	12	5	5	5	3	Kilomètres parcourus
Passengers carried	970	1114	1110	1102	206	159	159	110	Passagers transportés
Passenger – km	830	735	736	641	470	361	361	250	Passagers – km
Total ton – km	94	86	87	80	58	49	49	39	Total tonnes – km
Samoa									**Samoa**
Kilometres flown	4	3	4	3	4	3	3	3	Kilomètres parcourus
Passengers carried	270	75	149	92	270	75	77	77	Passagers transportés
Passenger – km	265	247	250	244	265	247	242	242	Passagers – km
Total ton – km	26	30	24	23	26	30	23	23	Total tonnes – km
Solomon Islands									**Iles Salomon**
Kilometres flown	3	3	3	4	1	1	1	1	Kilomètres parcourus
Passengers carried	94	94	94	98	28	28	28	23	Passagers transportés
Passenger – km	74	74	74	80	58	58	58	47	Passagers – km
Total ton – km	9	9	9	9	7	7	7	6	Total tonnes – km
Tonga									**Tonga**
Kilometres flown	1	1	1	1	...	...	...	...	Kilomètres parcourus
Passengers carried	56	49	49	91	...	...	...	...	Passagers transportés
Passenger – km	11	10	10	19	...	...	...	...	Passagers – km
Total ton – km	1	1	1	2	...	...	...	...	Total tonnes – km
Vanuatu									**Vanuatu**
Kilometres flown	2	2	3	3	2	2	3	3	Kilomètres parcourus
Passengers carried	73	75	89	86	73	75	89	86	Passagers transportés
Passenger – km	150	156	179	178	150	156	179	178	Passagers – km
Total ton – km	15	15	19	18	15	15	19	18	Total tonnes – km

Source:
International Civil Aviation Organization (ICAO), Montreal, "Digest of Statistics – Traffic, 1995 – 1999" and the ICAO database.

Source:
Organisation de l'aviation civile international (OACI), Montréal, "Recueil de statistiques – trafic, 1995 – 1999" et la base de données de l'OACI.

† For information on recent changes in country or area nomenclature pertaining to former Czechoslovakia, Germany, Hong Kong Special Administrative Region (SAR) of China, Macao Special Administrative Region (SAR) of China, SFR of Yugoslavia and the former USSR, see Annex I – Country or area nomenclature, regional and other groupings.

†† For statistical purposes, the data for China do not include those for the Hong Kong Special Administrative Region, (Hong Kong SAR), Macao Special Administrative Region (Macao SAR) and Taiwan Province of China.

1 The statistics of France, Netherlands, Portugal, United Kingdom and United States have been distributed between two or more regions – France (Europe, Africa, North America and Oceania), Netherlands (Europe and North America), Portugal (1997 only; Europe and Asia), United Kingdom (Europe, Asia and North America) and United States (North America and Oceania).

2 Includes apportionment (1/10) of the traffic of Air Afrique, a multinational airline with headquarters in Côte d'Ivoire and operated by 10 African States until 1991. From 1992 includes apportionment (1/11) of the traffic of Air Afrique operated by 11 African States.

3 Includes apportionment (1/4) of the traffic of Gulf Air, a multinational airline with headquarters in Bahrain and operated by four Gulf States.

4 Includes an apportionment of international operations performed by Scandinavian Airlines System (SAS); Denmark (2/7), Norway (2/7), Sweden (3/7).

5 Including data for airlines based in the territories and dependencies of France.

† Pour les modifications récentes de nomenclature de pays ou de zone concernant l'Allemagne, Hong Kong (Région administrative spéciale de Chine), Macao (Région administrative spéciale de Chine), l'ex– Tchécoslovaquie, l'ex–URSS et l'ex–Rfs de Yougoslavie, voir annexe I – Nomenclature des pays ou des zones, groupements régionaux et autres groupements.

†† Les données statistiques relatives à la Chine ne comprennent pas celles qui concernent la région administrative spéciale de Hong Kong (la RAS de Hong Kong (la RAS de Hong Kong), la région administrative spéciale de Macao (la RAS de Macao), et la province chinoise de Taiwan.

1 Les statistiques de la France, des Pays–Bas, du Portugal, du Royaume–Uni et des Etats–Unis concernent deux régions ou plus; France (Europe, Afrique, Amérique du Nord et Océanie), Pays–Bas (Europe et Amérique du Nord), Portugal (1997 seulement; Europe et Asie), Royaume–Uni (Europe, Asie et Amérique du Nord) et Etats–Unis (Amérique du Nord et Océanie).

2 Ces chiffres comprennent une partie du trafic (1/10) assurée par Air Afrique, compagnie aérienne multinationale dont le siège est situé en Côte d'Ivoire et est exploitée conjointement par 10 Etats Africains jusqu'à 1991. A partir de 1992 ces chiffres comprennent une partie du trafic (1/11) assurée par Air Afrique et exploitée conjointement par 11 Etats Africains.

3 Ces chiffres comprennent une partie du trafic (1/4) assurée par Gulf Air, compagnie aérienne multinationale dont le siège est situé en Bahreïn et est exploitée conjointement par 4 Etats Gulf.

4 Y compris une partie des vols internationaux effectués par le SAS; Danemark (2/7), Norvège (2/7) et Suède (3/7).

5 Y compris les données relatives aux compagnies aériennes ayant des bases d'opérations dans les territoires et

63
Civil Aviation
Passengers on scheduled services (thousands); Kilometres (millions) [*cont.*]
Aviation civile
Passagers sur les services réguliers (milliers); Kilomètres (millions) [*suite*]

Including data for airlines based in the territories and dependencies of Netherlands.

Including data for airlines based in the territories and dependencies of United Kingdom.

For 1997, data refer to the last six months of 1997.

Beginning the second half of 1997, data exlude those for Hong Kong Special Administrative Region (SAR) of China.

dépendances de France.

6   **Y compris les données relatives aux compagnies aériennes ayant des bases d'opérations dans les territoires et dépendances des Pays–Bas.**

7   **Y compris les données relatives aux compagnies aériennes ayant des bases d'opération dans les territoires et dépendances du Royaume–Uni.**

8   **Pour 1997, les données se rapportent au second semestre de 1997.**

9   **A partir du second semestre de 1997, les données ne comprennent pas celles relatives à la RAS de Hong Kong de la Chine.**

Technical notes, tables 59-63

Table 59: Data refer to domestic and international traffic on all railway lines within each country shown, except railways entirely within an urban unit, and plantation, industrial mining, funicular and cable railways. The figures relating to passenger-kilometres include all passengers except military, government and railway personnel when carried without revenue. Those relating to ton-kilometres are freight net ton-kilometres and include both fast and ordinary goods services but exclude service traffic, mail, baggage and non-revenue governmental stores.

Table 60: For years in which a census or registration took place, the census or registration figure is shown; for other years, unless otherwise indicated, the officially estimated number of vehicles in use is shown. The time of year to which the figures refer is variable. Special purpose vehicles such as two- or three-wheeled cycles and motorcycles, trams, trolley-buses, ambulances, hearses, military vehicles operated by police or other governmental security organizations are excluded. Passenger cars includes vehicles seating not more than nine persons (including the driver), such as taxis, jeeps and station wagons. Commercial vehicles include: vans, lorries (trucks), buses, tractor and semi-trailer combinations but excludes trailers and farm tractors.

Table 61: Data refer to merchant fleets registered in each country as at 31 December, except for data prior to 1992 which refer to 30 June of the year stated. They are given in gross registered tons (100 cubic feet or 2.83 cubic metres) and represent the total volume of all the permanently enclosed spaces of the vessels to which the figures refer. Vessels without mechanical means of propulsion are excluded, but sailing vessels with auxiliary power are included.

Part A of the table refers to the total of merchant fleets registered. Part B shows data for oil tanker fleets and part C data for ore/oil and bulk carrier fleets. The data are published by Lloyd's Register of Shipping in *World Fleet Statistics* [19].

Table 62: The figures for vessels entered and cleared, unless otherwise stated, represent the sum of the net registered tonnage of sea-going foreign and domestic merchant vessels (power and sailing) entered with cargo from or cleared with cargo to a foreign port and refer to only one entrance or clearance for each foreign voyage. Where possible, the data exclude vessels "in ballast", i.e. entering without unloading or clearing without loading goods.

Table 63: Data for total services cover both domestic and international scheduled services operated by airlines registered in each country. Scheduled services

Notes techniques, tableaux 59 à 63

Tableau 59: Les données se rapportent au trafic intérieur et international de toutes les lignes de chemins de fer du pays indiqué, à l'exception des lignes situées entièrement à l'intérieur d'une agglomération urbaine ou desservant une plantation ou un complexe industriel minier, des funiculaires et des téléfériques. Les chiffres relatifs aux voyageurs-kilomètres se rapportent à tous les voyageurs sauf les militaires, les fonctionnaires et le personnel des chemins de fer, qui sont transportés gratuitement. Les chiffres relatifs aux tonnes-kilomètres se rapportent aux tonnes-kilomètres nettes de fret et comprennent les services rapides et ordinaires de transport de marchandises, à l'exception des transports pour les besoins du service, du courrier, des bagages et des marchandises transportées gratuitement pour les besoins de l'Etat.

Tableau 60: Pour les années où a eu lieu un recensement ou un enregistrement des véhicules, le chiffre indiqué est le résultat de cette opération; pour les autres années, sauf indication contraire, le chiffre indiqué correspond à l'estimation officielle du nombre de véhicules en circulation. L'époque de l'année à laquelle se rapportent les chiffres varie. Les véhicules à usage spécial, tels que les cycles à deux ou trois roues et motocyclettes, les tramways, les trolley-bus, les ambulances, les corbillards, les véhicules militaires utilisés par la police ou par d'autres services publics de sécurité ne sont pas compris dans ces chiffres. Les voitures de tourisme comprennent les véhicules automobiles dont le nombre de places assises (y compris celle du conducteur) n'est pas supérieur à neuf, tels que les taxis, jeeps et breaks. Les véhicules utilitaires comprennent les fourgons, camions, autobus et autocars, les ensembles tracteurs-remorques et semi-remorques, mais ne comprennent pas les remorques et les tracteurs agricoles.

Tableau 61: Les données se rapportent à la flotte marchande enregistrée dans chaque pays au 31 décembre de l'année indiquée à l'exception des données qui se rapportent aux années avant 1992, qui se réfèrent à la flotte marchande au 30 juin. Elles sont exprimées en tonneaux de jauge brute (100 pieds cubes ou 2,83 mètres cubes) et représentent le volume total de tous les espaces clos en permanence dans les navires auxquels elle s'appliquent. Elles excluent les navires sans moteur, mais pas les voiliers avec moteurs auxiliaires.

Les données de la Partie A du tableau se rapportent au total de la flotte marchande enregistrée. Celles de la Partie B se rapportent à la flotte des pétroliers, et celles de la Partie C à la flotte des minéraliers et des transporteurs de vrac et d'huile. Les données sont publiées par Lloyd's Register of Shipping dans *World*

include supplementary services occasioned by overflow traffic on regularly scheduled trips and preparatory flights for newly scheduled services. Freight means all goods, except mail and excess baggage, carried for remuneration. The data are published by the International Civil Aviation Organization in *Civil Aviation Statistics of the World* [11] and in the *Digest of Statistics—Traffic* [12].

Fleet Statistics [19].

Tableau 62: Sauf indication contraire, les données relatives aux navires entrés et sortis représentent la jauge nette totale des navires marchands de haute mer (à moteur ou à voile) nationaux ou étrangers, qui entrent ou sortent chargés, en provenance ou à destination d'un port étranger. On ne compte qu'une seule entrée et une seule sortie pour chaque voyage international. Dans la mesure du possible, le tableau exclut les navires sur lest (c'est-à-dire les navires entrant sans décharger ou sortant sans avoir chargé).

Tableau 63: Les données relatives au total des services se rapportent aux services réguliers, intérieurs ou internationaux des compagnies de transport aérien enregistrées dans chaque pays. Les services réguliers comprennent aussi les vols supplémentaires nécessités par un surcroît d'activité des services réguliers et les vols préparatoires en vue de nouveaux services réguliers. Par fret, on entend toutes les marchandises transportées contre paiement, mais non le courrier et les excédents de bagage. Les données sont publiées par l'Organisation de l'aviation civile internationale dans les *Statistiques de l'Aviation civile dans le monde* [11] et dans le *Recueil de statistiques—trafic* [12].

64
Production, trade and consumption of commercial energy
Production, commerce et consommation d'énergie commerciale
Thousand metric tons of oil equivalent and kilograms per capita
Milliers de tonnes d'équivalent pétrole et kilogrammes par habitant

Region, country or area	Year	Primary energy production – Production d'énergie primaire					Changes in stocks Variations des stocks	Imports Importations	Exports Exporta
		Total Totale	Solids Solides	Liquids Liquides	Gas Gaz	Electricity Electricité			
World	1995	8 558 491	2 292 787	3 345 655	2 055 068	864 980	13 616	3 061 510	3 0
	1996	8 788 503	2 329 992	3 409 588	2 156 896	892 027	949	3 237 067	3 1
	1997	8 909 172	2 345 804	3 513 854	2 161 009	888 504	47 518	3 359 349	3 3
	1998	8 932 349	2 274 060	3 577 185	2 176 603	904 501	51 478	3 405 212	3 4
Africa	1995	555 652	114 928	348 268	84 269	8 187	7 473	56 208	3
	1996	569 305	114 464	355 267	90 888	8 686	7 809	54 443	3
	1997	594 925	121 643	363 505	100 499	9 278	6 448	53 626	3
	1998	606 353	124 042	369 565	102 673	10 073	7 953	56 568	3
Algeria	1995	119 420	15	61 288	58 101	17	163	933	
	1996	126 709	15	64 093	62 589	11	195	713	
	1997	137 134	16	66 487	70 624	6	− 327	760	
	1998	144 359	16	68 911	75 423	9	− 28	794	
Angola	1995	32 750	...	32 164	509	77	409	197	
	1996	35 400	...	34 812	509	80	831	225	
	1997	35 787	...	35 184	518	85	448	237	
	1998	37 027	...	36 418	527	82	153	51	
Benin	1995	131	...	131	...	...	...	200	
	1996	112	...	112	...	...	...	205	
	1997	90	...	90	...	...	...	208	
	1998	62	...	62	...	...	...	211	
Burkina Faso	1995	8	...	...	...	8	0	323	
	1996	10	...	...	...	10	0	326	
	1997	10	...	...	...	10	0	328	
	1998	10	...	...	...	10	0	334	
Burundi	1995	14	4	...	...	10	1	75	
	1996	14	4	...	...	10	1	77	
	1997	15	4	...	...	10	0	79	
	1998	15	4	...	...	10	0	80	
Cameroon	1995	5 633	1	5 403	...	229	− 350	83	
	1996	5 450	1	5 220	...	229	− 325	98	
	1997	5 746	1	5 516	...	229	− 95	98	
	1998	6 142	1	5 911	...	230	0	101	
Cape Verde	1995	...	...	...	...	...	0	38	
	1996	...	...	...	...	...	0	40	
	1997	...	...	...	...	...	0	40	
	1998	...	...	...	...	...	0	40	
Central African Rep.	1995	7	...	...	...	7	1	94	
	1996	7	...	...	...	7	1	95	
	1997	7	...	...	...	7	1	98	
	1998	7	...	...	...	7	1	99	
Chad	1995	...	...	...	...	...	3	55	
	1996	...	...	...	...	...	3	56	
	1997	...	...	...	...	...	0	57	
	1998	...	...	...	...	...	0	57	
Comoros	1995	0	...	...	...	0	...	23	
	1996	0	...	...	...	0	...	23	
	1997	0	...	...	...	0	...	23	
	1998	0	...	...	...	0	...	24	
Congo	1995	9 318	0	9 277	3	37	− 109	15	
	1996	10 421	0	10 380	3	37	− 229	16	1
	1997	11 650	0	11 610	3	38	− 566	16	1
	1998	12 764	0	12 723	3	38	− 465	16	1
Côte d'Ivoire	1995	401	...	314	...	86	...	3 504	
	1996	1 384	...	1 264	...	120	...	2 486	
	1997	1 419	...	1 273	...	146	...	2 498	
	1998	1 429	...	1 283	...	146	...	2 508	
Dem. Rep. of the Congo	1995	1 673	65	1 147	...	461	...	746	
	1996	1 680	67	1 149	...	464	...	754	
	1997	1 683	67	1 152	...	465	...	768	
	1998	1 689	67	1 156	...	465	...	782	
Djibouti	1995	...	...	...	...	...	...	545	
	1996	...	...	...	...	...	...	545	
	1997	...	...	...	...	...	...	550	
	1998	...	...	...	...	...	...	550	

nkers – Soutes		Unallocated	Consumption – Consommation							
Air Avion	Sea Maritime	Unallocated Nondistribué	Per capita Par habitant	Total Totale	Solids Solides	Liquids Liquides	Gas Gaz	Electricity Electricité	Année	Région, pays ou zone
2 535	120 953	313 237	1 427	8 083 847	2 307 316	2 865 021	2 046 775	864 735	1995	**Monde**
5 431	124 486	332 622	1 454	8 347 307	2 376 767	2 927 290	2 151 256	891 993	1996	
7 584	128 120	374 227	1 436	8 356 531	2 337 909	2 960 275	2 170 348	887 998	1997	
8 795	132 548	367 515	1 405	8 315 199	2 284 537	2 974 556	2 151 978	904 127	1998	
2 529	6 958	22 226	317	221 263	76 244	87 536	49 417	8 065	1995	**Afrique**
2 742	7 474	15 569	319	227 451	76 099	89 784	53 136	8 433	1996	
2 633	7 241	15 963	319	233 026	79 901	89 595	54 558	8 972	1997	
2 342	6 633	17 032	317	237 708	80 897	93 519	53 685	9 606	1998	
258	375	4 640	1 125	31 557	351	8 270	22 943	– 7	1995	Algérie
268	334	4 946	1 149	32 985	238	8 180	24 568	– 1	1996	
279	266	5 269	1 179	34 652	403	9 250	24 993	6	1997	
279	239	5 127	1 242	37 372	456	10 361	26 547	8	1998	
382	9	2 051	131	1 437	0	851	509	77	1995	Angola
334	7	1 514	133	1 510	0	921	509	80	1996	
341	2	313	131	1 538	0	934	518	85	1997	
220	0	264	119	1 444	0	835	527	82	1998	
21	...	1	32	172	...	149	...	23	1995	Bénin
22	...	2	32	177	...	151	...	25	1996	
22	...	3	32	179	...	153	...	25	1997	
23	...	2	31	181	...	154	...	26	1998	
...	...	...	32	331	0	323	...	8	1995	Burkina Faso
...	...	...	31	336	0	326	...	10	1996	
...	...	...	31	338	0	328	...	10	1997	
...	...	...	30	344	0	334	...	10	1998	
6	...	...	13	83	4	66	...	13	1995	Burundi
6	...	...	14	85	4	68	...	13	1996	
6	...	...	14	87	4	70	...	13	1997	
6	...	...	14	88	4	71	...	13	1998	
19	...	– 405	102	1 344	1	1 115	...	229	1995	Cameroun
21	...	– 513	101	1 368	1	1 138	...	229	1996	
21	...	– 770	99	1 373	1	1 143	...	229	1997	
21	...	– 575	97	1 385	1	1 155	...	230	1998	
0	0	...	100	38	...	38	...	...	1995	Cap–Vert
0	0	...	103	40	...	40	...	...	1996	
0	0	...	101	40	...	40	...	...	1997	
0	0	...	99	40	...	40	...	...	1998	
13	...	...	26	86	...	79	...	7	1995	Rép. centrafricaine
14	...	...	26	86	...	79	...	7	1996	
14	...	...	26	89	...	82	...	7	1997	
14	...	...	26	90	...	83	...	7	1998	
20	...	...	5	32	...	32	...	...	1995	Tchad
20	...	...	5	33	...	33	...	...	1996	
20	...	...	5	37	...	37	...	...	1997	
20	...	...	5	37	...	37	...	...	1998	
0	...	...	38	23	...	23	...	0	1995	Comores
0	...	...	37	23	...	23	...	0	1996	
0	...	...	36	23	...	23	...	0	1997	
0	...	...	36	24	...	24	...	0	1998	
0	10	21	216	553	0	504	3	47	1995	Congo
0	10	37	214	564	0	514	3	47	1996	
0	10	25	210	570	0	519	3	48	1997	
0	10	27	205	572	0	521	3	48	1998	
100	8	1 418	155	2 101	...	2 015	...	86	1995	Côte d'Ivoire
100	8	1 068	175	2 413	...	2 293	...	120	1996	
102	8	1 066	175	2 457	...	2 312	...	146	1997	
101	8	1 071	173	2 471	...	2 325	...	146	1998	
114	2	15	23	1 060	224	464	...	372	1995	Rép. Dém. du Congo
114	2	20	23	1 080	226	475	...	379	1996	
116	2	21	23	1 089	228	482	...	380	1997	
117	2	28	22	1 097	228	489	...	380	1998	
68	354	...	205	123	...	123	...	...	1995	Djibouti
68	356	...	199	121	...	121	...	...	1996	
69	360	...	197	121	...	121	...	...	1997	
69	360	...	195	121	...	121	...	...	1998	

64

Production, trade and consumption of commercial energy
Thousand metric tons of oil equivalent and kilograms per capita [*cont.*]
Production, commerce et consommation d'énergie commerciale
Milliers de tonnes d'équivalent pétrole et kilogrammes par habitant [*suite*]

| Region, country or area | Year | Primary energy production – Production d'énergie primaire | | | | | Changes in stocks | Imports | Exports |
		Total Totale	Solids Solides	Liquids Liquides	Gas Gaz	Electricity Electricité	Variations des stocks	Imports Importations	Exports Exportati
Egypt	1995	60 405	...	46 797	12 658	950	8 773	1 073	1
	1996	59 882	...	45 461	13 462	959	7 661	1 996	1
	1997	59 414	...	44 515	13 893	1 006	6 381	1 866	1
	1998	55 754	...	43 200	11 523	1 031	8 203	2 192	
Equatorial Guinea	1995	340	...	339	...	0	18	42	
	1996	858	...	858	...	0	4	43	
	1997	3 000	...	3 000	...	0	152	46	
	1998	4 103	...	4 103	...	0	− 36	46	
Ethiopia	1995	122	...	...	...	122	4	1 039	
	1996	130	...	...	...	130	2	608	
	1997	135	...	...	...	135	2	688	
	1998	136	...	...	...	136	2	697	
Gabon	1995	19 101	...	18 264	769	68	814	156	1
	1996	19 079	...	18 295	718	66	− 88	173	1
	1997	19 369	...	18 616	684	70	− 113	249	1
	1998	18 894	...	18 213	610	71	− 117	237	1
Gambia	1995	...	...	...	...	...	...	74	
	1996	...	...	...	...	...	...	74	
	1997	...	...	...	...	...	...	74	
	1998	...	...	...	...	...	...	78	
Ghana	1995	526	...		...	526	0	1 278	
	1996	570	...		...	570	0	1 283	
	1997	571	...		...	571	0	1 283	
	1998	572	...		...	572	0	1 290	
Guinea	1995	16	...	...	...	16	...	370	
	1996	16	...	...	...	16	...	374	
	1997	16	...	...	...	16	...	375	
	1998	16	...	...	...	16	...	376	
Guinea−Bissau	1995	...	...	...	...	...	...	82	
	1996	...	...	...	...	...	...	82	
	1997	...	...	...	...	...	...	82	
	1998	...	...	...	...	...	...	82	
Kenya	1995	518	...	...	...	518	...	2 496	
	1996	518	...	...	...	518	...	2 659	
	1997	628	...	...	...	628	...	2 815	
	1998	755	...	...	...	755	...	3 649	
Liberia	1995	15	...	...	...	15	...	123	
	1996	15	...	...	...	15	...	125	
	1997	16	...	...	...	16	...	128	
	1998	16	...	...	...	16	...	131	
Libyan Arab Jamah.	1995	75 232	...	69 320	5 913	...	− 762	7	59
	1996	75 102	...	69 115	5 987	...	0	7	59
	1997	77 202	...	71 075	6 127	...	0	7	58
	1998	75 121	...	69 190	5 931	...	0	7	60
Madagascar	1995	35	...	...	...	35	− 7	430	
	1996	38	...	...	...	38	1	431	
	1997	42	...	...	...	42	0	436	
	1998	44	...	...	...	44	0	439	
Malawi	1995	72	...	...	...	72	...	229	
	1996	74	...	...	...	74	...	233	
	1997	74	...	...	...	74	...	234	
	1998	74	...	...	...	74	...	236	
Mali	1995	19	...	...	...	19	...	173	
	1996	18	...	...	...	18	...	176	
	1997	20	...	...	...	20	...	176	
	1998	20	...	...	...	20	...	178	
Mauritania	1995	2	...	...	...	2	...	1 060	
	1996	2	...	...	...	2	...	1 063	
	1997	2	...	...	...	2	...	1 064	
	1998	2	...	...	...	2	...	1 065	
Mauritius	1995	12	...	...	...	12	− 21	785	
	1996	9	...	...	...	9	− 36	799	
	1997	9	...	...	...	9	− 15	809	
	1998	9	...	...	...	9	− 15	817	

...kers – Soutes			Consumption – Consommation							
Air vion	Sea Maritime	Unallocated Nondistribué	Per capita Par habitant	Total Totale	Solids Solides	Liquids Liquides	Gas Gaz	Electricity Electricité	Année	Région, pays ou zone
258	2 486	2 189	515	32 050	647	17 816	12 638	950	1995	Egypte
361	3 055	2 422	544	34 560	903	19 236	13 462	959	1996	
310	3 011	2 440	553	35 792	749	20 144	13 893	1 006	1997	
337	2 228	2 160	537	35 400	663	22 183	11 523	1 031	1998	
...	...	− 16	105	42	...	42	...	0	1995	Guinée équatoriale
...	...	− 2	105	43	...	43	...	0	1996	
...	...	− 150	110	46	...	46	...	0	1997	
...	...	38	107	46	...	46	...	0	1998	
53	14	9	15	891	0	770	...	122	1995	Ethiopie
55	14	1	10	630	0	501	...	130	1996	
55	14	27	10	633	0	499	...	135	1997	
57	14	25	10	639	0	503	...	136	1998	
26	310	90	1 120	1 206	...	369	769	68	1995	Gabon
39	318	101	1 052	1 164	...	381	718	66	1996	
34	290	2	1 141	1 297	...	544	684	70	1997	
35	285	15	1 022	1 192	...	511	610	71	1998	
...	...	...	65	72	...	72	...	...	1995	Gambie
...	...	...	63	72	...	72	...	...	1996	
...	...	...	61	72	...	72	...	...	1997	
...	...	...	62	76	...	76	...	...	1998	
29	24	66	90	1 597	2	1 088	...	507	1995	Ghana
29	25	55	91	1 654	2	1 102	...	550	1996	
29	25	54	89	1 657	2	1 103	...	552	1997	
30	26	41	87	1 674	2	1 119	...	553	1998	
14	...	...	52	372	...	356	...	16	1995	Guinée
14	...	...	52	377	...	361	...	16	1996	
14	...	...	52	378	...	362	...	16	1997	
15	...	...	52	378	...	362	...	16	1998	
6	...	...	70	76	...	76	...	...	1995	Guinée – Bissau
6	...	...	69	76	...	76	...	...	1996	
6	...	...	67	76	...	76	...	...	1997	
6	...	...	66	76	...	76	...	...	1998	
0	55	− 65	97	2 650	66	2 051	...	533	1995	Kenya
0	55	87	95	2 660	65	2 062	...	533	1996	
0	57	232	87	2 485	80	1 764	...	640	1997	
0	72	517	109	3 158	46	2 344	...	767	1998	
4	12	0	58	121	...	106	...	15	1995	Libéria
4	12	0	56	124	...	108	...	15	1996	
4	12	0	53	127	...	111	...	16	1997	
2	12	0	49	131	...	116	...	16	1998	
114	89	3 261	2 644	13 131	4	8 568	4 559	...	1995	Jamah. arabe libyenne
134	89	1 310	2 757	14 021	4	9 120	4 897	...	1996	
52	89	4 912	2 538	13 225	4	8 093	5 128	...	1997	
52	89	859	2 473	13 205	4	8 096	5 105	...	1998	
2	15	− 25	33	460	12	413	...	35	1995	Madagascar
2	15	− 50	34	480	12	431	...	38	1996	
2	15	− 105	37	545	12	490	...	42	1997	
2	15	− 47	33	491	12	435	...	44	1998	
17	...	...	29	285	12	201	...	72	1995	Malawi
18	...	...	29	289	12	204	...	73	1996	
18	...	...	29	290	12	205	...	74	1997	
19	...	...	28	291	12	205	...	74	1998	
17	...	...	18	176	...	157	...	19	1995	Mali
18	...	...	17	177	...	159	...	18	1996	
18	...	...	17	178	...	159	...	20	1997	
18	...	...	17	181	...	161	...	20	1998	
12	10	96	405	944	4	937	...	2	1995	Mauritanie
12	10	90	398	953	4	946	...	2	1996	
12	10	85	390	959	4	952	...	2	1997	
12	10	82	381	963	4	956	...	2	1998	
124	157	...	482	537	46	479	...	12	1995	Maurice
128	131	...	521	585	47	530	...	9	1996	
129	133	...	504	572	48	515	...	9	1997	
124	135	...	509	582	48	525	...	9	1998	

64
Production, trade and consumption of commercial energy
Thousand metric tons of oil equivalent and kilograms per capita [*cont.*]
Production, commerce et consommation d'énergie commerciale
Milliers de tonnes d'équivalent pétrole et kilogrammes par habitant [*suite*]

Region, country or area	Year	Primary energy production – Production d'énergie primaire					Changes in stocks Variations des stocks	Imports Importations	Exports Exportati
		Total Totale	Solids Solides	Liquids Liquides	Gas Gaz	Electricity Electricité			
Morocco	1995	525	455	5	13	52	212	8 633	
	1996	543	354	5	17	167	− 236	8 143	
	1997	484	263	12	32	177	178	8 843	
	1998	386	188	12	35	151	− 163	9 180	
Mozambique	1995	59	27	...	...	33	...	413	
	1996	52	14	...	...	38	...	410	
	1997	96	13	...	...	83	...	431	
	1998	600	13	...	...	587	...	410	
Niger	1995	121	121	...	...	...	0	247	
	1996	121	121	...	...	...	0	248	
	1997	122	122	...	...	...	0	248	
	1998	122	122	...	...	...	0	248	
Nigeria	1995	97 255	98	92 249	4 444	464	...	2 237	8
	1996	98 551	98	92 898	5 092	463	...	2 242	8
	1997	99 759	98	93 734	5 456	471	...	2 226	8
	1998	103 072	41	97 057	5 502	471	...	1 902	8
Réunion	1995	52	...	...	...	52	0	607	
	1996	54	...	...	...	54	1	635	
	1997	47	...	...	...	47	0	670	
	1998	48	...	...	...	48	0	712	
Rwanda	1995	14	...	...	0	14	...	172	
	1996	14	...	...	0	14	...	172	
	1997	14	...	...	0	14	...	176	
	1998	14	...	...	0	14	...	178	
Saint Helena	1995	...	...	...	...	...	...	2	
	1996							2	
	1997	...				...		2	
	1998	...				...		2	
Sao Tome and Principe	1995	1	...	...	...	1	...	26	
	1996	1	...	...	...	1	...	26	
	1997	1	...	...	...	1	...	26	
	1998	1	...	...	...	1	...	26	
Senegal	1995	...	...	...	...	...	...	1 213	
	1996	...	...	...	...	...	...	1 216	
	1997	...	...	...	...	...	...	1 225	
	1998	...	...	...	...	...	...	1 229	
Seychelles	1995	...	...	...	...	...	0	174	
	1996	...	...	...	...	...	0	175	
	1997	...	...	...	...	...	0	181	
	1998	...	...	...	...	...	0	181	
Sierra Leone	1995	...	...	...	...	...	...	287	
	1996	...	...	...	...	...	...	289	
	1997	...	...	...	...	...	...	293	
	1998	...	...	...	...	...	...	295	
Southern African Customs Union	1995	122 168	110 049	7 280	1 716	3 123	− 1 427	16 350	42
	1996	122 480	109 972	7 396	1 716	3 396	...	14 645	42
	1997	129 842	117 179	7 407	1 532	3 723	...	13 024	45
	1998	132 421	119 910	7 307	1 290	3 913	...	16 157	47
Sudan	1995	80	...	...	...	80	...	1 338	
	1996	81	...	...	...	81	...	1 345	
	1997	82	...	...	...	82	...	1 346	
	1998	82	...	...	...	82	...	1 353	
Togo	1995	1	...	...	...	1	0	224	
	1996	1	...	...	...	1	0	226	
	1997	1	...	...	...	1	0	234	
	1998	1	...	...	...	1	0	234	
Tunisia	1995	4 436	...	4 289	144	3	− 225	4 588	4
	1996	5 008	...	4 208	795	6	115	5 207	4
	1997	5 468	...	3 835	1 630	4	238	4 683	4
	1998	5 854	...	4 019	1 829	6	194	4 911	3
Uganda	1995	94	...	...	...	94	...	310	
	1996	100	...	...	...	100	...	315	
	1997	108	...	...	...	108	...	336	
	1998	109	...	...	...	109	...	397	

Air Avion	Sea Maritime	Unallocated Nondistribué	Per capita Par habitant	Total Totale	Solids Solides	Liquids Liquides	Gas Gaz	Electricity Electricité	Année	Région, pays ou zone
82	0	913	306	7 951	1 841	6 025	13	73	1995	Maroc
77	0	827	303	8 017	2 201	5 622	17	178	1996	
77	0	810	307	8 261	2 149	5 893	32	188	1997	
88	0	960	317	8 681	2 448	5 987	35	212	1998	
3	3	...	27	466	39	342	...	84	1995	Mozambique
2	3	...	25	457	25	342	...	90	1996	
2	2	...	26	481	24	357	...	100	1997	
2	1	...	27	518	24	365	...	129	1998	
22	...	...	38	347	121	209	...	17	1995	Niger
22	...	...	37	348	121	210	...	17	1996	
22	...	...	36	348	122	210	...	17	1997	
22	...	...	35	349	122	210	...	17	1998	
366	379	3 134	116	11 522	102	6 512	4 444	464	1995	Nigéria
377	379	2 062	120	12 183	102	6 525	5 092	463	1996	
372	369	− 96	120	12 485	102	6 455	5 456	471	1997	
377	359	1 119	125	13 262	46	7 243	5 502	471	1998	
0	15	...	982	643	...	592	...	52	1995	Réunion
0	10	...	1 020	677	...	624	...	54	1996	
0	11	...	1 048	705	...	658	...	47	1997	
0	14	...	1 093	745	...	697	...	48	1998	
9	...	...	34	176	...	161	0	15	1995	Rwanda
9	...	...	32	176	...	161	0	15	1996	
9	...	...	30	181	...	165	0	15	1997	
9	...	...	28	183	...	167	0	15	1998	
0	...	...	344	2	0	2	...	...	1995	Saint−Hélène
0	...	...	344	2	0	2	...	...	1996	
0	...	...	344	2	0	2	...	...	1997	
0	...	...	344	2	0	2	...	...	1998	
0	...	...	198	26	...	26	...	1	1995	Sao Tomé−et−Principe
0	...	...	195	26	...	26	...	1	1996	
0	...	...	191	26	...	26	...	1	1997	
0	...	...	186	26	...	26	...	1	1998	
109	144	4	110	917	...	917	...	...	1995	Sénégal
109	144	1	108	923	...	923	...	...	1996	
110	148	− 2	106	928	...	928	...	...	1997	
110	148	− 5	104	935	...	935	...	...	1998	
34	78	...	852	62	...	62	...	...	1995	Seychelles
34	78	...	855	63	...	63	...	...	1996	
35	80	...	871	65	...	65	...	...	1997	
35	80	...	859	65	...	65	...	...	1998	
19	83	53	31	130	0	130	...	...	1995	Sierra Leone
19	83	53	30	131	0	131	...	...	1996	
19	85	52	30	134	0	134	...	...	1997	
19	85	53	30	135	0	135	...	...	1998	
...	2 294	4 604	2 427	90 926	68 605	17 727	1 716	2 877	1995	Union douanière
...	2 304	1 405	2 381	90 780	68 204	17 941	1 716	2 918	1996	d'Afrique australe
...	2 210	1 612	2 402	93 115	72 211	16 217	1 532	3 154	1997	
...	2 334	3 807	2 417	95 114	73 369	16 727	1 290	3 728	1998	
37	8	158	44	1 178	0	1 097	...	80	1995	Soudan
38	8	151	44	1 188	0	1 106	...	81	1996	
38	8	146	43	1 192	0	1 111	...	82	1997	
38	8	142	43	1 203	0	1 121	...	82	1998	
...	...	...	54	218	0	190	...	28	1995	Togo
...	...	...	53	220	0	192	...	28	1996	
...	...	...	53	229	0	201	...	28	1997	
...	...	...	52	229	0	201	...	28	1998	
104	1	− 27	554	4 956	62	3 063	1 824	6	1995	Tunisie
196	0	− 67	592	5 379	63	3 155	2 154	7	1996	
217	0	− 43	618	5 696	68	3 304	2 320	4	1997	
4	74	1 395	643	6 005	55	3 400	2 543	6	1998	
0	...	...	20	384	...	307	...	77	1995	Ouganda
0	...	...	21	399	...	312	...	87	1996	
0	...	...	21	426	...	333	...	93	1997	
0	...	...	24	490	...	394	...	95	1998	

64

Production, trade and consumption of commercial energy
Thousand metric tons of oil equivalent and kilograms per capita [cont.]
Production, commerce et consommation d'énergie commerciale
Milliers de tonnes d'équivalent pétrole et kilogrammes par habitant [suite]

| Region, country or area | Year | Primary energy production – Production d'énergie primaire | | | | | Changes in stocks Variations des stocks | Imports Importations | Exports Exportati |
		Total Totale	Solids Solides	Liquids Liquides	Gas Gaz	Electricity Electricité			
United Rep. of Tanzania	1995	132	4	...	...	129	...	746	
	1996	133	4	...	...	129	...	751	
	1997	133	4	...	...	129	...	760	
	1998	133	4	...	...	130	...	765	
Western Sahara	1995	...	...	...	...	...	...	73	
	1996	...	...	...	...	...	...	73	
	1997	...	...	...	...	...	...	73	
	1998	...	...	...	...	...	...	73	
Zambia	1995	879	212	...	...	667	...	576	
	1996	859	192	...	...	667	...	586	
	1997	832	165	...	...	667	...	591	
	1998	794	144	...	...	651	20	397	
Zimbabwe	1995	4 065	3 877		...	187	− 23	1 746	
	1996	3 810	3 623	...	...	186	− 92	1 951	
	1997	3 900	3 713	...	...	187	163	2 166	
	1998	3 699	3 533	...	...	166	204	755	
America, North	**1995**	**2 226 789**	**573 336**	**682 520**	**675 141**	**295 793**	**− 11 056**	**652 072**	**354**
	1996	**2 261 860**	**590 071**	**675 909**	**695 631**	**300 249**	**− 6 874**	**688 103**	**368**
	1997	**2 287 219**	**605 486**	**694 972**	**704 578**	**282 182**	**19 847**	**738 037**	**384**
	1998	**2 271 834**	**612 686**	**679 463**	**692 328**	**287 357**	**39 432**	**778 860**	**394**
Antigua and Barbuda	1995	...	...	...	...	...	...	158	
	1996	...	...	...	...	...	...	158	
	1997	...	...	...	...	...	...	164	
	1998	...	...	...	...	...	...	164	
Aruba	1995	...	...	...	...	...	...	592	
	1996	...	...	...	...	...	...	602	
	1997	...	...	...	...	...	...	615	
	1998	...	...	...	...	...	...	619	
Bahamas	1995						− 18	2 878	2
	1996	...	...	...	...	...	− 18	2 876	2
	1997	...	...	...	...	...	− 5	2 888	2
	1998	...	...	...	...	...	2	2 912	2
Barbados	1995	88	...	63	24	...	− 1	327	
	1996	77	...	50	27	...	7	364	
	1997	67	...	45	22	...	5	416	
	1998	115	...	80	35	...	6	567	
Belize	1995	3	...	...	...	3	...	138	
	1996	5	...	...	...	5	...	117	
	1997	6	...	...	...	6	...	148	
	1998	6	...	...	...	6	...	150	
Bermuda	1995	...	...	...	...	...	...	168	
	1996	...	...	...	...	...	...	171	
	1997	...	...	...	...	...	...	171	
	1998	...	...	...	...	...	...	171	
British Virgin Islands	1995	...	...	...	...	...	...	17	
	1996	...	...	...	...	...	...	20	
	1997	...	...	...	...	...	...	20	
	1998	...	...	...	...	...	...	20	
Canada	1995	354 500	38 899	112 797	148 358	54 444	− 2 866	41 794	160
	1996	361 104	39 721	113 262	153 305	54 816	42	47 670	167
	1997	372 242	41 103	123 362	156 059	51 718	2 073	55 110	174
	1998	361 071	38 947	114 465	160 434	47 225	2 000	58 311	184
Cayman Islands	1995		...	...	...	...	...	110	
	1996	...	...	...	...	...	...	111	
	1997	...	...	...	...	...	...	111	
	1998	...	...	...	...	...	...	113	
Costa Rica	1995	714	...	...	...	714	8	1 694	
	1996	779	...	...	...	779	− 50	1 600	1
	1997	886	...	...	...	886	− 88	1 646	1
	1998	918	...	...	...	918	− 17	1 665	1
Cuba	1995	1 663	...	1 640	16	8	− 162	6 302	
	1996	1 674	...	1 646	18	10	59	6 701	
	1997	1 660	...	1 630	21	10	35	6 550	
	1998	1 904	...	1 871	22	11	133	6 639	

Energy   Energie

kers – Soutes | | | Consumption – Consommation

Air vion	Sea Maritime	Unallocated Nondistribué	Per capita Par habitant	Total Totale	Solids Solides	Liquids Liquides	Gas Gaz	Electricity Electricité	Année	Région, pays ou zone
28	23	− 2	27	800	4	668	...	129	1995	République–Unie de
31	23	− 2	26	803	4	670	...	129	1996	Tanzanie
31	24	− 2	26	808	4	675	...	129	1997	
31	24	− 1	25	812	4	679	...	130	1998	
4	0	...	277	69	...	69	...	...	1995	Sahara occidental
4	0	...	268	69	...	69	...	...	1996	
4	0	...	259	69	...	69	...	...	1997	
4	0	...	250	69	...	69	...	...	1998	
36	...	42	147	1 201	209	453	...	539	1995	Zambie
36	...	49	141	1 186	189	457	...	540	1996	
26	...	63	135	1 161	162	459	...	540	1997	
25	...	− 71	118	1 040	142	374	...	524	1998	
...	...	...	528	5 738	3 886	1 435	...	417	1995	Zimbabwe
...	...	...	520	5 739	3 673	1 560	...	506	1996	
...	...	...	516	5 788	3 513	1 703	...	571	1997	
...	...	...	360	4 098	3 208	457	...	432	1998	
504	33 058	56 966	5 357	2 443 699	510 638	949 620	687 576	295 865	1995	Amérique du Nord
769	31 362	61 189	5 402	2 494 134	534 259	964 128	695 450	300 297	1996	
828	27 687	78 207	5 381	2 513 683	539 512	987 612	704 358	282 201	1997	
754	27 873	69 689	5 329	2 517 520	554 019	1 002 323	673 741	287 437	1998	
43	0	...	1 632	108	...	108	...	...	1995	Antigua–et–Barbuda
43	0	...	1 632	108	...	108	...	...	1996	
44	0	...	1 710	113	...	113	...	...	1997	
44	0	...	1 684	113	...	113	...	...	1998	
...	...	312	3 407	279	...	279	...	...	1995	Aruba
...	...	315	3 333	287	...	287	...	...	1996	
...	...	321	3 264	294	...	294	...	...	1997	
...	...	322	3 159	297	...	297	...	...	1998	
38	184	...	2 045	572	1	571	...	...	1995	Bahamas
41	184	...	2 002	572	1	571	...	...	1996	
36	184	...	1 981	577	1	575	...	...	1997	
36	184	...	2 005	593	1	593	...	...	1998	
123	...	− 42	1 189	314	0	289	24	...	1995	Barbade
136	...	− 44	1 196	318	0	291	27	...	1996	
179	...	− 54	1 245	333	0	311	22	...	1997	
162	...	136	1 306	350	0	315	35	...	1998	
9	0	...	621	132	...	127	...	6	1995	Belize
7	4	...	506	111	...	103	...	7	1996	
5	9	...	622	139	...	131	...	8	1997	
5	8	...	619	142	...	135	...	8	1998	
17	0	...	2 446	152	0	152	...	...	1995	Bermudes
17	0	...	2 456	155	0	155	...	...	1996	
17	0	...	2 456	155	0	155	...	...	1997	
17	0	...	2 417	155	0	155	...	...	1998	
...	...	...	920	17	...	17	...	...	1995	Iles Vierges britanniques
...	...	...	1 031	20	...	20	...	...	1996	
...	...	...	979	20	...	20	...	...	1997	
...	...	...	979	20	...	20	...	...	1998	
844	628	6 530	7 775	230 284	23 463	77 881	77 592	51 347	1995	Canada
996	636	3 697	7 874	235 793	24 099	78 772	81 345	51 577	1996	
970	546	4 417	8 084	244 637	25 652	88 416	81 924	48 645	1997	
932	1 163	− 7 265	7 782	237 850	26 751	88 084	78 143	44 871	1998	
14	...	...	2 985	96	...	96	...	...	1995	Iles Caïmanes
17	...	...	2 862	94	...	94	...	...	1996	
17	...	...	2 778	94	...	94	...	...	1997	
17	...	...	2 681	97	...	97	...	...	1998	
...	...	59	608	2 160	...	1 444	...	716	1995	Costa Rica
...	...	51	606	2 214	...	1 422	...	792	1996	
...	...	46	640	2 398	...	1 501	...	897	1997	
...	...	− 114	663	2 548	...	1 636	...	912	1998	
183	...	744	650	7 128	44	7 060	16	8	1995	Cuba
266	...	881	644	7 093	8	7 057	18	10	1996	
304	...	792	633	7 010	29	6 950	21	10	1997	
277	...	1 621	584	6 438	11	6 394	22	11	1998	

64
Production, trade and consumption of commercial energy
Thousand metric tons of oil equivalent and kilograms per capita [*cont.*]
Production, commerce et consommation d'énergie commerciale
Milliers de tonnes d'équivalent pétrole et kilogrammes par habitant [*suite*]

Region, country or area	Year	Primary energy production – Production d'énergie primaire					Changes in stocks	Imports	Exports
		Total Totale	Solids Solides	Liquids Liquides	Gas Gaz	Electricity Electricité	Variations des stocks	Imports Importations	Exports Exporta
Dominica	1995	2	...	...	...	2	...	27	
	1996	2	...	...	...	2	...	27	
	1997	2	...	...	...	2	...	27	
	1998	2	...	...	...	2	...	28	
Dominican Republic	1995	171	...	...	...	171	− 9	3 995	
	1996	181	...	...	...	181	− 10	3 987	
	1997	192	...	...	...	192	− 130	3 982	
	1998	203	...	...	...	203	0	6 392	
El Salvador	1995	507	...	...	...	507	52	1 468	
	1996	533	...	...	...	533	8	1 542	
	1997	550	...	...	...	550	5	1 739	
	1998	547	...	...	...	547	12	2 039	
Greenland	1995	...	0	...	...	...	...	174	
	1996	...	0	...	...	...	...	178	
	1997	...	0	...	...	...	...	180	
	1998	...	0	...	...	...	...	182	
Grenada	1995	...	...	...	...	...	− 1	58	
	1996	...	...	...	...	...	0	59	
	1997	...	...	...	...	...	0	64	
	1998	...	...	...	...	...	0	64	
Guadeloupe	1995	...	...	...	...	...	0	541	
	1996	...	...	...	...	...	0	544	
	1997	...	...	...	...	...	0	551	
	1998	...	...	...	...	...	0	551	
Guatemala	1995	641	...	467	10	164	1	2 142	
	1996	938	...	730	10	198	4	1 922	
	1997	1 167	...	976	10	181	26	2 277	
	1998	1 462	...	1 273	10	179	58	2 841	
Haiti	1995	19	...	...	...	19	...	311	
	1996	22	...	...	...	22	...	357	
	1997	22	...	...	...	22	...	477	
	1998	24	...	...	...	24	...	437	
Honduras	1995	180	...	...	...	180	38	1 229	
	1996	186	...	...	...	186	28	1 219	
	1997	119	...	...	...	119	1	1 248	
	1998	166	...	...	...	166	− 22	1 487	
Jamaica	1995	10	...	...	...	10	− 81	3 049	
	1996	11	...	...	...	11	− 113	3 200	
	1997	12	...	...	...	12	− 122	3 390	
	1998	12	...	...	...	12	− 70	3 538	
Martinique	1995	...	...	...	...	...	0	855	
	1996	...	...	...	...	...	0	857	
	1997	...	...	...	...	...	0	862	
	1998	...	...	...	...	...	0	862	
Mexico	1995	200 530	2 876	160 552	26 808	10 294	− 377	9 093	7
	1996	209 175	3 157	165 847	30 462	9 709	423	9 272	8
	1997	219 534	3 222	175 160	31 424	9 728	334	15 162	9
	1998	225 078	3 501	178 222	33 927	9 427	− 474	17 175	9
Montserrat	1995	...	...	...	...	...	...	15	
	1996	...	...	...	...	...	...	14	
	1997	...	...	...	...	...	...	16	
	1998	...	...	...	...	...	...	16	
Netherland Antilles	1995		...	...	...	...	...	15 636	9
	1996		...	...	...	...	...	15 650	9
	1997	...	...	...	...	...	...	15 673	9
	1998	...	...	...	...	...	...	16 037	9
Nicaragua	1995	503	...	...	...	503	10	898	
	1996	547	...	...	...	547	45	959	
	1997	547	...	...	...	547	2	979	
	1998	600	...	...	...	600	38	1 135	
Panama	1995	208	...	...	...	208	− 40	1 753	
	1996	258	...	...	...	258	4	2 864	1
	1997	250	...	...	...	250	86	2 910	
	1998	275	...	...	...	275	45	3 260	1

Air Aviation	Sea Maritime	Unallocated Nondistribué	Per capita Par habitant	Total Totale	Solids Solides	Liquids Liquides	Gas Gaz	Electricity Electricité	Année	Région, pays ou zone
0	...	...	403	29	...	27	...	2	1995	Dominique
0	...	...	403	29	...	27	...	2	1996	
0	...	...	404	29	...	27	...	2	1997	
0	...	...	419	30	...	28	...	2	1998	
...	...	300	495	3 876	78	3 627	...	171	1995	Rép. dominicaine
...	...	152	506	4 026	90	3 755	...	181	1996	
...	...	16	530	4 288	97	3 999	...	192	1997	
...	...	1 156	661	5 439	57	5 179	...	203	1998	
...	...	33	332	1 883	...	1 378	...	504	1995	El Salvador
...	...	37	329	1 905	...	1 371	...	534	1996	
...	...	33	343	2 026	...	1 469	...	557	1997	
...	...	34	393	2 372	...	1 822	...	550	1998	
...	...	...	2 981	167	0	167	...	...	1995	Groenland
...	...	...	3 054	171	0	171	...	...	1996	
...	...	...	3 091	173	0	173	...	...	1997	
...	...	...	3 127	175	0	175	...	...	1998	
2	...	...	618	57	...	57	...	...	1995	Grenade
2	...	...	618	57	...	57	...	...	1996	
2	...	...	667	62	...	62	...	...	1997	
2	...	...	667	62	...	62	...	...	1998	
79	...	...	1 090	462	...	462	...	...	1995	Guadeloupe
79	...	...	1 080	465	...	465	...	...	1996	
80	...	...	1 079	472	...	472	...	...	1997	
80	...	...	1 065	472	...	472	...	...	1998	
...	...	50	233	2 322	...	2 145	10	167	1995	Guatemala
...	...	− 13	217	2 224	...	2 018	10	196	1996	
...	...	103	229	2 413	...	2 229	10	173	1997	
...	...	158	276	2 977	...	2 792	10	175	1998	
7	...	...	43	323	...	304	...	19	1995	Haïti
8	...	...	48	371	...	349	...	22	1996	
15	...	...	62	483	...	461	...	22	1997	
15	...	...	56	445	...	422	...	24	1998	
...	...	...	239	1 353	...	1 174	...	178	1995	Honduras
...	...	...	230	1 338	...	1 158	...	180	1996	
...	...	...	225	1 344	...	1 212	...	132	1997	
...	...	...	271	1 663	...	1 493	...	170	1998	
31	...	− 38	1 250	3 092	39	3 043	...	10	1995	Jamaïque
36	...	2	1 294	3 228	45	3 172	...	11	1996	
36	...	50	1 343	3 379	47	3 321	...	12	1997	
36	...	41	1 373	3 484	50	3 422	...	12	1998	
...	37	49	1 522	577	...	577	...	...	1995	Martinique
...	39	44	1 510	577	...	577	...	...	1996	
...	39	45	1 491	576	...	576	...	...	1997	
...	39	43	1 483	577	...	577	...	...	1998	
...	613	8 927	1 359	123 877	4 067	81 394	28 197	10 220	1995	Mexique
...	575	9 296	1 338	124 059	4 642	78 806	30 893	9 718	1996	
...	796	10 463	1 364	128 582	4 838	81 850	32 065	9 829	1997	
...	785	10 067	1 419	135 954	4 936	86 483	34 984	9 550	1998	
...	1	...	1 312	14	...	14	...	...	1995	Montserrat
...	1	...	1 217	13	...	13	...	...	1996	
...	1	...	1 405	15	...	15	...	...	1997	
...	1	...	1 405	15	...	15	...	...	1998	
61	1 710	3 643	4 217	864	...	864	...	...	1995	Antilles néerlandaises
63	1 714	3 629	4 167	867	...	867	...	...	1996	
65	1 720	3 618	4 142	874	...	874	...	...	1997	
68	1 726	3 925	4 228	901	...	901	...	...	1998	
...	...	16	309	1 367	...	865	...	501	1995	Nicaragua
...	...	20	316	1 439	...	892	...	547	1996	
...	...	5	325	1 519	...	958	...	561	1997	
...	...	− 1	353	1 699	...	1 095	...	604	1998	
0	...	− 43	480	1 263	25	966	56	215	1995	Panama
0	...	28	646	1 729	70	1 344	57	258	1996	
0	...	864	676	1 840	40	1 472	57	271	1997	
0	...	10	753	2 082	41	1 706	57	278	1998	

64

Production, trade and consumption of commercial energy
Thousand metric tons of oil equivalent and kilograms per capita [*cont.*]
Production, commerce et consommation d'énergie commerciale
Milliers de tonnes d'équivalent pétrole et kilogrammes par habitant [*suite*]

| Region, country or area | Year | Primary energy production – Production d'énergie primaire | | | | | Changes in stocks Variations des stocks | Imports Importations | Exports Exportatic |
		Total Totale	Solids Solides	Liquids Liquides	Gas Gaz	Electricity Electricité			
Puerto Rico	1995	9	...	...	...	9	− 34	7 967	
	1996	12	...	...	...	12	− 74	7 988	
	1997	8	...	...	...	8	− 79	8 003	
	1998	10	...	...	...	10	72	8 606	
Saint Kitts and Nevis	1995	...	...	...	...	...	0	32	
	1996	...	...	...	...	...	0	34	
	1997	...	...	...	...	...	0	34	
	1998	...	...	...	...	...	0	34	
Saint Lucia	1995	...	...	...	...	...	...	64	
	1996	...	...	...	...	...	...	64	
	1997	...	...	...	...	...	...	67	
	1998	...	...	...	...	...	...	67	
Saint Pierre and Miquelon	1995	...	...	...	...	...	...	28	
	1996	...	...	...	...	...	...	28	
	1997	...	...	...	...	...	...	19	
	1998	...	...	...	...	...	...	22	
Saint Vincent and the Grenadines	1995	2	...	...	...	2	...	43	
	1996	2	...	...	...	2	...	44	
	1997	2	...	...	...	2	...	44	
	1998	2	...	...	...	2	...	55	
Trinidad and Tobago	1995	13 084	...	6 791	6 293	...	− 342	1 861	6
	1996	13 829	...	6 717	7 112	...	87	2 303	7
	1997	13 789	...	6 218	7 572	...	33	2 065	6
	1998	14 294	...	6 391	7 903	...	100	3 760	8
United States	1995	1 653 954	531 560	400 209	493 631	228 554	− 7 434	529 219	82
	1996	1 672 525	547 193	387 656	504 696	232 979	− 7 432	557 012	80
	1997	1 676 165	561 161	387 581	509 471	217 952	17 496	592 685	79
	1998	1 665 145	570 237	377 161	489 996	227 751	37 360	621 110	75
U.S. Virgin Islands	1995	...	...	...	...	...	200	17 435	13
	1996	...	...	...	...	...	115	17 587	13
	1997	...	...	...	...	...	175	17 744	13
	1998	...	...	...	...	...	189	17 830	14
America, South	**1995**	**430 737**	**22 992**	**286 385**	**79 636**	**41 725**	**− 600**	**74 481**	**205 5**
	1996	**463 339**	**24 862**	**317 271**	**77 948**	**43 258**	**6 326**	**81 064**	**225 9**
	1997	**494 310**	**28 205**	**335 517**	**85 054**	**45 534**	**− 478**	**85 333**	**254 7**
	1998	**503 482**	**30 413**	**340 698**	**86 046**	**46 325**	**1 412**	**88 812**	**254 7**
Argentina	1995	67 015	180	37 282	25 387	4 165	− 14	6 164	17 3
	1996	70 526	183	41 758	24 661	3 924	− 67	4 890	19 4
	1997	78 041	148	44 358	29 034	4 501	241	4 529	21 4
	1998	77 995	171	43 758	29 835	4 232	315	5 482	22 4
Bolivia	1995	5 275	...	1 641	3 515	118	− 5	151	2 2
	1996	5 536	...	1 824	3 587	125	− 45	159	2 0
	1997	5 139	...	1 805	3 205	129	− 270	165	2 0
	1998	5 287	...	2 081	3 067	140	16	305	1 6
Brazil	1995	65 315	2 310	35 908	4 604	22 493	− 2 482	45 966	2 6
	1996	71 203	2 135	40 418	5 160	23 490	974	51 897	1 7
	1997	76 936	2 509	43 879	5 729	24 819	211	52 392	1 8
	1998	85 089	2 451	50 716	6 012	25 910	522	51 052	3 9
Chile	1995	4 864	743	864	1 673	1 583	34	10 846	1
	1996	4 701	718	877	1 653	1 452	511	13 047	
	1997	4 925	746	754	1 797	1 629	− 108	15 044	1
	1998	4 452	672	789	1 620	1 371	97	16 601	1
Colombia	1995	54 552	16 815	30 424	4 545	2 769	1 044	1 595	30 8
	1996	59 893	19 237	32 629	4 972	3 056	172	1 119	36 1
	1997	63 934	21 185	33 970	6 051	2 729	151	1 406	39 1
	1998	68 318	21 886	37 457	6 327	2 647	463	1 312	43 5
Ecuador	1995	21 206	...	20 261	365	580	...	848	14 2
	1996	20 727	...	19 431	618	679	...	731	12 8
	1997	21 517	...	20 313	581	624	...	906	15 4
	1998	21 856	...	20 866	368	622	...	1 514	14 7
Falkland Is. (Malvinas)	1995	3	3	...	...	...	...	9	
	1996	3	3	...	...	...	...	10	
	1997	3	3	...	...	...	...	11	
	1998	3	3	...	...	...	...	9	

Air vion	Sea Maritime	Unallocated Nondistribué	Per capita Par habitant	Total Totale	Solids Solides	Liquids Liquides	Gas Gaz	Electricity Electricité	Année	Région, pays ou zone
...	170	247	1 865	6 927	116	6 803	...	9	1995	Porto Rico
...	172	223	1 870	7 010	119	6 879	...	12	1996	
...	175	199	1 859	7 025	121	6 896	...	8	1997	
...	175	628	1 850	7 050	123	6 917	...	10	1998	
...	...	...	797	32	...	32	...	...	1995	Saint−Kitts−et−Nevis
...	...	...	847	34	...	34	...	...	1996	
...	...	...	869	34	...	34	...	...	1997	
...	...	...	869	34	...	34	...	...	1998	
0	...	...	444	64	...	64	...	...	1995	Saint−Lucie
0	...	...	438	64	...	64	...	...	1996	
0	...	...	453	67	...	67	...	...	1997	
0	...	...	447	67	...	67	...	...	1998	
...	4	...	3 908	23	0	23	...	...	1995	Saint−Pierre−et−
...	4	...	3 908	23	0	23	...	...	1996	Miquelon
...	4	...	2 185	15	0	15	...	...	1997	
...	4	...	2 625	18	0	18	...	...	1998	
0	...	...	412	45	...	43	...	2	1995	Saint−Vincent−et−les−
0	...	...	417	46	...	44	...	2	1996	Grenadines
0	...	...	414	46	...	44	...	2	1997	
0	...	...	505	57	...	55	...	2	1998	
53	171	640	5 950	7 509	...	1 216	6 293	...	1995	Trinité−et−Tobago
58	221	132	6 685	8 490	...	1 378	7 112	...	1996	
58	221	65	6 948	8 873	...	1 301	7 572	...	1997	
63	265	− 5	7 108	9 120	...	1 217	7 903	...	1998	
0	29 349	34 876	7 654	2 043 856	482 631	754 049	575 387	231 789	1995	Etats−Unis
0	27 620	41 923	7 745	2 086 685	505 010	769 438	575 988	236 248	1996	
0	23 798	56 355	7 695	2 091 250	508 509	779 172	582 688	220 881	1997	
0	23 325	58 027	7 633	2 091 686	521 873	787 172	552 586	230 054	1998	
...	191	662	25 512	2 475	175	2 300	...	...	1995	Iles Vierges américaines
...	193	816	26 243	2 519	175	2 344	...	...	1996	
...	195	868	26 635	2 530	176	2 354	...	...	1997	
...	198	905	27 009	2 539	178	2 361	...	...	1998	
783	2 527	16 761	874	280 216	19 608	139 294	79 591	41 723	1995	**Amérique du Sud**
893	2 821	22 077	879	286 357	20 749	144 864	77 502	43 241	1996	
978	3 186	22 459	904	298 769	21 922	147 013	84 284	45 550	1997	
115	3 092	24 187	917	307 704	21 923	154 074	85 604	46 104	1998	
0	479	1 881	1 538	53 482	977	20 789	27 369	4 348	1995	Argentine
0	579	4 480	1 447	50 951	818	19 441	26 480	4 213	1996	
0	704	5 658	1 527	54 480	733	18 995	29 804	4 948	1997	
0	701	5 750	1 503	54 291	826	19 306	29 466	4 693	1998	
0	...	22	426	3 157	0	1 439	1 600	119	1995	Bolivie
0	...	269	446	3 388	0	1 545	1 718	126	1996	
0	...	423	396	3 077	0	1 581	1 367	129	1997	
0	...	587	416	3 312	0	1 766	1 406	141	1998	
680	1 172	7 459	639	101 787	11 707	59 942	4 604	25 534	1995	Brésil
779	1 347	9 101	676	109 178	12 364	65 019	5 160	26 634	1996	
858	1 713	9 255	705	115 463	12 571	68 864	5 729	28 299	1997	
963	1 703	9 721	719	119 266	12 315	71 640	6 012	29 299	1998	
0	0	311	1 073	15 248	2 741	9 361	1 562	1 583	1995	Chili
0	0	519	1 153	16 632	3 823	10 100	1 258	1 452	1996	
6	0	556	1 322	19 330	4 928	10 678	2 095	1 629	1997	
27	0	712	1 354	20 073	4 685	10 811	3 207	1 371	1998	
...	185	1 895	575	22 167	3 730	11 092	4 545	2 801	1995	Colombie
...	191	1 975	574	22 534	3 301	11 191	4 972	3 070	1996	
...	207	2 454	583	23 333	3 242	11 294	6 051	2 746	1997	
...	203	2 829	554	22 623	2 678	10 969	6 327	2 649	1998	
43	211	1 136	563	6 449	...	5 504	365	580	1995	Equateur
46	223	1 118	615	7 189	...	5 892	618	679	1996	
41	151	− 184	586	7 001	...	5 796	581	624	1997	
36	143	1 272	585	7 121	...	6 130	368	622	1998	
...	0	...	6 291	13	3	9	...	...	1995	Iles Falkland (Malvinas)
...	0	...	6 825	14	3	10	...	...	1996	
...	0	...	7 332	15	3	11	...	...	1997	
...	0	...	5 959	12	3	9	...	...	1998	

64

Production, trade and consumption of commercial energy
Thousand metric tons of oil equivalent and kilograms per capita [*cont.*]
Production, commerce et consommation d'énergie commerciale
Milliers de tonnes d'équivalent pétrole et kilogrammes par habitant [*suite*]

Region, country or area	Year	Primary energy production – Production d'énergie primaire					Changes in stocks Variations des stocks	Imports Importations	Exports Exportatio
		Total Totale	Solids Solides	Liquids Liquides	Gas Gaz	Electricity Electricité			
French Guiana	1995	...	...	...	...	...	...	304	
	1996	...	...	...	...	...	...	304	
	1997	...	...	...	...	...	...	304	
	1998	...	...	...	...	...	...	309	
Guyana	1995	0	...	...	...	0	...	497	
	1996	0	...	...	...	0	...	516	
	1997	0	...	...	...	0	...	542	
	1998	0	...	...	...	0	...	559	
Paraguay	1995	3 620	...	...	...	3 620	− 88	1 124	3
	1996	4 131	...	...	...	4 131	− 138	952	3
	1997	4 373	...	...	...	4 373	− 61	1 120	3
	1998	4 375	...	...	...	4 375	2	1 376	3
Peru	1995	8 082	98	6 123	675	1 185	543	4 386	2
	1996	7 921	40	6 052	664	1 165	449	4 684	2
	1997	7 894	15	6 022	720	1 136	− 54	5 807	3
	1998	7 519	14	5 718	599	1 188	238	6 507	3
Suriname	1995	385	...	275	...	110	1	477	
	1996	356	...	245	...	110	0	483	
	1997	357	...	246	...	111	1	488	
	1998	360	...	248	...	111	1	493	
Uruguay	1995	504	...	...	...	504	79	2 032	
	1996	496	...	...	...	496	− 50	2 193	
	1997	558	...	...	...	558	− 15	2 152	
	1998	745	...	...	...	745	− 26	2 150	
Venezuela	1995	199 916	2 843	153 606	38 871	4 597	288	82	132 0
	1996	217 845	2 546	174 036	36 633	4 631	4 519	79	147 2
	1997	230 632	3 600	184 170	37 937	4 925	− 574	467	167 2
	1998	227 483	5 216	179 064	38 218	4 984	− 215	1 145	160 3
Asia	**1995**	**2 937 369**	**1 003 486**	**1 371 788**	**395 024**	**167 070**	**8 301**	**991 928**	**1 139 9**
	1996	**3 031 870**	**1 036 388**	**1 393 427**	**427 964**	**174 090**	**− 492**	**1 066 157**	**1 166 8**
	1997	**3 096 621**	**1 029 143**	**1 448 369**	**437 958**	**181 151**	**19 790**	**1 132 575**	**1 218 5**
	1998	**3 127 485**	**970 243**	**1 519 277**	**447 099**	**190 866**	**731**	**1 100 538**	**1 282 7**
Afghanistan	1995	196	4	...	157	36	10	303	
	1996	183	2	...	149	31	10	286	
	1997	166	1	...	137	28	10	268	
	1998	156	1	...	128	27	10	255	
Armenia	1995	244	...	...	...	244	0	1 530	
	1996	742	...	...	...	742	0	1 135	
	1997	537	...	...	...	537	171	1 455	
	1998	547	...	...	...	547	0	1 514	
Azerbaijan	1995	15 308	...	9 188	5 986	134	...	679	2 17
	1996	14 939	...	9 125	5 681	132	...	191	2 03
	1997	14 564	...	9 047	5 370	147	...	395	1 99
	1998	16 653	...	11 449	5 036	168	...	386	1 93
Bahrain	1995	8 759	...	2 447	6 312	...	− 291	10 549	10 47
	1996	8 913	...	2 378	6 536	...	− 381	11 089	10 85
	1997	9 252	...	2 364	6 888	...	− 33	10 604	10 08
	1998	9 708	...	2 287	7 421	...	− 488	10 540	10 25
Bangladesh	1995	6 372	...	10	6 330	32	− 23	2 798	
	1996	6 687	...	66	6 557	64	− 274	2 724	
	1997	6 551	...	45	6 444	62	− 25	3 276	
	1998	7 103	...	37	6 992	74	251	3 040	
Bhutan	1995	188	48	...	...	140	...	35	14
	1996	214	45	...	...	170	...	44	15
	1997	196	38	...	...	158	...	75	14
	1998	190	35	...	...	155	...	80	13
Brunei Darussalam	1995	18 899	...	8 970	9 928	...	− 33	7	16 98
	1996	18 640	...	8 679	9 962	...	89	59	16 62
	1997	18 524	...	8 563	9 961	...	25	80	16 46
	1998	18 116	...	8 472	9 644	...	− 50	14	16 06
Cambodia	1995	6	...	...	...	6	...	166	
	1996	7	...	...	...	7	...	166	
	1997	7	...	...	...	7	...	170	
	1998	7	...	...	...	7	...	170	

Energy Energie

...rs – Soutes			Consumption – Consommation							
...ir / ...on	Sea Maritime	Unallocated Nondistribué	Per capita Par habitant	Total Totale	Solids Solides	Liquids Liquides	Gas Gaz	Electricity Electricité	Année	Région, pays ou zone
17	...	...	1 957	288	...	288	...	...	1995	Guyane française
17	...	...	1 880	288	...	288	...	...	1996	
17	...	...	1 798	288	...	288	...	...	1997	
17	...	...	1 753	293	...	293	...	...	1998	
9	2	...	586	486	0	486	...	0	1995	Guyana
12	2	...	600	502	0	502	...	0	1996	
13	2	...	625	527	0	527	...	0	1997	
12	2	...	641	545	0	545	...	0	1998	
2	...	− 17	326	1 572	...	1 206	...	367	1995	Paraguay
2	...	− 3	351	1 740	...	1 072	...	668	1996	
2	...	7	317	1 611	...	1 153	...	458	1997	
2	...	8	354	1 848	...	1 362	...	487	1998	
...	...	447	378	8 890	368	6 662	675	1 185	1995	Pérou
...	...	− 14	395	9 464	347	7 288	664	1 165	1996	
...	...	738	400	9 745	333	7 556	720	1 136	1997	
...	...	− 226	411	10 193	412	7 995	599	1 188	1998	
0	...	212	1 456	596	0	486	...	110	1995	Suriname
0	...	189	1 469	602	0	492	...	110	1996	
0	...	189	1 475	608	0	497	...	111	1997	
0	...	191	1 481	613	0	502	...	111	1998	
32	408	12	602	1 937	0	1 437	...	500	1995	Uruguay
36	409	38	678	2 199	1	1 705	...	493	1996	
41	331	56	689	2 248	1	1 702	...	545	1997	
58	279	89	700	2 301	1	1 741	...	559	1998	
...	71	3 403	2 936	64 144	82	20 595	38 871	4 597	1995	Venezuela
...	70	4 406	2 764	61 675	92	20 319	36 633	4 631	1996	
...	78	3 305	2 680	61 045	111	18 072	37 937	4 925	1997	
...	61	3 252	2 806	65 212	1 002	21 007	38 218	4 984	1998	
812	39 021	163 614	746	2 562 637	1 112 775	889 681	392 727	167 454	1995	**Asie**
014	40 665	179 060	773	2 694 895	1 158 942	931 041	430 316	174 596	1996	
449	44 071	203 211	771	2 726 111	1 140 501	949 148	455 034	181 428	1997	
698	47 049	202 313	743	2 678 463	1 090 022	936 182	460 592	191 667	1998	
5	...	...	25	483	4	277	157	46	1995	Afghanistan
5	...	...	22	454	2	261	149	41	1996	
5	...	...	20	419	1	244	137	36	1997	
5	...	...	19	396	1	232	128	35	1998	
...	...	...	496	1 774	2	255	1 271	245	1995	Arménie
...	...	...	527	1 877	4	141	991	742	1996	
...	...	...	513	1 821	4	150	1 131	537	1997	
...	...	...	583	2 061	4	155	1 356	547	1998	
520	...	392	1 706	12 901	4	6 264	6 465	168	1995	Azerbaïdjan
544	...	1 479	1 455	11 074	4	5 197	5 703	170	1996	
464	...	1 950	1 381	10 552	4	4 993	5 370	184	1997	
543	...	3 911	1 389	10 655	1	5 428	5 036	190	1998	
0	...	1 949	12 857	7 174	...	862	6 312	...	1995	Bahreïn
0	...	2 164	12 925	7 367	...	831	6 536	...	1996	
0	...	1 973	13 439	7 835	...	947	6 888	...	1997	
0	...	2 128	14 042	8 355	...	934	7 421	...	1998	
0	12	665	72	8 516	321	1 833	6 330	32	1995	Bangladesh
0	14	775	74	8 897	179	2 097	6 557	64	1996	
0	9	622	75	9 222	323	2 393	6 444	62	1997	
0	7	221	77	9 664	86	2 511	6 992	74	1998	
...	...	...	45	83	20	35	...	28	1995	Bhoutan
...	...	...	55	104	25	43	...	36	1996	
...	...	...	65	127	50	41	...	36	1997	
...	...	...	65	131	48	44	...	39	1998	
...	...	− 349	7 845	2 306	...	978	1 329	...	1995	Brunéi Darussalam
...	...	− 338	7 711	2 321	...	949	1 372	...	1996	
...	...	− 288	7 798	2 402	...	977	1 424	...	1997	
...	...	− 272	7 582	2 388	...	906	1 482	...	1998	
...	...	0	17	173	...	166	...	6	1995	Cambodge
...	...	0	17	173	...	166	...	7	1996	
...	...	0	17	177	...	170	...	7	1997	
...	...	0	17	177	...	170	...	7	1998	

64

Production, trade and consumption of commercial energy
Thousand metric tons of oil equivalent and kilograms per capita [*cont.*]
Production, commerce et consommation d'énergie commerciale
Milliers de tonnes d'équivalent pétrole et kilogrammes par habitant [*suite*]

Region, country or area	Year	Primary energy production – Production d'énergie primaire					Changes in stocks Variations des stocks	Imports Importations	Exports Exportatic
		Total Totale	Solids Solides	Liquids Liquides	Gas Gaz	Electricity Electricité			
China ††	1995	868 198	679 685	150 194	18 581	19 739	5 025	35 525	44
	1996	895 837	697 802	157 491	20 824	19 720	− 4 499	43 578	46
	1997	890 748	685 724	160 902	23 504	20 618	10 429	63 451	51
	1998	831 205	624 375	161 161	24 101	21 568	− 6 938	54 879	48
China, Hong Kong SAR †	1995	...	...	...	...	...	− 382	21 742	8
	1996	...	...	...	...	...	− 5	23 138	8
	1997	...	...	...	...	...	177	25 326	10
	1998	...	...	...	...	...	75	26 309	8
China, Macao SAR †	1995	...	...	...	...	...	0	419	
	1996	...	...	...	...	...	2	480	
	1997	...	...	...	...	...	− 11	489	
	1998	...	...	...	...	...	10	561	
Cyprus	1995	...	...	...	...	...	174	2 056	
	1996	...	...	...	...	...	56	1 993	
	1997	...	...	...	...	...	− 8	1 999	
	1998	...	...	...	...	...	− 12	2 122	
Georgia	1995	538	25	47	9	457	0	984	
	1996	661	13	128	3	517	43	1 631	
	1997	657	3	134	0	520	63	1 858	
	1998	675	8	119	0	548	25	2 020	
India	1995	219 945	159 140	35 269	17 167	8 369	− 1 069	51 748	
	1996	240 182	170 750	36 653	24 404	8 374	− 1 026	60 943	
	1997	241 342	177 148	37 598	17 489	9 107	471	64 469	
	1998	249 632	178 145	37 343	23 811	10 334	985	70 725	1
Indonesia	1995	191 006	29 062	100 702	58 402	2 839	2 243	15 095	95
	1996	209 678	33 137	102 380	71 291	2 870	− 981	18 136	101
	1997	214 097	36 452	103 414	71 294	2 937	− 1 134	20 910	108
	1998	210 760	42 225	94 880	70 198	3 457	6 648	18 042	110
Iran (Islamic Rep. of)	1995	224 313	797	186 893	35 998	626	266	2 956	131
	1996	227 049	848	187 891	37 676	634	2 048	2 423	131
	1997	232 172	717	184 640	46 221	594	10 400	2 467	119
	1998	234 463	818	186 412	46 629	603	11 547	3 286	117 6
Iraq	1995	31 735	...	28 729	2 957	49	0	0	4 1
	1996	33 189	...	30 118	3 022	49	0	0	5 6
	1997	61 201	...	58 306	2 844	50	− 3 199	0	36 4
	1998	108 723	...	105 922	2 751	50	3 439	0	76 8
Israel	1995	131	103	7	18	2	− 103	18 130	1 8
	1996	110	93	4	12	2	− 805	16 971	1 8
	1997	118	104	0	12	2	251	19 764	2 4
	1998	111	98	0	11	2	− 254	21 019	2 8
Japan	1995	93 115	3 637	718	2 166	86 593	295	392 250	9 5
	1996	96 374	3 764	697	2 186	89 727	3 336	401 794	8 5
	1997	100 589	2 486	700	2 234	95 168	3 594	405 345	9 3
	1998	103 646	2 132	655	2 256	98 602	− 4 605	387 797	7 4
Jordan	1995	245	...	2	241	2	− 40	4 071	
	1996	239	...	2	235	2	72	4 450	
	1997	251	...	2	248	1	− 66	4 383	
	1998	254	...	2	251	1	175	4 719	
Kazakhstan	1995	63 444	36 642	20 755	5 330	716	...	11 880	22 4
	1996	64 362	33 761	24 092	5 878	630	...	7 271	27 2
	1997	66 009	32 009	26 130	7 311	559	...	6 769	29 10
	1998	64 818	30 804	26 325	7 161	528	...	7 019	32 1
Korea, Dem. People's Republic of	1995	62 598	60 620	...	...	1 978	...	5 528	28
	1996	61 925	59 990	...	...	1 935	...	5 441	2
	1997	57 714	55 911	...	...	1 803	...	5 071	2
	1998	54 828	53 115	...	...	1 713	...	4 818	2
Korea, Republic of	1995	20 539	2 573	...	...	17 966	2 142	141 169	14 16
	1996	21 969	2 227	...	...	19 741	1 985	158 552	17 70
	1997	22 614	2 030	...	...	20 584	2 331	179 829	26 36
	1998	25 895	1 962	...	...	23 933	1 245	167 414	33 86
Kuwait [1]	1995	115 086	...	106 433	8 652	...	0	1	89 10
	1996	114 874	...	106 199	8 675	...	0	1	88 37
	1997	115 041	...	106 396	8 645	...	0	1	87 92
	1998	118 029	...	109 178	8 851	...	0	1	89 33

Air Aviation	Sea Maritime	Unallocated Nondistribué	Per capita Par habitant	Total Totale	Solids Solides	Liquids Liquides	Gas Gaz	Electricity Electricité	Année	Région, pays ou zone
...	1 057	30 255	686	823 131	657 835	127 465	18 555	19 276	1995	Chine ††
...	983	37 899	709	858 455	683 981	135 884	19 179	19 411	1996	
...	990	45 659	692	845 643	658 145	146 556	20 936	20 006	1997	
...	2 067	45 236	635	797 460	605 843	149 332	20 972	21 314	1998	
783	2 319	...	1 426	8 877	4 874	3 456	26	521	1995	Chine, Hong Kong RAS †
359	2 389	...	1 426	9 074	3 623	3 183	1 645	623	1996	
991	2 159	...	1 487	9 680	3 055	3 427	2 568	629	1997	
708	2 891	...	1 807	12 037	3 800	5 213	2 409	615	1998	
...	...	...	973	419	0	403	...	15	1995	Chine, Macao RAS †
...	...		1 086	478	0	463	...	15	1996	
...	...		1 110	500	0	485	...	15	1997	
...	...		1 200	551	0	536	...	15	1998	
268	69	26	2 041	1 519	14	1 505	...	...	1995	Chypre
257	90	20	2 082	1 570	12	1 558	...	...	1996	
253	98	25	2 134	1 628	13	1 615	...	...	1997	
266	98	26	2 263	1 745	18	1 726	...	...	1998	
...	...	8	286	1 499	42	124	820	514	1995	Géorgie
...	...	4	408	2 115	42	844	705	524	1996	
...	...	8	443	2 267	8	872	851	536	1997	
...	...	18	494	2 501	17	1 179	765	540	1998	
666	0	20 036	270	251 996	165 947	60 381	17 167	8 500	1995	Inde
671	0	20 237	295	280 652	178 512	69 234	24 404	8 503	1996	
676	0	19 217	295	284 559	186 954	70 880	17 489	9 236	1997	
681	0	21 578	301	295 882	188 390	73 218	23 811	10 463	1998	
516	159	30 097	393	77 597	13 523	36 686	24 549	2 839	1995	Indonésie
619	168	31 591	473	94 772	11 088	40 018	40 796	2 870	1996	
645	178	32 014	466	94 701	7 299	44 659	39 806	2 937	1997	
722	184	30 584	388	80 161	9 886	42 805	24 013	3 457	1998	
5	846	8 843	1 370	85 355	1 082	47 650	35 998	626	1995	Iran (Rép. islamique d')
5	552	8 544	1 372	87 055	1 071	47 674	37 676	634	1996	
5	433	7 396	1 495	96 605	955	48 463	46 593	594	1997	
5	694	7 775	1 522	100 115	1 077	50 054	48 381	603	1998	
0	0	2 277	1 258	25 283	...	22 278	2 957	49	1995	Iraq
0	0	2 828	1 199	24 712	...	21 642	3 022	49	1996	
0	0	3 140	1 169	24 765	...	21 871	2 844	50	1997	
0	0	3 264	1 157	25 214	...	22 412	2 751	50	1998	
4	207	1 012	2 742	15 259	5 010	10 308	18	- 76	1995	Israël
4	93	887	2 628	15 038	5 559	9 550	12	- 82	1996	
4	180	1 254	2 685	15 732	6 152	9 666	12	- 98	1997	
4	153	1 420	2 829	16 931	6 597	10 411	11	- 89	1998	
5 567	6 231	16 507	3 564	447 194	87 496	215 253	57 852	86 593	1995	Japon
5 909	4 335	17 194	3 649	458 885	89 993	216 822	62 343	89 727	1996	
5 287	5 186	20 879	3 655	460 612	92 553	209 231	63 659	95 168	1997	
5 159	5 647	14 775	3 659	462 010	90 716	206 442	66 249	98 602	1998	
250	2	83	701	4 021	...	3 778	241	2	1995	Jordanie
303	1	89	711	4 221	...	3 985	235	2	1996	
280	2	62	711	4 357	...	4 108	248	1	1997	
226	1	80	712	4 490	...	4 238	251	1	1998	
354	...	2 078	3 059	50 491	28 433	9 489	11 217	1 352	1995	Kazakhstan
343	...	1 192	2 609	42 880	25 355	7 608	8 719	1 197	1996	
220	...	4 900	2 355	38 557	21 754	8 014	7 826	963	1997	
249	...	2 144	2 283	37 249	21 242	7 318	7 833	856	1998	
...	...	- 673	3 081	68 510	62 123	4 409	...	1 978	1995	Corée, Rép. populaire démocratique de
...	...	- 697	2 998	67 785	61 483	4 367	...	1 935	1996	
...	...	- 649	2 749	63 175	57 302	4 069	...	1 803	1997	
...	...	- 617	2 571	60 016	54 437	3 866	...	1 713	1998	
686	4 726	10 397	2 883	129 590	30 397	72 009	9 218	17 966	1995	Corée, République de
756	5 386	13 787	3 107	140 906	32 920	76 293	11 952	19 741	1996	
760	5 983	19 665	3 222	147 337	34 760	77 425	14 567	20 584	1997	
516	6 230	20 113	2 848	131 341	35 959	57 811	13 637	23 933	1998	
186	586	6 950	10 803	18 257	...	9 605	8 652	...	1995	Koweït [l]
103	554	6 379	11 542	19 461	...	10 786	8 675	...	1996	
181	662	5 717	11 869	20 558	...	11 913	8 645	...	1997	
196	621	5 066	12 595	22 809	...	13 958	8 851	...	1998	

64

Production, trade and consumption of commercial energy
Thousand metric tons of oil equivalent and kilograms per capita [*cont.*]
Production, commerce et consommation d'énergie commerciale
Milliers de tonnes d'équivalent pétrole et kilogrammes par habitant [*suite*]

Region, country or area	Year	Primary energy production – Production d'énergie primaire					Changes in stocks	Imports	Exports
		Total Totale	Solids Solides	Liquids Liquides	Gas Gaz	Electricity Electricité	Variations des stocks	Imports Importations	Exports Exportatio
Kyrgystan	1995	1 360	281	89	34	956	− 4	2 147	
	1996	1 416	238	100	24	1 054	...	2 506	
	1997	1 360	298	85	37	940	...	2 138	
	1998	1 202	253	77	17	855	...	2 377	
Lao People's Dem. Rep.	1995	87	1	...	...	86	...	107	
	1996	104	1	...	...	104	...	115	
	1997	102	1	...	...	101	...	120	
	1998	102	1	...	...	102	...	127	
Lebanon	1995	63	...	...	...	63	...	4 091	
	1996	69	...	...	...	69	...	4 171	
	1997	63	...	...	...	63	...	4 757	
	1998	68	...	...	...	68	...	4 957	
Malaysia	1995	68 837	78	35 538	32 690	530	95	10 135	35
	1996	68 732	58	35 341	32 891	442	573	11 544	36
	1997	72 558	70	34 811	37 213	464	700	13 047	38
	1998	72 167	246	35 722	35 788	411	877	11 501	39
Maldives	1995	...	...	...	...	...	...	144	
	1996	...	...	...	...	...	...	114	
	1997	...	...	...	...	...	...	173	
	1998	...	...	...	...	...	...	115	
Mongolia	1995	1 730	1 730	...	...	...	...	489	
	1996	1 828	1 828	...	...	...	...	437	
	1997	1 687	1 687	...	...	...	...	479	
	1998	1 632	1 632	...	...	...	...	467	
Myanmar	1995	2 009	31	483	1 356	140	− 159	666	
	1996	2 045	28	408	1 470	140	− 244	687	
	1997	2 168	28	402	1 588	150	− 297	941	
	1998	2 031	29	390	1 531	82	13	1 229	
Nepal	1995	82	4	...	...	78	− 26	589	
	1996	103	4	...	...	99	− 7	727	
	1997	106	6	...	...	100	− 4	837	
	1998	101	11	...	...	90	0	916	
Oman	1995	46 421	...	42 385	4 036	...	− 372	137	39 8
	1996	48 312	...	44 091	4 221	...	41	65	41 4
	1997	50 010	...	45 004	5 006	...	182	275	43 0
	1998	50 281	...	44 659	5 622	...	− 66	61	42 7
Pakistan	1995	20 311	1 439	2 765	14 008	2 099	...	13 376	3
	1996	21 687	1 720	2 959	14 885	2 122	...	15 117	2
	1997	22 123	1 680	2 980	15 579	1 884	...	14 796	4
	1998	21 965	1 494	2 889	15 587	1 995	...	15 757	2
Philippines	1995	6 436	624	135	...	5 677	652	20 041	3
	1996	6 661	524	47	...	6 090	1 395	21 916	6.
	1997	6 970	511	42	...	6 417	44	23 681	5
	1998	7 077	473	41	...	6 563	− 1	22 898	1
Qatar	1995	33 593	...	21 003	12 590	...	0	0	19 1.
	1996	34 073	...	21 296	12 776	...	− 1 783	0	20 9
	1997	45 104	...	28 878	16 227	...	731	0	25 0
	1998	50 060	...	31 800	18 260	...	− 1 769	0	30 4(
Saudi Arabia [1]	1995	467 085	...	431 610	35 475	...	65	0	365 09
	1996	471 435	...	432 882	38 553	...	− 1	0	358 87
	1997	485 275	...	442 992	42 283	...	33	0	368 73
	1998	500 685	...	457 022	43 663	...	94	0	380 95
Singapore	1995	...	...	...	...	...	− 4 800	76 439	41 56
	1996	...	...	...	...	...	− 4 575	83 779	43 0(
	1997	...	...	...	...	...	− 5 036	85 583	41 27
	1998	...	...	...	...	...	− 9 783	83 849	42 03
Sri Lanka	1995	388	...	...	...	388	− 13	2 489	9
	1996	280	...	...	...	280	− 14	2 902	7
	1997	296	...	...	...	296	28	3 023	7
	1998	337	...	...	...	337	15	3 084	2
Syrian Arab Republic	1995	33 354	...	30 987	2 151	216	− 444	468	19 77
	1996	33 146	...	30 489	2 438	219	327	616	18 97
	1997	32 145	...	28 575	3 346	224	− 1 485	800	19 14
	1998	33 089	...	28 077	4 780	232	− 1 926	780	18 46

	Bunkers – Soutes			Consumption – Consommation						
Air Aviation	Sea Maritime	Unallocated Nondistribué	Per capita Par habitant	Total Totale	Solids Solides	Liquids Liquides	Gas Gaz	Electricity Electricité	Année	Région, pays ou zone
...	...	71	573	2 620	426	532	823	839	1995	Kirghizistan
...	...	91	648	2 977	563	557	982	875	1996	
...	...	110	572	2 644	932	356	569	787	1997	
...	...	139	606	2 815	586	488	949	793	1998	
...	...	...	28	133	1	104	...	29	1995	Rép. démocratique
...	...	...	31	152	1	111	...	41	1996	populaire lao
...	...	...	31	156	1	116	...	39	1997	
...	...	...	32	163	1	123	...	39	1998	
169	0	...	1 324	3 985	133	3 785	...	67	1995	Liban
175	0	...	1 318	4 065	157	3 813	...	95	1996	
181	0	...	1 476	4 639	160	4 390	...	89	1997	
186	0	...	1 516	4 839	86	4 659	...	93	1998	
0	248	2 263	2 032	40 856	1 670	18 248	20 409	528	1995	Malaisie
0	162	3 286	1 919	39 443	2 041	19 348	17 612	441	1996	
0	156	3 319	2 041	42 829	1 928	20 753	19 688	461	1997	
0	405	3 899	1 817	38 897	1 852	18 798	17 837	411	1998	
...	...	...	380	95	...	95	...	...	1995	Maldives
...	...	...	386	99	...	99	...	...	1996	
...	...	...	468	123	...	123	...	...	1997	
...	...	...	402	109	...	109	...	...	1998	
...	...	...	876	2 148	1 772	343	...	33	1995	Mongolie
...	...	...	878	2 189	1 770	387	...	33	1996	
...	...	...	825	2 093	1 687	379	...	26	1997	
...	...	...	812	2 093	1 658	409	...	26	1998	
6	2	90	64	2 735	33	1 207	1 356	140	1995	Myanmar
12	5	67	67	2 893	32	1 251	1 470	140	1996	
17	4	132	74	3 253	33	1 481	1 588	150	1997	
13	2	132	71	3 100	33	1 454	1 531	82	1998	
...	...	...	32	686	90	512	...	84	1995	Népal
...	...	...	38	826	196	532	...	98	1996	
...	...	...	42	939	214	622	...	103	1997	
...	...	...	44	1 012	237	672	...	102	1998	
160	417	275	2 909	6 270	...	2 234	4 036	...	1995	Oman
131	454	− 139	2 870	6 400	...	2 179	4 221	...	1996	
36	396	− 304	3 017	6 954	...	1 948	5 006	...	1997	
25	150	97	3 119	7 429	...	1 807	5 622	...	1998	
138	15	854	238	32 372	2 198	14 067	14 008	2 099	1995	Pakistan
129	12	907	253	35 467	2 469	15 992	14 885	2 122	1996	
135	18	716	247	35 578	2 262	15 853	15 579	1 884	1997	
138	15	713	247	36 628	2 159	16 888	15 587	1 995	1998	
439	108	2 289	331	22 647	1 938	15 032	...	5 677	1995	Philippines
527	162	1 469	349	24 399	2 793	15 516	...	6 090	1996	
628	128	2 957	368	26 305	3 560	16 328	...	6 417	1997	
448	173	1 927	374	27 259	3 592	17 104	...	6 563	1998	
140	...	55	25 990	14 242	...	1 653	12 590	...	1995	Qatar
180	...	158	26 072	14 548	...	1 772	12 776	...	1996	
203	...	825	32 071	18 249	...	2 022	16 227	...	1997	
185	...	857	35 200	20 381	...	2 121	18 260	...	1998	
290	7 484	8 400	4 643	84 747	...	49 272	35 475	...	1995	Arabie saoudite [1]
393	8 009	9 932	4 951	93 229	...	54 677	38 553	...	1996	
264	7 932	12 131	4 886	95 182	...	52 899	42 283	...	1997	
238	6 994	12 779	4 887	98 628	...	54 965	43 663	...	1998	
903	11 346	7 050	6 137	20 380	23	20 358	...	...	1995	Singapour
187	14 199	7 227	6 737	22 738	0	22 737	...	...	1996	
027	16 115	7 441	7 225	24 760	0	24 760	...	...	1997	
032	17 120	8 065	7 301	25 378	0	25 378	...	...	1998	
79	336	165	124	2 214	1	1 825	...	388	1995	Sri Lanka
101	379	127	139	2 511	1	2 230	...	280	1996	
104	273	103	150	2 732	2	2 434	...	296	1997	
90	257	138	157	2 901	25	2 540	...	337	1998	
102	...	1 555	904	12 832	4	10 461	2 151	216	1995	Rép. arabe syrienne
98	...	748	935	13 617	3	10 957	2 438	219	1996	
108	...	954	951	14 222	3	10 650	3 346	224	1997	
108	...	831	1 069	16 388	0	11 376	4 780	232	1998	

64

Production, trade and consumption of commercial energy
Thousand metric tons of oil equivalent and kilograms per capita [*cont.*]
Production, commerce et consommation d'énergie commerciale
Milliers de tonnes d'équivalent pétrole et kilogrammes par habitant [*suite*]

Region, country or area	Year	Primary energy production – Production d'énergie primaire					Changes in stocks Variations des stocks	Imports Importations	Exports Exportatic
		Total Totale	Solids Solides	Liquids Liquides	Gas Gaz	Electricity Electricité			
Tajikistan	1995	1 322	7	24	35	1 255	...	2 363	
	1996	1 241	5	20	45	1 171	...	2 553	
	1997	1 244	5	25	35	1 179	...	2 254	
	1998	1 268	5	19	27	1 217	...	2 244	
Thailand	1995	21 835	8 105	3 683	9 469	578	− 639	33 656	1
	1996	25 043	9 449	4 223	10 740	632	1 199	41 632	4
	1997	29 368	10 291	5 060	13 398	620	228	41 307	5
	1998	28 478	8 870	5 266	13 896	446	− 1 057	36 430	5
Turkey	1995	18 839	12 022	3 520	167	3 130	1 137	38 609	1
	1996	19 601	12 356	3 504	189	3 553	565	42 916	1
	1997	20 287	13 107	3 452	232	3 496	− 427	44 563	1
	1998	21 938	14 490	3 226	517	3 705	− 132	45 794	1
Turkmenistan	1995	35 836	...	3 504	32 332	0	...	629	21
	1996	35 729	...	4 029	31 700	0	...	330	23
	1997	20 759	...	5 154	15 604	0	...	640	8
	1998	18 327	...	6 381	11 945	0	...	649	7
United Arab Emirates	1995	142 033	...	112 824	29 208	...	239	102	109
	1996	145 311	...	113 789	31 521	...	453	102	110
	1997	149 775	...	115 913	33 862	...	198	102	112
	1998	154 109	...	119 538	34 571	...	− 48	102	116
Uzbekistan	1995	51 441	837	7 668	42 404	532	2 232	2 763	6
	1996	51 688	779	7 729	42 619	561	135	5 060	9
	1997	53 499	806	8 020	44 176	497	− 481	3 609	10
	1998	54 491	801	8 330	44 865	495	0	4 963	8
Viet Nam	1995	14 908	5 845	7 628	5	1 430	541	4 927	9
	1996	17 261	6 876	8 812	7	1 566	490	5 833	11
	1997	19 628	7 972	10 100	11	1 546	1 644	6 142	12
	1998	22 199	8 170	12 513	12	1 504	2 013	6 982	14
Yemen	1995	17 516	...	17 516	...	...	− 502	190	14
	1996	17 747	...	17 747	...	...	− 500	200	14
	1997	18 582	...	18 582	...	...	− 691	153	14
	1998	19 032	...	19 032	...	...	− 691	127	15
Europe	**1995**	**2 201 597**	**444 526**	**621 597**	**788 902**	**346 572**	**7 279**	**1 258 192**	**870**
	1996	**2 253 196**	**428 408**	**633 610**	**831 033**	**360 146**	**− 5 036**	**1 315 486**	**925**
	1997	**2 217 410**	**416 225**	**637 164**	**799 276**	**364 745**	**− 77**	**1 317 037**	**941**
	1998	**2 191 875**	**382 325**	**631 183**	**814 261**	**364 107**	**3 687**	**1 347 825**	**954**
Albania	1995	950	41	522	26	362	0	95	
	1996	1 025	26	488	21	489	0	126	
	1997	865	19	366	17	464	0	133	
	1998	827	14	368	16	429	0	202	
Austria	1995	6 089	338	1 083	1 359	3 309	− 90	19 907	1
	1996	5 708	288	992	1 368	3 060	127	21 443	1
	1997	5 808	294	999	1 308	3 207	− 510	21 499	2
	1998	6 051	297	986	1 438	3 330	204	22 489	2
Belarus	1995	2 896	714	1 934	246	2	348	25 954	3
	1996	2 742	649	1 862	230	1	− 1 425	25 698	3
	1997	2 683	630	1 824	227	2	453	27 137	3
	1998	2 769	682	1 832	252	2	− 110	26 911	3
Belgium	1995	11 284	384	...	0	10 900	733	63 255	17
	1996	11 753	337	...	2	11 414	248	69 136	20
	1997	12 741	257	...	0	12 484	65	69 413	20
	1998	12 367	188	...	0	12 179	746	72 697	23
Bosnia & Herzegovina	1995	633	511	...	...	122	0	817	
	1996	653	527	...	...	126	11	841	
	1997	672	543	...	...	130	22	867	
	1998	693	559	...	...	134	0	893	
Bulgaria	1995	9 928	5 142	43	40	4 704	208	15 468	2
	1996	9 728	4 689	32	37	4 970	480	15 187	1
	1997	9 416	4 472	28	31	4 886	− 17	12 678	1
	1998	9 725	4 970	33	26	4 697	64	11 795	1
Croatia	1995	4 358	54	2 065	1 786	453	− 56	5 288	1
	1996	4 201	45	1 913	1 622	622	145	5 681	1
	1997	4 026	34	1 977	1 560	456	− 19	5 584	1
	1998	3 920	36	1 989	1 426	470	− 61	5 842	1

...ers – Soutes			Consumption – Consommation							
Air ...ion	Sea Maritime	Unallocated Nondistribué	Per capita Par habitant	Total Totale	Solids Solides	Liquids Liquides	Gas Gaz	Electricity Electricité	Année	Région, pays ou zone
...	...	24	574	3 300	7	1 167	813	1 312	1995	Tadjikistan
...	...	20	575	3 353	50	1 167	1 044	1 092	1996	
...	...	25	525	3 108	53	1 167	700	1 188	1997	
...	...	14	528	3 173	52	1 167	716	1 238	1998	
0	0	2 689	893	52 313	9 667	32 545	9 469	631	1995	Thaïlande
0	0	3 135	981	58 060	11 725	34 901	10 740	694	1996	
0	0	3 945	1 018	60 831	12 018	34 739	13 398	675	1997	
0	0	5 195	924	55 723	10 082	31 154	13 915	573	1998	
264	187	2 786	841	51 535	16 446	25 584	6 434	3 071	1995	Turquie
328	126	3 229	915	57 019	18 983	26 722	7 768	3 547	1996	
448	160	3 731	945	59 935	21 082	25 893	9 274	3 687	1997	
498	161	4 400	948	61 110	22 498	24 702	9 946	3 963	1998	
...	...	443	3 541	14 438	0	2 151	12 461	− 173	1995	Turkménistan
...	...	657	2 944	12 237	70	2 332	10 075	− 240	1996	
...	...	321	2 889	12 228	0	2 243	10 283	− 297	1997	
...	...	960	2 507	10 802	0	1 845	9 224	− 267	1998	
258	229	1 892	13 622	30 106	...	6 987	23 119	...	1995	Emirats arabes unis
310	214	1 882	14 265	32 240	...	7 004	25 236	...	1996	
464	207	1 735	14 924	34 430	...	7 385	27 045	...	1997	
392	91	2 069	15 028	35 362	...	7 058	28 304	...	1998	
...	...	1 660	1 942	43 646	832	5 989	36 405	421	1995	Ouzbékistan
...	...	1 584	1 980	45 246	932	5 923	37 736	655	1996	
...	...	1 661	1 954	45 358	767	6 158	37 856	577	1997	
...	...	1 667	2 093	49 342	800	5 937	42 032	573	1998	
...	...	1	131	9 658	3 311	4 912	5	1 430	1995	Viet Nam
...	...	1	151	11 336	3 891	5 872	7	1 566	1996	
...	...	1	158	12 060	4 322	6 181	11	1 546	1997	
...	...	1	165	12 795	4 313	6 966	12	1 504	1998	
53	100	247	223	3 345	...	3 345	...	...	1995	Yémen
63	100	524	227	3 560	...	3 560	...	...	1996	
63	100	121	271	4 422	...	4 422	...	...	1997	
63	100	92	263	4 435	...	4 435	...	...	1998	
997	37 908	54 679	3 380	2 460 350	543 353	756 459	814 546	345 992	1995	**Europe**
929	40 686	54 873	3 464	2 523 102	538 372	753 641	871 260	359 830	1996	
512	44 508	52 537	3 382	2 464 421	505 846	746 261	848 080	364 234	1997	
488	46 584	52 129	3 363	2 449 159	484 081	747 530	854 007	363 541	1998	
...	...	167	274	871	41	449	26	355	1995	Albanie
...	...	149	318	1 001	26	448	21	506	1996	
...	...	59	300	940	19	424	17	481	1997	
...	...	55	292	915	14	424	16	461	1998	
231	...	500	2 963	23 711	3 305	10 315	6 994	3 097	1995	Autriche
256	...	327	3 073	24 749	3 401	10 706	7 500	3 142	1996	
265	...	429	3 092	25 042	3 685	10 989	7 227	3 141	1997	
279	...	715	3 075	25 032	3 226	11 053	7 437	3 316	1998	
...	...	1 539	2 305	23 949	1 371	9 185	12 775	617	1995	Bélarus
...	...	1 834	2 346	24 349	1 308	8 828	13 478	736	1996	
...	...	1 364	2 400	24 846	1 076	7 793	15 320	657	1997	
...	...	1 139	2 396	24 713	1 075	7 317	15 400	920	1998	
884	3 984	2 398	4 869	49 121	9 302	16 771	11 798	11 250	1995	Belgique
998	4 591	2 726	5 128	51 835	8 785	18 139	13 137	11 774	1996	
281	5 197	3 226	5 113	51 778	8 604	17 884	12 524	12 765	1997	
512	5 563	1 158	5 199	52 722	8 667	17 888	13 869	12 299	1998	
...	...	...	420	1 434	511	541	242	140	1995	Bosnie–Herzégovine
...	...	...	429	1 467	527	547	249	144	1996	
...	...	...	426	1 501	543	553	257	148	1997	
...	...	...	427	1 569	559	592	265	153	1998	
...	274	1 307	2 540	21 589	7 216	5 097	4 585	4 690	1995	Bulgarie
...	238	1 098	2 519	21 282	6 795	4 354	5 200	4 932	1996	
...	9	898	2 300	19 306	7 082	3 530	4 113	4 580	1997	
...	71	929	2 256	18 803	7 187	3 752	3 480	4 383	1998	
59	33	1 098	1 469	6 601	185	3 426	2 151	839	1995	Croatie
56	37	1 084	1 521	6 824	150	3 442	2 410	822	1996	
59	24	989	1 595	7 150	265	3 591	2 498	795	1997	
63	26	931	1 630	7 302	255	3 887	2 401	759	1998	

64
Production, trade and consumption of commercial energy
Thousand metric tons of oil equivalent and kilograms per capita [*cont.*]
Production, commerce et consommation d'énergie commerciale
Milliers de tonnes d'équivalent pétrole et kilogrammes par habitant [*suite*]

Region, country or area	Year	Primary energy production – Production d'énergie primaire					Changes in stocks	Imports	Exports
		Total Totale	Solids Solides	Liquids Liquides	Gas Gaz	Electricity Electricité	Variations des stocks	Imports Importations	Exports Exportati
Czech Republic	1995	31 135	27 381	146	220	3 388	− 247	18 138	
	1996	31 444	27 529	152	202	3 561	636	20 107	
	1997	30 372	26 587	163	182	3 440	572	19 556	
	1998	28 779	24 809	179	188	3 602	222	19 619	
Denmark	1995	14 208	13	9 182	4 891	122	1 240	17 671	1
	1996	18 875	38	10 144	8 566	128	− 1 058	17 674	1
	1997	19 760	14	11 382	8 170	195	1 424	17 377	1
	1998	18 337	0	11 454	6 613	270	− 445	15 036	1
Estonia	1995	3 133	3 133	...	...	0	− 106	2 454	
	1996	3 481	3 481	...	...	0	− 84	2 288	
	1997	3 372	3 372	...	...	0	− 111	2 628	
	1998	2 846	2 845	...	...	0	− 55	2 602	
Faeroe Islands	1995	7	0	...	...	7	...	205	
	1996	7	0	...	...	7	...	210	
	1997	7	0	...	...	7	...	211	
	1998	7	0	...	...	7	...	213	
Finland	1995	8 160	2 032	...	...	6 128	− 644	19 168	
	1996	8 320	2 216	...	...	6 104	− 1 000	21 685	
	1997	9 134	2 627	...	...	6 508	503	21 642	
	1998	7 424	424	...	...	7 000	− 1 257	21 424	
France [2]	1995	117 972	6 045	3 733	3 105	105 088	201	138 507	1
	1996	121 191	5 360	3 307	2 676	109 848	− 1 831	149 941	2
	1997	119 201	4 501	3 202	2 365	109 134	691	148 029	2
	1998	115 749	3 790	2 860	2 043	107 056	− 1 189	158 928	2
Germany	1995	139 567	78 346	2 929	15 959	42 333	− 2 062	214 367	2
	1996	138 070	73 504	2 877	17 348	44 341	− 3 495	229 562	2
	1997	136 372	70 140	2 807	17 159	46 266	1 530	228 636	2
	1998	127 714	64 016	2 937	16 863	43 898	− 705	232 499	2
Gibraltar	1995	...	...	...	...	...	...	1 184	
	1996	...	...	...	...	...	...	1 739	
	1997	...	...	...	...	...	...	2 196	
	1998	...	...	...	...	...	...	2 207	
Greece	1995	8 371	7 508	459	48	357	161	22 141	3
	1996	8 763	7 783	517	50	412	− 83	23 229	3
	1997	8 620	7 709	468	49	395	274	22 656	2
	1998	8 712	7 976	317	44	375	937	24 259	2
Hungary	1995	13 890	2 970	3 038	4 207	3 675	236	14 557	1
	1996	13 705	3 123	2 863	4 000	3 719	757	16 323	1
	1997	13 326	3 214	2 712	3 735	3 664	596	16 014	1
	1998	12 551	3 021	2 579	3 297	3 654	760	16 761	1
Iceland	1995	652	...	...	...	652	2	733	
	1996	711	...	...	...	711	− 28	798	
	1997	770	...	...	...	770	− 12	794	
	1998	1 048	...	...	...	1 048	4	831	
Ireland	1995	4 376	1 785	...	2 499	92	786	8 644	
	1996	3 765	1 261	...	2 410	93	154	9 374	
	1997	2 949	740	...	2 119	90	− 57	10 896	1
	1998	2 489	813	...	1 564	112	15	12 010	1
Italy [3]	1995	30 066	88	5 243	18 175	6 560	305	152 838	16
	1996	31 008	69	5 459	18 194	7 287	1 950	153 701	17
	1997	30 896	24	5 956	17 544	7 372	− 996	156 263	19
	1998	30 429	44	5 629	17 309	7 447	− 379	163 808	21
Latvia	1995	331	79	...	...	253	− 10	3 571	
	1996	249	89	...	...	160	243	3 856	
	1997	343	89	...	...	254	− 105	3 030	
	1998	385	13	...	...	371	67	3 126	
Lithuania	1995	3 292	14	128	...	3 150	337	8 071	2
	1996	3 887	18	155	...	3 714	82	8 291	3
	1997	3 437	20	212	...	3 204	25	8 697	3
	1998	3 906	14	277	...	3 615	− 155	9 507	4
Luxembourg	1995	72	...	...	...	72	− 32	3 370	
	1996	75	...	...	...	75	16	3 508	
	1997	81	...	...	...	81	− 8	3 434	
	1998	90	...	...	...	90	36	3 508	

Air ion	Sea Maritime	Unallocated Nondistribué	Per capita Par habitant	Total Totale	Solids Solides	Liquids Liquides	Gas Gaz	Electricity Electricité	Année	Région, pays ou zone
186	...	1 585	3 781	39 041	22 260	6 073	7 284	3 424	1995	République tchèque
133	...	1 673	3 937	40 617	22 366	6 308	8 384	3 560	1996	
125	...	1 290	3 885	40 016	22 001	6 151	8 526	3 338	1997	
118	...	1 299	3 778	38 844	20 412	6 496	8 545	3 391	1998	
545	1 627	− 103	3 349	17 499	6 453	7 801	3 191	54	1995	Danemark
709	1 518	− 121	4 237	22 204	8 879	8 149	6 372	− 1 196	1996	
597	1 507	− 122	3 493	18 357	6 583	7 476	4 727	− 429	1997	
712	1 400	− 18	3 172	16 718	5 500	7 531	3 789	− 103	1998	
0	90	− 310	3 564	5 297	3 606	1 173	583	− 65	1995	Estonie
0	93	− 340	3 828	5 612	3 756	1 287	643	− 74	1996	
0	102	− 364	3 788	5 482	3 732	1 209	625	− 84	1997	
0	108	− 218	3 479	4 972	3 217	1 195	593	− 33	1998	
...	...	...	4 713	212	0	205	...	7	1995	Iles Féroé
...	...	...	4 917	216	0	210	...	7	1996	
...	...	...	4 940	217	0	211	...	7	1997	
...	...	...	5 106	220	0	213	...	7	1998	
293	336	− 2 487	5 066	25 879	6 144	9 737	3 270	6 728	1995	Finlande
314	380	− 2 391	5 434	27 856	7 487	10 652	3 299	6 419	1996	
326	413	− 1 330	5 249	26 983	6 821	9 764	3 232	7 166	1997	
334	528	− 1 229	5 043	25 991	4 715	9 767	3 709	7 800	1998	
380	2 547	8 057	3 823	221 800	16 252	71 950	34 516	99 082	1995	France [2]
138	2 749	9 014	4 023	234 369	16 749	74 709	38 981	103 931	1996	
247	2 993	8 849	3 878	226 773	14 773	72 729	35 762	103 510	1997	
528	2 894	6 942	4 015	235 636	17 204	76 309	40 017	102 106	1998	
503	2 056	5 687	3 949	322 477	91 114	115 276	73 338	42 748	1995	Allemagne
371	2 040	5 335	4 107	336 368	90 632	118 941	82 907	43 888	1996	
064	2 166	6 350	3 989	327 326	86 283	116 502	78 478	46 064	1997	
241	2 051	8 424	3 940	322 723	83 845	114 732	80 302	43 843	1998	
4	1 100	...	3 060	80	0	80	...	...	1995	Gibraltar
4	1 654	...	3 116	81	0	81	...	...	1996	
2	2 124	...	2 690	70	0	70	...	...	1997	
3	2 128	...	3 034	76	0	76	...	...	1998	
854	3 598	− 1 610	2 299	24 109	8 387	15 249	48	426	1995	Grèce
818	3 165	− 877	2 390	25 175	8 941	15 652	54	528	1996	
792	3 174	− 1 021	2 393	25 293	8 557	15 955	189	592	1997	
831	3 542	− 1 058	2 492	26 415	8 773	16 323	805	514	1998	
183	...	2 069	2 349	24 022	4 085	6 475	9 582	3 882	1995	Hongrie
194	...	1 676	2 512	25 602	4 191	6 133	11 370	3 908	1996	
185	...	1 708	2 467	25 055	4 062	6 349	10 795	3 849	1997	
193	...	1 922	2 467	24 955	4 007	6 361	10 870	3 718	1998	
67	46	...	4 741	1 271	55	564	...	652	1995	Islande
85	38	...	5 220	1 415	64	639	...	711	1996	
93	47	...	5 246	1 437	56	611	...	770	1997	
110	57	...	6 185	1 707	66	594	...	1 048	1998	
377	114	16	2 996	10 813	3 125	5 005	2 593	91	1995	Irlande
345	160	13	3 168	11 511	3 103	5 378	2 948	82	1996	
414	152	64	3 283	12 010	3 111	5 728	3 082	89	1997	
427	159	− 32	3 472	12 779	3 087	6 457	3 116	119	1998	
429	2 430	− 3 598	2 881	165 210	12 347	93 439	49 646	9 779	1995	Italie [3]
531	2 297	− 1 290	2 816	161 527	11 290	88 516	51 218	10 502	1996	
723	2 391	− 3 337	2 905	166 672	11 229	91 934	52 796	10 712	1997	
889	2 634	596	2 915	167 235	11 225	88 217	56 844	10 950	1998	
...	...	...	1 507	3 824	230	2 025	1 123	447	1995	Latvie
...	...	...	1 494	3 732	221	2 101	973	437	1996	
...	...	...	1 388	3 415	168	1 653	1 184	411	1997	
...	...	...	1 356	3 286	131	1 578	1 160	417	1998	
40	0	52	2 284	8 510	283	3 278	2 030	2 920	1995	Lettonie
33	0	− 311	2 448	9 095	255	3 400	2 170	3 270	1996	
32	55	− 429	2 354	8 723	198	3 620	2 003	2 901	1997	
29	29	− 292	2 413	8 913	168	3 899	1 755	3 092	1998	
190	...	...	7 907	3 218	514	1 583	619	502	1995	Luxembourg
206	...	...	7 976	3 286	485	1 624	679	497	1996	
252	...	...	7 657	3 193	312	1 658	696	527	1997	
284	...	...	7 540	3 182	205	1 718	703	555	1998	

64

Production, trade and consumption of commercial energy
Thousand metric tons of oil equivalent and kilograms per capita [*cont.*]
Production, commerce et consommation d'énergie commerciale
Milliers de tonnes d'équivalent pétrole et kilogrammes par habitant [*suite*]

| Region, country or area | Year | Primary energy production – Production d'énergie primaire | | | | | Changes in stocks Variations des stocks | Imports Importations | Exports Exportatio |
		Total Totale	Solids Solides	Liquids Liquides	Gas Gaz	Electricity Electricité			
Malta	1995	...	...	...	...	...	...	606	
	1996	...	...	...	...	...	...	615	
	1997	...	...	...	...	...	...	616	
	1998	...	...	...	...	...	...	633	
Netherlands	1995	71 675	...	3 542	67 049	1 084	− 1 551	95 359	8(
	1996	80 099	...	3 175	75 794	1 130	204	100 272	8;
	1997	70 930	...	3 000	67 253	677	1 103	105 908	83
	1998	67 747	...	2 738	63 950	1 060	− 442	108 630	8:
Norway [4]	1995	181 722	196	135 635	35 361	10 530	309	5 077	15:
	1996	209 757	154	153 922	46 734	8 946	1 632	5 840	184
	1997	211 536	259	153 692	48 045	9 540	− 43	6 093	19(
	1998	205 087	220	147 125	47 731	10 011	151	6 218	184
Poland	1995	94 588	90 475	292	3 488	332	− 1 187	24 296	2;
	1996	95 566	91 306	317	3 606	337	437	27 527	19
	1997	95 291	91 110	289	3 562	329	4 066	29 773	21
	1998	82 860	78 514	360	3 612	374	− 568	30 556	20
Portugal	1995	765	0	...	...	765	176	20 452	3
	1996	1 322	0	...	...	1 322	− 226	18 280	2
	1997	1 180	0	...	...	1 180	308	19 508	2
	1998	1 180	0	...	...	1 180	− 154	20 779	2
Republic of Moldova	1995	28	...	...	...	28	59	4 695	
	1996	31	...	...	...	31	− 156	4 712	
	1997	33	...	...	...	33	106	4 895	
	1998	7	...	...	...	7	− 112	4 179	
Romania	1995	30 231	7 364	6 976	14 455	1 436	20	19 288	4
	1996	29 897	7 531	6 876	13 773	1 717	− 61	18 742	3
	1997	27 836	6 229	6 776	11 916	2 915	1 094	17 579	2
	1998	25 588	4 844	6 579	11 157	3 009	− 450	14 814	3
Russian Federation	1995	981 646	110 331	305 412	524 655	41 248	13 414	25 084	355
	1996	978 189	107 146	299 797	529 133	42 113	343	22 432	371
	1997	956 124	102 266	304 172	507 641	42 046	− 12 855	23 156	379
	1998	964 936	96 682	301 707	525 736	40 811	2 621	22 555	385
Slovakia	1995	4 906	1 101	74	297	3 434	− 243	14 740	1
	1996	4 793	1 121	71	272	3 329	207	15 665	2
	1997	4 653	1 146	64	250	3 193	31	15 391	2
	1998	4 808	1 157	60	224	3 367	− 224	14 959	2
Slovenia	1995	2 605	1 062	2	16	1 526	− 40	3 345	
	1996	2 555	1 037	1	11	1 507	54	3 735	
	1997	2 664	1 077	1	10	1 576	55	3 872	
	1998	2 684	1 063	1	7	1 613	− 69	3 704	
Spain	1995	27 539	9 536	935	417	16 651	1 450	80 848	6
	1996	28 903	9 353	801	468	18 282	− 605	79 571	5
	1997	27 733	9 293	670	178	17 593	− 1 448	85 008	5
	1998	28 317	8 736	873	114	18 594	1 984	93 861	6
Sweden	1995	24 335	304	4	...	24 027	− 1 478	27 729	11
	1996	24 065	351	4	...	23 710	− 332	30 713	9
	1997	24 463	252	0	...	24 211	428	30 029	10
	1998	25 951	322	0	...	25 630	702	29 656	10
Switzerland [5]	1995	9 590	...	...	0	9 590	− 329	16 242	2
	1996	9 114	...	...	0	9 114	− 16	17 504	2
	1997	9 656	...	...	0	9 656	102	17 524	2.
	1998	9 721	...	...	0	9 721	19	18 208	3(
TFYR of Macedonia	1995	2 026	1 957	...	...	69	107	1 040	
	1996	2 002	1 929	...	...	73	− 6	1 293	
	1997	1 886	1 809	...	...	77	0	1 079	
	1998	2 301	2 208	...	...	93	90	1 201	
Ukraine	1995	84 586	44 230	4 062	16 937	19 358	0	92 081	3.
	1996	81 810	39 012	4 102	17 167	21 529	0	91 833	5;
	1997	82 255	39 613	4 138	16 909	21 595	0	79 033	4 !
	1998	81 381	39 715	3 904	16 756	21 006	0	71 704	4 -
United Kingdom	1995	262 630	32 870	133 089	72 869	23 803	− 4 739	70 321	102 !
	1996	274 914	30 244	132 750	86 746	25 174	− 2 356	72 737	102 (
	1997	275 087	29 218	131 285	88 427	26 156	2 657	73 700	103 (
	1998	280 468	24 956	135 483	93 236	26 794	1 438	74 989	107 ·

			Consumption – Consommation							
Air vion	Sea Maritime	Unallocated Nondistribué	Per capita Par habitant	Total Totale	Solids Solides	Liquids Liquides	Gas Gaz	Electricity Electricité	Année	Région, pays ou zone
52	30	...	1 397	524	179	345	...	...	1995	Malte
52	31	...	1 407	532	185	347	...	...	1996	
52	31	...	1 398	533	185	348	...	...	1997	
54	33	...	1 422	546	191	355	...	...	1998	
532	11 440	– 6 598	5 247	81 114	9 030	32 291	37 730	2 063	1995	Pays – Bas
705	11 646	– 9 118	5 643	87 694	9 239	34 970	41 444	2 041	1996	
930	12 354	– 6 293	5 311	82 919	8 898	33 088	39 170	1 764	1997	
191	12 446	– 7 432	5 317	83 366	8 879	33 663	38 748	2 076	1998	
92	711	– 636	6 142	26 709	1 058	7 903	7 791	9 957	1995	Norvège [4]
57	775	– 23	6 510	28 460	1 005	8 559	9 178	9 718	1996	
131	964	– 757	6 139	26 987	1 029	9 290	6 800	9 868	1997	
129	901	– 571	6 017	26 589	1 046	8 680	6 540	10 323	1998	
372	194	376	2 516	97 130	71 716	15 423	9 901	92	1995	Pologne
382	224	796	2 625	101 491	74 112	16 693	10 616	69	1996	
262	153	521	2 559	99 009	70 946	17 452	10 471	141	1997	
196	790	565	2 374	91 918	64 052	17 213	10 578	75	1998	
506	491	660	1 608	15 852	3 638	11 371	...	843	1995	Portugal
469	507	829	1 593	15 709	3 398	10 894	...	1 417	1996	
482	504	772	1 665	16 426	3 497	11 403	96	1 430	1997	
485	388	1 452	1 798	17 741	3 139	12 622	775	1 204	1998	
...	...	...	1 063	4 653	592	1 026	2 846	189	1995	Rép. de Moldova
...	...	...	1 120	4 899	523	952	3 255	170	1996	
...	...	...	1 101	4 820	263	878	3 478	201	1997	
...	...	...	982	4 298	259	721	3 145	172	1998	
185	...	2 854	1 838	41 769	10 073	10 982	19 253	1 461	1995	Roumanie
10	...	2 778	1 860	42 104	9 892	10 994	19 431	1 786	1996	
124	...	2 260	1 733	39 070	9 144	11 042	15 949	2 934	1997	
105	...	1 791	1 585	35 629	7 323	10 325	14 933	3 049	1998	
...	...	24 448	4 139	612 922	109 916	121 813	341 632	39 562	1995	Fédération de Russie
...	...	21 115	4 112	608 013	112 714	111 629	343 233	40 437	1996	
...	...	20 508	4 012	592 350	102 195	108 176	341 627	40 352	1997	
...	...	18 645	3 942	581 159	96 115	104 823	340 960	39 261	1998	
...	...	1 265	3 113	16 671	5 272	2 199	5 647	3 553	1995	Slovaquie
...	...	1 294	3 155	16 929	4 984	2 137	6 176	3 632	1996	
...	...	1 290	3 072	16 503	4 656	2 039	6 266	3 542	1997	
...	...	1 178	3 048	16 390	4 461	2 085	6 367	3 477	1998	
20	...	22	2 881	5 733	1 248	2 355	746	1 384	1995	Slovénie
18	...	61	2 975	5 935	1 207	2 657	707	1 364	1996	
19	...	66	3 095	6 174	1 283	2 665	795	1 430	1997	
17	...	54	3 000	5 978	1 325	2 389	818	1 447	1998	
2 038	3 237	7 649	2 218	87 753	18 978	43 156	8 581	17 037	1995	Espagne
2 150	4 727	7 967	2 241	88 718	18 339	42 403	9 603	18 373	1996	
2 322	5 830	7 464	2 351	93 142	17 968	45 275	12 570	17 328	1997	
2 450	6 138	6 515	2 480	98 290	17 258	49 238	12 907	18 887	1998	
436	1 084	160	4 617	40 631	2 902	13 093	756	23 880	1995	Suède
431	1 131	1 340	4 784	42 254	3 114	14 093	809	24 238	1996	
446	1 341	1 064	4 556	40 350	2 497	13 076	799	23 978	1997	
451	1 601	1 546	4 641	41 189	2 524	13 163	792	24 710	1998	
1 229	16	– 20	3 106	22 185	193	10 586	2 441	8 965	1995	Suisse [5]
1 287	14	46	3 132	22 542	146	10 721	2 642	9 032	1996	
1 343	13	– 82	3 161	22 917	111	11 180	2 551	9 075	1997	
1 440	11	– 17	3 214	23 462	92	11 535	2 626	9 209	1998	
...	...	7	1 480	2 906	2 069	769		69	1995	L'ex – Rép. yougoslave
...	...	– 23	1 664	3 287	2 011	1 203	...	73	1996	de Macédoine
...	...	12	1 483	2 947	1 879	991	...	77	1997	
...	...	23	1 678	3 354	2 385	876	...	93	1998	
918	...	2 057	3 303	169 856	52 513	22 097	76 142	19 104	1995	Ukraine
771	...	1 104	3 249	166 523	45 155	17 188	82 823	21 356	1996	
658	...	1 041	3 028	154 635	43 512	15 791	73 751	21 582	1997	
684	...	1 050	2 887	146 861	43 710	16 058	66 145	20 949	1998	
4 650	2 469	5 712	3 791	221 863	48 624	74 326	73 707	25 206	1995	Royaume – Uni
4 751	2 670	6 295	3 994	234 277	44 699	76 118	86 852	26 608	1996	
5 091	2 963	5 346	3 899	229 125	39 917	74 400	87 228	27 582	1997	
5 637	3 086	5 165	3 967	232 670	38 350	75 207	91 247	27 866	1998	

64
Production, trade and consumption of commercial energy
Thousand metric tons of oil equivalent and kilograms per capita [*cont.*]
Production, commerce et consommation d'énergie commerciale
Milliers de tonnes d'équivalent pétrole et kilogrammes par habitant [*suite*]

| Region, country or area | Year | Primary energy production – Production d'énergie primaire | | | | | Changes in stocks | Imports | Exports |
		Total Totale	Solids Solides	Liquids Liquides	Gas Gaz	Electricity Electricité	Variations des stocks	Imports Importations	Exports Exportation
Yugoslavia	1995	11 354	8 523	1 067	799	965	...	587	
	1996	10 818	8 193	1 031	605	989	...	3 617	
	1997	11 228	8 668	980	620	961	...	4 501	
	1998	12 024	9 398	914	659	1 054	...	4 014	
Oceania	**1995**	**206 347**	**133 519**	**35 097**	**32 096**	**5 635**	**2 219**	**28 629**	**113**
	1996	**208 933**	**135 798**	**34 105**	**33 432**	**5 597**	**− 783**	**31 814**	**115**
	1997	**218 687**	**145 102**	**34 328**	**33 644**	**5 613**	**1 988**	**32 741**	**122**
	1998	**231 319**	**154 352**	**36 999**	**34 195**	**5 773**	**− 1 737**	**32 609**	**134**
American Samoa	1995	...	...	...	...	...	...	183	
	1996	...	...	...	...	...	...	186	
	1997	...	...	...	...	...	...	186	
	1998	...	...	...	...	...	...	186	
Australia	1995	189 230	131 568	28 471	27 794	1 397	2 410	19 705	106
	1996	191 686	133 798	27 977	28 525	1 385	− 558	22 481	109
	1997	200 690	143 212	27 579	28 415	1 483	2 115	23 263	115
	1998	214 345	152 508	30 846	29 586	1 405	− 1 679	22 676	127
Cook Islands	1995	...	...	...		...	...	15	
	1996	...	...	...		...	...	15	
	1997	...	...	...		...	...	15	
	1998	...	...	...		...	...	15	
Fiji	1995	37	...	...		37	...	408	
	1996	37	...	...		37	...	416	
	1997	37	...	...		37	...	409	
	1998	37	...	...		37	...	377	
French Polynesia	1995	11		...		11	...	230	
	1996	12		...		12	...	230	
	1997	12		...		12	...	230	
	1998	12		...		12	...	230	
Guam	1995	...	...	...		...	...	1 481	
	1996	...	...	...		...	...	1 465	
	1997	...	...	...		...	...	1 465	
	1998	...	...	...		...	...	1 476	
Kiribati	1995	...	...	...		...	...	7	
	1996	...	...	...		...	...	7	
	1997	...	...	...		...	...	7	
	1998	...	...	...		...	...	7	
Nauru	1995	...	...	...		...	...	50	
	1996	...	...	...		...	...	50	
	1997	...	...	...		...	...	50	
	1998	...	...	...		...	...	50	
New Caledonia	1995	36	...	...		36	...	554	
	1996	41	...	...		41	...	567	
	1997	41	...	...		41	...	567	
	1998	41	...	...		41	...	568	
New Zealand	1995	11 904	1 951	1 621	4 225	4 107	− 191	4 594	1 7
	1996	13 028	2 000	2 124	4 829	4 075	− 224	4 990	2 2
	1997	13 817	1 889	2 785	5 151	3 992	− 127	5 132	2 5
	1998	12 856	1 845	2 249	4 531	4 231	− 58	5 633	2 3
Niue	1995	...	...	...	...	...	...	1	
	1996	...	...	...	...	...	...	1	
	1997	...	...	...	...	...	...	1	
	1998	...	...	...	...	...	...	1	
Palau	1995	3	...	...	...	3	...	95	
	1996	3	...	...	...	3	...	98	
	1997	3	...	...	...	3	...	96	
	1998	3	...	...	...	3	...	97	
Papua New Guinea	1995	5 124	...	5 005	76	43	...	724	4 9
	1996	4 124	...	4 004	78	43	...	724	3 9
	1997	4 085	...	3 964	78	43	...	736	3 9
	1998	4 025	...	3 904	78	43	...	709	3 8
Samoa	1995	2	...	...	...	2	...	44	
	1996	2	...	...	...	2	...	44	
	1997	2	...	...	...	2	...	44	
	1998	2	...	...	...	2	...	44	

Air Avion	Sea Maritime	Unallocated Nondistribué	Per capita Par habitant	Total Totale	Solids Solides	Liquids Liquides	Gas Gaz	Electricity Electricité	Année	Région, pays ou zone
43	...	356	1 092	11 541	8 567	1 029	980	965	1995	Yougoslavie
57	...	813	1 279	13 563	8 237	1 840	2 497	989	1996	
98	...	704	1 405	14 927	8 706	2 782	2 480	960	1997	
98	...	904	1 412	15 013	9 436	2 198	2 348	1 031	1998	
2 910	1 481	− 1 009	4 121	115 682	44 699	42 432	22 917	5 635	1995	**Oceanie**
3 084	1 477	− 146	4 265	121 368	48 347	43 831	23 593	5 597	1996	
3 183	1 426	1 849	4 181	120 520	50 227	40 647	24 033	5 613	1997	
3 398	1 317	2 165	4 271	124 645	53 596	40 928	24 350	5 773	1998	
...	91	...	1 608	92	...	92	...	...	1995	Samoa américaines
...	91	...	1 605	95	...	95	...	...	1996	
...	91	...	1 552	95	...	95	...	...	1997	
...	91	...	1 503	95	...	95	...	...	1998	
1 882	855	− 781	5 446	97 731	43 304	34 415	18 616	1 397	1995	Australie
2 029	871	− 18	5 649	102 480	46 846	35 563	18 687	1 385	1996	
2 102	805	1 969	5 512	101 053	48 643	32 123	18 804	1 483	1997	
2 325	708	2 307	5 699	105 544	52 191	32 207	19 741	1 405	1998	
8	...	...	378	7	...	7	...	...	1995	Iles Cook
8	...	...	378	7	...	7	...	...	1996	
8	...	...	378	7	...	7	...	...	1997	
8	...	...	378	7	...	7	...	...	1998	
26	29	...	352	270	14	220	...	37	1995	Fidji
26	29	...	357	277	15	225	...	37	1996	
26	29	...	345	271	15	219	...	37	1997	
21	27	...	329	262	14	211	...	37	1998	
5	38	...	920	198	...	187	...	11	1995	Polynésie française
5	38	...	907	199	...	187	...	12	1996	
5	38	...	891	199	...	187	...	12	1997	
5	38	...	907	199	...	187	...	12	1998	
8	90	...	9 155	1 382	...	1 382	...	...	1995	Guam
11	90	...	8 795	1 363	...	1 363	...	...	1996	
11	90	...	8 628	1 363	...	1 363	...	...	1997	
11	90	...	8 537	1 374	...	1 374	...	...	1998	
...	...	...	92	7	...	7	...	...	1995	Kiribati
...	...	...	91	7	...	7	...	...	1996	
...	...	...	89	7	...	7	...	...	1997	
...	...	...	88	7	...	7	...	...	1998	
5	...	...	4 093	45	...	45	...	...	1995	Nauru
5	...	...	4 093	45	...	45	...	...	1996	
5	...	...	4 093	45	...	45	...	...	1997	
5	...	...	4 093	45	...	45	...	...	1998	
15	9	...	2 871	554	116	402	...	36	1995	Nouvelle − Calédonie
17	9	...	2 879	570	118	411	...	41	1996	
17	9	...	2 822	570	118	411	...	41	1997	
18	9	...	2 767	570	116	413	...	41	1998	
518	353	− 232	3 893	14 291	1 265	4 695	4 225	4 107	1995	Nouvelle − Zélande
540	332	− 132	4 091	15 217	1 367	4 946	4 828	4 075	1996	
563	347	− 127	4 199	15 791	1 450	5 197	5 151	3 992	1997	
561	337	− 143	4 071	15 452	1 274	5 416	4 531	4 231	1998	
0	...	...	508	1	...	1	...	...	1995	Nioué
0	...	...	508	1	...	1	...	...	1996	
0	...	...	508	1	...	1	...	...	1997	
0	...	...	508	1	...	1	...	...	1998	
15	...	...	4 858	83	...	80	...	3	1995	Palaos
15	...	...	4 703	85	...	82	...	3	1996	
15	...	...	4 590	83	...	80	...	3	1997	
15	...	...	4 402	84	...	81	...	3	1998	
21	3	4	199	856	1	736	76	43	1995	Papouasie − Nouvelle − Guinée
21	3	4	195	857	1	736	78	43	1996	
23	3	7	193	869	1	747	78	43	1997	
21	3	1	183	840	1	719	78	43	1998	
...	...	...	277	46	0	44	...	2	1995	Samoa
...	...	...	273	46	0	44	...	2	1996	
...	...	...	270	46	0	44	...	2	1997	
...	...	...	267	46	0	44	...	2	1998	

64
Production, trade and consumption of commercial energy
Thousand metric tons of oil equivalent and kilograms per capita [*cont.*]
Production, commerce et consommation d'énergie commerciale
Milliers de tonnes d'équivalent pétrole et kilogrammes par habitant [*suite*]

| Region, country or area | Year | Primary energy production – Production d'énergie primaire | | | | | Changes in stocks Variations des stocks | Imports Importations | Exports Exportation |
		Total Totale	Solids Solides	Liquids Liquides	Gas Gaz	Electricity Electricité			
Solomon Islands	1995	...	...	...	...	...	...	55	
	1996	...	...	...	...	...	...	55	
	1997	...	...	...	...	...	...	55	
	1998	...	...	...	...	...	...	55	
Tonga	1995	...	...	...	...	...	...	41	
	1996	...	...	...	...	...	...	42	
	1997	...	...	...	...	...	...	43	
	1998	...	...	...	...	...	...	42	
Vanuatu	1995	...	...	...	...	...	...	20	
	1996	...	...	...	...	...	...	20	
	1997	...	...	...	...	...	...	20	
	1998	...	...	...	...	...	...	20	
Wake Island	1995	...	...	...	...	...	...	418	
	1996	...	...	...	...	...	...	421	
	1997	...	...	...	...	...	...	421	
	1998	...	...	...	...	...	...	421	

Source:
United Nations Statistics Division, New York, "Energy Statistics Yearbook 1998" and the energy statistics database.

Source:
Organisation des Nations Unies, Division de statistique, New York, "Annuaire des statistique de l'énergie 1998" et la base de données pour statistiques énergétiques.

† For information on recent changes in country or area nomenclature pertaining to former Czechoslovakia, Germany, Hong Kong Special Administrative Region (SAR) of China, Macao Special Administrative Region (SAR) of China, SFR of Yugoslavia and former USSR, see Annex I – Country or area nomenclature, regional and other groupings.

† Pour les modifications récentes de nomenclature de pays ou de zone concernant l'Allemagne, Hong Kong, région administrative spéciale (RAS) de Chine, Macao, région administrative spéciale (RAS) de Chine, l'ex–Tchécoslovaquie, l'ex–URSS et l'ex–Rfs de Yougoslavie, voir annex I – Nomenclature des pays ou des zones, groupements régionaux et autres groupements.

†† For statistical purposes, the data for China do not include those for Hong Kong Special Administrative Region (Hong Kong SAR), Macao Special Administrative Region (Macao SAR) and Taiwan province of China.

†† Les données statistiques relatives à la Chine ne comprennent pas ce qui concernent la région administrative spéciale de Hong Kong (la de Hong Kong), la région administrative spéciale de Macao (la RA Macao (la RAS de Macao), et la province chinoise de Taiwan.

1 Including part of the Neutral Zone.
2 Including Monaco.
3 Including San Marino.
4 Including Svalbard and Jan Mayen Islands.
5 Including Liechtenstein.

1 Y compris une partie de la Zone Neutrale.
2 Y compris Monaco.
3 Y compris Saint–Marin.
4 Y compris îles Svalbard et Jan Mayen.
5 Y compris Liechtenstein.

Energy   Energie

Air Avion	Sea Maritime	Unallocated Nondistribué	Per capita Par habitant	Total Totale	Solids Solides	Liquids Liquides	Gas Gaz	Electricity Electricité	Année	Région, pays ou zone
2	...	...	140	53	...	53	...	...	1995	Iles Salomon
2	...	...	136	53	...	53	...	...	1996	
2	...	...	132	53	...	53	...	...	1997	
2	...	...	128	53	...	53	...	...	1998	
3	...	...	394	38	0	38	...	...	1995	Tonga
3	...	...	405	39	0	39	...	...	1996	
3	...	...	411	40	0	40	...	...	1997	
3	...	...	400	39	0	39	...	...	1998	
...	0	...	121	20	0	20	...	...	1995	Vanuatu
...	0	...	118	20	0	20	...	...	1996	
...	0	...	116	20	0	20	...	...	1997	
...	0	...	112	20	0	20	...	...	1998	
400	12	...	6 125	6	0	6	...	...	1995	Ile de Wake
402	13	...	6 125	6	0	6	...	...	1996	
402	13	...	6 125	6	0	6	...	...	1997	
402	13	...	6 125	6	0	6	...	...	1998	

65
Production of selected energy commodities
Production des principaux biens de l'énergie
Thousand metric tons of oil equivalent
Milliers de tonnes d'équivalent pétrole

Region, country or area Région, pays ou zone	Year Anneé	Hard coal, lignite & peat Houille, lignite et tourbe	Briquettes & cokes Agglo- mérés et cokes	Crude petroleum & NGL Pétrole brut et GNL	Light petroleum products Produits pétroliers légers	Heavy petroleum products Produits pétroliers lourds	Other petroleum products Autres produits pétroliers	LPG & refinery gas GLP et gaz de raffinerie	Natural gas Gaz naturel	Electricity Electricité
World	1995	2 292 787	254 729	3 345 723	1 268 697	1 549 035	244 058	180 253	2 055 068	1 591 193
Monde	1996	2 329 992	244 165	3 409 545	1 311 223	1 592 687	245 048	180 264	2 156 896	1 643 317
	1997	2 345 804	244 118	3 513 678	1 351 397	1 630 384	253 778	185 751	2 161 009	1 664 550
	1998	2 274 060	233 125	3 577 331	1 370 595	1 632 261	257 633	187 955	2 176 603	1 705 079
Africa	1995	114 928	3 561	348 268	39 658	64 251	3 489	2 374	84 269	33 583
Afrique	1996	114 464	3 457	355 267	40 003	63 760	3 324	2 388	90 888	35 092
	1997	121 643	3 494	363 505	40 480	63 974	3 221	2 355	100 499	36 991
	1998	124 042	3 039	369 565	40 448	64 824	3 372	2 275	102 673	37 833
Algeria	1995	15	0	61 288	7 449	12 223	359	506	58 101	1 695
Algérie	1996	15	0	64 093	7 553	11 173	324	507	62 589	1 776
	1997	16	0	66 487	7 920	12 127	281	519	70 624	1 848
	1998	16	0	68 911	7 530	11 306	275	507	75 423	2 031
Angola	1995	...	...	32 164	602	1 136	0	36	509	83
Angola	1996	...	...	34 812	607	1 160	1	36	509	88
	1997	...	...	35 184	622	1 186	5	38	518	95
	1998	...	...	36 418	575	1 119	5	32	527	91
Benin	1995	...	...	131	...	...	...	...	...	1
Bénin	1996	...	...	112	...	...	...	...	...	1
	1997	...	...	90	...	...	...	...	...	1
	1998	...	...	62	...	...	...	...	...	1
Burkina Faso	1995	...	...	...	...	...	...	...	...	21
Burkina Faso	1996	...	...	...	...	...	...	...	...	23
	1997	...	...	...	...	...	...	...	...	25
	1998	...	...	...	...	...	...	...	...	26
Burundi	1995	4	0	...	...	...	...	...	...	10
Burundi	1996	4	0	...	...	...	...	...	...	10
	1997	4	0	...	...	...	...	...	...	10
	1998	4	0	...	...	...	...	...	...	11
Cameroon	1995	1	...	5 403	599	444	60	23	...	236
Cameroun	1996	1	...	5 220	606	448	63	24	...	237
	1997	1	...	5 516	611	449	67	24	...	237
	1998	1	...	5 911	613	455	68	24	...	238
Cape Verde	1995	...	...	...	...	...	...	...	...	3
Cap–Vert	1996	...	...	...	...	...	...	...	...	4
	1997	...	...	...	...	...	...	...	...	4
	1998	...	...	...	...	...	...	...	...	4
Central African Republic	1995	...	...	...	...	...	...	...	...	9
Rép. centrafricaine	1996	...	...	...	...	...	...	...	...	9
	1997	...	...	...	...	...	...	...	...	9
	1998	...	...	...	...	...	...	...	...	9
Chad	1995	...	...	...	...	...	...	...	...	8
Tchad	1996	...	...	...	...	...	...	...	...	8
	1997	...	...	...	...	...	...	...	...	8
	1998	...	...	...	...	...	...	...	...	8
Comoros	1995	...	...	...	...	...	...	...	...	1
Comores	1996	...	...	...	...	...	...	...	...	1
	1997	...	...	...	...	...	...	...	...	1
	1998	...	...	...	...	...	...	...	...	1
Congo	1995	0	...	9 277	179	347	11	4	3	37
Congo	1996	0	...	10 380	186	351	11	4	3	38
	1997	0	...	11 610	187	356	12	4	3	38
	1998	0	...	12 723	189	357	12	4	3	38
Côte d'Ivoire	1995	...	...	314	1 019	909	94	20	...	151
Côte d'Ivoire	1996	...	...	1 264	1 024	1 181	95	20	...	204
	1997	...	...	1 273	1 029	1 194	96	21	...	237
	1998	...	...	1 283	1 035	1 198	96	21	...	238

65
Production of selected energy commodities
Thousand metric tons of oil equivalent [*cont.*]
Production des principaux biens de l'énergie
Milliers de tonnes d'équivalent pétrole [*suite*]

Region, country or area Région, pays ou zone	Year Anneé	Hard coal, lignite & peat Houille, lignite et tourbe	Briquettes & cokes Agglo— mérés et cokes	Crude petroleum & NGL Pétrole brut et GNL	Light petroleum products Produits pétroliers légers	Heavy petroleum products Produits pétroliers lourds	Other petroleum products Autres produits pétroliers	LPG & refinery gas GLP et gaz de raffinerie	Natural gas Gaz naturel	Electricity Electricité
Dem. Rep. of the Congo	1995	65	...	1 147	23	26	13	0	...	463
Rép. dém. du Congo	1996	67	...	1 149	23	26	12	0	...	466
	1997	67	...	1 152	23	27	13	0	...	466
	1998	67	...	1 156	23	27	13	0	...	467
Djibouti	1995	...	...	...	...	...	...	...	...	16
Djibouti	1996	...	...	...	...	...	...	...	...	16
	1997	...	...	...	...	...	...	...	...	16
	1998	...	...	...	...	...	...	...	...	16
Egypt	1995	...	1 171	46 797	6 845	17 814	1 322	499	12 658	4 322
Egypte	1996	...	1 175	45 461	7 276	18 367	1 240	482	13 462	4 357
	1997	...	1 189	44 515	7 471	18 770	1 287	499	13 893	4 723
	1998	...	1 227	43 200	7 557	19 168	1 496	469	11 523	4 911
Equatorial Guinea	1995	...	...	339	...	...	...	...	...	2
Guinée équatoriale	1996	...	...	858	...	...	...	...	...	2
	1997	...	...	3 000	...	...	...	...	...	2
	1998	...	...	4 103	...	...	...	...	...	2
Ethiopia including Eritrea	1995	...	...	...	63	438	7	6	...	129
Ethiopie compris Erythrée	1996	...	...	...	24	57	2	3	...	137
	1997	...	...	...	19	113	2	4	...	143
	1998	...	...	...	19	118	2	4	...	144
Gabon	1995	...	...	18 264	163	484	29	12	769	98
Gabon	1996	...	...	18 295	184	473	33	12	718	104
	1997	...	...	18 616	186	516	28	11	684	108
	1998	...	...	18 213	182	512	31	11	610	110
Gambia	1995	...	...	...	...	...	...	...	...	6
Gambie	1996	...	...	...	...	...	...	...	...	7
	1997	...	...	...	...	...	...	...	...	7
	1998	...	...	...	...	...	...	...	...	7
Ghana	1995	...	...	0	361	549	59	20	...	528
Ghana	1996	...	...	0	367	557	59	20	...	570
	1997	...	...	0	368	557	59	20	...	572
	1998	...	...	0	377	561	60	20	...	573
Guinea	1995	...	...	...	...	...	...	...	...	46
Guinee	1996	...	...	...	...	...	...	...	...	47
	1997	...	...	...	...	...	...	...	...	47
	1998	...	...	...	...	...	...	...	...	47
Guinea—Bissau	1995	...	...	...	...	...	...	...	...	4
Guinée—Bissau	1996	...	...	...	...	...	...	...	...	4
	1997	...	...	...	...	...	...	...	...	5
	1998	...	...	...	...	...	...	...	...	5
Kenya	1995	...	...	...	706	1 005	119	35	...	547
Kenya	1996	...	...	...	707	1 012	117	35	...	547
	1997	...	...	...	632	912	106	26	...	667
	1998	...	...	...	675	937	110	32	...	807
Liberia	1995	...	...	...	0	...	0	...	...	42
Libéria	1996	...	...	...	0	...	0	...	...	42
	1997	...	...	...	0	...	0	...	...	43
	1998	...	...	...	0	...	0	...	...	43
Libyan Arab Jamahiriya	1995	...	...	69 320	4 920	8 935	102	256	5 913	1 548
Jamah. arabe libyenne	1996	...	...	69 115	4 991	9 063	103	259	5 987	1 574
	1997	...	...	71 075	4 938	9 127	106	286	6 127	1 632
	1998	...	...	69 190	4 938	9 127	106	286	5 931	1 677
Madagascar	1995	...	0	...	115	121	10	5	...	57
Madagascar	1996	...	0	...	131	122	10	5	...	59
	1997	...	0	...	188	124	10	5	...	63
	1998	...	0	...	131	124	10	7	...	68
Malawi	1995	...	...	...	...	...	...	...	...	74
Malawi	1996	...	...	...	...	...	...	...	...	75
	1997	...	...	...	...	...	...	...	...	75
	1998	...	...	...	...	...	...	...	...	75

65
Production of selected energy commodities
Thousand metric tons of oil equivalent [*cont.*]
Production des principaux biens de l'énergie
Milliers de tonnes d'équivalent pétrole [*suite*]

Region, country or area Région, pays ou zone	Year Anneé	Hard coal, lignite & peat Houille, lignite et tourbe	Briquettes & cokes Agglo- mérés et cokes	Crude petroleum & NGL Pétrole brut et GNL	Light petroleum products Produits pétroliers légers	Heavy petroleum products Produits pétroliers lourds	Other petroleum products Autres produits pétroliers	LPG & refinery gas GLP et gaz de raffinerie	Natural gas Gaz naturel	Electricity Electricité
Mali Mali	1995 1996 1997 1998	... ...	... ...	... ...	... ...	... ...	... ...	... ...	... ...	27 29 34 34
Mauritania Mauritanie	1995 1996 1997 1998	... ...	... ...	... ...	305 310 313 313	501 505 507 510	98 98 99 99	40 41 41 41	... ...	13 13 13 13
Mauritius Maurice	1995 1996 1997 1998	... ...	... ...	... ...	... ...	... ...	... ...	... ...	... ...	96 108 110 110
Morocco Maroc	1995 1996 1997 1998	455 354 263 188	0 0 0 0	5 5 12 12	1 120 981 1 062 1 140	4 359 3 893 4 126 4 170	269 254 260 260	256 264 260 274	13 17 32 35	1 042 1 067 1 136 1 156
Mozambique Mozambique	1995 1996 1997 1998	27 14 13 13	... ...	... ...	... ...	... ...	... ...	... ...	... ...	77 83 128 632
Niger Niger	1995 1996 1997 1998	121 121 122 122	... ...	... ...	... ...	... ...	... ...	... ...	... ...	20 20 20 20
Nigeria Nigéria	1995 1996 1997 1998	98 98 98 41	... ...	92 249 92 898 93 734 97 057	2 505 2 487 2 508 2 721	3 094 3 095 3 105 4 052	... ...	184 220 129 76	4 444 5 092 5 456 5 502	1 246 1 289 1 319 1 352
Réunion Réunion	1995 1996 1997 1998	... ...	... ...	... ...	... ...	... ...	... ...	... ...	... ...	112 119 127 135
Rwanda Rwanda	1995 1996 1997 1998	... ...	... ...	... ...	... ...	... ...	... ...	... ...	0 0 0 0	14 14 14 14
Saint Helena Sainte-Hélène	1995 1996 1997 1998	... ...	... ...	... ...	... ...	... ...	... ...	... ...	... ...	1 1 1 1
Sao Tome and Principe Sao Tomé-et-Principe	1995 1996 1997 1998	... ...	... ...	... ...	... ...	... ...	... ...	... ...	... ...	1 1 1 1
Senegal Sénégal	1995 1996 1997 1998	... ...	... ...	... ...	342 345 348 350	523 525 527 530	12 12 12 12	3 3 3 3	... ...	96 100 102 108
Seychelles Seychelles	1995 1996 1997 1998	... ...	... ...	... ...	... ...	... ...	... ...	... ...	... ...	11 11 13 14
Sierra Leone Sierra Leone	1995 1996 1997 1998	... ...	... ...	... ...	63 64 64 65	122 122 125 125	27 27 27 27	... ...	... ...	21 21 21 21
Somalia Somalie	1995 1996 1997 1998	... ...	... ...	... ...	... ...	... ...	... ...	... ...	... ...	23 24 24 24

65
Production of selected energy commodities
Thousand metric tons of oil equivalent [*cont.*]
Production des principaux biens de l'énergie
Milliers de tonnes d'équivalent pétrole [*suite*]

Region, country or area Région, pays ou zone	Year Anneé	Hard coal, lignite & peat Houille, lignite et tourbe	Briquettes & cokes Agglo- mérés et cokes	Crude petroleum & NGL Pétrole brut et GNL	Light petroleum products Produits pétroliers légers	Heavy petroleum products Produits pétroliers lourds	Other petroleum products Autres produits pétroliers	LPG & refinery gas GLP et gaz de raffinerie	Natural gas Gaz naturel	Electricity Electricité
South Africa Customs Union	1995	110 049	2 076	7 280	11 115	8 642	767	304	1 716	18 263
Union douanière d'Afrique	1996	109 972	1 962	7 396	10 944	9 051	732	279	1 716	19 389
australe	1997	117 179	1 962	7 407	10 594	7 540	621	311	1 532	20 394
	1998	119 910	1 497	7 307	10 871	7 899	562	309	1 290	20 165
Sudan	1995	...	...	...	251	647	107	8	...	114
Soudan	1996	...	...	...	257	650	107	8	...	115
	1997	...	...	...	259	652	107	8	...	115
	1998	...	...	...	264	655	107	8	...	116
Togo	1995	...	...	...	...	...	...	...	...	8
Togo	1996	...	...	...	...	...	...	...	...	8
	1997	...	...	...	...	...	...	...	...	8
	1998	...	...	...	...	...	...	...	...	8
Tunisia	1995	...	...	4 289	528	1 224	...	141	144	653
Tunisie	1996	...	...	4 208	546	1 217	...	154	795	674
	1997	...	...	3 835	756	1 220	...	133	1 630	721
	1998	...	...	4 019	507	1 198	...	138	1 829	770
Uganda	1995	...	...	...	...	...	...	...	...	94
Ouganda	1996	...	...	...	...	...	...	...	...	101
	1997	...	...	...	...	...	...	...	...	108
	1998	...	...	...	...	...	...	...	...	109
United Rep. of Tanzania	1995	4	...	...	190	394	2	7	...	148
Rép.-Unie de Tanzanie	1996	4	...	...	191	395	2	7	...	149
	1997	4	...	...	194	397	2	7	...	150
	1998	4	...	...	194	399	2	7	...	150
Western Sahara	1995	...	...	...	...	...	...	...	...	7
Sahara occidental	1996	...	...	...	...	...	...	...	...	7
	1997	...	...	...	...	...	...	...	...	7
	1998	...	...	...	...	...	...	...	...	7
Zambia	1995	212	20	...	195	312	20	11	...	670
Zambie	1996	192	9	...	199	316	20	5	...	670
	1997	165	3	...	190	317	18	5	...	670
	1998	144	0	...	183	276	15	4	...	654
Zimbabwe	1995	3 877	294	...	...	...	...	...	...	689
Zimbabwe	1996	3 623	311	...	...	...	...	...	...	672
	1997	3 713	340	...	...	...	...	...	...	673
	1998	3 533	315	...	...	...	...	...	...	574
America, North	1995	573 336	17 716	682 520	504 098	302 417	99 390	66 590	675 141	537 293
Amérique du Nord	1996	590 071	17 387	675 909	516 517	311 349	101 874	63 782	695 631	546 886
	1997	605 486	16 794	694 972	524 604	316 970	105 049	65 172	704 578	539 148
	1998	612 686	15 453	679 463	532 457	322 182	108 669	65 020	692 328	558 149
Antigua and Barbuda	1995	...	...	...	...	...	...	...	...	8
Antigua-et-Barbuda	1996	...	...	...	...	...	...	...	...	8
	1997	...	...	...	...	...	...	...	...	9
	1998	...	...	...	...	...	...	...	...	9
Aruba	1995	...	...	...	...	...	...	...	...	40
Aruba	1996	...	...	...	...	...	...	...	...	40
	1997	...	...	...	...	...	...	...	...	40
	1998	...	...	...	...	...	...	...	...	40
Bahamas	1995	...	...	...	...	...	...	...	...	112
Bahamas	1996	...	...	...	...	...	...	...	...	115
	1997	...	...	...	...	...	...	...	...	122
	1998	...	...	...	...	...	...	...	...	132
Barbados	1995	...	...	63	68	197	5	2	24	53
Barbade	1996	...	...	50	61	195	5	1	27	56
	1997	...	...	45	74	204	5	1	22	58
	1998	...	...	80	0	0	0	2	35	64
Belize	1995	...	...	...	...	...	...	...	...	13
Belize	1996	...	...	...	...	...	...	...	...	13
	1997	...	...	...	...	...	...	...	...	14
	1998	...	...	...	...	...	...	...	...	16

65
Production of selected energy commodities
Thousand metric tons of oil equivalent [cont.]
Production des principaux biens de l'énergie
Milliers de tonnes d'équivalent pétrole [suite]

Region, country or area Région, pays ou zone	Year Anneé	Hard coal, lignite & peat Houille, lignite et tourbe	Briquettes & cokes Agglo-mérés et cokes	Crude petroleum & NGL Pétrole brut et GNL	Light petroleum products Produits pétroliers légers	Heavy petroleum products Produits pétroliers lourds	Other petroleum products Autres produits pétroliers	LPG & refinery gas GLP et gaz de raffinerie	Natural gas Gaz naturel	Electricity Electricité
Bermuda	1995	...	...	...	...	...	...	...	...	45
Bermudes	1996	...	...	...	...	...	...	...	...	45
	1997	...	...	...	...	...	...	...	...	46
	1998	...	...	...	...	...	...	...	...	46
British Virgin Islands	1995	...	...	...	...	...	...	...	...	4
Iles Vierges britanniques	1996	...	...	...	...	...	...	...	...	4
	1997	...	...	...	...	...	...	...	...	4
	1998	...	...	...	...	...	...	...	...	4
Canada	1995	38 899	2 148	112 797	38 989	29 342	10 475	5 308	148 358	65 278
Canada	1996	39 721	2 196	113 262	40 705	31 944	10 216	5 285	153 305	65 501
	1997	41 103	2 205	123 362	40 409	34 685	11 739	6 103	156 059	63 767
	1998	38 947	2 055	114 465	40 417	32 939	12 561	6 331	160 434	60 827
Cayman Islands	1995	...	...	...	...	...	...	...	...	26
Iles Caïmanes	1996	...	...	...	...	...	...	...	...	26
	1997	...	...	...	...	...	...	...	...	26
	1998	...	...	...	...	...	...	...	...	26
Costa Rica	1995	...	...	...	152	523	25	2	...	778
Costa Rica	1996	...	...	...	128	485	23	2	...	814
	1997	...	...	...	135	501	26	2	...	895
	1998	...	...	...	6	165	12	0	...	956
Cuba	1995	...	...	1 640	1 241	826	151	148	16	1 071
Cuba	1996	...	...	1 646	1 343	1 076	146	146	18	1 138
	1997	...	...	1 630	694	1 182	135	142	21	1 211
	1998	...	...	1 871	450	619	169	134	22	1 270
Dominica	1995	...	...	...	...	...	...	...	...	3
Dominique	1996	...	...	...	...	...	...	...	...	3
	1997	...	...	...	...	...	...	...	...	3
	1998	...	...	...	...	...	...	...	...	3
Dominican Republic	1995	...	...	...	621	1 443	...	40	...	560
Rép. dominicaine	1996	...	...	...	642	1 489	...	42	...	589
	1997	...	...	...	664	1 567	...	39	...	631
	1998	...	...	...	249	1 081	...	45	...	650
El Salvador	1995	...	...	...	234	431	20	17	...	635
El Salvador	1996	...	...	...	288	414	28	15	...	630
	1997	...	...	...	228	502	35	15	...	648
	1998	...	...	...	224	641	31	17	...	704
Greenland	1995	0	...	...	...	...	...	...	...	22
Groenland	1996	0	...	...	...	...	...	...	...	22
	1997	0	...	...	...	...	...	...	...	22
	1998	0	...	...	...	...	...	...	...	22
Grenada	1995	...	...	...	...	...	...	...	...	8
Grenade	1996	...	...	...	...	...	...	...	...	8
	1997	...	...	...	...	...	...	...	...	9
	1998	...	...	...	...	...	...	...	...	9
Guadeloupe	1995	...	...	...	...	...	...	...	...	91
Guadeloupe	1996	...	...	...	...	...	...	...	...	97
	1997	...	...	...	...	...	...	...	...	104
	1998	...	...	...	...	...	...	...	...	104
Guatemala	1995	...	...	467	157	573	...	8	10	294
Guatemala	1996	...	...	730	147	526	...	8	10	318
	1997	...	...	976	154	564	...	5	10	355
	1998	...	...	1 273	141	591	...	5	10	383
Haiti	1995	...	...	...	...	...	...	...	...	45
Haïti	1996	...	...	...	...	...	...	...	...	54
	1997	...	...	...	...	...	...	...	...	54
	1998	...	...	...	...	...	...	...	...	59
Honduras	1995	...	...	...	...	...	...	...	...	244
Honduras	1996	...	...	...	...	...	...	...	...	257
	1997	...	...	...	...	...	...	...	...	266
	1998	...	...	...	...	...	...	...	...	317

65
Production of selected energy commodities
Thousand metric tons of oil equivalent [*cont.*]
Production des principaux biens de l'énergie
Milliers de tonnes d'équivalent pétrole [*suite*]

Region, country or area Région, pays ou zone	Year Anneé	Hard coal, lignite & peat Houille, lignite et tourbe	Briquettes & cokes Agglo- mérés et cokes	Crude petroleum & NGL Pétrole brut et GNL	Light petroleum products Produits pétroliers légers	Heavy petroleum products Produits pétroliers lourds	Other petroleum products Autres produits pétroliers	LPG & refinery gas GLP et gaz de raffinerie	Natural gas Gaz naturel	Electricity Electricité
Jamaica	1995	...	...	...	246	749	16	23	...	501
Jamaïque	1996	...	...	...	273	770	17	24	...	519
	1997	...	...	...	301	791	14	25	...	538
	1998	...	...	...	327	812	14	26	...	557
Martinique	1995	...	...	...	293	431	...	22	...	84
Martinique	1996	...	...	...	296	433	...	23	...	88
	1997	...	...	...	296	435	...	23	...	93
	1998	...	...	...	298	435	...	23	...	93
Mexico	1995	2 876	1 432	160 552	24 182	38 875	3 381	3 553	26 808	19 795
Mexique	1996	3 157	1 456	165 847	22 163	37 771	3 892	3 217	30 462	19 790
	1997	3 222	1 426	175 160	20 435	38 246	3 404	2 767	31 424	20 740
	1998	3 501	1 469	178 222	21 495	40 177	3 928	2 446	33 927	21 814
Montserrat	1995	...	...	...	...	...	...	...	...	1
Montserrat	1996	...	...	...	...	...	...	...	...	1
	1997	...	...	...	...	...	...	...	...	2
	1998	...	...	...	...	...	...	...	...	2
Netherlands Antilles	1995	...	...	...	2 771	7 213	2 388	66	...	126
Antilles néerlandaises	1996	...	...	...	2 775	7 219	2 394	69	...	127
	1997	...	...	...	2 785	7 223	2 400	70	...	128
	1998	...	...	...	2 809	7 231	2 410	74	...	128
Nicaragua	1995	...	...	...	139	403	23	30	...	580
Nicaragua	1996	...	...	...	144	424	24	32	...	629
	1997	...	...	...	137	575	24	30	...	628
	1998	...	...	...	147	675	24	28	...	694
Panama	1995	...	...	...	125	748	10	43	...	303
Panama	1996	...	...	...	277	1 700	10	61	...	340
	1997	...	...	...	314	1 125	10	57	...	360
	1998	...	...	...	361	1 916	10	70	...	387
Puerto Rico	1995	...	...	...	3 263	3 108	1 620	120	...	1 612
Porto Rico	1996	...	...	...	3 290	3 129	1 627	122	...	1 645
	1997	...	...	...	3 323	3 141	1 635	125	...	1 720
	1998	...	...	...	3 332	3 154	1 635	125	...	1 751
Saint Kitts and Nevis	1995	...	...	...	...	...	...	...	...	7
Saint-Kitts-et-Nevis	1996	...	...	...	...	...	...	...	...	7
	1997	...	...	...	...	...	...	...	...	8
	1998	...	...	...	...	...	...	...	...	8
Saint Lucia	1995	...	...	...	...	...	...	...	...	10
Sainte-Lucie	1996	...	...	...	...	...	...	...	...	10
	1997	...	...	...	...	...	...	...	...	10
	1998	...	...	...	...	...	...	...	...	10
St. Pierre and Miquelon	1995	...	...	...	...	...	...	...	...	4
St.-Pierre-et-Miquelon	1996	...	...	...	...	...	...	...	...	4
	1997	...	...	...	...	...	...	...	...	4
	1998	...	...	...	...	...	...	...	...	4
St. Vincent and Grenadines	1995	...	...	...	...	...	...	...	...	6
St.-Vincent-et-Grenad.	1996	...	...	...	...	...	...	...	...	7
	1997	...	...	...	...	...	...	...	...	7
	1998	...	...	...	...	...	...	...	...	7
Trinidad and Tobago	1995	...	...	6 791	1 485	3 261	37	473	6 293	370
Trinité-et-Tobago	1996	...	...	6 717	1 434	3 612	43	491	7 112	391
	1997	...	...	6 218	1 284	3 583	42	466	7 572	417
	1998	...	...	6 391	2 299	4 547	42	510	7 903	446
United States	1995	531 560	14 136	400 209	426 024	207 593	76 724	56 583	493 631	444 471
Etats-Unis	1996	547 193	13 735	387 656	438 424	213 455	78 934	54 091	504 696	453 495
	1997	561 161	13 163	387 581	449 229	215 933	81 045	55 144	509 471	446 117
	1998	570 237	11 929	377 161	455 748	220 478	83 292	55 026	489 996	466 513

65
Production of selected energy commodities
Thousand metric tons of oil equivalent [*cont.*]
Production des principaux biens de l'énergie
Milliers de tonnes d'équivalent pétrole [*suite*]

Region, country or area Région, pays ou zone	Year Anneé	Hard coal, lignite & peat Houille, lignite et tourbe	Briquettes & cokes Agglo— mérés et cokes	Crude petroleum & NGL Pétrole brut et GNL	Light petroleum products Produits pétroliers légers	Heavy petroleum products Produits pétroliers lourds	Other petroleum products Autres produits pétroliers	LPG & refinery gas GLP et gaz de raffinerie	Natural gas Gaz naturel	Electricity Electricité
U.S. Virgin Islands	1995	...	...	...	4 107	6 699	4 515	152	...	92
Iles Vierges américaines	1996	...	...	...	4 125	6 706	4 515	154	...	92
	1997	...	...	...	4 141	6 714	4 536	158	...	93
	1998	...	...	...	4 154	6 722	4 541	159	...	93
America, South	**1995**	**22 992**	**6 246**	**286 387**	**60 912**	**92 431**	**8 950**	**12 752**	**79 636**	**50 978**
Amérique du Sud	**1996**	**24 862**	**7 209**	**317 271**	**62 890**	**97 295**	**10 250**	**12 152**	**77 948**	**53 458**
	1997	**28 205**	**7 020**	**335 363**	**66 671**	**100 985**	**11 948**	**12 531**	**85 054**	**56 170**
	1998	**30 413**	**6 791**	**340 502**	**70 462**	**103 824**	**11 627**	**14 149**	**86 046**	**58 180**
Argentina	1995	180	379	37 282	9 006	11 018	1 868	1 545	25 387	7 006
Argentine	1996	183	467	41 758	7 766	11 536	1 849	1 507	24 661	7 316
	1997	148	478	44 358	7 489	13 082	2 070	1 466	29 034	7 671
	1998	171	473	43 758	6 850	13 544	2 080	1 575	29 835	7 680
Bolivia	1995	...	...	1 641	568	354	21	61	3 515	258
Bolivie	1996	...	...	1 824	620	340	22	59	3 587	277
	1997	...	...	1 805	704	344	19	60	3 205	291
	1998	...	...	2 031	655	419	19	56	3 067	319
Brazil	1995	2 310	5 249	35 908	19 473	34 432	3 307	6 504	4 604	24 143
Brésil	1996	2 135	6 096	40 418	20 595	36 929	3 919	6 528	5 160	25 472
	1997	2 509	5 949	43 726	22 567	39 481	4 576	6 798	5 729	27 041
	1998	2 451	5 770	50 570	24 687	42 905	4 727	6 917	6 012	28 228
Chile	1995	743	301	864	2 707	4 460	131	539	1 673	2 572
Chili	1996	718	319	877	2 850	4 505	130	629	1 653	2 797
	1997	746	301	754	3 165	4 629	133	616	1 797	2 863
	1998	672	328	789	3 277	5 028	126	762	1 620	3 053
Colombia	1995	16 815	317	30 424	5 239	5 893	280	1 269	4 545	3 891
Colombie	1996	19 237	328	32 629	6 029	6 254	280	1 354	4 972	3 858
	1997	21 185	293	33 970	5 635	6 355	294	1 363	6 051	3 989
	1998	21 886	220	37 457	5 607	5 949	285	1 325	6 327	3 953
Ecuador	1995	...	...	20 264	1 609	4 536	141	234	365	718
Equateur	1996	...	...	19 431	1 906	4 927	89	275	618	793
	1997	...	...	20 313	1 705	5 635	95	224	581	822
	1998	...	...	20 866	1 759	4 819	85	238	368	937
Falkland Is. (Malvinas)	1995	3	...	...	...	...	...	...	...	1
Iles Falkland (Malvinas)	1996	3	...	...	...	...	...	...	...	1
	1997	3	...	...	...	...	...	...	...	1
	1998	3	...	...	...	...	...	...	...	1
French Guiana	1995	...	...	...	...	...	...	...	...	39
Guyane française	1996	...	...	...	...	...	...	...	...	39
	1997	...	...	...	...	...	...	...	...	39
	1998	...	...	...	...	...	...	...	...	39
Guyana	1995	...	...	...	...	...	...	...	...	49
Guyana	1996	...	...	...	...	...	...	...	...	60
	1997	...	...	...	...	...	...	...	...	68
	1998	...	...	...	...	...	...	...	...	71
Paraguay	1995	...	...	...	66	155	...	1	...	3 632
Paraguay	1996	...	...	...	33	125	...	1	...	4 145
	1997	...	...	...	35	115	...	1	...	4 373
	1998	...	...	...	31	106	...	0	...	4 380
Peru	1995	98	...	6 123	2 193	4 306	92	228	675	1 500
Pérou	1996	40	...	6 052	2 439	4 428	128	228	664	1 486
	1997	15	...	6 022	2 353	4 435	265	280	720	1 544
	1998	14	...	5 718	2 714	5 394	185	356	599	1 598
Suriname	1995	...	...	275	...	...	...	...	...	139
Suriname	1996	...	...	245	...	...	...	...	...	139
	1997	...	...	246	...	...	...	...	...	140
	1998	...	...	248	...	...	...	...	...	139
Uruguay	1995	...	0	...	347	911	43	59	...	542
Uruguay	1996	...	0	...	348	1 199	61	70	...	573
	1997	...	0	...	360	920	80	81	...	615
	1998	...	0	...	483	1 167	60	105	...	823

65
Production of selected energy commodities
Thousand metric tons of oil equivalent [cont.]
Production des principaux biens de l'énergie
Milliers de tonnes d'équivalent pétrole [suite]

Region, country or area Région, pays ou zone	Year Anneé	Hard coal, lignite & peat Houille, lignite et tourbe	Briquettes & cokes Agglo- mérés et cokes	Crude petroleum & NGL Pétrole brut et GNL	Light petroleum products Produits pétroliers légers	Heavy petroleum products Produits pétroliers lourds	Other petroleum products Autres produits pétroliers	LPG & refinery gas GLP et gaz de raffinerie	Natural gas Gaz naturel	Electricity Electricité
Venezuela	1995	2 843	...	153 606	19 705	26 367	3 067	2 313	38 871	6 488
Venezuela	1996	2 546	...	174 036	20 303	27 052	3 772	1 499	36 633	6 501
	1997	3 600	...	184 170	22 659	25 988	4 416	1 642	37 937	6 714
	1998	5 216	...	179 064	24 398	24 492	4 060	2 815	38 218	6 958
Asia	1995	1 003 486	139 952	1 371 788	340 963	569 454	50 144	42 856	395 024	408 033
Asie	1996	1 036 388	139 800	1 393 427	363 807	589 968	52 148	45 198	427 964	430 268
	1997	1 029 143	141 093	1 448 369	384 992	614 109	54 825	47 703	437 958	450 368
	1998	970 243	136 008	1 519 277	389 504	602 813	54 912	48 462	447 099	465 968
Afghanistan	1995	4	...	...	...	...	...	...	157	54
Afghanistan	1996	2	...	...	...	...	...	...	149	49
	1997	1	...	...	...	...	...	...	137	43
	1998	1	...	...	...	...	...	...	128	42
Armenia	1995	...	...	...	...	...	...	...	...	531
Arménie	1996	...	...	...	...	...	...	...	...	941
	1997	...	...	...	...	...	...	...	...	798
	1998	...	...	...	...	...	...	...	...	810
Azerbaijan	1995	...	...	9 188	2 319	6 428	208	111	5 986	1 466
Azerbaïdjan	1996	...	...	9 125	1 474	6 068	360	104	5 681	1 470
	1997	...	...	9 047	1 460	5 793	212	103	5 370	1 448
	1998	...	...	11 449	1 388	6 080	134	161	5 036	1 547
Bahrain	1995	...	...	2 447	5 006	7 354	232	34	6 312	397
Bahreïn	1996	...	...	2 378	4 991	7 695	314	36	6 536	431
	1997	...	...	2 364	4 984	7 358	393	34	6 888	433
	1998	...	...	2 287	4 700	7 387	341	28	7 421	496
Bangladesh	1995	...	...	10	448	305	0	16	6 330	1 005
Bangladesh	1996	...	...	66	418	251	0	14	6 557	1 067
	1997	...	...	45	467	279	0	17	6 444	1 103
	1998	...	...	37	295	214	0	15	6 992	1 192
Bhutan	1995	48	...	...	...	...	...	...	...	140
Bhoutan	1996	45	...	...	...	...	...	...	...	170
	1997	38	...	...	...	...	...	...	...	158
	1998	35	...	...	...	...	...	...	...	155
Brunei Darussalam	1995	...	...	8 970	373	213	...	11	9 928	140
Brunéi Darussalam	1996	...	...	8 679	369	192	...	10	9 962	144
	1997	...	...	8 563	381	204	...	2	9 961	147
	1998	...	...	8 472	377	209	...	1	9 644	148
Cambodia	1995	...	...	...	0	0	...	...	...	17
Cambodge	1996	...	...	...	0	0	...	...	...	17
	1997	...	...	...	0	0	...	...	...	18
	1998	...	...	...	0	0	...	...	...	18
China ††	1995	679 685	89 989	150 194	51 517	69 662	8 781	10 168	18 581	88 910
Chine ††	1996	697 802	91 205	157 491	56 658	69 672	8 940	11 096	20 824	95 376
	1997	685 724	91 517	160 902	61 600	72 888	9 180	12 611	23 504	100 088
	1998	624 375	87 585	161 161	61 603	70 527	9 458	13 585	24 101	102 761
China, Hong Kong SAR †	1995	...	...	...	...	...	...	...	...	2 401
Chine, Hong Kong RAS †	1996	...	...	...	...	...	...	...	...	2 446
	1997	...	...	...	...	...	...	...	...	2 489
	1998	...	...	...	...	...	...	...	...	2 702
China, Macao SAR	1995	...	...	...	...	...	...	...	...	109
Chine, Macao RAS	1996	...	...	...	...	...	...	...	...	118
	1997	...	...	...	...	...	...	...	...	121
	1998	...	...	...	...	...	...	...	...	132
Cyprus	1995	...	...	...	138	619	37	46	...	213
Chypre	1996	...	...	...	120	575	30	45	...	223
	1997	...	...	...	174	789	37	56	...	233
	1998	...	...	...	177	826	37	56	...	254
Georgia	1995	25	...	47	10	29	1	...	9	598
Géorgie	1996	13	...	128	0	11	1	...	3	621
	1997	3	...	134	5	17	1	...	0	617
	1998	8	...	119	5	33	0	...	0	694

65
Production of selected energy commodities
Thousand metric tons of oil equivalent [*cont.*]
Production des principaux biens de l'énergie
Milliers de tonnes d'équivalent pétrole [*suite*]

Region, country or area Région, pays ou zone	Year Anneé	Hard coal, lignite & peat Houille, lignite et tourbe	Briquettes & cokes Agglo– mérés et cokes	Crude petroleum & NGL Pétrole brut et GNL	Light petroleum products Produits pétroliers légers	Heavy petroleum products Produits pétroliers lourds	Other petroleum products Autres produits pétroliers	LPG & refinery gas GLP et gaz de raffinerie	Natural gas Gaz naturel	Electricity Electricité
India	1995	159 140	6 997	35 269	18 115	30 043	5 384	1 674	17 167	37 349
Inde	1996	170 750	7 579	36 653	19 711	31 965	5 693	2 139	24 404	39 159
	1997	177 148	7 949	37 598	20 244	34 332	5 491	1 807	17 489	41 693
	1998	178 145	7 596	37 343	20 330	36 213	5 717	1 823	23 811	44 619
Indonesia	1995	29 062	...	100 702	13 674	22 015	1 539	3 499	58 402	7 593
Indonésie	1996	33 137	...	102 380	17 640	22 788	1 606	3 769	71 291	8 429
	1997	36 452	...	103 414	16 756	24 351	1 723	3 529	71 294	9 120
	1998	42 225	...	94 880	16 632	25 080	1 679	2 887	70 198	9 749
Iran (Islamic Republic of)	1995	797	108	186 893	15 370	33 311	3 064	2 093	35 998	7 307
Iran (Rép. islamique d')	1996	848	80	187 891	15 292	34 066	3 455	2 122	37 676	7 813
	1997	717	35	184 640	15 655	35 069	3 513	2 111	46 221	8 406
	1998	818	35	186 412	18 175	36 427	3 535	2 220	46 629	8 893
Iraq	1995	...	...	28 729	5 259	14 438	778	653	2 957	2 494
Iraq	1996	...	...	30 118	5 148	14 135	761	653	3 022	2 498
	1997	...	...	58 306	5 221	14 334	771	664	2 844	2 542
	1998	...	...	105 922	5 392	14 804	796	664	2 751	2 610
Israel	1995	103	...	7	4 197	6 394	392	500	18	2 613
Israël	1996	93	...	4	3 974	5 804	362	481	12	2 797
	1997	104	...	0	4 271	5 768	355	536	12	3 016
	1998	98	...	0	4 522	6 140	361	542	11	3 265
Japan	1995	3 637	26 937	718	82 494	107 502	11 239	13 938	2 166	138 555
Japon	1996	3 764	26 083	697	83 116	104 958	11 596	14 161	2 186	142 532
	1997	2 486	26 021	700	87 026	106 460	11 686	14 828	2 234	148 022
	1998	2 132	24 962	655	88 558	102 471	11 338	14 413	2 256	150 874
Jordan	1995	...	...	2	1 012	1 871	154	212	241	483
Jordanie	1996	...	...	2	1 075	1 877	168	209	235	521
	1997	...	...	2	1 069	2 125	157	223	248	539
	1998	...	...	2	1 013	2 184	172	212	251	580
Kazakhstan	1995	36 642	...	20 755	2 883	6 595	569	175	5 330	5 733
Kazakhstan	1996	33 761	...	24 092	3 011	6 462	239	180	5 878	5 045
	1997	32 009	...	26 130	2 321	5 854	660	160	7 311	4 472
	1998	30 804	...	26 325	2 261	5 557	893	160	7 161	4 226
Korea, Dem. People's Rep.	1995	60 620	2 205	...	1 220	1 655	...	...	...	3 096
Corée, Rép. pop. dém. de	1996	59 990	2 174	...	1 204	1 645	...	...	...	3 010
	1997	55 911	2 025	...	1 121	1 533	...	...	...	2 805
	1998	53 115	1 924	...	1 066	1 457	...	...	...	2 665
Korea, Republic of	1995	2 573	9 287	...	28 431	56 722	2 628	1 498	...	29 369
Corée, Rép. de	1996	2 227	8 286	...	33 258	62 557	2 950	1 498	...	32 506
	1997	2 030	8 496	...	43 596	72 727	3 403	1 948	...	34 874
	1998	1 962	8 565	...	44 785	64 092	2 845	2 569	...	36 386
Kuwait [1]	1995	...	...	106 433	17 848	22 069	1 833	348	8 652	2 075
Koweït [1]	1996	...	...	106 199	16 884	20 668	1 815	334	8 675	2 230
	1997	...	...	106 396	18 777	24 346	1 784	333	8 645	2 341
	1998	...	...	109 178	19 265	23 132	1 997	341	8 851	2 624
Kyrgyzstan	1995	281	...	89	...	...	...	...	34	1 062
Kirghizistan	1996	238	...	100	...	...	...	...	24	1 183
	1997	298	...	85	...	...	...	...	37	1 087
	1998	253	...	77	...	...	...	...	17	999
Lao People's Dem. Rep.	1995	1	...	...	...	...	...	...	...	90
Rép. dém. populaire lao	1996	1	...	...	...	...	...	...	...	107
	1997	1	...	...	...	...	...	...	...	105
	1998	1	...	...	...	...	...	...	...	105
Lebanon	1995	...	0	...	...	...	...	...	...	479
Liban	1996	...	0	...	...	...	...	...	...	644
	1997	...	0	...	...	...	...	...	...	716
	1998	...	0	...	...	...	...	...	...	775
Malaysia	1995	78	...	35 538	4 719	8 192	335	595	32 690	4 012
Malaisie	1996	58	...	35 341	5 048	9 047	350	538	32 891	4 558
	1997	70	...	34 811	5 222	9 841	365	544	37 213	5 046
	1998	246	...	35 722	6 111	8 291	148	642	35 788	5 201

65
Production of selected energy commodities
Thousand metric tons of oil equivalent [cont.]
Production des principaux biens de l'énergie
Milliers de tonnes d'équivalent pétrole [suite]

Region, country or area / Région, pays ou zone	Year / Anneé	Hard coal, lignite & peat / Houille, lignite et tourbe	Briquettes & cokes / Agglo-mérés et cokes	Crude petroleum & NGL / Pétrole brut et GNL	Light petroleum products / Produits pétroliers légers	Heavy petroleum products / Produits pétroliers lourds	Other petroleum products / Autres produits pétroliers	LPG & refinery gas / GLP et gaz de raffinerie	Natural gas / Gaz naturel	Electricity / Electricité
Maldives Maldives	1995	...	...	...	...	...	...	...	...	5
	1996	...	...	...	...	...	...	...	...	5
	1997	...	...	...	...	...	...	...	...	6
	1998	...	...	...	...	...	...	...	...	7
Mongolia Mongolie	1995	1 730	...	...	...	...	...	...	...	226
	1996	1 828	...	...	...	...	...	...	...	225
	1997	1 687	...	...	...	...	...	...	...	234
	1998	1 632	...	...	...	...	...	...	...	236
Myanmar Myanmar	1995	31	...	483	287	556	52	4	1 356	349
	1996	28	...	408	236	447	50	4	1 470	366
	1997	28	...	402	324	574	52	7	1 588	391
	1998	29	...	390	334	557	47	13	1 531	356
Nepal Népal	1995	4	...	...	...	...	...	...	...	86
	1996	4	...	...	...	...	...	...	...	104
	1997	6	...	...	...	...	...	...	...	108
	1998	11	...	...	...	...	...	...	...	103
Oman Oman	1995	...	...	42 385	754	2 831	0	66	4 036	722
	1996	...	...	44 091	906	2 835	0	38	4 221	772
	1997	...	...	45 004	856	2 648	0	39	5 006	831
	1998	...	...	44 659	905	2 712	0	39	5 622	918
Pakistan Pakistan	1995	1 439	...	2 765	2 147	3 346	454	40	14 008	4 694
	1996	1 720	...	2 959	2 320	3 618	470	39	14 885	4 982
	1997	1 680	...	2 980	2 149	3 398	436	45	15 579	5 145
	1998	1 494	...	2 889	2 278	3 622	401	60	15 587	5 407
Philippines Philippines	1995	624	...	135	3 975	10 786	83	407	...	7 489
	1996	524	...	47	4 467	11 729	88	450	...	8 107
	1997	511	...	42	4 587	11 146	83	494	...	8 669
	1998	473	...	41	4 268	10 750	58	465	...	8 883
Qatar Qatar	1995	...	...	21 003	991	1 573	...	86	12 590	517
	1996	...	...	21 296	1 131	1 694	...	97	12 776	569
	1997	...	...	28 878	999	1 547	...	75	16 227	594
	1998	...	...	31 800	1 106	1 652	...	85	18 260	703
Saudi Arabia [1] Arabie saoudite [1]	1995	...	...	431 610	23 718	46 368	2 152	990	35 475	8 586
	1996	...	...	432 882	26 257	52 991	2 212	1 001	38 553	8 888
	1997	...	...	442 992	25 176	49 492	2 234	1 001	42 283	9 227
	1998	...	...	457 022	25 579	49 964	2 257	1 003	43 663	9 691
Singapore Singapour	1995	...	...	...	22 342	34 641	1 872	761	...	1 897
	1996	...	...	...	24 298	35 542	1 817	952	...	2 017
	1997	...	...	...	22 309	36 640	2 366	1 050	...	2 252
	1998	...	...	...	20 871	37 585	2 366	1 050	...	2 432
Sri Lanka Sri Lanka	1995	...	...	...	549	1 204	70	59	...	413
	1996	...	...	...	593	1 382	68	68	...	389
	1997	...	...	...	508	1 235	67	55	...	442
	1998	...	...	...	595	1 441	94	70	...	489
Syrian Arab Republic Rép. arabe syrienne	1995	...	...	30 987	2 231	9 104	446	151	2 151	1 316
	1996	...	...	30 489	2 307	9 402	530	149	2 438	1 486
	1997	...	...	28 575	2 412	9 568	554	152	3 346	1 570
	1998	...	...	28 077	2 375	9 691	611	154	4 780	1 706
Tajikistan Tadjikistan	1995	7	0	24	23	...	...	...	35	1 270
	1996	5	0	20	19	...	...	...	45	1 196
	1997	5	3	25	24	...	...	...	35	1 204
	1998	5	1	19	13	...	...	...	27	1 240
Thailand Thaïlande	1995	8 105	...	3 683	6 664	14 325	280	770	9 469	7 196
	1996	9 449	...	4 223	8 807	19 859	341	1 017	10 740	7 867
	1997	10 291	...	5 060	9 900	23 035	591	1 147	13 398	8 390
	1998	8 870	...	5 266	9 246	21 447	653	1 059	13 896	8 151
Turkey Turquie	1995	12 022	2 193	3 520	6 984	17 521	1 584	1 478	167	7 484
	1996	12 356	2 249	3 504	6 820	16 678	1 723	1 449	189	8 223
	1997	13 107	2 253	3 452	7 389	16 089	1 968	1 492	232	8 948
	1998	14 490	2 140	3 226	7 568	16 228	2 488	1 522	517	9 614

65
Production of selected energy commodities
Thousand metric tons of oil equivalent [cont.]
Production des principaux biens de l'énergie
Milliers de tonnes d'équivalent pétrole [suite]

Region, country or area Région, pays ou zone	Year Anneé	Hard coal, lignite & peat Houille, lignite et tourbe	Briquettes & cokes Agglomérés et cokes	Crude petroleum & NGL Pétrole brut et GNL	Light petroleum products Produits pétroliers légers	Heavy petroleum products Produits pétroliers lourds	Other petroleum products Autres produits pétroliers	LPG & refinery gas GLP et gaz de raffinerie	Natural gas Gaz naturel	Electricity Electricité
Turkmenistan Turkmenistan	1995	...	...	3 504	673	2 387	...	...	32 332	843
	1996	...	...	4 029	711	2 561	...	...	31 700	869
	1997	...	...	5 154	804	3 128	...	...	15 604	817
	1998	...	...	6 381	728	3 793	...	...	11 945	810
United Arab Emirates Emirats arabes unis	1995	...	...	112 824	4 811	5 764	60	323	29 208	2 148
	1996	...	...	113 789	5 279	5 507	60	281	31 521	2 285
	1997	...	...	115 913	6 155	5 453	65	296	33 862	2 448
	1998	...	...	119 538	5 703	5 135	65	296	34 571	2 700
Uzbekistan Ouzbékistan	1995	837	...	7 668	1 573	4 200	695	220	42 404	4 081
	1996	779	...	7 729	1 648	4 050	723	213	42 619	3 906
	1997	806	...	8 020	1 773	4 027	829	232	44 176	3 961
	1998	801	...	8 330	1 876	4 138	823	230	44 865	3 947
Viet Nam Viet Nam	1995	5 845	...	7 628	11	27	1	...	5	1 729
	1996	6 876	...	8 812	11	27	1	...	7	1 937
	1997	7 972	...	10 100	11	27	1	...	11	2 135
	1998	8 170	...	12 513	11	27	1	...	12	2 361
Yemen Yémen	1995	...	...	17 516	1 732	1 611	58	63	...	204
	1996	...	...	17 747	1 882	2 329	60	21	...	201
	1997	...	...	18 582	2 123	2 937	59	22	...	220
	1998	...	...	19 032	2 123	2 966	59	22	...	216
Europe Europe	1995	444 526	84 140	621 663	302 398	505 852	78 944	53 409	788 902	541 274
	1996	428 408	73 272	633 566	306 659	515 420	74 112	54 333	831 033	557 047
	1997	416 225	72 812	637 141	313 025	518 920	75 492	55 513	799 276	560 704
	1998	382 325	68 662	631 524	315 783	522 846	75 530	55 720	814 261	562 560
Albania Albanie	1995	41	0	522	154	150	40	50	26	380
	1996	26	0	488	149	155	36	40	21	510
	1997	19	0	366	137	147	14	30	17	489
	1998	14	0	368	137	147	14	30	16	436
Austria Autriche	1995	338	986	1 083	2 824	4 923	1 339	370	1 359	4 866
	1996	288	1 061	992	2 912	5 066	1 519	381	1 368	4 716
	1997	294	1 109	999	3 053	5 501	1 577	400	1 308	4 889
	1998	297	1 137	1 167	2 824	5 285	809	381	1 438	4 940
Belarus Bélarus	1995	714	...	1 934	1 957	9 059	638	721	246	2 143
	1996	649	...	1 862	1 930	7 986	680	718	230	2 041
	1997	630	...	1 824	2 140	7 645	755	650	227	2 241
	1998	682	...	1 832	2 106	7 582	768	641	252	2 020
Belgium Belgique	1995	384	2 602	...	8 000	16 037	4 450	1 040	0	13 641
	1996	337	2 500	...	9 504	19 590	5 516	1 198	2	14 158
	1997	257	2 389	...	9 873	20 085	6 110	1 225	0	15 300
	1998	188	2 109	...	10 786	20 603	5 885	1 352	0	15 461
Bosnia and Herzegovina Bosnie–Herzégovine	1995	511	...	...	...	...	...	...	...	189
	1996	527	...	...	...	...	...	...	...	206
	1997	543	...	...	...	...	...	...	...	212
	1998	559	...	...	...	...	...	...	...	218
Bulgaria Bulgarie	1995	5 142	1 253	43	2 414	4 640	68	275	40	6 615
	1996	4 689	1 248	32	2 203	4 106	312	238	37	6 838
	1997	4 472	1 241	28	1 978	3 534	215	214	31	6 745
	1998	4 970	1 087	33	1 810	3 301	357	211	26	6 544
Croatia Croatie	1995	54	0	2 065	1 659	2 909	335	432	1 786	762
	1996	45	0	1 913	1 475	2 869	291	400	1 622	907
	1997	34	0	1 977	1 501	2 985	346	374	1 560	833
	1998	36	0	1 989	1 550	2 927	341	451	1 426	937
Czech Republic République tchèque	1995	27 381	3 378	146	1 838	3 865	1 495	198	220	7 373
	1996	27 529	3 414	152	1 970	4 239	1 524	246	202	7 775
	1997	26 587	2 955	163	1 856	4 001	1 386	306	182	7 742
	1998	24 809	2 692	179	1 715	4 017	1 233	254	188	7 906
Denmark Danemark	1995	13	0	9 178	2 676	6 707	...	533	4 891	3 267
	1996	38	0	10 131	3 319	6 933	...	588	8 566	4 707
	1997	14	0	11 371	2 973	5 408	...	528	8 170	4 141
	1998	0	0	11 443	2 688	4 839	...	442	6 613	3 940

65
Production of selected energy commodities
Thousand metric tons of oil equivalent [*cont.*]
Production des principaux biens de l'énergie
Milliers de tonnes d'équivalent pétrole [*suite*]

Region, country or area Région, pays ou zone	Year Anneé	Hard coal, lignite & peat Houille, lignite et tourbe	Briquettes & cokes Agglo− mérés et cokes	Crude petroleum & NGL Pétrole brut et GNL	Light petroleum products Produits pétroliers légers	Heavy petroleum products Produits pétroliers lourds	Other petroleum products Autres produits pétroliers	LPG & refinery gas GLP et gaz de raffinerie	Natural gas Gaz naturel	Electricity Electricité
Estonia	1995	3 133	24	...	...	310	...	...	...	748
Estonie	1996	3 481	26	...	...	340	...	...	...	783
	1997	3 372	25	...	...	364	...	...	...	793
	1998	2 845	16	...	...	218	...	...	...	733
Faeroe Islands	1995	0	0	...	...	...	...	...	...	15
Iles Féroé	1996	0	0	...	...	...	...	...	...	15
	1997	0	0	...	...	...	...	...	...	16
	1998	0	0	...	...	...	...	...	...	16
Finland	1995	2 032	580	...	5 652	5 111	264	832	...	8 858
Finlande	1996	2 216	573	...	5 669	5 942	274	968	...	9 374
	1997	2 627	554	...	5 049	5 535	335	864	...	9 606
	1998	424	575	...	5 571	6 627	377	945	...	9 859
France [2]	1995	6 045	4 023	3 733	29 215	41 824	9 736	5 099	3 105	108 381
France [2]	1996	5 360	4 022	3 307	30 184	44 258	9 710	5 440	2 676	113 554
	1997	4 501	3 897	3 202	32 798	46 591	10 394	5 491	2 365	112 961
	1998	3 790	3 911	2 861	33 377	48 568	10 129	5 724	2 043	111 183
Germany	1995	78 346	12 193	2 929	40 695	59 486	9 512	7 326	15 959	73 151
Allemagne	1996	73 504	11 653	2 877	40 784	61 404	8 819	7 105	17 348	75 946
	1997	70 140	10 943	2 807	39 659	58 310	8 831	6 762	17 159	77 239
	1998	64 016	9 904	2 937	41 556	62 007	9 361	6 887	16 863	76 050
Gibraltar	1995	...	...	...	...	...	...	...	...	9
Gibraltar	1996	...	...	...	...	...	...	...	...	9
	1997	...	...	...	...	...	...	...	...	10
	1998	...	...	...	...	...	...	...	...	10
Greece	1995	7 508	34	446	6 301	10 053	641	952	48	3 601
Grèce	1996	7 783	32	501	6 617	12 189	693	1 082	50	3 640
	1997	7 709	36	458	6 846	12 306	697	1 115	49	3 780
	1998	7 976	28	317	6 896	12 524	761	1 201	44	4 006
Hungary	1995	2 970	848	3 038	2 665	4 109	933	289	4 207	5 380
Hongrie	1996	3 123	823	2 863	2 647	3 806	671	281	4 000	5 499
	1997	3 214	763	2 712	2 820	3 971	775	283	3 735	5 488
	1998	3 021	756	2 579	2 898	3 847	901	282	3 297	5 639
Iceland	1995	...	...	...	...	...	...	...	...	653
Islande	1996	...	...	...	...	...	...	...	...	712
	1997	...	...	...	...	...	...	...	...	771
	1998	...	...	...	...	...	...	...	...	1 048
Ireland	1995	1 785	166	...	594	1 616	16	81	2 499	1 548
Irlande	1996	1 261	146	...	619	1 566	0	86	2 410	1 658
	1997	740	134	...	805	2 028	19	101	2 119	1 723
	1998	813	139	...	837	2 228	31	115	1 564	1 846
Italy [3]	1995	88	3 630	5 243	30 521	51 152	5 416	5 470	18 175	23 535
Italie [3]	1996	69	3 473	5 459	30 328	50 326	5 035	5 347	18 194	23 932
	1997	24	3 653	5 956	32 444	54 324	5 654	5 597	17 544	24 648
	1998	44	3 634	5 629	33 269	57 118	5 894	5 342	17 309	25 407
Latvia	1995	79	...	...	...	...	...	...	...	342
Lettonie	1996	89	...	...	...	...	...	...	...	269
	1997	89	...	...	...	...	...	...	...	387
	1998	13	...	...	...	...	...	...	...	498
Lithuania	1995	14	...	128	1 119	1 839	411	181	...	3 264
Lituanie	1996	18	...	155	1 628	2 195	139	255	...	3 884
	1997	20	...	212	1 979	3 018	70	455	...	3 382
	1998	14	...	277	2 603	3 587	120	473	...	3 888
Luxembourg	1995	...	...	...	...	...	...	...	...	102
Luxembourg	1996	...	...	...	...	...	...	...	...	101
	1997	...	...	...	...	...	...	...	...	100
	1998	...	...	...	...	...	...	...	...	100
Malta	1995	...	0	...	...	...	...	...	...	130
Malte	1996	...	0	...	...	...	...	...	...	130
	1997	...	0	...	...	...	...	...	...	130
	1998	...	0	...	...	...	...	...	...	131

65
Production of selected energy commodities
Thousand metric tons of oil equivalent [*cont.*]
Production des principaux biens de l'énergie
Milliers de tonnes d'équivalent pétrole [*suite*]

Region, country or area Région, pays ou zone	Year Anneé	Hard coal, lignite & peat Houille, lignite et tourbe	Briquettes & cokes Agglomérés et cokes	Crude petroleum & NGL Pétrole brut et GNL	Light petroleum products Produits pétroliers légers	Heavy petroleum products Produits pétroliers lourds	Other petroleum products Autres produits pétroliers	LPG & refinery gas GLP et gaz de raffinerie	Natural gas Gaz naturel	Electricity Electricité
Netherlands	1995	...	1 971	3 542	34 131	33 563	7 302	7 251	67 049	7 655
Pays–Bas	1996	...	1 988	3 175	33 927	36 035	5 161	7 888	75 794	8 045
	1997	...	1 977	3 000	33 595	34 645	5 532	7 767	67 253	7 872
	1998	...	1 931	2 738	32 960	35 888	5 780	7 515	63 950	8 485
Norway [4]	1995	196	...	135 718	4 678	7 656	145	913	35 361	10 590
Norvège [4]	1996	154	...	153 908	5 211	8 397	131	1 056	46 734	9 009
	1997	259	...	153 690	5 344	8 928	166	1 107	48 045	9 602
	1998	220	...	147 294	5 068	8 778	168	1 104	47 731	10 066
Poland	1995	90 475	7 743	292	4 111	8 682	1 365	477	3 488	11 955
Pologne	1996	91 306	6 927	317	4 375	9 248	1 557	506	3 606	12 313
	1997	91 110	7 153	289	4 551	9 480	1 913	610	3 562	12 280
	1998	78 514	6 613	360	4 672	10 316	1 834	758	3 612	12 280
Portugal	1995	0	222	...	4 945	7 754	473	459	...	2 893
Portugal	1996	0	222	...	4 596	6 827	777	413	...	3 007
	1997	0	228	...	5 039	7 025	791	494	...	2 978
	1998	0	236	...	5 028	7 590	1 263	446	...	3 398
Republic of Moldova	1995	...	...	...	...	...	...	...	...	522
République de Moldova	1996	...	...	...	...	...	...	...	...	526
	1997	...	...	...	...	...	...	...	...	454
	1998	...	...	...	...	...	...	...	...	394
Romania	1995	7 364	2 132	6 976	4 375	7 726	1 358	1 314	14 455	5 097
Roumanie	1996	7 531	1 986	6 876	4 048	6 644	1 661	1 088	13 773	5 519
	1997	6 229	2 089	6 776	3 998	6 073	1 267	1 148	11 916	5 860
	1998	4 844	1 973	6 579	3 997	6 019	1 981	1 213	11 157	5 529
Russian Federation	1995	110 331	22 071	305 412	39 251	115 271	17 794	9 445	524 655	91 404
Fédération de Russie	1996	107 146	13 813	299 797	37 980	112 386	15 580	9 424	529 133	92 234
	1997	102 266	13 996	304 172	38 229	111 246	14 424	10 165	507 641	90 826
	1998	96 682	12 589	301 707	36 954	101 969	12 224	10 249	525 736	89 307
Slovakia	1995	1 101	1 201	74	1 709	2 758	444	147	297	4 264
Slovaquie	1996	1 121	1 102	71	1 654	2 884	675	133	272	4 145
	1997	1 146	1 116	64	1 671	2 944	746	133	250	4 024
	1998	1 157	977	60	1 742	3 133	565	109	224	4 184
Slovenia	1995	1 062	...	2	232	369	4	...	16	1 924
Slovénie	1996	1 037	...	1	219	312	3	...	11	1 896
	1997	1 077	...	1	174	375	3	...	10	2 011
	1998	1 063	...	1	73	174	0	...	7	2 062
Spain	1995	9 536	1 763	935	16 545	30 576	5 719	3 471	417	24 077
Espagne	1996	9 353	1 745	801	16 206	29 972	5 066	3 148	468	24 865
	1997	9 293	1 914	670	16 653	32 310	5 089	3 364	178	26 042
	1998	8 736	1 903	873	18 319	35 191	6 399	3 283	114	27 117
Sweden	1995	304	770	4	5 915	12 178	1 112	251	...	24 884
Suède	1996	351	771	4	6 358	13 004	1 103	283	...	24 951
	1997	252	777	0	6 485	13 906	1 113	295	...	25 114
	1998	322	769	0	6 357	13 528	1 188	320	...	26 488
Switzerland [5]	1995	...	...	...	1 418	2 806	154	360	0	9 781
Suisse [5]	1996	...	...	...	1 590	3 214	134	420	0	9 307
	1997	...	...	...	1 682	2 872	126	425	0	9 847
	1998	...	...	...	1 723	2 845	144	471	0	9 929
TFYR Macedonia	1995	1 957	...	...	23	88	0	1	...	523
L'ex–R.y. Macédonie	1996	1 929	...	...	61	611	0	8	...	555
	1997	1 809	...	...	37	348	0	3	...	574
	1998	2 208	...	...	161	566	1	10	...	606
Ukraine	1995	44 230	12 393	4 062	3 677	11 187	1 431	460	16 937	29 105
Ukraine	1996	39 012	11 232	4 102	2 943	8 945	1 068	357	17 167	29 577
	1997	39 613	11 326	4 138	3 594	8 123	996	341	16 909	29 209
	1998	39 715	11 370	3 904	3 773	8 529	1 045	358	16 756	28 030
United Kingdom	1995	32 870	4 161	133 089	42 727	40 744	6 123	4 997	72 869	44 453
Royaume–Uni	1996	30 244	4 515	132 750	44 760	43 016	5 657	5 209	86 746	46 458
	1997	29 218	4 536	131 285	44 883	43 145	5 853	5 215	88 427	46 920
	1998	24 956	4 312	135 483	43 181	41 708	5 666	5 103	93 236	48 375

65
Production of selected energy commodities
Thousand metric tons of oil equivalent [*cont.*]
Production des principaux biens de l'énergie
Milliers de tonnes d'équivalent pétrole [*suite*]

Region, country or area / Région, pays ou zone	Year / Anneé	Hard coal, lignite & peat / Houille, lignite et tourbe	Briquettes & cokes / Agglo- mérés et cokes	Crude petroleum & NGL / Pétrole brut et GNL	Light petroleum products / Produits pétroliers légers	Heavy petroleum products / Produits pétroliers lourds	Other petroleum products / Autres produits pétroliers	LPG & refinery gas / GLP et gaz de raffinerie	Natural gas / Gaz naturel	Electricity / Electricité
Yugoslavia	1995	8 523	...	1 067	376	705	225	12	799	3 197
Yougoslavie	1996	8 193	...	1 031	795	954	321	29	605	3 276
	1997	8 668		980	1 179	1 746	293	51	620	3 467
	1998	9 398	...	914	1 156	1 188	289	49	659	3 496
Oceania	**1995**	**133 519**	**3 115**	**35 097**	**20 667**	**14 630**	**3 142**	**2 272**	**32 096**	**20 032**
Océanie	**1996**	**135 798**	**3 040**	**34 105**	**21 349**	**14 895**	**3 339**	**2 411**	**33 432**	**20 566**
	1997	**145 102**	**2 903**	**34 328**	**21 626**	**15 426**	**3 243**	**2 477**	**33 644**	**21 168**
	1998	**154 352**	**3 172**	**36 999**	**21 941**	**15 773**	**3 522**	**2 330**	**34 195**	**22 390**
American Samoa	1995	...	...	...	...	...	...	...	...	11
Samoa américaines	1996									11
	1997	...	...	...	...	...	...	...	...	11
	1998	...	...	...	...	...	...	...	...	11
Australia	1995	131 568	3 115	28 471	18 209	12 631	2 900	2 107	27 794	14 911
Australie	1996	133 798	3 040	27 977	18 990	12 946	3 105	2 220	28 525	15 280
	1997	143 212	2 903	27 579	19 123	13 271	3 044	2 226	28 415	15 754
	1998	152 508	3 172	30 846	19 414	13 453	3 314	2 087	29 586	16 756
Cook Islands	1995	...	...	...	...	...	...	...	...	1
Iles Cook	1996	...	...	...	...	...	...	...	...	1
	1997	...	...	...	...	...	...	...	...	1
	1998	...	...	...	...	...	...	...	...	1
Fiji	1995	...	...	...	...	...	...	...	...	47
Fidji	1996	...	...	...	...	...	...	...	...	47
	1997									47
	1998	...	...	...	...	...	...	...	...	46
French Polynesia	1995	...	...	...	...	...	...	...	...	30
Polynésie française	1996	...	...	...	...	...	...	...	...	31
	1997	...	...	...	...	...	...	...	...	31
	1998	...	...	...	...	...	...	...	...	31
Guam	1995	...	...	...	...	...	...	...	...	71
Guam	1996	...	...	...	...	...	...	...	...	71
	1997	...	...	...	...	...	...	...	...	71
	1998	...	...	...	...	...	...	...	...	71
Kiribati	1995	...	...	...	...	...	...	...	...	1
Kiribati	1996	...	...	...	...	...	...	...	...	1
	1997	...	...	...	...	...	...	...	...	1
	1998	...	...	...	...	...	...	...	...	1
Nauru	1995	...	...	...	...	...	...	...	...	3
Nauru	1996	...	...	...	...	...	...	...	...	3
	1997	...	...	...	...	...	...	...	...	3
	1998	...	...	...	...	...	...	...	...	3
New Caledonia	1995	...	...	...	...	...	...	...	...	142
Nouvelle – Caledonie	1996	...	...	...	...	...	...	...	...	135
	1997	...	...	...	...	...	...	...	...	135
	1998	...	...	...	...	...	...	...	...	135
New Zealand	1995	1 951	...	1 621	2 437	1 969	242	166	4 225	4 629
Nouvelle–Zélande	1996	2 000	...	2 124	2 338	1 919	234	191	4 829	4 800
	1997	1 889	...	2 785	2 482	2 122	198	250	5 151	4 929
	1998	1 845	...	2 249	2 509	2 289	208	243	4 531	5 149
Niue	1995	...	...	...	...	...	...	...	...	0
Niue	1996	...	...	...	...	...	...	...	...	0
	1997	...	...	...	...	...	...	...	...	0
	1998	...	...	...	...	...	...	...	...	0
Palau	1995	...	...	...	...	...	...	...	...	18
Palaos	1996	...	...	...	...	...	...	...	...	18
	1997	...	...	...	...	...	...	...	...	18
	1998	...	...	...	...	...	...	...	...	18
Papua New Guinea	1995	...	...	5 005	21	30	...	...	76	154
Papouasie–Nouv.–Guinée	1996	...	...	4 004	21	30	...	...	78	154
	1997	...	...	3 964	21	32	...	...	78	154
	1998	...	...	3 904	19	30	...	...	78	154

65
Production of selected energy commodities
Thousand metric tons of oil equivalent [*cont.*]
Production des principaux biens de l'énergie
Milliers de tonnes d'équivalent pétrole [*suite*]

Region, country or area Région, pays ou zone	Year Anneé	Hard coal, lignite & peat Houille, lignite et tourbe	Briquettes & cokes Agglo- mérés et cokes	Crude petroleum & NGL Pétrole brut et GNL	Light petroleum products Produits pétroliers légers	Heavy petroleum products Produits pétroliers lourds	Other petroleum products Autres produits pétroliers	LPG & refinery gas GLP et gaz de raffinerie	Natural gas Gaz naturel	Electricity Electricité
Samoa Samoa	1995	...	...	...	...	...	...	...	...	6
	1996	...	...	...	...	...	...	...	...	6
	1997	...	...	...	...	...	...	...	...	6
	1998	...	...	...	...	...	...	...	...	6
Solomon Islands Iles Salomon	1995	...	...	...	...	...	...	...	...	3
	1996	...	...	...	...	...	...	...	...	3
	1997	...	...	...	...	...	...	...	...	3
	1998	...	...	...	...	...	...	...	...	3
Tonga Tonga	1995	...	...	...	...	...	...	...	...	3
	1996	...	...	...	...	...	...	...	...	3
	1997	...	...	...	...	...	...	...	...	3
	1998	...	...	...	...	...	...	...	...	3
Vanuatu Vanuatu	1995	...	...	...	...	...	...	...	...	3
	1996	...	...	...	...	...	...	...	...	3
	1997	...	...	...	...	...	...	...	...	3
	1998	...	...	...	...	...	...	...	...	3

Source:
United Nations Statistics Division, New York, "Energy Statistics Yearbook 1998" and the energy statistics database.

Source:
Organisation des Nations Unies, Division de statistique, New York, "Annuaire des statistiques de l'énergie 1998" et la base de données pour les statistiques énergétiques.

† For information on recent changes in country or area nomenclature pertaining to former Czechoslovakia, Germany, Hong Kong Special Administrative Region (SAR) of China, Macao Special Administrative Region of China (SAR), SFR of Yugoslavia and former USSR, see Annex I – Country or area nomenclature, regional and other groupings.

†† For statistical purposes, the data for China do not include those for the Hong Kong Special Administrative Region (Hong Kong SAR), Macao Special Administrative Region (Macao SAR) and Taiwan province of China.

1 Including part of the Neutral Zone.
2 Including Monaco.
3 Including San Marino.
4 Including Svalbard and Jan Mayen Islands.
5 Including Liechtenstein.

† Pour les modifications récentes de nomenclature de pays ou de zone ou de zone concernant l'Allemagne, Hong Kong (Région administrative spéciale de Chine), Macao (Région administrative spéciale de Chine), l'ex-Tchécoslovaquie, Rfs de Yougoslavie et l'ex–URSS, voir annexe I – Nomenclature des pays ou des zones, groupements régionaux et autres groupements.

†† Les données statistiques relatives à la Chine ne comprennent pas celles qui concernent la région administrative spéciale de Hong Kong (la RAS de Hong Kong), la région administrative spéciale de Macao (la RAS de Macao) et la province chinoise de Taiwan.

1 Y compris une partie de la Zone Neutral.
2 Y compris Monaco.
3 Y compris Saint–Marin.
4 Y compris îles Svalbard et Jan Mayen.
5 Y compris Liechtenstein.

Technical notes, tables 64 and 65

Tables 64 and 65: Data are presented in metric tons of oil equivalent (TOE), to which the individual energy commodities are converted in the interests of international uniformity and comparability.

To convert from original units to TOE, the data in original units (metric tons, terajoules, kilowatt hours, cubic metres) are multiplied by conversion factors. For a list of the relevant conversion factors and a detailed description of methods, see the United Nations *Energy Statistics Yearbook* and related methodological publications [23, 44, 45].

Table 64: Included in the production of commercial primary energy for *solids* are hard coal, lignite, peat and oil shale; *liquids* are comprised of crude petroleum and natural gas liquids; *gas* comprises natural gas; and *electricity* is comprised of primary electricity generation from hydro, nuclear, geothermal, wind, tide, wave and solar sources.

In general, data on stocks refer to changes in stocks of producers, importers and/or industrial consumers at the beginning and end of each year.

International trade of energy commodities is based on the "general trade" system, that is, all goods entering and leaving the national boundary of a country are recorded as imports and exports.

Sea/air bunkers refer to the amounts of fuels delivered to ocean-going ships or aircraft of all flags engaged in international traffic. Consumption by ships engaged in transport in inland and coastal waters, or by aircraft engaged in domestic flights, is not included.

Data on consumption refer to "apparent consumption" and are derived from the formula "production + imports – exports – bunkers +/– stock changes". Accordingly, the series on apparent consumption may in some cases represent only an indication of the magnitude of actual gross inland availability.

Included in the consumption of commercial energy for *solids* are consumption of primary forms of solid fuels, net imports and changes in stocks of secondary fuels; *liquids* are comprised of consumption of energy petroleum products including feedstocks, natural gasolene, condensate, refinery gas and input of crude petroleum to thermal power plants; *gases* include the consumption of natural gas, net imports and changes in stocks of gasworks and coke-oven gas; and *electricity* is comprised of production of primary electricity and net imports of electricity.

Table 65: The definitions of the energy commodities are as follows:

— Hard coal: Coal that has a high degree of coalification with a gross calorific value above 23,865 KJ/kg (5,700 kcal/kg) on an ash-free but moist basis, and a mean random reflectance of vitrinite of at least 0.6. Slurries, middlings and

Notes techniques, tableaux 64 et 65

Tableaux 64 et 65: Les données relatives aux divers produits énergétiques ont été converties en tonnes d'équivalent pétrole (TEP), dans un souci d'uniformité et pour permettre les comparaisons entre la production de différents pays.

Pour passer des unités de mesure d'origine à l'unité commune, les données en unités d'origine (tonnes, kilowatt-heures, mètres cubes) sont multipliées pour les facteurs de conversion. Pour une liste des facteurs de conversion appropriée et pour des descriptions détaillées des méthodes appliquées, se reporter à *l'Annuaire des statistiques de l'énergie* des Nations Unies et aux publications méthodologiques connexes [23, 44, 45].

Tableau 64: Sont compris dans la production d'énergie primaire commerciale: pour *les solides*, la houille, le lignite, la tourbe et le schiste bitumineux; pour *les liquides*, le pétrole brut et les liquides de gaz naturel; pour *les gaz*, le gaz naturel; pour *l'électricité*, l'électricité primaire de source hydraulique, nucléaire, géothermique, éolienne, marémotrice, des vagues et solaire.

En général, les variations des stocks se rapportent aux différences entre les stocks des producteurs, des importateurs ou des consommateurs industriels au début et à la fin de chaque année.

Le commerce international des produits énergétiques est fondé sur le système du "commerce général", c'est-à-dire que tous les biens entrant sur le territoire national d'un pays ou en sortant sont respectivement enregistrés comme importations et exportations.

Les soutages maritimes/aériens se rapportent aux quantités de combustibles livrées aux navires de mer et aéronefs assurant des liaisons commerciales internationales, quel que soit leur pavillon. La consommation des navires effectuant des opérations de transport sur les voies navigables intérieures ou dans les eaux côtières n'est pas incluse, non plus que celle des aéronefs effectuant des vols intérieurs.

Les données sur la consommation se rapportent à la "consommation apparente" et sont obtenues par la formule "production + importations - exportations - soutage +/- variations des stocks". En conséquence, les séries relatives à la consommation apparente peuvent occasionnellement ne donner qu'une indication de l'ordre de grandeur des disponibilités intérieures brutes réelles.

Sont compris dans la consommation d'énergie commerciale: pour *les solides*, la consommation de combustibles solides primaires, les importations nettes et les variations de stocks de combustibles solides secondaires; pour *les liquides*, la consommation de produits pétroliers énergétiques y compris les charges d'alimentation des usines de traitement, l'essence naturelle, le condensat et le gaz de raffinerie ainsi que le pétrole brut consommé dans les centrales thermiques pour la production d'électricité; pour *les gaz*, la consommation de gaz naturel, les importations nettes et

other low-grade coal products, which cannot be classified according to the type of coal from which they are obtained, are included under hard coal.

— Lignite: Non-agglomerating coal with a low degree of coalification which retained the anatomical structure of the vegetable matter from which it was formed. Its gross calorific value is less than 17,435 KJ/kg (4,165 kcal/kg), and it contains greater than 31 per cent volatile matter on a dry mineral matter free basis.

— Peat: A solid fuel formed from the partial decomposition of dead vegetation under conditions of high humidity and limited air access (initial stage of coalification). Only peat used as fuel is included.

— Patent fuel (hard coal briquettes): A composition fuel manufactured from coal fines by shaping with the addition of a binding agent (pitch).

— Lignite briquettes: A composition fuel manufactured from lignite. The lignite is crushed, dried and molded under high pressure into an even-shaped briquette without the addition of binders.

— Peat briquettes: A composition fuel manufactured from peat. Raw peat, after crushing and drying, is molded under high pressure into an even-shaped briquette without the addition of binders.

— Coke: The solid residue obtained from coal or lignite by heating it to a high temperature in the absence or near absence of air. It is high in carbon and low in moisture and volatile matter. Several categories are distinguished: coke-oven coke; gas coke; and brown coal coke.

— Crude oil: A mineral oil consisting of a mixture of hydrocarbons of natural origin, yellow to black in color, of variable density and viscosity. Data in this category also includes lease or field condensate (separator liquids) which is recovered from gaseous hydrocarbons in lease separation facilities, as well as synthetic crude oil, mineral oils extracted from bituminous minerals such as shales and bituminous sand, and oils from coal liquefaction.

— Natural gas liquids (NGL): Liquid or liquefied hydrocarbons produced in the manufacture, purification and stabilization of natural gas. NGLs include, but are not limited to, ethane, propane, butane, pentane, natural gasolene, and plant condensate.

— Light petroleum products: Light products are defined in the table as liquid products obtained by distillation of crude petroleum at temperatures between 30°C and 350°C, and/or which have a specific gravity between 0.625 and 0.830. They comprise: aviation gasolene; motor gasolene; natural gasolene; jet fuel; kerosene; naphtha; and white spirit/industrial spirit.

— Heavy petroleum products: are defined in the table as products obtained by the distillation of crude petroleum at temperatures above 350°C, and which have a specific gravity higher than 0.83. Products which are

les variations de stocks de gaz d'usines à gaz et de gaz de cokerie; pour *l'électricité*, la production d'électricité primaire et les importations nettes d'électricité.

Tableau 65: Les définitions des produits énergétiques sont données ci-après :

— Houille: Charbon à haut degré de houillification et de pouvoir calorifique brut supérieur à 23 865 kJ/kg (5 700 kcal/kg), valeur mesurée pour un combustible exempt de cendres, mais humide et ayant un indice moyen de réflectance de la vitrinite au moins égal à 0,6. Les schlamms, les mixtes et autres produits du charbon de faible qualité qui ne peuvent être classés en fonction du type de charbon dont ils sont dérivés, sont inclus dans cette rubrique.

— Lignite: Le charbon non agglutinant d'un faible degré de houillification qui a gardé la structure anatomique des végétaux dont il est issu. Son pouvoir calorifique supérieur est inférieur à 17 435 kJ/kg (4 165 kcal/kg) et il contient plus de 31% de matières volatiles sur produit sec exempt de matières minérales.

— Tourbe: Combustible solide issu de la décomposition partielle de végétaux morts dans des conditions de forte humidité et de faible circulation d'air (phase initiale de la houillification). N'est prise en considération ici que la tourbe utilisée comme combustible.

— Agglomérés (briquettes de houille): Combustibles composites fabriqués par moulage au moyen de fines de charbon avec l'addition d'un liant (brai).

— Briquettes de lignite: Combustibles composites fabriqués au moyen de lignite. Le lignite est broyé, séché et moulé sous pression élevée pour donner une briquette de forme régulière sans l'addition d'un élément liant.

— Briquettes de tourbe: Combustibles composites fabriqués au moyen de tourbe. La tourbe brute, après broyage et séchage, est moulée sous pression élevée pour donner une briquette de forme régulière sans l'addition d'un élément liant.

— Coke: Résidu solide obtenu lors de la distillation de houille ou de lignite en l'absence totale ou presque total d'air. Il a un haut contenu de carbone, et a peu d'humidité et matières volatiles. On distingue plusieurs catégories de coke: coke de four; coke de gaz; et coke de lignite.

— Pétrole brut: Huile minérale constituée d'un mélange d'hydrocarbures d'origine naturelle, de couleur variant du jaune au noir, d'une densité et d'une viscosité variable. Figurent également dans cette rubrique les condensats directement récupérés sur les sites d'exploitation des hydrocarbures gazeux (dans les installations prévues pour la séparation des phases liquide et gazeuse), le pétrole brut synthétique, les huiles minérales brutes extraites des roches bitumineuses telles que schistes, sables asphaltiques et les huiles issues de la liquéfaction du charbon.

— Liquides de gaz naturel (LGN): Hydrocarbures liquides ou liquéfiés produits lors de la fabrication, de la purification et de la stabilisation du gaz naturel. Les liquides de gaz naturel comprennent l'éthane, le propane, le butane, le pentane, l'essence naturelle et les conden-

not used for energy purposes, such as insulating oils, lubricants, paraffin wax, bitumen and petroleum coke, are excluded. Heavy products comprise residual fuel oil and gas-diesel oil (distillate fuel oil).

— Liquefied petroleum gas (LPG): Hydrocarbons which are gaseous under conditions of normal temperature and pressure but are liquefied by compression or cooling to facilitate storage, handling and transportation. It comprises propane, butane, or a combination of the two. Also included is ethane from petroleum refineries or natural gas producers' separation and stabilization plants.

— Refinery gas: Non-condensable gas obtained during distillation of crude oil or treatment of oil products (e.g. cracking) in refineries. It consists mainly of hydrogen, methane, ethane and olefins.

— Natural gas: Gases consisting mainly of methane occurring naturally in underground deposits. It includes both non-associated gas (originating from fields producing only hydrocarbons in gaseous form) and associated gas (originating from fields producing both liquid and gaseous hydrocarbons), as well as methane recovered from coal mines and sewage gas. Production of natural gas refers to dry marketable production, measured after purification and extraction of natural gas liquids and sulphur. Extraction losses and the amounts that have been reinjected, flared, and vented are excluded from the data on production.

— Electricity production refers to gross production, which includes the consumption by station auxiliaries and any losses in the transformers that are considered integral parts of the station. Included also is total electric energy produced by pumping installations without deduction of electric energy absorbed by pumping.

le butane, le pentane, l'essence naturelle et les condensats d'usine, sans que la liste soit limitative.

— Produits pétroliers légers: Les produits légers sont définis ici comme des produits liquides obtenus par distillation du pétrole brut à des températures comprises entre 30°C et 350°C et/ou ayant une densité comprise entre 0,625 et 0,830. Ces produits sont les suivants: l'essence aviation; l'essence auto; l'essence naturelle; les carburéacteurs du type essence et du type kérosène; le pétrole lampant; les naphtas; et le white spirit/essences spéciales.

— Produits pétroliers lourds sont définis ici comme des produits obtenus par distillation du pétrole brut à des températures supérieures à 350°C et ayant une densité supérieure à 0,83. En sont exclus les produits qui ne sont pas utilisés à des fins énergétiques, tels que les huiles isolantes, les lubrifiants, les paraffines, le bitume et le coke de pétrole. Les produits lourds comprennent le mazout résiduel et le gazole/carburant diesel (mazout distillé).

— Gaz de pétrole liquéfiés (GPL): Hydrocarbures qui sont à l'état gazeux dans des conditions de température et de pression normales mais sont liquéfiés par compression ou refroidissement pour en faciliter l'entreposage, la manipulation et le transport. Dans cette rubrique figurent le propane et le butane ou un mélange de ces deux hydrocarbures. Est également inclus l'éthane produit dans les raffineries ou dans les installations de séparation et de stabilisation des producteurs de gaz naturel.

— Gaz de raffinerie: Comprend les gaz non condensables obtenus dans les raffineries lors de la distillation du pétrole brut ou du traitement des produits pétroliers (par craquage par exemple). Il s'agit principalement d'hydrogène, de méthane, d'éthane et d'oléfines.

— Gaz naturel: Est constitué de gaz, méthane essentiellement, extraits de gisements naturels souterrains. Il peut s'agir aussi bien de gaz non associé (provenant de gisements qui produisent uniquement des hydrocarbures gazeux) que de gaz associé (provenant de gisements qui produisent à la fois des hydrocarbures liquides et gazeux) ou de méthane récupéré dans les mines de charbon et le gaz de gadoues. La production de gaz naturel se rapporte à la production de gaz commercialisable sec, mesurée après purification et extraction des condensats de gaz naturel et du soufre. Les quantités réinjectées, brûlées à la torchère ou éventées et les pertes d'extraction sont exclus des données sur la production.

— Production d'électricité se rapporte à la production brute, qui comprend la consommation des équipements auxiliaires des centrales et les pertes au niveau des transformateurs considérés comme faisant partie intégrante de ces centrales, ainsi que la quantité totale d'énergie électrique produits par les installations de pompage sans déductions de l'énergie électrique absorbée par ces dernières.

66 Land
Terres

Country or area Pays ou zone	1999 Land area Superficie des terres	1999 Arable land Terres arables	Permanent crops Cultures permanentes	2000 Forest cover Superficie forestière	Net change − Variation nette 1990 − 1999 Arable land Terres arables	Net change − Variation nette 1990 − 1999 Permanent crops Cultures permanentes	Net change − Variation nette 1990−2000 Forest cover Superficie forestière	1997 Protected areas Aires protégées	Protected areas Aires protégées $\%$ [2]
			Area in thousand hectares − Superficie en milliers de hectares						
Africa · Afrique									
Algeria Algérie	238174	7700[1]	515[1]	2145	619	−39	27	5890.8	2.5
Angola Angola	124670	3000[1]	500[1]	69756	100	0	−124	8181.2	6.6
Benin Bénin	11062	1700[1]	150[1]	2650	85	45	−70	1262.5	11.2
Botswana Botswana	56673	343[1]	3[1]	12427	−75	0	−118	10498.7	18.3
Burkina Faso Burkina Faso	27360	3400[1]	50[1]	7089	−120	−5	−15	2855.2	10.4
Burundi Burundi	2568	770[1]	330[1]	94	−40	−10	−15	146.2	5.3
Cameroon Cameroun	46540	5960[1]	1200[1]	23858	20	−30	−222	2097.7	4.4
Cape Verde Cap−Vert	403	39[1]	2[1]	85	−2	0	5	0.0	0.0
Central African Republic République centrafricaine	62298	1930[1]	90[1]	22907	10	4	−30	5445.6	8.7
Chad Tchad	125920	3520[1]	30[1]	12692	247	3	−82	11494.0	9.0
Comoros Comores	223	78[1]	40[1]	8	0	5	...	0.0	0.0
Congo Congo	34150	175[1]	45[1]	22060	21	3	−17	1699.8	5.0
Côte d'Ivoire Côte d'Ivoire	31800	2950[1]	4400[1]	7117	520	900	−265	1985.5	6.2
Dem. Republic of the Congo République dém. du Congo	226705	6700[1]	1180[1]	135207	30	−10	−532	14637.4	6.2
Djibouti Djibouti	2318	...	...	6	...	...	...	10.0	0.4
Egypt Egypte	99545	2834[1]	466[1]	72	550	102	2	793.8	0.8
Equatorial Guinea Guinée équatoriale	2805	130[1]	100[1]	1752	0	0	−11	0.0	0.0
Eritrea Erythrée	10100	498[1]	2[1]	1585	...	...	−5	500.6	4.3
Ethiopia Ethiopie	100000	10000[1]	728[1]	4593	...	...	−40	18699.8	16.9
Gabon Gabon	25767	325[1]	170[1]	21826	30	8	−10	723.0	2.7
Gambia Gambie	1000	195[1]	5[1]	481	13	0	4	22.5	2.1
Ghana Ghana	22754	3600[1]	1700[1]	6335	900	200	−120	1268.4	5.3
Guinea Guinée	24572	885[1]	600[1]	6929	157	100	−35	163.5	0.7
Guinea−Bissau Guinée−Bissau	2812	300[1]	50[1]	2187	0	10	−22	0.0	0.0
Kenya Kenya	56914	4000[1]	520[1]	17096	0	20	−93	4538.3	7.8
Lesotho Lesotho	3035	325[1]	...	14	8	...	...	6.8	0.2
Liberia Libéria	9632	190[1]	200[1]	3481	20	−30	−76	129.2	1.2
Libyan Arab Jamahiriya Jamah. arabe libyenne	175954	1815[1]	335[1]	358	10	−15	5	173.0	0.1

66
Land [*cont.*]
Terres [*suite*]

Country or area Pays ou zone	1999 Land area Superficie des terres	1999 Arable land Terres arables	Permanent crops Cultures permanentes	2000 Forest cover Superficie forestière	Net change − Variation nette 1990 − 1999 Arable land Terres arables	Net change − Variation nette 1990 − 1999 Permanent crops Cultures permanentes	1990−2000 Forest cover Superficie forestière	1997 Protected areas Aires protégées	Protecte area Aire protégée %
				Area in thousand hectares − Superficie en milliers de hectares					
Madagascar Madagascar	58154	2565[1]	543[1]	11727	63	−57	−117	1231.9	2.
Malawi Malawi	9408	1875[1]	125[1]	2562	60	10	−71	1058.5	11.
Mali Mali	122019	4606[1]	44[1]	13186	2553	4	−99	4531.9	3.
Mauritania Mauritanie	102522	488[1]	12[1]	317	88	6	−10	1746.0	1.
Mauritius Maurice	203	100[1]	6[1]	16	0	0	...	15.7	8.
Mayotte Mayotte	...	...	...	...	...	...	...	4.5	12.
Morocco Maroc	44630	8500[1]	945[1]	3025	−207	209	−1	317.4	0.
Mozambique Mozambique	78409	3120[1]	230[1]	30601	50	0	−64	6979.0	8.
Namibia Namibie	82329	816[1]	4[1]	8040	156	2	−73	11215.8	13.6
Niger Niger	126670	4994[1]	6[1]	1328	1394	1	−62	9694.1	8.2
Nigeria Nigéria	91077	28200[1]	2538[1]	13517	−1339	3	−398	3021.4	3.3
Reunion Réunion	250	32	3	71	−15	−2	−1	13.0	5.2
Rwanda Rwanda	2467	866	250	307	−14	−55	−15	396.4	15.1
Saint Helena Sainte−Hélène	31	4[1]	...	2	2	...	...	7.6	18.5
Sao Tome and Principe Sao Tomé−et−Principe	96	2[1]	39[1]	27	0	−1	...	...	...
Senegal Sénégal	19253	2230[1]	36[1]	6205	−95	11	−45	2242.1	11.4
Seychelles Seychelles	45	1[1]	6[1]	30	0	1	...	44.9	99.8
Sierra Leone Sierra Leone	7162	484	56	1055	−2	2	−36	153.3	2.1
Somalia Somalie	62734	1043[1]	22[1]	7515	21	2	−77	524.5	0.8
South Africa Afrique du Sud	122104	14753	959	8917	1313	99	−8	6645.1	5.6
Sudan Soudan	237600	16700[1]	200[1]	61627	3700	−35	−959	12249.0	4.9
Swaziland Swaziland	1720	168[1]	12[1]	522	−12	0	6	60.0	3.5
Togo Togo	5439	2200[1]	100[1]	510	100	10	−21	429.1	7.6
Tunisia Tunisie	15536	2850[1]	2250[1]	510	−59	308	1	44.5	0.3
Uganda Ouganda	19710	5060[1]	1750[1]	4190	60	40	−91	4915.3	20.8
United Republic of Tanzania Rép.−Unie de Tanzanie	88359	3750	900[1]	38811	250	0	−91	26261.8	27.9
Zambia Zambie	74339	5260[1]	19[1]	31246	11	0	−851	22649.1	30.1
Zimbabwe Zimbabwe	38685	3220[1]	130[1]	19040	330	10	−320	4996.8	12.8
America, North · Amérique du Nord									
Antigua and Barbuda Antigua−et−Barbuda	44	8[1]	...	9	0	...	...	6.6	14.9
Aruba Aruba	19	2[1]	...	...	0	...	...	0.0	0.0

66
Land [*cont.*]
Terres [*suite*]

Country or area Pays ou zone	1999 Land area Superficie des terres	1999 Arable land Terres arables	Permanent crops Cultures permanentes	2000 Forest cover Superficie forestière	Net change – Variation nette 1990–1999 Arable land Terres arables	Net change – Variation nette 1990–1999 Permanent crops Cultures permanentes	Net change – Variation nette 1990–2000 Forest cover Superficie forestière	1997 Protected areas Aires protégées	Protected areas Aires protégées % [2]
	Area in thousand hectares – Superficie en milliers de hectares								
Bahamas Bahamas	1001	6	4	842	−2	2	...	145.7	10.5
Barbados Barbade	43	16[1]	1[1]	2	0	0	...	0.2	0.5
Belize Belize	2280	64[1]	25[1]	1348	14	7	−36	913.0	39.8
Bermuda Bermudes	5	...	...	...	...	...	...	12.5	231.5
British Virgin Islands Iles Vierges britanniques	15	3[1]	1[1]	3	0	0	...	2.0	13.1
Canada Canada	922097	45560[1]	140[1]	244571	−260	10	...	95310.3	9.6
Cayman Islands Iles Caïmanes	26	...	...	13	...	...	...	8.8	34.0
Costa Rica Costa Rica	5106	225[1]	280[1]	1968	−35	30	−16	1204.4	23.7
Cuba Cuba	10982	3630[1]	835[1]	2348	380	25	28	1908.9	16.7
Dominica Dominique	75	3[1]	12[1]	46	−2	1	...	17.0	22.6
Dominican Republic Rép. dominicaine	4838	1071[1]	500[1]	1376	21	50	...	8404.3	173.5
El Salvador El Salvador	2072	560[1]	250[1]	121	10	−10	−7	5.2	0.2
Greenland Groenland	34170[5]	...	...	...	...	...	...	98250.0	45.2
Grenada Grenade	34	1	10	5	−1	0	...	0.6	1.7
Guadeloupe Guadeloupe	169	19	7	82	−2	−1	2	21.0	11.8
Guatemala Guatemala	10843	1360[1]	545[1]	2850	60	60	−54	2166.6	19.9
Haiti Haïti	2756	560[1]	350[1]	88	5	0	−7	9.7	0.3
Honduras Honduras	11189	1468[1]	359[1]	5383	−142	149	−59	1130.9	10.1
Jamaica Jamaïque	1083	174[1]	100[1]	325	55	0	−5	98.2	8.6
Martinique Martinique	106	10	13	47	0	3	...	71.2	66.0
Mexico Mexique	190869	24800[1]	2500[1]	55205	800	600	−631	15975.9	8.1
Montserrat Montserrat	10	2[1]	...	3	0	...	...	1.0	9.6
Netherland Antilles Antilles néerlandaises	80	8[1]	...	1	0	...	...	7.7	9.6
Nicaragua Nicaragua	12140	2457[1]	289[1]	3278	494	38	−117	1637.5	11.1
Panama Panama	7443	500[1]	155[1]	2876	1	0	−52	1547.3	19.7
Puerto Rico Porto Rico	887	35[1]	46[1]	229	−30	−4	−1	29.5	3.3
Saint Kitts and Nevis Saint−Kitts−et−Nevis	36	7	1	4	−1	−1	...	2.6	10.0
Saint Lucia Sainte−Lucie	61	3[1]	12[1]	9	−2	1	−1	9.7	15.7
Saint Pierre and Miquelon Saint−Pierre−et−Miquelon	23	3[1]	...	...	0	...	...	0.0	0.0
Saint Vincent − Grenadines Saint−Vincent−Grenadines	39	4[1]	7[1]	6	0	0	...	8.2	21.1
Trinidad and Tobago Trinité−et−Tobago	513	75[1]	47[1]	259	1	1	−2	21.0	4.1

66
Land [*cont.*]
Terres [*suite*]

Country or area Pays ou zone	1999 Land area Superficie des terres	1999 Arable land Terres arables	1999 Permanent crops Cultures permanentes	2000 Forest cover Superficie forestière	Net change – Variation nette 1990 – 1999 Arable land Terres arables	Net change – Variation nette 1990 – 1999 Permanent crops Cultures permanentes	Net change – Variation nette 1990–2000 Forest cover Superficie forestière	1997 Protected areas Aires protégées	Protecte are Air protégé %
	Area in thousand hectares – Superficie en milliers de hectares								
Turks and Caicos Islands Iles Turques et Caïques	43	1[1]	...	...	0	...	...	71.6	166
United States Etats–Unis	915896	176950[1]	2050[1]	225993	–8792	16	388	198844.4	21
United States Virgin Islands Iles Vierges américaines	34	4[1]	1[1]	14	0	0	...	5.7	16
America, South · Amérique du Sud									
Argentina Argentine	273669	25000[1]	2200[1]	34648	0	0	–285	9126.1	3
Bolivia Bolivie	108438	1955[1]	250[1]	53068	55	29	–161	17818.5	16
Brazil Brésil	845651	53200[1]	12000[1]	543905	7600	1000	–2309	52671.7	6
Chile Chili	74880	1979[1]	315[1]	15536	–823	68	–20	14137.2	18
Colombia Colombie	103870	2088	2276	49601	–912	276	–190	9365.2	8
Ecuador Equateur	27684	1574[1]	1427[1]	10557	–30	106	–137	15551.7	33
Falkland Islands (Malvinas) Iles Falkland (Malvinas)	1217	...	...	...	...	...	...	11.1	C
French Guiana Guyane française	8815	9	3	7926	–1	1	...	100.1	1
Guyana Guyana	19685	480[1]	16[1]	16879	0	1	–49	58.5	0
Paraguay Paraguay	39730	2200[1]	85[1]	23372	90	–4	–123	1401.1	3
Peru Pérou	128000	3700[1]	510[1]	65215	200	90	–269	6760.4	5
Suriname Suriname	15600	57[1]	10[1]	14113	0	–1	...	804.2	4
Uruguay Uruguay	17502	1260[1]	47[1]	1292	0	2	50	47.5	0
Venezuela Venezuela	88205	2640[1]	850[1]	49506	–340	–65	–218	56040.4	61
Asia · Asie									
Afghanistan Afghanistan	65209	7910[1]	144[1]	1351	0	0	...	218.6	0
Armenia Arménie	2820	495[1]	65[1]	351	...	...	4	213.4	7
Azerbaijan Azerbaïdjan	8660	1720[1]	263[1]	1094	...	...	13	477.6	5
Bahrain Bahreïn	69	3[1]	3[1]	...	1	1	...	0.8	1
Bangladesh Bangladesh	13017	8100[1]	340[1]	1334	–1037	40	17	98.0	0
Bhutan Bhoutan	4700	140[1]	20[1]	3016	27	1	...	997.8	21
Brunei Darussalam Brunéi Darussalam	527	3[1]	4[1]	442	0	0	–1	121.2	21
Cambodia Cambodge	17652	3700[1]	107[1]	9335	5	7	–56	3267.1	18
China [3] Chine [3]	932742	124140	11221	163480	462	3502	1806	68240.7	7
China, Hong Kong SAR Chine, Hong Kong RAS	...	...	...	...	...	...	...	46.1	43
Cyprus Chypre	924	101	42	172	–5	–9	5	78.1	8
East Timor Timor oriental	1487	70[1]	10[1]	507	0	0	–3	...	
Georgia Géorgie	6970	795[1]	268[1]	2988	...	...	...	195.3	2

66
Land [*cont.*]
Terres [*suite*]

Country or area Pays ou zone	1999 Land area Superficie des terres	1999 Arable land Terres arables	Permanent crops Cultures permanentes	2000 Forest cover Superficie forestière	Net change – Variation nette 1990–1999 Arable land Terres arables	Net change – Variation nette 1990–1999 Permanent crops Cultures permanentes	Net change 1990–2000 Forest cover Superficie forestière	1997 Protected areas Aires protégées	Protected areas Aires protégées % [2]
	Area in thousand hectares – Superficie en milliers de hectares								
India Inde	297319	161750[1]	7950[1]	64113	−1388	1650	38	14312.0	4.5
Indonesia Indonésie	181157	17941[1]	13046[1]	104986	−2312	1326	−1312	34511.8	18.0
Iran (Islamic Rep. of) Iran (Rép. islamique d')	162200	17300[1]	1965[1]	7299	2110	655	...	8303.1	5.0
Iraq Iraq	43737	5200[1]	340[1]	799	−100	50	...	0.5	0.0
Israel Israël	2062	351[1]	89[1]	132	3	1	5	325.6	15.7
Japan Japon	36450[1]	4503	363	24081	−265	−112	3	2559.0	6.9
Jordan Jordanie	8893	244[1]	143[1]	86	−46	53	...	298.0	3.1
Kazakhstan Kazakhstan	269970	30000[1]	135[1]	12148	...	...	239	7337.3	2.7
Korea, Dem.People's Rep. Corée, R. p. dém. de	12041	1700[1]	300[1]	8210	...	...	...	315.8	2.6
Korea, Republic of Corée, République de	9873	1699	200	6248	...	...	−5	...	6.9
Kuwait Koweït	1782	6[1]	1[1]	5	2	0	...	27.2	1.1
Kyrgyzstan Kirghizistan	19180	1368	67	1003	...	...	23	693.9	3.5
Lao People's Dem. Rep. Rép. dém. pop. lao	23080	875[1]	80[1]	12561	...	...	−53	2756.3	11.6
Lebanon Liban	1023	180[1]	128[1]	36	−3	6	...	4.8	0.5
Malaysia Malaisie	32855	1820[1]	5785[1]	19292	120	585	−237	1527.4	4.6
Maldives Maldives	30	1[1]	2[1]	1	0	0	...	0.0	0.0
Mongolia Mongolie	156650	1321[1]	1[1]	10645	−49	0	−60	16129.1	10.3
Myanmar Myanmar	65755	9548[1]	595[1]	34419	−19	93	−517	173.5	0.3
Nepal Népal	14300	2898[1]	70[1]	3900	612	6	−78	1270.5	9.0
Occ. Palestinian Territory [4] Terr. palestinien occupé [4]	38	10[1]	15[1]	...	1	0	...	...	...
Oman Oman	21246	16[1]	61[1]	1	0	16	...	3428.0	12.6
Pakistan Pakistan	77088	21234	646	2361	750	190	−39	3744.7	4.7
Philippines Philippines	29817	5550[1]	4500[1]	5789	70	100	−89	1454.0	4.8
Qatar Qatar	1100	18[1]	3	1	8	2	...	1.6	0.1
Saudi Arabia Arabie saoudite	214969	3594[1]	191	1504	204	100	...	82562.0	34.4
Singapore Singapour	61	1[1]		2	0	0	...	2.9	4.7
Sri Lanka Sri Lanka	6463	880[1]	1020[1]	1940	5	−5	−35	869.4	13.3
Syrian Arab Republic Rep. arabe syrienne	18378	4701	801	461	−184	60	...	0.0	0.0
Tajikistan Tadjikistan	14060	730[1]	130[1]	400	...	...	2	587.0	4.1
Thailand Thaïlande	51089	14700[1]	3300[1]	14762	−2794	191	−112	7077.1	13.8
Turkey Turquie	76963	24138	2534	10225	−509	−496	22	1289.8	1.7

66
Land [*cont.*]
Terres [*suite*]

| | 1999 | | | 2000 | Net change − Variation nette | | | 1997 | |
| | Land area Superficie des terres | Arable land Terres arables | Permanent crops Cultures permanentes | Forest cover Superficie forestière | 1990 − 1999 Arable land Terres arables | 1990 − 1999 Permanent crops Cultures permanentes | 1990−2000 Forest cover Superficie forestière | Protected areas Aires protégées | Protect are Air protégé |
Country or area Pays ou zone	Area in thousand hectares − Superficie en milliers de hectares								%
Turkmenistan Turkménistan	46993	1630[1]	65[1]	3755	...	...	...	1977.3	4
United Arab Emirates Emirats arabes unis	8360	82[1]	52[1]	321	47	32	8	0.0	0
Uzbekistan Ouzbékistan	41424	4475[1]	375[1]	1969	...	...	5	818.4	1
Viet Nam Viet Nam	32549	5750[1]	1600[1]	9819	411	555	52	995.1	3
Yemen Yémen	52797	1545[1]	123	449	22	20	−9	0.0	0
Europe · Europe									
Albania Albanie	2740	577	122	991	−2	−3	−8	102.5	3
Andorra Andorre	45	1[1]	...	...	0	...	...	0.0	0
Austria Autriche	8273	1397[1]	82[1]	3886	−29	3	8	2451.2	29
Belarus Bélarus	20748	6182	124	9402	...	...	256	875.4	4
Belgium−Luxembourg Belgique−Luxembourg	3282	814	20	728	48	5	−1	85.9	2
Bosnia and Herzegovina Bosnie−Herzégovine	5100	500[1]	150[1]	2273	...	...	...	26.7	0
Bulgaria Bulgarie	11055	4297	214	3690	441	−86	20	499.8	4
Croatia Croatie	5592	1461	129	1783	...	...	2	396.4	7.
Czech Republic République tchèque	7728	3096	236	2632	...	...	1	1277.6	16.
Denmark Danemark	4243	2294	8	455	−267	−2	1	1379.6	32.
Estonia Estonie	4227	1120	15	2060	...	...	13	536.4	11
Faeroe Islands Iles Féroé	140	3[1]	...	...	0	...	...	...	
Finland Finlande	30459	2174	3	21935	−97	0	8	2840.7	8.
France France	55010	18361	1154	15341	362	−37	62	5572.3	10.
Germany Allemagne	35668	11821	217	10740	−150	−226	...	9619.3	27.
Gibraltar Gibraltar	1	...	...	...	...	...	...	0.0	0
Greece Grèce	12890	2762	1108	3599	−137	40	30	340.8	2.
Hungary Hongrie	9234	4815	224	1840	−239	−10	7	649.0	7.
Iceland Islande	10025	7	...	31	0	...	1	980.5	9.
Ireland Irlande	6889	1076	3	659	35	0	17	65.3	0.
Italy Italie	29411	8545	2877	10003	−467	−83	30	2203.7	7.
Latvia Lettonie	6205	1851	29	2923	...	...	13	821.7	12.
Liechtenstein Liechtenstein	16	4[1]	...	7	0	...	...	6.1	38.
Lithuania Lituanie	6480	2937	59	1994	...	...	5	645.4	9.
Malta Malte	32	8	1	...	−4	0	...	0.4	1.

66
Land [*cont.*]
Terres [*suite*]

Country or area Pays ou zone	1999 Land area Superficie des terres	1999 Arable land Terres arables	1999 Permanent crops Cultures permanentes	2000 Forest cover Superficie forestière	Net change – Variation nette 1990 – 1999 Arable land Terres arables	Net change – Variation nette 1990 – 1999 Permanent crops Cultures permanentes	Net change – Variation nette 1990 – 2000 Forest cover Superficie forestière	1997 Protected areas Aires protégées	Protected areas Aires protégées %[2]
	Area in thousand hectares – Superficie en milliers de hectares								
Netherlands Pays–Bas	3388	914[1]	35[1]	375	35	5	1	482.0	11.7
Norway Norvège	30683	877	...	8868	13	...	31	2086.5	6.4
Poland Pologne	30442	14072	329	9047	−316	−16	18	2929.1	9.4
Portugal Portugal	9150	1968	737	3666	−405	−63	57	603.6	6.5
Republic of Moldova République de Moldova	3291	1810	371	325	...	...	1	50.6	1.5
Romania Roumanie	23034	9332	513	6448	−118	−78	15	1089.4	4.6
Russian Federation Fédération de Russie	1688850	124975	1845	851392	...	...	135	51668.8	3.0
San Marino Saint–Marin	6	1[1]	...	...	0	...	...	...	...
Slovakia Slovaquie	4808	1461	133	2177	...	...	18	1060.5	21.6
Slovenia Slovénie	2012	171	31	1107	...	...	2	120.2	5.9
Spain Espagne	49944	13680[1]	4850[1]	14370	−1655	13	86	4241.8	8.4
Svalbard and Jan Mayen Islands Svalbard et Ile Jan–Mayen	...	...	...	...	...	...	...	7289.0	116.8
Sweden Suède	41162	2747	...	27134	−98	...	1	3654.7	8.3
Switzerland Suisse	3955	415	24	1199	24	3	4	744.7	18.0
TFYR of Macedonia L'ex–R.y. Macédoine	2543	587	48	906	...	...	...	181.3	7.1
Ukraine Ukraine	57935	32670	945	9584	...	...	31	898.5	1.5
United Kingdom Royaume–Uni	24088	5917	51	2794	−703	−15	17	5000.1	20.4
Yugoslavia Yougoslavie	10200	3402	331	2887	...	...	−1	338.9	3.3
Oceania · Océanie									
American Samoa Samoa américaines	20	2[1]	3[1]	12	0	1	...	4.3	21.8
Australia Australie	768230	47979[1 6]	250[1]	154539	79	69	−282	104568.6	13.6
Cook Islands Iles Cook	45	4[1]	3[1]	...	2	−1	...	0.2	0.9
Fiji Fidji	1827	200[1]	85[1]	815	40	5	−2	20.0	1.1
French Polynesia Polynésie française	366	1[1]	20[1]	105	−1	−1	...	19.8	5.0
Guam Guam	55	6[1]	6[1]	21	0	0	...	8.6	19.1
Kiribati Kiribati	73	...	37[1]	28	...	0	...	26.7	39.0
Micronesia (Federated States of) Micronésie (Etats fédérés de)	...	...	...	15	...	...	−1	...	...
New Caledonia Nouvelle–Calédonie	1828	7[1]	6[1]	372	0	0	...	115.4	6.0
New Zealand Nouvelle–Zélande	26799	1555[1]	1725[1]	7946	−1006	421	39	6333.8	23.9

66
Land [*cont.*]
Terres [*suite*]

Country or area Pays ou zone	1999 Land area Superficie des terres	1999 Arable land Terres arables	1999 Permanent crops Cultures permanentes	2000 Forest cover Superficie forestière	Net change – Variation nette 1990 – 1999 Arable land Terres arables	Net change – Variation nette 1990 – 1999 Permanent crops Cultures permanentes	Net change – Variation nette 1990–2000 Forest cover Superficie forestière	1997 Protected areas Aires protégées	1997 Protect are Ai protégé
			Area in thousand hectares – Superficie en milliers de hectares						
Niue Nioué	26	5[1]	2[1]	6	0	0	...	5.4	2
Northern Mariana Islands Iles Mariannes du Nord	...	...	...	14	...	...	...	1.7	3
Palau Palaos	46	10[1]		35	−15	−34	...	4.0	8
Papua New Guinea Papouasie–Nvl–Guinée	45286	60[1]	610[1]	30601	25	30	−113	1034.1	2
Samoa Samoa	283	55[1]	67[1]	105	0	0	−3	11.5	4
Solomon Islands Iles Salomon	2799	42[1]	18[1]	2536	2	1	−4	8.2	0
Tonga Tonga	72	17[1]	31[1]	4	0	0	...	3.6	5
Tuvalu Tuvalu	3	...	...	...	...	...	...	3.3	132
Vanuatu Vanuatu	1219	30[1]	90[1]	447	0	0	1	3.4	0
Wallis and Futuna Islands Iles Wallis et Futuna	20	1[1]	4[1]	...	0	0	...	...	

Sources:
Food and Agriculture Organization of the United Nations (FAO), Rome, "FAO Production Yearbook 2000", the FAOSTAT database and the "Global Forest Resources Assessment 2000;" and the United Nations Environment Programme (UNEP), World Conservation Monitoring Centre, "United Nations List of Protected Areas".

1   FAO estimate.
2   Calculated by the World Conservation Monitoring Centre based on total area which includes land area and inland waters. Percentages are inflated due to the inclusion of marine protected areas.
3   Data generally include those for Taiwan Province of China, except for data on protected areas.
4   Data refer to the Gaza Strip.
5   Area free from ice.
6   Includes about 27 million hectares of cultivated grassland.

Sources:
Organisation des Nations Unies pour l'alimentation et l'agriculture (FAO), R "Annuaire FAO de la production 2000" et la base de données de FAOSTAT e "Global Forest Resources Assessment 2000;" et le Programme des Nations Ur pour l'environnement (PNUE), Centre mondial de surveillance pour la conservation, "United Nations List of Protected Areas".

1   Estimation de la FAO.
2   Les pourcentages sont calculés par le Centre mondial de surveillance pour conservation par rapport à la superficie totale des pays, qui comprend la superficie des terres et celle des eaux intérieures. Les pourcentages sont majorés, du fait qu'on tient compte des zones marines protégées.
3   Les données comprennent en général les chiffres pour la province de Taiw les données sur les aires protégées exceptées.
4   Les données se rapportent à la Zone de Gaza.
5   Superficie non couverte de glace.
6   Y compris 27 millions d'hectares d'herbages cultivés.

67
CO₂ emission estimates
Estimations des émissions de CO₂

From fossil fuel combustion, cement production and gas flared (thousand metric tons of carbon dioxide)
Dues à la combustion de combustibles fossiles, à la production de ciment et au gaz brûlés à la torche
(milliers de tonnes de dioxyde de carbone)

Country or area Pays ou zone	1990	1992	1993	1994	1995	1996	1997	1998	1999	Change: 1990– latest year (%) Variation: 1990 à l'année la plus récente (%)
Africa · Afrique										
Algeria Algérie	80441	80888	82511	86127	94463	96563	99472	106613	...	33
Angola Angola	4646	4408	5873	4195	11296	9926	6251	5925	...	28
Benin Bénin	564	601	682	678	740	641	696	733	...	30
Botswana Botswana	2169	3268	3481	3477	3510	3111	3375	3778	...	74
Burkina Faso Burkina Faso	993	923	920	953	971	982	993	1011	...	2
Burundi Burundi	194	191	205	209	213	220	224	227	...	17
Cameroon Cameroun	1488	3547	3620	3572	2235	1990	1216	1762	...	18
Cape Verde Cap–Vert	84	106	106	117	114	121	121	121	...	43
Central African Rep. Rép. centrafricaine	198	216	220	234	234	234	245	249	...	26
Chad Tchad	143	77	92	95	95	99	110	110	...	−23
Comoros Comores	66	66	66	66	66	66	66	70	...	6
Congo Congo	2037	1326	1891	2074	1795	1854	1806	1817	...	−11
Côte d'Ivoire Côte d'Ivoire	11872	38553	11930	10596	10432	13271	13370	13198	...	11
Dem. Rep. of the Congo Rép. dém. du Congo	4096	3386	3459	2195	2360	2378	2400	2433	...	−41
Djibouti Djibouti	352	366	377	366	370	366	366	366	...	4
Egypt Egypte	75436	80906	92217	84709	94463	102890	105660	105759	...	40
Equatorial Guinea Guinée équatoriale	117	125	194	128	77	121	...	253	...	116
Ethiopia Ethiopie	2964	2898	2957	3206	2660	1858	1979	1990	...	−33
Gabon Gabon	6676	2818	3430	2682	3309	2895	3345	2821	...	−58
Gambia Gambie	191	198	209	209	216	216	216	227	...	19
Ghana Ghana	3528	3741	3910	4001	3997	4104	4203	4357	...	23
Guinea Guinée	1011	1030	1063	1187	1205	1220	1224	1224	...	21
Guinea–Bissau Guinée–Bissau	209	216	227	227	231	231	231	231	...	11
Kenya Kenya	5822	5459	6236	6522	6716	7343	6819	9131	...	57
Lesotho [1] Lesotho [1]	...	...	...	636	...	...	...	...	...	...
Liberia Libéria	465	278	315	311	322	333	337	352	...	−24
Libyan Arab Jamahiriya Jamah. arabe libyenne	37773	37960	39748	39220	44254	40781	48706	36446	...	−4
Madagascar Madagascar	945	1004	1030	1158	1209	1205	1242	1249	...	32
Malawi Malawi	601	645	682	703	711	700	747	747	...	24

67

CO$_2$ emission estimates
From fossil fuel combustion, cement production and gas flared (thousand metric tons of carbon dioxide) [*cont.*]

Estimations des émissions de CO$_2$
Dues à la combustion de combustibles fossiles, à la production de ciment et au gaz brûlés à la torche
(milliers de tonnes de dioxyde de carbone) [*suite*]

Country or area Pays ou zone	1990	1992	1993	1994	1995	1996	1997	1998	1999	Change: 1990– latest year (%) Variation: 1990 à l'année la plus récente (%)
Mali Mali	421	443	454	462	473	480	476	484	...	15
Mauritania Mauritanie	2634	2884	2906	3063	2942	2939	2931	2917	...	11
Mauritius Maurice	1154	1400	1528	1455	1513	1744	1704	1726	...	50
Morocco Maroc	23487	26022	28199	29628	29170	29620	30423	32035	...	36
Mozambique Mozambique	997	997	1066	1063	1205	1213	1271	1330		33
Namibia Namibia	0	0	0	11	11	11	11	11	...	...
Niger Niger	1048	1077	1096	1088	1099	1103	1110	1107	...	6
Nigeria Nigéria	88667	110959	112421	99857	92041	90744	75575	78458	...	−12
Réunion Réunion	1227	1491	1539	1733	1924	2012	2103	2231		82
Rwanda Rwanda	528	487	502	484	491	495	506	513	...	−3
Saint Helena Sainte−Hélène	7	7	7	7	7	7	7	7	...	0
Sao Tome and Principe Sao Tomé−et−Principe	66	73	73	73	77	77	77	77		17
Senegal Sénégal	2898	3059	3059	3107	3114	3184	3210	3298	...	14
Seychelles Seychelles	114	154	161	176	187	191	198	198	...	74
Sierra Leone Sierra Leone	333	407	436	502	506	539	491	524		57
Somalia Somalie	18	11	11	11	11	0	0	0	...	−100
South Africa Afrique du Sud	291113	305011	290138	321177	335507	321155	331751	343718	...	18
Sudan Soudan	3459	3507	3382	3499	3620	3624	3576	3598	...	4
Swaziland Swaziland	425	264	132	484	454	341	399	399	...	−6
Togo Togo	689	696	711	685	791	784	810	883	...	28
Tunisia Tunisie	13260	14997	16474	15928	15711	16371	16638	22362	...	69
Uganda Ouganda	813	857	817	744	953	1015	1092	1279	...	57
United Rep. of Tanzania Rép.−Unie de Tanzanie	2272	2261	2275	2169	2202	2198	2198	2228	...	−2
Western Sahara Sahara occidental	198	198	202	202	209	209	209	209	...	6
Zambia Zambie	2444	2455	2495	2418	2411	2385	2356	1557	...	−36
Zimbabwe Zimbabwe	16646	18053	17324	18533	19493	19071	18940	14070	...	−15
America, North • Amérique du Nord										
Antigua and Barbuda Antigua−et−Barbuda	300	289	304	311	322	322	337	337	...	12
Aruba Aruba	1839	1718	1766	1781	1799	1832	1872	1883	...	2
Bahamas Bahamas	1949	1792	1715	1718	1729	1729	1740	1792	...	−8

67

CO$_2$ emission estimates
From fossil fuel combustion, cement production and gas flared (thousand metric tons of carbon dioxide) [*cont.*]

Estimations des émissions de CO$_2$
Dues à la combustion de combustibles fossiles, à la production de ciment et au gaz brûlés à la torche
(milliers de tonnes de dioxyde de carbone) [*suite*]

Country or area Pays ou zone	1990	1992	1993	1994	1995	1996	1997	1998	1999	Change: 1990– latest year (%) Variation: 1990 à l'année la plus récente (%)
Barbados Barbade	1077	978	1114	747	828	850	898	1572	...	46
Belize Belize	311	355	377	374	377	308	388	399	...	28
Bermuda Bermudes	590	399	462	458	454	462	462	462	...	−22
British Virgin Islands Iles Vierges britanniques	48	51	51	51	51	59	59	59	...	23
Canada [1] Canada [1]	471563	475414	473976	488077	500626	513343	524505	533907	545652	16
Cayman Islands Iles Caïmanes	249	275	286	286	286	282	282	289	...	16
Costa Rica Costa Rica	2917	3741	3943	5232	4859	4730	5009	5086	...	74
Cuba Cuba	32050	30881	28990	31848	24168	24410	24146	24879	...	−22
Dominica Dominique	59	59	62	70	81	81	81	84	...	44
Dominican Republic Rép. dominicaine	9435	11197	11787	12623	12923	12996	13425	20259	...	115
El Salvador El Salvador	2616	3415	3891	4423	4668	4646	4961	6057	...	132
Greenland Groenland	553	480	498	502	502	517	520	528	...	−5
Grenada Grenade	121	128	143	165	169	169	183	183	...	52
Guadeloupe Guadeloupe	1282	1411	1440	1484	1506	1513	1532	1532	...	19
Guatemala Guatemala	5086	6013	5654	6863	7207	6603	7684	9669	...	90
Haiti Haïti	993	909	663	300	909	1048	1389	1264	...	27
Honduras Honduras	2590	3074	2847	3334	3895	3965	4137	5115	...	97
Jamaica Jamaïque	7958	8090	8413	8625	9541	10094	10725	10996	...	38
Martinique Martinique	2059	2045	2015	2037	2037	2023	2023	2019	...	−2
Mexico Mexique	305366	345631	327226	344268	319729	329402	353567	373998	...	22
Montserrat Montserrat	33	37	37	37	44	40	48	48	...	44
Netherlands Antilles Antilles néerlandaises	895	5454	7223	6977	6856	6801	6771	7766	...	767
Nicaragua Nicaragua	2601	2437	2297	2536	2788	2895	3019	3426	...	32
Panama Panama	3129	4008	4118	4778	3272	4833	7698	5815	...	86
Puerto Rico Porto Rico	11762	13275	14565	17434	16001	16206	16221	17565	...	49
Saint Lucia Sainte−Lucie	161	169	172	187	191	191	198	198	...	23
St. Kitts and Nevis Saint−Kitts−et−Nevis	66	73	84	88	95	103	103	103	...	56
St. Pierre and Miquelon Saint−Pierre−et−Miquelon	92	95	73	70	70	70	48	55	...	−40
St. Vincent and the Grenadines St. Vincent−Grenadines	81	84	103	121	128	132	132	161	...	100
Trinidad and Tobago Trinité−et−Tobago	16924	20698	16759	19255	20816	22234	21966	22395	...	32

67

CO$_2$ emission estimates
From fossil fuel combustion, cement production and gas flared (thousand metric tons of carbon dioxide) [*cont.*]

Estimations des émissions de CO$_2$
Dues à la combustion de combustibles fossiles, à la production de ciment et au gaz brûlés à la torche
(milliers de tonnes de dioxyde de carbone) [*suite*]

Country or area Pays ou zone	1990	1992	1993	1994	1995	1996	1997	1998	1999	Change: 1990– latest year (%) Variation: 1990 à l'année la plus récente (%)
United States [1] Etats–Unis [1]	4912947	4960930	5072932	5168817	5219811	5403200	5478677	5489730	5558150	13
US Virgin Islands Iles Vierges américaines	8446	8581	12150	12938	10761	11362	11564	11707	...	39
America, South · Amérique du Sud										
Argentina Argentine	109731	118895	123713	131433	130448	130701	137160	136915	...	25
Bolivia Bolivie	5500	6577	7962	8805	9999	10498	10886	12069	...	119
Brazil Brésil	202615	215088	224871	234683	249618	276464	288196	299566	...	48
Chile Chili	35333	35102	35754	41243	44269	50483	58130	60171	...	70
Colombia Colombie	55943	60680	63077	66272	66532	66349	67906	67836	...	21
Ecuador Equateur	16569	22801	25139	14455	23395	24487	20332	26264	...	59
Falkland Islands (Malvinas) Iles Falkland (Malvinas)	37	37	37	37	40	44	48	37	...	0
French Guiana Guyane française	804	873	866	884	903	899	899	914	...	14
Guyana Guyana	1132	1044	1048	1326	1473	1517	1594	1649	...	46
Paraguay Paraguay	2261	2620	2946	3496	3884	3602	3924	4569	...	102
Peru Pérou	21658	21039	24260	23890	25905	23325	30452	27858	...	29
Suriname Suriname	1810	2110	2125	2136	2154	2100	2118	2140	...	18
Uruguay Uruguay	3910	5075	4404	4016	4485	5397	5434	5848	...	50
Venezuela Venezuela	113754	136358	152930	191506	160691	149801	151403	155396	...	37
Asia · Asie										
Afghanistan Afghanistan	2612	1392	1341	1290	1238	1176	1096	1037		−60
Armenia Arménie	...	3679	2781	2851	3510	2620	2942	3430	...	...
Azerbaijan Azerbaïdjan	...	47138	44581	41719	33281	31287	31943	38777	...	...
Bahrain Bahreïn	11710	10270	14872	15004	16041	16675	17075	18687	...	60
Bangladesh Bangladesh	15360	16184	17111	18401	21878	23113	24018	23362	...	52
Bhutan Bhoutan	128	216	187	216	253	300	392	388	...	203
Brunei Darussalam Brunéi Darussalam	5819	5078	5280	5097	5207	5071	5569	5489	...	−6
Cambodia Cambodge	451	476	476	539	550	601	612	663	...	47
China †† Chine ††	2401779	2646124	2788612	2956759	3181271	3332094	3299305	3108096	...	29
China, Hong Kong SAR † Chine, Hong Kong RAS †	26183	31661	34867	29833	29869	27686	28125	35831	...	37
China, Macao SAR † Chine, Macao RAS †	1026	1081	1180	1271	1231	1407	1473	1631	...	59
Cyprus Chypre	4646	4979	5104	5258	5130	5284	5412	5917	...	27
Georgia Géorgie	...	15180	9842	6020	2286	4166	4426	5236	...	...

67

CO₂ emission estimates
From fossil fuel combustion, cement production and gas flared (thousand metric tons of carbon dioxide) [*cont.*]

Estimations des émissions de CO₂
Dues à la combustion de combustibles fossiles, à la production de ciment et au gaz brûlés à la torche
(milliers de tonnes de dioxyde de carbone) [*suite*]

Country or area Pays ou zone	1990	1992	1993	1994	1995	1996	1997	1998	1999	Change: 1990– latest year (%) Variation: 1990 à l'année la plus récente (%)
India Inde	675271	774135	807331	860222	908514	1002252	1025464	1061064	...	57
Indonesia Indonésie	165212	180931	199028	200241	233829	268711	267561	233602	...	41
Iran, Islamic Rep. of Iran, Rép. islamique d'	212358	234507	218887	283217	268542	270481	284441	289897	...	37
Iraq Iraq	49263	57222	64077	72717	78231	78176	80034	82379	...	67
Israel Israël	34629	41451	45493	47816	53759	53946	56426	60263	...	74
Japan [1] Japon [1]	1124350	1162218	1143968	1214078	1217764	1236191	1233525	1186964	1224980	9
Jordan Jordanie	10182	12260	12091	13623	13616	14173	14433	13920	...	37
Kazakhstan Kazakhstan	...	252699	214065	196819	165531	140454	136010	122893	...	...
Korea, Dem.People's Rep. Corée, R. p. dém. de	244638	255209	261929	259434	256990	254330	237610	226153	...	−8
Korea, Republic of Corée, République de	241183	290193	317348	342839	373609	407934	423818	363694	...	51
Kuwait [2] Koweït [2]	42206	18610	27462	33174	42935	45134	44789	49106	...	16
Kyrgyzstan Kirghizistan	...	11040	8350	6669	5280	6383	6452	6423	...	...
Lao People's Dem. Rep. Rép. dém. pop. lao	231	275	275	300	315	337	352	374	...	62
Lebanon Liban	9094	11348	11648	12733	13612	13890	15173	16345	...	80
Malaysia Malaisie	55280	74329	90411	92649	118994	122248	130539	120474	...	118
Maldives Maldives	154	253	216	220	286	297	370	330	...	114
Mongolia Mongolie	9981	11010	9277	7936	7914	8035	7709	7702	...	−23
Myanmar Myanmar	4148	4892	5390	6295	6980	7262	8435	8149	...	96
Nepal Népal	630	1334	1466	1696	2037	2484	2781	3045	...	383
Oman Oman	11538	12029	13301	15341	17239	16246	17752	20273	...	76
Pakistan Pakistan	67873	72673	77729	84493	85197	94331	94203	97112	...	43
Philippines Philippines	44306	50436	51385	56243	63040	66015	77114	75993	...	72
Qatar Qatar	13652	27052	31031	30577	31174	32343	42184	46772	...	243
Saudi Arabia [2] Arabie saoudite [2]	177897	247177	260350	259518	260522	285947	272983	283001	...	59
Singapore Singapour	41920	51322	57808	60351	63817	71618	78916	82287	...	96
Sri Lanka Sri Lanka	3855	5181	5031	5514	5910	7090	7673	8123	...	111
Syrian Arab Republic Rép. arabe syrienne	35845	42983	45841	43987	45665	45398	46306	50637	...	41
Tajikistan Tadjikistan	...	20614	13605	5093	5181	5793	5089	5111	...	...
Thailand Thaïlande	95742	126725	142437	158144	181404	202384	209841	192447	...	101

67

CO$_2$ emission estimates
From fossil fuel combustion, cement production and gas flared (thousand metric tons of carbon dioxide) [*cont.*]

Estimations des émissions de CO$_2$
Dues à la combustion de combustibles fossiles, à la production de ciment et au gaz brûlés à la torche
(milliers de tonnes de dioxyde de carbone) [*suite*]

Country or area Pays ou zone	1990	1992	1993	1994	1995	1996	1997	1998	1999	Change: 1990– latest year (%) Variation: 1990 à l'année la plus récente (%)
Turkey Turquie	143822	146504	159768	155649	170906	188171	198013	202040	...	40
Turkmenistan Turkménistan	...	28041	27642	33449	33838	30397	29331	27865	...	...
United Arab Emirates Emirats arabes unis	60886	63571	70350	76388	76231	79759	85189	88201	...	45
Uzbekistan [1] Ouzbékistan [1]	114559	...	...	102157	...	...	...	...	...	−11
Viet Nam Viet Nam	22464	23846	27414	29946	32859	38905	42151	43866	...	95
Yemen Yémen	...	13759	8589	10637	11282	12718	14217	14158	...	...
Europe • Europe										
Albania Albanie ·	7269	2374	2352	1924	2063	1953	1601	1568	...	−78
Austria [1] Autriche [1]	62132	60154	59901	61756	63754	64889	66829	65489	65778	6
Belarus Bélarus	...	94606	78396	69903	63231	64209	62476	60545	...	...
Belgium [1] Belgique [1]	113997	121591	119519	124312	125576	129654	121340	130762	126491	11
Bosnia and Herzegovina Bosnie−Herzégovine	...	4723	3741	4203	4258	4313	4434	4686	...	...
Bulgaria [1] Bulgarie [1]	84136	59183	61859	59178	62332	66825	58742	52277	48440	−42
Croatia Croatie	...	16807	17001	16932	17749	18493	19299	19804	...	...
Czech Republic [1] République tchèque [1]	165490	140220	134851	127745	128817	132538	137125	128268	121093	−27
Denmark [1] Danemark [1]	53045	58315	59985	63861	60686	74035	64540	60203	56976	7
Estonia [1] Estonie [1]	37797	27766	21979	22852	20859	21423	20716	19232	16989	−55
Faeroe Islands Iles Féroé	616	638	575	513	619	630	634	641	...	4
Finland [1] Finlande [1]	62466	58670	59172	65468	62684	68130	66911	64601	64186	3
France [1] France [1]	385490	401010	379660	375710	381996	395858	389579	410684	404695	5
Germany [1] Allemagne [1]	986860	928307	918268	904111	903737	924621	893524	888264	858511	−13
Gibraltar Gibraltar	62	48	293	355	238	242	209	227	...	265
Greece [1] Grèce [1]	84350	84939	86083	87464	88148	90279	94757	99345	98452	17
Hungary [1] Hongrie [1]	71673	60557	60826	59196	59758	60475	58894	57601	60117	−16
Iceland [1] Islande [1]	2144	2209	2309	2273	2309	2393	2468	2506	2737	28
Ireland [1] Irlande [1]	31575	32893	32421	33987	34501	35700	38071	40019	41887	33
Italy [1] Italie [1]	437750	435491	423527	417291	442457	437405	440170	454200	456533	4
Latvia [1] Lettonie [1]	23526	14924	12859	11911	10145	9549	8619	8287	7385	−69
Liechtenstein [1] Liechtenstein [1]	208	...	...	...	...	...	...	...	...	...
Lithuania [1] Lituanie [1]	39535	...	...	...	15200	16200	16200	16694	...	−58

67

CO$_2$ emission estimates
From fossil fuel combustion, cement production and gas flared (thousand metric tons of carbon dioxide) [*cont.*]

Estimations des émissions de CO$_2$
Dues à la combustion de combustibles fossiles, à la production de ciment et au gaz brûlés à la torche
(milliers de tonnes de dioxyde de carbone) [*suite*]

Country or area Pays ou zone	1990	1992	1993	1994	1995	1996	1997	1998	1999	Change: 1990– latest year (%) Variation: 1990 à l'année la plus récente (%)
Luxembourg [1] Luxembourg [1]	12750	...	...	11998	9545	...	...	...	...	−25
Malta Malte	1660	1660	1707	1715	1726	1755	1759	1803	...	9
Monaco [1] Monaco [1]	98	120	121	123	120	126	125	121	129	32
Netherlands [1] Pays−Bas [1]	161173	165170	167450	168380	177130	184721	181166	180913	174126	8
Norway [1] Norvège [1]	35079	34307	35810	37676	37794	40871	41176	41396	41650	18
Poland [1] Pologne [1]	380697	371591	363160	371588	348172	372530	361626	337450	329697	−13
Portugal [1] Portugal [1]	44134	49693	48531	49089	52019	50386	52633	55743	57882	31
Republic of Moldova République de Moldova	...	20889	15649	12135	11227	11575	10853	9658		...
Romania [1] Roumanie [1]	172510	130160	127086	125597	...	...	...	...	...	−27
Russian Federation [1] Fédération de Russie [1]	2372300	...	...	1660000	1590420	1495920	...	...	...	−37
Slovakia [1] Slovaquie [1]	59606	48892	46000	43051	44470	44877	45157	44723	44875	−25
Slovenia [1] Slovénie [1]	13935	...	...	...	...	...	...	...	...	...
Spain [1] Espagne [1]	226057	242275	250076	242279	252958	240312	257713	268479	260965	15
Sweden [1] Suède [1]	55074	54859	54879	59233	58521	63001	57088	58142	56458	3
Switzerland [1] Suisse [1]	44409	45990	43566	42928	43805	44212	43549	44814	44826	1
TFYR of Macedonia L'ex−R.y. Macédoine	...	10633	10201	10336	10747	11747	10688	12377		...
Ukraine [1] Ukraine [1]	703792	577916	504222	406838	380928	346768	322907	314445	...	−55
United Kingdom [1] Royaume−Uni [1]	583479	572770	558665	555752	547194	566383	541686	543729	531529	−9
Yugoslavia Yougoslavie	130455	...	...	...	...	...	...	...	...	...
Oceania · Océanie										
American Samoa Samoa américaines	286	300	297	282	275	282	282	282	...	−1
Australia [1] Australie [1]	278600	282699	286222	290290	302199	312203	319438	335971	340776	22
Cook Islands Iles Cook	22	22	22	22	22	22	22	22	...	0
French Polynesia Polynésie française	613	624	628	547	562	562	562	562	...	−8
Fiji Fidji	813	707	711	722	755	773	755	725	...	−11
Guam Guam	2268	2451	3554	4558	4137	4078	4078	4111	...	81
Kiribati Kiribati	22	22	22	22	22	22	22	22	...	0
Micronesia (Fed. States of) [1] Micron (États fédérés de) [1]	...	...	...	236	...	141	...	...	...	...
Nauru Nauru	132	136	136	136	139	139	139	139	...	6
New Caledonia Nouvelle−Calédonie	1612	1759	1759	1711	1715	1751	1751	1748	...	8

67

CO$_2$ emission estimates
From fossil fuel combustion, cement production and gas flared (thousand metric tons of carbon dioxide) [*cont.*]

Estimations des émissions de CO$_2$
Dues à la combustion de combustibles fossiles, à la production de ciment et au gaz brûlés à la torche
(milliers de tonnes de dioxyde de carbone) [*suite*]

Country or area Pays ou zone	1990	1992	1993	1994	1995	1996	1997	1998	1999	Change: 1990– latest year (%) Variation: 1990 à l'année la plus récente (%)
New Zealand [1] Nouvelle−Zélande [1]	25399	27763	27136	27199	27206	28223	30210	28824	30523	20
Niue Nioué	4	4	4	4	4	4	4	4	...	0
Palau Palaos	234	234	231	231	238	245	238	242	...	3
Papua New Guinea Papouasie−Nvl−Guinée	2429	2528	2528	2503	2407	2407	2451	2345	...	−3
Samoa Samoa	125	128	128	121	132	132	132	132	...	6
Solomon Islands Iles Salomon	161	161	158	154	161	161	161	161	...	0
Tonga Tonga	77	88	103	106	114	117	121	117	...	52
Tuvalu [1] Tuvalu [1]	...	...	...	5	...	...	...	...	...	...
Vanuatu Vanuatu	66	62	62	62	62	62	62	62	...	−6
Wake Island Ile de Wake	48	44	33	18	18	18	18	18	...	−62

Sources:
Carbon Dioxide Information Analysis Center (CDIAC) of the
Oak Ridge National Laboratory, Oak Ridge, Tennessee, U.S.A.,
database on national CO$_2$ emissions estimates from fossil fuel
burning, cement production and gas flaring: 1751−1998 and the
Secretariat of the United Nations Framework Convention on
Climate Change (UNFCCC), Bonn, Secretariat of the UNFCCC
database.

The majority of the data have been taken from the CDIAC database;
all other data have been taken from the UNFCCC database and are
footnoted accordingly.

† For information on recent changes in country or area
nomenclature pertaining to former Czechoslovakia, Germany,
Hong Kong Special Administrative Region (SAR) of China,
Macao Special Administrative Region (SAR) of China,
SFR of Yugoslavia and the former USSR, see Annex I − Country
or area nomenclature, regional and other groupings.

†† For statistical purposes, the data for China do not
include those for the Hong Kong Special Administrative
Region (Hong Kong SAR), Macao Special Administrative
Region (Macao SAR) and Taiwan province of China.

1   Source: Secretariat of the UNFCCC.
2   Including part of the Neutral Zone.

Sources:
"Carbon Dioxide Information Analysis Center (CDIAC) of the
Oak Ridge National Laboratory, Oak Ridge, Tennessee, U.S.A.,
database on national CO$_2$ emissions estimates from fossil fuel
burning, cement production and gas flaring: 1751−1998" et la
Secrétariat de la convention−cadre concernant les changements
climatiques (CCCC) des Nations Unies, Bonn, la base de données du
Secrétariat de la CCCC.

La majorité des données proviennent de la base de données du
CDIAC; les autres, qui proviennent de la base de données
du Secrétariat de la CCCC, sont signalées par une note.

† Pour les modifications récentes de nomenclature de pays
ou de zone concernant l'Allemagne, Hong Kong région
administrative spéciale (RAS) de Chine, Macao région administrative
spéciale (RAS) de Chine, l'ex−Tchécoslovaquie, l'ex−URSS et l'ex−
Rfs de Yougoslavie, voir annex I − Nomenclature des pays ou des
zones, groupements régionaux et autres groupments.

†† Les données statistiques relatives à la Chine ne comprennent
pas celles qui concernent la région administrative spéciale de
Hong Kong (la RAS de Hong Kong), la région administrative
spéciale de Macao (la RAS de Macao) et la province chinoise
de Taiwan.

1   Source: Secrétariat de la CCCC des Nations Unies.
2   Y compris une partie de la Zone Neutral.

Technical notes, tables 66-67

Table 66: The data on land and forest cover are compiled by the Food and Agriculture Organization of the United Nations (FAO). The protected areas data are taken from the United Nations Environment Programme (UNEP) World Conservation Monitoring Centre.

FAO's definitions of the land categories and forest cover are as follows:

Land area: Total area excluding area under inland water bodies. The definition of inland water bodies generally includes major rivers and lakes.

Arable land: Land under temporary crops (double-cropped areas are counted only once); temporary meadows for mowing or pasture; land under market and kitchen gardens; and land temporarily fallow (less than five years). Abandoned land resulting from shifting cultivation is not included in this category. Data for "arable land" are not meant to indicate the amount of land that is potentially cultivable.

Permanent crops: Land cultivated with crops that occupy the land for long periods and need not be replanted after each harvest, such as cocoa, coffee and rubber. This category includes land under flowering shrubs, fruit trees, nut trees and vines, but excludes land under trees grown for wood or timber.

Forest: In the *Global Forest Resources Assessment 2000* [10] the following definition is used for forest. Forest includes natural forests and forest plantations and is used to refer to land with a tree crown cover (or equivalent stocking level) of more than 10 per cent and area of more than 0.5 ha. The trees should be able to reach a minimum height of 5 m at maturity *in situ.* Forest may consist either of closed forest formations where trees of various storeys and undergrowth cover a high proportion of the ground; or open forest formations with a continuous vegetation cover in which the tree crown cover exceeds 10 per cent. Young natural stands and all plantations established for forestry purposes that have yet to reach a crown density of 10 per cent or tree height of 5 m are included under forest, as are areas normally forming part of the forest area that are temporarily unstocked as a result of human intervention or natural causes but that are expected to revert to forest.

The *United Nations List of Protected Areas* [32] is the definitive list of the world's national parks and reserves. It is compiled by the UNEP World Conservation Monitoring Centre working in close collaboration with the World Conservation Union (IUCN) World Commission on Protected Areas. Information is provided by national protected areas authorities and the secretariats of international conventions and programmes.

Notes techniques, tableaux 66 à 67

Tableau 66: Les données relatives aux terres et à la superficie forestière sont compilées par l'Organisation des Nations Unies pour l'alimentation et l'agriculture (FAO). Les données relatives aux aires protégées viennent du Centre mondial de surveillance pour la conservation du Programme des Nations Unies pour l'environnement (PNUE).

Les définitions de la FAO en ce qui concerne les terres et la superficie forestière sont les suivantes:

Superficie totale des terres: Superficie totale, à l'exception des eaux intérieures. Les eaux intérieures désignent généralement les principaux fleuves et lacs.

Terres arables: Terres affectées aux cultures temporaires (les terres sur lesquelles est pratiquée la double culture ne sont comptabilisées qu'une fois), prairies temporaires à faucher ou à pâturer, jardins maraîchers ou potagers et terres en jachère temporaire (moins de cinq ans). Cette définition ne comprend pas les terres abandonnées du fait de la culture itinérante. Les données relatives aux terres arables ne peuvent être utilisées pour calculer la superficie des terres aptes à l'agriculture.

Cultures permanentes: Superficie des terres avec des cultures qui occupent la terre pour de longues périodes et qui ne nécessitent pas d'être replantées après chaque récolte, comme le cacao, le café et le caoutchouc. Cette catégorie comprend les terres plantées d'arbustes à fleurs, d'arbres fruitiers, d'arbres à noix et de vignes, mais ne comprend pas les terres plantées d'arbres destinés à la coupe.

Superficie forestière: Dans *l'Évaluation des ressources forestières mondiales 2000* [10], la FAO a défini les forêts comme suit : les forêts, qui comprennent les forêts naturelles et les plantations forestières, sont des terres où le couvert arboré (ou la densité de peuplement équivalente) est supérieur à 10 % et représente une superficie de plus de 0,5 ha. Les arbres doivent être susceptibles d'atteindre sur place, à leur maturité, une hauteur de 5 m minimum. Il peut s'agir de forêts denses, où les arbres de différente hauteur et le sous-bois couvrent une proportion importante du sol, ou de forêts claires, avec un couvert végétal continu, où le couvert arboré est supérieur à 10 %. Les jeunes peuplements naturels et toutes les plantations d'exploitation forestière n'ayant pas encore atteint une densité de couvert arboré de 10 % ou une hauteur de 5 m sont inclus dans les forêts, de même que les aires formant naturellement partie de la superficie forestière mais temporairement déboisées du fait d'une intervention de l'homme ou de causes naturelles, mais devant redevenir boisées.

La *Liste des Nations Unies des zones protégées* [32] est la liste la plus fiable des parcs et réserves natu-

Countries vary considerably in their mechanisms for creating and maintaining systems of protected areas. In order to facilitate international comparisons for protected areas, IUCN has adopted a definition of a protected area which is, an area of land and/or sea especially dedicated to the protection and maintenance of biological diversity, and of natural and associated cultural resources, and managed through legal or other effective means.

IUCN has defined a series of six protected area management categories, based on primary management objectives. These categories are as follows:

Category Ia: Strict Nature Reserve;
Category Ib: Wilderness Area;
Category II: National Park;
Category III: Natural Monument;
Category IV: Habitat/Species Management Area;
Category V: Protected Landscape/Seascape;
Category VI: Managed Resource Protected Area.

Table 65: The sources of the data presented on the emissions of carbon dioxide (CO_2) are the Carbon Dioxide Information Analysis Center (CDIAC) of the Oak Ridge National Laboratory in the USA and the Secretariat of the United Nations Framework Convention on Climate Change (UNFCCC). The majority of the data have been taken from the CDIAC database. The data taken from the UNFCCC database are footnoted accordingly.

The CDIAC estimates of CO_2 emissions are derived primarily from United Nations energy statistics on the consumption of liquid and solid fuels and gas consumption and flaring, and from cement production estimates from the Bureau of Mines of the U.S. Department of Interior. The emissions presented in the table are in units of 1,000 metric tons of carbon dioxide (CO_2); to convert CO_2 into carbon, multiply the data by 0.272756. Full details of the procedures for calculating emissions are given in *Global, Regional, and National Annual CO_2 Emissions Estimates from Fossil Fuel Burning, Hydraulic Cement Production, and Gas Flaring* [3] and in the CDIAC Web site. Relative to other industrial sources for which CO_2 emissions are estimated, statistics on gas flaring activities are sparse and sporadic. In countries where gas flaring activities account for a considerable proportion of the total CO_2 emissions, the sporadic nature of gas flaring statistics may produce spurious or misleading trends in national CO_2 emissions over the period covered by the table.

The UNFCCC data in the table are indicated by a footnote, and cover (a) the countries that joined the convention (except for Belarus which joined in May 2000) and (b) countries which voluntarily reported time-series data on their emissions to the UNFCCC. The CO_2 data from national reports to the Secretariat of the UNFCCC

rels du monde. Elle est établie par le Centre mondial de surveillance pour la conservation du PNUE, en collaboration étroite avec la Commission mondiale des aires protégées de l'Union mondiale pour la nature (UICN). Les renseignements sont communiqués par les services nationaux responsables des aires protégées et les secrétariats des conventions et programmes internationaux.

Les mécanismes nationaux de création et d'entretien des systèmes de zones protégées sont très différents d'un pays à l'autre. Pour faciliter les comparaisons internationales, l'UICN a adopté une définition des aires protégées, zone terrestre ou marine (ou les deux) spécialement consacrée à la protection et à la sauvegarde de la diversité biologique et des ressources naturelles, ainsi que des ressources culturelles qui y sont associées, dont la gestion est assurée par des moyens juridiques ou autres moyens efficaces.

L'UICN a défini une série de six catégories de gestion des aires protégées, en fonction des objectifs principaux:

Catégorie Ia:: Réserve naturelle intégrale;
Catégorie Ib: Zone vierge;
Catégorie II: Parc national;
Catégorie III: Monument naturel;
Catégorie IV: Aire de gestion des habitats/des espèces;
Catégorie V: Paysage terrestre/marin protégé;
Catégorie VI: Aire protégée de ressources naturelles.

Tableau 65: Les données sur les émissions de dioxyde de carbone (CO_2) proviennent du Carbon Dioxide Information Analysis Center (CDIAC) du Oak Ridge National Laboratory (États-Unis) et du Secrétariat de la convention-cadre concernant les changements climatiques (CCCC) des Nations Unies. La majorité des données proviennent de la base de données du CDIAC. Les données qui proviennent du Secrétariat de la CCCC sont signalées par une note.

Les estimations du Carbon Dioxide Information Analysis Center sont obtenues essentiellement à partir des statistiques de l'énergie des Nations Unies relatives à la consommation de combustibles liquides et solides, à la production et à la consommation de gaz de torche, et des chiffres de production de ciment du Bureau of Mines du Department of Interior des États-Unis. Les émissions sont indiquées en milliers de tonnes de dioxyde de carbone (à multiplier par 0,272756 pour avoir les chiffres de carbone). On peut voir dans le détail les méthodes utilisées pour calculer les émissions dans *Global, Regional, and National Annual CO_2 Emissions Estimates from Fossil Fuel Burning, Hydraulic Cement Production, and Gas Flaring* [3] et sur le site Web du Carbon Dioxide Information Analysis Center. Par rapport à d'autres

are based on the methodology of the Intergovernmental Panel for Climate Change (IPCC) 1996 Guidebook.

sources industrielles pour lesquelles on calcule les émissions de CO_2, les statistiques sur la production de gaz de torche sont rares et sporadiques. Dans les pays où cette production représente une proportion considérable de l'ensemble des émissions de dioxyde de carbone, on peut voir apparaître de ce fait des chiffres parasites ou trompeurs pour ce qui est des tendances des émissions nationales de dioxyde de carbone durant la période visée par le tableau.

Les données provenant du secrétariat de la Convention-cadre, qui sont signalées par une note, couvrent (a) les pays qui ont adhéré à la Convention (sauf pour le Bélarus, qui y a adhéré en mai 2000), et (b) les pays qui ont bénévolement communiqué des séries chronologiques sur leurs émissions au secrétariat. Les données sur le CO_2 tirées des rapports de pays au secrétariat de la Convention-cadre ont été obtenues par les méthodes recommandées dans le Manuel de 1996 du Groupe intergouvernemental d'experts pour l'étude du changement climatique.

68
Researchers, technicians and other supporting staff engaged in research and development
Chercheurs, techniciens et autre personnel de soutien employés à des travaux de recherche et de développement

Full−time equivalent (FTE)
Equivalent plein temps (EPT)

Country or area Pays ou zone	Year Année	Total	Researchers Chercheurs Total M & W Total H & F	Women Femmes	Technicians Techniciens Total M & W Total H & F	Women Femmes	Other supporting staff Autre personnel de soutien Total M & W Total H & F	Women Femmes
Africa · Afrique								
Benin [1]	1989	2 687	794	100	242	64	1 651	339
Bénin [1]								
Burkino Faso	1996	738	162	32	158	13	418	...
Burkina Faso	1997	780	176	34	165	16	439	...
Burundi [2][3]	1984	515	114	10	90	...	311	...
Burundi [2][3]	1989	814	170	17	168	...	476	...
Central African Rep.	1990	...	162	16	92	5	...	...
Rép. centrafricaine	1996	...	162	16	92	5	...	...
Congo [3]	1999[4]	227	110	15	114	22	3	...
Congo [3]	2000[4]	217	102	14	111	22	4	...
Egypt	1990	89 154	24 599	8 055	17 150	1 200	47 405	25 471
Egypte	1991	102 296	26 415	...	19 607	...	56 274	...
Guinea	1996	1 995	...	...	...	...	...	...
Guinée	2000	2 152	...	...	...	...	...	...
Libyan Arab Jamahiriya Jamah. arabe libyenne	1980	3 600	1 100	...	1 500	...	1 000	...
Madagascar [5]								
Madagascar [5]	1994	1 047	159	45	483	175	405	85
Mauritius	1989	1 021	193	33	172	46	656	97
Maurice	1992	1 162	389	...	170	...	603	...
Nigeria	1986	12 845	1 499	...	6 005	...	5 341	...
Nigéria	1987	12 880	1 338	...	6 042	...	5 500	...
Rwanda	1984	164	69	...	60	...	35	...
Rwanda	1995	315	181	18	40	31	94	33
Senegal [6]	1995	76	19	5	28	7	29	...
Sénégal [6]	1996	78	19	5	29	7	30	...
South Africa	1991	22 223	12 102	...	5 006	...	5 115	...
Afrique du Sud	1993	60 464	37 192	...	11 343	...	11 929	...
Togo	1989	1 200	277	...	183	...	740	...
Togo	1994	1 473	387	...	249	...	837	...
Tunisia	1996	3 589	1 085	...	524	...	1 980	...
Tunisie	1997	3 680	1 145	...	524	...	2 011	...
Uganda	1999	1 102	503	189	309	25	...	...
Ouganda	2000	1 187	549	206	330	27	...	...
America, North · Amérique du Nord								
Canada [7]	1994	136 785	83 492	...	34 098	...	19 195	...
Canada [7]	1995	145 240	88 330	...	...	...	...	...
Costa Rica [8]	1988[3]	1 528	1 528	...	...	...	...	...
Costa Rica [8]	1996	1 866	1 866	...	...	...	...	...
Cuba	1992	35 996	14 770	6 383	9 465	5 251	11 761	...
Cuba	1995	44 119	17 667	...	12 288	...	14 164	...
El Salvador El Salvador	1992	1 775	102[9]	...	1 612[9]	...	61	...
Guatemala [10]								
Guatemala [10]	1988	2 575	858	...	925	...	792	...
Jamaica [11]	1985	121	21	...	31	...	69	...
Jamaïque [11]	1986	104	18	10	15	3	71	...
Mexico	1994[7]	30 501	17 061	...	9 437	...	4 003	...
Mexique	1995	33 297	19 434	...	6 675	...	7 188	...
Nicaragua [3]	1985	1 803	650	...	212	...	941	...
Nicaragua [3]	1987	2 005	725	...	302	...	978	...
Trinidad and Tobago Trinité−et−Tobago	1997	515	185	80	330	129	...	...
United States [7][8][12]	1995	...	987 700	...	...	...	...	...
Etats−Unis [7][8][12]	1997	...	1 114 100	...	...	...	...	...

68
Researchers, technicians and other supporting staff engaged in research and development
Full–time equivalent (FTE) [*cont.*]
Chercheurs, techniciens et autre personnel de soutien employés à des travaux de recherche
et de developpement
Equivalent plein temps (EPT) [*suite*]

Country or area Pays ou zone	Year Année	Total	Researchers Chercheurs Total M & W Total H & F	Women Femmes	Technicians Techniciens Total M & W Total H & F	Women Femmes	Other supporting staff Autre personnel de soutien Total M & W Total H & F	Women Femmes
America, South · Amérique du Sud								
Argentina	1998	36 852	25 419	11 120	6 157	...	...	...
Argentine	1999	36 939	26 004	11 825	5 707	...	...	...
Bolivia	1995	...	1 200	...	...	...	...	...
Bolivie	1996	...	1 300	...	...	...	...	...
Brazil								...
Brésil	1995	...	26 754[13]		9 327			
Chile	1999	...	5 549	...	...	...	...	...
Chili	2000	...	5 629	...	...	...	...	...
Colombia								
Colombie	1982	3 709[1]	1 083	...	1 024	...	1 602	
Ecuador	1995	...	1 517	472	...	...	...	...
Ecuador	1997	1 874	1 676	250	198[14]		...	...
Paraguay								
Paraguay	1981[3]	...	807	...	...		1 545	
Peru	1996	...	5 551	...	234		...	...
Pérou	1997	...	5 576	...	34		...	...
Uruguay [3]								
Uruguay [3]	1987	...	2 093	720	...		...	...
Venezuela	1992	*5 333	*4 258	*1 490	*650	*205	*425	...
Venezuela	2000[15]	...	4 688	1 969	...		...	...
Asia · Asie								
Armenia	1997	7 716	5 492	2 509	653	321	1 571	
Arménie	1999	6 528	4 971	...	903	...	764	...
Azerbaijan	1995	25 629	21 547	8 813	1 356	...	2 726	...
Azerbaïdjan	1996	25 556	21 234	8 889	1 428	...	2 894	...
Bangladesh	1994	15 010	5 418	568	2 055	404	7 537	...
Bangladesh	1995	16 629	6 097	851	3 825	728	6 707	
China ††	1995	665 600	422 700	...	242 900[14]	...	...	...
Chine ††	1996	787 000	559 000	...	228 000[14]	...	...	...
China, Hong Kong SAR † [16]								
Chine, Hong Kong RAS † [16]	1995	1 627	574	...	613	...	440	...
Cyprus	1998	564	237	69	168	60	159	...
Chypre	1999	681	278	81	198	71	205	...
India	1992[17]	315 448	117 586	7 737	98 202	7 096	99 660	...
Inde	1996	*357 172	*149 326	11 078	108 817	9 121	99 029	...
Indonesia [3]	1984	36 185	24 895	...	4 125	...	7 165	
Indonésie [3]	1985	...	21 160	...	3 888	...	...	
Iran, Islamic Rep. of	1985	5 048[18]	3 194	...	1 854	...	...	...
Iran, Rép. islamique d'	1994	50 326	34 256	...	10 104	...	5 966	...
Israel	1996[3]	12 267	7 920	...	3 558	...	789	...
Israël	1997[3]	13 110	9 161	...	3 023	...	926	...
Japan [7]	1996	891 783	617 365	...	83 906	...	190 512	...
Japon [7]	1997	894 003	625 442	...	83 539	...	185 022	...
Korea, Republic of	1998	128 669	92 541	...	...	...	...	...
Corée, République de	1999	137 874	100 210	...	...	...	...	...
Kuwait	1996	763	397	...	122	...	244	...
Koweït	1997	742	387	...	118	...	237	...
Kyrgzstan	1996	4 126	2 629	...	256	...	1 241	...
Kirghizistan	1997	4 161	2 685	1 249	226	...	1 250	...
Malaysia	1996	4 436	1 893	509	654	146	1 888	...
Malaisie	1998	6 656	3 416	936	966	202	2 274	...
Mongolia	1998	2 623	1 518	823	204	77	907	...
Mongolie	1999	2 141	1 114	557	219	96	808	...
Pakistan [19]	1990	29 040	6 626	464	9 314	...	13 100	...
Pakistan [19]	1997	36 706	9 977	859	1 749	27	24 980	...
Philippines								
Philippines	1992	14 578	9 960	5 260	1 399	374	3 219	1 338
Qatar [3][19]								
Qatar [3][19]	1986	290	229	58	61	2	...	...

68
Researchers, technicians and other supporting staff engaged in research and development
Full−time equivalent (FTE) [cont.]
Chercheurs, techniciens et autre personnel de soutien employés à des travaux de recherche
et de developpement
Equivalent plein temps (EPT) [suite]

Country or area Pays ou zone	Year Année	Total	Researchers Chercheurs Total M & W Total H & F	Women Femmes	Technicians Techniciens Total M & W Total H & F	Women Femmes	Other supporting staff Autre personnel de soutien Total M & W Total H & F	Women Femmes
Singapore [20]	1987[3]	5 876	3 361	649	1 526	...	989	...
Singapour [20]	1995	9 497	7 695	...	997	...	805	...
Sri Lanka	1985	3 483[18]	2 790	667	693	188	...	...
Sri Lanka	1996	4 281[18]	3 448	1 103	833	...	...	...
Syrian Arab Republic								
Rép. arabe syrienne	1997	804	440	...	364	...	...	...
Tajikistan [3]	1992	...	3 974	1 144	...	...	...	...
Tadjikistan [3]	1993	...	3 722	...	...	...	...	...
Thailand	1996	10 209	6 038	...	2 303	...	1 868	...
Thaïlande	1997	14 022	4 409	...	4 446	...	5 167	...
Turkey [7]	1996	21 995	18 092	...	2 037	...	1 866	...
Turquie [7]	1997	23 432	18 908	...	2 373	...	2 151	...
Uzbekistan								
Ouzbékistan	1992	...	*37 625	*17 005	*6 687	...	...	...
Viet Nam [21]								
Viet Nam [21]	1995	...	20 000	...	...	...	...	...
Europe • Europe								
Austria								
Autriche	1993	24 458	12 821	2 008	6 397	1 945	5 240	2 119
Belarus	1995	35 858	23 771	...	3 131	...	8 956	...
Bélarus	1996	34 898	23 324	...	2 758	...	8 816	...
Belgium [7]	1996	38 741	23 330	...	...	...	...	...
Belgique [7]	1997	39 080	23 486	...	...	...	...	...
Bulgaria	1998	19 116[22]	11 972	5 321	4 862	3 295	2 282	...
Bulgarie	1999	16 087[22]	10 580	4 656	3 829	2 578	1 678	...
Croatia	1995	15 953	8 911	3 418	3 134	1 903	3 908	2 634
Croatie	1996	15 787	8 597	3 364	3 204	2 033	3 986	...
Czech Republic [7]	1998	22 740	12 566	...	7 016	...	3 158	...
République tchèque [7]	1999	24 106	13 535	...	...	...	...	...
Denmark [7]	1997	31 467	16 766	...	...	...	...	...
Danemark [7]	1998	32 107	17 173	...	...	...	...	...
Estonia [23]	1998	4 713	3 045	1 239	782	547	886	...
Estonie [23]	1999	4 545	3 001	1 251	749	538	795	...
Finland [7]	1998	46 517	23 745	...	...	...	...	...
Finlande [7]	1999	50 604	25 398	...	...	...	...	...
France [7]	1997	306 178	154 742	...	...	...	...	...
France [7]	1998	309 515	156 857	...	...	...	...	...
Germany [7]	1996	453 679	230 189	...	...	...	...	...
Allemagne [7]	1997	460 411	235 793	...	111 749	...	112 869	...
Greece [7]	1995	17 571	9 705	...	...	...	...	...
Grèce [7]	1997	20 173	10 972	...	...	...	...	...
Hungary [7]	1998	20 315	11 731	...	4 907	...	3 677	...
Hongrie [7]	1999	21 329	12 579	...	...	...	...	...
Iceland [7]	1998	2 273	1 414	...	520	...	338	...
Islande [7]	1999	2 390	1 578	...	...	...	...	...
Ireland [7]	1996	10 838	6 801	...	2 106	...	1 931	...
Irlande [7]	1997	12 033	7 825	...	2 163	...	2 063	...
Italy [7]	1996	142 288	76 441	...	46 794	...	19 053	...
Italie [7]	1997	141 737	76 056	...	46 379	...	19 302	...
Latvia	1998	4 437	2 557	1 201	777	422	1 103	...
Lettonie	1999	4 301	2 626	1 277	726	419	949	...
Lithuania								
Lituanie	1996	12 569	7 532	3 129	2 344	1 546	2 693	...
Malta [16]								
Malte [16]	1988	46	34	...	5	...	7	...
Netherlands [7]	1997	83 967	38 055	...	22 843	...	23 069	...
Pays−Bas [7]	1998	85 486	39 081	...	...	...	...	...

68

Researchers, technicians and other supporting staff engaged in research and development
Full−time equivalent (FTE) [*cont.*]
Chercheurs, techniciens et autre personnel de soutien employés à des travaux de recherche
et de developpement
Equivalent plein temps (EPT) [*suite*]

Country or area Pays ou zone	Year Année	Total	Researchers Chercheurs Total M & W Total H & F	Women Femmes	Technicians Techniciens Total M & W Total H & F	Women Femmes	Other supporting staff Autre personnel de soutien Total M & W Total H & F	Women Femmes
Norway [7]	1997	24 877	17 490	...	...	...	...	...
Norvège [7]	1999	25 400	18 265	...	...	...	...	...
Poland [7]	1998	84 510	56 179	...	...	...	...	...
Pologne [7]	1999	82 368	56 433	...	...	...	...	...
Portugal [7]	1997	18 035	13 642	...	...	...	...	...
Portugal [7]	1999	20 909	15 816	...	...	...	...	...
Republic of Moldova	1996	10 697	1 096	...	7 142	3 118	2 459	...
République de Moldova	1997	10 667	1 442	...	7 181	3 250	2 044	...
Romania	1991	60 712	28 302	12 675[24]	11 248	6 085	21 162[24]	11 616[24]
Roumanie	1994	59 102	31 672	14 048	13 272	7 991	14 158	...
Russian Federation	1998	967 499	492 494	188 464	83 499	...	391 506	...
Fédération de Russie	1999	989 291	497 030	186 264	80 498	...	411 763	...
Slovakia [7]	1998	16 461	10 145	...	...	...	...	...
Slovaquie [7]	1999	14 849	9 204	...	...	...	...	...
Slovenia [7]	1997	7 985	4 022	1 331	1 723	730	2 240	...
Slovénie [7]	1998	8 290	4 285	1 430	1 739	751	2 266	...
Spain [7]	1999	102 237	61 568	...	...	...	...	...
Espagne [7]	2000	103 259	...	...	...	...	...	...
Sweden	1997[7]	65 495	36 878	...	3 576	...	1 107	...
Suède	1999	66 674	39 921	...	...	...	...	...
Switzerland	1992	47 870	17 710	...	...	...	...	...
Suisse	1996	50 265	21 635	...	...	...	...	...
TFYR of Macedonia	1998	965	770	333	82	...	114	47
L'ex−R.y. Macédoine	1999	929	781	329	58	...	90	36
Ukraine	1999	170 599	102 196	...	27 851	...	40 552	...
Ukraine	2000	170 079	104 970	...	29 465	...	35 664	...
United Kingdom [7]	1997	...	146 546	...	...	...	...	...
Royaume−Uni [7]	1998	...	158 671	...	...	...	...	...
Yugoslavia	1991	26 559	12 082	...	5 377	...	9 100	...
Yougoslavie	1995	25 392	11 611	4 150	5 436	2 950	8 345	4 713
Oceania · Océanie								
Australia [7]	1996	90 796	61 098	...	...	...	...	...
Australie [7]	1998	90 717	62 250	...	...	...	...	...
Fiji [6]								
Fidji [6]	1986	156	36	4	90	10	30	...
Guam	1989	*52[6 16]	*21	*4	*11	*4	*20	*2
Guam	1991	55[6 16]	23	5	11	5	21	1
New Caledonia [25]								
Nouvelle−Calédonie [25]	1985	334	77	7	71	11	186	37
New Zealand [7]	1995	10 547	6 104	...	2 838	...	1 606	...
Nouvelle−Zélande [7]	1997	12 908	8 264	...	2 754	...	1 890	...

Source:
United Nations Educational, Scientific and Cultural Organization (UNESCO) Institute for Statistics, Montreal, the UNESCO statistics database, January 2002.

Source:
L'Institut de statistique de l'Organisation des Nations Unies pour l'éducation, la science et la culture (UNESCO), Montréal, la base de données de l'UNESCO, janvier 2002.

† For information on recent changes in country or area nomenclature pertaining to former Czechoslovakia, Germany, Hong Kong Special Administrative Region (SAR) of China, Macao Special Administrative Region (SAR) of China, SFR Yugoslavia and former USSR, see Annex I − Country or area nomenclature, regional and other groupings.

† Pour les modifications récentes de nomenclature de pays ou de zone concernant l'Allemagne, Hong Kong (Région administrative spéciale de Chine), Macao (Région administrative spéciale de Chine), l'ex−Tchécoslovaquie, l'ex−URSS, Rfs de Yougoslavie, voir annexe I − Nomenclature des pays ou des zones, groupements zones, groupements régionaux et autres groupments.

68
Researchers, technicians and other supporting staff engaged in research and development
Full-time equivalent (FTE) [*cont.*]
Chercheurs, techniciens et autre personnel de soutien employés à des travaux de recherche
et de developpement
Equivalent plein temps (EPT) [*suite*]

†† For statistical purposes, the data for China do not include those for the Hong Kong Special Administrative Region (Hong Kong SAR), Macao Special Administrative Region (Hong Kong SAR) and Taiwan province of China.

1 Not including data for the productive sector (non-integrated R & D).
2 Not including data for the productive sector.
3 Data refer to full-time plus part-time personnel.
4 Data relate only to research units and centers under the General Delegation for the Scientific and Technological Research.
5 Data refer to the Ministry of Scientific Research only.

6 Data relate to one research institute only.
7 Data are from OECD.
8 Data refer to researchers only.
9 Data refer to researchers and technicians in public enterprises only.
10 Data relate to the productive sector (integrated R&D) and the higher education sector only.
11 Data relate to the Scientific Research Council only.
12 Not including data for law, humanities and education.
13 Data refer to researchers listed in the directory of research group in Brazil by the Conselho Nacional de Desenvolvimento Cientifico e Tecnológico (CNPq).
14 Technicians and equivalent staff and other supporting staff are counted together.
15 Number of people applying to the Researcher Promotion Program.
16 Data refer to the higher education sector only.

17 Not including data for the higher education sector.
18 Not including data for other supporting staff.
19 Not including social sciences and humanities in the higher education sector.
20 Data relate to R&D activities concentrated mainly in government-financed research establishments.
21 Not including general service sector.
22 Not including technicians and supporting staff in the higher education sector.
23 Not including business enterprise sector.
24 Due to methodological changes, data are not comparable with earlier years.
25 Data refer only to 6 out of 11 research institutes.

†† Les données statistiques relatives à la Chine ne comprennent pas celles qui concernent la région administrative spéciale de Hong Kong (la RAS de Hong Kong), la région administrative spéciale de Macao (la RAS de Macao) et la province chinoise de Taiwan.

1 Non compris les données relatives au secteur de la production (activités de R-D non intégrées).
2 Non compris les données relatives au secteur de la production.
3 Les données se réfèrent au personnel à plein temps et à temps partiel.
4 Les données ne concernent que les unités et centres de recherche sous la Délégation générale pour la recherche scientifique et technologique.
5 Les données concernent le Ministère de la Recherche Scientifique seulement.
6 Les données ne concernent qu'un institut de recherche.
7 Les données sont de l'OCDE.
8 Les données se réfèrent aux chercheurs seulement.
9 Les données se réfèrent aux chercheurs et techniciens dans les entreprises publiques seulement.
10 Les données se réfèrent au secteur de la production (activités de R-D intégrées) et au secteur de l'enseignement supérieur seulement.
11 Les données se réfèrent au 'Scientific Research Council' seulement.
12 Non compris les données pour le droit, les sciences humaines et les
13 Les données se réfèrent aux chercheurs figurant dans le répertoire du groupe de chercheurs brésiliens élaboré par le Conselho Nacional de Desenvo vimento Cientifico e Tecnológico (CNPq).
14 Les techniciens et personnel assimilé et les autres personnel de soutien sont comptés ensemble.
15 Nombre de candidats au programme de la promotion des chercheurs.
16 Les données se réfèrent au secteur de l'enseignement supérieur seulement.
17 Non compris les données pour le secteur de l'enseignement supérieur.
18 Non compris les données pour le personnel de soutien.
19 Non compris les sciences sociales et humaines dans le secteur de l'enseignement supérieur.
20 Les données se réfèrent pour la plupart aux activités de R-D dans les établissements de recherche financés par le gouvernement.
21 Non compris le secteur de service général.
22 Non compris les techniciens et le personnel de soutien dans le secteur de l'enseignement supérieur.
23 Non compris le secteur des entreprises.
24 Suite à des changements de méthodologie, les données ne sont pas comparables avec celles des années précédentes.
25 Les données concernent 6 des 11 instituts de recherche.

69
Patents
Brevets

Applications, grants, patents in force: number
Demandes, délivrances, brevets en vigueur : nombre

Country or area Pays ou zone	Applications for patents Demandes de brevets			Grants of patents Brevets délivrés			Patents in force Brevets en vigueur		
	1997	1998	1999	1997	1998	1999	1997	1998	1999
African Intellectual Prop. Org[1] Org. africaine de la prop. intel.[1]	26 088	34 995	41 098	242	265	380	...	1 229	1 494
Albania Albanie	26 005	35 159	89 519	...	...	52	...	...	...
Algeria Algérie	240	306	282	863	...	...	1 368	...	1 501
Antigua and Barbuda Antigua-et-Barbuda	...	...	3	...	...	...	...	...	...
Argentina Argentine	5 859	6 320	6 457	1 228	1 689	1 241	...	...	...
Armenia Arménie	25 122	33 899	40 272	143	85	205	187	261	279
Australia Australie	48 211	57 706	63 355	9 464	14 784	13 528	76 694	83 429	88 361
Austria Autriche	111 224	147 040	162 121	16 025	14 963	14 347	14 184	13 621	12 845
Azerbaijan Azerbaïdjan	24 308	33 507	40 042	...	19	...	...	...	...
Bangladesh Bangladesh	...	216	...	...	140	...	...	...	...
Barbados Barbade	26 322	35 001	41 272	...	...	3	...	...	9
Belarus Bélarus	26 035	35 269	41 792	483	687	550	...	...	...
Belgium Belgique	86 645	112 652	120 981	17 673	16 093	15 802	85 663	88 752	85 370
Bosnia and Herzegovina Bosnie-Herzégovine	23 197	34 441	41 224	...	...	5	...	...	79
Botswana Botswana	93	92	54	32	21	26	...	...	...
Brazil Brésil	31 983	41 621	52 295	...	...	3 219	...	...	22 375
Bulgaria Bulgarie	28 000	36 575	42 952	448	534	533	1 908	1 754	2 136
Canada Canada	54 446	65 682	69 777	7 283	9 572	13 778	246 900	235 916	209 333
Chile Chili	...	...	2 812	...	...	418	20 310	...	...
China †† Chine ††	61 382	82 289	89 042	3 494	4 735	7 637	...	...	49 402
China, Hong Kong SAR† Chine, Hong Kong RAS†	2 385	14 667	6 040	1 487	2 453	2 502	...	...	...
China, Macao SAR † Chine, Macao RAS †	...	...	...	19	4	9	...	...	...
Colombia Colombie	...	1 736	1 683	...	476	590	...	417	...
Costa Rica Costa Rica	...	...	9 105	...	...	...	...	...	...

69
Patents
Applications, grants, patents in force: number [*cont.*]
Brevets
Demandes, délivrances, brevets en vigueur : nombre [*suite*]

Country or area Pays ou zone	Applications for patents Demandes de brevets			Grants of patents Brevets délivrés			Patents in force Brevets en vigueur		
	1997	1998	1999	1997	1998	1999	1997	1998	1999
Croatia Croatie	712	12 906	40 279	119	244	275	...	...	...
Cuba Cuba	23 271	33 997	41 039	50	...	70	1 399	...	1 427
Cyprus Chypre	4	77 374	118 767	...	...	3	...	...	...
Czech Republic République tchèque	30 577	39 196	45 309	1 477	1 451	1 482	6 203	7 001	7 249
Denmark Danemark	109 061	146 357	161 564	12 103	11 018	10 754	29 322	...	...
Dominica Dominique	...	...	8 500	...	...	...	...	...	...
Ecuador Equateur	310	...	490	212	...	142	...	...	...
Egypt Egypte	...	1 633	1 682	...	118	410	...	...	...
Estonia Estonie	26 644	35 501	41 756	108	82	103	130	212	320
Ethiopia Ethiopie	4	...	12	...	...	1	...	...	1
European Patent Office[2] Office européen de brevets[2]	97 943	113 408	121 816	39 646	36 718	35 358	...	...	...
Finland Finlande	109 437	146 884	159 033	2 315	2 329	1 618	19 878	20 274	...
France France	112 631	130 015	138 455	50 448	46 213	44 287	324 341	326 447	345 808
Gambia Gambie	200	60 272	79 703	29	18	26	...	...	...
Georgia Géorgie	26 826	35 728	41 960	318	536	398	...	961	728
Germany † Allemagne †	175 595	202 771	220 761	55 053	51 685	49 548	337 227	354 879	371 816
Ghana Ghana	34 103	66 173	80 028	29	13	17	...	...	...
Greece Grèce	82 443	111 339	119 774	8 555	7 857	7 598	...	...	...
Grenada Grenade	...	3 330	34 698	...	...	...	...	...	...
Guatemala Guatemala	135	207	231	15	17	36	...	...	...
Guinea-Bissau Guinée-Bissau	25	15 568	1	...	...	...	...	...	...
Haiti Haïti	...	...	6	...	...	7	...	...	...
Honduras Honduras	...	151	156	...	58	77	...	...	198
Hungary Hongrie	30 105	38 707	44 974	1 189	1 257	1 881	10 951	10 896	11 438
Iceland Islande	26 298	35 182	41 570	41	35	27	261	275	248

69
Patents
Applications, grants, patents in force: number [*cont.*]
Brevets
Demandes, délivrances, brevets en vigueur : nombre [*suite*]

Country or area Pays ou zone	Applications for patents Demandes de brevets			Grants of patents Brevets délivrés			Patents in force Brevets en vigueur		
	1997	1998	1999	1997	1998	1999	1997	1998	1999
India Inde	10 155	282	41 496	...	...	2 160	...	...	8 639
Indonesia Indonésie	4 517	32 910	42 503	...	...	...			
Iran (Islamic Rep. of) Iran (Rép. islamique d')	418	496	543	258	241	322	...	...	
Ireland Irlande	83 430	112 344	120 795	6 889	7 088	7 288	18 513	...	23 209
Israel Israël	30 344	42 271	49 414	2 152	2 021	2 024	12 018	12 017	12 040
Italy Italie	91 410	123 606	128 260	28 096	38 988	32 476	...	...	...
Jamaica Jamaïque	...	...	...	...	...	17	...		...
Japan Japon	417 974	437 375	442 245	147 686	141 448	150 059	870 928	935 858	1 005 304
Kazakhstan Kazakhstan	26 169	35 338	41 828	1 525	1 192	1 553	5 337	5 830	6 658
Kenya Kenya	49 960	67 830	80 544	79	101	94	136	...	...
Kiribati Kiribati	...	...	2	...	...	2	...	...	17
Korea, Dem. P. R. Corée, R. p. dém. de	25 467	33 918	40 391	...	...	...	...	...	...
Korea, Republic of Corée, République de	129 982	46 517	133 127	24 579	...	62 635	...	...	...
Kyrgyzstan Kirghizistan	25 103	33 905	40 191	133	105	93	488	579	501
Latvia Lettonie	27 023	35 963	90 276	403	297	353	...	2 160	1 883
Lesotho Lesotho	49 483	67 491	80 315	26	36	43	...	...	...
Liberia Libéria	26 045	34 862	41 120	...	...	...	...		...
Lithuania Lituanie	26 798	35 838	90 417	183	165	440	1 296	1 219	1 137
Luxembourg Luxembourg	106 484	144 401	159 601	8 981	8 023	7 490	31 237	30 681	30 503
Madagascar Madagascar	26 174	34 941	41 246	...	...	35	...	...	81
Malawi Malawi	49 934	67 756	80 431	49	76	84	546	631	...
Malaysia Malaisie	6 451	...	...	786	...	...	...	...	...
Malta Malte	46	34	83	2	28	35	158	110	237
Mauritius Maurice	15	15	...	1	3	...	113	96	...

69
Patents
Applications, grants, patents in force: number [*cont.*]
Brevets
Demandes, délivrances, brevets en vigueur : nombre [*suite*]

Country or area Pays ou zone	Applications for patents Demandes de brevets			Grants of patents Brevets délivrés			Patents in force Brevets en vigueur		
	1997	1998	1999	1997	1998	1999	1997	1998	1999
Mexico Mexique	35 932	44 721	50 000	3 944	3 219	3 899	34 799	36 817	38 965
Monaco Monaco	81 270	111 088	119 539	3 791	4 061	4 137	3 907	241	6 287
Mongolia Mongolie	26 383	35 154	41 240	116	172	161	552	...	...
Morocco Maroc	...	...	3 649	...	...	...	...	6 331	...
Netherlands Pays-Bas	90 629	115 076	123 513	23 794	22 411	21 403	112 237	117 453	120 748
New Zealand Nouvelle-Zélande	35 137	39 734	47 640	3 823	4 058	2 463	...	...	...
Nicaragua Nicaragua	105	154	145	38	18	12	...	...	205
Norway Norvège	32 007	44 258	50 662	2 942	2 560	2 362	...	...	...
Peru Pérou	804	...	992	180	...	271	...	...	1 007
Philippines Philippines	3 565	3 443	3 361	916	565	648	...	...	...
Poland Pologne	32 538	41 352	47 480	2 330	2 416	2 236	13 704	13 589	13 614
Portugal Portugal	106 687	145 142	159 666	7 229	8 947	8 493	14 235	...	22 219
Republic of Moldova République de Moldova	25 325	34 111	40 455	225	220	231	653	774	1 006
Romania Roumanie	29 055	37 826	91 304	1 417	1 818	1 083	20 380	20 100	18 425
Russian Federation Fédération de Russie	48 220	58 532	67 876	29 692	23 368	19 508	155 247	173 081	191 129
Rwanda Rwanda	...	...	4	...	...	4	...	...	47
Saint Lucia Sainte-Lucie	22 899	34 087	40 901	...	...	...	...	...	...
Saudi Arabia Arabie saoudite	1 058	1 331	1 216	2	3	16	6	8	22
Sierra Leone Sierra Leone	9 506	33 154	72 449	...	...	1	...	...	...
Singapore Singapour	37 655	44 948	51 495	...	2 291	4 410	...	...	...
Slovakia Slovaquie	28 207	36 852	43 079	562	845	773	2 252	2 436	...
Slovenia Slovénie	27 447	36 297	90 972	623	466	871	2 518	2 905	3 218
South Africa Afrique du Sud	...	8	26 470	...	...	...	...	...	...
Spain Espagne	113 767	147 889	163 090	20 613	20 128	20 066	197 806	...	178 782

69

Patents
Applications, grants, patents in force: number [*cont.*]
        Brevets
        Demandes, délivrances, brevets en vigueur : nombre [*suite*]

Country or area Pays ou zone	Applications for patents Demandes de brevets			Grants of patents Brevets délivrés			Patents in force Brevets en vigueur		
	1997	1998	1999	1997	1998	1999	1997	1998	1999
Sri Lanka Sri Lanka	26 403	34 974	41 263	160	...	...	1 873	...	...
Sudan Soudan	49 920	67 719	80 426	37	64	59	...	...	...
Swaziland Swaziland	25 672	34 535	40 673	34	63	57	...	...	...
Sweden Suède	115 000	149 493	165 051	19 412	18 482	17 649	96 809	97 435	97 980
Switzerland Suisse	112 852	147 579	162 403	18 083	16 253	15 434	94 636	87 527	87 033
Tajikistan Tadjikistan	24 765	33 779	40 141	109	57	42	181	177	222
Thailand Thaïlande	5 443	5 071	...	729	723	...	...	...	...
TFYR of Macedonia L'ex-R.y. Macédoine	26 153	35 133	89 425	79	80	55	431	360	378
Trinidad and Tobago Trinité-et-Tobago	26 339	34 969	41 238	171	...	...	...	...	...
Turkey Turquie	28 218	37 386	43 833	458	796	1 122	11 952	12 786	21 183
Turkmenistan Turkménistan	24 636	33 705	40 114	206	154	95	...	...	...
Uganda Ouganda	49 760	67 610	80 421	30	66	74	...	...	...
Ukraine Ukraine	32 728	41 950	48 273	9 121	4 336	1 294	18 823	19 587	16 270
United Arab Emirates Emirats arabes unis	...	8	24 218	...	...	...	...	...	...
United Kingdom Royaume-Uni	148 209	176 187	192 875	44 754	43 181	40 683	...	...	...
United Rep. of Tanzania Rép.-Unie de Tanzanie	...	...	14 467	...	10	8	...	...	...
United States Etats-Unis	236 692	262 787	294 706	111 984	147 520	153 487	1 113 452	1 173 145	1 242 853
Uruguay Uruguay	402	496	552	52	73	113	367	386	356
Uzbekistan Ouzbékistan	27 307	35 110	42 365	2	...	512	1 644	...	727
Venezuela Venezuela	2 524	...	...	9 844	...	...	...	...	...
Viet Nam Viet Nam	27 440	35 748	42 212	111	...	490	363	...	...
Yugoslavia Yougoslavie	17 021	34 541	42 084	293	342	175	2 687	2 059	2 238
Zambia Zambie	96	93	92	33	20	67	...	...	1 346
Zimbabwe Zimbabwe	21 969	66 272	80 168	33	30	34	...	...	...

69

Patents
Applications, grants, patents in force: number [*cont.*]

Brevets
Demandes, délivrances, brevets en vigueur : nombre [*suite*]

Source:
World Intellectual Property Organization (WIPO), Geneva,
"Industrial Property Statistics 1999, Publication A" and
previous issues.

† For information on recent changes in country or
area nomenclature pertaining to former Czechoslovakia,
Germany, Hong Kong Special Administrative Region (SAR)
of China, Macao Special Administrative Region (SAR) of China,
SFR of Yugoslavia and the former USSR, see Annex I - Country
or area nomenclature, regional and other groupings.

†† For statistical purposes, the data for
China do not include those for Hong Kong Special
Administrative Region (Hong Kong SAR), Macao Special
Administrative Region (Macao SAR) and Taiwan province of
China.

1 Members of the African Intellectual Property Organization
(OAPI), which includes Benin, Burkina Faso, Cameroon,
Central African Republic, Chad, Congo, Côte d'Ivoire, Gabon,
Guinea, Mali, Mauritania, Niger, Senegal, Togo.
2 In 1992, the European Patent Office (EPO) was constituted by
the following member countries: Austria, Belgium, Denmark,
France, Germany, Greece, Ireland, Italy, Liechtenstein,
Luxembourg, Monaco, Netherlands, Portugal, Spain, Sweden,
Switzerland, United Kingdom.

Source:
Organisation mondiale de la propriété intellectuelle (OMPI),
Genève, "Statistiques de propriété industrielle 1999,
Publication A" et éditions précédentes.

† Pour les modifications récentes de nomenclature
de pays ou de zone concernant l'Allemagne, Hong Kong, région
administrative spéciale (RAS) de Chine, Macao, région
administrative spéciale (RAS) de Chine,
l'ex-Tchécoslovaquie, l'ex-URSS et l'ex-Rfs de Yougoslavie,
voir annexe I - Nomenclature des pays ou des zones,
groupements régionaux et autres groupements.

†† Les données statistiques relatives à
la Chine ne comprennent pas celles qui concernent la région
administrative spéciale de Hong Kong (la RAS de Hong Kong),
la région administrative spéciale de Macao (la RAS de Macao)
et la province chinoise de Taiwan.

1 Les membres de l'Organisation africaine de la propriété
intellectuelle (OAPI): Bénin, Burkina Faso, Cameroun, Congo,
Côte d'Ivoire, Gabon, Guinée, Mali, Mauritanie, Niger,
République centrafricaine, Sénégal, Tchad, Togo.
2 En 1992, l'Office européen de brevets (OEB) comprenait les
pays membres suivants: Allemagne, Autriche, Belgique,
Danemark, Espagne, France, Grèce, Irlande, Italie,
Liechtenstein, Luxembourg, Monaco, Pays-Bas, Portugal,
Royaume-Uni, Suède, Suisse.

Technical notes, tables 68 et 69

Table 68: The data presented on personnel engaged in research and experimental development (R&D) are compiled by UNESCO. The definitions and classifications applied by UNESCO in the table are based on those set out in the *Recommendation concerning the International Standardization of Statistics on Science and Technology* (for data covering the years prior to 1998) and in the *Frascati Manual* (for data referring to 1998 and on).

The three categories of personnel shown are defined as follows:

Researchers are professionals engaged in the conception or creation of new knowledge, products, processes, methods and systems, and in the planning and management of R&D projects. Post-graduate students engaged in R&D are considered as researchers. The data shown for researchers for the years prior to 1998 refer to "R&D scientists and engineers".

Technicians (and equivalent staff) comprise persons whose main tasks require technical knowledge and experience in one or more fields of engineering, physical and life sciences, or social sciences and humanities.

Other supporting staff includes skilled and unskilled craftsmen, secretarial and clerical staff participating in or directly associated with R&D projects.

Table 69: Data on patents include patent applications filed directly with the office concerned and grants made on the basis of such applications; inventors' certificates; patents of importation, including patents of introduction, revalidation patents and "patentes precaucionales"; petty patents; patents applied and granted under the Patent Cooperation Treaty (PCT), the European Patent Convention, the Havana Agreement, the Harare Protocol of the African Regional Industrial Property Organization (ARIPO) and the African Intellectual Property Organization (OAPI). The data are compiled and published by the World Intellectual Property Organization [36].

Notes techniques, tableaux 68 et 69

Le *tableau 68 :* Les données présentées sur le personnel employé à des travaux de recherche scientifique et le développement expérimental (R-D) sont compilées par l'UNESCO. Les définitions et classifications appliquées par l'UNESCO sont basées sur la *Recommandation concernant la normalisation internationale des statistiques relatives à la science et à la technologie* (pour les chiffres des années antérieures à 1998) et sur le *Manuel de Frascati* (à compter de 1998).

Les trois catégories du personnel présentées sont définies comme suivant:

Les chercheurs sont des spécialistes travaillant à la conception ou à la création de connaissances, de produits, de procédés, de méthodes et de systèmes, et dans la planification et la gestion de projets de R-D. Les étudiants diplômés ayant des activités de R-D sont également considérés comme des chercheurs. Les données relatives aux chercheurs pour les années antérieures à 1998 se rapportent aux « scientifiques et ingénieurs employés à des travaux de R-D ».

Techniciens (et personnel assimilé) comprend des personnes dont les tâches principales requièrent des connaissances et une expérience technique dans un ou plusieurs domaines de l'ingénierie, des sciences physiques et de la vie ou des sciences sociales et humaines.

Autre personnel de soutien comprend les travailleurs, qualifiés ou non, et le personnel de secrétariat et de bureau qui participent à l'exécution des projets de R-D ou qui sont directement associés à l'exécution de tels projets.

Tableau 69: Les données relatives aux brevets comprennent les demandes de brevet déposées directement auprès de l'office intéressé et brevets délivrés sur la base de telles demandes; les brevets d'invention; les brevets d'importation; y compris les brevets d'introduction, les brevets de revalidation et les brevets "precaucionales"; les petits brevets, les brevets demandés et délivrés en vertu du traité de coopération sur les brevets, de la Convention européenne relative aux brevets, de l'Accord de la Havane, du Protocole d'Hararé de l'Organisation régionale africaine de la propriété industrielle (ARIPO) et de l'Organisation africaine de la propriété intellectuelle (OAPI). Les données sont compilées et publiées par l'Organisation mondiale de la propriété intellectuelle [36].

Part Four
International Economic Relations

XVI
**International merchandise trade
(tables 70-72)**
XVII
International tourism (tables 73-75)
XVIII
Balance of payments (table 76)
XIX
International finance (tables 77 and 78)
XX
Development assistance (tables 79-81)

Part Four of the *Yearbook* presents statistics on international economic relations in areas of international merchandise trade, international tourism, balance of payments and assistance to developing countries. The series cover all countries or areas of the world for which data are available.

Quatrième partie
Relations économiques internationales

XVI
**Commerce international des marchandises
(tableaux 70 à 72)**
XVII
Tourisme international (tableaux 73 à 75)
XVIII
Balance des paiements (tableau 76)
XIX
Finances internationales (tableaux 77 et 78)
XX
Aide au développement (tableaux 79 à 81)

La quatrième partie de l'*Annuaire* présente des statistiques sur les relations économiques internationales dans les domaines du commerce international des marchandises, du tourisme international, de la balance des paiements et de l'assistance aux pays en développement. Les séries couvrent tous les pays ou les zones du monde pour lesquels des données sont disponibles.

70
Total imports and exports
Importations et exportations totales

Imports c.i.f. and exports f.o.b., value in million US dollars
Importations c.a.f. et exportations f.o.b., valeur en millions de dollars E.–U.

Country or area	Sys. [1]	1994	1995	1996	1997	1998	1999	2000	Pays ou zone
World									***Monde***
Imports		**4255437**	**5083736**	**5327562**	**5505782**	**5426033**	**5657959**	**6373078**	*Importations*
Exports		**4218527**	**5045095**	**5257102**	**5445992**	**5370673**	**5543173**	**6165070**	*Exportations*
Balance		**−36909**	**−38640**	**−70460**	**−59790**	**−55360**	**−114786**	**−208009**	*Balance*
Developed economies [23]									**Économies développées** [23]
Imports		2887852	3419135	3535905	3609845	3694581	3880360	4268050	Importations
Exports		2897898	3448040	3539584	3616789	3636032	3698134	3946862	Exportations
Balance		10047	28905	3678	6944	−58549	−182226	−321188	Balance
Developing economies [3]									**Écon. en dévelop.** [3]
Imports		1235565	1490145	1588753	1675576	1508052	1577075	1873979	Importations
Exports		1182399	1420452	1521958	1624059	1534101	1646291	1967705	Exportations
Balance		−53165	−69694	−66795	−51518	26050	69217	93725	Balance
Other [4]									**Autres** [4]
Imports		132020	174455	202904	220361	223400	200524	231049	Importations
Exports		138229	176604	195561	205144	200539	198748	250503	Exportations
Balance		6209	2149	−7343	−15217	−22861	−1776	19454	Balance
			America · Amérique						
Developed economies [3]									**Économies développées** [3]
Imports		800325	886786	939950	1037793	1085185	1208512	1412590	Importations
Exports		637824	728927	773940	845918	836244	874811	973908	Exportations
Balance		−162501	−157859	−166010	−191875	−248941	−333701	−438682	Balance
Canada [5]									**Canada** [5]
Imports	G	151293	163954	170694	195980	201061	214791	238812	Importations
Exports	G	165380	192204	201636	214428	214335	238422	276645	Exportations
Balance	G	14087	28250	30942	18448	13274	23631	37833	Balance
United States [6]									**Etats–Unis** [6]
Imports	G	689215	770852	822025	899019	944353	1059430	1257640	Importations
Exports	G	512627	584743	625073	688696	682138	702098	781125	Exportations
Balance	G	−176588	−186109	−196952	−210323	−262215	−357332	−476515	Balance
Developing economies [3]									**Écon. en dévelop.** [3]
Imports		218796	248336	272349	320756	335738	324052	372966	Importations
Exports		184054	225156	252430	277785	275358	293757	351656	Exportations
Balance		−34743	−23180	−19919	−42971	−60380	−30295	−21310	Balance
LAIA+ [7]									**ALAI +** [7]
Imports		185928	209170	232689	278762	290274	276715	322843	Importations
Exports		168153	205834	231973	256137	252742	270397	326361	Exportations
Balance		−17775	−3336	−716	−22626	−37532	−6318	3518	Balance
Argentina									**Argentine**
Imports	S	21527	20122	23762	30450	31404	25508	25243	Importations
Exports	S	15659	20967	23811	26370	26441	23333	26409	Exportations
Balance	S	−5868	846	49	−4080	−4962	−2175	1166	Balance
Bolivia									**Bolivie**
Imports	G	1209	1424	1635	1851	1983	1755	1830	Importations
Exports	G	1032	1101	1137	1167	1104	1051	1230	Exportations
Balance	G	−177	−323	−498	−684	−879	−704	−600	Balance
Brazil [5]									**Brésil** [5]
Imports	G	35997	53783	56947	64996	60631	51675	58532	Importations
Exports	G	43545	46506	47747	52994	51140	48011	55086	Exportations
Balance	G	7548	−7277	−9200	−12001	−9491	−3664	−3446	Balance
Chile									**Chili**
Imports	S	11820	15900	17823	19662	18779	15137	18107	Importations
Exports	S	11604	16024	15405	16663	14830	15616	18158	Exportations
Balance	S	−216	124	−2419	−2999	−3949	478	51	Balance
Colombia									**Colombie**
Imports	G	11883	13853	13684	15378	14635	10659	11539	Importations
Exports	G	8419	10056	10587	11522	10852	11576	13040	Exportations
Balance	G	−3464	−3797	−3097	−3855	−3782	918	1502	Balance
Ecuador									**Equateur**
Imports	G	3622	4153	3935	4955	5576	3017	3721	Importations
Exports	G	3820	4307	4900	5264	4203	4451	4927	Exportations
Balance	G	198	155	965	310	−1373	1434	1205	Balance

70

Total imports and exports
Imports c.i.f. and exports f.o.b., value in million US dollars
Importations et exportations totales
Importations c.a.f. et exportations f.o.b., valeur en millions de dollars E.−U.

Country or area	Sys.[1]	1994	1995	1996	1997	1998	1999	2000	Pays ou zone
Mexico[58]									**Mexique**[58]
Imports	G	79346	72453	89469	109808	125373	141975	...	Importations
Exports	G	60882	79542	96000	110431	117460	136391	...	Exportations
Balance	G	−18464	7089	6531	623	−7913	−5584	...	Balance
Paraguay									**Paraguay**
Imports	S	2140	2782	2850	3099	2471	1725	...	Importations
Exports	S	817	919	1044	1089	1014	741	...	Exportations
Balance	S	−1324	−1863	−1807	−2011	−1457	−984	...	Balance
Peru[5]									**Pérou**[5]
Imports	S	6691	9224	9473	10264	9867	8075	8797	Importations
Exports	S	4555	5575	5897	6841	5757	6113	7002	Exportations
Balance	S	−2136	−3649	−3575	−3423	−4110	−1962	−1795	Balance
Uruguay									**Uruguay**
Imports	G	2786	2867	3323	3727	3811	3357	3466	Importations
Exports	G	1913	2106	2397	2726	2771	2237	2295	Exportations
Balance	G	−873	−761	−926	−1001	−1040	−1120	−1171	Balance
Venezuela									**Venezuela**
Imports	G	8913	12619	9794	14577	15749	13835	16142	Importations
Exports	G	15913	18739	23053	21073	17175	20880	31738	Exportations
Balance	G	7000	6121	13260	6496	1425	7045	15597	Balance
CACM+[9]									**MCAC+**[9]
Imports		**10745**	**12817**	**13110**	**15348**	**17985**	**18421**	**19602**	**Importations**
Exports		**6412**	**8284**	**8568**	**9993**	**11506**	**11933**	**11855**	**Exportations**
Balance		**−4334**	**−4534**	**−4543**	**−5354**	**−6479**	**−6488**	**−7747**	**Balance**
Costa Rica									**Costa Rica**
Imports	S	3789	4036	4300	4924	6230	6320	6372	Importations
Exports	S	2869	3453	3730	4268	5511	6577	5865	Exportations
Balance	S	−920	−583	−569	−656	−719	257	−507	Balance
El Salvador									**El Salvador**
Imports	S	2249	2853	2671	2973	3112	3130	3796	Importations
Exports	S	844	998	1024	1359	1263	1164	1342	Exportations
Balance	S	−1405	−1855	−1646	−1614	−1850	−1966	−2454	Balance
Guatemala									**Guatemala**
Imports	S	2781	3293	3146	3852	4651	4382	4791	Importations
Exports	S	1522	2156	2031	2344	2582	2398	2696	Exportations
Balance	S	−1260	−1137	−1115	−1508	−2069	−1984	−2095	Balance
Honduras									**Honduras**
Imports	S	1056	1643	1840	2149	2500	2728	2885	Importations
Exports	S	842	1220	1316	1446	1577	1249	1322	Exportations
Balance	S	−214	−422	−524	−703	−923	−1479	−1562	Balance
Nicaragua									**Nicaragua**
Imports	G	870	993	1154	1450	1492	1862	1759	Importations
Exports	G	335	457	466	577	573	545	631	Exportations
Balance	G	−536	−536	−687	−873	−918	−1317	−1127	Balance
Other America									**Autres pays d'Amérique**
Imports		**22123**	**26349**	**26549**	**26646**	**27479**	**28916**	**30521**	**Importations**
Exports		**9490**	**11039**	**11889**	**11655**	**11110**	**11428**	**13440**	**Exportations**
Balance		**−12634**	**−15310**	**−14660**	**−14991**	**−16369**	**−17488**	**−17082**	**Balance**
Antigua and Barbuda									**Antigua−et−Barbuda**
Imports	G	341	346	365	370	385	414	...	Importations
Exports	G	44	53	38	38	36	38	...	Exportations
Balance	G	−297	−293	−328	−332	−349	−376	...	Balance
Aruba									**Aruba**
Imports	S	...	567	578	614	815	782	...	Importations
Exports	S	...	15	12	24	29	29	...	Exportations
Balance	S	...	−552	−566	−590	−786	−753	...	Balance
Bahamas[10]									**Bahamas**[10]
Imports	G	1056	1243	1366	1666	1873	1911	1421	Importations
Exports	G	167	176	180	181	300	450	400	Exportations
Balance	G	−889	−1067	−1186	−1484	−1573	−1461	−1022	Balance
Barbados									**Barbade**
Imports	G	611	766	834	996	1010	1108	1156	Importations
Exports	G	181	238	281	283	252	264	272	Exportations
Balance	G	−430	−529	−553	−713	−758	−844	−884	Balance

70
Total imports and exports
Imports c.i.f. and exports f.o.b., value in million US dollars
Importations et exportations totales
Importations c.a.f. et exportations f.o.b., valeur en millions de dollars E.–U.

Country or area	Sys.[1]	1994	1995	1996	1997	1998	1999	2000	Pays ou zone
Belize									**Belize**
Imports	G	260	257	255	286	325	375	480	Importations
Exports	G	151	162	168	176	191	169	210	Exportations
Balance	G	−109	−96	−88	−110	−134	−205	−270	Balance
Bermuda									**Bermudes**
Imports	G	550	550	569	619	629	...	...	Importations
Exports	G	32	56	68	57	45	...	...	Exportations
Balance	G	−518	−494	−501	−562	−584	...	...	Balance
Cayman Islands									**Iles Caïmanes**
Imports	G	327	399	378	...	...	...	...	Importations
Exports	G	3	4	3	...	...	...	...	Exportations
Balance	G	−325	−395	−375	...	...	...	...	Balance
Cuba									**Cuba**
Imports	S	2055	2805	3205	...	...	...	...	Importations
Exports	S	1465	1625	2015	...	...	...	...	Exportations
Balance	S	−590	−1180	−1190	...	...	...	...	Balance
Dominica									**Dominique**
Imports	S	96	117	130	125	136	141	147	Importations
Exports	S	47	45	51	53	63	54	53	Exportations
Balance	S	−49	−72	−79	−72	−73	−87	−94	Balance
Dominican Republic [11 12]									**Rép. dominicaine** [11 12]
Imports	G	2992	3164	3581	4192	4897	5207	6416	Importations
Exports	G	644	872	945	1017	880	805	966	Exportations
Balance	G	−2348	−2292	−2635	−3175	−4016	−4402	−5450	Balance
French Guiana [13]									**Guyane française** [13]
Imports	S	676	752	...	...	...	...	...	Importations
Exports	S	136	131	...	...	...	...	...	Exportations
Balance	S	−539	−622	...	...	...	...	...	Balance
Greenland									**Groenland**
Imports	G	364	435	469	397	409	...	...	Importations
Exports	G	285	373	369	293	254	...	...	Exportations
Balance	G	−79	−63	−100	−104	−155	...	...	Balance
Grenada									**Grenade**
Imports	S	119	124	152	173	200	...	...	Importations
Exports	S	24	22	20	23	27	...	...	Exportations
Balance	S	−95	−102	−132	−151	−173	...	...	Balance
Guadeloupe [13]									**Guadeloupe** [13]
Imports	S	1539	1890	...	...	...	...	...	Importations
Exports	S	152	159	...	...	...	...	...	Exportations
Balance	S	−1387	−1731	...	...	...	...	...	Balance
Guyana									**Guyana**
Imports	S	506	528	598	629	...	...	...	Importations
Exports	S	456	455	517	643	485	523	498	Exportations
Balance	S	−50	−73	−81	14	...	...	...	Balance
Haiti									**Haiti**
Imports	G	259	654	666	648	800	1035	1041	Importations
Exports	G	87	112	90	119	175	199	165	Exportations
Balance	G	−172	−542	−576	−528	−626	−836	−876	Balance
Jamaica									**Jamaique**
Imports	G	2221	2808	5217	3128	3033	2899	3217	Importations
Exports	G	1211	1420	2579	1382	1312	1241	1296	Exportations
Balance	G	−1010	−1388	−2638	−1746	−1721	−1658	−1920	Balance
Martinique [13]									**Martinique** [13]
Imports	S	1642	1963	...	...	...	...	...	Importations
Exports	S	218	224	...	...	...	...	...	Exportations
Balance	S	−1424	−1739	...	...	...	...	...	Balance
Netherlands Antilles									**Antilles néerlandaises**
Imports	S	1758	1841	2519	2083	...	...	...	Importations
Exports	S	1376	1522	1269	1488	...	...	...	Exportations
Balance	S	−382	−319	−1249	−594	...	...	...	Balance
Panama									**Panama**
Imports	S	2404	2511	2780	3002	3398	3516	3379	Importations
Exports	S	583	625	623	723	784	822	859	Exportations
Balance	S	−1821	−1886	−2157	−2279	−2614	−2694	−2519	Balance

70

Total imports and exports
Imports c.i.f. and exports f.o.b., value in million US dollars
Importations et exportations totales
Importations c.a.f. et exportations f.o.b., valeur en millions de dollars E.–U.

Country or area	Sys. [1]	1994	1995	1996	1997	1998	1999	2000	Pays ou zone
Saint Kitts and Nevis									**Saint–Kitts–et–Nevis**
Imports	S	128	133	149	148	148	...	...	Importations
Exports	S	22	19	22	36	...	...	...	Exportations
Balance	S	−105	−114	−127	−112	...	...	...	Balance
Saint Lucia									**Sainte–Lucie**
Imports	S	302	306	304	332	335	...	...	Importations
Exports	S	106	124	82	66	...	...	...	Exportations
Balance	S	−195	−182	−222	−266	...	...	...	Balance
Saint Pierre and Miquelon									**St. Pierre–et–Miquelon**
Imports	S	75	...	...	...	...	...	...	Importations
Exports	S	12	...	...	...	...	...	...	Exportations
Balance	S	−63	...	...	...	...	...	...	Balance
Saint Vincent–Grenadines									**St.Vincent–Grenadines**
Imports	S	130	136	132	182	193	201	163	Importations
Exports	S	50	43	46	46	50	49	47	Exportations
Balance	S	−80	−93	−85	−136	−143	−152	−116	Balance
Suriname									**Suriname**
Imports	G	423	585	501	657	551	...	...	Importations
Exports	G	449	477	433	700	435	...	...	Exportations
Balance	G	26	−108	−68	43	−116	...	...	Balance
Trinidad and Tobago									**Trinité–et–Tobago**
Imports	S	1130	1714	2144	2990	2999	2740	3308	Importations
Exports	S	1866	2456	2500	2542	2258	2803	4654	Exportations
Balance	S	736	742	356	−448	−741	63	1346	Balance
Europe · Europe									
Developed economies [3]									**Economies développées** [3]
Imports		1710699	2075555	2120077	2106273	2211027	2239232	2343603	**Importations**
Exports		1772035	2175460	2243807	2234715	2310435	2303293	2372697	**Exportations**
Balance		61335	99905	123730	128442	99407	64061	29095	**Balance**
EU+ [14]									**UE+** [14]
Imports		1615081	1960478	2004766	1994534	2095347	2123965	2228312	**Importations**
Exports		1667630	2051365	2114253	2109852	2191140	2178173	2235648	**Exportations**
Balance		52549	90887	109487	115317	95792	54209	7336	**Balance**
Austria									**Autriche**
Imports	S	55340	66398	67336	64786	68187	69557	68986	Importations
Exports	S	45031	57653	57822	58599	62747	64126	64167	Exportations
Balance	S	−10309	−8745	−9514	−6187	−5441	−5431	−4819	Balance
Belgium [15]									**Belgique** [15]
Imports	S	130081	159713	163615	157283	162212	164620	173444	Importations
Exports	S	143674	175881	175367	171906	177666	178965	186265	Exportations
Balance	S	13593	16168	11752	14623	15454	14345	12820	Balance
Denmark									**Danemark**
Imports	S	34882	45082	44434	44044	45427	44067	43711	Importations
Exports	S	41422	49769	50099	47720	47481	48698	53840	Exportations
Balance	S	6540	4687	5665	3676	2054	4631	10129	Balance
Finland									**Finlande**
Imports	G	23214	28114	29265	29786	32301	30727	32610	Importations
Exports	G	29658	39574	38435	39318	42963	40666	44533	Exportations
Balance	G	6444	11460	9171	9533	10662	9939	11923	Balance
France [13]									**France** [13]
Imports	S	234581	281497	281776	272721	290273	289799	301085	Importations
Exports	S	234043	284914	287643	290972	305991	300763	298899	Exportations
Balance	S	−538	3417	5867	18252	15718	10964	−2186	Balance
Germany [16]									**Allemagne** [16]
Imports	S	385385	464366	458808	445683	471448	473551	497902	Importations
Exports	S	429760	523909	524226	512503	543431	542883	549686	Exportations
Balance	S	44375	59544	65418	66820	71983	69333	51784	Balance
Greece									**Grèce**
Imports	S	18742	22929	24136	23644	23247	25433	...	Importations
Exports	S	9384	10961	11948	11128	10732	9815	...	Exportations
Balance	S	−9358	−11968	−12187	−12516	−12515	−15618	...	Balance
Ireland									**Irlande**
Imports	G	25910	33067	35895	39231	44620	46535	50553	Importations
Exports	G	34155	44637	48670	53515	64574	70552	76873	Exportations
Balance	G	8244	11570	12775	14284	19954	24017	26320	Balance

70

Total imports and exports
Imports c.i.f. and exports f.o.b., value in million US dollars
Importations et exportations totales
Importations c.a.f. et exportations f.o.b., valeur en millions de dollars E.‒U.

Country or area	Sys.[1]	1994	1995	1996	1997	1998	1999	2000	Pays ou zone
Italy									**Italie**
Imports	S	169179	206025	208097	210297	218460	220327	236671	Importations
Exports	S	191431	233980	252044	240440	245715	235067	238310	Exportations
Balance	S	22252	27955	43947	30144	27255	14740	1639	Balance
Luxembourg									**Luxembourg**
Imports	S	8389	9755	9668	9380	7409	10787	10616	Importations
Exports	S	6562	7755	7211	7000	7912	7849	7825	Exportations
Balance	S	−1827	−1999	−2457	−2380	503	−2937	−2790	Balance
Netherlands									**Pays‒Bas**
Imports	S	141317	176874	180642	178133	187754	187488	197290	Importations
Exports	S	155554	196276	197420	194909	201382	200290	208896	Exportations
Balance	S	14238	19402	16778	16776	13628	12802	11607	Balance
Portugal									**Portugal**
Imports	S	27304	33314	35179	35066	38539	39826	38257	Importations
Exports	S	18006	23211	24606	23974	24816	25228	23314	Exportations
Balance	S	−9298	−10103	−10572	−11092	−13723	−14599	−14943	Balance
Spain									**Espagne**
Imports	S	92191	113315	121792	122721	133164	144438	152900	Importations
Exports	S	72926	91040	102003	104368	109240	109966	113348	Exportations
Balance	S	−19264	−22275	−19788	−18353	−23923	−34473	−39553	Balance
Sweden									**Suède**
Imports	G	51732	64752	66932	65710	68634	68586	72643	Importations
Exports	G	61352	79813	84904	82956	85003	84796	86920	Exportations
Balance	G	9620	15061	17973	17246	16369	16210	14277	Balance
United Kingdom									**Royaume‒Uni**
Imports	G	226172	265322	287472	306592	314036	317969	334366	Importations
Exports	G	204009	242036	262130	281083	271851	268254	281550	Exportations
Balance	G	−22163	−23286	−25342	−25509	−42185	−49715	−52816	Balance
EFTA+ [17]									**AELE+** [17]
Imports		92859	111734	112118	108781	112570	111990	111327	**Importations**
Exports		102546	121861	127489	122905	117139	123020	134287	**Exportations**
Balance		9687	10128	15371	14124	4569	11030	22960	**Balance**
Iceland									**Islande**
Imports	G	1472	1755	2031	1992	2489	2503	2591	Importations
Exports	G	1623	1803	1638	1852	2050	2005	1891	Exportations
Balance	G	151	48	−393	−140	−438	−498	−700	Balance
Norway									**Norvège**
Imports	G	27303	32972	35616	35713	36196	34047	32655	Importations
Exports	G	34685	41997	49646	48547	39649	44892	57519	Exportations
Balance	G	7382	9024	14030	12834	3453	10845	24865	Balance
Switzerland									**Suisse**
Imports	S	64085	77006	74471	71075	73885	75440	76082	Importations
Exports	S	66238	78061	76205	72506	75439	76124	74876	Exportations
Balance	S	2154	1055	1735	1431	1554	684	−1206	Balance
Other Developed Europe [3]									**Autres pays dév. d'Eur.** [3]
Imports		2759	3343	3193	2958	3110	3277	3964	**Importations**
Exports		1858	2233	2065	1959	2156	2100	2763	**Exportations**
Balance		−901	−1110	−1128	−999	−954	−1178	−1201	**Balance**
Faeroe Islands									**Iles Féroé**
Imports	G	243	316	365	...	...	...	...	Importations
Exports	G	327	362	437	...	...	...	...	Exportations
Balance	G	85	46	71	...	...	...	...	Balance
Malta									**Malte**
Imports	G	2441	2942	2796	2552	2666	2841	3417	Importations
Exports	G	1572	1913	1731	1630	1833	1783	2337	Exportations
Balance	G	−869	−1029	−1064	−922	−833	−1058	−1080	Balance
Developing economies [3 18]									**Écon. en dévelop.** [3 18]
Imports		17883	21386	22940	25039	25030	23249	23099	**Importations**
Exports		14335	15684	15813	16148	17504	16281	16906	**Exportations**
Balance		−3549	−5702	−7127	−8891	−7526	−6969	−6193	**Balance**
Croatia									**Croatie**
Imports	G	5229	7510	7788	9104	8383	7799	7887	Importations
Exports	G	4260	4633	4512	4171	4541	4303	4432	Exportations
Balance	G	−969	−2877	−3276	−4933	−3842	−3496	−3455	Balance

70

Total imports and exports
Imports c.i.f. and exports f.o.b., value in million US dollars
Importations et exportations totales
Importations c.a.f. et exportations f.o.b., valeur en millions de dollars E.−U.

Country or area	Sys.[1]	1994	1995	1996	1997	1998	1999	2000	Pays ou zone
Slovenia									**Slovénie**
Imports	S	7304	9492	9423	9357	10110	9952	10107	Importations
Exports	S	6828	8316	8312	8372	9048	8604	8733	Exportations
Balance	S	−476	−1175	−1111	−985	−1062	−1348	−1374	Balance
TFYR of Macedonia									**L'ex−Ry de Macédonie**
Imports	S	1484	1719	1627	1779	1915	1796	...	Importations
Exports	S	1086	1204	1147	1237	1311	1192	...	Exportations
Balance	S	−398	−515	−479	−542	−604	−604	...	Balance
Yugoslavia [19]									**Yougoslavie [19]**
Imports	S	...	2666	4102	4799	4622	...	...	Importations
Exports	S	...	1531	1842	2368	2604	...	...	Exportations
Balance	S	...	−1135	−2260	−2431	−2018	...	...	Balance
Eastern Europe									**Europe de l'est**
Imports		**67976**	**89688**	**111182**	**118016**	**132612**	**131158**	**147226**	**Importations**
Exports		**57178**	**73776**	**82670**	**89230**	**100273**	**101311**	**116077**	**Exportations**
Balance		**−10798**	**−15912**	**−28512**	**−28785**	**−32339**	**−29847**	**−31149**	**Balance**
Albania									**Albanie**
Imports	G	603	713	841	649	829	1140	1091	Importations
Exports	G	139	202	208	139	205	264	261	Exportations
Balance	G	−464	−511	−633	−510	−624	−876	−829	Balance
Bulgaria									**Bulgarie**
Imports	S	4284	5651	6861	5223	5021	5454	6492	Importations
Exports	S	3964	5353	6602	5322	4302	3964	4810	Exportations
Balance	S	−320	−298	−259	99	−719	−1490	−1682	Balance
Czech Rep[5]									**République tchèque[5]**
Imports	S	17500	25306	27716	27188	28814	28784	32241	Importations
Exports	S	16234	21686	21917	22751	26417	26245	29057	Exportations
Balance	S	−1266	−3620	−5799	−4437	−2397	−2540	−3184	Balance
Hungary [22]									**Hongrie [22]**
Imports	S	14386	15046	15853	20668	25600	27923	31955	Importations
Exports	S	10689	12439	12652	18628	22958	24950	28013	Exportations
Balance	S	−3697	−2607	−3200	−2040	−2642	−2973	−3942	Balance
Poland									**Pologne**
Imports	S	21496	29064	37045	42237	46803	45778	48970	Importations
Exports	S	17213	22890	24389	25708	27370	27323	31684	Exportations
Balance	S	−4283	−6173	−12656	−16529	−19433	−18455	−17285	Balance
Romania									**Roumanie**
Imports	S	7109	10278	11435	11280	11821	10392	13055	Importations
Exports	S	6151	7910	8085	8431	8300	8505	10367	Exportations
Balance	S	−958	−2368	−3351	−2849	−3521	−1887	−2688	Balance
Slovakia[5]									**Slovaquie[5]**
Imports	G	6838	9226	11431	10770	13725	11688	13423	Importations
Exports	G	6711	8596	8818	8251	10721	10062	11885	Exportations
Balance	G	−127	−630	−2613	−2519	−3004	−1625	−1538	Balance
Former USSR−Europe [24]									**anc. URSS−Europe [24]**
Imports		**58443**	**77176**	**82814**	**92836**	**81369**	**61146**	**74342**	**Importations**
Exports		**81052**	**102827**	**112890**	**115914**	**100266**	**97437**	**134426**	**Exportations**
Balance		**22609**	**25651**	**30076**	**23078**	**18898**	**36290**	**60083**	**Balance**
Belarus [25]									**Belarus [25]**
Imports	G	3066	5563	6939	8689	8549	6674	8492	Importations
Exports	G	2510	4707	5652	7301	7070	5909	7331	Exportations
Balance	G	−556	−856	−1287	−1388	−1479	−765	−1161	Balance
Estonia [26]									**Estonie [26]**
Imports	G	1667	2545	3245	4429	4611	4094	4242	Importations
Exports	G	1313	1838	2087	2924	3130	2937	3132	Exportations
Balance	G	−354	−707	−1157	−1506	−1482	−1157	−1109	Balance
Latvia									**Lettonie**
Imports	S	1244	1818	2320	2721	3191	2945	3187	Importations
Exports	S	992	1305	1443	1672	1811	1723	1867	Exportations
Balance	S	−253	−513	−876	−1049	−1380	−1222	−1320	Balance
Lithuania									**Lituanie**
Imports	G	2353	3649	4559	5644	5794	4835	5457	Importations
Exports	G	2029	2705	3355	3860	3711	3004	3810	Exportations
Balance	G	−325	−943	−1204	−1784	−2083	−1831	−1647	Balance

70
Total imports and exports
Imports c.i.f. and exports f.o.b., value in million US dollars
Importations et exportations totales
Importations c.a.f. et exportations f.o.b., valeur en millions de dollars E.–U.

Country or area	Sys.[1]	1994	1995	1996	1997	1998	1999	2000	Pays ou zone
Republic of Moldova [25]									**Rép. de Moldova** [25]
Imports	G	703	841	1079	1200	1018	567	...	Importations
Exports	G	619	739	805	890	644	465	...	Exportations
Balance	G	−84	−102	−275	−310	−374	−103	...	Balance
Russian Federation [25]									**Fédération de Russie** [25]
Imports	G	38661	46709	46034	53039	43530	30185	33884	Importations
Exports	G	63285	78217	85107	85036	71265	71817	103070	Exportations
Balance	G	24624	31508	39073	31997	27735	41632	69186	Balance
Ukraine [25][27]									**Ukraine** [25][27]
Imports	G	10748	16052	18639	17114	14676	11846	...	Importations
Exports	G	10305	13317	14441	14232	12637	11582	...	Exportations
Balance	G	−443	−2735	−4198	−2882	−2038	−264	...	Balance

Africa · Afrique

Country or area	Sys.[1]	1994	1995	1996	1997	1998	1999	2000	Pays ou zone
South Africa [28][29]									**Afrique du Sud** [28][29]
Imports	G	22470	29608	29105	31939	28277	25890	28980	Importations
Exports	G	24415	26918	28145	29964	25396	25901	29267	Exportations
Balance	G	1945	−2690	−960	−1975	−2881	11	287	Balance
Developing economies [3]									**Écon. en dévelop.** [3]
Imports		72383	87054	85767	89398	94342	95028	93152	**Importations**
Exports		66476	79049	86150	86239	78504	82114	89820	**Exportations**
Balance		−5906	−8005	383	−3159	−15838	−12914	−3332	**Balance**
North Africa									**Afrique du Nord**
Imports		40476	46249	45609	46282	51031	51200	51393	**Importations**
Exports		33546	37801	38669	39643	37548	37234	38881	**Exportations**
Balance		−6930	−8449	−6939	−6639	−13483	−13966	−12511	**Balance**
Algeria									**Algérie**
Imports	S	9370	10250	8690	...	...	...	...	Importations
Exports	S	8840	10250	12621	...	...	...	...	Exportations
Balance	S	−530	0	3931	...	...	...	...	Balance
Egypt [30]									**Égypte** [30]
Imports	S	10218	11760	13038	13211	16166	16022	14010	Importations
Exports	S	3475	3450	3539	3921	3130	3559	4691	Exportations
Balance	S	−6743	−8310	−9499	−9290	−13036	−12463	−9319	Balance
Libyan Arab Jamah.									**Jamah. arabe libyenne**
Imports	G	...	...	...	5593	5692	...	...	Importations
Exports	G	...	...	...	9036	6131	...	...	Exportations
Balance	G	...	...	...	3444	440	...	...	Balance
Morocco									**Maroc**
Imports	S	8272	10024	9704	9526	10290	9925	11534	Importations
Exports	S	5556	6882	6881	7033	7153	7367	7429	Exportations
Balance	S	−2716	−3142	−2823	−2493	−3137	−2558	−4106	Balance
Sudan									**Soudan**
Imports	G	1227	1219	1548	1580	1915	1988	...	Importations
Exports	G	503	556	620	594	596	616	...	Exportations
Balance	G	−725	−663	−927	−985	−1319	−1372	...	Balance
Tunisia									**Tunisie**
Imports	G	6581	7903	7700	7914	8350	8474	8567	Importations
Exports	G	4657	5475	5517	5559	5738	5872	5850	Exportations
Balance	G	−1924	−2428	−2184	−2355	−2612	−2603	−2717	Balance
Other Africa									**Autres pays d'Afrique**
Imports		31906	40804	40158	43116	43311	43828	41759	**Importations**
Exports		32930	41248	47481	46596	40955	44880	50938	**Exportations**
Balance		1023	444	7323	3480	−2355	1052	9179	**Balance**
CACEU+ [31]									**UDEAC+** [31]
Imports		2453	3326	4223	3946	3791	3655	3727	**Importations**
Exports		5047	6090	7120	7436	7053	7250	7386	**Exportations**
Balance		2593	2764	2897	3490	3262	3594	3659	**Balance**
Cameroon									**Cameroun**
Imports	S	721	1201	1226	1359	1503	1314	...	Importations
Exports	S	1370	1654	1768	1860	1675	1595	...	Exportations
Balance	S	649	453	542	501	172	281	...	Balance
Cent. African Rep.									**Rép. centrafricaine**
Imports	S	139	174	141	145	...	...	...	Importations
Exports	S	151	171	147	154	...	...	...	Exportations
Balance	S	12	−3	5	9	...	...	...	Balance

70
Total imports and exports
Imports c.i.f. and exports f.o.b., value in million US dollars
Importations et exportations totales
Importations c.a.f. et exportations f.o.b., valeur en millions de dollars E.–U.

Country or area	Sys.[1]	1994	1995	1996	1997	1998	1999	2000	Pays ou zone
Chad									**Tchad**
Imports	S	177	365	332	335	356	317	291	Importations
Exports	S	148	243	238	238	262	202	184	Exportations
Balance	S	−29	−122	−94	−97	−94	−115	−108	Balance
Congo									**Congo**
Imports	S	634	670	1399	925	682	820	...	Importations
Exports	S	963	1176	1552	1666	1373	1555	...	Exportations
Balance	S	329	506	153	741	691	735	...	Balance
Equatorial Guinea									**Guinée équatoriale**
Imports	G	24	31	168	80	32	28	...	Importations
Exports	G	67	128	232	497	423	407	...	Exportations
Balance	G	42	97	64	417	392	378	...	Balance
Gabon									**Gabon**
Imports	S	758	884	956	1103	...	...	...	Importations
Exports	S	2348	2719	3183	3021	...	...	...	Exportations
Balance	S	1590	1835	2227	1918	...	...	...	Balance
ECOWAS+[32]		**13906**	**18980**	**18097**	**20955**	**21049**	**21719**	**20818**	**CEDEAO+**[32]
Imports		**16338**	**21683**	**26930**	**25800**	**20943**	**24093**	**30488**	**Importations**
Exports		**2432**	**2703**	**8833**	**4845**	**−106**	**2375**	**9670**	**Exportations**
Balance									**Balance**
Benin									**Benin**
Imports	S	431	746	654	681	674	824	699	Importations
Exports	S	398	417	653	681	414	422	184	Exportations
Balance	S	−33	−329	−1	0	−260	−402	−516	Balance
Burkina Faso									**Burkina Faso**
Imports	S	349	455	647	588	732	579	550	Importations
Exports	S	105	275	234	232	319	255	213	Exportations
Balance	S	−244	−180	−413	−355	−412	−324	−337	Balance
Cape Verde									**Cap–Vert**
Imports	S	210	252	...	...	...	...	...	Importations
Exports	S	5	9	...	...	...	...	...	Exportations
Balance	S	−205	−243	...	...	...	...	...	Balance
Côte d'Ivoire									**Côte d'Ivoire**
Imports	S	1927	2929	2900	2782	3002	3262	3003	Importations
Exports	S	2755	3812	4444	4460	4610	4739	3990	Exportations
Balance	S	829	883	1543	1679	1608	1478	987	Balance
Gambia									**Gambie**
Imports	G	212	182	258	174	245	192	...	Importations
Exports	G	35	16	21	15	27	7	...	Exportations
Balance	G	−177	−166	−237	−159	−218	−185	...	Balance
Ghana									**Ghana**
Imports	G	582	1895	2101	2310	2561	3533	3055	Importations
Exports	G	374	1753	1670	1636	1792	...	...	Exportations
Balance	G	−208	−142	−431	−674	−769	...	...	Balance
Guinea–Bissau[33]									**Guinée–Bissau**[33]
Imports	G	164	134	85	89	69	69	71	Importations
Exports	G	86	45	28	49	27	51	62	Exportations
Balance	G	−78	−89	−57	−40	−42	−18	−9	Balance
Mali									**Mali**
Imports	S	591	774	772	738	761	753	689	Importations
Exports	S	336	443	433	561	556	571	378	Exportations
Balance	S	−255	−331	−340	−177	−205	−182	−311	Balance
Niger									**Niger**
Imports	S	328	373	448	391	376	390	363	Importations
Exports	S	225	289	325	272	334	288	262	Exportations
Balance	S	−103	−85	−123	−120	−42	−102	−101	Balance
Nigeria[34]									**Nigeria**[34]
Imports	G	6613	7912	6438	9501	9211	8588	8721	Importations
Exports	G	9415	11725	16154	15207	9855	13856	20975	Exportations
Balance	G	2803	3813	9715	5706	644	5268	12254	Balance
Senegal									**Sénégal**
Imports	S	1021	1411	1435	1446	1406	1468	1365	Importations
Exports	S	790	993	987	904	968	1025	998	Exportations
Balance	S	−231	−419	−448	−542	−439	−443	−367	Balance

70
Total imports and exports
Imports c.i.f. and exports f.o.b., value in million US dollars
Importations et exportations totales
Importations c.a.f. et exportations f.o.b., valeur en millions de dollars E.–U.

Country or area	Sys.[1]	1994	1995	1996	1997	1998	1999	2000	Pays ou zone
Sierra Leone									**Sierra Leone**
Imports	S	151	134	211	92	95	80	149	Importations
Exports	S	116	42	47	17	7	6	13	Exportations
Balance	S	−35	−91	−164	−75	−88	−74	−136	Balance
Togo									**Togo**
Imports	S	221	593	664	645	589	593	520	Importations
Exports	S	327	378	441	424	969	389	329	Exportations
Balance	S	106	−215	−224	−221	381	−204	−191	Balance
Rest of Africa									**Afrique NDA**
Imports		**15548**	**18499**	**17838**	**18215**	**18471**	**18454**	**17215**	**Importations**
Exports		**11545**	**13476**	**13430**	**13360**	**12960**	**13537**	**13065**	**Exportations**
Balance		**−4002**	**−5023**	**−4408**	**−4855**	**−5512**	**−4917**	**−4150**	**Balance**
Angola									**Angola**
Imports	S	138	427	...	...	...	...	...	Importations
Exports	S	3018	3642	...	...	...	...	...	Exportations
Balance	S	2880	3215	...	...	...	...	...	Balance
Burundi									**Burundi**
Imports	S	225	234	127	121	158	118	148	Importations
Exports	S	121	106	40	87	65	54	50	Exportations
Balance	S	−104	−129	−87	−35	−93	−64	−98	Balance
Comoros									**Comores**
Imports	S	53	63	...	...	...	...	...	Importations
Exports	S	11	11	...	...	...	...	...	Exportations
Balance	S	−41	−51	...	...	...	...	...	Balance
Dem. Rep. of the Congo									**Rép. dém. du Congo**
Imports	S	382	397	424	...	...	...	...	Importations
Exports	S	419	438	592	...	...	...	...	Exportations
Balance	S	37	41	167	...	...	...	...	Balance
Djibouti									**Djibouti**
Imports	G	196	177	179	148	158	153	...	Importations
Exports	G	12	14	14	11	12	12	...	Exportations
Balance	G	−184	−163	−165	−137	−146	−140	...	Balance
Ethiopia									**Ethiopie**
Imports	G	1033	1142	1401	...	...	1317	...	Importations
Exports	G	372	422	417	587	560	...	...	Exportations
Balance	G	−661	−720	−984	...	...	...	...	Balance
Kenya									**Kenya**
Imports	G	2090	3006	2949	3296	3195	2833	272	Importations
Exports	G	1587	1889	2068	2054	2007	1747	156	Exportations
Balance	G	−503	−1116	−881	−1243	−1188	−1086	−116	Balance
Madagascar									**Madagascar**
Imports	S	447	543	507	467	514	377	...	Importations
Exports	S	375	370	299	222	243	221	...	Exportations
Balance	S	−73	−173	−208	−245	−271	−156	...	Balance
Malawi									**Malawi**
Imports	G	489	475	623	791	583	697	...	Importations
Exports	G	342	405	481	537	517	442	...	Exportations
Balance	G	−147	−69	−143	−255	−67	−256	...	Balance
Mauritius									**Maurice**
Imports	G	1930	1976	2289	2181	2073	2248	...	Importations
Exports	G	1347	1538	1802	1592	1645	1554	...	Exportations
Balance	G	−583	−438	−487	−588	−428	−694	...	Balance
Mozambique									**Mozambique**
Imports	S	524	704	759	739	790	1139	1158	Importations
Exports	S	157	168	217	222	230	263	364	Exportations
Balance	S	−367	−536	−542	−517	−560	−876	−794	Balance
Réunion [13]									**Reunion** [13]
Imports	S	2365	2625	...	...	...	...	...	Importations
Exports	S	171	207	...	...	...	...	...	Exportations
Balance	S	−2195	−2418	...	...	...	...	...	Balance
Rwanda									**Rwanda**
Imports	G	101	241	256	297	285	253	213	Importations
Exports	G	24	52	60	87	60	61	53	Exportations
Balance	G	−77	−189	−196	−210	−225	−192	−160	Balance

70
Total imports and exports
Imports c.i.f. and exports f.o.b., value in million US dollars
Importations et exportations totales
Importations c.a.f. et exportations f.o.b., valeur en millions de dollars E.–U.

Country or area	Sys.[1]	1994	1995	1996	1997	1998	1999	2000	Pays ou zone
Seychelles									**Seychelles**
Imports	G	207	233	379	340	384	434	...	Importations
Exports	G	52	53	139	113	122	145	...	Exportations
Balance	G	−155	−180	−239	−227	−261	−289	...	Balance
Uganda									**Ouganda**
Imports	G	879	1056	1190	1317	1414	1342	1512	Importations
Exports	G	410	461	587	555	501	517	469	Exportations
Balance	G	−469	−595	−603	−762	−913	−825	−1044	Balance
United Rep. of Tanzania									**Rép.–Unie de Tanzanie**
Imports	G	1504	1679	1386	1336	1453	1550	1523	Importations
Exports	G	519	685	783	752	589	543	663	Exportations
Balance	G	−985	−994	−603	−584	−864	−1007	−860	Balance
Zambia [35]									**Zambie** [35]
Imports	S	530	708	836	819	...	...	...	Importations
Exports	S	827	1055	1049	914	...	...	...	Exportations
Balance	S	297	347	213	96	...	...	...	Balance
Zimbabwe									**Zimbabwe**
Imports	G	2241	2661	2817	...	...	...	...	Importations
Exports	G	1881	2114	2397	...	...	...	...	Exportations
Balance	G	−360	−548	−420	...	...	...	...	Balance

Asia · Asie

Country or area	Sys.[1]	1994	1995	1996	1997	1998	1999	2000	Pays ou zone
Developed economies [3]									**Economies développées** [3]
Imports		**291700**	**355049**	**369841**	**356741**	**296393**	**327068**	**401268**	**Importations**
Exports		**406592**	**453078**	**422252**	**432379**	**399420**	**429392**	**496659**	**Exportations**
Balance		**114893**	**98028**	**52411**	**75638**	**103027**	**102324**	**95391**	**Balance**
Israel									**Israël**
Imports	S	23776	28287	29951	29084	27470	31090	35750	Importations
Exports	S	16884	19046	20610	22503	22993	25794	31404	Exportations
Balance	S	−6892	−9241	−9341	−6582	−4477	−5296	−4345	Balance
Japan									**Japon**
Imports	G	275264	335991	349174	338830	280631	310039	379491	Importations
Exports	G	397048	443261	410926	421050	388135	417659	479227	Exportations
Balance	G	121784	107269	61752	82220	107504	107620	99736	Balance
Developing economies [3][36]									**Econ. en dévelop.** [3][36]
Imports		**920858**	**1127566**	**1201410**	**1234153**	**1047180**	**1128617**	**1378996**	**Importations**
Exports		**913117**	**1095868**	**1162854**	**1239610**	**1158967**	**1250075**	**1505232**	**Exportations**
Balance		**−7742**	**−31698**	**−38556**	**5457**	**111786**	**121458**	**126235**	**Balance**
Asia Middle East									**Moyen–Orient d'Asie**
Imports		**114109**	**137038**	**153601**	**165622**	**159403**	**164172**	**197505**	**Importations**
Exports		**137649**	**153596**	**175960**	**186310**	**162139**	**186446**	**225430**	**Exportations**
Balance		**23539**	**16558**	**22359**	**20688**	**2737**	**22274**	**27925**	**Balance**
Bahrain									**Bahreïn**
Imports	G	3748	3716	4273	4026	3566	3698	4612	Importations
Exports	G	3617	4113	4702	4384	3270	4140	5701	Exportations
Balance	G	−131	397	429	358	−296	443	1089	Balance
Cyprus [37]									**Chypre** [37]
Imports	G	3019	3694	3983	3655	3687	3618	3846	Importations
Exports	G	969	1231	1391	1250	1062	997	954	Exportations
Balance	G	−2050	−2463	−2591	−2405	−2625	−2621	−2893	Balance
Iran (Islamic Rep. of) [38]									**Iran (Rép. islamique d')** [38]
Imports	S	13774	13882	16274	...	...	...	...	Importations
Exports	S	19434	18360	22391	...	...	...	...	Exportations
Balance	S	5660	4478	6117	...	...	...	...	Balance
Jordan									**Jordanie**
Imports	G	3382	3696	4293	4102	3828	3717	4539	Importations
Exports	G	1424	1769	1817	1836	1802	1832	1897	Exportations
Balance	G	−1958	−1928	−2476	−2266	−2026	−1885	−2641	Balance
Kuwait									**Koweït**
Imports	S	6680	7792	8373	8246	8617	7617	...	Importations
Exports	S	11231	12785	14889	14225	9553	12218	18156	Exportations
Balance	S	4551	4992	6515	5979	936	4601	...	Balance
Lebanon									**Liban**
Imports	S	2598	5480	7540	7467	7070	6207	6228	Importations
Exports	S	470	656	736	643	662	677	714	Exportations
Balance	S	−2128	−4825	−6804	−6824	−6408	−5530	−5514	Balance

70
Total imports and exports
Imports c.i.f. and exports f.o.b., value in million US dollars
Importations et exportations totales
Importations c.a.f. et exportations f.o.b., valeur en millions de dollars E.–U.

Country or area	Sys.[1]	1994	1995	1996	1997	1998	1999	2000	Pays ou zone
Oman									**Oman**
Imports	G	3915	4248	4578	5026	5682	4674	5040	Importations
Exports	G	5545	6068	7346	7630	5508	...	...	Exportations
Balance	G	1630	1821	2768	2604	−173	...	...	Balance
Qatar									**Qatar**
Imports	G	1927	3398	2868	3322	3409	2499	...	Importations
Exports	G	...	...	3752	...	...	...	...	Exportations
Balance	G	...	...	884	...	...	...	...	Balance
Saudi Arabia									**Arabe saoudite**
Imports	S	23338	28091	27744	28732	30013	28010	30267	Importations
Exports	S	42614	50040	60729	60732	38822	50760	...	Exportations
Balance	S	19276	21949	32985	32000	8809	22750	...	Balance
Syrian Arab Republic									**Rep. arabe syrienne**
Imports	S	5467	4709	5380	4028	3895	3832	16706	Importations
Exports	S	3047	3563	3999	3916	2890	3464	19260	Exportations
Balance	S	−2420	−1146	−1381	−111	−1005	−368	2553	Balance
Turkey									**Turquie**
Imports	S	23270	35709	43627	48559	45921	40692	53499	Importations
Exports	S	18106	21637	23224	26261	26974	26588	26572	Exportations
Balance	S	−5164	−14072	−20403	−22298	−18947	−14104	−26927	Balance
United Arab Emirates									**Emirats arabes unis**
Imports	G	21024	20984	22638	29952	24728	34745	...	Importations
Exports	G	26922	27753	28085	39613	42666	43307	...	Exportations
Balance	G	5898	6769	5447	9661	17938	8562	...	Balance
Yemen [39]									**Yémen [39]**
Imports	S	2087	1817	2442	2017	2172	2006	2326	Importations
Exports	S	934	1917	3206	2509	1501	2438	4078	Exportations
Balance	S	−1154	101	763	491	−671	432	1751	Balance
Non Petrol. Export [40]									**Pétrole non Compris [40]**
Imports		...	...	...	...	...	...	...	Importations
Exports		137649	153596	175960	186310	162139	186446	225430	Exportations
Balance		...	...	...	...	...	...	...	Balance
Other Asia									**Autres Pays d'Asie**
Imports		797513	979954	1033934	1054750	874737	953019	1168338	**Importations**
Exports		765374	929757	972076	1037724	983543	1049964	1262581	**Exportations**
Balance		−32139	−50196	−61858	−17026	108806	96945	94243	**Balance**
ASEAN+ [41]									**ANASE+ [41]**
Imports		280654	354169	375044	371431	281437	300880	367004	**Importations**
Exports		261705	320469	340148	352431	328904	359409	427039	**Exportations**
Balance		−18950	−33700	−34897	−19000	47467	58529	60035	**Balance**
Brunei Darussalam									**Brunéi Darussalam**
Imports	S	1854	2091	2494	2203	1552	...	...	Importations
Exports	S	2210	2402	2481	2467	2058	...	...	Exportations
Balance	S	356	311	−13	264	506	...	...	Balance
Indonesia									**Indonésie**
Imports	S	31983	40630	42929	41694	27337	24004	33515	Importations
Exports	S	40055	45417	49814	53443	48847	48665	62124	Exportations
Balance	S	8072	4787	6885	11749	21511	24661	28609	Balance
Lao People's Dem.Rep.									**Rép. dém. populaire lao**
Imports	S	564	589	690	706	553	525	...	Importations
Exports	S	301	311	323	359	370	311	...	Exportations
Balance	S	−264	−278	−367	−347	−183	−214	...	Balance
Malaysia									**Malaisie**
Imports	G	59600	77545	78408	79030	58325	64962	82199	Importations
Exports	G	58844	73779	78318	78741	73305	84451	98136	Exportations
Balance	G	−756	−3766	−90	−289	14980	19488	15936	Balance
Myanmar									**Myanmar**
Imports	G	878	1335	1355	2037	2667	2301	2371	Importations
Exports	G	792	851	744	866	1066	1125	1621	Exportations
Balance	G	−86	−484	−611	−1171	−1601	−1176	−750	Balance
Philippines									**Philippines**
Imports	G	22640	28328	34127	38604	31542	32569	33808	Importations
Exports	G	13306	17491	20408	24895	29449	36577	39794	Exportations
Balance	G	−9334	−10836	−13719	−13709	−2093	4008	5986	Balance

70
Total imports and exports
Imports c.i.f. and exports f.o.b., value in million US dollars
Importations et exportations totales
Importations c.a.f. et exportations f.o.b., valeur en millions de dollars E.–U.

Country or area	Sys.[1]	1994	1995	1996	1997	1998	1999	2000	Pays ou zone
Singapore									**Singapour**
Imports	G	102670	124502	131340	132443	104728	111062	134546	Importations
Exports	G	96825	118263	125016	124990	109905	114682	137806	Exportations
Balance	G	−5845	−6239	−6324	−7453	5177	3620	3259	Balance
Thailand									**Thaïlande**
Imports	S	54460	70787	72336	62880	42971	50343	61924	Importations
Exports	S	45262	56440	55721	57402	54458	58440	69057	Exportations
Balance	S	−9198	−14347	−16616	−5479	11487	8098	7133	Balance
Viet Nam									**Viet Nam**
Imports	G	5826	8155	11144	11592	11500	11742	...	Importations
Exports	G	4054	5449	7256	9185	9360	11541	...	Exportations
Balance	G	−1771	−2706	−3888	−2407	−2140	−201	...	Balance
Rest of Asia									**Asie NDA**
Imports		516859	625785	658889	683319	593300	652139	801334	**Importations**
Exports		503669	609288	631928	685294	654639	690554	835542	**Exportations**
Balance		−13190	−16496	−26961	1975	61339	38416	34208	**Balance**
Afghanistan									**Afghanistan**
Imports	G	142	50	...	...	...	...	...	Importations
Exports	G	24	26	...	...	...	...	...	Exportations
Balance	G	−118	−24	...	...	...	...	...	Balance
Bangladesh									**Bangladesh**
Imports	G	4602	6501	6621	6896	6978	7685	8358	Importations
Exports	G	2661	3173	3297	3778	3831	3919	4692	Exportations
Balance	G	−1942	−3328	−3324	−3117	−3147	−3766	−3667	Balance
China ††									**Chine ††**
Imports	S	115681	129113	138944	142189	140305	165788	206132	Importations
Exports	S	121047	148797	151197	182877	183589	195150	249297	Exportations
Balance	S	5366	19684	12253	40688	43284	29362	43165	Balance
China, Hong Kong SAR †									**Chine, Hong Kong RAS †**
Imports	G	161841	192751	198550	208614	184518	179520	212805	Importations
Exports	G	151399	173750	180750	188059	174002	173885	201860	Exportations
Balance	G	−10442	−19001	−17800	−20555	−10516	−5635	−10945	Balance
China, Macao SAR †									**Chine, Macao RAS †**
Imports	G	1978	2021	1979	2062	1937	2024	2249	Importations
Exports	G	1845	1977	1975	2128	2122	2181	2529	Exportations
Balance	G	−133	−44	−4	65	185	157	281	Balance
India									**Inde**
Imports	G	26843	34710	37944	41430	42999	46971	51507	Importations
Exports	G	25022	30628	33107	35006	33463	35666	42379	Exportations
Balance	G	−1821	−4082	−4837	−6425	−9536	−11305	−9128	Balance
Korea, Republic of									**Corée, République**
Imports	G	102348	135119	150339	144616	93282	119752	160481	Importations
Exports	G	96013	125058	129715	136164	132313	143686	172268	Exportations
Balance	G	−6335	−10061	−20624	−8452	39031	23934	11787	Balance
Maldives									**Maldives**
Imports	G	222	268	302	349	354	402	389	Importations
Exports	G	46	50	59	73	74	64	76	Exportations
Balance	G	−176	−218	−242	−276	−280	−338	−313	Balance
Mongolia									**Mongolie**
Imports	G	258	415	451	468	503	426	...	Importations
Exports	G	356	473	424	452	345	233	...	Exportations
Balance	G	98	58	−27	−17	−158	−192	...	Balance
Nepal									**Népal**
Imports	G	1155	1333	1398	1693	1245	1418	1572	Importations
Exports	G	362	346	385	406	474	600	804	Exportations
Balance	G	−793	−988	−1013	−1287	−772	−818	−768	Balance
Pakistan									**Pakistan**
Imports	G	8889	11461	12191	11652	9331	10163	11486	Importations
Exports	G	7365	7992	9367	8760	8515	8387	9174	Exportations
Balance	G	−1523	−3469	−2824	−2893	−816	−1776	−2312	Balance
Sri Lanka									**Sri Lanka**
Imports	G	4767	5307	5442	5864	5877	5961	7210	Importations
Exports	G	3208	3798	4095	4639	4787	4594	5416	Exportations
Balance	G	−1559	−1509	−1347	−1225	−1091	−1367	−1794	Balance

70
Total imports and exports
Imports c.i.f. and exports f.o.b., value in million US dollars
Importations et exportations totales
Importations c.a.f. et exportations f.o.b., valeur en millions de dollars E.–U.

Country or area	Sys.[1]	1994	1995	1996	1997	1998	1999	2000	Pays ou zone
Former USSR – Asia									**anc. URSS – Asie**
Imports		**9236**	**10574**	**13875**	**13781**	**13041**	**11426**	**13154**	**Importations**
Exports		**10094**	**12514**	**14818**	**15576**	**13284**	**13666**	**17222**	**Exportations**
Balance		**859**	**1940**	**943**	**1795**	**244**	**2240**	**4068**	**Balance**
Armenia[25]									**Arménie**[25]
Imports	S	394	674	856	892	902	800	882	Importations
Exports	S	216	271	290	233	221	232	294	Exportations
Balance	S	−178	−403	−565	−660	−682	−567	−588	Balance
Azerbaijan[25]									**Azerbaidjan**[25]
Imports	G	778	668	961	794	1077	1036	...	Importations
Exports	G	638	637	631	781	606	929	...	Exportations
Balance	G	−140	−30	−329	−13	−471	−106	...	Balance
Georgia[25]									**Géorgie**[25]
Imports	G	236	417	687	944	878	...	...	Importations
Exports	G	134	159	199	240	192	...	...	Exportations
Balance	G	−102	−257	−489	−704	−686	...	...	Balance
Kazakhstan[25]									**Kazakhstan**[25]
Imports	G	3561	3807	4241	4301	4350	3687	5052	Importations
Exports	G	3231	5250	5911	6497	5436	5598	9140	Exportations
Balance	G	−330	1444	1670	2196	1086	1912	4087	Balance
Kyrgyzstan[25]									**Kirghizistan**[25]
Imports	S	316	522	838	709	842	600	...	Importations
Exports	S	340	409	505	604	514	454	...	Exportations
Balance	S	24	−113	−332	−105	−328	−146	...	Balance
Tajikistan[25]									**Tadjikistan**[25]
Imports	G	578	810	763	750	771	664	...	Importations
Exports	G	483	749	651	746	602	689	...	Exportations
Balance	G	−95	−61	−112	−5	−170	25	...	Balance
Turkmenistan[25]									**Turkménistan**[25]
Imports	G	894	777	...	...	...	...	...	Importations
Exports	G	2010	1939	...	...	...	...	...	Exportations
Balance	G	1116	1162	...	...	...	...	...	Balance
Uzbekistan[25]									**Ouzbékistan**[25]
Imports	G	2479	2900	4721	4523	3289	...	...	Importations
Exports	G	3044	3100	4590	4388	3528	...	...	Exportations
Balance	G	565	200	−131	−135	240	...	...	Balance

Oceania · Océanie

Country or area	Sys.	1994	1995	1996	1997	1998	1999	2000	Pays ou zone
Developed economies[3]									**Economies développées**[3]
Imports		**62658**	**72138**	**76932**	**77098**	**73699**	**79659**	**81609**	**Importations**
Exports		**57032**	**63658**	**71439**	**73813**	**64538**	**64737**	**74331**	**Exportations**
Balance		**−5626**	**−8480**	**−5492**	**−3285**	**−9162**	**−14922**	**−7279**	**Balance**
Australia									**Australie**
Imports	G	53426	61283	65428	65892	64630	69158	71537	Importations
Exports	G	47529	53115	60300	62910	55893	56080	64898	Exportations
Balance	G	−5897	−8167	−5128	−2982	−8737	−13078	−6639	Balance
New Zealand									**Nouvelle–Zélande**
Imports	G	11913	13958	14724	14519	12496	14299	13906	Importations
Exports	G	12185	13645	14360	14215	12071	12455	13266	Exportations
Balance	G	271	−312	−364	−303	−425	−1844	−640	Balance
Developing economies[3]									**Econ. en dévelop.**[3]
Imports		**5644**	**5803**	**6288**	**6230**	**5762**	**6128**	**5766**	**Importations**
Exports		**4418**	**4694**	**4711**	**4276**	**3769**	**4064**	**4091**	**Exportations**
Balance		**−1226**	**−1108**	**−1577**	**−1953**	**−1992**	**−2064**	**−1675**	**Balance**
Cook Islands									**Iles Cook**
Imports	G	49	49	43	48	38	41	...	Importations
Exports	G	4	5	3	3	3	4	...	Exportations
Balance	G	−45	−44	−40	−45	−35	−38	...	Balance
Fiji									**Fidji**
Imports	G	842	892	987	965	721	...	830	Importations
Exports	G	573	619	749	619	510	...	585	Exportations
Balance	G	−269	−273	−239	−346	−211	...	−246	Balance

70
Total imports and exports
Imports c.i.f. and exports f.o.b., value in million US dollars
Importations et exportations totales
Importations c.a.f. et exportations f.o.b., valeur en millions de dollars E.−U.

Country or area	Sys.[1]	1994	1995	1996	1997	1998	1999	2000	Pa...
French Polynesia									**Polynésie française**
Imports	S	881	1019	1016	936	...	...	...	Importations
Exports	S	226	196	251	222	...	...	...	Exportations
Balance	S	−655	−823	−765	−714	...	...	...	Balance
Kiribati									**Kiribati**
Imports	G	26	35	38	39	33	...	...	Importations
Exports	G	5	7	5	6	6	...	...	Exportations
Balance	G	−21	−28	−33	−33	−27	...	...	Balance
New Caledonia									**Nouvelle−Calédonie**
Imports	S	876	912	995	928	...	...	...	Importations
Exports	S	366	515	487	522	...	...	...	Exportations
Balance	S	−510	−398	−508	−405	...	...	...	Balance
Papua New Guinea									**Papouaise−Nvl−Guinee**
Imports	G	1521	1452	1741	1709	1240	1236	1151	Importations
Exports	G	2630	2654	2531	2160	1772	1927	2021	Exportations
Balance	G	1109	1202	789	451	532	691	870	Balance
Samoa									**Samoa**
Imports	S	81	95	100	97	97	115	106	Importations
Exports	S	4	9	10	15	15	20	14	Exportations
Balance	S	−78	−86	−90	−82	−82	−95	−92	Balance
Solomon Islands									**Iles Salomon**
Imports	S	98	104	150	182	150	...	...	Importations
Exports	S	99	114	161	155	118	...	...	Exportations
Balance	S	0	10	11	−27	−32	...	...	Balance
Tonga									**Tonga**
Imports	G	69	77	75	73	69	73	70	Importations
Exports	G	14	15	13	10	8	12	9	Exportations
Balance	G	−55	−63	−61	−63	−61	−60	−61	Balance
Vanuatu									**Vanuatu**
Imports	G	89	95	97	94	88	96	89	Importations
Exports	G	25	28	30	35	34	26	26	Exportations
Balance	G	−64	−67	−67	−59	−54	−71	−63	Balance
ANCOM+									**ANCOM+**
Imports		32311	41263	38515	47021	47806	37338	42025	Importations
Exports		33732	39769	45570	45864	39087	44068	57934	Exportations
Balance		1421	−1494	7055	−1157	−8719	6730	15908	Balance
APEC+									**CEAP+**
Imports		1927844	2240439	2381917	2500890	2322651	2542641	3035768	Importations
Exports		1856531	2175469	2252630	2408956	2305573	2444697	2856363	Exportations
Balance		−71313	−64970	−129287	−91935	−17078	−97944	−179404	Balance
CARICOM+									**CARICOM+**
Imports		7097	8805	11874	11454	11591	11412	12118	Importations
Exports		4507	5381	6590	5888	5210	5934	7967	Exportations
Balance		−2591	−3424	−5284	−5566	−6381	−5478	−4151	Balance
CIS+									**CEI+**
Imports		62414	79739	86567	93822	80813	60699	74612	Importations
Exports		86813	109494	120823	123034	104900	103438	142838	Exportations
Balance		24399	29755	34256	29212	24087	42739	68227	Balance
COMESA+									**COMESA+**
Imports		23168	27226	31378	32059	34863	34563	31203	Importations
Exports		15411	17338	17435	17687	16252	17325	17977	Exportations
Balance		−7757	−9889	−13944	−14371	−18611	−17238	−13226	Balance
LDC+									**PMA+**
Imports		23635	29131	32882	33217	34672	37068	38734	Importations
Exports		16172	19691	21026	21047	20846	23629	26921	Exportations
Balance		−7464	−9440	−11856	−12170	−13826	−13439	−11813	Balance
MERCOSUR+									**MERCOSUR+**
Imports		62451	79554	86882	102272	98316	82265	90938	Importations
Exports		61935	70499	74998	83179	81366	74322	85027	Exportations
Balance		−516	−9055	−11884	−19093	−16950	−7943	−5911	Balance
NAFTA+									**ALENA+**
Imports		879671	959239	1029419	1147601	1210558	1350487	1584362	Importations
Exports		698707	808469	869940	956349	953704	1011202	1139151	Exportations
Balance		−180965	−150770	−159479	−191252	−256854	−339285	−445211	Balance

70
Total imports and exports
Imports c.i.f. and exports f.o.b., value in million US dollars
Importations et exportations totales
Importations c.a.f. et exportations f.o.b., valeur en millions de dollars E.−U.

Country or area	Sys. [1]	1994	1995	1996	1997	1998	1999	2000	Pays ou zone
OECD+									OCDE+
Imports		3097193	3670594	3837705	3938940	4001517	4225007	4698274	Importations
Exports		3073879	3683095	3796661	3902307	3938980	4029521	4336264	Exportations
Balance		−23315	12501	−41044	−36633	−62537	−195486	−362010	Balance
OPEC+									OPEP+
Imports		129026	151333	151392	167557	151004	157706	174870	Importations
Exports		188993	210820	241798	251131	216092	242303	294081	Exportations
Balance		59967	59488	90406	83574	65089	84597	119211	Balance

Source:
United Nations Statistics Division, New York, trade
statistics database.

+ For member states of this grouping, see Annex I − Other groupings.
The totals have been re−calculated for all periods shown according
to the current composition.

† For information on recent changes in country or area
nomenclature pertaining to former Czechoslovakia, Germany,
Hong Kong Special Administrative Region (SAR) of China,
Macao Special Administrative Region (SAR) of China,
SFR of Yugoslavia and the former USSR, see Annex I − Country
or area nomenclature, regional and other groupings.

††For statistical purposes, the data for China do not
include those for the Hong Kong Special Administrative
Region (Hong Kong SAR), Macao Special Administrative
Region (Hong Kong SAR) and Taiwan province of China.

1 Systems of trade: Two systems of recording trade, the General trade
system (G) and the Special trade system (S), are in common use. They
differ mainly in the way warehoused and re−exported goods are recorded.
See the Technical notes for an explanation of the trade systems.

2 United States, Canada, Developed Economies of Europe, Israel, Japan,
Australia, New Zealand and South African Customs Union.

3 This classification is intended for statistical convenience and
does not necessarily express a judgement about the stage
reached by a particular country in the development process.

4 Beginning January 1992, includes Eastern Europe and the
European countries of the former USSR.

5 Imports are f.o.b. Beginning 1998, imports for Brazil, Peru and Canada
are f.o.b.

6 Including the trade of the U.S. Virgin Islands and Puerto Rico, but
excluding shipments of merchandise between the United States
and its other possessions (Guam, American Samoa, etc). Data
include imports and exports of non−monetary gold.

7 Latin American Integration Association. Formerly Latin American
Free Trade Associztion.

8 Trade data exclude goods from custom−bonded warehouses.
Total exports include revaluation and exports of silver.

9 Central American Common Market.
10 Beginning 1990, trade statistics exclude certain oil and chemical products.

Source:
Organisation des Nations Unies, Division de statistique, New York, la
base de données pour les statistiques de commerce extérieur.

+ Pour les Etats membres de ce groupements, voir annexe I − Autres
groupements. Les totaux ont été récalculés pour toutes les périodes
données suivant la composition présente.

† Pour les modifications récentes de nomenclature de pays ou de
zone concernant l'Allemagne, Hong Kong région administrative
spéciale (RAS) de Chine, Macao région administrative
spéciale (RAS) de Chine, l'ex−Tchécoslovaquie, l'ex−URSS
et l'ex− Rfs de Yougoslavie, voir annexe I − Nomenclature des
pays ou des zones, groupements régionaux et autres groupements.

††Les données statistiques relatives à la Chine ne comprennent
pas celles qui concernent la région administrative spéciale de
Hong Kong (la RAS de Hong Kong), la région administrative
spéciale de Macao (la RAS de Macao) et la province chinoise
de Taiwan.

1 Systèmes de commerce: Deux systèmes d'enregistrement du
commerce sont couramment utilisés, le Commerce général (G) et le
Commerce spécial (S). Ils ne diffèrent que par la façon dont sont
enregistrées les marchandises entreposées et les marchandises
réexportées. Voir les Notes techniques pour une explication des
Systèmes de commerce.

2 Etats−Unis, Canada, Pays aux économies développés d'Europe,
Israël, Japon, Australie, Nouvelle−Zélande et l'Union douanière
de l'Afrique australe.

3 Cette classification est utilisée pour plus de commodité dans la
présentation des statistiques et n'implique pas nécessairement un
jugement quant au stage de développement auquel est parvenu un
pays donné.

4 A partir de janvier 1992, y compris l'Europe de l'est et les pays
européennes de l'ancienne URSS.

5 Importations f.o.b. A partir 1998, importations pour Brésil, Pérou
et Canada sont f.o.b.

6 Y compris le commerce des isles Vierges américaines et de Porto
Rico mais non compris les échanges de merchandises entre les
Etats−Unis et leurs autres possessions (Guam, Samoa américaines,
etc). Les données comprennent les importations et exportations
d'or non monétaire.

7 Association latino−américaine d'intégration. Antérieurement
Association latino−américaine de libre−échange.

8 Les statistiques du commerce extérieur ne comprennent pas les
marchandises provenant des entrepôts en douane. Les exportations
comprennent le réévaluation et les données sur les exportations
d'argent.

9 Marché commun de l'Amérique central.
10 A partir de l'année 1990, les statistiques commerciales font
exclusion de certains produits pétroliers et chimiques.

70
Total imports and exports
Imports c.i.f. and exports f.o.b., value in million US dollars
Importations et exportations totales
Importations c.a.f. et exportations f.o.b., valeur en millions de dollars E.–U.

11Export and import values exclude trade in the processing zone.

12Beinning January 1997, imports are f.o.b.
13Beginning January 1996, trade data for France include the import and
   export values of French Guiana, Guadeloupe, Martinique and Réunion.

14European Union. Prior to January 1995, excludes Austria, Finland and
   Sweden. Total EU re–calculated for all periods shown in the table
   according to the current composition.
15Economic Union of Belgium and Luxembourg. Inter–trade between the
   two countries is excluded. Beginning January 1993, data refer only to
   Belgium.
16Data prior to January 1991 pertaining to the territorial boundaries of the
   Federal Republic of Germany prior to 3 October 1990.

17Europen Free Trade Association. Prior to January 1995, includes Austria,
   Finland and Sweden. Total EFTA re–calculated for all periods shown in
   the table according to the current composition.

18Beginning January 1992, data refer to Bosnia and Herzegovina, Croatia,
   Slovenia, TFYR Macedonia and the Federal Republic of Yugoslavia.

19Prior to January 1992, data refer to Socialist Federal Republic of
   Yugoslavia. Beginning 1992, data refer to the Federal Republic of
   Yugoslavia.
20Prior to 1992, import values are f.o.b.
21Data excludes re–exports.
22Includes trade with the Czech Republic.
23For 1991, data for the former USSR are converted to US dollars using
   commercial exchange rate of rouble and are not comparable to those
   shown for prior periods.
24Excluding inter–trade among countries of the region, except for Estonia,
   Latvia and Lithuania.
25Beginning 1994, data includes inter–trade among the Commonwealth of
   Independent States (CIS).
26Beginning January 1994, foreign trade statistics exclude re–exports.

27Prior to 1994, the source for trade values is the CIS Yearbook.

28Exports include gold exports.
29The South African Customs Union comprising Botswana, Lesotho,
   Namibia, South Africa and Swaziland. Trade between the component
   countries is excluded.
30Imports exclude petroleum imported without stated value. Exports cover
   domestic exports.
31Central African Customs and Economic Union. Inter–trade among the
   members of the Union is excluded.
32Economic Community of West African States.
33Beginning May 1997, Guinea–Bissau has adopted as the national
   currency the CFA franc following its membership in the West African
   Monetary Union and the Central Bank of West African States (BCEAO).

34Beginning February 1995, trade data for Nigeria are valued at an average
   (unitary) exchange rate of 70.36 naira to the U.S. dollar. This exchange
   rate is the weighted average of the official rate and the market rate.

35Beginning January 1996, imports are f.o.b.
36Beginning January 1992, includes Armenia, Azerbaijan, Georgia,
   Kazakhstan, Kyrgyzstan, Tajikistan, Turkmenistan and Uzbekistan. Total
   developing Asia re–calculated for all periods shown in the table
   according to the current composition.

11Les valeurs à l'exportation et à l'importation excluent le commerce
   de la zone de transformation.
12A partir de janvier 1997, les valuers des importations sont f.o.b.
13A partir de janvier 1996 les valeurs de commerce pour la France
   comprennent les valeurs des importations et des exportations de la
   Guyane française, la Guadeloupe, la Martinique, et la Réunion.
14L'Union européenne. Avant janvier 1995, non compris Autriche,
   Finlande, et Suède. Total UE avait été recalculé pour toutes les
   périodes données au tableau, suivant la composition présente.
15L'Union économique belgo–luxembourgeoise. Non compris le
   commerce entre ces pays. A partir de janvier 1993, les données se
   rapportent à Belgique seulement.
16Les données relatives à la période précedant janvier 1991
   correspondent aux liimutes territoriales de la République fédérales
   d'Allemagne autérieur au 3 octobre 1990.

17Association européenne de libre–échange. Avant janvier 1995, y
   compris Autriche, Finlande, et Suède. Total AELE avait été
   recalculé pour toutes les périodes données au tableau, suivant la
   composition présente.
18A partir de janvier 1992, les données se rapportent aux Bosnie–
   Herzégovine, Croatie, Slovénie, l'ex–R.y. Macédonie et la
   République fédéral de Yougoslavie.
19Avant 1992, les données se rapportent à la République fédérative
   socialiste de Yougoslavie. A partir de l'année 1992, les données se
   rapportent à la République fédérative de Yougoslavie.
20Avant 1992 les valeurs des importations sont f.o.b.
21Les données non compris les réexportations.
22Y compris le commerce avec la République tchèque.
23Les données de 1991 de l'ancienne URSS sont converties en dollars
   des E.U. en utilisant le taux de change commercial de rouble et ne
   sont pas comparables aux données des périodes antérieures.
24Non compris le commerce avec les autres pays de la région, excepte
   pour Estonie, Lettonie et Lituanie.
25A partir de janvier 1994, les données compris le commerce avec les
   pays du Communauté des Etats indépandants (CEI).
26A partir de janvier 1994, les statistiques du commerce extérieur non
   compris les réexportations.
27Avant 1994, la source des valeurs de commerce est l'Annuaire
   statistique du CEI.
28Y compris les exportations d'or.
29L'Union douanière d'Afrique australe comprend Botswana,
   Lesotho, Namibie, Afrique du Sud et Swaziland. Non compris le
   commerce entre ces pays.
30Non compris le pétrole brute dont la valeur des importations ne sont
   pas stipulée. Les exportations sont les exportations d'intérieur.
31L'Union douanière et économique de l'Afrique centrale. Non
   compris le commerce avec les autres pays membres de l'UDEAC.
32Communauté économique des Etats de l'Afrique de l'Ouest.
33A partir de mai 1997, la Guinée–Bissau a adopté le franc CFA
   comme monnaie nationale après être devenue membre de l'Union
   monétaire ouest–africaine et le Banque centrale des états de
   l'Afrique de l'ouest (BCEAO).
34A partir de févier 1995 les valeurs de commerce pour la Nigéria
   sont évaluées au taux de change (unitaire) moyen de 70.36 naira
   pour 1 dollar E.U. Il s'agit de la moyenne pondérée du taux officiel
   et du taux du marché.
35A partir de janvier 1996, les valeurs des importations sont f.o.b.
36A partir de janvier 1992, données compris Arménie, Azerbaidjan,
   Géorgie, Kazakhstan, Kirghizistan, Tadjikistan, Turkménistan et
   Ouzbékistan. Total Asie en voie de développement avait été
   recalculé pour toutes les périodes données au tableau, suivant la

70
Total imports and exports
Imports c.i.f. and exports f.o.b., value in million US dollars
Importations et exportations totales
Importations c.a.f. et exportations f.o.b., valeur en millions de dollars E.–U.

37 Imports exclude military goods.

38 Data include oil and gas. Beginning October 1980, data on the value and volume of oil exports and on the value of total exports are rough estimates based on information published in various petroleum industry journals.

39 Comprises trade of the former Democratic Yemen and former Yemen Arab Republic including any inter–trade between them.

40 Data refer to total exports less petroleum exports of Asia Middle East countries where petroleum, in this case, is the sum of SITC groups 333, 334 and 335.

41 Association of Southeast Asian Nations.

composition présente.

37 Non compris les importations des economats militaires.

38 Les données comprennent le pétrole et le gaz. A partir d'octobre 1980 les données relatives à la valeur et au volume des exportations de pétrole et à la valeur des exportations totales sont des estimations approximatives établies sur la base des données de diverses publications consacrées à l'industrie pétrolière.

39 Y compris le commerce de l'ancienne République populaire démocratique de Yémen, le commerce de l'ancienne République arabe de Yémen et le commerce entre eux.

40 Les données se rapportent aux exportations totales moins les exportations pétroliers de moyen–orient d'Asie. Dans ce cas, le pétrole est la somme des groupes CTCI 333, 334 et 335.

41 Association des nations de l'Asie du Sud–Est.

71
Total imports and exports : index numbers
Importations et exportations : indices

1990 = 100

Country or area	1992	1993	1994	1995	1996	1997	1998	1999	2000	Pays ou zone
Argentina										**Argentine**
Imports: Quantum	387	448	569	503	603	782	857	733	794	Imp.: quantum
Imports: Unit value	94	92	93	98	104	95	90	98	107	Imp.: valeur unitaire
Exports: Quantum	97	104	122	152	162	181	202	202	221	Exp.: quantum
Exports: Unit value	102	102	105	111	129	114	104	106	122	Exp.: valeur unitaire
Terms of trade	109	111	113	113	124	120	116	108	114	Termes de l'échange
Purchasing power	105	115	138	172	201	217	233	218	252	Pouvoir d'achat
Australia										**Australie**
Imports: Quantum	107	114	133	148	161	180	201	223	...	Imp.: quantum
Imports: Unit value [1]	106	114	111	115	109	109	118	116	127	Imp.: valeur unitaire [1]
Exports: Quantum	121	128	139	141	157	179	189	196	...	Exp.: quantum
Exports: Unit value [1]	93	94	92	99	94	96	101	94	108	Exp.: valeur unitaire [1]
Terms of trade	88	82	83	86	86	88	86	81	85	Termes de l'échange
Purchasing power	106	106	115	121	135	158	162	159	...	Pouvoir d'achat
Austria										**Autriche**
Imports: Quantum	107	106	119	125	129	142	151	...	157	Imp.: quantum
Imports: Unit value	99	95	94	96	91	86	81	...	82	Imp.: valeur unitaire
Exports: Quantum	111	108	119	140	147	172	182	...	190	Exp.: quantum
Exports: Unit value	95	91	85	86	83	78	73	...	72	Exp.: valeur unitaire
Terms of trade	96	96	90	90	91	91	90	...	88	Termes de l'échange
Purchasing power	107	103	108	125	134	156	164	...	167	Pouvoir d'achat
Belgium										**Belgique**
Imports: Quantum	105	106	115	121	126	132	141	141	155	Imp.: quantum
Imports: Unit value	95	91	91	94	97	103	101	102	115	Imp.: valeur unitaire
Exports: Quantum	104	111	123	131	134	144	151	156	171	Exp.: quantum
Exports: Unit value	97	95	94	97	100	105	105	104	115	Exp.: valeur unitaire
Terms of trade	102	104	103	103	103	102	104	102	100	Termes de l'échange
Purchasing power	106	116	127	135	138	147	157	159	171	Pouvoir d'achat
Bolivia										**Bolivie**
Exports: Quantum	99	93	95	91	93	98	93	85	97	Exp.: quantum
Exports: Unit value [2]	76	64	66	73	72	55	49	48	61	Exp.: valeur unitaire [2]
Brazil										**Brésil**
Imports: Quantum	119	136	142	176	190	161	162	150	163	Imp.: quantum
Imports: Unit value [2]	86	91	112	136	133	180	167	153	160	Imp.: valeur unitaire [2]
Exports: Quantum	100	109	116	120	119	125	138	137	146	Exp.: quantum
Exports: Unit value [2]	114	113	119	124	128	136	119	112	120	Exp.: valeur unitaire [2]
Terms of trade	133	124	106	91	96	76	71	73	75	Termes de l'échange
Purchasing power	133	135	123	109	115	94	98	100	110	Pouvoir d'achat
Bulgaria										**Bulgarie**
Imports: Quantum	91	108	106	108	...	...	...	...	...	Imp.: quantum
Exports: Quantum	75	68	75	76	...	...	...	...	...	Exp.: quantum
Canada										**Canada**
Imports: Quantum	110	120	133	143	151	179	190	207	226	Imp.: quantum
Imports: Unit value	103	108	115	120	119	120	124	124	127	Imp.: valeur unitaire
Exports: Quantum	110	123	138	152	161	175	189	210	229	Exp.: quantum
Exports: Unit value	99	103	110	119	120	120	119	120	130	Exp.: valeur unitaire
Terms of trade	96	95	96	99	101	100	96	97	102	Termes de l'échange
Purchasing power	106	117	132	151	162	175	181	203	234	Pouvoir d'achat
China, Hong Kong SAR †										**Chine, Hong Kong RAS †**
Imports: Quantum	145	164	187	213	222	238	221	222	262	Imp.: quantum
Imports: Unit value	102	102	104	109	108	106	100	98	99	Imp.: valeur unitaire
Exports: Quantum	140	160	176	197	207	220	210	218	255	Exp.: quantum
Exports: Unit value	104	103	105	108	108	106	102	99	99	Exp.: valeur unitaire
Terms of trade	102	101	101	99	100	100	102	101	100	Termes de l'échange
Purchasing power	143	162	178	195	207	220	214	220	255	Pouvoir d'achat
Colombia										**Colombie**
Imports: Unit value	130	145	158	182	209	224	259	296	343	Imp.: valeur unitaire
Exports: Unit value	118	134	174	204	217	263	293	336	419	Exp.: valeur unitaire
Terms of trade	91	92	110	112	104	117	113	114	122	Termes de l'échange

71
Total imports and exports : index numbers
Importations et exportations : indices

1990 = 100

Country or area	1992	1993	1994	1995	1996	1997	1998	1999	2000	Pays ou zone
Denmark										**Danemark**
Imports: Quantum	113	114	118	126	128	139	145	148	156	Imp.: quantum
Imports: Unit value	96	93	95	97	98	101	100	100	108	Imp.: valeur unitaire
Exports: Quantum	116	113	122	116	119	127	128	135	144	Exp.: quantum
Exports: Unit value	98	96	97	97	99	100	100	100	110	Exp.: valeur unitaire
Terms of trade	102	103	102	100	101	99	100	100	102	Termes de l'échange
Purchasing power	118	117	125	116	120	126	128	135	147	Pouvoir d'achat
Dominica										**Dominique**
Exports: Quantum	97	94	107	68	...	...	...	...	...	Exp.: quantum
Exports: Unit value	100	89	97	100	...	...	...	...	...	Exp.: valeur unitaire
Dominican Republic										**Rép. dominicaine**
Exports: Quantum	91	95	92	96	101	104	99	...	...	Exp.: quantum
Exports: Unit value	...	...	...	101	102	106	83	...	...	Exp.: valeur unitaire
Ecuador										**Equateur**
Imports: Quantum	0	0	0	138	182	255	314	...	...	Imp.: quantum
Exports: Quantum	116	124	137	154	158	157	149	143	154	Exp.: quantum
Exports: Unit value [2]	89	74	83	84	96	94	70	85	111	Exp.: valeur unitaire [2]
Ethiopia										**Ethiopie**
Exports: Quantum	50	125	...	...	...	...	...	...	...	Exp.: quantum
Exports: Unit value	104	157	...	...	...	...	...	...	...	Exp.: valeur unitaire
Finland										**Finlande**
Imports: Quantum	81	79	95	102	110	119	128	...	...	Imp.: quantum
Imports: Unit value	113	127	123	123	125	129	129	...	...	Imp.: valeur unitaire
Exports: Quantum	99	117	133	143	151	169	178	...	...	Exp.: quantum
Exports: Unit value	106	113	113	121	121	123	125	...	...	Exp.: valeur unitaire
Terms of trade	94	89	92	98	97	95	97	...	...	Termes de l'échange
Purchasing power	93	104	122	141	146	161	172	...	...	Pouvoir d'achat
France										**France**
Imports: Quantum	104	107	117	123	126	135	146	152	168	Imp.: quantum
Imports: Unit value	95	90	94	96	96	98	98	...	...	Imp.: valeur unitaire
Exports: Quantum	108	110	120	129	134	147	157	166	185	Exp.: quantum
Exports: Unit value	97	94	100	102	102	103	104	...	...	Exp.: valeur unitaire
Terms of trade	102	104	106	106	106	105	106	...	...	Termes de l'échange
Purchasing power	110	115	128	137	142	155	167	...	...	Pouvoir d'achat
Germany										**Allemagne**
Imports: Quantum	115	104	113	115	122	133	146	153	...	Imp.: quantum
Imports: Unit value	99	93	95	98	96	98	96	94	105	Imp.: valeur unitaire
Exports: Quantum	102	98	112	116	125	140	152	159	...	Exp.: quantum
Exports: Unit value	99	94	93	95	93	94	93	92	95	Exp.: valeur unitaire
Terms of trade	100	101	98	97	97	96	97	98	90	Termes de l'échange
Purchasing power	102	99	110	112	121	134	147	156	...	Pouvoir d'achat
Greece										**Grèce**
Imports: Quantum	130	143	150	163	178	180	219	...	...	Imp.: quantum
Imports: Unit value	110	111	110	112	105	112	123	...	...	Imp.: valeur unitaire
Exports: Quantum	147	143	149	164	175	194	221	...	...	Exp.: quantum
Exports: Unit value	106	109	121	122	105	101	114	...	...	Exp.: valeur unitaire
Terms of trade	96	98	110	109	100	90	93	...	...	Termes de l'échange
Purchasing power	142	140	164	179	175	175	205	...	...	Pouvoir d'achat
Guatemala										**Guatemala**
Imports: Quantum	125	133	148	...	...	...	...	...	...	Imp.: quantum
Imports: Unit value	123	119	109	...	...	...	...	...	...	Imp.: valeur unitaire
Exports: Quantum	145	136	147	...	...	...	...	...	...	Exp.: quantum
Exports: Unit value	77	85	88	98	89	...	...	...	...	Exp.: valeur unitaire
Terms of trade	63	71	81	...	...	...	...	...	...	Termes de l'échange
Purchasing power	91	97	119	...	...	...	...	...	...	Pouvoir d'achat
Honduras										**Honduras**
Exports: Quantum	102	90	79	83	99	86	86	...	...	Exp.: quantum
Exports: Unit value [2]	77	78	89	123	115	119	116	...	...	Exp.: valeur unitaire [2]
Hungary										**Hongrie**
Imports: Quantum	98	119	136	131	138	175	218	...	...	Imp.: quantum
Imports: Unit value	161	176	203	269	324	367	409	...	...	Imp.: valeur unitaire
Exports: Quantum	96	84	97	106	110	143	175	...	...	Exp.: quantum
Exports: Unit value	143	160	189	254	299	343	388	...	...	Exp.: valeur unitaire
Terms of trade	89	91	93	94	92	93	95	...	...	Termes de l'échange
Purchasing power	85	76	90	100	102	134	166	...	...	Pouvoir d'achat

71
Total imports and exports : index numbers
Importations et exportations : indices

1990 = 100

Country or area	1992	1993	1994	1995	1996	1997	1998	1999	2000	Pays ou zone
Iceland										**Islande**
Imports: Quantum	97	84	90	96	111	118	...	...	...	Imp.: quantum
Imports: Unit value	104	113	118	123	128	127	...	...	...	Imp.: valeur unitaire
Exports: Quantum	91	96	108	105	115	117	...	...	...	Exp.: quantum
Exports: Unit value	104	107	113	120	119	122	...	...	...	Exp.: valeur unitaire
Terms of trade	100	95	96	98	93	96	...	...	...	Termes de l'échange
Purchasing power	91	91	103	102	107	112	...	...	...	Pouvoir d'achat
India										**Inde**
Imports: Quantum	120	138	168	261	186	198	...	...	...	Imp.: quantum
Imports: Unit value	125	117	122	110	168	212	...	...	...	Imp.: valeur unitaire
Exports: Quantum	116	140	154	189	236	205	...	...	...	Exp.: quantum
Exports: Unit value	142	155	168	167	157	...	...	...	...	Exp.: valeur unitaire
Terms of trade	114	132	138	152	93	...	...	...	...	Termes de l'échange
Purchasing power	132	185	212	287	221	...	...	...	...	Pouvoir d'achat
Indonesia										**Indonésie**
Exports: Quantum	141	148	163	170	179	230	214	...	...	Exp.: quantum
Exports: Unit value [2]	84	77	97	111	117	111	87	...	...	Exp.: valeur unitaire [2]
Ireland										**Irlande**
Imports: Quantum	106	113	128	146	161	185	218	236	268	Imp.: quantum
Imports: Unit value	100	105	108	113	111	112	115	118	130	Imp.: valeur unitaire
Exports: Quantum	121	133	153	184	202	232	289	336	406	Exp.: quantum
Exports: Unit value	97	104	104	106	105	106	109	109	113	Exp.: valeur unitaire
Terms of trade	97	99	96	94	95	95	95	92	87	Termes de l'échange
Purchasing power	117	132	147	173	191	220	274	310	353	Pouvoir d'achat
Israel										**Israël**
Imports: Quantum	130	146	166	182	194	197	197	226	257	Imp.: quantum
Imports: Unit value [2]	95	92	94	102	101	96	91	88	91	Imp.: valeur unitaire [2]
Exports: Quantum	107	121	140	150	161	177	188	204	256	Exp.: quantum
Exports: Unit value [2]	101	102	100	105	105	104	101	102	102	Exp.: valeur unitaire [2]
Terms of trade	106	111	106	103	104	108	111	116	112	Termes de l'échange
Purchasing power	114	134	149	154	167	192	209	236	287	Pouvoir d'achat
Italy										**Italie**
Imports: Quantum	107	114	108	119	113	124	135	145	157	Imp.: quantum
Imports: Unit value	99	110	115	100	100	101	99	98	112	Imp.: valeur unitaire
Exports: Quantum	102	112	125	141	138	145	149	149	165	Exp.: quantum
Exports: Unit value	136	151	156	131	136	137	138	138	146	Exp.: valeur unitaire
Terms of trade	137	137	136	131	136	136	139	141	130	Termes de l'échange
Purchasing power	140	154	170	185	188	197	208	210	215	Pouvoir d'achat
Japan										**Japon**
Imports: Quantum	104	107	121	136	141	145	137	150	166	Imp.: quantum
Imports: Unit value	84	74	69	68	80	84	79	69	73	Imp.: valeur unitaire
Exports: Quantum	104	101	103	107	107	117	116	118	129	Exp.: quantum
Exports: Unit value	100	96	95	94	101	105	105	97	96	Exp.: valeur unitaire
Terms of trade	119	130	138	138	126	125	133	141	132	Termes de l'échange
Purchasing power	124	131	142	148	135	146	154	166	170	Pouvoir d'achat
Jordan										**Jordanie**
Imports: Quantum	136	224	219	152	164	160	151	149	178	Imp.: quantum
Imports: Unit value	95	90	88	99	108	106	105	103	105	Imp.: valeur unitaire
Exports: Quantum	96	143	153	137	134	143	147	151	163	Exp.: quantum
Exports: Unit value	107	96	101	117	125	121	114	111	107	Exp.: valeur unitaire
Terms of trade	113	107	115	118	116	114	109	108	102	Termes de l'échange
Purchasing power	108	153	176	162	155	163	160	163	166	Pouvoir d'achat
Kenya										**Kenya**
Imports: Quantum	90	97	121	141	140	149	150	...	...	Imp.: quantum
Imports: Unit value	129	208	187	216	236	252	259	...	...	Imp.: valeur unitaire
Exports: Quantum	121	133	153	183	...	...	...	...	...	Exp.: quantum
Exports: Unit value	144	259	266	289	307	359	363	...	...	Exp.: valeur unitaire
Terms of trade	112	125	142	134	130	142	140	...	...	Termes de l'échange
Purchasing power	135	166	218	245	...	...	...	...	...	Pouvoir d'achat
Korea, Republic of										**Corée, République de**
Imports: Quantum	222	236	287	187	210	213	168	213	253	Imp.: quantum
Imports: Unit value	108	107	108	113	116	130	154	130	142	Imp.: valeur unitaire
Exports: Quantum	216	230	264	181	217	271	317	325	395	Exp.: quantum
Exports: Unit value	126	129	132	116	104	104	132	110	105	Exp.: valeur unitaire
Terms of trade	117	121	122	103	90	80	86	85	74	Termes de l'échange
Purchasing power	252	277	323	186	195	217	272	275	292	Pouvoir d'achat

71
Total imports and exports : index numbers
Importations et exportations : indices

1990 = 100

Country or area	1992	1993	1994	1995	1996	1997	1998	1999	2000	Pays ou zone
Malaysia										**Malaisie**
Exports: Quantum	96	86	84	84	...	...	...	...	...	Exp.: quantum
Mauritius										**Maurice**
Imports: Unit value	107	119	127	135	144	147	148	...	...	Imp.: valeur unitaire
Exports: Unit value	114	124	130	138	153	158	179	...	...	Exp.: valeur unitaire
Terms of trade	107	104	102	102	106	107	121	...	...	Termes de l'échange
Mexico										**Mexique**
Imports: Unit value [2]	101	102	...	...	...	...	...	...	...	Imp.: valeur unitaire [2]
Exports: Unit value [2]	92	89	...	...	...	...	...	...	...	Exp.: valeur unitaire [2]
Terms of trade	91	87	...	...	...	...	...	...	...	Termes de l'échange
Morocco										**Maroc**
Imports: Quantum	128	120	96	...	...	...	...	...	...	Imp.: quantum
Imports: Unit value	92	101	114	...	...	...	...	...	...	Imp.: valeur unitaire
Exports: Quantum	101	105	115	...	...	...	...	...	...	Exp.: quantum
Exports: Unit value	95	95	94	128	...	...	...	...	...	Exp.: valeur unitaire
Terms of trade	103	94	82	...	...	...	...	...	...	Termes de l'échange
Purchasing power	104	99	95	...	...	...	...	...	...	Pouvoir d'achat
Myanmar										**Myanmar**
Exports: Quantum	108	149	145	150	104	110	...	...	...	Exp.: quantum
Exports: Unit value	88	81	87	136	130	132	...	...	...	Exp.: valeur unitaire
Netherlands										**Pays−Bas**
Imports: Quantum	106	110	121	136	143	152	166	176	189	Imp.: quantum
Imports: Unit value	97	92	92	92	93	98	96	95	105	Imp.: valeur unitaire
Exports: Quantum	108	116	129	140	146	159	171	190	192	Exp.: quantum
Exports: Unit value	95	92	92	94	94	100	97	94	106	Exp.: valeur unitaire
Terms of trade	98	100	100	102	101	102	101	99	101	Termes de l'échange
Purchasing power	106	116	129	143	148	162	173	188	194	Pouvoir d'achat
New Zealand										**Nouvelle−Zélande**
Imports: Quantum	100	104	121	129	134	139	142	161	157	Imp.: quantum
Imports: Unit value	108	107	104	103	100	99	103	105	123	Imp.: valeur unitaire
Exports: Quantum	113	118	130	134	140	147	146	149	157	Exp.: quantum
Exports: Unit value	104	106	102	100	97	94	98	100	117	Exp.: valeur unitaire
Terms of trade	96	99	98	97	97	95	95	95	95	Termes de l'échange
Purchasing power	109	117	128	130	136	140	139	142	149	Pouvoir d'achat
Norway										**Norvège**
Imports: Quantum [3]	106	107	122	134	147	159	176	172	...	Imp.: quantum [3]
Imports: Unit value [3]	96	97	97	98	98	97	98	96	...	Imp.: valeur unitaire [3]
Exports: Quantum [3]	115	121	136	144	163	170	172	179	...	Exp.: quantum [3]
Exports: Unit value [3]	88	88	85	88	95	97	85	95	...	Exp.: valeur unitaire [3]
Terms of trade	92	91	88	90	97	100	87	99	...	Termes de l'échange
Purchasing power	105	110	119	129	158	170	149	177	...	Pouvoir d'achat
Pakistan										**Pakistan**
Imports: Quantum	122	124	119	129	127	130	130	140	138	Imp.: quantum
Imports: Unit value	110	118	138	156	172	89	86	102	119	Imp.: valeur unitaire
Exports: Quantum	124	112	139	110	130	123	119	134	150	Exp.: quantum
Exports: Unit value	106	116	136	171	189	217	243	249	247	Exp.: valeur unitaire
Terms of trade	96	98	99	110	110	244	283	244	208	Termes de l'échange
Purchasing power	119	110	137	121	143	300	336	327	311	Pouvoir d'achat
Papua New Guinea										**Papouasie−Nvl−Guinée**
Exports: Unit value	101	113	132	185	182	202	231	259	...	Exp.: valeur unitaire
Peru										**Pérou**
Exports: Quantum	111	120	132	133	141	153	132	148	168	Exp.: quantum
Exports: Unit value [2]	94	74	86	106	112	109	84	90	120	Exp.: valeur unitaire [2]
Poland										**Pologne**
Imports: Quantum	...	186	211	254	325	397	473	492	526	Imp.: quantum
Imports: Unit value [1]	152	177	225	254	298	338	356	379	391	Imp.: valeur unitaire [1]
Exports: Quantum	...	94	111	130	142	162	173	183	226	Exp.: quantum
Exports: Unit value [1]	...	190	245	297	321	362	390	417	424	Exp.: valeur unitaire [1]
Terms of trade	...	107	109	117	108	107	110	110	108	Termes de l'échange
Purchasing power	...	101	121	152	153	174	190	201	245	Pouvoir d'achat
Portugal										**Portugal**
Imports: Quantum	119	...	...	...	...	...	...	...	...	Imp.: quantum
Imports: Unit value	95	...	...	...	...	...	...	...	...	Imp.: valeur unitaire
Exports: Quantum	107	...	...	...	...	...	...	...	...	Exp.: quantum
Exports: Unit value	98	...	...	...	...	...	...	...	...	Exp.: valeur unitaire
Terms of trade	103	...	...	...	...	...	...	...	...	Termes de l'échange
Purchasing power	110	...	...	...	...	...	...	...	...	Pouvoir d'achat

71
Total imports and exports : index numbers
Importations et exportations : indices

1990 = 100

Country or area	1992	1993	1994	1995	1996	1997	1998	1999	2000	Pays ou zone
Rwanda										**Rwanda**
Exports: Quantum	83	73	30	51	49	121	129	...	...	Exp.: quantum
Exports: Unit value	105	127	124	429	400	602	400	...	...	Exp.: valeur unitaire
Seychelles										**Seychelles**
Imports: Quantum	107	147	124	135	227	200	...	...	...	Imp.: quantum
Imports: Unit value	92	85	85	83	84	86	...	...	...	Imp.: valeur unitaire
Exports: Quantum	126	106	172	139	256	421	...	...	...	Exp.: quantum
Exports: Unit value	101	102	91	112	110	111	...	...	...	Exp.: valeur unitaire
Terms of trade	110	120	107	135	131	129	...	...	...	Termes de l'échange
Purchasing power	138	127	184	188	335	543	...	...	...	Pouvoir d'achat
Singapore										**Singapour**
Imports: Quantum	114	137	157	177	188	203	184	194	220	Imp.: quantum
Imports: Unit value [1]	93	92	91	91	90	88	87	88	96	Imp.: valeur unitaire [1]
Exports: Quantum	123	145	187	216	229	245	248	261	302	Exp.: quantum
Exports: Unit value [1]	88	86	83	82	81	79	78	78	83	Exp.: valeur unitaire [1]
Terms of trade	95	93	91	90	90	90	90	89	86	Termes de l'échange
Purchasing power	116	136	171	195	206	220	222	231	261	Pouvoir d'achat
Solomon Islands										**Iles Salomon**
Exports: Quantum	136	...	...	...	...	...	...	...	...	Exp.: quantum
Exports: Unit value	103	...	...	...	...	...	...	...	...	Exp.: valeur unitaire
South Africa										**Afrique du Sud**
Imports: Quantum	103	108	125	136	155	...	...	...	...	Imp.: quantum
Imports: Unit value	117	125	138	157	166	...	...	...	...	Imp.: valeur unitaire
Exports: Quantum	88	109	115	119	169	...	...	...	...	Exp.: quantum
Exports: Unit value	112	122	137	161	177	...	...	...	...	Exp.: valeur unitaire
Terms of trade	96	98	99	103	107	...	...	...	...	Termes de l'échange
Purchasing power	84	106	114	122	180	...	...	...	...	Pouvoir d'achat
Spain										**Espagne**
Imports: Unit value [1]	96	101	107	112	112	116	114	113	128	Imp.: valeur unitaire [1]
Exports: Unit value [1]	100	105	110	117	118	122	122	121	128	Exp.: valeur unitaire [1]
Terms of trade	104	104	103	104	105	105	107	107	100	Termes de l'échange
Sri Lanka										**Sri Lanka**
Imports: Quantum	132	136	153	178	179	201	218	218	247	Imp.: quantum
Imports: Unit value	109	114	121	140	155	161	...	...	...	Imp.: valeur unitaire
Exports: Quantum	108	108	118	145	151	167	165	173	205	Exp.: quantum
Exports: Unit value	128	115	121	169	189	206	237	236	258	Exp.: valeur unitaire
Terms of trade	117	101	100	121	122	128	...	...	...	Termes de l'échange
Purchasing power	127	109	118	175	184	214	...	...	...	Pouvoir d'achat
Sweden										**Suède**
Imports: Quantum	95	97	108	109	102	110	110	103	112	Imp.: quantum
Imports: Unit value [1]	99	112	117	124	119	122	121	...	...	Imp.: valeur unitaire [1]
Exports: Quantum	99	107	114	112	106	111	100	106	110	Exp.: quantum
Exports: Unit value [1]	98	108	110	117	111	112	111	110	...	Exp.: valeur unitaire [1]
Terms of trade	99	96	94	94	93	92	92	...	...	Termes de l'échange
Purchasing power	98	103	107	106	99	102	92	...	...	Pouvoir d'achat
Switzerland										**Suisse**
Imports: Quantum	94	93	102	108	...	117	126	137	146	Imp.: quantum
Imports: Unit value	102	100	95	93	94	98	95	92	98	Imp.: valeur unitaire
Exports: Quantum	103	104	109	114	...	123	129	134	144	Exp.: quantum
Exports: Unit value	103	103	102	100	101	105	105	105	109	Exp.: valeur unitaire
Terms of trade	101	103	107	108	107	107	111	114	111	Termes de l'échange
Purchasing power	104	107	117	123	...	132	143	153	160	Pouvoir d'achat
Syrian Arab Republic										**Rép. arabe syrienne**
Imports: Quantum	143	225	276	248	250	218	...	...	...	Imp.: quantum
Imports: Unit value	98	93	105	118	125	107	...	...	...	Imp.: valeur unitaire
Exports: Quantum	105	158	171	167	164	183	...	...	...	Exp.: quantum
Exports: Unit value	68	67	72	90	95	75	...	...	...	Exp.: valeur unitaire
Terms of trade	69	72	69	76	76	70	...	...	...	Termes de l'échange
Purchasing power	73	114	117	127	125	128	...	...	...	Pouvoir d'achat
Thailand										**Thaïlande**
Imports: Quantum	117	130	151	170	154	137	100	124	150	Imp.: quantum
Imports: Unit value	105	106	109	122	138	163	198	176	197	Imp.: valeur unitaire
Exports: Quantum	134	149	177	243	219	235	254	284	346	Exp.: quantum
Exports: Unit value	104	106	109	118	130	156	178	157	163	Exp.: valeur unitaire
Terms of trade	99	100	100	97	94	96	90	89	83	Termes de l'échange
Purchasing power	133	149	177	235	206	225	228	253	286	Pouvoir d'achat

71
Total imports and exports : index numbers
Importations et exportations : indices

1990 = 100

Country or area	1992	1993	1994	1995	1996	1997	1998	1999	2000	Pays ou zone
Tunisia										**Tunisie**
Imports: Quantum	104	115	120	...	...	...	...	...	...	Imp.: quantum
Imports: Unit value	94	94	...	...	...	...	...	...	...	Imp.: valeur unitaire
Exports: Quantum	111	121	137	...	...	...	...	...	...	Exp.: quantum
Exports: Unit value	95	96	101	...	...	...	...	...	...	Exp.: valeur unitaire
Terms of trade	101	102	...	...	...	...	...	...	...	Termes de l'échange
Purchasing power	112	124	...	...	...	...	...	...	...	Pouvoir d'achat
Turkey										**Turquie**
Imports: Quantum	98	134	99	128	166	205	195	198	...	Imp.: quantum
Imports: Unit value	95	89	95	111	105	96	92	87	...	Imp.: valeur unitaire
Exports: Quantum	110	117	134	143	157	178	189	201	...	Exp.: quantum
Exports: Unit value	100	98	95	107	102	97	93	87	...	Exp.: valeur unitaire
Terms of trade	105	110	100	96	97	101	101	100	...	Termes de l'échange
Purchasing power	116	129	134	138	153	180	191	201	...	Pouvoir d'achat
United Kingdom										**Royaume−Uni**
Imports: Quantum	101	101	107	112	123	135	148	159	177	Imp.: quantum
Imports: Unit value [1]	102	112	115	127	127	119	114	114	118	Imp.: valeur unitaire [1]
Exports: Quantum	103	103	116	125	136	146	148	155	172	Exp.: quantum
Exports: Unit value [1]	103	116	118	126	127	120	110	109	113	Exp.: valeur unitaire [1]
Terms of trade	101	104	103	99	100	101	96	96	96	Termes de l'échange
Purchasing power	104	107	119	124	136	147	143	148	165	Pouvoir d'achat
United States										**Etats−Unis**
Imports: Quantum	106	117	131	140	148	166	185	206	230	Imp.: quantum
Imports: Unit value [1]	101	100	102	106	107	105	99	101	102	Imp.: valeur unitaire [1]
Exports: Quantum [4]	113	116	126	136	145	162	166	173	190	Exp.: quantum [4]
Exports: Unit value [1 4]	101	101	104	109	109	108	104	102	108	Exp.: valeur unitaire [1 4]
Terms of trade	100	101	102	103	102	103	105	101	106	Termes de l'échange
Purchasing power	113	117	128	140	148	167	174	175	201	Pouvoir d'achat
Uruguay										**Uruguay**
Exports: Unit value	99	93	95	105	102	...	...	...	...	Exp.: valeur unitaire
Venezuela										**Venezuela**
Imports: Unit value	140	189	341	514	1 098	1 338	1 547	1 724	1 894	Imp.: valeur unitaire
Exports: Unit value	108	127	...	...	...	...	...	...	...	Exp.: valeur unitaire
Terms of trade	77	67	...	...	...	...	...	...	...	Termes de l'échange

Source:
United Nations Statistics Division, New York, trade statistics
database.

Source:
Organisation des Nations Unies, Division de statistique, New York, la base de
données pour les statistiques du commerce extérieur.

† For information on recent changes in country or
area nomenclature pertaining to former Czechoslovakia,
Germany, Hong Kong Special Administrative Region (SAR) of
China, Macao Special Administrative Region (SAR) of China,
SFR of Yugoslavia and the former USSR, see Annex I − Country
or area nomenclature, regional and other groupings.

† Pour les modifications récentes de nomenclature de pays ou de zone
concernant l'Allemagne, Hong Kong, région administrative spéciale (RAS)
de Chine, Macao, région administrative spéciale (RAS) de Chine,
l'ex−Tchécoslovaquie, l'ex−URSS et l'ex−Rfs de Yougoslavie,
voir annexe I − Nomenclature des pays ou des zones,
groupements régionaux et autres groupements.

1 Price index numbers. For Australia beginning 1981, for the
United States beginning 1989, for the United Kingdom
starting 1999.
2 Calculated in terms of US dollars.
3 Excluding ships.
4 Excludes military exports.

1 Indices des prix. Pour l'Australie, à partir de 1981; pour les Etats−Unis
à partir de 1989; pour le Royaume−Uni, à partir de 1999.
2 Calculés en dollars des Etats−Unis.
3 Non compris les navires.
4 Non compris les exportations militaires.

72
Manufactured goods exports
Exportations des produits manufacturés

1990 = 100

Region, country or area Region, pays ou zone	1991	1992	1993	1994	1995	1996	1997	1998	1999	2000
Unit value indices in US dollars · Indices de valeur unitaire en dollars des E.-U.										
Total[1]	100	103	98	100	110	106	99	97	93	...
Developed economies Econ. développées	99	103	97	99	110	106	99	97	94	91
Northern America Amérique septentrionale	102	100	99	99	102	102	103	102	101	102
Canada Canada	99	91	88	84	87	88	89	85	83	84
United States[2] Etats-Unis[2]	102	103	103	104	107	106	108	108	108	109
Europe Europe	98	102	91	93	107	103	93	92	88	82
EU+ UE+	97	102	91	93	106	103	92	92	87	81
Austria Autriche	96	99	91	90	104	94	77	68	...	...
Belgium-Luxembourg Belgique-Luxembourg	97	99	87	91	105	103	94	93	88	83
Denmark Danemark	96	102	92	97	112	108	98	97	94	...
Finland Finlande	95	90	74	83	105	99	89	88	85	82
France France	96	100	94	98	111	107	96	96	90	80
Germany † Allemagne †	98	103	93	94	108	101	87	89	80	72
Greece Grèce	95	94	77	82	88	84	71	66	...	...
Ireland[3] Irlande[3]	95	97	96	89	98	97	81	75	...	...
Italy[3] Italie[3]	99	105	89	86	96	98	90	91	...	...
Netherlands[4] Pays-Bas[4]	96	102	92	92	109	102	91	89	85	77
Portugal[3] Portugal[3]	101	106	98	94	111	105	96	96	...	...
Spain[3] Espagne[3]	95	109	85	86	99	99	88	86	...	...
Sweden Suède	100	102	82	85	105	106	94	90	85	80
United Kingdom Royaume-Uni	100	102	98	103	114	113	113	112	106	...
EFTA+ AELE+	97	101	87	96	116	114	101	99	97	95
Iceland[3] Islande[3]	88	86	76	80	114	106	101	89	...	...
Norway Norvège	94	92	80	82	102	96	88	85	80	75

72
Manufactured goods exports
1990 = 100 [cont.]
   Exportations des produits manufacturés
   1990 = 100 [suite]

Region, country or area Region, pays ou zone	1991	1992	1993	1994	1995	1996	1997	1998	1999	2000
Switzerland[3] Suisse[3]	98	103	88	99	120	118	105	104	101	...
Other developed economies Autres écon. développées	105	113	120	129	138	128	121	115	113	118
Australia Australie	58	86	81	88	96	94	89	78	78	80
Israel Israël	101	101	102	101	105	105	102	105	114	137
Japan Japon	108	115	124	134	144	133	126	121	119	...
New Zealand Nouvelle-Zélande	94	89	89	98	112	109	102	84	80	83
South Africa Afrique du Sud	96	101	100	101	123	107	...	...	...	...
Developing economies Econ. en dévelop.	101	101	102	104	111	105	99	96	89	...
China, Hong Kong SAR† Chine, Hong Kong RAS†	102	104	104	105	108	108	104	101	99	...
India Inde	80	92	89	88	86	69	84	79	...	...
Korea, Republic of[4] Corée, République de[4]	100	97	96	98	102	86	85	76	76	77
Pakistan Pakistan	98	101	98	107	125	123	130	127	118	110
Singapore Singapour	101	103	99	108	112	109	102	92	90	...
Turkey[5] Turquie[5]	99	100	95	90	106	97	89	84	80	85

Unit value indices in 'SDR' • Indices de valeur unitaire en 'DTS'

	1991	1992	1993	1994	1995	1996	1997	1998	1999	2000
Total	99	99	96	95	99	99	97	97	92	...
Developed economies Econ. développées	99	99	94	94	98	99	97	97	93	93
Developing economies Econ. en dévelop.	100	97	99	99	99	98	97	96	88	...

Unit value indices in national currency • Indices de valeur unitaire en monnaie nationale

Northern America · Amérique septentrionale

	1991	1992	1993	1994	1995	1996	1997	1998	1999	2000
Canada Canada	97	94	98	99	102	103	105	108	106	106
United States[2] Etats-Unis[2]	102	103	103	104	107	106	108	108	108	109

Europe · Europe
EU+ · UE+

	1991	1992	1993	1994	1995	1996	1997	1998	1999	2000
Austria Autriche	98	96	93	91	92	88	83	74	...	...
Belgium-Luxembourg Belgique-Luxembourg	...	...	90	91	93	95	100	101	100	109
Denmark Danemark	99	100	97	100	102	102	105	105	106	...

72
Manufactured goods exports
1990 = 100 [cont.]

Exportations des produits manufacturés
1990 = 100 [suite]

Region, country or area Région, pays ou zone	1991	1992	1993	1994	1995	1996	1997	1998	1999	2000
Finland Finlande	100	106	112	112	120	119	121	123	124	138
France France	99	97	98	100	101	101	103	104	102	104
Germany † Allemagne †	100	100	95	94	96	94	94	97	92	95
Greece Grèce	110	114	112	127	128	128	123	123	...	...
Netherlands[4] Pays-Bas[4]	99	98	94	92	96	95	97	97	97	102
Sweden Suède	102	100	108	111	126	120	121	120	119	124
United Kingdom Royaume-Uni	101	104	117	120	129	129	123	121	117	...
EFTA+ · AELE+ Norway Norvège	98	92	92	93	104	99	100	103	100	107
Other developed economies · Autres écon. développées Australia Australie	58	91	94	94	102	94	94	97	94	108
Japan Japon	100	101	95	95	93	101	106	109	94	...
New Zealand Nouvelle-Zélande	97	99	98	99	101	94	92	93	90	109
South Africa Afrique du Sud	103	111	127	139	173	178	...	...	...	...
Developing economies · Econ. en dévelop. China, Hong Kong SAR† Chine, Hong Kong RAS†	102	103	103	105	107	107	103	100	98	97
India Inde	103	136	154	158	160	141	174	187	...	...
Korea, Republic of Corée, République de	104	106	108	111	112	107	114	150	122	120
Pakistan Pakistan	107	117	127	151	182	203	245	265	270	269

Quantum indices · Indices de volume

Total[1]	105	111	115	130	141	152	171	169	176	...
Developed economies **Econ. développées**	104	106	108	121	129	137	153	158	165	181
Northern America **Amérique septentrionale**	106	114	121	137	152	162	179	183	193	207
Canada Canada	102	119	135	164	187	193	204	223	253	254
United States Etats-Unis	107	113	117	130	142	153	172	172	176	194

72
Manufactured goods exports
1990 = 100 [*cont.*]

Exportations des produits manufacturés
1990 = 100 [*suite*]

Region, country or area Region, pays ou zone	1991	1992	1993	1994	1995	1996	1997	1998	1999	2000
Europe **Europe**	**103**	**104**	**106**	**119**	**126**	**135**	**153**	**160**	**165**	**182**
EU+ **UE+**	**103**	**105**	**106**	**120**	**128**	**137**	**156**	**162**	**167**	**186**
Austria Autriche	104	108	107	119	130	147	181	201	...	...
Belgium-Luxembourg Belgique-Luxembourg	102	104	116	128	133	137	147	163	170	192
Denmark Danemark	106	114	111	118	125	128	145	152	170	...
Finland Finlande	90	97	117	132	144	153	172	188	188	211
France France	107	112	104	116	122	129	143	154	163	189
Germany † Allemagne †	102	104	100	112	117	126	145	148	158	184
Greece Grèce	109	127	140	133	154	169	196	216	...	...
Ireland Irlande	108	122	124	166	193	232	320	434	...	...
Italy Italie	101	100	112	132	144	153	159	161	...	...
Netherlands Pays-Bas	105	105	107	121	130	139	184	170	180	205
Portugal Portugal	101	110	100	120	132	143	154	166	...	...
Spain Espagne	114	109	132	157	169	191	220	231	...	...
Sweden Suède	97	97	108	128	131	131	156	157	171	171
United Kingdom Royaume-Uni	100	101	95	108	116	128	139	139	140	...
EFTA+ **AELE+**	**99**	**101**	**111**	**108**	**106**	**108**	**119**	**125**	**134**	**133**
Iceland Islande	91	94	102	131	120	130	149	168	...	...
Norway Norvège	103	106	105	96	100	106	136	147	149	155
Switzerland Suisse	98	100	112	111	107	108	114	120	130	...
Other developed economies **Autres écon. développées**	**104**	**104**	**104**	**107**	**112**	**115**	**124**	**120**	**133**	**145**
Australia Australie	192	138	161	180	196	254	277	267	291	320
Israel Israël	98	111	126	146	155	170	194	197	203	207
Japan Japon	102	103	101	103	107	107	115	110	121	...

72
Manufactured goods exports
1990 = 100 [cont.]
Exportations des produits manufacturés
1990 = 100 [suite]

Region, country or area / Region, pays ou zone	1991	1992	1993	1994	1995	1996	1997	1998	1999	2000
New Zealand / Nouvelle-Zélande	112	120	132	152	155	162	178	203	221	222
South Africa / Afrique du Sud	108	107	114	126	134	159	...	...	...	...
Developing economies / Econ. en dévelop.	**112**	**133**	**146**	**171**	**196**	**218**	**250**	**221**	**226**	...
China, Hong Kong SAR† / Chine, Hong Kong RAS†	100	100	95	93	95	87	90	84	78	...
India / Inde	128	132	147	181	215	278	246	253	...	...
Korea, Republic of / Corée, République de	110	122	132	151	184	202	228	249	295	335
Pakistan / Pakistan	120	130	136	137	124	146	131	128	145	161
Singapore / Singapour	112	125	155	195	236	255	274	267	292	...
Turkey / Turquie	102	119	130	164	170	197	250	279	294	297

Value (thousand million US $) · Valeur (millards de dollars des E.-U.)

	1991	1992	1993	1994	1995	1996	1997	1998	1999	2000
Total[1]	**2 517.50**	**2 747.30**	**2 729.60**	**3 141.80**	**3 744.20**	**3 872.70**	**4 068.50**	**3 935.30**	**3 931.70**	...
Developed economies / Econ. développées	**2 014.90**	**2 148.10**	**2 064.30**	**2 346.20**	**2 774.60**	**2 847.20**	**2 959.80**	**2 993.30**	**3 031.70**	**3 211.20**
Northern America / Amérique septentrionale	**389.25**	**413.80**	**435.09**	**490.11**	**557.03**	**593.68**	**667.70**	**675.62**	**703.74**	**763.59**
Canada / Canada	79.42	84.61	93.80	109.17	128.22	134.01	142.90	148.67	165.60	167.30
United States / Etats-Unis	309.83	329.19	341.29	380.94	428.81	459.67	524.79	526.96	538.14	596.29
Europe / Europe	**1 290.50**	**1 372.70**	**1 244.10**	**1 432.40**	**1 741.30**	**1 803.10**	**1 830.80**	**1 894.10**	**1 866.90**	**1 922.00**
EU+ / UE+	**1 216.70**	**1 294.70**	**1 170.60**	**1 352.80**	**1 646.90**	**1 709.30**	**1 739.00**	**1 798.60**	**1 767.80**	**1 824.50**
Austria / Autriche	37.53	40.66	36.70	40.88	51.38	52.28	53.05	51.65	50.44	49.82
Belgium-Luxembourg / Belgique-Luxembourg	93.84	97.60	95.90	110.73	133.05	133.30	131.23	143.26	142.52	151.41
Denmark / Danemark	21.40	24.66	21.65	24.30	29.43	29.22	30.17	31.22	33.76	31.83
Finland / Finlande	19.65	20.05	20.05	25.11	34.68	34.77	35.12	38.00	36.70	39.71
France / France	169.44	184.58	162.83	187.22	222.89	229.44	225.78	244.30	242.53	249.20
Germany † / Allemagne †	361.85	387.53	334.59	380.38	455.79	459.69	455.26	477.85	461.09	481.03
Greece / Grèce	4.59	5.31	4.83	4.88	5.99	6.29	6.21	6.34	5.58	...
Ireland / Irlande	16.96	19.56	19.58	24.29	31.21	36.99	42.82	53.58	59.55	65.59
Italy / Italie	150.98	158.35	150.13	170.55	208.98	226.89	215.04	219.73	206.69	212.62

72
Manufactured goods exports
1990 = 100 [*cont.*]
Exportations des produits manufacturés
1990 = 100 [*suite*]

Region, country or area Région, pays ou zone	1991	1992	1993	1994	1995	1996	1997	1998	1999	2000
Netherlands Pays-Bas	80.89	85.31	79.18	89.86	113.91	114.03	133.46	121.70	122.17	127.52
Portugal Portugal	13.39	15.38	12.88	14.86	19.45	19.85	19.48	21.10	21.33	...
Spain Espagne	46.08	50.61	47.54	57.74	71.35	80.45	82.32	84.75	88.72	89.43
Sweden Suède	47.50	48.49	43.13	53.35	67.44	67.70	71.39	68.70	71.11	67.16
United Kingdom Royaume-Uni	152.62	156.62	141.64	168.65	201.32	218.42	237.73	236.39	225.63	232.53
EFTA+ **AELE+**	**72.60**	**76.60**	**72.26**	**78.21**	**92.70**	**92.26**	**90.34**	**93.84**	**97.39**	**95.38**
Iceland Islande	0.23	0.23	0.23	0.31	0.40	0.40	0.44	0.44	0.56	0.61
Norway Norvège	13.84	13.84	12.05	11.20	14.46	14.39	17.01	17.67	16.84	16.60
Switzerland Suisse	58.52	62.53	59.98	66.70	77.84	77.47	72.88	75.73	79.99	78.18
Other developed economies **Autres écon. développées**	**335.15**	**361.60**	**385.08**	**423.70**	**476.20**	**450.37**	**461.27**	**423.65**	**461.04**	**525.60**
Australia Australie	9.19	9.83	10.85	13.07	15.63	19.75	20.43	17.29	18.73	21.21
Israel Israël	10.47	11.74	13.48	15.50	17.09	18.79	20.84	21.67	24.22	29.71
Japan Japon	304.34	328.52	348.56	381.06	425.75	393.58	402.10	369.56	397.48	454.78
New Zealand Nouvelle-Zélande	2.67	2.73	2.98	3.78	4.38	4.46	4.60	4.32	4.50	4.69
South Africa Afrique du Sud	8.48	8.78	9.22	10.28	13.36	13.79	13.31	10.81	16.12	15.21
Developing economies **Econ. en dévelop.**	**502.63**	**599.24**	**665.29**	**795.55**	**969.59**	**1 025.50**	**1 108.70**	**942.00**	**900.00**	**...**
China, Hong Kong SAR† Chine, Hong Kong RAS†	28.16	28.42	27.12	27.11	28.22	25.83	25.69	23.26	21.16	22.43
India Inde	12.95	15.35	16.42	20.15	23.34	24.32	25.97	25.28	...	...
Korea, Republic of Corée, République de	66.90	71.38	76.79	89.86	115.54	115.97	119.96	116.33	130.55	156.87
Pakistan Pakistan	5.10	5.72	5.79	6.38	6.74	7.76	7.40	7.08	7.41	7.73
Singapore Singapour	43.36	49.33	58.74	80.54	100.99	105.95	106.55	94.15	99.68	119.26
Turkey Turquie	9.10	10.64	11.17	13.30	16.32	17.32	20.02	21.04	21.19	22.70

Source:
United Nations Statistics Division, New York, trade
statistics database.

Source:
Organisation des Nations Unies, Division de statistique, New
York, la base de données pour les statistiques du commerce
extérieur.

+   For Member States of this grouping, see

72
Manufactured goods exports
[*cont.*]

Exportations des produits manufacturés
1990 = 100 [*suite*]

Annex I - Other groupings.

† For information on recent changes in country or area nomenclature pertaining to former Czechoslovakia, Germany, Hong Kong Special Administrative Region (SAR) of China, Macao Special Administrative Region (SAR) of China, SFR of Yugoslavia and the former USSR, see Annex I - Country or area nomenclature, regional and other groupings.

1 Excludes trade of the countries of Eastern Europe and the former USSR.
2 Derived from price indices; national unit value index discontinued.
3 Indices are calculated by the United Nations Statistics Division.
4 Derived from sub-indices using current weights.

5 Industrial product.

+ Pour les Etats membres de ce groupement, voir annexe I - Autres groupements.

† Pour les modifications récentes de nomenclature de pays ou de zone concernant l'Allemagne, Hong Kong, région administrative spéciale (RAS) de Chine, Macao, région administrative spéciale (RAS) de Chine, l'ex-Tchécoslovaquie, l'ex-URSS et l'ex-Rfs de Yougoslavie, voir annexe I - Nomenclature des pays ou des zones, groupements régionaux et autres groupements.

1 Non compris le commerce des pays de l'Europe de l'Est et l'ex-URSS.
2 Calculés à partir des indices des prix; l'indice de la valeur unitaire nationale est discontinué.
3 Les indices sont calculés par la Division de statistique des Nations Unies.
4 Calculé à partir de sous-indices à coéfficients de pondération correspondant à la période en cours.
5 Produit industriel.

Technical notes, tables 70-72

Tables 70-72: Current data (annual, monthly and/or quarterly) for most of the series are published regularly by the Statistics Division in the United Nations *Monthly Bulletin of Statistics* [26]. More detailed descriptions of the tables and notes on methodology appear in the United Nations *1977 Supplement to the Statistical Yearbook and Monthly Bulletin of Statistics* [56], *International Trade Statistics: Concepts and Definitions* [50] and the *International Trade Statistics Yearbook* [25]. More detailed data including series for individual countries showing the value in national currencies for imports and exports and notes on these series can be found in the *International Trade Statistics Yearbook* [25] and in the *Monthly Bulletin of Statistics* [26].

Data are obtained from national published sources; from data supplied by the governments for publication in United Nations publications and from publications of other United Nations agencies.

Territory

The statistics reported by a country refer to the customs area of the country. In most cases, this coincides with the geographical area of the country.

Systems of trade

Two systems of recording trade are in common use, differing mainly in the way warehoused and re-exported goods are recorded:

(a)   Special trade (S): special imports are the combined total of imports for direct domestic consumption (including transformation and repair) and withdrawals from bonded warehouses or free zones for domestic consumption. Special exports comprise exports of national merchandise, namely, goods wholly or partly produced or manufactured in the country, together with exports of nationalized goods. (Nationalized goods are goods which, having been included in special imports, are then exported without transformation);

(b)   General trade (G): general imports are the combined total of imports for direct domestic consumption and imports into bonded warehouses or free zones. General exports are the combined total of national exports and re-exports. Re-exports, in the general trade system, consist of the outward movement of nationalized goods plus goods which, after importation, move outward from bonded warehouses or free zones without having been transformed.

Valuation

Goods are, in general, valued according to the transaction value. In the case of imports, the transaction value is the value at which the goods were purchased by

Notes techniques, tableaux 70 à 72

Tableaux 70-72: La Division de statistique des Nations Unies publie régulièrement dans le *Bulletin mensuel de statistique* [26] des données courantes (annuelles, mensuelles et/ou trimestrielles) pour la plupart des séries de ces tableaux. Des descriptions plus détaillées des tableaux et des notes méthodologiques figurent dans *1977 Supplément à l'Annuaire statistique et au Bulletin mensuel de statistique* des Nations Unies [56], dans la publication *Statistiques du commerce international, Concepts et définitions* [50] et dans l'*Annuaire statistique du Commerce international* [25]. Des données plus détaillées, comprenant des séries indiquant la valeur en monnaie nationale des importations et des exportations des divers pays et les notes accompagnant ces séries figurent dans l'*Annuaire statistique du Commerce international* [25] et dans le *Bulletin mensuel de statistique* [26].

Les données proviennent de publications nationales et des informations fournies par les gouvernements pour les publications des Nations Unies ainsi que de publications d'autres institutions des Nations Unies.

Territoire

Les statistiques fournies par pays se rapportent au territoire douanier de ce pays. Le plus souvent, ce territoire coïncide avec l'étendue géographique du pays.

Systèmes de commerce

Deux systèmes d'enregistrement du commerce sont couramment utilisés, qui ne diffèrent que par la façon dont sont enregistrées les marchandises entreposées et les marchandises réexportées:

(a)   Commerce spécial (S): les importations spéciales représentent le total combiné des importations destinées directement à la consommation intérieure (transformations et réparations comprises) et les marchandises retirées des entrepôts douaniers ou des zones franches pour la consommation intérieure. Les exportations spéciales comprennent les exportations de marchandises nationales, c'est-à-dire des biens produits ou fabriqués en totalité ou en partie dans le pays, ainsi que les exportations de biens nationalisés. (Les biens nationalisés sont des biens qui, ayant été inclus dans les importations spéciales, sont ensuite réexportés tels quels.)

(b)   Commerce général (G): les importations générales sont le total combiné des importations destinées directement à la consommation intérieure et des importations placées en entrepôt douanier ou destinées aux zones franches. Les exportations générales sont le total combiné des exportations de biens nationaux et des réexportations. Ces dernières, dans le système du com-

the importer plus the cost of transportation and insurance to the frontier of the importing country (c.i.f. valuation). In the case of exports, the transaction value is the value at which the goods were sold by the exporter, including the cost of transportation and insurance to bring the goods onto the transporting vehicle at the frontier of the exporting country (f.o.b. valuation).

Currency conversion

Conversion of values from national currencies into United States dollars is done by means of external trade conversion factors which are generally weighted averages of exchange rates, the weight being the corresponding monthly or quarterly value of imports or exports.

Coverage

The statistics relate to merchandise trade. Merchandise trade is defined to include, as far as possible, all goods which add to or subtract from the material resources of a country as a result of their movement into or out of the country. Thus, ordinary commercial transactions, government trade (including foreign aid, war reparations and trade in military goods), postal trade and all kinds of silver (except silver coins after their issue), are included in the statistics. Since their movement affects monetary rather than material resources, monetary gold, together with currency and titles of ownership after their issue into circulation, are excluded.

Commodity classification

The commodity classification of trade is in accordance with the United Nations *Standard International Trade Classification* (SITC) [55].

World and regional totals

The regional, economic and world totals have been adjusted: (a) to include estimates for countries or areas for which full data are not available; (b) to include insurance and freight for imports valued f.o.b.; (c) to include countries or areas not listed separately; (d) to approximate special trade; (e) to approximate calendar years; and (f) where possible, to eliminate incomparabilities owing to geographical changes, by adjusting the figures for periods before the change to be comparable to those for periods after the change.

Quantum and unit value index numbers

These index numbers show the changes in the volume of imports or exports (quantum index) and the average price of imports or exports (unit value index).

Description of tables

Table 70: World imports and exports are the sum of imports and exports of Developed economies, Developing economies and other. The regional totals for im-

merce général, comprennent les exportations de biens nationalisés et de biens qui, après avoir été importés, sortent des entrepôts de douane ou des zones franches sans avoir été transformés.

Evaluation

En général, les marchandises sont évaluées à la valeur de la transaction. Dans le cas des importations, cette valeur est celle à laquelle les marchandises ont été achetées par l'importateur plus le coût de leur transport et de leur assurance jusqu'à la frontière du pays importateur (valeur c.a.f.). Dans le cas des exportations, la valeur de la transaction est celle à laquelle les marchandises ont été vendues par l'exportateur, y compris le coût de transport et d'assurance des marchandises jusqu'à leur chargement sur le véhicule de transport à la frontière du pays exportateur (valeur f.à.b.).

Conversion des monnaies

Le conversion en dollars des Etats-Unis de valeurs exprimées en monnaie nationale se fait par application de coefficients de conversion du commerce extérieur, qui sont généralement les moyennes pondérées des taux de change, le poids étant la valeur mensuelle ou trimestrielle correspondante des importations ou des exportations.

Couverture

Les statistiques se rapportent au commerce des marchandises. Le commerce des marchandises se définit comme comprenant, dans toute la mesure du possible, toutes les marchandises qui ajoutent ou retranchent aux ressources matérielles d'un pays par suite de leur importation ou de leur exportation par ce pays. Ainsi, les transactions commerciales ordinaires, le commerce pour le compte de l'Etat (y compris l'aide extérieure, les réparations pour dommages de guerre et le commerce des fournitures militaires), le commerce par voie postale et les transactions de toutes sortes sur l'argent (à l'exception des transactions sur les pièces d'argent après leur émission) sont inclus dans ces statistiques. La monnaie or ainsi que la monnaie et les titres de propriété après leur mise en circulation sont exclus, car leurs mouvements influent sur les ressources monétaires plutôt que sur les ressources matérielles.

Classification par marchandise

La classification par marchandise du commerce extérieur est celle adoptée dans la *Classification type pour le commerce international* des Nations Unies (CTCI) [55].

Totaux mondiaux et régionaux

Les totaux économiques, régionaux et mondiaux ont été ajustés de manière: (a) à inclure les estimations

ports and exports and have been adjusted to exclude the re-exports of countries or areas comprising each region. Estimates for certain countries or areas not shown separately as well as for those shown separately but for which no data are yet available are included in the regional and world totals. Export and import values in terms of U.S. dollars are derived by the United Nations Statistics Division from data published in national publications, from data in the replies to the *Monthly Bulletin of Statistics* questionnaires and from data published by the International Monetary Fund (IMF) in the publication *International Financial Statistics* [15].

Table 71: These index numbers show the changes in the volume (quantum index) and the average price (unit value index) of total imports and exports. The terms of trade figures are calculated by dividing export unit value indices by the corresponding import unit value indices. The product of the net terms of trade and the quantum index of exports is called the index of the purchasing power of exports. The footnotes to countries appearing in table 70 also apply to the index numbers in this table.

Table 72: Manufactured goods are defined here to comprise sections 5 through 8 of the Standard International Trade Classification (SITC). These sections are: chemicals and related products, manufactured goods classified chiefly by material, machinery and transport equipment and miscellaneous manufactured articles. The economic and geographic groupings in this table are in accordance with those of table 70, although table 70 includes more detailed geographical sub-groups which make up the groupings "other developed market economies" and "developing market economies" of this table.

The unit value indices are obtained from national sources, except those of a few countries which the United Nations Statistics Division compiles using their quantity and value figures. For countries that do not compile indices for manufactured goods exports conforming to the above definition, sub-indices are aggregated to approximate an index of SITC sections 5-8. Unit value indices obtained from national indices are rebased, where necessary, so that 1990=100. Indices in national currency are converted into US dollars using conversion factors obtained by dividing the weighted average exchange rate of a given currency in the current period by the weighted average exchange rate in the base period. All aggregate unit value indices are current period weighted.

The indices in Special Drawing Rights (SDRs) are calculated by multiplying the equivalent aggregate indices in United States dollars by conversion factors obtained by dividing the SDR/US $ exchange rate in the current period by the rate in the base period.

pour les pays ou régions pour lesquels on ne disposait pas de données complètes; (b) à inclure l'assurance et le fret dans la valeur f.o.b. des importations; (c) à inclure les pays ou régions non indiqués séparément; (d) à donner une approximation du commerce spécial; (e) à les ramener à des années civiles; et (f) à éliminer, dans la mesure du possible, les données non comparables par suite de changements géographiques, en ajustant les chiffres correspondant aux périodes avant le changement de manière à les rendre comparables à ceux des périodes après le changement.

Indices de quantum et de valeur unitaire

Ces indices indiquent les variations du volume des importations ou des exportations (indice de quantum) et du prix moyen des importations ou des exportations (indice de valeur unitaire).

Description des tableaux

Tableau 70: Les importations et les exportations totales pour le monde se composent des importations et exportations des Economies développées, des Economies en développement et des autres. Les totaux régionaux pour importations et exportations ont été ajustés pour exclure les re-exportations des pays ou zones qui comprennent la région. Les totaux régionaux et mondiaux comprennent des estimations pour certains pays ou zones ne figurant pas séparément mais pour lesquels les données ne sont pas encore disponibles. Les valeurs en dollars des E.U. des exportations et des importations ont été obtenues par la Division de statistique des Nations Unies à partir des réponses aux questionnaires du *Bulletin Mensuel de Statistique*, des données publiées par le Fonds Monétaire International dans la publication *Statistiques financières internationales* [15].

Tableau 71: Ces indices indiquent les variations du volume (indice de quantum) et du prix moyen (indice de valeur unitaire) des importations et des exportations totales. Les chiffres relatifs aux termes de l'échange se calculent en divisant les indices de valeur unitaire des exportations par les indices correspondants de valeur unitaire des importations. Le produit de la valeur nette des termes de l'échange et de l'indice du quantum des exportations est appelé indice du pouvoir d'achat des exportations. Les notes figurant au bas du tableau 70 concernant certains pays s'appliquent également aux indices du présent tableau.

Tableau 72: Les produits manufacturés se définissent comme correspondant aux sections 5 à 8 de la Classification type pour le commerce international (CTCI). Ces sections sont: produits chimiques et produits connexes, biens manufacturés classés principalement par matière première, machines et équipements de transport et articles divers manufacturés. Les groupements éco-

The quantum indices are derived from the value data and the unit value indices. All aggregate quantum indices are base period weighted.

nomiques et géographiques de ce tableau sont conformes à ceux du tableau 70; toutefois, le tableau 70 comprend des subdivisions géographiques plus détaillées qui composent les groupements "autres pays développés à économie de marché" et "pays en développement à économie de marché" du présent tableau.

Les indices de valeur unitaire sont obtenus de sources nationales, à l'exception de ceux de certains pays que la Division de statistique des Nations Unies compile en utilisant les chiffres de ces pays relatifs aux quantités et aux valeurs. Pour les pays qui n'établissent pas d'indices conformes à la définition ci-dessus pour leurs exportations de produits manufacturés, on fait la synthèse de sous-indices de manière à établir un indice proche de celui des sections 5 à 8 de la CTCI. Le cas échéant, les indices de valeur unitaire obtenus à partir des indices nationaux sont ajustés sur la base 1990=100. On convertit les indices en monnaie nationale en indices en dollars des Etats-Unis en utilisant des facteurs de conversion obtenus en divisant la moyenne pondérée des taux de change d'une monnaie donnée pendant la période courante par la moyenne pondérée des taux de change de la période de base. Tous les indices globaux de valeur unitaire sont pondérés pour la période courante.

On calcule les indices en droits de tirages spécial (DTS) en multipliant les indices globaux équivalents en dollars des Etats-Unis par les facteurs de conversion obtenus en divisant le taux de change DTS/dollars E.U. de la période courante par le taux correspondant de la période de base.

On détermine les indices de quantum à partir des données de valeur et des indices de valeur unitaire. Tous les indices globaux de quantum sont pondérés par rapport à la période de base.

73
Tourist/visitor arrivals by region of origin
Arrivées de touristes/visiteurs par région de provenance

Country or area of destination and region of origin +	1995	1996	1997	1998	1999	Pays ou zone de destination et région de provenance+
Albania[1]	**40 175**	**56 276**	**19 154**	**27 709**	**38 963**	**Albanie**[1]
Africa	42	195	...	...	...	Afrique
Americas	4 580	4 752	1 177	1 545	2 150	Amériques
Europe	24 504	29 052	11 849	13 854	18 520	Europe
Asia, East and South East/Oceania	701	1 582	185	310	417	Asie, Est et Sud-Est et Océanie
Southern Asia	48	234	...	...	...	Asie du Sud
Western Asia	1 756	3 594	105	2 370	3 056	Asie occidentale
Region not specified	8 544	16 867	5 838	9 630	14 820	Région non spécifiée
Algeria[2][3]	**519 576**	**604 968**	**634 761**	**678 436**	**748 536**	**Algérie**[2][3]
Africa	42 878	35 029	34 027	37 373	51 303	Afrique
Americas	2 005	1 770	1 838	2 297	2 563	Amériques
Europe	37 831	45 570	48 440	56 509	72 573	Europe
Asia, East and South East/Oceania	1 661	1 107	1 342	2 609	4 414	Asie, Est et Sud-Est et Océanie
Western Asia	13 275	10 015	9 194	8 414	10 008	Asie occidentale
Region not specified	421 926	511 477	539 920	571 234	607 675	Région non spécifiée
American Samoa[4][5]	**17 522**	**21 366**	...	...	...	**Samoa américaines**[4][5]
Africa	2	19	...	...	...	Afrique
Americas	8 695	9 108	...	...	...	Amériques
Europe	888	3 036	...	...	...	Europe
Asia, East and South East/Oceania	7 848	8 618	...	...	...	Asie, Est et Sud-Est et Océanie
Southern Asia	62	531	...	...	...	Asie du Sud
Western Asia	18	29	...	...	...	Asie occidentale
Region not specified	9	25	...	...	...	Région non spécifiée
Angola[5]	**9 546**	**20 978**	**45 139**	**52 011**	**45 477**	**Angola**[5]
Africa	2 115	4 524	13 863	7 332	7 887	Afrique
Americas	1 145	2 133	3 154	7 509	6 074	Amériques
Europe	6 143	13 097	27 422	34 444	29 113	Europe
Asia, East and South East/Oceania	...	264	540	2 125	2 009	Asie, Est et Sud-Est et Océanie
Southern Asia	...	90	26	359	328	Asie du Sud
Western Asia	...	...	...	242	66	Asie occidentale
Region not specified	143	870	134	...	...	Région non spécifiée
Anguilla[5][6]	**38 531**	**37 498**	**43 181**	**43 874**	**46 782**	**Anguilla**[5][6]
Americas	35 272	33 748	36 642	34 658	33 449	Amériques
Europe	2 405	2 926	5 455	7 986	11 720	Europe
Region not specified	854	824	1 084	1 230	1 613	Région non spécifiée
Antigua and Barbuda[5][6][7]	**211 663**	**220 475**	**232 141**	**226 121**	...	**Antigua-et-Barbuda**[5][6][7]
Americas	123 680	128 266	138 028	133 607	...	Amériques
Europe	83 799	87 935	89 884	88 082	...	Europe
Region not specified	4 184	4 274	4 229	4 432	...	Région non spécifiée
Argentina[5][6][8]	**2 288 694**	**2 613 909**	**2 764 226**	**3 012 472**	**2 898 241**	**Argentine**[5][6][8]
Americas	1 988 119	2 252 082	2 378 327	2 595 379	2 490 667	Amériques
Europe	248 348	298 858	319 787	344 323	336 676	Europe
Region not specified	52 227	62 969	66 112	72 770	70 898	Région non spécifiée
Armenia[9]	**12 043**	**13 388**	**23 430**	**31 837**	**40 745**	**Arménie**[9]
Africa	15	44	10	32	43	Afrique
Americas	2 061	1 011	3 282	5 028	6 156	Amériques
Europe	8 376	11 245	16 109	23 099	26 880	Europe
Asia, East and South East/Oceania	141	232	602	906	923	Asie, Est et Sud-Est et Océanie
Southern Asia	1 181	638	2 203	1 300	4 845	Asie du Sud
Western Asia	269	218	1 224	1 472	1 898	Asie occidentale

73
Tourist/visitor arrivals by region of origin [*cont.*]
Arrivées de touristes/visiteurs par région de provenance[*suite*]

Country or area of destination and region of origin +	1995	1996	1997	1998	1999	Pays ou zone de destination et région de provenance +
Aruba[5]	**618 916**	**640 836**	**649 893**	**647 437**	**683 320**	**Aruba**[5]
Americas	564 985	582 140	587 776	595 186	629 597	Amériques
Europe	51 882	55 333	57 335	49 042	49 370	Europe
Asia, East and South East/Oceania	274	284	346	320	273	Asie, Est et Sud-Est et Océanie
Region not specified	1 775	3 079	4 436	2 889	4 080	Région non spécifiée
Australia[3 6 10]	**3 725 800**	**4 164 800**	**4 317 867**	**4 167 204**	**4 459 181**	**Australie**[3 6 10]
Africa	42 600	53 400	56 220	70 849	71 480	Afrique
Americas	381 800	401 300	420 040	473 551	533 953	Amériques
Europe	762 300	810 500	885 103	963 571	1 083 978	Europe
Asia, East and South East/Oceania	2 490 700	2 842 900	2 892 508	2 583 820	2 683 321	Asie, Est et Sud-Est et Océanie
Southern Asia	27 500	33 100	37 765	42 741	50 160	Asie du Sud
Western Asia	17 500	20 100	21 120	28 003	34 449	Asie occidentale
Region not specified	3 400	3 500	5 111	4 669	1 840	Région non spécifiée
Austria[9]	**17 172 968**	**17 089 973**	**16 647 281**	**17 352 477**	**17 466 714**	**Autriche**[9]
Africa	22 245	21 783	23 080	32 818	32 575	Afrique
Americas	672 779	707 509	718 578	827 764	767 196	Amériques
Europe	15 722 110	15 569 746	15 063 175	15 680 020	15 843 176	Europe
Asia, East and South East/Oceania	477 316	514 877	530 304	499 515	534 948	Asie, Est et Sud-Est et Océanie
Southern Asia	23 885	27 742	24 174	21 533	30 685	Asie du Sud
Western Asia	21 787	20 582	25 703	25 583	25 030	Asie occidentale
Region not specified	232 846	227 734	262 267	265 244	233 104	Région non spécifiée
Azerbaijan[5]	...	...	**305 830**	**483 163**	**602 047**	**Azerbaïdjan**[5]
Americas	...	...	4 895	3 350	1 815	Amériques
Europe	...	...	182 506	331 377	446 415	Europe
Southern Asia	...	...	106 183	140 459	122 231	Asie du Sud
Western Asia	...	...	405	208	94	Asie occidentale
Region not specified	...	...	11 841	7 769	31 492	Région non spécifiée
Bahamas[5]	**1 598 135**	**1 633 105**	**1 617 595**	**1 528 000**	**1 577 000**	**Bahamas**[5]
Americas	1 432 505	1 445 460	1 413 485	1 333 100	1 383 000	Amériques
Europe	114 950	127 600	130 365	118 000	140 800	Europe
Asia, East and South East/Oceania	20 450	25 680	...	...	...	Asie, Est et Sud-Est et Océanie
Region not specified	30 230	34 365	73 745	76 900	53 200	Région non spécifiée
Bahrain[3 6]	**2 310 828**	**1 987 604**	**2 600 320**	**2 897 562**	**3 280 452**	**Bahrein**[3 6]
Africa	10 069	11 713	18 389	21 910	26 396	Afrique
Americas	79 097	76 746	86 358	96 881	101 859	Amériques
Europe	156 142	147 574	173 258	179 472	191 040	Europe
Asia, East and South East/Oceania	74 774	84 318	82 767	96 886	100 646	Asie, Est et Sud-Est et Océanie
Southern Asia	209 067	193 465	221 615	260 817	299 168	Asie du Sud
Western Asia	1 781 522	1 473 748	2 017 933	2 241 596	2 561 343	Asie occidentale
Region not specified	157	40	...	...	...	Région non spécifiée
Bangladesh[5 6]	**156 231**	**165 887**	**182 420**	**171 961**	**172 781**	**Bangladesh**[5 6]
Africa	1 089	1 381	1 150	1 609	1 511	Afrique
Americas	13 110	13 984	15 435	15 653	12 444	Amériques
Europe	48 994	51 034	47 934	36 920	39 599	Europe
Asia, East and South East/Oceania	25 621	29 875	33 609	35 757	34 865	Asie, Est et Sud-Est et Océanie
Southern Asia	64 300	66 307	81 728	77 692	78 878	Asie du Sud
Western Asia	3 117	3 282	2 548	4 291	5 333	Asie occidentale
Region not specified	...	24	16	39	151	Région non spécifiée
Barbados[5]	**442 107**	**447 083**	**472 290**	**512 397**	**514 614**	**Barbade**[5]
Africa	...	...	...	...	563	Afrique

73
Tourist/visitor arrivals by region of origin [*cont.*]
Arrivées de touristes/visiteurs par région de provenance[*suite*]

Country or area of destination and region of origin +	1995	1996	1997	1998	1999	Pays ou zone de destination et région de provenance +
Americas	237 998	238 721	245 004	254 982	264 129	Amériques
Europe	195 268	200 960	220 618	251 735	245 143	Europe
Asia, East and South East/Oceania	2 556	1 615	1 490	1 515	4 242	Asie, Est et Sud-Est et Océanie
Southern Asia	...	...	...	...	363	Asie du Sud
Western Asia	...	...	...	...	174	Asie occidentale
Region not specified	6 285	5 787	5 178	4 165	...	Région non spécifiée
Belarus[5]	**161 397**	**234 226**	**254 023**	**355 342**	**...**	**Bélarus** [5]
Africa	305	171	235	703	...	Afrique
Americas	5 428	7 808	9 214	9 607	...	Amériques
Europe	153 682	222 177	241 549	339 587	...	Europe
Asia, East and South East/Oceania	1 179	2 883	2 311	4 388	...	Asie, Est et Sud-Est et Océanie
Southern Asia	373	502	508	676	...	Asie du Sud
Western Asia	430	685	206	381	...	Asie occidentale
Belgium[9]	**5 559 875**	**5 829 257**	**6 037 031**	**6 179 254**	**6 369 030**	**Belgique**[9]
Africa	55 984	63 451	63 003	61 028	57 058	Afrique
Americas	372 915	388 850	410 712	420 335	434 012	Amériques
Europe	4 826 574	5 046 096	5 197 330	5 363 775	5 522 422	Europe
Asia, East and South East/Oceania	230 481	266 218	286 455	266 801	287 214	Asie, Est et Sud-Est et Océanie
Southern Asia	22 451	30 305	27 946	17 149	19 211	Asie du Sud
Western Asia	14 861	16 036	18 083	19 275	17 898	Asie occidentale
Region not specified	36 609	18 301	33 502	30 891	31 215	Région non spécifiée
Belize[3 11]	**362 003**	**367 602**	**328 143**	**299 725**	**339 581**	**Belize**[3 11]
Americas	314 387	322 529	275 704	248 188	288 212	Amériques
Europe	40 777	38 808	47 489	45 130	44 364	Europe
Asia, East and South East/Oceania	4 724	4 975	3 780	3 972	3 917	Asie, Est et Sud-Est et Océanie
Region not specified	2 115	1 290	1 170	2 435	3 088	Région non spécifiée
Benin[1]	**138 000**	**...**	**...**	**...**	**...**	**Bénin**[1]
Africa	90 300	...	...	...	...	Afrique
Americas	4 640	...	...	...	...	Amériques
Europe	39 800	...	...	...	...	Europe
Asia, East and South East/Oceania	3 260	...	...	...	...	Asie, Est et Sud-Est et Océanie
Bermuda[5 12]	**387 412**	**390 395**	**380 060**	**368 756**	**354 026**	**Bermudes**[5 12]
Americas	348 841	351 229	338 727	323 609	311 015	Amériques
Europe	29 592	30 273	31 646	37 096	35 597	Europe
Asia, East and South East/Oceania	1 054	1 260	1 010	978	851	Asie, Est et Sud-Est et Océanie
Region not specified	7 925	7 633	8 677	7 073	6 563	Région non spécifiée
Bhutan[5]	**4 765**	**5 150**	**5 362**	**6 203**	**...**	**Bhoutan**[5]
Africa	...	...	5	8	...	Afrique
Americas	1 002	1 072	1 046	1 622	...	Amériques
Europe	2 229	2 365	2 576	3 145	...	Europe
Asia, East and South East/Oceania	1 521	1 597	1 679	1 403	...	Asie, Est et Sud-Est et Océanie
Southern Asia	6	15	33	24	...	Asie du Sud
Region not specified	7	101	23	1	...	Région non spécifiée
Bolivia[1 13]	**350 687**	**376 855**	**397 517**	**420 491**	**409 142**	**Bolivie**[1 13]
Africa	733	683	641	1 016	943	Afrique
Americas	211 866	226 084	257 203	269 344	242 075	Amériques
Europe	124 185	135 084	124 895	135 759	146 138	Europe
Asia, East and South East/Oceania	13 903	15 004	14 778	14 372	19 986	Asie, Est et Sud-Est et Océanie
Bonaire[5 14]	**59 410**	**65 080**	**62 776**	**61 737**	**61 495**	**Bonaire**[5 14]
Americas	38 819	41 650	40 495	39 976	40 883	Amériques

73
Tourist/visitor arrivals by region of origin [*cont.*]
Arrivées de touristes/visiteurs par région de provenance [*suite*]

Country or area of destination and region of origin +	1995	1996	1997	1998	1999	Pays ou zone de destination et région de provenance +
Europe	20 381	23 188	22 090	21 605	20 393	Europe
Asia, East and South East/Oceania	51	74	38	25	19	Asie, Est et Sud-Est et Océanie
Region not specified	159	168	153	131	200	Région non spécifiée
Botswana[3][15]	...	...	**606 790**	**749 535**	...	**Botswana**[3][15]
Africa	...	...	516 337	629 033	...	Afrique
Americas	...	...	8 614	10 714	...	Amériques
Europe	...	...	38 311	38 755	...	Europe
Asia, East and South East/Oceania	...	...	9 281	9 127	...	Asie, Est et Sud-Est et Océanie
Southern Asia	...	...	1 174	1 063	...	Asie du Sud
Region not specified	...	...	33 073	60 843	...	Région non spécifiée
Brazil[5][16]	**1 991 416**	**2 665 508**	**2 849 750**	**4 818 084**	**5 107 169**	**Brésil**[5][16]
Africa	18 933	23 187	23 747	40 959	41 294	Afrique
Americas	1 374 111	1 830 419	1 998 967	3 449 456	3 643 223	Amériques
Europe	516 722	681 340	713 059	1 160 673	1 246 155	Europe
Asia, East and South East/Oceania	66 845	109 638	95 228	121 692	130 070	Asie, Est et Sud-Est et Océanie
Western Asia	4 599	7 344	7 674	13 661	15 254	Asie occidentale
Region not specified	10 206	13 580	11 075	31 643	31 173	Région non spécifiée
British Virgin Islands[5]	**219 481**	**243 683**	**244 318**	**279 097**	**285 900**	**Iles Vierges britanniques**[5]
Americas	193 757	213 311	214 316	223 729	236 000	Amériques
Europe	21 478	23 043	22 137	21 457	32 600	Europe
Region not specified	4 246	7 329	7 865	33 911	17 300	Région non spécifiée
Brunei Darussalam[3]	...	...	...	**964 080**	...	**Brunéi Darussalam**[3]
Americas	...	...	...	10 184	...	Amériques
Europe	...	...	...	40 593	...	Europe
Asia, East and South East/Oceania	...	...	...	892 051	...	Asie, Est et Sud-Est et Océanie
Southern Asia	...	...	...	12 442	...	Asie du Sud
Region not specified	...	...	...	8 810	...	Région non spécifiée
Bulgaria[3][17]	**8 004 584**	**6 810 688**	**7 543 185**	**5 239 691**	**5 056 240**	**Bulgarie**[3][17]
Africa	4 406	3 254	6 838	6 675	4 418	Afrique
Americas	21 353	18 672	21 515	39 788	39 241	Amériques
Europe	7 687 351	6 406 574	7 247 812	4 821 516	4 911 853	Europe
Asia, East and South East/Oceania	13 319	13 812	19 054	20 715	21 275	Asie, Est et Sud-Est et Océanie
Southern Asia	9 715	10 086	15 963	14 778	14 570	Asie du Sud
Western Asia	24 665	18 201	21 438	19 840	17 964	Asie occidentale
Region not specified	243 775	340 089	210 565	316 379	46 919	Région non spécifiée
Burkina Faso[1]	**124 270**	**131 113**	**138 364**	**160 284**	...	**Burkina Faso**[1]
Africa	51 617	54 460	57 459	62 673	...	Afrique
Americas	7 374	7 780	8 209	10 062	...	Amériques
Europe	52 075	54 942	57 997	77 785	...	Europe
Asia, East and South East/Oceania	1 933	2 039	2 153	3 199	...	Asie, Est et Sud-Est et Océanie
Western Asia	608	642	677	1 016	...	Asie occidentale
Region not specified	10 663	11 250	11 869	5 549	...	Région non spécifiée
Burundi[2][5]	**34 125**	**27 391**	**10 553**	**15 404**	...	**Burundi**[2][5]
Africa	16 201	13 004	5 011	7 394	...	Afrique
Americas	2 068	1 660	639	1 092	...	Amériques
Europe	13 099	10 514	4 051	5 700	...	Europe
Asia, East and South East/Oceania	2 757	2 213	852	1 218	...	Asie, Est et Sud-Est et Océanie
Cambodia[5][12]	**219 680**	**260 489**	**218 843**	**186 333**	**262 907**	**Cambodge**[5][12]
Africa	...	...	...	...	4 592	Afrique
Americas	21 538	27 812	24 561	21 773	36 324	Amériques

73
Tourist/visitor arrivals by region of origin [cont.]
Arrivées de touristes/visiteurs par région de provenance [suite]

Country or area of destination and region of origin +	1995	1996	1997	1998	1999	Pays ou zone de destination et région de provenance +
Europe	37 907	53 761	43 331	46 165	60 031	Europe
Asia, East and South East/Oceania	155 820	174 406	147 470	105 422	135 502	Asie, Est et Sud-Est et Océanie
Southern Asia	1 158	3 609	2 735	1 999	2 445	Asie du Sud
Western Asia	...	...	...	...	24 013	Asie occidentale
Region not specified	3 257	901	746	10 974	...	Région non spécifiée
Cameroon[1]	**99 749**	**101 106**	**132 839**	**...**	**...**	**Cameroun**[1]
Africa	26 551	26 912	47 689	...	...	Afrique
Americas	7 624	7 728	14 080	...	...	Amériques
Europe	61 393	62 228	66 034	...	...	Europe
Asia, East and South East/Oceania	1 849	1 874	2 736	...	...	Asie, Est et Sud-Est et Océanie
Western Asia	1 310	1 328	1 308	...	...	Asie occidentale
Region not specified	1 022	1 036	992	...	...	Région non spécifiée
Canada[5]	**16 932 100**	**17 285 400**	**17 635 700**	**18 828 100**	**19 366 600**	**Canada**[5]
Africa	48 700	55 500	58 700	59 200	66 300	Afrique
Americas	13 294 400	13 240 500	13 741 900	15 256 000	15 564 300	Amériques
Europe	2 187 700	2 371 200	2 329 900	2 273 800	2 381 800	Europe
Asia, East and South East/Oceania	1 300 600	1 509 400	1 392 600	1 145 400	1 251 000	Asie, Est et Sud-Est et Océanie
Southern Asia	68 700	73 400	77 700	55 700	62 500	Asie du Sud
Western Asia	32 000	35 400	34 900	38 000	40 700	Asie occidentale
Cape Verde[5 12]	**27 785**	**37 000**	**45 000**	**...**	**...**	**Cap-Vert**[5 12]
Africa	981	...	...	...	...	Afrique
Americas	1 819	...	...	...	...	Amériques
Europe	18 496	31 108	37 834	...	...	Europe
Region not specified	6 489	5 892	7 166	...	...	Région non spécifiée
Cayman Islands[5 12]	**361 444**	**373 245**	**381 188**	**404 205**	**394 534**	**Iles Caïmanes**[5 12]
Africa	334	374	374	514	661	Afrique
Americas	320 271	335 548	344 391	365 319	355 605	Amériques
Europe	37 319	33 440	32 746	34 690	34 501	Europe
Asia, East and South East/Oceania	2 352	2 462	2 861	2 800	2 870	Asie, Est et Sud-Est et Océanie
Region not specified	1 168	1 421	816	882	897	Région non spécifiée
Central African Rep.[5]	**...**	**...**	**...**	**7 478**	**...**	**Rép. centrafricaine**[5]
Africa	...	...	...	3 439	...	Afrique
Americas	...	...	...	455	...	Amériques
Europe	...	...	...	3 054	...	Europe
Asia, East and South East/Oceania	...	...	...	313	...	Asie, Est et Sud-Est et Océanie
Western Asia	...	...	...	89	...	Asie occidentale
Region not specified	...	...	...	128	...	Région non spécifiée
Chad[1]	**18 821**	**19 962**	**26 980**	**41 244**	**46 603**	**Tchad**[1]
Africa	2 137	2 400	3 700	12 160	13 649	Afrique
Americas	643	1 023	615	3 963	4 546	Amériques
Europe	4 141	5 246	4 764	21 206	24 134	Europe
Asia, East and South East/Oceania	218	98	180	216	420	Asie, Est et Sud-Est et Océanie
Western Asia	243	124	116	139	591	Asie occidentale
Region not specified	11 439	11 071	17 605	3 560	3 263	Région non spécifiée
Chile[5]	**1 539 593**	**1 449 528**	**1 643 640**	**1 759 279**	**1 622 252**	**Chili**[5]
Africa	2 724	...	1 794	2 092	2 482	Afrique
Americas	1 345 445	1 242 865	1 402 868	1 492 699	1 356 414	Amériques
Europe	163 322	167 986	203 373	226 653	224 018	Europe
Asia, East and South East/Oceania	25 749	27 745	32 023	34 281	35 377	Asie, Est et Sud-Est et Océanie
Southern Asia	962	...	1 818	2 442	2 193	Asie du Sud

73
Tourist/visitor arrivals by region of origin [*cont.*]
Arrivées de touristes/visiteurs par région de provenance [*suite*]

Country or area of destination and region of origin +	1995	1996	1997	1998	1999	Pays ou zone de destination et région de provenance +
Western Asia	151	...	519	455	568	Asie occidentale
Region not specified	1 240	10 932	1 245	657	1 200	Région non spécifiée
China ††[5][18]	**5 886 716**	**6 744 334**	**7 428 006**	**7 107 747**	**8 432 296**	**Chine ††[5][18]**
Africa	33 073	38 663	38 099	39 385	43 097	Afrique
Americas	697 255	809 185	867 166	947 927	1 025 996	Amériques
Europe	1 609 431	1 770 216	2 039 424	1 896 160	2 148 520	Europe
Asia, East and South East/Oceania	3 405 199	3 972 408	4 312 645	4 057 595	5 022 581	Asie, Est et Sud-Est et Océanie
Southern Asia	108 425	119 692	130 716	132 853	160 990	Asie du Sud
Western Asia	16 460	17 769	21 644	20 993	26 051	Asie occidentale
Region not specified	16 873	16 401	18 312	12 834	5 061	Région non spécifiée
China, Hong Kong SAR†[3][19]	**10 199 994**	**12 973 764**	**11 273 377**	**10 159 646**	**11 328 272**	**Chine, Hong Kong RAS†[3][19]**
Africa	68 041	64 831	73 559	63 939	65 027	Afrique
Americas	986 342	1 083 247	1 125 138	1 104 888	1 155 313	Amériques
Europe	1 162 107	1 373 747	1 195 345	1 042 231	1 059 155	Europe
Asia, East and South East/Oceania	7 805 221	10 256 102	8 695 439	7 761 524	8 852 807	Asie, Est et Sud-Est et Océanie
Southern Asia	155 263	179 845	167 690	167 766	171 615	Asie du Sud
Western Asia	19 384	15 992	16 206	19 298	24 355	Asie occidentale
Region not specified	3 636	...	...	...	...	Région non spécifiée
China, Macao SAR †[3][20]	**7 752 495**	**8 151 055**	**7 000 370**	**6 948 535**	**7 443 924**	**Chine, Macao RAS †[3][20]**
Africa	5 998	6 595	5 579	4 786	4 101	Afrique
Americas	134 527	149 327	121 286	110 619	105 714	Amériques
Europe	241 352	293 355	239 364	262 783	163 450	Europe
Asia, East and South East/Oceania	7 188 065	7 493 180	6 434 682	6 498 013	7 154 937	Asie, Est et Sud-Est et Océanie
Southern Asia	14 628	18 489	16 221	12 532	14 010	Asie du Sud
Western Asia	561	562	586	719	682	Asie occidentale
Region not specified	167 364	189 547	182 652	59 083	1 030	Région non spécifiée
Colombia[5][21]	**1 398 997**	**756 606**	**639 250**	**674 425**	**546 035**	**Colombie[5][21]**
Americas	1 232 974	499 884	512 979	561 292	475 322	Amériques
Europe	166 023	61 372	69 797	69 664	70 617	Europe
Region not specified	...	195 350	56 474	43 469	96	Région non spécifiée
Comoros[5][12]	**22 838**	**23 775**	**26 219**	**27 474**	**24 479**	**Comores[5][12]**
Africa	7 949	11 355	14 202	11 155	14 420	Afrique
Americas	292	130	337	783	144	Amériques
Europe	14 151	10 623	11 143	12 799	9 083	Europe
Asia, East and South East/Oceania	446	215	537	460	210	Asie, Est et Sud-Est et Océanie
Region not specified	...	1 452	...	2 277	622	Région non spécifiée
Congo[1][22]	**37 432**	**39 114**	**25 811**	**25 082**	**4 753**	**Congo[1][22]**
Africa	16 872	14 337	9 477	9 194	2 354	Afrique
Americas	2 135	2 792	1 830	1 791	265	Amériques
Europe	17 375	20 926	13 806	13 410	2 032	Europe
Region not specified	1 050	1 059	698	687	102	Région non spécifiée
Cook Islands[5][23]	**48 500**	**48 819**	**49 964**	**48 629**	**55 599**	**Iles Cook[5][23]**
Americas	7 912	8 866	9 484	8 988	11 083	Amériques
Europe	18 630	17 914	19 924	19 291	18 382	Europe
Asia, East and South East/Oceania	21 713	21 793	20 400	20 239	25 974	Asie, Est et Sud-Est et Océanie
Region not specified	245	246	156	111	160	Région non spécifiée
Costa Rica[5]	**784 610**	**781 127**	**811 490**	**942 853**	**1 031 585**	**Costa Rica[5]**
Africa	489	714	689	748	897	Afrique
Americas	633 055	629 879	661 574	791 219	863 324	Amériques
Europe	134 656	132 435	130 713	131 657	145 586	Europe

73
Tourist/visitor arrivals by region of origin [*cont.*]
Arrivées de touristes/visiteurs par région de provenance[*suite*]

Country or area of destination and region of origin +	1995	1996	1997	1998	1999	Pays ou zone de destination et région de provenance +
Asia, East and South East/Oceania	13 165	14 638	14 484	14 447	15 885	Asie, Est et Sud-Est et Océanie
Region not specified	3 245	3 461	4 030	4 782	5 893	Région non spécifiée
Côte d'Ivoire[5 24]	**187 911**	**236 913**	**274 094**	**301 039**	**...**	**Côte d'Ivoire**[5 24]
Africa	104 739	113 324	137 886	158 808	...	Afrique
Americas	13 441	19 478	20 703	23 328	...	Amériques
Europe	63 750	96 620	107 304	109 176	...	Europe
Asia, East and South East/Oceania	3 360	5 440	5 649	6 172	...	Asie, Est et Sud-Est et Océanie
Southern Asia	702	720	...	1 000	...	Asie du Sud
Western Asia	1 919	1 331	2 552	2 555	...	Asie occidentale
Croatia[9]	**1 324 492**	**2 649 424**	**3 834 186**	**4 111 536**	**3 443 232**	**Croatie**[9]
Americas	23 535	65 229	60 072	51 743	45 660	Amériques
Europe	1 280 865	2 562 039	3 747 869	4 026 662	3 369 698	Europe
Asia, East and South East/Oceania	3 965	7 987	10 938	15 845	14 781	Asie, Est et Sud-Est et Océanie
Region not specified	16 127	14 169	15 307	17 286	13 093	Région non spécifiée
Cuba[3]	**745 495**	**1 004 336**	**1 170 083**	**1 415 832**	**1 602 781**	**Cuba**[3]
Africa	1 868	3 036	5 178	5 919	6 269	Afrique
Americas	357 189	418 378	496 913	594 354	696 521	Amériques
Europe	375 052	562 575	648 265	793 246	874 444	Europe
Asia, East and South East/Oceania	8 308	15 287	13 775	16 368	20 060	Asie, Est et Sud-Est et Océanie
Southern Asia	1 682	3 141	4 083	4 278	3 366	Asie du Sud
Western Asia	707	1 045	1 554	1 319	1 782	Asie occidentale
Region not specified	689	874	315	348	339	Région non spécifiée
Curaçao[2 5 12]	**232 276**	**218 969**	**208 828**	**...**	**...**	**Curaçao**[2 5 12]
Americas	141 467	130 846	128 009	...	...	Amériques
Europe	89 946	87 231	79 861	...	...	Europe
Asia, East and South East/Oceania	191	239	199	...	...	Asie, Est et Sud-Est et Océanie
Region not specified	672	653	759	...	...	Région non spécifiée
Cyprus[5]	**2 100 000**	**1 950 000**	**2 088 000**	**2 222 706**	**2 434 285**	**Chypre**[5]
Africa	...	...	...	5 769	8 509	Afrique
Americas	...	...	...	26 030	30 747	Amériques
Europe	1 840 000	1 772 500	1 978 509	2 111 879	2 312 058	Europe
Asia, East and South East/Oceania	...	...	...	9 921	11 358	Asie, Est et Sud-Est et Océanie
Southern Asia	...	...	...	11 304	13 053	Asie du Sud
Western Asia	105 000	105 000	52 825	51 133	55 674	Asie occidentale
Region not specified	155 000	72 500	56 666	6 670	2 886	Région non spécifiée
Czech Republic[9]	**3 381 186**	**4 558 322**	**4 975 658**	**5 482 080**	**5 609 700**	**République tchèque**[9]
Africa	12 246	15 321	15 538	22 089	26 317	Afrique
Americas	149 222	234 065	257 313	317 618	313 151	Amériques
Europe	3 107 277	4 149 631	4 507 425	4 925 570	5 037 345	Europe
Region not specified	112 441	159 305	195 382	216 803	232 887	Région non spécifiée
Dem. Rep. of the Congo[5 25]	**35 700**	**37 000**	**30 000**	**53 139**	**...**	**Rép. dém. du Congo**[5 25]
Africa	20 000	...	...	22 223	...	Afrique
Americas	500	...	...	1 231	...	Amériques
Europe	15 000	...	...	7 975	...	Europe
Asia, East and South East/Oceania	200	...	...	1 333	...	Asie, Est et Sud-Est et Océanie
Region not specified	...	37 000	30 000	20 377	...	Région non spécifiée
Denmark[9 26]	**...**	**2 124 572**	**2 157 665**	**2 072 800**	**2 023 056**	**Danemark**[9 26]
Americas	...	93 551	95 437	100 781	101 039	Amériques
Europe	...	1 823 769	1 850 525	1 792 981	1 748 024	Europe
Asia, East and South East/Oceania	...	55 673	51 230	55 921	60 947	Asie, Est et Sud-Est et Océanie

73
Tourist/visitor arrivals by region of origin [cont.]
Arrivées de touristes/visiteurs par région de provenance [suite]

Country or area of destination and region of origin +	1995	1996	1997	1998	1999	Pays ou zone de destination et région de provenance +
Region not specified	...	151 579	160 473	123 117	113 046	Région non spécifiée
Dominica[5]	**60 471**	**63 259**	**65 446**	**65 501**	**73 500**	**Dominique**[5]
Americas	46 676	50 542	52 295	52 776	60 400	Amériques
Europe	12 940	11 898	12 215	11 710	12 600	Europe
Asia, East and South East/Oceania	54	277	806	339	...	Asie, Est et Sud-Est et Océanie
Region not specified	801	542	130	676	500	Région non spécifiée
Dominican Republic[2 5 27]	**1 775 873**	**1 948 464**	**2 184 688**	**2 334 493**	**2 664 583**	**Rép. dominicaine**[2 5 27]
Americas	...	701 555	732 535	804 941	938 057	Amériques
Europe	...	863 492	1 013 863	1 063 766	1 207 678	Europe
Asia, East and South East/Oceania	...	2 790	2 553	2 455	...	Asie, Est et Sud-Est et Océanie
Region not specified	1 775 873	380 627	435 737	463 331	518 848	Région non spécifiée
Ecuador[3 6]	**439 523**	**493 727**	**529 492**	**510 626**	**508 713**	**Equateur**[3 6]
Africa	712	1 023	1 033	980	958	Afrique
Americas	330 857	373 652	406 379	387 560	393 258	Amériques
Europe	94 592	105 452	108 473	107 845	102 498	Europe
Asia, East and South East/Oceania	13 278	13 561	13 595	14 195	11 985	Asie, Est et Sud-Est et Océanie
Region not specified	84	39	12	46	14	Région non spécifiée
Egypt[3]	**3 133 461**	**3 895 942**	**3 961 416**	**3 453 866**	**4 796 520**	**Egypte**[3]
Africa	130 485	115 808	120 145	130 671	150 552	Afrique
Americas	228 896	259 057	256 668	217 403	276 769	Amériques
Europe	1 811 000	2 342 709	2 394 414	1 956 833	3 224 097	Europe
Asia, East and South East/Oceania	186 997	251 789	230 769	130 835	211 107	Asie, Est et Sud-Est et Océanie
Southern Asia	32 467	36 539	29 549	30 193	34 682	Asie du Sud
Western Asia	741 581	828 727	893 351	985 947	897 108	Asie occidentale
Region not specified	2 035	61 313	36 520	1 984	2 205	Région non spécifiée
El Salvador[5 6]	**235 364**	**282 835**	**387 052**	**541 863**	**658 191**	**El Salvador**[5 6]
Africa	115	150	...	...	...	Afrique
Americas	205 198	244 818	343 209	498 160	596 044	Amériques
Europe	25 340	32 613	27 401	27 107	26 469	Europe
Asia, East and South East/Oceania	4 682	5 224	3 719	3 965	3 406	Asie, Est et Sud-Est et Océanie
Western Asia	29	30	...	...	...	Asie occidentale
Region not specified	...	...	12 723	12 631	32 272	Région non spécifiée
Eritrea[2 3]	**315 417**	**416 596**	**409 544**	**187 647**	**56 699**	**Erythrée**[2 3]
Africa	181 955	254 996	279 666	119 357	3 729	Afrique
Americas	2 065	2 564	2 960	2 088	783	Amériques
Europe	8 959	11 611	11 948	7 757	3 605	Europe
Asia, East and South East/Oceania	2 367	1 521	1 614	1 406	2 126	Asie, Est et Sud-Est et Océanie
Southern Asia	193	167	475	408	345	Asie du Sud
Western Asia	3 259	1 302	1 403	1 543	1 501	Asie occidentale
Region not specified	116 619	144 435	111 478	55 088	44 610	Région non spécifiée
Estonia[3]	**2 110 926**	**2 443 871**	**2 618 484**	**2 908 819**	**3 180 530**	**Estonie**[3]
Americas	30 000	55 568	44 519	78 590	65 448	Amériques
Europe	2 072 426	2 364 836	2 547 620	2 783 501	3 090 765	Europe
Asia, East and South East/Oceania	7 000	16 196	24 338	28 156	14 142	Asie, Est et Sud-Est et Océanie
Region not specified	1 500	7 271	2 007	18 572	10 175	Région non spécifiée
Ethiopia[2 5 28]	**103 336**	**108 885**	**114 732**	**90 847**	**91 859**	**Ethiopie**[2 5 28]
Africa	30 595	27 658	29 255	25 368	28 496	Afrique
Americas	13 743	14 917	15 957	15 126	16 162	Amériques
Europe	35 652	39 198	40 905	29 536	25 704	Europe
Asia, East and South East/Oceania	3 925	4 246	4 705	4 297	4 462	Asie, Est et Sud-Est et Océanie

73
Tourist/visitor arrivals by region of origin [*cont.*]
Arrivées de touristes/visiteurs par région de provenance[*suite*]

Country or area of destination and region of origin +	1995	1996	1997	1998	1999	Pays ou zone de destination et région de provenance +
Southern Asia	2 172	2 069	2 066	1 642	1 755	Asie du Sud
Western Asia	9 300	12 739	13 538	14 814	15 221	Asie occidentale
Region not specified	7 949	8 058	8 306	64	59	Région non spécifiée
Fiji[5 6]	**318 495**	**339 560**	**359 441**	**371 342**	**409 955**	**Fidji**[5 6]
Americas	50 148	50 138	57 735	61 227	75 683	Amériques
Europe	55 377	60 782	67 825	68 675	67 394	Europe
Asia, East and South East/Oceania	211 618	227 211	232 157	239 600	263 734	Asie, Est et Sud-Est et Océanie
Region not specified	1 352	1 429	1 724	1 840	3 144	Région non spécifiée
Finland[9 29]	**1 779 000**	**1 724 000**	**1 831 500**	**1 866 842**	**1 830 560**	**Finlande**[9 29]
Africa	3 916	3 796	4 032	3 583	3 495	Afrique
Americas	111 462	108 015	114 740	113 959	113 986	Amériques
Europe	1 468 101	1 422 712	1 511 328	1 539 863	1 502 238	Europe
Asia, East and South East/Oceania	120 391	116 669	123 961	110 937	119 036	Asie, Est et Sud-Est et Océanie
Southern Asia	4 548	4 408	4 682	4 756	3 995	Asie du Sud
Western Asia	1 621	1 571	1 669	1 729	1 358	Asie occidentale
Region not specified	68 961	66 829	71 088	92 015	86 452	Région non spécifiée
France[5 30]	**60 033 000**	**62 406 000**	**67 310 000**	**70 040 300**	**73 042 300**	**France**[5 30]
Africa	...	996 000	1 086 000	1 117 800	986 700	Afrique
Americas	2 184 000	4 191 000	4 433 000	4 703 700	4 609 400	Amériques
Europe	46 438 000	54 788 000	59 180 000	61 556 000	64 784 600	Europe
Asia, East and South East/Oceania	965 000	1 986 000	2 133 000	2 229 000	2 235 700	Asie, Est et Sud-Est et Océanie
Western Asia	...	262 000	288 000	246 100	234 100	Asie occidentale
Region not specified	10 446 000	183 000	190 000	187 700	191 800	Région non spécifiée
French Polynesia[5 6 31]	**172 129**	**163 774**	**180 440**	**188 933**	**210 800**	**Polynésie française**[5 6 31]
Africa	268	171	207	161	212	Afrique
Americas	59 862	54 970	53 811	62 225	80 148	Amériques
Europe	74 228	73 827	83 697	87 454	91 785	Europe
Asia, East and South East/Oceania	37 209	34 138	42 020	38 381	37 780	Asie, Est et Sud-Est et Océanie
Southern Asia	36	14	32	33	44	Asie du Sud
Western Asia	137	199	186	213	283	Asie occidentale
Region not specified	389	455	487	466	548	Région non spécifiée
Gabon[5]	**124 685**	**144 509**	**167 197**	**195 323**	**177 834**	**Gabon**[5]
Africa	21 363	28 338	33 341	47 819	40 942	Afrique
Americas	18 598	20 911	24 094	26 562	24 516	Amériques
Europe	72 325	81 819	93 699	103 294	95 725	Europe
Asia, East and South East/Oceania	992	1 115	1 285	1 416	1 312	Asie, Est et Sud-Est et Océanie
Western Asia	2 479	2 788	3 212	3 541	...	Asie occidentale
Region not specified	8 928	9 538	11 566	12 691	15 339	Région non spécifiée
Gambia[5 32]	**45 401**	**76 814**	**84 751**	**91 106**	**...**	**Gambie**[5 32]
Africa	1 205	625	1 388	1 541	...	Afrique
Americas	356	528	575	779	...	Amériques
Europe	40 365	73 176	81 501	86 998	...	Europe
Region not specified	3 475	2 485	1 287	1 788	...	Région non spécifiée
Georgia[5]	**85 492**	**116 980**	**313 290**	**317 063**	**383 817**	**Géorgie**[5]
Africa	11	57	139	140	340	Afrique
Americas	2 858	2 918	4 248	5 278	8 919	Amériques
Europe	78 362	106 564	304 547	303 572	362 548	Europe
Asia, East and South East/Oceania	54	326	1 091	1 513	4 784	Asie, Est et Sud-Est et Océanie
Southern Asia	1 327	2 071	2 522	4 832	4 872	Asie du Sud
Western Asia	2	249	685	774	1 877	Asie occidentale

73
Tourist/visitor arrivals by region of origin [*cont.*]
Arrivées de touristes/visiteurs par région de provenance[*suite*]

Country or area of destination and region of origin +	1995	1996	1997	1998	1999	Pays ou zone de destination et région de provenance +
Region not specified	2 878	4 795	58	954	477	Région non spécifiée
Germany †[9][33]	**14 846 830**	**15 204 707**	**15 836 797**	**16 511 486**	**17 115 685**	**Allemagne †[9][33]**
Africa	124 057	124 108	133 811	136 740	141 843	Afrique
Americas	1 888 840	1 942 264	2 127 253	2 351 112	2 399 923	Amériques
Europe	10 820 216	11 112 158	11 490 712	11 979 093	12 497 088	Europe
Asia, East and South East/Oceania	1 546 058	1 573 285	1 589 968	1 514 879	1 567 293	Asie, Est et Sud-Est et Océanie
Western Asia	62 112	75 854	83 888	96 820	93 341	Asie occidentale
Region not specified	405 547	377 038	411 165	432 842	416 197	Région non spécifiée
Ghana[5]	**286 000**	**304 860**	**325 433**	**347 949**	**372 651**	**Ghana[5]**
Africa	97 309	103 726	110 725	118 384	126 788	Afrique
Americas	24 019	25 603	27 331	29 222	31 297	Amériques
Europe	70 897	75 572	80 672	86 255	92 378	Europe
Asia, East and South East/Oceania	13 756	14 663	15 652	16 736	17 924	Asie, Est et Sud-Est et Océanie
Western Asia	2 169	2 312	2 468	2 639	2 827	Asie occidentale
Region not specified	77 850	82 984	88 585	94 713	101 437	Région non spécifiée
Greece[5][34]	**10 130 177**	**9 233 295**	**10 070 325**	**10 916 046**	**12 164 088**	**Grèce[5][34]**
Africa	27 237	23 706	23 072	21 134	23 995	Afrique
Americas	323 780	298 144	314 057	291 507	305 261	Amériques
Europe	9 467 111	8 541 456	9 404 889	10 333 580	11 555 502	Europe
Asia, East and South East/Oceania	261 070	314 038	280 749	224 193	225 275	Asie, Est et Sud-Est et Océanie
Southern Asia	5 960	5 319	3 730	3 848	3 809	Asie du Sud
Western Asia	45 019	50 632	43 828	41 784	50 246	Asie occidentale
Grenada[5]	**108 007**	**108 230**	**110 749**	**115 794**	**...**	**Grenade[5]**
Africa	146	144	238	337	...	Afrique
Americas	51 718	49 753	51 727	54 578	...	Amériques
Europe	36 488	37 587	37 796	38 081	...	Europe
Asia, East and South East/Oceania	655	1 039	977	1 279	...	Asie, Est et Sud-Est et Océanie
Western Asia	27	49	75	104	...	Asie occidentale
Region not specified	18 973	19 658	19 936	21 415	...	Région non spécifiée
Guadeloupe[1]	**152 896**	**146 878**	**147 010**	**133 030**	**146 201**	**Guadeloupe[1]**
Americas	11 622	11 040	16 740	7 097	8 435	Amériques
Europe	140 641	134 799	129 436	125 231	137 030	Europe
Region not specified	633	1 039	834	702	736	Région non spécifiée
Guam[5][7]	**1 361 830**	**1 362 600**	**1 381 513**	**1 137 026**	**1 161 803**	**Guam[5][7]**
Americas	56 626	35 836	44 087	42 415	41 798	Amériques
Europe	...	1 278	1 786	1 890	1 628	Europe
Asia, East and South East/Oceania	1 275 948	1 307 561	1 323 597	1 079 175	1 105 064	Asie, Est et Sud-Est et Océanie
Region not specified	29 256	17 925	12 043	13 546	13 313	Région non spécifiée
Guatemala[5]	**563 478**	**520 085**	**576 361**	**636 278**	**822 695**	**Guatemala[5]**
Americas	446 012	409 374	457 156	504 757	692 626	Amériques
Europe	103 828	96 830	104 475	115 406	113 698	Europe
Asia, East and South East/Oceania	11 917	12 029	13 746	14 739	15 084	Asie, Est et Sud-Est et Océanie
Southern Asia	222	267	...	...	...	Asie du Sud
Western Asia	364	318	261	296	345	Asie occidentale
Region not specified	1 135	1 267	723	1 080	942	Région non spécifiée
Guinea[5][35]	**...**	**...**	**17 000**	**23 000**	**27 345**	**Guinée[5][35]**
Africa	...	...	2 886	4 400	9 098	Afrique
Americas	...	...	2 300	2 434	3 638	Amériques
Europe	...	...	8 966	11 562	11 173	Europe
Asia, East and South East/Oceania	...	...	353	489	2 408	Asie, Est et Sud-Est et Océanie

73
Tourist/visitor arrivals by region of origin [*cont.*]
Arrivées de touristes/visiteurs par région de provenance[*suite*]

Country or area of destination and region of origin +	1995	1996	1997	1998	1999	Pays ou zone de destination et région de provenance +
Southern Asia	...	...	...	...	229	Asie du Sud
Western Asia	...	...	2 495	4 115	409	Asie occidentale
Region not specified	...	...	...	...	390	Région non spécifiée
Guyana [5]	**105 537**	**91 971**	**75 732**	**68 469**	**...**	**Guyana** [5]
Africa	122	137	128	63	...	Afrique
Americas	97 648	84 533	69 419	62 930	...	Amériques
Europe	6 813	5 946	5 218	4 927	...	Europe
Asia, East and South East/Oceania	604	839	543	265	...	Asie, Est et Sud-Est et Océanie
Southern Asia	340	358	268	207	...	Asie du Sud
Western Asia	10	17	11	11	...	Asie occidentale
Region not specified	...	141	145	66	...	Région non spécifiée
Haiti [5]	**145 369**	**150 147**	**148 735**	**146 837**	**143 400**	**Haïti** [5]
Americas	129 266	133 475	132 706	131 385	125 100	Amériques
Europe	14 245	14 625	14 112	13 607	11 800	Europe
Region not specified	1 858	2 047	1 917	1 845	6 500	Région non spécifiée
Honduras [3]	**270 549**	**263 317**	**306 646**	**321 149**	**370 848**	**Honduras** [3]
Africa	206	237	231	168	222	Afrique
Americas	227 485	224 926	265 600	280 437	330 822	Amériques
Europe	33 523	31 666	32 954	32 892	33 702	Europe
Asia, East and South East/Oceania	8 157	6 462	7 823	7 618	5 767	Asie, Est et Sud-Est et Océanie
Southern Asia	...	...	...	...	157	Asie du Sud
Western Asia	...	...	...	...	142	Asie occidentale
Region not specified	1 178	26	38	34	36	Région non spécifiée
Hungary [5 6 36]	**20 689 886**	**20 674 199**	**17 248 257**	**...**	**...**	**Hongrie** [5 6 36]
Africa	19 698	29 757	26 219	...	...	Afrique
Americas	298 358	329 686	372 537	...	...	Amériques
Europe	20 163 497	20 054 714	16 575 893	...	...	Europe
Asia, East and South East/Oceania	208 333	260 042	273 608	...	...	Asie, Est et Sud-Est et Océanie
Iceland [5]	**189 796**	**200 835**	**201 666**	**232 219**	**262 604**	**Islande** [5]
Africa	374	294	407	487	706	Afrique
Americas	30 411	33 759	35 757	44 414	48 568	Amériques
Europe	152 812	160 370	158 767	179 783	204 837	Europe
Asia, East and South East/Oceania	5 811	6 129	6 187	7 001	7 701	Asie, Est et Sud-Est et Océanie
Southern Asia	210	185	205	421	615	Asie du Sud
Western Asia	128	77	314	82	133	Asie occidentale
Region not specified	50	21	29	31	44	Région non spécifiée
India [5 6]	**2 123 683**	**2 287 860**	**2 374 094**	**2 358 629**	**2 481 928**	**Inde** [5 6]
Africa	84 148	85 663	98 910	106 045	129 520	Afrique
Americas	283 860	322 240	339 875	348 621	372 857	Amériques
Europe	824 680	897 010	898 929	924 753	895 200	Europe
Asia, East and South East/Oceania	289 348	335 165	358 472	343 102	368 804	Asie, Est et Sud-Est et Océanie
Southern Asia	540 209	543 967	583 706	558 772	624 945	Asie du Sud
Western Asia	100 615	96 857	93 555	77 153	90 358	Asie occidentale
Region not specified	823	6 958	647	183	244	Région non spécifiée
Indonesia [5]	**4 324 229**	**5 034 472**	**5 185 243**	**4 606 416**	**4 727 520**	**Indonésie** [5]
Africa	38 128	29 051	24 253	52 312	37 551	Afrique
Americas	201 149	244 497	208 726	201 488	186 727	Amériques
Europe	793 842	754 412	820 340	641 374	688 234	Europe
Asia, East and South East/Oceania	3 212 997	3 936 282	4 061 865	3 608 283	3 747 388	Asie, Est et Sud-Est et Océanie
Southern Asia	50 901	46 370	39 580	58 707	35 484	Asie du Sud

73
Tourist/visitor arrivals by region of origin [*cont.*]
Arrivées de touristes/visiteurs par région de provenance[*suite*]

Country or area of destination and region of origin +	1995	1996	1997	1998	1999	Pays ou zone de destination et région de provenance +
Western Asia	27 212	23 860	30 479	44 252	32 136	Asie occidentale
Iran (Islamic Rep. of)[5]	**452 059**	**567 334**	**739 711**	**1 007 597**	**1 320 690**	**Iran (Rép. islamique d')[5]**
Africa	1 578	1 966	2 596	2 914	3 410	Afrique
Americas	2 794	3 350	2 640	2 986	1 825	Amériques
Europe	215 157	260 958	449 115	631 020	735 202	Europe
Asia, East and South East/Oceania	16 051	17 063	10 847	17 800	20 805	Asie, Est et Sud-Est et Océanie
Southern Asia	154 549	208 752	194 409	255 776	298 954	Asie du Sud
Western Asia	61 790	75 200	80 104	97 101	113 494	Asie occidentale
Region not specified	140	45	...	...	147 000	Région non spécifiée
Iraq[3]	**60 540**	**51 330**	**...**	**...**	**...**	**Iraq[3]**
Africa	756	777	...	...	...	Afrique
Americas	1 140	761	...	...	...	Amériques
Europe	3 869	3 052	...	...	...	Europe
Asia, East and South East/Oceania	2 051	1 541	...	...	...	Asie, Est et Sud-Est et Océanie
Southern Asia	11 049	9 087	...	...	...	Asie du Sud
Western Asia	39 910	34 812	...	...	...	Asie occidentale
Region not specified	1 765	1 300	...	...	...	Région non spécifiée
Ireland[5]	**4 821 000**	**5 282 000**	**5 587 000**	**6 064 000**	**...**	**Irlande[5]**
Americas	641 000	729 000	778 000	858 000	...	Amériques
Europe	3 977 000	4 368 000	4 600 000	4 985 000	...	Europe
Asia, East and South East/Oceania	119 000	121 000	143 000	150 000	...	Asie, Est et Sud-Est et Océanie
Region not specified	84 000	64 000	66 000	71 000	...	Région non spécifiée
Israel[5][6]	**2 215 285**	**2 100 051**	**2 010 242**	**1 941 620**	**2 312 411**	**Israël[5][6]**
Africa	57 302	42 172	42 837	37 085	36 173	Afrique
Americas	581 783	558 964	548 385	571 409	645 040	Amériques
Europe	1 289 425	1 246 091	1 178 934	1 117 249	1 340 682	Europe
Asia, East and South East/Oceania	101 926	111 002	107 478	66 303	98 734	Asie, Est et Sud-Est et Océanie
Southern Asia	9 931	12 834	14 480	12 715	17 152	Asie du Sud
Western Asia	151 710	106 039	94 094	100 507	111 684	Asie occidentale
Region not specified	23 208	22 949	24 034	36 352	62 946	Région non spécifiée
Italy[3][37]	**55 706 000**	**57 249 184**	**57 998 188**	**58 499 261**	**59 521 444**	**Italie[3][37]**
Africa	95 774	168 162	241 635	181 150	155 103	Afrique
Americas	2 403 313	2 034 016	2 645 989	2 474 646	2 004 432	Amériques
Europe	51 111 688	52 905 181	52 920 478	54 049 369	55 840 818	Europe
Asia, East and South East/Oceania	1 100 246	1 973 565	2 018 245	1 626 810	1 346 538	Asie, Est et Sud-Est et Océanie
Southern Asia	...	71 851	72 052	73 450	74 396	Asie du Sud
Western Asia	227 160	96 176	99 789	93 751	100 157	Asie occidentale
Region not specified	767 819	233	...	85	...	Région non spécifiée
Jamaica[2][5][12]	**1 147 001**	**1 162 449**	**1 192 194**	**1 225 287**	**1 248 397**	**Jamaïque[2][5][12]**
Africa	1 132	1 063	1 023	1 026	1 361	Afrique
Americas	920 391	925 859	959 027	995 137	1 024 015	Amériques
Europe	197 544	209 050	211 551	213 893	209 576	Europe
Asia, East and South East/Oceania	25 194	25 266	19 621	14 144	12 248	Asie, Est et Sud-Est et Océanie
Southern Asia	384	484	700	595	751	Asie du Sud
Western Asia	...	...	63	423	367	Asie occidentale
Region not specified	2 356	727	209	69	79	Région non spécifiée
Japan[5][6]	**3 345 274**	**3 837 113**	**4 218 208**	**4 106 057**	**4 437 863**	**Japon[5][6]**
Africa	11 534	10 914	11 928	12 556	12 939	Afrique
Americas	695 385	749 000	780 711	828 240	852 751	Amériques
Europe	442 559	484 394	545 783	577 278	580 135	Europe

73
Tourist/visitor arrivals by region of origin [*cont.*]
Arrivées de touristes/visiteurs par région de provenance[*suite*]

Country or area of destination and region of origin +	1995	1996	1997	1998	1999	Pays ou zone de destination et région de provenance +
Asia, East and South East/Oceania	2 148 885	2 540 221	2 817 089	2 622 286	2 925 323	Asie, Est et Sud-Est et Océanie
Southern Asia	42 392	47 123	55 525	57 662	60 114	Asie du Sud
Western Asia	2 642	2 659	2 841	3 095	3 317	Asie occidentale
Region not specified	1 877	2 802	4 331	4 940	3 284	Région non spécifiée
Jordan[5]	**1 073 549**	**1 102 752**	**1 127 028**	**1 256 428**	**1 357 822**	**Jordanie**[5]
Africa	2 300	2 313	2 338	2 750	2 811	Afrique
Americas	103 346	107 960	107 676	108 612	123 525	Amériques
Europe	355 575	373 016	365 036	338 706	418 285	Europe
Asia, East and South East/Oceania	45 767	46 806	47 877	33 933	51 603	Asie, Est et Sud-Est et Océanie
Western Asia	566 561	572 657	604 101	772 427	761 598	Asie occidentale
Kenya[3 6 38]	**973 600**	**1 003 000**	**1 000 599**	**894 300**	...	**Kenya**[3 6 38]
Africa	188 170	207 100	272 674	251 243	...	Afrique
Americas	58 770	59 200	85 161	79 864	...	Amériques
Europe	386 860	393 400	573 672	504 204	...	Europe
Asia, East and South East/Oceania	52 260	37 100	44 313	38 145	...	Asie, Est et Sud-Est et Océanie
Southern Asia	...	12 100	24 026	20 844	...	Asie du Sud
Region not specified	287 540	294 100	753	...	...	Région non spécifiée
Kiribati[5 39]	**3 153**	**3 406**	**5 007**	...	...	**Kiribati**[5 39]
Americas	358	278	1 163	...	...	Amériques
Europe	135	248	314	...	...	Europe
Asia, East and South East/Oceania	2 406	2 500	3 317	...	...	Asie, Est et Sud-Est et Océanie
Region not specified	254	380	213	...	...	Région non spécifiée
Korea, Republic of[3 40]	**3 753 197**	**3 683 779**	**3 908 140**	**4 250 176**	**4 659 785**	**Corée, République de**[3 40]
Africa	7 519	8 639	10 681	11 368	13 986	Afrique
Americas	417 087	464 509	493 942	471 317	463 937	Amériques
Europe	426 926	444 691	436 078	401 309	408 481	Europe
Asia, East and South East/Oceania	2 495 443	2 381 766	2 582 236	2 977 078	3 380 795	Asie, Est et Sud-Est et Océanie
Southern Asia	61 815	74 352	71 251	65 727	81 044	Asie du Sud
Western Asia	8 749	7 456	6 907	9 382	10 515	Asie occidentale
Region not specified	335 658	302 366	307 045	313 995	301 027	Région non spécifiée
Kuwait[3]	**1 443 069**	**1 555 285**	**1 637 805**	**1 762 641**	**1 883 633**	**Koweït**[3]
Africa	10 418	10 797	13 885	18 648	17 679	Afrique
Americas	23 159	26 311	31 807	33 428	39 191	Amériques
Europe	52 342	58 383	66 155	65 998	73 638	Europe
Asia, East and South East/Oceania	50 561	56 670	54 516	65 908	81 737	Asie, Est et Sud-Est et Océanie
Southern Asia	417 940	459 051	471 276	513 475	537 496	Asie du Sud
Western Asia	879 387	930 385	983 464	1 045 852	1 117 588	Asie occidentale
Region not specified	9 262	13 688	16 702	19 332	16 304	Région non spécifiée
Kyrgyzstan[5]	**36 423**	**41 650**	**87 386**	**59 363**	**68 863**	**Kirghizistan**[5]
Americas	...	...	...	1 386	3 224	Amériques
Europe	25 710	28 625	72 202	46 287	50 352	Europe
Asia, East and South East/Oceania	...	...	...	6 791	8 786	Asie, Est et Sud-Est et Océanie
Southern Asia	...	...	...	2 656	2 930	Asie du Sud
Western Asia	...	...	...	90	160	Asie occidentale
Region not specified	10 713	13 025	15 184	2 153	3 411	Région non spécifiée
Lao People's Dem. Rep.[3]	**345 460**	**403 000**	**463 200**	**500 200**	**614 278**	**Rép. dém. pop. lao**[3]
Americas	11 019	14 102	18 213	25 326	31 780	Amériques
Europe	20 635	30 582	39 096	52 749	70 755	Europe
Asia, East and South East/Oceania	300 955	337 437	397 253	410 888	503 324	Asie, Est et Sud-Est et Océanie
Southern Asia	12 515	20 255	6 528	10 308	7 379	Asie du Sud

73
Tourist/visitor arrivals by region of origin [*cont.*]
Arrivées de touristes/visiteurs par région de provenance[*suite*]

Country or area of destination and region of origin +	1995	1996	1997	1998	1999	Pays ou zone de destination et région de provenance +
Region not specified	336	624	2 110	929	1 040	Région non spécifiée
Latvia[9]	**184 783**	**188 269**	**219 939**	**238 835**	**240 799**	**Lettonie**[9]
Africa	...	...	68	144	77	Afrique
Americas	8 953	9 812	9 312	10 762	10 991	Amériques
Europe	160 919	165 829	199 147	214 066	217 050	Europe
Asia, East and South East/Oceania	1 691	2 707	4 010	4 097	5 928	Asie, Est et Sud-Est et Océanie
Southern Asia	103	84	214	286	793	Asie du Sud
Western Asia	18	46	79	106	157	Asie occidentale
Region not specified	13 099	9 791	7 109	9 374	5 803	Région non spécifiée
Lebanon[5 41]	**449 809**	**424 000**	**557 568**	**630 781**	**673 261**	**Liban**[5 41]
Africa	13 232	13 527	19 380	23 497	27 887	Afrique
Americas	50 568	46 917	59 404	68 321	84 516	Amériques
Europe	151 982	142 100	173 887	195 950	223 945	Europe
Asia, East and South East/Oceania	28 942	33 604	40 683	40 962	46 986	Asie, Est et Sud-Est et Océanie
Southern Asia	20 832	20 213	26 598	35 273	36 004	Asie du Sud
Western Asia	145 666	138 891	207 866	235 992	253 423	Asie occidentale
Region not specified	38 587	28 748	29 750	30 786	500	Région non spécifiée
Lesotho[3]	**208 906**	**311 802**	**323 868**	**289 819**	**...**	**Lesotho**[3]
Africa	202 007	304 368	313 323	285 734	...	Afrique
Americas	1 120	1 242	2 861	794	...	Amériques
Europe	4 706	4 708	5 682	2 311	...	Europe
Asia, East and South East/Oceania	1 073	1 484	2 002	980	...	Asie, Est et Sud-Est et Océanie
Libyan Arab Jamah.[3]	**1 831 884**	**1 276 000**	**913 251**	**850 292**	**858 452**	**Jamah. arabe libyenne**[3]
Africa	967 704	829 000	571 868	461 533	432 944	Afrique
Americas	1 821	3 030	861	456	307	Amériques
Europe	36 812	54 733	28 140	22 649	24 630	Europe
Asia, East and South East/Oceania	11 052	18 500	3 177	3 088	1 928	Asie, Est et Sud-Est et Océanie
Southern Asia	4 495	8 000	2 100	1 271	446	Asie du Sud
Western Asia	810 000	361 938	307 105	361 295	386 605	Asie occidentale
Region not specified	...	799	...	...	11 592	Région non spécifiée
Liechtenstein[1]	**59 447**	**56 168**	**57 077**	**59 228**	**59 502**	**Liechtenstein**[1]
Africa	161	209	155	173	176	Afrique
Americas	4 697	4 504	5 252	4 879	4 861	Amériques
Europe	52 183	49 031	49 237	52 319	52 554	Europe
Asia, East and South East/Oceania	2 074	1 733	2 433	1 857	1 911	Asie, Est et Sud-Est et Océanie
Region not specified	332	691	...	...	...	Région non spécifiée
Lithuania[9 42]	**210 781**	**255 301**	**288 028**	**306 228**	**293 120**	**Lituanie**[9 42]
Africa	269	170	234	208	166	Afrique
Americas	11 283	11 344	12 407	14 918	15 194	Amériques
Europe	195 181	237 682	267 822	284 489	270 082	Europe
Asia, East and South East/Oceania	4 048	6 105	7 565	6 613	7 678	Asie, Est et Sud-Est et Océanie
Luxembourg[9]	**767 519**	**723 965**	**771 153**	**789 176**	**833 161**	**Luxembourg**[9]
Americas	33 249	30 463	35 681	31 000	32 126	Amériques
Europe	713 156	671 456	712 614	721 519	765 213	Europe
Region not specified	21 114	22 046	22 858	36 657	35 822	Région non spécifiée
Madagascar[5]	**74 619**	**82 681**	**100 762**	**121 207**	**138 253**	**Madagascar**[5]
Africa	8 331	9 303	5 844	15 515	20 461	Afrique
Americas	5 235	5 606	2 015	2 424	6 913	Amériques
Europe	57 386	63 462	64 488	82 421	95 395	Europe
Asia, East and South East/Oceania	3 667	4 205	1 008	1 454	2 489	Asie, Est et Sud-Est et Océanie

73
Tourist/visitor arrivals by region of origin [cont.]
Arrivées de touristes/visiteurs par région de provenance [suite]

Country or area of destination and region of origin +	1995	1996	1997	1998	1999	Pays ou zone de destination et région de provenance +
Region not specified	...	105	27 407	19 393	12 995	Région non spécifiée
Malawi[5 36]	**192 169**	**193 628**	**207 259**	**219 570**	**254 352**	**Malawi**[5 36]
Africa	139 602	142 840	152 876	161 955	187 610	Afrique
Americas	6 397	9 681	10 362	10 979	12 718	Amériques
Europe	36 120	30 980	33 161	35 131	40 696	Europe
Asia, East and South East/Oceania	7 686	7 745	8 290	8 783	10 174	Asie, Est et Sud-Est et Océanie
Southern Asia	2 172	2 188	2 342	2 481	2 874	Asie du Sud
Region not specified	192	194	228	241	280	Région non spécifiée
Malaysia[5 43]	**7 468 749**	**7 138 452**	**6 210 921**	**5 550 748**	**7 931 149**	**Malaisie**[5 43]
Africa	29 171	30 039	23 502	25 519	29 863	Afrique
Americas	136 405	145 991	137 164	121 569	122 079	Amériques
Europe	404 285	407 537	386 790	367 660	308 713	Europe
Asia, East and South East/Oceania	6 660 317	6 335 909	5 449 937	4 696 660	6 826 835	Asie, Est et Sud-Est et Océanie
Southern Asia	63 673	62 985	53 644	56 117	68 992	Asie du Sud
Western Asia	28 923	31 371	16 460	19 571	19 128	Asie occidentale
Region not specified	145 975	124 620	143 424	263 652	555 539	Région non spécifiée
Maldives[5 12]	**314 869**	**338 733**	**365 563**	**395 725**	**429 666**	**Maldives**[5 12]
Africa	8 064	7 584	7 962	7 168	1 846	Afrique
Americas	3 624	4 125	6 101	6 119	6 082	Amériques
Europe	227 375	252 781	273 066	304 905	340 469	Europe
Asia, East and South East/Oceania	48 764	52 634	60 644	56 983	60 598	Asie, Est et Sud-Est et Océanie
Southern Asia	26 207	19 782	16 443	19 284	19 393	Asie du Sud
Western Asia	830	1 819	1 347	1 266	1 278	Asie occidentale
Region not specified	5	8	...	...	...	Région non spécifiée
Mali[1]	**42 897**	**53 893**	**65 649**	**83 000**	**87 000**	**Mali**[1]
Africa	12 026	11 541	14 321	18 000	17 000	Afrique
Americas	4 689	5 814	6 841	8 000	8 400	Amériques
Europe	22 155	31 137	38 278	49 000	51 450	Europe
Asia, East and South East/Oceania	728	1 467	1 621	2 000	2 100	Asie, Est et Sud-Est et Océanie
Western Asia	176	171	321	400	420	Asie occidentale
Region not specified	3 123	3 763	4 267	5 600	7 630	Région non spécifiée
Malta[5 36]	**1 115 971**	**1 053 788**	**1 111 161**	**1 182 240**	**1 214 230**	**Malte**[5 36]
Africa	4 969	4 383	5 730	6 342	7 387	Afrique
Americas	16 503	17 662	21 197	25 258	25 951	Amériques
Europe	1 033 734	952 940	1 023 222	1 087 709	1 107 725	Europe
Asia, East and South East/Oceania	10 583	11 952	13 930	15 706	17 620	Asie, Est et Sud-Est et Océanie
Southern Asia	1 307	1 336	1 250	1 987	2 054	Asie du Sud
Western Asia	39 485	53 328	42 117	41 067	48 480	Asie occidentale
Region not specified	9 390	12 187	3 715	4 171	5 013	Région non spécifiée
Marshall Islands[5 12]	**5 504**	**6 229**	**6 354**	**6 374**	**4 622**	**Iles Marshall**[5 12]
Americas	1 770	2 055	2 471	2 388	2 064	Amériques
Europe	299	367	354	229	220	Europe
Asia, East and South East/Oceania	3 262	3 664	3 411	3 497	2 234	Asie, Est et Sud-Est et Océanie
Region not specified	173	143	118	260	104	Région non spécifiée
Martinique[5]	**457 226**	**476 880**	**513 229**	**548 767**	**564 304**	**Martinique**[5]
Americas	73 534	66 226	77 759	77 270	85 291	Amériques
Europe	378 663	406 423	431 096	467 263	474 475	Europe
Region not specified	5 029	4 231	4 374	4 234	4 538	Région non spécifiée
Mauritius[5]	**422 463**	**486 867**	**536 125**	**558 195**	**578 085**	**Maurice**[5]
Africa	143 586	163 435	164 082	163 024	156 228	Afrique

73
Tourist/visitor arrivals by region of origin [*cont.*]
Arrivées de touristes/visiteurs par région de provenance[*suite*]

Country or area of destination and region of origin +	1995	1996	1997	1998	1999	Pays ou zone de destination et région de provenance +
Americas	3 617	4 265	5 509	5 842	5 820	Amériques
Europe	244 070	281 817	326 522	352 688	379 051	Europe
Asia, East and South East/Oceania	19 063	23 887	25 283	22 677	21 531	Asie, Est et Sud-Est et Océanie
Southern Asia	11 225	13 075	13 998	13 395	14 694	Asie du Sud
Western Asia	...	...	682	509	527	Asie occidentale
Region not specified	902	388	49	60	234	Région non spécifiée
Mexico[2 5]	**20 241 000**	**21 404 674**	**19 350 900**	**19 392 005**	**19 042 726**	**Mexique**[2 5]
Americas	19 862 286	21 019 950	18 940 859	18 550 480	18 182 563	Amériques
Europe	338 620	340 593	346 530	476 654	562 790	Europe
Region not specified	40 094	44 131	63 511	364 871	297 373	Région non spécifiée
Monaco[1]	**232 500**	**226 421**	**258 604**	**278 474**	**278 448**	**Monaco**[1]
Africa	398	466	576	555	2 326	Afrique
Americas	32 823	31 309	45 817	42 929	41 660	Amériques
Europe	166 881	159 163	172 201	194 000	202 394	Europe
Asia, East and South East/Oceania	12 622	12 051	14 202	12 061	11 689	Asie, Est et Sud-Est et Océanie
Western Asia	2 796	3 516	3 660	4 816	3 717	Asie occidentale
Region not specified	16 980	19 916	22 148	24 113	16 662	Région non spécifiée
Mongolia[5]	**108 434**	**70 853**	**82 084**	**197 424**	**158 734**	**Mongolie**[5]
Africa	...	...	81	72	115	Afrique
Americas	4 322	3 834	5 129	5 442	6 059	Amériques
Europe	42 187	21 800	25 956	79 818	72 430	Europe
Asia, East and South East/Oceania	61 116	44 733	50 328	111 493	79 421	Asie, Est et Sud-Est et Océanie
Southern Asia	680	464	526	490	584	Asie du Sud
Western Asia	129	22	64	109	115	Asie occidentale
Region not specified	...	...	...	...	10	Région non spécifiée
Montserrat[5 6 12]	**17 675**	**8 703**	**5 132**	**7 467**	**9 900**	**Montserrat**[5 6 12]
Americas	14 250	6 771	3 770	5 560	6 900	Amériques
Europe	2 749	1 631	1 085	1 496	2 300	Europe
Region not specified	676	301	277	411	700	Région non spécifiée
Morocco[2 5]	**2 601 641**	**2 693 338**	**3 071 668**	**3 242 105**	**3 816 641**	**Maroc**[2 5]
Africa	66 258	75 658	78 327	80 687	87 888	Afrique
Americas	117 453	119 534	129 530	141 676	178 642	Amériques
Europe	1 243 178	1 337 213	1 507 819	1 655 935	1 875 803	Europe
Asia, East and South East/Oceania	31 250	32 480	36 041	38 992	45 370	Asie, Est et Sud-Est et Océanie
Southern Asia	2 793	3 350	3 490	4 013	5 256	Asie du Sud
Western Asia	60 979	62 910	66 022	76 795	78 266	Asie occidentale
Region not specified	1 079 730	1 062 193	1 250 439	1 244 007	1 545 416	Région non spécifiée
Myanmar[5 44]	**117 000**	**172 000**	**189 000**	**201 000**	**198 210**	**Myanmar**[5 44]
Africa	...	...	...	...	316	Afrique
Americas	9 103	13 654	14 747	13 304	12 748	Amériques
Europe	33 880	50 818	54 859	51 659	51 627	Europe
Asia, East and South East/Oceania	65 586	98 377	113 927	119 721	126 136	Asie, Est et Sud-Est et Océanie
Southern Asia	1 204	1 805	1 948	10 816	5 967	Asie du Sud
Western Asia	...	...	...	...	1 416	Asie occidentale
Region not specified	7 227	7 346	3 519	5 500	...	Région non spécifiée
Namibia[5]	...	**461 310**	**502 012**	**559 674**	...	**Namibie**[5]
Africa	...	351 398	383 515	429 532	...	Afrique
Americas	...	8 452	9 181	10 074	...	Amériques
Europe	...	93 946	101 162	111 113	...	Europe
Region not specified	...	7 514	8 154	8 955	...	Région non spécifiée

73
Tourist/visitor arrivals by region of origin [cont.]
Arrivées de touristes/visiteurs par région de provenance [suite]

Country or area of destination and region of origin +	1995	1996	1997	1998	1999	Pays ou zone de destination et région de provenance +
Nepal[5]	**363 395**	**393 613**	**421 857**	**463 684**	**491 504**	**Népal**[5]
Africa	1 073	1 775	1 645	1 795	1 857	Afrique
Americas	32 751	34 865	40 855	48 975	53 006	Amériques
Europe	142 958	145 450	151 587	165 349	179 048	Europe
Asia, East and South East/Oceania	59 316	73 319	79 464	82 252	89 754	Asie, Est et Sud-Est et Océanie
Southern Asia	127 271	138 174	148 289	165 305	167 834	Asie du Sud
Region not specified	26	30	17	8	5	Région non spécifiée
Netherlands[9]	**6 573 700**	**6 580 300**	**7 834 000**	**9 322 000**	**9 881 000**	**Pays-Bas**[9]
Africa	49 800	55 000	70 000	80 000	107 000	Afrique
Americas	720 500	664 200	900 000	1 144 000	1 162 000	Amériques
Europe	5 307 200	5 340 000	6 089 000	7 381 000	7 912 000	Europe
Asia, East and South East/Oceania	496 200	521 100	775 000	717 000	700 000	Asie, Est et Sud-Est et Océanie
New Caledonia[2 5]	**86 256**	**91 121**	**105 137**	**103 835**	**99 735**	**Nouvelle-Calédonie**[2 5]
Africa	493	472	480	511	597	Afrique
Americas	1 193	1 355	1 311	1 529	1 738	Amériques
Europe	26 618	29 823	32 608	31 421	32 111	Europe
Asia, East and South East/Oceania	57 942	59 080	70 475	70 005	64 749	Asie, Est et Sud-Est et Océanie
Region not specified	10	391	263	369	540	Région non spécifiée
New Zealand[2 3]	**1 408 795**	**1 528 720**	**1 497 183**	**1 484 512**	**1 607 478**	**Nouvelle-Zélande**[2 3]
Africa	11 060	13 686	15 529	17 499	14 896	Afrique
Americas	190 885	187 490	185 257	205 738	228 612	Amériques
Europe	258 136	270 179	280 766	294 904	317 314	Europe
Asia, East and South East/Oceania	905 166	982 665	941 659	887 317	975 357	Asie, Est et Sud-Est et Océanie
Southern Asia	4 815	5 838	6 255	6 751	6 602	Asie du Sud
Western Asia	3 754	3 894	3 535	3 691	...	Asie occidentale
Region not specified	34 979	64 968	64 182	68 612	64 697	Région non spécifiée
Nicaragua[5]	**281 254**	**302 694**	**358 439**	**405 702**	**468 159**	**Nicaragua**[5]
Africa	110	106	121	155	192	Afrique
Americas	247 452	266 880	322 241	365 011	424 072	Amériques
Europe	29 263	29 761	30 315	33 639	35 521	Europe
Asia, East and South East/Oceania	3 842	5 474	5 318	6 170	7 763	Asie, Est et Sud-Est et Océanie
Southern Asia	502	410	359	647	461	Asie du Sud
Western Asia	85	63	85	80	97	Asie occidentale
Region not specified	...	...	...	...	53	Région non spécifiée
Niger[5 45]	**35 132**	**37 561**	**44 018**	**41 961**	**42 826**	**Niger**[5 45]
Africa	7 151	7 388	7 500	8 000	26 618	Afrique
Americas	1 701	1 923	2 030	3 000	1 383	Amériques
Europe	6 775	7 104	8 000	7 902	9 380	Europe
Asia, East and South East/Oceania	472	508	500	1 000	706	Asie, Est et Sud-Est et Océanie
Western Asia	...	...	500	...	...	Asie occidentale
Region not specified	19 033	20 638	25 488	22 059	4 739	Région non spécifiée
Nigeria[3]	**1 030 739**	**1 230 155**	**...**	**...**	**...**	**Nigéria**[3]
Africa	737 762	866 709	...	...	...	Afrique
Americas	33 198	48 018	...	...	...	Amériques
Europe	157 055	189 927	...	...	...	Europe
Asia, East and South East/Oceania	66 785	75 855	...	...	...	Asie, Est et Sud-Est et Océanie
Southern Asia	21 186	28 016	...	...	...	Asie du Sud
Western Asia	13 939	20 635	...	...	...	Asie occidentale
Region not specified	814	995	...	...	...	Région non spécifiée
Niue[5 12 46]	**2 161**	**1 522**	**1 820**	**1 736**	**2 252**	**Nioué**[5 12 46]

73
Tourist/visitor arrivals by region of origin [*cont.*]
Arrivées de touristes/visiteurs par région de provenance[*suite*]

Country or area of destination and region of origin +	1995	1996	1997	1998	1999	Pays ou zone de destination et région de provenance +
Africa	...	...	...	...	15	Afrique
Americas	32	55	98	86	247	Amériques
Europe	57	74	81	78	226	Europe
Asia, East and South East/Oceania	2 048	1 360	1 623	1 552	1 617	Asie, Est et Sud-Est et Océanie
Western Asia	...	...	...	...	1	Asie occidentale
Region not specified	24	33	18	20	146	Région non spécifiée
Northern Mariana Islands[3]	**676 161**	**736 117**	**694 888**	**490 165**	**501 788**	**Iles Mariannes du Nord**[3]
Africa	37	22	39	34	15	Afrique
Americas	99 373	84 856	76 217	61 491	49 892	Amériques
Europe	1 840	2 000	2 860	2 852	2 374	Europe
Asia, East and South East/Oceania	574 376	648 188	614 558	425 178	449 405	Asie, Est et Sud-Est et Océanie
Southern Asia	427	306	187	141	...	Asie du Sud
Western Asia	28	32	63	100	74	Asie occidentale
Region not specified	80	713	964	369	28	Région non spécifiée
Norway[9]	...	...	...	**4 538 221**	**4 481 400**	**Norvège**[9]
Africa	...	...	...	9 316	7 763	Afrique
Americas	...	...	...	277 624	302 965	Amériques
Europe	...	...	...	3 960 482	3 846 408	Europe
Asia, East and South East/Oceania	...	...	...	187 482	209 961	Asie, Est et Sud-Est et Océanie
Region not specified	...	...	...	103 317	114 303	Région non spécifiée
Oman[1]	**279 000**	**349 000**	**375 000**	**423 000**	**502 000**	**Oman**[1]
Africa	15 000	22 000	11 000	7 000	19 000	Afrique
Americas	18 000	25 000	23 000	32 000	58 000	Amériques
Europe	99 000	110 000	159 000	176 000	172 000	Europe
Asia, East and South East/Oceania	45 000	65 000	70 000	87 000	130 000	Asie, Est et Sud-Est et Océanie
Western Asia	40 000	58 000	74 000	62 000	115 000	Asie occidentale
Region not specified	62 000	69 000	38 000	59 000	8 000	Région non spécifiée
Pakistan[5]	**378 400**	**368 662**	**374 800**	**428 781**	**432 217**	**Pakistan**[5]
Africa	10 536	9 776	8 261	8 330	9 694	Afrique
Americas	57 789	54 070	54 169	61 073	60 676	Amériques
Europe	165 729	152 998	153 788	183 855	189 979	Europe
Asia, East and South East/Oceania	40 531	43 987	41 935	48 798	44 484	Asie, Est et Sud-Est et Océanie
Southern Asia	83 660	87 502	97 000	107 302	107 214	Asie du Sud
Western Asia	20 066	20 274	19 587	19 375	19 792	Asie occidentale
Region not specified	89	55	60	48	378	Région non spécifiée
Palau[5 47]	**53 229**	**69 330**	**73 719**	**64 194**	**55 493**	**Palaos**[5 47]
Americas	9 846	9 955	10 481	12 487	5 587	Amériques
Europe	2 508	2 870	1 767	2 044	1 764	Europe
Asia, East and South East/Oceania	40 434	55 897	59 909	45 667	46 831	Asie, Est et Sud-Est et Océanie
Region not specified	441	608	1 562	3 996	1 311	Région non spécifiée
Panama[3 48]	**359 575**	**376 672**	**418 846**	**422 228**	**445 957**	**Panama**[3 48]
Africa	363	215	276	216	228	Afrique
Americas	316 519	331 908	370 752	377 594	398 852	Amériques
Europe	31 822	29 985	32 415	30 934	33 729	Europe
Asia, East and South East/Oceania	10 809	14 504	15 338	13 426	13 098	Asie, Est et Sud-Est et Océanie
Western Asia	62	60	65	58	50	Asie occidentale
Papua New Guinea[5]	**42 328**	**61 385**	**66 143**	**67 465**	**67 357**	**Papouasie-Nvl-Guinée**[5]
Africa	...	...	...	310	320	Afrique
Americas	5 469	6 192	6 878	7 013	6 542	Amériques
Europe	6 565	5 770	5 984	6 646	7 282	Europe

73
Tourist/visitor arrivals by region of origin [*cont.*]
Arrivées de touristes/visiteurs par région de provenance [*suite*]

Country or area of destination and region of origin +	1995	1996	1997	1998	1999	Pays ou zone de destination et région de provenance +
Asia, East and South East/Oceania	29 894	44 391	53 019	53 316	53 055	Asie, Est et Sud-Est et Océanie
Southern Asia	...	...	...	162	142	Asie du Sud
Region not specified	400	5 032	262	18	16	Région non spécifiée
Paraguay[5 6 10]	**437 653**	**425 561**	**395 058**	**349 592**	**269 021**	**Paraguay**[5 6 10]
Africa	...	...	1 541	723	289	Afrique
Americas	354 019	349 283	316 244	282 668	213 662	Amériques
Europe	47 704	40 226	41 995	33 280	32 200	Europe
Asia, East and South East/Oceania	14 179	7 929	11 219	3 852	4 260	Asie, Est et Sud-Est et Océanie
Region not specified	21 751	28 123	24 059	29 069	18 610	Région non spécifiée
Peru[5]	**479 231**	**584 388**	**649 287**	**723 668**	**...**	**Pérou**[5]
Africa	862	1 088	1 435	1 541	...	Afrique
Americas	300 485	372 079	436 479	483 106	...	Amériques
Europe	140 479	166 648	172 204	199 495	...	Europe
Asia, East and South East/Oceania	35 745	42 643	36 940	36 054	...	Asie, Est et Sud-Est et Océanie
Southern Asia	1 306	1 626	1 888	2 566	...	Asie du Sud
Western Asia	199	248	271	349	...	Asie occidentale
Region not specified	155	56	70	557	...	Région non spécifiée
Philippines[2 5]	**1 760 063**	**2 049 367**	**2 222 523**	**2 149 357**	**2 170 514**	**Philippines**[2 5]
Africa	1 567	1 802	1 888	2 054	1 824	Afrique
Americas	391 309	434 828	496 213	540 596	534 480	Amériques
Europe	231 902	272 987	294 679	310 762	293 722	Europe
Asia, East and South East/Oceania	929 047	1 133 893	1 232 487	1 050 917	1 076 862	Asie, Est et Sud-Est et Océanie
Southern Asia	22 068	25 861	27 384	30 954	25 920	Asie du Sud
Western Asia	17 539	18 406	15 104	16 123	15 868	Asie occidentale
Region not specified	166 631	161 590	154 768	197 951	221 838	Région non spécifiée
Poland[3]	**82 243 621**	**87 438 583**	**87 817 369**	**88 592 355**	**89 117 875**	**Pologne**[3]
Africa	5 465	5 543	5 558	7 988	8 387	Afrique
Americas	235 273	251 164	276 272	307 205	297 944	Amériques
Europe	81 875 078	87 022 729	87 369 361	88 145 239	88 677 996	Europe
Asia, East and South East/Oceania	56 514	67 373	74 777	71 173	77 679	Asie, Est et Sud-Est et Océanie
Southern Asia	11 845	11 546	10 558	9 234	9 198	Asie du Sud
Western Asia	8 356	8 147	8 121	7 123	6 430	Asie occidentale
Region not specified	51 090	72 081	72 722	44 393	40 241	Région non spécifiée
Portugal[5 6 49]	**9 511 490**	**9 730 200**	**10 172 423**	**11 294 973**	**11 631 996**	**Portugal**[5 6 49]
Americas	350 077	337 004	373 915	408 580	417 122	Amériques
Europe	8 888 759	9 150 847	9 550 552	10 588 648	10 869 577	Europe
Asia, East and South East/Oceania	35 439	37 502	37 769	44 209	40 570	Asie, Est et Sud-Est et Océanie
Region not specified	237 215	204 847	210 187	253 536	304 727	Région non spécifiée
Puerto Rico[5 12]	**3 130 662**	**3 065 056**	**3 241 774**	**3 396 115**	**3 024 088**	**Porto Rico**[5 12]
Americas	2 278 344	2 237 540	2 474 433	2 569 596	2 284 058	Amériques
Region not specified	852 318	827 516	767 341	826 519	740 030	Région non spécifiée
Republic of Moldova[3 50]	**32 821**	**28 900**	**21 169**	**19 896**	**14 088**	**République de Moldova**[3 50]
Africa	5	23	13	42	10	Afrique
Americas	678	773	1 050	894	910	Amériques
Europe	31 481	27 642	19 692	18 634	12 832	Europe
Asia, East and South East/Oceania	305	220	277	187	224	Asie, Est et Sud-Est et Océanie
Southern Asia	178	52	48	75	23	Asie du Sud
Western Asia	174	190	89	64	89	Asie occidentale
Réunion[5]	**304 000**	**346 898**	**370 255**	**391 000**	**394 000**	**Réunion**[5]
Africa	40 119	40 073	40 626	43 000	53 000	Afrique

73
Tourist/visitor arrivals by region of origin [cont.]
Arrivées de touristes/visiteurs par région de provenance [suite]

Country or area of destination and region of origin +	1995	1996	1997	1998	1999	Pays ou zone de destination et région de provenance +
Americas	1 219	794	1 269	1 000	1 000	Amériques
Europe	259 568	303 772	325 045	345 000	338 000	Europe
Asia, East and South East/Oceania	1 287	1 402	1 351	1 000	1 000	Asie, Est et Sud-Est et Océanie
Southern Asia	608	77	285	1 000	1 000	Asie du Sud
Region not specified	1 199	780	1 679	...	...	Région non spécifiée
Romania[5]	**2 757 195**	**3 027 596**	**2 957 161**	**2 965 707**	**...**	**Roumanie**[5]
Africa	4 852	4 466	4 224	3 751	...	Afrique
Americas	56 997	66 866	70 933	79 351	...	Amériques
Europe	2 643 000	2 895 069	2 825 926	2 831 628	...	Europe
Asia, East and South East/Oceania	20 828	27 435	27 549	27 642	...	Asie, Est et Sud-Est et Océanie
Southern Asia	5 350	6 305	5 516	5 332	...	Asie du Sud
Western Asia	21 599	20 501	21 458	16 926	...	Asie occidentale
Region not specified	4 569	6 954	1 555	1 077	...	Région non spécifiée
Russian Federation[3 51]	**10 290 147**	**16 208 339**	**17 462 627**	**15 805 242**	**18 493 012**	**Fédération de Russie**[3 51]
Africa	22 857	25 378	33 593	31 321	28 616	Afrique
Americas	271 453	245 747	293 230	291 751	255 017	Amériques
Europe	9 142 771	15 196 814	16 034 061	14 286 682	16 780 247	Europe
Asia, East and South East/Oceania	736 233	652 297	757 046	754 049	747 677	Asie, Est et Sud-Est et Océanie
Southern Asia	52 040	34 726	51 155	51 851	43 137	Asie du Sud
Western Asia	51 424	45 004	39 429	64 264	28 290	Asie occidentale
Region not specified	13 369	8 373	254 113	325 324	610 028	Région non spécifiée
Saba[5 52]	**9 983**	**9 785**	**10 556**	**10 565**	**9 300**	**Saba**[5 52]
Americas	7 545	7 540	8 295	8 172	6 898	Amériques
Europe	1 306	990	994	1 110	850	Europe
Region not specified	1 132	1 255	1 267	1 283	1 552	Région non spécifiée
Saint Eustatius[3 12]	**20 556**	**19 912**	**19 128**	**19 072**	**19 065**	**Saint-Eustache**[3 12]
Americas	16 261	15 331	14 396	14 076	13 835	Amériques
Europe	3 703	3 816	4 125	4 309	4 293	Europe
Region not specified	592	765	607	687	937	Région non spécifiée
Saint Kitts and Nevis[5 7]	**78 868**	**84 176**	**88 297**	**93 190**	**84 002**	**Saint-Kitts-et-Nevis**[5 7]
Americas	68 613	71 365	74 662	77 056	67 684	Amériques
Europe	9 833	11 944	13 068	15 166	15 759	Europe
Asia, East and South East/Oceania	21	151	62	91	114	Asie, Est et Sud-Est et Océanie
Region not specified	401	716	505	877	445	Région non spécifiée
Saint Lucia[5 6]	**231 259**	**235 659**	**248 406**	**252 237**	**260 583**	**Sainte-Lucie**[5 6]
Americas	142 958	148 353	149 334	161 000	158 800	Amériques
Europe	85 802	84 376	96 398	88 642	98 555	Europe
Asia, East and South East/Oceania	...	...	207	179	...	Asie, Est et Sud-Est et Océanie
Region not specified	2 499	2 930	2 467	2 416	3 228	Région non spécifiée
Saint Maarten[5 53]	**460 070**	**364 706**	**439 234**	**458 486**	**444 814**	**Saint-Martin**[5 53]
Americas	308 046	224 612	285 827	303 465	296 705	Amériques
Europe	131 845	119 394	130 924	132 881	125 828	Europe
Region not specified	20 179	20 700	22 483	22 140	22 281	Région non spécifiée
St. Vincent-Grenadines[5]	**60 206**	**57 882**	**65 143**	**67 228**	**68 293**	**St. Vincent-Grenadines**[5]
Americas	41 836	39 186	45 722	46 186	46 980	Amériques
Europe	17 551	18 045	18 625	20 301	20 264	Europe
Region not specified	819	651	796	741	1 049	Région non spécifiée
Samoa[5]	**68 392**	**73 155**	**67 960**	**77 926**	**85 124**	**Samoa**[5]
Americas	6 456	8 434	6 956	8 037	8 252	Amériques
Europe	6 951	4 799	4 494	4 917	5 460	Europe

73
Tourist/visitor arrivals by region of origin [*cont.*]
Arrivées de touristes/visiteurs par région de provenance[*suite*]

Country or area of destination and region of origin +	1995	1996	1997	1998	1999	Pays ou zone de destination et région de provenance +
Asia, East and South East/Oceania	53 462	58 252	55 370	64 695	70 603	Asie, Est et Sud-Est et Océanie
Region not specified	1 523	1 670	1 140	277	809	Région non spécifiée
San Marino[3 54]	**3 368 159**	**3 345 381**	**3 307 983**	**3 264 385**	**3 148 477**	**Saint-Marin**[3 54]
Region not specified	3 368 159	3 345 381	3 307 983	3 264 385	3 148 477	Région non spécifiée
Sao Tome and Principe[5]	**6 160**	**6 436**	**4 924**	...	...	**Sao Tomé-et-Principe**[5]
Africa	1 657	1 742	1 109	...	...	Afrique
Americas	441	320	236	...	...	Amériques
Europe	3 832	4 101	3 395	...	...	Europe
Asia, East and South East/Oceania	166	219	146	...	...	Asie, Est et Sud-Est et Océanie
Southern Asia	13	17	17	...	...	Asie du Sud
Western Asia	51	37	21	...	...	Asie occidentale
Saudi Arabia[3]	**3 351 549**	...	...	...	...	**Arabie saoudite**[3]
Africa	585 114	...	...	...	...	Afrique
Americas	29 221	...	...	...	...	Amériques
Europe	79 345	...	...	...	...	Europe
Asia, East and South East/Oceania	2 657 869	...	...	...	...	Asie, Est et Sud-Est et Océanie
Senegal[1 55]	**280 000**	**282 169**	**313 642**	**352 389**	**369 116**	**Sénégal**[1 55]
Africa	56 651	67 267	70 224	84 244	81 101	Afrique
Americas	11 244	12 803	11 597	11 632	10 057	Amériques
Europe	205 521	194 705	224 971	247 533	269 692	Europe
Asia, East and South East/Oceania	2 933	3 542	3 583	2 588	2 680	Asie, Est et Sud-Est et Océanie
Western Asia	1 174	1 572	1 335	1 611	955	Asie occidentale
Region not specified	2 477	2 280	1 932	4 781	4 631	Région non spécifiée
Seychelles[5]	**120 716**	**130 955**	**130 070**	**128 258**	**124 865**	**Seychelles**[5]
Africa	14 202	13 330	13 966	12 675	14 188	Afrique
Americas	6 274	6 657	6 726	6 787	4 144	Amériques
Europe	93 827	103 495	102 510	102 736	101 320	Europe
Asia, East and South East/Oceania	4 413	4 408	3 523	2 916	2 543	Asie, Est et Sud-Est et Océanie
Southern Asia	905	1 828	1 875	1 782	1 251	Asie du Sud
Western Asia	1 095	1 237	1 470	1 362	1 419	Asie occidentale
Sierra Leone[5 12]	**13 765**	**21 877**	...	...	...	**Sierra Leone**[5 12]
Africa	5 087	7 313	...	...	...	Afrique
Americas	2 117	3 932	...	...	...	Amériques
Europe	2 553	4 481	...	...	...	Europe
Region not specified	4 008	6 151	...	...	...	Région non spécifiée
Singapore[3 56]	**7 136 538**	**7 292 366**	**7 197 871**	**6 242 152**	**6 958 201**	**Singapour**[3 56]
Africa	82 660	75 036	64 978	72 197	83 808	Afrique
Americas	425 707	459 471	460 435	425 424	444 252	Amériques
Europe	973 880	1 011 044	996 814	990 805	1 058 433	Europe
Asia, East and South East/Oceania	5 236 745	5 329 485	5 216 166	4 287 819	4 849 620	Asie, Est et Sud-Est et Océanie
Southern Asia	365 015	367 208	396 147	394 617	444 088	Asie du Sud
Western Asia	52 191	49 860	48 106	59 976	66 045	Asie occidentale
Region not specified	340	262	15 225	11 314	11 955	Région non spécifiée
Slovakia[9]	**902 975**	**951 355**	**814 138**	**896 100**	**975 105**	**Slovaquie**[9]
Africa	2 353	2 481	2 305	3 039	2 664	Afrique
Americas	25 867	28 189	25 982	30 206	30 683	Amériques
Europe	853 974	897 505	762 025	839 445	917 862	Europe
Asia, East and South East/Oceania	20 781	23 180	21 143	22 901	23 204	Asie, Est et Sud-Est et Océanie
Southern Asia	...	...	...	...	425	Asie du Sud
Western Asia	...	...	...	...	180	Asie occidentale

73
Tourist/visitor arrivals by region of origin [cont.]
Arrivées de touristes/visiteurs par région de provenance [suite]

Country or area of destination and region of origin +	1995	1996	1997	1998	1999	Pays ou zone de destination et région de provenance +
Region not specified	...	...	2 683	509	87	Région non spécifiée
Slovenia[9]	**732 103**	**831 895**	**974 350**	**976 514**	**884 048**	**Slovénie[9]**
Americas	15 361	16 926	17 193	20 510	22 290	Amériques
Europe	704 254	800 426	942 022	940 365	844 728	Europe
Asia, East and South East/Oceania	4 134	4 786	5 820	7 775	8 286	Asie, Est et Sud-Est et Océanie
Region not specified	8 354	9 757	9 315	7 864	8 744	Région non spécifiée
Solomon Islands[5]	**11 795**	**11 217**	**15 894**	**13 229**	**21 318**	**Iles Salomon[5]**
Americas	1 089	988	1 145	789	1 824	Amériques
Europe	1 504	1 517	1 356	1 073	2 193	Europe
Asia, East and South East/Oceania	9 158	8 664	13 318	11 278	16 247	Asie, Est et Sud-Est et Océanie
Region not specified	44	48	75	89	1 054	Région non spécifiée
South Africa[3 6 57]	**4 684 064**	**5 186 221**	**5 170 096**	**5 898 236**	**6 026 086**	**Afrique du Sud[3 6 57]**
Africa	3 449 460	3 790 167	3 676 810	4 304 878	4 362 677	Afrique
Americas	160 473	178 347	207 891	254 840	245 297	Amériques
Europe	738 287	817 071	924 497	1 015 942	1 048 633	Europe
Asia, East and South East/Oceania	173 320	180 213	190 022	199 248	187 576	Asie, Est et Sud-Est et Océanie
Southern Asia	24 588	27 008	29 918	33 666	38 656	Asie du Sud
Western Asia	8 007	8 058	7 095	10 614	10 582	Asie occidentale
Region not specified	129 929	185 357	133 863	79 048	132 665	Région non spécifiée
Spain[1 58]	**34 919 575**	**36 221 008**	**39 552 719**	**43 396 083**	**46 775 869**	**Espagne[1 58]**
Americas	...	...	1 904 078	2 165 477	2 238 148	Amériques
Europe	...	...	36 743 065	40 261 677	43 587 460	Europe
Asia, East and South East/Oceania	...	...	299 337	387 815	359 113	Asie, Est et Sud-Est et Océanie
Region not specified	34 919 575	36 221 008	606 239	581 114	591 148	Région non spécifiée
Sri Lanka[5 6]	**403 101**	**302 265**	**366 165**	**381 063**	**436 440**	**Sri Lanka[5 6]**
Africa	798	2 376	1 533	1 035	1 236	Afrique
Americas	15 177	12 798	16 455	17 937	18 849	Amériques
Europe	254 730	171 888	218 481	246 198	282 000	Europe
Asia, East and South East/Oceania	61 536	51 402	58 632	54 474	66 528	Asie, Est et Sud-Est et Océanie
Southern Asia	67 041	59 919	66 645	57 387	63 006	Asie du Sud
Western Asia	3 819	3 882	4 419	4 032	4 821	Asie occidentale
Sudan[5]	**63 040**	**...**	**...**	**...**	**...**	**Soudan[5]**
Africa	5 715	...	...	...	...	Afrique
Americas	8 472	...	...	...	...	Amériques
Europe	18 086	...	...	...	...	Europe
Asia, East and South East/Oceania	9 803	...	...	...	...	Asie, Est et Sud-Est et Océanie
Southern Asia	3 020	...	...	...	...	Asie du Sud
Western Asia	12 344	...	...	...	...	Asie occidentale
Region not specified	5 600	...	...	...	...	Région non spécifiée
Suriname[5 59]	**43 411**	**53 228**	**61 361**	**54 585**	**...**	**Suriname[5 59]**
Africa	155	74	70	62	...	Afrique
Americas	20 111	10 419	9 553	5 501	...	Amériques
Europe	17 600	39 149	49 929	46 061	...	Europe
Asia, East and South East/Oceania	5 149	3 390	1 744	1 714	...	Asie, Est et Sud-Est et Océanie
Southern Asia	394	159	59	45	...	Asie du Sud
Region not specified	2	37	6	1 202	...	Région non spécifiée
Swaziland[1]	**299 822**	**314 921**	**...**	**...**	**...**	**Swaziland[1]**
Africa	253 409	264 037	...	...	...	Afrique
Americas	5 764	6 464	...	...	...	Amériques
Europe	33 468	38 122	...	...	...	Europe

73
Tourist/visitor arrivals by region of origin [*cont.*]
Arrivées de touristes/visiteurs par région de provenance[*suite*]

Country or area of destination and region of origin +	1995	1996	1997	1998	1999	Pays ou zone de destination et région de provenance +
Asia, East and South East/Oceania	3 810	4 094	...	...	...	Asie, Est et Sud-Est et Océanie
Region not specified	3 371	2 204	...	...	...	Région non spécifiée
Switzerland[1]	**6 945 983**	**6 729 797**	**7 039 225**	**7 185 379**	**7 153 967**	**Suisse**[1]
Africa	83 102	79 804	81 015	82 431	73 139	Afrique
Americas	980 212	946 349	990 354	1 074 217	1 019 743	Amériques
Europe	4 784 799	4 556 622	4 846 684	5 050 341	5 029 798	Europe
Asia, East and South East/Oceania	1 008 010	1 057 519	1 026 559	879 624	923 645	Asie, Est et Sud-Est et Océanie
Southern Asia	36 555	37 276	42 190	55 102	64 543	Asie du Sud
Western Asia	53 305	52 227	52 423	43 664	43 099	Asie occidentale
Syrian Arab Republic[3 6]	**2 252 787**	**2 435 381**	**2 331 628**	**2 463 724**	**2 681 534**	**Rép. arabe syrienne**[3 6]
Africa	52 501	71 636	76 116	70 906	64 920	Afrique
Americas	19 208	21 375	26 265	27 766	30 591	Amériques
Europe	339 429	332 005	342 767	342 615	369 479	Europe
Asia, East and South East/Oceania	11 866	13 027	18 215	16 319	22 287	Asie, Est et Sud-Est et Océanie
Southern Asia	213 064	199 324	139 693	170 143	220 741	Asie du Sud
Western Asia	1 581 703	1 745 916	1 696 803	1 799 683	1 928 846	Asie occidentale
Region not specified	35 016	52 098	31 769	36 292	44 670	Région non spécifiée
Thailand[5 60]	**6 951 566**	**7 244 400**	**7 293 957**	**7 842 760**	**8 651 260**	**Thaïlande**[5 60]
Africa	47 258	47 449	50 963	72 097	73 233	Afrique
Americas	357 674	384 012	388 190	448 761	514 595	Amériques
Europe	1 618 379	1 651 788	1 635 581	1 946 154	2 055 430	Europe
Asia, East and South East/Oceania	4 582 307	4 765 104	4 840 429	4 931 506	5 546 527	Asie, Est et Sud-Est et Océanie
Southern Asia	274 932	275 966	235 623	258 815	280 422	Asie du Sud
Western Asia	71 016	67 826	70 559	107 597	110 125	Asie occidentale
Region not specified	...	52 255	72 612	77 830	70 928	Région non spécifiée
TFYR of Macedonia[9]	**147 007**	**136 137**	**121 337**	**156 670**	**180 788**	**L'ex-R.y. Macédoine**[9]
Americas	3 706	6 083	5 424	8 788	15 526	Amériques
Europe	141 010	126 679	112 752	143 830	158 754	Europe
Asia, East and South East/Oceania	1 034	1 672	1 644	2 280	2 440	Asie, Est et Sud-Est et Océanie
Region not specified	1 257	1 703	1 517	1 772	4 068	Région non spécifiée
Togo[1]	**53 061**	**58 049**	**92 081**	**69 461**	**69 818**	**Togo**[1]
Africa	28 016	30 650	52 275	39 026	41 268	Afrique
Americas	2 601	2 846	4 263	4 853	3 339	Amériques
Europe	20 733	22 683	30 488	21 857	21 336	Europe
Asia, East and South East/Oceania	675	731	1 739	1 091	1 453	Asie, Est et Sud-Est et Océanie
Western Asia	959	1 057	3 163	2 588	2 344	Asie occidentale
Region not specified	77	82	153	46	78	Région non spécifiée
Tonga[5 12]	**29 520**	**26 642**	**26 162**	**27 132**	**30 949**	**Tonga**[5 12]
Americas	6 253	5 681	5 166	6 093	6 153	Amériques
Europe	5 192	4 485	4 225	4 031	4 855	Europe
Asia, East and South East/Oceania	17 945	16 389	16 712	16 921	19 790	Asie, Est et Sud-Est et Océanie
Southern Asia	71	72	51	72	84	Asie du Sud
Region not specified	59	15	8	15	67	Région non spécifiée
Trinidad and Tobago[5 12]	**259 784**	**265 900**	**324 293**	**347 705**	**336 046**	**Trinité-et-Tobago**[5 12]
Africa	543	483	613	766	782	Afrique
Americas	203 802	208 398	249 552	265 427	257 730	Amériques
Europe	51 993	52 790	69 887	76 965	71 912	Europe
Asia, East and South East/Oceania	2 177	2 088	1 758	2 149	2 735	Asie, Est et Sud-Est et Océanie
Southern Asia	926	1 017	937	894	895	Asie du Sud
Western Asia	94	141	233	99	246	Asie occidentale

73
Tourist/visitor arrivals by region of origin [cont.]
Arrivées de touristes/visiteurs par région de provenance [suite]

Country or area of destination and region of origin +	1995	1996	1997	1998	1999	Pays ou zone de destination et région de provenance +
Region not specified	249	983	1 313	1 405	1 746	Région non spécifiée
Tunisia[56]	**4 119 847**	**3 884 593**	**4 263 107**	**4 717 705**	**4 831 658**	**Tunisie**[56]
Africa	1 034 479	719 410	671 432	750 322	670 987	Afrique
Americas	24 817	26 945	26 689	27 831	27 050	Amériques
Europe	2 357 242	2 522 893	2 845 952	3 011 383	3 460 857	Europe
Asia, East and South East/Oceania	3 738	4 706	5 506	8 354	9 314	Asie, Est et Sud-Est et Océanie
Western Asia	660 637	571 010	675 264	879 931	635 412	Asie occidentale
Region not specified	38 934	39 629	38 264	39 884	28 038	Région non spécifiée
Turkey[5]	**7 083 101**	**7 966 004**	**9 039 671**	**8 959 712**	**6 892 636**	**Turquie**[5]
Africa	103 766	90 714	95 596	95 504	82 332	Afrique
Americas	203 834	220 032	267 575	317 451	282 616	Amériques
Europe	5 979 640	6 854 575	7 874 694	7 786 373	5 786 258	Europe
Asia, East and South East/Oceania	155 766	169 973	204 510	194 838	166 139	Asie, Est et Sud-Est et Océanie
Southern Asia	384 300	398 671	348 318	320 779	366 621	Asie du Sud
Western Asia	247 076	218 971	233 183	231 436	199 750	Asie occidentale
Region not specified	8 719	13 068	15 795	13 331	8 920	Région non spécifiée
Turkmenistan[3]	**232 832**	**281 988**	**332 425**	**...**	**...**	**Turkménistan**[3]
Africa	91	248	109	...	...	Afrique
Americas	1 876	3 684	2 647	...	...	Amériques
Europe	124 518	162 804	150 705	...	...	Europe
Asia, East and South East/Oceania	2 370	2 668	2 189	...	...	Asie, Est et Sud-Est et Océanie
Southern Asia	102 803	108 502	175 542	...	...	Asie du Sud
Western Asia	1 174	4 082	1 233	...	...	Asie occidentale
Turks and Caicos Islands[5]	**78 957**	**87 794**	**93 011**	**110 855**	**120 898**	**Iles Turques et Caïques**[5]
Americas	67 767	73 446	78 736	90 321	98 316	Amériques
Europe	8 494	11 431	9 121	11 887	11 498	Europe
Region not specified	2 696	2 917	5 154	8 647	11 084	Région non spécifiée
Tuvalu[5]	**922**	**1 039**	**1 029**	**1 077**	**...**	**Tuvalu**[5]
Americas	70	89	76	118	...	Amériques
Europe	168	88	127	123	...	Europe
Asia, East and South East/Oceania	676	849	822	804	...	Asie, Est et Sud-Est et Océanie
Region not specified	8	13	4	32	...	Région non spécifiée
Uganda[5]	**159 899**	**...**	**...**	**...**	**...**	**Ouganda**[5]
Africa	102 129	...	...	...	...	Afrique
Americas	10 675	...	...	...	...	Amériques
Europe	31 977	...	...	...	...	Europe
Asia, East and South East/Oceania	5 241	...	...	...	...	Asie, Est et Sud-Est et Océanie
Southern Asia	6 474	...	...	...	...	Asie du Sud
Western Asia	2 452	...	...	...	...	Asie occidentale
Region not specified	951	...	...	...	...	Région non spécifiée
Ukraine[5]	**3 715 994**	**3 853 944**	**7 658 235**	**6 207 640**	**4 232 358**	**Ukraine**[5]
Africa	10 046	729	10 551	3 739	5 174	Afrique
Americas	58 698	26 116	79 638	63 940	58 934	Amériques
Europe	3 586 084	3 611 514	7 465 648	6 091 006	2 938 259	Europe
Asia, East and South East/Oceania	13 193	4 009	28 129	22 473	13 681	Asie, Est et Sud-Est et Océanie
Southern Asia	24 689	2 507	36 381	12 675	4 264	Asie du Sud
Western Asia	16 891	205 273	28 585	8 940	5 465	Asie occidentale
Region not specified	6 393	3 796	9 303	4 867	1 206 581	Région non spécifiée
United Arab Emirates[161]	**1 600 847**	**1 767 638**	**1 791 994**	**2 184 292**	**2 480 821**	**Emirats arabes unis**[161]

73
Tourist/visitor arrivals by region of origin [cont.]
Arrivées de touristes/visiteurs par région de provenance [suite]

Country or area of destination and region of origin +	1995	1996	1997	1998	1999	Pays ou zone de destination et région de provenance +
Africa	56 399	84 147	106 612	128 412	132 490	Afrique
Americas	66 617	51 465	49 016	82 778	93 669	Amériques
Europe	567 887	628 686	534 299	658 955	779 036	Europe
Asia, East and South East/Oceania	163 746	148 510	153 641	186 086	173 613	Asie, Est et Sud-Est et Océanie
Southern Asia	212 764	272 255	322 167	354 843	420 734	Asie du Sud
Western Asia	533 434	582 575	626 259	773 218	881 279	Asie occidentale
United Kingdom[3][36]	**23 537 000**	**25 163 000**	**25 515 000**	**25 744 000**	**25 396 000**	**Royaume-Uni**[3][36]
Africa	549 000	510 000	525 000	570 000	588 000	Afrique
Americas	4 101 000	4 017 000	4 509 000	5 053 000	5 000 000	Amériques
Europe	15 790 000	17 856 000	17 644 000	17 581 000	17 046 000	Europe
Asia, East and South East/Oceania	2 173 000	2 166 000	2 155 000	1 872 000	2 062 000	Asie, Est et Sud-Est et Océanie
Southern Asia	265 000	238 000	269 000	264 000	291 000	Asie du Sud
Western Asia	659 000	376 000	413 000	404 000	409 000	Asie occidentale
United Rep. of Tanzania[3]	**295 312**	**326 188**	**360 000**	**482 331**	**627 417**	**Rép.-Unie de Tanzanie**[3]
Africa	115 000	127 027	139 842	186 980	252 355	Afrique
Americas	65 800	72 681	80 014	105 720	136 902	Amériques
Europe	106 012	117 098	128 912	175 031	218 297	Europe
Asia, East and South East/Oceania	8 500	9 382	11 232	14 600	19 863	Asie, Est et Sud-Est et Océanie
United States[5]	**43 317 966**	**46 488 866**	**47 766 476**	**46 395 587**	**48 491 187**	**Etats-Unis**[5]
Africa	185 779	204 322	233 972	258 228	273 762	Afrique
Americas	26 680 595	27 948 103	28 155 272	27 512 761	28 746 665	Amériques
Europe	9 062 595	10 028 117	10 734 881	11 040 602	11 634 166	Europe
Asia, East and South East/Oceania	7 046 008	7 928 682	8 201 299	7 081 823	7 301 839	Asie, Est et Sud-Est et Océanie
Southern Asia	168 560	201 723	235 416	282 112	300 673	Asie du Sud
Western Asia	174 429	177 919	205 636	220 061	234 082	Asie occidentale
United States Virgin Is.[1]	**363 201**	**229 237**	**386 740**	**480 064**	**...**	**Iles Vierges américaines**[1]
Africa	165	254	248	539	...	Afrique
Americas	332 835	213 318	360 897	453 047	...	Amériques
Europe	12 216	11 868	14 875	14 570	...	Europe
Asia, East and South East/Oceania	735	395	1 063	764	...	Asie, Est et Sud-Est et Océanie
Region not specified	17 250	3 402	9 657	11 144	...	Région non spécifiée
Uruguay[2][3]	**2 176 930**	**2 258 616**	**2 462 532**	**2 323 993**	**2 186 997**	**Uruguay**[2][3]
Americas	1 743 468	1 749 878	1 888 852	1 809 579	1 759 517	Amériques
Europe	83 347	60 101	83 626	96 190	...	Europe
Asia, East and South East/Oceania	7 707	...	...	...	...	Asie, Est et Sud-Est et Océanie
Western Asia	323	...	...	...	...	Asie occidentale
Region not specified	342 085	448 637	490 054	418 224	427 480	Région non spécifiée
Vanuatu[5]	**43 712**	**46 123**	**49 605**	**52 085**	**50 484**	**Vanuatu**[5]
Americas	1 157	1 223	1 248	1 297	1 651	Amériques
Europe	2 352	2 644	2 788	2 337	2 758	Europe
Asia, East and South East/Oceania	39 993	42 199	44 623	47 547	45 283	Asie, Est et Sud-Est et Océanie
Region not specified	210	57	946	904	792	Région non spécifiée
Venezuela[5]	**699 837**	**758 503**	**813 862**	**685 429**	**586 900**	**Venezuela**[5]
Africa	799	866	929	3 364	860	Afrique
Americas	390 761	423 517	454 427	366 315	296 212	Amériques
Europe	297 865	322 606	346 182	301 795	277 014	Europe
Asia, East and South East/Oceania	5 877	6 597	7 065	9 179	5 069	Asie, Est et Sud-Est et Océanie
Southern Asia	813	900	966	462	686	Asie du Sud
Western Asia	1 507	1 619	1 716	1 051	519	Asie occidentale
Region not specified	2 215	2 398	2 577	3 263	6 540	Région non spécifiée

73

Tourist/visitor arrivals by region of origin [*cont.*]

Arrivées de touristes/visiteurs par région de provenance[*suite*]

Country or area of destination and region of origin +	1995	1996	1997	1998	1999	Pays ou zone de destination et région de provenance +
Viet Nam[2 3 62]	**1 351 296**	**1 607 155**	**1 715 637**	**1 520 128**	**1 781 754**	**Viet Nam**[2 3 62]
Africa	...	...	626	...	4 599	Afrique
Americas	189 090	146 488	176 159	176 578	243 549	Amériques
Europe	190 710	128 487	218 502	123 002	241 537	Europe
Asia, East and South East/Oceania	450 557	705 895	1 033 527	679 577	1 059 357	Asie, Est et Sud-Est et Océanie
Southern Asia	...	...	6 151		6 428	Asie du Sud
Region not specified	520 939	626 285	280 672	540 971	226 284	Région non spécifiée
Yemen[1]	**61 346**	**74 476**	**83 754**	**...**	**...**	**Yémen**[1]
Africa	1 611	1 610	2 138	...	...	Afrique
Americas	3 207	3 293	4 462	...	...	Amériques
Europe	41 474	48 597	58 868	...	...	Europe
Asia, East and South East/Oceania	5 335	5 475	8 082	...	...	Asie, Est et Sud-Est et Océanie
Western Asia	9 719	15 501	10 204	...	...	Asie occidentale
Yugoslavia[9]	**227 538**	**301 428**	**298 415**	**282 639**	**151 650**	**Yougoslavie**[9]
Americas	3 839	5 864	6 288	9 952	2 595	Amériques
Europe	218 412	285 005	280 363	258 992	140 806	Europe
Asia, East and South East/Oceania	1 119	2 073	1 942	2 156	1 525	Asie, Est et Sud-Est et Océanie
Region not specified	4 168	8 486	9 822	11 539	6 724	Région non spécifiée
Zambia[5]	**159 217**	**270 747**	**340 897**	**362 025**	**456 000**	**Zambie**[5]
Africa	120 092	192 923	203 777	260 162	319 200	Afrique
Americas	5 152	12 438	27 819	14 893	18 759	Amériques
Europe	22 934	44 023	71 427	67 055	84 461	Europe
Asia, East and South East/Oceania	6 962	16 364	34 419	17 494	22 035	Asie, Est et Sud-Est et Océanie
Southern Asia	3 901	4 560	3 455	2 421	10 083	Asie du Sud
Western Asia	176	353	...	...	1 462	Asie occidentale
Region not specified	...	86	...	...	...	Région non spécifiée
Zimbabwe[5 63]	**1 539 352**	**1 745 904**	**1 495 676**	**2 090 407**	**2 100 000**	**Zimbabwe**[5 63]
Africa	1 184 000	1 258 000	984 000	1 583 343	1 503 000	Afrique
Americas	40 309	48 000	62 224	121 104	116 000	Amériques
Europe	151 729	179 348	227 847	305 490	380 000	Europe
Asia, East and South East/Oceania	34 302	41 284	62 000	80 470	101 000	Asie, Est et Sud-Est et Océanie
Region not specified	129 012	219 272	159 605	...		Région non spécifiée

Source:

World Tourism Organization (WTO), Madrid, "Yearbook of Tourism Statistics", 53rd edition, 2001 and the WTO Statistics Database.

+   For a listing of the Member States of the regions of origin, see Annex I, with the following exceptions:

    Africa includes the countries and territories listed under Africa in Annex I but excludes Egypt, Guinea-Bissau, Liberia, Libyan Arab Jamahiriya, Mozambique and Western Sahara.

    Americas is as shown in Annex I, but excludes Falkland Islands (Malvinas), French Guyana, Greenland and Saint Pierre and Miquelon.

    Europe is as shown in Annex I, but excludes Andorra, Channel Islands, Faeroe Islands, Holy See, Isle of

Source:

Organisation mondiale du tourisme (OMT), Madrid, "Annuaire des statistiques du tourisme", 53e édition, 2001 et la base de données de l'OMT.

+   On se reportera à l'Annexe I pour les États Membres classés dans les différentes régions de provenance, avec les exceptions ci-après :

    Afrique - Comprend les États et territoires énumérés à l'Annexe I, sauf l'Égypte, la Guinée-Bissau, le Libéria, la Jamahiriya arabe libyenne, le Mozambique et le Sahara occidental.

    Amériques - Comprend les États et territoires énumérés à l'Annexe I, sauf les îles Falkland (Malvinas), le Groënland, la Guyane française et Saint-Pierre-et-Miquelon.

    Europe - Comprend les États et territoires énumérés à l'Annexe I, sauf l'Andorre, les îles

73
Tourist/visitor arrivals by region of origin
[*cont.*]

Arrivées de touristes/visiteurs par région de provenance
[*suite*]

Man and Svalbard and Jan Mayen Islands. The Europe group
also includes Armenia, Azerbaijan, Cyprus, Israel,
Kyrgyzstan, Turkey and Turkmenistan.

Asia, East and South East/Oceania includes the
countries and territories listed under Eastern Asia and
South-eastern Asia in Annex I (except for East Timor), and
under Oceania except for Christmas Island, Cocos Island,
Norfolk Island, Nauru, Wake Island, Johnston Island, Midway
Islands, Pitcairn, Tokelau and Wallis and Futuna Islands.
The Asia, East and South East/Oceania group also includes
Taiwan Province of China.

Southern Asia is as shown in Annex I under
South-central Asia, but excludes Kazakhstan, Kyrgyzstan,
Tajikistan, Turkmenistan and Uzbekistan.

Western Asia is as shown in Annex I but excludes
Armenia, Azerbaijan, Cyprus, Georgia, Israel, Occupied
Palestinian Territory, and Turkey. The Western Asia group
also includes Egypt and the Libyan Arab Jamahiriya.

† For information on recent changes in country or
area nomenclature pertaining to former Czechoslovakia,
Germany, Hong Kong Special Administrative Region (SAR) of
China, Macao Special Administrative Region (SAR) of China,
SFR of Yugoslavia and the former USSR, see Annex I - Country
or area nomenclature, regional and other groupings.

†† For statistical purposes, the data for
China do not include those for Hong Kong Special
Administrative Region (Hong Kong SAR), Macao Special
Administrative Region (Macao SAR) and Taiwan province of
China.

1 Arrivals of non-resident tourists at hotels and similar
  establishments.
2 Including nationals of the country residing abroad.
3 Arrivals of non-resident tourists at national borders
  (including tourists and same-day visitors).
4 1987 - 1989: including arrivals from Western Samoa.
  Beginning 1990, excluding arrivals from Western Samoa.
5 Arrivals of non-resident tourists at national borders
  (excluding same-day visitors).
6 Excluding nationals of the country residing abroad.
7 Air and sea arrivals.
8 Arrivals correspond to a new series and source of data from
  1990 to 1999.
9 Arrivals of non-resident tourists in all types of
  accommodation establishments.
10 Excluding crew members.
11 Including transit passengers, border permits and returning
   residents.
12 Air arrivals.
13 International tourist arrivals in hotels of regional
   capitals.
14 Excluding arrivals from the Netherlands Antilles.

Anglo-normandes, les îles Féroé, l'île de Man, le
Saint-Siège et les îles Svalbard et Jan Mayen. Le Groupe
comprend en revanche l'Arménie, l'Azerbaïdjan, Chypre,
Israël, l'Kirghizistan, la Turquie et le Turkménistan.

L'Asie de l'Est et du Sud-Est/Océanie - Comprend
les États et territoires énumérés à l'Annexe I dans les
Groupes Asie de l'Est et Asie du Sud-Est sauf le Timor
oriental, et les États et territoires énumérés dans le
Groupe Océanie sauf les îles Christmas, les îles Cocos,
l'île Johnston, les îles Midway, Nauru, l'île Norfolk,
Pitcairn, Tokélou, l'île Wake et Wallis-et-Futuna. Le
Groupe Asie de l'Est et du Sud-Est/Océanie comprend en
revanche la Province chinoise de Taiwan.

Asie du Sud - Comprend les États et territoires
énumérés à l'Annexe I, sauf le Kazakhstan, le Kirghizistan,
l'Ouzbékistan, le Tadjikistan et le Turkménistan.

Asie occidentale - Comprend les États et
territoires énumérés à l'Annexe I, sauf l'Arménie,
l'Azerbaïdjan, Chypre, la Géorgie, Israël, le territoire
Palestinien Occupé et la Turquie. Le Groupe comprend en
revanche l'Égypte et la Jamahiriya arabe libyenne.

† Pour les modifications récentes de nomenclature
de pays ou de zone concernant l'Allemagne, Hong Kong, région
administrative spéciale (RAS) de Chine, Macao, région
administrative spéciale (RAS) de Chine,
l'ex-Tchécoslovaquie, l'ex-URSS et l'ex-Rfs de Yougoslavie,
voir annexe I - Nomenclature des pays ou des zones,
groupements régionaux et autres groupements.

†† Les données statistiques relatives à
la Chine ne comprennent pas celles qui concernent la région
administrative spéciale de Hong Kong (la RAS de Hong Kong),
la région administrative spéciale de Macao (la RAS de Macao)
et la province chinoise de Taiwan.

1 Arrivées de touristes non résidents dans les hôtels et
  établissements assimilés.
2 Y compris les nationaux du pays résidant à l'étranger
3 Arrivées de visiteurs non résidents aux frontières
  nationales (y compris touristes et visiteurs de la journée).
4 1987-1989: y compris des arrivées en provenance de Samoa
  occidentale. A partir de 1990, à l'exclusion des arrivées
  en provenance de Samoa occidentale.
5 Arrivées de touristes non résidents aux frontières
  nationales (à l'exclusion de visiteurs de la journée).
6 A l'exclusion des nationaux du pays résidant à l'étranger.
7 Arrivées par voie aérienne et maritime.
8 Les arrivées constituent une nouvelle série et source de
  données de 1990 à 1999.
9 Arrivées de touristes non résidents dans tous les types
  d'établissements d'hébergement touristique.
10 A l'exclusion des membres des équipages.
11 Y compris passagers en transit, passages à la frontière et
   résidents de retour de voyage.
12 Arrivées par voie aérienne.
13 Arrivées de touristes internationaux dans les hôtels des
   capitales de département.
14 A l'exclusion des arrivées en provenance des Antilles
   Néerlandaises.

73
Tourist/visitor arrivals by region of origin
[*cont.*]

Arrivées de touristes/visiteurs par région de provenance
[*suite*]

15 1980-1994: excluding returning residents.

16 1998: Change in methodology.
17 1998: Excluding children without own passports.
18 Excluding ethnic Chinese arriving from "China, Hong Kong SAR", Macao SAR and Taiwan: 1987: 25,174,446; 1988: 29,852,598; 1989: 28,040,424; 1990: 25,714,506; 1991: 30,639,658; 1992: 34,108,578; 1993: 36,871,088; 1994: 38,502,396; 1995: 40,499,795; 1996: 44,383,182; 1997: 50,159,917; 1998: 56,370,654; 1999: 64,363,298. Also including stateless persons and employees of the United Nations Organizations.
19 From 1996 and onwards, figures adjusted to include non-Macanese arrivals via Macao.
20 Including arrivals by sea, land and by air (helicopter). 1995, Nov.: Arrivals by air began (Macao SAR International Airport). Including stateless and Chinese people who do not have permanent residency in Hong Kong SAR, China: 1992: 93,965; 1993: 92,679; 1994: 147,304; 1995: 167,361; 1996: 189,364; 1997: 182,344.

21 Beginning 1996, change in national source.

22 International tourist arrivals at HS in Brazzaville, Pointe Noire, Loubomo, Owando and Sibiti.
23 Air arrivals at Rarotonga.
24 Prior to 1997. air arrivals at the International FHB Airport at Port Bouet. Arrivals at land frontiers, Bouake Airport and Air Ivoire Airport at Abidjan are not taken into consideration. 1997-1998: Air arrivals at the International FHB Airport at Port Bouet and arrivals at land frontiers.

25 1991: January-June; 1992: Incomplete; 1993: July-December; 1994: January-June; 1995: estimate; 1998: Arrivals through "Ndjili" and "Beach" posts and including nationals of the country residing abroad
26 Beginning 1996, including camp sites with more than 74 units only.
27 1987-1995: Air arrivals. 1996-1999: Departures by air.

28 International tourist arrivals at Addis Ababa Airport.
29 Prior to 1997: estimates.
30 Since 1989 survey at frontiers and car study realized by SOFRES. 1992 and 1993: Estimates based on the frontier survey. 1994 and 1996: Frontier survey. 1997: Update of the frontier survey 1996. 1995, 1998 and 1999: Estimates.

31 1996-1999: Air arrivals.
32 Charter tourists only.
33 The data relate to the territory of the Federal Republic of Germany prior to 3 October 1990. As of 1990, tourists from the former German Democratic Republic will be regarded as domestic tourists.

34 Data based on surveys.
35 Air arrivals at Conakry airport.
36 Departures
37 Prior to 1996: travellers; 1996: New methodology, excluding seasonal and border workers.
38 1996: Departures.
39 Arrivals at Tarawa and Christmas Islands.
40 Including nationals residing abroad and from June 1988, also crew members.

15 1980-1994 : à l'exclusion des résidants qui retournent au pays.
16 1998: Changement de méthodologie.
17 1998: A l'exclusion d'enfants sans passeports personnels.
18 A l'exclusion des arrivées de personnes d'ethnie chinoise en provenance de "Chine, Hong Kong RAS", Macao et Taiwan: 1987: 25.174.446; 1988: 29.852.598; 1989: 28,040,424; 1990: 25,714,506; 1991: 30.639.658; 1992: 34,108,578; 1993: 36,871,088; 1994: 38,502,396; 1995: 40,499,795; 1996: 44,383,182; 1997: 50,159,917; 1998: 56,370,654; 1999: 64,363,298. Y compris également les apatrides et les employés des organisations des Nations Unis.
19 A partir de 1996, les chiffres ont été ajustés pour inclure les arrivées de non-macanais arrivant via Macao.
20 Y compris les arrivées par mer, terre et air (hélicoptère). 1995, Nov.: Début de l'inclusion des arrivées par air (Aéroport international de Macao SAR). Y compris les aptrides et les chinois qui ne résident pas de manière permanente à Hong Kong SAR, Chine: 1992: 93,965; 1993: 92,679; 1994: 147,304; 1995: 167,361; 1996: 189,364; 1997: 182,344.
21 A partir de 1996, changement de la source national des données.
22 Arrivées de touristes internationaux dans HA de Brazzaville, Pointe Noire, Loubomo et Sibiti.
23 Arrivées par voie aérienne à Rarotonga.
24 Avant 1997, arrivées par voie aérienne à l'aéroport international FHB de Port-Bouet. Les arrivées aux frontières terrestres, à l'aéroport de Bouaké, ainsi qu'à l'aéroport Air Ivoire d'Abidjan ne sont pas prises en compte. 1997-1998 : Arrivées par voie aérienne à l'aéroport international FHB de Port-Bouet et arrivées aux frontières terrestres.
25 1991: Janvier-juin; 1992: Incomplet; 1993: Juillet-décembre; 1994: Janvier-juin; 1995: estimation; 1998: Arrivées aux postes de "Ndjih" et "Beach" et y compris les nationaux du pays résidant à l'étranger.
26 A partir de 1996, y compris terrains de camping de plus de 74 unités seulement.
27 1987-1995: Arrivées par voie aérienne. 1996-1999: Départs par voie aérienne.
28 Arrivées par voie aérienne (Aéroport Addis-Ababa).
29 Avant 1997: estimations.
30 A partir de 1989 enquête aux frontières et étude autocar réalisée par la SOFRES. 1992 et 1993: Estimation sur la base des enquêtes aux frontières. 1994 et 1996: Enquêtes aux frontières. 1997 : Actualisation de l'enquête aux frontières 1996. 1995, 1998 et 1999: Estimation.
31 1996-1999: Arrivées par voie aérienne.
32 Arrivées en vols à la demande seulement.
33 Les données se référent au territoire de la République fédérale d'Allemagne avant le 3 octobre 1990. A partir de 1990, les touristes en provenance de l'ancienne République Démocratique Allemande seront considérés comme des touristes nationaux.
34 Données obtenues au moyen d'enquêtes.
35 Arrivées par voie aérienne à l'aéroport de Conakry.
36 Départs.
37 Avant 1996: voyageurs; 1996: Nouvelle méthodologie, à l'exclusion des travailleurs saisoniers et frontaliers.
38 1996: Départs.
39 Arrivées aux Iles Tarawa et Christmas.
40 Y compris les nationaux résidant à l'étranger, à partir de juin 1988, également membres des équipages.

73
Tourist/visitor arrivals by region of origin
[*cont.*]

Arrivées de touristes/visiteurs par région de provenance
[*suite*]

41 Excluding Syrian nationals, Palestinians and students.

42 1992: Excluding sanatoria and rest houses.
43 Foreign tourist departures; includes Singapore residents crossing the frontier by road through Johore Causeway.

44 Arrivals at Yangon by air.
45 Air arrivals (Niamey Airport).
46 Including Niuans residing usually in New Zealand.

47 Air arrivals (Palau International Airport).

48 Total number of visitors broken down by permanent residence who arrived in Panama at Tocumen International Airport and Paso Canoa border post.
49 Including arrivals from abroad to insular possessions of Madeira and the Azores.
50 Persons who enjoyed the services of the economic agents which carry out the tourist's activity in the republic (except left-bank Dniester river regions and municipality of Bender).
51 Data for 1992 correspond to all CIS countries. 1994: Excluding arrivals by road from Belarus, Kazakhstan and Uzbekistan.
52 Prior to 1994, air arrivals. Beginning 1994, air and sea arrivals.
53 Arrivals at Princess Juliana International airport. Including visitors to St. Maarten (the French side of the island).
54 Including Italian visitors.
55 Data for 1993 cannot be compared to previous years because one of the most important tourist regions, Zinginchor, did not open during that year, resulting in a drop in arrivals and nights.

56 Including Malaysian citizens arriving by land.
57 Beginning January 1992, contract and border traffic concession workers are excluded.
58 The 1995-1999 series have been technically adjusted and refer to arrivals of non-resident tourists at national borders (excluding same-day visitors). They now exclude passengers residing in Spain who enter the country by international air transport. This statistical improvement has resulted in the revision of the data published until now with a decrease in the number of arrivals.
59 Arrivals at Zanderij Airport.
60 Prior to 1996, excluding nationals of the country residing abroad. Beginning 1996, including nationals of the country residing abroad.
61 Data refer to Dubai only.
62 1992: air arrivals only.
63 Excluding transit passengers.

41 A l'exclusion des ressortissants syriens, palestiniens et sous-études.
42 1992: A l'exclusion des sanatoria et des maisons de repos.
43 Départs de touristes étrangers; y compris les résidents de Singapour traversant la frontière par voie terrestre à travers le Johore Causeway.
44 Arrivées à Yangon par voie aérienne.
45 Arrivées par voie aérienne (Aéroport de Niamey).
46 Y compris les nationaux de Niue résidant habituellement en Nouvelle-Zélande.
47 Arrivées par voie aérienne (Aéroport international de Palau).
48 Nombre total de visiteurs arrivées au Panama par l'aéroport international de Tocúmen et le poste frontière de Paso Canoa, classes selon leur résidence permanente.
49 Y compris les arrivées en provenance de l'étranger aux possessions insulaires de Madère et des Açores.
50 Personnes qui ont bénéficié des services des agents économiques chargés de l'activité touristique dans le pays (à l'exception des régions de la rive gauche du Dniester et la municipalité de Bender).
51 Les données de 1992 couvrent l'ensemble des pays CEI. 1994: Exception faite des arrivées per le route en provenance de Bélarus, Kazakhstan et Ouzbékistan.
52 Avant 1996, arrivées par voie aérienne. A partir de 1994, arrivées par voie aérienne et maritime.
53 Arrivées à l'aéroport international "Princess Juliana". Y compris les visiteurs à Saint-Martin (partie française de l'île).
54 Y compris les visiteurs italiens.
55 Les données de 1993 ne sont pas comparables à celles des années antérieures, étant donné que la région de Ziguinchor, la plus touristique, n'a pas ouvert durant toute l'année. D'ou les importantes baises en arrivées et nuitées.
56 Y compris les arrivées de malaysiens par voie terrestre.
57 A partir de janvier 1992, les données excluent les travailleurs contractuels et ceux de la zone frontière.
58 La série 1995-1999 a été modifiée. Cette série exclue maintenant les passagers résidents en Espagne qui rentrent dans le pays par vols internationaux. Cette amélioration statistique a donné lieu à une révision qui montre une diminution dans le chiffre des arrivées (par rapport aux chiffres publiés jusqu'à présent).

59 Arrivées à l'aéroport de Zanderij.
60 Avant 1996, à l'exclusion des nationaux du pays résidant à l'étranger. A partir de 1996, y compris les nationaux du pays résidant à l'étranger.
61 Les données se réfèrent au Dubai seulement.
62 1992: arrivées par voie aérienne seulement.
63 A l'exclusion des passagers en transit.

74

Tourist/visitor arrivals and tourism expenditure
Arrivées de touristes/visiteurs et dépenses touristiques

Region, country or area Région, pays ou zone	Number of tourist/visitor arrivals (thousands) Nombre d'arrivées de touristes/visiteurs (milliers)					Tourist expenditure (million US dollars) Dépenses touristiques (millions de dollars E. - U.)				
	1995	1996	1997	1998	1999	1995	1996	1997	1998	1999
World *Monde*	**550 272**	**584 322**	**608 576**	**626 655**	**650 154**[1]	**406 195**	**438 108**	**440 913**	**442 410**	**455 066**[1]
Africa **Afrique**	**23 009**	**25 279**	**26 155**	**28 249**	**30 959**[1]	**10 793**	**12 397**	**13 101**	**12 500**	**14 205**[1]
Algeria Algérie	520	605	635	678	749	27	24	6	24	...
Angola Angola	9	21	45	52	45	10	9	9	8	13
Benin Bénin	138	143	148	152	...	27	29	31	33	...
Botswana Botswana	521	512	607	750	...	162	93	136	175	234
Burkina Faso Burkina Faso	124	131	138	160	218	25	31	39	42	...
Burundi Burundi	34	27	11	15	26	1	1	1	1	1
Cameroon Cameroun	100	101	133	135	...	36	38	39	40	...
Cape Verde Cap-Vert	28	37	45	44	...	10	11	15	20	23
Central African Rep. Rép. centrafricaine	26	21	17	7	10	5	5	5	6	...
Chad Tchad	19	20	27	41	47	10	10	9	10	...
Comoros Comores	23	24	26	27	24	21	23	26	16	19
Congo Congo	37	39	26	25	5	14	10	10	9	12
Côte d'Ivoire Côte d'Ivoire	188	237	274	301	...	89	93	95	108	...
Dem. Rep. of the Congo Rép. dém. du Congo	35	37	30	53	...	5	5	2	2	...
Djibouti Djibouti	21	20	20	21	...	4	4	4	4	...
Egypt Egypte	2 871	3 528	3 657	3 213	4 489	2 684	3 204	3 727	2 565	3 903
Equatorial Guinea Guinée équatoriale	...	...	...	...	...	2	2	2	2	...
Eritrea Erythrée	315	417	410	188	57	58	69	90	34	28
Ethiopia Ethiopie	103	109	115	91	92	26[2]	28[2]	36[2]	16[2]	16[2]
Gabon Gabon	125	145	167	195	175	7	7	7	8	11
Gambia Gambie	45	77	85	91	...	23	31	32	33	...
Ghana Ghana	286	305	325	348	373	233	249	266	284	304

74
Tourist/visitor arrivals and tourism expenditure
[*cont.*]

Arrivées de touristes/visiteurs et dépenses touristiques
[*suite*]

Region, country or area Région, pays ou zone	Number of tourist/visitor arrivals (thousands) Nombre d'arrivées de touristes/visiteurs (milliers)					Tourist expenditure (million US dollars) Dépenses touristiques (millions de dollars E. - U.)				
	1995	1996	1997	1998	1999	1995	1996	1997	1998	1999
Guinea Guinée	...	12	17	23	27	1	6	5	1	7
Kenya Kenya	896	925	907	857	943	486	448	385	290	304
Lesotho Lesotho	87	134	144	150	186	27	32	22	18	19
Libyan Arab Jamah. Jamah. arabe libyenne	56	88	50	32	40	6	6	6	18	28
Madagascar Madagascar	75	83	101	121	138	58	65	74	91	100
Malawi Malawi	192	194	207	220	254	9	5	11	15	20
Mali Mali	42	98	75	83	87	25	29	26	50	50
Mauritania Mauritanie	...	...	...	...	24	11	19	21	20	28
Mauritius Maurice	422	487	536	558	578	430	452	485	503	545
Morocco Maroc	2 602	2 693	3 072	3 242	3 817	1 304	1 674	1 449	1 712	1 880
Namibia Namibie	399	461	502	614	...	278	293	333	288	...
Niger Niger	35	38	44	42	43	15	17	18	18	24
Nigeria Nigéria	656	822	611	739	...	54	85	118	142	...
Réunion Réunion	304	350	374	400	394	216	258	249	265	270
Rwanda Rwanda	1	1	1	2	...	2	4	17	19	17
Sao Tome and Principe Sao Tomé-et-Principe	6	6	5	5	...	2	2	2	2	...
Senegal Sénégal	280	282	314	352	369	161	149	153	178	166
Seychelles Seychelles	121	131	130	128	125	98	107	122	111	112
Sierra Leone Sierra Leone	38	22	23	6	6	6	10	...	8	8
Somalia Somalie	10	10	10	10	...	...	...	...	...	...
South Africa Afrique du Sud	4 684	5 186	5 170	5 898	6 026	2 125	2 575	2 769	2 738	2 526
Sudan Soudan	63	57	30	38	39	8	8	4	2	2
Swaziland Swaziland	300	339	340	319	...	48	38	40	37	35
Togo Togo	53	58	92	69	70	13	10	12	11	6
Tunisia Tunisie	4 120	3 885	4 263	4 718	4 832	1 393	1 411	1 361	1 557	1 560

74

Tourist/visitor arrivals and tourism expenditure
[*cont.*]

Arrivées de touristes/visiteurs et dépenses touristiques
[*suite*]

Region, country or area Région, pays ou zone	Number of tourist/visitor arrivals (thousands) Nombre d'arrivées de touristes/visiteurs (milliers)					Tourist expenditure (million US dollars) Dépenses touristiques (millions de dollars E. - U.)				
	1995	1996	1997	1998	1999	1995	1996	1997	1998	1999
Uganda Ouganda	188	205	227	238	...	78	117	135	144	149
United Rep. of Tanzania Rép.-Unie de Tanzanie	285	315	347	450	...	259	322	392	570	733
Zambia Zambie	163	264	341	362	456	47	60	75	75	85
Zimbabwe Zimbabwe	1 363	1 577	1 281	1 986	2 103	154	219	230	177	202
America, North **Amérique du Nord**	**97 138**	**102 160**	**103 017**	**104 058**	**107 124**[1]	**91 213**	**100 046**	**106 702**	**105 397**	**110 832**[1]
Anguilla Anguilla	39	37	43	44	47	49	48	57	58	56
Antigua and Barbuda Antigua-et-Barbuda	212	220	232	226	232	247	258	269	256	291
Aruba Aruba	619	641	650	647	683	521	613	668	730	782
Bahamas Bahamas	1 598	1 633	1 618	1 528	1 577	1 346	1 398	1 416	1 354	1 503
Barbados Barbade	442	447	472	512	515	612	644	657	703	677
Belize Belize	131	133	146	177	181	77	89	87	108	112
Bermuda Bermudes	387	390	380	369	354	488	472	478	484	480
British Virgin Islands Iles Vierges britanniques	219	244	244	279	286	205	268	210	232	300
Canada Canada	16 932	17 286	17 636	18 858	19 465	7 882	8 616	8 828	9 396	10 171
Cayman Islands Iles Caïmanes	361	373	381	404	395	394	368	436	450	...
Costa Rica Costa Rica	785	781	811	943	1 032	660	689	719	884	1 002
Cuba Cuba	742	999	1 153	1 390	1 561	977	1 185	1 326	1 571	1 714
Dominica Dominique	60	63	65	66	74	34	37	40	38	49
Dominican Republic Rép. dominicaine	1 776	1 926	2 211	2 309	2 649	1 576	1 763	2 099	2 142	2 524
El Salvador El Salvador	235	283	387	542	658	41	44	75	125	211
Grenada Grenade	108	108	111	116	125	54	55	55	59	63
Guadeloupe Guadeloupe	640	625	660	693	561	458	496	372	466	375
Guatemala Guatemala	566	520	576	636	823	277	284	325	394	570
Haiti Haïti	145	150	149	147	143	56	58	57	57	...

74
Tourist/visitor arrivals and tourism expenditure
[*cont.*]

Arrivées de touristes/visiteurs et dépenses touristiques
[*suite*]

Region, country or area Région, pays ou zone	Number of tourist/visitor arrivals (thousands) Nombre d'arrivées de touristes/visiteurs (milliers)					Tourist expenditure (million US dollars) Dépenses touristiques (millions de dollars E. - U.)				
	1995	1996	1997	1998	1999	1995	1996	1997	1998	1999
Honduras Honduras	264	255	303	318	371	80	115	146	168	195
Jamaica Jamaïque	1 147	1 162	1 192	1 225	1 248	1 069	1 092	1 131	1 197	1 279
Martinique Martinique	457	477	513	549	564	384	382	400	415	404
Mexico Mexique	20 241	21 405	19 351	19 392	19 043	6 179[3]	6 934[3]	7 593[3]	7 493[3]	7 223[3]
Montserrat Montserrat	19	9	5	7	10	20	10	5	8	3
Netherlands Antilles Antilles néerlandaises	775	669	726	751	726	565	554	624	749	774
Nicaragua Nicaragua	281	303	358	406	468	50	54	74	90	107
Panama Panama	345	362	421	431	457	367	425	457	494	538
Puerto Rico Porto Rico	3 131	3 065	3 242	3 396	3 024	1 828	1 898	2 046	2 233	2 138
Saint Kitts and Nevis Saint-Kitts-et-Nevis	79	84	88	93	84	65	67	72	76	70
Saint Lucia Sainte-Lucie	231	236	248	252	261	268	269	284	291	311
St. Vincent-Grenadines St. Vincent-Grenadines	60	58	65	67	68	41	64	70	72	77
Trinidad and Tobago Trinité-et-Tobago	260	266	324	348	336	73	108	193	201	...
Turks and Caicos Islands Iles Turques et Caïques	79	88	93	111	121	53	99	113	196	246
United States Etats-Unis	43 318	46 489	47 752	46 404	48 497	63 395	69 809	74 426	71 286	74 881
United States Virgin Is. Iles Vierges américaines	454	373	411	422	485	822	781	894	921	940
America, South Amérique du Sud	**11 793**	**12 439**	**13 190**	**15 417**	**15 099**[1]	**8 434**	**10 055**	**10 702**	**11 798**	**11 584**[1]
Argentina Argentine	2 289	2 614	2 764	3 012	2 898	2 144	2 542	2 693	2 888	2 812
Bolivia Bolivie	284	313	355	434	342	145	159	166	174	179
Brazil Brésil	1 991	2 666	2 850	4 818	5 107	2 097[4]	2 469[4]	2 595[4]	3 678[4 5]	3 994[4]
Chile Chili	1 540	1 450	1 644	1 759	1 622	900	905	1 020	1 062	894
Colombia Colombie	1 399	757	639	674	546	657	1 120	1 044	929	928
Ecuador Equateur	440	494	529	511	509	255	281	290	291	343
French Guiana Guyane française	...	...	...	68	70	...	...	...	51	50

74
Tourist/visitor arrivals and tourism expenditure
[*cont.*]

Arrivées de touristes/visiteurs et dépenses touristiques
[*suite*]

Region, country or area Région, pays ou zone	Number of tourist/visitor arrivals (thousands) Nombre d'arrivées de touristes/visiteurs (milliers)					Tourist expenditure (million US dollars) Dépenses touristiques (millions de dollars E. - U.)				
	1995	1996	1997	1998	1999	1995	1996	1997	1998	1999
Guyana Guyana	106	92	76	68	75	78	70	60	52	...
Paraguay Paraguay	438	426	395	350	269	137[6]	140[6]	128[6]	111[6]	81[6]
Peru Pérou	541	663	747	820	944	428	670	817	845	890
Suriname Suriname	43	53	61	55	57	31	38	44	61	53
Uruguay Uruguay	2 022	2 152	2 316	2 163	2 073	611	717	759	695	653
Venezuela Venezuela	700	759	814	685	587	951	944	1 086	961	656
Asia Asie	98 834	108 309	109 960	111 980	120 672[1]	79 806	88 941	84 188	80 758	82 808[1]
Afghanistan Afghanistan	4	4	4	4	...	1	1	1	1	...
Armenia Arménie	12	13	23	32	41	5	5	7	10	27
Azerbaijan Azerbaïdjan	93	90	306	483	602	70	46	162	125	81
Bahrain Bahreïn	1 396	1 201	1 571	1 750	1 991	247	263	311	366	408
Bangladesh Bangladesh	156	166	182	172	173	23	32	59	51	50
Bhutan Bhoutan	5	5	5	6	7	5	6	6	8	9
Brunei Darussalam Brunéi Darussalam	498	837	850	964	...	37	38	39	37	...
Cambodia Cambodge	220	260	219	186	263	100	118	103	166	190
China †† Chine ††	20 034	22 765	23 770	25 073	27 047	8 733	10 200	12 074	12 602	14 098
China, Hong Kong SAR† Chine, Hong Kong RAS†	10 200	12 974	11 273	10 160	11 328	9 604[7]	11 994[7]	9 979[7]	7 496[7]	7 210[7]
China, Macao SAR † Chine, Macao RAS †	4 202	4 690	3 836	4 517	5 050	3 090[8]	3 085[8]	2 947[8]	2 638[8]	2 466[8]
Cyprus Chypre	2 100	1 950	2 088	2 223	2 434	1 788	1 669	1 639	1 696	1 878
Georgia Géorgie	85	117	313	317	384	...	170	416	423	400
India Inde	2 124	2 288	2 374	2 359	2 482	2 583	2 832	2 889	2 948	3 009
Indonesia Indonésie	4 324	5 034	5 185	4 606	4 728	5 229	6 307	5 321	4 331	4 710
Iran (Islamic Rep. of) Iran (Rép. islamique d')	452	567	740	1 008	1 321	190	244	327	477	662
Iraq Iraq	61	51	51	51	...	13	13	13	13	...

74
Tourist/visitor arrivals and tourism expenditure
[*cont.*]

Arrivées de touristes/visiteurs et dépenses touristiques
[*suite*]

Region, country or area Région, pays ou zone	Number of tourist/visitor arrivals (thousands) Nombre d'arrivées de touristes/visiteurs (milliers)					Tourist expenditure (million US dollars) Dépenses touristiques (millions de dollars E. - U.)				
	1995	1996	1997	1998	1999	1995	1996	1997	1998	1999
Israel Israël	2 215	2 100	2 010	1 942	2 312	2 964	2 955	2 836	2 657	2 974
Japan Japon	3 345	3 837	4 218	4 106	4 438	3 226	4 078	4 326	3 742	3 428
Jordan Jordanie	1 074	1 103	1 127	1 256	1 358	652	743	774	773	795
Kazakhstan Kazakhstan	...	...	...	...	...	122	199	289	407	363
Korea, Dem. P. R. Corée, R. p. dém. de	128	127	128	130	...	...	...	...	...	...
Korea, Republic of Corée, République de	3 753	3 684	3 908	4 250	4 660	5 587[9]	5 430[9]	5 116[9]	6 865[9]	6 802[9]
Kuwait Koweït	69	73	76	77	...	121	184	188	207	243
Kyrgyzstan Kirghizistan	36	42	87	59	69	5	4	7	8	...
Lao People's Dem. Rep. Rép. dém. pop. lao	60	93	193	200	259	25	44	73	80	97
Lebanon Liban	450	424	558	631	673	710	715	1 000	1 221	673
Malaysia Malaisie	7 469	7 138	6 211	5 551	7 931	3 909	4 447	2 702	2 456	3 540
Maldives Maldives	315	339	366	396	430	210	266	286	303	325
Mongolia Mongolie	108	71	82	197	159	21	10	13	33	28
Myanmar Myanmar	117	172	189	201	198	38	33	34	35	35
Nepal Népal	363	394	422	464	492	117	117	116	153	168
Occupied Palestinian Terr. Terr. palestinien occupé	...	...	...	201	271	126	104	96	114	132
Oman Oman	279	349	375	423	502	92[10]	99[10]	108[10]	112[10]	104[10]
Pakistan Pakistan	378	369	375	429	432	114	146	117	98	76
Philippines Philippines	1 760	2 049	2 223	2 149	2 171	2 454	2 701	2 831	2 413	2 534
Qatar Qatar	294	327	435	451	...	...	...	...	...	...
Saudi Arabia Arabie saoudite	3 325	3 458	3 594	3 700	...	1 210	1 308	1 420	1 462	...
Singapore Singapour	6 422	6 608	6 531	5 631	6 258	8 390	8 012	6 073	5 402	5 974
Sri Lanka Sri Lanka	403	302	366	381	436	225	173	217	231	275
Syrian Arab Republic Rép. arabe syrienne	815	830	891	1 267	1 386	1 338	1 206	1 035	1 190	1 360

74
Tourist/visitor arrivals and tourism expenditure
[*cont.*]

Arrivées de touristes/visiteurs et dépenses touristiques
[*suite*]

Region, country or area Région, pays ou zone	Number of tourist/visitor arrivals (thousands) Nombre d'arrivées de touristes/visiteurs (milliers)					Tourist expenditure (million US dollars) Dépenses touristiques (millions de dollars E. - U.)				
	1995	1996	1997	1998	1999	1995	1996	1997	1998	1999
Tajikistan Tadjikistan	...	...	...	511	...	...	...	...	...	...
Thailand Thaïlande	6 952	7 244	7 294	7 843	8 651	7 664	8 664	7 048	5 934	6 695
Turkey Turquie	7 083	7 966	9 040	8 960	6 893	4 957	5 962	7 002	7 177	5 203
Turkmenistan Turkménistan	218	217	257	300	...	...	66	74	192	...
United Arab Emirates[11] Emirats arabes unis[11]	1 601	1 768	1 792	2 184	2 481	389[12]	459[12]	535[12]	562[12]	607[12]
Uzbekistan Ouzbékistan	92	174	253	272	...	...	15	19	21	...
Viet Nam Viet Nam	1 351	1 607	1 716	1 520	1 782	86	87	88	86	...
Yemen Yémen	61	74	81	88	...	50	55	70	64	...
Europe **Europe**	**309 559**	**325 430**	**345 225**	**356 384**	**367 446**[1]	**202 890**	**212 094**	**210 863**	**218 947**	**221 918**[1]
Albania Albanie	40	56	19	28	39	65	77	27	54	211
Andorra Andorre	...	...	...	...	2 347	...	...	...	...	...
Austria Autriche	17 173	17 090	16 647	17 352	17 467	14 586[13]	13 930[13]	12 248[13]	12 628[13]	12 533[13]
Belarus Bélarus	161	234	254	355	...	23	55	25	22	13
Belgium Belgique	5 560	5 829	6 037	6 179	6 369	...	...	...	...	...
Belgium-Luxembourg Belgique-Luxembourg	...	...	...	...	...	5 859	4 893	5 267	5 443	7 039
Bosnia and Herzegovina Bosnie-Herzégovine	37	99	100	90	89	7	16	15	21	21
Bulgaria Bulgarie	3 466	2 795	2 980	2 667	2 472	473	450	496	966[5]	932[5]
Croatia Croatie	1 485	2 914	4 178	4 499	3 805	1 349	2 014	2 523	2 733	2 493
Czech Republic République tchèque	3 381	4 558	4 976	5 482	5 610	2 875	4 075	3 647	3 719	3 035
Denmark Danemark	2 124	2 125	2 158	2 073	2 023	3 672	3 425	3 185	3 211	3 460
Estonia Estonie	530	665	730	825	950	353	470	465	534	560
Finland Finlande	1 779	1 724	1 832	2 644	2 454	1 643[14]	1 637[14]	1 644[14]	1 631[14]	1 517[14]
France France	60 033	62 406	67 310	70 040	73 042	27 527	28 357	28 009	29 931	31 507[15]
Germany † Allemagne †	14 847	15 205	15 837	16 511	17 116	18 135[16]	17 706[16]	16 696[16]	16 766[16]	16 730[16]

74
Tourist/visitor arrivals and tourism expenditure
[*cont.*]

Arrivées de touristes/visiteurs et dépenses touristiques
[*suite*]

Region, country or area Région, pays ou zone	Number of tourist/visitor arrivals (thousands) Nombre d'arrivées de touristes/visiteurs (milliers)					Tourist expenditure (million US dollars) Dépenses touristiques (millions de dollars E. - U.)				
	1995	1996	1997	1998	1999	1995	1996	1997	1998	1999
Greece Grèce	10 130	9 233	10 070	10 916	12 164	4 136	3 723	5 151	6 188[17]	8 783[17]
Hungary Hongrie	19 620	19 917	18 658	16 812	14 402	2 640[5]	3 222	3 440	3 514	3 394
Iceland Islande	190	201	202	232	263	185	176	173	207	222
Ireland Irlande	4 818	5 289	5 587	6 064	6 403	2 691	3 022	3 189	3 267	3 392
Italy Italie	31 052	32 943	34 692	34 933	36 516	28 729	30 017	29 714	29 866	28 359
Latvia Lettonie	523	560	625	567	490	20	215	192	182	118
Liechtenstein Liechtenstein	59	56	57	59	60	...	...	...	...	...
Lithuania Lituanie	650	832	1 012	1 416	1 422	77	316	360	460	550
Luxembourg Luxembourg	768	725	772	790	834	...	...	...	...	...
Malta Malte	1 116	1 054	1 111	1 182	1 214	660	635	648	661	675
Monaco Monaco	233	226	259	278	278	...	...	...	...	...
Netherlands Pays-Bas	6 574	6 580	7 834	9 320	9 881	6 563	6 548	6 304	6 788	7 092
Norway Norvège	2 880	2 746	2 702	4 538	4 481	2 362	2 356	2 216	2 212	2 229
Poland Pologne	19 215	19 410	19 520	18 780	17 950	6 614[18]	8 444[18]	8 679[18]	7 946[18]	6 100[18]
Portugal Portugal	9 511	9 730	10 172	11 295	11 632	4 339	4 265	4 619	5 302	5 131
Republic of Moldova République de Moldova	32	29	21	19	14	4[19]	4[19]	4[19]	4[19]	2[19]
Romania Roumanie	2 757	3 028	2 957	2 966	3 209	590	529	526	260	254
Russian Federation Fédération de Russie	10 290	16 208	17 463	15 805	18 496	4 312	6 868	7 164	6 508	7 510
San Marino Saint-Marin	535	530	532	532	...	...	...	...	...	...
Slovakia Slovaquie	903	951	814	896	975	* 620	* 673	* 546	* 489	* 461
Slovenia Slovénie	732	832	974	977	884	1 084[20]	1 240[20]	1 187[20]	1 088[20]	954[20]
Spain Espagne	34 917	36 220	39 553	43 396	46 776	25 388	27 600	26 900	29 839	32 400
Sweden Suède	2 310	2 376	2 388	2 573	2 595	3 464	3 657	3 730	4 189	3 894
Switzerland Suisse	11 500	10 600	10 600	10 900	10 700	9 365	8 826	7 915	7 973	7 739

74
Tourist/visitor arrivals and tourism expenditure
[*cont.*]

Arrivées de touristes/visiteurs et dépenses touristiques
[*suite*]

Region, country or area Région, pays ou zone	Number of tourist/visitor arrivals (thousands) Nombre d'arrivées de touristes/visiteurs (milliers)					Tourist expenditure (million US dollars) Dépenses touristiques (millions de dollars E. - U.)				
	1995	1996	1997	1998	1999	1995	1996	1997	1998	1999
TFYR of Macedonia L'ex-R.y. Macédoine	147	136	121	157	181	19	21	14	15	40
Ukraine Ukraine	3 716	3 854	7 658	6 208	4 232	3 865	3 416	3 865	3 317	2 124
United Kingdom Royaume-Uni	23 537	25 163	25 515	25 745	25 394	18 554	19 173	20 039	20 978	20 223
Yugoslavia Yougoslavie	228	301	298	283	152	42	43	41	35	17
Oceania **Océanie**	**8 079**	**8 759**	**8 923**	**8 327**	**8 855**[1]	**13 059**	**14 575**	**15 357**	**13 010**	**13 719**[1]
American Samoa Samoa américaines	18	21	22	21	...	10	9	10	10	...
Australia Australie	3 726	4 165	4 318	4 167	4 459	7 873	9 073	8 786	7 338	8 017
Cook Islands Iles Cook	48	48	50	49	56	28	50	35	34	37
Fiji Fidji	318	340	359	371	410	283	299	297	244	275
French Polynesia Polynésie française	172	164	180	189	211	326	322	345	354	394
Guam Guam	1 362	1 363	1 382	1 137	1 162	1 275	1 415	2 818	2 361	1 908
Kiribati Kiribati	3	3	5	2	1	1	1	2	2	2
Marshall Islands Iles Marshall	6	6	6	6	5	3	3	3	3	4
Micronesia (Fed. States of)[21] Micron (Etats fédérés de)[21]	11	11	11	11	...	...	...	...	...	...
New Caledonia Nouvelle-Calédonie	86	91	105	104	100	108	114	117	110	...
New Zealand Nouvelle-Zélande	1 409	1 529	1 497	1 485	1 607	2 318	2 432	2 093	1 726	2 083
Niue Nioué	2	2	2	2	2	2	1	2	1	...
Northern Mariana Islands Iles Mariannes du Nord	669	728	685	481	498	655	670	672	647	...
Palau Palaos	53	69	74	64	55	...	...	...	...	...
Papua New Guinea Papouasie-Nvl-Guinée	42	61	66	67	67	60	68	71	75	76
Samoa Samoa	68	73	68	78	85	33	41	37	38	42
Solomon Islands Iles Salomon	12	11	16	13	21	16	14	7	7	6
Tonga Tonga	29	27	26	27	31	10	13	16	8	9
Tuvalu Tuvalu	1	1	1	1	1	...	...	...	...	...

74

Tourist/visitor arrivals and tourism expenditure
[*cont.*]

Arrivées de touristes/visiteurs et dépenses touristiques
[*suite*]

Region, country or area Région, pays ou zone	Number of tourist/visitor arrivals (thousands) Nombre d'arrivées de touristes/visiteurs (milliers)					Tourist expenditure (million US dollars) Dépenses touristiques (millions de dollars E. - U.)				
	1995	1996	1997	1998	1999	1995	1996	1997	1998	1999
Vanuatu Vanuatu	44	46	50	52	50	58	50	46	52	56

Source:
World Tourism Organization (WTO), Madrid, "Yearbook of
Tourism Statistics", 53rd edition, 2001 and the WTO
Statistics Database.

† For information on recent changes in country or
area nomenclature pertaining to former Czechoslovakia,
Germany, Hong Kong Special Administrative Region (SAR) of
China, Macao Special Administrative Region (SAR) of China,
SFR of Yugoslavia and the former USSR, see Annex I - Country
or area nomenclature, regional and other groupings.

†† For statistical purposes, the data for
China do not include those for Hong Kong Special
Administrative Region (Hong Kong SAR), Macao Special
Administrative Region (Macao SAR) and Taiwan province of
China.

1 The 1999 World and regional totals are global estimates
prepared by WTO. The estimated part relates only to those
countries that were unable to provide the information
contained in the WTO Database as of 1.6.2001.

2 Including revenues from hotels services, tour operators and
travel agency services, duty free, gift articles and
souvenir sales. Excluding National Bank of Ethiopia foreign
currency earning report and revenue from private sector.

3 Including receipts from cruise passengers and frontier
visitors.
4 Data based on the sample survey conducted by EMBRATUR.

5 Change in methodology.
6 Beginning 1995 change in methodology. The data relate only
to expenditure by tourists; expenditure by same-day visitors
is no longer included.
7 Including receipts from servicemen, air crew members and
transit passengers.
8 Including gambling receipts.
9 Excluding expenses of students studying overseas.

10 Hotel sales.
11 Dubai.
12 Hotel receipts.
13 1995-1999: Including international transport.
14 Data collected by travel surveys.
15 Beginning 1999, excluding frontier workers paid in foreign
currency.
16 Including border merchandise transactions and including
purchases of inward-bound and outward-bound commuters.
17 1998-1999: Including registrations through new methodology.

18 Based on surveys and estimations by Institute of Tourism.

19 Sale of tourism products by travel agencies.
20 Data refer to the item "travel" of the Balance of Payments.

21 Data refer to the states of Pohnpei, Truk and Yap.

Source:
Organisation mondiale du tourisme (OMT), Madrid, "Annuaire
des statistiques du tourisme", 53e édition, 2001 et la base
de données de l'OMT.

† Pour les modifications récentes de nomenclature
de pays ou de zone concernant l'Allemagne, Hong Kong, région
administrative spéciale (RAS) de Chine, Macao, région
administrative spéciale (RAS) de Chine,
l'ex-Tchécoslovaquie, l'ex-URSS et l'ex-Rfs de Yougoslavie,
voir annexe I - Nomenclature des pays ou des zones,
groupements régionaux et autres groupements.

†† Les données statistiques relatives à
la Chine ne comprennent pas celles qui concernent la région
administrative spéciale de Hong Kong (la RAS de Hong Kong),
la région administrative spéciale de Macao (la RAS de Macao)
et la province chinoise de Taiwan.

1 Les chiffres de 1999 (chiffre mondial et chiffres régionaux)
sont des estimations globales de L'OMT. La partie
estimative ne concerne que les pays qui n'ont pas été en
mesure de communiquer les données intégrées à la base de
l'OMT au 1er juin 2001.
2 Y compris les recettes correspondant aux services hôteliers,
à ceux des organisateurs de voyages et des agences de
voyage, ainsi qu'aux ventes hors taxe et aux ventes de
cadeaux et souvenirs. Non compris les recette en devises de
la National Bank of Ethiopia et les recettes provenant du
secteur privé.
3 Y compris les recettes provenant des passagers de navires de
croisière et des visiteurs frontaliers.
4 Données basées sur une enquête sur échantillon réalisée par
EMBRATUR.
5 Changement de méthode.
6 A partir de 1995, changement de méthode : les données ne
concernent que les dépenses des touristes, à l'exclusion de
celles des visiteurs ne restant pas au-delà d'une journée.
7 Y compris les recettes provenant des militaires, des
équipages d'avions et des passagers en transit.
8 Y compris les recettes tirées des jeux de hasard.
9 Non compris les dépenses des étudiants poursuivant des
études à l'ètranger.
10 Chiffre d'affaires des hôtels.
11 Dubai.
12 Recettes des hôtels.
13 1995-1999 : Y compris les transports internationaux.
14 Données collectées au moyen d'enquêtes sur les voyages.
15 A partir de 1999, non compris les travailleurs frontaliers
rémunérés en devises.
16 Y compris les transactions frontalières en marchandises, et
les achats des migrants quotidiens entrant et sortant.
17 1998-1999 : y compris les mouvements enregistrés selon la
nouvelle méthode.
18 Chiffres basés sur des enquêtes et des estimations de
l'Institut du tourisme.
19 Vente de produits touristiques par les agences de voyage.
20 Données relatives à la rubrique " Voyages" de la balance de
paiements.
21 Les données se rapportent aux États de Pohnpei, Truk et Yap.

75
Tourism expenditure in other countries
Dépenses touristiques dans d'autres pays
Million US dollars
Millions de dollars E.-U.

Region, country or area Région, pays ou zone	1990	1991	1992	1993	1994	1995	1996	1997	1998	1999
World *Monde*	**244 065**	**249 634**	**286 495**	**280 489**	**313 373**	**363 679**	**384 163**	**378 517**	...	...
Africa **Afrique**	**4 666**	**5 594**	**5 529**	**6 013**	**6 452**	**7 233**	**7 697**	**8 418**	...	...
Algeria Algérie	149	140	163	163	24	42	40	40	...	...
Angola Angola	38	65	75	66	88	75	73	70	...	...
Benin Bénin	12	10	12	12	6	5	6	7	7	...
Botswana Botswana	56	67	75	79	76	145	78	92	126	143
Burkina Faso Burkina Faso	32	22	21	21	23	30	32	32	...	...
Burundi Burundi	17	18	21	20	18	25	12	12	11	8
Cameroon Cameroun	279	414	228	225	58	105	107	107	...	...
Cape Verde Cap-Vert	5	3	8	9	12	16	18	17	24	...
Central African Rep. Rép. centrafricaine	51	43	51	50	43	37	39	39		
Chad Tchad	70	63	80	86	26	23	24	24	...	...
Comoros Comores	6	7	7	6	6	7	8	8	3	...
Congo Congo	113	106	95	70	34	52	77	64	57	60
Côte d'Ivoire Côte d'Ivoire	169	163	168	169	157	190	221	215	237	...
Dem. Rep. of the Congo Rép. dém. du Congo	16	16	16	16	12	10	7	7	...	...
Djibouti Djibouti	...	...	3	5	3	4	5	5	...	...
Egypt Egypte	129	225	918	1 048	1 067	1 278	1 317	1 347	1 148	1 078
Equatorial Guinea Guinée équatoriale	8	9	9	9	8	7	8	8	...	...
Ethiopia Ethiopie	11	7	10	11	15	25	25	40	46	55
Gabon Gabon	137	112	143	154	143	173	176	178	180	183
Gambia Gambie	8	15	13	14	14	14	15	16	...	...
Ghana Ghana	13	14	17	20	20	21	22	23	24	36
Guinea Guinée	30	27	17	28	24	21	27	23	27	31

75
Tourism expenditure in other countries
Million US dollars [*cont.*]
Dépenses touristiques dans d'autres pays
Millions de dollars E.-U. [*suite*]

Region, country or area Région, pays ou zone	1990	1991	1992	1993	1994	1995	1996	1997	1998	1999
Kenya Kenya	38	24	29	48	114	145	167	194	147	115
Lesotho Lesotho	12	11	11	6	7	13	12	13	12	12
Libyan Arab Jamah. Jamah. arabe libyenne	424	877	154	206	210	212	215	154	143	150
Madagascar Madagascar	40	32	37	34	47	59	72	80	119	111
Malawi Malawi	16	27	24	11	15	16	17	17	...	...
Mali Mali	62	60	71	58	42	49	46	42	29	29
Mauritania Mauritanie	23	26	31	20	18	23	36	48	42	55
Mauritius Maurice	94	110	142	128	143	159	179	173	185	187
Morocco Maroc	184	190	242	245	303	304	300	316	424	440
Namibia Namibie	63	69	72	71	77	90	89	99	88	...
Niger Niger	44	40	30	29	21	21	23	24	25	26
Nigeria Nigéria	576	839	348	298	858	906	1 304	1 816	1 567	620
Rwanda Rwanda	23	17	17	18	18	10	12	13	17	18
Sao Tome and Principe Sao Tomé-et-Principe	2	2	2	2	1	1	1	1	...	...
Senegal Sénégal	105	105	112	50	48	72	53	53	...	...
Seychelles Seychelles	34	24	28	35	31	39	30	30	26	21
Sierra Leone Sierra Leone	4	4	3	4	4	2	2	...	4	4
South Africa Afrique du Sud	1 117	1 148	1 554	1 868	1 861	1 849	1 754	1 961	1 842	1 806
Sudan Soudan	51	12	33	15	47	43	28	33	29	35
Swaziland Swaziland	35	41	40	43	38	43	42	38	42	45
Togo Togo	40	29	30	20	18	18	3	5	3	2
Tunisia Tunisie	179	128	167	203	216	251	251	235	235	239
Uganda Ouganda	8	16	18	40	78	80	135	113	95	141
United Rep. of Tanzania Rép.-Unie de Tanzanie	23	60	73	180	206	360	412	407	493	550

75
Tourism expenditure in other countries
Million US dollars [*cont.*]
Dépenses touristiques dans d'autres pays
Millions de dollars E.-U. [*suite*]

Region, country or area Région, pays ou zone	1990	1991	1992	1993	1994	1995	1996	1997	1998	1999
Zambia Zambie	54	87	56	56	58	57	59	59	...	...
Zimbabwe Zimbabwe	66	70	55	44	96	106	118	120	131	110
America, North **Amérique du Nord**	**55 856**	**55 253**	**58 771**	**59 834**	**61 866**	**61 391**	**65 941**	**70 890**	**...**	**...**
Anguilla Anguilla	4	3	4	5	6	6	6	6	...	...
Antigua and Barbuda Antigua-et-Barbuda	18	20	23	23	24	23	26	26	...	...
Aruba Aruba	40	47	51	58	65	73	96	131	111	122
Bahamas Bahamas	196	200	187	171	193	213	235	250	256	309
Barbados Barbade	47	44	42	53	59	71	74	79	82	...
Belize Belize	7	8	14	20	19	25	26	34	24	24
Bermuda Bermudes	119	126	134	140	143	145	148	148	...	...
British Virgin Islands Iles Vierges britanniques	...	26	30	33	36	40	42	42	...	...
Canada Canada	10 931	12 002	11 796	11 133	10 014	10 267	11 253	11 464	10 765	11 345
Costa Rica Costa Rica	148	149	223	267	300	321	335	358	408	428
Dominica Dominique	4	5	6	5	6	6	7	7	8	...
Dominican Republic Rép. dominicaine	144	154	164	128	145	173	198	221	254	282
El Salvador El Salvador	61	57	58	61	70	72	73	75	77	80
Grenada Grenade	5	5	4	4	4	5	5	5	5	...
Guatemala Guatemala	100	67	103	117	151	141	135	119	157	183
Haiti Haïti	37	35	11	10	14	35	37	35	37	...
Honduras Honduras	38	37	38	55	57	57	60	62	81	94
Jamaica Jamaïque	114	71	87	82	81	148	157	181	198	227
Mexico[1] Mexique[1]	5 519	5 812	6 107	5 562	5 338	3 171	3 387	3 891	4 209	4 541
Montserrat Montserrat	2	2	1	3	3	2	3	3	...	...
Netherlands Antilles[2] Antilles néerlandaises[2]	82	95	105	125	147	221	250	255	138	149

75

Tourism expenditure in other countries
Million US dollars [*cont.*]

Dépenses touristiques dans d'autres pays
Millions de dollars E.-U. [*suite*]

Region, country or area Région, pays ou zone	1990	1991	1992	1993	1994	1995	1996	1997	1998	1999
Nicaragua Nicaragua	15	28	30	31	30	40	60	65	70	78
Panama Panama	99	109	120	123	123	128	136	164	176	184
Puerto Rico Porto Rico	630	689	736	776	797	833	821	869	874	815
Saint Kitts and Nevis Saint-Kitts-et-Nevis	4	5	5	5	6	5	6	6	6	...
Saint Lucia Sainte-Lucie	17	18	21	20	23	25	29	29	...	...
St. Vincent-Grenadines St. Vincent-Grenadines	4	4	4	5	6	7	8	7	8	...
Trinidad and Tobago Trinité-et-Tobago	122	113	115	106	90	69	76	72	67	...
Turks and Caicos Islands Iles Turques et Caïques	...	...	...	...	134	153	174	235	194	244
United States Etats-Unis	37 349	35 322	38 552	40 713	43 782	44 916	48 078	52 051	56 509	59 351
America, South **Amérique du Sud**	**5 793**	**6 317**	**7 392**	**9 230**	**10 632**	**11 197**	**14 587**	**15 116**	...	...
Argentina Argentine	1 505	2 145	2 613	3 117	3 306	3 190	3 497	3 874	3 993	4 107
Bolivia Bolivie	130	129	135	137	140	153	162	165	172	165
Brazil Brésil	1 559	1 224	1 332	1 892	2 931	3 412	5 825	5 446	5 731	3 059
Chile Chili	426	409	536	560	535	774	806	945	906	806
Colombia Colombie	454	509	641	694	841	878	1 116	1 209	1 120	1 078
Ecuador Equateur	175	177	178	190	203	235	219	227	241	271
Guyana Guyana	...	...	14	18	23	21	22	22	...	...
Paraguay Paraguay	103	118	135	138	177	133[3]	139[3]	139[3]	143[3]	109[3]
Peru Pérou	295	263	255	269	266	297	350	433	452	443
Suriname Suriname	12	16	21	3	3	3	8	11	11	...
Uruguay Uruguay	111	100	104	129	234	236	192	264	265	280
Venezuela Venezuela	1 023	1 227	1 428	2 083	1 973	1 865	2 251	2 381	2 451	1 646
Asia **Asie**	**44 835**	**46 978**	**55 462**	**57 816**	**64 589**	**76 073**	**82 335**	**78 538**	...	...
Afghanistan Afghanistan	1	1	1	1	1	1	1	1	...	...

75
Tourism expenditure in other countries
Million US dollars [*cont.*]
Dépenses touristiques dans d'autres pays
Millions de dollars E.-U. [*suite*]

Region, country or area Région, pays ou zone	1990	1991	1992	1993	1994	1995	1996	1997	1998	1999
Armenia Arménie	...	...	...	...	1	3	22	41	45	34
Azerbaijan Azerbaïdjan	...	...	...	...	...	146	100	186	170	139
Bahrain Bahreïn	94	98	141	130	146	122	109	122	142	159
Bangladesh Bangladesh	78	83	111	153	210	229	200	170	198	212
Cambodia Cambodge	...	...	...	4	8	8	15	13	7	8
China †† Chine ††	470	511	2 512	2 797	3 036	3 688	4 474	8 130	9 205	10 864
China, Macao SAR † Chine, Macao RAS †	39	49	59	71	102	137	159	172	146	131
Cyprus Chypre	111	113	132	133	176	241	263	278	276	289
Georgia Géorgie	...	...	...	...	...	...	92	228	262	270
India Inde	393	434	470	474	769	996	913	1 342	1 713	2 010
Indonesia Indonésie	836	969	1 166	1 539	1 900	2 172	2 399	2 411	2 102	2 353
Iran (Islamic Rep. of) Iran (Rép. islamique d')	340	734	1 109	862	149	241	529	677	788	918
Israel Israël	1 442	1 551	1 674	2 052	2 135	2 120	2 278	2 283	2 376	2 566
Japan Japon	24 928	23 983	26 837	26 860	30 715	36 792	37 040	33 041	28 815	32 808
Jordan[4] Jordanie [4]	336	281	350	344	394	420	381	398	353	355
Kazakhstan Kazakhstan	...	...	...	...	...	283	319	445	498	394
Korea, Republic of[5] Corée, République de[5]	3 166	3 784	3 794	3 259	4 088	5 903	6 963	6 262	2 640	3 975
Kuwait Koweït	1 837	2 012	1 797	1 819	2 146	2 248	2 492	2 377	2 517	2 510
Kyrgyzstan Kirghizistan	...	...	...	...	2	7	6	4	3	...
Lao People's Dem. Rep. Rép. dém. pop. lao	1	6	10	11	18	30	22	21	23	12
Malaysia Malaisie	1 450	1 584	1 770	1 838	1 994	2 314	2 569	2 590	1 785	1 973
Maldives Maldives	15	19	22	29	28	31	38	40	42	45
Mongolia Mongolie	1	2	4	3	3	20	19	14	45	41
Myanmar Myanmar	16	24	16	10	12	18	28	33	27	18

75
Tourism expenditure in other countries
Million US dollars [*cont.*]
Dépenses touristiques dans d'autres pays
Millions de dollars E.-U. [*suite*]

Region, country or area Région, pays ou zone	1990	1991	1992	1993	1994	1995	1996	1997	1998	1999
Nepal Népal	45	38	52	93	112	136	125	103	78	71
Oman Oman	47	47	47	47	47	47	47	47	47	47
Pakistan Pakistan	440	555	680	633	397	449	900	364	352	180
Philippines Philippines	111	61	102	130	196	422	1 266	1 935	1 950	1 308
Singapore Singapour	1 893	2 080	2 489	3 412	3 368	4 655	5 797	4 605	4 707	4 666
Sri Lanka Sri Lanka	74	97	111	121	170	186	176	180	202	219
Syrian Arab Republic Rép. arabe syrienne	249	256	260	300	512	498	513	545	580	630
Thailand Thaïlande	854	1 266	1 590	2 092	2 906	3 373	4 171	1 888	1 448	1 843
Turkey Turquie	520	592	776	934	886	912	1 265	1 716	1 754	1 471
Turkmenistan Turkménistan	...	...	...	...	...	...	73	125	...	...
Yemen Yémen	64	70	101	80	78	76	78	81	83	...
Europe **Europe**	**127 322**	**130 147**	**153 954**	**143 005**	**164 511**	**201 368**	**206 133**	**197 732**	**...**	**...**
Albania Albanie	4	3	1	7	6	7	12	5	5	5
Austria Autriche	7 748	7 362	7 891	7 776	8 788	11 663[6]	11 782[6]	10 712[6]	10 324[6]	9 803[6]
Belarus Bélarus	...	...	...	56	74	87	119	114	124	116
Belgium-Luxembourg Belgique-Luxembourg	5 477	5 543	6 714	6 338	7 773	9 003	8 562	8 281	8 794	10 057
Bulgaria Bulgarie	189	128	313	257	244	195	199	222	519[7]	526[7]
Croatia Croatie	729	231	158	375	396	422	510	530	600	751
Czech Republic République tchèque	455	274	467	527	1 585	1 633	2 953	2 380	1 869	1 474
Denmark[8] Danemark[8]	3 676	3 377	3 779	3 214	3 583	4 280	4 142	4 137	4 462	4 884
Estonia Estonie	...	...	19	25	48	90	98	118	133	217
Finland[9] Finlande[9]	2 791	2 677	2 386	1 617	1 608	2 272	2 287	2 082	2 063	2 021
France France	12 423	12 321	13 914	12 836	13 773	16 328	17 746	16 576	17 791	18 631[10]
Germany †[11] Allemagne †[11]	33 771	35 819	41 174	40 878	45 198	54 007	52 938	47 920	48 911	48 495

75
Tourism expenditure in other countries
Million US dollars [cont.]
Dépenses touristiques dans d'autres pays
Millions de dollars E.-U. [suite]

Region, country or area Région, pays ou zone	1990	1991	1992	1993	1994	1995	1996	1997	1998	1999
Greece Grèce	1 090	1 015	1 186	1 003	1 125	1 323	1 210	1 327	1 756 [12]	3 989 [12]
Hungary Hongrie	477	443	640	739	925	1 056 [7]	957	924	1 115	1 191
Iceland Islande	286	299	294	270	247	282	308	324	396	436
Ireland [13] Irlande [13]	1 163	1 128	1 361	1 220	1 615	2 034	2 198	2 210	2 374	2 620
Italy Italie	10 304	12 288	19 583	15 903	13 941	14 827	15 805	16 631	17 653	16 913
Latvia Lettonie	...	...	13	29	31	24	373	326	305	268
Lithuania Lituanie	...	...	...	12	50	106	266	277	292	341
Malta Malte	137	133	138	154	177	214	219	191	193	201
Netherlands Pays-Bas	7 376	8 149	9 634	8 920	9 371	11 661	11 528	10 309	10 975	11 366
Norway Norvège	3 679	3 413	3 870	3 364	3 712	4 247	4 509	4 496	4 608	4 751
Poland [14] Pologne [14]	423	143	132	181	316	5 500	6 240	5 750	4 430	3 600
Portugal Portugal	867	1 024	1 165	1 893	1 698	2 141	2 283	2 161	2 319	2 266
Romania Roumanie	103	143	260	195	449	697	666	783	451	395
Russian Federation Fédération de Russie	...	...	...	...	7 092	11 599	10 270	9 363	8 279	7 434
Slovakia * Slovaquie *	181	119	155	262	284	330	483	439	475	339
Slovenia [15] Slovénie [15]	...	...	282	305	369	573	602	518	558	539
Spain Espagne	4 254	4 544	5 542	4 735	4 129	4 461	4 919	4 467	5 001	5 523
Sweden Suède	6 286	6 286	7 059	4 483	4 864	5 624	6 448	6 898	7 723	7 557
Switzerland Suisse	5 873	5 735	6 099	5 954	6 370	7 346	7 570	6 960	6 798	6 842
TFYR of Macedonia L'ex-R.y. Macédoine	...	...	...	...	22	27	26	27	30	32
Ukraine Ukraine	...	...	...	...	2 650	3 041	2 596	2 564	2 021	1 774
United Kingdom Royaume-Uni	17 560	17 550	19 725	19 477	21 998	24 268	25 309	27 710	32 267	35 631
Oceania Océanie	5 593	5 345	5 387	4 591	5 323	6 417	7 470	7 823	...	...
Australia Australie	4 535	4 247	4 301	3 451	3 969	4 979	5 787	6 138	5 418	6 048

75
Tourism expenditure in other countries
Million US dollars [cont.]
Dépenses touristiques dans d'autres pays
Millions de dollars E.-U. [suite]

Region, country or area Région, pays ou zone	1990	1991	1992	1993	1994	1995	1996	1997	1998	1999
Fiji Fidji	32	36	34	47	62	64	70	69	52	66
Kiribati Kiribati	3	2	3	3	3	3	4	4	2	2
New Zealand Nouvelle-Zélande	958	987	977	1 002	1 194	1 289	1 510	1 512	1 438	1 493
Papua New Guinea Papouasie-Nvl-Guinée	50	57	57	69	71	58	72	78	52	53
Samoa Samoa	2	2	2	2	4	3	4	5	4	4
Solomon Islands Iles Salomon	11	12	11	12	13	13	15	9	6	7
Tonga Tonga	1	1	1	1	3	3	3	3	...	...
Vanuatu Vanuatu	1	1	1	4	4	5	5	5	8	9

Source:
World Tourism Organization (WTO), Madrid, "Yearbook of
Tourism Statistics", 53rd edition, 2001 and the WTO
Statistics Database.

† For information on recent changes in country or
area nomenclature pertaining to former Czechoslovakia,
Germany, Hong Kong Special Administrative Region (SAR) of
China, Macao Special Administrative Region (SAR) of China,
SFR of Yugoslavia and the former USSR, see Annex I - Country
or area nomenclature, regional and other groupings.

†† For statistical purposes, the data for
China do not include those for Hong Kong Special
Administrative Region (Hong Kong SAR), Macao Special
Administrative Region (Macao SAR) and Taiwan province of
China.

1 Including expenditure from frontier visitors.
2 Prior to 1995, data refer to Curaçao only; between 1995 and
1997, to Bonaire, Curaçao and Saint-Maarten; 1998 and 1999
to Bonaire and Saint Maarten.
3 Beginning 1995, change in methodology. The data reported
relate only to expenditure by tourists; expenditure by
same-day visitors are not included.

4 Including education payments.
5 Excluding expenses of students studying overseas.

6 1995-1999: Including international transport.
7 Change in methodology.
8 Including international fare expenditure.
9 Data collected by travel surveys.
10 New series since 1999 excluding frontier workers paid in
foreign currency.

Source:
Organisation mondiale du tourisme (OMT), Madrid, "Annuaire
des statistiques du tourisme", 53e édition, 2001 et la base
de données de l'OMT.

† Pour les modifications récentes de nomenclature
de pays ou de zone concernant l'Allemagne, Hong Kong, région
administrative spéciale (RAS) de Chine, Macao, région
administrative spéciale (RAS) de Chine,
l'ex-Tchécoslovaquie, l'ex-URSS et l'ex-Rfs de Yougoslavie,
voir annexe I - Nomenclature des pays ou des zones,
groupements régionaux et autres groupements.

†† Les données statistiques relatives à
la Chine ne comprennent pas celles qui concernent la région
administrative spéciale de Hong Kong (la RAS de Hong Kong),
la région administrative spéciale de Macao (la RAS de Macao)
et la province chinoise de Taiwan.

1 Y compris les dépenses des visiteurs frontaliers.
2 Avant 1995, données ne se rapportant qu'à Curaçao ; de 1995
à 1997, à Bonaire, Curaçao et Saint-Maarten ; 1998 et 1999,
à Bonaire et Saint-Maarten.
3 Avant 1995, changement de méthode : les données communiquées
ne se rapportent qu'aux dépenses des touristes, à
l'exclusion de celles des visiteurs ne restant pas au-delà
d'une journée.
4 Y compris les paiements pour l'éducation.
5 Non compris les dépenses des étudiants poursuivant leurs
études à l'étranger.
6 1995-1999 : y compris les transports internationaux.
7 Changement de méthode.
8 Y compris les dépenses de billets internationaux.
9 Données collectées au moyen d'enquêtes sur les voyages.
10 Série nouvelle à compter de 1999, à l'exclusion des
travailleurs frontaliers rémunérés en devises.

75
Tourism expenditure in other countries
Million US dollars [*cont.*]

Dépenses touristiques dans d'autres pays
Millions de dollars E.-U. [*suite*]

11 Including border merchandise transactions and purchases of inward-bound and outward-bound commuters.
12 1998-1999: Including registrations through new methodology.

13 Excluding fare paid to national carriers.

14 Based on surveys and estimations by the Institute of Tourism.
15 Data refer to the item "travel" of the Balance of Payments.

11 Y compris les transactions frontalières en marchandises, et les achats des migrants quotidiens entrant et sortant.
12 1998-1999 : y compris les mouvements enregistrés selon la nouvelle méthode.
13 Non compris les billets achetés à des transporteurs nationaux.
14 Chiffres basés sur des enquêtes et des estimations de l'Institut du tourisme.
15 Données relatives à la rubrique "Voyages" de la balance des paiements.

Technical notes, tables 73-75

The data on international tourism have been supplied by the World Tourism Organization (WTO), which publishes detailed tourism information in the *Yearbook of Tourism Statistics* [37]. Additional information on data collection methods and definitions can be found in the *Methodological Supplement to World Travel and Tourism Statistics* also published by the WTO [61; see also 53 and 54].

For statistical purposes, the term "international visitor" describes "any person who travels to a country other than that in which he/she has his/her usual residence but outside his/her usual environment for a period not exceeding 12 months and whose main purpose of visit is other than the exercise of an activity remunerated from within the country visited".

International visitors include:

(a) *Tourists* (overnight visitors): "visitors who stay at least one night in a collective or private accommodation in the country visited"; and

(b) *Same-day visitors*: "visitors who do not spend the night in a collective or private accommodation in the country visited".

The figures do not include immigrants, residents in a frontier zone, persons domiciled in one country or area and working in an adjoining country or area, members of the armed forces and diplomats and consular representatives when they travel from their country of origin to the country in which they are stationed and vice-versa.

The figures also exclude persons in transit who do not formally enter the country through passport control, such as air transit passengers who remain for a short period in a designated area of the air terminal or ship passengers who are not permitted to disembark. This category includes passengers transferred directly between airports or other terminals. Other passengers in transit through a country are classified as visitors.

Tables 73 and 74: Data on arrivals of international (or non-resident) visitors may be obtained from different sources. In some cases data are obtained from border statistics derived from administrative records (police, immigration, traffic and other type of controls applied at national borders), and eventually, completed by means of border statistical surveys. In other cases, data are obtained from different types of tourism accommodation establishments (hotels and similar establishments and/or all types of tourism accommodation establishments).

Unless otherwise stated, table 73 shows the number of tourist/visitor arrivals at frontiers classified by their region of origin. Totals correspond to the total

Notes techniques, tableaux 73 à 75

Les données sur le tourisme international ont été fournies par l'Organisation mondiale du tourisme (l'OMT) qui publie des renseignements détaillés sur le tourisme dans l'*Annuaire des statistiques du tourisme* [37]. On trouvera plus de renseignements sur les méthodes de collecte et sur les définitions dans « *Methodological Supplement to World Travel and Tourism Statistics* » publié par l'OMT [61; voir aussi 53 et 54].

A des fins statistiques, l'expression "*visiteur international*" désigne "toute personne qui se rend dans un pays autre que celui où elle a son lieu de résidence habituelle, mais différent de son environnement habituel, pour une période de 12 mois au maximum, dans un but principal autre que celui d'y exercer une profession rémunérée".

Entrent dans cette catégorie:

(a) Les *touristes* (visiteurs passant la nuit), c'est à dire "les visiteurs qui passent une nuit au moins en logement collectif ou privé dans le pays visité";

(b) Les *visiteurs ne restant que la journée*, c'est à dire "les visiteurs qui ne passent pas la nuit en logement collectif ou privé dans le pays visité".

Ces chiffres ne comprennent pas les immigrants, les résidents frontaliers, les personnes domiciliées dans une zone ou un pays donné et travaillant dans une zone ou pays limitrophe, les membres des forces armées et les membres des corps diplomatique et consulaire lorsqu'ils se rendent de leur pays d'origine au pays où ils sont en poste, et vice versa.

Ne sont pas non plus inclus les voyageurs en transit, qui ne pénètrent pas officiellement dans le pays en faisant contrôler leurs passeports, tels que les passagers d'un vol en escale, qui demeurent pendant un court laps de temps dans une aire distincte de l'aérogare, ou les passagers d'un navire qui ne sont pas autorisés à débarquer. Cette catégorie comprend également les passagers transportés directement d'une aérogare à l'autre ou à un autre terminal. Les autres passagers en transit dans un pays sont classés parmi les visiteurs.

Tableaux 73 et 74: Les données relatives aux arrivées des visiteurs internationaux (ou non résidents) peuvent être obtenues de différentes sources. Dans certains cas, elles proviennent des statistiques des frontières tirées des registres administratifs (contrôles de police, de l'immigration, de la circulation et autres effectués aux frontières nationales) et, éventuellement, complétées à l'aide d'enquêtes statistiques aux frontières. Dans d'autres cas, elles proviennent de différents types d'établissements d'hébergement touristique (hôtels et établissements assimilés et/ou tous types

number of arrivals from the regions indicated in the table. However, these totals may not correspond to the number of tourist arrivals shown in table 74. The latter excludes same-day visitors whereas they may be included in table 73. More detailed information can be found in the *Yearbook of Tourism Statistics* [37].

When a person visits the same country several times a year, an equal number of arrivals is recorded. Likewise, if a person visits several countries during the course of a single trip, his/her arrival in each country is recorded separately. Consequently, *arrivals* cannot be assumed to be equal to the number of persons traveling.

Tourism expenditure (in the country of reference) corresponds to the "expenditure of non-resident visitors (tourists and same-day visitors)" within the economic territory of the country of reference. International transport is excluded. The data are obtained by the WTO from the item "Travel receipts" of the Balance of Payments of each country shown in the *Balance of Payments Statistics Yearbook* published by the International Monetary Fund [14].

Table 75: The data on tourism expenditure in other countries are obtained from the item "Travel expenditure" of the Balance of Payments of each country and corresponds to the "expenditure of resident visitors (tourists and same-day visitors)" outside the economic territory of the country of reference.

For more information, see the *Yearbook of Tourism Statistics* published by the World Tourism Organization.[37] and the *Balance of Payments Statistics Yearbook* published by the International Monetary Fund [14].

d'établissements d'hébergement touristique).

Sauf indication contraire, le tableau 73 indique le nombre d'arrivées de touristes/visiteurs par région de provenance. Les totaux correspondent au nombre total d'arrivées de touristes des régions indiquées sur le tableau. Les chiffres totaux peuvent néanmoins, ne pas coïncider avec le nombre des arrivées de touristes indiqué dans le tableau 74, qui ne comprend pas les visiteurs ne restant que la journée, lesquels peuvent au contraire être inclus dans les chiffres du tableau 73. Pour plus de renseignements, consulter l'*Annuaire des statistiques du tourisme* [37].

Lorsqu'une personne visite le même pays plusieurs fois dans l'année, il est enregistré un nombre égal d'arrivées. En outre, si une personne visite plusieurs pays au cours d'un seul et même voyage, son arrivée dans chaque pays est enregistrée séparément. Par conséquent, on ne peut pas partir du postulat que les *arrivées* sont égales au nombre de personnes qui voyagent.

Dépenses touristiques (dans le pays de référence) correspondent aux «dépenses des visiteurs (touristes et visiteurs de la journée) non résidents» dans le territoire économique du pays dont il s'agit. Les données excluent les dépenses du transport international. Ils sont tirées par l'OMT du poste «recettes au titre des voyages» de la balance des paiements de chaque pays presentée dans le "*Balance of Payments Statistics Yearbook*" publié par le Fonds monétaire international [14].

Tableau 75: Les dépenses touristiques dans d'autres pays sont tirées du poste «dépenses au titre des voyages» de la balance des paiements de chaque pays et correspondent aux «dépenses des visiteurs (touristes et visiteurs de la journée) résidents» en dehors du territoire économique du pays de référence.

On trouvera plus de renseignements dans l'*Annuaire des statistiques du tourisme* publié par l'Organisation mondiale du tourisme [37] et dans "*Balance of Payments Statistics Yearbook*" publié par le Fonds monétaire international [14].

76
Summary of balance of payments
Résumé des balances des paiements
Millions of US dollars
Millions de dollars des E.−U.

Country or area	1994	1995	1996	1997	1998	1999	2000	Pays ou zone
Africa · Afrique								
Angola								**Angola**
Goods: Exports fob	3 016.6	3 722.7	5 095.0	5 006.8	3 542.9	5 156.5	...	Biens : exportations,fàb
Goods: Imports fob	−1 454.1	−1 467.7	−2 040.5	−2 597.0	−2 079.4	−3 109.1	...	Biens : importations,fàb
Serv. & Income: Credit	163.2	129.0	311.0	250.9	157.5	178.8	...	Serv. & revenu : crédit
Serv. & Income: Debit	−2 310.6	−2 834.6	−3 940.0	−3 638.6	−3 638.5	−3 990.7	...	Serv. & revenu : débit
Current Trans.,nie: Credit	333.2	312.2	3 949.4	187.7	246.6	161.2	...	Transf. cour.,nia : crédit
Current Transfers: Debit	−88.1	−156.7	−108.6	−81.9	−86.7	−98.8	...	Transf. courants : débit
Capital Acct.,nie: Credit	0.0	0.0	0.0	0.0	0.0	0.0	...	Compte de cap.,nia : crédit
Capital Account: Debit	0.0	0.0	0.0	0.0	0.0	0.0	...	Compte de capital : débit
Financial Account,nie	−443.4	−924.8	−654.5	489.5	496.4	1 498.7	...	Compte d'op. fin., nia
Net Errors and Omissions	−244.5	−19.4	149.2	−182.2	377.6	−80.9	...	Erreurs et omissions nettes
Reserves and Related Items	1 027.7	1 239.3	−2 761.0	564.8	983.6	284.3	...	Rés. et postes appareutés
Benin								**Bénin**
Goods: Exports fob	397.9	419.9	527.7	424.0	414.3	421.5	...	Biens : exportations,fàb
Goods: Imports fob	−451.5	−622.5	−559.7	−576.9	−572.6	−635.2	...	Biens : importations,fàb
Serv. & Income: Credit	161.0	217.8	162.7	141.4	173.4	206.0	...	Serv. & revenu : crédit
Serv. & Income: Debit	−203.1	−303.3	−246.3	−217.7	−235.9	−255.8	...	Serv. & revenu : débit
Current Trans.,nie: Credit	98.5	105.4	92.4	77.8	102.0	87.1	...	Transf. cour.,nia : crédit
Current Transfers: Debit	−25.9	−30.5	−34.2	−18.5	−32.7	−14.9	...	Transf. courants : débit
Capital Acct.,nie: Credit	75.2	85.6	6.4	84.5	66.6	69.9	...	Compte de cap.,nia : crédit
Capital Account: Debit	0.0	0.0	0.0	0.0	0.0	0.0	...	Compte de capital : débit
Financial Account,nie	−17.6	−126.3	−104.2	−21.3	−8.9	25.4	...	Compte d'op. fin., nia
Net Errors and Omissions	−16.3	−1.0	6.3	6.7	7.1	7.3	...	Erreurs et omissions nettes
Reserves and Related Items	−18.1	254.9	149.0	100.0	86.7	88.7	...	Rés. et postes appareutés
Botswana								**Botswana**
Goods: Exports fob	1 874.3	2 160.2	2 217.5	2 819.8	2 060.6	2 671.0	...	Biens : exportations,fàb
Goods: Imports fob	−1 364.3	−1 605.4	−1 467.7	−1 924.5	−1 983.1	−1 996.5	...	Biens : importations,fàb
Serv. & Income: Credit	416.9	743.6	664.7	832.3	878.0	802.4	...	Serv. & revenu : crédit
Serv. & Income: Debit	−777.1	−959.8	−1 098.4	−1 207.5	−1 025.5	−1 211.9	...	Serv. & revenu : débit
Current Trans.,nie: Credit	356.8	330.7	355.4	456.8	460.9	474.4	...	Transf. cour.,nia : crédit
Current Transfers: Debit	−295.1	−369.5	−176.6	−255.5	−220.8	−222.6	...	Transf. courants : débit
Capital Acct.,nie: Credit	19.6	15.4	18.0	29.4	44.2	33.5	...	Compte de cap.,nia : crédit
Capital Account: Debit	−0.4	−0.9	−11.9	−12.5	−12.4	−12.9	...	Compte de capital : débit
Financial Account,nie	41.1	−33.9	42.4	5.6	−202.4	−175.2	...	Compte d'op. fin., nia
Net Errors and Omissions	−136.7	−73.6	−32.9	−108.9	44.6	8.7	...	Erreurs et omissions nettes
Reserves and Related Items	−135.2	−206.6	−510.7	−635.1	−44.2	−371.0	...	Rés. et postes appareutés
Burkina Faso								**Burkina Faso**
Goods: Exports fob	215.6	...	...	...	...	...	...	Biens : exportations,fàb
Goods: Imports fob	−344.3	...	...	...	...	...	...	Biens : importations,fàb
Serv. & Income: Credit	65.1	...	...	...	...	...	...	Serv. & revenu : crédit
Serv. & Income: Debit	−176.5	...	...	...	...	...	...	Serv. & revenu : débit
Current Trans.,nie: Credit	308.0	...	...	...	...	...	...	Transf. cour.,nia : crédit
Current Transfers: Debit	−53.0	...	...	...	...	...	...	Transf. courants : débit
Capital Acct.,nie: Credit	0.0	...	...	...	...	...	...	Compte de cap.,nia : crédit
Capital Account: Debit	0.0	...	...	...	...	...	...	Compte de capital : débit
Financial Account,nie	−13.9	...	...	...	...	...	...	Compte d'op. fin., nia
Net Errors and Omissions	−8.3	...	...	...	...	...	...	Erreurs et omissions nettes
Reserves and Related Items	7.3	...	...	...	...	...	...	Rés. et postes appareutés
Burundi								**Burundi**
Goods: Exports fob	80.7	112.9	40.4	87.5	64.0	55.0	49.1	Biens : exportations,fàb
Goods: Imports fob	−172.6	−175.6	−100.0	−96.1	−123.5	−97.3	−107.9	Biens : importations,fàb
Serv. & Income: Credit	23.0	26.8	16.9	13.0	11.2	8.2	8.5	Serv. & revenu : crédit
Serv. & Income: Debit	−113.4	−106.3	−58.7	−62.2	−61.4	−43.9	−57.9	Serv. & revenu : débit
Current Trans.,nie: Credit	167.0	154.7	62.5	61.3	59.3	52.9	61.1	Transf. cour.,nia : crédit
Current Transfers: Debit	−1.6	−2.1	−1.1	−4.5	−3.3	−1.8	−1.8	Transf. courants : débit
Capital Acct.,nie: Credit	0.0	0.0	0.0	0.0	0.0	0.0	0.0	Compte de cap.,nia : crédit
Capital Account: Debit	−0.2	−0.8	−0.3	−0.1	0.0	0.0	0.0	Compte de capital : débit
Financial Account,nie	31.1	21.1	14.1	13.7	28.8	17.0	58.9	Compte d'op. fin., nia
Net Errors and Omissions	21.1	5.9	−9.2	−2.4	5.4	8.7	−6.2	Erreurs et omissions nettes
Reserves and Related Items	−35.2	−36.7	35.3	−10.2	19.5	1.2	−3.9	Rés. et postes appareutés

76
Summary of balance of payments
Millions of US dollars
Résumé des balances des paiements
Millions de dollars des E. – U.

Country or area	1994	1995	1996	1997	1998	1999	2000	Pays ou zone
Cameroon								**Cameroun**
Goods: Exports fob	1 454.2	1 735.9	...	...	...	...	...	Biens : exportations,fàb
Goods: Imports fob	−1 052.3	−1 109.0	...	...	...	...	...	Biens : importations,fàb
Serv. & Income: Credit	350.8	316.7	...	...	...	...	...	Serv. & revenu : crédit
Serv. & Income: Debit	−829.5	−923.3	...	...	...	...	...	Serv. & revenu : débit
Current Trans.,nie: Credit	83.8	100.7	...	...	...	...	...	Transf. cour.,nia : crédit
Current Transfers: Debit	−63.0	−31.2	...	...	...	...	...	Transf. courants : débit
Capital Acct.,nie: Credit	14.1	21.1	...	...	...	...	...	Compte de cap.,nia : crédit
Capital Account: Debit	0.0	−0.7	...	...	...	...	...	Compte de capital : débit
Financial Account,nie	−626.4	43.3	...	...	...	...	...	Compte d'op. fin., nia
Net Errors and Omissions	117.0	−138.1	...	...	...	...	...	Erreurs et omissions nettes
Reserves and Related Items	551.3	−15.4	...	...	...	...	...	Rés. et postes appareutés
Cape Verde								**Cap–Vert**
Goods: Exports fob	14.2	16.6	23.9	43.2	32.7	...	...	Biens : exportations,fàb
Goods: Imports fob	−195.3	−233.6	−207.5	−215.1	−218.3	...	...	Biens : importations,fàb
Serv. & Income: Credit	51.2	70.9	80.5	96.2	89.0	...	...	Serv. & revenu : crédit
Serv. & Income: Debit	−39.1	−67.1	−77.4	−80.4	−98.6	...	...	Serv. & revenu : débit
Current Trans.,nie: Credit	125.6	156.0	148.4	129.9	142.5	...	...	Transf. cour.,nia : crédit
Current Transfers: Debit	−2.3	−4.4	−2.9	−3.6	−5.1	...	...	Transf. courants : débit
Capital Acct.,nie: Credit	20.1	20.9	12.8	6.3	19.0	...	...	Compte de cap.,nia : crédit
Capital Account: Debit	0.0	0.0	0.0	0.0	0.0	...	...	Compte de capital : débit
Financial Account,nie	39.6	44.5	46.0	44.1	37.0	...	...	Compte d'op. fin., nia
Net Errors and Omissions	8.3	−35.6	−1.3	−20.4	12.8	...	...	Erreurs et omissions nettes
Reserves and Related Items	−22.2	31.9	−22.5	−0.2	−10.8	...	...	Rés. et postes appareutés
Central African Rep.								**Rép. centrafricaine**
Goods: Exports fob	145.9	...	...	...	...	...	...	Biens : exportations,fàb
Goods: Imports fob	−130.6	...	...	...	...	...	...	Biens : importations,fàb
Serv. & Income: Credit	33.1	...	...	...	...	...	...	Serv. & revenu : crédit
Serv. & Income: Debit	−136.5	...	...	...	...	...	...	Serv. & revenu : débit
Current Trans.,nie: Credit	92.6	...	...	...	...	...	...	Transf. cour.,nia : crédit
Current Transfers: Debit	−29.2	...	...	...	...	...	...	Transf. courants : débit
Capital Acct.,nie: Credit	0.0	...	...	...	...	...	...	Compte de cap.,nia : crédit
Capital Account: Debit	0.0	...	...	...	...	...	...	Compte de capital : débit
Financial Account,nie	52.8	...	...	...	...	...	...	Compte d'op. fin., nia
Net Errors and Omissions	−15.0	...	...	...	...	...	...	Erreurs et omissions nettes
Reserves and Related Items	−13.1	...	...	...	...	...	...	Rés. et postes appareutés
Chad								**Tchad**
Goods: Exports fob	135.3	...	...	...	...	...	...	Biens : exportations,fàb
Goods: Imports fob	−212.1	...	...	...	...	...	...	Biens : importations,fàb
Serv. & Income: Credit	59.8	...	...	...	...	...	...	Serv. & revenu : crédit
Serv. & Income: Debit	−211.8	...	...	...	...	...	...	Serv. & revenu : débit
Current Trans.,nie: Credit	209.4	...	...	...	...	...	...	Transf. cour.,nia : crédit
Current Transfers: Debit	−18.4	...	...	...	...	...	...	Transf. courants : débit
Capital Acct.,nie: Credit	0.0	...	...	...	...	...	...	Compte de cap.,nia : crédit
Capital Account: Debit	0.0	...	...	...	...	...	...	Compte de capital : débit
Financial Account,nie	76.3	...	...	...	...	...	...	Compte d'op. fin., nia
Net Errors and Omissions	−33.0	...	...	...	...	...	...	Erreurs et omissions nettes
Reserves and Related Items	−5.5	...	...	...	...	...	...	Rés. et postes appareutés
Comoros								**Comores**
Goods: Exports fob	10.8	11.3	...	...	...	...	...	Biens : exportations,fàb
Goods: Imports fob	−44.9	−53.5	...	...	...	...	...	Biens : importations,fàb
Serv. & Income: Credit	31.5	37.9	...	...	...	...	...	Serv. & revenu : crédit
Serv. & Income: Debit	−48.3	−52.2	...	...	...	...	...	Serv. & revenu : débit
Current Trans.,nie: Credit	50.0	41.1	...	...	...	...	...	Transf. cour.,nia : crédit
Current Transfers: Debit	−6.2	−3.5	...	...	...	...	...	Transf. courants : débit
Capital Acct.,nie: Credit	0.0	0.0	...	...	...	...	...	Compte de cap.,nia : crédit
Capital Account: Debit	0.0	0.0	...	...	...	...	...	Compte de capital : débit
Financial Account,nie	18.5	10.9	...	...	...	...	...	Compte d'op. fin., nia
Net Errors and Omissions	−6.3	−1.8	...	...	...	...	...	Erreurs et omissions nettes
Reserves and Related Items	−5.0	9.9	...	...	...	...	...	Rés. et postes appareutés
Congo								**Congo**
Goods: Exports fob	958.9	1 167.0	1 554.5	1 744.1	...	...	...	Biens : exportations,fàb
Goods: Imports fob	−612.7	−650.7	−1 361.0	−802.9	...	...	...	Biens : importations,fàb
Serv. & Income: Credit	69.0	79.3	102.8	60.8	...	...	...	Serv. & revenu : crédit
Serv. & Income: Debit	−1 286.9	−1 237.9	−1 391.3	−1 234.1	...	...	...	Serv. & revenu : débit
Current Trans.,nie: Credit	111.3	30.9	29.9	24.7	...	...	...	Transf. cour.,nia : crédit

76
Summary of balance of payments
Millions of US dollars
Résumé des balances des paiements
Millions de dollars des E.–U.

Country or area	1994	1995	1996	1997	1998	1999	2000	Pays ou zone
Current Transfers: Debit	−33.0	−38.3	−44.0	−44.5	...	...	...	Transf. courants : débit
Capital Acct.,nie: Credit	0.0	0.0	0.0	0.0	...	...	...	Compte de cap.,nia : crédit
Capital Account: Debit	0.0	0.0	0.0	0.0	...	...	...	Compte de capital : débit
Financial Account,nie	605.4	−80.3	657.2	−173.7	...	...	...	Compte d'op. fin., nia
Net Errors and Omissions	33.1	120.7	102.1	−122.1	...	...	...	Erreurs et omissions nettes
Reserves and Related Items	154.9	609.3	349.7	547.7	...	...	...	Rés. et postes appareutés
Côte d'Ivoire								**Côte d'Ivoire**
Goods: Exports fob	2 895.9	3 805.9	4 446.1	4 451.2	4 606.5	4 661.4	3 972.9	Biens : exportations,fàb
Goods: Imports fob	−1 606.8	−2 430.3	−2 622.4	−2 658.4	−2 886.5	−2 766.1	−2 175.5	Biens : importations,fàb
Serv. & Income: Credit	641.6	720.4	736.4	740.8	783.5	748.6	576.6	Serv. & revenu : crédit
Serv. & Income: Debit	−1 828.6	−2 351.8	−2 379.8	−2 307.8	−2 400.0	−2 378.4	−2 017.2	Serv. & revenu : débit
Current Trans.,nie: Credit	246.8	277.7	204.1	137.7	148.1	136.8	74.2	Transf. cour.,nia : crédit
Current Transfers: Debit	−362.6	−514.3	−546.6	−518.3	−541.7	−522.7	−443.8	Transf. courants : débit
Capital Acct.,nie: Credit	527.6	291.3	49.8	50.5	35.9	17.4	16.9	Compte de cap.,nia : crédit
Capital Account: Debit	0.0	0.0	0.0	0.0	0.0	0.0	0.0	Compte de capital : débit
Financial Account,nie	−523.1	−88.6	−717.8	−323.0	−417.0	−577.2	−673.6	Compte d'op. fin., nia
Net Errors and Omissions	−11.1	35.6	−15.4	−39.6	32.0	−23.9	59.6	Erreurs et omissions nettes
Reserves and Related Items	20.3	254.2	848.4	476.6	649.6	707.8	612.3	Rés. et postes appareutés
Djibouti								**Djibouti**
Goods: Exports fob	56.4	33.5	...	...	...	...	...	Biens : exportations,fàb
Goods: Imports fob	−237.1	−205.0	...	...	...	...	...	Biens : importations,fàb
Serv. & Income: Credit	176.0	177.3	...	...	...	...	...	Serv. & revenu : crédit
Serv. & Income: Debit	−96.7	−95.9	...	...	...	...	...	Serv. & revenu : débit
Current Trans.,nie: Credit	73.7	85.4	...	...	...	...	...	Transf. cour.,nia : crédit
Current Transfers: Debit	−18.3	−18.4	...	...	...	...	...	Transf. courants : débit
Capital Acct.,nie: Credit	0.0	0.0	...	...	...	...	...	Compte de cap.,nia : crédit
Capital Account: Debit	0.0	0.0	...	...	...	...	...	Compte de capital : débit
Financial Account,nie	39.1	−2.1	...	...	...	...	...	Compte d'op. fin., nia
Net Errors and Omissions	7.9	0.7	...	...	...	...	...	Erreurs et omissions nettes
Reserves and Related Items	−0.8	24.5	...	...	...	...	...	Rés. et postes appareutés
Egypt								**Egypte**
Goods: Exports fob	4 044.0	4 670.0	4 779.0	5 525.3	4 403.0	5 236.5	7 061.0	Biens : exportations,fàb
Goods: Imports fob	−9 997.0	−12 267.0	−13 169.0	−14 156.8	−14 617.0	−15 164.8	−15 382.0	Biens : importations,fàb
Serv. & Income: Credit	9 400.0	10 168.0	11 172.0	11 501.4	10 171.0	11 281.5	11 674.0	Serv. & revenu : crédit
Serv. & Income: Debit	−7 759.0	−6 856.0	−6 640.0	−7 955.0	−7 567.0	−7 496.4	−8 496.0	Serv. & revenu : débit
Current Trans.,nie: Credit	4 622.0	4 284.0	3 888.0	4 737.7	5 166.0	4 563.8	4 224.0	Transf. cour.,nia : crédit
Current Transfers: Debit	−279.0	−253.0	−222.0	−363.1	−122.0	−55.4	−52.0	Transf. courants : débit
Capital Acct.,nie: Credit	0.0	0.0	0.0	0.0	0.0	0.0	0.0	Compte de cap.,nia : crédit
Capital Account: Debit	0.0	0.0	0.0	0.0	0.0	0.0	0.0	Compte de capital : débit
Financial Account,nie	−1 450.0	−1 845.0	−1 459.0	1 957.8	1 901.0	−1 421.4	−1 646.0	Compte d'op. fin., nia
Net Errors and Omissions	255.4	272.0	−73.6	−1 882.3	−721.9	−1 557.6	586.8	Erreurs et omissions nettes
Reserves and Related Items	1 163.6	1 827.0	1 724.6	635.1	1 386.9	4 613.8	2 030.2	Rés. et postes appareutés
Equatorial Guinea								**Guinée équatoriale**
Goods: Exports fob	62.0	89.9	175.3	...	...	...	...	Biens : exportations,fàb
Goods: Imports fob	−36.9	−120.6	−292.0	...	...	...	...	Biens : importations,fàb
Serv. & Income: Credit	3.4	4.3	5.0	...	...	...	...	Serv. & revenu : crédit
Serv. & Income: Debit	−32.6	−100.6	−229.8	...	...	...	...	Serv. & revenu : débit
Current Trans.,nie: Credit	5.7	6.8	4.0	...	...	...	...	Transf. cour.,nia : crédit
Current Transfers: Debit	−1.9	−3.3	−6.6	...	...	...	...	Transf. courants : débit
Capital Acct.,nie: Credit	0.0	0.0	0.0	...	...	...	...	Compte de cap.,nia : crédit
Capital Account: Debit	0.0	0.0	0.0	...	...	...	...	Compte de capital : débit
Financial Account,nie	−15.0	101.6	313.8	...	...	...	...	Compte d'op. fin., nia
Net Errors and Omissions	−2.9	10.3	24.8	...	...	...	...	Erreurs et omissions nettes
Reserves and Related Items	18.4	11.5	5.5	...	...	...	...	Rés. et postes appareutés
Ethiopia								**Ethiopie**
Goods: Exports fob	372.0	423.0	417.5	588.3	560.3	467.4	486.0	Biens : exportations,fàb
Goods: Imports fob	−925.7	−1 136.7	−1 002.2	−1 001.6	−1 309.8	−1 387.2	−1 131.4	Biens : importations,fàb
Serv. & Income: Credit	337.5	412.9	418.4	415.0	449.8	490.3	522.4	Serv. & revenu : crédit
Serv. & Income: Debit	−385.0	−445.1	−424.9	−459.7	−540.3	−516.7	−541.1	Serv. & revenu : débit
Current Trans.,nie: Credit	728.5	737.3	679.0	425.5	589.8	500.8	697.9	Transf. cour.,nia : crédit
Current Transfers: Debit	−2.0	−1.1	−7.5	−7.6	−15.7	−19.7	−17.7	Transf. courants : débit
Capital Acct.,nie: Credit	3.7	0.0	0.0	0.0	0.0	0.0	0.0	Compte de cap.,nia : crédit
Capital Account: Debit	0.0	0.0	−1.7	−0.8	0.0	0.0	0.0	Compte de capital : débit
Financial Account,nie	−199.0	158.3	−499.6	241.2	−23.5	54.3	156.6	Compte d'op. fin., nia
Net Errors and Omissions	69.5	−49.0	−44.1	−627.9	−75.6	405.1	−212.3	Erreurs et omissions nettes
Reserves and Related Items	0.4	−99.6	465.0	427.7	364.9	5.8	39.6	Rés. et postes appareutés

76
Summary of balance of payments
Millions of US dollars
Résumé des balances des paiements
Millions de dollars des E.−U.

Country or area	1994	1995	1996	1997	1998	1999	2000	Pays ou zone
Gabon								**Gabon**
Goods: Exports fob	2 365.3	2 727.8	3 334.2	3 032.7	1 907.6	2 498.8	...	Biens : exportations,fàb
Goods: Imports fob	−776.7	−880.9	−961.6	−1 030.6	−1 163.2	−910.5	...	Biens : importations,fàb
Serv. & Income: Credit	231.4	252.1	276.7	271.9	277.1	365.1	...	Serv. & revenu : crédit
Serv. & Income: Debit	−1 336.6	−1 592.1	−1 723.6	−1 708.2	−1 563.5	−1 520.1	...	Serv. & revenu : débit
Current Trans.,nie: Credit	18.7	58.0	65.2	62.7	36.6	42.6	...	Transf. cour.,nia : crédit
Current Transfers: Debit	−184.8	−100.3	−102.1	−97.1	−90.0	−85.6	...	Transf. courants : débit
Capital Acct.,nie: Credit	0.0	5.6	9.6	7.5	3.6	5.7	...	Compte de cap.,nia : crédit
Capital Account: Debit	0.0	−0.8	−4.5	−1.7	−1.8	−0.3	...	Compte de capital : débit
Financial Account,nie	−745.0	−724.7	−1 047.6	−626.2	−165.8	−686.8	...	Compte d'op. fin., nia
Net Errors and Omissions	254.6	−181.1	−97.4	−108.4	92.5	−106.7	...	Erreurs et omissions nettes
Reserves and Related Items	173.0	436.3	251.2	197.4	667.0	397.8	...	Rés. et postes appareutés
Gambia								**Gambie**
Goods: Exports fob	125.0	123.0	118.7	119.6	...	...	...	Biens : exportations,fàb
Goods: Imports fob	−181.6	−162.5	−217.1	−207.1	...	...	...	Biens : importations,fàb
Serv. & Income: Credit	95.3	58.1	107.2	113.1	...	...	...	Serv. & revenu : crédit
Serv. & Income: Debit	−72.2	−78.8	−86.3	−86.0	...	...	...	Serv. & revenu : débit
Current Trans.,nie: Credit	45.9	55.8	35.1	45.0	...	...	...	Transf. cour.,nia : crédit
Current Transfers: Debit	−4.2	−3.7	−5.4	−8.2	...	...	...	Transf. courants : débit
Capital Acct.,nie: Credit	0.0	0.0	8.5	5.7	...	...	...	Compte de cap.,nia : crédit
Capital Account: Debit	0.0	0.0	0.0	0.0	...	...	...	Compte de capital : débit
Financial Account,nie	33.1	24.8	58.6	39.4	...	...	...	Compte d'op. fin., nia
Net Errors and Omissions	−35.1	−15.6	−4.9	−14.2	...	...	...	Erreurs et omissions nettes
Reserves and Related Items	−6.2	−0.9	−14.5	−7.4	...	...	...	Rés. et postes appareutés
Ghana								**Ghana**
Goods: Exports fob	1 237.7	1 431.2	1 570.1	1 489.9	2 090.8	2 005.5	1 898.4	Biens : exportations,fàb
Goods: Imports fob	−1 579.9	−1 687.8	−1 937.0	−2 128.2	−2 896.5	−3 228.1	−2 741.3	Biens : importations,fàb
Serv. & Income: Credit	159.3	164.3	180.3	191.6	465.3	482.8	519.9	Serv. & revenu : crédit
Serv. & Income: Debit	−543.5	−575.6	−619.8	−663.1	−836.6	−812.7	−720.5	Serv. & revenu : débit
Current Trans.,nie: Credit	487.3	538.9	497.9	576.5	751.0	637.8	649.3	Transf. cour.,nia : crédit
Current Transfers: Debit	−15.5	−15.7	−16.2	−16.4	−17.1	−17.8	−18.4	Transf. courants : débit
Capital Acct.,nie: Credit	0.0	0.0	0.0	0.0	0.0	0.0	0.0	Compte de cap.,nia : crédit
Capital Account: Debit	−1.0	−1.0	−1.0	−1.0	−1.0	−1.0	0.0	Compte de capital : débit
Financial Account,nie	481.7	462.1	285.1	493.8	449.9	554.5	265.8	Compte d'op. fin., nia
Net Errors and Omissions	−54.0	−65.6	20.2	83.6	102.1	289.4	−111.7	Erreurs et omissions nettes
Reserves and Related Items	−172.1	−250.8	20.4	−26.7	−107.9	89.6	258.5	Rés. et postes appareutés
Guinea								**Guinée**
Goods: Exports fob	515.7	582.8	636.5	630.1	693.0	677.9	...	Biens : exportations,fàb
Goods: Imports fob	−685.4	−621.7	−525.3	−512.5	−572.0	−583.4	...	Biens : importations,fàb
Serv. & Income: Credit	159.4	130.4	136.9	118.4	119.7	137.9	...	Serv. & revenu : crédit
Serv. & Income: Debit	−445.8	−486.8	−527.9	−442.9	−516.3	−449.0	...	Serv. & revenu : débit
Current Trans.,nie: Credit	280.6	258.3	137.8	131.4	116.2	80.1	...	Transf. cour.,nia : crédit
Current Transfers: Debit	−72.5	−79.3	−35.3	−15.6	−24.3	−15.1	...	Transf. courants : débit
Capital Acct.,nie: Credit	0.0	0.0	0.0	0.0	0.0	0.0	...	Compte de cap.,nia : crédit
Capital Account: Debit	0.0	0.0	0.0	0.0	0.0	0.0	...	Compte de capital : débit
Financial Account,nie	84.2	109.2	47.5	−89.3	8.0	117.2	...	Compte d'op. fin., nia
Net Errors and Omissions	39.7	34.8	69.9	49.8	17.8	−45.0	...	Erreurs et omissions nettes
Reserves and Related Items	124.1	72.5	59.9	130.6	157.8	79.5	...	Rés. et postes appareutés
Guinea−Bissau								**Guinée−Bissau**
Goods: Exports fob	33.2	23.9	21.6	48.9	...	...	...	Biens : exportations,fàb
Goods: Imports fob	−53.8	−59.3	−56.8	−62.5	...	...	...	Biens : importations,fàb
Serv. & Income: Credit	5.6	5.7	7.0	8.0	...	...	...	Serv. & revenu : crédit
Serv. & Income: Debit	−53.4	−51.0	−47.9	−40.5	...	...	...	Serv. & revenu : débit
Current Trans.,nie: Credit	21.8	31.4	15.7	15.8	...	...	...	Transf. cour.,nia : crédit
Current Transfers: Debit	−1.1	−1.3	0.0	0.0	...	...	...	Transf. courants : débit
Capital Acct.,nie: Credit	44.4	49.2	40.7	32.2	...	...	...	Compte de cap.,nia : crédit
Capital Account: Debit	0.0	0.0	0.0	0.0	...	...	...	Compte de capital : débit
Financial Account,nie	−27.0	−28.3	−12.3	2.0	...	...	...	Compte d'op. fin., nia
Net Errors and Omissions	−24.3	−10.9	−11.5	−19.2	...	...	...	Erreurs et omissions nettes
Reserves and Related Items	54.5	40.6	43.5	15.2	...	...	...	Rés. et postes appareutés
Kenya								**Kenya**
Goods: Exports fob	1 537.0	1 923.8	2 083.3	2 062.6	2 017.0	1 748.6	1 773.4	Biens : exportations,fàb
Goods: Imports fob	−1 775.3	−2 673.9	−2 598.2	−2 948.4	−3 028.7	−2 731.8	−3 044.0	Biens : importations,fàb
Serv. & Income: Credit	1 138.3	1 050.1	957.6	937.4	871.7	966.2	1 012.6	Serv. & revenu : crédit
Serv. & Income: Debit	−1 072.5	−1 218.6	−1 096.2	−1 080.9	−909.4	−761.3	−902.6	Serv. & revenu : débit
Current Trans.,nie: Credit	333.7	563.6	585.4	572.5	578.6	685.3	926.6	Transf. cour.,nia : crédit

76
Summary of balance of payments
Millions of US dollars
Résumé des balances des paiements
Millions de dollars des E.−U.

Country or area	1994	1995	1996	1997	1998	1999	2000	Pays ou zone
Current Transfers: Debit	−63.2	−45.5	−5.4	0.0	−4.5	−4.7	−4.2	Transf. courants : débit
Capital Acct.,nie: Credit	0.0	0.0	0.0	76.8	84.3	55.4	49.6	Compte de cap.,nia : crédit
Capital Account: Debit	−0.4	−0.4	−0.4	0.0	0.0	0.0	0.0	Compte de capital : débit
Financial Account,nie	−41.7	247.9	589.1	362.6	562.1	222.9	109.7	Compte d'op. fin., nia
Net Errors and Omissions	5.8	11.4	−128.2	32.8	−88.6	−214.6	43.0	Erreurs et omissions nettes
Reserves and Related Items	−61.6	141.6	−387.0	−15.5	−82.6	34.0	36.0	Rés. et postes appareutés
Lesotho								**Lesotho**
Goods: Exports fob	143.5	160.0	186.9	196.1	193.4	172.5	211.1	Biens : exportations,fàb
Goods: Imports fob	−810.2	−985.2	−998.6	−1 024.4	−866.0	−779.2	−727.6	Biens : importations,fàb
Serv. & Income: Credit	407.3	510.6	495.6	534.3	411.2	368.7	331.4	Serv. & revenu : crédit
Serv. & Income: Debit	−103.6	−218.5	−175.4	−177.6	−175.8	−130.7	−105.2	Serv. & revenu : débit
Current Trans.,nie: Credit	472.1	211.3	190.2	202.9	158.0	149.4	139.8	Transf. cour.,nia : crédit
Current Transfers: Debit	−0.9	−1.2	−1.1	−0.5	−1.2	−1.6	−1.0	Transf. courants : débit
Capital Acct.,nie: Credit	0.0	43.7	45.5	44.5	22.9	15.2	22.0	Compte de cap.,nia : crédit
Capital Account: Debit	0.0	0.0	0.0	0.0	0.0	0.0	0.0	Compte de capital : débit
Financial Account,nie	33.0	349.1	350.6	323.7	316.1	135.8	85.2	Compte d'op. fin., nia
Net Errors and Omissions	−20.3	28.1	23.3	42.1	56.8	29.0	62.1	Erreurs et omissions nettes
Reserves and Related Items	−120.9	−97.8	−116.9	−141.0	−115.6	40.8	−17.8	Rés. et postes appareutés
Libyan Arab Jamahiriya								**Jamahiriya arabe libyenne**
Goods: Exports fob	8 365.0	9 037.9	9 577.9	9 876.1	6 328.0	6 757.8	...	Biens : exportations,fàb
Goods: Imports fob	−7 339.0	−6 257.1	−7 059.2	−7 159.8	−5 857.1	−3 995.7	...	Biens : importations,fàb
Serv. & Income: Credit	526.7	563.0	603.9	673.3	680.0	561.9	...	Serv. & revenu : crédit
Serv. & Income: Debit	−1 218.0	−1 080.9	−1 306.8	−1 274.2	−1 274.5	−1 136.7	...	Serv. & revenu : débit
Current Trans.,nie: Credit	5.0	4.9	3.0	3.9	5.1	6.4	...	Transf. cour.,nia : crédit
Current Transfers: Debit	−311.0	−270.1	−342.0	−244.0	−271.9	−209.9	...	Transf. courants : débit
Capital Acct.,nie: Credit	0.0	0.0	0.0	0.0	0.0	0.0	...	Compte de cap.,nia : crédit
Capital Account: Debit	0.0	0.0	0.0	0.0	0.0	0.0	...	Compte de capital : débit
Financial Account,nie	159.9	−250.1	224.2	−884.0	−554.7	−970.8	...	Compte d'op. fin., nia
Net Errors and Omissions	106.3	299.1	−234.1	877.7	432.1	−371.8	...	Erreurs et omissions nettes
Reserves and Related Items	−294.8	−2 046.7	−1 467.0	−1 868.9	513.2	−641.3	...	Rés. et postes appareutés
Madagascar								**Madagascar**
Goods: Exports fob	450.1	506.6	509.3	516.1	538.2	584.0	823.7	Biens : exportations,fàb
Goods: Imports fob	−545.8	−628.1	−629.0	−694.1	−692.7	−742.5	−997.5	Biens : importations,fàb
Serv. & Income: Credit	208.0	249.6	299.5	292.0	315.6	346.7	386.5	Serv. & revenu : crédit
Serv. & Income: Debit	−486.2	−532.7	−542.4	−500.9	−538.6	−519.3	−586.2	Serv. & revenu : débit
Current Trans.,nie: Credit	113.7	141.1	94.4	156.3	109.5	110.9	121.9	Transf. cour.,nia : crédit
Current Transfers: Debit	−16.9	−12.4	−22.6	−35.3	−32.7	−31.8	−31.3	Transf. courants : débit
Capital Acct.,nie: Credit	61.9	45.1	5.1	115.4	102.7	128.8	115.0	Compte de cap.,nia : crédit
Capital Account: Debit	0.0	0.0	0.0	0.0	0.0	0.0	0.0	Compte de capital : débit
Financial Account,nie	−122.4	−197.5	133.3	109.7	−76.3	−13.6	−30.7	Compte d'op. fin., nia
Net Errors and Omissions	61.3	98.5	58.8	24.6	−25.0	32.4	38.6	Erreurs et omissions nettes
Reserves and Related Items	276.3	330.0	93.7	16.1	299.2	104.3	160.0	Rés. et postes appareutés
Malawi								**Malawi**
Goods: Exports fob	362.6	...	...	...	...	...	...	Biens : exportations,fàb
Goods: Imports fob	−639.0	...	...	...	...	...	...	Biens : importations,fàb
Serv. & Income: Credit	24.1	...	...	...	...	...	...	Serv. & revenu : crédit
Serv. & Income: Debit	−321.5	...	...	...	...	...	...	Serv. & revenu : débit
Current Trans.,nie: Credit	139.7	...	...	...	...	...	...	Transf. cour.,nia : crédit
Current Transfers: Debit	−15.4	...	...	...	...	...	...	Transf. courants : débit
Capital Acct.,nie: Credit	0.0	...	...	...	...	...	...	Compte de cap.,nia : crédit
Capital Account: Debit	0.0	...	...	...	...	...	...	Compte de capital : débit
Financial Account,nie	122.0	...	...	...	...	...	...	Compte d'op. fin., nia
Net Errors and Omissions	292.6	...	...	...	...	...	...	Erreurs et omissions nettes
Reserves and Related Items	35.0	...	...	...	...	...	...	Rés. et postes appareutés
Mali								**Mali**
Goods: Exports fob	334.9	441.8	433.5	561.6	...	...	...	Biens : exportations,fàb
Goods: Imports fob	−449.2	−556.8	−551.5	−551.9	...	...	...	Biens : importations,fàb
Serv. & Income: Credit	78.3	95.8	98.5	92.7	...	...	...	Serv. & revenu : crédit
Serv. & Income: Debit	−366.7	−483.5	−449.8	−407.3	...	...	...	Serv. & revenu : débit
Current Trans.,nie: Credit	281.3	266.8	246.1	170.0	...	...	...	Transf. cour.,nia : crédit
Current Transfers: Debit	−41.2	−48.0	−50.0	−43.5	...	...	...	Transf. courants : débit
Capital Acct.,nie: Credit	99.1	126.2	136.4	108.6	...	...	...	Compte de cap.,nia : crédit
Capital Account: Debit	0.0	0.0	0.0	0.0	...	...	...	Compte de capital : débit
Financial Account,nie	−7.0	118.6	174.6	52.7	...	...	...	Compte d'op. fin., nia
Net Errors and Omissions	5.6	−13.0	−8.8	7.9	...	...	...	Erreurs et omissions nettes
Reserves and Related Items	65.0	52.0	−29.0	9.2	...	...	...	Rés. et postes appareutés

76
Summary of balance of payments
Millions of US dollars
Résumé des balances des paiements
Millions de dollars des E.-U.

Country or area	1994	1995	1996	1997	1998	1999	2000	Pays ou zone
Mauritania								**Mauritanie**
Goods: Exports fob	399.7	476.4	480.0	423.6	358.6	...	...	Biens : exportations,fàb
Goods: Imports fob	−352.3	−292.6	−346.1	−316.5	−318.7	...	...	Biens : importations,fàb
Serv. & Income: Credit	27.1	29.2	32.5	36.3	36.4	...	...	Serv. & revenu : crédit
Serv. & Income: Debit	−228.7	−266.5	−277.2	−240.2	−186.6	...	...	Serv. & revenu : débit
Current Trans.,nie: Credit	113.3	94.7	217.5	157.9	198.3	...	...	Transf. cour.,nia : crédit
Current Transfers: Debit	−28.9	−19.2	−15.5	−13.3	−10.8	...	...	Transf. courants : débit
Capital Acct.,nie: Credit	0.0	0.0	0.0	0.0	0.0	...	...	Compte de cap.,nia : crédit
Capital Account: Debit	0.0	0.0	0.0	0.0	0.0	...	...	Compte de capital : débit
Financial Account,nie	−11.4	−10.2	−86.1	−17.3	−25.9	...	...	Compte d'op. fin., nia
Net Errors and Omissions	−23.5	−18.1	−1.0	−3.0	−8.1	...	...	Erreurs et omissions nettes
Reserves and Related Items	104.7	6.2	−4.2	−27.6	−43.2	...	...	Rés. et postes appareutés
Mauritius								**Maurice**
Goods: Exports fob	1 376.9	1 571.7	1 810.6	1 600.1	1 669.3	1 589.2	1 559.4	Biens : exportations,fàb
Goods: Imports fob	−1 773.9	−1 812.2	−2 136.3	−2 036.1	−1 933.3	−2 107.9	−1 953.3	Biens : importations,fàb
Serv. & Income: Credit	664.5	829.9	991.9	940.6	964.8	1 070.7	1 107.0	Serv. & revenu : crédit
Serv. & Income: Debit	−602.8	−712.6	−748.0	−720.9	−792.4	−786.8	−810.1	Serv. & revenu : débit
Current Trans.,nie: Credit	129.6	146.8	182.8	206.4	186.8	196.4	167.6	Transf. cour.,nia : crédit
Current Transfers: Debit	−26.3	−45.4	−67.0	−79.0	−91.8	−92.7	−103.8	Transf. courants : débit
Capital Acct.,nie: Credit	0.0	0.0	0.0	0.0	0.0	0.0	0.0	Compte de cap.,nia : crédit
Capital Account: Debit	−1.3	−1.1	−0.8	−0.5	−0.8	−0.5	−0.6	Compte de capital : débit
Financial Account,nie	41.4	25.1	91.9	−18.6	−26.0	134.0	182.0	Compte d'op. fin., nia
Net Errors and Omissions	148.5	106.7	−76.8	73.4	−41.9	187.3	82.5	Erreurs et omissions nettes
Reserves and Related Items	43.5	−108.8	−48.3	34.6	65.4	−189.7	−230.6	Rés. et postes appareutés
Morocco								**Maroc**
Goods: Exports fob	5 540.9	6 871.0	6 886.2	7 039.1	7 143.7	7 509.0	7 418.6	Biens : exportations,fàb
Goods: Imports fob	−7 647.6	−9 353.1	−9 079.6	−8 903.0	−9 462.6	−9 956.6	−10 653.6	Biens : importations,fàb
Serv. & Income: Credit	2 238.5	2 424.5	2 932.0	2 643.4	3 020.3	3 301.7	3 310.1	Serv. & revenu : crédit
Serv. & Income: Debit	−3 124.2	−3 458.7	−3 279.9	−3 071.8	−3 189.9	−3 174.9	−3 032.8	Serv. & revenu : débit
Current Trans.,nie: Credit	2 355.2	2 298.0	2 565.4	2 204.2	2 437.7	2 246.1	2 574.2	Transf. cour.,nia : crédit
Current Transfers: Debit	−85.6	−78.0	−82.5	−80.6	−95.0	−96.0	−117.6	Transf. courants : débit
Capital Acct.,nie: Credit	0.3	0.0	78.1	0.5	0.1	0.2	0.1	Compte de cap.,nia : crédit
Capital Account: Debit	−3.7	−5.7	−4.8	−5.0	−10.2	−8.8	−6.0	Compte de capital : débit
Financial Account,nie	1 247.7	−984.4	−896.6	−989.8	−644.1	−13.0	−719.4	Compte d'op. fin., nia
Net Errors and Omissions	−38.7	391.1	208.7	174.8	160.4	123.5	148.1	Erreurs et omissions nettes
Reserves and Related Items	−482.6	1 895.4	673.1	988.2	639.5	68.8	1 078.4	Rés. et postes appareutés
Mozambique								**Mozambique**
Goods: Exports fob	149.5	168.9	226.1	230.0	244.6	...	...	Biens : exportations,fàb
Goods: Imports fob	−916.7	−705.2	−704.4	−684.0	−735.6	...	...	Biens : importations,fàb
Serv. & Income: Credit	245.9	301.5	314.2	342.3	332.5	...	...	Serv. & revenu : crédit
Serv. & Income: Debit	−510.5	−549.1	−481.1	−496.8	−584.0	...	...	Serv. & revenu : débit
Current Trans.,nie: Credit	564.6	339.2	224.7	312.9	313.2	...	...	Transf. cour.,nia : crédit
Current Transfers: Debit	0.0	0.0	0.0	0.0	0.0	...	...	Transf. courants : débit
Capital Acct.,nie: Credit	0.0	0.0	0.0	0.0	0.0	...	...	Compte de cap.,nia : crédit
Capital Account: Debit	0.0	0.0	0.0	0.0	0.0	...	...	Compte de capital : débit
Financial Account,nie	344.4	366.7	235.0	182.2	300.4	...	...	Compte d'op. fin., nia
Net Errors and Omissions	−443.2	−308.6	−238.3	−364.8	−263.8	...	...	Erreurs et omissions nettes
Reserves and Related Items	566.0	386.6	423.8	478.2	392.7	...	...	Rés. et postes appareutés
Namibia								**Namibie**
Goods: Exports fob	1 320.4	1 418.4	1 403.7	1 343.3	1 278.3	...	...	Biens : exportations,fàb
Goods: Imports fob	−1 406.3	−1 548.2	−1 530.9	−1 615.0	−1 450.9	...	...	Biens : importations,fàb
Serv. & Income: Credit	472.9	689.3	656.5	632.1	553.8	...	...	Serv. & revenu : crédit
Serv. & Income: Debit	−628.2	−786.6	−829.6	−714.3	−622.8	...	...	Serv. & revenu : débit
Current Trans.,nie: Credit	349.2	426.9	437.3	462.2	418.2	...	...	Transf. cour.,nia : crédit
Current Transfers: Debit	−22.7	−23.9	−21.0	−18.0	−14.7	...	...	Transf. courants : débit
Capital Acct.,nie: Credit	43.8	40.7	42.5	33.9	24.2	...	...	Compte de cap.,nia : crédit
Capital Account: Debit	−0.6	−0.6	−0.5	−0.4	−0.4	...	...	Compte de capital : débit
Financial Account,nie	−102.1	−205.3	−174.0	−71.4	−145.6	...	...	Compte d'op. fin., nia
Net Errors and Omissions	48.5	13.4	39.1	15.3	15.7	...	...	Erreurs et omissions nettes
Reserves and Related Items	−75.0	−24.2	−22.9	−67.8	−55.8	...	...	Rés. et postes appareutés
Niger								**Niger**
Goods: Exports fob	226.8	288.1	...	...	...	...	...	Biens : exportations,fàb
Goods: Imports fob	−271.3	−305.6	...	...	...	...	...	Biens : importations,fàb
Serv. & Income: Credit	46.0	39.1	...	...	...	...	...	Serv. & revenu : crédit
Serv. & Income: Debit	−194.3	−204.7	...	...	...	...	...	Serv. & revenu : débit
Current Trans.,nie: Credit	115.1	60.6	...	...	...	...	...	Transf. cour.,nia : crédit

76
Summary of balance of payments
Millions of US dollars
Résumé des balances des paiements
Millions de dollars des E.−U.

Country or area	1994	1995	1996	1997	1998	1999	2000	Pays ou zone
Current Transfers: Debit	−48.5	−29.1	...	...	...	...	...	Transf. courants : débit
Capital Acct.,nie: Credit	88.2	65.3	...	...	...	...	...	Compte de cap.,nia : crédit
Capital Account: Debit	0.0	0.0	...	...	...	...	...	Compte de capital : débit
Financial Account,nie	29.9	−46.1	...	...	...	...	...	Compte d'op. fin., nia
Net Errors and Omissions	−67.8	114.4	...	...	...	...	...	Erreurs et omissions nettes
Reserves and Related Items	75.8	18.1	...	...	...	...	...	Rés. et postes appareutés
Nigeria								**Nigéria**
Goods: Exports fob	9 459.1	11 734.4	16 117.0	15 207.3	8 971.2	12 875.7	...	Biens : exportations,fàb
Goods: Imports fob	−6 511.5	−8 221.5	−6 438.4	−9 501.4	−9 211.3	−8 587.6	...	Biens : importations,fàb
Serv. & Income: Credit	419.5	708.3	847.5	1 044.9	1 216.6	1 219.3	...	Serv. & revenu : crédit
Serv. & Income: Debit	−5 993.0	−7 598.4	−7 964.1	−8 115.7	−6 789.5	−6 293.3	...	Serv. & revenu : débit
Current Trans.,nie: Credit	549.9	803.5	946.6	1 920.3	1 574.2	1 301.1	...	Transf. cour.,nia : crédit
Current Transfers: Debit	−52.0	−4.7	−1.7	−3.8	−4.7	−9.4	...	Transf. courants : débit
Capital Acct.,nie: Credit	0.0	0.0	0.0	0.0	0.0	0.0	...	Compte de cap.,nia : crédit
Capital Account: Debit	0.0	−66.2	−68.1	−49.4	−54.3	−47.7	...	Compte de capital : débit
Financial Account,nie	329.2	−46.2	−4 155.0	−424.9	1 502.5	−4 002.4	...	Compte d'op. fin., nia
Net Errors and Omissions	−139.2	−82.9	−44.8	−62.1	−77.5	6.8	...	Erreurs et omissions nettes
Reserves and Related Items	1 938.0	2 773.7	761.0	−15.1	2 872.8	3 537.6	...	Rés. et postes appareutés
Rwanda								**Rwanda**
Goods: Exports fob	32.2	56.7	61.7	93.2	64.5	62.3	69.1	Biens : exportations,fàb
Goods: Imports fob	−367.4	−219.1	−218.5	−278.2	−234.0	−249.7	−222.3	Biens : importations,fàb
Serv. & Income: Credit	0.0	42.2	27.0	59.2	57.2	59.2	72.7	Serv. & revenu : crédit
Serv. & Income: Debit	−109.6	−172.2	−168.5	−223.1	−206.5	−214.2	−207.0	Serv. & revenu : débit
Current Trans.,nie: Credit	398.6	354.9	293.9	311.6	252.6	283.2	297.8	Transf. cour.,nia : crédit
Current Transfers: Debit	0.0	−4.9	−4.1	−24.9	−16.9	−12.8	−17.2	Transf. courants : débit
Capital Acct.,nie: Credit	0.0	0.0	0.0	0.0	0.0	0.0	0.0	Compte de cap.,nia : crédit
Capital Account: Debit	0.0	0.0	0.0	0.0	0.0	0.0	0.0	Compte de capital : débit
Financial Account,nie	−12.5	−10.7	24.8	46.8	−15.2	−14.4	−23.0	Compte d'op. fin., nia
Net Errors and Omissions	62.4	5.8	4.1	46.0	35.9	−59.3	−109.5	Erreurs et omissions nettes
Reserves and Related Items	−3.7	−52.6	−20.3	−30.5	62.4	145.9	139.3	Rés. et postes appareutés
Senegal								**Sénégal**
Goods: Exports fob	818.8	993.3	988.0	904.6	967.7	1 027.1	...	Biens : exportations,fàb
Goods: Imports fob	−1 022.0	−1 242.9	−1 264.0	−1 176.0	−1 280.6	−1 372.8	...	Biens : importations,fàb
Serv. & Income: Credit	475.7	599.7	459.9	439.6	501.8	499.4	...	Serv. & revenu : crédit
Serv. & Income: Debit	−657.2	−789.7	−550.0	−531.5	−607.5	−632.9	...	Serv. & revenu : débit
Current Trans.,nie: Credit	267.0	284.7	244.3	258.8	254.7	225.4	...	Transf. cour.,nia : crédit
Current Transfers: Debit	−69.7	−89.6	−77.8	−80.3	−83.6	−66.3	...	Transf. courants : débit
Capital Acct.,nie: Credit	200.5	201.2	169.3	96.3	98.8	99.0	...	Compte de cap.,nia : crédit
Capital Account: Debit	−9.9	−14.2	−0.1	−0.3	−0.4	−0.5	...	Compte de capital : débit
Financial Account,nie	48.5	44.2	−179.1	3.5	−109.7	−54.8	...	Compte d'op. fin., nia
Net Errors and Omissions	−28.9	−19.6	7.6	−9.3	10.7	8.2	...	Erreurs et omissions nettes
Reserves and Related Items	−22.8	32.9	201.9	94.7	248.1	268.2	...	Rés. et postes appareutés
Seychelles								**Seychelles**
Goods: Exports fob	52.1	53.1	78.0	115.2	123.4	145.2	...	Biens : exportations,fàb
Goods: Imports fob	−188.6	−214.1	−262.7	−302.7	−351.6	−377.6	...	Biens : importations,fàb
Serv. & Income: Credit	201.7	223.9	241.9	247.5	284.5	321.7	...	Serv. & revenu : crédit
Serv. & Income: Debit	−99.0	−125.1	−129.1	−137.3	−172.7	−196.5	...	Serv. & revenu : débit
Current Trans.,nie: Credit	21.3	19.5	27.6	27.1	3.6	3.9	...	Transf. cour.,nia : crédit
Current Transfers: Debit	−13.4	−11.3	−12.1	−13.1	−11.7	−10.8	...	Transf. courants : débit
Capital Acct.,nie: Credit	0.0	0.0	0.0	0.0	21.7	16.5	...	Compte de cap.,nia : crédit
Capital Account: Debit	0.0	0.0	0.0	0.0	0.0	0.0	...	Compte de capital : débit
Financial Account,nie	7.4	16.7	22.9	49.6	73.3	82.5	...	Compte d'op. fin., nia
Net Errors and Omissions	6.8	23.1	20.6	8.4	−4.8	−23.0	...	Erreurs et omissions nettes
Reserves and Related Items	11.7	14.0	13.0	5.2	34.4	38.1	...	Rés. et postes appareutés
Sierra Leone								**Sierra Leone**
Goods: Exports fob	116.0	41.5	...	...	...	...	...	Biens : exportations,fàb
Goods: Imports fob	−188.7	−168.1	...	...	...	...	...	Biens : importations,fàb
Serv. & Income: Credit	101.6	87.6	...	...	...	...	...	Serv. & revenu : crédit
Serv. & Income: Debit	−164.6	−113.2	...	...	...	...	...	Serv. & revenu : débit
Current Trans.,nie: Credit	47.5	35.3	...	...	...	...	...	Transf. cour.,nia : crédit
Current Transfers: Debit	−0.9	−9.5	...	...	...	...	...	Transf. courants : débit
Capital Acct.,nie: Credit	0.1	0.0	...	...	...	...	...	Compte de cap.,nia : crédit
Capital Account: Debit	0.0	0.0	...	...	...	...	...	Compte de capital : débit
Financial Account,nie	−25.5	61.6	...	...	...	...	...	Compte d'op. fin., nia
Net Errors and Omissions	55.1	19.3	...	...	...	...	...	Erreurs et omissions nettes
Reserves and Related Items	59.5	45.6	...	...	...	...	...	Rés. et postes appareutés

76
Summary of balance of payments
Millions of US dollars
Résumé des balances des paiements
Millions de dollars des E.−U.

Country or area	1994	1995	1996	1997	1998	1999	2000	Pays ou zone
South Africa								**Afrique du Sud**
Goods: Exports fob	26 332.9	30 071.1	30 262.8	31 171.3	29 263.7	28 624.3	31 433.7	Biens : exportations,fàb
Goods: Imports fob	−21 852.4	−27 404.2	−27 567.7	−28 847.5	−27 207.6	−24 474.1	−27 202.3	Biens : importations,fàb
Serv. & Income: Credit	4 721.6	5 753.5	6 104.4	6 631.4	6 588.0	6 616.3	7 271.6	Serv. & revenu : crédit
Serv. & Income: Debit	−8 481.3	−9 980.0	−9 926.7	−10 525.0	−10 057.8	−10 393.0	−11 045.9	Serv. & revenu : débit
Current Trans.,nie: Credit	143.5	195.6	54.3	138.4	60.3	66.2	106.4	Transf. cour.,nia : crédit
Current Transfers: Debit	−752.5	−841.1	−807.5	−862.5	−803.8	−992.7	−1 032.9	Transf. courants : débit
Capital Acct.,nie: Credit	20.0	22.1	25.0	29.5	24.4	25.4	18.1	Compte de cap.,nia : crédit
Capital Account: Debit	−86.5	−62.0	−72.0	−222.1	−80.4	−67.9	−70.6	Compte de capital : débit
Financial Account,nie	1 087.1	4 003.5	3 018.0	8 131.1	4 851.9	3 641.0	−1 535.8	Compte d'op. fin., nia
Net Errors and Omissions	−449.3	−851.9	−2 362.7	−1 049.2	−1 718.5	1 169.8	2 457.4	Erreurs et omissions nettes
Reserves and Related Items	−683.2	−906.6	1 272.0	−4 595.4	−920.2	−4 215.2	−399.8	Rés. et postes appareutés
Sudan								**Soudan**
Goods: Exports fob	523.9	555.7	620.3	594.2	595.7	780.1	1 806.7	Biens : exportations,fàb
Goods: Imports fob	−1 045.4	−1 066.0	−1 339.5	−1 421.9	−1 732.2	−1 256.0	−1 366.3	Biens : importations,fàb
Serv. & Income: Credit	77.8	127.2	57.0	48.4	29.5	100.7	32.0	Serv. & revenu : crédit
Serv. & Income: Debit	−239.6	−177.2	−201.5	−178.1	−214.6	−398.1	−1 227.2	Serv. & revenu : débit
Current Trans.,nie: Credit	120.1	346.2	236.3	439.1	731.8	702.2	651.3	Transf. cour.,nia : crédit
Current Transfers: Debit	−38.5	−285.8	−199.4	−309.8	−366.7	−393.7	−453.3	Transf. courants : débit
Capital Acct.,nie: Credit	0.0	0.0	0.0	0.0	13.0	45.8	16.5	Compte de cap.,nia : crédit
Capital Account: Debit	0.0	0.0	0.0	0.0	−67.2	−68.7	−135.8	Compte de capital : débit
Financial Account,nie	276.0	473.7	136.8	195.0	333.4	435.3	431.6	Compte d'op. fin., nia
Net Errors and Omissions	344.8	89.3	727.5	651.2	750.5	167.2	368.4	Erreurs et omissions nettes
Reserves and Related Items	−19.1	−63.1	−37.5	−18.1	−73.2	−114.8	−123.9	Rés. et postes appareutés
Swaziland								**Swaziland**
Goods: Exports fob	790.9	867.8	850.5	961.3	969.9	896.9	810.8	Biens : exportations,fàb
Goods: Imports fob	−841.0	−1 064.4	−1 054.4	−1 088.6	−1 095.8	−1 018.6	−921.3	Biens : importations,fàb
Serv. & Income: Credit	251.3	314.4	301.6	307.1	268.3	268.1	204.3	Serv. & revenu : crédit
Serv. & Income: Debit	−356.8	−291.5	−309.4	−289.4	−343.6	−264.7	−229.9	Serv. & revenu : débit
Current Trans.,nie: Credit	252.6	257.2	268.7	231.2	243.4	232.0	212.7	Transf. cour.,nia : crédit
Current Transfers: Debit	−95.1	−113.3	−108.9	−112.7	−110.6	−107.4	−116.5	Transf. courants : débit
Capital Acct.,nie: Credit	0.1	0.3	0.1	0.1	0.1	0.0	0.1	Compte de cap.,nia : crédit
Capital Account: Debit	−0.3	−0.4	0.0	0.0	0.0	0.0	0.0	Compte de capital : débit
Financial Account,nie	−63.1	−74.5	−4.6	−2.9	96.4	6.0	8.4	Compte d'op. fin., nia
Net Errors and Omissions	48.8	134.1	71.8	19.3	22.3	13.9	25.0	Erreurs et omissions nettes
Reserves and Related Items	12.5	−29.8	−15.4	−25.3	−50.5	−26.3	6.6	Rés. et postes appareutés
Togo								**Togo**
Goods: Exports fob	328.4	377.4	440.6	422.5	420.3	391.5	...	Biens : exportations,fàb
Goods: Imports fob	−365.5	−506.5	−567.8	−530.6	−553.5	−489.4	...	Biens : importations,fàb
Serv. & Income: Credit	80.0	96.1	161.8	123.5	120.4	108.6	...	Serv. & revenu : crédit
Serv. & Income: Debit	−179.3	−206.6	−273.4	−231.7	−217.0	−209.1	...	Serv. & revenu : débit
Current Trans.,nie: Credit	91.3	129.7	106.8	120.2	101.8	73.6	...	Transf. cour.,nia : crédit
Current Transfers: Debit	−11.2	−12.1	−21.9	−20.8	−12.2	−2.2	...	Transf. courants : débit
Capital Acct.,nie: Credit	0.0	0.0	5.6	5.8	6.1	6.9	...	Compte de cap.,nia : crédit
Capital Account: Debit	0.0	0.0	0.0	0.0	0.0	0.0	...	Compte de capital : débit
Financial Account,nie	−40.5	−52.8	151.3	126.9	114.1	155.5	...	Compte d'op. fin., nia
Net Errors and Omissions	−0.2	−19.3	−27.9	−2.7	2.7	−3.7	...	Erreurs et omissions nettes
Reserves and Related Items	97.1	194.0	24.9	−13.1	17.2	−31.6	...	Rés. et postes appareutés
Tunisia								**Tunisie**
Goods: Exports fob	4 643.4	5 469.7	5 518.8	5 559.2	5 724.0	5 873.3	5 840.2	Biens : exportations,fàb
Goods: Imports fob	−6 210.3	−7 458.6	−7 279.6	−7 514.2	−7 875.5	−8 014.5	−8 092.3	Biens : importations,fàb
Serv. & Income: Credit	2 338.0	2 628.6	2 697.7	2 690.1	2 847.9	3 009.5	2 861.3	Serv. & revenu : crédit
Serv. & Income: Debit	−2 106.7	−2 187.7	−2 274.5	−2 121.3	−2 203.3	−2 212.1	−2 255.1	Serv. & revenu : débit
Current Trans.,nie: Credit	815.6	804.7	879.4	821.0	851.8	919.7	853.6	Transf. cour.,nia : crédit
Current Transfers: Debit	−16.8	−30.7	−19.5	−29.8	−20.2	−17.7	−29.2	Transf. courants : débit
Capital Acct.,nie: Credit	4.9	46.5	46.2	94.9	82.5	72.5	8.8	Compte de cap.,nia : crédit
Capital Account: Debit	−7.9	−14.8	−9.2	−18.1	−22.0	−13.5	−5.8	Compte de capital : débit
Financial Account,nie	1 143.8	958.0	815.7	699.0	489.1	1 083.3	647.9	Compte d'op. fin., nia
Net Errors and Omissions	−77.5	−118.9	67.0	205.6	−12.0	37.6	−34.3	Erreurs et omissions nettes
Reserves and Related Items	−526.5	−96.8	−442.0	−386.5	137.6	−738.1	205.0	Rés. et postes appareutés
Uganda								**Ouganda**
Goods: Exports fob	463.0	560.3	639.3	592.6	510.2	500.1	...	Biens : exportations,fàb
Goods: Imports fob	−714.2	−926.8	−986.9	−1 042.6	−1 166.3	−1 096.5	...	Biens : importations,fàb
Serv. & Income: Credit	77.9	121.7	174.4	205.1	227.0	222.8	...	Serv. & revenu : crédit
Serv. & Income: Debit	−507.3	−676.0	−753.8	−724.6	−788.0	−807.6	...	Serv. & revenu : débit
Current Trans.,nie: Credit	473.1	581.9	674.7	602.6	714.6	630.3	...	Transf. cour.,nia : crédit

76
Summary of balance of payments
Millions of US dollars
Résumé des balances des paiements
Millions de dollars des E.−U.

Country or area	1994	1995	1996	1997	1998	1999	2000	Pays ou zone
Current Transfers: Debit	0.0	0.0	0.0	0.0	0.0	0.0	...	Transf. courants : débit
Capital Acct.,nie: Credit	36.1	48.3	61.4	31.9	49.5	26.3	...	Compte de cap.,nia : crédit
Capital Account: Debit	0.0	0.0	0.0	0.0	0.0	0.0	...	Compte de capital : débit
Financial Account,nie	76.8	210.7	140.5	298.8	372.8	368.9	...	Compte d'op. fin., nia
Net Errors and Omissions	32.5	28.8	41.3	−4.8	39.7	49.7	...	Erreurs et omissions nettes
Reserves and Related Items	62.1	51.2	9.1	40.9	40.6	105.9	...	Rés. et postes appareutés
United Rep. Tanzania								**Rép.−Unie de Tanzanie**
Goods: Exports fob	519.4	682.5	764.1	715.3	589.5	542.9	665.7	Biens : exportations,fàb
Goods: Imports fob	−1 309.3	−1 340.0	−1 213.1	−1 164.5	−1 365.3	−1 368.3	−1 339.8	Biens : importations,fàb
Serv. & Income: Credit	449.1	614.4	658.4	539.0	590.0	679.3	674.1	Serv. & revenu : crédit
Serv. & Income: Debit	−656.7	−941.4	−1 058.7	−965.5	−1 161.8	−889.9	−809.4	Serv. & revenu : débit
Current Trans.,nie: Credit	311.5	370.5	370.9	313.6	426.6	413.4	406.0	Transf. cour.,nia : crédit
Current Transfers: Debit	−25.0	−32.3	−32.3	−67.7	−35.5	−123.3	−77.0	Transf. courants : débit
Capital Acct.,nie: Credit	262.6	190.9	191.0	360.6	422.9	322.5	331.7	Compte de cap.,nia : crédit
Capital Account: Debit	0.0	0.0	0.0	0.0	0.0	0.0	0.0	Compte de capital : débit
Financial Account,nie	−91.7	66.7	−92.8	3.6	77.6	80.8	−123.8	Compte d'op. fin., nia
Net Errors and Omissions	121.4	30.0	158.6	−31.9	−53.5	269.3	134.5	Erreurs et omissions nettes
Reserves and Related Items	418.6	358.7	254.0	297.5	509.4	73.4	138.0	Rés. et postes appareutés
Zimbabwe								**Zimbabwe**
Goods: Exports fob	1 961.1	...	...	...	...	...	...	Biens : exportations,fàb
Goods: Imports fob	−1 803.5	...	...	...	...	...	...	Biens : importations,fàb
Serv. & Income: Credit	410.8	...	...	...	...	...	...	Serv. & revenu : crédit
Serv. & Income: Debit	−1 032.9	...	...	...	...	...	...	Serv. & revenu : débit
Current Trans.,nie: Credit	69.4	...	...	...	...	...	...	Transf. cour.,nia : crédit
Current Transfers: Debit	−29.8	...	...	...	...	...	...	Transf. courants : débit
Capital Acct.,nie: Credit	285.4	...	...	...	...	...	...	Compte de cap.,nia : crédit
Capital Account: Debit	−1.0	...	...	...	...	...	...	Compte de capital : débit
Financial Account,nie	−25.5	...	...	...	...	...	...	Compte d'op. fin., nia
Net Errors and Omissions	80.2	...	...	...	...	...	...	Erreurs et omissions nettes
Reserves and Related Items	85.8	...	...	...	...	...	...	Rés. et postes appareutés
America, North · Amérique du Nord								
Anguilla								**Anguilla**
Goods: Exports fob	1.6	...	...	...	...	...	...	Biens : exportations,fàb
Goods: Imports fob	−38.3	...	...	...	...	...	...	Biens : importations,fàb
Serv. & Income: Credit	63.0	...	...	...	...	...	...	Serv. & revenu : crédit
Serv. & Income: Debit	−35.2	...	...	...	...	...	...	Serv. & revenu : débit
Current Trans.,nie: Credit	5.1	...	...	...	...	...	...	Transf. cour.,nia : crédit
Current Transfers: Debit	−6.7	...	...	...	...	...	...	Transf. courants : débit
Capital Acct.,nie: Credit	7.2	...	...	...	...	...	...	Compte de cap.,nia : crédit
Capital Account: Debit	−1.3	...	...	...	...	...	...	Compte de capital : débit
Financial Account,nie	8.4	...	...	...	...	...	...	Compte d'op. fin., nia
Net Errors and Omissions	−4.2	...	...	...	...	...	...	Erreurs et omissions nettes
Reserves and Related Items	0.2	...	...	...	...	...	...	Rés. et postes appareutés
Antigua and Barbuda								**Antigua−et−Barbuda**
Goods: Exports fob	44.4	53.1	54.0	...	...	...	...	Biens : exportations,fàb
Goods: Imports fob	−298.1	−301.8	−316.6	...	...	...	...	Biens : importations,fàb
Serv. & Income: Credit	400.6	353.9	373.3	...	...	...	...	Serv. & revenu : crédit
Serv. & Income: Debit	−165.7	−175.0	−178.4	...	...	...	...	Serv. & revenu : débit
Current Trans.,nie: Credit	10.4	77.9	31.5	...	...	...	...	Transf. cour.,nia : crédit
Current Transfers: Debit	−9.5	−8.7	−3.6	...	...	...	...	Transf. courants : débit
Capital Acct.,nie: Credit	6.5	7.0	3.6	...	...	...	...	Compte de cap.,nia : crédit
Capital Account: Debit	−0.6	0.0	0.0	...	...	...	...	Compte de capital : débit
Financial Account,nie	13.8	12.1	61.7	...	...	...	...	Compte d'op. fin., nia
Net Errors and Omissions	6.3	−5.0	−36.8	...	...	...	...	Erreurs et omissions nettes
Reserves and Related Items	−8.1	−13.6	11.3	...	...	...	...	Rés. et postes appareutés
Aruba								**Aruba**
Goods: Exports fob	1 296.8	1 347.2	1 735.7	1 728.7	1 164.8	1 413.5	2 582.1	Biens : exportations,fàb
Goods: Imports fob	−1 607.3	−1 772.5	−2 043.4	−2 115.9	−1 518.2	−2 005.2	−2 610.4	Biens : importations,fàb
Serv. & Income: Credit	633.8	661.5	789.1	836.5	932.6	1 027.0	1 078.7	Serv. & revenu : crédit
Serv. & Income: Debit	−250.9	−270.1	−546.9	−634.0	−593.2	−781.9	−732.2	Serv. & revenu : débit
Current Trans.,nie: Credit	47.5	71.5	18.4	18.4	29.3	59.3	46.2	Transf. cour.,nia : crédit
Current Transfers: Debit	−38.7	−37.9	−22.0	−29.5	−34.1	−45.9	−82.2	Transf. courants : débit
Capital Acct.,nie: Credit	0.3	3.1	28.7	21.6	10.2	0.9	10.5	Compte de cap.,nia : crédit
Capital Account: Debit	−4.4	−3.6	−0.7	−0.6	−5.0	−0.9	−0.6	Compte de capital : débit
Financial Account,nie	−75.4	41.6	10.7	158.9	64.2	336.4	−314.6	Compte d'op. fin., nia

76
Summary of balance of payments
Millions of US dollars
Résumé des balances des paiements
Millions de dollars des E.–U.

Country or area	1994	1995	1996	1997	1998	1999	2000	Pays ou zone
Net Errors and Omissions	−4.7	2.0	4.3	−2.5	0.6	−0.7	6.5	Erreurs et omissions nettes
Reserves and Related Items	3.2	−42.7	26.1	18.4	−51.3	−2.5	15.9	Rés. et postes appareutés
Bahamas								**Bahamas**
Goods: Exports fob	198.5	225.4	273.3	295.0	362.9	379.9	549.8	Biens : exportations,fàb
Goods: Imports fob	−1 013.8	−1 156.7	−1 287.4	−1 410.7	−1 737.1	−1 808.1	−1 905.0	Biens : importations,fàb
Serv. & Income: Credit	1 571.8	1 617.4	1 662.8	1 698.6	1 680.9	2 040.8	2 234.8	Serv. & revenu : crédit
Serv. & Income: Debit	−826.0	−849.9	−949.2	−1 094.3	−1 336.3	−1 321.0	−1 360.3	Serv. & revenu : débit
Current Trans.,nie: Credit	33.1	25.1	45.9	50.0	45.0	49.0	53.8	Transf. cour.,nia : crédit
Current Transfers: Debit	−5.8	−7.2	−8.7	−10.7	−10.8	−12.5	−10.6	Transf. courants : débit
Capital Acct.,nie: Credit	0.0	0.0	0.0	0.0	0.0	0.0	0.0	Compte de cap.,nia : crédit
Capital Account: Debit	−11.6	−12.5	−24.4	−12.9	−11.7	−14.5	−16.5	Compte de capital : débit
Financial Account,nie	66.8	104.6	181.1	412.0	817.7	611.4	429.3	Compte d'op. fin., nia
Net Errors and Omissions	−3.9	50.9	99.0	129.5	308.6	140.2	−36.3	Erreurs et omissions nettes
Reserves and Related Items	−9.1	2.9	7.6	−56.5	−119.2	−65.2	61.0	Rés. et postes appareutés
Barbados								**Barbade**
Goods: Exports fob	190.0	245.4	286.7	289.0	257.1	262.0	...	Biens : exportations,fàb
Goods: Imports fob	−544.7	−691.2	−743.0	−887.7	−901.1	−953.7	...	Biens : importations,fàb
Serv. & Income: Credit	859.7	915.0	981.0	1 019.7	1 087.1	1 092.0	...	Serv. & revenu : crédit
Serv. & Income: Debit	−405.7	−459.3	−493.4	−517.6	−551.8	−592.3	...	Serv. & revenu : débit
Current Trans.,nie: Credit	54.5	56.2	64.8	71.7	78.3	94.0	...	Transf. cour.,nia : crédit
Current Transfers: Debit	−20.2	−23.6	−26.6	−25.1	−26.2	−27.7	...	Transf. courants : débit
Capital Acct.,nie: Credit	0.0	0.0	0.4	0.0	0.7	3.8	...	Compte de cap.,nia : crédit
Capital Account: Debit	0.0	0.0	0.0	0.0	0.0	0.0	...	Compte de capital : débit
Financial Account,nie	−6.4	−26.4	−22.2	20.0	55.5	119.4	...	Compte d'op. fin., nia
Net Errors and Omissions	−89.4	26.0	38.5	47.4	−5.7	38.9	...	Erreurs et omissions nettes
Reserves and Related Items	−37.8	−42.1	−86.4	−17.4	6.1	−36.3	...	Rés. et postes appareutés
Belize								**Belize**
Goods: Exports fob	156.5	164.6	171.3	193.4	186.2	213.2	212.3	Biens : exportations,fàb
Goods: Imports fob	−231.9	−230.6	−229.5	−282.9	−290.9	−337.5	−403.7	Biens : importations,fàb
Serv. & Income: Credit	124.0	135.6	144.2	145.3	147.7	164.3	177.2	Serv. & revenu : crédit
Serv. & Income: Debit	−116.2	−120.0	−123.7	−122.5	−138.3	−154.7	−178.6	Serv. & revenu : débit
Current Trans.,nie: Credit	34.4	38.3	34.2	38.2	38.4	40.6	56.6	Transf. cour.,nia : crédit
Current Transfers: Debit	−6.9	−5.2	−3.1	−3.4	−2.8	−3.5	−3.2	Transf. courants : débit
Capital Acct.,nie: Credit	0.0	0.0	0.0	0.0	0.0	0.5	0.9	Compte de cap.,nia : crédit
Capital Account: Debit	0.0	0.0	−2.2	−3.4	−1.9	−2.4	−0.5	Compte de capital : débit
Financial Account,nie	3.6	−1.0	11.0	27.6	23.5	91.5	88.4	Compte d'op. fin., nia
Net Errors and Omissions	32.8	22.4	18.4	9.1	24.5	0.9	7.3	Erreurs et omissions nettes
Reserves and Related Items	3.6	−4.1	−20.6	−1.4	13.7	−12.9	43.3	Rés. et postes appareutés
Canada								**Canada**
Goods: Exports fob	166 990.0	193 373.0	205 443.0	217 739.0	217 406.0	242 820.0	281 148.0	Biens : exportations,fàb
Goods: Imports fob	−152 155.0	−167 517.0	−174 352.0	−200 516.0	−204 631.0	−220 064.0	−244 538.0	Biens : importations,fàb
Serv. & Income: Credit	39 401.6	45 015.6	48 446.4	53 908.5	53 678.5	56 136.9	63 361.9	Serv. & revenu : crédit
Serv. & Income: Debit	−66 912.2	−75 082.1	−76 660.9	−81 746.5	−78 094.3	−81 843.2	−88 146.0	Serv. & revenu : débit
Current Trans.,nie: Credit	2 625.1	2 878.2	3 593.5	3 653.3	3 341.5	3 654.4	3 865.7	Transf. cour.,nia : crédit
Current Transfers: Debit	−2 972.8	−2 995.0	−3 091.8	−3 103.8	−2 833.9	−2 977.6	−3 025.0	Transf. courants : débit
Capital Acct.,nie: Credit	7 875.8	5 415.9	6 262.1	5 862.3	3 793.7	3 886.8	3 862.0	Compte de cap.,nia : crédit
Capital Account: Debit	−377.6	−466.2	−428.7	−433.0	−458.7	−458.6	−497.8	Compte de capital : débit
Financial Account,nie	5 159.4	−1 277.4	−9 276.8	3 835.2	9 397.0	−1 868.4	−10 941.1	Compte d'op. fin., nia
Net Errors and Omissions	−26.0	3 366.2	5 562.8	−1 592.2	3 397.2	6 646.6	−1 369.1	Erreurs et omissions nettes
Reserves and Related Items	392.4	−2 710.8	−5 497.7	2 393.1	−4 996.3	−5 933.2	−3 719.9	Rés. et postes appareutés
Costa Rica								**Costa Rica**
Goods: Exports fob	2 122.0	3 481.8	3 774.1	4 220.6	5 538.3	6 667.7	...	Biens : exportations,fàb
Goods: Imports fob	−2 727.8	−3 804.4	−4 023.3	−4 718.2	−5 937.4	−6 008.1	...	Biens : importations,fàb
Serv. & Income: Credit	1 349.6	1 115.5	1 196.0	1 314.0	1 526.1	1 723.8	...	Serv. & revenu : crédit
Serv. & Income: Debit	−1 143.1	−1 284.9	−1 360.0	−1 422.8	−1 761.0	−3 135.1	...	Serv. & revenu : débit
Current Trans.,nie: Credit	164.5	165.2	192.7	191.2	190.5	190.7	...	Transf. cour.,nia : crédit
Current Transfers: Debit	−9.2	−31.3	−43.2	−65.7	−77.3	−88.6	...	Transf. courants : débit
Capital Acct.,nie: Credit	0.0	0.0	28.2	0.0	0.0	0.0	...	Compte de cap.,nia : crédit
Capital Account: Debit	0.0	0.0	0.0	0.0	0.0	0.0	...	Compte de capital : débit
Financial Account,nie	−108.4	517.3	47.5	129.7	199.0	576.6	...	Compte d'op. fin., nia
Net Errors and Omissions	249.1	57.1	118.7	157.8	−182.6	224.2	...	Erreurs et omissions nettes
Reserves and Related Items	103.3	−216.2	69.3	193.3	504.3	−151.3	...	Rés. et postes appareutés
Dominica								**Dominique**
Goods: Exports fob	47.8	46.1	52.7	53.8	62.3	...	...	Biens : exportations,fàb
Goods: Imports fob	−95.8	−103.2	−100.5	−104.3	−98.8	...	...	Biens : importations,fàb
Serv. & Income: Credit	56.0	57.2	64.1	78.1	80.4	...	...	Serv. & revenu : crédit

76
Summary of balance of payments
Millions of US dollars
Résumé des balances des paiements
Millions de dollars des E.–U.

Country or area	1994	1995	1996	1997	1998	1999	2000	Pays ou zone
Serv. & Income: Debit	−53.6	−57.7	−66.5	−71.6	−72.2	...	...	Serv. & revenu : débit
Current Trans.,nie: Credit	14.9	16.3	17.8	17.6	17.5	...	...	Transf. cour.,nia : crédit
Current Transfers: Debit	−7.8	−8.4	−7.7	−7.1	−6.7	...	...	Transf. courants : débit
Capital Acct.,nie: Credit	9.4	24.6	25.4	22.6	14.0	...	...	Compte de cap.,nia : crédit
Capital Account: Debit	−0.8	−0.1	−0.1	−0.1	−0.1	...	...	Compte de capital : débit
Financial Account,nie	29.8	45.0	9.7	15.3	2.2	...	...	Compte d'op. fin., nia
Net Errors and Omissions	−3.2	−11.8	7.1	−2.4	5.3	...	...	Erreurs et omissions nettes
Reserves and Related Items	3.2	−8.0	−2.2	−1.8	−4.0	...	...	Rés. et postes appareutés
Dominican Republic								**Rép. dominicaine**
Goods: Exports fob	3 452.5	3 779.5	4 052.8	4 613.7	4 980.5	5 136.7	5 736.7	Biens : exportations,fàb
Goods: Imports fob	−4 903.2	−5 170.4	−5 727.0	−6 608.7	−7 597.3	−8 041.1	−9 478.5	Biens : importations,fàb
Serv. & Income: Credit	1 889.3	2 079.4	2 270.3	2 587.0	2 669.7	3 068.6	3 527.3	Serv. & revenu : crédit
Serv. & Income: Debit	−1 704.4	−1 863.5	−1 976.5	−2 107.1	−2 377.8	−2 441.2	−2 714.3	Serv. & revenu : débit
Current Trans.,nie: Credit	996.8	1 007.7	1 187.6	1 373.1	2 016.9	1 997.1	2 095.6	Transf. cour.,nia : crédit
Current Transfers: Debit	−14.0	−15.5	−19.9	−21.0	−30.4	−149.3	−193.3	Transf. courants : débit
Capital Acct.,nie: Credit	0.0	0.0	0.0	0.0	0.0	0.0	0.0	Compte de cap.,nia : crédit
Capital Account: Debit	0.0	0.0	0.0	0.0	0.0	0.0	0.0	Compte de capital : débit
Financial Account,nie	368.0	253.6	64.1	447.6	688.1	1 061.0	1 596.6	Compte d'op. fin., nia
Net Errors and Omissions	−596.0	75.3	108.8	−193.7	−338.6	−480.4	−618.5	Erreurs et omissions nettes
Reserves and Related Items	511.0	−146.1	39.8	−90.9	−11.1	−151.4	48.4	Rés. et postes appareutés
El Salvador								**El Salvador**
Goods: Exports fob	1 252.3	1 651.1	1 787.4	2 437.1	2 459.5	2 534.3	2 971.6	Biens : exportations,fàb
Goods: Imports fob	−2 422.3	−3 113.5	−3 029.7	−3 580.3	−3 765.2	−3 879.4	−4 690.2	Biens : importations,fàb
Serv. & Income: Credit	422.7	442.6	458.5	550.9	699.8	741.9	815.3	Serv. & revenu : crédit
Serv. & Income: Debit	−559.1	−630.5	−639.1	−866.4	−1 011.7	−1 227.5	−1 343.3	Serv. & revenu : débit
Current Trans.,nie: Credit	1 290.9	1 393.2	1 258.6	1 363.6	1 534.1	1 565.5	1 830.4	Transf. cour.,nia : crédit
Current Transfers: Debit	−2.5	−4.6	−4.8	−2.7	−7.3	−9.0	−1.4	Transf. courants : débit
Capital Acct.,nie: Credit	0.0	0.0	0.0	11.6	28.9	32.1	109.7	Compte de cap.,nia : crédit
Capital Account: Debit	0.0	0.0	0.0	0.0	−0.3	−0.2	−0.5	Compte de capital : débit
Financial Account,nie	115.8	438.3	358.1	653.2	1 034.3	584.8	330.2	Compte d'op. fin., nia
Net Errors and Omissions	15.4	−28.4	−24.2	−204.4	−668.9	−143.2	−70.5	Rés. et postes appareutés
Reserves and Related Items	−113.3	−148.3	−164.8	−362.7	−303.3	−199.2	48.8	Rés. et postes appareutés
Grenada								**Grenade**
Goods: Exports fob	26.5	25.9	24.9	...	...	...	...	Biens : exportations,fàb
Goods: Imports fob	−115.6	−125.4	−147.5	...	...	...	...	Biens : importations,fàb
Serv. & Income: Credit	105.1	104.1	111.0	...	...	...	...	Serv. & revenu : crédit
Serv. & Income: Debit	−53.7	−56.9	−65.7	...	...	...	...	Serv. & revenu : débit
Current Trans.,nie: Credit	19.7	21.6	23.4	...	...	...	...	Transf. cour.,nia : crédit
Current Transfers: Debit	−3.9	−4.5	−4.1	...	...	...	...	Transf. courants : débit
Capital Acct.,nie: Credit	23.0	27.3	30.9	...	...	...	...	Compte de cap.,nia : crédit
Capital Account: Debit	−1.4	−1.4	−1.5	...	...	...	...	Compte de capital : débit
Financial Account,nie	4.1	3.1	26.2	...	...	...	...	Compte d'op. fin., nia
Net Errors and Omissions	0.7	12.3	2.6	...	...	...	...	Erreurs et omissions nettes
Reserves and Related Items	−4.5	−6.0	−0.3	...	...	...	...	Rés. et postes appareutés
Guatemala								**Guatemala**
Goods: Exports fob	1 550.1	2 157.5	2 236.9	2 602.9	2 846.9	2 780.6	3 082.3	Biens : exportations,fàb
Goods: Imports fob	−2 546.6	−3 032.6	−2 880.3	−3 542.7	−4 255.7	−4 225.7	−4 508.2	Biens : importations,fàb
Serv. & Income: Credit	761.1	712.5	599.2	661.2	731.3	775.7	882.2	Serv. & revenu : crédit
Serv. & Income: Debit	−838.5	−900.6	−929.8	−961.6	−1 066.9	−1 071.4	−1 195.6	Serv. & revenu : débit
Current Trans.,nie: Credit	456.4	508.2	537.1	628.8	742.9	754.4	869.2	Transf. cour.,nia : crédit
Current Transfers: Debit	−7.8	−17.0	−14.6	−22.1	−37.6	−39.5	−43.0	Transf. courants : débit
Capital Acct.,nie: Credit	0.0	61.6	65.0	85.0	71.0	68.4	69.1	Compte de cap.,nia : crédit
Capital Account: Debit	0.0	0.0	0.0	0.0	0.0	0.0	0.0	Compte de capital : débit
Financial Account,nie	655.2	494.8	672.3	737.4	1 136.7	637.5	1 768.4	Compte d'op. fin., nia
Net Errors and Omissions	−23.6	−136.2	−71.7	40.7	66.8	195.0	−269.3	Erreurs et omissions nettes
Reserves and Related Items	−6.3	151.8	−214.1	−229.6	−235.4	125.0	−655.0	Rés. et postes appareutés
Haiti								**Haïti**
Goods: Exports fob	60.3	88.3	82.5	205.4	299.3	...	...	Biens : exportations,fàb
Goods: Imports fob	−171.5	−517.2	−498.6	−559.6	−640.7	...	...	Biens : importations,fàb
Serv. & Income: Credit	6.7	104.1	109.1	173.7	180.0	...	...	Serv. & revenu : crédit
Serv. & Income: Debit	−75.1	−315.2	−293.2	−345.1	−392.3	...	...	Serv. & revenu : débit
Current Trans.,nie: Credit	156.2	552.9	462.5	477.9	515.6	...	...	Transf. cour.,nia : crédit
Current Transfers: Debit	0.0	0.0	0.0	0.0	0.0	...	...	Transf. courants : débit
Capital Acct.,nie: Credit	0.0	0.0	0.0	0.0	0.0	...	...	Compte de cap.,nia : crédit
Capital Account: Debit	0.0	0.0	0.0	0.0	0.0	...	...	Compte de capital : débit
Financial Account,nie	−15.8	99.2	67.9	61.5	193.1	...	...	Compte d'op. fin., nia

76
Summary of balance of payments
Millions of US dollars
Résumé des balances des paiements
Millions de dollars des E.–U.

Country or area	1994	1995	1996	1997	1998	1999	2000	Pays ou zone
Net Errors and Omissions	−10.5	125.0	19.4	16.0	−120.5	...	...	Erreurs et omissions nettes
Reserves and Related Items	49.7	−137.1	50.4	−29.8	−34.5	...	...	Rés. et postes appareutés
Honduras								**Honduras**
Goods: Exports fob	1 101.5	1 377.2	1 638.4	1 856.5	2 047.9	1 769.6	2 039.2	Biens : exportations,fàb
Goods: Imports fob	−1 351.1	−1 518.6	−1 925.8	−2 150.4	−2 370.5	−2 509.6	−2 697.6	Biens : importations,fàb
Serv. & Income: Credit	266.4	289.9	344.5	404.9	436.6	582.7	541.9	Serv. & revenu : crédit
Serv. & Income: Debit	−549.1	−591.9	−619.8	−642.7	−710.4	−738.1	−795.2	Serv. & revenu : débit
Current Trans.,nie: Credit	190.2	243.7	271.7	306.8	241.7	354.6	447.4	Transf. cour.,nia : crédit
Current Transfers: Debit	−1.2	−1.2	−44.4	−47.3	−40.1	−42.4	−45.4	Transf. courants : débit
Capital Acct.,nie: Credit	0.0	0.0	29.2	15.3	29.4	111.1	81.7	Compte de cap.,nia : crédit
Capital Account: Debit	0.0	0.0	−0.7	−0.7	−0.8	0.0	0.0	Compte de capital : débit
Financial Account,nie	157.5	114.6	70.2	243.3	113.9	275.1	73.1	Compte d'op. fin., nia
Net Errors and Omissions	115.5	45.0	157.9	196.5	96.1	6.4	16.6	Erreurs et omissions nettes
Reserves and Related Items	70.3	41.3	78.8	−182.2	155.4	190.6	338.3	Rés. et postes appareutés
Jamaica								**Jamaïque**
Goods: Exports fob	1 548.0	1 796.0	1 721.0	1 700.3	1 613.4	1 499.1	1 554.6	Biens : exportations,fàb
Goods: Imports fob	−2 099.2	−2 625.3	−2 715.2	−2 832.6	−2 743.9	−2 685.6	−2 908.1	Biens : importations,fàb
Serv. & Income: Credit	1 584.8	1 744.5	1 743.7	1 846.2	1 926.7	2 144.2	2 218.9	Serv. & revenu : crédit
Serv. & Income: Debit	−1 411.9	−1 620.9	−1 515.7	−1 670.9	−1 757.9	−1 821.3	−1 960.6	Serv. & revenu : débit
Current Trans.,nie: Credit	504.2	669.6	709.3	705.7	733.5	762.8	969.2	Transf. cour.,nia : crédit
Current Transfers: Debit	−44.3	−62.6	−85.7	−80.9	−99.6	−110.6	−148.6	Transf. courants : débit
Capital Acct.,nie: Credit	33.2	34.5	42.5	21.7	20.3	19.1	29.6	Compte de cap.,nia : crédit
Capital Account: Debit	−22.8	−24.0	−25.9	−33.3	−29.0	−30.0	−27.4	Compte de capital : débit
Financial Account,nie	256.1	108.4	388.6	163.5	337.2	94.8	841.7	Compte d'op. fin., nia
Net Errors and Omissions	9.6	6.8	8.8	9.9	43.2	−8.9	−50.9	Erreurs et omissions nettes
Reserves and Related Items	−357.7	−27.0	−271.4	170.4	−43.9	136.4	−518.4	Rés. et postes appareutés
Mexico								**Mexique**
Goods: Exports fob	60 882.2	79 541.6	96 000.0	110 431.0	117 459.0	136 392.0	166 455.0	Biens : exportations,fàb
Goods: Imports fob	−79 346.0	−72 453.0	−89 469.0	−109 808.0	−125 374.0	−141 973.0	−174 458.0	Biens : importations,fàb
Serv. & Income: Credit	13 667.9	13 492.8	14 932.6	15 830.0	16 976.0	16 208.0	19 803.4	Serv. & revenu : crédit
Serv. & Income: Debit	−28 648.1	−26 117.7	−28 321.6	−29 154.0	−30 799.0	−31 265.0	−36 950.8	Serv. & revenu : débit
Current Trans.,nie: Credit	3 821.7	3 995.0	4 560.2	5 272.0	6 042.0	6 341.0	7 023.1	Transf. cour.,nia : crédit
Current Transfers: Debit	−39.8	−35.0	−30.0	−25.0	−28.0	−27.0	−29.5	Transf. courants : débit
Capital Acct.,nie: Credit	0.0	0.0	0.0	0.0	0.0	0.0	0.0	Compte de cap.,nia : crédit
Capital Account: Debit	0.0	0.0	0.0	0.0	0.0	0.0	0.0	Compte de capital : débit
Financial Account,nie	15 786.8	−10 487.3	6 132.0	19 252.4	18 540.0	18 021.0	22 330.9	Compte d'op. fin., nia
Net Errors and Omissions	−3 323.5	−4 247.8	58.5	2 199.0	376.6	581.4	2 976.1	Erreurs et omissions nettes
Reserves and Related Items	17 198.8	16 311.5	−3 862.6	−13 997.4	−3 192.6	−4 278.4	−7 150.1	Rés. et postes appareutés
Montserrat								**Montserrat**
Goods: Exports fob	2.9	...	...	...	...	...	...	Biens : exportations,fàb
Goods: Imports fob	−30.0	...	...	...	...	...	...	Biens : importations,fàb
Serv. & Income: Credit	27.6	...	...	...	...	...	...	Serv. & revenu : crédit
Serv. & Income: Debit	−19.7	...	...	...	...	...	...	Serv. & revenu : débit
Current Trans.,nie: Credit	3.3	...	...	...	...	...	...	Transf. cour.,nia : crédit
Current Transfers: Debit	−3.4	...	...	...	...	...	...	Transf. courants : débit
Capital Acct.,nie: Credit	10.1	...	...	...	...	...	...	Compte de cap.,nia : crédit
Capital Account: Debit	0.0	...	...	...	...	...	...	Compte de capital : débit
Financial Account,nie	−4.3	...	...	...	...	...	...	Compte d'op. fin., nia
Net Errors and Omissions	15.1	...	...	...	...	...	...	Erreurs et omissions nettes
Reserves and Related Items	−1.6	...	...	...	...	...	...	Rés. et postes appareutés
Netherlands Antilles								**Antilles néerlandaises**
Goods: Exports fob	351.1	354.2	...	...	...	...	...	Biens : exportations,fàb
Goods: Imports fob	−1 271.6	−1 318.7	...	...	...	...	...	Biens : importations,fàb
Serv. & Income: Credit	1 547.9	1 809.4	...	...	...	...	...	Serv. & revenu : crédit
Serv. & Income: Debit	−769.9	−855.8	...	...	...	...	...	Serv. & revenu : débit
Current Trans.,nie: Credit	217.9	245.9	...	...	...	...	...	Transf. cour.,nia : crédit
Current Transfers: Debit	−173.3	−148.5	...	...	...	...	...	Transf. courants : débit
Capital Acct.,nie: Credit	1.0	1.4	...	...	...	...	...	Compte de cap.,nia : crédit
Capital Account: Debit	−1.7	−2.2	...	...	...	...	...	Compte de capital : débit
Financial Account,nie	−2.3	31.1	...	...	...	...	...	Compte d'op. fin., nia
Net Errors and Omissions	24.9	22.5	...	...	...	...	...	Erreurs et omissions nettes
Reserves and Related Items	75.9	−139.3	...	...	...	...	...	Rés. et postes appareutés
Nicaragua								**Nicaragua**
Goods: Exports fob	338.6	470.5	470.2	581.6	580.1	552.4	652.8	Biens : exportations,fàb
Goods: Imports fob	−781.4	−882.3	−1 044.3	−1 371.2	−1 397.1	−1 698.2	−1 647.3	Biens : importations,fàb
Serv. & Income: Credit	131.9	148.4	182.3	228.1	274.2	314.2	331.0	Serv. & revenu : crédit

76
Summary of balance of payments
Millions of US dollars
Résumé des balances des paiements
Millions de dollars des E.-U.

Country or area	1994	1995	1996	1997	1998	1999	2000	Pays ou zone
Serv. & Income: Debit	−651.8	−599.7	−587.6	−518.8	−479.0	−562.2	−570.7	Serv. & revenu : débit
Current Trans.,nie: Credit	248.4	285.5	350.2	407.4	518.0	696.5	729.2	Transf. cour.,nia : crédit
Current Transfers: Debit	0.0	0.0	0.0	0.0	0.0	0.0	0.0	Transf. courants : débit
Capital Acct.,nie: Credit	0.0	0.0	0.0	0.0	0.0	0.0	0.0	Compte de cap.,nia : crédit
Capital Account: Debit	0.0	0.0	0.0	0.0	0.0	0.0	0.0	Compte de capital : débit
Financial Account,nie	−901.9	−625.0	−355.0	3.2	197.1	488.2	260.7	Compte d'op. fin., nia
Net Errors and Omissions	50.4	158.8	174.1	355.1	−102.9	−251.2	−209.8	Erreurs et omissions nettes
Reserves and Related Items	1 565.8	1 043.8	810.1	314.6	409.6	460.3	454.1	Rés. et postes appareutés
Panama								**Panama**
Goods: Exports fob	6 044.8	6 090.9	5 822.9	6 655.4	6 349.7	5 299.5	5 748.8	Biens : exportations,fàb
Goods: Imports fob	−6 294.9	−6 679.8	−6 467.0	−7 355.7	−7 711.2	−6 714.5	−7 039.7	Biens : importations,fàb
Serv. & Income: Credit	2 606.6	3 163.5	2 980.7	3 084.4	3 453.3	3 261.2	3 388.6	Serv. & revenu : crédit
Serv. & Income: Debit	−2 489.6	−3 096.3	−2 773.2	−3 138.2	−3 426.7	−3 386.4	−3 190.7	Serv. & revenu : débit
Current Trans.,nie: Credit	185.5	184.1	167.7	185.2	195.2	202.7	206.4	Transf. cour.,nia : crédit
Current Transfers: Debit	−36.6	−31.5	−33.0	−34.6	−36.2	−38.5	−40.2	Transf. courants : débit
Capital Acct.,nie: Credit	0.0	8.5	2.5	72.7	50.9	3.0	1.7	Compte de cap.,nia : crédit
Capital Account: Debit	0.0	0.0	0.0	0.0	0.0	0.0	0.0	Compte de capital : débit
Financial Account,nie	−297.2	159.3	533.0	788.3	906.2	1 369.2	−61.1	Compte d'op. fin., nia
Net Errors and Omissions	−80.4	−130.0	33.2	85.8	−244.4	−144.0	659.5	Erreurs et omissions nettes
Reserves and Related Items	361.8	331.3	−266.8	−343.3	463.2	147.8	326.7	Rés. et postes appareutés
Saint Kitts and Nevis [1]								**Saint−Kitts−et−Nevis** [1]
Goods: Exports fob	29.3	...	...	...	...	...	...	Biens : exportations,fàb
Goods: Imports fob	−98.3	...	...	...	...	...	...	Biens : importations,fàb
Serv. & Income: Credit	94.5	...	...	...	...	...	...	Serv. & revenu : crédit
Serv. & Income: Debit	−61.5	...	...	...	...	...	...	Serv. & revenu : débit
Current Trans.,nie: Credit	15.2	...	...	...	...	...	...	Transf. cour.,nia : crédit
Current Transfers: Debit	−5.7	...	...	...	...	...	...	Transf. courants : débit
Capital Acct.,nie: Credit	2.6	...	...	...	...	...	...	Compte de cap.,nia : crédit
Capital Account: Debit	−0.9	...	...	...	...	...	...	Compte de capital : débit
Financial Account,nie	26.0	...	...	...	...	...	...	Compte d'op. fin., nia
Net Errors and Omissions	1.0	...	...	...	...	...	...	Erreurs et omissions nettes
Reserves and Related Items	−2.3	...	...	...	...	...	...	Rés. et postes appareutés
Saint Lucia								**Sainte−Lucie**
Goods: Exports fob	99.9	114.6	86.3	...	...	...	...	Biens : exportations,fàb
Goods: Imports fob	−265.6	−269.4	−270.7	...	...	...	...	Biens : importations,fàb
Serv. & Income: Credit	242.7	271.6	273.0	...	...	...	...	Serv. & revenu : crédit
Serv. & Income: Debit	−143.3	−169.2	−182.9	...	...	...	...	Serv. & revenu : débit
Current Trans.,nie: Credit	26.1	28.7	26.5	...	...	...	...	Transf. cour.,nia : crédit
Current Transfers: Debit	−8.3	−9.5	−12.5	...	...	...	...	Transf. courants : débit
Capital Acct.,nie: Credit	11.8	13.6	9.5	...	...	...	...	Compte de cap.,nia : crédit
Capital Account: Debit	−1.1	−0.4	−0.7	...	...	...	...	Compte de capital : débit
Financial Account,nie	41.7	28.1	61.2	...	...	...	...	Compte d'op. fin., nia
Net Errors and Omissions	−6.3	−2.8	3.5	...	...	...	...	Erreurs et omissions nettes
Reserves and Related Items	2.4	−5.3	6.9	...	...	...	...	Rés. et postes appareutés
St. Vincent−Grenadines								**St. Vincent−Grenadines**
Goods: Exports fob	48.9	61.9	52.3	...	...	...	...	Biens : exportations,fàb
Goods: Imports fob	−115.4	−119.4	−127.5	...	...	...	...	Biens : importations,fàb
Serv. & Income: Credit	67.4	78.2	98.2	...	...	...	...	Serv. & revenu : crédit
Serv. & Income: Debit	−70.6	−70.8	−69.7	...	...	...	...	Serv. & revenu : débit
Current Trans.,nie: Credit	19.4	16.8	18.5	...	...	...	...	Transf. cour.,nia : crédit
Current Transfers: Debit	−7.6	−7.9	−7.2	...	...	...	...	Transf. courants : débit
Capital Acct.,nie: Credit	5.4	6.9	5.2	...	...	...	...	Compte de cap.,nia : crédit
Capital Account: Debit	−1.4	−0.7	−1.1	...	...	...	...	Compte de capital : débit
Financial Account,nie	50.9	35.8	18.3	...	...	...	...	Compte d'op. fin., nia
Net Errors and Omissions	3.5	−1.1	13.2	...	...	...	...	Erreurs et omissions nettes
Reserves and Related Items	−0.5	0.3	−0.4	...	...	...	...	Rés. et postes appareutés
Trinidad and Tobago								**Trinité−et−Tobago**
Goods: Exports fob	1 777.6	2 456.1	2 354.1	2 448.0	2 258.0	...	...	Biens : exportations,fàb
Goods: Imports fob	−1 036.6	−1 868.5	−1 971.6	−2 976.6	−2 998.9	...	...	Biens : importations,fàb
Serv. & Income: Credit	383.3	419.2	500.3	610.3	735.8	...	...	Serv. & revenu : crédit
Serv. & Income: Debit	−906.8	−708.6	−770.6	−699.0	−660.7	...	...	Serv. & revenu : débit
Current Trans.,nie: Credit	28.3	34.0	34.2	37.0	58.4	...	...	Transf. cour.,nia : crédit
Current Transfers: Debit	−27.9	−38.5	−41.3	−33.2	−36.2	...	...	Transf. courants : débit
Capital Acct.,nie: Credit	1.1	1.1	0.0	0.0	0.0	...	...	Compte de cap.,nia : crédit
Capital Account: Debit	−7.5	−13.0	0.0	0.0	0.0	...	...	Compte de capital : débit
Financial Account,nie	−32.2	−214.7	43.0	697.2	471.5	...	...	Compte d'op. fin., nia

76
Summary of balance of payments
Millions of US dollars
Résumé des balances des paiements
Millions de dollars des E.–U.

Country or area	1994	1995	1996	1997	1998	1999	2000	Pays ou zone
Net Errors and Omissions	6.3	16.5	90.0	110.1	252.2	...	...	Erreurs et omissions nettes
Reserves and Related Items	−185.5	−83.7	−238.1	−193.6	−80.2	...	...	Rés. et postes appareutés
United States [2]								**Etats–Unis** [2]
Goods: Exports fob	504.9	577.1	614.0	680.3	672.4	686.9	774.9	Biens : exportations,fàb
Goods: Imports fob	−668.7	−749.4	−803.1	−876.5	−917.1	−1 030.0	−1 224.4	Biens : importations,fàb
Serv. & Income: Credit	364.5	429.0	464.0	515.3	519.6	555.9	643.8	Serv. & revenu : crédit
Serv. & Income: Debit	−280.7	−332.5	−355.8	−418.1	−447.9	−488.2	−584.8	Serv. & revenu : débit
Current Trans.,nie: Credit	6.5	7.7	8.9	8.5	9.2	9.3	10.2	Transf. cour.,nia : crédit
Current Transfers: Debit	−44.7	−41.8	−49.0	−49.3	−53.6	−58.2	−64.4	Transf. courants : débit
Capital Acct.,nie: Credit	0.3	0.7	0.7	0.4	0.6	0.5	0.7	Compte de cap.,nia : crédit
Capital Account: Debit	−0.8	−0.3	0.0	0.0	0.0	−4.0	0.0	Compte de capital : débit
Financial Account,nie	124.6	123.1	165.5	272.5	151.6	367.9	443.6	Compte d'op. fin., nia
Net Errors and Omissions	−11.3	−3.8	−51.9	−132.0	71.9	−48.8	0.7	Erreurs et omissions nettes
Reserves and Related Items	5.3	−9.7	6.7	−1.0	−6.7	8.7	−0.3	Rés. et postes appareutés
America, South · Amérique du Sud								
Argentina								**Argentine**
Goods: Exports fob	16 024.0	21 162.0	24 043.0	26 431.0	26 433.0	23 309.0	26 409.0	Biens : exportations,fàb
Goods: Imports fob	−20 163.0	−18 804.0	−22 283.0	−28 554.0	−29 532.0	−24 103.0	−23 851.0	Biens : importations,fàb
Serv. & Income: Credit	6 812.0	8 133.0	8 708.0	9 896.0	10 739.0	10 531.0	11 933.0	Serv. & revenu : crédit
Serv. & Income: Debit	−14 293.0	−16 251.0	−17 790.0	−20 570.0	−22 664.0	−22 158.0	−23 750.0	Serv. & revenu : débit
Current Trans.,nie: Credit	798.0	821.0	702.0	751.0	711.0	688.0	641.0	Transf. cour.,nia : crédit
Current Transfers: Debit	−336.0	−271.0	−257.0	−298.0	−313.0	−306.0	−352.0	Transf. courants : débit
Capital Acct.,nie: Credit	0.0	0.0	0.0	0.0	0.0	0.0	0.0	Compte de cap.,nia : crédit
Capital Account: Debit	0.0	0.0	0.0	0.0	0.0	0.0	0.0	Compte de capital : débit
Financial Account,nie	11 351.0	4 915.0	11 799.0	16 590.0	18 971.0	14 693.0	8 110.0	Compte d'op. fin., nia
Net Errors and Omissions	−886.8	−2 030.4	−1 715.3	−966.5	−327.7	−729.5	−402.8	Erreurs et omissions nettes
Reserves and Related Items	674.8	2 311.4	−3 257.7	−3 330.6	−4 090.3	−2 012.6	1 175.8	Rés. et postes appareutés
Bolivia								**Bolivie**
Goods: Exports fob	985.1	1 041.4	1 132.0	1 166.6	1 104.0	1 051.2	1 229.6	Biens : exportations,fàb
Goods: Imports fob	−1 015.3	−1 223.7	−1 368.0	−1 643.6	−1 759.4	−1 539.0	−1 610.1	Biens : importations,fàb
Serv. & Income: Credit	214.7	220.7	209.5	345.4	378.0	416.7	363.5	Serv. & revenu : crédit
Serv. & Income: Debit	−538.7	−585.1	−600.2	−713.4	−730.6	−803.0	−832.1	Serv. & revenu : débit
Current Trans.,nie: Credit	269.2	248.0	226.2	300.3	341.6	414.7	418.1	Transf. cour.,nia : crédit
Current Transfers: Debit	−5.2	−3.8	−3.8	−8.8	−11.7	−28.6	−33.2	Transf. courants : débit
Capital Acct.,nie: Credit	1.2	2.0	2.8	25.3	9.9	0.0	0.0	Compte de cap.,nia : crédit
Capital Account: Debit	0.0	0.0	0.0	0.0	0.0	0.0	0.0	Compte de capital : débit
Financial Account,nie	315.3	505.2	701.0	889.8	1 083.3	751.8	508.4	Compte d'op. fin., nia
Net Errors and Omissions	−315.8	−112.3	−31.6	−260.6	−314.2	−236.8	−84.3	Erreurs et omissions nettes
Reserves and Related Items	89.5	−92.4	−268.0	−101.0	−100.9	−26.9	40.1	Rés. et postes appareutés
Brazil								**Brésil**
Goods: Exports fob	44 102.0	46 506.0	47 851.0	53 189.0	51 136.0	48 011.0	55 087.0	Biens : exportations,fàb
Goods: Imports fob	−33 241.0	−49 663.0	−53 304.0	−59 841.0	−57 739.0	−49 272.0	−55 783.0	Biens : importations,fàb
Serv. & Income: Credit	7 110.0	9 592.0	10 005.0	11 333.0	12 545.0	11 125.0	13 002.0	Serv. & revenu : crédit
Serv. & Income: Debit	−21 547.0	−28 192.0	−30 241.0	−36 986.0	−41 207.0	−36 952.0	−38 460.0	Serv. & revenu : débit
Current Trans.,nie: Credit	2 577.0	3 861.0	2 699.0	2 130.0	1 795.0	1 969.0	1 828.0	Transf. cour.,nia : crédit
Current Transfers: Debit	−154.0	−240.0	−258.0	−316.0	−359.0	−281.0	−306.0	Transf. courants : débit
Capital Acct.,nie: Credit	175.0	363.0	507.0	519.0	488.0	361.0	300.0	Compte de cap.,nia : crédit
Capital Account: Debit	−2.0	−11.0	−13.0	−37.0	−113.0	−22.0	−28.0	Compte de capital : débit
Financial Account,nie	8 020.0	29 306.0	33 142.0	24 918.0	20 063.0	8 056.0	29 369.0	Compte d'op. fin., nia
Net Errors and Omissions	−441.8	1 446.7	−1 991.6	−3 160.2	−2 910.7	239.6	2 971.0	Erreurs et omissions nettes
Reserves and Related Items	−6 598.2	−12 968.7	−8 396.4	8 251.2	16 301.7	16 765.4	−7 980.0	Rés. et postes appareutés
Chile								**Chili**
Goods: Exports fob	11 604.1	16 025.0	15 405.0	16 663.0	14 831.0	15 616.0	18 159.0	Biens : exportations,fàb
Goods: Imports fob	−10 872.1	−14 644.0	−16 496.0	−18 221.0	−17 347.0	−13 952.0	−16 721.0	Biens : importations,fàb
Serv. & Income: Credit	3 396.3	4 201.4	4 456.0	5 195.3	5 257.0	4 893.0	5 540.0	Serv. & revenu : crédit
Serv. & Income: Debit	−6 044.5	−7 239.0	−7 382.0	−7 886.0	−7 343.0	−7 089.0	−8 506.0	Serv. & revenu : débit
Current Trans.,nie: Credit	449.2	482.0	664.0	877.0	815.0	793.0	870.0	Transf. cour.,nia : crédit
Current Transfers: Debit	−117.9	−175.0	−157.0	−356.0	−352.0	−341.0	−333.0	Transf. courants : débit
Capital Acct.,nie: Credit	0.0	0.0	0.0	0.0	0.0	0.0	0.0	Compte de cap.,nia : crédit
Capital Account: Debit	0.0	0.0	0.0	0.0	0.0	0.0	0.0	Compte de capital : débit
Financial Account,nie	5 293.6	2 356.6	6 664.6	7 355.2	3 181.0	−829.0	1 239.0	Compte d'op. fin., nia
Net Errors and Omissions	−557.9	131.5	−650.8	−443.1	−1 177.3	150.8	−15.5	Erreurs et omissions nettes
Reserves and Related Items	−3 150.8	−1 138.5	−2 503.8	−3 184.5	2 135.3	758.2	−232.5	Rés. et postes appareutés
Colombia								**Colombie**
Goods: Exports fob	9 059.1	10 594.0	10 966.2	12 065.0	11 480.2	12 029.9	13 619.8	Biens : exportations,fàb
Goods: Imports fob	−11 287.7	−13 139.0	−13 057.7	−14 702.6	−13 929.9	−10 254.8	−11 076.9	Biens : importations,fàb

76
Summary of balance of payments
Millions of US dollars
Résumé des balances des paiements
Millions de dollars des E.-U.

Country or area	1994	1995	1996	1997	1998	1999	2000	Pays ou zone
Serv. & Income: Credit	2 277.2	2 377.0	2 898.7	3 036.8	2 824.7	2 655.3	2 867.9	Serv. & revenu : crédit
Serv. & Income: Debit	−4 790.0	−5 157.0	−6 164.3	−6 880.8	−6 051.5	−5 384.4	−6 621.9	Serv. & revenu : débit
Current Trans.,nie: Credit	1 261.9	963.0	814.0	830.9	607.5	1 270.8	1 441.1	Transf. cour.,nia : crédit
Current Transfers: Debit	−193.1	−234.0	−217.3	−217.3	−161.9	−218.8	−188.9	Transf. courants : débit
Capital Acct.,nie: Credit	0.0	0.0	0.0	0.0	0.0	0.0	0.0	Compte de cap.,nia : crédit
Capital Account: Debit	0.0	0.0	0.0	0.0	0.0	0.0	0.0	Compte de capital : débit
Financial Account,nie	3 529.6	4 476.0	6 737.8	6 900.6	3 787.9	16.6	1 128.1	Compte d'op. fin., nia
Net Errors and Omissions	325.3	115.1	−247.9	−754.6	45.3	−426.5	−307.4	Erreurs et omissions nettes
Reserves and Related Items	−182.3	4.9	−1 729.5	−278.0	1 397.7	311.9	−861.8	Rés. et postes appareutés
Ecuador								**Equateur**
Goods: Exports fob	3 843.0	4 381.0	4 873.0	5 264.0	4 203.0	4 451.0	...	Biens : exportations,fàb
Goods: Imports fob	−3 282.0	−4 057.0	−3 680.0	−4 666.0	−5 198.0	−2 786.0	...	Biens : importations,fàb
Serv. & Income: Credit	797.0	936.0	931.0	928.0	890.0	861.0	...	Serv. & revenu : crédit
Serv. & Income: Debit	−2 184.0	−2 256.0	−2 330.0	−2 631.0	−2 840.0	−2 672.0	...	Serv. & revenu : débit
Current Trans.,nie: Credit	164.0	250.0	359.0	438.0	840.0	1 151.0	...	Transf. cour.,nia : crédit
Current Transfers: Debit	−19.0	−19.0	−69.0	−47.0	−64.0	−50.0	...	Transf. courants : débit
Capital Acct.,nie: Credit	0.0	0.0	0.0	0.0	0.0	0.0	...	Compte de cap.,nia : crédit
Capital Account: Debit	0.0	0.0	0.0	0.0	0.0	0.0	...	Compte de capital : débit
Financial Account,nie	998.0	1 883.0	1 514.0	1 454.0	2 114.0	743.0	...	Compte d'op. fin., nia
Net Errors and Omissions	21.7	−1 307.0	−1 343.5	−477.3	−352.4	−2 024.3	...	Erreurs et omissions nettes
Reserves and Related Items	−338.7	189.0	−254.5	−262.7	407.4	326.3	...	Rés. et postes appareutés
Guyana								**Guyane**
Goods: Exports fob	463.4	495.7	...	...	...	...	...	Biens : exportations,fàb
Goods: Imports fob	−504.0	−536.5	...	...	...	...	...	Biens : importations,fàb
Serv. & Income: Credit	129.4	145.7	...	...	...	...	...	Serv. & revenu : crédit
Serv. & Income: Debit	−275.7	−301.7	...	...	...	...	...	Serv. & revenu : débit
Current Trans.,nie: Credit	68.1	67.3	...	...	...	...	...	Transf. cour.,nia : crédit
Current Transfers: Debit	−6.2	−5.3	...	...	...	...	...	Transf. courants : débit
Capital Acct.,nie: Credit	11.0	12.5	...	...	...	...	...	Compte de cap.,nia : crédit
Capital Account: Debit	−2.7	−3.0	...	...	...	...	...	Compte de capital : débit
Financial Account,nie	126.9	71.1	...	...	...	...	...	Compte d'op. fin., nia
Net Errors and Omissions	−16.3	11.2	...	...	...	...	...	Erreurs et omissions nettes
Reserves and Related Items	6.0	43.0	...	...	...	...	...	Rés. et postes appareutés
Paraguay								**Paraguay**
Goods: Exports fob	3 360.1	4 218.6	3 796.9	3 327.5	3 548.6	2 681.3	2 373.3	Biens : exportations,fàb
Goods: Imports fob	−3 603.5	−4 489.0	−4 383.4	−4 192.4	−3 941.5	−3 041.5	−2 905.6	Biens : importations,fàb
Serv. & Income: Credit	674.1	856.4	881.4	933.1	891.8	780.6	829.4	Serv. & revenu : crédit
Serv. & Income: Debit	−727.5	−873.6	−830.0	−899.3	−836.2	−685.8	−611.2	Serv. & revenu : débit
Current Trans.,nie: Credit	25.6	199.7	183.0	182.2	178.3	176.7	178.3	Transf. cour.,nia : crédit
Current Transfers: Debit	−2.9	−4.4	−0.8	−1.3	−1.0	−1.5	−1.5	Transf. courants : débit
Capital Acct.,nie: Credit	8.8	10.6	14.2	7.5	5.4	19.6	3.0	Compte de cap.,nia : crédit
Capital Account: Debit	0.0	0.0	0.0	0.0	0.0	0.0	0.0	Compte de capital : débit
Financial Account,nie	212.9	232.5	152.4	421.3	312.9	134.1	53.2	Compte d'op. fin., nia
Net Errors and Omissions	353.0	−106.0	139.8	5.8	−141.6	−364.4	−260.9	Erreurs et omissions nettes
Reserves and Related Items	−300.6	−44.8	46.5	215.8	−16.7	300.9	342.0	Rés. et postes appareutés
Peru								**Pérou**
Goods: Exports fob	4 597.0	5 587.0	5 898.0	6 831.0	5 757.0	6 116.0	7 026.0	Biens : exportations,fàb
Goods: Imports fob	−5 595.0	−7 755.0	−7 884.0	−8 554.0	−8 219.0	−6 749.0	−7 349.0	Biens : importations,fàb
Serv. & Income: Credit	1 401.0	1 705.0	2 025.0	2 281.0	2 559.0	2 225.0	2 311.0	Serv. & revenu : crédit
Serv. & Income: Debit	−3 710.0	−4 474.0	−4 351.0	−4 535.0	−4 710.0	−4 510.0	−4 635.0	Serv. & revenu : débit
Current Trans.,nie: Credit	754.0	817.0	890.0	928.0	990.0	1 022.0	1 027.0	Transf. cour.,nia : crédit
Current Transfers: Debit	−7.0	−5.0	−8.0	−8.0	−11.0	−27.0	−8.0	Transf. courants : débit
Capital Acct.,nie: Credit	32.0	66.0	52.0	25.0	21.0	25.0	24.0	Compte de cap.,nia : crédit
Capital Account: Debit	−89.0	−33.0	−29.0	−74.0	−78.0	−79.0	−92.0	Compte de capital : débit
Financial Account,nie	3 908.0	3 017.0	3 372.0	5 590.0	1 900.0	1 066.0	1 097.0	Compte d'op. fin., nia
Net Errors and Omissions	156.4	491.4	896.6	−311.4	428.9	45.1	468.9	Erreurs et omissions nettes
Reserves and Related Items	−1 447.4	583.6	−861.6	−2 172.6	1 362.1	865.9	130.1	Rés. et postes appareutés
Suriname								**Suriname**
Goods: Exports fob	293.6	415.6	397.2	401.6	349.7	342.0	399.1	Biens : exportations,fàb
Goods: Imports fob	−194.3	−292.6	−398.8	−365.5	−376.9	−297.9	−246.1	Biens : importations,fàb
Serv. & Income: Credit	73.5	106.8	110.8	99.0	78.5	87.0	104.1	Serv. & revenu : crédit
Serv. & Income: Debit	−118.2	−166.7	−173.8	−203.8	−203.9	−158.7	−222.7	Serv. & revenu : débit
Current Trans.,nie: Credit	6.2	2.0	3.6	4.0	1.3	1.8	1.2	Transf. cour.,nia : crédit
Current Transfers: Debit	−2.2	−2.3	−2.5	−3.0	−3.6	−3.3	−3.3	Transf. courants : débit
Capital Acct.,nie: Credit	0.2	22.1	41.6	14.6	6.6	3.5	2.3	Compte de cap.,nia : crédit
Capital Account: Debit	−0.4	0.0	0.0	0.0	0.0	0.0	0.0	Compte de capital : débit

76
Summary of balance of payments
Millions of US dollars
Résumé des balances des paiements
Millions de dollars des E.−U.

Country or area	1994	1995	1996	1997	1998	1999	2000	Pays ou zone
Financial Account,nie	−84.1	−6.7	27.7	26.9	30.5	−21.6	−139.1	Compte d'op. fin., nia
Net Errors and Omissions	60.0	41.6	−7.5	45.3	125.9	42.8	114.3	Erreurs et omissions nettes
Reserves and Related Items	−34.3	−119.8	1.7	−19.1	−8.1	4.4	−9.8	Rés. et postes appareutés
Uruguay								**Uruguay**
Goods: Exports fob	1 917.6	2 147.6	2 448.5	2 793.1	2 829.3	2 290.6	2 379.6	Biens : exportations,fàb
Goods: Imports fob	−2 623.6	−2 710.6	−3 135.4	−3 497.5	−3 601.4	−3 187.2	−3 316.4	Biens : importations,fàb
Serv. & Income: Credit	1 613.2	1 763.5	1 859.2	1 971.4	1 927.1	1 997.1	2 114.7	Serv. & revenu : crédit
Serv. & Income: Debit	−1 386.7	−1 489.0	−1 488.2	−1 628.6	−1 689.5	−1 681.6	−1 836.8	Serv. & revenu : débit
Current Trans.,nie: Credit	49.2	84.0	90.7	83.0	75.0	78.4	71.0	Transf. cour.,nia : crédit
Current Transfers: Debit	−8.0	−8.0	−8.2	−8.8	−16.0	−4.9	−4.9	Transf. courants : débit
Capital Acct.,nie: Credit	0.0	0.0	0.0	0.0	0.0	0.0	0.0	Compte de cap.,nia : crédit
Capital Account: Debit	0.0	0.0	0.0	0.0	0.0	0.0	0.0	Compte de capital : débit
Financial Account,nie	537.2	421.7	233.6	608.7	545.1	147.1	790.3	Compte d'op. fin., nia
Net Errors and Omissions	10.2	18.6	152.2	78.8	285.5	250.9	36.9	Erreurs et omissions nettes
Reserves and Related Items	−109.1	−227.8	−152.4	−400.1	−355.1	109.6	−234.4	Rés. et postes appareutés
Venezuela								**Venezuela**
Goods: Exports fob	16 105.0	19 082.0	23 707.0	23 703.0	17 576.0	20 819.0	34 038.0	Biens : exportations,fàb
Goods: Imports fob	−8 480.0	−12 069.0	−9 937.0	−13 678.0	−15 105.0	−13 213.0	−16 073.0	Biens : importations,fàb
Serv. & Income: Credit	3 202.0	3 538.0	3 152.0	3 628.0	3 747.0	3 423.0	4 085.0	Serv. & revenu : crédit
Serv. & Income: Debit	−8 202.0	−8 646.0	−8 146.0	−10 042.0	−9 363.0	−7 410.0	−8 557.0	Serv. & revenu : débit
Current Trans.,nie: Credit	606.0	413.0	526.0	221.0	275.0	331.0	317.0	Transf. cour.,nia : crédit
Current Transfers: Debit	−690.0	−304.0	−388.0	−365.0	−383.0	−261.0	−460.0	Transf. courants : débit
Capital Acct.,nie: Credit	0.0	0.0	0.0	0.0	0.0	0.0	0.0	Compte de cap.,nia : crédit
Capital Account: Debit	0.0	0.0	0.0	0.0	0.0	0.0	0.0	Compte de capital : débit
Financial Account,nie	−3 204.0	−2 964.0	−1 784.0	1 067.0	1 764.0	−1 656.0	−3 915.0	Compte d'op. fin., nia
Net Errors and Omissions	−281.1	−494.2	−891.8	−1 458.6	−1 442.3	−992.0	−3 626.2	Erreurs et omissions nettes
Reserves and Related Items	944.1	1 444.2	−6 238.2	−3 075.4	2 931.3	−1 041.0	−5 808.8	Rés. et postes appareutés
Asia • Asie								
Armenia								**Arménie**
Goods: Exports fob	215.4	270.9	290.4	233.6	228.9	247.3	...	Biens : exportations,fàb
Goods: Imports fob	−393.6	−673.9	−759.6	−793.1	−806.3	−721.4	...	Biens : importations,fàb
Serv. & Income: Credit	13.7	83.2	155.8	235.6	234.3	229.4	...	Serv. & revenu : crédit
Serv. & Income: Debit	−44.7	−66.9	−161.8	−199.8	−252.2	−236.5	...	Serv. & revenu : débit
Current Trans.,nie: Credit	106.3	170.0	199.0	252.4	203.0	200.6	...	Transf. cour.,nia : crédit
Current Transfers: Debit	−0.8	−1.7	−14.4	−35.2	−25.6	−26.5	...	Transf. courants : débit
Capital Acct.,nie: Credit	5.7	8.1	13.4	10.9	9.7	16.9	...	Compte de cap.,nia : crédit
Capital Account: Debit	0.0	0.0	0.0	0.0	0.0	−4.3	...	Compte de capital : débit
Financial Account,nie	89.9	227.5	216.8	334.8	390.4	286.2	...	Compte d'op. fin., nia
Net Errors and Omissions	4.8	12.4	15.1	10.8	18.4	13.1	...	Erreurs et omissions nettes
Reserves and Related Items	3.3	−29.5	45.5	−50.0	−0.6	−4.8	...	Rés. et postes appareutés
Azerbaijan								**Azerbaïdjan**
Goods: Exports fob	...	612.3	643.7	808.3	677.8	1 025.2	1 858.3	Biens : exportations,fàb
Goods: Imports fob	...	−985.4	−1 337.6	−1 375.2	−1 723.9	−1 433.4	−1 539.0	Biens : importations,fàb
Serv. & Income: Credit	...	182.3	164.3	364.6	370.0	267.8	315.7	Serv. & revenu : crédit
Serv. & Income: Debit	...	−320.6	−468.1	−758.2	−752.3	−541.1	−875.9	Serv. & revenu : débit
Current Trans.,nie: Credit	...	129.3	107.2	95.7	145.0	134.5	135.0	Transf. cour.,nia : crédit
Current Transfers: Debit	...	−18.5	−40.7	−50.9	−80.9	−52.8	−62.0	Transf. courants : débit
Capital Acct.,nie: Credit	...	0.0	0.0	0.0	0.0	0.0	0.0	Compte de cap.,nia : crédit
Capital Account: Debit	...	−1.6	0.0	−10.2	−0.7	0.0	0.0	Compte de capital : débit
Financial Account,nie	...	400.3	822.5	1 092.1	1 326.0	690.2	493.4	Compte d'op. fin., nia
Net Errors and Omissions	...	59.7	23.6	−27.0	−20.1	42.4	0.1	Erreurs et omissions nettes
Reserves and Related Items	...	−57.8	85.0	−139.2	59.2	−132.9	−325.6	Rés. et postes appareutés
Bahrain								**Bahreïn**
Goods: Exports fob	3 617.0	4 114.4	4 702.1	4 383.0	3 270.2	4 140.4	5 700.5	Biens : exportations,fàb
Goods: Imports fob	−3 497.3	−3 488.3	−4 037.0	−3 778.2	−3 298.7	−3 468.4	−4 373.4	Biens : importations,fàb
Serv. & Income: Credit	3 931.1	4 770.2	4 481.4	4 908.0	5 488.6	5 842.8	6 732.4	Serv. & revenu : crédit
Serv. & Income: Debit	−3 976.9	−4 780.1	−4 452.9	−5 141.8	−5 577.9	−6 035.9	−6 956.4	Serv. & revenu : débit
Current Trans.,nie: Credit	101.1	120.7	126.3	232.7	65.2	36.7	22.3	Transf. cour.,nia : crédit
Current Transfers: Debit	−430.6	−499.7	−559.3	−634.8	−725.0	−856.1	−1 012.8	Transf. courants : débit
Capital Acct.,nie: Credit	319.1	156.9	50.0	125.0	100.0	100.0	50.0	Compte de cap.,nia : crédit
Capital Account: Debit	0.0	0.0	0.0	0.0	0.0	0.0	0.0	Compte de capital : débit
Financial Account,nie	1 301.1	−1 726.6	−510.4	15.4	22.3	287.2	−8.2	Compte d'op. fin., nia
Net Errors and Omissions	−1 412.2	1 501.4	193.3	−6.5	638.7	−21.6	45.6	Erreurs et omissions nettes
Reserves and Related Items	47.5	−168.9	6.4	−102.8	16.6	−25.3	−200.1	Rés. et postes appareutés

76
Summary of balance of payments
Millions of US dollars
Résumé des balances des paiements
Millions de dollars des E.–U.

Country or area	1994	1995	1996	1997	1998	1999	2000	Pays ou zone
Bangladesh								**Bangladesh**
Goods: Exports fob	2 934.4	3 733.3	4 009.3	4 839.9	5 141.5	5 458.3	6 399.2	Biens : exportations,fàb
Goods: Imports fob	−4 350.5	−6 057.4	−6 284.6	−6 550.7	−6 715.7	−7 535.5	−8 052.9	Biens : importations,fàb
Serv. & Income: Credit	740.3	968.3	734.2	773.9	815.4	872.0	893.4	Serv. & revenu : crédit
Serv. & Income: Debit	−1 213.8	−1 733.0	−1 359.1	−1 481.7	−1 443.2	−1 655.2	−1 965.0	Serv. & revenu : débit
Current Trans.,nie: Credit	2 091.4	2 266.8	1 912.8	2 136.5	2 172.9	2 501.4	2 426.5	Transf. cour.,nia : crédit
Current Transfers: Debit	−2.2	−1.8	−4.0	−4.3	−5.9	−5.3	−7.0	Transf. courants : débit
Capital Acct.,nie: Credit	0.0	0.0	371.2	366.8	238.7	364.1	248.7	Compte de cap.,nia : crédit
Capital Account: Debit	0.0	0.0	0.0	0.0	0.0	0.0	0.0	Compte de capital : débit
Financial Account,nie	748.8	178.8	92.4	−140.2	−116.0	−448.8	−144.9	Compte d'op. fin., nia
Net Errors and Omissions	−257.1	133.3	113.5	−75.5	201.0	259.9	171.3	Erreurs et omissions nettes
Reserves and Related Items	−691.3	511.7	414.3	135.1	−288.5	189.2	30.7	Rés. et postes appareutés
Cambodia								**Cambodge**
Goods: Exports fob	489.9	855.2	643.6	736.0	899.9	979.9	1 327.1	Biens : exportations,fàb
Goods: Imports fob	−744.4	−1 186.8	−1 071.8	−1 064.0	−1 073.2	−1 211.5	−1 525.1	Biens : importations,fàb
Serv. & Income: Credit	56.6	123.7	175.4	176.4	127.1	151.2	201.7	Serv. & revenu : crédit
Serv. & Income: Debit	−188.7	−254.8	−313.1	−246.5	−226.5	−266.5	−327.5	Serv. & revenu : débit
Current Trans.,nie: Credit	230.0	277.9	383.4	188.5	224.0	235.9	304.8	Transf. cour.,nia : crédit
Current Transfers: Debit	0.0	−0.9	−2.4	−0.3	−0.6	−1.6	−0.3	Transf. courants : débit
Capital Acct.,nie: Credit	73.2	78.0	75.8	65.2	42.0	44.1	38.1	Compte de cap.,nia : crédit
Capital Account: Debit	0.0	0.0	0.0	0.0	0.0	0.0	0.0	Compte de capital : débit
Financial Account,nie	54.0	122.4	259.1	219.8	154.5	126.3	107.2	Compte d'op. fin., nia
Net Errors and Omissions	65.6	11.5	−78.0	−41.2	−116.5	−7.9	−40.0	Erreurs et omissions nettes
Reserves and Related Items	−36.2	−26.2	−72.0	−33.9	−30.7	−49.9	−85.9	Rés. et postes appareutés
China ††								**Chine ††**
Goods: Exports fob	102 561.0	128 110.0	151 077.0	182 670.0	183 529.0	194 716.0	249 131.0	Biens : exportations,fàb
Goods: Imports fob	−95 271.0	−110 060.0	−131 542.0	−136 448.0	−136 915.0	−158 734.0	−214 657.0	Biens : importations,fàb
Serv. & Income: Credit	22 357.0	24 321.6	27 919.0	30 279.0	29 479.0	34 578.0	42 980.4	Serv. & revenu : crédit
Serv. & Income: Debit	−23 074.0	−42 187.9	−42 340.0	−44 682.0	−48 900.0	−54 389.0	−63 246.9	Serv. & revenu : débit
Current Trans.,nie: Credit	1 269.0	1 826.7	2 368.0	5 477.0	4 661.0	5 368.0	6 860.8	Transf. cour.,nia : crédit
Current Transfers: Debit	−934.0	−392.1	−239.0	−333.0	−382.0	−424.0	−549.5	Transf. courants : débit
Capital Acct.,nie: Credit	0.0	0.0	0.0	0.0	0.0	0.0	0.0	Compte de cap.,nia : crédit
Capital Account: Debit	0.0	0.0	0.0	−21.0	−47.0	−26.0	−35.3	Compte de capital : débit
Financial Account,nie	32 645.0	38 673.8	39 966.0	21 037.0	−6 275.0	5 204.0	1 957.9	Compte d'op. fin., nia
Net Errors and Omissions	−9 100.3	−17 823.2	−15 504.0	−22 121.8	−18 901.8	−17 640.5	−11 747.9	Erreurs et omissions nettes
Reserves and Related Items	−30 452.8	−22 469.0	−31 705.0	−35 857.2	−6 248.2	−8 652.5	−10 693.1	Rés. et postes appareutés
China, Hong Kong SAR †								**Chine, Hong Kong RAS †**
Goods: Exports fob	...	...	...	...	175 833.0	174 719.0	202 673.0	Biens : exportations,fàb
Goods: Imports fob	...	...	...	...	−183 666.0	−177 878.0	−210 891.0	Biens : importations,fàb
Serv. & Income: Credit	...	...	...	...	82 503.7	83 594.9	94 102.1	Serv. & revenu : crédit
Serv. & Income: Debit	...	...	...	...	−69 170.5	−67 414.2	−75 426.0	Serv. & revenu : débit
Current Trans.,nie: Credit	...	...	...	...	668.7	569.5	596.9	Transf. cour.,nia : crédit
Current Transfers: Debit	...	...	...	...	−2 265.0	−2 109.3	−2 228.5	Transf. courants : débit
Capital Acct.,nie: Credit	...	...	...	...	377.4	103.3	56.4	Compte de cap.,nia : crédit
Capital Account: Debit	...	...	...	...	−2 759.0	−1 883.3	−1 574.5	Compte de capital : débit
Financial Account,nie	...	...	...	...	−8 475.8	1 060.5	3 748.2	Compte d'op. fin., nia
Net Errors and Omissions	...	...	...	...	164.2	−734.7	−1 208.3	Erreurs et omissions nettes
Reserves and Related Items	...	...	...	...	6 789.1	−10 027.7	−9 848.0	Rés. et postes appareutés
Cyprus								**Chypre**
Goods: Exports fob	967.5	1 228.7	1 392.4	1 245.8	1 064.6	1 000.3	951.0	Biens : exportations,fàb
Goods: Imports fob	−2 703.0	−3 314.2	−3 575.7	−3 317.2	−3 490.4	−3 309.5	−3 556.5	Biens : importations,fàb
Serv. & Income: Credit	2 768.2	3 362.4	3 231.5	3 209.8	3 371.4	3 608.4	3 705.3	Serv. & revenu : crédit
Serv. & Income: Debit	−1 073.2	−1 469.7	−1 547.0	−1 502.4	−1 577.9	−1 603.8	−1 682.0	Serv. & revenu : débit
Current Trans.,nie: Credit	125.0	46.4	43.1	40.9	49.6	113.6	153.3	Transf. cour.,nia : crédit
Current Transfers: Debit	−10.2	−17.7	−9.9	−15.0	−20.3	−26.3	−27.5	Transf. courants : débit
Capital Acct.,nie: Credit	0.0	0.0	0.0	0.0	0.0	0.0	0.0	Compte de cap.,nia : crédit
Capital Account: Debit	0.0	0.0	0.0	0.0	0.0	0.0	0.0	Compte de capital : débit
Financial Account,nie	185.7	−140.8	419.0	383.7	657.9	1 006.4	301.4	Compte d'op. fin., nia
Net Errors and Omissions	−13.1	−58.2	−13.3	−92.5	−137.6	−150.0	147.0	Erreurs et omissions nettes
Reserves and Related Items	−246.9	363.1	59.8	47.0	82.5	−639.0	8.0	Rés. et postes appareutés
Georgia								**Géorgie**
Goods: Exports fob	...	...	...	376.5	299.9	329.5	459.0	Biens : exportations,fàb
Goods: Imports fob	...	...	...	−1 162.9	−994.5	−863.4	−970.5	Biens : importations,fàb
Serv. & Income: Credit	...	...	...	384.6	608.7	428.3	385.0	Serv. & revenu : crédit
Serv. & Income: Debit	...	...	...	−308.9	−397.9	−288.5	−277.4	Serv. & revenu : débit
Current Trans.,nie: Credit	...	...	...	205.5	219.9	228.7	163.2	Transf. cour.,nia : crédit

76
Summary of balance of payments
Millions of US dollars
Résumé des balances des paiements
Millions de dollars des E.−U.

Country or area	1994	1995	1996	1997	1998	1999	2000	Pays ou zone
Current Transfers: Debit	...	...	...	−9.0	−11.8	−33.0	−28.3	Transf. courants : débit
Capital Acct.,nie: Credit	...	...	...	0.0	0.0	0.0	0.0	Compte de cap.,nia : crédit
Capital Account: Debit	...	...	...	−6.5	−6.1	−7.1	−4.8	Compte de capital : débit
Financial Account,nie	...	...	...	322.7	348.8	135.5	92.8	Compte d'op. fin., nia
Net Errors and Omissions	...	...	...	136.0	−170.5	55.7	187.4	Erreurs et omissions nettes
Reserves and Related Items	...	...	...	62.0	103.5	14.3	−6.4	Rés. et postes appareutés
India								**Inde**
Goods: Exports fob	25 522.5	31 238.5	33 737.3	35 702.1	34 075.7	36 877.3	43 131.7	Biens : exportations,fàb
Goods: Imports fob	−29 672.6	−37 957.3	−43 789.0	−45 730.1	−44 828.0	−45 556.2	−55 324.6	Biens : importations,fàb
Serv. & Income: Credit	6 858.9	8 260.3	8 649.4	10 594.3	13 497.2	16 428.5	20 610.7	Serv. & revenu : crédit
Serv. & Income: Debit	−12 569.8	−15 487.0	−15 837.6	−17 444.4	−19 982.5	−22 900.6	−26 068.4	Serv. & revenu : débit
Current Trans.,nie: Credit	8 207.8	8 409.5	11 349.5	13 975.4	10 401.8	11 957.9	13 503.6	Transf. cour.,nia : crédit
Current Transfers: Debit	−23.1	−27.3	−65.8	−62.4	−67.4	−34.9	−51.3	Transf. courants : débit
Capital Acct.,nie: Credit	0.0	0.0	0.0	0.0	0.0	0.0	0.0	Compte de cap.,nia : crédit
Capital Account: Debit	0.0	0.0	0.0	0.0	0.0	0.0	0.0	Compte de capital : débit
Financial Account,nie	10 575.6	3 860.9	11 847.8	9 634.7	8 583.9	9 578.5	9 615.7	Compte d'op. fin., nia
Net Errors and Omissions	1 491.6	969.7	−1 934.1	−1 348.4	1 389.9	313.2	669.5	Erreurs et omissions nettes
Reserves and Related Items	−10 390.9	732.6	−3 957.6	−5 321.1	−3 070.7	−6 663.7	−6 086.9	Rés. et postes appareutés
Indonesia								**Indonésie**
Goods: Exports fob	40 223.0	47 454.0	50 188.0	56 298.0	50 371.0	51 242.0	65 406.0	Biens : exportations,fàb
Goods: Imports fob	−32 322.0	−40 921.0	−44 240.0	−46 223.0	−31 942.0	−30 598.0	−40 366.0	Biens : importations,fàb
Serv. & Income: Credit	5 845.0	6 775.0	7 809.0	8 796.0	6 389.0	6 470.0	7 669.0	Serv. & revenu : crédit
Serv. & Income: Debit	−17 157.0	−20 720.0	−22 357.0	−24 794.0	−22 060.0	−23 243.0	−26 539.0	Serv. & revenu : débit
Current Trans.,nie: Credit	619.0	981.0	937.0	1 034.0	1 338.0	1 914.0	1 816.0	Transf. cour.,nia : crédit
Current Transfers: Debit	0.0	0.0	0.0	0.0	0.0	0.0	0.0	Transf. courants : débit
Capital Acct.,nie: Credit	0.0	0.0	0.0	0.0	0.0	0.0	0.0	Compte de cap.,nia : crédit
Capital Account: Debit	0.0	0.0	0.0	0.0	0.0	0.0	0.0	Compte de capital : débit
Financial Account,nie	3 839.0	10 259.0	10 847.0	−603.0	−9 638.0	−5 941.0	−7 896.0	Compte d'op. fin., nia
Net Errors and Omissions	−263.4	−2 254.6	1 318.7	−2 645.4	1 849.5	2 127.5	3 640.1	Erreurs et omissions nettes
Reserves and Related Items	−783.6	−1 573.4	−4 502.7	8 137.4	3 692.5	−1 971.5	−3 730.1	Rés. et postes appareutés
Iran (Islamic Rep. of)								**Iran (Rép. islamique d')**
Goods: Exports fob	19 434.0	18 360.0	22 391.0	18 381.0	13 118.0	21 030.0	28 345.0	Biens : exportations,fàb
Goods: Imports fob	−12 617.0	−12 774.0	−14 989.0	−14 123.0	−14 286.0	−13 433.0	−15 207.0	Biens : importations,fàb
Serv. & Income: Credit	580.0	909.0	1 348.0	1 658.0	2 023.0	1 397.0	1 786.0	Serv. & revenu : crédit
Serv. & Income: Debit	−3 639.0	−3 133.0	−3 981.0	−4 096.0	−3 491.0	−2 930.0	−2 900.0	Serv. & revenu : débit
Current Trans.,nie: Credit	1 200.0	0.0	471.0	400.0	500.0	508.0	539.0	Transf. cour.,nia : crédit
Current Transfers: Debit	−2.0	−4.0	−8.0	−7.0	−3.0	17.0	82.0	Transf. courants : débit
Capital Acct.,nie: Credit	0.0	0.0	0.0	0.0	0.0	0.0	0.0	Compte de cap.,nia : crédit
Capital Account: Debit	0.0	0.0	0.0	0.0	0.0	0.0	0.0	Compte de capital : débit
Financial Account,nie	−346.0	−774.0	−5 508.0	−4 822.0	2 270.0	−5 894.0	−10 189.0	Compte d'op. fin., nia
Net Errors and Omissions	−3 701.9	201.8	2 717.3	−1 088.2	−1 121.7	−243.5	−1 372.5	Erreurs et omissions nettes
Reserves and Related Items	−908.1	−2 785.8	−2 441.3	3 697.2	990.7	−451.5	−1 083.5	Rés. et postes appareutés
Israel								**Israël**
Goods: Exports fob	17 241.8	19 662.5	21 332.6	22 698.1	22 974.2	25 576.5	30 837.0	Biens : exportations,fàb
Goods: Imports fob	−22 752.4	−26 923.7	−28 514.6	−27 937.1	−26 314.7	−30 090.9	−34 187.3	Biens : importations,fàb
Serv. & Income: Credit	7 798.0	9 498.0	9 812.4	10 470.3	12 039.0	13 604.6	18 584.9	Serv. & revenu : crédit
Serv. & Income: Debit	−11 275.8	−12 904.2	−14 329.5	−15 285.3	−16 220.8	−18 464.4	−23 252.1	Serv. & revenu : débit
Current Trans.,nie: Credit	5 850.0	5 941.1	6 441.4	6 373.6	6 690.4	7 139.3	7 534.8	Transf. cour.,nia : crédit
Current Transfers: Debit	−249.6	−267.9	−304.3	−324.6	−606.9	−809.8	−933.2	Transf. courants : débit
Capital Acct.,nie: Credit	1 762.8	1 908.9	1 942.2	2 050.2	1 630.5	1 672.0	1 210.4	Compte de cap.,nia : crédit
Capital Account: Debit	0.0	0.0	0.0	0.0	0.0	0.0	0.0	Compte de capital : débit
Financial Account,nie	−608.4	2 656.8	3 132.8	5 744.2	−1 777.6	1 361.5	660.0	Compte d'op. fin., nia
Net Errors and Omissions	123.0	908.2	1 690.1	3 287.1	1 475.0	38.1	−1 522.2	Erreurs et omissions nettes
Reserves and Related Items	2 110.6	−479.7	−1 203.1	−7 076.5	110.9	−26.9	1 067.7	Rés. et postes appareutés
Japan [2]								**Japon [2]**
Goods: Exports fob	385.7	428.7	400.3	409.2	374.0	403.7	459.5	Biens : exportations,fàb
Goods: Imports fob	−241.5	−296.9	−316.7	−307.6	−251.7	−280.4	−342.8	Biens : importations,fàb
Serv. & Income: Credit	213.5	257.7	292.8	291.5	272.0	249.3	276.2	Serv. & revenu : crédit
Serv. & Income: Debit	−221.3	−270.8	−301.5	−289.9	−264.8	−253.6	−266.2	Serv. & revenu : débit
Current Trans.,nie: Credit	1.8	2.0	6.0	6.0	5.5	6.2	7.4	Transf. cour.,nia : crédit
Current Transfers: Debit	−7.9	−9.7	−15.0	−14.8	−14.4	−18.4	−17.2	Transf. courants : débit
Capital Acct.,nie: Credit	0.0	0.0	1.2	1.5	1.6	0.7	0.8	Compte de cap.,nia : crédit
Capital Account: Debit	−1.8	−2.2	−4.5	−5.6	−16.0	−17.2	−10.0	Compte de capital : débit
Financial Account,nie	−85.1	−64.0	−28.1	−118.1	−116.8	−31.1	−75.5	Compte d'op. fin., nia
Net Errors and Omissions	−18.0	13.8	0.6	34.3	4.4	17.0	16.9	Erreurs et omissions nettes
Reserves and Related Items	−25.3	−58.6	−35.1	−6.6	6.2	−76.3	−49.0	Rés. et postes appareutés

76
Summary of balance of payments
Millions of US dollars
Résumé des balances des paiements
Millions de dollars des E.−U.

Country or area	1994	1995	1996	1997	1998	1999	2000	Pays ou zone
Jordan								**Jordanie**
Goods: Exports fob	1 424.5	1 769.6	1 816.9	1 835.5	1 802.4	1 831.9	...	Biens : exportations,fàb
Goods: Imports fob	−3 003.9	−3 287.8	−3 818.1	−3 648.5	−3 404.0	−3 292.0	...	Biens : importations,fàb
Serv. & Income: Credit	1 634.7	1 824.9	1 958.0	1 985.0	2 132.0	2 002.8	...	Serv. & revenu : crédit
Serv. & Income: Debit	−1 780.2	−2 009.5	−2 010.4	−1 994.2	−2 228.8	−2 153.6	...	Serv. & revenu : débit
Current Trans.,nie: Credit	1 447.4	1 591.8	1 970.2	2 096.1	1 984.3	2 321.3	...	Transf. cour.,nia : crédit
Current Transfers: Debit	−120.5	−147.6	−138.5	−244.6	−271.9	−305.5	...	Transf. courants : débit
Capital Acct.,nie: Credit	0.0	197.2	157.7	163.8	81.1	90.3	...	Compte de cap.,nia : crédit
Capital Account: Debit	0.0	0.0	0.0	0.0	0.0	0.0	...	Compte de capital : débit
Financial Account,nie	188.9	230.0	233.9	242.3	−177.3	487.9	...	Compte d'op. fin., nia
Net Errors and Omissions	−55.8	−339.9	−357.9	−160.8	−454.0	−10.2	...	Erreurs et omissions nettes
Reserves and Related Items	264.9	171.3	188.2	−274.6	536.1	−972.9	...	Rés. et postes appareutés
Kazakhstan								**Kazakhstan**
Goods: Exports fob	...	5 440.0	6 291.6	6 899.3	5 870.5	5 988.7	9 615.4	Biens : exportations,fàb
Goods: Imports fob	...	−5 325.9	−6 626.7	−7 175.7	−6 671.7	−5 645.0	−6 849.8	Biens : importations,fàb
Serv. & Income: Credit	...	579.7	731.1	915.7	999.8	1 041.1	1 274.3	Serv. & revenu : crédit
Serv. & Income: Debit	...	−965.9	−1 205.4	−1 513.2	−1 545.9	−1 712.5	−3 172.2	Serv. & revenu : débit
Current Trans.,nie: Credit	...	79.9	83.4	104.7	141.4	174.7	294.5	Transf. cour.,nia : crédit
Current Transfers: Debit	...	−20.9	−25.0	−30.1	−19.0	−18.0	−87.8	Transf. courants : débit
Capital Acct.,nie: Credit	...	116.1	87.9	58.3	65.9	61.1	66.2	Compte de cap.,nia : crédit
Capital Account: Debit	...	−496.7	−403.4	−498.1	−435.0	−295.1	−356.9	Compte de capital : débit
Financial Account,nie	...	1 162.5	2 005.1	2 901.6	2 229.1	1 299.2	1 324.0	Compte d'op. fin., nia
Net Errors and Omissions	...	−270.1	−780.0	−1 114.1	−1 078.4	−641.6	−1 537.4	Erreurs et omissions nettes
Reserves and Related Items	...	−298.7	−158.6	−548.4	443.3	−252.6	−570.3	Rés. et postes appareutés
Korea, Republic of								**Corée, République de**
Goods: Exports fob	94 964.3	124 632.0	129 968.0	138 619.0	132 122.0	145 164.0	175 782.0	Biens : exportations,fàb
Goods: Imports fob	−97 824.2	−129 076.0	−144 933.0	−141 798.0	−90 494.8	−116 793.0	−159 181.0	Biens : importations,fàb
Serv. & Income: Credit	19 640.9	26 313.1	27 078.5	30 179.5	28 239.5	29 773.4	36 542.0	Serv. & revenu : crédit
Serv. & Income: Debit	−21 928.4	−30 593.5	−35 073.4	−35 834.6	−32 853.7	−35 583.4	−42 716.0	Serv. & revenu : débit
Current Trans.,nie: Credit	3 672.3	4 104.0	4 279.0	5 287.9	6 736.6	6 421.3	6 410.8	Transf. cour.,nia : crédit
Current Transfers: Debit	−2 391.9	−3 885.9	−4 325.1	−4 620.9	−3 384.3	−4 505.5	−5 793.9	Transf. courants : débit
Capital Acct.,nie: Credit	8.0	14.5	18.9	16.6	463.6	95.1	32.5	Compte de cap.,nia : crédit
Capital Account: Debit	−444.5	−502.1	−616.5	−624.2	−292.5	−484.4	−572.2	Compte de capital : débit
Financial Account,nie	10 732.9	17 273.2	23 924.4	−9 195.0	−8 381.0	12 708.8	12 266.5	Compte d'op. fin., nia
Net Errors and Omissions	−1 815.9	−1 239.9	1 094.6	−5 009.6	−6 224.9	−3 536.0	1 438.1	Erreurs et omissions nettes
Reserves and Related Items	−4 613.6	−7 039.2	−1 415.7	22 979.4	−25 930.1	−33 260.2	−24 208.8	Rés. et postes appareutés
Kuwait								**Koweït**
Goods: Exports fob	11 284.4	12 833.1	14 946.1	14 280.6	9 617.5	12 276.0	19 576.1	Biens : exportations,fàb
Goods: Imports fob	−6 615.7	−7 254.2	−7 949.0	−7 750.2	−7 714.4	−6 704.7	−6 845.9	Biens : importations,fàb
Serv. & Income: Credit	5 588.3	7 525.6	7 929.0	9 503.9	8 925.2	7 654.0	9 571.3	Serv. & revenu : crédit
Serv. & Income: Debit	−5 534.4	−6 624.3	−6 329.1	−6 596.4	−6 838.3	−6 156.1	−5 551.7	Serv. & revenu : débit
Current Trans.,nie: Credit	94.3	53.6	53.4	79.1	98.4	98.5	104.3	Transf. cour.,nia : crédit
Current Transfers: Debit	−1 589.9	−1 517.9	−1 543.0	−1 585.6	−1 873.6	−2 102.4	−1 988.6	Transf. courants : débit
Capital Acct.,nie: Credit	0.0	0.0	3.3	115.4	288.8	716.1	1 978.8	Compte de cap.,nia : crédit
Capital Account: Debit	−205.5	−194.3	−207.1	−211.0	−210.0	−13.1	−19.6	Compte de capital : débit
Financial Account,nie	3 304.5	157.5	−7 631.7	−6 210.7	−2 920.4	−5 706.0	−14 174.3	Compte d'op. fin., nia
Net Errors and Omissions	−6 276.0	−5 119.3	704.5	−1 618.1	885.8	855.7	−382.2	Erreurs et omissions nettes
Reserves and Related Items	−50.0	140.2	23.6	−7.0	−259.0	−918.1	−2 268.2	Rés. et postes appareutés
Kyrgyzstan								**Kirghizistan**
Goods: Exports fob	340.0	408.9	531.2	630.8	535.1	462.6	510.9	Biens : exportations,fàb
Goods: Imports fob	−426.1	−531.0	−782.9	−646.1	−755.7	−546.9	−502.1	Biens : importations,fàb
Serv. & Income: Credit	32.7	42.9	35.9	51.8	75.4	75.9	78.8	Serv. & revenu : crédit
Serv. & Income: Debit	−93.1	−234.3	−292.9	−242.6	−267.4	−239.3	−246.0	Serv. & revenu : débit
Current Trans.,nie: Credit	63.4	80.4	85.9	69.8	2.2	1.2	2.2	Transf. cour.,nia : crédit
Current Transfers: Debit	−0.8	−1.7	−1.9	−2.2	−2.0	−1.2	−2.2	Transf. courants : débit
Capital Acct.,nie: Credit	0.3	2.2	9.0	6.2	3.9	14.6	22.8	Compte de cap.,nia : crédit
Capital Account: Debit	−62.7	−31.3	−25.0	−14.6	−12.0	−29.8	−34.1	Compte de capital : débit
Financial Account,nie	103.4	259.9	362.5	250.7	284.5	220.2	61.6	Compte d'op. fin., nia
Net Errors and Omissions	48.0	−76.9	58.4	−57.7	63.5	−7.0	11.2	Erreurs et omissions nettes
Reserves and Related Items	−5.0	80.7	19.8	−46.2	72.7	49.7	96.9	Rés. et postes appareutés
Lao People's Dem. Rep.								**Rép. dém. pop. lao**
Goods: Exports fob	305.5	310.9	322.8	318.3	342.1	338.2	...	Biens : exportations,fàb
Goods: Imports fob	−519.2	−626.8	−643.7	−601.3	−506.8	−527.7	...	Biens : importations,fàb
Serv. & Income: Credit	94.2	104.2	113.6	116.9	151.9	140.5	...	Serv. & revenu : crédit
Serv. & Income: Debit	−161.3	−134.5	−139.5	−139.4	−137.3	−101.7	...	Serv. & revenu : débit
Current Trans.,nie: Credit	0.0	0.0	0.0	0.0	0.0	80.2	...	Transf. cour.,nia : crédit

76
Summary of balance of payments
Millions of US dollars
Résumé des balances des paiements
Millions de dollars des E.−U.

Country or area	1994	1995	1996	1997	1998	1999	2000	Pays ou zone
Current Transfers: Debit	−3.2	0.0	0.0	0.0	0.0	−50.6	...	Transf. courants : débit
Capital Acct.,nie: Credit	9.5	21.7	44.9	40.3	49.4	0.0	...	Compte de cap.,nia : crédit
Capital Account: Debit	0.0	−8.5	−9.9	−6.9	−6.3	0.0	...	Compte de capital : débit
Financial Account,nie	24.3	90.0	135.7	3.5	−43.4	−46.9	...	Compte d'op. fin., nia
Net Errors and Omissions	71.8	92.4	17.7	−100.5	−103.8	−165.1	...	Erreurs et omissions nettes
Reserves and Related Items	178.4	150.6	158.4	369.1	254.2	333.1	...	Rés. et postes appareutés
Malaysia								**Malaisie**
Goods: Exports fob	56 897.3	71 767.2	76 985.1	77 538.3	71 882.8	84 051.8	...	Biens : exportations,fàb
Goods: Imports fob	−55 320.0	−71 870.6	−73 136.8	−74 028.7	−54 377.8	−61 404.2	...	Biens : importations,fàb
Serv. & Income: Credit	11 628.4	14 225.0	17 828.3	18 212.0	13 058.9	13 922.1	...	Serv. & revenu : crédit
Serv. & Income: Debit	−17 955.2	−21 747.7	−24 956.0	−26 147.6	−18 572.7	−22 235.8	...	Serv. & revenu : débit
Current Trans.,nie: Credit	411.2	700.0	765.9	944.1	727.8	800.8	...	Transf. cour.,nia : crédit
Current Transfers: Debit	−181.8	−1 717.4	−1 948.4	−2 453.4	−3 190.3	−2 529.0	...	Transf. courants : débit
Capital Acct.,nie: Credit	0.0	0.0	0.0	0.0	0.0	0.0	...	Compte de cap.,nia : crédit
Capital Account: Debit	−81.5	0.0	0.0	0.0	0.0	0.0	...	Compte de capital : débit
Financial Account,nie	1 288.0	7 642.5	9 476.8	2 197.5	−2 549.7	−6 619.0	...	Compte d'op. fin., nia
Net Errors and Omissions	153.6	−761.6	−2 501.6	−136.9	3 038.8	−1 275.0	...	Erreurs et omissions nettes
Reserves and Related Items	3 160.1	1 762.7	−2 513.3	3 874.7	−10 017.7	−4 711.9	...	Rés. et postes appareutés
Maldives								**Maldives**
Goods: Exports fob	75.4	85.0	80.0	93.0	95.6	91.4	108.7	Biens : exportations,fàb
Goods: Imports fob	−195.1	−235.8	−265.5	−307.0	−311.5	−353.9	−342.0	Biens : importations,fàb
Serv. & Income: Credit	201.2	237.3	294.9	319.6	339.9	351.8	358.8	Serv. & revenu : crédit
Serv. & Income: Debit	−86.8	−101.2	−115.6	−129.1	−135.6	−148.2	−150.1	Serv. & revenu : débit
Current Trans.,nie: Credit	16.3	23.0	26.2	17.2	18.9	17.7	17.7	Transf. cour.,nia : crédit
Current Transfers: Debit	−22.2	−26.6	−27.3	−27.9	−30.6	−40.5	−46.2	Transf. courants : débit
Capital Acct.,nie: Credit	0.0	0.0	0.0	0.0	0.0	0.0	0.0	Compte de cap.,nia : crédit
Capital Account: Debit	0.0	0.0	0.0	0.0	0.0	0.0	0.0	Compte de capital : débit
Financial Account,nie	27.4	67.6	52.2	71.0	60.3	76.2	40.0	Compte d'op. fin., nia
Net Errors and Omissions	−10.8	−32.2	−16.6	−14.6	−16.9	14.1	8.8	Erreurs et omissions nettes
Reserves and Related Items	−5.4	−17.1	−28.3	−22.2	−20.1	−8.6	4.3	Rés. et postes appareutés
Mongolia								**Mongolie**
Goods: Exports fob	367.0	451.0	423.4	568.5	462.4	454.3	...	Biens : exportations,fàb
Goods: Imports fob	−333.3	−425.7	−459.7	−453.1	−524.2	−510.7	...	Biens : importations,fàb
Serv. & Income: Credit	48.6	60.3	69.1	58.8	87.9	82.5	...	Serv. & revenu : crédit
Serv. & Income: Debit	−113.7	−123.8	−139.5	−123.2	−156.5	−152.3	...	Serv. & revenu : débit
Current Trans.,nie: Credit	77.8	77.1	6.2	4.2	5.5	17.6	...	Transf. cour.,nia : crédit
Current Transfers: Debit	0.0	0.0	0.0	0.0	−3.6	−3.6	...	Transf. courants : débit
Capital Acct.,nie: Credit	0.0	0.0	0.0	0.0	0.0	0.0	...	Compte de cap.,nia : crédit
Capital Account: Debit	0.0	0.0	0.0	0.0	0.0	0.0	...	Compte de capital : débit
Financial Account,nie	−39.0	−15.9	41.3	27.0	126.2	69.6	...	Compte d'op. fin., nia
Net Errors and Omissions	−1.0	9.1	−28.1	−75.6	−50.2	23.6	...	Erreurs et omissions nettes
Reserves and Related Items	−6.4	−32.1	87.3	−6.6	52.5	19.0	...	Rés. et postes appareutés
Myanmar								**Myanmar**
Goods: Exports fob	857.4	933.2	937.9	974.5	1 065.2	1 281.1	1 618.8	Biens : exportations,fàb
Goods: Imports fob	−1 466.8	−1 756.3	−1 869.1	−2 106.6	−2 451.2	−2 159.6	−2 134.9	Biens : importations,fàb
Serv. & Income: Credit	277.8	376.3	436.8	528.2	637.0	558.2	556.5	Serv. & revenu : crédit
Serv. & Income: Debit	−203.0	−368.0	−355.0	−463.6	−376.1	−342.2	−580.5	Serv. & revenu : débit
Current Trans.,nie: Credit	405.2	564.2	598.4	685.1	631.2	381.0	297.3	Transf. cour.,nia : crédit
Current Transfers: Debit	−0.6	−8.0	−28.8	−29.7	−0.3	−0.3	−0.1	Transf. courants : débit
Capital Acct.,nie: Credit	0.0	0.0	0.0	0.0	0.0	0.0	0.0	Compte de cap.,nia : crédit
Capital Account: Debit	0.0	0.0	0.0	0.0	0.0	0.0	0.0	Compte de capital : débit
Financial Account,nie	185.2	242.8	266.8	469.1	535.1	248.8	160.1	Compte d'op. fin., nia
Net Errors and Omissions	−10.3	−16.2	−11.7	−26.0	18.8	−12.3	59.6	Erreurs et omissions nettes
Reserves and Related Items	−45.0	31.8	24.7	−31.0	−59.7	45.4	23.3	Rés. et postes appareutés
Nepal								**Népal**
Goods: Exports fob	368.7	349.9	388.7	413.8	482.0	612.3	785.7	Biens : exportations,fàb
Goods: Imports fob	−1 158.9	−1 310.8	−1 494.7	−1 691.9	−1 239.1	−1 494.2	−1 578.3	Biens : importations,fàb
Serv. & Income: Credit	613.8	722.6	790.6	897.6	610.6	710.9	578.1	Serv. & revenu : crédit
Serv. & Income: Debit	−327.4	−348.1	−274.8	−253.1	−222.7	−240.9	−235.1	Serv. & revenu : débit
Current Trans.,nie: Credit	160.7	239.2	281.6	267.4	326.0	182.3	189.0	Transf. cour.,nia : crédit
Current Transfers: Debit	−8.7	−9.1	−18.0	−21.8	−24.1	−26.9	−16.7	Transf. courants : débit
Capital Acct.,nie: Credit	0.0	0.0	0.0	0.0	0.0	111.2	0.0	Compte de cap.,nia : crédit
Capital Account: Debit	0.0	0.0	0.0	0.0	0.0	0.0	0.0	Compte de capital : débit
Financial Account,nie	407.3	368.5	275.2	340.3	212.9	−24.5	76.1	Compte d'op. fin., nia
Net Errors and Omissions	7.1	2.8	82.3	216.6	134.0	58.3	124.6	Erreurs et omissions nettes
Reserves and Related Items	−62.5	−15.0	−30.9	−168.8	−279.7	222.7	76.8	Rés. et postes appareutés

76
Summary of balance of payments
Millions of US dollars
Résumé des balances des paiements
Millions de dollars des E.–U.

Country or area	1994	1995	1996	1997	1998	1999	2000	Pays ou zone
Oman								**Oman**
Goods: Exports fob	5 542.3	6 065.0	7 373.2	7 656.7	5 521.5	7 238.8	11 318.6	Biens : exportations,fàb
Goods: Imports fob	−3 693.1	−4 049.9	−4 231.5	−4 645.0	−5 214.6	−4 299.6	−4 593.0	Biens : importations,fàb
Serv. & Income: Credit	270.5	338.1	494.1	652.8	613.8	460.4	574.8	Serv. & revenu : crédit
Serv. & Income: Debit	−1 624.2	−1 684.3	−1 927.2	−2 236.7	−2 447.3	−2 330.6	−2 496.7	Serv. & revenu : débit
Current Trans.,nie: Credit	65.0	67.6	49.4	70.2	39.0	39.0	0.0	Transf. cour.,nia : crédit
Current Transfers: Debit	−1 365.4	−1 537.1	−1 370.6	−1 500.7	−1 466.8	−1 438.4	−1 456.4	Transf. courants : débit
Capital Acct.,nie: Credit	0.0	0.0	0.0	0.0	0.0	0.0	0.0	Compte de cap.,nia : crédit
Capital Account: Debit	0.0	0.0	−18.2	−23.4	−26.0	−18.2	−26.0	Compte de capital : débit
Financial Account,nie	229.9	−18.7	260.1	52.0	1 482.4	65.0	−405.7	Compte d'op. fin., nia
Net Errors and Omissions	−85.8	387.7	−420.1	520.6	750.9	521.5	−686.9	Erreurs et omissions nettes
Reserves and Related Items	660.8	431.6	−188.5	−531.0	765.4	−214.6	−2 262.4	Rés. et postes appareutés
Pakistan								**Pakistan**
Goods: Exports fob	7 116.8	8 356.4	8 507.3	8 350.7	...	...	...	Biens : exportations,fàb
Goods: Imports fob	−9 355.3	−11 247.8	−12 163.7	−10 750.2	...	...	...	Biens : importations,fàb
Serv. & Income: Credit	1 902.1	2 043.9	2 191.7	1 771.8	...	...	...	Serv. & revenu : crédit
Serv. & Income: Debit	−4 359.0	−5 062.9	−5 656.6	−5 024.6	...	...	...	Serv. & revenu : débit
Current Trans.,nie: Credit	2 918.6	2 610.7	2 739.5	3 980.6	...	...	...	Transf. cour.,nia : crédit
Current Transfers: Debit	−35.2	−49.0	−54.1	−39.9	...	...	...	Transf. courants : débit
Capital Acct.,nie: Credit	0.0	0.0	0.0	0.0	...	...	...	Compte de cap.,nia : crédit
Capital Account: Debit	0.0	0.0	0.0	0.0	...	...	...	Compte de capital : débit
Financial Account,nie	2 977.4	2 449.4	3 496.2	2 321.1	...	...	...	Compte d'op. fin., nia
Net Errors and Omissions	177.8	−304.2	159.6	−71.8	...	...	...	Erreurs et omissions nettes
Reserves and Related Items	−1 343.1	1 203.6	780.3	−537.7	...	...	...	Rés. et postes appareutés
Philippines								**Philippines**
Goods: Exports fob	13 483.0	17 447.0	20 543.0	25 228.0	29 496.0	34 209.6	37 298.0	Biens : exportations,fàb
Goods: Imports fob	−21 333.0	−26 391.0	−31 885.0	−36 355.0	−29 524.0	−29 252.0	−30 381.0	Biens : importations,fàb
Serv. & Income: Credit	10 550.0	15 415.0	19 006.0	22 835.0	13 917.0	12 883.0	11 972.0	Serv. & revenu : crédit
Serv. & Income: Debit	−6 586.0	−9 331.0	−12 206.0	−17 139.0	−12 778.0	−10 425.0	−10 241.0	Serv. & revenu : débit
Current Trans.,nie: Credit	1 041.0	1 147.0	1 185.0	1 670.0	758.0	610.0	551.0	Transf. cour.,nia : crédit
Current Transfers: Debit	−105.0	−267.0	−596.0	−590.0	−323.0	−116.0	−118.0	Transf. courants : débit
Capital Acct.,nie: Credit	0.0	0.0	0.0	0.0	0.0	44.0	74.0	Compte de cap.,nia : crédit
Capital Account: Debit	0.0	0.0	0.0	0.0	0.0	−53.0	−36.0	Compte de capital : débit
Financial Account,nie	5 120.0	5 309.0	11 277.0	6 498.0	483.0	−935.0	−6 794.0	Compte d'op. fin., nia
Net Errors and Omissions	156.8	−2 093.6	−2 986.0	−5 241.4	−749.9	−3 306.5	−2 700.6	Erreurs et omissions nettes
Reserves and Related Items	−2 326.8	−1 235.4	−4 338.0	3 094.4	−1 279.1	−3 659.1	375.5	Rés. et postes appareutés
Saudi Arabia								**Arabie saoudite**
Goods: Exports fob	42 614.2	50 040.9	60 728.7	60 731.4	38 821.9	50 756.7	78 973.3	Biens : exportations,fàb
Goods: Imports fob	−21 325.0	−25 650.5	−25 358.3	−26 369.8	−27 534.6	−25 717.5	−27 797.3	Biens : importations,fàb
Serv. & Income: Credit	7 378.9	8 467.6	7 899.1	10 012.3	10 539.1	11 191.2	8 136.2	Serv. & revenu : crédit
Serv. & Income: Debit	−20 452.9	−21 267.2	−26 975.7	−28 934.0	−19 923.1	−21 742.9	−28 234.8	Serv. & revenu : débit
Current Trans.,nie: Credit	0.0	0.0	0.0	0.0	0.0	0.0	0.0	Transf. cour.,nia : crédit
Current Transfers: Debit	−18 702.0	−16 916.0	−15 613.2	−15 134.4	−15 052.9	−14 075.6	−15 510.8	Transf. courants : débit
Capital Acct.,nie: Credit	0.0	0.0	0.0	0.0	0.0	0.0	0.0	Compte de cap.,nia : crédit
Capital Account: Debit	0.0	0.0	0.0	0.0	0.0	0.0	0.0	Compte de capital : débit
Financial Account,nie	10 340.7	6 542.1	5 068.6	343.1	12 430.7	2 402.9	−12 901.7	Compte d'op. fin., nia
Net Errors and Omissions	0.5	0.0	−0.1	−0.5	−0.1	−0.4	−0.1	Erreurs et omissions nettes
Reserves and Related Items	145.6	−1 216.9	−5 749.0	−648.1	718.9	−2 814.6	−2 664.8	Rés. et postes appareutés
Singapore								**Singapour**
Goods: Exports fob	97 919.0	118 456.0	126 010.0	125 746.0	110 561.0	115 518.0	138 931.0	Biens : exportations,fàb
Goods: Imports fob	−96 564.6	−117 480.0	−123 786.0	−124 628.0	−95 782.1	−104 361.0	−127 531.0	Biens : importations,fàb
Serv. & Income: Credit	32 827.0	42 606.4	42 491.2	44 386.5	32 118.4	38 959.9	42 292.7	Serv. & revenu : crédit
Serv. & Income: Debit	−22 120.5	−27 797.0	−30 825.6	−26 408.8	−25 465.8	−27 203.3	−30 537.6	Serv. & revenu : débit
Current Trans.,nie: Credit	144.9	155.9	156.7	150.5	136.1	133.7	131.9	Transf. cour.,nia : crédit
Current Transfers: Debit	−806.0	−1 041.5	−1 224.2	−1 319.4	−1 233.8	−1 297.2	−1 490.5	Transf. courants : débit
Capital Acct.,nie: Credit	0.0	0.0	0.0	0.0	0.0	0.0	0.0	Compte de cap.,nia : crédit
Capital Account: Debit	0.0	0.0	0.0	0.0	0.0	0.0	0.0	Compte de capital : débit
Financial Account,nie	−8 841.0	−878.0	−4 824.9	−10 976.2	−21 813.1	−18 280.2	−11 398.9	Compte d'op. fin., nia
Net Errors and Omissions	2 261.5	−5 351.6	−463.5	1 162.1	4 670.4	915.1	−3 429.0	Erreurs et omissions nettes
Reserves and Related Items	−4 736.1	−8 599.1	−7 395.6	−7 939.8	−2 965.4	−4 193.9	−6 806.0	Rés. et postes appareutés
Sri Lanka								**Sri Lanka**
Goods: Exports fob	3 208.3	3 797.9	4 095.2	4 638.7	4 808.0	4 596.2	5 439.6	Biens : exportations,fàb
Goods: Imports fob	−4 293.4	−4 782.6	−4 895.0	−5 278.3	−5 313.4	−5 365.5	−6 483.6	Biens : importations,fàb
Serv. & Income: Credit	897.8	1 042.5	940.6	1 108.6	1 130.8	1 131.1	1 087.7	Serv. & revenu : crédit
Serv. & Income: Debit	−1 364.3	−1 559.7	−1 582.5	−1 695.5	−1 756.2	−1 833.0	−2 069.9	Serv. & revenu : débit
Current Trans.,nie: Credit	882.3	846.7	881.4	966.5	1 054.5	1 078.1	1 166.5	Transf. cour.,nia : crédit

76
Summary of balance of payments
Millions of US dollars
Résumé des balances des paiements
Millions de dollars des E.−U.

Country or area	1994	1995	1996	1997	1998	1999	2000	Pays ou zone
Current Transfers: Debit	−88.1	−114.7	−122.4	−134.7	−151.3	−168.2	−182.7	Transf. courants : débit
Capital Acct.,nie: Credit	0.0	124.2	99.7	91.3	84.6	85.2	56.3	Compte de cap.,nia : crédit
Capital Account: Debit	0.0	−3.5	−3.8	−4.2	−4.7	−5.2	−5.7	Compte de capital : débit
Financial Account,nie	958.8	730.1	452.2	466.7	345.1	413.4	574.5	Compte d'op. fin., nia
Net Errors and Omissions	106.3	157.9	143.6	148.0	26.3	−27.3	56.4	Erreurs et omissions nettes
Reserves and Related Items	−307.7	−238.7	−9.0	−307.2	−223.6	95.2	360.8	Rés. et postes appareutés
Syrian Arab Republic								**Rép. arabe syrienne**
Goods: Exports fob	3 329.0	3 858.0	4 178.0	4 057.0	3 142.0	3 806.0	5 146.0	Biens : exportations,fàb
Goods: Imports fob	−4 604.0	−4 004.0	−4 516.0	−3 603.0	−3 320.0	−3 590.0	−3 723.0	Biens : importations,fàb
Serv. & Income: Credit	2 501.0	2 343.0	2 326.0	2 003.0	2 035.0	2 007.0	2 045.0	Serv. & revenu : crédit
Serv. & Income: Debit	−2 608.0	−2 541.0	−2 572.0	−2 495.0	−2 330.0	−2 511.0	−2 891.0	Serv. & revenu : débit
Current Trans.,nie: Credit	597.0	610.0	630.0	504.0	533.0	491.0	495.0	Transf. cour.,nia : crédit
Current Transfers: Debit	−6.0	−3.0	−6.0	−5.0	−2.0	−2.0	−10.0	Transf. courants : débit
Capital Acct.,nie: Credit	102.0	20.0	26.0	18.0	27.0	80.0	63.0	Compte de cap.,nia : crédit
Capital Account: Debit	0.0	0.0	0.0	0.0	0.0	0.0	0.0	Compte de capital : débit
Financial Account,nie	1 159.0	521.0	782.0	65.0	196.0	173.0	−392.0	Compte d'op. fin., nia
Net Errors and Omissions	96.0	35.0	139.0	−95.0	153.1	−195.0	−192.0	Erreurs et omissions nettes
Reserves and Related Items	−566.0	−839.0	−987.0	−449.0	−434.1	−259.0	−541.0	Rés. et postes appareutés
Thailand								**Thaïlande**
Goods: Exports fob	44 477.8	55 446.6	54 408.4	56 655.9	52 752.9	56 775.1	67 948.7	Biens : exportations,fàb
Goods: Imports fob	−48 204.1	−63 414.9	−63 896.6	−55 084.3	−36 514.9	−42 761.8	−56 192.1	Biens : importations,fàb
Serv. & Income: Credit	14 201.7	18 646.1	20 976.3	19 505.6	16 479.3	17 726.9	18 103.1	Serv. & revenu : crédit
Serv. & Income: Debit	−19 688.3	−24 718.3	−26 939.3	−24 577.0	−18 889.1	−19 665.6	−21 076.3	Serv. & revenu : débit
Current Trans.,nie: Credit	1 901.3	1 190.2	1 651.0	1 392.1	819.8	805.6	951.6	Transf. cour.,nia : crédit
Current Transfers: Debit	−773.7	−703.7	−891.3	−913.3	−405.4	−452.5	−365.7	Transf. courants : débit
Capital Acct.,nie: Credit	0.0	0.0	0.0	0.0	0.0	0.0	0.0	Compte de cap.,nia : crédit
Capital Account: Debit	0.0	0.0	0.0	0.0	0.0	0.0	0.0	Compte de capital : débit
Financial Account,nie	12 167.0	21 908.6	19 486.0	−12 055.7	−14 110.3	−11 073.0	−10 185.9	Compte d'op. fin., nia
Net Errors and Omissions	87.4	−1 196.0	−2 627.3	−3 173.0	−2 828.1	33.4	−989.8	Erreurs et omissions nettes
Reserves and Related Items	−4 169.1	−7 158.7	−2 167.3	18 249.8	2 696.0	−1 388.3	1 806.4	Rés. et postes appareutés
Turkey								**Turquie**
Goods: Exports fob	18 390.0	21 975.0	32 446.0	32 631.0	31 220.0	29 325.0	31 664.0	Biens : exportations,fàb
Goods: Imports fob	−22 606.0	−35 187.0	−43 028.0	−48 029.0	−45 440.0	−39 768.0	−54 041.0	Biens : importations,fàb
Serv. & Income: Credit	11 691.0	16 095.0	14 628.0	21 273.0	25 802.0	18 748.0	22 320.0	Serv. & revenu : crédit
Serv. & Income: Debit	−7 936.0	−9 717.0	−10 930.0	−13 420.0	−15 325.0	−14 840.0	−14 987.0	Serv. & revenu : débit
Current Trans.,nie: Credit	3 113.0	4 512.0	4 466.0	4 909.0	5 860.0	5 294.0	5 317.0	Transf. cour.,nia : crédit
Current Transfers: Debit	−21.0	−16.0	−19.0	−43.0	−133.0	−119.0	−92.0	Transf. courants : débit
Capital Acct.,nie: Credit	0.0	0.0	0.0	0.0	0.0	0.0	0.0	Compte de cap.,nia : crédit
Capital Account: Debit	0.0	0.0	0.0	0.0	0.0	0.0	0.0	Compte de capital : débit
Financial Account,nie	−4 194.0	4 643.0	8 763.0	8 616.0	448.0	4 670.0	9 445.0	Compte d'op. fin., nia
Net Errors and Omissions	1 765.8	2 355.3	−1 782.5	−2 593.8	−1 991.1	1 894.5	−2 559.5	Erreurs et omissions nettes
Reserves and Related Items	−202.8	−4 660.3	−4 543.5	−3 343.2	−440.9	−5 204.5	2 933.5	Rés. et postes appareutés
Turkmenistan								**Turkménistan**
Goods: Exports fob	...	...	1 692.0	774.2			...	Biens : exportations,fàb
Goods: Imports fob	...	...	−1 388.3	−1 005.1	...	...	...	Biens : importations,fàb
Serv. & Income: Credit	...	...	209.6	428.7	...	...	...	Serv. & revenu : crédit
Serv. & Income: Debit	...	...	−518.4	−746.6	...	...	...	Serv. & revenu : débit
Current Trans.,nie: Credit	...	...	4.8	49.9	...	...	...	Transf. cour.,nia : crédit
Current Transfers: Debit	...	...	0.0	−81.2	...	...	...	Transf. courants : débit
Capital Acct.,nie: Credit	...	...	2.8	14.0	...	...	...	Compte de cap.,nia : crédit
Capital Account: Debit	...	...	−159.7	−22.9	...	...	...	Compte de capital : débit
Financial Account,nie	...	...	113.4	1 060.0	...	...	...	Compte d'op. fin., nia
Net Errors and Omissions	...	...	51.6	−72.9	...	...	...	Erreurs et omissions nettes
Reserves and Related Items	...	...	−7.9	−398.0	...	...	...	Rés. et postes appareutés
Yemen								**Yémen**
Goods: Exports fob	1 796.2	1 980.1	2 262.7	2 274.0	1 503.7	2 478.3	...	Biens : exportations,fàb
Goods: Imports fob	−1 522.0	−1 831.5	−2 293.5	−2 406.5	−2 288.8	−2 120.4	...	Biens : importations,fàb
Serv. & Income: Credit	170.0	216.8	232.5	277.2	275.5	277.3	...	Serv. & revenu : crédit
Serv. & Income: Debit	−1 258.2	−1 237.7	−1 236.1	−1 348.0	−969.5	−1 289.5	...	Serv. & revenu : débit
Current Trans.,nie: Credit	1 062.3	1 080.5	1 140.1	1 177.6	1 223.5	1 262.1	...	Transf. cour.,nia : crédit
Current Transfers: Debit	−70.0	−64.5	−66.9	−43.1	−47.7	−30.7	...	Transf. courants : débit
Capital Acct.,nie: Credit	0.0	0.0	0.0	4 236.2	2.2	1.5	...	Compte de cap.,nia : crédit
Capital Account: Debit	0.0	0.0	0.0	0.0	0.0	0.0	...	Compte de capital : débit
Financial Account,nie	−710.7	−858.4	−367.8	−197.6	−468.0	−549.8	...	Compte d'op. fin., nia
Net Errors and Omissions	−189.2	186.5	−107.0	48.4	188.2	45.2	...	Erreurs et omissions nettes
Reserves and Related Items	721.6	528.2	436.0	−4 018.2	580.9	−74.0	...	Rés. et postes appareutés

76
Summary of balance of payments
Millions of US dollars
Résumé des balances des paiements
Millions de dollars des E.−U.

Country or area	1994	1995	1996	1997	1998	1999	2000	Pays ou zone
Europe · Europe								
Albania								**Albanie**
Goods: Exports fob	141.3	204.9	243.7	158.6	208.0	275.0	255.7	Biens : exportations,fàb
Goods: Imports fob	−601.0	−679.7	−922.0	−693.6	−811.7	−938.0	−1 070.0	Biens : importations,fàb
Serv. & Income: Credit	134.2	170.8	212.9	125.2	172.6	354.9	563.7	Serv. & revenu : crédit
Serv. & Income: Debit	−173.8	−184.9	−201.3	−127.0	−138.0	−173.3	−438.6	Serv. & revenu : débit
Current Trans.,nie: Credit	347.5	521.2	595.9	299.8	560.8	508.9	629.0	Transf. cour.,nia : crédit
Current Transfers: Debit	−5.5	−43.8	−36.5	−35.2	−56.9	−182.9	−96.1	Transf. courants : débit
Capital Acct.,nie: Credit	0.0	389.4	4.8	2.0	31.0	22.6	78.0	Compte de cap.,nia : crédit
Capital Account: Debit	0.0	0.0	0.0	0.0	0.0	0.0	0.0	Compte de capital : débit
Financial Account,nie	40.2	−411.0	61.5	151.4	15.4	33.7	188.4	Compte d'op. fin., nia
Net Errors and Omissions	123.9	53.7	96.9	158.4	71.1	206.2	9.8	Erreurs et omissions nettes
Reserves and Related Items	−6.8	−20.6	−55.9	−39.5	−52.4	−107.1	−119.9	Rés. et postes appareutés
Austria								**Autriche**
Goods: Exports fob	45 175.1	57 695.2	57 937.3	58 662.3	63 299.1	64 421.7	64 683.7	Biens : exportations,fàb
Goods: Imports fob	−53 089.4	−64 351.6	−65 251.9	−62 936.3	−66 983.3	−68 050.8	−67 415.4	Biens : importations,fàb
Serv. & Income: Credit	35 093.0	41 111.6	43 828.9	39 998.0	39 715.8	43 978.5	42 122.7	Serv. & revenu : crédit
Serv. & Income: Debit	−29 087.6	−38 201.1	−39 621.5	−39 251.5	−39 356.2	−44 973.7	−43 346.8	Serv. & revenu : débit
Current Trans.,nie: Credit	1 370.3	2 972.3	3 144.8	2 911.6	2 940.4	2 924.8	3 013.0	Transf. cour.,nia : crédit
Current Transfers: Debit	−2 453.3	−4 674.3	−4 928.0	−4 605.2	−4 874.0	−4 956.1	−4 262.1	Transf. courants : débit
Capital Acct.,nie: Credit	676.2	540.0	591.3	590.0	483.3	554.6	525.3	Compte de cap.,nia : crédit
Capital Account: Debit	−744.4	−601.7	−513.0	−563.7	−830.6	−820.0	−954.8	Compte de capital : débit
Financial Account,nie	4 311.1	7 365.0	5 324.9	1 665.9	9 534.8	4 788.7	4 310.6	Compte d'op. fin., nia
Net Errors and Omissions	−417.3	−464.0	562.1	475.5	−447.2	−39.7	576.7	Erreurs et omissions nettes
Reserves and Related Items	−833.8	−1 391.3	−1 075.0	3 053.3	−3 481.9	2 171.9	747.0	Rés. et postes appareutés
Belarus								**Bélarus**
Goods: Exports fob	2 510.0	4 803.0	5 790.1	6 918.7	6 172.3	5 646.4	6 986.8	Biens : exportations,fàb
Goods: Imports fob	−2 999.8	−5 468.7	−6 938.6	−8 325.7	−7 673.4	−6 216.4	−7 824.9	Biens : importations,fàb
Serv. & Income: Credit	251.9	468.0	982.1	950.0	951.9	774.1	1 019.5	Serv. & revenu : crédit
Serv. & Income: Debit	−228.6	−336.6	−440.8	−480.6	−562.9	−501.6	−500.4	Serv. & revenu : débit
Current Trans.,nie: Credit	50.9	107.2	135.5	106.1	120.9	137.0	177.1	Transf. cour.,nia : crédit
Current Transfers: Debit	−28.2	−31.2	−44.2	−27.7	−25.3	−33.2	−20.0	Transf. courants : débit
Capital Acct.,nie: Credit	23.8	7.3	257.2	248.0	261.3	131.1	111.3	Compte de cap.,nia : crédit
Capital Account: Debit	0.0	0.0	−156.1	−114.8	−91.2	−70.7	−69.4	Compte de capital : débit
Financial Account,nie	144.6	204.0	378.7	738.1	354.8	399.5	167.3	Compte d'op. fin., nia
Net Errors and Omissions	−41.6	168.6	−178.1	53.0	172.3	−246.3	129.0	Erreurs et omissions nettes
Reserves and Related Items	317.0	78.4	214.2	−65.1	319.3	−19.9	−176.3	Rés. et postes appareutés
Belgium−Luxembourg [3]								**Belgique−Luxembourg** [3]
Goods: Exports fob	122 795.0	155 219.0	154 695.0	149 497.0	153 558.0	154 352.0	162 508.0	Biens : exportations,fàb
Goods: Imports fob	−115 895.0	−145 664.0	−146 004.0	−141 794.0	−146 577.0	−147 710.0	−157 173.0	Biens : importations,fàb
Serv. & Income: Credit	129 843.0	110 264.0	97 586.0	93 740.0	103 332.0	111 924.0	121 254.0	Serv. & revenu : crédit
Serv. & Income: Debit	−120 666.0	−101 124.0	−87 907.0	−83 546.0	−93 726.0	−100 641.0	−110 615.0	Serv. & revenu : débit
Current Trans.,nie: Credit	4 501.0	7 822.0	7 474.0	7 142.0	7 006.0	6 738.0	6 085.0	Transf. cour.,nia : crédit
Current Transfers: Debit	−8 009.0	−12 285.0	−12 081.0	−11 124.0	−11 426.0	−11 289.0	−10 209.0	Transf. courants : débit
Capital Acct.,nie: Credit	0.0	734.0	673.0	783.0	323.0	449.0	224.0	Compte de cap.,nia : crédit
Capital Account: Debit	0.0	−356.0	−494.0	−379.0	−436.0	−442.0	−6 270.0	Compte de capital : débit
Financial Account,nie	−10 182.0	−12 912.0	−12 257.0	−12 091.0	−16 043.0	−15 948.0	−11 699.0	Compte d'op. fin., nia
Net Errors and Omissions	−2 169.0	−1 456.0	−1 091.0	−1 171.0	1 893.0	699.0	−1 307.0	Erreurs et omissions nettes
Reserves and Related Items	−219.0	−243.0	−593.0	−1 056.0	2 095.0	1 867.0	1 557.0	Rés. et postes appareutés
Bosnia and Herzegovina								**Bosnie−Herzégovine**
Goods: Exports fob	...	...	...	...	592.7	748.8	1 066.2	Biens : exportations,fàb
Goods: Imports fob	...	...	...	...	−2 722.9	−3 076.8	−2 896.0	Biens : importations,fàb
Serv. & Income: Credit	...	...	...	...	846.9	1 106.9	830.2	Serv. & revenu : crédit
Serv. & Income: Debit	...	...	...	...	−354.2	−436.5	−412.6	Serv. & revenu : débit
Current Trans.,nie: Credit	...	...	...	...	800.7	905.5	854.7	Transf. cour.,nia : crédit
Current Transfers: Debit	...	...	...	...	−6.5	−5.6	−7.2	Transf. courants : débit
Capital Acct.,nie: Credit	...	...	...	...	368.9	431.9	429.7	Compte de cap.,nia : crédit
Capital Account: Debit	...	...	...	...	0.0	0.0	0.0	Compte de capital : débit
Financial Account,nie	...	...	...	...	227.4	44.8	18.1	Compte d'op. fin., nia
Net Errors and Omissions	...	...	...	...	59.8	264.1	85.6	Erreurs et omissions nettes
Reserves and Related Items	...	...	...	...	187.4	17.1	31.4	Rés. et postes appareutés
Bulgaria								**Bulgarie**
Goods: Exports fob	3 935.1	5 345.0	4 890.2	4 939.6	4 193.5	4 006.4	4 812.2	Biens : exportations,fàb
Goods: Imports fob	−3 951.9	−5 224.0	−4 702.6	−4 559.3	−4 574.2	−5 087.4	−5 987.6	Biens : importations,fàb
Serv. & Income: Credit	1 341.5	1 581.1	1 547.0	1 548.2	2 094.5	2 051.8	2 497.7	Serv. & revenu : crédit
Serv. & Income: Debit	−1 523.2	−1 859.8	−1 823.1	−1 738.4	−2 005.4	−1 955.3	−2 313.0	Serv. & revenu : débit

76
Summary of balance of payments
Millions of US dollars
Résumé des balances des paiements
Millions de dollars des E.−U.

Country or area	1994	1995	1996	1997	1998	1999	2000	Pays ou zone
Current Trans.,nie: Credit	357.1	256.8	231.8	275.5	261.4	328.7	354.1	Transf. cour.,nia : crédit
Current Transfers: Debit	−190.4	−124.9	−127.6	−38.7	−31.6	−28.9	−64.4	Transf. courants : débit
Capital Acct.,nie: Credit	763.3	0.0	65.9	0.0	0.0	0.0	25.0	Compte de cap.,nia : crédit
Capital Account: Debit	0.0	0.0	0.0	0.0	0.0	−2.4	0.0	Compte de capital : débit
Financial Account,nie	−1 018.7	326.6	−715.0	462.0	266.7	777.4	883.3	Compte d'op. fin., nia
Net Errors and Omissions	71.6	143.8	−105.3	256.4	−299.2	6.1	−70.3	Erreurs et omissions nettes
Reserves and Related Items	215.6	−444.6	738.7	−1 145.4	94.3	−96.4	−137.0	Rés. et postes appareutés
Croatia								**Croatie**
Goods: Exports fob	4 260.4	4 632.7	4 545.9	4 210.4	4 604.5	4 394.7	4 567.0	Biens : exportations,fàb
Goods: Imports fob	−5 402.1	−7 892.0	−8 169.1	−9 406.6	−8 751.9	−7 693.4	−7 770.7	Biens : importations,fàb
Serv. & Income: Credit	3 006.1	2 673.3	3 566.3	4 367.9	4 358.8	3 975.4	4 452.9	Serv. & revenu : crédit
Serv. & Income: Debit	−1 537.1	−1 657.9	−2 056.8	−2 365.9	−2 448.4	−2 699.1	−2 506.1	Serv. & revenu : débit
Current Trans.,nie: Credit	669.2	971.1	1 173.1	963.8	919.1	967.3	1 065.3	Transf. cour.,nia : crédit
Current Transfers: Debit	−142.8	−168.9	−150.8	−94.5	−213.3	−334.9	−207.6	Transf. courants : débit
Capital Acct.,nie: Credit	0.0	0.0	18.0	23.5	24.1	28.3	24.1	Compte de cap.,nia : crédit
Capital Account: Debit	0.0	0.0	−1.8	−2.2	−5.0	−3.3	−3.6	Compte de capital : débit
Financial Account,nie	16.3	1 136.1	2 996.3	3 020.7	1 610.3	2 519.7	1 272.4	Compte d'op., nia
Net Errors and Omissions	−593.5	346.0	−903.8	−326.7	62.3	−744.7	−282.9	Erreurs et omissions nettes
Reserves and Related Items	−276.5	−40.4	−1 017.3	−390.4	−160.5	−410.0	−610.8	Rés. et postes appareutés
Czech Republic								**République tchèque**
Goods: Exports fob	15 964.0	21 476.8	21 693.4	22 736.9	26 394.7	26 258.9	29 019.3	Biens : exportations,fàb
Goods: Imports fob	−17 371.7	−25 162.2	−27 570.6	−27 324.5	−28 989.3	−28 161.3	−32 114.5	Biens : importations,fàb
Serv. & Income: Credit	5 957.9	7 922.5	9 350.6	8 536.6	8 941.4	8 572.9	8 541.8	Serv. & revenu : crédit
Serv. & Income: Debit	−5 496.9	−6 182.5	−8 156.2	−7 585.4	−8 141.5	−8 749.9	−7 980.9	Serv. & revenu : débit
Current Trans.,nie: Credit	297.8	664.1	616.6	866.0	780.9	1 072.3	722.8	Transf. cour.,nia : crédit
Current Transfers: Debit	−170.9	−92.1	−232.6	−500.6	−373.1	−563.4	−425.0	Transf. courants : débit
Capital Acct.,nie: Credit	0.0	11.7	1.0	16.7	13.8	18.4	5.8	Compte de cap.,nia : crédit
Capital Account: Debit	0.0	−4.9	−0.5	−5.5	−11.6	−20.5	−10.9	Compte de capital : débit
Financial Account,nie	4 503.8	8 224.6	4 202.5	1 122.2	2 908.2	3 079.9	3 355.6	Compte d'op. fin., nia
Net Errors and Omissions	−209.5	595.5	−729.3	379.1	367.0	131.9	−270.4	Erreurs et omissions nettes
Reserves and Related Items	−3 474.4	−7 453.4	825.2	1 758.4	−1 890.4	−1 639.3	−843.6	Rés. et postes appareutés
Denmark								**Danemark**
Goods: Exports fob	41 740.8	50 348.2	50 734.7	48 102.9	47 907.8	49 823.3	50 692.1	Biens : exportations,fàb
Goods: Imports fob	−34 299.5	−43 820.5	−43 202.5	−42 734.2	−44 021.5	−43 134.7	−43 493.2	Biens : importations,fàb
Serv. & Income: Credit	36 404.1	43 739.6	54 128.5	32 817.7	25 612.8	25 864.6	32 430.0	Serv. & revenu : crédit
Serv. & Income: Debit	−39 451.7	−47 021.5	−57 005.8	−35 929.8	−30 026.4	−26 593.0	−33 160.1	Serv. & revenu : débit
Current Trans.,nie: Credit	2 261.5	2 579.6	2 398.3	3 632.9	3 442.8	3 477.0	3 013.1	Transf. cour.,nia : crédit
Current Transfers: Debit	−3 465.9	−3 970.4	−3 963.4	−4 968.0	−4 923.7	−6 394.1	−6 128.6	Transf. courants : débit
Capital Acct.,nie: Credit	0.0	0.0	0.0	127.8	81.3	1 263.3	319.7	Compte de cap.,nia : crédit
Capital Account: Debit	0.0	0.0	0.0	0.0	−31.3	−247.0	−333.7	Compte de capital : débit
Financial Account,nie	−5 646.9	−431.6	1 882.0	8 495.5	−1 489.1	6 065.9	−6 153.5	Compte d'op. fin., nia
Net Errors and Omissions	606.4	1 074.7	−1 408.3	−3 012.5	−792.3	−687.4	−2 835.0	Erreurs et omissions nettes
Reserves and Related Items	1 851.2	−2 497.9	−3 563.3	−6 532.1	4 239.4	−9 437.3	5 649.3	Rés. et postes appareutés
Estonia								**Estonie**
Goods: Exports fob	1 225.0	1 696.3	1 812.4	2 289.6	2 690.1	2 453.1	3 291.6	Biens : exportations,fàb
Goods: Imports fob	−1 581.4	−2 362.3	−2 831.5	−3 413.7	−3 805.4	−3 330.6	−4 080.5	Biens : importations,fàb
Serv. & Income: Credit	552.6	940.4	1 220.5	1 433.1	1 613.2	1 623.5	1 616.5	Serv. & revenu : crédit
Serv. & Income: Debit	−477.1	−558.5	−700.2	−987.4	−1 124.7	−1 153.1	−1 280.8	Serv. & revenu : débit
Current Trans.,nie: Credit	120.3	134.5	116.8	135.3	172.9	153.7	167.4	Transf. cour.,nia : crédit
Current Transfers: Debit	−5.7	−8.2	−16.3	−18.6	−24.6	−41.3	−29.1	Transf. courants : débit
Capital Acct.,nie: Credit	0.5	1.4	0.2	0.7	2.1	1.4	16.8	Compte de cap.,nia : crédit
Capital Account: Debit	−1.1	−2.2	−0.8	−0.9	−0.3	−0.2	−0.2	Compte de capital : débit
Financial Account,nie	167.2	233.4	540.9	802.8	508.1	418.2	406.7	Compte d'op. fin., nia
Net Errors and Omissions	17.2	8.7	−35.6	−25.1	5.9	−5.5	19.2	Erreurs et omissions nettes
Reserves and Related Items	−17.5	−83.5	−106.3	−215.9	−37.3	−119.3	−127.6	Rés. et postes appareutés
Finland								**Finlande**
Goods: Exports fob	29 880.8	40 558.0	40 725.0	41 148.2	43 393.4	41 983.0	45 703.2	Biens : exportations,fàb
Goods: Imports fob	−22 157.9	−28 120.7	−29 410.6	−29 604.4	−30 902.9	−29 815.1	−32 018.9	Biens : importations,fàb
Serv. & Income: Credit	7 279.3	10 293.5	9 996.7	10 776.1	10 934.6	12 177.2	13 012.1	Serv. & revenu : crédit
Serv. & Income: Debit	−13 438.5	−16 902.4	−15 319.5	−14 834.7	−15 087.1	−15 651.3	−17 177.2	Serv. & revenu : débit
Current Trans.,nie: Credit	409.9	1 536.4	1 253.0	1 209.8	1 522.7	1 607.8	1 646.5	Transf. cour.,nia : crédit
Current Transfers: Debit	−863.2	−2 133.3	−2 242.0	−2 062.2	−2 521.1	−2 640.7	−2 277.6	Transf. courants : débit
Capital Acct.,nie: Credit	0.0	113.7	129.9	247.5	90.7	149.3	96.0	Compte de cap.,nia : crédit
Capital Account: Debit	0.0	−48.0	−74.3	0.0	0.0	−65.4	−7.4	Compte de capital : débit
Financial Account,nie	4 092.8	−4 284.3	−7 718.4	−2 975.8	−1 722.3	−5 065.5	−8 761.7	Compte d'op. fin., nia

76
Summary of balance of payments
Millions of US dollars
Résumé des balances des paiements
Millions de dollars des E.−U.

Country or area	1994	1995	1996	1997	1998	1999	2000	Pays ou zone
Net Errors and Omissions	−489.4	−1 384.5	−375.5	−1 600.3	−5 412.2	−2 666.5	144.4	Erreurs et omissions nettes
Reserves and Related Items	−4 713.9	371.7	3 035.7	−2 304.2	−295.8	−12.8	−359.5	Rés. et postes appareutés
France								**France**
Goods: Exports fob	230 811.0	278 627.0	281 846.0	286 071.0	303 025.0	300 052.0	295 533.0	Biens : exportations,fàb
Goods: Imports fob	−223 561.0	−267 629.0	−266 911.0	−259 172.0	−278 084.0	−282 064.0	−294 402.0	Biens : importations,fàb
Serv. & Income: Credit	117 081.6	129 272.1	131 078.2	137 920.6	151 623.9	147 348.3	153 137.8	Serv. & revenu : crédit
Serv. & Income: Debit	−105 990.3	−120 263.1	−117 529.5	−114 202.0	−125 732.4	−117 473.6	−120 275.8	Serv. & revenu : débit
Current Trans.,nie: Credit	18 223.3	22 005.7	22 759.8	19 614.0	19 653.9	18 880.0	17 346.3	Transf. cour.,nia : crédit
Current Transfers: Debit	−29 148.7	−31 172.6	−30 683.5	−32 430.6	−32 786.3	−31 703.6	−30 872.5	Transf. courants : débit
Capital Acct.,nie: Credit	986.0	1 163.1	1 883.4	2 412.6	2 098.5	1 885.7	1 923.2	Compte de cap.,nia : crédit
Capital Account: Debit	−5 164.7	−655.7	−648.9	−933.9	−632.4	−313.5	−528.3	Compte de capital : débit
Financial Account,nie	−4 775.6	−7 325.3	−22 344.5	−37 598.2	−29 289.9	−36 133.7	−30 282.3	Compte d'op. fin., nia
Net Errors and Omissions	3 986.5	−3 310.1	788.7	4 258.7	9 939.5	−1 869.6	5 987.1	Erreurs et omissions nettes
Reserves and Related Items	−2 447.5	−712.4	−239.3	−5 940.0	−19 815.1	1 392.3	2 432.6	Rés. et postes appareutés
Germany [2]								**Allemagne** [2]
Goods: Exports fob	430.5	523.6	522.6	510.0	542.6	542.7	549.2	Biens : exportations,fàb
Goods: Imports fob	−379.6	−458.5	−453.2	−439.9	−465.7	−472.7	−491.9	Biens : importations,fàb
Serv. & Income: Credit	134.8	166.7	166.9	164.8	168.9	173.6	181.0	Serv. & revenu : crédit
Serv. & Income: Debit	−167.6	−211.8	−210.2	−207.4	−222.1	−234.2	−232.2	Serv. & revenu : débit
Current Trans.,nie: Credit	13.9	16.9	17.9	16.5	16.5	17.3	15.8	Transf. cour.,nia : crédit
Current Transfers: Debit	−52.9	−55.8	−51.9	−46.9	−46.8	−44.7	−40.7	Transf. courants : débit
Capital Acct.,nie: Credit	1.6	1.7	2.8	2.8	3.3	3.0	17.1	Compte de cap.,nia : crédit
Capital Account: Debit	−1.4	−4.4	−4.9	−2.8	−2.6	−3.2	−3.2	Compte de capital : débit
Financial Account,nie	30.4	44.0	16.1	1.1	17.6	−40.5	13.2	Compte d'op. fin., nia
Net Errors and Omissions	−11.7	−15.1	−7.2	−2.0	−7.7	44.5	−13.6	Erreurs et omissions nettes
Reserves and Related Items	2.0	−7.2	1.2	3.8	−4.0	14.1	5.2	Rés. et postes appareutés
Greece								**Grèce**
Goods: Exports fob	5 338.0	5 918.0	5 890.0	5 576.0	...	8 544.7	10 201.5	Biens : exportations,fàb
Goods: Imports fob	−16 611.0	−20 343.0	−21 395.0	−20 951.0	...	−26 495.6	−30 440.4	Biens : importations,fàb
Serv. & Income: Credit	10 312.0	10 917.0	10 504.0	10 495.0	...	19 082.3	22 046.1	Serv. & revenu : crédit
Serv. & Income: Debit	−6 121.0	−7 364.0	−7 575.0	−7 490.0	...	−12 498.8	−14 978.5	Serv. & revenu : débit
Current Trans.,nie: Credit	6 964.0	8 039.0	8 053.0	7 538.0	...	4 956.5	4 115.8	Transf. cour.,nia : crédit
Current Transfers: Debit	−28.0	−31.0	−31.0	−28.0	...	−884.0	−764.2	Transf. courants : débit
Capital Acct.,nie: Credit	0.0	0.0	0.0	0.0	...	0.0	0.0	Compte de cap.,nia : crédit
Capital Account: Debit	0.0	0.0	0.0	0.0	...	0.0	0.0	Compte de capital : débit
Financial Account,nie	6 903.0	3 162.0	8 658.0	119.0	...	7 477.5	10 830.0	Compte d'op. fin., nia
Net Errors and Omissions	−447.9	−321.3	110.6	225.8	...	41.6	−549.8	Erreurs et omissions nettes
Reserves and Related Items	−6 309.2	23.3	−4 214.6	4 515.2	...	−2 435.5	−2 572.8	Rés. et postes appareutés
Hungary								**Hongrie**
Goods: Exports fob	7 648.2	12 864.1	14 183.8	19 639.9	20 746.6	21 848.1	25 365.7	Biens : exportations,fàb
Goods: Imports fob	−11 364.1	−15 297.2	−16 835.5	−21 601.7	−23 100.9	−24 036.8	−27 471.5	Biens : importations,fàb
Serv. & Income: Credit	3 792.5	5 980.1	7 181.8	7 115.2	7 032.2	6 423.8	7 193.6	Serv. & revenu : crédit
Serv. & Income: Debit	−5 039.8	−6 217.6	−6 164.2	−6 273.7	−7 130.5	−6 680.8	−6 991.6	Serv. & revenu : débit
Current Trans.,nie: Credit	2 871.0	363.6	159.8	334.9	379.4	582.0	698.9	Transf. cour.,nia : crédit
Current Transfers: Debit	−1 961.4	−222.5	−214.5	−196.6	−230.9	−242.7	−288.9	Transf. courants : débit
Capital Acct.,nie: Credit	0.0	79.5	266.2	266.5	408.0	509.0	456.6	Compte de cap.,nia : crédit
Capital Account: Debit	0.0	−20.5	−110.3	−149.4	−219.3	−479.5	−188.0	Compte de capital : débit
Financial Account,nie	3 369.7	7 080.3	−686.7	658.4	3 017.5	4 693.5	2 357.0	Compte d'op. fin., nia
Net Errors and Omissions	209.0	789.1	975.6	31.7	48.6	−281.5	−79.5	Erreurs et omissions nettes
Reserves and Related Items	474.9	−5 399.0	1 244.0	174.9	−950.7	−2 335.0	−1 052.2	Rés. et postes appareutés
Iceland								**Islande**
Goods: Exports fob	1 561.0	1 804.0	1 890.0	1 855.0	1 927.0	2 009.0	1 901.0	Biens : exportations,fàb
Goods: Imports fob	−1 288.0	−1 598.0	−1 871.0	−1 850.0	−2 279.0	−2 316.9	−2 377.1	Biens : importations,fàb
Serv. & Income: Credit	688.0	780.0	881.0	948.0	1 070.0	1 060.5	1 203.0	Serv. & revenu : crédit
Serv. & Income: Debit	−844.0	−927.0	−1 011.0	−1 073.0	−1 262.0	−1 333.0	−1 566.8	Serv. & revenu : débit
Current Trans.,nie: Credit	12.0	15.0	10.0	17.0	4.0	4.8	6.1	Transf. cour.,nia : crédit
Current Transfers: Debit	−20.0	−20.0	−16.0	−22.0	−20.0	−14.9	−15.6	Transf. courants : débit
Capital Acct.,nie: Credit	6.0	13.0	10.0	11.0	9.0	17.3	17.5	Compte de cap.,nia : crédit
Capital Account: Debit	−12.0	−16.0	−11.0	−10.0	−14.0	−18.1	−20.7	Compte de capital : débit
Financial Account,nie	−293.0	−17.0	303.0	195.0	679.0	907.5	785.7	Compte d'op. fin., nia
Net Errors and Omissions	40.0	−30.1	−32.1	−115.0	−82.0	−230.6	−1.8	Erreurs et omissions nettes
Reserves and Related Items	150.0	−3.9	−152.9	44.0	−32.0	−85.6	68.7	Rés. et postes appareutés
Ireland								**Irlande**
Goods: Exports fob	33 641.6	44 422.5	49 183.9	55 292.7	78 562.0	68 539.8	73 432.9	Biens : exportations,fàb
Goods: Imports fob	−24 275.3	−30 865.9	−33 429.7	−36 667.7	−53 172.1	−44 283.6	−48 016.9	Biens : importations,fàb
Serv. & Income: Credit	7 831.9	10 126.6	11 325.4	13 538.9	42 165.6	39 964.6	46 760.8	Serv. & revenu : crédit

76
Summary of balance of payments
Millions of US dollars
Résumé des balances des paiements
Millions de dollars des E.−U.

Country or area	1994	1995	1996	1997	1998	1999	2000	Pays ou zone
Serv. & Income: Debit	−17 371.2	−23 738.1	−27 220.2	−32 254.0	−68 425.3	−65 120.1	−73 719.3	Serv. & revenu : débit
Current Trans.,nie: Credit	2 849.5	3 009.0	3 538.2	3 083.4	7 428.5	5 308.1	4 303.7	Transf. cour.,nia : crédit
Current Transfers: Debit	−1 099.5	−1 233.1	−1 349.0	−1 127.7	−5 542.6	−4 054.9	−3 354.6	Transf. courants : débit
Capital Acct.,nie: Credit	476.9	913.6	880.8	961.7	1 326.7	674.4	1 167.1	Compte de cap.,nia : crédit
Capital Account: Debit	−89.8	−96.2	−96.0	−91.0	−108.3	−81.0	−70.2	Compte de capital : débit
Financial Account,nie	−3 962.7	−33.0	−2 779.7	−7 484.3	4 686.1	−3 892.6	8 901.2	Compte d'op. fin., nia
Net Errors and Omissions	1 823.1	−166.6	−106.0	3 639.4	−3 708.0	971.8	−9 283.6	Erreurs et omissions nettes
Reserves and Related Items	175.5	−2 338.8	52.3	1 108.7	−3 212.4	1 973.5	−121.2	Rés. et postes appareutés
Italy								**Italie**
Goods: Exports fob	191 421.0	233 998.0	252 039.0	240 404.0	242 572.0	235 856.0	238 736.0	Biens : exportations,fàb
Goods: Imports fob	−159 854.0	−195 269.0	−197 921.0	−200 527.0	−206 941.0	−212 420.0	−228 019.0	Biens : importations,fàb
Serv. & Income: Credit	82 280.2	95 787.2	105 801.3	112 725.1	118 867.5	105 148.5	94 789.6	Serv. & revenu : crédit
Serv. & Income: Debit	−93 526.7	−104 861.3	−112 706.0	−116 163.1	−127 015.2	−115 118.3	−106 848.8	Serv. & revenu : débit
Current Trans.,nie: Credit	12 254.5	14 287.1	14 320.3	15 551.5	14 402.3	16 776.2	15 790.3	Transf. cour.,nia : crédit
Current Transfers: Debit	−19 366.5	−18 866.1	−21 534.8	−19 587.9	−21 887.4	−22 132.3	−20 118.3	Transf. courants : débit
Capital Acct.,nie: Credit	2 212.9	2 796.6	1 414.0	4 582.4	3 359.4	4 571.9	4 172.1	Compte de cap.,nia : crédit
Capital Account: Debit	−1 187.3	−1 125.5	−1 348.0	−1 147.9	−1 001.5	−1 608.0	−1 296.5	Compte de capital : débit
Financial Account,nie	−14 207.0	−2 889.1	−7 982.2	−6 878.3	−18 074.0	−17 414.7	7 507.8	Compte d'op. fin., nia
Net Errors and Omissions	1 547.5	−21 054.2	−20 176.2	−15 809.8	−25 753.7	−1 710.8	−1 465.6	Erreurs et omissions nettes
Reserves and Related Items	−1 575.3	−2 803.6	−11 906.7	−13 149.7	21 471.9	8 051.1	−3 247.9	Rés. et postes appareutés
Latvia								**Lettonie**
Goods: Exports fob	1 021.7	1 367.6	1 487.6	1 838.1	2 011.2	1 889.1	2 058.1	Biens : exportations,fàb
Goods: Imports fob	−1 322.3	−1 947.2	−2 285.9	−2 686.0	−3 141.4	−2 916.1	−3 116.3	Biens : importations,fàb
Serv. & Income: Credit	707.9	791.2	1 266.0	1 210.0	1 315.8	1 182.0	1 427.4	Serv. & revenu : crédit
Serv. & Income: Debit	−338.9	−298.5	−841.0	−784.5	−959.6	−902.1	−961.0	Serv. & revenu : débit
Current Trans.,nie: Credit	135.7	75.4	98.1	90.9	137.3	113.8	202.8	Transf. cour.,nia : crédit
Current Transfers: Debit	−3.0	−4.6	−4.6	−13.6	−12.8	−21.0	−105.4	Transf. courants : débit
Capital Acct.,nie: Credit	0.0	0.0	0.0	13.7	14.1	12.6	38.5	Compte de cap.,nia : crédit
Capital Account: Debit	0.0	0.0	0.0	0.0	0.0	0.0	−8.9	Compte de capital : débit
Financial Account,nie	363.4	635.6	537.1	346.9	601.1	768.4	514.0	Compte d'op. fin., nia
Net Errors and Omissions	−508.0	−652.6	−46.3	86.5	96.9	38.3	−21.4	Erreurs et omissions nettes
Reserves and Related Items	−56.5	33.2	−211.1	−102.2	−62.6	−165.0	−27.8	Rés. et postes appareutés
Lithuania								**Lithuanie**
Goods: Exports fob	2 029.2	2 706.1	3 413.2	4 192.4	3 961.6	3 146.7	4 050.4	Biens : exportations,fàb
Goods: Imports fob	−2 234.1	−3 404.0	−4 309.3	−5 339.9	−5 479.9	−4 551.3	−5 154.1	Biens : importations,fàb
Serv. & Income: Credit	343.3	536.1	849.5	1 112.3	1 233.5	1 206.4	1 244.3	Serv. & revenu : crédit
Serv. & Income: Debit	−389.3	−561.8	−819.7	−1 176.1	−1 248.4	−1 158.6	−1 058.0	Serv. & revenu : débit
Current Trans.,nie: Credit	161.6	112.3	149.4	237.0	240.4	167.4	246.8	Transf. cour.,nia : crédit
Current Transfers: Debit	−4.8	−3.0	−5.6	−7.0	−5.4	−4.6	−4.3	Transf. courants : débit
Capital Acct.,nie: Credit	12.9	3.3	5.5	4.5	0.9	2.7	2.6	Compte de cap.,nia : crédit
Capital Account: Debit	0.0	−42.3	0.0	−0.4	−2.6	−6.0	−0.4	Compte de capital : débit
Financial Account,nie	240.9	534.4	645.6	1 005.6	1 443.9	1 060.7	702.4	Compte d'op. fin., nia
Net Errors and Omissions	−46.9	287.2	66.7	195.8	282.9	−42.1	128.3	Erreurs et omissions nettes
Reserves and Related Items	−112.8	−168.3	4.8	−224.2	−426.8	178.7	−158.0	Rés. et postes appareutés
Luxembourg								**Luxembourg**
Goods: Exports fob	...	9 243.7	8 476.8	8 472.7	9 010.0	8 358.2	8 614.5	Biens : exportations,fàb
Goods: Imports fob	...	−10 844.8	−10 211.1	−10 465.9	−11 008.6	−10 806.8	−10 436.4	Biens : importations,fàb
Serv. & Income: Credit	...	57 222.3	48 904.1	47 761.4	53 699.9	55 075.4	64 329.3	Serv. & revenu : crédit
Serv. & Income: Debit	...	−52 684.9	−44 350.9	−42 998.8	−49 048.7	−50 952.5	−60 625.9	Serv. & revenu : débit
Current Trans.,nie: Credit	...	1 741.7	2 225.0	1 935.0	2 124.0	2 281.7	2 155.0	Transf. cour.,nia : crédit
Current Transfers: Debit	...	−2 368.7	−2 725.7	−2 446.2	−2 474.6	−2 644.2	−2 445.6	Transf. courants : débit
Capital Acct.,nie: Credit	...	...	...	...	...	...	...	Compte de cap.,nia : crédit
Capital Account: Debit	...	...	...	...	...	...	...	Compte de capital : débit
Financial Account,nie	...	...	...	...	...	...	...	Compte d'op. fin., nia
Net Errors and Omissions	...	...	...	...	...	...	...	Erreurs et omissions nettes
Reserves and Related Items	...	...	...	...	...	...	...	Rés. et postes appareutés
Malta								**Malte**
Goods: Exports fob	1 618.5	1 949.4	1 772.8	1 663.2	1 824.3	2 017.0	2 476.2	Biens : exportations,fàb
Goods: Imports fob	−2 221.0	−2 673.1	−2 536.2	−2 320.7	−2 417.0	−2 588.4	−3 097.0	Biens : importations,fàb
Serv. & Income: Credit	1 214.0	1 336.4	1 381.0	1 471.7	1 692.0	2 453.6	2 072.2	Serv. & revenu : crédit
Serv. & Income: Debit	−837.1	−998.8	−1 051.6	−1 070.8	−1 378.8	−2 046.8	−1 981.8	Serv. & revenu : débit
Current Trans.,nie: Credit	101.2	80.5	87.1	122.4	114.9	120.1	104.1	Transf. cour.,nia : crédit
Current Transfers: Debit	−7.1	−54.3	−56.1	−66.9	−56.9	−77.8	−88.5	Transf. courants : débit
Capital Acct.,nie: Credit	0.0	16.8	64.2	32.9	33.1	38.0	24.0	Compte de cap.,nia : crédit
Capital Account: Debit	0.0	−4.3	−6.1	−24.5	−4.6	−5.5	−5.6	Compte de capital : débit
Financial Account,nie	480.9	23.3	205.4	107.2	294.6	405.5	168.5	Compte d'op. fin., nia

76
Summary of balance of payments
Millions of US dollars
Résumé des balances des paiements
Millions de dollars des E.–U.

Country or area	1994	1995	1996	1997	1998	1999	2000	Pays ou zone
Net Errors and Omissions	33.4	17.1	54.5	92.3	89.4	−77.1	106.2	Erreurs et omissions nettes
Reserves and Related Items	−382.8	307.1	84.9	−6.8	−190.9	−238.4	221.6	Rés. et postes appareutés
Netherlands								**Pays–Bas**
Goods: Exports fob	141 810.0	195 600.0	195 079.0	188 988.0	196 277.0	197 359.0	205 653.0	Biens : exportations,fàb
Goods: Imports fob	−123 124.0	−171 788.0	−172 312.0	−168 051.0	−175 222.0	−179 426.0	−187 107.0	Biens : importations,fàb
Serv. & Income: Credit	70 988.5	82 686.7	84 770.3	89 374.9	87 721.5	98 551.2	98 043.7	Serv. & revenu : crédit
Serv. & Income: Debit	−67 102.7	−74 302.5	−79 308.9	−79 033.3	−88 221.8	−94 964.6	−96 631.4	Serv. & revenu : débit
Current Trans.,nie: Credit	4 197.1	4 725.0	4 319.3	4 345.5	3 798.7	4 565.8	4 361.2	Transf. cour.,nia : crédit
Current Transfers: Debit	−9 474.3	−11 158.7	−11 089.3	−10 465.2	−10 980.6	−10 913.6	−10 554.7	Transf. courants : débit
Capital Acct.,nie: Credit	563.5	855.8	1 266.7	1 099.2	1 037.4	1 688.0	2 896.6	Compte de cap.,nia : crédit
Capital Account: Debit	−1 569.5	−1 954.9	−3 290.7	−2 396.3	−1 457.2	−1 902.1	−2 236.1	Compte de capital : débit
Financial Account,nie	−9 969.2	−18 817.5	−5 436.4	−14 478.2	−7 449.3	−24 940.0	−2 932.8	Compte d'op. fin., nia
Net Errors and Omissions	−5 819.0	−7 758.8	−19 688.6	−12 091.1	−7 842.5	5 371.8	−11 271.2	Erreurs et omissions nettes
Reserves and Related Items	−500.1	1 912.9	5 690.7	2 707.9	2 338.8	4 611.0	−220.5	Rés. et postes appareutés
Norway								**Norvège**
Goods: Exports fob	35 016.4	42 312.2	49 968.3	48 736.7	40 643.3	45 651.0	60 061.5	Biens : exportations,fàb
Goods: Imports fob	−27 520.4	−33 740.9	−37 037.4	−37 584.6	−38 843.9	−35 532.2	−34 561.6	Biens : importations,fàb
Serv. & Income: Credit	15 661.1	17 888.6	19 258.5	20 125.6	20 517.6	20 026.1	21 655.7	Serv. & revenu : crédit
Serv. & Income: Debit	−17 653.3	−19 542.8	−20 438.7	−21 842.7	−22 110.9	−22 514.3	−22 699.3	Serv. & revenu : débit
Current Trans.,nie: Credit	1 291.1	1 276.1	1 324.6	1 234.5	1 208.0	1 246.1	1 212.1	Transf. cour.,nia : crédit
Current Transfers: Debit	−3 034.7	−3 338.9	−2 835.2	−2 652.0	−2 732.0	−2 862.8	−2 682.7	Transf. courants : débit
Capital Acct.,nie: Credit	93.1	85.8	64.5	29.0	38.7	35.5	28.8	Compte de cap.,nia : crédit
Capital Account: Debit	−249.8	−255.4	−191.9	−212.4	−149.6	−146.0	−174.6	Compte de capital : débit
Financial Account,nie	−1 363.3	−639.9	−1 700.7	−7 413.2	−50.2	478.0	−11 824.3	Compte d'op. fin., nia
Net Errors and Omissions	−1 987.2	−3 470.0	−1 942.1	−1 619.4	−4 906.3	−421.4	−7 344.2	Erreurs et omissions nettes
Reserves and Related Items	−253.0	−574.8	−6 469.9	1 198.5	6 385.3	−5 960.1	−3 671.4	Rés. et postes appareutés
Poland								**Pologne**
Goods: Exports fob	18 355.0	25 041.0	27 557.0	30 731.0	32 467.0	30 060.0	35 902.0	Biens : exportations,fàb
Goods: Imports fob	−18 930.0	−26 687.0	−34 844.0	−40 553.0	−45 303.0	−45 132.0	−48 210.0	Biens : importations,fàb
Serv. & Income: Credit	7 245.0	11 764.0	11 274.0	10 382.0	13 066.0	10 200.0	12 640.0	Serv. & revenu : crédit
Serv. & Income: Debit	−6 968.0	−10 222.0	−8 945.0	−8 339.0	−10 028.0	−9 829.0	−12 709.0	Serv. & revenu : débit
Current Trans.,nie: Credit	2 174.0	2 459.0	2 825.0	2 700.0	3 520.0	2 898.0	3 008.0	Transf. cour.,nia : crédit
Current Transfers: Debit	−922.0	−1 501.0	−1 131.0	−665.0	−623.0	−684.0	−628.0	Transf. courants : débit
Capital Acct.,nie: Credit	9 215.0	285.0	5 833.0	91.0	117.0	95.0	108.0	Compte de cap.,nia : crédit
Capital Account: Debit	0.0	0.0	−5 739.0	−25.0	−54.0	−40.0	−76.0	Compte de capital : débit
Financial Account,nie	−9 065.0	9 260.0	6 673.0	7 410.0	13 282.0	10 462.0	10 196.0	Compte d'op. fin., nia
Net Errors and Omissions	−97.6	−563.6	321.3	1 309.3	−519.6	2 125.6	395.2	Erreurs et omissions nettes
Reserves and Related Items	−1 006.5	−9 835.4	−3 824.3	−3 041.3	−5 924.4	−155.6	−626.2	Rés. et postes appareutés
Portugal								**Portugal**
Goods: Exports fob	18 644.7	24 024.3	25 623.0	25 379.2	25 617.9	25 440.3	24 750.4	Biens : exportations,fàb
Goods: Imports fob	−26 965.6	−32 934.4	−35 344.8	−35 721.2	−37 828.9	−39 206.7	−38 891.3	Biens : importations,fàb
Serv. & Income: Credit	8 987.5	12 331.2	12 289.6	12 239.9	13 325.4	12 919.5	13 030.1	Serv. & revenu : crédit
Serv. & Income: Debit	−8 282.9	−10 685.1	−12 055.4	−12 316.3	−13 037.9	−12 794.1	−13 308.0	Serv. & revenu : débit
Current Trans.,nie: Credit	7 410.0	9 045.9	6 514.8	5 985.1	6 169.6	6 047.6	5 327.7	Transf. cour.,nia : crédit
Current Transfers: Debit	−1 989.5	−1 913.6	−2 243.2	−2 031.3	−2 079.5	−2 143.2	−1 921.2	Transf. courants : débit
Capital Acct.,nie: Credit	0.0	0.0	2 836.4	2 892.7	2 724.2	2 641.9	1 677.9	Compte de cap.,nia : crédit
Capital Account: Debit	0.0	0.0	−141.4	−188.9	−178.7	−183.1	−168.4	Compte de capital : débit
Financial Account,nie	1 052.2	3 024.7	3 835.2	6 662.3	5 980.3	8 955.3	11 138.3	Compte d'op. fin., nia
Net Errors and Omissions	−286.9	−3 192.8	−766.7	−1 927.7	−184.5	−1 461.7	−1 264.8	Erreurs et omissions nettes
Reserves and Related Items	1 430.4	299.8	−547.5	−973.7	−507.9	−215.6	−370.7	Rés. et postes appareutés
Republic of Moldova								**République de Moldova**
Goods: Exports fob	618.5	739.0	822.9	889.6	643.6	474.8	476.6	Biens : exportations,fàb
Goods: Imports fob	−672.4	−809.2	−1 082.5	−1 237.6	−1 031.7	−609.5	−783.2	Biens : importations,fàb
Serv. & Income: Credit	43.6	158.7	205.3	300.5	286.4	257.2	330.9	Serv. & revenu : crédit
Serv. & Income: Debit	−105.1	−228.7	−210.6	−281.4	−298.3	−255.3	−301.9	Serv. & revenu : débit
Current Trans.,nie: Credit	36.9	66.6	72.9	104.1	110.9	114.7	161.8	Transf. cour.,nia : crédit
Current Transfers: Debit	−3.6	−14.1	−2.8	−50.0	−45.5	−39.6	−15.3	Transf. courants : débit
Capital Acct.,nie: Credit	0.0	0.0	0.1	0.1	2.1	1.5	2.8	Compte de cap.,nia : crédit
Capital Account: Debit	−1.0	−0.4	−0.1	−0.3	−2.5	−0.4	−1.1	Compte de capital : débit
Financial Account,nie	211.1	−68.8	76.6	100.9	−10.1	−33.8	139.0	Compte d'op. fin., nia
Net Errors and Omissions	−115.2	−18.4	15.5	−8.6	−2.0	−29.1	9.3	Erreurs et omissions nettes
Reserves and Related Items	−12.9	175.4	102.7	182.8	347.0	119.4	−19.0	Rés. et postes appareutés
Romania								**Roumanie**
Goods: Exports fob	6 151.0	7 910.0	8 085.0	8 431.0	8 302.0	8 503.0	10 366.0	Biens : exportations,fàb
Goods: Imports fob	−6 562.0	−9 487.0	−10 555.0	−10 411.0	−10 927.0	−9 595.0	−12 050.0	Biens : importations,fàb
Serv. & Income: Credit	1 160.0	1 575.0	1 641.0	1 728.0	1 530.0	1 517.0	2 092.0	Serv. & revenu : crédit

76
Summary of balance of payments
Millions of US dollars
Résumé des balances des paiements
Millions de dollars des E.−U.

Country or area	1994	1995	1996	1997	1998	1999	2000	Pays ou zone
Serv. & Income: Debit	−1 460.0	−2 141.0	−2 335.0	−2 464.0	−2 576.0	−2 348.0	−2 627.0	Serv. & revenu : débit
Current Trans.,nie: Credit	317.0	473.0	667.0	731.0	886.0	804.0	1 079.0	Transf. cour.,nia : crédit
Current Transfers: Debit	−61.0	−110.0	−82.0	−152.0	−133.0	−178.0	−219.0	Transf. courants : débit
Capital Acct.,nie: Credit	0.0	32.0	152.0	43.0	39.0	46.0	37.0	Compte de cap.,nia : crédit
Capital Account: Debit	0.0	0.0	0.0	0.0	0.0	−1.0	−1.0	Compte de capital : débit
Financial Account,nie	535.0	812.0	1 486.0	2 458.0	2 042.0	697.0	1 943.0	Compte d'op. fin., nia
Net Errors and Omissions	90.8	456.4	358.6	1 094.9	194.4	794.5	286.0	Erreurs et omissions nettes
Reserves and Related Items	−170.8	479.6	582.4	−1 458.9	642.6	−239.5	−906.0	Rés. et postes appareutés
Russian Federation								**Fédération de Russie**
Goods: Exports fob	67 826.0	82 913.0	90 564.0	89 008.0	74 883.0	75 665.6	105 565.0	Biens : exportations,fàb
Goods: Imports fob	−50 451.0	−62 603.0	−68 093.0	−71 982.0	−58 014.0	−39 536.9	−44 861.7	Biens : importations,fàb
Serv. & Income: Credit	11 924.0	14 849.0	17 619.0	18 446.0	16 674.0	12 948.6	14 385.2	Serv. & revenu : crédit
Serv. & Income: Debit	−20 634.0	−27 828.0	−28 405.0	−33 056.0	−32 523.0	−24 948.3	−28 840.9	Serv. & revenu : débit
Current Trans.,nie: Credit	311.0	895.0	771.0	411.0	308.0	1 182.8	807.5	Transf. cour.,nia : crédit
Current Transfers: Debit	−542.0	−738.0	−701.0	−766.0	−645.0	−581.7	−738.2	Transf. courants : débit
Capital Acct.,nie: Credit	5 882.0	3 122.0	3 066.0	2 138.0	1 705.0	885.0	11 543.0	Compte de cap.,nia : crédit
Capital Account: Debit	−3 474.0	−3 470.0	−3 529.0	−2 934.0	−2 087.0	−1 213.0	−867.3	Compte de capital : débit
Financial Account,nie	−30 219.0	−7 463.0	−23 586.0	−2 902.0	−12 596.0	−19 129.1	−33 795.7	Compte d'op. fin., nia
Net Errors and Omissions	407.4	−7 974.7	−4 895.9	−4 854.6	−9 072.4	−6 976.6	−9 274.0	Erreurs et omissions nettes
Reserves and Related Items	18 969.6	8 297.7	17 189.9	6 491.6	21 367.4	1 703.6	−13 923.0	Rés. et postes appareutés
Slovakia								**Slovaquie**
Goods: Exports fob	6 706.1	8 590.8	8 823.8	9 640.7	10 720.2	10 201.3	11 896.1	Biens : exportations,fàb
Goods: Imports fob	−6 645.4	−8 820.0	−11 106.5	−11 725.2	−13 070.9	−11 310.3	−12 790.6	Biens : importations,fàb
Serv. & Income: Credit	2 416.8	2 628.1	2 289.1	2 482.5	2 729.4	2 167.7	2 508.9	Serv. & revenu : crédit
Serv. & Income: Debit	−1 875.1	−2 101.5	−2 297.8	−2 532.7	−2 870.8	−2 411.8	−2 428.5	Serv. & revenu : débit
Current Trans.,nie: Credit	165.8	242.5	482.9	540.4	645.0	466.0	343.8	Transf. cour.,nia : crédit
Current Transfers: Debit	−97.6	−149.9	−282.0	−367.1	−279.3	−268.1	−224.0	Transf. courants : débit
Capital Acct.,nie: Credit	84.0	45.6	30.3	0.0	82.8	171.0	105.7	Compte de cap.,nia : crédit
Capital Account: Debit	0.0	0.0	0.0	0.0	−12.4	−13.4	−14.8	Compte de capital : débit
Financial Account,nie	70.8	1 211.2	2 267.9	1 780.1	1 911.5	1 788.8	1 472.4	Compte d'op. fin., nia
Net Errors and Omissions	379.7	144.4	162.2	280.1	−333.1	−14.3	50.7	Erreurs et omissions nettes
Reserves and Related Items	−1 205.1	−1 791.3	−370.0	−98.9	477.6	−777.0	−919.7	Rés. et postes appareutés
Slovenia								**Slovénie**
Goods: Exports fob	6 831.7	8 350.2	8 352.6	8 407.4	9 090.9	8 622.7	8 805.9	Biens : exportations,fàb
Goods: Imports fob	−7 168.1	−9 303.3	−9 177.5	−9 183.8	−9 880.2	−9 867.9	−9 887.3	Biens : importations,fàb
Serv. & Income: Credit	2 143.6	2 438.0	2 547.7	2 444.2	2 444.6	2 309.4	2 280.9	Serv. & revenu : crédit
Serv. & Income: Debit	−1 330.8	−1 680.5	−1 782.1	−1 774.5	−1 924.3	−1 969.7	−1 915.2	Serv. & revenu : débit
Current Trans.,nie: Credit	237.2	247.7	250.9	259.5	299.8	334.4	342.5	Transf. cour.,nia : crédit
Current Transfers: Debit	−140.6	−151.5	−160.3	−141.5	−178.0	−211.2	−221.1	Transf. courants : débit
Capital Acct.,nie: Credit	2.7	3.1	5.5	5.0	3.5	3.3	4.5	Compte de cap.,nia : crédit
Capital Account: Debit	−5.8	−10.1	−7.4	−3.9	−5.0	−3.9	−3.4	Compte de capital : débit
Financial Account,nie	146.6	541.0	565.8	1 198.7	244.2	674.8	717.8	Compte d'op. fin., nia
Net Errors and Omissions	−70.0	−194.6	−5.2	77.3	62.4	26.9	54.0	Erreurs et omissions nettes
Reserves and Related Items	−646.5	−240.0	−590.1	−1 288.4	−157.8	81.3	−178.5	Rés. et postes appareutés
Spain								**Espagne**
Goods: Exports fob	73 924.9	93 439.2	102 735.0	106 926.0	111 986.0	112 664.0	115 081.0	Biens : exportations,fàb
Goods: Imports fob	−88 817.2	−111 854.0	−119 017.0	−120 333.0	−132 744.0	−143 002.0	−147 836.0	Biens : importations,fàb
Serv. & Income: Credit	42 546.2	53 897.8	58 482.4	57 322.2	63 928.4	66 053.9	68 302.7	Serv. & revenu : crédit
Serv. & Income: Debit	−35 321.8	−39 326.0	−44 185.9	−44 225.9	−49 555.1	−52 618.8	−54 382.6	Serv. & revenu : débit
Current Trans.,nie: Credit	9 171.3	12 055.0	11 111.8	11 738.0	12 690.5	13 434.6	11 623.3	Transf. cour.,nia : crédit
Current Transfers: Debit	−7 892.7	−7 419.6	−8 718.4	−8 915.9	−9 441.2	−10 291.7	−10 045.0	Transf. courants : débit
Capital Acct.,nie: Credit	3 571.4	7 374.1	7 713.0	7 274.6	7 159.8	8 060.4	5 802.4	Compte de cap.,nia : crédit
Capital Account: Debit	−1 266.1	−1 370.0	−1 123.8	−837.2	−829.5	−1 093.8	−975.9	Compte de capital : débit
Financial Account,nie	4 491.0	−7 950.5	20 138.2	8 547.4	−14 155.7	−10 997.2	17 032.8	Compte d'op. fin., nia
Net Errors and Omissions	−370.6	−5 259.8	−2 856.1	−5 740.9	−3 394.6	−5 059.2	−7 483.7	Erreurs et omissions nettes
Reserves and Related Items	−36.3	6 413.9	−24 278.8	−11 755.7	14 355.5	22 850.3	2 880.9	Rés. et postes appareutés
Sweden								**Suède**
Goods: Exports fob	60 199.0	79 903.4	84 689.6	83 193.7	85 179.0	87 568.0	87 431.0	Biens : exportations,fàb
Goods: Imports fob	−50 641.2	−63 925.6	−66 053.4	−65 194.8	−67 547.3	−71 854.2	−72 215.7	Biens : importations,fàb
Serv. & Income: Credit	23 285.5	30 527.6	31 268.4	32 173.3	34 515.3	39 774.8	40 325.8	Serv. & revenu : crédit
Serv. & Income: Debit	−30 220.3	−38 595.1	−41 396.3	−40 037.1	−44 069.9	−45 907.3	−45 577.0	Serv. & revenu : débit
Current Trans.,nie: Credit	543.9	1 554.6	2 524.0	2 318.6	2 266.0	2 340.6	2 602.5	Transf. cour.,nia : crédit
Current Transfers: Debit	−2 424.3	−4 524.6	−5 140.0	−5 048.1	−5 703.7	−5 939.6	−5 950.1	Transf. courants : débit
Capital Acct.,nie: Credit	37.5	32.3	31.3	210.9	1 502.2	1 288.6	1 225.7	Compte de cap.,nia : crédit
Capital Account: Debit	−14.4	−18.3	−22.4	−438.6	−634.0	−3 431.9	−841.2	Compte de capital : débit
Financial Account,nie	6 077.9	−5 052.5	−10 046.2	−10 121.2	5 960.7	−1 412.9	−3 296.6	Compte d'op. fin., nia

76
Summary of balance of payments
Millions of US dollars
Résumé des balances des paiements
Millions de dollars des E.−U.

Country or area	1994	1995	1996	1997	1998	1999	2000	Pays ou zone
Net Errors and Omissions	−4 462.2	−1 566.0	−2 240.6	−3 768.9	−8 214.5	−544.6	−3 533.9	Erreurs et omissions nettes
Reserves and Related Items	−2 381.4	1 664.1	6 385.6	6 712.1	−3 253.8	−1 881.4	−170.5	Rés. et postes appareutés
Switzerland								**Suisse**
Goods: Exports fob	82 624.9	97 138.5	95 543.6	95 039.5	93 781.7	91 823.4	93 293.6	Biens : exportations,fàb
Goods: Imports fob	−79 279.1	−93 880.1	−93 676.0	−92 302.1	−92 849.1	−91 008.6	−92 904.3	Biens : importations,fàb
Serv. & Income: Credit	49 366.0	57 601.5	59 246.6	60 366.3	72 657.3	77 432.7	89 131.8	Serv. & revenu : crédit
Serv. & Income: Debit	−31 700.3	−34 814.3	−36 074.4	−33 023.0	−43 134.8	−45 066.9	−53 164.1	Serv. & revenu : débit
Current Trans.,nie: Credit	2 526.1	2 995.1	2 960.7	2 625.4	2 785.9	6 761.6	6 036.7	Transf. cour.,nia : crédit
Current Transfers: Debit	−5 949.4	−7 237.0	−6 949.1	−6 027.3	−6 466.7	−11 783.7	−9 852.1	Transf. courants : débit
Capital Acct.,nie: Credit	0.0	0.0	0.0	0.0	0.0	0.0	0.0	Compte de cap.,nia : crédit
Capital Account: Debit	−380.5	−472.5	−233.0	−202.5	−616.1	−567.2	−1 867.7	Compte de capital : débit
Financial Account,nie	−11 852.2	−8 643.3	−24 252.6	−22 758.4	−22 988.3	−37 080.1	−30 131.0	Compte d'op. fin., nia
Net Errors and Omissions	−4 377.3	−12 669.2	5 937.1	−1 599.6	−2 745.5	6 951.6	−4 728.3	Erreurs et omissions nettes
Reserves and Related Items	−1 009.1	−29.1	−2 521.5	−2 153.9	−1 179.2	2 484.5	4 004.6	Rés. et postes appareutés
TFYR of Macedonia								**L'ex−R.y. Macédoine**
Goods: Exports fob	...	...	1 147.4	1 201.4	1 292.9	1 192.1	1 317.1	Biens : exportations,fàb
Goods: Imports fob	...	...	−1 464.0	−1 589.1	−1 713.2	−1 602.2	−1 875.2	Biens : importations,fàb
Serv. & Income: Credit	...	...	199.6	167.3	154.9	270.9	345.2	Serv. & revenu : crédit
Serv. & Income: Debit	...	...	−384.3	−345.4	−372.7	−390.1	−445.0	Serv. & revenu : débit
Current Trans.,nie: Credit	...	...	475.4	535.0	692.6	750.3	923.1	Transf. cour.,nia : crédit
Current Transfers: Debit	...	...	−262.3	−244.8	−366.2	−330.2	−372.4	Transf. courants : débit
Capital Acct.,nie: Credit	...	...	0.0	0.0	11.2	4.4	0.3	Compte de cap.,nia : crédit
Capital Account: Debit	...	...	0.0	0.0	−1.8	0.0	0.0	Compte de capital : débit
Financial Account,nie	...	...	174.3	186.8	449.2	189.6	385.2	Compte d'op. fin., nia
Net Errors and Omissions	...	...	18.8	−29.9	−114.8	34.5	−46.0	Erreurs et omissions nettes
Reserves and Related Items	...	...	95.1	118.6	−32.1	−119.2	−232.3	Rés. et postes appareutés
Ukraine								**Ukraine**
Goods: Exports fob	13 894.0	14 244.0	15 547.0	15 418.0	13 699.0	13 189.0	15 722.0	Biens : exportations,fàb
Goods: Imports fob	−16 469.0	−16 946.0	−19 843.0	−19 623.0	−16 283.0	−12 945.0	−14 943.0	Biens : importations,fàb
Serv. & Income: Credit	2 803.0	3 093.0	4 901.0	5 095.0	4 044.0	3 967.0	3 943.0	Serv. & revenu : crédit
Serv. & Income: Debit	−1 938.0	−2 015.0	−2 298.0	−3 070.0	−3 538.0	−3 259.0	−4 258.0	Serv. & revenu : débit
Current Trans.,nie: Credit	583.0	557.0	619.0	942.0	868.0	754.0	1 136.0	Transf. cour.,nia : crédit
Current Transfers: Debit	−36.0	−85.0	−110.0	−97.0	−86.0	−48.0	−119.0	Transf. courants : débit
Capital Acct.,nie: Credit	106.0	6.0	5.0	0.0	0.0	0.0	0.0	Compte de cap.,nia : crédit
Capital Account: Debit	−9.0	0.0	0.0	0.0	−3.0	−10.0	−8.0	Compte de capital : débit
Financial Account,nie	−557.0	−726.0	317.0	1 413.0	−1 340.0	−879.0	−321.0	Compte d'op. fin., nia
Net Errors and Omissions	423.5	248.2	259.3	−780.7	−817.9	−953.1	−148.2	Erreurs et omissions nettes
Reserves and Related Items	1 199.5	1 623.8	602.8	702.7	3 456.9	184.1	−1 003.8	Rés. et postes appareutés
United Kingdom [2]								**Royaume−Uni** [2]
Goods: Exports fob	207.4	242.6	261.6	281.3	271.8	268.9	283.2	Biens : exportations,fàb
Goods: Imports fob	−224.3	−261.1	−281.8	−300.8	−305.8	−311.3	−326.8	Biens : importations,fàb
Serv. & Income: Credit	194.4	231.4	242.9	270.9	282.6	285.1	322.5	Serv. & revenu : crédit
Serv. & Income: Debit	−172.5	−207.9	−216.3	−232.3	−238.1	−252.1	−297.7	Serv. & revenu : débit
Current Trans.,nie: Credit	19.6	21.1	33.4	25.1	25.5	30.2	31.6	Transf. cour.,nia : crédit
Current Transfers: Debit	−26.7	−32.0	−40.4	−33.3	−36.1	−36.9	−37.2	Transf. courants : débit
Capital Acct.,nie: Credit	1.9	1.8	2.2	2.8	2.4	2.6	4.2	Compte de cap.,nia : crédit
Capital Account: Debit	−1.9	−1.0	−1.0	−1.5	−1.6	−1.3	−1.3	Compte de capital : débit
Financial Account,nie	−7.7	1.2	2.4	−25.5	−7.8	17.5	31.2	Compte d'op. fin., nia
Net Errors and Omissions	11.2	3.1	−3.5	9.4	6.9	−3.8	−4.4	Erreurs et omissions nettes
Reserves and Related Items	−1.5	0.9	0.7	3.9	0.3	1.0	−5.3	Rés. et postes appareutés
Oceania · Océanie								
Australia								**Australie**
Goods: Exports fob	47 370.6	53 219.6	60 396.9	64 892.7	55 883.6	56 096.0	64 040.8	Biens : exportations,fàb
Goods: Imports fob	−50 648.0	−57 442.8	−61 031.7	−63 043.6	−61 215.2	−65 826.0	−68 751.8	Biens : importations,fàb
Serv. & Income: Credit	18 647.6	21 413.4	24 558.0	25 650.3	22 713.8	24 262.6	26 936.4	Serv. & revenu : crédit
Serv. & Income: Debit	−32 287.6	−36 403.6	−39 826.3	−39 844.2	−35 114.2	−37 515.5	−37 541.7	Serv. & revenu : débit
Current Trans.,nie: Credit	2 205.7	2 364.2	2 698.9	2 765.1	2 650.6	3 002.7	2 629.0	Transf. cour.,nia : crédit
Current Transfers: Debit	−2 434.0	−2 473.6	−2 606.2	−2 804.7	−2 932.7	−3 031.7	−2 628.8	Transf. courants : débit
Capital Acct.,nie: Credit	908.1	1 250.0	1 674.1	1 606.1	1 315.3	1 534.7	1 405.9	Compte de cap.,nia : crédit
Capital Account: Debit	−585.5	−691.7	−709.8	−703.3	−645.6	−715.5	−790.9	Compte de capital : débit
Financial Account,nie	15 897.2	18 631.8	16 069.5	16 820.4	15 116.5	27 968.6	14 723.7	Compte d'op. fin., nia
Net Errors and Omissions	−33.8	528.7	1 248.0	−2 465.6	187.8	929.4	−1 387.5	Erreurs et omissions nettes
Reserves and Related Items	959.8	−395.9	−2 471.5	−2 873.3	2 040.0	−6 705.5	1 364.7	Rés. et postes appareutés
Fiji								**Fidji**
Goods: Exports fob	490.2	519.6	672.2	535.6	428.9	537.7	...	Biens : exportations,fàb
Goods: Imports fob	−719.7	−761.4	−839.9	−818.9	−614.6	−653.3	...	Biens : importations,fàb

76
Summary of balance of payments
Millions of US dollars
Résumé des balances des paiements
Millions de dollars des E. – U.

Country or area	1994	1995	1996	1997	1998	1999	2000	Pays ou zone
Serv. & Income: Credit	583.8	619.5	676.2	729.7	557.8	572.4	...	Serv. & revenu : crédit
Serv. & Income: Debit	−471.7	−493.3	−504.5	−504.8	−462.6	−472.6	...	Serv. & revenu : débit
Current Trans.,nie: Credit	38.1	36.0	44.1	54.6	45.3	42.7	...	Transf. cour.,nia : crédit
Current Transfers: Debit	−33.5	−33.1	−34.6	−30.3	−14.7	−14.2	...	Transf. courants : débit
Capital Acct.,nie: Credit	76.0	120.1	114.5	88.9	100.6	59.3	...	Compte de cap.,nia : crédit
Capital Account: Debit	−32.6	−33.1	−43.8	−40.5	−40.0	−45.3	...	Compte de capital : débit
Financial Account,nie	61.0	88.3	3.6	−15.1	28.7	−104.0	...	Compte d'op. fin., nia
Net Errors and Omissions	30.9	30.4	−9.7	−24.3	−24.6	32.5	...	Erreurs et omissions nettes
Reserves and Related Items	−22.5	−93.0	−78.1	25.1	−4.9	44.9	...	Rés. et postes appareutés
Kiribati								**Kiribati**
Goods: Exports fob	6.1	...	...	...	...	...	...	Biens : exportations,fàb
Goods: Imports fob	−27.3	...	...	...	...	...	...	Biens : importations,fàb
Serv. & Income: Credit	34.6	...	...	...	...	...	...	Serv. & revenu : crédit
Serv. & Income: Debit	−19.4	...	...	...	...	...	...	Serv. & revenu : débit
Current Trans.,nie: Credit	9.0	...	...	...	...	...	...	Transf. cour.,nia : crédit
Current Transfers: Debit	−1.6	...	...	...	...	...	...	Transf. courants : débit
Capital Acct.,nie: Credit	2.5	...	...	...	...	...	...	Compte de cap.,nia : crédit
Capital Account: Debit	0.0	...	...	...	...	...	...	Compte de capital : débit
Financial Account,nie	−4.8	...	...	...	...	...	...	Compte d'op. fin., nia
Net Errors and Omissions	−5.1	...	...	...	...	...	...	Erreurs et omissions nettes
Reserves and Related Items	6.0	...	...	...	...	...	...	Rés. et postes appareutés
New Zealand								**Nouvelle–Zélande**
Goods: Exports fob	12 176.2	13 554.1	14 337.5	14 246.2	12 255.7	12 594.9	13 484.2	Biens : exportations,fàb
Goods: Imports fob	−10 768.5	−12 583.5	−13 813.8	−13 379.6	−11 333.0	−13 028.0	−12 847.8	Biens : importations,fàb
Serv. & Income: Credit	4 025.0	5 420.5	5 010.2	4 675.9	4 619.5	5 204.6	4 916.3	Serv. & revenu : crédit
Serv. & Income: Debit	−8 145.8	−9 589.3	−9 984.9	−10 160.3	−7 997.4	−8 611.6	−8 528.3	Serv. & revenu : débit
Current Trans.,nie: Credit	637.8	557.6	896.8	704.6	694.3	622.0	646.1	Transf. cour.,nia : crédit
Current Transfers: Debit	−309.1	−362.6	−409.4	−452.9	−401.6	−413.5	−404.0	Transf. courants : débit
Capital Acct.,nie: Credit	995.4	1 651.6	1 837.5	777.4	260.5	258.6	236.4	Compte de cap.,nia : crédit
Capital Account: Debit	−378.5	−427.2	−502.4	−541.1	−443.7	−476.8	−418.0	Compte de capital : débit
Financial Account,nie	2 219.6	4 664.9	3 571.4	4 045.4	1 580.4	1 973.6	3 335.3	Compte d'op. fin., nia
Net Errors and Omissions	280.6	−2 502.1	829.3	−1 357.9	279.2	2 064.6	−563.7	Erreurs et omissions nettes
Reserves and Related Items	−732.7	−384.0	−1 772.2	1 442.3	486.0	−188.4	143.7	Rés. et postes appareutés
Papua New Guinea								**Papouasie–Nvl–Guinée**
Goods: Exports fob	2 651.0	2 670.4	2 529.8	2 160.1	1 773.3	1 927.4	...	Biens : exportations,fàb
Goods: Imports fob	−1 324.9	−1 262.4	−1 513.3	−1 483.3	−1 078.3	−1 071.4	...	Biens : importations,fàb
Serv. & Income: Credit	257.9	343.9	464.3	432.1	339.0	266.4	...	Serv. & revenu : crédit
Serv. & Income: Debit	−1 031.5	−1 152.8	−1 239.7	−1 268.4	−1 073.6	−1 019.2	...	Serv. & revenu : débit
Current Trans.,nie: Credit	58.8	66.7	252.1	69.9	82.4	60.3	...	Transf. cour.,nia : crédit
Current Transfers: Debit	−209.3	−173.9	−304.2	−102.6	−71.6	−68.7	...	Transf. courants : débit
Capital Acct.,nie: Credit	19.9	15.7	15.2	13.9	9.7	7.8	...	Compte de cap.,nia : crédit
Capital Account: Debit	−19.9	−15.7	−15.2	−13.9	−9.7	−7.8	...	Compte de capital : débit
Financial Account,nie	−609.2	−444.7	46.6	8.0	−179.7	16.0	...	Compte d'op. fin., nia
Net Errors and Omissions	37.1	−86.6	−33.1	7.3	−12.5	14.3	...	Erreurs et omissions nettes
Reserves and Related Items	170.1	39.5	−202.5	177.0	221.0	−125.0	...	Rés. et postes appareutés
Samoa								**Samoa**
Goods: Exports fob	3.5	8.8	10.1	14.6	20.4	18.2	...	Biens : exportations,fàb
Goods: Imports fob	−68.8	−80.3	−90.8	−100.1	−96.9	−115.7	...	Biens : importations,fàb
Serv. & Income: Credit	47.0	60.4	70.6	70.8	68.5	64.1	...	Serv. & revenu : crédit
Serv. & Income: Debit	−32.6	−39.6	−36.8	−44.2	−31.5	−26.9	...	Serv. & revenu : débit
Current Trans.,nie: Credit	62.7	66.7	66.9	73.7	64.1	44.7	...	Transf. cour.,nia : crédit
Current Transfers: Debit	−6.1	−6.6	−7.8	−5.6	−4.6	−3.1	...	Transf. courants : débit
Capital Acct.,nie: Credit	0.0	0.0	0.0	0.0	0.0	27.1	...	Compte de cap.,nia : crédit
Capital Account: Debit	0.0	0.0	0.0	0.0	0.0	−2.7	...	Compte de capital : débit
Financial Account,nie	−5.5	−5.6	−3.6	−5.9	−5.0	−0.7	...	Compte d'op. fin., nia
Net Errors and Omissions	−4.2	−1.7	−1.3	7.9	−9.6	2.1	...	Erreurs et omissions nettes
Reserves and Related Items	3.9	−2.0	−7.4	−11.1	−5.5	−7.0	...	Rés. et postes appareutés
Solomon Islands								**Iles Salomon**
Goods: Exports fob	142.2	168.3	161.5	156.4	141.8	164.6	...	Biens : exportations,fàb
Goods: Imports fob	−142.2	−154.5	−150.5	−184.5	−159.9	−110.0	...	Biens : importations,fàb
Serv. & Income: Credit	51.5	43.0	55.5	73.0	57.2	61.8	...	Serv. & revenu : crédit
Serv. & Income: Debit	−110.4	−84.9	−94.9	−118.4	−64.5	−109.9	...	Serv. & revenu : débit
Current Trans.,nie: Credit	66.6	53.2	57.5	52.6	56.4	41.5	...	Transf. cour.,nia : crédit
Current Transfers: Debit	−11.1	−16.7	−14.5	−17.1	−22.9	−26.5	...	Transf. courants : débit
Capital Acct.,nie: Credit	2.9	1.5	0.5	0.3	6.9	9.2	...	Compte de cap.,nia : crédit
Capital Account: Debit	−0.2	−0.9	−2.7	−1.3	−0.3	0.0	...	Compte de capital : débit

76
Summary of balance of payments
Millions of US dollars
Résumé des balances des paiements
Millions de dollars des E.−U.

Country or area	1994	1995	1996	1997	1998	1999	2000	Pays ou zone
Financial Account,nie	1.5	−8.3	−1.4	45.7	16.9	−33.8	...	Compte d'op. fin., nia
Net Errors and Omissions	−2.8	−1.4	7.0	2.3	−14.4	−1.6	...	Erreurs et omissions nettes
Reserves and Related Items	2.0	0.8	−18.0	−9.1	−17.2	4.7	...	Rés. et postes appareutés
Vanuatu								**Vanuatu**
Goods: Exports fob	25.1	28.3	30.2	35.3	33.8	24.9	...	Biens : exportations,fàb
Goods: Imports fob	−74.7	−79.4	−81.1	−79.0	−76.2	−76.4	...	Biens : importations,fàb
Serv. & Income: Credit	88.1	94.7	108.6	103.2	134.9	135.8	...	Serv. & revenu : crédit
Serv. & Income: Debit	−80.8	−85.1	−84.0	−81.6	−76.8	−88.6	...	Serv. & revenu : débit
Current Trans.,nie: Credit	23.2	23.8	22.4	21.8	30.3	38.4	...	Transf. cour.,nia : crédit
Current Transfers: Debit	−0.7	−0.6	−22.9	−19.0	−31.2	−37.2	...	Transf. courants : débit
Capital Acct.,nie: Credit	41.4	38.3	43.4	23.8	25.2	23.9	...	Compte de cap.,nia : crédit
Capital Account: Debit	−4.2	−6.7	−38.5	−29.2	−35.1	−57.2	...	Compte de capital : débit
Financial Account,nie	−13.4	25.3	20.9	−16.7	−3.1	43.9	...	Compte d'op. fin., nia
Net Errors and Omissions	−10.2	−33.4	−4.1	39.4	6.3	−11.0	...	Erreurs et omissions nettes
Reserves and Related Items	6.1	−5.3	5.3	2.2	−8.1	3.5	...	Rés. et postes appareutés

Source:
International Monetary Fund (IMF), Washington, D.C., "International Financial Statistics," November 2001, and the IMF database.

† For information on recent changes in country or area nomenclature pertaining to former Czechoslovakia, Germany, Hong Kong Special Administrative Region (SAR) of China, Macao Special Administrative Region (SAR) of China, SFR of Yugoslavia and the former USSR, see Annex I − Country or area nomenclature, regional and other groupings.

††For statistical purposes, the data for China do not include those for the Hong Kong Special Administrative Region (Hong Kong SAR), Macao Special Administrative Region (Hong Kong SAR) and Taiwan province of China.

1 From 1980−1994, including Anguilla.
2 Billions of US Dollars.
3 BLEU trade data refer to the Belgium−Luxembourg Economic Union and exclude transactions between the two countries. Beginning in 1997, trade data are for Belgium only, which includes trade between Belgium and Luxembourg.

Source:
Fonds Monétaire International (FMI), Washington, D.C., "Statistiques Financières Internationales," novembre 2001 et la base de données du FMI.

† Pour les modifications récentes de nomenclature de pays ou de zone concernant l'Allemagne, Hong Kong région administrative spéciale (RAS) de Chine, Macao région administrative spéciale (RAS) de Chine, l'ex−Tchécoslovaquie, l'ex−URSS et l'ex−Rfs de Yougoslavie, voir annexe I − Nomenclature des pays ou des zones, groupements régionaux et autres groupements.

††Les données statistiques relatives à la Chine ne comprennent pas celles qui concernent la région administrative spéciale de Hong Kong (la RAS de Hong Kong), la région administrative spéciale de Macao (la RAS de Macao) et la province chinoise de Taiwan.

1 Dès 1980−1994, y compris Anguilla.
2 Milliards de dollars des E.−U.
3 Les données sur le commerce extérieur se rapportent à l'Union économique belgo−luxembourgeoise (UEBL) et ne couvrent pas les transactions entre les deux pays. A compter de 1997, les données sur le commerce extérieur ne se rapportent qu'à la Belgique, et recouvrent les échanges entre la Belgique et le Luxembourg.

Technical notes, table 76

A balance of payments can be broadly described as the record of an economy's international economic transactions. It shows (a) transactions in goods, services and income between an economy and the rest of the world, (b) changes of ownership and other changes in that economy's monetary gold, special drawing rights (SDRs) and claims on and liabilities to the rest of the world, and (c) unrequited transfers and counterpart entries needed to balance in the accounting sense any entries for the foregoing transactions and changes which are not mutually offsetting.

The balance of payments are presented on the basis of the methodology and presentation of the fifth edition of the *Balance of Payments Manual* (BPM5)[40], published by the International Monetary Fund in September 1993. The BPM5 incorporates several major changes to take account of developments in international trade and finance over the past decade, and to better harmonize the Fund's balance of payments methodology with the methodology of the 1993 *System of National Accounts* (SNA) [58]. The Fund's balance of payments has been converted for all periods from the BPM4 basis to the BPM5 basis; thus the time series conform to the BPM5 methodology with no methodological breaks.

The detailed definitions concerning the content of the basic categories of the balance of payments are given in the *Balance of Payments Manual (fifth edition)* [40]. Brief explanatory notes are given below to clarify the scope of the major items.

Goods: Exports f.o.b. and *Goods: Imports f.o.b.* are both measured on the "free-on-board" (f.o.b.) basis□that is, by the value of the goods at the border of the exporting country; in the case of imports, this excludes the cost of freight and insurance incurred beyond the border of the exporting country.

Services and income covers transactions in real resources between residents and non-residents other than those classified as merchandise, including (a) shipment and other transportation services, including freight, insurance and other distributive services in connection with the movement of commodities, (b) travel, i.e. goods and services acquired by non-resident travellers in a given country and similar acquisitions by resident travellers abroad, and (c) investment income which covers income of non-residents from their financial assets invested in the compiling economy (debit) and similar income of residents from their financial assets invested abroad (credit).

Current Transfers, n.i.e.: Credit comprises all current transfers received by the reporting country, except those made to the country to finance its "overall bal-

Notes techniques, tableau 76

La balance des paiements peut se définir d'une façon générale comme le relevé des transactions économiques internationales d'une économie. Elle indique (a) les transactions sur biens, services et revenus entre une économie et le reste du monde, (b) les transferts de propriété et autres variations intervenues dans les avoirs en or monétaire de cette économie, dans ses avoirs en droits de tirages spéciaux (DTS) ainsi que dans ses créances financières sur le reste du monde ou dans ses engagements financiers envers lui et (c) les "inscriptions de transferts sans contrepartie" et de "contrepartie" destinées à équilibrer, d'un point de vue comptable, les transactions et changements précités qui ne se compensent pas réciproquement.

Les données de balance des paiements sont présentées conformément à la méthodologie et à la classification recommandées dans la cinquième édition du *Manuel de la balance des paiements* [40], publiée en septembre 1993 par le Fonds monétaire international. La cinquième édition fait état de plusieurs changements importants qui ont été opérés de manière à rendre compte de l'évolution des finances et des changes internationaux pendant la décennie écoulée et à harmoniser davantage la méthodologie de la balance des paiements du FMI avec celle du *Système de comptabilité nationale* (SCN) [58] de 1993. Les statistiques incluses dans la balance des paiements du FMI ont été converties et sont désormais établies, pour toutes les périodes, sur la base de la cinquième et non plus de la quatrième édition; en conséquence, les séries chronologiques sont conformes aux principes de la cinquième édition, sans rupture due à des différences d'ordre méthodologique.

Les définitions détaillées relatives au contenu des postes fondamentaux de la balance des paiements figurent dans le *Manuel de la balance des paiements (cinquième édition)* [40]. De brèves notes explicatives sont présentées ci-après pour clarifier la portée de ces principales rubriques.

Les Biens: exportations, f.à.b. et *Biens: importations, f.à.b.* sont évalués sur la base f.à.b. (franco à bord)□c'est-à-dire à la frontière du pays exportateur; dans le cas des importations, cette valeur exclut le coût du fret et de l'assurance au-delà de la frontière du pays exportateur.

Services et revenus: transactions en ressources effectuées entre résidents et non résidents, autres que celles qui sont considérées comme des marchandises, notamment: (a) expéditions et autres services de transport, y compris le fret, l'assurance et les autres services de distribution liés aux mouvements de marchandises; (b) voyages, à savoir les biens et services acquis par des

ance", hence, the label "n.i.e." (not included elsewhere). (Note: some of the capital and financial accounts labeled "n.i.e." denote that *Exceptional Financing items* and *Liabilities Constituting Foreign Authorities' Reserves* (LCFARs) have been excluded.)

Capital Account, n.i.e.: *Credit* refers mainly to capital transfers linked to the acquisition of a fixed asset other than transactions relating to debt forgiveness plus the disposal of nonproduced, nonfinancial assets. *Capital Account*: *Debit* refers mainly to capital transfers linked to the disposal of fixed assets by the donor or to the financing of capital formation by the recipient, plus the acquisition of nonproduced, nonfinancial assets.

Financial Account, n.i.e. is the net sum of the balance of direct investment, portfolio investment, and other investment transactions.

Net Errors and Omissions is a residual category needed to ensure that all debit and credit entries in the balance of payments statement sum to zero and reflects statistical inconsistencies in the recording of the credit and debit entries.

Reserves and Related Items is the sum of transactions in reserve assets, LCFARs, exceptional financing, and use of Fund credit and loans.

For further information see *International Financial Statistics* [15].

voyageurs non résidents dans un pays donné et achats similaires faits par des résidents voyageant à l'étranger; et (c) revenus des investissements, qui correspondent aux revenus que les non résidents tirent de leurs avoirs financiers placés dans l'économie déclarante (débit) et les revenus similaires que les résidents tirent de leurs avoirs financiers placés à l'étranger (crédit).

Les transferts courants, n.i.a: *Crédit* englobent tous les transferts courants reçus par l'économie qui établit sa balance des paiements, à l'exception de ceux qui sont destinés à financer sa "balance globale"—c'est ce qui explique la mention "n.i.a." (non inclus ailleurs). (Note: comptes de capital et d'opérations financières portent la mention "n.i.a.", ce qui signifie que les postes de *Financement exceptionnel* et les *Engagements constituant des réserves pour les autorités étrangères* ont été exclus de ces composantes du compte de capital et d'opérations financières.

Le Compte de capital, n.i.a.: *crédit* retrace principalement les transferts de capital liés à l'acquisition d'un actif fixe autres que les transactions ayant trait à des remises de dettes plus les cessions d'actifs non financiers non produits. Le *Compte de capital*: *débit* retrace principalement les transferts de capital liés à la cession d'actifs fixes par le donateur ou au financement de la formation de capital par le bénéficiaire, plus les acquisitions d'actifs non financiers non produits.

Le solde du *Compte d'op. Fin., n.i.a* (compte d'opérations financières, n.i.a.) est la somme des soldes des investissements directs, des investissements de portefeuille et des autres investissements.

Le poste des *Erreurs et omissions* nettes est une catégorie résiduelle qui est nécessaire pour assurer que la somme de toutes les inscriptions effectuées au débit et au crédit est égal à zéro et qui laisse apparaître les écarts entre les montants portés au débit et ceux qui sont inscrits au crédit.

Le montant de *Réserves et postes apparent*és est égal à la somme de transactions afférentes aux avoirs de réserve, aux engagements constituant des réserves pour les autorités étrangères, au financement exceptionnel et à l'utilisation des crédits et des prêts du FMI.

Pour plus de renseignements, voir *Statistiques financières internationales* [15].

77
Exchange rates
Cours des changes
National currency per US dollar
Valeur du dollar des Etats-Unis en monnaie nationale

Country (monetary unit) Pays (unité monétaire)	1991	1992	1993	1994	1995	1996	1997	1998	1999	2000
Afghanistan: afghani Afghanistan : afghani										
End of period Fin de période[1]	50.600	50.600	50.600	500.000	1 000.000	3 000.000	3 000.000	3 000.000	3 000.000	3 000.000
Period average Moyenne sur période[1]	50.600	50.600	50.600	425.100	833.333	2 333.330	3 000.000	3 000.000	3 000.000	3 000.000
Albania: lek Albanie : lek										
End of period Fin de période	...	102.900	98.700	95.590	94.240	103.070	149.140	140.580	135.120	142.640
Period average Moyenne sur période	...	75.033	102.062	94.623	92.698	104.499	148.933	150.633	137.691	143.709
Algeria: Algerian dinar Algérie : dinar algérien										
End of period Fin de période	21.392	22.781	24.123	42.893	52.175	56.186	58.414	60.353	69.314	75.343
Period average Moyenne sur période	18.473	21.836	23.345	35.059	47.663	54.749	57.707	58.739	66.574	75.260
Angola: readjusted kwanza Angola : réajusté kwanza										
End of period Fin de période	0.000	0.000	0.000	0.001	0.006	0.202	0.262	0.697	5.580	16.818
Period average Moyenne sur période	0.000	0.000	0.000	0.000	0.003	0.128	0.229	0.393	2.791	10.041
Antigua and Barbuda: EC dollar Antigua-et-Barbuda : dollar des Caraïbes orientales										
End of period Fin de période	2.700	2.700	2.700	2.700	2.700	2.700	2.700	2.700	2.700	2.700
Argentina: Argentine peso Argentine : peso argentin										
End of period Fin de période[2]	0.999	0.991	0.999	1.000	1.000	1.000	1.000	1.000	1.000	1.000
Period average Moyenne sur période[2]	0.954	0.991	0.999	0.999	1.000	1.000	1.000	1.000	1.000	1.000
Armenia: dram Arménie : dram										
End of period Fin de période	...	2.070	75.000	405.510	402.000	435.070	494.980	522.030	523.770	552.180
Period average Moyenne sur période	...	...	9.105	288.651	405.908	414.041	490.847	504.915	535.062	539.526
Aruba: Aruban florin Aruba : florin de Aruba										
End of period Fin de période	1.790	1.790	1.790	1.790	1.790	1.790	1.790	1.790	1.790	1.790
Australia: Australian dollar Australie : dollar australien										
End of period Fin de période	1.316	1.452	1.477	1.287	1.342	1.256	1.532	1.629	1.530	1.805
Period average Moyenne sur période	1.284	1.362	1.471	1.368	1.349	1.278	1.347	1.592	1.550	1.725
Austria: Austrian schilling, euro Autriche : schilling autrichien, euro										
End of period Fin de période[3]	10.689	11.354	12.143	10.969	10.088	10.954	12.633	11.747	0.995	1.075
Period average Moyenne sur période[3]	11.676	10.989	11.632	11.422	10.082	10.587	12.204	12.379	0.939	1.085
Azerbaijan: manat Azerbaïdjan : manat										
End of period Fin de période	...	48.600	118.000	4 182.000	4 440.000	4 098.000	3 888.000	3 890.000	4 378.000	4 565.000
Period average Moyenne sur période	...	54.200	99.975	1 570.220	4 413.540	4 301.260	3 985.370	3 869.000	4 120.170	4 474.150
Bahamas: Bahamian dollar Bahamas : dollar des Bahamas										
End of period Fin de période[1]	1.000	1.000	1.000	1.000	1.000	1.000	1.000	1.000	1.000	1.000

77
Exchange rates
National currency per US dollar [*cont.*]
   Cours des changes
   Valeur du dollar des Etats-Unis en monnaie nationale [*suite*]

Country (monetary unit) Pays (unité monétaire)	1991	1992	1993	1994	1995	1996	1997	1998	1999	2000
Bahrain: Bahrain dinar Bahrein : dinar de Bahrein										
End of period										
Fin de période	0.376	0.376	0.376	0.376	0.376	0.376	0.376	0.376	0.376	0.376
Bangladesh: taka Bangladesh : taka										
End of period[1]										
Fin de période[1]	38.580	39.000	39.850	40.250	40.750	42.450	45.450	48.500	51.000	54.000
Period average[1]										
Moyenne sur période[1]	36.596	38.951	39.567	40.212	40.278	41.794	43.892	46.906	49.085	52.142
Barbados: Barbados dollar Barbade : dollar de la Barbade										
End of period										
Fin de période	2.000	2.000	2.000	2.000	2.000	2.000	2.000	2.000	2.000	2.000
Belarus: Belarussian rouble Bélarus : rouble bélarussien										
End of period										
Fin de période	...	0.015	0.699	10.600	11.500	15.500	30.740	106.000	320.000	1 180.000
Period average										
Moyenne sur période	...	...	...	...	11.521	13.230	26.020	46.127	248.795	876.750
Belgium: Belgian franc, euro Belgique : franc belge, euro										
End of period[3]										
Fin de période[3]	31.270	33.180	36.110	31.838	29.415	32.005	36.920	34.575	0.995	1.075
Period average[3]										
Moyenne sur période[3]	34.148	32.150	34.597	33.457	29.480	30.962	35.774	36.299	0.939	1.085
Belize: Belize dollar Belize : dollar du Belize										
End of period										
Fin de période	2.000	2.000	2.000	2.000	2.000	2.000	2.000	2.000	2.000	2.000
Benin: CFA franc Bénin : franc CFA										
End of period[4]										
Fin de période[4]	259.000	275.325	294.775	534.600	490.000	523.700	598.810	562.210	652.953	704.951
Period average[4]										
Moyenne sur période[4]	282.107	264.692	283.163	555.205	499.148	511.552	583.669	589.952	615.699	711.976
Bhutan: ngultrum Bhoutan : ngultrum										
End of period										
Fin de période	25.834	26.200	31.380	31.380	35.180	35.930	39.280	42.480	43.490	46.750
Period average										
Moyenne sur période	22.742	25.918	30.493	31.374	32.427	35.433	36.313	41.259	43.055	44.942
Bolivia: boliviano Bolivie : boliviano										
End of period[5]										
Fin de période[5]	3.745	4.095	4.475	4.695	4.935	5.185	5.365	5.645	5.990	6.390
Period average[5]										
Moyenne sur période[5]	3.581	3.901	4.265	4.621	4.800	5.075	5.254	5.510	5.812	6.184
Bosnia and Herzegovina: convertible mark Bosnie-Herzégovine : mark convertible										
End of period										
Fin de période	...	...	...	0.016	0.014	0.016	1.792	1.673	1.947	2.102
Period average										
Moyenne sur période	...	...	...	...	0.014	0.015	1.734	1.760	1.837	2.124
Botswana: pula Botswana : pula										
End of period										
Fin de période	2.073	2.257	2.565	2.717	2.822	3.644	3.810	4.458	4.632	5.362
Period average										
Moyenne sur période	2.022	2.110	2.423	2.685	2.772	3.324	3.651	4.226	4.624	5.102
Brazil: real Brésil : real										
End of period[1][6]										
Fin de période[1][6]	388.650	4 504.550	0.119	0.846	0.973	1.039	1.116	1.209	1.789	1.955

77

Exchange rates
National currency per US dollar [*cont.*]
Cours des changes
Valeur du dollar des Etats-Unis en monnaie nationale [*suite*]

Country (monetary unit) Pays (unité monétaire)	1991	1992	1993	1994	1995	1996	1997	1998	1999	2000
Period average[16] Moyenne sur période[16]	147.860	1 641.090	0.032	0.639	0.918	1.005	1.078	1.161	1.815	1.830
Brunei Darussalam: Brunei dollar Brunéi Darussalam : dollar du Brunéi										
End of period Fin de période	1.631	1.645	1.608	1.461	1.414	1.400	1.676	1.661	1.666	1.732
Period average Moyenne sur période	1.728	1.629	1.616	1.527	1.417	1.410	1.485	1.674	1.695	1.724
Bulgaria: lev Bulgarie : lev										
End of period Fin de période	0.022	0.025	0.033	0.066	0.071	0.487	1.777	1.675	1.947	2.102
Period average Moyenne sur période	0.018	0.023	0.028	0.054	0.067	0.178	1.682	1.760	1.836	2.123
Burkina Faso: CFA franc Burkina Faso : franc CFA										
End of period[4] Fin de période[4]	259.000	275.325	294.775	534.600	490.000	523.700	598.810	562.210	652.953	704.951
Period average[4] Moyenne sur période[4]	282.107	264.692	283.163	555.205	499.148	511.552	583.669	589.952	615.699	711.976
Burundi: Burundi franc Burundi : franc burundais										
End of period Fin de période	191.100	236.550	264.380	246.940	277.920	322.350	408.380	505.160	628.580	778.200
Period average Moyenne sur période	181.513	208.303	242.780	252.662	249.757	302.747	352.351	447.766	563.562	720.673
Cambodia: riel Cambodge : riel										
End of period Fin de période	520.000	2 000.000	2 305.000	2 575.000	2 526.000	2 713.000	3 452.000	3 770.000	3 770.000	3 905.000
Period average Moyenne sur période	...	1 266.580	2 689.000	2 545.250	2 450.830	2 624.080	2 946.250	3 744.420	3 807.830	3 840.750
Cameroon: CFA franc Cameroun : franc CFA										
End of period[4] Fin de période[4]	259.000	275.325	294.775	534.600	490.000	523.700	598.810	562.210	652.953	704.951
Period average[4] Moyenne sur période[4]	282.107	264.692	283.163	555.205	499.148	511.552	583.669	589.952	615.699	711.976
Canada: Canadian dollar Canada : dollar canadien										
End of period Fin de période	1.156	1.271	1.324	1.403	1.365	1.370	1.429	1.531	1.443	1.500
Period average Moyenne sur période	1.146	1.209	1.290	1.366	1.372	1.364	1.385	1.484	1.486	1.485
Cape Verde: Cape Verde escudo Cap-Vert : escudo du Cap-Vert										
End of period Fin de période	66.470	73.089	85.992	81.140	77.455	85.165	96.235	94.255	107.575	118.760
Period average Moyenne sur période	71.408	68.018	80.427	81.891	76.853	82.592	93.177	98.158	102.700	115.877
Central African Rep.: CFA franc Rép. centrafricaine : franc CFA										
End of period[4] Fin de période[4]	259.000	275.325	294.775	534.600	490.000	523.700	598.810	562.210	652.953	704.951
Period average[4] Moyenne sur période[4]	282.107	264.692	283.163	555.205	499.148	511.552	583.669	589.952	615.699	711.976
Chad: CFA franc Tchad : franc CFA										
End of period[4] Fin de période[4]	259.000	275.325	294.775	534.600	490.000	523.700	598.810	562.210	652.953	704.951
Period average[4] Moyenne sur période[4]	282.107	264.692	283.163	555.205	499.148	511.552	583.669	589.952	615.699	711.976
Chile: Chilean peso Chili : peso chilien										
End of period[1] Fin de période[1]	374.870	382.330	431.040	404.090	407.130	424.970	439.810	473.770	530.070	572.680

77
Exchange rates
National currency per US dollar [cont.]
Cours des changes
Valeur du dollar des Etats-Unis en monnaie nationale [suite]

Country (monetary unit) Pays (unité monétaire)	1991	1992	1993	1994	1995	1996	1997	1998	1999	2000
Period average[1] Moyenne sur période[1]	349.216	362.576	404.166	420.177	396.773	412.267	419.295	460.287	508.777	535.466
China ††: yuan Chine †† : yuan										
End of period[1] Fin de période[1]	5.434	5.752	5.800	8.446	8.317	8.298	8.280	8.279	8.280	8.277
Period average[1] Moyenne sur période[1]	5.323	5.515	5.762	8.619	8.351	8.314	8.290	8.279	8.278	8.278
China, Hong Kong SAR†: Hong Kong dollar Chine, Hong Kong RAS† : dollar de Hong Kong										
End of period Fin de période	7.781	7.743	7.726	7.738	7.732	7.736	7.746	7.746	7.771	7.796
Period average Moyenne sur période	7.771	7.741	7.736	7.728	7.736	7.734	7.742	7.745	7.758	7.791
Colombia: Colombian peso Colombie : peso colombien										
End of period Fin de période	706.860	811.770	917.330	831.270	987.650	1 005.330	1 293.580	1 507.520	1 873.770	2 187.020
Period average Moyenne sur période	633.045	759.282	863.065	844.836	912.826	1 036.690	1 140.960	1 426.040	1 756.230	2 087.900
Comoros: Comorian franc Comores : franc comorien										
End of period[7] Fin de période[7]	258.997	275.322	294.772	400.948	367.498	392.773	449.105	421.655	489.715	528.714
Period average[7] Moyenne sur période[7]	282.105	264.690	283.160	416.399	374.357	383.660	437.747	442.459	461.775	533.982
Congo: CFA franc Congo : franc CFA										
End of period[4] Fin de période[4]	259.000	275.325	294.775	534.600	490.000	523.700	598.810	562.210	652.953	704.951
Period average[4] Moyenne sur période[4]	282.107	264.692	283.163	555.205	499.148	511.552	583.669	589.952	615.699	711.976
Costa Rica: Costa Rican colón Costa Rica : colón costa-ricien										
End of period Fin de période	135.425	137.430	151.440	165.070	194.900	220.110	244.290	271.420	298.190	318.020
Period average Moyenne sur période	122.432	134.506	142.172	157.067	179.729	207.689	232.597	257.229	285.685	308.187
Côte d'Ivoire: CFA franc Côte d'Ivoire : franc CFA										
End of period[4] Fin de période[4]	259.000	275.325	294.775	534.600	490.000	523.700	598.810	562.210	652.953	704.951
Period average[4] Moyenne sur période[4]	282.107	264.692	283.163	555.205	499.148	511.552	583.669	589.952	615.699	711.976
Croatia: kuna Croatie : kuna										
End of period Fin de période	...	0.798	6.562	5.629	5.316	5.540	6.303	6.248	7.648	8.155
Period average Moyenne sur période	...	...	3.577	5.996	5.230	5.434	6.101	6.362	7.112	8.277
Cyprus: Cyprus pound Chypre : livre chypriote										
End of period Fin de période	0.439	0.483	0.520	0.476	0.457	0.470	0.526	0.498	0.575	0.617
Period average Moyenne sur période	0.464	0.450	0.497	0.492	0.452	0.466	0.514	0.518	0.543	0.622
Czech Republic: Czech koruna République tchèque : couronne tchèque										
End of period Fin de période	...	...	29.955	28.049	26.602	27.332	34.636	29.855	35.979	37.813
Period average[1] Moyenne sur période[1]	...	...	29.153	28.785	26.541	27.145	31.698	32.281	34.569	38.598
Dem. Rep. of the Congo: Congo franc Rép. dém. du Congo : franc congolais										
End of period[8] Fin de période[8]	0.212	6.633	350.000	# 32.500	148.310	1 156.000	1 060.000	# 2.450	4.500	50.000

77
Exchange rates
National currency per US dollar [*cont.*]
Cours des changes
Valeur du dollar des Etats-Unis en monnaie nationale [*suite*]

Country (monetary unit) Pays (unité monétaire)	1991	1992	1993	1994	1995	1996	1997	1998	1999	2000
Period average[6] Moyenne sur période[6]	0.052	2.151	25.144	# 11.941	70.245	501.849	1 313.448	# 1.607	4.018	21.818
Denmark: Danish krone Danemark : couronne danoise										
End of period Fin de période	5.914	6.256	6.773	6.083	5.546	5.945	6.826	6.387	7.399	8.021
Period average Moyenne sur période	6.397	6.036	6.484	6.361	5.602	5.799	6.605	6.701	6.976	8.083
Djibouti: Djibouti franc Djibouti : franc djiboutien										
End of period Fin de période	177.721	177.721	177.721	177.721	177.721	177.721	177.721	177.721	177.721	177.721
Dominica: EC dollar Dominique : dollar des Caraïbes orientales										
End of period Fin de période	2.700	2.700	2.700	2.700	2.700	2.700	2.700	2.700	2.700	2.700
Dominican Republic: Dominican peso Rép. dominicaine : peso dominicain										
End of period[1] Fin de période[1]	12.660	12.575	12.767	13.064	13.465	14.062	14.366	15.788	16.039	16.674
Period average[1] Moyenne sur période[1]	12.692	12.774	12.676	13.160	13.597	13.775	14.266	15.267	16.033	16.415
Ecuador: sucre Equateur : sucre										
End of period[1] Fin de période[1]	1 270.580	1 844.250	2 043.780	2 269.000	2 923.500	3 635.000	4 428.000	6 825.000	20 243.000	25 000.000
Period average[1] Moyenne sur période[1]	1 046.250	1 533.960	1 919.100	2 196.730	2 564.490	3 189.470	3 998.270	5 446.570	11 786.800	24 988.400
Egypt: Egyptian pound Egypte : livre égyptienne										
End of period[1] Fin de période[1]	3.332	3.339	3.372	3.391	3.390	3.388	3.388	3.388	3.405	3.690
Period average[1] Moyenne sur période[1]	3.138	3.322	3.353	3.385	3.392	3.392	3.389	3.388	3.395	3.472
El Salvador: El Salvadoran colón El Salvador : cólon salvadorien										
End of period[1] Fin de période[1]	8.080	9.170	8.670	8.750	8.755	8.755	8.755	8.755	8.755	8.755
Period average[1] Moyenne sur période[1]	8.017	8.361	8.703	8.729	8.755	8.755	8.756	8.755	8.755	8.755
Equatorial Guinea: CFA franc Guinée équatoriale : franc CFA										
End of period[4] Fin de période[4]	259.000	275.325	294.775	534.600	490.000	523.700	598.810	562.210	652.953	704.951
Period average[4] Moyenne sur période[4]	282.107	264.692	283.163	555.205	499.148	511.552	583.669	589.952	615.699	711.976
Estonia: Estonian kroon Estonie : couronne estonienne										
End of period Fin de période	...	12.912	13.878	12.390	11.462	12.440	14.336	13.410	15.562	16.820
Period average Moyenne sur période	...	...	13.223	12.991	11.465	12.034	13.882	14.075	14.678	16.969
Ethiopia: Ethiopian birr Ethiopie : birr éthiopien										
End of period Fin de période	2.070	5.000	5.000	5.950	6.320	6.426	6.864	7.503	8.134	8.314
Period average Moyenne sur période	2.070	2.803	5.000	5.465	6.158	6.352	6.709	7.116	7.942	8.217
Euro Area: euro Zone euro : euro										
End of period[9] Fin de période[9]	...	...	...	...	...	...	...	...	0.995	1.075
Period average[9] Moyenne sur période[9]	...	...	...	...	...	...	...	...	0.939	1.085

77
Exchange rates
National currency per US dollar [*cont.*]
Cours des changes
Valeur du dollar des Etats-Unis en monnaie nationale [*suite*]

Country (monetary unit) Pays (unité monétaire)	1991	1992	1993	1994	1995	1996	1997	1998	1999	2000
Fiji: Fiji dollar Fidji : dollar des Fidji										
End of period										
Fin de période	1.473	1.565	1.541	1.409	1.429	1.384	1.549	1.986	1.966	2.186
Period average										
Moyenne sur période	1.476	1.503	1.542	1.464	1.406	1.403	1.444	1.987	1.970	2.129
Finland: Finnish markka, euro Finlande : markka finlandais, euro										
End of period[3]										
Fin de période[3]	4.133	5.245	5.785	4.743	4.359	4.644	5.421	5.096	0.995	1.075
Period average[3]										
Moyenne sur période[3]	4.044	4.479	5.712	5.224	4.367	4.594	5.191	5.344	0.939	1.085
France: French franc, euro France : franc français, euro										
End of period[3]										
Fin de période[3]	5.180	5.507	5.896	5.346	4.900	5.237	5.988	5.622	0.995	1.075
Period average[3]										
Moyenne sur période[3]	5.642	5.294	5.663	5.552	4.992	5.116	5.837	5.900	0.939	1.085
Gabon: CFA franc Gabon : franc CFA										
End of period[4]										
Fin de période[4]	259.000	275.325	294.775	534.600	490.000	523.700	598.810	562.210	652.953	704.951
Period average[4]										
Moyenne sur période[4]	282.107	264.692	283.163	555.205	499.148	511.552	583.669	589.952	615.699	711.976
Gambia: dalasi Gambie : dalasi										
End of period										
Fin de période	8.957	9.217	9.535	9.579	9.640	9.892	10.530	10.991	11.547	14.888
Period average										
Moyenne sur période	8.803	8.887	9.129	9.576	9.546	9.789	10.200	10.643	11.395	12.788
Georgia: lari Géorgie : lari										
End of period										
Fin de période	...	...	...	...	1.230	1.276	1.304	1.800	1.930	1.975
Period average										
Moyenne sur période	...	...	...	...	...	1.263	1.298	1.390	2.025	1.976
Germany †: deutsche mark Allemagne † : deutsche mark										
End of period[3]										
Fin de période[3]	1.516	1.614	1.726	1.549	1.434	1.555	1.792	1.673	0.995	1.075
Period average[3]										
Moyenne sur période[3]	1.660	1.562	1.653	1.623	1.433	1.505	1.734	1.760	0.939	1.085
Ghana: cedi Ghana : cedi										
End of period[1]										
Fin de période[1]	390.625	* 520.833	819.672	1 052.630	1 449.280	1 754.390	2 272.730	2 325.580	3 535.140	7 047.650
Period average[1]										
Moyenne sur période[1]	367.831	* 437.087	649.061	956.711	1 200.430	1 637.230	2 050.170	2 314.150	2 669.300	5 455.060
Greece: drachma Grèce : drachme										
End of period										
Fin de période	175.280	214.580	249.220	240.100	237.040	247.020	282.610	282.570	328.440	365.620
Period average										
Moyenne sur période	182.266	190.624	229.250	242.603	231.663	240.712	273.058	295.529	305.647	365.399
Grenada: EC dollar Grenade : dollar des Caraïbes orientales										
End of period										
Fin de période	2.700	2.700	2.700	2.700	2.700	2.700	2.700	2.700	2.700	2.700
Guatemala: quetzal Guatemala : quetzal										
End of period										
Fin de période	5.043	5.274	5.815	5.649	6.042	5.966	6.177	6.848	7.821	7.731
Period average										
Moyenne sur période	5.029	5.171	5.635	5.751	5.810	6.050	6.065	6.395	7.386	7.763

77

Exchange rates
National currency per US dollar [*cont.*]
    Cours des changes
        Valeur du dollar des Etats-Unis en monnaie nationale [*suite*]

Country (monetary unit) Pays (unité monétaire)	1991	1992	1993	1994	1995	1996	1997	1998	1999	2000
Guinea: Guinean franc Guinée : franc guinéen										
End of period										
Fin de période	802.950	922.410	972.414	981.024	997.984	1 039.130	1 144.950	1 298.030	1 736.000	1 882.270
Period average										
Moyenne sur période	753.858	902.001	955.490	976.636	991.411	1 004.020	1 095.330	1 236.830	1 387.400	1 746.870
Guinea-Bissau: CFA franc Guinée-Bissau : franc CFA										
End of period[10]										
Fin de période[10]	76.295	133.162	176.366	236.451	337.366	537.482	598.810	562.210	652.953	704.951
Period average[10]										
Moyenne sur période[10]	56.286	106.676	155.106	198.341	278.039	405.745	583.669	589.952	615.699	711.976
Guyana: Guyana dollar Guyana : dollar guyanais										
End of period[1]										
Fin de période[1]	122.000	126.000	130.750	142.500	140.500	141.250	144.000	162.250	180.500	184.750
Period average[1]										
Moyenne sur période[1]	111.811	125.002	126.730	138.290	141.989	140.375	142.401	150.519	177.995	182.430
Haiti: gourde Haïti : gourde										
End of period[1]										
Fin de période[1]	8.240	10.953	12.805	12.947	16.160	15.093	17.311	16.505	17.965	22.524
Period average[1]										
Moyenne sur période[1]	6.034	9.802	12.823	15.040	15.110	15.701	16.655	16.766	16.938	21.171
Honduras: lempira Honduras : lempira										
End of period[1]										
Fin de période[1]	5.400	5.830	7.260	9.400	10.343	12.869	13.094	13.808	14.504	15.141
Period average[1]										
Moyenne sur période[1]	5.317	5.498	6.472	8.409	9.471	11.705	13.004	13.385	14.213	14.839
Hungary: forint Hongrie : forint										
End of period										
Fin de période	75.620	83.970	100.700	110.690	139.470	164.930	203.500	219.030	252.520	284.730
Period average										
Moyenne sur période	74.735	78.988	91.933	105.160	125.681	152.647	186.789	214.402	237.146	282.179
Iceland: Icelandic króna Islande : couronne islandaise										
End of period										
Fin de période	55.620	63.920	72.730	68.300	65.230	66.890	72.180	69.320	72.550	84.700
Period average										
Moyenne sur période	58.996	57.546	67.603	69.944	64.692	66.500	70.904	70.958	72.335	78.616
India: Indian rupee Inde : roupie indienne										
End of period										
Fin de période	25.834	26.200	31.380	31.380	35.180	35.930	39.280	42.480	43.490	46.750
Period average										
Moyenne sur période	22.742	25.918	30.493	31.374	32.427	35.433	36.313	41.259	43.055	44.942
Indonesia: Indonesian rupiah Indonésie : roupie indonésien										
End of period										
Fin de période	1 992.000	2 062.000	2 110.000	2 200.000	2 308.000	2 383.000	4 650.000	8 025.000	7 085.000	9 595.000
Period average										
Moyenne sur période	1 950.320	2 029.920	2 087.100	2 160.750	2 248.610	2 342.300	2 909.380	10 013.600	7 855.150	8 421.770
Iran (Islamic Rep. of): Iranian rial Iran (Rép. islamique d') : rial iranien										
End of period[1]										
Fin de période[1]	64.591	67.039	1 758.560	1 735.970	1 747.500	1 749.140	1 754.260	1 750.930	1 752.290	2 262.930
Period average[1]										
Moyenne sur période[1]	67.505	65.552	1 267.770	1 748.750	1 747.930	1 750.760	1 752.920	1 751.860	1 752.930	1 764.430
Iraq: Iraqi dinar Iraq : dinar iraquien										
End of period[1]										
Fin de période[1]	0.311	0.311	0.311	0.311	0.311	0.311	0.311	0.311	0.311	0.311

77
Exchange rates
National currency per US dollar [*cont.*]
Cours des changes
Valeur du dollar des Etats-Unis en monnaie nationale [*suite*]

Country (monetary unit) Pays (unité monétaire)	1991	1992	1993	1994	1995	1996	1997	1998	1999	2000
Ireland: Irish pound, euro Irlande : livre irlandaise, euro										
End of period[3]										
Fin de période[3]	0.572	0.614	0.709	0.646	0.623	0.595	0.699	0.672	0.995	1.075
Period average[3]										
Moyenne sur période[3]	0.621	0.588	0.677	0.669	0.624	0.625	0.660	0.702	0.939	1.085
Israel: new sheqel Israël : nouveau sheqel										
End of period										
Fin de période	2.283	2.764	2.986	3.018	3.135	3.251	3.536	4.161	4.153	4.041
Period average										
Moyenne sur période	2.279	2.459	2.830	3.011	3.011	3.192	3.449	3.800	4.140	4.077
Italy: Italian lira, euro Italie : lire italienne, euro										
End of period[3]										
Fin de période[3]	1 151.060	1 470.860	1 703.970	1 629.740	1 584.720	1 530.570	1 759.190	1 653.100	0.995	1.075
Period average[3]										
Moyenne sur période[3]	1 240.610	1 232.410	1 573.670	1 612.440	1 628.930	1 542.950	1 703.100	1 736.210	0.939	1.085
Jamaica: Jamaican dollar Jamaïque : dollar jamaïcain										
End of period										
Fin de période	21.493	22.185	32.475	33.202	39.616	34.865	36.341	37.055	41.291	45.415
Period average										
Moyenne sur période	12.116	22.960	24.949	33.086	35.142	37.120	35.405	36.550	39.044	42.701
Japan: yen Japon : yen										
End of period										
Fin de période	125.200	124.750	111.850	99.740	102.830	116.000	129.950	115.600	102.200	114.900
Period average										
Moyenne sur période	134.707	126.651	111.198	102.208	94.060	108.779	120.991	130.905	113.907	107.765
Jordan: Jordan dinar Jordanie : dinar jordanien										
End of period										
Fin de période	0.675	0.691	0.704	0.701	0.709	0.709	0.709	0.709	0.709	0.709
Period average										
Moyenne sur période	0.681	0.680	0.693	0.699	0.700	0.709	0.709	0.709	0.709	0.709
Kazakhstan: tenge Kazakhstan : tenge										
End of period										
Fin de période	...	...	6.310	54.260	63.950	73.300	75.550	83.800	138.200	144.500
Period average										
Moyenne sur période	...	...	...	35.538	60.950	67.303	75.438	78.303	119.523	142.133
Kenya: Kenya shilling Kenya : shilling du Kenya										
End of period										
Fin de période	28.074	36.216	68.163	44.839	55.939	55.021	62.678	61.906	72.931	78.036
Period average										
Moyenne sur période	27.508	32.217	58.001	56.051	51.430	57.115	58.732	60.367	70.326	76.176
Kiribati: Australian dollar Kiribati : dollar australien										
End of period										
Fin de période	1.316	1.452	1.477	1.287	1.342	1.256	1.532	1.629	1.530	1.805
Period average										
Moyenne sur période	1.284	1.362	1.471	1.368	1.349	1.278	1.347	1.592	1.550	1.725
Korea, Republic of: Korean won Corée, République de : won coréen										
End of period										
Fin de période	760.800	788.400	808.100	788.700	774.700	844.200	1 695.000	1 204.000	1 138.000	1 264.500
Period average										
Moyenne sur période	733.353	780.651	802.671	803.446	771.273	804.453	951.289	1 401.440	1 188.820	1 130.960
Kuwait: Kuwaiti dinar Koweït : dinar koweïtien										
End of period										
Fin de période	0.284	0.303	0.298	0.300	0.299	0.300	0.305	0.302	0.304	0.305
Period average										
Moyenne sur période	0.284	0.293	0.302	0.297	0.298	0.299	0.303	0.305	0.304	0.307

77
Exchange rates
National currency per US dollar [*cont.*]
Cours des changes
Valeur du dollar des Etats-Unis en monnaie nationale [*suite*]

Country (monetary unit) Pays (unité monétaire)	1991	1992	1993	1994	1995	1996	1997	1998	1999	2000
Kyrgyzstan: Kyrgyz som Kirghizistan : som kirghize										
End of period Fin de période	...	...	8.030	10.650	11.200	16.700	17.375	29.376	45.429	48.304
Period average Moyenne sur période	...	...	...	10.842	10.822	12.810	17.363	20.838	39.008	47.704
Lao People's Dem. Rep.: kip Rép. dém. pop. lao : kip										
End of period Fin de période	711.500	717.000	718.000	719.000	# 923.000	935.000	2 634.500	4 274.000	7 600.000	8 218.000
Period average Moyenne sur période	702.083	716.083	716.250	717.667	# 804.691	921.022	1 259.980	3 298.330	7 102.020	7 887.640
Latvia: lats Lettonie : lats										
End of period Fin de période	...	0.835	0.595	0.548	0.537	0.556	0.590	0.569	0.583	0.613
Period average Moyenne sur période	...	0.737	0.675	0.560	0.528	0.551	0.581	0.590	0.585	0.607
Lebanon: Lebanese pound Liban : livre libanaise										
End of period Fin de période	879.000	1 838.000	1 711.000	1 647.000	1 596.000	1 552.000	1 527.000	1 508.000	1 507.500	1 507.500
Period average Moyenne sur période	928.227	1 712.790	1 741.360	1 680.070	1 621.410	1 571.440	1 539.450	1 516.130	1 507.840	1 507.500
Lesotho: loti Lesotho : loti										
End of period[1] Fin de période[1]	2.743	3.053	3.398	3.544	3.648	4.683	4.868	5.860	6.155	7.569
Period average[1] Moyenne sur période[1]	2.761	2.852	3.268	3.551	3.627	4.299	4.608	5.528	6.110	6.940
Liberia: Liberian dollar Libéria : dollar libérien										
End of period[1] Fin de période[1]	1.000	1.000	1.000	1.000	1.000	1.000	1.000	43.250	39.500	42.750
Period average[1] Moyenne sur période[1]	1.000	1.000	1.000	1.000	1.000	1.000	1.000	41.508	41.903	40.953
Libyan Arab Jamah.: Libyan dinar Jamah. arabe libyenne : dinar libyen										
End of period Fin de période	0.268	0.301	0.325	0.360	0.353	0.365	0.389	0.379	0.540	0.540
Period average Moyenne sur période	* 0.281	0.285	0.305	0.321	0.346	0.362	0.382	0.394	0.499	0.510
Lithuania: litas Lituanie : litas										
End of period Fin de période	...	3.790	3.900	4.000	4.000	4.000	4.000	4.000	4.000	4.000
Period average Moyenne sur période	...	1.773	4.344	3.978	4.000	4.000	4.000	4.000	4.000	4.000
Luxembourg: Luxembourg franc, euro Luxembourg : franc luxembourgeois, euro										
End of period[3] Fin de période[3]	31.270	33.180	36.110	31.838	29.415	32.005	36.920	34.575	0.995	1.075
Period average[3] Moyenne sur période[3]	34.148	32.150	34.597	33.457	29.480	30.962	35.774	36.299	0.939	1.085
Madagascar: Malagasy franc Madagascar : franc malgache										
End of period Fin de période	1 832.660	1 910.170	1 962.670	3 871.080	3 422.970	4 328.470	5 284.670	5 402.210	6 543.200	6 550.440
Period average Moyenne sur période	1 835.360	1 863.970	1 913.780	3 067.340	4 265.630	4 061.250	5 090.890	5 441.400	6 283.770	6 767.480
Malawi: Malawi kwacha Malawi : kwacha malawien										
End of period Fin de période	2.664	4.396	4.494	15.299	15.303	15.323	21.228	43.884	46.438	80.076
Period average Moyenne sur période	2.803	3.603	4.403	8.736	15.284	15.309	16.444	31.073	44.088	59.544

77
Exchange rates
National currency per US dollar [*cont.*]
Cours des changes
Valeur du dollar des Etats-Unis en monnaie nationale [*suite*]

Country (monetary unit) Pays (unité monétaire)	1991	1992	1993	1994	1995	1996	1997	1998	1999	2000
Malaysia: ringgit Malaisie : ringgit										
End of period										
Fin de période	2.724	2.612	2.702	2.560	2.542	2.529	3.892	3.800	3.800	3.800
Period average										
Moyenne sur période	2.750	2.547	2.574	2.624	2.504	2.516	2.813	3.924	3.800	3.800
Maldives: rufiyaa Maldives : rufiyaa										
End of period										
Fin de période	10.320	10.535	11.105	11.770	11.770	11.770	11.770	11.770	11.770	11.770
Period average										
Moyenne sur période	10.253	10.569	10.957	11.586	11.770	11.770	11.770	11.770	11.770	11.770
Mali: CFA franc Mali : franc CFA										
End of period [4]										
Fin de période [4]	259.000	275.325	294.775	534.600	490.000	523.700	598.810	562.210	652.953	704.951
Period average [4]										
Moyenne sur période [4]	282.107	264.692	283.163	555.205	499.148	511.552	583.669	589.952	615.699	711.976
Malta: Maltese lira Malte : lire maltaise										
End of period										
Fin de période	0.306	0.374	0.395	0.368	0.352	0.360	0.391	0.377	0.412	0.438
Period average										
Moyenne sur période	0.323	0.319	0.382	0.378	0.353	0.361	0.386	0.389	0.399	0.438
Mauritania: ouguiya Mauritanie : ouguiya										
End of period										
Fin de période	77.820	115.100	124.160	128.370	137.110	142.450	168.350	205.780	225.000	252.300
Period average										
Moyenne sur période	81.946	87.027	120.806	123.575	129.768	137.222	151.853	188.476	209.514	238.923
Mauritius: Mauritian rupee Maurice : roupie mauricienne										
End of period										
Fin de période	14.794	16.998	18.656	17.863	17.664	17.972	22.265	24.784	25.468	27.882
Period average										
Moyenne sur période	15.652	15.563	17.648	17.960	17.386	17.948	21.057	23.993	25.186	26.250
Mexico: Mexican peso Mexique : peso mexicain										
End of period [1]										
Fin de période [1]	3.071	3.115	3.106	5.325	7.643	7.851	8.083	9.865	9.514	9.572
Period average [1]										
Moyenne sur période [1]	3.018	3.095	3.116	3.375	6.419	7.600	7.919	9.136	9.560	9.456
Micronesia (Fed. States of): US dollar Micron (Etats fédérés de) : dollar des Etats-Unis										
End of period										
Fin de période	1.000	1.000	1.000	1.000	1.000	1.000	1.000	1.000	1.000	1.000
Mongolia: togrog Mongolie : togrog										
End of period										
Fin de période	39.400	105.067	# 396.510	414.090	473.620	693.510	813.160	902.000	1 072.370	1 097.000
Period average										
Moyenne sur période	9.515	42.559	...	# 412.721	448.613	548.403	789.992	840.828	1 021.870	1 076.670
Morocco: Moroccan dirham Maroc : dirham marocain										
End of period										
Fin de période	8.150	9.049	9.651	8.960	8.469	8.800	9.714	9.255	10.087	10.619
Period average										
Moyenne sur période	8.707	8.538	9.299	9.203	8.540	8.716	9.527	9.604	9.804	10.626
Mozambique: metical Mozambique : metical										
End of period [1]										
Fin de période [1]	1 838.840	# 2 940.950	5 324.240	6 627.450	10 851.400	11 336.700	11 502.100	12 322.200	13 252.900	17 140.500
Period average [1]										
Moyenne sur période [1]	1 462.930	2 566.480	3 951.110	6 158.400	9 203.390	11 517.800	11 772.600	12 110.200	13 028.600	15 447.100

77
Exchange rates
National currency per US dollar [*cont.*]
Cours des changes
Valeur du dollar des Etats-Unis en monnaie nationale [*suite*]

Country (monetary unit) Pays (unité monétaire)	1991	1992	1993	1994	1995	1996	1997	1998	1999	2000
Myanmar: kyat Myanmar : kyat										
End of period										
Fin de période	6.014	6.241	6.246	5.903	5.781	5.988	6.363	6.109	6.268	6.599
Period average										
Moyenne sur période	6.284	6.105	6.157	5.975	5.667	5.918	6.242	6.343	6.286	6.517
Namibia: Namibia dollar Namibie : Dollar namibia										
End of period										
Fin de période	2.743	3.053	3.398	3.544	3.648	4.683	4.868	5.860	6.155	7.569
Period average										
Moyenne sur période	2.761	2.852	3.268	3.551	3.627	4.299	4.608	5.528	6.110	6.940
Nepal: Nepalese rupee Népal : roupie népalaise										
End of period										
Fin de période	42.700	43.200	49.240	49.880	56.000	57.030	63.300	67.675	68.725	74.300
Period average										
Moyenne sur période	37.255	42.718	48.607	49.398	51.890	56.692	58.010	65.976	68.239	71.094
Netherlands: Netherlands guilder, euro Pays-Bas : florin néerlandais, euro										
End of period[3]										
Fin de période[3]	1.710	1.814	1.941	1.735	1.604	1.744	2.017	1.889	0.995	1.075
Period average[3]										
Moyenne sur période[3]	1.870	1.759	1.857	1.820	1.606	1.686	1.951	1.984	0.939	1.085
Netherlands Antilles: Netherlands Antillean guilder Antilles néerlandaises : florin des Antilles néerlandaises										
End of period										
Fin de période	1.790	1.790	1.790	1.790	1.790	1.790	1.790	1.790	1.790	1.790
New Zealand: New Zealand dollar Nouvelle-Zélande : dollar néo-zélandais										
End of period										
Fin de période	1.848	1.944	1.790	1.556	1.531	1.416	1.719	1.898	1.921	2.272
Period average										
Moyenne sur période	1.734	1.862	1.851	1.687	1.524	1.455	1.512	1.868	1.890	2.201
Nicaragua: córdoba Nicaragua : córdoba										
End of period[1 11]										
Fin de période[1 11]	5.000	5.000	6.350	7.112	7.965	8.924	9.995	11.194	12.318	13.057
Period average[1 11]										
Moyenne sur période[1 11]	4.271	5.000	5.620	6.723	7.546	8.435	9.448	10.582	11.809	12.684
Niger: CFA franc Niger : franc CFA										
End of period[4]										
Fin de période[4]	259.000	275.325	294.775	534.600	490.000	523.700	598.810	562.210	652.953	704.951
Period average[4]										
Moyenne sur période[4]	282.107	264.692	283.163	555.205	499.148	511.552	583.669	589.952	615.699	711.976
Nigeria: naira Nigéria : naira										
End of period[1]										
Fin de période[1]	9.862	19.646	21.882	21.997	21.887	21.886	21.886	21.886	97.950	109.550
Period average[1]										
Moyenne sur période[1]	9.910	17.298	22.065	21.996	21.895	21.884	21.886	21.886	92.338	101.697
Norway: Norwegian krone Norvège : couronne norvégienne										
End of period										
Fin de période	5.973	6.925	7.518	6.762	6.319	6.443	7.316	7.600	8.040	8.849
Period average										
Moyenne sur période	6.483	6.215	7.094	7.058	6.335	6.450	7.073	7.545	7.799	8.802
Oman: rial Omani Oman : rial omani										
End of period										
Fin de période	0.385	0.385	0.385	0.385	0.385	0.385	0.385	0.385	0.385	0.385
Pakistan: Pakistan rupee Pakistan : roupie pakistanaise										
End of period										
Fin de période	24.658	25.636	30.045	30.723	34.165	40.020	43.940	45.885	# 51.785	58.029

77
Exchange rates
National currency per US dollar [*cont.*]
Cours des changes
Valeur du dollar des Etats-Unis en monnaie nationale [*suite*]

Country (monetary unit) Pays (unité monétaire)	1991	1992	1993	1994	1995	1996	1997	1998	1999	2000
Period average Moyenne sur période	23.689	24.965	27.975	30.423	31.494	35.909	40.918	44.943	49.118	53.648
Panama: balboa Panama : balboa										
End of period Fin de période	1.000	1.000	1.000	1.000	1.000	1.000	1.000	1.000	1.000	1.000
Papua New Guinea: kina Papouasie-Nvl-Guinée : kina										
End of period Fin de période	0.953	0.988	0.981	1.179	1.335	1.347	1.751	2.096	2.695	3.072
Period average Moyenne sur période	0.952	0.965	0.978	1.011	1.280	1.319	1.438	2.074	2.571	2.782
Paraguay: guaraní Paraguay : guaraní										
End of period Fin de période	1 380.000	1 630.000	1 880.000	1 924.700	1 979.660	2 109.670	2 360.000	2 840.190	3 328.860	3 526.900
Period average Moyenne sur période	1 325.180	1 500.260	1 744.350	1 904.760	1 963.020	2 056.810	2 177.860	2 726.490	3 119.070	3 486.350
Peru: new sol Pérou : nouveau sol										
End of period[12] Fin de période[12]	0.960	1.630	2.160	2.180	2.310	2.600	2.730	3.160	3.510	3.527
Period average[12] Moyenne sur période[12]	0.773	1.246	1.988	2.195	2.253	2.453	2.664	2.930	3.383	3.490
Philippines: Philippine peso Philippines : peso philippin										
End of period Fin de période	26.650	25.096	27.699	24.418	26.214	26.288	39.975	39.059	40.313	49.998
Period average Moyenne sur période	27.479	25.513	27.120	26.417	25.715	26.216	29.471	40.893	39.089	44.192
Poland: new zloty Pologne : nouveau zloty										
End of period[13] Fin de période[13]	1.096	1.577	2.134	2.437	2.468	2.876	3.518	3.504	4.148	4.143
Period average[13] Moyenne sur période[13]	1.058	1.363	1.812	2.272	2.425	2.696	3.279	3.475	3.967	4.346
Portugal: Portuguese escudo, euro Portugal : escudo portugais, euro										
End of period[3] Fin de période[3]	134.184	146.758	176.812	159.093	149.413	156.385	183.326	171.829	0.995	1.075
Period average[3] Moyenne sur période[3]	144.482	134.998	160.800	165.993	151.106	154.244	175.312	180.104	0.939	1.085
Qatar: Qatar riyal Qatar : riyal qatarien										
End of period Fin de période	3.640	3.640	3.640	3.640	3.640	3.640	3.640	3.640	3.640	3.640
Republic of Moldova: Moldovan leu République de Moldova : leu moldove										
End of period Fin de période	0.002	0.414	# 3.640	4.270	4.499	4.674	4.661	8.323	11.590	12.383
Period average Moyenne sur période	...	...	...	...	4.496	4.605	4.624	5.371	10.516	12.434
Romania: Romanian leu Roumanie : leu roumain										
End of period[1] Fin de période[1]	189.000	460.000	1 276.000	1 767.000	2 578.000	4 035.000	8 023.000	10 951.000	18 255.000	25 926.000
Period average[1] Moyenne sur période[1]	76.387	# 307.953	760.051	1 655.090	2 033.280	3 084.220	7 167.940	8 875.580	15 332.800	21 708.700
Russian Federation: ruble Fédération de Russie : ruble										
End of period[14] Fin de période[14]	...	0.415	1.247	3.550	4.640	5.560	5.960	20.650	27.000	28.160
Period average[14] Moyenne sur période[14]	...	...	0.992	2.191	4.559	5.121	5.785	9.705	24.620	28.129

77
Exchange rates
National currency per US dollar [*cont.*]
Cours des changes
Valeur du dollar des Etats-Unis en monnaie nationale [*suite*]

Country (monetary unit) Pays (unité monétaire)	1991	1992	1993	1994	1995	1996	1997	1998	1999	2000
Rwanda: Rwanda franc Rwanda : franc rwandais										
End of period										
Fin de période	119.790	146.270	146.370	138.330	299.811	304.164	304.672	320.338	349.530	430.486
Period average										
Moyenne sur période	125.140	133.350	144.307	220.000	262.197	306.820	301.530	312.314	333.942	389.696
Saint Kitts and Nevis: EC dollar Saint-Kitts-et-Nevis : dollar des Caraïbes orientales										
End of period										
Fin de période	2.700	2.700	2.700	2.700	2.700	2.700	2.700	2.700	2.700	2.700
Saint Lucia: EC dollar Sainte-Lucie : dollar des Caraïbes orientales										
End of period										
Fin de période	2.700	2.700	2.700	2.700	2.700	2.700	2.700	2.700	2.700	2.700
St. Vincent-Grenadines: EC dollar St. Vincent-Grenadines : dollar des Caraïbes orientales										
End of period										
Fin de période	2.700	2.700	2.700	2.700	2.700	2.700	2.700	2.700	2.700	2.700
Samoa: tala Samoa : tala										
End of period										
Fin de période	2.449	2.558	2.608	2.452	2.527	2.434	2.766	3.010	3.018	3.341
Period average										
Moyenne sur période	2.400	2.466	2.569	2.535	2.473	2.462	2.559	2.948	3.013	3.286
San Marino: Italian lira Saint-Marin : lire italienne										
End of period[3]										
Fin de période[3]	1 151.060	1 470.860	1 703.970	1 629.740	1 584.720	1 530.570	1 759.190	1 653.100	0.995	1.075
Period average[3]										
Moyenne sur période[3]	1 240.610	1 232.410	1 573.670	1 612.440	1 628.930	1 542.950	1 703.100	1 736.210	0.939	1.085
Sao Tome and Principe: dobra Sao Tomé-et-Principe : dobra										
End of period										
Fin de période	280.021	375.540	516.700	1 185.310	1 756.870	2 833.210	6 969.730	6 885.000	7 300.000	8 610.650
Period average										
Moyenne sur période	201.816	321.337	429.854	732.628	1 420.340	2 203.160	4 552.510	6 883.240	7 118.960	7 978.170
Saudi Arabia: Saudi Arabian riyal Arabie saoudite : riyal saoudien										
End of period										
Fin de période	3.745	3.745	3.745	3.745	3.745	3.745	3.745	3.745	3.745	3.745
Senegal: CFA franc Sénégal : franc CFA										
End of period[4]										
Fin de période[4]	259.000	275.325	294.775	534.600	490.000	523.700	598.810	562.210	652.953	704.951
Period average[4]										
Moyenne sur période[4]	282.107	264.692	283.163	555.205	499.148	511.552	583.669	589.952	615.699	711.976
Seychelles: Seychelles rupee Seychelles : roupie seychelloises										
End of period										
Fin de période	5.063	5.255	5.258	4.970	4.864	4.995	5.125	5.452	5.368	6.269
Period average										
Moyenne sur période	5.289	5.122	5.182	5.056	4.762	4.970	5.026	5.262	5.343	5.714
Sierra Leone: leone Sierra Leone : leone										
End of period										
Fin de période	434.783	526.316	577.634	613.008	943.396	909.091	1 333.330	1 590.760	2 276.050	1 666.670
Period average										
Moyenne sur période	295.344	499.442	567.459	586.740	755.216	920.732	981.482	1 563.620	1 804.190	2 092.120
Singapore: Singapore dollar Singapour : dollar singapourien										
End of period										
Fin de période	1.631	1.645	1.608	1.461	1.414	1.400	1.676	1.661	1.666	1.732
Period average										
Moyenne sur période	1.728	1.629	1.616	1.527	1.417	1.410	1.485	1.674	1.695	1.724

77

Exchange rates
National currency per US dollar [*cont.*]
Cours des changes
Valeur du dollar des Etats-Unis en monnaie nationale [*suite*]

Country (monetary unit) Pays (unité monétaire)	1991	1992	1993	1994	1995	1996	1997	1998	1999	2000
Slovakia: Slovak koruna Slovaquie : couronne slovaque										
End of period										
Fin de période	...	...	33.202	31.277	29.569	31.895	34.782	36.913	42.266	47.389
Period average [1]										
Moyenne sur période [1]	...	...	30.770	32.045	29.713	30.654	33.616	35.233	41.363	46.035
Slovenia: tolar Slovénie : tolar										
End of period										
Fin de période	56.693	98.701	131.842	126.458	125.990	141.480	169.180	161.200	196.770	227.377
Period average										
Moyenne sur période	27.571	81.287	113.242	128.809	118.518	135.364	159.688	166.134	181.769	222.656
Solomon Islands: Solomon Islands dollar Iles Salomon : dollar des Iles Salomon										
End of period										
Fin de période	2.795	3.100	3.248	3.329	3.476	3.622	4.748	4.859	5.076	5.099
Period average										
Moyenne sur période	2.715	2.928	3.188	3.291	3.406	3.566	3.717	4.816	4.838	5.089
South Africa: rand Afrique du Sud : rand										
End of period [1]										
Fin de période [1]	2.743	3.053	3.398	3.544	3.648	4.683	4.868	5.860	6.155	7.569
Period average [1]										
Moyenne sur période [1]	2.761	2.852	3.268	3.551	3.627	4.299	4.608	5.528	6.110	6.940
Spain: peseta, euro Espagne : peseta, euro										
End of period [3]										
Fin de période [3]	96.688	114.623	142.214	131.739	121.409	131.275	151.702	142.607	0.995	1.075
Period average [3]										
Moyenne sur période [3]	103.912	102.379	127.260	133.958	124.689	126.662	146.414	149.395	0.939	1.085
Sri Lanka: Sri Lanka rupee Sri Lanka : roupie sri-lankaise										
End of period										
Fin de période	42.580	46.000	49.562	49.980	54.048	56.705	61.285	68.297	72.170	82.580
Period average										
Moyenne sur période	41.372	43.830	48.322	49.415	51.252	55.271	58.995	64.450	70.635	77.005
Sudan: Sudanese pound Soudan : livre soudanaise										
End of period [1]										
Fin de période [1]	1.499	13.514	21.739	40.000	52.632	144.928	172.200	237.800	257.700	257.350
Period average [1]										
Moyenne sur période [1]	0.696	9.743	15.931	28.961	58.087	125.079	157.574	200.802	252.550	257.122
Suriname: Suriname guilder Suriname : florin surinamais										
End of period										
Fin de période	1.785	1.785	1.785	# 409.500	407.000	401.000	401.000	401.000	987.500	2 178.500
Period average										
Moyenne sur période	1.785	1.785	1.785	# 134.117	442.228	401.258	401.000	401.000	859.437	1 322.470
Swaziland: lilangeni Swaziland : lilangeni										
End of period										
Fin de période	2.743	3.053	3.398	3.544	3.648	4.683	4.868	5.860	6.155	7.569
Period average										
Moyenne sur période	2.761	2.852	3.268	3.551	3.627	4.299	4.608	5.528	6.110	6.940
Sweden: Swedish krona Suède : couronne suédoise										
End of period										
Fin de période	5.530	7.043	8.304	7.462	6.658	6.871	7.877	8.061	8.525	9.535
Period average										
Moyenne sur période	6.048	5.824	7.783	7.716	7.133	6.706	7.635	7.950	8.262	9.162
Switzerland: Swiss franc Suisse : franc suisse										
End of period										
Fin de période	1.356	1.456	1.480	1.312	1.151	1.346	1.455	1.377	1.600	1.637
Period average										
Moyenne sur période	1.434	1.406	1.478	1.368	1.183	1.236	1.451	1.450	1.502	1.689

77
Exchange rates
National currency per US dollar [*cont.*]
Cours des changes
Valeur du dollar des Etats-Unis en monnaie nationale [*suite*]

Country (monetary unit) Pays (unité monétaire)	1991	1992	1993	1994	1995	1996	1997	1998	1999	2000
Syrian Arab Republic: Syrian pound Rép. arabe syrienne : livre syrienne										
End of period[1]										
Fin de période[1]	11.225	11.225	11.225	11.225	11.225	11.225	11.225	11.225	11.225	11.225
Tajikistan: somoni Tadjikistan : somoni										
End of period										
Fin de période	...	0.005	0.014	0.039	0.294	0.328	0.747	0.978	1.436	2.200
Period average										
Moyenne sur période	...	0.003	0.010	0.025	0.123	0.296	0.562	0.777	1.238	2.076
Thailand: baht Thaïlande : baht										
End of period										
Fin de période	25.280	25.520	25.540	25.090	25.190	25.610	# 47.247	36.691	37.470	42.268
Period average										
Moyenne sur période	25.517	25.400	25.320	25.150	24.915	25.343	31.364	41.359	37.814	40.112
TFYR of Macedonia: TFYR Macedonian denar L'ex-R.y. Macédoine : denar de l'ex-R.Y. Macédoine										
End of period										
Fin de période	...	...	44.456	40.596	37.980	41.411	55.421	51.836	60.339	66.328
Period average										
Moyenne sur période	...	...	...	43.263	37.882	39.981	50.004	54.462	56.902	65.904
Togo: CFA franc Togo : franc CFA										
End of période[4]										
Fin de période[4]	259.000	275.325	294.775	534.600	490.000	523.700	598.810	562.210	652.953	704.951
Period average[4]										
Moyenne sur période[4]	282.107	264.692	283.163	555.205	499.148	511.552	583.669	589.952	615.699	711.976
Tonga: pa'anga Tonga : pa'anga										
End of period										
Fin de période	1.327	1.385	1.375	1.254	1.266	1.209	1.357	1.610	1.608	1.977
Period average										
Moyenne sur période	1.296	1.347	1.384	1.320	1.271	1.232	1.264	1.492	1.599	1.759
Trinidad and Tobago: Trinidad and Tobago dollar Trinité-et-Tobago : dollar de la Trinité-et-Tobago										
End of period										
Fin de période	4.250	4.250	5.814	5.933	5.997	6.195	6.300	6.597	6.300	6.300
Period average										
Moyenne sur période	4.250	4.250	5.351	5.925	5.948	6.005	6.252	6.298	6.299	6.300
Tunisia: Tunisian dinar Tunisie : dinar tunisien										
End of period										
Fin de période	0.865	0.951	1.047	0.991	0.951	0.999	1.148	1.101	1.253	1.385
Period average										
Moyenne sur période	0.925	0.884	1.004	1.012	0.946	0.973	1.106	1.139	1.186	1.371
Turkey: Turkish lira Turquie : livre turque										
End of period										
Fin de période	5 079.920	8 564.430	14 472.500	38 726.000	59 650.000	107 775.000	205 605.000	314 464.000	541 400.000	673 385.000
Period average										
Moyenne sur période	4 171.820	6 872.420	10 984.600	29 608.700	45 845.100	81 404.900	151 865.000	260 724.000	418 783.000	625 218.000
Turkmenistan: Turkmen manat Turkménistan : manat turkmene										
End of period										
Fin de période	...	...	1.990	75.000	200.000	4 070.000	4 165.000	5 200.000	5 200.000	...
Period average										
Moyenne sur période	...	...	...	19.198	110.917	3 257.670	4 143.420	4 890.170	5 200.000	...
Uganda: Uganda shilling Ouganda : shilling ougandais										
End of period[1]										
Fin de période[1]	915.000	1 217.150	1 130.150	926.770	1 009.450	1 029.590	1 140.110	1 362.690	1 506.040	1 766.680
Period average[1]										
Moyenne sur période[1]	734.010	1 133.830	1 195.020	979.445	968.917	1 046.080	1 083.010	1 240.310	1 454.830	1 644.480

77
Exchange rates
National currency per US dollar [*cont.*]
Cours des changes
Valeur du dollar des Etats-Unis en monnaie nationale [*suite*]

Country (monetary unit) Pays (unité monétaire)	1991	1992	1993	1994	1995	1996	1997	1998	1999	2000
Ukraine: hryvnia Ukraine : hryvnia										
End of period										
Fin de période	...	0.006	0.126	1.042	1.794	# 1.889	1.899	3.427	5.216	5.435
Period average										
Moyenne sur période	...	...	0.045	0.328	1.473	1.830	1.862	2.450	4.130	5.440
United Arab Emirates: UAE dirham Emirats arabes unis : dirham des EAU										
End of period										
Fin de période	3.671	3.671	3.671	3.671	3.671	3.671	3.673	3.673	3.673	3.673
United Kingdom: pound sterling Royaume-Uni : livre sterling										
End of period										
Fin de période	0.535	0.661	0.675	0.640	0.645	0.589	0.605	0.601	0.619	0.670
Period average										
Moyenne sur période	0.567	0.570	0.667	0.653	0.634	0.641	0.611	0.604	0.618	0.661
United Rep. of Tanzania: Tanzania shilling Rép.-Unie de Tanzanie : shilling tanzanien										
End of period										
Fin de période	233.900	335.000	479.871	523.453	550.360	595.640	624.570	681.000	797.330	803.260
Period average										
Moyenne sur période	219.157	297.708	405.274	509.631	574.762	579.977	612.122	664.671	744.759	800.409
United States: US dollar Etats-Unis : dollar des Etats-Unis										
End of period										
Fin de période	1.000	1.000	1.000	1.000	1.000	1.000	1.000	1.000	1.000	1.000
Uruguay: Uruguayan peso Uruguay : peso uruguayen										
End of period										
Fin de période	2.488	3.480	# 4.416	5.601	7.111	8.713	10.040	10.817	11.615	12.515
Period average										
Moyenne sur période	2.018	3.025	# 3.941	5.044	6.349	7.972	9.442	10.472	11.339	12.100
Uzbekistan: Uzbek sum Ouzbékistan : sum ouzbek										
Period average										
Moyenne sur période	...	...	...	...	29.775	40.067	62.917	94.492	124.625	236.608
Vanuatu: vatu Vanuatu : vatu										
End of period										
Fin de période	110.790	119.000	120.800	112.080	113.740	110.770	124.310	129.780	128.890	142.810
Period average										
Moyenne sur période	111.675	113.392	121.581	116.405	112.112	111.719	115.873	127.517	129.075	137.643
Venezuela: bolívar Venezuela : bolívar										
End of period										
Fin de période	61.554	79.450	105.640	# 170.000	290.000	476.500	504.250	564.500	648.250	699.750
Period average										
Moyenne sur période	56.816	68.376	90.826	148.503	# 176.842	417.332	488.635	547.556	605.717	679.960
Viet Nam: dong Viet Nam : dong										
End of period										
Fin de période	11 500.000	10 565.000	10 842.500	11 051.000	11 015.000	11 149.000	12 292.000	13 890.000	14 028.000	14 514.000
Period average										
Moyenne sur période	10 037.000	11 202.200	10 641.000	10 965.700	11 038.200	11 032.600	11 683.300	13 268.000	13 943.200	14 167.700
Yemen: Yemeni rial Yémen : rial yéménite										
End of period										
Fin de période	12.010	12.010	12.010	12.010	# 50.040	# 126.910	130.460	141.650	159.100	165.590
Period average										
Moyenne sur période	12.010	12.010	12.010	12.010	# 40.839	# 94.160	129.281	135.882	155.718	161.718
Zambia: Zambia kwacha Zambie : kwacha zambie										
End of period										
Fin de période	88.968	359.712	500.000	680.272	956.130	1 282.690	1 414.840	2 298.920	2 632.190	4 157.830
Period average										
Moyenne sur période	64.640	172.214	452.763	669.371	864.119	1 207.900	1 314.500	1 862.070	2 388.020	3 110.840

77
Exchange rates
National currency per US dollar [*cont.*]
Cours des changes
Valeur du dollar des Etats-Unis en monnaie nationale [*suite*]

Country (monetary unit) Pays (unité monétaire)	1991	1992	1993	1994	1995	1996	1997	1998	1999	2000
Zimbabwe: Zimbabwe dollar	**Zimbabwe : dollar zimbabwéen**									
End of period										
Fin de période	5.051	5.483	6.935	8.387	9.311	10.839	18.608	37.369	38.139	55.066
Period average										
Moyenne sur période	3.621	5.099	6.483	8.152	8.665	10.002	12.111	23.679	38.301	44.418

Source:
International Monetary Fund (IMF), Washington, D.C.,
"International Financial Statistics," November 2001 and the
IMF database.

† For information on recent changes in country or
area nomenclature pertaining to former Czechoslovakia,
Germany, Hong Kong Special Administrative Region (SAR) of
China, Macao Special Administrative Region (SAR) of China,
SFR of Yugoslavia and the former USSR, see Annex I - Country
or area nomenclature, regional and other groupings.

†† For statistical purposes, the data for
China do not include those for Hong Kong Special
Administrative Region (Hong Kong SAR), Macao Special
Administrative Region (Macao SAR) and Taiwan province of
China.

1 Principal rate.
2 Peso per million US dollars through 1983, per thousand US
dollars through 1988 and per US dollar thereafter.

3 Beginning 1999, Euros per US dollar.
4 Prior to January 1999, the official rate was pegged to the
French franc. On January 12, 1994, the CFA franc was
devalued to CFAF 100 per French franc from CFAF 50 at which
it had been fixed since 1948. From January 1, 1999, the
CFAF is pegged to the euro at a rate of CFA franc 655.957
per euro.

5 Bolivianos per million US dollars through 1983, per thousand
US dollars for 1984, and per US dollar thereafter.

6 Reals per trillion US dollars through 1983, per billion US
dollars 1984-1988, per million US dollars 1989-1992, and per
US dollar thereafter.

7 The official rate is pegged to the French franc. Beginning
January 12, 1994, the CFA franc was devalued to CFAF 75 per
French franc from CFAF 50 at which it had been fixed since
1948.
8 Congo francs per billion US dollars through 1990; per
million US dollars for 1991 - 1993; per thousand US dollars
for 1994-1997; and per US dollar thereafter.

9 "Euro Area" is an official descriptor for the European
Economic and Monetary Union (EMU). The participating member
states of the EMU are Austria, Belgium, Finland, France,
Germany, Ireland, Italy, Luxembourg, Netherlands, Portugal,
and Spain.

Source:
Fonds monétaire international (FMI), Washington,
D.C.,"Statistiques Financières Internationales," novembre
2001 et la base de données de FMI.

† Pour les modifications récentes de nomenclature
de pays ou de zone concernant l'Allemagne, Hong Kong, région
administrative spéciale (RAS) de Chine, Macao, région
administrative spéciale (RAS) de Chine,
l'ex-Tchécoslovaquie, l'ex-URSS et l'ex-Rfs de Yougoslavie,
voir annexe I - Nomenclature des pays ou des zones,
groupements régionaux et autres groupements.

†† Les données statistiques relatives à
la Chine ne comprennent pas celles qui concernent la région
administrative spéciale de Hong Kong (la RAS de Hong Kong),
la région administrative spéciale de Macao (la RAS de Macao)
et la province chinoise de Taiwan.

1 Taux principal.
2 Peso par million de dollars des États-Unis jusqu'en 1983,
par millier de dollars des États-Unis jusqu'en 1988 et par
dollar des États-Unis après cette date.
3 A partir de 1999, euros pour un dollar des États-Unis.
4 Avant janvier 1999, le taux officiel était établi par
référence au franc français. Le 12 janvier 1994, le franc
CFA a été dévalué; son taux par rapport au franc français,
auquel il est rattaché depuis 1948, est passé de 50 à 100
francs CFA pour 1 franc français. A compter du 1er janvier
1999, le taux officiel est établi par référence à l'euro à
un taux de 655 957 francs CFA pour un euro.

5 Bolivianos par million de dollars des États-Unis jusqu'en
1983, par millier de dollars des États-Unis en 1984, et par
dollar des États-Unis après cette date.
6 Reals par trillion de dollars des États-Unis jusqu'en 1983,
par millard de dollars des États-Unis 1984-1988, par million
de dollars des États-Unis 1989-1992, et par dollar des
États-Unis après cette date.

7 Le taux de change officiel est raccroché au taux de change
du franc français. Le 12 janvier 1994, le franc CFA a été
dévalué de 50 par franc français, valuer qu'il avait
conservée depuis 1948, à 75 par franc français.
8 Francs congolais par milliard de dollars des États-Unis
jusqu'en 1990; par million de dollars des États-Unis en 1991
- 1993; par millier de dollars des États-Unis en 1994 à
1997; et par dollar des États-Unis après cette date.
9 L'expression "zone euro" est un intitulé officiel pour
l'Union économique et monétaire (UEM) européenne. L'UEM est
composée des pays membres suivants : Allemagne, Autriche,
Belgique, Espagne, Finlande, France, Irlande, Italie,
Luxembourg, Pays-Bas et Portugal.

77
Exchange rates
National currency per US dollar [*cont.*]

Cours des changes
Valeur du dollar des Etats-Unis en monnaie nationale [*suite*]

10 Prior to January 1999, the official rate was pegged to the French franc at CFAF 100 per French franc. The CFA franc was adopted as national currency as of May 2, 1997. The Guinean peso and the CFA franc were set at PG65 per CFA franc. From January 1, 1999, the CFAF is pegged to the euro at a rate of CFA franc 655.957 per euro.

11 Gold córdoba per billion US dollars through 1987, per million US dollars for 1988, per thousand US dollars for 1989-1990 and per US dollar thereafter.

12 New soles per billion US dollars through 1987, per million US dollars for 1988-1989, and per US dollar thereafter.

13 Zlotys per thousand US dollars through 1989, and per US dollar thereafter.

14 The post-January 1, 1998 ruble is equal to 1,000 of the pre-January 1,1998 rubles.

10 Avant janvier 1999, le taux de change officiel était raccroché au taux de change du franc français à CFA 100 pour franc français. Le franc CFA été adopté comme monnaie nationale au 2 mai 1997. Le peso guinéen et le franc CFA a été établi à 65 pesos guinéen pour 1 franc CFA. A compter du 1er janvier 1999, le taux officiel est établi par référence à l'euro à un taux de 655 957 francs CFA pour un euro.

11 Cordobas or par milliard de dollars des États-Unis jusqu'en 1987, par million de dollars en 1988, par millier de dollars des États-Unis en 1989-1990 et par dollar des États-Unis après cette date.

12 Nouveaux soles par milliard de dollars des États-Unis jusqu'en 1987, par million de dollars des États-Unis en 1988-1989 et par dollar des États-Unis après cette date.

13 Zlotys par millier de dollars des États-Unis jusqu'en 1989, et par dollar des États-Unis après cette date.

14 Le rouble ayant cours après le 1er janvier 1998 vaut 1 000 roubles de la période antérieure à cette date.

78
Total external and public/publicly guaranteed long-term debt of developing countries
Total de la dette extérieure et dette publique extérieure à long terme garantie par l'Etat des pays en développement

Million US dollars
Millions de dollars E.-U.

A. Total external debt [1] • Total de la dette extérieure [1]

	1992	1993	1994	1995	1996	1997	1998	1999	
Total long-term debt (LDOD)	1284842	1404912	1564113	1668287	1722738	1798034	2063206	2077863	**Total de la dette à long terme (LDOD)**
Public and publicly guaranteed	1184355	1276918	1375278	1432698	1424307	1411209	1535453	1542386	**Dette publique ou garantie par l'Etat**
Official creditors	676631	760199	831353	863504	831681	794828	856573	877329	Créanciers publics
Multilateral	231211	248473	274479	290207	286250	289765	328221	344869	Multilatéraux
IBRD	97945	102691	110108	113869	107160	106036	115925	118960	BIRD
IDA	53607	58303	66505	71630	75218	77474	84159	86672	IDA
Bilateral	445421	511726	556874	573297	545432	505065	528353	532460	Bilatéraux
Private creditors	507724	516719	543925	569194	592625	616381	678879	665058	Créanciers privés
Bonds	127554	160999	234708	257369	293479	308145	345811	364962	Obligations
Commercial banks	240094	217175	168465	173594	173032	205924	236764	218777	Banques commerciales
Other private	140076	138545	140751	138231	126115	102312	96305	81317	Autres institutions privées
Private non-guaranteed	100487	127995	188836	235588	298432	386825	527753	535479	**Dette privée non garantie**
Undisbursed debt	241447	250767	255292	257108	243779	232085	253879	288889	**Dette (montants non versés)**
Official creditors	184270	190448	200762	205022	190883	182974	204061	248619	Créanciers publics
Private creditors	57176	60319	54529	52087	52896	49110	49817	40271	Créanciers privés
Commitments	136336	140284	120638	153593	172395	183780	192773	145131	**Engagements**
Official creditors	67909	62798	61913	80305	60989	70965	86189	68521	Créanciers publics
Private creditors	68427	77487	58725	73288	111407	112815	106584	76610	Créanciers privés
Disbursements	154152	175603	176719	212746	265801	301643	300116	255600	**Versements**
Public and publicly guaranteed	117417	126633	116036	144249	165070	177648	176969	151606	**Dette publique ou garantie par l'Etat**
Official creditors	52096	53989	50112	66216	56651	65562	68766	61822	Créanciers publics
Multilateral	27761	31495	29435	32298	33842	40986	46454	38525	Multilatéraux
IBRD	10429	13143	11580	13237	13358	17660	17561	15144	BIRD
IDA	5143	4860	6065	5474	6313	5934	5560	5396	IDA
Bilateral	24335	22494	20678	33917	22809	24576	22312	23297	Bilatéraux
Private creditors	65320	72643	65924	78033	108419	112087	108203	89784	Créanciers privés
Bonds	10722	26012	24143	29902	58726	61047	57431	50416	Obligations
Commercial banks	21796	17833	17638	26663	29582	32091	36529	25837	Banques commerciales
Other private	32752	28799	24143	21468	20111	18949	14243	13530	Autres institutions privées
Private non-guaranteed	36736	48971	60682	68497	100731	123995	123147	103994	**Dette privée non garantie**
Principal repayments	92689	101444	112754	128432	163696	190247	185650	239405	**Remboursements du principal**
Public and publicly guaranteed	77813	75196	83428	97349	120050	127987	109812	134101	**Dette publique ou garantie par l'Etat**
Official creditors	28235	29028	36612	44921	53217	51164	42244	44978	Créanciers publics
Multilateral	15634	16455	19198	21343	21013	19820	18750	19665	Multilatéraux
IBRD	10314	10384	11887	12134	11998	10934	10728	10055	BIRD
IDA	345	398	458	546	593	650	745	887	IDA
Bilateral	12601	12573	17413	23580	32204	31344	23494	25313	Bilatéraux
Private creditors	49578	46168	46816	52428	66834	76823	67568	89123	Créanciers privés
Bonds	8571	8943	7167	12887	21801	35199	24234	26704	Obligations
Commercial banks	18870	17605	19140	19768	27347	25424	26076	47321	Banques commerciales
Other private	22137	19621	20509	19773	17685	16200	17257	15098	Autres institutions privées
Private non-guaranteed	14876	26248	29326	31083	43646	62259	75838	105305	**Dette privée non garantie**

78
Total external and public/publicly guaranteed long-term debt of developing countries
Million US dollars [cont.]
Total de la dette extérieure et dette publique extérieure à long terme garantie par l'Etat des pays en développement
Millions de dollars E.-U. [suite]

A. Total external debt [1] · Total de la dette extérieure [1]

	1992	1993	1994	1995	1996	1997	1998	1999	
Net flows	**61463**	**74159**	**63965**	**84314**	**102105**	**111397**	**114466**	**16195**	**Apports nets**
Public and publicly									Dette publique ou
guaranteed	39603	51438	32609	46900	45020	49661	67157	17506	garantie par l'Etat
Official creditors	23861	24962	13501	21295	3436	14398	26521	16844	Créanciers publics
Multilateral	12127	15041	10236	10957	12830	21165	27703	18861	Multilatéraux
IBRD	115	2759	−306	1104	1360	6727	6833	5089	BIRD
IDA	4798	4462	5607	4928	5721	5284	4815	4508	IDA
Bilateral	11735	9921	3264	10339	−9394	−6768	−1182	−2017	Bilatéraux
Private creditors	15742	26475	19108	25605	41585	35264	40635	662	Créanciers privés
Bonds	2201	17069	16976	17015	36924	25848	33197	23712	Obligations
Commercial banks	2926	228	−1502	6896	2235	6666	10453	−21483	Banques commerciales
Other private	10615	9177	3634	1694	2426	2749	−3014	−1568	Autres institutions privées
Private non−guaranteed	**21860**	**22722**	**31356**	**37413**	**57085**	**61736**	**47309**	**−1311**	**Dette privée non garantie**
Interest payments (LINT)	**53891**	**52270**	**60719**	**77194**	**80591**	**87156**	**94976**	**100319**	**Paiements d'intérêts (LINT)**
Public and publicly									Dette publique ou
guaranteed	47884	45327	51240	63955	64595	65358	67296	71574	garantie par l'Etat
Official creditors	22328	23742	25571	30446	30494	28221	27841	29546	Créanciers publics
Multilateral	12375	12949	13587	13969	13754	12855	13653	16182	Multilatéraux
IBRD	7781	8004	8002	8139	7807	6894	7030	7880	BIRD
IDA	371	395	432	504	513	532	554	600	IDA
Bilateral	9952	10792	11984	16477	16740	15365	14189	13365	Bilatéraux
Private creditors	25556	21585	25668	33508	34099	37137	39456	42027	Créanciers privés
Bonds	7584	8524	11168	16901	16792	19666	21310	24958	Obligations
Commercial banks	11805	7641	7678	9345	10621	11458	12779	12341	Banques commerciales
Other private	6167	5420	6821	7261	6687	6013	5366	4728	Autres institutions privées
Private non−guaranteed	**6006**	**6943**	**9480**	**13239**	**15996**	**21798**	**27680**	**28746**	**Dette privée non garantie**
Net transfers	**7573**	**21888**	**3246**	**7120**	**21515**	**24241**	**19489**	**−84124**	**Transferts nets**
Public and publicly									Dette publique ou
guaranteed	−8281	6109	−18631	−17054	−19573	−15697	−140	−54068	garantie par l'Etat
Official creditors	1534	1220	−12071	−9151	−27058	−13824	−1320	−12703	Créanciers publics
Multilateral	−249	2092	−3351	−3012	−924	8310	14051	2679	Multilatéraux
IBRD	−7667	−5246	−8309	−7036	−6448	−167	−196	−2791	BIRD
IDA	4426	4067	5175	4425	5209	4753	4261	3908	IDA
Bilateral	1783	−871	−8719	−6139	−26134	−22134	−15371	−15382	Bilatéraux
Private creditors	−9814	4890	−6561	−7903	7484	−1873	1180	−41366	Créanciers privés
Bonds	−5382	8545	5807	114	20132	6183	11887	−1246	Obligations
Commercial banks	−8879	−7414	−9180	−2451	−8386	−4791	−2327	−33824	Banques commerciales
Other private	4447	3758	−3188	−5566	−4262	−3264	−8379	−6297	Autres institutions privées
Private non−guaranteed	**15853**	**15779**	**21876**	**24175**	**41089**	**39938**	**19629**	**−30056**	**Dette privée non garantie**
Total debt service (LTDS)	**146580**	**153714**	**173473**	**205626**	**244287**	**277403**	**280626**	**339724**	**Total du service de la dette (LTDS)**
Public and publicly									Dette publique ou
guaranteed	125697	120522	134667	161304	184645	193345	177108	205674	garantie par l'Etat
Official creditors	50562	52769	62182	75367	83710	79386	70086	74524	Créanciers publics
Multilateral	28010	29404	32786	35310	34767	32676	32403	35847	Multilatéraux
IBRD	18096	18389	19890	20273	19806	17826	17757	17935	BIRD
IDA	717	792	890	1050	1106	1181	1298	1487	IDA
Bilateral	22553	23366	29397	40056	48943	46710	37683	38679	Bilatéraux
Private creditors	75135	67753	72485	85937	100935	113960	107023	131150	Créanciers privés
Bonds	16155	17467	18336	29788	38594	54865	45544	51662	Obligations
Commercial banks	30675	25246	26818	29114	37968	36882	38856	59661	Banques commerciales
Other private	28305	25040	27331	27034	24373	22213	22623	19827	Autres institutions privées
Private non−guaranteed	**20882**	**33192**	**38806**	**44322**	**59642**	**84058**	**103518**	**134050**	**Dette privée non garantie**

78

Total external and public/publicly guaranteed long-term debt of developing countries
Million US dollars [*cont.*]

Total de la dette extérieure et dette publique extérieure à long terme garantie par l'Etat des pays en développement
Millions de dollars E.-U. [*suite*]

B. Public and publicly guaranteed long-term debt • Dette publique extérieure à long terme garantie par l'Etat

Country or area Pays ou zone	1990	1991	1992	1993	1994	1995	1996	1997	1998	1999
Albania Albanie	35.7	86.2	126.9	179.0	247.6	554.7	630.3	654.3	778.3	865.1
Algeria Algérie	26415.7	25969.0	25488.9	24847.1	28177.8	31042.4	31061.7	28709.8	28468.7	25913.3
Angola Angola	7605.1	7705.6	8139.6	8704.1	9001.2	9423.5	9256.5	8571.6	9513.3	9247.8
Argentina Argentine	48675.6	49374.1	49855.0	52545.8	63757.2	71316.4	81628.6	90554.6	105150.9	111887.3
Armenia Arménie	...	...	...	133.9	188.6	298.3	402.7	484.5	563.9	681.9
Azerbaijan Azerbaïdjan	...	...	...	35.5	103.2	206.1	247.9	235.9	385.5	599.8
Bangladesh Bangladesh	11987.0	12536.7	12962.5	13815.0	15391.6	15501.0	15327.2	14577.8	15804.1	16961.7
Barbados Barbade	504.1	482.8	400.6	348.8	374.0	372.1	383.7	367.6	387.8	359.1
Belarus Bélarus	...	...	...	866.1	1100.2	1274.8	720.1	674.5	766.0	864.5
Belize Belize	147.3	159.9	176.4	179.2	184.0	220.1	251.2	268.9	281.7	294.6
Benin Bénin	1218.5	1239.9	1324.1	1371.4	1487.3	1483.0	1448.4	1397.5	1471.4	1472.3
Bhutan Bhoutan	80.3	84.8	88.3	94.9	103.8	105.2	112.9	117.6	171.0	181.8
Bolivia Bolivie	3863.6	3671.5	3809.7	3879.2	4312.9	4697.5	4541.0	4555.3	4934.3	4507.5
Bosnia and Herzegovina Bosnie-Herzégovine	...	...	...	...	...	...	...	...	...	1828.5
Botswana Botswana	555.5	613.2	605.5	651.8	677.5	693.2	607.5	522.0	508.2	442.3
Brazil Brésil	94339.9	93372.8	103852.2	112903.4	119619.9	128431.0	145592.7	164091.3	209885.9	206325.9
Bulgaria Bulgarie	9809.1	9736.1	9629.7	9694.0	8371.7	9021.2	8525.6	8075.9	8266.4	8246.5
Burkina Faso Burkina Faso	749.6	882.6	978.9	1066.0	1039.9	1135.9	1159.5	1138.8	1233.8	1294.7
Burundi Burundi	851.0	901.2	947.0	998.0	1061.9	1095.1	1081.0	1022.1	1078.9	1049.6
Cambodia Cambodge	1688.0	1688.6	1679.8	1685.4	1745.2	1946.3	2012.5	2031.0	2101.7	2135.8
Cameroon Cameroun	5595.4	5784.7	6533.0	6511.6	7543.9	8356.7	8307.9	7960.5	8376.0	7968.5
Cape Verde Cap-Vert	130.6	130.3	136.1	140.8	166.4	185.0	196.0	200.1	237.3	265.1
Central African Rep. Rép. centrafricaine	624.1	716.9	729.6	773.2	802.4	853.9	850.4	801.5	845.8	830.1
Chad Tchad	463.9	559.6	671.1	713.4	758.5	833.4	914.2	938.5	1004.9	1045.0
Chile Chili	14687.3	14790.4	15180.8	16030.9	17999.2	18607.2	20414.4	21522.1	28565.2	32269.0
China †† Chine ††	45515.2	49479.2	58663.0	70631.7	82973.9	95764.3	103410.0	115233.0	126666.8	136540.8
Colombia Colombie	15783.8	15449.7	14726.1	15289.3	17448.1	19502.7	23015.8	26040.6	27031.6	30572.3
Comoros Comores	172.6	166.0	175.2	169.6	179.0	190.3	192.9	189.5	188.1	179.9
Congo Congo	4200.5	4041.3	3875.6	4114.2	4774.0	4955.4	4665.7	4283.8	4250.5	3932.2

78

Total external and public/publicly guaranteed long–term debt of developing countries
Million US dollars [*cont.*]
Total de la dette extérieure et dette publique extérieure à long terme garantie par l'Etat des pays en développement
Millions de dollars E.–U. [*suite*]

B. Public and publicly guaranteed long–term debt · Dette publique extérieure à long terme garantie par l'Etat

Country or area Pays ou zone	1990	1991	1992	1993	1994	1995	1996	1997	1998	1999
Costa Rica Costa Rica	3366.9	3595.8	3509.6	3410.8	3446.4	3347.6	3116.3	2938.4	3263.2	3402.0
Côte d'Ivoire Côte d'Ivoire	13223.1	13867.9	13859.6	13727.3	13852.3	14562.0	13215.6	12497.6	12632.2	11294.6
Croatia Croatie	...	...	...	1486.8	1685.4	3016.4	4291.6	6045.2	8276.3	8554.8
Czech Republic République tchèque	3983.4	4809.6	4550.3	6081.4	7791.9	11147.8	14470.1	15059.2	16391.6	15317.4
Dem. Rep. of the Congo Rép. dém. du Congo	9010.1	9285.0	8960.7	8780.9	9293.9	9635.8	9275.2	8628.3	9198.6	8187.5
Djibouti Djibouti	155.2	204.7	219.3	230.9	254.9	268.9	279.3	253.0	263.8	252.7
Dominica Dominique	80.2	87.8	88.6	92.4	88.7	94.1	97.8	90.6	90.9	89.0
Dominican Republic Rép. dominicaine	3518.3	3839.5	3802.5	3842.1	3654.5	3672.0	3528.7	3468.4	3533.3	3665.1
Ecuador Equateur	10029.1	10093.5	9931.5	10215.5	10776.6	12507.7	12763.8	12716.2	12799.0	13258.8
Egypt Egypte	28372.4	29316.5	28347.8	28303.1	30189.8	30792.2	28937.3	26858.3	27704.9	26109.7
El Salvador El Salvador	1938.4	2079.4	2159.7	1924.1	2022.2	2084.4	2318.3	2441.7	2783.2	2960.9
Equatorial Guinea Guinée équatoriale	209.2	215.5	214.4	214.8	219.3	229.6	222.2	208.6	216.5	207.9
Eritrea Erythrée	...	...	...	...	29.1	36.7	44.3	75.5	146.1	253.8
Estonia Estonie	...	...	47.8	96.1	117.0	164.9	336.6	1237.8	1586.9	1612.5
Ethiopia Ethiopie	8478.6	8842.9	9003.2	9286.6	9570.8	9776.0	9484.5	9426.8	9617.5	5360.4
Fiji Fidji	400.7	349.0	308.2	283.4	268.2	236.3	199.7	171.1	172.3	145.4
Gabon Gabon	3150.2	3224.5	3048.8	2933.3	3694.4	3976.4	3971.6	3664.9	3832.8	3290.2
Gambia Gambie	308.4	322.5	346.2	350.2	368.1	386.5	412.8	402.0	433.5	425.4
Georgia Géorgie	...	...	79.3	558.8	924.1	1039.4	1106.3	1189.5	1316.2	1324.8
Ghana Ghana	2816.3	3152.6	3354.2	3674.8	4188.9	4666.1	5243.1	5322.2	5833.3	5907.1
Grenada Grenade	89.9	99.7	94.1	92.5	100.2	98.9	105.8	113.8	115.7	122.2
Guatemala Guatemala	2604.7	2610.6	2517.5	2676.4	2899.9	2965.6	2876.4	2974.7	3171.4	3290.3
Guinea Guinée	2252.8	2399.2	2450.2	2659.2	2886.4	2987.1	2980.6	3008.8	3126.4	3057.0
Guinea–Bissau Guinée–Bissau	630.4	676.4	692.3	712.5	761.6	797.7	856.2	838.4	878.3	831.7
Guyana Guyana	1781.3	1784.2	1697.1	1755.5	1811.0	1805.8	1394.2	1370.3	1394.9	1242.5
Haiti Haïti	796.6	666.7	684.0	694.0	680.9	797.1	870.5	920.3	991.3	1049.3
Honduras Honduras	3486.6	3170.6	3322.0	3739.5	4001.9	4095.6	4061.7	4181.5	4358.2	4669.7
Hungary Hongrie	17931.4	19194.5	18537.8	21127.4	24736.9	28002.7	23678.1	20979.0	23529.6	25499.3
India Inde	72550.0	74900.7	79125.7	85675.9	93906.7	87045.8	85431.2	88609.5	93022.3	90323.7
Indonesia Indonésie	58242.3	65067.4	69945.1	71184.9	88366.9	98432.0	96710.2	100337.8	121681.2	119818.9
Iran (Islamic Rep. of) Iran (Rép. islamique d')	1796.8	2064.5	1780.1	5898.7	15921.7	15429.6	11948.0	8469.2	9496.0	6739.0

78
Total external and public/publicly guaranteed long-term debt of developing countries
Million US dollars [*cont.*]
Total de la dette extérieure et dette publique extérieure à long terme garantie par l'Etat des pays en développement
Millions de dollars E.-U. [*suite*]

B. Public and publicly guaranteed long-term debt • Dette publique extérieure à long terme garantie par l'Etat

Country or area Pays ou zone	1990	1991	1992	1993	1994	1995	1996	1997	1998	1999
Jamaica Jamaïque	3970.4	3740.3	3591.4	3480.9	3516.0	3537.2	3257.2	3111.7	3283.2	3070.8
Jordan Jordanie	7042.7	7457.5	6922.2	6770.0	6883.4	7073.1	7136.0	6975.3	7387.7	7574.0
Kazakhstan Kazakhstan	...	...	25.7	1621.1	2268.2	2936.5	2149.4	3217.6	5010.7	4830.0
Kenya Kenya	5641.7	6252.0	5728.0	5845.6	6118.5	6404.9	6059.6	5549.5	5888.4	5604.0
Korea, Republic of Corée, République de	24168.4	28532.9	32236.0	35001.8	40802.3	39197.4	49221.1	72128.4	94062.0	88915.8
Kyrgyzstan Kirghizistan	...	...	3.7	229.8	354.2	470.3	986.8	1143.0	1334.2	1449.0
Lao People's Dem. Rep. Rép. dém. pop. lao	1757.5	1849.6	1886.7	1948.2	2022.0	2091.2	2185.8	2246.8	2373.1	2471.3
Latvia Lettonie	...	...	30.0	123.6	207.5	271.1	758.4	940.9	1327.5	1499.0
Lebanon Liban	357.6	336.2	300.5	368.0	778.2	1600.5	2343.4	3237.7	4764.6	6239.3
Lesotho Lesotho	377.7	425.7	464.7	500.6	571.8	630.7	627.9	624.7	660.7	661.8
Liberia Libéria	1115.9	1106.3	1081.2	1101.9	1137.0	1161.4	1110.0	1061.2	1092.2	1062.2
Lithuania Lituanie	...	...	27.4	205.2	277.3	458.6	828.2	1971.9	2131.1	2806.2
Madagascar Madagascar	3334.7	3518.8	3469.0	3316.2	3536.6	3705.7	3552.0	3875.0	4106.5	4022.7
Malawi Malawi	1384.9	1520.1	1568.0	1729.5	1900.4	2083.0	2095.6	2099.2	2309.9	2595.7
Malaysia Malaisie	13422.0	15005.5	16378.5	19197.2	24146.9	27068.5	28605.0	32289.2	36113.0	38389.5
Maldives Maldives	64.0	78.0	90.5	109.3	122.5	151.9	163.5	164.3	183.4	192.5
Mali Mali	2335.8	2461.4	2777.0	2784.9	2544.7	2738.7	2762.2	2691.8	2827.4	2797.8
Mauritania Mauritanie	1788.6	1819.0	1825.3	1903.4	1989.5	2080.8	2125.0	2039.8	2213.9	2137.7
Mauritius Maurice	909.7	988.9	942.5	899.8	1097.5	1414.9	1398.5	1975.6	1908.6	1891.4
Mexico Mexique	81808.7	85444.7	81830.1	90681.7	97010.5	113745.0	114378.5	111747.7	125076.6	138424.0
Mongolia Mongolie	...	...	272.2	338.5	400.5	464.9	481.0	532.6	631.7	816.3
Morocco Maroc	23301.3	20991.7	21234.1	20859.6	21788.0	22415.6	21526.0	19930.5	20374.9	18876.6
Mozambique Mozambique	4230.6	4353.5	4718.1	4858.6	6871.0	6977.7	7203.2	7128.9	7742.3	6371.5
Myanmar Myanmar	4466.1	4579.7	5003.0	5389.8	6153.8	5377.7	4803.5	4628.7	5014.7	5332.9
Nepal Népal	1571.8	1712.5	1757.6	1939.6	2209.9	2346.5	2345.7	2332.3	2590.6	2909.9
Nicaragua Nicaragua	8280.5	9153.4	9312.0	9303.5	9624.2	8541.2	5124.7	5335.8	5636.4	5904.9
Niger Niger	1487.2	1362.6	1371.0	1390.9	1425.4	1463.4	1439.2	1424.1	1524.0	1473.3
Nigeria Nigéria	31935.3	32668.3	26809.1	26741.9	28265.8	28441.3	25730.5	22926.2	23740.0	22672.6
Oman Oman	2400.2	2473.5	2340.3	2314.7	2610.1	2639.9	2648.5	2569.7	2230.7	1767.6
Pakistan Pakistan	16643.2	18161.6	19396.6	21478.9	23887.3	25380.9	25613.2	26307.1	28799.4	30735.6

78

Total external and public/publicly guaranteed long-term debt of developing countries
Million US dollars [*cont.*]
Total de la dette extérieure et dette publique extérieure à long terme garantie par l'Etat des pays en développement
Millions de dollars E.-U. [*suite*]

B. Public and publicly guaranteed long-term debt • Dette publique extérieure à long terme garantie par l'Etat

Country or area Pays ou zone	1990	1991	1992	1993	1994	1995	1996	1997	1998	1999
Panama Panama	3987.9	4011.9	3771.2	3799.3	3930.3	3913.5	5210.6	5418.2	5767.9	6245.1
Papua New Guinea Papouasie-Nvl-Guinée	2461.2	2595.5	3317.8	2960.4	2677.7	2379.0	2423.9	2389.9	2515.7	2575.9
Paraguay Paraguay	1732.1	1704.9	1385.4	1308.2	1376.5	1457.5	1423.9	1500.6	1620.5	1762.4
Peru Pérou	13959.3	15660.2	15807.9	16948.8	18853.6	20215.4	21702.3	22482.7	23872.1	25193.7
Philippines Philippines	25241.2	26420.7	26648.5	29691.3	32632.0	31822.6	31770.2	33032.6	39039.6	44454.1
Poland Pologne	39262.7	45001.4	43142.2	41837.0	40367.0	42085.5	40810.3	36589.0	49303.3	48324.7
Republic of Moldova République de Moldova	...	...	38.5	190.2	326.4	449.5	554.5	801.4	811.9	735.6
Romania Roumanie	229.9	334.0	1446.7	2315.9	3243.3	4324.9	7052.3	7887.0	8326.1	7968.3
Russian Federation Fédération de Russie	47539.6	55154.7	64551.3	101681.1	108264.5	101749.9	101993.8	108357.9	143396.2	142957.7
Rwanda Rwanda	664.5	747.1	789.9	837.6	905.3	970.1	984.5	993.5	1119.8	1161.7
Saint Kitts and Nevis Saint-Kitts-et-Nevis	44.2	48.6	47.4	49.7	55.2	54.1	62.6	111.9	124.3	131.7
Saint Lucia Sainte-Lucie	72.1	76.1	89.8	96.5	103.6	111.3	121.4	119.9	128.2	125.6
St. Vincent-Grenadines St. Vincent-Grenadines	58.9	65.6	74.4	78.4	92.3	92.2	91.2	90.1	105.4	159.8
Samoa Samoa	91.0	113.4	117.8	140.4	156.7	168.1	162.8	148.3	154.3	156.5
Sao Tome and Principe Sao Tomé-et-Principe	132.9	149.8	168.5	181.3	200.7	231.6	223.4	223.6	240.1	233.2
Senegal Sénégal	3000.1	2937.9	3042.2	3096.6	3096.5	3234.2	3154.9	3156.1	3281.1	3124.8
Seychelles Seychelles	117.2	125.5	130.5	132.1	147.8	145.8	138.1	131.3	145.0	132.2
Sierra Leone Sierra Leone	603.8	616.3	677.1	763.8	848.9	905.8	903.0	888.5	956.8	937.8
Slovakia Slovaquie	1505.2	1764.0	1710.0	2121.4	2893.6	3650.0	4580.5	6371.8	7395.6	7440.3
Solomon Islands Iles Salomon	103.2	98.4	92.5	144.4	152.9	147.8	143.6	133.2	146.4	155.4
Somalia Somalie	1925.9	1945.2	1897.8	1897.0	1934.8	1960.8	1918.2	1852.5	1886.4	1859.4
South Africa Afrique du Sud	...	...	...	...	13035.0	14771.7	14334.5	13878.5	13267.5	10377.6
Sri Lanka Sri Lanka	5048.4	5768.9	5737.1	6062.4	6718.6	7084.8	6887.5	6778.4	7728.7	8268.4
Sudan Soudan	9651.2	9716.1	9479.6	9489.8	9895.9	10275.4	9865.2	9494.2	9721.9	9348.0
Swaziland Swaziland	249.2	240.5	215.7	200.0	210.2	223.0	219.6	210.1	222.5	205.5
Syrian Arab Republic Rép. arabe syrienne	14902.1	16343.2	15909.8	16234.4	16540.1	16756.8	16697.7	16253.8	16328.3	16142.4
Tajikistan Tadjikistan	...	...	9.7	384.9	562.0	590.4	656.8	797.0	824.4	697.3
Thailand Thaïlande	19842.0	25280.1	27137.6	30083.0	36417.5	55997.7	65164.4	69466.1	72044.4	69485.7
TFYR of Macedonia L'ex-R.y. Macédoine	...	...	...	913.5	926.8	1077.7	1481.3	1008.3	1515.9	1263.6
Togo Togo	1074.8	1130.0	1121.9	1112.1	1217.7	1274.2	1294.4	1195.4	1301.8	1262.5
Tonga Tonga	44.5	44.2	42.6	43.7	57.6	62.8	62.5	56.3	60.8	63.5

78
Total external and public/publicly guaranteed long-term debt of developing countries
Million US dollars [*cont.*]
Total de la dette extérieure et dette publique extérieure à long terme garantie par l'Etat des pays en développement
Millions de dollars E.-U. [*suite*]

B. Public and publicly guaranteed long-term debt • Dette publique extérieure à long terme garantie par l'Etat

Country or area Pays ou zone	1990	1991	1992	1993	1994	1995	1996	1997	1998	1999
Trinidad and Tobago Trinité-et-Tobago	2054.7	1991.1	1988.4	1970.4	2089.9	2040.2	1954.2	1587.1	1621.4	1628.9
Tunisia Tunisie	6879.6	7323.6	7409.9	7620.0	8205.2	9216.7	9565.8	9517.3	9680.5	10258.9
Turkey Turquie	39924.2	41756.5	43893.9	50074.8	54601.4	57404.6	61634.2	66182.4	75606.8	77433.3
Turkmenistan Turkménistan	...	...	...	276.4	346.3	384.9	464.2	1242.4	1747.5	1692.5
Uganda Ouganda	2160.9	2283.3	2433.2	2599.2	2869.1	3062.4	3151.0	3404.3	3482.3	3564.2
Ukraine Ukraine	...	...	457.7	3694.1	4854.8	6664.1	6831.9	7641.8	9796.6	11014.7
United Rep. of Tanzania Rép.-Unie de Tanzanie	5793.2	5802.3	5861.6	5819.5	6139.8	6247.3	6126.8	6056.0	6464.6	6627.6
Uruguay Uruguay	3114.0	2925.8	3174.9	3436.0	3812.1	3960.5	4231.4	4809.1	5428.1	5496.2
Uzbekistan Ouzbékistan	...	...	59.7	939.5	952.8	1417.6	2035.4	2104.4	2871.8	3745.3
Vanuatu Vanuatu	30.6	38.1	39.6	39.4	41.5	43.2	42.2	38.9	54.2	63.4
Venezuela Venezuela	28158.6	28588.6	29627.5	30177.3	30478.3	30514.1	30282.6	29545.8	33373.3	32842.2
Viet Nam Viet Nam	21378.1	21360.5	21648.5	21599.0	21854.5	21777.3	21964.3	18985.5	19918.0	20528.7
Yemen Yémen	5160.4	5255.5	5253.4	5341.1	5459.5	5527.8	5621.8	3418.2	3606.4	3729.2
Yugoslavia Yougoslavie	16801.5	15871.5	15194.9	10990.1	11269.7	11483.6	11238.6	10923.7	11079.7	10174.7
Zambia Zambie	4553.5	4707.5	4527.7	4410.5	5187.7	5298.4	5378.7	5257.2	5348.3	4570.5
Zimbabwe Zimbabwe	2649.2	2876.9	3137.3	3403.4	3650.8	3860.5	3737.3	3556.4	3531.8	3450.6

Source:
World Bank, Washington, D.C., "Global Development
Finance 2000", volumes 1 and 2.

Source:
Banque mondiale, Washington, D.C., "Global Development
Finance 2000", volumes 1 et 2.

†† For statistical purposes, the data for China do not
include those for the Hong Kong Special Administrative
Region (Hong Kong SAR) and Taiwan province of China.

†† Les données statistiques relatives à la Chine ne comprennent pas
celles qui concernent la région administrative spéciale de
Hong Kong (la RAS de Hong Kong) et la province chinoise
de Taiwan.

1   The following abbreviations have been used in the table:
    LDOD: Long-term debt outstanding and disbursed
    IBRD: International Bank for Reconstruction and Development
    IDA: International Development Association
    LINT: Loan Interest
    LTDS: Long-term debt service

1 Les abbréviations ci-après ont été utilisées dans le tableau:
    LDOD: Dette à long terme
    BIRD: Banque internationale pour la réconstruction et le
    développement
    IDA: Association internationale de développement
    LINT: Paiement d'intérêts
    LTDS: Service de la dette à long terme

Technical notes, tables 77 and 78

Table 77: Foreign exchange rates are shown in units of national currency per US dollar. The exchange rates are classified into three broad categories, reflecting both the role of the authorities in the determination of the exchange and/or the multiplicity of exchange rates in a country. The *market rate* is used to describe exchange rates determined largely by market forces; the *official rate* is an exchange rate determined by the authorities, sometimes in a flexible manner. For countries maintaining multiple exchange arrangements, the rates are labeled *principal rate*, *secondary rate*, and *tertiary rate*. Unless otherwise stated, the table refers to end of period and period averages of market exchange rates or official exchange rates. For further information see *International Financial Statistics* [15].

Table 78: Data were extracted from *Global Development Finance 2000* [34], published by the World Bank.

Long term external debt is defined as debt that has an original or extended maturity of more than one year and is owed to non-residents and repayable in foreign currency, goods, or services. A distinction is made between:

— Public debt which is an external obligation of a public debtor, which could be a national government, a political sub-division, an agency of either of the above or, in fact, any autonomous public body;

— Publicly guaranteed debt, which is an external obligation of a private debtor that is guaranteed for repayment by a public entity;

— Private non-guaranteed external debt, which is an external obligation of a private debtor that is not guaranteed for repayment by a public entity.

The data referring to public and publicly guaranteed debt do not include data for (a) transactions with the International Monetary Fund, (b) debt repayable in local currency, (c) direct investment and (d) short-term debt (that is, debt with an original maturity of less than a year).

The data referring to private non-guaranteed debt also exclude the above items but include contractual obligations on loans to direct-investment enterprises by foreign parent companies or their affiliates.

Data are aggregated by type of creditor. The breakdown is as follows:

Official creditors:

(a) Loans from international organizations (multilateral loans), excluding loans from funds administered by an international organization on behalf of a single donor government. The latter are classified as loans from governments;

(b) Loans from governments (bilateral loans) and

Notes techniques, tableaux 77 et 78

Tableau 77: Les taux des changes sont exprimés par nombre d'unités de monnaie nationale pour un dollar des Etats-Unis. Les taux de change sont classés en trois catégories, qui dénotent le rôle des autorités dans l'établissement des taux de change et/ou la multiplicité des taux de change dans un pays. Par *taux du marché*, on entend les taux de change déterminés essentiellement par les forces du marché; le *taux officiel* est un taux de change établi par les autorités, parfois selon des dispositions souples. Pour les pays qui continuent de mettre en œuvre des régimes de taux de change multiples, les taux sont désignés par les appellations suivantes: "taux principal", "taux secondaire" et "taux tertiaire". Sauf indication contraire, le tableau indique des taux de fin de période et les moyennes sur la période, des taux de change du marché ou des taux de change officiels. Pour plus de renseignements, voir *Statistiques financières internationales* [15].

Tableau 78: Les données sont extraites de *Global Development Finance 2000* [34] publié par la Banque mondiale.

La dette extérieure à long terme désigne la dette dont l'échéance initiale ou reportée est de plus d'un an, due à des non résidents et remboursable en devises, biens ou services. On établit les distinctions suivantes:

— La dette publique, qui est une obligation extérieure d'un débiteur public, pouvant être un gouvernement, un organe politique, une institution de l'un ou l'autre ou, en fait, tout organisme public autonome.

— La dette garantie par l'Etat, qui est une obligation extérieure d'un débiteur privé, dont le remboursement est garanti par un organisme public.

— La dette extérieure privée non garantie, qui est une obligation extérieure d'un débiteur privé, dont le remboursement n'est pas garanti par un organisme public.

Les statistiques relatives à la dette publique ou à la dette garantie par l'Etat ne comprennent pas les données concernant: (a) les transactions avec le Fonds monétaire international; (b) la dette remboursable en monnaie nationale; (c) les investissements directs; et (d) la dette à court terme (c'est-à-dire la dette dont l'échéance initiale est inférieure à un an).

Les statistiques relatives à la dette privée non garantie ne comprennent pas non plus les éléments précités, mais comprennent les obligations contractuelles au titre des prêts consentis par des sociétés mères étrangères ou leurs filiales à des entreprises créées dans le cadre d'investissements directs.

Les données sont groupées par type de créancier, comme suit:

Créanciers publics:

(a) Les prêts obtenus auprès d'organisations internationales (prêts multilatéraux), à l'exclusion des prêts au

from autonomous public bodies;

Private creditors:

(a) Suppliers: Credits from manufacturers, exporters, or other suppliers of goods;

(b) Financial markets: Loans from private banks and other private financial institutions as well as publicly issued and privately placed bonds;

(c) Other: External liabilities on account of nationalized properties and unclassified debts to private creditors.

A distinction is made between the following categories of external public debt:

— Debt outstanding (including undisbursed) is the sum of disbursed and undisbursed debt and represents the total outstanding external obligations of the borrower at year-end;

— Debt outstanding (disbursed only) is total outstanding debt drawn by the borrower at year end;

— Commitments are the total of loans for which contracts are signed in the year specified;

— Disbursements are drawings on outstanding loan commitments during the year specified;

— Service payments are actual repayments of principal amortization and interest payments made in foreign currencies, goods or services in the year specified;

— Net flows (or net lending) are disbursements minus principal repayments;

— Net transfers are net flows minus interest payments or disbursements minus total debt-service payments.

The countries included in the table are those for which data are sufficiently reliable to provide a meaningful presentation of debt outstanding and future service payments.

titre de fonds administrés par une organisation internationale pour le compte d'un gouvernement donateur précis, qui sont classés comme prêts consentis par des gouvernements;

(b) Les prêts consentis par des gouvernements (prêts bilatéraux) et par des organisations publiques autonomes.

Créanciers privés:

(a) Fournisseurs: Crédits consentis par des fabricants exportateurs et autre fournisseurs de biens;

(b) Marchés financiers: prêts consentis par des banques privées et autres institutions financières privées, et émissions publiques d'obligations placées auprès d'investisseurs privés;

(c) Autres créanciers: engagements vis-à-vis de l'extérieur au titre des biens nationalisés et dettes diverses à l'égard de créanciers privés.

On fait une distinction entre les catégories suivantes de dette publique extérieure:

— L'encours de la dette (y compris les fonds non décaissés) est la somme des fonds décaissés et non décaissés et représente le total des obligations extérieures en cours de l'emprunteur à la fin de l'année;

— L'encours de la dette (fonds décaissés seulement) est le montant total des tirages effectués par l'emprunteur sur sa dette en cours à la fin de l'année;

— Les engagements représentent le total des prêts dont les contrats ont été signés au cours de l'année considérée;

— Les décaissements sont les sommes tirées sur l'encours des prêts pendant l'année considérée;

— Les paiements au titre du service de la dette sont les remboursements effectifs du principal et les paiements d'intérêts effectués en devises, biens ou services pendant l'année considérée;

— Les flux nets (ou prêts nets) sont les décaissements moins les remboursements de principal;

— Les transferts nets désignent les flux nets moins les paiements d'intérêts, ou les décaissements moins le total des paiements au titre du service de la dette.

Les pays figurant sur ce tableau sont ceux pour lesquels les données sont suffisamment fiables pour permettre une présentation significative de l'encours de la dette et des paiements futurs au titre du service de la dette.

79
Disbursements of bilateral and multilateral official development assistance and official aid to individual recipients
Versements d'aide publique au développement et d'aide publique bilatérales et multilatérales aux bénéficiares

Region, country or area Région, pays ou zone	Year Année	Net disbursements (US $) — Versements nets ($ E.—U.)			
		Bilateral Bilatérale (millions)	Multilateral [1] Multilatérale [1] (millions)	Total (millions)	Per capita [2] Par habitant [2]
Total	**1997**	**36475.5**	**16870.8**	**53346.3**	...
Total	**1998**	**39724.1**	**17086.1**	**56810.2**	...
	1999	**42519.5**	**16371.4**	**58890.9**	...
Africa	**1997**	**11383.0**	**6366.0**	**17749.0**	...
Afrique	**1998**	**11218.7**	**5846.4**	**17065.1**	...
	1999	**10291.2**	**4788.0**	**15079.2**	...
Algeria	1997	192.6	44.1	236.7	8.1
Algérie	1998	121.9	252.7	374.6	12.5
	1999	37.1	20.6	57.7	1.9
Angola	1997	227.0	127.7	354.7	30.3
Angola	1998	214.5	120.7	335.2	27.7
	1999	251.8	135.7	387.5	31.1
Benin	1997	148.0	72.8	220.8	39.2
Bénin	1998	143.9	68.0	211.9	36.7
	1999	119.3	93.1	212.4	35.8
Botswana	1997	55.8	69.2	125.0	81.1
Botswana	1998	73.1	35.9	109.0	69.4
	1999	41.1	20.6	61.7	38.6
Burkina Faso	1997	217.9	146.8	364.7	33.2
Burkina Faso	1998	226.6	167.4	394.0	34.9
	1999	232.0	156.7	388.7	33.5
Burundi	1997	38.2	18.3	56.5	8.9
Burundi	1998	44.4	32.8	77.2	12.0
	1999	52.0	22.2	74.2	11.3
Cameroon	1997	330.2	170.6	500.8	36.0
Cameroun	1998	303.0	123.2	426.2	29.8
	1999	254.3	183.3	437.6	29.8
Cape Verde	1997	68.0	43.3	111.3	279.0
Cap–Vert	1998	85.2	44.7	129.9	318.4
	1999	88.7	48.1	136.8	327.3
Central African Republic	1997	61.3	29.7	91.0	26.6
République centrafricaine	1998	56.5	63.4	119.9	34.4
	1999	59.1	58.1	117.2	33.0
Chad	1997	96.4	126.3	222.7	31.4
Tchad	1998	74.5	88.2	162.7	22.4
	1999	64.5	116.5	181.0	24.3
Comoros	1997	15.3	11.9	27.2	42.5
Comores	1998	18.6	16.6	35.2	53.5
	1999	13.2	8.3	21.5	31.8
Congo	1997	260.1	8.7	268.8	99.2
Congo	1998	59.7	5.2	64.9	23.3
	1999	121.4	18.9	140.3	49.0
Côte d'Ivoire	1997	233.0	212.8	445.8	31.7
Côte d'Ivoire	1998	489.5	309.0	798.5	55.9
	1999	365.6	80.2	445.8	30.7
Dem. Republic of the Congo	1997	104.6	44.4	149.0	3.1
République dém. du Congo	1998	79.7	43.5	123.2	2.5
	1999	87.0	45.3	132.3	2.6
Djibouti	1997	62.2	18.6	80.8	131.0
Djibouti	1998	62.3	16.9	79.2	127.1
	1999	55.4	18.7	74.1	117.8
Egypt	1997	1496.6	388.1	1884.7	29.1
Egypte	1998	1472.3	267.3	1739.6	26.4
	1999	1298.1	210.2	1508.2	22.4
Equatorial Guinea	1997	17.8	6.5	24.3	57.9
Guinée équatoriale	1998	18.3	6.5	24.8	57.5
	1999	14.6	5.6	20.2	45.7
Eritrea	1997	80.9	25.7	106.6	31.1
Erythrée	1998	97.7	38.1	135.8	38.0
	1999	80.5	49.6	130.1	35.0

79
Disbursements of bilateral and multilateral official development assistance
and official aid to individual recipients [*cont.*]
Versements d'aide publique au développement et d'aide publique
bilatérales et multilatérales aux bénéficiares [*suite*]

Region, country or area Région, pays ou zone	Year Année	Net disbursements (US $) — Versements nets ($ E.—U.)			
		Bilateral Bilatérale (millions)	Multilateral[1] Multilatérale[1] (millions)	Total (millions)	Per capita[2] Par habitant[2]
Ethiopia Ethiopie	1997 1998 1999	373.7 365.1 325.0	197.6 282.2 303.1	571.3 647.3 628.1	9.3 10.2 9.7
Gabon Gabon	1997 1998 1999	30.2 37.4 34.5	11.2 8.6 13.1	41.4 46.0 47.6	36.4 39.4 39.8
Gambia Gambie	1997 1998 1999	17.4 13.5 13.2	23.0 24.6 19.0	40.4 38.1 32.2	34.0 31.0 25.4
Ghana Ghana	1997 1998 1999	291.9 374.5 355.6	188.6 324.1 247.7	480.5 698.6 603.3	25.8 36.5 30.7
Guinea Guinée	1997 1998 1999	125.5 148.5 111.1	221.6 187.1 108.7	347.1 335.6 219.8	47.4 45.7 29.9
Guinea–Bissau Guinée–Bissau	1997 1998 1999	58.5 64.8 32.1	65.5 31.0 20.3	124.0 95.8 52.4	109.2 82.5 44.1
Kenya Kenya	1997 1998 1999	301.0 275.8 253.7	144.8 200.8 53.2	445.8 476.6 306.9	15.7 16.4 10.4
Lesotho Lesotho	1997 1998 1999	44.6 32.5 25.6	39.9 34.9 6.6	84.5 67.4 32.2	41.9 32.7 15.3
Liberia Libéria	1997 1998 1999	31.0 31.3 44.6	43.8 41.3 49.4	74.8 72.6 94.0	31.1 27.2 32.1
Libyan Arab Jamahiriya Jamahiriya arabe libyenne	1997 1998 1999	1.8 3.6 3.3	5.2 3.4 3.9	7.0 7.0 7.2	1.3 1.3 1.3
Madagascar Madagascar	1997 1998 1999	549.0 333.7 192.4	284.4 161.0 165.7	833.4 494.7 358.1	57.0 32.9 23.1
Malawi Malawi	1997 1998 1999	174.1 203.6 227.7	170.7 230.1 214.2	344.8 433.7 441.9	34.3 41.9 41.5
Mali Mali	1997 1998 1999	256.6 236.2 237.3	177.5 115.9 117.0	434.1 352.1 354.3	41.6 32.9 32.3
Mauritania Mauritanie	1997 1998 1999	96.5 63.5 88.7	154.2 115.1 124.8	250.7 178.6 213.5	101.9 70.6 82.2
Mauritius Maurice	1997 1998 1999	2.8 19.9 5.1	28.8 21.1 36.4	31.6 41.0 41.5	27.9 35.8 36.1
Mayotte Mayotte	1997 1998 1999	102.3 104.4 109.3	1.9 ... 2.5	104.2 104.4 111.8	... ...
Morocco Maroc	1997 1998 1999	215.4 250.7 333.5	217.0 249.1 315.9	432.4 499.8 649.4	16.1 18.3 23.3
Mozambique Mozambique	1997 1998 1999	621.6 712.6 593.2	326.7 329.2 −472.6	948.3 1041.8 120.6	51.4 55.2 6.3
Namibia Namibie	1997 1998 1999	122.9 128.7 117.2	41.6 51.5 60.4	164.5 180.2 177.6	101.4 108.6 104.8
Niger Niger	1997 1998 1999	181.2 144.6 120.2	141.2 145.9 66.3	322.4 290.5 186.5	33.0 28.8 9.6
Nigeria Nigéria	1997 1998 1999	52.2 34.3 52.9	148.6 169.8 96.3	200.8 204.1 149.2	1.9 1.9 1.4

79
Disbursements of bilateral and multilateral official development assistance
and official aid to individual recipients [*cont.*]
Versements d'aide publique au développement et d'aide publique
bilatérales et multilatérales aux bénéficiares [*suite*]

Region, country or area Région, pays ou zone	Year Année	Net disbursements (US $) – Versements nets ($ E.−U.)			
		Bilateral Bilatérale (millions)	Multilateral [1] Multilatérale [1] (millions)	Total (millions)	Per capita [2] Par habitant [2]
Rwanda Rwanda	1997	178.7	50.4	229.1	38.4
	1998	209.0	140.9	349.9	53.0
	1999	180.5	192.4	372.9	51.5
Saint Helena Sainte−Hélène	1997	14.8	0.3	15.1	2516.7
	1998	14.4	1.4	15.8	2633.3
	1999	13.5	0.3	13.8	2300.0
Sao Tome and Principe Sao Tomé−et−Principe	1997	21.2	12.2	33.4	242.0
	1998	18.1	10.1	28.2	200.0
	1999	19.1	8.4	27.5	191.0
Senegal Sénégal	1997	292.0	121.6	413.6	47.2
	1998	289.0	211.0	500.0	55.5
	1999	416.2	114.7	530.9	57.5
Seychelles Seychelles	1997	6.3	5.8	12.1	161.3
	1998	17.2	5.8	23.0	302.6
	1999	4.8	6.1	10.9	141.6
Sierra Leone Sierra Leone	1997	41.4	76.2	117.6	26.6
	1998	53.2	50.5	103.7	22.7
	1999	59.9	13.3	73.2	15.5
Somalia Somalie	1997	46.0	33.9	79.9	9.1
	1998	41.7	38.3	80.0	8.7
	1999	75.9	38.7	114.6	11.9
South Africa Afrique du Sud	1997	415.2	80.0	495.2	12.8
	1998	420.7	91.6	512.3	13.0
	1999	386.1	152.4	538.5	13.5
Sudan Soudan	1997	85.8	52.4	138.2	5.0
	1998	150.2	58.5	208.7	7.4
	1999	158.5	58.2	216.7	7.5
Swaziland Swaziland	1997	16.3	10.3	26.6	28.8
	1998	16.8	13.6	30.4	31.9
	1999	14.9	14.1	29.0	29.6
Togo Togo	1997	75.7	50.6	126.3	29.5
	1998	66.1	61.2	127.3	29.0
	1999	47.0	21.2	68.2	15.1
Tunisia Tunisie	1997	69.6	144.1	213.7	23.2
	1998	102.3	76.4	178.7	19.1
	1999	102.0	160.9	262.9	27.8
Uganda Ouganda	1997	438.8	371.2	810.0	40.5
	1998	383.9	87.3	471.2	22.9
	1999	357.5	231.9	589.4	27.9
United Republic of Tanzania Rép.−Unie de Tanzanie	1997	569.1	372.9	942.0	30.0
	1998	769.1	228.3	997.4	31.1
	1999	613.4	375.8	989.2	30.2
Zambia Zambie	1997	367.1	242.9	610.0	71.1
	1998	256.5	93.2	349.7	39.8
	1999	340.0	283.4	623.4	69.5
Zimbabwe Zimbabwe	1997	222.5	115.6	338.1	30.2
	1998	216.3	64.5	280.8	24.7
	1999	219.2	25.5	244.7	21.2
Other and unallocated Autres et non−ventilés	1997	1166.7	426.3	1593.0	...
	1998	973.1	187.3	1160.4	...
	1999	770.7	247.1	1017.8	...
Americas **Amériques**	**1997**	**3917.1**	**1505.7**	**5422.8**	...
	1998	**4015.5**	**1587.3**	**5602.8**	...
	1999	**4241.2**	**1723.7**	**5964.9**	...
Anguilla Anguilla	1997	1.8	0.8	2.6	325.0
	1998	3.2	−0.2	3.0	375.0
	1999	2.7	−0.3	2.4	300.0
Antigua and Barbuda Antigua−et−Barbuda	1997	1.0	−0.4	0.6	9.1
	1998	5.0	2.1	7.1	106.0
	1999	8.2	0.8	9.0	134.3
Argentina Argentine	1997	56.9	25.8	82.7	2.3
	1998	28.9	46.4	75.3	2.1
	1999	31.3	59.2	90.5	2.5

79
Disbursements of bilateral and multilateral official development assistance
and official aid to individual recipients [cont.]
Versements d'aide publique au développement et d'aide publique
bilatérales et multilatérales aux bénéficiares [suite]

		Net disbursements (US $) – Versements nets ($ E.–U.)			
Region, country or area Région, pays ou zone	Year Année	Bilateral Bilatérale (millions)	Multilateral [1] Multilatérale [1] (millions)	Total (millions)	Per capita [2] Par habitant [2]
Aruba	1997	23.7	1.3	25.0	277.8
Aruba	1998	10.7	0.6	11.3	120.2
	1999	−7.1	−0.3	−7.4	−75.5
Bahamas	1997	1.1	2.3	3.4	11.7
Bahamas	1998	0.2	22.4	22.6	76.4
	1999	0.9	10.7	11.6	38.5
Barbados	1997	0.1	4.2	4.3	16.1
Barbade	1998	0.5	15.2	15.7	58.6
	1999	1.4	−3.5	−2.1	−7.8
Belize	1997	2.4	7.2	9.6	42.9
Belize	1998	2.6	8.8	11.4	49.6
	1999	37.5	8.6	46.1	196.2
Bermuda	1997	−8.2	...	−8.2	−130.2
Bermudes	1998	0.6	...	0.6	9.4
	1999	0.1	...	0.1	1.6
Bolivia	1997	453.5	244.9	698.4	89.8
Bolivie	1998	416.2	211.8	628.0	78.9
	1999	397.3	171.3	568.6	69.8
Brazil	1997	192.9	81.6	274.5	1.7
Brésil	1998	218.9	110.2	329.1	2.0
	1999	98.4	85.2	183.6	1.1
British Virgin Islands	1997	1.5	0.3	1.8	90.0
Iles Vierges britanniques	1998	1.5	−0.3	1.2	60.0
	1999	2.8	−0.2	2.6	123.8
Cayman Islands	1997	−2.9	−0.9	−3.8	−111.8
Iles Caïmanes	1998	−1.5	1.7	0.2	5.6
	1999	0.5	2.6	3.1	83.8
Chile	1997	113.1	14.2	127.3	8.7
Chili	1998	95.1	9.5	104.6	7.1
	1999	63.5	5.6	69.1	4.6
Colombia	1997	171.2	23.3	194.5	4.9
Colombie	1998	160.8	6.7	167.5	4.1
	1999	292.3	9.0	301.3	7.3
Costa Rica	1997	−2.1	−4.4	−6.5	−1.7
Costa Rica	1998	21.9	6.9	28.8	7.5
	1999	−4.3	−5.5	−9.8	−2.5
Cuba	1997	32.0	33.0	65.0	5.9
Cuba	1998	56.8	23.0	79.8	7.2
	1999	35.5	22.7	58.2	5.3
Dominica	1997	13.3	0.5	13.8	194.4
Dominique	1998	5.7	13.7	19.4	273.2
	1999	6.9	3.0	9.9	139.4
Dominican Republic	1997	31.5	39.5	71.0	8.8
République dominicaine	1998	60.4	60.0	120.4	14.6
	1999	151.9	42.8	194.7	23.3
Ecuador	1997	139.8	9.5	149.3	12.5
Equateur	1998	155.2	21.0	176.2	14.5
	1999	128.9	16.6	145.5	11.7
El Salvador	1997	234.0	38.5	272.5	46.1
El Salvador	1998	154.4	25.4	179.8	29.8
	1999	173.7	9.0	182.7	29.7
Falkland Islands	1997	...	−0.2	−0.2	−100.0
Iles Falkland	1998	...	−0.2	−0.2	−100.0
	1999	...	−0.2	−0.2	−100.0
Grenada	1997	3.8	2.5	6.3	67.7
Grenade	1998	3.4	2.6	6.0	64.5
	1999	2.4	3.0	5.4	58.1
Guatemala	1997	212.7	50.4	263.1	25.0
Guatemala	1998	181.7	50.9	232.6	21.5
	1999	230.7	62.3	293.0	26.4
Guyana	1997	206.0	58.4	264.4	313.6
Guyana	1998	51.8	41.2	93.0	109.4
	1999	39.6	−13.0	26.6	31.1

79
Disbursements of bilateral and multilateral official development assistance
and official aid to individual recipients [*cont.*]
Versements d'aide publique au développement et d'aide publique
bilatérales et multilatérales aux bénéficiares [*suite*]

Region, country or area Région, pays ou zone	Year Année	Net disbursements (US $) — Versements nets ($ E.—U.)			
		Bilateral Bilatérale (millions)	Multilateral[1] Multilatérale[1] (millions)	Total (millions)	Per capita[2] Par habitant[2]
Haiti Haïti	1997	175.8	148.8	324.6	41.5
	1998	250.9	156.2	407.1	51.2
	1999	157.2	105.6	262.8	32.5
Honduras Honduras	1997	155.0	131.4	286.4	47.9
	1998	192.9	125.0	317.9	51.7
	1999	355.1	459.6	814.7	129.0
Jamaica Jamaïque	1997	−5.0	76.3	71.3	28.3
	1998	3.5	15.1	18.6	7.3
	1999	−22.7	−0.6	−23.3	−9.1
Mexico Mexique	1997	88.8	10.3	99.1	1.1
	1998	3.9	10.9	14.8	0.2
	1999	21.9	12.6	34.5	0.4
Montserrat Montserrat	1997	42.8	0.0	42.8	3890.9
	1998	65.1	0.5	65.6	5963.6
	1999	40.5	0.4	40.9	3718.2
Netherlands Antilles Antilles néerlandaises	1997	108.9	1.7	110.6	524.2
	1998	125.7	3.4	129.1	606.1
	1999	126.2	0.8	127.0	590.7
Nicaragua Nicaragua	1997	261.6	148.5	410.1	87.7
	1998	323.5	248.9	572.4	119.1
	1999	323.4	351.3	674.7	136.6
Panama Panama	1997	43.0	−1.4	41.6	15.3
	1998	22.4	−0.6	21.8	7.9
	1999	15.2	−1.6	13.6	4.8
Paraguay Paraguay	1997	70.1	32.5	102.6	20.2
	1998	55.7	20.3	76.0	14.6
	1999	65.5	12.1	77.6	14.5
Peru Pérou	1997	364.2	29.2	393.4	16.1
	1998	381.6	119.9	501.5	20.2
	1999	407.3	44.9	452.2	17.9
Saint Kitts and Nevis Saint−Kitts−et−Nevis	1997	0.7	5.2	5.9	151.3
	1998	1.3	2.6	3.9	100.0
	1999	0.3	4.3	4.6	118.0
Saint Lucia Sainte−Lucie	1997	9.9	13.7	23.6	159.5
	1998	0.4	4.8	5.2	34.7
	1999	9.9	14.1	24.0	157.9
Saint Vincent & Grenadines St. Vincent−et−Grenadines	1997	5.4	−0.4	5.0	44.6
	1998	3.3	16.4	19.7	175.9
	1999	6.0	8.6	14.6	129.2
Suriname Suriname	1997	69.7	6.6	76.3	185.2
	1998	52.2	6.6	58.8	142.0
	1999	30.1	5.8	35.9	86.5
Trinidad and Tobago Trinité−et−Tobago	1997	−0.5	33.5	33.0	25.8
	1998	−2.3	16.0	13.7	10.7
	1999	0.2	26.1	26.3	20.4
Turks and Caicos Islands Iles Turques et Caiques	1997	4.1	0.1	4.2	280.0
	1998	4.9	1.1	6.0	375.0
	1999	5.4	2.0	7.4	462.5
Uruguay Uruguay	1997	29.5	4.1	33.6	10.3
	1998	19.4	4.7	24.1	7.3
	1999	19.0	2.6	21.6	6.5
Venezuela Venezuela	1997	−1.8	10.4	8.6	0.4
	1998	21.4	15.2	36.6	1.6
	1999	34.1	9.4	43.5	1.8
Other and unallocated Autres et non−ventilés	1997	615.8	222.9	838.7	...
	1998	855.8	140.7	996.5	...
	1999	951.9	176.6	1128.5	...
Asia **Asie**	**1997**	**9366.8**	**5721.4**	**15088.2**	...
	1998	**11515.2**	**5309.0**	**16824.2**	...
	1999	**13578.7**	**4680.5**	**18259.2**	...
Afghanistan Afghanistan	1997	123.3	106.5	229.8	11.0
	1998	88.2	65.7	153.9	7.2
	1999	104.1	38.3	142.4	6.5

79
Disbursements of bilateral and multilateral official development assistance
and official aid to individual recipients [*cont.*]
Versements d'aide publique au développement et d'aide publique
bilatérales et multilatérales aux bénéficiares [*suite*]

| Region, country or area
Région, pays ou zone | Year
Année | Net disbursements (US $) — Versements nets ($ E.—U.) | | | |
		Bilateral Bilatérale (millions)	Multilateral[1] Multilatérale[1] (millions)	Total (millions)	Per capita[2] Par habitant[2]
Armenia	1997	47.5	118.5	166.0	46.8
Arménie	1998	66.9	75.6	142.5	40.3
	1999	75.3	133.2	208.5	59.2
Azerbaijan	1997	15.7	160.9	176.6	23.1
Azerbaïdjan	1998	35.6	52.8	88.4	11.5
	1999	52.4	109.3	161.7	21.0
Bahrain	1997	1.6	0.4	2.0	3.4
Bahreïn	1998	1.1	0.7	1.8	3.0
	1999	1.6	0.6	2.2	3.6
Bangladesh	1997	560.0	452.3	1012.3	8.3
Bangladesh	1998	623.9	630.1	1254.0	10.1
	1999	607.3	588.2	1195.5	9.4
Bhutan	1997	45.0	21.2	66.2	34.0
Bhoutan	1998	41.0	16.0	57.0	28.4
	1999	53.0	14.7	67.7	32.8
Brunei Darussalam	1997	0.3	0.0	0.3	1.0
Brunéi Darussalam	1998	0.3	0.0	0.3	1.0
	1999	1.4	0.0	1.4	4.4
Cambodia	1997	228.4	105.1	333.5	31.8
Cambodge	1998	230.6	106.5	337.1	31.5
	1999	167.1	111.8	278.9	25.5
China ††	1997	1238.2	803.7	2041.9	1.7
Chine ††	1998	1731.7	639.5	2371.2	1.9
	1999	1821.6	512.2	2333.8	1.8
China, Hong Kong SAR †	1997	3.8	4.7	8.5	1.3
Chine, Hong Kong RAS †	1998	6.7	0.1	6.8	1.0
	1999	3.8	−0.1	3.7	0.5
China, Macao SAR†	1997	0.2	0.2	0.4	0.9
Chine, Macao RAS †	1998	0.1	0.4	0.5	1.1
	1999	0.3	0.0	0.3	0.6
East Timor	1997	0.4	...	0.4	0.5
Timor oriental	1998	1.7	...	1.7	2.0
	1999	147.2	5.6	152.8	175.4
Georgia	1997	70.3	167.6	237.9	46.5
Géorgie	1998	78.5	87.8	166.3	32.9
	1999	77.7	161.0	238.7	47.7
India	1997	928.4	730.6	1659.0	1.7
Inde	1998	915.1	700.2	1615.3	1.6
	1999	838.3	660.0	1498.3	1.5
Indonesia	1997	790.5	45.2	835.7	4.1
Indonésie	1998	1243.3	13.3	1256.6	6.1
	1999	2169.4	36.4	2205.8	10.5
Iran (Islamic Rep. of)	1997	165.3	33.0	198.3	3.1
Iran (Rép. islamique d')	1998	142.4	21.8	164.2	2.5
	1999	138.4	23.0	161.4	2.4
Iraq	1997	180.2	39.9	220.1	10.4
Iraq	1998	74.7	40.9	115.6	5.3
	1999	79.0	−3.1	75.9	3.4
Israel	1997	1186.0	10.3	1196.3	204.2
Israël	1998	1055.4	10.6	1066.0	178.1
	1999	901.5	4.1	905.6	148.4
Jordan	1997	288.9	172.3	461.2	75.3
Jordanie	1998	277.0	131.5	408.5	64.8
	1999	325.3	105.4	430.7	66.5
Kazakhstan	1997	93.8	35.6	129.4	7.9
Kazakhstan	1998	176.6	30.7	207.3	12.7
	1999	133.6	27.1	160.7	9.9
Korea, Dem. Poeple's Republic	1997	35.2	53.1	88.3	3.8
Corée, Rép. populaire dém. de	1998	23.5	83.4	106.9	4.6
	1999	165.1	35.6	200.7	8.5
Korea, Republic of	1997	−158.3	−1.1	−159.4	−3.5
Corée, République de	1998	−49.1	−1.3	−50.4	−1.1
	1999	−53.8	−1.4	−55.2	−1.2

79
Disbursements of bilateral and multilateral official development assistance
and official aid to individual recipients [*cont.*]
Versements d'aide publique au développement et d'aide publique
bilatérales et multilatérales aux bénéficiares [*suite*]

Region, country or area Région, pays ou zone	Year Année	Net disbursements (US $) – Versements nets ($ E.−U.)			
		Bilateral Bilatérale (millions)	Multilateral[1] Multilatérale[1] (millions)	Total (millions)	Per capita[2] Par habitant[2]
Kuwait Koweït	1997 1998 1999	0.5 4.9 5.6	−0.1 1.0 1.7	0.4 5.9 7.3	0.2 3.3 3.9
Kyrgyzstan Kirghizistan	1997 1998 1999	50.4 79.8 115.6	187.6 135.9 151.1	238.0 215.7 266.7	51.5 46.5 57.1
Lao People's Dem. Rep. République dém. pop. lao	1997 1998 1999	164.8 165.7 210.5	163.1 115.7 83.4	327.9 281.4 293.9	65.2 54.5 55.5
Lebanon Liban	1997 1998 1999	69.6 73.9 80.3	77.5 125.3 67.6	147.1 199.2 147.9	46.8 62.4 45.7
Malaysia Malaisie	1997 1998 1999	−243.7 198.1 140.1	4.5 4.0 5.0	−239.2 202.1 145.1	−11.4 9.4 6.7
Maldives Maldives	1997 1998 1999	16.9 16.6 25.5	11.1 9.1 6.5	28.0 25.7 32.0	106.5 94.8 115.1
Mongolia Mongolie	1997 1998 1999	118.1 141.4 138.2	127.0 60.2 79.3	245.1 201.6 217.5	96.6 78.2 83.0
Myanmar Myanmar	1997 1998 1999	23.6 27.4 44.7	10.0 31.3 28.6	33.6 58.7 73.3	0.8 1.3 1.7
Nepal Népal	1997 1998 1999	233.5 212.7 204.8	167.0 189.3 137.2	400.5 402.0 342.0	18.0 17.6 14.6
Occupied Palestinian Terr. Territoire palestinien occupé	1997 1998 1999	324.6 336.4 326.6	248.1 245.2 168.6	572.7 581.6 495.2	... ...
Oman Oman	1997 1998 1999	20.3 19.8 8.8	2.5 2.7 2.3	22.8 22.5 11.1	9.9 9.5 4.5
Pakistan Pakistan	1997 1998 1999	78.6 534.8 435.2	527.7 521.8 296.8	606.3 1056.6 732.0	4.2 7.1 4.8
Philippines Philippines	1997 1998 1999	567.3 528.0 616.0	115.0 79.6 74.4	682.3 607.6 690.4	9.6 8.3 9.3
Qatar Qatar	1997 1998 1999	0.6 1.1 4.7	0.3 0.2 0.2	0.9 1.3 4.9	1.6 2.3 8.3
Saudi Arabia Arabie saoudite	1997 1998 1999	−2.4 14.7 19.1	13.0 10.7 9.7	10.6 25.4 28.8	0.5 1.3 1.4
Singapore Singapour	1997 1998 1999	1.6 1.3 −1.5	1.2 0.3 0.4	2.8 1.6 −1.1	0.8 0.5 −0.3
Sri Lanka Sri Lanka	1997 1998 1999	228.3 282.3 207.7	103.4 209.9 42.6	331.7 492.2 250.3	18.2 26.7 13.4
Syrian Arab Republic Rép. arabe syrienne	1997 1998 1999	93.4 83.3 172.3	40.9 43.8 34.6	134.3 127.1 206.9	9.0 8.3 13.2
Tajikistan Tadjikistan	1997 1998 1999	35.9 40.0 35.1	49.3 65.1 87.0	85.2 105.1 122.1	14.4 17.5 20.0
Thailand Thaïlande	1997 1998 1999	600.8 675.7 994.8	23.5 14.8 11.7	624.3 690.5 1006.5	10.5 11.5 16.5
Turkmenistan Turkménistan	1997 1998 1999	2.2 8.2 11.5	8.3 8.4 9.0	10.5 16.6 20.5	2.5 3.9 4.7

79
Disbursements of bilateral and multilateral official development assistance
and official aid to individual recipients [cont.]
Versements d'aide publique au développement et d'aide publique
bilatérales et multilatérales aux bénéficiares [suite]

Region, country or area Région, pays ou zone	Year Année	Net disbursements (US $) — Versements nets ($ E.–U.)			
		Bilateral Bilatérale (millions)	Multilateral[1] Multilatérale[1] (millions)	Total (millions)	Per capita[2] Par habitant[2]
United Arab Emirates	1997	1.1	0.7	1.8	0.8
Emirats arabes unis	1998	3.5	0.5	4.0	1.7
	1999	2.9	1.2	4.1	1.7
Uzbekistan	1997	110.9	17.0	127.9	5.5
Ouzbékistan	1998	123.6	19.6	143.2	6.1
	1999	112.8	20.9	133.7	5.6
Viet Nam	1997	585.5	401.3	986.8	12.9
Viet Nam	1998	712.6	451.9	1164.5	15.0
	1999	1017.7	407.1	1424.8	18.1
Yemen	1997	174.5	181.5	356.0	21.9
Yémen	1998	166.8	143.3	310.1	18.4
	1999	177.3	278.9	456.2	26.1
Other and unallocated	1997	259.8	180.1	439.9	199.9
Autres et non–ventilés	1998	220.6	113.2	333.8	147.1
	1999	650.0	113.0	763.0	326.2
Europe	**1997**	**3798.3**	**2258.8**	**6057.1**	...
Europe	**1998**	**4499.0**	**3253.7**	**7752.7**	...
	1999	**6200.7**	**3995.8**	**10196.5**	...
Albania	1997	114.3	49.2	163.5	52.2
Albanie	1998	93.8	162.8	256.6	81.9
	1999	253.0	224.9	477.9	153.2
Belarus	1997	31.9	10.8	42.7	4.1
Bélarus	1998	20.9	7.5	28.4	2.8
	1999	15.5	8.6	24.1	2.4
Bosnia and Herzegovina	1997	520.5	291.8	812.3	230.8
Bosnie – Herzégovine	1998	599.1	284.5	883.6	240.4
	1999	734.5	325.2	1059.7	276.0
Bulgaria	1997	74.6	142.8	217.4	25.9
Bulgarie	1998	137.7	98.0	235.7	28.3
	1999	137.1	126.5	263.6	31.8
Croatia	1997	22.9	17.4	40.3	9.0
Croatie	1998	26.3	12.8	39.1	8.7
	1999	27.8	20.3	48.1	10.7
Cyprus	1997	−0.3	43.0	42.7	55.96
Chypre	1998	13.0	18.7	31.7	41.12
	1999	4.9	50.3	55.2	70.95
Czech Republic	1997	56.6	58.3	114.9	11.2
République tchèque	1998	48.9	398.3	447.2	43.5
	1999	29.8	288.2	318.0	31.0
Estonia	1997	35.1	29.6	64.7	44.7
Estonie	1998	35.9	54.1	90.0	63.0
	1999	28.6	54.1	82.7	58.6
Gibraltar	1997	0.4	...	0.4	15.4
Gibraltar	1998	0.2	...	0.2	8.0
	1999	1.1	...	1.1	44.0
Hungary	1997	85.4	78.2	163.6	16.1
Hongrie	1998	111.1	129.0	240.1	23.7
	1999	29.2	218.4	247.6	24.6
Latvia	1997	46.8	33.1	79.9	32.5
Lettonie	1998	47.0	49.9	96.9	40.0
	1999	44.1	52.3	96.4	40.4
Lithuania	1997	53.0	44.3	97.3	26.3
Lituanie	1998	66.7	54.3	121.0	32.8
	1999	61.3	67.2	128.5	34.9
Malta	1997	22.1	5.1	27.2	71.4
Malte	1998	23.8	1.6	25.4	66.2
	1999	23.8	3.2	27.0	70.0
Poland	1997	622.6	237.3	859.9	22.2
Pologne	1998	471.4	430.6	902.0	23.3
	1999	385.4	598.4	983.8	25.4
Republic of Moldova	1997	14.5	45.7	60.2	13.8
République de Moldova	1998	21.7	12.6	34.3	7.8
	1999	51.2	50.9	102.1	23.3

79

Disbursements of bilateral and multilateral official development assistance
and official aid to individual recipients [*cont.*]
Versements d'aide publique au développement et d'aide publique
bilatérales et multilatérales aux bénéficiares [*suite*]

Region, country or area Région, pays ou zone	Year Année	Net disbursements (US $) — Versements nets ($ E.—U.)			
		Bilateral Bilatérale (millions)	Multilateral[1] Multilatérale[1] (millions)	Total (millions)	Per capita[2] Par habitant[2]
Romania Roumanie	1997	77.5	134.2	211.7	9.4
	1998	176.1	181.0	357.1	15.9
	1999	122.5	250.9	373.4	16.7
Russian Federation Fédération de Russie	1997	550.5	183.5	734.0	5.0
	1998	871.4	146.7	1018.1	6.9
	1999	1599.9	216.4	1816.3	12.3
Slovakia Slovaquie	1997	30.5	39.8	70.3	13.1
	1998	39.0	115.7	154.7	28.8
	1999	35.0	283.3	318.3	59.1
Slovenia Slovenie	1997	−9.7	106.3	96.6	48.4
	1998	5.6	34.0	39.6	19.9
	1999	1.3	29.7	31.0	15.6
TFYR of Macedonia l'ex−République y. Macédoine	1997	30.4	67.9	98.3	49.5
	1998	32.1	60.2	92.3	46.2
	1999	136.5	134.3	270.8	134.7
Turkey Turquie	1997	−59.0	64.7	5.7	0.1
	1998	−80.5	86.1	5.6	0.1
	1999	−66.4	24.0	−42.4	−0.7
Ukraine Ukraine	1997	166.4	13.8	180.2	3.5
	1998	273.6	108.1	381.7	7.5
	1999	401.7	77.8	479.5	9.4
Yugoslavia Yougoslavie	1997	77.6	19.8	97.4	9.2
	1998	94.6	12.6	107.2	10.1
	1999	635.1	3.1	638.2	60.0
Yugoslavia, SFR †[3] Yougoslavie, Rfs †[3]	1997	71.2	−2.5	68.7	...
	1998	53.3	52.9	106.2	...
	1999	161.6	272.6	434.2	...
Other and unallocated Autres et non−ventilés	1997	1162.6	544.8	1707.4	...
	1998	1316.2	741.6	2057.8	...
	1999	1346.2	615.1	1961.3	...
Oceania **Océanie**	**1997**	**1433.0**	**121.5**	**1554.5**	...
	1998	**1525.8**	**124.4**	**1650.2**	...
	1999	**1370.0**	**51.5**	**1421.5**	...
Cook Islands Iles Cook	1997	7.1	2.9	10.0	526.3
	1998	5.9	2.1	8.0	421.1
	1999	4.5	1.4	5.9	310.5
Fiji Fidji	1997	39.1	4.4	43.5	55.3
	1998	35.8	0.6	36.4	45.7
	1999	37.8	−3.6	34.2	42.4
French Polynesia Polynésie française	1997	364.9	2.5	367.4	1647.5
	1998	368.7	1.7	370.4	1691.3
	1999	353.2	−1.7	351.5	1576.2
Kiribati Kiribati	1997	14.2	1.5	15.7	196.3
	1998	16.2	1.1	17.3	213.6
	1999	19.6	1.3	20.9	254.9
Marshall Islands Iles Marshall	1997	52.3	10.6	62.9	1084.5
	1998	42.1	8.2	50.3	838.3
	1999	58.7	4.2	62.9	1014.5
Micronesia (Fed. States of) Micronésie (Etats fédérés de)	1997	83.8	12.2	96.0	857.1
	1998	73.8	6.3	80.1	702.6
	1999	102.3	5.6	107.9	930.2
Nauru Nauru	1997	2.6	0.0	2.6	236.4
	1998	2.0	0.1	2.1	190.9
	1999	6.5	0.1	6.6	600.0
New Caledonia Nouvelle−Calédonie	1997	336.6	2.2	338.8	1677.2
	1998	336.3	2.1	338.4	1642.7
	1999	314.9	−0.4	314.5	1497.6
Niue Nioué	1997	5.2	0.1	5.3	2650.0
	1998	3.9	0.2	4.1	2050.0
	1999	3.9	0.2	4.1	2050.0
Northern Mariana Islands Iles Mariannes du Nord	1997	...	0.7	0.7	10.6
	1998	...	0.2	0.2	2.9
	1999	...	0.1	0.1	1.4

79
Disbursements of bilateral and multilateral official development assistance
and official aid to individual recipients [*cont.*]
Versements d'aide publique au développement et d'aide publique
bilatérales et multilatérales aux bénéficiares [*suite*]

Region, country or area Région, pays ou zone	Year Année	Net disbursements (US $) — Versements nets ($ E. — U.)			
		Bilateral Bilatérale (millions)	Multilateral[1] Multilatérale[1] (millions)	Total (millions)	Per capita[2] Par habitant[2]
Palau	1997	38.1	0.1	38.2	2122.2
Palaos	1998	89.0	0.1	89.1	4689.5
	1999	28.7	0.1	28.8	1515.8
Papua New Guinea	1997	291.9	54.1	346.0	76.9
Papouasie — Nvl — Guinée	1998	311.9	49.6	361.5	78.6
	1999	212.2	3.9	216.1	46.0
Samoa	1997	26.7	0.9	27.6	160.5
Samoa	1998	29.7	6.5	36.2	208.1
	1999	22.4	0.5	22.9	129.4
Solomon Islands	1997	36.1	5.6	41.7	103.2
Iles Salomon	1998	23.6	19.2	42.8	102.6
	1999	20.5	16.5	37.0	86.1
Tokelau	1997	4.2	0.2	4.4	4400.0
Tokélaou	1998	3.5	0.1	3.6	3600.0
	1999	4.6	0.1	4.7	4700.0
Tonga	1997	22.4	5.1	27.5	280.6
Tonga	1998	16.3	8.4	24.7	252.0
	1999	15.2	5.9	21.1	215.3
Tuvalu	1997	9.4	0.7	10.1	918.2
Tuvalu	1998	4.9	0.3	5.2	472.7
	1999	3.4	3.2	6.6	600.0
Vanuatu	1997	23.4	3.7	27.1	153.1
Vanuatu	1998	26.1	14.6	40.7	223.6
	1999	28.9	8.3	37.2	197.9
Wallis and Futuna Islands	1997	0.1	0.5	0.6	42.9
Iles Wallis et Futuna	1998	46.5	0.8	47.3	3378.6
	1999	50.1	0.3	50.4	3600.0
Other and unallocated	1997	74.9	13.4	88.3	...
Autres et non — ventilés	1998	89.7	2.2	91.9	...
	1999	82.6	5.5	88.1	...
Unspecified	**1997**	**6577.3**	**897.4**	**7474.7**	...
Non — specifiés	**1998**	**6949.9**	**965.3**	**7915.2**	...
	1999	**6837.7**	**1131.9**	**7969.6**	...

Source:
Organisation for Economic Co — operation and Development (OECD),
Paris, "Geographical Distribution of Financial Flows to Aid Recipients,
1995 — 1999" and the OECD Development Assistance Database. Per
capita calculated by the UN Statistics Division.

† For information on the recent changes in country or area
nomenclature pertaining to former Czechoslovakia,
Germany, Hong Kong Special Administrative Region (SAR)
of China, Macao Special Administrative Region (SAR) of
China, SFR of Yugoslavia and the former USSR, see Annex I
— Country or area nomenclature, regional and other groupings.

†† For statistical purposes, the data for China do not include
those for Hong Kong Special Administrative Region
(Hong Kong SAR), Macao Special Administrative
Region (Macao SAR) and Taiwan province of China.

1 As reported by OECD/DAC, covers agencies of the United Nations
family, the European Union, IDA and the concessional lending
facilities of regional development banks. Excludes non — concessional
flows (i.e., less than 25% grant elements).

2 Population based on estimates of mid — year population.

3 Data refer to Yugoslavia, SFR unspecified.

Source:
Organisation de coopération et de développement économiques
(OCDE), Paris, "Répartition géographique des ressources financières
allouées aux pays bénéficiaires de l'aide, 1995 — 1999" et la base de
données de l'OCDE sur l'aide au développement. Les données par
habitant ont été calculées par la Division de statistique de l'ONU.

† Pour les modifications récentes de nomenclature de pays ou de
zone concernant l'Allemagne, Hong Kong, région administrative
spéciale (RAS) de Chine, Macao, région administrative spéciale
(RAS) de Chine, l'ex — Tchécoslovaquie, l'ex — URSS et l'ex — Rfs
de Yougoslavie, voir annex I — Nomenclature des pays ou des
zones, groupements régionaux et autres groupements.

†† Les données statistiques relatives à la Chine ne comprennent pas
celles qui concernent la région administrative spéciale de Hong
Kong (la RAS de Hong Kong), la région administrative spéciale de
Macao (la RAS de Macao), et la province chinoise de Taiwan.

1 Communiqué par le Comité d'aide au développement de l'OCDE.
Comprend les institutions et organismes du système des Nations
Unies, l'Union européene, l'Association internationale de
développement, et les mécanismes de prêt à des conditions
privilégiées des banques régionales de développement. Les apports
aux conditions du marché (élément de libéralité inférieur à 25%)
en sont exclus.

2 Population d'après des estimations de la population au milieu
de l'année.

3 Les données concernent Yougoslavie, Rfs non spécifié.

80
Net official development assistance from DAC countries to developing countries and multilateral organizations
Aide publique au développement nette de pays du CAD aux pays en développement et aux organisations multilatérales

Net disbursements: million US dollars and as % of GNI
Versements nets: millions de dollars E.-U. et en % du RNB

Country or area / Pays ou zone	1994 Million US $ Millions $ E.-U.	1994 As % of GNI En % du RNB	1995 Million US $ Millions $ E.-U.	1995 As % of GNI En % du RNB	1996 Million US $ Millions $ E.-U.	1996 As % of GNI En % du RNB	1997 Million US $ Millions $ E.-U.	1997 As % of GNI En % du RNB	1998 Million US $ Millions $ E.-U.	1998 As % of GNI En % du RNB	1999 Million US $ Millions $ E.-U.	1999 As % of GNI En % du RNB
Total	59152	0.29	58926	0.27	55622	0.25	48497	0.22	52084	0.23	56378	0.24
Australia / Australie	1091	0.34	1194	0.36	1074	0.28	1061	0.28	960	0.27	982	0.26
Austria / Autriche	655	0.33	767	0.33	557	0.24	527	0.26	456	0.22	527	0.26
Belgium / Belgique	727	0.32	1034	0.38	913	0.34	764	0.31	883	0.35	760	0.30
Canada / Canada	2250	0.43	2067	0.38	1795	0.32	2045	0.34	1707	0.30	1699	0.28
Denmark / Danemark	1446	1.03	1623	0.96	1772	1.04	1637	0.97	1704	0.99	1733	1.01
Finland / Finlande	290	0.31	388	0.32	408	0.34	379	0.33	396	0.32	416	0.33
France / France	8466	0.64	8443	0.55	7451	0.48	6307	0.45	5742	0.40	5637	0.39
Germany / Allemagne	6818	0.33	7524	0.31	7601	0.32	5857	0.28	5581	0.26	5515	0.26
Greece / Grèce	...	...	...	...	184	0.15	173	0.14	179	0.15	194	0.15
Ireland / Irlande	109	0.25	153	0.29	179	0.31	187	0.31	199	0.30	245	0.31
Italy / Italie	2705	0.27	1623	0.15	2416	0.20	1266	0.11	2278	0.20	1806	0.15
Japan / Japon	13239	0.29	14489	0.28	9439	0.20	9358	0.22	10640	0.28	15323	0.35
Luxembourg / Luxembourg	59	0.40	65	0.36	82	0.44	95	0.55	112	0.65	119	0.66
Netherlands / Pays-Bas	2517	0.76	3226	0.81	3246	0.81	2947	0.81	3042	0.80	3134	0.79
New Zealand / Nouvelle-Zélande	110	0.24	123	0.23	122	0.21	154	0.26	130	0.27	134	0.27
Norway / Norvège	1137	1.05	1244	0.87	1311	0.85	1306	0.86	1321	0.91	1370	0.91
Portugal / Portugal	303	0.34	258	0.25	218	0.21	250	0.25	259	0.24	276	0.26
Spain / Espagne	1305	0.28	1348	0.24	1251	0.22	1234	0.24	1376	0.24	1363	0.23
Sweden / Suède	1819	0.96	1704	0.77	1999	0.84	1731	0.79	1573	0.72	1630	0.70
Switzerland / Suisse	982	0.36	1084	0.34	1026	0.34	911	0.34	898	0.32	969	0.35
United Kingdom / Royaume-Uni	3197	0.31	3202	0.29	3199	0.27	3433	0.26	3864	0.27	3401	0.23
United States / Etats-Unis	9927	0.14	7367	0.10	9377	0.12	6878	0.09	8786	0.10	9145	0.10

Source:
Organisation for Economic Co-operation and Development (OECD), Paris, "Development Co-operation, 2000 Report" and previous issues.

Source:
Organisation de Coopération et de Développement Economiques (OCDE), Paris, "Coopération pour le développement, Rapport 2000" et éditions précédentes.

81
Socio-economic development assistance through the United Nations system
Assistance en matière de développement socioéconomique fournie par le système des Nations Unies

Thousand US dollars
Milliers de dollars E.−U.

Development grant expenditures [1] • Aide au développement [1]

Country or area Pays ou zone	Year Année	UNDP PNUD Central resources Ressources centrales	Special funds Fonds gérés	UNFPA FNUAP	UNICEF	WFP PAM	Other UN system Autres organis. − ONU Regular budget Budget ordinaire	Extra−budgetary Extra−budgétaire	Total	Gov't self−supporting Auto−assistance gouverne−mentale
Total	**1999**	1631813	412303	187149	817890	1429777	**444007**	1123352	6046291	163629
Total	**2000**	1457911	459788	134132	884984	1491035	**469575**	1553320	6450745	589022
Regional programmes	**1999**	117342	59055	36072	31804	0	**157710**	612083	1014066	27510
Totaux régionaux	**2000**	99186	73780	17653	35947	0	**195373**	865210	1287149	287868
Africa	1999	54810	13263	4235	3386	0	32430	35808	143932	536
Afrique	2000	22346	12191	2897	5233	0	41093	203534	287294	164559
Asia and the Pacific	1999	0	7397	4679	2556	0	25135	37182	76949	558
Asie et le Pacifique	2000	15094	8214	1085	2909	0	33268	57134	117704	17911
Europe	1999	0	2480	1232	0	0	23329	28015	55056	175
Europe	2000	2680	4939	566	586	0	22454	23752	54977	15966
Latin America	1999	0	4877	1547	1871	0	27069	21173	56537	546
Amérique latine	2000	4176	6204	1159	1353	0	30844	23233	66970	2559
Western Asia	1999	0	2027	887	5389	0	26972	281468	316743	27
Asie occidentale	2000	3281	2647	666	852	0	25177	302403	335026	8513
Interregional	1999	13109	10772	23493	0	0	14358	95790	157522	905
Interrégional	2000	11928	10426	11281	0	0	11235	102318	147188	346
Global	1999	49423	18239	0	18602	0	8415	112646	207326	24764
Global	2000	39681	29159	0	25014	0	31301	152835	277991	78014
Country programmes	**1999**	1509666	313429	147102	750673	1414095	**265614**	454420	4854999	136107
Programmes, pays	**2000**	1351401	353539	113615	783001	1457918	**268069**	666593	4994136	283500
Afghanistan	1999	14161	565	510	11115	41918	3829	2645	74742	33
Afghanistan	2000	8475	2631	755	13544	62491	3361	5468	96725	4912
Albania	1999	2715	121	611	7532	0	1002	2818	14800	0
Albanie	2000	4260	761	220	5759	1	445	2309	13755	1556
Algeria	1999	1555	180	754	1437	2733	1665	899	9223	−2
Algérie	2000	912	280	425	878	4312	2167	984	9959	144
Andorra	1999	0	0	0	0	0	30	0	30	0
Andorre	2000	0	0	0	0	0	87	0	87	0
Angola	1999	7835	2373	2127	15069	94265	1511	1464	124644	50
Angola	2000	2763	3543	1313	13762	108493	1979	6766	138619	4457
Anguilla	1999	79	0	0	0	0	0	0	79	0
Anguilla	2000	10	7	0	0	0	0	7	24	0
Antigua and Barbuda	1999	122	0	0	0	0	153	0	275	0
Antigua−et−Barbuda	2000	76	242	0	0	0	172	0	490	0
Argentina	1999	197537	774	58	2378	...	2125	25540	228411	22728
Argentine	2000	179021	1919	0	2815	0	2126	26615	212496	23516
Aruba	1999	246	0	0	0	0	29	0	275	0
Aruba	2000	179	0	0	0	0	88	0	267	0
Azerbaijan	1999	3029	2881	487	1667	8119	162	350	16696	0
Azerbaïdjan	2000	3983	500	620	1680	3515	370	448	11116	287
Bahamas	1999	41	59	0	0	0	610	0	710	0
Bahamas	2000	0	76	0	0	0	329	41	446	41
Bahrain	1999	652	0	14	0	0	399	30	1095	17
Bahreïn	2000	1029	288	1	0	0	127	79	1523	22
Bangladesh	1999	13994	636	5950	36291	61422	6339	5804	130435	29
Bangladesh	2000	19601	335	3680	34771	23135	5483	5332	92336	3569
Barbados	1999	3	215	0	0	0	721	43	982	43
Barbade	2000	14	14	0	0	0	354	11	393	11
Belize	1999	148	480	21	669	0	579	19	1915	0
Belize	2000	33	1156	22	629	45	571	10	2466	0
Benin	1999	3359	1020	1439	2997	859	1830	671	12175	18
Bénin	2000	3327	1200	715	2769	1978	1873	752	12615	147
Bermuda	1999	0	0	0	0	0	3	0	3	0
Bermudes	2000	0	0	0	0	0	0	0	0	0
Bhutan	1999	4239	1738	1274	2040	1321	1968	191	12770	24
Bhoutan	2000	3407	1542	1431	2077	1623	1775	392	12247	173
Bolivia	1999	11692	830	1036	7576	6304	1941	8254	37633	1220
Bolivie	2000	9366	2111	1108	7748	6255	1674	5159	33421	2591

81
Socio—economic development assistance through the United Nations system
Thousand US dollars [*cont.*]

Assistance en matière de développement socioéconomique fournie par le système des Nations Unies
Milliers de dollars E.—U. [*suite*]

Development grant expenditures [1] • Aide au développement [1]

Country or area Pays ou zone	Year Année	UNDP PNUD Central resources Ressources centrales	Special funds Fonds gérés	UNFPA FNUAP	UNICEF	WFP PAM	Other UN system Autres organis. — ONU Regular budget Budget ordinaire	Extra-budgetary Extra-budgétaire	Total	Gov't self-supporting Auto-assistance gouvernementale
Botswana	1999	2825	904	496	1474	3	1040	112	6854	23
Botswana	2000	3555	485	350	1066	0	1745	238	7439	90
Brazil	1999	143223	6731	1325	9542	0	2549	66332	229702	62527
Brésil	2000	186244	8132	847	8048	0	3131	96169	302573	90154
British Virgin Islands	1999	60	0	0	0	0	39	0	99	0
Iles Vierges britanniques	2000	−7	0	0	0	0	98	0	91	0
Brunei Darussalam	1999	2	0	0	0	0	44	0	46	0
Brunéi Darussalam	2000	0	0	0	0	0	14	0	14	0
Bulgaria	1999	5818	714	7	0	0	1368	260	8167	0
Bulgarie	2000	14178	373	74	0	0	743	365	15734	19
Burkina Faso	1999	5280	3627	1597	5789	5052	2906	1295	25546	1
Burkina Faso	2000	4226	1357	1129	5975	1000	2624	1981	18292	1087
Burundi	1999	9327	1434	679	8496	2958	2126	3508	28528	38
Burundi	2000	6400	1413	674	6598	4186	2897	2618	24786	69
Cambodia	1999	10393	21044	3295	11980	13624	2183	6256	68775	17
Cambodge	2000	4598	16053	3231	12380	23679	2628	8329	70898	2543
Cameroon	1999	1745	301	669	2343	5498	2275	1253	14084	107
Cameroun	2000	1098	−22	1510	2591	406	1826	1402	8811	614
Cape Verde	1999	856	983	778	820	97	1498	2342	7375	908
Cap-Vert	2000	583	760	329	767	893	1782	1484	6598	173
Cayman Islands	1999	110	0	0	0	0	0	0	110	0
Iles Caïmanes	2000	73	0	0	0	0	0	0	73	0
Central African Rep.	1999	3709	1325	1124	1267	1178	1603	9	10215	5
Rép. centrafricaine	2000	1961	1717	740	1716	1635	1951	202	9921	112
Chad	1999	6138	522	1331	3750	2291	1824	292	16148	0
Tchad	2000	5236	878	1029	4016	3896	2215	753	18022	587
Chile	1999	14692	564	51	1196	0	1620	959	19082	313
Chili	2000	18598	726	62	1002	0	1438	1374	23200	389
China ††	1999	30361	10439	5458	20835	59469	6324	21130	154016	220
Chine ††	2000	22875	17641	3497	23796	13938	5461	16776	103985	4323
China, Hong Kong SAR †	1999	24	0	0	0	0	61	0	85	0
Chine, Hong Kong RAS †	2000	0	0	0	0	0	106	0	106	0
China, Macao SAR †	1999	0	0	0	0	0	19	23	42	23
Chine, Macao RAS †	2000	0	0	0	0	0	10	0	10	0
Colombia	1999	75041	743	316	4469	2737	1942	1502	86750	501
Colombie	2000	83981	1248	340	3223	4146	2647	1507	97091	397
Comoros	1999	693	384	274	598	150	1097	24	3220	0
Comores	2000	557	328	86	659	7	1469	41	3148	40
Congo	1999	149	19	267	1986	5008	2179	77	9685	1
Congo	2000	1001	178	235	3199	5361	2510	922	13407	95
Cook Islands	1999	215	0	100	0	0	323	0	638	0
Iles Cook	2000	140	47	55	0	0	360	0	602	0
Costa Rica	1999	1569	1099	152	870	0	1234	2598	7521	870
Costa Rica	2000	3495	1537	160	692	0	1501	1217	8602	416
Côte d'Ivoire	1999	1972	595	1459	4200	2990	1782	1247	14245	229
Côte d'Ivoire	2000	1502	4035	1071	3203	1485	1704	1848	14848	1076
Cuba	1999	1313	431	349	1532	5464	2886	888	12862	43
Cuba	2000	1110	1752	269	1439	2868	1622	1194	10255	17
Cyprus	1999	8943	0	2	0	0	406	61	9411	56
Chypre	2000	6610	0	0	0	0	169	90	6869	76
Czech Republic	1999	473	0	0	0	0	1503	1289	3265	1173
République tchèque	2000	346	304	0	0	0	476	108	1234	113
Dem. Rep. of the Congo	1999	22581	83	217	22744	14348	2453	952	63378	15
Rép. dém. du Congo	2000	3242	173	646	29143	22685	3171	8648	67708	6413
Djibouti	1999	1211	357	437	626	2242	1367	0	6240	0
Djibouti	2000	764	75	277	940	5979	1221	33	9289	8
Dominica	1999	74	204	0	0	0	250	155	683	7
Dominique	2000	81	68	0	0	0	277	99	525	37
Dominican Republic	1999	9206	696	703	1968	5491	1723	5694	25481	5390
Rép. dominicaine	2000	10581	774	580	1610	1108	1549	6562	22764	6325

81

Socio—economic development assistance through the United Nations system
Thousand US dollars [cont.]

Assistance en matière de développement socioéconomique fournie par le système des Nations Unies
Milliers de dollars E.—U. [suite]

Development grant expenditures [1] • Aide au développement [1]

Country or area / Pays ou zone	Year / Année	UNDP PNUD Central resources / Ressources centrales	Special funds / Fonds gérés	UNFPA FNUAP	UNICEF	WFP PAM	Other UN system Autres organis.—ONU Regular budget / Budget ordinaire	Extra-budgetary / Extra-budgétaire	Total	Gov't self-supporting / Auto-assistance gouvernementale
Ecuador	1999	18741	668	702	3249	3089	1852	2920	31221	149
Equateur	2000	16001	1301	622	3604	2628	2052	2812	29020	324
Egypt	1999	15313	2511	3240	5967	3749	3773	3995	38548	1614
Egypte	2000	16148	2729	1899	6585	9131	2083	2148	40723	727
El Salvador	1999	22709	1011	463	2655	5562	907	1172	34479	139
El Salvador	2000	17077	2976	561	2762	874	1334	1181	26765	28
Equatorial Guinea	1999	1171	25	420	484	3	1004	12	3120	0
Guinée équatoriale	2000	924	62	508	979	0	1363	48	3884	9
Eritrea	1999	4593	1185	1574	5581	2444	1467	1392	18236	0
Erythrée	2000	2455	1861	637	10357	41434	2317	1478	60538	163
Ethiopia	1999	9610	1394	865	30475	89117	2724	2841	137026	228
Ethiopia	2000	20326	2226	2956	33108	236953	4443	9912	309923	6830
Fiji	1999	348	160	74	0	0	1897	43	2522	7
Fidji	2000	274	108	109	0	0	1653	231	2375	1
French Guiana	1999	0	0	0	0	0	48	0	48	0
Guyane française	2000	0	0	0	0	0	19	0	19	0
French Polynesia	1999	0	0	0	0	0	36	0	36	0
Polynésie française	2000	0	0	0	0	0	0	0	0	0
Gabon	1999	1120	357	464	931	0	1409	130	4411	17
Gabon	2000	804	245	161	721	588	1434	182	4136	104
Gambia	1999	2573	230	677	1198	1250	1606	565	8099	10
Gambie	2000	1702	1265	371	1232	1562	2054	856	9042	103
Ghana	1999	3275	649	3299	8868	1344	2263	750	20447	3
Ghana	2000	5388	855	1800	6699	1549	2573	2234	21098	736
Greece	1999	0	0	0	0	0	349	0	349	0
Grèce	2000	0	0	0	0	0	221	142	363	142
Grenada	1999	224	26	0	0	0	127	17	394	9
Grenade	2000	62	124	0	0	0	164	44	394	13
Guam	1999	0	0	0	0	0	42	0	42	0
Guam	2000	0	0	0	0	0	5	0	5	0
Guatemala	1999	43846	2939	731	6155	4442	1155	2685	61953	116
Guatemala	2000	29847	5182	267	3757	3076	1160	3822	47112	176
Guinea	1999	3757	624	709	2776	5452	2436	215	15969	−1
Guinée	2000	1680	763	565	4104	996	2200	280	10588	144
Guinea—Bissau	1999	2256	1228	71	2572	6569	1201	1009	14906	0
Guinée—Bissau	2000	1147	−264	195	2300	1181	1697	1184	7440	131
Guyana	1999	1270	219	20	782	1005	679	367	4343	20
Guyana	2000	1866	410	282	956	46	727	82	4369	13
Haiti	1999	4949	2107	1949	3223	3703	1079	1633	18643	120
Haïti	2000	4434	1597	1198	4519	6068	620	1494	19932	90
Honduras	1999	39347	1026	934	7130	4990	600	5126	59153	1651
Honduras	2000	36671	7832	759	2385	978	781	5248	54654	997
Hungary	1999	385	0	0	0	0	394	168	947	0
Hongrie	2000	131	0	0	0	0	379	250	760	0
India	1999	16437	6913	6957	69941	27383	6815	8525	142972	5997
Inde	2000	22028	9206	8974	85507	29968	9024	27468	192174	22548
Indonesia	1999	53737	5890	4074	18898	13411	6646	1991	104647	25
Indonésie	2000	4658	6799	2505	19346	57899	6633	5716	103556	3389
Iran (Islamic Rep. of)	1999	1566	1070	1232	1765	896	3654	2780	12963	281
Iran (Rép. islamique d')	2000	1536	2141	1135	2309	1043	2222	1989	12376	184
Iraq	1999	−37567	83417	252	5311	25013	1959	120866	199251	0
Iraq	2000	926	87837	326	6886	20078	1565	200144	317763	1274
Jamaica	1999	1240	371	218	1865	0	1746	569	6008	42
Jamaïque	2000	921	192	197	1052	0	2003	72	4437	0
Jordan	1999	1519	3231	590	1070	2889	1878	1236	12413	5
Jordanie	2000	1604	2217	438	1158	3728	1103	1478	11725	4
Kazakhstan	1999	1554	549	201	1389	0	663	694	5050	170
Kazakhstan	2000	1735	656	785	761	0	784	747	5469	366
Kenya	1999	5767	1068	3027	5513	35716	2032	1234	54357	10
Kenya	2000	5337	1542	1855	8407	115714	2260	3071	138187	2200

81

Socio—economic development assistance through the United Nations system
Thousand US dollars [cont.]

Assistance en matière de développement socioéconomique fournie par le système des Nations Unies
Milliers de dollars E.—U. [suite]

Development grant expenditures [1] • Aide au développement [1]

Country or area Pays ou zone	Year Année	UNDP PNUD		UNFPA FNUAP	UNICEF	WFP PAM	Other UN system Autres organis. — ONU		Total	Gov't self— supporting Auto— assistance gouverne— mentale
		Central resources Ressources centrales	Special funds Fonds gérés				Regular budget Budget ordinaire	Extra— budgetary Extra— budgétaire		
Kiribati	1999	72	73	94	0	0	437	6	681	0
Kiribati	2000	402	121	72	0	0	565	−1	1160	0
Korea, Dem. P. R.	1999	1321	276	459	10813	214056	2693	4128	233746	0
Corée, Rep. dém. de	2000	1783	310	354	4126	123069	2233	5329	137205	1886
Korea, Republic of	1999	1964	0	0	0	0	1412	127	3503	125
Corée, République de	2000	864	0	0	0	0	1621	169	2654	125
Kuwait	1999	1269	0	0	0	0	326	144	1739	0
Koweït	2000	2328	0	0	95	0	205	47	2675	47
Kyrgyzstan	1999	3148	756	585	1050	0	231	231	6001	0
Kirghizistan	2000	2111	827	434	907	0	308	283	4870	85
Lao People's Dem. Rep.	1999	8844	5434	983	4403	0	1753	1310	22727	0
Rép. dém. pop. lao	2000	6436	10905	1432	4866	1369	1741	1403	28151	183
Lebanon	1999	7364	843	487	1091	0	2212	1767	13765	383
Liban	2000	5501	1525	261	1905	0	1991	2056	13239	424
Lesotho	1999	1749	196	148	1077	1762	1130	213	6275	118
Lesotho	2000	1194	300	183	849	1192	1334	439	5491	27
Liberia	1999	4726	476	925	8324	45658	1716	323	62147	63
Libéria	2000	4325	105	740	4529	37711	2390	376	50175	376
Libyan Arab Jamahiriya	1999	1570	0	0	0	0	763	3054	5386	2659
Jamah. arabe libyenne	2000	2493	16	0	0	0	895	1709	5113	1666
Lithuania	1999	707	606	24	0	0	508	368	2213	32
Lithuanie	2000	...	...	...	...	...	...	...	...	...
Madagascar	1999	5500	1639	2008	6728	1322	2000	1849	21045	119
Madagascar	2000	6053	2066	1395	10187	6251	2468	2010	30431	518
Malawi	1999	12845	3754	1751	9317	11095	1913	351	41026	0
Malawi	2000	3493	1734	1130	6474	2543	1959	663	17997	117
Malaysia	1999	714	676	249	671	0	1437	239	3986	0
Malaisie	2000	374	2592	154	435	0	1270	352	5177	0
Maldives	1999	856	140	485	719	0	1430	104	3734	5
Maldives	2000	1048	214	576	599	0	1671	133	4241	120
Mali	1999	8101	6686	1085	6814	2169	2244	1732	28832	0
Mali	2000	2323	5271	810	8001	3295	2408	1884	23992	512
Malta	1999	204	0	0	0	0	298	52	554	43
Malte	2000	53	0	0	0	0	111	21	185	1
Marshall Islands	1999	44	142	107	0	0	156	105	553	0
Iles Marshall	2000	95	30	105	0	0	144	212	585	0
Mauritania	1999	2510	2026	844	2442	2871	2164	579	13435	302
Mauritanie	2000	2042	3513	722	3041	2260	2482	1166	15226	508
Mauritius	1999	372	160	72	674	63	989	187	2517	49
Maurice	2000	531	98	88	631	0	862	163	2372	87
Mexico	1999	3184	1092	1360	3252	0	1650	2843	13380	1192
Mexique	2000	8251	3095	1190	1768	0	2425	2201	18931	1415
Micronesia (Fed. States of)	1999	362	3	83	0	0	285	155	888	63
Micronésie (Etats féd. de)	2000	257	100	58	0	0	268	83	766	77
Mongolia	1999	4214	895	1456	1197	0	2827	888	11478	27
Mongolie	2000	3882	661	1494	1831	0	1844	908	10620	66
Montserrat	1999	15	0	0	0	0	0	0	15	0
Montserrat	2000	38	2	0	0	0	1	4	45	3
Morocco	1999	4566	125	1956	2168	2617	2386	1968	15786	554
Maroc	2000	3465	512	1268	1517	2189	1994	3007	13952	464
Mozambique	1999	31122	12390	3268	11388	3600	2126	6454	70348	0
Mozambique	2000	18600	8743	3408	21877	31024	2212	8088	93952	943
Myanmar	1999	15572	0	872	12605	1490	4168	176	34883	58
Myanmar	2000	14938	0	821	11217	1865	5435	1641	35918	1173
Namibia	1999	1591	31	726	3506	502	2103	1191	9651	422
Namibie	2000	1246	136	439	1994	730	1752	918	7215	378
Nauru	1999	0	0	0	0	0	74	0	74	0
Nauru	2000	0	0	0	0	0	91	0	91	0
Nepal	1999	9190	3982	3913	10053	11356	3816	2763	45073	1081
Népal	2000	8577	3010	2478	10647	9961	4135	4124	42933	2339

81
Socio—economic development assistance through the United Nations system
Thousand US dollars [cont.]
Assistance en matière de développement socioéconomique fournie par le système des Nations Unies
Milliers de dollars E.—U. [suite]

Development grant expenditures [1] • Aide au développement [1]

Country or area Pays ou zone	Year Année	UNDP PNUD		UNFPA FNUAP	UNICEF	WFP PAM	Other UN system Autres organis. —ONU		Total	Gov't self— supporting Auto— assistance gouverne— mentale
		Central resources Ressources centrales	Special funds Fonds gérés				Regular budget Budget ordinaire	Extra— budgetary Extra— budgétaire		
Netherlands Antilles	1999	393	0	0	0	0	66	0	459	0
Antilles néerlandaises	2000	395	0	0	0	0	114	0	509	0
Nicaragua	1999	10544	1517	1765	9901	65600	1525	2676	93528	49
Nicaragua	2000	8260	3962	1198	3032	12657	1162	2162	32434	341
Niger	1999	5401	1389	1357	7591	1907	2445	3103	23193	26
Niger	2000	5889	1141	985	7860	3302	2583	3524	25283	2510
Nigeria	1999	3871	3021	3433	22613	0	3059	2112	38109	200
Nigéria	2000	6542	1701	3684	31556	0	3269	12645	59397	11131
Niue	1999	63	12	2	0	0	127	0	204	0
Nioué	2000	123	84	0	0	0	102	21	330	0
Oman	1999	0	15	0	701	0	780	754	2249	754
Oman	2000	0	0	10	805	0	947	667	2429	595
Pakistan	1999	8123	715	5529	18298	12630	4292	2389	51976	148
Pakistan	2000	5231	1670	652	22268	5112	3790	12505	51228	10340
Palau	1999	0	0	0	0	0	67	0	67	0
Palaos	2000	0	0	0	0	0	152	0	152	0
Panama	1999	123348	808	244	1069	0	1014	505	126987	369
Panama	2000	94849	976	213	904	0	1000	527	98468	487
Papua New Guinea	1999	1210	580	697	786	0	1992	185	5450	30
Papouasie—Nvl—Guinée	2000	2132	525	686	1547	0	2416	74	7379	27
Paraguay	1999	19298	176	459	1297	0	1188	53	22472	7
Paraguay	2000	28936	415	546	1057	0	971	424	32349	226
Peru	1999	81134	1457	2884	4523	9415	2672	7245	109329	6351
Pérou	2000	54678	1144	1394	4819	3841	1949	4526	72352	3468
Philippines	1999	8038	1676	2559	6641	0	1882	5290	26086	879
Philippines	2000	4170	2228	997	8115	0	1029	5620	22159	2298
Poland	1999	2238	152	163	0	0	952	673	4178	0
Pologne	2000	1864	431	113	0	0	1668	91	4167	0
Portugal	1999	0	0	0	0	0	168	34	202	33
Portugal	2000	0	0	0	0	0	155	6	161	0
Qatar	1999	38	0	4	0	0	174	208	424	0
Qatar	2000	29	0	0	0	0	146	297	472	0
Réunion	1999	0	0	0	0	0	45	0	45	0
Réunion	2000	0	0	0	0	0	35	0	35	0
Romania	1999	1038	74	544	1892	0	1099	1161	5808	54
Roumanie	2000	1052	49	280	1446	0	510	1957	5294	143
Rwanda	1999	12238	17763	1740	6333	90369	1849	2294	132586	0
Rwanda	2000	5474	20905	724	5900	73263	2877	2278	111420	564
Saint Helena	1999	128	0	0	0	0	0	2	130	0
Sainte—Hélène	2000	259	0	0	0	0	0	0	259	0
Saint Kitts and Nevis	1999	2	1	0	0	49	158	6	216	6
Saint—Kitts—et—Nevis	2000	0	27	0	0	0	336	13	376	13
Saint Lucia	1999	152	1	0	0	0	207	26	386	10
Sainte—Lucie	2000	1	60	0	0	0	354	67	482	9
Saint Vincent—Grenadines	1999	73	77	5	0	0	167	20	342	0
Saint Vincent—Grenadines	2000	38	58	0	0	0	163	9	268	0
Samoa	1999	197	28	80	0	0	1352	336	1993	0
Samoa	2000	665	49	24	0	0	1021	138	1897	0
Sao Tome and Principe	1999	672	401	520	552	189	1126	62	3521	9
Sao Tomé—et—Principe	2000	572	366	278	404	1166	1672	89	4547	81
Saudi Arabia	1999	4288	0	0	0	0	1104	7051	12444	6783
Arabie saoudite	2000	3033	0	0	0	0	840	9205	13079	9086
Senegal	1999	2277	1026	1782	4073	12447	3278	4632	29515	71
Sénégal	2000	3368	1489	1037	4527	12741	3195	4869	31225	292
Seychelles	1999	41	44	86	57	0	700	179	1108	25
Seychelles	2000	32	24	52	0	0	874	−2	980	−2
Sierra Leone	1999	3234	0	196	5736	3582	1842	334	14924	0
Sierra Leone	2000	890	1	225	10424	4007	2342	2420	20309	1768
Singapore	1999	0	0	0	0	0	301	0	301	0
Singapour	2000	0	0	0	0	0	316	17	333	17

81

Socio—economic development assistance through the United Nations system
Thousand US dollars [*cont.*]

Assistance en matière de développement socioéconomique fournie par le système des Nations Unies
Milliers de dollars E.—U. [*suite*]

Development grant expenditures [1] • Aide au développement [1]

Country or area Pays ou zone	Year Année	UNDP PNUD Central resources Ressources centrales	Special funds Fonds gérés	UNFPA FNUAP	UNICEF	WFP PAM	Other UN system Autres organis. — ONU Regular budget Budget ordinaire	Extra— budgetary Extra— budgétaire	Total	Gov't self— supporting Auto— assistance gouverne— mentale
Solomon Islands	1999	1115	0	158	0	0	594	97	1963	57
Iles Salomon	2000	570	0	58	0	0	637	144	1409	150
Somalia	1999	16957	191	616	17068	15111	3494	559	53995	0
Somalie	2000	9424	779	365	16782	14732	3707	4667	50456	2822
South Africa	1999	3210	1400	881	3480	0	2800	1760	13531	9
Afrique du Sud	2000	3476	567	334	3210	0	2754	1336	11677	222
Sri Lanka	1999	6552	526	961	5671	4712	4216	1073	23711	546
Sri Lanka	2000	6488	1251	554	3848	3925	3348	1771	21186	545
Sudan	1999	10663	1222	2866	17422	133492	4331	1237	171233	73
Soudan	2000	6622	204	1567	15821	102923	3928	6084	137149	5008
Suriname	1999	259	87	63	361	0	519	1406	2695	950
Suriname	2000	293	2627	573	179	0	539	256	4467	34
Swaziland	1999	530	360	247	1217	15	1165	45	3579	0
Swaziland	2000	929	207	199	732	0	1557	73	3697	64
Syrian Arab Republic	1999	1654	1296	1293	797	6305	2677	3166	17188	27
Rép. arabe syrienne	2000	1273	1873	944	1064	5952	2408	3580	17095	508
Tajikistan	1999	6063	669	700	2381	9653	380	1420	21266	0
Tajikistan	2000	5519	868	369	1801	11860	380	1845	22642	1187
Thailand	1999	2167	1932	393	3590	0	4102	1732	13916	42
Thaïlande	2000	2019	1378	570	3059	289	5091	1660	14066	151
TFYR of Macedonia	1999	1091	117	30	7628	0	690	305	9861	0
L'ex—R.y. Macédoine	2000	1875	399	−11	5079	0	431	1317	9090	779
Togo	1999	3769	950	715	1361	0	1402	449	8646	2
Togo	2000	2829	1241	493	1629	0	1503	376	8072	203
Tokelau	1999	23	0	0	0	0	54	0	77	0
Tokélaou	2000	76	0	0	0	0	57	0	133	0
Tonga	1999	48	0	9	0	0	701	30	788	0
Tonga	2000	124	0	46	0	0	794	6	970	0
Trinidad and Tobago	1999	107	453	0	0	0	897	160	1617	18
Trinité—et—Tobago	2000	107	248	0	0	0	838	138	1331	32
Tunisia	1999	945	285	601	1197	8	1565	1222	5823	202
Tunisie	2000	743	485	361	1045	0	1125	1156	4916	406
Turkey	1999	2230	310	794	4946	0	1468	1817	11566	175
Turquie	2000	2327	2404	502	11156	0	864	1842	19094	331
Turkmenistan	1999	1106	112	532	1224	0	85	61	3119	0
Turkménistan	2000	1231	88	426	943	0	110	27	2826	27
Turks and Caicos Islands	1999	173	10	0	0	0	8	10	200	0
Iles Turques et Caïques	2000	363	42	0	0	0	39	42	486	0
Tuvalu	1999	233	9	64	0	0	30	9	345	0
Tuvalu	2000	165	1	35	0	0	21	1	223	0
Uganda	1999	6734	4317	4062	20083	14894	2708	2491	55290	474
Ouganda	2000	5174	5586	2619	22549	20463	2678	5711	64779	2352
Ukraine	1999	3505	8	151	53	0	887	92	4695	0
Ukraine	2000	...	...	...	...	...	...	...	...	...
United Arab Emirates	1999	3602	0	0	0	0	240	828	4670	826
Emirats arabes unis	2000	3954	10	8	0	0	98	755	4825	755
United Rep. of Tanzania	1999	12464	2744	3281	15425	6687	3150	4068	47818	201
Rép.— Unie de Tanzanie	2000	10305	3209	2388	22443	4598	3021	5461	51424	2676
Uruguay	1999	31128	1222	231	733	0	542	563	34419	299
Uruguay	2000	26232	1145	107	676	0	526	320	29005	23
Uzbekistan	1999	1852	1383	900	2416	0	370	224	7145	0
Ouzbékistan	2000	9669	1478	553	1549	0	732	466	14447	159
Vanuatu	1999	373	32	52	0	0	655	44	1156	0
Vanuatu	2000	111	0	79	0	0	1049	13	1251	1
Venezuela	1999	62590	1014	267	1379	0	1337	802	67390	81
Venezuela	2000	38659	3814	322	4070	635	2017	1083	50601	180
Viet Nam	1999	17129	4651	5299	11602	8802	3844	3676	55003	153
Viet Nam	2000	15325	2936	4202	10799	10125	3353	3945	50686	387
Yemen	1999	9414	3024	1803	4643	7705	3135	2529	32253	811
Yémen	2000	9827	1976	1824	5063	7197	2406	3436	31729	2076

81
Socio—economic development assistance through the United Nations system
Thousand US dollars [*cont.*]

Assistance en matière de développement socioéconomique fournie par le système des Nations Unies
Milliers de dollars E.—U. [*suite*]

Development grant expenditures [1] • Aide au développement [1]

Country or area Pays ou zone	Year Année	UNDP PNUD Central resources Ressources centrales	Special funds Fonds gérés	UNFPA FNUAP	UNICEF	WFP PAM	Other UN system Autres organis. — ONU Regular budget Budget ordinaire	Extra— budgetary Extra— budgétaire	Total	Gov't self— supporting Auto— assistance gouverne— mentale
Yugoslavia	1999	1393	2442	0	26735	110059	24	2180	142833	0
Yougoslavie	2000	3856	6098	69	11610	67551	386	10778	100348	1136
Zambia	1999	5873	1465	1020	7545	6935	2658	2232	27728	505
Zambie	2000	3402	2150	3421	10864	7447	2831	1652	31767	458
Zimbabwe	1999	5056	2057	1671	6500	0	2160	1809	19254	103
Zimbabwe	2000	3607	602	451	5160	13	2446	4014	16293	2231
Other countries	1999	28773	21868	1337	11807	11397	7892	11776	94851	221
Autres pays	2000	28476	10183	894	11717	20043	8394	16456	96164	4367
Not elsewhere classified	**1999**	**4805**	**39819**	**3976**	**35413**	**15682**	**20683**	**56849**	**177227**	**12**
Non—classé ailleurs	**2000**	**7324**	**32469**	**2969**	**66036**	**33116**	**6134**	**21518**	**169566**	**17654**

Source: United Nations, "Operational activities of the United Nations for international development cooperation, Report of the Secretary—General, Addendum, Comprehensive statistical data on operational activities for development for the year 1999" (A/56/70/Add.1) and "Operational activities of the United Nations for international development cooperation, Report of the Secretary—General, Addendum, Comprehensive statistical data on operational activities for development for the year 2000" (A/56/320/Add.2).

Source: Nations Unies, "Activités opérationnelles du système des Nations Unies au service de la coopération internationale pour le développement, Rapport du Secrétaire général, Additif, Données statistiques globales sur les activités opérationnelles au service du développement pour 1999" (A/56/70/Add.1) et "Activités opérationnelles du système des Nations Unies au service de la coopération internationale pour le développement, Rapport du Secrétaire général, Additif, Données statistiques globales sur les activités opérationnelles au service du développement pour 2000" (A/56/320/Add.2).

† For information on the recent changes in country or area nomenclature pertaining to former Czechoslovakia, Germany, Hong Kong Special Administrative Region (SAR) of China, Macao Special Administrative Region (SAR) of China, SFR of Yugoslavia and the former USSR, see Annex I — Country or area nomenclature, regional and other groupings.

† Pour les modifications récentes de nomenclature de pays ou de zone concernant l'Allemagne, Hong Kong, région administrative spéciale (RAS) de Chine, Macao, région administrative spéciale (RAS) de Chine, l'ex—Tchécoslovaquie, l'ex—URSS et l'ex—Rfs de Yougoslavie, voir annex I — Nomenclature des pays ou des zones, groupements régionaux et autres groupements.

†† For statistical purposes, the data for China do not include those for Hong Kong Special Administrative Region (Hong Kong SAR), Macao Special Administrative Region (Macao SAR) and Taiwan province of China.

†† Les données statistiques relatives à la Chine ne comprennent pas celles qui concernent la région administrative spéciale de Hong Kong (la RAS de Hong Kong), la région administrative spéciale de Macao (la RAS de Macao), et la province chinoise de Taiwan.

1 The following abbreviations have been used in the table:
UNDP: United Nations Development Programme
UNFPA: United Nations Population Fund
UNICEF: United Nations Children's Fund
WFP: World Food Programme

1 Les abbréviations ci—après ont été utilisées dans le tableau:
PNUD : Programme des Nations Unies pour le développement
FNUAP : Fonds des Nations Unies pour la population
UNICEF : Fonds des Nations Unies pour l'enfance
PAM : Programme alimentaire mondial.

Technical notes, tables 79-81

Table 79 presents estimates of flows of financial resources to individual recipients either directly (bilaterally) or through multilateral institutions (multilaterally).

The multilateral institutions include the World Bank Group, regional banks, financial institutions of the European Union and a number of United Nations institutions, programmes and trust funds.

The main source of data is the Development Assistance Committee of OECD to which member countries reported data on their flow of resources to developing countries and territories and countries and territories in transition, and multilateral institutions.

Additional information on definitions, methods and sources can be found in OECD's *Geographical Distribution of Financial Flows to Aid Recipients* [21].

Table 80 presents the development assistance expenditures of donor countries. This table includes donors' contributions to multilateral agencies, so the overall totals differ from those in table 79, which include disbursements by multilateral agencies.

Table 81 includes data on expenditures on operational activities for development undertaken by the organizations of the United Nations system. Operational activities encompass, in general, those activities of a development cooperation character that seek to mobilize or increase the potential and capacity of countries to promote economic and social development and welfare, including the transfer of resources to developing countries or regions in a tangible or intangible form. The table also covers, as a memo item, expenditures on activities of an emergency character, the purpose of which is immediate relief in crisis situations, such as assistance to refugees, humanitarian work and activities in respect of disasters.

Expenditures on operational activities for development are financed from contributions from governments and other official and non-official sources to a variety of funding channels in the United Nations system. These include United Nations funds and programmes such as contributions to the United Nations Development Programme, contributions to funds administered by the United Nations Development Programme, and regular (assessed) and other extrabudgetary contributions to specialized agencies.

Data are taken from the 1999 and 2000 reports of the Secretary-General to the General Assembly on operational activities for development [28].

Notes techniques, tableaux 79 à 81

Le *Tableau 79* présente les estimations des flux de ressources financières mises à la disposition des pays soit directement (aide bilatérale) soit par l'intermédiaire d'institutions multilatérales (aide multilatérale).

Les institutions multilatérales comprennent le Groupe de la Banque mondiale, les banques régionales, les institutions financières de l'Union européenne et un certain nombre d'institutions, de programmes et de fonds d'affectation spéciale des Nations Unies.

La principale source de données est le Comité d'aide au développement de l'OCDE, auquel les pays membres ont communiqué des données sur les flux de ressources qu'ils mettent à la disposition des pays et territoires en développement et en transition et des institutions multilatérales.

Pour plus de renseignements sur les définitions, méthodes et sources, se reporter à la publication de l'OCDE, la *Répartition géographique des ressources financières de aux pays bénéficiaires de l'Aide* [21].

Le *Tableau 80* présente les dépenses que les pays donateurs consacrent à l'aide publique au développement (APD). Ces chiffres incluent les contributions des donateurs à des agences multilatérales, de sorte que les totaux diffèrent de ceux du tableau 79, qui incluent les dépenses des agences multilatérales.

Le *Tableau 81* présente des données sur les dépenses consacrées à des activités opérationnelles pour le développement par les organisations du système des Nations Unies. Par "activités opérationnelles", on entend en général les activités ayant trait à la coopération au développement, qui visent à mobiliser ou à accroître les potentialités et aptitudes que présentent les pays pour promouvoir le développement et le bien-être économiques et sociaux, y compris les transferts de ressources vers les pays ou régions en développement sous forme tangible ou non. Ce tableau indique également, pour mémoire, les dépenses liées à des activités revêtant un caractère d'urgence, qui ont pour but d'apporter un secours immédiat dans les situations de crise, telles que l'aide aux réfugiés, l'assistance humanitaire et les secours en cas de catastrophe.

Les dépenses consacrées aux activités opérationnelles pour le développement sont financées au moyen de contributions que les gouvernements et d'autres sources officielles et non officielles apportent à divers organes de financement, tels que fonds et programmes du système des Nations Unies. On peut citer notamment les contributions au Programme des Nations Unies pour le développement, les contributions aux fonds gérés par le Programme des Nations Unies pour le développement, les contributions régulières (budgétaires) et les contributions extrabudgétaires aux institutions spécialisées.

Les données sont extraites des rapports annuels de 1999 et de 2000 du Secrétaire général à la session de l'Assemblée générale sur les activités opérationnelles pour le développement [28].

Annex I

Country and area nomenclature, regional and other groupings

A.   Changes in country or area names

In the periods covered by the statistics in the present issue of the *Statistical Yearbook* (in general, 1990-1999 or 1991-2000), and as indicated at the end of each table, the following major changes in designation have taken place:

Czech Republic, Slovakia: Since 1 January 1993, data for the Czech Republic and Slovakia, where available, are shown separately under the appropriate country name. For periods prior to 1 January 1993, where no separate data are available for the Czech Republic and Slovakia, unless otherwise indicated, data for the former Czechoslovakia are shown under the country name "former Czechoslovakia";

Germany: Through the accession of the German Democratic Republic to the Federal Republic of Germany with effect from 3 October 1990, the two German States have united to form one sovereign State. As from the date of unification, the Federal Republic of Germany acts in the United Nations under the designation "Germany". All data shown which pertain to Germany prior to 3 October 1990 are indicated separately for the Federal Republic of Germany and the former German Democratic Republic based on their respective territories at the time indicated;

Hong Kong Special Administrative Region of China: Pursuant to a Joint Declaration signed on 19 December 1984, the United Kingdom restored Hong Kong to the People's Republic of China with effect from 1 July 1997; the People's Republic of China resumed the exercise of sovereignty over the territory with effect from that date;

Macao Special Administrative Region of China: Pursuant to the joint declaration signed on 13 April 1987, Portugal restored Macao to the People's Republic of China with effect from 20 December 1999; the People's Republic of China resumed the exercise of sovereignty over the territory with effect from that date;

Former USSR: In 1991, the Union of Soviet Socialist Republics formally dissolved into fifteen independent countries (Armenia, Azerbaijan, Belarus, Estonia, Georgia, Kazakhstan, Kyrgyzstan, Latvia, Lithuania, Republic of Moldova, Russian Federation, Tajikistan, Turkmenistan, Ukraine and Uzbekistan). Whenever possible, data are shown for the individual countries. Otherwise, data are shown for the former USSR;

Yemen: On 22 May 1990 Democratic Yemen and Yemen merged to form a single State. Since that date they have been represented as one Member with the name 'Yemen';

Yugoslavia: Unless otherwise indicated, data provided for Yugoslavia prior to 1 January 1992 refer to the Socialist Federal Republic of Yugoslavia which was composed of six republics. Data provided for Yugoslavia after that date refer to the Federal Republic of

Annexe I

Nomenclature des pays ou zones, groupements régionaux et autres groupements

A.   Changements dans le nom des pays ou zones

Au cours des périodes sur lesquelles portent les statistiques, dans cette édition de l'*Annuaire Statistique* (1990-1999 ou 1991-2000, en générale), et comme indiqués à la fin de chaque tableau les changements principaux de désignation suivants ont eu lieu:

République tchèque, Slovaquie: Depuis le 1er janvier 1993, les données relatives à la République tchèque, et à la Slovaquie, lorsqu'elles sont disponibles, sont présentées séparément sous le nom de chacun des pays. En ce qui concerne la période précédant le 1er janvier 1993, pour laquelle on ne possède pas de données séparées pour les deux Républiques, les données relatives à l'ex-Tchécoslovaquie sont, sauf indication contraire, présentées sous le titre "l'ex-Tchécoslovaquie";

Allemagne: En vertu de l'adhésion de la République démocratique allemande à la République fédérale d'Allemagne, prenant effet le 3 octobre 1990, les deux Etats allemands se sont unis pour former un seul Etat souverain. A compter de la date de l'unification, la République fédérale d'Allemagne est désigné à l'ONU sous le nom d'"Allemagne". Toutes les données se rapportant à l'Allemagne avant le 3 octobre figurent dans deux rubriques séparées basées sur les territoires respectifs de la République fédérale d'Allemagne et l'ex-République démocratique allemande selon la période indiquée;

Hong Kong, région administrative spéciale de Chine: Conformément à une Déclaration commune signée le 19 décembre 1984, le Royaume-Uni a rétrocédé Hong Kong à la République populaire de Chine, avec effet au 1er juillet 1997; la souveraineté de la République populaire de Chine s'exerce à nouveau sur le territoire à compter de cette date;

Macao, région administrative spéciale de Chine: Conformément à une Déclaration commune signée le 13 avril 1987, le Portugal a rétrocédé Macao à la République populaire de Chine, avec effet au 20 décembre 1999; la souveraineté de la République populaire de Chine s'exerce à nouveau sur le territoire à compter de cette date;

L'ex-URSS: En 1991, l'Union des républiques socialistes soviétiques s'est séparé en 15 pays distincts (Arménie, Azerbaïdjan, Bélarus, Estonie, Géorgie, Kazakhstan, Kirghizistan, Lettonie, Lituanie, République de Moldova, Fédération de Russie, Tadjikistan, Turkménistan, Ukraine, Ouzbékistan). Les données sont présentées pour ces pays pris séparément quand cela est possible. Autrement, les données sont présentées pour l'ex-URSS;

Yémen: Le Yémen et le Yémen démocratique ont fusionné le 22 mai 1990 pour ne plus former qu'un seul Etat, qui est depuis lors représenté comme tel à l'Organisation, sous le nom 'Yémen';

Yougoslavie: Sauf indication contraire, les données fournies pour la Yougoslavie avant le 1er janvier 1992 se rapportent à la République fédérative socialiste de Yougoslavie, qui était composée de six républiques. Les données fournies pour la Yougoslavie après cette date se rapportent à la République fédérative de Yougoslavie, qui est composée de deux républiques (Serbie et Monténégro);

Yugoslavia which is composed of two republics (Serbia and Montenegro);

Other changes in designation during the periods are listed below:

Brunei Darussalam was formerly listed as Brunei;

Burkina Faso was formerly listed as Upper Volta;

Cambodia was formerly listed as Democratic Kampuchea;

Cameroon was formerly listed as United Republic of Cameroon;

Côte d'Ivoire was formerly listed as Ivory Coast;

Democratic Republic of the Congo was formerly listed as Zaire;

Myanmar was formerly listed as Burma;

Palau was formerly listed as Pacific Islands and includes data for Federated States of Micronesia, Marshall Islands and Northern Mariana Islands;

Saint Kitts and Nevis was formerly listed as Saint Christopher and Nevis.

Data relating to the People's Republic of China generally include those for Taiwan Province in the field of statistics relating to population, area, natural resources and natural conditions such as climate. In other fields of statistics, they do not include Taiwan Province unless otherwise stated.

B. Regional groupings

The scheme of regional groupings given below presents seven regions based mainly on continents. Five of the seven continental regions are further subdivided into 21 regions that are so drawn as to obtain greater homogeneity in sizes of population, demographic circumstances and accuracy of demographic statistics [22, 59]. This nomenclature is widely used in international statistics and is followed to the greatest extent possible in the present *Yearbook* in order to promote consistency and facilitate comparability and analysis. However, it is by no means universal in international statistical compilation, even at the level of continental regions, and variations in international statistical sources and methods dictate many unavoidable differences in particular fields in the present *Yearbook*. General differences are indicated in the footnotes to the classification presented below. More detailed differences are given in the footnotes and technical notes to individual tables.

Neither is there international standardization in the use of the terms "developed" and "developing" countries, areas or regions. These terms are used in the present publication to refer to regional groupings generally considered as "developed": these are Europe and the former USSR, the United States of America and Canada in Northern America, and Australia, Japan and New Zealand in Asia and Oceania. These designations are intended for statistical convenience and do not necessarily express a judgement about the stage reached by a parlicular country or area in the development process. Differences from this usage are indicated in the notes to individual tables.

Les autres changements de désignation couvrant les périodes mentionnées sont énumérés ci-dessous:

Le *Brunéi Darussalam* apparaissait antérieurement sous le nom de Brunéi;

Le *Burkino Faso* apparaissait antérieurement sous le nom de la Haute-Volta;

Le *Cambodge* apparaissait antérieurement sous le nom de la Kampuchea démocratique;

Le *Cameroun* apparaissait antérieurement sous le nom de République-Unie du Cameroun;

La *République démocratique du Congo* apparaissait antérieurement sous le nom de Zaïre;

Le *Myanmar* apparaissait antérieurement sous le nom de Birmanie;

Les *Palaos* apparaissait antérieurement sous le nom de Iles du Pacifique y compris les données pour les Etats fédérés de Micronésie, les îles Marshall et îles Mariannes du Nord;

Saint-Kitts-et-Nevis apparaissait antérieurement sous le nom de Saint-Christophe-et-Nevis.

Les données relatives à la République populaire de Chine comprennent en général les données relatives à la province de Taïwan lorsqu'il s'agit de statistiques concernant la population, la superficie, les ressources naturelles, et les conditions naturelles telles que le climat, etc. Dans les statistiques relatives à d'autres domaines, la province de Taïwan n'est pas comprise, sauf indication contraire.

B. Groupements régionaux

Le système de groupements régionaux présenté ci-dessous comporte sept régions basés principalement sur les continents. Cinq des sept régions continentales sont elles-mêmes subdivisées, formant ainsi 21 régions délimitées de manière à obtenir une homogénéité accrue dans les effectifs de population, les situations démographiques et la précision des statistiques démographiques [22, 59]. Cette nomenclature est couramment utilisée aux fins des statistiques internationales et a été appliquée autant qu'il a été possible dans le présent *Annuaire* en vue de renforcer la cohérence et de faciliter la comparaison et l'analyse. Son utilisation pour l'établissement des statistiques internationales n'est cependant rien moins qu'universelle, même au niveau des régions continentales, et les variations que présentent les sources et méthodes statistiques internationales entraînent inévitablement de nombreuses différences dans certains domaines de cet *Annuaire*. Les différences d'ordre général sont indiquées dans les notes figurant au bas de la classification présentée ci-dessous. Les différences plus spécifiques sont mentionnées dans les notes techniques et notes infrapaginales accompagnant les divers tableaux.

L'application des expressions "développés" et "en développement" aux pays, zones ou régions n'est pas non plus normalisée à l'échelle internationale. Ces expressions sont utilisées dans la présente publication en référence aux groupements régionaux généralement considérés comme "développés", à savoir l'Europe et l'ex-URSS, les Etats-Unis d'Amérique et le Canada en Amérique septentrionale, et l'Australie, le Japon et la Nouvelle-Zélande dans la région de l'Asie et du Pacifique. Ces appellations sont employées pour des raisons de commodité statistique et n'expriment pas nécessairement un jugement sur le stade de développement atteint par tel ou tel pays ou zone. Les cas différant de cet usage sont signalés dans les notes accompagnant les tableaux concernés.

Africa	**Afrique**
Eastern Africa	*Afrique orientale*
Burundi	Burundi
Comoros	Comores
Djibouti	Djibouti
Eritrea	Erythrée
Ethiopia	Ethiopie
Kenya	Kenya
Madagascar	Madagascar
Malawi	Malawi
Mauritius	Maurice
Mozambique	Mozambique
Réunion	Réunion
Rwanda	Rwanda
Seychelles	Seychelles
Somalia	Somalie
Uganda	Ouganda
United Republic of Tanzania	République-Unie de Tanzanie
Zambia	Zambie
Zimbabwe	Zimbabwe
Middle Africa	*Afrique centrale*
Angola	Angola
Cameroon	Cameroun
Central African Republic	République centrafricaine
Chad	Tchad
Congo	Congo
Democratic Republic of the Congo	République démocratique du Congo
Equatorial Guinea	Guinée équatoriale
Gabon	Gabon
Sao Tome and Principe	Sao Tomé-et-Principe
Northern Africa	*Afrique septentrionale*
Algeria	Algérie
Egypt	Egypte
Libyan Arab Jamahiriya	Jamahiriya arabe libyenne
Morocco	Maroc
Sudan	Soudan
Tunisia	Tunisie
Western Sahara	Sahara occidental
Southern Africa	*Afrique australe*
Botswana	Botswana
Lesotho	Lesotho
Namibia	Namibie
South Africa	Afrique du Sud
Swaziland	Swaziland
Western Africa	*Afrique occidentale*
Benin	Bénin
Burkina Faso	Burkina Faso
Cape Verde	Cap-Vert
Côte d'Ivoire	Côte d'Ivoire
Gambia	Gambie
Ghana	Ghana
Guinea	Guinée

Guinea-Bissau	Guinée-Bissau
Liberia	Libéria
Mali	Mali
Mauritania	Mauritanie
Niger	Niger
Nigeria	Nigéria
Saint Helena	Sainte-Hélène
Senegal	Sénégal
Sierra Leone	Sierra Leone
Togo	Togo

Americas   **Amériques**
Latin America and the Caribbean   **Amérique latine et Caraïbes**

Caribbean	*Caraïbes*
Anguilla	Anguilla
Antigua and Barbuda	Antigua-et-Barbuda
Aruba	Aruba
Bahamas	Bahamas
Barbados	Barbade
British Virgin Islands	Iles Vierges britanniques
Cayman Islands	Iles Caïmanes
Cuba	Cuba
Dominica	Dominique
Dominican Republic	République dominicaine
Grenada	Grenade
Guadeloupe	Guadeloupe
Haiti	Haïti
Jamaica	Jamaïque
Martinique	Martinique
Montserrat	Montserrat
Netherlands Antilles	Antilles néerlandaises
Puerto Rico	Porto Rico
Saint Kitts and Nevis	Saint-Kitts-et-Nevis
Saint Lucia	Sainte-Lucie
Saint Vincent and the Grenadines	Saint-Vincent-et-les Grenadines
Trinidad and Tobago	Trinité-et-Tobago
Turks and Caicos Islands	Iles Turques et Caïques
United States Virgin Islands	Iles Vierges américaines

Central America	*Amérique centrale*
Belize	Belize
Costa Rica	Costa Rica
El Salvador	El Salvador
Guatemala	Guatemala
Honduras	Honduras
Mexico	Mexique
Nicaragua	Nicaragua
Panama	Panama

South America	*Amérique du Sud*
Argentina	Argentine
Bolivia	Bolivie
Brazil	Brésil
Chile	Chili
Colombia	Colombie
Ecuador	Equateur

Falkland Islands (Malvinas)	Iles Falkland (Malvinas)
French Guiana	Guyane française
Guyana	Guyana
Paraguay	Paraguay
Peru	Pérou
Suriname	Suriname
Uruguay	Uruguay
Venezuela	Venezuela

Northern America [a]

Bermuda
Canada
Greenland
Saint Pierre and Miquelon
United States of America

Amérique septentrionale [a]

Bermudes
Canada
Groenland
Saint-Pierre-et-Miquelon
Etats-Unis d'Amérique

Asia

Eastern Asia

China
Hong Kong Special Administrative Region of China
Democratic People's Republic of Korea
Japan
Macao Special Administrative Region of China
Mongolia
Republic of Korea

Asie

Asie orientale

Chine
Hong Kong, région administrative spéciale de Chine
République populaire démocratique de Corée
Japon
Macao, région administrative spéciale de Chine
Mongolie
République de Corée

South-central Asia

Afghanistan
Bangladesh
Bhutan
India
Iran (Islamic Republic of)
Kazakhstan
Kyrgyzstan
Maldives
Nepal
Pakistan
Sri Lanka
Tajikistan
Turkmenistan
Uzbekistan

Asie centrale et du Sud

Afghanistan
Bangladesh
Bhoutan
Inde
Iran (République islamique d')
Kazakhstan
Kirghizistan
Maldives
Népal
Pakistan
Sri Lanka
Tadjikistan
Turkménistan
Ouzbékistan

South-eastern Asia

Brunei Darussalam
Cambodia
East Timor
Indonesia
Lao People's Democratic Republic
Malaysia
Myanmar
Philippines
Singapore
Thailand
Viet Nam

Asie du Sud-Est

Brunéi Darussalam
Cambodge
Timor oriental
Indonésie
République démocratique populaire lao
Malaisie
Myanmar
Philippines
Singapour
Thaïlande
Viet Nam

Western Asia	*Asie occidentale*
Armenia	Arménie
Azerbaijan	Azerbaïdjan
Bahrain	Bahreïn
Cyprus	Chypre
Georgia	Géorgie
Iraq	Iraq
Israel	Israël
Jordan	Jordanie
Kuwait	Koweït
Lebanon	Liban
Occupied Palestinian Territory	Territoire palestinien occupé
Oman	Oman
Qatar	Qatar
Saudi Arabia	Arabie saoudite
Syrian Arab Republic	République arabe syrienne
Turkey	Turquie
United Arab Emirates	Emirats arabes unis
Yemen	Yémen
Europe	**Europe**
Eastern Europe	*Europe orientale*
Belarus	Bélarus
Bulgaria	Bulgarie
Czech Republic	République tchèque
Hungary	Hongrie
Poland	Pologne
Republic of Moldova	République de Moldova
Romania	Roumanie
Russian Federation	Fédération de Russie
Slovakia	Slovaquie
Ukraine	Ukraine
Northern Europe	*Europe septentrionale*
Channel Islands	Iles Anglo-Normandes
Denmark	Danemark
Estonia	Estonie
Faeroe Islands	Iles Féroé
Finland	Finlande
Iceland	Islande
Ireland	Irlande
Isle of Man	Ile de Man
Latvia	Lettonie
Lithuania	Lituanie
Norway	Norvège
Svalbard and Jan Mayen Islands	Iles Svalbard et Jan Mayen
Sweden	Suède
United Kingdom	Royaume-Uni
Southern Europe	*Europe méridionale*
Albania	Albanie
Andorra	Andorre
Bosnia and Herzegovina	Bosnie-Herzégovine
Croatia	Croatie
Gibraltar	Gibraltar
Greece	Grèce

Holy See	Saint-Siège
Italy	Italie
Malta	Malte
Portugal	Portugal
San Marino	Saint-Marin
Slovenia	Slovénie
Spain	Espagne
The former Yugoslav Republic of Macedonia	Ex-République yougoslave de Macédoine
Yugoslavia	Yougoslavie

Western Europe	*Europe occidentale*
Austria	Autriche
Belgium	Belgique
France	France
Germany	Allemagne
Liechtenstein	Liechtenstein
Luxembourg	Luxembourg
Monaco	Monaco
Netherlands	Pays-Bas
Switzerland	Suisse

Oceania	**Océanie**
Australia and New Zealand	*Australie et Nouvelle-Zélande*
Australia	Australie
New Zealand	Nouvelle-Zélande
Norfolk Island	Ile Norfolk

Melanesia	*Mélanésie*
Fiji	Fidji
New Caledonia	Nouvelle-Calédonie
Papua New Guinea	Papouasie-Nouvelle-Guinée
Solomon Islands	Iles Salomon
Vanuatu	Vanuatu

Micronesia-Polynesia	*Micronésie-Polynésie*
Micronesia	*Micronésie*
Guam	Guam
Kiribati	Kiribati
Marshall Islands	Iles Marshall
Micronesia (Federated States of)	Micronésie (Etats fédérés de)
Nauru	Nauru
Northern Mariana Islands	Iles Mariannes septentrionales
Palau	Palaos

Polynesia	*Polynésie*
American Samoa	Samoa américaines
Cook Islands	Iles Cook
French Polynesia	Polynésie française
Niue	Nioué
Pitcairn	Pitcairn
Samoa	Samoa
Tokelau	Tokélaou
Tonga	Tonga
Tuvalu	Tuvalu
Wallis and Futuna Islands	Iles Wallis-et-Futuna

C. Other groupings

Following is a list of other groupings and their compositions presented in the *Yearbook*. These groupings are organized mainly around economic and trade interests in regional associations.

Andean Common Market (ANCOM)
  Bolivia
  Colombia
  Ecuador
  Peru
  Venezuela

Asia-Pacific Economic Cooperation (APEC)
  Australia
  Brunei Darussalam
  Canada
  Chile
  China
  Hong Kong Special Administrative Region
      of China
  Indonesia
  Japan
  Malaysia
  Mexico
  New Zealand
  Papua New Guinea
  Peru
  Philippines
  Republic of Korea
  Russian Federation
  Singapore
  Taiwan Province of China
  Thailand
  United States of America
  Viet Nam

Association of Southeast Asian Nations (ASEAN)
  Brunei Darussalam
  Cambodia
  Indonesia
  Lao People's Democratic Republic
  Malaysia
  Myanmar
  Philippines
  Singapore
  Thailand
  Viet Nam

Caribbean Community and Common Market
(CARICOM)
  Antigua and Barbuda
  Bahamas (member of the Community only)
  Barbados
  Belize
  Dominica
  Grenada
  Guyana
  Jamaica

C. Autres groupements

On trouvera ci-après une liste des autres groupements et de leur composition, présentée dans l'*Annuaire*. Ces groupements correspondent essentiellement à des intérêts économiques et commerciaux d'après les associations régionales.

Marché commun andin (ANCOM)
  Bolivie
  Colombie
  Equateur
  Pérou
  Vénézuela

Coopération économique Asie-Pacifique (CEAP)
  Australie
  Brunéi Darussalam
  Canada
  Chili
  Chine
  Hong Kong, région administrative spéciale
      de Chine
  Indonésie
  Japon
  Malaisie
  Mexique
  Nouvelle-Zélande
  Papouasie-Nouvelle-Guinée
  Pérou
  Philippines
  République de Corée
  Fédération de Russie
  Singapour
  Province chinoise de Taiwan
  Thaïlande
  Etats-Unis d'Amérique
  Viet Nam

Association des nations de l'Asie du Sud-Est (ANASE)
  Brunéi Darussalam
  Cambodge
  Indonésie
  République démocratique populaire lao
  Malaisie
  Myanmar
  Philippines
  Singapour
  Thaïlande
  Viet Nam

*Communauté des Caraïbes et Marché commun des Caraï-
bes* (CARICOM)
  Antigua-et-Barbuda
  Bahamas (membre de la communauté seulement)
  Barbade
  Belize
  Dominique
  Grenade
  Guyana
  Jamaïque

Montserrat	Montserrat
Saint Kitts and Nevis	Saint-Kitts-et-Nevis
Saint Lucia	Sainte-Lucie
Saint Vincent and the Grenadines	Saint-Vincent-et-les Grenadines
Suriname	Suriname
Trinidad and Tobago	Trinité-et-Tobago

Central African Customs and Economic Union (CACEU)	*Union douanière et économique de l'Afrique centrale* (UDEAC)
Cameroon	Cameroun
Central African Republic	République centrafricaine
Chad	Tchad
Congo	Congo
Equatorial Guinea	Guinée équatoriale
Gabon	Gabon

Central American Common Market (CACM)	*Marché commun centraméricain* (MCC)
Costa Rica	Costa Rica
El Salvador	El Salvador
Guatemala	Guatemala
Honduras	Honduras
Nicaragua	Nicaragua

Common Market for Eastern and Southern Africa (COMESA)	*Marché commun de l'Afrique de l'Est et de l'Afrique australe* (COMESA)
Angola	Angola
Burundi	Burundi
Comoros	Comores
Democratic Republic of the Congo	République démocratique du Congo
Djibouti	Djibouti
Egypt	Egypte
Eritrea	Erythrée
Ethiopia	Ethiopie
Kenya	Kenya
Madagascar	Madagascar
Malawi	Malawi
Mauritius	Maurice
Namibia	Namibie
Rwanda	Rwanda
Seychelles	Seychelles
Sudan	Soudan
Swaziland	Swaziland
Uganda	Ouganda
United Republic of Tanzania	République-Unie de Tanzanie
Zambia	Zambie
Zimbabwe	Zimbabwe

Commonwealth of Independent States (CIS)	*Communauté d'Etats indépendants* (CEI)
Armenia	Arménie
Azerbaijan	Azerbaïdjan
Belarus	Bélarus
Georgia	Géorgie
Kazakhstan	Kazakhstan
Kyrgyzstan	Kirghizistan
Republic of Moldova	République de Moldova
Russian Federation	Fédération de Russie
Tajikistan	Tadjikistan
Turkmenistan	Turkménistan
Ukraine	Ukraine
Uzbekistan	Ouzbékistan

Economic Community of West African States (ECOWAS)	*Communauté économique des Etats de l'Afrique de l'Ouest* (CEDEAO)
Benin	Bénin
Burkina Faso	Burkina Faso
Cape Verde	Cap-Vert
Côte d'Ivoire	Côte d'Ivoire
Gambia	Gambie
Ghana	Ghana
Guinea	Guinée
Guinea-Bissau	Guinée-Bissau
Liberia	Libéria
Mali	Mali
Mauritania	Mauritanie
Niger	Niger
Nigeria	Nigéria
Senegal	Sénégal
Sierra Leone	Sierra Leone
Togo	Togo

European Free Trade Association (EFTA)	*Association européenne de libre-échange* (AELE)
Iceland	Islande
Liechtenstein	Liechtenstein
Norway	Norvège
Switzerland	Suisse

European Union (EU)	*Union européenne* (UE)
Austria	Autriche
Belgium	Belgique
Denmark	Danemark
Finland	Finlande
France	France
Germany	Allemagne
Greece	Grèce
Ireland	Irlande
Italy	Italie
Luxembourg	Luxembourg
Netherlands	Pays-Bas
Portugal	Portugal
Spain	Espagne
Sweden	Suède
United Kingdom	Royaume-Uni

Latin American Integration Association (LAIA)	*Association latino-américaine pour l'intégration* (ALAI)
Argentina	Argentine
Bolivia	Bolivie
Brazil	Brésil
Chile	Chili
Colombia	Colombie
Ecuador	Equateur
Mexico	Mexique
Paraguay	Paraguay
Peru	Pérou
Uruguay	Uruguay
Venezuela	Venezuela

Least developed countries (LDCs) [b]	*Pays les moins avancés* (PMA) [b]
Afghanistan	Afghanistan
Angola	Angola
Bangladesh	Bangladesh
Benin	Bénin

Bhutan	Bhoutan
Burkina Faso	Burkina Faso
Burundi	Burundi
Cambodia	Cambodge
Cape Verde	Cap-Vert
Central African Republic	République centrafricaine
Chad	Tchad
Comoros	Comores
Democratic Republic of the Congo	République démocratique du Congo
Djibouti	Djibouti
Equatorial Guinea	Guinée équatoriale
Eritrea	Erythrée
Ethiopia	Ethiopie
Gambia	Gambie
Guinea	Guinée
Guinea-Bissau	Guinée-Bissau
Haiti	Haïti
Kiribati	Kiribati
Lao People's Democratic Republic	République démocratique populaire lao
Lesotho	Lesotho
Liberia	Libéria
Madagascar	Madagascar
Malawi	Malawi
Maldives	Maldives
Mali	Mali
Mauritania	Mauritanie
Mozambique	Mozambique
Myanmar	Myanmar
Nepal	Népal
Niger	Niger
Rwanda	Rwanda
Samoa	Samoa
Sao Tome and Principe	Sao Tomé-et-Principe
Sierra Leone	Sierra Leone
Solomon Islands	Iles Salomon
Somalia	Somalie
Sudan	Soudan
Togo	Togo
Tuvalu	Tuvalu
Uganda	Ouganda
United Republic of Tanzania	République-Unie de Tanzanie
Vanuatu	Vanuatu
Yemen	Yémen
Zambia	Zambie

Mercado Común Sudamericano (MERCOSUR)	*Marché commun sud-américain* (Mercosur)
Argentina	Argentine
Brazil	Brésil
Paraguay	Paraguay
Uruguay	Uruguay

North American Free Trade Agreement (NAFTA)	*Accord de libre-échange nord-américain* (ALENA)
Canada	Canada
Mexico	Mexique
United States of America	Etats-Unis d'Amérique

Organisation for Economic Cooperation and Development (OECD)	*Organisation de coopération et de développement économiques* (OCDE)
Australia	Australie
Austria	Autriche

Belgium	Belgique
Canada	Canada
Czech Republic	République tchèque
Denmark	Danemark
Finland	Finlande
France	France
Germany	Allemagne
Greece	Grèce
Hungary	Hongrie
Iceland	Islande
Ireland	Irlande
Italy	Italie
Japan	Japon
Luxembourg	Luxembourg
Mexico	Mexique
Netherlands	Pays-Bas
New Zealand	Nouvelle-Zélande
Norway	Norvège
Poland	Pologne
Portugal	Portugal
Republic of Korea	République de Corée
Spain	Espagne
Sweden	Suède
Switzerland	Suisse
Turkey	Turquie
United Kingdom	Royaume-Uni
United States of America	Etats-Unis d'Amérique

Organization of Petroleum Exporting Countries (OPEC) *Organisation des pays exportateurs de pétrole* (OPEP)

Algeria	Algérie
Indonesia	Indonésie
Iran (Islamic Republic of)	Iran (République islamique d')
Iraq	Iraq
Kuwait	Koweït
Libyan Arab Jamahiriya	Jamahiriya arabe libyenne
Nigeria	Nigéria
Qatar	Qatar
Saudi Arabia	Arabie saoudite
United Arab Emirates	Emirats arabes unis
Venezuela	Venezuela

Southern African Customs Union (SACU) *Union douanière d'Afrique australe*

Botswana	Botswana
Lesotho	Lesotho
Namibia	Namibie
South Africa	Afrique du Sud
Swaziland	Swaziland

---

a   The continent of North America comprises Northern America, Caribbean and Central America.

b   As determined by the General Assembly in its resolution 49/133.

---

a   Le continent de l'Amérique du Nord comprend l'Amérique septentrionale, les Caraïbes et l'Amérique centrale.

b   Comme déterminé par l'Assemblée générale dans sa résolution 49/133.

Annex II

Conversion coefficients and factors

The metric system of weights and measures is employed in the *Statistical Yearbook*. In this system, the relationship between units of volume and capacity is: 1 litre = 1 cubic decimetre (dm^3) exactly (as decided by the 12th International Conference of Weights and Measures, New Delhi, November 1964).

Section A shows the equivalents of the basic metric, British imperial and United States units of measurements. According to an agreement between the national standards institutions of English-speaking nations, the British and United States units of length, area and volume are now identical, and based on the yard = 0.9144 metre exactly. The weight measures in both systems are based on the pound = 0.45359237 kilogram exactly (Weights and Measures Act 1963 (London), and *Federal Register* announcement of 1 July 1959: *Refinement of Values for the Yard and Pound* (Washington D.C.)).

Section B shows various derived or conventional conversion coefficients and equivalents.

Section C shows other conversion coefficients or factors which have been utilized in the compilation of certain tables in the *Statistical Yearbook*. Some of these are only of an approximate character and have been employed solely to obtain a reasonable measure of international comparability in the tables.

For a comprehensive survey of international and national systems of weights and measures and of units weights for a large number of commodities in different countries, see *World Weights and Measures* (United Nations publication, Sales No. E.66.XVII.3).

Annexe II

Coefficients et facteurs de conversion

L'*Annuaire statistique* utilise le système métrique pour les poids et mesures. La relation entre unités métriques de volume et de capacité est: 1 litre = 1 décimètre cube (dm^3) exactement (comme fut décidé à la Conférence internationale des poids et mesures, New Delhi, novembre 1964).

La section A fournit les équivalents principaux des systèmes de mesure métrique, britannique et américain. Suivant un accord entre les institutions de normalisation nationales des pays de langue anglaise, les mesures britanniques et américaines de longueur, superficie et volume sont désormais identiques, et sont basées sur le yard = 0:9144 mètre exactement. Les mesures de poids se rapportent, dans les deux systèmes, à la livre (pound) = 0.45359237 kilogramme exactement ("Weights and Measures Act 1963" (Londres), et "Federal Register Announcement of 1 July 1959: Refinement of Values for the Yard and Pound" (Washington, D.C.)).

La section B fournit divers coefficients et facteurs de conversion conventionnels ou dérivés.

La section C fournit d'autres coefficients ou facteurs de conversion utilisés dans l'élaboration de certains tableaux de l'*Annuaire statistique*. D'aucuns ne sont que des approximations et n'ont été utilisés que pour obtenir un degré raisonnable de comparabilité sur le plan international.

Pour une étude d'ensemble des systèmes internationaux et nationaux de poids et mesures, et d'unités de poids pour un grand nombre de produits dans différents pays, voir "*World Weights and Measures*" (publication des Nations Unies, No de vente E.66.XVII.3).

A. Equivalents of metric, British imperial and United States units of measure
A. Equivalents des unités métriques, britanniques et des Etats-Unis

Metric units / Unités métriques	British imperial and US equivalents / Equivalents en mesures britanniques et des Etats-Unis	British imperial and US units / Unités britanniques et des Etats-Unis	Metric equivalents / Equivalents en mesures métriques	
Length — Longeur				
1 centimetre – centimètre (cm)	0.3937008 inch	1 inch	2.540	cm
1 metre – mètre (m)	3.280840 feet	1 foot	30.480	cm
	1.093613 yard	1 yard	0.9144	m
1 kilometre – kilomètre (km)	0.6213712 mile	1 mile	1609.344	m
	0.5399568 int. naut. mile	1 international nautical mile	1852.000	m
Area — Superficie				
1 square centimetre – (cm²)	0.1550003 square inch	1 square inch	6.45160	cm²
1 square metre – (m²)	10.763910 square feet	1 square foot	9.290304	dm²
	1.195990 square yards	1 square yard	0.83612736	m²
1 hectare – (ha)	2.471054 acres	1 acre	0.4046856	ha
1 square kilometre – (km²)	0.3861022 square mile	1 square mile	2.589988	km²
Volume				
1 cubic centimetre – (cm³)	0.06102374 cubic inch	1 cubic inch	16.38706	cm³
1 cubic metre – (m³)	35.31467 cubic feet	1 cubic foot	28.316847	dm³
	1.307951 cubic yards	1 cubic yard	0.76455486	m³
Capacity — Capacité				
1 litre (l)	0.8798766 imp. quart	1 British imperial quart	1.136523	l
	1.056688 U.S. liq. quart	1 U.S. liquid quart	0.9463529	l
	0.908083 U.S. dry quart	1 U.S. dry quart	1.1012208	l
1 hectolitre (hl)	21.99692 imp. gallons	1 imperial gallon	4.546092	l
	26.417200 U.S. gallons	1 U.S. gallon	3.785412	l
	2.749614 imp. bushels	1 imperial bushel	36.368735	l
	2.837760 U.S. bushels	1 U.S. bushel	35.239067	l
Weight or mass — Poids				
1 kilogram (kg)	35.27396 av. ounces	1 av. ounce	28.349523	g
	32.15075 troy ounces	1 troy ounce	31.10348	g
	2.204623 av. pounds	1 av. pound	453.59237	g
		1 cental (100 lb.)	45.359237	kg
		1 hundredweight (112 lb.)	50.802345	kg
1 ton – tonne (t)	1.1023113 short tons	1 short ton (2 000 lb.)	0.9071847	t
	0.9842065 long tons	1 long ton (2 240 lb.)	1.0160469	t

B. Various conventional or derived coefficients	**B. Divers coefficients conventionnels ou dérivés**

Railway and air transport

1 passenger-mile = 1.609344 voyageur (passager) - kilomètre

1 short ton-mile = 1.459972 tonne-kilomètre

1 long ton-mile = 1.635169 tonne kilomètre

Ship tonnage

1 register ton (100 cubic feet) — tonne de jauge = 2.83m³

1 British shipping ton (42 cubic feet) = 1.19m³

1 U.S. shipping ton (40 cubic feet) = 1.13m³

1 deadweight ton (dwt ton = long ton) = 1.016047 metric ton — tonne métrique

Electric energy

1 Kilowatt (kW) =   1.34102 British horsepower (hp)

1.35962 cheval vapeur (cv)

C.   Other coefficients or conversion factors employed in *Statistical Yearbook* tables

Roundwood

Equivalent in solid volume without bark.

Sugar

1 metric ton raw sugar = 0.9 metric ton refined sugar.

For the United States and its possessions:

1 metric ton refined sugar = 1.07 metric tons raw sugar.

Transport ferroviaire et aérien

1 voyageur (passager) - kilomètre = 0.621371) passenger-mile

1 tonne-kilomètre =   0.684945 short ton-mile

0.611558 long ton-mile

Tonnage de navire

1 cubic metre – m³ = 0.353 register ton - tonne de jauge

0.841 British shipping ton

0.885 US shipping ton

1 metric ton — tonne métrique — 0.984 dwt ton

Energie électrique

1 British horsepower (hp) = 0.7457 kW

1 cheval vapeur (cv) = 0.735499 kW

C.   Autres coefficients ou facteurs de conversion utilisés dans les tableaux de l'*Annuaire statistique*

Bois rond

Equivalences en volume solide sans écorce.

Sucre

1 tonne métrique de sucre brut = 0.9 tonne métrique de sucre raffiné.

Pour les Etats-Unis et leurs possessions:

1 tonne métrique de sucre raffiné = 1.07 t.m. de sucre brut.

Annex III

Tables added and omitted

A.   Tables added

The present issue of the *Statistical Yearbook* (1999) includes the following tables which were not presented in the previous issue:

Table 9: Population in urban and rural areas, rates of growth and largest urban agglomeration population;

Table 11: Selected indicators of life expectancy, childbearing and mortality;

Table 14: Book production: number of titles by UDC classes;

Table 15: Daily newspapers;

Table 16: Non-daily newspapers and periodicals;

Table 17: Television and radio receivers;

Table 68: Researchers, technicians and other supporting staff engaged in research and development.

B.   Tables omitted

The following tables have been deleted from the present issue:

Table 45: Tires;

Table 48: Soap, washing powders and detergents.

C.   The following tables which were presented in the previous issues (44th and 45th) are not presented in the present issue. They will be updated in future issues of the *Yearbook* when new data become available:

Table 9: Education at the primary, secondary and tertiary levels (45th issue);

Table 10: Public expenditure on education: total and current (45th issue);

Table 26: Government final consumption expenditure by function at current prices (44th issue);

Table 27: Private final consumption expenditure by type and purpose at current prices (44th issue);

Table 66: Water supply and sanitation coverage (45th issue);

Table 67: Threatened species (45th issue);

Table 72: Gross domestic expenditure on R&D by source of funds (44th issue).

Annexe III

Tableaux ajoutés et supprimés

A.   Tableaux ajoutés

Dans ce numéro de l'*Annuaire statistique* (1999), les tableaux suivants qui n'ont pas été présentés dans le numéro antérieur, ont été ajoutés:

Tableau 9: Population urbaine, population rurale, taux d'accroissement et population de l'agglomération urbaine la plus peuplée;

Tableau 11: Choix d'indicateurs de l'espérance de vie, de maternité et de la mortalité;

Tableau 14: Production de livres: nombre de titres classés d'après la CDU;

Tableau 15: Journaux quotidiens;

Tableau 16: Journaux non quotidiens et périodiques;

Tableau 17: Récepteurs de télévision et de radiodiffusion sonore;

Tableau 68: Chercheurs, techniciens et autre personnel de soutien employés à des travaux de recherche et de développement.

B.   Tableaux supprimés

Les tableaux suivants ont été supprimés dans la présente édition:

Tableau 45: Pneumatiques;

Tableau 48: Savons, poudres pour lessives et détersifs.

C.   Les tableaux suivants qui ont été repris dans les éditions antérieures (la 44ème et la 45ème éditions) n'ont pas été repris dans la présente édition. Ils seront actualisés dans les futures livraisons de l'*Annuaire* à mesure que des données nouvelles deviendront disponibles:

Tableau 9: Enseignement primaire, secondaire et supérieur (45ème édition);

Tableau 10: Dépenses publiques afférentes à l'éducation: totales et ordinaires (45ème édition);

Tableau 26: Consommation finale des administrations publiques par fonction aux prix courants (44ème édition);

Tableau 27: Consommation finale privée par catégorie de dépenses et par fonction aux prix courants (44ème édition);

Tableau 66: Accès à l'eau et à l'assainissement (45ème édition);

Tableau 67: Espèces menacées (45ème édition);

Tableau 72: Dépenses intérieures brutes de recherche et développement par source de fonds (44ème édition).

Statistical sources and references

A.   Statistical sources

1.   American Automobile Manufacturers Association, *Motor Vehicle Facts and Figures 1997* (Detroit, USA).

2.   Auto and Truck International, *2000-2001 World Automotive Market Report* (Illinois, USA).

3.   Carbon Dioxide Information Analysis Center, *Global, Regional, and National CO_2 Emissions Estimates from Fossil-Fuel Burning, Hydraulic Cement Production, and Gas Flaring* (Oak Ridge, Tennessee, USA).

4.   Food and Agriculture Organization of the United Nations, *FAO Fertilizer Yearbook 2000* (Rome).

5.   _____, *FAO Food balance sheets, 1997-1999 average*, (Rome).

6.   _____, *FAO Production Yearbook 2000* (Rome).

7.   _____, *FAO Trade Yearbook 2000* (Rome).

8.   _____, *FAO Yearbook of Fishery Statistics, Capture production 1999* (Rome).

9.   _____, *FAO Yearbook of Forest Products 2000* (Rome).

10.   _____, *Global Forest Resources Assessment 2000* (Rome).

11.   International Civil Aviation Organization, *Civil Aviation Statistics of the World 1998* (Montreal).

12.   _____, *Digest of statistics — Traffic 1995-1999* (Montreal).

13.   International Labour Office, *Yearbook of Labour Statistics 2000* (Geneva).

14.   International Monetary Fund, *Balance of Payments Statistics Yearbook 2000* (Washington, D.C.).

15.   _____, *International Financial Statistics*, November 2001 (Washington, D.C.).

16.   International Sugar Organization, *Sugar Yearbook 2000* (London).

17.   International Telecommunication Union, *World Telecommunication Development Report 1998* (Geneva).

18.   _____, *Yearbook of Statistics, Telecommunication Services, Chronological Time Series 1990-1999* (Geneva).

19.   Lloyd's Register of Shipping, *World Fleet Statistics 2000* (London).

20.   Organisation for Economic Cooperation and Development, *Development Cooperation, 2000 Report* (Paris).

21.   _____, *Geographical Distribution of Financial Flows to Aid Recipients, 1995-1999* (Paris).

22.   United Nations, *Demographic Yearbook 1999* (United Nations publication, Sales No. E/F.01.XIII.1.

23.   _____, *Energy Statistics Yearbook 1998*

Sources statistiques et références

A.   Sources statistiques

1.   "American Automobile Manufacturers Association, *Motor Vehicle Facts and Figures 1997*" (Detroit, USA).

2.   "Auto and Truck International, *2000-2001 World Automotive Market Report*" (Illinois, USA).

3.   "Carbon Dioxide Information Analysis Center, *Global, Regional, and National CO_2 Emissions Estimates from Fossil-Fuel Burning, Hydraulic Cement Production, and Gas Flaring*" (Oak Ridge, Tennessee, USA).

4.   Organisation des Nations Unies pour l'alimentation et l'agriculture, *Annuaire FAO des engrais 2000* (Rome).

5.   _____, *Bilans alimentaires de la FAO, moyenne 1997-1999* (Rome).

6.   _____, *Annuaire FAO de la production 2000* (Rome).

7.   _____, *Annuaire FAO du commerce 2000* (Rome).

8.   _____, *Annuaire statistique des pêches, captures 1999* (Rome).

9.   _____, *Annuaire FAO des produits forestiers 2000* (Rome).

10.   _____, *Evaluation des ressources forestières mondiales 2000* (Rome).

11.   Organisation de l'aviation civile internationale, *Statistiques de l'aviation civile dans le monde 1998* (Montréal).

12.   _____, *Recueil de statistiques — trafic 1995-1999* (Montréal).

13.   Bureau international du Travail, *Annuaire des statistiques du Travail 2000* (Genève).

14.   Fonds monétaire international, "*Balance of Payments Statistics Yearbook 2000*", (Washington, D.C.).

15.   _____, *Statistiques financières internationales*, novembre 2001 (Washington, D.C.).

16.   Organisation internationale du sucre, *Annuaire du sucre 2000* (Londres).

17.   Union international de télécommunication, "*World Telecommunication Development Report 1998*" (Genève).

18.   _____, "*Yearbook of Statistics, Telecommunication Services, Chronological Time Series 1990-1999*" (Genève).

19.   "Lloyd's Register of Shipping, *World Fleet Statistics 2000*" (Londres).

20.   Organisation de Coopération et de Développement Economiques, *Coopération pour le développement, Rapport 2000* (Paris).

21.   _____, *Répartition géographique des*

(United Nations publication, Sales No. E/F.01.XVII.12).

24. _____, *Industrial Commodity Statistics Yearbook 1999* (United Nations publications, Sales No. E/F.02.XVII.2).

25. _____, *International Trade Statistics Yearbook 1999*, vols. I and II (United Nations publication, Sales No. E/F.01.XVII.2).

26. _____, *Monthly Bulletin of Statistics*, various issues up to November 2001 (United Nations publication, Series Q).

27. _____, *National Accounts Statistics: Main Aggregates and Detailed Tables, 1999* (United Nations publication, Sales No. E.02.XVII.6).

28. _____, *Operational activities of the United Nations for international development cooperation , Report of the Secretary-General, Addendum, Comprehensive statistical data on operational activities for development for the year 1999* (A/56/70/Add.1) and *Operational activities ... for the year 2000* (A/56/320/Add.2).

29. _____, *World Population Prospects: The 2000 Revision*, vols. I and II (United Nations publication, Sales No. E.01.XIII.8 and E.01.XIII.9).

30. _____, *World Urbanization Prospects: The 2001 Revision, Data Tables and Highlights* (ESA/P/WP.173, 20 March 2002).

31. United Nations Educational, Scientific and Cultural Organization Institute for Statistics, *Statistical Yearbook 1999* (Paris).

32. United Nations Environment Programme, World Conservation Monitoring Centre, *United Nations List of Protected Areas* (Nairobi).

33. United Nations Programme on HIV/AIDS and the World Health Organization, *Aids epidemic update: December 2001* (Geneva).

34. World Bank, *Global Development Finance*, vols. I and II, 2000 (Washington, D.C.).

35. World Health Organization and United Nations Children's Fund, *Revised 1990 Estimates of Maternal Mortality, A New Approach by WHO and UNICEF"* (Geneva).

36. World Intellectual Property Organization, *Industrial Property Statistics 1999, Publication A* (Geneva).

37. World Tourism Organization, *Yearbook of Tourism Statistics 2001 edition* (Madrid).

ressources financières allouées aux pays bénéficiaires de l'aide, 1995-1999 (Paris).

22. Nations Unies, *Annuaire démographique 1999* (publication des Nations Unies, No de vente E/F.01.XIII.1).

23. _____, *Annuaire des statistiques de l'énergie 1998* (publication des Nations Unies, No de vente E/F.01.XVII.12).

24. _____, *Annuaire des statistiques industrielles par produit 1999* (publications des Nations Unies, No de vente E/F.02.XVII.2).

25. _____, *Annuaire statistique du commerce international 1999*, Vols. I et II (publication des Nations Unies, No de vente E/F.01.XVII.2).

26. _____, *Bulletin mensuel de statistique*, différentes éditions, jusqu'à novembre 2001 (publication des Nations Unies, Série Q).

27. _____, *"National Accounts Statistics: Main Aggregates and Detailed Tables 1999"* (publication des Nations Unies, No de vente E.02.XVII.6).

28. _____, *Activités opérationnelles du système des Nations Unies au service de la coopération internationale pour le développement, Rapport du Secrétaire général, Additif, Données statistiques globales sur les activités opérationnelles au service du développement pour 1999* (A/56/70/Add.1) et *Activités ... pour 2000* (A/56/320/Add.2).

29. _____, *"World Population Prospects: The 2000 Revision"*, Vols. I et II (publication des Nations Unies, No de vente E.01.XIII.8 et E.01.XIII.9).

30. _____, *World Urbanization Prospects: The 2001 Revision, Data Tables and Highlights* (ESA/P/WP.173, 20 mars 2002).

31. Institut de statististique de l'Organisation des Nations Unies pour l'éducation, la science et la culture, *Annuaire statistique 1999* (Paris).

32. Programme des Nations Unies pour l'environnement, Centre mondial de surveillance pour la conservation, *"United Nations List of Protected Areas"* (Nairobi).

33. Programme des Nations Unies sur le VIH/SIDA et l'Organisation mondiale de la santé, *Le point sur l'épidémie de SIDA: décembre 2001* (Genève)

34. Banque mondiale, *"Global Development Finance, Vols. I et II, 2000"* (Washington, D.C.).

35. Organisation mondiale de la santé et Fonds des Nations Unies pour l'enfance, *"Revised 1990 Estimates of Maternal Mortality, A New Approach by WHO and UNICEF"* (Genève).

36. Organisation mondiale de la propriété intellectuelle, *Statistiques de propriété industrielle 1999, Publication A* (Genève).

37. Organisation mondiale du tourisme, *Annuaire des statistiques du tourisme 2001 édition* (Madrid).

B.   References

38.   Food and Agriculture Organization of the United Nations, *The Fifth World Food Survey 1985* (Rome 1985).

39.   International Labour Office, *International Standard Classification of Occupations, Revised Edition 1968* (Geneva, 1969); revised edition, 1988, *ISCO-88* (Geneva, 1990).

40.   International Monetary Fund, *Balance of Payments Manual, Fifth Edition* (Washington, D.C., 1993).

41.   Stanton, C. et al, *Modelling maternal mortality in the developing world*, mimeo, November 1995 (Geneva and New York, WHO, UNICEF).

42.   United Nations, *Basic Methodological Principles Governing the Compilation of the System of Statistical Balances of the National Economy*, Studies in Methods, Series F, No. 17, Rev. 1, vols. 1 and 2 (United Nations publications, Sales No. E.89.XVII.5 and E.89.XVII.3).

43.   _____, *Classifications of Expenditure According to Purpose: Classification of the Functions of Government (COFOG), Classification of Individual Consumption According to Purpose (COICOP), Classification of the Purposes of Non-Profit Institutions Serving Households (COPNI), Classification of the Outlays of Producers According to Purpose (COPP)*, Series M, No. 84 (United Nations publication, Sales No. E.00.XVII.6).

44.   _____, *Energy Statistics: Definitions, Units of Measure and Conversion Factors*, Series F, No. 44 (United Nations publication, Sales No. E.86.XVII.21).

45.   _____, *Energy Statistics: Manual for Developing Countries*, Series F, No. 56 (United Nations publication, Sales No. E.91.XVII.10).

46.   _____, *Handbook of Vital Statistics Systems and Methods*, vol. I, *Legal, Organization and Technical Aspects*, Series F, No. 35, vol. I (United Nations publication, Sales No. E.91.XVII.5).

47.   _____, *Handbook on Social Indicators*, Studies in Methods, Series F, No. 49 (United Nations publication, Sales No. E.89.XVII.6).

48.   _____, *International Recommendations for Industrial Statistics*, Series M, No. 48, Rev. 1 (United Nations publication, Sales No. E.83.XVII.8).

49.   _____, *International Standard Industrial Classification of All Economic Activities*, Statistical Papers, Series M, No. 4, Rev. 2 (United Nations publication, Sales No. E.68.XVII.8); Rev. 3 (United Nations publication, Sales No. E.90.XVII.11).

50.   _____, *International Trade Statistics: Concepts and Definitions*, Series M, No. 52, Rev. 1 (United Nations publication, Sales No. E.82.XVII.14).

B.   Références

38.   Organisation des Nations Unies pour l'alimentation et l'agriculture, *Cinquième enquête mondiale sur l'alimentation 1985* (Rome, 1985).

39.   Organisation internationale du Travail, *Classification internationale type des professions, édition révisée* 1968 (Genève, 1969); édition révisée 1988, *CITP-88* (Genève, 1990).

40.   Fonds monétaire international, *Manuel de la balance des paiements, cinquième édition* (Washington, D.C., 1993).

41.   Stanton, C, et al, "*Modelling maternal mortality in the developing world*", novembre 1995 (Genève et New York, WHO, UNICEF).

42.   Organisation des Nations Unies, *Principes méthodologiques de base régissant l'établissement des balances statistiques de l'économie nationale*, Série F, No 17, Rev.1 Vol. 1 et Vol. 2 (publication des Nations Unies, No de vente F.89.XVII.5 et F.89.XVII.3).

43.   _____, "*Classifications of Expenditure According to Purpose: Classification of the Functions of Government (COFOG), Classification of Individual Consumption According to Purpose (COICOP), Classification of the Purposes of Non-Profit Institutions Serving Households (COPNI), Classification of the Outlays of Producers According to Purpose (COPP)*", Série M, No 84 (publication des Nations Unies, No de vente E. 00.XVII.6).

44.   _____, *Statistiques de l'énergie: définitions, unités de mesures et facteurs de conversion*, Série F, No 44 (publication des Nations Unies, No de vente F.86.XVII.21).

45.   _____, *Statistiques de l'énergie: Manuel pour les pays en développement*, Série F, No 56 (publication des Nations Unies, No de vente F.91.XVII.10).

46.   _____, "*Handbook of Vital Statistics System and Methods, Vol. 1, Legal, Organization and Technical Aspects*", Série F, No 35, Vol. 1 (publication des Nations Unies, No de vente E.91.XVII.5).

47.   _____, *Manuel des indicateurs sociaux*, Série F, No 49 (publication des Nations Unies, No de vente F.89.XVII.6).

48.   _____, *Recommandations internationales concernant les statistiques industrielles*, Série M, No 48, Rev. 1 (publication des Nations Unies, No de vente F.83.XVII.8).

49.   _____, *Classification internationale type, par industrie, de toutes les branches d'activité économique*, Série M, No 4, Rev. 2 (publication des Nations Unies, No de vente F.68.XVII.8); Rev. 3 (publication des Nations Unies, No de vente F.90.XVII.11).

51. _____, *Methods Used in Compiling the United Nations Price Indexes for External Trade*, volume 1, Statistical Papers, Series M, No. 82 (United Nations Publication, Sales No. E.87.XVII.4).

52. _____, *Principles and Recommendations for Population and Housing Censuses*, Statistical Papers, Series M, No. 67 (United Nations publication, Sales No. E.80.XVII.8).

53. _____, *Provisional Guidelines on Statistics of International Tourism*, Statistical Papers, Series M, No. 62 (United Nations publication, Sales No. E.78.XVII.6).

54. _____ and World Tourism Organization, *Recommendations on Tourism Statistics*, Statistical Papers, Series M, No. 83 (United Nations publication, Sales No. E.94.XVII.6).

55. _____, *Standard International Trade Classification, Revision 3*, Statistical Papers, Series M, No. 34, Rev. 3 (United Nations publication, Sales No. E.86.XVII.12), *Revision 2*, Series M, No. 34, Rev. 2 (United Nations publication), *Revision*, Series M, No. 34, Revision (United Nations publication, Sales No. E.61.XVII.6).

56. _____, *Supplement to the Statistical Yearbook and the Monthly Bulletin of Statistics, 1977*, Series S and Series Q, Supplement 2 (United Nations publication, Sales No. E.78.XVII.10).

57. _____, *System of National Accounts, Studies in Methods*, Series F, No. 2, Rev. 3 (United Nations publication, Sales No. E.69.XVII.3).

58. _____, *System of National Accounts 1993*, Studies in Methods, Series F, No. 2, Rev. 4 (United Nations publication, Sales No. E.94.XVII.4).

59. _____, *Towards a System of Social and Demographic Statistics, Studies in Methods*, Series F, No. 18 (United Nations publication, Sales No. E.74.XVII.8).

60. World Health Organization, *Manual of the International Statistical Classification of Diseases, Injuries and Causes of Death*, vol. 1 (Geneva, 1977).

61. World Tourism Organization, *Methodological Supplement to World Travel and Tourism Statistics* (Madrid, 1985).

50. _____, *Statistiques du commerce international: Concepts et définitions*, Série M, No 52, Rev. 1 (publication des Nations Unies, No de vente F.82.XVII.14).

51. _____, *Méthodes utilisées par les Nations Unies pour établir les indices des prix des produits de base entrant dans le commerce international*, Série M, No 82, Vol. 1 (publication des Nations Unies, No de vente F.87.XVII.4).

52. _____, *Principes et recommandations concernant les recensements de la population et de l'habitation*, Série M, No 67 (publication des Nations Unies, No de vente F.80.XVII.8).

53. _____, *Directives provisoires pour l'établissement des statistiques du tourisme international*, Série M, No 62 (publication des Nations Unies, No de vente 78.XVII.6).

54. _____ et l'Organisation mondiale du tourisme, *"Recommendations on Tourism Statistics*, Statistical Papers"*, Série M, No. 83 (publication des Nations Unies, No. de vente E.94.XVII.6).

55. _____, *Classification type pour le commerce international (troisième version révisée)*, Série M, No 34, Rev. 3 (publication des Nations Unies, No de vente F.86.XVII.12), *Révision 2*, Série M, No 34, Rev. 2 (publication des Nations Unies), *Révision*, Série M, No. 34, Révision (publication des Nations Unies, No de vente F.61.XVII.6).

56. _____, *Supplément à l'Annuaire statistique et au bulletin mensuel de statistique, 1977*, Série S et Série Q, supplément 2 (publication des Nations Unies, No de vente F.78.XVII.10).

57. _____, *Système de comptabilité nationale*, Série F, No 2, Rev. 3 (publication des Nations Unies, No de vente F.69.XVII.3).

58. _____, *Système de comptabilité nationale 1993*, Série F, No 2, Rev. 4 (publication des Nations Unies, No de vente F.94.XVII.4).

59. _____, *Vers un système de statistiques démographiques et sociales, Etudes méthodologiques*, Série F, No 18 (publication des Nations Unies, No. de vente F.74.XVII.8).

60. Organisation mondiale de la santé, *Manuel de la classification statistique internationale des maladies, traumatismes et causes de décès*, Vol. 1 (Genève, 1977).

61. Organisation mondiale du tourisme, *Supplément méthodologique aux statistiques des voyages et du tourisme mondiaux* (Madrid, 1985).

Index

Note: References to tables are indicated by **boldface** type. For citations of organizations, see the Index of Organizations.

aggregates, national account (e.g., GDP), relationships between, **199–208**, 238
agricultural production, 14, **333–341**
  method of calculating series, 28, 414
  per capita, **15**
  sources of information, 414
agricultural products, nonfood:
  defined, 414
  external trade in, **10**
  price indexes, **10**
  prices, 308–315, **333–341**
  See also food
agriculture, hunting, forestry, fishing:
  employment, **256–259**, **260–274**
  production, 9, **333–416**
  value added by, **188–198**
AIDS:
  cumulative cases, **73–80**
  deaths, **73–80**
  reported cases, by year, **73–80**
  sources of data, 88
AIDS epidemic update (UN, WHO), 88
airline traffic. *See* civil aviation
aluminium:
  defined, 534
  production, **10**, **506–510**
apparel industry. *See* textile, apparel, leather industry
arable lands, as percentage of total land area, **657–664**
asses, number raised, **358–376**
automobiles. *See* motor vehicles, passenger
aviation. *See* civil aviation

balance of payments:
  by category of payment, **775–807**
  definition of terms, 806–807
Balance of Payments Manual (IMF), 806
Balance of Payments Statistics Yearbook (IMF), 28, 774
beef, veal, and buffalo, production, **428–452**
beer:
  defined, 533
  production, **453–458**
beverage industry. *See* food, beverages, tobacco industries
beverages, alcoholic. *See* beer
births, rate of, **12–13**
book production:
  method of calculating series, 155

by UDC class, **91–97**
boring machines. *See* drilling and boring machines
briquettes:
  defined, 654
  production, **638–652**
brown coal. *See* lignite and brown coal
buffalo. *See* beef, veal, and buffalo
business services industry. *See* finance, insurance, real estate, business service industries; real estate, renting, and business activities

call money rates. *See* money market rate
capital account:
  in balance of payments, **775–807**
  defined, 807
capital goods, prices, **308–315**
carbon dioxide emissions, **665–672**
  method of calculating series, 674–675
cars. *See* motor vehicles, passenger
cattle and buffaloes, number raised, **358–376**
cellulosic and non-cellulosic fibre:
  defined, 534
  production, **9**
cellulosic and non-cellulosic fibre fabrics, production, **470–471**
cement:
  defined, 534
  production, **10**, **490–496**
central banks, discount rates, **239–244**
cereals (grain):
  defined, 414
  production, 9, **342–349**
chemical industry, production, **16–22**, **209–235**, **490–499**
child mortality, **65–72**
  defined, 87
cigarettes, production, **459–465**
cinemas:
  definition of terms, 155
  method of calculating series, 156
  number, attendance, and receipts, **121–126**
civil aviation:
  definition of terms, 608–609
  passengers and freight carried, **593–607**
Civil Aviation Statistics of the World (ICAO), 609
clothing and footwear. *See* textile, apparel, leather industry
coal:
  defined, 653
  production, **9**, **16–22**, **638–652**

coke:
    defined, 654
    production, **638–652**
commodities:
    classification of, 722
    conversion tables for, 868–869
    exports, **10**
    value of, **10**
commodities, primary. *See* primary commodities
communication industry. *See* transportation, storage
        and communication industries
communications, **91–156**
community, social and personal service industries,
        employment, **256–259**
construction industry:
    employment, **256–259**, **260–274**
    value added by, **188–198**
consumer prices, **308–315**
    indexes of, **316–330**
consumption. *See* final consumption expenditures
consumption of fixed capital, as percentage of GDP,
        199–208
conversion factors, currency, 176, 237
conversion tables:
    for selected commodities, 868–869
    for units of measure and weight, 868–869
cotton, production, **9**
cotton fabrics, production, **466–468**
countries and areas:
    boundaries and legal status of, not implied by this
        publication, ii
    changes in designation, 856–857
    customs areas, 721
    economic and regional associations, 863–867
    regional groupings for statistical purposes, 3, 856–867
    surface area, **33–41**, 721
    See also developed countries or areas; developing
    countries or areas
credit:
    in balance of payments, **775–807**
    defined, 807
croplands, permanent, as percentage of total land area,
        657–664
crops:
    production, **9**
    See also agricultural production
crude oil. *See* petroleum, crude
cultural indicators, **91–156**
    sources of information, 155–156
currency:
    conversion factors, 176, 237
    exchange rates, 176, **809–826**

method of calculating series, 175, 237, 722, 723
current transfers:
    in balance of payments, **775–807**
    defined, 806

death, rate of, **12–13**, **65–72**
debit:
    in balance of payments, **775–807**
    defined, 807
Demographic Yearbook (UN), 13, 28, 41, 53, **65–72**, 87
developed countries or areas:
    defined, ii, 3, 857
    development assistance from, **837–846**, **847**
developing countries or areas:
    defined, ii, 3, 857
    development assistance to, **837–846**, **847**
    external debt of, **827–833**
development assistance, **837–855**
    bilateral and multilateral, to individuals, **837–846**
    bilateral and multilateral, to organisations, **847**
    United Nations system, **848–854**, **855**
Development Assistance Committee (DAC) countries,
        development assistance from, **847**
Digest of Statistics - Traffic (ICAO), 609
discount rates, **239–244**
    defined, 254
domestic production, prices, **308–315**
domestic service, employment, **260–274**
domestic supply, prices, **308–315**
drilling and boring machines:
    defined, 535
    production, **10**, **523–524**

earnings. *See* wages
economic activity, kind of. *See* industry
economic associations, country lists, 863–867
economic relations, international. *See* international
        economic relations
economic statistics, **157–688**
education, **55–63**
    employment, **260–274**
    literacy rate, **55–63**
electrical products. *See* office and related electrical
        products
electricity:
    consumption, **24–25**, **610–637**
    defined, 655
    production, 10, 24–25, 610–637, 638–652
electricity, gas, water utilities:
    employment, **256–259**, **260–274**
    production, **16–22**, **209–235**
    value added by, **188–198**
employment:

defined, 293
by industry, **256–274**
method of calculating series, 294
See also unemployment
energy, **610–655**
by category, production, trade, and consumption, **24–25**
consumption, **24–25, 610–637**
definition of terms, 653–655
method of calculating series, 653
production, **24–25, 610–637**
stocks, 24–25, **610–637**
trade, 24–25, **610–637**
energy commodities (solid, liquid, and gas):
consumption, **610–637**
definition of terms, 653–655
production, **610–637, 638–652**
Energy Statistics: Definitions, Units of Measure and Conversion Factors (UN), 653
Energy Statistics: Manual for Developing Countries (UN), 653
Energy Statistics Yearbook (UN), 24, 28, 653
environment, **657–675**
European Patent Convention, 688
exchange rates, 175, **809–826**
definition of terms, 834
exports:
in balance of payments, **775–807**
defined, 806
index numbers, **708–713, 714–720**
as percentage of GDP, **177–187**
prices, **308–315**
purchasing power of, **708–713**
value of, 10, **26–27, 691–707, 708–713, 714–716, 718–719**
volume of, **26–27, 708–713, 716–718**
See also external trade
external debt:
definition of terms, 834–835
of developing countries or areas, **827–833**
external trade (international trade), **691–724**
by commodity classes, **10**
definition of terms, 722
in energy, **24–25, 610–637**
method of calculating series, 721–722
as percentage of GDP, **177–187**
sources of information, 28, 721
systems for recording of, 721
value of, 10, **26–27, 691–707**
volume of, 10, **26–27**
See also exports; imports
extraterritorial organisations, employment by, **260–274**

fabrics:
defined, 534
production, **9, 16–22, 466–472**
See also fibres
factor income, **199–208**
FAO Fertilizer Yearbook, 414, 415–416
FAO Food Balance Sheets, 88
FAO Production Yearbook, 14, 15, 28, 29, 414
FAOSTAT database, 14, 15
FAO Trade Yearbook, 414
FAO Yearbook of Fishery Statistics, 28, 414
FAO Yearbook of Forest Products, 28, 414
ferro-alloys, production, **9**
fertility rate, **65–72**
total, defined, 87
fertilizer:
consumption, **394–413**
production, 10, **394–413**
types of, defined, 415–416
fibres:
production, **9**
See also cellulosic and non-cellulosic fibre; fabrics
final consumption expenditures, as percentage of GDP, **177–187, 199–208**
finance, insurance, real estate, business service industries:
employment, **256–259, 260–274**
See also real estate, renting, and business activities
finance, international. *See* international finance
financial account:
in balance of payments, **775–807**
defined, 807
financial intermediation, **260–274**
financial statistics, **239–254**
sources of information, 254
finished goods, prices, **308–315**
fish:
aquaculture, **384–393**
captures, **9, 384–393**
defined, 415
production, **9, 384–393**
fishing:
sources of information, 414
See also agriculture, hunting, forestry, fishing
fixed capital. *See* gross fixed capital formation
food:
defined, 414
external trade in, **10**
price indexes, **10**
prices, **316–330**
production, **9, 14, 333–341**
production per capita, **15**

supply, method of calculating series, 88–89
supply and composition of, in terms of calories, protein, and fats, **81–86**
food, beverages, tobacco industries, production, **16–22, 209–235, 417–465**
footwear, leather:
 defined, 534
 production, **9, 473–477**
footwear industry. *See* textile, apparel, leather industry
foreign exchange reserves, **11**
forestry. *See* agriculture, hunting, forestry, fishing
forests, as percentage of total land area, **657–664**
Frascati Manual, 688
freight traffic:
 air, **593–607**
 rail, **537–547**
furniture industry. *See* wood and wood products

gas. *See* liquified petroleum gas; natural gas; refinery gas
gas utilities. *See* electricity, gas, water utilities
Geographical Distribution of Financial Flows to Aid Recipients (OECD), 855
Global, Regional, and National Annual CO₂ Emissions . . . (Carbon Dioxide Information Analysis Center), 674
Global Development Finance (World Bank), 834
Global Forest Resources Assessment (FAO), 673
government final consumption, as percentage of GDP, **177–187**
government finance, **11**
 sources of information, 28
grain. *See* cereals
gross domestic product:
 distribution by expenditure (government final consumption, household final consumption, changes in inventories, gross fixed capital formation, exports, imports), **177–187**, 237
 method of calculating series, 236
 related to other national accounting aggregates, **199–208**
 total and per capita, **159–176**
gross fixed capital formation, as percentage of GDP, **177–187**
gross national disposable income, as percentage of GDP, **199–208**
gross national product, as percentage of GDP, **199–208**
gross savings, as percentage of GDP, **199–208**

Handbook on Social Indicators, iv
Harare Protocol, 688
Havana Agreement, 688
health, **65–89**

health and social work, employment, **260–274**
heavy petroleum products:
 defined, 654
 production, **638–652**
HIV infection:
 cumulative, **73–80**
 See also AIDS
horses, number raised, **358–376**
hotel industry. *See* trade (wholesale/retail), restaurants, hotel industries
household final consumption, as percentage of GDP, **177–187**
hunting. *See* agriculture, hunting, forestry, fishing

illiteracy, **55–63**
 defined, 63
imports:
 in balance of payments, **775–807**
 defined, 806
 index numbers, **708–713**
 as percentage of GDP, **177–187**
 prices, **308–315**
 value of, 10, 26–27, **691–707, 708–713**
 volume of, **26–27, 708–713**
 See also external trade
income:
 in balance of payments, **775–807**
 defined, 806
individuals, development assistance, bilateral and multilateral, to, **837–846**
Industrial Commodity Statistics Yearbook (UN), 22, 28, 533, 534, 535
industrial production, **9–10, 159–238**
 indexes of, **209–235**
 method of calculating series, 29
 prices, **308–315**
 by region, **16–22**
 sources of information, 533
industry (economic activity):
 employment by, **256–274**
 value added by kind of, **188–198**
infant mortality, **65–72**
 defined, 87
insurance industry. *See* finance, insurance, real estate, business service industries
intellectual property, **677–688**
interest rates. *See* rates
intermediate products, prices, **308–315**
international economic relations, **689–855**
international finance, **809–835**
 sources of information, 834
International Financial Statistics (IMF), 236, 254, 723, 807, 834

International Recommendations for Industrial Statistics (UN), 533
international reserves minus gold, **11**
International Standard Industrial Classification of All Economic Activities (ISIC) (UN), iv, 29, 237, 238, 533
    Rev. 2 and Rev. 3, 294, 331
international trade. *See* external trade
International Trade Statistics: Concepts and Definitions (UN), 721
International Trade Statistics Yearbook (UN), 28, 721
Internet, statistics available on the, iii
Internet users, **146–154**
    method of calculating series, 156
inventories (stocks), changes in, as percentage of GDP, **177–187**
iron. *See* pig iron

labour force, **256–294**
    sources of information, 293–294
    wages, **295–307**
lands:
    categories of, arable, croplands, forested, and protected, area of, **657–664**
    definition of terms, 673
lathes:
    defined, 535
    production, **10, 524–525**
leather footwear. *See* footwear, leather
leather industry. *See* textile, apparel, leather industry
life expectancy, **65–72**
    defined, 87
light petroleum products:
    defined, 654
    production, **638–652**
lignite and brown coal:
    defined, 654
    production, **9, 638–652**
liquified petroleum gas (LPG):
    defined, 655
    production, **638–652**
literacy, **55–63**
    defined, 63
livestock:
    defined, 415
    production, **9, 358–376**
lorries (trucks):
    assembly, **10, 529–530**
    assembly, defined, 535
    production, **10, 530–531**
    production, defined, 535

machinery and equipment, production, **511–531**

machine tools:
    defined, 535
    production, **10, 523–528**
manufactured goods:
    defined, 723
    exports, **10, 714–720**
    value of, **10**
manufacturing industries:
    employment, **256–259, 260–274**
    production, 9, 16–22, 209–235, 417–536
    value added by, **188–198**
    wages, **295–307**
maritime transport, international:
    definition of terms, 608
    vessels entered and cleared, **584–591**
market exchange rates (MERs), 175, 236
maternal mortality, **65–72**
    method of calculating series, 87
meat:
    defined, 533
    production, **9, 428–452**
merchant vessels:
    defined, 608
    tonnage registered, **566–583**
metal ores, production, **16–22**
metal products industries, production, **16–22, 511–531**
metals, basic:
    defined, 534
    production, 16–22, 209–235, 500–510
    sources of information, 534
metal-working presses:
    defined, 535
    production, **526–527**
Methodological Supplement to World Travel and Tourism Statistics (WTO), 773
milling machines:
    defined, 535
    production, **525–526**
mineral products, non-metallic, production, **16–22**
minerals:
    external trade in, **10**
    price indexes, **10**
mining and quarrying:
    employment, **256–259, 260–274**
    production, **9, 16–22, 209–235**
    value added by, **188–198**
mobile cellular telephones:
    defined, 156
    subscribers, **127–135**
Modelling maternal mortality in the developing world (WHO, UNICEF), 88
money market rate, **245–253**

defined, 254

Monthly Bulletin of Statistics (UN), iii, 254, 332, 721, 723

Internet access to (*MBS On-Line*), iii

mortality, **12–13, 65–72**

Motor Vehicle Facts and Figures (AAMA), 28

motor vehicles, commercial:
 defined, 608
 number in use, **10, 548–565**
 production, **10, 529–531**

motor vehicles, passenger:
 defined, 535, 608
 number in use, **10, 548–565**
 production, **10, 514–515**

mules, number raised, **358–376**

multilateral institutions:
 defined, 855
 development assistance by, **837–846**
 development contributions to, **847**

mutton, lamb, and goat, production, **428–452**

national accounts, **159–238**
 definition of terms, 238
 relationships between principal aggregates of, **199–208**, 238
 sources of information, 236–238

National Accounts Statistics: Main Aggregates and Detailed Tables (UN), 236

national income, as percentage of GDP, **199–208**

natural gas:
 defined, 655
 production, **9, 16–22, 638–652**

natural gas liquids (NGL):
 defined, 654
 production, **638–652**

net current transfers from the rest of the world, as percentage of GDP, **199–208**

net errors and omissions:
 in balance of payments, **775–807**
 defined, 807

net factor income from the rest of the world, as percentage of GDP, **199–208**

newspapers:
 daily, numbers and circulation, **98–104**
 non-daily, numbers and circulation, **105–112**
 types of, defined, 155

nitrogenous fertilizers, production and consumption, **394–413**

office and related electrical products, **16–22**

oil crops:
 defined, 414–415
 production, **9, 350–357**

oil tankers, tonnage registered, **573–579**

Operational activities of the United Nations for international development cooperation . . . (UN), 53, 855

ore and bulk carriers, tonnage registered, **579–583**

"other activities," value added by, **188–198**

paper, printing, publishing, recorded media industries, production, **16–22**

paper and paperboard:
 defined, 534
 production, **485–489**

passenger traffic:
 air, **593–607**
 rail, **537–547**

Patent Cooperation Treaty (PCT), 688

patents:
 applied for, granted, and in force, **682–686**
 sources of information, 688

peat:
 defined, 654
 production, **638–652**

periodicals:
 numbers and circulation, **105–112**
 types of, defined, 155

personal service industry. *See* community, social and personal service industries

petroleum, crude:
 defined, 654
 production, **9, 16–22, 638–652**

petroleum products:
 defined, 654
 production, **638–652**

phosphate fertilizers, production and consumption, **394–413**

pig iron:
 defined, 534
 production, **9, 500–505**

pigs, number raised, **358–376**

population, **33–53**
 definition of terms, 28
 density, **12–13, 33–41**
 method of calculating series, 28, 53
 numbers, **9, 12–13, 33–41**
 rate of increase, **12–13, 33–41, 45–52**
 by sex, **33–41**
 sources of information, 28
 urban and rural, **45–52**

pork, production, **428–452**

potash fertilizers, production and consumption, **394–413**

prices:
 consumer, **308–315, 316–330**
 indexes of, **10, 316–330**, 331

method of calculating series, 29, 331
producer and wholesale, **308–315**
types of, defined, 331
primary commodities (raw materials):
price indexes, **10**
prices, **308–315**
printing industry. *See* paper, printing, publishing,
recorded media industries
producer prices, **308–315**
indexes of, **209–235**
production, sources of information, 28
protected lands, as percentage of land area, **657–664**
*Provisional Guidelines on Statistics of International
Tourism* (UN), 773
public administration, employment, **260–274**
publishing industry. *See* paper, printing, publishing,
recorded media industries

radio receivers:
number in use, **113–120**
production, **511–513**
railway traffic:
definition of terms, 608
passengers and freight carried, **537–547**
rates:
discount, **239–244**
money market, **245–253**
treasury bills, **245–253**
raw materials. *See* primary commodities
real estate, renting, and business activities:
employment, **260–274**
See also finance, insurance, real estate, business
service industries
receivers, radio and television:
defined, 155
number in use, **113–120**
production, **511–513**
*Recommendation concerning the International
Standardization of Statistics on Science and
Technology*, 688
Recommendations on Tourism Statistics (UN, WTO),
773
refinery gas:
defined, 655
production, **638–652**
refrigerators, household:
defined, 535
production, **9, 516–519**
regional associations, country lists, **863–867**
regions, statistical:
countries included, 3, **857–862**
purpose of, 28
surface area, **12–13**

renting activities. *See* real estate, renting, and business
activities
repair services, employment, **260–274**
research and development, sources of information, 688
researchers:
defined, 688
number of, **677–681**
reserved and related items:
in balance of payments, **775–807**
defined, 807
reserve positions in IMF, **11**
restaurant industry. *See* trade (wholesale/retail),
restaurants, hotel industries
rest of the world, factor and transfer income from, **199–
208**
retail trade. *See* trade (wholesale/retail), restaurants,
hotel industries
Revised 1990 Estimates of Maternal Mortality . . .
(WHO, UNICEF), **65–72**, 87
roundwood:
defined, 415
production, **9, 377–383**
rural population, **45–52**

savings, as percentage of GDP, **199–208**
sawnwood:
defined, 534
production, **10, 478–484**
science and technology, **677–688**
scientists. *See* researchers
service activities, other, employment, **260–274**
services:
in balance of payments, **775–807**
defined, 806
sex, population by, **33–41**
sheep and goats, number raised, **358–376**
shipping. *See* maritime transport, international
short term rates, **245–253**
defined, 254
social service industry. *See* community, social and
personal service industries
social statistics, **31–156**
special drawing rights (SDRs), **11**
method of calculating series, 723
Standard International Trade Classification (SITC)
(UN), 722
Statbase Locator on Disk (United Nations Statistics
Division), iv
Statistical Yearbook (UN), **1–6**
CD-ROM version, iii–iv
contents of, iii
explanation of use, iv, xiv
organisation of, iv, 2–3

sources and references, iii, iv, 871–874

tables added and omitted in present edition, iv, 870

Statistical Yearbook (UNESCO), 155

statistics:

comparability of, iv, 4–5

on the Internet, iii

reliability of, 5

sources of, iii, iv, 871–874

timeliness of, iii, 5

units and symbols used, xiv

steel, crude:

defined, 534

production, **500–505**

stocks, changes in, as percentage of GDP, **177–187**

storage industry. *See* transportation, storage and communication industries

sugar:

consumption, **417–427**

defined, 533

production, **10**, **417–427**

Sugar Yearbook (ISO), 533

sulphuric acid:

defined, 534

production, **9**, **497–499**

Supplement to the Statistical Yearbook and the Monthly Bulletin of Statistics, 1977 (UN), 332, 721

System of National Accounts, Rev. 3 (1968, UN), 236

System of National Accounts, Rev. 4 (1993, UN), 236, 806

technicians:

defined, 688

number of, **677–681**

telephones:

definition of terms, 156

number in use and per capita, **136–145**

See also mobile cellular telephones

television receivers:

number in use, **113–120**

production, **511–513**

terms of trade, **26–27**, **708–713**

textile, apparel, leather industry, production, **16–22**, **209–235**, **466–477**

textiles. *See* fabrics; fibres

tobacco industry. *See* food, beverages, tobacco industries

tobacco products, production, **459–465**

ton of oil equivalent (TOE), defined, 653

tourism, international, **725–774**

definition of terms, 773–774

method of calculating series, 773–774

sources of information, 773

tourists:

arrivals, **725–753**, **754–763**

inbound, receipts from, **754–763**

origin and destination of, **725–753**

outbound, expenditures of, **764–772**

trade, international. *See* external trade

trade (wholesale/retail), restaurants, hotel industries:

employment, **256–259**, **260–274**

value added by, **188–198**

transfer income, **199–208**

transportation, **537–608**

transportation, storage and communication industries:

employment, **256–259**, **260–274**

value added by, **188–198**

transportation equipment:

number of vehicles in use, **10**

production, **16–22**

sources of information, 28

See also motor vehicles, commercial; motor vehicles, passenger

treasury bill rate, **245–253**

defined, 254

trucks. *See* lorries; motor vehicles, commercial

unemployment:

defined, 293

numbers and percentages, **275–292**

United Nations List of Protected Areas (UNEP), 673

units of measure and weight, conversion tables, 868–869

urban agglomeration, largest, by country, **45–52**

urban population, **45–52**

value added, by industry (kind of economic activity), **188–198**

veal. *See* beef, veal, and buffalo

vessels in international transport, **584–591**

visitors, international, defined, 773

wages:

in manufacturing, **295–307**

method of calculating series, 331

washing machines, household:

defined, 535

production, **9**, **520–522**

water utilities. *See* electricity, gas, water utilities

wearing apparel, leather, footwear industries. *See* textile, apparel, leather industry

wholesale prices, **308–315**

wholesale trade. *See* trade (wholesale/retail), etc.

wood and wood products:

production, **16–22**, **478–489**

See also roundwood; sawnwood

woodpulp, production, **10**

wool, production, **9**

wool fabrics, production, **468–470**

World Debt Tables. See Global Development Finance

World Fleet Statistics (Lloyd's Register of Shipping), 608
World Population Prospects (UN), 28, 53, 87
world statistics:
    selected, **9–11**
    summary, **7–30**
World Weights and Measures, 868
World Wide Web, statistics available on the, iii

Yearbook of Labour Statistics (ILO), 293
Yearbook of Statistics, Telecommunication Services . . . (ITU), 156
Yearbook of Tourism Statistics (WTO), 773, 774

Index of Organizations

African Intellectual Property Organization (OAPI), 688

African Regional Industrial Property Organization (ARIPO), 688

Carbon Dioxide Information Analysis Center (CDIAC) (Oak Ridge National Laboratory, USA), 672, 674

Development Assistance Committee (DAC) (OECD), 855

Food and Agriculture Organization of the United Nations (FAO), 11, 14, 15, 86, 88, 341, 349, 357, 376, 383, 393, 413, 414, 452, 484, 489, 664, 673
　Internet address, 414

International Civil Aviation Organization (ICAO), 606, 609

International Labour Office (ILO), 272, 290, 305, 330

International Monetary Fund (IMF), 11, 175, 236, 244, 253, 723, 774, 805, 806, 825, 834

International Sugar Organization (ISO), 427

International Telecommunications Union (ITU), 135, 145, 154

Joint United Nations Programme on HIV/AIDS (UNAIDS), 80, 88

Latin American Iron and Steel Institute, 534

Lloyd's Register of Shipping, 583

Organization for Economic Cooperation and Development (OECD), 846, 847, 855

Statistics Division, UN. *See* United Nations Statistics Division

United Nations:
　development assistance programs, **848–854**, 854, 855
　document symbols, ii

United Nations Children's Fund (UNICEF), 88

United Nations Development Programme (UNDP), 88, 855

United Nations Economic Commission for Europe (ECE), 534

United Nations Educational, Scientific, and Cultural Organization (UNESCO), 88, 688
　Institute for Statistics, 61, 96, 104, 112, 120, 126, 680

United Nations Environment Programme (UNEP), 39

United Nations Framework Convention on Climate Change (UNFCCC), 674

United Nations International Drug Control Programme, 88

United Nations Population Division, 28, 88

United Nations Population Fund, 88

United Nations Statistical Commission, 4

United Nations Statistics Division, iii, 1, 11, 236, 721, 723, 846
　demographic statistics database, 13, 41
　energy statistics database, 24, 636, 652
　how to contact, v
　industrial statistics database, 22, 234, 457, 464, 471, 477, 496, 499, 505, 510, 513, 515, 518, 522, 527, 531
　Internet addresses, iii
　national accounts database, 175, 186, 197, 208
　price statistics database, 315
　trade statistics database, 27, 705, 713, 719
　transport statistics database, 546, 563, 591

United States of America, Bureau of Mines, 534, 674

World Bank, 88, 833, 834

World Conservation Monitoring Center (WCMC), 664, 673

World Conservation Union (IUCN), 673–674

World Health Organization (WHO), 80, 88

World Intellectual Property Organization (WIPO), 687, 688

World Tourism Organization (WTO), 750, 763, 771, 773

Litho in United Nations, New York
01-70322—May 2002—5,760
ISBN 92-1-061191-8
ISSN 0082-8459

United Nations publication
Sales No. E/F.01.XVII.1
ST/ESA/STAT/SER.S/22